The Oxford Dictionary of
Quotations

The Oxford Dictionary of Quotations

FIFTH EDITION

Edited by **Elizabeth Knowles**

OXFORD
UNIVERSITY PRESS

OXFORD
UNIVERSITY PRESS

Great Clarendon Street, Oxford OX2 6DP

Oxford University Press is a department of the University of Oxford.
It furthers the University's objective of excellence in research, scholarship,
and education by publishing worldwide in

Oxford New York

Athens Auckland Bangkok Bogotá Buenos Aires Calcutta
Cape Town Chennai Dar es Salaam Delhi Florence Hong Kong Istanbul
Karachi Kuala Lumpur Madrid Melbourne Mexico City Mumbai
Nairobi Paris São Paulo Singapore Taipei Tokyo Toronto Warsaw

with associated companies in Berlin Ibadan

Oxford is a registered trade mark of Oxford University Press
in the UK and in certain other countries

Published in the United States
by Oxford University Press Inc., New York

First published 1999

British Library Cataloguing in Publication Data
Data available

Library of Congress Cataloging in Publication Data
The Oxford dictionary of quotations /
edited by Elizabeth Knowles. — 5th ed.
Rev. ed. of: The Oxford dictionary of quotations /
Angela Partington, 4th ed., 1992.
Includes indexes.
I. Knowles, Elizabeth (Elizabeth M.)
II. Partington, Angela.
Oxford dictionary of quotations.
PN6080.095 1999 082—dc21 99-12096

ISBN 0-19-860173-5

5 7 9 10 8 6 4

Designed by Jane Stevenson
Typeset in Photina and Gill Sans
by Interactive Sciences Ltd, Gloucester
printed in Great Britain on acid-free paper by
Biddles Ltd, www.Biddles.co.uk

Project Team

Managing Editor	Elizabeth Knowles
Associate Editor	Susan Ratcliffe
Index Editor	Christina Malkowska Zaba
Library Research	Ralph Bates Marie G. Diaz
Reading Programme	Charlotte Graves Taylor Jean Harker Verity Mason Penelope Newsome Helen Rappaport
Data Capture	Sandra Vaughan
Proof-reading	Kim Allen Fabia Claris Penny Trumble

We are grateful to Gerald Blick for additional research.

Contents

Introduction ix

How to Use the Dictionary xiii

Dictionary 1

SPECIAL CATEGORIES

- Advertising slogans 7
- Borrowed titles 144
- Catchphrases 195
- Closing lines 222
- Epitaphs 302
- Film lines 311
- Film titles 312
- Last words 455
- Military sayings, slogans, and songs 508
- Misquotations 521
- Mottoes 535
- Newspaper headlines and leaders 544
- Official advice 554
- Opening lines 555
- Political slogans and songs 581
- Prayers 592
- Sayings and Slogans 647
- Songs, spirituals, and shanties 729
- Telegrams 758
- Toasts 778

Thematic Index 843

Administration, Age, America, Art, Books, Britain, Business, Computing, Drinks, Education, Environment, Europe, Family, Fashion, Film, Food, Future, Gardening, Health and Fitness, Law, Literature, Love, Marriage, Men and Women, Music, Past, Photography, Politics, Present, Press, Quotations, Religion, Royalty, Science, Seasons, Sex, Sport, Technology, Television, Transport, Travel, War, Weather, Youth

Keyword Index 853

Introduction

Since 1953, all updated editions of the *Oxford Dictionary of Quotations* have built on their predecessors, and the fifth edition is no exception to this rule. The character of the *Dictionary*, responding to its readership, changes with each new edition, but without the work of earlier editors it would not have been possible to compile what is the most comprehensive, as well as the most extensive, version of the *Dictionary*.

The text now runs to well over 20,000 quotations, and represents over 3,000 authors: over 2,000 quotations are completely new additions, and we have also drawn on our other recent texts, in particular the *Oxford Dictionary of Twentieth Century Quotations* published last year. Certain categories of material have, after a gap of many years, been restored: proverbs and nursery rhymes will now be found here. (It has been clear from correspondents over the years that many of our readers expect to be able to find this material in the *Dictionary*.)

For the first time, the *Oxford Dictionary of Quotations* gives proper place to the sacred texts of world religions. This is of course appropriate to a multicultural age, but it has also been fascinating to see how words and phrases from these sources are already permeating the English language. When the American physicist Robert Oppenheimer witnessed the explosion of the first atomic bomb in New Mexico in 1945, he commented, 'I remembered the line from the Hindu scripture, the *Bhagavad Gita*, "I am become death, the destroyer of worlds."' We now have the relevant verse from the *Bhagavadgita*: 'I [Krishna] am all-powerful Time which destroys all things.' The closing words of Eliot's *The Waste Land*, 'Shantih, shantih, shantih', are cross-referred to their source, the *Upanishads*, with the translation: 'Peace! Peace! Peace!'

In 1992, Brian Keenan's account of his time as a hostage, *An Evil Cradling*, received wide publicity. It may however be less well known that the title of the book was taken from a verse of the Koran: 'You shall be . . . mustered into Gehenna—an evil cradling!' The heroine of an earlier book, Nevil Shute's *A Town Like Alice* (first published in 1950, and subsequently twice filmed) quotes directly from the Koran: 'if ye be kind towards women and fear to wrong them, God is well acquainted with what ye do.'

Sometimes the relationship is an echo rather than a direct borrowing. Confucius tells us that 'A ruler who governs his state by virtue is like the north polar star, which remains in its place while all the other stars revolve around it,' and we are at once reminded of the assertion of Shakespeare's Julius Caesar: 'I am constant as the northern star.' At other times, we are made aware of a common tradition: the 12th-century rabbi Eleazar of Worms states that 'The highest sacrifice is a broken and contrite heart,' and we recall the words of the psalm, 'a broken and a contrite heart, O God, thou shalt not despise.'

Oxford dictionaries draw their strength from a constant monitoring of the language, and it is appropriate that the most up-to-date quotations in the news can be found here, with politicians as always to the fore. Bill Clinton reflects on the relationship that should not have occurred ('[It] was not appropriate. In fact, it was wrong'), and his wife Hillary on the nature of marriage ('the only people who count . . . are the two that are in it'). George Mitchell looks forward somewhat ruefully to the peace negotiations in Northern Ireland ('Nobody ever said it would be easy—and that was an understatement'), and Bertie Ahern celebrates his achievement ('It is a day we should treasure'). Tony Benn, whose entry spans 30 years, comments crisply, 'When I think of Cool Britannia, I think of old people dying of hypothermia.' Barbara Castle gives her recipe for longevity, 'I will fight for what I believe in until I drop dead. And that's what keeps you alive.' Seamus Heaney, in his funeral address, reflects movingly on the death of Ted Hughes: 'No death outside my immediate family has left me more bereft. No death in my lifetime has hurt poets more.' Jeremy Paxman takes a firm line on conformity to an official line: 'Speaking for myself, if there is a message I want to be off it.'

While it is important that we cover the up to date, the *Oxford Dictionary of Quotations* should also be the source in which references to older writers likely to be encountered today can be checked. Two books recently published in the Oxford World's Classics editions make the point. Robert Fraser's abridgement of Fraser's *The Golden Bough*, published in 1994, carried the original epigraph from Macaulay's *The Battle of Lake Regillus*, and the often-quoted lines

> The priest who slew the slayer,
> And shall himself be slain

can now be found in these pages.

In another book now available in the World's Classics, Rider Haggard's *King Solomon's Mines*, an allusion is made to the figure of 'Hamilton Tighe'. The origin, and explanation, of this reference can now be found in quotations from 'The Legend of Hamilton Tighe' by Richard Barham. The growth in popularity of audio cassettes is another trend of which we have taken note, since through this medium our readers may well come into contact with the prose and poetry of an earlier age.

It is pleasing that in some cases we have been able to improve on the information provided in the last edition, as for example for the quotation then attributed to Robert Burton: 'Every thing, saith Epictetus, hath two handles, the one to be held by, the other not.' We now have an entry for the Stoic philosopher, where the original quotation is to be found. The *Dictionary* can also provide the origin of what are now established phrases in our language: 'cruel and unusual punishment' and the 'sins of the fathers' are both for the first time found here.

Chronologically the *Dictionary* spans the ages, and it is exciting that we have been able to enrich the text with quotations from earlier centuries which bring the speakers vividly to life. 'Everybody's quick to blame the alien,' says Aeschylus, and Plutarch comments on Cicero's ability 'to see beneath the surface of Caesar's public policy and to fear it, as one might fear the smiling surface of the sea.' The historian Thucydides reflects that 'Happiness depends on being free, and freedom depends on being courageous.' Pliny the Elder is concerned about standards of scholarship: 'I have found that the most professedly reliable and modern writers have copied the old authors word for word, without acknowledgement.'

New quotations are spread through the centuries. The 16th-century merchant and writer Robert Thorne gives his view on exploration: 'There is no land unhabitable, nor sea innavigable.' Francis Bacon looks nearer home, to his garden: 'Nothing is more pleasant to the eye than green grass kept finely shorn.' William Wycherley has a sardonic view of the law: 'A man without money needs no more fear a crowd of lawyers than a crowd of pickpockets.' Edward Gibbon, considering the Roman penal system, gives the view that:

> Whenever the offence inspires less horror than the punishment, the rigour of penal law is obliged to give way to the common feelings of mankind.

Some quotations signal moments of technological and cultural change. 'Mr Watson, come here, I want you!' says Alexander Graham Bell to his assistant in the next room; the first words spoken on the telephone. Towards the end of his life Walt Disney reflects wryly, 'Fancy being remembered around the world for the invention of a mouse!' There are some highly individual indications of personal sources of pleasure: 'There is nothing worth living for but Christian architecture and a boat', asserts the architect Augustus Welby Pugin in 1852, while two centuries earlier the Puritan Margaret Hoby reflects ruefully that she has spent too long in the garden 'to the detriment of spiritual exercise'. Lady Mary Wortley Montagu, in a letter to her daughter, describes herself as 'a rake in reading'. Some older quotations surprise us with their topicality: the statement 'I want the whole of Europe to have one currency' is attributable not to a current Europhile but to Napoleon.

Quotations have always clustered around royal figures. 'My dear firstborn is . . . the greatest beast in the whole world,' says Caroline of Ansbach of her son, Frederick, Prince of Wales. A later Prince of Wales, George, the Prince Regent, inspires Leigh Hunt's regretful comment, 'This Adonis in loveliness was a corpulent man of fifty.' The Prince Regent (in view of his marital troubles) was looked on less kindly by Jane Austen, who found her sympathies with Caroline of Brunswick: 'Poor woman, I shall support her as long as I can, because she is a woman and because I hate her husband.' There are however indications of happier relationships, as when Queen Victoria records her first meeting with her future husband: 'It was with some emotion . . . that I beheld Albert—who is beautiful.' It is their eldest daughter Vicky, on her marriage to Prince Frederick William of Prussia, who inspires Bismarck's cautious comment, 'If the Princess can leave the English woman at home and become a Prussian, then she may be a blessing to the country.' In our own time, the present Princess Royal comments briskly on the way in which she works for children's charities: 'The very idea that all children want to be cuddled by a complete stranger, I find completely amazing.'

Some notable figures appear for the first time. 'Let no man write my epitaph,' runs Robert Emmet's speech from the dock, and a later Irish nationalist, Eamonn de Valera, asserts that 'Whenever I wanted to know what the Irish people wanted, I had only to examine my own heart.' The American labour activist Mary Harris 'Mother' Jones advises, 'Pray for the dead, and fight like hell for the living.' The blind and deaf Helen Keller recalls the moment when language became a mode of communication for her:

> The mystery of language was revealed to me. I knew then that 'w-a-t-e-r' meant the wonderful cool something that was flowing over my hand.

It has been an object to provide readers with as much access as possible to the riches of the *Dictionary*, and we have thus followed the pattern set by the *Oxford Dictionary of Twentieth Century Quotations* (1998) in providing a number of special category sections integrated into the main author sequence. **Advertising slogans** span a chronological range from 1859 ('Worth a guinea a box'—Beecham's pills) to 1998 ('Maybe, just maybe'—the British national lottery.) **Borrowed titles** gives the origins of, among others, *The Golden Bough* (Virgil) and *Ring of Bright Water* (Kathleen Raine). **Film lines** make their usual strong showing, with some new additions ('And call off Christmas!' snarls Alan Rickman in *Robin Hood*). **Last words** range from Socrates to Timothy Leary, by way of the martyred William Tyndale ('Lord, open the king of England's eyes'). **Newspaper headlines and leaders** now include the sentence from which the *Times* derived its nickname of 'The Thunderer': 'Unless the people . . . come forward and petition, ay, thunder for reform!'

We have also improved the accessibility of information by including a selective thematic index, through which can be found the best quotations on given topics such as **Age** ('Although I am 92, my brain is 30 years old', says the photographer Alfred Eisenstaedt). At **America** ('God's crucible', 'From sea to shining sea') the Puritan John Winthrop sees the new settlement as 'a city upon a hill'; three centuries later, the Sioux leader Sitting Bull says simply, 'the Black Hills belong to me.' Diane Arbus and Robert Capa give their views on **Photography**: 'a secret about a secret', 'if your pictures aren't good enough, you aren't close enough'. The **Press** ('the men with the muck-rakes'—Theodore Roosevelt) have always elicited strong views ('ferocious, it forgives nothing'—Diana, Princess of Wales), but the importance of journalism is stated, with dignity, by Amy Goodman: 'Go to where the silence is, and say something.' Views of the **Present** range from Cicero ('*O tempora! O mores!*') to Tom Wolfe ('We are now in the Me decade').

As well as author descriptions, we have included biographical cross-references: directions to quotations *about* that author elsewhere in the *Dictionary*, so that anyone consulting the entry for Richard Crossman can also find Hugh Dalton's assessment of him: 'loyal to his own career but only incidentally to anything or anyone else'. Authors mentioned in source notes who have their own entries appear in bold type, further to facilitate movement sideways through the text.

In compiling this book we have as always drawn on the substantial resources of Oxford Quotations Dictionaries: our existing published texts, and our growing bank of new quotations. Fed by our reading programme, this is constantly enhanced by the generosity of those who write to us with questions, comments, and suggestions, a practice which we continue to welcome. Among those who have contributed particularly to our resources and replied to specific questions, thanks are due to Pauline Adams, Ralph Bates, Archie Burnett, Glynnis Chantrell, Margot Charlton, Mike Clark, Robert Franklin, Henry Hardy, Peter Hennessy, Simon Hornblower, Antony Jay, Richard Judd, Peter Kemp, John McNeill, Bernard O'Donoghue, Nigel Rees, Brenda Richardson, Ned Sherrin, Robin Sawers, Hilary Spurling, Jeffery Triggs, and Norman Vance. Colleagues in the Dictionary Department have, as always, supplied us with quotations that they have come across. We hope once more that our contributors, as well as those who read and use the book, will share in the pleasure and interest felt by the editorial staff in working on the text.

ELIZABETH KNOWLES

Oxford 1999

How to use the Dictionary

The sequence of entries is by alphabetical order of author, usually by surname but with occasional exceptions such as members of royal families (e.g. **Diana, Princess of Wales** and **Elizabeth II**) and Popes (**John Paul II**), or authors known by a pseudonym ('**Saki**') or a nickname (**Caligula**). In general authors' names are given in the form by which they are best known, so that we have **Harold Macmillan** (not Lord Stockton), **George Eliot** (not Mary Ann Evans), and **H. G. Wells** (not Herbert George Wells). Collections such as **Anonymous**, the **Bible**, the **Book of Common Prayer**, the **Missal**, and so forth, are included in the alphabetical sequence. Some **Anonymous** quotations may be included in one of the special category sections (see below).

Author names are followed by dates of birth and death (where known) and brief descriptions; where appropriate, cross-references are then given to quotations about that author elsewhere in the text (*on Byron: see* ***Lamb*** 448:8). Cross-references are also made to other entries in which the author appears, e.g. '*see also* ***Epitaphs*** 304:7' and '*see also* ***Lennon and McCartney***'. Within each author entry, quotations are separated by literary form (novels, plays, poems: see further below) and within each group arranged by order of title, 'a' and 'the' being ignored. Foreign-language text is given for most literary quotations, or if it is felt that the quotation is familiar in the language of origin.

Quotations from diaries, letters, and speeches are given in chronological order and usually follow the literary or published works quoted, with the form for which the author is best known taking precedence. Thus in the case of political figures, speeches appear first, just as poetry quotations precede those in prose for poets, and poetry quotations come second for an author regarded primarily as a novelist.

Quotations from secondary sources such as biographies and other writer's works, to which a date in the author's lifetime can be assigned, are arranged in sequence with diary entries, letters, and speeches. Other quotations from secondary sources and attributed quotations which cannot be so dated are arranged in alphabetical order of quotation text.

Within the alphabetical sequence there are a number of special category entries, such as **Advertising slogans**, **Catchphrases**, **Film lines**, **Misquotations**, and **Newspaper headlines and leaders**. Quotations in these sections are arranged alphabetically according to the first word of the quotation (ignoring 'a' and 'the').

Contextual information regarded as essential to a full appreciation of the quotation precedes the text in an italicized note; information seen as providing useful amplification follows in an italicized note. Each quotation is accompanied by a bibliographical note of the source from which the quotation is taken. Titles of published volumes (*Don Juan* by Byron and *David Copperfield* by Charles Dickens) appear in italics; titles of short stories and poems not published as volumes in their own right, and individual song titles, are given in roman type inside inverted commas ('Ode to a Nightingale' by John Keats and 'Both Sides Now' by Joni Mitchell).

All numbers in source references are given in arabic, with the exception of lower-case roman numerals denoting quotations from prefatory matter, whose page numbering is separate from the main text. The numbering itself relates to the beginning of the quotation, whether or not it runs on to another stanza or line in the original. Where possible, chapter numbers have been offered for prose works.

A date in brackets indicates first publication in volume form of the work cited. Unless otherwise stated, the dates thus offered are intended as chronological guides only and do not necessarily indicate the date of the text cited; where the latter is of significance, this has been stated. Where neither date of publication nor of composition is known, an approximate date (e.g. '*c.*1625') may indicate the likely date of composition. Where there is a large discrepancy between date of composition (or performance) and of publication, in most cases the former only has been given (e.g. 'written 1725', 'performed 1622').

Spellings have been Anglicized and modernized except in those cases, such as **Burns** or **Chaucer**, where this would have been inappropriate; capitalization has been retained only for personifications; with rare exceptions, verse has been aligned with the left hand margin. Italic type has been used for all foreign-language originals.

Sub-headings have been used as a guide to novel titles under **Dickens**, for the names of books under the **Bible** (arranged canonically, not alphabetically), and for plays and poems under **Shakespeare**. **Anonymous** quotations are grouped by language.

Cross-references to specific quotations are used to direct the reader to another related item. In each case a reference is given to an author's name or to the title of a special category entry, followed by the page number and then the unique quotation number on that page ('see **Last words** 456:8' and 'cf. **Tennyson** 761:17'). The use of 'see' indicates that following up the cross-reference will supply essential information; 'cf.' indicates information that will amplify what is already given. In some cases, the quotation may exist in two forms, or may depend on an earlier source not quoted in its own right; when this happens, the subordinate quotation is given directly below the quotation to which it relates. Authors who have their own entries are typographically distinguished by the use of bold ('*of William* **Shakespeare**', '*by Mae* **West**') in context or source notes.

Indexes

Thematic index

A selection of quotations on designated subjects can be traced through the thematic index. Each subject heading is followed by a short line from each of the quotations on the theme. References are to the author's name and the page and quotation number, as in the keyword index (see below). There is a list of subjects which are included in the thematic index on page vii.

Keyword index

The most significant words from each quotation appear in the keyword index, allowing individual quotations to be traced. Both the keywords and the context lines following each keyword, including those in foreign languages, are in strict alphabetical order. Singular and plural nouns (with their possessive forms) are grouped separately: for 'some old lover's ghost' see **lover**; for 'at lovers' perjuries' see **lovers**. Variant forms of common words (fresshe/fresh, luve/love) are grouped under a single heading: **fresh**, **love**.

References are to the author's name (usually in abbreviated form, as AUST for Jane Austen) followed by the page number and the number of the unique quotation on the page. Thus AUST 38:7 means quotation number 7 on page 38, in the entry for Jane Austen.

Diane Abbott 1953–
British Labour politician

1 Being an MP is the sort of job all working-class parents want for their children—clean, indoors and no heavy lifting.
in *Independent* 18 January 1994

George Abbott 1887–1995
American director, producer, and dramatist

2 If you want to be adored by your peers and have standing ovations wherever you go—live to be over ninety.
in *The Times* 2 February 1995; obituary

Peter Abelard 1079–1142
French scholar, theologian, and philosopher, lover of **Héloise**

3 *O quanta qualia sunt illa sabbata,*
Quae semper celebrat superna curia.
O what their joy and glory must be,
Those endless sabbaths the blessèd ones see!
Hymnarius Paraclitensis bk. 1, pars altera 'Hymni Diurni' no. 29 'Sabbato. Ad Vesperas' (translated by J. M. Neale, 1854)

4 *Non enim facile de his quos plurimum diligimus turpitudinem suspicamur.*
For we do not easily expect evil of those whom we love most.
Historia Calamitatum Mearum ch. 6

Dannie Abse 1923–
Welsh-born doctor and poet

5 Are all men in disguise except those crying?
'Encounter at a greyhound bus station' (1986)

6 I know the colour rose, and it is lovely,
But not when it ripens in a tumour;
And healing greens, leaves and grass, so springlike,
In limbs that fester are not springlike.
'Pathology of Colours' (1968)

7 So in the simple blessing of a rainbow,
In the bevelled edge of a sunlit mirror,
I have seen visible, Death's artifact
Like a soldier's ribbon on a tunic tacked.
'Pathology of Colours' (1968)

Accius 170–*c.*86 BC
Latin poet and dramatist

8 *Oderint, dum metuant.*
Let them hate, so long as they fear.
from *Atreus*, in Seneca *Dialogues* bks. 3–5 *De Ira* bk. 1, sect. 20, subsect. 4

Goodman Ace 1899–1982
American humorist

9 TV—a clever contraction derived from the words Terrible Vaudeville . . . we call it a medium because nothing's well done.
letter to Groucho Marx, in *The Groucho Letters* (1967)

Chinua Achebe 1930–
Nigerian novelist

10 In such a regime, I say, you died a good death if your life had inspired someone to come forward and shoot your murderer in the chest—without asking to be paid.
A Man of the People (1966)

Dean Acheson 1893–1971
American politician

11 I will undoubtedly have to seek what is happily known as gainful employment, which I am glad to say does not describe holding public office.
in *Time* 22 December 1952

12 Great Britain has lost an empire and has not yet found a role.
speech at the Military Academy, West Point, 5 December 1962, in *Vital Speeches* 1 January 1963

13 The first requirement of a statesman is that he be dull.
in *Observer* 21 June 1970

14 A memorandum is written not to inform the reader but to protect the writer.
in *Wall Street Journal* 8 September 1977

Lord Acton 1834–1902
British historian

15 Liberty is not a means to a higher political end. It is itself the highest political end.
The History of Freedom in Antiquity (1907), lecture delivered 26 February 1877

16 Power tends to corrupt and absolute power corrupts absolutely.
letter to Bishop Mandell Creighton, 3 April 1887, in Louise Creighton *Life and Letters of Mandell Creighton* (1904) vol. 1, ch. 13; cf. **Pitt** 576:22

17 Great men are almost always bad men, even when they exercise influence and not authority.
letter to Bishop Mandell Creighton, 3 April 1887

Abigail Adams 1744–1818
American letter writer, wife of John **Adams** *and mother of John Quincy* **Adams**

18 In the new code of laws which I suppose it will be necessary for you to make I desire you would remember the ladies, and be more generous and favourable to them than your ancestors. Do not put such unlimited power into the hands of the husbands. Remember all men would be tyrants if they could.
letter to John Adams, 31 March 1776, in Butterfield et al. (eds.) *The Book of Abigail and John Adams* (1975); cf. **Defoe** 255:8

19 It is really mortifying, sir, when a woman possessed of a common share of understanding considers the difference of education between the male and female sex, even in those families where education is attended to . . . Nay why should your sex wish for such a disparity in those whom they one day intend for companions and associates.

Pardon me, sir, if I cannot help sometimes suspecting that this neglect arises in some measure from an ungenerous jealousy of rivals near the throne.

letter to John Thaxter, 15 February 1778, in *Adams Family Correspondence* vol. 2 (1963)

1 These are times in which a genius would wish to live. It is not in the still calm of life, or the repose of a pacific station, that great characters are formed . . . Great necessities call out great virtues.

letter to John Quincy Adams, 19 January 1780

2 Patriotism in the female sex is the most disinterested of all virtues. Excluded from honours and from offices, we cannot attach ourselves to the State or Government from having held a place of eminence . . . Yet all history and every age exhibit instances of patriotic virtue in the female sex; which considering our situation equals the most heroic of yours.

letter to John Adams, 17 June 1782

Charles Francis Adams 1807–86

American lawyer and diplomat

3 It would be superfluous in me to point out to your lordship that this is war.

of the situation in the United States during the American Civil War

dispatch to Earl Russell, 5 September 1863, in C. F. Adams *Charles Francis Adams* (1900) ch. 17

Douglas Adams 1952–

English science fiction writer

4 The Answer to the Great Question Of . . . Life, the Universe and Everything . . . [is] Forty-two.

The Hitch Hiker's Guide to the Galaxy (1979) ch. 27

Frank Adams and Will M. Hough

5 I wonder who's kissing her now.

title of song (1909)

Franklin P. Adams 1881–1960

American journalist and humorist

6 When the political columnists say 'Every thinking man' they mean themselves, and when candidates appeal to 'Every intelligent voter' they mean everybody who is going to vote for them.

Nods and Becks (1944)

7 Years ago we discovered the exact point, the dead centre of middle age. It occurs when you are too young to take up golf and too old to rush up to the net.

Nods and Becks (1944)

8 Elections are won by men and women chiefly because most people vote against somebody rather than for somebody.

Nods and Becks (1944); cf. **Fields** 310:22

Gerry Adams 1948–

Northern Irish politician; President of Sinn Féin

9 It might or might not be right to kill, but sometimes it is necessary.

view of the protagonist in a short story; *Before the Dawn* (1996)

10 We want him to be the last British Prime Minister with jurisdiction in Ireland.

of Tony ***Blair***

in *Irish Times* 18 October 1997

11 Peace cannot be built on exclusion. That has been the price of the past 30 years.

in *Daily Telegraph* 11 April 1998

12 Well done, David.

at the Sinn Féin annual conference, on hearing that the Ulster Unionist Council had given its support to David Trimble and the Northern Ireland peace agreement

in *Independent on Sunday* 19 April 1998

Henry Brooks Adams 1838–1918

American man of letters

13 Politics, as a practice, whatever its professions, has always been the systematic organization of hatreds.

The Education of Henry Adams (1907) ch. 1

14 Accident counts for much in companionship as in marriage.

The Education of Henry Adams (1907) ch. 4; cf. **Ustinov** 788:22

15 Women have, commonly, a very positive moral sense; that which they will, is right; that which they reject, is wrong; and their will, in most cases, ends by settling the moral.

The Education of Henry Adams (1907) ch. 6

16 All experience is an arch to build upon.

The Education of Henry Adams (1907) ch. 6

17 A friend in power is a friend lost.

The Education of Henry Adams (1907) ch. 7

18 [Charles] Sumner's mind had reached the calm of water which receives and reflects images without absorbing them; it contained nothing but itself.

The Education of Henry Adams (1907) ch. 13

19 Chaos often breeds life, when order breeds habit.

The Education of Henry Adams (1907) ch. 16

20 A teacher affects eternity; he can never tell where his influence stops.

The Education of Henry Adams (1907) ch. 20

21 Morality is a private and costly luxury.

The Education of Henry Adams (1907) ch. 22

22 Practical politics consists in ignoring facts.

The Education of Henry Adams (1907) ch. 22

23 Nothing in education is so astonishing as the amount of ignorance it accumulates in the form of inert facts.

The Education of Henry Adams (1907) ch. 25

24 Symbol or energy, the Virgin had acted as the greatest force the Western world had ever felt, and had drawn man's activities to herself more strongly

than any other power, natural or supernatural, had ever done.
The Education of Henry Adams (1907) ch. 25

1 Modern politics is, at bottom, a struggle not of men but of forces.
The Education of Henry Adams (1907) ch. 28

2 No one means all he says, and yet very few say all they mean, for words are slippery and thought is viscous.
The Education of Henry Adams (1907) ch. 31

John Adams 1735–1826

American statesman, 2nd President of the US; husband of Abigail ***Adams*** *and father of John Quincy* ***Adams***
see also ***Last Words*** *457:12*

3 The law, in all vicissitudes of government . . . will preserve a steady undeviating course; it will not bend to the uncertain wishes, imaginations, and wanton tempers of men . . . On the one hand it is inexorable to the cries of the prisoners; on the other it is deaf, deaf as an adder to the clamours of the populace.
argument in defence of the British soldiers in the Boston Massacre Trials, 4 December 1770; cf. **Sidney** 718:5

4 There is danger from all men. The only maxim of a free government ought to be to trust no man living with power to endanger the public liberty.
Notes for an Oration at Braintree (Spring 1772), in *Diary and Autobiography of John Adams* vol. 2 (1960)

5 A government of laws, and not of men.
in *Boston Gazette* (1774) no. 7, 'Novanglus' papers; later incorporated in the Massachusetts Constitution (1780); cf. **Ford** 319:13

6 I agree with you that in politics the middle way is none at all.
letter to Horatio Gates, 23 March 1776, in R. J. Taylor (ed.) *Papers of John Adams* 3rd series (1979) vol. 4

7 You bid me burn your letters. But I must forget you first.
letter to Abigail Adams, 28 April 1776

8 Yesterday, the greatest question was decided which ever was debated in America, and a greater perhaps never was nor will be decided among men. A resolution was passed without one dissenting colony, 'that these United Colonies are, and of right ought to be, free and independent States.'
letter to Abigail Adams, 3 July 1776

9 My country has in its wisdom contrived for me the most insignificant office that ever the invention of man contrived or his imagination conceived.
of the vice-presidency
letter to Abigail Adams, 19 December 1793

10 You and I ought not to die before we have explained ourselves to each other.
letter to Thomas Jefferson, 15 July 1813, in L. J. Cappon (ed.) *The Adams–Jefferson Letters* (1959) vol. 2

11 The fundamental article of my political creed is that despotism, or unlimited sovereignty, or absolute power, is the same in a majority of a popular assembly, an aristocratic council, an oligarchical junto, and a single emperor.
letter to Thomas Jefferson, 13 November 1815, in P. Wilstach (ed.) *Correspondence of John Adams and Thomas Jefferson* (1925)

12 Liberty cannot be preserved without a general knowledge among the people, who have a right . . . and a desire to know; but besides this, they have a right, an indisputable, unalienable, indefeasible, divine right to that most dreaded and envied kind of knowledge, I mean of the characters and conduct of their rulers.
A Dissertation on the Canon and Feudal Law (1765), in M. J. Kline (ed.) *Papers of John Adams* vol. 1 (1977)

13 The jaws of power are always opened to devour, and her arm is always stretched out, if possible, to destroy the freedom of thinking, speaking, and writing.
A Dissertation on the Canon and the Feudal Law (1765), in Charles Francis Adams (ed.) *Works of John Adams* (1851) vol. 3

14 The happiness of society is the end of government.
Thoughts on Government (1776)

15 Fear is the foundation of most governments.
Thoughts on Government (1776)

John Quincy Adams 1767–1848

American statesman, 6th President of the US; son of Abigail ***Adams*** *and John* ***Adams***

16 Think of your forefathers! Think of your posterity!
Oration at Plymouth 22 December 1802

17 *Fiat justitia, pereat coelum* [Let justice be done, though heaven fall]. My toast would be, may our country be always successful, but whether successful or otherwise, always right.
letter to John Adams, 1 August 1816, in A. Koch and W. Peden (eds.) *The Selected Writings of John and John Quincy Adams* (1946); cf. **Decatur** 254:10, **Mansfield** 494:10, **Mottoes** 535:8, **Schurz** 649:14, **Watson** 805:1

Samuel Adams 1722–1803

American revolutionary leader

18 What a glorious morning is this.
on hearing gunfire at Lexington, 19 April 1775; traditionally quoted as, 'What a glorious morning for America'
J. K. Hosmer *Samuel Adams* (1886) ch. 19

19 A nation of shopkeepers are very seldom so disinterested.
Oration in Philadelphia 1 August 1776 (the authenticity of this publication is doubtful); cf. **Napoleon** 539:4, **Smith** 723:10

20 We cannot make events. Our business is wisely to improve them . . . Mankind are governed more by their feelings than by reason. Events which excite those feelings will produce wonderful effects.
J. N. Rakove *The Beginnings of National Politics* (1979) ch. 5

Sarah Flower Adams 1805–48

English hymn-writer

21 Nearer, my God, to thee,
Nearer to thee!

E'en though it be a cross
That raiseth me:
Still all my song would be,
'Nearer, my God, to thee,
Nearer to thee!'

'Nearer My God to Thee' in W. G. Fox *Hymns and Anthems* (1841)

Harold Adamson 1906–80

American songwriter

1 Comin' in on a wing and a pray'r.
words derived from the contemporary comment of a war pilot, speaking from a disabled plane to ground control

title of song (1943)

Jane Addams 1860–1935

American social worker

2 The new growth in the plant swelling against the sheath, which at the same time imprisons and protects it, must still be the truest type of progress.

Democracy and Social Ethics (1907) 'Filial Relations'

3 A city is in many respects a great business corporation, but in other respects it is enlarged housekeeping . . . May we not say that city housekeeping has failed partly because women, the traditional housekeepers, have not been consulted as to its multiform activities?

Newer Ideals of Peace (1907) 'Utilization of Women in City Government'

4 Perhaps I may record here my protest against the efforts, so often made, to shield children and young people from all that has to do with death and sorrow, to give them a good time at all hazards on the assumption that the ills of life will come soon enough. Young people themselves often resent this attitude on the part of their elders; they feel set aside and belittled as if they were denied the common human experiences.

Twenty Years at Hull House (1910)

Joseph Addison 1672–1719

English poet, dramatist, and essayist; co-founder of The Spectator

on Addison: see **Johnson** *409:24,* **Pope** *583:7,* **Tickell** *777:11; see also* **Closing lines** *222:9,* **Last words** *457:3*

5 He more had pleased us, had he pleased us less.
of Abraham **Cowley**

An Account of the Greatest English Poets (1694)

6 'Twas then great Marlbro's mighty soul was proved.

The Campaign (1705) l. 279

7 And, pleased th' Almighty's orders to perform,
Rides in the whirlwind, and directs the storm.

The Campaign (1705) l. 291

8 And those who paint 'em truest praise 'em most.

The Campaign (1705) l. 476

9 'Tis not in mortals to command success,
But we'll do more, Sempronius; we'll deserve it.

Cato (1713) act 1, sc. 2, l. 43; cf. **Churchill** 215:13

10 'Tis pride, rank pride, and haughtiness of soul;
I think the Romans call it stoicism.

Cato (1713) act 1, sc. 4, l. 82

11 The pale, unripened beauties of the north.

Cato (1713) act 1, sc. 4, l. 135

12 The woman that deliberates is lost.

Cato (1713) act 4, sc. 1, l. 31

13 Curse on his virtues! they've undone his country.
Such popular humanity is treason.

Cato (1713) act 4, sc. 1, l. 205

14 What pity is it
That we can die but once to serve our country!

Cato (1713) act 4, sc. 1, l. 258; cf. **Last words** 456:8

15 Content thyself to be obscurely good.
When vice prevails, and impious men bear sway,
The post of honour is a private station.

Cato (1713) act 4, sc. 1, l. 319

16 It must be so—Plato, thou reason'st well!—
Else whence this pleasing hope, this fond desire,
This longing after immortality?
Or whence this secret dread, and inward horror,
Of falling into naught? Why shrinks the soul
Back on herself, and startles at destruction?
'Tis the divinity that stirs within us;
'Tis heaven itself, that points out an hereafter,
And intimates eternity to man.
Eternity! thou pleasing, dreadful thought!

Cato (1713) act 5, sc. 1, l. 1

17 I should think my self a very bad woman, if I had done what I do, for a farthing less.

The Drummer (1716) act 1, sc. 1

18 There is nothing more requisite in business than dispatch.

The Drummer (1716) act 5, sc. 1

19 Our Grubstreet biographers . . . watch for the death of a great man, like so many undertakers, on purpose to make a penny of him.

The Freeholder (1751) no. 35

20 Poetic fields encompass me around,
And still I seem to tread on classic ground.

Letter from Italy (1704)

21 A painted meadow, or a purling stream.

Letter from Italy (1704)

22 Music, the greatest good that mortals know,
And all of heaven we have below.

'A Song for St Cecilia's Day' (1694)

23 Should the whole frame of nature round him break,
In ruin and confusion hurled,
He, unconcerned, would hear the mighty crack,
And stand secure amidst a falling world.

translation of Horace *Odes* bk. 3, no. 3; cf. **Horace** 388:16, **Pope** 583:2

24 A reader seldom peruses a book with pleasure until he knows whether the writer of it be a black man

or a fair man, of a mild or choleric disposition, married or a bachelor.
The Spectator no. 1 (1 March 1711)

1 In all thy humours, whether grave or mellow,
Thou'rt such a touchy, testy, pleasant fellow;
Hast so much wit, and mirth, and spleen about thee,
There is no living with thee, nor without thee.
The Spectator no. 68 (18 May 1711); cf. **Martial** 498:4

2 As Sir Roger is landlord to the whole congregation, he keeps them in very good order, and will suffer nobody to sleep in it [the church] besides himself; for if by chance he has been surprised into a short nap at sermon, upon recovering out of it, he stands up, and looks about him; and if he sees anybody else nodding, either wakes them himself, or sends his servant to them.
The Spectator no. 112 (9 July 1711)

3 Sir Roger told them, with the air of a man who would not give his judgement rashly, that much might be said on both sides.
The Spectator no. 122 (20 July 1711)

4 I have often thought, says Sir Roger, it happens very well that Christmas should fall out in the Middle of Winter.
The Spectator no. 269 (8 January 1712)

5 A true critic ought to dwell rather upon excellencies than imperfections, to discover the concealed beauties of a writer, and communicate to the world such things as are worth their observation.
The Spectator no. 291 (2 February 1712); cf. **Horace** 386:4

6 These widows, Sir, are the most perverse creatures in the world.
The Spectator no. 335 (25 March 1712)

7 Mirth is like a flash of lightning that breaks through a gloom of clouds, and glitters for a moment: cheerfulness keeps up a kind of day-light in the mind.
The Spectator no. 381 (17 May 1712)

8 The Knight in the triumph of his heart made several reflections on the greatness of the British Nation; as, that one Englishman could beat three Frenchmen; that we could never be in danger of Popery so long as we took care of our fleet; that the Thames was the noblest river in Europe; that London Bridge was a greater piece of work than any of the Seven Wonders of the World; with many other honest prejudices which naturally cleave to the heart of a true Englishman.
The Spectator no. 383 (20 May 1712)

9 Wide and undetermined prospects are as pleasing to the fancy, as the speculations of eternity or infinitude are to the understanding.
The Spectator no. 412 (23 June 1712)

10 Through all Eternity to Thee
A joyful Song I'll raise,
For oh! Eternity's too short
To utter all thy Praise.
The Spectator no. 453 (9 August 1712)

11 We have in England a particular bashfulness in every thing that regards religion.
The Spectator no. 458 (15 August 1712)

12 The spacious firmament on high,
With all the blue ethereal sky,
And spangled heavens, a shining frame,
Their great Original proclaim.
The Spectator no. 465 (23 August 1712) 'Ode'

13 In Reason's ear they all rejoice,
And utter forth a glorious voice,
For ever singing, as they shine:
'The hand that made us is divine.'
The Spectator no. 465 (23 August 1712) 'Ode'

14 A woman seldom asks advice before she has bought her wedding clothes.
The Spectator no. 475 (4 September 1712)

15 Our disputants put me in mind of the skuttle fish, that when he is unable to extricate himself, blackens all the water about him, till he becomes invisible.
The Spectator no. 476 (5 September 1712)

16 If we may believe our logicians, man is distinguished from all other creatures by the faculty of laughter.
The Spectator no. 494 (26 September 1712)

17 'We are always doing', says he, 'something for Posterity, but I would fain see Posterity do something for us.'
The Spectator no. 583 (20 August 1714)

18 There is sometimes a greater judgement shewn in deviating from the rules of art, than in adhering to them; and . . . there is more beauty in the works of a great genius who is ignorant of all the rules of art, than in the works of a little genius, who not only knows but scrupulously observes them.
The Spectator no. 592 (10 September 1714); cf. **Pope** 584:14

19 I remember when our whole island was shaken with an earthquake some years ago, there was an impudent mountebank who sold pills which (as he told the country people) were very good against an earthquake.
The Tatler no. 240 (21 October 1710)

George Ade 1866–1944
American humorist and dramatist

20 After being turned down by numerous publishers, he had decided to write for posterity.
Fables in Slang (1900)

21 R-E-M-O-R-S-E!
Those dry Martinis did the work for me;
Last night at twelve I felt immense,
Today I feel like thirty cents.
My eyes are bleared, my coppers hot,
I'll try to eat, but I cannot.
It is no time for mirth and laughter,
The cold, grey dawn of the morning after.
The Sultan of Sulu (1903) act 2

1 'Whom are you?' he asked, for he had attended business college.
'The Steel Box' in *Chicago Record* 16 March 1898

Konrad Adenauer 1876–1967
German statesman, first Chancellor of the Federal Republic of Germany

2 A thick skin is a gift from God.
in *New York Times* 30 December 1959

3 It was at the Congress of Vienna, when you so foolishly put Prussia on the Rhine as a safeguard against France and another Napoleon.
identifying England's greatest mistake in its relations with Germany
answering his own question to Noel Annan in 1945; Noel Annan *Changing Enemies: the Defeat and Regeneration of Germany* (1989)

Adi Granth see **Sikh Scriptures**

Alfred Adler 1870–1937
Austrian psychologist and psychiatrist

4 The truth is often a terrible weapon of aggression. It is possible to lie, and even to murder, for the truth.
The Problems of Neurosis (1929) ch. 2

5 To be a human being means to possess a feeling of inferiority which constantly presses towards its own conquest . . . The greater the feeling of inferiority that has been experienced, the more powerful is the urge for conquest and the more violent the emotional agitation.
Heinz and Rowens Ansbacher (eds.) *The Individual Psychology of Alfred Adler* (1956) ch. 4, sect. 3

Polly Adler 1900–62
American writer

6 A house is not a home.
title of book (1954)

Theodor Adorno 1903–69
German philosopher, sociologist, and musicologist

7 It is barbarous to write a poem after Auschwitz.
I. Buruma *Wages of Guilt* (1994)

□ Advertising slogans
see box opposite

Æ (George William Russell) 1867–1935
Irish poet and essayist

8 In ancient shadows and twilights
Where childhood had strayed,
The world's great sorrows were born
And its heroes were made.
In the lost boyhood of Judas
Christ was betrayed.
'Germinal' (1931)

Aeschylus *c.*525–456 BC
Greek tragedian

9 Hell to ships, hell to men, hell to cities.
of Helen (literally 'Ship-destroyer, man-destroyer, city-destroyer')
Agamemnon

10 And from your policy do not wholly banish fear
For what man living, freed from fear, will still be just?
The Eumenides

11 Countless chuckles of the waves of the sea.
Prometheus Bound

12 Everyone's quick to blame the alien.
The Suppliant Maidens

13 The saying of the noble and glorious Aeschylus, who declared that his tragedies were large cuts taken from Homer's mighty dinners.
Athenaeus *Deipnosophistae*

Herbert Agar 1897–1980
American poet and writer

14 The truth which makes men free is for the most part the truth which men prefer not to hear.
A Time for Greatness (1942) ch. 7; cf. **Bible** 101:35

James Agate 1877–1947
British drama critic and novelist

15 Shaw's plays are the price we pay for Shaw's prefaces.
diary, 10 March 1933

16 This was an actress who, for twenty years, had the world at her feet. She kicked it away, and the ball rolled out of her reach.
of Mrs Patrick ***Campbell***
diary, 12 April 1940

17 My mind is not a bed to be made and re-made.
diary, 9 June 1943

18 A professional is a man who can do his job when he doesn't feel like it. An amateur is a man who can't do his job when he does feel like it.
diary, 19 July 1945

19 Diary-writing isn't wholly good for one . . . It leads to living for one's diary instead of living for the fun of living as ordinary people do.
letter, 7 December 1946

Agathon b. *c.*445 BC
Athenian tragic poet

20 Even a god cannot change the past.
literally 'The one thing which even God cannot do is to make undone what has been done'
Aristotle *Nicomachaean Ethics* bk. 6; cf. **Butler** 172:17

Advertising slogans

1 Access—your flexible friend.
Access credit card, 1981 onwards

2 An ace caff with quite a nice museum attached.
the Victoria and Albert Museum, February 1989

3 All human life is there.
the *News of the World*; used by Maurice Smelt in the late 1950s; cf. **James** 403:7

4 All the news that's fit to print.
motto of the *New York Times*, from 1896; coined by its proprietor Adolph S. Ochs (1858–1935)

5 American Express? . . . That'll do nicely, sir.
American Express credit card, 1970s

6 And all because the lady loves Milk Tray.
Cadbury's Milk Tray chocolates, 1968 onwards

7 Australians wouldn't give a XXXX for anything else.
Castlemaine lager, 1986 onwards

8 Beanz meanz Heinz.
Heinz baked beans, *c.*1967; coined by Maurice Drake

9 Bovril . . . Prevents that sinking feeling.
Bovril, 1920; coined by H. H. Harris (1920)

10 . . . But I know a man who can.
Automobile Association, 1980s

11 Can you tell Stork from butter?
Stork margarine, from *c.*1956

12 Cool as a mountain stream.
Consulate menthol cigarettes, early 1960s onwards

13 A diamond is forever.
De Beers Consolidated Mines, 1940s onwards; coined by Frances Gerety; cf. **Loos** 475:11

14 Does she . . . or doesn't she?
Clairol hair colouring, 1950s

15 Don't be vague, ask for Haig.
Haig whisky, *c.*1936

16 Don't forget the fruit gums, Mum.
Rowntree's Fruit gums, 1958–61

17 Drinka Pinta Milka Day.
British Milk Marketing Board, 1958; coined by Bertrand Whitehead

18 Even your closest friends won't tell you.
Listerine mouthwash, US, in *Woman's Home Companion* November 1923

19 Every picture tells a story.
advertisement for Doan's Backache Kidney Pills (early 1900s); cf. **Proverbs** 599:37

20 Full of Eastern promise.
Fry's Turkish Delight, 1950s onwards

21 Go to work on an egg.
British Egg Marketing Board, from 1957; perhaps written by Fay Weldon or Mary Gowing

22 Guinness is good for you.
reply universally given to researchers asking people why they drank Guinness
adopted by Oswald Greene, *c.*1929; cf. **Advertising slogans** 8:1

23 Happiness is a cigar called Hamlet.
Hamlet cigars; cf. **Lennon** 463:14

24 Have a break, have a Kit-Kat.
Rowntree's Kit-Kat, from *c.*1955

25 Heineken refreshes the parts other beers cannot reach.
Heineken lager, 1975 onwards; coined by Terry Lovelock

26 High o'er the fence leaps Sunny Jim
'Force' is the food that raises him.
advertising slogan for breakfast cereal (1903); coined by Minnie Hanff (1880–1942)

27 Horlicks guards against night starvation.
Horlicks malted milk drink, 1930s

28 If you want to get ahead, get a hat.
the Hat Council, 1965

29 I'm only here for the beer.
Double Diamond beer, 1971 onwards; coined by Ros Levenstein

30 It beats as it sweeps as it cleans.
Hoover vacuum cleaners, devised in 1919 by Gerald Page-Wood

31 It could be you.
British national lottery, from 1994

32 It's finger lickin' good.
Kentucky fried chicken, from 1958

33 It's good to listen.
British Telecom, from 1997

34 It's good to talk.
British Telecom, from 1994

35 It's tingling fresh. It's fresh as ice.
Gibbs toothpaste; the first advertising slogan heard on British television, 22 September 1955

36 I was a seven-stone weakling.
Charles Atlas body-building, originally in US

37 Just when you thought it was safe to go back in the water.
Jaws 2 (1978 film) advertising copy

38 Keep that schoolgirl complexion.
Palmolive soap,from 1917; coined by Charles S. Pearce

39 Kills all known germs.
Domestos bleach, 1959

40 Let the train take the strain.
British Rail, 1970 onwards

41 Let your fingers do the walking.
Bell system Telephone Directory Yellow Pages, 1960s

42 The man you love to hate.
billing for Erich von Stroheim in the film *The Heart of Humanity* (1918)

43 A Mars a day helps you work, rest and play.
Mars bar, *c.*1960 onwards

44 Maybe, just maybe.
British national lottery, from 1998

45 The mint with the hole.
Life-Savers, US, 1920; and for Rowntree's Polo mints, UK from 1947

Advertising slogans *continued*

1 My Goodness, My Guinness.
Guinness stout, 1935; coined by Dicky Richards; cf. **Advertising slogans** 7:22

2 Never knowingly undersold.
motto of the John Lewis Partnership, from *c.*1920; coined by John Spedan Lewis (1885–1963)

3 Nice one, Cyril.
taken up by supporters of Cyril Knowles, Tottenham Hotspur footballer; the Spurs team later made a record featuring the line
Wonderloaf, 1972

4 No manager ever got fired for buying IBM.
IBM

5 Oxo gives a meal man-appeal.
Oxo beef extract, *c.*1960

6 Persil washes whiter—and it shows.
Persil washing powder, 1970s

7 Put a tiger in your tank.
Esso petrol, 1964

8 Say it with flowers.
Society of American Florists, 1917, coined by Patrick O'Keefe (1872–1934)

9 Sch . . . you know who.
Schweppes mineral drinks, 1960s

10 Someone, somewhere, wants a letter from you.
British Post Office, 1960s

11 Stop me and buy one.
Wall's ice cream, from spring 1922; coined by Cecil Rodd

12 Tell Sid.
privatization of British Gas, 1986

13 They come as a boon and a blessing to men,
The Pickwick, the Owl, and the Waverley pen.
advertisement by MacNiven and H. Cameron Ltd., current by 1879; almost certainly inspired by the following:
It came as a boon and a blessing to men,
The peaceful, the pure, the victorious PEN!
J. C. Prince (1808–66) 'The Pen and the Press'

14 Things go better with Coke.
Coca-Cola, 1963

15 Top people take *The Times*.
The Times newspaper, from January 1959

16 *Vorsprung durch Technik.*
Progress through technology.
Audi motors (advertising slogan, from 1986)

17 We are the Ovaltineys,
Little [*or* Happy] girls and boys.
'We are the Ovaltineys' (song from *c.*1935); Ovaltine drink

18 We're number two. We try harder.
Avis car rentals

19 We won't make a drama out of a crisis.
Commercial Union insurance

20 Where's the beef?
Wendy's Hamburgers, from January 1984; coined by Cliff Freeman; cf. **Mondale** 526:1

21 Worth a guinea a box.
Beecham's pills, from *c.*1859, from the chance remark of a lady purchaser

22 You're never alone with a Strand.
Strand cigarettes, 1960; coined by John May

Agesilaus 444–360 BC
King of Sparta

23 Every honourable action has its proper time and season, or rather it is this propriety or observance which distinguishes an honourable action from its opposite.
Plutarch *Lives* 'Agesilaus'

Spiro T. Agnew 1918–96
American Republican politician

24 I didn't say I wouldn't go into ghetto areas. I've been in many of them and to some extent I would have to say this: If you've seen one city slum you've seen them all.
in *Detroit Free Press* 19 October 1968; cf. **Burton** 170:11

25 In the United States today, we have more than our share of the nattering nabobs of negativism.
speech in San Diego, 11 September 1970

Agnolo di Tura b. *c.*1300
Sienese chronicler

26 No one wept for the dead, because everyone expected death itself.
Rerum Italicarum scriptores; M. Meiss *Painting in Florence and Siena after the Black Death* (1951)

Bertie Ahern 1951–
Irish Fianna Fáil statesman, Taoiseach since 1997

27 If we are talking about setting up north–south bodies that are not executive and are really ad-hoc 'chat shows', then I am not in the business of negotiating.
in *Daily Telegraph* 2 April 1998

28 It is a day we should treasure. Today is about the promise of a bright future, a day when we hope a line will be drawn under the bloody past.
in *Guardian* 11 April 1998

29 This is the first time since 1918 in an act of self-determination that everyone on this island, on the one issue, has had the opportunity to pass their verdict.
opening the Fianna Fáil referendum campaign
in *Irish Times* 9 May 1998 'This Week They Said'

Maria, Marchioness of Ailesbury
d. 1902
British peeress

1 My dear, my dear, you never know when any beautiful young lady may not blossom into a Duchess!
Duke of Portland *Men, Women, and Things* (1937) ch. 3; cf. **Mitford** 524:6

Alfred Ainger 1837–1904
English lecturer

2 No flowers, by request.
summarizing the principle of conciseness for contributors to the Dictionary of National Biography
Supplement to the Dictionary of National Biography 1901–1911 (1912)

Arthur Campbell Ainger 1841–1919
English schoolmaster

3 God is working his purpose out as year succeeds to year;
God is working his purpose out and the time is drawing near;
Nearer and nearer draws the time, the time that shall surely be,
When the earth shall be filled with the glory of God as the waters cover the sea.
'God is working his purpose out' (1894 hymn); **Bible** 86:21

Max Aitken see **Lord Beaverbrook**

Mark Akenside 1721–70
English poet and physician

4 Mind, mind alone, bear witness, earth and heaven!
The living fountains in itself contains
Of beauteous and sublime.
The Pleasures of Imagination (1744) bk. 1, l. 481

5 Nor ever yet
The melting rainbow's vernal-tinctured hues
To me have shone so pleasing, as when first
The hand of science pointed out the path
In which the sun-beams gleaming from the west
Fall on the wat'ry cloud.
The Pleasures of Imagination (1744) bk. 2, l. 103

Anna Akhmatova 1889–1966
Russian poet

6 All has been looted, betrayed, sold; black death's wing flashed ahead.
'All has been Looted' (1921) (translated by Dmitri Obolensky)

7 As if I were a river
The harsh age changed my course,
Replaced one life with another,
Flowing in a different channel
And I do not recognize my shores.
'As if I were a River' (1944) (translated by Amanda Haight)

8 Memories have three epochs,
And the first is like yesterday.
The soul is under their blessed vault,
and the body is in the bliss of their shadow.
Northern Elegies (1953) (translated by Richard McKane)

9 It was a time when only the dead smiled, happy in their peace.
Requiem (1935–40) (translated by Richard McKane)

10 Stars of death stood over us,
and innocent Russia squirmed
under the bloody boots,
under the wheels of black Marias.
Requiem (1935–40) (translated by Richard McKane)

11 I'd like to name the names of all that host
but they snatched up the list and now it's lost.
I've woven them a garment that's prepared
out of poor words, those that I overheard,
and will hold fast to every word and glance
all of my days, even in new mischance.
Requiem (1935–40) (translated by Stanley Kunitz and Max Hayward)

12 In the young century's cool nursery,
In its chequered silence, I was born.
'Willow' (1940)

Zoë Akins 1886–1958
American poet and dramatist

13 The Greeks had a word for it.
title of play (1930)

William Alabaster 1567–1640
English divine and Latin poet

14 Tell them, my soul, the fears that make me quake:
The smouldering brimstone and the burning lake,
Life feeding death, death ever life devouring,
Torments not moved, unheard, yet still roaring,
God lost, hell found,—ever, never begun.
Now bid me into flame from smoke to run!
'Away, fear, with thy projects' (written 1597–8)

Alain (Émile-Auguste Chartier) 1868–1951
French poet and philosopher

15 *Rien n'est plus dangereux qu'une idée, quand on n'a qu'une idée.*
Nothing is more dangerous than an idea, when you have only one idea.
Propos sur la religion (1938) no. 74

Alain-Fournier (Henri Alban) 1886–1914
French novelist

16 *Mais quelqu'un est venu qui m'a enlevé à tous ces plaisirs d'enfant paisible. Quelqu'un a soufflé la bougie qui éclairait pour moi le doux visage maternel penché sur le repas du soir. Quelqu'un a éteint la lampe autour de laquelle nous étions une famille heureuse, à la nuit, lorsque mon père avait accroché les volets de bois aux portes vitrées. Et celui-là, ce fut Augustin Meaulnes, que les autres élèves appelèrent bientôt le grand Meaulnes.*

But someone came and put an end to these mild and childish pleasures. Someone blew out the candle which illumined for me the sweet maternal face bent over the evening meal. Someone extinguished the lamp around which we had been a happy family group at night-time when my father had closed all the wooden shutters. And that someone was Augustin Meaulnes, whom in no time the other boys began to call le grand Meaulnes.

Le Grand Meaulnes (1912) pt. 1, ch. 2 (translated by Frank Davison)

1 *Quand on a, disait-il, commis quelque lourde faute impardonnable, on songe parfois, au milieu d'une grande amertume: 'Il y a pourtant par le monde des gens qui me pardonneraient'. On imagine de vieilles gens, des grandparents pleins d'indulgence, qui sont persuadés à l'avance que tout ce que vous faites est bien fait.*

When you've done something inexcusable, you try to ease your conscience by telling yourself that someone, somewhere would forgive you. You think of old people, perhaps indulgent grandparents, who are convinced that whatever you do is right.

Le Grand Meaulnes (1912) pt. 1, ch. 14

2 *Notre aventure est finie. L'hiver de cette année est mort comme la tombe. Peut-être quand nous mourrons, peut-être la mort seule nous donnera la clef et la suite et la fin de cette aventure manquée.*

Our adventure is ended. The winter of this year is as dead as the grave. Perhaps when we come to die, death will provide the meaning and the sequel and the ending of this unsuccessful adventure.

Le Grand Meaulnes (1912) pt. 2, ch. 12

3 *Un homme qui a fait une fois un bond dans le paradis, comment pourrait-il s'accommoder ensuite de la vie de tout le monde?*

How can a man who has once strayed into Heaven ever hope to make terms with the earth!

Le Grand Meaulnes (1912) pt. 3, ch. 4

4 *C'est d'abord comme une voix tremblante qui, de très loin, ose à peine chanter sa joie . . . Cet air que je ne connais pas, c'est aussi une prière, une supplication au bonheur de ne pas être trop cruel, un salut et comme un agenouillement devant le bonheur.*

It is at first like some far-away tentative voice intimidated by an excess of joy . . . This melody, which I've never heard before, is a kind of prayer to happiness, an entreaty asking fate not to be too cruel, a salutation to happiness and at the same time a genuflexion.

Le Grand Meaulnes (1912) pt. 3, ch. 7

Edward Albee 1928–

American dramatist

5 I have a fine sense of the ridiculous, but no sense of humour.

Who's Afraid of Virginia Woolf? (1962) act 1

Prince Albert (Albert Francis Charles Augustus Emmanuel of Saxe-Coburg-Gotha) 1819–61

Consort of Queen ***Victoria*** *from 1840*

on Albert: see ***Tennyson*** *759:11,* ***Victoria*** *792:2*

6 The works of art, by being publicly exhibited and offered for sale, are becoming articles of trade, following as such the unreasoning laws of markets and fashion; and public and even private patronage is swayed by their tyrannical influence.

speech at the Royal Academy Dinner, 3 May 1851, in *Addresses* (1857)

Scipione Alberti

7 *I pensieri stretti ed il viso sciolto* [Secret thoughts and open countenance] will go safely over the whole world.

letter from Henry Wotton to John Milton, 13 April 1638, prefixed to *Comus* in Milton *Poems* (1645 ed.)

Mary Alcock *c.*1742–98

English poet

8 A masquerade, a murdered peer,
His throat just cut from ear to ear—
A rake turned hermit—a fond maid
Run mad, by some false loon betrayed—
These stores supply the female pen,
Which writes them o'er and o'er again,
And readers likewise may be found
To circulate them round and round.

'A Receipt for Writing a Novel' l. 65

Louisa May Alcott 1832–88

American novelist

see also ***Opening lines*** *555:11*

9 I am angry nearly every day of my life . . . but I have learned not to show it; and I still hope to learn not to feel it, though it may take me another forty years to do so.

Little Women (1868–9) ch. 8

Alcuin *c.*735–804

English scholar and theologian

10 *Nec audiendi qui solent dicere, Vox populi, vox Dei, quum tumultuositas vulgi semper insaniae proxima sit.*

And those people should not be listened to who keep saying the voice of the people is the voice of God, since the riotousness of the crowd is always very close to madness.

letter 164 in *Works* (1863) vol. 1; cf. **Pope** 586:15, **Proverbs** 613:35, **Sherman** 716:26

Richard Aldington 1892–1962

English poet, novelist, and biographer

11 Patriotism is a lively sense of collective responsibility. Nationalism is a silly cock crowing on its own dunghill.

The Colonel's Daughter (1931) pt. 1, ch. 6

Brian Aldiss 1925–
English science fiction writer
see also **Closing lines** *222:16*

1 Science Fiction is no more written for scientists than ghost stories are written for ghosts.
introduction to *Penguin Science Fiction* (1962)

Henry Aldrich 1647–1710
English scholar; Dean of Christ Church, Oxford, from 1689

2 If all be true that I do think,
There are five reasons we should drink;
Good wine—a friend—or being dry—
Or lest we should be by and by—
Or any other reason why.
'Reasons for Drinking' (1689)

Thomas Bailey Aldrich 1836–1907
American writer

3 The fair, frail palaces,
The fading alps and archipelagoes,
And great cloud-continents of sunset-seas.
'Miracles' (1874)

'Buzz' Aldrin (Edwin Eugene Aldrin Jnr) 1930–
American astronaut; second man on the moon

4 Beautiful! Beautiful! Magnificent desolation.
of the lunar landscape
on the first moon walk, 20 July 1969

Alexander the Great 356–323 BC
King of Macedon from 336 BC
see also **Diogenes** *268:1*

5 If I were not Alexander, I would be Diogenes.
Plutarch *Parallel Lives* 'Alexander' ch. 14, sect. 3

6 Is it not worthy of tears that, when the number of worlds is infinite, we have not yet become lords of a single one?
when asked why he wept on hearing from Anaxarchus that there was an infinite number of worlds
Plutarch *Moralia* 'On Tranquillity of the Mind'

Alexander II ('the Liberator') 1818–81
Tsar of Russia from 1855

7 Better to abolish serfdom from above than to wait till it begins to abolish itself from below.
speech in Moscow, 30 March 1856

Cecil Frances Alexander 1818–95
Irish poet and hymn writer

8 All things bright and beautiful,
All creatures great and small,
All things wise and wonderful,
The Lord God made them all.
'All Things Bright and Beautiful' (1848)

9 The rich man in his castle,
The poor man at his gate,
God made them, high or lowly,
And ordered their estate.
'All Things Bright and Beautiful' (1848)

10 Once in royal David's city
Stood a lowly cattle-shed,
Where a mother laid her baby
In a manger for his bed:
Mary was that mother mild,
Jesus Christ her little child.
'Once in royal David's city' (1848)

11 I bind unto myself to-day
The strong name of the Trinity,
By invocation of the same
The Three in One and One in Three.
'St Patrick's Breastplate' (1889); cf. **Patrick** 570:2

12 There is a green hill far away,
Without a city wall,
Where the dear Lord was crucified,
Who died to save us all.
'There is a green hill far away' (1848)

William Alexander, Lord Stirling *c.*1567–1640
Scottish poet and courtier

13 The weaker sex, to piety more prone.
'Doomsday' 5th Hour (1637)

Alfonso 'the Wise' 1221–84
King of Castile and León from 1252

14 Had I been present at the Creation, I would have given some useful hints for the better ordering of the universe.
on studying the Ptolemaic system
attributed

Alfred the Great AD 849–99
King of Wessex from AD 871

15 *Ða ic ða gemunde hu sio lar Lædengeðiodes ær ðissum afeallen wæs giond Angelcynn, ond ðeah monige cuðon Englisc gewrit arædan, ða ongan ic on gemang oðrum mislicum ond manigfealdum bisgum ðisses kynerices ða boc on Englisc ðe is genemned on Læden* Pastoralis, *ond on Englisc* Hierdeboc, *hwilum word be worde, hwilum andgit of andgite.*

When I recalled how knowledge of Latin had previously decayed throughout England, and yet many could still read things written in English, I then began, amidst the various and multifarious afflictions of this kingdom, to translate into English the book which in Latin is called *Pastoralis*, in English 'Shepherd-book', sometimes word for word, sometimes sense for sense.
preface to the Anglo-Saxon version of St Gregory's *Pastoral Care* (translated by S. Keynes and M. Lapidge, 1983)

Nelson Algren 1909–
American novelist

16 A walk on the wild side.
title of novel (1956)

1 Never play cards with a man called Doc. Never eat at a place called Mom's. Never sleep with a woman whose troubles are worse than your own.
in *Newsweek* 2 July 1956

Ali ibn-Abi-Talib *c.*602–661
fourth Islamic caliph

2 He who has a thousand friends has not a friend to spare,
And he who has one enemy will meet him everywhere.
A Hundred Sayings

Muhammad Ali (Cassius Clay) 1942–
American boxer

3 I'm the greatest.
adopted as his catchphrase from 1962, in *Louisville Times* 16 November 1962

4 Float like a butterfly, sting like a bee.
summary of his boxing strategy (probably originated by his aide Drew 'Bundini' Brown)
G. Sullivan *Cassius Clay Story* (1964) ch. 8

5 I ain't got no quarrel with the Viet Cong.
refusing to be drafted to fight in Vietnam
at a press conference in Miami, Florida, February 1966

Abbé d'Allainval 1700–53
French dramatist

6 *L'embarras des richesses.*
The embarrassment of riches.
title of comedy (1726)

Fred Allen (John Florence Sullivan) 1894–1956
American humorist

7 Committee—a group of men who individually can do nothing but as a group decide that nothing can be done.
attributed

William Allen see **Last words**

Woody Allen (Allen Stewart Konigsberg) 1935–
American film director, writer, and actor

8 That was the most fun I ever had without laughing.
of sex
Annie Hall (1977 film, with Marshall Brickman)

9 Don't knock masturbation. It's sex with someone I love.
Annie Hall (1977 film, with Marshall Brickman)

10 Is sex dirty? Only if it's done right.
Everything You Always Wanted to Know about Sex (1972 film)

11 If it turns out that there is a God, I don't think that he's evil. But the worst that you can say about him is that basically he's an underachiever.
Love and Death (1975 film)

12 My brain? It's my second favourite organ.
Sleeper (1973 film, with Marshall Brickman)

13 A fast word about oral contraception. I asked a girl to go to bed with me and she said 'no'.
Woody Allen Volume Two (Colpix CP 488) side 4, band 6

14 It's not that I'm afraid to die. I just don't want to be there when it happens.
Death (1975)

15 If only God would give me some clear sign! Like making a large deposit in my name at a Swiss bank.
'Selections from the Allen Notebooks' in *New Yorker* 5 November 1973

16 On bisexuality: It immediately doubles your chances for a date on Saturday night.
in *New York Times* 1 December 1975

17 I don't want to achieve immortality through my work . . . I want to achieve it through not dying.
Eric Lax *Woody Allen and his Comedy* (1975) ch. 12

18 I recently turned sixty. Practically a third of my life is over.
in *Observer* 10 March 1996 'Sayings of the Week'

Isabel Allende 1942–
Chilean novelist

19 I repent of my diets, the delicious dishes rejected out of vanity, as much as I lament the opportunities for making love that I let go by because of pressing tasks or puritanical virtue.
in *The Times* 25 April 1998

Svetlana Alliluyeva 1925–
daughter of Joseph ***Stalin***

20 He is gone, but his shadow still stands over all of us. It still dictates to us and we, very often, obey.
of her father, Joseph ***Stalin***
Twenty Letters to a Friend (1967)

William Allingham 1824–89
Irish poet

21 Up the airy mountain,
Down the rushy glen,
We daren't go a-hunting,
For fear of little men.
'The Fairies' (1850)

St Alphonsus (Alfonso Maria de' Liguori) 1696–1787
Italian theologian, founder of the Redemptorists

22 O Mother blest, whom God bestows
On sinners and on just,
What joy, what hope thou givest those
Who in thy mercy trust!
'O Mother Blest', translated by E. Vaughan

Joseph Alsop b. 1910
American journalist

23 Gratitude, like love, is never a dependable international emotion.
in *Observer* 30 November 1952

Robert Altman 1922–
American film director

1 What's a cult? It just means not enough people to make a minority.
in *Guardian* 11 April 1981

Luis Walter Alvarez 1911–88
American physicist

2 There is no democracy in physics. We can't say that some second-rate guy has as much right to opinion as Fermi.
D. S. Greenberg *The Politics of Pure Science* (1969)

St Ambrose *c.*339–97
French-born bishop of Milan
see also **Prayers** 592:7

3 *Ubi Petrus, ibi ergo ecclesia.*
Where Peter is, there must be the Church.
'Explanatio psalmi 40' in *Corpus Scriptorum Ecclesiasticorum Latinorum* (1919) vol. 64

4 *Cum Romanum venio, ieiuno Sabbato; cum hic sum, non ieiuno: sic etiam tu, ad quam forte ecclesiam veneris, eius morem serva, si cuiquam non vis esse scandalum nec quemquam tibi.*
When I go to Rome, I fast on Saturday, but here [Milan] I do not. Do you also follow the custom of whatever church you attend, if you do not want to give or receive scandal.
St Augustine: Letters vol. 1 (translated by Sister W. Parsons, 1951) 'Letter 54 to Januarius' (AD *c.*400); cf. **Proverbs** 614:22

Leo Amery 1873–1955
British Conservative politician

5 For twenty years he has held a season-ticket on the line of least resistance and has gone wherever the train of events has carried him, lucidly justifying his position at whatever point he has happened to find himself.
of Herbert **Asquith**
in *Quarterly Review* July 1914

6 Speak for England.
to Arthur Greenwood in the House of Commons, 2 September 1939; see **Boothby** 142:20

7 I will quote certain other words. I do it with great reluctance, because I am speaking of those who are old friends and associates of mine, but they are words which, I think, are applicable to the present situation. This is what Cromwell said to the Long Parliament when he thought it was no longer fit to conduct the affairs of the nation: 'You have sat too long here for any good you have been doing. Depart, I say, and let us have done with you. In the name of God, go.'
speech, House of Commons, 7 May 1940; cf. **Cromwell** 254:14

Fisher Ames 1758–1808
American politician

8 A monarchy is a merchantman which sails well, but will sometimes strike on a rock, and go to the bottom; whilst a republic is a raft which would never sink, but then your feet are always in the water.
attributed to Ames, speaking in the House of Representatives, 1795; quoted by R. W. Emerson in *Essays* (2nd series, 1844) no. 7, but not traced in Ames's speeches

Hardy Amies 1909–
English couturier

9 It is totally impossible to be well dressed in cheap shoes.
The Englishman's Suit (1994)

10 She is only 5ft 4in, and to make someone that height look regal is difficult. Fortunately she holds herself very well.
of the Queen
interview in *Sunday Telegraph* 9 February 1997

Kingsley Amis 1922–95
English novelist and poet

11 If there's one word that sums up everything that's gone wrong since the War, it's Workshop.
Jake's Thing (1979) ch. 14

12 His mouth had been used as a latrine by some small creature of the night, and then as its mausoleum.
Lucky Jim (1953) ch. 6

13 Alun's life was coming to consist more and more exclusively of being told at dictation speed what he knew.
The Old Devils (1986) ch. 7

14 Outside every fat man there was an even fatter man trying to close in.
One Fat Englishman (1963) ch. 3; cf. **Connolly** 234:1, **Orwell** 558:9

15 He was of the faith chiefly in the sense that the church he currently did not attend was Catholic.
One Fat Englishman (1963) ch. 8

16 Should poets bicycle-pump the human heart
Or squash it flat?
Man's love is of man's life a thing apart;
Girls aren't like that.
'A Bookshop Idyll' (1956); cf. **Byron** 176:7

17 We men have got love well weighed up; our stuff
Can get by without it.
Women don't seem to think that's good enough;
They write about it.
'A Bookshop Idyll' (1956)

18 Women are really much nicer than men:
No wonder we like them.
'A Bookshop Idyll' (1956)

19 Death has got something to be said for it:
There's no need to get out of bed for it;
Wherever you may be,
They bring it to you, free.
'Delivery Guaranteed' (1979)

20 The delusion that there are thousands of young people about who are capable of benefiting from university training, but have somehow failed to

find their way there, is . . . a necessary component of the expansionist case . . . More will mean worse.
in *Encounter* July 1960

1 If you can't annoy somebody with what you write, I think there's little point in writing.
in *Radio Times* 1 May 1971

2 A bad review may spoil your breakfast but you shouldn't allow it to spoil your lunch.
Giles Gordon *Aren't We Due a Royalty Statement?* (1993); attributed

3 No pleasure is worth giving up for the sake of two more years in a geriatric home in Weston-super-Mare.
in *The Times* 21 June 1994; attributed

Martin Amis 1949–
English novelist

4 To be more interested in the writer than the writing is just eternal human vulgarity.
on BBC2 *Bookmark*, 9 March 1996

5 You are living in a land you no longer recognize. You don't know the language.
on his 'cataclysmic mid-life crisis'
in *Times* 21 August 1997

Anacharsis
Scythian prince of the sixth century BC

6 Written laws are like spiders' webs; they will catch, it is true, the weak and poor, but would be torn in pieces by the rich and powerful.
Plutarch *Parallel Lives* 'Solon' bk. 5, sect. 2; cf. **Shenstone** 715:7, **Swift** 747:14

Anatolius
8th-century hymn-writer

7 Fierce was the wild billow,
Dark was the night;
Oars laboured heavily,
Foam glimmered white;
Trembled the mariners,
Peril was nigh:
Then said the God of God,
'Peace! it is I.'
'Fierce was the wild billow' (translated by John Mason Neale, 1862)

Hans Christian Andersen 1805–75
Danish novelist and writer of fairy stories

8 The Emperor's new clothes.
title of story in *Danish Fairy Legends and Tales* (1846)

9 'But the Emperor has nothing on at all!' cried a little child.
Danish Fairy Legends and Tales (1846) 'The Emperor's New Clothes'

Maxwell Anderson 1888–1959
American dramatist

10 But it's a long, long while
From May to December;
And the days grow short
When you reach September.
'September Song' (1938 song)

Maxwell Anderson 1888–1959 and Lawrence Stallings 1894–1968
American dramatists

11 What price glory?
title of play (1924)

Robert Anderson 1917–
American dramatist

12 Tea and sympathy.
title of play (1957)

Lancelot Andrewes 1555–1626
English preacher and writer of sermons; bishop, successively, of Chichester, Ely, and Winchester

13 What shall become of me (said Righteousness)? What use of Justice, if God will do no justice, if he spare sinners? And what use of me (saith Mercy), if he spare them not? Hard hold there was, inasmuch as, *Perii, nisi homo moriatur* (said Righteousness) I die, if he die not: And *Perii, nisi Misericordiam consequature* (said Mercy) if he die, I die too.
Of the Nativity (1616) Sermon 11; cf. **Milton** 516:2

14 *Verbum infans*, the Word without a word, not able to speak a word . . . He, that . . . taketh the vast body of the main Sea, turns it to and fro, as a little child, and rolls it about with the swaddling bands of darkness; He, to come thus into clouts, himself!
Of the Nativity (1618) Sermon 12

15 It was no summer progress. A cold coming they had of it, at this time of the year; just, the worst time of the year, to take a journey, and specially a long journey, in. The ways deep, the weather sharp, the days short, the sun farthest off *in solstitio brumali*, the very dead of Winter.
Of the Nativity (1622) Sermon 15; cf. **Eliot** 294:27

Norman Angell 1872–1967
English pacifist

16 The great illusion.
on the futility of war
title of book (1910), first published as 'Europe's optical illusion' (1909)

Maya Angelou 1928–
American writer
see also **Dunbar** *285:2*

17 Children's talent to endure stems from their ignorance of alternatives.
I Know Why The Caged Bird Sings (1969) ch.17

18 The sadness of the women's movement is that they don't allow the necessity of love. See, I don't personally trust any revolution where love is not allowed.
in *California Living* 14 May 1975

Noel Annan 1916–
English historian and writer

1 The day of the jewelled epigram is passed and, whether one likes it or not, one is moving into the stern puritanical era of the four-letter word.
in the House of Lords, 1966; George Greenfield *Scribblers for Bread* (1989)

2 The cardinal virtue was no longer to love one's country. It was to feel compassion for one's fellow men and women.
of his own generation
Our Age (1990)

Anne, Princess Royal 1950–
British princess; daughter of **Elizabeth II**

3 I don't work that way . . . The very idea that all children want to be cuddled by a complete stranger, I find completely amazing.
on her work for Save the Children
in *Daily Telegraph* 17 January 1998

Anonymous
ENGLISH

4 An abomination unto the Lord, but a very present help in time of trouble.
definition of a lie
an amalgamation of Proverbs 12.22 and Psalms 46.1, often attributed to Adlai **Stevenson**; Bill Adler *The Stevenson Wit* (1966); cf. **Bible** 82:26, **Book of Common Prayer** 134:18

5 Adam
Had 'em.
on the antiquity of microbes
noted as an example of a short poem

6 All human beings are born free and equal in dignity and rights.
Universal Declaration of Human Rights (1948) article 1

7 The almighty dollar is the only object of worship.
Philadelphia Public Ledger 2 December 1836

8 Along the electric wire the message came:
He is not better—he is much the same.
parodic poem on the illness of the Prince of Wales, later King **Edward VII**
F. H. Gribble *Romance of the Cambridge Colleges* (1913); sometimes attributed to Alfred Austin (1835–1913), Poet Laureate

9 And they lived happily ever after.
traditional ending to a fairy story
recorded (with slight variations) from the 1850s

10 Anyone here been raped and speaks English?
shouted by a British TV reporter in a crowd of Belgian civilians waiting to be airlifted out of the Belgian Congo, c.1960
Edward Behr *Anyone Here been Raped and Speaks English?* (1981)

11 Appeal from Philip drunk to Philip sober.
paraphrase of the words of an unidentified woman in Valerius Maximus *Facta ac Dicta Memorabilia* (AD *c.*32) bk. 6, ch. 2

12 Back and side go bare, go bare,
Both foot and hand go cold:
But belly God send thee good ale enough,
Whether it be new or old.
Gammer Gurton's Needle (1575) act 2 'Song', the play being attributed to William Stevenson (*c.*1530–75) and also to John Still (1543–1608), the song possibly of earlier origin

13 A beast, but a just beast.
a schoolboy's description of Dr Temple, Headmaster of Rugby School
F.E. Kitchener *Rugby Memoir of Archbishop Temple 1857–1869* (1907) ch. 3

14 The best defence against the atom bomb is not to be there when it goes off.
contributor to *British Army Journal*, in *Observer* 20 February 1949

15 Bigamy is having one husband too many. Monogamy is the same.
Erica Jong *Fear of Flying* (1973) ch. 1 (epigraph)

16 Cathedral time is five minutes later than standard time.
order of service leaflet, Christ Church Cathedral, Oxford

17 The cloud of unknowing.
title of mystical prose work (14th century)

18 Collapse of Stout Party.
supposed standard dénouement in Victorian humour
R. Pearsall *Collapse of Stout Party* (1975) introduction

19 A committee is a group of the unwilling, chosen from the unfit, to do the unnecessary.
various attributions (origin unknown)

20 A community in which power, wealth and opportunity are in the hands of the many not the few, where the rights we enjoy reflect the duties we owe . . . in which the enterprise of the market and the rigour of competition are joined with the forces of partnership and cooperation.
new Clause Four of the Labour Party constitution, passed at a special conference 29 April 1995; cf. **Anonymous** 19:9

21 A Company for carrying on an undertaking of Great Advantage, but no one to know what it is.
The South Sea Company Prospectus (1711), in Virginia Cowles *The Great Swindle* (1963) ch. 5

22 [Death is] nature's way of telling you to slow down.
American life insurance proverb, in *Newsweek* 25 April 1960

23 Do not fold, spindle or mutilate.
instruction on punched cards (found in this form in the 1950s, and in differing forms from the 1930s)

24 Do not stand at my grave and weep:
I am not there. I do not sleep.
I am a thousand winds that blow.
I am the diamond glints on snow.
I am the gentle autumn's rain.
When you awaken in the morning's hush,
I am the swift uplifting rush
Of quiet birds in circled flight.
I am the soft stars that shine at night.
Do not stand at my grave and cry;
I am not there, I did not die.
quoted in letter left by British soldier Stephen Cummins when killed by the IRA, March 1989
origin uncertain; attributed to various authors

1 Earned a precarious living by taking in one another's washing.
attributed to Mark **Twain** by William **Morris**, in *The Commonweal* 6 August 1887

2 The eternal triangle.
book review title, in *Daily Chronicle* 5 December 1907

3 Every country has its own constitution; ours is absolutism moderated by assassination.
Ernst Friedrich Herbert, Count Münster, quoting 'an intelligent Russian', in *Political Sketches of the State of Europe, 1814–1867* (1868)

4 Everyman, I will go with thee, and be thy guide,
In thy most need to go by thy side.
spoken by Knowledge
Everyman (*c.*1509–19) l. 522

5 Expletive deleted.
in *Submission of Recorded Presidential Conversations to the Committee on the Judiciary of the House of Representatives by President Richard M. Nixon* 30 April 1974, appendix 1

6 Exterminate . . . the treacherous English, walk over General French's contemptible little army.
allegedly a copy of Orders issued by the Kaiser ***Wilhelm II*** *but most probably fabricated by the British*
annexe to BEF [British Expeditionary Force] Routine Orders of 24 September 1914, in Arthur Ponsonby *Falsehood in Wartime* (1928) ch. 10; cf. **Cromwell** 245:18

7 Faster than a speeding bullet! . . . Look! Up in the sky! It's a bird! It's a plane! It's Superman! Yes, it's Superman! Strange visitor from another planet . . . Who can change the course of mighty rivers, bend steel with his bare hands, and who—disguised as Clark Kent, mild-mannered reporter for a great metropolitan newspaper—fights a never ending battle for truth, justice and the American way!
Superman (US radio show, 1940 onwards) preamble

8 The fault is great in man or woman
Who steals a goose from off a common;
But what can plead that man's excuse
Who steals a common from a goose?
in *The Tickler Magazine* 1 February 1821

9 A form of statuary which no careful father would wish his daughter, or no discerning young man his fiancée, to see.
on Jacob ***Epstein****'s sculptures for the former BMA building in the Strand, London*
in *Evening Standard* 19 June 1908

10 A gentleman haranguing on the perfection of our law, and that it was equally open to the poor and the rich, was answered by another, 'So is the London Tavern'.
Tom Paine's Jests (1794) no. 23; also attributed to John Horne Tooke (1736–1812) in W. Hazlitt *The Spirit of the Age* (1825) 'Mr Horne Tooke'; cf. **Mathew** 501:12

11 Good at a fight, but better at a play,
Godlike in giving, but—the devil to pay!
lines written on a cast from ***Sheridan****'s hand*
Thomas Moore *Memoirs of the Life of . . . Richard Brinsley Sheridan* (1825) ch. 21

12 Great Chatham with his sabre drawn
Stood waiting for Sir Richard Strachan;
Sir Richard, longing to be at 'em,
Stood waiting for the Earl of Chatham.
'At Walcheren, 1809'; attributed to Joseph Jekyll (1753–1837)

13 Have you heard? The Prime Minister has resigned and Northcliffe has sent for the King.
joke circulating in 1919, suggesting that Lord ***Northcliffe***, ***Lloyd George****'s implacable enemy, would succeed him as Prime Minister*
Hamilton Fyfe *Northcliffe, an Intimate Biography* (1930) ch. 16

14 He may be one of its [the Church's] buttresses, but certainly not one of its pillars, for he is never found within it.
of John Scott, Lord Eldon (1751–1838)
H. Twiss *Public and Private Life of Eldon* (1844) vol. 3 (later attributed to Lord **Melbourne**)

15 He talked shop like a tenth muse.
on ***Gladstone****'s Budget speeches*
G. W. E. Russell *Collections and Recollections* (1898) ch. 12

16 He tickles this age that can
Call Tullia's ape a marmasyte
And Leda's goose a swan.
'Fara diddle dyno', in Thomas Weelkes *Airs or Fantastic Spirits* (1608); reprinted in N. Ault *Elizabethan Lyrics* (1925)

17 Hierusalem, my happy home
When shall I come to thee?
When shall my sorrows have an end,
Thy joys when shall I see?
'Hierusalem' (*c.*1600 hymn)

18 How different, how very different from the home life of our own dear Queen!
comment overheard at a performance of Cleopatra by Sarah Bernhardt
Irvin S. Cobb *A Laugh a Day* (1924) (probably apocryphal)

19 Icham of Irlaunde
Ant of the holy londe of irlonde
Gode sir pray ich ye
for of saynte charite,
come ant daunce wyt me,
in irlaunde.
fourteenth century

20 I don't like the family Stein!
There is Gert, there is Ep, there is Ein.
Gert's writings are punk,
Ep's statues are junk,
Nor can anyone understand Ein.
rhyme current in the US in the 1920s; R. Graves and A. Hodge *The Long Weekend* (1940) ch. 12

21 I feel no pain dear mother now
But oh, I am so dry!
O take me to a brewery
And leave me there to die.
parody of 'The Collier's Dying Child'; cf. **Farmer** 307:2

22 If you really want to make a million . . . the quickest way is to start your own religion.
previously attributed to L. Ron Hubbard (1911–86) in B. Corydon and L. Ron Hubbard Jr. *L. Ron Hubbard* (1987), but attribution subsequently rejected by L. Ron Hubbard Jr., who also dissociated himself from this book

1 I'm armed with more than complete steel—The justice of my quarrel.

Lust's Dominion (1657) act 4, sc. 3 (attributed to **Marlowe**, though of doubtful authorship)

2 In Affectionate Remembrance
of
ENGLISH CRICKET,
Which Died at The Oval
on
29th August, 1882.
Deeply lamented by a large circle of
sorrowing friends and acquaintances.
R. I. P.
N. B.—The body will be cremated and
the ashes taken to Australia.

following England's defeat by the Australians

in *Sporting Times* September 1882

3 I saw my lady weep,
And Sorrow proud to be exalted so
In those fair eyes where all perfections keep.
Her face was full of woe;
But such a woe, believe me, as wins more hearts,
Than Mirth can do with her enticing parts.

lute song set by John Dowland, in *New Oxford Book of Sixteenth-Century Verse* (1991)

4 It became necessary to destroy the town to save it.

statement by unidentified US Army Major, referring to Ben Tre in Vietnam

in Associated Press Report, *New York Times* 8 February 1968

5 It's taking your face in your hands.

on the dangers of sitting for one's portrait to John Singer **Sargent**

W. Graham Robertson *Time Was* (1931) ch. 21

6 Jacques Brel is alive and well and living in Paris.

title of musical entertainment (1968–72) which triggered numerous imitations

7 Liberty is always unfinished business.

title of 36th Annual Report of the American Civil Liberties Union, 1 July 1955–30 June 1956

8 Like Caesar's wife, all things to all men.

impartiality, as described by a newly-elected mayor

G. W. E. Russell *Collections and Recollections* (1898) ch. 30; cf. **Caesar** 180:17

9 Little Englanders.

term applied to anti-imperialists

in *Westminster Gazette* 1 August 1895; in *Pall Mall Gazette* 16 September 1884 the phrase 'believe in a little England' occurs

10 Lizzie Borden took an axe
And gave her mother forty whacks;
When she saw what she had done
She gave her father forty-one!

after the acquittal of Lizzie Borden, in June 1893, from the charge of murdering her father and stepmother at Fall River, Massachusetts on 4 August 1892

popular rhyme

11 Lloyd George knew my father,
My father knew Lloyd George.

two-line comic song, sung to the tune of 'Onward, Christian Soldiers' and possibly by Tommy Rhys Roberts (1910–75)

12 London, thou art of townes *A per se*.

'London' (poem of unknown authorship, previously attributed to William Dunbar, *c.*1465–*c.*1530)

13 London, thou art the flower of cities all!
Gemme of all joy, jasper of jocunditie.

'London' l. 16

14 Love me little, love me long,
Is the burden of my song.

'Love me little, love me long' (1569–70)

15 CHILD: Mamma, are Tories born wicked, or do they grow wicked afterwards?
MOTHER: They are born wicked, and grow worse.

G. W. E. Russell *Collections and Recollections* (1898) ch. 10

16 The ministry of all the talents.

name given ironically to William Grenville's coalition of 1806, and also applied to later coalitions

G. W. Cooke *The History of Party* (1837) vol. 3

17 Miss Buss and Miss Beale
Cupid's darts do not feel.
How different from us,
Miss Beale and Miss Buss.

of the Headmistress of the North London Collegiate School and the Principal of the Ladies' College, Cheltenham

rhyme, *c.*1884

18 Most Gracious Queen, we thee implore
To go away and sin no more,
But if that effort be too great,
To go away at any rate.

epigram on Caroline of Brunswick, wife of **George IV**

letter from Francis Burton to Lord Colchester, 15 November 1820; in *Diary and Correspondence of Lord Colchester* (1861) vol. 3

19 Multiplication is vexation,
Division is as bad;
The Rule of Three doth puzzle me,
And Practice drives me mad.

Lean's Collectanea vol. 4 (1904) (possibly 16th-century)

20 My name is George Nathaniel Curzon,
I am a most superior person.

of Lord **Curzon**

The Masque of Balliol (*c.*1870), in W. G. Hiscock *The Balliol Rhymes* (1939); cf. **Beeching** 61:9, **Spring-Rice** 735:9

21 The nature of God is a circle of which the centre is everywhere and the circumference is nowhere.

said to have been traced to a lost treatise of Empedocles; quoted in the *Roman de la Rose*, and by St Bonaventura in *Itinerarius Mentis in Deum* ch. 5, closing line

22 The nearest thing to death in life
Is David Patrick Maxwell Fyfe,
Though underneath that gloomy shell
He does himself extremely well.

on Lord **Kilmuir**

E. Grierson *Confessions of a Country Magistrate* (1972), said to have been current on the Northern circuit in the late 1930s

23 No beauty she doth miss,
When all her robes are on;
But beauty's self she is,
When all her robes are gone.

'Madrigal', in F. Davison (ed.) *Poetical Rhapsody* (1602)

1 The noise, my dear! And the people!
of the retreat from Dunkirk, May 1940; the saying has also been attributed to Ernest Thesiger of the First World War
Anthony Rhodes *Sword of Bone* (1942) ch. 22

2 No more Latin, no more French,
No more sitting on a hard board bench.
No more beetles in my tea
Making googly eyes at me;
No more spiders in my bath
Trying hard to make me laugh.
children's rhyme for the end of term
Iona and Peter Opie *Lore and Language of Schoolchildren* (1959) ch. 13

3 Not so much a programme, more a way of life!
title of BBC television series, 1964

4 O God, if there be a God, save my soul, if I have a soul!
prayer of a common soldier before the battle of Blenheim, 1704
in *Notes and Queries* vol. 173, no. 15 (9 October 1937); quoted in John Henry Newman *Apologia pro Vita Sua* (1864)

5 One Cartwright brought a Slave from Russia, and would scourge him, for which he was questioned. and it was resolved, That England was too pure an Air for Slaves to breathe in.
'In the 11th of Elizabeth' (17 November 1568–16 November 1569), in John Rushworth *Historical Collections* (1680–1722) vol. 2; cf. **Cowper** 241:20

6 On Waterloo's ensanguined plain
Full many a gallant man was slain,
But none, by sabre or by shot,
Fell half so flat as Walter Scott.
on Sir Walter **Scott***'s poem 'The Field of Waterloo' (1815)*
U. Pope-Hennessy *The Laird of Abbotsford* (1932) ch. 9

7 A place within the meaning of the Act.
usually taken to be a reference to the Betting Act 1853, sect. 2, which banned off-course betting on horse-races

8 Please do not shoot the pianist. He is doing his best.
printed notice in a dancing saloon
Oscar Wilde *Impressions of America* 'Leadville' (*c.*1882–3)

9 Please to remember the Fifth of November,
Gunpowder Treason and Plot.
We know no reason why gunpowder treason
Should ever be forgot.
traditional rhyme on the Gunpowder Plot (1605)

10 *Puella Rigensis ridebat*
Quam tigris in tergo vehebat;
Externa profecta,
Interna revecta,
Risusque cum tigre manebat.

There was a young lady of Riga
Who smiled as she rode on a tiger;
They returned from the ride
With the lady inside,
And the smile on the face of the tiger.
variants exist from 1924 or earlier

11 The [*or* A] quick brown fox jumps over the lazy dog.
used by keyboarders to ensure that all letters of the alphabet are functioning
R. Hunter Middleton's introduction to *The Quick Brown Fox* (1945) by Richard H. Templeton Jr.

12 The rabbit has a charming face:
Its private life is a disgrace.
I really dare not name to you
The awful things that rabbits do.
'The Rabbit', in *The Week-End Book* (1925)

13 Raise the stone, and there thou shalt find me,
cleave the wood and there am I.
Oxyrhynchus Papyri, in B. P. Grenfell and A. S. Hunt (eds.) *Sayings of Our Lord* (1897) Logion 5, l. 23

14 Say it ain't so, Joe.
'Shoeless' Joe Jackson and seven other Chicago players were charged with being bribed to lose the 1919 World Baseball Series
plea said to have been made by a boy as Jackson emerged from the hearing, September 1920

15 Says Tweed to Till—
'What gars ye rin sae still?'
Says Till to Tweed—
'Though ye rin with speed
And I rin slaw,
For ae man that ye droon
I droon twa'.
'Two Rivers' (traditional rhyme)

16 Science finds, industry applies, man conforms.
subtitle of guidebook to 1933 Chicago World's Fair

17 See the happy moron,
He doesn't give a damn,
I wish I were a moron,
My God! perhaps I am!
in *Eugenics Review* July 1929

18 Seven wealthy towns contend for HOMER dead
Through which the living HOMER begged his bread.
epilogue to *Aesop at Tunbridge; or, a Few Selected Fables in Verse* By No Person of Quality (1698); cf. **Heywood** 376:8

19 Since first I saw your face, I resolved to honour and renown ye;
If now I be disdained, I wish my heart had never known ye.
What? I that loved and you that liked, shall we begin to wrangle?
No, no, no, my heart is fast, and cannot disentangle.
song set by Thomas Ford in *Music of Sundry Kinds* (1607)

20 So cryptic as to be almost meaningless. If there is a meaning, it is doubtless objectionable.
banning the film The Seashell and the Clergyman *(1929)*
The British Board of Film Censors; J. C. Robertson *Hidden Cinema* (1989) ch. 1

21 So much chewing gum for the eyes.
small boy's definition of certain television programmes
James Beasley Simpson *Best Quotes of '50, '55, '56* (1957)

22 Sumer is icumen in,
Lhude sing cuccu!

Groweth sed, and bloweth med,
And springth the wude nu.

'Cuckoo Song' (*c.*1250), sung annually at Reading Abbey gateway and first recorded by John Fornset, a monk of Reading Abbey; cf. **Pound** 589:6

1 The Sun himself cannot forget
His fellow traveller.
on Sir Francis **Drake**

Wit's Recreations (1640) epigram no. 146

2 There is a lady sweet and kind,
Was never face so pleased my mind;
I did but see her passing by,
And yet I love her till I die.

found on the reverse of leaf 53 of 'Popish Kingdome or reigne of Antichrist', in Latin verse by Thomas Naogeorgus, and Englished by Barnabe Googe; printed in 1570; sometimes attributed to Thomas Forde

3 There is one thing stronger than all the armies in the world; and that is an idea whose time has come.

in *Nation* 15 April 1943; cf. **Hugo** 393:18

4 There is so much good in the worst of us,
And so much bad in the best of us,
That it hardly becomes any of us
To talk about the rest of us.

attributed, among others, to Edward Wallis Hoch (1849–1945) on the grounds of it having appeared in his Kansas publication, the *Marion Record*, though in fact disclaimed by him ('behooves' sometimes substituted for 'becomes')

5 This fictional account of the day-by-day life of an English gamekeeper is still of considerable interest to outdoor-minded readers, as it contains many passages on pheasant raising, the apprehending of poachers, ways to control vermin, and other chores and duties of the professional gamekeeper. Unfortunately one is obliged to wade through many pages of extraneous material in order to discover and savour these sidelights on the management of a Midlands shooting estate, and in this reviewer's opinion this book cannot take the place of J. R. Miller's *Practical Gamekeeping*.

review of D. H. Lawrence *Lady Chatterley's Lover*; attributed to *Field and Stream*, *c.*1928

6 This is a rotten argument, but it should be good enough for their lordships on a hot summer afternoon.
annotation to a ministerial brief, said to have been read out inadvertently in the House of Lords

Lord Home *The Way the Wind Blows* (1976)

7 Though I yield to no one in my admiration for Mr Coolidge, I do wish he did not look as if he had been weaned on a pickle.

anonymous remark, in Alice Roosevelt Longworth *Crowded Hours* (1933) ch. 21

8 Too small to live in and too large to hang on a watch-chain.
Chiswick House described by a guest

Cecil Roberts *And so to Bath* (1940) ch. 4

9 To secure for the workers by hand or by brain the full fruits of their industry and the most equitable distribution thereof that may be possible upon the basis of the common ownership of the means of production, distribution, and exchange.

Clause Four of the Labour Party's Constitution of 1918 (revised 1929); the commitment to common ownership of services was largely removed in 1995; cf. **Anonymous** 15:20

10 Weep you no more, sad fountains;
What need you flow so fast?

lute song (1603) set to music by John Dowland, in *New Oxford Book of Sixteenth-Century Verse* (1991)

11 We hold these truths to be self-evident, that all men are created equal, that they are endowed by their Creator with certain unalienable rights, that among these are life, liberty and the pursuit of happiness.

The American Declaration of Independence, 4 July 1776; cf. **Jefferson** 405:3

12 We want eight, and we won't wait.
on the construction of Dreadnoughts

George Wyndham, speech in *The Times* 29 March 1909

13 Western wind, when will thou blow,
The small rain down can rain?
Christ, if my love were in my arms
And I in my bed again!

'Western Wind' (published 1790) in *New Oxford Book of Sixteenth-Century Verse* (1991)

14 When I was a little boy, I had but a little wit,
'Tis a long time ago, and I have no more yet;
Nor ever ever shall, until that I die,
For the longer I live the more fool am I.

Wit and Mirth, an Antidote against Melancholy (1684 ed.)

15 Where is the man who has the power and skill
To stem the torrent of a woman's will?
For if she will, she will, you may depend on't;
And if she won't, she won't; so there's an end on't.

inscription on the pillar erected on the mount in the Dane John Field, Canterbury, in *Examiner* 31 May 1829

16 Whilst Adam slept, Eve from his side arose:
Strange his first sleep should be his last repose.

'The Consequence'

17 With a heart of furious fancies,
Whereof I am commander;
With a burning spear,
And a horse of air,
To the wilderness I wander.

'Tom o' Bedlam'

18 Would you like to sin
With Elinor Glyn
On a tigerskin?
Or would you prefer
To err
With her
On some other fur?

1907 rhyme, in A. Glyn *Elinor Glyn* (1955) bk. 2, sect. 30

19 Yet, if his majesty our sovereign lord
Should of his own accord
Friendly himself invite,
And say 'I'll be your guest tomorrow night',
How should we stir ourselves, call and command
All hands to work! . . .

But at the coming of the King of Heaven

All's set at six and seven:
We wallow in our sin.
Christ cannot find a chamber in the inn.
We entertain Him always like a stranger,
And as at first still lodge Him in the manger.

from Christ Church MS

1 You should make a point of trying every experience once, excepting incest and folk-dancing.

Arnold Bax (1883–1953), quoting 'a sympathetic Scot' in *Farewell My Youth* (1943)

FRENCH

2 *Ça ira.*

Things will work out.

refrain of 'Carillon national', popular song of the French Revolution (*c.*July 1790), translated by William Doyle; the phrase is believed to originate with Benjamin **Franklin**, who may have uttered it in 1776 when asked for news of the American Revolution

3 *Cet animal est très méchant,*
Quand on l'attaque il se défend.

This animal is very bad; when attacked it defends itself.

'La Ménagerie' (1868 song) by 'Théodore P. K.'

4 *Chevalier sans peur et sans reproche.*

Fearless, blameless knight.

description in contemporary chronicles of Pierre Bayard (1476–1524)

5 *Il y avait un jeune homme de Dijon,*
Qui n'avait que peu de religion.
Il dit: 'Quant à moi,
Je déteste tous les trois,
Le Père, et le Fils, et le Pigeon.'

There was a young man of Dijon,
Who ,
He said: 'As for me,
I detest all the three,
The Father, the Son, and the Pigeon.'

The Norman Douglas Limerick Book (1969, privately printed, 1928, as *Some Limericks*) introduction

6 RIDDLE: *Je suis le capitaine de vingt-quatre soldats, et sans moi Paris serait pris?*
ANSWER: *A.*

RIDDLE: I am the captain of twenty-four soldiers, and without me Paris would be taken?
ANSWER: A [i.e. 'Paris' minus 'a' = *pris* taken].

the saying ' With twenty-six lead soldiers [the characters of the alphabet set up for printing] *I can conquer the world' may derive from this riddle, but probably arose independently*

Hugh Rowley *Puniana: or, Thoughts wise and otherwise* (1867)

7 *Laissez-nous-faire.*

Allow us to do [it].

remark dating from *c.*1664, in *Journal Oeconomique* Paris, April 1751: 'Monsieur Colbert assembled several deputies of commerce at his house to ask what could be done for commerce; the most rational and the least flattering among them answered him in one word: "Laissez-nous-faire"'; cf. **Argenson** 24:5, **Quesnay** 618:23

8 *L'amour est aveugle; l'amitié ferme les yeux.*

Love is blind; friendship closes its eyes.

proverbial saying; cf. **Proverbs** 606:4

9 *Le monde est plein de fous, et qui n'en veut pas voir*
Doit se tenir tout seul, et casser son miroir.

The world is full of fools, and he who would see none should live alone and smash his mirror.

adaptation from an original form attributed to Claude Le Petit (1640–65) in *Discours satiriques* (1686)

10 *L'ordre règne à Varsovie.*

Order reigns in Warsaw.

after the brutal suppression of an uprising, the newspaper *Moniteur* reported, 16 September 1831, '*L'ordre et la tranquillité sont entièrement rétablis dans la capitale* [Order and calm are completely restored in the capital]'; on the same day Count Sebastiani, minister of foreign affairs, declared: '*La tranquillité règne à Varsovie* [Peace reigns in Warsaw]'

11 *Nous n'irons plus aux bois, les lauriers sont coupés.*

We'll to the woods no more,
The laurels all are cut.

old nursery rhyme, quoted by Théodore de Banville in *Les Cariatides, les stalactites* (1842–6); translated by A. E. Housman in *Last Poems* (1922) introductory

12 *Revenons à ces moutons.*

Let us get back to these sheep [i.e. 'Let us get back to the subject'].

Maistre Pierre Pathelin l. 1191 (often quoted as '*Retournons à nos moutons* [Let us return to our sheep]')

13 *Si le Roi m'avait donné,*
Paris, sa grand'ville,
Et qu'il me fallût quitter
L'amour de ma mie,
Je dirais au roi Henri:
'Reprenez votre Paris:
J'aime mieux ma mie, au gué,
J'aime mieux ma mie.'

If the king had given me Paris, his great city, and if I were required to give up my darling's love, I would say to King Henry: 'Take your Paris back; I prefer my darling, by the ford, I prefer my darling.'

popular song, attributed to Antoine de Navarre (1518–62); quoted in this form by Molière in *Le Misanthrope* act 1, sc. 2

14 *Toujours perdrix!*

Always partridge!

attributed to a confessor of **Henri IV**, *who rebuked the king for his sexual liaisons and thereafter was served nothing but partridge*

G. Büchmann *Geflügelte Worte* (1874 ed.)

15 *Tout passe, tout casse, tout lasse.*

Everything passes, everything perishes, everything palls.

Charles Cahier *Quelques six mille proverbes* (1856) no. 1718

GERMAN

16 *Arbeit macht frei.*

Work liberates.

words inscribed on the gates of Dachau concentration camp, 1933, and subsequently on those of Auschwitz

17 *Jedem das Seine.*

To each his own.

often quoted as 'Everyone gets what he deserves'

inscription on the gate of Buchenwald concentration camp, *c.*1937; cf. **Bold** 124:10

18 *Kommt der Krieg ins Land*
Gibt's Lügen wie Sand.

When war enters a country
It produces lies like sand.
epigraph to Arthur Ponsonby *Falsehood in Wartime* (1928)

GREEK

1 Nothing in excess.
inscribed on the temple of Apollo at Delphi
variously ascribed to the Seven Wise Men

2 Whenever God prepares evil for a man, He first damages his mind, with which he deliberates.
scholiastic annotation to Sophocles's *Antigone* l. 622; cf. **Proverbs** 615:4

3 Let no one enter who does not know geometry [mathematics].
inscription on **Plato***'s door, probably at the Academy at Athens*
Elias Philosophus *In Aristotelis Categorias Commentaria*; in A. Busse (ed.) *Commentaria in Aristotelem Graeca* (1900) vol. 18, pt. 1

LATIN

4 *Adeste, fideles,*
laeti triumphantes;
venite, venite in Bethlehem;
natum videte regem angelorum . . .
venite, adoremus Dominum.

O come, all ye faithful,
Joyful and triumphant,
O come ye, O come ye to Bethlehem;
Come and behold him,
Born the King of angels:
O come, let us adore him . . . Christ the Lord!
French or German hymn (*c.*1743) in *Murray's Hymnal* (1852); translation based on that of F. Oakeley (1841)

5 *Ave Caesar, morituri te salutant.*

Hail Caesar, those who are about to die salute you.
gladiators saluting the Roman Emperor
Suetonius *Lives of the Caesars* 'Claudius' ch. 21

6 *Ave verum corpus,*
natum ex Maria Virgine.

Hail the true body, born of the Virgin Mary.
Eucharistic hymn, probably dating from the 14th century

7 *Caveant consules ne quid res publica detrimenti capiat.*

Let the consuls see to it that no harm come to the state.
senatorial 'ultimate decree' in the Roman Republic; cf. Cicero *Pro Milone* ch. 70

8 *Cras amet qui nunquam amavit, quique amavit cras amet!*

Let those love now, who never loved before:
Let those who always loved, now love the more.
Pervigilium Veneris (translated by Thomas Parnell, 1722)

9 *Gaudeamus igitur,*
Juvenes dum sumus
Post jucundam juventutem,
Post molestam senectutem,
Nos habebit humus.

Let us then rejoice,
While we are young.
After the pleasures of youth
And the burdens of old age
Earth will hold us.
medieval students' song, traced to 1267, but revised in the 18th century

10 *Meum est propositum*
In taberna mori,
Ut sint vina proxima
Morientis ori.
Tunc cantabunt laetius
Angelorum chori:
'Sit Deus propitius
Huic potatori!'
I desire to end my days in a tavern drinking,
May some Christian hold for me the glass when I am shrinking;
That the Cherubim may cry, when they see me sinking,
'God be merciful to a soul of this gentleman's way of thinking.'
The Arch-poet (fl. 1159–67) 'Estuans intrinsecus ira vehementi' (translated by Leigh Hunt)

11 *Omnia dispono solus meritos*[que] *corono. Quos scelus exercet me judice poena coercet.*

I alone dispose of all things and crown the just.
Those who follow crime I judge and punish.
around the mandorla enclosing the figure of Christ
inscription on the western portal of St-Lazare, Autun; carved by Gislebertus, *c.*1130

12 *Quidquid agis, prudenter agas, et respice finem.*

Whatever you do, do cautiously, and look to the end.
Gesta Romanorum no. 103

13 *Sic transit gloria mundi.*

Thus passes the glory of the world.
said during the coronation of a new Pope, while flax is burned to represent the transitoriness of earthly glory
used at the coronation of Alexander V in Pisa, 7 July 1409, but earlier in origin; cf. **Thomas à Kempis** 770:20

14 *Vox et praeterea nihil.*

A voice and nothing more.
describing a nightingale
Plutarch *Moralia* sect. 233a, no. 15

OLD ENGLISH

15 *Hige sceal þe heardra, heorte þe cenre,*
mod sceal þe mare, þe ure mægen lytlað.

Thought shall be the harder, heart the keener,
courage the greater, as our might lessens.
The Battle of Maldon (translated by R. K. Gordon, 1926)

16 *Hwæt! wē Gārdena in gēardagum*
þēodcyninga þrym gefrūnon,
hū ðā æþelingas ellen fremedon.

Listen!
The fame of Danish kings
in days gone by, the daring feats
worked by those heroes are well known to us.
Beowulf, translated by Kevin Crossley-Holland

17 *þæs oferēode, þisses swā mæg.*

That passed over, so may this.
Deor

1 King Harold was killed and Earl Leofwine his brother and Earl Gyrth his brother . . . and the French remained masters of the field.
Anglo-Saxon Chronicle for 1066

2 There was no single hide nor a yard of land nor indeed was one ox or one cow or one pig left out, that was not put down in his record.
of William the Conqueror's commissioning of the Domesday Book
Anglo-Saxon Chronicle for 1087

3 Men said openly that Christ slept and His saints.
of England during the civil war between Stephen and Matilda
Anglo-Saxon Chronicle for 1137

OLD NORSE

4 *Deyr fé, deyja frændr,*
deyr sjalfr et sama;
en orðstirr deyr aldrigi
hveims sér góðar getr.
Cattle die, kinsmen die,
the self must also die;
but glory never dies,
for the man who is able to achieve it.
Hávamál ('Sayings of the High One'), *c.*10th century

5 The morning work has been unequal; I have spun twelve ells of yarn, and you have killed Kjartan.
Laxdæla Saga (*c.*12 century); the words of Gudrun

6 I did the worst to him I loved the most.
Laxdæla Saga (*c.*12 century); the words of Gudrun

Jean Anouilh 1910–87
French dramatist

7 *Dieu est avec tout le monde . . . Et, en fin de compte, il est toujours avec ceux qui ont beaucoup d'argent et de grosses armées.*
God is on everyone's side . . . And, in the last analysis, he is on the side of those with plenty of money and large armies.
L'Alouette (1953); cf. **Bussy-Rabutin** 171:7, **Voltaire** 798:4

8 *Maintenant le ressort est bandé. Cela n'a plus qu'à se dérouler tout seul. C'est cela qui est commode dans la tragédie. On donne le petit coup de pouce pour que cela démarre.*
The spring is wound up tight. It will uncoil of itself. That is what is so convenient in tragedy. The least little turn of the wrist will do the job. Anything will set it going.
Antigone (1944, translated by Lewis Galantiere, 1957)

9 *C'est propre, la tragédie. C'est reposant, c'est sûr.*
Tragedy is clean, it is restful, it is flawless.
Antigone (1944, translated by Lewis Galantiere, 1957)

10 *Il y a l'amour bien sûr. Et puis il y a la vie, son ennemie.*
There is love of course. And then there's life, its enemy.
Ardèle (1949)

11 *Vous savez bien que l'amour, c'est avant tout le don de soi!*
You know very well that love is, above all, the gift of oneself!
Ardèle (1949)

12 *Mourir, mourir . . . Mourir ce n'est rien. Commence donc par vivre. C'est moins drôle et c'est plus long.*
Dying is nothing. So start by living. It's less fun and it lasts longer.
Roméo et Jeannette (1946) act 3

13 *Il y a aura toujours un chien perdu quelquepart qui m'empêchera d'être heureux.*
There will always be a lost dog somewhere that will prevent me from being happy.
La Sauvage (1938) act 3

Christopher Anstey 1724–1805
English writer

14 If ever I ate a good supper at night,
I dreamed of the devil, and waked in a fright.
The New Bath Guide (1766) Letter 4 'A Consultation of the Physicians'

15 You may go to Carlisle's, and to Almack's too;
And I'll give you my head if you find such a host,
For coffee, tea, chocolate, butter, and toast:
How he welcomes at once all the world and his wife,
And how civil to folk he ne'er saw in his life.
The New Bath Guide (1766) Letter 13 'A Public Breakfast'

F. Anstey (Thomas Anstey Guthrie) 1856–1934
English writer

16 Drastic measures is Latin for a whopping.
Vice Versa (1882) ch. 7

Susan Brownell Anthony 1820–1906
American feminist and political activist

17 Join the union, girls, and together say, 'Equal Pay for Equal Work!'
in *The Revolution* 8 October 1869

18 Marriage, to women as to men, must be a luxury, not a necessity; an incident of life, not all of it.
speech, 1875

Minna Antrim 1861–1950
American writer

19 A fool bolts pleasure, then complains of moral indigestion.
Naked Truth and Veiled Allusions (1902)

Guillaume Apollinaire 1880–1918
French poet

20 *Les souvenirs sont cors de chasse*
Dont meurt le bruit parmi le vent.
Memories are hunting horns
Whose sound dies on the wind.
'Cors de Chasse' (1912)

21 *Sous le pont Mirabeau coule la Seine.*
Et nos amours, faut-il qu'il m'en souvienne?

La joie venait toujours après la peine.
Vienne la nuit, sonne l'heure,
Les jours s'en vont, je demeure.

Under Mirabeau Bridge flows the Seine.
And our loves, must I remember them?
Joy always came after pain.
Let night come, ring out the hour,
The days go by, I remain.

'Le Pont Mirabeau' (1912)

1 When man wanted to make a machine that would walk he created the wheel, which does not resemble a leg.

Les Mamelles de Tirésias (1918)

2 *On ne peut pas porter partout le cadavre de son père.*

One can't carry one's father's corpse about everywhere.

Les peintres cubistes (1965) 'Méditations esthétiques: Sur la peinture' pt. 1

Edward Appleton 1892–1965

English physicist

3 I do not mind what language an opera is sung in so long as it is a language I don't understand.

in *Observer* 28 August 1955

Thomas Gold Appleton 1812–84

American epigrammatist

4 Good Americans, when they die, go to Paris.

Oliver Wendell Holmes *The Autocrat of the Breakfast Table* (1858) ch. 6; cf. **Proverbs** 601:22, **Wilde** 818:23

5 A Boston man is the east wind made flesh.

attributed

Arabian Nights Entertainments, or the Thousand and one Nights

A collection of stories written in Arabic

6 Who will change old lamps for new ones? . . . new lamps for old ones?

'The History of Aladdin'

7 Open Sesame!

'The History of Ali Baba'

William Arabin 1773–1841

English judge

8 If ever there was a case of clearer evidence than this of persons acting together, this case is that case.

H. B. Churchill *Arabiniana* (1843)

9 Prisoner, God has given you good abilities, instead of which you go about the country stealing ducks.

also attributed to a Revd Mr Alderson, in Frederick Pollock *Essays in the Law* (1922)

10 They will steal the very teeth out of your mouth as you walk through the streets. *I know it from experience.*

on the citizens of Uxbridge

Sir W. Ballantine *Some Experiences of a Barrister's Life* (1882) vol. 1, ch. 6

Louis Aragon 1897–1982

French poet, essayist, and novelist

11 *Ô mois des floraisons mois des métamorphoses*
Mai qui fut sans nuage et Juin poignardé
Je n'oublierai jamais les lilas ni les roses
Ni ceux que le printemps dans ses plis a gardé.

O month of flowerings, month of metamorphoses,
May without cloud and June that was stabbed,
I shall never forget the lilac and the roses
Nor those whom spring has kept in its folds.

'Les lilas et les roses' (1940)

Diane Arbus 1923–71

American photographer

12 Most people go through life dreading they'll have a traumatic experience. Freaks are born with their trauma. They've already passed it. They're aristocrats.

Diane Arbus (1972)

13 A photograph is a secret about a secret. The more it tells you the less you know.

Patricia Bosworth *Diane Arbus: a Biography* (1985)

John Arbuthnot 1667–1735

Scottish physician and pamphleteer

14 He [the writer] warns the heads of parties against believing their own lies.

The Art of Political Lying (1712)

15 Law is a bottomless pit.

The History of John Bull (1712) title of first pamphlet

16 Curle (who is one of the new terrors of Death) has been writing letters to every body for memoirs of his life.

letter to Jonathan Swift, 13 January 1733, in H. Williams (ed.) *The Correspondence of Jonathan Swift* vol. 4 (1965); cf. **Lyndhurst** 480:20, **Wetherell** 812:22

Archilochus

Greek poet of the 7th century BC

17 The fox knows many things—the hedgehog one *big* one.

E. Diehl (ed.) *Anthologia Lyrica Graeca* (3rd ed., 1949–52) vol. 1, no. 103; cf. **Berlin** 68:15

Archimedes *c.*287–212 BC

Greek mathematician and inventor

18 Eureka! [I've got it!]

Vitruvius Pollio *De Architectura* bk. 9, preface, sect. 10

19 Give me but one firm spot on which to stand, and I will move the earth.

on the action of a lever

Pappus *Synagoge* bk. 8, proposition 10, sect. 11

Robert Ardrey 1908–80

American dramatist and evolutionist

20 Not in innocence, and not in Asia, was mankind born.

African Genesis (1961)

Hannah Arendt 1906–75
American political philosopher

1 It was as though in those last minutes he was summing up the lessons that this long course in human wickedness had taught us—the lesson of the fearsome, word-and-thought-defying *banality of evil*.
of Adolf Eichmann, responsible for the administration of the Nazi concentration camps
Eichmann in Jerusalem (1963) ch. 15

2 Only crime and the criminal, it is true, confront us with the perplexity of radical evil; but only the hypocrite is really rotten to the core.
On Revolution (1963) ch. 2, pt. 5

3 The most radical revolutionary will become a conservative on the day after the revolution.
in *New Yorker* 12 September 1970

4 Under conditions of tyranny it is far easier to act than to think.
W. H. Auden *A Certain World* (1970)

Marquis d'Argenson (René Louis de Voyer d'Argenson) 1694–1757
French politician and political essayist

5 *Laisser-faire.*
No interference.
Mémoires et Journal Inédit du Marquis d'Argenson (1858 ed.) vol. 5; cf. **Anonymous** 20:7, **Quesnay** 618:23

Comte d'Argenson (Marc Pierre de Voyer d'Argenson) 1696–1764
French statesman; founder of the École Militaire, Paris

6 DESFONTAINES: I must live.
D'ARGENSON: I do not see the necessity.
on Desfontaines having produced a pamphlet satirizing D'Argenson, his benefactor
Voltaire *Alzire* (1736) 'Discours Préliminaire' footnote, in *Oeuvres Complètes Théâtre* (1877) vol. 2

Ludovico Ariosto 1474–1533
Italian poet and dramatist

7 *Natura il fece, e poi roppe la stampa.*
Nature made him, and then broke the mould.
Orlando Furioso (1532) canto 10, st. 84

Aristophanes *c.*450–*c.*385 BC
Athenian comic dramatist

8 How about 'Cloudcuckooland'?
naming the capital city of the Birds
The Birds (414 BC) l. 819

9 This Second Logic then, I mean the Worse one,
They teach to talk unjustly, and—prevail.
The Clouds (423 BC) l. 113; cf. **Milton** 515:9

10 The old are in a second childhood.
The Clouds (423 BC) l. 1417

11 But he was contented there, is contented here.
on ***Sophocles*** (there = *on earth and* here = *in Hades*)
The Frogs (405 BC) l. 82

12 Brekekekex koax koax.
cry of the Frogs
The Frogs (405 BC) l. 209 and *passim*

13 Under every stone lurks a politician.
Thesmophoriazusae l. 530

Aristotle 384–322 BC
Greek philosopher
see also ***Ascham*** *30:9,* ***Dante*** *249:11*

14 Now, we may say that the most important subjects about which all men deliberate and deliberative orators harangue, are five in number, to wit: ways and means, war and peace, the defence of the country, imports and exports, legislation.
The Art of Rhetoric bk. 1, 1359b 19–23

15 Every art and every investigation, and likewise every practical pursuit or undertaking, seems to aim at some good: hence it has been well said that the Good is That at which all things aim.
Nicomachean Ethics bk. 1, 1094a 1–3

16 Therefore, the good of man must be the end [i.e. objective] of the science of politics.
Nicomachean Ethics bk. 1, 1094b 6–7

17 The Good of man is the active exercise of his soul's faculties in conformity with excellence or virtue . . . Moreover this activity must occupy a complete lifetime; for one swallow does not make spring, nor does one fine day; and similarly one day or a brief period of happiness does not make a man supremely blessed and happy.
Nicomachean Ethics bk. 1, 1098a 16–20

18 Now some think that all justice is of this sort, because that which is by nature is unchangeable and has everywhere the same force (as fire burns both here and in Persia), while they see change in the things recognized as just.
Nicomachean Ethics bk. 5, 1134b 26

19 We make war that we may live in peace.
Nicomachean Ethics bk. 10, 1177b 5–6 (translated by M. Ostwald); cf. **Vegetius** 791:4

20 Politicians also have no leisure, because they are always aiming at something beyond political life itself, power and glory, or happiness.
Nicomachean Ethics bk. 10, 1177b 12–14

21 Tragedy is thus a representation of an action that is worth serious attention, complete in itself and of some amplitude . . . by means of pity and fear bringing about the purgation of such emotions.
Poetics ch. 6, 1449b 24–8

22 A whole is that which has a beginning, a middle, and an end.
Poetics ch. 7

23 So poetry is something more philosophical and more worthy of serious attention than history, for while poetry is concerned with universal truth, history treats of particular facts . . . The particular facts of the historian are what, say, Alcibiades did, or what happened to him.
Poetics ch. 9, 1451b 5–6

1 Probable impossibilities are to be preferred to improbable possibilities.
Poetics ch. 24, 1460a 26–7

2 Man is by nature a political animal.
Politics bk. 1, 1253a 2–3

3 He who is unable to live in society, or who has no need because he is sufficient for himself, must be either a beast or a god.
Politics bk. 1, 1253a 27–9; cf. **Bacon** 42:34

4 Nature does nothing without purpose or uselessly.
Politics bk. 1, 1256b 20–21

5 For if liberty and equality, as is thought by some, are chiefly to be found in democracy, they will be best attained when all persons alike share in the government to the utmost.
Politics bk. 4, 1291b 35

6 Where some people are very wealthy and others have nothing, the result will be either extreme democracy or absolute oligarchy, or despotism will come from either of those excesses.
Politics bk. 4, 1296a 1–3

7 No tyrant need fear till men begin to feel confident in each other.
Politics bk. 5, 1314a

8 Whereas then a rattle is a suitable occupation for infant children, education serves as a rattle for young people when older.
Politics bk. 8, 1340b 29–31

9 *Amicus Plato, sed magis amica veritas.*
Plato is dear to me, but dearer still is truth.
Latin translation of a Greek original ascribed to Aristotle

10 When he was asked 'What is a friend?' he said 'One soul inhabiting two bodies.'
Diogenes Laertius *Lives of Philosophers* bk. 5, sect. 20

11 This realization, according to [Aristotle], is twofold. Either it is potential, as that of Hermes in the wax, provided the wax be adapted to receive the proper mouldings, or as that of the statue implicit in the bronze; or again it is determinate, which is the case with the completed figure of Hermes or the finished statue.
Diogenes Laertius *Lives of the Philosophers* bk. 5, sect. 33

Lewis Addison Armistead 1817–63
American army officer

12 Give them the cold steel, boys!
during the American Civil War, 1863
attributed

Harry Armstrong 1879–1951
American songwriter

13 There's an old mill by the stream, Nellie Dean,
Where we used to sit and dream, Nellie Dean.
And the waters as they flow
Seem to murmur sweet and low,
'You're my heart's desire; I love you, Nellie Dean.'
'Nellie Dean' (1905 song)

John Armstrong 1709–79
Scottish poet and physician

14 Much had he read,
Much more had seen; he studied from the life,
And in th'original perused mankind.
The Art of Preserving Health (1744) bk. 4, l. 231

15 'Tis not for mortals always to be blest.
The Art of Preserving Health (1744) bk. 4, l. 260

16 'Tis not too late tomorrow to be brave.
The Art of Preserving Health (1744) bk. 4, l. 460

Louis Armstrong 1901–71
American singer and jazz musician

17 If you still have to ask . . . shame on you.
when asked what jazz is
Max Jones et al. *Salute to Satchmo* (1970); cf. **Misquotations** 522:1

18 All music is folk music, I ain't never heard no horse sing a song.
in *New York Times* 7 July 1971

Neil Armstrong 1930–
American astronaut; first man on the moon

19 That's one small step for a man, one giant leap for mankind.
as the craft touched down, he had radioed 'Houston. Tranquillity Base here. The Eagle has landed'
in *New York Times* 21 July 1969; interference in the transmission obliterated 'a'

Robert Armstrong 1927–
British civil servant; Head of the Civil Service, 1981–7

20 It contains a misleading impression, not a lie. It was being economical with the truth.
during the 'Spycatcher' trial in New South Wales
in *Daily Telegraph* 19 November 1986; cf. **Burke** 164:22, **Clark** 219:3, **Twain** 786:7

William Armstrong 1915–80
British civil servant, Head of the Civil Service 1968–74

21 The business of the Civil Service is the orderly management of decline.
in 1973: Peter Hennessy *Whitehall* (1990)

Arnald-Amaury d. 1225
French abbot of Citeaux

22 Kill them all; God will recognize his own.
when asked how the true Catholics could be distinguished from the heretics at the massacre of Béziers, 1209
Jonathan Sumption *The Albigensian Crusade* (1978)

Edwin Arnold 1832–1904
English poet and journalist

23 Nor ever once ashamed
So we be named
Press-men; Slaves of the Lamp; Servants of Light.
'The Tenth Muse' (1895) st. 18

George Arnold 1834–65

American humorist

1 The living need charity more than the dead.
'The Jolly Old Pedagogue' (1866)

Matthew Arnold 1822–88

English poet and essayist; son of Thomas ***Arnold***

2 And we forget because we must
And not because we will.
'Absence' (1852)

3 A bolt is shot back somewhere in our breast,
And a lost pulse of feeling stirs again.
The eye sinks inward, and the heart lies plain,
And what we mean, we say, and what we would, we know.
'The Buried Life' (1852) l. 84

4 The Sea of Faith
Was once, too, at the full, and round earth's shore
Lay like the folds of a bright girdle furled.
But now I only hear
Its melancholy, long, withdrawing roar,
Retreating, to the breath
Of the night-wind, down the vast edges drear
And naked shingles of the world.

Ah, love, let us be true
To one another!
'Dover Beach' (1867) l. 21

5 And we are here as on a darkling plain
Swept with confused alarms of struggle and flight,
Where ignorant armies clash by night.
'Dover Beach' (1867) l. 35

6 Be neither saint nor sophist-led, but be a man.
Empedocles on Etna (1852) act 1, sc. 2, l. 136

7 Is it so small a thing
To have enjoyed the sun,
To have lived light in the spring,
To have loved, to have thought, to have done.
Empedocles on Etna (1852) act 1, sc. 2, l. 397

8 Because thou must not dream, thou needst not then despair!
Empedocles on Etna (1852) act 1, sc. 2, l. 426

9 Come to me in my dreams, and then
By day I shall be well again!
For then the night will more than pay
The hopeless longing of the day.
'Faded Leaves' (1855) no. 5 (first published, 1852, as 'Longing')

10 Come, dear children, let us away;
Down and away below!
'The Forsaken Merman' (1849) l. 1

11 Now the great winds shorewards blow;
Now the salt tides seawards flow;
Now the wild white horses play,
Champ and chafe and toss in the spray.
'The Forsaken Merman' (1849) l. 4

12 Sand-strewn caverns, cool and deep,
Where the winds are all asleep;
Where the spent lights quiver and gleam;
Where the salt weed sways in the stream;
'The Forsaken Merman' (1849) l. 35

13 Where great whales come sailing by,
Sail and sail, with unshut eye,
Round the world for ever and aye.
'The Forsaken Merman' (1849) l. 43

14 Creep into thy narrow bed,
Creep, and let no more be said!
Vain thy onset! all stands fast.
Thou thyself must break at last.
Let the long contention cease!
Geese are swans, and swans are geese.
Let them have it how they will!
Thou art tired; best be still.
'The Last Word' (1867)

15 Calm soul of all things! make it mine
To feel, amid the city's jar,
That there abides a peace of thine,
Man did not make, and cannot mar.
'Lines written in Kensington Gardens' (1852)

16 He spoke, and loosed our heart in tears.
He laid us as we lay at birth
On the cool flowery lap of earth.
of William ***Wordsworth***
'Memorial Verses, April 1850' (1852) l. 47

17 Ere the parting hour go by,
Quick, thy tablets, Memory!
'A Memory Picture' (1849)

18 With aching hands and bleeding feet
We dig and heap, lay stone on stone;
We bear the burden and the heat
Of the long day, and wish 'twere done.
Not till the hours of light return,
All we have built do we discern.
'Morality' (1852); cf. **Bible** 96:18

19 Say, has some wet bird-haunted English lawn
Lent it the music of its trees at dawn?
'Parting' (1852) l. 19

20 Hark! ah, the Nightingale!
The tawny-throated!
Hark! from that moonlit cedar what a burst!
What triumph! hark—what pain!
'Philomela' (1853) l. 1

21 Eternal Passion!
Eternal Pain!
of the nightingale
'Philomela' (1853) l. 31

22 Cruel, but composed and bland,
Dumb, inscrutable and grand,
So Tiberius might have sat,
Had Tiberius been a cat.
'Poor Matthias' (1885) l. 40

23 Her cabined ample Spirit,
It fluttered and failed for breath.
To-night it doth inherit
The vasty hall of death.
'Requiescat' (1853)

24 Not deep the Poet sees, but wide.
'Resignation' (1849) l. 214

25 Yet they, believe me, who await
No gifts from chance, have conquered fate.
'Resignation' (1849) l. 247

1 Not milder is the general lot
Because our spirits have forgot,
In action's dizzying eddy whirled,
The something that infects the world.
'Resignation' (1849) l. 275

2 Coldly, sadly descends
The autumn evening. The Field
Strewn with its dank yellow drifts
Of withered leaves, and the elms,
Fade into dimness apace,
Silent;—hardly a shout
From a few boys late at their play!
'Rugby Chapel, November 1857' (1867)

3 Go, for they call you, Shepherd, from the hill.
'The Scholar-Gipsy' (1853) l. 1

4 All the live murmur of a summer's day.
'The Scholar-Gipsy' (1853) l. 20

5 Tired of knocking at Preferment's door.
'The Scholar-Gipsy' (1853) l. 35

6 Crossing the stripling Thames at Bab-lock-hithe.
'The Scholar-Gipsy' (1853) l. 74

7 Rapt, twirling in thy hand a withered spray,
And waiting for the spark from heaven to fall.
'The Scholar-Gipsy' (1853) l. 119

8 The line of festal light in Christ-Church hall.
'The Scholar-Gipsy' (1853) l. 129

9 Thou waitest for the spark from heaven! and we,
Light half-believers in our casual creeds . . .
Who hesitate and falter life away,
And lose to-morrow the ground won to-day—
Ah, do not we, Wanderer, await it too?
'The Scholar-Gipsy' (1853) l. 171

10 O born in days when wits were fresh and clear,
And life ran gaily as the sparkling Thames;
Before this strange disease of modern life,
With its sick hurry, its divided aims,
Its heads o'ertaxed, its palsied hearts, was rife—
Fly hence, our contact fear!
'The Scholar-Gipsy' (1853) l. 201

11 Still nursing the unconquerable hope,
Still clutching the inviolable shade.
'The Scholar-Gipsy' (1853) l. 211

12 Resolve to be thyself: and know, that he
Who finds himself, loses his misery.
'Self-Dependence' (1852) l. 31

13 Others abide our question. Thou art free.
We ask and ask: Thou smilest and art still,
Out-topping knowledge.
'Shakespeare' (1849)

14 And thou, who didst the stars and sunbeams know,
Self-schooled, self-scanned, self-honoured, self-secure,
Didst tread on Earth unguessed at.
'Shakespeare' (1849)

15 Curled minion, dancer, coiner of sweet words!
'Sohrab and Rustum' (1853) l. 458

16 No horse's cry was that, most like the roar
Of some pained desert lion, who all day
Hath trailed the hunter's javelin in his side,
And comes at night to die upon the sand.
'Sohrab and Rustum' (1853) l. 501

17 Truth sits upon the lips of dying men.
'Sohrab and Rustum' (1853) l. 656

18 But the majestic river floated on,
Out of the mist and hum of that low land,
Into the frosty starlight.
'Sohrab and Rustum' (1853) l. 875

19 The longed-for dash of waves is heard, and wide
His luminous home of waters opens, bright
And tranquil, from whose floor the new-bathed stars
Emerge, and shine upon the Aral Sea.
'Sohrab and Rustum' (1853) l. 889

20 For rigorous teachers seized my youth,
And purged its faith, and trimmed its fire,
Showed me the high, white star of Truth,
There bade me gaze, and there aspire.
'Stanzas from the Grande Chartreuse' (1855) l. 67

21 Wandering between two worlds, one dead,
The other powerless to be born,
With nowhere yet to rest my head,
Like these, on earth I wait forlorn.
'Stanzas from the Grande Chartreuse' (1855) l. 85

22 What helps it now, that Byron bore,
With haughty scorn which mocked the smart,
Through Europe to the Aetolian shore
The pageant of his bleeding heart?
That thousands counted every groan,
And Europe made his woe her own?
'Stanzas from the Grande Chartreuse' (1855) l. 133

23 Still bent to make some port he knows not where,
Still standing for some false impossible shore.
'A Summer Night' (1852) l. 68

24 The signal-elm, that looks on Ilsley downs,
The Vale, the three lone weirs, the youthful Thames.
'Thyrsis' (1866) l. 14

25 And that sweet City with her dreaming spires.
of Oxford
'Thyrsis' (1866) l. 19; cf. **Raphael** 622:4

26 So have I heard the cuckoo's parting cry,
From the wet field, through the vext garden-trees,
Come with the volleying rain and tossing breeze:
'The bloom is gone, and with the bloom go I.'
'Thyrsis' (1866) l. 57

27 Too quick despairer, wherefore wilt thou go?
Soon will the high Midsummer pomps come on,
Soon will the musk carnations break and swell.
'Thyrsis' (1866) l. 61

28 For Time, not Corydon, hath conquered thee.
'Thyrsis' (1866) l. 80

29 The foot less prompt to meet the morning dew,
The heart less bounding at emotion new,
And hope, once crushed, less quick to spring again.
'Thyrsis' (1866) l. 138

30 Who saw life steadily, and saw it whole:
The mellow glory of the Attic stage;

Singer of sweet Colonus, and its child.
*of **Sophocles***
'To a Friend' (1849)

1 France, famed in all great arts, in none supreme.
'To a Republican Friend—Continued' (1849)

2 Yes! in the sea of life enisled,
With echoing straits between us thrown,
Dotting the shoreless watery wild,
We mortal millions live *alone*.
'To Marguerite—Continued' (1852) l. 1

3 A God, a God their severance ruled!
'To Marguerite—Continued' (1852) l. 22

4 And bade betwixt their shores to be
The unplumbed, salt, estranging sea.
'To Marguerite—Continued' (1852) l. 23

5 Nor bring, to see me cease to live,
Some doctor full of phrase and fame,
To shake his sapient head and give
The ill he cannot cure a name.
'A Wish' (1867)

6 And sigh that one thing only has been lent
To youth and age in common—discontent.
'Youth's Agitations' (1852)

7 Our society distributes itself into Barbarians, Philistines, and Populace; and America is just ourselves, with the Barbarians quite left out, and the Populace nearly.
Culture and Anarchy (1869) preface

8 The pursuit of perfection, then, is the pursuit of sweetness and light . . . He who works for sweetness and light united, works to make reason and the will of God prevail.
Culture and Anarchy (1869) ch. 1; cf. **Forster** 320:13, **Swift** 747:12

9 The men of culture are the true apostles of equality.
Culture and Anarchy (1869) ch. 1

10 When I want to distinguish clearly the aristocratic class from the Philistines proper, or middle class, [I] name the former, in my own mind *the Barbarians*.
Culture and Anarchy (1869) ch. 3

11 Marching where it likes, meeting where it likes, bawling what it likes, breaking what it likes—to this vast residuum we may with great propriety give the name of Populace.
of the working class
Culture and Anarchy (1869) ch. 3

12 Hebraism and Hellenism—between these two points of influence moves our world.
Culture and Anarchy (1869) ch. 4

13 No man, who knows nothing else, knows even his Bible.
Culture and Anarchy (1869) ch. 5

14 Nothing could moderate, in the bosom of the great English middle class, their passionate, absorbing, almost blood-thirsty clinging to life.
Essays in Criticism First Series (1865) preface

15 Whispering from her towers the last enchantments of the Middle Age . . . Home of lost causes, and forsaken beliefs, and unpopular names, and impossible loyalties!
of Oxford
Essays in Criticism First Series (1865) preface; cf. **Beerbohm** 61:13

16 The gloom, the smoke, the cold, the strangled illegitimate child! . . . And the final touch,—short, bleak and inhuman: *Wragg is in custody.*
prompted by a newspaper report of the murder of her illegitimate child by a girl named Wragg
Essays in Criticism First Series (1865) 'The Function of Criticism at the Present Time'

17 I am bound by my own definition of criticism: *a disinterested endeavour to learn and propagate the best that is known and thought in the world.*
Essays in Criticism First Series (1865) 'The Function of Criticism at the Present Time'

18 Philistinism!—We have not the expression in English. Perhaps we have not the word because we have so much of the thing.
Essays in Criticism First Series (1865) 'Heinrich Heine'

19 The great apostle of the Philistines, Lord Macaulay.
Essays in Criticism First Series (1865) 'Joubert'

20 The absence, in this country, of any force of educated literary and scientific opinion.
Essays in Criticism First Series (1865) 'The Literary Influence of Academies'

21 In poetry, no less than in life, he is 'a beautiful and ineffectual angel, beating in the void his luminous wings in vain'.
Essays in Criticism Second Series (1888) 'Shelley' (quoting from his own essay on Byron in the same work)

22 More and more mankind will discover that we have to turn to poetry to interpret life for us, to console us, to sustain us. Without poetry, our science will appear incomplete; and most of what now passes with us for religion and philosophy will be replaced by poetry.
Essays in Criticism Second Series (1888) 'The Study of Poetry'

23 The difference between genuine poetry and the poetry of Dryden, Pope, and all their school, is briefly this: their poetry is conceived and composed in their wits, genuine poetry is conceived and composed in the soul.
Essays in Criticism Second Series (1888) 'Thomas Gray'

24 Poetry is at bottom a criticism of life.
Essays in Criticism Second Series (1888) 'Wordsworth'

25 His expression may often be called bald . . . but it is bald as the bare mountain tops are bald, with a baldness full of grandeur.
Essays in Criticism Second Series (1888) 'Wordsworth'

26 I am past thirty, and three parts iced over.
Howard Foster Lowry (ed.) *The Letters of Matthew Arnold to Arthur Hugh Clough* (1932) 12 February 1853

27 Terms like grace, new birth, justification . . . terms, in short, which with St Paul are literary terms, theologians have employed as if they were scientific terms.
Literature and Dogma (1873) ch. 1

1 The true meaning of religion is thus not simply morality, but morality touched by emotion.
Literature and Dogma (1873) ch. 1

2 Conduct is three-fourths of our life and its largest concern.
Literature and Dogma (1873) ch. 1

3 But there remains the question: what righteousness really is. The method and secret and sweet reasonableness of Jesus.
Literature and Dogma (1873) ch. 12

4 So we have the Philistine of genius in religion—Luther; the Philistine of genius in politics—Cromwell; the Philistine of genius in literature—Bunyan.
Mixed Essays (1879) 'Lord Falkland'

5 Wordsworth says somewhere that wherever Virgil seems to have composed 'with his eye on the object', Dryden fails to render him. Homer invariably composes 'with his eye on the object', whether the object be a moral or a material one: Pope composes with his eye on his style, into which he translates his object, whatever it is.
On Translating Homer (1861) Lecture 1

6 Of these two literatures [French and German], as of the intellect of Europe in general, the main effort, for now many years, has been a *critical* effort; the endeavours, in all branches of knowledge—theology, philosophy, history, art, science—to see the object as in itself it really is.
On Translating Homer (1861) Lecture 2

7 He [the translator] will find one English book and one only, where, as in the *Iliad* itself, perfect plainness of speech is allied with perfect nobleness; and that book is the Bible.
On Translating Homer (1861) Lecture 3

8 Nothing has raised more questioning among my critics than these words—noble, the grand style ... I think it will be found that the grand style arises in poetry, when a noble nature, poetically gifted, treats with simplicity or with severity a serious subject.
On Translating Homer. Last Words (1862)

9 Have something to say, and say it as clearly as you can. That is the only secret of style.
G. W. E. Russell *Collections and Recollections* (1898) ch. 13

Roseanne Arnold 1953-
American comedian

10 I used to think I was an interesting person, but I must tell you how sobering a thought it is to realize your life's story fills about thirty-five pages and you have, actually, not much to say.
Roseanne (1990)

11 If I were Her what would really piss me off the worst is that they cannot even get My gender right for Christsakes.
Roseanne (1990)

Samuel James Arnold
English organist and composer

12 England, home and beauty.
'The Death of Nelson' (1811 song)

Thomas Arnold 1795–1842
English historian and educator; Headmaster of Rugby School from 1828; father of Matthew **Arnold**

13 My object will be, if possible, to form Christian men, for Christian boys I can scarcely hope to make.
on appointment to the Headmastership of Rugby School
letter to Revd John Tucker, 2 March 1828; Arthur Penrhyn Stanley *The Life and Correspondence of Thomas Arnold* (1844) vol. 1, ch. 2

14 What we must look for here is, 1st, religious and moral principles: 2ndly, gentlemanly conduct: 3rdly, intellectual ability.
address to the praepostors [prefects] *of Rugby School*
Arthur Penrhyn Stanley *The Life and Correspondence of Thomas Arnold* (1844) vol. 1, ch. 3

15 As for rioting, the old Roman way of dealing with that is always the right one; flog the rank and file, and fling the ringleaders from the Tarpeian rock.
from an unpublished letter written before 1828, quoted by Matthew **Arnold** in *Cornhill Magazine* August 1868 'Anarchy and Authority'

16 It is quite awful to watch the strength of evil in such young minds, and how powerless is every effort against it. It would give the vainest man alive a very fair notion of his own insufficiency, to see how little he can do and how his most earnest addresses are as a cannon ball on a bolster.
David Newsome *Godliness and Good Learning* (1961)

17 My love for any place, or person, or institution, is exactly the measure of my desire to reform them.
David Newsome *Godliness and Good Learning* (1961); **Tusa** 786:1

Raymond Aron 1905-
French sociologist and political journalist

18 *La pensée politique, en France, est rétrospective ou utopique.*
Political thought, in France, is retrospective or utopian.
The Opium of the Intellectuals (1955) ch. 1

Antonin Artaud 1896–1948
French actor, director, and dramatic theorist

19 *Il faut nous laver de la littérature. Nous voulons être hommes avant tout, être humains.*
We must wash literature off ourselves. We want to be men above all, to be human.
Les Oeuvres et les Hommes (unpublished MS, 17 May 1922)

L. A. Artsimovich 1909–73

20 The joke definition according to which 'Science is the best way of satisfying the curiosity of individuals at government expense' is more or less correct.
in *Novy Mir* January 1967

Roger Ascham 1515–68
English scholar, writer, and courtier

1 I said . . . how, and why, young children, were sooner allured by love, than driven by beating, to attain good learning.
The Schoolmaster (1570) preface

2 There is no such whetstone, to sharpen a good wit and encourage a will to learning, as is praise.
The Schoolmaster (1570) bk. 1

3 Mark all mathematical heads which be only and wholly bent on these sciences, how solitary they be themselves, how unfit to live with others, and how unapt to serve the world.
The Schoolmaster (1570) bk. 1

4 To laugh, to lie, to flatter, to face
Four ways in court to win men grace.
The Schoolmaster (1570) bk. 1

5 Learning teacheth more in one year than experience in twenty.
The Schoolmaster (1570) bk. 1

6 We know by experience itself, that . . . we find out but a short way, by long wandering.
The Schoolmaster (1570) bk. 1

7 *Inglese Italianato, è un diavolo incarnato*, that is to say, you remain men in shape and fashion, but become devils in life and condition.
of Englishmen travelling in Italy
The Schoolmaster (1570) bk. 1

8 What toys, the daily reading of such a book, may work in the will of a young gentleman, or a young maid . . . wise men can judge, and honest men do pity.
of Malory's Le Morte D'Arthur *as unsuitable reading for the young*
The Schoolmaster (1570) bk. 1

9 He that will write well in any tongue, must follow this counsel of Aristotle, to speak as the common people do, to think as wise men do; and so should every man understand him, and the judgement of wise men allow him.
Toxophilus (1545) 'To all gentlemen and yeomen of England'

Daisy Ashford 1881–1972
English child author

10 Mr Salteena was an elderly man of 42.
The Young Visiters (1919) ch. 1

11 I am not quite a gentleman but you would hardly notice it but can't be helped anyhow.
The Young Visiters (1919) ch. 1

12 Bernard always had a few prayers in the hall and some whiskey afterwards as he was rarther pious but Mr Salteena was not very addicted to prayers so he marched up to bed.
The Young Visiters (1919) ch. 3

13 It was a sumpshous spot all done up in gold with plenty of looking glasses.
The Young Visiters (1919) ch. 5

14 Oh I see said the Earl but my own idear is that these things are as piffle before the wind.
The Young Visiters (1919) ch. 5

15 My life will be sour grapes and ashes without you.
The Young Visiters (1919) ch. 8

Isaac Asimov 1920–92
Russian-born biochemist and science fiction writer

16 The three fundamental Rules of Robotics . . . One, a robot may not injure a human being, or, through inaction, allow a human being to come to harm . . . Two . . . a robot must obey the orders given it by human beings except where such orders would conflict with the First Law . . . three, a robot must protect its own existence as long as such protection does not conflict with the First or Second Laws.
I, Robot (1950) 'Runaround'

17 Science fiction writers foresee the inevitable, and although problems and catastrophes may be inevitable, solutions are not.
'How Easy to See the Future' in *Natural History* April 1975

18 When, however, the lay public rallies around an idea that is denounced by distinguished but elderly scientists and supports that idea with great fervour and emotion—the distinguished but elderly scientists are then, after all, probably right.
corollary to Arthur C. **Clarke***'s law; cf.* **Clarke** *219:8*
Arthur C. Clarke 'Asimov's Corollary' in K. Frazier (ed.) *Paranormal Borderlands of Science* (1981)

19 The first law of dietetics seems to be: if it tastes good, it's bad for you.
attributed

Anne Askew 1521–46
English martyr

20 Like as the armèd knight
Appointed to the field,
With this world will I fight,
And faith shall be my shield . . .

I am not she that list
My anchor to let fall,
For every drizzling mist
My ship substantial.
'The Ballad which Anne Askew made and sang when she was in Newgate' (1546)

Cynthia Asquith 1887–1960
English writer

21 I am beginning to rub my eyes at the prospect of peace . . . One will at last fully recognize that the dead are not only dead for the duration of the war.
diary, 7 October 1918

Herbert Asquith, Earl of Oxford and Asquith 1852–1928

British Liberal statesman; Prime Minister, 1908–16; husband of Margot **Asquith**
on Asquith: see **Telegrams** *758:6*

1 We had better wait and see.
phrase used repeatedly in speeches in 1910, referring to the rumour that the House of Lords was to be flooded with new Liberal peers to ensure the passage of the Finance Bill
Roy Jenkins *Asquith* (1964)

2 We shall never sheathe the sword which we have not lightly drawn until Belgium recovers in full measure all and more than all that she has sacrificed, until France is adequately secured against the menace of aggression, until the rights of the smaller nationalities of Europe are placed upon an unassailable foundation, and until the military domination of Prussia is wholly and finally destroyed.
speech at the Guildhall, London, 9 November 1914, in *The Times* 10 November 1914

3 Youth would be an ideal state if it came a little later in life.
in *Observer* 15 April 1923

4 The office of the Prime Minister is what its holder chooses and is able to make of it.
Fifty Years of Parliament (1926) vol. 2

5 It is fitting that we should have buried the Unknown Prime Minister by the side of the Unknown Soldier.
of Andrew **Bonar Law**
Robert Blake *The Unknown Prime Minister* (1955)

6 [The War Office kept three sets of figures:] one to mislead the public, another to mislead the Cabinet, and the third to mislead itself.
Alistair Horne *Price of Glory* (1962) ch. 2

Margot Asquith 1864–1945

British political hostess; wife of Herbert **Asquith**

7 Kitchener is a great poster.
More Memories (1933) ch. 6

8 The *t* is silent, as in *Harlow*.
to Jean Harlow, who had been mispronouncing 'Margot'
T. S. Matthews *Great Tom* (1973) ch. 7

9 Lord Birkenhead is very clever but sometimes his brains go to his head.
in *Listener* 11 June 1953 'Margot Oxford' by Lady Violet Bonham Carter

10 He can't see a belt without hitting below it.
of **Lloyd George**
in *Listener* 11 June 1953 'Margot Oxford' by Lady Violet Bonham Carter

Mary Astell 1668–1731

English poet and feminist

11 Their sophistry I can control
Who falsely say that women have no soul.
'Ambition' (written 1684) l. 7

12 Happy am I who out of danger sit,
Can see and pity them who wade thro it;
Need take no thought my treasure to dispose,
What I ne'er had I cannot fear to lose.
'Awake my Lute' l. 18

13 Our opposers usually miscall our quickness of thought, fancy and flash, and christen their own heaviness by the specious names of judgement and solidity; but it is easy to retort upon them the reproachful ones of dullness and stupidity.
An Essay in Defence of the Female Sex (1696)

14 Fetters of gold are still fetters, and the softest lining can never make them so easy as liberty.
An Essay in Defence of the Female Sex (1696); cf. **Bacon** 42:1

15 If all men are born free, how is it that all women are born slaves?
Some Reflections upon Marriage (1706 ed.) preface

16 If marriage be such a blessed state, how comes it, may you say, that there are so few happy marriages? Now in answer to this, it is not to be wondered that so few succeed; we should rather be surprised to find so many do, considering how imprudently men engage, the motives they act by, and the very strange conduct they observe throughout.
Some Reflections upon Marriage (1700) preface

17 'Tis less to be wondered at that women marry off in haste, for if they took time to consider and reflect upon it, they seldom would.
Some Reflections upon Marriage (1700)

Jacob Astley 1579–1652

English soldier and royalist

18 O Lord! thou knowest how busy I must be this day: if I forget thee, do not thou forget me.
prayer before the Battle of Edgehill, 1642
Philip Warwick *Memoires* (1701)

Nancy Astor 1879–1964

American-born British Conservative politician
see also **Churchill** *216:23*

19 I married beneath me, all women do.
in *Dictionary of National Biography 1961–1970* (1981)

Brooks Atkinson 1894–1984

American journalist and critic

20 After each war there is a little less democracy to save.
Once Around the Sun (1951) 7 January

David Attenborough 1926–

English naturalist and broadcaster

21 I'm not over-fond of animals. I am merely astounded by them.
in *Independent* 14 January 1995

Clement Attlee 1883–1967

British Labour statesman; Prime Minister, 1945–51
see also **de Gaulle** 255:23

1 The voice we heard was that of Mr Churchill but the mind was that of Lord Beaverbrook.
speech on radio, 5 June 1945; Francis Williams *A Prime Minister Remembers* (1961)

2 A period of silence on your part would be welcome.
letter to Harold Laski, 20 August 1945; Francis Williams *A Prime Minister Remembers* (1961)

3 Few thought he was even a starter
There were many who thought themselves smarter
But he ended PM
CH and OM
An earl and a knight of the garter.
describing himself in a letter to Tom Attlee, 8 April 1956
Kenneth Harris *Attlee* (1982)

4 [Russian Communism is] the illegitimate child of Karl Marx and Catherine the Great.
speech at Aarhus University, 11 April 1956, in *The Times* 12 April 1956

5 Democracy means government by discussion, but it is only effective if you can stop people talking.
speech at Oxford, 14 June 1957, in *The Times* 15 June 1957

6 A monologue is not a decision.
to Winston **Churchill**, *who had complained that a matter had been raised several times in Cabinet*
Francis Williams *A Prime Minister Remembers* (1961) ch. 7

7 If the King asks you to form a Government you say 'Yes' or 'No', not 'I'll let you know later!'
Kenneth Harris *Attlee* (1982)

Margaret Atwood 1939–

Canadian novelist

8 Nobody dies from lack of sex. It's lack of love we die from.
The Handmaid's Tale (1986)

9 I tried for the longest time to find out what *deconstructionism* was. Nobody was able to explain it to me clearly. The best answer I got was from a writer, who said, 'Honey, it's bad news for you and me.'
in an interview, December 1986; Earl G. Ingersoll (ed.) *Margaret Atwood: Conversations* (1990)

Henriette Auber 1773–1862

English hymn-writer

10 Our blest Redeemer, ere he breathed
His tender last farewell,
A Guide, a Comforter, bequeathed
With us to dwell.

He came in tongues of living flame,
To teach, convince, subdue;
All-powerful as the wind he came,
As viewless too.
'Our blest Redeemer, ere he breathed' (1829 hymn)

John Aubrey 1626–97

English antiquary and biographer

11 The Bishop sometimes would take the key of the wine-cellar, and he and his chaplain would go and lock themselves in and be merry. Then first he lays down his episcopal hat—*There lies the Doctor*. Then he puts off his gown—*There lies the Bishop*. Then 'twas, *Here's to thee, Corbet*, and *Here's to thee, Lushington*.
Brief Lives 'Richard Corbet'

12 How these curiosities would be quite forgot, did not such idle fellows as I am put them down.
Brief Lives 'Venetia Digby'

13 He was wont to say that if he had read as much as other men, he should have known no more than other men.
Brief Lives 'Thomas Hobbes'

14 As they were reading of inscribing and circumscribing figures, said he, I will show you how to inscribe a triangle in a quadrangle. Bring a pig into the quadrangle and I will set the college dog at him, and he will take the pig by the ear, then I come and take the dog by the tail and the hog by the tail, and so there you have a triangle in a quadrangle, *quod erat faciendum*.
Brief Lives 'Ralph Kettel'

15 And when he saw the cheese-cakes:—'What have we here, *crinkum crankum*?'
Brief Lives 'Ralph Kettel'

16 His harmonical and ingenious soul did lodge in a beautiful and well proportioned body. He was a spare man.
Brief Lives 'John Milton'

17 Oval face. His eye a dark grey. He had auburn hair. His complexion exceeding fair—he was so fair that they called him *the lady of* Christ's College.
Brief Lives 'John Milton'

18 He pronounced the letter R (*littera canina*) very hard—a certain sign of a satirical wit.
Brief Lives 'John Milton'

19 Sciatica: he cured it, by boiling his buttock.
Brief Lives 'Sir Jonas Moore'

20 She was when a child much against the Bishops, and prayed to God to take them to him, but afterwards was reconciled to them. Prayed aloud, as the hypocritical fashion then was, and was overheard.
Brief Lives 'Katherine Philips'

21 Sir Walter, being strangely surprised and put out of his countenance at so great a table, gives his son a damned blow over the face. His son, as rude as he was, would not strike his father, but strikes over the face the gentleman that sat next to him and said 'Box about: 'twill come to my father anon'.
Brief Lives 'Sir Walter Raleigh'

22 He was a handsome, well-shaped man: very good company, and of a very ready and pleasant smooth wit.
Brief Lives 'William Shakespeare'

1 Anno 1670, not far from Cirencester, was an apparition; being demanded whether a good spirit or a bad? returned no answer, but disappeared with a curious perfume and most melodious twang. Mr W. Lilly believes it was a fairy.
Miscellanies (1696) 'Apparitions'

Auctoritates Aristotelis

A compilation of medieval propositions drawn from diverse classical and other sources (ed. J. Hamesse, 1974)

2 *Consuetudo est altera natura.*
Habit is second nature.

3 *Contra negantem principia non est disputandum.*
You cannot argue with someone who denies the first principles.

4 *Deus et natura nihil faciunt frustra.*
God and nature do nothing in vain.

5 *Ignorantia excusat peccatum.*
Ignorance excuses from sin.

6 *Melius est esse quam non esse.*
It is better to be than not to be.

7 *Natura dat unicuique quod sibi conveniens est.*
Nature gives to each what is appropriate.

8 *Natura desiderat semper quod melius est.*
Nature always desires what is better.

9 *Non est idem bonus homo et bonus civis.*
A good man and a good citizen are not the same thing.

10 *Omnes homines naturaliter scire desiderant.*
All men naturally desire to know.

11 *Oportet inquisitores veritatis non esse inimicos.*
There should be no enmity among seekers after truth.

12 *Parentes plus amant filios quam e converso.*
Parents love their children more than children love their parents.

13 *Signum scientis est posse docere.*
The touchstone of knowledge is the ability to teach.

14 *Silentium mulieri praestat ornatum.*
Silence is a woman's finest ornament.

15 *Tempus est mensura motus rerum mobilium.*
Time is the measure of movement.

W. H. Auden 1907–73

English poet
on Auden: see **Orwell** *559:6*

16 Sob, heavy world,
Sob as you spin
Mantled in mist, remote from the happy.
The Age of Anxiety (1947) pt. 4 'The Dirge'

17 Blessed Cecilia, appear in visions
To all musicians, appear and inspire:
Translated Daughter, come down and startle
Composing mortals with immortal fire.
Anthem for St Cecilia's Day (1941) pt. 1

18 I'll love you, dear, I'll love you
Till China and Africa meet
And the river jumps over the mountain
And the salmon sing in the street,
I'll love you till the ocean
Is folded and hung up to dry
And the seven stars go squawking
Like geese about the sky.
'As I Walked Out One Evening' (1940)

19 The glacier knocks in the cupboard,
The desert sighs in the bed,
And the crack in the teacup opens
A lane to the land of the dead.
'As I Walked Out One Evening' (1940)

20 At the far end of the enormous room
An orchestra is playing to the rich.
'At the far end of the enormous room' (1933)

21 Make intercession
For the treason of all clerks.
'At the Grave of Henry James' (1945); cf. **Benda** 64:22

22 August for the people and their favourite islands.
title of poem (1936)

23 The desires of the heart are as crooked as corkscrews
Not to be born is the best for man.
'Death's Echo' (1937); cf. **Sophocles** 728:15

24 Happy the hare at morning, for she cannot read
The Hunter's waking thoughts.
Dog beneath the Skin (with Christopher **Isherwood**, 1935) act 2, sc. 2

25 To save your world you asked this man to die:
Would this man, could he see you now, ask why?
'Epitaph for the Unknown Soldier' (1955)

26 When he laughed, respectable senators burst with laughter,
And when he cried the little children died in the streets.
'Epitaph on a Tyrant' (1940); cf. **Motley** 534:7

27 Altogether elsewhere, vast
Herds of reindeer move across
Miles and miles of golden moss,
Silently and very fast.
'The Fall of Rome' (1951)

28 He was my North, my South, my East and West,
My working week and my Sunday rest,
My noon, my midnight, my talk, my song;
I thought that love would last for ever: I was wrong.
'Funeral Blues' (1936)

29 To us he is no more a person
now but a whole climate of opinion.
'In Memory of Sigmund Freud' (1940) st. 17

30 The mercury sank in the mouth of the dying day.
What instruments we have agree
The day of his death was a dark cold day.
'In Memory of W. B. Yeats' (1940) pt. 1

31 You were silly like us; your gift survived it all:
The parish of rich women, physical decay,
Yourself. Mad Ireland hurt you into poetry.
'In Memory of W. B. Yeats' (1940) pt. 2

1 For poetry makes nothing happen: it survives
In the valley of its saying where executives
Would never want to tamper.
'In Memory of W. B. Yeats' (1940) pt. 2

2 Earth, receive an honoured guest:
William Yeats is laid to rest.
Let the Irish vessel lie
Emptied of its poetry.
In the nightmare of the dark
All the dogs of Europe bark,
And the living nations wait,
Each sequestered in its hate;
Intellectual disgrace
Stares from every human face,
And the seas of pity lie
Locked and frozen in each eye.
'In Memory of W. B. Yeats' (1940) pt. 3

3 Time that with this strange excuse
Pardoned Kipling and his views,
And will pardon Paul Claudel,
Pardons him for writing well.
'In Memory of W. B. Yeats' (1940) pt. 3

4 In the deserts of the heart
Let the healing fountain start,
In the prison of his days
Teach the free man how to praise.
'In Memory of W. B. Yeats' (1940) pt. 3

5 I see it often since you've been away:
The island, the veranda, and the fruit;
The tiny steamer breaking from the bay;
The literary mornings with its hoot;
Our ugly comic servant; and then you,
Lovely and willing every afternoon.
'I see it often since you've been away' (1933)

6 Look, stranger, at this island now.
title of poem (1936)

7 The leaping light for your delight discovers,
Stand stable here
And silent be,
That through the channels of the ear
May wander like a river
The swaying sound of the sea.
'Look, stranger, at this island now' (1936)

8 Lay your sleeping head, my love,
Human on my faithless arm.
'Lullaby' (1940)

9 About suffering they were never wrong,
The Old Masters: how well they understood
Its human position; how it takes place
While someone else is eating or opening a window
or just walking dully along.
'Musée des Beaux Arts' (1940)

10 They never forgot
That even the dreadful martyrdom must run its
course
Anyhow in a corner, some untidy spot
Where the dogs go on with their doggy life and the
torturer's horse
Scratches its innocent behind on a tree.
'Musée des Beaux Arts' (1940)

11 To the man-in-the-street, who, I'm sorry to say,
Is a keen observer of life,
The word 'Intellectual' suggests straight away
A man who's untrue to his wife.
New Year Letter (1941) l. 1277 n.

12 This is the Night Mail crossing the Border,
Bringing the cheque and the postal order,
Letters for the rich, letters for the poor,
The shop at the corner, the girl next door.
Pulling up Beattock, a steady climb:
The gradient's against her, but she's on time.
Past cotton-grass and moorland border,
Shovelling white steam over her shoulder.
'Night Mail' (1936) pt. 1

13 Letters of thanks, letters from banks,
Letters of joy from girl and boy,
Receipted bills and invitations
To inspect new stock or to visit relations,
And applications for situations,
And timid lovers' declarations,
And gossip, gossip from all the nations.
'Night Mail' (1936) pt. 3

14 And make us as Newton was, who in his garden
watching
The apple falling towards England, became aware
Between himself and her of an eternal tie.
'O Love, the interest itself' (1936)

15 Private faces in public places
Are wiser and nicer
Than public faces in private places.
Orators (1932) dedication

16 Out on the lawn I lie in bed,
Vega conspicuous overhead.
'Out on the lawn I lie in bed' (1936)

17 O what is that sound which so thrills the ear
Down in the valley drumming, drumming?
Only the scarlet soldiers, dear,
The soldiers coming.
'O what is that sound' (1936)

18 O it's broken the lock and splintered the door,
O it's the gate where they're turning, turning;
Their boots are heavy on the floor
And their eyes are burning.
'O what is that sound' (1936)

19 Some thirty inches from my nose
The frontier of my Person goes,
And all the untilled air between
Is private *pagus* or demesne.
Stranger, unless with bedroom eyes
I beckon you to fraternize,
Beware of rudely crossing it:
I have no gun, but I can spit.
'Prologue: the Birth of Architecture' (1966) postscript

20 My Dear One is mine as mirrors are lonely.
'The Sea and the Mirror' (1944) pt. 2 (Miranda)

21 I and the public know
What all schoolchildren learn,
Those to whom evil is done
Do evil in return.
'September 1, 1939' (1940)

1 But who can live for long
In an euphoric dream;
Out of the mirror they stare,
Imperialism's face
And the international wrong.
'September 1, 1939' (1940)

2 All I have is a voice
To undo the folded lie,
The romantic lie in the brain
Of the sensual man-in-the-street
And the lie of Authority
Whose buildings grope the sky:
There is no such thing as the State
And no one exists alone;
Hunger allows no choice
To the citizen or the police;
We must love one another or die.
'September 1, 1939' (1940)

3 A shilling life will give you all the facts.
title of poem (1936)

4 Each year brings new problems of Form and Content,
new foes to tug with: at Twenty I tried to
vex my elders, past Sixty it's the young whom
I hope to bother.
'Shorts I' (1969)

5 A poet's hope: to be,
like some valley cheese,
local, but prized elsewhere.
'Shorts II' (1976)

6 Harrow the house of the dead; look shining at
New styles of architecture, a change of heart.
'Sir, No Man's Enemy' (1930)

7 To-morrow for the young the poets exploding like bombs,
The walks by the lake, the weeks of perfect communion;
To-morrow the bicycle races
Through the suburbs on summer evenings: but to-day the struggle.
'Spain 1937' (1937) st. 20

8 The stars are dead; the animals will not look:
We are left alone with our day, and the time is short and
History to the defeated
May say Alas but cannot help or pardon.
'Spain 1937' (1937) st. 23

9 To ask the hard question is simple.
title of poem (1933)

10 Was he free? Was he happy? The question is absurd:
Had anything been wrong, we should certainly have heard.
'The Unknown Citizen' (1940)

11 The sky is darkening like a stain;
Something is going to fall like rain,
And it won't be flowers.
'The Witnesses' (1935) l. 67

12 All sin tends to be addictive, and the terminal point of addiction is what is called damnation.
A Certain World (1970) 'Hell'

13 Man is a history-making creature who can neither repeat his past nor leave it behind.
The Dyer's Hand (1963) 'D. H. Lawrence'

14 When I find myself in the company of scientists, I feel like a shabby curate who has strayed by mistake into a drawing room full of dukes.
The Dyer's Hand (1963) 'The Poet and the City'

15 Some books are undeservedly forgotten; none are undeservedly remembered.
The Dyer's Hand (1963) 'Reading'

16 Art is born of humiliation.
Stephen Spender *World Within World* (1951) ch. 2

17 LSD? Nothing much happened, but I did get the distinct impression that some birds were trying to communicate with me.
George Plimpton (ed.) *The Writer's Chapbook* (1989)

18 My face looks like a wedding-cake left out in the rain.
Humphrey Carpenter *W. H. Auden* (1981) pt. 2, ch. 6

19 Nothing I wrote in the thirties saved one Jew from Auschwitz.
attributed

Stan Augarten

20 Computers are composed of nothing more than logic gates stretched out to the horizon in a vast numerical irrigation system.
State of the Art: A Photographic History of the Integrated Circuit (1983)

Émile Augier 1820–89

French poet and playwright

21 MARQUIS: *Mettez un canard sur un lac au milieu des cygnes, vous verrez qu'il regrettera sa mare et finira par y retourner.*
MONTRICHARD: *La nostalgie de la boue!*
MARQUIS: Put a duck on a lake in the midst of some swans, and you'll see he'll miss his pond and eventually return to it.
MONTRICHARD: Longing to be back in the mud!
Le Mariage d'Olympe (1855) act 1, sc. 1

St Augustine of Hippo AD 354–430

Early Christian theologian
see also **Prayers** 592:7

22 *Tu excitas, ut laudare te delectet, quia fecisti nos, ad te et inquietum est cor nostrum, donec requiescat in te.*
You stir man to take pleasure in praising you, because you have made us for yourself, and our heart is restless until it rests in you.
Confessions (AD 397–8) bk. 1, ch. 1

23 *Nondum amabam, et amare amabam . . . quaerebam quid amarem, amans amare.*
I loved not yet, yet I loved to love . . . I sought what I might love, loving to love.
Confessions (AD 397–8) bk. 3, ch. 1

1 *Et illa erant fercula, in quibus mihi esurienti te inferebantur sol et luna.*

And these were the dishes wherein to me, hunger-starven for thee, the sun and moon were served up.

Confessions (AD 397–8) bk. 3, ch. 6

2 When he was reading, he drew his eyes along over the leaves, and his heart searched into the sense, but his voice and tongue were silent.

of St Ambrose

Confessions (AD 397–8) bk. 6, ch. 3

3 *Da mihi castitatem et continentiam, sed noli modo.*

Give me chastity and continency—but not yet!

Confessions (AD 397–8) bk. 8, ch. 7

4 *Tolle lege, tolle lege.*

Take up and read, take up and read.

Confessions (AD 397–8) bk. 8, ch. 12

5 *Sero te amavi, pulchritudo tam antiqua et tam nova, sero te amavi! et ecce intus eras et ego foris, et ibi te quaerebam.*

Too late came I to love thee, O thou Beauty both so ancient and so fresh, yea too late came I to love thee. And behold, thou wert within me, and I out of myself, where I made search for thee.

Confessions (AD 397–8) bk. 10, ch. 27

6 *Continentiam iubes; da quod iubes et iube quod vis.*

You command continence; give what you command, and command what you will.

Confessions (AD 397–8) bk. 10, ch. 29

7 *Salus extra ecclesiam non est.*

There is no salvation outside the church.

De Baptismo contra Donatistas bk. 4, ch. 17, sect. 24; cf. **Cyprian** 248:10, 248:12

8 *Audi partem alteram.*

Hear the other side.

De Duabus Animabus contra Manicheos ch. 14

9 *Dilige et quod vis fac.*

Love and do what you will.

often quoted as 'Ama et fac quod vis'

In Epistolam Joannis ad Parthos (AD 413) tractatus 7, sect. 8

10 *Multi quidem facilius se abstinent ut non utantur, quam temperent ut bene utantur.*

To many, total abstinence is easier than perfect moderation.

On the Good of Marriage (AD 401) ch. 21

11 *Cum dilectione hominum et odio vitiorum.*

With love for mankind and hatred of sins.

often quoted as 'Love the sinner but hate the sin'

letter 211 in J.-P. Migne (ed.) *Patrologiae Latinae* (1845) vol. 33; cf. **Pope** 582:23

12 *Roma locuta est; causa finita est.*

Rome has spoken; the case is concluded.

traditional summary of words found in *Sermons* (Antwerp, 1702) no. 131, sect. 10

13 *De vitiis nostris scalam nobis facimus, si vitia ipsa calcamus.*

We make ourselves a ladder out of our vices if we trample the vices themselves underfoot.

sermon no. 176 ('On the Ascension of the Lord' no. 1) in J.-P. Migne (ed.) *Patrologiae Latinae* (1845) vol. 38

14 It is a singing to the praise of God. If you praise God, and do not sing, you utter no hymn. If you sing, and praise no God, you utter no hymn. If you praise anything which does not pertain to the praise of God, though in singing you praise, you utter no hymn.

defining a hymn

note to Psalm 148; J. R. Watson *The English Hymn: a Critical and Historical Study* (1997) ch. 1

Augustus 63 BC–AD 14

first Roman emperor

15 Quintilius Varus, give me back my legions.

on Varus' loss of three legions in battle with Germanic tribes, AD 9

Suetonius *Lives of the Caesars* 'Divus Augustus' sect. 23

16 *Festina lente.*

Make haste slowly.

Suetonius *Lives of the Caesars* 'Divus Augustus' sect. 25; cf. **Proverbs** 606:11

17 He could boast that he inherited it brick and left it marble.

referring to the city of Rome

Suetonius *Lives of the Caesars* 'Divus Augustus' sect. 28

18 That they would pay at the Greek Kalends.

meaning never

Suetonius *Lives of the Caesars* 'Divus Augustus' sect. 87

Aung San Suu Kyi 1945–

Burmese political leader

19 It's very different from living in academia in Oxford. We called someone vicious in the *Times Literary Supplement*. We didn't know what vicious was.

on returning to Burma (Myanmar)

in *Observer* 25 September 1988 'Sayings of the Week'

20 In societies where men are truly confident of their own worth, women are not merely tolerated but valued.

videotape speech at NGO Forum on Women, China, early September 1995

Marcus Aurelius AD 121–80

Roman emperor from AD 161

21 Nowhere can a man find a quieter or more untroubled retreat than in his own soul.

Meditations bk. 4, sect. 3

22 Everything is fitting for me, my universe, which fits thy purpose. Nothing in its good time is too early or too late for me; everything is fruit for me which thy seasons, Nature, bear; from thee, in thee, to thee, are all things. The poet sings 'Dear city of Cecrops', and you will not say 'Dear city of God'?

Meditations bk. 4, sect. 23

1 Time is a violent torrent; no sooner is a thing brought to sight than it is swept by and another takes its place, and this too will be swept away.
Meditations bk. 4, sect. 43

2 Be like a headland of rock on which the waves break incessantly: but it stands fast and around it the seething of the waters sinks to rest.
Meditations bk. 4, sect. 49

3 Nothing happens to anybody which he is not fitted by nature to bear.
Meditations bk. 5, sect. 18

4 Sexual intercourse . . . is merely internal attrition and the spasmodic excretion of mucus.
Meditations bk 6, sect. 13

5 Every instant of time is a pinprick of eternity. All things are petty, easily changed, vanishing away.
Meditations bk. 6, sect. 36

6 He who sees what is now has seen all things, whatsoever comes to pass from everlasting and whatsoever shall be unto everlasting time.
Meditations bk. 6, sect. 37

7 To change your mind and to follow him who sets you right is to be nonetheless the free agent that you were before.
Meditations bk. 8, sect. 16

8 Mankind have been created for the sake of one another. Either instruct them, therefore, or endure them.
Meditations bk. 8, sect. 59

9 Whatever befalls you was prepared for you beforehand from eternity, and the thread of causes was spinning from everlasting both your existence and this which befalls you.
Meditations bk. 10, sect. 5

10 Man, you have been a citizen in this world city, what does it matter whether for five years or fifty?
Meditations bk. 12, sect. 36

Decius Magnus Ausonius *c.*309–392 AD
Latin poet

11 *Nemo bonus Britto est.*
No good man is a Briton.
Epigrams 119

Jane Austen 1775–1817
English novelist
on Austen: see ***Harding*** *360:4,* ***Mitford*** *524:4,* ***Scott*** *652:12; see also* ***Borrowed titles*** *144:12,* ***Clarke*** *219:15*

12 Miss Bates stood in the very worst predicament in the world for having much of the public favour; and she had no intellectual superiority to make atonement for herself, or frighten those who might hate her, into outward respect.
Emma (1816) ch. 3

13 An egg boiled very soft is not unwholesome.
Emma (1816) ch. 3

14 One half of the world cannot understand the pleasures of the other.
Emma (1816) ch. 9

15 With men he can be rational and unaffected, but when he has ladies to please, every feature works.
Emma (1816) ch. 13

16 The folly of people's not staying comfortably at home when they can! . . . five dull hours in another man's house, with nothing to say or to hear that was not said and heard yesterday, and may not be said and heard again tomorrow . . . four horses and four servants taken out for nothing but to convey five idle, shivering creatures into colder rooms and worse company than they might have had at home.
Emma (1816) ch. 13

17 The sooner every party breaks up the better.
Emma (1816) ch. 25

18 Surprises are foolish things. The pleasure is not enhanced, and the inconvenience is often considerable.
Emma (1816) ch. 26

19 One has no great hopes from Birmingham. I always say there is something direful in the sound.
Emma (1816) ch. 36

20 One of Edward's Mistresses was Jane Shore, who has had a play written about her, but it is a tragedy and therefore not worth reading.
The History of England (written 1791)

21 Nothing can be said in his vindication, but that his abolishing Religious Houses and leaving them to the ruinous depredations of time has been of infinite use to the landscape of England in general.
The History of England (written 1791)

22 It was too pathetic for the feelings of Sophia and myself—we fainted Alternately on a Sofa.
Love and Freindship (written 1790) 'Letter the 8th'

23 She was nothing more than a mere good-tempered, civil and obliging young woman; as such we could scarcely dislike her—she was only an Object of Contempt.
Love and Freindship (written 1790) 'Letter the 13th'

24 There is not one in a hundred of either sex who is not taken in when they marry. Look where I will, I see that it *is* so; and I feel that it *must* be so, when I consider that it is, of all transactions, the one in which people expect most from others, and are least honest themselves.
Mansfield Park (1814) ch. 5

25 We do not look in great cities for our best morality.
Mansfield Park (1814) ch. 9

26 A large income is the best recipe for happiness I ever heard of. It certainly may secure all the myrtle and turkey part of it.
Mansfield Park (1814) ch. 22

27 Shakespeare one gets acquainted with without knowing how. It is part of an Englishman's constitution. His thoughts and beauties are so spread abroad that one touches them everywhere, one is intimate with him by instinct.
Mansfield Park (1814) ch. 34

1 Let other pens dwell on guilt and misery. I quit such odious subjects as soon as I can.
Mansfield Park (1814) ch. 48

2 'Oh! it is only a novel! . . . only Cecilia, or Camilla, or Belinda:' or, in short, only some work in which the most thorough knowledge of human nature, the happiest delineation of its varieties, the liveliest effusions of wit and humour are conveyed to the world in the best chosen language.
Northanger Abbey (1818) ch. 5

3 Oh! who can ever be tired of Bath?
Northanger Abbey (1818) ch. 10

4 Where people wish to attach, they should always be ignorant. To come with a well-informed mind, is to come with an inability of administering to the vanity of others, which a sensible person would always wish to avoid. A woman especially, if she have the misfortune of knowing any thing, should conceal it as well as she can.
Northanger Abbey (1818) ch. 14

5 From politics, it was an easy step to silence.
Northanger Abbey (1818) ch. 14

6 A country like this, where . . . every man is surrounded by a neighbourhood of voluntary spies, and where roads and newspapers lay every thing open.
Northanger Abbey (1818) ch. 34

7 Sir Walter Elliot, of Kellynch-hall, in Somersetshire, was a man who, for his own amusement, never took up any book but the Baronetage; there he found occupation for an idle hour, and consolation in a distressed one.
Persuasion (1818) ch. 1

8 She had been forced into prudence in her youth, she learned romance as she grew older—the natural sequel of an unnatural beginning.
Persuasion (1818) ch. 4

9 She ventured to hope he did not always read only poetry; and to say, that she thought it was the misfortune of poetry, to be seldom safely enjoyed by those who enjoyed it completely; and that the strong feelings which alone could estimate it truly, were the very feelings which ought to taste it but sparingly.
Persuasion (1818) ch. 11

10 'My idea of good company, Mr Elliot, is the company of clever, well-informed people, who have a great deal of conversation; that is what I call good company.' 'You are mistaken,' said he gently, 'that is not good company, that is the best.'
Persuasion (1818) ch. 16

11 Men have had every advantage of us in telling their own story. Education has been theirs in so much higher a degree; the pen has been in their hands.
Persuasion (1818) ch. 23; cf. **Hardy** 360:10

12 All the privilege I claim for my own sex . . . is that of loving longest, when existence or when hope is gone.
Persuasion (1818) ch. 23

13 It was, perhaps, one of those cases in which advice is good or bad only as the event decides.
Persuasion (1818) ch. 23

14 It is a truth universally acknowledged, that a single man in possession of a good fortune, must be in want of a wife.
Pride and Prejudice (1813) ch. 1; cf. **Burney** 165:26

15 She was a woman of mean understanding, little information, and uncertain temper.
Pride and Prejudice (1813) ch. 1

16 May I ask whether these pleasing attentions proceed from the impulse of the moment, or are the result of previous study?
Pride and Prejudice (1813) ch. 14

17 Mr Collins had only to change from Jane to Elizabeth—and it was soon done—done while Mrs Bennet was stirring the fire.
Pride and Prejudice (1813) ch. 15

18 In his library he had been always sure of leisure and tranquillity; and though prepared . . . to meet with folly and conceit in every other room in the house, he was used to be free of them there.
Pride and Prejudice (1813) ch. 15

19 From this day you must be a stranger to one of your parents.—Your mother will never see you again if you do *not* marry Mr Collins, and I will never see you again if you *do*.
Pride and Prejudice (1813) ch. 20

20 Without thinking highly either of men or matrimony, marriage had always been her object; it was the only honourable provision for well-educated young women of small fortune, and however uncertain of giving happiness, must be their pleasantest preservative from want.
Pride and Prejudice (1813) ch. 22

21 What is the difference in matrimonial affairs, between the mercenary and the prudent move? Where does discretion end, and avarice begin?
Pride and Prejudice (1813) ch. 27

22 Loss of virtue in a female is irretrievable . . . one false step involves her in endless ruin.
Pride and Prejudice (1813) ch. 47

23 Are the shades of Pemberley to be thus polluted?
Pride and Prejudice (1813) ch. 56

24 You ought certainly to forgive them as a Christian, but never to admit them in your sight, or allow their names to be mentioned in your hearing.
Pride and Prejudice (1813) ch. 57

25 For what do we live, but to make sport for our neighbours, and laugh at them in our turn?
Pride and Prejudice (1813) ch. 57

26 An annuity is a very serious business.
Sense and Sensibility (1811) vol. 1, ch. 2

27 On every formal visit a child ought to be of the party, by way of provision for discourse.
Sense and Sensibility (1811) vol. 2, ch. 6

1 A man who has nothing to do with his own time has no conscience in his intrusion on that of others.
Sense and Sensibility (1811) vol. 2, ch. 9

2 A person and face, of strong, natural, sterling insignificance, though adorned in the first style of fashion.
Sense and Sensibility (1811) vol. 2, ch. 11

3 It is not time or opportunity that is to determine intimacy; it is disposition alone. Seven years would be insufficient to make some people acquainted with each other, and seven days are more than enough for others.
Sense and Sensibility (1811) vol. 2, ch. 12

4 To be so bent on marriage, to pursue a man merely for the sake of situation, is a sort of thing that shocks me; I cannot understand it. Poverty is a great evil; but to a woman of education and feeling it ought not, it cannot be the greatest.
The Watsons (c.1804)

5 I would rather be teacher at a school (and I can think of nothing worse) than marry a man I did not like.
The Watsons (c.1804)

6 We met . . . Dr Hall in such very deep mourning that either his mother, his wife, or himself must be dead.
letter to Cassandra Austen, 17 May 1799, in R. W. Chapman (ed.) *Jane Austen's Letters* (1952)

7 How horrible it is to have so many people killed!—And what a blessing that one cares for none of them!
letter to Cassandra Austen, 31 May 1811, after the battle of Albuera, 16 May 1811, in R. W. Chapman (ed.) *Jane Austen's Letters* (1952)

8 I suppose all the world is sitting in judgement upon the Princess of Wales's letter. Poor woman, I shall support her as long as I can, because she *is* a woman and because I hate her husband.
letter to Martha Lloyd, 16 February 1813; *Selected Letters* (1985)

9 3 or 4 families in a country village is the very thing to work on.
letter to Anna Austen, 9 September 1814, in R. W. Chapman (ed.) *Jane Austen's Letters* (1952)

10 I think I may boast myself to be, with all possible vanity, the most unlearned and uninformed female who ever dared to be an authoress.
letter, 11 December 1815, in R. W. Chapman (ed.) *Jane Austen's Letters* (1952)

11 What should I do with your strong, manly, spirited sketches, full of variety and glow?—How could I possibly join them on to the little bit (two inches wide) of ivory on which I work with so fine a brush, as produces little effect after much labour?
letter to J. Edward Austen, 16 December 1816, in R. W. Chapman (ed.) *Jane Austen's Letters* (1952)

12 Single women have a dreadful propensity for being poor—which is one very strong argument in favour of matrimony.
letter to Fanny Knight, 13 March 1817, in R. W. Chapman (ed.) *Jane Austen's Letters* (1952)

13 He and I should not in the least agree of course, in our ideas of novels and heroines;—pictures of perfection as you know make me sick and wicked.
letter to Fanny Knight, 23 March 1817, in R. W. Chapman (ed.) *Jane Austen's Letters* (1952)

14 I am going to take a heroine whom no-one but myself will much like.
on starting Emma
J. E. Austen-Leigh *A Memoir of Jane Austen* (1926 ed.)

15 When I asked if there was anything she wanted, her answer was that she wanted nothing but death.
of Jane Austen in her last illness
Cassandra Austen, letter to Fanny Knight, July 1817, in R. W. Chapman (ed.) *Jane Austen's Letters* (1952)

George Austin 1931–
British Anglican clergyman, Archdeacon of York

16 We're now paying the price for the Eighties and Lord Runcie's kind of effete, liberal elitism amongst bishops which also spread into the theological colleges. There is now a big gap between the faith of those in the pulpit and those in the pews.
in *Guardian* 7 February 1997

J. L. Austin 1911–60
English philosopher

17 In such cases we should not know what to say. This is when we say 'words fail us' and mean this literally. We should need new words. The old ones just would not fit. They aren't meant to cover this kind of case.
on being asked how one might describe the predicament of the character in **Kafka**'s Metamorphosis *who wakes to find himself transformed into a giant cockroach; cf.* **Kafka** *425:9*
Isaiah Berlin 'Austin and the Early Beginnings of Oxford Philosophy' in *Essays on J. L. Austin* (1973)

18 When asked to state his 'criterion' of philosophical correctness, [he] replied that, well, if you could get a collection of 'more or less cantankerous colleagues' all to accept something after argument, that, he thought, would be 'a bit of a criterion'.
G. J. Warnock 'Saturday Mornings' in *Essays on J. L. Austin* (1973)

Earl of Avon see Anthony Eden

Revd Awdry (Wilbert Vere Awdry) 1911–97
English writer of children's books

19 You've a lot to learn about trucks, little Thomas. They are silly things and must be kept in their place. After pushing them about here for a few weeks you'll know almost as much about them as Edward. Then you'll be a Really Useful Engine.
Thomas the Tank Engine (1946)

20 I should like my epitaph to say, 'He helped people see God in the ordinary things of life, and he made children laugh.'
in *Independent* 22 March 1997, obituary

Alan Ayckbourn 1939–
English dramatist

1 My mother used to say, Delia, if S-E-X ever rears its ugly head, close your eyes before you see the rest of it.
Bedroom Farce (1978) act 2

2 This place, you tell them you're interested in the arts, you get messages of sympathy.
Chorus of Disapproval (1986) act 2

3 If you gave Ruth a rose, she'd peel all the petals off to make sure there weren't any greenfly. And when she'd done that, she'd turn round and say, do you call that a rose? Look at it, it's all in bits.
Table Manners (1975) act 1, sc. 2

A. J. Ayer 1910–89
English philosopher

4 The criterion which we use to test the genuineness of apparent statements of fact is the criterion of verifiability. We say that a sentence is factually significant to any given person, if, and only if, he knows how to verify the proposition which it purports to express—that is, if he knows what observations would lead him, under certain conditions, to accept the proposition as being true, or reject it as being false.
Language, Truth, and Logic (1936) ch. 1

5 If now I . . . say 'Stealing money is wrong,' I produce a sentence which has no factual meaning—that is, expresses no proposition which can be either true or false. It is as if I had written 'Stealing money!!'—where the shape and thickness of the exclamation marks show, by a suitable convention, that a special sort of moral disapproval is the feeling which is being expressed.
Language, Truth, and Logic (1936) ch. 6

6 We offer the theist the same comfort as we gave to the moralist. His assertions cannot possibly be valid, but they cannot be invalid either. As he says nothing at all about the world, he cannot justly be accused of saying anything false, or anything for which he has insufficient grounds. It is only when the theist claims that in asserting the existence of a transcendent god he is expressing a genuine proposition that we are entitled to disagree with him.
Language, Truth, and Logic (1936) ch. 6

7 Why should you mind being wrong if someone can show you that you are?
attributed

Pam Ayres 1947–
English writer of humorous verse

8 Medicinal discovery,
It moves in mighty leaps,
It leapt straight past the common cold
And gave it us for keeps.
'Oh no, I got a cold' (1976)

Robert Aytoun 1570–1638
Scottish poet and courtier

9 I loved thee once. I'll love no more,
Thine be the grief, as is the blame;
Thou art not what thou wast before,
What reason I should be the same?
'To an Inconstant Mistress'

W. E. Aytoun 1813–65
Scottish lawyer and writer of ballads

10 'He is coming! he is coming!'
Like a bridegroom from his room,
Came the hero from his prison
To the scaffold and the doom.
'The Execution of Montrose' (1849) st. 14

11 The grim Geneva ministers
With anxious scowl drew near,
As you have seen the ravens flock
Around the dying deer.
'The Execution of Montrose' (1849) st. 17

12 The deep, unutterable woe
Which none save exiles feel.
'The Island of the Scots' (1849) st. 12

13 The earth is all the home I have,
The heavens my wide roof-tree.
'The Wandering Jew' (1867) l. 49

Charles Babbage 1792–1871
English mathematician and inventor; pioneer of machine computing

14 Every moment dies a man,
Every moment $1\frac{1}{16}$ is born.
parody of **Tennyson**'s 'Vision of Sin', in an unpublished letter to the poet, in *New Scientist* 4 Dec 1958; cf. **Tennyson** 767:13

Isaac Babel 1894–1940
Russian short-story writer

15 A phrase is born into the world both good and bad at the same time. The secret lies in a slight, an almost invisible twist. The lever should rest in your hand, getting warm, and you can only turn it once, not twice.
Guy de Maupassant (1932)

16 No iron can stab the heart with such force as a full stop put just at the right place.
Guy de Maupassant (1932)

17 On Sabbath eves I am oppressed . . . O the rotted Talmuds of my childhood! O the dense melancholy of memories!
Red Cavalry (1926) 'Gedali' (translated by Walter Morison)

18 Beyond the window, night stands like a black column . . . A shadowy radiance lies on the earth, and hanging from the bushes are necklaces of gleaming fruit.
Red Cavalry (1926) 'Pan Apolek' (translated by Walter Morison)

19 The bee of sorrow had stung his heart.
Red Cavalry (1926) 'Pan Apolek' (translated by Walter Morison)

1 Both of us looked on the world as a meadow in May—a meadow traversed by women and horses.
Red Cavalry (1926) 'The Story of a Horse' (translated by Walter Morison)

2 Now a man talks frankly only with his wife, at night, with the blanket over his head.
remark *c.*1937; Solomon Volkov *St Petersburg* (1996)

3 They didn't let me finish.
to his wife, on the day of his arrest by the NKVD, 16 May 1939

Lauren Bacall 1924–

American actress

4 I think your whole life shows in your face and you should be proud of that.
in *Daily Telegraph* 2 March 1988

Johann Sebastian Bach 1685–1750

German composer

on Bach: see **Barth** *56:6,* **Beecham** *61:6,* **Beethoven** *61:20,* **Fry** *326:28*

5 There is nothing to it. You only have to hit the right notes at the right time and the instrument plays itself.
when complimented on his organ playing
K. Geiringer *The Bach Family* (1954)

Francis Bacon 1561–1626

English lawyer, courtier, philosopher, and essayist

on Bacon: see **Jonson** *421:3,* **Strachey** *744:6,* **Walton** *803:1; see also* **Last words** *455:14*

6 For all knowledge and wonder (which is the seed of knowledge) is an impression of pleasure in itself.
The Advancement of Learning (1605) bk. 1, ch. 1, sect. 3

7 So let great authors have their due, as time, which is the author of authors, be not deprived of his due, which is further and further to discover truth.
The Advancement of Learning (1605) bk. 1, ch. 4, sect. 12

8 If a man will begin with certainties, he shall end in doubts; but if he will be content to begin with doubts, he shall end in certainties.
The Advancement of Learning (1605) bk. 1, ch. 5, sect. 8

9 [Knowledge is] a rich storehouse for the glory of the Creator and the relief of man's estate.
The Advancement of Learning (1605) bk. 1, ch. 5, sect. 11

10 Antiquities are history defaced, or some remnants of history which have casually escaped the shipwreck of time.
The Advancement of Learning (1605) bk. 2, ch. 2, sect. 1

11 Poesy was ever thought to have some participation of divineness, because it doth raise and erect the mind, by submitting the shows of things to the desires of the mind; whereas reason doth buckle and bow the mind unto the nature of things.
The Advancement of Learning (1605) bk. 2, ch. 4, sect. 2

12 The knowledge of man is as the waters, some descending from above, and some springing from beneath; the one informed by the light of nature, the other inspired by divine revelation.
The Advancement of Learning (1605) bk. 2, ch. 5, sect. 1

13 They are ill discoverers that think there is no land, when they can see nothing but sea.
The Advancement of Learning (1605) bk. 2, ch. 7, sect. 5

14 Words are the tokens current and accepted for conceits, as moneys are for values.
The Advancement of Learning (1605) bk. 2, ch. 16, sect. 3

15 A dance is a measured pace, as a verse is a measured speech.
The Advancement of Learning (1605) bk. 2, ch. 16, sect. 5

16 But men must know, that in this theatre of man's life it is reserved only for God and angels to be lookers on.
The Advancement of Learning (1605) bk. 2, ch. 20, sect. 8

17 Did not one of the fathers in great indignation call poesy *vinum daemonum?*
vinum daemonum = *the wine of devils*
The Advancement of Learning (1605) bk. 2, ch. 22, sect. 13

18 All good moral philosophy is but an handmaid to religion.
The Advancement of Learning (1605) bk. 2, ch. 22, sect. 14

19 It is in life as it is in ways, the shortest way is commonly the foulest, and surely the fairer way is not much about.
The Advancement of Learning (1605) bk. 2, ch. 23, sect. 45

20 Alonso of Aragon was wont to say in commendation of old age, that age appears to be best in four things,—old wood best to burn, old wine to drink, old friends to trust, and old authors to read.
Apophthegms New and Old (1625) no. 97

21 That all things are changed, and that nothing really perishes, and that the sum of matter remains exactly the same, is sufficiently certain.
Cogitationes de Natura Rerum Cogitatio 5 in J. Spedding (ed.) *The Works of Francis Bacon* vol. 5 (1858)

22 *Antiquitas saeculi juventus mundi.*
Ancient times were the youth of the world.
De Dignitate et Augmentis Scientiarum (1623) bk. 1 (translated by Gilbert Watts, 1640)

23 *Divitiae bona ancilla, pessima domina.*
Riches are a good handmaid, but the worst mistress.
De Dignitate et Augmentis Scientiarum (1623) bk. 6, ch. 3, pt. 3 'The Antitheta of Things' no. 6 (translated by Gilbert Watts, 1640)

24 *Nil moderatum vulgo gratum est.*
No term of moderation takes place with the vulgar.
De Dignitate et Augmentis Scientiarum (1623) bk. 6, ch. 3, pt. 3 'The Antitheta of Things' no. 30 (translated by Gilbert Watts, 1640)

25 *Silentium, stultorum virtus.*
Silence is the virtue of fools.
De Dignitate et Augmentis Scientiarum (1623) bk. 6, ch. 3, pt. 3 'The Antitheta of Things' no. 31 (translated by Gilbert Watts, 1640)

26 I hold every man a debtor to his profession.
The Elements of the Common Law (1596) preface

1 Why should a man be in love with his fetters, though of gold?
Essay of Death para. 4 in *The Remaines of . . . Lord Verulam* (1648); cf. **Astell** 31:14

2 He is the fountain of honour.
An Essay of a King (1642); attribution doubtful; cf. **Bagehot** 46:7

3 Prosperity is the blessing of the Old Testament, adversity is the blessing of the New.
Essays (1625) 'Of Adversity'

4 The pencil of the Holy Ghost hath laboured more in describing the afflictions of Job than the felicities of Solomon.
Essays (1625) 'Of Adversity'

5 Prosperity doth best discover vice, but adversity doth best discover virtue.
Essays (1625) 'Of Adversity'

6 I had rather believe all the fables in the legend, and the Talmud, and the Alcoran, than that this universal frame is without a mind.
Essays (1625) 'Of Atheism'

7 A little philosophy inclineth man's mind to atheism, but depth in philosophy bringeth men's minds about to religion.
Essays (1625) 'Of Atheism'

8 They that deny a God destroy man's nobility; for certainly man is of kin to the beasts by his body; and, if he be not of kin to God by his spirit, he is a base and ignoble creature.
Essays (1625) 'Of Atheism'

9 Virtue is like a rich stone, best plain set.
Essays (1625) 'Of Beauty'

10 There is no excellent beauty that hath not some strangeness in the proportion.
Essays (1625) 'Of Beauty'

11 He said it that knew it best.
referring to ***Demosthenes***
Essays (1625) 'Of Boldness'; cf. **Demosthenes** 257:4

12 In civil business; what first? boldness; what second and third? boldness: and yet boldness is a child of ignorance and baseness.
Essays (1625) 'Of Boldness'; cf. **Danton** 250:6, **Demosthenes** 257:4

13 Boldness is an ill keeper of promise.
Essays (1625) 'Of Boldness'

14 Houses are built to live in and not to look on; therefore let use be preferred before uniformity, except where both may be had.
Essays (1625) 'Of Building'

15 Light gains make heavy purses.
Essays (1625) 'Of Ceremonies and Respects'

16 He that is too much in anything, so that he giveth another occasion of satiety, maketh himself cheap.
Essays (1625) 'Of Ceremonies and Respects'

17 Books will speak plain when counsellors blanch.
Essays (1625) 'Of Counsel'

18 [Some] there be that can pack the cards and yet cannot play well; so there are some that are good in canvasses and factions, that are otherwise weak men.
Essays (1625) 'Of Cunning'

19 In things that are tender and unpleasing, it is good to break the ice by some whose words are of less weight, and to reserve the more weighty voice to come in as by chance.
Essays (1625) 'Of Cunning'

20 I knew one that when he wrote a letter he would put that which was most material in the postscript, as if it had been a bymatter.
Essays (1625) 'Of Cunning'; cf. **Steele** 736:16

21 Nothing doth more hurt in a state than that cunning men pass for wise.
Essays (1625) 'Of Cunning'

22 Men fear death as children fear to go in the dark; and as that natural fear in children is increased with tales, so is the other.
Essays (1625) 'Of Death'

23 Revenge triumphs over death; love slights it; honour aspireth to it; grief flieth to it.
Essays (1625) 'Of Death'

24 It is as natural to die as to be born; and to a little infant, perhaps, the one is as painful as the other.
Essays (1625) 'Of Death'

25 Death . . . openeth the gate to good fame, and extinguisheth envy.
Essays (1625) 'Of Death'

26 If you dissemble sometimes your knowledge of that you are thought to know, you shall be thought, another time, to know that you know not.
Essays (1625) 'Of Discourse'

27 I knew a wise man that had it for a by-word, when he saw men hasten to a conclusion. 'Stay a little, that we may make an end the sooner.'
Essays (1625) 'Of Dispatch'

28 To choose time is to save time.
Essays (1625) 'Of Dispatch'

29 Riches are for spending.
Essays (1625) 'Of Expense'

30 A man ought warily to begin charges which once begun will continue.
Essays (1625) 'Of Expense'

31 There is little friendship in the world, and least of all between equals.
Essays (1625) 'Of Followers and Friends'

32 Chiefly the mould of a man's fortune is in his own hands.
Essays (1625) 'Of Fortune'

33 If a man look sharply, and attentively, he shall see Fortune: for though she be blind, yet she is not invisible.
Essays (1625) 'Of Fortune'

34 It had been hard for him that spake it to have put more truth and untruth together, in a few words, than in that speech: 'Whosoever is delighted in solitude is either a wild beast, or a god.'
Essays (1625) 'Of Friendship'; cf. **Aristotle** 25:3

1 A crowd is not company, and faces are but a gallery of pictures, and talk but a tinkling cymbal, where there is no love.
Essays (1625) 'Of Friendship'

2 It redoubleth joys, and cutteth griefs in halves.
Essays (1625) 'Of Friendship'

3 Cure the disease and kill the patient.
Essays (1625) 'Of Friendship'

4 God Almighty first planted a garden; and, indeed, it is the purest of human pleasures.
Essays (1625) 'Of Gardens'

5 Nothing is more pleasant to the eye than green grass kept finely shorn.
Essays (1625) 'Of Gardens'

6 If a man be gracious and courteous to strangers, it shows he is a citizen of the world.
Essays (1625) 'Of Goodness, and Goodness of Nature'

7 The inclination to goodness is imprinted deeply in the nature of man: insomuch, that if it issue not towards men, it will take unto other living creatures.
Essays (1625) 'Of Goodness, and Goodness of Nature'

8 Men in great place are thrice servants: servants of the sovereign or state, servants of fame, and servants of business.
Essays (1625) 'Of Great Place'

9 It is a strange desire to seek power and to lose liberty.
Essays (1625) 'Of Great Place'

10 The rising unto place is laborious, and by pains men come to greater pains; and it is sometimes base, and by indignities men come to dignities. The standing is slippery, and the regress is either a downfall, or at least an eclipse.
Essays (1625) 'Of Great Place'

11 Severity breedeth fear, but roughness breedeth hate. Even reproofs from authority ought to be grave, and not taunting.
Essays (1625) 'Of Great Place'

12 All rising to great place is by a winding stair.
Essays (1625) 'Of Great Place'

13 As the births of living creatures at first are ill-shapen, so are all innovations, which are the births of time.
Essays (1625) 'Of Innovations'

14 He that will not apply new remedies must expect new evils; for time is the greatest innovator.
Essays (1625) 'Of Innovations'

15 The speaking in a perpetual hyperbole is comely in nothing but in love.
Essays (1625) 'Of Love'

16 It has been well said that 'the arch-flatterer with whom all the petty flatterers have intelligence is a man's self.'
Essays (1625) 'Of Love'

17 He that hath wife and children hath given hostages to fortune; for they are impediments to great enterprises, either of virtue or mischief.
Essays (1625) 'Of Marriage and the Single Life'; cf. **Lucan** 478:16

18 A single life doth well with churchmen, for charity will hardly water the ground where it must first fill a pool.
Essays (1625) 'Of Marriage and the Single Life'

19 Wives are young men's mistresses, companions for middle age, and old men's nurses.
Essays (1625) 'Of Marriage and the Single Life'

20 He was reputed one of the wise men that made answer to the question when a man should marry? 'A young man not yet, an elder man not at all.'
Essays (1625) 'Of Marriage and the Single Life'; cf. **Punch** 617:2

21 It is generally better to deal by speech than by letter.
Essays (1625) 'Of Negotiating'

22 New nobility is but the act of power, but ancient nobility is the act of time.
Essays (1625) 'Of Nobility'

23 Nobility of birth commonly abateth industry.
Essays (1625) 'Of Nobility'

24 The joys of parents are secret, and so are their griefs and fears.
Essays (1625) 'Of Parents and Children'

25 Children sweeten labours, but they make misfortunes more bitter.
Essays (1625) 'Of Parents and Children'

26 Fame is like a river, that beareth up things light and swollen, and drowns things weighty and solid.
Essays (1625) 'Of Praise'

27 Age will not be defied.
Essays (1625) 'Of Regimen of Health'

28 Revenge is a kind of wild justice, which the more man's nature runs to, the more ought law to weed it out.
Essays (1625) 'Of Revenge'

29 A man that studieth revenge keeps his own wounds green.
Essays (1625) 'Of Revenge'

30 Defer not charities till death; for certainly, if a man weigh it rightly, he that doth so is rather liberal of another man's than of his own.
Essays (1625) 'Of Riches'

31 The four pillars of government . . . (which are religion, justice, counsel, and treasure).
Essays (1625) 'Of Seditions and Troubles'

32 The surest way to prevent seditions (if the times do bear it) is to take away the matter of them.
Essays (1625) 'Of Seditions and Troubles'

33 Money is like muck, not good except it be spread.
Essays (1625) 'Of Seditions and Troubles'

34 The remedy is worse than the disease.
Essays (1625) 'Of Seditions and Troubles'

1 The French are wiser than they seem, and the Spaniards seem wiser than they are.
Essays (1625) 'Of Seeming Wise'

2 Studies serve for delight, for ornament, and for ability.
Essays (1625) 'Of Studies'

3 To spend too much time in studies is sloth.
Essays (1625) 'Of Studies'

4 They perfect nature and are perfected by experience.
Essays (1625) 'Of Studies'

5 Read not to contradict and confute, nor to believe and take for granted, nor to find talk and discourse, but to weigh and consider.
Essays (1625) 'Of Studies'

6 Some books are to be tasted, others to be swallowed, and some few to be chewed and digested.
Essays (1625) 'Of Studies'

7 Reading maketh a full man; conference a ready man; and writing an exact man.
Essays (1625) 'Of Studies'

8 Histories make men wise; poets, witty; the mathematics, subtile; natural philosophy, deep; moral, grave; logic and rhetoric, able to contend.
Essays (1625) 'Of Studies'

9 There is a superstition in avoiding superstition.
Essays (1625) 'Of Superstition'

10 Suspicions amongst thoughts are like bats amongst birds, they ever fly by twilight.
Essays (1625) 'Of Suspicion'

11 There is nothing makes a man suspect much, more than to know little.
Essays (1625) 'Of Suspicion'

12 Neither is money the sinews of war (as it is trivially said).
Essays (1625) 'Of the True Greatness of Kingdoms'; cf. **Cicero** 217:23

13 Neither will it be, that a people overlaid with taxes should ever become valiant and martial.
Essays (1625) 'Of the True Greatness of Kingdoms'

14 Travel, in the younger sort, is a part of education; in the elder, a part of experience. He that travelleth into a country before he hath some entrance into the language, goeth to school, and not to travel.
Essays (1625) 'Of Travel'

15 What is truth? said jesting Pilate; and would not stay for an answer.
Essays (1625) 'Of Truth'; cf. **Bible** 102:30

16 A mixture of a lie doth ever add pleasure.
Essays (1625) 'Of Truth'

17 It is not the lie that passeth through the mind, but the lie that sinketh in, and settleth in it, that doth the hurt.
Essays (1625) 'Of Truth'

18 The inquiry of truth, which is the love-making, or wooing of it, the knowledge of truth, which is the presence of it, and the belief of truth, which is the enjoying of it, is the sovereign good of human nature.
Essays (1625) 'Of Truth'

19 All colours will agree in the dark.
Essays (1625) 'Of Unity in Religion'

20 It was prettily devised of Aesop, 'The fly sat upon the axle-tree of the chariot-wheel and said, what a dust do I raise.'
Essays (1625) 'Of Vain-Glory'

21 In the youth of a state arms do flourish; in the middle age of a state, learning; and then both of them together for a time; in the declining age of a state, mechanical arts and merchandise.
Essays (1625) 'Of Vicissitude of Things'

22 Be so true to thyself as thou be not false to others.
Essays (1625) 'Of Wisdom for a Man's Self'; cf. **Shakespeare** 662:13

23 It is the nature of extreme self-lovers, as they will set a house on fire, and it were but to roast their eggs.
Essays (1625) 'Of Wisdom for a Man's Self'

24 It is the wisdom of the crocodiles, that shed tears when they would devour.
Essays (1625) 'Of Wisdom for a Man's Self'

25 Young men are fitter to invent than to judge, fitter for execution than for counsel, and fitter for new projects than for settled business.
Essays (1625) 'Of Youth and Age'

26 For they thought generally that he was a Prince as ordained, and sent down from heaven to unite and put to an end the long dissensions of the two houses; which although they had had, in the times of Henry the Fourth, Henry the Fifth, and a part of Henry the Sixth on the one side, and the times of Edward the Fourth on the other, lucid intervals and happy pauses; yet they did ever hang over the kingdom, ready to break forth into new perturbations and calamities.
History of King Henry VII (1622) para. 3 in J. Spedding (ed.) *The Works of Francis Bacon* vol. 6 (1858)

27 I have rather studied books than men.
A Letter of Advice . . . to the Duke of Buckingham, When he became Favourite to King James (1661)

28 I have taken all knowledge to be my province.
'To My Lord Treasurer Burghley' (1592) in J. Spedding (ed.) *The Letters and Life of Francis Bacon* vol. 1 (1861)

29 Universities incline wits to sophistry and affectation.
Valerius Terminus of the Interpretation of Nature ch. 26 in *Letters and Remains of the Lord Chancellor Bacon* (collected by Robert Stephens, 1734)

30 *Nam et ipsa scientia potestas est.*
For also knowledge itself is power.
Meditationes Sacrae (1597) 'Of Heresies'; cf. **Proverbs** 605:7

31 I would live to study, and not study to live.
Memorial of Access to King James I (*c.*1622) in *Letters, Speeches, Charges, Advices, etc. of Francis Bacon* (1763)

32 God's first Creature, which was Light.
New Atlantis (1627)

1 The end of our foundation is the knowledge of causes, and secret motions of things; and the enlarging of the bounds of human Empire, to the effecting of all things possible.
New Atlantis (1627)

2 *Quod enim mavult homo verum esse, id potius credit.*
For what a man would like to be true, that he more readily believes.
Novum Organum (1620) bk. 1, Aphorism 49 (translated by J. Spedding); cf. **Caesar** 180:16

3 *Magna ista scientiarum mater.*
That great mother of sciences.
of natural philosophy
Novum Organum (1620) bk. 1, Aphorism 80 (translated by J. Spedding)

4 *Vim et virtutem et consequentias rerum inventarum notare juvat; quae non in aliis manifestius occurrunt, quam in illis tribus quae antiquis incognitae, et quarum primordia, licet recentia, obscura et ingloria sunt: Artis nimirum Imprimendi, Pulveris Tormentarii, et Acus Nauticae. Haec enim tria rerum faciem et statum in orbe terrarum mutaverunt.*
It is well to observe the force and virtue and consequence of discoveries, and these are to be seen nowhere more conspicuously than in those three which were unknown to the ancients, and of which the origins, though recent, are obscure and inglorious; namely, printing, gunpowder, and the mariner's needle [compass] . . . these three have changed the whole face and state of things throughout the world.
Novum Organum (1620) bk. 1, Aphorism 129 (translated by J. Spedding); cf. **Carlyle** 187:19

5 *Natura enim non imperatur, nisi parendo.*
Nature cannot be ordered about, except by obeying her.
Novum Organum (1620) bk. 1, Aphorism 129 (translated by J. Spedding)

6 Books must follow sciences, and not sciences books.
Resuscitatio (1657) 'Proposition touching Amendment of Laws'

7 Wise nature did never put her precious jewels into a garret four stories high: and therefore . . . exceeding tall men had ever very empty heads.
J. Spedding (ed.) *The Works of Francis Bacon* vol. 7 (1859) 'Additional Apophthegms' no. 17

8 Hope is a good breakfast, but it is a bad supper.
J. Spedding (ed.) *The Works of Francis Bacon* vol. 7 (1859) 'Apophthegms contained in *Resuscitatio*' no. 36; cf. **Proverbs** 602:49

9 Anger makes dull men witty, but it keeps them poor.
often attributed to Queen **Elizabeth I** *from a misreading of the text*
J. Spedding (ed.) *The Works of Francis Bacon* vol. 7 (1859) 'Baconiana'

10 The world's a bubble; and the life of man
Less than a span.
The World (1629)

11 Who then to frail mortality shall trust,
But limns the water, or but writes in dust.
The World (1629)

12 What is it then to have or have no wife,
But single thraldom, or a double strife?
The World (1629)

13 What then remains, but that we still should cry,
Not to be born, or being born, to die?
The World (1629)

14 There be three things which make a nation great and prosperous: a fertile soil, busy workshops, easy conveyance for men and goods from place to place.
attributed; S. Platt (ed.) *Respectfully Quoted* (1989)

Francis Bacon 1909–92
Irish painter

15 What I see is a marvellous painting. But how are you going to make it? And, of course, as I don't know how to make it, I rely then on chance and accident making it for me.
David Sylvester (ed.) *Interviews with Francis Bacon: the brutality of fact* (ed. 3, 1987)

Roger Bacon *c.*1220–*c.*1292
English philosopher, scientist, Franciscan friar

16 If in other sciences we should arrive at certainty without doubt and truth without error, it behoves us to place the foundations of knowledge in mathematics.
Opus Majus bk. 1, ch. 4

Lord Baden-Powell see **Mottoes** 535:7

Karl Baedeker 1801–59
German publisher

17 Oxford is on the whole more attractive than Cambridge to the ordinary visitor; and the traveller is therefore recommended to visit Cambridge first, or to omit it altogether if he cannot visit both.
Great Britain (1887) Route 30 'From London to Oxford'

18 The traveller need have no scruple in limiting his donations to the smallest possible sums, as liberality frequently becomes a source of annoyance and embarrassment.
Northern Italy (1895) 'Gratuities'

19 PASSPORTS. On arrival at a Syrian port the traveller's passport is sometimes asked for, but an ordinary visiting-card will answer the purpose equally well.
Palestine and Syria (1876) 'Passports and Custom House'

Joan Baez 1941–
American singer and songwriter

20 The only thing that's been a worse flop than the organization of non-violence has been the organization of violence.
Daybreak (1970) 'What Would You Do If?'; cf. **Péguy** 572:4

Walter Bagehot 1826–77

English economist and essayist
see also ***Disraeli*** *268:12*

1 A constitutional statesman is in general a man of common opinion and uncommon abilities.
Biographical Studies (1881) 'Sir Robert Peel'

2 He believes, with all his heart and soul and strength, that there *is* such a thing as truth; he has the soul of a martyr with the intellect of an advocate.
Biographical Studies (1881) 'Mr Gladstone'

3 Capital must be propelled by self-interest; it cannot be enticed by benevolence.
Economic Studies (1880) ch. 2

4 The mystic reverence, the religious allegiance, which are essential to a true monarchy, are imaginative sentiments that no legislature can manufacture in any people.
The English Constitution (1867) 'The Cabinet'

5 In such constitutions [as England's] there are two parts . . . first, those which excite and preserve the reverence of the population—the *dignified* parts . . . and next, the *efficient* parts—those by which it, in fact, works and rules.
The English Constitution (1867) 'The Cabinet'

6 No orator ever made an impression by appealing to men as to their plainest physical wants, except when he could allege that those wants were caused by some one's tyranny.
The English Constitution (1867) 'The Cabinet'

7 The Crown is, according to the saying, the 'fountain of honour'; but the Treasury is the spring of business.
The English Constitution (1867) 'The Cabinet'; cf. **Bacon** 42:2

8 A cabinet is a combining committee—a *hyphen* which joins, a *buckle* which fastens, the legislative part of the state to the executive part of the state.
The English Constitution (1867) 'The Cabinet'

9 It has been said that England invented the phrase, 'Her Majesty's Opposition'; that it was the first government which made a criticism of administration as much a part of the polity as administration itself. This critical opposition is the consequence of cabinet government.
The English Constitution (1867) 'The Cabinet'; cf. **Hobhouse** 379:6

10 *The Times* has made many ministries.
The English Constitution (1867) 'The Cabinet'

11 The great qualities, the imperious will, the rapid energy, the eager nature fit for a great crisis are not required—are impediments—in common times.
The English Constitution (1867) 'The Cabinet'

12 We often want, at the sudden occurrence of a grave tempest, to change the helmsman—to replace the pilot of the calm by the pilot of the storm.
The English Constitution (1867) 'The Cabinet'

13 It has been said, not truly, but with a possible approximation to truth, that in 1802 every hereditary monarch was insane.
The English Constitution (1867) 'Checks and Balances'

14 The soldier—that is, the great soldier—of to-day is not a romantic animal, dashing at forlorn hopes, animated by frantic sentiment, full of fancies as to a love-lady or a sovereign; but a quiet, grave man, busied in charts, exact in sums, master of the art of tactics, occupied in trivial detail; thinking, as the Duke of Wellington was said to do, *most* of the shoes of his soldiers; despising all manner of *éclat* and eloquence; perhaps, like Count Moltke, 'silent in seven languages'.
The English Constitution (1867) 'Checks and Balances'

15 The finest brute votes in Europe.
view of 'a cynical politician'; sometimes attributed to ***Disraeli***
The English Constitution (1867) 'The House of Commons'

16 The order of nobility is of great use, too, not only in what it creates, but in what it prevents. It prevents the rule of wealth—the religion of gold. This is the obvious and natural idol of the Anglo-Saxon.
The English Constitution (1867) 'The House of Lords'

17 The House of Commons lives in a state of perpetual potential choice: at any moment it can choose a ruler and dismiss a ruler. And therefore party is inherent in it, is bone of its bone, and breath of its breath.
The English Constitution (1867) 'The House of Commons'

18 An Opposition, on coming into power, is often like a speculative merchant whose bills become due. Ministers have to make good their promises, and they find a difficulty in so doing.
The English Constitution (1867) 'The House of Commons'

19 A severe though not unfriendly critic of our institutions said that 'the cure for admiring the House of Lords was to go and look at it.'
The English Constitution (1867) 'The House of Lords'

20 Nations touch at their summits.
The English Constitution (1867) 'The House of Lords'

21 As soon as we see that England is a disguised republic we must see too that the classes for whom the disguise is necessary must be tenderly dealt with.
The English Constitution (1867) 'Its History'

22 It is nice to trace how the actions of a retired widow and an unemployed youth become of such importance.
of Queen ***Victoria*** *and the future* ***Edward VII***
The English Constitution (1867) 'The Monarchy'

23 Women—one half the human race at least—care fifty times more for a marriage than a ministry.
The English Constitution (1867) 'The Monarchy'

24 Royalty is a government in which the attention of the nation is concentrated on one person doing interesting actions. A Republic is a government in which that attention is divided between many, who are all doing uninteresting actions. Accordingly, so long as the human heart is strong

and the human reason weak, Royalty will be strong because it appeals to diffused feeling, and Republics weak because they appeal to the understanding.
The English Constitution (1867) 'The Monarchy'

1 Throughout the greater part of his life George III was a kind of 'consecrated obstruction'.
The English Constitution (1867) 'The Monarchy'

2 There are arguments for not having a Court, and there are arguments for having a splendid Court; but there are no arguments for having a mean Court.
The English Constitution (1867) 'The Monarchy'

3 The Queen . . . must sign her own death-warrant if the two Houses unanimously send it up to her.
The English Constitution (1867) 'The Monarchy'

4 Above all things our royalty is to be reverenced, and if you begin to poke about it you cannot reverence it . . . Its mystery is its life. We must not let in daylight upon magic.
The English Constitution (1867) 'The Monarchy (continued)'

5 The Sovereign has, under a constitutional monarchy such as ours, three rights—the right to be consulted, the right to encourage, the right to warn.
The English Constitution (1867) 'The Monarchy (continued)'

6 The only fit material for a constitutional king is a prince who begins early to reign—who in his youth is superior to pleasure—who in his youth is willing to labour—who has by nature a genius for discretion. Such kings are among God's greatest gifts, but they are also among His rarest.
The English Constitution (1867) 'The Monarchy' (continued)

7 It is an inevitable defect, that bureaucrats will care more for routine than for results.
The English Constitution (1867) 'On Changes of Ministry' .

8 The worst families are those in which the members never really speak their minds to one another; they maintain an atmosphere of unreality, and everyone always lives in an atmosphere of suppressed ill-feeling.
The English Constitution (ed. 2, 1872) introduction

9 No real English gentleman, in his secret soul, was ever sorry for the death of a political economist.
Estimates of some Englishmen and Scotchmen (1858) 'The First Edinburgh Reviewers'

10 Writers, like teeth, are divided into incisors and grinders.
Estimates of some Englishmen and Scotchmen (1858) 'The First Edinburgh Reviewers'

11 To a great experience one thing is essential, an experiencing nature.
Estimates of some Englishmen and Scotchmen (1858) 'Shakespeare—the Individual'

12 One of the greatest pains to human nature is the pain of a new idea.
Physics and Politics (1872) 'The Age of Discussion'

13 The most melancholy of human reflections, perhaps, is that, on the whole, it is a question whether the benevolence of mankind does most good or harm.
Physics and Politics (1872) 'The Age of Discussion'

14 Civilized ages inherit the human nature which was victorious in barbarous ages, and that nature is, in many respects, not at all suited to civilized circumstances.
Physics and Politics (1872) 'The Age of Discussion'

15 The truth is that the propensity of man to imitate what is before him is one of the strongest parts of his nature.
Physics and Politics (1872) 'Nation-Making'

16 One of the most common defects of half-instructed minds is to think much of that in which they differ from others, and little of that in which they agree with others.
on the evils of sectarianism
in *Economist* 11 June 1870

17 A great Premier must add the vivacity of an idle man to the assiduity of a very laborious one.
in *The Economist* 2 January 1875

18 In every country the extreme party is most irritated against the party which comes nearest to itself, but does not go so far.
in *The Economist* 2 January 1875

19 Small sciences are the labours of our manhood; but the round universe is the plaything of the boy.
in *National Review* January 1856 'Edward Gibbon'

20 The great breeding people had gone out and multiplied; colonies in every clime attest our success; French is the *patois* of Europe; English is the language of the world.
in *National Review* January 1856 'Edward Gibbon'

21 The purchaser [of a newspaper] desires an article which he can appreciate at sight; which he can lay down and say, 'An excellent article, very excellent; exactly *my own* sentiments.'
in *National Review* July 1856 'The Character of Sir Robert Peel'

22 He describes London like a special correspondent for posterity.
in *National Review* 7 October 1858 'Charles Dickens'

23 To be commonly above others, still more to think yourself above others, is to be below them every now and then, and sometimes much below.
in *National Review* July 1859 'John Milton'

24 Wordsworth, Tennyson and Browning; or, pure, ornate, and grotesque art in English poetry.
in *National Review* November 1864, essay title

Abdul Baha 1844–1921

Persian co-founder (with his father) of the Baha'i faith

25 In this century, which is the century of light and the revelation of mysteries . . . it is well established that mankind and womankind as parts of composite humanity are coequal and that no difference in estimate is allowable, for all are human.
at a woman's suffrage meeting in New York, 1912; *The Promulgation of Universal Peace* (2nd ed., 1982)

Bahya ibn Paquda fl. 1080
Jewish philosopher, born in Spain

1 We are obliged to serve God both outwardly and inwardly. Outward service is expressed in the duties of the members, such as prayer, fasting, almsgiving, learning and teaching the Torah . . . all of which can be wholly performed by man's physical body. Inward service, however, is expressed in the duties of the heart, in the heart's assertion of the unity of God, in belief in him and in his Book, in constant obedience to him and fear of him, in humility before him, love for him and complete reliance upon him, submission to him and abstinence from the things hateful to him.
The Duties of the Heart introduction

2 You should know, O man, that the greatest enemy you have in the world is your inclination.
The Duties of the Heart Gate 5, ch. 5

David Bailey 1938–
English photographer
see also ***Sayings*** *647:26*

3 It takes a lot of imagination to be a good photographer. You need less imagination to be a painter, because you can invent things. But in photography everything is so ordinary; it takes a lot of looking before you learn to see the ordinary.
interview in *The Face* December 1984

4 I never cared for fashion much. Amusing little seams and witty little pleats. It was the girls I liked.
in *Independent* 5 November 1990

5 Women love scallywags, but some marry them and then try to make them wear a blazer.
in *Mail on Sunday* 16 February 1997 'Quotes of the Week'

Philip James Bailey 1816–1902
English poet

6 We should count time by heart-throbs.
Festus (1839) sc. 5

7 America, thou half-brother of the world;
With something good and bad of every land.
Festus (1839) sc. 10

Beryl Bainbridge 1933–
English novelist

8 Nobody ever, unless he is very wicked, deliberately tries to hurt anybody. It's just that men cannot help not loving you or behaving badly.
interview in *Daily Telegraph* 10 September 1996

9 Women are programmed to love completely, and men are programmed to spread it around.
interview in *Daily Telegraph* 10 September 1996

10 I have to smoke more [cigarettes] than most people—because the ones I smoke are very small and full of holes.
in *Daily Telegraph* 28 February 1998

Bruce Bairnsfather 1888–1959
British cartoonist

11 Well, if you knows of a better 'ole, go to it.
Fragments from France (1915)

Henry Williams Baker 1821–77
English clergyman and hymn-writer

12 Lord, thy word abideth,
And our footsteps guideth;
Who its truth believeth
Light and joy receiveth.
'Lord, thy word abideth' (1861 hymn)

13 The King of love my shepherd is,
Whose goodness faileth never;
I nothing lack if I am his
And he is mine for ever . . .
Perverse and foolish oft I strayed,
But yet in love he sought me,
And on his shoulder gently laid,
And home, rejoicing, brought me.
'The King of love my shepherd is' (1868 hymn)

14 O praise ye the Lord, all things that give sound;
Each jubilant chord re-echo around;
Loud organs, his glory forth tell in deep tone,
And, sweet harp, the story of what he hath done.
'O praise ye the Lord!' (1875 hymn)

Joan Bakewell 1933–
English broadcaster and writer
on Bakewell: see ***Muir*** *535:24*

15 I'm afraid I'm addicted to fat and love British beef. BSE holds no terror for me because . . . I am as likely to get it as win the National Lottery.
on her main difficulty in following a healthy diet
in *Independent* 30 August 1997 'Quote Unquote'

Michael Bakunin 1814–76
Russian revolutionary and anarchist

16 The urge for destruction is also a creative urge!
Jahrbuch für Wissenschaft und Kunst (1842) 'Die Reaktion in Deutschland' (under the pseudonym 'Jules Elysard')

17 Everything will pass, and the world will perish but the Ninth Symphony will remain.
of ***Beethoven****'s Ninth Symphony*
Edmund Wilson *To The Finland Station* (1940)

James Baldwin 1924–87
American novelist and essayist

18 Children have never been very good at listening to their elders, but they have never failed to imitate them. They must, they have no other models.
Nobody Knows My Name (1961) 'Fifth Avenue, Uptown: a letter from Harlem'

19 Anyone who has ever struggled with poverty knows how extremely expensive it is to be poor.
Nobody Knows My Name (1961) 'Fifth Avenue, Uptown: a letter from Harlem'

1 Freedom is not something that anybody can be given; freedom is something people take and people are as free as they want to be.

Nobody Knows My Name (1961) 'Notes for a Hypothetical Novel'

2 Money, it turned out, was exactly like sex, you thought of nothing else if you didn't have it and thought of other things if you did.

in *Esquire* May 1961 'Black Boy looks at the White Boy'

3 It comes as a great shock around the age of 5, 6 or 7 to discover that the flag to which you have pledged allegiance, along with everybody else, has not pledged allegiance to you. It comes as a great shock to see Gary Cooper killing off the Indians and, although you are rooting for Gary Cooper, that the Indians are you.

speaking for the proposition that 'The American Dream is at the expense of the American Negro'

speech at the Cambridge Union, England, 17 February 1965; in *New York Times Magazine* 7 March 1965

4 If they take you in the morning, they will be coming for us that night.

in *New York Review of Books* 7 January 1971 'Open Letter to my Sister, Angela Davis'

Stanley Baldwin 1867–1947

British Conservative statesman; Prime Minister, 1923–4, 1924–9, 1935–7

on Baldwin: see **Beaverbrook** *59:1,* **Churchill** *216:5,* **Curzon** *248:6,* **Trevelyan** *781:10; see also* **Kipling**

5 They [parliament] are a lot of hard-faced men who look as if they had done very well out of the war.

J. M. Keynes *Economic Consequences of the Peace* (1919) ch. 5

6 A platitude is simply a truth repeated until people get tired of hearing it.

speech in the House of Commons, 29 May 1924

7 There are three classes which need sanctuary more than others—birds, wild flowers, and Prime Ministers.

in *Observer* 24 May 1925

8 I think it is well also for the man in the street to realize that there is no power on earth that can protect him from being bombed. Whatever people may tell him, the bomber will always get through. The only defence is in offence, which means that you have to kill more women and children more quickly than the enemy if you want to save yourselves.

speech in the House of Commons, 10 November 1932

9 Since the day of the air, the old frontiers are gone. When you think of the defence of England you no longer think of the chalk cliffs of Dover; you think of the Rhine. That is where our frontier lies.

speech in the House of Commons, 30 July 1934

10 I shall be but a short time tonight. I have seldom spoken with greater regret, for my lips are not yet unsealed. Were these troubles over I would make a case, and I guarantee that not a man would go into the lobby against us.

on the Abyssinian crisis

speech in the House of Commons, 10 December 1935; cf. **Misquotations** 522:4

11 This House today is a theatre which is being watched by the whole world. Let us conduct ourselves with that dignity which His Majesty is showing in this hour of his trial.

speech, House of Commons, 10 December 1936

12 Do not run up your nose dead against the Pope or the NUM!

R. A. Butler *The Art of Memory* (1982) 'Iain Macleod'; cf. **Macmillan** 487:21

Arthur James Balfour 1848–1930

British Conservative statesman; Prime Minister, 1902–5

on Balfour: see **Churchill** *214:21, 216:11,* **Lloyd George** *470:16*

13 It is unfortunate, considering that enthusiasm moves the world, that so few enthusiasts can be trusted to speak the truth.

letter to Mrs Drew, 19 May 1891; L. March-Phillips and B. Christian (eds.) *Some Hawarden Letters* (1917) ch. 7

14 The tyranny of majorities may be as bad as the tyranny of Kings . . . and I do not think that any rational or sober man will say that what is justifiable against a tyrannical King may not under certain circumstances be justifiable against a tyrannical majority.

watching the Belfast march past of Ulster Loyalists in 1893

in *Times* 5 April 1893

15 When it comes I shall not be sorry. Only let us have separation as well as Home Rule: England cannot afford to go on with the Irishmen in her Parliament.

Wilfrid Scawen Blunt *The Land War in Ireland* (1912)

16 His Majesty's Government view with favour the establishment in Palestine of a national home for the Jewish people, and will use their best endeavours to facilitate the achievement of this object, it being clearly understood that nothing shall be done which may prejudice the civil and religious rights of existing non-Jewish communities in Palestine, or the rights and political status enjoyed by Jews in any other country.

known as the 'Balfour Declaration'

letter to Lord Rothschild 2 November 1917

17 I make it a rule never to stare at people when they are in obvious distress.

on being asked what he thought of the behaviour of the German delegation at the signing of the Treaty of Versailles

Max Egremont *Balfour* (1980)

18 Zionism, be it right or wrong, good or bad, is rooted in age-long traditions, in present need, in future hopes, of far profounder import than the desires and prejudices of the seven hundred

thousand Arabs who now inhabit that ancient land.
in August 1919; Max Egremont *Balfour* (1980)

1 Christianity, of course . . . but why journalism?
replying to Frank Harris, who had claimed that 'all the faults of the age come from Christianity and journalism'
Margot Asquith *Autobiography* (1920) vol. 1, ch. 10

2 I thought he was a young man of promise, but it appears he is a young man of promises.
of Winston **Churchill**
Winston Churchill *My Early Life* (1930) ch. 17

3 I am more or less happy when being praised, not very uncomfortable when being abused, but I have moments of uneasiness when being explained.
K. Young *A. J. Balfour* (1963)

Ballads

4 There was a youth, and a well-beloved youth,
And he was an esquire's son,
He loved the bailiff's daughter dear,
That lived in Islington.
'The Bailiff's Daughter of Islington'

5 All in the merry month of May,
When green buds they were swellin',
Young Jemmy Grove on his death-bed lay,
For love of Barbara Allen.
'Barbara Allen's Cruelty'

6 O mother, mother, make my bed,
O make it saft and narrow:
My love has died for me to-day,
I'll die for him to-morrow.
'Barbara Allen's Cruelty'

7 It fell about the Lammastide,
When the muir-men win tound him to ride
Into England, to drive ound him to ride
Into England, to drive a prey.
'Battle of Otterburn'

8 There were twa sisters sat in a bour;
Binnorie, O Binnorie!
There came a knight to be their wooer,
By the bonnie milldams o' Binnorie.
'Binnorie'

9 Ye Highlands and ye Lawlands,
O where hae ye been?
They hae slain the Earl of Murray,
And hae laid him on the green.
'The Bonny Earl of Murray'

10 He was a braw gallant,
And he played at the gluve;
And the bonny Earl of Murray,
O he was the Queen's luve!

O lang will his Lady
Look owre the Castle Downe,
Ere she see the Earl of Murray
Come sounding through the town!
'The Bonny Earl of Murray'

11 Is there any room at your head, Sanders?
Is there any room at your feet?
Or any room at your twa sides,
Where fain, fain I would sleep?

There is na room at my head, Margaret,
There is na room at my feet;
My bed it is the cold, cold grave;
Among the hungry worms I sleep.
'Clerk Sanders'

12 She hadna sailed a league, a league,
A league but barely three,
Till grim, grim grew his countenance
And gurly grew the sea.
'The Daemon Lover'

13 'What hills are yon, yon pleasant hills,
The sun shines sweetly on?'—
'O yon are the hills o' Heaven,' he said,
'Where you will never won.'
'The Daemon Lover'

14 Let me have length and breadth enough,
And under my head a sod;
That they may say when I am dead,
—Here lies bold Robin Hood!
'The Death of Robin Hood'

15 There were three lords drinking at the wine
On the dowie dens o' Yarrow;
They made a compact them between
They would go fight tomorrow.
'Dowie Dens of Yarrow'

16 O well's me o' my gay goss-hawk,
That he can speak and flee!
He'll carry a letter to my love,
Bring another back to me.
'The Gay Goss Hawk'

17 I am a man upon the land,
I am a selkie in the sea;
When I am far and far from land,
My home it is the Sule Skerry.
'The Great Selkie of Sule Skerry'

18 I wish I were where Helen lies,
Night and day on me she cries;
O that I were where Helen lies,
On fair Kirkconnell lea!

Curst be the heart that thought the thought,
And curst the hand that fired the shot,
When in my arms burd Helen dropt,
And died to succour me!
'Helen of Kirkconnell'

19 Blair Atholl's mine, Jeanie,
Little Dunkeld is mine, lassie,
St Johnston's bower, and Huntingtower,
And all that's mine is thine, lassie.
'Huntingtower'

20 Where are your eyes that looked so mild
When my poor heart you first beguiled?
Why did you run from me and the child?
Och, Johnny, I hardly knew ye!
'Johnny, I hardly knew Ye'

21 I was but seven years auld
When my mither she did die;
My father married the ae warst woman
The warld did ever see.

For she has made me the laily worm
That lies at the fit o' the tree
And my sister Masery she's made
The machrel of the sea.
An' evry Saturday at noon
The machrel comes to me
An' she takes my laily head
An' lays it on her knee;
An' she kaims it wi' a siller kaim
An' washes 't in the sea.
'The Laily Worm and the Machrel'

1 'What gat ye to your dinner, Lord Randal, my Son?
What gat ye to your dinner, my handsome young man?'
'I gat eels boil'd in broo'; mother, make my bed soon,
For I'm weary wi' hunting, and fain wald lie down.'
'Lord Randal'

2 This ae nighte, this ae nighte,
—*Every nighte and alle,*
Fire and fleet and candle-lighte,
And Christe receive thy saule.
fleet = *corruption of* flet, *meaning house-room*
'Lyke-Wake Dirge'

3 From Brig o' Dread when thou may'st pass,
—*Every nighte and alle,*
To Purgatory fire thou com'st at last;
And Christe receive thy saule.
'Lyke-Wake Dirge'

4 If ever thou gavest meat or drink,
—*Every nighte and alle,*
The fire sall never make thee shrink
And Christe receive thy saule.
'Lyke-Wake Dirge'

5 When captains courageous whom death could not daunt,
Did march to the siege of the city of Gaunt,
They mustered their soldiers by two and by three,
And the foremost in battle was Mary Ambree.
'Mary Ambree'

6 For in my mind, of all mankind
I love but you alone.
'The Nut Brown Maid'

7 For I must to the greenwood go
Alone, a banished man.
'The Nut Brown Maid'

8 Marie Hamilton's to the kirk gane
Wi' ribbons on her breast;
The King thought mair o' Marie Hamilton
Than he listen'd to the priest.
'The Queen's Maries'

9 Yestreen the Queen had four Maries,
The night she'll hae but three;
There was Marie Seaton, and Marie Beaton,
And Marie Carmichael, and me.
'The Queen's Maries'

10 'O what is longer than the wave?
And what is deeper than the sea?
What is greener than the grass?
And what is more wicked than a woman once was?'
'Love is longer than the wave,
And hell is deeper than the sea.
Envy's greener than the grass,
And the de'il more wicked than a woman e'er was.'
As soon as she the fiend did name,
He flew awa' in a bleezing flame.
'Riddles Wisely Expounded'

11 There are twelve months in all the year,
As I hear many men say,
But the merriest month in all the year
Is the merry month of May.
'Robin Hood and the Widow's Three Sons'

12 Fight on, my men, sayes Sir Andrew Bartton,
I am hurt but I am not slain;
Ile lay mee downe and bleed a while
And then Ile rise and fight againe.
'Sir Andrew Bartton'

13 The king sits in Dunfermline town
Drinking the blude-red wine.
'Sir Patrick Spens'

14 To Noroway, to Noroway,
To Noroway o'er the faem;
The king's daughter o' Noroway,
'Tis thou must bring her hame.
'Sir Patrick Spens'

15 I saw the new moon late yestreen
Wi' the auld moon in her arm;
And if we gang to sea master,
I fear we'll come to harm.
'Sir Patrick Spens'

16 O lang, lang may the ladies sit,
Wi' their fans into their hand,
Before they see Sir Patrick Spens
Come sailing to the strand!
And lang, lang may the maidens sit
Wi' their gowd kames in their hair,
A-waiting for their ain dear loves!
For them they'll see nae mair.
'Sir Patrick Spens'

17 Half-owre, half-owre to Aberdour,
'Tis fifty fathoms deep;
And there lies good Sir Patrick Spens,
Wi' the Scots lords at his feet!
'Sir Patrick Spens'

18 And she has kilted her green kirtle
A little abune her knee;
And she has braided her yellow hair
A little abune her bree.
'Tam Lin'

19 But what I ken this night, Tam Lin,
Gin I had kent yestreen,
I wad ta'en out thy heart o' flesh,
And put in a heart o' stane.
'Tam Lin'

20 She's mounted on her milk-white steed,
She's ta'en true Thomas up behind.
'Thomas the Rhymer'

1 And see ye not yon braid, braid road,
That lies across the lily leven?
That is the Path of Wickedness,
Though some call it the Road to Heaven.
'Thomas the Rhymer'

2 It was mirk, mirk night, there was nae starlight,
They waded thro' red blude to the knee;
For a' the blude that's shed on the earth
Rins through the springs o' that countrie.
'Thomas the Rhymer'

3 There were three ravens sat on a tree,
They were as black as they might be.
The one of them said to his make,
'Where shall we our breakfast take?'
'The Three Ravens'

4 God send every gentleman
Such hounds, such hawks, and such leman.
'The Three Ravens' (*leman* sweetheart)

5 As I was walking all alane,
I heard twa corbies making a mane:
The tane unto the tither did say,
'Where sall we gang and dine the day?'

'—In behint yon auld fail dyke
I wot there lies a new-slain knight;
And naebody kens that he lies there
But his hawk, his hound, and his lady fair.

'His hound is to the hunting gane,
His hawk to fetch the wild-fowl hame,
His lady's ta'en anither mate,
So we may make our dinner sweet

'Ye'll sit on his white hause-bane,
And I'll pike out his bonny blue e'en:
Wi' ae lock o' his gowden hair
We'll theek our nest when it grows bare.'
'The Twa Corbies' (*corbies* ravens; *fail* turf; *hause* neck; *theek* thatch)

6 The wind doth blow to-day, my love,
And a few small drops of rain;
I never had but one true love;
In cold grave she was lain.

I'll do as much for my true-love
As any young man may;
I'll sit and mourn all at her grave
For a twelvemonth and a day.
'The Unquiet Grave'

7 O waly, waly, up the bank,
And waly, waly, doun the brae,
And waly, waly, yon burn-side,
Where I and my Love wont to gae!
'Waly, Waly'

8 O waly, waly, gin love be bonnie
A little time while it is new!
But when 'tis auld it waxeth cauld,
And fades awa' like morning dew.
'Waly, Waly'

9 But had I wist, before I kist,
That love had been sae ill to win,
I had locked my heart in a case o' gowd,
And pinned it wi' a siller pin.
And O! if my young babe were born,
And set upon the nurse's knee;
And I mysel' were dead and gane,
And the green grass growing over me!
'Waly, Waly'

10 Tom Pearse, Tom Pearse, lend me your grey mare,
All along, down along, out along, lee.
For I want for to go to Widdicombe Fair,
Wi' Bill Brewer, Jan Stewer, Peter Gurney, Peter Davey, Dan'l Whiddon, Harry Hawk,
Old Uncle Tom Cobbleigh and all.
Old Uncle Tom Cobbleigh and all.
'Widdicombe Fair'

J. G. Ballard 1930–
British writer

11 Everything is becoming science fiction. From the margins of an almost invisible literature has sprung the intact reality of the 20th century.
'Fictions of Every Kind' in *Books and Bookmen* February 1971

12 A car crash harnesses elements of eroticism, aggression, desire, speed, drama, kinaesthetic factors, the stylizing of motion, consumer goods, status—all these in one event. I myself see the car crash as a tremendous sexual event really: a liberation of human and machine libido (if there is such a thing).
interview in *Penthouse* September 1970

13 Some refer to it as a cultural Chernobyl. I think of it as a cultural Stalingrad.
of Euro Disney
in *Daily Telegraph* 2 July 1994; cf. **Mnouchkine** 524:14

Whitney Balliett 1926–
American writer

14 A critic is a bundle of biases held loosely together by a sense of taste.
Dinosaurs in the Morning (1962) introductory note

15 The sound of surprise.
title of book on jazz (1959)

Pierre Balmain 1914–82
French couturier

16 The trick of wearing mink is to look as though you were wearing a cloth coat. The trick of wearing a cloth coat is to look as though you are wearing mink.
in *Observer* 25 December 1955

Honoré de Balzac 1799–1850
French novelist
on Balzac: see ***Zola*** *841:2*

17 *L'homme n'est ni bon ni méchant, il naît avec des instincts et des aptitudes.*
Man is neither good nor bad; he is born with instincts and abilities.
La Comédie Humaine (1842) vol. 1, foreword

18 *La haine est un tonique, elle fait vivre, elle inspire la vengeance; mais la pitié tue, elle affaiblit encore notre faiblesse.*

Hatred is a tonic, it makes one live, it inspires vengeance; but pity kills, it makes our weakness weaker.
La Peau de Chagrin (1831) ch. 1

1 *Le despotisme fait illégalement de grandes choses, la liberté ne se donne même pas la peine d'en faire légalement de très petites.*
Despotism accomplishes great things illegally; liberty doesn't even go to the trouble of accomplishing small things legally.
La Peau de Chagrin (1831) ch. 3

2 If I'm not a genius, I'm done for.
letter to his sister Laure, 1819; Graham Robb *Balzac* (1994) ch. 3

3 I am not deep, but I am very wide, and it takes time to walk round me.
letter to Countess Maffei, 1837

George Bancroft 1800–91

4 Calvinism [in Switzerland] . . . established a religion without a prelate, a government without a king.
History of the United States (1855 ed.) vol. 3, ch. 6

Lord Bancroft 1922–96
British civil servant; Head of the Civil Service 1978–81

5 Conviction politicians, certainly: conviction civil servants, no.
'Whitehall: Some Personal Reflections', lecture at the London School of Economics 1 December 1983

Tallulah Bankhead 1903–68
American actress

6 Cocaine habit-forming? Of course not. I ought to know. I've been using it for years.
Tallulah (1952)

7 I'm as pure as the driven slush.
in *Saturday Evening Post* 12 April 1947

8 I read Shakespeare and the Bible and I can shoot dice. That's what I call a liberal education.
attributed

9 They used to shoot her through gauze. You should shoot me through linoleum.
on Shirley Temple
attributed

Théodore Faullain de Banville 1823–91
French poet

10 *Jeune homme sans mélancolie,*
Blond comme un soleil d'Italie,
Garde bien ta belle folie.
Young man untroubled by melancholy, fair as an Italian sun, take good care of your fine carelessness.
'A Adolphe Gaiffe' (1856)

11 LICENCES POÉTIQUES. *Il n'y en a pas.*
POETIC LICENCE. There's no such thing.
Petit traité de poésie française (1872) ch. 4

Imamu Amiri Baraka (Everett LeRoi Jones) 1934–
American poet and dramatist

12 A man is either free or he is not. There cannot be any apprenticeship for freedom.
in *Kulchur* Spring 1962 'Tokenism'

13 God has been replaced, as he has all over the West, with respectability and airconditioning.
Midstream (1963)

Yevgeny Baratynsky 1800–44
Russian poet

14 Providence has given human wisdom the choice between two fates: either hope and agitation, or hopelessness and calm.
'Two Fates' (1823) (translated by Dmitri Obolensky)

Anna Laetitia Barbauld 1743–1825
English poet and literary editor

15 If e'er thy breast with freedom glowed,
And spurned a tyrant's chain,
Let not thy strong oppressive force
A free-born mouse detain.
'The Mouse's Petition to Doctor Priestley Found in the Trap where he had been confined all Night' (1773) l. 9

16 Beware, lest in the worm you crush
A brother's soul you find.
'The Mouse's Petition' (1773) l. 33

17 Yes, injured Woman! rise, assert thy right!
'The Rights of Woman' (written *c.*1795, published 1825) l. 1

Mary Barber *c.*1690–1757
Irish poet

18 What is it our mammas bewitches
To plague us little boys with breeches?
'Written for My Son, and Spoken by Him at His First Putting on Breeches' (1731) l. 1

19 A husband's first praise is a Friend and Protector:
Then change not these titles for Tyrant and Hector.
'Conclusion of a Letter to the Revd Mr C—' (1734) l. 67

John Barbour *c.*1320–95
Scottish poet

20 Storys to rede ar delitabill,
Suppos that thai be nocht bot fabill.
The Bruce (1375) bk. 1, l. 1

21 A! fredome is a noble thing!
Fredome mayse man to haiff liking.
The Bruce (1375) bk. 1, l. 225

Alexander Barclay *c.*1475–1552
Scottish poet and priest

22 Thy bread is black, of ill sapour and taste,
And hard as flint because thou none should waste,
That scant be thy teeth able it to break.
Dip it in pottage if thou no shift can make,
And though white and brown be both at one price,

With brown shalt thou feed lest white might make thee nice.
The lords will alway that people note and see
Between them and servants some diversity,
Though it to them turn to no profit at all;
If they have pleasure, the servant shall have small.

Eclogues (1514) no. 2, l. 790

R. H. Barham ('Thomas Ingoldsby') 1788–1845

English clergyman

1 Though I've always considered Sir Christopher Wren,
As an architect, one of the greatest of men;
And, talking of Epitaphs,—much I admire his,
'Circumspice, si Monumentum requiris';
Which an erudite Verger translated to me,
'If you ask for his Monument, Sir-come-spy-see!'

The Ingoldsby Legends (First Series, 1840) 'The Cynotaph'; cf. **Epitaphs** 304:4

2 What *was* to be done?—'twas perfectly plain
That they could not well hang the man over again;
What *was* to be done?—The man was dead!
Nought *could* be done—nought could be said;
So—my Lord Tomnoddy went home to bed!

The Ingoldsby Legends (First Series, 1840) 'Hon. Mr Sucklethumbkin's Story'

3 The Jackdaw sat on the Cardinal's chair!
Bishop, and abbot, and prior were there;
Many a monk, and many a friar,
Many a knight, and many a squire,
With a great many more of lesser degree,—
In sooth a goodly company;
And they served the Lord Primate on bended knee.

The Ingoldsby Legends (First Series, 1840) 'The Jackdaw of Rheims'

4 And six little Singing-boys,—dear little souls!
In nice clean faces, and nice white stoles.

The Ingoldsby Legends (First Series, 1840) 'The Jackdaw of Rheims'

5 He cursed him in sleeping, that every night
He should dream of the devil, and wake in a fright.

The Ingoldsby Legends (First Series, 1840) 'The Jackdaw of Rheims'

6 Never was heard such a terrible curse!
But what gave rise
To no little surprise,
Nobody seemed one penny the worse!

The Ingoldsby Legends (First Series, 1840) 'The Jackdaw of Rheims'

7 Heedless of grammar, they all cried, 'That's him!'

The Ingoldsby Legends (First Series, 1840) 'The Jackdaw of Rheims'

8 Here's a corpse in the case with a sad swelled face,
And a 'Crowner's Quest' is a queer sort of thing!

in later editions: 'a Medical Crowner's a queer sort of thing!'

The Ingoldsby Legends (First Series, 1840) 'A Lay of St Gengulphus'

9 Now haste ye, my handmaidens, haste and see
How he sits there and glowers with his head on his knee!

The Ingoldsby Legends (First Series, 1840) 'The Legend of Hamilton Tighe'

10 But wherever they live, or whenever they die
They'll never get rid of young Hamilton Tighe.

The Ingoldsby Legends (First Series, 1840) 'The Legend of Hamilton Tighe'

11 A servant's too often a negligent elf;
—If it's business of consequence, DO IT YOURSELF!

The Ingoldsby Legends (Second Series, 1842) 'The Ingoldsby Penance!—Moral'

Maurice Baring 1874–1945

English man of letters

12 In Mozart and Salieri we see the contrast between the genius which does what it must and the talent which does what it can.

Outline of Russian Literature (1914) ch. 3

Sabine Baring-Gould 1834–1924

English clergyman

13 Onward, Christian soldiers,
Marching as to war,
With the cross of Jesus
Going on before.

'Onward, Christian Soldiers' (1864 hymn)

14 Through the night of doubt and sorrow
Onward goes the pilgrim band,
Singing songs of expectation,
Marching to the Promised Land.

'Through the night of doubt and sorrow' (1867 hymn); translated from the Danish of B. S. Ingemann (1789–1862)

Pat Barker 1943–

English novelist

15 The Somme is like the Holocaust. It revealed things about mankind that we cannot come to terms with and cannot forget. It can never become the past.

on winning the Booker Prize 1995

in *Athens News* 9 November 1995

Frederick R. Barnard

16 One picture is worth ten thousand words.

in *Printers' Ink* 10 March 1927

Julian Barnes 1946–

English novelist

17 The land of embarrassment and breakfast.

of Britain

Flaubert's Parrot (1984) ch. 7

18 Do not imagine that Art is something which is designed to give gentle uplift and self-confidence. Art is not a *brassière*. At least, not in the English sense. But do not forget that *brassière* is the French for life-jacket.

Flaubert's Parrot (1984) ch. 10

1 Books say: she did this because. Life says: she did this. Books are where things are explained to you; life is where things aren't.
Flaubert's Parrot (1984) ch. 13

2 All novelists know their art proceeds by indirection. When tempted by didacticism, the writer should imagine a spruce sea-captain eyeing the storm ahead, bustling from instrument to instrument in a catherine wheel of gold braid, expelling crisp orders down the speaking tube. But there is nobody below decks; the engine-room was never installed, and the rudder broke off centuries ago.
A History of the World in 10½ Chapters (1989) 'Parenthesis'

3 Does history repeat itself, the first time as tragedy, the second time as farce? No, that's too grand, too considered a process. History just burps, and we taste again that raw-onion sandwich it swallowed centuries ago.
A History of the World in 10½ Chapters (1989) 'Parenthesis'; cf. **Marx** 500:1, **Proverbs** 602:40

4 Love is just a system for getting someone to call you darling after sex.
Talking It Over (1991) ch. 16

Peter Barnes 1931–
English dramatist

5 CLAIRE: How do you know you're . . . God?
EARL OF GURNEY: Simple. When I pray to Him I find I'm talking to myself.
The Ruling Class (1969) act 1, sc. 4

William Barnes 1801–86
English poet

6 An' there vor me the apple tree
Do leän down low in Linden Lea.
Hwomely Rhymes (1859) 'My Orcha'd in Linden Lea'

7 But still the neäme do bide the seäme—
'Tis Pentridge—Pentridge by the river.
Hwomely Rhymes (1859) 'Pentridge by the River'

Richard Barnfield 1574–1627
English poet

8 The waters were his winding sheet, the sea was made his tomb;
Yet for his fame the ocean sea, was not sufficient room.
on the death of Sir John Hawkins
The Encomion of Lady Pecunia (1598) 'To the Gentlemen Readers'

9 My flocks feed not, my ewes breed not,
My rams speed not, all is amiss:
Love in dying, Faith is defying,
Heart's renying, causer of this.
'The Unknown Shepherd's Complaint' in Nicholas Ling (ed.) *England's Helicon* (1600)

10 Man's life is well comparèd to a feast,
Furnished with choice of all variety;
To it comes Time; and as a bidden guest
He sets him down, in pomp and majesty;
The three-fold Age of man the waiters be.
Then with an earthen voider (made of clay)
Comes Death, and takes the table clean away.
'Man's life' (1598)

Phineas T. Barnum 1810–91
American showman
see also **Lincoln** 469:5

11 There's a sucker born every minute.
attributed

Amelia E. Barr 1831–1919
American author and journalist

12 The fate of love is that it always seems too little or too much.
The Belle of Bolling Green (1904) ch. 4

J. M. Barrie 1860–1937
Scottish writer and dramatist
on Barrie: see **Guedalla** 354:11

13 His lordship may compel us to be equal upstairs, but there will never be equality in the servants' hall.
The Admirable Crichton (performed 1902, published 1914) act 1

14 When the first baby laughed for the first time, the laugh broke into a thousand pieces and they all went skipping about, and that was the beginning of fairies.
Peter Pan (1928) act 1

15 Every time a child says 'I don't believe in fairies' there is a little fairy somewhere that falls down dead.
Peter Pan (1928) act 1

16 To die will be an awfully big adventure.
Peter Pan (1928) act 3; cf. **Last words** 457:18

17 Do you believe in fairies? Say quick that you believe! If you believe, clap your hands!
Peter Pan (1928) act 4

18 That is ever the way. 'Tis all jealousy to the bride and good wishes to the corpse.
Quality Street (performed 1901, published 1913) act 1

19 Charm . . . it's a sort of bloom on a woman. If you have it, you don't need to have anything else; and if you don't have it, it doesn't much matter what else you have.
What Every Woman Knows (performed 1908, published 1918) act 1

20 There are few more impressive sights in the world than a Scotsman on the make.
What Every Woman Knows (performed 1908, published 1918) act 2

21 The tragedy of a man who has found himself out.
What Every Woman Knows (performed 1908, published 1918) act 4

Sebastian Barry 1955–
Irish writer and dramatist

1 Do you not feel that this island is moored only lightly to the sea-bed, and might be off for the Americas at any moment?
Prayers of Sherkin (1991)

2 I haven't really written my plays and books—I've heard them. The stories are there already, singing in your genes and in your blood.
in *Irish Times* 19 February 1998

Ethel Barrymore 1879–1959
American actress

3 For an actress to be a success, she must have the face of a Venus, the brains of a Minerva, the grace of Terpsichore, the memory of a Macaulay, the figure of Juno, and the hide of a rhinoceros.
George Jean Nathan *The Theatre in the Fifties* (1953)

Karl Barth 1886–1968
Swiss Protestant theologian

4 Men have never been good, they are not good and they never will be good.
Christian Community (1948)

5 He will not be like an ant which has foreseen everything in advance, but like a child in a forest, or on Christmas Eve: one who is always rightly astonished by events, by the encounters and experiences which overtake him.
of the justified man
Church Dogmatics (1936)

6 It may be that when the angels go about their task of praising God, they play only Bach. I am sure, however, that when they are together *en famille*, they play Mozart.
Wolfgang Amadeus Mozart (1956)

Roland Barthes 1915–80
French writer and critic

7 What the public wants is the image of passion, not passion itself.
Mythologies (1957) 'Le monde où l'on catche'

8 I think that cars today are almost the exact equivalent of the great Gothic cathedrals: I mean the supreme creation of an era, conceived with passion by unknown artists, and consumed in image if not in usage by a whole population which appropriates them as a purely magical object.
Mythologies (1957) 'La nouvelle Citroën'

Bernard Baruch 1870–1965
American financier and presidential adviser

9 Let us not be deceived—we are today in the midst of a cold war.
'cold war' was suggested to him by H. B. Swope, former editor of the New York World
speech to South Carolina Legislature, 16 April 1947; in *New York Times* 17 April 1947

10 To me old age is always fifteen years older than I am.
in *Newsweek* 29 August 1955

11 Vote for the man who promises least; he'll be the least disappointing.
Meyer Berger *New York* (1960)

12 A political leader must keep looking over his shoulder all the time to see if the boys are still there. If they aren't still there, he's no longer a political leader.
in *New York Times* 21 June 1965

Jacques Barzun 1907–
American historian and educationist

13 If it were possible to talk to the unborn, one could never explain to them how it feels to be alive, for life is washed in the speechless real.
The House of Intellect (1959) ch. 6

Matsuo Basho 1644–94
Japanese poet

14 Early autumn—
rice field, ocean,
one green.
translated by Lucien Stryk

15 Friends part
forever—wild geese
lost in cloud.
translated by Lucien Stryk

16 How pleasant—
just once *not* to see
Fuji through mist.
translated by Lucien Stryk

17 Old pond,
leap-splash—
a frog.
translated by Lucien Stryk

18 Rainy days—
silkworms droop
on mulberries.
translated by Lucien Stryk

19 Under the cherry—
blossom soup,
blossom salad.
translated by Lucien Stryk

20 You, the butterfly—
I, Chuang Tzu's
dreaming heart.
translated by Lucien Stryk; cf. **Chuang Tzu** 213:2

William Basse d. c.1653
English poet

21 The first men that our Saviour dear
Did choose to wait upon him here,
Blest fishers were; and fish the last
Food was, that he on earth did taste:
I therefore strive to follow those
Whom he to follow him hath chose.
'The Angler's Song' (1653)

1 Renownèd Spenser, lie a thought more nigh
To learnèd Chaucer, and rare Beaumont lie
A little nearer Spenser, to make more room
For Shakespeare, in your threefold, fourfold tomb.
'On Mr Wm. Shakespeare' (1633)

Thomas Bastard 1566–1618
English poet

2 Age is deformed, youth unkind,
We scorn their bodies, they our mind.
Chrestoleros (1598) bk. 7, epigram 9

Edgar Bateman and **George Le Brunn**
British songwriters

3 Wiv a ladder and some glasses,
You could see to 'Ackney Marshes,
If it wasn't for the 'ouses in between.
'If it wasn't for the 'Ouses in between' (1894 song)

Katherine Lee Bates 1859–1929
American writer and educationist

4 America! America!
God shed His grace on thee
And crown thy good with brotherhood
From sea to shining sea!
'America the Beautiful' (1893)

Charles Baudelaire 1821–67
French poet and critic

5 *Le poète est semblable au prince des nuées*
Qui hante la tempête et se rit de l'archer;
Exilé sur le sol, au milieu des huées,
Ses ailes de géant l'empêchent de marcher.

The poet is like the prince of the clouds, who rides out the tempest and laughs at the archer. But when he is exiled on the ground, amidst the clamour, his giant's wings prevent him from walking.
Les fleurs du mal (1857) 'L'Albatross'—'Spleen et idéal' no. 2

6 *Hypocrite lecteur,—mon semblable,—mon frère.*

Hypocrite reader—my likeness—my brother.
Les fleurs du mal (1857) 'Au Lecteur'

7 *La nature est un temple où de vivants piliers*
Laissent parfois sortir de confuses paroles;
L'homme y passe à travers des forêts de symboles
Qui l'observent avec des regards familiers.

Nature is a temple, where, from living pillars, confused words are sometimes allowed to escape; here man passes, through forests of symbols, which watch him with looks of recognition.
Les fleurs du mal (1857) 'Correspondances' no. 4

8 *Là, tout n'est qu'ordre et beauté,*
Luxe, calme et volupté.

Everything there is simply order and beauty, luxury, peace and sensual indulgence.
Les fleurs du mal (1857) 'L'Invitation au voyage'—'Spleen et idéal' no. 56

9 *Quelle est cette île triste et noire? C'est Cythère,*
Nous dit-on, un pays fameux dans les chansons,
Eldorado banal de tous les vieux garçons.
Regardez, après tout, c'est un pauvre terre.

What sad, black isle is that? It's Cythera, so they say, a land celebrated in song, the banal Eldorado of all the old fools. Look, after all, it's a land of poverty.
Les fleurs du mal (1857) 'Un voyage à Cythère'—'Les fleurs du mal' no. 121

10 *Nous voulons, tant ce feu nous brûle le cerveau,*
Plonger au fond du gouffre, Enfer ou Ciel, qu'importe?
Au fond de l'Inconnu pour trouver du nouveau!

We want, this fire so burns our brain tissue,
to drown in the abyss—heaven or hell,
who cares? Through the unknown, we'll find the new.
Les fleurs du mal (1857) 'Le voyage' no. 126 (translated by Robert Lowell)

11 *Il y a dans tout changement quelque chose d'infâme et d'agréable à la fois, quelque chose qui tient de l'infidelité et du déménagement. Cela suffit à expliquer la Révolution Française.*

There is in all change something at once sordid and agreeable, which smacks of infidelity and household removals. This is sufficient to explain the French Revolution.
Journaux intimes (1887) 'Mon coeur mis à nu' no. 4 (translated by Christopher Isherwood)

12 *La croyance au progrès est une doctrine de paresseux, une doctrine de Belges. C'est l'individu qui compte sur ses voisins pour faire sa besogne.*

Belief in progress is a doctrine of idlers and Belgians. It is the individual relying upon his neighbours to do his work.
Journaux intimes (1887) 'Mon coeur mis à nu' no. 9 (translated by Christopher Isherwood)

13 *Il faut épater le bourgeois.*

One must astonish the bourgeois.
attributed; also attributed to Privat d'Anglemont (*c.*1820–59) in the form '*Je les ai épatés, les bourgeois* [I flabbergasted them, the bourgeois]'

Jean Baudrillard 1929–
French sociologist and cultural critic

14 To love someone is to isolate him from the world, wipe out every trace of him, dispossess him of his shadow, drag him into a murderous future. It is to circle around the other like a dead star and absorb him into a black light.
Fatal Strategies (1983)

L. Frank Baum 1856–1919
American writer

15 The road to the City of Emeralds is paved with yellow brick.
The Wonderful Wizard of Oz (1900) ch. 2; cf. **Harburg** 359:19

Beverley Baxter 1891–1964
British journalist and Conservative politician

16 Beaverbrook is so pleased to be in the Government that he is like the town tart who has finally married the Mayor!
Henry Channon *Chips: the Diaries* (1967) 12 June 1940

John Bayley 1925–
English academic

1 It is rather like falling from stair to stair in a series of bumps.
on his wife Iris **Murdoch***'s progressive loss of memory from Alzheimer's disease*
in an interview, *Daily Telegraph* 8 February 1997

Thomas Haynes Bayly 1797–1839
English poet and dramatist

2 Oh! no! we never mention her,
Her name is never heard;
My lips are now forbid to speak
That once familiar word.
'Oh! No! We Never Mention Her' (1844)

Beachcomber see J. B. Morton

James Beattie 1735–1803
Scottish philosopher and poet

3 Some deemed him wondrous wise, and some believed him mad.
The Minstrel bk. 1 (1771) st. 16

4 Fancy a thousand wondrous forms descries
More wildly great than ever pencil drew,
Rocks, torrents, gulfs, and shapes of giant size,
And glittering cliffs on cliffs, and fiery ramparts rise.
The Minstrel bk. 1 (1771) st. 53

5 In the deep windings of the grove, no more
The hag obscene, and grisly phantom dwell;
Nor in the fall of mountain-stream, or roar
Of winds, is heard the angry spirit's yell.
The Minstrel bk. 2 (1774) st. 48

David Beatty 1871–1936
British Admiral of the Fleet, 1916–19

6 There's something wrong with our bloody ships today.
at the Battle of Jutland, 1916
Winston Churchill *The World Crisis 1916–1918* (1927) pt. 1

Topham Beauclerk 1739–80
English dandy

7 Then he does not wear them out in practice.
on hearing that a certain person was 'a man of good principles'
James Boswell *The Life of Samuel Johnson* (1791) 14 April 1778

Pierre-Augustin Caron de Beaumarchais 1732–99
French dramatist

8 *Aujourd'hui ce qui ne vaut pas la peine d'être dit, on le chante.*
Today if something is not worth saying, people sing it.
Le Barbier de Séville (1775) act 1, sc. 2

9 *Je me presse de rire de tout, de peur d'être obligé d'en pleurer.*
I hurry to laugh at everything, for fear of having to weep at it.
Le Barbier de Séville (1775) act 1, sc. 2

10 *Boire sans soif et faire l'amour en tout temps, madame, il n'y a que ça qui nous distingue des autres bêtes.*
Drinking when we are not thirsty and making love all year round, madam; that is all there is to distinguish us from other animals.
Le Mariage de Figaro (1785) act 2, sc. 21

11 *Parce que vous êtes un grand seigneur, vous vous croyez un grand génie! . . . Vous vous êtes donné la peine de naître, et rien de plus.*
Because you are a great lord, you believe yourself to be a great genius! . . . You took the trouble to be born, but no more.
Le Mariage de Figaro (1785) act 5, sc. 3

Francis Beaumont 1584–1616
English poet and dramatist

12 Nose, nose, jolly red nose,
Who gave thee this jolly red nose? . . .
Nutmegs and ginger, cinnamon and cloves,
And they gave me this jolly red nose.
The Knight of the Burning Pestle (c.1607) act 1

13 What things have we seen,
Done at the Mermaid! heard words that have been
So nimble, and so full of subtil flame,
As if that every one from whence they came,
Had meant to put his whole wit in a jest,
And had resolved to live a fool, the rest
Of his dull life.
'Letter to Ben Jonson'

14 Here are sands, ignoble things,
Dropt from the ruined sides of kings;
Here's a world of pomp and state,
Buried in dust, once dead by fate.
'On the Tombs in Westminster Abbey'

Francis Beaumont 1584–1616 and John Fletcher 1579–1625
English dramatists
see also ***John Fletcher***

15 Those have most power to hurt us that we love.
The Maid's Tragedy (written 1610–11) act 5

16 PHILASTER: Oh, but thou dost not know
What 'tis to die.
BELLARIO: Yes, I do know, my Lord:
'Tis less than to be born; a lasting sleep;
A quiet resting from all jealousy,
A thing we all pursue; I know besides,
It is but giving over of a game,
That must be lost.
Philaster (written 1609) act 3

17 There is no other purgatory but a woman.
The Scornful Lady (1616) act 3

18 It would talk: Lord how it talk't!
The Scornful Lady (1616) act 4

Lord Beaverbrook (Max Aitken, Lord Beaverbrook) 1879–1964

Canadian-born British newspaper proprietor and Conservative politician

on Beaverbrook: see **Attlee** *32:1,* **Baxter** *57:16,* **Kipling** *441:25*

1 The Flying Scotsman is no less splendid a sight when it travels north to Edinburgh than when it travels south to London. Mr Baldwin denouncing sanctions was as dignified as Mr Baldwin imposing them.
in *Daily Express* 29 May 1937

2 He did not seem to care which way he travelled providing he was in the driver's seat.
of **Lloyd George**
The Decline and Fall of Lloyd George (1963) ch. 7

3 Now who is responsible for this work of development on which so much depends? To whom must the praise be given? To the boys in the back rooms. They do not sit in the limelight. But they are the men who do the work.
in *Listener* 27 March 1941

4 I ran the paper [*Daily Express*] purely for propaganda, and with no other purpose.
evidence to Royal Commission on the Press, 18 March 1948, in A. J. P. Taylor *Beaverbrook* (1972)

5 With the publication of his Private Papers in 1952, he committed suicide 25 years after his death.
of Earl **Haig**
Men and Power (1956)

6 Our cock won't fight.
to Winston **Churchill** *of* **Edward VIII***, during the abdication crisis of 1936*
Frances Donaldson *Edward VIII* (1974) ch. 22

7 I have had two masters and one of them betrayed me.
of **Bonar Law** *and* **Churchill**
A. J. P. Taylor, letter, 16 December 1973; *Letters to Eva* (1991)

Carl Becker 1873–1945

American historian

8 The significance of man is that he is that part of the universe that asks the question, What is the significance of Man? He alone can stand apart imaginatively and, regarding himself and the universe in their eternal aspects, pronounce a judgement: The significance of man is that he is insignificant and is aware of it.
Progress and Power (1936) ch. 3

Samuel Beckett 1906–89

Irish dramatist, novelist, and poet

9 It is suicide to be abroad. But what is it to be at home, Mr Tyler, what is it to be at home? A lingering dissolution.
All That Fall (1957)

10 We could have saved sixpence. We have saved fivepence. (*Pause*) But at what cost?
All That Fall (1957)

11 I shall state silence more competently than ever a better man spangled the butterflies of vertigo.
A Dream of Fair to Middling Women (written 1932)

12 CLOV: Do you believe in the life to come?
HAMM: Mine was always that.
Endgame (1958)

13 Let us pray to God . . . the bastard! He doesn't exist!
Endgame (1958)

14 Perhaps my best years are gone . . . but I wouldn't want them back. Not with the fire that's in me now.
Krapp's Last Tape (1959)

15 There is no use indicting words, they are no shoddier than what they peddle.
Malone Dies (1958)

16 If I had the use of my body I would throw it out of the window.
Malone Dies (1958)

17 The sun shone, having no alternative, on the nothing new.
Murphy (1938)

18 His writing is not *about* something; it is that something itself.
Our Exagmination Round the Factification for Incamination of Work in Progress (1929)

19 To find a form that accommodates the mess, that is the task of the artist now.
Proust (1961)

20 Where I am, I don't know, I'll never know, in the silence you don't know, you must go on, I can't go on, I'll go on.
The Unnamable (1959)

21 Nothing to be done.
Waiting for Godot (1955) act 1

22 There's a man all over for you, blaming on his boots the faults of his feet.
Waiting for Godot (1955) act 1

23 One of the thieves was saved. (*Pause*) It's a reasonable percentage.
Waiting for Godot (1955) act 1

24 ESTRAGON: Charming spot. Inspiring prospects. Let's go.
VLADIMIR: We can't.
ESTRAGON: Why not?
VLADIMIR: We're waiting for Godot.
Waiting for Godot (1955) act 1

25 Nothing happens, nobody comes, nobody goes, it's awful!
Waiting for Godot (1955) act 1

26 He can't think without his hat.
Waiting for Godot (1955) act 1

27 All my lousy life I've crawled about in the mud! And you talk to me about scenery!
Waiting for Godot (1955) act 2

28 VLADIMIR: That passed the time.
ESTRAGON: It would have passed in any case.

VLADIMIR: Yes, but not so rapidly.
Waiting for Godot (1955) act 1

1 We are not saints, but we have kept our appointment. How many people can boast as much?
Waiting for Godot (1955) act 2

2 We all are born mad. Some remain so.
Waiting for Godot (1955) act 2

3 They give birth astride of a grave, the light gleams an instant, then it's night once more.
Waiting for Godot (1955) act 2

4 Habit is a great deadener.
Waiting for Godot (1955) act 2

5 Ever tried. Ever failed. No matter. Try again. Fail again. Fail better.
Worstward Ho (1983)

6 Time like a last oozing, so precious and worthless together.
letter to Kay Boyle, 23 August 1973; James Knowlson *Damned to Fame* (1996)

7 I couldn't have done it otherwise, gone on I mean. I could not have gone on through the awful wretched mess of life without having left a stain upon the silence.
Deirdre Bair *Samuel Beckett* (1978)

8 Even death is unreliable: instead of zero it may be some ghastly hallucination, such as the square root of minus one.
attributed

9 I am what her savage loving has made me.
of his mother
James Knowlson *Damned to Fame* (1996)

10 INTERVIEWER: You are English, Mr Beckett?
BECKETT: *Au contraire.*
attributed

William Beckford 1759–1844

English writer and collector
on Beckford: see **Borges** *143:5*

11 When he was angry, one of his eyes became so terrible, that no person could bear to behold it; and the wretch upon whom it was fixed, instantly fell backward, and sometimes expired. For fear, however, of depopulating his dominions and making his palace desolate, he but rarely gave way to his anger.
Vathek (1782; 3rd ed., 1816) opening para.

12 He did not think, with the Caliph Omar Ben Adalaziz, that it was necessary to make a hell of this world to enjoy Paradise in the next.
Vathek (1782; 3rd ed., 1816) para. 2

13 I am not over-fond of resisting temptation.
Vathek (1782; 3rd ed., 1816) para. 215

Thomas Lovell Beddoes 1803–49

English poet and dramatist

14 If thou wilt ease thine heart
Of love and all its smart,
Then sleep, dear, sleep.
Death's Jest Book 1825–8 (1850) act 2, sc. 2 'Dirge'

15 But wilt thou cure thine heart
Of love and all its smart,
Then die, dear, die.
Death's Jest Book 1825–8 (1850) act 2, sc. 2 'Dirge'

16 I have a bit of FIAT in my soul,
And can myself create my little world.
Death's Jest Book 1825–8 (1850) act 5, sc. 1, l. 39

17 King Death hath asses' ears.
Death's Jest Book 1825–8 (1850) act 5, sc. 4, l. 245

18 If there were dreams to sell,
What would you buy?
Some cost a passing bell;
Some a light sigh,
That shakes from Life's fresh crown
Only a rose-leaf down.
If there were dreams to sell,
Merry and sad to tell,
And the crier rung the bell,
What would you buy?
'Dream-Pedlary' (written 1830, published 1851)

The Venerable Bede AD 673–735

English historian and scholar; monk of Jarrow

19 *Talis, inquiens, mihi videtur, rex, vita hominum praesens in terris, ad conparationem eius, quod nobis incertum est, temporis, quale cum te residente ad caenam cum ducibus ac ministris tuis tempore brumali, . . . adveniens unus passerum domum citissime pervolaverit; qui cum per unum ostium ingrediens, mox per aliud exierit. Ipso quidem tempore, quo intus est, hiemis tempestate non tangitur, sed tamen parvissimo spatio serenitatis ad momentum excurso, mox de hieme in hiemem regrediens, tuis oculis elabitur. Ita haec vita hominum ad modicum apparet; quid autem sequatur, quidve praecesserit, prorsus ignoramus.*

'Such,' he said, 'O King, seems to me the present life of men on earth, in comparison with that time which to us is uncertain, as if when on a winter's night you sit feasting with your ealdormen and thegns,—a single sparrow should fly swiftly into the hall, and coming in at one door, instantly fly out through another. In that time in which it is indoors it is indeed not touched by the fury of the winter, but yet, this smallest space of calmness being passed almost in a flash, from winter going into winter again, it is lost to your eyes. Somewhat like this appears the life of man; but of what follows or what went before, we are utterly ignorant.'
Ecclesiastical History of the English People (translated by B. Colgrave, 1969) bk. 2, ch. 13

Harry Bedford and Terry Sullivan

British songwriters

20 I'm a bit of a ruin that Cromwell knocked about a bit.
'It's a Bit of a Ruin that Cromwell Knocked about a Bit' (1920 song; written for Marie Lloyd)

Barnard Elliott Bee 1823–61
American Confederate general

1 There is Jackson with his Virginians, standing like a stone wall. Let us determine to die here, and we will conquer.
referring to General T. J. ('Stonewall') Jackson at the battle of Bull Run, 21 July, 1861 (in which Bee himself was killed)
B. Perley Poore *Perley's Reminiscences* (1886) vol. 2, ch. 7

Thomas Beecham 1879–1961
English conductor

2 A kind of musical Malcolm Sargent.
of Herbert von Karajan
Harold Atkins and Archie Newman *Beecham Stories* (1978)

3 Like two skeletons copulating on a corrugated tin roof.
describing the harpsichord
Harold Atkins and Archie Newman *Beecham Stories* (1978)

4 The musical equivalent of the Towers of St Pancras Station.
of ***Elgar****'s 1st Symphony*
Neville Cardus *Sir Thomas Beecham* (1961) p. 113

5 There are two golden rules for an orchestra: start together and finish together. The public doesn't give a damn what goes on in between.
Harold Atkins and Archie Newman *Beecham Stories* (1978)

6 Too much counterpoint; what is worse, Protestant counterpoint.
of J. S. Bach
in *Guardian* 8 March 1971

7 Why do we have to have all these third-rate foreign conductors around—when we have so many second-rate ones of our own?
L. Ayre *Wit of Music* (1966) p. 70

H. C. Beeching 1859–1919
English clergyman

8 Not when the sense is dim,
But now from the heart of joy,
I would remember Him:
Take the thanks of a boy.
In a Garden and Other Poems (1895) 'Prayers'

9 First come I; my name is Jowett.
There's no knowledge but I know it.
I am Master of this college:
What I don't know isn't knowledge.
The Masque of Balliol (composed by and current among members of Balliol College in the late 1870s) in W. G. Hiscock (ed.) *The Balliol Rhymes* (1939); cf. **Anonymous** 17:20, **Spring-Rice** 735:9

Max Beerbohm 1872–1956
English critic, essayist, and caricaturist
on Beerbohm: see ***Shaw*** *709:23; see also* ***Telegrams*** *758:4, 758:9*

10 Mankind is divisible into two great classes: hosts and guests.
And Even Now (1920) 'Hosts and Guests'

11 I was not unpopular [at school] . . . It is Oxford that has made me insufferable.
More (1899) 'Going Back to School'

12 Enter Michael Angelo. Andrea del Sarto appears for a moment at a window. Pippa passes.
Seven Men (1919) 'Savonarola Brown' act 3

13 The fading signals and grey eternal walls of that antique station, which, familiar to them and insignificant, does yet whisper to the tourist the last enchantments of the Middle Age.
Zuleika Dobson (1911) ch. 1. cf. **Arnold** 28:15

14 The dullard's envy of brilliant men is always assuaged by the suspicion that they will come to a bad end.
Zuleika Dobson (1911) ch. 4

15 Women who love the same man have a kind of bitter freemasonry.
Zuleika Dobson (1911) ch. 4

16 The Socratic manner is not a game at which two can play.
Zuleika Dobson (1911) ch. 15

17 Fate wrote her a most tremendous tragedy, and she played it in tights.
of Caroline of Brunswick, wife of ***George IV***
The Yellow Book (1894) vol. 3

Ethel Lynn Beers 1827–79
American poet

18 All quiet along the Potomac to-night,
No sound save the rush of the river,
While soft falls the dew on the face of the dead—
The picket's off duty forever.
'The Picket Guard' (1861) st. 6; cf. **McClellan** 484:7

Ludwig van Beethoven 1770–1827
German composer
on Beethoven: see ***Bakunin*** *48:17*

19 *Muss es sein? Es muss sein.*
Must it be? It must be.
String Quartet in F Major, Opus 135, epigraph

20 The immortal god of harmony.
of J. S. ***Bach***
letter to Breitkopf und Härtel, 22 April 1801; Michael Hamburger (ed.) *Beethoven: Letters, Journals and Correspondence* (1951)

Brendan Behan 1923–64
Irish dramatist

21 So many belonging to me lay buried in Kilbarrock, the healthiest graveyard in Ireland, they said, because it was so near the sea.
Borstal Boy (1958)

22 PAT: He was an Anglo-Irishman.
MEG: In the blessed name of God what's that?
PAT: A Protestant with a horse.
Hostage (1958) act 1

23 Meanwhile I'll sing that famous old song, 'The Hound that Caught the Pubic Hare'.
Hostage (1958) act 1

1 When I came back to Dublin, I was courtmartialled in my absence and sentenced to death in my absence, so I said they could shoot me in my absence.
Hostage (1958) act 1

2 We're here because we're queer
Because we're queer because we're here.
Hostage (1958) act 3; cf. **Military sayings** 508:15

3 Other people have a nationality. The Irish and the Jews have a psychosis.
Richard's Cork Leg (1961)

on being asked 'What was the message of your play' after a performance of The Hostage*:*

4 Message? Message? What the hell do you think I am, a bloody postman?
Dominic Behan *My Brother Brendan* (1965); cf. **Goldwyn** 346:6

5 There's no such thing as bad publicity except your own obituary.
Dominic Behan *My Brother Brendan* (1965); cf. **Proverbs** 595:9

Aphra Behn 1640–89

English dramatist, poet, and novelist

6 Oh, what a dear ravishing thing is the beginning of an Amour!
The Emperor of the Moon (1687) act 1, sc. 1

7 Love ceases to be a pleasure, when it ceases to be a secret.
The Lover's Watch (1686) 'Four o' Clock. General Conversation'

8 All I ask, is the privilege for my masculine part the poet in me . . . If I must not, because of my sex, have this freedom . . . I lay down my quill, and you shall hear no more of me.
preface to *The Lucky Chance* (1686)

9 Since man with that inconstancy was born,
To love the absent, and the present scorn,
Why do we deck, why do we dress
For such a short-lived happiness?
Why do we put attraction on,
Since either way 'tis we must be undone?
Lycidus (1688) 'To Alexis, in Answer to his Poem against Fruition'

10 I owe a duty, where I cannot love.
The Moor's Revenge (1677) act 3, sc. 3

11 Be just, my lovely swain, and do not take
Freedoms you'll not to me allow;
Or give Amynta so much freedom back
That she may rove as well as you.
Let us then love upon the honest square,
Since interest neither have designed.
For the sly gamester, who ne'er plays me fair,
Must trick for trick expect to find.
Poems upon Several Occasions (1684) 'To Lysander, on some Verses he writ, and asking more for his Heart than 'twas worth'

12 A brave world, Sir, full of religion, knavery, and change: we shall shortly see better days.
The Roundheads (1682) act 1, sc. 1

13 Variety is the soul of pleasure.
The Rover pt. 2 (1681) act 1; cf. **Cowper** 241:23

14 Come away; poverty's catching.
The Rover pt. 2 (1681) act 1

15 Money speaks sense in a language all nations understand.
The Rover pt. 2 (1681) act 3

16 Do you not daily see fine clothes, rich furniture, jewels and plate are more inviting than beauty unadorned?
The Rover pt. 2 (1681) act 4

17 The soft, unhappy sex.
The Wandering Beauty (1698) para. 1

John Hay Beith see **Ian Hay**

Alexander Graham Bell 1847–1922

Scottish inventor of the telephone

18 Mr Watson, come here, I want you!
to his assistant, Thomas Watson, in the next room; the first words spoken on the telephone, 10 March 1876
Thomas A. Watson *Exploring Life* (1926)

Clive Bell 1881–1964

English art critic

19 Art and Religion are, then, two roads by which men escape from circumstance to ecstasy. Between aesthetic and religious rapture there is a family alliance. Art and Religion are means to similar states of mind.
Art (1914) pt. 2, ch. 1

20 I will try to account for the degree of my aesthetic emotion. That, I conceive, is the function of the critic.
Art (1914) pt. 3 ch. 3

21 Only reason can convince us of those three fundamental truths without a recognition of which there can be no effective liberty: that what we believe is not necessarily true; that what we like is not necessarily good; and that all questions are open.
Civilization (1928) ch. 5

George Bell 1883–1958

Anglican clergyman, Bishop of Chichester

22 The policy is obliteration, openly acknowledged. This is not a justifiable act of war.
speech, House of Lords, 9 February 1944

Gertrude Bell 1868–1926

English traveller, archaeologist, and government servant

23 I feel at times like the Creator about the middle of the week. He must have wondered what it was going to be like, as I do.
creating Iraq, at the Cairo Conference 1921; attributed

Francis Bellamy 1856–1931

American clergyman and editor

24 I pledge allegiance to the flag of the United States of America and to the republic for which it stands,

one nation under God, indivisible, with liberty and justice for all.
The Pledge of Allegiance to the Flag (1892)

St Robert Bellarmine 1542–1621
Italian cardinal and theologian

1 Nobody can remember more than seven of anything.
reason for omitting the eight beatitudes from his catechism
John Bossy *Christianity in the West 1400–1700* (1985)

Hilaire Belloc 1870–1953
British poet, essayist, historian, novelist, and Liberal politician

2 Child! do not throw this book about;
Refrain from the unholy pleasure
Of cutting all the pictures out!
Preserve it as your chiefest treasure.
A Bad Child's Book of Beasts (1896) dedication

3 I shoot the Hippopotamus
With bullets made of platinum,
Because if I use leaden ones
His hide is sure to flatten 'em.
A Bad Child's Book of Beasts (1896) 'The Hippopotamus'; cf. **Forster** 320:8

4 And mothers of large families (who claim to common sense)
Will find a Tiger well repay the trouble and expense.
A Bad Child's Book of Beasts (1896) 'The Tiger'

5 Believing Truth is staring at the sun
Which but destroys the power that could perceive.
So naught of our poor selves can be at one
With burning Truth, nor utterly believe.
'Believing Truth is staring at the sun' (1938)

6 Physicians of the Utmost Fame
Were called at once; but when they came
They answered, as they took their Fees,
'There is no Cure for this Disease.'
Cautionary Tales (1907) 'Henry King'

7 And always keep a-hold of Nurse
For fear of finding something worse.
Cautionary Tales (1907) 'Jim'

8 Sir! you have disappointed us!
We had intended you to be
The next Prime Minister but three:
The stocks were sold; the Press was squared;
The Middle Class was quite prepared.
But as it is! . . . My language fails!
Go out and govern New South Wales!
Cautionary Tales (1907) 'Lord Lundy'

9 Matilda told such Dreadful Lies,
It made one Gasp and Stretch one's Eyes.
Cautionary Tales (1907) 'Matilda'

10 For every time She shouted 'Fire!'
They only answered 'Little Liar!'
Cautionary Tales (1907) 'Matilda'

11 A Trick that everyone abhors
In Little Girls is slamming Doors.
Cautionary Tales (1907) 'Rebecca'

12 She was not really bad at heart,
But only rather rude and wild:
She was an aggravating child.
Cautionary Tales (1907) 'Rebecca'

13 Of Courtesy, it is much less
Than Courage of Heart or Holiness,
Yet in my Walks it seems to me
That the Grace of God is in Courtesy.
'Courtesy' (1910)

14 Here richly, with ridiculous display,
The Politician's corpse was laid away.
While all of his acquaintance sneered and slanged
I wept: for I had longed to see him hanged.
'Epitaph on the Politician Himself' (1923)

15 I said to Heart, 'How goes it ?' Heart replied:
'Right as a Ribstone Pippin!' But it lied.
'The False Heart' (1910)

16 I'm tired of Love: I'm still more tired of Rhyme.
But Money gives me pleasure all the time.
'Fatigued' (1923)

17 Strong brother in God and last companion, Wine.
'Heroic Poem upon Wine' (1926)

18 Remote and ineffectual Don
That dared attack my Chesterton.
'Lines to a Don' (1910)

19 Whatever happens we have got
The Maxim Gun, and they have not.
The Modern Traveller (1898) pt. 6

20 The Llama is a woolly sort of fleecy hairy goat,
With an indolent expression and an undulating throat
Like an unsuccessful literary man.
More Beasts for Worse Children (1897) 'The Llama'

21 The Microbe is so very small
You cannot make him out at all.
But many sanguine people hope
To see him through a microscope.
More Beasts for Worse Children (1897) 'The Microbe'

22 Oh! let us never, never doubt
What nobody is sure about!
More Beasts for Worse Children (1897) 'The Microbe'

23 Lord Finchley tried to mend the Electric Light
Himself. It struck him dead: And serve him right!
It is the business of the wealthy man
To give employment to the artisan.
More Peers (1911) 'Lord Finchley'

24 Like many of the Upper Class
He liked the Sound of Broken Glass.
New Cautionary Tales (1930) 'About John'. cf. **Waugh** 806:3

25 And even now, at twenty-five,
He has to WORK to keep alive!
Yes! All day long from 10 till 4!
For half the year or even more;
With but an hour or two to spend
At luncheon with a city friend.
New Cautionary Tales (1930) 'Peter Goole'

1 A smell of burning fills the startled Air—
The Electrician is no longer there!
'Newdigate Poem' (1910)

2 The accursed power which stands on Privilege
(And goes with Women, and Champagne, and
Bridge)
Broke—and Democracy resumed her reign:
(Which goes with Bridge, and Women and
Champagne).
'On a Great Election' (1923)

3 I am a sundial, and I make a botch
Of what is done much better by a watch.
'On a Sundial' (1938)

4 When I am dead, I hope it may be said:
'His sins were scarlet, but his books were read.'
'On His Books' (1923)

5 Pale Ebenezer thought it wrong to fight,
But Roaring Bill (who killed him) thought it right.
'The Pacifist' (1938)

6 When I am living in the Midlands
That are sodden and unkind . . .
And the great hills of the South Country
Come back into my mind.
'The South Country' (1910)

7 Do you remember an Inn,
Miranda?
Do you remember an Inn?
'Tarantella' (1923)

8 And the fleas that tease in the High Pyrenees
And the wine that tasted of the tar?
'Tarantella' (1923)

9 Balliol made me, Balliol fed me,
Whatever I had she gave me again:
And the best of Balliol loved and led me.
God be with you, Balliol men.
'To the Balliol Men Still in Africa' (1910)

10 There's nothing worth the wear of winning,
But laughter and the love of friends.
Verses (1910) 'Dedicatory Ode'

11 Is there no Latin word for Tea? Upon my soul, if I had known that I would have let the vulgar stuff alone.
On Nothing (1908) 'On Tea'

12 Gentlemen, I am a Catholic . . . If you reject me on account of my religion, I shall thank God that He has spared me the indignity of being your representative.
Speech to voters of South Salford, 1906, in R. Speaight *Life of Hilaire Belloc* (1957) ch. 10

Saul Bellow 1915–

American novelist
see also **Opening lines** *555:13*

13 It is sometimes necessary to repeat what we all know. All mapmakers should place the Mississippi in the same location, and avoid originality.
Mr Sammler's Planet (1969)

14 Art has something to do with the achievement of stillness in the midst of chaos. A stillness which characterizes prayer, too, and the eye of the storm . . . an arrest of attention in the midst of distraction.
George Plimpton *Writers at Work* (1967) 3rd series

15 A novel is balanced between a few true impressions and the multitude of false ones that make up most of what we call life. It tells us that for every human being there is a diversity of existences, that the single existence is itself an illusion in part . . . it promises us meaning, harmony, and even justice.
speech on receiving the Nobel Prize, 1976
in *The American Scholar* Summer 1977, no. 46

16 Nobody likes being written about in their lifetime, it's as though the FBI and the CIA were suddenly to splash your files in the paper.
in *Guardian* 10 September 1997

Du Belloy (Pierre-Laurent Buirette du Belloy) 1725–75

French dramatist

17 *Plus je vis d'étrangers, plus j'aimai ma patrie.*
The more foreigners I saw, the more I loved my homeland.
Le Siège de Calais (1765) act 2, sc. 3

Robert Benchley 1889–1945

American humorist
see also **Film lines** *311:19*, **Telegrams** *758:10*

18 The biggest obstacle to professional writing is the necessity for changing a typewriter ribbon.
Chips off the old Benchley (1949) 'Learn to Write'

19 The surest way to make a monkey of a man is to quote him.
My Ten Years in a Quandary (1936)

20 In America there are two classes of travel—first class, and with children.
Pluck and Luck (1925)

21 It took me fifteen years to discover that I had no talent for writing, but I couldn't give it up because by that time I was too famous.
Nathaniel Benchley *Robert Benchley* (1955) ch. 1

Julien Benda 1867–1956

French philosopher and novelist

22 *La trahison des clercs.*
The treachery of the intellectuals.
title of book (1927)

Stephen Vincent Benét 1898–1943

American poet and novelist

23 I have fallen in love with American names,
The sharp, gaunt names that never get fat,
The snakeskin-titles of mining-claims,
The plumed war-bonnet of Medicine Hat,
Tucson and Deadwood and Lost Mule Flat.
'American Names' (1927)

24 I shall not rest quiet in Montparnasse.
I shall not lie easy at Winchelsea.

You may bury my body in Sussex grass,
You may bury my tongue at Champmédy.
I shall not be there, I shall rise and pass.
Bury my heart at Wounded Knee.
'American Names' (1927)

1 And kept his heart a secret to the end
From all the picklocks of biographers.
of Robert E. **Lee**
John Brown's Body (1928)

2 We thought we were done with these things but we were wrong.
We thought, because we had power, we had wisdom.
'Litany for Dictatorships' (1935)

William Rose Benét 1886–1950

American poet

3 Blake saw a treefull of angels at Peckham Rye,
And his hands could lay hold on the tiger's terrible heart.
Blake knew how deep is Hell, and Heaven how high,
And could build the universe from one tiny part.
'Mad Blake' (1918)

Tony Benn (Anthony Wedgwood Benn) 1925–

British Labour politician

4 Not a reluctant peer but a persistent commoner.
at a Press Conference, 23 November 1960

5 Some of the jam we thought was for tomorrow, we've already eaten.
attributed, 1969; cf. **Carroll** 190:23

6 Office is something that builds up a man only if he is somebody in his own right.
on seeing Harold **Wilson**, *who had recently resigned as Prime Minister*
diary, 12 April 1976

7 It is as wholly wrong to blame Marx for what was done in his name, as it is to blame Jesus for what was done in his.
Alan Freeman *The Benn Heresy* (1982) 'Interview with Tony Benn'

8 A faith is something you die for; a doctrine is something you kill for: there is all the difference in the world.
in *Observer* 16 April 1989 'Sayings of the Week'

questions habitually asked by Tony Benn on meeting somebody in a position of power:

9 What power have you got? Where did you get it from? In whose interests do you exercise it? To whom are you accountable? How do we get rid of you?
'The Independent Mind', lecture at Nottingham, 18 June 1993

10 If you file your waste-paper basket for 50 years, you have a public library.
in *Daily Telegraph* 5 March 1994

11 A quotation is what a speaker wants to say—unlike a soundbite which is all that an interviewer allows you to say.
letter to Antony Jay, August 1996

12 We should put the spin-doctors in spin clinics, where they can meet other spin patients and be treated by spin consultants. The rest of us can get on with the proper democratic process.
in *Independent* 25 October 1997 'Quote Unquote'

13 When I think of Cool Britannia, I think of old people dying of hypothermia.
at the Labour Party Conference, in *Daily Star* 30 September 1998

George Bennard 1873–1958

American Methodist minister and hymn-writer

14 I will cling to the old rugged cross,
And exchange it some day for a crown.
'The Old Rugged Cross' (1913 hymn)

Alan Bennett 1934–

English actor and dramatist

15 The real solvent of class distinction is a proper measure of self-esteem—a kind of unselfconsciousness. Some people are at ease with themselves, so the world is at ease with them. My parents thought this kind of ease was produced by education . . . they didn't see that what disqualified them was temperament—just as, though educated up to the hilt, it disqualifies me. What keeps us in our place is embarrassment.
Dinner at Noon (BBC television, 1988)

16 I don't want to give you the idea I'm trying to hide anything, or that anything unorthodox goes on between my wife and me. It doesn't. Nothing goes on at all . . . No foreplay. No afterplay. And fuck all in between.
Enjoy (1980) act 1

17 I have never understood this liking for war. It panders to instincts already catered for within the scope of any respectable domestic establishment.
Forty Years On (1969) act 1

18 Memories are not shackles, Franklin, they are garlands.
Forty Years On (1969) act 2

19 Standards are always out of date. That is what makes them standards.
Forty Years On (1969) act 2

20 Sapper, Buchan, Dornford Yates, practitioners in that school of Snobbery with Violence that runs like a thread of good-class tweed through twentieth-century literature.
Forty Years On (1969) act 2

21 We started off trying to set up a small anarchist community, but people wouldn't obey the rules.
Getting On (1972) act 1

22 To be Prince of Wales is not a position. It is a predicament.
The Madness of King George (1995 film); in the 1992 play *The Madness of George III* the line was 'To be heir to the throne . . . '

1 We were put to Dickens as children but it never quite took. That unremitting humanity soon had me cheesed off.
The Old Country (1978) act 2

2 Here I sit, alone and sixty,
Bald, and fat, and full of sin,
Cold the seat and loud the cistern,
As I read the Harpic tin.
'Place Names of China' (1966)

3 People always complain about muck-raking biographers saying 'Leave us our heroes.' 'Leave us our villains' is just as important.
of an attempt to rehabilitate ***Haig***
diary, 11 February 1996

Arnold Bennett 1867–1931
English novelist

4 His opinion of himself, having once risen, remained at 'set fair'.
The Card (1911) ch. 1

5 'What great cause is he identified with?' 'He's identified . . . with the great cause of cheering us all up.'
The Card (1911) ch. 12

6 The price of justice is eternal publicity.
Things that have Interested Me (2nd series, 1923) 'Secret Trials'

7 A cause may be inconvenient, but it's magnificent. It's like champagne or high heels, and one must be prepared to suffer for it.
The Title (1918) act 1

8 Being a husband is a whole-time job. That is why so many husbands fail. They cannot give their entire attention to it.
The Title (1918) act 1

9 Journalists say a thing that they know isn't true, in the hope that if they keep on saying it long enough it *will* be true.
The Title (1918) act 1

10 Literature's always a good card to play for Honours.
The Title (1918) act 3

Jill Bennett 1931–90
English actress; former wife of John ***Osborne***

11 Never marry a man who hates his mother, because he'll end up hating you.
in *Observer* 12 September 1982 'Sayings of the Week'

Tony Bennett 1926–
American singer

12 We all fell in love, fell out of love, and fell in love again to the sound of his voice.
of Frank Sinatra
at Sinatra's funeral, Beverley Hills, 20 May 1998

A. C. Benson 1862–1925
English writer

13 Land of Hope and Glory, Mother of the Free,
How shall we extol thee who are born of thee?
Wider still and wider shall thy bounds be set;
God who made thee mighty, make thee mightier yet.
'Land of Hope and Glory' written to be sung as the Finale to **Elgar**'s *Coronation Ode* (1902)

Stella Benson 1892–1933
English novelist

14 Call no man foe, but never love a stranger.
This is the End (1917)

Henry A. Bent 1926–

15 The important point is not the bigness of Avogadro's number but the bigness of Avogadro.
Avogadro's number is equal to 6.023×10^{23} *(named after the Italian chemist and physicist Amedeo Avrogadro (1776–1856), who in 1811 formulated a law for deriving molecular weights)*
The Second Law (1965)

Jeremy Bentham 1748–1832
English philosopher

16 Right . . . is the child of law: from real laws come real rights; but from imaginary laws, from laws of nature, fancied and invented by poets, rhetoricians, and dealers in moral and intellectual poisons, come imaginary rights, a bastard brood of monsters.
Anarchical Fallacies in J. Bowring (ed.) *Works* vol. 2 (1843)

17 Natural rights is simple nonsense: natural and imprescriptible rights, rhetorical nonsense—nonsense upon stilts.
Anarchical Fallacies in J. Bowring (ed.) *Works* vol. 2 (1843)

18 The greatest happiness of the greatest number is the foundation of morals and legislation.
Bentham claimed to have acquired the 'sacred truth' either from Joseph ***Priestley*** *or Cesare Beccaria (1738–94)*
The Commonplace Book in J. Bowring (ed.) *Works* vol. 10 (1843); cf. **Hutcheson** 396:15

19 The Fool had stuck himself up one day, with great gravity, in the King's throne; with a stick, by way of a sceptre, in one hand, and a ball in the other: being asked what he was doing? he answered '*reigning*'. Much of the same sort of reign, I take it would be that of our Author's [Blackstone's] Democracy.
A Fragment on Government (1776) ch. 2, para. 34, footnote (e)

20 All punishment is mischief: all punishment in itself is evil.
Principles of Morals and Legislation (1789) ch. 13, para. 2

21 Every law is contrary to liberty.
Principles of the Civil Code (1843)

22 He rather hated the ruling few than loved the suffering many.
of James Mill
H. N. Pym (ed.) *Memories of Old Friends, being Extracts from the Journals and Letters of Caroline Fox* (1882) p. 113, 7 August 1840

1 Prose is when all the lines except the last go on to the end. Poetry is when some of them fall short of it.
M. St. J. Packe *The Life of John Stuart Mill* (1954) bk. 1, ch. 2

Edmund Clerihew Bentley 1875–1956
English writer

2 The Art of Biography
Is different from Geography.
Geography is about Maps,
But Biography is about Chaps.
Biography for Beginners (1905) introduction

3 What I like about Clive
Is that he is no longer alive.
There is a great deal to be said
For being dead.
Biography for Beginners (1905) 'Clive'

4 Sir Humphrey Davy
Abominated gravy.
He lived in the odium
Of having discovered Sodium.
Biography for Beginners (1905) 'Sir Humphrey Davy'

5 John Stuart Mill,
By a mighty effort of will,
Overcame his natural *bonhomie*
And wrote 'Principles of Political Economy'.
Biography for Beginners (1905) 'John Stuart Mill'

6 Sir Christopher Wren
Said, 'I am going to dine with some men.
If anybody calls
Say I am designing St Paul's.'
Biography for Beginners (1905) 'Sir Christopher Wren'

7 George the Third
Ought never to have occurred.
One can only wonder
At so grotesque a blunder.
More Biography (1929) 'George the Third'

Eric Bentley 1916–

8 Ours is the age of substitutes: instead of language, we have jargon; instead of principles, slogans; and, instead of genuine ideas, Bright Ideas.
in *New Republic* 29 December 1952

Richard Bentley 1662–1742
English classical scholar

9 I hold it as certain, that no man was ever written out of reputation but by himself.
William Warburton (ed.) *The Works of Alexander Pope* (1751) vol. 4

10 It is a pretty poem, Mr Pope, but you must not call it Homer.
when pressed by **Pope** *to comment on* 'My Homer' [i.e. his translation of **Homer**'s Iliad]
John Hawkins (ed.) *The Works of Samuel Johnson* (1787) vol. 4 'The Life of Pope'

11 It would be port if it could.
on claret
R. C. Jebb *Bentley* (1902) ch. 12

Lloyd Bentsen 1921–
American Democratic politician

responding to Dan **Quayle***'s claim to have 'as much experience in the Congress as Jack* **Kennedy** *had when he sought the presidency':*

12 Senator, I served with Jack Kennedy. I knew Jack Kennedy. Jack Kennedy was a friend of mine. Senator, you're no Jack Kennedy.
in the vice-presidential debate, 5 October 1988

Pierre-Jean de Béranger 1780–1857
French poet

13 *Nos amis, les ennemis.*
Our friends, the enemy.
'L'Opinion de ces demoiselles' (written 1815) in *Chansons de De Béranger* (1832)

14 *Il était un roi d'Yvetot*
Peu connu dans l'histoire.
There was a king of Yvetot
Little known to history.
'Le Roi d'Yvetot' (written 1813) in *Chansons de De Béranger* (1832)

Ingmar Bergman 1918–
Swedish film director

15 After years of playing with images of life and death, life has made me shy.
message sent when his daughter Linn Ullman collected the Palme of Palmes for him at the Cannes Film Festival
in *Observer* 18 May 1997 'Soundbites'

Henri Bergson 1859–1941
French philosopher

16 The present contains nothing more than the past, and what is found in the effect was already in the cause.
L'Évolution créatrice (1907) ch. 1

17 *L'élan vital.*
The vital spirit.
L'Évolution créatrice (1907) ch. 2 (section title)

George Berkeley 1685–1753
Irish philosopher and Anglican bishop
on Berkeley: see **Byron** *177:16,* **Johnson** *413:20,* **Smith** *725:5*

18 They are neither finite quantities, or quantities infinitely small, nor yet nothing. May we not call them the ghosts of departed quantities?
on **Newton***'s infinitesimals*
The Analyst (1734) sect. 35

19 [Tar water] is of a nature so mild and benign and proportioned to the human constitution, as to warm without heating, to cheer but not inebriate.
Siris (1744) para. 217; cf. **Cowper** 241:31

20 Truth is the cry of all, but the game of the few.
Siris (1744) para. 368

1 The same principles which at first lead to scepticism, pursued to a certain point bring men back to common sense.
Three Dialogues between Hylas and Philonous (1734) Dialogue 3

2 We have first raised a dust and then complain we cannot see.
A Treatise Concerning the Principles of Human Knowledge (1710) introduction, sect. 3

3 All the choir of heaven and furniture of earth—in a word, all those bodies which compose the mighty frame of the world—have not any subsistence without a mind.
A Treatise Concerning the Principles of Human Knowledge (1710) pt. 1, sect. 6

4 Westward the course of empire takes its way;
The first four acts already past,
A fifth shall close the drama with the day:
Time's noblest offspring is the last.
'On the Prospect of Planting Arts and Learning in America' (1752) st. 6.

Irving Berlin (Israel Baline) 1888–1989
American songwriter

5 Must you dance ev'ry dance
With the same fortunate man?
You have danced with him since the music began.
Won't you change partners and dance with me?
'Change Partners' (1938 song) in *Carefree*

6 Heaven—I'm in Heaven—And my heart beats so
that I can hardly speak;
And I seem to find the happiness I seek
When we're out together dancing cheek-to-cheek.
'Cheek-to-Cheek' (1935 song) in *Top Hat*

7 God bless America,
Land that I love,
Stand beside her and guide her
Thru the night with a light from above.
From the mountains to the prairies,
To the oceans white with foam,
God bless America,
My home sweet home.
'God Bless America' (1939 song)

8 There may be trouble ahead,
But while there's moonlight and music and love
and romance,
Let's face the music and dance.
'Let's Face the Music and Dance' (1936 song) in *Follow the Fleet*

9 A pretty girl is like a melody
That haunts you night and day.
'A Pretty Girl is like a Melody' (1919 song)

10 The song is ended (but the melody lingers on).
title of song (1927)

11 There's no business like show business.
title of song in *Annie Get Your Gun* (1946)

12 I'm dreaming of a white Christmas,
Just like the ones I used to know,
Where the tree-tops glisten
And children listen
To hear sleigh bells in the snow.
'White Christmas' (1942 song) in *Holiday Inn*

13 Listen, kid, take my advice, never hate a song that has sold half a million copies.
to Cole **Porter**, *of the song 'Rosalie'*
Philip Furia *Poets of Tin Pan Alley* (1990)

Isaiah Berlin 1909–97
British philosopher

14 Injustice, poverty, slavery, ignorance—these may be cured by reform or revolution. But men do not live only by fighting evils. They live by positive goals, individual and collective, a vast variety of them, seldom predictable, at times incompatible.
Four Essays on Liberty (1969) 'Political Ideas in the Twentieth Century'

15 There exists a great chasm between those, on one side, who relate everything to a single central vision . . . and, on the other side, those who pursue many ends, often unrelated and even contradictory . . . The first kind of intellectual and artistic personality belongs to the hedgehogs, the second to the foxes.
The Hedgehog and the Fox (1953) sect. 1; cf. **Archilochus** 23:17

16 Liberty is liberty, not equality or fairness or justice or human happiness or a quiet conscience.
Two Concepts of Liberty (1958)

17 Few new truths have ever won their way against the resistance of established ideas save by being overstated.
Vico and Herder (1976)

18 Rousseau was the first militant lowbrow.
in *Observer* 9 November 1952

J. D. Bernal 1901–71
Irish-born physicist

19 Men will not be content to manufacture life: they will want to improve on it.
The World, the Flesh and the Devil (1929)

Georges Bernanos 1888–1948
French novelist and essayist

20 The wish for prayer is a prayer in itself.
Journal d'un curé de campagne (1936) ch. 2

21 Hell, madam, is to love no more.
Journal d'un curé de campagne (1936) ch. 2

Bernard of Chartres d. *c.*1130
French philosopher

22 We are like dwarfs on the shoulders of giants, so that we can see more than they, and things at a greater distance, not by virtue of any sharpness of sight on our part, or any physical distinction, but

because we are carried high and raised up by their giant size.
John of Salisbury *The Metalogicon* (1159) bk. 3, ch. 4, quoted in R. K. Merton *On the Shoulders of Giants* (1965) ch. 9; cf. **Coleridge** 227:14, **Newton** 543:9

St Bernard of Clairvaux 1090–1153

French theologian, monastic reformer, and abbot
see also ***Caswall*** *194:1*

1 You will find something more in woods than in books. Trees and stones will teach you that which you can never learn from masters.
Epistles no. 106; cf. **Shakespeare** 658:14, **Wordsworth** 832:6

2 I am a kind of chimaera of my age, neither cleric nor layman.
Epistles no. 250

3 *Liberavi animam meam.*
I have freed my soul.
Epistles no. 371

4 In the cloister, under the eyes of the brethren who read there, what profit is there in those ridiculous monsters, in that marvellous and deformed beauty, that beautiful deformity? To what purpose are those unclean apes, those fierce lions, those monstrous centaurs, those half-men, those striped tigers, those fighting knights, those hunters winding their horns. Many bodies are there seen under one head, or again, many heads to a single body. Here is a four-footed beast with a serpent's tail; there, a fish with a beast's head. Here again the forepart of a horse trails half a goat behind it, or a horned beast bears the hind quarters of a horse. In short so many and so marvellous are the varieties of diverse shapes on every hand, that we are more tempted to read in the marble than in our books, and to spend the whole day in wondering at these things rather than in meditating the law of God. For God's sake, if men are not ashamed of these follies, why at least do they not shrink from the expense?
letter to William, Abbot of St-Thierry, *c.*1125

5 I spoke; and at once the Crusaders have multiplied to infinity. Villages and towns are now deserted. You will scarcely find one man for every seven women. Everywhere you see widows whose husbands are still alive.
of the effects of his preaching the Second Crusade
letter to Pope Eugenius III, 1146

6 Will the light only shine if it is in a candelabrum of gold or silver?
on Pope Urban II's conferring the title of Lux Mundi [light of the world] *on the abbey of Cluny*
attributed

Claude Bernard 1813–78

French physiologist

7 [The science of life] is a superb and dazzlingly lighted hall which may be reached only by passing through a long and ghastly kitchen.
An Introduction to the Study of Experimental Medicine (1865, translated Henry Copley Green, 1949)

Eric Berne 1910–70

American psychiatrist

8 Games people play: the psychology of human relationships.
title of book (1964)

9 Human life [as] . . . a process of filling in time until the arrival of death, or Santa Claus, with very little choice, if any, of what kind of business one is going to transact during the long wait, is a commonplace but not the final answer.
Games People Play (1964) ch. 18

Yogi Berra 1925–

American baseball player

10 The future ain't what it used to be.
attributed

11 If people don't want to come out to the ball park, nobody's going to stop 'em.
of baseball games
attributed

12 It ain't over till it's over.
comment on National League pennant race, 1973, quoted in many versions

13 It was déjà vu all over again.
attributed

Wendell Berry 1934–

American poet and novelist

14 I come into the peace of wild things
who do not tax their lives with forethought
of grief. I come into the presence of still water.
And I feel above me the day-blind stars
waiting with their light.
'The Peace of Wild Things' (1968)

15 Our hair
turns white with our ripening
as though to fly away in some
coming wind, bearing the seed
of what we know.
'Ripening' (1980)

16 Radiances know him. Grown lighter
than breath, he is set free
in our remembering. Grown brighter
than vision, he goes dark
into the life of the hill
that holds his peace.
'Three Elegiac Poems' (1969)

John Berryman 1914–72

American poet

17 People will take balls,
Balls will be lost always, little boy,
And no one buys a ball back.
'The Ball Poem' (1948)

18 We must travel in the direction of our fear.
'A Point of Age' (1942)

19 Life, friends, is boring. We must not say so . . .
And moreover my mother taught me as a boy

(repeatingly) 'Ever to confess you're bored
means you have no

Inner Resources.' I conclude now I have no
inner resources, because I am heavy bored.

77 Dream Songs (1964) no. 14

1 I seldom go to films. They are too exciting,
said the Honourable Possum.

77 Dream Songs (1964) no. 53

Charles Best fl. 1602

English poet

2 Look how the pale Queen of the silent night
Doth cause the Ocean to attend upon her,
And he, as long as she is in his sight,
With his full tide is ready her to honour.

'Of the Moon' (1602) in N. Ault (ed.) *Elizabethan Lyrics from the Original Texts* (1925)

Theobald von Bethmann Hollweg 1856–1921

Chancellor of Germany, 1909–17

3 Just for a word 'neutrality'—a word which in wartime has so often been disregarded—just for a scrap of paper, Great Britain is going to make war on a kindred nation who desires nothing better than to be friends with her.

summary of a report by Sir Edward Goschen to Sir Edward **Grey**

British Documents on Origins of the War 1898–1914 (1926) vol. 11; *The Diary of Edward Goschen 1900–1914* (1980) Appendix B discusses the contentious origins of this statement

John Betjeman 1906–84

English poet

4 He sipped at a weak hock and seltzer
As he gazed at the London skies
Through the Nottingham lace of the curtains
Or was it his bees-winged eyes?

He rose, and he put down *The Yellow Book*.
He staggered—and, terrible-eyed,
He brushed past the palms on the staircase
And was helped to a hansom outside.

'The Arrest of Oscar Wilde at the Cadogan Hotel' (1937)

5 And girls in slacks remember Dad,
And oafish louts remember Mum,
And sleepless children's hearts are glad,
And Christmas-morning bells say 'Come!'
Even to shining ones who dwell
Safe in the Dorchester Hotel.

And is it true? And is it true,
This most tremendous tale of all,
Seen in a stained-glass window's hue,
A Baby in an ox's stall?
The Maker of the stars and sea
Become a Child on earth for me?

'Christmas' (1954)

6 Oh! Chintzy, Chintzy cheeriness,
Half dead and half alive!

'Death in Leamington' (1931)

7 Spirits of well-shot woodcock, partridge, snipe
Flutter and bear him up the Norfolk sky.

'Death of King George V' (1937)9

8 Old men who never cheated, never doubted,
Communicated monthly, sit and stare
At the new suburb stretched beyond the run-way
Where a young man lands hatless from the air.

'Death of King George V' (1937)

9 And low the mists of evening lie
And lightly skims the midge.

'Henley-on-Thames' (1945)

10 Phone for the fish-knives, Norman
As Cook is a little unnerved;
You kiddies have crumpled the serviettes
And I must have things daintily served.

'How to get on in Society' (1954)

11 Milk and then just as it comes dear?
I'm afraid the preserve's full of stones;
Beg pardon, I'm soiling the doileys
With afternoon tea-cakes and scones.

'How to get on in Society' (1954)

12 The Church's Restoration
In eighteen-eighty-three
Has left for contemplation
Not what there used to be.

'Hymn' (1931)

13 Think of what our Nation stands for,
Books from Boots' and country lanes,
Free speech, free passes, class distinction,
Democracy and proper drains.
Lord, put beneath Thy special care
One-eighty-nine Cadogan Square.

'In Westminster Abbey' (1940)

14 Stony seaboard, far and foreign,
Stony hills poured over space,
Stony outcrop of the Burren,
Stones in every fertile place,
Little fields with boulders dotted,
Grey-stone shoulders saffron-spotted,
Stone-walled cabins thatched with reeds,
Where a Stone Age people breeds
The last of Europe's stone age race.

'Ireland with Emily' (1945)

15 In the licorice fields at Pontefract
My love and I did meet
And many a burdened licorice bush
Was blooming round our feet.

'The Licorice Fields at Pontefract' (1954)

16 Belbroughton Road is bonny, and pinkly bursts the spray
Of prunus and forsythia across the public way.

'May-Day Song for North Oxford' (1945)

17 Gaily into Ruislip Gardens
Runs the red electric train,
With a thousand Ta's and Pardon's
Daintily alights Elaine;
Hurries down the concrete station
With a frown of concentration,
Out into the outskirt's edges
Where a few surviving hedges

Keep alive our lost Elysium—rural Middlesex
again.
'Middlesex' (1954)

1 Official designs are aggressively neuter,
The Puritan work of an eyeless computer.
'The Newest Bath Guide' (1974)

2 Pam, I adore you, Pam, you great big mountainous
sports girl,
Whizzing them over the net, full of the strength of
five:
That old Malvernian brother, you zephyr and khaki
shorts girl,
Although he's playing for Woking,
Can't stand up to your wonderful backhand drive.
'Pot Pourri from a Surrey Garden' (1940)

3 The gas was on in the Institute,
The flare was up in the gymn,
A man was running a mineral line,
A lass was singing a hymn,
When Captain Webb the Dawley man,
Captain Webb from Dawley,
Came swimming along in the old canal
That carries the bricks to Lewley.
'A Shropshire Lad' (1940)

4 Come, friendly bombs, and fall on Slough!
It isn't fit for humans now,
There isn't grass to graze a cow.
Swarm over, Death!
'Slough' (1937)

5 Miss J. Hunter Dunn, Miss J. Hunter Dunn,
Furnish'd and burnish'd by Aldershot sun.
'A Subaltern's Love-Song' (1945)

6 Love-thirty, love-forty, oh! weakness of joy,
The speed of a swallow, the grace of a boy,
With carefullest carelessness, gaily you won,
I am weak from your loveliness, Joan Hunter
Dunn.
Miss Joan Hunter Dunn, Miss Joan Hunter Dunn,
How mad I am, sad I am, glad that you won.
'A Subaltern's Love-Song' (1945)

7 By roads 'not adopted', by woodlanded ways,
She drove to the club in the late summer haze.
'A Subaltern's Love-Song' (1945)

8 The dread of beatings! Dread of being late!
And, greatest dread of all, the dread of games!
Summoned by Bells (1960) ch. 7

9 Broad of Church and 'broad of Mind',
Broad before and broad behind,
A keen ecclesiologist,
A rather dirty Wykehamist.
'The Wykehamist' (1931)

10 Ghastly good taste, or a depressing story of the rise and fall of English architecture.
title of book (1933)

Bruno Bettelheim 1903–90
Austrian-born American psychologist

11 The most extreme agony is to feel that one has been utterly forsaken.
Surviving and other essays (1979)

Aneurin Bevan 1897–1960
British Labour politician

12 This island is made mainly of coal and surrounded by fish. Only an organizing genius could produce a shortage of coal and fish at the same time.
speech at Blackpool 24 May 1945, in *Daily Herald* 25 May 1945

13 No amount of cajolery, and no attempts at ethical or social seduction, can eradicate from my heart a deep burning hatred for the Tory Party . . . So far as I am concerned they are lower than vermin.
speech at Manchester, 4 July 1948, in *The Times* 5 July 1948

14 The language of priorities is the religion of Socialism.
speech at Labour Party Conference in Blackpool, 8 June 1949, in *Report of the 48th Annual Conference* (1949)

15 Why read the crystal when he can read the book?
of Robert **Boothby**, *during a debate on the Sterling Exchange Rate*
in the House of Commons, 29 September 1949

16 He does not talk the language of the 20th century but that of the 18th. He is still fighting Blenheim all over again. His only answer to a difficult situation is send a gun-boat.
of Winston **Churchill**
speech at Labour Party Conference, Scarborough, 2 October 1951, in *Daily Herald* 3 October 1951

17 We know what happens to people who stay in the middle of the road. They get run down.
in *Observer* 6 December 1953

18 Damn it all, you can't have the crown of thorns *and* the thirty pieces of silver.
on his position in the Labour Party, c.1956
Michael Foot *Aneurin Bevan* (1973) vol. 2, ch. 13

19 I am not going to spend any time whatsoever in attacking the Foreign Secretary . . . If we complain about the tune, there is no reason to attack the monkey when the organ grinder is present.
during a debate on the Suez crisis
in the House of Commmons, 16 May 1957

20 If you carry this resolution you will send Britain's Foreign Secretary naked into the conference chamber.
speaking against a motion proposing unilateral nuclear disarmament by the UK at Labour Party Conference in Brighton, 3 October 1957
in *Daily Herald* 4 October 1957

21 I know that the right kind of leader for the Labour Party is a desiccated calculating machine who must not in any way permit himself to be swayed by indignation. If he sees suffering, privation or injustice he must not allow it to move him, for that would be evidence of the lack of proper education or of absence of self-control. He must speak in calm and objective accents and talk about a dying child

in the same way as he would about the pieces inside an internal combustion engine.
generally taken as referring to Hugh **Gaitskell**, *although Bevan specifically denied it in an interview with Robin Day on 28 April 1959*
Michael Foot *Aneurin Bevan* (1973) vol. 2, ch. 11

1 This so-called affluent society is an ugly society still. It is a vulgar society. It is a meretricious society. It is a society in which priorities have gone all wrong.
speech in Blackpool, 29 November 1959

2 I read the newspapers avidly. It is my one form of continuous fiction.
in *The Times* 29 March 1960

3 I stuffed their mouths with gold.
of his handling of the consultants during the establishment of the National Health Service
Brian Abel-Smith *The Hospitals 1800–1948* (1964) ch. 29

4 Listening to a speech by Chamberlain is like paying a visit to Woolworth's: everything in its place and nothing above sixpence.
Michael Foot *Aneurin Bevan* (1962) vol. 1, ch. 8

William Henry Beveridge 1879–1963
British economist

5 Ignorance is an evil weed, which dictators may cultivate among their dupes, but which no democracy can afford among its citizens.
Full Employment in a Free Society (1944) pt. 7

6 Want is one only of five giants on the road of reconstruction . . . the others are Disease, Ignorance, Squalor and Idleness.
Social Insurance and Allied Services (1942) pt. 7

Ernest Bevin 1881–1951
British Labour politician and trade unionist
on Bevin: see **Foot** *318:26*

7 The most conservative man in this world is the British Trade Unionist when you want to change him.
speech, 8 September 1927, in *Report of Proceedings of the Trades Union Congress* (1927)

8 I hope you will carry no resolution of an emergency character telling a man with a conscience like Lansbury what he ought to do . . . It is placing the Executive in an absolutely wrong position to be taking your conscience round from body to body to be told what you ought to do with it.
of the Labour politician George Lansbury (1859–1940); often quoted as 'hawking his conscience round the Chancellories of Europe'
in *Labour Party Conference Report* (1935)

9 There never has been a war yet which, if the facts had been put calmly before the ordinary folk, could not have been prevented . . . The common man, I think, is the great protection against war.
speech in the House of Commons, 23 November 1945

10 My [foreign] policy is to be able to take a ticket at Victoria Station and go anywhere I damn well please.
in *Spectator* 20 April 1951

11 If you open that Pandora's Box, you never know what Trojan 'orses will jump out.
on the Council of Europe
Roderick Barclay *Ernest Bevin and the Foreign Office* (1975) ch. 3

12 I didn't ought never to have done it. It was you, Willie, what put me up to it.
to Lord Strang, after officially recognizing Communist China
C. Parrott *Serpent and Nightingale* (1977) ch. 3

on the observation that Aneurin **Bevan** *was sometimes his own worst enemy:*

13 Not while I'm alive 'e ain't!
also attributed to Bevin of Herbert **Morrison**
Roderick Barclay *Ernest Bevin and Foreign Office* (1975)

Bhagavadgita
Hindu poem composed between the 2nd century BC *and the 2nd century* AD *and incorporated into the Mahabharata*
textual translations are those of J. Mascaro, 1978

14 As the Spirit of our mortal body wanders on in childhood, and youth and old age, the Spirit wanders on to a new body: of this the sage has no doubts.
ch. 2, v. 13

15 If any man thinks he slays, and if another thinks he is slain, neither knows the ways of truth. The Eternal in man cannot kill: the Eternal in man cannot die.
He is never born, and he never dies. He is in Eternity, he is for evermore. Never-born and eternal, beyond times gone or to come, he does not die when the body dies.
ch. 2, v. 19; cf. **Emerson** 299:5, **Upanishads** 787:21

16 As a man leaves an old garment and puts on one that is new, the spirit leaves his mortal body and puts on one that is new.
ch. 2, v. 22

17 Invisible before birth are all beings and after death invisible again. They are seen between two unseens. Why in this truth find sorrow?
ch. 2, v. 28

18 Set thy heart upon thy work but never upon its reward. Work not for a reward: but never cease to do thy work.
Do thy work in the peace of Yoga and, free from selfish desires, be not moved in success or in failure. Yoga is evenness of mind—a peace that is ever the same.
ch. 2, v. 47

19 When in recollection he withdraws all his senses from the attractions of the pleasures of sense, even as a tortoise withdraws all its limbs, then his is a serene wisdom.
ch. 2, v. 58

1 And do thy duty, even if it be humble, rather than another's, even if it be great. To die in one's duty is life: to live in another's is death.
ch. 3, v. 35

2 I [Krishna] am all-powerful Time which destroys all things, and I have come here to slay these men. Even if thou does not fight, all the warriors facing thee shall die.
ch. 11, v. 32; cf. **Oppenheimer** 557:2

3 Only by love can men see me, and know me, and come unto me.
He who works for me, who loves me, whose End Supreme I am, free from attachment to all things, and with love for all creation, he in truth comes unto me.
ch. 11, v. 54

4 God dwells in the heart of all beings, Arjuna: thy God dwells in thy heart. And his power of wonder moves all things—puppets in a play of shadows—whirling them onwards on the stream of time.
ch. 18, v. 61

5 Leave all things behind, and come unto me for thy salvation. I will make thee free from the bondage of sins. Fear no more.
ch. 18, v. 66

Benazir Bhutto 1953–

Pakistani stateswoman; Prime Minister 1988–90 and 1993–96

6 Every dictator uses religion as a prop to keep himself in power.
interview on *60 Minutes*, CBS-TV, 8 August 1986

The Bible (Authorized Version, 1611)

many phrases derive from ***Tyndale****'s translation of the early 16th century*
see also ***Book of Common Prayer*** *(Psalms)*

7 Upon the setting of that bright Occidental Star, Queen Elizabeth of most happy memory.
The Epistle Dedicatory

8 The appearance of Your Majesty, as of the Sun in his strength.
The Epistle Dedicatory

9 Translation it is that openeth the window, to let in the light; that breaketh the shell, that we may eat the kernel; that putteth aside the curtain, that we may look into the most holy place; that removeth the cover of the well, that we may come by the water.
The Translators to the Reader

OLD TESTAMENT: GENESIS

10 In the beginning God created the heaven and the earth. And the earth was without form, and void; and darkness was upon the face of the deep. And the Spirit of God moved upon the face of the waters.
And God said, Let there be light: and there was light.
Genesis ch. 1, v. 1; cf. **Byron** 177:13

11 And the evening and the morning were the first day.
Genesis ch. 1, v. 5

12 And God saw that it was good.
Genesis ch. 1, v. 10

13 And God made two great lights; the greater light to rule the day, and the lesser light to rule the night.
Genesis ch. 1, v. 16

14 And God said, Let us make man in our image, after our likeness: and let them have dominion over the fish of the sea, and over the fowl of the air, and over the cattle, and over all the earth and over every creeping thing that creepeth upon the earth.
Genesis ch. 1, v. 26

15 Male and female created he them.
Genesis ch. 1, v. 27

16 Be fruitful, and multiply, and replenish the earth, and subdue it.
Genesis ch. 1, v. 28

17 And the Lord God formed man of the dust of the ground, and breathed into his nostrils the breath of life; and man became a living soul.
And the Lord God planted a garden eastward in Eden.
Genesis ch. 2, v. 7

18 And out of the ground made the Lord God to grow every tree that is pleasant to the sight, and good for food; the tree of life also in the midst of the garden, and the tree of knowledge of good and evil.
Genesis ch. 2, v. 9

19 But of the tree of the knowledge of good and evil, thou shalt not eat of it: for in the day that thou eatest thereof thou shalt surely die.
Genesis ch. 2, v. 17

20 It is not good that the man should be alone; I will make him an help meet for him.
Genesis ch. 2, v. 18

21 And the Lord God caused a deep sleep to fall upon Adam, and he slept: and he took one of his ribs, and closed up the flesh instead thereof;
And the rib, which the Lord God had taken from man, made he a woman.
Genesis ch. 2, v. 21

22 This is now bone of my bones, and flesh of my flesh: she shall be called Woman, because she was taken out of Man.
Genesis ch. 2, v. 23; cf. **Milton** 517:19

23 Therefore shall a man leave his father and his mother, and shall cleave unto his wife: and they shall be one flesh.
Genesis ch. 2, v. 24

24 Now the serpent was more subtil than any beast of the field.
Genesis ch. 3, v. 1

25 Ye shall be as gods, knowing good and evil.
Genesis ch. 3, v. 5

26 And they sewed fig leaves together, and made themselves aprons.

And they heard the voice of the Lord God walking in the garden in the cool of the day.
'and made themselves breeches' in the Geneva Bible, 1560, known for that reason as the 'Breeches Bible'
Genesis ch. 3, v. 7

1 The woman whom thou gavest to be with me, she gave me of the tree, and I did eat.
Genesis ch. 3, v. 12

2 What is this that thou hast done?
Genesis ch. 3, v. 13

3 The serpent beguiled me, and I did eat.
Genesis ch. 3, v. 13

4 It shall bruise thy head, and thou shalt bruise his heel.
Genesis ch. 3, v. 15

5 In sorrow thou shalt bring forth children.
Genesis ch. 3, v. 16

6 In the sweat of thy face shalt thou eat bread.
Genesis ch. 3, v. 19

7 For dust thou art, and unto dust shalt thou return.
Genesis ch. 3, v. 19; cf. **Longfellow** 474:3

8 Am I my brother's keeper?
Genesis ch. 4, v. 9

9 The voice of thy brother's blood crieth unto me from the ground.
Genesis ch. 4, v. 10

10 My punishment is greater than I can bear.
Genesis ch. 4, v. 13

11 And the Lord set a mark upon Cain.
Genesis ch. 4, v. 15

12 And Cain went out from the presence of the Lord, and dwelt in the land of Nod, on the east of Eden.
Genesis ch. 4, v. 16

13 And Enoch walked with God: and he was not; for God took him.
Genesis ch. 5, v. 24

14 And all the days of Methuselah were nine hundred sixty and nine years: and he died.
Genesis ch. 5, v. 27

15 There were giants in the earth in those days; and also after that, when the sons of God came in unto the daughters of men, and they bare children to them, the same became mighty men which were of old, men of renown.
Genesis ch. 6, v. 4

16 There went in two and two unto Noah into the Ark, the male and the female.
Genesis ch. 7, v. 9

17 But the dove found no rest for the sole of her foot.
Genesis ch. 8, v. 9

18 For the imagination of man's heart is evil from his youth.
Genesis ch. 8, v. 21

19 While the earth remaineth, seedtime and harvest, and cold and heat, and summer and winter, and day and night shall not cease.
Genesis ch. 8, v. 22

20 At the hand of every man's brother will I require the life of man.
Genesis ch. 9, v. 5

21 Whoso sheddeth man's blood, by man shall his blood be shed.
Genesis ch. 9, v. 6

22 I do set my bow in the cloud, and it shall be for a token of a covenant between me and the earth. And it shall come to pass, when I bring a cloud over the earth, that the bow shall be seen in the cloud.
Genesis ch. 9, v. 13

23 Even as Nimrod the mighty hunter before the Lord.
Genesis ch. 10, v. 9

24 Let there be no strife, I pray thee, between thee and me . . . for we be brethren.
Genesis ch. 13, v. 8

25 An horror of great darkness fell upon him.
Genesis ch. 15, v. 12

26 Thou shalt be buried in a good old age.
Genesis ch. 15, v. 15

27 His [Ishmael's] hand will be against every man, and every man's hand against him.
Genesis ch. 16, v. 12

28 Now Abraham and Sarah were old and well stricken in age; and it ceased to be with Sarah after the manner of women.
Genesis ch. 18, v. 11

29 Shall not the Judge of all the earth do right.
Genesis ch. 18, v. 25

30 But his [Lot's] wife looked back from behind him, and she became a pillar of salt.
Genesis ch. 19, v. 26

31 Take now thy son, thine only son Isaac, whom thou lovest.
Genesis ch. 22, v. 2

32 My son, God will provide himself a lamb.
Genesis ch. 22, v. 8

33 Behold behind him a ram caught in a thicket by his horns.
Genesis ch. 22, v. 13

34 Esau selleth his birthright for a mess of pottage.
chapter heading in Geneva Bible, 1560
Genesis ch. 25

35 Esau was a cunning hunter, a man of the field; and Jacob was a plain man, dwelling in tents.
Genesis ch. 25, v. 27

36 And he sold his birthright unto Jacob.
Genesis ch. 25, v. 33

37 Behold, Esau my brother is a hairy man, and I am a smooth man.
Genesis ch. 27, v. 11

38 The voice is Jacob's voice, but the hands are the hands of Esau.
Genesis ch. 27, v. 22

39 Thy brother came with subtilty, and hath taken away thy blessing.
Genesis ch. 27, v. 35

1 And he dreamed, and behold a ladder set up on the earth, and the top of it reached to heaven: and behold the angels of God ascending and descending on it.
Genesis ch. 28, v. 12

2 Surely the Lord is in this place; and I knew it not.
Genesis ch. 28, v. 16

3 This is none other but the house of God, and this is the gate of heaven.
Genesis ch. 28, v. 17

4 And Jacob served seven years for Rachel; and they seemed unto him but a few days, for the love he had to her.
Genesis ch. 29, v. 20

5 The Lord watch between me and thee, when we are absent one from another.
Genesis ch. 31, v. 49

6 I will not let thee go, except thou bless me.
Genesis ch. 32, v. 26

7 For I have seen God face to face, and my life is preserved.
Genesis ch. 32, v. 30

8 Now Israel loved Joseph more than all his children, because he was the son of his old age; and he made him a coat of many colours.
Genesis ch. 37, v. 3

9 Behold, your sheaves stood round about, and made obeisance to my sheaf.
Genesis ch. 37, v. 7

10 Behold, this dreamer cometh.
Genesis ch. 37, v. 19

11 Some evil beast hath devoured him.
Genesis ch. 37, v. 20

12 And she caught him by his garment, saying, Lie with me; and he left his garment in her hand, and fled.
Genesis ch. 39, v. 12

13 And the lean and the ill favoured kine did eat up the first seven fat kine.
Genesis ch. 41, v. 20

14 And the thin ears devoured the seven good ears.
Genesis ch. 41, v. 24

15 Jacob saw that there was corn in Egypt.
Genesis ch. 42, v. 1

16 Ye are spies; to see the nakedness of the land ye are come.
Genesis ch. 42, v. 9

17 My son shall not go down with you; for his brother is dead, and he is left alone: if mischief befall him by the way in which ye go, then shall ye bring down my grey hairs with sorrow to the grave.
Genesis ch. 42, v. 38

18 Ye shall eat the fat of the land.
Genesis ch. 45, v. 18

19 See that ye fall not out by the way.
Genesis ch. 45, v. 24

20 Few and evil have the days of the years of my life been.
Genesis ch. 47, v. 9

21 Unstable as water, thou shalt not excel.
Genesis ch. 49, v. 4

EXODUS

22 She took for him an ark of bulrushes, and daubed it with slime.
Exodus ch. 2, v. 3

23 Who made thee a prince and a judge over us?
Exodus ch. 2, v. 14

24 I have been a stranger in a strange land.
Exodus ch. 2, v. 22

25 Behold, the bush burned with fire, and the bush was not consumed.
Exodus ch. 3, v. 2

26 Put off thy shoes from off thy feet, for the place whereon thou standest is holy ground.
Exodus ch. 3, v. 5

27 And Moses hid his face; for he was afraid to look upon God.
Exodus ch. 3, v. 6

28 A land flowing with milk and honey.
Exodus ch. 3, v. 8

29 I AM THAT I AM.
Exodus ch. 3, v. 14

30 The Lord God of your fathers, the God of Abraham, the God of Isaac, and the God of Jacob.
Exodus ch. 3, v. 15

31 But I am slow of speech, and of a slow tongue.
Exodus ch. 4, v. 10

32 I know not the Lord, neither will I let Israel go.
Exodus ch. 5, v. 2

33 And I will harden Pharaoh's heart, and multiply my signs and my wonders in the land of Egypt.
Exodus ch. 7, v. 3

34 Aaron's rod swallowed up their rods.
And he hardened Pharaoh's heart, that he hearkened not.
Exodus ch. 7, v. 12

35 Let my people go.
Exodus ch. 7, v. 16

36 A boil breaking forth with blains.
Exodus ch. 9, v. 10

37 Stretch out thine hand toward heaven, that there may be darkness over the land of Egypt, even darkness which may be felt.
Exodus ch. 10, v. 21

38 Your lamb shall be without blemish.
Exodus ch. 12, v. 5

39 And they shall eat the flesh in that night, roast with fire, and unleavened bread; and with bitter herbs they shall eat it.
Eat not of it raw, nor sodden at all with water, but roast with fire; his head with his legs, and with the purtenance thereof.
Exodus ch. 12, v. 8

1 Ye shall eat it in haste; it is the Lord's passover.
Exodus ch. 12, v. 11

2 For I will pass through the land of Egypt this night, and will smite all the firstborn in the land of Egypt, both man and beast.
Exodus ch. 12, v. 12

3 And Pharaoh rose up in the night, he, and all his servants, and all the Egyptians; and there was a great cry in Egypt; for there was not a house where there was not one dead.
Exodus ch. 12, v. 30

4 And they spoiled the Egyptians.
Exodus ch. 12, v. 36

5 And the Lord went before them by day in a pillar of a cloud, to lead them the way; and by night in a pillar of fire, to give them light.
Exodus ch. 13, v. 21

6 The Lord is a man of war.
Exodus ch. 15, v. 3

7 Would to God we had died by the hand of the Lord in the land of Egypt, when we sat by the flesh pots, and when we did eat bread to the full.
Exodus ch. 16, v. 3

8 I am the Lord thy God, which have brought thee out of the land of Egypt, out of the house of bondage.
Thou shalt have no other gods before me.
Thou shalt not make unto thee any graven image, or any likeness of any thing that is in heaven above, or that is in the earth beneath, or that is in the water under the earth.
Exodus ch. 20, v. 2

9 I the Lord thy God am a jealous God, visiting the iniquity of the fathers upon the children unto the third and fourth generation of them that hate me.
Exodus ch. 20, v. 5; cf. **Book of Common Prayer** 129:5, **French** 324:5

10 Thou shalt not take the name of the Lord thy God in vain.
Exodus ch. 20, v. 7

11 Remember the sabbath day, to keep it holy.
Six days shalt thou labour, and do all thy work:
But the seventh day is the sabbath of the Lord thy God: in it thou shalt not do any work.
Exodus ch. 20, v. 8

12 For in six days the Lord made heaven and earth, the sea, and all that in them is, and rested the seventh day: wherefore the Lord blest the sabbath day, and hallowed it.
Exodus ch. 20, v. 11

13 Honour thy father and thy mother: that thy days may be long upon the land which the Lord thy God giveth thee.
Thou shalt not kill.
Thou shalt not commit adultery.
Thou shalt not steal.
Thou shalt not bear false witness against thy neighbour.
Thou shalt not covet thy neighbour's house, thou shalt not covet thy neighbour's wife, nor his manservant, nor his maidservant, nor his ox, nor his ass, nor any thing that is thy neighbour's.
Exodus ch. 20, v. 12; cf. **Book of Common Prayer** 129:7

14 Life for life,
Eye for eye, tooth for tooth, hand for hand, foot for foot,
Burning for burning, wound for wound, stripe for stripe.
Exodus ch. 21, v. 23

15 And thou shalt put in the breastplate of judgement the Urim and the Thummim.
sacred symbols worn on the breastplate of the high priest
Exodus ch. 28, v. 30

16 These be thy gods, O Israel.
Exodus ch. 32, v. 4

17 And the people sat down to eat and to drink, and rose up to play.
Exodus ch. 32, v. 6

18 I will not go up in the midst of thee; for thou art a stiffnecked people: lest I consume thee in the way.
Exodus ch. 33, v. 3

19 There shall no man see me and live.
Exodus ch. 33, v. 20

LEVITICUS

20 And the swine, though he divide the hoof, and be cloven-footed, yet he cheweth not the cud; .
Leviticus ch. 11, v. 7

21 Let him go for a scapegoat into the wilderness.
Leviticus ch. 16, v. 10

22 Ye shall therefore keep my statutes and my judgments: which if a man do, he shall live in them: I am the Lord.
Leviticus ch. 18, v. 5; cf. **Talmud** 754:7

23 Thou shalt love thy neighbour as thyself.
Leviticus ch. 19, v. 18; cf. **Bible** 96:24

NUMBERS

24 The Lord bless thee, and keep thee:
The Lord make his face shine upon thee, and be gracious unto thee:
The Lord lift up his countenance upon thee, and give thee peace.
Numbers ch. 6, v. 24

25 These are the names of the men which Moses sent to spy out the land.
Numbers ch. 13, v. 16

26 And there we saw the giants, the sons of Anak, which come of the giants: and we were in our own sight as grasshoppers, and so we were in their sight.
Numbers ch. 13, v. 33

27 And Israel smote him with the edge of the sword, and possessed his land.
Numbers ch. 21, v. 24

28 He whom thou blessest is blessed, and he whom thou cursest is cursed.
Numbers ch. 22, v. 6

29 God is not a man, that he should lie.
Numbers ch. 23, v. 19

1 What hath God wrought!
quoted by Samuel Morse in the first electric telegraph message, 24 May 1844
Numbers ch. 23, v. 23

2 I called thee to curse mine enemies, and, behold, thou hast altogether blessed them these three times.
Numbers ch. 24, v. 10

3 Be sure your sin will find you out.
Numbers ch. 32, v. 23

DEUTERONOMY

4 I call heaven and earth to witness against you this day.
Deuteronomy ch. 4, v. 26

5 Remember that thou wast a servant in the land of Egypt, and that the Lord thy God brought thee out thence through a mighty hand and by a stretched out arm.
Deuteronomy ch. 5, v. 15

6 Hear, O Israel: The Lord our God is one Lord.
Deuteronomy ch. 6, v. 4; cf. **Siddur** 717:17

7 If there arise among you a prophet, or a dreamer of dreams . . . Thou shalt not hearken.
Deuteronomy ch. 13, v. 1

8 If thy brother, the son of thy mother, or thy son, or thy daughter, or the wife of thy bosom, or thy friend, which is as thine own soul, entice thee secretly . . . Thou shalt not consent.
Deuteronomy ch. 13, v. 6

9 The secret things belong unto the Lord our God.
Deuteronomy ch. 29, v. 29

10 I have set before you life and death, blessing and cursing: therefore choose life that both thou and thy seed may live.
Deuteronomy ch. 30, v. 19

11 He found him in a desert land, and in the waste howling wilderness; he led him about, he instructed him, he kept him as the apple of his eye.
Deuteronomy ch. 32, v. 10

12 For they are a very froward generation, children in whom is no faith.
Deuteronomy ch. 32, v. 20

13 I will heap mischiefs upon them; I will spend mine arrows upon them.
Deuteronomy ch. 32, v. 23

14 The eternal God is thy refuge, and underneath are the everlasting arms.
Deuteronomy ch. 33, v. 27

15 No man knoweth of his [Moses's] sepulchre unto this day.
Deuteronomy ch. 34, v. 6

JOSHUA

16 As I was with Moses, so I will be with thee: I will not fail thee, nor forsake thee.
Joshua ch. 1, v. 5

17 Be strong and of a good courage; be not afraid, neither be thou dismayed: for the Lord thy God is with thee, whithersoever thou goest.
Joshua ch. 1, v. 9

18 This line of scarlet thread.
Joshua ch. 2, v. 18

19 All the Israelites passed over on dry ground.
Joshua ch. 3, v. 17

20 When the people heard the sound of the trumpet, and the people shouted with a great shout, that the wall fell down flat, so that the people went up into the city.
Joshua ch. 6, v. 20

21 Let them live; but let them be hewers of wood and drawers of water unto all the congregation.
Joshua ch. 9, v. 21

22 Sun, stand thou still upon Gibeon; and thou, Moon, in the valley of Ajalon.
Joshua ch. 10, v. 12

23 I am going the way of all the earth.
Joshua ch. 23, v. 14

JUDGES

24 He delivered them into the hands of spoilers.
Judges ch. 2, v. 14

25 Then Jael Heber's wife took a nail of the tent, and took an hammer in her hand, and went softly unto him, and smote the nail into his temples, and fastened it into the ground: for he was fast asleep and weary.
Judges ch. 4, v. 21

26 I arose a mother in Israel.
Judges ch. 5, v. 7

27 The stars in their courses fought against Sisera.
Judges ch. 5, v. 20

28 He asked water, and she gave him milk; she brought forth butter in a lordly dish.
Judges ch. 5, v. 25

29 At her feet he bowed, he fell, he lay down.
Judges ch. 5, v. 27

30 The mother of Sisera looked out at a window, and cried through the lattice, Why is his chariot so long in coming? why tarry the wheels of his chariots?
Judges ch. 5, v. 28

31 The Lord is with thee, thou mighty man of valour.
Judges ch. 6, v. 12

32 The Spirit of the Lord came upon Gideon, and he blew a trumpet.
Judges ch. 6, v. 34

33 The host of Midian was beneath him in the valley.
Judges ch. 7, v. 8

34 Is not the gleaning of the grapes of Ephraim better than the vintage of Abi-ezer?
Judges ch. 8, v. 2

35 Faint, yet pursuing.
Judges ch. 8, v. 4

36 Let fire come out of the bramble and devour the cedars of Lebanon.
Judges ch. 9, v. 15

37 Then said they unto him, Say now Shibboleth: and he said Sibboleth: for he could not frame to

pronounce it right. Then they took him, and slew him.
Judges ch. 12, v. 6

1 Out of the eater came forth meat, and out of the strong came forth sweetness.
Judges ch. 14, v. 14

2 If ye had not plowed with my heifer, ye had not found out my riddle.
Judges ch. 14, v. 18

3 He smote them hip and thigh.
Judges ch. 15, v. 8

4 With the jawbone of an ass, heaps upon heaps, with the jaw of an ass have I slain a thousand men.
Judges ch. 15, v. 16

5 The Philistines be upon thee, Samson.
Judges ch. 16, v. 9

6 He wist not that the Lord was departed from him.
Judges ch. 16, v. 20

7 He did grind in the prison house.
Judges ch. 16, v. 21

8 The dead which he slew at his death were more than they which he slew in his life.
Judges ch. 16, v. 30

9 In those days there was no king in Israel, but every man did that which was right in his own eyes.
Judges ch. 17, v. 6

10 From Dan even to Beer-sheba.
Judges ch. 20, v. 1

11 The people arose as one man.
Judges ch. 20, v. 8

RUTH

12 Intreat me not to leave thee, or to return from following after thee: for whither thou goest, I will go; and where thou lodgest, I will lodge: thy people shall be my people, and thy God my God:
Where thou diest, will I die, and there will I be buried: the Lord do so to me, and more also, if ought but death part thee and me.
Ruth ch. 1, v. 16

I SAMUEL

13 All the increase of thy house shall die in the flower of their age.
I Samuel ch. 2, v. 33

14 The Lord called Samuel: and he answered, Here am I.
I Samuel ch. 3, v. 4

15 Speak, Lord; for thy servant heareth.
I Samuel ch. 3, v. 9

16 The ears of every one that heareth it shall tingle.
I Samuel ch. 3, v. 11

17 Quit yourselves like men, and fight.
I Samuel ch. 4, v. 9

18 He fell from off the seat backward by the side of the gate, and his neck brake.
I Samuel ch. 4, v. 18

19 And she named the child I-chabod, saying, The glory is departed from Israel.
I Samuel ch. 4, v. 21

20 And the asses of Kish Saul's father were lost. And Kish said to Saul his son, Take now one of the servants with thee, and arise, go seek the asses.
I Samuel ch. 9, v. 3; cf. **Milton** 518:6

21 Is Saul also among the prophets?
I Samuel ch. 10, v. 11

22 God save the king.
I Samuel ch. 10, v. 24

23 A man after his own heart.
I Samuel ch. 13, v. 14

24 I did but taste a little honey with the end of the rod that was in mine hand, and, lo, I must die.
I Samuel ch. 14, v. 43

25 To obey is better than sacrifice, and to hearken than the fat of rams.
I Samuel ch. 15, v. 22

26 For rebellion is as the sin of witchcraft.
I Samuel ch. 15, v. 23

27 For the Lord seeth not as man seeth: for man looketh on the outward appearance, but the Lord looketh on the heart.
I Samuel ch. 16, v. 7

28 Now he was ruddy, and withal of a beautiful countenance, and goodly to look to.
I Samuel ch. 16, v. 12

29 I know thy pride, and the naughtiness of thine heart.
I Samuel ch. 17, v. 28

30 Let no man's heart fail because of him.
I Samuel ch. 17, v. 32

31 Go, and the Lord be with thee.
I Samuel ch. 17, v. 37

32 And he took his staff in his hand and chose him five smooth stones out of the brook.
I Samuel ch. 17, v. 40

33 Am I a dog, that thou comest to me with staves?
I Samuel ch. 17, v. 43

34 Saul hath slain his thousands, and David his ten thousands.
I Samuel ch. 18, v. 7; cf. **Porteus** 588:14

35 David therefore departed thence, and escaped to the cave Adullam: and when his brethren and all his father's house heard it, they went down thither to him.
And every one that was in distress, and every one that was in debt, and every one that was discontented, gathered themselves unto him.
I Samuel ch. 22, v. 1; cf. **Bright** 148:14

36 And Saul said, God hath delivered him into mine hand.
I Samuel ch. 23, v. 7

37 Behold, I have played the fool, and have erred exceedingly.
I Samuel ch. 26, v. 21

II SAMUEL

1 The beauty of Israel is slain upon thy high places: how are the mighty fallen!
Tell it not in Gath, publish it not in the streets of Askelon; lest the daughters of the Philistines rejoice, lest the daughters of the uncircumcised triumph.
Ye mountains of Gilboa, let there be no dew, neither let there be rain, upon you, nor fields of offerings: for there the shield of the mighty is vilely cast away.
II Samuel ch. 1, v. 19

2 Saul and Jonathan were lovely and pleasant in their lives, and in their death they were not divided: they were swifter than eagles, they were stronger than lions.
Ye daughters of Israel, weep over Saul, who clothed you in scarlet, with other delights, who put on ornaments of gold upon your apparel.
II Samuel ch. 1, v. 23

3 I am distressed for thee, my brother Jonathan: very pleasant hast thou been unto me: thy love to me was wonderful, passing the love of women.
How are the mighty fallen, and the weapons of war perished!
II Samuel ch. 1, v. 26

4 And David danced before the Lord with all his might.
II Samuel ch. 6, v. 14

5 The poor man had nothing, save one little ewe lamb.
II Samuel ch. 12, v. 3

6 Thou art the man.
II Samuel ch. 12, v. 7

7 While the child was yet alive, I fasted and wept . . . But now he is dead, wherefore should I fast? can I bring him back again? I shall go to him but he shall not return to me.
II Samuel ch. 12, v. 22

8 For we needs must die, and are as water spilt on the ground, which cannot be gathered up again; neither doth God respect any person.
II Samuel ch. 14, v. 14

9 Come out, come out, thou bloody man, and thou man of Belial.
II Samuel ch. 16, v. 7

10 And when Ahithophel saw that his counsel was not followed, he saddled his ass, and arose, and gat him home to his house, to his city, and put his household in order, and hanged himself.
II Samuel ch. 17, v. 23

11 And the king was much moved, and went up to the chamber over the gate, and wept: and as he went, thus he said, O my son Absalom, my son, my son Absalom! would God I had died for thee, O Absalom, my son, my son!
II Samuel ch. 18, v. 33

12 By my God have I leaped over a wall.
II Samuel ch. 22, v. 30; cf. **Book of Common Prayer** 132:13

13 David . . . the sweet psalmist of Israel.
II Samuel ch. 23, v. 1

14 Went in jeopardy of their lives.
II Samuel ch. 23, v. 17

I KINGS

15 And Zadok the priest took an horn of oil out of the tabernacle, and anointed Solomon. And they blew the trumpet; and all the people said, God save king Solomon.
I Kings ch. 1, v. 39

16 Then will I cut off Israel out of the land which I have given them; and this house, which I have hallowed for my name, will I cast out of my sight; and Israel shall be a proverb and a byword among all people.
I Kings ch. 9, v. 7

17 And when the queen of Sheba had seen all Solomon's wisdom . . . there was no more spirit in her.
I Kings ch. 10, v. 4

18 Behold, the half was not told me.
I Kings ch. 10, v. 7

19 Once in three years came the navy of Tharshish, bringing gold, and silver, ivory, and apes, and peacocks.
I Kings ch. 10, v. 22; cf. **Masefield** 500:13

20 But king Solomon loved many strange women.
I Kings ch. 11, v. 1

21 My little finger shall be thicker than my father's loins.
I Kings ch. 12, v. 10

22 My father hath chastised you with whips, but I will chastise you with scorpions.
I Kings ch. 12, v. 11

23 To your tents, O Israel: now see to thine own house, David.
I Kings ch. 12, v. 16

24 He slept with his fathers.
I Kings ch. 14, v. 20

25 He went and dwelt by the brook Cherith, that is before Jordan.
And the ravens brought him bread and flesh in the morning, and bread and flesh in the evening; and he drank of the brook.
I Kings ch. 17, v. 5

26 An handful of meal in a barrel, and a little oil in a cruse.
I Kings ch. 17, v. 12

27 How long halt ye between two opinions?
I Kings ch. 18, v. 21

28 He is talking, or he is pursuing, or he is in a journey, or peradventure he sleepeth, and must be awaked.
I Kings ch. 18, v. 27

29 There is a sound of abundance of rain.
I Kings ch. 18, v. 41

30 There ariseth a little cloud out of the sea, like a man's hand.
I Kings ch. 18, v. 44

1 He girded up his loins, and ran before Ahab.
I Kings ch. 18, v. 46

2 He himself went a day's journey into the wilderness, and came and sat down under a juniper tree.
I Kings ch. 19, v. 4

3 But the Lord was not in the wind: and after the wind an earthquake; but the Lord was not in the earthquake:
And after the earthquake a fire: but the Lord was not in the fire: and after the fire a still small voice.
I Kings ch. 19, v. 11

4 Elijah passed by him, and cast his mantle upon him.
I Kings ch. 19, v. 19

5 Let not him that girdeth on his harness boast himself as he that putteth it off.
I Kings ch. 20, v. 11

6 A vineyard, which was in Jezreel.
I Kings ch. 21, v. 1

7 And Ahab spake unto Naboth, saying, Give me thy vineyard, that I may have it for a garden of herbs, because it is near unto my house.
I Kings ch. 21, v. 2

8 Hast thou found me, O mine enemy?
I Kings ch. 21, v. 20

9 I saw all Israel scattered upon the hills, as sheep that have not a shepherd.
I Kings ch. 22, v. 17

10 Feed him with bread of affliction and with water of affliction, until I come in peace.
I Kings ch. 22, v. 27

11 And a certain man drew a bow at a venture, and smote the king of Israel between the joints of the harness.
I Kings ch. 22, v. 34

II KINGS

12 Elijah went up by a whirlwind into heaven.
And Elisha saw it, and he cried, My father, my father, the chariot of Israel, and the horsemen thereof.
II Kings ch. 2, v. 11

13 The spirit of Elijah doth rest on Elisha.
II Kings ch. 2, v. 15

14 Go up, thou bald head.
II Kings ch. 2, v. 23

15 Is it well with the child? And she answered, It is well.
II Kings ch. 4, v. 26

16 There is death in the pot.
II Kings ch. 4, v. 40

17 He shall know that there is a prophet in Israel.
II Kings ch. 5, v. 8

18 Are not Abana and Pharpar, rivers of Damascus, better than all the waters of Israel?
II Kings ch. 5, v. 12

19 I bow myself in the house of Rimmon.
II Kings ch. 5, v. 18

20 Whence comest thou, Gehazi?
II Kings ch. 5, v. 25

21 Is thy servant a dog, that he should do this great thing?
II Kings ch. 8, v. 13

22 Is it peace? And Jehu said, What hast thou to do with peace? turn thee behind me.
II Kings ch. 9, v. 18

23 The driving is like the driving of Jehu, the son of Nimshi; for he driveth furiously.
II Kings ch. 9, v. 20

24 She painted her face, and tired her head, and looked out at a window.
II Kings ch. 9, v. 30

25 Had Zimri peace, who slew his master?
II Kings ch. 9, v. 31

26 Who is on my side? who?
II Kings ch. 9, v. 32

27 They found no more of her than the skull, and the feet, and the palms of her hands.
II Kings ch. 9, v. 35

28 Thou trustest upon the staff of this bruised reed, even upon Egypt, on which if a man lean, it will go into his hand, and pierce it.
II Kings ch. 18, v. 21

I CHRONICLES

29 For we are strangers before thee, and sojourners, as were all our fathers: our days on the earth are as a shadow, and there is none abiding.
I Chronicles ch. 29, v. 15

30 He died in a good old age, full of days, riches, and honour.
I Chronicles ch. 29, v. 28

NEHEMIAH

31 Every one with one of his hands wrought in the work, and with the other hand held a weapon.
Nehemiah ch. 4, v. 17

ESTHER

32 And if I perish, I perish.
Esther ch. 4, v. 16

33 Thus shall it be done to the man whom the king delighteth to honour.
Esther ch. 6, v. 9

JOB

34 And the Lord said unto Satan, Whence comest thou? Then Satan answered the Lord, and said, From going to and fro in the earth, and from walking up and down in it.
Job ch. 1, v. 7

35 Doth Job fear God for naught?
Job ch. 1, v. 9

36 The Lord gave, and the Lord hath taken away; blessed be the name of the Lord.
Job ch. 1, v. 21

37 All that a man hath will he give for his life.
Job ch. 2, v. 4

1 And he took him a potsherd to scrape himself withal.
Job ch. 2, v. 8

2 Curse God, and die.
Job ch. 2, v. 9

3 Let the day perish wherein I was born, and the night in which it was said, There is a man child conceived.
Job ch. 3, v. 3

4 For now should I have lain still and been quiet, I should have slept: then had I been at rest,
With kings and counsellors of the earth, which built desolate places for themselves.
Job ch. 3, v. 13

5 There the wicked cease from troubling, and there the weary be at rest.
Job ch. 3, v. 17

6 Wherefore is light given to him that is in misery, and life unto the bitter in soul?
Job ch. 3, v. 20

7 Then a spirit passed before my face; the hair of my flesh stood up.
Job ch. 4, v. 15

8 Shall mortal man be more just than God? shall a man be more pure than his maker?
Job ch. 4, v. 17

9 Man is born unto trouble, as the sparks fly upward.
Job ch. 5, v. 7

10 My days are swifter than a weaver's shuttle.
Job ch. 7, v. 6

11 He shall return no more to his house, neither shall his place know him any more.
Job ch. 7, v. 10

12 Let me alone, that I may take comfort a little,
Before I go whence I shall not return, even to the land of darkness and the shadow of death.
Job ch. 10, v. 20

13 A land . . . where the light is as darkness.
Job ch. 10, v. 22

14 Canst thou by searching find out God?
Job ch. 11, v. 7

15 No doubt but ye are the people, and wisdom shall die with you.
Job ch. 12, v. 2

16 With the ancient is wisdom; and in length of days understanding.
Job ch. 12, v. 12

17 Though he slay me, yet will I trust in him: but I will maintain mine own ways before him.
Job ch. 13, v. 15

18 Man that is born of a woman is of few days, and full of trouble.
He cometh forth like a flower, and is cut down: he fleeth also as a shadow, and continueth not.
Job ch. 14, v. 1; cf. **Book of Common Prayer** 131:12

19 Miserable comforters are ye all.
Job ch. 16, v. 2

20 I also could speak as ye do: if your soul were in my soul's stead.
Job ch. 16, v. 4

21 I am escaped with the skin of my teeth.
Job ch. 19, v. 20

22 I know that my redeemer liveth, and that he shall stand at the latter day upon the earth:
And though after my skin worms destroy this body, yet in my flesh shall I see God.
Job ch. 19, v. 25

23 Ye should say, Why persecute we him, seeing the root of the matter is found in me?
Job ch. 19, v. 28

24 But where shall wisdom be found?
Job ch. 28, v. 12

25 The price of wisdom is above rubies.
Job ch. 28, v. 18

26 I was eyes to the blind, and feet was I to the lame.
Job ch. 29, v. 15

27 For I know that thou wilt bring me to death, and to the house appointed for all living.
Job ch. 30, v. 23

28 I am a brother to dragons, and a companion to owls.
Job ch. 30, v. 29

29 Great men are not always wise.
Job ch. 32, v. 9

30 Who is this that darkeneth counsel by words without knowledge?
Job ch. 38, v. 2

31 Where wast thou when I laid the foundations of the earth? declare, if thou hast understanding.
Job ch. 38, v. 4

32 When the morning stars sang together, and all the sons of God shouted for joy.
Job ch. 38, v. 7

33 Hath the rain a father? or who hath begotten the drops of dew?
Job ch. 38, v. 28

34 Canst thou bind the sweet influences of Pleiades, or loose the bands of Orion?
Job ch. 38, v. 31

35 He paweth in the valley, and rejoiceth in his strength: he goeth on to meet the armed men.
Job ch. 39, v. 21

36 He swalloweth the ground with fierceness and rage: neither believeth he that it is the sound of the trumpet.
Job ch. 39, v. 24

37 He saith among the trumpets, Ha, ha; and he smelleth the battle afar off, the thunder of the captains, and the shouting.
Job ch. 39, v. 25

38 Behold now behemoth, which I made with thee; he eateth grass as an ox.
Job ch. 40, v. 15

1 He is the chief of the ways of God: he that made him can make his sword to approach unto him.
Job ch. 40, v. 19

2 The shady trees cover him with their shadow; the willows of the brook compass him about.
Job ch. 40, v. 22

3 Canst thou draw out leviathan with an hook?
Job ch. 41, v. 1

4 I have heard of thee by the hearing of the ear: but now mine eye seeth thee.
Job ch. 42, v. 5

5 So the Lord blessed the latter end of Job more than his beginning.
Job ch. 42, v. 12

PROVERBS

6 Surely in vain the net is spread in the sight of any bird.
Proverbs ch. 1, v. 17; cf. **Proverbs** 604:2

7 For whom the Lord loveth he correcteth.
Proverbs ch. 3, v. 12

8 Length of days is in her right hand; and in her left hand riches and honour.
Proverbs ch. 3, v. 16

9 Her ways are ways of pleasantness, and all her paths are peace.
Proverbs ch. 3, v. 17; cf. **Spring-Rice** 735:8

10 Wisdom is the principal thing; therefore get wisdom: and with all thy getting get understanding.
Proverbs ch. 4, v. 7

11 The path of the just is as the shining light, that shineth more and more unto the perfect day.
Proverbs ch. 4, v. 18

12 For the lips of a strange woman drop as an honeycomb, and her mouth is smoother than oil:
But her end is bitter as wormwood, sharp as a two-edged sword.
Her feet go down to death; her steps take hold on hell.
Proverbs ch. 5, v. 3

13 Go to the ant thou sluggard; consider her ways, and be wise.
Proverbs ch. 6, v. 6

14 How long wilt thou sleep, O sluggard? When wilt thou arise out of thy sleep?
So shall thy poverty come as one that travelleth, and thy want as an armed man.
Yet a little sleep, a little slumber, a little folding of the hands to sleep.
Proverbs ch. 6, v. 9

15 Can a man take fire in his bosom, and his clothes not be burned?
Proverbs ch. 6, v. 27

16 Come, let us take our fill of love until the morning: let us solace ourselves with loves.
For the goodman is not at home, he is gone a long journey.
Proverbs ch. 7, v. 18

17 He goeth after her straightway, as an ox goeth to the slaughter.
Proverbs ch. 7, v. 22

18 Wisdom hath builded her house, she hath hewn out her seven pillars.
Proverbs ch. 9, v. 1; cf. **Borrowed titles** 144:15

19 Stolen waters are sweet, and bread eaten in secret is pleasant.
Proverbs ch. 9, v. 17; cf. **Proverbs** 611:25

20 A wise son maketh a glad father: but a foolish son is the heaviness of his mother.
Proverbs ch. 10, v. 1

21 The destruction of the poor is their poverty.
Proverbs ch. 10, v. 15

22 He that is surety for a stranger shall smart for it.
Proverbs ch. 11, v. 15

23 As a jewel of gold in a swine's snout, so is a fair woman which is without discretion.
Proverbs ch. 11, v. 22

24 A virtuous woman is a crown to her husband.
Proverbs ch. 12, v. 4

25 A righteous man regardeth the life of his beast: but the tender mercies of the wicked are cruel.
Proverbs ch. 12, v. 10

26 Lying lips are abomination to the Lord.
Proverbs ch. 12, v. 22; cf. **Anonymous** 15:4

27 Hope deferred maketh the heart sick: but when the desire cometh, it is a tree of life.
Proverbs ch. 13, v. 12; cf. **Proverbs** 602:47

28 The way of transgressors is hard.
Proverbs ch. 13, v. 15

29 The desire accomplished is sweet to the soul.
Proverbs ch. 13, v. 19

30 He that spareth his rod hateth his son.
Proverbs ch. 13, v. 24; cf. **Proverbs** 611:14

31 Even in laughter the heart is sorrowful.
Proverbs ch. 14, v. 13

32 In all labour there is profit.
Proverbs ch. 14, v. 23

33 Righteousness exalteth a nation.
Proverbs ch. 14, v. 34

34 A soft answer turneth away wrath.
Proverbs ch. 15, v. 1; cf. **Proverbs** 611:4

35 A merry heart maketh a cheerful countenance.
Proverbs ch. 15, v. 13

36 Better is a dinner of herbs where love is, than a stalled ox and hatred therewith.
'*Better is a mess of pottage with love, than a fat ox with evil will*' *in Matthew's Bible* (1535)
Proverbs ch. 15, v. 17; cf. **Proverbs** 596:3

37 A word spoken in due season, how good is it!
Proverbs ch. 15, v. 23

38 Pride goeth before destruction, and an haughty spirit before a fall.
Proverbs ch. 16, v. 18; cf. **Proverbs** 609:42

1 He that is slow to anger is better than the mighty; and he that ruleth his spirit than he that taketh a city.
Proverbs ch. 16, v. 32

2 He that repeateth a matter separateth very friends.
Proverbs ch. 17, v. 9

3 A friend loveth at all times, and a brother is born for adversity.
Proverbs ch. 17, v. 17

4 A merry heart doeth good like a medicine.
Proverbs ch. 17, v. 22

5 A wounded spirit who can bear?
Proverbs ch. 18, v. 14

6 There is a friend that sticketh closer than a brother.
Proverbs ch. 18, v. 24; cf. **Kipling** 440:11

7 Wine is a mocker, strong drink is raging.
Proverbs ch. 20, v. 1

8 Every fool will be meddling.
Proverbs ch. 20, v. 3

9 Even a child is known by his doings.
Proverbs ch. 20, v. 11

10 The hearing ear, and the seeing eye, the Lord hath made even both of them.
Proverbs ch. 20, v. 12

11 It is naught, it is naught, saith the buyer: but when he is gone his way, then he boasteth.
Proverbs ch. 20, v. 14

12 It is better to dwell in a corner of the housetop, than with a brawling woman in a wide house.
Proverbs ch. 21, v. 9

13 A good name is rather to be chosen than great riches.
Proverbs ch. 22, v. 1

14 Train up a child in the way he should go: and when he is old, he will not depart from it.
Proverbs ch. 22, v. 6

15 Remove not the ancient landmark, which thy fathers have set.
Proverbs ch. 22, v. 28

16 Look not thou upon the wine when it is red, when it giveth his colour in the cup . . . At the last it biteth like a serpent, and stingeth like an adder.
Proverbs ch. 23, v. 31

17 The heart of kings is unsearchable.
Proverbs ch. 25, v. 3

18 A word fitly spoken is like apples of gold in pictures of silver.
Proverbs ch. 25, v. 11

19 Whoso boasteth himself of a false gift is like clouds and wind without rain.
Proverbs ch. 25, v. 14

20 Withdraw thy foot from thy neighbour's house; lest he be weary of thee, and so hate thee.
Proverbs ch. 25, v. 17

21 If thine enemy be hungry, give him bread to eat; and if he be thirsty, give him water to drink.
For thou shalt heap coals of fire upon his head, and the Lord shall reward thee.
Proverbs ch. 25, v. 21

22 As cold waters to a thirsty soul, so is good news from a far country.
Proverbs ch. 25, v. 25

23 Answer not a fool according to his folly, lest thou also be like unto him.
Answer a fool according to his folly, lest he be wise in his own conceit.
Proverbs ch. 26, v. 4

24 As a dog returneth to his vomit, so a fool returneth to his folly.
Proverbs ch. 26, v. 11; cf. **Proverbs** 598:24

25 Seest thou a man wise in his own conceit? There is more hope of a fool than of him.
Proverbs ch. 26, v. 12

26 The sluggard is wiser in his own conceit than seven men that can render a reason.
Proverbs ch. 26, v. 16

27 Boast not thyself of to morrow; for thou knowest not what a day may bring forth.
Proverbs ch. 27, v. 1

28 Open rebuke is better than secret love.
Proverbs ch. 27, v. 5

29 Faithful are the wounds of a friend.
Proverbs ch. 27, v. 6

30 A continual dropping in a very rainy day and a contentious woman are alike.
Proverbs ch. 27, v. 15

31 The wicked flee when no man pursueth: but the righteous are bold as a lion.
Proverbs ch. 28, v. 1

32 He that maketh haste to be rich shall not be innocent.
Proverbs ch. 28, v. 20

33 A fool uttereth all his mind.
Proverbs ch. 29, v. 11

34 Where there is no vision, the people perish.
Proverbs ch. 29, v. 18

35 Give me neither poverty nor riches; feed me with food convenient for me.
Proverbs ch. 30, v. 8

36 There be three things which are too wonderful for me, yea, four which I know not:
The way of an eagle in the air; the way of a serpent upon a rock; the way of a ship in the midst of the sea; and the way of a man with a maid.
Proverbs ch. 30, v. 18

37 Give strong drink unto him that is ready to perish, and wine unto those that be of heavy hearts.
Proverbs ch. 31, v. 6

38 Who can find a virtuous woman? for her price is far above rubies.
Proverbs ch. 31, v. 10

ECCLESIASTES

39 Vanity of vanities, saith the Preacher, vanity of vanities; all is vanity.

What profit hath a man of all his labour which he taketh under the sun?
One generation passeth away, and another generation cometh.
Ecclesiastes ch. 1, v. 2; cf. **Bible** 113:26

1 All the rivers run into the sea; yet the sea is not full.
Ecclesiastes ch. 1, v. 7

2 All things are full of labour; man cannot utter it: the eye is not satisfied with seeing, nor the ear filled with hearing.
Ecclesiastes ch. 1, v. 8

3 The thing that hath been, it is that which shall be; and that which is done is that which shall be done: and there is no new thing under the sun.
Ecclesiastes ch. 1, v. 9; cf. **Proverbs** 612:20

4 All is vanity and vexation of spirit.
Ecclesiastes ch. 1, v. 14

5 He that increaseth knowledge increaseth sorrow.
Ecclesiastes ch. 1, v. 18

6 Wisdom excelleth folly, as far as light excelleth darkness.
Ecclesiastes ch. 2, v. 13

7 To every thing there is a season, and a time to every purpose under the heaven:
A time to be born, and a time to die; a time to plant, and a time to pluck up that which is planted;
A time to kill, and a time to heal; a time to break down, and a time to build up;
A time to weep, and a time to laugh; a time to mourn, and a time to dance;
A time to cast away stones, and a time to gather stones together; a time to embrace, and a time to refrain from embracing;
A time to get, and a time to lose; a time to keep, and a time to cast away;
A time to rend, and a time to sew; a time to keep silence, and a time to speak;
A time to love, and a time to hate; a time of war, and a time of peace.
Ecclesiastes ch. 3, v. 1; cf. **Proverbs** 612:6

8 For that which befalleth the sons of men befalleth beasts; even one thing befalleth them: as the one dieth, so dieth the other; yea, they have all one breath; so that a man hath no preeminence above a beast: for all is vanity.
Ecclesiastes ch. 3, v. 19

9 Wherefore I praised the dead which are already dead more than the living which are yet alive.
Ecclesiastes ch. 4, v. 2

10 A threefold cord is not quickly broken.
Ecclesiastes ch. 4, v. 12; cf. **Burke** 162:10

11 God is in heaven, and thou upon earth: therefore let thy words be few.
Ecclesiastes ch. 5, v. 2

12 The sleep of a labouring man is sweet.
Ecclesiastes ch. 5, v. 12; cf. **Bunyan** 161:7

13 As the crackling of thorns under a pot, so is the laughter of a fool.
Ecclesiastes ch. 7, v. 6

14 Better is the end of a thing than the beginning thereof.
Ecclesiastes ch. 7, v. 8

15 Say not thou, What is the cause that the former days were better than these? for thou dost not enquire wisely concerning this.
Ecclesiastes ch. 7, v. 10

16 In the day of prosperity be joyful, but in the day of adversity consider.
Ecclesiastes ch. 7, v. 14

17 God hath made man upright; but they have sought out many inventions.
Ecclesiastes ch. 7, v. 29

18 There is no man that hath power over the spirit to retain the spirit; neither hath he power in the day of death; there is no discharge in that war.
Ecclesiastes ch. 8, v. 8

19 A man hath no better thing under the sun, than to eat, and to drink, and to be merry.
Ecclesiastes ch. 8, v. 15; cf. **Bible** 87:9, 99:21

20 A living dog is better than a dead lion.
Ecclesiastes ch. 9, v. 4; cf. **Proverbs** 605:47

21 Go thy way, eat thy bread with joy, and drink thy wine with a merry heart; for God now accepteth thy works.
Ecclesiastes ch. 9, v. 7

22 Whatsoever thy hand findeth to do, do it with thy might; for there is no work, nor device, nor knowledge, nor wisdom, in the grave, whither thou goest.
Ecclesiastes ch. 9, v. 10

23 The race is not to the swift, nor the battle to the strong.
Ecclesiastes ch. 9, v. 11; cf. **Davidson** 251:13, **Proverbs** 610:4

24 He that diggeth a pit shall fall into it.
Ecclesiastes ch. 10, v. 8

25 Woe to thee, O land, when thy king is a child, and thy princes eat in the morning!
Ecclesiastes ch. 10, v. 16; cf. **Shakespeare** 696:19

26 Wine maketh merry: but money answereth all things.
Ecclesiastes ch. 10, v. 19

27 Cast thy bread upon the waters: for thou shalt find it after many days.
Ecclesiastes ch. 11, v. 1

28 In the place where the tree falleth, there it shall be.
Ecclesiastes ch. 11, v. 3; cf. **Proverbs** 595:18

29 He that observeth the wind shall not sow; and he that regardeth the clouds shall not reap.
Ecclesiastes ch. 11, v. 4

30 In the morning sow thy seed, and in the evening withhold not thine hand.
Ecclesiastes ch. 11, v. 6

31 Truly the light is sweet, and a pleasant thing it is for the eyes to behold the sun.
Ecclesiastes ch. 11, v. 7

1 Rejoice, O young man, in thy youth; and let thy heart cheer thee in the days of thy youth.
Ecclesiastes ch. 11, v. 9

2 Remember now thy Creator in the days of thy youth, while the evil days come not, nor the years draw nigh, when thou shalt say, I have no pleasure in them;
While the sun, or the light, or the moon, or the stars, be not darkened, nor the clouds return after the rain:
In the day when the keepers of the house shall tremble, and the strong men shall bow themselves, and the grinders cease because they are few, and those that look out of the windows be darkened,
And the doors shall be shut in the streets, when the sound of the grinding is low, and he shall rise up at the voice of the bird, and all the daughters of music shall be brought low;
Also when they shall be afraid of that which is high, and fears shall be in the way, and the almond tree shall flourish, and the grasshopper shall be a burden, and desire shall fail: because man goeth to his long home, and the mourners go about the streets:
Or ever the silver cord be loosed, or the golden bowl be broken, or the pitcher be broken at the fountain, or the wheel broken at the cistern.
Then shall the dust return to the earth as it was: and the spirit shall return unto God who gave it.
Ecclesiastes ch. 12, v. 1

3 The words of the wise are as goads.
Ecclesiastes ch. 12, v. 11

4 Of making many books there is no end; and much study is a weariness of the flesh.
Ecclesiastes ch. 12, v. 12

5 Fear God, and keep his commandments: for this is the whole duty of man.
For God shall bring every work into judgement, with every secret thing, whether it be good, or whether it be evil.
Ecclesiastes ch. 12, v. 13

SONG OF SOLOMON

6 The song of songs, which is Solomon's.
Let him kiss me with the kisses of his mouth: for thy love is better than wine.
Song of Solomon ch. 1, v. 1

7 I am black, but comely, O ye daughters of Jerusalem,
as the tents of Kedar, as the curtains of Solomon.
Song of Solomon ch. 1, v. 5

8 A bundle of myrrh is my wellbeloved unto me; he shall lie all night betwixt my breasts.
Song of Solomon ch. 1, v. 13

9 I am the rose of Sharon, and the lily of the valleys.
Song of Solomon ch. 2, v. 1

10 Rise up, my love, my fair one, and come away.
For, lo, the winter is past, the rain is over and gone;
The flowers appear on the earth; the time of the singing of birds is come, and the voice of the turtle is heard in our land.
Song of Solomon ch. 2, v. 10

11 Take us the foxes, the little foxes, that spoil the vines.
Song of Solomon ch. 2, v. 15

12 My beloved is mine, and I am his: he feedeth among the lilies.
Until the day break, and the shadows flee away.
Song of Solomon ch. 2, v. 16

13 By night on my bed I sought him whom my soul loveth.
Song of Solomon ch. 3, v. 1

14 Behold, thou art fair, my love; behold, thou art fair; thou hast doves' eyes within thy locks: thy hair is as a flock of goats, that appear from mount Gilead.
Thy teeth are like a flock of sheep that are even shorn, which came up from the washing; whereof every one bear twins, and none is barren among them.
Thy lips are like a thread of scarlet, and thy speech is comely: thy temples are like a piece of a pomegranate within thy locks.
Thy neck is like the tower of David builded for an armoury, whereon there hang a thousand bucklers, all shields of mighty men.
Thy two breasts are like two young roes that are twins, which feed among the lilies.
Song of Solomon ch. 4, v. 1

15 Thou art all fair, my love; there is no spot in thee.
Song of Solomon ch. 4, v. 7

16 A garden inclosed is my sister, my spouse; a spring shut up, a fountain sealed.
Song of Solomon ch. 4, v. 12

17 Awake, O north wind; and come, thou south; blow upon my garden, that the spices thereof may flow out. Let my beloved come into his garden, and eat his pleasant fruits.
Song of Solomon ch. 4, v. 16

18 I sleep, but my heart waketh: it is the voice of my beloved that knocketh, saying, Open to me, my sister, my love, my dove, my undefiled.
Song of Solomon ch. 5, v. 2

19 The watchmen that went about the city found me, they smote me, they wounded me; the keepers of the walls took away my veil from me.
I charge you, O daughters of Jerusalem, if ye find my beloved, that ye tell him, that I am sick of love.
What is thy beloved more than another beloved, O thou fairest among women?
Song of Solomon ch. 5, v. 7

20 My beloved is white and ruddy, the chiefest among ten thousand.
Song of Solomon ch. 5, v. 10

21 His hands are as gold rings set with the beryl: his belly is as bright ivory overlaid with sapphires.
His legs are as pillars of marble, set upon sockets of fine gold: his countenance is as Lebanon, excellent as the cedars.

His mouth is most sweet: yea, he is altogether lovely. This is my beloved, and this is my friend, O daughters of Jerusalem.
Song of Solomon ch. 5, v. 14

1 Who is she that looketh forth as the morning, fair as the moon, clear as the sun, and terrible as an army with banners?
Song of Solomon ch. 6, v. 10

2 Return, return, O Shulamite; return, return, that we may look upon thee.
Song of Solomon ch. 6, v. 13

3 How beautiful are thy feet with shoes, O prince's daughter!
Song of Solomon ch. 7, v. 1

4 Thy navel is like a round goblet, which wanteth not liquor: thy belly is like an heap of wheat set about with lilies.
Song of Solomon ch. 7, v. 2

5 Thy neck is as a tower of ivory; thine eyes like the fishpools in Heshbon.
Song of Solomon ch. 7, v. 4

6 Like the best wine, for my beloved, that goeth down sweetly, causing the lips of those that are asleep to speak.
Song of Solomon ch. 7, v. 9

7 Set me as a seal upon thine heart, as a seal upon thine arm: for love is strong as death; jealousy is cruel as the grave.
Song of Solomon ch. 8, v. 6

8 Many waters cannot quench love, neither can the floods drown it: if a man would give all the substance of his house for love, it would utterly be contemned.
Song of Solomon ch. 8, v. 7

9 Make haste, my beloved, and be thou like to a roe or to a young hart upon the mountains of spices.
Song of Solomon ch. 8, v. 14

ISAIAH

10 The daughter of Zion is left as a cottage in a vineyard, as a lodge in a garden of cucumbers, as a besieged city.
Isaiah ch. 1, v. 8

11 Bring no more vain oblations; incense is an abomination unto me; the new moons and sabbaths, the calling of assemblies, I cannot away with.
Isaiah ch. 1, v. 13

12 Though your sins be as scarlet, they shall be as white as snow.
Isaiah ch. 1, v. 18

13 They shall beat their swords into plowshares, and their spears into pruninghooks: nation shall not lift up sword against nation, neither shall they learn war any more.
Micah ch. 4, v. 3, Joel ch. 3, v. 10 have same image
Isaiah ch. 2, v. 4; cf. **Rendall** 624:13

14 What mean ye that ye beat my people to pieces, and grind the faces of the poor?
Isaiah ch. 3, v. 15

15 My well-beloved hath a vineyard in a very fruitful hill.
Isaiah ch. 5, v. 1

16 And he looked that it should bring forth grapes, and it brought forth wild grapes.
Isaiah ch. 5, v. 2

17 And he looked for judgement, but behold oppression; for righteousness, but behold a cry.
Isaiah ch. 5, v. 7

18 Woe unto them that join house to house, that lay field to field, till there be no place.
Isaiah ch. 5, v. 8

19 Woe unto them that call evil good, and good evil.
Isaiah ch. 5, v. 20

20 For all this his anger is not turned away, but his hand is stretched out still.
Isaiah ch. 5, v. 25

21 In the year that king Uzziah died I saw also the Lord sitting upon a throne, high and lifted up, and his train filled the temple.
Above it stood the seraphims: each one had six wings; with twain he covered his face, and with twain he covered his feet, and with twain he did fly.
And one cried unto another, and said, Holy, holy, holy, is the Lord of hosts: the whole earth is full of his glory.
Isaiah ch. 6, v. 1

22 Then said I, Woe is me! for I am undone; because I am a man of unclean lips, and I dwell in the midst of a people of unclean lips.
Isaiah ch. 6, v. 5

23 Then flew one of the seraphims unto me, having a live coal in his hand, which he had taken with the tongs from off the altar.
And he laid it upon my mouth, and said, Lo, this hath touched thy lips.
Isaiah ch. 6, v. 6

24 Whom shall I send, and who will go for us? Then said I, Here am I; send me.
Isaiah ch. 6, v. 8

25 Then said I, Lord, how long?
Isaiah ch. 6, v. 11

26 Behold, a virgin shall conceive, and bear a son, and shall call his name Immanuel.
Butter and honey shall he eat, that he may know to refuse the evil, and choose the good.
Isaiah ch. 7, v. 14

27 Sanctify the Lord of hosts himself; and let him be your fear, and let him be your dread.
And he shall be for a sanctuary; but for a stone of stumbling and for a rock of offence to both the houses of Israel.
Isaiah ch. 8, v. 13

28 The people that walked in darkness have seen a great light: they that dwell in the land of the shadow of death, upon them hath the light shined.
Thou hast multiplied the nation, and not increased the joy: they joy before thee according to the joy in

harvest, and as men rejoice when they divide the spoil.
Isaiah ch. 9, v. 2; cf. **Scottish Metrical Psalms** 652:23

1 For unto us a child is born, unto us a son is given: and the government shall be upon his shoulder: and his name shall be called Wonderful, Counsellor, The mighty God, The everlasting Father, The Prince of Peace.
Of the increase of his government and peace there shall be no end.
Isaiah ch. 9, v. 6

2 The zeal of the Lord of hosts will perform this.
Isaiah ch. 9, v. 7

3 And there shall come forth a rod out of the stem of Jesse, and a branch shall grow out of his roots:
And the spirit of the Lord shall rest upon him, the spirit of wisdom and understanding, the spirit of counsel and might, the spirit of knowledge and of the fear of the Lord.
Isaiah ch. 11, v. 1

4 The wolf also shall dwell with the lamb, and the leopard shall lie down with the kid; and the calf and the young lion and the fatling together; and a little child shall lead them.
Isaiah ch. 11, v. 6

5 And the lion shall eat straw like the ox.
And the sucking child shall play on the hole of the asp, and the weaned child shall put his hand on the cockatrice' den.
They shall not hurt nor destroy in all my holy mountain: for the earth shall be full of the knowledge of the Lord, as the waters cover the sea.
Isaiah ch. 11, v. 7

6 And the wild beasts of the islands shall cry in their desolate houses, and dragons in their pleasant palaces.
Isaiah ch. 13, v. 22

7 How art thou fallen from heaven, O Lucifer, son of the morning!
Isaiah ch. 14, v. 12

8 Watchman, what of the night? Watchman, what of the night?
The watchman said, The morning cometh, and also the night.
Isaiah ch. 21, v. 11

9 Let us eat and drink; for to morrow we shall die.
Isaiah ch. 22, v. 13; cf. **Bible** 84:19, 99:21

10 In this mountain shall the Lord of hosts make unto all people a feast of fat things, a feast of wine on the lees, of fat things full of marrow, of wine on the lees well refined.
Isaiah ch. 25, v. 6

11 He will swallow up death in victory; and the Lord God will wipe away tears from off all faces.
Isaiah ch. 25, v. 8

12 We have as it were brought forth wind.
Isaiah ch. 26, v. 18

13 For precept must be upon precept, precept upon precept; line upon line, line upon line; here a little, and there a little.
Isaiah ch. 28, v. 10

14 We have made a covenant with death, and with hell are we at agreement.
Isaiah ch. 28, v. 15; cf. **Garrison** 330:11

15 Speak unto us smooth things, prophesy deceits.
Isaiah ch. 30, v. 10

16 In quietness and in confidence shall be your strength.
Isaiah ch. 30, v. 15

17 The bread of adversity, and the waters of affliction.
Isaiah ch. 30, v. 20

18 This is the way, walk ye in it.
Isaiah ch. 30, v. 21

19 And a man shall be as an hiding place from the wind, and a covert from the tempest; as rivers of water in a dry place, as the shadow of a great rock in a weary land.
Isaiah ch. 32, v. 2

20 And thorns shall come up in her palaces, nettles and brambles in the fortresses thereof: and it shall be an habitation of dragons, and a court for owls.
Isaiah ch. 34, v. 13

21 The wilderness and the solitary place shall be glad for them; and the desert shall rejoice, and blossom as the rose.
Isaiah ch. 35, v. 1

22 Strengthen ye the weak hands, and confirm the feeble knees.
Isaiah ch. 35, v. 3

23 Then shall the lame man leap as an hart, and the tongue of the dumb sing: for in the wilderness shall waters break out, and streams in the desert.
Isaiah ch. 35, v. 6

24 They shall obtain joy and gladness, and sorrow and sighing shall flee away.
Isaiah ch. 35, v. 10

25 Set thine house in order: for thou shalt die, and not live.
Isaiah ch. 38, v. 1

26 I shall go softly all my years in the bitterness of my soul.
Isaiah ch. 38, v. 15

27 Comfort ye, comfort ye my people, saith your God.
Speak ye comfortably to Jerusalem, and cry unto her, that her warfare is accomplished.
Isaiah ch. 40, v. 1

28 The voice of him that crieth in the wilderness, Prepare ye the way of the Lord, make straight in the desert a highway for our God.
Every valley shall be exalted, and every mountain and hill shall be made low: and the crooked shall be made straight, and the rough places plain:
And the glory of the Lord shall be revealed, and all flesh shall see it together: for the mouth of the Lord hath spoken it.
Isaiah ch. 40, v. 3; cf. **Bible** 92:27

1 The voice said, Cry. And he said, What shall I cry? All flesh is grass, and all the goodliness thereof is as the flower of the field:
The grass withereth, the flower fadeth: because the spirit of the Lord bloweth upon it: surely the people is grass.
Isaiah ch. 40, v. 6; cf. **Bible** 110:26

2 He shall feed his flock like a shepherd: he shall gather the lambs with his arm, and carry them in his bosom, and shall gently lead those that are with young.
Isaiah ch. 40, v. 11

3 The nations are as a drop of a bucket, and are counted as the small dust of the balance: behold, he taketh up the isles as a very little thing.
Isaiah ch. 40, v. 15

4 Have ye not known? have ye not heard? hath it not been told you from the beginning?
Isaiah ch. 40, v. 21

5 But they that wait upon the Lord shall renew their strength: they shall mount up with wings as eagles; they shall run, and not be weary; and they shall walk, and not faint.
Isaiah ch. 40, v. 31

6 A bruised reed shall he not break, and the smoking flax shall he not quench.
Isaiah ch. 42, v. 3

7 Woe unto him that striveth with his maker! Let the potsherd strive with the potsherds of the earth. Shall the clay say to him that fashioneth it, What makest thou?
Isaiah ch. 45, v. 9

8 I have chosen thee in the furnace of affliction.
Isaiah ch. 48, v. 10

9 O that thou hadst hearkened to my commandments! then had thy peace been as a river, and thy righteousness as the waves of the sea.
Isaiah ch. 48, v. 18

10 There is no peace, saith the Lord, unto the wicked.
Isaiah ch. 48, v. 22

11 Can a woman forget her sucking child, that she should not have compassion on the son of her womb? yea, they may forget, yet will I not forget thee.
Isaiah ch. 49, v. 15

12 How beautiful upon the mountains are the feet of him that bringeth good tidings, that publisheth peace; that bringeth good tidings of good, that publisheth salvation; that saith unto Zion, Thy God reigneth!
Isaiah ch. 52, v. 7

13 For they shall see eye to eye, when the Lord shall bring again Zion.
Break forth into joy, sing together, ye waste places of Jerusalem: for the Lord hath comforted his people, he hath redeemed Jerusalem.
Isaiah ch. 52, v. 8

14 Who hath believed our report? and to whom is the arm of the Lord revealed?
Isaiah ch. 53, v. 1

15 He hath no form nor comeliness; and when we shall see him there is no beauty that we should desire him.
Isaiah ch. 53, v. 2

16 He is despised and rejected of men; a man of sorrows, and acquainted with grief: and we hid as it were our faces from him; he was despised, and we esteemed him not.
Surely he hath borne our griefs, and carried our sorrows.
Isaiah ch. 53, v. 3

17 But he was wounded for our transgressions, he was bruised for our iniquities: the chastisement of our peace was upon him; and with his stripes we are healed.
All we like sheep have gone astray; we have turned every one to his own way; and the Lord hath laid on him the iniquity of us all.
He was oppressed, and he was afflicted, yet he opened not his mouth: he is brought as a lamb to the slaughter, and as a sheep before her shearers is dumb, so he openeth not his mouth.
Isaiah ch. 53, v. 5

18 He was cut off out of the land of the living.
Isaiah ch. 53, v. 8

19 He was numbered with the transgressors; and he bare the sin of many, and made intercession for the transgressors.
Isaiah ch. 53, v. 12

20 Ho, every one that thirsteth, come ye to the waters, and he that hath no money; come ye, buy, and eat; yea, come, buy wine and milk without money and without price.
Wherefore do ye spend money for that which is not bread? and your labour for that which satisfieth not?
Isaiah ch. 55, v. 1

21 Seek ye the Lord while he may be found, call ye upon him while he is near.
Isaiah ch. 55, v. 6

22 For my thoughts are not your thoughts, neither are your ways my ways, saith the Lord.
Isaiah ch. 55, v. 8

23 Instead of the thorn shall come up the fir tree, and instead of the brier shall come up the myrtle tree.
Isaiah ch. 55, v. 13

24 I will give them an everlasting name, that shall not be cut off.
Isaiah ch. 56, v. 5

25 Mine house shall be called an house of prayer for all people.
Isaiah ch. 56, v. 7; cf. **Bible** 96:20

26 The righteous perisheth, and no man layeth it to heart.
Isaiah ch. 57, v. 1

27 Peace to him that is far off, and to him that is near.
Isaiah ch. 57, v. 19

1 Is not this the fast that I have chosen? to loose the bands of wickedness, to undo the heavy burdens, and to let the oppressed go free, and that ye break every yoke?
Isaiah ch. 58, v. 6

2 Then shall thy light break forth as the morning, and thine health shall spring forth speedily.
Isaiah ch. 58, v. 8

3 They make haste to shed innocent blood.
Isaiah ch. 59, v. 7

4 Arise, shine; for thy light is come, and the glory of the Lord is risen upon thee.
Isaiah ch. 60, v. 1

5 The Spirit of the Lord God is upon me . . . To bind up the brokenhearted, to proclaim liberty to the captives, and the opening of the prison to them that are bound;
To proclaim the acceptable year of the Lord, and the day of vengeance of our God; to comfort all that mourn.
Isaiah ch. 61, v. 1

6 To give unto them beauty for ashes, the oil of joy for mourning, the garment of praise for the spirit of heaviness.
Isaiah ch. 61, v. 3

7 All our righteousnesses are as filthy rags; and we all do fade as a leaf.
Isaiah ch. 64, v. 6

8 Stand by thyself, come not near to me; for I am holier than thou.
Isaiah ch. 65, v. 5

9 For, behold, I create new heavens and a new earth.
Isaiah ch. 65, v. 17

JEREMIAH

10 Can a maid forget her ornaments, or a bride her attire?
Jeremiah ch. 2, v. 32

11 They were as fed horses in the morning: every one neighed after his neighbour's wife.
Jeremiah ch. 5, v. 8

12 This people hath a revolting and a rebellious heart.
Jeremiah ch. 5, v. 23

13 The prophets prophesy falsely, and the priests bear rule by their means; and my people love to have it so: and what will ye do in the end thereof?
Jeremiah ch. 5, v. 31

14 They have healed also the hurt of the daughter of my people slightly, saying, Peace, peace; when there is no peace.
Jeremiah ch. 6, v. 14

15 The harvest is past, the summer is ended, and we are not saved.
Jeremiah ch. 8, v. 20

16 Is there no balm in Gilead?
Jeremiah ch. 8, v. 22

17 Can the Ethiopian change his skin, or the leopard his spots?
Jeremiah ch. 13, v. 23; cf. **Proverbs** 605:16

18 Woe is me, my mother, that thou hast borne me a man of strife and a man of contention to the whole earth!
Jeremiah ch. 15, v. 10

19 The heart is deceitful above all things, and desperately wicked.
Jeremiah ch. 17, v. 9

20 As the partridge sitteth on eggs, and hatcheth them not; so he that getteth riches, and not by right, shall leave them in the midst of his days.
Jeremiah ch. 17, v. 11

21 Behold, I will make thee a terror to thyself, and to all thy friends.
Jeremiah ch. 20, v. 4

LAMENTATIONS

22 How doth the city sit solitary, that was full of people!
Lamentations ch. 1, v. 1

23 Is it nothing to you, all ye that pass by? behold, and see if there be any sorrow like unto my sorrow.
Lamentations ch. 1, v. 12

24 And I said, My strength and my hope is perished from the Lord:
Remembering mine affliction and my misery, the wormwood and the gall.
Lamentations ch. 3, v. 18

25 It is good for a man that he bear the yoke in his youth.
Lamentations ch. 3, v. 27

26 He giveth his cheek to him that smiteth him.
Lamentations ch. 3, v. 30

27 O Lord, thou hast seen my wrong: judge thou my cause.
Lamentations ch. 4, v. 59

EZEKIEL

28 As is the mother, so is her daughter.
Ezekiel ch. 16, v. 44; cf. **Proverbs** 605:32

29 The fathers have eaten sour grapes, and the children's teeth are set on edge.
Ezekiel ch. 18, v. 2

30 When the wicked man turneth away from his wickedness that he hath committed, and doeth that which is lawful and right, he shall save his soul alive.
Ezekiel ch. 18, v. 27

31 The king of Babylon stood at the parting of the ways.
Ezekiel ch. 21, v. 21

32 The hand of the Lord was upon me, and carried me out in the spirit of the Lord, and set me down in the midst of the valley which was full of bones.
Ezekiel ch. 37, v. 1

33 Can these bones live?
Ezekiel ch. 37, v. 3

34 Again he said unto me, Prophesy upon these bones, and say unto them, O ye dry bones, hear the word of the Lord.
Ezekiel ch. 37, v. 4

DANIEL

1 To you it is commanded, O peoples, nations, and languages,
That at what time ye hear the sound of the cornet, flute, harp, sackbut, psaltery, dulcimer, and all kinds of music, ye fall down and worship the golden image that Nebuchadnezzar the king hath set up:
And whoso falleth not down and worshippeth shall the same hour be cast into the midst of a burning fiery furnace.
Daniel ch. 3, v. 4

2 Shadrach, Meshach, and Abed-nego, ye servants of the most high God, come forth and come hither.
Daniel ch. 3, v. 26

3 In the same hour came forth fingers of a man's hand, and wrote over against the candlestick upon the plaister of the wall of the king's palace.
Daniel ch. 5, v. 5

4 And this is the writing that was written, MENE, MENE, TEKEL, UPHARSIN.
This is the interpretation of the thing: MENE; God hath numbered thy kingdom, and finished it.
TEKEL; Thou art weighed in the balances and art found wanting.
PERES; Thy kingdom is divided, and given to the Medes and Persians.
Daniel ch. 5, v. 25

5 Now, O king, establish the decree, and sign the writing, that it be not changed, according to the law of the Medes and Persians, which altereth not.
Daniel ch. 6, v. 8

6 The Ancient of days did sit, whose garment was white as snow, and the hair of his head like the pure wool: his throne was like the fiery flame, and his wheels as burning fire.
A fiery stream issued and came forth from behind him: thousand thousands ministered unto him, and ten thousand times ten thousand stood before him: the judgement was set, and the books were opened.
Daniel ch. 7, v. 9

7 O Daniel, a man greatly beloved.
Daniel ch. 10, v. 11

8 Many shall run to and fro, and knowledge shall be increased.
Daniel ch. 12, v. 4

HOSEA

9 Like people, like priest.
Hosea ch. 4, v. 9; cf. **Proverbs** 605:33

10 They have sown the wind, and they shall reap the whirlwind.
Hosea ch. 8, v. 7; cf. **Proverbs** 612:36

11 I drew them . . . with bands of love.
Hosea ch. 11, v. 4

JOEL

12 That which the palmerworm hath left hath the locust eaten.
Joel ch. 1, v. 4

13 I will restore to you the years that the locust hath eaten, the cankerworm, and the caterpillar, and the palmerworm, my great army which I sent among you.
Joel ch. 2, v. 25

14 And it shall come to pass afterward, that I will pour out my spirit upon all flesh; and your sons and your daughters shall prophesy, your old men shall dream dreams, your young men shall see visions.
Joel ch. 2, v. 28

15 Multitudes, multitudes in the valley of decision: for the day of the Lord is near in the valley of decision.
Joel ch. 3, v. 14

AMOS

16 Can two walk together, except they be agreed?
Amos ch. 3, v. 3

17 Shall there be evil in a city, and the Lord hath not done it?
Amos ch. 3, v. 6

18 I have overthrown some of you, as God overthrew Sodom and Gomorrah, and ye were as a firebrand plucked out of the burning.
Amos ch. 4, v. 11

MICAH

19 But thou, Bethlehem Ephratah, though thou be little among the thousands of Judah, yet out of thee shall he come forth unto me that is to be ruler in Israel.
Micah ch. 5, v. 2

20 What doth the Lord require of thee, but to do justly, and to love mercy, and to walk humbly with thy God?
Micah ch. 6, v. 8

NAHUM

21 Woe to the bloody city! it is all full of lies and robbery; the prey departeth not.
Nahum ch. 3, v. 1

HABAKKUK

22 Write the vision, and make it plain upon tables, that he may run that readeth it.
Habakkuk ch. 2, v. 2

ZEPHANIAH

23 Woe to her that is filthy and polluted, to the oppressing city!
Zephaniah ch. 3, v. 1

HAGGAI

24 Ye have sown much, and bring in little; ye eat but ye have not enough . . . and he that earneth wages earneth wages to put it into a bag with holes.
Haggai ch. 1, v. 6

MALACHI

25 But unto you that fear my name shall the Sun of righteousness arise with healing in his wings.
Malachi ch. 4, v. 2; cf. **Wesley** 810:23

APOCRYPHA

26 The first wrote, Wine is the strongest. The second wrote, The king is strongest. The third wrote,

Women are strongest: but above all things Truth beareth away the victory.
I Esdras ch. 3, v. 10

1 Great is Truth, and mighty above all things.
I Esdras ch. 4, v. 41; cf. **Bible** 114:12

2 Nourish thy children, O thou good nurse; stablish their feet.
II Esdras ch. 2, v. 25

3 For the world has lost his youth, and the times begin to wax old.
II Esdras ch. 14, v. 10

4 I shall light a candle of understanding in thine heart, which shall not be put out.
II Esdras ch. 14, v. 25; cf. **Last words** 455:4

5 The ear of jealousy heareth all things.
Wisdom of Solomon ch. 1, v. 10

6 Let us crown ourselves with rosebuds, before they be withered.
Wisdom of Solomon ch. 2, v. 8

7 Through envy of the devil came death into the world.
Wisdom of Solomon ch. 2, v. 24

8 But the souls of the righteous are in the hand of God, and there shall no torment touch them.
In the sight of the unwise they seemed to die: and their departure is taken for misery,
And their going from us to be utter destruction: but they are in peace.
For though they be punished in the sight of men, yet is their hope full of immortality.
And having been a little chastised, they shall be greatly rewarded: for God proved them, and found them worthy for himself.
Wisdom of Solomon ch. 3, v. 1

9 And in the time of their visitation they shall shine, and run to and fro like sparks among the stubble.
Wisdom of Solomon ch. 3, v. 7

10 He, being made perfect in a short time, fulfilled a long time.
Wisdom of Solomon ch. 4, v. 13

11 We fools accounted his life madness, and his end to be without honour:
How is he numbered among the children of God, and his lot is among the saints!
Wisdom of Solomon ch. 5, v. 4

12 Even so we in like manner, as soon as we were born, began to draw to our end.
Wisdom of Solomon ch. 5, v. 13

13 For the hope of the ungodly . . . passeth away as the remembrance of a guest that tarrieth but a day.
Wisdom of Solomon ch. 5, v. 14

14 And love is the keeping of her laws; and the giving heed unto her laws is the assurance of incorruption.
Wisdom of Solomon ch. 6, v. 18

15 For the same things uttered in Hebrew, and translated into another tongue, have not the same force in them: and not only these things, but the law itself, and the prophets, and the rest of the books, have no small difference, when they are spoken in their own language.
Ecclesiasticus: The Prologue

16 For the Lord is full of compassion and mercy, long-suffering, and very pitiful, and forgiveth sins, and saveth in time of affliction.
Ecclesiasticus ch. 2, v. 11

17 We will fall into the hands of the Lord, and not into the hands of men: for as his majesty is, so is his mercy.
Ecclesiasticus ch. 2, v. 18

18 Be not curious in unnecessary matters: for more things are shewed unto thee than men understand.
Ecclesiasticus ch. 3, v. 23

19 Be not ignorant of any thing in a great matter or a small.
Ecclesiasticus ch. 5, v. 15

20 A faithful friend is the medicine of life.
Ecclesiasticus ch. 6, v. 16

21 Laugh no man to scorn in the bitterness of his soul.
Ecclesiasticus ch. 7, v. 11

22 Miss not the discourse of the elders.
Ecclesiasticus ch. 8, v. 9

23 Open not thine heart to every man.
Ecclesiasticus ch. 8, v. 19

24 Forsake not an old friend; for the new is not comparable to him; a new friend is as new wine; when it is old, thou shalt drink it with pleasure.
Ecclesiasticus ch. 9, v. 10

25 Many kings have sat down upon the ground; and one that was never thought of hath worn the crown.
Ecclesiasticus ch. 11, v. 5

26 Judge none blessed before his death.
Ecclesiasticus ch. 11, v. 28; cf. **Solon** 727:9

27 He that toucheth pitch shall be defiled therewith.
Ecclesiasticus ch. 13, v. 1; cf. **Proverbs** 602:17

28 For how agree the kettle and the earthen pot together?
Ecclesiasticus ch. 13, v. 2

29 When a rich man is fallen, he hath many helpers: he speaketh things not to be spoken, and yet men justify him: the poor man slipped, and yet they rebuked him too; he spake wisely, and could have no place.
Ecclesiasticus ch. 14, v. 22

30 When thou hast enough, remember the time of hunger.
Ecclesiasticus ch. 18, v. 25

31 Be not made a beggar by banqueting upon borrowing.
Ecclesiasticus ch. 18, v. 33

32 He that contemneth small things shall fall by little and little.
Ecclesiasticus ch. 19, v. 1

1 Neither [give] a wicked woman liberty to gad abroad.
Ecclesiasticus ch. 25, v. 25

2 A merchant shall hardly keep himself from doing wrong.
Ecclesiasticus ch. 26, v. 29

3 Many have fallen by the edge of the sword: but not so many as have fallen by the tongue.
Ecclesiasticus ch. 28, v. 18

4 And weigh thy words in a balance, and make a door and bar for thy mouth.
Ecclesiasticus ch. 28, v. 25

5 Envy and wrath shorten the life.
Ecclesiasticus ch. 30, v. 24

6 Leave off first for manners' sake.
Ecclesiasticus ch. 31, v. 17

7 Wine is as good as life to a man, if it be drunk moderately: what life is then to a man that is without wine? for it was made to make men glad.
Ecclesiasticus ch. 31, v. 27

8 Leave not a stain in thine honour.
Ecclesiasticus ch. 33, v. 22

9 Honour a physician with the honour due unto him for the uses which ye may have of him: for the Lord hath created him.
Ecclesiasticus ch. 38, v. 1

10 He that sinneth before his Maker, let him fall into the hand of the physician.
Ecclesiasticus ch. 38, v. 15

11 The wisdom of a learned man cometh by opportunity of leisure: and he that hath little business shall become wise.
Ecclesiasticus ch. 38, v. 24

12 How can he get wisdom . . . whose talk is of bullocks?
Ecclesiasticus ch. 38, v. 25

13 Let us now praise famous men, and our fathers that begat us.
Ecclesiasticus ch. 44, v. 1

14 Such as did bear rule in their kingdoms.
Ecclesiasticus ch. 44, v. 3

15 Such as found out musical tunes, and recited verses in writing:
Rich men furnished with ability, living peaceably in their habitations.
Ecclesiasticus ch. 44, v. 5

16 There be of them, that have left a name behind them.
Ecclesiasticus ch. 44, v. 8

17 And some there be, which have no memorial . . . and are become as though they had never been born . . .
But these were merciful men, whose righteousness hath not been forgotten . . .
Their seed shall remain for ever, and their glory shall not be blotted out.
Their bodies are buried in peace; but their name liveth for evermore.
Ecclesiasticus ch. 44, v. 9

18 As the flower of roses in the spring of the year, as lilies by the rivers of waters, and as the branches of the frankincense tree in the time of summer.
Ecclesiasticus ch. 50, v. 8

19 Get learning with a great sum of money, and get much gold by her.
Ecclesiasticus ch. 51, v. 28

20 It is a foolish thing to make a long prologue, and to be short in the story itself.
II Maccabees ch. 2, v. 32

21 When he was at the last gasp.
II Maccabees ch. 7, v. 9

NEW TESTAMENT: ST MATTHEW

22 There came wise men from the east to Jerusalem, Saying, Where is he that is born King of the Jews? for we have seen his star in the east, and are come to worship him.
St Matthew ch. 2, v. 1

23 They presented unto him gifts; gold, and frankincense, and myrrh.
St Matthew ch. 2, v. 11

24 They departed into their own country another way.
St Matthew ch. 2, v. 12

25 In Rama was there a voice heard, lamentation, and weeping, and great mourning, Rachel weeping for her children, and would not be comforted, because they are not.
referring to Jeremiah ch. 31, v. 15
St Matthew ch. 2, v. 18

26 Repent ye: for the kingdom of heaven is at hand.
St Matthew ch. 3, v. 2

27 The voice of one crying in the wilderness, Prepare ye the way of the Lord, make his paths straight.
St Matthew ch. 3, v. 3; cf. **Bible** 87:28

28 John had his raiment of camel's hair, and a leathern girdle about his loins; and his meat was locusts and wild honey.
St Matthew ch. 3, v. 4

29 O generation of vipers, who hath warned you to flee from the wrath to come?
St Matthew ch. 3, v. 7

30 And now also the axe is laid unto the root of the trees.
St Matthew ch. 3, v. 10

31 This is my beloved Son, in whom I am well pleased.
St Matthew ch. 3, v. 17

32 Man shall not live by bread alone, but by every word that proceedeth out of the mouth of God.
echoing Deuteronomy ch. 8, v. 3
St Matthew ch. 4, v. 4; cf. **Proverbs** 606:13

33 Thou shalt not tempt the Lord thy God.
echoing Deuteronomy ch. 6, v. 16
St Matthew ch. 4, v. 7

34 The devil taketh him up into an exceeding high mountain, and sheweth him all the kingdoms of the world, and the glory of them.
St Matthew ch. 4, v. 8

1 Angels came and ministered unto him.
St Matthew ch. 4, v. 11

2 Follow me, and I will make you fishers of men.
St Matthew ch. 4, v. 19

3 Blessed are the poor in spirit: for theirs is the kingdom of heaven.
Blessed are they that mourn: for they shall be comforted.
Blessed are the meek: for they shall inherit the earth.
Blessed are they which do hunger and thirst after righteousness: for they shall be filled.
Blessed are the merciful: for they shall obtain mercy.
Blessed are the pure in heart: for they shall see God.
Blessed are the peacemakers: for they shall be called the children of God.
St Matthew ch. 5, v. 3; cf. **Smith** 724:1

4 Ye are the salt of the earth: but if the salt have lost his savour, wherewith shall it be salted?
St Matthew ch. 5, v. 13

5 Ye are the light of the world. A city that is set on an hill cannot be hid.
St Matthew ch. 5, v. 14

6 Let your light so shine before men, that they may see your good works.
St Matthew ch. 5, v. 16

7 Think not that I am come to destroy the law, or the prophets: I am come not to destroy, but to fulfil.
St Matthew ch. 5, v. 17

8 Except your righteousness shall exceed the righteousness of the scribes and Pharisees, ye shall in no case enter into the kingdom of heaven.
St Matthew ch. 5, v. 20

9 Whosoever shall say, Thou fool, shall be in danger of hell fire.
St Matthew ch. 5, v. 22

10 Till thou hast paid the uttermost farthing.
St Matthew ch. 5, v. 26

11 Swear not at all; neither by heaven; for it is God's throne:
Nor by the earth; for it is his footstool.
St Matthew ch. 5, v. 34

12 Resist not evil: but whosoever shall smite thee on thy right cheek, turn to him the other also.
St Matthew ch. 5, v. 39

13 Whosoever shall compel thee to go a mile, go with him twain.
St Matthew ch. 5, v. 41

14 He maketh his sun to rise on the evil and on the good, and sendeth rain on the just and on the unjust.
St Matthew ch. 5, v. 45; cf. **Bowen** 145:20

15 For if ye love them which love you, what reward have ye? do not even the publicans the same?
St Matthew ch. 5, v. 46

16 Be ye therefore perfect, even as your Father which is in heaven is perfect.
St Matthew ch. 5, v. 48

17 When thou doest alms, let not thy left hand know what thy right hand doeth.
That thine alms may be in secret: and thy Father which seeth in secret himself shall reward you openly.
St Matthew ch. 6, v. 3

18 Use not vain repetitions, as the heathen do: for they think that they shall be heard for their much speaking.
St Matthew ch. 6, v. 7

19 After this manner therefore pray ye: Our Father which art in heaven, Hallowed be thy name.
Thy kingdom come. Thy will be done in earth, as it is in heaven.
Give us this day our daily bread.
And forgive us our debts, as we forgive our debtors.
And lead us not into temptation, but deliver us from evil: For thine is the kingdom, and the power, and the glory, for ever. Amen.
St Matthew ch. 6, v. 9; cf. **Book of Common Prayer** 125:18, **Missal** 522:17

20 Lay not up for yourselves treasures upon earth, where moth and rust doth corrupt, and where thieves break through and steal:
But lay up for yourselves treasures in heaven.
St Matthew ch. 6, v. 19

21 Where your treasure is, there will your heart be also.
St Matthew ch. 6, v. 21

22 No man can serve two masters . . . Ye cannot serve God and mammon.
St Matthew ch. 6, v. 24; cf. **Proverbs** 607:47

23 Is not the life more than meat, and the body than raiment?
Behold the fowls of the air: for they sow not, neither do they reap, nor gather into barns.
St Matthew ch. 6, v. 25

24 Which of you by taking thought can add one cubit unto his stature?
St Matthew ch. 6, v. 27

25 Consider the lilies of the field, how they grow; they toil not, neither do they spin:
And yet I say unto you, That even Solomon in all his glory was not arrayed like one of these.
St Matthew ch. 6, v. 28

26 Seek ye first the kingdom of God, and his righteousness; and all these things shall be added unto you.
St Matthew ch. 6, v. 33

27 Take therefore no thought for the morrow: for the morrow shall take thought for the things of itself. Sufficient unto the day is the evil thereof.
St Matthew ch. 6, v. 34; cf. **Proverbs** 611:34

28 Judge not, that ye be not judged.
St Matthew ch. 7, v. 1; cf. **Proverbs** 604:46

1 Why beholdest thou the mote that is in thy brother's eye, but considerest not the beam that is in thine own eye?
St Matthew ch. 7, v. 3

2 Neither cast ye your pearls before swine.
St Matthew ch. 7, v. 6; cf. **Proverbs** 598:29

3 Ask, and it shall be given you; seek, and ye shall find; knock, and it shall be opened unto you.
St Matthew ch. 7, v. 7; cf. **Proverbs** 610:28

4 Every one that asketh receiveth; and he that seeketh findeth.
St Matthew ch. 7, v. 8

5 Or what man is there of you, whom if his son ask bread, will he give him a stone?
St Matthew ch. 7, v. 9

6 Therefore all things whatsoever ye would that men should do to you, do ye even so to them: for this is the law and the prophets.
St Matthew ch. 7, v. 12

7 Wide is the gate, and broad is the way, that leadeth to destruction, and many there be that go in thereat.
St Matthew ch. 7, v. 13

8 Strait is the gate, and narrow is the way, which leadeth unto life, and few there be that find it.
St Matthew ch. 7, v. 14

9 Beware of false prophets, which come to you in sheep's clothing, but inwardly they are ravening wolves.
St Matthew ch. 7, v. 15

10 Do men gather grapes of thorns, or figs of thistles?
St Matthew ch. 7, v. 16

11 By their fruits ye shall know them.
St Matthew ch. 7, v. 20

12 The winds blew, and beat upon that house; and it fell not: for it was founded upon a rock.
St Matthew ch. 7, v. 25

13 Every one that heareth these sayings of mine, and doeth them not, shall be likened unto a foolish man, which built his house upon the sand:
And the rain descended, and the floods came, and the winds blew, and beat upon that house; and it fell: and great was the fall of it.
St Matthew ch. 7, v. 27

14 For he taught them as one having authority, and not as the scribes.
St Matthew ch. 7, v. 29

15 Lord I am not worthy that thou shouldest come under my roof.
St Matthew ch. 8, v. 8; cf. **Missal** 522:20

16 I am a man under authority, having soldiers under me: and I say to this man, Go, and he goeth; and to another, Come, and he cometh; and to my servant, Do this, and he doeth it.
St Matthew ch. 8, v. 9

17 I have not found so great faith, no, not in Israel.
St Matthew ch. 8, v. 10

18 But the children of the kingdom shall be cast out into outer darkness: there shall be weeping and gnashing of teeth.
St Matthew ch. 8, v. 12

19 The foxes have holes, and the birds of the air have nests; but the Son of man hath not where to lay his head.
St Matthew ch. 8, v. 20

20 Let the dead bury their dead.
St Matthew ch. 8, v. 22; cf. **Longfellow** 474:5, **Proverbs** 605:21

21 The whole herd of swine ran violently down a steep place into the sea, and perished in the waters.
St Matthew ch. 8, v. 32

22 He saw a man, named Matthew, sitting at the receipt of custom: and he saith unto him, Follow me. And he arose and followed him.
St Matthew ch. 9, v. 9

23 Why eateth your Master with publicans and sinners?
St Matthew ch. 9, v. 11

24 They that be whole need not a physician, but they that are sick.
St Matthew ch. 9, v. 12

25 I am not come to call the righteous, but sinners to repentance.
St Matthew ch. 9, v. 13

26 Neither do men put new wine into old bottles.
St Matthew ch. 9, v. 17; cf. **Proverbs** 615:29

27 Thy faith hath made thee whole.
St Matthew ch. 9, v. 22

28 The maid is not dead, but sleepeth.
St Matthew ch. 9, v. 24

29 He casteth out devils through the prince of the devils.
St Matthew ch. 9, v. 34

30 The harvest truly is plenteous, but the labourers are few.
St Matthew ch. 9, v. 37

31 Go rather to the lost sheep of the house of Israel.
St Matthew ch. 10, v. 6

32 Freely ye have received, freely give.
St Matthew ch. 10, v. 8

33 When ye depart out of that house or city, shake off the dust of your feet.
St Matthew ch. 10, v. 14

34 Be ye therefore wise as serpents, and harmless as doves.
St Matthew ch. 10, v. 16

35 The disciple is not above his master, nor the servant above his lord.
St Matthew ch. 10, v. 24

36 Are not two sparrows sold for a farthing? and one of them shall not fall on the ground without your Father.
The very hairs of your head are all numbered.
Fear ye not therefore, ye are of more value than many sparrows.
St Matthew ch. 10, v. 29; cf. **Bible** 99:20

1 I came not to send peace, but a sword.
St Matthew ch. 10, v. 34

2 A man's foes shall be they of his own household.
St Matthew ch. 10, v. 36

3 He that findeth his life shall lose it: and he that loseth his life for my sake shall find it.
St Matthew ch. 10, v. 39

4 Whosoever shall give to drink unto one of these little ones a cup of cold water only in the name of a disciple, verily I say unto you, he shall in no wise lose his reward.
St Matthew ch. 10, v. 42

5 Art thou he that should come, or do we look for another?
St Matthew ch. 11, v. 3

6 What went ye out into the wilderness to see? A reed shaken with the wind?
But what went ye out for to see? A man clothed in soft raiment? . . .
But what went ye out for to see? A prophet? yea, I say unto you, and more than a prophet.
St Matthew ch. 11, v. 7

7 We have piped unto you, and ye have not danced; we have mourned unto you, and ye have not lamented.
St Matthew ch. 11, v. 17

8 Wisdom is justified of her children.
St Matthew ch. 11, v. 19

9 Come unto me, all ye that labour and are heavy laden, and I will give you rest.
Take my yoke upon you, and learn of me; for I am meek and lowly in heart: and ye shall find rest unto your souls.
For my yoke is easy, and my burden is light.
St Matthew ch. 11, v. 28

10 He that is not with me is against me.
St Matthew ch. 12, v. 30 and St Luke ch. 11, v. 23

11 The blasphemy against the Holy Ghost shall not be forgiven unto men.
St Matthew ch. 12, v. 31

12 The tree is known by his fruit.
St Matthew ch. 12, v. 33; cf. **Proverbs** 613:17

13 Out of the abundance of the heart the mouth speaketh.
St Matthew ch. 12, v. 34; cf. **Proverbs** 609:16

14 Every idle word that men shall speak, they shall give account thereof in the day of judgement.
St Matthew ch. 12, v. 36

15 An evil and adulterous generation seeketh after a sign.
St Matthew ch. 12, v. 39

16 Behold, a greater than Solomon is here.
St Matthew ch. 12, v. 42

17 When the unclean spirit is gone out of a man, he walketh through dry places, seeking rest, and findeth none.
Then he saith, I will return into my house from whence I came out; and when he is come, he findeth it empty, swept, and garnished.
St Matthew ch. 12, v. 43

18 Then goeth he, and taketh with himself seven other spirits more wicked than himself, and they enter in and dwell there: and the last state of that man is worse than the first.
St Matthew ch. 12, v. 45

19 Behold my mother and my brethren!
St Matthew ch. 12, v. 49

20 Behold, a sower went forth to sow;
And when he sowed, some seeds fell by the wayside, and the fowls came and devoured them up:
Some fell upon stony places, where they had not much earth: and forthwith they sprung up, because they had no deepness of earth:
And when the sun was up, they were scorched; and because they had no root, they withered away.
And some fell among thorns; and the thorns sprang up and choked them:
But other fell into good ground, and brought forth fruit, some an hundredfold, some sixtyfold, some thirtyfold.
St Matthew ch. 13, v. 3

21 He also that received the seed among the thorns is he that heareth the word; and the care of this world, and the deceitfulness of riches, choke the word, and he becometh unfruitful.
St Matthew ch. 13, v. 22

22 The kingdom of heaven is like to a grain of mustard seed, which a man took, and sowed in his field:
Which indeed is the least of all seeds: but when it is grown, it is the greatest among herbs, and becometh a tree, so that the birds of the air come and lodge in the branches thereof.
St Matthew ch. 13, v. 31

23 The kingdom of heaven is like unto a merchant man, seeking goodly pearls:
Who, when he had found one pearl of great price, went and sold all that he had, and bought it.
St Matthew ch. 13, v. 45

24 A prophet is not without honour, save in his own country, and in his own house.
St Matthew ch. 13, v. 57; cf. **Proverbs** 609:46

25 In the fourth watch of the night Jesus went unto them, walking on the sea.
St Matthew ch. 14, v. 25

26 Be of good cheer; it is I; be not afraid.
St Matthew ch. 14, v. 27

27 O thou of little faith, wherefore didst thou doubt?
St Matthew ch. 14, v. 31

28 Not that which goeth into the mouth defileth a man; but that which cometh out of the mouth, this defileth a man.
St Matthew ch. 15, v. 11

29 They be blind leaders of the blind. And if the blind lead the blind, both shall fall into the ditch.
St Matthew ch. 15, v. 14; cf. **Proverbs** 614:25

1 Truth, Lord: yet the dogs eat of the crumbs which fall from their masters' table.
St Matthew ch. 15, v. 27

2 When it is evening, ye say, It will be fair weather: for the sky is red.
St Matthew ch. 16, v. 2

3 Ye can discern the face of the sky; but can ye not discern the signs of the times?
St Matthew ch. 16, v. 3

4 Thou art Peter, and upon this rock I will build my church; and the gates of hell shall not prevail against it.
St Matthew ch. 16, v. 18

5 Get thee behind me, Satan.
St Matthew ch. 16, v. 23

6 If ye have faith as a grain of mustard seed, ye shall say unto this mountain, Remove hence to yonder place; and it shall remove.
St Matthew ch. 17, v. 20; cf. **Proverbs** 600:10

7 Except ye be converted, and become as little children, ye shall not enter into the kingdom of heaven.
St Matthew ch. 18, v. 3

8 Whoso shall receive one such little child in my name receiveth me.
But whoso shall offend one of these little ones which believe in me, it were better for him that a millstone were hanged about his neck, and that he were drowned in the depth of the sea.
St Matthew ch. 18, v. 5

9 If thine eye offend thee, pluck it out, and cast it from thee: it is better for thee to enter into life with one eye, rather than having two eyes to be cast into hell fire.
St Matthew ch. 18, v. 9

10 For where two or three are gathered together in my name, there am I in the midst of them.
St Matthew ch. 18, v. 20

11 Lord, how oft shall my brother sin against me, and I forgive him? till seven times?
Jesus saith unto him I say not unto thee, Until seven times: but Until seventy times seven.
St Matthew ch. 18, v. 21

12 What therefore God hath joined together, let not man put asunder.
St Matthew ch. 19, v. 6; cf. **Book of Common Prayer** 131:7

13 If thou wilt be perfect, go and sell that thou hast, and give to the poor, and thou shalt have treasure in heaven.
St Matthew ch. 19, v. 21

14 He went away sorrowful: for he had great possessions.
St Matthew ch. 19, v. 22

15 It is easier for a camel to go through the eye of a needle, than for a rich man to enter into the kingdom of God.
St Matthew ch. 19, v. 24. See also St Luke ch. 18, v. 24

16 With men this is impossible; but with God all things are possible.
St Matthew ch. 19, v. 26; cf. **Proverbs** 595:4

17 But many that are first shall be last; and the last shall be first.
St Matthew ch. 19, v. 30

18 These last have wrought but one hour, and thou hast made them equal unto us, which have borne the burden and heat of the day.
St Matthew ch. 20, v. 12

19 I will give unto this last, even as unto thee.
Is it not lawful for me to do what I will with mine own?
St Matthew ch. 20, v. 14

20 It is written, My house shall be called the house of prayer; but ye have made it a den of thieves.
St Matthew ch. 21, v. 13; cf. **Bible** 88:25

21 For many are called, but few are chosen.
St Matthew ch. 22, v. 14; cf. **Proverbs** 606:25

22 Render therefore unto Caesar the things which are Caesar's; and unto God the things that are God's.
St Matthew ch. 22, v. 21; cf. **Crashaw** 244:13

23 For in the resurrection they neither marry, nor are given in marriage.
St Matthew ch. 22, v. 30

24 Thou shalt love the Lord thy God with all thy heart, and with all thy soul, and with all thy mind.
This is the first and great commandment.
And the second is like unto it, Thou shalt love thy neighbour as thyself.
St Matthew ch. 22, v. 38; cf. **Bible** 76:23

25 They make broad their phylacteries, and enlarge the borders of their garments,
And love the uppermost rooms at feasts, and the chief seats in the synagogues.
St Matthew ch. 23, v. 5

26 Woe unto you, scribes and Pharisees, hypocrites! for ye pay tithe of mint and anise and cummin, and have omitted the weightier matters of the law, judgement, mercy, and faith: these ought ye to have done, and not to leave the other undone.
St Matthew ch. 23, v. 23

27 Ye blind guides, which strain at a gnat, and swallow a camel.
St Matthew ch. 23, v. 24

28 Ye are like unto whited sepulchres, which indeed appear beautiful outward, but are within full of dead men's bones, and of all uncleanness.
St Matthew ch. 23, v. 27

29 O Jerusalem, Jerusalem, thou that killest the prophets, and stonest them which are sent unto thee, how often would I have gathered thy children together, even as a hen gathereth her chickens under her wings, and ye would not!
St Matthew ch. 23, v. 37

30 Ye shall hear of wars and rumours of wars: see that ye be not troubled: for all these things must come to pass but the end is not yet.
St Matthew ch. 24, v. 6

1 For nation shall rise against nation, and kingdom against kingdom.
St Matthew ch. 24, v. 7

2 When ye therefore shall see the abomination of desolation, spoken of by Daniel the prophet, stand in the holy place.
referring to Daniel ch. 12, v. 11
St Matthew ch. 24, v. 15

3 Wheresoever the carcase is, there will the eagles be gathered together.
St Matthew ch. 24, v. 28; cf. **Proverbs** 614:39

4 Heaven and earth shall pass away, but my words shall not pass away.
St Matthew ch. 24, v. 35

5 For as in the days that were before the flood they were eating and drinking, marrying and giving in marriage, until the day that Noe entered into the ark,
And knew not until the flood came, and took them all away; so shall also the coming of the Son of Man be.
St Matthew ch. 24, v. 38

6 One shall be taken, and the other left.
St Matthew ch. 24, v. 40

7 Watch therefore: for ye know not what hour your Lord doth come.
St Matthew ch. 24, v. 42

8 Well done, thou good and faithful servant: thou hast been faithful over a few things, I will make thee a ruler over many things: enter thou into the joy of thy lord.
St Matthew ch. 25, v. 21

9 Lord, I knew thee that thou art an hard man, reaping where thou hast not sown, and gathering where thou hast not strawed.
St Matthew ch. 25, v. 24

10 Unto every one that hath shall be given, and he shall have abundance: but from him that hath not shall be taken away even that which he hath.
St Matthew ch. 25, v. 29

11 And he shall set the sheep on his right hand, but the goats on the left.
St Matthew ch. 25, v. 33

12 For I was an hungred, and ye gave me meat: I was thirsty and ye gave me drink: I was a stranger, and ye took me in:
Naked, and ye clothed me: I was sick, and ye visited me: I was in prison, and ye came unto me.
St Matthew ch. 25, v. 35

13 Inasmuch as ye have done it unto one of the least of these my brethren, ye have done it unto me.
St Matthew ch. 25, v. 40

14 There came unto him a woman having an alabaster box of very precious ointment, and poured it on his head, as he sat at meat.
St Matthew ch. 26, v. 7

15 To what purpose is this waste?
For this ointment might have been sold for much, and given to the poor.
St John ch. 12, v. 5 attributes this to Judas Iscariot
St Matthew ch. 26, v. 8

16 What will ye give me, and I will deliver him unto you? And they covenanted with him [Judas Iscariot] for thirty pieces of silver.
St Matthew ch. 26, v. 15

17 It had been good for that man if he had not been born.
St Matthew ch. 26, v. 24

18 Jesus took bread, and blessed it, and brake it, and gave it to the disciples, and said, Take, eat; this is my body.
St Matthew ch. 26, v. 26

19 This night, before the cock crow, thou shalt deny me thrice.
to St Peter
St Matthew ch. 26, v. 34

20 Though I should die with thee, yet will I not deny thee.
said by St Peter
St Matthew ch. 26, v. 35

21 If it be possible, let this cup pass from me.
St Matthew ch. 26, v. 39

22 What, could ye not watch with me one hour?
St Matthew ch. 26, v. 40

23 Watch and pray, that ye enter not into temptation: the spirit indeed is willing but the flesh is weak.
St Matthew ch. 26, v. 41

24 Friend, wherefore art thou come?
St Matthew ch. 26, v. 50

25 All they that take the sword shall perish with the sword.
St Matthew ch. 26, v. 52; cf. **Proverbs** 602:30

26 Thy speech bewrayeth thee.
Then began he [St Peter] to curse and to swear, saying, I know not the man. And immediately the cock crew.
St Matthew ch. 26, v. 73

27 He [Pilate] took water, and washed his hands before the multitude, saying, I am innocent of the blood of this just person: see ye to it.
St Matthew ch. 27, v. 24

28 He saved others; himself he cannot save.
St Matthew ch. 27, v. 42

29 Eli, Eli, lama sabachthani? . . . My God, my God, why hast thou forsaken me?
St Matthew ch. 27, v. 46; cf. **Book of Common Prayer** 132:21

30 And, lo, I am with you alway, even unto the end of the world.
St Matthew ch. 28, v. 20

ST MARK

31 The sabbath was made for man, and not man for the sabbath.
St Mark ch. 2, v. 27

1 How can Satan cast out Satan?
St Mark ch. 3, v. 23; cf. **Sorley** 728:20

2 If a house be divided against itself, that house cannot stand.
St Mark ch. 3, v. 25; cf. **Lincoln** 468:5, **Proverbs** 603:3

3 He that hath ears to hear, let him hear.
St Mark ch. 4, v. 9

4 With what measure ye mete, it shall be measured to you.
St Mark ch. 4, v. 24

5 My name is Legion: for we are many.
St Mark ch. 5, v. 9

6 Jesus, immediately knowing in himself that virtue had gone out of him, turned him about in the press, and said, Who touched my clothes?
St Mark ch. 5, v. 30

7 I see men as trees, walking.
St Mark ch. 8, v. 24

8 For what shall it profit a man, if he shall gain the whole world, and lose his own soul?
St Mark ch. 8, v. 36; cf. **Bolt** 124:21

9 Lord, I believe; help thou mine unbelief.
St Mark ch. 9, v. 24

10 Suffer the little children to come unto me, and forbid them not: for of such is the kingdom of God.
St Mark ch. 10, v. 14

11 Beware of the scribes, which love to go in long clothing, and love salutations in the marketplaces,
And the chief seats in the synagogues, and the uppermost rooms at feasts:
Which devour widows' houses, and for a pretence make long prayers.
St Mark ch. 12, v. 38

12 And there came a certain poor widow, and she threw in two mites.
St Mark ch. 12, v. 42

13 Watch ye therefore: for ye know not when the master of the house cometh . . . Lest coming suddenly he find you sleeping.
St Mark ch. 13, v. 35

14 Go ye into all the world, and preach the gospel to every creature.
St Mark ch. 16, v. 15

ST LUKE

15 Hail, thou that art highly favoured, the Lord is with thee: blessed art thou among women.
the angel to the Virgin Mary
St Luke ch. 1, v. 28; cf. **Prayers** 592:1

16 And Mary said,
My soul doth magnify the Lord,
And my spirit hath rejoiced in God my Saviour.
For he hath regarded the low estate of his handmaiden: for, behold, from henceforth all generations shall call me blessed.
known as the Magnificat; beginning 'Tell out my soul, the greatness of the Lord' in New English Bible
St Luke ch. 1, v. 46; cf. **Bible** 114:3

17 He hath shewed strength with his arm; he hath scattered the proud in the imagination of their hearts.
He hath put down the mighty from their seats, and exalted them of low degree.
He hath filled the hungry with good things; and the rich he hath sent empty away.
the Magnificat
St Luke ch. 1, v. 51

18 To give light to them that sit in darkness and in the shadow of death, to guide our feet into the way of peace.
St Luke ch. 1, v. 79

19 And it came to pass in those days, that there went out a decree from Caesar Augustus, that all the world should be taxed.
St Luke ch. 2, v. 1

20 She brought forth her firstborn son, and wrapped him in swaddling clothes, and laid him in a manger; because there was no room for them in the inn.
And there were in the same country shepherds abiding in the field, keeping watch over their flock by night.
And, lo, the angel of the Lord came upon them, and the glory of the Lord shone round about them: and they were sore afraid.
St Luke ch. 2, v. 7

21 Behold, I bring you good tidings of great joy.
the angel to the shepherds
St Luke ch. 2, v. 10

22 Glory to God in the highest, and on earth peace, good will toward men.
the angels to the shepherds
St Luke ch. 2, v. 14; cf. **Missal** 520:13

23 But Mary kept all these things, and pondered them in her heart.
St Luke ch. 2, v. 19

24 Lord, now lettest thou thy servant depart in peace, according to thy word.
said by Simeon
St Luke ch. 2, v. 29; cf. **Bible** 114:5

25 A light to lighten the Gentiles, and the glory of thy people Israel.
said by Simeon
St Luke ch. 2, v. 32

26 Yea, a sword shall pierce through thy own soul also.
said by Simeon to the Virgin Mary
St Luke ch. 2, v. 35

27 Wist ye not that I must be about my Father's business?
St Luke ch. 2, v. 49

28 And the devil, taking him up into a high mountain, shewed unto him all the kingdoms of the world in a moment of time.
St Luke ch. 4, v. 5

29 Physician, heal thyself.
St Luke ch. 4, v. 23; cf. **Proverbs** 609:25

1 Master, we have toiled all the night, and have taken nothing: nevertheless at thy word I will let down the net.
said by St Peter
St Luke ch. 5, v. 5

2 No man . . . having drunk old wine straightway desireth new: for he saith, The old is better.
St Luke ch. 5, v. 39

3 Woe unto you, when all men shall speak well of you!
St Luke ch. 6, v. 26

4 Love your enemies, do good to them which hate you.
St Luke ch. 6, v. 27

5 Give, and it shall be given unto you; good measure, pressed down, and shaken together, and running over, shall men give into your bosom.
St Luke ch. 6, v. 38

6 Her sins, which are many, are forgiven; for she loved much.
St Luke ch. 7, v. 47

7 No man, having put his hand to the plough, and looking back, is fit for the kingdom of God.
St Luke ch. 9, v. 62

8 For the labourer is worthy of his hire.
St Luke ch. 10, v. 7; cf. **Proverbs** 605:8

9 I beheld Satan as lightning fall from heaven.
St Luke ch. 10, v. 18

10 Blessed are the eyes which see the things which ye see:
For I tell you, that many prophets and kings have desired to see those things which ye see, and have not seen them; and to hear those things which ye hear, and have not heard them.
St Luke ch. 10, v. 23

11 A certain man went down from Jerusalem to Jericho, and fell among thieves.
St Luke ch. 10, v. 30

12 He passed by on the other side.
St Luke ch. 10, v. 31

13 He took out two pence, and gave them to the host, and said unto him, Take care of him; and whatsoever thou spend more, when I come again, I will repay thee.
St Luke ch. 10, v. 35

14 Go, and do thou likewise.
St Luke ch. 10, v. 37

15 But Martha was cumbered about much serving, and came to him, and said, Lord, dost thou not care that my sister hath left me to serve alone? bid her therefore that she help me.
St Luke ch. 10, v. 40

16 Mary hath chosen that good part, which shall not be taken away from her.
St Luke ch. 10, v. 42

17 When a strong man armed keepeth his palace, his goods are in peace. But when a stronger than he shall come upon him, and overcome him, he taketh from him all his armour wherein he trusted, and divideth his spoils.
St Luke ch. 11, v. 21

18 No man, when he hath lighted a candle, putteth it in a secret place, neither under a bushel, but on a candlestick, that they which come in may see the light.
St Luke ch. 11, v. 33

19 Woe unto you, lawyers! for ye have taken away the key of knowledge.
St Luke ch. 11, v. 52

20 Are not five sparrows sold for two farthings, and not one of them is forgotten before God?
St Luke ch. 12, v. 6; cf. **Bible** 94:36

21 Soul, thou hast much goods laid up for many years; take thine ease, eat, drink, and be merry.
St Luke ch. 12, v. 19; cf. **Bible** 84:19, 87:9

22 Thou fool, this night thy soul shall be required of thee.
St Luke ch. 12, v. 20

23 Let your loins be girded about, and your lights burning.
St Luke ch. 12, v. 35

24 When thou art bidden of any man to a wedding, sit not down in the highest room; lest a more honourable man than thou be bidden of him;
And he that bade thee and him come and say to thee, Give this man place; and thou begin with shame to take the lowest room.
St Luke ch. 14, v. 8

25 Friend, go up higher.
St Luke ch. 14, v. 10

26 For whosoever exalteth himself shall be abased; and he that humbleth himself shall be exalted.
St Matthew ch. 23, v. 12 is similar
St Luke ch. 14, v. 11

27 They all with one consent began to make excuse . . . I pray thee have me excused.
St Luke ch. 14, v. 18

28 I have married a wife, and therefore I cannot come.
St Luke ch. 14, v. 20

29 Go out quickly into the streets and lanes of the city, and bring in hither the poor, and the maimed, and the halt, and the blind.
St Luke ch. 14, v. 21

30 Go out into the highways and hedges, and compel them to come in.
St Luke ch. 14, v. 23

31 For which of you, intending to build a tower, sitteth not down first, and counteth the cost, whether he have sufficient to finish it?
St Luke ch. 14, v. 28

32 Leave the ninety and nine in the wilderness.
St Luke ch. 15, v. 4

33 Rejoice with me; for I have found my sheep which was lost.
St Luke ch. 15, v. 6

1 Joy shall be in heaven over one sinner that repenteth, more than over ninety and nine just persons, which need no repentance.
St Luke ch. 15, v. 7

2 The younger son gathered all together, and took his journey into a far country, and there wasted his substance with riotous living.
St Luke ch. 15, v. 13

3 He would fain have filled his belly with the husks that the swine did eat: and no man gave unto him.
And when he came to himself, he said, How many hired servants of my father's have bread enough and to spare, and I perish with hunger!
St Luke ch. 15, v. 16

4 I will arise and go to my father, and will say unto him, Father, I have sinned against heaven, and before thee,
And am no more worthy to be called thy son: make me as one of thy hired servants.
St Luke ch. 15, v. 18

5 Bring hither the fatted calf, and kill it.
St Luke ch. 15, v. 23

6 This my son was dead, and is alive again; he was lost, and is found.
St Luke ch. 15, v. 24

7 And the Lord commended the unjust steward, because he had done wisely: for the children of this world are in their generation wiser than the children of light.
St Luke ch. 16, v. 8

8 Make to yourselves friends of the mammon of unrighteousness; that, when ye fail, they may receive you into everlasting habitations.
St Luke ch. 16, v. 9

9 He that is faithful in that which is least is faithful also in much.
St Luke ch. 16, v. 10

10 There was a certain rich man, which was clothed in purple and fine linen, and fared sumptuously every day:
And there was a certain beggar named Lazarus, which was laid at his gate, full of sores,
And desiring to be fed with the crumbs which fell from the rich man's table: moreover the dogs licked his sores.
And it came to pass that the beggar died, and was carried by the angels into Abraham's bosom.
St Luke ch. 16, v. 19

11 Between us and you there is a great gulf fixed.
St Luke ch. 16, v. 26

12 The kingdom of God is within you.
St Luke ch. 17, v. 21

13 Remember Lot's wife.
St Luke ch. 17, v. 32

14 Men ought always to pray, and not to faint.
St Luke ch. 18, v. 1

15 God, I thank thee, that I am not as other men are.
St Luke ch. 18, v. 11

16 God be merciful to me a sinner.
St Luke ch. 18, v. 13

17 Out of thine own mouth will I judge thee.
St Luke ch. 19, v. 22

18 If these should hold their peace, the stones would immediately cry out.
St Luke ch. 19, v. 40

19 If thou hadst known, even thou, at least in this thy day, the things which belong unto thy peace! but now they are hid from thine eyes.
St Luke ch. 19, v. 42

20 And when they heard it, they said, God forbid.
St Luke ch. 20, v. 16

21 He shall show you a large upper room furnished.
St Luke ch. 22, v. 12

22 I am among you as he that serveth.
St Luke ch. 22, v. 27

23 Nevertheless, not my will, but thine, be done.
St Luke ch. 22, v. 42

24 And the Lord turned, and looked upon Peter.
St Luke ch. 22, v. 61

25 For if they do these things in a green tree, what shall be done in the dry?
St Luke ch. 23, v. 31

26 Father, forgive them: for they know not what they do.
St Luke ch. 23, v. 34

27 Lord, remember me when thou comest into thy kingdom.
said by the Penitent Thief
St Luke ch. 23, v. 42

28 To day shalt thou be with me in paradise.
to the Penitent Thief
St Luke ch. 23, v. 43

29 Father, into thy hands I commend my spirit.
St Luke ch. 23, v. 46; cf. **Book of Common Prayer** 133:16

30 He was a good man, and a just.
of Joseph of Arimathea
St Luke ch. 23, v. 50

31 Why seek ye the living among the dead?
St Luke ch. 24, v. 5

32 Their words seemed to them as idle tales.
St Luke ch. 24, v. 11

33 Abide with us: for it is toward evening, and the day is far spent.
St Luke ch. 24, v. 29; cf. **Lyte** 480:23

34 Did not our heart burn within us, while he talked with us by the way?
the disciples on the road to Emmaus
St Luke ch. 24, v. 32

35 He was known of them in breaking of bread.
St Luke ch. 24, v. 35

36 They gave him a piece of a broiled fish, and of an honeycomb.
St Luke ch. 24, v. 42

ST JOHN

1 In the beginning was the Word, and the Word was with God, and the Word was God.
St John ch. 1, v. 1; cf. **Missal** 522:22

2 All things were made by him; and without him was not any thing made that was made.
St John ch. 1, v. 3

3 And the light shineth in darkness; and the darkness comprehended it not.
St John ch. 1, v. 5

4 There was a man sent from God, whose name was John.
St John ch. 1, v. 6

5 He was not that Light, but was sent to bear witness of that Light.
That was the true Light, which lighteth every man that cometh into the world.
St John ch. 1, v. 8

6 He was in the world, and the world was made by him, and the world knew him not.
He came unto his own, and his own received him not.
St John ch. 1, v. 10

7 And the Word was made flesh, and dwelt among us, (and we beheld his glory, the glory as of the only begotten of the Father), full of grace and truth.
St John ch. 1, v. 14; cf. **Missal** 523:1

8 No man hath seen God at any time.
St John ch. 1, v. 18

9 I baptize with water: but there standeth one among you, whom ye know not;
He it is, who coming after me is preferred before me, whose shoe's latchet I am not worthy to unloose.
said by St John the Baptist
St John ch. 1, v. 26

10 Behold the Lamb of God, which taketh away the sin of the world.
St John ch. 1, v. 29; cf. **Missal** 522:19

11 Can there any good thing come out of Nazareth?
St John ch. 1, v. 46

12 Behold an Israelite indeed, in whom is no guile!
St John ch. 1, v. 47

13 Woman, what have I to do with thee? mine hour is not yet come.
St John ch. 2, v. 4

14 Every man at the beginning doth set forth good wine; and when men have well drunk, then that which is worse: but thou hast kept the good wine until now.
St John ch. 2, v. 10

15 When he had made a scourge of small cords, he drove them all out of the temple.
St John ch. 2, v. 15

16 Verily, verily, I say unto thee, Except a man be born again, he cannot see the kingdom of God.
St John ch. 3, v. 3

17 The wind bloweth where it listeth, and thou hearest the sound thereof, but canst not tell whence it cometh, and whither it goeth.
St John ch. 3, v. 8

18 God so loved the world, that he gave his only begotten Son, that whosoever believeth in him should not perish, but have everlasting life.
St John ch. 3, v. 16

19 Men loved darkness rather than light, because their deeds were evil.
St John ch. 3, v. 19

20 God is a Spirit: and they that worship him must worship him in spirit and in truth.
St John ch. 4, v. 24

21 Except ye see signs and wonders, ye will not believe.
St John ch. 4, v. 48

22 Rise, take up thy bed, and walk.
St John ch. 5, v. 8

23 He was a burning and a shining light.
St John ch. 5, v. 35

24 Search the scriptures; for in them ye think ye have eternal life: and they are which testify of me.
St John ch. 5, v. 39

25 There is a lad here, which hath five barley loaves, and two small fishes: but what are they among so many?
St John ch. 6, v. 9

26 Gather up the fragments that remain, that nothing be lost.
St John ch. 6, v. 12

27 Verily, verily, I say unto you . . . my Father giveth you the true bread from heaven.
For the bread of God is he which cometh down from heaven, and giveth life to the world.
St John ch. 6, v. 32

28 I am the bread of life: he that cometh to me shall never hunger; and he that believeth on me shall never thirst.
St John ch. 6, v. 35

29 Him that cometh to me I will in no wise cast out.
St John ch. 6, v. 37

30 Verily, verily, I say unto you, He that believeth on me hath everlasting life.
St John ch. 6, v. 47

31 It is the spirit that quickeneth.
St John ch. 6, v. 63

32 And the scribes and the Pharisees brought unto him a woman taken in adultery.
St John ch. 8, v. 3

33 He that is without sin among you, let him first cast a stone at her.
St John ch. 8, v. 7

34 Neither do I condemn thee: go, and sin no more.
St John ch. 8, v. 11

35 And ye shall know the truth, and the truth shall make you free.
St John ch. 8, v. 32

1 Ye are of your father the devil, and the lusts of your father ye will do. He was a murderer from the beginning, and abode not in the truth, because there is no truth in him. When he speaketh a lie, he speaketh of his own: for he is a liar, and the father of it.
St John ch. 8, v. 44

2 The night cometh, when no man can work.
St John ch. 9, v. 4

3 He is of age; ask him: he shall speak for himself.
St John ch. 9, v. 21

4 One thing I know, that, whereas I was blind, now I see.
St John ch. 9, v. 25

5 I am the door.
St John ch. 10, v. 9

6 I am the good shepherd: the good shepherd giveth his life for the sheep.
St John ch. 10, v. 11

7 The hireling fleeth, because he is an hireling, and careth not for the sheep.
St John ch. 10, v. 13

8 Other sheep I have, which are not of this fold.
St John ch. 10, v. 16

9 Though ye believe not me, believe the works.
St John ch. 10, v. 38

10 I am the resurrection, and the life.
St John ch. 11, v. 25

11 Jesus wept.
St John ch. 11, v. 35; cf. **Hugo** 394:1

12 It is expedient for us, that one man should die for the people.
said by Caiaphas
St John ch. 11, v. 50

13 The poor always ye have with you.
St John ch. 12, v. 8

14 Lord, dost thou wash my feet?
said by St Peter
St John ch. 13, v. 6

15 That thou doest, do quickly.
St John ch. 13, v. 27

16 Let not your heart be troubled.
St John ch. 14, v. 1

17 In my Father's house are many mansions . . . I go to prepare a place for you.
St John ch. 14, v. 2

18 I am the way, the truth, and the life: no man cometh unto the Father, but by me.
St John ch. 14, v. 6

19 Have I been so long time with you, and yet hast thou not known me, Philip?
St John ch. 14, v. 9

20 Judas saith unto him, not Iscariot.
St John ch. 14, v. 22

21 Peace I leave with you, my peace I give unto you: not as the world giveth, give I unto you.
St John ch. 14, v. 27

22 Greater love hath no man than this, that a man lay down his life for his friends.
St John ch. 15, v. 13; cf. **Joyce** 422:16, **Thorpe** 776:21

23 Ye have not chosen me, but I have chosen you.
St John ch. 15, v. 16

24 It is expedient for you that I go away: for if I go not away, the Comforter will not come unto you.
St John ch. 16, v. 7

25 I have yet many things to say unto you, but ye cannot bear them now.
St John ch. 16, v. 12

26 A little while, and ye shall not see me: and again, a little while, and ye shall see me, because I go to the Father.
St John ch. 16, v. 16

27 In the world ye shall have tribulation: but be of good cheer; I have overcome the world.
St John ch. 16, v. 33

28 While I was with them in the world, I kept them in thy name: those that thou gavest me I have kept, and none of them is lost but the son of perdition.
St John ch. 17, v. 12

29 Put up thy sword into the sheath.
to St Peter
St John ch. 18, v. 11

30 Pilate saith unto him, What is truth?
St John ch. 18, v. 38; cf. **Bacon** 44:15

31 Now Barabbas was a robber.
St John ch. 18, v. 40; cf. **Campbell** 183:20

32 A place called the place of a skull, which is called in the Hebrew Golgotha.
St John ch. 19, v. 17

33 And Pilate wrote a title and put it on the cross. And the writing was, JESUS OF NAZARETH THE KING OF THE JEWS.
St John ch. 19, v. 19

34 What I have written I have written.
said by Pilate
St John ch. 19, v. 22

35 Woman, behold thy son! . . .
Behold thy mother!
to the Virgin Mary and, traditionally, St John
St John ch. 19, v. 26

36 I thirst.
St John ch. 19, v. 28

37 It is finished.
St John ch. 19, v. 30; cf. **Bible** 114:9

38 The first day of the week cometh Mary Magdalene early, when it was yet dark, unto the sepulchre, and seeth the stone taken away from the sepulchre.
St John ch. 20, v. 1

39 So they ran both together: and the other disciple did outrun Peter, and came first to the sepulchre.
St John ch. 20, v. 4

40 They have taken away my Lord, and I know not where they have laid him.
said by St Mary Magdalene
St John ch. 20, v. 13

1 Jesus saith unto her, Woman, why weepest thou? whom seekest thou? She supposing him to be the gardener saith unto him, Sir, if thou have borne him hence, tell me where thou hast laid him, and I will take him away.
St John ch. 20, v. 15

2 Touch me not.
to St Mary Magdalene
St John ch. 20, v. 17; cf. **Bible** 114:10

3 Except I shall see in his hands the print of the nails, and put my finger into the print of the nails, and thrust my hand into his side, I will not believe.
said by St Thomas
St John ch. 20, v. 25

4 Be not faithless, but believing.
to St Thomas
St John ch. 20, v. 27

5 Thomas answered and said unto him, My Lord and my God.
St John ch. 20, v. 28

6 Thomas, because thou hast seen me, thou hast believed: blessed are they that have not seen, and yet have believed.
St John ch. 20, v. 29

7 Simon Peter saith unto them, I go a fishing.
St John ch. 21, v. 3

8 Simon, son of Jonas, lovest thou me more than these? . . . Feed my lambs.
St John ch. 21, v. 15

9 Feed my sheep.
St John ch. 21, v. 16

10 Lord, thou knowest all things; thou knowest that I love thee.
said by St Peter
St John ch. 21, v. 17

11 When thou wast young, thou girdedst thyself, and walkedst whither thou wouldest: but when thou shalt be old, thou shalt stretch forth thy hands, and another shall gird thee, and carry thee whither thou wouldest not.
to St Peter
St John ch. 21, v. 18

12 Peter, turning about, seeth the disciple whom Jesus loved following; which also leaned on his breast at supper, and said Lord, which is he that betrayeth thee?
traditionally St John
St John ch. 21, v. 20

13 Jesus saith unto him, If I will that he tarry till I come, what is that to thee?
to St Peter, of St John
St John ch. 21, v. 22

ACTS OF THE APOSTLES

14 Ye men of Galilee, why stand ye gazing up into heaven?
Acts of the Apostles ch. 1, v. 11

15 And suddenly there came a sound from heaven as of a rushing mighty wind, and it filled all the house where they were sitting.
And there appeared unto them cloven tongues like as of fire.
Acts of the Apostles ch. 2, v. 2

16 Parthians, and Medes, and Elamites, and the dwellers in Mesopotamia, and in Judaea, and Cappadocia, in Pontus, and Asia,
Phrygia, and Pamphylia, in Egypt, and in the parts of Libya about Cyrene, and strangers of Rome, Jews and proselytes,
Cretes and Arabians, we do hear them speak in our tongues the wonderful works of God.
Acts of the Apostles ch. 2, v. 9

17 And all that believed were together, and had all things common.
Acts of the Apostles ch. 2, v. 44

18 Silver and gold have I none, but such as I have give I thee.
Acts of the Apostles ch. 3, v. 6

19 Walking, and leaping, and praising God.
Acts of the Apostles ch. 3, v. 8

20 It is not reason that we should leave the word of God, and serve tables.
Acts of the Apostles ch. 6, v. 2

21 The witnesses laid down their clothes at a young man's feet, whose name was Saul.
Acts of the Apostles ch. 7, v. 58

22 Saul was consenting unto his death.
Acts of the Apostles ch. 8, v. 1

23 Thy money perish with thee, because thou hast thought that the gift of God may be purchased with money.
to Simon Magus
Acts of the Apostles ch. 8, v. 20

24 Saul, Saul, why persecutest thou me?
Acts of the Apostles ch. 9, v. 4

25 It is hard for thee to kick against the pricks.
Acts of the Apostles ch. 9, v. 5

26 The street which is called Straight.
Acts of the Apostles ch. 9, v. 11

27 Dorcas: this woman was full of good works.
Acts of the Apostles ch. 9, v. 36

28 He fell into a trance,
And saw heaven opened, and a certain vessel descending unto him, as it had been a great sheet knit at the four corners, and let down to the earth:
Wherein were all manner of four-footed beasts of the earth, and wild beasts, and creeping things, and fowls of the air.
Acts of the Apostles ch. 10, v. 10

29 What God hath cleansed, that call not thou common.
Acts of the Apostles ch. 10, v. 15

30 God is no respecter of persons.
Acts of the Apostles ch. 10, v. 34

31 He was eaten of worms, and gave up the ghost.
Acts of the Apostles ch. 12, v. 23

32 The gods are come down to us in the likeness of men.
Acts of the Apostles ch. 14, v. 11

1 We also are men of like passions with you.
Acts of the Apostles ch. 14, v. 15

2 Come over into Macedonia, and help us.
Acts of the Apostles ch. 16, v. 9

3 What must I do to be saved?
Acts of the Apostles ch. 16, v. 30

4 The Jews which believed not, moved with envy, took unto them certain lewd fellows of the baser sort, and gathered a company, and set all the city on an uproar.
Acts of the Apostles ch. 17, v. 5

5 Those that have turned the world upside down are come hither also;
Whom Jason hath received: and these all do contrary to the decrees of Caesar, saying that there is another king, one Jesus.
Acts of the Apostles ch. 17, v. 6

6 What will this babbler say?
Acts of the Apostles ch. 17, v. 18

7 For all the Athenians and strangers which were there spent their time in nothing else, but either to tell, or to hear some new thing.
Acts of the Apostles ch. 17, v. 21

8 Ye men of Athens, I perceive that in all things ye are too superstitious.
For as I passed by, and beheld your devotions, I found an altar with this inscription, TO THE UNKNOWN GOD. Whom therefore ye ignorantly worship, him declare I unto you.
Acts of the Apostles ch. 17, v. 22

9 God that made the world and all things therein, seeing that he is Lord of Heaven and earth, dwelleth not in temples made with hands.
Acts of the Apostles ch. 17, v. 24

10 For in him we live, and move, and have our being.
Acts of the Apostles ch. 17, v. 28

11 We have not so much as heard whether there be any Holy Ghost.
Acts of the Apostles ch. 19, v. 2

12 All with one voice about the space of two hours cried out, Great is Diana of the Ephesians.
Acts of the Apostles ch. 19, v. 34

13 I go bound in the spirit unto Jerusalem.
Acts of the Apostles ch. 20, v. 22

14 It is more blessed to give than to receive.
Acts of the Apostles ch. 20, v. 35; cf. **Proverbs** 604:11

15 But Paul said, I am a man which am a Jew of Tarsus, a city in Cilicia, a citizen of no mean city.
Acts of the Apostles ch. 21, v. 39

16 And the chief captain answered, With a great sum obtained I this freedom. And Paul said, But I was free born.
Acts of the Apostles ch. 22, v. 28

17 A conscience void of offence toward God, and toward men.
Acts of the Apostles ch. 24, v. 16

18 I appeal unto Caesar.
Acts of the Apostles ch. 25, v. 11

19 Hast thou appealed unto Caesar? unto Caesar shalt thou go.
Acts of the Apostles ch. 25, v. 12

20 Paul, thou art beside thyself; much learning doth make thee mad.
Acts of the Apostles ch. 26, v. 24

21 For this thing was not done in a corner.
Acts of the Apostles ch. 26, v. 26

22 Almost thou persuadest me to be a Christian.
Acts of the Apostles ch. 26, v. 28

23 I would to God, that not only thou, but also all that hear me this day, were both almost, and altogether such as I am, except these bonds.
Acts of the Apostles ch. 26, v. 29

ROMANS

24 Without ceasing I make mention of you always in my prayers.
Romans ch. 1, v. 9

25 I am debtor both to the Greeks, and to the Barbarians; both to the wise, and to the unwise.
Romans ch. 1, v. 14

26 The just shall live by faith.
Romans ch. 1, v. 17

27 Worshipped and served the creature more than the Creator.
Romans ch. 1, v. 25

28 Patient continuance in well doing.
Romans ch. 2, v. 7

29 A law unto themselves.
Romans ch. 2, v. 14

30 Let God be true, but every man a liar.
Romans ch. 3, v. 4

31 Let us do evil, that good may come.
Romans ch. 3, v. 8

32 For all have sinned, and come short of the glory of God.
Romans ch. 3, v. 23

33 For where no law is, there is no transgression.
Romans ch. 4, v. 15

34 Who against hope believed in hope, that he might become the father of many nations.
of Abraham
Romans ch. 4, v. 18

35 Hope maketh not ashamed; because the love of God is shed abroad in our hearts by the Holy Ghost which is given unto us.
Romans ch. 5, v. 5

36 Where sin abounded, grace did much more abound.
Romans ch. 5, v. 20

37 Shall we continue in sin, that grace may abound? God forbid. How shall we, that are dead to sin, live any longer in sin?
Romans ch. 6, v. 1

38 We also should walk in newness of life.
Romans ch. 6, v. 4

1 Christ being raised from the dead dieth no more; death hath no more dominion over him.
For in that he died, he died unto sin once: but in that he liveth, he liveth unto God.
Romans ch. 6, v. 9; cf. **Thomas** 772:1

2 The wages of sin is death.
Romans ch. 6, v. 23

3 Is the law sin? God forbid. Nay, I had not known sin, but by the law.
Romans ch. 7, v. 7

4 For the good that I would I do not: but the evil which I would not, that I do.
Romans ch. 7, v. 19; cf. **Ovid** 561:17

5 O wretched man that I am! who shall deliver me from the body of this death?
Romans ch. 7, v. 24

6 They that are after the flesh do mind the things of the flesh; but they that are after the Spirit the things of the Spirit.
For to be carnally minded is death.
Romans ch. 8, v. 5

7 For ye have not received the spirit of bondage again to fear; but ye have received the Spirit of adoption, whereby we cry, Abba, Father.
Romans ch. 8, v. 15

8 We are the children of God:
And if the children, then heirs; heirs of God, and joint-heirs with Christ.
Romans ch. 8, v. 16

9 For we know that the whole creation groaneth and travaileth in pain together until now.
Romans ch. 8, v. 22

10 All things work together for good to them that love God.
Romans ch. 8, v. 28

11 If God be for us, who can be against us?
Romans ch. 8, v. 31

12 For I am persuaded, that neither death, nor life, nor angels, nor principalities, nor powers, nor things present, nor things to come,
Nor height, nor depth, nor any other creature, shall be able to separate us from the love of God, which is in Christ Jesus our Lord.
Romans ch. 8, v. 38

13 Shall the thing formed say to him that formed it, Why hast thou made me thus?
Hath not the potter power over the clay, of the same lump to make one vessel unto honour, and another unto dishonour?
Romans ch. 9, v. 20

14 I beseech you therefore, brethren, by the mercies of God, that ye present your bodies a living sacrifice, holy, acceptable unto God.
Romans ch. 12, v. 1

15 Rejoice with them that do rejoice, and weep with them that weep.
Romans ch. 12, v. 15

16 Mind not high things, but condescend to men of low estate. Be not wise in your own conceits.
Romans ch. 12, v. 16

17 Vengeance is mine; I will repay, saith the Lord.
Romans ch. 12, v. 19

18 Be not overcome of evil, but overcome evil with good.
Romans ch. 12, v. 21

19 Let every soul be subject unto the higher powers . . . the powers that be are ordained of God.
Romans ch. 13, v. 1

20 Render therefore to all their dues: tribute to whom tribute is due; custom to whom custom; fear to whom fear; honour to whom honour.
Owe no man anything, but to love one another: for he that loveth another hath fulfilled the law.
Romans ch. 13, v. 7

21 Now it is high time to awake out of sleep: for now is our salvation nearer than when we believed.
The night is far spent, the day is at hand: let us therefore cast off the works of darkness, and let us put on the armour of light.
Romans ch. 13, v. 11

22 Make not provision for the flesh, to fulfil the lusts thereof.
Romans ch. 13, v. 14

23 Doubtful disputations.
Romans ch. 14, v. 1

24 Let every man be fully persuaded in his own mind.
Romans ch. 14, v. 5

25 Salute one another with an holy kiss.
Romans ch. 16, v. 16

I CORINTHIANS

26 The foolishness of preaching to save them that believe.
I Corinthians ch. 1, v. 21

27 For the Jews require a sign, and the Greeks seek after wisdom.
I Corinthians ch. 1, v. 22

28 We preach Christ crucified, unto the Jews a stumbling-block, and unto the Greeks foolishness.
I Corinthians ch. 1, v. 23

29 God hath chosen the foolish things of the world to confound the wise; and God hath chosen the weak things of the world to confound the things which are mighty.
I Corinthians ch. 1, v. 27

30 I have planted, Apollos watered; but God gave the increase.
I Corinthians ch. 3, v. 6

31 Stewards of the mysteries of God.
I Corinthians ch. 4, v. 1

32 We are made a spectacle unto the world, and to angels.
I Corinthians ch. 4, v. 9

33 Absent in body, but present in spirit.
I Corinthians ch. 5, v. 3

1 Know ye not that a little leaven leaveneth the whole lump?
I Corinthians ch. 5, v. 6

2 Christ our passover is sacrificed for us:
Therefore let us keep the feast, not with the old leaven, neither with the leaven of malice and wickedness; but with the unleavened bread of sincerity and truth.
I Corinthians ch. 5, v. 7

3 Your body is the temple of the Holy Ghost.
I Corinthians ch. 6, v. 19

4 It is better to marry than to burn.
I Corinthians ch. 7, v. 9

5 The unbelieving husband is sanctified by the wife.
I Corinthians ch. 7, v. 14

6 The fashion of this world passeth away.
I Corinthians ch. 7, v. 31

7 Knowledge puffeth up, but charity edifieth.
I Corinthians ch. 8, v. 1

8 Who goeth a warfare any time at his own charges? who planteth a vineyard, and eateth not of the fruit thereof?
I Corinthians ch. 9, v. 7

9 I am made all things to all men.
I Corinthians ch. 9, v. 22

10 Know ye not that they which run in a race run all, but one receiveth the prize.
I Corinthians ch. 9, v. 24

11 Now they do it to obtain a corruptible crown; but we an incorruptible.
I therefore so run, not as uncertainly; so fight I, not as one that beateth the air.
But I keep under my body, and bring it into subjection; lest that by any means, when I have preached to others, I myself should be a castaway.
I Corinthians ch. 9, v. 25

12 All things are lawful for me, but all things are not expedient.
I Corinthians ch. 10, v. 23

13 For the earth is the Lord's and the fulness thereof.
I Corinthians ch. 10, v. 26; cf. **Book of Common Prayer** 133:2

14 Doth not even nature itself teach you, that if a man have long hair, it is a shame unto him?
But if a woman have long hair, it is a glory to her.
I Corinthians ch. 11, v. 14

15 Now there are diversities of gifts, but the same Spirit.
I Corinthians ch. 12, v. 4

16 Though I speak with the tongues of men and of angels, and have not charity, I am become as sounding brass, or a tinkling cymbal.
And though I have the gift of prophecy, and understand all mysteries, and all knowledge; and though I have all faith; so that I could remove mountains; and have not charity, I am nothing.
And though I bestow all my goods to feed the poor, and though I give my body to be burned, and have not charity, it profiteth me nothing.
Charity suffereth long, and is kind; charity envieth not; charity vaunteth not itself, is not puffed up,
Doth not behave itself unseemly, seeketh not her own, is not easily provoked, thinketh no evil;
Rejoiceth not in iniquity, but rejoiceth in the truth;
Beareth all things, believeth all things, hopeth all things, endureth all things.
Charity never faileth: but whether there be prophecies, they shall fail; whether there be tongues, they shall cease; whether there be knowledge, it shall vanish away.
For we know in part, and we prophesy in part.
But when that which is perfect is come, then that which is in part shall be done away.
When I was a child, I spake as a child, I understood as a child, I thought as a child: but when I became a man, I put away childish things.
For now we see through a glass, darkly; but then face to face: now I know in part; but then shall I know even as also I am known.
And now abideth faith, hope, charity, these three; but the greatest of these is charity.
I Corinthians ch. 13, v. 1

17 If the trumpet give an uncertain sound, who shall prepare himself to the battle?
I Corinthians ch. 14, v. 8

18 Let all things be done decently and in order.
I Corinthians ch. 14, v. 40

19 Last of all he was seen of me also, as of one born out of due time.
For I am the least of the apostles, that am not meet to be called an apostle, because I persecuted the church of God.
But by the grace of God I am what I am.
I Corinthians ch. 15, v. 8

20 I laboured more abundantly than they all: yet not I, but the grace of God which was with me.
I Corinthians ch. 15, v. 10

21 If in this life only we have hope in Christ, we are of all men most miserable.
I Corinthians ch. 15, v. 19

22 But now is Christ risen from the dead, and become the first fruits of them that slept.
For since by man came death, by man came also the resurrection of the dead.
For as in Adam all die, even so in Christ shall all be made alive.
I Corinthians ch. 15, v. 20

23 The last enemy that shall be destroyed is death.
I Corinthians ch. 15, v. 26

24 If after the manner of men I have fought with beasts at Ephesus, what advantageth it me, if the dead rise not? let us eat and drink; for to morrow we die.
I Corinthians ch. 15, v. 32; cf. **Bible** 84:19, 87:9, 99:21

25 Evil communications corrupt good manners.
I Corinthians ch. 15, v. 33; cf. **Proverbs** 599:44

26 One star differeth from another star in glory.
I Corinthians ch. 15, v. 41

1 So also is the resurrection of the dead. It is sown in corruption; it is raised in incorruption.
I Corinthians ch. 15, v. 42

2 The first man is of the earth, earthy.
I Corinthians ch. 15, v. 47

3 Behold, I shew you a mystery; We shall not all sleep, but we shall all be changed,
In a moment, in the twinkling of an eye, at the last trump; for the trumpet shall sound, and the dead shall be raised incorruptible, and we shall be changed.
For this corruptible must put on incorruption, and this mortal must put on immortality.
I Corinthians ch. 15, v. 51

4 O death, where is thy sting? O grave, where is thy victory?
I Corinthians ch. 15, v. 55: cf. **Military sayings** 508:13

II CORINTHIANS

5 Our sufficiency is of God;
Who also hath made us able ministers of the new testament; not of the letter, but of the spirit: for the letter killeth, but the spirit giveth life.
II Corinthians ch. 3, v. 5

6 We have this treasure in earthen vessels.
II Corinthians ch. 4, v. 7

7 We know that if our earthly house of this tabernacle were dissolved, we have a building of God, an house not made with hands, eternal in the heavens.
II Corinthians ch. 5, v. 1; cf. **Browning** 155:17

8 For he saith, I have found thee in a time accepted, and in the day of salvation have I succoured thee: behold, now is the accepted time; behold, now is the day of salvation.
II Corinthians ch. 6, v. 2

9 As having nothing, and yet possessing all things.
II Corinthians ch. 6, v. 10

10 God loveth a cheerful giver.
II Corinthians ch. 9, v. 7

11 For ye suffer fools gladly, seeing ye yourselves are wise.
II Corinthians ch. 11, v. 19

12 Are they Hebrews? so am I. Are they Israelites? so am I. Are they the seed of Abraham? so am I.
Are they ministers of Christ? (I speak as a fool) I am more.
II Corinthians ch. 11, v. 22

13 Of the Jews five times received I forty stripes save one.
Thrice was I beaten with rods, once was I stoned, thrice I suffered shipwreck, a night and a day have I been in the deep;
In weariness and painfulness, in watchings often, in hunger and thirst, in fastings often, in cold and nakedness.
Beside those things that are without, that which cometh upon me daily, the care of all the churches.
II Corinthians ch. 11, v. 24

14 In journeyings often, in perils of waters, in perils of robbers, in perils by mine own countrymen, in perils by the heathen, in perils of the city, in perils in the wilderness, in perils in the sea, in perils among false brethren.
II Corinthians ch. 11, v. 26

15 I knew a man in Christ above fourteen years ago (whether in the body, I cannot tell; or whether out of the body, I cannot tell: God knoweth)—such an one caught up to the third heaven.
II Corinthians ch. 12, v. 2

16 There was given to me a thorn in the flesh, the messenger of Satan to buffet me.
II Corinthians ch. 12, v. 7

17 My strength is made perfect in weakness.
II Corinthians ch. 12, v. 9

GALATIANS

18 The right hands of fellowship.
Galatians ch. 2, v. 9

19 It is written, that Abraham had two sons, the one by a bondmaid, the other by a freewoman.
But he who was of the bondwoman was born after the flesh; but he of the freewoman was by promise.
Which things are an allegory.
Galatians ch. 4, v. 22

20 Ye are fallen from grace.
Galatians ch. 5, v. 4

21 But the fruit of the Spirit is love, joy, peace, longsuffering, gentleness, goodness, faith,
Meekness, temperance.
Galatians ch. 5, v. 22

22 Be not deceived; God is not mocked: for whatsoever a man soweth, that shall he also reap.
Galatians ch. 6, v. 7; cf. **Proverbs** 595:22

23 Let us not be weary in well doing: for in due season we shall reap, if we faint not.
'*Be not weary in well doing*' in *II Thessalonians ch. 3, v. 13*
Galatians ch. 6, v. 9

24 Ye see how large a letter I have written unto you with mine own hand.
Galatians ch. 6, v. 11

EPHESIANS

25 [Christ] came and preached peace to you which were afar off, and to them that were nigh.
Ephesians ch. 2, v. 17

26 Unto me, who am less than the least of all saints, is this grace given, that I should preach among the Gentiles the unsearchable riches of Christ.
Ephesians ch. 3, v. 8

27 I bow my knees unto the Father of our Lord Jesus Christ,
Of whom the whole family in heaven and earth is named,
That he would grant you, according to the riches of his glory, to be strengthened with might by his Spirit in the inner man.
Ephesians ch. 3, v. 14

28 The love of Christ, which passeth knowledge.
Ephesians ch. 3, v. 19

1 Now unto him that is able to do exceeding abundantly above all that we ask or think, according to the power that worketh in us,
Unto him be glory in the church by Christ Jesus throughout all ages, world without end. Amen.
Ephesians ch. 3, v. 20

2 I therefore, the prisoner of the Lord, beseech you that ye walk worthy of the vocation wherewith ye are called.
Ephesians ch. 4, v. 1

3 He gave some, apostles; and some, prophets; and some, evangelists; and some, pastors and teachers;
For the perfecting of the saints, for the work of the ministry, for the edifying of the body of Christ:
Till we all come in the unity of the faith, and of the knowledge of the Son of God, unto a perfect man, unto the measure of the stature of the fulness of Christ:
That we henceforth be no more children, tossed to and fro, and carried about with every wind of doctrine, by the sleight of men, and cunning craftiness, whereby they lie in wait to deceive.
Ephesians ch. 4, v. 11

4 We are members one of another.
Ephesians ch. 4, v. 25

5 Be ye angry and sin not: let not the sun go down upon your wrath.
Ephesians ch. 4, v. 26; cf. **Proverbs** 607:31

6 Fornication, and all uncleanness, or covetousness, let it not be once named among you, as becometh saints;
Neither filthiness, nor foolish talking, nor jesting, which are not convenient.
Ephesians ch. 5, v. 3

7 Let no man deceive you with vain words: for because of these things cometh the wrath of God upon the children of disobedience.
Ephesians ch. 5, v. 6

8 See then that ye walk circumspectly, not as fools, but as wise,
Redeeming the time, because the days are evil.
Ephesians ch. 5, v. 15

9 Be not drunk with wine, wherein is excess; but be filled with the Spirit;
Speaking to yourselves in psalms and hymns and spiritual songs, singing and making melody in your heart to the Lord.
Ephesians ch. 5, v. 18

10 Ye fathers, provoke not your children to wrath.
Ephesians ch. 6, v. 4

11 Not with eyeservice, as menpleasers.
Ephesians ch. 6, v. 6

12 Put on the whole armour of God.
Ephesians ch. 6, v. 11

13 For we wrestle not against flesh and blood, but against principalities, against powers, against the rulers of the darkness of this world, against spiritual wickedness in high places.
Wherefore take unto you the whole armour of God, that ye may be able to withstand in the evil day, and having done all, to stand.
Stand therefore, having your loins girt about with truth, and having on the breastplate of righteousness;
And your feet shod with the preparation of the gospel of peace;
Above all, taking the shield of faith, wherewith ye shall be able to quench all the fiery darts of the wicked.
Ephesians ch. 6, v. 12

PHILIPPIANS

14 For me to live is Christ, and to die is gain.
Philippians ch. 1, v. 21

15 Having a desire to depart, and to be with Christ; which is far better.
Philippians ch. 1, v. 23

16 Let this mind be in you, which was also in Christ Jesus:
Who, being in the form of God, thought it not robbery to be equal with God:
But made himself of no reputation, and took upon him the form of a servant and was made in the likeness of men.
Philippians ch. 2, v. 5

17 God hath also highly exalted him, and given him a name which is above every name:
That at the name of Jesus every knee should bow, of things in heaven, and things in earth, and things under the earth.
Philippians ch. 2, v. 9; cf. **Noel** 546:12

18 Work out your own salvation with fear and trembling.
Philippians ch. 2, v. 12

19 If any other man thinketh that he hath whereof he might trust in the flesh, I more:
Circumcised the eighth day, of the stock of Israel, of the tribe of Benjamin, an Hebrew of the Hebrews; as touching the law, a Pharisee.
Philippians ch. 3, v. 4

20 But what things were gain to me, those I counted loss for Christ.
Philippians ch. 3, v. 7

21 Forgetting those things which are behind, and reaching forth unto those things which are before, I press toward the mark.
Philippians ch. 3, v. 13

22 Whose God is their belly, and whose glory is in their shame.
Philippians ch. 3, v. 19

23 Rejoice in the Lord alway: and again I say, Rejoice.
Philippians ch. 4, v. 4

24 The peace of God, which passeth all understanding, shall keep your hearts and minds through Christ Jesus.
Philippians ch. 4, v. 7; cf. **James I** 402:17

25 Whatsoever things are true, whatsoever things are honest, whatsoever things are just, whatsoever things are pure, whatsoever things are lovely,

whatsoever things are of good report; if there be any virtue and if there be any praise, think on these things.
Philippians ch. 4, v. 8

1 I can do all things through Christ which strengtheneth me.
Philippians ch. 4, v. 13

COLOSSIANS

2 For by him were all things created, that are in heaven, and that are in earth, visible and invisible, whether they be thrones, or dominions, or principalities, or powers.
Colossians ch. 1, v. 16; cf. **Milton** 517:1

3 Set your affection on things above, not on things on the earth.
Colossians ch. 3, v. 2

4 Ye have put off the old man with his deeds:
And have put on the new man, which is renewed in knowledge after the image of him that created him:
Where there is neither Greek nor Jew, circumcision nor uncircumcision, Barbarian, Scythian, bond nor free: but Christ is all, and in all.
Colossians ch. 3, v. 9

5 Husbands, love your wives, and be not bitter against them.
Colossians ch. 3, v. 19

6 Let your speech be alway with grace, seasoned with salt.
Colossians ch. 4, v. 6

I THESSALONIANS

7 We give thanks to God always for you all, making mention of you in our prayers;
Remembering without ceasing your work of faith and labour of love, and patience of hope in our Lord Jesus Christ.
I Thessalonians ch. 1, v. 2

8 Study to be quiet, and to do your own business.
I Thessalonians ch. 4, v. 11

9 But let us, who are of the day, be sober, putting on the breastplate of faith and love; and for an helmet, the hope of salvation.
I Thessalonians ch. 5, v. 8

10 Rejoice evermore. Pray without ceasing. In everything give thanks.
I Thessalonians ch. 5, v. 16

11 Prove all things; hold fast that which is good.
I Thessalonians ch. 5, v. 21

II THESSALONIANS

12 If any would not work, neither should he eat.
II Thessalonians ch. 3, v. 10; cf. **Proverbs** 603:32

I TIMOTHY

13 Sinners; of whom I am chief.
I Timothy ch. 1, v. 15

14 A bishop then must be blameless, the husband of one wife, vigilant, sober, of good behaviour, given to hospitality, apt to teach;
Not given to wine, no striker, not greedy of filthy lucre; but patient, not a brawler, not covetous.
I Timothy ch. 3, v. 2

15 Refuse profane and old wives' fables, and exercise thyself rather unto godliness.
I Timothy ch. 4, v. 7

16 Use a little wine for thy stomach's sake.
I Timothy ch. 5, v. 23

17 For we brought nothing into this world, and it is certain we can carry nothing out.
I Timothy ch. 6, v. 7

18 The love of money is the root of all evil.
I Timothy ch. 6, v. 10; cf. **Proverbs** 606:45

19 Fight the good fight of faith, lay hold on eternal life.
I Timothy ch. 6, v. 12; cf. **Monsell** 526:10

II TIMOTHY

20 For God hath not given us the spirit of fear; but of power, and of love, and of a sound mind.
II Timothy ch. 1, v. 7

21 Hold fast the form of sound words.
II Timothy ch. 1, v. 13

22 Be instant in season, out of season.
II Timothy ch. 4, v. 2

23 I have fought a good fight, I have finished my course, I have kept the faith.
II Timothy ch. 4, v. 7

TITUS

24 Unto the pure all things are pure.
Titus ch. 1, v. 15; cf. **Lawrence** 454:15, **Proverbs** 613:14

HEBREWS

25 God, who at sundry times and in divers manners spake in time past unto the fathers by the prophets,
Hath in these last days spoken unto us by his Son, whom he hath appointed heir of all things, by whom he also made the worlds:
Who being the brightness of his glory, and the express image of his person, and upholding all things by the word of his power, when he had by himself purged our sins, sat down on the right hand of the Majesty on high.
Hebrews ch. 1, v. 1

26 Without shedding of blood is no remission.
Hebrews ch. 9, v. 22

27 It is a fearful thing to fall into the hands of the living God.
Hebrews ch. 10, v. 31

28 Faith is the substance of things hoped for, the evidence of things not seen.
Hebrews ch. 11, v. 1

29 For he looked for a city which hath foundations, whose maker and builder is God.
Hebrews ch. 11, v. 10

30 These all died in faith, not having received the promises, but having seen them afar off, and were persuaded of them, and embraced them, and confessed that they were strangers and pilgrims on the earth.
Hebrews ch. 11, v. 13

1 Of whom the world was not worthy.
Hebrews ch. 11, v. 38

2 Wherefore seeing we also are compassed about with so great a cloud of witnesses, let us lay aside every weight, and the sin which doth so easily beset us, and let us run with patience the race that is set before us,
Looking unto Jesus the author and finisher of our faith; who for the joy that was set before him endured the cross, despising the shame, and is set down at the right hand of God.
Hebrews ch. 12, v. 1

3 Whom the Lord loveth he chasteneth.
Hebrews ch. 12, v. 6

4 The spirits of just men made perfect.
Hebrews ch. 12, v. 23

5 Let brotherly love continue.
Hebrews ch. 13, v. 1

6 Be not forgetful to entertain strangers: for thereby some have entertained angels unawares.
Hebrews ch. 13, v. 2

7 Jesus Christ the same yesterday, and to day, and for ever.
Hebrews ch. 13, v. 8

8 For here have we no continuing city, but we seek one to come.
Hebrews ch. 13, v. 14

9 To do good and to communicate forget not.
Hebrews ch. 13, v. 16

JAMES

10 Let patience have her perfect work.
James ch. 1, v. 4

11 Blessed is the man that endureth temptation: for when he is tried, he shall receive the crown of life.
James ch. 1, v. 12

12 Every good gift and every perfect gift is from above, and cometh down from the Father of lights, with whom is no variableness, neither shadow of turning.
James ch. 1, v. 17

13 Be swift to hear, slow to speak, slow to wrath:
For the wrath of man worketh not the righteousness of God.
Wherefore lay apart all filthiness and superfluity of naughtiness, and receive with meekness the engrafted word, which is able to save your souls,
For if any be a hearer of the word, and not a doer, he is like unto a man beholding his natural face in a glass:
For he beholdeth himself, and goeth his way, and straightway forgetteth what manner of man he was.
James ch. 1, v. 19

14 But be ye doers of the word, and not hearers only, deceiving your own selves.
James ch. 1, v. 22

15 If any man among you seem to be religious, and bridleth not his tongue, but deceiveth his own heart, this man's religion is vain.
James ch. 1, v. 26

16 Pure religion and undefiled before God and the Father is this, To visit the fatherless and widows in their affliction, and to keep himself unspotted from the world.
James ch. 1, v. 27

17 Faith without works is dead.
James ch. 2, v. 20

18 How great a matter a little fire kindleth.
James ch. 3, v. 5

19 The tongue can no man tame; it is an unruly evil.
James ch. 3, v. 8

20 Doth a fountain send forth at the same place sweet water and bitter?
James ch. 3, v. 11

21 For what is your life? It is even a vapour, that appeareth for a little time, and then vanisheth away.
James ch. 4, v. 14

22 Ye have heard of the patience of Job.
James ch. 5, v. 11

23 Let your yea be yea; and your nay, nay.
James ch. 5, v. 12

24 The effectual fervent prayer of a righteous man availeth much.
James ch. 5, v. 16

I PETER

25 Jesus Christ: Whom having not seen, ye love; in whom, though now ye see him not, yet believing, ye rejoice with joy unspeakable and full of glory.
I Peter ch. 1, v. 7

26 All flesh is as grass, and all the glory of man as the flower of grass. The grass withereth, and the flower thereof falleth away.
I Peter ch. 1, v. 24; cf. **Bible** 88:1

27 As newborn babes, desire the sincere milk of the word, that ye may grow thereby:
If so be ye have tasted that the Lord is gracious.
I Peter ch. 2, v. 2

28 But ye are a chosen generation, a royal priesthood, an holy nation, a peculiar people.
I Peter ch. 2, v. 9

29 Abstain from fleshly lusts, which war against the soul.
I Peter ch. 2, v. 11

30 Honour all men. Love the brotherhood. Fear God. Honour the king.
I Peter ch. 2, v. 17

31 For what glory is it, if, when ye be buffeted for your faults, ye shall take it patiently? but if, when ye do well, and suffer for it, ye take it patiently, this is acceptable with God.
I Peter ch. 2, v. 20

1 Ye were as sheep going astray; but are now returned unto the Shepherd and Bishop of your souls.
I Peter ch. 2, v. 25

2 The ornament of a meek and quiet spirit.
I Peter ch. 3, v. 4

3 Giving honour unto the wife, as unto the weaker vessel.
I Peter ch. 3, v. 7

4 Not rendering evil for evil, or railing for railing: but contrariwise blessing.
I Peter ch. 3, v. 9

5 The end of all things is at hand.
I Peter ch. 4, v. 7

6 Charity shall cover the multitude of sins.
I Peter ch. 4, v. 8; cf. **Proverbs** 597:12

7 Be sober, be vigilant; because your adversary the devil, as a roaring lion, walketh about, seeking whom he may devour.
I Peter ch. 5, v. 8

II PETER

8 And the day star arise in your hearts.
II Peter ch. 1, v. 19

9 They are not afraid to speak evil of dignities.
II Peter ch. 2, v. 10

10 The dog is turned to his own vomit again.
II Peter ch. 2, v. 22

I JOHN

11 If we say that we have no sin, we deceive ourselves, and the truth is not in us.
I John ch. 1, v. 8

12 But whoso hath this world's good, and seeth his brother have need, and shutteth up his bowels of compassion from him, how dwelleth the love of God in him?
I John ch. 3, v. 17

13 He that loveth not knoweth not God; for God is love.
I John ch. 4, v. 8

14 There is no fear in love; but perfect love casteth out fear.
I John ch. 4, v. 18; cf. **Connolly** 234:3

15 If a man say, I love God, and hateth his brother, he is a liar: for he that loveth not his brother whom he hath seen, how can he love God whom he hath not seen?
I John ch. 4, v. 20

III JOHN

16 He that doeth good is of God: but he that doeth evil hath not seen God.
III John v. 11

REVELATION

17 John to the seven churches which are in Asia: Grace be unto you, and peace, from him which is, and which was, and which is to come.
Revelation ch. 1, v. 4

18 Behold, he cometh with clouds; and every eye shall see him, and they also which pierced him: and all kindreds of the earth shall wail because of him.
Even so, Amen.
I am Alpha and Omega, the beginning and the ending, saith the Lord.
Revelation ch. 1, v. 7

19 I was in the Spirit on the Lord's day, and heard behind me a great voice as of a trumpet.
Revelation ch. 1, v. 10

20 What thou seest, write in a book, and send it unto the seven churches which are in Asia.
Revelation ch. 1, v. 11

21 Being turned, I saw seven golden candlesticks.
Revelation ch. 1, v. 12

22 His head and his hairs were white like wool, as white as snow; and his eyes were as a flame of fire;
And his feet like unto fine brass, as if they burned in a furnace; and his voice as the sound of many waters.
And he had in his right hand seven stars: and out of his mouth went a sharp two-edged sword: and his countenance was as the sun shineth in his strength.
And when I saw him, I fell at his feet as dead.
Revelation ch. 1, v. 14

23 I am he that liveth, and was dead; and, behold, I am alive for evermore, Amen; and have the keys of hell and of death.
Revelation ch. 1, v. 18

24 I have somewhat against thee, because thou hast left thy first love.
Revelation ch. 2, v. 4

25 Be thou faithful unto death, and I will give thee a crown of life.
Revelation ch. 2, v. 10

26 I will not blot out his name out of the book of life.
Revelation ch. 3, v. 5

27 I will write upon him my new name.
Revelation ch. 3, v. 12

28 I know thy works, that thou art neither cold nor hot: I would thou wert cold or hot.
So then, because thou art lukewarm, and neither cold nor hot, I will spew thee out of my mouth.
Revelation ch. 3, v. 15

29 Behold, I stand at the door, and knock.
Revelation ch. 3, v. 20

30 And he that sat was to look upon like a jasper and a sardine stone: and there was a rainbow round about the throne, in sight like unto an emerald.
Revelation ch. 4, v. 3

31 And before the throne there was a sea of glass like unto crystal: and in the midst of the throne, and round about the throne, were four beasts full of eyes before and behind.
Revelation ch. 4, v. 6

32 They were full of eyes within: and they rest not day and night, saying, Holy, holy, holy, Lord God Almighty, which was, and is, and is to come.
Revelation ch. 4, v. 8; cf. **Book of Common Prayer** 129:20, **Missal** 520:21

1 Thou hast created all things, and for thy pleasure they are and were created.
Revelation ch. 4, v. 11

2 Who is worthy to open the book, and to loose the seals thereof?
Revelation ch. 5, v. 2

3 The four beasts and four and twenty elders fell down before the Lamb, having every one of them harps, and golden vials full of odours, which are the prayers of saints.
Revelation ch. 5, v. 8

4 He went forth conquering, and to conquer.
Revelation ch. 6, v. 2

5 And I looked, and behold a pale horse: and his name that sat on him was Death.
Revelation ch. 6, v. 8

6 The kings of the earth, and the great men, and the rich men, and the chief captains, and the mighty men, and every bondman, and every free man, hid themselves in the dens and in the rocks of the mountains;
And said to the mountains and rocks, Fall on us, and hide us from the face of him that sitteth upon the throne, and from the wrath of the Lamb:
For the great day of his wrath is come; and who shall be able to stand?
Revelation ch. 6, v. 15

7 A great multitude, which no man could number, of all nations, and kindreds, and people, and tongues, stood before the throne, and before the Lamb.
Revelation ch. 7, v. 9

8 And all the angels stood round about the throne, and about the elders and the four beasts, and fell before the throne on their faces, and worshipped God.
Revelation ch. 7, v. 11

9 And one of the elders answered, saying unto me, What are these which are arrayed in white robes? and whence came they?
Revelation ch. 7, v. 13

10 These are they which came out of great tribulation, and have washed their robes, and made them white in the blood of the Lamb.
Revelation ch. 7, v. 14; cf. **Lindsay** 469:8

11 They shall hunger no more, neither thirst any more; neither shall the sun light on them, nor any heat.
Revelation ch. 7, v. 16

12 God shall wipe away all tears from their eyes.
Revelation ch. 7, v. 17

13 And when he had opened the seventh seal, there was silence in heaven about the space of half an hour.
Revelation ch. 8, v. 1

14 And the name of the star is called Wormwood.
Revelation ch. 8, v. 11

15 And in those days shall men seek death, and shall not find it; and shall desire to die, and death shall flee from them.
Revelation ch. 9, v. 6

16 And there were stings in their tails.
Revelation ch. 9, v. 10

17 It was in my mouth sweet as honey: and as soon as I had eaten it, my belly was bitter.
Revelation ch. 10, v. 10

18 And there appeared a great wonder in heaven; a woman clothed with the sun, and the moon under her feet, and upon her head a crown of twelve stars.
Revelation ch. 12, v. 1

19 And there was war in heaven: Michael and his angels fought against the dragon; and the dragon fought and his angels.
Revelation ch. 12, v. 7

20 Who is like unto the beast? who is able to make war with him?
Revelation ch. 13, v. 4

21 And that no man might buy or sell, save he that had the mark, or the name of the beast, or the number of his name.
Revelation ch. 13, v. 17

22 Let him that hath understanding count the number of the beast: for it is the number of a man; and his number is Six hundred threescore and six.
Revelation ch. 13, v. 18

23 And I heard a voice from heaven, as the voice of many waters, and as the voice of a great thunder: and I heard the voice of harpers harping with their harps:
And they sung as it were a new song . . . and no man could learn that song but the hundred and forty and four thousand, which were redeemed from the earth.
Revelation ch. 14, v. 2

24 Babylon is fallen, is fallen, that great city.
Revelation ch. 14, v. 8

25 And the smoke of their torment ascendeth up for ever and ever: and they have no rest day or night, who worship the beast and his image.
Revelation ch. 14, v. 11

26 Blessed are the dead which die in the Lord from henceforth: Yea, saith the Spirit, that they may rest from their labours; and their works do follow them.
Revelation ch. 14, v. 13

27 And I saw as it were a sea of glass mingled with fire.
Revelation ch. 15, v. 2

28 Behold, I come as a thief.
Revelation ch. 16, v. 15

29 And he gathered them together into a place called in the Hebrew tongue Armageddon.
Revelation ch. 16, v. 16

30 I will shew unto thee the judgement of the great whore that sitteth upon many waters.
Revelation ch. 17, v. 1

31 And upon her forehead was a name written, MYSTERY, BABYLON THE GREAT, THE MOTHER OF HARLOTS AND ABOMINATIONS OF THE EARTH.
Revelation ch. 17, v. 5

1 And a mighty angel took up a stone like a great millstone, and cast it into the sea, saying, Thus with violence shall that great city Babylon be thrown down, and shall be found no more at all.
Revelation ch. 18, v. 21

2 And I saw heaven opened, and behold a white horse; and he that sat upon him was called Faithful and True.
Revelation ch. 19, v. 11

3 And he hath on his vesture and on his thigh a name written, KING OF KINGS, AND LORD OF LORDS.
Revelation ch. 19, v. 16

4 And he laid hold on the dragon, that old serpent, which is the Devil, and Satan, and bound him a thousand years.
Revelation ch. 20, v. 2

5 And I saw a great white throne.
Revelation ch. 20, v. 11

6 And the sea gave up the dead which were in it; and death and hell delivered up the dead which were in them: and they were judged every man according to their works.
Revelation ch. 20, v. 13

7 And I saw a new heaven and a new earth: for the first heaven and the first earth were passed away; and there was no more sea.
And I John saw the holy city, new Jerusalem, coming down from God out of heaven, prepared as a bride adorned for her husband.
Revelation ch. 21, v. 1

8 And God shall wipe away all tears from their eyes; and there shall be no more death, neither sorrow, nor crying, neither shall there be any more pain: for the former things are passed away.
And he that sat upon the throne said, Behold, I make all things new. And he said unto me, Write: for these words are true and faithful.
Revelation ch. 21, v. 4; cf. **Pound** 589:8

9 I will give unto him that is athirst of the fountain of the water of life freely.
Revelation ch. 21, v. 6

10 The street of the city was pure gold.
Revelation ch. 21, v. 21

11 And the gates of it shall not be shut at all by day: for there shall be no night there.
Revelation ch. 21, v. 25

12 And he shewed me a pure river of water of life, clear as crystal, proceeding out of the throne of God and of the Lamb.
Revelation ch. 22, v. 1

13 And the leaves of the tree were for the healing of the nations.
Revelation ch. 22, v. 2

14 And, behold, I come quickly.
Revelation ch. 22, v. 12

15 For without are dogs, and sorcerers, and whoremongers, and murderers, and idolaters, and whosoever loveth and maketh a lie.
Revelation ch. 22, v. 15

16 Amen. Even so, come, Lord Jesus.
Revelation ch. 22, v. 20

VULGATE

17 *Dominus illuminatio mea, et salus mea, quem timebo?*
The Lord is the source of my light and my safety, so whom shall I fear?
Psalm 26, v. 1; cf. **Book of Common Prayer** 133:10, **Mottoes** 535:7

18 *Asperges me hyssopo, et mundabor; lavabis me, et super nivem dealbabor.*
You will sprinkle me with hyssop, and I shall be made clean; you will wash me and I shall be made whiter than snow.
Psalm 50, v. 9 (Psalm 51, v. 7 in the Authorized Version); cf. **Book of Common Prayer** 135:6

19 *Cantate Domino canticum novum, quia mirabilia fecit.*
Sing to the Lord a new song, because he has done marvellous things.
Psalm 97, v. 1 (Psalm 98, v. 1 in the Authorized Version); cf. **Book of Common Prayer** 138:9

20 *Jubilate Deo, omnis terra; servite Domino in laetitia.*
Sing joyfully to God, all the earth; serve the Lord with gladness.
Psalm 99, v. 2 (Psalm 100, v. 2 in the Authorized Version); cf. **Book of Common Prayer** 138:13

21 *Beatus vir qui timet Dominum, in mandatis ejus volet nimis!*
Happy is the man who fears the Lord, who is only too willing to follow his orders.
Psalm 111, v. 1 (Psalm 112, v. 1 in the Authorized Version)

22 *Non nobis, Domine, non nobis; sed nomini tuo da gloriam.*
Not unto us, Lord, not unto us; but to thy name give glory.
Psalm 113 (second part), v. 1 (Psalm 115, v. 1 in the Authorized Version); cf. **Book of Common Prayer** 139:22

23 *Laudate Dominum, omnes gentes; laudate eum, omnes populi.*
Praise the Lord, all nations; praise him, all people.
Psalm 116, v. 1 (Psalm 117, v. 1 in the Authorized Version)

24 *Nisi Dominus aedificaverit domum, in vanum laboraverunt qui aedificant eam.*
Nisi Dominus custodierit civitatem, frustra vigilat qui custodit eam.
Unless the Lord has built the house, its builders have laboured in vain. Unless the Lord guards the city, the watchman watches in vain.
Psalm 126, v. 1 (Psalm 127, v. 1 in the Authorized Version); cf. **Book of Common Prayer** 140:21, **Mottoes** 535:11

25 *De profundis clamavi ad te, Domine; Domine, exaudi vocem meam.*
Up from the depths I have cried to thee, Lord; Lord, hear my voice.
Psalm 129, v. 1 (Psalm 130, v. 1 in the Authorized Version); cf. **Book of Common Prayer** 141:1

26 *Vanitas vanitatum, dixit Ecclesiastes; vanitas vanitatum, et omnia vanitas.*
Vanity of vanities, said the preacher; vanity of vanities, and everything is vanity.
Ecclesiastes ch. 1, v. 2; cf. **Bible** 83:39, **Ménage** 504:11

1 *Rorate, coeli, desuper, et nubes pluant Justum; aperiatur terra, et germinet Salvatorem.*

Drop down dew, heavens, from above, and let the clouds rain down righteousness; let the earth be opened, and a saviour spring to life.

Isaiah ch. 45, v. 8

2 *Benedicite, omnia opera Domini, Domino; laudate et superexaltate eum in secula.*

Bless the Lord, all the works of the Lord; praise him and exalt him above all things for ever.

Daniel ch. 3, v. 57; cf. **Book of Common Prayer** 126:3

3 *Magnificat anima mea Dominum; Et exsultavit spiritus meus in Deo salutari meo.*

My soul doth magnify the Lord: and my spirit hath rejoiced in God my Saviour.

St Luke ch. 1, v. 46; cf. **Bible** 98:16

4 *Esurientes implevit bonis, et divites dimisit inanes.*

He hath filled the hungry with good things: and the rich he hath sent empty away.

St Luke ch. 1, v. 53; cf. **Bible** 98:17

5 *Nunc dimittis servum tuum, Domine, secundum verbum tuum in pace.*

Lord, now lettest thou thy servant depart in peace: according to thy word.

St Luke ch. 2, v. 29; cf. **Bible** 98:24

6 *Pax Vobis.*

Peace be unto you.

St Luke ch. 24, v. 36

7 *Quo vadis?*

Where are you going?

St John ch. 16, v. 5

8 *Ecce homo.*

Behold the man.

St John ch. 19, v. 5

9 *Consummatum est.*

It is achieved.

St John ch. 19, v. 30; cf. **Bible** 102:37

10 *Noli me tangere.*

Do not touch me.

St John ch. 20, v. 17; cf. **Bible** 103:2

11 *Sicut modo geniti infantes, rationabile, sine dolo lac concupiscite.*

After the fashion of newborn babes, desire the sincere milk of the word.

I Peter ch. 2, v. 2; cf. **Bible** 110:27

12 *Magna est veritas, et praevalet.*

Great is truth, and it prevails.

III Esdras ch. 4, v. 41; cf. **Bible** 91:1, **Brooks** 151:10

Isaac Bickerstaffe 1733–*c.*1808

Irish dramatist

13 Perhaps it was right to dissemble your love,
But—why did you kick me downstairs?

'An Expostulation' (1789); cf. **Carroll** 189:13

14 There was a jolly miller once,
Lived on the river Dee;
He worked and sang from morn till night;
No lark more blithe than he.

Love in a Village (a comic opera with music by Thomas Arne, 1762) act 1, sc. 2

15 And this the burthen of his song,
For ever used to be,
I care for nobody, not I,
If no one cares for me.

Love in a Village (1762) act 1, sc. 2

E. H. Bickersteth 1825–1906

English clergyman

16 Peace, perfect peace, in this dark world of sin?
The Blood of Jesus whispers peace within.

Songs in the House of Pilgrimage (1875) 'Peace, perfect peace'

Ambrose Bierce 1842–*c.*1914

American writer

17 ALLIANCE, *n.* In international politics, the union of two thieves who have their hands so deeply inserted in each other's pocket that they cannot separately plunder a third.

The Cynic's Word Book (1906)

18 APPLAUSE, *n.* The echo of a platitude.

The Cynic's Word Book (1906)

19 BATTLE, *n.* A method of untying with the teeth a political knot that would not yield to the tongue.

The Cynic's Word Book (1906)

20 CALAMITY, *n.* . . . Calamities are of two kinds: misfortune to ourselves, and good fortune to others.

The Cynic's Word Book (1906)

21 CONSERVATIVE, *n.* A statesman who is enamoured of existing evils, as distinguished from the Liberal, who wishes to replace them with others.

The Cynic's Word Book (1906)

22 HISTORY, *n.* An account, mostly false, of events, mostly unimportant, which are brought about by rulers, mostly knaves, and soldiers, mostly fools.

The Cynic's Word Book (1906)

23 PEACE, *n.* In international affairs, a period of cheating between two periods of fighting.

The Devil's Dictionary (1911)

24 PREJUDICE, *n.* A vagrant opinion without visible means of support.

The Devil's Dictionary (1911)

25 SAINT, *n.* A dead sinner revised and edited.

The Devil's Dictionary (1911)

Roger Bigod, Earl of Norfolk 1245–1306

Marshal of England, 1270–1301

26 EDWARD I: By God, earl, you shall either go or hang.
BIGOD: By God, O King, I will neither go nor hang!

on the King's requiring the barons to invade France through Gascony while he himself took command in Flanders, 24 February 1297

Harry Rothwell (ed.) *The Chronicle of Walter of Guisbrough* Camden Society Series 3, vol. 89 (1957)

Steve Biko 1946–77
South African anti-apartheid campaigner

1 The liberal must understand that the days of the Noble Savage are gone; that the blacks do not need a go-between in this struggle for their own emancipation. No true liberal should feel any resentment at the growth of black consciousness. Rather, all true liberals should realize that the place for their fight for justice is within their white society. The liberals must realize that they themselves are oppressed if they are true liberals and therefore they must fight for their own freedom and not that of the nebulous 'they' with whom they can hardly claim identification. The liberal must apply himself with absolute dedication to the idea of educating his white brothers.
'Black Souls in White Skins?' (written 1970), in *Steve Biko—I Write What I Like* (1978); cf. **Dryden** 281:5

Josh Billings (Henry Wheeler Shaw) 1818–85
American humorist

2 Love iz like the meazles; we kant have it bad but onst, and the latter in life we hav it the tuffer it goes with us.
Josh Billings' Wit and Humour (1874)

Maeve Binchy 1940–
Irish novelist

3 The Anglo-Irish might consider themselves Irish . . . but of course they were nothing of the sort. They were as English as the people who lived across the sea. Their only problem was that they didn't realise it.
Circle of Friends (1990)

4 Those lighting devils that go by the wrong name of innocent children.
The Copper Beech (1992)

5 My mother tells me she's worn out pouring tinned sauce over the frozen chicken.
Evening Class (1996)

6 Advent. What was there to say about it except that it went on for ever and was nearly as bad as Lent?
The Glass Lake (1994)

7 It's not perfect, but to me on balance Right Now is a lot better than the Good Old Days.
in *Irish Times* 15 November 1997

Laurence Binyon 1869–1943
English poet

8 They shall grow not old, as we that are left grow old.
Age shall not weary them, nor the years condemn.
At the going down of the sun and in the morning
We will remember them.
regularly recited as part of the ritual for Remembrance Day parades
'For the Fallen' (1914)

9 Now is the time for the burning of the leaves.
'The Ruins' (1942)

Bion *c.*325–*c.*255 BC
Greek popular philosopher, born in Olbia, Scythia

10 Boys throw stones at frogs for fun, but the frogs don't die for 'fun', but in sober earnest.
Plutarch *Moralia*

Nigel Birch 1906–81
British Conservative politician

11 My God! They've shot our fox!
on hearing of the resignation of Hugh Dalton, Labour Chancellor of the Exchequer, after the leak of Budget secrets
comment, 13 November 1947; Harold Macmillan *Tides of Fortune* (1969) ch. 3

Lord Birkenhead see **F. E. Smith**

Earle Birney 1904–
Canadian poet

12 We French, we English, never lost our civil war,
endure it still, a bloodless civil bore;
no wounded lying about, no Whitman wanted.
It's only by our lack of ghosts we're haunted.
'Can.Lit.' (1962)

Augustine Birrell 1850–1933
British essayist

13 That great dust-heap called 'history'.
Obiter Dicta (1884) 'Carlyle'; cf. **Trotsky** 783:17

Harrison Birtwhistle 1934–
English composer and clarinettist

14 You can't stop. Composing's not voluntary, you know. There's no choice, you're not free. You're landed with an idea and you have responsibility to that idea.
in *Observer* 14 April 1996 'Sayings of the Week'

Elizabeth Bishop 1911–79
American poet

15 The state with the prettiest name,
the state that floats in brackish water,
held together by mangrove roots.
'Florida' (1946)

16 This iceberg cuts its facets from within.
Like jewelry from a grave
it saves itself perpetually and adorns
only itself.
'The Imaginary Iceberg' (1946)

17 Topography displays no favourites; North's as near as West.
More delicate than the historians' are the map-makers' colours.
'The Map' (1946)

18 The armoured cars of dreams, contrived to let us do so many a dangerous thing.
'Sleeping Standing Up' (1946)

19 Lullaby.
Let nations rage,

let nations fall.
The shadow of the crib makes an enormous cage
upon the wall.

'Songs for a Coloured Singer' (1946)

1 If she speaks of a chair you can practically sit on it.
of Marianne ***Moore***

notebook, *c.*1934/5; D. Kalstone *Becoming a Poet* (1989)

2 I am overcome by my own amazing sloth . . . Can you please forgive me and believe that it is really because I want to do something well that I don't do it at all?

letter to Marianne Moore, 25 February 1937

3 I am sorry for people who can't write letters. But I suspect also that you and I . . . love to write them because it's kind of like working without really doing it.

letter to Kit and Ilse Barker, 5 September 1953

Otto von Bismarck 1815–98

German statesman
on Bismarck: see ***Taylor*** *756:9,* ***Tenniel*** *757:9*

4 If the Princess can leave the Englishwoman at home and become a Prussian, then she may be a blessing to the country.
on the marriage of Victoria, Princess Royal, to Prince Frederick William of Prussia

letter, *c.*1857; Hannah Pakula *An Uncommon Woman: The Empress Frederick* (1996)

5 The secret of politics? Make a good treaty with Russia.
in 1863, when first in power

A. J. P. Taylor *Bismarck* (1955) ch. 7

6 Politics is the art of the possible.

in conversation with Meyer von Waldeck, 11 August 1867, in H. Amelung *Bismarck-Worte* (1918); cf. **Butler** 171:16, **Galbraith** 328:11, **Medawar** 503:6

7 Let us . . . put Germany in the saddle! She will know well enough how to ride!

in 1867; Alan Palmer *Bismarck* (1976) ch. 9

8 We will not go to Canossa.
during his quarrel with Pope Pius IX regarding papal authority over German subjects, in allusion to the Emperor Henry IV's submission to Pope Gregory VII at Canossa in Modena in 1077

speech to the Reichstag, 14 May 1872

9 Not worth the healthy bones of a single Pomeranian grenadier.
of possible German involvement in the Balkans; cf. ***Harris*** *362:13*

speech to the Reichstag, 5 December 1876

10 Whoever speaks of Europe is wrong, [it is] a geographical concept.

marginal note on a letter from the Russian Chancellor Gorchakov, November 1876; cf. **Metternich** 506:9

11 I do not regard the procuring of peace as a matter in which we should play the role of arbiter between different opinions . . . more that of an honest broker who really wants to press the business forward.

speech to the Reichstag, 19 February 1878, in Ludwig Hahn (ed.) *Fürst Bismarck. Sein politisches Leben und Wirken* vol. 3 (1881)

12 This policy cannot succeed through speeches, and shooting-matches, and songs; it can only be carried out through blood and iron.

speech in the Prussian House of Deputies, 28 January 1886, in *Fürst Bismarck als Redner. Vollständige Sammlung der parliamentarischen Reden* (1885–91) vol. 15; in a speech on 30 September 1862, Bismarck had used the form 'Iron and blood' (in *Fürst Bismarck. Sein politisches Leben und Wirken* (1878) vol. 4)

13 I am bored; the great things are done. The German *Reich* is made.

A. J. P. Taylor *Bismarck* (1955) ch. 4

14 Jena came twenty years after the death of Frederick the Great; the crash will come twenty years after my departure if things go on like this.
to Kaiser ***Wilhelm II*** *at their last meeting in 1895*

A. J. P. Taylor *Bismarck* (1955) ch. 10

15 If there is ever another war in Europe, it will come out of some damned silly thing in the Balkans.

attributed by Herr Ballen and quoted by Winston S. **Churchill** in the House of Commons, 16 August 1945

16 A lath of wood painted to look like iron.
describing Lord ***Salisbury***

attributed, but vigorously denied by Sidney Whitman in *Personal Reminiscences of Prince Bismarck* (1902) ch. 14

17 The old Jew! That is the man.
of ***Disraeli*** *at the Congress of Berlin*

attributed

18 A statesman . . . must wait until he hears the steps of God sounding through events; then leap up and grasp the hem of his garment.

A. J. P. Taylor *Bismarck* (1955) ch. 5

Björk 1965–

Icelandic pop star

19 Icelandic peoples were the ones who memorized sagas . . . We were the first rappers of Europe.

attributed, January 1996

James Black 1924–

British analytical pharmacologist; winner of the Nobel prize for medicine

20 In the culture I grew up in you did your work and you did not put your arm around it to stop other people from looking—you took the earliest possible opportunity to make knowledge available.
on modern scientific research

in *Daily Telegraph* 11 December 1995

Valentine Blacker 1728–1823

Anglo-Indian soldier

21 Put your trust in God, my boys, and keep your powder dry.
often attributed to Oliver ***Cromwell*** *himself*

'Oliver's Advice' in E. Hayes *Ballads of Ireland* (1856) vol. 1; cf. **Proverbs** 610:1

William Blackstone 1723–80

English jurist

1 Man was formed for society.
Commentaries on the Laws of England (1765) introduction, sect. 2; cf. **Aristotle** 25:3

2 The king never dies.
Commentaries on the Laws of England (1765) bk. 1, ch. 7

3 The royal navy of England hath ever been its greatest defence and ornament; it is its ancient and natural strength; the floating bulwark of the island.
Commentaries on the Laws of England (1765) bk. 1, ch. 13; cf. **Coventry** 238:8

4 That the king can do no wrong, is a necessary and fundamental principle of the English constitution.
Commentaries on the Laws of England (1765) bk. 3, ch. 17

5 It is better that ten guilty persons escape than one innocent suffer.
Commentaries on the Laws of England (1765) bk. 4, ch. 27

Robert Blair 1699–1746

Scottish poet

6 Oft, in the lone church-yard at night I've seen,
The schoolboy with a satchel in his hand,
Whistling aloud to keep his courage up . . .
Sudden he starts! and hears, or thinks he hears,
The sound of something purring at his heels;
Full fast he flies, and dares not look behind him,
Till out of breath, he overtakes his fellows.
The Grave (1743) l. 57; cf. **Coleridge** 226:24

Tony Blair 1953–

British Labour statesman; Prime Minister since 1997

7 Labour is the party of law and order in Britain today. Tough on crime and tough on the causes of crime.
as Shadow Home Secretary
speech at the Labour Party Conference, 30 September 1993

8 The art of leadership is saying no, not yes. It is very easy to say yes.
in *Mail on Sunday* 2 October 1994

9 Those who seriously believe we cannot improve on words written for the world of 1918 when we are now in 1995 are not learning from our history but living it.
on the proposed revision of Clause IV
in *Independent* 11 January 1995

10 We need to build a relationship of trust not just within a firm but within a society. By trust, I mean the recognition of a mutual purpose for which we work together and in which we all benefit. It is a Stakeholder Economy in which opportunity is available to all, advancement is through merit and from which no group or class is set apart or excluded.
speech (press release) in Singapore, 8 January 1996

11 Ask me my three main priorities for Government, and I tell you: education, education and education.
speech at the Labour Party Conference, 1 October 1996; cf. **Michelet** 506:16

12 We are not the masters. The people are the masters. We are the servants of the people . . . What the electorate gives, the electorate can take away.
addressing Labour MPs on the first day of the new Parliament, 7 May 1997; cf. **Burke** 165:1
in *Guardian* 8 May 1997

13 She was the People's Princess, and that is how she will stay . . . in our hearts and in our memories forever.
on hearing of the death of **Diana**, *Princess of Wales, 31 August 1997*
in *The Times* 1 September 1997

14 I am from the Disraeli school of Prime Ministers in their relations with the Monarch.
at the Queen's golden wedding celebration, 20 November 1997; cf. ***Disraeli*** *270:37,* ***Elizabeth II*** *297:19*
in *Daily Telegraph* 21 November 1997

Eubie Blake (James Hubert Blake) 1883–1983

American ragtime pianist

15 If I'd known I was gonna live this long, I'd have taken better care of myself.
on reaching the age of 100
in *Observer* 13 February 1983 'Sayings of the Week'

William Blake 1757–1827

English poet
on Blake: see **Benét** 65:3

16 When Sir Joshua Reynolds died
All Nature was degraded:
The King dropped a tear into the Queen's ear;
And all his pictures faded.
Annotations to The Works of Sir Joshua Reynolds 'When Sir Joshua Reynolds died' (*c.*1808)

17 To see a world in a grain of sand
And a heaven in a wild flower,
Hold infinity in the palm of your hand
And eternity in an hour.
'Auguries of Innocence' (*c.*1803) l. 1

18 A robin red breast in a cage
Puts all Heaven in a rage.
'Auguries of Innocence' (*c.*1803) l. 5

19 A dog starved at his master's gate
Predicts the ruin of the State.
A horse misused upon the road
Calls to Heaven for human blood.
Each outcry of the hunted hare
A fibre from the brain does tear.
A skylark wounded in the wing,
A cherubim does cease to sing.
'Auguries of Innocence' (*c.*1803) l. 9

20 He who shall hurt the little wren
Shall never be beloved by men
He who the ox to wrath has moved
Shall never be by woman loved.
'Auguries of Innocence' (*c.*1803) l. 29

21 The caterpillar on the leaf
Repeats to thee thy mother's grief.

Kill not the moth nor butterfly,
For the Last Judgement draweth nigh.
'Auguries of Innocence' (*c.*1803) l. 37

1 A truth that's told with bad intent
Beats all the lies you can invent.
'Auguries of Innocence' (*c.*1803) l. 53

2 Man was made for joy and woe;
And when this we rightly know
Thro' the world we safely go.
'Auguries of Innocence' (*c.*1803) l. 56

3 The strongest poison ever known
Came from Caesar's laurel crown.
'Auguries of Innocence' (*c.*1803) l. 97

4 If the Sun and Moon should doubt,
They'd immediately go out.
To be in a passion you good may do,
But no good if a passion is in you.
'Auguries of Innocence' (*c.*1803) l. 109

5 The whore and gambler, by the State
Licensed, build that nation's fate.
The harlot's cry from street to street
Shall weave old England's winding sheet.
'Auguries of Innocence' (*c.*1803) l. 113

6 Every night and every morn
Some to misery are born,
Every morn and every night
Some are born to sweet delight.
Some are born to sweet delight,
Some are born to endless night.
'Auguries of Innocence' (*c.*1803) l. 119

7 God appears and God is Light
To those poor souls who dwell in night
But does a human form display
To those who dwell in realms of day.
'Auguries of Innocence' (*c.*1803) l. 129

8 Does the eagle know what is in the pit?
Or wilt thou go ask the mole:
Can wisdom be put in a silver rod?
Or love in a golden bowl?
The Book of Thel (1789) plate i 'Thel's Motto'

9 Everything that lives,
Lives not alone, nor for itself.
The Book of Thel (1789) plate 3, l. 26

10 The Vision of Christ that thou dost see
Is my vision's greatest enemy;
Thine has a great hook nose like thine,
Mine has a snub nose like to mine.
The Everlasting Gospel (*c.*1818) (a) l. 1

11 Both read the Bible day and night,
But thou read'st black where I read white.
The Everlasting Gospel (*c.*1818) (a) l. 13

12 Was Jesus gentle, or did he
Give any marks of gentility?
When twelve years old he ran away
And left his parents in dismay.
The Everlasting Gospel (*c.*1818) (b) l. 1

13 Was Jesus humble or did he
Give any proofs of humility
Boast of high things with humble tone
And give with charity a stone.
The Everlasting Gospel (*c.*1818) (d) l. 1

14 Humility is only doubt
And does the sun and moon blot out
Rooting over with thorns and stems
The buried soul and all its gems
This life's dim windows of the soul
Distorts the heavens from pole to pole
And leads you to believe a lie
When you see with, not through, the eye.
The Everlasting Gospel (*c.*1818) (d) l. 99

15 Was Jesus chaste? or did he
Give any lessons of chastity?
The morning blushed fiery red:
Mary was found in adulterous bed.
The Everlasting Gospel (*c.*1818) (e) l. 1

16 Jesus was sitting in Moses' chair,
They brought the trembling woman there.
Moses commands she be stoned to death,
What was the sound of Jesus breath?
He laid His hand on Moses' Law:
The ancient Heavens, in silent awe
Writ with curses from pole to pole,
All away began to roll.
The Everlasting Gospel (*c.*1818) (e) l. 7

17 I am sure this Jesus will not do
Either for Englishman or Jew.
The Everlasting Gospel (*c.*1818) (f) l. 1

18 Mutual Forgiveness of each vice,
Such are the Gates of Paradise.
For the Sexes: The Gates of Paradise 'Mutual Forgiveness of each Vice' [prologue]

19 Truly, my Satan, thou art but a dunce,
And dost not know the garment from the man;
Every harlot was a virgin once,
Nor can'st thou ever change Kate into Nan.

Tho' thou art worshipped by the names divine
Of Jesus and Jehovah, thou art still
The Son of Morn in weary Night's decline,
The lost traveller's dream under the hill.
For the Sexes: The Gates of Paradise 'To the Accuser who is The God of This World' [epilogue]

20 I must create a system, or be enslaved by another man's.
I will not reason and compare: my business is to create.
Jerusalem (1815) 'Chapter 1' (plate 10, l. 20)

21 Near mournful
Ever weeping Paddington.
Jerusalem (1815) 'Chapter 1' (plate 12, l. 27)

22 The fields from Islington to Marybone,
To Primrose Hill and Saint John's Wood
Were builded over with pillars of gold;
And there Jerusalem's pillars stood.
Jerusalem (1815) 'To the Jews' (plate 27, l. 1) "The fields from Islington to Marybone"

23 Pancras and Kentish-town repose
Among her golden pillars high
Among her golden arches which

Shine upon the starry sky.
Jerusalem (1815) 'To the Jews' (plate 27, l. 9) "The fields from Islington to Marybone"

1 For a tear is an intellectual thing;
And a sigh is the sword of an Angel King
And the bitter groan of the martyr's woe
Is an arrow from the Almighty's bow!
Jerusalem (1815) 'To the Deists' (plate 52, l. 25) "I saw a Monk of Charlemaine"

2 He who would do good to another, must do it in minute particulars
General good is the plea of the scoundrel, hypocrite and flatterer:
For Art and Science cannot exist but in minutely organized particulars.
Jerusalem (1815) 'Chapter 3' (plate 55, l. 60)

3 I give you the end of a golden string;
Only wind it into a ball:
It will lead you in at Heaven's gate,
Built in Jerusalem's wall.
Jerusalem (1815) 'To the Christians' (plate 77) "I give you the end of a golden string"

4 England! awake! awake! awake!
Jerusalem thy sister calls!
Why wilt thou sleep the sleep of death,
And close her from thy ancient walls?
Jerusalem (1815) 'To the Christians' (plate 77) "England! awake! . . . "

5 And now the time returns again:
Our souls exult, and London's towers,
Receive the Lamb of God to dwell
In England's green and pleasant bowers.
Jerusalem (1815) 'To the Christians' (plate 77)

6 I care not whether a man is good or evil; all that I care
Is whether he is a wise man or a fool. Go! put off holiness
And put on Intellect.
Jerusalem (1815) 'Chapter 4' (plate 91, l. 54)

7 May God us keep
From Single vision and Newton's sleep!
'Letter to Thomas Butts, 22 November 1802'

8 O why was I born with a different face?
Why was I not born like the rest of my race?
'Letter to Thomas Butts, 16 August 1803'

9 Without contraries is no progression. Attraction and repulsion, reason and energy, love and hate, are necessary to human existence.
The Marriage of Heaven and Hell (1790–3) 'The Argument'

10 Energy is Eternal Delight.
The Marriage of Heaven and Hell (1790–3) 'The voice of the Devil'

11 The reason Milton wrote in fetters when he wrote of Angels and God, and at liberty when of Devils and Hell, is because he was a true Poet, and of the Devil's party without knowing it.
The Marriage of Heaven and Hell (1790–3) 'The voice of the Devil' (note)

12 The road of excess leads to the palace of wisdom.
The Marriage of Heaven and Hell (1790–3) 'Proverbs of Hell'

13 Prudence is a rich, ugly, old maid courted by Incapacity.
The Marriage of Heaven and Hell (1790–3) 'Proverbs of Hell'

14 He who desires but acts not, breeds pestilence.
The Marriage of Heaven and Hell (1790–3) 'Proverbs of Hell'

15 A fool sees not the same tree that a wise man sees.
The Marriage of Heaven and Hell (1790–3) 'Proverbs of Hell'

16 Eternity is in love with the productions of time.
The Marriage of Heaven and Hell (1790–3) 'Proverbs of Hell'

17 Bring out number weight and measure in a year of dearth.
The Marriage of Heaven and Hell (1790–3) 'Proverbs of Hell'

18 If the fool would persist in his folly he would become wise.
The Marriage of Heaven and Hell (1790–3) 'Proverbs of Hell'

19 Prisons are built with stones of Law, brothels with bricks of Religion.
The Marriage of Heaven and Hell (1790–3) 'Proverbs of Hell'

20 The pride of the peacock is the glory of God.
The lust of the goat is the bounty of God.
The wrath of the lion is the wisdom of God.
The nakedness of woman is the work of God.
The Marriage of Heaven and Hell (1790–3) 'Proverbs of Hell'

21 The tygers of wrath are wiser than the horses of instruction.
The Marriage of Heaven and Hell (1790–3) 'Proverbs of Hell'

22 Damn braces: Bless relaxes.
The Marriage of Heaven and Hell (1790–3) 'Proverbs of Hell'

23 Exuberance is beauty.
The Marriage of Heaven and Hell (1790–3) 'Proverbs of Hell'

24 Sooner murder an infant in its cradle than nurse unacted desires.
The Marriage of Heaven and Hell (1790–3) 'Proverbs of Hell'

25 Truth can never be told so as to be understood, and not be believed.
The Marriage of Heaven and Hell (1790–3) 'Proverbs of Hell'

26 How do you know but every bird that cuts the airy way
Is an immense world of delight, closed by your senses five?
The Marriage of Heaven and Hell (1790–3) 'A Memorable Fancy' plate 7

27 Then I asked: 'Does a firm persuasion that a thing is so, make it so?'
He replied: 'All Poets believe that it does, and in ages of imagination this firm persuasion removed mountains; but many are not capable of a firm persuasion of anything.'
The Marriage of Heaven and Hell (1790–3) 'A Memorable Fancy' plates 12–13

28 If the doors of perception were cleansed everything would appear to man as it is, infinite.
The Marriage of Heaven and Hell (1790–3) 'A Memorable Fancy' plate 14

29 I was in a printing house in Hell, and saw the method in which knowledge is transmitted from generation to generation.
The Marriage of Heaven and Hell (1790–3) 'A Memorable Fancy' plates 15–17

1 And did those feet in ancient time
Walk upon England's mountains green?
And was the holy Lamb of God
On England's pleasant pastures seen?
And did the Countenance Divine
Shine forth upon our clouded hills?
And was Jerusalem builded here
Among these dark Satanic mills?

Bring me my bow of burning gold:
Bring me my arrows of desire:
Bring me my spear: O clouds, unfold!
Bring me my chariot of fire.

I will not cease from mental fight,
Nor shall my sword sleep in my hand,
Till we have built Jerusalem,
In England's green and pleasant land.
Milton (1804–10) preface 'And did those feet in ancient time'

2 Mock on, mock on Voltaire, Rousseau:
Mock on, mock on: tis all in vain!
You throw the sand against the wind,
And the wind blows it back again.
MS Note-Book

3 The atoms of Democritus
And Newton's particles of light
Are sands upon the Red sea shore,
Where Israel's tents do shine so bright.
MS Note-Book

4 He has observed the golden rule
Till he's become the golden fool.
MS Note-Book

5 To forgive enemies H— does pretend,
Who never in his life forgave a friend.
MS Note-Book

6 The errors of a wise man make your rule
Rather than the perfections of a fool.
MS Note-Book

7 Great things are done when men and mountains meet;
This is not done by jostling in the street.
MS Note-Book

8 He who binds to himself a joy
Doth the winged life destroy;
But he who kisses the joy as it flies
Lives in Eternity's sunrise.
MS Note-Book 'Several Questions Answered'—"He who binds to himself a joy"

9 What is it men in women do require?
The lineaments of gratified desire.
What is it women do in men require?
The lineaments of gratified desire.
MS Note-Book 'Several Questions Answered'—"What is it men in women do require"

10 The sword sung on the barren heath,
The sickle in the fruitful field:
The sword he sung a song of death,
But could not make the sickle yield.
MS Note-Book

11 Never pain to tell thy love
Love that never told can be;
For the gentle wind does move
Silently, invisibly.
MS Note-Book

12 Piping down the valleys wild,
Piping songs of pleasant glee,
On a cloud I saw a child,
And he laughing said to me.

'Pipe a song about a Lamb!'
So I piped with merry cheer.
'Piper pipe that song again;'
So I piped: he wept to hear.
Songs of Innocence (1789) introduction

13 When my mother died I was very young,
And my father sold me while yet my tongue
Could scarcely cry "weep! 'weep! 'weep! 'weep!'
So your chimneys I sweep, and in soot I sleep.
Songs of Innocence (1789) 'The Chimney Sweeper'

14 To Mercy, Pity, Peace, and Love,
All pray in their distress.
Songs of Innocence (1789) 'The Divine Image'

15 For Mercy has a human heart,
Pity a human face,
And Love, the human form divine,
And Peace, the human dress.
Songs of Innocence (1789) 'The Divine Image'; cf. **Blake** 121:11

16 Then cherish pity, lest you drive an angel from your door.
Songs of Innocence (1789) 'Holy Thursday'

17 Little Lamb who made thee?
Dost thou know who made thee?
Gave thee life and bid thee feed.
By the stream and o'er the mead;
Gave thee clothing of delight,
Softest clothing woolly bright;
Gave thee such a tender voice,
Making all the vales rejoice!
Songs of Innocence (1789) 'The Lamb'

18 My mother bore me in the southern wild,
And I am black, but O! my soul is white;
White as an angel is the English child:
But I am black as if bereaved of light.
Songs of Innocence (1789) 'The Little Black Boy'

19 When the voices of children are heard on the green
And laughing is heard on the hill.
Songs of Innocence (1789) 'Nurse's Song'

20 Can I see another's woe,
And not be in sorrow too?
Can I see another's grief,
And not seek for kind relief?
Songs of Innocence (1789) 'On Another's Sorrow'

21 Hear the voice of the Bard!
Who present, past, and future, sees.
Songs of Experience (1794) introduction

22 Ah, Sun-flower! weary of time,
Who countest the steps of the Sun;
Seeking after that sweet golden clime
Where the traveller's journey is done.

Where the Youth pined away with desire,
And the pale Virgin shrouded in snow:

Arise from their graves and aspire,
Where my Sun-flower wishes to go.
Songs of Experience (1794) 'Ah, Sun-flower!'

1 Love seeketh not itself to please,
Nor for itself hath any care;
But for another gives its ease,
And builds a Heaven in Hell's despair.
Songs of Experience (1794) 'The Clod and the Pebble'

2 Love seeketh only Self to please,
To bind another to its delight,
Joys in another's loss of ease,
And builds a Hell in Heaven's despite.
Songs of Experience (1794) 'The Clod and the Pebble'

3 My mother groaned! my father wept.
Into the dangerous world I leapt:
Helpless, naked, piping loud;
Like a fiend hid in a cloud.
Songs of Experience (1794) 'Infant Sorrow'

4 Children of the future age,
Reading this indignant page:
Know that in a former time
Love! sweet love! was thought a crime.
Songs of Experience (1794) 'A Little Girl Lost'

5 I was angry with my friend;
I told my wrath, my wrath did end.
I was angry with my foe:
I told it not, my wrath did grow.
Songs of Experience (1794) 'A Poison Tree'

6 In the morning glad I see,
My foe outstretched beneath the tree
Songs of Experience (1794) 'A Poison Tree'

7 O Rose, thou art sick!
The invisible worm
That flies in the night,
In the howling storm:

Has found out thy bed
Of crimson joy:
And his dark secret love
Does thy life destroy.
Songs of Experience (1794) 'The Sick Rose'

8 Tyger Tyger, burning bright,
In the forests of the night;
What immortal hand or eye,
Could frame thy fearful symmetry?
Songs of Experience (1794) 'The Tiger'

9 What the hand dare seize the fire?
And what shoulder, and what art,
Could twist the sinews of thy heart?
And when thy heart began to beat,
What dread hand? and what dread feet?
Songs of Experience (1794) 'The Tiger'

10 When the stars threw down their spears
And watered heaven with their tears:
Did he smile his work to see?
Did he who made the Lamb make thee?
Songs of Experience (1794) 'The Tiger'

11 Cruelty has a human heart,
And Jealousy a human face;
Terror the human form divine,
And Secrecy the human dress.
'A Divine Image'; etched but not included in *Songs of Experience* (1794); cf. **Blake** 120:15

12 Vision or Imagination is a Representation of what Eternally Exists, Really and Unchangeably.
A Vision of the Last Judgement (1810) in *MS Note-Book*

13 What it will be questioned when the sun rises do you not see a round disc of fire somewhat like a guinea O no no I see an innumerable company of the heavenly host crying Holy, Holy, Holy is the Lord God Almighty.
A Vision of the Last Judgement (1810) in *MS Note-Book*

Susanna Blamire 1747–94
English poet

14 I've gotten a rock, I've gotten a reel,
I've gotten a wee bit spinning-wheel;
An' by the whirling rim I've found
How the weary, weary warl goes round.
'I've Gotten a Rock, I've Gotten a Reel' (*c.*1790) l. 1

15 Should we miss but a tree where we used to be playing,
Or find the wood cut where we sauntered a-Maying,—
If the yew-seat's away, or the ivy's a-wanting,
We hate the fine lawn and the new-fashioned planting.
Each thing called improvement seems blackened with crimes,
If it tears up one record of blissful old times.
'When Home We Return' (*c.*1790) l. 7

Jean Joseph Louis Blanc 1811–82
French utopian socialist

16 *Dans la doctrine saint-simonienne, le problème de la répartition des bénéfices est résolu par cette fameuse formule:* à chacun suivant sa capacité; à chaque capacité suivant ses oeuvres.

In the Saint-Simonian doctrine, the problem of the distribution of benefits is resolved by this famous saying: *To each according to his ability; to each ability according to its fruits.*

Blanc cites Saint-Simon in order to disagree with his ideas
Organisation du travail (1841 ed.); cf. **Marx** 499:15, **Morelly** 531:17

Lesley Blanch 1907–
British writer

17 She was an Amazon. Her whole life was spent riding at breakneck speed towards the wilder shores of love.
of Jane Digby El Mezrab (1807–81)
The Wilder Shores of Love (1954) pt. 2, ch. 1

Danny Blanchflower 1926–93
English footballer

18 The great fallacy is that the game is first and last about winning. It is nothing of the kind. The game is about glory, it is about doing things in style and

with a flourish, about going out and beating the lot, not waiting for them to die of boredom.
attributed, 1972

Arthur Bliss 1891–1975
English composer

1 What is called the serenity of age is only perhaps a euphemism for the fading power to feel the sudden shock of joy or sorrow.
As I Remember (1970) foreword

Philip Paul Bliss 1838–76
American evangelist

2 Hold the fort, for I am coming.
suggested by a flag message from General **Sherman**; *see* **Sherman** *716:27*
Gospel Hymns and Sacred Songs (1875) no. 14

Karen Blixen see **Isak Dinesen**

Alexander Blok 1880–1921
Russian poet

3 When rowan leaves are dank and rusting
And rowan berries red as blood,
When in my palm the hangman's thrusting
The final nail with bony thud . . .

Then, through the blood and weeping, stretches
My dying sight to space remote;
I see upon the river's reaches
Christ sailing to me in a boat.
'Autumn Love' (1907) (translated by Maurice Bowra)

4 The wind plays up; snow flutters down.
Twelve men are marching through the town.
'The Twelve' (1918) (translated by Jon Stallworthy and Peter France)

5 Caps tilted, fag drooping, every one
looks like a jailbird on the run.
'The Twelve' (1918) (translated by Jon Stallworthy and Peter France)

6 So they march with sovereign tread
Behind them limps the hungry dog,
and wrapped in wild snow at their head
carrying a blood-red flag—
soft-footed where the blizzard swirls,
invulnerable where bullets crossed—
crowned with a crown of snowflake pearls,
a flowery diadem of frost,
ahead of them goes Jesus Christ.
'The Twelve' (1918) (translated by Jon Stallworthy and Peter France)

Reginald Blomfield 1856–1942
English architect

7 Architecture should be at the head of the arts, not at the foot of the professions.
R. N. Shaw and T. G. Jackson (eds.) *Architecture* (1892)

Gebhard Lebrecht Blücher 1742–1819
Prussian field marshal

8 *Was für Plunder!*
What rubbish!
of London, as seen from the Monument in June 1814
Evelyn Princess Blücher *Memoirs of Prince Blücher* (1932); cf. **Misquotations** 522:13

Judy Blume 1938–
American writer

9 Are you there God? It's me, Margaret.
I just told my mother I want a bra.
Please help me grow God. You know where.
I want to be like everyone else.
Are You There God? It's Me, Margaret (1970)

Edmund Blunden 1896–1974
English poet

10 All things they have in common being so poor,
And their one fear, Death's shadow at the door.
'Almswomen' (1920)

11 I am for the woods against the world,
But are the woods for me?
'The Kiss' (1931)

12 I have been young, and now am not too old;
And I have seen the righteous forsaken,
His health, his honour and his quality taken.
This is not what we were formerly told.
'Report on Experience' (1929); cf. **Book of Common Prayer** 133:26

13 This was my country and it may be yet,
But something flew between me and the sun.
'The Resignation' (1928)

Wilfrid Scawen Blunt 1840–1922
English poet

14 To the Grafton Gallery to look at . . . the Post-Impressionist pictures sent over from Paris . . . The drawing is on the level of that of an untaught child of seven or eight years old, the sense of colour that of a tea-tray painter, the method that of a schoolboy who wipes his fingers on a slate after spitting on them . . . These are not works of art at all, unless throwing a handful of mud against a wall may be called one. They are the works of idleness and impotent stupidity, a pornographic show.
My Diaries (1920) 15 November 1910

Robert Bly 1926–
American poet

15 Terror just before death,
Shoulders torn, shot
From helicopters, the boy
Tortured with the telephone generator,
'I felt sorry for him
And blew his head off with a shotgun.'
These instants become crystals,
Particles
The grass cannot dissolve. Our own gaiety

Will end up
In Asia, and in your cup you will look down
And see
Black Starfighters.
We were the ones we intended to bomb!

'Driving Through Minnesota During the Hanoi Bombings' (1968)

1 Alive, we are like a sleek black water beetle.
Skating across still water in any direction
We choose, and soon to be swallowed
Suddenly from beneath.

'Night' (1962)

2 Every modern male has, lying at the bottom of his psyche, a large, primitive being covered with hair down to his feet. Making contact with this Wild Man is the step the Eighties male or the Nineties male has yet to take.

Iron John (1990)

Ronald Blythe 1922–

English writer

3 An industrial worker would sooner have a £5 note but a countryman must have praise.

Akenfield (1969)

4 With full-span lives having become the norm, people may need to learn how to be aged as they once had to learn how to be adult.

The View in Winter (1979)

Boccaccio 1313–75

Italian writer, poet, and humanist

5 *E infinite volte avvenne che, andando due preti con una croce per alcuno, si misero tre o quatro bare, da'portatori portate, di dietro a quella: e, dove un morto credevano avere i preti a seppilire, n'avevano sei o otto e tal fiate piú.*

And times without number it happened that two priests would be on their way to bury someone, holding a cross before them, only to find that bearers carrying three or four additional biers would fall in behind them; so that whereas the priests had thought they only had one burial to attend to, they in fact had six or eight, and sometimes more.

during the Black Death

Decameron (1348–58) introduction

6 *Fosse grandissime nelle quali a centinaia si mettevano i sopravegnenti; e in quelle stivati, come si mettono le mercantie nelle navi a suolo a suolo.*

They dug for each graveyard a huge trench, in which they laid the corpses as they arrived by hundreds at a time, piling them up tier upon tier as merchandise is stowed in a ship.

Decameron (1348–58) introduction

7 *In tanto che molto volte nelle cose da lui fatte si truova che il visivo denso degli uomini vi prese errore, quello credendo esser vero che era dipinto.*

Mortal sight was often puzzled, face to face with his creations, and took the painted thing for the actual object.

of the painting of Giotto (c.1267–1337)

Decameron (1348–58) bk. 6

John Ernest Bode 1816–74

English clergyman

8 O Jesus, I have promised
To serve thee to the end;
Be thou for ever near me,
My Master and my Friend.

'O Jesus, I have promised' (1869 hymn); written for the confirmation of Bode's three children

9 O let me hear thee speaking
In accents clear and still,
Above the storms of passion,
The murmurs of self-will.

'O Jesus, I have promised' (1869 hymn)

Ivan F. Boesky 1937–

American businessman

10 Greed is all right . . . Greed is healthy. You can be greedy and still feel good about yourself.

commencement address, Berkeley, California, 18 May 1986; cf. **Film lines** 311:9

Boethius AD c.476–524

Roman statesman and philosopher

11 *Nam in omni adversitate fortunae infelicissimum est genus infortunii, fuisse felicem.*

For in every ill-turn of fortune the most unhappy sort of unfortunate man is the one who has been happy.

De Consolatione Philosophiae bk. 2, prose 4; cf. **Chaucer** 207:12, **Dante** 249:12, **Tennyson** 762:24

Louise Bogan 1897–1970

American poet

12 Women have no wilderness in them,
They are provident instead,
Content in the tight hot cell of their hearts
To eat dusty bread.

'Women' (1923)

Humphrey Bogart see Catchphrases 195:3, Film lines 311:10, 311:12, 312:4, Telegrams 758:8

John B. Bogart 1848–1921

American journalist

13 When a dog bites a man, that is not news, because it happens so often. But if a man bites a dog, that is news.

often attributed to Charles A. Dana

F. M. O'Brien *The Story of the* [New York] *Sun* (1918) ch. 10

Niels Bohr 1885–1962
Danish physicist

1 Anybody who is not shocked by this subject has failed to understand it.
of quantum mechanics
attributed; in *Nature* 23 August 1990

2 Never express yourself more clearly than you think.
Abraham Pais *Einstein Lived Here* (1994)

3 One of the favourite maxims of my father was the distinction between the two sorts of truths, profound truths recognized by the fact that the opposite is also a profound truth, in contrast to trivialities where opposites are obviously absurd.
S. Rozental *Niels Bohr* (1967)

Nicolas Boileau 1636–1711
French critic and poet

4 *Enfin Malherbe vint, et, le premier en France,*
Fit sentir dans les vers une juste cadence.
At last came Malherbe, and he was the first in France to give poetry a proper flow.
L'Art poétique (1674) canto 1, l. 131

5 *Un sot trouve toujours un plus sot qui l'admire.*
A fool can always find a greater fool to admire him.
L'Art poétique (1674) canto 1, l. 232

6 *Qu'en un lieu, qu'en un jour, un seul fait accompli*
Tienne jusqu'à la fin le théâtre rempli.
Let a single completed action, all in one place, all in one day, keep the theatre packed to the end of your play.
L'Art poétique (1674) canto 3, l. 45

7 *Si j'écris quatre mots, j'en effacerai trois.*
Of every four words I write, I strike out three.
Satire (2). *A M. Molière* (1665)

Eavan Boland 1944–
Irish poet

8 Imagine how they stood there, what they stood with
that their possessions may become our power.
Cardboard. Iron. Their hardships parcelled in them.
'The Emigrant Irish' (1987)

9 I think of what great art removes:
Hazard and death, the future and the past.
'From the painting *Back from Market* by Chardin' (1967)

Alan Bold 1943–
Scottish poet

10 This happened near the core
Of a world's culture. This
Occurred among higher things.
This was a philosophical conclusion.
Everybody gets what he deserves.
The bare drab rubble of the place.
The dull damp stone. The rain.
The emptiness. The human lack.
'June 1967 at Buchenwald' (1969); cf. **Anonymous** 20:17

11 Scotland, land of the omnipotent No.
'A Memory of Death' (1969)

12 Our job is to try
To change things.
After Hiroshima
You ask a poet to sing.
'Recitative' (1965)

Henry St John, Lord Bolingbroke 1678–1751
English politician

13 They make truth serve as a stalking-horse to error.
Letters on the Study and Use of History (1752) No. 4, pt. 1

14 They [Thucydides and Xenophon] maintained the dignity of history.
Letters on the Study and Use of History (1752) No. 5, pt. 2

15 Nations, like men, have their infancy.
On the Study of History letter 5, in *Works* (1809) vol. 3

16 Truth lies within a little and certain compass, but error is immense.
Reflections upon Exile (1716)

17 What a world is this, and how does fortune banter us!
letter to Jonathan Swift, 3 August 1714, in Harold Williams (ed.) *Correspondence of Jonathan Swift* (1963) vol. 2

18 The great mistake is that of looking upon men as virtuous, or thinking that they can be made so by laws.
comment (*c.*1728), in Joseph Spence *Observations, Anecdotes, and Characters* (1820, ed. J. M. Osborn, 1966) Anecdote 882

19 The greatest art of a politician is to render vice serviceable to the cause of virtue.
comment (*c.*1728), in Joseph Spence *Observations, Anecdotes, and Characters* (1820, ed. J. M. Osborn, 1966) Anecdote 882

Robert Bolt 1924–95
English dramatist
see also **Borrowed titles** 144:11

20 This country's planted thick with laws from coast to coast—Man's laws, not God's—and if you cut them down—and you're just the man to do it—d'you really think you could stand upright in the winds that would blow then?
A Man for All Seasons (1960) act 1

21 It profits a man nothing to give his soul for the whole world . . . But for Wales—!
A Man for All Seasons (1960) act 2; cf. **Bible** 98:8

Edmund Bolton *c.*1575–*c.*1633
English poet

22 The withered primrose by the mourning river,
The faded summer's sun from weeping fountains,
The light-blown bubble vanished for ever,
The molten snow upon the naked mountains,
Are emblems that the treasures we up-lay
Soon wither, vanish, fade, and melt away.
'A Palinode' (1600)

Elizabeth Patterson Bonaparte
1785–1879

American-born wife of Jérôme Bonaparte, youngest brother of **Napoleon**

1 Even quarrels with one's husband are preferable to the ennui of a solitary existence.

Eugene L. Didier *The Life and Letters of Madame Bonaparte* (1879)

Andrew Bonar Law 1858–1923

Canadian-born British Conservative statesman, Prime Minister 1922–3

on Bonar Law: see **Asquith** 31:5, **Beaverbrook** 59:7

2 There are things stronger than parliamentary majorities. I can imagine no length of resistance to which Ulster will not go, in which I shall not be ready to support them.

at a Unionist meeting at Blenheim in 1912

Robert Blake *The Unknown Prime Minister* (1955)

3 In war it is necessary not only to be active but to seem active.

letter to **Asquith**, 1916; Robert Blake *The Unknown Prime Minister* (1955)

4 If I am a great man, then all great men are frauds.

Lord Beaverbrook *Politicians and the War* (1932)

St Bonaventura (Giovanni di Fidanza)
1221–74

Franciscan theologian, born in Tuscany

5 Reason is the natural image of the Creator.

Itinerarium Mentis in Deum

Carrie Jacobs Bond 1862–1946

American songwriter

6 When you come to the end of a perfect day.

'A Perfect Day' (1910 song)

David Bone 1874–1959

Scottish naval officer and writer

7 It's 'Damn you, Jack — I'm all right!' with you chaps.

Brassbounder (1910) ch. 3

Dietrich Bonhoeffer 1906–45

German Lutheran theologian and martyr

8 In me there is darkness, but with you there is light.

prayer written for fellow-prisoners in a Nazi prison, 1943

Letters and Papers from Prison (1971)

9 It is the nature, and the advantage, of strong people that they can bring out the crucial questions and form a clear opinion about them. The weak always have to decide between alternatives that are not their own.

Widerstand und Ergebung (Resistance and Submission, 1951) 'Ein paar Gedanken über Verschiedenes'

10 Jesus is there only for others . . . God in human form! not . . . in the Greek divine-human form of 'man in himself', but 'the man for others', and therefore the crucified.

Widerstand und Ergebung (Resistance and Submission, 1951) 'Entwurf einer Arbeit'

The Book of Common Prayer 1662

11 It hath been the wisdom of the Church of England, ever since the first compiling of her Publick Liturgy, to keep the mean between the two extremes, of too much stiffness in refusing, and of too much easiness in admitting any variation from it.

The Preface

12 There was never any thing by the wit of man so well devised, or so sure established, which in continuance of time hath not been corrupted.

The Preface Concerning the Service of the Church

13 Dearly beloved brethren, the Scripture moveth us in sundry places to acknowledge and confess our manifold sins and wickedness; and that we should not dissemble nor cloke them before the face of Almighty God our heavenly Father; but confess them with an humble, lowly, penitent, and obedient heart.

Morning Prayer Sentences of the Scriptures

14 I pray and beseech you, as many as are here present, to accompany me with a pure heart, and humble voice, unto the throne of the heavenly grace.

Morning Prayer Sentences of the Scriptures

15 We have erred, and strayed from thy ways like lost sheep. We have followed too much the devices and desires of our own hearts.

Morning Prayer General Confession

16 We have left undone those things which we ought to have done; And we have done those things which we ought not to have done; And there is no health in us.

Morning Prayer General Confession

17 Restore thou them that are penitent; According to thy promises declared unto mankind in Christ Jesu our Lord. And grant, O most merciful Father, for his sake; That we may hereafter live a godly, righteous, and sober life.

Morning Prayer General Confession

18 And forgive us our trespasses, As we forgive them that trespass against us.

Morning Prayer The Lord's Prayer; cf. **Bible** 93:19, **Missal** 522:17

19 Glory be to the Father, and to the Son: and to the Holy Ghost; As it was in the beginning, is now, and ever shall be: world without end. Amen.

Morning Prayer Gloria; cf. **Missal** 520:10

20 We praise thee, O God: we acknowledge thee to be the Lord.
All the earth doth worship thee: the Father everlasting.
To thee all Angels cry aloud: the Heavens, and all the Powers therein.
To thee Cherubin, and Seraphin: continually do cry,

Holy, Holy, Holy: Lord God of Sabaoth;
Heaven and earth are full of the Majesty: of thy Glory.
The glorious company of the Apostles: praise thee.
The goodly fellowship of the Prophets: praise thee.
The noble army of Martyrs: praise thee.
Morning Prayer Te Deum; cf. **Prayers** 592:7

1 When thou hadst overcome the sharpness of death: thou didst open the Kingdom of Heaven to all believers.
Morning Prayer Te Deum

2 Day by day: we magnify thee;
And we worship thy Name: ever world without end.
Vouchsafe, O Lord: to keep us this day without sin.
O Lord, have mercy upon us: have mercy upon us.
O Lord, let thy mercy lighten upon us: as our trust is in thee.
O Lord, in thee have I trusted: let me never be confounded.
Morning Prayer Te Deum; cf. **Prayers** 592:8

3 O all ye Works of the Lord, bless ye the Lord.
Morning Prayer Benedicite

4 O ye Waters that be above the Firmament, bless ye the Lord.
Morning Prayer Benedicite

5 O ye Showers, and Dew, bless ye the Lord: praise him, and magnify him for ever.
O ye Winds of God, bless ye the Lord: praise him, and magnify him for ever.
Morning Prayer Benedicite

6 O ye Dews, and Frosts, bless ye the Lord: praise him, and magnify him for ever.
O ye Frost and Cold, bless ye the Lord: praise him and magnify him for ever.
O ye Ice and Snow, bless ye the Lord: praise him and magnify him for ever.
O ye Nights, and Days, bless ye the Lord: praise him, and magnify him for ever.
Morning Prayer Benedicite

7 O let the Earth bless the Lord: yea, let it praise him, and magnify him for ever.
Morning Prayer Benedicite

8 O all ye Green Things upon the Earth, bless ye the Lord: praise him, and magnify him for ever.
Morning Prayer Benedicite

9 O ye Whales, and all that move in the Waters, bless ye the Lord: praise him, and magnify him for ever.
Morning Prayer Benedicite

10 I believe in God the Father Almighty, Maker of heaven and earth:
And in Jesus Christ his only Son our Lord, Who was conceived by the Holy Ghost, Born of the Virgin Mary, Suffered under Pontius Pilate, Was crucified, dead, and buried, He descended into hell; The third day he rose again from the dead, He ascended into heaven, And sitteth on the right hand of God the Father Almighty; From thence he shall come to judge the quick and the dead.
I believe in the Holy Ghost; The holy Catholic Church; The Communion of Saints; The Forgiveness of sins; The Resurrection of the body, And the life everlasting. Amen.
Morning Prayer The Apostles' Creed; cf. **Book of Common Prayer** 129:8, **Missal** 520:16

11 Give peace in our time, O Lord.
Morning Prayer Versicle

12 O God, who art the author of peace and lover of concord, in knowledge of whom standeth our eternal life, whose service is perfect freedom; Defend us thy humble servants in all assaults of our enemies.
Morning Prayer The Second Collect, for Peace

13 Grant that this day we fall into no sin, neither run into any kind of danger.
Morning Prayer The Third Collect, for Grace

14 In Quires and Places where they sing, here followeth the Anthem.
Morning Prayer rubric following Third Collect

15 Endue her plenteously with heavenly gifts; grant her in health and wealth long to live.
Morning Prayer Prayer for the Queen's Majesty

16 Almighty God, the fountain of all goodness.
Morning Prayer Prayer for the Royal Family

17 Almighty and everlasting God, who alone workest great marvels; Send down upon our Bishops, and Curates, and all Congregations committed to their charge, the healthful Spirit of thy grace; and that they may truly please thee, pour upon them the continual dew of thy blessing.
Morning Prayer Prayer for the Clergy and People

18 Almighty God, who hast given us grace at this time with one accord to make our common supplications unto thee; and dost promise, that when two or three are gathered together in thy Name thou wilt grant their requests: Fulfil now, O Lord, the desires and petitions of thy servants, as may be most expedient for them.
Morning Prayer Prayer of St Chrysostom

19 O God, from whom all holy desires, all good counsels, and all just works do proceed; Give unto thy servants that peace which the world cannot give.
Evening Prayer Second Collect

20 Lighten our darkness, we beseech thee, O Lord; and by thy great mercy defend us from all perils and dangers of this night.
Evening Prayer Third Collect

21 Whosoever will be saved: before all things it is necessary that he hold the Catholic Faith.
At Morning Prayer Athanasian Creed 'Quicunque vult'

22 And the Catholic Faith is this: That we worship one God in Trinity, and Trinity in Unity;
Neither confounding the Persons: nor dividing the Substance.
At Morning Prayer Athanasian Creed 'Quicunque vult'

23 There are not three incomprehensibles, nor three uncreated: but one uncreated, and one incomprehensible.
At Morning Prayer Athanasian Creed 'Quicunque vult'

1 Perfect God, and perfect Man: of a reasonable soul and human flesh subsisting;
Equal to the Father, as touching his Godhead: and inferior to the Father, as touching his Manhood.
At Morning Prayer Athanasian Creed 'Quicunque vult'

2 Have mercy upon us miserable sinners.
The Litany

3 From all evil and mischief; from sin, from the crafts and assaults of the devil; from thy wrath, and from everlasting damnation,
Good Lord, deliver us.
The Litany

4 From envy, hatred, and malice, and from all uncharitableness,
Good Lord, deliver us.
The Litany

5 From all the deceits of the world, the flesh, and the devil,
Good Lord, deliver us.
The Litany

6 From lightning and tempest; from plague, pestilence, and famine; from battle and murder, and from sudden death,
Good Lord, deliver us.
The Litany

7 By thine Agony and bloody Sweat; by thy Cross and Passion; by thy precious Death and Burial; by thy glorious Resurrection and Ascension; and by the coming of the Holy Ghost,
Good Lord, deliver us.
The Litany

8 In all time of our tribulation; in all time of our wealth; in the hour of death, and in the day of judgement,
Good Lord, deliver us.
The Litany

9 That it may please thee to illuminate all Bishops, Priests, and Deacons, with true knowledge and understanding of thy Word; and that both by their preaching and living they may set it forth, and show it accordingly;
We beseech thee to hear us, good Lord.
The Litany

10 That it may please thee to strengthen such as do stand; and to comfort and help the weak-hearted; and to raise up them that fall; and finally to beat down Satan under our feet;
We beseech thee to hear us, good Lord.
The Litany

11 That it may please thee to preserve all that travel by land or by water, all women labouring of child, all sick persons, and young children; and to shew thy pity upon all prisoners and captives;
We beseech thee to hear us, good Lord.
The Litany; cf. **Swift** 748:18

12 Defend, and provide for, the fatherless children, and widows, and all that are desolate and oppressed.
The Litany

13 That it may please thee to give and preserve to our use the kindly fruits of the earth, so as in due time we may enjoy them;
We beseech thee to hear us, good Lord.
The Litany

14 O God, merciful Father, that despisest not the sighing of a contrite heart, not the desire of such as be sorrowful; Mercifully assist our prayers that we make before thee in all our troubles and adversities, whensoever they oppress us.
The Litany

15 O God, whose nature and property is ever to have mercy and to forgive, receive our humble petitions; and though we be tied and bound with the chain of our sins, yet let the pitifulness of thy great mercy loose us; for the honour of Jesus Christ, our Mediator and Advocate.
Prayers . . . upon Several Occasions A prayer

16 O God, the Creator and Preserver of all mankind, we humbly beseech thee for all sorts and conditions of men.
Prayers . . . upon Several Occasions 'Collect or Prayer for all Conditions of Men'

17 We pray for the good estate of the Catholick Church; that it may be so guided and governed by thy good Spirit, that all who profess and call themselves Christians may be led into the way of truth.
Prayers . . . upon Several Occasions 'Collect or Prayer for all Conditions of Men'

18 We commend to thy fatherly goodness all those, who are any ways afflicted, or distressed, in mind, body, or estate; that it may please thee to comfort and relieve them, according to their several necessities, giving them patience under their sufferings, and a happy issue out of all their afflictions.
Prayers . . . upon Several Occasions 'Collect or Prayer for all Conditions of Men'

19 We bless thee for our creation, preservation, and all the blessings of this life; but above all, for thine inestimable love in the redemption of the world by our Lord Jesus Christ; for the means of grace, and for the hope of glory.
Thanksgivings General Thanksgiving

20 O God our heavenly Father, who by thy gracious providence dost cause the former and the latter rain to descend upon the earth, that it may bring forth fruit for the use of man; We give thee humble thanks that it hath pleased thee, in our great necessity, to send us at the last a joyful rain upon thine inheritance, and to refresh it when it was dry.
Thanksgivings For Rain

21 Almighty God, give us grace that we may cast away the works of darkness, and put upon us the armour of light, now in the time of this mortal life, in which thy Son Jesus Christ came to visit us in great humility.
Collects The first Sunday in Advent

22 Blessed Lord, who hast caused all holy Scriptures to be written for our learning; Grant that we may in

such wise hear them, read, mark, learn, and inwardly digest them, that by patience, and comfort of thy holy Word, we may embrace, and ever hold fast the blessed hope of everlasting life.
Collects The second Sunday in Advent

1 That whereas, through our sins and wickedness, we are sore let and hindered in running the race that is set before us, thy bountiful grace and mercy may speedily help and deliver us.
Collects The fourth Sunday in Advent

2 O Lord, we beseech thee mercifully to receive the prayers of thy people which call upon thee; and grant that they may both perceive and know what things they ought to do, and also may have grace and power faithfully to fulfil the same.
Collects The first Sunday after the Epiphany

3 O God, who knowest us to be set in the midst of so many and great dangers, that by reason of the frailty of our nature we cannot always stand upright; Grant to us such strength and protection, as may support us in all dangers, and carry us through all temptations.
Collects The fourth Sunday after the Epiphany

4 Almighty God, who seest that we have no power of ourselves to help ourselves; Keep us both outwardly in our bodies, and inwardly in our souls; that we may be defended from all adversities which may happen to the body, and from all evil thoughts which may assault and hurt the soul.
Collects The second Sunday in Lent

5 We humbly beseech thee, that, as by thy special grace preventing us thou dost put into our minds good desires, so by thy continued help we may bring the same to good effect.
Collects Easter-Day

6 Grant us so to put away the leaven of malice and wickedness, that we may alway serve thee in pureness of living and truth.
Collects The first Sunday after Easter

7 O Almighty God, who alone canst order the unruly wills and affections of sinful men; Grant unto thy people, that they may love the thing which thou commandest, and desire that which thou dost promise; that so, among the sundry and manifold changes of the world, our hearts may surely there be fixed, where true joys are to be found.
Collects The fourth Sunday after Easter

8 We beseech thee, leave us not comfortless; but send to us thine Holy Ghost to comfort us, and exalt us unto the same place whither our Saviour Christ is gone before.
Collects Sunday after Ascension Day

9 God, who as at this time didst teach the hearts of thy faithful people, by the sending to them the light of thy Holy Spirit; Grant us by the same Spirit to have a right judgement in all things.
Collects Whit-Sunday

10 Because through the weakness of our mortal nature we can do no good thing without thee, grant us the help of thy grace, that in keeping of thy commandments we may please thee, both in will and deed.
Collects The first Sunday after Trinity

11 O God, the protector of all that trust in thee, without whom nothing is strong, nothing is holy; Increase and multiply upon us thy mercy; that, thou being our ruler and guide, we may so pass through things temporal, that we finally lose not the things eternal.
Collects The fourth Sunday after Trinity

12 Grant, O Lord, we beseech thee, that the course of this world may be so peaceably ordered by thy governance, that thy Church may joyfully serve thee in all godly quietness.
Collects The fifth Sunday after Trinity

13 O God, who hast prepared for them that love thee such good things as pass man's understanding; Pour into our hearts such love toward thee, that we, loving thee above all things, may obtain thy promises, which exceed all that we can desire.
Collects The sixth Sunday after Trinity

14 Lord of all power and might, who art the author and giver of all good things; Graft in our hearts the love of thy Name, increase in us true religion, nourish us with all goodness, and of thy great mercy keep us in the same.
Collects The seventh Sunday after Trinity

15 Pour down upon us the abundance of thy mercy; forgiving us those things whereof our conscience is afraid.
Collects The twelfth Sunday after Trinity

16 O God, forasmuch as without thee we are not able to please thee; Mercifully grant, that thy Holy Spirit may in all things direct and rule our hearts.
Collects The nineteenth Sunday after Trinity

17 Grant, we beseech thee, merciful Lord, to thy faithful people pardon and peace, that they may be cleansed from all their sins, and serve thee with a quiet mind.
Collects The one and twentieth Sunday after Trinity

18 Lord, we beseech thee to keep thy household the Church in continual godliness.
Collects The two and twentieth Sunday after Trinity

19 Grant that those things which we ask faithfully we may obtain effectually.
Collects The three and twentieth Sunday after Trinity

20 Stir up, we beseech thee, O Lord, the wills of thy faithful people; that they, plenteously bringing forth the fruit of good works, may of thee be plenteously rewarded.
Collects The five and twentieth Sunday after Trinity

21 Give us grace, that, being not like children carried away with every blast of vain doctrine, we may be established in the truth of thy holy Gospel.
Collects St Mark's Day

22 O Almighty God, who hast knit together thine elect in one communion and fellowship, in the mystical body of thy Son Christ our Lord; Grant us grace so to follow thy blessed Saints in all virtuous and godly living, that we may come to those

unspeakable joys, which thou hast prepared for them that unfeignedly love thee.
Collects All Saints' Day

1 And if any of those be an open and notorious evil liver, or have done any wrong to his neighbours by word or deed, so that the Congregation be thereby offended; the Curate, having knowledge thereof, shall call him and advertise him, that in any wise he presume not to come to the Lord's Table.
Holy Communion introductory rubric

2 Until he have openly declared himself to have truly repented and amended his former naughty life.
Holy Communion introductory rubric

3 The Table, at the Communion-time having a fair white linen cloth upon it, shall stand in the Body of the Church, or in the Chancel.
Holy Communion introductory rubric

4 Almighty God, unto whom all hearts be open, all desires known, and from whom no secrets are hid; Cleanse the thoughts of our hearts by the inspiration of thy Holy Spirit, that we may perfectly love thee, and worthily magnify thy holy Name.
Holy Communion The Collect

5 I the Lord thy God am a jealous God, and visit the sins of the fathers upon the children unto the third and fourth generation of them that hate me.
the phrase 'sins of the fathers' is also used in the Douay/Rheims Bible (1609) in Numbers ch. 14, v. 18
Holy Communion The Ten Commandments; cf. **Bible** 76:9

6 Incline our hearts to keep this law.
Holy Communion The Ten Commandments (response)

7 Thou shalt do no murder.
Holy Communion The Ten Commandments; cf. **Bible** 76:13

8 I believe in one God the Father Almighty, Maker of heaven and earth, And of all things visible and invisible:
And in one Lord Jesus Christ, the only-begotten Son of God, Begotten of his Father before all worlds, God of God, Light of Light, Very God of very God, Begotten, not made, Being of one substance with the Father, By whom all things were made.
Holy Communion Nicene Creed; cf. **Book of Common Prayer** 126:10, **Missal** 520:16

9 And I believe in the Holy Ghost, the Lord and giver of life, Who proceedeth from the Father and the Son, Who with the Father and the Son together is worshipped and glorified, Who spake by the Prophets. And I believe one Catholick and Apostolick Church.
Holy Communion Nicene Creed; cf. **Missal** 520:16

10 Let us pray for the whole state of Christ's Church militant here in earth.
Holy Communion Prayer for the Church Militant

11 We humbly beseech thee most mercifully to accept our alms and oblations, and to receive these our prayers, which we offer unto thy Divine Majesty; beseeching thee to inspire continually the universal Church with the spirit of truth, unity, and concord: And grant, that all they that do confess thy holy Name may agree in the truth of thy holy Word, and live in unity, and godly love.
Holy Communion Prayer for the Church Militant

12 Grant unto her [the Queen's] whole Council, and to all that are put in authority under her, that they may truly and indifferently minister justice.
Holy Communion Prayer for the Church Militant

13 Give grace, O heavenly Father, to all Bishops and Curates, that they may both by their life and doctrine set forth thy true and lively Word.
Holy Communion Prayer for the Church Militant

14 We most humbly beseech thee of thy goodness, O Lord, to comfort and succour all them, who in this transitory life are in trouble, sorrow, need, sickness, or any other adversity. And we also bless thy holy Name for all thy servants departed this life in thy faith and fear.
Holy Communion Prayer for the Church Militant

15 Ye that do truly and earnestly repent you of your sins, and are in love and charity with your neighbours, and intend to lead a new life, following the commandments of God, and walking from henceforth in his holy ways; Draw near with faith, and take this holy Sacrament to your comfort; and make your humble confession to Almighty God, meekly kneeling upon your knees.
Holy Communion The Invitation

16 We do earnestly repent, And are heartily sorry for these our misdoings; The remembrance of them is grievous unto us; The burden of them is intolerable.
Holy Communion General Confession

17 Hear what comfortable words our Saviour Christ saith unto all that truly turn to him.
Holy Communion Comfortable Words (preamble)

18 Lift up your hearts.
Holy Communion versicles and responses; cf. **Missal** 520:19

19 It is meet and right so to do.
Holy Communion versicles and responses

20 It is very meet, right, and our bounden duty, that we should at all times, and in all places, give thanks unto thee, O Lord, Holy Father, Almighty, Everlasting God.
Therefore with Angels and Archangels, and with all the company of heaven, we laud and magnify thy glorious Name; evermore praising thee, and saying, Holy, holy, holy, Lord God of hosts, heaven and earth are full of thy glory: Glory be to thee, O Lord most High.
Holy Communion Hymn of Praise; cf. **Bible** 111:32, **Missal** 520:21

21 Almighty God, our heavenly Father, who of thy tender mercy didst give thine only Son Jesus Christ to suffer death upon the cross for our redemption; who made there (by his one oblation of himself once offered) a full, perfect, and sufficient sacrifice, oblation, and satisfaction, for the sins of the whole world.
Holy Communion Prayer of Consecration

22 Who, in the same night that he was betrayed, took Bread; and, when he had given thanks, he brake it,

and gave it to his disciples, saying, Take, eat, this is my Body which is given for you: Do this in remembrance of me. Likewise after supper he took the Cup; and, when he had given thanks, he gave it to them, saying, Drink ye all of this; for this is my Blood of the New Testament, which is shed for you and for many for the remission of sins: Do this, as oft as ye shall drink it, in remembrance of me.
Holy Communion Prayer of Consecration

1 Although we be unworthy, through our manifold sins, to offer unto thee any sacrifice, yet we beseech thee to accept this our bounden duty and service; not weighing our merits, but pardoning our offences.
Holy Communion First Prayer of Oblation

2 We are very members incorporate in the mystical body of thy Son, which is the blessed company of all faithful people; and are also heirs through hope of thy everlasting kingdom.
Holy Communion Second (alternative) Prayer of Oblation

Father of all, We give you thanks and praise, that when we were still far off you met us in your Son and brought us home. Dying and living, he declared your love, gave us grace, and opened the gate of glory.
Alternative Service Book Post-Communion prayer

3 The blessing of God Almighty, the Father, the Son, and the Holy Ghost, be amongst you and remain with you always.
Holy Communion The Blessing

4 Assist us mercifully, O Lord, in these our supplications and prayers, and dispose the way of thy servants towards the attainment of everlasting salvation; that, among all the changes and chances of this mortal life, they may ever be defended by thy most gracious and ready help.
Holy Communion Collects after the Offertory

5 Prevent us, O Lord, in all our doings with thy most gracious favour, and further us with thy continual help; that in all our works, begun, continued, and ended in thee, we may glorify thy holy Name.
Holy Communion Collects after the Offertory

6 Those things, which for our unworthiness we dare not, and for our blindness we cannot ask, vouchsafe to give us, for the worthiness of thy Son Jesus Christ our Lord.
Holy Communion Collects after the Offertory

7 It is expedient that Baptism be administered in the vulgar tongue.
Public Baptism of Infants introductory rubric

8 O merciful God, grant that the old Adam in this Child may be so buried, that the new man may be raised up in him.
Public Baptism of Infants Invocation of blessing on the child

9 It is your part and duty also . . . to walk answerably to your Christian calling, and as becometh the children of light.
Baptism of Such as are of Riper Years Priest's final address

10 QUESTION: Who gave you this Name?
ANSWER: My Godfathers and Godmothers in my Baptism; wherein I was made a member of Christ, the child of God, and an inheritor of the kingdom of heaven.
Catechism

11 I should renounce the devil and all his works, the pomps and vanity of this wicked world, and all the sinful lusts of the flesh.
Catechism

12 QUESTION: What dost thou chiefly learn by these Commandments?
ANSWER: I learn two things: my duty towards God, and my duty to my Neighbour.
Catechism

13 My duty towards my Neighbour, is to love him as myself, and to do to all men, as I would they should do unto me.
Catechism

14 To submit myself to all my governors, teachers, spiritual pastors and masters.
Catechism

15 To keep my hands from picking and stealing, and my tongue from evil-speaking, lying, and slandering.
Catechism

16 Not to covet nor desire other men's goods; but to learn and labour truly to get mine own living, and to do my duty in that state of life, unto which it shall please God to call me.
Catechism

17 QUESTION: How many Sacraments hath Christ ordained in his Church?
ANSWER: Two only, as generally necessary to salvation, that is to say, Baptism, and the Supper of the Lord.
QUESTION: What meanest thou by this word *Sacrament?*
ANSWER: I mean an outward and visible sign of an inward and spiritual grace.
Catechism

18 Our help is in the name of the Lord;
Who hath made heaven and earth.
Order of Confirmation

19 Lord, hear our prayers.
And let our cry come unto thee.
Order of Confirmation

20 Defend, O Lord, this thy Child [*or* this thy Servant] with thy heavenly grace, that he may continue thine for ever; and daily increase in thy holy Spirit more and more, until he come unto thy everlasting kingdom.
Order of Confirmation

21 If any of you know cause, or just impediment, why these two persons should not be joined together in holy Matrimony, ye are to declare it. This is the first [*second*, or *third*] time of asking.
Solemnization of Matrimony The Banns

22 Dearly beloved, we are gathered together here in the sight of God, and in the face of this

congregation, to join together this Man and this Woman in holy Matrimony.
Solemnization of Matrimony Exhortation

1 Which holy estate Christ adorned and beautified with his presence, and first miracle that he wrought, in Cana of Galilee; and is commended of Saint Paul to be honourable among all men: and therefore not by any to be enterprised, nor taken in hand, unadvisedly, lightly, or wantonly, to satisfy men's carnal lusts and appetites, like brute beasts that have no understanding.
Solemnization of Matrimony Exhortation

2 First, It was ordained for the procreation of children, to be brought up in the fear and nurture of the Lord, and to the praise of his holy Name.
Solemnization of Matrimony Exhortation

3 If any man can shew any just cause, why they may not lawfully be joined together, let him now speak, or else hereafter for ever hold his peace.
Solemnization of Matrimony Exhortation

4 Wilt thou have this Woman to thy wedded wife, to live together after God's ordinance in the holy estate of Matrimony? Wilt thou love her, comfort her, honour, and keep her in sickness and in health; and, forsaking all other, keep thee only unto her, so long as ye both shall live?
Solemnization of Matrimony Betrothal

5 I *N.* take thee *M.* to my wedded husband, to have and to hold from this day forward, for better for worse, for richer for poorer, in sickness and in health, to love, cherish, and to obey, till death us do part, according to God's holy ordinance; and thereto I give thee my troth.
the man having used the words 'I plight thee my troth' and not having promised 'to obey'; the woman may also omit the promise 'to obey'
Solemnization of Matrimony Betrothal

6 With this Ring I thee wed, with my body I thee worship, and with all my worldly goods I thee endow.
Solemnization of Matrimony Wedding

All that I am I give to you, and all that I have I share with you.
Alternative Service Book

7 Those whom God hath joined together let no man put asunder.
Solemnization of Matrimony Wedding; cf. **Bible** 96:12

8 Forasmuch as *M.* and *N.* have consented together in holy wedlock, and have witnessed the same before God and this company, and thereto have given and pledged their troth either to other, and have declared the same by giving and receiving of a Ring, and by joining of hands; I pronounce that they be Man and Wife together.
Solemnization of Matrimony Minister's Declaration

9 Peace be to this house, and to all that dwell in it.
The Visitation of the Sick

10 Unto God's gracious mercy and protection we commit thee.
The Visitation of the Sick

11 The Office ensuing is not to be used for any that die unbaptized, or excommunicate, or have laid violent hands upon themselves.
The Burial of the Dead introductory rubric

12 Man that is born of a woman hath but a short time to live, and is full of misery.
The Burial of the Dead First Anthem; cf. **Bible** 81:18

13 In the midst of life we are in death.
The Burial of the Dead First Anthem; cf. **Mumford** 536:5

14 Forasmuch as it hath pleased Almighty God of his great mercy to take unto himself the soul of our dear brother here departed, we therefore commit his body to the ground; earth to earth, ashes to ashes, dust to dust; in sure and certain hope of the Resurrection to eternal life, through our Lord Jesus Christ; who shall change our vile body, that it may be like unto his glorious body, according to the mighty working, whereby he is able to subdue all things to himself.
The Burial of the Dead Interment

15 Blessed is the man that hath not walked in the counsel of the ungodly, nor stood in the way of sinners: and hath not sat in the seat of the scornful.
Psalm 1, v. 1

16 Why do the heathen so furiously rage together: and why do the people imagine a vain thing?
Psalm 2, v. 1

17 Thou shalt bruise them with a rod of iron: and break them in pieces like a potter's vessel.
Psalm 2, v. 9

18 Blessed are all they that put their trust in him.
Psalm 2, v. 12

19 Stand in awe, and sin not: commune with your own heart, and in your chamber, and be still.
Psalm 4, v. 4

20 Lord, lift thou up: the light of thy countenance upon us.
Psalm 4, v. 7

21 I will lay me down in peace, and take my rest.
Psalm 4, v. 9

22 Make thy way plain before my face.
Psalm 5, v. 8

23 Let them perish through their own imaginations.
Psalm 5, v. 11

24 I am weary of my groaning; every night wash I my bed: and water my couch with my tears.
Psalm 6, v. 6

25 Away from me, all ye that work vanity.
Psalm 6, v. 8

26 Out of the mouth of very babes and sucklings hast thou ordained strength, because of thine enemies.
Psalm 8, v. 2; cf. **Proverbs** 609:17

27 What is man, that thou art mindful of him: and the son of man, that thou visitest him?
Thou madest him lower than the angels: to crown him with glory and worship.
Psalm 8, v. 4

1 Up, Lord, and let not man have the upper hand.
Psalm 9, v. 19

2 He that said in his heart, Tush, I shall never be cast down: there shall no harm happen unto me.
Psalm 10, v. 6

3 Upon the ungodly he shall rain snares, fire and brimstone, storm and tempest: this shall be their portion to drink.
Psalm 11, v. 7

4 How long wilt thou forget me, O Lord, for ever: how long wilt thou hide thy face from me?
Psalm 13, v. 1

5 The fool hath said in his heart: There is no God.
They are corrupt, and become abominable in their doings: there is none that doeth good, no not one.
Psalm 14, v. 1

6 They are all gone out of the way, they are altogether become abominable.
Psalm 14, v. 4

7 Lord, who shall dwell in thy tabernacle: or who shall rest upon thy holy hill?
Even he, that leadeth an uncorrupt life: and doeth the thing which is right, and speaketh the truth from his heart.
He that hath used no deceit in his tongue, nor done evil to his neighbour: and hath not slandered his neighbour.
Psalm 15, v. 1

8 He that sweareth unto his neighbour, and disappointeth him not: though it were to his own hindrance.
He that hath not given his money upon usury: nor taken reward against the innocent.
Whoso doeth these things: shall never fall.
Psalm 15, v. 5

9 The lot is fallen unto me in a fair ground: yea, I have a goodly heritage.
Psalm 16, v. 7

The lines are fallen unto me in pleasant places.
Psalm 16, v. 6 in Authorized Version of the Bible

10 Thou shalt not leave my soul in hell: neither shalt thou suffer thy Holy One to see corruption.
Psalm 16, v. 11

11 He rode upon the cherubims, and did fly: he came flying upon the wings of the wind.
Psalm 18, v. 10

12 At the brightness of his presence his clouds removed: hailstones, and coals of fire.
Psalm 18, v. 12

13 With the help of my God I shall leap over the wall.
Psalm 18, v. 29; cf. **Bible** 79:12

14 The heavens declare the glory of God: and the firmament sheweth his handy-work.
Psalm 19, v. 1

15 There is neither speech nor language: but their voices are heard among them.
Their sound is gone out into all lands: and their words into the ends of the world.
In them hath he set a tabernacle for the sun: which cometh forth as a bridegroom out of his chamber, and rejoiceth as a giant to run his course.
Psalm 19, v. 3

16 The statutes of the Lord are right, and rejoice the heart: the commandment of the Lord is pure, and giveth light unto the eyes.
Psalm 19, v. 8

17 The judgements of the Lord are true, and righteous altogether.
More to be desired are they than gold, yea, than much fine gold: sweeter also than honey, and the honey-comb.
Psalm 19, v. 10; cf. **Lincoln** 468:17

18 Let the words of my mouth, and the meditation of my heart: be alway acceptable in thy sight, O Lord: my strength, and my redeemer.
Psalm 19, v. 14

19 Some put their trust in chariots, and some in horses: but we will remember the Name of the Lord our God.
Psalm 20, v. 7

20 They intended mischief against thee: and imagined such a device as they are not able to perform.
Psalm 21, v. 11

21 My God, my God, look upon me; why hast thou forsaken me: and art so far from my health, and from the words of my complaint?
O my God, I cry in the day-time, but thou hearest not: and in the night-season also I take no rest.
Psalm 22, v. 1

22 But as for me, I am a worm, and no man; a very scorn of men, and the out-cast of the people.
All they that see me laugh me to scorn: they shoot out their lips, and shake their heads, saying,
He trusted in God, that he would deliver him: let him deliver him, if he will have him.
Psalm 22, v. 6

23 Many oxen are come about me: fat bulls of Basan close me in on every side.
Psalm 22, v. 12

24 I am poured out like water, and all my bones are out of joint: my heart also in the midst of my body is even like melting wax.
Psalm 22, v. 14

25 They pierced my hands and my feet; I may tell all my bones: they stand staring and looking upon me.
They part my garments among them: and cast lots upon my vesture.
Psalm 22, v. 17

26 The Lord is my shepherd: therefore can I lack nothing.
He shall feed me in a green pasture: and lead me forth beside the waters of comfort.
Psalm 23, v. 1; cf. **Herbert** 373:14, **Scottish Metrical Psalms** 652:20, and below:

The Lord is my shepherd; I shall not want.
He maketh me to lie down in green pastures: he leadeth me beside the still waters.
Bible (Authorized Version, 1611) Psalm 23, v. 1

1 Yea, though I walk through the valley of the shadow of death, I will fear no evil: for thou art with me; thy rod and thy staff comfort me.
Thou shalt prepare a table before me against them that trouble me: thou hast anointed my head with oil, and my cup shall be full.
But thy loving-kindness and mercy shall follow me all the days of my life: and I will dwell in the house of the Lord for ever.
Psalm 23, v. 4; cf. **Scottish Metrical Psalms** 652:20

2 The earth is the Lord's, and all that therein is: the compass of the world, and they that dwell therein.
Psalm 24, v. 1

3 Lift up your heads, O ye gates, and be ye lift up, ye everlasting doors: and the King of glory shall come in.
Who is the King of glory: it is the Lord strong and mighty, even the Lord mighty in battle.
Psalm 24, v. 7

4 Even the Lord of hosts, he is the King of glory.
Psalm 24, v. 10

5 O remember not the sins and offences of my youth.
Psalm 25, v. 6

6 Deliver Israel, O God: out of all his troubles.
Psalm 25, v. 21

7 Examine me, O Lord, and prove me: try out my reins and my heart.
Psalm 26, v. 2

8 I will wash my hands in innocency, O Lord: and so will I go to thine altar;
That I may shew the voice of thanksgiving: and tell of all thy wondrous works.
Psalm 26, v. 6

9 My foot standeth right: I will praise the Lord in the congregation.
Psalm 26, v. 12

10 The Lord is my light, and my salvation; whom then shall I fear: the Lord is the strength of my life; of whom then shall I be afraid?
Psalm 27, v. 1; cf. **Bible** 113:17

11 Teach me thy way, O Lord: and lead me in the right way, because of mine enemies.
Psalm 27, v. 13

12 I should utterly have fainted: but that I believe verily to see the goodness of the Lord in the land of the living.
Psalm 27, v. 15

13 The voice of the Lord breaketh the cedar-trees: yea, the Lord breaketh the cedars of Libanus.
He maketh them also to skip like a calf: Libanus also, and Sirion, like a young unicorn.
Psalm 29, v. 5

14 The Lord shall give strength unto his people: the Lord shall give his people the blessing of peace.
Psalm 29, v. 10

15 Heaviness may endure for a night, but joy cometh in the morning.
Psalm 30, v. 5

16 Into thy hands I commend my spirit.
Psalm 31, v. 6; cf. **Bible** 100:29

17 Blessed is the man unto whom the Lord imputeth no sin: and in whose spirit there is no guile.
For while I held my tongue: my bones consumed away through my daily complaining.
Psalm 32, v. 2

18 Great plagues remain for the ungodly: but whoso putteth his trust in the Lord, mercy embraceth him on every side.
Psalm 32, v. 11

19 Sing unto the Lord a new song: sing praises lustily unto him with a good courage.
Psalm 33, v. 3

20 O taste and see, how gracious the Lord is: blessed is the man that trusteth in him.
Psalm 34, v. 8

21 The lions do lack, and suffer hunger: but they who seek the Lord shall want no manner of thing that is good.
Psalm 34, v. 10

22 Keep thy tongue from evil: and thy lips, that they speak no guile.
Eschew evil, and do good: seek peace, and ensue it.
Psalm 34, v. 13

23 They rewarded me evil for good: to the great discomfort of my soul.
Psalm 35, v. 12

24 O deliver my soul from the calamities which they bring on me, and my darling from the lions.
Psalm 35, v. 17

25 Fret not thyself because of the ungodly.
Psalm 37, v. 1

26 I have been young, and now am old: and yet saw I never the righteous forsaken, nor his seed begging their bread.
Psalm 37, v. 25; cf. **Blunden** 122:12

27 I myself have seen the ungodly in great power: and flourishing like a green bay-tree.
Psalm 37, v. 36

28 I held my tongue, and spake nothing: I kept silence, yea, even from good words; but it was pain and grief to me.
Psalm 39, v. 3

29 Lord, let me know mine end, and the number of my days: that I may be certified how long I have to live.
Psalm 39, v. 5

30 For man walketh in a vain shadow, and disquieteth himself in vain: he heapeth up riches, and cannot tell who shall gather them.
Psalm 39, v. 7

31 I waited patiently for the Lord: and he inclined unto me, and heard my calling.

He brought me also out of the horrible pit, out of the mire and clay: and set my feet upon the rock, and ordered my goings.
Psalm 40, v. 1

1 In the volume of the book it is written of me, that I should fulfil thy will, O my God.
Psalm 40, v. 10

2 Thou art my helper and redeemer: make no long tarrying, O my God.
Psalm 40, v. 21

3 Blessed is he that considereth the poor and needy: the Lord shall deliver him in the time of trouble.
Psalm 41, v. 1

4 Yea, even mine own familiar friend, whom I trusted: who did also eat of my bread, hath laid great wait for me.
Psalm 41, v. 9

. . . hath lifted up his heel against me.
Psalm 41, v. 9 in the Authorized Version of the Bible

5 Like as the hart desireth the water-brooks: so longeth my soul after thee, O God.
My soul is a thirst for God, yea, even for the living God.
Psalm 42, v. 1; cf. **Tate** 755:8

As the hart panteth after the water brooks, so panteth my soul after thee, O God.
My soul thirsteth for God, the living God.
Psalm 42, v. 1 in the Authorized Version of the Bible

6 Why art thou so full of heaviness, O my soul: and why art thou so disquieted within me?
Psalm 42, v. 6

7 One deep calleth another, because of the noise of the water-pipes: all thy waves and storms are gone over me.
Psalm 42, v. 9

8 I will say unto the God of my strength, Why hast thou forgotten me: why go I thus heavily, while the enemy oppresseth me?
My bones are smitten asunder as with a sword: while mine enemies that trouble me cast me in the teeth;
Namely, while they say daily unto me: Where is now thy God?
Psalm 42, v. 11

9 Give sentence with me, O God, and defend my cause against the ungodly people: O deliver me from the deceitful and wicked man.
Psalm 43, v. 1

10 O send out thy light and thy truth, that they may lead me: and bring me unto thy holy hill, and to thy dwelling.
And that I may go unto the altar of God, even unto the God of my joy and gladness: and upon the harp will I give thanks unto thee, O God, my God.
Psalm 43, v. 3

11 O put thy trust in God: for I will yet give him thanks, which is the help of my countenance, and my God.
Psalm 43, v. 6

12 We have heard with our ears, O God, our fathers have told us: what thou hast done in their time of old.
Psalm 44, v. 1

13 My heart is inditing of a good matter: I speak of the things which I have made unto the King.
My tongue is the pen: of a ready writer.
Psalm 45, v. 1

14 Thou hast loved righteousness, and hated iniquity: wherefore God, even thy God, hath anointed thee with the oil of gladness above thy fellows.
Psalm 45, v. 8

15 Kings' daughters were among thy honourable women: upon thy right hand did stand the queen in a vesture of gold, wrought about with divers colours.
Psalm 45, v. 10

16 The King's daughter is all glorious within: her clothing is of wrought gold.
Psalm 45, v. 14

17 Instead of thy fathers thou shalt have children: whom thou mayest make princes in all lands.
Psalm 45, v. 17

18 God is our hope and strength: a very present help in trouble. Therefore will we not fear, though the earth be moved: and though the hills be carried into the midst of the sea.
Psalm 46, v. 1; cf. **Anonymous** 15:4

19 The heathen make much ado, and the kingdoms are moved: but God hath shewed his voice, and the earth shall melt away.
The Lord of hosts is with us: the God of Jacob is our refuge.
Psalm 46, v. 6

20 He maketh wars to cease in all the world: he breaketh the bow, and knappeth the spear in sunder, and burneth the chariots in the fire.
Be still then, and know that I am God: I will be exalted among the heathen, and I will be exalted in the earth.
Psalm 46, v. 9

21 O clap your hands together, all ye people: O sing unto God with the voice of melody.
Psalm 47, v. 1

22 He shall subdue the people under us: and the nations under our feet.
Psalm 47, v. 3

23 God is gone up with a merry noise: and the Lord with the sound of the trump.
Psalm 47, v. 5

24 For lo, the kings of the earth: are gathered, and gone by together.
They marvelled to see such things: they were astonished, and suddenly cast down.
Psalm 48, v. 3

25 Thou shalt break the ships of the sea: through the east-wind.
Psalm 48, v. 6

26 Walk about Sion, and go round about her: and tell the towers thereof.

Mark well her bulwarks, set up her houses: that ye may tell them that come after.
Psalm 48, v. 11

1 Man will not abide in honour: seeing he may be compared unto the beasts that perish.
Psalm 49, v. 12

2 All the beasts of the forest are mine: and so are the cattle upon a thousand hills.
Psalm 50, v. 10

3 Thinkest thou that I will eat bulls' flesh: and drink the blood of goats?
Psalm 50, v. 13

4 Wash me throughly from my wickedness: and cleanse me from my sin.
For I acknowledge my faults: and my sin is ever before me.
Against thee only have I sinned, and done this evil in thy sight.
Psalm 51, v. 2

5 Behold, I was shapen in wickedness: and in sin hath my mother conceived me.
Psalm 51, v. 5

6 Thou shalt purge me with hyssop, and I shall be clean: thou shalt wash me, and I shall be whiter than snow.
Thou shalt make me hear of joy and gladness: that the bones which thou hast broken may rejoice.
Psalm 51, v. 7; cf. **Bible** 113:18

7 Make me a clean heart, O God: and renew a right spirit within me.
Cast me not away from thy presence: and take not thy holy Spirit from me.
O give me the comfort of thy help again: and stablish me with thy free Spirit.
Psalm 51, v. 10

8 Deliver me from blood-guiltiness, O God.
Psalm 51, v. 14

9 Thou shalt open my lips, O Lord: and my mouth shall shew thy praise.
For thou desirest no sacrifice, else would I give it thee: but thou delightest not in burnt-offerings.
The sacrifice of God is a troubled spirit: a broken and contrite heart, O God, shalt thou not despise.
O be favourable and gracious unto Sion: build thou the walls of Jerusalem.
Psalm 51, v. 15

10 O that I had wings like a dove: for then would I flee away, and be at rest.
Psalm 55, v. 6

11 It was even thou, my companion: my guide, and mine own familiar friend.
We took sweet counsel together: and walked in the house of God as friends.
Psalm 55, v. 14

12 The words of his mouth were softer than butter, having war in his heart: his words were smoother than oil, and yet they be very swords.
Psalm 55, v. 22

13 Thou tellest my flittings; put my tears into thy bottle: are not these things noted in thy book?
Psalm 56, v. 8

14 Under the shadow of thy wings shall be my refuge, until this tyranny be over-past.
Psalm 57, v. 1

15 God shall send forth his mercy and truth: my soul is among lions.
And I lie even among the children of men, that are set on fire: whose teeth are spears and arrows, and their tongue a sharp sword.
Set up thyself, O God, above the heavens: and thy glory above all the earth.
Psalm 57, v. 4

16 They have laid a net for my feet, and pressed down my soul: they have digged a pit before me, and are fallen into the midst of it themselves.
Psalm 57, v. 7

17 Awake up, my glory; awake, lute and harp: I myself will awake right early.
Psalm 57, v. 9

18 They are as venomous as the poison of a serpent: even like the deaf adder that stoppeth her ears;
Which refuseth to hear the voice of the charmer: charm he never so wisely.
Psalm 58, v. 4

19 Gilead is mine, and Manasses is mine: Ephraim also is the strength of my head; Judah is my law-giver;
Philistia, be thou glad of me.
Psalm 60, v. 7

20 Moab is my wash-pot; over Edom will I cast out my shoe.
Psalm 60, v. 8

21 Their delight is in lies; they give good words with their mouth, but curse with their heart.
Psalm 62, v. 4

22 As for the children of men, they are but vanity: the children of men are deceitful upon the weights, they are altogether lighter than vanity itself.
O trust not in wrong and robbery, give not yourselves unto vanity: if riches increase, set not your heart upon them.
Psalm 62, v. 9

23 God spake once, and twice I have also heard the same: that power belongeth unto God;
And that thou, Lord, art merciful: for thou rewardest every man according to his work.
Psalm 62, v. 11

24 My soul thirsteth for thee, my flesh also longeth after thee: in a barren and dry land where no water is.
Psalm 63, v. 2

25 These also that seek the hurt of my soul: they shall go under the earth.
Let them fall upon the edge of the sword: that they may be a portion for foxes.
Psalm 63, v. 10

26 Thou, O God, art praised in Sion: and unto thee shall the vow be performed in Jerusalem.

Thou that hearest the prayer: unto thee shall all flesh come.
Psalm 65, v. 1

1 Thou that art the hope of all the ends of the earth, and of them that remain in the broad sea.
Who in his strength setteth fast the mountains: and is girded about with power.
Who stilleth the raging of the sea: and the noise of his waves, and the madness of the people.
Psalm 65, v. 5

2 Thou crownest the year with thy goodness: and thy clouds drop fatness.
They shall drop upon the dwellings of the wilderness: and the little hills shall rejoice on every side.
The folds shall be full of sheep: the valleys also shall stand so thick with corn, that they shall laugh and sing.
Psalm 65, v. 12

3 God be merciful unto us, and bless us: and shew us the light of his countenance, and be merciful unto us;
That thy way may be known upon earth: thy saving health among all nations.
Let the people praise thee, O God: yea, let all the people praise thee.
Psalm 67, v. 1

4 Then shall the earth bring forth her increase: and God, even our own God, shall give us his blessing.
Psalm 67, v. 6

5 Let God arise, and let his enemies be scattered: let them also that hate him flee before him.
Psalm 68, v. 1

6 O sing unto God, and sing praises unto his name: magnify him that rideth upon the heavens, as it were upon an horse; praise him in his name JAH, and rejoice before him.
He is a Father of the fatherless, and defendeth the cause of the widows: even God in his holy habitation.
He is the God that maketh men to be of one mind in an house, and bringeth the prisoners out of captivity: but letteth the runagates continue in scarceness.
O God, when thou wentest forth before the people: when thou wentest through the wilderness,
The earth shook, and the heavens dropped at the presence of God.
Psalm 68, v. 4

7 The Lord gave the word: great was the company of the preachers.
Kings with their armies did flee, and were discomfited: and they of the household divided the spoil.
Though ye have lien among the pots, yet shall ye be as the wings of a dove: that is covered with silver wings, and her feathers like gold.
Psalm 68, v. 11

8 Why hop ye so, ye high hills? this is God's hill, in which it pleaseth him to dwell.
Psalm 68, v. 16

9 Thou art gone up on high, thou hast led captivity captive, and received gifts for men.
Psalm 68, v. 18

10 The zeal of thine house hath even eaten me.
Psalm 69, v. 9

11 Thy rebuke hath broken my heart; I am full of heaviness: I looked for some to have pity on me, but there was no man, neither found I any to comfort me.
They gave me gall to eat: and when I was thirsty they gave me vinegar to drink.
Psalm 69, v. 21

12 Let their habitation be void: and no man to dwell in their tents.
Psalm 69, v. 26

13 Let them be wiped out of the book of the living: and not be written among the righteous.
Psalm 69, v. 29

14 Let them be ashamed and confounded that seek after my soul: let them be turned backward and put to confusion that wish me evil.
Let them for their reward be soon brought to shame: that cry over me, There, there.
Psalm 70, v. 2

15 I am become as it were a monster unto many: but my sure trust is in thee.
Psalm 71, v. 6

16 Cast me not away in the time of age: forsake me not when my strength faileth me.
Psalm 71, v. 8

17 The mountains also shall bring peace: and the little hills righteousness unto the people.
Psalm 72, v. 3

18 His dominion shall be also from the one sea to the other: and from the flood unto the world's end.
They that dwell in the wilderness shall kneel before him: his enemies shall lick the dust.
The Kings of Tharsis and of the isles shall give presents: the kings of Arabia and Saba shall bring gifts.
All kings shall fall down before him: all nations shall do him service.
Psalm 72, v. 8

19 He shall live, and unto him shall be given of the gold of Arabia.
Psalm 72, v. 15

20 Then thought I to understand this: but it was too hard for me.
Until I went into the sanctuary of God: then understood I the end of these men.
Psalm 73, v. 15

21 O deliver not the soul of thy turtle-dove unto the multitude of the enemies: and forget not the congregation of the poor for ever.
Psalm 74, v. 20

22 For promotion cometh neither from the east, nor from the west: nor yet from the south.
Psalm 75, v. 7

1 In Jewry is God known: his Name is great in Israel.
At Salem is his tabernacle: and his dwelling in Sion.
Psalm 76, v. 1

2 I have considered the days of old: and the years that are past.
Psalm 77, v. 5

3 Hear my law, O my people: incline your ears unto the words of my mouth.
I will open my mouth in a parable: I will declare hard sentences of old;
Which we have heard and known: and such as our fathers have told us.
Psalm 78, v. 1

4 Not to be as their forefathers, a faithless and stubborn generation: a generation that set not their heart aright, and whose spirit cleaveth not stedfastly unto God.
Psalm 78, v. 9

5 He divided the sea, and let them go through: he made the waters to stand on an heap.
Psalm 78, v. 14

6 He rained down manna also upon them for to eat: and gave them food from heaven.
So man did eat angels' food: for he sent them meat enough.
Psalm 78, v. 25

7 So the Lord awaked as one out of sleep: and like a giant refreshed with wine.
Psalm 78, v. 66

8 Turn us again, O God: shew the light of thy countenance, and we shall be whole.
Psalm 80, v. 3

9 Sing we merrily unto God our strength: make a cheerful noise unto the God of Jacob.
Take the psalm, bring hither the tabret: the merry harp with the lute.
Blow up the trumpet in the new-moon: even in the time appointed, and upon our solemn feast-day.
Psalm 81, v. 1

10 I have said, Ye are gods: and ye are all children of the most Highest.
But ye shall die like men: and fall like one of the princes.
Psalm 82, v. 6

11 O how amiable are thy dwellings: thou Lord of hosts!
My soul hath a desire and longing to enter into the courts of the Lord: my heart and my flesh rejoice in the living God.
Yea, the sparrow hath found her an house, and the swallow a nest where she may lay her young: even thy altars, O Lord of hosts, my King and my God.
Psalm 84, v. 1

12 Blessed is the man whose strength is in thee: in whose heart are thy ways.
Who going through the vale of misery use it for a well: and the pools are filled with water.
They will go from strength to strength.
Psalm 84, v. 5

13 For one day in thy courts: is better than a thousand.
I had rather be a door-keeper in the house of my God: than to dwell in the tents of ungodliness.
Psalm 84, v. 10

14 Wilt thou not turn again, and quicken us: that thy people may rejoice in thee?
Psalm 85, v. 6

15 Mercy and truth are met together: righteousness and peace have kissed each other.
Truth shall flourish out of the earth: and righteousness hath looked down from heaven.
Psalm 85, v. 10

16 Very excellent things are spoken of thee: thou city of God.
Psalm 87, v. 2

17 Lord, thou hast been our refuge: from one generation to another.
Before the mountains were brought forth, or ever the earth and the world were made: thou art God from everlasting, and world without end.
Psalm 90, v. 1

18 For a thousand years in thy sight are but as yesterday: seeing that is past as a watch in the night.
As soon as thou scatterest them they are even as a sleep: and fade away suddenly like the grass.
In the morning it is green, and groweth up: but in the evening it is cut down, dried up, and withered.
Psalm 90, v. 4

19 The days of our age are threescore years and ten; and though men be so strong that they come to fourscore years: yet is their strength then but labour and sorrow; so soon passeth it away, and we are gone.
Psalm 90, v. 10

20 So teach us to number our days: that we may apply our hearts unto wisdom.
Psalm 90, v. 12

21 For he shall deliver thee from the snare of the hunter and from the noisome pestilence.
He shall defend thee under his wings, and thou shalt be safe under his feathers: his faithfulness and truth shall be thy shield and buckler.
Psalm 91, v. 3

22 Thou shalt not be afraid for any terror by night: nor for the arrow that flieth by day;
For the pestilence that walketh in darkness: nor for the sickness that destroyeth in the noon-day.
A thousand shall fall beside thee, and ten thousand at thy right hand: but it shall not come nigh thee.
Psalm 91, v. 5

23 For thou, Lord, art my hope: thou hast set thine house of defence very high.
There shall no evil happen unto thee: neither shall any plague come nigh thy dwelling.
For he shall give his angels charge over thee: to keep thee in all thy ways.
They shall bear thee in their hands: that thou hurt not thy foot against a stone.

Thou shalt go upon the lion and adder: the young lion and the dragon shalt thou tread under thy feet.
Psalm 91, v. 9

1 With long life will I satisfy him: and shew him my salvation.
Psalm 91, v. 16

2 The Lord is King, and hath put on glorious apparel: the Lord hath put on his apparel, and girded himself with strength.
He hath made the round world so sure: that it cannot be moved.
Psalm 93, v. 1

3 The floods are risen, O Lord, the floods have lift up their voice: the floods lift up their waves.
The waves of the sea are mighty, and rage horribly: but yet the Lord, who dwelleth on high, is mightier.
Thy testimonies, O Lord, are very sure: holiness becometh thine house for ever.
Psalm 93, v. 4

4 He that planted the ear, shall he not hear: or he that made the eye, shall he not see?
Psalm 94, v. 9

5 O come, let us sing unto the Lord: let us heartily rejoice in the strength of our salvation.
Let us come before his presence with thanksgiving: and shew ourselves glad in him with psalms.
Psalm 95, v. 1

6 In his hand are all the corners of the earth: and the strength of the hills is his also.
The sea is his, and he made it: and his hands prepared the dry land.
O come, let us worship and fall down: and kneel before the Lord our Maker.
For he is the Lord our God: and we are the people of his pasture, and the sheep of his hand.
To-day if ye will hear his voice, harden not your hearts: as in the provocation, and as in the day of temptation in the wilderness;
When your fathers tempted me: proved me, and saw my works.
Forty years long was I grieved with this generation, and said It is a people that do err in their hearts, for they have not known my ways;
Unto whom I sware in my wrath: that they should not enter into my rest.
Psalm 95, v. 4

7 Ascribe unto the Lord the honour due unto his Name: bring presents, and come into his courts.
O worship the Lord in the beauty of holiness: let the whole earth stand in awe of him.
Psalm 96, v. 8

8 The Lord is King, the earth may be glad thereof: yea, the multitude of the isles may be glad thereof.
Psalm 97, v. 1

9 O sing unto the Lord a new song: for he hath done marvellous things.
With his own right hand, and with his holy arm: hath he gotten himself the victory.
Psalm 98, v. 1; cf. **Bible** 113:19

10 Praise the Lord upon the harp: sing to the harp with a psalm of thanksgiving.
With trumpets also, and shawms: O shew yourselves joyful before the Lord the King.
Psalm 98, v. 6

11 With righteousness shall he judge the world: and the people with equity.
Psalm 98, v. 10

12 The Lord is King, be the people never so impatient: he sitteth between the cherubims, be the earth never so unquiet.
Psalm 99, v. 1

13 O be joyful in the Lord, all ye lands: serve the Lord with gladness, and come before his presence with a song.
Be ye sure that the Lord he is God: it is he that hath made us, and not we ourselves; we are his people, and the sheep of his pasture.
Psalm 100, v. 1; cf. **Bible** 113:20

14 I am become like a pelican in the wilderness: and like an owl that is in the desert.
I have watched, and am even as it were a sparrow: that sitteth alone upon the house-top.
Psalm 102, v. 6

15 Thou, Lord, in the beginning hast laid the foundation of the earth: and the heavens are the work of thy hands.
They shall perish, but thou shalt endure: they all shall wax old as doth a garment;
And as a vesture shalt thou change them, and they shall be changed: but thou art the same, and thy years shall not fail.
Psalm 102, v. 25

16 Praise the Lord, O my soul: and forget not all his benefits.
Psalm 103, v. 2

17 Who satisfieth thy mouth with good things: making thee young and lusty as an eagle.
Psalm 103, v. 5

18 The Lord is full of compassion and mercy: long-suffering, and of great goodness.
He will not alway be chiding: neither keepeth he his anger for ever.
Psalm 103, v. 8

19 For look how high the heaven is in comparison of the earth: so great is his mercy also toward them that fear him.
Look how wide also the east is from the west: so far hath he set our sins from us.
Yea, like as a father pitieth his own children: even so is the Lord merciful unto them that fear him.
For he knoweth whereof we are made: he remembereth that we are but dust.
Psalm 103, v. 11

20 The days of man are but as grass: for he flourisheth as a flower of a field.
For as soon as the wind goeth over it, it is gone: and the place thereof shall know it no more.
Psalm 103, v. 15

1 Who layeth the beams of his chambers in the waters: and maketh the clouds his chariot, and walketh upon the wings of the wind.
He maketh his angels spirits: and his ministers a flaming fire.
He laid the foundations of the earth: that it never should move at any time.
Thou coveredst it with the deep like as with a garment: the waters stand in the hills.
Psalm 104, v. 3

2 Thou hast set them their bounds which they shall not pass: neither turn again to cover the earth.
He sendeth the springs into the rivers: which run among the hills.
All beasts of the field drink thereof: and the wild asses quench their thirst.
Beside them shall the fowls of the air have their habitation: and sing among the branches
Psalm 104, v. 9

3 He bringeth forth grass for the cattle: and green herb for the service of men;
That he may bring food out of the earth, and wine that maketh glad the heart of man: and oil to make him a cheerful countenance, and bread to strengthen man's heart.
The trees of the Lord also are full of sap: even the cedars of Libanus which he hath planted.
Psalm 104, v. 14

4 The high hills are a refuge for the wild goats: and so are the stony rocks for the conies.
He appointed the moon for certain seasons: and the sun knoweth his going down.
Psalm 104, v. 18

5 Thou makest darkness that it may be night: wherein all the beasts of the forest do move.
The lions roaring after their prey: do seek their meat from God.
Psalm 104, v. 20

6 There go the ships, and there is that Leviathan: whom thou hast made to take his pastime therein.
Psalm 104, v. 26

7 The earth shall tremble at the look of him: if he do but touch the hills, they shall smoke.
Psalm 104, v. 32

8 He had sent a man before them: even Joseph, who was sold to be a bond-servant;
Whose feet they hurt in the stocks: the iron entered into his soul.
Psalm 105, v. 17

9 The king sent, and delivered him: the prince of the people let him go free.
He made him lord also of his house: and ruler of all his substance;
That he might inform his princes after his will: and teach his senators wisdom.
Psalm 105, v. 20

10 Yea, they thought scorn of that pleasant land: and gave no credence to his word;
But murmured in their tents: and hearkened not unto the voice of the Lord.
Psalm 106, v. 24

11 Thus were they stained with their own works: and went a whoring with their own inventions.
Psalm 106, v. 38

12 Such as sit in darkness, and in the shadow of death: being fast bound in misery and iron.
Psalm 107, v. 10

13 Their soul abhorred all manner of meat: and they were even hard at death's door.
Psalm 107, v. 18

14 They that go down to the sea in ships: and occupy their business in great waters;
These men see the works of the Lord: and his wonders in the deep.
Psalm 107, v. 23

15 They reel to and fro, and stagger like a drunken man: and are at their wit's end.
So when they cry unto the Lord in their trouble: he delivereth them out of their distress.
For he maketh the storm to cease: so that the waves thereof are still.
Then are they glad, because they are at rest: and so he bringeth them unto the heaven where they would be.
Psalm 107, v. 27

16 The Lord said unto my Lord: Sit thou on my right hand, until I make thine enemies thy footstool.
Psalm 110, v. 1

17 Thou art a Priest for ever after the order of Melchisedech.
Psalm 110, v. 4

18 The fear of the Lord is the beginning of wisdom: a good understanding have all they that do thereafter; the praise of it endureth for ever.
Psalm 111, v. 10

19 A good man is merciful, and lendeth: and will guide his words with discretion.
For he shall never be moved: and the righteous shall be had in everlasting remembrance.
Psalm 112, v. 5

20 He maketh the barren woman to keep house: and to be a joyful mother of children.
Psalm 113, v. 8

21 When Israel came out of Egypt: and the house of Jacob from among the strange people,
Judah was his sanctuary: and Israel his dominion.
The sea saw that, and fled: Jordan was driven back.
The mountains skipped like rams: and the little hills like young sheep.
Psalm 114, v. 1

22 Not unto us, O Lord, not unto us, but unto thy Name give the praise.
Psalm 115, v. 1; cf. **Bible** 113:22

23 They have mouths, and speak not: eyes have they, and see not.
They have ears, and hear not: noses have they, and smell not.
They have hands, and handle not: feet have they, and walk not: neither speak they through their throat.
Psalm 115, v. 5

1 The snares of death compassed me round about: and the pains of hell gat hold upon me.
Psalm 116, v. 3

2 And why? thou hast delivered my soul from death: mine eyes from tears, and my feet from falling.
Psalm 116, v. 8

3 I said in my haste, All men are liars.
Psalm 116, v. 10

4 I will pay my vows now in the presence of all his people: right dear in the sight of the Lord is the death of his saints.
Psalm 116, v. 13

5 The right hand of the Lord hath the pre-eminence: the right hand of the Lord bringeth mighty things to pass.
Psalm 118, v. 16

6 The same stone which the builders refused: is become the head-stone in the corner.
This is the Lord's doing: and it is marvellous in our eyes.
This is the day which the Lord hath made: we will rejoice and be glad in it.
Psalm 118, v. 22

7 Blessed be he that cometh in the Name of the Lord: we have wished you good luck, ye that are of the house of the Lord.
Psalm 118, v. 26

8 The law of thy mouth is dearer unto me: than thousands of gold and silver.
Psalm 119, v. 72

9 Thy word is a lantern unto my feet: and a light unto my paths.
Psalm 119, v. 105

10 Woe is me that I am constrained to dwell with Mesech: and to have my habitation among the tents of Kedar.
Psalm 120, v. 4

11 I labour for peace, but when I speak unto them therof: they make them ready to battle.
Psalm 120, v. 6

12 I will lift up mine eyes unto the hills: from whence cometh my help.
My help cometh even from the Lord: who hath made heaven and earth.
He will not suffer thy foot to be moved: and he that keepeth thee will not sleep.
Behold, he that keepeth Israel: shall neither slumber nor sleep.
The Lord himself is thy keeper: the Lord is thy defence upon thy right hand;
So that the sun shall not burn thee by day: neither the moon by night.
Psalm 121, v. 1; cf. **Scottish Metrical Psalms** 652:22

13 The Lord shall preserve thy going out, and thy coming in: from this time forth for evermore.
Psalm 121, v. 8

14 I was glad when they said unto me: We will go into the house of the Lord.
Our feet shall stand in thy gates: O Jerusalem.
Jerusalem is built as a city: that is at unity in itself.
For thither the tribes go up, even the tribes of the Lord.
Psalm 122, v. 1

15 O pray for the peace of Jerusalem: they shall prosper that love thee.
Peace be within thy walls: and plenteousness with thy palaces.
Psalm 122, v. 6

16 If the Lord himself had not been on our side, now may Israel say: if the Lord himself had not been on our side, when men rose up against us;
They had swallowed us up quick: when they were so wrathfully displeased at us.
Psalm 124, v. 1

17 Our soul is escaped even as a bird out of the snare of the fowler: the snare is broken, and we are delivered.
Our help standeth in the Name of the Lord: who hath made heaven and earth.
Psalm 124, v. 6; cf. **Book of Common Prayer** 130:18

18 The hills stand about Jerusalem: even so standeth the Lord round about his people, from this time forth for evermore.
Psalm 125, v. 2

19 When the Lord turned again the captivity of Sion: then were we like unto them that dream.
Then was our mouth filled with laughter: and our tongue with joy.
Psalm 126, v. 1

20 Turn our captivity, O Lord: as the rivers in the south.
They that sow in tears: shall reap in joy.
He that now goeth on his way weeping, and beareth forth good seed: shall doubtless come again with joy, and bring his sheaves with him.
Psalm 126, v. 5

21 Except the Lord build the house: their labour is but lost that build it.
Except the Lord keep the city: the watchman waketh but in vain.
Psalm 127, v. 1; cf. **Bible** 113:24

22 Like as the arrows in the hand of the giant: even so are the young children.
Happy is the man that hath his quiver full of them: they shall not be ashamed when they speak with their enemies in the gate.
Psalm 127, v. 5

23 Thy wife shall be as the fruitful vine: upon the walls of thine house.
Thy children like the olive-branches: round about thy table.
Psalm 128, v. 3

24 Many a time have they fought against me from my youth up: may Israel now say.
Psalm 129, v. 1

25 But they have not prevailed against me.
The plowers plowed upon my back: and made long furrows.
Psalm 129, v. 2

1 Out of the deep have I called unto thee, O Lord: Lord, hear my voice.
O let thine ears consider well: the voice of my complaint.
If thou, Lord, wilt be extreme to mark what is done amiss: O Lord, who may abide it?
Psalm 130, v. 1; cf. **Bible** 113:25

2 My soul fleeth unto the Lord: before the morning watch, I say, before the morning watch.
Psalm 130, v. 6

3 Lord, I am not high-minded: I have no proud looks.
I do not exercise myself in great matters: which are too high for me.
Psalm 131, v. 1

4 Behold, how good and joyful a thing it is: brethren, to dwell together in unity!
Psalm 133, v. 1

5 He smote divers nations: and slew mighty kings;
Sehon king of the Amorites, and Og the king of Basan: and all the kingdoms of Canaan;
And gave their land to be an heritage: even an heritage unto Israel his people.
Psalm 135, v. 10

6 O give thanks unto the Lord, for he is gracious: and his mercy endureth for ever.
Psalm 136, v. 1; cf. **Milton** 512:25

7 By the waters of Babylon we sat down and wept: when we remembered thee, O Sion.
As for our harps, we hanged them up: upon the trees that are therein.
Psalm 137, v. 1

8 How shall we sing the Lord's song: in a strange land?
If I forget thee, O Jerusalem: let my right hand forget her cunning.
Psalm 137, v. 4

9 O Lord, thou hast searched me out, and known me: thou knowest my down-sitting, and mine up-rising; thou understandest my thoughts long before.
Psalm 139, v. 1

10 Such knowledge is too wonderful and excellent for me: I cannot attain unto it.
Psalm 139, v. 5

11 If I climb up into the heaven, thou art there: if I go down to hell, thou art there also.
If I take the wings of the morning: and remain in the uttermost parts of the sea;
Even there also shall thy hand lead me: and thy right hand shall hold me.
Psalm 139, v. 7

12 I will give thanks unto thee, for I am fearfully and wonderfully made.
Psalm 139, v. 13

13 Thine eyes did see my substance, yet being imperfect: and in thy book were all my members written;
Which day by day were fashioned: when as yet there were none of them.
Psalm 139, v. 15

14 Try me, O God, and seek the ground of my heart: prove me, and examine my thoughts.
Psalm 139, v. 23

15 Let the lifting up of my hands be an evening sacrifice.
Set a watch, O Lord, before my mouth: and keep the door of my lips.
Psalm 141, v. 2

16 Let the ungodly fall into their own nets together: and let me ever escape them.
Psalm 141, v. 11

17 Enter not into judgement with thy servant: for in thy sight shall no man living be justified.
Psalm 143, v. 2

18 Save me, and deliver me from the hand of strange children: whose mouth talketh of vanity, and their right hand is a right hand of iniquity.
That our sons may grow up as the young plants: and that our daughters may be as the polished corners of the temple.
Psalm 144, v. 11

19 The Lord upholdeth all such as fall: and lifteth up all those that are down.
Psalm 145, v. 14

20 Thou givest them their meat in due season.
Thou openest thine hand: and fillest all things living with plenteousness.
Psalm 145, v. 15

21 O put not your trust in princes, nor in any child of man: for there is no help in them.
Psalm 146, v. 2

22 The Lord looseth men out of prison: the Lord giveth sight to the blind.
Psalm 146, v. 7

23 The Lord careth for the strangers; he defendeth the fatherless and widow: as for the way of the ungodly, he turneth it upside down.
Psalm 146, v. 9

24 A joyful and pleasant thing it is to be thankful.
The Lord doth build up Jerusalem: and gather together the out-casts of Israel.
He healeth those that are broken in heart: and giveth medicine to heal their sickness.
He telleth the number of the stars: and calleth them all by their names.
Psalm 147, v. 1

25 He hath no pleasure in the strength of an horse: neither delighteth he in any man's legs.
Psalm 147, v. 10

26 He giveth snow like wool: and scattereth the hoar-frost like ashes.
He casteth forth his ice like morsels: who is able to abide his frost?
Psalm 147, v. 16

27 Praise the Lord upon earth: ye dragons, and all deeps;

Fire and hail, snow and vapours: wind and storm, fulfilling his word.
Psalm 148, v. 7

1 Young men and maidens, old men and children, praise the Name of the Lord: for his Name only is excellent, and his praise above heaven and earth.
Psalm 148, v. 12

2 Let the saints be joyful with glory: let them rejoice in their beds.
Let the praises of God be in their mouth: and a two-edged sword in their hands;
To be avenged of the heathen: and to rebuke the people;
To bind their kings in chains: and their nobles with links of iron.
Psalm 149, v. 5; cf. **Macaulay** 482:20

3 Praise him upon the well-tuned cymbals: praise him upon the loud cymbals.
Let every thing that hath breath: praise the Lord.
Psalm 150, v. 5

4 Be pleased to receive into thy Almighty and most gracious protection the persons of us thy servants, and the Fleet in which we serve.
Forms of Prayer to be Used at Sea First Prayer

5 That we may be . . . a security for such as pass on the seas upon their lawful occasions.
Forms of Prayer to be Used at Sea First Prayer

6 We therefore commit his body to the deep, to be turned into corruption, looking for the resurrection of the body (when the Sea shall give up her dead).
Forms of Prayer to be Used at Sea At the Burial of their Dead at Sea

7 Come, Holy Ghost, our souls inspire,
And lighten with celestial fire.
Thou the anointing Spirit art,
Who dost thy seven-fold gifts impart.
Ordering of Priests 'Veni, Creator Spiritus'; translation by Bishop John Cosin, 1627, from the *c.*9th century original, possibly by Rabanus Maurus (776–856)

8 Holy Scripture containeth all things necessary to salvation.
Articles of Religion (1562) no. 6

9 Man is very far gone from original righteousness.
Articles of Religion (1562) no. 9

10 It is a thing plainly repugnant to the Word of God, and the custom of the Primitive Church, to have publick Prayer in the Church, or to minister the Sacraments in a tongue not understanded of the people.
Articles of Religion (1562) no. 24

11 The sacrifices of Masses, in the which it was commonly said, that the Priest did offer Christ for the quick and the dead, to have remission of pain or guilt, were blasphemous fables, and dangerous deceits.
Articles of Religion (1562) no. 31

12 The Bishop of Rome hath no jurisdiction in this Realm of England.
Articles of Religion (1562) no. 37

13 It is lawful for Christian men, at the commandment of the Magistrate, to wear weapons, and serve in the wars.
Articles of Religion (1562) no. 37

14 The Riches and Goods of Christians are not common, as touching the right, title, and possession of the same, as certain Anabaptists do falsely boast.
Articles of Religion (1562) no. 38

15 A Man may not marry his Mother.
A Table of Kindred and Affinity

John Wilkes Booth 1838–65
American actor and assassin

16 *Sic semper tyrannis!* The South is avenged.
having shot President ***Lincoln****, 14 April 1865*
in *New York Times* 15 April 1865; the second part of the statement does not appear in any contemporary source, and is possibly apocryphal; cf. **Mottoes** 535:17

Paul Booth

17 Who put the colours in the rainbow?
Who put the salt into the sea?
Who put the cold into the snowflake?
Who made you and me?
Who put the hump upon the camel?
Who put the neck on the giraffe? . . .
God made all of these.
'Who put the colours in the rainbow?'

William Booth 1829–1912
founder of the Salvation Army, 1878
on Booth: see ***Lindsay*** *469:8*

18 The submerged tenth.
defined by Booth as 'three million men, women, and children, a vast despairing multitude in a condition nominally free, but really enslaved'
In Darkest England (1890) pt. 1, title of ch. 2

Frances Boothby fl. 1670
English dramatist

19 I'm hither come, but what d'ye think to say?
A woman's pen presents you with a play:
Who smiling told me I'd be sure to see
That once confirmed, the house would empty be.
Marcelia (1670) prologue

Robert Boothby 1900–86
British Conservative politician

20 *You* speak for Britain!
to Arthur Greenwood, acting Leader of the Labour Party, after Neville ***Chamberlain*** *had failed to announce an ultimatum to Germany; perhaps taking up an appeal already voiced by Leo* ***Amery***
Harold Nicolson, diary, 2 September 1939; cf. **Amery** 13:6

Betty Boothroyd 1929–

Labour politician; Speaker of the House of Commons since 1992

1 My desire to get here was like miners' coal dust, it was under my fingers and I couldn't scrub it out.
of Parliament
Glenys Kinnock and Fiona Millar (eds.) *By Faith and Daring* (1993)

James H. Boren 1925–

American bureaucrat

2 Guidelines for bureaucrats: (1) When in charge, ponder. (2) When in trouble, delegate. (3) When in doubt, mumble.
in *New York Times* 8 November 1970

Jorge Luis Borges 1899–1986

Argentinian writer

3 The universe (which others call the Library) is composed of an indefinite, perhaps an infinite number of hexagonal galleries.
Ficciones (1956) 'The Library of Babel'

4 On those remote pages [of the *Celestial Emporium of Benevolent Knowledge*] it is written that animals are divided into (a) those that belong to the Emperor, (b) embalmed ones, (c) those that are trained, (d) suckling pigs, (e) mermaids, (f) fabulous ones, (g) stray dogs, (h) those that are included in this classification, (i) those that tremble as if they were mad, (j) innumerable ones, (k) those drawn with a very fine camel's hair brush, (l) others, (m) those that have just broken a flower vase, (n) those that resemble flies from a distance.
Other Inquisitions (1966)

5 The original is unfaithful to the translation.
of Henley's translation of ***Beckford****'s* Vathek
Sobre el 'Vathek' de William Beckford (1943)

6 For one of those gnostics, the visible universe was an illusion or, more precisely, a sophism. Mirrors and fatherhood are abominable because they multiply it and extend it.
Tlön, Uqbar, Orbis Tertius (1941)

7 The Falklands thing was a fight between two bald men over a comb.
application of a proverbial phrase
in *Time* 14 February 1983

Cesare Borgia see **Mottoes** 535:2

George Borrow 1803–81

English writer

8 There are no countries in the world less known by the British than these selfsame British Islands.
Lavengro (1851) preface

9 There's night and day, brother, both sweet things; sun, moon, and stars, brother, all sweet things: there's likewise a wind on the heath. Life is very sweet, brother; who would wish to die?
Lavengro (1851) ch. 25

10 Let no one sneer at the bruisers of England—what were the gladiators of Rome, or the bull-fighters of Spain, in its palmiest days, compared to England's bruisers?
Lavengro (1851) ch. 26

11 A losing trade, I assure you, sir: literature is a drug.
Lavengro (1851) ch. 30

12 Youth will be served, every dog has his day, and mine has been a fine one.
Lavengro (1851) ch. 92

13 Fear God, and take your own part.
The Romany Rye (1857) ch. 16

□ Borrowed titles

see box overleaf

Pierre Bosquet 1810–61

French general

14 *C'est magnifique, mais ce n'est pas la guerre.*
It is magnificent, but it is not war.
on the charge of the Light Brigade at Balaclava, 25 October 1854
Cecil Woodham-Smith *The Reason Why* (1953) ch. 12

John Collins Bossidy 1860–1928

American oculist

15 And this is good old Boston,
The home of the bean and the cod,
Where the Lowells talk to the Cabots
And the Cabots talk only to God.
verse spoken at Holy Cross College alumni dinner in Boston, Massachusetts, 1910, in *Springfield Sunday Republican* 14 December 1924

Jacques-Bénigne Bossuet 1627–1704

French preacher

16 *L'Angleterre, ah, la perfide Angleterre, que le rempart de ses mers rendait inaccessible aux Romains, la foi du Sauveur y est abordée.*
England, ah, faithless England, which the protection afforded by its seas rendered inaccessible to the Romans, the faith of the Saviour spread even there.
first sermon on the feast of the Circumcision, in *Oeuvres de Bossuet* (1816) vol. 11; cf. **Ximénèz** 834:18

James Boswell 1740–95

Scottish lawyer; biographer of Samuel ***Johnson***
on Boswell: see ***Macaulay*** *481:13,* ***Walpole*** *801:11*

17 I think there is a blossom about me of something more distinguished than the generality of mankind.
Boswell's London Journal (ed. F. A. Pottle, 1950) 20 January 1763

18 I am, I flatter myself, completely a citizen of the world. In my travels through Holland, Germany, Switzerland, Italy, Corsica, France, I never felt myself from home.
Journal of a Tour to the Hebrides (ed. F. A. Pottle, 1936) 14 August 1773

continued

Borrowed titles

1 Brave new world.
novel (1932) by Aldous **Huxley**; see **Shakespeare** 699:12

2 By Grand Central Station I sat down and wept.
book (1945) by Elizabeth Smart (1913–86); see **Book of Common Prayer** 141:7

3 The catcher in the rye.
novel (1951) by J. D. **Salinger**; see **Burns** 166:20, **Salinger** 642:12

'You know that song "If a body catch a body comin' through the rye"? I'd like—'
'It's "If a body *meet* a body coming through the rye"!' old Phoebe said.
The Catcher in the Rye (1951) ch. 22

4 An evil cradling.
book (1992) by Brian **Keenan**; see **Koran** 443:23

5 Far from the madding crowd.
novel (1874) by Thomas **Hardy**; see **Gray** 350:13

6 For whom the bell tolls.
novel (1940) by Ernest **Hemingway**; see **Donne** 275:3

7 The glittering prizes.
novel (1976) by Frederic **Raphael**; see **Smith** 723:19

8 The golden bough.
book (1890–1915) by James George Frazer (1854–1941); from William Pitt's 1743 translation:

A mighty tree, that bears a golden bough.
Virgil *Aeneid* bk. 6

9 The grapes of wrath.
novel (1939) by John **Steinbeck**; see **Howe** 391:15

10 The heart is a lonely hunter.
novel (1940) by Carson McCullers (1917–67)

My heart is a lonely hunter that hunts on a lonely hill.
Fiona McLeod (William Sharp) (1855–1905) 'The Lonely Hunter' (1896) st. 6

11 A man for all seasons.
play (1960) by Robert **Bolt**; see **Whittington** 816:9

12 Pride and prejudice.
novel (1813) by Jane **Austen**; cf. **Burney** 165:26

13 Remembrance of things past.
translation by C. K. Scott-Moncrieff and S. Hudson of *À la recherche du temps perdu* (1913–27) by Marcel **Proust**; see **Shakespeare** 704:16

14 Ring of bright water.
book (1960) by Gavin Maxwell (1914–69); see **Raine** 620:8

15 The seven pillars of wisdom.
book (1926) by T. E. **Lawrence**; see **Bible** 82:18

16 The singer not the song.
novel (1959) by Audrey Erskine Lindop

The singer not the song.
West Indian calypso

James Boswell *continued*

17 We [Boswell and Johnson] are both *Tories*; both convinced of the utility of monarchical power, and both lovers of that reverence and affection for a sovereign which constitute loyalty, a principle which I take to be absolutely extinguished in Britain.
Journal of a Tour to the Hebrides (ed. F. A. Pottle, 1936) 13 September 1773

18 A page of my Journal is like a cake of portable soup. A little may be diffused into a considerable portion.
Journal of a Tour to the Hebrides (ed. F. A. Pottle, 1936) 13 September 1773

19 I have never yet exerted ambition in rising in the state. But sure I am, no man has made his way better to the best company.
Journal of a Tour to the Hebrides (ed. F. A. Pottle, 1936) 16 September 1773

20 JOHNSON: Well, we had a good talk.
BOSWELL: Yes, Sir; you tossed and gored several persons.
The Life of Samuel Johnson (1791) Summer 1768

21 A man, indeed, is not genteel when he gets drunk; but most vices may be committed very genteelly: a man may debauch his friend's wife genteelly: he may cheat at cards genteelly.
The Life of Samuel Johnson (1791) 6 April 1775

Horatio Bottomley 1860–1933
British newspaper proprietor and financier

reply to a prison visitor who asked if he were sewing:
22 No, reaping.
S. T. Felstead *Horatio Bottomley* (1936) ch. 16

23 What poor education I have received has been gained in the University of Life.
speech at the Oxford Union, 2 December 1920; Beverley Nichols 25 (1926) ch. 7

Dion Boucicault (Dionysius Lardner Boursiquot) 1820–90
Irish dramatist

24 Men talk of killing time, while time quietly kills them.
London Assurance (1841) act 2, sc. 1; cf. **Sitwell** 721:7

Antoine Boulay de la Meurthe 1761–1840
French statesman

25 *C'est pire qu'un crime, c'est une faute.*
It is worse than a crime, it is a blunder.
on hearing of the execution of the Duc d'Enghien, captured in Baden by Napoleon's forces, in 1804
C.-A. Sainte-Beuve *Nouveaux Lundis* (1870) vol. 12

Harold Edwin Boulton 1859–1935
British songwriter

1 Devon, glorious Devon!
'Glorious Devon' (1902)

2 Speed, bonnie boat, like a bird on the wing,
'Onward,' the sailors cry;
Carry the lad that's born to be king,
Over the sea to Skye.
'Skye Boat Song' (1908)

Matthew Boulton 1728–1809
British engineer

3 I sell here, Sir, what all the world desires to have—POWER.
speaking to ***Boswell*** *of his engineering works*
James Boswell *Life of Samuel Johnson* (1791) 22 March 1776

F. W. Bourdillon 1852–1921
English poet

4 The night has a thousand eyes,
And the day but one.
Among the Flowers (1878) 'Light'; cf. **Lyly** 480:17

Paul Bourget 1852–1935
French author

5 *La pensée est à la littérature ce que la lumière est à la peinture.*
Ideas are to literature what light is to painting.
La Physiologie de l'Amour Moderne (1890)

Louis Bousquet
French songwriter

6 *Nous en rêvons la nuit, nous y pensons le jour,*
Ce n'est que Madelon, mais pour nous, c'est l'amour.
We dream of her by night, we think of her by day,
It's only Madelon, but for us, it's love.
'Quand Madelon' (1914), French soldiers' song of the First World War

E. E. Bowen 1836–1901
English schoolmaster

7 Forty years on, when afar and asunder
Parted are those who are singing to-day.
'Forty Years On' (Harrow School Song, published 1886)

Elizabeth Bowen 1899–1973
Anglo-Irish novelist

8 Books, in Mallow, were heard of and even owned; they were the proper fittings of a gentleman's house.
Bowen's Court (1942)

9 My family got their position and drew their power from a situation that shows an inherent wrong. In the grip of that situation, England and Ireland each turned to the other a closed, harsh, distorted face—a face that, in each case, their lovers would hardly know.
Bowen's Court (afterword, ed. 2, 1964)

10 The innocent are so few that two of them seldom meet—when they do, their victims lie strewn around.
The Death of the Heart (1938) pt. 1, ch. 8

11 It is about five o'clock in an evening that the first hour of spring strikes—autumn arrives in the early morning, but spring at the close of a winter day.
The Death of the Heart (1938) pt. 2, ch. 1

12 There is no end to the violations committed by children on children, quietly talking alone.
The House in Paris (1935) pt. 1, ch. 2

13 Fate is not an eagle, it creeps like a rat.
The House in Paris (1935) pt. 2, ch. 2

14 Jealousy is no more than feeling alone against smiling enemies.
The House in Paris (1935) pt. 2, ch. 8

15 She could not conceive of her country emotionally: it was a way of living, an abstract of several landscapes, or an oblique frayed island, moored at the north but with an air of being detached and washed out west from the British coast.
The Last September (1929)

16 I could wish that the English kept history in mind more, that the Irish kept it in mind less.
'Notes on Eire' 9 November 1949

17 A high altar on the move.
of Edith ***Sitwell***
V. Glendinning *Edith Sitwell* (1981) ch. 25

Lord Bowen 1835–94
English judge

18 The man on the Clapham omnibus.
the average man
in *Law Reports* (1903); attributed

19 When I hear of an 'equity' in a case like this, I am reminded of a blind man in a dark room—looking for a black hat—which isn't there.
John Alderson Foote *Pie-Powder* (1911)

20 The rain, it raineth on the just
And also on the unjust fella:
But chiefly on the just, because
The unjust steals the just's umbrella.
Walter Sichel *Sands of Time* (1923) ch. 4: cf. **Bible** 93:14

David Bowie (David Jones) 1947–
English rock musician

21 Ground control to Major Tom.
'Space Oddity' (1969 song)

22 We have created a child who will be so exposed to the media that he will be lost to his parents by the time he is 12.
in *Melody Maker* 22 January 1972

23 The 1970s for me started the 21st century—it was the beginning of a true pluralism in social attitudes.
An Earthling at 50 ITV programme; in *Sunday Times* 12 January 1997

William Lisle Bowles 1762–1850
English clergyman and poet

1 The cause of Freedom is the cause of God!
A Poetical Address to the Right Honourable Edmund Burke (1791) l. 78

Maurice Bowra 1898–1971
English scholar and literary critic

2 I'm a man more dined against than dining.
John Betjeman *Summoned by Bells* (1960) ch. 9; cf. **Shakespeare** 678:25

Boy George 1961–
English pop singer and songwriter

3 She's a gay man trapped in a woman's body.
of ***Madonna***
Take It Like a Man (1995)

4 Sex has never been an obsession with me. It's just like eating a bag of crisps. Quite nice, but nothing marvellous. Sex is not simply black and white. There's a lot of grey.
in *Sun* 21 October 1982

John Bradford *c.*1510–55
English Protestant martyr

5 But for the grace of God there goes John Bradford.
on seeing a group of criminals being led to their execution; usually quoted 'There but for the grace of God go I'
in *Dictionary of National Biography* (1917–)

F. H. Bradley 1846–1924
English philosopher

6 Metaphysics is the finding of bad reasons for what we believe upon instinct; but to find these reasons is no less an instinct.
Appearance and Reality (1893) preface

7 The world is the best of all possible worlds, and everything in it is a necessary evil.
Appearance and Reality (1893) preface

8 Where everything is bad it must be good to know the worst.
Appearance and Reality (1893) preface

Omar Bradley 1893–1981
American general

9 The way to win an atomic war is to make certain it never starts.
speech on Armistice Day, 1948

10 We have grasped the mystery of the atom and rejected the Sermon on the Mount.
speech on Armistice Day, 1948
Collected Writings (1967) vol. 1

11 The world has achieved brilliance without wisdom, power without conscience. Ours is a world of nuclear giants and ethical infants.
speech on Armistice Day, 1948
Collected Writings (1967) vol. 1

John Bradshaw 1602–59
English judge at the trial of Charles I

12 Rebellion to tyrants is obedience to God.
suppositious epitaph; Henry S. Randall *Life of Thomas Jefferson* (1865) vol. 3, appendix 4; cf. **Mottoes** 535:15

Anne Bradstreet *c.*1612–72
English-born first poet of the New World

13 Thou ill-form'd offspring of my feeble brain,
Who after birth did'st by my side remain,
Till snatched from thence by friends, less wise than true
Who thee abroad expos'd to public view,
Made thee in rags, halting to th' press to trudge,
Where errors were not lessened (all may judge)
At thy return my blushing was not small,
My rambling brat (in print) should mother call.
'The Author to her Book' (1650)

14 I am obnoxious to each carping tongue,
Who says my hand a needle better fits,
A poet's pen, all scorn, I should thus wrong;
For such despite they cast on female wits:
If what I do prove well, it won't advance,
They'll say it's stolne, or else, it was by chance.
'The Prologue' (1650)

15 Let Greeks be Greeks, and Women what they are,
Men have precedency, and still excel.
'The Prologue' (1650)

16 This mean and unrefinèd stuff of mine,
Will make your glistering gold but more to shine.
'The Prologue' (1650)

Ernest Bramah (Ernest Bramah Smith) 1868–1942
English writer

17 It is a mark of insincerity of purpose to spend one's time in looking for the sacred Emperor in the low-class tea-shops.
The Wallet of Kai Lung (1900)

James Bramston *c.*1694–1744
English clergyman and poet

18 What's not destroyed by Time's devouring hand?
Where's Troy, and where's the Maypole in the Strand?
The Art of Politics (1729) l. 71

Louis D. Brandeis 1856–1941
American jurist

19 Fear of serious injury alone cannot justify suppression of free speech and assembly. Men feared witches and burned women. It is the function of speech to free men from the bondage of irrational fears.
in *Whitney v. California* (1927)

20 The greatest dangers to liberty lurk in insidious encroachment by men of zeal, well-meaning but without understanding.
dissenting opionion in *Olmstead v. United States* (1928)

Richard Branson 1950–
English businessman

1 We spend most of our lives working. So why do so few people have a good time doing it? Virgin is the possibility of good times.
interview in *New York Times* 28 February 1993

Georges Braque 1882–1963
French painter

2 Art is meant to disturb, science reassures.
Le Jour et la nuit: Cahiers 1917–52

3 Truth exists; only lies are invented.
Le Jour et la nuit: Cahiers 1917–52

Richard Brathwaite c.1588–1673
English poet

4 To Banbury came I, O profane one!
Where I saw a Puritane-one
Hanging of his cat on Monday
For killing of a mouse on Sunday.
Barnabee's Journal (1638) pt. 1, st. 4

John W. Bratton and James B. Kennedy
British songwriters

5 If you go down in the woods today
You're sure of a big surprise
If you go down in the woods today
You'd better go in disguise
For every Bear that ever there was
Will gather there for certain because,
Today's the day the Teddy Bears have their Picnic.
'The Teddy Bear's Picnic' (1932 song)

Werner von Braun 1912–77
German-born American rocket engineer

6 Don't tell me that man doesn't belong out there. Man belongs wherever he wants to go—and he'll do plenty well when he gets there.
on space
in *Time* 17 February 1958

7 Basic research is what I am doing when I don't know what I am doing.
R. L. Weber *A Random Walk in Science* (1973)

Bertolt Brecht 1898–1956
German dramatist

8 Terrible is the temptation to be good.
The Caucasian Chalk Circle (1948)

9 The aim of science is not to open the door to infinite wisdom, but to set a limit to infinite error.
The Life of Galileo (1939) sc. 9

10 ANDREA: Unhappy the land that has no heroes! . . .
GALILEO: No. Unhappy the land that needs heroes.
The Life of Galileo (1939) sc. 13

11 One observes, they have gone too long without a war here. Where is morality to come from in such a case, I ask? Peace is nothing but slovenliness, only war creates order.
Mother Courage (1939) sc. 1

12 Because I don't trust him, we are friends.
Mother Courage (1939) sc. 3

13 The finest plans are always ruined by the littleness of those who ought to carry them out, for the Emperors can actually do nothing.
Mother Courage (1939) sc. 6

14 War always finds a way.
Mother Courage (1939) sc. 6

15 Don't tell me peace has broken out, when I've just bought some new supplies.
Mother Courage (1939) sc. 8

16 The resistible rise of Arturo Ui.
title of play (1941)

17 Oh, the shark has pretty teeth, dear,
And he shows them pearly white.
Just a jackknife has Macheath, dear
And he keeps it out of sight.
The Threepenny Opera (1928) prologue

18 Food comes first, then morals.
The Threepenny Opera (1928) act 2, sc. 3

19 What is robbing a bank compared with founding a bank?
The Threepenny Opera (1928) act 3, sc. 3

20 Who built Thebes of the seven gates?
In the books you will find the names of kings.
Did the kings haul up the lumps of rock? . . .
Where, the evening that the wall of China was finished
Did the masons go?
'Questions From A Worker Who Reads' (1935)

21 Would it not be easier
In that case for the government
To dissolve the people
And elect another?
on the uprising against the Soviet occupying forces in East Germany in 1953
'The Solution' (1953)

Gerald Brenan 1894–1987
British travel writer and novelist

22 Those who have some means think that the most important thing in the world is love. The poor know that it is money.
Thoughts in a Dry Season (1978); cf. **Baldwin** 48:19

23 Religions are kept alive by heresies, which are really sudden explosions of faith. Dead religions do not produce them.
Thoughts in a Dry Season (1978)

24 You can't get at the truth by writing history; only the novelist can do that.
in *Times Literary Supplement* 28 November 1986

Sydney Brenner 1927–
British scientist

25 A modern computer hovers between the obsolescent and the nonexistent.
attributed in *Science* 5 January 1990

Jane Brereton (née Hughes) 1685–1740

English poet

1 The picture, placed the busts between,
Adds to the thought much strength:
Wisdom and Wit are little seen,
But Folly's at full length.

'On Mr Nash's Picture at Full Length, between the Busts of Sir Isaac Newton and Mr Pope' (1744)

Nicholas Breton c.1545–1626

English writer and poet

2 We rise with the lark and go to bed with the lamb.

The Court and Country (1618) para. 8

3 I wish my deadly foe, no worse
Than want of friends, and empty purse.

'A Farewell to Town' (1577)

4 Come little babe, come silly soul,
Thy father's shame, thy mother's grief,
Born as I doubt to all our dole,
And to thy self unhappy chief.

'A Sweet Lullaby' (1597)

Aristide Briand 1862–1932

French statesman

5 *Les hautes parties contractantes déclarent solennellement . . . qu'elles condamnent le recours à la guerre . . . et y renoncent en tant qu'instrument de politique nationale dans leurs relations mutuelles . . . le règlement ou la solution de tous les différends ou conflits de quelque nature ou de quelque origine qu'ils puissent être—qui pourront surgir entre elles ne devra jamais être cherché que par des moyens pacifiques.*

The high contracting powers solemnly declare . . . that they condemn recourse to war and renounce it . . . as an instrument of their national policy towards each other . . . The settlement or the solution of all disputes or conflicts of whatever nature or of whatever origin they may be which may arise . . . shall never be sought by either side except by pacific means.

draft, 20 June 1927, later incorporated into the Kellogg Pact, 1928, in *Le Temps* 13 April 1928

Edward Bridges 1892–1969

British civil servant, Cabinet Secretary and Head of the Civil Service

6 I confidently expect that we shall continue to be grouped with mothers-in-law and Wigan Pier as one of the recognized objects of ridicule.

of civil servants

Portrait of a Profession (1950)

Robert Bridges 1844–1930

English poet

7 All my hope on God is founded.

'All my hope on God is founded' (1899 hymn)

8 When men were all asleep the snow came flying,
In large white flakes falling on the city brown,
Stealthily and perpetually settling and loosely
lying,
Hushing the latest traffic of the drowsy town.

'London Snow' (1890)

John Bright 1811–89

English Liberal politician and reformer

9 The angel of death has been abroad throughout the land; you may almost hear the beating of his wings.

on the effects of the war in the Crimea

speech in the House of Commons, 23 February 1855

10 I am for 'Peace, retrenchment, and reform', the watchword of the great Liberal party 30 years ago.

speech at Birmingham, 28 April 1859, in *The Times* 29 April 1859; the phrase occurs earlier as

An immense yellow banner . . . 'Peace! Retrenchment!! Reform!!'

Samuel Warren *Ten Thousand a Year* (1841) bk. 7, ch. 1

11 A gigantic system of outdoor relief for the aristocracy of Great Britain.

of British foreign policy

speech at Birmingham, 29 October 1858; G. Barnett Smith *Life and Speeches of John Bright* (1881) vol. 1 ch. 16

12 My opinion is that the Northern States will manage somehow to muddle through.

during the American Civil War

Justin McCarthy *Reminiscences* (1899) vol. 1, ch. 5

13 England is the mother of Parliaments.

speech at Birmingham, 18 January 1865, in *The Times* 19 January 1865

14 The right hon Gentleman . . . has retired into what may be called his political Cave of Adullam—and he has called about him every one that was in distress and every one that was discontented.

referring to Robert **Lowe**, *leader of the dissident Whigs opposed to the Reform Bill of 1866*

speech in the House of Commons, 13 March 1866; cf. **Bible** 78:35

15 Force is not a remedy.

speech to the Birmingham Junior Liberal Club, 16 November 1880, in *The Times* 17 November 1880

16 The knowledge of the ancient languages is mainly a luxury.

letter in *Pall Mall Gazette* 30 November 1886

Anthelme Brillat-Savarin 1755–1826

French jurist and gourmet

17 Tell me what you eat and I will tell you what you are.

Physiologie du Goût (1825) aphorism no. 4; cf. **Feuerbach** 309:4

18 The discovery of a new dish does more for human happiness than the discovery of a star.

Physiologie du Goût (1825) aphorism no. 9

19 Cooking is the most ancient of the arts, for Adam was born hungry.

Physiologie du Goût (1825) pt. 1

Vera Brittain 1893–1970

English writer

1 Politics are usually the executive expression of human immaturity.

Rebel Passion (1964)

Russell Brockbank 1913–

British cartoonist

2 Fog in Channel—Continent isolated.

newspaper placard in cartoon, *Round the Bend with Brockbank* (1948); the phrase 'Continent isolated' was quoted as already current by John Gunther *Inside Europe* (1938)

3 Meek wifehood is no part of my profession;
I am your friend, but never your possession.

'Married Love' (1926)

Harold Brodkey 1930–96

American writer

4 The American daydream, as in Twain (and Hemingway), is about re-building after the flood, about being better off than before, about outwitting this or that challenge, up to and including death. Well, how do you manage to be optimistic for the moment? Without hope?

This Wild Darkness: The Story of My Death (1996)

Joseph Brodsky 1940–96

Russian-born American poet

5 As a form of moral insurance, at least, literature is much more dependable than a system of beliefs or a philosophical doctrine.

'Uncommon Visage', Nobel lecture 1987, in *On Grief and Reason* (1996)

Alexander Brome 1620–66

English poet

6 I have been in love, and in debt, and in drink,
This many and many a year.

Songs and Other Poems (2nd ed., 1664) pt. 1 'The Mad Lover'

7 Come, blessed peace, we once again implore,
And let our pains be less, or power more.

Songs and Other Poems (1661) 'The Riddle' (written 1644)

Jacob Bronowski 1908–74

Polish-born mathematician and humanist

8 The world can only be grasped by action, not by contemplation . . . The hand is the cutting edge of the mind.

The Ascent of Man (1973) ch. 3

9 The essence of science: ask an impertinent question, and you are on the way to a pertinent answer.

The Ascent of Man (1973) ch. 4

10 The wish to hurt, the momentary intoxication with pain, is the loophole through which the pervert climbs into the minds of ordinary men.

The Face of Violence (1954) ch. 5

11 Therapy has become what I think of as the tenth American muse.

attributed

Charlotte Brontë 1816–55

English novelist; daughter of Patrick **Brontë**, *sister of Emily* **Brontë**

see also **Opening lines** 556:21

12 We wove a web in childhood,
A web of sunny air;
We dug a spring in infancy
Of water pure and fair;
We sowed in youth a mustard seed,
We cut an almond rod;
We are now grown up to riper age—
Are they withered in the sod?

'We wove a web in childhood' (written 1835)

13 Conventionality is not morality. Self-righteousness is not religion. To attack the first is not to assail the last. To pluck the mask from the face of the Pharisee, is not to lift an impious hand to the Crown of Thorns.

Jane Eyre (2nd ed., 1848) preface

14 As his curate, his comrade, all would be right . . . There would be recesses in my mind which would be only mine, to which he never came; and sentiments growing there, fresh and sheltered, which his austerity could never blight, nor his measured warrior-march trample down. But as his wife . . . forced to keep the fire of my nature continually low, to compel it to burn inwardly and never utter a cry . . . *this* would be unendurable.

Jane Eyre (1847) ch. 34

15 Reader, I married him.

Jane Eyre (1847) ch. 38

16 Of late years an abundant shower of curates has fallen upon the North of England.

Shirley (1849) ch. 1

17 Be a governess! Better be a slave at once!

Shirley (1849) ch. 13

18 It is rustic all through. It is moorish, and wild, and knotty as a root of heath.

on the setting of Emily **Brontë**'s Wuthering Heights

in Charlotte's preface to the 1850 edition

19 I shall soon be 30—and I have done nothing yet . . . I feel as if we were all buried here.

letter to Ellen Nussey, 24 March 1845; *The Letters of Charlotte Brontë* (1995) vol. 1

20 You are not to suppose any of the characters in *Shirley* intended as literal portraits . . . We only suffer reality to *suggest*, never to *dictate*.

letter to Ellen Nussey, 16 November 1849, in Elizabeth Gaskell *The Life of Charlotte Bronte* (1857) ch. 18

Emily Brontë 1818–48

English novelist and poet; daughter of Patrick **Brontë**, *sister of Charlotte* **Brontë**

on Brontë: see **Brontë** 149:18; *see also* **Closing lines** 222:14

21 No coward soul is mine,
No trembler in the world's storm-troubled sphere:
I see Heaven's glories shine,
And faith shines equal, arming me from fear.

'No coward soul is mine' (1846)

1 Oh! dreadful is the check—intense the agony—
When the ear begins to hear, and the eye begins to see;
When the pulse begins to throb, the brain to think again;
The soul to feel the flesh, and the flesh to feel the chain.
'The Prisoner' (1846)

2 Cold in the earth—and fifteen wild Decembers,
From those brown hills, have melted into spring.
'Remembrance' (1846)

3 My love for Linton is like the foliage in the woods; time will change it, I'm well aware, as winter changes the trees—My love for Heathcliff resembles the eternal rocks beneath:—a source of little visible delight, but necessary.
Wuthering Heights (1847) ch. 9

Patrick Brontë 1777–1861

Anglo-Irish clergyman, perpetual curate of Haworth, Yorkshire from 1820; father of Charlotte and Emily **Brontë**

4 Charlotte has been writing a book, and it is much better than likely.
to his younger daughters, on first reading Jane Eyre; *in a letter of August 1850, Mrs Gaskell gives the wording as 'Charlotte has been writing a book—and it is better than I expected'*
Elizabeth Gaskell *The Life of Charlotte Brontë* (1857)

5 No quailing, Mrs Gaskell! no drawing back!
apropos her undertaking to write the life of Charlotte **Brontë**
letter from Mrs Gaskell to Ellen Nussey, 24 July 1855, in J. A. V. Chapple and A. Pollard (eds.) *The Letters of Mrs Gaskell* (1966) no. 257

Henry Brooke 1703–83

Irish poet and dramatist

6 For righteous monarchs,
Justly to judge, with their own eyes should see;
To rule o'er freemen, should themselves be free.
Earl of Essex (performed 1750, published 1761) act 1; cf. **Johnson** 417:13

Rupert Brooke 1887–1915

English poet
on Brooke: see **Cornford** *237:3,* **James** *403:22,* **Leavis** *461:6*

7 Blow out, you bugles, over the rich Dead!
There's none of these so lonely and poor of old,
But, dying, has made us rarer gifts than gold.
These laid the world away; poured out the red
Sweet wine of youth; gave up the years to be
Of work and joy, and that unhoped serene, That men call age; and those that would have been,
Their sons, they gave, their immortality.
'The Dead' (1914)

8 . . . The cool kindliness of sheets, that soon
Smooth away trouble; and the rough male kiss
Of blankets.
'The Great Lover' (1914)

9 Fish say, they have their stream and pond;
But is there anything beyond?
'Heaven' (1915)

10 Just now the lilac is in bloom,
All before my little room.
'The Old Vicarage, Grantchester' (1915)

11 Unkempt about those hedges blows
An English unofficial rose.
'The Old Vicarage, Grantchester' (1915)

12 Curates, long dust, will come and go
On lissom, clerical, printless toe;
And oft between the boughs is seen
The sly shade of a Rural Dean.
'The Old Vicarage, Grantchester' (1915)

13 God! I will pack, and take a train,
And get me to England once again!
For England's the one land, I know,
Where men with Splendid Hearts may go.
'The Old Vicarage, Grantchester' (1915)

14 For Cambridge people rarely smile,
Being urban, squat, and packed with guile.
'The Old Vicarage, Grantchester' (1915)

15 Stands the Church clock at ten to three?
And is there honey still for tea?
'The Old Vicarage, Grantchester' (1915)

16 Now, God be thanked Who has matched us with His hour,
And caught our youth, and wakened us from sleeping,
With hand made sure, clear eye, and sharpened power,
To turn, as swimmers into cleanness leaping.
'Peace' (1914)

17 If I should die, think only this of me:
That there's some corner of a foreign field
That is for ever England. There shall be
In that rich earth a richer dust concealed;
A dust whom England bore, shaped, made aware,
Gave, once, her flowers to love, her ways to roam,
A body of England's, breathing English air,
Washed by the rivers, blest by suns of home.
And think, this heart, all evil shed away,
A pulse in the eternal mind, no less
Gives somewhere back the thoughts by England given;
Her sights and sounds; dreams happy as her day;
And laughter, learnt of friends; and gentleness,
In hearts at peace, under an English heaven.
'The Soldier' (1914)

18 A play of Webster's is full of the feverish and ghastly turmoil of a nest of maggots.
John Webster and the Elizabethan Drama (1916)

Anita Brookner 1938–

British novelist and art historian

19 Good women always think it is their fault when someone else is being offensive. Bad women never take the blame for anything.
Hotel du Lac (1984) ch. 7

1 They were reasonable people, and no one was to be hurt, not even with words.
Hotel du Lac (1984) ch. 9

2 I have reached the age when a woman begins to perceive that she is growing into the person she least plans to resemble: her mother.
Incidents in the Rue Laugier (1995) ch. 1

3 They were privileged children . . . they would always expect to be greeted with smiles.
Lewis Percy (1989) ch. 9

4 Dr Weiss, at forty, knew that her life had been ruined by literature.
A Start in Life (1981) ch. 1

Gwendolyn Brooks 1917–
American poet

5 Exhaust the little moment. Soon it dies.
And be it gash or gold it will not come
Again in this identical disguise.
'Exhaust the little moment' (1949)

6 Abortions will not let you forget.
You remember the children you got that you did not get . . .
'The Mother' (1945)

7 The time
cracks into furious flower. Lifts its face
all unashamed. And sways in wicked grace.
'The Second Sermon on the Warpland' (1968)

J. Brooks

8 A four-legged friend, a four-legged friend,
He'll never let you down.
sung by Roy Rogers about his horse Trigger
'A Four Legged Friend' (1952)

Phillips Brooks 1835–93
American clergyman

9 O little town of Bethlehem,
How still we see thee lie!
Above thy deep and dreamless sleep
The silent stars go by.
Yet in thy dark streets shineth
The everlasting light;
The hopes and fears of all the years
Are met in thee to-night.
'O Little Town of Bethlehem' (1868 hymn)

Thomas Brooks 1608–80
English Puritan divine

10 For (*magna est veritas et praevalebit*) great is truth, and shall prevail.
The Crown and Glory of Christianity (1662); cf. **Bible** 114:12

Robert Barnabas Brough 1828–60
English satirical writer

11 My Lord Tomnoddy is thirty-four;
The Earl can last but a few years more.
My Lord in the Peers will take his place:
Her Majesty's councils his words will grace.
Office he'll hold and patronage sway;
Fortunes and lives he will vote away;
And what are his qualifications?—ONE!
He's the Earl of Fitzdotterel's eldest son.
Songs of the Governing Classes (1855) 'My Lord Tomnoddy'

Lord Brougham 1778–1868
Scottish lawyer and politician; Lord Chancellor
on Brougham: see **Melbourne** *503:16*

12 All we see about us, King, Lords, and Commons, the whole machinery of the State, all the apparatus of the system, and its varied workings, end in simply bringing twelve good men into a box.
in the House of Commons, 7 February 1828

13 The schoolmaster is abroad! and I trust more to the schoolmaster, armed with his primer, than I do to the soldier in full military array, for upholding and extending the liberties of his country.
sometimes quoted as 'Look out, gentlemen, the schoolmaster is abroad!', which Brougham is said to have used in a speech at the Mechanics' Instute, London, in 1825
in the House of Commons, 29 January 1828

14 Education makes a people easy to lead, but difficult to drive; easy to govern, but impossible to enslave.
attributed

Heywood Broun 1888–1939
American journalist

15 Men build bridges and throw railroads across deserts, and yet they contend successfully that the job of sewing on a button is beyond them. Accordingly, they don't have to sew buttons.
Seeing Things at Night (1921) 'Holding a Baby'

16 Posterity is as likely to be wrong as anybody else.
Sitting on the World (1924) 'The Last Review'

17 Everybody favours free speech in the slack moments when no axes are being ground.
in *New York World* 23 October 1926

18 Just as every conviction begins as a whim so does every emancipator serve his apprenticeship as a crank. A fanatic is a great leader who is just entering the room.
in *New York World* 6 February 1928

Christy Brown 1932–81
Irish writer

19 Painting became everything to me . . . Through it I made articulate all that I saw and felt, all that went on inside the mind that was housed within my useless body like a prisoner in a cell.
My Left Foot (1954)

H. Rap Brown (Hubert Geroid Brown) 1943–
American Black Power leader

20 I say violence is necessary. It is as American as cherry pie.
speech at Washington, 27 July 1967, in *Washington Post* 28 July 1967

John Brown 1715–66
English clergyman and writer

1 I have seen some extracts from Johnson's Preface to his 'Shakespeare' . . . No feeling nor pathos in him! Altogether upon the high horse, and blustering about Imperial Tragedy!
letter to Garrick, 27 October 1765, in *The Private Correspondence of David Garrick* (1831) vol. 1

John Brown 1800–59
American abolitionist
on Brown: see **Songs** *729:13*

2 Now, if it is deemed necessary that I should forfeit my life for the furtherance of the ends of justice, and mingle my blood further with the blood of my children, and with the blood of millions in this slave country whose rights are disregarded by wicked, cruel, and unjust enactments, I say let it be done.
last speech to the court, 2 November 1859, in *The Life, Trial and Execution of Captain John Brown* (1859)

3 I, John Brown, am now quite certain that the crimes of this guilty land will never be purged away but with blood.
written on the day of his execution, 2 December 1859, in R. J. Hinton *John Brown and His Men* (1894) ch. 12

Joseph Brown 1821–94
American politician; Confederate Governor of Georgia during the Civil War

4 I entered into this Revolution to contribute my mite to sustain the rights of states and prevent the consolidation of the Government, and I am *still* a rebel . . . no matter who may be in power
refusing to accept the Confederate President Jefferson **Davis***'s call for a day of national fasting*
in 1863; Geoffrey C. Ward *The Civil War* (1991)

Lew Brown (Louis Brownstein) 1893–1958
American songwriter

5 Life is just a bowl of cherries.
title of song (1931)

Thomas Brown 1663–1704
English satirist

6 A little before you made a leap into the dark.
Letters from the Dead to the Living (1702) 'Answer to Mr Joseph Haines'; cf. **Last words** 455:19

7 I do not love thee, Dr Fell.
The reason why I cannot tell;
But this I know, and know full well,
I do not love thee, Dr Fell.
written while an undergraduate at Christ Church, Oxford, of which Dr Fell was Dean
A. L. Hayward (ed.) *Amusements Serious and Comical by Tom Brown* (1927); cf. **Martial** 497:23, **Watkyns** 804:14

T. E. Brown 1830–97
Manx schoolmaster and poet

8 A garden is a lovesome thing, God wot!
'My Garden' (1893)

Cecil Browne 1932–
American businessman

9 But not so odd
As those who choose
A Jewish God,
But spurn the Jews.
reply to verse by William Norman **Ewer**; cf. **Ewer** 305:12

Sir Thomas Browne 1605–82
English writer and physician

10 He who discommendeth others obliquely commendeth himself.
Christian Morals (1716) pt. 1, sect. 34

11 As for that famous network of Vulcan, which enclosed Mars and Venus, and caused that unextinguishable laugh in heaven, since the gods themselves could not discern it, we shall not pry into it.
The Garden of Cyrus (1658) ch. 2

12 Life itself is but the shadow of death, and souls departed but the shadows of the living: all things fall under this name. The sun itself is but the dark *simulacrum*, and light but the shadow of God.
The Garden of Cyrus (1658) ch. 4

13 Flat and flexible truths are beat out by every hammer; but Vulcan and his whole forge sweat to work out Achilles his armour.
The Garden of Cyrus (1658) ch. 5

14 The quincunx of heaven runs low, and 'tis time to close the five ports of knowledge.
The Garden of Cyrus (1658) ch. 5

15 All things began in order, so shall they end, and so shall they begin again; according to the ordainer of order and mystical mathematics of the city of heaven.
The Garden of Cyrus (1658) ch. 5

16 Nor will the sweetest delight of gardens afford much comfort in sleep; wherein the dullness of that sense shakes hands with delectable odours; and though in the bed of Cleopatra, can hardly with any delight raise up the ghost of a rose.
The Garden of Cyrus (1658) ch. 5

17 Though Somnus in Homer be sent to rouse up Agamemnon, I find no such effects in these drowsy approaches of sleep. To keep our eyes open longer were but to act our Antipodes. The huntsmen are up in America, and they are already past their first sleep in Persia. But who can be drowsy at that hour which freed us from everlasting sleep? or have slumbering thoughts at that time, when sleep itself must end, and as some conjecture all shall awake again?
The Garden of Cyrus (1658) ch. 5

18 Old mortality, the ruins of forgotten times.
Hydriotaphia (Urn Burial, 1658) Epistle Dedicatory

19 With rich flames and hired tears they solemnized their obsequies.
Hydriotaphia (Urn Burial, 1658) ch. 3

1 Men have lost their reason in nothing so much as their religion, wherein stones and clouts make martyrs.
Hydriotaphia (Urn Burial, 1658) ch. 4

2 Were the happiness of the next world as closely apprehended as the felicities of this, it were a martyrdom to live.
Hydriotaphia (Urn Burial, 1658) ch. 4

3 The long habit of living indisposeth us for dying.
Hydriotaphia (Urn Burial, 1658) ch. 5

4 What song the Syrens sang, or what name Achilles assumed when he hid himself among women, though puzzling questions, are not beyond all conjecture.
Hydriotaphia (Urn Burial, 1658) ch. 5

5 But to subsist in bones, and be but pyramidally extant, is a fallacy in duration.
Hydriotaphia (Urn Burial, 1658) ch. 5

6 Generations pass while some trees stand, and old families last not three oaks.
Hydriotaphia (Urn Burial, 1658) ch. 5

7 To be nameless in worthy deeds exceeds an infamous history.
Hydriotaphia (Urn Burial, 1658) ch. 5

8 The iniquity of oblivion blindly scattereth her poppy, and deals with the memory of men without distinction to merit perpetuity.
Hydriotaphia (Urn Burial, 1658) ch. 5

9 The night of time far surpasseth the day, and who knows when was the equinox?
Hydriotaphia (Urn Burial, 1658) ch. 5

10 Man is a noble animal, splendid in ashes, and pompous in the grave.
Hydriotaphia (Urn Burial, 1658) ch. 5

11 Ready to be any thing, in the ecstasy of being ever.
Hydriotaphia (Urn Burial, 1658) ch. 5

12 At my devotion I love to use the civility of my knee, my hat, and hand.
Religio Medici (1643) pt. 1, sect. 3

13 Many from . . . an inconsiderate zeal unto truth, have too rashly charged the troops of error, and remain as trophies unto the enemies of truth.
Religio Medici (1643) pt. 1, sect. 6

14 A man may be in as just possession of truth as of a city, and yet be forced to surrender.
Religio Medici (1643) pt. 1, sect. 6

15 As for those wingy mysteries in divinity and airy subtleties in religion, which have unhinged the brains of better heads, they never stretched the *pia mater* of mine; methinks there be not impossibilities enough in religion for an active faith.
Religio Medici (1643) pt. 1, sect. 9

16 I love to lose myself in a mystery, to pursue my reason to an *O altitudo*!
Religio Medici (1643) pt. 1, sect. 9

17 Who can speak of eternity without a solecism, or think thereof without an ecstasy? Time we may comprehend, 'tis but five days elder than ourselves.
Religio Medici (1643) pt. 1, sect. 11

18 I have often admired the mystical way of Pythagoras, and the secret magic of numbers.
Religio Medici (1643) pt. 1, sect. 12

19 We carry within us the wonders we seek without us: there is all Africa and her prodigies in us.
Religio Medici (1643) pt. 1, sect. 15; cf. **Pliny** 578:17

20 All things are artificial, for nature is the art of God.
Religio Medici (1643) pt. 1, sect. 16

21 Obstinacy in a bad cause, is but constancy in a good.
Religio Medici (1643) pt. 1, sect. 25

22 Persecution is a bad and indirect way to plant religion.
Religio Medici (1643) pt. 1, sect. 25

23 Not wrung from speculations and subtleties, but from common sense, and observation; not picked from the leaves of any author, but bred among the weeds and tares of mine own brain.
Religio Medici (1643) pt. 1, sect. 36

24 I am not so much afraid of death, as ashamed thereof; 'tis the very disgrace and ignominy of our natures, that in a moment can so disfigure us that our nearest friends, wife, and children, stand afraid and start at us.
Religio Medici (1643) pt. 1, sect. 40

25 Certainly there is no happiness within this circle of flesh, nor is it in the optics of these eyes to behold felicity; the first day of our Jubilee is death.
Religio Medici (1643) pt. 1, sect. 44

26 He forgets that he can die who complains of misery, we are in the power of no calamity, while death is in our own.
Religio Medici (1643) pt. 1, sect. 44

27 All places, all airs make unto me one country: I am in England, everywhere, and under any meridian.
Religio Medici (1643) pt. 2, sect. 1

28 If there be any among those common objects of hatred I do condemn and laugh at, it is that great enemy of reason, virtue and religion, the multitude, that numerous piece of monstrosity, which taken asunder seem men, and the reasonable creatures of God; but confused together, make but one great beast, and a monstrosity more prodigious than Hydra.
Religio Medici (1643) pt. 2, sect. 1

29 This trivial and vulgar way of coition; it is the foolishest act a wise man commits in all his life, nor is there any thing that will more deject his cooled imagination, when he shall consider what an odd and unworthy piece of folly he hath committed.
Religio Medici (1643) pt. 2, sect. 9

30 Sure there is music even in the beauty, and the silent note which Cupid strikes, far sweeter than the sound of an instrument. For there is music wherever there is a harmony, order or proportion; and thus far we may maintain the music of the spheres; for those well-ordered motions, and regular paces, though they give no sound unto the

ear, yet to the understanding they strike a note most full of harmony.
Religio Medici (1643) pt. 2, sect. 9

1 We all labour against our own cure, for death is the cure of all diseases.
Religio Medici (1643) pt. 2, sect. 9

2 For the world, I count it not an inn, but an hospital, and a place, not to live, but to die in.
Religio Medici (1643) pt. 2, sect. 11

3 There is surely a piece of divinity in us, something that was before the elements, and owes no homage unto the sun.
Religio Medici (1643) pt. 2, sect. 11

4 We term sleep a death, and yet it is waking that kills us, and destroys those spirits which are the house of life.
Religio Medici (1643) pt. 2, sect. 12

5 Half our days we pass in the shadow of the earth; and the brother of death exacteth a third part of our lives.
S. Wilkin (ed.) *Sir Thomas Browne's Works* (1835) vol. 4, p. 355 'On Dreams'

6 That children dream not in the first half year, that men dream not in some countries, are to me sick men's dreams, dreams out of the ivory gate, and visions before midnight.
S. Wilkin (ed.) *Sir Thomas Browne's Works* (1835) vol. 4 'On Dreams'

William Browne 1692–1774

English physician and writer

7 The King to Oxford sent a troop of horse,
For Tories own no argument but force:
With equal skill to Cambridge books he sent,
For Whigs admit no force but argument.
reply to **Trapp**'s epigram on **George I**, in J. Nichols *Literary Anecdotes* vol. 3 (1812); cf. **Trapp** 781:1

Elizabeth Barrett Browning 1806–61

English poet; wife of Robert **Browning**
on Browning: see **Fitzgerald** *315:4*

8 Some people always sigh in thanking God.
Aurora Leigh (1857) bk. 1, l. 445

9 The works of women are symbolical.
We sew, sew, prick our fingers, dull our sight,
Producing what? A pair of slippers, sir,
To put on when you're weary.
Aurora Leigh (1857) bk. 1, l. 456

10 Nay, if there's room for poets in this world
A little overgrown (I think there is)
Their sole work is to represent the age,
Their age, not Charlemagne's.
Aurora Leigh (1857) bk. 5, l. 200

11 And Camelot to minstrels seemed as flat
As Fleet Street to our poets.
Aurora Leigh (1857) bk. 5, l. 212

12 The devil's most devilish when respectable.
Aurora Leigh (1857) bk. 7, l. 105

13 Earth's crammed with heaven,
And every common bush afire with God.
Aurora Leigh (1857) bk. 7, l. 821

14 And kings crept out again to feel the sun.
'Crowned and Buried' (1844) st. 11

15 Do ye hear the children weeping, O my brothers,
Ere the sorrow comes with years?
'The Cry of the Children' (1844) st. 1

16 And lips say, 'God be pitiful,'
Who ne'er said, 'God be praised.'
'The Cry of the Human' (1844) st. 1

17 I tell you, hopeless grief is passionless.
'Grief' (1844)

18 Or from Browning some 'Pomegranate', which, if cut deep down the middle,
Shows a heart within blood-tinctured, of a veined humanity.
'Lady Geraldine's Courtship' (1844) st. 41

19 'Yes,' I answered you last night;
'No,' this morning, sir, I say.
Colours seen by candle-light
Will not look the same by day.
'The Lady's Yes' (1844)

20 What was he doing, the great god Pan,
Down in the reeds by the river?
'A Musical Instrument' (1862)

21 How do I love thee? Let me count the ways.
I love thee to the depth and breadth and height
My soul can reach, when feeling out of sight
For the ends of Being and ideal Grace.
Sonnets from the Portuguese (1850) no. 43

22 I love thee with the breath,
Smiles, tears, of all my life!—and if God choose,
I shall but love thee better after death.
Sonnets from the Portuguese (1850) no. 43

23 Thou large-brained woman and large-hearted man.
'To George Sand—A Desire' (1844)

Frederick 'Boy' Browning 1896–1965

British soldier

24 I think we might be going a bridge too far.
expressing reservations about the Arnhem 'Market Garden' operation to Field Marshal **Montgomery**
on 10 September 1944; R. E. Urquhart *Arnhem* (1958)

Robert Browning 1812–89

English poet; husband of Elizabeth Barrett **Browning**
on Browning: see **Bagehot** *47:24,* **Browning** *154:18,* **Wilde** *817:26, 818:7*

25 The high that proved too high, the heroic for earth too hard,
The passion that left the ground to lose itself in the sky,
Are music sent up to God by the lover and the bard;
Enough that he heard it once: we shall hear it by-and-by.
'Abt Vogler' (1864) st. 10

1 . . . I feel for the common chord again . . .
The C Major of this life.
'Abt Vogler' (1864) st. 12

2 Ah, but a man's reach should exceed his grasp,
Or what's a heaven for?
'Andrea del Sarto' (1855) l. 97

3 Still, what an arm! and I could alter it:
But all the play, the insight and the stretch—
Out of me, out of me!
'Andrea del Sarto' (1855) l. 115

4 One who never turned his back but marched breast forward,
Never doubted clouds would break,
Never dreamed, though right were worsted, wrong would triumph,
Held we fall to rise, are baffled to fight better,
Sleep to wake.
Asolando (1889) 'Epilogue'

5 Greet the unseen with a cheer!
Asolando (1889) 'Epilogue'

6 There spoke up a brisk little somebody,
Critic and whippersnapper, in a rage
To set things right.
Balaustion's Adventure (1871) l. 306

7 Just when we are safest, there's a sunset-touch,
A fancy from a flower-bell, some one's death,
A chorus-ending from Euripides.
'Bishop Blougram's Apology' (1855) l. 182

8 The grand Perhaps!
'Bishop Blougram's Apology' (1855) l. 190

9 Our interest's on the dangerous edge of things.
The honest thief, the tender murderer,
The superstitious atheist, demirep
That loves and saves her soul in new French books.
'Bishop Blougram's Apology' (1855) l. 395

10 You, for example, clever to a fault,
The rough and ready man who write apace,
Read somewhat seldomer, think perhaps even less.
'Bishop Blougram's Apology' (1855) l. 420

11 He said true things, but called them by wrong names.
'Bishop Blougram's Apology' (1855) l. 996

12 Shrewd was that snatch from out the corner South
He graced his carrion with, God curse the same!
'The Bishop Orders his Tomb' (1845) l. 18

13 And have I not Saint Praxed's ear to pray
Horses for ye, and brown Greek manuscripts,
And mistresses with great smooth marbly limbs?
—That's if ye carve my epitaph aright.
'The Bishop Orders his Tomb' (1845) l. 73

14 And then how I shall lie through centuries,
And hear the blessed mutter of the mass,
And see God made and eaten all day long,
And feel the steady candle-flame, and taste
Good strong thick stupefying incense-smoke!
'The Bishop Orders his Tomb' (1845) l. 80

15 Boot, saddle, to horse, and away!
'Boot and Saddle' (1842)

16 And I turn the page, and I turn the page,
Not verse now, only prose!
'By the Fireside' (1855) st. 2

17 When earth breaks up and heaven expands,
How will the change strike me and you
In the house not made with hands?
'By the Fireside' (1855) st. 27; cf. **Bible** 107:7

18 Oh, the little more, and how much it is!
And the little less, and what worlds away!
'By the Fireside' (1855) st. 39

19 Setebos, Setebos, and Setebos!
'Thinketh, He dwelleth i' the cold o' the moon.
'Caliban upon Setebos' (1864) l. 24; cf. **Shakespeare** 698:25

20 'Let twenty pass, and stone the twenty-first,
Loving not, hating not, just choosing so.
'Caliban upon Setebos' (1864) l. 102

21 Dauntless the slug-horn to my lips I set,
And blew. '*Childe Roland to the Dark Tower came.*'
'Childe Roland to the Dark Tower Came' (1855) st. 34; cf. **Shakespeare** 679:9

22 We loved, sir—used to meet:
How sad and bad and mad it was—
But then, how it was sweet!
'Confessions' (1864) st. 9

23 Stung by the splendour of a sudden thought.
'A Death in the Desert' (1864) l. 59

24 . . . Progress, man's distinctive mark alone,
Not God's, and not the beasts': God is, they are,
Man partly is and wholly hopes to be.
'A Death in the Desert' (1864) l. 586

25 Open my heart and you will see
Graved inside of it, 'Italy'.
'De Gustibus' (1855) pt. 2, l. 43

26 'Tis well averred,
A scientific faith's absurd.
'Easter-Day' (1850) l. 123

27 Karshish, the picker-up of learning's crumbs,
The not-incurious in God's handiwork.
'An Epistle . . . of Karshish' (1855)

28 Beautiful Evelyn Hope is dead!
'Evelyn Hope' (1855)

29 If you get simple beauty and naught else,
You get about the best thing God invents.
'Fra Lippo Lippi' (1855) l. 217

30 This world's no blot for us,
Nor blank; it means intensely, and means good:
To find its meaning is my meat and drink.
'Fra Lippo Lippi' (1855) l. 313

31 This is our master, famous calm and dead,
Borne on our shoulders.
'A Grammarian's Funeral' (1855) l. 27

32 Yea, but we found him bald too, eyes like lead,
Accents uncertain:
'Time to taste life,' another would have said,
'Up with the curtain!'
'A Grammarian's Funeral' (1855) l. 53

33 He said, 'What's time? Leave Now for dogs and apes!

Man has Forever.'
'A Grammarian's Funeral' (1855) l. 83

1 That low man seeks a little thing to do,
Sees it and does it:
This high man, with a great thing to pursue,
Dies ere he knows it.
That low man goes on adding one to one,
His hundred's soon hit:
This high man, aiming at a million,
Misses an unit.
'A Grammarian's Funeral' (1855) l. 113

2 Oh, to be in England
Now that April's there,
And whoever wakes in England
Sees, some morning, unaware,
That the lowest boughs and the brushwood sheaf
Round the elm-tree bole are in tiny leaf,
While the chaffinch sings on the orchard bough
In England—now!
'Home-Thoughts, from Abroad' (1845); cf. **cummings** 247:6

3 That's the wise thrush; he sings each song twice over,
Lest you should think he never could recapture
The first fine careless rapture!
'Home-Thoughts, from Abroad' (1845)

4 Nobly, nobly Cape Saint Vincent to the North-west died away;
Sunset ran, one glorious blood-red, reeking into Cadiz Bay.
'Home-Thoughts, from the Sea' (1845)

5 'Here and here did England help me: how can I help England?'—say,
Whoso turns as I, this evening, turn to God to praise and pray,
While Jove's planet rises yonder, silent over Africa.
'Home-Thoughts, from the Sea' (1845)

6 'With this same key
Shakespeare unlocked his heart,' once more!
Did Shakespeare? If so, the less Shakespeare he!
'House' (1876); cf. **Wordsworth** 831:18

7 How they brought the good news from Ghent to Aix.
title of poem (1845)

8 I sprang to the stirrup, and Joris, and he;
I galloped, Dirck galloped, we galloped all three.
'How they brought the Good News from Ghent to Aix' (1845) l. 1

9 A man can have but one life and one death,
One heaven, one hell.
'In a Balcony' (1855) l. 13

10 I count life just a stuff
To try the soul's strength on, educe the man.
'In a Balcony' (1855) l. 651

11 'You're wounded!' 'Nay,' the soldier's pride
Touched to the quick, he said:
'I'm killed, Sire!' And his chief beside,
Smiling the boy fell dead.
'Incident of the French Camp' (1842) st. 5

12 Ignorance is not innocence but sin.
The Inn Album (1875) canto 5

13 The swallow has set her six young on the rail,
And looks sea-ward.
'James Lee's Wife' (1864) pt. 3, st. 1

14 Who knows but the world may end tonight?
'The Last Ride Together' (1855) st. 2

15 Had I said that, had I done this,
So might I gain, so might I miss.
Might she have loved me? just as well
She might have hated, who can tell!
'The Last Ride Together' (1855) st. 4

16 'Tis an awkward thing to play with souls,
And matter enough to save one's own.
'A Light Woman' (1855) st. 12

17 Just for a handful of silver he left us,
Just for a riband to stick in his coat.
of ***Wordsworth***
'The Lost Leader' (1845)

18 We that had loved him so, followed him, honoured him,
Lived in his mild and magnificent eye,
Learned his great language, caught his clear accents,
Made him our pattern to live and to die!
Shakespeare was of us, Milton was for us,
Burns, Shelley, were with us—they watch from their graves!
'The Lost Leader' (1845)

19 Never glad confident morning again!
'The Lost Leader' (1845)

20 Kentish Sir Byng stood for his King,
Bidding the crop-headed Parliament swing.
'Marching Along' (1842)

21 Marched them along, fifty-score strong,
Great-hearted gentlemen, singing this song.
God for King Charles! Pym and such carles
To the Devil that prompts 'em their treasonous parles!
'Marching Along' (1842)

22 A tap at the pane, the quick sharp scratch
And blue spurt of a lighted match,
And a voice less loud, through its joys and fears,
Than the two hearts beating each to each!
'Meeting at Night' (1845)

23 Ah, did you once see Shelley plain,
And did he stop and speak to you
And did you speak to him again?
How strange it seems, and new!
'Memorabilia' (1855)

24 That's my last Duchess painted on the wall,
Looking as if she were alive.
'My Last Duchess' (1842) l. 1

25 She had
A heart—how shall I say?—too soon made glad,
Too easily impressed; she liked whate'er
She looked on, and her looks went everywhere.
'My Last Duchess' (1842) l. 21

1 Never the time and the place
And the loved one all together!
'Never the Time and the Place' (1883)

2 What's come to perfection perishes.
Things learned on earth, we shall practise in heaven:
Works done least rapidly, Art most cherishes.
'Old Pictures in Florence' (1855) st. 17

3 Dante, who loved well because he hated,
Hated wickedness that hinders loving.
'One Word More' (1855) st. 5

4 Measure your mind's height by the shade it casts!
Paracelsus (1835) pt. 3, l. 821

5 I give the fight up: let there be an end,
A privacy, an obscure nook for me.
I want to be forgotten even by God.
Paracelsus (1835) pt. 5, l. 363

6 Round the cape of a sudden came the sea,
And the sun looked over the mountain's rim:
And straight was a path of gold for him,
And the need of a world of men for me.
'Parting at Morning' (1849)

7 It was roses, roses, all the way.
'The Patriot' (1855)

8 The air broke into a mist with bells.
'The Patriot' (1855)

9 Sun-treader, life and light be thine for ever!
of **Shelley**
Pauline (1833) l. 151

10 Rats!
They fought the dogs and killed the cats,
And bit the babies in the cradles,
And ate the cheeses out of the vats,
And licked the soup from the cooks' own ladles,
Split open the kegs of salted sprats,
Made nests inside men's Sunday hats,
And even spoiled the women's chats
By drowning their speaking
With shrieking and squeaking
In fifty different sharps and flats.
'The Pied Piper of Hamelin' (1842) st. 2

11 So munch on, crunch on, take your nuncheon,
Breakfast, supper, dinner, luncheon!
'The Pied Piper of Hamelin' (1842) st. 7

12 The year's at the spring
And day's at the morn;
Morning's at seven;
The hill-side's dew-pearled;
The lark's on the wing;
The snail's on the thorn:
God's in his heaven—
All's right with the world!
Pippa Passes (1841) pt. 1, l. 221; cf. **Proverbs** 601:16

13 All service ranks the same with God—
With God, whose puppets, best and worst,
Are we: there is no last nor first.
Pippa Passes (1841) epilogue

14 That moment she was mine, mine, fair,
Perfectly pure and good.
'Porphyria's Lover' (1842) l. 36

15 All her hair
In one long yellow string I wound
Three times her little throat around,
And strangled her. No pain felt she;
I am quite sure she felt no pain.
'Porphyria's Lover' (1842) l. 38

16 Fear death?—to feel the fog in my throat,
The mist in my face.
'Prospice' (1864)

17 I was ever a fighter, so—one fight more,
The best and the last!
I would hate that death bandaged my eyes, and forbore,
And bade me creep past.
No! let me taste the whole of it, fare like my peers
The heroes of old,
Bear the brunt, in a minute pay glad life's arrears
Of pain, darkness and cold.
'Prospice' (1864)

18 Grow old along with me!
The best is yet to be,
The last of life, for which the first was made.
'Rabbi Ben Ezra' (1864) st. 1

19 Fancies that broke through language and escaped.
'Rabbi Ben Ezra' (1864) st. 25

20 Time's wheel runs back or stops: potter and clay endure.
'Rabbi Ben Ezra' (1864) st. 27

21 O lyric Love, half-angel and half-bird.
The Ring and the Book (1868–9) bk. 1, l. 1391

22 So, Pietro craved an heir,
(The story always old and always new).
The Ring and the Book (1868–9) bk. 2, l. 213

23 Go practise if you please
With men and women: leave a child alone
For Christ's particular love's sake!
The Ring and the Book (1868–9) bk. 3, l. 88

24 In the great right of an excessive wrong.
The Ring and the Book (1868–9) bk. 3, l. 1055

25 Faultless to a fault.
The Ring and the Book (1868–9) bk. 9, l. 1175

26 White shall not neutralize the black, nor good
Compensate bad in man, absolve him so:
Life's business being just the terrible choice.
The Ring and the Book (1868–9) bk. 10, l. 1235

27 I want to know a butcher paints,
A baker rhymes for his pursuit,
Candlestick-maker much acquaints
His soul with song, or, haply mute,
Blows out his brains upon the flute!
'Shop' (1876) st. 21

28 Gr-r-r—there go, my heart's abhorrence!
Water your damned flowerpots, do!
If hate killed men, Brother Lawrence,
God's blood, would not mine kill you!
'Soliloquy of the Spanish Cloister' (1842) st. 1

29 There's a great text in Galatians,
Once you trip on it, entails
Twenty-nine distinct damnations,

One sure, if another fails.
'Soliloquy of the Spanish Cloister' (1842) st. 7

1 Sidney's self, the starry paladin.
Sordello (1840) bk. 1, l. 69

2 Still more labyrinthine buds the rose.
Sordello (1840) bk. 1, l. 476

3 Any nose
May ravage with impunity a rose.
Sordello (1840) bk. 6, l. 881

4 And the sin I impute to each frustrate ghost
Is—the unlit lamp and the ungirt loin,
Though the end in sight was a vice, I say.
'The Statue and the Bust' (1863 revision) l. 246

5 Oh Galuppi, Baldassaro, this is very sad to find!
I can hardly misconceive you; it would prove me deaf and blind;
But although I take your meaning, 'tis with such a heavy mind!
'A Toccata of Galuppi's' (1855) st. 1

6 Hark, the dominant's persistence till it must be answered to!
'A Toccata of Galuppi's' (1855) st. 8

7 Then they left you for their pleasure: till in due time, one by one,
Some with lives that came to nothing, some with deeds as well undone,
Death stepped tacitly and took them where they never see the sun.
'A Toccata of Galuppi's' (1855) st. 10

8 In you come with your cold music till I creep through every nerve.
'A Toccata of Galuppi's' (1855) st. 11

9 Dust and ashes, dead and done with, Venice spent what Venice earned.
'A Toccata of Galuppi's' (1855) st. 12

10 What of soul was left, I wonder, when the kissing had to stop?
'A Toccata of Galuppi's' (1855) st. 14

11 Dear dead women, with such hair, too—what's become of all the gold
Used to hang and brush their bosoms? I feel chilly and grown old.
'A Toccata of Galuppi's' (1855) st. 15

12 I would that you were all to me,
You that are just so much, no more.
'Two in the Campagna' (1855) st. 8

13 I pluck the rose
And love it more than tongue can speak—
Then the good minute goes.
'Two in the Campagna' (1855) st. 10

14 Let's contend no more, Love,
Strive nor weep:
All be as before, Love,
—Only sleep!
'A Woman's Last Word' (1855) st. 1

15 Ay, dead! and were yourself alive, good Fitz,
How to return your thanks would pass my wits.
Kicking you seems the common lot of curs—
While more appropriate greeting lends you grace:
Surely to spit there glorifies your face—
Spitting from lips once sanctified by Hers.
rejoinder to Edward **Fitzgerald**, *who had 'thanked God my wife was dead'*
in *Athenaeum* 13 July 1889; cf. **Fitzgerald** 315:4

16 When it was written, God and Robert Browning knew what it meant; now only God knows.
on Sordello
attributed; cf. **Klopstock** 442:5

Lenny Bruce 1925–66
American comedian

17 The liberals can understand everything but people who don't understand them.
John Cohen (ed.) *The Essential Lenny Bruce* (1967)

18 I'll die young, but it's like kissing God.
on his drug addiction
attributed

Robert Bruce 1554–1631
Scottish minister and laird of Kinnaird

19 Now, God be with you, my children: I have breakfasted with you and shall sup with my Lord Jesus Christ this night.
Robert Fleming *The Fulfilling of the Scripture* (3rd ed., 1693)

Cathal Brugha 1874–1922
Irish nationalist
on Brugha: see **Collins** *229:4*

20 Don't you realize that, if you sign this thing, you will split Ireland from top to bottom?
to **de Valera**, *December 1921, on the Treaty*
Jim Ring *Erskine Childers* (1996)

Beau Brummell (George Bryan Brummell) 1778–1840
English dandy

21 Who's your fat friend?
referring to the Prince of Wales, later **George IV**
Capt. Jesse *Life of George Brummell* (1844) vol. 1

22 [Brummell] used to say that, whether it was summer or winter, he always liked to have the morning well-aired before he got up.
Charles Macfarlane *Reminiscences of a Literary Life* (1917) ch. 27

23 No perfumes, but very fine linen, plenty of it, and country washing.
Memoirs of Harriette Wilson (1825) vol. 1

Gro Harlem Brundtland 1939–
Norwegian stateswoman; Prime Minister 1981, 1986–89, and 1990–96

24 I do not know of any environmental group in any country that does not view its government as an adversary.
in *Time* 25 September 1989

Frank Bruno 1961–
English boxer

1 Boxing's just show business with blood.
in *Guardian* 20 November 1991

2 Know what I mean, Harry?
supposed to have been said in interview with sports commentator Harry Carpenter, possibly apocryphal

William Jennings Bryan 1860–1925
American Democratic politician

3 You shall not press down upon the brow of labour this crown of thorns, you shall not crucify mankind upon a cross of gold.
opposing the gold standard
speech at the Democratic National Convention, Chicago, 1896, in *The First Battle. A Story of the Campaign of 1896* (1896) vol. 1, ch. 10

Bill Bryson 1951–
American travel writer

4 I had always thought that once you grew up you could do anything you wanted—stay up all night or eat ice-cream straight out of the container.
The Lost Continent (1989)

5 What an odd thing tourism is. You fly off to a strange land, eagerly abandoning all the comforts of home, and then expend vast quantities of time and money in a largely futile attempt to recapture the comforts that you wouldn't have lost if you hadn't left home in the first place.
Neither Here Nor There (1991)

Zbigniew Brzezinski 1928–
US Secretary of State and National Security Advisor

6 Russia can be an empire or a democracy, but it cannot be both.
in *Foreign Affairs* March/April 1994 'The Premature Partnership'

Martin Buber 1878–1965
Austrian-born religious philosopher and Zionist

7 Through the Thou a person becomes I.
I and Thou (1923)

John Buchan (Lord Tweedsmuir) 1875–1940
Scottish novelist and brother of O. **Douglas**; *Governor-General of Canada, 1935–40*

8 It's a great life if you don't weaken.
Mr Standfast (1919) ch. 5

9 An atheist is a man who has no invisible means of support.
H. E. Fosdick *On Being a Real Person* (1943) ch. 10

Frank Buchman 1878–1961
American evangelist; founder of the Moral Re-Armament movement

10 I thank heaven for a man like Adolf Hitler, who built a front line of defence against the anti-Christ of Communism.
in *New York World-Telegram* 26 August 1936

11 There is enough in the world for everyone's need, but not enough for everyone's greed.
Remaking the World (1947)

Gene Buck (Edward Eugene Buck) 1885–1957 and **Herman Ruby** 1891–1959

12 That Shakespearian rag,—
Most intelligent, very elegant.
'That Shakespearian Rag' (1912 song); cf. **Eliot** 296:5

George Villiers, 2nd Duke of Buckingham 1628–87
English courtier and writer

13 The world is made up for the most part of fools and knaves, both irreconcilable foes to truth.
The Dramatic Works (1715) vol. 2 'To Mr Clifford On his Humane Reason'

14 What a devil is the plot good for, but to bring in fine things?
The Rehearsal (1672) act 3, sc. 1

15 Ay, now the plot thickens very much upon us.
The Rehearsal (1672) act 3, sc. 2

John Sheffield, 1st Duke of Buckingham and Normanby 1648–1721
English poet and politician

16 Learn to write well, or not to write at all.
'An Essay upon Satire' (1689)

H. J. Buckoll 1803–71
English clergyman; master at Rugby School from 1826

17 Lord, dismiss us with Thy blessing,
Thanks for mercies past receive.
Pardon all, their faults confessing;
Time that's lost may all retrieve.
Psalms and Hymns for the Use of Rugby School Chapel (1850) 'Lord, Dismiss us with Thy Blessing'

J. B. Buckstone 1802–79
English comedian and dramatist

18 And we won't go home till morning.
Billy Taylor (performed 1829) act 1, sc. 2

Comte de Buffon (George-Louis Leclerc) 1707–88
French naturalist

19 Style is the man himself.
Discours sur le style (address given to the Académie Française, 25 August 1753); cf. **Proverbs** 611:31

20 Genius is only a greater aptitude for patience.
Hérault de Séchelles *Voyage à Montbar* (1803); **Carlyle** 187:20

Edward Bullard 1907–80
English geophysicist

21 Rutherford was a disaster. He started the 'something for nothing' tradition . . . the notion that research can always be done on the cheap . . . The war taught us differently. If you want quick and effective results you must put the money in.

P. Grosvenor and J. McMillan *The British Genius* (1973); cf. **Rutherford** 640:17

Arthur Buller 1874–1944

British botanist and mycologist

1 There was a young lady named Bright,
Whose speed was far faster than light;
She set out one day
In a relative way
And returned on the previous night.

'Relativity' in *Punch* 19 December 1923

Gerald Bullett 1894–1958

British writer

2 My Lord Archbishop, what a scold you are!
And when your man is down how bold you are!
Of charity how oddly scant you are!
How Lang, O Lord, how full of Cantuar!

on the role of Cosmo Gordon Lang, Archbishop of Canterbury, in the abdication of ***Edward VIII***

composed *c.*1936

Ivor Bulmer-Thomas 1905–93

British Conservative politician

3 If he ever went to school without any boots it was because he was too big for them.

of Harold ***Wilson****, who had claimed in a speech the previous year that more than half the children with whom he went to school had been unable to afford boots or shoes (and had therefore worn clogs)*

speech at the Conservative Party Conference, in *Manchester Guardian* 13 October 1949

Bernhard von Bülow 1849–1929

German statesman, Chancellor of Germany 1900–9

4 We desire to throw no one into the shade [in East Asia], but we also demand our own place in the sun.

in the Reichstag, 6 December 1897, in *Graf Bülows Reden* (1903); cf. **Wilhelm II** 819:18

Edward George Bulwer-Lytton

(1st Baron Lytton) 1803–73

British novelist and politician

5 Here Stanley meets,—how Stanley scorns, the glance!
The brilliant chief, irregularly great,
Frank, haughty, rash,—the Rupert of Debate!

on Edward Stanley, 14th Earl of ***Derby***

The New Timon (1846) pt. 1, sect. 3, l. 202; cf. **Disraeli** 268:9

6 Out-babying Wordsworth and out-glittering Keats.

on ***Tennyson***

The New Timon (1846) pt. 2, sect. 1, l. 62

7 Beneath the rule of men entirely great
The pen is mightier than the sword.

Richelieu (1839) act 2, sc. 2, l. 307; cf. **Burton** 170:10, **Proverbs** 609:22

8 In science, read, by preference, the newest works; in literature, the oldest.

Caxtoniana (1863) 'Hints on Mental Culture'

9 There is no man so friendless but what he can find a friend sincere enough to tell him disagreeable truths.

What will he do with it? (1857) vol. 1, bk. 3, ch. 15

Edward Robert Bulwer, Earl of Lytton

see **Owen Meredith**

Alfred 'Poet' Bunn *c.*1796–1860

English theatrical manager and librettist

10 I dreamed that I dwelt in marble halls
With vassals and serfs at my side.

The Bohemian Girl (1843) act 2 'The Gipsy Girl's Dream'

Basil Bunting 1900–85

English poet

11 Praise the green earth. Chance has appointed her
home, workshop, larder, middenpit.
Her lousy skin scabbed here and there by
cities provides us with name and nation.

'Attis: or, Something Missing' (1931) pt. 1

12 Dance tiptoe, bull,
black against may.
Ridiculous and lovely
chase hurdling shadows
morning into noon.

'Briggflatts' (1965) pt. 1

Luis Buñuel 1900–83

Spanish film director

see also ***Film titles*** *312:18*

13 Thanks to God, I am still an atheist.

in *Le Monde* 16 December 1959

John Bunyan 1628–88

English writer and Nonconformist preacher

on Bunyan: see ***Arnold*** *29:4,* ***Hill*** *376:13*

14 As I walked through the wilderness of this world.

The Pilgrim's Progress (1678) pt. 1, opening words

15 The name of the slough was Despond.

The Pilgrim's Progress (1678) pt. 1

16 CHRISTIAN: Gentlemen, Whence came you, and whither do you go?
FORMALIST AND HYPOCRISY: We were born in the land of Vainglory, and we are going for praise to Mount Sion.

The Pilgrim's Progress (1678) pt. 1

17 It is an hard matter for a man to go down into the valley of Humiliation . . . and to catch no slip by the way.

The Pilgrim's Progress (1678) pt. 1

18 A foul Fiend coming over the field to meet him; his name is Apollyon.

The Pilgrim's Progress (1678) pt. 1

1 It beareth the name of Vanity-Fair, because the town where 'tis kept, is lighter than vanity.
The Pilgrim's Progress (1678) pt. 1; cf. **Book of Common Prayer** 135:22

2 Hanging is too good for him, said Mr Cruelty.
The Pilgrim's Progress (1678) pt. 1

3 Yet my great-grandfather was but a water-man, looking one way, and rowing another: and I got most of my estate by the same occupation.
The Pilgrim's Progress (1678) pt. 1; cf. **Burton** 170:6

4 They are for religion when in rags and contempt; but I am for him when he walks in his golden slippers, in the sunshine and with applause.
The Pilgrim's Progress (1678) pt. 1

5 Now Giant Despair had a wife, and her name was Diffidence.
The Pilgrim's Progress (1678) pt. 1

6 They came to the Delectable Mountains.
The Pilgrim's Progress (1678) pt. 1

7 Sleep is sweet to the labouring man.
The Pilgrim's Progress (1678) pt. 1; cf. **Bible** 84:12

8 Then I saw that there was a way to Hell, even from the gates of heaven.
The Pilgrim's Progress (1678) pt. 1

9 So I awoke, and behold it was a dream.
The Pilgrim's Progress (1678) pt. 1

10 A man that could look no way but downwards, with a muckrake in his hand.
The Pilgrim's Progress (1684) pt. 2; cf. **Roosevelt** 633:7

11 One leak will sink a ship, and one sin will destroy a sinner.
The Pilgrim's Progress (1684) pt. 2

12 He that is down needs fear no fall,
He that is low no pride.
He that is humble ever shall
Have God to be his guide.
The Pilgrim's Progress (1684) pt. 2 'Shepherd Boy's Song'

13 Difficulties, lions, or Vanity-Fair, he feared not at all: 'twas only sin, death, and Hell that was to him a terror.
of Mr Fearing
The Pilgrim's Progress (1684) pt. 2

14 A man there was, tho' some did count him mad,
The more he cast away, the more he had.
The Pilgrim's Progress (1684) pt. 2

15 Mercy . . . laboured much for the poor . . . an ornament to her profession.
The Pilgrim's Progress (1684) pt. 2

16 Who would true valour see,
Let him come hither;
One here will constant be,
Come wind, come weather.
There's no discouragement
Shall make him once relent
His first avowed intent
To be a pilgrim.

Who so beset him round
With dismal stories,
Do but themselves confound—
His strength the more is.
The Pilgrim's Progress (1684) pt. 2

17 The last words of Mr Despondency were, Farewell night, welcome day. His daughter went through the river singing, but none could understand what she said.
The Pilgrim's Progress (1684) pt. 2

18 I am going to my Fathers, and tho' with great difficulty I am got hither, yet now I do not repent me of all the trouble I have been at to arrive where I am. My sword, I give to him that shall succeed me in my pilgrimage, and my courage and skill to him that can get it. My marks and scars I carry with me, to be a witness for me, that I have fought his battles, who will now be my rewarder.
Mr Valiant-for-Truth
The Pilgrim's Progress (1684) pt. 2

19 So he passed over, and the trumpets sounded for him on the other side.
Mr Valiant-for-Truth
The Pilgrim's Progress (1684) pt. 2

20 I have formerly lived by hearsay and faith, but now I go where I shall live by sight, and shall be with Him in whose company I delight myself.
Mr Standfast
The Pilgrim's Progress (1684) pt. 2

Samuel Dickinson Burchard 1812–91
American Presbyterian minister

21 We are Republicans and don't propose to leave our party and identify ourselves with the party whose antecedents are rum, Romanism, and rebellion.
speech at the Fifth Avenue Hotel, New York, 29 October 1884, in *New York World* 30 October 1884

Julie Burchill 1960–
English journalist and writer

22 The freedom women were supposed to have found in the Sixties largely boiled down to easy contraception and abortion: things to make life easier for men, in fact.
Damaged Goods (1986) 'Born Again Cows'

23 Now, at last, this sad, glittering century has an image worthy of it: a wandering, wondering girl, a silly Sloane turned secular saint, coming home in her coffin to RAF Northolt like the good soldier she was.
in *Guardian* 2 September 1997

Anthony Burgess 1917–93
English novelist and critic
see also **Opening lines** 555:27

24 A clockwork orange.
title of novel (1962)

25 He said it was artificial respiration, but now I find I am to have his child.
Inside Mr Enderby (1963) pt. 1, ch. 4

26 The ideal reader of my novels is a lapsed Catholic and a failed musician, short-sighted, colour-blind,

auditorily biased, who has read the books that I have read. He should also be about my age.
George Plimpton (ed.) *Writers at Work* (4th Series, 1977)

1 The US presidency is a Tudor monarchy plus telephones.
George Plimpton (ed.) *Writers at Work* (4th Series, 1977)

Gelett Burgess 1866–1951

American humorist and illustrator

2 I never saw a Purple Cow,
I never hope to see one;
But I can tell you, anyhow,
I'd rather see than be one!
The Burgess Nonsense Book (1914) 'The Purple Cow'

3 Ah, yes! I wrote the 'Purple Cow'—
I'm sorry, now, I wrote it!
But I can tell you anyhow,
I'll kill you if you quote it!
The Burgess Nonsense Book (1914) 'Confessional'

Lord Burghley see William Cecil

John William Burgon 1813–88

English clergyman; Dean of Chichester from 1876

4 Match me such marvel, save in Eastern clime,—
A rose-red city—half as old as Time!
Petra (1845) l. 131; cf. **Plomer** 579:5, **Rogers** 631:14

John Burgoyne 1722–92

English general and dramatist

5 You have only, when before your glass, to keep pronouncing to yourself nimini-pimini—the lips cannot fail of taking their plie.
The Heiress (1786) act 3, sc. 2

Edmund Burke 1729–97

Irish-born Whig politician and man of letters
on Burke: see ***Goldsmith*** *345:1,* ***Johnson*** *417:9,* ***Paine*** *563:18, 563:19; see also* ***Misquotations*** *521:17*

6 The conduct of a losing party never appears right: at least it never can possess the only infallible criterion of wisdom to vulgar judgements—success.
Letter to a Member of the National Assembly (1791)

7 Those who have been once intoxicated with power, and have derived any kind of emolument from it, even though for but one year, can never willingly abandon it.
Letter to a Member of the National Assembly (1791)

8 Tyrants seldom want pretexts.
Letter to a Member of the National Assembly (1791)

9 You can never plan the future by the past.
Letter to a Member of the National Assembly (1791)

10 The king, and his faithful subjects, the lords and commons of this realm,—the triple cord, which no man can break.
A Letter to a Noble Lord (1796); cf. **Bible** 84:10

11 Many have been taught to think that moderation, in a case like this, is a sort of treason.
Letter to the Sheriffs of Bristol (1777)

12 Between craft and credulity, the voice of reason is stifled.
Letter to the Sheriffs of Bristol (1777)

13 Liberty too must be limited in order to be possessed.
Letter to the Sheriffs of Bristol (1777)

14 Nothing in progression can rest on its original plan. We may as well think of rocking a grown man in the cradle of an infant.
Letter to the Sheriffs of Bristol (1777)

15 Among a people generally corrupt, liberty cannot long exist.
Letter to the Sheriffs of Bristol (1777)

16 There is, however, a limit at which forbearance ceases to be a virtue.
Observations on a late Publication on the Present State of the Nation (2nd ed., 1769)

17 It is a general popular error to imagine the loudest complainers for the public to be the most anxious for its welfare.
Observations on a late Publication on the Present State of the Nation (2nd ed., 1769)

18 It is the nature of all greatness not to be exact; and great trade will always be attended with considerable abuses.
On American Taxation (1775)

19 Falsehood has a perennial spring.
On American Taxation (1775)

20 To tax and to please, no more than to love and to be wise, is not given to men.
On American Taxation (1775); cf. **Proverbs** 608:34

21 I have in general no very exalted opinion of the virtue of paper government.
On Conciliation with America (1775)

22 The concessions of the weak are the concessions of fear.
On Conciliation with America (1775)

23 When we speak of the commerce with our colonies, fiction lags after truth; invention is unfruitful, and imagination cold and barren.
On Conciliation with America (1775)

24 The use of force alone is but *temporary*. It may subdue for a moment; but it does not remove the necessity of subduing again; and a nation is not governed, which is perpetually to be conquered.
On Conciliation with America (1775)

25 Nothing less will content me, than *whole America.*
On Conciliation with America (1775)

26 All Protestantism, even the most cold and passive, is a sort of dissent. But the religion most prevalent in our northern colonies is a refinement on the principle of resistance; it is the dissidence of dissent, and the Protestantism of the Protestant religion.
On Conciliation with America (1775)

27 I do not know the method of drawing up an indictment against an whole people.
On Conciliation with America (1775)

1 It is not, what a lawyer tells me I *may* do; but what humanity, reason, and justice, tells me I ought to do.
On Conciliation with America (1775)

2 Freedom and not servitude is the cure of anarchy; as religion, and not atheism, is the true remedy for superstition.
On Conciliation with America (1775)

3 Instead of a standing revenue, you will have therefore a perpetual quarrel.
On Conciliation with America (1775)

4 Parties must ever exist in a free country.
On Conciliation with America (1775)

5 Slavery they can have anywhere. It is a weed that grows in every soil.
On Conciliation with America (1775)

6 Deny them this participation of freedom, and you break that sole bond, which originally made, and must still preserve the unity of the empire.
On Conciliation with America (1775)

7 It is the love of the people; it is their attachment to their government, from the sense of the deep stake they have in such a glorious institution, which gives you your army and your navy, and infuses into both that liberal obedience, without which your army would be a base rabble, and your navy nothing but rotten timber.
On Conciliation with America (1775)

8 Magnanimity in politics is not seldom the truest wisdom; and a great empire and little minds go ill together.
On Conciliation with America (1775)

9 By adverting to the dignity of this high calling, our ancestors have turned a savage wilderness into a glorious empire: and have made the most extensive, and the only honourable conquests; not by destroying, but by promoting the wealth, the number, the happiness of the human race.
On Conciliation with America (1775)

10 No passion so effectually robs the mind of all its powers of acting and reasoning as fear.
On the Sublime and Beautiful (1757) pt. 2, sect. 2

11 Custom reconciles us to everything.
On the Sublime and Beautiful (1757) pt. 4, sect. 18

12 I flatter myself that I love a manly, moral, regulated liberty as well as any gentleman.
Reflections on the Revolution in France (1790)

13 Whenever our neighbour's house is on fire, it cannot be amiss for the engines to play a little on our own.
Reflections on the Revolution in France (1790)

14 A state without the means of some change is without the means of its conservation.
Reflections on the Revolution in France (1790)

15 Make the Revolution a parent of settlement, and not a nursery of future revolutions.
Reflections on the Revolution in France (1790)

16 People will not look forward to posterity, who never look backward to their ancestors.
Reflections on the Revolution in France (1790)

17 Those who attempt to level never equalize.
Reflections on the Revolution in France (1790)

18 Whatever each man can separately do, without trespassing upon others, he has a right to do for himself; and he has a right to a fair portion of all which society, with all its combinations of skill and force, can do in his favour.
Reflections on the Revolution in France (1790)

19 Government is a contrivance of human wisdom to provide for human *wants*. Men have a right that these wants should be provided for by this wisdom.
Reflections on the Revolution in France (1790)

20 I thought ten thousand swords must have leapt from their scabbards to avenge even a look that threatened her with insult.
of ***Marie-Antoinette***
Reflections on the Revolution in France (1790)

21 The age of chivalry is gone.— That of sophisters, economists, and calculators, has succeeded; and the glory of Europe is extinguished for ever.
Reflections on the Revolution in France (1790)

22 This barbarous philosophy, which is the offspring of cold hearts and muddy understandings.
Reflections on the Revolution in France (1790)

23 In the groves of *their* academy, at the end of every vista, you see nothing but the gallows.
Reflections on the Revolution in France (1790); cf. **Horace** 387:8

24 Kings will be tyrants from policy when subjects are rebels from principle.
Reflections on the Revolution in France (1790)

25 Learning will be cast into the mire, and trodden down under the hoofs of a swinish multitude.
Reflections on the Revolution in France (1790)

26 Because half a dozen grasshoppers under a fern make the field ring with their importunate chink, whilst thousands of great cattle, reposed beneath the shadow of the British oak, chew the cud and are silent, pray do not imagine that those who make the noise are the only inhabitants of the field.
Reflections on the Revolution in France (1790)

27 Man is by his constitution a religious animal; atheism is against not only our reason, but our instincts.
Reflections on the Revolution in France (1790); cf. **Aristotle** 25:2

28 A perfect democracy is therefore the most shameless thing in the world.
Reflections on the Revolution in France (1790)

29 Society is indeed a contract . . . it becomes a partnership not only between those who are living, but between those who are living, those who are dead, and those who are to be born.
Reflections on the Revolution in France (1790)

30 Nobility is a graceful ornament to the civil order. It is the Corinthian capital of polished society.
Reflections on the Revolution in France (1790)

1 Superstition is the religion of feeble minds.
Reflections on the Revolution in France (1790)

2 He that wrestles with us strengthens our nerves, and sharpens our skill. Our antagonist is our helper.
Reflections on the Revolution in France (1790)

3 Our patience will achieve more than our force.
Reflections on the Revolution in France (1790)

4 By hating vices too much, they come to love men too little.
Reflections on the Revolution in France (1790)

5 We begin our public affections in our families. No cold relation is a zealous citizen.
Reflections on the Revolution in France (1790)

6 Good order is the foundation of all good things.
Reflections on the Revolution in France (1790)

7 Every politician ought to sacrifice to the graces; and to join compliance with reason.
Reflections on the Revolution in France (1790)

8 Never, no never, did Nature say one thing and Wisdom say another.
Third Letter . . . on the Proposals for Peace with the Regicide Directory (1797)

9 Ambition can creep as well as soar.
Third Letter . . . on the Proposals for Peace . . . (1797)

10 And having looked to government for bread, on the very first scarcity they will turn and bite the hand that fed them.
Thoughts and Details on Scarcity (1800)

11 To complain of the age we live in, to murmur at the present possessors of power, to lament the past, to conceive extravagant hopes of the future, are the common dispositions of the greatest part of mankind.
Thoughts on the Cause of the Present Discontents (1770)

12 I am not one of those who think that the people are never in the wrong. They have been so, frequently and outrageously, both in other countries and in this. But I do say, that in all disputes between them and their rulers, the presumption is at least upon a par in favour of the people.
Thoughts on the Cause of the Present Discontents (1770)

13 The power of the crown, almost dead and rotten as Prerogative, has grown up anew, with much more strength, and far less odium, under the name of Influence.
Thoughts on the Cause of the Present Discontents (1770)

14 We must soften into a credulity below the milkiness of infancy to think all men virtuous. We must be tainted with a malignity truly diabolical, to believe all the world to be equally wicked and corrupt.
Thoughts on the Cause of the Present Discontents (1770)

15 When . . . [people] imagine that their food is only a cover for poison, and when they neither love nor trust the hand that serves it, it is not the name of the roast beef of old England that will persuade them to sit down to the table that is spread for them.
Thoughts on the Cause of the Present Discontents (1770)

16 When bad men combine, the good must associate; else they will fall, one by one, an unpitied sacrifice in a contemptible struggle.
Thoughts on the Cause of the Present Discontents (1770); cf. **Misquotations** 521:17

17 Of this stamp is the cant of *Not men, but measures*; a sort of charm by which many people get loose from every honourable engagement.
Thoughts on the Cause of the Present Discontents (1770); cf. **Canning** 185:5, **Goldsmith** 345:15

18 It is therefore our business carefully to cultivate in our minds, to rear to the most perfect vigour and maturity, every sort of generous and honest feeling that belongs to our nature. To bring the dispositions that are lovely in private life into the service and conduct of the commonwealth;
Thoughts on the Cause of the Present Discontents (1770)

19 So to be patriots, as not to forget we are gentlemen.
Thoughts on the Cause of the Present Discontents (1770)

20 Laws, like houses, lean on one another.
A Tract on the Popery Laws (planned *c.*1765) ch. 3, pt. 1 in *The Works* vol. 5 (1812)

21 In all forms of Government the people is the true legislator.
A Tract on the Popery Laws ch. 3, pt. 1 in *The Works* vol. 5 (1812)

22 Falsehood and delusion are allowed in no case whatsoever: But, as in the exercise of all the virtues, there is an economy of truth.
Two Letters on the Proposals for Peace with the Regicide Directory (1796) pt. 1; cf. **Armstrong** 25:20

23 All men that are ruined are ruined on the side of their natural propensities.
Two Letters on the Proposals for Peace with the Regicide Directory (9th ed., 1796)

24 Example is the school of mankind, and they will learn at no other.
Two Letters on the Proposals for Peace with the Regicide Directory (9th ed., 1796)

25 The greater the power, the more dangerous the abuse.
speech on the Middlesex Election, 7 February 1771, in *The Speeches* (1854)

26 Your representative owes you, not his industry only, but his judgement; and he betrays, instead of serving you, if he sacrifices it to your opinion.
speech, 3 November 1774, in *Speeches at his Arrival at Bristol* (1774)

27 People crushed by law have no hopes but from power. If laws are their enemies, they will be enemies to laws; and those, who have much to hope and nothing to lose, will always be dangerous, more or less.
letter to Charles James Fox, 8 October 1777, in *The Correspondence of Edmund Burke* vol. 3 (1961)

28 Bad laws are the worst sort of tyranny.
Speech at Bristol, previous to the Late Election (1780)

29 Individuals pass like shadows; but the commonwealth is fixed and stable.
speech, House of Commons, 11 February 1780

1 The people are the masters.
speech, House of Commons, 11 February 1780; cf. **Blair** 117:12

2 Not merely a chip of the old 'block', but the old block itself.
*on the younger **Pitt**'s maiden speech, February 1781*
N. W. Wraxall *Historical Memoirs of My Own Time* (1904 ed.) pt. 2

3 Every other conqueror of every other description has left some monument, either of state or beneficence, behind him. Were we to be driven out of India this day, nothing would remain to tell that it had been possessed, during the inglorious period of our dominion, by anything better than the orang-outang or the tiger.
speech on Fox's East India Bill, House of Commons, 1 December 1783

4 Your governor [Warren Hastings] stimulates a rapacious and licentious soldiery to the personal search of women, lest these unhappy creatures should avail themselves of the protection of their sex to secure any supply for their necessities.
speech on Fox's East India Bill, House of Commons, 1 December 1783

5 The people never give up their liberties but under some delusion.
speech at County Meeting of Buckinghamshire, 1784, attributed in E. Latham *Famous Sayings* (1904), with 'except' substituted for 'but'

6 Religious persecution may shield itself under the guise of a mistaken and over-zealous piety.
speech, 18 February 1788, in E. A. Bond (ed.) *Speeches . . . in the Trial of Warren Hastings* (1859) vol. 1

7 An event has happened, upon which it is difficult to speak, and impossible to be silent.
speech, 5 May 1789, in E. A. Bond (ed.) *Speeches . . . in the Trial of Warren Hastings* (1859) vol. 2

8 At last dying in the last dyke of prevarication.
speech, 7 May 1789, in E. A. Bond (ed.) *Speeches . . . in the Trial of Warren Hastings* (1859) vol. 2

9 Old religious factions are volcanoes burnt out.
speech on the Petition of the Unitarians, 11 May 1792, in *The Works* vol. 5 (1812); cf. **Disraeli** 269:9

10 Dangers by being despised grow great.
speech on the Petition of the Unitarians, 11 May 1792, in *The Works* vol. 5 (1812)

11 There is but one law for all, namely, that law which governs all law—the law of our Creator, the law of humanity, justice, equity, the law of nature and of nations.
speech, 28 May 1794, in E. A. Bond (ed.) *Speeches . . . in the Trial of Warren Hastings* (1859) vol. 4

12 The cold neutrality of an impartial judge.
J. P. Brissot *To his Constituents* (1794) 'Translator's Preface' (written by Burke)

13 The silent touches of time.
letter to William Smith, 29 January 1795, in *The Correspondence of Edmund Burke* vol. 8 (1969)

14 Somebody has said, that a king may make a nobleman but he cannot make a gentleman.
letter to William Smith, 29 January 1795, in *The Correspondence of Edmund Burke* vol. 8 (1969)

15 His virtues were his arts.
inscription on the pedestal of the statue of the Marquis of Rockingham in Wentworth Park

Johnny Burke 1908–64
American songwriter

16 Every time it rains, it rains
Pennies from heaven.
Don't you know each cloud contains
Pennies from heaven?
'Pennies from Heaven' (1936 song)

17 Like Webster's Dictionary, we're Morocco bound.
The Road to Morocco (1942 film) title song

Fanny Burney (Mme d'Arblay) 1752–1840
English novelist and diarist

18 A little alarm now and then keeps life from stagnation.
Camilla (1796) bk. 3, ch. 11

19 There is nothing upon the face of the earth so insipid as a medium. Give me love or hate! a friend that will go to jail for me, or an enemy that will run me through the body!
Camilla (1796) bk. 3, ch. 12

20 It's a delightful thing to think of perfection; but it's vastly more amusing to talk of errors and absurdities.
Camilla (1796) bk. 3, ch. 12

21 Vice is detestable; I banish all its appearances from my coteries; and I would banish its reality, too, were I sure I should then have any thing but empty chairs in my drawing-room.
Camilla (1796) bk. 5, ch. 6

22 The cure of a romantic first flame is a better surety to subsequent discretion, than all the exhortations of all the fathers, and mothers, and guardians, and maiden aunts in the universe.
Camilla (1796) bk. 5, ch. 6

23 O, we all acknowledge our faults, now; 'tis the mode of the day: but the acknowledgement passes for current payment; and therefore we never amend them.
Camilla (1796) bk. 6, ch. 2

24 No man is in love when he marries. He may have loved before; I have even heard he has sometimes loved after: but at the time never. There is something in the formalities of the matrimonial preparations that drive away all the little cupidons.
Camilla (1796) bk. 6, ch. 10

25 Travelling is the ruin of all happiness! There's no looking at a building here after seeing Italy.
Cecilia (1782) bk. 4, ch. 2

26 'The whole of this unfortunate business,' said Dr Lyster, 'has been the result of PRIDE AND PREJUDICE.'
Cecilia (1782) bk. 10, ch. 10

27 'Do you come to the play without knowing what it is?' 'O yes, Sir, yes, very frequently; I have no time to read play-bills; one merely comes to meet one's friends, and show that one's alive.'
Evelina (1778) Letter 20

1 The freedom with which Dr Johnson condemns whatever he disapproves is astonishing.
Diary and Letters of Madame D'Arblay (1842) pt. 2 (23 August 1778)

2 The delusive seduction of martial music.
Joyce Hemlow et al. (eds.) *Journals and Letters of Fanny Burney* vol. 5 (1975) 'Paris Journal'

3 Such a set of tittle tattle, prittle prattle visitants! Oh dear! I am so sick of the ceremony and fuss of these fall lall people! So much dressing—chit chat—complimentary nonsense—In short, a country town is my detestation.
diary, 17 July 1768 in *Early Journals and Letters of Fanny Burney* (ed. L. E. Troide, 1988) vol. 1

4 O! how short a time does it take to put an end to a woman's liberty!
of a wedding
diary, 20 July 1768 in *Early Journals and Letters of Fanny Burney* (ed. L. E. Troide, 1988) vol. 1

John Burns 1858–1943
British Liberal politician

5 The Thames is liquid history.
to an American who had compared the Thames disparagingly with the Mississippi
in *Daily Mail* 25 January 1943

Robert Burns 1759–96
Scottish poet
see also: ***Last words*** *455:11*

6 O thou! whatever title suit thee,
Auld Hornie, Satan, Nick, or Clootie.
'Address to the Deil' (1786)

7 Address to the unco guid.
title of poem, 1787

8 Then gently scan your brother man,
Still gentler sister woman;
Tho' they may gang a kennin wrang,
To step aside is human.
'Address to the Unco Guid' (1787)

9 Ae fond kiss, and then we sever;
Ae fareweel, and then for ever!
'Ae fond Kiss' (1792)

10 Flow gently, sweet Afton, among thy green braes,
Flow gently, I'll sing thee a song in thy praise.
'Afton Water' (1792)

11 Should auld acquaintance be forgot
And never brought to mind?
'Auld Lang Syne' (1796)

12 We'll tak a cup o' kindness yet,
For auld lang syne.
'Auld Lang Syne' (1796)

13 Auld Scotland has a raucle tongue.
raucle *meaning 'rash, impetuous'*
'The Author's Earnest Cry' (1786)

14 Freedom and Whisky gang thegither!
'The Author's Earnest Cry and Prayer' (1786) l. 185

15 Ay waukin, Oh,
Waukin still and weary:
Sleep I can get nane,
For thinking on my dearie.
'Ay Waukin O' (1790)

16 Ye banks and braes o' bonny Doon,
How can ye bloom sae fresh and fair;
How can ye chant, ye little birds,
And I sae weary fu' o' care!
'The Banks o' Doon' (1792)

17 And my fause luver stole my rose,
But ah! he left the thorn wi' me.
'The Banks o' Doon' (1792)

18 Thou minds me o' departed joys,
Departed, never to return.
'The Banks o' Doon' (1792)

19 O saw ye bonnie Lesley,
As she gaed o'er the border?
She's gane, like Alexander,
To spread her conquests farther.

To see her is to love her,
And love but her for ever;
For Nature made her what she is
And never made anither!
'Bonnie Lesley' (1798)

20 Gin a body meet a body
Comin thro' the rye,
Gin a body kiss a body
Need a body cry?
'Comin thro' the rye' (1796)

21 Contented wi' little and cantie wi' mair,
Whene'er I forgather wi' Sorrow and Care,
I gie them a skelp, as they're creeping alang,
Wi' a cog o' gude swats and an auld Scotish sang.
'Contented wi' little' (1796)

22 Th' expectant wee-things, toddlin', stacher through
To meet their Dad, wi' flichterin' noise an' glee.
'The Cotter's Saturday Night' (1786) st. 3

23 They never sought in vain that sought the Lord aright.
'The Cotter's Saturday Night' (1786) st. 6

24 The healsome porritch, chief of Scotia's food.
'The Cotter's Saturday Night' (1786) st. 11

25 The sire turns o'er, wi' patriarchal grace,
The big ha'-Bible, ance his father's pride.
'The Cotter's Saturday Night' (1786) st. 12

26 From scenes like these old Scotia's grandeur springs,
That makes her loved at home, revered abroad:
Princes and Lords are but the breath of kings,
'An honest man's the noblest work of God.'
'The Cotter's Saturday Night' (1786) st. 19; cf. **Pope** 586:1

27 I wasna fou, but just had plenty.
'Death and Dr Hornbook' (1787) st. 3

28 On ev'ry hand it will allow'd be,
He's just—nae better than he shou'd be.
'A Dedication to G[avin] H[amilton]' (1786) l. 25

29 There's threesome reels, there's foursome reels,
There's hornpipes and strathspeys, man,

But the ae best dance e'er cam to the land
Was, the deil's awa wi' th'Exciseman.
'The Deil's awa wi' th'Exciseman' (1792)

1 Perhaps it may turn out a sang;
Perhaps, turn out a sermon.
'Epistle to a Young Friend' (1786) st. 1

2 I waive the quantum o' the sin;
The hazard of concealing;
But och! it hardens a' within,
And petrifies the feeling!
'Epistle to a Young Friend' (1786) st. 6

3 An atheist-laugh's a poor exchange
For Deity offended!
'Epistle to a Young Friend' (1786) st. 9

4 Gie me ae spark o' Nature's fire,
That's a' the learning I desire.
'Epistle to J. L[aprai]k' (1786) st. 13

5 For thus the royal mandate ran,
When first the human race began,
'The social, friendly, honest man,
Whate'er he be,
'Tis he fulfils great Nature's plan,
And none but he.'
'To the same [John Lapraik]' st. 15

6 The rank is but the guinea's stamp,
The man's the gowd for a' that!
'For a' that and a' that' (1790)

7 A man's a man for a' that.
'For a' that and a' that' (1790)

8 Green grow the rashes, O,
Green grow the rashes, O;
The sweetest hours that e'er I spend,
Are spent among the lasses, O.
'Green Grow the Rashes' (1787); cf. **Songs** 729:11

9 Auld nature swears, the lovely dears
Her noblest work she classes, O;
Her prentice han' she tried on man,
An' then she made the lasses, O.
'Green Grow the Rashes' (1787)

10 O, gie me the lass that has acres o' charms,
O, gie me the lass wi' the weel-stockit farms.
'Hey for a Lass wi' a Tocher' (1799)

11 Here, some are thinkin' on their sins,
An' some upo' their claes.
'The Holy Fair' (1786) st. 10

12 There's some are fou o' love divine;
There's some are fou o' brandy.
'The Holy Fair' (1786) st. 27

13 O L--d thou kens what zeal I bear,
When drinkers drink, and swearers swear,
And singin' there, and dancin' here,
Wi' great an' sma';
For I am keepet by thy fear,
Free frae them a'.
But yet—O L--d—confess I must—
At times I'm fash'd wi' fleshly lust . . .
O L--d—yestreen—thou kens—wi' Meg—
Thy pardon I sincerely beg!
O may 't ne'er be a living plague,
To my dishonour!
And I'll ne'er lift a lawless leg
Again upon her.
'Holy Willie's Prayer' (1785)

14 There's death in the cup—so beware!
'Inscription on a Goblet' (published 1834)

15 It was a' for our rightfu' King
We left fair Scotland's strand.
'It was a' for our Rightfu' King' (1796)

16 Corn rigs, an' barley rigs,
An' corn rigs are bonnie.
'It was upon a Lammas Night' (1796)

17 John Anderson my jo, John,
When we were first acquent,
Your locks were like the raven,
Your bonny brow was brent.
'John Anderson my Jo' (1790)

18 I once was a maid, tho' I cannot tell when,
And still my delight is in proper young men.
'The Jolly Beggars' (1799) l. 57, also known as 'Love and Liberty—A Cantata'

19 Partly wi' LOVE o'ercome sae sair,
And partly she was drunk.
'The Jolly Beggars' (1799) l. 183

20 A fig for those by law protected!
LIBERTY's a glorious feast!
Courts for cowards were erected,
Churches built to please the PRIEST.
'The Jolly Beggars' (1799) l. 254

21 Life is all a VARIORUM,
We regard not how it goes;
Let them cant about DECORUM,
Who have characters to lose.
'The Jolly Beggars' (1799) l. 270

22 Some have meat and cannot eat,
Some cannot eat that want it:
But we have meat and we can eat,
Sae let the Lord be thankit.
'The Kirkudbright Grace' (1790), also known as 'The Selkirk Grace'

23 I've seen sae mony changefu' years,
On earth I am a stranger grown:
I wander in the ways of men,
Alike unknowing and unknown.
'Lament for James, Earl of Glencairn' (1793)

24 May coward shame distain his name,
The wretch that dares not die!
'McPherson's Farewell' (1788)

25 Nature's law,
That man was made to mourn!
'Man was made to Mourn' (1786) st. 4

26 Man's inhumanity to man
Makes countless thousands mourn!
'Man was made to Mourn' (1786) st. 7

27 O Death! the poor man's dearest friend,
The kindest and the best!
'Man was made to Mourn' (1786) st. 11

28 Go fetch to me a pint o' wine,
An' fill it in a silver tassie.
'My Bonnie Mary' (1790)

1 My heart's in the Highlands, my heart is not here;
My heart's in the Highlands a-chasing the deer;
Chasing the wild deer, and following the roe,
My heart's in the Highlands, wherever I go.
'My Heart's in the Highlands' (1790)

2 My love she's but a lassie yet.
title of poem, 1787

3 The minister kiss'd the fiddler's wife,
An' could na preach for thinkin' o't.
'My Love She's but a Lassie yet' (1790)

4 The wan moon sets behind the white wave,
And time is setting with me, Oh.
'Open the door to me, Oh' (1793)

5 O whistle, an' I'll come to you, my lad:
O whistle, an' I'll come to you, my lad:
Tho' father and mither should baith gae mad,
O whistle, and I'll come to you, my lad.
'O Whistle, an' I'll come to you, my Lad' (1788); cf. **Fletcher** 318:11

6 O, my Luve's like a red, red rose
That's newly sprung in June;
O my Luve's like the melodie
That's sweetly play'd in tune.
'A Red Red Rose' (1796), derived from various folk-songs

7 Scots, wha hae wi' Wallace bled,
Scots, wham Bruce has aften led,
Welcome to your gory bed,—
Or to victorie.

Now's the day, and now's the hour;
See the front o' battle lour;
See approach proud Edward's power,
Chains and slaverie.
'Robert Bruce's March to Bannockburn' (1799), also known as 'Scots, Wha Hae'

8 Liberty's in every blow!
Let us do—or die!!!
'Robert Bruce's March to Bannockburn' (1799)

9 Good Lord, what is man! for as simple he looks,
Do but try to develop his hooks and his crooks,
With his depths and his shallows, his good and his evil,
All in all he's a problem must puzzle the devil.
'Sketch' inscribed to Charles James Fox (1800)

10 This day Time winds th'exhausted chain,
To run the twelvemonth's length again.
'Sketch. New Year's Day. To Mrs Dunlop' (1789)

11 His ancient, trusty, drouthy crony,
Tam lo'ed him like a vera brither;
They had been fou for weeks thegither.
'Tam o' Shanter' (1791) l. 42

12 Kings may be blest, but Tam was glorious,
O'er a' the ills o' life victorious!
'Tam o' Shanter' (1791) l. 57

13 But pleasures are like poppies spread,
You seize the flow'r, its bloom is shed;
Or like the snow falls in the river,
A moment white—then melts for ever.
'Tam o' Shanter' (1791) l. 59

14 Nae man can tether time or tide.
'Tam o' Shanter' (1791) l. 67

15 Inspiring, bold John Barleycorn,
What dangers thou canst make us scorn!
Wi' tippenny, we fear nae evil;
Wi' usquebae, we'll face the devil!
'Tam o' Shanter' (1791) l. 105

16 As Tammie glowr'd, amaz'd, and curious,
The mirth and fun grew fast and furious.
'Tam o' Shanter' (1791) l. 143

17 Tam tint his reason a' thegither,
And roars out—'Weel done, Cutty-sark!'
'Tam o' Shanter' (1791) l. 185

18 Ah Tam! ah Tam! thou'll get thy fairin'!
In hell they'll roast thee like a herrin!
'Tam o' Shanter' (1791) l. 201

19 A man may drink and no be drunk;
A man may fight and no be slain;
A man may kiss a bonnie lass,
And aye be welcome back again.
'There was a Lass' (1788)

20 Fair fa' your honest, sonsie face,
Great chieftain o' the puddin'-race!
Aboon them a' ye tak your place,
Painch, tripe, or thairm:
Weel are ye wordy o' a grace
As lang's my arm.
'To a Haggis' (1787)

21 O wad some Pow'r the giftie gie us
To see oursels as others see us!
It wad frae mony a blunder free us,
And foolish notion.
'To a Louse' (1786)

22 Wee, sleekit, cow'rin', tim'rous beastie,
O what a panic's in thy breastie!
Thou need na start awa sae hasty,
Wi' bickering brattle!
I wad be laith to rin an' chase thee,
Wi' murd'ring pattle!
'To a Mouse' (1786)

23 I'm truly sorry Man's dominion
Has broken Nature's social union,
An' justifies that ill opinion
Which makes thee startle,
At me, thy poor, earth-born companion,
An' fellow-mortal!
'To a Mouse' (1786)

24 The best laid schemes o' mice an' men
Gang aft a-gley.
'To a Mouse' (1786); cf. **Proverbs** 596:1

25 Come, Firm Resolve, take thou the van,
Thou stalk o' carl-hemp in man!
And let us mind, faint heart ne'er wan
A lady fair;
Wha does the utmost that he can,
Will whyles do mair.
'To Dr Blacklock' (1800)

1 Some rhyme a neebor's name to lash;
Some rhyme (vain thought!) for needfu' cash;
Some rhyme to court the countra clash,
An' raise a din;
For me, an aim I never fash;
I rhyme for fun.
'To J. S[mith]' (1786) st. 5

2 An' fareweel dear, deluding woman,
The joy of joys!
'To J. S[mith]' (1786) st. 14

3 Their sighan', cantan', grace-proud faces,
Their three-mile prayers, and half-mile graces.
'To the Rev. John M'Math' (1808)

4 We labour soon, we labour late,
To feed the titled knave, man;
And a' the comfort we're to get,
Is that ayont the grave, man.
'The Tree of Liberty' (1838)

5 His lockèd, lettered, braw brass collar,
Shew'd him the gentleman and scholar.
'The Twa Dogs' (1786) l. 13

6 An' there began a lang digression
About the lords o' the creation.
'The Twa Dogs' (1786) l. 45

7 Rejoiced they were na men, but dogs.
'The Twa Dogs' (1786) l. 236

8 All in this mottie, misty clime,
I backward mus'd on wasted time,
How I had spent my youthfu' prime
An' done nae-thing,
But stringing blethers up to rhyme
For fools to sing.
'The Vision' (1785)

9 What can a young lassie, what shall a young lassie,
What can a young lassie do wi' an auld man?
'What can a Young Lassie do wi' an Auld Man' (1792)

10 It is the moon, I ken her horn,
That's blinkin in the lift sae hie;
She shines sae bright to wyle us hame,
But by my sooth she'll wait a wee!
'Willie Brew'd a Peck o' Maut' (1790)

11 The Poetic Genius of my country found me as the prophetic bard Elijah did Elisha—at the plough; and threw her inspiring mantle over me. She bade me sing the loves, the joys, the rural scenes and rural pleasures of my native soil, in my native tongue; I tuned my wild, artless notes, as she inspired.
preface to *Poems* (1787 2nd ed.)

Burnum Burnum 1936–97
Australian political activist

12 We wish no harm to England's native people. We are here to bring you good manners, refinement and an opportunity to make a *Koompartoo*, a fresh start.
in 1988, the year of Australia's bicentenary, on planting an Aboriginal flag on the white cliffs of Dover and claiming England for the Aboriginal people
on 26 January 1988; in obituary, *Independent* 20 August 1997

Aaron Burr 1756–1836
American politician

13 Law is whatever is boldly asserted and plausibly maintained.
James Parton *The Life and Times of Aaron Burr* (1857); attributed

William S. Burroughs 1914–97
American novelist
see also ***Last words*** *456:14*

14 Junk is the ideal product . . . the ultimate merchandise. No sales talk necessary. The client will crawl through a sewer and beg to buy.
The Naked Lunch (1959) introduction

15 The face of 'evil' is always the face of total need.
The Naked Lunch (1959) introduction

16 In homosexual sex you know exactly what the other person is feeling, so you are identifying with the other person completely. In heterosexual sex you have no idea what the other person is feeling.
Victor Bockris *With William Burroughs: A Report from the Bunker* (1981) 'On Men'

Benjamin Hapgood Burt 1880–1950
American songwriter

17 One evening in October, when I was one-third sober,
An' taking home a 'load' with manly pride;
My poor feet began to stutter, so I lay down in the gutter,
And a pig came up an' lay down by my side;
Then we sang 'It's all fair weather when good fellows get together,'
Till a lady passing by was heard to say:
'You can tell a man who "boozes" by the company he chooses'
And the pig got up and slowly walked away.
'The Pig Got Up and Slowly Walked Away' (1933 song)

18 When you're all dressed up and no place to go.
title of song (1913)

Nat Burton

19 There'll be bluebirds over the white cliffs of Dover,
Tomorrow, just you wait and see.
'The White Cliffs of Dover' (1941 song)

Richard Burton 1821–90
English explorer, anthropologist, and translator

20 Don't be frightened; I am recalled. Pay, pack, and follow at convenience.
note to his wife, 19 August 1871, on being replaced as British Consul to Damascus
Isabel Burton *Life of Captain Sir Richard F. Burton* (1893) vol. 1, ch. 21

Robert Burton 1577–1640

English clergyman and scholar
see also **Closing lines** 222:5

1 All my joys to this are folly,
Naught so sweet as Melancholy.

The Anatomy of Melancholy (1621–51) 'The Author's Abstract of Melancholy'

2 I write of melancholy, by being busy to avoid melancholy.

The Anatomy of Melancholy (1621–51) 'Democritus to the Reader'

3 They lard their lean books with the fat of others' works.

The Anatomy of Melancholy (1621–51) 'Democritus to the Reader'

4 A loose, plain, rude writer . . . I call a spade a spade.

The Anatomy of Melancholy (1621–51) 'Democritus to the Reader'

5 I had not time to lick it into form, as she [a bear] doth her young ones.

The Anatomy of Melancholy (1621–51) 'Democritus to the Reader'

6 Like watermen, that row one way and look another.

The Anatomy of Melancholy (1621–51) 'Democritus to the Reader'; cf. **Bunyan** 161:3

7 All poets are mad.

The Anatomy of Melancholy (1621–51) 'Democritus to the Reader'; cf. **Wordsworth** 831:12

8 What, if a dear year come or dearth, or some loss? And were it not that they are loath to lay out money on a rope, they would be hanged forthwith, and sometimes die to save charges.

The Anatomy of Melancholy (1621–51) pt. 1, sect. 2, member 3, subsect. 12

9 I may not here omit those two main plagues, and common dotages of human kind, wine and women, which have infatuated and besotted myriads of people. They go commonly together.

The Anatomy of Melancholy (1621–51) pt. 1, sect. 2, member 3, subsect. 13

10 *Hinc quam sit calamus saevior ense patet.*

From this it is clear how much the pen is worse than the sword.

The Anatomy of Melancholy (1621–51) pt. 1, sect. 2, member 4, subsect. 4; cf. **Bulwer-Lytton** 160:7, **Proverbs** 609:22

11 See one promontory (said Socrates of old), one mountain, one sea, one river, and see all.

The Anatomy of Melancholy (1621–51) pt. 1, sect. 2, member 4, subsect. 7

12 One was never married, and that's his hell: another is, and that's his plague.

The Anatomy of Melancholy (1621–51) pt. 1, sect. 2, member 4, subsect. 7

13 The gods are well pleased when they see great men contending with adversity.

The Anatomy of Melancholy (1621–51) pt. 2, sect. 3, member 1, subsect. 1

14 Who cannot give good counsel? 'tis cheap, it costs them nothing.

The Anatomy of Melancholy (1621–51) pt. 2, sect. 3, member 3, subsect. 1

15 What is a ship but a prison?

The Anatomy of Melancholy (1621–51) pt. 2, sect. 3, member 4, subsect. 1; cf. **Johnson** 412:22

16 All places are distant from Heaven alike.

The Anatomy of Melancholy (1621–51) pt. 2, sect. 3, member 4, subsect. 1

17 'Let me not live,' saith Aretine's Antonia, 'if I had not rather hear thy discourse than see a play!'

The Anatomy of Melancholy (1621–51) pt. 3, sect. 1, member 1, subsect. 1

18 To enlarge or illustrate this power and effect of love is to set a candle in the sun.

The Anatomy of Melancholy (1621–51) pt. 3, sect. 2, member 1, subsect. 2; cf. **Sidney** 718:4, **Young** 839:1

19 No cord nor cable can so forcibly draw, or hold so fast, as love can do with a twined thread.

The Anatomy of Melancholy (1621–51) pt. 3, sect. 2, member 1, subsect. 2

20 To these crocodile's tears they will add sobs, fiery sighs, and sorrowful countenance, pale colour, leanness.

The Anatomy of Melancholy (1621–51) pt. 3, sect. 2, member 2, subsect. 4

21 Diogenes struck the father when the son swore.

The Anatomy of Melancholy (1621–51) pt. 3, sect. 2, member 5, subsect. 5

22 One religion is as true as another

The Anatomy of Melancholy (1621–51) pt. 3, sect. 4, member 2, subsect. 1

Wilhelm Busch 1832–1908

German satirical poet and illustrator

23 *Ach, das war ein schlimmes Ding,*
Wie es Max und Moritz ging!
Drum est hier, was sie getrieben,
Abgemalt und aufgeschrieben.

Oh, that was a bad business,
What happened to Max and Moritz!
Which is why their doings are here
Pictured and written down.

Max und Moritz (1865)

24 *Vater werden ist nicht schwer*
Vater sein dagegen sehr.

Becoming a father isn't difficult,
But it's very difficult to be a father.

Julchen (1877)

Hermann Busenbaum 1600–68

German theologian

25 *Cum finis est licitus, etiam media sunt licita.*

The end justifies the means.

Medulla Theologiae Moralis (1650); literally 'When the end is allowed, the means also are allowed'; cf. **Proverbs** 599:12

Barbara Bush 1925–
wife of George Bush; First Lady, 1989–93

1 Somewhere out in this audience may even be someone who will one day follow in my footsteps, and preside over the White House as the President's spouse. I wish him well!
remarks at Wellesley College Commencement, 1 June 1990

George Bush 1924–
American Republican statesman; 41st President of the US, 1989–93

2 Oh, the vision thing.
responding to the suggestion that he turn his attention from short-term campaign objectives and look to the longer term.
in *Time* 26 January 1987

3 Read my lips: no new taxes.
campaign pledge on taxation
in *New York Times* 19 August 1988

4 And now, we can see a new world coming into view. A world in which there is the very real prospect of a new world order.
speech, in *New York Times* 7 March 1991

Comte de Bussy-Rabutin 1618–93
French soldier and poet

5 *L'amour vient de l'aveuglement,*
L'amitié de la connaissance.
Love comes from blindness,
Friendship from knowledge.
Histoire Amoureuse des Gaules: Maximes d'Amour (1665) pt. 1; cf. **Proverbs** 606:4

6 *L'absence est à l'amour ce qu'est au feu le vent;*
Il éteint le petit, il allume le grand.
Absence is to love what wind is to fire;
It extinguishes the small, it kindles the great.
Histoire Amoureuse des Gaules: Maximes d'Amour (1665) pt. 2; cf. **Francis** 323:2, **La Rochefoucauld** 453:18

7 As you know, God is usually on the side of the big squadrons against the small.
letter to the Comte de Limoges, 18 October 1677, in *Lettres de . . . Comte de Bussy* (1697) vol. 4; cf. **Anouilh** 22:7, **Proverbs** 609:47, **Tacitus** 752:17, **Voltaire** 798:4

Joseph Butler 1692–1752
English bishop and theologian

8 It has come, I know not how, to be taken for granted, by many persons, that Christianity is not so much as a subject of inquiry; but that it is, now at length, discovered to be fictitious.
The Analogy of Religion (1736) 'Advertisement'

9 But to us, probability is the very guide of life.
The Analogy of Religion (1736) 'Introduction'

10 Everything is what it is, and not another thing.
preface to *Fifteen Sermons preached at the Rolls Chapel* (ed. 2, 1729)

11 Things and actions are what they are, and the consequences of them will be what they will be: why then should we desire to be deceived?
Fifteen Sermons preached at the Rolls Chapel (1726) no. 7

12 Sir, the pretending to extraordinary revelations and gifts of the Holy Ghost is a horrid thing—a very horrid thing.
to John **Wesley**, 16 August 1739; John Wesley *Journal* (ed. N. Curnock) note

Nicholas Murray Butler 1862–1947
President of Columbia University, 1901–45

13 An expert is one who knows more and more about less and less.
Commencement address at Columbia University (attributed)

R. A. ('Rab') Butler 1902–82
British Conservative politician

14 REPORTER: Mr Butler, would you say that this [Anthony Eden] is the best Prime Minister we have?
R. A. BUTLER: Yes.
interview at London Airport, 8 January 1956; R. A. Butler *The Art of the Possible*

15 I think a Prime Minister has to be a butcher and know the joints. That is perhaps where I have not been quite competent, in knowing all the ways that you can cut up a carcass.
in *Listener* 28 June 1966

16 Politics is the Art of the Possible. That is what these pages show I have tried to achieve—not more—and that is what I have called my book.
The Art of the Possible (1971); cf. **Bismarck** 116:6

17 In politics you must always keep running with the pack. The moment that you falter and they sense that you are injured, the rest will turn on you like wolves.
Dennis Walters *Not Always with the Pack* (1989)

Samuel Butler 1612–80
English poet

18 He'd run in debt by disputation,
And pay with ratiocination.
Hudibras pt. 1 (1663), canto 1, l. 77

19 For rhetoric he could not ope
His mouth, but out there flew a trope.
Hudibras pt. 1 (1663), canto 1, l. 81

20 A Babylonish dialect
Which learned pedants much affect.
Hudibras pt. 1 (1663), canto 1, l. 93

21 What ever sceptic could inquire for;
For every why he had a wherefore.
Hudibras pt. 1 (1663), canto 1, l. 131

22 He knew what's what, and that's as high
As metaphysic wit can fly.
Hudibras pt. 1 (1663), canto 1, l. 149

23 Such as take lodgings in a head
That's to be let unfurnished.
Hudibras pt. 1 (1663), canto 1, l. 159

24 And still be doing, never done:
As if Religion were intended
For nothing else but to be mended.
Hudibras pt. 1 (1663), canto 1, l. 202

1 Compound for sins, they are inclined to,
By damning those they have no mind to.
Hudibras pt. 1 (1663), canto 1, l. 213

2 The trenchant blade, Toledo trusty,
For want of fighting was grown rusty,
And eat into it self, for lack
Of some body to hew and hack.
Hudibras pt. 1 (1663), canto 1, l. 357

3 For rhyme the rudder is of verses,
With which like ships they steer their courses.
Hudibras pt. 1 (1663), canto 1, l. 457

4 Great actions are not always true sons
Of great and mighty resolutions.
Hudibras pt. 1 (1663), canto 1, l. 877

5 Cleric before, and Lay behind;
A lawless linsy-woolsy brother,
Half of one order, half another.
Hudibras pt. 1 (1663), canto 3, l. 1226

6 Learning, that cobweb of the brain,
Profane, erroneous, and vain.
Hudibras pt. 1 (1663), canto 3, l. 1339

7 She that with poetry is won,
Is but a desk to write upon.
Hudibras pt. 2 (1664), canto 1, l. 591

8 Love is a boy, by poets styled,
Then spare the rod, and spoil the child.
Hudibras pt. 2 (1664), canto 1, l. 843; **Proverbs** 611:14

9 Oaths are but words, and words but wind.
Hudibras pt. 2 (1664), canto 2, l. 107

10 Doubtless the pleasure is as great
Of being cheated, as to cheat.
As lookers-on feel most delight,
That least perceive a juggler's sleight;
And still the less they understand,
The more th' admire his sleight of hand.
Hudibras pt. 2 (1664), canto 3, l. 1

11 What makes all doctrines plain and clear?
About two hundred pounds a year.
And that which was proved true before,
Prove false again? Two hundred more.
Hudibras pt. 3 (1680), canto 1, l. 1277

12 He that complies against his will,
Is of his own opinion still.
Hudibras pt. 3 (1680), canto 3, l. 547; cf. **Proverbs** 602:11

13 For Justice, though she's painted blind,
Is to the weaker side inclined.
Hudibras pt. 3 (1680), canto 3, l. 709

14 For money has a power above
The stars and fate, to manage love.
Hudibras pt. 3 (1680) 'The Lady's Answer to the Knight' l. 131

15 All love at first, like generous wine,
Ferments and frets, until 'tis fine;
But when 'tis settled on the lee,
And from th' impurer matter free,
Becomes the richer still, the older,
And proves the pleasanter, the colder.
Genuine Remains (1759) 'Miscellaneous Thoughts'

16 The law can take a purse in open court,
Whilst it condemns a less delinquent for't.
Genuine Remains (1759) 'Miscellaneous Thoughts'

Samuel Butler 1835–1902
English novelist

17 It has been said that though God cannot alter the past, historians can; it is perhaps because they can be useful to Him in this respect that He tolerates their existence.
Erewhon Revisited (1901) ch. 14; cf. **Agathon** 6:20

18 All animals, except man, know that the principal business of life is to enjoy it.
The Way of All Flesh (1903) ch. 19

19 The advantage of doing one's praising for oneself is that one can lay it on so thick and exactly in the right places.
The Way of All Flesh (1903) ch. 34

20 Young as he was, his instinct told him that the best liar is he who makes the smallest amount of lying go the longest way.
The Way of All Flesh (1903) ch. 39

21 'Tis better to have loved and lost than never to have lost at all.
The Way of All Flesh (1903) ch. 67; cf. **Tennyson** 761:4

22 It was very good of God to let Carlyle and Mrs Carlyle marry one another and so make only two people miserable instead of four.
Letters between Samuel Butler and Miss E. M. A. Savage 1871–1885 (1935) 21 November 1884

23 All progress is based upon a universal innate desire on the part of every organism to live beyond its income.
Notebooks (1912) ch. 1

24 The history of art is the history of revivals.
Notebooks (1912) ch. 8

25 An apology for the Devil: It must be remembered that we have only heard one side of the case. God has written all the books.
Notebooks (1912) ch. 14

26 A definition is the enclosing a wilderness of idea within a wall of words.
Notebooks (1912) ch. 14

27 To live is like to love — all reason is against it, and all healthy instinct for it.
Notebooks (1912) ch. 14

28 The public buys its opinions as it buys its meat, or takes in its milk, on the principle that it is cheaper to do this than to keep a cow. So it is, but the milk is more likely to be watered.
Notebooks (1912) ch. 17

29 The three most important things a man has are, briefly, his private parts, his money, and his religious opinions.
Further Extracts from Notebooks (1934)

30 Jesus! with all thy faults I love thee still.
Further Extracts from Notebooks (1934)

1 Conscience is thoroughly well-bred and soon leaves off talking to those who do not wish to hear it.
Further Extracts from Notebooks (1934)

2 Yet meet we shall, and part, and meet again
Where dead men meet, on lips of living men.
'Not on sad Stygian shore' (1904)

3 Dusty, cobweb-covered, maimed, and set at naught,
Beauty crieth in an attic, and no man regardeth.
O God! O Montreal!
'Psalm of Montreal', in *Spectator* 18 May 1878

William Butler 1535–1618
English physician

4 Doubtless God could have made a better berry, but doubtless God never did.
of the strawberry
Izaak Walton *The Compleat Angler* (3rd ed., 1661) pt. 1, ch. 5

A. S. Byatt 1936–
English novelist

5 What literature can and should do is change the people who teach the people who don't read the books.
interview in *Newsweek* 5 June 1995

William Byrd 1543–1623
English composer

6 The exercise of singing is delightful to Nature, and good to preserve the health of man. It doth strengthen all parts of the breast, and doth open the pipes.
Psalms, Sonnets and Songs (1588)

John Byrom 1692–1763
English poet

7 I am content, I do not care,
Wag as it will the world for me.
'Careless Content' (1773)

8 Christians, awake! Salute the happy morn,
Whereon the Saviour of the world was born.
Hymn (*c.*1750)

9 Some say, that Signor Bononcini,
Compared to Handel's a mere ninny;
Others aver, that to him Handel
Is scarcely fit to hold a candle.
Strange! that such high dispute should be
'Twixt Tweedledum and Tweedledee.
'On the Feuds between Handel and Bononcini' (1727)

10 God bless the King, I mean the Faith's Defender;
God bless—no harm in blessing—the Pretender;
But who Pretender is, or who is King,
God bless us all—that's quite another thing.
'To an Officer in the Army, Extempore, Intended to allay the Violence of Party-Spirit' (1773)

Lord Byron 1788–1824
English poet
on Byron: see ***Arnold*** *27:22,* ***Lamb*** *448:8; see also* ***Campbell*** *183:20*

11 Proud Wellington, with eagle beak so curled,
That nose, the hook where he suspends the world!
'The Age of Bronze' (1823) st. 13

12 For what were all these country patriots born?
To hunt, and vote, and raise the price of corn?
'The Age of Bronze' (1823) st. 14

13 Year after year they voted cent per cent
Blood, sweat, and tear-wrung millions—why? for rent!
'The Age of Bronze' (1823) st. 14; cf. **Churchill** 215:7

14 Did'st ever see a gondola? . . .
It glides along the water looking blackly,
Just like a coffin clapt in a canoe.
Beppo (1818) st. 19

15 In short, he was a perfect cavaliero,
And to his very valet seemed a hero.
Beppo (1818) st. 33; cf. **Cornuel** 237:7

16 His heart was one of those which most enamour us,
Wax to receive, and marble to retain.
Beppo (1818) st. 34

17 Our cloudy climate, and our chilly women.
Beppo (1818) st. 49

18 A pretty woman as was ever seen,
Fresh as the Angel o'er a new inn door.
Beppo (1818) st. 57

19 Where the virgins are soft as the roses they twine,
And all, save the spirit of man, is divine.
The Bride of Abydos (1813) canto 1, st. 1

20 Such was Zuleika, such around her shone
The nameless charms unmarked by her alone—
The light of love, the purity of grace,
The mind, the Music breathing from her face,
The heart whose softness harmonized the whole,
And oh! that eye was in itself a Soul!
The Bride of Abydos (1813) canto 1, st. 6

21 I have looked out
In the vast desolate night in search of him;
And when I saw gigantic shadows in
The umbrage of the walls of Eden, chequered
By the far-flashing of the cherubs' swords,
I watched for what I thought his coming: for
With fear rose longing in my heart to know
What 'twas which shook us all—but nothing came.
Cain (1821) act 1, sc. 1, l. 266

22 Adieu, adieu! my native shore
Fades o'er the waters blue.
Childe Harold's Pilgrimage (1812–18) canto 1, st. 13

23 Lo! where the Giant on the mountain stands,
His blood-red tresses deep'ning in the sun,
With death-shot glowing in his fiery hands,
And eye that scorcheth all it glares upon.
Childe Harold's Pilgrimage (1812–18) canto 1, st. 39

1 Here all were noble, save Nobility.
Childe Harold's Pilgrimage (1812–18) canto 1, st. 85

2 Cold is the heart, fair Greece! that looks on thee,
Nor feels as lovers o'er the dust they loved;
Dull is the eye that will not weep to see
Thy walls defaced, thy mouldering shrines removed
By British hands.
Childe Harold's Pilgrimage (1812–18) canto 2, st. 15

3 None are so desolate but something dear,
Dearer than self, possesses or possessed
A thought, and claims the homage of a tear.
Childe Harold's Pilgrimage (1812–18) canto 2, st. 24

4 Dark Sappho! could not verse immortal save
That breast imbued with such immortal fire?
Could she not live who life eternal gave?
Childe Harold's Pilgrimage (1812–18) canto 2, st. 39

5 Fair Greece! sad relic of departed worth!
Immortal, though no more! though fallen, great!
Childe Harold's Pilgrimage (1812–18) canto 2, st. 73

6 Hereditary bondsmen! know ye not
Who would be free themselves must strike the blow?
Childe Harold's Pilgrimage (1812–18) canto 2, st. 76

7 What is the worst of woes that wait on age?
What stamps the wrinkle deeper on the brow?
To view each loved one blotted from life's page,
And be alone on earth, as I am now.
Childe Harold's Pilgrimage (1812–18) canto 2, st. 98

8 Once more upon the waters! yet once more!
And the waves bound beneath me as a steed
That knows his rider.
Childe Harold's Pilgrimage (1812–18) canto 3, st. 2

9 The wandering outlaw of his own dark mind.
Childe Harold's Pilgrimage (1812–18) canto 3, st. 3

10 Years steal
Fire from the mind as vigour from the limb;
And life's enchanted cup but sparkles near the brim.
Childe Harold's Pilgrimage (1812–18) canto 3, st. 8

11 Where rose the mountains, there to him were friends;
Where rolled the ocean, thereon was his home;
Where a blue sky, and glowing clime, extends,
He had the passion and the power to roam.
Childe Harold's Pilgrimage (1812–18) canto 3, st. 13

12 The very knowledge that he lived in vain,
That all was over on this side the tomb,
Had made Despair a smilingness assume.
Childe Harold's Pilgrimage (1812–18) canto 3, st. 16

13 There was a sound of revelry by night,
And Belgium's capital had gathered then
Her beauty and her chivalry, and bright
The lamps that shone o'er fair women and brave men;
A thousand hearts beat happily; and when
Music arose with its voluptuous swell,
Soft eyes looked love to eyes which spake again,
And all went merry as a marriage bell;
But hush! hark! a deep sound strikes like a rising knell!
Childe Harold's Pilgrimage (1812–18) canto 3, st. 21

14 On with the dance! let joy be unconfined;
No sleep till morn, when Youth and Pleasure meet
To chase the glowing Hours with flying feet.
Childe Harold's Pilgrimage (1812–18) canto 3, st. 22

15 He rushed into the field, and, foremost fighting, fell.
Childe Harold's Pilgrimage (1812–18) canto 3, st. 23

16 But life will suit
Itself to Sorrow's most detested fruit,
Like to the apples on the Dead Sea's shore,
All ashes to the taste.
Childe Harold's Pilgrimage (1812–18) canto 3, st. 34

17 Quiet to quick bosoms is a hell.
Childe Harold's Pilgrimage (1812–18) canto 3, st. 42

18 To fly from, need not be to hate, mankind.
Childe Harold's Pilgrimage (1812–18) canto 3, st. 69

19 I live not in myself, but I become
Portion of that around me; and to me,
High mountains are a feeling, but the hum
Of human cities torture.
Childe Harold's Pilgrimage (1812–18) canto 3, st. 72

20 His love was passion's essence:—as a tree
On fire by lightning, with ethereal flame
Kindled he was, and blasted.
Childe Harold's Pilgrimage (1812–18) canto 3, st. 78

21 Sapping a solemn creed with solemn sneer.
of Edward **Gibbon**
Childe Harold's Pilgrimage (1812–18) canto 3, st. 107

22 I have not loved the world, nor the world me;
I have not flattered its rank breath, nor bowed
To its idolatries a patient knee.
Childe Harold's Pilgrimage (1812–18) canto 3, st. 113

23 I stood
Among them, but not of them; in a shroud
Of thoughts which were not their thoughts.
Childe Harold's Pilgrimage (1812–18) canto 3, st. 113

24 I stood in Venice, on the Bridge of Sighs:
A palace and a prison on each hand.
Childe Harold's Pilgrimage (1812–18) canto 4, st. 1

25 The moon is up, and yet it is not night;
Sunset divides the sky with her—a sea
Of glory streams along the Alpine height
Of blue Friuli's mountains; Heaven is free
From clouds, but of all colours seems to be
Melted to one vast Iris of the West,
Where the day joins the past eternity.
Childe Harold's Pilgrimage (1812–18) canto 4, st. 27

26 Italia! oh Italia! thou who hast
The fatal gift of beauty.
Childe Harold's Pilgrimage (1812–18) canto 4, st. 42

27 Oh Rome! my country! city of the soul!
Childe Harold's Pilgrimage (1812–18) canto 4, st. 78

28 Alas! our young affections run to waste,
Or water but the desert.
Childe Harold's Pilgrimage (1812–18) canto 4, st. 120

29 Of its own beauty is the mind diseased.
Childe Harold's Pilgrimage (1812–18) canto 4, st. 122

1 Time, the avenger! unto thee I lift
My hands, and eyes, and heart, and crave of thee a gift.
Childe Harold's Pilgrimage (1812–18) canto 4, st. 130

2 But I have lived, and have not lived in vain:
My mind may lose its force, my blood its fire,
And my frame perish even in conquering pain;
But there is that within me which shall tire
Torture and Time, and breathe when I expire.
Childe Harold's Pilgrimage (1812–18) canto 4, st. 137

3 *There* were his young barbarians all at play,
There was their Dacian mother— he, their sire,
Butchered to make a Roman holiday.
Childe Harold's Pilgrimage (1812–18) canto 4, st. 141

4 A ruin—yet what ruin! from its mass
Walls, palaces, half-cities, have been reared.
Childe Harold's Pilgrimage (1812–18) canto 4, st. 143

5 While stands the Coliseum, Rome shall stand;
When falls the Coliseum, Rome shall fall;
And when Rome falls—the World.
Childe Harold's Pilgrimage (1812–18) canto 4, st. 145

6 The Lord of the unerring bow,
The God of life, and poesy, and light.
Childe Harold's Pilgrimage (1812–18) canto 4, st. 161

7 Oh! that the desert were my dwelling-place,
With one fair spirit for my minister,
That I might all forget the human race,
And, hating no one, love but only her!
Childe Harold's Pilgrimage (1812–18) canto 4, st. 177

8 There is a pleasure in the pathless woods,
There is a rapture on the lonely shore,
There is society, where none intrudes,
By the deep sea, and music in its roar:
I love not man the less, but nature more.
Childe Harold's Pilgrimage (1812–18) canto 4, st. 178

9 Roll on, thou deep and dark blue Ocean—roll!
Ten thousand fleets sweep over thee in vain;
Man marks the earth with ruin—his control
Stops with the shore.
Childe Harold's Pilgrimage (1812–18) canto 4, st. 179

10 Without a grave, unknelled, uncoffined, and unknown.
Childe Harold's Pilgrimage (1812–18) canto 4, st. 179

11 Dark-heaving;—boundless, endless, and sublime—
The image of eternity.
of the sea
Childe Harold's Pilgrimage (1812–18) canto 4, st. 183

12 The glory and the nothing of a name.
'Churchill's Grave' (1816)

13 Such hath it been—shall be—beneath the sun
The many still must labour for the one.
The Corsair (1814) canto 1, st. 8

14 There was a laughing devil in his sneer,
That raised emotions both of rage and fear;
And where his frown of hatred darkly fell,
Hope withering fled, and Mercy sighed farewell!
The Corsair (1814) canto 1, st. 9

15 Deep in my soul that tender secret dwells,
Lonely and lost to light for evermore,
Save when to thine my heart responsive swells,
Then trembles into silence as before.
The Corsair (1814) canto 1, st. 14 'Medora's Song'

16 The spirit burning but unbent,
May writhe, rebel—the weak alone repent!
The Corsair (1814) canto 2, st. 10

17 Oh! too convincing—dangerously dear—
In woman's eye the unanswerable tear!
The Corsair (1814) canto 2, st. 15

18 And she for him had given
Her all on earth, and more than all in heaven!
The Corsair (1814) canto 3, st. 17

19 He left a Corsair's name to other times,
Linked with one virtue, and a thousand crimes.
The Corsair (1814) canto 3, st. 24

20 Slow sinks, more lovely ere his race be run,
Along Morea's hills the setting sun;
Not, as in northern climes, obscurely bright,
But one unclouded blaze of living light.
'The Curse of Minerva' (1812) l. 1 and *The Corsair* (1814) canto 3, st. 1

21 A land of meanness, sophistry, and mist.
of Scotland
'The Curse of Minerva' (1812) l. 138

22 Each breeze from foggy mount and marshy plain
Dilutes with drivel every drizzly brain,
Till, burst at length, each wat'ry head o'erflows,
Foul as their soil, and frigid as their snows.
of Scotland
'The Curse of Minerva' (1812) l. 139

23 The Assyrian came down like the wolf on the fold,
And his cohorts were gleaming in purple and gold;
And the sheen of their spears was like stars on the sea,
When the blue wave rolls nightly on deep Galilee.
'The Destruction of Sennacherib' (1815) st. 1

24 For the Angel of Death spread his wings on the blast,
And breathed in the face of the foe as he passed.
'The Destruction of Sennacherib' (1815) st. 3

25 And Coleridge, too, has lately taken wing,
But, like a hawk encumbered with his hood,
Explaining metaphysics to the nation—
I wish he would explain his explanation.
Don Juan (1819–24) canto 1, dedication st. 2

26 The intellectual eunuch Castlereagh.
Don Juan (1819–24) canto 1, dedication st. 11

27 My way is to begin with the beginning.
Don Juan (1819–24) canto 1, st. 7

28 But—Oh! ye lords of ladies intellectual,
Inform us truly, have they not hen-pecked you all?
Don Juan (1819–24) canto 1, st. 22

29 Married, charming, chaste, and twenty-three.
Don Juan (1819–24) canto 1, st. 59

30 What men call gallantry, and gods adultery,
Is much more common where the climate's sultry.
Don Juan (1819–24) canto 1, st. 63

1 Christians have burnt each other, quite persuaded
That all the Apostles would have done as they did.
Don Juan (1819–24) canto 1, st. 83

2 He thought about himself, and the whole earth,
Of man the wonderful, and of the stars,
And how the deuce they ever could have birth;
And then he thought of earthquakes, and of wars,
How many miles the moon might have in girth,
Of air-balloons, and of the many bars
To perfect knowledge of the boundless skies;
And then he thought of Donna Julia's eyes.
Don Juan (1819–24) canto 1, st. 92

3 'Twas strange that one so young should thus concern
His brain about the action of the sky;
If *you* think 'twas philosophy that this did,
I can't help thinking puberty assisted.
Don Juan (1819–24) canto 1, st. 93

4 A little still she strove, and much repented,
And whispering 'I will ne'er consent'—consented.
Don Juan (1819–24) canto 1, st. 117

5 Sweet is revenge—especially to women.
Don Juan (1819–24) canto 1, st. 124

6 Pleasure's a sin, and sometimes sin's a pleasure.
Don Juan (1819–24) canto 1, st. 133

7 Man's love is of man's life a thing apart,
'Tis woman's whole existence.
Don Juan (1819–24) canto 1, st. 194; cf. **Amis** 13:16

8 A panoramic view of hell's in training,
After the style of Virgil and of Homer,
So that my name of Epic's no misnomer.
Don Juan (1819–24) canto 1, st. 200

9 Prose poets like blank-verse, I'm fond of rhyme,
Good workmen never quarrel with their tools.
Don Juan (1819–24) canto 1, st. 201

10 So for a good old-gentlemanly vice,
I think I must take up with avarice.
Don Juan (1819–24) canto 1, st. 216

11 There's nought, no doubt, so much the spirit calms
As rum and true religion.
Don Juan (1819–24) canto 2, st. 34

12 A solitary shriek, the bubbling cry
Of some strong swimmer in his agony.
Don Juan (1819–24) canto 2, st. 53

13 Let us have wine and women, mirth and laughter,
Sermons and soda-water the day after.
Don Juan (1819–24) canto 2, st. 178

14 Man, being reasonable, must get drunk;
The best of life is but intoxication.
Don Juan (1819–24) canto 2, st. 179

15 They looked up to the sky, whose floating glow
Spread like a rosy ocean, vast and bright;
They gazed upon the glittering sea below,
Whence the broad moon rose circling into sight;
They heard the wave's splash, and the wind so low,
And saw each other's dark eyes darting light
Into each other—and, beholding this,
Their lips drew near, and clung into a kiss.
Don Juan (1819–24) canto 2, st. 185

16 And thus they form a group that's quite antique,
Half naked, loving, natural, and Greek.
Don Juan (1819–24) canto 2, st. 194

17 Alas! the love of women! it is known
To be a lovely and a fearful thing!
Don Juan (1819–24) canto 2, st. 199

18 In her first passion woman loves her lover,
In all the others all she loves is love.
Don Juan (1819–24) canto 3, st. 3

19 Love and marriage rarely can combine,
Although they both are born in the same clime;
Marriage from love, like vinegar from wine—
A sad, sour, sober beverage—by time
Is sharpened from its high celestial flavour,
Down to a very homely household savour.
Don Juan (1819–24) canto 3, st. 5

20 Think you, if Laura had been Petrarch's wife,
He would have written sonnets all his life?
Don Juan (1819–24) canto 3, st. 8

21 All tragedies are finished by a death,
All comedies are ended by a marriage;
The future states of both are left to faith.
Don Juan (1819–24) canto 3, st. 9

22 Dreading that climax of all human ills,
The inflammation of his weekly bills.
Don Juan (1819–24) canto 3, st. 35

23 . . . He was the mildest mannered man
That ever scuttled ship or cut a throat.
Don Juan (1819–24) canto 3, st. 41

24 But Shakespeare also says, 'tis very silly
'To gild refined gold, or paint the lily.'
Don Juan (1819–24) canto 3, st. 76; cf. **Shakespeare** 677:15

25 The isles of Greece, the isles of Greece!
Where burning Sappho loved and sung,
Where grew the arts of war and peace,
Where Delos rose, and Phoebus sprung!
Eternal summer gilds them yet,
But all, except their sun, is set!
Don Juan (1819–24) canto 3, st. 86 (1)

26 The mountains look on Marathon—
And Marathon looks on the sea;
And musing there an hour alone,
I dreamed that Greece might still be free.
Don Juan (1819–24) canto 3, st. 86 (3)

27 For what is left the poet here?
For Greeks a blush—for Greece a tear.
Don Juan (1819–24) canto 3, st. 86 (6)

28 Earth! render back from out thy breast
a remnant of our Spartan dead!
Of the three hundred grant but three,
To make a new Thermopylae!
Don Juan (1819–24) canto 3, st. 86 (7)

29 Milton's the prince of poets—so we say;
A little heavy, but no less divine.
Don Juan (1819–24) canto 3, st. 91

30 A drowsy frowzy poem, called the 'Excursion',
Writ in a manner which is my aversion.
Don Juan (1819–24) canto 3, st. 94

1 We learn from Horace, Homer sometimes sleeps;
We feel without him: Wordsworth sometimes wakes.
Don Juan (1819–24) canto 3, st. 98; cf. **Horace** 386:5

2 Ave Maria! 'tis the hour of prayer!
Ave Maria! 'tis the hour of love!
Don Juan (1819–24) canto 3, st. 103; cf. **Prayers** 592:1

3 Now my sere fancy 'falls into the yellow
Leaf,' and imagination droops her pinion,
And the sad truth which hovers o'er my desk
Turns what was once romantic to burlesque.
Don Juan (1819–24) canto 4, st. 3; cf. **Byron** 178:22, **Shakespeare** 685:17

4 And if I laugh at any mortal thing,
'Tis that I may not weep.
Don Juan (1819–24) canto 4, st. 4

5 'Whom the gods love die young' was said of yore.
And many deaths do they escape by this.
Don Juan (1819–24) canto 4, st. 12; cf. **Menander** 504:12

6 I've stood upon Achilles' tomb,
And heard Troy doubted; time will doubt of Rome.
Don Juan (1819–24) canto 4, st. 101

7 When amatory poets sing their loves
In liquid lines mellifluously bland,
And pair their rhymes as Venus yokes her doves.
They little think what mischief is in hand.
Don Juan (1819–24) canto 5, st. 1

8 And is this blood, then, formed but to be shed?
Can every element our elements mar?
And air—earth—water—fire live—and we dead?
We, whose minds comprehend all things?
Don Juan (1819–24) canto 5, st. 39

9 . . . That all-softening, overpowering knell,
The tocsin of the soul—the dinner bell.
Don Juan (1819–24) canto 5, st. 49

10 Why don't they knead two virtuous souls for life
Into that moral centaur, man and wife?
Don Juan (1819–24) canto 5, st. 158

11 There is a tide in the affairs of women,
Which, taken at the flood, leads—God knows where.
Don Juan (1819–24) canto 6, st. 2; cf. **Shakespeare** 676:28

12 A lady of a 'certain age', which means
Certainly aged.
Don Juan (1819–24) canto 6, st. 69

13 'Let there be light!' said God, and there was light!'
'Let there be blood!' says man, and there's a sea!
Don Juan (1819–24) canto 7, st. 41; cf. **Bible** 73:10

14 Read your own hearts and Ireland's present story,
Then feed her famine fat with Wellesley's glory.
Don Juan (1819–24) canto 8, st. 125

15 That water-land of Dutchmen and of ditches.
Don Juan (1819–24) canto 10, st. 63

16 When Bishop Berkeley said 'there was no matter',
And proved it—'twas no matter what he said.
Don Juan (1819–24) canto 11, st. 1

17 And, after all, what is a lie? 'Tis but
The truth in masquerade.
Don Juan (1819–24) canto 11, st. 37

18 'Tis strange the mind, that very fiery particle,
Should let itself be snuffed out by an article.
on ***Keats*** *'who was killed off by one critique'*
Don Juan (1819–24) canto 11, st. 60

19 For talk six times with the same single lady,
And you may get the wedding dresses ready.
Don Juan (1819–24) canto 12, st. 59

20 Merely innocent flirtation,
Not quite adultery, but adulteration.
Don Juan (1819–24) canto 12, st. 63

21 Now hatred is by far the longest pleasure;
Men love in haste, but they detest at leisure.
Don Juan (1819–24) canto 13, st. 4; cf. **Proverbs** 606:31

22 Cervantes smiled Spain's chivalry away.
Don Juan (1819–24) canto 13, st. 11

23 The English winter—ending in July,
To recommence in August.
Don Juan (1819–24) canto 13, st. 42

24 Society is now one polished horde,
Formed of two mighty tribes, the *Bores* and *Bored*.
Don Juan (1819–24) canto 13, st. 95

25 Of all the horrid, hideous notes of woe,
Sadder than owl-songs or the midnight blast,
Is that portentous phrase, 'I told you so.'
Don Juan (1819–24) canto 14, st. 50

26 'Tis strange—but true; for truth is always strange;
Stranger than fiction.
Don Juan (1819–24) canto 14, st. 101; cf. **Proverbs** 613:19

27 All present life is but an Interjection,
An 'Oh!' or 'Ah!' of joy or misery,
Or a 'Ha! ha!' or 'Bah!'—a yawn, or 'Pooh!'
Of which perhaps the latter is most true.
Don Juan (1819–24) canto 15, st. 1

28 A lovely being, scarcely formed or moulded,
A rose with all its sweetest leaves yet folded.
Don Juan (1819–24) canto 15, st. 43

29 'Tis wonderful what fable will not do!
'Tis said it makes reality more bearable:
But what's reality? Who has its clue?
Philosophy? No; she too much rejects.
Religion? Yes; but which of all her sects?
Don Juan (1819–24) canto 15, st. 89

30 How little do we know that which we are!
How less what we may be!
Don Juan (1819–24) canto 15, st. 99

31 The worlds beyond this world's perplexing waste
Had more of her existence for in her
There was a depth of feeling to embrace
Thoughts, boundless, deep, but silent too as space.
Don Juan (1819–24) canto 16, st. 48

32 The mind can make
Substance, and people planets of its own
With beings brighter than have been, and give
A breath to forms which can outlive all flesh.
'The Dream' (1816) st. 1

33 I'll publish, right or wrong:
Fools are my theme, let satire be my song.
English Bards and Scotch Reviewers (1809) l. 5

1 A man must serve his time to every trade
Save censure—critics all are ready made.
Take hackneyed jokes from Miller, got by rote,
With just enough of learning to misquote.
English Bards and Scotch Reviewers (1809) l. 63

2 Each country Book-club bows the knee to Baal,
And, hurling lawful Genius from the throne,
Erects a shrine and idol of its own.
English Bards and Scotch Reviewers (1809) l. 138

3 Who, both by precept and example, shows
That prose is verse, and verse is merely prose,
Convincing all by demonstration plain,
Poetic souls delight in prose insane;
And Christmas stories tortured into rhyme,
Contain the essence of the true sublime.
of ***Wordsworth***
English Bards and Scotch Reviewers (1809) l. 241

4 Be warm, but pure; be amorous, but be chaste.
English Bards and Scotch Reviewers (1809) l. 306

5 The petrifactions of a plodding brain.
English Bards and Scotch Reviewers (1809) l. 416

6 Then let Ausonia, skilled in every art
To soften manners, but corrupt the heart,
Pour her exotic follies o'er the town,
To sanction Vice, and hunt Decorum down.
Ausonia = *Italy*
English Bards and Scotch Reviewers (1809) l. 618

7 Let simple Wordsworth chime his childish verse,
And brother Coleridge lull the babe at nurse.
English Bards and Scotch Reviewers (1809) l. 917

8 And glory, like the phoenix midst her fires,
Exhales her odours, blazes, and expires.
English Bards and Scotch Reviewers (1809) l. 959

9 Dusky like night, but night with all her stars,
Or cavern sparkling with its native spars;
With eyes that were a language and a spell,
A form like Aphrodite's in her shell,
With all her loves around her on the deep,
Voluptuous as the first approach of sleep.
'The Island' (1823) canto 2, st. 7

10 Beside the jutting rock the few appeared,
Like the last remnant of the red-deer's herd;
Their eyes were feverish, and their aspect worn,
But still the hunter's blood was on their horn,
A little stream came tumbling from the height,
And straggling into ocean as it might,
Its bounding crystal frolicked in the ray,
And gushed from cliff to crag with saltless spray . . .
To this young spring they rushed,—all feelings first
Absorbed in passion's and in nature's thirst,—
Drank as they do who drink their last, and threw
Their arms aside to revel in its dew;
Cooled their scorched throats, and washed the gory stains
From wounds whose only bandage might be chains.
'The Island' (1823) canto 3, st. 3

11 Friendship is Love without his wings!
'L'Amitié est l'amour sans ailes' (written 1806, published 1831)

12 So he has cut his throat at last!—He! Who?
The man who cut his country's long ago.
on Castlereagh's suicide, c.1822
'Epigram on Lord Castlereagh'

13 Sorrow is knowledge: they who know the most
Must mourn the deepest o'er the fatal truth,
The Tree of Knowledge is not that of Life.
Manfred (1817) act 1, sc. 1, l. 10

14 How beautiful is all this visible world!
How glorious in its action and itself!
But we, who name ourselves its sovereigns, we,
Half dust, half deity, alike unfit
To sink or soar, with our mixed essence make
A conflict of its elements, and breathe
The breath of degradation and of pride.
Manfred (1817) act 1, sc. 2, l. 37

15 I linger yet with nature, for the night
Hath been to me a more familiar face
Than that of man; and in her starry shade
Of dim and solitary loveliness
I learned the language of another world.
Manfred (1817) act 3, sc. 4, l. 2

16 Old man! 'tis not so difficult to die.
Manfred (2nd ed., 1819) act 3, sc. 4, l. 151

17 You have deeply ventured;
But all must do so who would greatly win.
Marino Faliero (1821) act 1, sc. 2

18 'Tis done—but yesterday a King!
And armed with Kings to strive—
And now thou art a nameless thing:
So abject—yet alive!
'Ode to Napoleon Bonaparte' (1814) st. 1

19 The arbiter of others' fate
A suppliant for his own!
'Ode to Napoleon Bonaparte' (1814) st. 5

20 The Cincinnatus of the West.
of George ***Washington***
'Ode to Napoleon Bonaparte' (1814) st. 19

21 It is not in the storm nor in the strife
We feel benumbed, and wish to be no more,
But in the after-silence on the shore,
When all is lost, except a little life.
'On hearing that Lady Byron was ill' (written 1816)

22 My days are in the yellow leaf;
The flowers and fruits of love are gone;
The worm, the canker, and the grief
Are mine alone!
'On This Day I Complete my Thirty-Sixth Year' (1824); cf. **Byron** 177:3, **Shakespeare** 685:17

23 My hair is grey, but not with years,
Nor grew it white
In a single night,
As men's have grown from sudden fears.
The Prisoner of Chillon (1816) st. 1

24 She walks in beauty, like the night
Of cloudless climes and starry skies;
And all that's best of dark and bright
Meet in her aspect and her eyes:
Thus mellowed to that tender light

Which heaven to gaudy day denies.
'She Walks in Beauty' (1815) st. 1

1 A mind at peace with all below,
A heart whose love is innocent!
'She Walks in Beauty' (1815)

2 Born in the garret, in the kitchen bred,
Promoted thence to deck her mistress' head.
'A Sketch from Private Life' (1816)

3 Eternal spirit of the chainless mind!
Brightest in dungeons, Liberty! thou art.
'Sonnet on Chillon' (1816)

4 So, we'll go no more a-roving
So late into the night,
Though the heart be still as loving,
And the moon be still as bright.
'So we'll go no more a-roving' (written 1817)

5 There's not a joy the world can give like that it takes away.
'Stanzas for Music' (1816)

6 Oh, talk not to me of a name great in story;
The days of our youth are the days of our glory;
And the myrtle and ivy of sweet two-and-twenty
Are worth all your laurels, though ever so plenty.
'Stanzas Written on the Road between Florence and Pisa, November 1821'

7 I knew it was love, and I felt it was glory.
'Stanzas Written on the Road between Florence and Pisa, November 1821'

8 I am ashes where once I was fire.
'To the Countess of Blessington' (written 1823)

9 Still I can't contradict, what so oft has been said,
'Though women are angels, yet wedlock's the devil.'
'To Eliza' (1806)

10 And when we think we lead, we are most led.
The Two Foscari (1821) act 2, sc. 1, l. 361

11 The angels all were singing out of tune,
And hoarse with having little else to do,
Excepting to wind up the sun and moon,
Or curb a runaway young star or two.
The Vision of Judgement (1822) st. 2

12 And when the gorgeous coffin was laid low,
It seemed the mockery of hell to fold
The rottenness of eighty years in gold.
on the burial of **George III**
The Vision of Judgement (1822) st. 10

13 In whom his qualities are reigning still,
Except that household virtue, most uncommon,
Of constancy to a bad, ugly woman.
The Vision of Judgement (1822) st. 12

14 As he drew near, he gazed upon the gate
Ne'er to be entered more by him or Sin,
With such a glance of supernatural hate,
As made Saint Peter wish himself within;
He pattered with his keys at a great rate,
And sweated through his apostolic skin:
Of course his perspiration was but ichor,
Or some such other spiritual liquor.
The Vision of Judgement (1822) st. 25

15 Yet still between his Darkness and his Brightness
There passed a mutual glance of great politeness.
The Vision of Judgement (1822) st. 35

16 Satan met his ancient friend
With more hauteur, as might an old Castilian
Poor noble meet a mushroom rich civilian.
The Vision of Judgement (1822) st. 36

17 And when the tumult dwindled to a calm,
I left him practising the hundredth psalm.
The Vision of Judgement (1822) st. 106

18 When we two parted
In silence and tears,
Half broken-hearted
To sever for years,
Pale grew thy cheek and cold,
Colder thy kiss.
'When we two parted' (1816)

19 If I should meet thee
After long years,
How should I greet thee?—
With silence and tears.
'When we two parted' (1816)

20 Near this spot are deposited the remains of one who possessed beauty without vanity, strength without insolence, courage without ferocity, and all the virtues of Man, without his vices.
'Inscription on the Monument of a Newfoundland Dog' (1808)

21 The man is mad, Sir, mad, frightful as a Mandrake, and lean as a rutting Stag, and all about a bitch not worth a Bank token.
of the Revd Robert Bland
letter to John Cam Hobhouse, 16 November 1811; in L. A. Marchand (ed.) *Byron's Letters and Journals* vol. 2 (1973)

22 My Princess of Parallelograms.
of his future wife Annabella Milbanke, a keen amateur mathematician; Byron explains: 'Her proceedings are quite rectangular, or rather we are two parallel lines prolonged to infinity side by side but never to meet'
letter to Lady Melbourne, 18 October 1812; in L. A. Marchand (ed.) *Byron's Letters and Journals* vol. 2 (1973)

23 The place is very well and quiet and the children only scream in a low voice.
letter to Lady Melbourne, 21 September 1813, in L. A. Marchand (ed.) *Byron's Letters and Journals* vol. 3 (1974)

24 We have progressively improved into a less spiritual species of tenderness—but the seal is not yet fixed though the wax is preparing for the impression.
of his relationship with Lady Frances Webster
letter to Lady Melbourne, 14 October 1813; in L. A. Marchand (ed.) *Byron's Letters and Journals* vol. 3 (1974)

25 I by no means rank poetry high in the scale of intelligence—this may look like affectation—but it is my real opinion—it is the lava of the imagination whose eruption prevents an earthquake.
letter to Annabella Milbanke, 29 November 1813, in L. A. Marchand (ed.) *Byron's Letters and Journals* vol. 3 (1974)

1 I prefer the talents of action—of war—of the senate—or even of science—to all the speculations of those mere dreamers of another existence.
letter to Annabella Milbanke, 29 November 1813, in L. A. Marchand (ed.) *Byron's Letters and Journals* vol. 3 (1974)

2 What is hope? nothing but the paint on the face of Existence; the least touch of truth rubs it off, and then we see what a hollow-cheeked harlot we have got hold of.
letter to Thomas Moore, 28 October 1815, in L. A. Marchand (ed.) *Byron's Letters and Journals* vol. 4 (1975)

3 Like other parties of the kind, it was first silent, then talky, then argumentative, then disputatious, then unintelligible, then altogethery, then inarticulate, and then drunk.
letter to Thomas Moore, 31 October 1815, in L. A. Marchand (ed.) *Byron's Letters and Journals* vol. 4 (1975)

4 Wordsworth—stupendous genius! damned fool! These poets run about their ponds though they cannot fish.
fragment of a letter to James Hogg, recorded in the diary of Henry Crabb Robinson, 1 December 1816; in L. A. Marchand (ed.) *Byron's Letters and Journals* vol. 5 (1976)

5 Love in this part of the world is no sinecure.
letter to John Murray from Venice, 27 December 1816, in L. A. Marchand (ed.) *Byron's Letters and Journals* vol. 5 (1976)

6 I hate things all *fiction* . . . there should always be some foundation of fact for the most airy fabric and pure invention is but the talent of a liar.
letter to John Murray from Venice, 2 April 1817; in L. A. Marchand (ed.) *Byron's Letters and Journals* vol. 5 (1976)

7 Without means, without connection, without character . . . he beat them all, in all he ever attempted.
of Richard Brinsley ***Sheridan***
letter to Thomas Moore, 1 June 1818, in L. A. Marchand (ed.) *Byron's Letters and Journals* vol. 6 (1978)

8 Is it not *life*, is it not *the thing?*—Could any man have written it—who has not lived in the world?—and tooled in a post-chaise? in a hackney coach? in a gondola? Against a wall? in a court carriage? in a *vis-à-vis?*—on a table?—and under it?
of Don Juan
letter to Douglas Kinnaird, 26 October 1819; in L. A. Marchand (ed.) *Byron's Letters and Journals* vol. 6 (1978)

9 The reading or non-reading a book—will never keep down a single petticoat.
letter to Richard Hoppner, 29 October 1819, in L. A. Marchand (ed.) *Byron's Letters and Journals* vol. 6 (1978)

10 Such writing is a sort of mental masturbation—he is always f—gg—g his *imagination.*—I don't mean that he is indecent but viciously soliciting his own ideas into a state which is neither poetry nor any thing else but a Bedlam vision produced by raw pork and opium.
of ***Keats***
letter to John Murray, 9 November 1820; in L. A. Marchand (ed.) *Byron's Letters and Journals* vol. 7 (1979)

11 I awoke one morning and found myself famous.
on the instantaneous success of Childe Harold
Thomas Moore *Letters and Journals of Lord Byron* (1830) vol. 1

12 You should have a softer pillow than my heart.
to his wife, who had rested her head on his breast
E. C. Mayne (ed.) *The Life and Letters of Anne Isabella, Lady Noel Byron* (1929) ch. 11

James Branch Cabell 1879–1958

American novelist and essayist

13 The optimist proclaims that we live in the best of all possible worlds; and the pessimist fears this is true.
The Silver Stallion (1926) bk. 4, ch. 26

Augustus Caesar see Augustus

Irving Caesar 1895–

American songwriter

14 Picture you upon my knee,
Just tea for two and two for tea.
'Tea for Two' (1925 song)

Julius Caesar 100–44 BC

Roman general and statesman
see also ***Plutarch*** *579:8*

15 *Gallia est omnis divisa in partes tres.*
Gaul as a whole is divided into three parts.
De Bello Gallico bk. 1, sect. 1

16 Men are nearly always willing to believe what they wish.
De Bello Gallico bk. 3, sect. 18; cf. **Bacon** 45:2

17 Caesar's wife must be above suspicion.
divorcing his wife Pompeia after unfounded allegations were made against her
oral tradition, based on Plutarch *Parallel Lives* 'Julius Caesar' ch. 10, sect. 9; cf. **Proverbs** 596:46

18 Caesar had rather be first in a village than second at Rome.
Francis Bacon *The Advancement of Learning* pt. 2, ch. 23, sect. 36; based on Plutarch

I should rather be first among these people than second at Rome.
Parallel Lives 'Julius Caesar' ch. 11

19 Thou hast Caesar and his fortune with thee.
Plutarch *Parallel Lives* 'Julius Caesar' ch. 38, sect. 3 (translated by T. North, 1579; literally 'You are carrying Caesar, and his fortune is in the same boat')

20 *Iacta alea est.*
The die is cast.
at the crossing of the Rubicon, the boundary beyond which he was forbidden to lead his army
Suetonius *Lives of the Caesars* 'Divus Julius' sect. 32; originally spoken in Greek, Plutarch *Parallel Lives* 'Pompey' ch. 60, sect. 2

21 *Veni, vidi, vici.*
I came, I saw, I conquered.
inscription displayed in Caesar's Pontic triumph, according to Suetonius *Lives of the Caesars* 'Divus Julius' sect. 37; or, according to Plutarch *Parallel Lives* 'Julius Caesar' ch. 50, sect. 2, written in a letter by Caesar, announcing the victory of Zela which concluded the Pontic campaign

22 *Et tu, Brute?*
You too, Brutus?
traditional rendering of Suetonius; cf. **Shakespeare** 675:16

Some have written that when Marcus Brutus rushed at him, he said in Greek, 'You too, my child?'
Suetonius *Lives of the Caesars* 'Divus Julius' sect. 82

John Cage 1912–
American composer, pianist, and writer

1 I have nothing to say
and I am saying it and that is
poetry.
'Lecture on nothing' (1961)

James Cagney see **Misquotations** 522:16

James M. Cain 1892–1977
American novelist

2 The postman always rings twice.
title of novel (1934)

Joseph Cairns 1920–
British industrialist and politician

3 The betrayal of Ulster, the cynical and entirely undemocratic banishment of its properly elected Parliament and a relegation to the status of a fuzzy-wuzzy colony is, I hope, a last betrayal contemplated by Downing Street because it is the last that Ulster will countenance.
speech on retiring as Lord Mayor of Belfast, 31 May 1972
in *Daily Telegraph* 1 June 1972

Pedro Calderón de La Barca 1600–81
Spanish dramatist and poet

4 . . . *Aun en sueños*
no se pierde el hacer bien.
Even in dreams good works are not wasted.
La Vida es Sueño (1636) 'Segunda Jornada' l. 2146

5 *¿Qué es la vida? Un frenesí.*
¿Qué es la vida? Una ilusión,
una sombra, una ficción,
y el mayor bien es pequeño;
que toda la vida es sueño,
y los sueños, sueños son.
What is life? a frenzy. What is life? An illusion, a shadow, a fiction. And the greatest good is of slight worth, as all life is a dream, and dreams are dreams.
La Vida es Sueño (1636) 'Segunda Jornada' l. 2183; cf. **Montaigne** 528:3

Caligula (Gaius Julius Caesar Germanicus) AD 12–41
Roman emperor from AD 37

6 *Utinam populus Romanus unam cervicem haberet!*
Would that the Roman people had but one neck!
Suetonius *Lives of the Caesars* 'Gaius Caligula' sect. 30

7 *Ita feri ut se mori sentiat.*
Strike him so that he can feel that he is dying.
Suetonius *Lives of the Caesars* 'Gaius Caligula' sect. 30

Antônio Callado 1917–97
Brazilian novelist

8 To live beyond eighty is an exaggeration, almost an excess.
in *Independent* 1 February 1997; obituary

James Callaghan 1912–
British Labour statesman; Prime Minister 1976–9
see also **Misquotations** 521:7

9 You cannot now, if you ever could, spend your way out of a recession.
speech at Labour Party Conference, 28 September 1976

10 You never reach the promised land. You can march towards it.
in a television interview, 20 July 1978

11 I had known it was going to be a 'winter of discontent'.
television interview, 8 February 1979; in *Daily Telegraph* 9 February 1979; cf. **Newspaper headlines** 544:20

12 It's the first time in recorded history that turkeys have been known to vote for an early Christmas.
in the debate resulting in the fall of the Labour government, when the pact between Labour and the Liberals had collapsed, and the Scottish and Welsh Nationalists had also withdrawn their support
in the House of Commons, 28 March 1979

13 There are times, perhaps once every thirty years, when there is a sea-change in politics. It then does not matter what you say or what you do. There is a shift in what the public wants and what it approves of. I suspect there is now such a sea-change—and it is for Mrs Thatcher.
during the election campaign of 1979
Kenneth O. Morgan *Callaghan* (1997)

14 I certainly didn't go down on one knee. I think she said it's about time we got married.
on his diamond wedding day, remembering his proposal
in *Daily Telegraph* 29 July 1998

Callimachus *c.*305–*c.*240 BC
Hellenistic poet and scholar

15 Someone spoke of your death, Heraclitus. It brought me
Tears, and I remembered how often together
We ran the sun down with talk.
R. Pfeiffer (ed) *Callimachus* (1949–53) Epigram 2; translated by Peter Jay

16 I abhor, too, the roaming lover, nor do I drink from every well; I loathe all things held in common.
R. Pfeiffer (ed.) *Callimachus* (1949–53) Epigram 28

17 A great book is like great evil.
R. Pfeiffer (ed.) *Callimachus* (1949–53) Fragment 465; cf. **Proverbs** 601:33

Charles Alexandre de Calonne
1734–1802
French statesman

1 *Madame, si c'est possible, c'est fait; impossible? cela se fera.*

Madam, if a thing is possible, consider it done; the impossible? that will be done.

in J. Michelet *Histoire de la Révolution Française* (1847) vol. 1, pt. 2, sect. 8; cf. **Military sayings** 508:6, **Nansen** 538:7

C. S. Calverley (born Blayds) 1831–84
English writer

2 The farmer's daughter hath soft brown hair;
(*Butter and eggs and a pound of cheese*)
And I met with a ballad, I can't say where,
Which wholly consisted of lines like these.

'Ballad' (1872)

3 O Beer! O Hodgson, Guinness, Allsopp, Bass!
Names that should be on every infant's tongue!

'Beer' (1861)

4 Life is with such all beer and skittles;
They are not difficult to please
About their victuals.

'Contentment' (1872)

5 For king-like rolls the Rhine,
And the scenery's divine,
And the victuals and the wine
Rather good.

'Dover to Munich' (1861)

6 For I've read in many a novel that, unless they've souls that grovel,
Folks *prefer* in fact a hovel to your dreary marble halls.

'In the Gloaming' (1872); cf. **Bunn** 160:10

7 How Eugene Aram, though a thief, a liar, and a murderer,
Yet, being intellectual, was amongst the noblest of mankind.

'Of Reading' (1861); cf. **Hood** 382:17

Italo Calvino 1923–85
Italian novelist and short-story writer

8 The gaze of dogs who don't understand and who don't know that they may be right not to understand.

Il Barone Rampante (1957) ch. 10

9 Revolutionaries are more formalistic than conservatives.

Il Barone Rampante (1957) ch. 28

Helder Camara 1909–
Brazilian priest

10 When I give food to the poor they call me a saint. When I ask why the poor have no food they call me a communist.

attributed

Pierre, Baron de Cambronne
1770–1842
French general

11 *La Garde meurt, mais ne se rend pas.*

The Guards die but do not surrender.

attributed to Cambronne when called upon to surrender at Waterloo, 1815, but later denied by him

H. Houssaye *La Garde meurt et ne se rend pas* (1907); an alternative version is that he replied:

Merde!

Shit!

attributed, known in French as the '*mot de Cambronne*'

Lord Camden 1714–94
British Whig politician; Lord Chancellor, 1766–70

12 Taxation and representation are inseparable . . . whatever is a man's own, is absolutely his own; no man hath a right to take it from him without his consent either expressed by himself or representative; whoever attempts to do it, attempts an injury; whoever does it, commits a robbery; he throws down and destroys the distinction between liberty and slavery.

on the taxation of Americans by the British parliament

speech in the House of Lords, 10 February 1766; cf. **Otis** 560:21

Julia Margaret Cameron 1815–79
English photographer

13 I longed to arrest all beauty that came before me.

Annals of my Glass House 1874

Jane Montgomery Campbell 1817–78
English hymn-writer

14 We plough the fields, and scatter
The good seed on the land,
But it is fed and watered
By God's almighty hand;
He sends the snow in winter,
The warmth to swell the grain,
The breezes and the sunshine,
And soft refreshing rain.

'We plough the fields, and scatter' (1861 hymn); translated from the German of Matthias Claudius (1740–1815)

Mrs Patrick Campbell (Beatrice Stella Tanner) 1865–1940
English actress

on Campbell: see ***Agate*** *6:16,* ***Woollcott*** *827:6*

15 The deep, deep peace of the double-bed after the hurly-burly of the chaise-longue.

on her recent marriage

Alexander Woollcott *While Rome Burns* (1934) 'The First Mrs Tanqueray'

16 It doesn't matter what you do in the bedroom as long as you don't do it in the street and frighten the horses.

Daphne Fielding *The Duchess of Jermyn Street* (1964) ch. 2

Roy Campbell 1901–57
South African poet

1 Giraffes!—a People
Who live between the earth and skies,
Each in his lone religious steeple,
Keeping a lighthouse with his eyes.
'Dreaming Spires' (1946)

2 You praise the firm restraint with which they write—
I'm with you there, of course:
They use the snaffle and the curb all right,
But where's the bloody horse?
'On Some South African Novelists' (1930)

Thomas Campbell 1777–1844
Scottish poet

3 There was silence deep as death,
And the boldest held his breath
For a time.
'Battle of the Baltic' (1809)

4 Let us think of them that sleep,
Full many a fathom deep,
By thy wild and stormy steep,
Elsinore!
'Battle of the Baltic' (1809)

5 O leave this barren spot to me!
Spare, woodman, spare the beechen tree.
'The Beech-Tree's Petition' (1800); cf. **Morris** 532:9

6 To-morrow let us do or die!
'Gertrude of Wyoming' (1809) pt. 3, st. 37

7 On the green banks of Shannon, when Sheelah was nigh,
No blithe Irish lad was so happy as I;
No harp like my own could so cheerily play,
And wherever I went was my poor dog Tray.
'The Harper' (1799)

8 On Linden, when the sun was low,
All bloodless lay the untrodden snow,
And dark as winter was the flow
Of Iser, rolling rapidly.
'Hohenlinden' (1802)

9 Better be courted and jilted
Than never be courted at all.
'The Jilted Nymph' (1843)

10 'Tis the sunset of life gives me mystical lore,
And coming events cast their shadows before.
Lochiel's Warning (1801)

11 A chieftain to the Highlands bound
Cries, 'Boatman, do not tarry!
And I'll give thee a silver pound
To row us o'er the ferry.'
'Lord Ullin's Daughter' (1809)

12 O, I'm the chief of Ulva's isle
And this Lord Ullin's daughter.
'Lord Ullin's Daughter' (1809)

13 'Tis distance lends enchantment to the view,
And robes the mountain in its azure hue.
Pleasures of Hope (1799) pt. 1, l. 7; cf. **Proverbs** 598:19

14 Hope, for a season, bade the world farewell,
And Freedom shrieked—as Kosciuszko fell!
Pleasures of Hope (1799) pt. 1, l. 381

15 What millions died—that Caesar might be great!
Pleasures of Hope (1799) pt. 2, l. 174

16 What though my wingèd hours of bliss have been,
Like angel-visits, few and far between?
Pleasures of Hope (1799) pt. 2, l. 375

17 An original something, fair maid, you would win me
To write—but how shall I begin?
For I fear I have nothing original in me—
Excepting Original Sin.
'To a Young Lady, Who Asked Me to Write Something Original for Her Album' (1843)

18 Ye Mariners of England
That guard our native seas,
Whose flag has braved, a thousand years
The battle and the breeze.
'Ye Mariners of England' (1801)

19 With thunders from her native oak
She quells the floods below.
'Ye Mariners of England' (1801)

20 Now Barabbas was a publisher.
also attributed, wrongly, to **Byron**
attributed, in Samuel Smiles *A Publisher and his Friends: Memoir and Correspondence of the late John Murray* (1891) vol. 1, ch. 14; see **Bible** 102:31

Thomas Campion 1567–1620
English poet and musician

21 My sweetest Lesbia let us live and love,
And though the sager sort our deeds reprove,
Let us not weigh them: Heav'n's great lamps do dive
Into their west, and straight again revive,
But soon as once set is our little light,
Then must we sleep one ever-during night.
A Book of Airs (1601) no. 1 'My sweetest Lesbia' (translation of Catullus *Carmina* no. 5); cf. **Catullus** 197:2

22 When to her lute Corinna sings,
Her voice revives the leaden strings,
And both in highest notes appear,
As any challenged echo clear.
But when she doth of mourning speak,
Ev'n with her sighs the strings do break.
A Book of Airs (1601) no. 6

23 Follow your Saint, follow with accents sweet;
Haste you, sad notes, fall at her flying feet.
A Book of Airs (1601) no. 10

24 Good thoughts his only friends,
His wealth a well-spent age,
The earth his sober inn
And quiet pilgrimage.
A Book of Airs (1601) no. 18

25 There is a garden in her face
Where roses and white lilies grow;
A heavenly paradise is that place,
Wherein all pleasant fruits do flow.
There cherries grow, which none may buy

Till 'Cherry ripe' themselves do cry.
The Fourth Book of Airs (c.1617) no. 7; music by Richard Alison, who published the song in *An Hour's Recreation in Music* (1606)

1 Rose-cheeked Laura, come;
Sing thou smoothly with thy beauty's
Silent music, either other
Sweetly gracing.
'Rose-cheeked Laura' (1602)

2 Kind are her answers,
But her performance keeps no day;
Breaks time, as dancers
From their own music when they stray.
The Third Book of Airs (1617) no. 7

Albert Camus 1913–60

French novelist, dramatist, and essayist
see also **Opening lines** 555:8

3 *Intellectuel = celui qui se dédouble.*
An intellectual is someone whose mind watches itself.
Carnets, 1935–42 (1962)

4 *La politique et le sort des hommes sont formés par des hommes sans idéal et sans grandeur.*
Politics and the fate of mankind are formed by men without ideals and without greatness.
Carnets, 1935–42 (1962)

5 *Vous savez ce qu'est le charme: une manière de s'entendre répondre oui sans avoir posé aucune question claire.*
You know what charm is: a way of getting the answer yes without having asked any clear question.
The Fall (1956)

6 *Nous sommes tous des cas exceptionnels. Nous voulons tous faire appel de quelque chose! Chacun exige d'être innocent, à tout prix, même si, pour cela, il faut accuser le genre humain et le ciel.*
We are all special cases. We all want to appeal against something! Everyone insists on his innocence, at all costs, even if it means accusing the rest of the human race and heaven.
The Fall (1956)

7 *Nous nous confions rarement à ceux qui sont meilleurs que nous.*
We seldom confide in those who are better than ourselves.
The Fall (1956)

8 *Je vais vous dire un grand secret, mon cher. N'attendez pas le jugement dernier. Il a lieu tous les jours.*
I'll tell you a great secret, my friend. Don't wait for the last judgement. It happens every day.
The Fall (1956)

9 *Sisyphe, prolétaire des dieux, impuissant et révolté, connaît toute l'entendue de sa misérable condition: c'est à elle qu'il pense pendant sa descente. La clairvoyance qui devait faire son tourment consomme du même coup sa victoire. Il n'est pas de destin que ne se surmonte par le mépris.*
Sisyphus, proletarian of the gods, powerless and rebellious, knows the whole extent of his wretched condition; it is what he thinks of during his descent. The lucidity that was to constitute his torture at the same time crowns his victory. There is no fate that cannot be surmounted by scorn.
The Myth of Sisyphus (1942) (translated by Justin O'Brien)

10 *La lutte elle-même vers les sommets suffit à remplir un cœur d'homme. Il faut imaginer Sisyphe heureux.*
The struggle itself towards the heights is enough to fill a human heart. One must imagine that Sisyphus is happy.
The Myth of Sisyphus (1942)

11 *Qu'est-ce qu'un homme révolté ? Un homme qui dit non.*
What is a rebel? A man who says no.
The Rebel (1951)

12 *Toutes les révolutions modernes ont abouti à un renforcement de l'État.*
All modern revolutions have ended in a reinforcement of the State.
The Rebel (1951)

13 *Tout révolutionnaire finit en oppresseur ou en hérétique.*
Every revolutionary ends as an oppressor or a heretic.
The Rebel (1951)

14 When the imagination sleeps, words are emptied of their meaning.
Resistance, Rebellion and Death (1961) 'Reflections on the Guillotine'

15 One sometimes sees more clearly in the man who lies than in the man who tells the truth. Truth, like the light, blinds. Lying, on the other hand, is a beautiful twilight, which gives to each object its value.
attributed; Lord Trevelyan *Diplomatic Channels* (1973)

16 What I know most surely about morality and the duty of man I owe to sport.
often quoted as '. . . *I owe to football*'
Herbert R. Lottman *Albert Camus* (1979)

17 Without work, all life goes rotten, but when work is soulless, life stifles and dies.
attributed; E. F. Schumacher *Good Work* (1979)

Elias Canetti 1905–94

Bulgarian-born writer and novelist

18 All the things one has forgotten scream for help in dreams.
Die Provinz der Menschen (1973)

George Canning 1770–1827

British Tory statesman; Prime Minister, 1827

19 In matters of commerce the fault of the Dutch
Is offering too little and asking too much.
The French are with equal advantage content,
So we clap on Dutch bottoms just twenty per cent.
dispatch, in cipher, to the English ambassador at the Hague, 31 January 1826
Sir Harry Poland *Mr Canning's Rhyming 'Dispatch' to Sir Charles Bagot* (1905)

1 A steady patriot of the world alone,
The friend of every country but his own.
on the Jacobin
'New Morality' (1821) l. 113; cf. **Disraeli** 269:17, **Overbury** 561:1

2 And finds, with keen discriminating sight,
Black's not so black;—nor white so very white.
'New Morality' (1821) l. 199

3 Give me the avowed, erect and manly foe;
Firm I can meet, perhaps return the blow;
But of all plagues, good Heaven, thy wrath can send,
Save me, oh, save me, from the candid friend.
'New Morality' (1821) l. 207

4 Pitt is to Addington
As London is to Paddington.
'The Oracle' (*c.*1803)

5 Away with the cant of 'Measures not men'!—the idle supposition that it is the harness and not the horses that draw the chariot along. If the comparison must be made, if the distinction must be taken, men are everything, measures comparatively nothing.
speech on the Army estimates, 8 December 1802, in *Speeches of . . . Canning* (1828) vol. 2; the phrase 'measures not men' may be found as early as 1742 (in a letter from Chesterfield to Dr Chevenix, 6 March); cf. **Burke** 164:17, **Goldsmith** 345:15

6 I called the New World into existence, to redress the balance of the Old.
speech on the affairs of Portugal, in House of Commons 12 December 1826

7 You well know how soon one of these stupendous masses, now reposing on their shadows in perfect stillness, would upon any call of patriotism or of necessity, assume the likeness of an animated thing, instinct with life and motion: how soon it would ruffle, as it were its swelling plumage, how quickly it would put forth all its beauty and its bravery, collect its scattered elements of strength and waken its dormant thunder . . . Such is England herself; while apparently passive and motionless, she silently concentrates the power to be put forth on an adequate occasion.
on the men-of-war lying at anchor in the harbour
speech at Plymouth, 12 December 1823; in R. W. Seton-Watson *Britain in Europe 1789–1914* (1945)

8 [The Whip's duty is] to make a House, and keep a House, and cheer the minister.
J. E. Ritchie *Modern Statesmen* (1861) ch. 7; attributed

Hughie Cannon 1877–1912
American songwriter

9 Won't you come home Bill Bailey, won't you come home?
'Bill Bailey, Won't You Please Come Home' (1902 song)

Moya Cannon 1956–
Irish poet

10 Our windy, untidy loft
where old people had flung up old junk
they'd thought might come in handy
ploughs, ladles, bears, lions, a clatter of heroes.
'The Stars' (1997)

11 There is something about winter
which pares things down to their essentials
a bare tree
a black hedge
hold their own stark throne in our hearts.
'Winter Paths' (1997)

Eric Cantona 1966–
French footballer

12 When seagulls follow a trawler, it is because they think sardines will be thrown into the sea.
to the media at the end of a press conference, 31 March 1995

Robert Capa 1913–54
Hungarian-born American photojournalist

13 If your pictures aren't good enough, you aren't close enough.
Russell Miller *Magnum: Fifty years at the Front Line of History* (1997)

14 I would say that the war correspondent gets more drinks, more girls, better pay and greater freedom than the soldier, but that at this stage of the game having the freedom to choose his spot and being allowed to be a coward and not be executed for it, is his torture. The war correspondent has his stake—his life—in his hands, and he can put it on this horse or that horse, or he can put it back in his pocket at the very last minute.
Cornell Capa (ed.) *The Concerned Photographer* (1972)

Truman Capote 1924–84
American writer and novelist

15 Other voices, other rooms.
title of novel (1948)

Al Capp (Alfred Gerard Caplin) 1907–79
American cartoonist

16 A product of the untalented, sold by the unprincipled to the utterly bewildered.
of abstract art
in *National Observer* 1 July 1963; cf. **Zappa** 839:24

Francesco Caracciolo 1752–99
Neapolitan diplomat

17 In England there are sixty different religions, and only one sauce.
attributed

Ethna Carbery 1866–1902
Irish poet

18 I met the Love-Talker one eve in the glen,
He was handsomer than any of our handsome young men,
His eyes were blacker than the sloe, his voice sweeter far

Than the crooning of old Kevin's pipes beyond in Coolnagar.
'The Love-Talker' (1902)

1 Oh, Kathaleen Ní Houlihan, your road's a thorny way,
And 'tis a faithful soul would walk the flints with you for aye,
Would walk the sharp and cruel flints until his locks grew grey.
'The Passing of the Gael' (1902)

2 Young Rody MacCorley goes to die
On the Bridge of Toome today.
'Rody MacCorley' (1902)

Neville Cardus 1889–1975

English critic and writer

3 If everything else in this nation of ours were lost but cricket—her Constitution and the laws of England of Lord Halsbury—it would be possible to reconstruct from the theory and practice of cricket all the eternal Englishness which has gone to the establishment of that Constitution and the laws aforesaid.
Cricket (1930)

Richard Carew 1555–1620

English poet

4 Will you have all in all for prose and verse? Take the miracle of our age, Sir Philip Sidney.
William Camden *Remains concerning Britain* (1614) 'The Excellency of the English Tongue'

Thomas Carew *c.*1595–1640

English poet and courtier

5 He that loves a rosy cheek,
Or a coral lip admires,
Or, from star-like eyes, doth seek
Fuel to maintain his fires;
As old Time makes these decay,
So his flames must waste away.
'Disdain Returned' (1640)

6 The Muses' garden with pedantic weeds
O'erspread, was purged by thee; the lazy seeds
Of servile imitation thrown away,
And fresh invention planted.
'An Elegy upon the Death of Dr John Donne' (1640)

7 Here lies a king, that ruled as he thought fit
The universal monarchy of wit.
'An Elegy upon the Death of Dr John Donne' (1640)

8 The purest soul that e'er was sent
Into a clayey tenement.
'Epitaph On the Lady Mary Villiers' (1640)

9 Good to the poor, to kindred dear,
To servants kind, to friendship clear,
To nothing but herself severe.
'Inscription on the Tomb of Lady Mary Wentworth' (1640)

10 So though a virgin, yet a bride
To every Grace, she justified
A chaste polygamy, and died.
'Inscription on the Tomb of Lady Mary Wentworth' (1640)

11 Give me more love or more disdain;
The torrid or the frozen zone:
Bring equal ease unto my pain;
The temperate affords me none.
'Mediocrity in Love Rejected' (1640)

12 Though a stranger to this place,
Bewail in theirs thine own hard case:
For thou perhaps at thy return
Mayst find thy darling in an urn.
'On the Lady Mary Villiers' (1640)

13 Ask me no more where Jove bestows,
When June is past, the fading rose;
For in your beauty's orient deep
These flowers, as in their causes, sleep.
'A Song' (1640)

14 Ask me no more whither doth haste
The nightingale when May is past;
For in your sweet dividing throat
She winters and keeps warm her note.
'A Song' (1640)

15 Ask me no more if east or west
The Phoenix builds her spicy nest;
For unto you at last she flies,
And in your fragrant bosom dies.
'A Song' (1640)

16 When thou, poor excommunicate
From all the joys of love, shalt see
The full reward and glorious fate
Which my strong faith shall purchase me,
Then curse thine own inconstancy.
'To My Inconstant Mistress' (1640)

George Carey 1935–

Archbishop of Canterbury from 1991

17 I see it as an elderly lady, who mutters away to herself in a corner, ignored most of the time.
on the Church of England
in *Readers Digest* (British ed.) March 1991

18 We must recall that the Church is always 'one generation away from extinction.'
Working Party Report *Youth A Part: Young People and the Church* (1996) foreword

Henry Carey *c.*1687–1743

English comic dramatist and songwriter
see also **Songs** *729:7*

19 Let your little verses flow
Gently, sweetly, row by row;
Let the verse the subject fit,
Little subject, little wit.
'Namby-Pamby: or, A Panegyric on the New Versification' (1725)

20 As an actor does his part,
So the nurses get by heart
Namby-pamby's little rhymes,
Little jingle, little chimes.
'Namby-Pamby' (1725)

21 Of all the girls that are so smart
There's none like pretty Sally,
She is the darling of my heart,

And she lives in our alley.
'Sally in our Alley' (1729)

Jane Carlyle (née Welsh) 1801–66

wife of Thomas Carlyle
on Carlyle: see **Butler** *172:22*

1 I am not at all the sort of person you and I took me for.
letter to Thomas Carlyle, 7 May 1822, in C. R. Sanders et al. (eds.) *Collected Letters of Thomas and Jane Welsh Carlyle* (1970) vol. 2

Thomas Carlyle 1795–1881

Scottish historian and political philosopher
on Carlyle: see **Butler** *172:22,* **Clough** *223:5*

2 A witty statesman said, you might prove anything by figures.
Chartism (1839) ch. 2

3 Surely of all 'rights of man', this right of the ignorant man to be guided by the wiser, to be, gently or forcibly, held in the true course by him, is the indisputablest.
Chartism (1839) ch. 6

4 In epochs when cash payment has become the sole nexus of man to man.
Chartism (1839) ch. 6

5 The 'golden-calf of self-love.'
Critical and Miscellaneous Essays (1838) 'Burns'

6 The foul sluggard's comfort: 'It will last my time.'
Critical and Miscellaneous Essays (1838) 'Count Cagliostro. Flight Last'

7 Thou wretched fraction, wilt thou be the ninth part even of a tailor?
Critical and Miscellaneous Essays (1838) 'Francia'; cf. **Proverbs** 607:44

8 What is all knowledge too but recorded experience, and a product of history; of which, therefore, reasoning and belief, no less than action and passion, are essential materials?
Critical and Miscellaneous Essays (1838) 'On History'

9 History is the essence of innumerable biographies.
Critical and Miscellaneous Essays (1838) 'On History'

10 A well-written Life is almost as rare as a well-spent one.
Critical and Miscellaneous Essays (1838) 'Jean Paul Friedrich Richter'

11 There is no life of a man, faithfully recorded, but is a heroic poem of its sort, rhymed or unrhymed.
Critical and Miscellaneous Essays (1838) 'Sir Walter Scott'

12 Under all speech that is good for anything there lies a silence that is better. Silence is deep as Eternity; speech is shallow as Time.
Critical and Miscellaneous Essays (1838) 'Sir Walter Scott'

13 To the very last he [Napoleon] had a kind of idea; that, namely, of *La carrière ouverte aux talents*, The tools to him that can handle them.
Critical and Miscellaneous Essays (1838) 'Sir Walter Scott' (*La carrière . . .* Career open to the talents)

14 It can be said of him, when he departed, he took a man's life along with him.
Critical and Miscellaneous Essays (1838) 'Sir Walter Scott'

15 This idle habit of 'accounting for the moral sense' . . . The moral sense, thank God, is a thing you will never 'account for' . . . By no greatest happiness principle, greatest nobleness principle, or any principle whatever, will you make that in the least clearer than it already is.
Critical and Miscellaneous Essays (1838) 'Shooting Niagara: and After?'

16 It is the Age of Machinery, in every outward and inward sense of that word.
Critical and Miscellaneous Essays (1838) 'Signs of the Times'

17 The Bible-Society . . . is found, on inquiry, to be . . . a machine for converting the Heathen.
Critical and Miscellaneous Essays (1838) 'Signs of the Times'

18 Thought, he [Dr Cabanis] is inclined to hold, is still secreted by the brain; but then Poetry and Religion (and it is really worth knowing) are 'a product of the smaller intestines'!
Critical and Miscellaneous Essays (1838) 'Signs of the Times'

19 The three great elements of modern civilization, Gunpowder, Printing, and the Protestant Religion.
Critical and Miscellaneous Essays (1838) 'The State of German Literature'; cf. **Bacon** 45:4

20 'Genius' (which means transcendent capacity of taking trouble, first of all).
History of Frederick the Great (1858–65) bk. 4, ch. 3; cf. **Buffon** 159:20, **Proverbs** 601:3

21 A whiff of grapeshot.
History of the French Revolution (1837) vol. 1, bk. 5, ch. 3

22 History a distillation of rumour.
History of the French Revolution (1837) vol. 1, bk. 7, ch. 5

23 The difference between Orthodoxy or My-doxy and Heterodoxy or Thy-doxy.
History of the French Revolution (1837) vol. 2, bk. 4, ch. 2; cf. **Warburton** 803:4

24 The seagreen Incorruptible.
describing ***Robespierre***
History of the French Revolution (1837) vol. 2, bk. 4, ch. 4

25 France was long a despotism tempered by epigrams.
History of the French Revolution (1837) vol. 3, bk. 7, ch. 7

26 Aristocracy of the Moneybag.
History of the French Revolution (1837) vol. 3, bk. 7, ch. 7

27 Worship is transcendent wonder.
On Heroes, Hero-Worship, and the Heroic (1841) 'The Hero as Divinity'

28 I hope we English will long maintain our *grand talent pour le silence.*
On Heroes, Hero-Worship, and the Heroic (1841) 'The Hero as King'

29 In books lies the *soul* of the whole Past Time; the articulate audible voice of the Past, when the body and material substance of it has altogether vanished like a dream.
On Heroes, Hero-Worship, and the Heroic (1841) 'The Hero as Man of Letters'

1 The true University of these days is a collection of books.
On Heroes, Hero-Worship, and the Heroic (1841) 'The Hero as Man of Letters'

2 Adversity is sometimes hard upon a man; but for one man who can stand prosperity, there are a hundred that will stand adversity.
On Heroes, Hero-Worship, and the Heroic (1841) 'The Hero as Man of Letters'

3 Maid-servants, I hear people complaining, are getting instructed in the 'ologies'.
Inaugural Address at Edinburgh, 2 April 1866, on being installed as Rector of the University

4 A Parliament speaking through reporters to Buncombe and the twenty-seven millions mostly fools.
Latter-Day Pamphlets (1850) 'Parliaments'; cf. **Walker** 799:12

5 The Dismal Science.
on political economy
Latter-Day Pamphlets (1850) 'The Present Time'

6 Little other than a redtape talking-machine, and unhappy bag of parliamentary eloquence.
describing himself
Latter-Day Pamphlets (1850) 'The Present Time'

7 Transcendental moonshine.
on the influence of a romantic imagination in motivating Sterling to enter the priesthood
The Life of John Sterling (1851) pt. 1, ch. 15

8 Captains of industry.
Past and Present (1843) bk. 4, ch. 4 (title)

9 He who first shortened the labour of copyists by device of *Movable Types* was disbanding hired armies, and cashiering most Kings and Senates, and creating a whole new democratic world: he had invented the art of printing.
Sartor Resartus (1834) bk. 1, ch. 5

10 Man is a tool-using animal . . . Without tools he is nothing, with tools he is all.
Sartor Resartus (1834) bk. 1, ch. 5

11 Whoso has sixpence is sovereign (to the length of sixpence) over all men; commands cooks to feed him, philosophers to teach him, kings to mount guard over him,—to the length of sixpence.
Sartor Resartus (1834) bk. 1, ch. 5

12 Language is called the garment of thought: however, it should rather be, language is the flesh-garment, the body, of thought.
Sartor Resartus (1834) bk. 1, ch. 11

13 The end of man is an action and not a thought, though it were the noblest.
Sartor Resartus (1834) bk. 2, ch. 6

14 The everlasting No.
Sartor Resartus (1834) bk. 2, ch. 7 (title)

15 Be no longer a chaos, but a world, or even worldkin. Produce! Produce! Were it but the pitifullest infinitesimal fraction of a product, produce it in God's name! 'Tis the utmost thou hast in thee: out with it, then.
Sartor Resartus (1834) bk. 2, ch. 9

16 Does it not stand on record that the English Queen Elizabeth, receiving a deputation of eighteen tailors, address them with a 'Good morning, gentlemen both!'
Sartor Resartus (1834) bk. 3, ch. 11, quoting an imaginary work by Diogenes Teufelsdröctch; cf. **Proverbs** 607:44

17 What a sad want I am in of libraries, of books to gather facts from! Why is there not a Majesty's library in every county town? There is a Majesty's jail and gallows in every one.
diary, 18 May 1832

18 A good book is the purest essence of a human soul.
speech in support of the London Library, 24 June 1840, in F. Harrison *Carlyle and the London Library* (1907)

19 'Gad! she'd better!'
on hearing that Margaret Fuller 'accept[ed] *the universe'*
William James *Varieties of Religious Experience* (1902) lecture 2

20 Macaulay is well for a while, but one wouldn't *live* under Niagara.
R. M. Milnes *Notebook* (1838)

21 Cobden is an inspired bagman, who believes in a calico millennium.
T. W. Reid *Life, Letters and Friendships of Richard Monckton* (1890) vol. 1, ch. 10

22 If Jesus Christ were to come to-day, people would not even crucify him. They would ask him to dinner, and hear what he had to say, and make fun of it.
D. A. Wilson *Carlyle at his Zenith* (1927)

Stokely Carmichael 1941–98
American Black Power leader

23 The only position for women in SNCC is prone.
response to a question about the position of women
at a Student Nonviolent Coordinating Committee conference, November 1964

Stokely Carmichael 1941–98 and **Charles Vernon Hamilton** 1929–
American Black Power leaders

24 The adoption of the concept of Black Power is one of the most legitimate and healthy developments in American politics and race relations in our time. . . . It is a call for black people in this country to unite, to recognize their heritage, to build a sense of community. It is a call for black people to begin to define their own goals, to lead their own organizations and to support those organizations. It is a call to reject the racist institutions and values of this society.
Black Power (1967)

Andrew Carnegie 1835–1919
American industrialist and philanthropist
see also **Proverbs** *600:48*

25 The man who dies . . . rich dies disgraced.
North American Review June 1889 'Wealth'

Dale Carnegie 1888–1955
American writer and lecturer

1 How to win friends and influence people.
title of book (1936)

Julia A. Carney 1823–1908

2 Little drops of water,
Little grains of sand,
Make the mighty ocean
And the beauteous land.
'Little Things' (1845)

Caroline of Ansbach 1683–1737
Queen of Great Britain and Ireland from 1727, wife of **George II**
see also **George II** *333:11*

3 My dear firstborn is the greatest ass, and the greatest liar, and the greatest *canaille*, and the greatest beast in the whole world, and I heartily wish he was out of it.
of her eldest son, Frederick, Prince of Wales, father of **George III**
in *Dictionary of National Biography* (1917–)

Joseph Edwards Carpenter 1813–85
English poet and songwriter

4 What are the wild waves saying
Sister, the whole day long,
That ever amid our playing,
I hear but their low lone song?
'What are the Wild Waves Saying?' (1850 song)

Emily Carr 1871–1945
Canadian artist

5 You come into the world alone and you go out of the world alone yet it seems to me you are more alone while living than even going and coming.
Hundreds and Thousands: The Journals of Emily Carr (1966) 16 July 1933

J. L. Carr 1912–
English novelist

6 *You* have not had thirty years' experience . . . *You* have had one year's experience 30 times.
The Harpole Report (1972)

Lewis Carroll (Charles Lutwidge Dodgson) 1832–98
English writer and logician

7 'What is the use of a book', thought Alice, 'without pictures or conversations?'
Alice's Adventures in Wonderland (1865) ch. 1

8 'Curiouser and curiouser!' cried Alice.
Alice's Adventures in Wonderland (1865) ch. 2

9 How doth the little crocodile
Improve his shining tail,
And pour the waters of the Nile
On every golden scale!
Alice's Adventures in Wonderland (1865) ch. 2; cf. **Watts** 805:5

10 How cheerfully he seems to grin,
How neatly spreads his claws,
And welcomes little fishes in
With gently smiling jaws!
Alice's Adventures in Wonderland (1865) ch. 2

11 'I'll be judge, I'll be jury,' said cunning old Fury;
'I'll try the whole cause, and condemn you to death.'
Alice's Adventures in Wonderland (1865) ch. 3

12 'You are old, Father William,' the young man said,
'And your hair has become very white;
And yet you incessantly stand on your head—
Do you think, at your age, it is right?'
Alice's Adventures in Wonderland (1865) ch. 5; cf. **Southey** 730:21

13 'I have answered three questions, and that is enough,'
Said his father; 'don't give yourself airs!
Do you think I can listen all day to such stuff?
Be off, or I'll kick you downstairs!'
Alice's Adventures in Wonderland (1865) ch. 5; cf. **Bickerstaffe** 114:13

14 'If everybody minded their own business,' said the Duchess in a hoarse growl, 'the world would go round a good deal faster than it does.'
Alice's Adventures in Wonderland (1865) ch. 6

15 Speak roughly to your little boy,
And beat him when he sneezes;
He only does it to annoy,
Because he knows it teases.
Alice's Adventures in Wonderland (1865) ch. 6

16 This time it vanished quite slowly, beginning with the end of the tail, and ending with the grin, which remained some time after the rest of it had gone.
the Cheshire Cat
Alice's Adventures in Wonderland (1865) ch. 6

17 'Then you should say what you mean,' the March Hare went on. 'I do,' Alice hastily replied; 'at least—at least I mean what I say—that's the same thing, you know.' 'Not the same thing a bit!' said the Hatter. 'Why, you might just as well say that "I see what I eat" is the same thing as "I eat what I see!" '
Alice's Adventures in Wonderland (1865) ch. 7

18 Twinkle, twinkle, little bat!
How I wonder what you're at!
Up above the world you fly!
Like a teatray in the sky.
Alice's Adventures in Wonderland (1865) ch. 7; cf. **Taylor** 756:13

19 'Take some more tea,' the March Hare said to Alice, very earnestly. 'I've had nothing yet,' Alice replied in an offended tone, 'so I can't take more.' 'You mean you can't take *less*,' said the Hatter: 'it's very easy to take *more* than nothing.'
Alice's Adventures in Wonderland (1865) ch. 7

20 Off with her head!
the Queen of Hearts
Alice's Adventures in Wonderland (1865) ch. 8

21 Everything's got a moral, if you can only find it.
Alice's Adventures in Wonderland (1865) ch. 9

1 Take care of the sense, and the sounds will take care of themselves.
Alice's Adventures in Wonderland (1865) ch. 9; cf. **Proverbs** 611:38

2 'That's nothing to what I could say if I chose,' the Duchess replied.
Alice's Adventures in Wonderland (1865) ch. 9

3 'That's the reason they're called lessons,' the Gryphon remarked: 'because they lessen from day to day.'
Alice's Adventures in Wonderland (1865) ch. 9

4 'Will you walk a little faster?' said a whiting to a snail,
'There's a porpoise close behind us, and he's treading on my tail.'
Alice's Adventures in Wonderland (1865) ch. 10

5 Will you, won't you, will you, won't you, will you join the dance?
Alice's Adventures in Wonderland (1865) ch. 10

6 'Tis the voice of the Lobster: I heard him declare
'You have baked me too brown, I must sugar my hair.'
Alice's Adventures in Wonderland (1865) ch. 10; cf. **Watts** 805:11

7 Soup of the evening, beautiful Soup!
Alice's Adventures in Wonderland (1865) ch. 10

8 'Where shall I begin, please your Majesty?' he asked. 'Begin at the beginning,' the King said, gravely, 'and go on till you come to the end: then stop.'
Alice's Adventures in Wonderland (1865) ch. 12

9 'That's not a regular rule: you invented it just now.'
'It's the oldest rule in the book,' said the King.
'Then it ought to be Number One,' said Alice.
Alice's Adventures in Wonderland (1865) ch. 12

10 No! No! Sentence first—verdict afterwards.
Alice's Adventures in Wonderland (1865) ch. 12

11 What a comfort a Dictionary is!
Sylvie and Bruno Concluded (1893)

12 'Twas brillig, and the slithy toves
Did gyre and gimble in the wabe;
All mimsy were the borogoves,
And the mome raths outgrabe.

'Beware the Jabberwock, my son!
The jaws that bite, the claws that catch!'
Through the Looking-Glass (1872) ch. 1

13 And as in uffish thought he stood,
The Jabberwock, with eyes of flame,
Came whiffling through the tulgey wood,
And burbled as it came!

One, two! One, two! And through and through
The vorpal blade went snicker-snack!
He left it dead, and with its head
He went galumphing back.

'And hast thou slain the Jabberwock?
Come to my arms, my beamish boy!
O frabjous day! Callooh! Callay!'
He chortled in his joy.
Through the Looking-Glass (1872) ch. 1

14 Curtsey while you're thinking what to say. It saves time.
Through the Looking-Glass (1872) ch. 2

15 Now, *here*, you see, it takes all the running *you* can do, to keep in the same place. If you want to get somewhere else, you must run at least twice as fast as that!
Through the Looking-Glass (1872) ch. 2

16 Speak in French when you can't think of the English for a thing.
Through the Looking-Glass (1872) ch. 2

17 If you think we're wax-works, you ought to pay, you know. Wax-works weren't made to be looked at for nothing. Nohow!
Through the Looking-Glass (1872) ch. 4

18 'Contrariwise,' continued Tweedledee, 'if it was so, it might be; and if it were so, it would be: but as it isn't, it ain't. That's logic.'
Through the Looking-Glass (1872) ch. 4

19 The Walrus and the Carpenter
Were walking close at hand;
They wept like anything to see
Such quantities of sand:
'If this were only cleared away,'
They said, 'it would be grand!'

'If seven maids with seven mops
Swept it for half a year,
Do you suppose,' the Walrus said,
'That they could get it clear?'
'I doubt it,' said the Carpenter,
And shed a bitter tear.
Through the Looking-Glass (1872) ch. 4

20 'The time has come,' the Walrus said,
'To talk of many things:
Of shoes—and ships—and sealing wax—
Of cabbages—and kings—
And why the sea is boiling hot—
And whether pigs have wings.'
Through the Looking-Glass (1872) ch. 4

21 But answer came there none—
And this was scarcely odd because
They'd eaten every one.
Through the Looking-Glass (1872) ch. 4; cf. **Scott** 650:10

22 'You know,' he said very gravely, 'it's one of the most serious things that can possibly happen to one in a battle—to get one's head cut off.'
Through the Looking-Glass (1872) ch. 4

23 The rule is, jam to-morrow and jam yesterday—but never jam today.
Through the Looking-Glass (1872) ch. 5; cf. **Benn** 65:5

24 'It's a poor sort of memory that only works backwards,' the Queen remarked.
Through the Looking-Glass (1872) ch. 5

25 Why, sometimes I've believed as many as six impossible things before breakfast.
Through the Looking-Glass (1872) ch. 5

26 With a name like yours, you might be any shape, almost.
Through the Looking-Glass (1872) ch. 6

1 They gave it me,—for an un-birthday present.
Through the Looking-Glass (1872) ch. 6

2 'There's glory for you!' 'I don't know what you mean by "glory",' Alice said. 'I meant, "there's a nice knock-down argument for you!" ' 'But "glory" doesn't mean "a nice knock-down argument",' Alice objected. 'When *I* use a word,' Humpty Dumpty said in a rather scornful tone, 'it means just what I choose it to mean—neither more nor less.'
Through the Looking-Glass (1872) ch. 6

3 'The question is,' said Humpty Dumpty, 'which is to be master—that's all.'
Through the Looking-Glass (1872) ch. 6; cf. **Shawcross** 709:27

4 You see it's like a portmanteau—there are two meanings packed up into one word
Through the Looking-Glass (1872) ch. 6

5 '*I* can repeat poetry as well as other folk if it comes to that—' 'Oh, it needn't come to that!' Alice hastily said.
Through the Looking-Glass (1872) ch. 6

6 The little fishes of the sea,
They sent an answer back to me.
The little fishes' answer was
'We cannot do it, Sir, because—'
Through the Looking-Glass (1872) ch. 6

7 He's an Anglo-Saxon Messenger—and those are Anglo-Saxon attitudes.
Through the Looking-Glass (1872) ch. 7

8 The other Messenger's called Hatta. I must have *two* you know—to come and go. One to come, and one to go.
Through the Looking-Glass (1872) ch. 7

9 'There's nothing like eating hay when you're faint' . . . 'I didn't say there was nothing *better*,' the King replied, 'I said there was nothing *like* it.'
Through the Looking-Glass (1872) ch. 7

10 'I'm sure nobody walks much faster than I do!' 'He can't do that,' said the King, 'or else he'd have been here first.'
Through the Looking-Glass (1872) ch. 7

11 It's as large as life, and twice as natural!
Through the Looking-Glass (1872) ch. 7

12 It's my own invention.
the White Knight
Through the Looking-Glass (1872) ch. 8

13 I'll tell thee everything I can:
There's little to relate.
I saw an aged, aged man,
A-sitting on a gate.
Through the Looking-Glass (1872) ch. 8

14 He said, 'I look for butterflies
That sleep among the wheat:
I make them into mutton-pies,
And sell them in the street.'
Through the Looking-Glass (1872) ch. 8

15 Or madly squeeze a right-hand foot
Into a left-hand shoe.
Through the Looking-Glass (1872) ch. 8

16 No admittance till the week after next!
Through the Looking-Glass (1872) ch. 9

17 It isn't etiquette to cut any one you've been introduced to. Remove the joint.
Through the Looking-Glass (1872) ch. 9

18 Un-dish-cover the fish, or dishcover the riddle.
Through the Looking-Glass (1872) ch. 9

19 What I tell you three times is true.
The Hunting of the Snark (1876) 'Fit the First: The Landing'

20 He would answer to 'Hi!' or to any loud cry,
Such as 'Fry me!' or 'Fritter-my-wig!'
The Hunting of the Snark (1876) 'Fit the First: The Landing'

21 His intimate friends called him 'Candle-ends',
And his enemies, 'Toasted-cheese'.
The Hunting of the Snark (1876) 'Fit the First: The Landing'

22 'What's the good of *Mercator's* North Poles and Equators,
Tropics, Zones and Meridian lines?'
So the Bellman would cry: and the crew would reply,
'They are merely conventional signs!'
The Hunting of the Snark (1876) 'Fit the Second: The Bellman's Speech'

23 But the principal failing occurred in the sailing,
And the Bellman, perplexed and distressed,
Said he *had* hoped, at least, when the wind blew due East,
That the ship would *not* travel due West!
The Hunting of the Snark (1876) 'Fit the Second: The Bellman's Speech'

24 But oh, beamish nephew, beware of the day,
If your Snark be a Boojum! For then
You will softly and suddenly vanish away,
And never be met with again!
The Hunting of the Snark (1876) 'Fit the Third: The Baker's Tale'

25 They sought it with thimbles, they sought it with care;
They pursued it with forks and hope;
They threatened its life with a railway-share;
They charmed it with smiles and soap.
The Hunting of the Snark (1876) 'Fit the Fifth: The Beaver's Lesson'

26 For the Snark *was* a Boojum, you see.
The Hunting of the Snark (1876) 'Fit the Eighth: The Vanishing'

27 I never loved a dear Gazelle—
Nor anything that cost me much:
High prices profit those who sell,
But why should I be fond of such?
Phantasmagoria (1869) 'Theme with Variations'; cf. **Moore** 530:18

28 He thought he saw an Elephant,
That practised on a fife:
He looked again, and found it was
A letter from his wife.
'At length I realize,' he said,

'The bitterness of life!'
Sylvie and Bruno (1889) ch. 5

1 He thought he saw a Rattlesnake
That questioned him in Greek,
He looked again and found it was
The Middle of Next Week.
'The one thing I regret,' he said,
'Is that it cannot speak!'
Sylvie and Bruno (1889) ch. 6

William Herbert Carruth 1859–1924

2 Some call it evolution,
And others call it God.
'Each In His Own Tongue' (1908)

Edward Carson 1854–1935

British lawyer and politician

3 I now enter into compact with you, and with the help of God you and I joined together . . . will yet defeat the most nefarious conspiracy that has ever been hatched against a free people . . . We must be prepared . . . the morning Home Rule passes, ourselves to become responsible for the government of the Protestant Province of Ulster.
speech at Craigavon, 23 September 1911

4 My one affection left me is my love for Ireland.
after the death of his wife in 1913
Montgomery Hyde *Carson* (1953)

5 From the day I first entered parliament up to the present, devotion to the union has been the guiding star of my political life.
in *Dictionary of National Biography* (1917–)

6 My only great qualification for being put at the head of the Navy is that I am very much at sea.
Ian Colvin *Life of Lord Carson* (1936) vol. 3, ch. 23

Rachel Carson 1907–64

American zoologist

7 Over increasingly large areas of the United States, spring now comes unheralded by the return of the birds, and the early mornings are strangely silent where once they were filled with the beauty of bird song.
The Silent Spring (1962)

Angela Carter 1940–92

English novelist

8 Clothes are our weapons, our challenges, our visible insults.
Nothing Sacred (1982) 'Notes for a Theory of Sixties Style'

9 Comedy is tragedy that happens to *other* people.
Wise Children (1991) ch. 4

10 If *Miss* means respectably unmarried, and *Mrs* respectably married, then *Ms* means nudge, nudge, wink, wink.
'The Language of Sisterhood' in Christopher Ricks (ed.) *The State of the Language* (1980); cf. **Monty Python's Flying Circus** 529:5

Henry Carter d. 1806

11 True patriots we; for be it understood,
We left our country for our country's good . . .
And none will doubt but that our emigration
Has proved most useful to the British nation.
prologue, written for, but not recited at, the opening of the Playhouse, Sydney, New South Wales, 16 January 1796, when the actors were principally convicts
A. W. Jose and H. J. Carter (eds.) *The Australian Encyclopaedia* (1927); previously attributed to George Barrington (b. 1755); cf. **Fitzgeffrey** 314:6

Howard Carter 1874–1939

English archaeologist

12 Yes, wonderful things.
when asked what he could see on first looking into the tomb of Tutankhamun, 26 November 1922; his notebook records the words as 'Yes, it is wonderful'
The Tomb of Tut-ankh-amen (1933)

James Earl 'Jimmy' Carter 1924–

American Democratic statesman, 39th President of the US, 1977–81

13 I'm Jimmy Carter, and I'm going to be your next president.
I'll Never Lie to You (1976)

14 I've looked on a lot of women with lust. I've committed adultery in my heart many times. This is something that God recognizes I will do—and I have done it—and God forgives me for it.
in *Playboy* November 1976

Sydney Carter 1915–

English folk-song writer

15 It's God they ought to crucify
Instead of you and me,
I said to the carpenter
A-hanging on the tree.
'Friday Morning' (1967)

16 I danced in the morning
When the world was begun
And I danced in the moon
And the stars and the sun
And I came down from heaven
And I danced on the earth—
At Bethlehem I had my birth.
Dance then wherever you may be,
I am the Lord of the Dance, said he,
And I'll lead you all, wherever you may be
And I'll lead you all in the dance, said he.
'Lord of the Dance' (1967)

17 One more step along the world I go.
'One More Step'

Jacques Cartier 1491–1557

French navigator and explorer

18 *J'estime mieux que autrement, que c'est la terre que Dieu donne à Caïn.*

I am rather inclined to believe that this is the land God gave to Cain.
on discovering the northern shore of the Gulf of St Lawrence (now Labrador and Quebec) in 1534; after the murder of Abel, Cain was exiled to the desolate land of Nod (cf. **Bible** *74:12)*
La Première Relation; H. P. Biggar (ed.) *The Voyages of Jacques Cartier* (1924)

Henri Cartier-Bresson 1908–
French photographer and artist

1 To me, photography is the simultaneous recognition, in a fraction of a second, of the significance of an event as well as of a precise organisation of forms which give that event its proper expression.
The Decisive Moment (1952)

Barbara Cartland 1901–
English writer

2 After forty a woman has to choose between losing her figure or her face. My advice is to keep your face, and stay sitting down.
Libby Purves 'Luncheon à la Cartland'; in *The Times* 6 October 1993; similar remarks have been attributed since *c.*1980

3 I was shown round Tutankhamun's tomb in the 1920s. I saw all this wonderful pink on the walls and the artefacts. I was so impressed that I vowed to wear it for the rest of my life.
in *Irish Times* 28 March 1998 'This Week They Said'

John Cartwright 1740–1824
English political reformer

4 One man shall have one vote.
The People's Barrier Against Undue Influence (1780) ch. 1 'Principles, maxims, and primary rules of politics' no. 68

Elizabeth Tanfield Cary 1585–1639
English woman of letters, poet, and dramatist

5 I know I could enchain him with a smile:
And lead him captive with a gentle word,
I scorn my look should ever man beguile,
Or other speech, than meaning to afford.
The Tragedy of Mariam (1613)

Joyce Cary 1888–1957
Irish novelist and short-story writer

6 Sara could commit adultery at one end and weep for her sins at the other, and enjoy both operations at once.
The Horse's Mouth (1944)

Roger Casement 1864–1916
Irish nationalist; executed for treason in 1916
on Casement: see **Yeats** *836:4*

7 Self-government is our right, a thing born in us at birth, a thing no more to be doled out to us, or withheld from us, by another people than the right to life itself—than the right to feel the sun, or smell the flowers, or to love our kind.
statement at the conclusion of his trial, the Old Bailey, London, 29 June 1916

8 Where all your rights become only an accumulated wrong; where men must beg with bated breath for leave to subsist in their own land, to think their own thoughts, to sing their own songs, to garner the fruits of their own labours . . . then surely it is a braver, a saner and truer thing, to be a rebel in act and deed against such circumstances as these than tamely to accept it as the natural lot of men.
statement at the conclusion of his trial, the Old Bailey, London, 29 June 1916

A. M. Cassandre 1901–68
French illustrator

9 A good poster is a visual telegram.
attributed

Mary Cassatt 1844–1926
American artist

10 Why do people so love to wander? I think the civilized parts of the world will suffice for me in the future.
letter to Louisine Havemeyer, 11 February 1911

Hugh Casson 1910–
English architect

11 We have now to plan no longer for soft little animals pottering about on their own two legs, but for hard steel canisters hurtling about with these same little animals inside them.
C. Williams-Ellis *Around the World in 90 Years* (1978)

Barbara Castle 1910–
British Labour politician

12 I will fight for what I believe in until I drop dead. And that's what keeps you alive.
in *Guardian* 14 January 1998

Ted Castle 1907–79
British journalist

13 In place of strife.
title of Government White Paper, 17 January 1969, suggested by Castle to his wife, Barbara **Castle**, *then Secretary of State for Employment*
Barbara Castle, diary, 15 January 1969

Fidel Castro 1927–
Cuban statesman, Prime Minister 1959–76 and President since 1976

14 *La historia me absolverá.*
History will absolve me.
title of pamphlet (1953)

15 Capitalism is using its money; we socialists throw it away.
in *Observer* 8 November 1964 'Sayings of the Week'

Edward Caswall 1814–78
English hymn-writer

1 Jesu, the very thought of Thee
With sweetness fills the breast.
translation of 'Jesu dulcis memoria, dans vera cordis gaudia', *usually attributed to St* **Bernard**
'Jesu, the very thought of thee' (1849 hymn)

2 My God, I love Thee; not because
I hope for heaven thereby.
'My God, I Love Thee' (1849 hymn); translation of '*O deus ego amo te, nec amo te ut salves me*'; usually attributed to St Francis Xavier (1506–52)

3 See, amid the winter's snow,
Born for us on earth below,
See, the Lamb of God appears,
Promised from eternal years!
Hail, thou ever-blessèd morn!
Hail, redemption's happy dawn!
Sing through all Jerusalem:
Christ is born in Bethlehem!
'See, amid the winter's snow' (1858 hymn)

4 When morning gilds the skies.
Title of hymn (1854)

□ Catchphrases
see box opposite
see also **Laurel** *454:8*

A Catechism of Christian Doctrine 1898
Popularly known as the 'Penny Catechism'

5 Who made you? God made me.
Why did God make you? God made me to know Him, love him, and serve Him in this world, and to be happy with Him for ever in the next.
ch. 1

Willa Cather 1873–1947
American novelist

6 Oh, the Germans classify, but the French arrange!
Death Comes For the Archbishop (1927)

7 Men travel faster now, but I do not know if they go to better things.
Death Comes for the Archbishop (1927)

8 That is happiness: to be dissolved into something complete and great.
on her gravestone in Jaffrey, New Hampshire
My Ántonia (1918)

9 Winter lies too long in country towns; hangs on until it is stale and shabby, old and sullen.
My Ántonia (1918)

10 I like trees because they seem more resigned to the way they have to live than other things do.
O Pioneers! (1913)

11 I tell you there is such a thing as creative hate!
The Song of the Lark (1915)

Catherine the Great 1729–96
Empress of Russia from 1762

12 *Moi, je serai autocrate: c'est mon métier. Et le bon Dieu me pardonnera: c'est son métier.*
I shall be an autocrat: that's my trade. And the good Lord will forgive me: that's his.
attributed; cf. **Last words** 455:9

Cato the Elder (or 'the Censor') 234–149 BC
Roman statesman, orator, and writer

13 *Delenda est Carthago.*
Carthage must be destroyed.
words concluding every speech Cato made in the Senate
Pliny the Elder *Naturalis Historia* bk. 15, ch. 74

14 A farm is like a man—however great the income, if there is extravagance but little is left.
On Agriculture bk 2, sect. 6

15 Even though work stops, expenses run on.
On Agriculture bk 39, sect. 2

16 *Rem tene; verba sequentur.*
Grasp the subject, the words will follow.
Caius Julius Victor *Ars Rhetorica* 'De inventione'

Carrie Chapman Catt 1859–1947
American feminist

17 No written law has ever been more binding than unwritten custom supported by popular opinion.
speech at Senate hearing on woman's suffrage, 13 February 1900
Why We Ask for the Submission of an Amendment (1900)

18 When a just cause reaches its flood-tide . . . whatever stands in the way must fall before its overwhelming power.
speech at Stockholm, *Is Woman Suffrage Progressing?* (1911)

Catullus c.84–c.54 BC
Roman poet
on Catullus: see **Tennyson** *758:20*

19 *Cui dono lepidum novum libellum*
Arido modo pumice expolitum?
To whom shall I give my nice new little book polished dry with pumice?
Carmina no. 1

20 *Namque tu solebas*
Meas esse aliquid putare nugas.
For you used to think my trifles were worth something.
Carmina no. 1

21 *Plus uno maneat perenne saeclo.*
May it live and last for more than a century.
Carmina no. 1

22 *Lugete, O Veneres Cupidinesque,*
Et quantum est hominum venustiorum.
Passer mortuus est meae puellae,
Passer, deliciae meae puellae.
Mourn, you powers of Charm and Desire, and all you who are endowed with charm. My lady's

continued

Catchphrases

1 CECIL: After you, Claude.
CLAUDE: No, after you, Cecil.
ITMA (BBC radio programme, 1939–49), written by Ted Kavanagh (1892–1958)

2 And now for something completely different.
Monty Python's Flying Circus (BBC TV programme, 1969–74)

3 Anyone for tennis?
said to be typical of drawing-room comedies, much associated with Humphrey Bogart (1899–1957); perhaps from George Bernard Shaw 'Anybody on for a game of tennis?' *Misalliance* (1914)

4 Are you sitting comfortably? Then I'll begin.
sometimes 'Then we'll begin'
Listen with Mother (BBC radio programme for children, 1950–82), used by Julia Lang (1921–)

5 The butler did it!
a solution for detective stories
Nigel Rees, in *Sayings of the Century* (1984), quotes a correspondent who recalls hearing it at a cinema *c.*1916 but the origin of the phrase has not been traced

6 Can I do you now, sir?
spoken by 'Mrs Mopp'
ITMA (BBC radio programme, 1939–49), written by Ted Kavanagh (1892–1958)

7 Can you hear me, mother?
used by Sandy Powell (1900–82)

8 The day war broke out.
customary preamble to radio monologues in the role of a Home Guard
used by Robb Wilton (1881–1957) from *c.*1940

9 Didn't she [*or* he *or* they] do well?
used by Bruce Forsyth (1928–) in 'The Generation Game' on BBC Television, 1973 onwards

10 Don't forget the diver.
spoken by 'The Diver'; based on 'a memory of the pier at New Brighton where Tommy Handley used to go as a child . . . A man in a bathing suit . . . whined "Don't forget the diver, sir."'
ITMA (BBC radio programme, 1939–49), written by Ted Kavanagh (1892–1958)

11 Eat my shorts!
The Simpsons (American TV series, 1990–), created by Matt Groening

12 Ee, it was agony, Ivy.
Ray's a Laugh (BBC radio programme, 1949–61), written by Ted Ray (1906–77)

13 Evening, all.
opening words spoken by Jack Warner as Sergeant Dixon in *Dixon of Dock Green* (BBC television series, 1956–76), written by Ted Willis (1918–)

14 Everybody wants to get inta the act!
used by Jimmy Durante (1893–1980)

15 An everyday story of country folk.
introduction to *The Archers* (BBC radio serial, 1950 onwards), written by Geoffrey Webb and Edward J. Mason

16 Give him the money, Barney.
Have a Go! (BBC radio quiz programme, 1946–67), used by Wilfred Pickles (1904–78)

17 A good idea—son.
Educating Archie, 1950–3 BBC radio comedy series, written by Eric Sykes and Max Bygraves (1922–)

18 Good morning, sir—was there something?
used by Sam Costa in radio comedy series *Much-Binding-in-the-Marsh*, written by Richard Murdoch (1907–90) and Kenneth Horne (1900–69), started 2 January 1947

19 Goodnight, children . . . everywhere.
closing words normally spoken by 'Uncle Mac' in the 1930s and 1940s
on *Children's Hour* (BBC Radio programme); written by Derek McCulloch (1892–1978)

20 Have you read any good books lately?
used by Richard Murdoch in radio comedy series *Much-Binding-in-the-Marsh*, written by Richard Murdoch (1907–90) and Kenneth Horne (1900–69), started 2 January 1947

21 Hello, good evening, and welcome.
used by David **Frost** in 'The Frost Programme' on BBC Television, 1966 onwards

22 Here come de judge.
from the song-title 'Here comes the judge' (1968); written by Dewey 'Pigmeat' Markham, Dick Alen, Bob Astor, and Sarah Harvey

23 Here's one I made earlier.
culmination to directions for making a model out of empty yoghurt pots, coat-hangers, and similar domestic items
children's BBC television programme *Blue Peter*, 1963 onwards

24 I didn't get where I am today without . . . .
used by the manager C. J. in BBC television series *The Fall and Rise of Reginald Perrin*, 1976–80); based on David Nobbs *The Death of Reginald Perrin* (1975)

25 I don't like this game, let's play another game—let's play doctor and nurses.
phrase first used by Bluebottle in 'The Phantom Head-Shaver' in *The Goon Show* (BBC radio series) 15 October 1954, written by Spike **Milligan**; the catchphrase was often 'I do not like this game'

26 I don't mind if I do.
spoken by 'Colonel Chinstrap'
ITMA (BBC radio programme, 1939–49), written by Ted Kavanagh (1892–1958)

27 I go—I come back.
spoken by 'Ali Oop'
ITMA (BBC radio programme, 1939–49), written by Ted Kavanagh (1892–1958)

28 I have a cunning plan.
Baldrick's habitual overoptimistic promise in *Blackadder II* (1987 television series), written by Richard Curtis and Ben Elton (1959–)

Catchphrases *continued*

1 I'm Bart Simpson: who the hell are you?
The Simpsons (American TV series, 1990–), created by Matt Groening

2 I'm in charge.
used by Bruce Forsyth (1928–) in 'Sunday Night at the London Palladium' on ITV, 1958 onwards

3 I'm worried about Jim.
frequent line in *Mrs Dale's Diary*, BBC radio series 1948–69

4 It all depends what you mean by . . .
habitually used by C. E. M. Joad (1891–1953) when replying to questions on 'The Brains Trust' (formerly 'Any Questions'), BBC radio (1941–8)

5 It's being so cheerful as keeps me going.
spoken by 'Mona Lott'
ITMA (BBC radio programme, 1939–49), written by Ted Kavanagh (1892–1958)

6 I've arrived and to prove it I'm here!
Educating Archie, 1950–3 BBC radio comedy series, written by Eric Sykes (1923–) and Max Bygraves (1922–)

7 I've started so I'll finish.
said when a contestant's time runs out while a question is being put
Magnus Magnusson (1929–) *Mastermind*, BBC television (1972–97)

8 Just like that!
used by Tommy Cooper (1921–84)

9 Keep on truckin'.
used by Robert Crumb (1943–) in cartoons from *c.*1972

10 Left hand down a bit!
The Navy Lark (BBC radio series, 1959–77), written by Laurie Wyman

11 Let's be careful out there.
Hill Street Blues (television series, 1981 onwards), written by Steven Bochco and Michael Kozoll

12 Meredith, we're in!
originating in a stage sketch by Fred Kitchen (1872–1950), *The Bailiff* (1907); J. P. Gallagher *Fred Karno* (1971) ch. 9

13 Mind my bike!
used by Jack Warner (1895–1981) in the BBC radio series *Garrison Theatre*, 1939 onwards

14 Nice to see you—to see you, nice.
used by Bruce Forsyth (1928–) in 'The Generation Game' on BBC Television, 1973 onwards

15 Oh, calamity!
used by Robertson Hare (1891–1979)

16 Ohhh, I don't *believe* it!
Victor Meldrew in *One Foot in the Grave* (BBC television series, 1989–), written by David Renwick

17 Once again we stop the mighty roar of London's traffic.
In Town Tonight (BBC radio series, 1933–60) preamble

18 Pass the sick bag, Alice.
used by John **Junor**; in *Sunday Express* and elsewhere, from 1980 or earlier

19 Seriously, though, he's doing a grand job!
popularized by David **Frost** in 'That Was The Week That Was', on BBC Television, 1962–3; originally deriving from a sketch written for Roy Kinnear

20 Shome mishtake, shurely?
in *Private Eye* magazine, 1980s

21 So farewell then . . .
frequent opening of poems by 'E. J. Thribb' in Private Eye *magazine, usually as an obituary*
1970s onwards

22 Take me to your leader.
from science-fiction stories

23 The truth is out there.
The X Files (American television series, 1993–), created by Chris Carter

24 Very interesting . . . but stupid.
Rowan and Martin's Laugh-In (American television series, 1967–73), written by Dan Rowan (1922–87) and Dick Martin (1923–)

25 The weekend starts here.
Ready, Steady, Go, British television series, *c.*1963

26 We have ways of making you talk.
perhaps originating in the line 'We have ways of making men talk' in *Lives of a Bengal Lancer* (1935 film), written by Waldemar Young et al.

27 What's up, Doc?
Bugs Bunny cartoons, written by Tex Avery (1907–80) from *c.*1940

28 Who loves ya, baby?
used by Telly Savalas (1926–) in American TV series *Kojak* (1973–8)

29 You bet your sweet bippy.
Rowan and Martin's Laugh-In (American television series, 1967–73), written by Dan Rowan (1922–87) and Dick Martin (1923–)

30 You might very well think that. I couldn't possibly comment.
the Chief Whip's habitual response to questioning
House of Cards (televised 1990); written by Michael Dobbs (1948–)

31 You're going to like this . . . not a lot . . . but you'll like it!
used by Paul Daniels (1938–) in his conjuring act, especially on television from 1981 onwards

32 You rotten swines. I told you I'd be deaded.
phrase first used by Bluebottle in 'Hastings Flyer' in *The Goon Show* (BBC radio series) 3 January 1956, written by Spike **Milligan**

33 Your starter for ten.
phrase often used by Bamber Gascoigne (1935–) in *University Challenge* (ITV quiz series, 1962–87)

34 You silly twisted boy.
phrase first used in 'The Dreaded Batter Pudding Hurler' in *The Goon Show* (BBC radio series) 12 October 1954, written by Spike **Milligan**

Catullus *continued*

sparrow is dead, the sparrow which was my lady's darling.

Carmina no. 3; cf. **Millay** 509:15

1 *Qui nunc it per iter tenebricosum*
Illuc, unde negant redire quemquam.

Now he goes along the darksome road, thither whence they say no one returns.

Carmina no. 4

2 *Vivamus, mea Lesbia, atque amemus,*
Rumoresque senum severiorum
Omnes unius aestimemus assis.
Soles occidere et redire possunt:
Nobis cum semel occidit brevis lux
Nox est perpetua una dormienda.

Let us live, my Lesbia, and let us love, and let us reckon all the murmurs of more censorious old men as worth one farthing. Suns can set and come again: for us, when once our brief light has set, one everlasting night is to be slept.

Carmina no. 5; cf. **Campion** 183:21, **Jonson** 420:10, 420:12

3 *Da mi basia mille, deinde centum,*
Dein mille altera, dein secunda centum,
Deinde usque altera mille, deinde centum.

Give me a thousand kisses, then a hundred, then another thousand, then a second hundred, then yet another thousand, then a hundred.

Carmina no. 5

4 *Miser Catulle, desinas ineptire,*
Et quod vides perisse perditum ducas.

Poor Catullus, drop your silly fancies, and what you see is lost let it be lost.

Carmina no. 8

5 *Paene insularum, Sirmio, insularumque*
Ocelle.

Sirmio, bright eye of peninsulas and islands.

Carmina no. 31; cf. **Tennyson** 758:20

6 *Nam risu inepto res ineptior nulla est.*

For there is nothing sillier than a silly laugh.

Carmina no. 39; cf. **Chesterfield** 209:16, **Congreve** 232:10

7 *Iam ver egelidos refert tepores.*

Now Spring restores balmy warmth.

Carmina no. 46

8 *Gratias tibi maximas Catullus*
Agit pessimus omnium poeta,
Tanto pessimus omnium poeta,
Quanto tu optimus omnium's patronum.

Catullus gives you warmest thanks,
And he the worst of poets ranks;
As much the worst of bards confessed,
As you of advocates the best.

letter of thanks to **Cicero**

Carmina no. 49 (translated by Sir William Marris)

9 *Ille mi par esse deo videtur,*
Ille, si fas est, superare divos,
Qui sedens adversus identidem te
Spectat et audit
Dulce ridentem, misero quod omnis
Eripit sensus mihi.

Like a god he seems to me, above the gods, if so may be, who sitting often close to you may see and hear you sweetly laughing, which snatches away all the senses from poor me.

Carmina no. 51 (a translation of Sappho); cf. **Sappho** 644:14

10 *Caeli, Lesbia nostra, Lesbia illa,*
Illa Lesbia, quam Catullus unam
Plus quam se atque suos amavit omnes,
Nunc in quadriviis et angiportis
Glubit magnanimos Remi nepotes.

O Caelius, our Lesbia, that Lesbia whom Catullus once loved uniquely, more than himself and more than all his own, now at the crossroads and in the alleyways has it off with the high-minded descendants of Remus.

Carmina no. 58

11 *Ut flos in saeptis secretus nascitur hortis,*
Ignotus pecori, nullo contusus aratro,
Quem mulcent aurae, firmat sol, educat imber;
Multi illum pueri, multae optavere puellae.

As a flower grows concealed in an enclosed garden, unknown to the cattle, bruised by no plough, and which the breezes caress, the sun makes strong, and the rain brings out; many boys and many girls long for it.

Carmina no. 62

12 *Sed mulier cupido quod dicit amanti,*
In vento et rapida scribere oportet aqua.

But what a woman says to her lusting lover it is best to write in wind and swift-flowing water.

Carmina no. 70

13 *Desine de quoquam quicquam bene velle mereri,*
Aut aliquem fieri posse putare pium.

Give up wanting to deserve any thanks from anyone, or thinking that anybody can be grateful.

Carmina no. 73

14 *Siqua recordanti benefacta priora voluptas*
Est homini.

If a man can take any pleasure in recalling the thought of kindnesses done.

Carmina no. 76

15 *Difficile est longum subito deponere amorem.*

It is difficult suddenly to lay aside a long-cherished love.

Carmina no. 76

16 *Si vitam puriter egi.*

If I have led a pure life.

Carmina no. 76

17 *O di, reddite mi hoc pro pietate mea.*

O gods, grant me this in return for my piety.

Carmina no. 76

18 *Chommoda dicebat, si quando commoda vellet*
Dicere, et insidias Arrius hinsidias.

Arrius, if he wanted to say 'amenities' used to say 'hamenities', and for 'intrigue' 'hintrigue'.

Carmina no. 84

19 *Odi et amo: quare id faciam, fortasse requiris.*
Nescio, sed fieri sentio et excrucior.

I hate and I love: why I do so you may well ask. I
do not know, but I feel it happen and am in agony.
Carmina no. 85

1 *Multas per gentes et multa per aequora vectus*
Advenio has miseras, frater, ad inferias,
Ut te postremo donarem munere mortis
Et mutam nequiquam alloquerer cinerem . . .
Nunc tamen interea haec prisco quae more parentum
Tradita sunt tristi munere ad inferias,
Accipe fraterno multum manantia fletu,
Atque in perpetuum, frater, ave atque vale.
By many lands and over many a wave
I come, my brother, to your piteous grave,
To bring you the last offering in death
And o'er dumb dust expend an idle breath . . .
Yet take these gifts, brought as our fathers bade
For sorrow's tribute to the passing shade;
A brother's tears have wet them o'er and o'er;
And so, my brother, hail, and farewell evermore!
Carmina no. 101 (translated by Sir William Marris); cf. **Tennyson** 758:20

2 *At non effugies meos iambos.*
But you shall not escape my iambics.
R. A. B. Mynors (ed.) *Catulli Carmina* (1958) Fragment 3

Charles Causley 1917–
English poet and schoolmaster

3 Timothy Winters comes to school
With eyes as wide as a football-pool,
Ears like bombs and teeth like splinters:
A blitz of a boy is Timothy Winters.
'Timothy Winters' (1957)

Constantine Cavafy 1863–1933
Greek poet

4 Body, remember not only how much you were loved,
not only the beds you lay on,
but also those desires glowing openly
in eyes that looked at you,
trembling for you in voices.
'Body, Remember' (1918)

5 When you set out for Ithaka
ask that your way be long.
'Ithaka' (1911) (translated by E. Keeley and P. Sherrard)

6 Ithaka gave you the splendid journey.
Without her you would not have set out.
She hasn't anything else to give you.
'Ithaka' (1911)

7 What are we waiting for, gathered in the market-place?
The barbarians are to arrive today.
'Waiting for the Barbarians' (1904) (translated by E. Keeley and P. Sherrard)

8 And now, what will become of us without the barbarians?
Those people were a kind of solution.
'Waiting for the Barbarians' (1904)

9 New places you will not find, you will not find another sea
The city will follow you.
'The Town' (1911) (translated by E. Keeley and P. Sherrard)

Edith Cavell 1865–1915
English nurse, executed by the Germans for assisting in the escape of British soldiers from occupied Belgium

10 Standing, as I do, in view of God and eternity, I realize that patriotism is not enough. I must have no hatred or bitterness towards anyone.
on the eve of her execution
in *The Times* 23 October 1915

Margaret Cavendish (Duchess of Newcastle) *c.*1624–74
English woman of letters

11 Greek, Latin poets, I could never read,
Nor their historians, but our English Speed;
I could not steal their wit, nor plots out take;
All my plays' plots, my own poor brain did make.
Plays (1662) 'To the Readers'

12 Marriage is the grave or tomb of wit.
Plays (1662) 'Nature's Three Daughters' pt. 2, act 5, sc. 20

13 If Nature had not befriended us with beauty, and other good graces, to help us to insinuate our selves into men's affections, we should have been more enslaved than any other of Nature's creatures she hath made.
Sociable Letters (1664)

14 But for the most part, women are not educated as they should be, I mean those of quality; oft their education is only to dance, sing, and fiddle, to write complimental letters, to read romances, to speak some languages that is not their native . . . their parents take more care of their feet than their head, more of their words than their reason.
Sociable Letters (1664)

Count Cavour (Camillo Benso di Cavour) 1810–61
Italian statesman

15 We are ready to proclaim throughout Italy this great principle: a free church in a free state.
speech, 27 March 1861, in William de la Rive *Reminiscences of the Life and Character of Count Cavour* (1862) ch. 13

William Caxton *c.*1421–91
first English printer

16 The worshipful father and first founder and embellisher of ornate eloquence in our English, I mean Master Geoffrey Chaucer.
Caxton's edition (*c.*1478) of Chaucer's translation of Boethius *De Consolacione Philosophie* epilogue

17 It is notoriously known through the universal world that there be nine worthy and the best that ever were. That is to wit three paynims, three Jews, and three Christian men. As for the paynims they were . . . the first Hector of Troy . . . the second Alexander the Great; and the third Julius Caesar . . . As for the three Jews . . . the first was Duke Joshua . . . the second David, King of

Jerusalem; and the third Judas Maccabaeus . . . And sith the said Incarnation . . . was first the noble Arthur . . . The second was Charlemagne or Charles the Great . . . and the third and last was Godfrey of Bouillon.

Thomas Malory *Le Morte D'Arthur* (1485) prologue

1 I, according to my copy, have done set it in imprint, to the intent that noble men may see and learn the noble acts of chivalry, the gentle and virtuous deeds that some knights used in those days.

Thomas Malory *Le Morte D'Arthur* (1485) prologue

Nicolae Ceauşescu 1918–89

Romanian Communist statesman, first President of the Socialist Republic of Romania 1974–89

2 Fidel Castro is right. You do not quieten your enemy by talking with him like a priest, but by burning him.

at a Communist Party meeting 17 December 1989

in *Guardian* 11 January 1990

Lord Edward Cecil 1867–1918

British soldier and civil servant

3 An agreement between two men to do what both agree is wrong.

definition of a compromise

letter, 3 September 1911; Kenneth Rose *The Later Cecils* (1975) ch. 7

Lord Hugh Cecil 1869–1956

British Conservative politician and clergyman, Provost of Eton

4 There is no more ungraceful figure than that of a humanitarian with an eye to the main chance.

in *The Times* 24 June 1901

5 The two dangers which beset the Church of England are good music and bad preaching.

Kenneth Rose *The Later Cecils* (1975)

Robert Cecil 1563–1612

English courtier and statesman, son of William **Cecil**, *Lord Burghley*

6 Rest content, and give heed to one that hath sorrowed in the bright lustre of a court, and gone heavily even on the best-seeming fair ground . . . I know it bringeth little comfort on earth; and he is, I reckon, no wise man that looketh this way to Heaven.

letter to John Harington; Algernon Cecil *A Life of Robert Cecil* (1915) ch. 12

William Cecil (Lord Burghley) 1520–98

English courtier and politician, father of Robert **Cecil**

on Cecil: see **Elizabeth I** *297:2, 297:3*

7 What! all this for a song?

to Queen **Elizabeth I**, *on being ordered to make a gratuity of £100 to* **Spenser** *in return for some poems*

Edmund Spenser *The Faerie Queene* (1751) 'The Life of Mr Edmund Spenser' by Thomas Birch

Paul Celan 1920–70

German poet

8 A man lives in the house he plays with his vipers
he writes
he writes when it grows dark to Deutschland your
golden hair Margareta
Your ashen hair Shulamith we shovel a grave in
the air there you won't lie too cramped.

'Deathfugue' (written 1944)

9 He shouts play death more sweetly this Death is a
master from Deutschland
he shouts scrape your strings darker you'll rise
then as smoke to the sky
you'll have a grave then in the clouds there you
won't lie too cramped.

'Deathfugue' (written 1944)

10 *Der Tod ist ein Meister aus Deutschland.*

Death is a master from Germany.

'Deathfugue' (written 1944)

11 There's nothing in the world for which a poet will give up writing, not even when he is a Jew and the language of his poems is German.

letter to relatives, 2 August 1948

Susannah Centlivre c.1669–1723

English actress and dramatist

12 For he or she, who drags the marriage chain,
And finds in spouse occasion to complain,
Should hide their frailties with a lover's care,
And let th'ill-judging world conclude 'em fair;
Better th'offence ne'er reach the offender's ear.
For they who sin with caution, whilst concealed,
Grow impudently careless, when revealed.

The Artifice (1722) act 5, sc. 3

13 The real Simon Pure.

A Bold Stroke for a Wife (1718) act 5, sc. 1

14 Nothing to be done without a bribe I find, in love as well as law.

The Perjured Husband (1700) act 3, sc. 2

15 The carping malice of the vulgar world; who think it a proof of sense to dislike every thing that is writ by Women.

The Platonic Lady (1707) dedication

Cervantes (Miguel de Cervantes Saavedra) 1547–1616

Spanish novelist

on Cervantes: see **Byron** *177:22*

16 *El Caballero de la Triste Figura.*

The Knight of the Doleful Countenance.

Don Quixote (1605) pt. 1, ch. 19

17 *El pan comido y la compañía deshecha.*

With the bread eaten up, up breaks the company.

Don Quixote (1605) pt. 2, ch. 7

18 *No todos podemos ser frailes, y muchos son los caminos por donde lleva Dios a los suyos al cielo: religión es la caballería.*

We cannot all be friars, and many are the ways by which God leads his own to eternal life. Knight-errantry *is* religion.
to Sancho, on his asking whether, to get to heaven, we ought not all to become monks
Don Quixote (1605) pt. 2, ch. 8

1 *Es un entreverado loco, lleno de lúcidos intervalos.*
He's a muddle-headed fool, with frequent lucid intervals.
Don Quixote (1605) pt. 2, ch. 18 (Don Lorenzo of Don Quixote)

2 *Dos linajes solos hay en el mundo, como decía una abuela mía, que son el tener y el no tener.*
There are only two families in the world, as a grandmother of mine used to say: the haves and the have-nots.
Don Quixote (1605) pt. 2, ch. 20

3 *Digo, paciencia y barajar.*
What I say is, patience, and shuffle the cards.
Don Quixote (1605) pt. 2, ch. 23

4 *La diligencia es madre de la buena ventura y la pereza, su contrario, jamás llegó al término que pide un buen deseo.*
Diligence is the mother of good fortune, and idleness, its opposite, never led to good intention's goal.
Don Quixote (1605) pt. 2, ch. 43

5 *Bien haya el que inventó el sueño, capa que cubre todos los humanos pensamientos, manjar que quita la hambre, agua que ahuyenta la sed, fuego que calienta el frío, frío que templa el ardor, y, finalmente, moneda general con que todas las cosas se compran, balanza y peso que iguala al pastor con el rey y al simple con el discreto.*
Blessings on him who invented sleep, the mantle that covers all human thoughts, the food that satisfies hunger, the drink that slakes thirst, the fire that warms cold, the cold that moderates heat, and, lastly, the common currency that buys all things, the balance and weight that equalizes the shepherd and the king, the simpleton and the sage.
Don Quixote (1605) pt. 2, ch. 68

6 *Los buenos pintores imitan la naturaleza, pero los malos la vomitan.*
Good painters imitate nature, bad ones spew it up.
El Licenciado Vidriera in *Novelas Ejemplares* (1613)

7 *Puesto ya el pie en el estribo.*
With one foot already in the stirrup.
apprehending his own imminent death
Los Trabajos de Persiles y Sigismunda (1617) preface

Paul Cézanne 1839–1906
French painter

8 Treat nature in terms of the cylinder, the sphere, the cone, all in perspective.
letter to Emile Bernard, 1904; Emile Bernard *Paul Cézanne* (1925)

9 Monet is only an eye, but what an eye!
attributed

John Chalkhill *c.*1600–42
English poet

10 Oh, the gallant fisher's life,
It is the best of any
'Tis full of pleasure, void of strife,
And 'tis beloved of many.
'Piscator's Song', in Izaak Walton *The Compleat Angler* (1653–76)

Jason Chamberlain fl. 1811
American clergyman

11 Morals and manners will rise or decline with our attention to grammar.
inaugural address, University of Vermont, 1811

Joseph Chamberlain 1836–1914
British Liberal politician, father of Neville **Chamberlain**

12 In politics, there is no use looking beyond the next fortnight.
letter from A. J. Balfour to 3rd Marquess of Salisbury, 24 March 1886; A. J. Balfour *Chapters of Autobiography* (1930) ch. 16; cf. **Wilson** 821:16

13 Provided that the City of London remains, as it is at present, the clearing-house of the world, any other nation may be its workshop.
speech at the Guildhall, 19 January 1904, in *The Times* 20 January 1904; cf. **Disraeli** 268:7

14 The day of small nations has long passed away. The day of Empires has come.
speech at Birmingham, 12 May 1904, in *The Times* 13 May 1904

15 We are not downhearted. The only trouble is we cannot understand what is happening to our neighbours.
referring to a constituency which had remained unaffected by an electoral landslide
speech at Smethwick, 18 January 1906, in *The Times* 19 January 1906

Neville Chamberlain 1869–1940
British Conservative statesman; Prime Minister, 1937–40, son of Joseph **Chamberlain**
on Chamberlain: see **Bevan** *72:4*

16 In war, whichever side may call itself the victor, there are no winners, but all are losers.
speech at Kettering, 3 July 1938, in *The Times* 4 July 1938

17 How horrible, fantastic, incredible it is that we should be digging trenches and trying on gas-masks here because of a quarrel in a far away country between people of whom we know nothing.
on Germany's annexation of the Sudetenland
radio broadcast, 27 September 1938, in *The Times* 28 September 1938

18 This is the second time in our history that there has come back from Germany to Downing Street peace with honour. I believe it is peace for our time.
speech from 10 Downing Street, 30 September 1938, in *The Times* 1 October 1938; cf. **Disraeli** 269:18, **Russell** 640:10

1 This morning, the British Ambassador in Berlin handed the German government a final Note stating that, unless we heard from them by eleven o'clock that they were prepared at once to withdraw their troops from Poland, a state of war would exist between us. I have to tell you now that no such undertaking has been received, and that consequently this country is at war with Germany.
radio broadcast, 3 September 1939

2 Whatever may be the reason—whether it was that Hitler thought he might get away with what he had got without fighting for it, or whether it was that after all the preparations were not sufficiently complete—however, one thing is certain—he missed the bus.
speech at Central Hall, Westminster, 4 April 1940, in *The Times* 5 April 1940

Haddon Chambers 1860–1921
English dramatist

3 The long arm of coincidence.
Captain Swift (1888) act 2

William Chambers 1726–96
British architect

4 In the constructive part of architecture, the ancients were no great proficients.
Treatise on Decorative Civil Architecture (ed. 3, 1791)

Nicolas-Sébastien Chamfort 1741–94
French writer

5 *Vivre est une maladie dont le sommeil nous soulage toutes les 16 heures. C'est un palliatif. La mort est le remède.*
Living is an illness to which sleep provides relief every sixteen hours. It's a palliative. The remedy is death.
Maximes et Pensées (1796) ch. 2

6 *Des qualités trop supérieures rendent souvent un homme moins propre à la société. On ne va pas au marché avec des lingots; on y va avec de l'argent ou de la petite monnaie.*
Qualities too elevated often unfit a man for society. We don't take ingots with us to market; we take silver or small change.
Maximes et Pensées (1796) ch. 3

7 *L'amour, tel qu'il existe dans la société, n'est que l'échange de deux fantaisies et le contact de deux épidermes.*
Love, in the form in which it exists in society, is nothing but the exchange of two fantasies and the superficial contact of two bodies.
Maximes et Pensées (1796) ch. 6

8 *Je dirais volontiers des métaphysiciens ce que Scaliger disait des Basques, on dit qu'ils s'entendent, mais je n'en crois rien.*
I am tempted to say of metaphysicians what Scaliger used to say of the Basques: they are said to understand one another, but I don't believe a word of it.
Maximes et Pensées (1796) ch. 7

9 *Les pauvres sont les nègres de l'Europe.*
The poor are Europe's blacks.
Maximes et Pensées (1796) ch. 8

10 *Sois mon frère, ou je te tue.*
Be my brother, or I kill you.
his interpretation of 'Fraternité ou la mort [Fraternity or death]'
P. R. Anguis (ed.) *Oeuvres Complètes* (1824) vol. 1 'Notice Historique sur la Vie et les Écrits de Chamfort'; cf. **Political slogans** 581:24

John Chandler 1806–76
English clergyman

11 Conquering kings their titles take
From the foes they captive make.
hymn (1837); translation from a Latin original: '*Victis sibi cognomina sumant tyranni gentibus . . .*'

Raymond Chandler 1888–1959
American writer of detective fiction

12 It was a blonde. A blonde to make a bishop kick a hole in a stained glass window.
Farewell, My Lovely (1940) ch. 13

13 A big hard-boiled city with no more personality than a paper cup.
of Los Angeles
The Little Sister (1949) ch. 26

14 I let go of her wrists, closed the door with my elbow and slid past her. It was like the first time. 'You ought to carry insurance on those,' I said.
The Little Sister (1949) ch. 34

15 Crime isn't a disease, it's a symptom. Cops are like a doctor that gives you aspirin for a brain tumour.
The Long Good-Bye (1953) ch. 47

16 Down these mean streets a man must go who is not himself mean, who is neither tarnished nor afraid.
in *Atlantic Monthly* December 1944 'The Simple Art of Murder'

17 If my books had been any worse, I should not have been invited to Hollywood, and if they had been any better, I should not have come.
letter to Charles W. Morton, 12 December 1945, in Dorothy Gardiner and Katherine S. Walker *Raymond Chandler Speaking* (1962)

18 Would you convey my compliments to the purist who reads your proofs and tell him or her that I write in a sort of broken-down patois which is something like the way a Swiss waiter talks, and that when I split an infinitive, God damn it, I split it so it will stay split.
letter to Edward Weeks, 18 January 1947, in F. MacShane *Life of Raymond Chandler* (1976) ch. 7

19 When in doubt have a man come through the door with a gun in his hand.
attributed

Coco Chanel (Gabrielle Bonheur) 1883–1971
French couturière

1 Clothes by a man who doesn't know women, never had one, and dreams of being one!
of Dior's New Look
in *Vanity Fair* June 1994

2 Passion always goes, and boredom stays.
Frances Kennett *Coco: the Life and Loves of Gabrielle Chanel* (1989)

3 You ask if they were happy. This is not a characteristic of a European. To be contented—that's for the cows.
A. Madsen *Coco Chanel* (1990) ch. 35

4 Youth is something very new: twenty years ago no one mentioned it.
Marcel Haedrich *Coco Chanel, Her Life, Her Secrets* (1971)

Henry ('Chips') Channon 1897–1958
American-born British Conservative politician and diarist

5 I like my 'abroad' to be Catholic and sensual.
diary, 18 January 1924; Robert Rhodes James (ed.) *Chips: the Diaries* (1967)

6 What is more dull than a discreet diary? One might just as well have a discreet soul.
diary, 26 July 1935

7 We saw Queen Mary looking like the Jungfrau, white and sparkling in the sun.
diary, 22 June 1937

8 There is nowhere in the world where sleep is so deep as in the libraries of the House of Commons.
diary, 15 January 1939

Charlie Chaplin (Charles Spencer Chaplin) 1889–1977
English film actor and director

9 All I need to make a comedy is a park, a policeman and a pretty girl.
My Autobiography (1964) ch. 10

10 Words are cheap. The biggest thing you can say is 'elephant'.
on the universality of silent films
B. Norman *The Movie Greats* (1981)

Arthur Chapman 1873–1935
American poet

11 Out where the handclasp's a little stronger,
Out where the smile dwells a little longer,
That's where the West begins.
Out Where the West Begins (1916)

George Chapman *c.*1559–1634
English scholar, poet, and dramatist

12 An Englishman,
Being flattered, is a lamb; threatened, a lion.
Alphonsus, Emperor of Germany (1654) act 1

13 Man is a torch borne in the wind; a dream
But of a shadow, summed with all his substance.
Bussy D'Ambois (1607–8) act 1, sc. 1

14 Who to himself is law, no law doth need,
Offends no law, and is a king indeed.
Bussy D'Ambois (1607–8) act 2, sc. 1

15 Oh my fame,
Live in despite of murder! Take thy wings
And haste thee where the grey eyed Morn perfumes
Her rosy chariot with Sabaean spices!
Fly, where the Evening from th'Iberian vales
Takes on her swarthy shoulders Hecate,
Crowned with a grove of oaks; fly where men feel
The burning axletree, and those that suffer
Beneath the chariot of the snowy Bear.
Bussy D'Ambois (1607–8) act 5, sc. 3

16 There is no danger to a man, that knows
What life and death is; there's not any law,
Exceeds his knowledge; neither is it lawful
That he should stoop to any other law,
He goes before them, and commands them all,
That to himself is a law rational.
The Conspiracy of Charles, Duke of Byron (1608) act 3, sc. 3

17 Come, come, dear Night, Love's mart of kisses,
Sweet close of his ambitious line,
The fruitful summer of his blisses,
Love's glory doth in darkness shine.
O come, soft rest of cares, come Night,
Come naked Virtue's only tire,
The reapèd harvest of the light,
Bound up in sheaves of sacred fire.
Hero and Leander (1598)

18 We have watered our houses in Helicon.
occasionally misread 'We have watered our horses in Helicon', following an 1814 edition
May-Day (1611) act 3, sc. 3

19 For one heat, all know, doth drive out another,
One passion doth expel another still.
Monsieur D'Olive (1606) act 5, sc. 1

20 I am ashamed the law is such an ass.
Revenge for Honour (1654) act 3, sc. 2; cf. **Dickens** 264:19

21 They're only truly great who are truly good.
Revenge for Honour (1654) act 5, sc. 2, last line

22 A poem, whose subject is not truth, but things like truth.
The Revenge of Bussy D'Ambois (1613) dedication

23 Danger, the spur of all great minds.
The Revenge of Bussy D'Ambois (1613) act 5, sc. 1

24 And let a scholar all Earth's volumes carry,
He will be but a walking dictionary.
The Tears of Peace (1609) l. 530

Charles I 1600–49
King of England, Scotland, and Ireland from 1625, son of ***James I*** *and father of* ***Charles II***
on Charles I: see ***Marvell*** *498:19*

25 Never make a defence or apology before you be accused.
letter to Lord Wentworth, 3 September 1636, in Sir Charles Petrie (ed.) *Letters of King Charles I* (1935)

1 I see all the birds are flown.
*after attempting to arrest five members of the Long Parliament (**Pym**, Hampden, Haselrig, Holles, and Strode)*
in the House of Commons, 4 January 1642

2 Sweet-heart, now they will cut off thy father's head. Mark, child, what I say: they will cut off my head, and perhaps make thee a king. But mark what I say: you must not be a king, so long as your brothers Charles and James do live.
said to Prince Henry
Reliquiae Sacrae Carolinae (1650)

3 You manifestly wrong even the poorest ploughman, if you demand not his free consent.
The King's Reasons for declining the jurisdiction of the High Court of Justice, 21 January 1649, in S. R. Gardiner *Constitutional Documents of the Puritan Revolution* (1906 ed.)

4 As to the King, the laws of the land will clearly instruct you for that . . . For the people; and truly I desire their liberty and freedom, as much as any body: but I must tell you, that their liberty and freedom consists in having the government of those laws, by which their life and their goods may be most their own; 'tis not for having share in government [sirs] that is nothing pertaining to 'em. A subject and a sovereign are clean different things.
speech on the scaffold, 30 January 1649; J. Rushworth *Historical Collections* pt. 4, vol. 2 (1701)

5 If I would have given way to an arbitrary way, for to have all laws changed according to the power of the sword, I needed not to have come here; and therefore I tell you (and I pray God it be not laid to your charge) that I am the martyr of the people.
speech on the scaffold, 30 January 1649; J. Rushworth *Historical Collections* pt. 4, vol. 2 (1701)

6 I die a Christian, according to the profession of the Church of England, as I found it left me by my father.
speech on the scaffold, 30 January 1649; J. Rushworth *Historical Collections* pt. 4, vol. 2 (1701)

Charles II 1630–85

*King of England, Scotland and Ireland from 1660, son of **Charles I***

*on Charles: see **Defoe** 255:13, **Epitaphs** 302:14, **Rochester** 630:17, **Sellar and Yeatman** 654:11; see also **Last words** 456:11*

7 Better than a play.
on the debates in the House of Lords on Lord Ross's Divorce Bill, 1670
A. Bryant *King Charles II* (1931)

8 He [Charles II] said once to myself, he was no atheist, but he could not think God would make a man miserable only for taking a little pleasure out of the way.
Bishop Gilbert Burnet *History of My Own Time* (1724) vol. 1, bk. 2, p. 93

9 He [Lauderdale] told me, the king spoke to him to let that [Presbytery] go, for it was not a religion for gentlemen.
Bishop Gilbert Burnet *History of My Own Time* (1724) vol. 1, bk. 2

10 His nonsense suits their nonsense.
said of Woolly, afterwards Bishop of Clonfert ('a very honest man, but a very great blockhead') who had gone from house to house trying to persuade Nonconformists to go to church
Bishop Gilbert Burnet *History of My Own Time* (1724) vol. 1, bk. 2

11 I am sure no man in England will take away my life to make you King.
to his brother James
William King *Political & Literary Anecdotes* (1818)

12 I am weary of travelling and am resolved to go abroad no more. But when I am dead and gone I know not what my brother will do: I am much afraid that when he comes to wear the crown he will be obliged to travel again.
on the difference between himself and his brother (later James II)
attributed

13 It is upon the navy under the good Providence of God that the safety, honour, and welfare of this realm do chiefly depend.
'Articles of War' preamble (probably a popular paraphrase); Geoffrey Callender *The Naval Side of British History* (1952) pt. 1, ch. 8

14 This is very true: for my words are my own, and my actions are my ministers'.
*reply to Lord **Rochester**'s epitaph on him*
Thomas Hearne: Remarks and Collections (1885–1921) 17 November 1706; see **Epitaphs** 302:14

15 He had been, he said, an unconscionable time dying; but he hoped that they would excuse it.
Lord Macaulay *History of England* (1849) vol. 1, ch. 4

Charles V 1500–58

Holy Roman Emperor, 1519–56; King of Spain from 1516

16 To God I speak Spanish, to women Italian, to men French, and to my horse—German.
attributed; Lord Chesterfield *Letters to his Son* (ed. Dobrée, 1932) vol. 4

Charles, Prince of Wales 1948–

*Heir apparent to the British throne; son of **Elizabeth II** and former husband of **Diana**, Princess of Wales*

when asked if he was 'in love':

17 Yes . . . whatever that may mean.
after the announcement of his engagement
interview, 24 February 1981; cf. **Duffy** 284:10

18 A monstrous carbuncle on the face of a much-loved and elegant friend.
on the proposed extension to the National Gallery
speech to the Royal Institute of British Architects, 30 May 1984, in *The Times* 31 May 1984; cf. **Spencer** 732:15

19 I just come and talk to the plants, really—very important to talk to them, they respond I find.
television interview, 21 September 1986

1 I begin to tire of needing to issue denials of false stories about all manner of thoughts which I am alleged to be having.
on the suggestion in a forthcoming television programme that he wished the Queen to abdicate
in joint statement issued by Buckingham Palace and St James's Palace, 6 November 1998

Pierre Charron 1541–1603
French philosopher and theologian

2 The true science and study of man is man.
De la Sagesse (1601) bk. 1, preface; cf. **Pope** 585:18

Salmon Portland Chase 1808–73
American lawyer and politician

3 The Constitution, in all its provisions, looks to an indestructible Union composed of indestructible States.
decision in Texas v. White, 1868, in *Cases Argued and Decided in the Supreme Court of the United States* (1926) bk. 19

François-René Chateaubriand (Vicomte de Chateaubriand) 1768–1848
French writer and diplomat

4 *L'écrivain original n'est pas celui qui n'imite personne, mais celui que personne ne peut imiter.*
The original writer is not he who refrains from imitating others, but he who can be imitated by none.
Le Génie du Christianisme (1802) pt. 2, bk. 1, ch. 3

Geoffrey Chaucer c.1343–1400
English poet
on Chaucer: see **Caxton** *198:16*, **Dryden** *283:11, 283:12*, **Dunbar** *285:5*, **Lydgate** *480:9*, **Spenser** *734:23*, **Ward** *803:5*
line references are to The Riverside Chaucer (ed. F. N. Robinson, 1987)

5 Ful craftier to pley she was
Than Athalus, that made the game
First of the ches, so was his name.
The Book of the Duchess l. 662

6 Whan that Aprill with his shoures soote
The droghte of March hath perced to the roote.
The Canterbury Tales 'The General Prologue' l. 1

7 And smale foweles maken melodye,
That slepen al the nyght with open ye
(So priketh hem nature in hir corages),
Thanne longen folk to goon on pilgrimages.
The Canterbury Tales 'The General Prologue' l. 9

8 He loved chivalrie,
Trouthe and honour, fredom and curteisie.
The Canterbury Tales 'The General Prologue' l. 45

9 He was a verray, parfit gentil knyght.
The Canterbury Tales 'The General Prologue' l. 72

10 He was as fressh as is the month of May.
The Canterbury Tales 'The General Prologue' l. 92

11 Curteis he was, lowely, and servysable,
And carf biforn his fader at the table.
The Canterbury Tales 'The General Prologue' l. 99

12 Hire gretteste ooth was but by Seinte Loy.
The Canterbury Tales 'The General Prologue' l. 120

13 Ful weel she soong the service dyvyne,
Entuned in hir nose ful semely;
And Frenssh she spak ful faire and fetisly,
After the scole of Stratford atte Bowe,
For Frenssh of Parys was to hire unknowe.
The Canterbury Tales 'The General Prologue' l. 122

14 She wolde wepe, if that she saugh a mous
Kaught in a trappe, if it were deed or bledde.
Of smale houndes hadde she that she fedde
With rosted flessh, or milk and wastel-breed.
But soore wepte she if oon of hem were deed.
The Canterbury Tales 'The General Prologue' l. 144

15 Of smal coral aboute hire arm she bar
A peire of bedes, gauded al with grene,
And theron heng a brooch of gold ful sheene,
On which ther was first write a crowned A,
And after *Amor vincit omnia*.
The Canterbury Tales 'The General Prologue' l. 158; cf. **Virgil** 796:12

16 He yaf nat of that text a pulled hen,
That seith that hunters ben nat hooly men.
The Canterbury Tales 'The General Prologue' l. 177

17 Somwhat he lipsed, for his wantownesse,
To make his Englissh sweete upon his tonge.
The Canterbury Tales 'The General Prologue' l. 264

18 A Clerk there was of Oxenford also,
That unto logyk hadde longe ygo.
As leene was his hors as is a rake,
And he was nat right fat, I undertake,
But looked holwe, and therto sobrely.
The Canterbury Tales 'The General Prologue' l. 285

19 For hym was levere have at his beddes heed
Twenty bookes, clad in blak or reed,
Of Aristotle and his philosophie
Than robes riche, or fithele, or gay sautrie.
But al be that he was a philosophre,
Yet hadde he but litel gold in cofre.
The Canterbury Tales 'The General Prologue' l. 293

20 And gladly wolde he lerne and gladly teche.
The Canterbury Tales 'The General Prologue' l. 308

21 Nowher so bisy a man as he ther nas,
And yet he semed bisier than he was.
The Canterbury Tales 'The General Prologue' l. 321

22 For he was Epicurus owene sone.
The Canterbury Tales 'The General Prologue' l. 336

23 Housbondes at chirche dore she hadde fyve,
Withouten oother compaignye in youthe—
But thereof nedeth nat to speke as nowthe.
The Canterbury Tales 'The General Prologue' l. 460

24 This noble ensample to his sheep he yaf,
That first he wroghte, and afterward he taughte.
The Canterbury Tales 'The General Prologue' l. 496

25 If gold ruste, what shall iren do?
The Canterbury Tales 'The General Prologue' l. 500

1 But Cristes loore and his apostels twelve
He taughte; but first he folwed it hymselve.
The Canterbury Tales 'The General Prologue' l. 527

2 His nosethirles blake were and wyde.
A swerd and a bokeler bar he by his syde.
His mouth as greet was as a greet forneys.
He was a janglere and a goliardeys,
And that was moost of synne and harlotries.
The Canterbury Tales 'The General Prologue' l. 557

3 A Somonour was ther with us in that place,
That hadde a fyr-reed cherubynnes face,
For saucefleem he was, with eyen narwe.
As hoot he was and lecherous as a sparwe.
The Canterbury Tales 'The General Prologue' l. 623

4 Wel loved he garleek, oynons, and eek lekes,
And for to drynken strong wyn, reed as blood.
The Canterbury Tales 'The General Prologue' l. 634

5 His walet, biforn him in his lappe,
Bretful of pardoun, comen from Rome al hoot.
The Canterbury Tales 'The General Prologue' l. 686

6 He hadde a croys of latoun ful of stones,
And in a glas he hadde pigges bones.
But with thise relikes, whan that he fond
A povre person dwellynge upon lond,
Upon a day he gat hym moore moneye
Than that the person gat in monthes tweye;
And thus, with feyned flaterye and japes,
He made the person and the peple his apes.
The Canterbury Tales 'The General Prologue' l. 699

7 O stormy peple! Unsad and evere untrewe!
The Canterbury Tales 'The Clerk's Tale' l. 995

8 Grisilde is deed, and eek hire pacience,
And bothe atones buryed in Ytaille;
For which I crie in open audience
No wedded man so hardy be t'assaille
His wyves pacience in trust to fynde
Grisildis, for in certein he shal faille.
The Canterbury Tales 'The Clerk's Tale: Lenvoy de Chaucer' l. 1177

9 Ye archewyves, stondeth at defense,
Syn ye be strong as is a greet camaille;
Ne suffreth nat that men yow doon offense.
And sklendre wyves, fieble as in bataille,
Beth egre as is a tygre yond in Ynde;
Ay clappeth as a mille, I yow consaille.
The Canterbury Tales 'The Clerk's Tale: Lenvoy de Chaucer' l. 1195

10 Be ay of chiere as light as leef on lynde,
And lat hym care, and wepe, and wrynge, and waille!
The Canterbury Tales 'The Clerk's Tale: Lenvoy de Chaucer' l. 1211

11 Love wol nat been constreyned by maistrye.
When maistrie comth, the God of Love anon
Beteth his wynges, and farewel, he is gon!
Love is a thyng as any spirit free.
The Canterbury Tales 'The Franklin's Tale' l. 764

12 Wommen, of kynde, desiren libertee,
And nat to been constreyned as a thral;
And so doon men, if I sooth seyen shal.
The Canterbury Tales 'The Franklin's Tale' l. 768

13 Til that the brighte sonne loste his hewe;
For th'orisonte hath reft the sonne his lyght—
This is as muche to seye as it was nyght.
The Canterbury Tales 'The Franklin's Tale' l. 1016

14 Trouthe is the hyeste thyng that man may kepe.
The Canterbury Tales 'The Franklin's Tale' l. 1479

15 And therefore, at the kynges court, my brother,
Ech man for hymself, ther is noon oother.
The Canterbury Tales 'The Knight's Tale' l. 1181

16 And whan a beest is deed he hath no peyne;
But man after his deeth moot wepe and pleyne.
The Canterbury Tales 'The Knight's Tale' l. 1319

17 The bisy larke, messager of day.
The Canterbury Tales 'The Knight's Tale' l. 1491

18 For pitee renneth soone in gentil herte.
The Canterbury Tales 'The Knight's Tale' l. 1761

19 The smylere with the knyf under the cloke.
The Canterbury Tales 'The Knight's Tale' l. 1999

20 Up roos the sonne, and up roos Emelye.
The Canterbury Tales 'The Knight's Tale' l. 2273

21 What is this world? what asketh men to have?
Now with his love, now in his colde grave.
The Canterbury Tales 'The Knight's Tale' l. 2777

22 She is mirour of alle curteisye.
The Canterbury Tales 'The Man of Law's Tale' l. 166

23 Lat take a cat, and fostre hym wel with milk
And tendre flessh, and make his couche of silk,
And lay hym seen a mous go by the wal,
Anon he weyveth milk and flessh and al,
And every deyntee that is in that hous,
Swich appetit hath he to ete a mous.
The Canterbury Tales 'The Manciple's Tale' l. 175

24 Kepe wel they tonge, and thenk upon the crowe.
The Canterbury Tales 'The Manciple's Tale' l. 362

25 And what is bettre than wisedoom? Womman. And
what is bettre than a good womman? Nothyng.
The Canterbury Tales 'The Tale of Melibee' l. 1107

26 She was a prymerole, a piggesnye,
For any lord to leggen in his bedde,
Or yet for any good yeman to wedde.
The Canterbury Tales 'The Miller's Tale' l. 3268

27 Derk was the nyght as pich, or as the cole,
And at the wyndow out she putte hir hole,
And Absolon, hym fil no bet be wers,
But with his mouth he kiste hir naked ers
Ful savourly, er he were war of this.
Abak he stirte, and thoughte it was amys,
For wel he wiste a womman hath no berd.
He felte a thyng al rough and long yherd,
And seyde, 'Fy! allas! what have I to do?'
'Tehee!' quod she, and clapte the wyndow to.
The Canterbury Tales 'The Miller's Tale' l. 3730

28 For certein, whan that Fortune list to flee,
Ther may no man the cours of hire withholde.
The Canterbury Tales 'The Monk's Tale' l. 1995

29 Ful wys is he that kan hymselven knowe!
The Canterbury Tales 'The Monk's Tale' l. 2139

1 Redeth the grete poete of Ytaille
That highte Dant, for he kan al devyse
Fro point to point; nat o word wol he faille.
The Canterbury Tales 'The Monk's Tale' l. 2460

2 His coomb was redder than the fyn coral,
And batailled as it were a castel wal;
His byle was blak, and as the jeet it shoon;
Lyk asure were his legges and his toon;
His nayles whitter than the lylye flour,
And lyk the burned gold was his colour,
This gentil cok hadde in his governaunce
Sevene hennes for to doon al his plesaunce,
Whiche were his sustres and his paramours,
And wonder lyk to hym, as of colours;
Of whiche the faireste hewed on hir throte
Was cleped fair damoysele Pertelote.
The Canterbury Tales 'The Nun's Priest's Tale' l. 2859

3 Mordre wol out; that se we day by day.
The Canterbury Tales 'The Nun's Priest's Tale' l. 3052; cf. **Proverbs** 607:16

4 Whan that the month in which the world bigan,
That highte March, whan God first maked man.
The Canterbury Tales 'The Nun's Priest's Tale' l. 3187

5 And on a Friday fil al this meschaunce.
The Canterbury Tales 'The Nun's Priest's Tale' l. 3341

6 Thanne peyne I me to strecche forth the nekke,
And est and west upon the peple I bekke.
The Canterbury Tales 'The Pardoner's Prologue' l. 395

7 O wombe! O bely! O stynkyng cod
Fulfilled of dong and of corrupcioun!
The Canterbury Tales 'The Pardoner's Tale' l. 534

8 And lightly as it comth, so wol we spende.
The Canterbury Tales 'The Pardoner's Tale' l. 781

9 Yet in oure asshen olde is fyr yreke.
The Canterbury Tales 'The Reeve's Prologue' l. 3882

10 The gretteste clerkes been noght wisest men.
The Canterbury Tales 'The Reeve's Tale' l. 4054

11 So was hir joly whistle wel ywet.
The Canterbury Tales 'The Reeve's Tale' l. 4155

12 Thou lookest as thou woldest fynde an hare,
For evere upon the ground I se thee stare.
The Canterbury Tales 'Prologue to Sir Thopas' l. 696

13 He hadde a semely nose.
The Canterbury Tales 'Sir Thopas' l. 729

14 'By God,' quod he, 'for pleynly, at a word,
Thy drasty rymyng is nat worth a toord!'
The Canterbury Tales 'Sir Thopas' l. 929

15 Experience, though noon auctoritee
Were in this world, is right ynogh for me
To speke of wo that is in mariage.
The Canterbury Tales 'The Wife of Bath's Prologue' l. 1

16 Yblessed be god that I have wedded fyve!
Welcome the sixte, whan that evere he shal.
For sothe, I wol nat kepe me chaast in al.
Whan myn housbonde is fro the world ygon,
Som Cristen man shall wedde me anon.
The Canterbury Tales 'The Wife of Bath's Prologue' l. 44

17 And after wyn on Venus moste I thynke,
For al so siker as cold engendreth hayl,
A likerous mouth moste han a likerous tayl.
The Canterbury Tales 'The Wife of Bath's Prologue' l. 464

18 But—Lord Crist!—what that it remembreth me
Upon my yowthe, and on my jolitee,
It tikleth me aboute myn herte roote.
Unto this day it dooth myn herte boote
That I have had my world as in my time.
The Canterbury Tales 'The Wife of Bath's Prologue' l. 469

19 And for to se, and eek for to be seye
Of lusty folk.
The Canterbury Tales 'The Wife of Bath's Prologue' l. 552

20 But yet I hadde alwey a coltes tooth.
Gat-tothed I was, and that bicam me weel.
The Canterbury Tales 'The Wife of Bath's Prologue' l. 602

21 Of which mayde anon, maugree hir heed,
By verray force, he rafte hire maydenhed.
The Canterbury Tales 'The Wife of Bath's Tale' l. 887

22 Wommen desiren to have sovereynetee
As wel over hir housbond as hir love.
The Canterbury Tales 'The Wife of Bath's Tale' l. 1038

23 Venus clerk Ovide,
That hath ysowen wonder wide
The grete god of Loves name.
The House of Fame l. 1487

24 And as for me, though that I konne but lyte,
On bokes for to rede I me delyte,
And to hem yive I feyth and ful credence,
And in myn herte have hem in reverence
So hertely, that ther is game noon
That fro my bokes maketh me to goon,
But yt be seldom on the holyday,
Save, certeynly, whan that the month of May
Is comen, and that I here the foules synge,
And that the floures gynnen for to sprynge,
Farewel my bok and my devocioun!
The Legend of Good Women 'The Prologue' l. 29

25 Of al the floures in the mede,
Thanne love I most thise floures white and rede,
Swiche as men callen daysyes in our toun.
The Legend of Good Women 'The Prologue' l. 41

26 That wel by reson men it calle may
The 'dayesye,' or elles the 'ye of day,'
The emperice and flour of floures alle.
The Legend of Good Women 'The Prologue' l. 183

27 And she was fayr as is the rose in May.
The Legend of Good Women 'Cleopatra' l. 613

28 That lyf so short,
the craft so long to lerne,
Th'assay so hard, so sharp the conquerynge.
The Parliament of Fowls l. 1; cf. **Hippocrates** 377:15, **Proverbs** 595:17

29 Thou shalt make castels thanne in Spayne
And dreme of joye, all but in vayne.
The Romaunt of the Rose l. 2573

30 O blynde world, O blynde entencioun!
How often falleth al the effect contraire
Of surquidrie and foul presumpcioun;
For kaught is proud, and kaught is debonaire.
This Troilus is clomben on the staire,

And litel weneth that he moot descenden;
But alday faileth thing that fooles wenden.
Troilus and Criseyde bk. 1, l. 211

1 For evere it was, and evere it shal byfalle,
That Love is he that alle thing may bynde,
For may no man fordon the lawe of kynde.
Troilus and Criseyde bk. 1, l. 236

2 But love a womman that she woot it nought,
And she wol quyte it that thow shalt nat fele;
Unknowe, unkist, and lost, that is unsought.
Troilus and Criseyde bk. 1, l. 807

3 O wynd, O wynd, the weder gynneth clere.
Troilus and Criseyde bk. 2, l. 2

4 Ye knowe ek that in forme of speche is chaunge
Withinne a thousand yeer, and wordes tho
That hadden pris, now wonder nyce and straunge
Us thinketh hem, and yet thei spake hem so.
Troilus and Criseyde bk. 2, l. 22

5 So longe mote ye lyve, and alle proude,
Til crowes feet be growe under youre yë.
Troilus and Criseyde bk. 2, l. 402

6 And we shall speek of the somwhat, I trowe,
Whan thow art gon, to don thyn eris glowe!
Troilus and Criseyde bk. 2, l. 1021

7 God loveth, and to love wol nought werne,
And in this world no lyves creature
Withouten love is worth, or may endure.
Troilus and Criseyde bk. 3, l. 12

8 It is nought good a slepyng hound to wake.
Troilus and Criseyde bk. 3, l. 764; cf. **Proverbs** 605:18

9 For I have seyn of a ful misty morwe
Folowen ful ofte a myrie someris day.
Troilus and Criseyde bk. 3, l. 1060

10 Right as an aspes leef she gan to quake.
Troilus and Criseyde bk. 3, l. 1200

11 And as the newe abaysed nyghtyngale,
That stynteth first whan she bygynneth to synge.
Troilus and Criseyde bk. 3, l. 1233

12 For of fortunes sharpe adversitee
The worst kynde of infortune is this,
A man to han ben in prosperitee,
And it remembren, whan it passed is.
Troilus and Criseyde bk. 3, l. 1625; cf. **Boethius** 123:11, **Dante** 249:12

13 Oon ere it herde, at tother out it wente.
Troilus and Criseyde bk. 4, l. 434

14 But manly sette the world on six and sevene;
And if thow deye a martyr, go to hevene!
Troilus and Criseyde bk. 4, l. 622

15 For tyme ylost may nought recovered be.
Troilus and Criseyde bk. 4, l. 1283

16 Ye, fare wel al the snow of ferne yere!
Troilus and Criseyde bk. 5, l. 1176

17 Ek gret effect men write in place lite;
Th' entente is al, and nat the lettres space.
Troilus and Criseyde bk. 5, l. 1629

18 Go, litel bok, go, litel myn tragedye,
Ther God thi makere yet, er that he dye,
So sende myght to make in som comedye!
But litel bok, no makyng thow n'envie,
But subgit be to alle poesye;
And kis the steppes, where as thow seest pace
Virgile, Ovide, Omer, Lucan, and Stace.
And for ther is so gret diversite
In Englissh and in writyng of oure tonge,
So prey I God that non myswrite the,
Ne the mysmetre for defaute of tonge;
And red wherso thow be, or elles songe,
That thow be understonde, God I biseche!
Troilus and Criseyde bk. 5, l. 1786; cf. **Stevenson** 743:3

19 And whan that he was slayn in this manere,
His lighte goost ful blisfully is went
Up to the holughnesse of the eighthe spere,
In convers letyng everich element;
And ther he saugh, with ful avysement
The erratik sterres, herkenyng armonye
With sownes ful of hevenyssh melodie.
And down from thennes faste he gan avyse
This litel spot of erthe, that with the se
Embraced is, and fully gan despise
This wrecched world, and held al vanite
To respect of the pleyn felicite
That is in hevene above.
Troilus and Criseyde bk. 5, l. 1811

20 O yonge, fresshe folkes, he or she,
In which that love up groweth with youre age.
Repeyreth hom fro worldly vanyte,
And of youre herte up casteth the visage
To thilke God that after his ymage
Yow made, and thynketh al nys but a faire,
This world that passeth soone as floures faire.
And loveth hym the which that right for love
Upon a crois, our soules for to beye,
First start, and roos, and sit in hevene above;
For he nyl falsen no wight, dar I seye,
That wol his herte al holly on hym leye.
And syn he best to love is, and most meke,
What nedeth feynede loves for to seke?
Troilus and Criseyde bk. 5, l. 1835

21 Lo here, of payens corsed olde rites!
Lo here, what alle hire goddes may availle!
Lo here, thise wrecched worldes appetites!
Lo here, the fyn and guerdoun for travaille
Of Jove, Appollo, of Mars, of swich rascaille!
Troilus and Criseyde bk. 5, l. 1849

22 O moral Gower, this book I directe
To the.
Troilus and Criseyde bk. 5, l. 1856

23 Flee fro the prees, and dwelle with sothfastnesse.
'Truth: Balade de Bon Conseyle' l. 1

24 Forth, pilgrim, forth! Forth, beste, out of thy stal!
Know thy contree, look up, thank God of al;
Hold the heye wey, and lat thy gost thee lede,
And trowth thee shal delivere, it is no drede.
'Truth: Balade de Bon Conseyle' l. 18

Anton Chekhov 1860–1904

Russian dramatist and short-story writer

1 If a lot of cures are suggested for a disease, it means that the disease is incurable.
The Cherry Orchard (1904) act 1 (translated by Elisaveta Fen)

2 The Lord God has given us vast forests, immense fields, wide horizons; surely we ought to be giants, living in such a country as this.
The Cherry Orchard (1904) act 2 (translated by Elisaveta Fen)

3 To begin to live in the present, we must first atone for our past and be finished with it, and we can only atone for it by suffering, by extraordinary, unceasing exertion.
The Cherry Orchard (1904) act 2 (translated by Elisaveta Fen)

4 MEDVEDENKO: Why do you wear black all the time?
MASHA: I'm in mourning for my life, I'm unhappy.
The Seagull (1896) act 1

5 NINA: Your play's hard to act, there are no living people in it.
TREPLEV: Living people! We should show life neither as it is nor as it ought to be, but as we see it in our dreams.
The Seagull (1896) act 1

6 Women can't forgive failure.
The Seagull (1896) act 2

7 I'm a seagull. No, that's wrong. Remember you shot a seagull? A man happened to come along, saw it and killed it, just to pass the time. A plot for a short story.
The Seagull (1896) act 4

8 Man must work by the sweat of his brow whatever his class, and that should make up the whole meaning and purpose of his life and happiness and contentment.
The Three Sisters (1901) act 1 (translated by Elisaveta Fen)

9 People who don't even notice whether it's summer or winter are lucky! If I lived in Moscow I don't think I'd care what the weather was like.
The Three Sisters (1901) act 2 (translated by Elisaveta Fen)

10 Life isn't finished for us yet! We're going to live! . . . Maybe, if we wait a little longer, we shall find out why we live, why we suffer.
The Three Sisters (1901) act 4 (translated by Elisaveta Fen)

11 Forests keep disappearing, rivers dry up, wild life's become extinct, the climate's ruined and the land grows poorer and uglier every day.
Uncle Vanya (1897) act 1

12 When a woman isn't beautiful, people always say, 'You have lovely eyes, you have lovely hair.'
Uncle Vanya (1897) act 3

13 A writer must be as objective as a chemist: he must abandon the subjective line; he must know that dung-heaps play a very reasonable part in a landscape, and that evil passions are as inherent in life as good ones.
letter to M. V. Kiselev, 14 January 1887, in L. S. Friedland (ed.) *Anton Chekhov: Letters on the Short Story . . .* (1964)

14 Medicine is my lawful wife and literature is my mistress. When I get tired of one I spend the night with the other.
letter to A. S. Suvorin, 11 September 1888, in L. S. Friedland (ed.) *Anton Chekhov: Letters on the Short Story . . .* (1964)

15 Brevity is the sister of talent.
letter to Alexander Chekhov, 11 April 1889, in L. S. Friedland (ed.) *Anton Chekhov: Letters on the Short Story . . .* (1964)

16 In *Anna Karenina* and *Onegin* not a single problem is solved, but they satisfy you completely just because all their problems are correctly presented. The court is obliged to submit the case fairly, but let the jury do the deciding, each according to its own judgement.
letter to Alexei Suvorin, 27 October 1888, in L. Hellman (ed.) *Selected Letters of Anton Chekhov* (1955, translated by S. Lederer)

17 I couldn't stand a happiness that went on morning noon and night . . . I promise to be a splendid husband, but give me a wife who, like the moon, does not rise every night in my sky.
on being urged to marry
letter, 23 March 1895; Donald Rayfield *Anton Chekhov* (1997)

18 Between 'God exists' and 'There is no God' lies a whole enormous field which a true sage has great difficulty in crossing. But a Russian knows only one of these two extremes and the middle between them doesn't interest him, which is why he knows nothing or very little . . . A good man's indifference is as good as any religion.
diary, 1897; Donald Rayfield *Anton Chekhov* (1997)

19 Women deprived of the company of men pine, men deprived of the company of women become stupid.
Notebooks (1921)

20 Love, friendship, respect do not unite people as much as common hatred for something.
Notebooks (1921)

21 Things on stage should be as complicated and as simple as in life. People dine, just dine, while their happiness is made and their lives are smashed. If in Act 1 you have a pistol hanging on the wall, then it must fire in the last act.
his rules for writing drama, as noted by an aspiring writer, Alia Gurliand
Donald Rayfield *Anton Chekhov* (1997); attributed

Cher 1946–

American singer and actress

22 If grass can grow through cement, love can find you at every time in your life.
in *The Times* 30 May 1998

Mary Chesnut 1823–86

American diarist and Confederate supporter

23 Atlanta is gone. That agony is over. There is no hope but we will try to have no fear.
after the fall of Atlanta to ***Sherman****'s army in 1864*
Geoffrey C. Ward *The Civil War* (1991) ch. 4

Lord Chesterfield (Philip Dormer Stanhope, Earl of Chesterfield) 1694–1773

English writer and politician
on Chesterfield: see **Johnson** *412:13, 412:17,* **Walpole** *801:15; see also* **Last words** *455:15*

1 Unlike my subject will I frame my song,
It shall be witty and it sha'n't be long.
epigram on 'Long' Sir Thomas Robinson in the *Dictionary of National Biography* (1917–) vol. 17

2 In scandal, as in robbery, the receiver is always thought as bad as the thief.
Advice to his Son (1775) 'Rules for Conversation: Private Scandal'

3 In matters of religion and matrimony I never give any advice; because I will not have anybody's torments in this world or the next laid to my charge.
Letters to Arthur Charles Stanhope, Esq. (1817) 12 October 1765

4 Religion is by no means a proper subject of conversation in a mixed company.
Letters . . . to his Godson and Successor (1890) Letter 142

5 Cunning is the dark sanctuary of incapacity.
Letters . . . to his Godson and Successor (1890) 'Letter . . . to be delivered after his own death'

6 Parsons are very like men, and neither the better nor the worse for wearing a black gown.
Letters to his Son (1774) 5 April 1746

7 The knowledge of the world is only to be acquired in the world, and not in a closet.
Letters to his Son (1774) 4 October 1746

8 An injury is much sooner forgotten than an insult.
Letters to his Son (1774) 9 October 1746

9 Courts and camps are the only places to learn the world in.
Letters to his Son (1774) 2 October 1747

10 Take the tone of the company that you are in.
Letters to his Son (1774) 16 October 1747

11 Do as you would be done by is the surest method that I know of pleasing.
Letters to his Son (1774) 16 October 1747

12 I recommend to you to take care of minutes: for hours will take care of themselves.
Letters to his Son (1774) 6 November 1747; cf. **Lowndes** 478:9

13 Advice is seldom welcome; and those who want it the most always like it the least.
Letters to his Son (1774) 29 January 1748

14 Wear your learning, like your watch in a private pocket: and do not merely pull it out and strike it, merely to show that you have one.
Letters to his Son (1774) 22 February 1748

15 Speak of the moderns without contempt, and of the ancients without idolatry.
Letters to his Son (1774) 27 February 1748

16 In my mind, there is nothing so illiberal and so ill-bred, as audible laughter.
Letters to his Son (1774) 9 March 1748; cf. **Catullus** 197:6, **Congreve** 232:10

17 Women, then, are only children of a larger growth.
Letters to his Son (1774) 5 September 1748; cf. **Dryden** 280:27

18 It must be owned, that the Graces do not seem to be natives of Great Britain; and I doubt, the best of us here have more of rough than polished diamond.
Letters to his Son (1774) 18 November 1748

19 Idleness is only the refuge of weak minds.
Letters to his Son (1774) 20 July 1749

20 Putting moral virtues at the highest, and religion at the lowest, religion must still be allowed to be a collateral security, at least, to virtue; and every prudent man will sooner trust to two securities than to one.
Letters to his Son (1774) 8 January 1750

21 It is commonly said, and more particularly by Lord Shaftesbury, that ridicule is the best test of truth.
Letters to his Son (1774) 6 February 1752; cf. **Shaftesbury** 655:18

22 Knowledge may give weight, but accomplishments give lustre, and many more people see than weigh.
Maxims, in *Letters to his Son* (3rd ed., 1774) vol. 4

23 The chapter of knowledge is a very short, but the chapter of accidents is a very long one.
letter to Solomon Dayrolles, 16 February 1753, in M. Maty (ed.) *Miscellaneous Works* vol. 2 (1778) no. 79

24 I . . . could not help reflecting in my way upon the singular ill-luck of this my dear country, which, as long as ever I remember it, and as far back as I have read, has always been governed by the only two or three people, out of two or three millions, totally incapable of governing, and unfit to be trusted.
in *The World* 7 October 1756); M. Maty (ed.) *Miscellaneous Works* vol. 2 (1778) 'Miscellaneous Pieces' no. 45

25 Tyrawley and I have been dead these two years; but we don't choose to have it known.
James Boswell *Life of Samuel Johnson* (1934 ed.) vol. 2, 3 April 1773

26 The pleasure is momentary, the position ridiculous, and the expense damnable.
of sex
attributed

G. K. Chesterton 1874–1936

English essayist, novelist, and poet
on Chesterton: see **Epitaphs** *304:2; see also* **Telegrams** *758:1*

27 Are they clinging to their crosses, F. E. Smith?
satirizing F. E. **Smith***'s response to the Welsh Disestablishment Bill*
'Antichrist' (1915)

28 Talk about the pews and steeples
And the Cash that goes therewith!
But the souls of Christian peoples . . .
Chuck it, Smith!
'Antichrist' (1915)

29 The gallows in my garden, people say,
Is new and neat and adequately tall.

I tie the noose on in a knowing way
As one that knots his necktie for a ball;
But just as all the neighbours—on the wall—
Are drawing a long breath to shout 'Hurray!'
The strangest whim has seized me . . . . After all
I think I will not hang myself today.
'Ballade of Suicide' (1915)

1 I tell you naught for your comfort,
Yea, naught for your desire,
Save that the sky grows darker yet
And the sea rises higher.
The Ballad of the White Horse (1911) bk. 1

2 For the great Gaels of Ireland
Are the men that God made mad,
For all their wars are merry,
And all their songs are sad.
The Ballad of the White Horse (1911) bk. 2

3 The thing on the blind side of the heart,
On the wrong side of the door,
The green plant groweth, menacing
Almighty lovers in the Spring;
There is always a forgotten thing,
And love is not secure.
The Ballad of the White Horse (1911) bk. 3

4 When fishes flew and forests walked
And figs grew upon thorn,
Some moment when the moon was blood
Then surely I was born.

With monstrous head and sickening cry
And ears like errant wings,
The devil's walking parody
On all four-footed things.
'The Donkey' (1900)

5 Fools! For I also had my hour;
One far fierce hour and sweet:
There was a shout about my ears,
And palms before my feet.
'The Donkey' (1900)

6 They died to save their country and they only saved the world.
'English Graves' (1922)

7 Why do you rush through the fields in trains,
Guessing so much and so much.
Why do you flash through the flowery meads,
Fat-head poet that nobody reads;
And why do you know such a frightful lot
About people in gloves and such?
'The Fat White Woman Speaks' (1933); an answer to Frances Cornford; cf. **Cornford** 237:2

8 From all that terror teaches,
From lies of tongue and pen,
From all the easy speeches
That comfort cruel men,
From sale and profanation
Of honour and the sword,
From sleep and from damnation,
Deliver us, good Lord!
'A Hymn' (1915)

9 White founts falling in the courts of the sun,
And the Soldan of Byzantium is smiling as they run.
'Lepanto' (1915)

10 The cold queen of England is looking in the glass;
The shadow of the Valois is yawning at the Mass.
'Lepanto' (1915)

11 Strong gongs groaning as the guns boom far,
Don John of Austria is going to the war.
'Lepanto' (1915)

12 The folk that live in Liverpool, their heart is in their boots;
They go to hell like lambs, they do, because the hooter hoots.
'Me Heart' (1914)

13 Before the Roman came to Rye or out to Severn strode,
The rolling English drunkard made the rolling English road.
A reeling road, a rolling road, that rambles round the shire,
And after him the parson ran, the sexton and the squire;
'The Rolling English Road' (1914)

14 A merry road, a mazy road, and such as we did tread
The night we went to Birmingham by way of Beachy Head.
'The Rolling English Road' (1914)

15 For there is good news yet to hear and fine things to be seen,
Before we go to Paradise by way of Kensal Green.
'The Rolling English Road' (1914)

16 Smile at us, pay us, pass us; but do not quite forget.
For we are the people of England, that never have spoken yet.
'The Secret People' (1915)

17 We only know the last sad squires ride slowly towards the sea,
And a new people takes the land: and still it is not we.
'The Secret People' (1915)

18 God made the wicked Grocer
For a mystery and a sign,
That men might shun the awful shops
And go to inns to dine.
'The Song Against Grocers' (1914)

19 He keeps a lady in a cage
Most cruelly all day,
And makes her count and calls her 'Miss'
Until she fades away.
'The Song Against Grocers' (1914)

20 Tea, although an Oriental,
Is a gentleman at least;
Cocoa is a cad and coward,
Cocoa is a vulgar beast.
'Song of Right and Wrong' (1914)

21 Lancashire merchants whenever they like
Can water the beer of a man in Klondike

Or poison the meat of a man in Bombay;
And that is the meaning of Empire Day.
'Songs of Education: II Geography' (1922)

1 And Noah he often said to his wife when he sat down to dine,
'I don't care where the water goes if it doesn't get into the wine.'
'Wine and Water' (1914)

2 An adventure is only an inconvenience rightly considered. An inconvenience is only an adventure wrongly considered.
All Things Considered (1908) 'On Running after one's Hat'

3 Literature is a luxury; fiction is a necessity.
The Defendant (1901) 'A Defence of Penny Dreadfuls'

4 The rich are the scum of the earth in every country.
The Flying Inn (1914) ch. 15

5 Bigotry may be roughly defined as the anger of men who have no opinions.
Heretics (1905) ch. 20

6 After the first silence the small man said to the other: 'Where does a wise man hide a pebble?'
And the tall man answered in a low voice: 'On the beach.'
The small man nodded, and after a short silence said: 'Where does a wise man hide a leaf?'
And the other answered: 'In the forest.'
The Innocence of Father Brown (1911)

7 One sees great things from the valley; only small things from the peak.
The Innocence of Father Brown (1911)

8 Thieves respect property. They merely wish the property to become their property that they may more perfectly respect it.
The Man who was Thursday (1908) ch. 4

9 Tradition means giving votes to the most obscure of all classes, our ancestors. It is the democracy of the dead.
Orthodoxy (1908) ch. 4

10 Democrats object to men being disqualified by the accident of birth; tradition objects to their being disqualified by the accident of death.
Orthodoxy (1908) ch. 4

11 All conservatism is based upon the idea that if you leave things alone you leave them as they are. But you do not. If you leave a thing alone you leave it to a torrent of change.
Orthodoxy (1908) ch. 7

12 It isn't that they can't see the solution. It is that they can't see the problem.
The Scandal of Father Brown (1935)

13 They say travel broadens the mind; but you must have the mind.
'The Shadow of the Shark' (1921)

14 Lying in bed would be an altogether perfect and supreme experience if only one had a coloured pencil long enough to draw on the ceiling.
Tremendous Trifles (1909)

15 Hardy went down to botanize in the swamp, while Meredith climbed towards the sun. Meredith became, at his best, a sort of daintily dressed Walt Whitman: Hardy became a sort of village atheist brooding and blaspheming over the village idiot.
Victorian Age in Literature (1912)

16 He could not think up to the height of his own towering style.
of ***Tennyson***
The Victorian Age in Literature (1912) ch. 3

17 The Christian ideal has not been tried and found wanting. It has been found difficult; and left untried.
What's Wrong with the World (1910) pt. 1 'The Unfinished Temple'

18 The prime truth of woman, the universal mother . . . that if a thing is worth doing, it is worth doing badly.
What's Wrong with the World (1910) pt. 4 'Folly and Female Education'

19 To be clever enough to get all that money, one must be stupid enough to want it.
The Wisdom of Father Brown (1914)

20 Journalism largely consists in saying 'Lord Jones Dead' to people who never knew that Lord Jones was alive.
The Wisdom of Father Brown (1914)

21 Democracy means government by the uneducated, while aristocracy means government by the badly educated.
in *New York Times* 1 February 1931, pt. 5

22 When men stop believing in God they don't believe in nothing; they believe in anything.
widely attributed, although not traced in his works; first recorded as 'The first effect of not believing in God is to believe in anything' in Emile Cammaerts *Chesterton: The Laughing Prophet* (1937)

Maurice Chevalier 1888–1972
French singer and actor

23 Considering the alternative, it's not too bad at all.
on being asked what he felt about the advancing years, on his seventy-second birthday
Michael Freedland *Maurice Chevalier* (1981)

Lydia Maria Child 1802–80
American abolitionist and suffragist

24 We first crush people to the earth, and then claim the right of trampling on them forever, because they are prostrate.
An Appeal on Behalf of That Class of Americans Called Africans (1833)

25 Woman stock is rising in the market. I shall not live to see women vote, but I'll come and rap at the ballot box.
letter to Sarah Shaw, 3 August 1856

Erskine Childers 1870–1922

Anglo-Irish writer and political activist
see also **Last words** 455:6

1 The riddle of the sands.
title of novel (1903)

2 It seems perfectly simple and inevitable, like lying down after a long day's work.
shortly before his execution by Free State forces
letter to his wife, November 1922

William Chillingworth 1602–44

English scholar

3 The Bible and the Bible only is the religion of Protestants.
The Religion of Protestants (1637)

4 I once knew a man out of courtesy help a lame dog over a stile, and he for requital bit his fingers.
The Religion of Protestants (1637)

Charles Chilton see Joan Littlewood

Jaques Chirac 1932–

French statesman, Prime Minister 1974–6 and 1986–8, President since 1995

5 For its part, France wants you to take part in this great undertaking.
on European Monetary Union
speech to both Houses of Parliament, 15 May 1996

Melanie ('Mel C.') Chisholm 1974–

English pop singer, member ('Sporty Spice') of The Spice Girls
see also **Rowbottom** 636:8

6 If Oasis are bigger than God, what does that make us? Bigger than Buddha?
asserting that the Spice Girls are 'a darn sight bigger than Oasis'
in *Independent* 16 August 1997 'Quote Unquote'; cf. **Gallagher** 328:16, **Lennon** 463:17

Thomas O. Chisholm 1866–1960

7 Great is thy faithfulness! Great is thy faithfulness!
Morning by morning new mercies I see;
All I have needed thy hand has provided.
Great is thy faithfulness, Lord, unto me.
'Great is thy faithfulness' (hymn)

Rufus Choate 1799–1859

American lawyer and politician

8 Its constitution the glittering and sounding generalities of natural right which make up the Declaration of Independence.
letter to the Maine Whig State Central Committee, 9 August 1856, in S. G. Brown *The Works of Rufus Choate with a Memoir of his Life* (1862) vol. 1; cf. **Emerson** 300:2

Duc de Choiseul 1719–85

French politician

9 A minister who moves about in society is in a position to read the signs of the times even in a festive gathering, but one who remains shut up in his office learns nothing.
Jack F. Bernard *Talleyrand* (1973)

Noam Chomsky 1928–

American linguistics scholar

10 The notion 'grammatical' cannot be identified with 'meaningful' or 'significant' in any semantic sense. Sentences (1) and (2) are equally nonsensical, but . . . only the former is grammatical.
(1) Colourless green ideas sleep furiously.
(2) Furiously sleep ideas green colourless.
Syntactic Structures (1957) ch. 2

11 The empiricist view is so deep-seated in our way of looking at the human mind that it almost has the character of a superstition.
radio discussion, in *Listener* 30 May 1968

12 As soon as questions of will or decision or reason or choice of action arise, human science is at a loss.
television interview, in *Listener* 6 April 1978

13 The Internet is an élite organization; most of the population of the world has never even made a phone call.
on the limitations of the World Wide Web
in *Observer* 18 February 1996

Agatha Christie 1890–1976

English writer of detective fiction

14 War settles *nothing* . . . to win a war is as disastrous as to lose one!
An Autobiography (1977) pt. 10

15 He [Hercule Poirot] tapped his forehead. 'These little grey cells. It is "up to them".'
The Mysterious Affair at Styles (1920) ch. 10

16 I'm a sausage machine, a perfect sausage machine.
G. C. Ramsey *Agatha Christie* (1972)

David Christy 1802–c.68

17 Cotton is King; or, the economical relations of slavery.
title of book, 1855

Chuang Tzu (Zhuangzi) c.369–286 BC

Chinese philosopher

18 Without them [feelings] there would not be I. And without me who will experience them? They are right near by. But we don't know what causes them. It seems there is a True Lord who does so, but there is no indication of his existence.
Chuang Tzu ch. 2

19 When one is at ease with himself, one is near Tao.
Chuang Tzu ch. 2

20 The sage harmonizes the right and wrong and rests in natural equalization. This is called following two courses at the same time.
Chuang Tzu ch. 2

21 The universe and I exist together, and all things and I are one.
Chuang Tzu ch. 2

1 The sage has the sun and moon by his side. He grasps the universe under the arm. He blends everything into a harmonious whole, casts aside whatever is confused or obscured, and regards the humble as honourable.
Chuang Tzu ch. 2

2 Once I, Chang Chou, dreamed that I was a butterfly and was happy as a butterfly. I was conscious that I was quite pleased with myself but I did not know that I was Chou. Suddenly I awoke and there I was, visibly Chou. I do not know whether it was Chou dreaming that he was a butterfly or the butterfly dreaming that it was Chou.
Chuang Tzu ch. 2; cf. **Basho** 56:20

3 If the Universe is hidden in the universe itself, then there can be no escape from it. This is the great truth of things in general.
Chuang Tzu ch. 6

4 Tao has reality and evidence but no action or physical form. It may be transmitted but cannot be received. It may be obtained but cannot be seen. It is based in itself, rooted in itself. Before heaven and earth came into being, Tao existed by itself from all time.
Chuang Tzu ch. 6

5 Those who are contented and at ease when the occasion comes and live in accord with the course of Nature cannot be affected by sorrow or joy. This is what the ancients called release from bondage. Those who cannot release themselves are so because they are bound by material things.
Chuang Tzu ch. 6

6 Do not be the possessor of fame. Do not be the storehouse of schemes. Do not take over the function of things. Do not be the master of knowledge [to manipulate things]. Personally realize the infinite to the highest degree and travel in the realm of which there is no sign. Exercise fully what you have received from Nature without any subjective viewpoint. In one word; be absolutely vacuous.
Chuang Tzu ch. 7

7 The mind of the perfect man is like a mirror. It does not lean forward or backward in its response to things. It responds to things but conceals nothing of its own. Therefore it is able to deal with things without injury to [its reality].
Chuang Tzu ch. 7

Mary, Lady Chudleigh (née Leigh) 1656–1710
English poet

8 'Tis hard we should be by the men despised,
Yet kept from knowing what would make us prized;
Debarred from knowledge, banished from the schools,
And with the utmost industry bred fools.
The Ladies Defence (1701)

9 Wife and Servant are the same,
But only differ in the name.
Poems (1703) 'To the Ladies'

10 Then shun, oh! shun that wretched state
And all the fawning flatterers hate:
Value yourselves, and men despise
You must be proud if you'll be wise.
on marriage
Poems (1703) 'To the Ladies'

Francis Pharcellus Church 1839–1906
American journalist

11 Yes, Virginia, there is a Santa Claus.
replying to a letter from eight-year-old Virginia O'Hanlon
editorial in New York *Sun*, 21 September 1897

Charles Churchill 1731–64
English poet

12 Though by whim, envy, or resentment led,
They damn those authors whom they never read.
The Candidate (1764) l. 57

13 The danger chiefly lies in acting well;
No crime's so great as daring to excel.
An Epistle to William Hogarth (1763) l. 51

14 Be England what she will,
With all her faults, she is my country still.
The Farewell (1764) l. 27; cf. **Cowper** 241:21

15 It can't be Nature, for it is not sense.
The Farewell (1764) l. 200

16 England—a happy land we know,
Where follies naturally grow.
The Ghost (1763) bk. 1, l. 111

17 And adepts in the speaking trade
Keep a cough by them ready made.
The Ghost (1763) bk. 2, l. 545

18 Just to the windward of the law.
The Ghost (1763) bk. 3, l. 56

19 . . . He for subscribers baits his hook,
And takes your cash; but where's the book?
No matter where; wise fear, you know,
Forbids the robbing of a foe;
But what, to serve our private ends,
Forbids the cheating of our friends?
satirizing Samuel ***Johnson***
The Ghost (1763) bk. 3, l. 801

20 A joke's a very serious thing.
The Ghost (1763) bk. 4, l. 1386

21 Happy, thrice happy now the savage race,
Since Europe took their gold, and gave them grace!
Pastors she sends to help them in their need,
Some who can't write, with others who can't read.
Gotham (1764) bk. 1, l. 67

22 Our vices, with more zeal than holy prayers,
She teaches them, and in return takes theirs.
Gotham (1764) bk. 1, l. 73

23 Old-age, a second child, by Nature cursed
With more and greater evils than the first,

Weak, sickly, full of pains; in ev'ry breath
Railing at life, and yet afraid of death.
Gotham (1764) bk. 1, l. 215

1 Keep up appearances; there lies the test;
The world will give thee credit for the rest.
Outward be fair, however foul within;
Sin if thou wilt, but then in secret sin.
Night (1761) l. 311

2 Stay out all night, but take especial care
That Prudence bring thee back to early prayer
As one with watching and with study faint,
Reel in a drunkard, and reel out a saint.
Night (1761) l. 321

3 Grave without thought, and without feeling gay.
on pretentious poets
The Prophecy of Famine (1763) l. 60

4 No merit but mere knack of rhyme,
Short gleams of sense, and satire out of time.
The Prophecy of Famine (1763) l. 81

5 Apt Alliteration's artful aid.
The Prophecy of Famine (1763) l. 86

6 He sickened at all triumphs but his own.
of Thomas Franklin, Professor of Greek at Cambridge University
The Rosciad (1761) l. 64

7 To mischief trained, e'en from his mother's womb,
Grown old in fraud, tho' yet in manhood's bloom.
Adopting arts, by which gay villains rise,
And reach the heights, which honest men despise;
Mute at the bar, and in the senate loud,
Dull 'mongst the dullest, proudest of the proud;
A pert, prim prater of the northern race,
Guilt in his heart, and famine in his face.
of Alexander Wedderburn, later Lord Loughborough
The Rosciad (1761) l. 69

8 Ne'er blushed unless, in spreading Vice's snares,
She blundered on some virtue unawares.
The Rosciad (1761) l. 137

9 Learned without sense, and venerably dull.
of Arthur Murphy
The Rosciad (1761) l. 592

10 But, spite of all the criticizing elves,
Those who would make us feel, must feel themselves.
The Rosciad (1761) l. 961

11 Where he falls short, 'tis Nature's fault alone;
Where he succeeds, the merit's all his own.
of the actor, Thomas Sheridan
The Rosciad (1761) l. 1025

Lord Randolph Churchill 1849–94

British Conservative politician

12 The forest laments in order that Mr Gladstone may perspire.
on ***Gladstone****'s hobby of felling trees*
speech on Financial Reform, delivered in Blackpool, 24 January 1884, in F. Banfield (ed.) *Life and Speeches of Lord Randolph Churchill* (1884)

13 I decided some time ago that if the G. O. M. went for Home Rule, the Orange card would be the one to play. Please God it may turn out the ace of trumps and not the two.
G. O. M. = *Grand Old Man* (***Gladstone***)
letter to Lord Justice FitzGibbon, 16 February 1886, in Robert Rhodes James *Lord Randolph Churchill* (1959) ch. 8; cf. **Shapiro** 706:11

14 Ulster will fight; Ulster will be right.
public letter, 7 May 1886, in R. F. Foster *Lord Randolph Churchill* (1981)

15 An old man in a hurry.
on ***Gladstone***
address to the electors of South Paddington, 19 June 1886; in W. S. Churchill *Lord Randolph Churchill* (1906) vol. 2

16 All great men make mistakes. Napoleon forgot Blücher, I forgot Goschen.
when Lord Randolph suddenly resigned the position of Chancellor of the Exchequer in 1886, ***Goschen*** *had been appointed in his place*
Leaves from the Notebooks of Lady Dorothy Nevill (1907)

17 I never could make out what those damned dots [decimal points] meant.
W. S. Churchill *Lord Randolph Churchill* (1906) vol. 2

Winston Churchill 1874–1965

British Conservative statesman; Prime Minister, 1940–5, 1951–5
on Churchill: see **Attlee** 32:1, **Balfour** 50:2, **Bevan** 71:16, **de Valera** 259:5, **Murrow** 537:8; *see also* **Johnson** 417:7

18 It cannot in the opinion of His Majesty's Government be classified as slavery in the extreme acceptance of the word without some risk of terminological inexactitude.
speech in the House of Commons, 22 February 1906

19 He is one of those orators of whom it was well said, 'Before they get up, they do not know what they are going to say; when they are speaking, they do not know what they are saying; and when they have sat down, they do not know what they have said.'
of Lord Charles Beresford
speech in the House of Commons, 20 December 1912

20 Business carried on as usual during alterations on the map of Europe.
on the self-adopted 'motto' of the British people
speech at Guildhall, 9 November 1914, *Complete Speeches* (1974) vol. 3

21 The difference between him and Arthur is that Arthur is wicked and moral, Asquith is good and immoral.
comparing H. H. ***Asquith*** *with Arthur* ***Balfour***
E. T. Raymond *Mr Balfour* (1920)

22 The whole map of Europe has been changed . . . but as the deluge subsides and the waters fall short we see the dreary steeples of Fermanagh and Tyrone emerging once again.
speech in the House of Commons, 16 February 1922

1 Anyone can rat, but it takes a certain amount of ingenuity to re-rat.
on rejoining the Conservatives twenty years after leaving them for the Liberals, c.1924
Kay Halle *Irrepressible Churchill* (1966)

2 I remember, when I was a child, being taken to the celebrated Barnum's circus, which contained an exhibition of freaks and monstrosities, but the exhibit on the programme which I most desired to see was the one described as 'The Boneless Wonder'. My parents judged that that spectacle would be too revolting and demoralizing for my youthful eyes, and I have waited 50 years to see the boneless wonder sitting on the Treasury Bench.
of Ramsay **MacDonald**
speech in the House of Commons, 28 January 1931

3 [The Government] go on in strange paradox, decided only to be undecided, resolved to be irresolute, adamant for drift, solid for fluidity, all-powerful to be impotent.
speech in the House of Commons, 12 November 1936

4 Dictators ride to and fro upon tigers which they dare not dismount. And the tigers are getting hungry.
letter, 11 November 1937, in *Step by Step* (1939); cf. **Proverbs** 602:32

5 The utmost he [Neville Chamberlain] has been able to gain for Czechoslovakia and in the matters which were in dispute has been that the German dictator, instead of snatching his victuals from the table, has been content to have them served to him course by course.
speech in the House of Commons, 5 October 1938

6 I cannot forecast to you the action of Russia. It is a riddle wrapped in a mystery inside an enigma.
radio broadcast, 1 October 1939, in *Into Battle* (1941)

7 I have nothing to offer but blood, toil, tears and sweat.
speech in the House of Commons, 13 May 1940; cf. **Byron** 173:13

8 What is our policy? . . . to wage war against a monstrous tyranny, never surpassed in the dark, lamentable catalogue of human crime.
speech in the House of Commons, 13 May 1940

9 What is our aim? . . . Victory, victory at all costs, victory in spite of all terror; victory, however long and hard the road may be; for without victory, there is no survival.
speech in the House of Commons, 13 May 1940

10 We shall not flag or fail. We shall go on to the end. We shall fight in France, we shall fight on the seas and oceans, we shall fight with growing confidence and growing strength in the air, we shall defend our island, whatever the cost may be. We shall fight on the beaches, we shall fight on the landing grounds, we shall fight in the fields and in the streets, we shall fight in the hills; we shall never surrender.
speech in the House of Commons, 4 June 1940

11 Let us therefore brace ourselves to our duty, and so bear ourselves that, if the British Commonwealth and its Empire lasts for a thousand years, men will still say, 'This was their finest hour.'
speech in the House of Commons, 18 June 1940

12 Never in the field of human conflict was so much owed by so many to so few.
on the Battle of Britain
speech in the House of Commons, 20 August 1940

13 No one can guarantee success in war, but only deserve it.
letter to Lord Wavell, 26 November 1940, in *The Second World War* vol. 2 (1949) ch. 27; cf. **Addison** 4:9

14 Give us the tools and we will finish the job.
radio broadcast, 9 February 1941, in *Complete Speeches* (1974) vol. 6

15 When I warned them [the French Government] that Britain would fight on alone whatever they did, their generals told their Prime Minister and his divided Cabinet, 'In three weeks England will have her neck wrung like a chicken.' Some chicken! Some neck!
speech to Canadian Parliament, 30 December 1941, in *Complete Speeches* (1974) vol. 6

16 A medal glitters, but it also casts a shadow.
a reference to the envy caused by the award of honours in 1941; Kenneth Rose *King George V* (1983) p. 7

17 Now this is not the end. It is not even the beginning of the end. But it is, perhaps, the end of the beginning.
on the Battle of Egypt
speech at the Mansion House, London, 10 November 1942, in *The End of the Beginning* (1943)

18 We make this wide encircling movement in the Mediterranean, having for its primary object the recovery of the command of that vital sea, but also having for its object the exposure of the underbelly of the Axis, especially Italy, to heavy attack.
speech in the House of Commons, 11 November 1942; cf. **Misquotations** 522:8

19 National compulsory insurance for all classes for all purposes from the cradle to the grave.
radio broadcast, 21 March 1943, in *Complete Speeches* (1974) vol. 7

20 There is no finer investment for any community than putting milk into babies.
radio broadcast, 21 March 1943, in *Complete Speeches* (1974) vol. 7

21 The empires of the future are the empires of the mind.
speech at Harvard, 6 September 1943, in *Onwards to Victory* (1944)

22 The Prime Minister has nothing to hide from the President of the United States
on stepping from his bath in the presence of a startled President **Roosevelt**
recalled by Roosevelt's son in *Churchill* (BBC television series presented by Martin Gilbert, 1992) pt. 3

1 From Stettin in the Baltic to Trieste in the Adriatic an iron curtain has descended across the Continent.
'iron curtain' previously had been applied by others to the Soviet Union or her sphere of influence, e.g. Ethel Snowden Through Bolshevik Russia *(1920), Dr* **Goebbels** Das Reich *(25 February 1945), and by Churchill himself in a cable to President* **Truman** *(4 June 1945)*
speech at Westminster College, Fulton, Missouri, 5 March 1946, in *Complete Speeches* (1974) vol. 7

2 Democracy is the worst form of Government except all those other forms that have been tried from time to time.
speech in the House of Commons, 11 November 1947

3 This is the sort of English up with which I will not put.
Ernest Gowers *Plain Words* (1948) 'Troubles with Prepositions'

4 Naval tradition? Monstrous. Nothing but rum, sodomy, prayers, and the lash.
often quoted as 'rum, sodomy, and the lash', as in Peter Gretton Former Naval Person *(1968)*
Harold Nicolson, diary, 17 August 1950

5 The candle in that great turnip has gone out.
in reply to the comment 'One never hears of **Baldwin** *nowadays — he might as well be dead'*
Harold Nicolson: Diaries and Letters 1945–62 (1968) diary 17 August 1950

6 To jaw-jaw is always better than to war-war.
speech at White House, 26 June 1954, in *New York Times* 27 June 1954

7 I have never accepted what many people have kindly said—namely, that I inspired the nation . . . It was the nation and the race dwelling all round the globe that had the lion's heart. I had the luck to be called upon to give the roar. I also hope that I sometimes suggested to the lion the right place to use his claws.
speech at Westminster Hall, 30 November 1954

8 I still have the ideas, Walter, but I can't find the words to clothe them.
to Walter **Monckton**
Tony Benn, diary, 15 December 1956

9 I have taken more out of alcohol than alcohol has taken out of me.
Quentin Reynolds *By Quentin Reynolds* (1964) ch. 11

10 In defeat unbeatable: in victory unbearable.
of Lord **Montgomery**
Edward Marsh *Ambrosia and Small Beer* (1964) ch. 5

11 Like a powerful graceful cat walking delicately and unsoiled across a rather muddy street.
of **Balfour***'s moving from* **Asquith***'s Cabinet to that of* **Lloyd George**
Great Contemporaries (1937)

of the career of Lord **Curzon***:*

12 The morning had been golden; the noontide was bronze; and the evening lead. But all were solid, and each was polished till it shone after its fashion.
Great Contemporaries (1937)

13 Headmasters have powers at their disposal with which Prime Ministers have never yet been invested.
My Early Life (1930) ch. 2

14 Mr Gladstone read Homer for fun, which I thought served him right.
My Early Life (1930) ch. 2

15 It is a good thing for an uneducated man to read books of quotations.
My Early Life (1930) ch. 9

16 In war: resolution. In defeat: defiance. In victory: magnanimity. In peace: goodwill.
The Second World War vol. 1 (1948) epigraph, which according to Edward Marsh in *A Number of People* (1939), occurred to Churchill shortly after the conclusion of the First World War

17 The loyalties which centre upon number one are enormous. If he trips he must be sustained. If he makes mistakes they must be covered. If he sleeps he must not be wantonly disturbed. If he is no good he must be pole-axed. But this last extreme process cannot be carried out every day; and certainly not in the days just after he has been chosen.
The Second World War (1949) vol. 2 ch. 1

18 If Hitler invaded hell I would make at least a favourable reference to the devil in the House of Commons.
The Second World War (1950) vol. 3 ch. 20

19 I did not suffer from any desire to be relieved of my responsibilities. All I wanted was compliance with my wishes after reasonable discussion.
The Second World War (1951) vol. 4 ch. 5

20 Jellicoe was the only man on either side who could lose the war in an afternoon.
The World Crisis (1927) pt. 1, ch. 5

21 The ability to foretell what is going to happen tomorrow, next week, next month, and next year. And to have the ability afterwards to explain why it didn't happen.
describing the qualifications desirable in a prospective politician
B. Adler *Churchill Wit* (1965)

22 I am fond of pigs. Dogs look up to us. Cats look down on us. Pigs treat us as equals.
attributed, in M. Gilbert *Never Despair* (1988)

23 NANCY ASTOR: If I were your wife I would put poison in your coffee!
CHURCHILL: And if I were your husband I would drink it.
Consuelo Vanderbilt Balsan *Glitter and Gold* (1952)

24 A remarkable example of modern art. It certainly combines force with candour.
on the notorious 80th birthday portrait by Graham Sutherland, later destroyed by Lady Churchill
Martin Gilbert *Churchill: A Life* (1991)

25 The only recorded instance in history of a rat swimming *towards* a sinking ship.
of a former Conservative who proposed to stand as a Liberal
Leon Harris *The Fine Art of Political Wit* (1965)

1 A sheep in sheep's clothing.
of Clement ***Attlee***
Lord Home *The Way the Wind Blows* (1976) ch. 6; cf. **Gosse** 347:7

2 Take away that pudding—it has no theme.
Lord Home *The Way the Wind Blows* (1976) ch. 16

Count Galeazzo Ciano 1903–44
Italian fascist politician; son-in-law of Mussolini

3 *La vittoria trova cento padri, e nessuno vuole riconoscere l'insuccesso.*
Victory has a hundred fathers, but defeat is an orphan.
literally 'no-one wants to recognise defeat as his own'
Diary (1946) vol. 2, 9 September 1942

Colley Cibber 1671–1757
English dramatist

4 Oh! how many torments lie in the small circle of a wedding-ring!
The Double Gallant (1707) act 1, sc. 2

5 Off with his head—so much for Buckingham.
Richard III (1700) act 4 (adapted from Shakespeare); cf. **Shakespeare** 696:21

6 Perish the thought!
Richard III (1700) act 5 (adapted from Shakespeare)

7 Conscience avaunt, Richard's himself again:
Hark! the shrill trumpet sounds, to horse, away,
My soul's in arms, and eager for the fray.
Richard III (1700) act 5 (adapted from Shakespeare)

8 Stolen sweets are best.
The Rival Fools (1709) act 1, sc. 1; cf. **Proverbs** 611:24

Cicero (Marcus Tullius Cicero) 106–43 BC
Roman orator and statesman
on Cicero: see ***Catullus*** *197:8,* ***Cromwell*** *246:3,* ***Dickens*** *262:12,* ***Stevenson*** *740:16*

9 *Dicit enim tamquam in Platonis πολιτείᾳ, non tamquam in Romuli faece sententiam.*
For he delivers his opinions as though he were living in Plato's Republic rather than among the dregs of Romulus.
of M. Porcius Cato, the Younger
Ad Atticum bk. 2, letter 1, sect. 8

10 *Sed nescio quo modo nihil tam absurde dici potest quod non dicatur ab aliquo philosophorum.*
There is nothing so absurd but some philosopher has said it.
De Divinatione bk. 2, ch. 119

11 *Vulgo enim dicitur: Iucundi acti labores.*
For it is commonly said: completed labours are pleasant.
De Finibus bk. 2, ch. 105

12 *Salus populi suprema est lex.*
The good of the people is the chief law.
De Legibus bk. 3, ch. 8; cf. **Selden** 653:21

13 *'Ipse dixit.' 'Ipse' autem erat Pythagoras.*
'He himself said', and this 'himself' was Pythagoras.
De Natura Deorum bk. 1, ch. 10

14 *Summum bonum.*
The highest good.
De Officiis bk. 1, ch. 5

15 *Cedant arma togae, concedant laurea laudi.*
Let war yield to peace, laurels to paeans.
De Officiis bk. 1, ch. 77

16 *Numquam se minus otiosum esse quam cum otiosus, nec minus solum quam cum solus esset.*
Never less idle than when wholly idle, nor less alone than when wholly alone.
De Officiis bk. 3, ch. 1

17 *Mens cuiusque is est quisque.*
The spirit is the true self.
De Republica bk. 6, ch. 26

18 *Quousque tandem abutere, Catilina, patientia nostra?*
How long will you abuse our patience, Catiline?
In Catilinam Speech 1, ch. 1

19 *O tempora, O mores!*
Oh, the times! Oh, the manners!
In Catilinam Speech 1, ch. 1

20 *Abiit, excessit, evasit, erupit.*
He departed, he withdrew, he strode off, he broke forth.
In Catilinam Speech 2, ch. 1

21 *Civis Romanus sum.*
I am a Roman citizen.
In Verrem Speech 5, ch. 147; **Kennedy** 433:17, **Palmerston** 566:3

22 *Quod di omen avertant.*
May the gods avert this omen.
Third Philippic ch. 35

23 *Nervos belli, pecuniam infinitam.*
The sinews of war, unlimited money.
Fifth Philippic ch. 5; cf. **Bacon** 44:12, **Farquhar** 307:18

24 *Silent enim leges inter arma.*
Laws are silent in time of war.
Pro Milone ch. 11

25 *Cui bono?*
To whose profit?
Pro Roscio Amerino ch. 84 and *Pro Milone* ch. 12, sect. 32, quoting L. Cassius Longinus Ravilla

26 *Id quod est praestantissimum maximeque optabile omnibus sanis et bonis et beatis cum dignitate otium.*
The thing which is the most outstanding and chiefly to be desired by all healthy and good and well-off persons, is leisure with honour.
Pro Sestio ch. 98

27 *Errare mehercule malo cum Platone . . . quam cum istis vera sentire.*

I would rather be wrong, by God, with Plato . . .
than be correct with those men.
on Pythagoreans
Tusculanae Disputationes bk. 1, ch. 39

1 *O fortunatam natam me consule Romam!*
O happy Rome, born when I was consul!
Juvenal *Satires* poem 10, l. 122

2 The young man should be praised, decorated, and got rid of.
of Octavian, the future Emperor ***Augustus***
referred to in a letter from Decimus Brutus to Cicero; Sulpicius *Epistulae ad Familiares* bk. 9

E. M. Cioran 1911–95
Romanian-born French philosopher

3 Without the possibility of suicide, I would have killed myself long ago.
in *Independent* 2 December 1989

4 I do nothing, granted. But I see the hours pass—which is better than trying to fill them.
in *Guardian* 11 May 1993

Claire Clairmont 1798–1879
lover of ***Byron*** *and stepsister of Mary* ***Shelley***

5 I shall ever remember the gentleness of your manners and the wild originality of your countenance.
letter to Lord Byron, 16 April 1816; M. K. Stocking (ed.) *The Clairmont Correspondence* (1995)

John Clare 1793–1864
English poet

6 When badgers fight and everyone's a foe.
'Badger' (written *c.*1836)

7 He could not die when the trees were green,
For he loved the time too well.
'The Dying Child'

8 My life hath been one chain of contradictions,
Madhouses, prisons, whore-shops.
'Child Harold' (written 1841) l. 146

9 They took me from my wife, and to save trouble
I wed again, and made the error double.
'Child Harold' (written 1841) l. 152

10 God hath often saw
Things here too dirty for the light of day;
For in a madhouse there exists no law
Now stagnant grows my too refinèd clay;
I envy birds their wings to fly away.
'Child Harold' (written 1841) l. 158

11 Pale death, the grand physician, cures all pain;
The dead rest well who lived for joys in vain.
'Child Harold' (written 1841) l. 215

12 When words refuse before the crowd
My Mary's name to give,
The muse in silence sings aloud:
And there my love will live.
'Child Harold' (written 1841) l. 513

13 Hopeless hope hopes on and meets no end,
Wastes without springs and homes without a friend.
'Child Harold' (written 1841) l. 1018

14 A quiet, pilfering, unprotected race.
'The Gipsy Camp' (1841)

15 I am—yet what I am, none cares or knows;
My friends forsake me like a memory lost:
I am the self-consumer of my woes.
'I Am' (1848)

16 I long for scenes where man hath never trod
A place where woman never smiled or wept
There to abide with my Creator God
And sleep as I in childhood sweetly slept,
Untroubling and untroubled where I lie
The grass below, above, the vaulted sky.
'I Am' (1848)

17 The present is the funeral of the past,
And man the living sepulchre of life.
'The present is the funeral of the past' (written 1845)

18 Summers pleasures they are gone like to visions every one
And the cloudy days of autumn and of winter cometh on
I tried to call them back but unbidden they are gone
Far away from heart and eye and for ever far away.
'Remembrances'

Edward Hyde, Earl of Clarendon 1609–74
English statesman and historian

19 Without question, when he first drew the sword, he threw away the scabbard.
of Hampden
The History of the Rebellion (1703, ed. W. D. Macray, 1888) vol. 3, bk. 7, sect. 84; cf. **Proverbs** 615:5

20 He had a head to contrive, a tongue to persuade, and a hand to execute any mischief.
of Hampden
The History of the Rebellion (1703, ed. W. D. Macray, 1888) vol. 3, bk. 7, sect. 84; cf. **Gibbon** 335:12

21 He . . . would, with a shrill and sad accent, ingeminate the word *Peace, Peace.*
of ***Falkland***
The History of the Rebellion (1703, ed. W. D. Macray, 1888) vol. 3, bk. 7, sect. 233

22 So enamoured on peace that he would have been glad the King should have bought it at any price.
of ***Falkland***
The History of the Rebellion (1703, ed. W. D. Macray, 1888) vol. 3, bk. 7, sect. 233

23 He will be looked upon by posterity as a brave bad man.
of ***Cromwell***
The History of the Rebellion (1703, ed. W. D. Macray, 1888) vol. 6, bk. 15

Claribel (Mrs Charlotte Alington Barnard) 1840–69
English writer of ballads

1 I cannot sing the old songs
I sang long years ago,
For heart and voice would fail me,
And foolish tears would flow.
'The Old Songs' (1865)

Alan Clark 1928–
British Conservative politician, son of Kenneth **Clark**

2 There are no true friends in politics. We are all sharks circling, and waiting, for traces of blood to appear in the water.
diary, 30 November 1990

3 Our old friend economical . . . with the *actualité*.
under cross-examination at the Old Bailey during the Matrix Churchill case
in *Independent* 10 November 1992; cf. **Armstrong** 25:20

4 If you have bright plumage, people will take pot shots at you.
in *Independent* 25 June 1994

5 Safe is spelled D-U-L-L. Politics has got to be a fun activity, otherwise people turn their back on it.
on being selected as parliamentary candidate for Kensington and Chelsea, 24 January 1997
in *Daily Telegraph* 25 January 1997

Kenneth Clark 1903–83
English art historian, father of Alan **Clark**

6 Medieval marriages were entirely a matter of property, and, as everyone knows, marriage without love means love without marriage.
Civilisation (1969) ch. 3

7 It's a curious fact that the all-male religions have produced no religious imagery—in most cases have positively forbidden it. The great religious art of the world is deeply involved with the female principle.
Civilisation (1969) ch. 7

Arthur C. Clarke 1917–
English science fiction writer

8 When a distinguished but elderly scientist states that something is possible, he is almost certainly right. When he states that something is impossible, he is very probably wrong.
Profiles of the Future (1962) ch. 2; cf. **Asimov** 30:18

9 Any sufficiently advanced technology is indistinguishable from magic.
Profiles of the Future (1962) ch. 2

10 How inappropriate to call this planet Earth when it is clearly Ocean.
in *Nature* 8 March 1990

11 The only genuine consciousness-expanding drug.
of science fiction
letter claiming coinage in *New Scientist* 2 April 1994

Austin Clarke 1896–1974
Irish poet, dramatist, and novelist

12 For the house of the planter
Is known by the trees.
'The Planter's Daughter' (1929)

13 And O! She was the Sunday
In every week.
'The Planter's Daughter' (1929)

Grant Clarke 1891–1931 and **Edgar Leslie** 1885–1976

14 He'd have to get under, get out and get under
And fix up his automobile.
He'd Have to Get Under—Get Out and Get Under (1913 song)

James Stanier Clarke *c.*1765–1834
English clergyman, chaplain and private secretary to Prince Leopold of Coburg

15 Perhaps when you again appear in print you may choose to dedicate your volumes to Prince Leopold: any historical romance, illustrative of the history of the august House of Coburg, would just now be very interesting.
letter to Jane Austen, 27 March 1816, in R. W. Chapman (ed.) *Jane Austen's Letters* (1952)

John Clarke d. 1658

16 He that would thrive
Must rise at five;
He that hath thriven
May lie till seven.
Paraemiologia Anglo-Latina (1639) 'Diligentia'

Claudian 370–*c.*404
Alexandrian-born Latin poet

17 *Erret, et extremos alter scrutetur Hiberos:*
Plus habet hic vitae, plus habet ille viae.
Let who will be a wanderer and explore farthest Spain: such may have more of a journey: he of Verona has more of a life.
of the old man of Verona who never left his home
De Sene Veronensi

Appius Claudius Caecus fl. 312–279 BC
Roman censor, orator, and prose writer

18 *Faber est suae quisque fortunae.*
Each man is the smith of his own fortune.
Sallust *Ad Caesarem Senem de Re Publica Oratio* ch. 1, sect. 2; cf. **Proverbs** 599:34

Karl von Clausewitz 1780–1831
Prussian soldier and military theorist

19 War is nothing but a continuation of politics with the admixture of other means.
commonly rendered as 'War is the continuation of politics by other means'
On War (1832–4) bk. 8, ch. 6, sect. B

Henry Clay 1777–1852

American politician

on Clay: see **Glascock** *341:17*

1 If you wish to avoid foreign collision, you had better abandon the ocean.

speech in the House of Representatives, 22 January 1812, in C. Colton *The Life, Correspondence and Speeches of Henry Clay* (1864) vol. 5

2 The gentleman [Josiah Quincy] can not have forgotten his own sentiment, uttered even on the floor of this House, 'peaceably if we can, forcibly if we must'.

speech in Congress, 8 January 1813, in C. Colton (ed.) *The Works of Henry Clay* (1904) vol. 1; cf. **Quincy** 619:3

3 The arts of power and its minions are the same in all countries and in all ages. It marks a victim; denounces it; and excites the public odium and the public hatred, to conceal its own abuses and encroachments.

speech in the Senate, 14 March 1834, in C. Colton (ed.) *The Works of Henry Clay* (1904) vol. 5

4 It has been my invariable rule to do all for the Union. If any man wants the key of my heart, let him take the key of the Union, and that is the key to my heart.

speech in Norfolk, 22 April 1844; Robert V. Rimini *Henry Clay* (1991)

5 I had rather be right than be President.

to Senator Preston of South Carolina, 1839

attributed; S. W. McCall *Life of Thomas Brackett Reed* (1914) ch. 14

Philip 'Tubby' Clayton 1885–1972

Australian-born British clergyman, founder of Toc H

6 CHAIRMAN: What is service?

CANDIDATE: The rent we pay for our room on earth.

admission ceremony of Toc H, a society founded after the First World War to provide Christian fellowship and social service

Tresham Lever *Clayton of Toc H* (1971)

Eldridge Cleaver 1935–98

American political activist

7 What we're saying today is that you're either part of the solution or you're part of the problem.

speech in San Francisco, 1968, in R. Scheer *Eldridge Cleaver, Post Prison Writings and Speeches* (1969)

John Cleland 1710–89

English writer

8 Truth! stark naked truth, is the word.

Memoirs of a Woman of Pleasure a.k.a. *Fanny Hill* (1749) vol. 1

Georges Clemenceau 1841–1929

French statesman; Prime Minister of France, 1906–9, 1917–20

9 War is too serious a matter to entrust to military men.

attributed to Clemenceau, e.g. in Hampden Jackson *Clemenceau and the Third Republic* (1946), but also to Briand and Talleyrand; cf. **de Gaulle** 255:23

10 My home policy: I wage war; my foreign policy: I wage war. All the time I wage war.

speech to French Chamber of Deputies, 8 March 1918, in *Discours de Guerre* (1968)

11 It is easier to make war than to make peace.

speech at Verdun, 20 July 1919, in *Discours de Paix* (1938)

12 What do you expect when I'm between two men of whom one [Lloyd George] thinks he is Napoleon and the other [Woodrow Wilson] thinks he is Jesus Christ?

to André Tardieu, on being asked why he always gave in to **Lloyd George** *at the Paris Peace Conference, 1918*

James Lees-Milne *Harold Nicolson* (1980) vol. 1, ch. 7, letter from Nicolson to his wife, 20 May 1919

Clement XIII 1693–1769

Pope, 1758–69

13 *Sint ut sunt aut non sint.*

Let them be as they are or not be at all.

replying to a request for changes in the constitutions of the Society of Jesus

J. A. M. Crétineau-Joly *Clément XIV et les Jésuites* (1847)

Grover Cleveland 1837–1908

22nd and 24th President of the US

14 I have considered the pension list of the republic a roll of honour.

Veto of Dependent Pension Bill, 5 July 1888, in *A Compilation of the Messages and Papers of the Presidents* vol. 11 (1897)

15 The lessons of paternalism ought to be unlearned and the better lesson taught that, while the people should patriotically and cheerfully support their government, its functions do not include the support of the people.

inaugural address, 4 March 1893, in *New York Times* 5 March 1893

Harlan Cleveland 1918–

American government official

16 The revolution of rising expectations.

phrase coined, 1950; Arthur Schlesinger *A Thousand Days* (1965) ch. 16

John Cleveland 1613–58

English poet

see also **Epitaphs** *303:6*

17 Had Cain been Scot, God would have changed his
doom
Nor forced him wander, but confined him home.

'The Rebel Scot' (1647)

Hillary Rodham Clinton 1947–

American lawyer, wife of Bill **Clinton**, *First Lady of the US since 1993*

18 I am not standing by my man, like Tammy Wynette. I am sitting here because I love him, I respect him, and I honour what he's been through and what we've been through together.

interview on *60 Minutes*, CBS-TV, 27 January 1992

1 I could have stayed home and baked cookies and had teas. But what I decided was to fulfil my profession, which I entered before my husband was in public life.
comment on questions raised by rival Democratic contender Edmund G. Brown Jr.; in *Albany Times-Union* 17 March 1992

2 There is no such thing as other people's children.
in *Newsweek* 15 January 1996

3 I learnt a long time ago that the only people who count in any marriage are the two that are in it.
television interview with NBC, 27 January 1998

William Jefferson ('Bill') Clinton 1946–

American Democratic statesman; 42nd President of the US from 1993; husband of Hillary Rodham **Clinton**

4 I experimented with marijuana a time or two. And I didn't like it, and I didn't inhale.
in *Washington Post* 30 March 1992

5 The comeback kid!
description of himself after coming second in the New Hampshire primary in the 1992 presidential election (since 1952, no presidential candidate had won the election without first winning in New Hampshire)
Michael Barone and Grant Ujifusa *The Almanac of American Politics 1994*

6 I did not have sexual relations with that woman.
television interview, in *Daily Telegraph* 27 January 1998

7 Peace is no longer a dream. It is a reality.
of the Northern Ireland referendum on the Good Friday agreement
in *Sunday Times* 24 May 1998

8 I did have a relationship with Ms Lewinsky that was not appropriate. In fact, it was wrong.
broadcast to the American people, 18 August 1998
in *Times* 19 August 1998

Lord Clive 1725–74

British general; Governor of Bengal
on Clive: see **Bentley** *67:3*

9 By God, Mr Chairman, at this moment I stand astonished at my own moderation!
reply during Parliamentary cross-examination, 1773
G. R. Gleig *The Life of Robert, First Lord Clive* (1848) ch. 29

10 I feel that I am reserved for some end or other.
when his pistol twice failed to fire, while attempting to take his own life
G. R. Gleig *The Life of Robert, First Lord Clive* (1848) ch. 1

□ Closing lines

see box overleaf

Arthur Hugh Clough 1819–61

English poet
on Clough: see **Swinburne** *751:15*

11 Rome, believe me, my friend, is like its own Monte Testaceo,
Merely a marvellous mass of broken and castaway wine-pots.
Amours de Voyage (1858) canto 1, pt. 2

12 Am I prepared to lay down my life for the British female?
Really, who knows? . . .
Ah, for a child in the street I could strike; for the full-blown lady—
Somehow, Eustace, alas! I have not felt the vocation.
Amours de Voyage (1858) canto 2, pt. 4

13 I do not like being moved: for the will is excited; and action
Is a most dangerous thing: I tremble for something factitious,
Some malpractice of heart and illegitimate process;
We are so prone to these things with our terrible notions of duty.
Amours de Voyage (1858) canto 2, pt. 11

14 Mild monastic faces in quiet collegiate cloisters.
Amours de Voyage (1858) canto 3, pt. 9

15 Whither depart the souls of the brave that die in the battle,
Die in the lost, lost fight, for the cause that perishes with them?
Amours de Voyage (1858) canto 5, pt. 6

16 Sesquipedalian blackguard.
The Bothie of Tober-na-Vuolich (1848) pt. 2, l. 223

17 Good, too, Logic, of course; in itself, but not in fine weather.
The Bothie of Tober-na-Vuolich (1848) pt. 2, l. 249

18 Grace is given of God, but knowledge is bought in the market.
The Bothie of Tober-na-Vuolich (1848) pt. 4, l. 159

19 Afloat. We move: Delicious! Ah,
What else is like the gondola?
Dipsychus (1865) sc. 5

20 This world is bad enough may-be;
We do not comprehend it;
But in one fact can all agree
God won't, and we can't mend it.
Dipsychus (1865) sc. 5

21 I drive through the street, and I care not a d–mn;
The people they stare, and they ask who I am;
And if I should chance to run over a cad,
I can pay for the damage if ever so bad.
Dipsychus (1865) sc. 5

22 My pleasure of thought is the pleasure of thinking
How pleasant it is to have money, heigh ho!
How pleasant it is to have money.
Dipsychus (1865) sc. 5

23 And almost every one when age,
Disease, or sorrows strike him,
Inclines to think there is a God,
Or something very like Him.
Dipsychus (1865) sc. 6

24 Thou shalt have one God only; who
Would be at the expense of two?
'The Latest Decalogue' (1862); cf. **Bible** 76:13

continued

Closing lines

1 After all, tomorrow is another day.
Margaret **Mitchell** *Gone with the Wind* (1936)

2 *L'amor che muove il sole e l'altre stelle.*
The love that moves the sun and the other stars.
Dante Alighieri *Divina Commedia* 'Paradiso'

3 And so I betake myself to that course, which is almost as much as to see myself go into my grave—for which, and all the discomforts that will accompany my being blind, the good God prepare me!
Samuel **Pepys** *Diary* 31 May 1669

4 And when they buried him the little port
Had seldom seen a costlier funeral.
Alfred, Lord **Tennyson** 'Enoch Arden' (1864)

5 Be not solitary, be not idle.
Robert **Burton** *The Anatomy of Melancholy* (1621–51)

6 The creatures outside looked from pig to man, and from man to pig, and from pig to man again, but already it was impossible to say which was which.
George **Orwell** *Animal Farm* (1945)

7 *Das Ewig-Weibliche zieht uns hinan.*
Eternal Woman draws us upward.
Johann Wolfgang von **Goethe** *Faust* pt. 2 (1832) 'Hochgebirg'

8 For ne'er
Was flattery lost on poet's ear:
A simple race! they waste their toil
For the vain tribute of a smile.
Sir Walter **Scott** *The Lay of the Last Minstrel* (1805) canto 4

9 From hence, let fierce contending nations know
What dire effects from civil discord flow.
Joseph **Addison** *Cato* (1713)

10 The gladsome light of Jurisprudence.
Edward **Coke** *The First Part of the Institutes of the Laws of England* (1628) 'Epilogus'

11 Goddess, allow this aged man his right,
To be your beadsman now that was your knight.
George **Peele** *Polyhymnia* (1590) 'Sonnet'

12 He will be looked upon by posterity as a brave bad man.
of ***Cromwell***
Edward Hyde, Earl of **Clarendon** *The History of the Rebellion* (1703)

13 *Hört ihr das Glöckchen klingeln? Kniet nieder—Man bringt die Sakramente einem sterbenden Gotte.*
Do you hear the little bell tinkle? Kneel down. They are bringing the sacraments to a dying god.
Heinrich **Heine** *Zur Geschichte der Religion und Philosophie in Deutschland* (1834) bk. 2

14 I lingered round them, under that benign sky: watched the moths fluttering among the heath and hare-bells; listened to the soft wind breathing through the grass; and wondered how any one could ever imagine unquiet slumbers for the sleepers in that quiet earth.
Emily **Brontë** *Wuthering Heights* (1847)

15 'Justice' was done, and the President of the Immortals (in Aeschylean phrase) had ended his sport with Tess.
Thomas **Hardy** *Tess of the D'Urbervilles* (1891)

16 Keep violence in the mind
Where it belongs.
Brian **Aldiss** *Barefoot in the Head* (1969) 'Charteris'

17 Learn to write well, or not to write at all.
John Sheffield, 1st Duke of **Buckingham** 'An Essay upon Satire' (1689)

18 Oh my grief, I've lost him surely. I've lost the only Playboy of the Western World.
John Millington **Synge** *The Playboy of the Western World* (1907) act 3

19 The proletarians have nothing to lose but their chains. They have a world to win. WORKING MEN OF ALL COUNTRIES, UNITE!
commonly rendered as 'Workers of the world, unite!'
Karl **Marx** and Friedrich **Engels** *The Communist Manifesto* (1848)

20 Silent, upon a peak in Darien.
John **Keats** 'On First Looking into Chapman's Homer' (1817)

21 So that, in the end, there was no end.
Patrick **White** *The Tree of Man* (1955)

22 They hand in hand, with wandering steps and slow,
Through Eden took their solitary way.
John **Milton** *Paradise Lost*

23 *Zwei Seelen und ein Gedanke,*
Zwei Herzen und ein Schlag!
Two souls with but a single thought,
Two hearts that beat as one.
Friedrich **Halm** *Der Sohn der Wildnis* (1842) act 2; translated by Maria Lovell as *Ingomar the Barbarian* (1854)

Arthur Hugh Clough *continued*

24 Thou shalt not kill; but need'st not strive
Officiously to keep alive.
'The Latest Decalogue' (1862)

25 Do not adultery commit;
Advantage rarely comes of it.
'The Latest Decalogue' (1862)

26 Thou shalt not steal; an empty feat,
When it's so lucrative to cheat.
'The Latest Decalogue' (1862)

27 Thou shalt not covet; but tradition
Approves all forms of competition.
'The Latest Decalogue' (1862)

1 'Tis better to have fought and lost,
Than never to have fought at all.
'Peschiera' (1854); cf. **Tennyson** 761:4

2 Say not the struggle naught availeth,
The labour and the wounds are vain,
The enemy faints not, nor faileth,
And as things have been, things remain.
'Say not the struggle naught availeth' (1855)

3 If hopes were dupes, fears may be liars.
'Say not the struggle naught availeth' (1855)

4 In front the sun climbs slow, how slowly,
But westward, look, the land is bright.
'Say not the struggle naught availeth' (1855)

5 What shall we do without you? Think where we are. Carlyle has led us all out into the desert, and he has left us there.
parting words to Ralph Waldo **Emerson**, *15 July 1848*
E. E. Hale *James Russell Lowell and his Friends* (1889) ch. 9

Kurt Cobain 1967–94

American rock singer, guitarist, and songwriter, husband of Courtney **Love**
see also **Young** *839:17*

6 I'd rather be dead than cool.
'Stay Away' (1991 song)

Thomas W. Cobb fl. 1820

American politician

7 If you persist, the Union will be dissolved. You have kindled a fire which all the waters of the ocean cannot put out, which seas of blood can only extinguish.
to James Tallmadge, on his amendment to the bill to admit Missouri to the Union as a slave state in 1820
Robert V. Remini *Henry Clay* (1991) ch. 11

William Cobbett 1762–1835

English political reformer and radical journalist

8 Free yourselves from the slavery of the tea and coffee and other slop-kettle.
Advice to Young Men (1829) letter 1, sect. 31

9 From a very early age, I had imbibed the opinion, that it was every man's duty to do all that lay in his power to leave his country as good as he had found it.
Political Register 22 December 1832

10 Nouns of number, or multitude, such as Mob, Parliament, Rabble, House of Commons, Regiment, Court of King's Bench, Den of Thieves, and the like.
English Grammar (1817) letter 17 'Syntax as Relating to Pronouns'

11 But what is to be the fate of the great wen of all? The monster, called . . . 'the metropolis of the empire'?
of London
Rural Rides: The Kentish Journal in *Cobbett's Weekly Political Register* 5 January 1822, vol. 40

Alison Cockburn (née Rutherford) 1713–94

Scottish poet and songwriter

12 I've seen the smiling of Fortune beguiling,
I've felt all its favours and found its decay;
Sweet was its blessing, kind its caressing,
But now it is fled, fled far, far away.
'The Flowers of the Forest' (1765); cf. **Elliot** 298:9

13 O fickle Fortune, why this cruel sporting?
Why thus torment us poor sons of day?
Nae mair your smiles can cheer me, nae mair your frowns can fear me,
For the flowers of the forest are a' wade away.
wade *weeded (often quoted as 'For the flowers of the forest are withered away')*
'The Flowers of the Forest' (1765)

Claud Cockburn 1904–81

British writer and journalist

14 Reality goes bounding past the satirist like a cheetah laughing as it lopes ahead of the greyhound.
Crossing the Line (1958)

15 Small earthquake in Chile. Not many dead.
winning entry for a dullest headline competition at The Times
In Time of Trouble (1956) ch. 10

Jean Cocteau 1889–1963

French dramatist and film director

16 History is a combination of reality and lies. The reality of History becomes a lie. The unreality of the fable becomes the truth.
Journal d'un inconnu (1953) 'De la prééminence des fables'

17 Life is a horizontal fall.
Opium (1930)

18 Victor Hugo was a madman who thought he was Victor Hugo.
Opium (1930)

19 Being tactful in audacity is knowing how far one can go too far.
Le Rappel à l'ordre (1926) 'Le Coq et l'Arlequin'

20 If it has to choose who is to be crucified, the crowd will always save Barabbas.
Le Rappel à l'ordre (1926) 'Le Coq et l'Arlequin'

21 My method is simple: not to bother about poetry. It must come of its own accord. Merely whispering its name drives it away.
on 26 August 1945; *Professional Secrets* (1972)

George M. Cohan 1878–1942

American songwriter, dramatist, and producer

22 Over there, over there,
Send the word, send the word over there
That the Yanks are coming, the Yanks are coming,
The drums rum-tumming everywhere.
So prepare, say a prayer,
Send the word, send the word to beware.

We'll be over, we're coming over
And we won't come back till it's over, over there.
'Over There' (1917 song)

1 I'm a Yankee Doodle Dandy,
A Yankee Doodle, do or die;
A real live nephew of my Uncle Sam's,
Born on the fourth of July.
I've got a Yankee Doodle sweetheart,
She's my Yankee Doodle joy.
Yankee Doodle came to London,
Just to ride the ponies;
I am the Yankee Doodle Boy.
'Yankee Doodle Boy' (1904 song); cf. **Songs** 730:9

2 I don't care what you say about me, as long as you say *something* about me, and as long as you spell my name right.
to a newspaperman who wanted some information about Broadway Jones *in 1912*
John McCabe *George M. Cohan* (1973)

Leonard Cohen 1934–

Canadian singer and writer

3 A woman watches her body uneasily, as though it were an unreliable ally in the battle for love.
The Favourite Game (1963) bk. 3, ch. 8

4 I don't consider myself a pessimist. I think of a pessimist as someone who is waiting for it to rain. And I feel soaked to the skin.
in *Observer* 2 May 1993 'Sayings of the Week'

Aston Cokayne 1608–84

English poet

5 Sydney, whom we yet admire
Lighting our little torches at his fire.
Funeral Elegies, no. 1 'On the Death of my very good Friend Mr Michael Drayton' (1658)

Edward Coke 1552–1634

English jurist

6 How long soever it hath continued, if it be against reason, it is of no force in law.
The First Part of the Institutes of the Laws of England (1628) bk. 1, ch. 10, sect. 80

7 Reason is the life of the law, nay the common law itself is nothing else but reason.
The First Part of the Institutes of the Laws of England (1628) bk. 2, ch. 6, sect. 138

8 Law . . . is the perfection of reason.
The First Part of the Institutes of the Laws of England (1628) bk. 2, ch. 6, sect. 138

9 The gladsome light of Jurisprudence.
The First Part of the Institutes of the Laws of England (1628) 'Epilogus'

10 For a man's house is his castle, *et domus sua cuique est tutissimum refugium* [and each man's home is his safest refuge].
The Third Part of the Institutes of the Laws of England (1628) ch. 73; cf. **Proverbs** 599:16

11 Six hours in sleep, in law's grave study six,
Four spend in prayer, the rest on Nature fix.
translation of a quotation from Justinian *The Pandects* (or *Digest*) bk. 2, ch. 4 'De in Jus Vocando'; cf. **Jones** 419:5

12 They [corporations] cannot commit treason, nor be outlawed, nor excommunicate, for they have no souls.
The Reports of Sir Edward Coke (1658) vol. 5, pt. 10 'The case of Sutton's Hospital'; cf. **Proverbs** 597:37, **Thurlow** 777:4

13 Magna Charta is such a fellow, that he will have no sovereign.
on the Lords' Amendment to the Petition of Right, 17 May 1628
J. Rushworth *Historical Collections* (1659) vol. 1

David Coleman 1926–

British sports commentator

14 He just can't believe what isn't happening to him.
in *Guardian* 24 December 1980 'Sports Quotes of the Year'

15 That's the fastest time ever run—but it's not as fast as the world record.
Barry Fantoni (ed.) *Private Eye's Colemanballs 3* (1986)

Hartley Coleridge 1796–1849

English poet; eldest son of Samuel Taylor ***Coleridge***

16 But what is Freedom? Rightly understood,
A universal licence to be good.
'Liberty' (1833)

17 She is not fair to outward view
As many maidens be;
Her loveliness I never knew
Until she smiled on me.
Oh! then I saw her eye was bright,
A well of love, a spring of light.
'She is not fair' (1833)

Mary Coleridge 1861–1907

English poet, novelist, and essayist

18 Egypt's might is tumbled down
Down a-down the deeps of thought;
Greece is fallen and Troy town,
Glorious Rome hath lost her crown,
Venice' pride is nought.
But the dreams their children dreamed
Fleeting, unsubstantial, vain
Shadowy as the shadows seemed
Airy nothing, as they deemed,
These remain.
'Egypt's might is tumbled down' (1908); cf. **Shakespeare** 690:19

Samuel Taylor Coleridge 1772–1834

English poet, critic, and philosopher, father of Hartley ***Coleridge***
on Coleridge: see ***Byron*** *175:25, 178:7,* ***Hazlitt*** *365:5,* ***Hunt*** *395:18,* ***Lamb*** *449:3,* ***Shelley*** *711:23*

19 O softly tread, said Christabel.
'Christabel' (1816) pt. 1, l. 164

20 Behold! her bosom and half her side—
A sight to dream of, not to tell!
'Christabel' (1816) pt. 1, l. 252

1 A little child, a limber elf,
Singing, dancing to itself,
A fairy thing with red round cheeks,
That always finds, and never seeks,
Makes such a vision to the sight
As fills a father's eyes with light.
'Christabel' (1816) pt. 2, conclusion, l. 656

2 I see them all so excellently fair,
I see, not feel, how beautiful they are!
'Dejection: an Ode' (1802) st. 2

3 O Lady! we receive but what we give,
And in our life alone does Nature live.
'Dejection: an Ode' (1802) st. 4

4 Ah! from the soul itself must issue forth
A light, a glory, a fair luminous cloud
Enveloping the Earth—
And from the soul itself must there be sent
A sweet and potent voice, of its own birth,
Of all sweet sounds the life and element!
'Dejection: an Ode' (1802) st. 4

5 For hope grew round me, like the twining vine,
And fruits, and foliage, not my own, seemed mine.
'Dejection: an Ode' (1802) st. 6

6 But oh! each visitation
Suspends what nature gave me at my birth,
My shaping spirit of imagination.
'Dejection: an Ode' (1802) st. 6; cf. **Coleridge** 227:11

7 And the Devil did grin, for his darling sin
Is pride that apes humility.
'The Devil's Thoughts' (1799)

8 And what if all animated nature
Be but organic harps diversely framed,
That tremble into thought, as o'er them sweeps,
Plastic and vast, one intellectual breeze,
At once the soul of each, and god of all?
'The Eolian Harp' (1796) l. 44

9 What is an Epigram? a dwarfish whole,
Its body brevity, and wit its soul.
'Epigram' (1809)

10 O, lift one thought in prayer for S. T. C.;
That he who many a year with toil of breath
Found death in life, may here find life in death.
'Epitaph for Himself' (1834)

11 Forth from his dark and lonely hiding-place
(Portentous sight!) the owlet Atheism,
Sailing on obscene wings athwart the noon,
Drops his blue-fringèd lids, and holds them close,
And hooting at the glorious sun in Heaven,
Cries out, 'Where is it?'
'Fears in Solitude' (1798)

12 The frost performs its secret ministry,
Unhelped by any wind.
'Frost at Midnight' (1798) l. 1

13 Sea, and hill, and wood,
With all the numberless goings-on of life,
Inaudible as dreams!
'Frost at Midnight' (1798) l. 11

14 The thin blue flame
Lies on my low-burnt fire, and quivers not;
Only that film, which fluttered on the grate,
Still flutters there, the sole unquiet thing
'Frost at Midnight' (1798) l. 13

15 For I was reared
In the great city, pent 'mid cloisters dim,
And saw nought love but the sky and stars.
But *thou*, my babe! shalt wander like a breeze
By lakes and sandy shores, beneath the crags
Of ancient mountain, and beneath the clouds,
Which image in their bulk both lakes and shores
And mountain crags.
'Frost at Midnight' (1798) l. 51

16 Therefore all seasons shall be sweet to thee.
'Frost at Midnight' (1798) l. 65

17 Whether the eave-drops fall
Heard only in the trances of the blast,
Or if the secret ministry of frost
Shall hang them up in silent icicles,
Quietly shining to the quiet moon.
'Frost at Midnight' (1798) l. 70

18 O struggling with the darkness all the night,
And visited all night by troops of stars.
'Hymn before Sunrise, in the Vale of Chamouni' (1809) l. 30

19 On awaking he . . . instantly and eagerly wrote down the lines that are here preserved. At this moment he was unfortunately called out by a person on business from Porlock.
'Kubla Khan' (1816) preliminary note; cf. **Smith** 724:25

20 In Xanadu did Kubla Khan
A stately pleasure-dome decree:
Where Alph, the sacred river, ran
Through caverns measureless to man
Down to a sunless sea.
So twice five miles of fertile ground
With walls and towers were girdled round.
'Kubla Khan' (1816)

21 A savage place! as holy and enchanted
As e'er beneath a waning moon was haunted
By woman wailing for her demon-lover!
And from this chasm, with ceaseless turmoil seething,
As if this earth in fast thick pants were breathing,
A mighty fountain momently was forced.
'Kubla Khan' (1816)

22 It was a miracle of rare device,
A sunny pleasure-dome with caves of ice.
'Kubla Khan' (1816)

23 And 'mid this tumult Kubla heard from far
Ancestral voices prophesying war!
'Kubla Khan' (1816)

24 A damsel with a dulcimer
In a vision once I saw:
It was an Abyssinian maid,
And on her dulcimer she played,
Singing of Mount Abora.
'Kubla Khan' (1816)

25 And all who heard should see them there,
And all should cry, Beware! Beware!
His flashing eyes, his floating hair!

Weave a circle round him thrice,
And close your eyes with holy dread,
For he on honey-dew hath fed,
And drunk the milk of Paradise.
'Kubla Khan' (1816)

1 All thoughts, all passions, all delights,
Whatever stirs this mortal frame,
All are but ministers of Love,
And feed his sacred flame.
'Love' (1800)

2 With Donne, whose muse on dromedary trots,
Wreathe iron pokers into true-love knots.
Rhyme's sturdy cripple, fancy's maze and clue,
Wit's forge and fire-blast, meaning's press and screw.
'On Donne's Poetry' (1818)

3 It is an ancient Mariner,
And he stoppeth one of three.
'By thy long grey beard and glittering eye,
Now wherefore stopp'st thou me?'
'The Rime of the Ancient Mariner' (1798) pt. 1

4 He holds him with his glittering eye—
The Wedding-Guest stood still.
'The Rime of the Ancient Mariner' (1798) pt. 1

5 The Wedding-Guest sat on a stone:
He cannot choose but hear.
'The Rime of the Ancient Mariner' (1798) pt. 1

6 The Wedding-Guest here beat his breast,
For he heard the loud bassoon.
'The Rime of the Ancient Mariner' (1798) pt. 1

7 And ice, mast-high, came floating by,
As green as emerald.
'The Rime of the Ancient Mariner' (1798) pt. 1

8 'God save thee, ancient Mariner!
From the fiends that plague thee thus!—
Why look'st thou so?'—With my cross-bow
I shot the Albatross.
'The Rime of the Ancient Mariner' (1798) pt. 1

9 Nor dim nor red, like God's own head,
The glorious Sun uprist.
'The Rime of the Ancient Mariner' (1798) pt. 2

10 We were the first that ever burst
Into that silent sea.
'The Rime of the Ancient Mariner' (1798) pt. 2

11 As idle as a painted ship
Upon a painted ocean.
'The Rime of the Ancient Mariner' (1798) pt. 2

12 Water, water, everywhere,
And all the boards did shrink;
Water, water, everywhere,
Nor any drop to drink.

The very deep did rot: O Christ!
That ever this should be!
Yes, slimy things did crawl with legs
Upon the slimy sea.
'The Rime of the Ancient Mariner' (1798) pt. 2

13 *Her* lips were red, *her* looks were free,
Her locks were yellow as gold:
Her skin was white as leprosy,
The Night-mare LIFE-IN-DEATH was she,
Who thicks man's blood with cold.
'The Rime of the Ancient Mariner' (1798) pt. 3

14 The Sun's rim dips; the stars rush out;
At one stride comes the dark.
'The Rime of the Ancient Mariner' (1798) pt. 3

15 The hornèd Moon, with one bright star
Within the nether tip.
'The Rime of the Ancient Mariner' (1798) pt. 3; cf. **Wordsworth** 827:10

16 I fear thee, ancient Mariner!
I fear thy skinny hand!
And thou art long, and lank, and brown,
As is the ribbed sea-sand.
'The Rime of the Ancient Mariner' (1798) pt. 4

17 Alone, alone, all, all alone,
Alone on a wide wide sea!
And never a saint took pity on
My soul in agony.
'The Rime of the Ancient Mariner' (1798) pt. 4

18 And a thousand thousand slimy things
Lived on; and so did I.
'The Rime of the Ancient Mariner' (1798) pt. 4

19 A spring of love gushed from my heart,
And I blessed them unaware.
'The Rime of the Ancient Mariner' (1798) pt. 4

20 Oh Sleep! it is a gentle thing,
Beloved from pole to pole.
To Mary Queen the praise be given!
She sent the gentle sleep from Heaven,
That slid into my soul.
'The Rime of the Ancient Mariner' (1798) pt. 5

21 Sure I had drunken in my dreams,
And still my body drank.
'The Rime of the Ancient Mariner' (1798) pt. 5

22 We were a ghastly crew.
'The Rime of the Ancient Mariner' (1798) pt. 5

23 It ceased; yet still the sails made on
A pleasant noise till noon,
A noise like of a hidden brook
In the leafy month of June,
That to the sleeping woods all night
Singeth a quiet tune.
'The Rime of the Ancient Mariner' (1798) pt. 5

24 Like one, that on a lonesome road
Doth walk in fear and dread,
And having once turned round walks on,
And turns no more his head;
Because he knows, a frightful fiend
Doth close behind him tread.
'The Rime of the Ancient Mariner' (1798) pt. 6; cf. **Blair** 117:6

25 No voice; but oh! the silence sank
Like music on my heart.
'The Rime of the Ancient Mariner' (1798) pt. 6

26 I pass, like night, from land to land;
I have strange power of speech.
'The Rime of the Ancient Mariner' (1798) pt. 7

27 He prayeth well, who loveth well
Both man and bird and beast.

He prayeth best, who loveth best
All things both great and small.
'The Rime of the Ancient Mariner' (1798) pt. 7

1 He went like one that hath been stunned,
And is of sense forlorn:
A sadder and a wiser man,
He rose the morrow morn.
'The Rime of the Ancient Mariner' (1798) pt. 7

2 So for the mother's sake the child was dear,
And dearer was the mother for the child.
'Sonnet to a Friend Who Asked How I Felt When the Nurse First Presented My Infant to Me' (1797)

3 Well, they are gone, and here must I remain,
This lime-tree bower my prison!
'This Lime-Tree Bower my Prison' (1800) l. 1

4 When the last rook
Beat its straight path along the dusky air.
'This Lime-Tree Bower my Prison' (1800) l. 68

5 A charm
For thee, my gentle-hearted Charles, to whom
No sound is dissonant which tells of life.
*of Charles **Lamb***
'This Lime-Tree Bower my Prison' (1800) l. 74

6 Work without hope draws nectar in a sieve,
And hope without an object cannot live.
'Work without Hope' (1828)

7 He who begins by loving Christianity better than Truth will proceed by loving his own sect or church better than Christianity, and end by loving himself better than all.
Aids to Reflection (1825) 'Moral and Religious Aphorisms' no. 25

8 Evidences of Christianity! I am weary of the word. Make a man feel the want of it; rouse him, if you can, to the self-knowledge of his need of it; and you may safely trust it to his own Evidence.
Aids to Reflection (1825) 'Conclusion'

9 If a man could pass through Paradise in a dream, and have a flower presented to him as a pledge that his soul had really been there, and if he found the flower in his hand when he awoke—Aye! and what then?
Anima Poetae (E. H. Coleridge ed., 1895)

10 Until you understand a writer's ignorance, presume yourself ignorant of his understanding.
Biographia Literaria (1817) ch. 12

11 The primary imagination I hold to be the living Power and prime Agent of all human Perception, and as a repetition in the finite mind of the eternal act of creation in the infinite I AM.
Biographia Literaria (1817) ch. 13

12 That willing suspension of disbelief for the moment, which constitutes poetic faith.
Biographia Literaria (1817) ch. 14

13 Our *myriad-minded* Shakespeare.
Footnote. *Ἀνὴρ μυριόνους*, a phrase which I have borrowed from a Greek monk, who applies it to a Patriarch of Constantinople.
Biographia Literaria (1817) ch. 15

14 The dwarf sees farther than the giant, when he has the giant's shoulder to mount on.
The Friend (1818) vol. 2 'On the Principles of Political Knowledge'; cf. **Bernard** 68:22, **Newton** 543:9

15 Iago's soliloquy— the motive-hunting of motiveless malignity.
The Literary Remains of Samuel Taylor Coleridge (1836) bk. 2 'Notes on the Tragedies of Shakespeare: Othello'

16 State policy, a cyclops with one eye, and that in the back of the head!
On the Constitution of the Church and State (1839)

17 Reviewers are usually people who would have been poets, historians, biographers, &c., if they could; they have tried their talents at one or at the other, and have failed; therefore they turn critics.
Seven Lectures on Shakespeare and Milton (delivered 1811–12, published 1856) Lecture 1; cf. **Disraeli** 270:22

18 You abuse snuff! Perhaps it is the final cause of the human nose.
Table Talk (1835) 4 January 1823

19 To see him act, is like reading Shakespeare by flashes of lightning.
of Edmund Kean
Table Talk (1835) 27 April 1823

20 Prose = words in their best order;—poetry = the *best* words in the best order.
Table Talk (1835) 12 July 1827

21 The man's desire is for the woman; but the woman's desire is rarely other than for the desire of the man.
Table Talk (1835) 23 July 1827

22 Poetry is certainly something more than good sense, but it must be good sense at all events; just as a palace is more than a house, but it must be a house, at least.
Table Talk (1835) 9 May 1830

23 Swift was *anima Rabelaisii habitans in sicco*—the soul of Rabelais dwelling in a dry place.
Table Talk (1835) 15 June 1830

24 In politics, what begins in fear usually ends in folly.
Table Talk (1835) 5 October 1830

25 If men could learn from history, what lessons it might teach us! But passion and party blind our eyes, and the light which experience gives is a lantern on the stern, which shines only on the waves behind us!
Table Talk (1835) 18 December 1831

26 That passage is what I call the sublime dashed to pieces by cutting too close with the fiery four-in-hand round the corner of nonsense.
Table Talk (1835) 20 January 1834 (on lines excluded from his own poem *Limbo*, written 1817)

27 Shakespeare . . . is of no age—nor of any religion, or party or profession. The body and substance of his works came out of the unfathomable depths of his own oceanic mind.
Table Talk (1835) 15 March 1834

28 Bygone images and scenes of early life have stolen into my mind, like breezes blown from the spice-

islands of Youth and Hope—those twin realities of this phantom world!

Table Talk (1835) 10 July 1834

1 Summer has set in with its usual severity.

Alfred Ainger (ed.) *Letters of Charles Lamb* (1888) vol. 2, letter to Vincent Novello, 9 May 1826

Colette (Sidonie-Gabrielle Colette) 1873–1954

French novelist

2 *Le monde des émotions qu'on nomme, à la légère, physiques.*

The world of the emotions that are so lightly called physical.

Le Blé en herbe (1923)

3 *Son enfance, son adolescence lui avaient appris la patience, l'espoir, le silence, le maniement aisé des armes et des vertus des prisonniers.*

Her childhood, then her adolescence, had taught her patience, hope, silence and the easy manipulation of the weapons and virtues of all prisoners.

Chéri (1920) pt. 2 (translated by Janet Flanner, 1930)

4 *Allons acheter des cartes à jouer, du bon vin, des marques de bridge, des aiguilles à tricoter, tous les bibelots qu'il faut pour boucher un grand trou, tout ce qu'il faut pour déguiser le monstre—la vieille femme.*

Let's buy a pack of cards, good wine, bridge scores, knitting needles, all the paraphernalia needed to fill an enormous void, everything needed to hide that horror—the old woman.

Chéri (1920) pt. 2 (translated by Janet Flanner, 1930)

5 *Si on voulait être sincère, on avouerait qu'il y a l'amour bien nourri, et l'amour mal nourri. Et le reste c'est de la littérature.*

If we want to be sincere, we must admit that there is a well-nourished love and an ill-nourished love. And the rest is literature.

La Fin de Chéri (1926) (translated by Viola Gerard Garvin)

Mary Collier *c.*1690–*c.*1762

English washerwoman and poet

6 Though we all day with care our work attend,
Such is our fate, we know not when 'twill end.
When evening's come, you homeward take your way;
We, till our work is done, are forced to stay.

The Woman's Labour (1739)

7 So the industrious bees do hourly strive
To bring their loads of honey to the hive;
Their sordid owners always reap the gains,
And poorly recompense their toils and pains.

The Woman's Labour (1739)

8 The greatest heroes that the world can know,
To *women* their original must owe.

'The Three Wise Sentences, from the First Book of Esdras' (1740) l. 132

William Collingbourne d. 1484

English landowner; conspirator against Richard III

9 The Cat, the Rat, and Lovell our dog
Rule all England under a hog.

referring to Sir William Catesby (d. 1485), Sir Richard Ratcliffe (d. 1485), Lord Lovell (1454–c.1487), whose crest was a dog, and King Richard III, whose emblem was a wild boar

Robert Fabyan *The Concordance of Chronicles* (ed. H. Ellis, 1811)

Lord Collingwood 1748–1810

English naval commander

10 Now, gentlemen, let us do something today which the world may talk of hereafter.

before the Battle of Trafalgar, 21 October 1805

G. L. Newnham Collingwood (ed.) *A Selection from the Correspondence of Lord Collingwood* (1828) vol. 1

R. G. Collingwood 1889–1943

English philosopher and archaeologist

11 Perfect freedom is reserved for the man who lives by his own work and in that work does what he wants to do.

Speculum Mentis (1924); cf. **Gill** 339:14

Charles Collins

English songwriter

12 Any old iron, any old iron,
Any any old old iron?
You look neat
Talk about a treat,
You look dapper from your napper to your feet.
Dressed in style, brand new tile,
And your father's old green tie on,
But I wouldn't give you tuppence for your old watch chain;
Old iron, old iron?

'Any Old Iron' (1911 song, with E. A. Sheppard and Fred Terry); the second line often sung 'Any any any old iron?'

13 My old man said, 'Follow the van,
Don't dilly-dally on the way!'
Off went the cart with the home packed in it,
I walked behind with my old cock linnet.
But I dillied and dallied, dallied and dillied,
Lost the van and don't know where to roam.
You can't trust the 'specials' like the old time 'coppers'
When you can't find your way home.

'Don't Dilly-Dally on the Way' (1919 song, with Fred Leigh); popularized by Marie Lloyd

Joan Collins 1933–

British actress

14 I've never yet met a man who could look after me.
I don't need a husband. What I need is a wife.

in *Sunday Times* 27 December 1987

Michael Collins 1890–1922

Irish revolutionary

1 That volley which we have just heard is the only speech which it is proper to make over the grave of a dead Fenian.
at the funeral of Thomas Ashe, who had died in prison while on hunger strike
Glasnevin cemetery, 30th September 1917

2 Think—what I have got for Ireland? Something which she has wanted these past seven hundred years. Will anyone be satisfied at the bargain? Will anyone? I tell you this—early this morning I signed my death warrant. I thought at the time how odd, how ridiculous—a bullet may just as well have done the job five years ago.
on signing the treaty establishing the Irish Free State; he was shot from ambush in the following year
letter, 6 December 1921, in T. R. Dwyer *Michael Collins and the Treaty* (1981) ch. 4

3 We've been waiting seven hundred years, you can have the seven minutes.
arriving at Dublin Castle for the handover by British forces on 16 January 1922, and being told that he was seven minutes late
Tim Pat Coogan *Michael Collins* (1990); attributed

4 Because of his sincerity, I would forgive him anything.
after the death of Cathal **Brugha**, *July 1922*
Robert Kee *Ourselves Alone* (1976)

5 My own fellow-countymen won't kill me.
before leaving for Cork where he was ambushed and killed, 20 August 1922
James Mackay *Michael Collins* (1996)

6 I found out that those fellows we put on the spot were going to put a lot of us on the spot, so we got in first.
of the elimination of undercover British Intelligence officers (the 'Cairo Gang') in 1920
Diana Norman *Terrible Beauty* (1987)

William Collins 1721–59

English poet

7 To fair Fidele's grassy tomb
Soft maids and village hinds shall bring
Each opening sweet of earliest bloom,
And rifle all the breathing spring.
'Dirge' (1744); occasionally included in 18th-century performances of Shakespeare's *Cymbeline*

8 Now air is hushed, save where the weak-eyed bat,
With short shrill shriek flits by on leathern wing,
Or where the beetle winds
His small but sullen horn,
As oft he rises 'midst the twilight path,
Against the pilgrim borne in heedless hum.
'Ode to Evening' (1747)

9 How sleep the brave, who sink to rest,
By all their country's wishes blest!
'Ode Written in the Year 1746' (1748)

10 By fairy hands their knell is rung,
By forms unseen their dirge is sung.
'Ode Written in the Year 1746' (1748)

11 With eyes up-raised, as one inspired,
Pale Melancholy sate retired,
And from her wild sequestered seat,
In notes by distance made more sweet,
Poured thro' the mellow horn her pensive soul.
'The Passions, an Ode for Music' (1747)

12 Love of peace, and lonely musing,
In hollow murmurs died away.
'The Passions, an Ode for Music' (1747)

13 Too nicely Jonson knew the critic's part,
Nature in him was almost lost in Art.
'Verses addressed to Sir Thomas Hanmer' (1743)

George Colman, the Elder 1732–94 and David Garrick 1717–79

English dramatists

14 Love and a cottage! Eh, Fanny! Ah, give me indifference and a coach and six!
The Clandestine Marriage (1766) act 1; cf. **Keats** 428:15

George Colman, the Younger 1762–1836

English dramatist

15 Oh, London is a fine town,
A very famous city,
Where all the streets are paved with gold,
And all the maidens pretty.
The Heir at Law (performed 1797, published 1808) act 1, sc. 2

16 Says he, 'I am a handsome man, but I'm a gay deceiver.'
Love Laughs at Locksmiths (1808) act 2; cf. **Proverbs** 606:5

17 My father was an eminent button maker . . . but I had a soul above buttons . . . I panted for a liberal profession.
New Hay at the Old Market (1795) sc. 1

18 Johnson's style was grand and Gibbon's elegant; the stateliness of the former was sometimes pedantic, and the polish of the latter was occasionally finical. Johnson marched to kettle-drums and trumpets; Gibbon moved to flute and hautboys: Johnson hewed passages through the Alps, while Gibbon levelled walks through parks and gardens.
Random Records (1830) vol. 1

19 As the lone Angler, patient man,
At Mewry-Water, or the Banne,
Leaves off, against his placid wish,
Impaling worms to torture fish.
The Lady of the Wreck (1813) canto 2, st. 18

20 And, on the label of the stuff,
He wrote this verse;
Which one would think was clear enough,
And terse:—

When taken,
To be well shaken.
'The Newcastle Apothecary' (1797)

John Robert Colombo 1936–
Canadian writer

1 Canada could have enjoyed:
English government,
French culture,
and American know-how.
Instead it ended up with:
English know-how,
French government,
and American culture.
'O Canada' (1965)

Charles Caleb Colton *c.*1780–1832
English clergyman and writer

2 When you have nothing to say, say nothing.
Lacon (1820) vol. 1, no. 183

3 Examinations are formidable even to the best prepared, for the greatest fool may ask more than the wisest man can answer.
Lacon (1820) vol. 1, no. 322

4 If you would be known, and not know, vegetate in a village; if you would know, and not be known, live in a city.
Lacon (1820) vol. 1, no. 334

5 Man is an embodied paradox, a bundle of contradictions.
Lacon (1820) vol. 1, no. 408

St Colum Cille ?521–597
Irish cleric and missionary, founder of Iona

6 To every cow her calf, to every book its copy.
traditionally attributed

Betty Comden 1919– and **Adolph Green** 1915–

7 New York, New York,—a helluva town.
New York, New York (1945 song)

8 The party's over, it's time to call it a day.
'The Party's Over' (1956); cf. **Crosland** 246:7

Henry Steele Commager 1902–
American historian

9 It was observed half a century ago that what is a stone wall to a layman, to a corporate lawyer is a triumphant arch. Much the same might be said of civil rights and freedoms. To the layman the Bill of Rights seems to be a stone wall against the misuse of power. But in the hands of a congressional committee, or often enough of a judge, it turns out to be so full of exceptions and qualifications that it might be a whole series of arches.
'The Right to Dissent' in *Current History* October 1955; cf. **Dunne** 285:14

Denis Compton 1918–97
British cricketer

10 I couldn't bat for the length of time required to score 500. I'd get bored and fall over.
to Brian Lara, who had recently scored 501 not out, a world record in first-class cricket
in *Daily Telegraph* 27 June 1994

Ivy Compton-Burnett 1884–1969
English novelist

11 Time has too much credit . . . It is not a great healer. It is an indifferent and perfunctory one. Sometimes it does not heal at all. And sometimes when it seems to, no healing has been necessary.
Darkness and Day (1951) ch. 7; cf. **Proverbs** 613:1

12 Being cruel to be kind is just ordinary cruelty with an excuse made for it . . . And it is right that it should be more resented, as it is.
Daughters and Sons (1937) ch. 6

13 Well, of course, people are only human . . . But it really does not seem much for them to be.
A Family and a Fortune (1939) ch. 2

14 People don't resent having nothing nearly as much as too little.
A Family and a Fortune (1939) ch. 4

15 There are different kinds of wrong. The people sinned against are not always the best.
The Mighty and their Fall (1961) ch. 7

16 A leopard does not change his spots, or change his feeling that spots are rather a credit.
More Women than Men (1933) ch. 4

17 My point is that it [wickedness] is not punished, and that is why it is natural to be guilty of it. When it is likely to be punished, most of us avoid it.
in *Orion* (1945) 'A Conversation between I. Compton-Burnett and M. Jourdain'

18 A plot is like the bones of a person, not interesting like expression or signs of experience, but the support of the whole.
in *Orion* (1945) 'A Conversation between I. Compton-Burnett and M. Jourdain'

19 There's not much to say. I haven't been at all deedy.
on being asked about herself
in *The Times* 30 August 1969

Auguste Comte 1798–1857
French philosopher

20 M. Comte used to reproach his early English admirers with maintaining the 'conspiracy of silence' concerning his later performances.
J. S. Mill *Auguste Comte and Positivism* (1865)

Prince de Condé (the Great Condé) 1621–86

French general

1 *Silence! Voilà l'ennemi!*

Hush! Here comes the enemy!

as the Jesuit preacher Louis Bourdaloue mounted the pulpit at St Sulpice

P. M. Lauras *Bourdaloue: sa vie et ses oeuvres* (1881) vol. 2

Marquis de Condorcet 1743–94

French philosopher

2 As one meditates about the nature of the moral sciences one really cannot avoid the conclusion that since, like the physical sciences, they rest upon observation of the facts, they ought to follow the same methods, acquire a language no less exact and precise, and so attain to the same degree of certainty. If some being alien to our species were to set himself to study us he would find no difference between these two studies, and would examine human society as we do that of bees or beavers.

Discours prononcé dans l'Académie Française 21 February 1782; A. Condorcet O'Connor and M. F. Arago (eds.) *Oeuvres de Condorcet* vol. 1 (1847–9)

Confucius (K'ung Fu-tzu) 551–479 BC

Chinese philosopher

textual translations are those of Wing-Tsit Chan, 1963

3 Is it not a pleasure to learn and to repeat or practice from time to time what has been learned? Is it not delightful to have friends coming from afar? Is one not a superior man if he does not feel hurt even though he does not feel recognized?

Analects ch. 1, v. 1

4 When a man's father is alive, look at the bent of his will. When his father is dead, look at his conduct. If for three years [of mourning] he does not change from the way of his father, he may be called filial.

Analects ch. 1, v. 11

5 A ruler who governs his state by virtue is like the north polar star, which remains in its place while all the other stars revolve around it.

Analects ch. 2, v. 1

6 At fifteen my mind was set on learning. At thirty my character had been formed. At forty I had no more perplexities. At fifty I knew the Mandate of Heaven. At sixty I was at ease with whatever I heard. At seventy I could follow my heart's desire without transgressing moral principles.

Analects ch. 2, v. 4

7 A man who reviews the old so as to find out the new is qualified to teach others.

Analects ch. 2, v. 11

8 The superior man is broadminded but not partisan; the inferior man is partisan but not broadminded.

Analects ch. 2, v. 14

9 A superior man in dealing with the world is not for anything or against anything. He follows righteousness as the standard.

Analects ch. 4, v. 10

10 The Way of our Master is none other than conscientiousness and altruism.

the 'one thread' of Confucius' doctrines

Analects ch. 4, v. 15

11 The superior man understands righteousness; the inferior man understands profit.

Analects ch. 4, v. 16

12 Man is born with uprightness. If one loses it he will be lucky if he escapes with his life.

Analects ch. 6, v. 17

13 The man of wisdom delights in water; the man of humanity delights in mountains. The man of wisdom is active; the man of humanity is tranquil. The man of wisdom enjoys happiness; the man of humanity enjoys long life.

Analects ch. 6, v. 21

14 The superior man extensively studies literature and restrains himself with the rules of propriety. Thus he will not violate the Way.

Analects ch. 6, v. 25

15 I transmit but do not create. I believe in and love the ancients.

Analects ch. 7, v. 1

16 Set your will on the Way. Have a firm grasp on virtue. Rely on humanity. Find recreation in the arts.

Analects ch. 7, v. 6

17 Let a man be stimulated by poetry, established by the rules of propriety, and perfected by music.

Analects ch. 8, v. 8

18 I have never yet seen anyone whose desire to build up his moral power was as strong as sexual desire.

Analects ch. 9, v. 17; translated by Arthur Waley

19 The commander of three armies may be taken away but the will of even a common man may not be taken away from him.

Analects ch. 9, v. 25

20 If we are not yet able to serve man, how can we serve spiritual beings? . . . If we do not yet know about life how can we know about death?

Analects ch. 11, v. 11

21 To go too far is the same as not to go far enough.

Analects ch. 11, v. 15

22 No state can exist without the confidence of the people.

Analects ch. 12, v. 7

23 The way of the superior man is threefold, but I have not been able to attain it. The man of wisdom has no perplexities; the man of humanity has no worry; the man of courage has no fear.

Analects ch. 14, v. 30

1 It is the word altruism. Do not do to others what you do not want them to do to you.
replying to Tzu-hung's question 'Is there one word which can serve as the guiding principle for conduct throughout life?'
Analects ch. 15, v. 23

2 It is man that can make the Way great, and not the Way that can make man great.
Analects ch. 15, v. 28

3 In education there should be no class distinction.
Analects ch. 15, v. 38

4 By nature men are alike. Through practice they have become far apart.
Analects ch. 17, v. 2

5 Only the most intelligent and the most stupid do not change.
Analects ch. 17, v. 3

6 Does Heaven say anything? The four seasons run their course and all things are produced. Does Heaven say anything?
Analects ch. 17, v. 19

7 Women and servants are most difficult to deal with. If you are familiar with them, they cease to be humble. If you keep a distance from them, they resent it.
Analects ch. 17, v. 25

William Congreve 1670–1729

English dramatist

8 It is the business of a comic poet to paint the vices and follies of human kind.
The Double Dealer (1694) epistle dedicatory

9 Retired to their tea and scandal, according to their ancient custom.
The Double Dealer (1694) act 1, sc. 1

10 There is nothing more unbecoming a man of quality than to laugh; Jesu, 'tis such a vulgar expression of the passion!
The Double Dealer (1694) act 1, sc. 4; cf. **Catullus** 197:6, **Chesterfield** 209:16

11 Tho' marriage makes man and wife one flesh, it leaves 'em still two fools.
The Double Dealer (1694) act 2, sc. 3

12 She lays it on with a trowel.
The Double Dealer (1694) act 3, sc. 10

13 See how love and murder will out.
The Double Dealer (1694) act 4, sc. 6; cf. **Proverbs** 607:16

14 No mask like open truth to cover lies,
As to go naked is the best disguise.
The Double Dealer (1694) act 5, sc. 6

15 Invention flags, his brain goes muddy,
And black despair succeeds brown study.
An Impossible Thing (1720)

16 I am always of the opinion with the learned, if they speak first.
Incognita (1692)

17 Has he not a rogue's face? . . . a hanging-look to me . . . has a damned Tyburn-face, without the benefit o' the Clergy.
Love for Love (1695) act 2, sc. 7

18 I came upstairs into the world; for I was born in a cellar.
Love for Love (1695) act 2, sc. 7

19 I know that's a secret, for it's whispered every where.
Love for Love (1695) act 3, sc. 3

20 He that first cries out stop thief, is often he that has stolen the treasure.
Love for Love (1695) act 3, sc. 14

21 Women are like tricks by sleight of hand,
Which, to admire, we should not understand.
Love for Love (1695) act 4, sc. 21

22 A branch of one of your antediluvian families, fellows that the flood could not wash away.
Love for Love (1695) act 5, sc. 2

23 Aye, 'tis well enough for a servant to be bred at an University. But the education is a little too pedantic for a gentleman.
Love for Love (1695) act 5, sc. 3

24 Nay, for my part I always despised Mr Tattle of all things; nothing but his being my husband could have made me like him less.
Love for Love (1695) act 5, sc. 11

25 Music has charms to sooth a savage breast.
The Mourning Bride (1697) act 1, sc. 1

26 Heaven has no rage, like love to hatred turned,
Nor Hell a fury, like a woman scorned.
The Mourning Bride (1697) act 3, sc. 8; cf. **Proverbs** 602:37

27 Is he then dead?
What, dead at last, quite, quite for ever dead!
The Mourning Bride (1697) act 5, sc. 11

28 In my conscience I believe the baggage loves me, for she never speaks well of me herself, nor suffers any body else to rail at me.
The Old Bachelor (1693) act 1, sc. 1

29 Man was by Nature Woman's cully made:
We never are, but by ourselves, betrayed.
The Old Bachelor (1693) act 3, sc. 1

30 Bilbo's the word, and slaughter will ensue.
The Old Bachelor (1693) act 3, sc. 7

31 If this be not love, it is madness, and then it is pardonable.
The Old Bachelor (1693) act 3, sc. 10

32 Eternity was in that moment.
The Old Bachelor (1693) act 4, sc. 7

33 Now am I slap-dash down in the mouth.
The Old Bachelor (1693) act 4, sc. 9

34 SHARPER: Thus grief still treads upon the heels of pleasure:
Married in haste, we may repent at leisure.
SETTER: Some by experience find those words misplaced:
At leisure married, they repent in haste.
The Old Bachelor (1693) act 5, sc. 1; cf. **Byron** 177:21; cf. **Proverbs** 606:13

1 Courtship to marriage, as a very witty prologue to a very dull play.
The Old Bachelor (1693) act 5, sc. 10

2 I could find it in my heart to marry thee, purely to be rid of thee.
The Old Bachelor (1693) act 5, sc. 10

3 They come together like the Coroner's Inquest, to sit upon the murdered reputations of the week.
The Way of the World (1700) act 1, sc. 1

4 Ay, ay, I have experience: I have a wife, and so forth.
The Way of the World (1700) act 1, sc. 3

5 I always take blushing either for a sign of guilt, or of ill breeding.
The Way of the World (1700) act 1, sc. 9

6 Say what you will, 'tis better to be left than never to have been loved.
The Way of the World (1700) act 2, sc. 1; cf. **Tennyson** 761:4; cf. **Proverbs** 613:6

7 Here she comes i' faith full sail, with her fan spread and streamers out, and a shoal of fools for tenders.
The Way of the World (1700) act 2, sc. 4

8 WITWOUD: Madam, do you pin up your hair with all your letters?
MILLAMANT: Only with those in verse, Mr Witwoud. I never pin up my hair with prose.
The Way of the World (1700) act 2, sc. 4

9 Beauty is the lover's gift.
The Way of the World (1700) act 2, sc. 4

10 A little disdain is not amiss; a little scorn is alluring.
The Way of the World (1700) act 3, sc. 5

11 O, nothing is more alluring than a levee from a couch in some confusion.
The Way of the World (1700) act 4, sc. 1

12 Don't let us be familiar or fond, nor kiss before folks, like my Lady Fadler and Sir Francis: nor go to Hyde-Park together the first Sunday in a new chariot, to provoke eyes and whispers, and then never be seen there together again; as if we were proud of one another the first week, and ashamed of one another ever after . . . Let us be very strange and well-bred: Let us be as strange as if we had been married a great while, and as well-bred as if we were not married at all.
The Way of the World (1700) act 4, sc. 5

13 These articles subscribed, if I continue to endure you a little longer, I may by degrees dwindle into a wife.
The Way of the World (1700) act 4, sc. 5

14 I hope you do not think me prone to any iteration of nuptials.
The Way of the World (1700) act 4, sc. 12

15 Careless she is with artful care,
Affecting to seem unaffected.
'Amoret'

16 Music alone with sudden charms can bind
The wand'ring sense, and calm the troubled mind.
'Hymn to Harmony'

17 Would I were free from this restraint,
Or else had hopes to win her;
Would she could make of me a saint,
Or I of her a sinner.
'Pious Selinda Goes to Prayers' (song)

18 For 'tis some virtue, virtue to commend.
'To Sir Godfrey Kneller'

19 I confess freely to you, I could never look long upon a monkey, without very mortifying reflections.
letter to John Dennis, 10 July 1695

Gerry Conlon 1954–

first member of the Guildford Four to be released from prison

20 I felt the rush of happiness and warmth coming out of the people and I was carried out among them on a surge of joy. I suppose when you die and go to heaven you get a feeling like that.
Proved Innocent (1990)

21 The life sentence goes on. It's like a runaway train that you can't just get off.
of life after his conviction was quashed by the Court of Appeal
in *Irish Post* 13 September 1997

James M. Connell 1852–1929

Irish socialist songwriter

22 The people's flag is deepest red;
It shrouded oft our martyred dead.
'The Red Flag' (1889) in H. E. Piggott *Songs that made History* (1937) ch. 6

23 Then raise the scarlet standard high!
Within its shade we'll live or die.
Tho' cowards flinch and traitors sneer,
We'll keep the red flag flying here.
'The Red Flag' (1889) in H. E. Piggott *Songs that made History* (1937) ch. 6

Billy Connolly 1942–

Scottish comedian

24 Marriage is a wonderful invention; but, then again, so is a bicycle repair kit.
Duncan Campbell *Billy Connolly* (1976)

Cyril Connolly 1903–74

English writer

25 Whom the gods wish to destroy they first call promising.
Enemies of Promise (1938) ch. 13; **Proverbs** 615:4

26 There is no more sombre enemy of good art than the pram in the hall.
Enemies of Promise (1938) ch. 14

27 The Mandarin style . . . is beloved by literary pundits, by those who would make the written word as unlike as possible to the spoken one. It is the style of those writers whose tendency is to make their language convey more than they mean or more than they feel, it is the style of most artists and all humbugs.
Enemies of Promise (1938) ch. 20

1 Imprisoned in every fat man a thin one is wildly signalling to be let out.
The Unquiet Grave (1944) pt. 2; cf. **Orwell** 558:9

2 Our memories are card-indexes consulted, and then put back in disorder by authorities whom we do not control.
The Unquiet Grave (1944) pt. 3

3 Perfect fear casteth out love.
remark to Philip Toynbee during the Blitz
in *Observer* 1 December 1974; obituary notice by Toynbee; cf. **Bible** 111:14

4 It is closing time in the gardens of the West and from now on an artist will be judged only by the resonance of his solitude or the quality of his despair.
in *Horizon* December 1949—January 1950

James Connolly 1868–1916

Irish labour leader and nationalist; executed after the Easter Rising, 1916

5 The worker is the slave of capitalist society, the female worker is the slave of that slave.
The Re-conquest of Ireland (1915)

6 The time for Ireland's battle is NOW, the place for Ireland's battle is HERE.
in *The Workers' Republic* 22 January 1916

Jimmy Connors 1952–

American tennis player

7 New Yorkers love it when you spill your guts out there. Spill your guts at Wimbledon and they make you stop and clean it up.
at Flushing Meadow
in *Guardian* 24 December 1984 'Sports Quotes of the Year'

Joseph Conrad (Teodor Josef Konrad Korzeniowski) 1857–1924

Polish-born English novelist

8 As I waited I thought that there's nothing like a confession to make one look mad; and that of all confessions a written one is the most detrimental all round. Never confess! Never, never!
Chance (1913) ch. 7

9 The opening was barred by a black bank of clouds, and the tranquil waterway leading to the uttermost ends of the earth flowed sombre under an overcast sky—seemed to lead into the heart of an immense darkness.
Heart of Darkness (1902) ch. 1

10 The conquest of the earth, which mostly means the taking it away from those who have a different complexion or slightly flatter noses than ourselves, is not a pretty thing when you look into it.
Heart of Darkness (1902) ch. 1

11 We live, as we dream—alone.
Heart of Darkness (1902) ch. 1

12 Exterminate all the brutes!
Heart of Darkness (1902) ch. 2

13 The horror! The horror!
Heart of Darkness (1902) ch. 3

14 Mistah Kurtz—he dead.
Heart of Darkness (1902) ch. 3

15 A man that is born falls into a dream like a man who falls into the sea. If he tries to climb out into the air as inexperienced people endeavour to do, he drowns . . . and with the exertions of your hands and feet in the water make the deep, deep sea keep you up.
Lord Jim (1900) ch. 20

16 To the destructive element submit yourself.
Lord Jim (1900) ch. 20

17 My task which I am trying to achieve is by the power of the written word, to make you hear, to make you feel—it is, before all, to make you *see*. That—and no more, and it is everything.
The Nigger of the Narcissus (1897) preface

18 Action is consolatory. It is the enemy of thought and the friend of flattering illusions.
Nostromo (1904) pt. 1, ch. 6

19 It's only those who do nothing that make no mistakes, I suppose.
Outcast of the Islands (1896) pt. 3, ch. 2

20 The perfect delight of writing tales where so many lives come and go at the cost of one which slips imperceptibly away.
A Personal Record (1912)

21 The terrorist and the policeman both come from the same basket.
The Secret Agent (1907) ch. 4

22 Only in men's imagination does every truth find an effective and undeniable existence. Imagination, not invention, is the supreme master of art, as of life.
Some Reminiscences (1912) ch. 1

23 The scrupulous and the just, the noble, humane, and devoted natures; the unselfish and the intelligent may begin a movement—but it passes away from them. They are not the leaders of a revolution. They are its victims.
Under Western Eyes (1911) pt. 2, ch. 3

24 A belief in a supernatural source of evil is not necessary; men alone are quite capable of every wickedness.
Under Western Eyes (1911) pt. 2, ch. 4

25 I remember my youth and the feeling that will never come back any more—the feeling that I could last for ever, outlast the sea, the earth, and all men; the deceitful feeling that lures us on to joys, to perils, to love, to vain effort—to death; the triumphant conviction of strength, the heat of life in the handful of dust, the glow in the heart that with every year grows dim, grows cold, grows small, and expires—and expires, too soon, too soon—before life itself.
Youth (1902); cf. **Eliot** 295:28

26 One writes only half the book; the other half is with the reader.
letter to Cunninghame Graham, 1897

1 For me, writing—*the only possible writing*—is just simply the conversion of nervous force into phrases.
letter, October 1903

2 Reality, as usual, beats fiction out of sight.
commenting on 'this wartime atmosphere'
letter, 11 August 1915

Shirley Conran 1932–
English writer

3 Life is too short to stuff a mushroom.
Superwoman (1975)

Henry Constable 1562–1613
English poet

4 I did not know that thou wert dead before;
I did not feel the grief I did sustain;
The greater stroke astonisheth the more;
Astonishment takes from us sense of pain.
I stood amazed when others' tears begun,
And now begin to weep when they have done.
'To Sir Philip Sidney's Soul' (1595)

5 When thee (O holy sacrificial Lamb)
In severed signs I white and liquid see:
As on thy body slain I think on thee,
Which pale by shedding of thy blood became;
And when again I do behold the same
Veiled in white to be received of me,
Thou seemest in thy sindon wrapped to be
Like to a corse, whose monument I am.
'To the Blessed Sacrament' (first published 1815)

John Constable 1776–1837
English painter

6 The sound of water escaping from mill-dams, etc., willows, old rotten planks, slimy posts, and brickwork . . . those scenes made me a painter and I am grateful.
letter to John Fisher, 23 October 1821, in C. R. Leslie *Memoirs of the Life of John Constable* (1843) ch. 5

7 A gentleman's park—is my aversion. It is not beauty because it is not nature.
of Fonthill
letter to John Fisher, 7 October 1822, in *Correspondence* (1968) vol. 6

8 In Claude's landscape all is lovely—all amiable—all is amenity and repose;—the calm sunshine of the heart.
lecture, 2 June 1836, in C. R. Leslie *Memoirs of the Life of John Constable* (1843) ch. 18

9 There is nothing ugly; *I never saw an ugly thing in my life*: for let the form of an object be what it may,—light, shade, and perspective will always make it beautiful.
C. R. Leslie *Memoirs of the Life of John Constable* (1843) ch. 17

Benjamin Constant (Henri Benjamin Constant de Rebecque) 1767–1834
French novelist, political philosopher, and politician

10 Art for art's sake, with no purpose, for any purpose perverts art. But art achieves a purpose which is not its own.
describing a conversation with Crabb Robinson about the latter's work on ***Kant****'s aesthetics*
Journal intime 11 February 1804, in *Revue Internationale* 10 January 1887; cf. **Cousin** 238:6

Constantine the Great AD *c.*288–337
Roman emperor from AD *306*

11 *In hoc signo vinces.*
In this sign shalt thou conquer.
traditional form of Constantine's vision (AD 312), reported in Greek
τούτῳ νίκα.
By this, conquer.
Eusebius *Life of Constantine* bk. 1, ch. 28

Constitution of the United States 1787
the first ten amendments are known as the Bill of Rights

12 Congress shall make no law respecting an establishment of religion, or prohibiting the free exercise thereof; or abridging the freedom of speech, or of the press; or the right of the people peaceably to assemble, and to petition the government for a redress of grievances.
First Amendment (1791)

13 A well-regulated militia, being necessary to the security of a free State, the right of the people to keep and bear arms, shall not be infringed.
Second Amendment (1791)

14 Excessive bail shall not be required, nor excessive fines imposed, nor cruel and unusual punishment inflicted.
Eighth Amendment (1791)

A. J. Cook 1885–1931
English labour leader; Secretary of the Miners' Federation of Great Britain, 1924–31

15 Not a penny off the pay, not a second on the day.
often quoted with 'minute' substituted for 'second'
speech at York, 3 April 1926, in *The Times* 5 April 1926

Eliza Cook 1818–89
English poet

16 Better build schoolrooms for 'the boy',
Than cells and gibbets for 'the man'.
'A Song for the Ragged Schools' (1853)

Calvin Coolidge 1872–1933
30th President of the US
on Coolidge: see ***Anonymous*** *19:17,* ***Lippmann*** *470:1,* ***Parker*** *567:13*

17 There is no right to strike against the public safety by anybody, anywhere, any time.
telegram to Samuel Gompers, 14 September 1919

1 Civilization and profits go hand in hand.
speech in New York, 27 November 1920, in *New York Times* 28 November 1920

2 The chief business of the American people is business.
speech in Washington, 17 January 1925, in *New York Times* 18 January 1925

when asked by Mrs Coolidge what a sermon had been about:

3 'Sins,' he said. 'Well, what did he say about sin?' 'He was against it.'
John H. McKee *Coolidge: Wit and Wisdom* (1933); perhaps apocryphal

4 They hired the money, didn't they?
on war debts incurred by England and others
John H. McKee *Coolidge: Wit and Wisdom* (1933)

5 Nothing in the world can take the place of persistence. Talent will not; nothing is more common than unsuccessful men with talent. Genius will not; unrewarded genius is almost a proverb. Education will not; the world is full of educated derelicts. Persistence and determination are omnipotent. The slogan 'press on' has solved and always will solve the problems of the human race.
attributed in the programme of a memorial service for Coolidge in 1933

Duff Cooper, Lord Norwich 1890–1954
British Conservative politician, diplomat, and writer

6 Your two stout lovers frowning at one another across the hearth rug, while your small, but perfectly formed one kept the party in a roar.
letter to Lady Diana Manners, later his wife, October 1914; in Artemis Cooper *Durable Fire* (1983)

Elizabeth Cooper fl. 1730
English writer and dramatist

7 Regularity and Decorum. 'Tis what we women-authors, in particular, have been thought greatly deficient in; and I should be concerned to find it an objection not to be removed.
preface to *The Rival Widows* (1735)

Wendy Cope 1945–
English poet

8 Making cocoa for Kingsley Amis.
title of poem (1986)

9 I used to think all poets were Byronic—
Mad, bad and dangerous to know.
And then I met a few. Yes it's ironic—
I used to think all poets were Byronic.
They're mostly wicked as a ginless tonic
And wild as pension plans.
'Triolet' (1986); cf. **Lamb** 448:8

Aaron Copland 1900–90
American composer, pianist, and conductor

10 The whole problem can be stated quite simply by asking, 'Is there a meaning to music?' My answer to that would be, 'Yes.' And 'Can you state in so many words what the meaning is?' My answer to that would be, 'No.'
What to Listen for in Music (1939)

Richard Corbet 1582–1635
English poet and prelate; Chaplain to James I

11 Farewell, rewards and Fairies,
Good housewives now may say,
For now foul sluts in dairies
Do fare as well as they.
'The Fairies' Farewell'

12 Who of late for cleanliness,
Finds sixpence in her shoe?
'The Fairies' Farewell'

13 By which we note the Fairies
Were of the old profession;
Their songs were Ave Marys,
Their dances were procession.
'The Fairies' Farewell'

14 I wish thee all thy mother's graces,
Thy father's fortunes, and his places.
I wish thee friends, and one at Court,
Not to build on, but support;
To keep thee, not in doing many
Oppressions, but from suffering any.
'To his Son, Vincent Corbet'

Pierre Corneille 1606–84
French dramatist
on Corneille: see **Johnson** 418:1

15 *A vaincre sans péril, on triomphe sans gloire.*
When there is no peril in the fight, there is no glory in the triumph.
Le Cid (1637) act 2, sc. 2

16 *Faites votre devoir et laissez faire aux dieux.*
Do your duty, and leave the outcome to the Gods.
Horace (1640) act 2, sc. 8

17 *Un premier mouvement ne fut jamais un crime.*
A first impulse was never a crime.
Horace (1640) act 5, sc. 3; cf. **Montrond** 528:17

Ralph Cornes

18 Computers are anti-Faraday machines. He said he couldn't understand anything until he could count it, while computers count everything and understand nothing.
in *Guardian* 28 March 1991

Bernard Cornfeld 1927–
American businessman

19 Do you sincerely want to be rich?
stock question to salesmen
C. Raw et al. *Do You Sincerely Want to be Rich?* (1971)

Frances Cornford (née Darwin) 1886–1960

English poet; wife of Francis M. **Cornford**

1 How long ago Hector took off his plume,
Not wanting that his little son should cry,
Then kissed his sad Andromache goodbye —
And now we three in Euston waiting-room.

'Parting in Wartime' (1948)

2 O fat white woman whom nobody loves,
Why do you walk through the fields in gloves . . .
Missing so much and so much?

'To a Fat Lady seen from the Train' (1910); cf. **Chesterton** 210:7

3 A young Apollo, golden-haired,
Stands dreaming on the verge of strife,
Magnificently unprepared
For the long littleness of life.

of Rupert **Brooke**

'Youth' (1910)

Francis M. Cornford 1874–1943

English academic; husband of Frances **Cornford**

4 Every public action, which is not customary, either is wrong, or, if it is right, is a dangerous precedent. It follows that nothing should ever be done for the first time.

Microcosmographia Academica (1908) ch. 7

5 Another sport which wastes unlimited time is comma-hunting. Once start a comma and the whole pack will be off, full cry, especially if they have had a literary training . . . But comma-hunting is so exciting as to be a little dangerous. When attention is entirely concentrated on punctuation, there is some fear that the conduct of business may suffer, and a proposal get through without being properly obstructed on its demerits. It is therefore wise, when a kill has been made, to move at once for adjournment.

Microcosmographia Academica (1908) ch. 8

6 That branch of the art of lying which consists in very nearly deceiving your friends without quite deceiving your enemies.

of propaganda

Microcosmographia Academica (1922 ed.)

Mme Cornuel 1605–94

French society hostess

7 No man is a hero to his valet.

Lettres de Mlle Aïssé à Madame C (1787) Letter 13 'De Paris, 1728'; cf. **Byron** 173:15, **Proverbs** 607:48

Coronation Service 1689

8 We present you with this Book, the most valuable thing that this world affords. Here is wisdom; this is the royal Law; these are the lively Oracles of God.

The Presenting of the Holy Bible; L. G. Wickham Legge *English Coronation Records* (1901)

Correggio (Antonio Allegri Correggio) c.1489–1534

Italian painter

9 *Son pittore ancor io!*

I, too, am a painter!

on seeing Raphael's St Cecilia *at Bologna, c.1525*

L. Pungileoni *Memorie Istoriche de . . . Correggio* (1817) vol. 1

Gregory Corso 1930–

American poet

10 O God, and the wedding! All her family and her friends
and only a handful of mine all scroungy and bearded
just wait to get at the drinks and food.

'Marriage' (1960)

William Cory (born Johnson) 1823–92

English poet; assistant master at Eton College, 1845–72

11 Jolly boating weather,
And a hay harvest breeze,
Blade on the feather,
Shade off the trees
Swing, swing together
With your body between your knees.

'Eton Boating Song' in *Eton Scrap Book* (1865); E. Parker *Floreat* (1923)

12 Nothing in life shall sever
The chain that is round us now.

'Eton Boating Song' in *Eton Scrap Book* (1865); E. Parker *Floreat* (1923)

13 They told me, Heraclitus, they told me you were dead,
They brought me bitter news to hear and bitter tears to shed.
I wept as I remembered how often you and I
Had tired the sun with talking and sent him down the sky.

'Heraclitus' (1858); translation of Callimachus 'Epigram 2'; cf. **Callimachus** 181:15

14 Your chilly stars I can forgo,
This warm kind world is all I know.

'Mimnermus in Church' (1858)

Bill Cosby 1937–

American comedian and actor

15 The heart of marriage is memories.

Love and Marriage (1989)

Charles Cotton 1630–87

English poet

16 The shadows now so long do grow,
That brambles like tall cedars show,
Molehills seem mountains, and the ant
Appears a monstrous elephant.

'Evening Quatrains' (1689) st. 3

John Cotton 1584–1652
English-born New England puritan preacher and theologian

1 If you pinch the sea of its liberty, though it be walls of stone or brass, it will beat them down.
'Limitations of Government'; Perry Miller *The American Puritans* (1956)

2 There is never peace where full liberty is not given, nor never stable peace where more than full liberty is granted.
'Limitations of Government'; Perry Miller *The American Puritans* (1956)

Baron Pierre de Coubertin 1863–1937
French sportsman and educationist

3 The important thing in life is not the victory but the contest; the essential thing is not to have won but to have fought well.
speech at a government banquet in London, 24 July 1908, in T. A. Cook *Fourth Olympiad* (1909)

Émile Coué 1857–1926
French psychologist
on Coué: see **Inge** *399:2*

4 Every day, in every way, I am getting better and better.
to be said 15 to 20 times, morning and evening
De la suggestion et de ses applications (1915)

Douglas Coupland 1961–
Canadian author

5 Generation X: tales for an accelerated culture.
title of book (1991)

Victor Cousin 1792–1867
French philosopher

6 We must have religion for religion's sake, morality for morality's sake, as with art for art's sake . . . the beautiful cannot be the way to what is useful, or to what is good, or to what is holy; it leads only to itself.
Du Vrai, du beau, et du bien [Sorbonne lecture, 1818] (1853) pt. 2; cf. **Constant** 235:10

Jacques Cousteau 1910–97
French naval officer and underwater explorer
see also ***Epitaphs*** *302:2*

7 Mankind has probably done more damage to the earth in the 20th century than in all of previous human history.
'Consumer Society is the Enemy' in *New Perspectives Quarterly* Summer 1996

Thomas Coventry 1578–1640
English judge

8 The dominion of the sea, as it is an ancient and undoubted right of the crown of England, so it is the best security of the land . . . The wooden walls are the best walls of this kingdom.
wooden walls = *ships*
speech to the Judges, 17 June 1635, in J. Rushworth *Historical Collections* (1680) vol. 2; cf. **Blackstone** 117:3, **Themistocles** 770:16

Noël Coward 1899–1973
English dramatist, actor, and composer

9 Dance, dance, dance, little lady!
Leave tomorrow behind.
'Dance, Little Lady' (1928 song)

10 Don't let's be beastly to the Germans
When our Victory is ultimately won.
'Don't Let's Be Beastly to the Germans' (1943 song)

11 There's sand in the porridge and sand in the bed,
And if this is pleasure we'd rather be dead.
'The English Lido' (1928)

12 I believe that since my life began
The most I've had is just
A talent to amuse.
'If Love Were All' (1929 song)

13 I'll see you again,
Whenever spring breaks through again.
'I'll See You Again' (1929 song)

14 Mad about the boy.
title of song (1932)

15 Mad dogs and Englishmen
Go out in the midday sun.
The Japanese don't care to,
The Chinese wouldn't dare to,
The Hindus and Argentines sleep firmly from
twelve to one,
But Englishmen detest a siesta.
'Mad Dogs and Englishmen' (1931 song)

16 Don't put your daughter on the stage, Mrs
Worthington,
Don't put your daughter on the stage.
'Mrs Worthington' (1935 song)

17 Poor little rich girl.
title of song (1925)

18 Someday I'll find you,
Moonlight behind you,
True to the dream I am dreaming.
'Someday I'll Find You' (1930 song)

19 The Stately Homes of England,
How beautiful they stand,
To prove the upper classes
Have still the upper hand.
'The Stately Homes of England' (1938 song); cf. **Hemans** 369:6

20 There are bad times just around the corner,
There are dark clouds travelling through the sky
And it's no good whining
About a silver lining
For we know from experience that they won't roll
by.
'There are Bad Times Just Around the Corner' (1953 song); cf. **Proverbs** 599:21

1 I believe we should all behave quite differently if we lived in a warm, sunny climate all the time.
Brief Encounter (1945)

2 Very flat, Norfolk.
Private Lives (1930) act 1

3 Extraordinary how potent cheap music is.
Private Lives (1930) act 1

4 Certain women should be struck regularly, like gongs.
Private Lives (1930) act 3

5 Dear 338171 (May I call you 338?).
letter to T. E. Lawrence, 25 August 1930

6 Just say the lines and don't trip over the furniture.
advice on acting
D. Richards *The Wit of Noël Coward* (1968)

7 Television is for appearing on, not looking at.
D. Richards *The Wit of Noël Coward* (1968)

8 It would be nice if sometimes the kind things I say were considered worthy of quotation. It isn't difficult, you know, to be witty or amusing when one has something to say that is destructive, but damned hard to be clever and quotable when you are singing someone's praises.
William Marchant *The Pleasure of His Company* (1981)

9 Two wise acres and a cow.
of Edith, Osbert, and Sacheverell **Sitwell**
John Pearson *Façades* (1978) ch. 10; cf. **Political slogans** 582:1

Abraham Cowley 1618–67

English poet and essayist
on Cowley: see **Addison** *4:5,* **Dryden** *283:13,* **Pope** *586:14*

10 The thirsty earth soaks up the rain,
And drinks, and gapes for drink again.
The plants suck in the earth, and are
With constant drinking fresh and fair.
'Drinking' (1656)

11 Fill all the glasses there, for why
Should every creature drink but I,
Why, man of morals, tell me why?
'Drinking' (1656)

12 God the first garden made, and the first city Cain.
Essays, in Verse and Prose (1668) 'The Garden'; cf. **Cowper** 241:19

13 Hence, ye profane; I hate ye all;
Both the great vulgar, and the small.
Essays, in Verse and Prose (1668) 'Of Greatness' (translation of Horace *Odes* bk. 3, no. 1); cf. **Horace** 388:11

14 This only grant me, that my means may lie
Too low for envy, for contempt too high.
Essays, in Verse and Prose (1668) 'Of Myself'

15 Acquaintance I would have, but when't depends
Not on the number, but the choice of friends.
Essays, in Verse and Prose (1668) 'Of Myself'

16 Love in her sunny eyes does basking play;
Love walks the pleasant mazes of her hair;
Love does on both her lips for ever stray;
And sows and reaps a thousand kisses there.
In all her outward parts Love's always seen;
But, oh, he never went within.
The Mistress: or . . . Love Verses (1647) 'The Change'

17 The world's a scene of changes, and to be
Constant, in Nature were inconstancy.
The Mistress: or . . . Love Verses (1647) 'Inconstancy'

18 Lukewarmness I account a sin
As great in love as in religion.
The Mistress: or . . . Love Verses 'The Request'

19 The stings,
The crowd, and buzz, and murmurings
Of this great hive, the city.
The Mistress: or . . . Love Verses (1647) 'The Wish'

20 Nothing so soon the drooping spirits can raise
As praises from the men, whom all men praise.
'Ode upon a Copy of Verses of My Lord Broghill's' (1663)

21 Poet and Saint! to thee alone are given
The two most sacred names of earth and Heaven.
'On the Death of Mr Crashaw' (1656)

22 Ye fields of Cambridge, our dear Cambridge, say,
Have ye not seen us walking every day?
Was there a tree about which did not know
The love betwixt us two?
'On the Death of Mr William Hervey' (1656)

23 Life is an incurable disease.
'To Dr Scarborough' (1656) st. 6

Hannah Cowley (née Parkhouse) 1743–1809

English dramatist

24 Five minutes! Zounds! I have been five minutes too late all my life-time!
The Belle's Stratagem (1780) act 1, sc. 1

25 Vanity, like murder, will out.
The Belle's Stratagem (1780) act 1, sc. 4

26 But what is woman?—only one of Nature's agreeable blunders.
Who's the Dupe? (1779) act 2; cf. **Nietzsche** 545:12

William Cowper 1731–1800

English poet

27 No voice divine the storm allayed,
No light propitious shone;
When snatched from all effectual aid,
We perished, each alone:
But I beneath a rougher sea,
And whelmed in deeper gulfs than he.
'The Castaway' (written 1799) l. 61

28 Grief is itself a med'cine.
'Charity' (1782) l. 159

29 He found it inconvenient to be poor.
of a burglar
'Charity' (1782) l. 189

30 A tale should be judicious, clear, succinct;
The language plain, and incidents well linked;
Tell not as new what ev'ry body knows,
And new or old, still hasten to a close.
'Conversation' (1782) l. 235

1 The pipe with solemn interposing puff,
Makes half a sentence at a time enough;
The dozing sages drop the drowsy strain,
Then pause, and puff—and speak, and pause again.
'Conversation' (1782) l. 245

2 Pernicious weed! whose scent the fair annoys,
Unfriendly to society's chief joys.
on tobacco
'Conversation' (1782) l. 251

3 His wit invites you by his looks to come,
But when you knock it never is at home.
'Conversation' (1782) l. 303

4 . . . Thousands, careless of the damning sin,
Kiss the book's outside who ne'er look within.
on oath-taking
'Expostulation' (1782) l. 388

5 The man that hails you Tom or Jack,
And proves by thumps upon your back
How he esteems your merit,
Is such a friend, that one had need
Be very much his friend indeed
To pardon or to bear it.
'Friendship' (1782) l. 169

6 Damned below Judas; more abhorred than he was.
'Hatred and vengeance, my eternal portion' (written c.1774)

7 Man disavows, and Deity disowns me.
'Hatred and vengeance, my eternal portion' (written c.1774)

8 Men deal with life, as children with their play,
Who first misuse, then cast their toys away.
'Hope' (1782) l. 127

9 Could he with reason murmur at his case,
Himself sole author of his own disgrace?
'Hope' (1782) l. 316

10 And differing judgements serve but to declare
That truth lies somewhere, if we knew but where.
'Hope' (1782) l. 423

11 John Gilpin was a citizen
Of credit and renown,
A train-band captain eke was he
Of famous London town.
'John Gilpin' (1785) l. 1

12 My sister and my sister's child,
Myself and children three,
Will fill the chaise; so you must ride
On horseback after we.
'John Gilpin' (1785) l. 13

13 O'erjoy'd was he to find
That, though on pleasure she was bent,
She had a frugal mind.
'John Gilpin' (1785) l. 30

14 Beware of desperate steps. The darkest day
(Live till tomorrow) will have passed away.
'The Needless Alarm' (written c.1790) l. 132

15 No dancing bear was so genteel,
Or half so dégagé.
'Of Himself' (written 1752)

16 God moves in a mysterious way
His wonders to perform;
He plants his footsteps in the sea,
And rides upon the storm.
Olney Hymns (1779) 'Light Shining out of Darkness'

17 Ye fearful saints fresh courage take,
The clouds ye so much dread
Are big with mercy, and shall break
In blessings on your head.
Olney Hymns (1779) 'Light Shining out of Darkness'

18 Behind a frowning providence
He hides a smiling face.
Olney Hymns (1779) 'Light Shining out of Darkness'

19 Hark, my soul! it is the Lord;
'Tis thy Saviour, hear his word;
Jesus speaks, and speaks to thee;
'Say, poor sinner, lov'st thou me?'
Olney Hymns (1779) 'Lovest Thou Me?'

20 There is a fountain filled with blood
Drawn from Emmanuel's veins,
And sinners, plunged beneath that flood,
Lose all their guilty stains.
Olney Hymns (1779) 'Praise for the Fountain Opened'

21 Oh! for a closer walk with God,
A calm and heav'nly frame;
A light to shine upon the road
That leads me to the Lamb!
Olney Hymns (1779) 'Walking with God'

22 My dog! what remedy remains,
Since, teach you all I can,
I see you, after all my pains,
So much resemble man!
'On a Spaniel called Beau, killing a young bird' (written 1793)

23 Toll for the brave—
The brave! that are no more:
All sunk beneath the wave,
Fast by their native shore.
'On the Loss of the Royal George' (written 1782)

24 His sword was in the sheath,
His fingers held the pen,
When Kempenfeld went down
With twice four hundred men.
'On the Loss of the Royal George' (written 1782)

25 Oh, fond attempt to give a deathless lot
To names ignoble, born to be forgot!
'On Observing Some Names of Little Note Recorded in the Biographia Britannica' (1782)

26 Thy morning bounties ere I left my home,
The biscuit, or confectionary plum.
'On the Receipt of My Mother's Picture out of Norfolk' (1798) l. 60

27 Me howling winds drive devious, tempest-tossed,
Sails ripped, seams op'ning wide, and compass lost.
'On the Receipt of My Mother's Picture out of Norfolk' (1798) l. 102

28 I shall not ask Jean Jacques Rousseau,
If birds confabulate or no.
'Pairing Time Anticipated' (1795)

1 The poplars are felled, farewell to the shade
And the whispering sound of the cool colonnade.
'The Poplar-Field' (written 1784)

2 Oh, laugh or mourn with me the rueful jest,
A cassocked huntsman and a fiddling priest!
'The Progress of Error' (1782) l. 110

3 Himself a wand'rer from the narrow way,
His silly sheep, what wonder if they stray?
'The Progress of Error' (1782) l. 118

4 Remorse, the fatal egg by pleasure laid.
'The Progress of Error' (1782) l. 239

5 As creeping ivy clings to wood or stone,
And hides the ruin that it feeds upon,
So sophistry, cleaves close to, and protects
Sin's rotten trunk, concealing its defects.
'The Progress of Error' (1782) l. 285

6 How much a dunce that has been sent to roam
Excels a dunce that has been kept at home.
'The Progress of Error' (1782) l. 415

7 Thou god of our idolatry, the press . . .
Thou fountain, at which drink the good and wise;
Thou ever-bubbling spring of endless lies;
Like Eden's dread probationary tree,
Knowledge of good and evil is from thee.
'The Progress of Error' (1782) l. 461

8 Laugh at all you trembled at before.
'The Progress of Error' (1782) l. 592

9 The disencumbered Atlas of the state.
of the statesman
'Retirement' (1782) l. 394

10 He likes the country, but in truth must own,
Most likes it, when he studies it in town.
'Retirement' (1782) l. 573

11 Philologists, who chase
A panting syllable through time and space,
Start it at home, and hunt it in the dark,
To Gaul, to Greece, and into Noah's ark.
'Retirement' (1782) l. 691

12 'Till authors hear at length, one gen'ral cry,
Tickle and entertain us, or we die.
The loud demand from year to year the same,
Beggars invention and makes fancy lame.
'Retirement' (1782) l. 707

13 Admirals extolled for standing still,
Or doing nothing with a deal of skill.
'Table Talk' (1782) l. 192

14 Freedom has a thousand charms to show,
That slaves, howe'er contented, never know.
'Table Talk' (1782) l. 260

15 Stamps God's own name upon a lie just made,
To turn a penny in the way of trade.
'Table Talk' (1782) l. 420 (Perjury)

16 I sing the sofa.
The Task (1785) bk. 1 'The Sofa' l. 1

17 Thus first necessity invented stools,
Convenience next suggested elbow-chairs,
And luxury the accomplished sofa last.
The Task (1785) bk. 1 'The Sofa' l. 86

18 The nurse sleeps sweetly, hired to watch the sick,
Whom, snoring, she disturbs.
The Task (1785) bk. 1 'The Sofa' l. 89

19 God made the country, and man made the town.
The Task (1785) bk. 1 'The Sofa' l. 749; cf. **Cowley** 239:12, **Proverbs** 601:13

20 Slaves cannot breathe in England, if their lungs
Receive our air, that moment they are free;
They touch our country, and their shackles fall.
The Task (1785) bk. 2 'The Timepiece' l. 40; cf. **Anonymous** 18:5

21 England, with all thy faults, I love thee still—
My country!
The Task (1785) bk. 2 'The Timepiece' l. 206; cf. **Churchill** 213:14

22 There is a pleasure in poetic pains
Which only poets know.
The Task (1785) bk. 2 'The Timepiece' l. 285

23 Variety's the very spice of life,
That gives it all its flavour.
The Task (1785) bk. 2 'The Timepiece' l. 606; cf. **Behn** 62:13, **Proverbs** 613:33

24 I was a stricken deer, that left the herd
Long since.
The Task (1785) bk. 3 'The Garden' l. 108; cf. **Shakespeare** 665:1

25 Great contest follows, and much learned dust
Involves the combatants.
The Task (1785) bk. 3 'The Garden' l. 161

26 Defend me, therefore, common sense, say I,
From reveries so airy, from the toil
Of dropping buckets into empty wells,
And growing old in drawing nothing up!
The Task (1785) bk. 3 'The Garden' l. 187

27 Newton, childlike sage!
Sagacious reader of the works of God.
The Task (1785) bk. 3 'The Garden' l. 252

28 Detested sport,
That owes its pleasures to another's pain.
of hunting
The Task (1785) bk. 3 'The Garden' l. 326

29 Studious of laborious ease.
The Task (1785) bk. 3 'The Garden' l. 361

30 To combat may be glorious, and success
Perhaps may crown us; but to fly is safe.
The Task (1785) bk. 3 'The Garden' l. 686

31 Now stir the fire, and close the shutters fast,
Let fall the curtains, wheel the sofa round,
And, while the bubbling and loud-hissing urn
Throws up a steamy column, and the cups,
That cheer but not inebriate, wait on each,
So let us welcome peaceful evening in.
The Task (1785) bk. 4 'The Winter Evening' l. 34; cf. **Berkeley** 67:19

32 'Tis pleasant through the loopholes of retreat
To peep at such a world; to see the stir
Of the great Babel, and not feel the crowd.
The Task (1785) bk. 4 'The Winter Evening' l. 88

1 I crown thee king of intimate delights,
Fire-side enjoyments, home-born happiness.
The Task (1785) bk. 4 'The Winter Evening' l. 139

2 A Roman meal . . .
. . . a radish and an egg.
The Task (1785) bk. 4 'The Winter Evening' l. 168

3 The slope of faces, from the floor to th' roof,
(As if one master-spring controlled them all),
Relaxed into a universal grin.
of the theatre
The Task (1785) bk. 4 'The Winter Evening' l. 202

4 Shaggy, and lean, and shrewd, with pointed ears
And tail cropped short, half lurcher and half cur.
The Task (1785) bk. 5 'The Winter Morning Walk' l. 45

5 But war's a game, which, were their subjects wise,
Kings would not play at.
The Task (1785) bk. 5 'The Winter Morning Walk' l. 187

6 Knowledge dwells
In heads replete with thoughts of other men;
Wisdom in minds attentive to their own.
The Task (1785) bk. 6 'The Winter Walk at Noon' l. 89

7 Knowledge is proud that he has learned so much;
Wisdom is humble that he knows no more.
The Task (1785) bk. 6 'The Winter Walk at Noon' l. 96

8 Nature is but a name for an effect,
Whose cause is God.
The Task (1785) bk. 6 'The Winter Walk at Noon' l. 223

9 A cheap but wholesome salad from the brook.
The Task (1785) bk. 6 'The Winter Walk at Noon' l. 304

10 I would not enter on my list of friends
(Tho' graced with polished manners and fine sense,
Yet wanting sensibility) the man
Who needlessly sets foot upon a worm.
The Task (1785) bk. 6 'The Winter Walk at Noon' l. 560

11 Public schools 'tis public folly feeds.
'Tirocinium' (1785) l. 250

12 The parson knows enough who knows a duke.
'Tirocinium' (1785) l. 403

13 As a priest,
A piece of mere church furniture at best.
'Tirocinium' (1785) l. 425

14 Tenants of life's middle state,
Securely placed between the small and great.
'Tirocinium' (1785) l. 807

15 He has no hope that never had a fear.
'Truth' (1782) l. 298

16 But what is man in his own proud esteem?
Hear him, himself the poet and the theme;
A monarch clothed with majesty and awe,
His mind his kingdom and his will his law.
'Truth' (1782) l. 403

17 I am monarch of all I survey,
My right there is none to dispute;
From the centre all round to the sea
I am lord of the foul and the brute.
'Verses Supposed to be Written by Alexander Selkirk' (1782)

18 Oh! I could thresh his old jacket till I made his
pension jingle in his pockets.
on Samuel ***Johnson****'s inadequate treatment of* Paradise Lost
letter to the Revd William Unwin, 31 October 1779; J. King and C. Ryskamp (eds.) *Letters and Prose Writings of William Cowper* vol. 1 (1979)

19 Our severest winter, commonly called the spring.
letter to the Revd William Unwin, 8 June 1783, in J. King and C. Ryskamp (eds.) *Letters and Prose Writings of William Cowper* vol. 2 (1981)

George Crabbe 1754–1832

English poet

20 'What is a church?'—Our honest sexton tells,
''Tis a tall building, with a tower and bells.'
The Borough (1810) Letter 2 'The Church' l. 11

21 Virtues neglected then, adored become,
And graces slighted, blossom on the tomb.
The Borough (1810) Letter 2 'The Church' l. 133

22 The Town small-talk flows from lip to lip;
Intrigues half-gathered, conversation-scraps,
Kitchen-cabals, and nursery-mishaps.
The Borough (1810) Letter 3 'The Vicar' l. 70

23 Habit with him was all the test of truth,
'It must be right: I've done it from my youth.'
The Borough (1810) Letter 3 'The Vicar' l. 138

24 There anchoring, Peter chose from man to hide,
There hang his head, and view the lazy tide
In its hot slimy channel slowly glide;
Where the small eels that left the deeper way
For the warm shore, within the shallows play;
Where gaping mussels, left upon the mud,
Slope their slow passage to the fallen flood;—
Here dull and hopeless he'd lie down and trace
How sidelong crabs had scrawled their crooked
race.
The Borough (1810) Letter 22 'Peter Grimes' l. 185

25 He nursed the feelings these dull scenes produce,
And loved to stop beside the opening sluice;
Where the small stream, confined in narrow
bound,
Ran with a dull, unvaried, sad'ning sound;
Where all presented to the eye or ear,
Oppressed the soul! with misery, grief, and fear.
The Borough (1810) Letter 22 'Peter Grimes' l. 199

26 Lo! the poor toper whose untutored sense,
Sees bliss in ale, and can with wine dispense;
Whose head proud fancy never taught to steer,
Beyond the muddy ecstasies of beer.
'Inebriety' (in imitation of Pope, 1775) pt. 1, l. 132; cf. **Pope** 585:10

27 With awe, around these silent walks I tread;
These are the lasting mansions of the dead.
'The Library' (1808) l. 105

28 Lo! all in silence, all in order stand,
And mighty folios first, a lordly band;
Then quartos their well-ordered ranks maintain,
And light octavos fill a spacious plain;
See yonder, ranged in more frequented rows,

A humbler band of duodecimos.
'The Library' (1808) l. 128

1 Fashion, though Folly's child, and guide of fools,
Rules e'en the wisest, and in learning rules.
'The Library' (1808) l. 167

2 Coldly profane and impiously gay.
'The Library' (1808) l. 265

3 The murmuring poor, who will not fast in peace.
'The Newspaper' (1785) l. 158

4 A master passion is the love of news.
'The Newspaper' (1785) l. 279

5 Our farmers round, well pleased with constant gain,
Like other farmers, flourish and complain.
'The Parish Register' (1807) pt. 1, l. 273

6 The one so worn as you behold,
So thin and pale—is yet of gold.
these lines were printed by Crabbe's son from a paper which he had found wrapped round his mother's wedding-ring (with 'ring' instead of 'one')
'A Ring to Me Cecilia Sends' (written *c.*1813–14)

7 That all was wrong because not all was right.
Tales (1812) 'The Convert' l. 313

8 He tried the luxury of doing good.
Tales of the Hall (1819) 'Boys at School' l. 139

9 'The game,' said he, 'is never lost till won.'
Tales of the Hall (1819) 'Gretna Green' l. 334

10 The face the index of a feeling mind.
Tales of the Hall (1819) 'Lady Barbara' l. 124

11 Secrets with girls, like loaded guns with boys,
Are never valued till they make a noise.
Tales of the Hall (1819) 'The Maid's Story' l. 84

12 Yes, thus the Muses sing of happy swains,
Because the Muses never knew their pains:
They boast their peasants' pipes, but peasants now
Resign their pipes and plod behind the plough.
The Village (1783) bk. 1, l. 21

13 I grant indeed that fields and flocks have charms,
For him that gazes or for him that farms.
The Village (1783) bk. 1, l. 39

14 I paint the cot,
As truth will paint it, and as bards will not.
The Village (1783) bk. 1, l. 53

15 Where Plenty smiles—alas! she smiles for few,
And those who taste not, yet behold her store,
Are as the slaves that dig the golden ore,
The wealth around them makes them doubly poor.
The Village (1783) bk. 1, l. 136

16 The cold charities of man to man.
The Village (1783) bk. 1, l. 245

17 A potent quack, long versed in human ills,
Who first insults the victim whom he kills;
Whose murd'rous hand a drowsy bench protect,
And whose most tender mercy is neglect.
The Village (1783) bk. 1, l. 282

Maurice James Craig 1919–
Irish poet and architectural historian

18 O the bricks they will bleed and the rain it will weep
And the damp Lagan fog lull the city to sleep;
It's to hell with the future and live on the past:
May the Lord in His mercy be kind to Belfast.
based on the traditional refrain 'May God in His mercy look down on Belfast'
'Ballad to a Traditional Refrain' (1974)

Hart Crane 1899–1932
American poet

19 Stars scribble on our eyes the frosty sagas,
The gleaming cantos of unvanquished space.
'Cape Hatteras' (1930)

20 Cowslip and shad-blow, flaked like tethered foam
Around bared teeth of stallions, bloomed that spring.
'Cape Hatteras' (1930)

21 We have seen
The moon in lonely alleys make
A grail of laughter of an empty ash can.
'Chaplinesque' (1926)

22 The apple on its bough is her desire,—
Shining suspension, mimic of the sun.
'Garden Abstract' (1926)

23 Ah, madame! truly it's not right
When one isn't the real Gioconda,
To adapt her methods and deportment
For snaring the poor world in a blue funk.
'Locutions des Pierrots' (1933)

24 So the 20th Century—so
whizzed the Limited—roared by and left
three men, still hungry on the tracks, ploddingly
watching the tail lights wizen and converge, slipping
gimleted and neatly out of sight.
'The River' (1930)

25 O Sleepless as the river under thee,
Vaulting the sea, the prairies' dreaming sod,
Unto us lowliest sometime sweep, descend
And of the curveship lend a myth to God.
'To Brooklyn Bridge' (1930)

26 You who desired so much—in vain to ask—
Yet fed your hunger like an endless task,
Dared dignify the labor, bless the quest—
Achieved that stillness ultimately best,
Being, of all, least sought for: Emily, hear!
'To Emily Dickinson' (1927)

Stephen Crane 1871–1900
American writer

27 The red badge of courage.
title of novel (1895)

Thomas Cranmer 1489–1556

Anglican prelate and martyr; Archbishop of Canterbury from 1553

on Cranmer: see **Henry VIII** *370:10*

1 This was the hand that wrote it [his recantation], therefore it shall suffer first punishment.

at the stake, Oxford, 21 March 1556

John Richard Green *A Short History of the English People* (1874) ch. 7, sect. 2

Richard Crashaw c.1612–49

English poet

on Crashaw: see **Cowley** *239:21*

2 Lord, what is man? Why should he cost thee
So dear? What had his ruin lost thee?
Lord, what is man, that thou hast overbought
So much a thing of nought?

'Caritas Nimia, or The Dear Bargain' (1648)

3 *Nympha pudica Deum vidit, et erubuit.*

The conscious water saw its God, and blushed.

literally, 'the chaste nymph saw . . . '; the translation above is attributed to **Dryden**, *when a schoolboy*

Epigrammata Sacra (1634) 'Aquae in vinum versae [Water changed into wine]'; the translation is discussed in *Notes and Queries* 4th series (1869) vol. 4

4 Love's passives are his activ'st part.
The wounded is the wounding heart.

'The Flaming Heart upon the Book of Saint Teresa' (1652) l. 73

5 By all the eagle in thee, all the dove.

'The Flaming Heart upon the Book of Saint Teresa' (1652) l. 95

6 Love, thou art absolute sole Lord
Of life and death.

'Hymn to the Name and Honour of the Admirable Saint Teresa' (1652) l. 1

7 Poor World (said I) what wilt thou do
To entertain this starry stranger?
Is this the best thou canst bestow?
A cold, and not too cleanly, manger?
Contend, ye powers of heav'n and earth
To fit a bed for this huge birth.

'Hymn of the Nativity' (1652)

8 Welcome, all wonders in one sight!
Eternity shut in a span.

'Hymn of the Nativity' (1652)

9 Lo here a little volume, but large book.

'On a Prayer book' (1646)

10 It is love's great artillery
Which here contracts itself and comes to lie
Close couched in your white bosom.

'On a Prayer book' (1646)

11 I would be married, but I'd have no wife,
I would be married to a single life.

'On Marriage' (1646)

12 Two walking baths; two weeping motions;
Portable, and compendious oceans.

'Saint Mary Magdalene, or The Weeper' (1652) st. 19

13 All is Caesar's; and what odds
So long as Caesar's self is God's?

Steps to the Temple (1646) 'Mark 12'; cf. **Bible** 96:22

14 And when life's sweet fable ends,
Soul and body part like friends;
No quarrels, murmurs, no delay;
A kiss, a sigh, and so away.

'Temperance' (1652)

15 Whoe'er she be,
That not impossible she
That shall command my heart and me.

'Wishes to His (Supposed) Mistress' (1646)

Julia Crawford ?1800–?55

Irish poet and composer

16 Kathleen Mavourneen! the grey dawn is breaking,
The horn of the hunter is heard on the hill.

'Kathleen Mavourneen' in *Metropolitan Magazine*, London (1835)

17 Oh! hast thou forgotten this day we must part?
It may be for years, and it may be for ever,
Oh! why art thou silent, thou voice of my heart?

'Kathleen Mavourneen' in *Metropolitan Magazine*, London (1835)

Robert Crawford 1959–

Scottish poet

18 In Scotland we live between and across languages.

Identifying Poets (1993)

Crazy Horse (Ta-Sunko-Witko) c.1849–77

Oglala Sioux leader

19 One does not sell the earth upon which the people walk.

Dee Brown *Bury My Heart at Wounded Knee* (1970) ch. 12

Mandell Creighton 1843–1901

English prelate

20 No people do so much harm as those who go about doing good.

in *The Life and Letters of Mandell Creighton* by his wife (1904) vol. 2

Michel Guillaume Jean de Crèvecoeur 1735–1813

French-born immigrant to America

21 What then is the American, this new man? He is either a European, or the descendant of a European, hence that strange mixture of blood, which you will find in no other country . . . Here individuals of all nations are melted into a new race of men, whose labours and posterity will one day cause great changes in the world.

Letters from an American Farmer (1782)

Ranulphe Crewe 1558–1646

English judge

22 And yet time hath his revolution; there must be a period and an end to all temporal things, *finis*

rerum, an end of names and dignities and whatsoever is terrene; and why not of De Vere? Where is Bohun, where's Mowbray, where's Mortimer? Nay, which is more and most of all, where is Plantagenet? They are entombed in the urns and sepulchres of mortality. And yet let the name and dignity of De Vere stand so long as it pleaseth God.

speech in Oxford Peerage Case, 22 March 1626; in *Dictionary of National Biography* (1917–) vol. 5

Francis Crick 1916–

English biophysicist

1 'You' your joys and your sorrows, your memories and ambitions, your sense of personal identity and free will, are in fact no more than the behaviour of a vast assembly of nerve cells and their associated molecules.

The Astonishing Hypothesis: The Scientific Search for the Soul (1994) ch. 1

2 Almost all aspects of life are engineered at the molecular level, and without understanding molecules we can only have a very sketchy understanding of life itself.

What Mad Pursuit (1988) ch. 5

Francis Crick 1916– and **James D. Watson** 1928–

English biophysicist; American biologist

3 It has not escaped our notice that the specific pairing we have postulated immediately suggests a possible copying mechanism for the genetic material.

proposing the double helix as the structure of DNA, and hence the chemical mechanism of heredity

in *Nature* 25 April 1953

Quentin Crisp 1908–99

English writer

4 There was no need to do any housework at all. After the first four years the dirt doesn't get any worse.

The Naked Civil Servant (1968) ch. 15

5 An autobiography is an obituary in serial form with the last instalment missing.

The Naked Civil Servant (1968) ch. 29

Julian Critchley 1930–

British Conservative politician and journalist

6 The only safe pleasure for a parliamentarian is a bag of boiled sweets.

in *Listener* 10 June 1982

Richmal Crompton (Richmal Crompton Lamburn) 1890–1969

English author of books for children

7 I'll thcream and thcream and thcream till I'm thick.

Violet Elizabeth's habitual threat

Still—William (1925) ch. 8

Oliver Cromwell 1599–1658

English soldier and statesman; Lord Protector from 1653

on Cromwell: see **Arnold** *29:4*, **Blacker** *116:21*, **Clarendon** *218:23*, **Dryden** *281:15*, **Hill** *376:13*, **Milton** *519:3*, **Pope** *586:3; see also* **Last words** *456:16*, **Misquotations** *522:11*

8 A few honest men are better than numbers.

letter to William Spring, September 1643, in Thomas Carlyle *Oliver Cromwell's Letters and Speeches* (2nd ed., 1846)

9 I would rather have a plain russet-coated captain that knows what he fights for, and loves what he knows, than that which you call 'a gentleman' and is nothing else.

letter to William Spring, September 1643, in Thomas Carlyle *Oliver Cromwell's Letters and Speeches* (2nd ed., 1846)

10 Cruel necessity.

on the execution of **Charles I**

Joseph Spence *Anecdotes* (1820)

11 It has pleased God to bless our endeavours at Drogheda . . . I believe we put to the sword the whole number of the defendants.

letter to Bradshaw, September 1649

12 I beseech you, in the bowels of Christ, think it possible you may be mistaken.

letter to the General Assembly of the Kirk of Scotland, 3 August 1650, in Thomas Carlyle *Oliver Cromwell's Letters and Speeches* (1845)

13 The dimensions of this mercy are above my thoughts. It is, for aught I know, a crowning mercy.

letter to William Lenthall, Speaker of the Parliament of England, 4 September 1651, in Thomas Carlyle *Oliver Cromwell's Letters and Speeches* (1845)

14 You have sat too long here for any good you have been doing. Depart, I say, and let us have done with you. In the name of God, go!

addressing the Rump Parliament, 20 April 1653; oral tradition, based on Bulstrode Whitelock *Memorials of the English Affairs* (1732 ed.); cf. **Amery** 13:7

15 Take away that fool's bauble, the mace.

at the dismissal of the Rump Parliament, 20 April 1653; in Bulstrode Whitelock *Memorials of the English Affairs* (1732 ed.); cf. **Misquotations** 522:10

16 It's a maxim not to be despised, 'Though peace be made, yet it's interest that keeps peace.'

speech to Parliament, 4 September 1654, in Thomas Carlyle *Oliver Cromwell's Letters and Speeches* (1845)

17 Necessity hath no law. Feigned necessities, imaginary necessities . . . are the greatest cozenage that men can put upon the Providence of God, and make pretences to break known rules by.

speech to Parliament, 12 September 1654, in Thomas Carlyle *Oliver Cromwell's Letters and Speeches* (1845); cf. **Proverbs** 607:24

18 Your poor army, those poor contemptible men, came up hither.

speech to Parliament, 21 April 1657, in Thomas Carlyle *Oliver Cromwell's Letters and Speeches* (1845); cf. **Anonymous** 16:6

1 You have accounted yourselves happy on being environed with a great ditch from all the world besides.

speech to Parliament, 25 January 1658, in Thomas Carlyle *Oliver Cromwell's Letters and Speeches* (1845)

2 Hell or Connaught.

summary of the choice offered to the Catholic population of Ireland, transported to the western counties to make room for settlers

traditionally attributed

3 There is no one I am more at a loss how to manage than that Marcus Tullius Cicero, the little man with three names.

of Anthony Ashley Cooper, Lord **Shaftesbury**

B. Martyn and Dr Kippis *The Life of the First Earl of Shaftesbury* (1836) vol. 1 ch. 5

Bing Crosby 1903–77

American singer and film actor
see also **Epitaphs** *303:8*

4 Where the blue of the night
Meets the gold of the day,
Someone waits for me.

'Where the Blue of the Night meets the Gold of the Day' (1931 song, with Roy Turk and Fred Ahlert)

Anthony Crosland 1918–77

British Labour politician

5 Total abstinence and a good filing system are not now the right signposts to the socialist Utopia; or at least, if they are, some of us will fall by the wayside.

The Future of Socialism (1956)

6 If it's the last thing I do, I'm going to destroy every fucking grammar school in England. And Wales, and Northern Ireland.

c.1965, while Secretary of State for Education and Science

Susan Crosland *Tony Crosland* (1982)

7 The party's over.

cutting back central government's support for rates, as Minister of the Environment in the 1970s

Anthony Sampson *The Changing Anatomy of Britain* (1982); cf. **Comden** 230:8

Amanda Cross 1926–

American crime writer and academic

8 'What . . . is a text course?' 'One that uses books, of course . . . You remember books? They're what we used to read before we started discussing what we ought to read.'

Poetic Justice (1970)

9 In former days, everyone found the assumption of innocence so easy; today we find fatally easy the assumption of guilt.

Poetic Justice (1970)

Douglas Cross

American songwriter

10 I left my heart in San Francisco
High on a hill it calls to me.
To be where little cable cars climb half-way to the
  stars,
The morning fog may chill the air—
I don't care!

'I Left My Heart in San Francisco' (1954 song)

Richard Assheton, Lord Cross 1823–1914

British Conservative politician

11 I hear a smile.

when the House of Lords laughed at his speech in favour of Spiritual Peers

G. W. E. Russell *Collections and Recollections* (1898) ch. 29

Richard Crossman 1907–74

British Labour politician
on Crossman: see **Dalton** *248:14*

12 While there is death there is hope.

on the death of Hugh **Gaitskell** *in 1963, according to Crossman; this was a favourite phrase of Harold* **Laski**

Tam Dalyell *Dick Crossman* (1989)

13 The Civil Service is profoundly deferential — 'Yes, Minister! No, Minister! If you wish it, Minister!'

Diaries of a Cabinet Minister vol. 1 (1975) 22 October 1964

14 [To strip away] the thick masses of foliage which we call the myth of democracy.

introduction to *Diaries of a Cabinet Minister* vol. 1 (1975)

Samuel Crossman 1624–83

English clergyman

15 My song is love unknown,
My saviour's love for me,
Love to the loveless shown,
That they might lovely be.
O, who am I,
That for my sake
My Lord should take
Frail flesh and die?

'My song is love unknown' (1664); set to music as a hymn from 1868, and by John Ireland in 1919

Crowfoot c.1830–90

chief of the Blackfoot Indians

16 A little while and I will be gone from among you, whither I cannot tell. From nowhere we came, into nowhere we go. What is life? It is a flash of a firefly in the night. It is a breath of a buffalo in the winter time. It is as the little shadow that runs across the grass and loses itself in the sunset.

attributed farewell to his people, 25 April 1890; John Peter Turner *The North-West Mounted Police: 1873–93* (1950); cf. **Haggard** 356:4

Aleister Crowley 1875–1947

English diabolist

17 Do what thou wilt shall be the whole of the Law.

Book of the Law (1909) l. 40; cf. **Rabelais** 619:11

Ralph Cudworth 1617–88

English Puritan divine and scholar

1 Some who are far from atheists, may make themselves merry with that conceit of thousands of spirits dancing at once upon a needle's point.

The True Intellectual System of the Universe (1678)

Richard Cumberland 1631–1718

English divine

2 It is better to wear out than to rust out.

George Horne *The Duty of Contending for the Faith* (1786); cf. **Proverbs** 596:13

e. e. cummings (Edward Estlin Cummings) 1894–1962

American poet

3 anyone lived in a pretty how town
(with up so floating many bells down)
spring summer autumn winter
he sang his didn't he danced his did.

50 Poems (1949) no. 29

4 'next to of course god america i
love you land of the pilgrims' and so forth oh
say can you see by the dawn's early my
country 'tis of centuries come and go
and are no more what of it we should worry
in every language even deafanddumb
thy sons acclaim your glorious name by gorry
by jingo by gee by gosh by gum.

is 5 (1926) p. 62

5 Humanity i love you because
when you're hard up you pawn your
intelligence to buy a drink.

'La Guerre' no. 2 (1925)

6 o to be a metope
now that triglyph's here.

'Memorabilia' (1926); cf. **Browning** 156:2

7 a politician is an arse upon
which everyone has sat except a man.

1 x 1 (1944) no. 10

8 plato told
him: he couldn't
believe it (jesus

told him; he
wouldn't believe
it) lao

tsze
certainly told
him, and general
(yes

mam)
sherman.

1 x 1 (1944) no. 13

9 pity this busy monster, manunkind,
not. Progress is a comfortable disease.

1 x 1 (1944) no. 14

10 We doctors know
a hopeless case if—listen: there's a hell
of a good universe next door; let's go.

1 x 1 (1944) no. 14

11 when man determined to destroy
himself he picked the was
of shall and finding only why
smashed it into because.

1 x 1 (1944) no. 26

12 i like my body when it is with your
body. It is so quite new a thing.
Muscles better and nerves more.

'Sonnets–Actualities' no. 8 (1925)

13 the Cambridge ladies who live in furnished souls
are unbeautiful and have comfortable minds.

'Sonnets–Realities' no. 1 (1923)

William Thomas Cummings 1903–45

American priest

14 There are no atheists in the foxholes.

Carlos P. Romulo *I Saw the Fall of the Philippines* (1943) ch. 15

Allan Cunningham 1784–1842

Scottish poet

15 A wet sheet and a flowing sea,
A wind that follows fast
And fills the white and rustling sail
And bends the gallant mast.

'A Wet Sheet and a Flowing Sea' (1825)

16 It's hame and it's hame, hame fain wad I be,
O, hame, hame, hame to my ain countree!

'It's hame and It's hame', in James Hogg *Jacobite Relics of Scotland* (1819) vol. 1; in his notes, Hogg says he took it from R. H. Cromek's *Remains of Nithsdale and Galloway Song* (1810) and supposes that it owed much to Cunningham

J. V. Cunningham 1911–

American poet

17 And all's coherent.
Search in this gloss
No text inherent:
The text was loss.
The gain is gloss.

'To the Reader' (1947)

Mario Cuomo 1932–

American Democratic politician

18 You campaign in poetry. You govern in prose.

in *New Republic*, Washington, DC, 8 April 1985

Marie Curie 1867–1934

Polish-born French physicist

19 In science, we must be interested in things, not in persons.

to an American journalist, c.1904, after she and her husband Pierre had shared the Nobel Prize for Physics with A.-H. Becquerel

Eve Curie *Madame Curie* (1937)

Don Cupitt 1934–
British theologian

1 Christmas is the Disneyfication of Christianity.
in *Independent* 19 December 1996

John Philpot Curran 1750–1817
Irish judge

2 The condition upon which God hath given liberty to man is eternal vigilance; which condition if he break, servitude is at once the consequence of his crime, and the punishment of his guilt.
speech on the right of election of the Lord Mayor of Dublin, 10 July 1790, in Thomas Davis (ed.) *Speeches* (1845)

3 Like the silver plate on a coffin.
describing Robert **Peel***'s smile*
quoted by Daniel O'Connell, House of Commons, 26 February 1835

Michael Curtiz 1888–1962
Hungarian-born American film director

4 Bring on the empty horses!
while directing The Charge of the Light Brigade *(1936 film)*
David Niven *Bring on the Empty Horses* (1975) ch. 6

Lord Curzon 1859–1925
British Conservative politician; Viceroy of India 1898–1905

on Curzon: see **Anonymous** *17:20,* **Churchill** *216:12,* **Nehru** *540:9*

5 When a group of Cabinet Ministers begins to meet separately and to discuss independent action, the death-tick is audible in the rafters.
in November 1922, shortly before the fall of **Lloyd George***'s Coalition Government*
David Gilmour *Curzon* (1994)

6 Not even a public figure. A man of no experience. And of the utmost insignificance.
of Stanley **Baldwin***, appointed Prime Minister in 1923 in succession to* **Bonar Law**
Harold Nicolson *Curzon: the Last Phase* (1934)

7 Dear me, I never knew that the lower classes had such white skins.
supposedly said by Curzon when watching troops bathing during the First World War
K. Rose *Superior Person* (1969)

8 Gentlemen do not take soup at luncheon.
E. L. Woodward *Short Journey* (1942) ch. 7

Astolphe Louis Léonard, Marquis de Custine 1790–1857
French author and traveller

9 This empire, vast as it is, is only a prison to which the emperor holds the key.
of Russia
La Russie en 1839; at Peterhof, 23 July 1839

St Cyprian c.AD 200–258
Latin Christian writer and martyr; Bishop of Carthage

10 He cannot have God for his father who has not the church for his mother.
De Ecclesiae Catholicae Unitate sect. 6; cf. **Augustine** 36:7

11 *Fratres nostros non esse lugendos arcessitione dominica de saeculo liberatos, cum sciamus non amitti sed praemitti.*
Our brethren who have been freed from the world by the summons of the Lord should not be mourned, since we know that they are not lost but sent before.
De Mortalite ch. 20 (ed. M. L. Hannam, 1933); cf. **Norton** 547:1, **Rogers** 631:13

12 There cannot be salvation for any, except in the Church.
Epistle Ad Pomponium, De Virginibus sect. 4; cf. **Augustine** 36:7, **Cyprian** 248:10

Salvador Dali 1904–89
Spanish painter

13 Picasso is Spanish, I am too. Picasso is a genius. I am too. Picasso will be seventy-two and I about forty-eight. Picasso is known in every country of the world; so am I. Picasso is a Communist; I am not.
lecture in Madrid, 12 October 1951; Meredith Etherington Smith *Dali* (1992)

Hugh Dalton 1887–1962
British Labour politician

14 He is loyal to his own career but only incidentally to anything or anyone else.
of Richard **Crossman**
diary, 17 September 1941

15 How I love a colleague-free day! Then I can really get on with the job.
diary, 15 May 1946

Samuel Daniel 1563–1619
English poet and dramatist

16 And look, how Thames, enriched with many a flood . . .
Glides on, with pomp of waters, unwithstood,
Unto the ocean.
The Civil Wars (1595) bk. 2, st. 7

17 Custom that is before all law, Nature that is above all art.
A Defence of Rhyme (1603)

18 Men do not weigh the stalk for that it was,
When once they find her flower, her glory, pass.
Delia (1592) Sonnet 32

19 Fresh shalt thou see in me the wounds thou madest,
Though spent thy flame, in me the heat remaining;
I that have loved thee thus before thou fadest,
My faith shall wax, when thou art in thy waning.
The world shall find this miracle in me,
That fire can burn when all the matter's spent.
Delia (1592) Sonnet 33

1 Care-charmer Sleep, son of the sable Night,
Brother to Death, in silent darkness born.
Delia (1592) Sonnet 54; cf. **Fletcher** 318:9, **Shelley** 713:17

2 Tiring thy wits and toiling to no end,
But to attain that idle smoke of praise.
Musophilus (1599) l. 1

3 And who, in time, knows whither we may vent
The treasure of our tongue, to what strange shores
This gain of our best glory shall be sent,
T'enrich unknowing nations with our stores?
What worlds in th'yet unformed Occident
May come refined with th'accents that are ours?
Musophilus (1599) l. 957

4 But years hath done this wrong,
To make me write too much, and live too long.
Philotas (1605) 'To the Prince' (dedication) l. 108

5 Princes in this case
Do hate the traitor, though they love the treason.
The Tragedy of Cleopatra (1594) act 4, sc. 1; cf. **Dryden** 281:10

Dante Alighieri 1265–1321

Italian poet
on Dante: see **Browning** 157:3

6 *Nel mezzo del cammin di nostra vita.*
Midway along the path of our life.
Divina Commedia 'Inferno' canto 1, l. 1

7 PER ME SI VA NELLA CITTÀ DOLENTE,
PER ME SI VA NELL' ETERNO DOLORE,
PER ME SI VA TRA LA PERDUTA GENTE . . .
LASCIATE OGNI SPERANZA VOI CH'ENTRATE!
Through me is the way to the sorrowful city.
Through me is the way to eternal suffering.
Through me is the way to join the lost people . . .
Abandon all hope, you who enter!
inscription at the entrance to Hell
Divina Commedia 'Inferno' canto 3, l. 1

8 *Non ragioniam di lor, ma guarda, e passa.*
Let us not speak of them, but look, and pass on.
Divina Commedia 'Inferno' canto 3, l. 51

9 *Il gran rifiuto.*
The great refusal.
Divina Commedia 'Inferno' canto 3, l. 60

10 *Onorate l'altissimo poeta.*
Honour the greatest poet.
Divina Commedia 'Inferno' canto 4, l. 80

11 *Il maestro di color che sanno.*
The master of those who know.
of ***Aristotle***
Divina Commedia 'Inferno' canto 4, l. 131

12 *. . . Nessun maggior dolore,*
Che ricordarsi del tempo felice
Nella miseria.
There is no greater pain than to remember a happy time when one is in misery.
Divina Commedia 'Inferno' canto 5, l. 121; cf. **Boethius** 123:11, **Tennyson** 762:24

13 *Noi leggiavamo un giorno per diletto*
Di Lancialotto, come amor lo strinse:
Soli eravamo, e sanza alcun sospetto.
One day, we were reading for pleasure about Lancelot, and how love constrained him: we were alone and completely unsuspecting.
Divina Commedia 'Inferno' canto 5, l. 127

14 *Galeotto fu il libro e chi lo scrisse:*
Quel giorno più non vi leggemmo avante.
A Galeotto [a pander] was the book and writer too: that day we did not read any more.
Divina Commedia 'Inferno' canto 5, l. 137

15 *Siete voi qui, ser Brunetto?*
Are *you* here, Advocate Brunetto?
of Brunetto Latini, an old and respected friend of Dante, encountered in hell
Divina Commedia 'Inferno' canto 15, l. 30

16 *La cara e buona imagine paterna.*
The dear and kindly paternal image.
Divina Commedia 'Inferno' canto 15, l. 83

17 *Considerate la vostra semenza:*
Fatti non foste a viver come bruti,
Ma per seguir virtute e conoscenza.
Consider your origins: you were not made to live as brutes, but to follow virtue and knowledge.
Divina Commedia 'Inferno' canto 26, l. 118

18 *E quindi uscimmo a riveder le stelle.*
Thence we came forth to see the stars again.
Divina Commedia 'Inferno' canto 34, l. 139

19 *O dignitosa coscienza e netta,*
Come t'è picciol fallo amaro morso!
O pure and noble conscience, how bitter a sting to thee is a little fault!
Divina Commedia 'Purgatorio' canto 3, l. 8

20 *Che ti fa ciò che quivi pispiglia?*
Vien dietro a me, e lascia dir le genti.
What is it to thee what they whisper there? Come after me and let the people talk.
Divina Commedia 'Purgatorio' canto 5, l. 12

21 *O vana gloria dell'umane posse*
Com'poco verde in su la cima dura
se non è giunta dall'etati grosse!
Credette Cimabue nella pittura
tener lo campo, ed ora ha Giotto il grido
si che la fama di colui è oscura.
O vain renown of human enterprise, no longer lasting than the greenery of the trees, unless succeeded by an uncouth age.
In painting Cimabue was thought to hold the field; now Giotto has the palm, so that he has obscured the other's fame.
Divina Commedia 'Purgatorio' canto 11, l. 91

22 *Non è il mondan romore altro che un fiato*
di vento, ch'or vien quinci ed or qien quindi,
e muta nome perchè muta lato.
The reputation which the world bestows
is like the wind, that shifts now here now there,
its name changed with the quarter whence it blows.
Divina Commedia 'Purgatorio' canto 11, l. 100

1 *Men che dramma*
Di sangue m'è rimaso, che no tremi;
Conosco i segni dell' antica fiamma.

Less than a drop of blood remains in me that does not tremble; I recognize the signals of the ancient flame.

Divina Commedia 'Purgatorio' canto 30, l. 46; cf. **Virgil** 794:10

2 *Puro e disposto a salire alle stelle.*

Pure and ready to mount to the stars.

Divina Commedia 'Purgatorio' canto 33, l. 145

3 *E'n la sua volontade è nostra pace.*

In His will is our peace.

Divina Commedia 'Paradiso' canto 3, l. 85

4 *Tu proverai sì come sa di sale*
Lo pane altrui, e com'è duro calle
Lo scendere e'l salir per l'altrui scale.

You shall find out how salt is the taste of another man's bread, and how hard is the way up and down another man's stairs.

Divina Commedia 'Paradiso' canto 17, l. 58

5 *L'amor che muove il sole e l'altre stelle.*

The love that moves the sun and the other stars.

Divina Commedia 'Paradiso' canto 33, l. 145

Georges Jacques Danton 1759–94

French revolutionary

6 *De l'audace, et encore de l'audace, et toujours de l'audace!*

Boldness, and again boldness, and always boldness!

speech to the Legislative Committee of General Defence, 2 September 1792, in *Le Moniteur* 4 September 1792; cf. **Bacon** 42:12

7 Thou wilt show my head to the people: it is worth showing.

to his executioner, 5 April 1794

Thomas Carlyle *History of the French Revolution* (1837) vol. 3, bk. 6, ch. 2

Joe Darion 1917–

American songwriter

8 Dream the impossible dream.

'The Impossible Dream' (1965 song)

George Darley 1795–1846

Irish-born poet

9 O blest unfabled Incense Tree,
That burns in glorious Araby.

'Nepenthe' (1835) l. 147

Bill Darnell

Canadian environmentalist

10 Make it a *green* peace.

at a meeting of the Don't Make a Wave Committee, which preceded the formation of Greenpeace

in Vancouver, 1970; Robert Hunter *The Greenpeace Chronicle* (1979); cf. **Hunter** 396:8

Clarence Darrow 1857–1938

American lawyer

11 I do not consider it an insult, but rather a compliment to be called an agnostic. I do not pretend to know where many ignorant men are sure—that is all that agnosticism means.

speech at the trial of John Thomas Scopes for teaching Darwin's theory of evolution in school, 15 July 1925, in *The World's Most Famous Court Trial* (1925) ch. 4

12 I would like to see a time when man loves his fellow man and forgets his colour or his creed. We will never be civilized until that time comes. I know the Negro race has a long road to go. I believe that the life of the Negro race has been a life of tragedy, of injustice, of oppression. The law has made him equal, but man has not.

speech in Detroit, 19 May 1926

13 When I was a boy I was told that anybody could become President. I'm beginning to believe it.

Irving Stone *Clarence Darrow for the Defence* (1941)

Charles Darwin 1809–82

English natural historian; grandson of Erasmus ***Darwin****, father of Francis* ***Darwin***

14 The highest possible stage in moral culture is when we recognize that we ought to control our thoughts.

The Descent of Man (1871) ch. 4

15 False views, if supported by some evidence, do little harm, for everyone takes a salutary pleasure in proving their falseness.

The Descent of Man (1871) ch. 21

16 A hairy quadruped, furnished with a tail and pointed ears, probably arboreal in its habits.

on man's probable ancestors

The Descent of Man (1871) ch. 21

17 Man with all his noble qualities . . . still bears in his bodily frame the indelible stamp of his lowly origin.

The Descent of Man (1871), closing words

18 I have called this principle, by which each slight variation, if useful, is preserved, by the term of Natural Selection.

On the Origin of Species (1859) ch. 3

19 We will now discuss in a little more detail the Struggle for Existence.

On the Origin of Species (1859) ch. 3

20 The expression often used by Mr Herbert Spencer of the Survival of the Fittest is more accurate [than 'Struggle for Existence'], and is sometimes equally convenient.

On the Origin of Species (1869 ed.) ch. 3; cf. **Spencer** 732:5

21 From the war of nature, from famine and death, the most exalted object which we are capable of conceiving, namely, the production of the higher animals, directly follows.

On the Origin of Species (1859) ch. 3

22 There is a grandeur in this view of life.

On the Origin of Species (1859) ch. 14

1 What a book a devil's chaplain might write on the clumsy, wasteful, blundering, low, and horridly cruel works of nature!
letter to J. D. Hooker, 13 July 1856, in *Correspondence of Charles Darwin* vol. 6 (1990)

2 Animals, whom we have made our slaves, we do not like to consider our equal.
Notebook B (1837–8) in P. H. Barrett et al. (eds.) *Charles Darwin's Notebooks 1836–1844* (1987)

3 He who understands baboon [will] would do more towards metaphysics than Locke.
Notebook M (16 August 1838) in P. H. Barrett et al. (eds.) *Charles Darwin's Notebooks 1836–1844* (1987)

Erasmus Darwin 1731–1802

English physician; grandfather of Charles **Darwin**, *great-grandfather of Francis* **Darwin**

4 A fool . . . is a man who never tried an experiment in his life.
F. V. Barry (ed.) *Maria Edgeworth: Chosen Letters* (1931) To Sophy Ruxton, 9 March 1792

5 No, Sir, because I have time to think before I speak, and don't ask impertinent questions.
when asked if he found his stammering very inconvenient
'Reminiscences of My Father's Everyday Life', an appendix by Francis Darwin to his edition of Charles Darwin *Autobiography* (1877)

Francis Darwin 1848–1925

English botanist; son of Charles **Darwin**, *great-grandson of Erasmus* **Darwin**

6 In science the credit goes to the man who convinces the world, not to the man to whom the idea first occurs.
in *Eugenics Review* April 1914 'Francis Galton'

Charles D'Avenant 1656–1714

English dramatist and political economist

7 Custom, that unwritten law,
By which the people keep even kings in awe.
Circe (1677) act 2, sc. 3

William D'Avenant 1606–68

English dramatist and poet

8 In every grave make room, make room!
The world's at an end, and we come, we come.
The Law against Lovers (1673) act 3, sc. 1 'Viola's Song'

9 Had laws not been, we never had been blamed;
For not to know we sin is innocence.
'The Philosopher's Disquisition directed to the Dying Christian' (1672) st. 76

10 For I must go where lazy Peace
Will hide her drowsy head;
And, for the sport of kings, increase
The number of the dead.
'The Soldier Going to the Field' (1673); cf. **Somerville** 727:17, **Surtees** 746:16

11 The lark now leaves his wat'ry nest
And, climbing, shakes his dewy wings.
'Song: The Lark' (1638)

John Davidson 1857–1909

Scottish poet

12 A runnable stag, a kingly crop.
'A Runnable Stag' (1906)

13 In anguish we uplift
A new unhallowed song:
The race is to the swift,
The battle to the strong.
'War Song' (1899) st. 1; cf. **Bible** 84:23

John Davies 1569–1626

English poet

14 Wedlock, indeed, hath oft compared been
To public feasts where meet a public rout,
Where they that are without would fain go in
And they that are within would fain go out.
'A Contention Betwixt a Wife, a Widow, and a Maid for Precedence' (1608) l. 193

15 Skill comes so slow, and life so fast doth fly,
We learn so little and forget so much.
'Nosce Teipsum' (1599) st. 19

16 For this, the wisest of all moral men
Said *he knew nought, but that he nought did know*;
And the great mocking master mocked not then,
When he said, *Truth was buried deep below.*
'Nosce Teipsum' (1599) st. 20; cf. **Milton** 518:9, **Socrates** 726:21

17 I know my life's a pain and but a span,
I know my sense is mocked in every thing;
And to conclude, I know myself a man,
Which is a proud and yet a wretched thing.
'Nosce Teipsum' (1599) st. 45

18 This wondrous miracle did Love devise,
For dancing is love's proper exercise.
'Orchestra, or a Poem of Dancing' (1596) st. 18

19 What makes the vine about the elm to dance
With turnings, windings, and embracements round?
What makes the lodestone to the north advance
His subtle point, as if from thence he found
His chief attractive virtue to redound?
Kind nature first doth cause all things to love;
Love makes them dance, and in just order move.
'Orchestra, or a Poem of Dancing' (1596) st. 56

20 Since all the world's great fortune and affairs
Forward and backward rapt and whirlèd are,
According to the music of the spheres;
And Chance herself her nimble feet upbears
On a round slippery wheel, that rolleth aye.
And turns all states with her imperious sway;
'Orchestra, or a Poem of Dancing' (1596) st. 60

21 Learn then to dance, you that are princes born,
And lawful lords of earthly creatures all;
Imitate them, and thereof take no scorn,
(For this new art to them is natural)
And imitate the stars celestial.
For when pale death your vital twist shall sever,

Your better parts must dance with them forever.
'Orchestra, or a Poem of Dancing' (1596) st. 61

Robertson Davies 1913–95
Canadian novelist

1 A great many complimentary things have been said about the faculty of memory, and if you look in a good quotation book you will find them neatly arranged.
The Enthusiasms of Robertson Davies (1990)

2 I see Canada as a country torn between a very northern, rather extraordinary, mystical spirit which it fears and its desire to present itself to the world as a Scotch banker.
The Enthusiasms of Robertson Davies (1990)

3 It's an excellent life of somebody else. But I've really lived inside myself, and she can't get in there.
on a biography of himself
interview in *The Times* 4 April 1995

Scrope Davies c.1783–1852
English conversationalist

4 Babylon in all its desolation is a sight not so awful as that of the human mind in ruins.
***Addison**, in* The Spectator *no. 421 (3 July 1712), also remarked of 'a distracted person' that 'Babylon in ruins is not so melancholy a spectacle'*
letter to Thomas Raikes, May 1835, in *A Portion of the Journal kept by Thomas Raikes* (1856) vol. 2; cf. **Doyle** 277:14

W. H. Davies 1871–1940
Welsh poet

5 And hear the pleasant cuckoo, loud and long—
The simple bird that thinks two notes a song.
'April's Charms' (1916)

6 A rainbow and a cuckoo's song
May never come together again;
May never come
This side the tomb.
'A Great Time' (1914)

7 It was the Rainbow gave thee birth,
And left thee all her lovely hues.
'Kingfisher' (1910)

8 What is this life if, full of care,
We have no time to stand and stare.
'Leisure' (1911)

9 Come, lovely Morning, rich in frost
On iron, wood and glass.
'Silver Hours' (1932)

10 Sweet Stay-at-Home, sweet Well-content,
Thou knowest of no strange continent:
Thou hast not felt thy bosom keep
A gentle motion with the deep.
'Sweet Stay-At-Home' (1913)

Bette Davis see Film lines 311:3, 311:6, 312:10

Jefferson Davis 1808–89
American statesman; President of the Confederate states 1861–5
*on Davis: see **Yancey** 834:19*

11 If the Confederacy fails, there should be written on its tombstone: *Died of a Theory*.
in 1865; Geoffrey C. Ward *The Civil War* (1991) ch. 5

Sammy Davis Jnr. 1925–90
American entertainer

12 Being a star has made it possible for me to get insulted in places where the average Negro could never *hope* to go and get insulted.
Yes I Can (1965) pt. 3, ch. 23

Thomas Davis 1814–45
Irish poet and nationalist

13 But the land of their heart's hope they never saw more,
For in far, foreign fields, from Dunkirk to Belgrade
Lie the soldiers and chiefs of the Irish Brigade.
'The Battle-Eve of the Brigade' (1846)

14 Viva la the New Brigade!
Viva la the Old One, too!
Viva la, the Rose shall fade,
And the shamrock shine for ever new.
'Clare's Dragoons' (1846)

15 And then I prayed I yet might see
Our fetters rent in twain,
And Ireland, long a province, be
A Nation once again.
'A Nation Once Again' (1846)

16 Come in the evening, or come in the morning,
Come when you're looked for, or come without warning.
'The Welcome' (1846)

17 But—hark!—some voice like thunder spake:
The West's awake! the West's awake!
'The West's Asleep' (1846)

18 This country of ours is no sandbank, thrown up by some recent caprice of earth. It is an ancient land, honoured in the archives of civilisation, traceable into antiquity by its piety, its valour, and its sufferings. Every great European race has sent its stream to the river of Irish mind.
Literary and Historical Essays (1846)

19 If we live influenced by wind, and sun, and tree, and not by the passions and deeds of the past, we are a thriftless and hopeless people.
Literary and Historical Essays (1846)

Michael Davitt 1846–1905
Irish nationalist

20 An Englishman of the strongest type moulded for an Irish purpose.
*of Charles Stewart **Parnell***
The Fall of Feudalism in Ireland (1906)

Richard Dawkins
English biologist

1 [Natural selection] has no vision, no foresight, no sight at all. If it can be said to play the role of watchmaker in nature, it is the *blind* watchmaker.
The Blind Watchmaker (1986) ch. 1; cf. **Paley** 564:11

2 However many ways there may be of being alive, it is certain that there are vastly more ways of being dead.
The Blind Watchmaker (1986) ch. 1

3 The essence of life is statistical improbability on a colossal scale.
The Blind Watchmaker (1986) ch. 11

4 They are in you and in me; they created us, body and mind; and their preservation is the ultimate rationale for our existence . . . they go by the name of genes, and we are their survival machines.
The Selfish Gene (1976) ch. 2

5 Science offers the best answers to the meaning of life. Science offers the privilege of understanding before you die why you were ever born in the first place.
in *Break the Science Barrier with Richard Dawkins* (Channel Four) 1 September 1996

6 I think it is likely that there is life out there. I fear we shall never know about it.
in *Seven Wonders of the World* (BBC TV) 9 April 1997

Christopher Dawson 1889–1970
English historian of ideas and social culture

7 As soon as men decide that all means are permitted to fight an evil, then their good becomes indistinguishable from the evil that they set out to destroy.
The Judgement of the Nations (1942)

Lord Dawson of Penn 1864–1945
Physician to King ***George V***

8 The King's life is moving peacefully towards its close.
bulletin, drafted on a menu card at Buckingham Palace on the eve of the king's death, 20 January 1936, in Kenneth Rose *King George V* (1983) ch. 10

Robin Day 1923–
British broadcaster
on Day: see **Howerd** *392:2*

9 Television . . . thrives on unreason, and unreason thrives on television . . . [Television] strikes at the emotions rather than the intellect.
Grand Inquisitor (1989)

Moshe Dayan 1915–81
Israeli statesman and general

10 War is the most exciting and dramatic thing in life. In fighting to the death you feel terribly relaxed when you manage to come through.
in *Observer* 13 February 1972 'Sayings of the Week'

C. Day-Lewis 1904–72
Anglo-Irish poet and critic

11 Do not expect again a phoenix hour,
The triple-towered sky, the dove complaining,
Sudden the rain of gold and heart's first ease
Traced under trees by the eldritch light of
sundown.
'From Feathers to Iron' (1935)

12 Tempt me no more; for I
Have known the lightning's hour,
The poet's inward pride,
The certainty of power.
The Magnetic Mountain (1933) pt. 3, no. 24

13 And when the Treaty emptied the British jails,
A haggard woman returned and Dublin went wild
to greet her.
But still it was not enough: an iota
Of compromise, she cried, and the Cause fails.
'Remembering Con Markievicz' (1970)

14 It is the logic of our times,
No subject for immortal verse—
That we who lived by honest dreams
Defend the bad against the worse.
'Where are the War Poets?' (1943)

15 Every good poem, in fact, is a bridge built from the known, familiar side of life over into the unknown. Science too, is always making expeditions into the unknown. But this does not mean that science can supersede poetry. For poetry enlightens us in a different way from science; it speaks directly to our feelings or imagination. The findings of poetry are no more and no less true than science.
Poetry for You (1944)

James Dean see **Film titles** 313:1

John Dean 1938–
American lawyer and White House counsel during the Watergate affair

16 We have a cancer within, close to the Presidency, that is growing.
from the [Nixon] Presidential Transcripts, 21 March 1973

Millvina Dean 1911–
English youngest survivor of the Titanic disaster

17 I can't bear iced drinks . . . the iceberg, you know. Perhaps some champagne, though.
while visiting the house in Kansas City, Missouri, in which her family would have lived if her father had not drowned
in *Times* 20 August 1997

Seamus Deane 1940–
Irish poet and novelist

18 Meningitis. It was a word you had to bite on to say it. It had a fright and a hiss in it.
Reading in the Dark (1996)

19 The doctor came and gave her pills and medicines. She'd take them and become calmer, but her grief just collected under the drugs like a thrombosis.
Reading in the Dark (1996)

Percy Dearmer 1867–1936
English clergyman

1 Jesu, good above all other,
Gentle Child of gentle Mother,
In a stable born our Brother,
Give us grace to persevere.
'Jesu, good above all other' (1906 hymn)

Simone de Beauvoir 1908–86
French novelist and feminist

2 Garbo's visage had a kind of emptiness into which anything could be projected—nothing can be read into Bardot's face.
Brigitte Bardot and the Lolita Syndrome (1959)

3 It is not in giving life but in risking life that man is raised above the animal; that is why superiority has been accorded in humanity not to the sex that brings forth but to that which kills.
The Second Sex (1949) vol. 1, pt. 2, ch. 1

4 One is not born a woman: one becomes one.
The Second Sex (1949) vol. 2, pt. 1, ch. 1

5 Few tasks are more like the torture of Sisyphus than housework, with its endless repetition ... The housewife wears herself out marking time: she makes nothing, simply perpetuates the present.
The Second Sex (1949) pt. 5, ch. 1

Edward de Bono 1933–
British writer and physician

6 Some people are aware of another sort of thinking which ... leads to those simple ideas that are obvious only after they have been thought of ... the term 'lateral thinking' has been coined to describe this other sort of thinking; 'vertical thinking' is used to denote the conventional logical process.
The Use of Lateral Thinking (1967) foreword

Louis de Bernières 1954–
British novelist and short-story writer

7 The human heart likes a little disorder in its geometry.
Captain Corelli's Mandolin (1994) ch. 26

Eugene Victor Debs 1855–1926
founder of the Socialist party of America

8 When great changes occur in history, when great principles are involved, as a rule the majority are wrong. The minority are right.
speech at his trial for sedition in Cleveland, Ohio, 11 September 1918; in *Speeches* (1928); cf. **Dillon** 267:15

9 While there is a lower class, I am in it; while there is a criminal element, I am of it; while there is a soul in prison, I am not free.
speech at his trial for sedition in Cleveland, Ohio, 14 September 1918; in *Liberator* November 1918

Stephen Decatur 1779–1820
American naval officer

10 Our country! In her intercourse with foreign nations, may she always be in the right; but our country, right or wrong.
Decatur's toast at Norfolk, Virginia, April 1816, in A. S. Mackenzie *Life of Stephen Decatur* (1846) ch. 14; cf. **Adams** 3:17, **Schurz** 649:14

Daniel Defoe 1660–1731
English novelist and journalist

11 We must distinguish between a man of polite learning and a mere scholar: the first is a gentleman and what a gentleman should be; the last is a mere book-case, a bundle of letters, a head stuffed with the jargon of languages, a man that understands every body but is understood by no body.
The Complete English Gentleman (written 1728–9) ch. 5

12 Pleasure is a thief to business.
The Complete English Tradesman (1725) vol. 1, ch. 9

13 The soul is placed in the body like a rough diamond, and must be polished, or the lustre of it will never appear.
An Essay Upon Projects (1697) 'Of Academies: An Academy for Women'

14 Why then should women be denied the benefits of instruction? If knowledge and understanding had been useless additions to the sex, God almighty would never have given them capacities.
An Essay Upon Projects (1697) 'Of Academies: An Academy for Women'

15 Things as certain as death and taxes, can be more firmly believed.
History of the Devil (1726) bk. 2, ch. 6; cf. **Franklin** 323:15

16 Vice came in always at the door of necessity, not at the door of inclination.
Moll Flanders (1721)

17 Give me not poverty lest I steal.
Review vol. 8, no. 75 (15 September 1711); later incorporated into *Moll Flanders* (1721)

18 He told me ... that mine was the middle state, or what might be called the upper station of low life, which he had found by long experience was the best state in the world, the most suited to human happiness.
Robinson Crusoe (1719)

19 I never saw them afterwards, or any sign of them, except three of their hats, one cap, and two shoes that were not fellows.
Robinson Crusoe (1719, ed. J. D. Crowley, 1972) (on his shipmates)

20 It happened one day, about noon, going towards my boat, I was exceedingly surprised with the print of a man's naked foot on the shore, which was very plain to be seen in the sand. I stood like one thunderstruck, or as if I had seen an apparition.
Robinson Crusoe (1719)

21 My man Friday.
Robinson Crusoe (1719)

1 My island was now peopled, and I thought my self very rich in subjects; and it was a merry reflection which I frequently made, how like a king I looked.
Robinson Crusoe (1719)

2 In trouble to be troubled
Is to have your trouble doubled.
The Farther Adventures of Robinson Crusoe (1719, ed. G. Aitken, 1895)

3 Necessity makes an honest man a knave.
The Serious Reflections of Robinson Crusoe (1720) ch. 2

4 The best of men cannot suspend their fate:
The good die early, and the bad die late.
'Character of the late Dr S. Annesley' (1697)

5 We loved the doctrine for the teacher's sake.
'Character of the late Dr S. Annesley' (1697)

6 Actions receive their tincture from the times,
And as they change are virtues made or crimes.
A Hymn to the Pillory (1703) l. 29

7 Fools out of favour grudge at knaves in place.
The True-Born Englishman (1701) introduction, l. 7

8 Nature has left this tincture in the blood,
That all men would be tyrants if they could.
The History of the Kentish Petition (1712–13) addenda, l. 11

9 Wherever God erects a house of prayer,
The Devil always builds a chapel there;
And 'twill be found, upon examination,
The latter has the largest congregation.
The True-Born Englishman (1701) pt. 1, l. 1; cf. **Proverbs** 614:36

10 In their religion they are so uneven,
That each one goes his own by-way to heaven.
The True-Born Englishman (1701) pt. 1, l. 104

11 From this amphibious ill-born mob began
That vain, ill-natured thing, an Englishman.
The True Born Englishman (1701) pt.1, l. 132

12 Your Roman-Saxon-Danish-Norman English.
The True-Born Englishman (1701) pt. 1, l. 139

13 His lazy, long, lascivious reign.
of ***Charles II***
The True-Born Englishman (1701) pt. 1, l. 236

14 Great families of yesterday we show,
And lords whose parents were the Lord knows who.
The True-Born Englishman (1701) pt. 1, l. 374

15 And of all plagues with which mankind are curst,
Ecclesiastic tyranny's the worst.
The True-Born Englishman (1701) pt. 2, l. 299

16 When kings the sword of justice first lay down,
They are no kings, though they possess the crown.
Titles are shadows, crowns are empty things,
The good of subjects is the end of kings.
The True-Born Englishman (1701) pt. 2, l. 313

Edgar Degas 1834–1917
French artist

17 Art is vice. You don't marry it legitimately, you rape it.
Paul Lafond *Degas* (1918)

Charles de Gaulle 1890–1970
French soldier and statesman; President of France, 1959–69

18 France has lost a battle. But France has not lost the war!
proclamation, 18 June 1940, in *Discours, messages et déclarations du Général de Gaulle* (1941)

19 Faced by the bewilderment of my countrymen, by the disintegration of a government in thrall to the enemy, by the fact that the instutions of my country are incapable, at the moment, of functioning, I General de Gaulle, a French soldier and military leader, realize that I now speak for France.
speech in London, 19 June 1940

20 Since they whose duty it was to wield the sword of France have let it fall shattered to the ground, I have taken up the broken blade.
speech, 13 July 1940, in *Discours et Messages* (1942)

21 *Je vous ai compris.*
I have understood you.
speech to French colonists at Algiers, 4 June 1958, in *Discours et Messages* vol. 3 (1970); by 1962 Algeria had achieved independence

22 Yes, it is Europe, from the Atlantic to the Urals, it is Europe, it is the whole of Europe, that will decide the fate of the world.
speech to the people of Strasbourg, 23 November 1959, in *Le Monde* 24 November 1959

23 Politics are too serious a matter to be left to the politicians.
replying to ***Attlee****'s remark that 'De Gaulle is a very good soldier and a very bad politician'*
Clement Attlee *A Prime Minister Remembers* (1961) ch. 4; cf. **Clemenceau** 220:9

24 *Europe des patries.*
A Europe of nations.
widely associated with De Gaulle, c.1962, and taken as encapsulating his views, although perhaps not coined by him
J. Lacouture *De Gaulle: the Ruler* (1991)

25 How can you govern a country which has 246 varieties of cheese?
Ernest Mignon *Les Mots du Général* (1962)

26 Since a politician never believes what he says, he is quite surprised to be taken at his word.
Ernest Mignon *Les Mots du Général* (1962)

27 Treaties, you see, are like girls and roses: they last while they last.
speech at Elysée Palace, 2 July 1963, in André Passeron *De Gaulle parle 1962–6* (1966)

28 *Vive Le Québec Libre.*
Long Live Free Quebec.
speech in Montreal, 24 July 1967, in *Discours et messages* (1970)

29 The sword is the axis of the world and its power is absolute.
Vers l'armée de métier (1934) 'Comment?' Commandement 3

1 And now she is like everyone else.
on the death of his daughter, who had been born with Down's syndrome
Jean Lacouture *De Gaulle* (1965)

2 One does not put Voltaire in the Bastille.
when asked to arrest **Sartre**, *in the 1960s*
in *Encounter* June 1975

Thomas Dekker 1570–1641

English dramatist

3 That great fishpond (the sea).
The Honest Whore (1604) pt. 1, act 1, sc. 2

4 The best of men
That e'er wore earth about him, was a sufferer,
A soft, meek, patient, humble, tranquil spirit,
The first true gentleman that ever breathed.
The Honest Whore (1604) pt. 1, act 1, sc. 2

5 Art thou poor, yet hast thou golden slumbers?
O sweet content!
Art thou rich, yet is thy mind perplexed?
O, punishment!
Dost thou laugh to see how fools are vexed
To add to golden numbers, golden numbers?
O, sweet content, O, sweet, O, sweet content!
Work apace, apace, apace, apace;
Honest labour bears a lovely face;
Then hey nonny, nonny; hey nonny, nonny.
Patient Grissil (1603) act 1, sc. 1

6 Golden slumbers kiss your eyes,
Smiles awake you when you rise:
Sleep, pretty wantons, do not cry,
And I will sing a lullaby:
Rock them, rock them, lullaby.
Patient Grissil (1603) act 4, sc. 2

7 Prince I am not, yet I am nobly born.
The Shoemaker's Holiday (1600) sc. 7

Walter de la Mare 1873–1956

English poet and novelist

8 Ann, Ann!
Come! quick as you can!
There's a fish that *talks*
In the frying-pan.
'Alas, Alack' (1913)

9 Oh, no man knows
Through what wild centuries
Roves back the rose.
'All That's Past' (1912)

10 He is crazed with the spell of far Arabia,
They have stolen his wits away.
'Arabia' (1912)

11 But beauty vanishes; beauty passes;
However rare—rare it be;
'Epitaph' (1912)

12 Look thy last on all things lovely,
Every hour.
'Fare Well' (1918)

13 Hi! handsome hunting man
Fire your little gun.
Bang! Now the animal
Is dead and dumb and done.
Nevermore to peep again, creep again, leap again,
Eat or sleep or drink again, Oh, what fun!
'Hi!' (1930)

14 Three jolly gentlemen,
In coats of red,
Rode their horses
Up to bed.
'The Huntsmen' (1913)

15 'Is there anybody there?' said the Traveller,
Knocking on the moonlit door;
And his horse in the silence champed the grasses
Of the forest's ferny floor.
'The Listeners' (1912)

16 'Tell them I came, and no one answered,
That I kept my word,' he said.
'The Listeners' (1912)

17 Ay, they heard his foot upon the stirrup,
And the sound of iron on stone,
And how the silence surged softly backward,
When the plunging hoofs were gone.
'The Listeners' (1912)

18 What is the world, O soldiers?
It is I:
I, this incessant snow,
This northern sky;
Soldiers, this solitude
Through which we go
Is I.
'Napoleon' (1906)

19 Softly along the road of evening,
In a twilight dim with rose,
Wrinkled with age, and drenched with dew,
Old Nod, the shepherd, goes.
'Nod' (1912)

20 Slowly, silently, now the moon
Walks the night in her silver shoon.
'Silver' (1913)

21 Behind the blinds I sit and watch
The people passing—passing by;
And not a single one can see
My tiny watching eye.
'The Window' (1913)

Shelagh Delaney 1939–

English dramatist

22 Women never have young minds. They are born three thousand years old.
A Taste of Honey (1959) act 1, sc. 2

Frederick Delius 1862–1934

English composer, of German and Scandinavian descent

23 It is only that which cannot be expressed otherwise that is worth expressing in music.
in *Sackbut* September 1920 'At the Crossroads'

24 No artist should ever marry . . . if ever you do have to marry, marry a girl who is more in love with your art than with you.
Eric Fenby *Delius as I Knew Him* (1936)

Agnes de Mille 1908–
American dancer and choreographer

1 The truest expression of a people is in its dances and its music. Bodies never lie.
in *New York Times Magazine* 11 May 1975

Democritus *c.*460–*c.*370 BC
Greek philosopher

2 By convention there is colour, by convention sweetness, by convention bitterness, but in reality there are atoms and space.
fragment 125

Demosthenes *c.*384—*c.*322 BC
Athenian orator and statesman
on Demosthenes, see **Stevenson** *740:16*

3 There is one safeguard known generally to the wise, which is an advantage and security to all, but especially to democracies against despots—suspicion.
Philippic

4 When asked what was first in oratory, [he] replied to his questioner, 'action,' what second, 'action,' and again third, 'action'.
Cicero *Brutus* ch. 37, sect. 142

Jack Dempsey 1895–1983
American boxer

5 Honey, I just forgot to duck.
to his wife, on losing the World Heavyweight title, 23 September 1926; after a failed attempt on his life in 1981, Ronald **Reagan** *quipped 'I forgot to duck'*
J. and B. P. Dempsey *Dempsey* (1977)

Catherine Deneuve 1943–
French actress

6 Sexuality is such a part of life, but sexuality in the movies—I have a hard time finding it.
in *Première* April 1993

7 Why would I talk about the men in my life? For me, life is not about men.
on writing her autobiography
in *Independent* 26 April 1997 'Quote Unquote'

8 The paparazzi are nothing but dogs of war.
after the death in a car crash of **Diana**, *Princess of Wales*
in *Daily Telegraph* 3 September 1997

Deng Xiaoping 1904–97
Chinese Communist statesman, from 1977 paramount leader of China

9 It doesn't matter if a cat is black or white, as long as it catches mice.
in the early 1960s; in *Daily Telegraph* 20 February 1997, obituary

10 I should love to be around in 1997 to see with my own eyes Hong Kong's return to China.
in 1984; in *Daily Telegraph* 20 February 1997, obituary

John Denham 1615–69
English poet

11 Thames, the most loved of all the Ocean's sons,
By his old sire, to his embraces runs,
Hasting to pay his tribute to the Sea,
Like mortal life to meet eternity.
'Cooper's Hill' (1642)

12 Youth, what man's age is like to be doth show;
We may our ends by our beginnings know.
'Of Prudence' (1668) l. 225

13 Old Mother Wit, and Nature gave
Shakespeare and Fletcher all they have;
In Spenser, and in Jonson, Art,
Of slower Nature got the start.
'On Mr Abraham Cowley' (1667)

14 Such is our pride, our folly, or our fate,
That few, but such as cannot write, translate.
'To Richard Fanshaw' (1648)

Lord Denman 1779–1854
English politician and lawyer; Lord Chief Justice, 1832–50

15 Trial by jury itself, instead of being a security to persons who are accused, will be a delusion, a mockery, and a snare.
on a case involving the fraudulent omission of sixty names from the list of jurors in Dublin
speech in the House of Lords, 4 September 1844; in E. W. Cox (ed.) *Reports of Cases in Criminal Law* (1846) vol. 1

Lord Denning 1899–1999
British judge

16 The Treaty [of Rome] is like an incoming tide. It flows into the estuaries and up the rivers. It cannot be held back.
in 1975; Anthony Sampson *The Essential Anatomy of Britain* (1992)

17 To every subject of this land, however powerful, I would use Thomas Fuller's words over three hundred years ago, 'Be ye never so high, the law is above you.'
in a High Court ruling against the Attorney-General, January 1977

18 The keystone of the rule of law in England has been the independence of judges. It is the only respect in which we make any real separation of powers.
The Family Story (1981)

19 We shouldn't have all these campaigns to get the Birmingham Six released if they'd been hanged. They'd have been forgotten and the whole community would be satisfied.
in *Spectator* 18 August 1990

John Dennis 1657–1734

English critic, poet, and dramatist

1 A man who could make so vile a pun would not scruple to pick a pocket.
in *The Gentleman's Magazine* (1781) editorial note

2 The great design of art is to restore the decays that happened to human nature by the fall, by restoring order.
The Grounds of Criticism in Poetry (1704) ch. 2

3 Damn them! They will not let my play run, but they steal my thunder!
on hearing his new thunder effects used at a performance of Macbeth, *following the withdrawal of one of his own plays after only a short run*
William S. Walsh *A Handy-Book of Literary Curiosities* (1893)

Christine de Pisan 1364–*c.*1430

Italian writer, resident in France from 1369

4 Where true love is, it showeth; it will not feign.
'The Epistle of Othea to Hector'

Thomas De Quincey 1785–1859

English essayist and critic

5 The burden of the incommunicable.
Confessions of an English Opium Eater (1856 ed.) pt. 1

6 Oxford Street, stony-hearted stepmother, thou that listenest to the sighs of orphans, and drinkest the tears of children.
Confessions of an English Opium Eater (1822, ed. 1856) pt. 1

7 A duller spectacle this earth of ours has not to show than a rainy Sunday in London.
Confessions of an English Opium Eater (1822, ed. 1856) pt. 2

8 Thou hast the keys of Paradise, oh just, subtle, and mighty opium!
Confessions of an English Opium Eater (1822, ed. 1856) pt. 2

9 Books, we are told, propose to *instruct* or to *amuse*. Indeed! . . . The true antithesis to knowledge, in this case, is not *pleasure*, but *power*. All that is literature seeks to communicate power; all that is not literature, to communicate knowledge.
De Quincey adds that he is indebted for this distinction to 'many years' conversation with Mr **Wordsworth**'
Letters to a Young Man whose Education has been Neglected no. 3, in the *London Magazine* January–July 1823

10 Murder considered as one of the fine arts.
title of essay in *Blackwood's Magazine* February 1827

11 If once a man indulges himself in murder, very soon he comes to think little of robbing; and from robbing he comes next to drinking and sabbath-breaking, and from that to incivility and procrastination.
'On Murder Considered as One of the Fine Arts' (Supplementary Paper) in *Blackwood's Magazine* November 1839

12 There is first the literature of *knowledge*, and secondly, the literature of *power*.
review of the *Works of Pope* (1847 ed.) in *North British Review* August 1848, vol. 9

Edward Stanley, 14th Earl of Derby 1799–1869

British Conservative statesman; Prime Minister, 1852, 1858–9, 1866–8
on Derby: see **Bulwer-Lytton** *160:5*, **Disraeli** *268:9*

13 The duty of an Opposition [is] very simple . . . to oppose everything, and propose nothing.
quoting 'Mr Tierney, a great Whig authority'
in the House of Commons, 4 June 1841

14 Meddle and muddle.
summarizing Lord John **Russell**'*s foreign policy*
Speech on the Address, House of Lords, 4 February 1864

Jacques Derrida 1930–

Algerian-born French philosopher and critic

15 *Il n'y a pas de hors-texte.*
There is nothing outside of the text.
Of Grammatology (1967)

René Descartes 1596–1650

French philosopher and mathematician
on Descartes: see **Ryle** *640:20*

16 *La lecture de tous les bons livres est comme une conversation avec les plus honêttes gens des siècles passés, qui en ont été les auteurs, et même une conversation étudiée en laquelle ils nous découvrent que les meilleures de leurs pensées.*
The reading of good books is like a conversation with the best men of past centuries—in fact like a prepared conversation, in which they reveal only the best of their thoughts.
Le Discours de la méthode (1637) pt. 1

17 *Le bon sens est la chose du monde la mieux partagée, car chacun pense en être bien pourvu.*
Common sense is the best distributed commodity in the world, for every man is convinced that he is well supplied with it.
Le Discours de la méthode (1637) pt. 1

18 *Je pense, donc je suis.*
I think, therefore I am.
usually quoted as, 'Cogito, ergo sum', *from the 1641 Latin edition*
Le Discours de la méthode (1637) pt. 4

19 *Agnoscam fieri non posse ut existam talis naturae qualis sum, nempe ideam Dei in me habens, nisi revera Deus etiam existeret, Deus, inquam, ille idem cujus idea in me est.*
I could not possibly exist with the nature I actually have, that is, one endowed with the idea of God, unless there really is a God; the very God, I mean, of whom I have an idea.
Meditationes (ed. 2, 1642) pt. 3

20 *Repugnare ut detur vacuum sive in quo nulla plane sit res.*
It is contrary to reason to say that there is a vacuum or space in which there is absolutely nothing.
Principia Philosophiae (1644) pt. 2, sect. 16 (translated by E. S. Haldane and G. R. T. Ross)

Camille Desmoulins 1760–94
French revolutionary

1 My age is that of the *bon Sansculotte Jésus*; an age fatal to Revolutionists.
reply given at his trial
Thomas Carlyle *History of the French Revolution* (1837) bk. 6, ch. 2

Philippe Néricault Destouches 1680–1754
French dramatist

2 *Les absents ont toujours tort.*
The absent are always in the wrong.
L'Obstacle imprévu (1717) act 1, sc. 6

Buddy De Sylva 1895–1950 and Lew Brown 1893–1958

3 The moon belongs to everyone,
The best things in life are free,
The stars belong to everyone,
They gleam there for you and me.
'The Best Things in Life are Free' (1927 song); cf. **Proverbs** 595:49

Eamonn de Valera 1882–1975
American-born Irish statesman, Taoiseach 1937–48, 1951–4, and 1957–9, and President of the Republic of Ireland 1959–73
on de Valera: see **Lloyd George** *471:8*

4 Whenever I wanted to know what the Irish people wanted, I had only to examine my own heart and it told me straight off what the Irish people wanted.
speech in Dáil Éireann, 6 January 1922

5 Further sacrifice of life would now be in vain . . . Military victory must be allowed to rest for the moment with those who have destroyed the Republic.
message to the Republican armed forces, 24 May 1923

6 That Ireland which we dreamed of would be the home of a people who valued material wealth only as a basis of right living, of a people who were satisfied with frugal comfort and devoted their leisure to the things of the spirit; a land whose countryside would be bright with cosy homesteads, whose fields and villages would be joyous with sounds of industry, the romping of sturdy children, the contests of athletic youths, the laughter of comely maidens; whose firesides would be the forums of the wisdom of serene old age.
St Patrick's Day broadcast, 17 March 1943

7 Mr Churchill is proud of Britain's stand alone, after France had fallen, and before America had entered the war. Could he not find in his heart the generosity to acknowledge that there is a small nation that stood alone, not for one year or two, but for several hundred years, against aggression; that endured spoliation, famines, massacres in endless succession; that was clubbed many times into insensibility but each time, on returning consciousness, took up the fight anew; a small nation that could never be got to accept defeat and has never surrendered her soul?
radio broadcast, 16 May 1945

8 I sometimes admit that when I think of television and radio and their immense power, I feel somewhat afraid.
at the inauguration of Telefís Éireann in 1961

9 Women are at once the boldest and most unmanageable revolutionaries.
in conversation, *c.*1975

Edward De Vere, Earl of Oxford see Oxford

Robert Devereux, Earl of Essex see Essex

Bernard De Voto 1897–1955
American writer

10 The proper union of gin and vermouth is a great and sudden glory; it is one of the happiest marriages on earth, and one of the shortest lived.
in *Harper's Magazine* December 1949

Peter De Vries 1910–
American novelist and humorist

11 Gluttony is an emotional escape, a sign something is eating us.
Comfort Me With Apples (1956)

12 It is the final proof of God's omnipotence that he need not exist in order to save us.
The Mackerel Plaza (1958) ch. 1

13 The value of marriage is not that adults produce children but that children produce adults.
The Tunnel of Love (1954) ch. 8

James Dewar 1842–1923
Scottish physicist

14 Minds are like parachutes. They only function when they are open.
attributed

Lord Dewar 1864–1930
British industrialist

15 [There are] only two classes of pedestrians in these days of reckless motor traffic—the quick, and the dead.
George Robey *Looking Back on Life* (1933) ch. 28

George Dewey 1837–1917
American naval officer

16 You may fire when you are ready, Gridley.
to the captain of his flagship at Manila, 1 May 1898, in *Autobiography* (1913) ch. 15

Sergei Diaghilev 1872–1929

Russian ballet impresario

1 *Étonne-moi.*
Astonish me.
to Jean ***Cocteau***
Wallace Fowlie (ed.) *Journals of Jean Cocteau* (1956) ch. 1

2 Tchaikovsky thought of committing suicide for fear of being discovered as a homosexual, but today, if you are a composer and *not* homosexual, you might as well put a bullet through your head.
Vernon Duke *Listen Here!* (1963)

Diana, Princess of Wales 1961–97

former wife of ***Charles****, Prince of Wales*
on Diana: see ***Blair*** *117:13,* ***Duffy*** *284:10,* ***Elizabeth II*** *297:17,* ***John*** *408:2,* ***Spencer*** *732:12*

3 If men had to have babies, they would only ever have one each.
in *Observer* 29 July 1984 'Sayings of the Week'

4 I'd like to be a queen in people's hearts but I don't see myself being Queen of this country.
interview on *Panorama*, BBC1 TV, 20 November 1995

5 There were three of us in this marriage, so it was a bit crowded.
interview on *Panorama*, BBC1 TV, 20 November 1995

6 You are going to get a big surprise with the next thing I do.
to reporters at St Tropez
in *Guardian* 16 July 1997

7 The press is ferocious. It forgives nothing, it only hunts for mistakes . . . In my position anyone sane would have left a long time ago.
contrasting British and foreign press reporting
in *Le Monde* 27 August 1997

Diane de Poitiers 1499–1566

mistress of Henry II of France

8 *Adieu doulx baisers colombins.*
Adieu ce qu'en secret faisons
Quand entre nous deux nous jouons.
Farewell sweet kisses, pigeon-wise,
With lip and tongue; farewell again
The secret sports betwixt us twain.
'To Henry II Upon His Leaving for a Trip' (*c.*1552)

Porfirio Diaz 1830–1915

Mexican revolutionary and statesman; President of Mexico, 1877–80, 1884–1911

9 Poor Mexico, so far from God and so close to the United States.
attributed

Charles Dibdin 1745–1814

English songwriter and dramatist

10 Did you ever hear of Captain Wattle?
He was all for love, and a little for the bottle.
'Captain Wattle and Miss Roe' (1797)

11 For a soldier I listed, to grow great in fame,
And be shot at for sixpence a-day.
'Charity' (1791)

12 In every mess I finds a friend,
In every port a wife.
'Jack in his Element' (1790)

13 But the standing toast that pleased the most
Was—The wind that blows, the ship that goes,
And the lass that loves a sailor!
'The Lass that Loves a Sailor' (1811)

14 Here, a sheer hulk, lies poor Tom Bowling,
The darling of our crew.
'Tom Bowling' (1790)

Thomas Dibdin 1771–1841

English songwriter

15 Oh! what a snug little Island,
A right little, tight little Island!
'The Snug Little Island' (1833)

Charles Dickens 1812–70

English novelist
on Dickens: see ***Bagehot*** *47:22,* ***Bennett*** *66:1*

BARNABY RUDGE

16 Something will come of this. I hope it mayn't be human gore.
Simon Tappertit
Barnaby Rudge (1841) ch. 4

17 There are strings . . . in the human heart that had better not be wibrated.
Mr Tappertit
Barnaby Rudge (1841) ch. 22

BLEAK HOUSE

18 Jarndyce and Jarndyce still drags its dreary length before the Court, perennially hopeless.
Bleak House (1853) ch. 1

19 This is a London particular . . . A fog, miss.
Bleak House (1853) ch. 3

20 The wind's in the east . . . I am always conscious of an uncomfortable sensation now and then when the wind is blowing in the east.
Mr Jarndyce
Bleak House (1853) ch. 6

21 'Not to put too fine a point upon it'—a favourite apology for plain-speaking with Mr Snagsby.
Bleak House (1853) ch. 11

22 He wos wery good to me, he wos!
Jo
Bleak House (1853) ch. 11

23 He is celebrated, almost everywhere, for his Deportment.
Caddy Jellyby of Mr Turveydrop
Bleak House (1853) ch. 14

24 You are a human boy, my young friend. A human boy. O glorious to be a human boy! . . . O running stream of sparkling joy
To be a soaring human boy!
Mr Chadband
Bleak House (1853) ch. 19

1 Jobling, there *are* chords in the human mind.
Mr Guppy
Bleak House (1853) ch. 20

2 'It is,' says Chadband, 'the ray of rays, the sun of suns, the moon of moons, the star of stars. It is the light of Terewth.'
Bleak House (1853) ch. 25

3 It's my old girl that advises. She has the head. But I never own to it before her. Discipline must be maintained.
Mr Bagnet
Bleak House (1853) ch. 27

4 The one great principle of the English law is, to make business for itself.
Bleak House (1853) ch. 39

5 Dead, your Majesty, Dead, my lords and gentlemen. Dead, Right Reverends and Wrong Reverends of every Order. Dead, men and women, born with heavenly compassion in your hearts. And dying thus around us, every day.
on the death of Jo
Bleak House (1853) ch. 47

6 I call them the Wards in Jarndyce. They are caged up with all the others. With Hope, Joy, Youth, Peace, Rest, Life, Dust, Ashes, Waste, Want, Ruin, Despair, Madness, Death, Cunning, Folly, Words, Wigs, Rags, Sheepskin, Plunder, Precedent, Jargon, Gammon, and Spinach!
Miss Flite's birds
Bleak House (1853) ch. 60

THE CHIMES

7 O let us love our occupations,
Bless the squire and his relations,
Live upon our daily rations,
And always know our proper stations.
The Chimes (1844) 'The Second Quarter'

A CHRISTMAS CAROL

8 'Bah,' said Scrooge. 'Humbug!'
A Christmas Carol (1843) stave 1

9 I am the Ghost of Christmas Past.
A Christmas Carol (1843) stave 2

10 'God bless us every one!' said Tiny Tim, the last of all.
A Christmas Carol (1843) stave 3

11 It *was* a turkey! He could never have stood upon his legs, that bird. He would have snapped 'em off short in a minute, like sticks of sealing-wax.
A Christmas Carol (1843) stave 5

DAVID COPPERFIELD

12 I am a lone lorn creetur . . . and everythink goes contrairy with me.
Mrs Gummidge
David Copperfield (1850) ch. 3

13 I'd better go into the house, and die and be a riddance!
Mrs Gummidge
David Copperfield (1850) ch. 3

14 She's been thinking of the old 'un!
Mr Peggotty of Mrs Gummidge
David Copperfield (1850) ch. 3

15 Barkis is willin'.
David Copperfield (1850) ch. 5

16 I live on broken wittles—and I sleep on the coals.
The Waiter
David Copperfield (1850) ch. 5

17 Experientia does it—as papa used to say.
Mrs Micawber
David Copperfield (1850) ch. 11; see **Tacitus** 752:18

18 I have known him come home to supper with a flood of tears, and a declaration that nothing was now left but a jail; and go to bed making a calculation of the expense of putting bow-windows to the house, 'in case anything turned up,' which was his favourite expression.
of Mr Micawber
David Copperfield (1850) ch. 11

19 Annual income twenty pounds, annual expenditure nineteen nineteen six, result happiness. Annual income twenty pounds, annual expenditure twenty pounds nought and six, result misery.
Mr Micawber
David Copperfield (1850) ch. 12

20 Mr. Dick had been for upwards of ten years endeavouring to keep King Charles the First out of the Memorial; but he had been constantly getting into it, and was there now.
David Copperfield (1850) ch. 14

21 We live in a numble abode.
Uriah Heep
David Copperfield (1850) ch. 16

22 The mistake was made of putting some of the trouble out of King Charles's head into my head.
Mr Dick
David Copperfield (1850) ch. 17

23 We are so very 'umble.
Uriah Heep
David Copperfield (1850) ch. 17

24 I only ask for information.
Miss Rosa Dartle
David Copperfield (1850) ch. 20

25 It was as true . . . as taxes is. And nothing's truer than them.
Mr Barkis
David Copperfield (1850) ch. 21; cf. **Franklin** 323:15

26 What a world of gammon and spinnage it is, though, ain't it!
Miss Mowcher
David Copperfield (1850) ch. 22

27 Other things are all very well in their way, but give me Blood!
Mr Waterbrook
David Copperfield (1850) ch. 25

1 I assure you she's the dearest girl.
Mr Traddles
David Copperfield (1850) ch. 27

2 Accidents will occur in the best-regulated families.
David Copperfield (1850) ch. 28 (Mr Micawber); cf. **Proverbs** 594:13

3 He told me, only the other day, that it was provided for. That was Mr Micawber's expression, 'Provided for.'
Mr Traddles
David Copperfield (1850) ch. 28

4 'People can't die, along the coast,' said Mr Peggotty, 'except when the tide's pretty nigh out. They can't be born, unless it's pretty nigh in—not properly born, till flood. He's a going out with the tide.'
David Copperfield (1850) ch. 30

5 Mrs Crupp had indignantly assured him that there wasn't room to swing a cat there; but, as Mr Dick justly observed to me, sitting down on the foot of the bed, nursing his leg, 'You know, Trotwood, I don't want to swing a cat. I never do swing a cat. Therefore, what does that signify to *me*!'
David Copperfield (1850) ch. 35

6 It's only my child-wife.
of Dora
David Copperfield (1850) ch. 44

7 Circumstances beyond my individual control.
Mr Micawber
David Copperfield (1850) ch. 49

8 I'm Gormed—and I can't say no fairer than that!
Mr Peggotty
David Copperfield (1850) ch. 63

DOMBEY AND SON

9 He's tough, ma'am, tough is J.B. Tough, and devilish sly!
Major Bagstock
Dombey and Son (1848) ch. 7

10 Papa! What's money?
Paul Dombey
Dombey and Son (1848) ch. 8

11 There was no light nonsense about Miss Blimber . . . she was dry and sandy with working in the graves of deceased languages. None of your live languages for Miss Blimber. They must be dead—stone dead—and then Miss Blimber dug them up like a Ghoul.
Dombey and Son (1848) ch. 11

12 If I could have known Cicero, and been his friend, and talked with him in his retirement at Tusculum (beau-ti-ful Tusculum), I could have died contented.
Mrs Blimber
Dombey and Son (1848) ch. 11

13 In the Proverbs of Solomon you will find the following words, 'May we never want a friend in need, nor a bottle to give him!' When found, make a note of.
Captain Cuttle
Dombey and Son (1848) ch. 15

14 What the waves were always saying.
Dombey and Son (1848) title of ch. 16

15 Cows are my passion.
Mrs Skewton
Dombey and Son (1848) ch. 21

16 If you could see my legs when I take my boots off, you'd form some idea of what unrequited affection is.
Mr Toots
Dombey and Son (1848) ch. 48

GREAT EXPECTATIONS

17 Your sister is given to government.
Joe Gargery
Great Expectations (1861) ch. 7

18 'He calls the knaves, Jacks, this boy,' said Estella with disdain, before our first game was out.
Great Expectations (1861) ch. 8

19 In the little world in which children have their existence, whosoever brings them up, there is nothing so finely perceived and so finely felt, as injustice.
Great Expectations (1861) ch. 8

20 Her bringing me up by hand, gave her no right to bring me up by jerks.
Great Expectations (1861) ch. 8

21 It is a most miserable thing to feel ashamed of home.
Great Expectations (1861) ch. 14

22 On the Rampage, Pip, and off the Rampage, Pip; such is Life!
Joe Gargery
Great Expectations (1861) ch. 15

HARD TIMES

23 Now, what I want is, Facts . . . Facts alone are wanted in life.
Mr Gradgrind
Hard Times (1854) bk. 1, ch. 1

24 People mutht be amuthed. They can't be alwayth a learning, nor yet they can't be alwayth a working, they an't made for it.
Mr Sleary
Hard Times (1854) bk. 3, ch. 8

LITTLE DORRIT

25 Whatever was required to be done, the Circumlocution Office was beforehand with all the public departments in the art of perceiving—HOW NOT TO DO IT.
Little Dorrit (1857) bk. 1, ch. 10

26 There's milestones on the Dover Road!
Mr F.'s Aunt
Little Dorrit (1857) bk. 1, ch. 23

27 As to marriage on the part of a man, my dear, Society requires that he should retrieve his fortunes

by marriage. Society requires that he should gain by marriage. Society requires that he should found a handsome establishment by marriage. Society does not see, otherwise, what he has to do with marriage.
Mrs Merdle
Little Dorrit (1857) bk. 1, ch. 33

1 Father is rather vulgar, my dear. The word Papa, besides, gives a pretty form to the lips. Papa, potatoes, poultry, prunes, and prism, are all very good words for the lips: especially prunes and prism.
Mrs General
Little Dorrit (1857) bk. 2, ch. 5

2 Once a gentleman, and always a gentleman.
Rigaud
Little Dorrit (1857) bk. 2, ch. 28

MARTIN CHUZZLEWIT

3 Affection beaming in one eye, and calculation shining out of the other.
Mrs Todgers
Martin Chuzzlewit (1844) ch. 8

4 Charity and Mercy. Not unholy names, I hope?
Mr Pecksniff
Martin Chuzzlewit (1844) ch. 9

5 Here's the rule for bargains: 'Do other men, for they would do you.' That's the true business precept.
Jonas Chuzzlewit
Martin Chuzzlewit (1844) ch. 11

6 'Mrs Harris,' I says, 'leave the bottle on the chimley-piece, and don't ask me to take none, but let me put my lips to it when I am so dispoged.'
Mrs Gamp
Martin Chuzzlewit (1844) ch. 19

7 Some people . . . may be Rooshans, and others may be Prooshans; they are born so, and will please themselves. Them which is of other naturs thinks different.
Mrs Gamp
Martin Chuzzlewit (1844) ch. 19

8 Brought reg'lar and draw'd mild.
Mrs Gamp on her 'half a pint of porter'
Martin Chuzzlewit (1844) ch. 25

9 He'd make a lovely corpse.
Mrs Gamp
Martin Chuzzlewit (1844) ch. 25

10 'Sairey,' says Mrs Harris, 'sech is life. Vich likeways is the hend of all things!'
Mrs Gamp
Martin Chuzzlewit (1844) ch. 29

11 'The Ankworks package . . . I wish it was in Jonadge's belly, I do,' cried Mrs Gamp; appearing to confound the prophet with the whale in this miraculous aspiration.
Martin Chuzzlewit (1844) ch. 40

12 'Who deniges of it?' Mrs Gamp enquired.
Martin Chuzzlewit (1844) ch. 49

13 No, Betsey! Drink fair, wotever you do!
Mrs Gamp
Martin Chuzzlewit (1844) ch. 49

14 The words she spoke of Mrs Harris, lambs could not forgive . . . nor worms forget.
Mrs Gamp
Martin Chuzzlewit (1844) ch. 49

15 Farewell! Be the proud bride of a ducal coronet, and forget me! . . . Unalterably, never yours, Augustus.
Augustus Moddle
Martin Chuzzlewit (1844) ch. 54

NICHOLAS NICKLEBY

16 United Metropolitan Improved Hot Muffin and Crumpet Baking and Punctual Delivery Company.
Nicholas Nickleby (1839) ch. 2

17 EDUCATION.—At Mr Wackford Squeers's Academy, Dotheboys Hall, at the delightful village of Dotheboys, near Greta Bridge in Yorkshire, Youth are boarded, clothed, booked, furnished with pocket-money, provided with all necessaries, instructed in all languages living and dead, mathematics, orthography, geometry, astronomy, trigonometry, the use of the globes, algebra, single stick (if required), writing, arithmetic, fortification, and every other branch of classical literature. Terms, twenty guineas per annum. No extras, no vacations, and diet unparalleled.
Nicholas Nickleby (1839) ch. 3

18 He had but one eye, and the popular prejudice runs in favour of two.
Mr Squeers
Nicholas Nickleby (1839) ch. 4

19 Here's richness!
Mr Squeers
Nicholas Nickleby (1839) ch. 5

20 Subdue your appetites my dears, and you've conquered human natur.
Mr Squeers
Nicholas Nickleby (1839) ch. 5

21 C-l-e-a-n, clean, verb active, to make bright, to scour. W-i-n, win, d-e-r, der, winder, a casement. When the boy knows this out of the book, he goes and does it.
Mr Squeers
Nicholas Nickleby (1839) ch. 8

22 As she frequently remarked when she made any such mistake, it would be all the same a hundred years hence.
Mrs Squeers
Nicholas Nickleby (1839) ch. 9

23 There are only two styles of portrait painting; the serious and the smirk.
Miss La Creevy
Nicholas Nickleby (1839) ch. 10

24 Sir, My pa requests me to write to you, the doctors considering it doubtful whether he will ever

recuvver the use of his legs which prevents his holding a pen.
Fanny Squeers
Nicholas Nickleby (1839) ch. 15

1 I pity his ignorance and despise him.
Fanny Squeers
Nicholas Nickleby (1839) ch. 15

2 'It's very easy to talk,' said Mrs Mantalini. 'Not so easy when one is eating a demnition egg,' replied Mr Mantalini; 'for the yolk runs down the waistcoat, and yolk of egg does not match any waistcoat but a yellow waistcoat, demmit.'
Nicholas Nickleby (1839) ch. 17

3 Language was not powerful enough to describe the infant phenomenon.
Nicholas Nickleby (1839) ch. 23

4 The unities, sir . . . are a completeness—a kind of universal dovetailedness with regard to place and time.
Mr Curdle
Nicholas Nickleby (1839) ch. 24

5 She's the only sylph I ever saw, who could stand upon one leg, and play the tambourine on her other knee, like a sylph.
Mr Crummles
Nicholas Nickleby (1839) ch. 25

6 Bring in the bottled lightning, a clean tumbler, and a corkscrew.
The Gentleman in the Small-clothes
Nicholas Nickleby (1839) ch. 49

7 All is gas and gaiters.
The Gentleman in the Small-clothes
Nicholas Nickleby (1839) ch. 49

8 My life is one demd horrid grind!
Mr Mantalini
Nicholas Nickleby (1839) ch. 64

9 He has gone to the demnition bow-wows.
Mr Mantalini
Nicholas Nickleby (1839) ch. 64

THE OLD CURIOSITY SHOP

10 Codlin's the friend, not Short.
Codlin
The Old Curiosity Shop (1841) ch. 19

11 I never nursed a dear Gazelle, to glad me with its soft black eye, but when it came to know me well, and love me, it was sure to marry a market-gardener.
Dick Swiveller
The Old Curiosity Shop (1841) ch. 56; cf. **Moore** 530:18

12 It was a maxim with Foxey—our revered father, gentlemen—'Always suspect everybody.'
Sampson Brass
The Old Curiosity Shop (1841) ch. 66

OLIVER TWIST

13 Please, sir, I want some more.
Oliver
Oliver Twist (1838) ch. 2

14 Known by the *sobriquet* of 'The artful Dodger'.
Oliver Twist (1838) ch. 8

15 There is a passion for hunting something deeply implanted in the human breast.
Oliver Twist (1838) ch. 10

16 I only know two sorts of boys. Mealy boys, and beef-faced boys.
Mr Grimwig
Oliver Twist (1838) ch. 14

17 Oh, Mrs Corney, what a prospect this opens! What a opportunity for a jining of hearts and house-keepings!
Bumble
Oliver Twist (1838) ch. 27

18 This ain't the shop for justice.
The Artful Dodger
Oliver Twist (1838) ch. 43

19 'If the law supposes that,' said Mr Bumble . . . 'the law is a ass—a idiot.'
Bumble
Oliver Twist (1838) ch. 51; cf. **Chapman** 202:20

20 Strike them all dead! What right have they to butcher me?
Fagin
Oliver Twist (1838) ch. 52

OUR MUTUAL FRIEND

21 A literary man—*with* a wooden leg.
Mr Boffin, of Silas Wegg
Our Mutual Friend (1865) bk. 1, ch. 5

22 Professionally he declines and falls, and as a friend he drops into poetry.
Mr Boffin, of Silas Wegg
Our Mutual Friend (1865) bk. 1, ch. 5

23 Meaty jelly, too, especially when a little salt, which is the case when there's ham, is mellering to the organ.
Silas Wegg
Our Mutual Friend (1865) bk. 1, ch. 5

24 There is in the Englishman a combination of qualities, a modesty, an independence, a responsibility, a repose, combined with an absence of everything calculated to call a blush into the cheek of a young person, which one would seek in vain among the Nations of the Earth.
Mr Podsnap
Our Mutual Friend (1865) bk. 1, ch. 11

25 I think . . . that it is the best club in London.
Mr Twemlow, on the House of Commons
Our Mutual Friend (1865) bk. 2, ch. 3

26 A slap-up gal in a bang-up chariot.
Our Mutual Friend (1865) bk. 2, ch. 8

27 He'd be sharper than a serpent's tooth, if he wasn't as dull as ditch water.
Fanny Cleaver
Our Mutual Friend (1865) bk. 3, ch. 10

1 I want to be something so much worthier than the doll in the doll's house.
Bella
Our Mutual Friend (1865) bk. 4, ch. 5

PICKWICK PAPERS

2 He had used the word in its Pickwickian sense . . . He had merely considered him a humbug in a Pickwickian point of view.
Mr Blotton
Pickwick Papers (1837) ch. 1

3 Kent, sir—everybody knows Kent—apples, cherries, hops, and women.
Jingle
Pickwick Papers (1837) ch. 2

4 I wants to make your flesh creep.
The Fat Boy
Pickwick Papers (1837) ch. 8

5 'It's always best on these occasions to do what the mob do.' 'But suppose there are two mobs?' suggested Mr Snodgrass. 'Shout with the largest,' replied Mr Pickwick.
Pickwick Papers (1837) ch. 13

6 Battledore and shuttlecock's a wery good game, vhen you an't the shuttlecock and two lawyers the battledores, in which case it gets too excitin' to be pleasant.
Mr Weller
Pickwick Papers (1837) ch. 20

7 Be wery careful o' vidders all your life.
Mr Weller
Pickwick Papers (1837) ch. 20

8 Poverty and oysters always seem to go together.
Sam Weller
Pickwick Papers (1837) ch. 22

9 Dumb as a drum vith a hole in it, sir.
Sam Weller
Pickwick Papers (1837) ch. 25

10 'Eccentricities of genius, Sam,' said Mr Pickwick.
Pickwick Papers (1837) ch. 30

11 A double glass o' the inwariable.
Mr Weller
Pickwick Papers (1837) ch. 33

12 It's my opinion, sir, that this meeting is drunk, sir!
Mr Stiggins
Pickwick Papers (1837) ch. 33

13 'Do you spell it with a "V" or a "W"?' inquired the judge. 'That depends upon the taste and fancy of the speller, my Lord,' replied Sam [Weller].
Pickwick Papers (1837) ch. 34

14 'Little to do, and plenty to get, I suppose?' said Sergeant Buzfuz, with jocularity. 'Oh, quite enough to get, sir, as the soldier said ven they ordered him three hundred and fifty lashes,' replied Sam. 'You must not tell us what the soldier, or any other man, said, sir,' interposed the judge; 'it's not evidence.'
Pickwick Papers (1837) ch. 34; cf. **Proverbs** 614:10

15 A good uniform must work its way with the women, sooner or later.
The Gentleman in Blue
Pickwick Papers (1837) ch. 37

16 'And a bird-cage, sir,' says Sam. 'Veels vithin veels, a prison in a prison.'
Pickwick Papers (1837) ch. 40

17 The have-his-carcase, next to the perpetual motion, is vun of the blessedest things as wos ever made.
Sam Weller
Pickwick Papers (1837) ch. 43

18 Anythin' for a quiet life, as the man said wen he took the sitivation at the lighthouse.
Sam Weller
Pickwick Papers (1837) ch. 43; cf. **Middleton** 507:3

19 'Never . . . see . . . a dead postboy, did you?' inquired Sam . . . 'No,' rejoined Bob, 'I never did.' 'No!' rejoined Sam triumphantly. 'Nor never vill; and there's another thing that no man never see, and that's a dead donkey.'
Pickwick Papers (1837) ch. 51

SKETCHES BY BOZ

20 Minerva House . . . where some twenty girls . . . acquired a smattering of everything, and a knowledge of nothing.
Sketches by Boz (1839) Tales, ch. 3 'Sentiment'

A TALE OF TWO CITIES

21 It was the best of times, it was the worst of times, it was the age of wisdom, it was the age of foolishness, it was the epoch of belief, it was the epoch of incredulity, it was the season of Light, it was the season of Darkness, it was the spring of hope, it was the winter of despair, we had everything before us, we had nothing before us, we were all going direct to Heaven, we were all going direct the other way.
A Tale of Two Cities (1859) bk. 1, ch. 1

22 I pass my whole life, miss, in turning an immense pecuniary Mangle.
Mr Lorry
A Tale of Two Cities (1859) bk. 1, ch. 4

23 A likely thing . . . If it was ever intended that I should go across salt water, do you suppose Providence would have cast my lot in an island?
Miss Pross
A Tale of Two Cities (1859) bk. 1, ch. 4

24 If you must go flopping yourself down, flop in favour of your husband and child, and not in opposition to 'em.
Jerry Cruncher
A Tale of Two Cities (1859) bk. 2, ch. 1

1 'It is possible—that it may not come, during our lives . . . We shall not see the triumph.' 'We shall have helped it,' returned madame.
Monsieur and Madame Defarge
A Tale of Two Cities (1859) bk. 2, ch. 16

2 There might be medical doctors . . . a cocking their medical eyes.
A Tale of Two Cities (1859) bk. 3, ch. 9 (Jerry Cruncher)

3 It is a far, far better thing that I do, than I have ever done; it is a far, far better rest that I go to, than I have ever known.
Sydney Carton's thoughts on the scaffold
A Tale of Two Cities (1859) bk. 3, ch. 15

4 My faith in the people governing is, on the whole, infinitesimal; my faith in The People governed is, on the whole, illimitable.
speech at Birmingham and Midland Institute, 27 September 1869, in K. J. Fielding (ed.) *Speeches of Charles Dickens* (1960)

Emily Dickinson 1830–86

American poet
on Dickinson: see **Crane** *243:26*

5 After great pain, a formal feeling comes.
'After great pain, a formal feeling comes' (1862)

6 Because I could not stop for Death—
He kindly stopped for me—
The Carriage held but just Ourselves—
And Immortality.
'Because I could not stop for Death' (*c.*1863)

7 Since then—'tis Centuries—and yet
Feels shorter than the Day
I first surmised the Horses Heads
Were toward Eternity.
'Because I could not stop for Death' (*c.*1863)

8 What fortitude the Soul contains,
That it can so endure
The accent of a coming Foot—
The opening of a Door.
'Elysium is as far as to' (*c.*1882)

9 There interposed a Fly—
With Blue—uncertain stumbling Buzz—
Between the light—and me—
And then the Windows failed—and then
I could not see to see.
'I heard a Fly buzz—when I died' (*c.*1862)

10 There is no Frigate like a Book
To take us Lands away
Nor any Coursers like a Page
Of prancing Poetry.
'A Book (2)' (*c.*1873)

11 The Bustle in a House
The Morning after Death
Is solemnest of industries
Enacted upon Earth—
The Sweeping up the Heart
And putting Love away
We shall not want to use again
Until Eternity.
'The Bustle in a House' (*c.*1866)

12 Heaven is what I cannot reach
The apple on the tree
'Forbidden Fruit' (*c.*1861)

13 Parting is all we know of heaven,
And all we need of hell.
'My life closed twice before its close'

14 The Soul selects her own Society—
Then—shuts the Door—
To her divine Majority—
Present no more.
'The Soul selects her own Society' (*c.*1862)

15 Success is counted sweetest
By those who ne'er succeed.
To comprehend a nectar
Requires sorest need.
'Success is counted sweetest' (1859)

16 There's a certain Slant of light,
Winter Afternoons—
That oppresses like the Heft
Of Cathedral Tunes—
'There's a certain Slant of light' (*c.*1861)

17 They shut me up in prose—
As when a little girl
They put me in the closet—
Because they liked me 'still'.
'They shut me up in prose' (*c.*1862)

18 This is my letter to the world
That never wrote to me.
'This is my letter to the world' (*c.*1862)

19 This quiet Dust was Gentlemen and Ladies
And Lads and Girls—
Was laughter and ability and Sighing
And Frocks and Curls.
'This quiet Dust was Gentlemen and Ladies' (*c.*1864)

20 Will you tell me my fault, frankly as to yourself, for I had rather wince, than die. Men do not call the surgeon to commend the bone, but to set it, Sir.
letter to T. W. Higginson, July 1862

21 Friday I tasted life. It was a vast morsel. A Circus passed the house—still I feel the red in my mind though the drums are out. The Lawn is full of south and the odors tangle, and I hear to-day for the first time the river in the tree.
letter to Mrs J. G. Holland, May 1866, in T. H. Johnson (ed.) *The Letters of Emily Dickinson* vol. 2 (1958)

John Dickinson 1732–1808

American politician

22 We have counted the cost of this contest, and find nothing so dreadful as voluntary slavery . . . Our cause is just, our union is perfect.
declaration of reasons for taking up arms against England, presented to Congress, 8 July 1775
C. J. Stillé *The Life and Times of John Dickinson* (1891) ch. 5

23 Then join hand in hand, brave Americans all,—
By uniting we stand, by dividing we fall.
'The Liberty Song' (1768), in *The Writings of John Dickinson* vol. 1 (1895); cf. **Proverbs** 613:32

Paul Dickson 1939–
American writer

1 Rowe's Rule: the odds are five to six that the light at the end of the tunnel is the headlight of an oncoming train.
in *Washingtonian* November 1978; cf. **Lowell** 478:5

Denis Diderot 1713–84
French philosopher and man of letters

2 *Et des boyaux du dernier prêtre*
Serrons le cou du dernier roi.
And [with] the guts of the last priest
Let's shake the neck of the last king.
Dithrambe sur fête de rois; cf. **Meslier** 506:5

3 Poetry wants something enormous, barbarous, savage.
Discours de la poésie dramatique (1758)

4 There are two sorts of laws, those of absolute equity and universality, and the bizarre ones which owe their autonomy only to blindness or to the force of circumstance. The latter merely cover the man who is breaking them with a passing disgrace, which time then transfers to the judges and the nations, on whom it remains forever.
Oeuvres romanesques (ed. H. Bénac, revised L. Perol, 1981) (translated by Peter France)

5 The first vows sworn by two creatures of flesh and blood were made at the foot of a rock that was crumbling to dust; they called as witness to their constancy a heaven which never stays the same for one moment; everything within them and around them was changing, and they thought their hearts were exempt from vicissitudes. Children!
Oeuvres romanesques (ed. H. Bénac, revised L. Perol, 1981) (translated by Peter France)

6 *L'esprit de l'escalier.*
Staircase wit.
the witty riposte one thinks of only when one has left the drawing-room and is already on the way downstairs
Paradoxe sur le Comédien (written 1773–8, published 1830)

7 See this egg. It is with this that all the schools of theology and all the temples of the earth are to be overturned.
on how life develops from an insensitive mass
Le Rêve de d'Alembert (written 1769, published 1830) pt. 1

8 Oh Richardson! thou singular genius.
Isaac D'Israeli *Curiosities of Literature* (1849 ed.)

Joan Didion 1934–
American writer

9 Was there ever in anyone's life span a point free in time, devoid of memory, a night when choice was any more than the sum of all the choices gone before?
Run River (1963) ch. 4

10 When we start deceiving ourselves into thinking not that we want something or need something, not that it is a pragmatic necessity for us to have it, but that it is a *moral imperative* that we have it, then is when we join the fashionable madmen, and then is when the thin whine of hysteria is heard in the land, and then is when we are in bad trouble.
Slouching towards Bethlehem (1968) 'On Morality'

Howard Dietz 1896–1983
American songwriter

11 *Ars gratia artis.*
Art for art's sake.
motto of Metro-Goldwyn-Mayer film studios, apparently intended to say 'Art is beholden to the artists'
Bosley Crowthier *The Lion's Share* (1957); cf. **Constant** 235:10

Wentworth Dillon, Lord Roscommon c.1633–1685
Irish poet and critic

12 But words once spoke can never be recalled.
Art of Poetry (1680) l. 438; cf. **Horace** 387:1

13 Choose an author as you choose a friend.
Essay on Translated Verse (1684) l. 96

14 Immodest words admit of no defence,
For want of decency is want of sense.
Essay on Translated Verse (1684) l. 113

15 The multitude is always in the wrong.
Essay on Translated Verse (1684) l. 183; cf. **Debs** 254:8, **Ibsen** 398:6

Ernest Dimnet
French priest, writer, and lecturer

16 [The word moral] is gradually getting to resemble the word *righteous* . . . But, for all that, moral is not preaching, it is beauty of a rare kind.
What We Live By (1932) pt. 1

17 Architecture, of all the arts, is the one which acts the most slowly, but the most surely, on the soul.
What We Live By (1932) pt. 2, ch. 12

Isak Dinesen (Karen Blixen) 1885–1962
Danish novelist and short-story writer

18 A herd of elephant . . . pacing along as if they had an appointment at the end of the world.
Out of Africa (1937) pt. 1, ch. 1

19 The giraffe, in their queer, inimitable, vegetative gracefulness . . . a family of rare, long-stemmed, speckled gigantic flowers slowly advancing.
Out of Africa (1937) pt. 1, ch. 1

20 What is man, when you come to think upon him, but a minutely set, ingenious machine for turning, with infinite artfulness, the red wine of Shiraz into urine?
Seven Gothic Tales (1934) 'The Dreamers'

Diogenes c.400–c.325 BC

Greek Cynic philosopher
on Diogenes: see **Alexander** *11:5*

1 Alexander . . . asked him if he lacked anything. 'Yes,' said he, 'that I do: that you stand out of my sun a little.'
Plutarch *Parallel Lives* 'Alexander' ch. 14, sect. 4 (translated by T. North, 1579)

2 To get practice in being refused.
on being asked why he was begging for alms from a statue
Diogenes Laertius *Lives of the Philosophers*

Dionysius of Halicarnassus fl. 30–7 BC

Greek historian, resident in Rome from 30 BC

3 History is philosophy from examples.
Ars Rhetorica ch. 11, sect. 2

Pseudo-Dionysius fl. 6th century

unidentified author of theological and Neoplatonist works

4 The most holy mysteries are set forth in two modes: one by means of similar and sacred representations akin to their nature, and the other through unlike forms designed with every possible discordance and difference.
The Celestial Hierarchies

Walt Disney 1901–66

American animator and film producer

5 Fancy being remembered around the world for the invention of a mouse!
during his last illness
Leonard Mosley *Disney's World* (1985)

Benjamin Disraeli, Lord Beaconsfield 1804–81

British Tory statesman and novelist; Prime Minister, 1868, 1874–80
on Disraeli: see **Foot** *319:2,* **Salisbury** *642:13, 642:18*

6 Though I sit down now, the time will come when you will hear me.
maiden speech in the House of Commons, 7 December 1837

7 The Continent will [not] suffer England to be the workshop of the world.
speech, House of Commons, 15 March 1838; cf. **Chamberlain** 200:13

8 Thus you have a starving population, an absentee aristocracy, and an alien Church, and in addition the weakest executive in the world. That is the Irish Question.
speech, House of Commons, 16 February 1844

9 The noble Lord is the Prince Rupert of Parliamentary discussion.
of Edward Stanley, later Lord **Derby**
speech, House of Commons, 24 April 1844; cf. **Bulwer-Lytton** 160:5

10 The right hon. Gentleman caught the Whigs bathing, and walked away with their clothes.
on Sir Robert **Peel***'s abandoning protection in favour of free trade, traditionally the policy of the Whig Opposition*
speech, House of Commons, 28 February 1845

11 Protection is not a principle, but an expedient.
speech, House of Commons, 17 March 1845

12 A Conservative Government is an organized hypocrisy.
Bagehot, *quoting Disraeli in* The English Constitution *(1867) 'The House of Lords', elaborated on the theme with the words 'so much did the ideas of its "head" differ from the sensations of its "tail" '*
speech, House of Commons, 17 March 1845

13 He traces the steam-engine always back to the tea-kettle.
of Robert **Peel**
speech, House of Commons, 11 April 1845

14 Justice is truth in action.
speech, House of Commons, 11 February 1851

15 I read this morning an awful, though monotonous, manifesto in the great organ of public opinion, which always makes me tremble: Olympian bolts; and yet I could not help fancying amid their rumbling terrors I heard the plaintive treble of the Treasury Bench.
speech, House of Commons, 13 February 1851

16 These wretched colonies will all be independent, too, in a few years, and are a millstone round our necks.
letter to Lord Malmesbury, 13 August 1852, in W. Monypenny and G. Buckle *Life of Benjamin Disraeli* vol. 3 (1914) ch. 12

17 Petulance is not sarcasm, and . . . insolence is not invective.
speech, House of Commons, 16 December 1852

18 England does not love coalitions.
speech, House of Commons, 16 December 1852

19 Finality is not the language of politics.
speech, House of Commons, 28 February 1859

20 It was a melancholy day for human nature when that stupid Lord Anson, after beating about for three years, found himself again at Greenwich. The circumnavigation of our globe was accomplished, but the illimitable was annihilated and a fatal blow [dealt] to all imagination.
written 1860, in *Reminiscences* (ed. H. and M. Swartz, 1975) ch. 6

21 You are not going, I hope, to leave the destinies of the British Empire to prigs and pedants.
speech, House of Commons, 5 February 1863

22 Party is organized opinion.
speech at Oxford, 25 November 1864, in *The Times* 26 November 1864

23 I hold that the characteristic of the present age is craving credulity.
speech at Oxford, 25 November 1864, in *The Times* 26 November 1864

1 Man, my Lord, is a being born to believe.
speech at Oxford, 25 November 1864, in *The Times* 26 November 1864

2 Is man an ape or an angel? Now I am on the side of the angels.
speech at Oxford, 25 November 1864, in *The Times* 26 November 1864

3 Assassination has never changed the history of the world.
speech, House of Commons, 1 May 1865

4 I had to prepare the mind of the country, and . . . to educate our party.
speech at Edinburgh, 29 October 1867, in *The Times* 30 October 1867

5 Change is inevitable in a progressive country. Change is constant.
speech at Edinburgh, 29 October 1867, in *The Times* 30 October 1867

6 There can be no economy where there is no efficiency.
Address to his Constituents, 1 October 1868, in *The Times* 3 October 1868

7 We have legalized confiscation, consecrated sacrilege, and condoned high treason.
speech, House of Commons, 27 February 1871

8 I believe that without party Parliamentary government is impossible.
speech at Manchester, 3 April 1872, in *The Times* 4 April 1872

9 You behold a range of exhausted volcanoes.
of the Treasury Bench
speech at Manchester, 3 April 1872, in *The Times* 4 April 1872; cf. **Burke** 165:9

10 Increased means and increased leisure are the two civilizers of man.
speech at Manchester, 3 April 1872, in *The Times* 4 April 1872

11 A University should be a place of light, of liberty, and of learning.
speech, House of Commons, 11 March 1873

12 An author who speaks about his own books is almost as bad as a mother who talks about her own children.
at a banquet given in Glasgow on his installation as Lord Rector, 19 November 1873, in *The Times* 20 November 1873

13 Upon the education of the people of this country the fate of this country depends.
speech, House of Commons, 15 June 1874

14 He is a great master of gibes and flouts and jeers.
of the Marquess of ***Salisbury***
speech, House of Commons, 5 August 1874

15 Mr Gladstone not only appeared but rushed into the debate . . . the new members trembled and fluttered like small birds when a hawk is in the air.
of Gladstone in the House of Commons, 15 March 1875
letter to Queen Victoria, March 1875; Roy Jenkins *Gladstone* (1995)

16 Coffee house babble.
on the Bulgarian Atrocities, 1876
in R. W. Seton-Watson *Britain in Europe 1789–1914* (1955)

17 Cosmopolitan critics, men who are the friends of every country save their own.
speech at Guildhall, 9 November 1877, in *The Times* 10 November 1877; cf. **Canning** 185:1, **Overbury** 561:1

18 Lord Salisbury and myself have brought you back peace—but a peace I hope with honour.
speech on returning from the Congress of Berlin, 16 July 1878, in *The Times* 17 July 1878; cf. **Chamberlain** 200:18, **Russell** 640:10

19 A series of congratulatory regrets.
describing Lord Harrington's Resolution on the Berlin Treaty
at a banquet, Knightsbridge, 27 July 1878; in *The Times* 29 July 1878

20 A sophistical rhetorician, inebriated with the exuberance of his own verbosity.
of ***Gladstone***
in *The Times* 29 July 1878

21 I admit that there is gossip . . . But the government of the world is carried on by sovereigns and statesmen, and not by anonymous paragraph writers . . . or by the hare-brained chatter of irresponsible frivolity.
speech at Guildhall, London, 9 November 1878, in *The Times* 11 November 1878

22 One of the greatest of Romans, when asked what were his politics, replied, *Imperium et Libertas*. That would not make a bad programme for a British Ministry.
speech at Mansion House, London, 10 November 1879

Here the two great interests Imperium & Libertas, res olim insociabiles (saith Tacitus), began to incounter each other.
Winston Churchill (*c.*1620–88) *Divi Britannici* (1675); see **Tacitus** 752:6

23 The key of India is London.
speech, House of Commons, 4 March 1881

24 Take away that emblem of mortality.
on being offered an air cushion to sit on, 1881
Robert Blake *Disraeli* (1966) ch. 32

25 No it is better not. She would only ask me to take a message to Albert.
on his death-bed, declining a proposed visit from Queen ***Victoria***
Robert Blake *Disraeli* (1966) ch. 32

26 I will not go down to posterity talking bad grammar.
while correcting proofs of his last Parliamentary speech, 31 March 1881
Robert Blake *Disraeli* (1966) ch. 32

27 No Government can be long secure without a formidable Opposition.
Coningsby (1844) bk. 2, ch. 1

28 A government of statesmen or of clerks? Of Humbug or Humdrum?
Coningsby (1844) bk. 2, ch. 4

1 Conservatism discards Prescription, shrinks from Principle, disavows Progress; having rejected all respect for antiquity, it offers no redress for the present, and makes no preparation for the future.
Coningsby (1844) bk. 2, ch. 5

2 'A sound Conservative government,' said Taper, musingly. 'I understand: Tory men and Whig measures.'
Coningsby (1844) bk. 2, ch. 6

3 Youth is a blunder; Manhood a struggle; Old Age a regret.
Coningsby (1844) bk. 3, ch. 1

4 It seems to me a barren thing this Conservatism—an unhappy cross-breed, the mule of politics that engenders nothing.
Coningsby (1844) bk. 3, ch. 5; cf. **Power** 591:1

5 Where can we find faith in a nation of sectaries?
Coningsby (1844) bk. 4, ch. 13

6 Man is only truly great when he acts from the passions.
Coningsby (1844) bk. 4, ch. 13

7 Read no history: nothing but biography, for that is life without theory.
Contarini Fleming (1832) pt. 1, ch. 23; cf. **Emerson** 299:20

8 The practice of politics in the East may be defined by one word—dissimulation.
Contarini Fleming (1832) pt. 5, ch. 10

9 His Christianity was muscular.
Endymion (1880) ch. 14

10 An insular country, subject to fogs, and with a powerful middle class, requires grave statesmen.
Endymion (1880) ch. 37

11 As for our majority . . . one is enough.
Endymion (1880) ch. 64

12 'Sensible men are all of the same religion.' 'And pray what is that?' . . . 'Sensible men never tell.'
Endymion (1880) ch. 81; cf. **Shaftesbury** 655:16

13 The sweet simplicity of the three per cents.
Endymion (1880) ch. 91; cf. **Stowell** 744:4

14 I believe they went out, like all good things, with the Stuarts.
Endymion (1880) ch. 99

15 Time is the great physician.
Henrietta Temple (1837) bk. 6, ch. 9; cf. **Proverbs** 613:1

16 They mean well; their feelings are strong, but their hearts are in the right place.
The Infernal Marriage (1834) pt. 1, 1 (of the Furies)

17 The blue ribbon of the turf.
of the Derby
Lord George Bentinck (1852) ch. 26

18 A Protestant, if he wants aid or advice on any matter, can only go to his solicitor.
Lothair (1870) ch. 27

19 London: a nation, not a city.
Lothair (1870) ch. 27

20 The gondola of London.
a hansom cab
Lothair (1870) ch. 27

21 When a man fell into his anecdotage it was a sign for him to retire from the world.
Lothair (1870) ch. 28

22 You know who the critics are? The men who have failed in literature and art.
Lothair (1870) ch. 35; cf. **Coleridge** 227:17

23 'Two nations; between whom there is no intercourse and no sympathy; who are as ignorant of each other's habits, thoughts, and feelings, as if they were dwellers in different zones, or inhabitants of different planets; who are formed by a different breeding, are fed by a different food, are ordered by different manners, and are not governed by the same laws.' 'You speak of—' said Egremont, hesitatingly, 'THE RICH AND THE POOR.'
Sybil (1845) bk. 2, ch. 5; cf. **Foster** 321:11

24 Mr Kremlin himself was distinguished for ignorance, for he had only one idea,—and that was wrong.
Sybil (1845) bk. 4, ch. 5; cf. **Johnson** 414:8

25 I was told that the Privileged and the People formed Two Nations.
Sybil (1845) bk. 4, ch. 8

26 The Youth of a Nation are the trustees of Posterity.
Sybil (1845) bk. 6, ch. 13

27 That fatal drollery called a representative government.
Tancred (1847) bk. 2, ch. 13

28 A majority is always the best repartee.
Tancred (1847) bk. 2, ch. 14

29 The East is a career.
Tancred (1847) bk. 2, ch. 14

30 London is a modern Babylon.
Tancred (1847) bk. 5, ch. 5

31 There is no act of treachery or meanness of which a political party is not capable; for in politics there is no honour.
Vivian Grey (1826) bk. 4 ch. 1

32 Experience is the child of Thought, and Thought is the child of Action. We cannot learn men from books.
Vivian Grey (1826) bk. 5, ch. 1

33 All power is a trust . . . from the people, and for the people, all springs, and all must exist.
Vivian Grey (1826) bk. 6, ch. 7; cf. **Dryden** 280:6

34 All Paradise opens! Let me die eating ortolans to the sound of soft music!
The Young Duke (1831) bk. 1, ch. 10; cf. **Smith** 726:4

35 'The age of chivalry is past,' said May Dacre. 'Bores have succeeded to dragons.'
The Young Duke (1831) bk. 2, ch. 5

36 Damn your principles! Stick to your party.
attributed to Disraeli and believed to have been said to Edward ***Bulwer-Lytton***
E. Latham *Famous Sayings and their Authors* (1904)

37 Everyone likes flattery; and when you come to Royalty you should lay it on with a trowel.
to Matthew ***Arnold***
G. W. E. Russell *Collections and Recollections* (1898) ch. 23

1 I am dead; dead, but in the Elysian fields.
to a peer, on his elevation to the House of Lords
W. Monypenny and G. Buckle *Life of Benjamin Disraeli* vol. 5 (1920) ch. 13

2 I have climbed to the top of the greasy pole.
on becoming Prime Minister
W. Monypenny and G. Buckle *Life of Benjamin Disraeli* vol. 4 (1916) ch. 16

3 I never deny; I never contradict; I sometimes forget.
said to Lord Esher of his relations with Queen **Victoria**
Elizabeth Longford *Victoria R. I* (1964) ch. 27

4 Never complain and never explain.
J. Morley *Life of William Ewart Gladstone* (1903) vol. 1; cf. **Fisher** 313:15, **Hubbard** 392:10

5 The palace is not safe when the cottage is not happy.
Robert Blake *Disraeli* (1966)

6 Pray remember, Mr Dean, no dogma, no Dean.
W. Monypenny and G. Buckle *Life of Benjamin Disraeli* vol. 4 (1916) ch. 10

7 The school of Manchester.
describing the free trade politics of Cobden and **Bright**
Robert Blake *Disraeli* (1966) ch. 10

8 There are three kinds of lies: lies, damned lies and statistics.
attributed to Disraeli in Mark Twain *Autobiography* (1924) vol. 1

9 We came here for fame.
to John **Bright**, *in the House of Commons*
Robert Blake *Disraeli* (1966) ch. 4

10 When I want to read a novel, I write one.
W. Monypenny and G. Buckle *Life of Benjamin Disraeli* vol. 6 (1920) ch. 17; cf. **Punch** 617:15

Isaac D'Israeli 1766–1848
British literary historian; father of Benjamin **Disraeli**

11 He wreathed the rod of criticism with roses.
of Pierre Bayle
Curiosities of Literature (9th ed., 1834) vol. 1

William Chatterton Dix 1837–98
English clergyman

12 Alleluia! sing to Jesus,
His the sceptre, his the throne;
Alleluia! his the triumph,
His the victory alone:
Hark! the songs of peaceful Zion
Thunder like a mighty flood;
Jesus, out of every nation,
Hath redeemed us by his blood.
'Alleluia! sing to Jesus' (1867 hymn)

13 As with gladness men of old
Did the guiding star behold.
'As with gladness men of old' (1861 hymn)

Henry Austin Dobson 1840–1921
English poet, biographer, and essayist

14 All passes. Art alone
Enduring stays to us;
The Bust outlasts the throne,—
The Coin, Tiberius.
'Ars Victrix' (1876); translation of Gautier's 'L'Art'; cf. **Gautier** 331:6

15 Fame is a food that dead men eat,—
I have no stomach for such meat.
'Fame is a Food' (1906)

16 The ladies of St James's!
They're painted to the eyes;
Their white it stays for ever,
Their red it never dies:
But Phyllida, my Phyllida!
Her colour comes and goes;
It trembles to a lily, —
It wavers to a rose.
'The Ladies of St James's' (1883)

17 Time goes, you say? Ah no!
Alas, Time stays, *we* go.
'The Paradox of Time' (1877)

Ken Dodd 1931–
British comedian

18 Freud's theory was that when a joke opens a window and all those bats and bogeymen fly out, you get a marvellous feeling of relief and elation. The trouble with Freud is that he never had to play the old Glasgow Empire on a Saturday night after Rangers and Celtic had both lost.
in *Guardian* 30 April 1991; quoted in many, usually much contracted, forms since the mid-1960s

Philip Doddridge 1702–51
English Nonconformist divine

19 Ye servants of the Lord,
Each in his office wait,
Observant of his heavenly word
And watchful at his gate.
Hymns (1755) 'The active Christian'

20 O God of Bethel, by whose hand
Thy people still are fed,
Who through this weary pilgrimage
Hast all our fathers led.
Hymns (1755) 'O God of Bethel'

Bubb Dodington, Lord Melcombe 1691–1762
English politician

21 Love thy country, wish it well,
Not with too intense a care,
'Tis enough, that when it fell,
Thou its ruin didst not share.
'Ode' (written 1761) in Joseph Spence *Anecdotes* (1820)

Robert ('Bob') Dole 1923–

American Republican politician

announcing his decision to relinquish his Senate seat and step down as majority leader:

1 I will seek the presidency with nothing to fall back on but the judgement of the people and with nowhere to go but the White House or home.
on Capitol Hill, 15 May 1996; in *Daily Telegraph* 16 May 1996

2 It's a lot more fun winning. It hurts to lose.
conceding the US presidential election, 6 November 1996
in *Daily Telegraph* 7 November 1996

Aelius Donatus

4th-century Latin grammarian

3 *Pereant, inquit, qui ante nos nostra dixerunt.*
Confound those who have said our remarks before us.
St Jerome *Commentary on Ecclesiastes* bk 1; J.-P. Migne *Patrologiae Latinae* vol. 23

J. P. Donleavy 1926–

Irish-American novelist

4 I got disappointed in human nature as well and gave it up because I found it too much like my own.
A Fairy Tale of New York (1973)

5 When you don't have any money, the problem is food. When you have money, it's sex. When you have both it's health.
The Ginger Man (1955) ch. 5

6 Writing is turning one's worst moments into money.
in *Playboy* May 1979

John Donne 1572–1631

English poet and divine
on Donne: see **Carew** *186:6*, **Coleridge** *226:2*, **James I** *402:17*, **Jonson** *421:1*, **McEwan** *485:6*, **Walton** *803:2*

Verse dates are those of composition

7 And new philosophy calls all in doubt,
The element of fire is quite put out;
The sun is lost, and th'earth, and no man's wit
Can well direct him, where to look for it.
An Anatomy of the World: The First Anniversary (1611) l. 205

8 She, she is dead; she's dead; when thou know'st this,
Thou know'st how dry a cinder this world is.
An Anatomy of the World: The First Anniversary (1611) l. 427

9 Love built on beauty, soon as beauty, dies.
Elegies 'The Anagram' (c.1595)

10 No spring, nor summer beauty hath such grace,
As I have seen in one autumnal face.
Elegies 'The Autumnal' (c.1600)

11 Whoever loves, if he do not propose
The right true end of love, he's one that goes
To sea for nothing but to make him sick.
Elegies 'Love's Progress' (c.1600)

12 . . . The straight Hellespont between
The Sestos and Abydos of her breasts.
Elegies 'Love's Progress' (c.1600)

13 By our first strange and fatal interview,
By all desires which thereof did ensue.
Elegies 'On His Mistress' (c.1600)

14 Nurse, O my love is slain; I saw him go
O'er the white Alps, alone; I saw him, I,
Assailed, fight, taken, stabbed, bleed, fall, and die.
Elegies 'On His Mistress' (c.1600)

15 We easily know
By this these angels from an evil sprite,
They set our hairs, but these our flesh upright.
Elegies 'To His Mistress Going to Bed' (c.1595)

16 License my roving hands, and let them go,
Behind, before, above, between, below.
O my America, my new found land,
My kingdom, safeliest when with one man manned.
Elegies 'To His Mistress Going to Bed' (c.1595)

17 Hail, Bishop Valentine, whose day this is,
All the air is thy Diocese.
'An Epithalamion . . . on the Lady Elizabeth and Count Palatine being Married on St Valentine's Day' (1613)

18 The household bird, with the red stomacher.
'An Epithalamion . . . on the Lady Elizabeth and Count Palatine . . . ' (1613)

19 Clothed in her virgin white integrity.
'A Funeral Elegy' (1610) l. 75

20 At the round earth's imagined corners, blow
Your trumpets, angels, and arise, arise
From death, you numberless infinities
Of souls, and to your scattered bodies go.
Holy Sonnets (1609) no. 4 (ed. J. Carey, 1990)

21 All whom war, dearth, age, agues, tyrannies,
Despair, law, chance, hath slain.
Holy Sonnets (1609) no. 4 (ed. J. Carey, 1990)

22 Death be not proud, though some have called thee
Mighty and dreadful, for thou art not so,
For, those, whom thou think'st, thou dost overthrow,
Die not, poor death, nor yet canst thou kill me.
Holy Sonnets (1609) no. 6 (ed. J. Carey, 1990)

23 One short sleep past, we wake eternally,
And death shall be no more; Death thou shalt die.
Holy Sonnets (1609) no. 6 (ed. J. Carey, 1990)

24 Batter my heart, three-personed God; for, you
As yet but knock, breathe, shine, and seek to mend.
Holy Sonnets (after 1609) no. 10 (ed. J. Carey, 1990)

25 Take me to you, imprison me, for I
Except you enthral me, never shall be free,
Nor ever chaste, except you ravish me.
Holy Sonnets (after 1609) no. 10 (ed. J. Carey, 1990)

26 I am a little world made cunningly
Of elements, and an angelic sprite.
Holy Sonnets (after 1609) no. 15 (ed. J. Carey, 1990)

1 What if this present were the world's last night?
Holy Sonnets (after 1609) no. 19 (ed. J. Carey, 1990)

2 As thou
Art jealous, Lord, so I am jealous now,
Thou lov'st not, till from loving more, thou free
My soul; who ever gives, takes liberty:
O, if thou car'st not whom I love
Alas, thou lov'st not me.
'A Hymn to Christ, at the Author's last going into Germany' (1619)

3 Seal then this bill of my divorce to all.
'A Hymn to Christ, at the Author's last going into Germany' (1619)

4 To see God only, I go out of sight:
And to 'scape stormy days, I choose
An everlasting night.
'A Hymn to Christ, at the Author's last going into Germany' (1619)

5 Since I am coming to that holy room,
Where, with thy choir of saints for evermore,
I shall be made thy music; as I come
I tune the instrument here at the door,
And what I must do then, think now before.
'Hymn to God my God, in my Sickness' (1623)

6 Wilt thou forgive that sin where I begun,
Which is my sin, though it were done before?
Wilt thou forgive those sins, through which I run
And do them still: though still I do deplore?
When thou hast done, thou hast not done,
For, I have more.
'A Hymn to God the Father' (1623)

7 Immensity cloistered in thy dear womb,
Now leaves his well-belovèd imprisonment.
La Corona (1609) 'Nativity'

8 Think then, my soul, that death is but a groom,
Which brings a taper to the outward room.
Of the Progress of the Soul: The Second Anniversary (1612) l. 85

9 Her pure and eloquent blood
Spoke in her cheeks, and so distinctly wrought,
That one might almost say, her body thought.
Of the Progress of the Soul: The Second Anniversary (1612) l. 244

10 I sing the progress of a deathless soul.
'The Progress of the Soul' (1601) st. 1

11 Great Destiny the commissary of God.
'The Progress of the Soul' (1601) st. 4

12 So, of a lone unhaunted place possessed,
Did this soul's second inn, built by the guest,
This living buried man, this quiet mandrake, rest.
'The Progress of the Soul' (1601) st. 16

13 Nature's great masterpiece, an elephant,
The only harmless great thing.
'The Progress of the Soul' (1601) st. 39

14 On a huge hill,
Cragged, and steep, Truth stands, and he that will
Reach her, about must, and about must go.
Satire no. 3 (1594–5) l. 79

15 Air and angels.
title of poem, *Songs and Sonnets*

16 Twice or thrice had I loved thee,
Before I knew thy face or name;
So in a voice, so in a shapeless flame,
Angels affect us oft, and worshipped be.
Songs and Sonnets 'Air and Angels'

17 Just such disparity
As is 'twixt air and angels' purity,
'Twixt women's love, and men's will ever be.
Songs and Sonnets 'Air and Angels'

18 All other things, to their destruction draw,
Only our love hath no decay;
This, no tomorrow hath, nor yesterday,
Running it never runs from us away,
But truly keeps his first, last, everlasting day.
Songs and Sonnets 'The Anniversary'

19 Come live with me, and be my love,
And we will some new pleasures prove
Of golden sands, and crystal brooks,
With silken lines, and silver hooks.
Songs and Sonnets 'The Bait'; cf. **Marlowe** 496:19, **Ralegh** 620:9

20 A naked thinking heart, that makes no show,
Is to a woman, but a kind of ghost.
Songs and Sonnets 'The Blossom' l. 27

21 For God's sake hold your tongue, and let me love.
Songs and Sonnets 'The Canonization'

22 Dear love, for nothing less than thee
Would I have broke this happy dream,
It was a theme
For reason, much too strong for fantasy.
Songs and Sonnets 'The Dream' ('Dear love, for nothing less than thee')

23 So, if I dream I have you, I have you,
For, all our joys are but fantastical.
Songs and Sonnets 'The Dream' ('Image of her whom I love')

24 Where, like a pillow on a bed,
A pregnant bank swelled up, to rest
The violet's reclining head,
Sat we two, one another's best.
Songs and Sonnets 'The Ecstasy'

25 But O alas, so long, so far
Our bodies why do we forbear?
They're ours, though they're not we, we are
The intelligencies, they the sphere.
Songs and Sonnets 'The Ecstasy'

26 So must pure lovers' souls descend
T'affections, and to faculties,
Which sense may reach and apprehend,
Else a great prince in prison lies.
Songs and Sonnets 'The Ecstasy'

27 So, so, break off this last lamenting kiss,
Which sucks two souls, and vapours both away,
Turn thou ghost that way, and let me turn this,
And let our selves benight our happiest day.
We asked none leave to love; nor will we owe
Any, so cheap a death, as saying, Go.
Songs and Sonnets 'The Expiration'

28 Oh wrangling schools, that search what fire
Shall burn this world, had none the wit
Unto this knowledge to aspire,

That this her fever might be it?
Songs and Sonnets 'A Fever'

1 Whoever comes to shroud me, do not harm
Nor question much
That subtle wreath of hair, which crowns my arm;
The mystery, the sign you must not touch,
For 'tis my outward soul,
Viceroy to that, which then to heaven being gone,
Will leave this to control,
And keep these limbs, her provinces, from dissolution.
Songs and Sonnets 'The Funeral'

2 I wonder by my troth, what thou, and I
Did, till we loved, were we not weaned till then?
But sucked on country pleasures, childishly?
Or snorted we in the seven sleepers den?
Songs and Sonnets 'The Good-Morrow'

3 And now good morrow to our waking souls,
Which watch not one another out of fear.
Songs and Sonnets 'The Good-Morrow'

4 Stand still, and I will read to thee
A lecture, love, in love's philosophy.
Songs and Sonnets 'A Lecture in the Shadow'

5 Love is a growing or full constant light;
And his first minute, after noon, is night.
Songs and Sonnets 'A Lecture in the Shadow'

6 If yet I have not all thy love,
Dear, I shall never have it all.
Songs and Sonnets 'Lovers' Infiniteness'

7 I long to talk with some old lover's ghost,
Who died before the god of love was born.
Songs and Sonnets 'Love's Deity'

8 'Tis the year's midnight, and it is the day's.
Songs and Sonnets 'A Nocturnal upon St Lucy's Day'

9 The world's whole sap is sunk:
The general balm th'hydroptic earth hath drunk.
Songs and Sonnets 'A Nocturnal upon St Lucy's Day'

10 When my grave is broke up again
Some second guest to entertain,
(For graves have learnt that woman-head
To be to more than one a bed)
And he that digs it, spies
A bracelet of bright hair about the bone,
Will he not let us alone?
Songs and Sonnets 'The Relic'

11 Go, and catch a falling star,
Get with child a mandrake root,
Tell me, where all past years are,
Or who cleft the Devil's foot,
Teach me to hear mermaids singing.
Songs and Sonnets 'Song: Go and catch a falling star'

12 And swear
No where
Lives a woman true and fair.
Songs and Sonnets 'Song: Go and catch a falling star'

13 Sweetest love, I do not go,
For weariness of thee,
Nor in hope the world can show
A fitter love for me;
But since that I
Must die at last, 'tis best,
To use my self in jest
Thus by feigned deaths to die.
Songs and Sonnets 'Song: Sweetest love, I do not go'

14 Busy old fool, unruly sun,
Why dost thou thus,
Through windows, and through curtains call on us?
Must to thy motions lovers' seasons run?
Songs and Sonnets 'The Sun Rising'

15 Love, all alike, no season knows, nor clime,
Nor hours, days, months, which are the rags of time.
Songs and Sonnets 'The Sun Rising'

16 This bed thy centre is, these walls thy sphere.
Songs and Sonnets 'The Sun Rising'

17 I am two fools, I know,
For loving, and for saying so
In whining poetry.
Songs and Sonnets 'The Triple Fool'

18 I have done one braver thing
Than all the Worthies did,
And yet a braver thence doth spring,
Which is, to keep that hid.
Songs and Sonnets 'The Undertaking'

19 So let us melt, and make no noise,
No tear-floods, nor sigh-tempests move,
'Twere profanation of our joys
To tell the laity our love.
Songs and Sonnets 'A Valediction: forbidding mourning'

20 Thy firmness makes my circle just,
And makes me end, where I begun.
Songs and Sonnets 'A Valediction: forbidding mourning'

21 O more than moon,
Draw not up seas to drown me in thy sphere,
Weep me not dead, in thine arms, but forbear
To teach the sea what it may do too soon.
Songs and Sonnets 'A Valediction: of Weeping'

22 Sir, more than kisses, letters mingle souls.
'To Sir Henry Wotton' (1597–8)

23 And seeing the snail, which everywhere doth roam,
Carrying his own house still, still is at home,
Follow (for he is easy paced) this snail,
Be thine own palace, or the world's thy gaol.
'To Sir Henry Wotton' (1597–8)

24 We have a winding sheet in our mother's womb, which grows with us from our conception, and we come into the world, wound up in that winding sheet, for we come to seek a grave.
Death's Duel (1632)

25 That which we call life, is but *hebdomada mortium*, a week of death, seven days, seven periods of our life spent in dying, a dying seven times over; and there is an end.
Death's Duel (1632)

26 There we leave you, in that blessed dependancy, to hang upon him that hangs upon the Cross, there

bathe in his tears, there suck at his wounds, and lie down in peace in his grave, till he vouchsafe you a resurrection, and an ascension into that Kingdom, which he hath prepared for you, with the inestimable price of his incorruptible blood. Amen.

Death's Duel (1632)

1 My God, my God, thou art a direct God, may I not say a literal God, a God that wouldst be understood literally and according to the plain sense of all that thou sayest? But thou art also . . . a figurative, a metaphorical God too.

Devotions upon Emergent Occasions (1624) 'Expostulation XIX'

2 But I do nothing upon my self, and yet I am mine own Executioner.

Devotions upon Emergent Occasions (1624) 'Meditation XII'

3 No man is an Island, entire of it self; every man is a piece of the Continent, a part of the main; if a clod be washed away by the sea, Europe is the less, as well as if a promontory were, as well as if a manor of thy friends or of thine own were; any man's death diminishes me, because I am involved in Mankind; And therefore never send to know for whom the bell tolls; it tolls for thee.

Devotions upon Emergent Occasions (1624) 'Meditation XVII'

4 From this I testify her holy cheerfulness, and religious alacrity, (one of the best evidences of a good conscience), that as she came to this place, God's house of Prayer . . . she ever hastened her family, and her company hither, with that cheerful provocation, For God's sake let's go, For God's sake let's be there at the Confession.

A Sermon of Commemoration of the Lady Danvers [mother of George Herbert] (1627)

5 [Death] comes equally to us all, and makes us all equal when it comes. The ashes of an Oak in the Chimney, are no epitaph of that Oak, to tell me how high or how large that was; It tells me not what flocks it sheltered while it stood, nor what men it hurt when it fell.

LXXX Sermons (1640) 8 March 1621/2

6 When a whirlwind hath blown the dust of the Churchyard into the Church, and the man sweeps out the dust of the Church into the Churchyard, who will undertake to sift those dusts again, and to pronounce, This is the Patrician, this is the noble flower, and this the yeomanly, this the Plebeian bran.

LXXX Sermons (1640) 8 March 1621/2

7 A day that hath no *pridie*, nor *postridie*, yesterday doth not usher it in, nor tomorrow shall not drive it out. *Methusalem*, with all his hundreds of years, was but a mushroom of a night's growth, to this day, And all the four Monarchies, with all their thousands of years, and all the powerful Kings and all the beautiful Queens of this world, were but as a bed of flowers, some gathered at six, some at seven, some at eight, All in one Morning, in respect of this Day.

LXXX Sermons (1640) 30 April 1626 'Eternity'

8 I throw myself down in my Chamber, and I call in, and invite God, and his Angels thither, and when they are there, I neglect God and his Angels, for the noise of a fly, for the rattling of a coach, for the whining of a door.

LXXX Sermons (1640) 12 December 1626 'At the Funeral of Sir William Cokayne'

9 A memory of yesterday's pleasures, a fear of tomorrow's dangers, a straw under my knee, a noise in mine ear, a light in mine eye, an anything, a nothing, a fancy, a chimera in my brain, troubles me in my prayer. So certainly is there nothing, nothing in spiritual things, perfect in this world.

LXXX Sermons (1640) 12 December 1626 'At the Funeral of Sir William Cokayne'

10 There is nothing that God hath established in a constant course of nature, and which therefore is done every day, but would seem a Miracle, and exercise our admiration, if it were done but once.

LXXX Sermons (1640) Easter Day, 25 March 1627

11 Man is but earth; 'Tis true; but earth is the centre. That man who dwells upon himself, who is always conversant in himself, rests in his true centre.

LXXX Sermons (1640) Christmas Day, 1627

12 Poor intricated soul! Riddling, perplexed, labyrinthical soul!

LXXX Sermons (1640) 25 January 1628/9

13 They shall awake as Jacob did, and say as Jacob said, *Surely the Lord is in this place*, and *this is no other but the house of God, and the gate of heaven*, And into that gate they shall enter, and in that house they shall dwell, where there shall be no Cloud nor Sun, no darkness nor dazzling, but one equal light, no noise nor silence, but one equal music, no fears nor hopes, but one equal possession, no foes nor friends, but one equal communion and identity, no ends nor beginnings, but one equal eternity.

XXVI Sermons (1660) 29 February 1627/8

14 John Donne, Anne Donne, Un-done.

in a letter to his wife, on being dismissed from the service of his father-in-law, Sir George More

Izaak Walton *The Life of Dr Donne* (first printed in *LXXX Sermons*, 1640)

Fedor Dostoevsky 1821–81

Russian novelist

15 If you were to destroy in mankind the belief in immortality, not only love but every living force maintaining the life of the world would at once be dried up.

The Brothers Karamazov (1879–80) bk. 2, ch. 6

16 Beauty is mysterious as well as terrible. God and devil are fighting there, and the battlefield is the heart of man.

The Brothers Karamazov (1879–80) bk. 3, ch. 3

17 If the devil doesn't exist, but man has created him, he has created him in his own image and likeness.

The Brothers Karamazov (1879–80) bk. 5, ch. 4

18 Too high a price is asked for harmony; it's beyond our means to pay so much to enter. And so I hasten to give back my entrance ticket . . . It's not

God that I don't accept, Alyosha, only I most respectfully return Him the ticket.
The Brothers Karamazov (1879–80) bk. 5, ch. 4

1 Imagine that you are creating a fabric of human destiny with the object of making men happy in the end, giving them peace and rest at last, but that it was essential and inevitable to torture to death only one tiny creature . . . and to found that edifice on its unavenged tears, would you consent to be the architect on those conditions?
The Brothers Karamazov (1879–80) bk. 5, ch. 4

2 Men reject their prophets and slay them, but they love their martyrs and honour those whom they have slain.
The Brothers Karamazov (1879–80) bk. 6, ch. 3

3 Power is given only to him who dares to stoop and take it . . . one must have the courage to dare.
Crime and Punishment (1866) pt. 5, ch. 4 (translated by David Magarshak)

4 I wanted to murder, for my own satisfaction . . . At that moment I did not care a damn whether I would become the benefactor of someone, or would spend the rest of my life like a spider catching them all in my web and sucking the living juices out of them.
Crime and Punishment (1866) pt. 5, ch. 4 (translated by David Magarshak)

5 Some new sorts of microbes were attacking the bodies of men, but these microbes were endowed with intelligence and will . . . Men attacked by them became at once mad and furious.
Crime and Punishment (1866) epilogue (translated by Constance Garnett)

6 To crush, to annihilate a man utterly, to inflict on him the most terrible punishment so that the most ferocious murderer would shudder at it beforehand, one need only give him work of an absolutely, completely useless and irrational character.
House of the Dead (1862) pt. 1, ch. 1 (translated by Constance Garnett)

7 Petersburg, the most abstract and premeditated city on earth.
Notes from Underground (1864) pt. 1, ch. 2 (translated by Andrew R. McAndrew)

8 In despair there are the most intense enjoyments, especially when one is very acutely conscious of the hopelessness of one's position.
Notes from Underground (1864) pt. 1, ch. 2 (translated by Andrew R. McAndrew)

9 What man wants is simply *independent* choice, whatever that independence may cost and wherever it may lead.
Notes from Underground (1864) pt. 1, ch. 7 (translated by Constance Garnett)

Mark Doty 1953–
American poet

10 and I swear sometimes
when I put my head to his chest
I can hear the virus humming
like a refrigerator.
'Atlantis' (1996)

Lord Alfred Douglas 1870–1945
poet and intimate of Oscar Wilde

11 I am the Love that dare not speak its name.
'Two Loves' (1896)

Gavin Douglas c.1475–1522
Scottish poet and prelate

12 And all small fowlys singis on the spray:
Welcum the lord of lycht and lamp of day.
Eneados (1553) bk. 12, prologue l. 251

James Douglas, Earl of Morton c.1516–81
Scottish courtier

13 Here lies he who neither feared nor flattered any flesh.
of John **Knox**, *said as he was buried, 26 November 1572*
George R. Preedy *The Life of John Knox* (1940) ch. 7

Keith Douglas 1920–44
English poet

14 And all my endeavours are unlucky explorers
come back, abandoning the expedition.
'On Return from Egypt, 1943–4' (1946)

15 Remember me when I am dead
And simplify me when I'm dead.
'Simplify me when I'm Dead' (1941)

16 But she would weep to see today
how on his skin the swart flies move;
the dust upon the paper eye
and the burst stomach like a cave.

For here the lover and killer are mingled
who had one body and one heart.
And death, who had the soldier singled
has done the lover mortal hurt.
'Vergissmeinnicht, 1943'

Norman Douglas 1868–1952
Scottish-born novelist and essayist

17 To find a friend one must close one eye. To keep him—two.
Almanac (1941)

18 You can tell the ideals of a nation by its advertisements.
South Wind (1917) ch. 6

19 Many a man who thinks to found a home discovers that he has merely opened a tavern for his friends.
South Wind (1917) ch. 20

O. Douglas (Anna Buchan) 1877–1948
Scottish writer, sister of John **Buchan**

20 It is wonderful how much news there is when people write every other day; if they wait for a month, there is nothing that seems worth telling.
Penny Plain (1920)

21 I know heaps of quotations, so I can always make quite a fair show of knowledge.
The Setons (1917)

Alec Douglas-Home see Lord Home

Frederick Douglass c.1818–95

American former slave and civil rights campaigner

1 Every tone [of the songs of the slaves] was a testimony against slavery, and a prayer to God for deliverance from chains.

Narrative of the Life of Frederick Douglass (1845) ch. 2

2 The life of the nation is secure only while the nation is honest, truthful, and virtuous.

speech on the 23rd anniversary of Emancipation in the District of Columbia, Washington DC, April 1885

Lorenzo Dow 1777–1834

American divine

3 You will be damned if you do—And you will be damned if you don't.

on the Calvinist doctrine of 'Particular Election'

Reflections on the Love of God (1836) ch. 6

Maureen Dowd 1952–

American journalist

4 The Princess of Wales was the queen of surfaces, ruling over a kingdom where fame was the highest value and glamour the most cherished attribute.

in *New York Times* 3 September 1997

Ernest Dowson 1867–1900

English poet

5 I have forgot much, Cynara! gone with the wind,
Flung roses, roses, riotously, with the throng,
Dancing, to put thy pale, lost lilies out of mind;
But I was desolate and sick of an old passion,
Yea, all the time, because the dance was long:
I have been faithful to thee, Cynara! in my fashion.

'Non Sum Qualis Eram' (1896) (also known as 'Cynara'); cf. **Horace** 389:2

6 They are not long, the weeping and the laughter,
Love and desire and hate.

'Vitae Summa Brevis' (1896)

7 They are not long, the days of wine and roses.

'Vitae Summa Brevis' (1896)

Arthur Conan Doyle 1859–1930

Scottish-born writer of detective fiction

8 Singularity is almost invariably a clue. The more featureless and commonplace a crime is, the more difficult is it to bring it home.

The Adventures of Sherlock Holmes (1892) 'The Boscombe Valley Mystery'

9 It is my belief, Watson, founded upon my experience, that the lowest and vilest alleys in London do not present a more dreadful record of sin than does the smiling and beautiful countryside.

The Adventures of Sherlock Holmes (1892) 'The Copper Beeches'

10 A man should keep his little brain attic stocked with all the furniture that he is likely to use, and the rest he can put away in the lumber room of his library, where he can get it if he wants it.

The Adventures of Sherlock Holmes (1892) 'The Five Orange Pips'

11 It is quite a three-pipe problem, and I beg that you won't speak to me for fifty minutes.

The Adventures of Sherlock Holmes (1892) 'The Red-Headed League'

12 You see, but you do not observe.

The Adventures of Sherlock Holmes (1892) 'Scandal in Bohemia'

13 The giant rat of Sumatra, a story for which the world is not yet prepared.

The Case-Book of Sherlock Homes (1927) 'The Sussex Vampire'

14 Of all ruins that of a noble mind is the most deplorable.

His Last Bow (1917) 'The Dying Detective'; cf. **Davies** 252:4

15 Good old Watson! You are the one fixed point in a changing age.

His Last Bow (1917) title story

16 'Excellent,' I cried. 'Elementary,' said he.

The Memoirs of Sherlock Holmes (1894) 'The Crooked Man'; cf. **Misquotations** 521:9

17 Ex-Professor Moriarty of mathematical celebrity . . . is the Napoleon of crime, Watson.

The Memoirs of Sherlock Holmes (1894) 'The Final Problem'

18 'Is there any other point to which you would wish to draw my attention?'
'To the curious incident of the dog in the night-time.'
'The dog did nothing in the night-time.'
'That was the curious incident,' remarked Sherlock Holmes.

The Memoirs of Sherlock Holmes (1894) 'Silver Blaze'

19 What one man can invent another can discover.

The Return of Sherlock Holmes (1905) 'The Dancing Men'

20 I didn't think there was a soul in England who didn't know Godfrey Staunton, the back three-quarter, Cambridge, Blackheath, and five Internationals. Good Lord! Mr Holmes where *have* you lived.

The Return of Sherlock Holmes (1905) 'The Missing Three-Quarter'

21 You live in a different world to me, Mr Overton, a sweeter and a healthier one. My ramifications stretch out into many sections of society, but never, I am happy to say, into amateur sport, which is the best and soundest thing in England.

The Return of Sherlock Holmes (1905) 'The Missing Three-Quarter'

22 Detection is, or ought to be, an exact science, and should be treated in the same cold and unemotional manner. You have attempted to tinge it with romanticism, which produces much the same effect as if you worked a love-story or an elopement into the fifth proposition of Euclid.

The Sign of Four (1890) ch. 1

1 How often have I said to you that when you have eliminated the impossible, whatever remains, *however improbable*, must be the truth?
The Sign of Four (1890) ch. 6

2 You know my methods. Apply them.
The Sign of Four (1890) ch. 6

3 It is the unofficial force—the Baker Street irregulars.
The Sign of Four (1890) ch. 8

4 London, that great cesspool into which all the loungers and idlers of the Empire are irresistibly drained.
A Study in Scarlet (1888) ch. 1

5 It is a capital mistake to theorize before you have all the evidence. It biases the judgement.
A Study in Scarlet (1888) ch. 3

6 Where there is no imagination there is no horror.
A Study in Scarlet (1888) ch. 5

7 The vocabulary of 'Bradshaw' is nervous and terse, but limited.
The Valley of Fear (1915) ch. 1

8 Mediocrity knows nothing higher than itself, but talent instantly recognizes genius.
The Valley of Fear (1915) ch. 1

9 What of the bow?
The bow was made in England,
Of true wood, of yew wood,
The wood of English bows.
The White Company (1891) 'Song of the Bow'

Francis Doyle 1810–88
English poet

10 Last night, among his fellow roughs,
He jested, quaffed, and swore.
'The Private of the Buffs' (1866)

Roddy Doyle 1958–
Irish novelist

11 They'd been in the folk mass choir when they were in school but that, they knew now, hadn't really been singing. Jimmy said that real music was sex . . . They were starting to agree with him. And there wasn't much sex in Morning Has Broken or The Lord Is My Shepherd.
The Commitments (1987)

12 I said one Hail Mary and four Our Fathers, because I preferred the Our Fathers to the Hail Mary and it was longer and better.
Paddy Clarke Ha Ha Ha (1993)

Margaret Drabble 1939–
English novelist

13 Lord knows what incommunicable small terrors infants go through, unknown to all. We disregard them, we say they forget, because they have not the words to make us remember . . . By the time they learn to speak they have forgotten the details of their complaints, and so we never know. They forget so quickly we say, because we cannot contemplate the fact that they never forget.
The Millstone (1965)

14 England's not a bad country . . . It's just a mean, cold, ugly, divided, tired, clapped-out, post-imperial, post-industrial slag-heap covered in polystyrene hamburger cartons.
A Natural Curiosity (1989)

15 Perhaps the rare and simple pleasure of being seen for what one is compensates for the misery of being it.
A Summer Bird-Cage (1963) ch. 7

16 In the past, in old novels, the price of love was death, a price which virtuous women paid in childbirth, and the wicked, like Nana, with the pox. Nowadays it is paid in thrombosis or neurosis: one can take one's pick.
The Waterfall (1969)

Francis Drake *c.*1540–96
English sailor and explorer
on Drake: see **Anonymous** *19:1*

17 There must be a beginning of any great matter, but the continuing unto the end until it be thoroughly finished yields the true glory.
dispatch to Francis Walsingham, 17 May 1587, in *Navy Records Society* vol. 11 (1898)

18 The singeing of the King of Spain's Beard.
on the expedition to Cadiz, 1587
Francis Bacon *Considerations touching a War with Spain* (1629)

19 I must have the gentleman to haul and draw with the mariner, and the mariner with the gentleman . . . I would know him, that would refuse to set his hand to a rope, but I know there is not any such here.
J. S. Corbett *Drake and the Tudor Navy* (1898) vol. 1, ch. 9

20 There is plenty of time to win this game, and to thrash the Spaniards too.
attributed, in *Dictionary of National Biography* (1917–) vol. 5

Joseph Rodman Drake 1795–1820
American poet

21 Forever float that standard sheet!
Where breathes the foe but falls before us,
With Freedom's soil beneath our feet,
And Freedom's banner streaming o'er us?
'The American Flag' in *New York Evening Post*, 29 May 1819 (also attributed to Fitz-Greene Halleck)

Michael Drayton 1563–1631
English poet

22 Ill news hath wings, and with the wind doth go,
Comfort's a cripple and comes ever slow.
The Barons' Wars (1603) canto 2, st. 28

23 The mind is free, whate'er afflict the man,
A King's a King, do Fortune what she can.
The Barons' Wars (1603) canto 5, st. 36

1 Thus when we fondly flatter our desires,
Our best conceits do prove the greatest liars.
The Barons' Wars (1603) canto 6, st. 94

2 All men to some one quality incline:
Only to love is naturally mine.
England's Heroical Epistles (1597) 'Owen Tudor to Queen Katharine'

3 Since there's no help, come let us kiss and part,
Nay, I have done: you get no more of me,
And I am glad, yea glad with all my heart,
That thus so cleanly, I myself can free,
Shake hands for ever, cancel all our vows,
And when we meet at any time again,
Be it not seen in either of our brows,
That we one jot of former love retain.
Idea (1619) Sonnet 61

4 That shire which we the Heart of England well may call.
of Warwickshire
Poly-Olbion (1612–22) Song 13, l. 2

5 But when the bowels of the earth were sought,
And men her golden entrails did espy,
This mischief then into the world was brought,
This framed the mint which coined our misery.

Then lofty pines were by ambition hewn,
And men sea-monsters swam the brackish flood
In wainscot tubs to seek out worlds unknown,
For certain ill to leave assurèd good.
The Shepherd's Garland (1593) Eclogue 8

6 For that fine madness still he did retain
Which rightly should possess a poet's brain.
on ***Marlowe***
'To Henry Reynolds, of Poets and Poesy' (1627) l. 109

7 Next these, learn'd Jonson, in this list I bring,
Who had drunk deep of the Pierian spring.
'To Henry Reynolds, of Poets and Poesy' (1627) l. 129; cf. **Pope** 584:15

8 These poor half-kisses kill me quite.
'To His Coy Love' (1619)

9 Fair stood the wind for France
When we our sails advance,
Nor now to prove our chance
Longer will tarry.
To the Cambro-Britons (1619) 'Agincourt'

William Drennan 1754–1820
Irish writer of patriotic verse

10 Nor one feeling of vengeance presume to defile
The cause, or the men, of the Emerald Isle.
Erin (1795) st. 3

John Drinkwater 1882–1937
English poet and dramatist

11 Deep is the silence, deep
On moon-washed apples of wonder.
'Moonlit Apples' (1917)

William Driver 1803–86
American sailor

12 I name thee Old Glory.
saluting a new flag hoisted on his ship, the Charles Doggett
attributed

Thomas Drummond 1797–1840
British government official; Under-secretary of State for Ireland, 1835–40

13 Property has its duties as well as its rights.
letter to the Earl of Donoughmore, 22 May 1838, in R. Barry O'Brien *Thomas Drummond . . . Life and Letters* (1889)

William Drummond of Hawthornden 1585–1649
Scottish poet

14 Phoebus, arise,
And paint the sable skies,
With azure, white, and red.
'Song: Phoebus, arise' (1614)

15 A morn
Of bright carnations did o'erspread her face.
'Sonnet: Alexis here she stayed' (1614)

16 In all nations it is observed that there are some families fatal to the ruin of the Commonwealth and some persons fatal to the ruin of the house and race of which they are descended.
Agnes Mure *Scottish Pageant* (1946) vol. 1

John Dryden 1631–1700
English poet, critic, and playwright
on Dryden: see ***Arnold*** *28:23, 29:5,* ***Johnson*** *410:2,* ***Macaulay*** *482:16,* ***Pope*** *586:17; see also* ***Crashaw*** *244:3*

17 In pious times, ere priestcraft did begin,
Before polygamy was made a sin.
Absalom and Achitophel (1681) pt. 1, l. 1

18 Then Israel's monarch, after Heaven's own heart,
His vigorous warmth did, variously, impart
To wives and slaves: and, wide as his command,
Scattered his Maker's image through the land.
Absalom and Achitophel (1681) pt. 1, l. 7

19 Whate'er he did was done with so much ease,
In him alone, 'twas natural to please.
Absalom and Achitophel (1681) pt. 1, l. 27

20 Plots, true or false, are necessary things,
To raise up commonwealths and ruin kings.
Absalom and Achitophel (1681) pt. 1, l. 83

21 Of these the false Achitophel was first,
A name to all succeeding ages curst.
For close designs and crooked counsels fit,
Sagacious, bold, and turbulent of wit,
Restless, unfixed in principles and place,

In power unpleased, impatient of disgrace;
A fiery soul, which working out its way,
Fretted the pigmy body to decay.
Absalom and Achitophel (1681) pt. 1, l. 150

1 A daring pilot in extremity;
Pleased with the danger, when the waves went high
He sought the storms; but for a calm unfit.
Absalom and Achitophel (1681) pt. 1, l. 159

2 Great wits are sure to madness near allied,
And thin partitions do their bounds divide.
Absalom and Achitophel (1681) pt. 1, l. 163

3 Why should he, with wealth and honour blest,
Refuse his age the needful hours of rest?
Punish a body which he could not please;
Bankrupt of life, yet prodigal of ease?
And all to leave what with his toil he won
To that unfeathered two-legged thing, a son.
Absalom and Achitophel (1681) pt. 1, l. 165

4 In friendship false, implacable in hate:
Resolved to ruin or to rule the state.
Absalom and Achitophel (1681) pt. 1, l. 173

5 The people's prayer, the glad diviner's theme,
The young men's vision and the old men's dream!
Absalom and Achitophel (1681) pt. 1, l. 238

6 All empire is no more than power in trust.
Absalom and Achitophel (1681) pt. 1, l. 411; cf. **Disraeli** 270:33

7 Better one suffer, than a nation grieve.
Absalom and Achitophel (1681) pt. 1, l. 416

8 But far more numerous was the herd of such
Who think too little and who talk too much.
Absalom and Achitophel (1681) pt. 1, l. 533

9 A man so various that he seemed to be
Not one, but all mankind's epitome.
Stiff in opinions, always in the wrong;
Was everything by starts, and nothing long.
But, in the course of one revolving moon:
Was chemist, fiddler, statesman, and buffoon.
Absalom and Achitophel (1681) pt. 1, l. 545

10 In squandering wealth was his peculiar art:
Nothing went unrewarded, but desert.
Beggared by fools, whom still he found too late:
He had his jest, and they had his estate.
Absalom and Achitophel (1681) pt. 1, l. 559

11 Youth, beauty, graceful action seldom fail:
But common interest always will prevail:
And pity never ceases to be shown
To him, who makes the people's wrongs his own.
Absalom and Achitophel (1681) pt. 1, l. 723

12 For who can be secure of private right,
If sovereign sway may be dissolved by might?
Nor is the people's judgement always true:
The most may err as grossly as the few.
Absalom and Achitophel (1681) pt. 1, l. 779

13 Never was patriot yet, but was a fool.
Absalom and Achitophel (1681) pt. 1, l. 968

14 Beware the fury of a patient man.
Absalom and Achitophel (1681) pt. 1, l. 1005

15 Free from all meaning, whether good or bad,
And in one word, heroically mad.
Absalom and Achitophel (1681) pt. 2, l. 416

16 Rhyme is the rock on which thou art to wreck.
Absalom and Achitophel (1681) pt. 2, l. 486

17 Happy, happy, happy, pair!
None but the brave,
None but the brave,
None but the brave deserves the fair.
Alexander's Feast (1697) l. 4; cf. **Proverbs** 608:9

18 Drinking is the soldier's pleasure;
Rich the treasure;
Sweet the pleasure;
Sweet is pleasure after pain.
Alexander's Feast (1697) l. 57

19 Fallen from his high estate,
And welt'ring in his blood:
Deserted at his utmost need
By those his former bounty fed;
On the bare earth exposed he lies,
With not a friend to close his eyes.
Alexander's Feast (1697) l. 78

20 War, he sung, is toil and trouble;
Honour but an empty bubble.
Never ending, still beginning,
Fighting still, and still destroying,
If the world be worth thy winning,
Think, oh think, it worth enjoying.
Alexander's Feast (1697) l. 97

21 Sighed and looked, and sighed again.
Alexander's Feast (1697) l. 120

22 Revenge, revenge! Timotheus cries.
Alexander's Feast (1697) l. 131

23 Let old Timotheus yield the prize,
Or both divide the crown:
He raised a mortal to the skies;
She drew an angel down.
of 'Divine Cecilia'
Alexander's Feast (1697) l. 177

24 Errors, like straws, upon the surface flow;
He who would search for pearls must dive below.
All for Love (1678) prologue

25 My love's a noble madness.
All for Love (1678) act 2, sc. 1

26 Give, you gods,
Give to your boy, your Caesar,
The rattle of a globe to play withal,
This gewgaw world, and put him cheaply off:
I'll not be pleased with less than Cleopatra.
All for Love (1678) act 2, sc. 1

27 Men are but children of a larger growth;
Our appetites as apt to change as theirs,
And full as craving too, and full as vain.
All for Love (1678) act 4, sc. 1; cf. **Chesterfield** 209:17

28 By viewing nature, nature's handmaid art,
Makes mighty things from small beginnings grow:
Thus fishes first to shipping did impart,
Their tail the rudder, and their head the prow.
Annus Mirabilis (1667) st. 155

1 An horrid stillness first invades the ear,
And in that silence we the tempest fear.
Astraea Redux (1660) l. 7

2 Death, in itself, is nothing; but we fear,
To be we know not what, we know not where.
Aureng-Zebe (1675) act 4, sc. 1

3 None would live past years again,
Yet all hope pleasure in what yet remain;
And, from the dregs of life, think to receive,
What the first sprightly running could not give.
Aureng-Zebe (1675) act 4, sc. 1

4 Refined himself to soul, to curb the sense
And made almost a sin of abstinence.
'The Character of a Good Parson' (1700) l. 10

5 I am as free as nature first made man,
Ere the base laws of servitude began,
When wild in woods the noble savage ran.
The Conquest of Granada (1670) pt. 1, act 1, sc. 1

6 Forgiveness to the injured does belong;
But they ne'er pardon, who have done the wrong.
The Conquest of Granada (1670) pt. 2, act 1, sc. 2

7 Thou strong seducer, opportunity!
The Conquest of Granada (1670) pt. 2, act 4, sc. 3

8 Bold knaves thrive without one grain of sense,
But good men starve for want of impudence.
Constantine the Great (1684) epilogue

9 He trudged along unknowing what he sought,
And whistled as he went, for want of thought.
Cymon and Iphigenia (1700) l. 84

10 She hugged the offender, and forgave the offence.
Cymon and Iphigenia (1700) l. 367; cf. **Augustine** 36:11, **Dryden** 281:25

11 Of seeming arms to make a short essay,
Then hasten to be drunk, the business of the day.
Cymon and Iphigenia (1700) l. 407

12 His colours laid so thick on every place,
As only showed the paint, but hid the face.
Epistle 'To my honoured friend Sir Robert Howard' (1660) l. 75

13 Better to hunt in fields, for health unbought,
Than fee the doctor for a nauseous draught.
The wise, for cure, on exercise depend;
God never made his work, for man to mend.
Epistle 'To my honoured kinsman John Driden' (1700) l. 92

14 Even victors are by victories undone.
Epistle 'To my honoured kinsman John Driden' (1700) l. 164

15 For he was great, ere fortune made him so.
on the death of Oliver ***Cromwell***
Heroic Stanzas (1659) st. 6

16 And doomed to death, though fated not to die.
The Hind and the Panther (1687) pt. 1, l. 8

17 For truth has such a face and such a mien
As to be loved needs only to be seen.
The Hind and the Panther (1687) pt. 1, l. 33

18 Good life be now my task: my doubts are done;
(What more could fright my faith than Three in One?)
The Hind and the Panther (1687) pt. 1, l. 75

19 Reason to rule, but mercy to forgive:
The first is law, the last prerogative.
The Hind and the Panther (1687) pt. 1, l. 261

20 My manhood, long misled by wandering fires,
Followed false lights.
The Hind and the Panther (1687) pt. 1, l. 72

21 Either be wholly slaves or wholly free.
The Hind and the Panther (1687) pt. 2, l. 285

22 Much malice mingled with a little wit
Perhaps may censure this mysterious writ.
The Hind and the Panther (1687) pt. 3, l. 1

23 For present joys are more to flesh and blood
Than a dull prospect of a distant good.
The Hind and the Panther (1687) pt. 3, l. 364

24 By education most have been misled;
So they believe, because they so were bred.
The priest continues what the nurse began,
And thus the child imposes on the man.
The Hind and the Panther (1687) pt. 3, l. 389

25 T'abhor the makers, and their laws approve,
Is to hate traitors and the treason love.
The Hind and the Panther (1687) pt. 3, l. 706; cf. **Augustine** 36:11, **Dryden** 281:10

26 For those whom God to ruin has designed,
He fits for fate, and first destroys their mind.
The Hind and the Panther (1687) pt. 3, l. 1093; cf. **Anonymous** 21:2, **Proverbs** 615:4

27 And love's the noblest frailty of the mind.
The Indian Emperor (1665) act 2, sc. 2; cf. **Shadwell** 655:11

28 Repentance is the virtue of weak minds.
The Indian Emperor (1665) act 3, sc. 1

29 For all the happiness mankind can gain
Is not in pleasure, but in rest from pain.
The Indian Emperor (1665) act 4, sc. 1

30 That fairy kind of writing which depends only upon the force of imagination.
King Arthur (1691) dedication

31 War is the trade of kings.
King Arthur (1691) act 2, sc. 2

32 Fairest Isle, all isles excelling,
Seat of pleasures, and of loves;
Venus here will choose her dwelling,
And forsake her Cyprian groves.
King Arthur (1691) act 5 'Song of Venus'; cf. **Wesley** 811:7

33 Ovid, the soft philosopher of love.
Love Triumphant (1694) act 2, sc. 1

34 Thou tyrant, tyrant Jealousy,
Thou tyrant of the mind!
Love Triumphant (1694) act 3, sc. 1 'Song of Jealousy'

35 All human things are subject to decay,
And, when fate summons, monarchs must obey.
MacFlecknoe (1682) l. 1

36 The rest to some faint meaning make pretence,
But Shadwell never deviates into sense.
Some beams of wit on other souls may fall,
Strike through and make a lucid interval;
But Shadwell's genuine night admits no ray,
His rising fogs prevail upon the day.
MacFlecknoe (1682) l. 19

1 Thy genius calls thee not to purchase fame
In keen iambics, but mild anagram:
Leave writing plays, and choose for thy command
Some peaceful province in Acrostic Land.
There thou mayest wings display and altars raise,
And torture one poor word ten thousand ways.
MacFlecknoe (1682) l. 203

2 I am resolved to grow fat and look young till forty, and then slip out of the world with the first wrinkle and the reputation of five-and-twenty.
The Maiden Queen (1668) act 3, sc. 1

3 I am to be married within these three days; married past redemption.
Marriage à la Mode (1672) act 1, sc. 1

4 We loathe our manna, and we long for quails.
The Medal (1682) l. 131

5 But treason is not owned when 'tis descried;
Successful crimes alone are justified.
The Medal (1682) l. 207

6 Whatever is, is in its causes just.
Oedipus (with Nathaniel Lee, 1679) act 3, sc. 1

7 But love's a malady without a cure.
Palamon and Arcite (1700) bk. 2, l. 110

8 Fool, not to know that love endures no tie,
And Jove but laughs at lovers' perjury.
Palamon and Arcite (1700) bk. 2, l. 148; cf. **Ovid** 561:6, **Proverbs** 604:45

9 And Antony, who lost the world for love.
Palamon and Arcite (1700) bk. 2, l. 607

10 Repentance is but want of power to sin.
Palamon and Arcite (1700) bk. 3, l. 813

11 Like pilgrims to th'appointed place we tend;
The world's an inn, and death the journey's end.
Palamon and Arcite (1700) bk. 3, l. 887

12 A virgin-widow, and a *mourning bride*.
Palamon and Arcite (1700) bk. 3, l. 927

13 But 'tis the talent of our English nation,
Still to be plotting some new reformation.
'The Prologue at Oxford, 1680' (prologue to Nathaniel Lee *Sophonisba*, 2nd ed., 1681)

14 So poetry, which is in Oxford made
An art, in London only is a trade.
'Prologue to the University of Oxon . . . at the Acting of *The Silent Woman*' (1673)

15 And this unpolished rugged verse I chose
As fittest for discourse and nearest prose.
Religio Laici (1682) l. 453

16 A very merry, dancing, drinking,
Laughing, quaffing, and unthinking time.
The Secular Masque (1700) l. 39

17 Joy ruled the day, and Love the night.
The Secular Masque (1700) l. 81

18 All, all of a piece throughout;
Thy chase had a beast in view;
Thy wars brought nothing about;
Thy lovers were all untrue.
'Tis well an old age is out,
And time to begin a new.
The Secular Masque (1700) l. 92

19 For secrets are edged tools,
And must be kept from children and from fools.
Sir Martin Mar-All (1667) act 2, sc. 2

20 From harmony, from heavenly harmony
This universal frame began:
From harmony to harmony
Through all the compass of the notes it ran,
The diapason closing full in Man.
A Song for St Cecilia's Day (1687) st. 1

21 What passion cannot Music raise and quell?
A Song for St Cecilia's Day (1687) st. 2

22 The soft complaining flute.
A Song for St Cecilia's Day (1687) st. 4

23 The trumpet shall be heard on high,
The dead shall live, the living die,
And Music shall untune the sky.
A Song for St Cecilia's Day (1687) 'Grand Chorus'

24 There is a pleasure sure,
In being mad, which none but madmen know!
The Spanish Friar (1681) act 1, sc. 1

25 And, dying, bless the hand that gave the blow.
The Spanish Friar (1681) act 2, sc. 2

26 Mute and magnificent, without a tear.
Threnodia Augustalis (1685) st. 2

27 Freedom which in no other land will thrive,
Freedom an English subject's sole prerogative.
Threnodia Augustalis (1685) st. 10

28 Wit will shine
Through the harsh cadence of a rugged line.
'To the Memory of Mr Oldham' (1684)

29 Thou youngest virgin-daughter of the skies,
Made in the last promotion of the blest.
'To the pious Memory of . . . Mrs Anne Killigrew' (1686) l. 1

30 And he, who servilely creeps after sense,
Is safe, but ne'er will reach an excellence.
Tyrannic Love (1669) prologue

31 All delays are dangerous in war.
Tyrannic Love (1669) act 1, sc. 1

32 Happy the man, and happy he alone,
He, who can call to-day his own:
He who, secure within, can say,
Tomorrow do thy worst, for I have lived today.
translation of Horace *Odes* bk. 3, no. 29; cf. **Horace** 388:23, **Smith** 725:22

33 Not Heaven itself upon the past has power;
But what has been, has been, and I have had my hour.
translation of Horace *Odes* bk. 3, no. 29

34 I can enjoy her while she's kind;
But when she dances in the wind,
And shakes the wings, and will not stay,
I puff the prostitute away.
of Fortune
translation of Horace *Odes* bk. 3, no. 29

35 Look round the habitable world! how few
Know their own good; or knowing it, pursue.
Translation of Juvenal *Satires* no. 10

36 She knows her man, and when you rant and swear,

Can draw you to her *with a single hair*.
Translation of Persius *Satires* no. 5, l. 246

1 Arms, and the man I sing, who, forced by fate,
And haughty Juno's unrelenting hate,
Expelled and exiled, left the Trojan shore.
translation of Virgil *Aeneid* (*Aeneis*, 1697) bk. 1, l. 1; cf. **Virgil** 793:4

2 We must beat the iron while it is hot, but we may polish it at leisure.
Aeneis (1697) dedication

3 Every age has a kind of universal genius, which inclines those that live in it to some particular studies.
An Essay of Dramatic Poesy (1668)

4 The famous rules, which the French call *Des Trois Unitez*, or, the Three Unities, which ought to be observed in every regular play; namely, of Time, Place, and Action.
A Essay of Dramatic Poesy (1668)

5 A thing well said will be wit in all languages.
An Essay of Dramatic Poesy (1668)

6 He was naturally learn'd; he needed not the spectacles of books to read Nature: he looked inwards, and found her there . . . He is many times flat, insipid; his comic wit degenerating into clenches, his serious swelling into bombast. But he is always great.
on ***Shakespeare***
An Essay of Dramatic Poesy (1668)

7 He invades authors like a monarch; and what would be theft in other poets, is only victory in him.
on Ben ***Jonson***
An Essay of Dramatic Poesy (1668)

8 If by the people you understand the multitude, the *hoi polloi*, 'tis no matter what they think; they are sometimes in the right, sometimes in the wrong: their judgement is a mere lottery.
An Essay of Dramatic Poesy (1668)

9 [Shakespeare] is the very Janus of poets; he wears almost everywhere two faces; and you have scarce begun to admire the one, ere you despise the other.
Essay on the Dramatic Poetry of the Last Age (1672)

10 What judgement I had increases rather than diminishes; and thoughts, such as they are, come crowding in so fast upon me, that my only difficulty is to choose or reject; to run them into verse or to give them the other harmony of prose.
Fables Ancient and Modern (1700) preface

11 'Tis sufficient to say, according to the proverb, that here is God's plenty.
of ***Chaucer***
Fables Ancient and Modern (1700) preface

12 [Chaucer] is a perpetual fountain of good sense.
Fables Ancient and Modern (1700) preface

13 One of our late great poets is sunk in his reputation, because he could never forgive any conceit which came in his way; but swept like a drag-net, great and small. There was plenty enough, but the dishes were ill-sorted; whole pyramids of sweetmeats, for boys and women; but little of solid meat for men.
on Abraham ***Cowley***
Fables Ancient and Modern (1700) preface

14 Sure the poet . . . spewed up a good lump of clotted nonsense at once.
Notes and Observations on the Empress of Morocco [by Elkanah Settle] (1674) 'The First Act'

15 How easy it is to call rogue and villain, and that wittily! But how hard to make a man appear a fool, a blockhead, or a knave, without using any of those opprobrious terms! To spare the grossness of the names, and to do the thing yet more severely, is to draw a full face, and to make the nose and cheeks stand out, and yet not to employ any depth of shadowing.
Of Satire (1693)

16 A man may be capable, as Jack Ketch's wife said of his servant, of a plain piece of work, a bare hanging; but to make a malefactor die sweetly was only belonging to her husband.
Of Satire (1693)

17 I find all your trade are sharpers.
to the publisher Jacob Tonson, c.1697
Ian Hamilton *Keepers of the Flame* (1992) ch. 4

18 Cousin Swift, you will never be a poet.
Samuel Johnson *Lives of the English Poets* (1779–81) 'Dryden'

Diane Duane

American writer

19 Reading one book is like eating one crisp.
So You Want to Be a Wizard (1983)

Alexander Dubček 1921–92

Czechoslovak statesman; First Secretary of the Czechoslovak Communist Party, 1968–9

20 In the service of the people we followed such a policy that socialism would not lose its human face.
in *Rudé Právo* 19 July 1968; a resolution by the party group in the Ministry of Foreign Affairs, 1968, referred to Czechoslovakian foreign policy acquiring 'its own defined face'; in *Rudé Právo* 14 March 1968

Joachim Du Bellay 1522–60

French poet

21 *France, mère des arts, des armes et des lois.*
France, mother of arts, of warfare, and of laws.
Les Regrets (1558) sonnet no. 9

22 *Heureux qui comme Ulysse a fait un beau voyage*
Ou comme celui-là qui conquit la toison,
Et puis est retourné, plein d'usage et raison,
Vivre entre ses parents le reste de son âge!
Happy he who like Ulysses has made a great journey, or like that man who won the Fleece and then came home, full of experience and good sense, to live the rest of his time among his family!
Les Regrets (1558) Sonnet no. 31

23 *Plus que le marbre dur me plaît l'ardoise fine,*
Plus mon Loire Gaulois, que le Tibre Latin,

Plus mon petit Lyré, que le mont Palatin,
Et plus que l'air marin la douceur angevine.

I love thin slate more than hard marble, my Gallic Loire more than the Latin Tiber, my little Liré more than the Palatine Hill, and more than the sea air the sweetness of Anjou.

Les Regrets (1558) Sonnet no. 31

W. E. B. Du Bois 1868–1963

American social reformer and political activist

1 One thing alone I charge you. As you live, believe in life!

last message, written 26 June, 1957, and read at his funeral, 1963, in *Journal of Negro History* April 1964

2 The problem of the twentieth century is the problem of the colour line—the relation of the darker to the lighter races of men in Asia and Africa, in America and the islands of the sea.

The Souls of Black Folk (1905) ch. 2

3 Herein lies the tragedy of the age: not that men are poor . . . not that men are wicked . . . but that men know so little of men.

The Souls of Black Folk (1905) ch. 12

Stephen Duck 1705–56

English poet and clergyman

4 Let those who feast at ease on dainty fare,
Pity the reapers, who their feasts prepare.

'The Thresher's Labour' (1730)

5 Like Sisyphus, our work is never done;
Continually rolls back the restless stone.

'The Thresher's Labour' (1730)

Mme Du Deffand (Marie de Vichy-Chamrond) 1697–1780

French literary hostess

6 *La distance n'y fait rien; il n'y a que le premier pas qui coûte.*

The distance is nothing; it is only the first step that is difficult.

commenting on the legend that St Denis, carrying his head in his hands, walked two leagues

letter to Jean Le Rond d'Alembert, 7 July 1763, in Gaston Maugras *Trois mois à la cour de Frédéric* (1886); cf. **Proverbs** 604:26

Helen, Lady Dufferin 1807–67

Irish writer

7 Is the cabin still left standing? Has the rich man need of all?
Is the children's birthplace taken now within the new park wall?

'The Emigrant Ship'

George Duffield 1818–88

American Presbyterian minister

8 Stand up!—stand up for Jesus!
Ye soldiers of the Cross.

'Stand Up, Stand Up for Jesus' (1858 hymn); the opening line inspired by the dying words of the American evangelist, Dudley Atkins Tyng; cf. **Last words** 457:7

Carol Ann Duffy 1965–

English poet

9 You roll the waistband
of your skirt over and over, all leg, all
dumb insolence, smoke-rings. You won't pass.
You could do better. But there's the wall you climb
into dancing, lovebites, marriage, the Cheltenham
and Gloucester, today. The day you'll be sorry one day.

'The Good Teachers' (1993)

10 Whatever 'in love' means,
true love is talented.
Someone vividly gifted in love has gone.

on the death of **Diana**, *Princess of Wales*

'September, 1997' (1997); cf. **Charles** 203:17

Charles Gavan Duffy 1816–1903

Irish nationalist and (later) Australian politician

11 I am still an Irish rebel to the backbone and the spinal marrow, a rebel for the same reason that John Hampden and Algernon Sidney, George Washington and Charles Carrol of Carroltown, were rebels—because tyranny had supplanted the law.

arriving in Australia in 1856

Cyril Pearl *The Three Lives of Gavan Duffy* (1979)

Georges Duhamel 1884–1966

French novelist

12 I have too much respect for the idea of God to make it responsible for such an absurd world.

Le désert de Bièvres (1937)

John Foster Dulles 1888–1959

American international lawyer and politician

13 The ability to get to the verge without getting into the war is the necessary art . . . We walked to the brink and we looked it in the face.

in *Life* 16 January 1956; cf. **Stevenson** 740:14

Alexandre Dumas ('Dumas père') 1802–70

French novelist and dramatist

14 *Cherchons la femme.*

Let us look for the woman.

attributed to Joseph Fouché (1763–1820) in the form 'Cherchez la femme'

Les Mohicans de Paris (1854–5) *passim*

15 *Tous pour un, un pour tous.*

All for one, one for all.

Les Trois Mousquetaires (1844) ch. 9

Alexandre Dumas ('Dumas fils') 1824–95

French writer

16 All generalizations are dangerous, even this one.

attributed

Daphne Du Maurier 1907–89

English novelist

17 Last night I dreamt I went to Manderley again.

Rebecca (1938) ch. 1

Charles François du Périer Dumouriez 1739–1823
French general

1 The courtiers who surround him have forgotten nothing and learnt nothing.
of Louis XVIII, at the time of the Declaration of Verona, September 1795; quoted by **Napoleon** *in his Declaration to the French on his return from Elba, 1815*
Examen impartial d'un Écrit intitulé Déclaration de Louis XVIII (1795); cf. **Talleyrand** 753:7

Paul Lawrence Dunbar 1872–1906
American poet

2 I know why the caged bird sings!
adopted by Maya **Angelou** *as the title of her autobiography, 1969*
'Sympathy' st. 3; cf. **Webster** 808:15

William Dunbar c.1465–c.1513
Scottish poet and priest
see also **Anonymous** *17:12*

3 All women of us suld have honouring,
Service and love above all other thing.
'In Praise of Women'

4 I that in heill wes and gladnes
Am trublit now with gret seiknes
And feblit with infirmitie:
Timor mortis conturbat me.
makaris = *makers, i.e. poets*
'Lament for the Makaris'

5 He hes done petuously devour,
The noble Chaucer, of makaris flouir,
The Monk of Bery, and Gower, all three;
Timor mortis conturbat me.
'Lament for the Makaris'

6 All love is lost but upon God alone.
'The Merle and the Nightingale' st. 2

Isadora Duncan see Last words 455:1

Ian Dunlop 1940–
British art historian

7 The shock of the new: seven historic exhibitions of modern art.
title of book (1972)

Helen Dunmore 1952–

8 That killed head straining through the windscreen
with its frill of bubbles in the eye-sockets
is not trying to tell you something—
it is telling you something.
'Poem on the Obliteration of 100,000 Iraqi Soldiers' (1994)

Douglas Dunn 1942–
Scottish poet

9 In a country like this
Our ghosts outnumber us . . .
'At Falkland Palace' (1988)

10 My poems should be Clyde-built, crude and sure,
With images of those dole-deployed
To honour the indomitable Reds,
Clydesiders of slant steel and angled cranes;
A poetry of nuts and bolts, born, bred,
Embattled by the Clyde, tight and impure.
'Clydesiders' (1974)

11 They ruined us. They conquered continents.
We filled their uniforms. We cruised the seas.
We worked their mines and made their histories.
You work, we rule, they said. We worked; they ruled.
They fooled the tenements. All men were fooled.
'Empires' (1979)

12 I am light with meditation, religiose
And mystic with a day of solitude.
'Reading Pascal in the Lowlands' (1985)

13 As well as between tongue and teeth, poetry happens between the ears and behind the left nipple.
in *Observer* 23 March 1997

Finlay Peter Dunne 1867–1936
American humorous writer

14 A law, Hinnissey, that might look like a wall to you or me wud look like a triumphal arch to th'expeeryenced eye iv a lawyer.
'Mr Dooley on the Power of the Press' in *American Magazine* no. 62 1906; cf. **Commager** 230:9

Sean Dunne 1956–97
Irish poet

15 The country wears their going like a scar,
Today their relatives save to support and
Send others in planes for the new diaspora.
'Letter from Ireland' (1991)

John Dunning, Lord Ashburton 1731–83
English lawyer and politician

16 The influence of the Crown has increased, is increasing, and ought to be diminished.
resolution passed in the House of Commons, 6 April 1780

Richard Duppa 1770–1831
English artist and writer

17 In language, the ignorant have prescribed laws to the learned.
Maxims (1830) no. 252

Marguerite Duras 1914–
French writer

18 Men like women who write. Even though they don't say so. A writer is a foreign country.
Practicalities (1987) 'The M. D. Uniform'

19 In heterosexual love there's no solution. Man and woman are irreconcilable, and it's the doomed attempt to do the impossible, repeated in each new affair, that lends heterosexual love its grandeur.
Practicalities (1990) 'Men'

Paul Durcan 1944–
Irish poet

1 Poetry's another word
For losing everything
Except purity of heart.
'Christmas Day' (1996)

2 Some of us made it
To the forest edge, but many of us did not
Make it, although their unborn children did—
Such as you whom the camp commandant branded
Sid Vicious of the Sex Pistols. Jesus, break his fall:
There—but for the clutch of luck—go we all.
'The Death by Heroin of Sid Vicious' (1980)

Ray Durem 1915–63
American poet

3 Some of my best friends are white boys.
when I meet 'em
I treat 'em
just the same as if they was people.
'Broadminded' (written 1951)

Albrecht Dürer 1471–1528
German painter and engraver

4 He that would be a painter must have a natural turn thereto. Love and delight therein are better teachers of the Art of Painting than compulsion is.
Third Book of Human Proportions (written *c.*1512–3) introduction; William Martin Conway *Literary remains of Albrecht Dürer* (1889)

John George Lambton, Lord Durham 1792–1840
English Whig politician

5 £40,000 a year a moderate income—such a one as a man *might jog on with.*
Herbert Maxwell (ed.) *The Creevey Papers* (1903) vol. 2, from a letter from Mr Creevey to Miss Elizabeth Ord, 13 September 1821

6 I expected to find a contest between a government and a people: I found two nations warring in the bosom of a single state.
of Canada
Report of the Affairs of British North America (1839)

Leo Durocher 1906–91
American baseball coach

7 I called off his players' names as they came marching up the steps behind him . . . All nice guys. They'll finish last. Nice guys. Finish last.
casual remark at a practice ground in the presence of a number of journalists, July 1946, generally quoted as 'Nice guys finish last'
Nice Guys Finish Last (1975) pt. 1

Lawrence Durrell 1912–90
English novelist, poet, and travel writer

8 No history much? Perhaps. Only this ominous
Dark beauty flowering under veils,
Trapped in the spectrum of a dying style:
A village like an instinct left to rust,
Composed around the echo of a pistol-shot.
'Sarajevo' (1951)

Ian Dury 1942–2000
British rock singer and songwriter

9 Sex and drugs and rock and roll.
title of song (1977)

10 I could be the catalyst that sparks the revolution.
I could be an inmate in a long term institution
I could lean to wild extremes I could do or die,
I could yawn and be withdrawn and watch them gallop by,
What a waste, what a waste, what a waste, what a waste.
'What a Waste' (1978 song)

Andrea Dworkin 1946–
American feminist and writer

11 Seduction is often difficult to distinguish from rape. In seduction, the rapist bothers to buy a bottle of wine.
speech to women at Harper & Row, 1976; in *Letters from a War Zone* (1988)

Edward Dyer d. 1607
English poet

12 Silence augmenteth grief, writing increaseth rage,
Staled are my thoughts, which loved and lost, the wonder of our age.
previously attributed to Fulke **Greville**
'Elegy on the Death of Sir Philip Sidney' (1593)

13 My mind to me a kingdom is.
Such perfect joy therein I find
That it excels all other bliss
That world affords or grows by kind.
Though much I want which most would have,
Yet still my mind forbids to crave.
'In praise of a contented mind' (1588), attributed

John Dyer 1700–58
Welsh clergyman and poet

14 The care of sheep, the labours of the loom,
And arts of trade, I sing.
The Fleece (1757) bk. 1, l. 1

15 Industry,
Which dignifies the artist, lifts the swain,
And the straw cottage to a palace turns.
The Fleece (1757) bk. 3, l. 332

16 But transient is the smile of fate:
A little rule, a little sway,
A sunbeam in a winter's day,
Is all the proud and mighty have
Between the cradle and the grave.
Grongar Hill (1726) l. 88

17 The town and village, dome and farm,
Each give each a double charm,
As pearls upon an Ethiop's arm.
Grongar Hill (1726) l. 111

1 The pilgrim oft
At dead of night, mid his orison hears
Aghast the voice of Time, disparting tow'rs.
The Ruins of Rome (1740) l. 38

John Dyer
English poet

2 And he that will this health deny,
Down among the dead men let him lie.
'Down among the Dead Men' (*c.*1700)

Bob Dylan (Robert Zimmerman) 1941–
American singer and songwriter

3 How many roads must a man walk down
Before you can call him a man? . . .
The answer, my friend, is blowin' in the wind,
The answer is blowin' in the wind.
'Blowin' in the Wind' (1962 song)

4 Praise be to Nero's Neptune
The Titanic sails at dawn
And everybody's shouting
'Which Side Are You On?'
And Ezra Pound and T. S. Eliot
Fighting in the captain's tower
While calypso singers laugh at them
And fishermen hold flowers.
'Desolation Row' (1965 song)

5 Don't think twice, it's all right.
title of song (1963)

6 I saw ten thousand talkers whose tongues were all broken,
I saw guns and sharp swords, in the hands of young children . . .
And it's a hard rain's a gonna fall.
'A Hard Rain's A Gonna Fall' (1963 song)

7 Money doesn't talk, it swears.
'It's Alright, Ma (I'm Only Bleeding)' (1965 song)

8 She takes just like a woman, yes, she does
She makes love just like a woman, yes, she does
And she aches just like a woman
But she breaks like a little girl.
'Just Like a Woman' (1966 song)

9 How does it feel
To be on your own
With no direction home
Like a complete unknown
Like a rolling stone?
'Like a Rolling Stone' (1965 song)

10 She knows there's no success like failure
And that failure's no success at all.
'Love Minus Zero / No Limit' (1965 song)

11 Hey! Mr Tambourine Man, play a song for me.
I'm not sleepy and there is no place I'm going to.
'Mr Tambourine Man' (1965 song)

12 Ah, but I was so much older then,
I'm younger than that now.
'My Back Pages' (1964 song)

13 Señor, señor, do you know where we're headin'?
Lincoln County Road or Armageddon?
'Señor (Tale of Yankee Power)' (1978 song)

14 All that foreign oil controlling American soil.
'Slow Train' (1979 song)

15 The times they are a-changin'.
title of song (1964)

16 Come mothers and fathers,
Throughout the land
And don't criticize
What you can't understand.
'The Times They Are A-Changing' (1964 song)

17 But I can't think for you
You'll have to decide,
Whether Judas Iscariot
Had God on his side.
'With God on our Side' (1963 song)

18 I think that's just another word for a washed-up has-been.
on being described as an 'icon'
in *Mail on Sunday* 18 January 1998 'Quotes of the Week'

Esther Dyson
American businesswoman

19 The important thing to remember is that this is not a new form of life. It is just a new activity.
of the Internet
in *New York Times* 7 July 1996 'The Cyber-Maxims of Esther Dyson'

Clint Eastwood see **Film lines** 311:8

Abba Eban 1915–
Israeli diplomat

20 History teaches us that men and nations behave wisely once they have exhausted all other alternatives.
speech in London, 16 December 1970, in *The Times* 17 December 1970

Arthur Eddington 1882–1944
British astrophysicist

21 Let us draw an arrow arbitrarily. If as we follow the arrow we find more and more of the random element in the world, then the arrow is pointing towards the future; if the random element decreases the arrow points towards the past . . . I shall use the phrase 'time's arrow' to express this one-way property of time which has no analogue in space.
The Nature of the Physical World (1928) ch. 4

22 If an army of monkeys were strumming on typewriters they *might* write all the books in the British Museum.
The Nature of the Physical World (1928); cf. **Wilensky** 819:17

23 If someone points out to you that your pet theory of the universe is in disagreement with Maxwell's equations—then so much the worse for Maxwell's equations. If it is found to be contradicted by observation—well, these experimentalists do bungle things sometimes. But if your theory is found to be against the second law of thermodynamics I can give you no hope; there is

nothing for it but to collapse in deepest humiliation.

The Nature of the Physical World (1928) ch. 14

1 I am standing on the threshold about to enter a room. It is a complicated business. In the first place I must shove against an atmosphere pressing with a force of fourteen pounds on every square inch of my body. I must make sure of landing on a plank travelling at twenty miles a second round the sun— a fraction of a second too early or too late, the plank would be miles away. I must do this whilst hanging from a round planet, head outward into space, and with a wind of aether blowing at no one knows how many miles a second through every interstice of my body.

The Nature of the Physical World (1928) ch. 15

2 I ask you to look both ways. For the road to a knowledge of the stars leads through the atom; and important knowledge of the atom has been reached through the stars.

Stars and Atoms (1928) Lecture 1

3 Science is one thing, wisdom is another. Science is an edged tool, with which men play like children, and cut their own fingers.

attributed in Robert L. Weber *More Random Walks in Science* (1982)

Mary Baker Eddy 1821–1910

American religious leader and founder of the Christian Science movement

4 Jesus of Nazareth was the most scientific man that ever trod the globe. He plunged beneath the material surface of things, and found the spiritual cause.

Science and Health with Key to the Scriptures (1875)

5 Disease is an experience of so-called mortal mind. It is fear made manifest on the body.

Science and Health with Key to the Scriptures (1875)

Anthony Eden, Earl of Avon 1897–1977

British Conservative statesman; Prime Minister, 1955–7

on Eden: see **Muggeridge** *534:17*

6 We are in an armed conflict; that is the phrase I have used. There has been no declaration of war.

on the Suez crisis

speech in the House of Commons, 1 November 1956

7 Long experience has taught me that to be criticized is not always to be wrong.

during the Suez crisis

speech at Lord Mayor's Guildhall banquet; in *Daily Herald* 10 November 1956

Clarissa Eden 1920–

wife of Anthony **Eden**

8 For the past few weeks I have really felt as if the Suez Canal was flowing through my drawing-room.

speech at Gateshead, 20 November 1956

Marriott Edgar 1880–1951

9 There's a famous seaside place called Blackpool,
That's noted for fresh air and fun,
And Mr and Mrs Ramsbottom
Went there with young Albert, their son.

'The Lion and Albert' (1932)

Maria Edgeworth 1767–1849

Anglo-Irish novelist

10 Well! some people talk of morality, and some of religion, but give me a little snug property.

The Absentee (1812) ch. 2

11 It was her settled purpose to make the Irish and Ireland ridiculous and contemptible to Lord Colambre; to disgust him with his native country; to make him abandon the wish of residing on his own estate. To confirm him an absentee was her object.

The Absentee (1812) ch. 7

12 Your Irish ortolans are famous good eating.

The Absentee (1812) ch. 8

13 We cannot judge either of the feelings or of the character of men with perfect accuracy, from their actions or their appearance in public; it is from their careless conversation, their half-finished sentences, that we may hope with the greatest probability of success to discover their real character.

Castle Rackrent (1800) preface

14 To be sure a love match was the only thing for happiness, where the parties could any way afford it.

Castle Rackrent (1800) 'Continuation of Memoirs'

15 Business was his aversion; pleasure was his business.

The Contrast (1804) ch. 2

16 What a misfortune it is to be born a woman! . . . Why seek for knowledge, which can prove only that our wretchedness is irremediable? If a ray of light break in upon us, it is but to make darkness more visible; to show us the new limits, the Gothic structure, the impenetrable barriers of our prison.

Leonora (1806) Letter 1

17 Man is to be held only by the *slightest* chains, with the idea that he can break them at pleasure, he submits to them in sport.

Letters for Literary Ladies (1795) 'Letters of Julia and Caroline' no. 1

18 They are now disfigured by all manner of crooked marks of Papa's critical indignation, besides various abusive margin notes.

of the draft pages of her first book, Letters for Literary Ladies

letter to Sophy Ruxton, February 1794

19 All that I crave for my own part is, that if I am to have my throat cut, it may not be by a man with his face blackened by charcoal.

letter to Mrs Ruxton, January 1796

Richard Lovell Edgeworth 1744–1817

Irish landowner and writer, father of Maria **Edgeworth**

1 We hear from good authority that the King was much pleased with Castle Rackrent—he rubbed his hands and said what—what—I know something now of my Irish subjects.

letter to D. A. Beaufort, 26 April 1800

Thomas Alva Edison 1847–1931

American inventor

2 Genius is one per cent inspiration, ninety-nine per cent perspiration.

said *c.*1903, in *Harper's Monthly Magazine* September 1932; cf. **Buffon** 159:20

James Edmeston 1791–1867

English architect and hymn-writer

3 Lead us, Heavenly Father, lead us
O'er the world's tempestuous sea;
Guard us, guide us, keep us, feed us,
For we have no help but Thee;
Yet possessing every blessing,
If our God our Father be.

'Lead us, heavenly Father, lead us' (1821)

John Maxwell Edmonds see **Epitaphs** 304:14

Edward III 1312–77

King of England from 1327
see also **Mottoes** *535:9*

4 Also say to them, that they suffre hym this day to wynne his spurres, for if god be pleased, I woll this journey be his, and the honoure therof.

speaking of the Black Prince at Crécy, 1346; commonly quoted 'Let the boy win his spurs'

The Chronicle of Froissart (translated by Sir John Bourchier, Lord Berners, 1523–5) ch. 130

Edward VII 1841–1910

King of the United Kingdom from 1901

5 I thought everyone must know that a *short* jacket is always worn with a silk hat at a private view in the morning.

to Frederick Ponsonby, who had proposed accompanying him in a tailcoat

Philip Magnus *Edward VII* (1964) ch. 19

Edward VIII, afterwards Duke of Windsor 1894–1972

King of the United Kingdom, 1936
on Edward: see **Beaverbrook** *59:6,* **George V** *334:3,* **Hardie** *360:2,* **Mary** *500:8, 500:9,* **Newspaper headlines** *544:12*

6 These works brought all these people here. Something should be done to get them at work again.

speaking at the derelict Dowlais Iron and Steel Works, 18 November 1936

in *Western Mail* 19 November 1936; cf. **Misquotations** 522:9

7 At long last I am able to say a few words of my own . . . you must believe me when I tell you that I have found it impossible to carry the heavy burden of responsibility and to discharge my duties as King as I would wish to do without the help and support of the woman I love.

radio broadcast following his abdication, 11 December 1936, in *The Times* 12 December 1936

8 The thing that impresses me most about America is the way parents obey their children.

in *Look* 5 March 1957

Jonathan Edwards 1703–58

American theologian

9 Of all Insects no one is more wonderful than the spider especially with Respect to their sagacity and admirable way of working . . . I . . . once saw a very large spider to my surprise swimming in the air . . . and others have assured me that they often have seen spiders fly, the appearance is truly very pretty and pleasing.

The Flying Spider—Observations by Jonathan Edwards when a boy 'Of Insects' in *Andover Review* vol. 13 (1890); cf. **Lowell** 478:2

10 The bodies of those that made such a noise and tumult when alive, when dead, lie as quietly among the graves of their neighbours as any others.

Sermon on procrastination (*Miscellaneous Discourses*) in *Works* (1834) vol. 2

Oliver Edwards 1711–91

English lawyer

11 I have tried too in my time to be a philosopher; but, I don't know how, cheerfulness was always breaking in.

James Boswell *Life of Samuel Johnson* (1791) 17 April 1778

12 For my part now, I consider supper as a turnpike through which one must pass, in order to get to bed.

Boswell *notes: 'I am not absolutely sure but this was my own suggestion, though it is truly in the character of Edwards'*

James Boswell *Life of Samuel Johnson* (1791) 17 April 1778

Richard Edwards *c.*1523–66

English poet and playwright

13 The falling out of faithful friends, renewing is of love.

The Paradise of Dainty Devices (1576) 'Amantium Irae'; cf. **Proverbs** 610:2

Sarah Egerton 1670–1723

English poet

14 From the first dawn of life unto the grave,
Poor womankind's in every state a slave.

'The Emulation' (1703)

15 We will our rights in learning's world maintain;
Wit's empire now shall know a female reign.

'The Emulation' (1703)

Barbara Ehrenreich 1941–
American sociologist and writer

1 Exercise is the yuppie version of bulimia.
The Worst Years of Our Lives (1991) 'Food Worship'

2 Personally, I can't see why it would be any less romantic to find a husband in a nice four-colour catalogue than in the average downtown bar at happy hour.
The Worst Years of Our Lives (1991) 'Tales of the Man Shortage'

Paul Ralph Ehrlich 1932–
American biologist

3 The first rule of intelligent tinkering is to save all the parts.
in *Saturday Review* 5 June 1971

John Ehrlichman 1925–99
Presidential assistant to Richard Nixon

4 I think we ought to let him hang there. Let him twist slowly, slowly in the wind.
Richard **Nixon** *had withdrawn his support for Patrick Gray, nominated as director of the FBI, although Gray himself had not been informed*
in a telephone conversation with John Dean; in *Washington Post* 27 July 1973

Max Ehrmann 1872–1945

5 Go placidly amid the noise and the haste, and
remember what peace there may be in silence.
often wrongly dated to 1692, the date of foundation of a church in Baltimore whose vicar circulated the poem in 1956
'Desiderata' (1948)

Joseph von Eichendorff 1788–1857
German poet

6 *Wem Gott will rechte Gunst erweisen,*
Den schickt er in die weite Welt.

Those whom God wishes to show true favour
He sends out into the great wide world.
Der frohe Wandersmann (1826)

Einhard c.770–840
Frankish chronicler, friend and biographer of Charlemagne

7 He was large and strong and of lofty stature, though not disproportionately tall; the upper part of his head was round, his eyes very large and animated, nose a little long, hair fair, and face laughing and merry. Thus his appearance was always stately and dignified, whether he was standing or sitting; although his neck was somewhat short, and his belly rather prominent; but the symmetry of the rest of his body concealed these defects.
of Charlemagne
The Life of Charlemagne (ed. S. Painter, 1960)

Albert Einstein 1879–1955
German-born theoretical physicist; originator of the theory of relativity
on Einstein: see **Anonymous** *16:20,* **Squire** *735:16*

8 Science without religion is lame, religion without science is blind.
Science, Philosophy and Religion: a Symposium (1941) ch. 13

9 $E = mc^2$.
the usual form of Einstein's original statement: 'If a body releases the energy L in the form of radiation, its mass is decreased by L/V^2'
in *Annalen der Physik* 18 (1905)

10 God is subtle but he is not malicious.
remark made during a week at Princeton beginning 9 May 1921, later carved above the fireplace of the Common Room of Fine Hall (the Mathematical Institute), Princeton University; R. W. Clark *Einstein* (1973) ch. 14

11 I am convinced that *He* [God] does not play dice.
often quoted as: 'God does not play dice'
letter to Max Born, 4 December 1926; in *Einstein und Born Briefwechsel* (1969)

12 If my theory of relativity is proven correct, Germany will claim me as a German and France will declare that I am a citizen of the world. Should my theory prove untrue, France will say that I am a German and Germany will declare that I am a Jew.
address at the Sorbonne, Paris, possibly early December 1929, in *New York Times* 16 February 1930

13 I never think of the future. It comes soon enough.
in an interview, given on the *Belgenland*, December 1930

14 The eternal mystery of the world is its comprehensibility . . . The fact that it is comprehensible is a miracle.
usually quoted as 'The most incomprehensible fact about the universe is that it is comprehensible'
in *Franklin Institute Journal* March 1936 'Physics and Reality'

15 Some recent work by E. Fermi and L. Szilard, which has been communicated to me in manuscript, leads me to expect that the element uranium may be turned into a new and important source of energy in the immediate future. Certain aspects of the situation which has arisen seem to call for watchfulness and, if necessary, quick action on the part of the Administration.
warning of the possible development of an atomic bomb, and leading to the setting up of the Manhattan Project
letter to Franklin **Roosevelt**, 2 August 1939, drafted by Leo Szilard and signed by Einstein

16 The unleashed power of the atom has changed everything save our modes of thinking and we thus drift toward unparalleled catastrophe.
telegram to prominent Americans, 24 May 1946, in *New York Times* 25 May 1946

17 If *A* is a success in life, then *A* equals *x* plus *y* plus *z*. Work is *x*; *y* is play; and *z* is keeping your mouth shut.
in *Observer* 15 January 1950

1 Common sense is nothing more than a deposit of prejudices laid down in the mind before you reach eighteen.
Lincoln Barnett *The Universe and Dr Einstein* (1950 ed.)

2 The grand aim of all science [is] to cover the greatest number of empirical facts by logical deduction from the smallest possible number of hypotheses or axioms.
Lincoln Barnett *The Universe and Dr Einstein* (1950 ed.)

3 If I would be a young man again and had to decide how to make my living, I would not try to become a scientist or scholar or teacher. I would rather choose to be a plumber or a peddler in the hope to find that modest degree of independence still available under present circumstances.
in *Reporter* 18 November 1954

4 The distinction between past, present and future is only an illusion, however persistent.
letter to Michelangelo Besso, 21 March 1955

5 Nationalism is an infantile sickness. It is the measles of the human race.
Helen Dukas and Banesh Hoffman *Albert Einstein, the Human Side* (1979)

6 One must divide one's time between politics and equations. But our equations are much more important to me.
C. P. Snow 'Einstein' in M. Goldsmith et al. (eds.) *Einstein* (1980)

7 When I was young, I found out that the big toe always ends up making a hole in a sock. So I stopped wearing socks.
to Philippe Halsman; A. P. French *Einstein: A Centenary Volume* (1979)

Dwight D. Eisenhower 1890–1969

American Republican statesman; 34th President of the US

8 This world in arms is not spending money alone. It is spending the sweat of its labourers, the genius of its scientists, the hopes of its children.
speech in Washington, 16 April 1953, in *Public Papers of Presidents* 1953 (1960)

9 You have broader considerations that might follow what you might call the 'falling domino' principle. You have a row of dominoes set up. You knock over the first one, and what will happen to the last one is that it will go over very quickly. So you have the beginning of a disintegration that would have the most profound influences.
speech at press conference, 7 April 1954, in *Public Papers of Presidents* 1954 (1960)

10 I think that people want peace so much that one of these days governments had better get out of the way and let them have it.
broadcast discussion, 31 August 1959, in *Public Papers of Presidents* 1959 (1960)

11 In preparing for battle I have always found that plans are useless, but planning is indispensable.
Richard Nixon *Six Crises* (1962); attributed

Alfred Eisenstaedt 1898–1995

German-born American photographer and photojournalist

12 Although I am 92, my brain is 30 years old.
to a reporter in 1991; in *Life* 24 August 1995 (electronic edition), obituary

13 It's more important to click with people than to click the shutter
in *Life* 24 August 1995 (electronic edition), obituary

Eleazar of Worms 1176–1238

Jewish rabbi

14 No crown carries such royalty with it as doth humility; no monument gives such glory as an unsullied name; no worldly gain can equal that which comes from observing God's laws.
Sefer Rokeah

15 The highest sacrifice is a broken and contrite heart; the highest wisdom is that which is found in the Torah; the noblest of all ornaments is modesty; and the most beautiful thing that man can do, is to forgive a wrong.
Sefer Rokeah; cf. **Book of Common Prayer** 135:7

16 If the means of thy support in life be measured out scantily to thee, remember that thou hast to be thankful and grateful even for the mere privilege to breathe, and that thou must look upon that suffering as a test of thy piety and a preparation for better things.
Sefer Rokeah

Edward Elgar 1857–1934

English composer
on Elgar: see **Beecham** *61:4; see also* **Shelley** *713:24*

17 To my friends pictured within.
Enigma Variations (1899) dedication

18 I essay much, I hope little, I ask nothing.
inscribed at the end of *Enigma Variations* (1899)

19 There is music in the air.
R. J. Buckley *Sir Edward Elgar* (1905) ch. 4

George Eliot (Mary Ann Evans) 1819–80

English novelist
on Eliot: see **Gaskell** *330:23*

20 Our deeds determine us, as much as we determine our deeds; and until we know what has been or will be the peculiar combination of outward with inward facts, which constitute a man's critical actions, it will be better not to think ourselves wise about his character.
Adam Bede (1859) ch. 29

21 He was like a cock who thought the sun had risen to hear him crow.
Adam Bede (1859) ch. 33

22 Deep, unspeakable suffering may well be called a baptism, a regeneration, the initiation into a new state.
Adam Bede (1859) ch. 42

23 We hand folks over to God's mercy, and show none ourselves.
Adam Bede (1859) ch. 42

1 The mother's yearning, that completest type of the life in another life which is the essence of real human love, feels the presence of the cherished child even in the debased, degraded man.
Adam Bede (1859) ch. 43

2 Vanity is as ill at ease under indifference as tenderness is under a love which it cannot return.
Daniel Deronda (1876) bk. 1 ch. 10

3 Gossip is a sort of smoke that comes from the dirty tobacco-pipes of those who diffuse it: it proves nothing but the bad taste of the smoker.
Daniel Deronda (1876) bk. 2, ch. 13

4 A difference of taste in jokes is a great strain on the affections.
Daniel Deronda (1876) bk. 2, ch. 15

5 There is a great deal of unmapped country within us which would have to be taken into account in an explanation of our gusts and storms.
Daniel Deronda (1876) bk. 3, ch. 24

6 Friendships begin with liking or gratitude—roots that can be pulled up.
Daniel Deronda (1876) bk. 4, ch. 32

7 Half the sorrows of women would be averted if they could repress the speech they know to be useless; nay, the speech they have resolved not to make.
Felix Holt (1866) ch. 2

8 There is no private life which has not been determined by a wider public life.
Felix Holt (1866) ch. 3

9 An election is coming. Universal peace is declared, and the foxes have a sincere interest in prolonging the lives of the poultry.
Felix Holt (1866) ch. 5

10 A little daily embroidery had been a constant element in Mrs Transome's life; that soothing occupation of taking stitches to produce what neither she nor any one else wanted, was then the resource of many a well-born and unhappy woman.
Felix Holt (1866) ch. 7

11 Speech is often barren; but silence also does not necessarily brood over a full nest. Your still fowl, blinking at you without remark, may all the while be sitting on one addled egg; and when it takes to cackling will have nothing to announce but that addled delusion.
Felix Holt (1866) ch. 15

12 A woman can hardly ever choose . . . she is dependent on what happens to her. She must take meaner things, because only meaner things are within her reach.
Felix Holt (1866) ch. 27

13 There's many a one who would be idle if hunger didn't pinch him; but the stomach sets us to work.
Felix Holt (1866) ch. 30

14 'Abroad', that large home of ruined reputations.
Felix Holt (1866) epilogue

15 Debasing the moral currency.
The Impressions of Theophrastus Such (1879) essay title

16 Many Theresas have been born who found for themselves no epic life wherein there was a constant unfolding of far-resonant action; perhaps only a life of mistakes, the offspring of a certain spiritual grandeur ill-matched with the meanness of opportunity; perhaps a tragic failure which found no sacred poet and sank unwept into oblivion.
Middlemarch (1871–2) Prelude

17 A woman dictates before marriage in order that she may have an appetite for submission afterwards.
Middlemarch (1871–2) bk. 1, ch. 9

18 He said he should prefer not to know the sources of the Nile, and that there should be some unknown regions preserved as hunting-grounds for the poetic imagination.
Middlemarch (1871–2) bk. 1, ch. 9

19 Among all forms of mistake, prophecy is the most gratuitous.
Middlemarch (1871–2) bk. 1, ch. 10

20 Plain women he regarded as he did the other severe facts of life, to be faced with philosophy and investigated by science.
Middlemarch (1871–2) bk. 1, ch. 11

21 Any one watching keenly the stealthy convergence of human lots, sees a slow preparation of effects from one life on another, which tells like a calculated irony on the indifference or the frozen stare with which we look at our unintroduced neighbour.
Middlemarch (1871–2) bk. 1, ch. 11

22 Fred's studies are not very deep . . . he is only reading a novel.
Middlemarch (1871–2) bk 1, ch. 11

23 If we had a keen vision and feeling of all ordinary human life, it would be like hearing the grass grow and the squirrel's heart beat, and we should die of that roar which lies on the other side of silence.
Middlemarch (1871–2) bk. 2, ch. 20

24 We do not expect people to be deeply moved by what is not unusual. That element of tragedy which lies in the very fact of frequency, has not yet wrought itself into the coarse emotion of mankind.
Middlemarch (1871–2) bk. 2, ch. 20

25 A woman, let her be as good as she may, has got to put up with the life her husband makes for her.
Middlemarch (1871–2) bk. 3, ch. 25

26 It is an uneasy lot at best, to be what we call highly taught and yet not to enjoy: to be present at this great spectacle of life and never to be liberated from a small hungry shivering self.
Middlemarch (1871–2) bk. 3, ch. 29

27 A man is seldom ashamed of feeling that he cannot love a woman so well when he sees a certain greatness in her: nature having intended greatness for men.
Middlemarch (1871–2) bk. 4, ch. 39

1 'I am going to London,' said Dorothea.
'How can you always live in a street? And you will be so poor.'
Middlemarch (1871–2) bk. 8, ch. 84

2 Anger and jealousy can no more bear to lose sight of their objects than love.
The Mill on the Floss (1860) bk. 1, ch. 10

3 Our instructed vagrancy, which has hardly time to linger by the hedgerows, but runs away early to the tropics, and is at home with palms and banyans—which is nourished on books of travel, and stretches the theatre of its imagination to the Zambesi.
The Mill on the Floss (1860) bk. 3, ch. 9

4 The dead level of provincial existence.
The Mill on the Floss (1860) bk. 5, ch. 3

5 The happiest women, like the happiest nations, have no history.
The Mill on the Floss (1860) bk. 6, ch. 3; cf. **Montesquieu** 528:11

6 I should like to know what is the proper function of women, if it is not to make reasons for husbands to stay at home, and still stronger reasons for bachelors to go out.
The Mill on the Floss (1860) bk. 6, ch. 6

7 'Character' says Novalis, in one of his questionable aphorisms—'character is destiny.'
The Mill on the Floss (1860) bk. 6, ch. 6; cf. **Heraclitus** 371:9, **Novalis** 547:3

8 In every parting there is an image of death.
Scenes of Clerical Life (1858) 'Amos Barton' ch. 10

9 Cruelty, like every other vice, requires no motive outside itself—it only requires opportunity.
Scenes of Clerical Life (1858) 'Janet's Repentance' ch. 13

10 Errors look so very ugly in persons of small means—one feels they are taking quite a liberty in going astray; whereas people of fortune may naturally indulge in a few delinquencies.
Scenes of Clerical Life (1858) 'Janet's Repentance' ch. 25

11 Oh may I join the choir invisible
Of those immortal dead who live again
In minds made better by their presence.
'Oh May I Join the Choir Invisible' (1867)

12 Life is too precious to be spent in this weaving and unweaving of false impressions, and it is better to live quietly under some degree of misrepresentation than to attempt to remove it by the uncertain process of letter-writing.
letter to Mrs Peter Taylor, 8 June 1856, in G. S. Haight (ed.) *The George Eliot Letters* vol. 2 (1954)

13 Whatever may be the success of my stories, I shall be resolute in preserving my incognito, having observed that a *nom de plume* secures all the advantages without the disagreeables of reputation.
letter to William Blackwood, 4 February 1857, in G. S. Haight (ed.) *The George Eliot Letters* vol. 3 (1954)

14 If art does not enlarge men's sympathies, it does nothing morally.
letter to Charles Bray, 5 July 1859, in G. S. Haight (ed.) *The George Eliot Letters* vol. 3 (1954)

15 Beginnings are always troublesome . . . Even Macaulay's few pages of introduction to his 'Introduction' in the English History are the worst bit of writing in the book.
letter to Sara Hennell, 15 August 1859, in G. S. Haight (ed.) *The George Eliot Letters* vol. 3 (1954)

16 The idea of God, so far as it has been a high spiritual influence, is the ideal of a goodness entirely human.
letter to the Hon. Mrs H. F. Ponsonby, 10 December 1874, in G. S. Haight (ed.) *The George Eliot Letters* vol. 6 (1956)

17 She, stirred somewhat beyond her wont, and taking as her text the three words which have been used so often as the inspiring trumpet-calls of men—the words *God, Immortality, Duty*—pronounced, with terrible earnestness, how inconceivable was the *first*, how unbelievable the *second*, and yet how peremptory and absolute the third. Never, perhaps, have sterner accents affirmed the sovereignty of impersonal and unrecompensing Law.
F. W. H. Myers 'George Eliot', in *Century Magazine* November 1881

T. S. Eliot (Thomas Stearns Eliot) 1888–1965

Anglo-American poet, critic, and dramatist
on Eliot: see **Leavis** *461:7*

18 The pain of living and the drug of dreams
Curl up the small soul in the window seat
Behind the *Encyclopedia Britannica.*
'Animula' (1929)

19 Because I do not hope to turn again
Because I do not hope
Because I do not hope to turn.
Ash-Wednesday (1930) pt. 1

20 Teach us to care and not to care
Teach us to sit still.
Ash-Wednesday (1930) pt. 1

21 Lady, three white leopards sat under a juniper-tree
In the cool of the day.
Ash-Wednesday (1930) pt. 2

22 You've missed the point completely, Julia:
There *were* no tigers. *That* was the point.
The Cocktail Party (1950) act 1, sc. 1

23 What is hell?
Hell is oneself,
Hell is alone, the other figures in it
Merely projections. There is nothing to escape from
And nothing to escape to. One is always alone.
The Cocktail Party (1950) act 1, sc. 3; cf. **Sartre** 645:4

24 Over buttered scones and crumpets
Weeping, weeping multitudes
Droop in a hundred A.B.C.'s.
'Cooking Egg' (1920)

25 Success is relative:
It is what we can make of the mess we have made of things.
The Family Reunion (1939) pt. 2, sc. 3

26 Round and round the circle
Completing the charm

So the knot be unknotted
The cross be uncrossed
The crooked be made straight
And the curse be ended.
The Family Reunion (1939) pt. 2, sc. 3

1 Time present and time past
Are both perhaps present in time future,
And time future contained in time past.
Four Quartets 'Burnt Norton' (1936) pt. 1

2 Footfalls echo in the memory
Down the passage which we did not take
Towards the door we never opened
Into the rose-garden.
Four Quartets 'Burnt Norton' (1936) pt. 1

3 Human kind
Cannot bear very much reality.
Four Quartets 'Burnt Norton' (1936) pt. 1.

4 At the still point of the turning world.
Four Quartets 'Burnt Norton' (1936) pt. 2

5 Words strain,
Crack and sometimes break, under the burden,
Under the tension, slip, slide, perish,
Decay with imprecision, will not stay in place,
Will not stay still.
Four Quartets 'Burnt Norton' (1936) pt. 5

6 In my beginning is my end.
Four Quartets 'East Coker' (1940) pt. 1; cf. **Mary** 500:11

7 That was a way of putting it—not very satisfactory:
A periphrastic study in a worn-out poetical fashion,
Leaving one still with the intolerable wrestle
With words and meanings. The poetry does not matter.
Four Quartets 'East Coker' (1940) pt. 2

8 The houses are all gone under the sea.
The dancers are all gone under the hill.
Four Quartets 'East Coker' (1940) pt. 2

9 O dark dark dark. They all go into the dark,
The vacant interstellar spaces, the vacant into the vacant.
Four Quartets 'East Coker' (1940) pt. 3

10 The wounded surgeon plies the steel
That questions the distempered part;
Beneath the bleeding hands we feel
The sharp compassion of the healer's art
Resolving the enigma of the fever chart.
Four Quartets 'East Coker' (1940) pt. 4

11 Each venture
Is a new beginning, a raid on the inarticulate
With shabby equipment always deteriorating
In the general mess of imprecision of feeling.
Four Quartets 'East Coker' (1940) pt. 5

12 I think that the river
Is a strong brown god—sullen, untamed and intractable.
Four Quartets 'The Dry Salvages' (1941) pt. 1

13 The communication
Of the dead is tongued with fire beyond the language of the living.
Four Quartets 'Little Gidding' (1942) pt. 1

14 Ash on an old man's sleeve
Is all the ash the burnt roses leave.
Four Quartets 'Little Gidding' (1942) pt. 2

15 This is the death of air.
Four Quartets 'Little Gidding' (1942) pt. 2

16 Since our concern was speech, and speech impelled us
To purify the dialect of the tribe
And urge the mind to aftersight and foresight.
Four Quartets 'Little Gidding' (1942) pt. 2

17 We shall not cease from exploration
And the end of all our exploring
Will be to arrive where we started
And know the place for the first time.
Four Quartets 'Little Gidding' (1942) pt. 5

18 What we call the beginning is often the end
And to make an end is to make a beginning.
The end is where we start from.
Four Quartets 'Little Gidding' (1942) pt. 5

19 So, while the light fails
On a winter's afternoon, in a secluded chapel
History is now and England.
Four Quartets 'Little Gidding' (1942) pt. 5

20 And all shall be well and
All manner of thing shall be well
When the tongues of flame are in-folded
Into the crowned knot of fire
And the fire and the rose are one.
Four Quartets 'Little Gidding' (1942) pt. 5; cf. **Julian** 423:3

21 Here I am, an old man in a dry month
Being read to by a boy, waiting for rain.
'Gerontion' (1920)

22 After such knowledge, what forgiveness?
'Gerontion' (1920)

23 Tenants of the house,
Thoughts of a dry brain in a dry season.
'Gerontion' (1920)

24 We are the hollow men
We are the stuffed men
Leaning together
Headpiece filled with straw. Alas!
'The Hollow Men' (1925)

25 *Here we go round the prickly pear*
Prickly pear prickly pear
Here we go round the prickly pear
At five o'clock in the morning.

Between the idea
And the reality
Between the motion
And the act
Falls the Shadow.
'The Hollow Men' (1925)

26 This is the way the world ends
Not with a bang but a whimper.
'The Hollow Men' (1925)

27 A cold coming we had of it,
Just the worst time of the year
For a journey, and such a long journey:
The ways deep and the weather sharp,

The very dead of winter.
'Journey of the Magi' (1927); cf. **Andrewes** 14:15

1 I had seen birth and death
But had thought they were different.
'Journey of the Magi' (1927)

2 An alien people clutching their gods.
'Journey of the Magi' (1927)

3 Let us go then, you and I,
When the evening is spread out against the sky
Like a patient etherized upon a table.
'The Love Song of J. Alfred Prufrock' (1917); cf. **Lewis** 466:22

4 In the room the women come and go
Talking of Michelangelo.
'The Love Song of J. Alfred Prufrock' (1917)

5 The yellow fog that rubs its back upon the window-panes.
'The Love Song of J. Alfred Prufrock' (1917)

6 I have measured out my life with coffee spoons.
'The Love Song of J. Alfred Prufrock' (1917)

7 I should have been a pair of ragged claws
Scuttling across the floors of silent seas.
'The Love Song of J. Alfred Prufrock' (1917)

8 I have seen the moment of my greatness flicker,
And I have seen the eternal Footman hold my coat, and snicker,
And in short, I was afraid.
'The Love Song of J. Alfred Prufrock' (1917)

9 No! I am not Prince Hamlet, nor was meant to be;
Am an attendant lord, one that will do
To swell a progress, start a scene or two,
Advise the prince.
'The Love Song of J. Alfred Prufrock' (1917)

10 I grow old . . . I grow old . . .
I shall wear the bottoms of my trousers rolled.
'The Love Song of J. Alfred Prufrock' (1917)

11 Shall I part my hair behind? Do I dare to eat a peach?
I shall wear white flannel trousers, and walk upon the beach.
I have heard the mermaids singing, each to each.

I do not think that they will sing to me.
'The Love Song of J. Alfred Prufrock' (1917); cf. **Donne** 274:11

12 I am aware of the damp souls of housemaids
Sprouting despondently at area gates.
'Morning at the Window' (1917)

13 Polyphiloprogenitive
The sapient sutlers of the Lord.
'Mr Eliot's Sunday Morning Service' (1919)

14 Yet we have gone on living,
Living and partly living.
Murder in the Cathedral (1935) pt. 1

15 The last temptation is the greatest treason:
To do the right deed for the wrong reason.
Murder in the Cathedral (1935) pt. 1

16 Clear the air! clean the sky! wash the wind! take the stone from stone, take the skin from the arm, take the muscle from bone, and wash them.
Murder in the Cathedral (1935) pt. 2

17 The Naming of Cats is a difficult matter,
It isn't just one of your holiday games;
You may think at first I'm as mad as a hatter
when I tell you, a cat must have THREE DIFFERENT NAMES.
Old Possum's Book of Practical Cats (1939) 'The Naming of Cats'

18 He always has an alibi, and one or two to spare:
At whatever time the deed took place — MACAVITY WASN'T THERE!
Old Possum's Book of Practical Cats (1939) 'Macavity: the Mystery Cat'

19 The winter evening settles down
With smell of steaks in passageways.
Six o'clock.
The burnt-out ends of smoky days.
'Preludes' (1917)

20 Midnight shakes the memory
As a madman shakes a dead geranium.
'Rhapsody on a Windy Night' (1917)

21 Where is the wisdom we have lost in knowledge?
Where is the knowledge we have lost in information?
The Rock (1934) pt. 1

22 And the wind shall say: 'Here were decent godless people:
Their only monument the asphalt road
And a thousand lost golf balls.'
The Rock (1934) pt. 1

23 Birth, and copulation, and death.
That's all the facts when you come to brass tacks.
Sweeney Agonistes (1932) 'Fragment of an Agon'

24 I gotta use words when I talk to you.
Sweeney Agonistes (1932) 'Fragment of an Agon'

25 The nightingales are singing near
The Convent of the Sacred Heart,

And sang within the bloody wood
When Agamemnon cried aloud
And let their liquid siftings fall
To stain the stiff dishonoured shroud.
'Sweeney among the Nightingales' (1919)

26 April is the cruellest month, breeding
Lilacs out of the dead land.
The Waste Land (1922) pt. 1

27 I read, much of the night, and go south in the winter.
The Waste Land (1922) pt. 1

28 I will show you fear in a handful of dust.
The Waste Land (1922) pt. 1; cf. **Conrad** 234:25

29 Madame Sosostris, famous clairvoyante,
Had a bad cold, nevertheless
Is known to be the wisest woman in Europe,
With a wicked pack of cards.
The Waste Land (1922) pt. 1

1 A crowd flowed over London Bridge, so many,
I had not thought death had undone so many.
The Waste Land (1922) pt. 1

2 The Chair she sat in, like a burnished throne,
Glowed on the marble.
The Waste Land (1922) pt. 2; cf. **Shakespeare** 656:23

3 And still she cried, and still the world pursues,
'Jug Jug' to dirty ears.
The Waste Land (1922) pt. 2; cf. **Lyly** 480:16

4 I think we are in rats' alley
Where the dead men lost their bones.
The Waste Land (1922) pt. 2

5 O O O O that Shakespeherian Rag—
It's so elegant
So intelligent.
The Waste Land (1922) pt. 2; cf. **Buck** 159:12

6 Hurry up please it's time.
The Waste Land (1922) pt. 2

7 But at my back from time to time I hear
The sound of horns and motors, which shall bring
Sweeney to Mrs Porter in the spring.
O the moon shone bright on Mrs Porter
And on her daughter
They wash their feet in soda water.
The Waste Land (1922) pt. 3; cf. **Marvell** 499:2

8 At the violet hour, when the eyes and back
Turn upward from the desk, when the human
engine waits
Like a taxi throbbing waiting.
The Waste Land (1922) pt. 3

9 I Tiresias, old man with wrinkled dugs,
The Waste Land (1922) pt. 3

10 One of the low on whom assurance sits
As a silk hat on a Bradford millionaire.
The Waste Land (1922) pt. 3

11 When lovely woman stoops to folly and
Paces about her room again, alone,
She smoothes her hair with automatic hand,
And puts a record on the gramophone.
The Waste Land (1922) pt. 3; cf. **Goldsmith** 345:30

12 Phlebas the Phoenician, a fortnight dead,
Forgot the cry of gulls, and the deep sea swell
And the profit and loss.
The Waste Land (1922) pt. 4

13 Who is the third who walks always beside you?
When I count, there are only you and I together
But when I look ahead up the white road
There is always another one walking beside you.
The Waste Land (1922) pt. 5

14 These fragments I have shored against my ruins.
The Waste Land (1922) pt. 5

15 Shantih, shantih, shantih.
The Waste Land (1922) closing words; cf. **Upanishads** 787:19

16 Webster was much possessed by death
And saw the skull beneath the skin.
'Whispers of Immortality' (1919)

17 The only way of expressing emotion in the form of art is by finding an 'objective correlative'; in other words, a set of objects, a situation, a chain of events which shall be the formula of that *particular* emotion; such that when the external facts, which must terminate in sensory experience, are given, the emotion is immediately evoked.
The Sacred Wood (1920) 'Hamlet and his Problems'

18 Immature poets imitate; mature poets steal.
The Sacred Wood (1920) 'Philip Massinger'

19 Someone said: 'The dead writers are remote from us because we *know* so much more than they did.' Precisely, and they are that which we know.
The Sacred Wood (1920) 'Tradition and Individual Talent'

20 In the seventeenth century a dissociation of sensibility set in, from which we have never recovered; and this dissociation, as is natural, was due to the influence of the two most powerful poets of the century, Milton and Dryden.
Selected Essays (1932) 'The Metaphysical Poets' (1921)

21 Poets in our civilization, as it exists at present, must be *difficult*.
Selected Essays (1932) 'The Metaphysical Poets' (1921)

22 To me . . . [*The Waste Land*] was only the relief of a personal and wholly insignificant grouse against life; it is just a piece of rhythmical grumbling.
The Waste Land (ed. Valerie Eliot, 1971) epigraph

Elizabeth I 1533–1603

Queen of England and Ireland from 1558
on Elizabeth: see **Bible** *73:7; see also* **Bacon** *45:9,* **Last words** *455:2,* **Mottoes** *535:16*

23 The queen of Scots is this day leichter of a fair son, and I am but a barren stock.
to her ladies, June 1566, in Sir James Melville *Memoirs of His Own Life* (1827 ed.)

24 I am your anointed Queen. I will never be by violence constrained to do anything. I thank God that I am endued with such qualities that if I were turned out of the Realm in my petticoat, I were able to live in any place in Christome.
speech to Members of Parliament, 5 November 1566, in J. E. Neale *Elizabeth I and her Parliaments 1559–1581* (1953) pt. 3, ch. 1

25 I know what it is to be a subject, what to be a Sovereign, what to have good neighbours, and sometimes meet evil-willers.
speech to a Parliamentary deputation at Richmond, 12 November 1586, in Sir John Neale *Elizabeth I and her Parliaments 1584–1601* (1957, from a report 'which the Queen herself heavily amended in her own hand'; cf. **Misquotations** 521:15

26 I will make you shorter by the head.
to the leaders of her Council, who were opposing her course towards **Mary** *Queen of Scots*
F. Chamberlin *Sayings of Queen Elizabeth* (1923)

27 I know I have the body of a weak and feeble woman, but I have the heart and stomach of a king, and of a king of England too; and think foul scorn that Parma or Spain, or any prince of Europe, should dare to invade the borders of my realm.

speech to the troops at Tilbury on the approach of the Armada, 1588, in Lord Somers *A Third Collection of Scarce and Valuable Tracts* (1751)

1 The daughter of debate, that eke discord doth sow.

on **Mary** *Queen of Scots*

George Puttenham (ed.) *The Art of English Poesie* (1589) bk. 3, ch. 20

2 My lord, we make use of you, not for your bad legs, but for your good head.

to William **Cecil**, *who suffered from gout*

F. Chamberlin *Sayings of Queen Elizabeth* (1923)

3 I do entreat heaven daily for your longer life, else will my people and myself stand in need of cordials too. My comfort hath been in my people's happiness and their happiness in thy discretion.

to William **Cecil** *on his death-bed, 1598*

F. Chamberlin *Sayings of Queen Elizabeth* (1923)

4 Though God hath raised me high, yet this I count the glory of my crown: that I have reigned with your loves.

The Golden Speech, 1601, in *The Journals of All the Parliaments . . .* Collected by Sir Simonds D'Ewes (1682)

5 God may pardon you, but I never can.

to the dying Countess of Nottingham, February 1603, for her part in the death of the Earl of **Essex**; *the story is almost certainly apocryphal*

David Hume *The History of England under the House of Tudor* (1759) vol. 2, ch. 7

6 Must! Is *must* a word to be addressed to princes? Little man, little man! thy father, if he had been alive, durst not have used that word.

to Robert **Cecil**, *on his saying she must go to bed, shortly before her death*

J. R. Green *A Short History of the English People* (1874) ch. 7; *Dodd's Church History of England* vol. 3 (ed. M. A. Tierney, 1840) adds: 'but thou knowest I must die, and that maketh thee so presumptuous'

7 If thy heart fails thee, climb not at all.

lines after Sir Walter **Ralegh**, *written on a window-pane*

Thomas Fuller *Worthies of England* vol. 1; cf. **Ralegh** 621:3

8 I think that, at the worst, God has not yet ordained that England shall perish.

F. Chamberlin *Sayings of Queen Elizabeth* (1923)

9 I would not open windows into men's souls.

oral tradition, in J. B. Black *Reign of Elizabeth 1558–1603* (1936); the words very possibly originating in a letter drafted by Bacon

10 Like strawberry wives, that laid two or three great strawberries at the mouth of their pot, and all the rest were little ones.

describing the tactics of the Commission of Sales, in their dealings with her

Francis Bacon *Apophthegms New and Old* (1625) no. 54

11 Madam I may not call you; mistress I am ashamed to call you; and so I know not what to call you; but howsoever, I thank you.

to the wife of the Archbishop of Canterbury, the Queen disapproving of marriage among the clergy

Sir John Harington *A Brief View of the State of the Church of England* (1653)

12 My Lord, I had forgot the fart.

to Edward de Vere, Earl of **Oxford**, *on his return from seven years self-imposed exile, occasioned by the acute embarrassment to himself of breaking wind in the presence of the Queen*

John Aubrey *Brief Lives* 'Edward de Vere'

13 'Twas God the word that spake it,
He took the bread and brake it;
And what the word did make it;
That I believe, and take it.

answer on being asked her opinion of Christ's presence in the Sacrament

S. Clarke *The Marrow of Ecclesiastical History* (1675) pt. 2, bk. 1 'The Life of Queen Elizabeth'

Elizabeth II 1926–

Queen of the United Kingdom from 1952; daughter of **George VI** *and Queen* **Elizabeth** *the Queen Mother, mother of Prince* **Charles**

14 I declare before you all that my whole life, whether it be long or short, shall be devoted to your service and the service of our great Imperial family to which we all belong.

broadcast speech, as Princess Elizabeth, to the Commonwealth from Cape Town, 21 April 1947, in *The Times* 22 April 1947

15 I think everybody really will concede that on this, of all days, I should begin my speech with the words 'My husband and I'.

speech at Guildhall, London, on her 25th wedding anniversary

in *The Times* 21 November 1972

16 In the words of one of my more sympathetic correspondents, it has turned out to be an 'annus horribilis'.

speech at Guildhall, London, 24 November 1992

17 I for one believe that there are lessons to be drawn from her life and from the extraordinary and moving reaction to her death.

broadcast from Buckingham Palace on the evening before the funeral of **Diana**, *Princess of Wales, 5 September 1997*

in *The Times* 6 September 1997

18 I sometimes sense the world is changing almost too fast for its inhabitants, at least for us older ones.

on her tour of Pakistan, 8 October 1997

in *Times* 9 October 1997

19 Please don't be too effusive.

adjuration to the Prime Minister on the speech he was to make to celebrate her golden wedding, 18 November 1997

in *Daily Telegraph* 21 November 1997; cf. **Blair** 117:14

20 Think what we would have missed if we had never . . . used a mobile phone or surfed the Net—

or, to be honest, listened to other people talking about surfing the Net.
reflecting on developments in the past 50 years
in *Daily Telegraph* 21 November 1997

Queen Elizabeth, the Queen Mother 1900–
Queen Consort of ***George VI****, mother of* ***Elizabeth II***

1 I'm glad we've been bombed. It makes me feel I can look the East End in the face.
to a London policeman, 13 September 1940
John Wheeler-Bennett *King George VI* (1958) pt. 3, ch. 6

2 The Princesses would never leave without me and I couldn't leave without the King, and the King will never leave.
on the suggestion that the royal family be evacuated during the Blitz
Penelope Mortimer *Queen Elizabeth* (1986) ch. 25

3 How small and selfish is sorrow. But it bangs one about until one is senseless.
letter to Edith ***Sitwell****, shortly after the death of* ***George VI***
Victoria Glendinning *Edith Sitwell* (1983) ch. 25

Elizabeth, Countess von Arnim 1866–1941
Australian-born British writer

4 Guests can be, and often are, delightful, but they should never be allowed to get the upper hand.
All the Dogs in My Life (1936)

Alf Ellerton

5 Belgium put the kibosh on the Kaiser.
title of song (1914)

John Ellerton 1826–93
English clergyman

6 The day Thou gavest, Lord, is ended,
The darkness falls at Thy behest.
Hymn (1870), the first line borrowed from an earlier, anonymous hymn

Duke Ellington 1899–1974
American jazz pianist, composer, and band-leader
see also ***Mills*** 510:9

7 Playing 'Bop' is like scrabble with all the vowels missing.
in *Look* 10 August 1954

Emily Elizabeth Steele Elliot 1836–97
English hymn-writer

8 O come to my heart, Lord Jesus!
There is room in my heart for thee.
'Thou didst leave thy throne and thy kingly crown' (1870 hymn)

Jane Elliot 1727–1805
Scottish poet

9 I've heard them lilting, at the ewe milking.
Lasses a' lilting, before dawn of day;
But now they are moaning, on ilka green loaning;
The flowers of the forest are a' wede away.
'The Flowers of the Forest' (1769), the most popular version of the traditional lament for the Battle of Flodden in 1513; cf. **Cockburn** 223:12

Charlotte Elliott 1789–1871
English hymn-writer

10 Just as I am, without one plea
But that Thy blood was shed for me,
And that Thou bidd'st me come to Thee,
O Lamb of God, I come!
Invalid's Hymn Book (1834) 'Just as I am'

11 'Christian! seek not yet repose,'
Hear thy guardian angel say;
Thou art in the midst of foes—
'Watch and pray.'
Morning and Evening Hymns (1836) 'Christian! seek not yet repose'; cf. **Bible** 97:23

Ebenezer Elliott 1781–1849
English poet known as the 'Corn Law Rhymer'

12 What is a communist? One who hath yearnings
For equal division of unequal earnings.
'Epigram' (1850)

13 When wilt thou save the people?
Oh, God of Mercy! when?
The people, Lord, the people!
Not thrones and crowns, but men!
'The People's Anthem' (1850)

George Ellis 1753–1815
English poet and journalist

14 Snowy, Flowy, Blowy,
Showery, Flowery, Bowery,
Hoppy, Croppy, Droppy,
Breezy, Sneezy, Freezy.
'The Twelve Months'

Havelock Ellis (Henry Havelock Ellis) 1859–1939
English sexologist

15 What we call 'progress' is the exchange of one nuisance for another nuisance.
Impressions and Comments (1914) 31 July 1912

16 All civilization has from time to time become a thin crust over a volcano of revolution.
Little Essays of Love and Virtue (1922) ch. 7

Friar Elstow
English Franciscan

17 With thanks to God we know the way to heaven, to be as ready by water as by land, and therefore we care not which way we go.
when threatened with drowning by Henry VIII
John Stow *The Annals of England* (1615); cf. **Gilbert** 337:3

Paul Éluard 1895–1952

French poet

1 *L'espoir ne fait pas de poussière.*
Hope raises no dust.
'Ailleurs, ici, partout' (1946)

2 *Adieu tristesse*
Bonjour tristesse
Tu es inscrite dans les lignes du plafond.
Farewell sadness
Good-day sadness
You are inscribed in the lines of the ceiling.
'À peine défigurée' (1932)

Buchi Emecheta 1944–

Nigerian writer

3 I am a woman and a woman of Africa. I am a daughter of Nigeria and if she is in shame, I shall stay and mourn with her in shame.
Destination Biafra (1982)

4 The whole world seemed so unequal, so unfair. Some people were created with all the good things ready-made for them, others were just created like mistakes. God's mistakes.
Second-Class Citizen (1974) ch.9

Ralph Waldo Emerson 1803–82

American philosopher and poet
see also **Clough** *223:5*

5 If the red slayer think he slays,
Or if the slain think he is slain,
They know not well the subtle ways
I keep, and pass, and turn again.
'Brahma' (1867); cf. **Lang** 450:10, **Upanishads** 787:21

6 I am the doubter and the doubt.
'Brahma' (1867)

7 By the rude bridge that arched the flood,
Their flag to April's breeze unfurled,
Here once the embattled farmers stood,
And fired the shot heard round the world.
'Concord Hymn' (1837)

8 Things are in the saddle,
And ride mankind.
'Ode' inscribed to W. H. Channing (1847)

9 He builded better than he knew;—
The conscious stone to beauty grew.
'The Problem' (1847)

10 The frolic architecture of the snow.
'The Snowstorm' (1847)

11 When Duty whispers low, *Thou must*,
The youth replies, *I can*.
'Voluntaries' no. 3 (1867)

12 Make yourself necessary to someone.
The Conduct of Life (1860) 'Considerations by the way'

13 All sensible people are selfish, and nature is tugging at every contract to make the terms of it fair.
The Conduct of Life (1860) 'Considerations by the way'

14 Art is a jealous mistress.
The Conduct of Life (1860) 'Wealth'

15 The louder he talked of his honour, the faster we counted our spoons.
The Conduct of Life (1860) 'Worship'; cf. **Johnson** 413:8, **Shaw** 708:10

16 I feel in regard to this aged England . . . that she sees a little better on a cloudy day, and that, in storm of battle and calamity, she has a secret vigour and a pulse like a cannon.
speech at Manchester, November 1847 in *English Traits* (1883 ed.)

17 The only reward of virtue is virtue; the only way to have a friend is to be one.
Essays (1841) 'Friendship'

18 We need books of this tart cathartic virtue, more than books of political science or of private economy.
on ***Plutarch****'s* Lives
Essays (1841) 'Heroism'

19 It was a high counsel that I once heard given to a young person, 'Always do what you are afraid to do.'
Essays (1841) 'Heroism'

20 There is properly no history; only biography.
Essays (1841) 'History'; cf. **Disraeli** 270:7

21 In skating over thin ice, our safety is in our speed.
Essays (1841) 'Prudence'

22 Whoso would be a man must be a nonconformist.
Essays (1841) 'Self-Reliance'

23 A foolish consistency is the hobgoblin of little minds, adored by little statesmen and philosophers and divines. With consistency a great soul has simply nothing to do.
Essays (1841) 'Self-Reliance'

24 Is it so bad, then, to be misunderstood? Pythagoras was misunderstood, and Socrates, and Jesus, and Luther, and Copernicus, and Galileo, and Newton, and every pure and wise spirit that ever took flesh. To be great is to be misunderstood.
Essays (1841) 'Self-Reliance'

25 To fill the hour—that is happiness.
Essays. Second Series (1844) 'Experience'

26 Every man is wanted, and no man is wanted much.
Essays. Second Series (1844) 'Nominalist and Realist'

27 Language is fossil poetry.
Essays. Second Series (1844) 'The Poet'

28 What is a weed? A plant whose virtues have not been discovered.
Fortune of the Republic (1878)

29 Every hero becomes a bore at last.
Representative Men (1850) 'Uses of Great Men'

30 Hitch your wagon to a star.
Society and Solitude (1870) 'Civilization'

31 We boil at different degrees.
Society and Solitude (1870) 'Eloquence'

32 America is a country of young men.
Society and Solitude (1870) 'Old Age'

1 I hate quotations. Tell me what you know.
Journals and Miscellaneous Notebooks (1961) May 1849

2 Glittering generalities! They are blazing ubiquities.
on Rufus **Choate**
attributed; cf. **Choate** 212:8

3 If a man write a better book, preach a better sermon, or make a better mouse-trap than his neighbour, tho' he build his house in the woods, the world will make a beaten path to his door.
attributed to Emerson in Sarah S. B. Yule *Borrowings* (1889); Mrs Yule states in *The Docket* February 1912 that she copied this in her handbook from a lecture delivered by Emerson; the quotation was the occasion of a long controversy owing to Elbert Hubbard's claim to its authorship

Robert Emmet 1778–1803

Irish nationalist

4 Let no man write my epitaph . . . When my country takes her place among the nations of the earth, *then*, and *not till then*, let my epitaph be written.
speech from the dock when condemned to death, 19 September 1803

William Empson 1906–84

English poet and literary critic

5 Waiting for the end, boys, waiting for the end.
'Just a smack at Auden' (1940)

6 You don't want madhouse and the whole thing there.
'Let it Go' (1955)

7 Slowly the poison the whole blood stream fills.
It is not the effort nor the failure tires.
The waste remains, the waste remains and kills.
'Missing Dates' (1935)

8 The central function of imaginative literature is to make you realize that other people act on moral convictions different from your own.
Milton's God (1981) ch. 7

9 Seven types of ambiguity.
title of book (1930)

10 Learning French is some trouble, but after that you have a clear and beautiful language; in English the undergrowth is part of the language.
in *Spectator* 14 June 1935

Friedrich Engels 1820–95

German socialist; founder, with Karl **Marx***, of modern Communism*
see also **Marx and Engels**

11 *Der Staat wird nicht 'abgeschafft'*, er stirbt ab.
The State is not 'abolished', *it withers away.*
Anti-Dühring (1878) pt. 3, ch. 2

12 Naturally, the workers are perfectly free; the manufacturer does not force them to take his materials and his cards, but he says to them . . . 'If you don't like to be frizzled in my frying-pan, you can take a walk into the fire'.
The Condition of the Working Class in England in 1844 (1892) ch. 7

Thomas Dunn English 1819–1902

American physician, lawyer, and writer

13 Oh! don't you remember sweet Alice, Ben Bolt,
Sweet Alice, whose hair was so brown,
Who wept with delight when you gave her a smile,
And trembled with fear at your frown?
'Ben Bolt' (1885)

Ennius 239–169 BC

Roman writer
on Ennius: see **Horace** *389:18*

14 *O Tite tute Tati tibi tanta tyranne tulisti!*
O tyrant Titus Tatius, what a lot you brought upon yourself!
Annals bk. 1 (l. 104 in O. Skutsch (ed.) *Annals of Q. Ennius*, 1985)

15 *Moribus antiquis res stat Romana virisque.*
The Roman state survives by its ancient customs and its manhood.
Annals bk. 5 (l. 156 in O. Skutsch (ed.) *Annals of Q. Ennius*, 1985)

16 *Unus homo nobis cunctando restituit rem.*
One man by delaying put the state to rights for us.
referring to the Roman general Fabius Cunctator ('The Delayer')
Annals bk. 12 (l. 363 in O. Skutsch (ed.) *Annals of Q. Ennius*, 1985)

17 *At tuba terribili sonitu taratantara dixit.*
And the trumpet in terrible tones went taratantara.
Annals (l. 451 in O. Skutsch (ed.) *Annals of Q. Ennius*, 1985)

Ephelia

17th-century poet

18 And yet I love this false, this worthless man,
With all the passion that a woman can;
Dote on his imperfections, though I spy
Nothing to love; I love, and know not why.
Female Poems (1679) 'To one that asked me why I loved J.G.'

Nora Ephron 1941–

American screenwriter and director
see also **Film lines** *311:14*

19 The anecdote is a particularly dehumanising sort of descriptive narrative.
Scribble, Scribble (1978)

Epictetus AD c.50–120

Phrygian Stoic philosopher

20 Everything has two handles, by one of which it ought to be carried and by the other not.
The Encheiridion sect. 43

Epicurus 341–271 BC

Greek philosopher

21 Death, therefore, the most awful of evils, is nothing to us, seeing that, when we are death is not come, and when death is come, we are not.
Diogenes Laertius *Lives of Eminent Philosophers* bk. 10

□ Epitaphs
see box overleaf

Jacob Epstein 1880–1959
British sculptor
on Epstein: see **Anonymous** *16:9, 16:20*

1 Why don't they stick to murder and leave art to us?
on hearing that his statue of Lazarus in New College chapel, Oxford, kept **Khrushchev** *awake at night*
attributed

Olaudah Equiano *c.*1745–*c.*1797
African writer and former slave

2 We are . . . a nation of dancers, singers and poets.
of the Ibo people
Narrative of the Life of Olaudah Equiano (1789) ch. 1

3 When I recovered a little I found some black people about me . . . I asked them if we were not to be eaten by those white men with horrible looks, red faces, and loose hair.
Narrative of the Life of Olaudah Equiano (1789) ch. 3

Erasmus (Desiderius Erasmus) *c.*1469–1536
Dutch Christian humanist

4 *In regione caecorum rex est luscus.*
In the country of the blind the one-eyed man is king.
Adages bk. 3, century 4, no. 96; cf. **Proverbs** 604:1

Ludwig Erhard 1897–1977
German statesman, Chancellor of West Germany (1963–6)

5 Without Britain Europe would remain only a torso.
remark on W. German television, 27 May 1962; in *The Times* 28 May 1962

Susan Ertz 1894–1985
American writer

6 Millions long for immortality who don't know what to do with themselves on a rainy Sunday afternoon.
Anger in the Sky (1943)

Lord Esher 1913–
English architect and planner

7 When politicians and civil servants hear the word 'culture' they feel for their blue pencils.
speech, House of Lords, 2 March 1960; cf. **Johst** 418:17

8 Who would guess that those gloomy bunkers were built to celebrate the pleasures of the senses?
of the Hayward Gallery complex, London
A Broken Wave (1987)

Robert Devereux, Earl of Essex 1566–1601
English soldier and courtier, executed for treason

9 Reasons are not like garments, the worse for wearing.
letter to Lord Willoughby, 4 January 1599, in *Notes and Queries* 10th Series, vol. 2 (1904)

Henri Estienne 1531–98
French printer and publisher

10 *Si jeunesse savait; si vieillesse pouvait.*
If youth knew; if age could.
Les Prémices (1594) bk. 4, epigram 4

George Etherege *c.*1635–91
English dramatist

11 I walk within the purlieus of the Law.
Love in a Tub (1664) act 1, sc. 3; cf. **Tennyson** 761:23

12 When love grows diseased, the best thing we can do is put it to a violent death; I cannot endure the torture of a lingering and consumptive passion.
The Man of Mode (1676) act 2, sc. 2

13 Writing, Madam, 's a mechanic part of wit! A gentleman should never go beyond a song or a billet.
The Man of Mode (1676) act 4, sc. 1

14 Fear not, though love and beauty fail,
My reason shall my heart direct:
Your kindness now will then prevail,
And passion turn into respect:
Chloris, at worst, you'll in the end
But change your Lover for a friend.
New Academy of Compliments (1671) 'Chloris, 'tis not in your power'

Euclid fl. *c.*300 BC
Greek mathematician

15 *Quod erat demonstrandum.*
Which was to be proved.
often abbreviated to QED
Latin translation from the Greek of *Elementa* bk. 1, proposition 5 and *passim*

16 A line is length without breadth.
Elementa bk. 1, definition 2

17 There is no 'royal road' to geometry.
addressed to Ptolemy I, in Proclus *Commentary on the First Book of Euclid's Elementa* prologue, pt. 2; cf. **Proverbs** 612:17

Infanta Eulalia of Spain 1864–1958
Spanish princess

18 We could not go anywhere without sending word ahead so that life might be put on parade for us.
Court Life from Within (1915)

Epitaphs

1 The body of
Benjamin Franklin, printer,
(Like the cover of an old book,
Its contents worn out,
And stripped of its lettering and gilding)
Lies here, food for worms!
Yet the work itself shall not be lost,
For it will, as he believed, appear once more
In a new
And more beautiful edition,
Corrected and amended
By its Author!

Benjamin **Franklin**'s epitaph for himself (1728); cf. **Turgot** 785:9

2 Commander Jacques-Yves Cousteau has rejoined the world of silence.

announcement by the Cousteau Foundation, Paris, 25 June 1997; Cousteau (1910–97) published The Silent World *in 1953*

in *Daily Telegraph* 26 June 1997

3 *Et in Arcadia ego.*
And I too in Arcadia.

tomb inscription, of disputed meaning, often depicted in classical paintings, notably by Poussin in 1655; E. Panofsky 'Et in Arcadia ego' in R. K. Klibansky and H. J. Paton (eds.) *Philosophy and History: Essays Presented to E. Cassirer* (1936)

4 Excuse my dust.

Dorothy **Parker** *(1893–1967); suggested epitaph for herself (1925)*

Alexander Woollcott *While Rome Burns* (1934) 'Our Mrs Parker'

5 *Ex umbris et imaginibus in veritatem.*
From shadows and types to the reality.

John Henry **Newman** *(1801–90)*

motto on his memorial tablet, in Owen Chadwick *Newman* (1983)

6 Farewell, great painter of mankind!
Who reached the noblest point of art,
Whose pictured morals charm the mind
And through the eye correct the heart.

epitaph on William Hogarth (1697–1764)

monument in Chiswick churchyard (1772), by David **Garrick**

7 Free at last, free at last
Thank God almighty
We are free at last.

epitaph of Martin Luther **King** *(1929–68), Atlanta, Georgia*

anonymous spiritual, with which he ended his 'I have a dream' speech; cf. **King** 436:14

8 From Moses to Moses there was none like unto Moses.

later inscription on the tomb of the Jewish scholar Moses **Maimonides** (1135–1204)

9 God damn you all: I told you so.

H. G. **Wells**' *suggestion for his own epitaph, in conversation with Ernest Barker, 1939*

Ernest Barker *Age and Youth* (1953)

10 Good friend, for Jesu's sake forbear
To dig the dust enclosed here.
Blest be the man that spares these stones,
And curst be he that moves my bones.

William **Shakespeare** *(1564–1616)*

insciption on his grave, Stratford upon Avon, probably composed by himself

11 Go, tell the Spartans, thou who passest by,
That here obedient to their laws we lie.

epitaph for the 300 Spartans killed at Thermopylae, 480 BC

attributed to **Simonides**; Herodotus *Histories* bk. 7, ch. 228

12 Hereabouts died a very gallant gentleman, Captain L. E. G. Oates of the Inniskilling Dragoons. In March 1912, returning from the Pole, he walked willingly to his death in a blizzard to try and save his comrades, beset by hardships.

epitaph on cairn erected in the Antarctic, 15 November 1912, by E. L. Atkinson (1882–1929) and Apsley Cherry-Garrard (1882–1959)

Apsley Cherry-Garrard *The Worst Journey in the World* (1922); cf. **Last words** 456:1

13 Here lie I, Martin Elginbrodde:
Hae mercy o' my soul, Lord God;
As I wad do, were I Lord God,
And ye were Martin Elginbrodde.

George MacDonald *David Elginbrod* (1863) bk. 1, ch. 13

14 Here lies a great and mighty king
Whose promise none relies on;
He never said a foolish thing,
Nor ever did a wise one.

of **Charles II** *(1630–85); an alternative first line reads: 'Here lies our sovereign lord the King'*

John Wilmot, Earl of Rochester 'The King's Epitaph'; in C. E. Doble et al. *Thomas Hearne: Remarks and Collections* (1885–1921) 17 November 1706; cf. **Charles II** 203:14

15 Here lies a poor woman who always was tired,
For she lived in a place where help wasn't hired.
Her last words on earth were, Dear friends I am going
Where washing ain't done nor sweeping nor sewing,
And everything there is exact to my wishes,
For there they don't eat and there's no washing of dishes . . .
Don't mourn for me now, don't mourn for me never,
For I'm going to do nothing for ever and ever.

epitaph in Bushey churchyard, before 1860; destroyed by 1916

16 Here lies a valiant warrior
Who never drew a sword;
Here lies a noble courtier
Who never kept his word;
Here lies the Earl of Leicester
Who governed the estates
Whom the earth could never living love,

Epitaphs *continued*

And the just heaven now hates.
of Robert Dudley, Earl of Leicester (c.1532–88)
attributed to Ben **Jonson** in Silvester Tissington *A Collection of Epitaphs and Monumental Inscriptions* (1857)

1 Here lies Fred,
Who was alive and is dead:
Had it been his father,
I had much rather;
Had it been his brother,
Still better than another;
Had it been his sister,
No one would have missed her;
Had it been the whole generation,
Still better for the nation:
But since 'tis only Fred,
Who was alive and is dead,—
There's no more to be said.
of Frederick Louis, Prince of Wales (1707–1751), son of ***George II*** *and* ***Caroline*** *of Ansbach*
in Horace Walpole *Memoirs of George II* (1847) vol. 1

2 Here lies Groucho Marx—and lies and lies and lies. P.S. He never kissed an ugly girl.
his own suggestion for his epitaph
B. Norman *The Movie Greats* (1981)

3 Here lies one whose name was writ in water.
epitaph for himself by John ***Keats*** *(1795–1821)*
Richard Monckton Milnes *Life, Letters and Literary Remains of John Keats* (1848) vol. 2; cf. **Shakespeare** 673:22

4 Here lies that peerless paper peer Lord Peter,
Who broke the laws of God and man and metre.
epitaph for Patrick ('Peter'), Lord Robertson (1794–1855) by John Gibson ***Lockhart***
The Journal of Sir Walter Scott (1890) vol. 1

5 Here lies W. C. Fields. I would rather be living in Philadelphia.
W. C. **Fields**' suggested epitaph for himself, in *Vanity Fair* June 1925

6 Here lies wise and valiant dust,
Huddled up, 'twixt fit and just:
Strafford, who was hurried hence
'Twixt treason and convenience.
He spent his time here in a mist,
A Papist, yet a Calvinist . . .
Riddles lie here, or in a word,
Here lies blood; and let it lie
Speechless still, and never cry.
John Cleveland (1613–58) 'Epitaph on the Earl of Strafford' (1647)

7 Here Skugg
Lies snug
As a bug
In a rug.
letter to Georgiana Shipley on the death of her squirrel, 26 September 1772; skugg = *squirrel*
Benjamin **Franklin**, in W. B. Willcox (ed.) *Papers of Benjamin Franklin* vol. 19 (1975)

8 He was an average guy who could carry a tune.
Bing ***Crosby****'s suggested epitaph for himself*
in *Newsweek* 24 October 1977

9 His foe was folly and his weapon wit.
W. S. ***Gilbert*** *(1836–1911)*
inscription by Anthony **Hope** on memorial on the Victoria Embankment, London, 1915

10 I will return. And I will be millions.
inscription on the tomb of Eva **Perón**, Buenos Aires

11 John Le Mesurier wishes it to be known that he conked out on November 15th. He sadly misses family and friends.
obituary notice on the death of John Le Mesurier (1912–83), in *The Times* 16 November 1983

12 Life is a jest; and all things show it.
I thought so once; but now I know it.
John ***Gay*** *(1685–1732)*
'My Own Epitaph' (1720)

13 Long night succeeds thy little day
Oh blighted blossom! can it be,
That this grey stone and grassy clay
Have closed our anxious care of thee?
Thomas Love ***Peacock****'s epitaph on his daughter Margaret, who died at the age of three*
H. Cole (ed.) *Works of Peacock* (1875)

14 Love made me poet,
And this I writ;
My heart did do it,
And not my wit.
Elizabeth, Lady Tanfield (*c.*1565–1628); epitaph for her husband, in Burford Parish Church, Oxfordshire

15 My friend, judge not me,
Thou seest I judge not thee.
Betwixt the stirrup and the ground
Mercy I asked, mercy I found.
epitaph for 'A gentleman falling off his horse [who] *brake his neck'*
William Camden *Remains Concerning Britain* (1605) 'Epitaphs'

16 My sledge and anvil lie declined
My bellows too have lost their wind
My fire's extinct, my forge decayed,
And in the dust my vice is laid
My coals are spent, my iron's gone
My nails are drove, my work is done.
blacksmith's epitaph
in Nettlebed churchyard, commemorating William Strange, d. 6 June 1746

17 *Olivarii Goldsmith,*
Poetae, Physici, Historici,
Qui nullum fere scribendi genus
Non tetigit,
Nullum quod tetigit non ornavit.
To Oliver Goldsmith, A Poet, Naturalist, and Historian, who left scarcely any style of writing

Epitaphs *continued*

untouched, and touched none that he did not adorn.
epitaph on **Goldsmith** *(1728–74) by Samuel* **Johnson**
James Boswell *Life of Samuel Johnson* (1791) 22 June 1776

1 O rare Ben Jonson.
inscription on the tomb of Ben **Jonson** in Westminster Abbey

2 Poor G.K.C., his day is past—
Now God will know the truth at last.
mock epitaph for G. K. **Chesterton**, *by E. V. Lucas (1868–1938)*
Dudley Barker *G. K. Chesterton* (1973)

3 Rest in peace. The mistake shall not be repeated.
inscription on the cenotaph at Hiroshima, Japan

4 *Si monumentum requiris, circumspice.*
If you seek a monument, gaze around.
inscription in St Paul's Cathedral, London, attributed to the son of Sir Christopher Wren (1632–1723), its architect; cf. **Barham** 54:1

5 A soldier of the Great War known unto God.
standard epitaph for the unidentified dead of World War One
adopted by the War Graves Commission

6 Their name liveth for evermore.
standard inscription on the Stone of Sacrifice in each military cemetery of World War One, proposed by Rudyard **Kipling** *as a member of the War Graves Commission*
Charles Carrington *Rudyard Kipling* (rev. ed. 1978); cf. **Bible** 92:17, **Sassoon** 645:23

7 Timothy has passed . . .
message on his Internet web page announcing the death of Timothy **Leary**, *31 May 1996*
in *Guardian* 1 June 1996

8 *Ubi saeva indignatio ulterius cor lacerare nequit.*
Where fierce indignation can no longer tear his heart.
Jonathan **Swift** *(1667–1745)*
Shane Leslie *The Skull of Swift* (1928) ch. 15; cf. **Yeats** 837:15

9 Underneath this sable hearse
Lies the subject of all verse;
Sidney's sister, Pembroke's mother,
Death, ere thou hast slain another,
Fair and learn'd, and good as she,
Time shall throw a dart at thee.
William Browne (*c.*1590–1643) 'Epitaph on the Countess Dowager of Pembroke' (1623)

10 Under this stone, Reader, survey
Dead Sir John Vanbrugh's house of clay.
Lie heavy on him, Earth! for he
Laid many heavy loads on thee!
Abel Evans (1679–1737) 'Epitaph on Sir John Vanbrugh, Architect of Blenheim Palace'

11 Were there but a few hearts and intellects like hers this earth would already become the hoped-for heaven.
epitaph (1859) inscribed by John Stuart **Mill** *on the tomb of his wife, Harriet (d. 1858), at the cemetery of St Véran, near Avignon*
M. St J. Packe *Life of John Stuart Mill* (1954) bk. 7, ch. 3

12 What Cato did, and Addison approved,
Cannot be wrong.
lines found on the desk of Eustace Budgell (1686–1737), after he, too, had taken his own life
Colley Cibber *Lives of the Poets* (1753) vol. 5 'Life of Eustace Budgell'

13 What wee gave, wee have;
What wee spent, wee had;
What wee kept, wee lost.
epitaph on Edward Courtenay, Earl of Devonshire (d. 1419) and his wife
at Tiverton, in Thomas Westcote *A View of Devonshire in 1630* (ed. G. Oliver and P. Jones, 1845); variants appear in Tristram Risdon *Survey of the County of Devon* (1714) and Edmund Spenser *The Shepherd's Calendar* (1579)

14 When you go home, tell them of us and say,
'For your tomorrow we gave our today.'
Kohima memorial to the Burma campaign of the Second World War; in recent years used at Remembrance Day parades in the UK; cf. **Binyon** 115:8

When you go home, tell them of us and say,
'For your tomorrows these gave their today.'
John Maxwell Edmonds (1875–1958) *Inscriptions Suggested for War Memorials* (1919)

15 Without you, Heaven would be too dull to bear,
And Hell would not be Hell if you are there.
epitaph for Maurice **Bowra**
John **Sparrow**, in *Times Literary Supplement* 30 May 1975

Euripides *c.*485–*c.*406 BC
Greek dramatist

16 Never shall I say that marriage brings more joy than pain.
Alcestis l. 238

17 Be happy, drink, think each day your own as you live it and leave the rest to fortune.
Alcestis l. 788

18 Nothing have I found stronger than Necessity.
Alcestis l. 965

19 My tongue swore, but my mind's unsworn.
Hippolytus lamenting his breaking of an oath
Hippolytus l. 612

20 Better a life of wretchedness than a noble death.
Iphigenia in Tauris l. 1252

1 When passions come upon men in strength beyond due measure their gift is neither one of glory nor of greatness.
Medea l. 627

2 The man is to be envied who has been fortunate in his children, and has avoided dire calamity.
Orestes l. 542

3 You mention a slave's condition; not to say what one thinks.
The Phoenician Women l. 392

John Evelyn 1620–1706
English diarist

4 This knight was indeed a valiant Gent: but not a little given to romance, when he spake of himself.
E. S. de Beer (ed.) *Diary of John Evelyn* (1955) 6 September 1651

5 Mulberry Garden, now the only place of refreshment about the town for persons of the best quality to be exceedingly cheated at.
E. S. de Beer (ed.) *Diary of John Evelyn* (1955) 10 May 1654

6 That miracle of a youth, Mr Christopher Wren.
E. S. de Beer (ed.) *Diary of John Evelyn* (1955) 11 July 1654

7 I saw Hamlet Prince of Denmark played, but now the old play began to disgust this refined age.
E. S. de Beer (ed.) *Diary of John Evelyn* (1955) 26 November 1661

Lord Eversley see **Charles Shaw-Lefevre**

Gavin Ewart 1916–95
British poet

8 So the last date slides into the bracket,
that will appear in all future anthologies—
And in quiet Cornwall and in London's ghastly
racket
We are now Betjemanless.
'In Memoriam, Sir John Betjeman (1906–84)' (1985)

9 The path of true love isn't smooth,
the ruffled feathers sex can soothe
ruffle again—for couples never
spend all their lives in bed together.
'24th March 1986' (1987)

10 Is it Colman's smile
That makes life worth while
Or Crawford's significant form?
Is it Lombard's lips
Or Mae West's hips
That carry you through the storm?
'Verse from an Opera' (1939)

William Norman Ewer 1885–1976
British writer

11 I gave my life for freedom—This I know:
For those who bade me fight had told me so.
'Five Souls' (1917)

12 How odd
Of God
To choose
The Jews.
Week-End Book (1924); cf. **Browne** 152:9

Richard Eyre 1943–
English theatre director

13 We exercise the ultimate sanction of switching off only in an extreme case, like a heroin addict rejecting the needle in the face of death.
on television as an agent of cultural destruction
attributed, 1995

Frederick William Faber 1814–63
English priest

14 Faith of our Fathers! living still
In spite of dungeon, fire, and sword:
Oh, how our hearts beat fast with joy
Whene'er they hear that glorious word.
Faith of our Fathers! Holy Faith!
We will be true to thee till death.
'Faith of our Fathers'

15 Faith of our Fathers! Mary's prayers
Shall win our country back to thee
And by the truth that comes from God
England shall then indeed be free.
'Faith of our Fathers'

16 My God, how wonderful Thou art!
Thy Majesty how bright!
Oratory Hymns (1854) 'The Eternal Father'

17 The music of the Gospel leads us home.
Oratory Hymns (1854) 'The Pilgrims of the Night'

18 There's a wideness in God's mercy
Like the wideness of the sea.
Oratory Hymns (1854) 'Souls of men, why will ye scatter'

19 Dark night hath come down on us, Mother! and
we
Look out for thy shining, sweet Star of the Sea!
'O Purest of Creatures'

Quintus Fabius Maximus *c.*275–203 BC
Roman politician and general

20 To be turned from one's course by men's opinions, by blame, and by misrepresentation shows a man unfit to hold an office.
Plutarch *Parallel Lives* 'Fabius Maximus'

Robert Fabyan d. 1513
English chronicler

21 Finally he paid the debt of nature.
The New Chronicles of England and France (1516) vol. 1, ch. 41

22 King Henry [I] being in Normandy, after some writers, fell from or with his horse, whereof he caught his death; but Ranulphe says he took a surfeit by eating of a lamprey, and thereof died.
The New Chronicles of England and France (1516) vol. 1, ch. 229

23 The Duke of Clarence . . . then being a prisoner in the Tower, was secretly put to death and drowned

in a barrel of Malmesey wine within the said Tower.

The New Chronicles of England and France (1516) vol. 2 '1478'; 'malvesye' for 'malmesey' in early editions

Clifton Fadiman 1904–

American critic

1 Milk's leap toward immortality.

of cheese

Any Number Can Play (1957)

2 The mama of dada.

of Gertrude **Stein**

Party of One (1955)

Émile Faguet 1847–1916

French writer and critic

3 It would be equally reasonable to say that sheep are born carnivorous, and everywhere nibble grass.

in response to Rousseau (see **Rousseau** *636:5)*

paraphrasing Joseph de Maistre; *Politiques et Moralistes du Dix-Neuvième Siècle* (1899)

Thomas Fairfax 1621–71

English Parliamentary general, appointed commander of the New Model Army in 1645, and replaced in 1650 by Oliver **Cromwell** *for refusing to march against the Scots, who had proclaimed the future* **Charles II** *king*

4 Human probabilities are not sufficient grounds to make war upon a neighbour nation.

to the proposal in 1650 to forestall an expected Scottish attack by invading Scotland

in *Dictionary of National Biography* (1917–)

Marianne Faithfull 1946–

British singer

5 Maybe the most that you can expect from a relationship that goes bad is to come out of it with a few good songs.

Faithfull (1994) 'Colston Hall'

Lucius Cary, Lord Falkland 1610–43

English royalist politician

on Falkland: see **Clarendon** *218:21, 218:22*

6 When it is not necessary to change, it is necessary not to change.

Discourses of Infallibility (1660) 'A Speech concerning Episcopacy' delivered in 1641

Frantz Fanon 1925–61

French West Indian psychoanalyst and writer

7 Leave this Europe where they are never done talking of Man, yet murder men everywhere they find them.

The Wretched of the Earth (1961)

8 The shape of Africa resembles a revolver, and Zaire is the trigger.

attributed

Richard Fanshawe 1605–66

English diplomat and translator

9 Ten years the world upon him falsely smiled,
Sheathing in fawning looks the deadly knife
Long aimed at his head; that so beguiled
It more securely might bereave his life:
Then threw him to a scaffold from a throne.
Much doctrine lies under this little stone.

The Faithful Shepherd (1648) 'The Fall'; translation of G. B. Guarini's *Il pastor fido*, 1589

10 White Peace (the beautiful'st of things)
Seems here her everlasting rest
To fix, and spreads her downy wings over the nest.

The Faithful Shepherd (1648) 'An Ode, upon occasion of His Majesty's Proclamation in the Year 1630'

Michael Faraday 1791–1867

English physicist and chemist

11 The most prominent requisite to a lecturer, though perhaps not really the most important, is a good delivery; for though to all true philosophers science and nature will have charms innumerable in every dress, yet I am sorry to say that the generality of mankind cannot accompany us one short hour unless the path is strewed with flowers.

Advice to a Lecturer (1960); from his letters and notebook written at age 21

12 Nothing is too wonderful to be true, if it be consistent with the laws of nature, and in such things as these, experiment is the best test of such consistency.

diary, 19 March 1849; *Faraday's Diary* (1934 ed.) vol. 5

13 Tyndall, I must remain plain Michael Faraday to the last; and let me now tell you, that if I accepted the honour which the Royal Society desires to confer upon me, I would not answer for the integrity of my intellect for a single year.

on being offered the Presidency of the Royal Society

J. Tyndall *Faraday as a Discoverer* (1868) 'Illustrations of Character'

14 Why sir, there is every possibility that you will soon be able to tax it!

to Gladstone, when asked about the usefulness of electricity

W. E. H. Lecky *Democracy and Liberty* (1899 ed.)

Eleanor Farjeon 1881–1965

English writer for children

15 Morning has broken
Like the first morning,
Blackbird has spoken
Like the first bird.

Children's Bells (1957) 'A Morning Song (for the First Day of Spring)'

Herbert Farjeon 1887–1945

English writer and theatre critic

16 For I've danced with a man.
I've danced with a man
Who—well, you'll never guess.

I've danced with a man who's danced with a girl
Who's danced with the Prince of Wales!
'I've danced with a man who's danced with a girl'; first written for Elsa Lanchester and sung at private parties; later sung on stage by Mimi Crawford (1928)

James Farley 1888–1976
American Democratic politician

1 As Maine goes, so goes Vermont.
*after predicting correctly that Franklin **Roosevelt** would carry all but two states in the election of 1936; cf. **Political slogans** 581:5*
statement to the press, 4 November 1936

Edward Farmer *c.*1809–76
English poet

2 I have no pain, dear mother, now;
But oh! I am so dry:
Just moisten poor Jim's lips once more;
And, mother, do not cry!
'The Collier's Dying Child'; cf. **Anonymous** 16:21

Farouk 1920–65
King of Egypt, 1936–52

3 The whole world is in revolt. Soon there will be only five Kings left—the King of England, the King of Spades, the King of Clubs, the King of Hearts and the King of Diamonds.
said to Lord Boyd-Orr at a conference in Cairo, 1948; *As I Recall* (1966) ch. 21

George Farquhar 1678–1707
Irish dramatist

4 Sir, you shall taste my *Anno Domini*.
The Beaux' Stratagem (1707) act 1, sc. 1

5 I have fed purely upon ale; I have eat my ale, drank my ale, and I always sleep upon ale.
The Beaux' Stratagem (1707) act 1, sc. 1

6 My Lady Bountiful.
The Beaux' Stratagem (1707) act 1, sc. 1

7 There is no scandal like rags, nor any crime so shameful as poverty.
The Beaux' Stratagem (1707) act 1, sc. 1

8 There's some diversion in a talking blockhead; and since a woman must wear chains, I would have the pleasure of hearing 'em rattle a little.
The Beaux' Stratagem (1707) act 2, sc. 2

9 No woman can be a beauty without a fortune.
The Beaux' Stratagem (1707) act 2, sc. 2

10 I believe they talked of me, for they laughed consumedly.
The Beaux' Stratagem (1707) act 3, sc. 1

11 'Twas for the good of my country that I should be abroad.—Anything for the good of one's country—I'm a Roman for that.
The Beaux' Stratagem (1707) act 3, sc. 2

12 AIMWELL: Then you understand Latin, Mr Bonniface?
BONNIFACE: Not I, Sir, as the saying is, but he talks it so very fast that I'm sure it must be good.
The Beaux' Stratagem (1707) act 3, sc. 2

13 Spare all I have, and take my life.
The Beaux' Stratagem (1707) act 5, sc. 2

14 I hate all that don't love me, and slight all that do.
The Constant Couple (1699) act 1, sc. 2

15 Grant me some wild expressions, Heavens, or I shall burst— . . . Words, words or I shall burst.
The Constant Couple (1699) act 5, sc. 3

16 Charming women can true converts make,
We love the precepts for the teacher's sake.
The Constant Couple (1699) act 5, sc. 3; cf. **Defoe** 255:5

17 Crimes, like virtues, are their own rewards.
The Inconstant (1702) act 4, sc. 2

18 Money is the sinews of love, as of war.
Love and a Bottle (1698) act 2, sc. 1; cf. **Cicero** 217:23

19 Poetry's a mere drug, Sir.
Love and a Bottle (1698) act 3, sc. 2; cf. **Lowell** 477:10

20 Hanging and marriage, you know, go by Destiny
The Recruiting Officer (1706) act 3, sc. 2

21 I could be mighty foolish, and fancy my self mighty witty; Reason still keeps its throne, but it nods a little, that's all.
The Recruiting Officer (1706) act 3, sc. 2

22 I'm privileged to be very impertinent, being an Oxonian.
Sir Harry Wildair (1701) act 2, sc. 1

23 A lady, if undressed at Church, looks silly,
One cannot be devout in dishabilly.
The Stage Coach (1704) prologue

David Glasgow Farragut 1801–70
American admiral

24 Damn the torpedoes! Full speed ahead.
at the battle of Mobile Bay, 5 August 1864
(torpedoes *mines*)
A. T. Mahan *Great Commanders: Admiral Farragut* (1892) ch. 10

William Faulkner 1897–1962
American novelist
*see also **Film titles** 312:22*

25 The past is never dead. It's not even past.
Requiem for a Nun (1951) act 1

26 He made the books and he died.
his own 'sum and history of my life'
letter to Malcolm Cowley, 11 February 1949

27 I believe man will not merely endure, he will prevail. He is immortal, not because he, alone among creatures, has an inexhaustible voice but because he has a soul, a spirit capable of compassion and sacrifice and endurance.
Nobel Prize acceptance speech, Stockholm, 10 December 1950

28 The poet's voice need not merely be the record of man; it can be one of the props, the pillars, to help him endure and prevail.
Nobel prize speech, Stockholm, 10 December 1950

1 The writer's only responsibility is to his art. He will be completely ruthless if he is a good one. He has a dream. It anguishes him so much he must get rid of it. He has no peace until then. Everything goes by the board . . . If a writer has to rob his mother, he will not hesitate; the *Ode on a Grecian Urn* is worth any number of old ladies.
in *Paris Review* Spring 1956

2 A man shouldn't fool with booze until he's fifty; then he's a damn fool if he doesn't.
James M. Webb and A. Wigfall Green *William Faulkner of Oxford* (1965)

Guy Fawkes 1570–1606
English conspirator in the Gunpowder Plot, 1605

3 A desperate disease requires a dangerous remedy.
6 November 1605, in *Dictionary of National Biography* (1917–); cf. **Proverbs** 598:5, **Shakespeare** 665:26

Vicki Feaver 1943–
British poet

4 Sometimes I have wanted
to throw you off
like a heavy coat.
Sometimes I have said
you would not let me
breathe or move.
'Coat'

Ellen Fein and **Sherrie Schneider**

5 Rule 1. Be a 'creature unlike any other'.
The Rules: Time Tested Secrets for Capturing the Heart of Mr Right (1995)

Dianne Feinstein 1933–
American Democratic politician, Mayor of San Francisco

6 Toughness doesn't have to come in a pinstripe suit.
in *Time* 4 June 1984

7 There was a time when you could say the least government was the best—but not in the nation's most populous state.
campaign speech, 15 March 1990

James Fenton 1949–
English poet

8 It is not what they built. It is what they knocked down.
It is not the houses. It is the spaces between the houses.
It is not the streets that exist. It is the streets that no longer exist.
German Requiem (1981)

9 'I didn't exist at Creation
I didn't exist at the Flood,
And I won't be around for Salvation
To sort out the sheep from the cud—
'Or whatever the phrase is. The fact is
In soteriological terms
I'm a crude existential malpractice
And you are a diet of worms.'
'God, A Poem' (1983)

10 Yes
You have come upon the fabled lands where myths
Go when they die.
'The Pitt-Rivers Museum' (1983)

11 Windbags can be right. Aphorists can be wrong. It is a tough world.
in *Times* 21 February 1985

Edna Ferber 1887–1968
American writer

12 Being an old maid is like death by drowning, a really delightful sensation after you cease to struggle.
R. E. Drennan *Wit's End* (1973)

13 Only amateurs say that they write for their own amusement. Writing is not an amusing occupation. It is a combination of ditch-digging, mountain-climbing, treadmill and childbirth. Writing may be interesting, absorbing, exhilarating, racking, relieving. But amusing? Never!
A Peculiar Treasure (1939)

14 Roast Beef, Medium, is not only a food. It is a philosophy.
foreword to *Roast Beef, Medium* (1911)

Robert Fergusson 1750–74
Scottish poet

15 For thof ye had as wise a snout on
As Shakespeare or Sir Isaac Newton,
Your judgement fouk woud hae a doubt on,
I'll tak my aith,
Till they could see ye wi' a suit on
O' gude Braid Claith.
'Braid Claith' (1773)

16 The Lawyers may revere that tree
Where thieves so oft have swung,
Since, by the Law's most wise decree,
Her thieves are never hung.
'Epigram on a Lawyer's desiring one of the Tribe to look with respect to a Gibbet' (1779)

Samuel Ferguson 1810–86
Irish poet

17 I walked through Ballinderry in the springtime,
When the bud was on the tree,
And I said, in every fresh-ploughed field beholding
The sowers striding free,
Scattering broadcast forth the corn in golden plenty
On the quick, seed-clasping soil
Even such, this day, among the fresh-stirred hearts of Erin,
Thomas Davis, is thy toil.
'Lament for the Death of Thomas Davis'

18 As I heard the sweet lark sing
In the clear air of the day.
'The Lark in the Clear Air'

Pierre de Fermat 1601–65

French mathematician

1 *Cuius rei demonstrationem mirabilem sane detexi hanc marginis exiguitas non caperet.*

I have a truly marvellous demonstration of this proposition which this margin is too narrow to contain.

of 'Fermat's last theorem', written in the margin of his copy of Diophantus' Arithmetica, *and subsequently published by his son in 1670 in an edition of the book containing Fermat's annotations*

Simon Singh *Fermat's Last Theorem* (1997)

Enrico Fermi 1901–54

Italian-born American atomic physicist

2 If I could remember the names of all these particles I'd be a botanist.

R. L. Weber *More Random Walks in Science* (1973)

3 Whatever Nature has in store for mankind, unpleasant as it may be, men must accept, for ignorance is never better than knowledge.

Laura Fermi *Atoms in the Family* (1955)

Ludwig Feuerbach 1804–72

German philosopher

4 *Der Mensch ist, was er isst.*

Man is what he eats.

Jacob Moleschott *Lehre der Nahrungsmittel: Für das Volk* (1850) 'Advertisement'; cf. **Brillat-Savarin** 148:17, **Proverbs** 615:22

Paul Feyerabend 1924–94

Austrian philosopher

5 The time is overdue for adding the separation of state and science to the by now customary separation of state and church. Science is only *one* of the many instruments man has invented to cope with his surroundings. It is not the only one, it is not infallible, and it has become too powerful, too pushy, and too dangerous to be left on its own.

Against Method (1975)

Richard Phillips Feynman 1918–88

American theoretical physicist

6 For a successful technology, reality must take precedence over public relations, for nature cannot be fooled.

appendix to the *Rogers Commission Report on the Space Shuttle Challenger Accident* 6 June 1986

7 What I cannot create, I do not understand.

attributed

Eugene Field 1850–95

American poet and journalist

8 But I, when I undress me
Each night, upon my knees,
Will ask the Lord to bless me,
With apple pie and cheese.

'Apple Pie and Cheese' (1889)

9 Wynken, Blynken, and Nod one night
Sailed off in a wooden shoe—
Sailed on a river of crystal light,
Into a sea of dew.

'Wynken, Blynken, and Nod' (1889)

10 He played the King as though under momentary apprehension that someone else was about to play the ace.

of Creston Clarke as King Lear

review attributed to Field, in the *Denver Tribune* c.1880

Frank Field 1942–

British Labour politician

11 The archbishop is usually to be found nailing his colours to the fence.

of Archbishop **Runcie**; *a similar comment has been recorded on A. J.* **Balfour**, *c.1904*

attributed in *Crockfords 1987/88* (1987)

Helen Fielding 1958–

British writer

12 I will not . . . sulk about having no boyfriend, but develop inner poise and authority and sense of self as woman of substance, complete *without* boyfriend, as best way to obtain boyfriend.

Bridget Jones's Diary (1996)

13 When someone leaves you . . . the worst is the thought that they tried you out and, in the end, the whole sum of parts which adds up to you got stamped REJECT by the one you love. How can you not be left with the personal confidence of a passed-over British Rail sandwich?

Bridget Jones's Diary (1996)

Henry Fielding 1707–54

English novelist and dramatist

on Fielding: see **Richardson** *627:8*

14 It hath been often said, that it is not death, but dying, which is terrible.

Amelia (1751) bk. 3, ch. 4

15 One fool at least in every married couple.

Amelia (1751) bk. 9, ch. 4

16 The dusky night rides down the sky,
And ushers in the morn;
The hounds all join in glorious cry,
The huntsman winds his horn:
And a-hunting we will go.

Don Quixote in England (1733) act 2, sc. 5 'A-Hunting We Will Go'

17 Oh! The roast beef of England,
And old England's roast beef.

The Grub Street Opera (1731) act 3, sc. 3

18 He in a few minutes ravished this fair creature, or at least would have ravished her, if she had not, by a timely compliance, prevented him.

Jonathan Wild (1743) bk. 3, ch. 7

19 To whom nothing is given, of him can nothing be required.

Joseph Andrews (1742) bk. 2, ch. 8

1 I describe not men, but manners; not an individual, but a species.
Joseph Andrews (1742) bk. 3, ch. 1

2 Public schools are the nurseries of all vice and immorality.
Joseph Andrews (1742) bk. 3, ch. 5

3 A lottery is a taxation
Upon all the fools in creation
And Heaven be praised
It is easily rais'd,
Credulity's always in fashion.
The Lottery (1732) sc. 1

4 Love and scandal are the best sweeteners of tea.
Love in Several Masques (1728) act 4, sc. 11

5 Necessity is a bad recommendation to favours . . . which as seldom fall to those who really want them, as to those who really deserve them.
The Modern Husband (1732) act 2, sc. 5

6 Map me no maps, sir, my head is a map, a map of the whole world.
Rape upon Rape (1730) act 2, sc. 5

7 When I mention religion, I mean the Christian religion; and not only the Christian religion, but the Protestant religion; and not only the Protestant religion but the Church of England.
Tom Jones (1749) bk. 3, ch. 3

8 Thwackum was for doing justice, and leaving mercy to heaven.
Tom Jones (1749) bk. 3, ch. 10

9 What is commonly called love, namely the desire of satisfying a voracious appetite with a certain quantity of delicate white human flesh.
Tom Jones (1749) bk. 6, ch. 1

10 O! more than Gothic ignorance.
Tom Jones (1749) bk. 7, ch. 3

11 The only supernatural agents which can in any manner be allowed to us moderns, are ghosts; but of these I would advise an author to be extremely sparing. These are indeed like arsenic, and other dangerous drugs in physic, to be used with the utmost caution; nor would I advise the introduction of them at all in those works, or by those authors, to which or to whom a horse-laugh in the reader would be any great prejudice or mortification.
Tom Jones (1749) bk. 8, ch. 1

12 His designs were strictly honourable, as the phrase is; that is, to rob a lady of her fortune by way of marriage.
Tom Jones (1749) bk. 11, ch. 4

13 That monstrous animal, a husband and wife.
Tom Jones (1749) bk. 15, ch. 9

14 All Nature wears one universal grin.
Tom Thumb the Great (1731) act 1, sc. 1

15 When I'm not thanked at all, I'm thanked enough,
I've done my duty, and I've done no more.
Tom Thumb the Great (1731) act 1, sc. 3

Dorothy Fields 1905–74

American songwriter

16 A fine romance with no kisses.
A fine romance, my friend, this is.
'A Fine Romance' (1936 song)

17 Grab your coat, and get your hat,
Leave your worry on the doorstep,
Just direct your feet
To the sunny side of the street.
'On the Sunny Side of the Street' (1930 song)

W. C. Fields (William Claude Dukenfield) 1880–1946

American humorist
on Fields: see **Rosten** *635:17; see also* **Epitaphs** *303:5*

18 Never give a sucker an even break.
title of a W. C. Fields film (1941); the catchphrase (Fields's own) is said to have originated in the musical comedy *Poppy* (1923); cf. **Proverbs** 607:29

19 Some weasel took the cork out of my lunch.
You Can't Cheat an Honest Man (1939 film)

20 It ain't a fit night out for man or beast.
adopted by Fields but claimed by him not to be original; letter, 8 February 1944, in *W. C. Fields by Himself* (1974) pt. 2

21 Fish fuck in it.
on being asked why he never drank water
attributed

22 Hell, I never vote *for* anybody. I always vote *against*.
Robert Lewis Taylor *W. C. Fields* (1950); cf. **Adams** 2:8

23 Never cry over spilt milk, because it may have been poisoned.
Carlotta Monti with Cy Rice *W. C. Fields and Me* (1971)

□ Film lines

see box opposite
see also Woody **Allen**, *W. C.* **Fields**, *Greta* **Garbo**, *Stan* **Laurel**, *Mae* **West**

□ Film titles

see box overleaf

Alain Finkielkraut

French philosopher

24 Civilized people must get off their high horse and learn with humble lucidity that they too are an indigenous variety.
describing **Lévi-Strauss**'s *views*
The Undoing of Thought (1988)

25 Is there a culture where there is corporal punishment for delinquency . . . where female circumcision is practised, where mixed marriages
continued

Film lines

1 Anyway, Ma, I made it . . . Top of the world!

White Heat (1949 film) written by Ivan Goff (1910–) and Ben Roberts (1916–84); last lines—spoken by James Cagney

2 Cancel the kitchen scraps for lepers and orphans. No more merciful beheadings. And call off Christmas!

Robin Hood, Prince of Thieves (1991 film), written by Pen Densham and John Watson; spoken by Alan Rickman

3 Don't let's ask for the moon! We have the stars!

Now, Voyager (1942 film), from the novel (1941) by Olive Higgins Prouty (1882–1974); spoken by Bette Davis

4 Either he's dead, or my watch has stopped.

A Day at the Races (1937 film) written by Robert Pirosh, George Seaton, and George Oppenheimer; spoken by Groucho **Marx**

5 E.T. phone home.

E.T. (1982 film) written by Melissa Mathison (1950–)

6 Fasten your seat-belts, it's going to be a bumpy night.

All About Eve (1950 film) written by Joseph L. Mankiewicz (1909–); spoken by Bette Davis

7 Frankly, my dear, I don't give a damn!

Gone with the Wind (1939 film) written by Sidney Howard; spoken by Clark Gable; cf. **Mitchell** 524:2

8 Go ahead, make my day.

Sudden Impact (1983 film) written by Joseph C. Stinson (1947–); spoken by Clint Eastwood

9 Greed—for lack of a better word—is good. Greed is right. Greed works.

Wall Street (1987 film) written by Stanley Weiser and Oliver Stone (1946–); cf. **Boesky** 123:10

10 Here's looking at you, kid.

Casablanca (1942 film) written by Julius J. Epstein (1909–), Philip G. Epstein (1909–52), and Howard Koch (1902–95); spoken by Humphrey Bogart to Ingrid Bergman

11 I could have had class. I could have been a contender.

On the Waterfront (1954 film) written by Budd **Schulberg**; spoken by Marlon Brando

12 If she can stand it, I can. Play it!

usually quoted as 'Play it again, Sam'

Casablanca (1942 film) written by Julius J. Epstein (1909–), Philip G. Epstein (1909–52), and Howard Koch (1902–95); spoken by Humphrey Bogart; cf. **Misquotations** 522:6

13 If you can't leave in a taxi you can leave in a huff. If that's too soon, you can leave in a minute and a huff.

Duck Soup (1933 film) written by Bert Kalmar (1884–1947), Harry Ruby (1895–1974), Arthur Sheekman (1891–1978), and Nat Perrin; spoken by Groucho **Marx**

14 I'll have what she's having.

woman to waiter, seeing Sally acting an orgasm

When Harry Met Sally (1989 film) written by Nora Ephron (1941–)

15 I love the smell of napalm in the morning. It smells like victory.

Apocalypse Now (1979 film) written by John Milius and Francis Ford Coppola (1939–); spoken by Robert Duvall

16 In Italy for thirty years under the Borgias they had warfare, terror, murder, bloodshed—they produced Michelangelo, Leonardo da Vinci and the Renaissance. In Switzerland they had brotherly love, five hundred years of democracy and peace and what did that produce . . . ? The cuckoo clock.

The Third Man (1949 film); words added by Orson **Welles** to Graham **Greene**'s screenplay

17 It's a funny old world—a man's lucky if he gets out of it alive.

You're Telling Me (1934 film), written by Walter de Leon and Paul M. Jones; spoken by W. C. **Fields**; cf. **Thatcher** 770:13

18 DRIFTWOOD (Groucho Marx): It's all right. That's—that's in every contract. That's—that's what they call a sanity clause.

FIORELLO (Chico Marx): You can't fool me. There ain't no Sanity Claus.

Night at the Opera (1935 film) written by George S. Kaufman (1889–1961) and Morrie Ryskind (1895–1985)

19 Let's get out of these wet clothes and into a dry Martini.

line coined in the 1920s by Robert **Benchley**'s press agent and adopted by Mae **West** in *Every Day's a Holiday* (1937 film)

20 Madness! Madness!

The Bridge on the River Kwai (1957 film of the novel by Pierre Boulle) written by Carl Foreman (1914–84), closing line

21 Major Strasser has been shot. Round up the usual suspects.

Casablanca (1942 film) written by Julius J. Epstein (1909–), Philip G. Epstein (1909–52), and Howard Koch (1902–95); spoken by Claude Rains

22 The man you love to hate.

anonymous billing for Erich von Stroheim in the film *The Heart of Humanity* (1918)

23 Man your ships, and may the force be with you.

Star Wars (1977 film) written by George Lucas (1944–)

24 Marriage isn't a word . . . it's a *sentence*!

The Crowd (1928 film) written by King Vidor (1895–1982)

25 Maybe just whistle. You know how to whistle, don't you, Steve? You just put your lips together and blow.

To Have and Have Not (1944 film) written by Jules Furthman (1888–1960) and William **Faulkner**; spoken by Lauren **Bacall**

Film lines *continued*

1 Mr Kane was a man who got everything he wanted, and then lost it. Maybe Rosebud was something he couldn't get or something he lost. Anyway, it wouldn't have explained anything. I don't think any word can explain a man's life. No, I guess Rosebud is just a piece in a jigsaw puzzle, a missing piece.

Citizen Kane (1941 film) written by Herman J. Mankiewicz (1897–1953) and Orson **Welles**

2 My momma always said life was like a box of chocolates . . . you never know what you're gonna get.

Forrest Gump (1994 film), written by Eric Ross, based on the novel (1986) by Winston Groom; spoken by Tom Hanks

3 Nature, Mr Allnutt, is what we are put into this world to rise above.

The African Queen (1951 film) written by James Agee 1909–55; spoken by Katharine Hepburn; not in the novel by C. S. Forester

4 Of all the gin joints in all the towns in all the world, she walks into mine.

Casablanca (1942 film) written by Julius J. Epstein (1909–), Philip G. Epstein (1909–52), and Howard Koch (1902–95); spoken by Humphrey Bogart

5 Oh no, it wasn't the aeroplanes. It was Beauty killed the Beast.

King Kong (1933 film) written by James Creelman (1901–41) and Ruth Rose, final words

6 The pellet with the poison's in the vessel with the pestle. The chalice from the palace has the brew that is true.

The Court Jester (1955 film) written by Norman Panama (1914–) and Melvin Frank (1913–88; spoken by Danny Kaye)

7 Remember, you're fighting for this woman's honour . . . which is probably more than she ever did.

Duck Soup (1933 film) written by Bert Kalmar (1884–1947), Harry Ruby (1895–1974), Arthur Sheekman (1891–1978), and Nat Perrin; spoken by Groucho **Marx**

8 The son of a bitch stole my watch!

The Front Page (1931 film), from the play (1928) by Charles MacArthur (1895–1956) and Ben **Hecht**

9 GERRY: We can't get married at all....I'm a man.
OSGOOD: Well, nobody's perfect.

Some Like It Hot (1959 film) written by Billy **Wilder** and I. A. L. Diamond; closing words spoken by Jack Lemmon and Joe E. Brown

10 What a dump!

Beyond the Forest (1949 film) written by Lenore Coffee (?1897–1984); line spoken by Bette Davis, entering a room

11 Why, a four-year-old child could understand this report. Run out and find me a four-year-old child. I can't make head or tail of it.

Duck Soup (1933 film) written by Bert Kalmar (1884–1947), Harry Ruby (1895–1974), Arthur Sheekman (1891–1978), and Nat Perrin; spoken by Groucho **Marx**

12 NINOTCHKA: Why should you carry other people's bags?
PORTER: Well, that's my business, Madame.
NINOTCHKA: That's no business. That's social injustice.
PORTER: That depends on the tip.

Ninotchka (1939 film) written by Charles Brackett (1892–1969), Billy **Wilder**, and Walter Reisch (1903–1983)

13 You're going out a youngster but you've *got* to come back a star.

42nd Street (1933 film) written by James Seymour and Rian James

14 You're here to stay until the rustle in your dying throat relieves you!

Beau Hunks (1931 film; re-named *Beau Chumps* for British audiences) written by H. M. Walker; addressed to **Laurel** and Hardy

15 JOE GILLIS: You used to be in pictures. You used to be big.
NORMA DESMOND: I am big. It's the pictures that got small.

Sunset Boulevard (1950 film) written by Charles Brackett (1892–1969), Billy **Wilder**, and D. M. Marshman Jr

Film titles

16 Back to the future.

written by Robert Zemeckis and Bob Gale, 1985

17 Close encounters of the third kind.

written by Steven Spielberg (1947–), 1977

18 The discreet charm of the bourgeoisie.

written by Luis **Buñuel**, 1972

19 The Empire strikes back.

written by George Lucas (1944–), 1980

20 Every which way but loose.

written by Jeremy Joe Kronsberg, 1978; starring Clint Eastwood

21 The good, the bad, and the ugly.

written by Age Scarpelli, Luciano Vincenzoni (1926–), and Sergio Leone (1921–), 1966

22 The long hot summer.
based on stories by William ***Faulkner***

written by Irving Ravetch and Harriet Frank, 1958; 'The Long Summer' is the title of bk. 3 of Faulkner's *The Hamlet* (1940)

23 Naughty but nice.

written by Jerry Wald (1911–62) and Richard Macaulay, 1939

24 Never on Sunday.

written by Jules Dassin (1911–), 1959

Film titles *continued*

1 Rebel without a cause.

written by R. M. Lindner (1914–56), 1959, based on his book (1944); starring James Dean

2 Sunday, bloody Sunday.

written by Penelope **Gilliatt**, 1971

3 Suppose they gave a war and nobody came?

written by Don McGuire and Hal Captain, 1969; 'Suppose They Gave a War and No One Came?' was the title of a piece by Charlotte Keyes in *McCall's* October 1966; see **Ginsberg** 339:19, **Sandburg** 644:2

4 Sweet smell of success.

written by Ernest Lehman (1920–), 1957

Alain Finkielkraut *continued*

are forbidden and polygamy authorized? Multiculturalism requires that we respect all these practices . . . In a world which has lost its transcendental significance, cultural identity serves to sanction those barbarous traditions which God is no longer in a position to endorse. Fanaticism is indefensible when it appeals to heaven, but beyond reproach when it is grounded in antiquity and cultural distinctiveness.

The Undoing of Thought (1988)

Ronald Firbank 1886–1926

English novelist

5 'O! help me, heaven,' she prayed, 'to be decorative and to do right!'

The Flower Beneath the Foot (1923) ch. 2

6 There was a pause—just long enough for an angel to pass, flying slowly.

Vainglory (1915) ch. 6

7 The world is disgracefully managed, one hardly knows to whom to complain.

Vainglory (1915) ch. 10

L'Abbé Edgeworth de Firmont 1745–1807

Irish-born confessor to Louis XVI

8 *Fils de Saint Louis, montez au ciel.*

Son of Saint Louis, ascend to heaven.

to Louis XVI as he mounted the steps of the guillotine, 1793

attributed

Michael Fish 1944–

British weather forecaster

9 A woman rang to say she heard there was a hurricane on the way. Well don't worry, there isn't.

weather forecast on the night before serious gales in southern England

BBC TV, 15 October 1987

Carrie Fisher 1956–

American actress and writer

10 Here's how men think. Sex, work—and those are reversible, depending on age—sex, work, food, sports and lastly, begrudgingly, relationships. And here's how women think. Relationships, relationships, relationships, work, sex, shopping, weight, food.

Surrender the Pink (1990)

H. A. L. Fisher 1856–1940

English historian

11 Men wiser and more learned than I have discerned in history a plot, a rhythm, a predetermined pattern. These harmonies are concealed from me. I can see only one emergency following upon another as wave follows upon wave.

A History of Europe (1935)

12 Purity of race does not exist. Europe is a continent of energetic mongrels.

A History of Europe (1935) ch. 1

John Arbuthnot Fisher 1841–1920

British admiral

13 The best scale for an experiment is 12 inches to a foot.

Memories (1919)

14 Sack the lot!

on government overmanning and overspending

letter to *The Times*, 2 September 1919

15 Never contradict
Never explain
Never apologize.

letter to *The Times*, 5 September 1919; cf. **Disraeli** 271:4, **Hubbard** 392:10

16 Yours till Hell freezes.

attributed to Fisher, but not original; see below

Once an officer in India wrote to me and ended his letter "Yours till Hell freezes". I used this forcible expression in a letter to Fisher, and he adopted it.

F. Ponsonby *Reflections of Three Reigns* (1951)

Marve Fisher

American songwriter

17 I like Chopin and Bizet, and the voice of Doris Day,
Gershwin songs and old forgotten carols.
But the music that excels is the sound of oil wells
As they slurp, slurp, slurp into the barrels.

'An Old-Fashioned Girl' (1954 song)

18 I want an old-fashioned house
With an old-fashioned fence
And an old-fashioned millionaire.

'An Old-Fashioned Girl' (1954 song)

R. A. Fisher 1890–1962
English statistician and geneticist

1 The best causes tend to attract to their support the worst arguments.
Statistical Methods and Scientific Inference (1956)

2 It was Darwin's chief contribution, not only to Biology but to the whole of natural science, to have brought to light a process by which contingencies *a priori* improbable are given, in the process of time, an increasing probability, until it is their non-occurrence, rather than their occurence, which becomes highly probable.
sometimes quoted as 'Natural selection is a mechanism for generating an exceedingly high degree of improbability'
'Retrospect of the criticisms of the Theory of Natural Selection' in Julian Huxley *Evolution as a Process* (1954)

Gerry Fitt 1926–
Northern Irish politician

3 People [in Northern Ireland] don't march as an alternative to jogging. They do it to assert their supremacy. It is pure tribalism, the cause of troubles all over the world.
referring to the 'marching season' in Northern Ireland, leading up to the anniversary of the Battle of the Boyne on 12 July, when parades by Orange communities traditionally take place
in *The Times* 5 August 1994

4 The people have spoken and the politicians have had to listen.
on the outcome of the referendum on the Good Friday agreement
in *Sunday Telegraph* 24 May 1998

Albert H. Fitz

5 You are my honey, honeysuckle, I am the bee.
'The Honeysuckle and the Bee' (1901 song)

Charles Fitzgeffrey c.1575–1638
English poet

6 And bold and hard adventures t' undertake,
Leaving his country for his country's sake.
Sir Francis Drake (1596) st. 213

Edward Fitzgerald 1809–83
English scholar and poet

7 Awake! for Morning in the bowl of night
Has flung the stone that puts the stars to flight:
And Lo! the Hunter of the East has caught
The Sultan's turret in a noose of light.
The Rubáiyát of Omar Khayyám (1859) st. 1

8 Each morn a thousand roses brings, you say;
Yes, but where leaves the rose of yesterday?
The Rubáiyát of Omar Khayyám (4th ed., 1879) st. 9

9 Here with a loaf of bread beneath the bough,
A flask of wine, a book of verse—and Thou
Beside me singing in the wilderness—
And wilderness is paradise enow.
The Rubáiyát of Omar Khayyám (1859) st. 11

A book of verses underneath the bough,
A jug of wine, a loaf of bread—and Thou
Beside me singing in the wilderness—
Oh, wilderness were paradise enow!
The Rubáiyát of Omar Khayyám (4th ed., 1879) st. 12

10 Ah, take the cash in hand and waive the rest;
Oh, the brave music of a *distant* drum!
The Rubáiyát of Omar Khayyám (1859) st. 12

Ah, take the cash and let the credit go,
Nor heed the rumble of a distant drum!
The Rubáiyát of Omar Khayyám (4th ed., 1879) st. 13

11 I sometimes think that never blows so red
The rose as where some buried Caesar bled.
The Rubáiyát of Omar Khayyám (1859) st. 18

12 Dust into dust, and under dust, to lie,
Sans wine, sans song, sans singer, and—sans End!
The Rubáiyát of Omar Khayyám (1859) st. 23

13 One thing is certain, and the rest is lies;
The flower that once hath blown for ever dies.
The Rubáiyát of Omar Khayyám (1859) st. 26

One thing is certain and the rest is lies;
The flower that once has blown for ever dies.
The Rubáiyát of Omar Khayyám (4th ed., 1879) st. 63

14 Ah, fill the cup:—what boots it to repeat
How time is slipping underneath our feet:
Unborn TOMORROW, and dead YESTERDAY,
Why fret about them if TODAY be sweet!
The Rubáiyát of Omar Khayyám (1859) st. 37

15 'Tis all a chequer-board of nights and days
Where Destiny with Men for pieces plays:
Hither and thither moves, and mates, and slays,
And one by one back in the closet lays.
The Rubáiyát of Omar Khayyám (1859) st. 49

But helpless pieces of the game he plays
Upon this chequerboard of nights and days;
Hither and thither moves, and checks, and slays,
And one by one back in the closet lays.
The Rubáiyát of Omar Khayyám (4th ed., 1879) st. 69

16 The ball no question makes of Ayes and Noes,
But here or there as strikes the player goes;
And he that tossed you down into the field,
He knows about it all—HE knows—HE knows!
The Rubáiyát of Omar Khayyám (4th ed., 1879) st. 70

17 The moving finger writes; and, having writ,
Moves on: nor all thy piety nor wit
Shall lure it back to cancel half a line,
Nor all thy tears wash out a word of it.
The Rubáiyát of Omar Khayyám (1859) st. 51; 'all your tears' in 4th ed. (1879) st. 71

18 That inverted bowl we call The Sky.
The Rubáiyát of Omar Khayyám (1859) st. 52; 'they call the Sky' in 4th ed. (1879) st. 72

19 They sneer at me for leaning all awry;
What! did the hand then of the potter shake?
The Rubáiyát of Omar Khayyám (4th ed., 1879) st. 86

20 Who *is* the potter, pray, and who the pot?
The Rubáiyát of Omar Khayyám (1859) st. 60

21 Then said another—'Surely not in vain
My substance from the common earth was ta'en,

That He who subtly wrought me into shape,
Should stamp me back to common earth again.'
The Rubáiyát of Omar Khayyám (1859) st. 61

1 Indeed the idols I have loved so long
Have done my credit in this world much wrong:
Have drowned my glory in a shallow cup
And sold my reputation for a song.
The Rubáiyát of Omar Khayyám (4th ed., 1879) st. 93

2 Alas, that spring should vanish with the rose!
That youth's sweet-scented manuscript should close!
The Rubáiyát of Omar Khayyám (1859) st. 72

3 And when Thyself with shining foot shall pass
Among the guests star-scattered on the grass,
And in thy joyous errand reach the spot
Where I made one—turn down an empty glass!
The Rubáiyát of Omar Khayyám (1859) st. 75

And when like her, O Saki, you shall pass
Among the guests star-scattered on the grass,
And in your joyous errand reach the spot
Where I made one—turn down an empty glass!
The Rubáiyát of Omar Khayyám (4th ed., 1879) st. 101

4 Mrs Browning's death is rather a relief to me, I must say: no more Aurora Leighs, thank God! A woman of real genius, I know; but what is the upshot of it all? She and her sex had better mind the kitchen and their children; and perhaps the poor: except in such things as little novels, they only devote themselves to what men do much better, leaving that which men do worse or not at all.
letter to W. H. Thompson, 15 July 1861, in A. M. and A. B. Terhune (eds.) *Letters of Edward Fitzgerald* (1980) vol. 2; cf. **Browning** 158:15

5 Taste is the feminine of genius.
letter to J. R. Lowell, October 1877, in A. M. and A. B. Terhune (eds.) *Letters of Edward Fitzgerald* (1980) vol. 4

F. Scott Fitzgerald 1896–1940

American novelist

6 Let me tell you about the very rich. They are different from you and me.
to which Ernest **Hemingway** *replied, 'Yes, they have more money' (in* Esquire *August 1936 'The Snows of Kilimanjaro')*
All the Sad Young Men (1926) 'Rich Boy'

7 The beautiful and damned.
title of novel (1922)

8 At eighteen our convictions are hills from which we look; at forty-five they are caves in which we hide.
'Bernice Bobs her Hair' (1920)

9 No grand idea was ever born in a conference, but a lot of foolish ideas have died there.
Edmund Wilson (ed.) *The Crack-Up* (1945) 'Note-Books E'

10 Show me a hero and I will write you a tragedy.
Edmund Wilson (ed.) *The Crack-Up* (1945) 'Note-Books E'

11 I've been drunk for about a week now, and I thought it might sober me up to sit in a library.
The Great Gatsby (1925) ch. 3

12 Her voice is full of money.
The Great Gatsby (1925) ch. 7

13 They were careless people, Tom and Daisy—they smashed up things and creatures and then retreated back into their money or their vast carelessness, or whatever it was that kept them together, and let other people clean up the mess they had made.
The Great Gatsby (1925) ch. 9

14 In a real dark night of the soul it is always three o'clock in the morning.
'Handle with Care' in *Esquire* March 1936; cf. **Misquotations** 521:11

15 See that little stream—we could walk to it in two minutes. It took the British a month to walk it—a whole empire walking very slowly, dying in front and pushing forward behind. And another empire walked very slowly backward a few inches a day, leaving the dead like a million bloody rugs.
Tender is the Night (1934)

16 There are no second acts in American lives.
Edmund Wilson (ed.) *The Last Tycoon* (1941) 'Hollywood, etc.'

17 An author ought to write for the youth of his own generation, the critics of the next, and the schoolmasters of ever after.
letter to the Booksellers' Convention, April 1920; Andrew Turnbull (ed.) *Selected Letters of F. Scott Fitzgerald* (1963)

18 All good writing is *swimming under water* and holding your breath.
letter (undated) to his daughter, Frances Scott Fitzgerald; Andrew Turnbull (ed.) *Selected Letters of F. Scott Fitzgerald* (1963)

Garret Fitzgerald 1926–

Irish Fine Gael statesman, Taoiseach 1981–2, 1983–7

19 Living in history is a bit like finding oneself in a shuttered mansion to which one has been brought blindfold, and trying to imagine what it might look like from the outside.
in *Irish Times* 9 May 1998

Robert Fitzsimmons 1862–1917

New Zealand boxer

20 The bigger they are, the further they have to fall.
prior to a fight
in *Brooklyn Daily Eagle* 11 August 1900; cf. **Proverbs** 596:20

Bud Flanagan 1896–1968

British comedian

21 Underneath the Arches,
I dream my dreams away,
Underneath the Arches,
On cobble-stones I lay.
'Underneath the Arches' (1932 song)

Michael Flanders 1922–75 and **Donald Swann** 1923–94

English songwriters

1 Have Some Madeira, M'dear.
title of song (*c.*1956)

2 Mud! Mud! Glorious mud!
Nothing quite like it for cooling the blood.
So, follow me, follow,
Down to the hollow,
And there let us wallow
In glorious mud.
'The Hippopotamus' (1952)

3 Ma's out, Pa's out—let's talk rude:
Pee, po, belly, bum, drawers.
'P**, P*, B****, B**, D******' (*c.*1956)

4 Eating people is wrong!
'The Reluctant Cannibal' (1956 song); adopted as the title of a novel (1959) by Malcolm Bradbury

5 That monarch of the road,
Observer of the Highway Code,
That big six-wheeler
Scarlet-painted
London Transport
Diesel-engined
Ninety-seven horse power
Omnibus!
'A Transport of Delight' (*c.*1956 song)

Thomas Flatman 1637–88

English poet

6 There's an experienced rebel, Time,
And in his squadrons Poverty;
There's Age that brings along with him
A terrible artillery:
And if against all these thou keep'st thy crown,
Th'usurper Death will make thee lay it down.
'The Defiance' (1686)

Gustave Flaubert 1821–80

French novelist

7 *La parole humaine est comme un chaudron fêlé où nous battons des mélodies à faire danser les ours, quand on voudrait attendrir les étoiles.*

Human speech is like a cracked kettle on which we tap crude rhythms for bears to dance to, while we long to make music that will melt the stars.
Madame Bovary (1857) pt. 1, ch. 12 (translated by F. Steegmuller)

8 From time to time, in the towns, I open a newspaper. Things seem to be going at a dizzy rate. We are dancing not on a volcano, but on the rotten seat of a latrine.
letter to Louis Bouilhet, 14 November 1850, in M. Nadeau (ed.) *Correspondence 1846–51* (1964) (translated by F. Steegmuller)

9 Read. Do not brood. Immerse yourself in long study: only the habit of persistent work can make one continually content; it produces an opium that numbs the soul.
letter to Louise Colet, 26 July 1851, in *Letters of Gustave Flaubert* (1980) vol. 1 (translated by F. Steegmuller)

10 What a heavy oar the pen is, and what a strong current ideas are to row in!
letter to Louise Colet, 23 October 1851, in *Letters of Gustave Flaubert* (1980) vol. 1 (translated by F. Steegmuller)

11 It is splendid to be a great writer, to put men into the frying pan of your words and make them pop like chestnuts.
letter to Louise Colet, 3 November 1851, in *Letters of Gustave Flaubert* (1980) vol. 1 (translated by F. Steegmuller)

12 Prose was born yesterday—this is what we must tell ourselves. Poetry is pre-eminently the medium of past literatures. All the metrical combinations have been tried but nothing like this can be said of prose.
letter to Louise Colet, 24 April 1852, in M. Nadeau (ed.) *Correspondence 1852* (1964)

13 You can calculate the worth of a man by the number of his enemies, and the importance of a work of art by the harm that is spoken of it.
letter to Louise Colet, 14 June 1853, in M. Nadeau (ed.) *Correspondence 1853–56* (1964)

14 Unless one is a moron, one always dies unsure of one's own value and that of one's works. Virgil himself, as he lay dying, wanted the Aeneid burned.
letter to Louise Colet, 19 September 1852, in *Letters of Gustave Flaubert* (1980) vol. 1 (translated by F. Steegmuller)

15 Poetry is a subject as precise as geometry.
letter to Louise Colet, 14 August 1853, in M. Nadeau (ed.) *Correspondence 1853–56* (1964)

16 Style is life! It is the very life-blood of thought!
letter to Louise Colet, 7 September 1853, in M. Nadeau (ed.) *Correspondence 1853–56* (1964)

17 The artist must be in his work as God is in creation, invisible and all-powerful; one must sense him everywhere but never see him.
letter to Mademoiselle Leroyer de Chantepie, 18 March 1857, in M. Nadeau (ed.) *Correspondence 1857–64* (1965)

18 Books are made not like children but like pyramids . . . and they're just as useless! and they stay in the desert! . . . Jackals piss at their foot and the bourgeois climb up on them.
letter to Ernest Feydeau, November/December 1857, in M. Nadeau (ed.) *Correspondence 1857–64* (1965)

19 Life is short and Art is long, indeed nearly impossible when one is writing in a language that is worn to the point of being threadbare, so worm-eaten that it frays at every touch.
letter to Mademoiselle Leroyer de Chantepie, 18 February 1859, in *Letters of Gustave Flaubert* (1980) vol. 2 (translated by F. Steegmuller)

20 Human life is a sad show, undoubtedly: ugly, heavy and complex. Art has no other end, for people of feeling, than to conjure away the burden and bitterness.
letter to Amelie Bosquet, July 1864, in M. Nadeau (ed.) *Correspondence 1857–64* (1965)

James Elroy Flecker 1884–1915
English poet

1 West of these out to seas colder than the Hebrides I must go
Where the fleet of stars is anchored and the young Star captains glow.
'The Dying Patriot' (1913)

2 The dragon-green, the luminous, the dark, the serpent-haunted sea.
'The Gates of Damascus' (1913)

3 We who with songs beguile your pilgrimage
And swear that beauty lives though lilies die.
The Golden Journey to Samarkand (1913) 'Prologue'

4 For lust of knowing what should not be known,
We take the Golden Road to Samarkand.
The Golden Journey to Samarkand (1913) pt. 1, 'Epilogue'

5 I have seen old ships sail like swans asleep
Beyond the village which men still call Tyre,
With leaden age o'ercargoed, dipping deep
For Famagusta and the hidden sun
That rings black Cyprus with a lake of fire.
'Old Ships' (1915)

6 A ship, an isle, a sickle moon—
With few but with how splendid stars
The mirrors of the sea are strewn
Between their silver bars!
'A Ship, an Isle, and a Sickle Moon' (1913)

7 O friend unseen, unborn, unknown,
Student of our sweet English tongue,
Read out my words at night, alone:
I was a poet, I was young.
'To a Poet a Thousand Years Hence' (1910)

Richard Flecknoe d. *c.*1678
Irish poet

8 Still-born Silence! thou that art
Floodgate of the deeper heart.
'Invocation of Silence' (1653)

Ian Fleming 1908–64
English thriller writer
see also ***Misquotations*** *521:18*

9 A medium Vodka dry Martini—with a slice of lemon peel. Shaken and not stirred.
Dr No (1958) ch. 14

Marjory Fleming 1803–11
English child writer

10 A direful death indeed they had
That would put any parent mad
But she was more than usual calm
She did not give a singel dam.
Journals, Letters and Verses (ed. A. Esdaile, 1934)

11 The most devilish thing is 8 times 8 and 7 times 7 it is what nature itselfe cant endure.
Journals, Letters and Verses (ed. A. Esdaile, 1934)

12 To-day I pronunced a word which should never come out of a lady's lips it was that I called John a Impudent Bitch.
Journals, Letters and Verses (ed. A. Esdaile, 1934)

13 I am going to turn over a new life and am going to be a very good girl and be obedient to Isa Keith, here there is planty of goosaberys which makes my teath watter.
Journals, Letters and Verses (ed. A. Esdaile, 1934)

14 I hope I will be religious again but as for reganing my charecter I despare for it.
Journals, Letters and Verses (ed. A. Esdaile, 1934)

15 An annibabtist is a thing I am not a member of.
Journals, Letters and Verses (ed. A. Esdaile, 1934)

16 Sentiment is what I am not acquainted with.
Journals, Letters and Verses (ed. A. Esdaile, 1934)

17 My dear Isa, I now sit down on my botom to answer all your kind and beloved letters which you was so good as to write to me.
Journals, Letters and Verses (ed. A. Esdaile, 1934) Letter to Isabella

18 O lovely O most charming pug
Thy graceful air and heavenly mug . . .
His noses cast is of the roman
He is a very pretty weoman
I could not get a rhyme for roman
And was obligded to call it weoman.
'Sonnet'

Peter Fleming 1907–71
English journalist and travel writer

19 São Paulo is like Reading, only much farther away.
Brazilian Adventure (1933)

20 Last night we went to a Chinese dinner at six and a French dinner at nine, and I can feel the sharks' fins navigating unhappily in the Burgundy.
letter from Yunnanfu, 20 March 1938

Robert, Marquis de Flers 1872–1927 and Arman de Caillavet 1869–1915
French dramatists

21 Democracy is the name we give the people whenever we need them.
L'habit vert act 1, sc. 12, in *La petite Illustration série théâtre* 31 May 1913

Andrew Fletcher of Saltoun 1655–1716
Scottish patriot and anti-Unionist

22 If a man were permitted to make all the ballads, he need not care who should make the laws of a nation.
'An Account of a Conversation concerning a Right Regulation of Government for the Good of Mankind. In a Letter to the Marquis of Montrose' (1704) in *Political Works* (1732) pt. 7

John Fletcher 1579–1625

English dramatist

see also **Beaumont and Fletcher**, **Shakespeare** *Henry VIII*

1 Best while you have it use your breath,
There is no drinking after death.
The Bloody Brother, or *Rollo Duke of Normandy* (with Ben Jonson and others, performed *c.*1616) act 2, sc. 2 'Song'

2 And he that will go to bed sober,
Falls with the leaf still in October.
The Bloody Brother act 2, sc. 2 'Song'

3 Three merry boys, and three merry boys,
And three merry boys are we,
As ever did sing in a hempen string
Under the Gallows-Tree.
The Bloody Brother act 3, sc. 2

4 Death hath so many doors to let out life.
The Custom of the Country (with Massinger) act 2, sc. 2; cf. **Massinger** 501:6, **Seneca** 654:20, **Webster** 808:1

5 Our acts our angels are, or good or ill,
Our fatal shadows that walk by us still.
The Honest Man's Fortune epilogue

6 Nothing's so dainty sweet, as lovely melancholy.
The Nice Valour (with Middleton) act 3, sc. 3, 'Song'

7 Are you at ease now? Is your heart at rest?
Now you have got a shadow, an umbrella
To keep the scorching world's opinion
From your fair credit.
Rule a Wife and Have a Wife (performed 1624) act 3, sc. 1

8 Daisies smell-less, yet most quaint,
And sweet thyme true,
Primrose first born child of Ver,
Merry Springtime's Harbinger.
Two Noble Kinsmen (with Shakespeare) act 1, sc. 1

9 Care-charming Sleep, thou easer of all woes,
Brother to Death.
Valentinian (performed *c.*1610–14) act 5, sc. 7 'Song'; cf. **Daniel** 249:1, **Shelley** 713:17

10 Come sing now, sing; for I know ye sing well,
I see ye have a singing face.
The Wild-Goose Chase (performed 1621) act 2, sc. 2

11 Whistle and she'll come to you.
Wit Without Money act 4, sc. 4; cf. **Burns** 168:5

12 Charity and beating begins at home.
Wit Without Money act 5, sc. 2; cf. **Proverbs** 597:11

Phineas Fletcher 1582–1650

English clergyman and poet

13 Drop, drop, slow tears,
And bathe those beauteous feet,
Which brought from Heaven
The news and Prince of Peace.
Poetical Miscellanies (1633) 'An Hymn'

14 In your deep floods
Drown all my faults and fears;
Not let His eye
See sin, but through my tears.
Poetical Miscellanies (1633) 'An Hymn'

15 Love's tongue is in the eyes.
Piscatory Eclogues (1633) no. 5, st. 13

16 His little son into his bosom creeps,
The lively picture of his father's face.
The Purple Island (1633) canto 12, st. 6

17 Poorly (poor man) he lived; poorly (poor man) he died.
The Purple Island (1633) canto 1, st. 19

18 Love is like linen often changed, the sweeter.
Sicelides (performed 1614) act 3, sc. 5

19 The coward's weapon, poison.
Sicelides (performed 1614) act 5, sc. 3

Jean-Pierre Claris de Florian 1755–94

French writer and poet

20 *Plaisir d'amour ne dure qu'un moment,*
Chagrin d'amour dure toute la vie.
Love's pleasure lasts but a moment;
Love's sorrow lasts all through life.
Célestine (1784); cf. **Malory** 492:11

Dario Fo 1926–

Italian dramatist

21 *Non si paga, non si paga.*
We won't pay, we won't pay.
title of play (1975; translated by Lino Pertile in 1978 as 'We Can't Pay? We Won't Pay!' and performed in London in 1981 as '*Can't Pay? Won't Pay!*'); cf. **Political slogans** 581:10

Ferdinand Foch 1851–1929

French Marshal

22 My centre is giving way, my right is retreating, situation excellent, I am attacking.
message during the first Battle of the Marne, September 1914
R. Recouly *Foch* (1919) ch. 6

23 This is not a peace treaty, it is an armistice for twenty years.
at the signing of the Treaty of Versailles, 1919
Paul Reynaud *Mémoires* (1963) vol. 2

J. Foley 1906–1970

British songwriter

24 Old soldiers never die,
They simply fade away.
'Old Soldiers Never Die' (1920 song); copyrighted by Foley but possibly a 'folk-song' from the First World War; cf. **Proverbs** 608:26

Jane Fonda 1937–

American actress

25 A man has every season, while a woman has only the right to spring.
in *Daily Mail* 13 September 1989

Michael Foot 1913–

British Labour politician

26 A speech from Ernest Bevin on a major occasion had all the horrific fascination of a public

execution. If the mind was left immune, eyes and ears and emotions were riveted.
Aneurin Bevan (1962) vol. 1, ch. 13

1 Think of it! A second Chamber selected by the Whips. A seraglio of eunuchs.
speech in the House of Commons, 3 February 1969

2 Disraeli was my favourite Tory. He was an adventurer pure and simple, or impure and complex. I'm glad to say Gladstone got the better of him.
in *Observer* 16 March 1975 'Sayings of the Week'

3 It is not necessary that every time he rises he should give his famous imitation of a semi-house-trained polecat.
*of Norman **Tebbit***
speech in the House of Commons, 2 March 1978

4 He's passed from rising hope to elder statesman without any intervening period whatsoever.
*of David **Steel***
in the House of Commons, 28 March 1979

Samuel Foote 1720–77
English actor and dramatist

5 Born in a cellar . . . and living in a garret.
The Author (1757) act 2

6 God's revenge against vanity.
*to David **Garrick**, who had asked him what he thought of a heavy shower of rain falling on the day of the **Shakespeare** Jubilee, organized by and chiefly starring Garrick himself*
W. Cooke *Memoirs of Samuel Foote* (1805) vol. 2

7 He is not only dull in himself, but the cause of dullness in others.
on a dull law lord
James Boswell *Life of Samuel Johnson* (1791) 1783; cf. **Shakespeare** 669:22

8 So she went into the garden to cut a cabbage-leaf to make an apple-pie; and at the same time a great she-bear coming up the street, pops its head into the shop. 'What! no soap?' So he died, and she very imprudently married the barber; and there were present the Picninnies, and the Joblillies, and the Garyulies, and the grand Panjandrum himself, with the little round button at top; and they all fell to playing the game of catch as catch can, till the gun powder ran out at the heels of their boots.
nonsense composed to test the vaunted memory of the actor Charles Macklin (1697?–1797)
Maria Edgeworth *Harry and Lucy* (1825) vol. 2

Miss C. F. Forbes 1817–1911
English writer

9 The sense of being well-dressed gives a feeling of inward tranquillity which religion is powerless to bestow.
R. W. Emerson *Letters and Social Aims* (1876)

Anna Ford 1943–
English journalist and broadcaster

10 Let's face it, there are no plain women on television.
in *Observer* 23 September 1979

Gerald Ford 1909–
American Republican statesman, 38th President of the US, 1974–7
*on Ford: see **Johnson** 408:20*

11 If the Government is big enough to give you everything you want, it is big enough to take away everything you have.
John F. Parker *If Elected* (1960)

12 I am a Ford, not a Lincoln.
on taking the vice-presidential oath, 6 December 1973
in *Washington Post* 7 December 1973

13 Our long national nightmare is over. Our Constitution works; our great Republic is a Government of laws and not of men.
on being sworn in as President, 9 August 1974
G. J. Lankevich *Gerald R. Ford* (1977); cf. **Adams** 3:5

Henry Ford 1863–1947
American car manufacturer

14 Any customer can have a car painted any colour that he wants so long as it is black.
on the Model T Ford, 1909
Henry Ford with Samuel Crowther *My Life and Work* (1922) ch. 2

15 History is more or less bunk.
in *Chicago Tribune* 25 May 1916 (interview with Charles N. Wheeler)

16 What we call evil is simply ignorance bumping its head in the dark.
in *Observer* 16 March 1930

17 Exercise is bunk. If you are healthy, you don't need it: if you are sick you shouldn't take it.
attributed

John Ford 1586–after 1639
English dramatist

18 Tempt not the stars, young man, thou canst not play
With the severity of fate.
The Broken Heart (1633) act 1, sc. 3

19 I am . . . a mushroom
On whom the dew of heaven drops now and then.
The Broken Heart (1633) act 1, sc. 3

20 The joys of marriage are the heaven on earth,
Life's paradise, great princess, the soul's quiet,
Sinews of concord, earthly immortality,
Eternity of pleasures; no restoratives
Like to a constant woman.
The Broken Heart (1633) act 2, sc. 2

21 There's not a hair
Sticks on my head but, like a leaden plummet,
It sinks me to the grave: I must creep thither;

The journey is not long.
The Broken Heart (1633) act 4, sc. 2

1 He hath shook hands with time.
The Broken Heart (1633) act 5, sc. 2

2 Tell us, pray, what devil
This melancholy is, which can transform
Men into monsters.
The Lady's Trial (1639) act 3, sc. 1

3 Brother, even by our mother's dust, I charge you,
Do not betray me to your mirth or hate.
'Tis Pity She's a Whore (1633) act 1, sc. 2

4 View but her face, and in that little round,
You may observe a world of variety.
'Tis Pity She's a Whore (1633) act 2

5 Why, I hold fate
Clasped in my fist, and could command the course
Of time's eternal motion, hadst thou been
One thought more steady than an ebbing sea.
'Tis Pity She's a Whore (1633) act 5, sc. 4

Lena Guilbert Ford 1870–1916

English songwriter

6 Keep the Home-fires burning,
While your hearts are yearning,
Though your lads are far away
They dream of Home.
There's a silver lining
Through the dark cloud shining;
Turn the dark cloud inside out,
Till the boys come Home.
'Till the Boys Come Home!' (1914 song); music by Ivor Novello; cf. **Proverbs** 599:21

Howell Forgy 1908–83

American naval chaplain

7 Praise the Lord and pass the ammunition.
at Pearl Harbor, 7 December 1941, while Forgy moved along a line of sailors passing ammunition by hand to the deck
in *New York Times* 1 November 1942; later the title of a song by Frank Loesser, 1942

E. M. Forster 1879–1970

English novelist
on Forster: see ***Mansfield*** *494:8*

8 American women shoot the hippopotamus with eyebrows made of platinum.
Abinger Harvest (1936) 'Mickey and Minnie'; cf. **Belloc** 63:3

9 [Public schoolboys] go forth into a world that is not entirely composed of public-school men or even of Anglo-Saxons, but of men who are as various as the sands of the sea; into a world of whose richness and subtlety they have no conception. They go forth into it with well-developed bodies, fairly developed minds, and undeveloped hearts.
Abinger Harvest (1936) 'Notes on English Character'

10 It is not that the Englishman can't feel—it is that he is afraid to feel. He has been taught at his public school that feeling is bad form. He must not express great joy or sorrow, or even open his mouth too wide when he talks—his pipe might fall out if he did.
Abinger Harvest (1936) 'Notes on English Character'

11 Yes—oh dear yes—the novel tells a story.
Aspects of the Novel (1927) ch. 2

12 The test of a round character is whether it is capable of surprising in a convincing way. If it never surprises, it is flat. If it does not convince, it is flat pretending to be round.
on fictional characters
Aspects of the Novel (1927) ch. 4

13 A dogged attempt to cover the universe with mud, an inverted Victorianism, an attempt to make crossness and dirt succeed where sweetness and light failed.
of James ***Joyce****'s* Ulysses
Aspects of the Novel (1927) ch. 6; cf. **Arnold** 28:8, **Swift** 747:12

14 It is a period between two wars—the long week-end it has been called.
The Development of English Prose between 1918 and 1939 (1945)

15 Railway termini. They are our gates to the glorious and the unknown. Through them we pass out into adventure and sunshine, to them, alas! we return.
Howards End (1910) ch. 2

16 To trust people is a luxury in which only the wealthy can indulge; the poor cannot afford it.
Howards End (1910) ch. 5

17 Personal relations are the important thing for ever and ever, and not this outer life of telegrams and anger.
Howards End (1910) ch. 19

18 Only connect! . . . Only connect the prose and the passion, and both will be exalted, and human love will be seen at its height.
Howards End (1910) ch. 22

19 Of all means to regeneration Remorse is surely the most wasteful. It cuts away healthy tissue with the poisoned. It is a knife that probes far deeper than the evil.
Howards End (1910) ch. 41

20 It's the worst thing that can ever happen to you in all your life, and you've got to mind it . . . They'll come saying, 'Bear up—trust to time.' No, no; they're wrong. Mind it.
The Longest Journey (1907) ch. 5

21 The so-called white races are really pinko-grey.
A Passage to India (1924) ch. 7

22 Nothing in India is identifiable, the mere asking of a question causes it to disappear or to merge in something else.
A Passage to India (1924) ch. 8

23 Pathos, piety, courage—they exist, but are identical, and so is filth. Everything exists, nothing has value.
A Passage to India (1924) ch. 14

1 Where there is officialism every human relationship suffers.
A Passage to India (1924) ch. 24

2 Like all gossip—it's merely one of those half-alive things that try to crowd out real life.
A Passage to India (1924) ch. 31

3 God si [is] Love. Is this the final message of India?
A Passage to India (1924) ch. 33

4 If I had to choose between betraying my country and betraying my friend, I hope I should have the guts to betray my country.
Two Cheers for Democracy (1951) 'What I Believe'

5 So Two cheers for Democracy: one because it admits variety and two because it permits criticism. Two cheers are quite enough: there is no occasion to give three. Only Love the Beloved Republic deserves that.
Two Cheers for Democracy (1951) 'What I Believe'; cf. **Swinburne** 751:1

Venantius Fortunatus AD *c.*530–*c.*610

Poet and priest; Bishop of Poitiers from AD 599

6 *Pange, lingua, gloriosi*
Proelium certaminis.
Sing, my tongue, of the battle in the glorious struggle.
Passiontide hymn, most commonly sung as: 'Sing, my tongue, the glorious battle'
'Pange lingua gloriosi'; cf. **Thomas Aquinas** 771:10

7 *Vexilla regis prodeunt,*
Fulget crucis mysterium;
Qua vita mortem pertulit,
Et morte vitam protulit.
The banners of the king advance, the mystery of the cross shines bright; where his life went through with death, and from death brought forth life.
hymn, usually sung as 'The royal banners forward go'
'Vexilla Regis'

8 *Regnavit a ligno Deus.*
God reigned from the wood.
'Vexilla Regis'

Harry Emerson Fosdick 1878–1969

American Baptist minister

9 I renounce war for its consequences, for the lies it lives on and propagates, for the undying hatred it arouses, for the dictatorships it puts in the place of democracy, for the starvation that stalks after it.
Armistice Day Sermon in New York, 1933, in *The Secret of Victorious Living* (1934)

Charles Foster 1828–1904

American politician

10 Isn't this a billion dollar country?
responding to a Democratic gibe about a 'million dollar Congress'
at the 51st Congress; also attributed to Thomas B. Reed, who reported the exchange in *North American Review* March 1892, vol. 154

John Foster 1770–1843

English Baptist minister

11 But the two classes [the educated and the uneducated] so beheld in contrast, might they not seem to belong to two different nations?
Essay on the Evils of Popular Ignorance (1820); cf. **Disraeli** 270:23, 270:25

12 They [the wealthy] are in a religious diving-bell; religion is not circumambient, but a little is conveyed down into the worldly depth, where they breathe by a sort of artificial inlet—a tube.
Journal Item 420 in *Life and Correspondence* (1846)

13 Is not the pleasure of feeling and exhibiting *power* over other beings, a principal part of the gratification of cruelty?
Journal Item 772 in *Life and Correspondence* (1846)

Stephen Collins Foster 1826–64

American songwriter

14 Beautiful dreamer, wake unto me,
Starlight and dewdrop are waiting for thee.
'Beautiful Dreamer' (1864 song)

15 Gwine to run all night!
Gwine to run all day!
I'll bet my money on de bobtail nag—
Somebody bet on de bay.
'De Camptown Races' (1850) chorus

16 I dream of Jeanie with the light brown hair,
Floating, like a vapour, on the soft summer air.
'Jeanie with the Light Brown Hair' (1854)

17 Way down upon the Swanee River,
Far, far, away,
There's where my heart is turning ever;
There's where the old folks stay.
'The Old Folks at Home' (1851)

18 All the world is sad and dreary
Everywhere I roam,
Oh! darkies, how my heart grows weary,
Far from the old folks at home.
'The Old Folks at Home' (1851) chorus

Charles Fourier 1772–1837

French social theorist

19 The extension of women's rights is the basic principle of all social progress.
Théorie des Quatre Mouvements (1808) vol. 2, ch. 4

Gene Fowler 1890–1960

American writer

20 Will Hays is my shepherd, I shall not want, He maketh me to lie down in clean postures.
on the establishment of the 'Hays Office' in 1922 to monitor the Hollywood film industry
Clive Marsh and Gaye Ortiz (eds.) *Explorations in Theology and Film* (1997); cf. **Scottish Metrical Psalms** 652:20

H. W. Fowler 1858–1933

English lexicographer and grammarian

21 The English speaking world may be divided into (1) those who neither know nor care what a split

infinitive is; (2) those who do not know, but care very much; (3) those who know and condemn; (4) those who know and approve; and (5) those who know and distinguish. Those who neither know nor care are the vast majority and are a happy folk, to be envied by most of the minority classes.
Modern English Usage (1926)

H. W. Fowler 1858–1933 and F. G. Fowler 1870–1918
English lexicographers and grammarians

1 Pretentious quotations being the surest road to tedium.
The King's English (1906)

Norman Fowler 1938–
British Conservative politician

2 I have a young family and for the next few years I should like to devote more time to them.
often quoted as 'spend more time with my family'
resignation letter to the Prime Minister, in *Guardian* 4 January 1990; cf. **Thatcher** 770:10

Caroline Fox d. 1774
wife of Henry Fox, Lord **Holland**, *and mother of Charles James* **Fox**

3 That little boy will be a thorn in Charles's side as long as he lives.
seeing in the young William **Pitt** *a prospective rival for her son Charles James* **Fox**
attributed

Charles James Fox 1749–1806
English Whig politician
on Fox: see **Shaw-Lefevre** *709:28; see also* **Last words** *456:2*

4 He was uniformly of an opinion which, though not a popular one, he was ready to aver, that the right of governing was not property but a trust.
on **Pitt** *the Younger's scheme of Parliamentary Reform, 1785*
J. L. Hammond *Charles James Fox* (1903) ch. 4

5 How much the greatest event it is that ever happened in the world! and how much the best!
on the fall of the Bastille
letter to Richard Fitzpatrick, 30 July 1789, in Lord John Russell *Life and Times of C. J. Fox* vol. 2 (1859)

6 I will not close my politics in that foolish way.
in the last year of his life it had been suggested that he should accept a peerage
in *Dictionary of National Biography* (1917–)

George Fox 1624–91
English founder of the Society of Friends (Quakers)

7 I saw also that there was an ocean of darkness and death, but an infinite ocean of light and love, which flowed over the ocean of darkness.
Journal 1647

8 I told them I lived in the virtue of that life and power that took away the occasion of all wars.
on being offered a captaincy in the army of the Commonwealth, against the forces of the King
Journal 1651

9 I . . . espied three steeple-house spires, and they struck at my life.
on seeing the spires of Lichfield
Journal 1651

10 Walk cheerfully over the world, answering that of God in every one.
Journal 1656

11 Be still and cool in thy own mind and spirit from thy own thoughts, and then thou wilt feel the principle of God to turn thy mind to the Lord God.
Journal 1952) 1658

12 All bloody principles and practices, we, as to our own particulars, do utterly deny, with all outward wars and strife and fightings with outward weapons, for any end or under any pretence whatsoever. And this is our testimony to the whole world.
Journal 1661

Henry Fox see Lord Holland

Anatole France (Jacques-Anatole-François Thibault) 1844–1924
French novelist and man of letters

13 Imitation lies at the root of most human actions. A respectable person is one who conforms to custom. People are called good when they do as others do.
Crainquebille (1923)

14 In every well-governed state, wealth is a sacred thing; in democracies it is the only sacred thing.
L'Île des pingouins (1908) pt. 6, ch. 2

15 They [the poor] have to labour in the face of the majestic equality of the law, which forbids the rich as well as the poor to sleep under bridges, to beg in the streets, and to steal bread.
Le Lys rouge (1894) ch. 7

16 Without lies humanity would perish of despair and boredom.
La Vie en fleur (1922)

17 The good critic is he who relates the adventures of his soul in the midst of masterpieces.
La Vie littéraire (1888) dedicatory letter

18 Make hatred hated!
to public school teachers
speech in Tours, August 1919; Carter Jefferson *Anatole France: The Politics of Scepticism.*

19 You think you are dying for your country; you die for the industrialists.
in *L'Humanité* 18 July 1922

Francis I 1494–1547
King of France from 1515

1 *De toutes choses ne m'est demeuré que l'honneur et la vie qui est saulve.*

Of all I had, only honour and life have been spared.
letter to his mother following his defeat at Pavia, 1525; usually quoted as 'Tout est perdu fors l'honneur [All is lost save honour]'
in *Collection des Documents Inédits sur l'Histoire de France* (1847) vol. 1

St Francis de Sales 1567–1622
French bishop of Geneva; leader of the Counter-Reformation

2 Big fires flare up in a wind, but little ones are blown out unless they are carried in under cover.
Introduction à la vie dévote (1609) pt. 3, ch. 34; cf. **Bussy-Rabutin** 171:6, **La Rochefoucauld** 453:18

3 *On a beau dire, mais le coeur parle au coeur, et la langue ne parle qu'aux oreilles.*

It has been well said, that heart speaks to heart, whereas language only speaks to the ears.
letter to the Archbishop of Bourges, 5 October 1604, in *Oeuvres de Saint François de Sales* (1834) vol. 3; cf. **Mottoes** 535:5

St Francis of Assisi 1181–1226
Italian monk, founder of the Franciscan Order

4 Praised be You, my Lord, with all your creatures,
especially Sir Brother Sun,
Who is the day and through whom You give us light.
'The Canticle of Brother Sun'

5 Lord, make me an instrument of Your peace!
Where there is hatred let me sow love;
Where there is injury, pardon;
Where there is doubt, faith;
Where there is despair, hope;
Where there is darkness, light;
Where there is sadness, joy.

O divine Master, grant that I may not so much seek
To be consoled as to console;
To be understood as to understand;
To be loved as to love.
'Prayer of St Francis' (attributed)

Anne Frank 1929–45
German-born Jewish diarist

6 I want to go on living even after death!
diary, 4 April 1944

Felix Frankfurter 1882–1965
American judge

7 It is a fair summary of history to say that the safeguards of liberty have been forged in controversies involving not very nice people.
dissenting opinion in *United States v. Rabinowitz* (1950)

Benjamin Franklin 1706–90
American politician, inventor, and scientist
on Franklin: see **Turgot** *785:9; see also* **Anonymous** *20:2,* **Epitaphs** *302:1, 303:7,* **Toasts** *778:1*

8 Remember that time is money.
Advice to a Young Tradesman (1748); cf. **Proverbs** 613:2

9 Some are weather-wise, some are otherwise.
Poor Richard's Almanac (1735) February

10 Necessity never made a good bargain.
Poor Richard's Almanac (1735) April

11 At twenty years of age, the will reigns; at thirty, the wit; and at forty, the judgement.
Poor Richard's Almanac (1741) June

12 He that lives upon hope will die fasting.
Poor Richard's Almanac (1758) preface

13 We must indeed all hang together, or, most assuredly, we shall all hang separately.
at the signing of the Declaration of Independence, 4 July 1776 (possibly not original); P. M. Zall *Ben Franklin* (1980)

14 There never was a good war, or a bad peace.
letter to Josiah Quincy, 11 September 1783, in *Works* (1882) vol. 10

15 In this world nothing can be said to be certain, except death and taxes.
letter to Jean Baptiste Le Roy, 13 November 1789, in *Works of Benjamin Franklin* (1817) ch. 6.; cf. **Defoe** 254:15, **Proverbs** 608:12

16 Man is a tool-making animal.
James Boswell *Life of Samuel Johnson* (1791) 7 April 1778

17 What is the use of a new-born child?
when asked what was the use of a new invention
J. Parton *Life and Times of Benjamin Franklin* (1864) pt. 4, ch. 17

Lord Franks 1905–92
British philosopher and administrator

18 The Pentagon, that immense monument to modern man's subservience to the desk.
in *Observer* 30 November 1952

on the composition of such bodies as royal commissions and committees of inquiry:

19 There is a fashion in these things and when you are in fashion you are asked to do a lot.
in conversation, 24 January 1977; Peter Hennessy *Whitehall* (1990)

20 A secret in the Oxford sense: you may tell it to only one person at a time.
in *Sunday Telegraph* 30 January 1977

Frederick the Great 1712–86
King of Prussia from 1740
see also **Napoleon** *539:1*

21 Drive out prejudices through the door, and they will return through the window.
letter to Voltaire, 19 March 1771, in *Oeuvres Complètes* (1790) vol. 12

1 My people and I have come to an agreement which satisfies us both. They are to say what they please, and I am to do what I please.
his interpretation of benevolent despotism
attributed

2 Rascals, would you live for ever?
to hesitant Guards at Kolin, 18 June 1757
attributed

E. A. Freeman 1823–92
English historian
on Freeman: see **Rogers** *631:17*

3 History is past politics, and politics is present history.
Methods of Historical Study (1886)

John Freeth *c.*1731–1808
English poet

4 The loss of America what can repay?
New colonies seek for at Botany Bay.
'Botany Bay' in *New London Magazine* (1786)

Marilyn French 1929–
American writer

5 The truth is that it is not the sins of the fathers that descend unto the third generation, but the sorrows of the mothers.
Her Mother's Daughter (1987); cf. **Bible** 76:9

6 Whatever they may be in public life, whatever their relations with men, in their relations with women, all men are rapists, and that's all they are. They rape us with their eyes, their laws, and their codes.
The Women's Room (1977)

7 'I hate discussions of feminism that end up with who does the dishes,' she said. So do I. But at the end, there are always the damned dishes.
The Women's Room (1977)

Percy French 1854–1920
Irish songwriter

8 Come back, Paddy Reilly, to Ballyjamesduff;
Come home, Paddy Reilly, to me.
'Come Back, Paddy Reilly'

9 Oh Mary, this London's a wonderful sight,
With the people all working by day and by
night . . .
But for all I found there, I might as well be
Where the Mountains of Mourne sweep down to
the sea.
'The Mountains of Mourne'

John Hookham Frere 1769–1846
English poet

10 The feathered race with pinions skim the air—
Not so the mackerel, and still less the bear!
'The Progress of Man' (1798) canto 1, l. 34

11 Ah! who has seen the mailed lobster rise,
Clap her broad wings, and soaring claim the skies?
'The Progress of Man' (1798) canto 1, l. 44

Sigmund Freud 1856–1939
Austrian psychiatrist; originator of psychoanalysis
on Freud: see **Auden** *33:29,* **Dodd** *271:18; see also* **Riviere** *628:16*

12 Anatomy is destiny.
Collected Writings (1924) vol. 5

13 The interpretation of dreams is the royal road to a knowledge of the unconscious activities of the mind.
The Interpretation of Dreams (2nd ed., 1909) ch. 7, sect. E; cf. **Misquotations** 521:8

14 Intolerance of groups is often, strangely enough, exhibited more strongly against small differences than against fundamental ones.
Moses and Monotheism (1938)

15 Analogies decide nothing, that is true, but they can make one feel more at home.
New Introductory Lectures on Psychoanalysis (1933)

16 'Itzig, where are you riding to?' 'Don't ask me, ask the horse.'
letter to Wilhelm Fliess, 7 July 1898, in *Origins of Psychoanalysis* (1950)

17 The great question that has never been answered and which I have not yet been able to answer, despite my thirty years of research into the feminine soul, is 'What does a woman want?'
letter to Marie Bonaparte, in Ernest Jones *Sigmund Freud: Life and Work* (1955) vol. 2, pt. 3, ch. 16

18 All that matters is love and work.
attributed

19 Frozen anger.
his definition of depression
attributed

Nancy Friday 1937–
American writer

20 The older I get the more of my mother I see in myself.
My Mother, My Self (1977) ch.1

21 It was the promise of men, that around each corner there was yet another man, more wonderful than the last, that sustained me. You see, I had men confused with life . . . You can't get what I wanted from a man, not in this life.
My Mother, My Self (1977) ch.8

Betty Friedan 1921–
American feminist

22 The problem that has no name.
being the fact that American women are kept from growing to their full human capacities
The Feminine Mystique (1963) ch. 14

23 It is easier to live through someone else than to become complete yourself.
The Feminine Mystique (1963) ch. 14

24 Today the problem that has no name is how to juggle work, love, home and children.
The Second Stage (1987); cf. **Douglas** 276:11

Milton Friedman 1912–

*American economist and exponent of monetarism; policy adviser to President **Reagan** 1981–9*
*see also **Sayings** 648:4*

1 There is an invisible hand in politics that operates in the opposite direction to the invisible hand in the market. In politics, individuals who seek to promote only the public good are led by an invisible hand to promote special interests that it was no part of their intention to promote.
Bright Promises, Dismal Performance: An Economist's Protest (1983)

2 Inflation is the one form of taxation that can be imposed without legislation.
in *Observer* 22 September 1974

3 Thank heavens we do not get all of the government that we are made to pay for.
attributed; quoted by Lord Harris of High Cross in the House of Lords, 24 November 1994

Brian Friel 1929–

Irish dramatist

4 Two such wonderful phrases—'I understand perfectly' and 'That is a lie'—a précis of life, aren't they?
The Communication Cord (1983)

5 Do you want the whole countryside to be laughing at us?—women of our years?—mature women, *dancing?*
Dancing at Lughnasa (1990)

6 People with a culture of poverty suffer much less repression than we of the middle class suffer and indeed, if I may make the suggestion with due qualification, they often have a lot more fun than we have.
The Freedom of the City (1973)

7 Wordsworth? . . . no, I'm afraid we're not familiar with your literature, Lieutenant. We feel closer to the warm Mediterranean. We tend to overlook your island.
Translations (1980)

Max Frisch 1911–91

Swiss novelist and dramatist

8 Technology . . . the knack of so arranging the world that we need not experience it.
Homo Faber (1957) pt. 2

Erich Fromm 1900–80

American philosopher and psychologist

9 Immature love says: 'I love you because I need you.' Mature love says: 'I need you because I love you.'
The Art of Loving (1956) ch. 2

10 Love is often nothing but a favourable exchange between two people who get the most out of what they can expect, considering their value on the personality market.
The Sane Society (1955) ch. 5

11 In the nineteenth century the problem was that *God is dead*; in the twentieth century the problem is that *man is dead*. In the nineteenth century inhumanity meant cruelty; in the twentieth century it means schizoid self-alienation. The danger of the past was that men became slaves. The danger of the future is that men may become robots.
The Sane Society (1955) ch. 9

David Frost 1939–

English broadcaster and writer
*see also **Catchphrases** 195:21, 196:19*

12 Having one child makes you a parent; having two you are a referee.
in *Independent* 16 September 1989

Robert Frost 1874–1963

American poet

13 I have been one acquainted with the night.
'Acquainted with the Night' (1928)

14 . . . Life is too much like a pathless wood
Where your face burns and tickles with the cobwebs
Broken across it, and one eye is weeping
From a twig's having lashed across it open.
'Birches' (1916)

15 I'd like to get away from earth awhile
And then come back to it and begin over.
May no fate wilfully misunderstand me
And half grant what I wish and snatch me away
Not to return. Earth's the right place for love:
I don't know where it's likely to go better.
'Birches' (1916)

16 Most of the change we think we see in life
Is due to truths being in and out of favour.
'The Black Cottage' (1914)

17 Forgive, O Lord, my little jokes on Thee
And I'll forgive Thy great big one on me.
'Cluster of Faith' (1962)

18 And nothing to look backward to with pride,
And nothing to look forward to with hope.
'The Death of the Hired Man' (1914)

19 'Home is the place where, when you have to go there,
They have to take you in.'
'I should have called it
Something you somehow haven't to deserve.'
'The Death of the Hired Man' (1914)

20 They cannot scare me with their empty spaces
Between stars—on stars where no human race is.
I have it in me so much nearer home
To scare myself with my own desert places.
'Desert Places' (1936)

21 Some say the world will end in fire,
Some say in ice.
From what I've tasted of desire
I hold with those who favour fire.
But if it had to perish twice,
I think I know enough of hate

To say that for destruction ice
Is also great
And would suffice.
'Fire and Ice' (1923)

1 The land was ours before we were the land's.
She was our land more than a hundred years
Before we were her people.
'The Gift Outright' (1942)

2 Happiness makes up in height for what it lacks in length.
title of poem (1942)

3 And were an epitaph to be my story
I'd have a short one ready for my own.
I would have written of me on my stone:
I had a lover's quarrel with the world.
'The Lesson for Today' (1942)

4 Something there is that doesn't love a wall,
That sends the frozen-ground-swell under it.
'Mending Wall' (1914)

5 My apple trees will never get across
And eat the cones under his pines, I tell him.
He only says, 'Good fences make good neighbours.'
'Mending Wall' (1914)

6 Before I built a wall I'd ask to know
What I was walling in or walling out,
And to whom I was like to give offence.
'Mending Wall' (1914)

7 I never dared be radical when young
For fear it would make me conservative when old.
'Precaution' (1936)

8 No memory of having starred
Atones for later disregard,
Or keeps the end from being hard.
'Provide Provide' (1936)

9 Two roads diverged in a wood, and I—
I took the one less travelled by,
And that has made all the difference.
'The Road Not Taken' (1916)

10 We dance round in a ring and suppose,
But the Secret sits in the middle and knows.
'The Secret Sits' (1942)

11 I've broken Anne of gathering bouquets.
It's not fair to the child. It can't be helped though:
Pressed into service means pressed out of shape.
'The Self-Seeker' (1914)

12 The woods are lovely, dark and deep.
But I have promises to keep,
And miles to go before I sleep,
And miles to go before I sleep.
'Stopping by Woods on a Snowy Evening' (1923)

13 The figure a poem makes. It begins in delight and ends in wisdom. The figure is the same as for love.
Collected Poems (1939) 'The Figure a Poem Makes'

14 No tears in the writer, no tears in the reader. No surprise for the writer, no surprise for the reader.
Collected Poems (1939) 'The Figure a Poem Makes'

15 Like a piece of ice on a hot stove the poem must ride on its own melting. A poem may be worked over once it is in being, but may not be worried into being.
Collected Poems (1939) 'The Figure a Poem Makes'

16 Poetry is a way of taking life by the throat.
Elizabeth S. Sergeant *Robert Frost* (1960) ch. 18

17 You can be a little ungrammatical if you come from the right part of the country.
in *Atlantic Monthly* January 1962

18 I'd as soon write free verse as play tennis with the net down.
Edward Lathem *Interviews with Robert Frost* (1966)

19 Poetry is what is lost in translation. It is also what is lost in interpretation.
Louis Untermeyer *Robert Frost* (1964)

Christopher Fry 1907–
English dramatist

20 The dark is light enough.
title of play (1954)

21 The lady's not for burning.
title of play (1949); cf. **Thatcher** 769:24

22 What after all
Is a halo? It's only one more thing to keep clean.
The Lady's not for Burning (1949) act 1

23 Where in this small-talking world can I find
A longitude with no platitude?
The Lady's not for Burning (1949) act 3

24 The best
Thing we can do is to make wherever we're lost in
Look as much like home as we can.
The Lady's not for Burning (1949) act 3

Elizabeth Fry 1780–1845
English Quaker prison reformer

25 Does capital punishment tend to the security of the people?

By no means. It hardens the hearts of men, and makes the loss of life appear light to them; and it renders life insecure, inasmuch as the law holds out that property is of greater value than life.
note found among her papers; Rachel E. Cresswell and Katharine Fry *Memoir of the Life of Elizabeth Fry* (1848)

26 Punishment is not for revenge, but to lessen crime and reform the criminal.
note found among her papers; Rachel E. Cresswell and Katharine Fry *Memoir of the Life of Elizabeth Fry* (1848)

Roger Fry 1866–1934
English art critic

27 Art is significant deformity.
Virginia Woolf *Roger Fry* (1940) ch. 8

28 Bach almost persuades me to be a Christian.
Virginia Woolf *Roger Fry* (1940) ch. 11

Carlos Fuentes 1928–
Mexican novelist and writer

29 High on the agenda for the 21st century will be the need to restore some kind of tragic consciousness.
Rushworth M. Kidder *An Agenda for the 21st Century* (1987)

Francis Fukuyama 1952–
American historian

1 What we may be witnessing is not just the end of the Cold War but the end of history as such: that is, the end point of man's ideological evolution and the universalism of Western liberal democracy.
in *Independent* 20 September 1989

J. William Fulbright 1905–95
American politician

2 The Soviet Union has indeed been our greatest menace, not so much because of what it has done, but because of the excuses it has provided us for our failures.
in *Observer* 21 December 1958 'Sayings of the Year'

R. Buckminster Fuller 1895–1983
American designer and architect

3 Either war is obsolete or men are.
in *New Yorker* 8 January 1966

4 God, to me, it seems,
is a verb
not a noun,
proper or improper.
No More Secondhand God (1963) (untitled poem written in 1940); cf. **Hugo** 393:16

5 Now there is one outstandingly important fact regarding Spaceship Earth, and that is that no instruction book came with it.
Operating Manual for Spaceship Earth (1969) ch. 4

Sam Fuller 1912–
American film director

6 When you're in the battlefield, survival is all there is. Death is the only great emotion.
in *Guardian* 26 February 1991

Thomas Fuller 1608–61
English preacher and historian

7 But our captain counts the Image of God nevertheless his image, cut in ebony as if done in ivory.
The Holy State and the Profane State (1642) bk. 2 'The Good Sea-Captain'

8 Know most of the rooms of thy native country before thou goest over the threshold thereof.
The Holy State and the Profane State bk. 3 'Of Travelling'

9 Anger is one of the sinews of the soul.
The Holy State and the Profane State bk. 3 'Of Anger'

10 Light (God's eldest daughter) is a principal beauty in building.
The Holy State and the Profane State bk. 3 'Of Building'

11 He was one of a lean body and visage, as if his eager soul, biting for anger at the clog of his body, desired to fret a passage through it.
The Holy State and the Profane State bk. 5 'Life of the Duke of Alva'

Thomas Fuller 1654–1734
English writer and physician
see also **Denning** 257:17

12 He that plants trees loves others beside himself.
Gnomologia (1732) no. 2247

13 We are all Adam's children but silk makes the difference.
Gnomologia (1732) no. 5425

Alfred Funke b. 1869
German writer

14 *Gott strafe England!*
God punish England!
Schwert und Myrte (1914)

Henry Fuseli (Johann Heinrich Füssli) 1741–1825
Swiss-born British painter and art critic

15 The Greeks were gods! The Greeks were gods!
on first seeing the Elgin marbles
J. Mordaunt Crook *The Greek Revival* (1995)

David Maxwell Fyfe see **Lord Kilmuir**

Rose Fyleman 1877–1957
English writer for children

16 There are fairies at the bottom of our garden!
Fairies and Chimneys (1918) 'The Fairies' (first published in *Punch* 23 May 1917)

Clark Gable see **Film lines** 311:7

Thomas Gainsborough 1727–88
English painter
see also **Last words** 457:15

17 Damn gentlemen. There is not such a set of enemies to a real artist in the world as they are, if not kept at a proper distance.
letter to the musician William Jackson, 2 September 1767; Mary Woodall (ed.) *The Letters of Thomas Gainsborough* (1961)

18 Recollect that painting and punctuality mix like oil and vinegar, and that genius and regularity are utter enemies, and must be to the end of time.
speech to the Edward Stratford, 1 May 1772; Mary Woodall (ed.) *The Letters of Thomas Gainsborough* (1961)

Thomas Gaisford 1779–1855
English classicist; Dean of Christ Church, Oxford, from 1831

19 Nor can I do better, in conclusion, than impress upon you the study of Greek literature, which not only elevates above the vulgar herd, but leads not infrequently to positions of considerable emolument.
Christmas Day Sermon in the Cathedral, Oxford, in W. Tuckwell *Reminiscences of Oxford* (2nd ed., 1907)

Hugh Gaitskell 1906–63

British Labour politician
on Gaitskell: see **Bevan** *71:21*

1 There are some of us . . . who will fight and fight and fight again to save the Party we love.
speech at Labour Party Conference, 5 October 1960, in *Report of 59th Annual Conference*

2 It means the end of a thousand years of history.
on a European federation
speech at Labour Party Conference, 3 October 1962, in *Report of 61st Annual Conference*

3 The subtle terrorism of words.
in a warning given to his Party, c.1957
Harry Hopkins *The New Look* (1963); attributed

Gaius (or Caius) AD c.110–c.180

Roman jurist

4 *Damnosa hereditas.*
Ruinous inheritance.
The Institutes bk. 2, ch. 163

J. K. Galbraith 1908–

American economist

5 The affluent society.
title of book (1958)

6 These are the days when men of all social disciplines and all political faiths seek the comfortable and the accepted; when the man of controversy is looked upon as a disturbing influence; when originality is taken to be a mark of instability; and when, in minor modification of the scriptural parable, the bland lead the bland.
The Affluent Society (1958) ch. 1, sect. 3

7 The greater the wealth, the thicker will be the dirt.
The Affluent Society (1958) ch. 18, sect. 2

8 The salary of the chief executive of the large corporation is not a market reward for achievement. It is frequently in the nature of a warm personal gesture by the individual to himself.
Annals of an Abiding Liberal (1979)

9 Trickle-down theory—the less than elegant metaphor that if one feeds the horse enough oats, some will pass through to the road for the sparrows.
The Culture of Contentment (1992)

10 A wrong decision isn't forever; it can always be reversed. The losses from a delayed decision *are* forever; they can never be retrieved.
A Life in our Times (1981)

11 Politics is not the art of the possible. It consists in choosing between the disastrous and the unpalatable.
speech to President Kennedy, 2 March 1962, in *Ambassador's Journal* (1969); cf. **Bismarck** 116:6

Galen AD 129–199

Greek physician

12 That which *is* grows, while that which *is not* becomes.
On the Natural Faculties bk. 2, sect. 3

Galileo Galilei 1564–1642

Italian astronomer and physicist

13 Philosophy is written in that great book which ever lies before our eyes—I mean the universe . . . This book is written in mathematical language and its characters are triangles, circles and other geometrical figures, without whose help . . . one wanders in vain through a dark labyrinth.
often quoted as 'The book of nature is written . . .'
The Assayer (1623)

14 *Eppur si muove.*
But it does move.
after his recantation, that the earth moves around the sun, in 1632
attributed; Baretti *Italian Library* (1757) is possibly the earliest appearance of the phrase

Noel Gallagher 1967–

English pop singer

15 Drugs is like getting up and having a cup of tea in the morning.
in a radio interview, 28 January 1997
in *Daily Telegraph* 31 January 1997

16 I would hope we mean more to people than putting money in a church basket and saying ten Hail Marys on a Sunday. Has God played Knebworth recently?
on the drawing power of Oasis
in *New Musical Express* 12 July 1997; cf. **Chisholm** 212:6, **Lennon** 463:17

John Galsworthy 1867–1933

English novelist

17 He was afflicted by the thought that where Beauty was, nothing ever ran quite straight, which, no doubt, was why so many people looked on it as immoral.
In Chancery (1920) pt. 1, ch. 13

18 A man of action forced into a state of thought is unhappy until he can get out of it.
Maid in Waiting (1931) ch. 3

John Galt 1779–1839

Scottish writer

19 From the lone shieling of the misty island
Mountains divide us, and the waste of seas—
Yet still the blood is strong, the heart is Highland,
And we in dreams behold the Hebrides!
'Canadian Boat Song' translated from the Gaelic in *Blackwoods Edinburgh Magazine* September 1829 'Noctes Ambrosianae' no. 46, and later attributed to Galt

Ray Galton 1930– and Alan Simpson 1929–

English scriptwriters

20 I came in here in all good faith to help my country. I don't mind giving a reasonable amount [of blood], but a pint . . . why that's very nearly an armful.
Hancock's Half Hour 'The Blood Donor' (1961 television programme); words spoken by Tony Hancock

Patrick Galvin 1927–

Irish poet

1 Tonight
with London's ghost
I walk the streets
As easy as November fog
Among the reeds.

'Christ in London'

George Gamow 1904–68

Russian-born American physicist

2 We do not know why they [elementary particles] have the masses they do; we do not know why they transform into another the way they do; we do not know anything! The one concept that stands like the Rock of Gibraltar in our sea of confusion is the Pauli [exclusion] principle.

in *Scientific American* July 1959

3 With five free parameters, a theorist could fit the profile of an elephant.

attributed; in *Nature* 21 June 1990

Mahatma Gandhi (Mohandas Karamchand Gandhi) 1869–1948

Indian statesman

on Gandhi: see ***Naidhu*** *538:4*

4 What difference does it make to the dead, the orphans and the homeless, whether the mad destruction is wrought under the name of totalitarianism or the holy name of liberty or democracy?

Non-Violence in Peace and War (1942) vol. 1, ch. 142

5 The moment the slave resolves that he will no longer be a slave, his fetters fall. He frees himself and shows the way to others. Freedom and slavery are mental states.

Non-Violence in Peace and War (1949) vol. 2, ch. 5

6 Non-violence is the first article of my faith. It is also the last article of my creed.

speech at Shahi Bag, 18 March 1922, on a charge of sedition, in *Young India* 23 March 1922

7 In my humble opinion, non-cooperation with evil is as much a duty as is cooperation with good.

speech in Ahmadabad, 23 March 1922

on being asked what he thought of modern civilization:

8 That would be a good idea.

while visiting England in 1930

E. F. Schumacher *Good Work* (1979)

Greta Garbo (Greta Lovisa Gustafsson) 1905–90

Swedish film actress

9 I want to be alone.

Grand Hotel (1932 film), the phrase already being associated with Garbo

Federico García Lorca 1899–1936

Spanish poet and dramatist

10 *A las cinco de la tarde.*
Eran las cinco en punto de la tarde.
Un niño trajo la blanca sábana
a las cinco de la tarde.

At five in the afternoon.
It was exactly five in the afternoon.
A boy brought the white sheet
at five in the afternoon.

Llanto por Ignacio Sánchez Mejías (1935) 'La Cogida y la muerte'

11 *Verde que te quiero verde.*
Verde viento. Verdes ramas.
El barco sobre la mar
y el caballo en la montaña.

Green how I love you green.
Green wind.
Green boughs.
The ship on the sea
and the horse on the mountain.

Romance sonámbulo (1924–7)

Gabriel García Márquez 1928–

Colombian novelist

12 The world must be all fucked up when men travel first class and literature goes as freight.

One Hundred Years of Solitude (1967)

13 A famous writer who wants to continue writing has to be constantly defending himself against fame.

in *Writers at Work* (6th series, 1984)

Richard Gardiner b. *c.*1533

English writer

14 Sowe Carrets in your Gardens, and humbly praise God for them, as for a singular and great blessing.

Profitable Instructions for the Manuring, Sowing and Planting of Kitchen Gardens (1599)

Ed Gardner 1901–63

American radio comedian

15 Opera is when a guy gets stabbed in the back and, instead of bleeding, he sings.

in *Duffy's Tavern* (US radio programme, 1940s)

James A. Garfield 1831–81

American Republican statesman; 20th President of the US

on Garfield: see ***Thayer*** *770:15*

16 Fellow-citizens: God reigns, and the Government at Washington lives!

speech on the assassination of President Lincoln, 17 April 1865; in *Death of President Garfield* (1881)

Giuseppe Garibaldi 1807–82

Italian patriot and military leader

17 Men, I'm getting out of Rome. Anyone who wants to carry on the war against the outsiders, come with me. I can offer you neither honours nor wages; I offer you hunger, thirst, forced marches, battles and death. Anyone who loves his country, follow me.

Giuseppe Guerzoni *Garibaldi* (1882) vol. 1 (not a verbatim record)

John Nance Garner 1868–1967
American Democratic politician; vice-president 1933–41

1 The vice-presidency isn't worth a pitcher of warm piss.
O. C. Fisher *Cactus Jack* (1978) ch. 11

David Garrick 1717–79
English actor-manager
on Garrick: see **Foote** *319:6,* **Goldsmith** *345:2, 345:3, 345:4,* **Johnson** *410:8; see also* **Colman and Garrick, Epitaphs** *302:6*

2 They smile with the simple, and feed with the poor.
Florizel and Perdita (performed 1756) act 2, sc. 1; cf. **Johnson** 414:1

3 Heart of oak are our ships,
Heart of oak are our men:
We always are ready;
Steady, boys, steady;
We'll fight and we'll conquer again and again.
Harlequin's Invasion (1759) 'Heart of Oak' (song)

4 Here lies Nolly Goldsmith, for shortness called Noll,
Who wrote like an angel, but talked like poor Poll.
'Impromptu Epitaph' (written 1773/4); cf. **Goldsmith** 344:23, **Johnson** 416:15

5 A fellow-feeling makes one wond'rous kind.
'An Occasional Prologue on Quitting the Theatre' 10 June 1776

6 Are these the choice dishes the Doctor has sent us?
Is this the great poet whose works so content us?
This Goldsmith's fine feast, who has written fine books?
Heaven sends us good meat, but the Devil sends cooks.
'On Doctor Goldsmith's Characteristical Cookery' (1777)

7 Prologues precede the piece—in mournful verse;
As undertakers—walk before the hearse.
prologue to Arthur Murphy's *The Apprentice* (1756)

8 Kitty, a fair, but frozen maid,
Kindled a flame I still deplore.
'A Riddle' (1762)

William Lloyd Garrison 1805–79
American anti-slavery campaigner

9 I am in earnest—I will not equivocate—I will not excuse—I will not retreat a single inch—and I will be heard!
in *The Liberator* 1 January 1831 'Salutatory Address'

10 Our country is the world—our countrymen are all mankind.
The Liberator 15 December 1837 'Prospectus'

11 The compact which exists between the North and the South is 'a covenant with death and an agreement with hell'.
resolution adopted by the Massachusetts Anti-Slavery Society, 27 January 1843, in Archibald H. Grimke *William Lloyd Garrison: The Abolitionist* (1891) ch. 16; cf. **Bible** 87:14

Samuel Garth 1661–1719
English poet and physician

12 Hard was their lodging, homely was their food;
For all their luxury was doing good.
'Claremont' (1715) l. 148

13 A barren superfluity of words.
The Dispensary (1699) canto 2, l. 82

George Gascoigne c.1534–77
English soldier and poet

14 The common speech is, spend and God will send.
But what sends he? a bottle and a bag,
A staff, a wallet and a woeful end,
For such as list in bravery so to brag.
'*Magnum vectigal parsimonia* [Thrift makes a good income]' (1573)

15 The carrion crow, that loathsome beast,
Which cries against the rain.
'Gascoigne's Good Morrow' (1573)

16 As busy brains must beat on tickle toys,
As rash invention breeds a raw device,
So sudden falls do hinder hasty joys;
And as swift baits do fleetest fish entice,
So haste makes waste.
'No haste but good' (1573)

Elizabeth Gaskell 1810–65
English novelist

17 A man . . . is *so* in the way in the house!
Cranford (1853) ch. 1

18 Economy was always 'elegant', and money-spending always 'vulgar' and ostentatious— a sort of sour-grapeism, which made us very peaceful and satisfied.
Cranford (1853) ch. 1

19 Bombazine would have shown a deeper sense of her loss.
Cranford (1853) ch. 7

20 I'll not listen to reason . . . Reason always means what someone else has got to say.
Cranford (1853) ch. 14

21 That kind of patriotism which consists in hating all other nations.
Sylvia's Lovers (1863) ch. 1

22 I never *did* write a biography, and I don't exactly know how to set about it; you see I have to be accurate and keep to facts; a most difficult thing for a writer of fiction.
while writing her Life of Charlotte Brontë
letter to Harriet Anderson, 15 March 1856; *The Letters of Mrs Gaskell* (1966)

23 It is a noble grand book, whoever wrote it—but Miss Evans' life taken at the best construction, does so jar against the beautiful book that one cannot help hoping against hope.
on first hearing of the true identity of 'George **Eliot**', *author of* Adam Bede
letter to George Smith, 4 August 1859; *The Letters of Mrs Gaskell* (1966)

1 I look at them as a child looks at a cake,—with glittering eyes and watering mouth, imagining the pleasure that awaits him!
on the books she was planning to read
letter to George Smith, 4 August 1859; *The Letters of Mrs Gaskell* (1966)

Bill Gates 1955–
American computer entrepreneur
on Gates: see **Stross** *745:1*

2 If they want we will give them a sleeping bag, but there is something romantic about sleeping under the desk. They want to do it.
on his young software programmers
in *Independent* 18 November 1995 'Quote Unquote'

3 Technology is just a tool. In terms of getting the kids working together and motivating them, the teacher is the most important.
in *Independent on Sunday* 12 October 1997 'For the Record'

Paul Gauguin 1848–1903
French painter

4 A hint—don't paint too much direct from nature. Art is an abstraction! study nature then brood on it and treasure the creation which will result, which is the only way to ascend towards God—to create like our Divine Master.
letter to Emile Schuffenecker, 14 August 1888; *Paul Gauguin: Letters to his wife and friends* (1946, ed. Maurice Malingue, trans. Henry J. Stenning)

Alan Gaunt 1935–
hymnwriter

5 We pray for peace,
But not the easy peace
Built on complacency
And not the truth of God.
'We pray for peace' (hymn)

Théophile Gautier 1811–72
French poet, novelist, and critic

6 *Toute passe.—L'art robuste*
Seul à l'éternité,
Le Buste
Survit à la cité.

Everything passes. Robust art alone is eternal, the bust survives the city.
'L'Art' (1857); cf. **Dobson** 271:14

Gavarni (Guillaume Sulpice Chevalier) 1804–66
French lithographer

7 *Les enfants terribles.*

The little terrors.
title of a series of prints (1842)

John Gay 1685–1732
English poet and dramatist
on Gay: see **Johnson** *410:3; see also* **Epitaphs** *303:12*

8 O ruddier than the cherry,
O sweeter than the berry.
Acis and Galatea (performed 1718, published 1732) pt. 2

9 How, like a moth, the simple maid
Still plays about the flame!
The Beggar's Opera (1728) act 1, sc. 4, air 4

10 Our Polly is a sad slut! nor heeds what we have taught her.
I wonder any man alive will ever rear a daughter!
The Beggar's Opera (1728) act 1, sc. 8, air 7

11 Do you think your mother and I should have lived comfortably so long together, if ever we had been married?
The Beggar's Opera (1728) act 1, sc. 8

12 Can Love be controlled by advice?
The Beggar's Opera (1728) act 1, sc. 8, air 8

13 POLLY: Then all my sorrows are at an end.
MRS PEACHUM: A mighty likely speech, in troth, for a wench who is just married!
The Beggar's Opera (1728) act 1, sc. 8

14 Money, wife, is the true fuller's earth for reputations, there is not a spot or a stain but what it can take out.
The Beggar's Opera (1728) act 1, sc. 9

15 The comfortable estate of widowhood, is the only hope that keeps up a wife's spirits.
The Beggar's Opera (1728) act 1, sc. 10

16 If with me you'd fondly stray.
Over the hills and far away.
The Beggar's Opera (1728) act 1, sc. 13, air 16

17 Fill ev'ry glass, for wine inspires us,
And fires us
With courage, love and joy.
Women and wine should life employ.
Is there ought else on earth desirous?
The Beggar's Opera (1728) act 2, sc. 1, air 19

18 If the heart of a man is deprest with cares,
The mist is dispelled when a woman appears.
The Beggar's Opera (1728) act 2, sc. 3, air 21

19 I must have women. There is nothing unbends the mind like them.
The Beggar's Opera (1728) act 2, sc. 3

20 Youth's the season made for joys;
Love is then our duty.
The Beggar's Opera (1728) act 2, sc. 4, air 22

21 To cheat a man is nothing; but the woman must have fine parts indeed who cheats a woman!
The Beggar's Opera (1728) act 2, sc. 4

22 I am ready, my dear Lucy, to give you satisfaction—if you think there is any in marriage?
The Beggar's Opera (1728) act 2, sc. 9

23 In one respect indeed, our employment may be reckoned dishonest, because, like great Statesmen, we encourage those who betray their friends.
The Beggar's Opera (1728) act 2, sc. 10

1 How happy could I be with either,
Were t'other dear charmer away!
The Beggar's Opera (1728) act 2, sc. 13, air 35

2 She who has never loved, has never lived.
The Captives (1724) act 2, sc. 2

3 She who trifles with all
Is less likely to fall
Than she who but trifles with one.
'The Coquet Mother and the Coquet Daughter' (1727)

4 Behold the victim of Parthenia's pride!
He saw, he sighed, he loved, was scorned and died.
Dione (1720) act 1, sc. 1

5 A woman's friendship ever ends in love.
Dione (1720) act 4, sc. 6

6 Whence is thy learning? Hath thy toil
O'er books consumed the midnight oil?
Fables (1727) introduction, l. 15; cf. **Quarles** 618:16

7 Envy's a sharper spur than pay,
No author ever spared a brother,
Wits are gamecocks to one another.
Fables (1727) 'The Elephant and the Bookseller' l. 74

8 And when a lady's in the case,
You know, all other things give place.
Fables (1727) 'The Hare and Many Friends' l. 41

9 Those who in quarrels interpose,
Must often wipe a bloody nose.
Fables (1727) 'The Mastiffs' l. 1

10 An open foe may prove a curse,
But a pretended friend is worse.
Fables (1727) 'The Shepherd's Dog and the Wolf' l. 33

11 I know you lawyers can, with ease,
Twist words and meanings as you please;
That language, by your skill made pliant,
Will bend to favour ev'ry client.
Fables (1738) 'The Dog and the Fox' l. 1

12 Studious of elegance and ease,
Myself alone I seek to please.
Fables (1738) 'The Man, the Cat, the Dog, and the Fly' l. 127

13 That politician tops his part,
Who readily can lie with art.
Fables (1738) 'The Squire and his Cur' l. 27

14 Give me, kind heaven, a private station,
A mind serene for contemplation.
Fables (1738) 'The Vulture, the Sparrow, and Other Birds' l. 69

15 Behold the bright original appear.
'A Letter to a Lady' (1714) l. 85

16 Praising all alike, is praising none.
'A Letter to a Lady' (1714) l. 114

17 Whether we can afford it or no, we must have superfluities.
'Polly' (1729) act 1, sc. 1

18 No, sir, tho' I was born and bred in England, I can dare to be poor, which is the only thing now-a-days men are ashamed of.
'Polly' (1729) act 1, sc. 11

19 An inconstant woman, tho' she has no chance to be very happy, can never be very unhappy.
'Polly' (1729) act 1, sc. 14

20 All in the Downs the fleet was moored,
The streamers waving in the wind,
When black-eyed Susan came aboard.
'Sweet William's Farewell to Black-Eyed Susan' (1720)

21 They'll tell thee, sailors, when away,
In ev'ry port a mistress find.
'Sweet William's Farewell to Black-Eyed Susan' (1720)

22 Adieu, she cries! and waved her lily hand.
'Sweet William's Farewell to Black-Eyed Susan' (1720)

23 A miss for pleasure, and a wife for breed.
'The Toilette' (1716)

Noel Gay (Richard Moxon Armitage) 1898–1954

British songwriter

24 I'm leaning on a lamp post at the corner of the street,
In case a certain little lady comes by.
'Leaning on a Lamp Post' (1937); sung by George Formby in the film *Father Knew Best*

Eric Geddes 1875–1937

British politician and administrator

25 The Germans, if this Government is returned, are going to pay every penny; they are going to be squeezed as a lemon is squeezed—until the pips squeak.
speech at Cambridge, 10 December 1918, in *Cambridge Daily News* 11 December 1918

Bob Geldof 1954–

Irish rock musician

26 Sex was a competitive event in those days and the only thing you could take as a certainty was that everyone else was lying, just as you were.
Is That It? (1986)

27 Most people get into bands for three very simple rock and roll reasons: to get laid, to get fame, and to get rich.
in *Melody Maker* 27 August 1977

Bob Geldof 1954– and **Midge Ure** 1953–

Irish rock musician; Scottish rock musician

28 Do they know it's Christmas?
title of song (1984)

Martha Gellhorn 1908–98

American journalist

1 I believed that all one did about a war was go to it, as a gesture of solidarity, and get killed, or survive if lucky until the war was over . . . I had no idea you could be what I became, an unscathed tourist of wars.

The Face of War (1959)

of the defeat of the Spanish Republic:

2 I daresay we all became more competent press tourists because of it, since we never again cared so much. You can only love one war; afterward, I suppose, you do your duty.

The Honeyed Peace (1953)

3 Never believe governments, not any of them, not a word they say; keep an untrusting eye on all they do.

in obituary, *Daily Telegraph* 17 February 1998

Jean Genet 1910–86

French novelist, poet, and dramatist

4 What we need is hatred. From it our ideas are born.

The Blacks (1959); epigraph

5 Are you there . . . Africa of the millions of royal slaves, deported Africa, drifting continent, are you there? Slowly you vanish, you withdraw into the past, into the tales of castaways, colonial museums, the works of scholars.

The Blacks (1959)

6 Anyone who hasn't experienced the ecstasy of betrayal knows nothing about ecstasy at all.

Prisoner of Love (1986)

Genghis Khan (Temujin) 1162–1227

founder of the Mongol empire, who took the name Genghis Khan ('ruler of all') in 1206 after uniting the nomadic tribes

7 Happiness lies in conquering one's enemies, in driving them in front of oneself, in taking their property, in savouring their despair, in outraging their wives and daughters.

Witold Rodzinski *The Walled Kingdom: A History of China* (1979)

Máire Geoghegan-Quinn 1950–

Irish politician and writer

8 I've kept political diaries ever since I went into politics . . . I'd love to do a political memoir, but a lot of people will have to be dead first.

in *Irish Times* 6 November 1997

George I 1660–1727

King of Great Britain and Ireland from 1714
on George I: see **Johnson** *414:28,* **Landor** *450:4*

9 I hate all Boets and Bainters.

John Campbell *Lives of the Chief Justices* (1849) 'Lord Mansfield'

George II 1683–1760

King of Great Britain and Ireland from 1727, husband of **Caroline** *of Ansbach*
on George II: see **Landor** *450:4*

10 We are come for your good, for all your goods.

speech at Portsmouth, probably 1716, in Joseph Spence *Anecdotes* (ed. J. M. Osborn, 1966) no. 903

11 *Non, j'aurai des maîtresses.*

No, I shall have mistresses.

when Queen **Caroline***, on her deathbed in 1737, urged him to marry again; the Queen replied,* 'Ah! mon dieu! cela n'empêche pas [Oh, my God! That won't make any difference]'

John Hervey *Memoirs of the Reign of George II* (1848) vol. 2.

12 Mad, is he? Then I hope he will *bite* some of my other generals.

replying to the Duke of Newcastle, who had complained that General **Wolfe** *was a madman*

Henry Beckles Willson *Life and Letters of James Wolfe* (1909) ch. 17

George III 1738–1820

King of Great Britain and Ireland from 1760
on George III: see **Bagehot** *47:1,* **Bentley** *67:7,* **Byron** *179:12,* **Landor** *450:4,* **Shelley** *713:28,* **Walpole** *801:23; see also* **Edgeworth** *289:1*

13 Born and educated in this country, I glory in the name of Briton.

The King's Speech on Opening the Session House of Lords, 18 November 1760

14 Was there ever such stuff as great part of Shakespeare? Only one must not say so! But what think you?—what?—Is there not sad stuff? what?—what?

to Fanny Burney, in *Diary and Letters of Madame d'Arblay* vol. 2 (1842) diary, 19 December 1785

George IV 1762–1830

King of Great Britain and Ireland from 1820
on George IV: see **Brummell** *158:21,* **Hunt** *396:5,* **Landor** *450:4*

15 Harris, I am not well; pray get me a glass of brandy.

on first seeing Caroline of Brunswick, his future wife

Earl of Malmesbury *Diaries and Correspondence* (1844) vol. 3, 5 April 1795

George V 1865–1936

King of Great Britain and Ireland from 1910
on George V: see **Betjeman** *70:7,* **Dawson** *253:8,* **Nicolson** *545:3; see also* **Last words** *455:5, 455:18*

16 Wake up, England.

title of 1911 reprint of speech below

I venture to allude to the impression which seemed generally to prevail among their brethren across the seas, that the Old Country must wake up if she intends to maintain her old position of pre-eminence in her Colonial trade against foreign competitors.

speech at Guildhall, 5 December 1901, in Harold Nicolson *King George V* (1952)

1 I pray that my coming to Ireland today may prove to be the first step towards an end of strife among her people, whatever their race or creed. In that hope I appeal to all Irishmen to pause, to stretch out the hand of forbearance and conciliation, to forgive and forget, and to join with me in making for the land they love a new era of peace, contentment and goodwill.

speech to the new Ulster Parliament at Stormont, 22 June 1921; Kenneth Rose *King George V* (1983)

2 I have many times asked myself whether there can be more potent advocates of peace upon earth through the years to come than this massed multitude of silent witnesses to the desolation of war.

message read at Terlincthun Cemetery, Boulogne, 13 May 1922, in *The Times* 15 May 1922

3 After I am dead, the boy will ruin himself in twelve months.

of his son, the future ***Edward VIII***

Keith Middlemas and John Barnes *Baldwin* (1969) ch. 34

4 Anything except that damned Mouse.

on being asked what film he would like to see

George Lyttelton, letter to Rupert Hart-Davis, 12 November 1959

on H. G. ***Wells****'s comment on 'an alien and uninspiring court':*

5 I may be uninspiring, but I'll be damned if I'm an alien!

Sarah Bradford *George VI* (1989); attributed

6 My father was frightened of his mother; I was frightened of my father, and I am damned well going to see to it that my children are frightened of me.

attributed in Randolph S. Churchill *Lord Derby* (1959), but said by Kenneth Rose in *George V* (1983) to be almost certainly apocryphal; cf. **Morshead** 533:7

George VI 1895–1952

King of Great Britain and Northern Ireland from 1936
see also ***Haskins*** *363:16*

7 Personally I feel happier now that we have no allies to be polite to and to pamper.

to Queen Mary, 27 June 1940, in John Wheeler-Bennett *King George VI* (1958) pt. 3, ch. 6

8 Abroad is bloody.

W. H. Auden *A Certain World* (1970) 'Royalty'; cf. **Mitford** 524:9

9 The family firm.

description of the British monarchy

attributed

Daniel George (Daniel George Bunting)

English writer

10 O Freedom, what liberties are taken in thy name!

The Perpetual Pessimist (1963); cf. **Last words** 456:19

Lloyd George see David Lloyd George

Geronimo c.1829–1909

Apache leader

11 Once I moved about like the wind. Now I surrender to you and that is all.

surrendering to General Crook, 25 March 1886; Dee Brown *Bury My Heart at Wounded Knee* (1970) ch. 17

Ira Gershwin 1896–1983

American songwriter
see also ***Heyward and Gershwin***

12 A foggy day in London Town
Had me low and had me down.
I viewed the morning with alarm,
The British Museum had lost its charm.
How long, I wondered, could this thing last?
But the age of miracles hadn't passed,
For, suddenly, I saw you there
And through foggy London town the sun was shining everywhere.

'A Foggy Day' (1937 song) in *Damsel in Distress*

13 I don't think I'll fall in love today.

title of song (1928, from *Treasure Girl*); cf. **Chesterton** 209:29

14 I got rhythm.

title of song (1930, from *Girl Crazy*)

15 In time the Rockies may crumble,
Gibraltar may tumble,
They're only made of clay,
But our love is here to stay.

'Love is Here to Stay' (1938 song) in *The Goldwyn Follies*

16 Holding hands at midnight
'Neath a starry sky,
Nice work if you can get it,
And you can get it if you try.

'Nice Work If You Can Get It' (1937 song) in *Damsel in Distress*

17 Ev'ry corner that you turn you meet a notable
With a statement that is eminently quotable!

'Of Thee I Sing' (title of song and show, 1931)

18 They all laughed at Christopher Columbus
When he said the world was round
They all laughed when Edison recorded sound
They all laughed at Wilbur and his brother
When they said that man could fly;
They told Marconi
Wireless was a phony—
It's the same old cry!

'They All Laughed' (1937 song)

19 A good lyric should be rhymed conversation.

Philip Furia *Ira Gershwin* (1966)

20 I now belong, I see, to the rank of Brothers of the Great.

thanking a friend for clippings about his brother George's success

Philip Furia *Ira Gershwin* (1966)

21 The Show Must Go On—but not too long after eleven p.m.

on axing a skit and a song from a late running show

Philip Furia *Ira Gershwin* (1966)

Gervase of Canterbury c.1141–c.1210

English monastic chronicler

1 Him, therefore, they retained, on account of his lively genius and good reputation, and dismissed the others.
on the appointment of William of Sens as architect of the new work at Canterbury cathedral in 1174
Chronica Gervasii; F. Woodman *The Architectural History of Canterbury Cathedral* (1981)

J. Paul Getty 1892–1976

American industrialist

2 If you can actually count your money, then you are not really a rich man.
in *Observer* 3 November 1957

Giuseppe Giacosa 1847–1906 and Luigi Illica 1857–1919

Italian librettists

3 *Che gelida manina.*
Your tiny hand is frozen.
Rodolfo to Mimi
La Bohème (1896) act 1; music by Puccini

Edward Gibbon 1737–94

English historian

on Gibbon: see **Byron** *174:21*, **Colman** *229:18*, **Gloucester** *341:19*

4 The various modes of worship, which prevailed in the Roman world, were all considered by the people as equally true; by the philosopher, as equally false; and by the magistrate, as equally useful. And thus toleration produced not only mutual indulgence, but even religious concord.
The Decline and Fall of the Roman Empire (1776–88) ch. 2

5 In elective monarchies, the vacancy of the throne is a moment big with danger and mischief.
The Decline and Fall of the Roman Empire (1776–88) ch. 3

6 History . . . is, indeed, little more than the register of the crimes, follies, and misfortunes of mankind.
The Decline and Fall of the Roman Empire (1776–88) ch. 3; cf. **Voltaire** 797:18

7 In every age and country, the wiser, or at least the stronger, of the two sexes, has usurped the powers of the state, and confined the other to the cares and pleasures of domestic life.
The Decline and Fall of the Roman Empire (1776–88) ch. 6

8 Twenty-two acknowledged concubines, and a library of sixty-two thousand volumes, attested the variety of his inclinations, and from the productions which he left behind him, it appears that the former as well as the latter were designed for use rather than ostentation. [Footnote] By each of his concubines the younger Gordian left three or four children. His literary productions were by no means contemptible.
The Decline and Fall of the Roman Empire (1776–88) ch. 7

9 All taxes must, at last, fall upon agriculture.
quoting Artaxerxes, in *The Decline and Fall of the Roman Empire* (1776–88) ch. 8

10 Whenever the offence inspires less horror than the punishment, the rigour of penal law is obliged to give way to the common feelings of mankind.
The Decline and Fall of the Roman Empire (1776–88) ch. 14

11 Corruption, the most infallible symptom of constitutional liberty.
The Decline and Fall of the Roman Empire (1776–88) ch. 21

12 In every deed of mischief he had a heart to resolve, a head to contrive, and a hand to execute.
of Comnenus
The Decline and Fall of the Roman Empire (1776–88) ch. 48; cf. **Clarendon** 218:19

13 Our sympathy is cold to the relation of distant misery.
The Decline and Fall of the Roman Empire (1776–88) ch. 49

14 Persuasion is the resource of the feeble; and the feeble can seldom persuade.
The Decline and Fall of the Roman Empire (1776–88) ch. 68

15 All that is human must retrograde if it does not advance.
The Decline and Fall of the Roman Empire (1776–88) ch. 71

16 The satirist may laugh, the philosopher may preach, but Reason herself will respect the prejudices and habits which have been consecrated by the experience of mankind.
Memoirs of My Life (1796) ch. 1

17 To the University of Oxford I acknowledge no obligation; and she will as cheerfully renounce me for a son, as I am willing to disclaim her for a mother. I spent fourteen months at Magdalen College: they proved the fourteen months the most idle and unprofitable of my whole life.
Memoirs of My Life (1796) ch. 3

18 Their dull and deep potations excused the brisk intemperance of youth.
on the dons at Oxford
Memoirs of My Life (1796) ch. 3

19 Dr— well remembered that he had a salary to receive, and only forgot that he had a duty to perform.
Memoirs of My Life (1796) ch. 3

20 It was here that I suspended my religious inquiries (aged 17).
Memoirs of My Life (1796) ch. 4

21 I saw and loved.
Memoirs of My Life (1796) ch. 4

22 I sighed as a lover, I obeyed as a son.
Memoirs of My Life (1796) ch. 4 n.

23 Crowds without company, and dissipation without pleasure.
of London
Memoirs of My Life (1796) ch. 5

24 The captain of the Hampshire grenadiers . . . has not been useless to the historian of the Roman empire.
of his own army service
Memoirs of My Life (1796) ch. 5

25 It was at Rome, on the fifteenth of October, 1764, as I sat musing amidst the ruins of the Capitol,

while the barefoot friars were singing vespers in the Temple of Jupiter, that the idea of writing the decline and fall of the city first started to my mind.
Memoirs of My Life (1796) ch. 6 n.

1 I will not dissemble the first emotions of joy on the recovery of my freedom, and, perhaps, the establishment of my fame. But my pride was soon humbled, and a sober melancholy was spread over my mind, by the idea that I had taken an everlasting leave of an old and agreeable companion, and that whatsoever might be the future date of my History, the life of the historian must be short and precarious.
on the completion of The Decline and Fall of the Roman Empire
Memoirs of My Life (1796) ch. 8

2 My English text is chaste, and all licentious passages are left in the obscurity of a learned language.
parodied as 'decent obscurity' in the Anti-Jacobin, *1797–8*
Memoirs of My Life (1796) ch. 8

3 The abbreviation of time, and the failure of hope, will always tinge with a browner shade the evening of life.
Memoirs of My Life (1796) ch. 8

Orlando Gibbons 1583–1625
English organist and composer

4 The silver swan, who, living had no note,
When death approached unlocked her silent
throat.
The First Set of Madrigals and Motets of Five Parts (1612) 'The Silver Swan'

Stella Gibbons 1902–89
English novelist

5 When the sukebind hangs heavy from the wains.
Cold Comfort Farm (1932) ch. 5

6 'Tes the hand of Nature and we women cannot escape it.
Cold Comfort Farm (1932) ch. 5

7 Something nasty in the woodshed.
Cold Comfort Farm (1932) ch. 10

8 By god, D. H. Lawrence was right when he had said there must be a dumb, dark, dull, bitter belly-tension between a man and a woman, and how else could this be achieved save in the long monotony of marriage?
Cold Comfort Farm (1932) ch. 20

Wolcott Gibbs 1902–58
American critic

9 Backward ran sentences until reeled the mind.
satirizing the style of Time *magazine*
in *New Yorker* 28 November 1936 'Time . . . Fortune . . . Life . . . Luce'

Kahlil Gibran 1883–1931
Syrian writer and painter

10 Are you a politician who says to himself: 'I will use my country for my own benefit'? . . . Or are you a devoted patriot, who whispers in the ear of his inner self: 'I love to serve my country as a faithful servant.'
The New Frontier (1931), translated by Anthony R. Ferris in *The Voice of the Master* (1958); cf. **Kennedy** 433:14

11 Your children are not your children.
They are the sons and daughters of Life's longing
for itself.
They came through you but not from you
And though they are with you yet they belong not
to you.
You may give them your love but not your
thoughts,
For they have their own thoughts.
You may house their bodies but not their souls.
The Prophet (1923) 'On Children'

12 You shall be together when the white wings of
death scatter your days.
Ay, you shall be together even in the silent
memory of God.
But let there be spaces in your togetherness,
And let the winds of the heavens dance between
you.
The Prophet (1923) 'On Marriage'

13 Work is love made visible.
The Prophet (1923) 'On Work'

14 An exaggeration is a truth that has lost its temper.
Sand and Foam (1926)

Wilfrid Wilson Gibson 1878–1962
English poet

15 Nor feel the heart-break in the heart of things.
'Lament' (1918)

André Gide 1869–1951
French novelist and critic

16 The whole effect of Christianity was to transfer the drama onto the moral plane.
Les Faux Monnayeurs (1925) pt. 1, ch. 13 (translated by Dorothy Bussy)

17 What cleanliness everywhere! You dare not throw your cigarette into the lake. No graffiti in the urinals. Switzerland is proud of this; but I believe this is just what she lacks: manure.
diary, Lucerne, 10 August 1917; *Journals 1889–1949* (1967, translated by Justin O'Brien)

18 The great secret of Stendhal, his great shrewdness, consisted in writing *at once* . . . thought charged with emotion.
Journal (1939) vol. 3, 3 September 1937 (translated by Justin O'Brien)

19 Hugo—alas!
when asked who was the greatest 19th-century poet
Claude Martin *La Maturité d'André Gide* (1977)

Thomas Gilbart fl. c.1583

English poet

1 Shall silence shroud such sin
As Satan seems to show
Even in his imps, in these our days
That all men might it know?
No, no, it cannot be.
'A declaration of the death of John Lewes' (1583)

2 And when the fire did compass him
About on every side,
The people looked he then would speak,
And therefore loud they cried:
'Now call on Christ to save thy soul;
Now trust in Christ his death.'
But all in vain; no words he spake,
But thus yields up his breath.
Oh, woeful state, oh danger deep,
That he was drownèd in!
Oh grant us, God, for Christ his sake,
We fall not in such sin.
'A declaration of the death of John Lewes' (1583)

Humphrey Gilbert c.1537–83

English explorer

3 We are as near to heaven by sea as by land!
Richard Hakluyt *Third and Last Volume of the Voyages . . . of the English Nation* (1600); cf. **Elstow** 298:17

W. S. Gilbert (Sir William Schwenck Gilbert) 1836–1911

English writer of comic and satirical verse
on Gilbert: see ***Epitaphs*** *303:19*

4 Then they began to sing
That extremely lovely thing,
'*Scherzando! ma non troppo ppp.*'
The 'Bab' Ballads (1869) 'Story of Prince Agib'

5 That celebrated,
Cultivated,
Underrated
Nobleman,
The Duke of Plaza Toro!
The Gondoliers (1889) act 1

6 Of that there is no manner of doubt—
No probable, possible shadow of doubt—
No possible doubt whatever.
The Gondoliers (1889) act 1

7 But the privilege and pleasure
That we treasure beyond measure
Is to run on little errands for the Ministers of State.
The Gondoliers (1889) act 2

8 Take a pair of sparkling eyes,
Hidden, ever and anon,
In a merciful eclipse.
The Gondoliers (1889) act 2

9 Ambassadors cropped up like hay,
Prime Ministers and such as they
Grew like asparagus in May,
And dukes were three a penny.
The Gondoliers (1889) act 2

10 When every one is somebodee,
Then no one's anybody.
The Gondoliers (1889) act 2

11 Bow, bow, ye lower middle classes!
Bow, bow, ye tradesmen, bow, ye masses.
Iolanthe (1882) act 1

12 The Law is the true embodiment
Of everything that's excellent.
It has no kind of fault or flaw,
And I, my Lords, embody the Law.
Iolanthe (1882) act 1

13 Hearts just as pure and fair
May beat in Belgrave Square
As in the lowly air
Of Seven Dials.
Iolanthe (1882) act 1

14 I often think it's comical
How Nature always does contrive
That every boy and every gal,
That's born into the world alive,
Is either a little Liberal,
Or else a little Conservative!
Iolanthe (1882) act 2

15 When in that House MPs divide,
If they've a brain and cerebellum too,
They have to leave that brain outside,
And vote just as their leaders tell 'em to.
Iolanthe (1882) act 2

16 The prospect of a lot
Of dull MPs in close proximity,
All thinking for themselves is what
No man can face with equanimity.
Iolanthe (1882) act 2

17 The House of Peers, throughout the war,
Did nothing in particular,
And did it very well.
Iolanthe (1882) act 2

18 When you're lying awake with a dismal headache, and repose is taboo'd by anxiety,
I conceive you may use any language you choose to indulge in, without impropriety.
Iolanthe (1882) act 2

19 For you dream you are crossing the Channel, and tossing about in a steamer from Harwich—
Which is something between a large bathing machine and a very small second class carriage.
Iolanthe (1882) act 2

20 The shares are a penny, and ever so many are taken by Rothschild and Baring,
And just as a few are allotted to you, you awake with a shudder despairing.
Iolanthe (1882) act 2

21 A wandering minstrel I—
A thing of shreds and patches.
Of ballads, songs and snatches,
And dreamy lullaby!
The Mikado (1885) act 1; cf. **Shakespeare** 665:19

22 I can trace my ancestry back to a protoplasmal primordial atomic globule. Consequently, my

family pride is something in-conceivable. I can't help it. I was born sneering.
The Mikado (1885) act 1

1 As some day it may happen that a victim must be found,
I've got a little list—I've got a little list
Of society offenders who might well be under ground
And who never would be missed—who never would be missed!
The Mikado (1885) act 1

2 The idiot who praises, with enthusiastic tone,
All centuries but this, and every country but his own.
The Mikado (1885) act 1; cf. **Canning** 185:1, **Disraeli** 269:7, **Overbury** 561:1

3 Three little maids from school are we,
Pert as a schoolgirl well can be,
Filled to the brim with girlish glee.
The Mikado (1885) act 1

4 Three little maids who, all unwary,
Come from a ladies' seminary.
The Mikado (1885) act 1

5 Modified rapture!
The Mikado (1885) act 1

6 Awaiting the sensation of a short, sharp shock,
From a cheap and chippy chopper on a big black block.
The Mikado (1885) act 1

7 Here's a how-de-doo!
The Mikado (1885) act 2

8 Here's a state of things!
The Mikado (1885) act 2

9 My object all sublime
I shall achieve in time—
To let the punishment fit the crime—
The punishment fit the crime.
The Mikado (1885) act 2

10 And there he plays extravagant matches
In fitless fingerstalls
On a cloth untrue
With a twisted cue
And elliptical billiard balls.
on the billiard sharp
The Mikado (1885) act 2

11 I have a left shoulder-blade that is a miracle of loveliness. People come miles to see it. My right elbow has a fascination that few can resist.
The Mikado (1885) act 2

12 Something lingering, with boiling oil in it, I fancy.
The Mikado (1885) act 2

13 Merely corroborative detail, intended to give artistic verisimilitude to an otherwise bald and unconvincing narrative.
The Mikado (1885) act 2

14 The flowers that bloom in the spring,
Tra la,
Have nothing to do with the case.
The Mikado (1885) act 2

15 On a tree by a river a little tom-tit
Sang 'Willow, titwillow, titwillow!'
And I said to him, 'Dicky-bird, why do you sit
Singing Willow, titwillow, titwillow?'
The Mikado (1885) act 2

16 There's a fascination frantic
In a ruin that's romantic;
Do you think you are sufficiently decayed?
The Mikado (1885) act 2

17 If you're anxious for to shine in the high aesthetic line as a man of culture rare.
Patience (1881) act 1

18 The meaning doesn't matter if it's only idle chatter of a transcendental kind.
Patience (1881) act 1

19 An attachment à la Plato for a bashful young potato, or a not too French French bean!
Patience (1881) act 1

20 If you walk down Piccadilly with a poppy or a lily in your medieval hand.
Patience (1881) act 1

21 Francesca di Rimini, miminy, piminy,
Je-ne-sais-quoi young man!
Patience (1881) act 2

22 A greenery-yallery, Grosvenor Gallery,
Foot-in-the-grave young man!
Patience (1881) act 2

23 I'm called Little Buttercup—dear Little Buttercup,
Though I could never tell why.
HMS Pinafore (1878) act 1

24 What, never?
No, never!
What, *never*?
Hardly ever!
HMS Pinafore (1878) act 1

25 Though 'Bother it' I may
Occasionally say,
I never use a big, big D—
HMS Pinafore (1878) act 1

26 And so do his sisters, and his cousins and his aunts!
His sisters and his cousins,
Whom he reckons up by dozens,
And his aunts!
HMS Pinafore (1878) act 1

27 I cleaned the windows and I swept the floor,
And I polished up the handle of the big front door.
I polished up that handle so carefullee
That now I am the Ruler of the Queen's Navee!
HMS Pinafore (1878) act 1

28 I always voted at my party's call,
And I never thought of thinking for myself at all.
HMS Pinafore (1878) act 1

29 Stick close to your desks and never go to sea,
And you all may be Rulers of the Queen's Navee!
HMS Pinafore (1878) act 1

30 He is an Englishman!
For he himself has said it,

And it's greatly to his credit,
That he is an Englishman!
HMS Pinafore (1878) act 2

1 For he might have been a Roosian,
A French, or Turk, or Proosian,
Or perhaps Ital-ian!
But in spite of all temptations
To belong to other nations,
He remains an Englishman!
HMS Pinafore (1878) act 2

2 It is, it is a glorious thing
To be a Pirate King.
The Pirates of Penzance (1879) act 1

3 I'm very good at integral and differential calculus,
I know the scientific names of beings animalculous;
In short, in matters vegetable, animal, and mineral,
I am the very model of a modern Major-General.
The Pirates of Penzance (1879) act 1

4 About binomial theorem I'm teeming with a lot of news,
With many cheerful facts about the square on the hypotenuse.
The Pirates of Penzance (1879) act 1

5 When constabulary duty's to be done,
A policeman's lot is not a happy one.
The Pirates of Penzance (1879) act 2

6 Man is Nature's sole mistake!
Princess Ida (1884) act 2

7 He combines the manners of a Marquis with the morals of a Methodist.
Ruddigore (1887) act 1

8 Some word that teems with hidden meaning—like Basingstoke.
Ruddigore (1887) act 2

9 This particularly rapid, unintelligible patter
Isn't generally heard, and if it is it doesn't matter.
Ruddigore (1887) act 2

10 I was a pale young curate then.
The Sorcerer (1877) act 1

11 So I fell in love with a rich attorney's
Elderly ugly daughter.
Trial by Jury (1875)

12 She may very well pass for forty-three
In the dusk with a light behind her!
Trial by Jury (1875)

13 'Tis ever thus with simple folk—an accepted wit has but to say 'Pass the mustard', and they roar their ribs out!
The Yeoman of the Guard (1888) act 2

Eric Gill 1882–1940

English sculptor, engraver, and typographer

14 That state is a state of slavery in which a man does what he likes to do in his spare time and in his working time that which is required of him.
Art-nonsense and Other Essays (1929) 'Slavery and Freedom'; cf. **Collingwood** 228:11

Charlotte Perkins Gilman 1860–1935

American writer and feminist

15 The labour of women in the house, certainly enables men to produce more wealth than they otherwise could; and in this way women are economic factors in society. But so are horses.
Women and Economics (1898) ch. 1

16 There is no female mind. The brain is not an organ of sex. As well speak of a female liver.
Women and Economics (1898) ch. 8

17 The people people choose for friends
Your common sense appal,
But the people people marry
Are the queerest ones of all.
'Queer People'

Newton Gingrich 1943–

American Republican politician; Speaker of the House of Representatives from 1995

18 No society can survive, no civilization can survive, with 12-year-olds having babies, with 15-year-olds killing each other, with 17-year-olds dying of Aids, with 18-year-olds getting diplomas they can't read.
in *The Times* 9 February 1995

Allen Ginsberg 1926–97

American poet and novelist
see also ***Last Words*** *456:6*

19 What if someone gave a war & Nobody came?
Life would ring the bells of Ecstasy and Forever be Itself again.
'Graffiti' (1972); cf. **Film titles** 313:3, **Sandburg** 644:2

20 I saw the best minds of my generation destroyed by madness, starving hysterical naked,
dragging themselves through the negro streets at dawn looking for an angry fix,
angelheaded hipsters burning for the ancient heavenly connection to the starry dynamo in the machinery of the night.
Howl (1956)

21 What thoughts I have of you tonight, Walt Whitman, for I walked
down the sidestreets under the trees with a headache self-
conscious looking at the full moon.
'A Supermarket in California' (1956)

22 What peaches and what penumbras! Whole
families shopping at night! Aisles full of husbands!
Wives in the avocados, babies in the tomatoes!—
and you, Garcia Lorca what were you doing down
by the watermelons?
'A Supermarket in California' (1956)

23 Ah, dear father, graybeard, lonely old courage-teacher, what
America did you have when Charon quit poling his ferry and you
got out on a smoking bank and stood watching the boat
disappear on the black waters of Lethe?
'A Supermarket in California' (1956)

Nikki Giovanni 1943–

American poet

1 it's a sex object if you're pretty
and no love
or love and no sex if you're fat

'Woman Poem' (1970)

George Gipp 1895–1920

American footballer

2 Tell them to go in there with all they've got and win just one for the Gipper.

the catchphrase 'Win one for the Gipper' was later used by Ronald ***Reagan****, who played Gipp in the 1940 film* Knute Rockne, All American

Knut Rockne 'Gipp the Great' in *Collier's* 22 November 1930

Giraldus Cambrensis (Gerald of Wales) c.1146–c.1223

Welsh cleric and historian

3 The well of poisons brims over in the East.

The History and Topography of Ireland pt. 1, ch. 32

4 The Isle of Man . . . is equidistant from the north of Ireland and Britain. There was a great controversy in antiquity concerning the question, to which of the two countries should the island properly belong? . . . All agreed that since it allowed poisonous reptiles to live in it, it should belong to Britain.

The History and Topography of Ireland pt. 2, ch. 48

5 Just as the men of this country are during their mortal life more prone to anger and revenge than any other race, so in eternal death the saints of this land that have been elevated by their merits are more vindictive than the saints of any other region.

The History and Topography of Ireland pt. 2, ch. 83

6 The clergy of this country are on the whole to be commended for their observance. Among their other virtues chastity shines out as a kind of special prerogative.

The History and Topography of Ireland pt. 3, ch. 104

Jean Giraudoux 1882–1944

French dramatist

7 As soon as war is declared it will be impossible to hold the poets back. Rhyme is still the most effective drum.

La Guerre de Troie n'aura pas lieu (1935) act 2, sc. 4 (translated by Christopher Fry as *Tiger at the Gates*, 1955)

8 All of us here know there's no better way of exercising the imagination than the study of law. No poet ever interpreted nature as freely as a lawyer interprets the truth.

La Guerre de Troie n'aura pas lieu (1935) act 2, sc. 5

George Gissing 1857–1903

English novelist

9 Imagine the future historian writing in wonderment of the absurd reticence with which our novelists treat sexual subjects, and comparing this with their licence to describe in detail the most hideous of murders.

Commonplace Book (1962)

10 Mr Quarmby laughed in a peculiar way, which was the result of long years of mirth-subdual in the Reading-room.

New Grub Street (1891)

Edna Gladney

American philanthropist

11 There are no illegitimate children, only illegitimate parents.

MGM paid her a large sum for the line for the 1941 film based on her life, 'Blossoms in the Dust'

A. Loos *Kiss Hollywood Good-Bye* (1978)

W. E. Gladstone 1809–98

British Liberal statesman; Prime Minister, 1868–74, 1880–5, 1886, 1892–4

on Gladstone: see ***Anonymous*** *16:15,* ***Churchill*** *214:12, 214:13, 214:15,* ***Disraeli*** *269:15, 269:20,* ***Foot*** *319:2,* ***Labouchere*** *446:13,* ***Sellar and Yeatman*** *654:15,* ***Victoria*** *792:5, 792:7*

12 Ireland, Ireland! that cloud in the west, that coming storm.

letter to his wife, 12 October 1845

13 This is the negation of God erected into a system of Government.

A Letter to the Earl of Aberdeen on the State Prosecutions of the Neapolitan Government (1851)

14 Finance is, as it were, the stomach of the country, from which all the other organs take their tone.

article on finance, 1858, in H. C. G. Matthew *Gladstone 1809–1874* (1986) ch. 5

15 I am come among you 'unmuzzled'.

speech in Manchester, 18 July 1865, after his parliamentary defeat at Oxford University

John Morley *Life of Gladstone* (1903) vol. 2

16 You cannot fight against the future. Time is on our side.

speech on the Reform Bill, in House of Commons, 27 April 1866

17 My mission is to pacify Ireland.

on receiving news that he was to form his first cabinet, 1st December 1868

H. C. G. Matthew *Gladstone 1809–1874* (1986) ch. 5

18 Swimming for his life, a man does not see much of the country through which the river winds.

diary, 31 December 1868 in M. R. D. Foot and H. C. G. Matthew (eds.) *The Gladstone Diaries* (1978) vol. 6

19 Let the Turks now carry away their abuses in the only possible manner, namely by carrying off themselves . . . one and all, bag and baggage, shall I hope clear out from the province they have desolated and profaned.

Bulgarian Horrors and the Question of the East (1876)

1 [An] Established Clergy will always be a Tory Corps d'Armée.

letter to Bishop Goodwin, 8 September 1881

2 There never was a Churchill from John of Marlborough down that had either morals or principles.

in conversation in 1882, recorded by Captain R. V. Briscoe; R. F. Foster *Lord Randolph Churchill* (1981)

3 Our first site in Egypt, be it by larceny or be it by emption, will be the almost certain egg of a North African Empire, that will grow and grow . . . till we finally join hands across the Equator with Natal and Cape Town, to say nothing of the Transvaal and the Orange River on the south, or of Abyssinia or Zanzibar to be swallowed by way of *viaticum* on our journey.

Aggression on Egypt and Freedom in the East (1884)

4 Ideal perfection is not the true basis of English legislation. We look at the attainable; we look at the practical, and we have too much English sense to be drawn away by those sanguine delineations of what might possibly be attained in Utopia, from a path which promises to enable us to effect great good for the people of England.

speech on the Reform Bill, in House of Commons, 28 February 1884

5 It is perfectly true that these gentlemen wish to march through rapine to disintegration and dismemberment of the Empire, and, I am sorry to say, even to the placing of different parts of the Empire in direct hostility one with the other.

on the Irish Land League

speech at Knowsley, 27 October 1881, in *The Times*, 28 October 1881

6 I would tell them of my own intention to keep my counsel . . . and I will venture to recommend them, as an old Parliamentary hand, to do the same.

speech, House of Commons, 21 January 1886

7 This, if I understand it, is one of those golden moments of our history, one of those opportunities which may come and may go, but which rarely returns.

speech on the Second Reading of the Home Rule Bill, in House of Commons, 7 June 1886

8 I will venture to say, that upon the one great class of subjects, the largest and the most weighty of them all, where the leading and determining considerations that ought to lead to a conclusion are truth, justice, and humanity—upon these, gentlemen, all the world over, I will back the masses against the classes.

speech in Liverpool, 28 June 1886, in *The Times* 29 June 1886

9 One prayer absorbs all others: Ireland, Ireland, Ireland.

diary, 10 April 1887

10 The blubbering Cabinet.

of the colleagues who wept at his final Cabinet meeting

diary, 1 March 1894; note

11 What that Sicilian mule was to me, I have been to the Queen.

of a mule on which Gladstone rode, which he 'could neither love nor like', although it had rendered him 'much valuable service'

memorandum, 20 March 1894; H. C. G. Matthew *The Gladstone Diaries* vol. 8 (1994)

12 The God-fearing and God-sustaining University of Oxford. I served her, perhaps mistakenly, but to the best of my ability.

farewell message, just before his death, May 1898

Roy Jenkins *Gladstone* (1995)

13 I absorb the vapour and return it as a flood.

on public speaking

Lord Riddell *Some Things That Matter* (1927 ed.)

14 It is not a Life at all. It is a Reticence, in three volumes.

on J. W. Cross's Life of George Eliot

E. F. Benson *As We Were* (1930) ch. 6

15 [Money should] fructify in the pockets of the people.

H. G. C. Matthew *Gladstone 1809–1874* (1986)

16 We are bound to lose Ireland in consequence of years of cruelty, stupidity and misgovernment and I would rather lose her as a friend than as a foe.

Margot Asquith *More Memories* (1933) ch. 8

Thomas Glascock

American politician

17 No, sir! I am his adversary, and choose not to subject myself to his fascination.

when Thomas Glascock of Georgia took his seat in the US Senate, a mutual friend expressed the wish to introduce him to Henry **Clay** *of Virginia*

Robert V. Remini *Henry Clay* (1991) ch. 6

Hannah Glasse fl. 1747

English cook

18 Take your hare when it is cased.

cased = *skinned*

The Art of Cookery Made Plain and Easy (1747) ch. 1; cf. **Proverbs** 600:26

William Henry, Duke of Gloucester 1743–1805

19 Another damned, thick, square book! Always scribble, scribble, scribble! Eh! Mr Gibbon?

Henry Best *Personal and Literary Memorials* (1829); D. M. Low *Edward Gibbon* (1937) notes alternative attributions to the Duke of Cumberland and King George III

Jean-Luc Godard 1930–

French film director

20 Photography is truth. The cinema is truth 24 times per second.

Le Petit Soldat (1960 film)

21 *Ce n'est pas une image juste, c'est juste une image.*

This is not a just image, it is just an image.

Colin MacCabe *Godard: Images, Sounds, Politics* (1980)

1 GEORGES FRANJU: Movies should have a beginning, a middle and an end.
JEAN-LUC GODARD: Certainly, but not necessarily in that order.
in *Time* 14 September 1981; cf. **Aristotle** 24:22

A. D. Godley 1856–1925

English classicist

2 What is this that roareth thus?
Can it be a Motor Bus?
Yes, the smell and hideous hum
Indicat Motorem Bum!...
How shall wretches live like us
Cincti Bis Motoribus?
Domine, defende nos
Contra hos Motores Bos!
letter to C. R. L. Fletcher, 10 January 1914, in *Reliquiae* (1926) vol. 1

Sidney Godolphin 1610–43

English poet

3 Or love me less, or love me more
And play not with my liberty;
Either take all, or all restore,
Bind me at least, or set me free.
'Song'

William Godwin 1756–1836

English philosopher and novelist; husband of Mary ***Wollstonecraft*** *and father of Mary* ***Shelley***

4 Perfectibility is one of the most unequivocal characteristics of the human species.
An Enquiry concerning the Principles of Political Justice (1793) bk. 1, ch. 2

5 The illustrious bishop of Cambrai was of more worth than his chambermaid, and there are few of us that would hesitate to pronounce, if his palace were in flames, and the life of only one of them could be preserved, which of the two ought to be preferred.
An Enquiry concerning the Principles of Political Justice (1793) bk. 2, ch. 2

6 Love of our country is another of those specious illusions, which have been invented by impostors in order to render the multitude the blind instruments of their crooked designs.
An Enquiry concerning the Principles of Political Justice (1793) bk. 5, ch. 16

7 It is a most mistaken way of teaching men to feel they are brothers, by imbuing their mind with perpetual hatred.
on the subject of war
An Enquiry concerning the Principles of Political Justice (1793) bk. 5, ch. 18

8 What . . . can be more shameless than for society to make an example of those whom she has goaded to the breach of order, instead of amending her own institutions which, by straining order into tyranny, produced the mischief?
on the penal laws
An Enquiry concerning the Principles of Political Justice (1793) bk. 7, ch. 3

Joseph Goebbels 1897–1945

German Nazi leader

9 We can manage without butter but not, for example, without guns. If we are attacked we can only defend ourselves with guns not with butter.
speech in Berlin, 17 January 1936, in *Deutsche Allgemeine Zeitung* 18 January 1936; cf. **Goering** 342:11

10 Making noise is an effective means of opposition.
Ernest K. Bramsted *Goebbels and National Socialist Propaganda 1925–45* (1965)

Hermann Goering 1893–1946

German Nazi leader
see also ***Johst*** *418:17*

11 We have no butter . . . but I ask you—would you rather have butter or guns? . . . preparedness makes us powerful. Butter merely makes us fat.
speech at Hamburg, 1936, in W. Frischauer *Goering* (1951) ch. 10; cf. **Goebbels** 342:9

12 I herewith commission you to carry out all preparations with regard to . . . a *total solution* of the Jewish question in those territories of Europe which are under German influence.
instructions to Heydrich, 31 July 1941, in W. L. Shirer *The Rise and Fall of the Third Reich* (1962) bk. 5, ch. 27; cf. **Heydrich** 376:2

Johann Wolfgang von Goethe 1749–1832

German poet, novelist, and dramatist
see also ***Last words*** *456:15*

13 *Glücklich allein*
Ist die Seele, die liebt.
Only the soul that loves is happy.
Egmont (1788) 'Clärchens Lied'

14 *Es irrt der Mensch, so lang er strebt.*
Man will err while yet he strives.
Faust pt. 1 (1808) 'Prolog im Himmel'

15 *Welch Schauspiel! Aber ach, ein Schauspiel nur!*
What a show! But alas, only a show!
Faust pt. 1 (1808) 'Nacht'

16 *Was du ererbt von deinen Vätem hast,*
Erwirb es, um es zu besitzen.
What you have inherited from your fathers
Work on, that you may possess it.
Faust pt. 1 (1808) 'Nacht'

17 *Zwei Seelen wohnen, ach! in meiner Brust.*
Two souls dwell, alas! in my breast.
Faust pt. 1 (1808) 'Vor dem Thor'

18 *Ich bin der Geist der stets verneint.*
I am the spirit that always denies.
Faust pt. 1 (1808) 'Studierzimmer'

19 *Entbehren sollst Du! sollst entbehren!*
Das ist der ewige Gesang.
Deny yourself! You must deny yourself!
That is the song that never ends.
Faust pt. 1 (1808) 'Studierzimmer'

20 *Grau, teurer Freund, ist alle Theorie*
Und grün des Lebens goldner Baum.

All theory, dear friend, is grey, but the golden tree
of actual life springs ever green.
Faust pt. 1 (1808) 'Studierzimmer'

1 *Meine Ruh' ist hin,*
Mein Herz ist schwer.
My peace is gone,
My heart is heavy.
Faust pt. 1 (1808) 'Gretchen am Spinnrad'

2 *Das ist der Weisheit letzer Schluss:*
Nur der verdient sich Freiheit wie das Leben,
Der täglich sie erobem muss.
This is wisdom's final thought:
Freedom alone he earns as well as life
Who day by day must conquer them anew.
Faust pt. 2 (1832) act 5 'Grosser Vorhof des Palastes'

3 *Die Tat ist alles, nichts der Ruhm.*
The deed is all, the glory nothing.
Faust pt. 2 (1832) 'Hochgebirg'

4 *Das Ewig-Weibliche zieht uns hinan.*
Eternal Woman draws us upward.
Faust pt. 2 (1832) 'Hochgebirg' closing words

5 *Du musst herrschen und gewinnen,*
Oder dienen und verlieren,
Leiden oder triumphieren
Amboss oder Hammer sein.
You must be master and win, or serve and lose,
grieve or triumph, be the anvil or the hammer.
Der Gross-Cophta (1791) act 2

6 *Wenn es eine Freude ist das Gute zu geniessen, so ist es eine grössere das Bessere zu empfinden, und in der Kunst ist das Beste gut genug.*
Since it is a joy to have the benefit of what is good, it is a greater one to experience what is better, and in art the best is good enough.
Italienische Reise (1816–17) 3 March 1787

7 *Der Aberglaube ist die Poesie des Lebens.*
Superstition is the poetry of life.
Maximen und Reflexionen (1819) 'Literatur und Sprache' no. 908

8 *Es bildet ein Talent sich in der Stille,*
Sich ein Charakter in dem Strom der Welt.
Talent develops in quiet places, character in the full current of human life.
Torquato Tasso (1790) act 1, sc. 2

9 *Die Wahlverwandtschaften.*
Elective affinities.
title of novel (1809)

10 *Über allen Gipfeln*
Ist Ruh'.
Over all the mountain tops is peace.
Wanderers Nachtlied (1821)

11 *Wer nie sein Brot mit Tränen ass,*
Wer nie die kummervollen Nächte
Auf seinem Bette weinend sass,
Der kennt euch nicht, ihr himmlischen Mächte.
Who never ate his bread in sorrow,
Who never spent the darksome hours
Weeping and watching for the morrow
He knows ye not, ye heavenly powers.
Wilhelm Meisters Lehrjahre (1795–6) bk. 2, ch. 13 (translated by Carlyle)

12 *Kennst du das Land, wo die Zitronen blühn?*
Im dunkeln Laub die Gold-Orangen glühn,
Ein sanfter Wind vom blauen Himmel weht,
Die Myrte still und hoch der Lorbeer steht—
Kennst du es wohl?
Dahin! Dahin
Möcht ich mit dir, o mein Geliebter, ziehn!
Know you the land where the lemon-trees bloom? In the dark foliage the gold oranges glow; the myrtle is still and the laurel stands tall—do you know it well? There, there, I would go, O my beloved, with thee!
Wilhelm Meisters Lehrjahre (1795–6) bk. 3, ch. 1

13 If I love you, what does that matter to you!
Wilhelm Meisters Lehrjahre (1795–6) bk. 4, ch. 9

14 *Nur, wer die Sehnsucht kennt,*
Weiss, was ich leide!
None but the lonely heart
Knows what I suffer!
Wilhelm Meisters Lehrjahre (1795–6) bk. 4, ch. 11 'Mignons Lied'

15 *Ohne Hast, aber ohne Rast.*
Without haste, but without rest.
Zahme Xenien (with Schiller, 1796) sect. 2, no. 6, l. 281

16 For the rest of it, the last and greatest art is to limit and isolate oneself.
J. P. Eckermann *Conversations with Goethe in the Last Years of his Life* (1836–48) 20 April 1825

17 Classicism is health, romanticism is disease.
J. P. Eckermann *Conversations with Goethe in the Last Years of his Life* (1836–48) 2 April 1829

18 I do not know myself, and God forbid that I should.
J. P. Eckermann *Conversations with Goethe in the Last Years of his Life* (1836–48) 10 April 1829; cf. **Proverbs** 605:6

Oliver St John Gogarty 1878–1957
Irish writer and surgeon

19 Politics is the chloroform of the Irish people, or, rather, the hashish.
As I Was Going Down Sackville Street (1937)

20 I said, 'It is most extraordinary weather for this time of year!' He replied, 'Ah, it isn't this time of year at all.'
It Isn't This Time of Year at All (1954)

21 You might as well try to employ a boa constrictor as a tape-measure as to go to a lawyer for legal advice.
Tumbling in the Hay (1939)

22 Golden stockings you had on
In the meadow where you ran.
'Golden Stockings'

23 Only the Lion and the Cock;
As Galen says, withstand Love's shock.
So, dearest, do not think me rude
If I yield now to lassitude,
But sympathize with me. I know

You would not have me roar or crow.
'After Galen' (1957)

Nikolai Gogol 1809–52
Russian writer

1 As you pass from the tender years of youth into harsh and embittered manhood, make sure you take with you on your journey all the human emotions! Don't leave them on the road, for you will not pick them up afterwards!
Dead Souls (1842) pt. 1, ch. 6 (translated by David Magarshak)

2 [Are not] you too, Russia, speeding along like a spirited *troika* that nothing can overtake? . . . Everything on earth is flying past, and looking askance, other nations and states draw aside and make way.
Dead Souls (1842) pt. 1, ch. 11 (translated by David Magarshak)

Isaac Goldberg 1887–1938

3 Diplomacy is to do and say
The nastiest thing in the nicest way.
in *The Reflex* October 1927

Whoopi Goldberg 1949–
American actress

4 I dislike this idea that if you're a black person in America then you must be called an African-American. I'm not an African. I'm an American. Just call me black, if you want to call me anything.
in *Irish Times* 25 April 1998 'Quotes of the Week'

Emma Goldman 1869–1940
American anarchist

5 Anarchism, then, really, stands for the liberation of the human mind from the dominion of religion; the liberation of the human body from the dominion of property; liberation from the shackles and restraints of government.
Anarchism and Other Essays (1910)

William Golding 1911–93
English novelist

6 Nothing is so impenetrable as laughter in a language you don't understand.
An Egyptian Journal (1985)

Oliver Goldsmith 1728–74
Anglo-Irish writer, poet, and dramatist
on Goldsmith: see ***Epitaphs*** *303:17,* ***Garrick*** *330:4, 330:6,* ***Johnson*** *414:19*

7 Sweet Auburn, loveliest village of the plain.
The Deserted Village (1770) l. 1

8 Ill fares the land, to hast'ning ills a prey,
Where wealth accumulates, and men decay;
Princes and lords may flourish, or may fade;
A breath can make them, as a breath has made;
But a bold peasantry, their country's pride,
When once destroyed, can never be supplied.
The Deserted Village (1770) l. 51

9 How happy he who crowns in shades like these,
A youth of labour with an age of ease.
The Deserted Village (1770) l. 99

10 The watchdog's voice that bayed the whisp'ring wind,
And the loud laugh that spoke the vacant mind.
The Deserted Village (1770) l. 121; cf. **Chesterfield** 209:16

11 A man he was to all the country dear,
And passing rich with forty pounds a year.
Remote from towns he ran his godly race,
Nor e'er had changed nor wished to change his place.
The Deserted Village (1770) l. 141

12 Truth from his lips prevailed with double sway,
And fools, who came to scoff, remained to pray.
The Deserted Village (1770) l. 179

13 A man severe he was, and stern to view;
I knew him well, and every truant knew;
Well had the boding tremblers learned to trace
The day's disasters in his morning face;
Full well they laughed with counterfeited glee,
At all his jokes, for many a joke had he.
The Deserted Village (1770) l. 197

14 The village all declared how much he knew;
'Twas certain he could write and cypher too.
The Deserted Village (1770) l. 207

15 In arguing too, the parson owned his skill,
For e'en though vanquished, he could argue still;
While words of learned length, and thund'ring sound
Amazed the gazing rustics ranged around,
And still they gazed, and still the wonder grew,
That one small head could carry all he knew.
The Deserted Village (1770) l. 211

16 How wide the limits stand
Between a splendid and a happy land.
The Deserted Village (1770) l. 267

17 In all the silent manliness of grief.
The Deserted Village (1770) l. 384

18 I see the rural virtues leave the land.
The Deserted Village (1770) l. 398

19 Thou source of all my bliss, and all my woe,
That found'st me poor at first, and keep'st me so.
of poetry
The Deserted Village (1770) l. 413

20 Man wants but little here below,
Nor wants that little long.
'Edwin and Angelina, or the Hermit' (1766); cf. **Holmes** 381:8, **Young** 839:11

21 The doctor found, when she was dead,—
Her last disorder mortal.
'Elegy on Mrs Mary Blaize' (1759)

22 The man recovered of the bite,
The dog it was that died.
'Elegy on the Death of a Mad Dog' (1766)

23 Our Garrick's a salad; for in him we see
Oil, vinegar, sugar, and saltness agree.
Retaliation (1774) l. 11; cf. **Garrick** 330:4

1 Too nice for a statesman, too proud for a wit.
of Edmund **Burke**
Retaliation (1774) l. 32

2 An abridgement of all that was pleasant in man.
of David **Garrick**
Retaliation (1774) l. 94

3 On the stage he was natural, simple, affecting;
'Twas only that when he was off he was acting.
of David **Garrick**
Retaliation (1774) l. 101

4 Of praise a mere glutton, he swallowed what came,
And the puff of a dunce he mistook it for fame.
of David **Garrick**
Retaliation (1774) l. 101

5 When they talked of their Raphaels, Correggios, and stuff,
He shifted his trumpet, and only took snuff.
of Joshua **Reynolds**
Retaliation (1774) l. 145

6 Where'er I roam, whatever realms to see,
My heart untravelled fondly turns to thee;
Still to my brother turns with ceaseless pain,
And drags at each remove a lengthening chain.
The Traveller (1764) l. 7

7 Such is the patriot's boast, where'er we roam,
His first, best country ever is, at home.
The Traveller (1764) l. 73

8 And honour sinks where commerce long prevails.
The Traveller (1764) l. 92

9 Pride in their port, defiance in their eye,
I see the lords of human kind pass by.
The Traveller (1764) l. 327

10 Laws grind the poor, and rich men rule the law.
The Traveller (1764) l. 386

11 How small, of all that human hearts endure,
That part which laws or kings can cause or cure!
The Traveller (1764) l. 429; cf. **Johnson** 411:12

12 The true use of speech is not so much to express our wants as to conceal them.
The Bee no. 3 (20 October 1759) 'On the Use of Language'

13 Friendship is a disinterested commerce between equals; love, an abject intercourse between tyrants and slaves.
The Good-Natured Man (1768) act 1

14 Silence is become his mother tongue.
The Good-Natured Man (1768) act 2

15 Measures not men, have always been my mark.
The Good Natured Man (1768) act 2; cf. **Burke** 164:17, **Canning** 185:5

16 You, that are going to be married, think things can never be done too fast; but we, that are old, and know what we are about, must elope methodically, madam.
The Good-Natured Man (1768) act 2

17 Let schoolmasters puzzle their brain,
With grammar, and nonsense, and learning,
Good liquor, I stoutly maintain,
Gives genius a better discerning.
She Stoops to Conquer (1773) act 1, sc. 1 'Song'

18 Is it one of my well-looking days, child? Am I in face to-day?
She Stoops to Conquer (1773) act 1

19 The very pink of perfection.
She Stoops to Conquer (1773) act 1

20 I'll be with you in the squeezing of a lemon.
She Stoops to Conquer (1773) act 1

21 It's a damned long, dark, boggy, dirty, dangerous way.
She Stoops to Conquer (1773) act 1

22 This is Liberty-Hall, gentlemen.
She Stoops to Conquer (1773) act 2

23 The first blow is half the battle.
She Stoops to Conquer (1773) act 2

24 A man who leaves home to mend himself and others is a philosopher; but he who goes from country to country, guided by a blind impulse of curiosity, is a vagabond.
The Citizen of the World (1762)

25 I was ever of opinion, that the honest man who married and brought up a large family, did more service than he who continued single and only talked of population.
The Vicar of Wakefield (1766) ch. 1

26 I . . . chose my wife, as she did her wedding gown, not for a fine glossy surface, but such qualities as would wear well.
The Vicar of Wakefield (1766) ch. 1

27 All our adventures were by the fire-side, and all our migrations from the blue bed to the brown.
The Vicar of Wakefield (1766) ch. 1

28 The virtue which requires to be ever guarded is scarce worth the sentinel.
The Vicar of Wakefield (1766) ch. 5

29 It seemed to me pretty plain, that they had more of love than matrimony in them.
The Vicar of Wakefield (1766) ch. 16

30 When lovely woman stoops to folly
And finds too late that men betray,
What charm can soothe her melancholy,
What art can wash her guilt away?
The Vicar of Wakefield (1766) ch. 29; cf. **Eliot** 296:11

31 There is no arguing with Johnson; for when his pistol misses fire, he knocks you down with the butt end of it.
James Boswell *Life of Samuel Johnson* (1791) 26 October 1769

32 As I take my shoes from the shoemaker, and my coat from the tailor, so I take my religion from the priest.
James Boswell *Life of Samuel Johnson* (1791) 9 April 1773

Barry Goldwater 1909–98
American Republican politician

33 I would remind you that extremism in the defence of liberty is no vice! And let me remind you also

that moderation in the pursuit of justice is no virtue!

accepting the presidential nomination, 16 July 1964, in *New York Times* 17 July 1964

Sam Goldwyn (Samuel Goldfish) 1882–1974

American film producer

on Goldwyn: see ***Hand*** *359:7*

1 Gentlemen, include me out.

resigning from the Motion Picture Producers and Distributors of America, October 1933

Michael Freedland *The Goldwyn Touch* (1986) ch. 10

2 That's the way with these directors, they're always biting the hand that lays the golden egg.

Alva Johnston *The Great Goldwyn* (1937) ch. 1

3 A verbal contract isn't worth the paper it is written on.

Alva Johnston *The Great Goldwyn* (1937) ch. 1

4 Why should people go out and pay to see bad movies when they can stay at home and see bad television for nothing?

in *Observer* 9 September 1956

5 Any man who goes to a psychiatrist should have his head examined.

Norman Zierold *Moguls* (1969) ch. 3

6 Pictures are for entertainment, messages should be delivered by Western Union.

Arthur Marx *Goldwyn* (1976) ch. 15; cf. **Behan** 62:4

Ivan Goncharov 1812–91

Russian novelist

7 No devastating or redeeming fires have ever burnt in my life . . . My life began by flickering out.

Obolomov (1859) pt. 2, ch. 4 (translated by David Magarshak)

8 You lost your ability for doing things in childhood . . . It all began with your inability to put on your socks and ended by your inability to live.

Obolomov (1859) pt. 4, ch. 2 (translated by David Magarshak)

Maud Gonne (Maud Gonne MacBride) 1867–1953

Irish nationalist and actress

9 The Famine Queen.

of Queen ***Victoria***

in *L'Irlande libre* 1900

10 This war is an inconceivable madness which has taken hold of Europe—It is unlike any other war that has ever been.

letter to W. B. Yeats, 26 August 1914

11 Poets should never marry. The world should thank me for not marrying you.

to W. B. ***Yeats***

Nancy Cardozo *Maud Gonne* (1978)

Amy Goodman 1957–

American journalist

12 Go to where the silence is and say something.

accepting an award from Columbia University for her coverage of the 1991 massacre in East Timor by Indonesian troops

in *Columbia Journalism Review* March/April 1994

Barnabe Googe 1540–94

English poet

13 Fair face show friends
When riches do abound:
Come time of proof,
Farewell, they must away.

'Of Money' (1563)

14 Gold never starts
Aside, but in distress
Finds ways enough
To ease thine heaviness.

'Of Money' (1563)

Thomas Goold 1766–1846

Irish lawyer and politician

15 The God of nature never intended that Ireland should be a province, and by God she never will.

speech opposing the Act of Union at a meeting of the Irish Bar, 9 December 1799

Mikhail Sergeevich Gorbachev 1931–

Soviet politician, General Secretary of the Communist Party of the USSR 1985–91 and President 1988–91

on Gorbachev: see ***Gromyko*** *354:1,* ***Thatcher*** *770:5,* ***Zhvanetsky*** *840:2*

16 The guilt of Stalin and his immediate entourage before the Party and the people for the mass repressions and lawlessness they committed is enormous and unforgivable.

speech on the seventieth anniversary of the Russian Revolution, 2 November 1987

17 The idea of restructuring [perestroika] . . . combines continuity and innovation, the historical experience of Bolshevism and the contemporaneity of socialism.

speech on the seventieth anniversary of the Russian Revolution, 2 November 1987

18 After leaving the Kremlin . . . my conscience was clear. The promise I gave to the people when I started the process of perestroika was kept: I gave them freedom.

Memoirs (1995)

Adam Lindsay Gordon 1833–70

Australian poet

19 Life is mostly froth and bubble,
Two things stand like stone,
Kindness in another's trouble,
Courage in your own.

Ye Wearie Wayfarer (1866) 'Fytte 8'

Mack Gordon 1904–59
American songwriter

1 Pardon me boy is that the Chattanooga Choo-choo,
Track twenty nine,
Boy you can gimme a shine.
I can afford to board a Chattanooga Choo-choo,
I've got my fare and just a trifle to spare.
You leave the Pennsylvania station 'bout a quarter to four,
Read a magazine and then you're in Baltimore,
Dinner in the diner nothing could be finer
Than to have your ham'n eggs in Carolina.
'Chattanooga Choo-choo' (1941 song)

Eva Gore-Booth 1870–1926
Irish poet, sister of Constance ***Markievicz***

2 The little waves of Breffny go stumbling through my soul.
'The Waves of Breffny' (1920)

Maxim Gorky 1868–1936
Russian writer and revolutionary

3 The proletarian state must bring up thousands of excellent 'mechanics of culture', 'engineers of the soul'.
speech at the Writers' Congress 1934; cf. **Kennedy** 433:18, **Stalin** 736:2

Stuart Gorrell 1902–63
American songwriter

4 Georgia, Georgia, no peace I find,
Just an old sweet song keeps Georgia on my mind.
'Georgia on my Mind' (1930 song)

George Joachim, Lord Goschen 1831–1907
British Liberal Unionist politician
on Goschen: see ***Churchill*** *214:16*

5 I have the courage of my opinions, but I have not the temerity to give a political blank cheque to Lord Salisbury.
speech in the House of Commons, 19 February 1884

Edmund Gosse 1849–1928
English poet and man of letters

6 Man was the animal he studied less than any other, understood most imperfectly, and, on the whole, was least interested in.
of his father, the naturalist Philip Gosse
Life of P. H. Gosse (1890) ch. 12

7 A sheep in sheep's clothing.
of the 'woolly-bearded poet' Sturge ***Moore***
F. Greenslet *Under the Bridge* (1943) ch. 10; cf. **Churchill** 217:1

Stephen Jay Gould 1941–
American palaeontologist

8 A man does not attain the status of Galileo merely because he is persecuted; he must also be right.
Ever since Darwin (1977)

9 Science is an integral part of culture. It's not this foreign thing, done by an arcane priesthood. It's one of the glories of human intellectual tradition.
in *Independent* 24 January 1990

John Gower *c.*1330–1408
English poet

10 It hath and schal ben evermor
That love is maister wher he wile.
Confessio Amantis (1386–90) prologue, l. 34

Ernest Gowers 1880–1966
British public servant

11 It is not easy nowadays to remember anything so contrary to all appearances as that officials are the servants of the public; and the official must try not to foster the illusion that it is the other way round.
Plain Words (1948) ch. 3

Goya (Francisco José de Goya y Lucientes) 1746–1828
Spanish painter

12 *No se puede mirar.*
One cannot look at this.
The Disasters of War (1863) title of etching, no. 26

13 *El sueño de la razón produce monstruos.*
The dream of reason produces monsters.
Los Caprichos (1799) plate 43 (title)

Baltasar Gracián 1601–58
Spanish philosopher

14 Never open the door to the least of evils, for many other, greater ones lurk outside.
The Art of Worldly Wisdom (translated by Christopher Maurer, 1994)

15 Renew your brilliance. It is the privilege of the Phoenix. Excellence grows old and so does fame. Custom wears down our admiration, and a mediocre novelty can conquer the greatest eminence in its old age. So be reborn in courage, in intellect, in happiness, and in all else. Dare to renew your brilliance, dawning many times, like the sun, only changing your surroundings. Withhold it and make people miss it; renew it and make them applaud.
The Art of Worldly Wisdom (translated by Christopher Maurer, 1994)

16 Don't express your ideas too clearly. Most people think little of what they understand, and venerate what they do not.
The Art of Worldly Wisdom (translated by Christopher Maurer, 1994)

Clementina Stirling Graham 1782–1877
Scottish writer

17 The best way to get the better of temptation is just to yield to it.
Mystifications (1859) 'Soirée at Mrs Russel's'; cf. **Wilde** 818:8

D. M. Graham 1911–

1 That this House will in no circumstances fight for its King and Country.

motion worded by Graham for a debate at the Oxford Union, of which he was Librarian, 9 February 1933 (passed by 275 votes to 153)

Harry Graham 1874–1936

British writer and journalist

2 Weep not for little Léonie
Abducted by a French Marquis!
Though loss of honour was a wrench
Just think how it's improved her French.

More Ruthless Rhymes for Heartless Homes (1930) 'Compensation'

3 O'er the rugged mountain's brow
Clara threw the twins she nursed,
And remarked, 'I wonder now
Which will reach the bottom first?'

Ruthless Rhymes for Heartless Homes (1899) 'Calculating Clara'

4 'There's been an accident,' they said,
'Your servant's cut in half; he's dead!'
'Indeed!' said Mr Jones, 'and please,
Send me the half that's got my keys.'

Ruthless Rhymes for Heartless Homes (1899) 'Mr Jones' (attributed to 'G.W.')

5 Billy, in one of his nice new sashes,
Fell in the fire and was burnt to ashes;
Now, although the room grows chilly,
I haven't the heart to poke poor Billy.

Ruthless Rhymes for Heartless Homes (1899) 'Tender-Heartedness'

James Graham see **Marquess of Montrose**

Kenneth Grahame 1859–1932

Scottish-born writer

6 The curate faced the laurels—hesitatingly. But Aunt Maria flung herself on him. 'O Mr Hodgitts!' I heard her cry, 'you are brave! for my sake do not be rash!' He was not rash.

The Golden Age (1895) 'The Burglars'

7 There is *nothing*—absolutely nothing—half so much worth doing as simply messing about in boats.

The Wind in the Willows (1908) ch. 1

8 The poetry of motion! The *real* way to travel! The *only* way to travel! Here today—in next week tomorrow! Villages skipped, towns and cities jumped—always somebody else's horizon!

The Wind in the Willows (1908) ch. 2; cf. **Kaufman and Anthony** 426:5

9 O bliss! O poop-poop! O my!

The Wind in the Willows (1908) ch. 2

10 The clever men at Oxford
Know all that there is to be knowed.
But they none of them know one half as much
As intelligent Mr Toad!

The Wind in the Willows (1908) ch. 10

James Grainger c.1721–66

English physician and man of letters

11 What is fame? an empty bubble;
Gold? a transient, shining trouble.

'Solitude' (1755) l. 96

12 Knock off the chains
Of heart-debasing slavery; give to man,
Of every colour and of every clime,
Freedom, which stamps him image of his God.

The Sugar Cane (1764) bk. 4

Phil Gramm 1942–

American Republican politician

13 I did not come to Washington to be loved, and I have not been disappointed.

Michael Barone and Grant Ujifusa *The American Political Almanac 1994*

Bernie Grant 1944–

British Labour politician

14 The police were to blame for what happened on Sunday night and what they got was a bloody good hiding.

after a riot in which a policeman was killed

speech as leader of Haringey Council outside Tottenham Town Hall, 8 October 1985

Robert Grant 1785–1838

British lawyer and politician

15 O worship the King, all-glorious above;
O gratefully sing his power and his love:
Our Shield and Defender, the Ancient of Days,
Pavilioned in splendour, and girded with praise.

'O worship the King, all glorious above' (1833 hymn)

Ulysses S. Grant 1822–85

American Unionist general and statesman; 18th President of the US

16 No terms except unconditional and immediate surrender can be accepted. I propose to move immediately upon your works.

to Simon Bolivar Buckner, under siege at Fort Donelson, 16 February 1862; in P. C. Headley *The Life and Campaigns of General U. S. Grant* (1869) ch. 6

17 I purpose to fight it out on this line, if it takes all summer.

dispatch to Washington, from head-quarters in the field, 11 May 1864, in P. C. Headley *The Life and Campaigns of General U. S. Grant* (1869) ch. 23

18 The war is over—the rebels are our countrymen again.

preventing his men from cheering after **Lee**'s *surrender at Appomattox*

on 9 April, 1865

1 Let us have peace.
letter to General Joseph R. Hawkey, 29 May 1868, accepting the presidential nomination, in P. C. Headley *The Life and Campaigns of General U. S. Grant* (1869) ch. 29

2 I know no method to secure the repeal of bad or obnoxious laws so effective as their stringent execution.
inaugural address, 4 March 1869, in P. C. Headley *The Life and Campaigns of General U. S. Grant* (1869) ch. 29

3 Let no guilty man escape, if it can be avoided . . . No personal consideration should stand in the way of performing a public duty.
on the implication of his private secretary in a tax fraud
endorsement of a letter relating to the Whiskey Ring received 29 July 1875, in E. P. Oberholtzer *History of the United States Since the Civil War* (1937) vol. 3, ch. 19

George Granville, Lord Lansdowne 1666–1735
English poet and dramatist

4 Bright as the day, and like the morning, fair,
Such Cloe is . . . and common as the air.
'Cloe' (1712)

5 Cowards in scarlet pass for men of war.
The She Gallants (1696) act 5

Henry Grattan 1746–1820
Irish nationalist leader

6 The thing he proposes to buy is what cannot be sold—liberty.
speech in the Irish Parliament against the proposed union, 16 January 1800
in *Dictionary of National Biography* (1917–)

7 He [Gladstone] quoted as I have heard him do before, a saying of Grattan about 'the Channel forbidding Union, the Ocean forbidding separation.'
as recalled by Lord Derby; R. F. Foster *Paddy and Mr Punch* (1993)

Arthur Percival Graves 1846–1931
Irish songwriter

8 Trottin' to the fair,
Me and Moll Maloney,
Seated, I declare
On a single pony.
'Ridin' Double'

John Woodcock Graves 1795–1886
British huntsman and songwriter

9 D'ye ken John Peel with his coat so grey?
D'ye ken John Peel at the break of the day?
D'ye ken John Peel when he's far far away
With his hounds and his horn in the morning?
an alternative version 'coat so gay' is often sung
'John Peel' (1820)

10 For Peel's view-hollo would waken the dead,
Or a fox from his lair in the morning.
'John Peel' (1820)

Robert Graves 1895–1985
English poet

11 Beware, madam, of the witty devil,
The arch intriguer who walks disguised
In a poet's cloak, his gay tongue oozing evil.
'Beware, Madam!'

12 There's a cool web of language winds us in,
Retreat from too much joy or too much fear.
'The Cool Web' (1927)

13 Truth-loving Persians do not dwell upon
The trivial skirmish fought near Marathon.
'The Persian Version' (1945)

14 As you are woman, so be lovely:
As you are lovely, so be various,
Merciful as constant, constant as various,
So be mine, as I yours for ever.
'Pygmalion to Galatea' (1927)

15 Love is a universal migraine.
A bright stain on the vision
Blotting out reason.
'Symptoms of Love'

16 To evoke posterity
Is to weep on your own grave,
Ventriloquizing for the unborn.
'To Evoke Posterity' (1938)

17 Goodbye to all that.
title of autobiography (1929)

18 Imaginative readers rewrite books to suit their own taste, omitting and mentally altering what they read.
The Reader over your Shoulder (1947)

19 The award of a pure gold medal for poetry would flatter the recipient unduly: no poem ever attains such carat purity.
Address to the Oxford University Philological Society January 1960

20 If there's no money in poetry, neither is there poetry in money.
speech at London School of Economics, 6 December 1963

21 Science has lost its virgin purity, has become dogmatic instead of seeking for enlightenment and has gradually fallen into the hands of the traders.
Bruno Friedman *Flawed science, damaged human life* (1969)

22 LSD reminds me of the minks that escape from mink-farms and breed in the forest and become dangerous and destructive. It has escaped from the drug factory and gets made in college laboratories.
George Plimpton (ed.) *The Writer's Chapbook* (1989)

John Gray 1951–

23 Men are from Mars, women are from Venus.
title of book (1992)

John Chipman Gray 1839–1915
American lawyer

24 Dirt is only matter out of place; and what is a blot on the escutcheon of the Common Law may be a jewel in the crown of the Social Republic.
Restraints on the Alienation of Property (2nd ed., 1895) preface

Patrick, Lord Gray d. 1612

1 A dead woman bites not.
*pressing for the execution of **Mary** Queen of Scots in 1587*
oral tradition; see below; cf. **Proverbs** 597:49
Mortua non mordet.
Being dead, she will bite no more.
A. Darcy's 1625 translation of William Camden's *Annals of the Reign of Queen Elizabeth* (1615) vol. 1

Thomas Gray 1716–71

English poet
*on Gray: see **Johnson** 410:4, 414:25, 416:14, **Wolfe** 825:7*

2 Ruin seize thee, ruthless King!
Confusion on thy banners wait,
Tho' fanned by Conquest's crimson wing
They mock the air with idle state.
The Bard (1757) l. 1

3 Loose his beard, and hoary hair
Streamed, like a meteor, to the troubled air.
The Bard (1757) l. 19; cf. **Milton** 514:28

4 Weave the warp, and weave the woof,
The winding-sheet of Edward's race.
Give ample room, and verge enough
The characters of hell to trace.
The Bard (1757) l. 49

5 In gallant trim the gilded vessel goes;
Youth on the prow, and Pleasure at the helm.
'The Bard' (1757) l. 73

6 The curfew tolls the knell of parting day,
The lowing herd wind slowly o'er the lea,
The ploughman homeward plods his weary way,
And leaves the world to darkness and to me.
Now fades the glimmering landscape on the sight,
And all the air a solemn stillness holds,
Save where the beetle wheels his droning flight,
And drowsy tinklings lull the distant folds.
Elegy Written in a Country Churchyard (1751) l. 1

7 Save that from yonder ivy-mantled tow'r,
The moping owl does to the moon complain.
Elegy Written in a Country Churchyard (1751) l. 9

8 Beneath those rugged elms, that yew-tree's shade,
Where heaves the turf in many a mouldering heap,
Each in his narrow cell for ever laid,
The rude forefathers of the hamlet sleep.
Elegy Written in a Country Churchyard (1751) l. 13

9 Let not ambition mock their useful toil,
Their homely joys, and destiny obscure;
Nor grandeur hear with a disdainful smile,
The short and simple annals of the poor.
The boast of heraldry, the pomp of pow'r,
And all that beauty, all that wealth e'er gave,
Awaits alike th' inevitable hour,
The paths of glory lead but to the grave.
Elegy Written in a Country Churchyard (1751) l. 29

10 Can storied urn or animated bust
Back to its mansion call the fleeting breath?
Can honour's voice provoke the silent dust,
Or flatt'ry soothe the dull cold ear of death?
Elegy Written in a Country Churchyard (1751) l. 41

11 Full many a gem of purest ray serene,
The dark unfathomed caves of ocean bear:
Full many a flower is born to blush unseen,
And waste its sweetness on the desert air.
Some village-Hampden, that with dauntless breast
The little tyrant of his fields withstood;
Some mute inglorious Milton here may rest,
Some Cromwell guiltless of his country's blood.
Elegy Written in a Country Churchyard (1751) l. 53

12 Forbad to wade through slaughter to a throne,
And shut the gates of mercy on mankind.
Elegy Written in a Country Churchyard (1751) l. 67

13 Far from the madding crowd's ignoble strife,
Their sober wishes never learned to stray;
Along the cool sequestered vale of life
They kept the noiseless tenor of their way.
Elegy Written in a Country Churchyard (1751) l. 73

14 Here rests his head upon the lap of Earth
A youth to fortune and to fame unknown.
Fair Science frowned not on his humble birth,
And Melancholy marked him for her own.
Elegy Written in a Country Churchyard (1751) l. 117

15 Ye distant spires, ye antique towers,
That crown the wat'ry glade.
Ode on a Distant Prospect of Eton College (1747) l. 1

16 Alas, regardless of their doom,
The little victims play!
No sense have they of ills to come,
Nor care beyond to-day.
Ode on a Distant Prospect of Eton College (1747) l. 51

17 To each his suff'rings, all are men,
Condemned alike to groan;
The tender for another's pain,
Th' unfeeling for his own.
Ode on a Distant Prospect of Eton College (1747) l. 91

18 Thought would destroy their paradise.
No more; where ignorance is bliss,
'Tis folly to be wise.
Ode on a Distant Prospect of Eton College (1747) l. 98; cf. **Proverbs** 614:13

19 Demurest of the tabby kind,
The pensive Selima reclined.
'Ode on the Death of a Favourite Cat' (1748)

20 What female heart can gold despise?
What cat's averse to fish?
'Ode on the Death of a Favourite Cat' (1748)

21 A favourite has no friend!
'Ode on the Death of a Favourite Cat' (1748)

22 Not all that tempts your wand'ring eyes
And heedless hearts, is lawful prize;
Nor all, that glisters, gold.
'Ode on the Death of a Favourite Cat' (1748)

23 The Attic warbler pours her throat,
Responsive to the cuckoo's note,
The untaught harmony of spring.
'Ode on the Spring' (1748) l. 5

1 In thy green lap was Nature's darling laid.
of ***Shakespeare***
The Progress of Poesy (1757) l. 84

2 Nor second he, that rode sublime
Upon the seraph-wings of ecstasy,
The secrets of th' abyss to spy.
He passed the flaming bounds of place and time:
The living throne, the sapphire-blaze,
Where angels tremble, while they gaze,
He saw; but blasted with excess of light,
Closed his eyes in endless night.
of ***Milton***
The Progress of Poesy (1757) l. 95

3 Thoughts, that breathe, and words, that burn.
The Progress of Poesy (1757) l. 110

4 Beyond the limits of a vulgar fate,
Beneath the good how far—but far above the great.
The Progress of Poesy (1757) l. 122

5 Too poor for a bribe, and too proud to importune,
He had not the method of making a fortune.
'Sketch of his own Character' (written 1761)

6 The language of the age is never the language of poetry, except among the French, whose verse, where the thought or image does not support it, differs in nothing from prose.
letter to Richard West, 8 April 1742, in H. W. Starr (ed.) *Correspondence of Thomas Gray* (1971) vol. 1

7 It has been usual to catch a mouse or two (for form's sake) in public once a year.
on refusing the Laureateship
letter to William Mason, 19 December 1757; in H. W. Starr (ed.) *Correspondence of Thomas Gray* (1971) vol. 2

8 I shall be but a shrimp of an author.
letter to Horace Walpole, 25 February 1768, in H. W. Starr (ed.) *Correspondence of Thomas Gray* (1971) vol. 3

9 Any fool may write a most valuable book by chance, if he will only tell us what he heard and saw with veracity.
letter to Horace Walpole, 25 February 1768, in H. W. Starr (ed.) *Correspondence of Thomas Gray* (1971) vol. 3

Horace Greeley 1811–72
American founder and editor of the New York Tribune

10 Go West, young man, and grow up with the country.
Hints toward Reforms (1850); cf. **Newspaper headlines** 544:7

Matthew Green 1696–1737
English poet

11 They politics like ours profess,
The greater prey upon the less.
The Grotto (1732) l. 69

12 To cure the mind's wrong bias, spleen,
Some recommend the bowling-green,
Some, hilly walks; all, exercise.
The Spleen (1737) l. 89

13 Or to some coffee-house I stray
For news, the manna of a day.
The Spleen (1737) l. 168

14 By happy alchemy of mind
They turn to pleasure all they find.
The Spleen (1737) l. 610

Graham Greene 1904–91
English novelist

15 Catholics and Communists have committed great crimes, but at least they have not stood aside, like an established society, and been indifferent. I would rather have blood on my hands than water like Pilate.
The Comedians (1966) pt. 3, ch. 4

16 He gave her a bright fake smile; so much of life was a putting-off of unhappiness for another time. Nothing was ever lost by delay.
The Heart of the Matter (1948) bk. 1, pt. 1, ch. 1

17 Against the beautiful and the clever and the successful, one can wage a pitiless war, but not against the unattractive.
The Heart of the Matter (1948) bk. 1, pt. 1, ch. 2

18 They had been corrupted by money, and he had been corrupted by sentiment. Sentiment was the more dangerous, because you couldn't name its price. A man open to bribes was to be relied upon below a certain figure, but sentiment might uncoil in the heart at a name, a photograph, even a smell remembered.
The Heart of the Matter (1948) bk. 1, pt. 1, ch. 2

19 He felt the loyalty we all feel to unhappiness—the sense that that is where we really belong.
The Heart of the Matter (1948) bk. 2, pt. 2, ch. 1

20 His hilarity was like a scream from a crevasse.
The Heart of the Matter (1948) bk. 3, pt. 1, ch. 1

21 The dreaded essential opening sentences.
In Search of a Character (1961)

22 What do we ever get nowadays from reading to equal the excitement and the revelation in those first fourteen years?
The Lost Childhood and Other Essays (1951) title essay

23 There is always one moment in childhood when the door opens and lets the future in.
The Power and the Glory (1940) pt. 1, ch. 1

24 Innocence always calls mutely for protection, when we would be so much wiser to guard ourselves against it: innocence is like a dumb leper who has lost his bell, wandering the world meaning no harm.
The Quiet American (1955) pt. 1, ch. 3

25 The beastly adverb—far more damaging to a writer than an adjective.
Ways of Escape (1980)

26 What's writing? A way of escape, like travelling to a war, or to see the Mau Mau. Escaping what? Boredom. Death.
interview with John Mortimer, in *Sunday Times* 16 March 1980

1 [I wanted] to discover what lies behind the dark, thick leaf of the aspidistra that guards . . . the vulnerable gap between the lace curtains.
on early attempts to experience life outside his own social class
Norman Sherry *Life of Graham Greene 1904–39* (1989) ch. 39

Robert Greene *c.*1560–92
English poet and dramatist

2 Hangs in the uncertain balance of proud time.
Friar Bacon and Friar Bungay (1594) act 3, sc. 1

3 'Men, when they lust, can many fancies feign,'
Said Phillis. This not Coridon denied,
That lust had lies. 'But love,' quoth he, 'says truth.'
Perimedes (1588) 'Phillis kept sheep'

4 Ah! what is love! It is a pretty thing,
As sweet unto a shepherd as a king,
And sweeter too;
For kings have cares that wait upon a crown,
And cares can make the sweetest love to frown.
Ah then, ah then,
If country loves such sweet desires do gain,
What lady would not love a shepherd swain?
'The Shepherd's Wife's Song' (1590)

5 For there is an upstart crow, beautified with our feathers, that with his tiger's heart wrapped in a player's hide, supposes he is as well able to bumbast out a blank verse as the best of you; and being an absolute *Johannes fac totum*, is in his own conceit the only Shake-scene in a country.
Groatsworth of Wit Bought with a Million of Repentance (1592); cf. **Shakespeare** 672:26

Germaine Greer 1939–
Australian feminist

6 The female eunuch.
title of book (1970)

7 Women have very little idea of how much men hate them.
The Female Eunuch (1970)

8 Is it too much to ask that women be spared the daily struggle for superhuman beauty in order to offer it to the caresses of a subhumanly ugly mate?
The Female Eunuch (1970)

9 You can now see the Female Eunuch the world over . . . spreading herself wherever blue jeans and Coca-Cola may go. Wherever you see nail varnish, lipstick, brassieres, and high heels, the Eunuch has set up her camp.
The Female Eunuch (20th anniversary ed., 1991) foreword

10 Human beings have an inalienable right to invent themselves; when that right is pre-empted it is called brain-washing.
in *The Times* 1 February 1986

11 I didn't fight to get women out from behind the vacuum cleaner to get them onto the board of Hoover.
in *Guardian* 27 October 1986

12 Football is an art more central to our culture than anything the Arts Council deigns to recognize.
in *Independent* 28 June 1996

Gregory the Great AD *c.*540–604
Pope from 590

13 *Non Angli sed Angeli.*
Not Angles but Angels.
on seeing English slaves in Rome
oral tradition, based on
Responsum est, quod Angli vocarentur. At ille: 'Bene,' inquit; 'nam et angelicam habent faciem, et tales angelorum in caelis decet esse coheredes'.
They answered that they were called Angles. 'It is well,' he said, 'for they have the faces of angels, and such should be the co-heirs of the angels of heaven'
Bede *Historia Ecclesiastica* bk. 2, sect. 1

Stephen Grellet 1773–1855
French missionary

14 I expect to pass through this world but once; any good thing therefore that I can do, or any kindness that I can show to any fellow-creature, let me do it now; let me not defer or neglect it, for I shall not pass this way again.
attributed; some of the many other claimants to authorship are given in John o' London *Treasure Trove* (1925)

Joyce Grenfell 1910–79
English comedy actress and writer

15 Stately as a galleon, I sail across the floor,
Doing the Military Two-step, as in the days of yore . . .
So gay the band,
So giddy the sight,
Full evening dress is a must,
But the zest goes out of a beautiful waltz
When you dance it bust to bust.
'Stately as a Galleon' (1978 song)

16 George—don't do that.
recurring line in monologues about a nursery school, from the 1950s, in *George—Don't Do That* (1977)

Julian Grenfell 1888–1915
English soldier and poet

17 And Life is Colour and Warmth and Light
And a striving evermore for these;
And he is dead, who will not fight;
And who dies fighting has increase.
'Into Battle' in *The Times* 28 May 1915

George Grenville 1712–70
British Whig statesman; Prime Minister 1763–5

18 A wise government knows how to enforce with temper, or to conciliate with dignity.
speaking against the expulsion of John **Wilkes**
in the House of Commons, 3 February 1769

Jean-Baptiste-Louis Gresset 1709–77

French poet and dramatist

1 *Les sots sont ici-bas pour nos menus plaisirs.*

Fools are here below for our minor pleasures.

Le Méchant (1747) act 2, sc. 1

Frances Greville (née Macartney) c.1724–89

Irish poet

2 Far as distress the soul can wound
'Tis pain in each degree;
Bliss goes but to a certain bound,
Beyond is agony.

'A Prayer for Indifference' (1759)

Fulke Greville, Lord Brooke 1554–1628

English poet, writer, and politician
see also **Dyer** *286:12*

3 Life is a top which whipping Sorrow driveth.

Caelica (1633) 'The earth with thunder torn, with fire blasted'

4 O wearisome condition of humanity!
Born under one law, to another bound;
Vainly begot, and yet forbidden vanity;
Created sick, commanded to be sound.

Mustapha (1609) act 5, sc. 4

Edward Grey, Lord Grey of Fallodon 1862–1933

British Liberal politician

5 The lamps are going out all over Europe; we shall not see them lit again in our lifetime.

on the eve of the First World War

25 Years (1925) vol. 2, ch. 18

Lady Jane Grey 1537–54

niece of **Henry VIII**, *queen of England 9–19 June 1553*

6 One of the greatest benefits that God ever gave me is that he sent me so sharp and severe parents and so gentle a schoolmaster.

Roger Ascham *The Schoolmaster* (1570) bk. 1

Arthur Griffith 1871–1922

Irish statesman

7 The Irish leader who would connive in the name of Home Rule at the acceptance of any measure which alienated for a day—for an hour—for one moment of time—a square inch of the soil of Ireland would act the part of a traitor and would deserve a traitor's fate.

in *Sinn Féin* 21 February 1914

8 What I have signed I will stand by, in the belief that the end of the conflict of centuries is at hand.

statement to Dáil Éireann before the debate on the Treaty, December 1921

9 We have brought back the flag; we have brought back the evacuation of Ireland after 700 years by British troops and the formation of an Irish army. We have brought back to Ireland her full rights.

when moving acceptance of the Treaty in the Dáil, December 1921

Mervyn Griffith-Jones 1909–79

British lawyer

10 Is it a book you would even wish your wife or your servants to read?

of D. H. **Lawrence***'s* Lady Chatterley's Lover, *while appearing for the prosecution at the Old Bailey, 20 October 1960*

in *The Times* 21 October 1960

Philip Jones Griffiths

Welsh photojournalist

11 There are very few professions where even when you are at the top, a household name, you might still be standing on a draughty street corner with your feet getting wet and cold, waiting for something to happen.

of working as a photojournalist

Russell Miller *Magnum: Fifty Years at the Front Line of History* (1997)

John Grigg 1924–

British writer and journalist, who as Lord Altrincham disclaimed his hereditary title in 1963

12 The personality conveyed by the utterances which are put into her mouth is that of a priggish schoolgirl, captain of the hockey team, a prefect, and a recent candidate for confirmation. It is not thus that she will be able to come into her own as an independent and distinctive character.

of Queen **Elizabeth II**

in *National and English Review* August 1958

13 Autobiography is now as common as adultery and hardly less reprehensible.

in *Sunday Times* 28 February 1962

Nicholas Grimald 1519–62

English poet

14 Of all the heavenly gifts that mortal men
commend,
What trusty treasure in the world can countervail
a friend?

'Of Friendship' (1557)

Joseph ('Jo') Grimond 1913–93

British Liberal politician, Leader of the Liberal Party (1956–67)

15 In bygone days, commanders were taught that when in doubt, they should march their troops towards the sound of gunfire. I intend to march my troops towards the sound of gunfire.

speech to the Liberal Party Assembly, 14 September 1963

Andrei Gromyko 1909–89
Soviet statesman, President of the USSR 1985–8

1 Comrades, this man has a nice smile, but he's got iron teeth.
of Mikhail **Gorbachev**
speech to Soviet Communist Party Central Committee, 11 March 1985

George Grossmith 1847–1912
English actor, singer, and writer

2 You should see me dance the Polka,
You should see me cover the ground,
You should see my coat-tails flying,
As I jump my partner round.
'See me Dance the Polka' (*c.*1887 song)

George and Weedon Grossmith 1847–1912, 1854–1919
English writers

3 What's the good of a home if you are never in it?
The Diary of a Nobody (1894) ch. 1

4 I . . . recognized her as a woman who used to work years ago for my old aunt at Clapham. It only shows how small the world is.
The Diary of a Nobody (1894) ch. 2

5 He suggested we should play 'Cutlets', a game we never heard of. He sat on a chair, and asked Carrie to sit on his lap, an invitation which dear Carrie rightly declined.
The Diary of a Nobody (1894) ch. 7

6 I left the room with silent dignity, but caught my foot in the mat.
The Diary of a Nobody (1894) ch. 12

7 I am a poor man, but I would gladly give ten shillings to find out who sent me the insulting Christmas card I received this morning.
The Diary of a Nobody (1894) ch. 13

Andrew Grove 1936–
American businessman

8 Only the paranoid survive.
dictum on which he has long run his company, the Intel Corporation
in *New York Times* 18 December 1994

Philip Guedalla 1889–1944
British historian and biographer

9 Any stigma, as the old saying is, will serve to beat a dogma.
Masters and Men (1923) 'Ministers of State'; cf. **Proverbs** 604:16

10 The little ships, the unforgotten Homeric catalogue of *Mary Jane* and *Peggy IV*, of *Folkestone Belle*, *Boy Billy*, and *Ethel Maud*, of *Lady Haig* and *Skylark* . . . the little ships of England brought the Army home.
on the evacuation of Dunkirk
Mr Churchill (1941) ch. 7

11 The cheerful clatter of Sir James Barrie's cans as he went round with the milk of human kindness.
Supers and Supermen (1920) 'Some Critics'

12 The work of Henry James has always seemed divisible by a simple dynastic arrangement into three reigns: James I, James II, and the Old Pretender.
Supers and Supermen (1920) 'Some Critics'

13 History repeats itself. Historians repeat each other.
Supers and Supermen (1920) 'Some Historians'; cf. **Proverbs** 602:40

Edgar A. Guest 1881–1959
American writer, journalist, and poet

14 The best of all the preachers are the men who live their creeds.
'Sermons we See' (1926)

Ernesto ('Che') Guevara 1928–67
Argentinian revolutionary and guerrilla leader

15 The Revolution is made by man, but man must forge his revolutionary spirit from day to day.
Socialism and Man in Cuba (1968)

Hervé Guibert 1955–91
French writer

16 [Aids was] an illness in stages, a very long flight of steps that led assuredly to death, but whose every step represented a unique apprenticeship. It was a disease that gave death time to live and its victims time to die, time to discover time, and in the end to discover life.
To the Friend who did not Save my Life (1991) ch. 61 (translated by Linda Coverdale)

François Guizot 1787–1874
French historian and politician

17 *L'humanité ne se passe pas longtemps de grandeur.*
Humanity cannot for long dispense with greatness.
in 1832; E. Percy *The Heresy of Democracy* (1954)

Nubar Gulbenkian 1896–1972
British industrialist and philanthropist

18 The best number for a dinner party is two—myself and a dam' good head waiter.
in *Daily Telegraph* 14 January 1965

Nikolai Gumilev 1886–1921
Russian poet

19 Our freedom is but a light that breaks through from another world.
'The Tram that Lost its Way' (1921) (tr. Dmitri Obolensky)

Thom Gunn 1929–
English poet

20 My thoughts are crowded with death
and it draws so oddly on the sexual
that I am confused
confused to be attracted
by, in effect, my own annihilation.
'In Time of Plague' (1992)

1 Their relationship consisted
In discussing if it existed.
'Jamesian' (1992)

Dorothy Frances Gurney 1858–1932
English poet

2 The kiss of the sun for pardon,
The song of the birds for mirth,
One is nearer God's Heart in a garden
Than anywhere else on earth.
'God's Garden' (1913)

Ivor Gurney 1890–1937
English poet

3 I paid the prices of life
Standing where Rome immortal heard October's strife,
A war poet whose right of honour cuts falsehood like a knife.
'Poem for End' (*c.*1922–5)

4 War told me truth: I have Severn's right of maker,
As of Cotswold: war told me: I was elect, I was born fit
To praise the three hundred feet depth of every acre
Between Tewkesbury and Stroudway, Side and Wales Gate.
'While I Write' (*c.*1922–5)

John Hampden Gurney 1802–62
English clergyman

5 Ye holy angels bright,
Who wait at God's right hand,
Or through the realms of light
Fly at your Lord's command,
Assist our song,
Or else the theme
Too high doth seem
For mortal tongue.
'Ye holy angels bright' (1838 hymn); based on a poem by Richard Baxter (1615–91)

6 My soul, bear thou thy part,
Triumph in God above,
And with a well-tuned heart
Sing thou the songs of love.
'Ye holy angels bright' (1838 hymn)

Woody Guthrie (Woodrow Wilson Guthrie) 1912–67
American folksinger and songwriter

7 This land is your land, this land is my land,
From California to the New York Island.
From the redwood forest to the Gulf Stream waters
This land was made for you and me.
'This Land is Your Land' (1956 song)

Nell Gwyn 1650–87
English actress and courtesan
on Gwyn: see **Last words** *456:11,* **Pepys** *573:7*

8 Pray, good people, be civil. I am the Protestant whore.
at Oxford, during the Popish Terror, 1681; in B. Bevan *Nell Gwyn* (1969) ch. 13

William Habington 1605–54
English poet

9 Direct your eyesight inward, and you'll find
A thousand regions in your mind
Yet undiscover'd. Travel them, and be
Expert in home cosmography.
'To my honoured friend Sir Ed. P. Knight', in *Castara* (1634)

Alan Hackney
British novelist

10 Miles of cornfields, and ballet in the evening.
describing Russia
Private Life (1958) ch. 11 (later filmed as *I'm All Right Jack*, 1959)

Hadrian AD 76–138
Roman emperor from 117

11 *Animula vagula blandula,*
Hospes comesque corporis,
Quae nunc abibis in loca
Pallidula rigida nudula,
Nec ut soles dabis iocos!

Ah! gentle, fleeting, wav'ring sprite,
Friend and associate of this clay!
To what unknown region borne,
Wilt thou now wing thy distant flight?
No more with wonted humour gay,
But pallid, cheerless, and forlorn.
J. W. Duff (ed.) *Minor Latin Poets* (1934); translated by Byron as 'Adrian's Address to His Soul When Dying'; cf. **Pope** 582:15

Ernst Haeckel 1834–1919
German biologist and philosopher

12 Ontogenesis, or the development of the individual, is a short and quick recapitulation of phylogenesis, or the development of the tribe to which it belongs, determined by the laws of inheritance and adaptation.
this discredited theory is often summarized as, 'ontogeny recapitulates phylogeny'
The History of Creation (1868)

Haggadah
the text recited at the Seder on the first two nights of the Jewish Passover

13 This is the bread of poverty which our fathers ate in the land of Egypt. Let all who are hungry come and eat; let all who are in need come to our Passover feast. Now we are here; next year may we be in the land of Israel! Now we are slaves; next year may we be free!
The narration

14 It is this promise which has stood by our fathers and by us. For it is not simply a matter of one man rising up against us to destroy us. Rather, in every generation men have risen up against us to destroy us, but the Holy One, blessed be he, has saved us from their hands.
In every generation

1 Rabban Gamaliel says: 'Whoever does not mention the following three things at Passover has not fulfilled his duty—the Passover sacrifice, unleavened bread, and bitter herbs.'
The three essentials of the Seder

2 Therefore, we are duty-bound to thank, praise, laud, glorify, exalt, honour, bless, extol, and adore him who performed all these miracles for our fathers and for us. He has brought us out from slavery to freedom, from sorrow to joy, from mourning to holiday, from darkness to great light, and from bondage to redemption. Let us, then, sing before him a new song. Hallelujah!
Praise to the Redeemer of Israel

3 Next year in Jerusalem!
Accepted

H. Rider Haggard 1856–1925
English writer
on Haggard: see **Stephen** 738:1

4 Out of the dark we came, into the dark we go . . . Life is nothing. Life is all. It is the hand with which we hold off death. It is the glow-worm that shines in the night-time and is black in the morning; it is the white breath of the oxen in winter; it is the little shadow that runs across the grass and loses itself at sunset.
King Solomon's Mines (1886) ch. 5; cf. **Crowfoot** 246:16

5 She who must be obeyed.
She (1887) ch. 6 and *passim*

William Hague 1961–
British Conservative politician; Leader of the Conservative party since 1997

6 It was inevitable the Titanic was going to set sail, but that doesn't mean it was a good idea to be on it.
on his opposition to joining the single currency
in *Mail on Sunday* 11 January 1998 'Quotes of the Week'

7 Feather-bedding, pocket-lining, money-grabbing cronies.
on the influence of lobbyists
in the House of Commons, 8 July 1998

C. F. S. Hahnemann see **Mottoes** 535:18

Earl Haig 1861–1928
Commander of British armies in France, 1915–18
on Haig: see **Beaverbrook** 59:5

8 A very weak-minded fellow I am afraid, and, like the feather pillow, bears the marks of the last person who has sat on him!
describing Lord **Derby**
letter to Lady Haig, 14 January 1918; in R. Blake *Private Papers of Douglas Haig* (1952) ch. 16

9 Every position must be held to the last man: there must be no retirement. With our backs to the wall, and believing in the justice of our cause, each one of us must fight on to the end.
order to British troops, 12 April 1918; A. Duff Cooper *Haig* (1936) vol. 2, ch. 23

Quintin Hogg, Lord Hailsham 1907–
British Conservative politician

10 Conservatives do not believe that the political struggle is the most important thing in life . . . The simplest of them prefer fox-hunting—the wisest religion.
The Case for Conservatism (1947) pt. 1

11 A great party is not to be brought down because of a scandal by a woman of easy virtue and a proved liar.
in a BBC television interview on the Profumo affair, in *The Times* 14 June 1963

12 The elective dictatorship.
title of the Dimbleby Lecture, 19 October 1976

13 The English and, more latterly, the British, have the habit of acquiring their institutions by chance or inadvertence, and shedding them in a fit of absent-mindedness.
'The Granada Guildhall Lecture 1987' 10 November 1987; cf. **Seeley** 653:8

Hakuin 1686–1769
Japanese monk, writer and artist; founder of modern Japanese Zen

14 If someone claps his hand a sound arises. Listen to the sound of the single hand!
attributed

J. B. S. Haldane 1892–1964
Scottish mathematical biologist

15 Now, my own suspicion is that the universe is not only queerer than we suppose, but queerer than we *can* suppose . . . I suspect that there are more things in heaven and earth than are dreamed of, or can be dreamed of, in any philosophy.
Possible Worlds and Other Essays (1927) 'Possible Worlds'; cf. **Shakespeare** 663:4

16 If my mental processes are determined wholly by the motions of atoms in my brain, I have no reason for supposing that my beliefs are true. They may be sound chemically, but that does not make them sound logically. And hence I have no reason for supposing my brain to be composed of atoms.
Possible Worlds (1927) 'When I am Dead'

17 I wish I had the voice of Homer
To sing of rectal carcinoma,
Which kills a lot more chaps, in fact,
Than were bumped off when Troy was sacked.
'Cancer's a Funny Thing'; Ronald Clark *J. B. S.* (1968)

18 The Creator, if He exists, has a special preference for beetles.
on observing that there are 400,000 species of beetle on this planet, but only 8,000 species of mammals
report of lecture, 7 April 1951, in *Journal of the British Interplanetary Society* (1951) vol. 10

H. R. Haldeman 1929–93

Presidential assistant to Richard Nixon

1 Once the toothpaste is out of the tube, it is awfully hard to get it back in.

on the Watergate affair

to John Dean on the Watergate affair, 8 April 1973, in *Hearings Before the Select Committee on Presidential Campaign Activities of US Senate: Watergate and Related Activities* (1973) vol. 4

Edward Everett Hale 1822–1909

American Unitarian clergyman; Senate chaplain for 1903

2 'Do you pray for the senators, Dr Hale?' 'No, I look at the senators and I pray for the country.'

Van Wyck Brooks *New England Indian Summer* (1940)

Matthew Hale 1609–76

English judge

3 Christianity is part of the laws of England.

William Blackstone's summary of Hale's words (Taylor's case, 1676) in *Commentaries* (1769) vol. 4; Holdsworth's *History of English Law* (1937 ed.) vol. 8 traces the origin of the expression to Sir John Prisot (d. 1460)

Nathan Hale see **Last Words** 456:8

Sarah Josepha Hale 1788–1879

American writer

4 Mary had a little lamb,
Its fleece was white as snow,
And everywhere that Mary went
The lamb was sure to go.

Poems for Our Children (1830) 'Mary's Little Lamb'

Judah Ha-Levi *c.*1075–1141

Jewish poet and philosopher, born in Spain

5 Israel amidst the nations is like the heart amidst the organs; it is the most sick and the most healthy of them all.

The Kuzari 2.36

6 I understand the difference between the God and the Lord and I see how great is the difference between the God of Abraham and the God of Aristotle.

The Kuzari 4.16

George Savile, Lord Halifax ('the Trimmer') 1633–95

English politician and essayist

7 Love is a passion that hath friends in the garrison.

Advice to a Daughter (1688) 'Behaviour and Conversation'

8 This innocent word *Trimmer* signifieth no more than this, that if men are together in a boat, and one part of the company would weigh it down on one side, another would make it lean as much to the contrary.

Character of a Trimmer (1685, printed 1688)

9 Men in business are in as much danger from those that work under them, as from those that work against them.

Political, Moral, and Miscellaneous Thoughts and Reflections (1750) 'Instruments of State: Ministers'

10 A known liar should be outlawed in a well-ordered government.

Political, Moral, and Miscellaneous Thoughts and Reflections (1750) 'Miscellaneous: Lying'

11 Anger is never without an argument, but seldom with a good one.

Political, Moral, and Miscellaneous Thoughts and Reflections (1750) 'Of Anger'

12 After a revolution, you see the same men in the drawing-room, and within a week the same flatterers.

Political, Moral, and Miscellaneous Thoughts and Reflections (1750) 'Of Courts'

13 Most men make little other use of their speech than to give evidence against their own understanding.

Political, Moral, and Miscellaneous Thoughts and Reflections (1750) 'Of Folly and Fools'

14 There is . . . no fundamental, but that *every supreme power must be arbitrary.*

Political, Moral, and Miscellaneous Thoughts and Reflections (1750) 'Of Fundamentals'

15 In corrupted governments the place is given for the sake of the man; in good ones the man is chosen for the sake of the place.

Political, Moral, and Miscellaneous Thoughts and Reflections (1750) 'Of Fundamentals'

16 It is in a disorderly government as in a river, the lightest things swim at the top.

Political, Moral, and Miscellaneous Thoughts and Reflections (1750) 'Of Government'

17 The best definition of the best government is, that it has no inconveniences but such as are supportable; but inconveniences there must be.

Political, Moral, and Miscellaneous Thoughts and Reflections (1750) 'Of Government'

18 Malice is of a low stature, but it hath very long arms.

Political, Moral, and Miscellaneous Thoughts and Reflections (1750) 'Of Malice and Envy'

19 The best party is but a kind of conspiracy against the rest of the nation.

Political, Moral, and Miscellaneous Thoughts and Reflections (1750) 'Of Parties'

20 When the people contend for their liberty, they seldom get anything by their victory but new masters.

Political, Moral, and Miscellaneous Thoughts and Reflections (1750) 'Of Prerogative, Power and Liberty'

21 Power is so apt to be insolent and Liberty to be saucy, that they are very seldom upon good terms.

Political, Moral, and Miscellaneous Thoughts and Reflections (1750) 'Of Prerogative, Power and Liberty'

22 Men are not hanged for stealing horses, but that horses may not be stolen.

Political, Moral, and Miscellaneous Thoughts and Reflections (1750) 'Of Punishment'

1 Wherever a knave is not punished, an honest man is laughed at.
Political, Moral, and Miscellaneous Thoughts and Reflections (1750) 'Of Punishment'

2 State business is a cruel trade; good nature is a bungler in it.
Political, Moral, and Miscellaneous Thoughts and Reflections (1750) 'Wicked Ministers'

3 To the question, What shall we do to be saved in this World? there is no other answer but this, Look to your Moat.
A Rough Draft of a New Model at Sea (1694)

4 Lord Rochester was made Lord president: which being a post superior in rank, but much inferior both in advantage and credit to that he held formerly, drew a jest from Lord Halifax . . . he had heard of many kicked down stairs, but never of any that was kicked up stairs before.
Gilbert Burnet *History of My Own Time* (written 1683–6) vol. 1 (1724)

Joseph Hall 1574–1656
English bishop

5 I first adventure, follow me who list
And be the second English satirist.
Virgidemiae (1597) prologue

6 Perfection is the child of Time.
Works (1625)

Radclyffe Hall 1883–1943
English novelist

7 The well of loneliness
title of novel (1928)

8 You're neither unnatural, nor abominable, nor mad; you're as much a part of what people call nature as anyone else; only you're unexplained as yet—you've not got your niche in creation.
of lesbianism
The Well of Loneliness (1928) bk. 2, ch. 20, sect. 3

Fitz-Greene Halleck 1790–1867
American poet

9 They love their land because it is their own,
And scorn to give aught other reason why;
Would shake hands with a king upon his throne,
And think it kindness to his Majesty.
'Connecticut' (1847)

10 Green be the turf above thee,
Friend of my better days!
None knew thee but to love thee,
Nor named thee but to praise.
'On the Death of Joseph Rodman Drake' (1820)

Friedrich Halm see **Closing lines** 222:23

Margaret Halsey 1910–
American writer

11 The English never smash in a face. They merely refrain from asking it to dinner.
With Malice Toward Some (1938) pt. 3

W. F. ('Bull') Halsey 1882–1959
American admiral

12 The Third Fleet's sunken and damaged ships have been salvaged and are retiring at high speed toward the enemy.
on hearing claims that the Japanese had virtually annihilated the US fleet
report, 14 October 1944; E. B. Potter *Bull Halsey* (1985) ch. 17

Alexander Hamilton *c.*1755–1804
American politician

13 A national debt, if it is not excessive, will be to us a national blessing.
letter to Robert Morris, 30 April 1781, in John C. Hamilton (ed.) *Works of Alexander Hamilton* vol. 1 (1850)

William Hamilton 1788–1856
Scottish metaphysician

14 Truth, like a torch, the more it's shook it shines.
Discussions on Philosophy (1852) title page (epigram)

15 On earth there is nothing great but man; in man there is nothing great but mind.
Lectures on Metaphysics and Logic (ed. Mamsel and Veitch, 1859) vol. 1; attributed in a Latin form to Favorinus in Pico di Mirandola (1463–94) *Disputationes Adversus Astrologiam Divinatricem* (ed. E. Garin, 1946) bk. 3, ch. 27

Oscar Hammerstein II 1895–1960
American songwriter

16 Fish got to swim and birds got to fly
I got to love one man till I die,
Can't help lovin' dat man of mine.
'Can't Help Lovin' Dat Man of Mine' (1927 song) in *Showboat*

17 Climb ev'ry mountain, ford ev'ry stream
Follow ev'ry rainbow, till you find your dream.
'Climb Ev'ry Mountain' (1959 song) in *The Sound of Music*

18 I'm gonna wash that man right outa my hair.
title of song (1949) from *South Pacific*

19 June is bustin' out all over.
title of song (1945) in *Carousel*

20 The last time I saw Paris
Her heart was warm and gay,
I heard the laughter of her heart in ev'ry street café.
'The Last Time I saw Paris' (1941 song) in *Lady Be Good*

21 The corn is as high as an elephant's eye,
An' it looks like it's climbin' clear up to the sky.
'Oh, What a Beautiful Mornin' ' (1943 song) in *Oklahoma!*

22 Ol' man river, dat ol' man river,
He must know sumpin', but don't say nothin',
He jus' keeps rollin',
He jus' keeps rollin' along.
'Ol' Man River' (1927 song) in *Showboat*

23 Some enchanted evening,
You may see a stranger,
You may see a stranger,
Across a crowded room.
'Some Enchanted Evening' (1949 song) in *South Pacific*

1 The hills are alive with the sound of music,
With songs they have sung for a thousand years.
The hills fill my heart with the sound of music,
My heart wants to sing ev'ry song it hears.
'The Sound of Music' (1959 title-song in show)

2 There is nothin' like a dame.
title of song (1949) in *South Pacific*

3 I'm as corny as Kansas in August,
High as a flag on the Fourth of July!
'A Wonderful Guy' (1949 song) in *South Pacific*

4 You'll never walk alone.
title of song (1945) in *Carousel*

5 You've got to be taught to be afraid
Of people whose eyes are oddly made,
Of people whose skin is a different shade.
You've got to be carefully taught.
'You've Got to be Carefully Taught' (1949 song) in *South Pacific*

Richard Hampden 1631–95
English politician

6 To tie a popish successor with laws for the preservation of the Protestant religion was binding Samson with withes.
moving a bill to exclude the Duke of York by name from the succession, 11 May 1679
in *Dictionary of National Biography* (1917–)

Learned Hand 1872–1961
American judge

7 A self-made man may prefer a self-made name.
on Samuel Goldfish's changing his name to Samuel **Goldwyn**
Bosley Crowther *Lion's Share* (1957) ch. 7

George Frederick Handel 1685–1759
German-born composer and organist, resident in England from 1712

8 Whether I was in my body or out of my body as I wrote it I know not. God knows.
of the 'Hallelujah Chorus' in his Messiah; *echoing St Paul*
Romain Rolland *A Musical Tour Through the Land of the Past* (1922); cf. **Bible** 107:15

Kate Hankey 1834–1911
English evangelist

9 Tell me the old, old story
Of unseen things above,
Of Jesus and his glory,
Of Jesus and his love.
'Tell me the old, old story' (1867 hymn)

Sophie Hannah 1971–
British poet

10 The end of love should be a big event.
It should involve the hiring of a hall.
Why the hell not? It happens to us all.
Why should it pass without acknowledgement?
'The End of Love'

Brian Hanrahan 1949–
British journalist

11 I counted them all out and I counted them all back.
on the number of British aeroplanes joining the raid on Port Stanley in the Falkland Islands
BBC broadcast report, 1 May 1982, in *Battle for the Falklands* (1982)

Lorraine Hansberry 1930–65
American dramatist

12 Though it be a thrilling and marvellous thing to be merely young and gifted in such times, it is doubly so, doubly dynamic—to be young, gifted and *black*.
To be young, gifted and black: Lorraine Hansberry in her own words (1969) adapted by Robert Nemiroff; cf. **Irvine** 400:1

Edmond Haraucourt 1856–1941
French poet

13 *Partir c'est mourir un peu,*
C'est mourir à ce qu'on aime:
On laisse un peu de soi-même
En toute heure et dans tout lieu.

To go away is to die a little, it is to die to that which one loves: everywhere and always, one leaves behind a part of oneself.
Seul (1891) 'Rondel de l'Adieu'

Otto Harbach 1873–1963
American songwriter

14 Now laughing friends deride tears I cannot hide,
So I smile and say 'When a lovely flame dies,
Smoke gets in your eyes.'
'Smoke Gets in your Eyes' (1933 song)

E. Y. ('Yip') Harburg 1898–1981
American songwriter

15 Brother can you spare a dime?
title of song (1932)

16 Say, it's only a paper moon,
Sailing over a cardboard sea.
'It's Only a Paper Moon' (1933 song, with Billy Rose)

17 Wanna cry, wanna croon.
Wanna laugh like a loon.
It's that Old Devil Moon in your eyes.
'Old Devil Moon' (1946 song) in *Finian's Rainbow*

18 Somewhere over the rainbow
Way up high,
There's a land that I heard of
Once in a lullaby.
'Over the Rainbow' (1939 song) in *The Wizard of Oz*

19 Follow the yellow brick road.
'We're Off to See the Wizard' (1939 song); cf. **Baum** 57:15, **John** 408:4

William Harcourt 1827–1904
British Liberal politician

1 We are all socialists now.
during the passage of Lord **Goschen**'s *1888 budget, noted for the reduction of the national debt*
attributed; Hubert Bland 'The Outlook' in G. B. Shaw (ed.) *Fabian Essays in Socialism* (1889)

Keir Hardie 1856–1915
Scottish Labour politician

2 From his childhood onward this boy will be surrounded by sycophants and flatterers by the score—[*Cries of* 'Oh, oh!']—and will be taught to believe himself as of a superior creation. [*Cries of* 'Oh, oh!'] A line will be drawn between him and the people whom he is to be called upon some day to reign over. In due course, following the precedent which has already been set, he will be sent on a tour round the world, and probably rumours of a morganatic alliance will follow—[*Loud cries of* 'Oh, oh!' *and* 'Order!']—and the end of it all will be that the country will be called upon to pay the bill. [*Cries of* Divide!]
of the future **Edward VIII**
speech in the House of Commons, 28 June 1894

3 Woman, even more than the working class, is the great unknown quantity of the race.
speech at Bradford, 11 April 1914

D. W. Harding 1906–
British psychologist and critic

4 Regulated hatred.
title of an article on the novels of Jane **Austen**
in *Scrutiny* March 1940

Warren G. Harding 1865–1923
American Republican statesman; 29th President of the US, 1921–3

5 America's present need is not heroics, but healing; not nostrums but normalcy; not revolution, but restoration.
speech at Boston, 14 May 1920, in Frederick E. Schortemeier *Rededicating America* (1920) ch. 17

Philip Yorke, Lord Hardwicke 1690–1764
English judge
on Hardwicke: see **Pulteney** *617:1*

6 His doubts are better than most people's certainties.
of Lord Dirleton's Law Doubts *(1698)*
James Boswell *Life of Samuel Johnson* (1791)

Godfrey Harold Hardy 1877–1947
English mathematician

7 Beauty is the first test: there is no permanent place in the world for ugly mathematics.
A Mathematician's Apology (1940)

Thomas Hardy 1840–1928
English novelist and poet
see also **Borrowed titles** *144:5*

8 A local thing called Christianity.
The Dynasts (1904) pt. 1, act 1, sc. 6

9 War makes rattling good history; but Peace is poor reading.
The Dynasts (1904) pt. 1, act 2, sc. 5

10 It is hard for a woman to define her feelings in language which is chiefly made by men to express theirs.
Far from the Madding Crowd (1874) ch. 81; cf. **Austen** 38:11

11 A lover without indiscretion is no lover at all.
The Hand of Ethelberta (1876) ch. 20

12 Done because we are too menny.
Jude the Obscure (1896) pt. 6, ch. 2

13 Dialect words—those terrible marks of the beast to the truly genteel.
The Mayor of Casterbridge (1886) ch. 20

14 She whose youth had seemed to teach that happiness was but the occasional episode in a general drama of pain.
The Mayor of Casterbridge (1886) ch. 45, closing words

15 The regular resource of people who don't go enough into the world to live a novel is to write one.
A Pair of Blue Eyes (1873) ch. 12

16 It was at present a place perfectly accordant with man's nature—neither ghastly, hateful, nor ugly: neither commonplace, unmeaning, nor tame; but, like man, slighted and enduring; and withal singularly colossal and mysterious in its swarthy monotony. As with some persons who have long lived a past, solitude seemed to look out of its countenance. It had a lonely face, suggesting tragical possibilities.
of Egdon Heath
The Return of the Native (1878) bk. 1, ch. 1

17 Human beings, in their generous endeavour to construct a hypothesis that shall not degrade a First Cause, have always hesitated to conceive a dominant power of a lower moral quality than their own.
The Return of the Native (1878) bk. 6, ch. 1

18 A novel is an impression, not an argument.
Tess of the D'Urbervilles (5th ed., 1892) preface

19 Why it was that upon this beautiful feminine tissue, sensitive as gossamer, and practically blank as snow as yet, there should have been traced such a coarse pattern as it was doomed to receive; why so often the coarse appropriates the finer thus, the wrong man the woman, the wrong woman the man, many thousand years of analytical philosophy have failed to explain to our sense of order.
Tess of the D'Urbervilles (1891) ch. 11

1 The two forces were at work here as everywhere, the inherent will to enjoy, and the circumstantial will against enjoyment.
Tess of the D'Urbervilles (1891) ch. 43

2 'Justice' was done, and the President of the Immortals (in Aeschylean phrase) had ended his sport with Tess.
Tess of the D'Urbervilles (1891) ch. 59

3 Good, but not religious-good.
Under the Greenwood Tree (1872) ch. 2

4 It was one of those sequestered spots outside the gates of the world . . . where, from time to time, dramas of a grandeur and unity truly Sophoclean are enacted in the real, by virtue of the concentrated passions and closely knit interdependence of the lives therein.
The Woodlanders (1887) ch. 1

5 The business of the poet and novelist is to show the sorriness underlying the grandest things, and the grandeur underlying the sorriest things.
notebook entry for 19 April 1885, in Florence Hardy *The Early Life of Thomas Hardy 1840–91* (1928) ch. 13

6 When the Present has latched its postern behind
my tremulous stay,
And the May month flaps its glad green leaves like
wings,
Delicate-filmed as new-spun silk, will the
neighbours say,
'He was a man who used to notice such things'?
'Afterwards' (1917)

7 The bower we shrined to Tennyson,
Gentlemen,
Is roof-wrecked; damps there drip upon
Sagged seats, the creeper-nails are rust,
The spider is sole denizen.
'An Ancient to Ancients' (1922)

8 'Peace upon earth!' was said. We sing it,
And pay a million priests to bring it.
After two thousand years of mass
We've got as far as poison-gas.
'Christmas: 1924' (1928)

9 In a solitude of the sea
Deep from human vanity,
And the Pride of Life that planned her, stilly
couches she.

Steel chambers, late the pyres
Of her salamandrine fires,
Cold currents thrid, and turn to rhythmic tidal
lyres.

Over the mirrors meant
To glass the opulent
The sea-worm crawls—grotesque, slimed, dumb,
indifferent.
'Convergence of the Twain' (1914)

10 The Immanent Will that stirs and urges everything.
'Convergence of the Twain' (1914)

11 An aged thrush, frail, gaunt, and small,
In blast-beruffled plume.
'The Darkling Thrush' (1902)

12 So little cause for carollings
Of such ecstatic sound
Was written on terrestrial things
Afar or nigh around,
That I could think there trembled through
His happy good-night air
Some blessed Hope, whereof he knew
And I was unaware.
'The Darkling Thrush' (1902)

13 If way to the Better there be, it exacts a full look at
the worst.
'De Profundis' (1902)

14 Well, World, you have kept faith with me,
Kept faith with me;
Upon the whole you have proved to be
Much as you said you were.
'He Never Expected Much' (1928)

15 I am the family face;
Flesh perishes, I live on,
Projecting trait and trace
Through time to times anon,
And leaping from place to place
Over oblivion.
'Heredity' (1917)

16 Only a man harrowing clods
In a slow silent walk
With an old horse that stumbles and nods
Half asleep as they stalk.
'In Time of "The Breaking of Nations" ' (1917)

17 Yonder a maid and her wight
Come whispering by:
War's annals will cloud into night
Ere their story die.
'In Time of "The Breaking of Nations" ' (1917)

18 Yes; quaint and curious war is!
You shoot a fellow down
You'd treat if met where any bar is,
Or help to half-a-crown.
'The Man he Killed' (1909)

19 What of the faith and fire within us
Men who march away
Ere the barn-cocks say
Night is growing grey,
To hazards whence no tears can win us;
What of the faith and fire within us
Men who march away?
'Men Who March Away' (1914)

20 In the third-class seat sat the journeying boy
And the roof-lamp's oily flame
Played down on his listless form and face,
Bewrapt past knowing to what he was going,
Or whence he came.
'Midnight on the Great Western' (1917)

21 Woman much missed, how you call to me, call to
me.
'The Voice' (1914)

22 This is the weather the cuckoo likes,
And so do I.
'Weathers' (1922)

23 And drops on gate-bars hang in a row,
And rooks in families homeward go,

And so do I.
'Weathers' (1922)

1 When I set out for Lyonnesse,
A hundred miles away,
The rime was on the spray,
And starlight lit my lonesomeness
When I set out for Lyonnesse
A hundred miles away.
'When I set out for Lyonnesse' (1914)

2 If this sort of thing continues no more novel-writing for me. A man must be a fool to deliberately stand up and be shot at.
of a hostile review of Tess of the D'Urbervilles, *1891*
Florence Hardy *The Early Life of Thomas Hardy* (1928)

Julius Hare 1795–1855 and Augustus Hare 1792–1834

English writers and clergymen

3 The ancients dreaded death: the Christian can only fear dying.
Guesses at Truth (1827) Series 1

Maurice Evan Hare 1886–1967

English limerick writer

4 There once was an old man who said, 'Damn!
It is borne in upon me I am
An engine that moves
In determinate grooves,
I'm not even a bus, I'm a tram.'
'Limerick' (1905)

W. F. Hargreaves 1846–1919

British songwriter

5 I'm Burlington Bertie
I rise at ten thirty and saunter along like a toff,
I walk down the Strand with my gloves on my hand,
Then I walk down again with them off.
'Burlington Bertie from Bow' (1915 song)

6 I acted so tragic the house rose like magic,
The audience yelled 'You're sublime.'
They made me a present of Mornington Crescent
They threw it a brick at a time.
'The Night I Appeared as Macbeth' (1922 song)

John Harington d. 1582

English poet

7 There was a battle fought of late,
Yet was the slaughter small;
The strife was, whether I should write,
Or send nothing at all.
Of one side were the captains' names
Short Time and Little Skill;
One fought alone against them both,
Whose name was Great Good-will.
'To his mother' (written 1540)

John Harington 1561–1612

English writer and courtier

8 When I make a feast,
I would my guests should praise it, not the cooks.
Epigrams (1618) bk. 1, no. 5

9 Treason doth never prosper, what's the reason?
For if it prosper, none dare call it treason.
Epigrams (1618) bk. 4, no. 5

David Ormsby Gore, Lord Harlech 1918–85

British diplomat; Ambassador to Washington, 1961–5

10 Britain will be honoured by historians more for the way she disposed of an empire than for the way in which she acquired it.
in *New York Times* 28 October 1962, sect. 4

Harold II *c.*1019–66

King of England, 1066

11 He will give him seven feet of English ground, or as much more as he may be taller than other men.
his offer to Harald Hardrada of Norway, invading England, before the battle of Stamford Bridge
King Harald's Saga sect. 91, in Snorri Sturluson *Heimskringla* (*c.*1260, first translated by Samuel Laing as *History of the Norse Kings*, 1844)

Jimmy Harper, Will E. Haines, and Tommy Connor

12 The biggest aspidistra in the world.
title of song (1938); popularized by Gracie Fields

Arthur Harris 1892–1984

British Air Force Marshal

13 I would not regard the whole of the remaining cities of Germany as worth the bones of one British Grenadier.
supporting the continued strategic bombing of German cities
letter to Norman Bottomley, deputy Chief of Air Staff, 29 March 1945; Max Hastings *Bomber Command* (1979); cf. **Bismarck** 116:9

Joel Chandler Harris 1848–1908

American writer

14 Hit look lak sparrer-grass, hit feel like sparrer-grass, hit tas'e lak sparrer-grass, en I bless ef 'taint sparrer-grass.
Nights with Uncle Remus (1883) ch. 27

15 All by my own-alone self.
Nights with Uncle Remus (1883) ch. 36

16 You know w'at de jay-bird say ter der squinch-owl! 'I'm sickly but sassy.'
Nights with Uncle Remus (1883) ch. 50

17 Bred en bawn in a brier-patch!
Uncle Remus and His Legends of the Old Plantation (1881) 'How Mr Rabbit was too Sharp for Mr Fox'

18 Lounjun 'roun' en suffer'n'.
Uncle Remus and His Legends of the Old Plantation (1881) 'Mr Wolf tackles Old Man Tarrypin'

1 Tar-baby ain't sayin' nuthin', en Brer Fox, he lay low.
Uncle Remus and His Legends of the Old Plantation (1881) 'The Wonderful Tar-Baby Story'

Tony Harrison 1953–
British poet

2 The ones we choose to love become our anchor
when the hawser of the blood-tie's hacked, or frays.
v (1985)

Josephine Hart

3 Damaged people are dangerous. They know they can survive.
Damage (1991) ch. 12

Lorenz Hart 1895–1943
American songwriter

4 I'm wild again
Beguiled again
A simpering, whimpering child again,
Bewitched, bothered, and bewildered am I.
'Bewitched' (1941 song) in *Pal Joey* (1941)

5 When love congeals
It soon reveals
The faint aroma of performing seals,
The double crossing of a pair of heels.
I wish I were in love again!
'I Wish I Were in Love Again' (1937 song) in *Babes in Arms*

6 I get too hungry for dinner at eight.
I like the theatre, but never come late.
I never bother with people I hate.
That's why the lady is a tramp.
'The Lady is a Tramp' (1937 song) in *Babes in Arms*

7 In a mountain greenery
Where God paints the scenery—
Just two crazy people together.
'Mountain Greenery' (1926 song)

8 Thou swell! Thou witty!
Thou sweet! Thou grand!
Wouldst kiss me pretty?
Wouldst hold my hand?
'Thou Swell' (1927 song)

Bret Harte 1836–1902
American poet

9 And on that grave where English oak and holly
And laurel wreaths entwine
Deem it not all a too presumptuous folly,—
This spray of Western pine!
'Dickens in Camp' (1870)

10 If, of all words of tongue and pen,
The saddest are, 'It might have been,'
More sad are these we daily see:
'It is, but hadn't ought to be!'
'Mrs Judge Jenkins' (1867); cf. **Whittier** 816:6

11 And he smiled a kind of sickly smile, and curled up on the floor,
And the subsequent proceedings interested him no more.
'The Society upon the Stanislaus' (1868) st. 7

12 All you know about it [luck] for certain is that it's bound to change.
'The Outcasts of Poker Flat' (1871) in *The Luck of the Roaring Camp and Other Stories* (1922)

L. P. Hartley 1895–1972
English novelist

13 The past is a foreign country: they do things differently there.
The Go-Between (1953) prologue; cf. **Morley** 532:2

F. W. Harvey b. 1888
English poet

14 From troubles of the world
I turn to ducks
Beautiful comical things.
'Ducks' (1919)

Molly Haskell 1940–
American writer and film critic

15 Being alone and liking it is, for a woman, an act of treachery, an infidelity far more threatening than adultery.
Love and Other Infectious Diseases (1990)

Minnie Louise Haskins 1875–1957
English teacher and writer

16 And I said to the man who stood at the gate of the year: 'Give me a light that I may tread safely into the unknown.'
And he replied:
'Go out into the darkness and put your hand into the Hand of God. That shall be to you better than light and safer than a known way.'
quoted by **George VI** *in his Christmas broadcast,* 1939
Desert (1908) 'God Knows'

Edwin Hatch 1835–89
English clergyman and scholar

17 Breathe on me, Breath of God,
Fill me with life anew,
That I may love what thou dost love,
And do what thou wouldst do.
'Breathe on me, Breath of God' (1878 hymn)

Helen Hathaway 1893–1932
American writer

18 More tears have been shed over men's lack of manners than their lack of morals.
Manners for Men (1928)

Charles Haughey 1925–

Irish Fianna Fáil statesman; Taoiseach 1979–81, 1982, and 1987–92

on Haughey: see **O'Brien** *552:7*

1 It was a bizarre happening, an unprecedented situation, a grotesque situation, an almost unbelievable mischance.

on the series of events leading to the resignation of the Attorney General; the acronym GUBU *was subsequently coined by Conor Cruise* **O'Brien** *to describe Haughey's style of government*

at a press conference in 1982; T. Ryle Dwyer *Charlie: the Political Biography of Charles Haughey* (1987) ch. 12

Václav Havel 1936–

Czech dramatist and statesman; President of Czechoslovakia 1989–92 and of the Czech Republic since 1993

2 That special time caught me up in its wild vortex and—in the absence of leisure to reflect on the matter—compelled me to do what had to be done.

on his election to the Presidency

Summer Meditations (1992)

3 Truth is not merely what we are thinking, but also why, to whom and under what circumstances we say it.

Temptation (1985)

4 I really do inhabit a system in which words are capable of shaking the entire structure of government, where words can prove mightier than ten military divisions.

speech in Germany accepting a peace prize, October 1989, in *Independent* 9 December 1989

Stephen Hawes d. *c.*1523

English poet

5 The end of joy and all prosperity
Is death at last, thorough his course and might;
After the day there cometh the dark night;
For though the day be never so long,
At last the bells ringeth to evensong.

The Pastime of Pleasure (1509) ch. 42, st. 10

R. S. Hawker 1803–75

English clergyman and poet

6 And have they fixed the where and when?
And shall Trelawny die?
Here's twenty thousand Cornish men
Will know the reason why!

the last three lines have been in existence since the imprisonment by James II, in 1688, of seven bishops, including Trelawny, Bishop of Bristol

'The Song of the Western Men'

Jacquetta Hawkes 1910–96

English archaeologist and writer

7 I was conscious of this vanished being and myself as part of an unbroken stream of consciousness . . . With an imaginative effort it is possible to see the eternal present in which all days, all the seasons of the plain, stand in enduring unity.

discovering a Neanderthal skeleton

in *New York Times Biographical Service* 21 March 1996

Stephen Hawking 1942–

English theoretical physicist

8 Each equation . . . in the book would halve the sales.

A Brief History of Time (1988)

9 In effect, we have redefined the task of science to be the discovery of laws that will enable us to predict events up to the limits set by the uncertainty principle.

A Brief History of Time (1988) ch. 11

10 What is it that breathes fire into the equations and makes a universe for them to describe . . . Why does the universe go to all the bother of existing?

A Brief History of Time (1988)

11 If we find the answer to that [why it is that we and the universe exist], it would be the ultimate triumph of human reason—for then we would know the mind of God.

A Brief History of Time (1988) ch. 11

Nathaniel Hawthorne 1804–64

American novelist

12 Dr Johnson's morality was as English an article as a beefsteak.

Our Old Home (1863) 'Lichfield and Uttoxeter'

13 The scarlet letter.

title of novel (1850)

14 America is now given over to a damned mob of scribbling women.

letter, 1855; Caroline Ticknor *Hawthorne and his Publisher* (1913)

Ian Hay (John Hay Beith) 1876–1952

Scottish novelist and dramatist

15 War is hell, and all that, but it has a good deal to recommend it. It wipes out all the small nuisances of peace-time.

The First Hundred Thousand (1915)

16 What do you mean, funny? Funny-peculiar or funny ha-ha?

The Housemaster (1938) act 3

17 The dawn of legibility in his handwriting has revealed his utter inability to spell.

attributed; perhaps used in a dramatization of *The Housemaster* (1938)

Franz Joseph Haydn 1732–1809

Austrian composer

18 But all the world understands my language.

on being advised by **Mozart***, in 1790, not to visit England because he knew too little of the world and too few languages*

Rosemary Hughes *Haydn* (1950) ch. 6

Alfred Hayes 1911–85
American songwriter

1 I dreamed I saw Joe Hill last night
Alive as you and me.
Says I, 'But Joe, you're ten years dead.'
'I never died,' says he.
'I Dreamed I Saw Joe Hill Last Night' (1936 song)

J. Milton Hayes 1884–1940
British writer

2 There's a one-eyed yellow idol to the north of Khatmandu,
There's a little marble cross below the town,
There's a broken-hearted woman tends the grave of Mad Carew,
And the Yellow God forever gazes down.
The Green Eye of the Yellow God (1911)

Eliza Haywood c.1693–1756
English actress, dramatist, and novelist

3 One has no sooner left off one's bib and apron, than people cry—'Miss will soon be married!'—and this man, and that man, is presently picked out for a husband. Mighty ridiculous! they want to deprive us of all the pleasures of life, just when one begins to have a relish for them.
The History of Miss Betty Thoughtless (1751)

William Hazlitt 1778–1830
English essayist
see also **Last words** 457:16

4 His sayings are generally like women's letters; all the pith is in the postscript.
of Charles **Lamb**
Conversations of James Northcote (1826–7)

5 He talked on for ever; and you wished him to talk on for ever.
of **Coleridge**
Lectures on the English Poets (1818) 'On the Living Poets'

6 So have I loitered my life away, reading books, looking at pictures, going to plays, hearing, thinking, writing on what pleased me best. I have wanted only one thing to make me happy, but wanting that have wanted everything.
Literary Remains (1836) 'My First Acquaintance with Poets'

7 The dupe of friendship, and the fool of love; have I not reason to hate and to despise myself? Indeed I do; and chiefly for not having hated and despised the world enough.
The Plain Speaker (1826) 'On the Pleasure of Hating'

8 The love of liberty is the love of others; the love of power is the love of ourselves.
Political Essays (1819) 'The Times Newspaper'

9 There is nothing good to be had in the country, or if there is, they will not let you have it.
The Round Table (1817) 'Observations on Mr Wordsworth's Poem *The Excursion*'

10 Comedy naturally wears itself out—destroys the very food on which it lives; and by constantly and successfully exposing the follies and weaknesses of mankind to ridicule, in the end leaves itself nothing worth laughing at.
The Round Table (1817) 'On Modern Comedy'

11 The art of pleasing consists in being pleased.
The Round Table (1817) 'On Manner'

12 A nickname is the heaviest stone that the devil can throw at a man.
Sketches and Essays (1839) 'Nicknames'

13 There is an unseemly exposure of the mind, as well as of the body.
Sketches and Essays (1839) 'On Disagreeable People'

14 Rules and models destroy genius and art.
Sketches and Essays (1839) 'On Taste'

15 Death cancels everything but truth; and strips a man of everything but genius and virtue. It is a sort of natural canonization.
The Spirit of the Age (1825) 'Lord Byron'

16 The present is an age of talkers, and not of doers; and the reason is, that the world is growing old. We are so far advanced in the Arts and Sciences, that we live in retrospect, and dote on past achievement.
The Spirit of the Age (1825) 'Mr Coleridge'

17 He writes as fast as they can read, and he does not write himself down . . . His worst is better than any other person's best.
The Spirit of the Age (1825) 'Sir Walter Scott'

18 His works (taken together) are almost like a new edition of human nature. This is indeed to be an author!
The Spirit of the Age (1825) 'Sir Walter Scott'

19 Mr Wordsworth's genius is a pure emanation of the Spirit of the Age. Had he lived in any other period of the world, he would never have been heard of.
The Spirit of the Age (1825) 'Mr Wordsworth'

20 You will hear more good things on the outside of a stagecoach from London to Oxford than if you were to pass a twelvemonth with the undergraduates, or heads of colleges, of that famous university.
Table Talk vol. 1 (1821) 'The Ignorance of the Learned'

21 The English (it must be owned) are rather a foul-mouthed nation.
Table Talk vol. 2 (1822) 'On Criticism'

22 We can scarcely hate any one that we know.
Table Talk vol. 2 (1822) 'On Criticism'

23 Give me the clear blue sky over my head, and the green turf beneath my feet, a winding road before me, and a three hours' march to dinner—and then to thinking! It is hard if I cannot start some game on these lone heaths.
Table Talk vol. 2 (1822) 'On Going a Journey'

Bessie Head 1937–86
South African-born writer

24 And if the white man thought that Asians were a low, filthy nation, Asians could still smile with relief—at least, they were not Africans. And if the

white man thought that Africans were a low, filthy nation, Africans in southern Africa could still smile—at least, they were not bushmen. They all have their monsters.

Maru (1971) pt. 1

1 Love is mutually feeding each other, not one living on another like a ghoul.

A Question of Power (1973)

Denis Healey 1917–

British Labour politician, husband of Edna **Healey**

2 I warn you there are going to be howls of anguish from the 80,000 people who are rich enough to pay over 75% [tax] on the last slice of their income.

speech at Labour Party Conference, 1 October 1973

3 Like being savaged by a dead sheep.

on being criticized by Geoffrey **Howe** *in the House of Commons*

in the House of Commons, 14 June 1978

4 While the rest of Europe is marching to confront the new challenges, the Prime Minister is shuffling along in the gutter in the opposite direction, like an old bag lady, muttering imprecations at anyone who catches her eye.

of Margaret **Thatcher**

in the House of Commons, 22 February 1990

Edna Healey 1918–

British writer, wife of Denis **Healey**

5 She has no hinterland; in particular she has no sense of history.

of Margaret **Thatcher**

Denis Healey *The Time of My Life* (1989)

Timothy Michael Healy 1855–1931

Irish nationalist politician

6 REDMOND: Gladstone is now master of the Party!
HEALY: Who is to be mistress of the Party?

at the meeting of the Irish Parliamentary Party on 6 December 1890, when the Party split over **Parnell***'s involvement in the O'Shea divorce; Healy's reference to Katherine O'Shea was particularly damaging to Parnell*

Robert Kee *The Laurel and the Ivy* (1993)

7 The Sinns won in three years what we did not win in forty. You cannot make revolutions with rosewater, or omelettes without making eggs.

letter to his brother; Frank Callanan *T. M. Healy* (1996)

Seamus Heaney 1939–

Irish poet

8 All agog at the plasterer on his ladder
Skimming our gable and writing our name there
With his trowel point, letter by strange letter.

'Alphabets' (1987)

9 And found myself thinking: if it were nowadays,
This is how Death would summon Everyman.

'A Call' (1996)

10 How culpable was he
That last night when he broke
Our tribe's complicity?
'Now you're supposed to be
An educated man,'
I hear him say. 'Puzzle me
The right answer to that one.

'Casualty' (1979)

11 Between my finger and my thumb
The squat pen rests.
I'll dig with it.

'Digging' (1966)

12 Me waiting until I was nearly fifty
To credit marvels.

'Fosterling' (1991)

13 The annals say: when the monks of Clonmacnoise
Were all at prayers inside the oratory
A ship appeared above them in the air.

'Lightenings viii' (1991)

14 Don't be surprised
If I demur, for, be advised
My passport's green.
No glass of ours was ever raised
To toast *The Queen.*

rebuking the editors of The Penguin Book of Contemporary British Poetry *for including him among its authors*

Open Letter (Field Day pamphlet no. 2, 1983)

15 Who would connive
in civilised outrage
yet understand the exact
and tribal, intimate revenge.

'Punishment' (1975)

16 Until, on Vinegar Hill, the fatal conclave.
Terraced thousands died, shaking scythes at
cannon.

'Requiem for the Croppies' (1969)

17 My heart besieged by anger, my mind a gap of
danger,
I walked among their old haunts, the home ground
where they bled;
And in the dirt lay justice like an acorn in the
winter
Till its oak would sprout in Derry where the
thirteen men lay dead.

of Bloody Sunday, Londonderry, 30 January 1972

'The Road to Derry'

18 HERE IS THE NEWS,
Said the absolute speaker. Between him and us
A great gulf was fixed where pronunciation
Reigned tyrannically

'A Sofa in the Forties' (1996)

19 The famous
Northern reticence, the tight gag of place
And times: yes, yes. Of the 'wee six' I sing
Where to be saved you only must save face
And whatever you say, you say nothing.

'Whatever You Say Say Nothing' (1975)

20 The dead-pan cloudiness of a word processor.

The Redress of Poetry (1995)

21 If revolution is the kicking down of a rotten door, evolution is more like pushing the stone from the

mouth of the tomb. There is an Easter energy about it, a sense of arrival rather than wreckage.
in *Observer* 12 April 1998

1 No death outside my immediate family has left me more bereft. No death in my lifetime has hurt poets more.
funeral oration for Ted **Hughes**, 3 November 1998, in *Guardian* 4 November 1998

William Randolph Hearst 1863–1951
American newspaper publisher and tycoon

2 You furnish the pictures and I'll furnish the war.
message to the artist Frederic Remington in Havana, Cuba, during the Spanish-American War of 1898
attributed

Edward Heath 1916–
British Conservative statesman; Prime Minister, 1970–4

3 The unpleasant and unacceptable face of capitalism.
on the Lonrho affair
in the House of Commons, 15 May 1973

John Heath-Stubbs 1918–
English poet

4 Venerable Mother Toothache
Climb down from the white battlements,
Stop twisting in your yellow fingers
The fourfold rope of nerves;
And tomorrow I will give you a tot of whisky
To hold in your cupped hands,
A garland of anise flowers,
And three cloves like nails.
'A Charm Against the Toothache' (1954)

Reginald Heber 1783–1826
English clergyman; Bishop of Calcutta from 1823

5 Brightest and best of the sons of the morning,
Dawn on our darkness and lend us thine aid;
Star of the east, the horizon adorning,
Guide where our infant Redeemer is laid.
'Brightest and best of the sons of the morning' (1827 hymn)

6 From Greenland's icy mountains,
From India's coral strand,
Where Afric's sunny fountains
Roll down their golden sand.
'From Greenland's icy mountains' (1821 hymn)

7 What though the spicy breezes
Blow soft o'er Ceylon's isle;
Though every prospect pleases,
And only man is vile:
In vain with lavish kindness
The gifts of God are strown;
The heathen in his blindness
Bows down to wood and stone.
'From Greenland's icy mountains' (1821 hymn); Heber later altered 'Ceylon's isle' to 'Java's isle'; cf. **Kipling** 438:11

8 Holy, Holy, Holy! Lord God Almighty!
Early in the morning our song shall rise to thee:
Holy, Holy, Holy! merciful and mighty!
God in Three Persons, blessèd Trinity!
Holy, Holy, Holy! all the saints adore thee,
Casting down their golden crowns around the glassy sea,
Cherubim and Seraphim falling down before thee,
Which wert, and art, and evermore shalt be.
'Holy, Holy, Holy! Lord God Almighty!' (1826 hymn)

Ben Hecht 1894–1964
American screenwriter
see also ***Film lines*** *312:8*

9 [Goldwyn] filled the room with wonderful panic and beat at your mind like a man in front of a slot machine, shaking it for a jackpot.
A. Scott Berg *Goldwyn* (1989) ch. 15

G. W. F. Hegel 1770–1831
German idealist philosopher
see also ***Marx*** *500:1*

10 What experience and history teach is this—that nations and governments have never learned anything from history, or acted upon any lessons they might have drawn from it.
Lectures on the Philosophy of World History: Introduction (1830, translated by H. B. Nisbet, 1975) introduction

11 Only in the state does man have a rational existence . . . Man owes his entire existence to the state, and has his being within it alone. Whatever worth and spiritual reality he possesses are his solely by virtue of the state.
Lectures on the Philosophy of World History: Introduction (1830, translated by H. B. Nisbet, 1975)

12 It is a land of desire for all those who are weary of the historical arsenal of old Europe.
of America
Lectures on the Philosophy of World History: Introduction (1830, translated by H. B. Nisbet, 1975) introduction

13 In history, we are concerned with what has been and what is; in philosophy, however, we are concerned not with what belongs exclusively to the past or to the future, but with that which *is*, both now and eternally—in short, with reason.
Lectures on the Philosophy of World History: Introduction (1830, translated by H. B. Nisbet, 1975)

14 What is rational is actual and what is actual is rational.
Philosophy of Right (1821, translated by T. M. Knox, 1952)

15 When philosophy paints its grey on grey, then has a shape of life grown old. By philosophy's grey on grey it cannot be rejuvenated but only understood. The owl of Minerva spreads its wings only with the falling of the dusk.
Philosophy of Right (1821, translated by T. M. Knox, 1952)

16 Thus to be independent of public opinion is the first formal condition of achieving anything great or rational whether in life or in science. Great achievement is assured, however, of subsequent recognition and grateful acceptance by public opinion, which in due course will make it one of its own prejudices.
Philosophy of Right (1821, translated by T. M. Knox, 1952) sect. 318

Heikhalot Rabbati

Jewish mystical text of c.5th–6th century AD

1 I may tell them the mysteries that are hidden and concealed, the wonders of the weaving of the web on which depends the perfection and glory of the world . . . the wonders of the path of the celestial ladder, one end of which rests on earth and the other by the right foot of the Throne of Glory.

16:1

Piet Hein 1905–

poet and cartoonist

2 Problems worthy
of attack
prove their worth
by hitting back.

'Problems' (1969)

Heinrich Heine 1797–1856

German poet
see also **Last words** 455:9

3 *Dort, wo man Bücher*
Verbrennt, verbrennt man auch am Ende Menschen.

Wherever books will be burned, men also, in the end, are burned.

Almansor (1823) l. 245

4 *Auf Flügeln des Gesanges.*

On wings of song.

title of song (1823)

5 *Ich weiss nicht, was soll es bedeuten,*
Dass ich so traurig bin;
Ein Märchen aus alten Zeiten,
Das kommt mir nicht aus dem Sinn.

I know not why I am so sad; I cannot get out of my head a fairy-tale of olden times.

'Die Lorelei' (1826–31)

6 *Es ist eine alte Geschichte,*
Doch bleibt sie immer neu.

It is so old a story,
Yet somehow always new.

Lyrisches Intermezzo (1823) no. 39 (translated by Hal Draper)

7 Wild, dark times are rumbling towards us, and the prophet who wishes to write a new apocalypse will have to invent entirely new beasts, and beasts so terrible that the ancient animal symbols of Saint John will seem like cooing doves and cupids in comparison.

Lutezia (1855)

8 *Sie hatten sich beide so herzlich lieb,*
Spitzbübin war sie, er war ein Dieb.

They loved each other beyond belief—
She was a strumpet, he was a thief.

Neue Gedichte (1852) 'Ein Weib' (translated by Louis Untermeyer, 1938)

9 *Hört ihr das Glöckchen klingeln? Kniet nieder—Man bringt die Sakramente einem sterbenden Gotte.*

Do you hear the little bell tinkle? Kneel down. They are bringing the sacraments to a dying god.

Zur Geschichte der Religion und Philosophie in Deutschland (1834) bk. 2, closing words

10 Maximilien Robespierre was nothing but the hand of Jean Jacques Rousseau, the bloody hand that drew from the womb of time the body whose soul Rousseau had created.

Zur Geschichte der Religion und Philosophie in Deutschland (1834) bk. 3, para. 3

Werner Heisenberg 1901–76

German mathematical physicist

11 An expert is someone who knows some of the worst mistakes that can be made in his subject and who manages to avoid them.

Der Teil und das Ganze (1969) ch. 17 (translated by A. J. Pomerans as *Physics and Beyond*, 1971)

on Felix Bloch's stating that space was the field of linear operations:

12 Nonsense. Space is blue and birds fly through it.

Felix Bloch 'Heisenberg and the early days of quantum mechanics' in *Physics Today* December 1976

Joseph Heller 1923–99

American novelist

13 There was only one catch and that was Catch-22, which specified that a concern for one's own safety in the face of dangers that were real and immediate was the process of a rational mind . . . Orr would be crazy to fly more missions and sane if he didn't, but if he was sane he had to fly them. If he flew them he was crazy and didn't have to; but if he didn't want to he was sane and had to.

Catch-22 (1961) ch. 5

14 Some men are born mediocre, some men achieve mediocrity, and some men have mediocrity thrust upon them. With Major Major it had been all three.

Catch-22 (1961) ch. 9; cf. **Shakespeare** 701:28

15 When I read something saying I've not done anything as good as *Catch-22* I'm tempted to reply, 'Who has?'

in *The Times* 9 June 1993

Lillian Hellman 1905–84

American dramatist
on Hellman: see **McCarthy** *484:4*

16 I cannot and will not cut my conscience to fit this year's fashions.

letter to John S. Wood, 19 May 1952, in *US Congress Committee Hearing on Un-American Activities* (1952) pt. 8

Leona Helmsley *c.*1920–

American hotelier

17 Only the little people pay taxes.

comment made to her housekeeper in 1983, and reported at her trial for tax evasion

in *New York Times* 12 July 1989

Héloise c.1098–1164
French abbess, lover of ***Abelard***

1 God knows I never sought anything in you except yourself; I wanted simply you, nothing of yours.
letter to Peter Abelard, *c.*1132; Betty Radice *The Letters of Abelard and Heloise* (1974)

2 My heart was not in me but with you, and now, even more, if it is not with you it is nowhere.
letter to Peter Abelard, *c.*1132; Betty Radice *The Letters of Abelard and Heloise* (1974)

Helvétius (Claude Arien Helvétius) 1715–71
French philosopher
on Helvétius: see ***Misquotations*** *521:14*

3 [We must] substitute the language of interest for the tone of injury. Do not complain, appeal to interest.
De l'esprit (1758) 'Discours 2' ch. 15

4 *L'éducation nous faisait ce que nous sommes.*
Education made us what we are.
De l'esprit (1758) 'Discours 3' ch. 30

Felicia Hemans 1793–1835
English poet
on Hemans: see ***Scott*** *652:16*

5 The boy stood on the burning deck
Whence all but he had fled;
The flame that lit the battle's wreck
Shone round him o'er the dead.
'Casabianca' (1849)

6 The stately homes of England,
How beautiful they stand!
Amidst their tall ancestral trees,
O'er all the pleasant land.
'The Homes of England' (1849); cf. **Coward** 238:19

John Heming 1556–1630 and **Henry Condell** d. 1627
joint editors of the First Folio

7 Well! it is now public, and you will stand for your privileges we know: to read, and censure. Do so, but buy it first. That doth best commend a book, the stationer says.
First Folio Shakespeare (1623) preface

8 Who, as he was a happy imitator of Nature, was a most gentle expresser of it. His mind and hand went together: And what he thought, he uttered with that easiness, that we have scarce received from him a blot.
First Folio Shakespeare (1623) preface; cf. **Jonson** 421:2, **Pope** 586:18

Ernest Hemingway 1899–1961
American novelist
see also ***Borrowed titles*** *144:6,* ***Fitzgerald*** *315:6,* ***Stein*** *737:9*

9 Where do the noses go? I always wondered where the noses would go.
For Whom the Bell Tolls (1940) ch. 7

10 But did thee feel the earth move?
For Whom the Bell Tolls (1940) ch. 13

11 Paris is a movable feast.
A Movable Feast (1964) epigraph

12 The sun also rises.
title of novel (1926)

13 Grace under pressure.
when asked what he meant by 'guts' in an interview with Dorothy ***Parker***
in *New Yorker* 30 November 1929

14 The most essential gift for a good writer is a built-in, shock-proof shit detector. This is the writer's radar, and all great writers have had it.
in *Paris Review* Spring 1958

Arthur Henderson 1863–1935
Labour politician

15 The first forty-eight hours decide whether a Minister is going to run his office or whether his office is going to run him.
Susan Crosland *Tony Crosland* (1982) ch. 16

Jimi Hendrix (James Marshall Hendrix) 1942–70
American rock musician

16 Purple haze is in my brain
Lately things don't seem the same.
'Purple Haze' (1967 song)

17 A musician, if he's a messenger, is like a child who hasn't been handled too many times by man, hasn't had too many fingerprints across his brain.
in *Life Magazine* (1969)

Arthur W. D. Henley

18 Nobody loves a fairy when she's forty.
title of song (1934)

W. E. Henley 1849–1903
English poet and dramatist
on Henley: see ***Wilde*** *819:10*

19 A deal of Ariel, just a streak of Puck,
Much Antony, of Hamlet most of all,
And something of the Shorter-Catechist.
of Robert Louis ***Stevenson***
'In Hospital' (1888)

20 Out of the night that covers me,
Black as the Pit from pole to pole,
I thank whatever gods may be
For my unconquerable soul.

In the fell clutch of circumstance,
I have not winced nor cried aloud:
Under the bludgeonings of chance
My head is bloody, but unbowed.
'Invictus. In Memoriam R.T.H.B.' (1888)

21 It matters not how strait the gate,
How charged with punishments the scroll,
I am the master of my fate:

I am the captain of my soul.
'Invictus. In Memoriam R.T.H.B.' (1888)

1 What have I done for you,
England, my England?
'Pro Rege Nostro' (1900); cf. **MacDonell** 485:4

2 Or ever the knightly years were gone
With the old world to the grave,
I was a King in Babylon
And you were a Christian slave.
'To W. A.' (1888)

Peter Hennessy 1947–
English historian

3 The model of a modern Prime Minister would be a kind of grotesque composite freak—someone with the dedication to duty of a Peel, the physical energy of a Gladstone, the detachment of a Salisbury, the brains of an Asquith, the balls of a Lloyd George, the word-power of a Churchill, the administrative gifts of an Attlee, the style of a Macmillan, the managerialism of a Heath, and the sleep requirements of a Thatcher. Human beings do not come like that.
The Hidden Wiring (1995); cf. **Gilbert** 339:3

Henri IV (of Navarre) 1553–1610
King of France from 1589

4 I want there to be no peasant in my kingdom so poor that he is unable to have a chicken in his pot every Sunday.
Hardouin de Péréfixe *Histoire de Henry le Grand* (1681); cf. **Hoover** 383:11

5 Hang yourself, brave Crillon; we fought at Arques and you were not there.
traditional form given by Voltaire to a letter from Henri to Crillon, 20 September 1597; Henri's actual words were

My good man, Crillon, hang yourself for not having been at my side last Monday at the greatest event that's ever been seen and perhaps ever will be seen.
Lettres missives de Henri IV, Collection des documents inédits de l'histoire de France vol. 4 (1847)

6 *Paris vaut bien une messe.*

Paris is well worth a mass.
attributed to Henri IV; alternatively to his minister Sully, in conversation with Henri

7 The wisest fool in Christendom.
of ***James I*** *of England*
attributed both to Henri IV and Sully

Henry I 1068–1135
King of England from 1100

8 An illiterate king is a crowned ass.
described as a proverbial usage on the part of Henry by William of Malmesbury in *De Gestis Regum Anglorum*, and probably first coined by Count Foulques II of Anjou, *c.*950

Henry II 1133–89
King of England from 1154

9 Will no one rid me of this turbulent priest?
of Thomas Becket, Archbishop of Canterbury, murdered in Canterbury Cathedral, December 1170
oral tradition, conflating a number of variant forms, including G. Lyttelton *History of the Life of King Henry the Second* (1769) pt. 4: 'so many cowardly and ungrateful men in his court, none of whom would revenge him of the injuries he sustained from one turbulent priest'

Henry VIII 1491–1547
King of England from 1509
on Henry VIII: see ***More*** *531:6*

10 That man hath the sow by the right ear.
of Thomas ***Cranmer****, June 1529*
Acts and Monuments of John Foxe ['Foxe's Book of Martyrs'] (1570)

11 The King found her so different from her picture . . . that . . . he swore they had brought him a Flanders mare.
of Anne of Cleves
Tobias Smollett *A Complete History of England* (3rd ed., 1759) vol. 6

Henry of Huntingdon *c.*1084–1155
English chronicler

12 They beheaded priests at the very altar, and then cutting off the heads of the crucifixes on the roodbeams they put the priest's head on the trunk of the crucifix, and the head of the crucifix on the trunk of the priest.
description of atrocities occurring during the invasion of King David of Scotland in 1138
Historia Anglorum (ed. T. Arnold, Rolls series, 1879)

13 A new kind of monster, compounded of purity and corruption, a monk and a knight.
of Henry of Blois (1101–71), bishop of Winchester and brother of King Stephen
Historia Anglorum (ed. T. Arnold, Rolls series, 1879)

Matthew Henry 1662–1714
English divine

14 The better day, the worse deed.
An Exposition on the Old and New Testament (1710) Genesis ch. 3, v. 6, gloss 2

15 He rolls it under his tongue as a sweet morsel.
An Exposition on the Old and New Testament (1710) Psalm 36, v. 2, gloss 1

16 They that die by famine die by inches.
An Exposition on the Old and New Testament (1710) Psalm 59, v. 15, gloss 5 (referring incorrectly to v. 13)

O. Henry (William Sydney Porter) 1862–1910
American short-story writer
see also ***Last words*** *457:13*

17 It was beautiful and simple as all truly great swindles are.
Gentle Grafter (1908) 'Octopus Marooned'

Patrick Henry 1736–99
American statesman

1 Caesar had his Brutus—Charles the First, his Cromwell—and George the Third—('Treason,' cried the Speaker) . . . *may profit by their example.* If *this* be treason, make the most of it.
speech in the Virginia assembly, May 1765, in William Wirt *Patrick Henry* (1818) sect. 2

2 I am not a Virginian, but an American.
in [John Adams's] Notes of Debates in the Continental Congress, Philadelphia, 6 September 1774; in L. H. Butterfield (ed.) *Diary and Autobiography of John Adams* (1961) vol. 2

3 I know not what course others may take; but as for me, give me liberty, or give me death!
speech in Virginia Convention, 23 March 1775, in William Wirt *Patrick Henry* (1818) sect. 4

Philip Henry 1631–96
English clergyman

4 All this, and heaven too!
in Matthew Henry *Life of Mr Philip Henry* (1698) ch. 5

Joseph Henshaw 1603–79
English divine; Bishop of Peterborough from 1663

5 One doth but breakfast here, another dines, he that liveth longest doth but sup; we must all go to bed in another world.
Horae Succisivae (1631) pt. 1

Barbara Hepworth 1903–75
English sculptor

6 Carving is interrelated masses conveying an emotion: a perfect relationship between the mind and the colour, light and weight which is the stone, made by the hand which feels.
Herbert Read (ed.) *Unit One* (1934)

Heraclitus *c.*540–*c.*480 BC
Greek philosopher

7 Everything flows and nothing stays.
Plato *Cratylus* 402a

8 You can't step twice into the same river.
Plato *Cratylus* 402a

9 A man's character is his fate.
On the Universe fragment 121 (translated by W. H. S. Jones); cf. **Eliot** 293:7, **Novalis** 547:3

10 The road up and the road down are one and the same.
H. Diels and W. Kranz *Die Fragmente der Vorsokratiker* (7th ed., 1954) fragment 60

A. P. Herbert (Sir Alan Patrick Herbert) 1890–1971
English writer and humorist

11 Don't let's go to the dogs tonight,
For mother will be there.
'Don't Let's Go to the Dogs Tonight' (1926)

12 The Farmer will never be happy again;
He carries his heart in his boots;
For either the rain is destroying his grain
Or the drought is destroying his roots.
'The Farmer' (1922)

13 As my poor father used to say
In 1863,
Once people start on all this Art
Goodbye, moralitee!
'Lines for a Worthy Person' (1930)

14 Other people's babies—
That's my life!
Mother to dozens,
And nobody's wife.
'Other People's Babies' (1930)

15 This high official, all allow,
Is grossly overpaid;
There wasn't any Board, and now
There isn't any Trade.
'The President of the Board of Trade' (1922)

16 Nothing is wasted, nothing is in vain:
The seas roll over but the rocks remain.
Tough at the Top (operetta *c.*1949)

17 Holy deadlock.
title of novel (1934)

18 People must not do things for fun. We are not here for fun. There is no reference to fun in any Act of Parliament.
Uncommon Law (1935) 'Is it a Free Country?'

19 The critical period in matrimony is breakfast-time.
Uncommon Law (1935) 'Is Marriage Lawful?'

20 'Was the cow crossed?'
'No, your worship, it was an open cow.'
on an attempt to write a cheque on a cow
Uncommon Law (1935) 'The Negotiable Cow'

21 The Common Law of England has been laboriously built about a mythical figure—the figure of 'The Reasonable Man'.
Uncommon Law (1935) 'The Reasonable Man'

Lord Herbert of Cherbury 1583–1648
English philosopher and poet; brother of George **Herbert**

22 Now that the April of your youth adorns
The garden of your face.
'Ditty: Now that the April' (1665)

George Herbert 1593–1633
English poet and clergyman

23 Whereas my birth and spirit rather took
The way that takes the town;
Thou didst betray me to a lingering book,
And wrap me in a gown.
'Affliction (1)' (1633) l. 37

24 Now I am here, what thou wilt do with me
None of my books will show:
I read, and sigh, and wish I were a tree;
For then I should grow
To fruit or shade: at least some bird would trust
Her household to me, and I should be just.
'Affliction (1)' (1633) l. 55

1 Ah, my dear God! though I am clean forgot,
Let me not love Thee, if I love Thee not.
'Affliction (1)' (1633) l. 65

2 Love is that liquor sweet and most divine,
Which my God feels as blood; but I, as wine.
'The Agonie' (1633) l. 17

3 Let all the world in ev'ry corner sing
My God and King.
The heavens are not too high,
His praise may thither fly;
The earth is not too low,
His praises there may grow.
Let all the world in ev'ry corner sing
My God and King.
The Church with psalms must shout,
No door can keep them out:
But above all, the heart
Must bear the longest part.
'Antiphon: Let all the world in ev'ry corner sing' (1633)

4 Hearken unto a Verser, who may chance
Rhyme thee to good, and make a bait of pleasure.
A verse may find him, who a sermon flies,
And turn delight into a sacrifice.
'The Church Porch' (1633) st. 1

5 Judge not the preacher, for he is thy Judge:
If thou mislike him, thou conceiv'st him not.
God calleth preaching folly. Do not grudge
To pick out treasures from an earthen pot.
The worst speaks something good: if all want sense,
God takes a text, and preacheth patience.
'The Church Porch' (1633) st. 72

6 I struck the board, and cried, 'No more.
I will abroad.'
What? shall I ever sigh and pine?
My lines and life are free; free as the road,
Loose as the wind, as large as store.
Shall I be still in suit?
Have I no harvest but a thorn
To let me blood, and not restore
What I have lost with cordial fruit?
Sure there was wine
Before my sighs did dry it; there was corn
Before my tears did drown it;
Is the year only lost to me?
Have I no bays to crown it?
'The Collar' (1633)

7 Away; take heed:
I will abroad.
Call in thy death's-head there: tie up thy fears.
'The Collar' (1633)

8 But as I raved and grew more fierce and wild
At every word,
Methought I heard one calling, 'Child';
And I replied, 'My Lord.'
'The Collar' (1633)

9 O that thou shouldst give dust a tongue
To cry to thee,
And then not hear it crying!
'Denial' (1633) l. 16

10 Love is swift of foot;
Love's a man of war,
And can shoot,
And can hit from far.
'Discipline' (1633)

11 I got me flowers to strew Thy way;
I got me boughs off many a tree:
But Thou wast up by break of day,
And brought'st Thy sweets along with Thee.
'Easter' (1633)

12 Teach me, my God and King,
In all things Thee to see,
And what I do in any thing
To do it as for Thee.
'The Elixir' (1633)

13 A man that looks on glass,
On it may stay his eye;
Or if he pleaseth, through it pass,
And then the heaven espy.
'The Elixir' (1633)

14 A servant with this clause
Makes drudgery divine:
Who sweeps a room as for Thy laws
Makes that and th' action fine.
'The Elixir' (1633)

15 Oh that I were an orange-tree,
That busy plant!
Then I should ever laden be,
And never want
Some fruit for Him that dressed me.
'Employment: He that is weary, let him sit' (1633)

16 Who would have thought my shrivelled heart
Could have recovered greenness?
'The Flower' (1633)

17 And now in age I bud again,
After so many deaths I live and write;
I once more smell the dew and rain,
And relish versing.
'The Flower' (1633)

18 Lovely enchanting language, sugar-cane,
Honey of roses!
'The Forerunners' (1633)

19 Death is still working like a mole,
And digs my grave at each remove.
'Grace' (1633)

20 Who says that fictions only and false hair
Become a verse? Is there in truth no beauty?
Is all good structure in a winding stair?
'Jordan (1)' (1633)

21 I made a posy while the day ran by:
Here will I smell my remnant out, and tie
My life within this band.
But Time did beckon to the flowers, and they
By noon most cunningly did steal away,
And withered in my hand.
'Life' (1633)

22 Love bade me welcome: yet my soul drew back,
Guilty of dust and sin.
But quick-eyed Love, observing me grow slack
From my first entrance in,

Drew nearer to me, sweetly questioning,
If I lacked any thing.
'Love: Love bade me welcome' (1633)

1 'You must sit down,' says Love, 'and taste my meat.'
So I did sit and eat.
'Love: Love bade me welcome' (1633)

2 For us the winds do blow,
The earth doth rest, heaven move, and fountains flow.
Nothing we see, but means our good,
As our delight or as our treasure:
The whole is either our cupboard of food,
Or cabinet of pleasure.
'Man' (1633)

3 When boys go first to bed,
They step into their voluntary graves.
'Mortification' (1633)

4 Prayer: prayer the Church's banquet.
title of poem (1633)

5 Exalted manna, gladness of the best,
Heaven in ordinary, man well drest,
The Milky Way, the bird of Paradise,
Church-bells beyond the stars heard, the soul's blood,
The land of spices; something understood.
'Prayer: Prayer the Church's banquet' (1633)

6 When God at first made man,
Having a glass of blessings standing by;
Let us (said he) pour on him all we can:
Let the world's riches, which dispersed lie,
Contract into a span.
'The Pulley' (1633)

7 He would adore my gifts instead of Me,
And rest in Nature, not the God of Nature:
So both should losers be.
'The Pulley' (1633)

8 Yet let him keep the rest,
But keep them with repining restlessness:
Let him be rich and weary, that at least,
If goodness lead him not, yet weariness
May toss him to My breast.
'The Pulley' (1633)

9 But who does hawk at eagles with a dove?
'The Sacrifice' (1633) l. 91

10 Man stole the fruit, but I must climb the tree.
'The Sacrifice' (1633) l. 202

11 Lord, with what care Thou hast begirt us round!
Parents first season us: then schoolmasters
Deliver us to laws; they send us bound
To rules of reason, holy messengers,
Pulpits and Sundays, sorrow dogging sin,
Afflictions sorted, anguish of all sizes,
Fine nets and stratagems to catch us in,
Bibles laid open, millions of surprises.
'Sin: Lord, with what care Thou hast begirt us round!' (1633)

12 Yet all these fences and their whole array
One cunning bosom—sin blows quite away.
'Sin: Lord, with what care Thou hast begirt us round!' (1633)

13 Grasp not at much, for fear thou losest all.
'The Size' (1633)

14 The God of love my Shepherd is,
And He that doth me feed:
While He is mine, and I am His,
What can I want or need?
'The 23rd Psalm' (1633); cf. **Book of Common Prayer** 132:26

15 Lord, make me coy and tender to offend:
In friendship, first I think, if that agree
Which I intend,
Unto my friend's intent and end.
I would not use a friend, as I use Thee.
'Unkindness' (1633)

16 My friend may spit upon my curious floor:
Would he have gold? I lend it instantly;
But let the poor,
And Thou within them, starve at door.
I cannot use a friend, as I use Thee.
'Unkindness' (1633)

17 Sweet day, so cool, so calm, so bright,
The bridal of the earth and sky,
The dew shall weep thy fall to-night;
For thou must die.

Sweet rose, whose hue angry and brave
Bids the rash gazer wipe his eye:
Thy root is ever in its grave,
And thou must die.

Sweet spring, full of sweet days and roses,
A box where sweets compacted lie;
My music shows ye have your closes,
And all must die.
'Virtue' (1633)

18 Only a sweet and virtuous soul,
Like seasoned timber, never gives;
But though the whole world turn to coal,
Then chiefly lives.
'Virtue' (1633)

19 He that makes a good war makes a good peace.
Outlandish Proverbs (1640) no. 420

20 He that lives in hope danceth without music.
Outlandish Proverbs (1640) no. 1006; cf. **Proverbs** 602:16

Johann Gottfried von Herder

1744–1803
German critic and philosopher

21 I am not here to think, but to be, feel, live!
Bernhard Suphan (ed.) J. G. Herder *Sämmtliche Werke* (1877–1913)

Herodotus c.485–c.425

Greek historian

22 In peace, children inter their parents; war violates the order of nature and causes parents to inter their children.
Histories bk. 1 sect. 87

1 The most hateful torment for men is to have knowledge of everything but power over nothing.
Histories bk. 9 sect. 16

Robert Herrick 1591–1674
English poet and clergyman

2 Here a little child I stand,
Heaving up my either hand;
Cold as paddocks though they be,
Here I lift them up to Thee,
For a benison to fall
On our meat, and on us all. Amen.
'Another Grace for a Child' (1647)

3 I sing of brooks, of blossoms, birds, and bowers:
Of April, May, of June, and July-flowers.
I sing of May-poles, Hock-carts, wassails, wakes,
Of bride-grooms, brides, and of their bridal-cakes.
'The Argument of his Book' from *Hesperides* (1648)

4 And once more yet (ere I am laid out dead)
Knock at a star with my exalted head.
'The Bad Season Makes the Poet Sad' (1648)

5 Cherry-ripe, ripe, ripe, I cry,
Full and fair ones; come and buy:
If so be, you ask me where
They do grow? I answer, there,
Where my Julia's lips do smile;
There's the land, or cherry-isle.
'Cherry-Ripe' (1648)

6 Get up, sweet Slug-a-bed, and see
The dew bespangling herb and tree.
'Corinna's Going a-Maying' (1648)

7 So when or you or I are made
A fable, song, or fleeting shade;
All love, all liking, all delight
Lies drowned with us in endless night.
Then while time serves, and we are but decaying;
Come, my Corinna, come, let's go a-Maying.
'Corinna's Going a-Maying' (1648)

8 A sweet disorder in the dress
Kindles in clothes a wantonness:
A lawn about the shoulders thrown
Into a fine distraction . . .
A careless shoe-string, in whose tie
I see a wild civility:
Do more bewitch me, than when Art
Is too precise in every part.
'Delight in Disorder' (1648)

9 It is the end that crowns us, not the fight.
'The End' (1648)

10 In prayer the lips ne'er act the winning part,
Without the sweet concurrence of the heart.
'The Heart' (1647)

11 When the artless doctor sees
No one hope, but of his fees,
And his skill runs on the lees;
Sweet Spirit, comfort me!

When his potion and his pill,
Has, or none, or little skill,
Meet for nothing, but to kill;
Sweet Spirit, comfort me!
'His Litany to the Holy Spirit' (1647)

12 Only a little more
I have to write,
Then I'll give o'er,
And bid the world Good-night.
'His Poetry his Pillar' (1648)

13 Love is a circle that doth restless move
In the same sweet eternity of love.
'Love What It Is' (1648)

14 Her eyes the glow-worm lend thee,
The shooting-stars attend thee;
And the elves also,
Whose little eyes glow,
Like the sparks of fire, befriend thee.
'The Night-Piece, to Julia' (1648)

15 Night makes no difference 'twixt the Priest and Clerk;
Joan as my Lady is as good i' th' dark.
'No Difference i' th' Dark' (1648)

16 Made us nobly wild, not mad.
'An Ode for him [Ben Jonson]' (1648)

17 And yet each verse of thine
Out-did the meat, out-did the frolic wine.
'An Ode for him [Ben Jonson]' (1648)

18 Fain would I kiss my Julia's dainty leg,
Which is as white and hairless as an egg.
'On Julia's Legs' (1648)

19 Praise they that will times past, I joy to see
My self now live: this age best pleaseth me.
'The Present Time Best Pleaseth' (1648)

20 But, for Man's fault, then was the thorn,
Without the fragrant rose-bud, born;
But ne'er the rose without the thorn.
'The Rose' (1647)

21 A little saint best fits a little shrine,
A little prop best fits a little vine,
As my small cruse best fits my little wine.
'A Ternary of Littles, upon a Pipkin of Jelly sent to a Lady' (1648)

22 For my Embalming (Sweetest) there will be
No Spices wanting, when I'm laid by thee.
'To Anthea: Now is the Time' (1648)

23 Bid me to live, and I will live
Thy Protestant to be:
Or bid me love, and I will give
A loving heart to thee.
'To Anthea, Who May Command Him Anything' (1648)

24 Bid me despair, and I'll despair,
Under that cypress tree:
Or bid me die, and I will dare
E'en Death, to die for thee.

Thou art my life, my love, my heart,
The very eyes of me:
And hast command of every part,
To live and die for thee.
'To Anthea, Who May Command Him Anything' (1648)

25 Fair daffodils, we weep to see
You haste away so soon.

As yet the early-rising sun
Has not attained his noon.
Stay, stay,
Until the hasting day
Has run
But to the even-song;
And, having prayed together, we
Will go with you along.

We have short time to stay, as you,
We have as short a Spring;
As quick a growth to meet decay,
As you or any thing.
'To Daffodils' (1648)

1 If any thing delight me for to print
My book, 'tis this; that Thou, my God, art in't.
'To God' (1647)

2 Gather ye rosebuds while ye may,
Old Time is still a-flying:
And this same flower that smiles to-day,
To-morrow will be dying.
'To the Virgins, to Make Much of Time' (1648)

3 Then be not coy, but use your time;
And while ye may, go marry:
For having lost but once your prime,
You may for ever tarry.
'To the Virgins, to Make Much of Time' (1648)

4 Whenas in silks my Julia goes,
Then, then (methinks) how sweetly flows
That liquefaction of her clothes.
Next, when I cast mine eyes and see
That brave vibration each way free;
O how that glittering taketh me!
'Upon Julia's Clothes' (1648)

5 So smooth, so sweet, so silvery is thy voice,
As, could they hear, the damned would make no noise,
But listen to thee (walking in thy chamber)
Melting melodious words, to lutes of amber.
'Upon Julia's Voice' (1648)

6 To work a wonder, God would have her shown,
At once, a bud, and yet a rose full-blown.
'The Virgin Mary' (1647)

Lord Hervey 1696–1743
English politician and writer
on Hervey: see **Montagu** *526:18,* **Pope** *583:9, 583:10*

7 Whoever would lie usefully should lie seldom.
Memoirs of the Reign of George II (ed. J. W. Croker, 1848) vol. 1, ch. 19

8 I am fit for nothing but to carry candles and set chairs all my life.
letter to Robert Walpole, 1737, in *Memoirs of the Reign of George II* (ed. J. W. Croker, 1848) vol. 2, ch. 40

Theodor Herzl 1860–1904
Hungarian-born journalist, dramatist, and Zionist leader

9 At Basle I founded the Jewish state.
of the first Zionist congress, held in Basle in 1897
diary, 3 September 1897

Hesiod c.700 BC
Greek poet

10 Then potter is potter's enemy, and
craftsman is craftsman's
rival; tramp is jealous of tramp
and singer of singer.
Works and Days l.25, translated by R. Lattimore

11 The half is greater than the whole.
Works and Days l. 40

12 Often a whole city is paid punishment
for one bad man.
Works and Days l. 240, translated by R. Lattimore

13 The man who does evil to another does evil
to himself,
and the evil counsel is most evil
for him who counsels it.
Works and Days l. 265, translated by R. Lattimore

14 When the bottle has just been opened, and when
it's giving out, drink deep;
be sparing when it's half-full; but it's useless
to spare the fag end.
Works and Days l. 368, translated by R. Lattimore

Hermann Hesse 1877–1962
German novelist and poet

15 If you hate a person, you hate something in him that is part of yourself. What isn't part of ourselves doesn't disturb us.
Demian (1919) ch. 6

16 The bourgeois prefers comfort to pleasure, convenience to liberty, and a pleasant temperature to the deathly inner consuming fire.
Der Steppenwolf (1927) 'Tractat vom Steppenwolf', translated by Basil Creighton

Gordon Hewart 1870–1943
British lawyer and politician

17 A long line of cases shows that it is not merely of some importance, but is of fundamental importance that justice should not only be done, but should manifestly and undoubtedly be seen to be done.
Rex v Sussex Justices, 9 November 1923, in *Law Reports King's Bench Division* (1924) vol. 1

Robert Hewison 1943–
British historian

18 The turn of the century raises expectations. The end of a millennium promises apocalypse and revelation. But at the close of the twentieth century the golden age seems behind us, not ahead. The end game of the 1990s promises neither nirvana nor Armageddon, but entropy.
Future Tense (1990)

John Hewitt 1907–87
Northern Irish poet

19 We would be strangers in the Capitol;
this is our country also, no-where else;

and we shall not be outcast on the world.
'The Colony' (1950)

1 I'm an Ulsterman, of planter stock. I was born in the island of Ireland, so secondarily I'm an Irishman. I was born in the British archipelago and English is my native tongue, so I am British. The British archipelago consists of offshore islands to the continent of Europe, so I'm European. This is my hierarchy of values and so far as I am concerned, anyone who omits one step in that sequence of values is falsifying the situation.
in *The Irish Times* 4 July 1974

Reinhard Heydrich 1904–42
German Nazi leader

2 Now the rough work has been done we begin the period of finer work. We need to work in harmony with the civil administration. We count on you gentlemen as far as the final solution is concerned.
on the planned mass murder of all European Jews; cf. **Goering** *342:12*
speech in Wannsee, 20 January 1942

Du Bose Heyward 1885–1940 and Ira Gershwin 1896–1983
American songwriter

3 It ain't necessarily so,
It ain't necessarily so,
De t'ings dat yo' li'ble
To read in de Bible
It ain't necessarily so.
'It ain't necessarily so' (1935 song) in *Porgy and Bess*

4 Summer time an' the livin' is easy,
Fish are jumpin' an' the cotton is high.
Oh, yo' daddy's rich, and yo' ma' is good-lookin',
So hush, little baby, don' yo' cry.
'Summertime' (1935 song) in *Porgy and Bess*

5 A woman is a sometime thing.
title of song (1935) in *Porgy and Bess*

John Heywood *c.*1497–*c.*1580
English dramatist

6 All a green willow, willow;
All a green willow is my garland.
'The Green Willow'; cf. **Shakespeare** 693:19

7 I never heard thy fire once spark,
I never heard thy dog once bark.
I never heard once in thy house
So much as one peep of one mouse.
I never heard thy cat once mew.
These praises are not small nor few.
'A quiet neighbour' (1556)

Thomas Heywood *c.*1574–1641
English dramatist

8 Seven cities warred for Homer, being dead,
Who, living, had no roof to shroud his head.
'The Hierarchy of the Blessed Angels' (1635); cf. **Anonymous** 18:18

J. R. Hicks 1904–
British economist

9 The best of all monopoly profits is a quiet life.
Econometrica (1935) 'The Theory of Monopoly'

David Hilbert 1862–1943
German mathematician

10 The importance of a scientific work can be measured by the number of previous publications it makes it superfluous to read.
attributed; Lewis Wolpert *The Unnatural Nature of Science* (1993)

Aaron Hill 1685–1750
English poet and dramatist

11 Tender-handed stroke a nettle,
And it stings you for your pains;
Grasp it like a man of mettle,
And it soft as silk remains.
'Verses Written on a Window in Scotland'

Christopher Hill 1912–
British historian

12 Only very slowly and late have men come to realize that unless freedom is universal it is only extended privilege.
Century of Revolution (1961)

13 Just as Oliver Cromwell aimed to bring about the kingdom of God on earth and founded the British Empire, so Bunyan wanted the millennium and got the novel.
A Turbulent, Seditious, and Factious People: John Bunyan and his Church, 1628–1688 (1988)

Damon Hill 1960–
English motor-racing driver

14 Winning is everything. The only ones who remember you when you come second are your wife and your dog.
in *Sunday Times* 18 December 1994 'Quotes of the Year'

Geoffrey Hill 1932–
English poet

15 Poetry
Unearths from among the speechless dead

Lazarus mystified, common man
Of death. The lily rears its gouged face
From the provided loam.
'History as Poetry' (1968)

16 She kept the siege. And every day
We watched her brooding over death
Like a strong bird above its prey.
The room filled with the kettle's breath.

Damp curtains glued against the pane
Sealed time away. Her body froze
As if to freeze us all, and chain
Creation to a stunned repose.
'In Memory of Jane Fraser' (1959)

17 I love my work and my children. God
Is distant, difficult. Things happen.

Too near the ancient troughs of blood
Innocence is no earthly weapon.
'Ovid in the Third Reich' (1968)

Joe Hill (Joel Hägglund) 1879–1915

Swedish-born American labour leader and songwriter
see also **Last words** 456:10

1 You will eat, bye and bye,
In that glorious land above the sky;
Work and pray, live on hay,
You'll get pie in the sky when you die.
'Preacher and the Slave' in *Songs of the Workers* (Industrial Workers of the World, 1911)

Pattie S. Hill 1868–1946

American educationist

2 Happy birthday to you.
title of song (1935)

Rowland Hill 1744–1833

English clergyman

3 He did not see any reason why the devil should have all the good tunes.
E. W. Broome *The Rev. Rowland Hill* (1881) ch. 7; cf. **Proverbs** 615:8

Selima Hill 1945–

4 All we're allowed's anxiety like fishbones
lodged in our throats
as beauty parlours hum;
all we're allowed is having pretty faces
and cold and glittery hearts like water-ices . . .
Mine's more like a centrally-heated boiler-room,
evil and warm;
like kidneys on a plate.
'Do It Again' (1993)

Edmund Hillary 1919–

New Zealand mountaineer

5 Well, we knocked the bastard off!
on conquering Mount Everest, 1953
Nothing Venture, Nothing Win (1975) ch. 10; cf. **Mallory** 492:6

Fred Hillebrand 1893–1963

6 Home James, and don't spare the horses.
title of song (1934)

Hillel 'The Elder' *c.*60 BC–AD *c.*9

Jewish scholar and teacher

7 What is hateful to you do not do to your neighbour: that is the whole Torah.
in *Talmud* Shabbat 31a

8 A name made great is a name destroyed.
in *Talmud* Mishnah 'Pirqei Avot' 1:13

9 If I am not for myself who is for me? and being for my own self what am I? If not now when?
in *Talmud* Mishnah 'Pirqei Avot' 1:14

10 Keep not aloof from the congregation.
in *Talmud* Mishnah 'Pirqei Avot' 2:5

11 Say not, When I have leisure I will study; perchance thou wilt never have leisure.
in *Talmud* Mishnah 'Pirqei Avot' 2:5

James Hilton 1900–54

English novelist

12 Nothing really wrong with him—only anno domini, but that's the most fatal complaint of all, in the end.
Goodbye, Mr Chips (1934) ch. 1

Paul von Hindenburg 1847–1934

German Field Marshal and statesman, President of the Weimar Republic 1925–34

13 That man for a Chancellor? I'll make him a postmaster and he can lick the stamps with my head on them.
on ***Hitler***
to Meissner, 13 August 1932; J. W. Wheeler-Bennett *Hindenburg: the Wooden Titan* (1936)

Hippocleides

6th-century Athenian aristocrat

14 Hippocleides doesn't care.
on being told that he had ruined his marriage chances with the daughter of a tyrant, concluding a dance by standing on his head and gesticulating with his legs
Herodotus *Histories* bk. 6, sect. 129

Hippocrates *c.*460–357 BC

Greek physician

15 Life is short, the art long.
often quoted as 'Ars longa, vita brevis', *after* ***Seneca****'s rendering in* De Brevitate Vitae *sect. 1*
Aphorisms sect. 1, para. 1 (translated by W. H. S. Jones); cf. **Chaucer** 206:28, **Longfellow** 474:4, **Proverbs** 595:17

16 Time is that wherein there is opportunity, and opportunity is that wherein there is no great time.
Precepts ch. 1 (translated by W. H. S. Jones, 1923)

17 Healing is a matter of time, but it is sometimes also a matter of opportunity.
Precepts ch. 1 (translated by W. H. S. Jones, 1923)

Emperor Hirohito 1901–89

Emperor of Japan from 1926

18 The war situation has developed not necessarily to Japan's advantage.
announcing Japan's surrender, in a broadcast to his people after atom bombs had destroyed Hiroshima and Nagasaki
on 15 August 1945

Damien Hirst 1965–

English artist

19 It's amazing what you can do with an E in A-level art, twisted imagination and a chainsaw.
after winning the 1995 Turner Prize
in *Observer* 3 December 1995 'Sayings of the Week'

Alfred Hitchcock 1899–1980

British-born film director

1 Actors are cattle.
in *Saturday Evening Post* 22 May 1943

2 Television has brought back murder into the home—where it belongs.
in *Observer* 19 December 1965

3 There is no terror in a bang, only in the anticipation of it.
Leslie Halliwell (ed.) *Halliwell's Filmgoer's Companion* (1984); attributed

Adolf Hitler 1889–1945

German dictator

on Hitler: see **Buchman** *159:10*, **Chamberlain** *201:2*, **Hindenburg** *377:13*

4 The broad mass of a nation . . . will more easily fall victim to a big lie than to a small one.
Mein Kampf (1925) vol. 1, ch. 10

5 The night of the long knives.
referring to the massacre of Ernst Roehm and his associates by Hitler on 29–30 June 1934 (subsequently associated with Harold **Macmillan***'s Cabinet dismissals of 13 July 1962)*
S. H. Roberts *The House Hitler Built* (1937) pt. 2, ch. 3

6 I go the way that Providence dictates with the assurance of a sleepwalker.
speech in Munich, 15 March 1936, in Max Domarus (ed.) *Hitler: Reden und Proklamationen 1932–1945* (1962)

7 It is the last territorial claim which I have to make in Europe, but it is the claim from which I will not recede and which, God-willing, I will make good.
on the Sudetenland
speech at Berlin Sportpalast, 26 September 1938; in Max Domarus (ed.) *Hitler: Reden und Proklamationen 1932–1945* (1962)

8 With regard to the problem of the Sudeten Germans, my patience is now at an end!
speech at Berlin Sportpalast, 26 September 1938, in Max Domarus (ed.) *Hitler: Reden und Proklamationen 1932–1945* (1962)

9 Is Paris burning?
on 25 August 1944, in Larry Collins and Dominique Lapierre *Is Paris Burning?* (1965) ch. 5

Lady Ho fl. 300 BC

Chinese poet

10 When a pair of magpies fly together
They do not envy the pair of phoenixes.
'A Song of Magpies'; K. Rexroth and Chung (eds.) *The Orchid Boat: Women Poets of China* (1972)

Thomas Hobbes 1588–1679

English philosopher

on Hobbes: see **Aubrey** *32:13*, **Swift** *749:18*; *see also* **Last words** *455:19*

11 Laughter is nothing else but sudden glory arising from some sudden conception of some eminency in ourselves, by comparison with the infirmity of others, or with our own formerly.
Human Nature (1650) ch. 9, sect. 13

12 By art is created that great Leviathan, called a commonwealth or state, (in Latin *civitas*) which is but an artificial man . . . and in which, the sovereignty is an artificial soul.
Leviathan (1651); introduction

13 True and False are attributes of speech, not of things. And where speech is not, there is neither Truth nor Falsehood.
Leviathan (1651) pt. 1, ch. 4

14 In Geometry (which is the only science that it hath pleased God hitherto to bestow on mankind) men begin at settling the significations of their words; which . . . they call Definitions.
Leviathan (1651) pt. 1, ch. 4

15 Words are wise men's counters, they do but reckon by them: but they are the money of fools, that value them by the authority of an Aristotle, a Cicero, or a Thomas, or any other doctor whatsoever, if but a man.
Leviathan (1651) pt. 1, ch. 4

16 The power of a man, to take it universally, is his present means, to obtain some future apparent good; and is either original or instrumental.
Leviathan (1651) pt. 1, ch. 10

17 I put for a general inclination of all mankind, a perpetual and restless desire of power after power, that ceaseth only in death.
Leviathan (1651) pt. 1, ch. 11

18 They that approve a private opinion, call it opinion; but they that mislike it, heresy: and yet heresy signifies no more than private opinion.
Leviathan (1651) pt. 1, ch. 11

19 During the time men live without a common power to keep them all in awe, they are in that condition which is called war; and such a war as is of every man against every man.
Leviathan (1651) pt. 1, ch. 13

20 For as the nature of foul weather, lieth not in a shower or two of rain; but in an inclination thereto of many days together: so the nature of war consisteth not in actual fighting, but in the known disposition thereto during all the time there is no assurance to the contrary.
Leviathan (1651) pt. 1, ch. 13

21 No arts; no letters; no society; and which is worst of all, continual fear and danger of violent death; and the life of man, solitary, poor, nasty, brutish, and short.
Leviathan (1651) pt. 1, ch. 13

22 Force, and fraud, are in war the two cardinal virtues.
Leviathan (1651) pt. 1, ch. 13

23 Liberties . . . depend on the silence of the law.
Leviathan (1651) pt. 2, ch. 16

24 I put down for one of the most effectual seeds of the death of any state, that the conquerors require not only a submission of men's actions to them for the

future, but also an approbation of all their actions past.

Leviathan (1651) pt. 2, ch. 17

1 They that are discontented under *monarchy*, call it *tyranny*; and they that are displeased with *aristocracy*, call it *oligarchy*: so also, they which find themselves grieved under a *democracy*, call it *anarchy*, which signifies the want of government; and yet I think no man believes, that want of government, is any new kind of government.

Leviathan (1651) pt. 2, ch. 19

2 Whereas some have attributed the dominion [of the family] to the man only, as being of the more excellent sex; they misreckon in it. For there is not always that difference of strength, or prudence between the man and the woman, as that the right can be determined without war.

Leviathan (1651) pt. 2, ch. 20

3 For it is with the mysteries of our religion, as with wholesome pills for the sick, which swallowed whole, have the virtue to cure; but chewed, are for the most part cast up again without effect.

Leviathan (1651) pt. 3, ch. 32

4 The papacy is not other than the ghost of the deceased Roman Empire, sitting crowned upon the grave thereof.

Leviathan (1651) pt. 4, ch. 47

5 The praise of ancient authors proceeds not from the reverence of the dead, but from the competition, and mutual envy of the living.

Leviathan (1651) 'A Review and Conclusion'

John Cam Hobhouse, Lord Broughton 1786–1869

English politician

6 When I invented the phrase 'His Majesty's Opposition' [Canning] paid me a compliment on the fortunate hit.

Recollections of a Long Life (1865) vol. 2, ch. 12; see below; cf. **Bagehot** 46:9

It is said to be very hard on his majesty's ministers to raise objections to this proposition. For my own part, I think it is more hard on his majesty's opposition (a laugh) to compel them to take this course.

speech, House of Commons, 10 April 1826

Eric Hobsbawm 1917–

British historian

7 For 80 per cent of humanity the Middle Ages ended suddenly in the 1950s; or perhaps better still, they were *felt* to end in the 1960s.

Age of Extremes (1994)

8 This was the kind of war which existed in order to produce victory parades.

of the Falklands War

in *Marxism Today* January 1983

Margaret Hoby 1571–1633

English diarist

9 This day I bestowed too much time in the garden, and thereby was worse able to perform spiritual duties.

diary, 6 April 1605; Dorothy M. Meads (ed.) *Diary of Lady Margaret Hoby* (1930)

David Hockney 1937–

British artist

10 All you can do with most ordinary photographs is stare at them—they stare back, blankly—and presently your concentration begins to fade. They stare you down. I mean, photography is all right if you don't mind looking at the world from the point of view of a paralysed cyclops—*for a split second.*

as told to Lawrence Weschler, *Cameraworks* (1984)

11 All painting, no matter what you're painting, is abstract in that it's got to be organized.

David Hockney (1976)

12 The thing with high-tech is that you always end up using scissors.

in *Observer* 10 July 1994 'Sayings of the Week'

Ralph Hodgson 1871–1962

English poet

13 'Twould ring the bells of Heaven
The wildest peal for years,
If Parson lost his senses
And people came to theirs,
And he and they together
Knelt down with angry prayers
For tamed and shabby tigers
And dancing dogs and bears,
And wretched, blind, pit ponies,
And little hunted hares.

'Bells of Heaven' (1917)

14 Time, you old gipsy man,
Will you not stay,
Put up your caravan
Just for one day?

'Time, You Old Gipsy Man' (1917)

Al Hoffman 1902–60 and **Dick Manning** 1912–

15 Takes two to tango.

title of song (1952); cf. **Proverbs** 604:41

August Heinrich Hoffman (Hoffman von Fallersleben) 1798–1874

German poet

16 *Deutschland über alles.*

Germany above all.

title of poem (1841)

Heinrich Hoffmann 1809–94

German writer for children

17 Augustus was a chubby lad;
Fat ruddy cheeks Augustus had:

And everybody saw with joy
The plump and hearty, healthy boy.
He ate and drank as he was told,
And never let his soup get cold.
But one day, one cold winter's day,
He screamed out, 'Take the soup away!
O take the nasty soup away!
I won't have any soup today.'
Struwwelpeter (1848) 'Augustus'

1 But fidgety Phil,
He won't sit still.
Struwwelpeter (1848) 'Fidgety Philip'

2 Look at little Johnny there,
Little Johnny Head-In-Air!
Struwwelpeter (1848) 'Johnny Head-In-Air'; cf. **Pudney** 616:14

3 The door flew open, in he ran,
The great, long, red-legged scissor-man.
Struwwelpeter (1848) 'The Little Suck-a-Thumb'

4 Snip! Snap! Snip! They go so fast.
That both his thumbs are off at last.
Struwwelpeter (1848) 'The Little Suck-a-Thumb'

5 The hare sits snug in leaves and grass,
And laughs to see the green man pass.
Struwwelpeter (1848) 'The Man Who Went Out Shooting'

6 And now she's trying all she can,
To shoot the sleepy, green-coat man.
Struwwelpeter (1848) 'The Man Who Went Out Shooting'

7 The hare's own child, the little hare.
Struwwelpeter (1848) 'The Man Who Went Out Shooting'

8 Anything to me is sweeter
Than to see Shock-headed Peter.
Struwwelpeter (1848) 'Shock-Headed Peter' (title poem)

Gerard Hoffnung 1925–59
English humorist

9 Standing among savage scenery, the hotel offers stupendous revelations. There is a French widow in every bedroom, affording delightful prospects.
supposedly quoting a letter from a Tyrolean landlord
speech at the Oxford Union, 4 December 1958

Lancelot Hogben 1895–1975
English scientist

10 This is not the age of pamphleteers. It is the age of the engineers. The spark-gap is mightier than the pen. Democracy will not be salvaged by men who talk fluently, debate forcefully and quote aptly.
Science for the Citizen (1938) epilogue; cf. **Proverbs** 609:22

James Hogg 1770–1835
Scottish poet
see also ***Songs*** *729:7*

11 Where the pools are bright and deep
Where the gray trout lies asleep,
Up the river and o'er the lea
That's the way for Billy and me.
'A Boy's Song' (1838)

12 Cock up your beaver, and cock it fu' sprush;
We'll over the Border and gi'e them a brush;
There's somebody there we'll teach better behaviour.
Hey, Johnnie lad, cock up your beaver!
'Cock Up Your Beaver' in *Jacobite Relics of Scotland* Second Series (1821)

13 We'll o'er the water, we'll o'er the sea,
We'll o'er the water to Charlie;
Come weel, come wo, we'll gather and go,
And live or die wi' Charlie.
'O'er the Water to Charlie' in *Jacobite Relics of Scotland* Second Series (1821)

14 Bird of the wilderness,
Blithesome and cumberless,
Sweet be thy matin o'er moorland and lea!
'The Skylark'

15 The private memoirs and confessions of a justified sinner.
title of novel (1824)

Paul Henri, Baron d'Holbach 1723–89
French philosopher

16 Art is only Nature operating with the aid of the instruments she has made.
Système de la Nature (1780 ed.) pt. 1, ch. 1

17 If ignorance of nature gave birth to the Gods, knowledge of nature is destined to destroy them.
Système de la Nature (1770) pt. 2, ch. 1

Johann Christian Friedrich Hölderlin 1770–1843
German lyric poet

18 *So zu harren und was zu thun indess und zu sagen?*
Weiss ich nicht und wozu Dich ter in durftiger Zeit?
Always waiting and what to do or to say in the meantime
I don't know, and who wants poets at all in lean years?
'Bread and Wine' (1800–01), translated by Michael Hamburger in *Poems and Fragments* (1994)

Billie Holiday (Eleanor Fagan) 1915–59
American singer
see also ***Opening lines*** *555:5*

19 Mama may have, papa may have,
But God bless the child that's got his own!
That's got his own.
'God Bless the Child' (1941 song, with Arthur Herzog Jnr)

20 Southern trees bear strange fruit,
Blood on the leaves and blood at the root,
Black bodies swinging in the Southern breeze,
Strange fruit hanging from the poplar trees.
'Strange Fruit' (1939)

21 You can be up to your boobies in white satin, with gardenias in your hair and no sugar cane for miles, but you can still be working on a plantation.
Lady Sings the Blues (1956, with William Duffy) ch. 11

22 In this country, don't forget, a habit is no damn private hell. There's no solitary confinement outside of jail. A habit is hell for those you love.
of a drug habit
Lady Sings the Blues (1956, with William Duffy) ch. 24

Henry Fox, Lord Holland 1705–74

English Whig politician
on Holland: see **Walpole** 801:17

1 If Mr Selwyn calls again, shew him up: if I am alive I shall be delighted to see him; and if I am dead he would like to see me.
during his last illness
J. H. Jesse *George Selwyn and his Contemporaries* (1844) vol. 3

Henry Scott Holland 1847–1918

English theologian and preacher

2 Death is nothing at all; it does not count. I have only slipped away into the next room.
sermon preached on Whitsunday 1910, in *Facts of the Faith* (1919) 'The King of Terrors'

Stanley Holloway 1890–1982

English actor and singer

3 Sam, Sam, pick up tha' musket.
'Pick Up Tha' Musket' (1930 recorded monologue)

John H. Holmes 1879–1964

American Unitarian minister

4 This, now, is the judgement of our scientific age—the third reaction of man upon the universe! This universe is not hostile, nor yet is it friendly. It is simply indifferent.
The Sensible Man's View of Religion (1932) ch. 4

Oliver Wendell Holmes 1809–94

American physician, poet, and essayist

5 The axis of the earth sticks out visibly through the centre of each and every town or city.
The Autocrat of the Breakfast-Table (1858) ch. 6

6 It is the province of knowledge to speak and it is the privilege of wisdom to listen.
The Poet at the Breakfast-Table (1872) ch. 10

7 Fate tried to conceal him by naming him Smith.
of Samuel Francis **Smith**
'The Boys' (1858)

8 Lean, hungry, savage anti-everythings.
'A Modest Request' (1848)

9 Man wants but little drink below,
But wants that little strong.
'A Song of other Days' (1848); cf. **Goldsmith** 344:20

10 We pause to . . . recall what our country has done for each of us and to ask ourselves what we can do for our country in return.
speech, Keene, New Hampshire, 30 May 1884; cf. **Kennedy** 433:14

11 It is better to be seventy years young than forty years old!
reply to invitation from Julia Ward **Howe** *to her seventieth birthday party, 27 May 1889*
Laura Richards and Maud Howe Elliott *Julia Ward Howe* (1916) vol. 2

12 Blank cheques of intellectual bankruptcy.
definition of catchphrases
attributed

Oliver Wendell Holmes Jr. 1841–1935

American lawyer

13 Certitude is not the test of certainty. We have been cocksure of many things that were not so.
'Natural Law' (1918)

14 The most stringent protection of free speech would not protect a man falsely shouting fire in a theatre and causing a panic.
sometimes quoted as, 'shouting fire in a crowded theatre'
in *Schenck v. United States* (1919)

15 The minute a phrase becomes current it becomes an apology for not thinking accurately to the end of the sentence.
letter to Harold Laski, 2 July 1917

16 But I have long thought that if you knew a column of advertisements by heart, you could achieve unexpected felicities with them. You can get a happy quotation anywhere if you have the eye.
letter to Harold Laski, 31 May 1923

John Home 1722–1808

Scottish dramatist

17 My name is Norval; on the Grampian hills
My father feeds his flocks.
Douglas (1756) act 2, sc. 1

18 Like Douglas conquer, or like Douglas die.
Douglas (1756) act 5

Alec Douglas-Home, Lord Home 1903–95

British Conservative statesman; Prime Minister, 1963–4

19 As far as the fourteenth earl is concerned, I suppose Mr Wilson, when you come to think of it, is the fourteenth Mr Wilson.
replying to Harold **Wilson***'s remark (on Home's becoming leader of the Conservative party) that 'the whole* [democratic] *process has ground to a halt with a fourteenth Earl'*
in *Daily Telegraph* 22 October 1963

Homer

Greek poet of the 8th century BC
on Homer: see **Anonymous** 18:18, **Arnold** 29:5, **Horace** 386:5, **Keats** 430:14

20 Achilles' cursed anger sing, O goddess, that son of Peleus, which started a myriad sufferings for the Achaeans.
The Iliad bk. 1, l. 1; cf. **Pope** 586:6

21 Winged words.
The Iliad bk. 1, l. 201

22 The son of Kronos [Zeus] spoke, and nodded with his darkish brows, and immortal locks fell forward from the lord's deathless head, and he made great Olympus tremble.
The Iliad bk. 1, l. 528

23 It is no cause for anger that the Trojans and the well-greaved Achaeans have suffered for so long

over *such* a woman: she is wondrously like the immortal goddesses to look upon.
of Helen
The Iliad bk. 3, l. 156

1 Son of Atreus, what manner of speech has escaped the barrier of your teeth?
The Iliad bk. 4, l. 350

2 Like that of leaves is a generation of men.
The Iliad bk. 6, l. 146

3 Always to be best, and to be distinguished above the rest.
The Iliad bk. 6, l. 208

4 Smiling through her tears.
The Iliad bk. 6, l. 484

5 Hateful to me as the gates of Hades is that man who hides one thing in his heart and speaks another.
The Iliad bk. 9, l. 312

6 This is the one best omen, to fight in defence of one's country.
The Iliad bk. 12, l. 243

7 He lay great and greatly fallen, forgetful of his horsemanship.
The Iliad bk. 16, l. 776

8 It lies in the lap of the gods.
The Iliad bk. 17, l. 514 and elsewhere

9 Tell me, Muse, of the man of many devices, who wandered far and wide after he had sacked Troy's sacred city, and saw the towns of many men and knew their mind.
of Odysseus
The Odyssey bk. 1, l. 1

10 Rosy-fingered dawn.
The Odyssey bk. 2, l. 1 and *passim*

11 I would rather be tied to the soil as another man's serf, even a poor man's, who hadn't much to live on himself, than be King of all these the dead and destroyed.
The Odyssey bk. 11, l. 489

Arthur Honegger 1892–1955
Swiss composer

12 The first requirement for a composer is to be dead.
Je suis compositeur (1951)

Thomas Hood 1799–1845
English poet and humorist

13 Take her up tenderly,
Lift her with care;
Fashioned so slenderly,
Young, and so fair!
'The Bridge of Sighs' (1844)

14 Or was there a dearer one
Still, and a nearer one
Yet, than all other?
'The Bridge of Sighs' (1844)

15 The bleak wind of March
Made her tremble and shiver;
But not the dark arch,
Or the black flowing river.
'The Bridge of Sighs' (1844)

16 Mad from life's history,
Glad to death's mystery,
Swift to be hurled—
Anywhere, anywhere,
Out of the world!
'The Bridge of Sighs' (1844)

17 Two stern-faced men set out from Lynn,
Through the cold and heavy mist;
And Eugene Aram walked between,
With gyves upon his wrist.
'The Dream of Eugene Aram' (1829)

18 Ben Battle was a soldier bold,
And used to war's alarms:
But a cannon-ball took off his legs,
So he laid down his arms!
'Faithless Nelly Gray' (1826)

19 For here I leave my second leg,
And the Forty-second Foot!
'Faithless Nelly Gray' (1826)

20 They went and told the sexton, and
The sexton tolled the bell.
'Faithless Sally Brown' (1826)

21 I remember, I remember,
The house where I was born,
The little window where the sun
Came peeping in at morn.
'I Remember' (1826)

22 But evil is wrought by want of thought,
As well as want of heart!
'The Lady's Dream' (1844)

23 Home-made dishes that drive one from home.
Miss Kilmansegg and her Precious Leg (1841–3) 'Her Misery'

24 No sun—no moon!
No morn—no noon
No dawn—no dusk—no proper time of day.
'No!' (1844)

25 No warmth, no cheerfulness, no healthful ease,
No comfortable feel in any member—
No shade, no shine, no butterflies, no bees,
No fruits, no flowers, no leaves, no birds,—
November!
'No!' (1844)

26 I saw old Autumn in the misty morn
Stand shadowless like Silence, listening
To silence.
'Ode: Autumn' (1823)

27 She stood breast high amid the corn,
Clasped by the golden light of morn,
Like the sweetheart of the sun,
Who many a glowing kiss had won.
'Ruth' (1827); cf. **Keats** 429:15

28 With fingers weary and worn,
With eyelids heavy and red,
A woman sat, in unwomanly rags,
Plying her needle and thread—
Stitch! stitch! stitch!

In poverty, hunger, and dirt.
And still with a voice of dolorous pitch
She sang the 'Song of the Shirt'.
'The Song of the Shirt' (1843)

1 Oh! God! that bread should be so dear,
And flesh and blood so cheap!
'The Song of the Shirt' (1843)

2 What is a modern poet's fate?
To write his thoughts upon a slate;
The critic spits on what is done,
Gives it a wipe—and all is gone.
'To the Reviewers', dedication of *Whims and Oddities* (1826)

3 The sedate, sober, silent, serious, sad-coloured sect.
of Quakers
Comic Annual (1839) 'The Doves and the Crows'

4 Holland . . . lies so low they're only saved by being dammed.
Up the Rhine (1840) 'Letter from Martha Penny to Rebecca Page'

Richard Hooker *c.*1554–1600

English theologian

5 He that goeth about to persuade a multitude, that they are not so well governed as they ought to be, shall never want attentive and favourable hearers.
Of the Laws of Ecclesiastical Polity (1593) bk. 1, ch. 1, sect. 1

6 Of Law there can be no less acknowledged, than that her seat is the bosom of God, her voice the harmony of the world: all things in heaven and earth do her homage, the very least as feeling her care, and the greatest as not exempted from her power.
Of the Laws of Ecclesiastical Polity (1593) bk. 1, ch. 16, sect. 8

7 Alteration though it be from worse to better hath in it inconveniences, and those weighty.
Of the Laws of Ecclesiastical Polity (1593) bk. 4, ch. 14, sect. 1; cf. **Johnson** 409:3

Ellen Sturgis Hooper 1816–41

American poet

8 I slept, and dreamed that life was beauty;
I woke, and found that life was duty.
'Beauty and Duty' (1840)

Herbert Hoover 1874–1964

American Republican statesman, 31st President of the US, 1929–33

9 Our country has deliberately undertaken a great social and economic experiment, noble in motive and far-reaching in purpose.
on the Eighteenth Amendment enacting Prohibition
letter to Senator W. H. Borah, 23 February 1928; in Claudius O. Johnson *Borah of Idaho* (1936) ch. 21

10 The American system of rugged individualism.
speech in New York City, 22 October 1928, in *New Day* (1928) p. 154

11 The slogan of progress is changing from the full dinner pail to the full garage.
sometimes paraphrased as, 'a car in every garage and a chicken in every pot'
speech, 22 October 1928; cf. **Henri IV** 370:4

12 The grass will grow in the streets of a hundred cities, a thousand towns.
on proposals 'to reduce the protective tariff to a competitive tariff for revenue'
speech, 31 October 1932, in *State Papers of Herbert Hoover* (1934) vol. 2

13 Older men declare war. But it is youth who must fight and die.
speech at the Republican National Convention, Chicago, 27 June 1944, in *Addresses upon the American Road* (1946)

Anthony Hope (Anthony Hope Hawkins) 1863–1933

English novelist
see also ***Epitaphs*** *303:9*

14 Economy is going without something you do want in case you should, some day, want something you probably won't want.
The Dolly Dialogues (1894) no. 12

15 'You oughtn't to yield to temptation.' 'Well, somebody must, or the thing becomes absurd,' said I.
The Dolly Dialogues (1894) no. 14

16 Oh, for an hour of Herod!
at the first night of J. M. ***Barrie****'s* Peter Pan *in 1904*
Denis Mackail *The Story of JMB* (1941) ch. 17

Bob Hope 1903–

American comedian

17 A bank is a place that will lend you money if you can prove that you don't need it.
In Alan Harrington *Life in the Crystal Palace* (1959) 'The Tyranny of Farms'

18 Well, I'm still here.
after erroneous reports of his death, marked by tributes paid to him in Congress
in *Mail on Sunday* 7 June 1998 'Quotes of the Week'

Francis Hope 1938–74

British journalist and poet

19 And scribbled lines like fallen hopes
On backs of tattered envelopes.
'Instead of a Poet' (1965)

Laurence Hope (Adela Florence Nicolson) 1865–1904

Anglo-Indian poet

20 Pale hands I loved beside the Shalimar,
Where are you now? Who lies beneath your spell?
The Garden of Kama (1901) 'Kashmiri Song'

21 Less than the dust, beneath thy Chariot wheel,
Less than the rust, that never stained thy
Sword . . .

Less than the need thou hast in life of me.
Even less am I.
The Garden of Kama (1901) 'Less than the Dust'

Gerard Manley Hopkins 1844–89

English poet and priest

1 Ten or twelve, only ten or twelve
Strokes of havoc únselve.
'Binsey Poplars' (written 1879)

2 Not, I'll not, carrion comfort, Despair, not feast on thee;
Not untwist—slack they may be—these last strands of man
In me or, most weary, cry *I can no more*. I can;
Can something, hope, wish day come, not choose not to be.
'Carrion Comfort' (written 1885)

3 That night, that year
Of now done darkness I wretch lay wrestling with (my God!) my God.
'Carrion Comfort' (written 1885)

4 Towery city and branchy between towers;
Cuckoo-echoing, bell-swarmèd, lark-charmèd, rook-racked, river-rounded.
'Duns Scotus's Oxford' (written 1879)

5 The world is charged with the grandeur of God.
It will flame out like shining from shook foil . . .
Generations have trod, have trod, have trod;
And all is seared with trade; bleared, smeared with toil;
And wears man's smudge and shares man's smell: the soil
Is bare now, nor can foot feel, being shod.
'God's Grandeur' (written 1877)

6 Because the Holy Ghost over the bent
World broods with warm breast and with ah! bright wings.
'God's Grandeur' (written 1877)

7 Elected Silence, sing to me
And beat upon my whorlèd ear,
Pipe me to pastures still and be
The music that I care to hear.
'The Habit of Perfection' (written 1866)

8 Palate, the hutch of tasty lust,
Desire not to be rinsed with wine.
'The Habit of Perfection' (written 1866)

9 I have desired to go
Where springs not fail,
To fields where flies no sharp and sided hail
And a few lilies blow.
'Heaven-Haven' (written 1864)

10 What would the world be, once bereft
Of wet and wildness? Let them be left,
O let them be left, wildness and wet;
Long live the weeds and the wilderness yet.
'Inversnaid' (written 1881)

11 No worst, there is none. Pitched past pitch of grief,
More pangs will, schooled at forepangs, wilder wring.
Comforter, where, where is your comforting?
'No worst, there is none' (written 1885)

12 O the mind, mind has mountains; cliffs of fall
Frightful, sheer, no-man-fathomed. Hold them cheap
May who ne'er hung there.
'No worst, there is none' (written 1885)

13 All
Life death does end and each day dies with sleep.
'No worst, there is none' (written 1885)

14 Glory be to God for dappled things.
'Pied Beauty' (written 1877)

15 All things counter, original, spare, strange;
Whatever is fickle, freckled (who knows how?)
With swift, slow; sweet, sour; adazzle, dim;
He fathers-forth whose beauty is past change:
Praise him.
'Pied Beauty' (written 1877)

16 The glassy peartree leaves and blooms, they brush
The descending blue; that blue is all in a rush
With richness.
'Spring' (written 1877)

17 Márgarét, áre you grieving
Over Goldengrove unleaving?
'Spring and Fall: to a young child' (written 1880)

18 Áh! ás the heart grows older
It will come to such sights colder
By and by, nor spare a sigh
Though worlds of wanwood leafmeal lie;
And yet you *will* weep and know why.
'Spring and Fall: to a young child' (written 1880)

19 It is the blight man was born for,
It is Margaret you mourn for.
'Spring and Fall: to a young child' (written 1880)

20 Look at the stars! look, look up at the skies!
O look at all the fire-folk sitting in the air!
The bright boroughs, the circle-citadels there!
'The Starlight Night' (written 1877)

21 This piece-bright paling shuts the spouse
Christ home, Christ and his mother and all his hallows.
'The Starlight Night' (written 1877)

22 I am all at once what Christ is, since he was what I am, and
This Jack, joke, poor potsherd, patch, matchwood, immortal diamond,
Is immortal diamond.
'That Nature is a Heraclitean Fire' (written 1888)

23 Thou art indeed just, Lord, if I contend
With thee; but, sir, so what I plead is just.
Why do sinners' ways prosper? and why must
Disappointment all I endeavour end?
'Thou art indeed just, Lord' (written 1889)

24 Birds build—but not I build; no, but strain,
Time's eunuch, and not breed one work that wakes.
Mine, O thou lord of life, send my roots rain.
'Thou art indeed just, Lord' (written 1889); cf. **Hopkins** 385:8

1 I caught this morning morning's minion, kingdom of daylight's dauphin, dapple-dawn-drawn Falcon.
'The Windhover' (written 1877)

2 My heart in hiding
Stirred for a bird,—the achieve of, the mastery of the thing!
'The Windhover' (written 1877)

3 I did say yes
O at lightning and lashed rod;
Thou heardst me truer than tongue confess
Thy terror, O Christ, O God.
'The Wreck of the Deutschland' (written 1876) pt. 1

4 On Saturday sailed from Bremen,
American-outward-bound,
Take settler and seamen, tell men with women,
Two hundred souls in the round.
'The Wreck of the Deutschland' (written 1876) pt. 2

5 Time has three dimensions and one positive pitch or direction. It is therefore not so much like any river or any sea as like the Sea of Galilee, which has the Jordan running through it and giving a current to the whole.
'Creation and Redemption The Great Sacrifice' (written 1881), in Christopher Devlin (ed.) *The Sermons and Devotional Writings of Gerard Manley Hopkins* (1959) ch. 8

6 To lift up the hands in prayer gives God glory, but a man with a dungfork in his hand, a woman with a slop-pail, give him glory too. He is so great that all things give him glory if you mean they should.
G. Roberts (ed.) *Gerard Manley Hopkins. Selected Prose* (1980) 'The Principle or Foundation' (1882)

7 I am surprised you should say fancy and aesthetic tastes have led me to my present state of mind; these would be better satisfied in the Church of England, for bad taste is always meeting one in the accessories of Catholicism.
on his adoption of the Catholic faith
letter to his father, 16 October 1866; in G. Roberts (ed.) *Gerard Manley Hopkins. Selected Prose* (1980)

8 The fine pleasure is not to do a thing but to feel that you could . . . If I could but get on, if I could but produce a work I should not mind its being buried, silenced, and going no further; but it kills me to be time's eunuch and never to beget.
letter to Robert Bridges, 1 September 1885, in C. C. Abbott (ed.) *The Correspondence of Gerard Manley Hopkins and Robert Bridges* (1935); cf. **Hopkins** 384:24

Joseph Hopkinson 1770–1842
American politician

9 Hail, Columbia! happy land!
Hail, ye heroes! heaven-born band!
'Hail, Columbia!' in *Porcupine's Gazette* 20 April 1798

Horace (Quintus Horatius Flaccus) 65–8 BC
Roman poet

10 *Ut turpiter atrum*
Desinat in piscem mulier formosa superne.
So that what is a beautiful woman on top ends in a black and ugly fish.
Ars Poetica l. 3

11 *'Pictoribus atque poetis*
Quidlibet audendi semper fuit aequa potestas.'
Scimus, et hanc veniam petimusque damusque vicissim.
'Painters and poets alike have always had licence to dare anything.' We know that, and we both claim and permit others this indulgence.
Ars Poetica l. 9

12 *Inceptis gravibus plerumque et magna professis*
Purpureus, late qui splendeat, unus et alter
Adsuitur pannus.
Works of serious purpose and grand promises often have a purple patch or two stitched on, to shine far and wide.
Ars Poetica l. 14

13 *Brevis esse laboro,*
Obscurus fio.
I strive to be brief, and I become obscure.
Ars Poetica l. 25

14 *Dixeris egregie notum si callida verbum*
Reddiderit iunctura novum.
You will have written exceptionally well if, by skilful arrangement of your words, you have made an ordinary one seem original.
Ars Poetica l. 47

15 *Multa renascentur quae iam cecidere, cadentque*
Quae nunc sunt in honore vocabula, si volet usus,
Quem penes arbitrium est et ius et norma loquendi.
Many terms which have now dropped out of favour will be revived, and those that are at present respectable will drop out, if usage so choose, with whom lies the decision, the judgement, and the rule of speech.
Ars Poetica l. 70

16 *Grammatici certant et adhuc sub iudice lis est.*
Scholars dispute, and the case is still before the courts.
Ars Poetica l. 78

17 *Proicit ampullas et sesquipedalia verba.*
He throws aside his paint-pots and his words a foot and a half long.
Ars Poetica l. 97; cf. **Wells** 810:8

18 *Si vis me flere, dolendum est*
Primum ipsi tibi.
If you want me to weep, you must first feel grief yourself.
Ars Poetica l. 102

19 *Difficile est proprie communia dicere.*
It is hard to utter common notions in an individual way.
Ars Poetica l. 128

20 *Parturient montes, nascetur ridiculus mus.*
Mountains will go into labour, and a silly little mouse will be born.
Ars Poetica l. 139

21 *Non fumum ex fulgore, sed ex fumo dare lucem*
Cogitat.
His thinking does not produce smoke after the flame, but light after smoke.
Ars Poetica l. 143

1 *Semper ad eventum festinat et in medias res*
Non secus ac notas auditorem rapit.

He always hurries to the main event and whisks his audience into the middle of things as though they knew already.

Ars Poetica l. 148

2 *Difficilis, querulus, laudator temporis acti*
Se puero, castigator censorque minorum.

Tiresome, complaining, a praiser of past times, when he was a boy, a castigator and censor of the young generation.

Ars Poetica l. 173

3 *Omne tulit punctum qui miscuit utile dulci,*
Lectorem delectando pariterque monendo.

He has gained every point who has mixed profit with pleasure, by delighting the reader at the same time as instructing him.

Ars Poetica l. 343

4 *Verum ubi plura nitent in carmine, non ego paucis*
Offendar maculis.

When many beauties grace a poem, I shall not take offence at a few faults.

Ars Poetica l. 351

5 *Indignor quandoque bonus dormitat Homerus.*

I'm aggrieved when sometimes even excellent Homer nods.

Ars Poetica l. 359; cf. **Byron** 177:1, **Proverbs** 602:44

6 *Ut pictura poesis.*

A poem is like a painting.

Ars Poetica l. 361

7 *Mediocribus esse poetis*
Non homines, non di, non concessere columnae.

Not gods, nor men, nor even booksellers have put up with poets being second-rate.

Ars Poetica l. 372

8 *Nullius addictus iurare in verba magistri,*
Quo me cumque rapit tempestas, deferor hospes.

Not bound to swear allegiance to any master, wherever the wind takes me I travel as a visitor.

Epistles bk. 1, no. 1, l. 14; cf. **Mottoes** 535:12

9 *Condicio dulcis sine pulvere palmae.*

The happy state of winning the palm without the dust of racing.

Epistles bk. 1, no. 1, l. 51

10 *O cives, cives, quarenda pecunia primum est;*
Virtus post nummos.

Citizens, citizens, the first thing to acquire is money. Cash before conscience!

Epistles bk. 1, no. 1, l. 53

11 *Si possis recte, si non, quocumque modo rem.*

If possible honestly, if not, somehow, make money.

Epistles bk. 1, no. 1, l. 66; cf. **Pope** 586:10

12 *Olim quod vulpes aegroto cauta leoni*
Respondit referam: 'quia me vestigia terrent,
Omnia te adversum spectantia, nulla retrorsum.'

Let me remind you what the wary fox said once upon a time to the sick lion: 'Because those footprints scare me, all directed your way, none coming back.'

explaining why he did not follow popular opinion

Epistles bk. 1, no. 1, l. 73

13 *Quidquid delirant reges plectuntur Achivi.*

Whatever madness their kings commit, the Greeks take the beating.

Epistles bk. 1, no. 2, l. 14

14 *Nos numerus sumus et fruges consumere nati.*

We are just statistics, born to consume resources.

Epistles bk. 1, no. 2, l. 27

15 *Dimidium facti qui coepit habet: sapere aude.*

To have begun is half the job: be bold and be sensible.

Epistles bk. 1, no. 2, l. 40

16 *Ira furor brevis est.*

Anger is a short madness.

Epistles bk. 1, no. 2, l. 62

17 *Omnem crede diem tibi diluxisse supremum.*
Grata superveniet quae non sperabitur hora.
Me pinguem et nitidum bene curata cute vises
Cum ridere voles Epicuri de grege porcum.

Believe each day that has dawned is your last. Some hour to which you have not been looking forward will prove lovely. As for me, if you want a good laugh, you will come and find me fat and sleek, in excellent condition, one of Epicurus's herd of pigs.

Epistles bk. 1, no. 4, l. 13

18 *Nil admirari prope res est una, Numici,*
Solaque quae possit facere et servare beatum.

To marvel at nothing is just about the one and only thing, Numicius, that can make a man happy and keep him that way.

Epistles bk. 1, no. 6, l. 1; cf. **Pope** 586:11

19 *Naturam expelles furca, tamen usque recurret.*

You may drive out nature with a pitchfork, yet she'll be constantly running back.

Epistles bk. 1, no. 10, l. 24; cf. **Proverbs** 615:24

20 *Caelum non animum mutant qui trans mare currunt.*
Strenua nos exercet inertia: navibus atque
Quadrigis petimus bene vivere. Quod petis hic est,
Est Ulubris, animus si te non deficit aequus.

They change their clime, not their frame of mind, who rush across the sea. We strain at achieving nothing: we seek happiness in boats and carriage rides. What you seek is here, at Ulubrae, so long as peace of mind does not desert you.

Epistles bk. 1, no. 11, l. 27

21 *Concordia discors.*

Discordant harmony.

Epistles bk. 1, no. 12, l. 19

22 *Principibus placuisse viris non ultima laus est.*
Non cuivis homini contingit adire Corinthum.

It is not the least praise to have pleased leading men. Not everyone is lucky enough to get to Corinth.

Epistles bk. 1, no. 17, l. 35

1 *Et semel emissum volat irrevocabile verbum.*

And once sent out a word takes wing beyond recall.

Epistles bk. 1, no. 18, l. 71; cf. **Dillon** 267:12

2 *Nam tua res agitur, paries cum proximus ardet.*

For it is your business, when the wall next door catches fire.

Epistles bk. 1, no. 18, l. 84

3 *Fallentis semita vitae.*

The pathway of a life unnoticed.

Epistles bk. 1, no. 18, l. 103

4 *Nulla placere diu nec vivere carmina possunt*
Quae scribuntur aquae potoribus.

No verse can give pleasure for long, nor last, that is written by drinkers of water.

Epistles bk. 1, no. 19, l. 2

5 *O imitatores, servum pecus.*

O imitators, you slavish herd.

Epistles bk. 1, no. 19, l. 19

6 *Scribimus indocti doctique poemata passim.*

Skilled or unskilled, we all scribble poems.

Epistles bk. 2, no. 1, l. 117; cf. **Pope** 586:16

7 *Si foret in terris, rideret Democritus.*

If he were on earth, Democritus would laugh at the sight.

Epistles bk. 2, no. 1, l. 194

8 *Atque inter silvas Academi quaerere verum.*

And seek for truth in the groves of Academe.

Epistles bk. 2, no. 2, l. 45

9 *Multa fero, ut placem genus irritabile vatum.*

I have to put up with a lot, to please the touchy breed of poets.

Epistles bk. 2, no. 2, l. 102

10 *Quid te exempta iuvat spinis de pluribus una?*
Vivere si recte nescis, decede peritis.
Lusisti satis, edisti satis atque bibisti:
Tempus abire tibi est.

What pleasure does it give to be rid of one thorn out of many? If you don't know how to live right, give way to those who are expert at it. You have had enough fun, eaten and drunk enough: it is time for you to go.

Epistles bk. 2, no. 2, l. 212

11 *Beatus ille, qui procul negotiis,*
Ut prisca gens mortalium,
Paterna rura bubus exercet suis,
Solutus omni faenore.

Happy the man who, far away from business, like the race of men of old, tills his ancestral fields with his own oxen, unbound by any interest to pay.

Epodes epode 2, l. 1

12 *Indocilis pauperiem pati.*

Untaught to bear poverty.

Odes bk. 1, no. 1, l. 18

13 *Quodsi me lyricis vatibus inseres,*
Sublimi feriam sidera vertice.

And if you include me among the lyric poets, I'll hold my head so high it'll strike the stars.

Odes bk. 1, no. 1, l. 35

14 *Animae dimidium meae.*

Half my own soul.

of **Virgil**

Odes bk. 1, no. 3, l. 8

15 *Illi robur et aes triplex*
Circa pectus erat, qui fragilem truci
Commisit pelago ratem
Primus.

Oak was round his breast, and triple bronze, who first launched his frail boat on the rough sea.

Odes bk. 1, no. 3, l. 9

16 *Pallida Mors aequo pulsat pede pauperum tabernas*
Regumque turris.

Pale Death breaks into the cottages of the poor as into the castles of kings.

Odes bk. 1, no. 4, l. 13

17 *Vitae summa brevis spem nos vetat incohare longam.*

Life's short span forbids us to enter on far-reaching hopes.

Odes bk. 1, no. 4, l. 15

18 *Nil desperandum.*

Never despair.

Odes bk. 1, no. 7, l. 27

19 *Cras ingens iterabimus aequor.*

Tomorrow we shall sail again on the vast ocean.

Odes bk. 1, no. 7, l. 32

20 *Quid sit futurum cras fuge quaerere et*
Quem Fors dierum cumque dabit lucro
Appone.

Drop the question what tomorrow may bring, and count as profit every day that Fate allows you.

Odes bk. 1, no. 9, l. 13

21 *Tu ne quaesieris, scire nefas, quem mihi, quem tibi*
Finem di dederint.

Do not try to find out—we're forbidden to know—what end the gods may bestow on me or you.

Odes bk. 1, no. 11, l. 1

22 *Dum loquimur, fugerit invida*
Aetas: carpe diem, quam minimum credula postero.

While we're talking, envious time is fleeing: seize the day, put no trust in the future.

Odes bk. 1, no. 11, l. 7

23 *Felices ter et amplius*
Quos irrupta tenet copula nec malis
Divulsus querimoniis
Suprema citius solvet amor die.

Thrice blessed (and more) are they whom an unbroken bond holds and whose love, never strained by nasty quarrels, will not slip until their dying day.

Odes bk. 1, no. 13, l. 17

24 *Integer vitae scelerisque purus.*

Wholesome of life and free of crimes.

Odes bk. 1, no. 22, l. 1

1 *Dulce ridentem Lalagen amabo,*
Dulce loquentem.

I will go on loving Lalage, who laughs so sweetly and talks so sweetly.
Odes bk. 1, no. 22, l. 23

2 *Parcus deorum cultor et infrequens.*

A grudging and irregular worshipper of the gods.
Odes bk. 1, no. 34, l. 1

3 *Nunc est bibendum, nunc pede libero*
Pulsanda tellus.

Now for drinking, now the Earth must shake beneath a lively foot.
Odes bk. 1, no. 37, l. 1

4 *Persicos odi, puer, apparatus.*

I hate all that Persian gear, boy.
Odes bk. 1, no. 38, l. 1

5 *Mitte sectari, rosa quo locorum*
Sera moretur.

Stop looking for the place where a late rose may yet linger.
Odes bk. 1, no. 38, l. 3

6 *Aequam memento rebus in arduis*
Servare mentem.

When the going gets rough, remember to keep calm.
Odes bk. 2, no. 3, l. 1

7 *Auream quisquis mediocritatem*
Diligit.

Someone who loves the golden mean.
Odes bk. 2, no. 10, l. 5

8 *Eheu fugaces, Postume, Postume,*
Labuntur anni.

Ah me, Postumus, Postumus, the fleeting years are slipping by.
Odes bk. 2, no. 14, l. 1; cf. **Smart** 722:14

9 *Nihil est ab omni*
Parte beatum.

Nothing is an unmixed blessing.
Odes bk. 2, no. 16, l. 27

10 *Credite posteri.*

Believe me, you who come after me!
Odes bk. 2, no. 19, l. 2

11 *Odi profanum vulgus et arceo;*
Favete linguis; carmina non prius
Audita Musarum sacerdos
Virginibus puerisque canto.

I hate the common herd and keep them off. Hush your tongues; as a priest of the Muses, I sing songs never heard before to virgin girls and boys.
Odes bk. 3, no. 1, l. 1; cf. **Cowley** 239:13

12 *Omne capax movet urna nomen.*

The enormous tombola shakes up everyone's name.
Odes bk. 3, no. 1, l. 16

13 *Post equitem sedet atra Cura.*

Black Care sits behind the horseman.
Odes bk. 3, no. 1, l. 40

14 *Dulce et decorum est pro patria mori.*

Lovely and honourable it is to die for one's country.
Odes bk. 3, no. 2, l. 13; cf. **Owen** 562:8, **Pound** 589:16

15 *Iustum et tenacem propositi virum*
Non civium ardor prava iubentium,
Non vultus instantis tyranni
Mente quatit solida.

The just man having a firm grasp of his intentions, neither the heated passions of his fellow men ordaining something awful, nor a tyrant staring him in the face, will shake in his convictions.
Odes bk. 3, no. 3, l. 1

16 *Si fractus illabatur orbis,*
Impavidum ferient ruinae.

If the world should break and fall on him, its ruins would strike him unafraid.
Odes bk. 3, no. 3, l. 7; cf. **Addison** 4:23, **Pope** 583:2

17 *Opaco*
Pelion imposuisse Olympo.

To pile Pelion on top of shady Olympus.
Odes bk. 3, no. 4, l. 52

18 *Vis consili expers mole ruit sua.*

Force, unaided by judgement, collapses through its own weight.
Odes bk. 3, no. 4, l. 65

19 *Damnosa quid non imminuit dies?*
Aetas parentum peior avis tulit
Nos nequiores, mox daturos
Progeniem vitiosiorem.

What do the ravages of time not injure? Our parents' age (worse than our grandparents') has produced us, more worthless still, who will soon give rise to a yet more vicious generation.
Odes bk. 3, no. 6, l. 45

20 *Splendide mendax et in omne virgo*
Nobilis aevum.

Gloriously deceitful and a virgin renowned for ever.
of the Danaid Hypermestra
Odes bk. 3, no. 11, l. 35

21 *Magnas inter opes inops.*

A beggar amidst great riches.
Odes bk. 3, no. 16, l. 28

22 *Fumum et opes strepitumque Romae.*

The smoke and wealth and din of Rome.
Odes bk. 3, no. 29, l. 12

23 *Ille potens sui*
Laetusque deget, cui licet in diem
Dixisse Vixi: cras vel atra
Nube polum pater occupato
Vel sole puro.

That man shall live as his own master and in happiness who can say each day 'I have lived': tomorrow let the Father fill the sky with a black cloud or clear sunshine.
Odes bk. 3, no. 29, l. 41; cf. **Dryden** 282:32

24 *Exegi monumentum aere perennius.*

I have erected a monument more lasting than bronze.
Odes bk. 3, no. 30, l. 1

1 *Non omnis moriar.*
I shall not altogether die.
Odes bk. 3, no. 30, l. 6

2 *Non sum qualis eram bonae*
Sub regno Cinarae.
I am not as I was when good Cinara was my queen.
Odes bk. 4, no. 1, l. 3; cf. **Dowson** 277:5

3 *Quod spiro et placeo, si placeo, tuum est.*
That I make poetry and give pleasure (if I give pleasure) are because of you.
Odes bk. 4, no. 3, l. 24

4 *Merses profundo: pulchrior evenit.*
Plunge it in deep water: it comes up more beautiful.
Odes bk. 4, no. 4, l. 65

5 *Occidit, occidit*
Spes omnis et fortuna nostri
Nominis Hasdrubale interempto.
All our hope is fallen, fallen, and the luck of our name lost with Hasdrubal.
Odes bk. 4, no. 4, l. 70

6 *Diffugere nives, redeunt iam gramina campis*
Arboribusque comae.
The snows have dispersed, now grass returns to the fields and leaves to the trees.
Odes bk. 4, no. 7, l. 1

7 *Immortalia ne speres, monet annus et almum*
Quae rapit hora diem.
The year and the hour which robs us of the fair day warn us not to hope for things to last for ever.
Odes bk. 4, no. 7, l. 7

8 *Dignum laude virum Musa vetat mori.*
The man worthy of praise the Muse forbids to die.
Odes bk. 4, no. 8, l. 28

9 *Vixere fortes ante Agamemnona*
Multi; sed omnes illacrimabiles
Urgentur ignotique longa
Nocte, carent quia vate sacro.
Many brave men lived before Agamemnon's time; but they are all, unmourned and unknown, covered by the long night, because they lack their sacred poet.
Odes bk. 4, no. 9, l. 25; cf. **Proverbs** 596:37

10 *Non possidentem multa vocaveris*
Recte beatum: rectius occupat
Nomen beati, qui deorum
Muneribus sapienter uti
Duramque callet pauperiem pati
Peiusque leto flagitium timet.
It is not he who has many possessions that you should call blessed: he more rightly deserves that name who knows how to use the gods' gifts wisely and to endure harsh poverty, and who fears dishonour more than death.
Odes bk. 4, no. 9, l. 45

11 *Misce stultitiam consiliis brevem:*
Dulce est desipere in loco.
Mix a little foolishness with your prudence: it's good to be silly at the right moment.
Odes bk. 4, no. 12, l. 27

12 *Qui fit, Maecenas, ut nemo, quam sibi sortem*
Seu ratio dederit seu fors obiecerit, illa
Contentus vivat, laudet diversa sequentis?
How is it, Maecenas, that no one lives contented with his lot, whether he has planned it for himself or fate has flung him into it, but yet he praises those who follow different paths?
Satires bk. 1, no. 1, l. 1

13 *Quamquam ridentem dicere verum*
Quid vetat?
Why should truth not be impress'd
Beneath the cover of a jest.
Satires bk 1, no. 1, l. 24

14 *. . . Mutato nomine de te*
Fabula narratur.
Change the name and it's about you, that story.
Satires bk. 1, no. 1, l. 69

15 *Est modus in rebus.*
There is moderation in everything.
Satires bk. 1, no. 1, l. 106; cf. **Proverbs** 606:41, 612:14

16 *Hoc genus omne.*
All that tribe.
Satires bk. 1, no. 2, l. 2

17 *. . . Ab ovo*
Usque ad mala.
From the egg right through to the apples.
from the start to the finish of a meal
Satires bk. 1, no. 3, l. 6

18 *Etiam disiecti membra poetae.*
Even though broken up, the limbs of a poet.
of ***Ennius***
Satires bk. 1, no. 4, l. 62

19 *. . . Ad unguem*
Factus homo.
An accomplished man to his fingertips.
Satires bk. 1, no. 5, l. 32

20 *. . . Credat Iudaeus Apella,*
Non ego.
Let Apella the Jew believe it; I shan't.
Satires bk. 1, no. 5, l. 100

21 *In silvam . . . ligna feras insanius.*
It's insane to carry timber to the forest.
Satires bk. 1, no. 10, l. 34

22 *Solventur risu tabulae, tu missus abibis.*
The case will be dismissed with a laugh. You will get off scot-free.
Satires bk. 2, no. 1, l. 86 (translated by H. R. Fairclough)

23 *Par nobile fratrum.*
A noble pair of brothers.
Satires bk. 2, no. 3, l. 243 (i.e. notorious villains)

24 *Hoc erat in votis: modus agri non ita magnus,*
Hortus ubi et tecto vicinus iugis aquae fons
Et paulum silvae super his foret.

This was among my prayers: a piece of land not so very large, where a garden should be and a spring of ever-flowing water near the house, and a bit of woodland as well as these.
Satires bk. 2, no. 6, l. 1; cf. **Mallet** 492:5, **Swift** 749:7

1 *O noctes cenaeque deum!*
O nights and feasts divine!
Satires bk. 2, no. 6, l. 65

2 *Responsare cupidinibus, contemnere honores*
Fortis, et in se ipso totus, teres, atque rotundus.
Strong enough to answer back to desires, to despise honours, and a whole man in himself, polished and well-rounded.
Satires bk. 2, no. 7, l. 85

Samuel Horsley 1733–1806

English bishop

3 In this country . . . the individual subject . . . 'has nothing to do with the laws but to obey them.'
defending a maxim he had used earlier in committee
speech, House of Lords, 13 November 1795

A. E. Housman 1859–1936

English poet

4 Oh who is that young sinner with the handcuffs on his wrists?
And what has he been after that they groan and shake their fists?
And wherefore is he wearing such a conscience-stricken air?
Oh they're taking him to prison for the colour of his hair.
first drafted in summer 1895, following the trial and imprisonment of Oscar **Wilde**
Collected Poems (1939) 'Additional Poems' no. 18

5 Mud's sister, not himself, adorns my legs.
Fragment of a Greek Tragedy (*Bromsgrovian* vol. 2, no. 5, 1883)

6 The Grizzly Bear is huge and wild;
He has devoured the infant child.
The infant child is not aware
He has been eaten by the bear.
'Infant Innocence' (1938)

7 And how am I to face the odds
Of man's bedevilment and God's?
I, a stranger and afraid
In a world I never made.
Last Poems (1922) no. 12

8 The candles burn their sockets,
The blinds let through the day,
The young man feels his pockets
And wonders what's to pay.
Last Poems (1922) no. 21

9 These, in the day when heaven was falling,
The hour when earth's foundations fled,
Followed their mercenary calling
And took their wages and are dead.

Their shoulders held the sky suspended;
They stood, and earth's foundations stay;
What God abandoned, these defended,
And saved the sum of things for pay.
Last Poems (1922) no. 37 'Epitaph on an Army of Mercenaries'

10 For nature, heartless, witless nature,
Will neither care nor know
What stranger's feet may find the meadow
And trespass there and go,
Nor ask amid the dews of morning
If they are mine or no.
Last Poems (1922) no. 40

11 The rainy Pleiads wester,
Orion plunges prone,
The stroke of midnight ceases,
And I lie down alone.
More Poems (1936) no. 11

12 Life, to be sure, is nothing much to lose;
But young men think it is, and we were young.
More Poems (1936) no. 36

13 Good-night. Ensured release
Imperishable peace,
Have these for yours,
While earth's foundations stand
And sky and sea and land
And heaven endures.
More Poems (1936) no. 48 'Alta Quies'

14 Loveliest of trees, the cherry now
Is hung with bloom along the bough,
And stands about the woodland ride
Wearing white for Eastertide.
A Shropshire Lad (1896) no. 2

15 And since to look at things in bloom
Fifty springs are little room,
About the woodlands I will go
To see the cherry hung with snow.
A Shropshire Lad (1896) no. 2

16 Clay lies still, but blood's a rover;
Breath's a ware that will not keep.
Up, lad: when the journey's over
There'll be time enough to sleep.
A Shropshire Lad (1896) no. 4

17 And naked to the hangman's noose
The morning clocks will ring
A neck God made for other use
Than strangling in a string.
A Shropshire Lad (1896) no. 9

18 When I was one-and-twenty
I heard a wise man say,
'Give crowns and pounds and guineas
But not your heart away;
Give pearls away and rubies,
But keep your fancy free.'
But I was one-and-twenty,
No use to talk to me.
A Shropshire Lad (1896) no. 13

19 In summertime on Bredon
The bells they sound so clear;
Round both the shires they ring them
In steeples far and near,
A happy noise to hear.
Here of a Sunday morning

My love and I would lie,
And see the coloured counties,
And hear the larks so high
About us in the sky.
A Shropshire Lad (1896) no. 21

1 The lads in their hundreds to Ludlow come in for the fair,
There's men from the barn and the forge and the mill and the fold,
The lads for the girls and the lads for the liquor are there,
And there with the rest are the lads that will never be old.
A Shropshire Lad (1896) no. 23

2 On Wenlock Edge the wood's in trouble;
His forest fleece the Wrekin heaves;
The wind it plies the saplings double,
And thick on Severn snow the leaves.
A Shropshire Lad (1896) no. 31

3 The gale, it plies the saplings double,
It blows so hard, 'twill soon be gone:
To-day the Roman and his trouble
Are ashes under Uricon.
A Shropshire Lad (1896) no. 31

4 From far, from eve and morning
And yon twelve-winded sky,
The stuff of life to knit me
Blew hither: here am I.
A Shropshire Lad (1896) no. 32

5 Into my heart an air that kills
From yon far country blows:
What are those blue remembered hills,
What spires, what farms are those?

That is the land of lost content,
I see it shining plain,
The happy highways where I went
And cannot come again.
A Shropshire Lad (1896) no. 40

6 And bound for the same bourn as I,
On every road I wandered by,
Trod beside me, close and dear,
The beautiful and death-struck year.
A Shropshire Lad (1896) no. 41

7 Clunton and Clunbury,
Clungunford and Clun,
Are the quietest places
Under the sun.
A Shropshire Lad (1896) no. 50 (epigraph)

8 By brooks too broad for leaping
The lightfoot boys are laid;
The rose-lipt girls are sleeping
In fields where roses fade.
A Shropshire Lad (1896) no. 54

9 Say, for what were hop-yards meant,
Or why was Burton built on Trent?
Oh many a peer of England brews
Livelier liquor than the Muse,
And malt does more than Milton can
To justify God's ways to man.
Ale, man, ale's the stuff to drink
For fellows whom it hurts to think.
A Shropshire Lad (1896) no. 62; cf. **Milton** 514:9

10 I tell the tale that I heard told.
Mithridates, he died old.
A Shropshire Lad (1896) no. 62

11 Cambridge has seen many strange sights. It has seen Wordsworth drunk and Porson sober. It is now destined to see a better scholar than Wordsworth and a better poet than Porson betwixt and between.
speech at University College, London, 29 March 1911, in R. W. Chambers *Man's Unconquerable Mind* (1939)

Samuel Houston 1793–1863
American politician and military leader

12 The North is determined to preserve this Union. They are not a fiery, impulsive people as you are, for they live in colder climates. But when they begin to move in a given direction . . . they move with the steady momentum and perseverance of a mighty avalanche.
in 1861, warning the people of Texas against secession
Geoffrey C. Ward *The Civil War* (1991) ch. 1

Geoffrey Howe 1926–
British Conservative politician
on Howe: see **Healey** *366:3*

13 It is rather like sending your opening batsmen to the crease only for them to find the moment that the first balls are bowled that their bats have been broken before the game by the team captain.
on the difficulties caused him as Foreign Secretary by the Margaret **Thatcher***'s anti-European views*
resignation speech as Deputy Prime Minister, in the House of Commons, 13 November 1990

14 The time has come for others to consider their own response to the tragic conflict of loyalties with which I have myself wrestled for perhaps too long.
resignation speech
in the House of Commons, 13 November 1990

Julia Ward Howe 1819–1910
American Unitarian lay preacher

15 Mine eyes have seen the glory of the coming of the Lord:
He is trampling out the vintage where the grapes of wrath are stored;
He hath loosed the fateful lightning of his terrible swift sword:
His truth is marching on.
'Battle Hymn of the Republic' (1862)

James Howell *c.*1594–1666
Anglo-Welsh man of letters

16 Some hold translations not unlike to be
The wrong side of a Turkey tapestry.
Familiar Letters (1645–55) bk. 1, no. 6

17 One hair of a woman can draw more than a hundred pair of oxen.
Familiar Letters (1645–55) bk. 2, no. 4; cf. **Proverbs** 595:37

1 The Netherlands have been for many years, as one may say, the very cockpit of Christendom.
Instructions for Foreign Travel (1642)

Frankie Howerd (Francis Alex Howard) 1922–92
British comedian

2 Such cruel glasses.
of Robin Day
in *That Was The Week That Was* (BBC television series, from 1963)

3 It's television, you see. If you are not on the thing every week, the public think you are either dead or deported.
attributed

Mary Howitt 1799–1888
English writer for children

4 Buttercups and daisies,
Oh, the pretty flowers;
Coming ere the springtime,
To tell of sunny hours.
'Buttercups and Daisies' (1838)

5 'Will you walk into my parlour?' said a spider to a fly:
''Tis the prettiest little parlour that ever you did spy.'
'The Spider and the Fly' (1834)

Edmond Hoyle 1672–1769
English writer on card-games

6 When in doubt, win the trick.
Hoyle's Games Improved (ed. Charles Jones, 1790) 'Twenty-four Short Rules for Learners'; though attributed to Hoyle, this may well have been an editorial addition by Jones, since it is not found in earlier editions

Fred Hoyle 1915–
English astrophysicist

7 Space isn't remote at all. It's only an hour's drive away if your car could go straight upwards.
in *Observer* 9 September 1979 'Sayings of the Week'

8 When I was young, the old regarded me as an outrageous young fellow, and now that I'm old the young regard me as an outrageous old fellow.
in *Scientific American* March 1995

9 There is a coherent plan to the universe, though I don't know what it's a plan for.
attributed

Elbert Hubbard 1859–1915
American writer
see also **Emerson** *300:3*

10 Never explain—your friends do not need it and your enemies will not believe you anyway.
The Motto Book (1907); cf. **Wodehouse** 824:21

11 Life is just one damned thing after another.
Philistine December 1909; often attributed to Frank Ward O'Malley

12 Editor: a person employed by a newspaper, whose business it is to separate the wheat from the chaff, and to see that the chaff is printed.
The Roycroft Dictionary (1914)

Frank McKinney ('Kin') Hubbard 1868–1930
American humorist

13 Classic music is th'kind that we keep thinkin'll turn into a tune.
Comments of Abe Martin and His Neighbors (1923)

14 It's no disgrace t'be poor, but it might as well be.
Short Furrows (1911)

Howard Hughes Jr. 1905–76
American industrialist, aviator and film producer

15 That man's ears make him look like a taxi-cab with both doors open.
of Clark Gable
Charles Higham and Joel Greenberg *Celluloid Muse* (1969)

Jimmy Hughes and **Frank Lake**

16 You'll get no promotion this side of the ocean,
So cheer up, my lads, Bless 'em all!
Bless 'em all! Bless 'em all! The long and the short and the tall.
'Bless 'Em All' (1940 song)

Langston Hughes 1902–67
American writer and poet

17 I, too, sing America.
I am the darker brother.
They send me to eat in the kitchen
When company comes.
But I laugh,
And eat well,
And grow strong.

Tomorrow
I'll sit at the table
When company comes
Nobody'll dare
Say to me,
'Eat in the kitchen'
Then.

Besides, they'll see how
beautiful I am
And be ashamed,—

I, too, am America.
'I, Too' in *Survey Graphic* March 1925

18 I've known rivers:
I've known rivers ancient as the world and older than the flow of human blood in human veins.
'The Negro Speaks of Rivers' (1921)

19 I bathed in the Euphrates when dawns were young.
I built my hut near the Congo and it lulled me to sleep.
I looked upon the Nile and raised the pyramids above it.

I heard the singing of the Mississippi when Abe Lincoln went down to New Orleans, and I've seen its muddy bosom turn all golden in the sunset.
'The Negro Speaks of Rivers' (1921)

1 'It's powerful,' he said.
'What?'
'That one drop of Negro blood—because just *one* drop of black blood makes a man coloured. *One* drop—you are a Negro!'
Simple Takes a Wife (1953)

2 I got the Weary Blues
And I can't be satisfied.
'Weary Blues' (1926)

Ted Hughes 1930–98

English poet
on Hughes: see **Heaney** *367:1*

3 Daylong this tomcat lies stretched flat
As an old rough mat, no mouth and no eyes,
Continual wars and wives are what
Have tattered his ears and battered his head.
'Esther's Tomcat' (1960)

4 It took the whole of Creation
To produce my foot, my each feather:
Now I hold Creation in my foot.
'Hawk Roosting' (1960)

5 Fourteen centuries have learned,
From charred remains, that what took place
When Alexandria's library burned
Brain-damaged the human race.
'Hear it Again' (1997)

6 I saw the horses:
Huge in the dense grey—ten together—
Megalith-still. They breathed, making no move,
With draped manes and tilted hind-hooves,
Making no sound.
I passed: not one snorted or jerked its head.
Grey silent fragments
Of a grey silent world.
'The Horses' (1957)

7 Adam ate the apple.
Eve ate Adam.
The serpent ate Eve.
This is the dark intestine.

The serpent, meanwhile,
Sleeps his meal off in Paradise—
Smiling to hear
God's querulous calling.
'Theology' (1967)

8 . . . With a sudden sharp hot stink of fox,
It enters the dark hole of the head.
'The Thought-Fox' (1957)

9 Ten years after your death
I meet on a page of your journal, as never before,
The shock of your joy.
'Visit' (1998)

10 Grape is my mulatto mother
In this frozen whited country.
'Wino' (1967)

11 Christianity deposes Mother Nature and begets, on her prostrate body, Science, which proceeds to destroy Nature.
in *Your Environment* Summer 1970

Thomas Hughes 1822–96

English lawyer, politician, and writer

12 Tom and his younger brothers as they grew up, went on playing with the village boys without the idea of equality or inequality (except in wrestling, running, and climbing) ever entering their heads, as it doesn't till it's put there by Jack Nastys or fine ladies' maids.
Tom Brown's Schooldays (1857) pt. 1, ch. 3

13 'I don't care a straw for Greek particles, or the digamma, no more does his mother. What is he sent to school for? . . . If he'll only turn out a brave, helpful, truth-telling Englishman, and a gentleman, and a Christian, that's all I want,' thought the Squire.
Tom Brown's Schooldays (1857) pt. 1, ch. 4

14 He never wants anything but what's right and fair; only when you come to settle what's right and fair, it's everything that he wants and nothing that you want. And that's his idea of a compromise. Give me the Brown compromise when I'm on his side.
Tom Brown's Schooldays (1857) pt. 2, ch. 2

15 It's more than a game. It's an institution.
of cricket
Tom Brown's Schooldays (1857) pt. 2, ch. 7

Victor Hugo 1802–85

French poet, novelist, and dramatist
on Hugo: see **Cocteau** *223:18,* **Gide** *336:19*

16 *Le mot, c'est le Verbe, et le Verbe, c'est Dieu.*
The word is the Verb, and the Verb is God.
Contemplations (1856) bk. 1, no. 8

17 *Souffrons, mais souffrons sur les cimes.*
If suffer we must, let's suffer on the heights.
Contemplations (1856) bk. 5, no. 26 'Les Malheureux'

18 *On résiste à l'invasion des armées; on ne résiste pas à l'invasion des idées.*
A stand can be made against invasion by an army; no stand can be made against invasion by an idea.
Histoire d'un Crime (written 1851–2, published 1877) pt. 5, sect. 10

19 *La symétrie, c'est l'ennui, et l'ennui est le fond même du deuil. Le désespoir baîlle.*
Symmetry is tedious, and tedium is the very basis of mourning. Despair yawns.
Les Misérables (1862) vol. 2, bk. 4, ch. 1

20 *Otez* Times is money, *que reste-t-il de l'Angleterre? ôtez* Cotton is king, *que reste-t-il d l'Amerique?*
Take away *time is money*, and what is left of England? take away *cotton is king*, and what is left of America?
Les Misérables (1862) 'Marius' bk. 4 ch. 4

21 *Étourdir de grelots l'esprit qui veut penser.*
To daze with little bells the spirit that would think.
Le Roi s'amuse (1833) act 2, sc. 2

1 *Jésus a pleuré, Voltaire a souri; c'est de cette larme divine et de ce sourire humain qu'est faite la douceur de la civilisation actuelle.* (Applaudissements prolongés.)

Jesus wept; Voltaire smiled. Of that divine tear and of that human smile the sweetness of present civilisation is composed. (*Hearty applause.*)

transcript of centenary oration on **Voltaire**, 30 May 1878, *Centenaire de Voltaire* (1878); cf. **Bible** 102:11

Hui-neng 638–713

Chinese philosopher, 6th Zen Patriarch

textual translations are those of Wong Mou-Lam, 1969

2 There is no Bodhi-tree,
Nor stand of mirror bright.
Since all is void,
Where can the dust alight?

Platform Scripture ch. 1

3 When you are thinking of neither good nor evil, what is at that particular moment, Venerable Sir, your real nature [original face]?

Platform Scripture ch. 1

4 When a pennant was blown about by the wind, two Bhikkus [monks] entered into a dispute as to what it was that was in motion, the wind or the pennant. As they could not settle their difference I submitted to them that it was neither, and that what actually moved was their own mind.

Platform Scripture ch. 1

5 Should we be so fortunate as to be followers of the Sudden School in this life,
In a sudden we shall see the Bhagavat of our Essence of Mind.
He who seeks the Buddha [from without] by practising certain doctrines
Knows not where the real Buddha is to be found.
He who is able to realize the Truth within his own mind
Has sown the seed of Buddhahood.

Platform Scripture ch. 1

David Hume 1711–76

Scottish philosopher

on Hume: see **Smith** *725:5*

6 Custom, then, is the great guide of human life.

An Enquiry Concerning Human Understanding (1748) sect. 5, pt. 1

7 If we take in our hand any volume; of divinity or school metaphysics, for instance; let us ask, *Does it contain any abstract reasoning concerning quantity or number?* No. *Does it contain any experimental reasoning, concerning matter of fact and existence?* No. Commit it then to the flames: for it can contain nothing but sophistry and illusion.

An Enquiry Concerning Human Understanding (1748) sect. 12, pt. 3

8 We soon learn that there is nothing mysterious or supernatural in the case, but that all proceeds from the usual propensity of mankind towards the marvellous, and that, though this inclination may at intervals receive a check from sense and learning, it can never be thoroughly extirpated from human nature.

An Enquiry Concerning Human Understanding (1748) 'Of Miracles' pt. 2

9 The Christian religion not only was at first attended with miracles, but even at this day cannot be believed by any reasonable person without one. Mere reason is insufficient to convince us of its veracity: and whoever is moved by faith to assent to it, is conscious of a continued miracle in his own person, which subverts all the principles of his understanding, and gives him a determination to believe what is most contrary to custom and experience.

An Enquiry Concerning Human Understanding (1748) 'Of Miracles' pt. 2

10 Avarice, the spur of industry, is so obstinate a passion, and works its way through so many real dangers and difficulties, that it is not likely to be scared by an imaginary danger, which is so small that it scarcely admits of calculation.

Essays: Moral and Political (1741–2) 'Of Civil Liberty'

11 Money . . . is none of the wheels of trade: it is the oil which renders the motion of the wheels more smooth and easy.

Essays: Moral and Political (1741–2) 'Of Money'

12 How many frivolous quarrels and disgusts are there, which people of common prudence endeavour to forget, when they lie under the necessity of passing their lives together; but which would soon inflame into the most deadly hatred, were they pursued to the utmost, under the prospect of an easy separation?

Essays: Moral and Political (1741–2) 'Of Polygamy and Divorces'

13 A little miss, dressed in a new gown for a dancing school ball, receives as complete enjoyment as the greatest orator, who triumphs in the splendour of his eloquence, while he governs the passions and resolutions of a numerous assembly.

Essays: Moral and Political (1741–2) 'The Sceptic'

14 Should it be said, that, by living under the dominion of a prince, which one might leave, every individual has given a tacit assent to his authority . . . We may as well assert, that a man by remaining in a vessel, freely consents to the dominion of the master; though he was carried on board while asleep, and must leap into the ocean, and perish, the moment he leaves her.

Essays, Moral, Political, and Literary (ed. T. H. Green and T. H. Grose, 1875) 'Of the Original Contract' (1748)

15 In all ages of the world, priests have been enemies of liberty.

Essays, Moral, Political, and Literary (ed. T. H. Green and T. H. Grose, 1875) 'Of the Parties of Great Britain' (1741–2)

16 The heart of man is made to reconcile the most glaring contradictions.

Essays, Moral, Political, and Literary (ed. T. H. Green and T. H. Grose, 1875) 'Of the Parties of Great Britain' (1741–2)

17 In all matters of opinion and science . . . the difference between men is . . . oftener found to lie in generals than in particulars; and to be less in reality than in appearance. An explanation of the terms commonly ends the controversy, and the disputants are surprised to find that they had been quarrelling, while at bottom they agreed in their judgement.

Essays, Moral, Political, and Literary (ed. T. H. Green and T. H. Grose, 1875) 'Of the Standard of Taste' (1757)

1 Beauty is no quality in things themselves. It exists merely in the mind which contemplates them.

Essays, Moral, Political, and Literary (ed. T. H. Green and T. H. Grose, 1875) 'Of the Standard of Taste' (1757)

2 Opposing one species of superstition to another, set them a quarrelling; while we ourselves, during their fury and contention, happily make our escape into the calm, though obscure, regions of philosophy.

Four Dissertations (1757) 'The Natural History of Religion' sect. 15

3 Never literary attempt was more unfortunate than my Treatise of Human Nature. It fell *dead-born from the press.*

My Own Life (1777) ch. 1

4 It is a just political maxim, that every man must be supposed a knave.

Political Discourses (1751) essay 6

5 Poets . . . though liars by profession, always endeavour to give an air of truth to their fictions.

A Treatise upon Human Nature (1739) bk. 1, pt. 3

6 Reason is, and ought only to be the slave of the passions, and can never pretend to any other office than to serve and obey them.

A Treatise upon Human Nature (1739) bk. 2, pt. 3

7 It is not contrary to reason to prefer the destruction of the whole world to the scratching of my finger.

A Treatise upon Human Nature (1739) bk. 2, pt. 3

8 In every system of morality, which I have hitherto met with, I have always remarked, that the author proceeds for some time in the ordinary way of reasoning, and establishes the being of a god, or makes observations concerning human affairs; when of a sudden I am surprized to find that instead of the usual copulations of proposition, *is* and *is not*, I meet with no proposition that is not connected with an *ought* or an *ought not*. This change is imperceptible; but it is, however, of the last consequence.

A Treatise upon Human Nature (1739) bk. 3, pt. 1

Hubert Humphrey 1911–78

American Democratic politician

9 Here we are the way politics ought to be in America, the politics of happiness, the politics of purpose and the politics of joy.

speech in Washington, 27 April 1968, in *New York Times* 28 April 1968

G. W. Hunt *c.*1829–1904

English composer of music-hall songs

10 We don't want to fight, but, by jingo if we do,
We've got the ships, we've got the men, we've got the money too.
We've fought the Bear before, and while Britons shall be true,
The Russians shall not have Constinople.

'We Don't Want to Fight' (1878 music hall song)

Leigh Hunt 1784–1859

English poet and essayist

on Hunt: see **Shelley** *711:24*

11 Abou Ben Adhem (may his tribe increase!)
Awoke one night from a deep dream of peace,
And saw, within the moonlight in his room,
Making it rich, and like a lily in bloom,
An angel writing in a book of gold:—
Exceeding peace had made Ben Adhem bold,
And to the presence in the room he said,
'What writest thou?'—The vision raised its head,
And with a look made of all sweet accord,
Answered, 'The names of those who love the Lord.'

'Abou Ben Adhem' (1838)

12 Write me as one that loves his fellow-men.

'Abou Ben Adhem' (1838)

13 You strange, astonished-looking, angle-faced,
Dreary-mouthed, gaping wretches of the sea.

'The Fish, the Man, and the Spirit' (1836)

14 The laughing queen that caught the world's great hands.

referring to Cleopatra

'The Nile' (1818)

15 Jenny kissed me when we met,
Jumping from the chair she sat in;
Time, you thief, who love to get
Sweets into your list, put that in:
Say I'm weary, say I'm sad,
Say that health and wealth have missed me,
Say I'm growing old, but add,
Jenny kissed me.

'Rondeau' (1838)

16 Stolen sweets are always sweeter,
Stolen kisses much completer,
Stolen looks are nice in chapels,
Stolen, stolen, be your apples.

'Song of Fairies Robbing an Orchard' (1830)

17 The two divinest things this world has got,
A lovely woman in a rural spot!

'The Story of Rimini' (1816) canto 3, l. 257

18 His forehead was prodigious—a great piece of placid marble; and his fine eyes, in which all the activity of his mind seemed to concentrate, moved under it with a sprightly ease, as if it was pastime to them to carry all that thought.

of **Coleridge**

Autobiography (1850) ch. 16

19 It is the entire man that writes and thinks, and not merely the head. His leg has often as much to do with it as his head—the state of his calves, his vitals and his nerves.

Stories in Verse (1855) preface

20 Poetry, in the most comprehensive application of the term, I take to be the flower of any kind of

experience, rooted in truth, and issuing forth into beauty.
The Story of Rimini (1832 ed.) preface

1 The pretension is nothing; the performance every thing. A good apple is better than an insipid peach.
The Story of Rimini (1832 ed.) preface

2 A mere gossiping entertainment: a few child's squalls, a few mumbled amens, and a few mumbled cakes, and a few smirks accompanied by a few fees.
on the christening of his godson
letter to Marianne Kent, February 1806; in T. L. Hunt *Correspondence of Leigh Hunt* (1862) vol. 1

3 Never lay yourself open to what is called conviction: you might as well open your waist-coat to receive a knock-down blow.
in *The Examiner* 6 March 1808 'Rules for the Conduct of Newspaper Editors'

4 A playful moderation in politics is just as absurd as a remonstrative whisper to a mob.
in *The Examiner* 6 March 1808 'Rules for the Conduct of Newspaper Editors'

5 This Adonis in loveliness was a corpulent man of fifty.
of the Prince Regent
in *The Examiner* 22 March 1812

6 A pleasure so exquisite as almost to amount to pain.
on receiving 'a glorious batch of Examiners'
letter to Alexander Ireland, 2 June 1848, in T. L. Hunt *Correspondence of Leigh Hunt* (1862) vol. 2

Anne Hunter 1742–1821
Scottish poet

7 My mother bids me bind my hair
With bands of rosy hue,
Tie up my sleeves with ribbons rare,
And lace my bodice blue.
'A Pastoral Song' (1794)

Robert Hunter 1941–
Canadian writer

8 The word *Greenpeace* had a ring to it—it conjured images of Eden; it said ecology and antiwar in two syllables; it fit easily into even a one-column headline.
Warriors of the Rainbow (1979); cf. **Darnell** 250:10

William Hunter 1718–83
Scottish obstetrician

9 Some physiologists will have it that the stomach is a mill;—others, that it is a fermenting vat;—others again that it is a stew-pan;—but in my view of the matter, it is neither a mill, a fermenting vat, nor a stew-pan—but a *stomach*, gentlemen, a *stomach*.
MS note from his lectures, in J. A. Paris *A Treatise on Diet* (1824) epigraph

Herman Hupfeld 1894–1951
American songwriter

10 You must remember this, a kiss is still a kiss,
A sigh is just a sigh;
The fundamental things apply,
As time goes by.
'As Time Goes By' (1931 song); cf. **Misquotations** 522:6

Zora Neale Hurston *c.*1901–60
American writer

11 I do not weep at the world—I am too busy sharpening my oyster knife.
How It Feels to Be Colored Me (1928)

John Huss *c.*1372–1415
Bohemian preacher and reformer

12 *O sancta simplicitas!*
O holy simplicity!
at the stake, seeing an aged peasant bringing a bundle of twigs to throw on the pile
J. W. Zincgreff and J. L. Weidner *Apophthegmata* (Amsterdam, 1653) pt. 3; cf. **Jerome** 406:14

Saddam Hussein 1937–
President of Iraq from 1979

13 The mother of battles.
popular interpretation of his description of the approaching Gulf War; in The Times *7 January 1991 it was reported that he had no intention of relinquishing Kuwait and was ready for the 'mother of all wars'*
speech in Baghdad, 6 January 1991

Francis Hutcheson 1694–1746
Scottish philosopher

14 Wisdom denotes the pursuing of the best ends by the best means.
An Inquiry into the Original of our Ideas of Beauty and Virtue (1725) Treatise 1, sect. 5, subsect. 16

15 That action is best, which procures the greatest happiness for the greatest numbers.
An Inquiry into the Original of our Ideas of Beauty and Virtue (1725) Treatise 2, sect. 3, subsect. 8; cf. **Bentham** 66:18

Aldous Huxley 1894–1963
English novelist
see also ***Borrowed titles*** *144:1*

16 There are few who would not rather be taken in adultery than in provincialism.
Antic Hay (1923) ch. 10

17 Official dignity tends to increase in inverse ratio to the importance of the country in which the office is held.
Beyond the Mexique Bay (1934)

18 The proper study of mankind is books.
Crome Yellow (1921) ch. 28; cf. **Pope** 585:19

1 Too much consistency is as bad for the mind as it is for the body. Consistency is contrary to nature, contrary to life. The only completely consistent people are the dead.
Do What You Will (1929) 'Wordsworth in the Tropics'

2 The end cannot justify the means, for the simple and obvious reason that the means employed determine the nature of the ends produced.
Ends and Means (1937) ch. 1

3 So long as men worship the Caesars and Napoleons, Caesars and Napoleons will duly arise and make them miserable.
Ends and Means (1937) ch. 8

4 Chastity—the most unnatural of all the sexual perversions.
Eyeless in Gaza (1936) ch. 27

5 Several excuses are always less convincing than one.
Point Counter Point (1928) ch. 1

6 A million million spermatozoa,
All of them alive:
Out of their cataclysm but one poor Noah
Dare hope to survive.
And among that billion minus one
Might have chanced to be
Shakespeare, another Newton, a new Donne—
But the One was Me.
'Fifth Philosopher's Song' (1920)

7 Ragtime . . . but when the wearied Band
Swoons to a waltz, I take her hand,
And there we sit in peaceful calm,
Quietly sweating palm to palm.
'Frascati's' (1920)

8 Beauty for some provides escape,
Who gain a happiness in eyeing
The gorgeous buttocks of the ape
Or Autumn sunsets exquisitely dying.
'Ninth Philosopher's Song' (1920)

Julian Huxley 1887–1975
English biologist

9 Operationally, God is beginning to resemble not a ruler but the last fading smile of a cosmic Cheshire cat.
Religion without Revelation (1957 ed.) ch. 3; cf. **Carroll** 189:16

T. H. Huxley 1825–95
English biologist

10 Most of my colleagues [in the Metaphysical Society] were *-ists* of one sort or another; and, however kind and friendly they might be, I, the man without a rag of a label to cover himself with, could not fail to have some of the uneasy feelings which must have beset the historical fox when, after leaving the trap in which his tail remained, he presented himself to his normally elongated companions. So I took thought, and invented what I conceived to be the appropriate title of 'agnostic'.
Collected Essays (1893–4) 'Agnosticism'

11 The great tragedy of Science—the slaying of a beautiful hypothesis by an ugly fact.
Collected Essays (1893–4) 'Biogenesis and Abiogenesis'

12 Science is nothing but trained and organized common sense, differing from the latter only as a veteran may differ from a raw recruit: and its methods differ from those of common sense only as far as the guardsman's cut and thrust differ from the manner in which a savage wields his club.
Collected Essays (1893–4) 'The Method of Zadig'

13 If some great Power would agree to make me always think what is true and do what is right, on condition of being turned into a sort of clock and wound up every morning before I got out of bed, I should instantly close with the offer.
Collected Essays (1893–4) 'On Descartes' *Discourse on Method*' (written 1870)

14 If a little knowledge is dangerous, where is the man who has so much as to be out of danger?
Collected Essays vol. 3 (1895) 'On Elementary Instruction in Physiology' (written 1877)

15 The chessboard is the world; the pieces are the phenomena of the universe; the rules of the game are what we call the laws of Nature. The player on the other side is hidden from us. We know that his play is always fair, just, and patient. But also we know, to our cost, that he never overlooks a mistake, or makes the smallest allowance for ignorance.
Lay Sermons, Addresses, and Reviews (1870) 'A Liberal Education'

16 The necessity of making things plain to uninstructed people was one of the very best means of clearing up the obscure corners in one's own mind.
Man's Place in Nature (1894 ed.) preface

17 It is the customary fate of new truths to begin as heresies and to end as superstitions.
Science and Culture and Other Essays (1881) 'The Coming of Age of the Origin of Species'

18 Irrationally held truths may be more harmful than reasoned errors.
Science and Culture and Other Essays (1881) 'The Coming of Age of the Origin of Species'

19 Logical consequences are the scarecrows of fools and the beacons of wise men.
Science and Culture and Other Essays (1881) 'On the Hypothesis that Animals are Automata'

20 I asserted—and I repeat—that a man has no reason to be ashamed of having an ape for his grandfather. If there were an ancestor whom I should feel shame in recalling it would rather be a *man*—a man of restless and versatile intellect—who, not content with an equivocal success in his own sphere of activity, plunges into scientific questions with which he has no real acquaintance, only to obscure them by an aimless rhetoric, and distract the attention of his hearers from the real point at issue by eloquent digressions and skilled appeals to religious prejudice.

replying to Bishop Samuel ***Wilberforce*** *in the debate on* ***Darwin****'s theory of evolution; see* ***Wilberforce*** *817:2*

meeting of the British Association in Oxford, 30 June 1860; letter from J. R. Green to Professor Boyd Dawkins in Leonard Huxley (ed.) *Life and Letters of Thomas Henry Huxley* (1900)

1 I am too much of a sceptic to deny the possibility of anything.

letter to Herbert Spencer, 22 March 1886, in Leonard Huxley *Life and Letters of Thomas Henry Huxley* (1900) vol. 2, ch. 8

Edward Hyde see **Earl of Clarendon**

Nicholas Hytner 1956–

English theatre and film director

2 If you gave him a good script, actors and technicians, Mickey Mouse could direct a movie.

in an interview, *Daily Telegraph* 24 February 1994, prior to the UK release of his film *The Crucible*

Dolores Ibarruri ('La Pasionaria') 1895–1989

Spanish Communist leader

3 *Il vaut mieux mourir debout que de vivre à genoux!*

It is better to die on your feet than to live on your knees.

also attributed to Emiliano ***Zapata***

speech in Paris, 3 September 1936, in *L'Humanité* 4 September 1936

4 *No pasarán.*

They shall not pass.

radio broadcast, Madrid, 19 July 1936, in *Speeches and Articles 1936–38* (1938); cf. **Military sayings** 508:10

Henrik Ibsen 1828–1906

Norwegian dramatist

5 The worst enemy of truth and freedom in our society is the compact majority. Yes, the damned, compact, liberal majority.

An Enemy of the People (1882) act 4

6 The majority never has right on its side.

An Enemy of the People (1882) act 4; cf. **Dillon** 267:15

7 You should never have your best trousers on when you go out to fight for freedom and truth.

An Enemy of the People (1882) act 5

8 Mother, give me the sun.

Ghosts (1881) act 3

9 But good God, people don't do such things!

Hedda Gabler (1890) act 4

10 Castles in the air—they are so easy to take refuge in. And easy to build, too.

The Master Builder (1892) act 3

11 What ought a man to be? Well, my short answer is 'himself'.

Peer Gynt (1867) act 4

12 Take the life-lie away from the average man and straight away you take away his happiness.

The Wild Duck (1884) act 5

13 Prose is for ideas, verse for visions.

'Rhymed Letter for Fru Heiberg' (1871)

Ice Cube 1970–

American rap musician

14 If I'm more of an influence to your son as a rapper than you are as a father . . . you got to look at yourself as a parent.

to Mike Sager in *Rolling Stone* 4 October 1990

Ice-T 1958–

American rap musician

15 Passion makes the world go round. Love just makes it a safer place.

The Ice Opinion (as told to Heidi Sigmund, 1994) ch. 4

16 When they call you articulate, that's another way of saying 'He talks good for a black guy'.

in *Independent* 30 December 1995 'Interviews of the Year'

St Ignatius Loyola 1491–1556

Spanish theologian, founder of the Jesuits

17 Teach us, good Lord, to serve Thee as Thou deservest:
To give and not to count the cost;
To fight and not to heed the wounds;
To toil and not to seek for rest;
To labour and not to ask for any reward
Save that of knowing that we do Thy will.

'Prayer for Generosity' (1548)

I-Hsüan d. 867

Chinese monk and Zen master

18 Seekers of the Way. In Buddhism no effort is necessary. All one has to do is to do nothing except to move his bowels, urinate, put on his clothing, eat his meals, and lie down if he is tired. The stupid will laugh at him, but the wise will understand.

Recorded Conversations of Zen Master I-Hsüan v. 5

19 Kill anything that you happen on. Kill the Buddha if you happen to meet him . . . Kill your parents or relatives if you happen to meet them. Only then can you be free, not bound by material things, and absolutely free and at ease.

Recorded Conversations of Zen Master I-Hsüan v. 6

Francis Iles see **Opening lines** 555:26

Ivan Illich 1926–

American sociologist

20 In a consumer society there are inevitably two kinds of slaves: the prisoners of addiction and the prisoners of envy.

Tools for Conviviality (1973) ch. 3

Mick Imlah 1956–

British poet

21 Oh, foolish boys!
The English elephant

Never lies!
'Tusking' (1988)

Gary Indiana
American writer

1 We used to say: How can we live like this? And now the question really is: How can we die like this?
of Aids
Horse Crazy (1989)

Charles Inge 1868–1957

2 This very remarkable man
Commends a most practical plan:
You can do what you want
If you don't think you can't,
So don't think you can't think you can.
'On Monsieur Coué' (1928); cf. **Coué** 238:4

William Ralph Inge 1860–1954
English writer; Dean of St. Paul's, 1911–34

3 The enemies of Freedom do not argue; they shout and they shoot.
End of an Age (1948) ch. 4

4 The effect of boredom on a large scale in history is underestimated. It is a main cause of revolutions, and would soon bring to an end all the static Utopias and the farmyard civilization of the Fabians.
End of an Age (1948) ch. 6

5 To become a popular religion, it is only necessary for a superstition to enslave a philosophy.
Idea of Progress (Romanes Lecture delivered at Oxford, 27 May 1920)

6 Many people believe that they are attracted by God, or by Nature, when they are only repelled by man.
More Lay Thoughts of a Dean (1931) pt. 4, ch. 1

7 It takes in reality only one to make a quarrel. It is useless for the sheep to pass resolutions in favour of vegetarianism, while the wolf remains of a different opinion.
Outspoken Essays: First Series (1919) 'Patriotism'

8 The nations which have put mankind and posterity most in their debt have been small states—Israel, Athens, Florence, Elizabethan England.
Outspoken Essays: Second Series (1922) 'State, visible and invisible'

9 A man may build himself a throne of bayonets, but he cannot sit on it.
a similar image was used by Boris Yeltsin at the time of the failed military coup in Russia, August 1991
Philosophy of Plotinus (1923) vol. 2, Lecture 22

Jean Ingelow 1820–97
English poet

10 Play uppe 'The Brides of Enderby'.
'The High Tide on the Coast of Lincolnshire, 1571' (1863)

11 'Cusha! Cusha! Cusha!' calling
E'er the early dews were falling,
Farre away I heard her song.
'The High Tide on the Coast of Lincolnshire, 1571' (1863)

12 But each will mourn her own (she saith)
And sweeter woman ne'er drew breath
Than my sonne's wife, Elizabeth.
'The High Tide on the Coast of Lincolnshire, 1571' (1863)

Robert G. Ingersoll 1833–99
American agnostic

13 An honest God is the noblest work of man.
The Gods (1876) pt. 1; cf. **Pope** 586:1

14 In nature there are neither rewards nor punishments—there are consequences.
Some Reasons Why (1881) pt. 8 'The New Testament'

Bernard Ingham 1932–
British journalist and public relations specialist

15 Blood sport is brought to its ultimate refinement in the gossip columns.
speech, 5 February 1986

16 The media . . . is like an oil painting. Close up, it looks like nothing on earth. Stand back and you get the drift.
speech to the Parliamentary Press Gallery, February 1990

John Kells Ingram 1823–1907
Irish social philosopher and songwriter

17 They rose in dark and evil days.
'The Memory of the Dead' (1843)

18 Who fears to speak of Ninety-Eight?
Who blushes at the name?
'The Memory of the Dead' (1843)

J. A. D. Ingres 1780–1867
French painter

19 *Le dessin est la probité de l'art.*
Drawing is the true test of art.
Pensées d'Ingres (1922)

Eugène Ionesco 1912–94
French dramatist

20 *C'est une chose anormale de vivre.*
Living is abnormal.
Le Rhinocéros (1959) act 1

21 *Tu ne prévois les événements que lorsqu'ils sont déjà arrivés.*
You can only predict things after they have happened.
Le Rhinocéros (1959) act 3

22 *Un fonctionnaire ne plaisante pas.*
A civil servant doesn't make jokes.
Tueur sans gages (The Killer, 1958) act 1

St Irenaeus *c.*130–*c.*200 AD
Greek theologian

23 The glory of God is a man fully alive.
attributed

Weldon J. Irvine

American songwriter

1 Young, gifted and black.
title of song (1969); cf. **Hansberry** 359:12

Washington Irving 1783–1859

American writer

2 A sharp tongue is the only edged tool that grows keener with constant use.
The Sketch Book (1820) 'Rip Van Winkle'

3 There is a certain relief in change, even though it be from bad to worse . . . it is often a comfort to shift one's position and be bruised in a new place.
Tales of a Traveller (1824) 'To the Reader'

4 The almighty dollar, that great object of universal devotion.
Wolfert's Roost (1855) 'The Creole Village'

Anne Ingram, Lady Irwin c.1696–1764

English poet

5 A female mind like a rude fallow lies;
No seed is sown, but weeds spontaneous rise.
As well might we expect, in winter, spring,
As land untilled a fruitful crop should bring.
'An Epistle to Mr Pope. Occasioned by his Characters of Women' in the *Gentleman's Magazine* (1736)

6 Untaught the noble end of glorious truth,
Bred to deceive even from their earliest youth.
'An Epistle to Mr Pope. Occasioned by his Characters of Women' in the *Gentleman's Magazine* (1736)

Christopher Isherwood 1904–86

English novelist
see also **Auden** *33:24*

7 The common cormorant (or shag)
Lays eggs inside a paper bag,
You follow the idea, no doubt?
It's to keep the lightning out.

But what these unobservant birds
Have never thought of, is that herds
Of wandering bears might come with buns
And steal the bags to hold the crumbs.
'The Common Cormorant' (written c.1925)

8 I am a camera with its shutter open, quite passive, recording, not thinking.
Goodbye to Berlin (1939) 'Berlin Diary' Autumn 1930

9 Here, gossip achieves the epigrammatic significance of poetry. To keep such a diary is to render a real service to the future.
of the Goncourt Brothers' Journals
diary, 5 July 1940

Alec Issigonis 1906–88

British engineer

10 A camel is a horse designed by a committee.
on his dislike of working in teams
in *Guardian* 14 January 1991 'Notes and Queries'; attributed

Charles Ives 1874–1954

American composer

11 Beauty in music is too often confused with something that lets the ears lie back in an easy chair.
Joseph Machlis *Introduction to Contemporary Music* (1963)

Alija Izetbegović 1925–

Bosnian statesman; President of Bosnia and Herzegovina since 1990

12 And to my people I say, this may not be a just peace, but it is more just than a continuation of war.
after signing the Dayton accord with representatives of Serbia and Croatia
in Dayton, Ohio, 21 November 1995

Andrew Jackson 1767–1845

American Democratic statesman; 7th President of the US, 1829–37

13 Our Federal Union: it must be preserved.
toast given on the Jefferson Birthday Celebration, 13 April 1830; in Thomas Hart Benton *Thirty Years' View* (1856) vol. 1

14 Each public officer who takes an oath to support the constitution swears that he will support it as he understands it, and not as it is understood by others.
vetoing the bill to re-charter the Bank of the United States
Presidential message, 10 July 1832, in H. S. Commager (ed.) *Documents of American History* vol. 1 (1963)

15 You are uneasy; you never sailed with *me* before, I see.
James Parton *Life of Jackson* (1860) vol. 3, ch. 35

Holbrook Jackson 1874–1948

English writer and critic

16 Pedantry is the dotage of knowledge.
Anatomy of Bibliomania (1930) vol. 1

Jesse Jackson 1941–

American Democratic politician and clergyman

17 When I look out at this convention, I see the face of America, red, yellow, brown, black, and white. We are all precious in God's sight—the real rainbow coalition.
speech at Democratic National Convention, Atlanta, 19 July 1988

Michael Jackson 1958–

American pop singer

18 Before you judge me, try hard to love me, look within your heart
Then ask,—have you seen my childhood?
'Childhood' (1995 song)

Robert H. Jackson 1892–1954

American lawyer and judge

19 That four great nations, flushed with victory and stung with injury, stay the hands of vengeance and

voluntarily submit their captive enemies to the judgement of the law, is one of the most significant tributes that Power has ever paid to Reason.
opening statement for the prosecution at Nuremberg
before the International Military Tribunal in Nuremberg, 21 November 1945

Joe Jacobs 1896–1940
American boxing manager

1 We was robbed!
after Jack Sharkey beat Max Schmeling (of whom Jacobs was manager) in the heavyweight title fight, 21 June 1932
Peter Heller *In This Corner* (1975)

2 I should of stood in bed.
after leaving his sick-bed to attend the World Baseball Series in Detroit, 1935, and betting on the losers
John Lardner *Strong Cigars* (1951)

Jacopone da Todi c.1230–1306
Franciscan lay brother

3 *Stabat Mater dolorosa,*
Iuxta crucem lacrimosa,
Dum pendebat filius.

At the cross her station keeping,
Stood the mournful Mother weeping,
Where he hung, the dying Lord.
'Stabat Mater dolorosa', ascribed also to Pope Innocent III and others (translation based on that of E. Caswall in *Lyra Catholica*, 1849)

Mick Jagger 1943– and Keith Richards 1943–
English rock musicians

4 Get off of my cloud.
title of song (1966)

5 Mother needs something today to calm her down,
And though she's not really ill,
There's a little yellow pill:
She goes running for the shelter
Of a mother's little helper,
And it helps her on her way,
Gets her through her busy day.
'Mother's Little Helper' (1966 song)

6 I can't get no satisfaction
I can't get no girl reaction.
'(I Can't Get No) Satisfaction' (1965 song)

7 Ev'rywhere I hear the sound of marching, charging feet, boy,
'Cause summer's here and the time is right for fighting in the street, boy.
But what can a poor boy do
Except to sing for a rock 'n' roll band,
'Cause in sleepy London town
There's just no place for a street fighting man!
'Street Fighting Man' (1968 song)

8 Please allow me to introduce myself
I'm a man of wealth and taste
I've been around for a long, long year
Stole many a man's soul and faith
And I was round when Jesus Christ
Had his moments of doubt and pain
Made damn sure that Pilate
Washed his hands and sealed his fate
Pleased to meet you, hope you guess my name
But what's puzzling you
Is the nature of my game.
'Sympathy for the Devil' (1968 song)

9 I shouted out 'Who killed the Kennedys?'
When after all, it was you and me.
'Sympathy for the Devil' (1968 song)

Richard Jago 1715–81
English poet

10 With leaden foot time creeps along
While Delia is away.
'Absence'

Jaina Sutras
Indian tradition, founded in the 6th century BC
textual translations are those of H. Jacobi, 1884

11 He believes in soul, believes in the world, believes in reward, believes in action . . . these are all the causes of sin, which must be comprehended and renounced.
Ācārānga Sutra bk. 1, lecture 1, lesson 1, v. 5

12 There are some who, of a truth, know this [causing injury] to be the bondage, the delusion, the death, the hell.
Ācārānga Sutra bk. 1, lecture 1, lesson 2, v. 4

13 He who sees by himself, needs no instruction. But the miserable, afflicted fool who delights in pleasures and whose miseries do not cease, is turned round in the whirl of pains.
Ācārānga Sutra bk. 1, lecture 2, lesson 3, v. 6

14 The world is greatly troubled by women.
Ācārānga Sutra bk. 1, lecture 2, lesson 4, v. 3

15 A wise man should avoid wrath, pride, deceit, greed, love, hate, delusion, conception, birth, death, hell, animal existence, and pain.
Ācārānga Sutra bk. 1, lecture 3, lesson 4, v. 4

16 All breathing, existing, living, sentient creatures should not be slain, nor treated with violence, nor abused, nor tormented, nor driven away.
This is the pure, unchangeable, eternal law.
Ācārānga Sutra bk. 1, lecture 4, lesson 1, v 1.

17 All the professors, conversant with pain, preach renunciation.
Ācārānga Sutra bk. 1, lecture 4, lesson 3, v. 2

18 Four things of paramount value are difficult to obtain here by a living being: human birth, instruction in the Law, belief in it, and energy in self-control.
Uttarādhyayana lecture 3, v. 1

19 These two ways of life ending with death have been declared: death with one's will and death against one's will.
Death against one's will is that of ignorant men . . . death with one's will is that of wise men.
Uttarādhyayana lecture 5, v. 2

1 There are five causes which render wholesome discipline impossible: egoism, delusion, carelessness, illness, and idleness.
Uttarādhyayana lecture 11, v. 3

2 He who adopts the law in the intention to live as a monk, should live in company, upright, and free from desire; he should abandon his former connections, and not longing for pleasures, he should wander about as an unknown beggar; then he is a true monk.
Uttarādhyayana lecture 15, v. 1

3 By the adoration of the twenty-four Jinas the soul arrives at purity of faith.
Uttarādhyayana lecture 29, v. 9

4 By renouncing his body he acquires the pre-eminent virtues of the Siddhas, by the possession of which he goes to the highest region of the universe, and becomes absolutely happy.
Uttarādhyayana lecture 29, v. 38

5 A monk destroys by austerities the bad karma which he had acquired by love and hatred.
Uttarādhyayana lecture 30, v. 1

6 There are three ways of committing sins: by one's own activity, by commission, by approval.
Sūtrakritānga bk. 1, lecture 1, ch. 3, v. 26

7 This is the quintessence of wisdom: not to kill anything. Know this to be the legitimate conclusion from the principle of the reciprocity with regard to non-killing.
Sūtrakritānga bk. 1, lecture 1, ch. 4, v. 10

8 Exert and control yourself! For it is not easy to walk on ways where there are minutely small animals.
Sūtrakritānga bk. 1, lecture 2, ch. 1, v. 11

9 Know this to be thus as I [Mahāvīra] have told you, because I am the Saviour.
Sūtrakritānga bk. 1, lecture 16, v. 6

10 This creed of the Nirgranthas [Jains] is true, supreme, excellent, full of virtues, right, pure, it removes doubts, it is the road to perfection, liberation, Nirvana.
Sūtrakritānga bk. 2, lecture 7, v. 15

James I (James VI of Scotland) 1566–1625

King of Scotland from 1567 and of England from 1603
on James: see ***Henri IV*** *370:7*

11 A branch of the sin of drunkenness, which is the root of all sins.
A Counterblast to Tobacco (1604)

12 A custom loathsome to the eye, hateful to the nose, harmful to the brain, dangerous to the lungs, and in the black, stinking fume thereof, nearest resembling the horrible Stygian smoke of the pit that is bottomless.
A Counterblast to Tobacco (1604)

13 No bishop, no King.
to a deputation of Presbyterians from the Church of Scotland, seeking religious tolerance in England
W. Barlow *Sum and Substance of the Conference* (1604)

14 The state of monarchy is the supremest thing upon earth; for kings are not only God's lieutenants upon earth, and sit upon God's throne, but even by God himself they are called gods.
speech to Parliament, 21 March 1610, in *Works* (1616)

15 The king is truly *parens patriae*, the politique father of his people.
speech to Parliament, 21 March 1610, in *Works* (1616)

16 I will govern according to the common weal, but not according to the common will.
December, 1621, in J. R. Green *History of the English People* vol. 3 (1879) bk. 7, ch. 4

17 Dr Donne's verses are like the peace of God; they pass all understanding.
remark recorded by Archdeacon Plume (1630–1704); cf. **Bible** 108:24

18 I made the carles lords, but who made the carlines ladies?
E. Grenville Murray *Embassies and Foreign Courts* (1855) ch. 14

19 You cannot name any example in any heathen author but I will better it in Scripture.
'Crumms Fal'n From King James's Table' no. 10, in E. F. Rimbault (ed.) *Miscellaneous Works of Sir Thomas Overbury* (1856)

James V 1512–42

King of Scotland from 1513

20 It came with a lass, and it will pass with a lass.
of the crown of Scotland, on learning of the birth of ***Mary*** *Queen of Scots, December 1542*
Robert Lindsay of Pitscottie (*c.*1500–65) *History of Scotland* (1728)

Evan James

Welsh bard

21 The land of my fathers, how fair is thy fame.
'Land of My Fathers' (1856), translated by W. G. Rothery

22 Wales, Wales, sweet are thy hills and vales,
Thy speech, thy song,
To thee belong,
O may they live ever in Wales.
'Land of My Fathers' (1856)

Henry James 1843–1916

American novelist, brother of William ***James***
on James: see ***Guedalla*** *354:12,* ***Maugham*** *501:16,* ***Wells*** *810:6*

23 The ever-importunate murmur, 'Dramatize it, dramatize it!'
The Altar of the Dead (1909 ed.) preface

24 The Story is just the spoiled child of art.
The Ambassadors (1909 ed.) preface

25 Live all you can; it's a mistake not to. It doesn't so much matter what you do in particular, so long as you have your life. If you haven't had that, what *have* you had?
The Ambassadors (1903) bk. 5, ch. 11

26 The balloon of experience is in fact of course tied to the earth, and under that necessity we swing,

thanks to a rope of remarkable length, in the more or less commodious car of the imagination; but it is by the rope we know where we are, and from the moment that cable is cut we are at large and unrelated.
The American (1909 ed.) preface

1 The historian, essentially, wants more documents than he can really use; the dramatist only wants more liberties than he can really take.
The Aspern Papers (1909 ed.) preface

2 Most English talk is a quadrille in a sentry-box.
The Awkward Age (1899) bk. 5, ch. 19

3 Vereker's secret, my dear man—the general intention of his books: the string the pearls were strung on, the buried treasure, the figure in the carpet.
The Figure in the Carpet (1896) ch. 11

4 One might enumerate the items of high civilization, as it exists in other countries, which are absent from the texture of American life, until it should become a wonder to know what was left. No State, in the European sense of the word, and indeed barely a specific national name. No sovereign, no court, no personal loyalty, no aristocracy, no church, no clergy, no army, no diplomatic service, no country gentlemen, no palaces, no castles, nor manors, nor old country houses, nor parsonages, nor thatched cottages, nor ivied ruins; no cathedrals nor abbeys, nor little Norman churches; no great universities nor public schools—no Oxford, nor Eton, nor Harrow; no literature, no novels, no museums, no pictures, no political society, no sporting class—no Epsom nor Ascot! . . . The natural remark in the almost lurid light of such an indictment, would be that if these things are left out, everything is left out.
Hawthorne (1879) ch. 2

5 He was worse than provincial—he was parochial.
of ***Thoreau***
Hawthorne (1879) ch. 4

6 The black and merciless things that are behind the great possessions.
The Ivory Tower (1917) notes

7 Cats and monkeys—monkeys and cats—all human life is there!
The Madonna of the Future (1879) vol. 1; cf. **Advertising slogans** 7:3

8 We work in the dark—we do what we can—we give what we have. Our doubt is our passion and our passion is our task. The rest is the madness of art.
'The Middle Years' (short story, 1893)

9 Experience is never limited, and it is never complete; it is an immense sensibility, a kind of huge spider-web of the finest silken threads suspended in the chamber of consciousness, and catching every air-borne particle in its tissue.
Partial Portraits (1888) 'The Art of Fiction'

10 What is character but the determination of incident? What is incident but the illustration of character?
Partial Portraits (1888) 'The Art of Fiction'

11 The house of fiction has in short not one window, but a million . . . but they are, singly or together, as nothing without the posted presence of the watcher.
The Portrait of a Lady (1908 ed.) preface

12 The note I wanted; that of the strange and sinister embroidered on the very type of the normal and easy.
Prefaces (1909) 'The Altar of the Dead'

13 The fatal futility of Fact.
The Spoils of Poynton (1909 ed.) preface

14 The time-honoured bread-sauce of the happy ending.
Theatricals (1894) 2nd series

15 The turn of the screw
title of novel (1898)

16 We were alone with the quiet day, and his little heart, dispossessed, had stopped.
The Turn of the Screw (1898)

17 There is no difficulty in beginning; the trouble is to leave off!
in 1891; Leon Edel (ed.) *The Diary of Alice James* (1965)

18 I could come back to America . . . to die—but never, never to live.
letter to Mrs William James, 1 April 1913, in Leon Edel (ed.) *Letters* vol. 4 (1984)

19 The war has used up words.
in *New York Times* 21 March 1915

20 Adjectives are the sugar of literature and adverbs the salt.
Theodora Bosanquet *Henry James at Work* (1924)

21 I should so much have loved to be popular!
Alfred Sutro *Celebrities and Simple Souls* (1933)

22 Of course, of course.
on hearing that Rupert ***Brooke*** *had died on a Greek island*
C. Hassall *Rupert Brooke* (1964) ch. 14

23 Summer afternoon—summer afternoon . . . the two most beautiful words in the English language.
Edith Wharton *A Backward Glance* (1934) ch. 10

24 So here it is at last, the distinguished thing!
on experiencing his first stroke
Edith Wharton *A Backward Glance* (1934) ch. 14

P. D. James 1920–
English writer of detective stories

25 What the detective story is about is not murder but the restoration of order.
in *Face* December 1986

26 I had an interest in death from an early age. It fascinated me. When I heard 'Humpty Dumpty sat on a wall,' I thought, 'Did he fall or was he pushed?'
in *Paris Review* 1995

William James 1842–1910
*American philosopher; brother of Henry **James***

1 There is no more miserable human being than one in whom nothing is habitual but indecision.
The Principles of Psychology (1890) vol. 1, ch. 4

2 The art of being wise is the art of knowing what to overlook.
The Principles of Psychology (1890) vol. 2, ch. 22

3 There is no worse lie than a truth misunderstood by those who hear it.
The Varieties of Religious Experience (1902)

4 Man, biologically considered, and whatever else he may be into the bargain, is simply the most formidable of all the beasts of prey, and, indeed, the only one that preys systematically on its own species.
in *Atlantic Monthly* December 1904

5 The moral flabbiness born of the exclusive worship of the bitch-goddess *success*.
letter to H. G. Wells, 11 September 1906, in *Letters* (1920) vol. 2

6 Hogamus, higamous
Man is polygamous
Higamus, hogamous
Woman monogamous.
in *Oxford Book of Marriage* (1990)

Randall Jarrell 1914–65
American poet

7 From my mother's sleep I fell into the State,
And I hunched in its belly till my wet fur froze.
Six miles from earth, loosed from its dream of life,
I woke to black flak and the nightmare fighters.
When I died they washed me out of the turret with a hose.
'The Death of the Ball Turret Gunner' (1945)

8 As I look, the world contracts around you:
I see Brünnhilde had brown braids and glasses
She used for studying; Salome straight brown bangs,
A calf's brown eyes, and sturdy light-brown limbs
Dusted with cinnamon, an apple-dumpling's . . .
'A Girl in a Library' (1951)

9 The firelight of a long, blind, dreaming story
Lingers upon your lips; and I have seen
Firm, fixed forever in your closing eyes,
The Corn King beckoning to his Spring Queen.
'A Girl in a Library' (1951)

10 In bombers named for girls, we burned
The cities we had learned about in school—
Till our lives wore out; our bodies lay among
The people we had killed and never seen.
When we lasted long enough they gave us medals;
When we died they said, 'Our casualties were low.'
'Losses' (1963)

11 To Americans, English manners are far more frightening than none at all.
Pictures from an Institution (1954) pt. 1, ch. 4

12 It is better to entertain an idea than to take it home to live with you for the rest of your life.
Pictures from an Institution (1954) pt. 1, ch. 4

Maria Jastrzebska 1953–
Polish-born British poet

13 I do
And then again
She does
And then sometimes
Neither of us
Wears any trousers at all.
'Which of Us Wears the Trousers'

Douglas Jay 1907–96
British Labour politician
*see also **Political slogans** 581:12*

14 In the case of nutrition and health, just as in the case of education, the gentleman in Whitehall really does know better what is good for people than the people know themselves.
The Socialist Case (1939) ch. 30

15 He never used one syllable where none would do.
*of **Attlee***
Peter Hennessy *Muddling Through* (1996)

Marianne Jean-Baptiste
British actress

16 The old men running the industry just have not got a clue . . . Britain is no longer totally a white place where people ride horses, wear long frocks and drink tea. The national dish is no longer fish and chips, it's curry.
having been excluded from the group of actors invited to promote British talent at Cannes
in *Observer* 18 May 1997 'Soundbites'

Jean Paul see **Johann Paul Friedrich Richter**

James Jeans 1877–1946
English astronomer, physicist, and mathematician

17 Taking a very gloomy view of the future of the human race, let us suppose that it can only expect to survive for two thousand million years longer, a period about equal to the past age of the earth. Then, regarded as a being destined to live for three-score years and ten, humanity, although it has been born in a house seventy years old, is itself only three days old.
Eos (1928)

18 If we assume that the last breath of, say, Julius Caesar has by now become thoroughly scattered through the atmosphere, then the chances are that each of us inhales one molecule of it with every breath we take.
now usually quoted as the 'dying breath of Socrates'
An Introduction to the Kinetic Theory of Gases (1940)

19 Life exists in the universe only because the carbon atom possesses certain exceptional properties.
The Mysterious Universe (1930) ch. 1

1 From the intrinsic evidence of his creation, the Great Architect of the Universe now begins to appear as a pure mathematician.
The Mysterious Universe (1930) ch. 5

Thomas Jefferson 1743–1826

American Democratic Republican statesman; 3rd President of the US, 1801–9
see also **Mottoes** 535:15

2 When in the course of human events, it becomes necessary for one people to dissolve the political bonds which have connected them with another, and to assume among the powers of the earth the separate and equal station to which the laws of nature and of Nature's God entitle them, a decent respect to the opinions of mankind requires that they should declare the causes which impel them to the separation.
American Declaration of Independence, 4 July 1776, preamble

3 We hold these truths to be sacred and undeniable; that all men are created equal and independent, that from that equal creation they derive rights inherent and inalienable, among which are the preservation of life, and liberty, and the pursuit of happiness.
'Rough Draft' of the American Declaration of Independence, in J. P. Boyd et al. *Papers of Thomas Jefferson* (1950) vol. 1; cf. **Anonymous** 19:11

4 Experience declares that man is the only animal which devours its own kind, for I can apply no milder term to the governments of Europe, and to the general prey of the rich on the poor.
letter to Colonel Edward Carrington, 16 January 1787, in *Papers of Thomas Jefferson* (1955) vol. 11

5 A little rebellion now and then is a good thing.
letter to James Madison, 30 January 1787, in *Papers of Thomas Jefferson* (1955) vol. 11

6 State a moral case to a ploughman and a professor. The former will decide it as well, and often better than the latter, because he has not been led astray by artificial rules.
letter to Peter Carr, 10 August 1787, in *Papers of Thomas Jefferson* (1955) vol. 12

7 The tree of liberty must be refreshed from time to time with the blood of patriots and tyrants. It is its natural manure.
letter to W. S. Smith, 13 November 1787, in *Papers of Thomas Jefferson* (1955) vol. 12

8 I think our governments will remain virtuous for many centuries; as long as they are chiefly agricultural; and this will be as long as there shall be vacant lands in any part of America. When they get piled upon one another in large cities, as in Europe, they will become corrupt as in Europe.
letter to James Madison, 20 December 1787, in *Papers of Thomas Jefferson* (1955) vol. 12

9 Whenever a man has cast a longing eye on them [official positions], a rottenness begins in his conduct.
letter to Tench Coxe, 21 May 1799, in P. L. Ford (ed.) *Writings of Thomas Jefferson* (1896) vol. 7

10 If the principle were to prevail, of a common law [i.e. a single government] being in force in the U.S. . . . it would become the most corrupt government on the earth.
letter to Gideon Granger, 13 August 1800, in P. L. Ford (ed.) *Writings of Thomas Jefferson* (1896) vol. 7

11 Though the will of the majority is in all cases to prevail, that will to be rightful must be reasonable; . . . the minority possess their equal rights, which equal law must protect, and to violate would be oppression.
first inaugural address, 4 March 1801

12 Would the honest patriot, in the full tide of successful experiment, abandon a government which has so far kept us free and firm?
first inaugural address, 4 March 1801

13 Peace, commerce, and honest friendship with all nations—entangling alliances with none.
first inaugural address, 4 March 1801

14 Freedom of religion; freedom of the press, and freedom of person under the protection of *habeas corpus*, and trial by juries impartially selected. These principles form the bright constellation which has gone before us, and guided our steps through an age of revolution and reformation.
first inaugural address, 4 March 1801

15 If a due participation of office is a matter of right, how are vacancies to be obtained? Those by death are few; by resignation none.
letter to E. Shipman and others, 12 July 1801, in P. L. Ford (ed.) *Writings of Thomas Jefferson* (1897) vol. 8; cf. **Misquotations** 521:12

16 When a man assumes a public trust, he should consider himself as public property.
to Baron von Humboldt, 1807, in B. L. Rayner *Life of Jefferson* (1834)

17 But though an old man, I am but a young gardener.
letter to Charles Willson Peale, 20 August 1811, in *Thomas Jefferson's Garden Book* (1944)

18 I agree with you that there is a natural aristocracy among men. The grounds of this are virtue and talents.
letter to John Adams, 28 October 1813, in P. L. Ford (ed.) *Writings of Thomas Jefferson* (1898) vol. 9

19 If a nation expects to be ignorant and free, in a state of civilization, it expects what never was and never will be.
letter to Colonel Charles Yancey, 6 January 1816, in P. L. Ford (ed.) *Writings of Thomas Jefferson* (1899) vol. 10

20 We have the wolf by the ears; and we can neither hold him, nor safely let him go. Justice is in one scale, and self-preservation in the other.
on slavery
letter to John Holmes, 22 April 1820; in A. A. Lipscome and A. E. Berg (eds.) *Writings of Thomas Jefferson* (1903) vol. 15

21 I know no safe depository of the ultimate powers of the society but the people themselves; and if we think them not enlightened enough to exercise their control with a wholesome discretion, the

remedy is not to take it from them, but to inform their discretion by education.

letter to William Charles Jarvis, 28 September 1820, in P. L. Ford (ed.) *Writings of Thomas Jefferson* (1899) vol. 10

1 To attain all this [universal republicanism], however, rivers of blood must yet flow, and years of desolation pass over; yet the object is worth rivers of blood, and years of desolation.

letter to John Adams, 4 September 1823, in P. L. Ford *Writings of Thomas Jefferson* (1899) vol. 10; cf. **Powell** 590:15, **Virgil** 794:16

2 Millions of innocent men, women, and children, since the introduction of Christianity, have been burnt, tortured, fined, imprisoned; yet we have not advanced one inch towards uniformity [of opinion]. What has been the effect of coercion? To make one half the world fools, and the other half hypocrites.

Notes on the State of Virginia (1781–5) Query 17

3 Indeed I tremble for my country when I reflect that God is just.

Notes on the State of Virginia (1781–5) Query 18

4 No duty the Executive had to perform was so trying as to put the right man in the right place.

J. B. MacMaster *History of the People of the United States* (1883–1913) vol. 2, ch. 13

Francis, Lord Jeffrey 1773–1850

Scottish critic

5 This will never do.

on ***Wordsworth****'s* The Excursion *(1814)*

in *Edinburgh Review* November 1814

David Jenkins 1925–

English theologian; Bishop of Durham from 1984

6 I am not clear that God manoeuvres physical things . . . After all, a conjuring trick with bones only proves that it is as clever as a conjuring trick with bones.

on the Resurrection

in 'Poles Apart' (BBC radio, 4 October 1984)

Roy Jenkins 1920–

British politician; co-founder of the Social Democratic Party, 1981

7 The politics of the left and centre of this country are frozen in an out-of-date mould which is bad for the political and economic health of Britain and increasingly inhibiting for those who live within the mould. Can it be broken?

speech to Parliamentary Press Gallery, 9 June 1980, in *The Times* 10 June 1980

8 A First Minister whose self-righteous stubbornness has not been equalled, save briefly by Neville Chamberlain, since Lord North.

of Margaret ***Thatcher***

in *Observer* 11 March 1990

9 Nearly all Prime Ministers are dissatisfied with their successors, perhaps even more so if they come from their own party.

Gladstone (1995)

Elizabeth Jennings 1926–

English poet

10 I hate a word like 'pets': it sounds so much
Like something with no living of its own.

'My Animals' (1966)

Soame Jenyns 1704–87

English politician and writer

11 Those who profess outrageous zeal for the liberty and prosperity of their country, and at the same time infringe her laws, affront her religion and debauch her people, are but despicable quacks.

A Free Enquiry into the Nature and Origin of Evil (1757) Letter 5

12 Thousands are collected from the idle and the extravagant for seeing dogs, horses, men and monkeys perform feats of activity, and, in some places, for the privilege only of seeing one another.

Works (1790) vol. 2 'Thoughts on the National Debt'

St Jerome c.AD 342–420

Christian monk and scholar; translator of the original Bible texts into Latin (the Vulgate)

13 *Aliorum vulnus nostra sit cautio.*

Let us take warning from another's wound.

letter 54, To Furia, AD 394

14 *Venerationi mihi semper fuit non verbosa rusticitas, sed sancta simplicitas.*

I have revered always not crude verbosity, but holy simplicity.

letter 57, To Pammachius

15 *Romanus orbit ruit et tamen cervix nostra erecta non flectitur.*

The Roman world is falling, yet we hold our heads erect instead of bowing our necks.

letter 60, To Heliodorus, AD 396

16 *Cotidie morimur, cotidie communtamur, et tamen aeternos esse nos credimus.*

Every day we die, every day we are changed, and yet we believe ourselves to be eternal.

letter 60, To Heliodorus, AD 396

17 *Fuint, non nascuntur Christiani.*

Christians are not born but made.

letter 107, To Laeta, AD 403

Jerome K. Jerome 1859–1927

English writer

18 It is impossible to enjoy idling thoroughly unless one has plenty of work to do.

Idle Thoughts of an Idle Fellow (1886) 'On Being Idle'

19 The passing of the third floor back.

title of story (1907) and play (1910)

20 I want a house that has got over all its troubles; I don't want to spend the rest of my life bringing up a young and inexperienced house.

They and I (1909) ch. 11

21 It is a most extraordinary thing, but I never read a patent medicine advertisement without being

impelled to the conclusion that I am suffering from the particular disease therein dealt with in its most virulent form.
Three Men in a Boat (1889) ch. 1

1 I like work: it fascinates me. I can sit and look at it for hours. I love to keep it by me: the idea of getting rid of it nearly breaks my heart.
Three Men in a Boat (1889) ch. 15

William Jerome 1865–1932
American songwriter

2 Any old place I can hang my hat is home sweet home to me.
title of song (1901)

Douglas Jerrold 1803–57
English dramatist and journalist

3 Religion's in the heart, not in the knees.
The Devil's Ducat (1830) act 1, sc. 2

4 The best thing I know between France and England is—the sea.
The Wit and Opinions of Douglas Jerrold (1859) 'The Anglo-French Alliance'

5 Earth is here so kind, that just tickle her with a hoe and she laughs with a harvest.
of Australia
The Wit and Opinions of Douglas Jerrold (1859) 'A Land of Plenty'

6 Love's like the measles—all the worse when it comes late in life.
The Wit and Opinions of Douglas Jerrold (1859) 'Love'

W. Stanley Jevons 1835–82
English economist

7 All classes of society are trades unionists at heart, and differ chiefly in the boldness, ability, and secrecy with which they pursue their respective interests.
The State in Relation to Labour (1882)

John Jewel 1522–71
English bishop

8 In old time we had treen chalices and golden priests, but now we have treen priests and golden chalices.
Certain Sermons Preached Before the Queen's Majesty (1609)

John XXIII (Angelo Giuseppe Roncalli) 1881–1963
Pope from 1958

9 If civil authorities legislate for or allow anything that is contrary to that order and therefore contrary to the will of God, neither the laws made or the authorizations granted can be binding on the consciences of the citizens, since God has more right to be obeyed than man.
Pacem in Terris (1963)

10 The social progress, order, security and peace of each country are necessarily connected with the social progress, order, security and peace of all other countries.
Pacem in Terris (1963)

11 [In the universal *Declaration of Human Rights* (December, 1948)] in most solemn form, the dignity of a person is acknowledged to all human beings; and as a consequence there is proclaimed, as a fundamental right, the right of free movement in search for truth and in the attainment of moral good and of justice, and also the right to a dignified life.
Pacem in Terris (1963)

12 I want to throw open the windows of the Church so that we can see out and the people can see in.
attributed

13 Signora, do you believe my blessing cannot pass through plastic?
to a pilgrim who asked him to bless again some medals and rosaries which he had blessed before she had time to remove them from her purse, 1959
Laureano López Rodó *Memorias* (1990)

John of Salisbury c.1115–80
English ecclesiastical scholar; supporter of Thomas Becket

14 The brevity of our life, the dullness of our senses, the torpor of our indifference, the futility of our occupation, suffer us to know but little: and that little is soon shaken and then torn from the mind by that traitor to learning, that hostile and faithless stepmother to memory, oblivion.
Prologue to the Policraticus (ed. C. C. I. Webb, 1909) vol. 1, translated by Helen Waddell

St John of the Cross 1542–91
Spanish mystic and poet
see also **Misquotations** 521:11

15 *Muero porque no muero.*
I die because I do not die.
the same words occur in St **Teresa** *of Ávila 'Versos nacidos del fuego del amor de Dios' (c.1571–3)*
'Coplas del alma que pena por ver a Dios' (*c.*1578)

16 *Con un no saber sabiendo.*
With a knowing ignorance.
'Coplas hechas sobre un éxtasis de alta contemplación'

Elton John 1947– and Bernie Taupin 1950–
English pop singer and songwriter; songwriter

17 It seems to me you lived your life
Like a candle in the wind.
Never knowing who to cling to
When the rain set in.
And I would have liked to have known you
But I was just a kid
The candle burned out long before
Your legend ever did.
Goodbye Norma Jean.
of Marilyn **Monroe**
'Candle in the Wind' (song, 1973)

1 Even when you died
Oh the press still hounded you.
'Candle in the Wind' (song, 1973)

2 Goodbye England's rose;
May you ever grow in our hearts.
rewritten for and sung at the funeral of **Diana**, *Princess of Wales, 7 September 1997*
'Candle in the Wind' (song, revised version, 1997)

3 And it seems to me you lived your life
Like a candle in the wind:
Never fading with the sunset
When the rain set in.
And your footsteps will always fall here
On England's greenest hills;
Your candle's burned out long before
Your legend ever will.
'Candle in the Wind' (song, revised version, 1997)

4 Goodbye yellow brick road.
title of song (1973); cf. **Harburg** 359:19

John Paul II 1920–

Polish cleric, Pope since 1978

5 Love is never defeated, and I could add, the history of Ireland proves it.
speech in Galway, 30 September 1979

6 It would be simplistic to say that Divine Providence caused the fall of communism. It fell by itself as a consequence of its own mistakes and abuses. It fell by itself because of its own inherent weaknesses.
when asked if the fall of the USSR could be ascribed to God
Carl Bernstein and Marco Politi *His Holiness: John Paul II and the Hidden History of our Time* (1996)

Hiram Johnson see Sayings 648:10

Linton Kwesi Johnson 1952–

Anglo-Jamaican poet

7 Brothers and sisters rocking,
a dread beat pulsing fire, burning.
'Dread Beat an Blood' (1975)

8 Cold lights hurting, breaking, hurting;
fire in the head and a dread beat bleeding, beating
fire: dread.
'Dread Beat an Blood' (1975)

Lyndon Baines Johnson 1908–73

36th President of the US

to a reporter who had queried his embracing Richard **Nixon** *on the vice-president's return from a controversial tour of South America in 1958:*

9 Son, in politics you've got to learn that overnight chicken shit can turn to chicken salad.
Fawn Brodie *Richard Nixon* (1983) ch. 25

10 I am a free man, an American, a United States Senator, and a Democrat, in that order.
in *Texas Quarterly* Winter 1958

11 I'll tell you what's at the bottom of it. If you can convince the lowest white man that he's better than the best coloured man, he won't notice you're picking his pocket. Hell, give him someone to look down on and he'll empty his pockets for you.
during the 1960 Presidential campaign, to Bill Moyers
Robert Dallek *Lone Star Rising* (1991) ch. 16

12 All I have I would have given gladly not to be standing here today.
following the assassination of J. F. **Kennedy**
first speech to Congress as President, 27 November 1963, in *Public Papers of . . . Lyndon B. Johnson 1963–64* vol. 1

13 We have talked long enough in this country about equal rights. We have talked for a hundred years or more. It is time now to write the next chapter, and to write it in the books of law.
speech to Congress, 27 November 1963, in *Public Papers of . . . Lyndon B. Johnson 1963–64* vol. 1

14 We hope that the world will not narrow into a neighbourhood before it has broadened into a brotherhood.
speech at the lighting of the Nation's Christmas Tree, 22 December 1963, in *Public Papers of . . . Lyndon B. Johnson 1963–64* vol. 1

15 In your time we have the opportunity to move not only toward the rich society and the powerful society, but upward to the Great Society.
speech at University of Michigan, 22 May 1964, in *Public Papers of . . . Lyndon B. Johnson 1963–64* vol. 1

16 We still seek no wider war.
speech on radio and television, 4 August 1964, in *Public Papers of . . . Lyndon B. Johnson 1963–64* vol. 2

17 We are not about to send American boys 9 or 10,000 miles away from home to do what Asian boys ought to be doing for themselves.
speech at Akron University, 21 October 1964, in *Public Papers of . . . Lyndon B. Johnson 1963–64* vol. 2; cf. **Roosevelt** 632:16

18 I don't want loyalty. I want *loyalty*. I want him to kiss my ass in Macy's window at high noon and tell me it smells like roses. I want his pecker in my pocket.
discussing a prospective assistant
David Halberstam *The Best and the Brightest* (1972) ch. 20

19 Better to have him inside the tent pissing out, than outside pissing in.
of J. Edgar Hoover
David Halberstam *The Best and the Brightest* (1972) ch. 20

20 So dumb he can't fart and chew gum at the same time.
of Gerald **Ford**
Richard Reeves *A Ford, not a Lincoln* (1975) ch. 2

Philander Chase Johnson 1866–1939

21 Cheer up! the worst is yet to come!
in *Everybody's Magazine* May 1920

Philip Johnson 1906–

American architect

22 Architecture is the art of how to waste space.
New York Times 27 December 1964

Samuel Johnson 1709–84

English poet, critic, and lexicographer
on Johnson: see **Brown** *152:1*, **Burney** *166:1*, **Churchill** *213:19*, **Colman** *229:18*, **Cowper** *242:18*, **Goldsmith** *345:31*, **Hawthorne** *364:12*, **Knowles** *442:9*, **Macaulay** *481:13*, **Pembroke** *572:11*, **Smollett** *726:16*, **Walpole** *801:11*; *see also* **Epitaphs** *303:17*, **Swift** *750:3*

1 In all pointed sentences, some degree of accuracy must be sacrificed to conciseness.
'The Bravery of the English Common Soldier' in *The British Magazine* January 1760

2 Liberty is, to the lowest rank of every nation, little more than the choice of working or starving.
'The Bravery of the English Common Soldier' in *The British Magazine* January 1760

3 Change is not made without inconvenience, even from worse to better.
A Dictionary of the English Language (1755) preface; cf. **Hooker** 383:7

4 I am not yet so lost in lexicography as to forget that words are the daughters of earth, and that things are the sons of heaven. Language is only the instrument of science, and words are but the signs of ideas: I wish, however, that the instrument might be less apt to decay, and that signs might be permanent, like the things which they denote.
A Dictionary of the English Language (1755) preface; cf. **Madden** 489:1

5 Every quotation contributes something to the stability or enlargement of the language.
on citations of usage in a dictionary
A Dictionary of the English Language (1755) preface

6 But these were the dreams of a poet doomed at last to wake a lexicographer.
A Dictionary of the English Language (1755) preface

7 If the changes we fear be thus irresistible, what remains but to acquiesce with silence, as in the other insurmountable distresses of humanity? It remains that we retard what we cannot repel, that we palliate what we cannot cure.
A Dictionary of the English Language (1755) preface

8 *Dull*. To make dictionaries is dull work.
A Dictionary of the English Language (1755) 'dull' (8th definition)

9 *Excise*. A hateful tax levied upon commodities.
A Dictionary of the English Language (1755)

10 *Lexicographer*. A writer of dictionaries, a harmless drudge.
A Dictionary of the English Language (1755)

11 *Network*. Anything reticulated or decussated at equal distances, with interstices between the intersections.
A Dictionary of the English Language (1755)

12 *Oats*. A grain, which in England is generally given to horses, but in Scotland supports the people.
A Dictionary of the English Language (1755)

13 *Patron*. Commonly a wretch who supports with insolence, and is paid with flattery.
A Dictionary of the English Language (1755)

14 *Pension*. Pay given to a state hireling for treason to his country.
A Dictionary of the English Language (1755)

15 The only end of writing is to enable the readers better to enjoy life, or better to endure it.
A Free Enquiry (1757, ed. D. Greene, 1984)

16 When two Englishmen meet, their first talk is of the weather.
in *The Idler* no. 11 (24 June 1758)

17 Among the calamities of war may be jointly numbered the diminution of the love of truth, by the falsehoods which interest dictates and credulity encourages.
in *The Idler* no. 30 (11 November 1758); see **Sayings** 648:10

18 Promise, large promise, is the soul of an advertisement.
The Idler no. 40 (20 January 1759)

19 I directed them to bring a bundle [of hay] into the room, and slept upon it in my riding coat. Mr Boswell, being more delicate, laid himself sheets with hay over and under him, and lay in linen like a gentleman.
A Journey to the Western Islands of Scotland (1775) 'Glenelg'

20 A Scotchman must be a very sturdy moralist, who does not love Scotland better than truth.
A Journey to the Western Islands of Scotland (1775) 'Ostig in Sky'

21 At seventy-seven it is time to be in earnest.
A Journey to the Western Islands of Scotland (1775) 'Col'

22 A hardened and shameless tea-drinker, who has for twenty years diluted his meals with only the infusion of this fascinating plant; whose kettle has scarcely time to cool; who with tea amuses the evening, with tea solaces the midnight, and with tea welcomes the morning.
review in the *Literary Magazine* vol. 2, no. 13 (1757)

23 About things on which the public thinks long it commonly attains to think right.
Lives of the English Poets (1779–81) 'Addison'

24 Whoever wishes to attain an English style, familiar but not coarse, and elegant but not ostentatious, must give his days and nights to the volumes of Addison.
Lives of the English Poets (1779–81) 'Addison'

25 The great source of pleasure is variety. Uniformity must tire at last, though it be uniformity of excellence. We love to expect; and, when expectation is disappointed or gratified, we want to be again expecting.
Lives of the English Poets (1779–81) 'Butler'

26 A man, doubtful of his dinner, or trembling at a creditor, is not much disposed to abstracted meditation, or remote enquiries.
Lives of the English Poets (1779–81) 'Collins'

27 The true genius is a mind of large general powers, accidentally determined to some particular direction.
Lives of the English Poets (1779–81) 'Cowley'

1 Language is the dress of thought.
Lives of the English Poets (1779–81) 'Cowley'; cf. **Pope** 584:19, **Wesley** 812:1

2 The father of English criticism.
Lives of the English Poets (1779–81) 'Dryden'

3 This play . . . was first offered to Cibber and his brethren at Drury-Lane, and rejected; it being then carried to Rich had the effect, as was ludicrously said, of making Gay *rich*, and Rich *gay*.
of ***Gay****'s* The Beggar's Opera
Lives of the English Poets (1779–81) 'John Gay'

4 In the character of his Elegy I rejoice to concur with the common reader; for by the common sense of readers uncorrupted with literary prejudices . . . must be finally decided all claim to poetical honours.
Lives of the English Poets (1779–81) 'Gray'

5 An exotic and irrational entertainment, which has been always combated, and always has prevailed.
of Italian opera
Lives of the English Poets (1779–81) 'Hughes'

6 We are perpetually moralists, but we are geometricians only by chance. Our intercourse with intellectual nature is necessary; our speculations upon matter are voluntary and at leisure.
Lives of the English Poets (1779–81) 'Milton'

7 An acrimonious and surly republican.
Lives of the English Poets (1779–81) 'Milton'

8 I am disappointed by that stroke of death, which has eclipsed the gaiety of nations and impoverished the public stock of harmless pleasure.
on the death of ***Garrick***
Lives of the English Poets (1779–81) 'Edmund Smith'

9 He washed himself with oriental scrupulosity.
Lives of the English Poets (1779–81) 'Swift'

10 Friendship is not always the sequel of obligation.
Lives of the English Poets (1779–81) 'James Thomson'

11 Nothing can please many, and please long, but just representations of general nature.
Plays of William Shakespeare . . . (1765) preface

12 He that tries to recommend him by select quotations, will succeed like the pedant in Hierocles, who, when he offered his house to sale, carried a brick in his pocket as a specimen.
of ***Shakespeare***
Plays of William Shakespeare . . . (1765) preface

13 Love is only one of many passions.
Plays of William Shakespeare . . . (1765) preface

14 Shakespeare has united the powers of exciting laughter and sorrow not only in one mind but in one composition . . . That this is a practice contrary to the rules of criticism will be readily allowed; but there is always an appeal open from criticism to nature.
Plays of William Shakespeare . . . (1765) preface

15 A quibble is to Shakespeare, what luminous vapours are to the traveller; he follows it at all adventures, it is sure to lead him out of his way and sure to engulf him in the mire.
Plays of William Shakespeare . . . (1765) preface

16 We fix our eyes upon his graces, and turn them from his deformities, and endure in him what we should in another loathe or despise.
of ***Shakespeare***
Plays of William Shakespeare . . . (1765) preface

17 I have always suspected that the reading is right, which requires many words to prove it wrong; and the emendation wrong, that cannot without so much labour appear to be right.
Plays of William Shakespeare . . . (1765) preface

18 Notes are often necessary, but they are necessary evils.
Plays of William Shakespeare . . . (1765) preface

19 It is better to suffer wrong than to do it, and happier to be sometimes cheated than not to trust.
in *Rambler* no. 79 (18 December 1750)

20 There are minds so impatient of inferiority, that their gratitude is a species of revenge, and they return benefits, not because recompense is a pleasure, but because obligation is a pain.
in *The Rambler* no. 87 (15 January 1751)

21 No place affords a more striking conviction of the vanity of human hopes, than a public library.
in *The Rambler* no. 106 (23 March 1751)

22 I have laboured to refine our language to grammatical purity, and to clear it from colloquial barbarisms, licentious idioms, and irregular combinations.
in *The Rambler* no. 208 (14 March 1752)

23 Ye who listen with credulity to the whispers of fancy, and pursue with eagerness the phantoms of hope; who expect that age will perform the promises of youth, and that the deficiencies of the present day will be supplied by the morrow; attend to the history of Rasselas prince of Abyssinia.
Rasselas (1759) ch. 1

24 The business of a poet, said Imlac, is to examine, not the individual, but the species; to remark general properties and appearances: he does not number the streaks of the tulip, or describe the different shades in the verdure of the forest.
Rasselas (1759) ch. 10

25 He [the poet] must write as the interpreter of nature, and the legislator of mankind, and consider himself as presiding over the thoughts and manners of future generations; as a being superior to time and place.
Rasselas (1759) ch. 10; cf. **Shelley** 714:24

26 Human life is everywhere a state in which much is to be endured, and little to be enjoyed.
Rasselas (1759) ch. 11

27 Marriage has many pains, but celibacy has no pleasures.
Rasselas (1759) ch. 26

28 Example is always more efficacious than precept.
Rasselas (1759) ch. 30

1 I consider this mighty structure as a monument of the insufficiency of human enjoyments.
of the Pyramids
Rasselas (1759) ch. 32

2 Integrity without knowledge is weak and useless, and knowledge without integrity is dangerous and dreadful.
Rasselas (1759) ch. 41

3 There is perhaps no class of men, to whom the precept given by the Apostle to his converts against too great confidence in their understandings, may be more properly inculcated, than those who are dedicated to the profession of literature.
Sermons (1788) no. 8

4 In this state of temporary honour, a proud man is too willing to exert his prerogative; and too ready to forget that he is dictating to those, who may one day dictate to him.
on schoolmasters
Sermons (1788) no. 8

5 He [God] will not leave his promises unfulfilled, nor his threats unexecuted . . . Neither can he want power to execute his purposes; he who spoke, and the world was made, can speak again, and it will perish.
Sermons (1788) no. 10

6 How is it that we hear the loudest yelps for liberty among the drivers of negroes?
Taxation No Tyranny (1775)

7 A generous and elevated mind is distinguished by nothing more certainly than an eminent degree of curiosity.
dedication of his English translation of Fr. J. Lobo's *Voyage to Abyssinia* (1735), signed 'the editor' but attributed to Johnson in James Boswell *Life of Samuel Johnson* (1791) 1734

8 There Poetry shall tune her sacred voice,
And wake from ignorance the Western World.
Demetrius forecasting the Renaissance
Irene (1749) act 4, sc. 1, l. 122

9 Here falling houses thunder on your head,
And here a female atheist talks you dead.
London (1738) l. 17

10 Of all the griefs that harrass the distressed,
Sure the most bitter is a scornful jest;
Fate never wounds more deep the gen'rous heart,
Than when a blockhead's insult points the dart.
London (1738) l. 166

11 The stage but echoes back the public voice.
The drama's laws the drama's patrons give,
For we that live to please, must please to live.
'Prologue spoken at the Opening of the Theatre in Drury Lane' (1747)

12 How small of all that human hearts endure,
That part which laws or kings can cause or cure.
Still to ourselves in every place consigned,
Our own felicity we make or find.
lines added to Oliver Goldsmith's *The Traveller* (1764) l. 429; cf. **Goldsmith** 345:11

13 Let observation with extensive view,
Survey mankind, from China to Peru.
The Vanity of Human Wishes (1749) l. 1

14 There mark what ills the scholar's life assail,
Toil, envy, want, the patron, and the jail.
The Vanity of Human Wishes (1749) l. 159

15 A frame of adamant, a soul of fire,
No dangers fright him, and no labours tire.
of Charles XII of Sweden
The Vanity of Human Wishes (1749) l. 193

16 His fall was destined to a barren strand,
A petty fortress, and a dubious hand;
He left the name, at which the world grew pale,
To point a moral, or adorn a tale.
of Charles XII of Sweden
The Vanity of Human Wishes (1749) l. 219

17 Enlarge my life with multitude of days,
In health, in sickness, thus the suppliant prays;
Hides from himself his state, and shuns to know,
That life protracted is protracted woe.
Time hovers o'er, impatient to destroy,
And shuts up all the passages of joy.
The Vanity of Human Wishes (1749) l. 255

18 In life's last scene what prodigies surprise,
Fears of the brave, and follies of the wise?
From Marlb'rough's eyes the streams of dotage flow,
And Swift expires a driv'ler and a show.
The Vanity of Human Wishes (1749) l. 315

19 Must helpless man, in ignorance sedate,
Roll darkling down the torrent of his fate?
The Vanity of Human Wishes (1749) l. 345

20 Still raise for good the supplicating voice,
But leave to heaven the measure and the choice.
The Vanity of Human Wishes (1749) l. 351

21 A lawyer has no business with the justice or injustice of the cause which he undertakes, unless his client asks his opinion, and then he is bound to give it honestly. The justice or injustice of the cause is to be decided by the judge.
James Boswell *Journal of a Tour to the Hebrides* (1785) 15 August 1773

22 Let him go abroad to a distant country; let him go to some place where he is *not* known. Don't let him go to the devil where he is known!
Boswell having asked if someone should commit suicide to avoid certain disgrace
James Boswell *Tour to the Hebrides* (1785) 18 August 1773

23 I have, all my life long, been lying till noon; yet I tell all young men, and tell them with great sincerity, that nobody who does not rise early will ever do any good.
James Boswell *Tour to the Hebrides* (1785) 14 September 1773

24 I inherited a vile melancholy from my father, which has made me mad all my life, at least not sober.
James Boswell *Tour to the Hebrides* (1785) 16 September 1773; cf. **Johnson** 417:7

1 I am always sorry when any language is lost, because languages are the pedigree of nations.
James Boswell *Tour to the Hebrides* (1785) 18 September 1773

2 I do not much like to see a Whig in any dress; but I hate to see a Whig in a parson's gown.
James Boswell *Tour to the Hebrides* (1785) 24 September 1773

3 A cucumber should be well sliced, and dressed with pepper and vinegar, and then thrown out, as good for nothing.
James Boswell *Tour to the Hebrides* (1785) 5 October 1773

4 I am sorry I have not learned to play at cards. It is very useful in life: it generates kindness and consolidates society.
James Boswell *Tour to the Hebrides* (1785) 21 November 1773

5 JOHNSON: I had no notion that I was wrong or irreverent to my tutor.
BOSWELL: That, Sir, was great fortitude of mind.
JOHNSON: No, Sir; stark insensibility.
James Boswell *Life of Samuel Johnson* (1791) 31 October 1728

6 Sir, we are a nest of singing birds.
of Pembroke College, Oxford
James Boswell *Life of Samuel Johnson* (1791) 1730

7 He was a vicious man, but very kind to me. If you call a dog *Hervey*, I shall love him.
of his former patron Henry Hervey
James Boswell *Life of Samuel Johnson* (1791) 1737

8 My old friend, Mrs Carter, could make a pudding, as well as translate Epictetus.
James Boswell *Life of Samuel Johnson* (1791) Spring 1738

9 Tom Birch is as brisk as a bee in conversation; but no sooner does he take a pen in his hand, than it becomes a torpedo to him, and benumbs all his faculties.
James Boswell *Life of Samuel Johnson* (1791) 1743

10 I'll come no more behind your scenes, David; for the silk stockings and white bosoms of your actresses excite my amorous propensities.
to **Garrick**; *John* **Wilkes** *recalled the remark in the form: 'the silk stockings and white bosoms of your actresses do make my genitals to quiver'*
James Boswell *Life of Samuel Johnson* (1791) 1750

11 A man may write at any time, if he will set himself doggedly to it.
James Boswell *Life of Samuel Johnson* (1791) March 1750

12 A fly, Sir, may sting a stately horse and make him wince; but one is but an insect, and the other is a horse still.
James Boswell *Life of Samuel Johnson* (1791) 1754

13 This man I thought had been a Lord among wits; but, I find, he is only a wit among Lords.
of Lord **Chesterfield**
James Boswell *Life of Samuel Johnson* (1791) 1754

14 They teach the morals of a whore, and the manners of a dancing master.
of the Letters *of Lord* **Chesterfield**
James Boswell *Life of Samuel Johnson* (1791) 1754

15 I had done all that I could; and no man is well pleased to have his all neglected, be it ever so little.
James Boswell *Life of Samuel Johnson* (1791) letter to Lord Chesterfield, 7 February 1755

16 The shepherd in Virgil grew at last acquainted with Love, and found him a native of the rocks.
James Boswell *Life of Samuel Johnson* (1791) letter to Lord Chesterfield, 7 February 1755

17 Is not a Patron, my Lord, one who looks with unconcern on a man struggling for life in the water, and, when he has reached ground, encumbers him with help? The notice which you have been pleased to take of my labours, had it been early, had been kind; but it has been delayed till I am indifferent, and cannot enjoy it; till I am solitary, and cannot impart it; till I am known, and do not want it.
James Boswell *Life of Samuel Johnson* (1791) letter to Lord Chesterfield, 7 February 1755

18 There are two things which I am confident I can do very well: one is an introduction to any literary work, stating what it is to contain, and how it should be executed in the most perfect manner; the other is a conclusion, shewing from various causes why the execution has not been equal to what the author promised to himself and to the public.
James Boswell *Life of Samuel Johnson* (1791) 1755

19 Ignorance, madam, pure ignorance.
on being asked why he had defined pastern *as the 'knee' of a horse*
James Boswell *Life of Samuel Johnson* (1791) 1755

20 I have protracted my work till most of those whom I wished to please have sunk into the grave; and success and miscarriage are empty sounds.
James Boswell *Life of Samuel Johnson* (1791) 1755

21 If a man does not make new acquaintance as he advances through life, he will soon find himself left alone. A man, Sir, should keep his friendship in constant repair.
James Boswell *Life of Samuel Johnson* (1791) 1755

22 No man will be a sailor who has contrivance enough to get himself into a jail; for being in a ship is being in a jail, with the chance of being drowned . . . A man in a jail has more room, better food, and commonly better company.
James Boswell *Life of Samuel Johnson* (1791) 16 March 1759; cf. **Burton** 170:15

23 No, Sir, I am not a botanist; and (alluding, no doubt, to his near sightedness) should I wish to become a botanist, I must first turn myself into a reptile.
James Boswell *Life of Samuel Johnson* (1791) 20 July 1762

24 BOSWELL: I do indeed come from Scotland, but I cannot help it . . .
JOHNSON: That, Sir, I find, is what a very great many of your countrymen cannot help.
James Boswell *Life of Samuel Johnson* (1791) 16 May 1763

25 The notion of liberty amuses the people of England, and helps to keep off the *taedium vitae*. When a

butcher tells you that *his heart bleeds for his country* he has, in fact, no uneasy feeling.
James Boswell *Life of Samuel Johnson* (1791) 16 May 1763

1 Yes, Sir, many men, many women, and many children.
on Dr Blair's asking whether any man of a modern age could have written Ossian
James Boswell *Life of Samuel Johnson* (1791) 24 May 1763

2 I did not think he ought to be shut up. His infirmities were not noxious to society. He insisted on people praying with him; and I'd as lief pray with Kit Smart as any one else. Another charge was, that he did not love clean linen; and I have no passion for it.
James Boswell *Life of Samuel Johnson* (1791) 24 May 1763

3 You *may* abuse a tragedy, though you cannot write one. You may scold a carpenter who has made you a bad table, though you cannot make a table. It is not your trade to make tables.
on literary criticism
James Boswell *Life of Samuel Johnson* (1791) 25 June 1763

4 I am afraid he has not been in the inside of a church for many years; but he never passes a church without pulling off his hat. This shows that he has good principles.
of Dr John Campbell
James Boswell *Life of Samuel Johnson* (1791) 1 July 1763

5 Great abilities are not requisite for an historian . . . imagination is not required in any high degree.
James Boswell *Life of Samuel Johnson* (1791) 6 July 1763

6 The noblest prospect which a Scotchman ever sees, is the high road that leads him to England!
James Boswell *Life of Samuel Johnson* (1791) 6 July 1763

7 A man ought to read just as inclination leads him; for what he reads as a task will do him little good.
James Boswell *Life of Samuel Johnson* (1791) 14 July 1763

8 But if he does really think that there is no distinction between virtue and vice, why, Sir, when he leaves our houses, let us count our spoons.
James Boswell *Life of Samuel Johnson* (1791) 14 July 1763; cf. **Emerson** 299:15

9 All the arguments which are brought to represent poverty as no evil, show it to be evidently a great evil. You never find people labouring to convince you that you may live very happily upon a plentiful fortune.
James Boswell *Life of Samuel Johnson* (1791) 20 July 1763

10 Truth, Sir, is a cow, that will yield such people [sceptics] no more milk, and so they are gone to milk the bull.
James Boswell *Life of Samuel Johnson* (1791) 21 July 1763

11 Young men have more virtue than old men; they have more generous sentiments in every respect.
James Boswell *Life of Samuel Johnson* (1791) 21 July 1763

12 In my early years I read very hard. It is a sad reflection, but a true one, that I knew almost as much at eighteen as I do now.
James Boswell *Life of Samuel Johnson* (1791) 21 July 1763

13 Your levellers wish to level *down* as far as themselves; but they cannot bear levelling *up* to themselves.
James Boswell *Life of Samuel Johnson* (1791) 21 July 1763

14 It is no matter what you teach them [children] first, any more than what leg you shall put into your breeches first.
James Boswell *Life of Samuel Johnson* (1791) 26 July 1763

15 Why, Sir, Sherry is dull, naturally dull; but it must have taken him a great deal of pains to become what we now see him. Such an excess of stupidity, Sir, is not in Nature.
of Thomas Sheridan
James Boswell *Life of Samuel Johnson* (1791) 28 July 1763

16 It is burning a farthing candle at Dover, to shew light at Calais.
on Thomas Sheridan's influence on the English language
James Boswell *Life of Samuel Johnson* (1791) 28 July 1763; cf. **Young** 839:1

17 A woman's preaching is like a dog's walking on his hinder legs. It is not done well; but you are surprised to find it done at all.
James Boswell *Life of Samuel Johnson* (1791) 31 July 1763

18 We could not have had a better dinner had there been a *Synod of Cooks*.
James Boswell *Life of Samuel Johnson* (1791) 5 August 1763

19 Don't, Sir, accustom yourself to use big words for little matters. It would *not* be *terrible*, though I *were* to be detained some time here.
when Boswell said it would be 'terrible' if Johnson should not be able to return speedily from Harwich
James Boswell *Life of Samuel Johnson* (1791) 6 August 1763

20 I refute it *thus*.
on Boswell observing of Bishop **Berkeley***'s theory of the non-existence of matter that though they were satisfied it was not true, they were unable to refute it, Johnson struck his foot against a large stone, till he rebounded from it, with these words*
James Boswell *Life of Samuel Johnson* (1791) 6 August 1763

21 Sir John, Sir, is a very unclubbable man.
of Sir John Hawkins
James Boswell *Life of Samuel Johnson* (1791) Spring 1764

22 That all who are happy, are equally happy, is not true. A peasant and a philosopher may be equally *satisfied*, but not equally *happy*. Happiness consists in the multiplicity of agreeable consciousness.
James Boswell *Life of Samuel Johnson* (1791) February 1766

23 Our tastes greatly alter. The lad does not care for the child's rattle, and the old man does not care for the young man's whore.
James Boswell *Life of Samuel Johnson* (1791) Spring 1766

24 It was not for me to bandy civilities with my Sovereign.
James Boswell *Life of Samuel Johnson* (1791) February 1767

25 There was as great a difference between them as between a man who knew how a watch was made, and a man who could tell the hour by looking on the dial-plate.
James Boswell *Life of Samuel Johnson* (1791) Spring 1768

1 Let me smile with the wise, and feed with the rich.
responding to ***Garrick***
James Boswell *Life of Samuel Johnson* (1791) 6 October 1769; cf. **Garrick** 330:2

2 We *know* our will is free, and *there's* an end on't.
James Boswell *Life of Samuel Johnson* (1791) 16 October 1769

3 In the description of night in Macbeth, the beetle and the bat detract from the general idea of darkness,—inspissated gloom.
James Boswell *Life of Samuel Johnson* (1791) 16 October 1769

4 Most schemes of political improvement are very laughable things.
James Boswell *Life of Samuel Johnson* (1791) 26 October 1769

5 It matters not how a man dies, but how he lives. The act of dying is not of importance, it lasts so short a time.
James Boswell *Life of Samuel Johnson* (1791) 26 October 1769

6 Burton's *Anatomy of Melancholy*, he said, was the only book that ever took him out of bed two hours sooner than he wished to rise.
James Boswell *Life of Samuel Johnson* (1791) 1770

7 Want of tenderness, he always alleged, was want of parts, and was no less a proof of stupidity than depravity.
James Boswell *Life of Samuel Johnson* (1791) 1770

8 That fellow seems to me to possess but one idea, and that is a wrong one.
of a chance-met acquaintance
James Boswell *Life of Samuel Johnson* (1791) 1770; cf. **Disraeli** 270:24

9 Johnson observed, that 'he did not care to speak ill of any man behind his back, but he believed the gentleman was an *attorney*.'
James Boswell *Life of Samuel Johnson* (1791) 1770

10 The triumph of hope over experience.
of a man who remarried immediately after the death of a wife with whom he had been unhappy
James Boswell *Life of Samuel Johnson* (1791) 1770

11 Every man has a lurking wish to appear considerable in his native place.
James Boswell *Life of Samuel Johnson* (1791) letter to Sir Joshua Reynolds, 17 July 1771

12 It is so far from being natural for a man and woman to live in a state of marriage, that we find all the motives which they have for remaining in that connection, and the restraints which civilized society imposes to prevent separation, are hardly sufficient to keep them together.
James Boswell *Life of Samuel Johnson* (1791) 31 March 1772

13 Nobody can write the life of a man, but those who have eat and drunk and lived in social intercourse with him.
James Boswell *Life of Samuel Johnson* (1791) 31 March 1772

14 I would not give half a guinea to live under one form of government rather than another. It is of no moment to the happiness of an individual.
James Boswell *Life of Samuel Johnson* (1791) 31 March 1772

15 If a sovereign oppresses his people to a great degree, they will rise and cut off his head. There is a remedy in human nature against tyranny, that will keep us safe under every form of government.
James Boswell *Life of Samuel Johnson* (1791) 31 March 1772

16 A man who is good enough to go to heaven, is good enough to be a clergyman.
James Boswell *Life of Samuel Johnson* (1791) 5 April 1772

17 Why, Sir, if you were to read Richardson for the story, your impatience would be so much fretted that you would hang yourself.
James Boswell *Life of Samuel Johnson* (1791) 6 April 1772

18 Grief is a species of idleness.
letter to Mrs Thrale, 17 March 1773, in R. W. Chapman (ed.) *Letters of Samuel Johnson* (1952) vol. 1

19 He has, indeed, done it very well; but it is a foolish thing well done.
on ***Goldsmith****'s apology in the* London Chronicle *for physically assaulting Thomas Evans, who had published a damaging open letter to Goldsmith in the* London Packet *24 March 1773*
James Boswell *Life of Samuel Johnson* (1791) 3 April 1773

20 All intellectual improvement arises from leisure.
James Boswell *Life of Samuel Johnson* (1791) 13 April 1773

21 ELPHINSTON: What, have you not read it through?
JOHNSON: No, Sir, do *you* read books *through*?
James Boswell *Life of Samuel Johnson* (1791) 19 April 1773

22 Read over your compositions, and where ever you meet with a passage which you think is particularly fine, strike it out.
quoting a college tutor
James Boswell *Life of Samuel Johnson* (1791) 30 April 1773

23 I hope I shall never be deterred from detecting what I think a cheat, by the menaces of a ruffian ['Ossian'].
James Boswell *Life of Samuel Johnson* (1791) letter to James Macpherson, 20 January 1775

24 There are few ways in which a man can be more innocently employed than in getting money.
James Boswell *Life of Samuel Johnson* (1791) 27 March 1775

25 He was dull in a new way, and that made many people think him *great*.
of Thomas ***Gray***
James Boswell *Life of Samuel Johnson* (1791) 28 March 1775

26 I never think I have hit hard, unless it rebounds.
James Boswell *Life of Samuel Johnson* (1791) 2 April 1775

27 Fleet-street has a very animated appearance; but I think the full tide of human existence is at Charing-Cross.
James Boswell *Life of Samuel Johnson* (1791) 2 April 1775

28 George the First knew nothing, and desired to know nothing; did nothing, and desired to do nothing; and the only good thing that is told of him is, that he wished to restore the crown to its hereditary successor.
James Boswell *Life of Samuel Johnson* (1791) 6 April 1775

1 It is wonderful, when a calculation is made, how little the mind is actually employed in the discharge of any profession.
James Boswell *Life of Samuel Johnson* (1791) 6 April 1775

2 The greatest part of a writer's time is spent in reading, in order to write: a man will turn over half a library to make one book.
James Boswell *Life of Samuel Johnson* (1791) 6 April 1775

3 Patriotism is the last refuge of a scoundrel.
James Boswell *Life of Samuel Johnson* (1791) 7 April 1775

4 Knowledge is of two kinds. We know a subject ourselves, or we know where we can find information upon it.
James Boswell *Life of Samuel Johnson* (1791) 18 April 1775

5 Politics are now nothing more than means of rising in the world.
James Boswell *Life of Samuel Johnson* (1791) 18 April 1775

6 Players, Sir! I look upon them as no better than creatures set upon tables and joint-stools to make faces and produce laughter, like dancing dogs.
James Boswell *Life of Samuel Johnson* (1791) 1775

7 In lapidary inscriptions a man is not upon oath.
James Boswell *Life of Samuel Johnson* (1791) 1775

8 There is now less flogging in our great schools than formerly, but then less is learned there; so that what the boys get at one end they lose at the other.
James Boswell *Life of Samuel Johnson* (1791) 1775

9 Nothing odd will do long. *Tristram Shandy* did not last.
James Boswell *Life of Samuel Johnson* (1791) 20 March 1776

10 There is nothing which has yet been contrived by man, by which so much happiness is produced as by a good tavern or inn.
James Boswell *Life of Samuel Johnson* (1791) 21 March 1776; cf. **Shenstone** 715:6

11 Marriages would in general be as happy, and often more so, if they were all made by the Lord Chancellor, upon a due consideration of characters and circumstances, without the parties having any choice in the matter.
James Boswell *Life of Samuel Johnson* (1791) 22 March 1776

12 He is gone, and we are going.
on the death of her son, Harry
letter to Mrs Thrale, 25 March 1776, in R. W. Chapman (ed.) *Letters of Samuel Johnson* (1952) vol. 3

13 Questioning is not the mode of conversation among gentlemen. It is assuming a superiority.
James Boswell *Life of Samuel Johnson* (1791) 25 March 1776

14 Fine clothes are good only as they supply the want of other means of procuring respect.
James Boswell *Life of Samuel Johnson* (1791) 27 March 1776

15 If a madman were to come into this room with a stick in his hand, no doubt we should pity the state of his mind; but our primary consideration would be to take care of ourselves. We should knock him down first, and pity him afterwards.
James Boswell *Life of Samuel Johnson* (1791) 3 April 1776

16 We would all be idle if we could.
James Boswell *Life of Samuel Johnson* (1791) 1776

17 No man but a blockhead ever wrote, except for money.
James Boswell *Life of Samuel Johnson* (1791) 5 April 1776

18 A man who has not been in Italy, is always conscious of an inferiority, from his not having seen what it is expected a man should see.
James Boswell *Life of Samuel Johnson* (1791) 11 April 1776

19 BOSWELL: Sir, what is poetry?
JOHNSON: Why Sir, it is much easier to say what it is not. We all *know* what light is; but it is not easy to *tell* what it is.
James Boswell *Life of Samuel Johnson* (1791) 12 April 1776

20 Every man of any education would rather be called a rascal, than accused of deficiency in *the graces.*
James Boswell *Life of Samuel Johnson* (1791) May 1776

21 Sir, you have but two topics, yourself and me. I am sick of both.
James Boswell *Life of Samuel Johnson* (1791) May 1776

22 If I had no duties, and no reference to futurity, I would spend my life in driving briskly in a post-chaise with a pretty woman.
James Boswell *Life of Samuel Johnson* (1791) 19 September 1777

23 Depend upon it, Sir, when a man knows he is to be hanged in a fortnight, it concentrates his mind wonderfully.
on the execution of Dr Dodd for forgery, 27 June 1777
James Boswell *Life of Samuel Johnson* (1791) 19 September 1777

24 When a man is tired of London, he is tired of life.
James Boswell *Life of Samuel Johnson* (1791) 20 September 1777

25 All argument is against it; but all belief is for it.
of the existence of ghosts
James Boswell *Life of Samuel Johnson* (1791) 31 March 1778

26 John Wesley's conversation is good, but he is never at leisure. He is always obliged to go at a certain hour. This is very disagreeable to a man who loves to fold his legs and have out his talk, as I do.
James Boswell *Life of Samuel Johnson* (1791) 31 March 1778

27 Though we cannot out-vote them we will out-argue them.
on the practical value of speeches in the House of Commons
James Boswell *Life of Samuel Johnson* (1791) 3 April 1778

28 Every man thinks meanly of himself for not having been a soldier, or not having been at sea.
James Boswell *Life of Samuel Johnson* (1791) 10 April 1778

29 Johnson had said that he could repeat a complete chapter of 'The Natural History of Iceland', from the Danish of Horrebow, the whole of which was exactly thus:—'CHAP. LXXII. *Concerning snakes.* There are no snakes to be met with throughout the whole island.'
James Boswell *Life of Samuel Johnson* (1791) 13 April 1778

30 The more contracted that power is, the more easily it is destroyed. A country governed by a despot is an inverted cone.
James Boswell *Life of Samuel Johnson* (1791) 14 April 1778

1 So it is in travelling; a man must carry knowledge with him, if he would bring home knowledge.
James Boswell *Life of Samuel Johnson* (1791) 17 April 1778

2 Sir, the insolence of wealth will creep out.
James Boswell *Life of Samuel Johnson* (1791) 18 April 1778

3 All censure of a man's self is oblique praise. It is in order to shew how much he can spare.
James Boswell *Life of Samuel Johnson* (1791) 25 April 1778

4 I have always said, the first Whig was the Devil.
James Boswell *Life of Samuel Johnson* (1791) 28 April 1778

5 Mutual cowardice keeps us in peace. Were one half of mankind brave and one half cowards, the brave would be always beating the cowards. Were all brave, they would lead a very uneasy life; all would be continually fighting: but being all cowards, we go on very well.
James Boswell *Life of Samuel Johnson* (1791) 28 April 1778

6 Were it not for imagination, Sir, a man would be as happy in the arms of a chambermaid as of a Duchess.
James Boswell *Life of Samuel Johnson* (1791) 9 May 1778

7 Madam, before you flatter a man so grossly to his face, you should consider whether or not your flattery is worth his having.
remark to Hannah **More**
Charlotte Barrett (ed.) *Diary and Letters of Madame D'Arblay* [Fanny Burney] (1842) vol. 1, pt. 2, August 1778

8 Claret is the liquor for boys; port, for men; but he who aspires to be a hero (smiling) must drink brandy.
James Boswell *Life of Samuel Johnson* (1791) 7 April 1779

9 A man who exposes himself when he is intoxicated, has not the art of getting drunk.
James Boswell *Life of Samuel Johnson* (1791) 24 April 1779

10 Worth seeing, yes; but not worth going to see.
on the Giant's Causeway
James Boswell *Life of Samuel Johnson* (1791) 12 October 1779

11 If you are idle, be not solitary; if you are solitary, be not idle.
James Boswell *Life of Samuel Johnson* (1791) letter to Boswell, 27 October 1779; cf. **Closing lines** 222:5

12 Among the anfractuosities of the human mind, I know not if it may not be one, that there is a superstitious reluctance to sit for a picture.
James Boswell *Life of Samuel Johnson* (1791) 1780

13 Every man has a right to utter what he thinks truth, and every other man has a right to knock him down for it. Martyrdom is the test.
James Boswell *Life of Samuel Johnson* (1791) 1780

14 They are forced plants, raised in a hot-bed; and they are poor plants; they are but cucumbers after all.
of Thomas Gray's Odes
James Boswell *Life of Samuel Johnson* (1791) 1780

15 No man was more foolish when he had not a pen in his hand, or more wise when he had.
of Oliver **Goldsmith**
James Boswell *Life of Samuel Johnson* (1791) 1780; cf. **Garrick** 330:4

16 If a man talks of his misfortunes there is something in them that is not disagreeable to him; for where there is nothing but pure misery, there never is any recourse to the mention of it.
James Boswell *Life of Samuel Johnson* (1791) 1780

17 I believe that is true. The dogs don't know how to write trifles with dignity.
to Fowke, who had observed that in writing biography Johnson infinitely exceeded his contemporaries
James Boswell *Life of Samuel Johnson* (1791) 1781

18 Mrs Montagu has dropt me. Now, Sir, there are people whom one should like very well to drop, but would not wish to be dropped by.
James Boswell *Life of Samuel Johnson* (1791) March 1781

19 This merriment of parsons is mighty offensive.
James Boswell *Life of Samuel Johnson* (1791) March 1781

20 We are not here to sell a parcel of boilers and vats, but the potentiality of growing rich, beyond the dreams of avarice.
at the sale of Thrale's brewery
James Boswell *Life of Samuel Johnson* (1791) 6 April 1781; cf. **Moore** 529:10

21 Classical quotation is the *parole* of literary men all over the world.
James Boswell *Life of Samuel Johnson* (1791) 8 May 1781

22 Why, that is, because, dearest, you're a dunce.
to Miss Monckton, later Lady Corke, who said that **Sterne***'s writings affected her*
James Boswell *Life of Samuel Johnson* (1791) May 1781

23 Sir, I have two very cogent reasons for not printing any list of subscribers;—one, that I have lost all the names,—the other, that I have spent all the money.
James Boswell *Life of Samuel Johnson* (1791) May 1781

24 Always, Sir, set a high value on spontaneous kindness. He whose inclination prompts him to cultivate your friendship of his own accord, will love you more than one whom you have been at pains to attach to you.
James Boswell *Life of Samuel Johnson* (1791) May 1781

25 A wise Tory and a wise Whig, I believe, will agree. Their principles are the same, though their modes of thinking are different.
James Boswell *Life of Samuel Johnson* (1791) May 1781, written statement given to Boswell

26 I hate a fellow whom pride, or cowardice, or laziness drives into a corner, and who does nothing when he is there but sit and *growl*; let him come out as I do, and *bark*.
of Jeremiah Markland
James Boswell *Life of Samuel Johnson* (1791) 10 October 1782

27 Resolve not to be poor: whatever you have, spend less. Poverty is a great enemy to human happiness; it certainly destroys liberty, and it makes some virtues impracticable, and others extremely difficult.
James Boswell *Life of Samuel Johnson* (1791) letter to Boswell, 7 December 1782

1 How few of his friends' houses would a man choose to be at when he is sick.
James Boswell *Life of Samuel Johnson* (1791) 1783

2 There is a wicked inclination in most people to suppose an old man decayed in his intellects. If a young or middle-aged man, when leaving a company, does not recollect where he laid his hat, it is nothing; but if the same inattention is discovered in an old man, people will shrug up their shoulders, and say, 'His memory is going.'
James Boswell *Life of Samuel Johnson* (1791) 1783

3 A man might write such stuff for ever, if he would *abandon* his mind to it.
of Ossian
James Boswell *Life of Samuel Johnson* (1791) 1783

4 Sir, there is no settling the point of precedency between a louse and a flea.
on the relative merits of two minor poets
James Boswell *Life of Samuel Johnson* (1791) 1783

5 When I observed he was a fine cat, saying, 'Why yes, Sir, but I have had cats whom I liked better than this'; and then as if perceiving Hodge to be out of countenance, adding, 'but he is a very fine cat, a very fine cat indeed.'
James Boswell *Life of Samuel Johnson* (1791) 1783

6 Clear your mind of cant.
James Boswell *Life of Samuel Johnson* (1791) 15 May 1783

7 The black dog I hope always to resist, and in time to drive, though I am deprived of almost all those that used to help me . . . When I rise my breakfast is solitary, the black dog waits to share it, from breakfast to dinner he continues barking, except that Dr Brocklesby for a little keeps him at a distance . . . Night comes at last, and some hours of restlessness and confusion bring me again to a day of solitude. What shall exclude the black dog from a habitation like this?
on his attacks of melancholia; more recently associated with Winston **Churchill**, *who used the phrase 'black dog' when alluding to his own periodic bouts of depression*
letter to Mrs Thrale, 28 June 1783, in R. W. Chapman (ed.) *Letters of Samuel Johnson* (1952) vol. 3

8 As I know more of mankind I expect less of them, and am ready now to call a man *a good man*, upon easier terms than I was formerly.
James Boswell *Life of Samuel Johnson* (1791) September 1783

9 If a man were to go by chance at the same time with Burke under a shed, to shun a shower, he would say—'this is an extraordinary man.'
on Edmund **Burke**
James Boswell *Life of Samuel Johnson* (1791) 15 May 1784

10 It is as bad as bad can be: it is ill-fed, ill-killed, ill-kept, and ill-drest.
on the roast mutton he had been served at an inn
James Boswell *Life of Samuel Johnson* (1791) 3 June 1784

11 JOHNSON: As I cannot be sure that I have fulfilled the conditions on which salvation is granted, I am afraid I may be one of those who shall be damned (looking dismally).
DR ADAMS: What do you mean by damned?
JOHNSON: (passionately and loudly) Sent to Hell, Sir, and punished everlastingly.
James Boswell *Life of Samuel Johnson* (1791) 12 June 1784

12 Milton, Madam, was a genius that could cut a Colossus from a rock; but could not carve heads upon cherry-stones.
to Hannah **More**, *who had expressed a wonder that the poet who had written* Paradise Lost *should write such poor sonnets*
James Boswell *Life of Samuel Johnson* (1791) 13 June 1784

13 It might as well be said 'Who drives fat oxen should himself be fat.'
parodying Henry **Brooke**
James Boswell *Life of Samuel Johnson* (1791) June 1784; cf. **Brooke** 150:6

14 Sir, I have found you an argument; but I am not obliged to find you an understanding.
James Boswell *Life of Samuel Johnson* (1791) June 1784

15 No man is a hypocrite in his pleasures.
James Boswell *Life of Samuel Johnson* (1791) June 1784; cf. **Pope** 584:2

16 Talking of the Comedy of 'The Rehearsal,' he said, 'It has not wit enough to keep it sweet.' This was easy;—he therefore caught himself, and pronounced a more rounded sentence; 'It has not vitality enough to preserve it from putrefaction.'
James Boswell *Life of Samuel Johnson* (1791) June 1784

17 Who can run the race with Death?
James Boswell *Life of Samuel Johnson* (1791) letter to Dr Burney, 2 August 1784

18 Dictionaries are like watches, the worst is better than none, and the best cannot be expected to go quite true.
James Boswell *Life of Samuel Johnson* (1791) letter to Francesco Sastres, 21 August 1784

19 Sir, I look upon every day to be lost, in which I do not make a new acquaintance.
James Boswell *Life of Samuel Johnson* (1791) November 1784

20 I will be conquered; I will not capitulate.
on his illness
James Boswell *Life of Samuel Johnson* (1791) November 1784

21 Long-expected one-and-twenty,
Ling'ring year, at length is flown;
Pride and pleasure, pomp and plenty,
Great [Sir John], are now your own.
James Boswell *Life of Samuel Johnson* (1791) December 1784

22 An odd thought strikes me:—we shall receive no letters in the grave.
James Boswell *Life of Samuel Johnson* (1791) December 1784

23 Abstinence is as easy to me, as temperance would be difficult.
William Roberts (ed.) *Memoirs of the Life and Correspondence of Mrs Hannah More* (1834) vol. 1

24 As with my hat upon my head
I walked along the Strand,
I there did meet another man
With his hat in his hand.
in *European Magazine* January 1785 'Anecdotes by George Steevens'

1 Corneille is to Shakespeare . . . as a clipped hedge is to a forest.

Hester Lynch Piozzi *Anecdotes of . . . Johnson* (1786)

2 Difficult do you call it, Sir? I wish it were impossible.

on the performance of a celebrated violinist

William Seward *Supplement to the Anecdotes of Distinguished Persons* (1797)

3 Every man has, some time in his life, an ambition to be a wag.

Joyce Hemlow (ed.) *Journals and Letters of Fanny Burney* vol. 1 (1972)

4 [Goldsmith] seeming to repine at the success of Beattie's Essay on Truth—'Here's such a stir (said he) about a fellow that has written one book, and I have written many.' Ah, Doctor (says his friend [Johnson]), there go two-and-forty sixpences you know to one guinea.

Hester Lynch Piozzi *Anecdotes of . . . Johnson* (1786)

5 He hated a fool, and he hated a rogue, and he hated a whig; he was a very good hater.

of Bathurst

Hester Lynch Piozzi *Anecdotes of . . . Johnson* (1786)

6 I dogmatise and am contradicted, and in this conflict of opinions and sentiments I find delight.

on his conversation in taverns

John Hawkins *Life of Samuel Johnson* (1787) p. 87

7 *Iam moriturus.*

I who am about to die.

to Francesco Sastres, shortly before his death on 13 December 1784, in John Hawkins *Life of Samuel Johnson* (1787); cf. **Anonymous** 21:3

8 If the man who turnips cries,
Cry not when his father dies,
'Tis a proof that he had rather
Have a turnip than his father.

burlesque of Lope de Vega's lines 'si a quien los leones vence [He who can conquer a lion . . .]'

Hester Lynch Piozzi *Anecdotes of . . . Johnson* (1786)

9 It is very strange, and very melancholy, that the paucity of human pleasures should persuade us ever to call hunting one of them.

Hester Lynch Piozzi *Anecdotes of . . . Johnson* (1786)

10 Love is the wisdom of the fool and the folly of the wise.

William Cooke *Life of Samuel Foote* (1805) vol. 2

11 A man is in general better pleased when he has a good dinner upon his table, than when his wife talks Greek.

John Hawkins (ed.) *The Works of Samuel Johnson* (1787) 'Apophthegms, Sentiments, Opinions, etc.' vol. 11

12 Of music Dr Johnson used to say that it was the only sensual pleasure without vice.

in *European Magazine* (1795)

13 One day at Streatham . . . a young gentleman called to him suddenly, and I suppose he thought disrespectfully, in these words: 'Mr Johnson, would you advise me to marry?' 'I would advise no man to marry, Sir,' returns for answer in a very angry tone Dr Johnson, 'who is not likely to propagate understanding.'

Hester Lynch Piozzi *Anecdotes of . . . Johnson* (1786)

14 Was there ever yet anything written by mere man that was wished longer by its readers, excepting *Don Quixote*, *Robinson Crusoe*, and the *Pilgrim's Progress*?

Hester Lynch Piozzi *Anecdotes of . . . Johnson* (1786)

15 What is written without effort is in general read without pleasure.

William Seward *Biographia* (1799)

Samuel Johnson 1822–82

American nonconformist minister

16 City of God, how broad and far.

title of hymn (1864)

Hanns Johst 1890–1978

German dramatist

17 Whenever I hear the word culture . . . I release the safety-catch of my Browning!

often attributed to Hermann **Goering**, *and quoted as 'Whenever I hear the word culture, I reach for my pistol!'*

Schlageter (1933) act 1, sc. 1

Jean de Joinville *c.*1224–1319

French historian, biographer of Louis IX of France

18 A *prudhomme* is so grand and good a thing that even to pronounce the word fills the mouth pleasantly.

prudhomme *'a man of valour and dignity'*

The Life of St Louis

19 Just like the writer who has finished his book and illuminates it with gold and azure, so the king illuminated his kingdom with the beautiful abbeys he made.

The Life of St Louis

Al Jolson (Asa Yoelson) 1886–1950

American singer

see also **Lewis** *467:5*

20 You think that's noise—you ain't heard nuttin' yet!

in a café, competing with the din from a neighbouring building site, in 1906; subsequently an aside in the 1927 film The Jazz Singer

Martin Abramson *The Real Story of Al Jolson* (1950) (later the title of a Jolson song, 1919, in the form 'You Ain't Heard Nothing Yet')

Henry Arthur Jones 1851–1929 and **Henry Herman** 1832–94

English dramatists

21 O God! Put back Thy universe and give me yesterday.

The Silver King (1907) act 2, sc. 4

John Paul Jones 1747–92
American admiral

1 I have not yet begun to fight.
when asked whether he had lowered his flag, as his ship was sinking, 23 September 1779
Mrs Reginald De Koven *Life and Letters of John Paul Jones* (1914) vol. 1

LeRoi Jones see **Imamu Amiri Baraka**

Mary Harris 'Mother' Jones 1830–1930
Irish-born American labour activist

2 Pray for the dead and fight like hell for the living!
The Autobiography of Mother Jones (1925)

Steve Jones 1944–
English geneticist

3 Sex and taxes are in many ways the same. Tax does to cash what males do to genes. It dispenses assets among the population as a whole. Sex, not death, is the great leveller.
speech to the Royal Society; in *Independent* 25 January 1997

William Jones 1746–94
English jurist

4 My opinion is, that power should always be distrusted, in whatever hands it is placed.
letter to Lord Althorpe, 5 October 1782, in Lord Teignmouth *Life of Sir W. Jones* (1835) vol. 1

5 Seven hours to law, to soothing slumber seven,
Ten to the world allot, and *all* to Heaven.
lines in substitution for Sir Edward Coke's lines 'Six hours in sleep . . .', in Lord Teignmouth *Life of Sir W. Jones* (1835) vol. 2; cf. **Coke** 224:11

Erica Jong 1942–
American novelist

6 The zipless fuck is absolutely pure. It is free of ulterior motives. There is no power game. The man is not 'taking' and the woman is not 'giving' . . . The zipless fuck is the purest thing there is. And it is rarer than the unicorn.
Fear of Flying (1973) ch. 1

7 Jealousy is all the fun you *think* they had.
How to Save Your Own Life (1977)

Ben Jonson *c.*1573–1637
English dramatist and poet
on Jonson: see **Dryden** *283:7,* **Epitaphs** *304:1,* **Milton** *512:24; see also* **Epitaphs** *302:16*

8 Fortune, that favours fools.
The Alchemist (1610) prologue

9 We will eat our mullets,
Soused in high-country wines, sup pheasants' eggs,
And have our cockles boiled in silver shells;
Our shrimps to swim again, as when they lived,
In a rare butter made of dolphins' milk,
Whose cream does look like opals.
The Alchemist (1610) act 4, sc. 1

10 Think
What a young wife and a good brain may do:
Stretch age's truth sometimes, and crack it too.
The Alchemist (1610) act 5, sc. 2

11 The very womb and bed of enormity.
of Ursula, the 'pig-woman'
Bartholomew Fair (1614) act 2, sc. 1

12 The lungs of the tobacconist are rotted, the liver spotted, the brain smoked like the backside of the pig-woman's booth here, and the whole body within, black as her pan you saw e'en now without.
Bartholomew Fair (1614) act 2, sc. 1

13 Neither do thou lust after that tawney weed tobacco.
Bartholomew Fair (1614) act 2, sc. 6

14 PEOPLE: The Voice of Cato is the voice of Rome.
CATO: The voice of Rome is the consent of heaven!
Catiline his Conspiracy (1611) act 3, sc. 1

15 Where it concerns himself,
Who's angry at a slander makes it true.
Catiline his Conspiracy (1611) act 3, sc. 1

16 Slow, slow, fresh fount, keep time with my salt tears.
Cynthia's Revels (1600) act 1, sc. 1

17 Queen and huntress, chaste and fair,
Now the sun is laid to sleep,
Seated in thy silver chair,
State in wonted manner keep:
Hesperus entreats thy light,
Goddess, excellently bright.
Cynthia's Revels (1600) act 5, sc. 3

18 This is Mab, the Mistress-Fairy
That doth nightly rob the dairy.
The Entertainment at Althorpe (1603)

19 Still to be neat, still to be drest,
As you were going to a feast;
Still to be powdered, still perfumed,
Lady, it is to be presumed,
Though art's hid causes are not found,
All is not sweet, all is not sound.
Epicene (1609) act 1, sc. 1

20 Such sweet neglect more taketh me,
Than all the adulteries of art;
They strike mine eyes, but not my heart.
Epicene (1609) act 1, sc. 1

21 And to these courteous eyes oppose a mirror,
As large as is the stage whereon we act;
Where they shall see the time's deformity
Anatomised in every nerve, and sinew.
Every Man out of His Humour (1600) Induction

22 Blind Fortune still
Bestows her gifts on such as cannot use them.
Every Man out of His Humour (1599) act 2, sc. 2

23 Ramp up my genius, be not retrograde;
But boldly nominate a spade a spade.
The Poetaster (1601) act 5, sc. 1

1 Detraction is but baseness' varlet;
And apes are apes, though clothed in scarlet.
The Poetaster (1601) act 5, sc. 1; cf. **Proverbs** 595:10

2 Tell proud Jove,
Between his power and thine there is no odds:
'Twas only fear first in the world made gods.
Sejanus (1603) act 2, sc. 2

3 Riches, the dumb god that giv'st all men tongues,
That canst do nought, and yet mak'st men do all things;
The price of souls; even hell, with thee to boot,
Is made worth heaven! Thou art virtue, fame,
Honour, and all things else.
Volpone (1606) act 1, sc. 1

4 I glory
More in the cunning purchase of my wealth
Than in the glad possession.
Volpone (1606) act 1, sc. 1

5 Give 'em words;
Pour oil into their ears, and send them hence.
Volpone (1606) act 1, sc. 4

6 What a rare punishment
Is avarice to itself!
Volpone (1606) act 1, sc. 4

7 I have been at my book, and am now past the craggy paths of study, and come to the flowery plains of honour and reputation.
Volpone (1606) act 2, sc. 1

8 Calumnies are answered best with silence.
Volpone (1606) act 2, sc. 2

9 Almost
All the wise world is little else in nature
But parasites or sub-parasites.
Volpone (1606) act 3, sc. 1

10 Suns, that set, may rise again;
But if once we lose this light,
'Tis with us perpetual night.
Volpone (1606) act 3, sc. 5; cf. **Catullus** 197:2

11 Our drink shall be prepared gold and amber;
Which we will take, until my roof whirl around
With the *vertigo*: and my dwarf shall dance.
Volpone (1606) act 3, sc. 5

12 Come, my Celia, let us prove,
While we can, the sports of love.
Volpone (1606) act 3, sc. 5; cf. **Catullus** 197:2

13 Honour! tut, a breath,
There's no such thing in nature; a mere term
Invented to awe fools.
Volpone (1606) act 3, sc. 7

14 You have a gift, sir, (thank your education),
Will never let you want, while there are men,
And malice, to breed causes.
to a lawyer
Volpone (1606) act 5, sc. 1

15 Mischiefs feed
Like beasts, till they be fat, and then they bleed.
Volpone (1606) act 5, sc. 8

16 The voice so sweet, the words so fair,
As some soft chime had stroked the air;
And though the sound were parted thence,
Still left an echo in the sense.
'Eupheme' (1640) no. 4 'The Mind'

17 Rest in soft peace, and, asked, say here doth lie
Ben Jonson his best piece of poetry.
'On My First Son' (1616)

18 This figure that thou here seest put,
It was for gentle Shakespeare cut,
Wherein the graver had a strife
With Nature, to out-do the life:
O could he but have drawn his wit
As well in brass, as he has hit
His face; the print would then surpass
All that was ever writ in brass:
But since he cannot, reader, look
Not on his picture, but his book.
on the portrait of ***Shakespeare***
First Folio Shakespeare (1623) 'To the Reader'

19 Follow a shadow, it still flies you;
Seem to fly it, it will pursue:
So court a mistress, she denies you;
Let her alone, she will court you.
Say, are not women truly then
Styled but the shadows of us men?
'That Women are but Men's Shadows' (1616)

20 Drink to me only with thine eyes,
And I will pledge with mine;
Or leave a kiss but in the cup,
And I'll not look for wine.
'To Celia' (1616)

21 In small proportions we just beauty see,
And in short measures life may perfect be.
'To the Immortal Memory . . . of . . . Sir Lucius Carey and Sir H. Morison' (1640)

22 Soul of the Age!
The applause, delight, the wonder of our stage!
'To the Memory of My Beloved, the Author, Mr William Shakespeare' (1623)

23 How far thou didst our Lyly outshine,
Or sporting Kyd, or Marlowe's mighty line.
'To the Memory of . . . Shakespeare' (1623)

24 Thou hadst small Latin, and less Greek.
'To the Memory of . . . Shakespeare' (1623)

25 He was not of an age, but for all time!
'To the Memory of . . . Shakespeare' (1623)

26 Sweet Swan of Avon! What a sight it were
To see thee in our waters yet appear,
And make those flights upon the banks of Thames
That so did take Eliza, and our James!
'To the Memory of . . . Shakespeare' (1623)

27 Thou art not, Penshurst, built to envious show
Of touch or marble, nor canst boast a row
Of polished pillars, or a roof of gold;
Thou hast no lantern whereof tales are told,
Or stair, or courts; but standst an ancient pile,
And these grudged at, art reverenced the while.
'To Penshurst' (1616) l. 1

28 The blushing apricot and woolly peach
Hang on thy walls, that every child may reach.
'To Penshurst' (1616) l. 43

1 Donne, for not keeping of accent, deserved hanging . . . Shakespeare wanted art.
in *Conversations with William Drummond of Hawthornden* (written 1619) no. 3

2 The players have often mentioned it as an honour to Shakespeare that in his writing, whatsoever he penned, he never blotted out a line. My answer hath been 'Would he had blotted a thousand' . . . But he redeemed his vices with his virtues. There was ever more in him to be praised than to be pardoned.
Timber, or Discoveries made upon Men and Matter (1641) l. 658 'De Shakespeare Nostrati'; cf. **Heming** 369:8, **Pope** 586:18

3 The fear of every man that heard him was, lest he should make an end.
on Francis ***Bacon***
Timber, or Discoveries made upon Men and Matter (1641) l. 906 'Dominus Verulamius'

4 Talking and eloquence are not the same: to speak, and to speak well, are two things.
Timber, or Discoveries made upon Men and Matter (1641) l. 1882 'Praecept[a] Element[aria]'

Janis Joplin 1943–70
American singer

5 Fourteen heart attacks and he had to die in my week. In MY week.
when ex-President ***Eisenhower****'s death prevented her photograph appearing on the cover of* Newsweek
in *New Musical Express* 12 April 1969

Thomas Jordan *c.*1612–85
English poet and dramatist

6 They plucked communion tables down
And broke our painted glasses;
They threw our altars to the ground
And tumbled down the crosses.
They set up Cromwell and his heir—
The Lord and Lady Claypole—
Because they hated Common Prayer,
The organ and the maypole.
'How the War began' (1664)

Joseph II 1741–90
Holy Roman Emperor

7 Too beautiful for our ears, and much too many notes, dear Mozart.
of The Abduction from the Seraglio *(1782)*
attributed; Franz Xaver Niemetschek *Life of Mozart* (1798)

Chief Joseph (Hinmaton-Yalaktit) *c.*1840–1904
Nez Percé leader

8 From where the sun now stands I will fight no more forever.
speech at the end of the Nez Percé war in 1877; Dee Brown *Bury My Heart at Wounded Knee* (1970) ch. 13

9 Good words do not last long unless they amount to something. Words do not pay for my dead people.
on a visit to Washington in 1879; Chester Anders Fee *Chief Joseph* (1936)

Jenny Joseph 1932–
English poet

10 When I am an old woman I shall wear purple
With a red hat which doesn't go, and doesn't suit me.
And I shall spend my pension on brandy and summer gloves
And satin sandals, and say we've got no money for butter.
'Warning' (1974)

11 I was raised to feel that doing nothing was a sin. I had to learn to do nothing.
in *Observer* 19 April 1998 'Sayings of the Week'

Benjamin Jowett 1817–93
English classicist; Master of Balliol College, Oxford, from 1870
on Jowett: see ***Beeching*** *61:9*

12 The lie in the soul is a true lie.
introduction to his translation (1871) of Plato's *Republic* bk. 2

13 Nowhere probably is there more true feeling, and nowhere worse taste, than in a churchyard.
Evelyn Abbott and Lewis Campbell (eds.) *Letters of Benjamin Jowett* (1899) ch. 6

14 One man is as good as another until he has written a book.
Evelyn Abbott and Lewis Campbell (eds.) *Life and Letters of Benjamin Jowett* (1897) vol. 1

James Joyce 1882–1941
Irish novelist
on Joyce: see ***Forster*** *320:13,* ***Lawrence*** *458:23,* ***Woolf*** *827:3; see also* ***Opening lines*** *556:9, 556:12*

15 His soul swooned slowly as he heard the snow falling faintly through the universe and faintly falling, like the descent of their last end, upon all the living and the dead.
Dubliners (1914) 'The Dead'

16 Dear, dirty Dublin.
Dubliners (1914) 'A Little Cloud'

17 riverrun, past Eve and Adam's, from swerve of shore to bend of bay, brings us by a commodious vicus of recirculation back to Howth Castle and Environs.
Finnegans Wake (1939) pt. 1

18 That ideal reader suffering from an ideal insomnia.
Finnegans Wake (1939) pt. 1

19 The flushpots of Euston and the hanging garments of Marylebone.
Finnegans Wake (1939) pt. 1

20 All moanday, tearsday, wailsday, thumpsday, frightday, shatterday till the fear of the Law.
Finnegans Wake (1939) pt. 2

21 Three quarks for Muster Mark!
Finnegans Wake (1939) pt. 2

22 A portrait of the artist as a young man.
title of book (1916)

1 Poor Parnell! he cried loudly. My dead king!
A Portrait of the Artist as a Young Man (1916) ch. 1

2 When the soul of a man is born in this country, there are nets flung at it to hold it back from flight. You talk to me of nationality, language, religion. I shall try to fly by those nets.
A Portrait of the Artist as a Young Man (1916) ch. 5

3 Ireland is the old sow that eats her farrow.
A Portrait of the Artist as a Young Man (1916) ch. 5

4 The artist, like the God of the creation, remains within or behind or beyond or above his handiwork, invisible, refined out of existence, indifferent, paring his fingernails.
A Portrait of the Artist as a Young Man (1916) ch. 5

5 The only arms I allow myself to use, silence, exile, and cunning.
A Portrait of the Artist as a Young Man (1916) ch. 5

6 By an epiphany he meant a sudden spiritual manifestation, whether in vulgarity of speech or of gesture or in a memorable phase of the mind itself. He believed that it was for the man of letters to recover these epiphanies with extreme care, seeing that they themselves are the most delicate and evanescent of moments.
Stephen Hero (1944) ch. 25 (part of a first draft of *A Portrait of the Artist as a Young Man*)

7 The snotgreen sea. The scrotumtightening sea.
Ulysses (1922)

8 It is a symbol of Irish art. The cracked lookingglass of a servant.
Ulysses (1922)

9 I fear those big words, Stephen said, which make us so unhappy.
Ulysses (1922)

10 History, Stephen said, is a nightmare from which I am trying to awake.
Ulysses (1922)

11 Lawn Tennyson, gentleman poet.
Ulysses (1922)

12 Mr Leopold Bloom ate with relish the inner organs of beasts and fowls. He liked thick giblet soup, nutty gizzards, a stuffed roast heart, liverslices fried with crustcrumbs, fried hencod's roes. Most of all he liked grilled mutton kidneys which gave to his palate a fine tang of faintly scented urine.
Ulysses (1922)

13 He . . . saw the dark tangled curls of his bush floating, floating hair of the stream around the limp father of thousands, a languid floating flower.
Ulysses (1922)

14 Come forth, Lazarus! And he came fifth and lost the job.
Ulysses (1922)

15 Plenty to see and hear and feel yet. Feel live warm beings near you. They aren't going to get me this innings. Warm beds: warm full blooded life.
Ulysses (1922)

16 Greater love than this, he said, no man hath that a man lay down his wife for his friend. Go thou and do likewise. Thus, or words to that effect, saith Zarathustra, sometime regius professor of French letters to the university of Oxtail.
Ulysses (1922); cf. **Bible** 102:22

17 The heaventree of stars hung with humid nightblue fruit.
Ulysses (1922)

18 O, father forsaken,
Forgive your son!
'Ecce Puer'

19 Writing in English is the most ingenious torture ever devised for sins committed in previous lives. The English reading public explains the reason why.
letter, 5 September 1918; Richard Ellmann (ed.) *Selected Letters of James Joyce* (1975)

William Joyce (Lord Haw-Haw) 1906–46

wartime broadcaster from Nazi Germany, executed for treason

20 Germany calling! Germany calling!
habitual introduction to propaganda broadcasts to Britain during the Second World War

Juan Carlos I 1938–

King of Spain from 1975

21 The Crown, the symbol of the permanence and unity of Spain, cannot tolerate any actions by people attempting to disrupt by force the democratic process.
on the occasion of the attempted coup in 1981
television broadcast at 1.15 a.m., 24 February 1981

22 I will neither abdicate the Crown nor leave Spain. Whoever rebels will provoke a new civil war and will be responsible.
on the occasion of the attempted coup in 1981
television broadcast at 1.15 a.m., 24 February 1981

Judah ben Samuel the Hasid d. 1217

Jewish mystic

23 In thy intercourse with non-Jews, be careful to be as wholly sincere as in that with Jews. In most places, Jews are not unlike Christians in their morals and usages.
Sefer Hasidim

24 There are three [sorts of people] for whom we should sternly close our hearts: a cruel person who commits vile things; the fool who rushes into ruin in spite of warning; and the ingrate. Ingratitude is the blackest of faults.
Sefer Hasidim

25 Sweet hymns shall be my chant and woven songs.
For Thou art all for which my spirit longs—
To be within the shadow of Thy hand
And all Thy mystery to understand.
The while Thy glory is upon my tongue,
My inmost heart with love of Thee is wrung.
'Hymn of Glory'

Jack Judge 1878–1938 and **Harry Williams** 1874–1924

British songwriters

1 It's a long way to Tipperary,
It's a long way to go;
It's a long way to Tipperary,
To the sweetest girl I know!
Goodbye, Piccadilly,
Farewell, Leicester Square,
It's a long, long way to Tipperary,
But my heart's right there!
'It's a Long Way to Tipperary' (1912 song)

Julian of Norwich 1343–after 1416

English anchoress

2 He showed me something small, no bigger than a hazelnut, lying in the palm of my hand, as it seemed to me, and it was as round as a ball. I looked at it with the eye of my understanding, and thought: What can this be? I was amazed that it could last, for I thought that because of its littleness it would suddenly have fallen into nothing. And I was answered in my understanding: It lasts and always will, because God loves it; and thus every thing has being through the love of God.
Revelations of Divine Love (the long text) ch. 5

3 Sin is behovely, but all shall be well and all shall be well and all manner of thing shall be well.
Revelations of Divine Love (the long text) ch. 27, Revelation 13; cf. **Eliot** 294:20

4 Wouldest thou wit thy Lord's meaning in this thing? Wit it well: Love was his meaning. Who shewed it thee? Love. What shewed He thee? Love. Wherefore shewed it He? for Love . . . Thus was I learned that Love is our Lord's meaning.
Revelations of Divine Love (the long text) ch. 86, Revelation 16

Julian the Apostate see **Last words**

Carl Gustav Jung 1875–1961

Swiss psychologist

5 A more or less superficial layer of the unconscious is undoubtedly personal. I call it the *personal unconscious*. But this personal unconscious rests upon a deeper layer, which does not derive from personal experience and is not a personal acquisition but is inborn. This deeper layer I call the *collective unconscious* . . . The contents of the personal unconscious are chiefly the *feeling-toned complexes* . . . The contents of the collective unconscious, on the other hand, are known as *archetypes*.
Eranos Jahrbuch (1934)

6 A man who has not passed through the inferno of his passions has never overcome them.
Memories, Dreams, Reflections (1962) ch. 9

7 As far as we can discern, the sole purpose of human existence is to kindle a light in the darkness of mere being.
Memories, Dreams, Reflections (1962) ch. 11

8 Every form of addiction is bad, no matter whether the narcotic be alcohol or morphine or idealism.
Memories, Dreams, Reflections (1962) ch. 12

9 The meeting of two personalities is like the contact of two chemical substances: if there is any reaction, both are transformed.
Modern Man in Search of a Soul (1933)

10 The afternoon of human life must also have a significance of its own and cannot be merely a pitiful appendage to life's morning.
The Stages of Life (1930)

11 If there is anything that we wish to change in the child, we should first examine it and see whether it is not something that could better be changed in ourselves.
'Vom Werden der Persönlichkeit' (1932)

'Junius'

18th-century pseudonymous writer

12 The liberty of the press is the *Palladium* of all the civil, political, and religious rights of an Englishman.
The Letters of Junius (1772 ed.) 'Dedication to the English Nation'

13 The right of election is the very essence of the constitution.
in *Public Advertiser* 24 April 1769, letter 11

14 There is a holy mistaken zeal in politics as well as in religion. By persuading others, we convince ourselves.
in *Public Advertiser* 19 December 1769, letter 35

15 However distinguished by rank or property, in the rights of freedom we are all equal.
in *Public Advertiser* 19 March 1770, letter 37

16 The injustice done to an individual is sometimes of service to the public.
in *Public Advertiser* 14 November 1770, letter 41

17 As for Mr Wedderburne, there is something about him, which even treachery cannot trust.
in *Public Advertiser* 22 June 1771, letter 49

John Junor 1919–97

British journalist
see also ***Catchphrases*** *196:18*

18 Such a graceful exit. And then he had to go and do this on the doorstep.
on Harold ***Wilson****'s 'Lavender List' (the honours list he drew up on resigning the British premiership in 1976)*
in *Observer* 23 January 1990

Donald Justice 1925–

American poet

19 Men at forty
Learn to close softly
The doors to rooms they will not be
Coming back to.
'Men at Forty' (1967)

Justinian AD 483–565

Roman emperor from AD 527

1 Justice is the constant and perpetual wish to render to every one his due.
Institutes bk. 1, ch. 1, para. 1

2 Solomon, I have vanquished thee.
at the dedication of Hagia Sophia in Constantinople, 27 December AD 537
attributed (according to a late tradition)

Juvenal AD *c.*60–*c.*130

Roman satirist

3 *Difficile est saturam non scribere.*
It's hard not to write satire.
Satires no. 1, l. 30

4 *Probitas laudatur et alget.*
Honesty is praised and left to shiver.
Satires no. 1, l. 74 (translation by G. G. Ramsay)

5 *Si natura negat, facit indignatio versum.*
Even if nature says no, indignation makes me write verse.
Satires no. 1, l. 79

6 *Quidquid agunt homines, votum timor ira voluptas*
Gaudia discursus nostri farrago libelli est.
Everything mankind does, their hope, fear, rage, pleasure, joys, business, are the hotch-potch of my little book.
Satires no. 1, l. 85

7 *Quis tulerit Gracchos de seditione querentes?*
Who would put up with the Gracchi complaining about subversion?
Satires no. 2, l. 24

8 *Nemo repente fuit turpissimus.*
No one ever suddenly became depraved.
Satires no. 2, l. 83

9 *Iam pridem Syrus in Tiberim defluxit Orontes*
Et linguam et mores.
The Syrian Orontes has now for long been pouring into the Tiber, with its own language and ways of behaving.
Satires no. 3, l. 62

10 *Grammaticus, rhetor, geometres, pictor, aliptes,*
Augur, schoenobates, medicus, magus, omnia novit
Graeculus esuriens: in caelum iusseris ibit.
Scholar, public speaker, geometrician, painter, physical training instructor, diviner of the future, rope-dancer, doctor, magician, the hungry little Greek can do everything: send him to—heaven (and he'll go there).
Satires no. 3, l. 76

11 *Nil habet infelix paupertas durius in se*
Quam quod ridiculos homines facit.
The misfortunes of poverty carry with them nothing harder to bear than that it makes men ridiculous.
Satires no. 3, l. 152

12 *Haud facile emergunt quorum virtutibus obstat*
Res angusta domi.
They do not easily rise out of obscurity whose talents straitened circumstances obstruct at home.
Satires no. 3, l. 164

13 *. . . Omnia Romae*
Cum pretio.
Everything in Rome has its price.
Satires no. 3, l. 183

14 *Rara avis in terris nigroque simillima cycno.*
A rare bird on this earth, like nothing so much as a black swan.
Satires no. 6, l. 165

15 *Hoc volo, sic iubeo, sit pro ratione voluntas.*
I will have this done, so I order it done; let my will replace reasoned judgement.
Satires no. 6, l. 223

16 *'Pone seram, cohibe.' Sed quis custodiet ipsos*
Custodes? Cauta est et ab illis incipit uxor.
'Bolt her in, keep her indoors.' But who is to guard the guards themselves? Your wife is prudent and begins with them.
Satires no. 6, l. 347

17 *Tenet insanabile multos*
Scribendi cacoethes et aegro in corde senescit.
Many suffer from the incurable disease of writing, and it becomes chronic in their sick minds.
Satires no. 7, l. 51

18 *Summum crede nefas animam praeferre pudori*
Et propter vitam vivendi perdere causas.
Count it the greatest sin to prefer mere existence to honour, and for the sake of life to lose the reasons for living.
Satires no. 8, l. 83 to honour

19 *Cantabit vacuus coram latrone viator.*
Travel light and you can sing in the robber's face.
Satires no. 10, l. 22

20 *. . . Verbosa et grandis epistula venit*
A Capreis.
A huge wordy letter came from Capri.
on the Emperor Tiberius's letter to the Senate, which caused the downfall of Sejanus in AD 31
Satires no. 10, l. 71

21 *. . . Duas tantum res anxius optat,*
Panem et circenses.
Only two things does he [the modern citizen] anxiously wish for—bread and circuses.
Satires no. 10, l. 80

22 *Expende Hannibalem: quot libras in duce summo*
Invenies?
Weigh Hannibal: how many pounds will you find in that great general?
Satires no. 10, l. 147

23 *. . . I, demens, et saevas curre per Alpes*
Ut pueris placeas et declamatio fias.
Off you go, madman, and hurry across the horrible Alps, duly to delight schoolboys and become a subject for practising speech-making.
on Hannibal
Satires no. 10, l. 166

1 *Mors sola fatetur*
Quantula sint hominum corpuscula.

Death alone reveals how small are men's poor bodies.
on Hannibal
Satires no. 10, l. 172

2 *Mens sana in corpore sano.*

A sound mind in a sound body.
Satires no. 10, l. 356

3 . . . *Prima est haec ultio, quod se*
Iudice nemo nocens absolvitur.

This is the first of punishments, that no guilty man is acquitted if judged by himself.
Satires no. 13, l. 2

4 *Quippe minuti*
Semper et infirmi est animi exiguique voluptas
Ultio.

Indeed, revenge is always the pleasure of a paltry, feeble, tiny mind.
Satires no. 13, l. 189

5 *Maxima debetur puero reverentia, siquid*
Turpe paras, nec tu pueri contempseris annos.

A child is owed the greatest respect; if you ever have something disgraceful in mind, don't ignore your son's tender years.
Satires no. 14, l. 47

Pauline Kael 1919–
American film critic

6 The words 'Kiss Kiss Bang Bang' which I saw on an Italian movie poster, are perhaps the briefest statement imaginable of the basic appeal of movies.
Kiss Kiss Bang Bang (1968) 'Note on the Title'

Franz Kafka 1883–1924
Czech novelist
see also **Opening lines** 556:17

7 You may object that it is not a trial at all; you are quite right, for it is only a trial if I recognize it as such.
The Trial (1925) ch. 2

8 It's often better to be in chains than to be free.
The Trial (1925) ch. 8

9 When Gregor Samsa awoke one morning from uneasy dreams he found himself transformed in his bed into a gigantic insect.
The Metamorphosis (1915) ch. 1; cf. **Austin** 39:17

Gus Kahn 1886–1941 and Raymond B. Egan 1890–1952
American songwriters

10 There's nothing surer,
The rich get rich and the poor get children.
In the meantime, in between time,
Ain't we got fun.
'Ain't We Got Fun' (1921 song)

Nicholas Kaldor 1908–86
British economist

11 There is no need for the economist to prove . . . that as a result of the adoption of a certain measure nobody is going to suffer. In order to establish his case, it is quite sufficient for him to show that even if all those who suffer as a result are fully compensated for their loss, the rest of the community will still be better off than before.
'Welfare Propositions of Economics' in *Economic Journal* September 1939

Immanuel Kant 1724–1804
German philosopher

12 Two things fill the mind with ever new and increasing wonder and awe, the more often and the more seriously reflection concentrates upon them: the starry heaven above me and the moral law within me.
Critique of Practical Reason (1788)

13 Nothing in the world—indeed nothing even beyond the world—can possibly be conceived which could be called good without qualification except a *good will.*
Foundation of the Metaphysics of Morals (1785) sect. 1

14 I am never to act otherwise than so that I could also will that my maxim should become a universal law.
Fundamental Principles of the Metaphysics of Ethics (1785) sect. 1 (translated by T. K. Abbott)

15 There is an imperative which commands a certain conduct immediately, without having as its condition any other purpose to be attained by it. This imperative is Categorical . . . This imperative may be called that of Morality.
Fundamental Principles of the Metaphysics of Ethics (1785) sect. 2 (translated by T. K. Abbott)

16 Whoever wills the end, wills also (so far as reason decides his conduct) the means in his power which are indispensably necessary thereto.
Fundamental Principles of the Metaphysics of Ethics (1785) sect. 2 (translated by T. K. Abbott)

17 Happiness is not an ideal of reason but of imagination.
Fundamental Principles of the Metaphysics of Ethics (1785) sect. 2 (translated by T. K. Abbott)

18 So act as to treat humanity, whether in thine own person or in that of any other, in every case as an end withal, never as means only.
Fundamental Principles of the Metaphysics of Ethics (1785) sect. 2 (translated by T. K. Abbott)

19 Out of the crooked timber of humanity no straight thing can ever be made.
Idee zu einer allgemeinen Geschichte in weltbürgerlicher Absicht (1784) proposition 6

Alphonse Karr 1808–90
French novelist and journalist

20 *Si l'on veut abolir la peine de mort en ce cas, que MM les assassins commencent.*

In that case, if we are to abolish the death penalty, let the murderers take the first step.
Les Guêpes January 1849 (6th series, 1859)

1 *Plus ça change, plus c'est la même chose.*
The more things change, the more they are the same.
Les Guêpes January 1849 (6th series, 1859)

George S. Kaufman 1889–1961
American dramatist

2 Satire is what closes Saturday night.
Scott Meredith *George S. Kaufman and his Friends* (1974) ch. 6

Gerald Kaufman 1930–
British Labour politician

3 The longest suicide note in history.
on the Labour Party manifesto New Hope for Britain (1983)
Denis Healey *The Time of My Life* (1989) ch. 23

4 We would prefer to see the House run by a philistine with the requisite financial acumen than by the succession of opera and ballet lovers who have brought a great and valuable institution to its knees.
report of the Commons' Culture, Media and Sport select committee on Covent Garden, 3 December 1997

Paul Kaufman and **Mike Anthony**
American songwriters

5 Poetry in motion.
title of song (1960); cf. **Grahame** 340:8

Christoph Kaufmann 1753–95
German man of letters

6 *Sturm und Drang.*
Storm and stress.
title suggested by Kaufmann for a romantic drama of the American War of Independence by the German dramatist, F. M. Klinger (1775), and thereafter given to a period of literary ferment which prevailed in Germany during the latter part of the 18th century

Kenneth Kaunda 1924–
Zambian statesman, President 1964–91

7 Westerners have aggressive problem-solving minds; Africans experience people.
attributed, 1990

Patrick Kavanagh 1904–67
Irish poet

8 Cassiopeia was over
Cassidy's hanging hill,
I looked and three whin bushes rode across
The horizon — the Three Wise Kings.
'A Christmas Childhood' (1947)

9 Clay is the word and clay is the flesh
Where the potato-gatherers like mechanized scarecrows move
Along the side-fall of the hill—Maguire and his men.
'The Great Hunger' (1947)

10 The weak, washy way of true tragedy—
A sick horse nosing around the meadow for a clean place to die.
'The Great Hunger' (1947)

11 I hate what every poet hates in spite
Of all the solemn talk of contemplation.
Oh, Alexander Selkirk knew the plight
Of being king and government and nation.
A road, a mile of kingdom, I am king
Of banks and stones and every blooming thing.
'Inniskeen Road: July Evening' (1936); cf. **Cowper** 242:17

Danny Kaye see **Film lines** 312:6

Paul Keating 1944–
Australian Labor statesman; Prime Minister 1991–6

12 Even as it [Great Britain] walked out on you and joined the Common Market, you were still looking for your MBEs and your knighthoods, and all the rest of the regalia that comes with it. You would take Australia right back down the time tunnel to the cultural cringe where you have always come from.
addressing Australian Conservative supporters of Great Britain
speech, House of Representatives (Australia) 27 February 1992; cf. **Phillips** 575:12

13 I'm a bastard. But I'm a bastard who gets the mail through. And they appreciate that.
in 1994, to a senior colleague
in *Sunday Telegraph* 20 November 1994

John Keats 1795–1821
English poet
on Keats: see **Bulwer-Lytton** *160:6,* **Byron** *177:18, 180:10,* **Lockhart** *472:10,* **Yeats** *836:1; see also* **Epitaphs** *303:3*

14 Bright star, would I were steadfast as thou art—
Not in lone splendour hung aloft the night,
And watching, with eternal lids apart,
Like nature's patient, sleepless Eremite,
The moving waters at their priestlike task
Of pure ablution round earth's human shores.
'Bright star, would I were steadfast as thou art' (written 1819)

15 The imagination of a boy is healthy, and the mature imagination of a man is healthy; but there is a space of life between, in which the soul is in a ferment, the character undecided, the way of life uncertain, the ambition thick-sighted: thence proceeds mawkishness.
Endymion (1818) preface

16 A thing of beauty is a joy for ever:
Its loveliness increases; it will never
Pass into nothingness.
Endymion (1818) bk. 1, l. 1; cf. **Rowland** 636:13

17 They alway must be with us, or we die.
Endymion (1818) bk. 1, l. 33

1 Who, of men, can tell
That flowers would bloom, or that green fruit would swell
To melting pulp, that fish would have bright mail,
The earth its dower of river, wood, and vale,
The meadows runnels, runnels pebble-stones,
The seed its harvest, or the lute its tones,
Tones ravishment, or ravishment its sweet,
If human souls did never kiss and greet?
Endymion (1818) bk. 1, l. 835

2 Their smiles,
Wan as primroses gathered at midnight
By chilly fingered spring.
Endymion (1818) bk. 4, l. 969

3 St Agnes' Eve—Ah, bitter chill it was!
The owl, for all his feathers, was a-cold;
The hare limped trembling through the frozen grass,
And silent was the flock in woolly fold.
'The Eve of St Agnes' (1820) st. 1

4 The sculptured dead, on each side, seem to freeze,
Emprisoned in black, purgatorial rails.
'The Eve of St Agnes' (1820) st. 2

5 The silver, snarling trumpets 'gan to chide.
'The Eve of St Agnes' (1820) st. 4

6 And soft adorings from their loves receive
Upon the honeyed middle of the night.
'The Eve of St Agnes' (1820) st. 6

7 A poor, weak, palsy-stricken, churchyard thing.
'The Eve of St Agnes' (1820) st. 18

8 Out went the taper as she hurried in;
Its little smoke, in pallid moonshine, died.
'The Eve of St Agnes' (1820) st. 23

9 A casement high and triple-arched there was,
All garlanded with carven imag'ries
Of fruits, and flowers, and bunches of knot-grass,
And diamonded with panes of quaint device,
Innumerable of stains and splendid dyes,
As are the tiger-moth's deep-damasked wings.
'The Eve of St Agnes' (1820) st. 24

10 By degrees
Her rich attire creeps rustling to her knees.
'The Eve of St Agnes' (1820) st. 26

11 Trembling in her soft and chilly nest.
'The Eve of St Agnes' (1820) st. 27

12 As though a rose should shut, and be a bud again.
'The Eve of St Agnes' (1820) st. 27

13 And still she slept an azure-lidded sleep,
In blanchèd linen, smooth, and lavendered,
While he from forth the closet brought a heap
Of candied apple, quince, and plum, and gourd;
With jellies soother than the creamy curd,
And lucent syrops, tinct with cinnamon;
Manna and dates, in argosy transferred
From Fez; and spiced dainties, every one,
From silken Samarcand to cedared Lebanon.
'The Eve of St Agnes' (1820) st. 30

14 He played an ancient ditty, long since mute,
In Provence called, 'La belle dame sans mercy.'
'The Eve of St Agnes' (1820) st. 33

15 And the long carpets rose along the gusty floor.
'The Eve of St Agnes' (1820) st. 40

16 And they are gone: aye, ages long ago
These lovers fled away into the storm.
'The Eve of St Agnes' (1820) st. 42

17 Fanatics have their dreams, wherewith they weave
A paradise for a sect.
'The Fall of Hyperion' (written 1819) l. 1

18 'None can usurp this height,' returned that shade,
'But those to whom the miseries of the world
Are misery, and will not let them rest.'
'The Fall of Hyperion' (written 1819) l. 147

19 The poet and the dreamer are distinct,
Diverse, sheer opposite, antipodes.
The one pours out a balm upon the world,
The other vexes it.
'The Fall of Hyperion' (written 1819) l. 199

20 Ever let the fancy roam,
Pleasure never is at home.
'Fancy' (1820) l. 1

21 O sweet Fancy! let her loose;
Summer's joys are spoilt by use.
'Fancy' (1820) l. 9

22 Deep in the shady sadness of a vale
Far sunken from the healthy breath of morn,
Far from the fiery noon, and eve's one star,
Sat grey-haired Saturn, quiet as a stone.
'Hyperion: A Fragment' (1820) bk. 1, l. 1

23 No stir of air was there,
Not so much life as on a summer's day
Robs not one light seed from the feathered grass,
But where the dead leaf fell, there did it rest.
'Hyperion: A Fragment' (1820) bk. 1, l. 7

24 The Naiad 'mid her reeds
Pressed her cold finger closer to her lips.
'Hyperion: A Fragment' (1820) bk. 1, l. 13

25 That large utterance of the early gods!
'Hyperion: A Fragment' (1820) bk. 1, l. 51

26 O aching time! O moments big as years!
'Hyperion: A Fragment' (1820) bk. 1, l. 64

27 As when, upon a trancèd summer-night,
Those green-robed senators of mighty woods,
Tall oaks, branch-charmèd by the earnest stars,
Dream, and so dream all night without a stir.
'Hyperion: A Fragment' (1820) bk. 1, l. 72

28 Sometimes eagle's wings,
Unseen before by gods or wondering men,
Darkened the place.
'Hyperion: A Fragment' (1820) bk. 1, l. 182

29 And still they were the same bright, patient stars.
'Hyperion: A Fragment' (1820) bk. 1, l. 353

30 Knowledge enormous makes a god of me.
'Hyperion: A Fragment' (1820) bk. 3, l. 113

31 I had a dove and the sweet dove died;
And I have thought it died of grieving:
O, what could it grieve for? Its feet were tied,
With a silken thread of my own hand's weaving.
'I had a dove and the sweet dove died' (written 1818)

1 In drear nighted December
Too happy, happy tree
Thy branches ne'er remember
Their green felicity.
'In drear nighted December' (written 1817)

2 So the two brothers and their murdered man
Rode past fair Florence.
'Isabella; or, The Pot of Basil' (1820) st. 27

3 And she forgot the stars, the moon, and sun,
And she forgot the blue above the trees,
And she forgot the dells where waters run,
And she forgot the chilly autumn breeze;
She had no knowledge when the day was done,
And the new morn she saw not: but in peace
Hung over her sweet Basil evermore,
And moistened it with tears unto the core.
'Isabella; or, The Pot of Basil' (1820) st. 53

4 'For cruel 'tis,' said she,
'To steal my Basil-pot away from me.'
'Isabella; or, The Pot of Basil' (1820) st. 62

5 And then there crept
A little noiseless noise among the leaves,
Born of the very sigh that silence heaves.
'I stood tip-toe upon a little hill' (1817) l. 10

6 Here are sweet peas, on tip-toe for a flight.
'I stood tip-toe upon a little hill' (1817) l. 57

7 Oh, what can ail thee knight at arms
Alone and palely loitering?
The sedge has withered from the lake
And no birds sing!
'La belle dame sans merci' (1820) st. 1

8 I see a lily on thy brow
With anguish moist and fever dew,
And on thy cheeks a fading rose
Fast withereth too.
'La belle dame sans merci' (1820) st. 3

9 I met a lady in the meads
Full beautiful, a faery's child
Her hair was long, her foot was light
And her eyes were wild.
'La belle dame sans merci' (1820) st. 4

10 She looked at me as she did love
And made sweet moan.
'La belle dame sans merci' (1820) st. 5

11 I set her on my pacing steed
And nothing else saw all day long
For sidelong would she bend and sing
A faery's song.
'La belle dame sans merci' (1820) st. 6

12 . . . La belle dame sans merci
Thee hath in thrall.
'La belle dame sans merci' (1820) st. 10

13 I saw their starved lips in the gloam
With horrid warning gapèd wide
And I awoke and found me here
On the cold hill's side.
'La belle dame sans merci' (1820) st. 11

14 She was a gordian shape of dazzling hue,
Vermilion-spotted, golden, green, and blue;
Striped like a zebra, freckled like a pard,
Eyed like a peacock, and all crimson barred.
'Lamia' (1820) pt. 1, l. 47

15 Love in a hut, with water and a crust,
Is—Love, forgive us!—cinders, ashes, dust;
Love in a palace is perhaps at last
More grievous torment than a hermit's fast.
'Lamia' (1820) pt. 2, l. 1; cf. **Colman** 229:14

16 That purple-linèd palace of sweet sin.
'Lamia' (1820) pt. 2, l. 31

17 In pale contented sort of discontent.
'Lamia' (1820) pt. 2, l. 135

18 Do not all charms fly
At the mere touch of cold philosophy?
'Lamia' (1820) pt. 2, l. 229

19 Philosophy will clip an Angel's wings.
'Lamia' (1820) pt. 2, l. 234

20 Souls of poets dead and gone,
What Elysium have ye known,
Happy field or mossy cavern,
Choicer than the Mermaid Tavern?
Have ye tippled drink more fine
Than mine host's Canary wine?
'Lines on the Mermaid Tavern' (1820)

21 Thou still unravished bride of quietness,
Thou foster-child of silence and slow time.
'Ode on a Grecian Urn' (1820) st. 1

22 What men or gods are these? What maidens loth?
What mad pursuit? What struggle to escape?
What pipes and timbrels? What wild ecstasy?
'Ode on a Grecian Urn' (1820) st. 1

23 Heard melodies are sweet, but those unheard
Are sweeter.
'Ode on a Grecian Urn' (1820) st. 2

24 For ever wilt thou love, and she be fair!
'Ode on a Grecian Urn' (1820) st. 2

25 For ever piping songs for ever new.
'Ode on a Grecian Urn' (1820) st. 3

26 For ever warm and still to be enjoyed,
For ever panting, and for ever young;
All breathing human passion far above,
That leaves a heart high-sorrowful and cloyed,
A burning forehead, and a parching tongue.
'Ode on a Grecian Urn' (1820) st. 3

27 Who are these coming to the sacrifice?
To what green altar, O mysterious priest,
Lead'st thou that heifer lowing at the skies,
And all her silken flanks with garlands dressed?
What little town by river or sea shore,
Or mountain-built with peaceful citadel,
Is emptied of this folk, this pious morn?
'Ode on a Grecian Urn' (1820) st. 4

28 O Attic shape! Fair attitude!
'Ode on a Grecian Urn' (1820) st. 5

29 Thou, silent form, dost tease us out of thought
As doth eternity: Cold Pastoral!
'Ode on a Grecian Urn' (1820) st. 5

1 'Beauty is truth, truth beauty,'—that is all
Ye know on earth, and all ye need to know.
'Ode on a Grecian Urn' (1820) st. 5

2 No, no, go not to Lethe, neither twist
Wolf's-bane, tight-rooted, for its poisonous wine.
'Ode on Melancholy' (1820) st. 1

3 Nor let the beetle, nor the death-moth be
Your mournful Psyche.
'Ode on Melancholy' (1820) st. 1

4 But when the melancholy fit shall fall
Sudden from heaven like a weeping cloud,
That fosters the droop-headed flowers all,
And hides the green hill in an April shroud;
Then glut thy sorrow on a morning rose,
Or on the rainbow of the salt sand-wave,
Or on the wealth of globèd peonies.
'Ode on Melancholy' (1820) st. 2

5 She dwells with Beauty—Beauty that must die;
And Joy, whose hand is ever at his lips
Bidding adieu; and aching Pleasure nigh,
Turning to poison while the bee-mouth sips:
Ay, in the very temple of Delight
Veiled Melancholy has her sovran shrine,
Though seen of none save him whose strenuous tongue
Can burst Joy's grape against his palate fine;
His soul shall taste the sadness of her might,
And be among her cloudy trophies hung.
'Ode on Melancholy' (1820) st. 3

6 My heart aches, and a drowsy numbness pains
My sense, as though of hemlock I had drunk,
Or emptied some dull opiate to the drains
One minute past, and Lethe-wards had sunk:
'Tis not through envy of thy happy lot,
But being too happy in thine happiness,—
That thou, light-wingèd Dryad of the trees,
In some melodious plot
Of beechen green, and shadows numberless,
Singest of summer in full-throated ease.
'Ode to a Nightingale' (1820) st. 1

7 O, for a draught of vintage! that hath been
Cooled a long age in the deep-delvèd earth,
Tasting of Flora and the country green.
'Ode to a Nightingale' (1820) st. 2

8 O for a beaker full of the warm South,
Full of the true, the blushful Hippocrene,
With beaded bubbles winking at the brim,
And purple-stainèd mouth;
That I might drink, and leave the world unseen,
And with thee fade away into the forest dim.
'Ode to a Nightingale' (1820) st. 2

9 Fade far away, dissolve, and quite forget
What thou among the leaves hast never known,
The weariness, the fever, and the fret.
'Ode to a Nightingale' (1820) st. 3

10 Where youth grows pale, and spectre-thin, and dies.
'Ode to a Nightingale' (1820) st. 3

11 Away! away! for I will fly to thee,
Not charioted by Bacchus and his pards,
But on the viewless wings of Poesy,
Though the dull brain perplexes and retards:
Already with thee! tender is the night.
'Ode to a Nightingale' (1820) st. 4

12 Fast fading violets covered up in leaves;
And mid-May's eldest child,
The coming musk-rose, full of dewy wine,
The murmurous haunt of flies on summer eves.
'Ode to a Nightingale' (1820) st. 5

13 Darkling I listen; and, for many a time
I have been half in love with easeful Death,
Called him soft names in many a musèd rhyme,
To take into the air my quiet breath;
Now more than ever seems it rich to die,
To cease upon the midnight with no pain.
'Ode to a Nightingale' (1820) st. 6

14 Thou wast not born for death, immortal bird!
No hungry generations tread thee down;
The voice I hear this passing night was heard
In ancient days by emperor and clown:
Perhaps the self-same song that found a path
Through the sad heart of Ruth, when, sick for home,
She stood in tears amid the alien corn;
The same that oft-times hath
Charmed magic casements, opening on the foam
Of perilous seas, in faery lands forlorn.
'Ode to a Nightingale' (1820) st. 7; cf. **Hood** 382:27

15 Forlorn! the very word is like a bell
To toll me back from thee to my sole self!
Adieu! the fancy cannot cheat so well
As she is famed to do, deceiving elf.
'Ode to a Nightingale' (1820) st. 8

16 Was it a vision, or a waking dream?
Fled is that music:—do I wake or sleep?
'Ode to a Nightingale' (1820) st. 8

17 'Mid hushed, cool-rooted flowers, fragrant-eyed,
Blue, silver-white, and budded Tyrian.
'Ode to Psyche' (1820) st. 1

18 Nor virgin-choir to make delicious moan
Upon the midnight hours.
'Ode to Psyche' (1820) st. 2

19 A bright torch, and a casement ope at night,
To let the warm Love in!
'Ode to Psyche' (1820) st. 4

20 Much have I travelled in the realms of gold,
And many goodly states and kingdoms seen.
'On First Looking into Chapman's Homer' (1817)

21 Then felt I like some watcher of the skies
When a new planet swims into his ken;
Or like stout Cortez when with eagle eyes
He stared at the Pacific—and all his men
Looked at each other with a wild surmise—
Silent, upon a peak in Darien.
'On First Looking into Chapman's Homer' (1817)

22 Mortality
Weighs heavily on me like unwilling sleep.
'On Seeing the Elgin Marbles' (1817)

23 The poetry of earth is never dead:
When all the birds are faint with the hot sun,

And hide in cooling trees, a voice will run
From hedge to hedge about the new-mown mead.
'On the Grasshopper and Cricket' (1817)

1 It keeps eternal whisperings around
Desolate shores,—and with its mighty swell
Gluts twice ten thousand Caverns.
'On the Sea' (1817)

2 O fret not after knowledge—I have none,
And yet my song comes native with the warmth.
O fret not after knowledge—I have none,
And yet the Evening listens.
'O thou whose face hath felt the winter's wind' (written 1818)

3 O for ten years, that I may overwhelm
Myself in poesy; so I may do the deed
That my own soul has to itself decreed.
'Sleep and Poetry' (1817) l. 96

4 They swayed about upon a rocking horse,
And thought it Pegasus.
'Sleep and Poetry' (1817) l. 186

5 And they shall be accounted poet kings
Who simply tell the most heart-easing things.
'Sleep and Poetry' (1817) l. 267

6 O soft embalmer of the still midnight,
Shutting, with careful fingers and benign
Our gloom-pleased eyes.
'Sonnet to Sleep' (written 1819)

7 Turn the key deftly in the oilèd wards,
And seal the hushèd casket of my soul.
'Sonnet to Sleep' (written 1819)

8 Season of mists and mellow fruitfulness,
Close bosom friend of the maturing sun;
Conspiring with him how to load and bless
With fruit the vines that round the thatch-eaves run.
'To Autumn' (1820) st. 1

9 Who hath not seen thee oft amid thy store?
Sometimes whoever seeks abroad may find
Thee sitting careless on a granary floor,
Thy hair soft-lifted by the winnowing wind;
Or on a half-reaped furrow sound asleep,
Drowsed with the fume of poppies while thy hook
Spares the next swath and all its twinèd flowers.
'To Autumn' (1820) st. 2

10 Where are the songs of Spring? Ay, where are they?
Think not of them, thou hast thy music too.
'To Autumn' (1820) st. 3

11 Then in a wailful choir the small gnats mourn
Among the river sallows, borne aloft
Or sinking as the light wind lives or dies.
'To Autumn' (1820) st. 3

12 The red-breast whistles from a garden-croft;
And gathering swallows twitter in the skies.
'To Autumn' (1820) st. 3

13 How soon the film of death obscured that eye,
Whence genius wildly flashed.
'To Chatterton' (written 1815)

14 Aye on the shores of darkness there is light,
And precipices show untrodden green,
There is a budding morrow in midnight,
There is a triple sight in blindness keen.
'To Homer' (written 1818)

15 It is a flaw
In happiness, to see beyond our bourn.
'To J. H. Reynolds, Esq.' (written 1818)

16 To one who has been long in city pent,
'Tis very sweet to look into the fair
And open face of heaven.
'To one who has been long in city pent' (1817); cf. **Milton** 517:14

17 When I have fears that I may cease to be
Before my pen has gleaned my teeming brain.
'When I have fears that I may cease to be' (written 1818)

18 When I behold, upon the night's starred face
Huge cloudy symbols of a high romance.
'When I have fears that I may cease to be' (written 1818)

19 Then on the shore
Of the wide world I stand alone and think
Till love and fame to nothingness do sink.
'When I have fears that I may cease to be' (written 1818)

20 A long poem is a test of invention which I take to be the polar star of poetry, as fancy is the sails, and imagination the rudder.
letter to Benjamin Bailey, 8 October 1817, in H. E. Rollins (ed.) *Letters of John Keats* (1958) vol. 1

21 I am certain of nothing but the holiness of the heart's affections and the truth of imagination—what the imagination seizes as beauty must be truth—whether it existed before or not.
letter to Benjamin Bailey, 22 November 1817, in H. E. Rollins (ed.) *Letters of John Keats* (1958) vol. 1; cf. **Keats** 429:1

22 O for a life of sensations rather than of thoughts!
letter to Benjamin Bailey, 22 November 1817, in H. E. Rollins (ed.) *Letters of John Keats* (1958) vol. 1

23 A man should have the fine point of his soul taken off to become fit for this world.
letter to J. H. Reynolds, 22 November 1817, in H. E. Rollins (ed.) *Letters of John Keats* (1958) vol. 1

24 Negative Capability, that is when man is capable of being in uncertainties, mysteries, doubts, without any irritable reaching after fact and reason—Coleridge, for instance, would let go by a fine isolated verisimilitude caught from the penetralium of mystery, from being incapable of remaining content with half knowledge.
letter to George and Thomas Keats, 21 December 1817, in H. E. Rollins (ed.) *Letters of John Keats* (1958) vol. 1

25 There is nothing stable in the world—uproar's your only music.
letter to George and Thomas Keats, 13 January 1818, in H. E. Rollins (ed.) *Letters of John Keats* (1958) vol. 1

26 For the sake of a few fine imaginative or domestic passages, are we to be bullied into a certain philosophy engendered in the whims of an egotist?
on the overbearing influence of ***Wordsworth*** *upon his contemporaries*
letter to J. H. Reynolds, 3 February 1818, in H. E. Rollins (ed.) *Letters of John Keats* (1958) vol. 1

1 We hate poetry that has a palpable design upon us—and if we do not agree, seems to put its hand in its breeches pocket. Poetry should be great and unobtrusive, a thing which enters into one's soul, and does not startle it or amaze it with itself, but with its subject.
letter to J. H. Reynolds, 3 February 1818, in H. E. Rollins (ed.) *Letters of John Keats* (1958) vol. 1

2 If poetry comes not as naturally as the leaves to a tree it had better not come at all.
letter to John Taylor, 27 February 1818, in H. E. Rollins (ed.) *Letters of John Keats* (1958) vol. 1

3 Scenery is fine—but human nature is finer.
letter to Benjamin Bailey, 13 March 1818, in H. E. Rollins (ed.) *Letters of John Keats* (1958) vol. 1

4 It is impossible to live in a country which is continually under hatches . . . Rain! Rain! Rain!
letter to J. H. Reynolds from Devon, 10 April 1818, in H. E. Rollins (ed.) *Letters of John Keats* (1958) vol. 1

5 I am in that temper that if I were under water I would scarcely kick to come to the top.
letter to Benjamin Bailey, 25 May 1818, in H. E. Rollins (ed.) *Letters of John Keats* (1958) vol. 1

6 O the flummery of a birth place! Cant! Cant! Cant! It is enough to give a spirit the guts-ache.
letter to John Hamilton Reynolds, 11 July 1818 in M. B. Forman (ed.) *Letters of John Keats* (1952)

7 I do think better of womankind than to suppose they care whether Mister John Keats five feet high likes them or not.
letter to Benjamin Bailey, 18 July 1818, in H. E. Rollins (ed.) *Letters of John Keats* (1958) vol. 1

8 There is an awful warmth about my heart like a load of immortality.
letter to J. H. Reynolds, 22 September 1818, in H. E. Rollins (ed.) *Letters of John Keats* (1958) vol. 1

9 In Endymion, I leaped headlong into the sea, and thereby have become better acquainted with the soundings, the quicksands, and the rocks, than if I had stayed upon the green shore, and piped a silly pipe, and took tea and comfortable advice.
letter to James Hessey, 8 October 1818, in H. E. Rollins (ed.) *Letters of John Keats* (1958) vol. 1

10 As to the poetical character itself, (I mean that sort of which, if I am any thing, I am a member; that sort distinguished from the Wordsworthian or egotistical sublime; which is a thing *per se* and stands alone) it is not itself—it has no self . . . It has as much delight in conceiving an Iago as an Imogen.
letter to Richard Woodhouse, 27 October 1818, in H. E. Rollins (ed.) *Letters of John Keats* (1958) vol. 1

11 The roaring of the wind is my wife and the stars through the window pane are my children.
letter to George and Georgiana Keats, 24 October 1818, in H. E. Rollins (ed.) *Letters of John Keats* (1958) vol. 1

12 I have come to this resolution—never to write for the sake of writing, or making a poem, but from running over with any little knowledge or experience which many years of reflection may perhaps give me—otherwise I shall be dumb.
letter to B. R. Haydon, 8 March 1819, in H. E. Rollins (ed.) *Letters of John Keats* (1958) vol. 2

13 I go among the fields and catch a glimpse of a stoat or a fieldmouse peeping out of the withered grass—The creature hath a purpose and its eyes are bright with it—I go amongst the buildings of a city and I see a man hurrying along—to what? The Creature has a purpose and his eyes are bright with it.
letter to George and Georgiana Keats, 19 March 1819, in H. E. Rollins (ed.) *Letters of John Keats* (1958) vol. 2

14 Call the world if you please 'The vale of soul-making'.
letter to George and Georgiana Keats, 21 April 1819, in H. E. Rollins (ed.) *Letters of John Keats* (1958) vol. 2

15 I have met with women whom I really think would like to be married to a poem and to be given away by a novel.
letter to Fanny Brawne, 8 July 1819, in H. E. Rollins (ed.) *Letters of John Keats* (1958) vol. 2

16 I have two luxuries to brood over in my walks, your loveliness and the hour of my death. O that I could have possession of them both in the same minute.
letter to Fanny Brawne, 25 July 1819, in H. E. Rollins (ed.) *Letters of John Keats* (1958) vol. 2

17 Fine writing is next to fine doing the top thing in the world.
letter to J. H. Reynolds, 24 August 1819, in H. E. Rollins (ed.) *Letters of John Keats* (1958) vol. 2

18 All clean and comfortable I sit down to write.
letter to George and Georgiana Keats, 17 September 1819, in H. E. Rollins (ed.) *Letters of John Keats* (1958) vol. 2

19 The only means of strengthening one's intellect is to make up one's mind about nothing—to let the mind be a thoroughfare for all thoughts. Not a select party.
letter to George and Georgiana Keats, 24 September 1819, in H. E. Rollins (ed.) *Letters of John Keats* (1958) vol. 2

20 If you should have a boy do not christen him John . . . 'Tis a bad name and goes against a man. If my name had been Edmund I should have been more fortunate.
letter to George and Georgiana Keats, 13 January 1820, in H. E. Rollins (ed.) *Letters of John Keats* (1958) vol. 2

21 'If I should die,' said I to myself, 'I have left no immortal work behind me—nothing to make my friends proud of my memory—but I have loved the principle of beauty in all things, and if I had had time I would have made myself remembered.'
letter to Fanny Brawne, *c.*February 1820, in H. E. Rollins (ed.) *Letters of John Keats* (1958) vol. 2

22 I wish you could invent some means to make me at all happy without you. Every hour I am more and more concentrated in you; every thing else tastes like chaff in my mouth.
letter to Fanny Brawne, August 1820, in H. E. Rollins (ed.) *Letters of John Keats* (1958) vol. 2

23 'Load every rift' of your subject with ore.
letter to Shelley, August 1820, in H. E. Rollins (ed.) *Letters of John Keats* (1958) vol. 2; cf. **Spenser** 733:25

1 I shall soon be laid in the quiet grave—thank God for the quiet grave—O! I can feel the cold earth upon me—the daisies growing over me—O for this quiet—it will be my first.

letter from Joseph Severn to John Taylor, 6 March 1821, in H. E. Rollins (ed.) *Letters of John Keats* (1958) vol. 2

2 In disease Medical Men guess: if they cannot ascertain a disease, they call it nervous.

J. A. Gere and John Sparrow (eds.) *Geoffrey Madan's Notebooks* (1981); attributed

John Keble 1792–1866

English clergyman; leader of the Oxford Movement

3 Blessed are the pure in heart,
For they shall see our God,
The secret of the Lord is theirs,
Their soul is Christ's abode.

The Christian Year (1827) 'Blessed are the pure in heart'

4 New every morning is the love
Our wakening and uprising prove;
Through sleep and darkness safely brought,
Restored to life, and power, and thought.

The Christian Year (1827) 'Morning'

5 The trivial round, the common task,
Would furnish all we ought to ask.

The Christian Year (1827) 'Morning'

6 There is a book, who runs may read,
Which heavenly truth imparts,
And all the lore its scholars need,
Pure eyes and Christian hearts.

The Christian Year (1827) 'Septuagesima'

7 The voice that breathed o'er Eden,
That earliest wedding-day,
The primal marriage blessing,
It hath not passed away.

'Holy Matrimony' (1857 hymn)

8 If the Church of England were to fail, it would be found in my parish.

D. Newsome *The Parting of Friends* (1966) ch. 8, pt. 3

Brian Keenan 1950–

Irish writer and teacher
see also **Borrowed titles** 144:4

9 Politics can only be a small part of what we are. It's a *way* of seeing, it's not all-seeing in itself.

An Evil Cradling (1992)

Garrison Keillor 1942–

American humorous writer and broadcaster

10 Years ago, manhood was an opportunity for achievement, and now it is a problem to be overcome.

The Book of Guys (1994)

11 Ronald Reagan, the President who never told bad news to the American people.

We Are Still Married (1989)

Helen Keller 1880–1968

American writer and social reformer, blind and deaf from the age of 19 months

12 The mystery of language was revealed to me. I knew then that 'w-a-t-e-r' meant the wonderful cool something that was flowing over my hand. That living word awakened my soul, gave it light, joy, set it free!

The Story of My Life (1902) ch. 4

13 Everything has its wonders, even darkness and silence, and I learn, whatever state I may be in, therein to be content.

The Story of My Life (1902) ch. 22

Frank B. Kellogg see Aristide Briand

Hugh Kelly 1739–77

Irish dramatist

14 Of all the stages in a woman's life, none is so dangerous as the period between her acknowledgment of a passion for a man, and the day set apart for her nuptials.

Memoirs of a Magdalen (1767, ed. 1782)

15 Your people of refined sentiments are the most troublesome creatures in the world to deal with.

False Delicacy (performed 1768) act 5, sc. 1

Thomas Kelly 1769–1855

Irish clergyman and hymn-writer

16 The head that once was crowned with thorns
Is crowned with glory now.

'The head that once was crowned with thorns' (1820 hymn)

Lord Kelvin 1824–1907

British scientist

17 When you can measure what you are speaking about, and express it in numbers, you know something about it; but when you cannot measure it, when you cannot express it in numbers, your knowledge is of a meagre and unsatisfactory kind: it may be the beginning of knowledge, but you have scarcely, in your thoughts, advanced to the stage of *science*, whatever the matter may be.

often quoted as 'If you cannot measure it, then it is not science'

Popular Lectures and Addresses vol. 1 (1889) 'Electrical Units of Measurement', delivered 3 May 1883

Thomas à Kempis see Thomas

Thomas Ken 1637–1711

English divine; Bishop of Bath and Wells, 1684–91, and formerly chaplain to **Charles II**

18 Awake, my soul, and with the sun
Thy daily stage of duty run.
Shake off dull sloth, and joyful rise
To pay thy morning sacrifice.

'Morning Hymn' in Winchester College *Manual of Prayers* (1695) but already in use by 1674

1 Redeem thy mis-spent time that's past,
And live this day as if thy last.
'Morning Hymn' (1709 ed.) v. 2

2 All praise to thee, my God, this night,
For all the blessings of the light;
Keep me, O keep me, King of Kings,
Beneath thy own almighty wings.
the first line later changed to 'Glory to thee, my God this night'
'Evening Hymn' in Winchester College *Manual of Prayers* (1695) but already in use by 1674

3 Teach me to live, that I may dread
The grave as little as my bed.
'Evening Hymn' (1695) v. 3

Jaan Kenbrovin and William Kellette

4 I'm forever blowing bubbles.
title of song (1919)

Florynce Kennedy 1916–

American lawyer

5 If men could get pregnant, abortion would be a sacrament.
in *Ms.* March 1973

Jimmy Kennedy and Michael Carr

British songwriters

6 We're gonna hang out the washing on the Siegfried Line.
title of song (1939)

John F. Kennedy 1917–63

American Democratic statesman, 35th President of the US, 1961–3

7 Don't buy a single vote more than necessary. I'll be damned if I'm going to pay for a landslide.
telegraphed message from his father, read at a Gridiron dinner in Washington, 15 March 1958, and almost certainly JFK's invention; J. F. Cutler *Honey Fitz* (1962)

8 We stand today on the edge of a new frontier.
speech accepting the Democratic nomination in Los Angeles, 15 July 1960, in *Vital Speeches* 1 August 1960

9 Let the word go forth from this time and place, to friend and foe alike, that the torch has been passed to a new generation of Americans—born in this century, tempered by war, disciplined by a hard and bitter peace.
inaugural address, 20 January 1961, in *Vital Speeches* 1 February 1961

10 Let every nation know, whether it wishes us well or ill, that we shall pay any price, bear any burden, meet any hardship, support any friend, oppose any foe to assure the survival and the success of liberty.
inaugural address, 20 January 1961, in *Vital Speeches* 1 February 1961

11 If a free society cannot help the many who are poor, it cannot save the few who are rich.
inaugural address, 20 January 1961, in *Vital Speeches* 1 February 1961

12 Let us never negotiate out of fear. But let us never fear to negotiate.
inaugural address, 20 January 1961, in *Vital Speeches* 1 February 1961

13 All this will not be finished in the first 100 days. Nor will it be finished in the first 1,000 days, nor in the life of this Administration, nor even perhaps in our lifetime on this planet. But let us begin.
inaugural address, 20 January 1961, in *Vital Speeches* 1 February 1961

14 And so, my fellow Americans: ask not what your country can do for you—ask what you can do for your country. My fellow citizens of the world: ask not what America will do for you, but what together we can do for the freedom of man.
inaugural address, 20 January 1961, in *Vital Speeches* 1 February 1961; cf. **Gibran** 336:10, **Holmes** 381:10

15 Mankind must put an end to war or war will put an end to mankind.
speech to United Nations General Assembly, 25 September 1961, in *New York Times* 26 September 1961

16 No one has been barred on account of his race from fighting or dying for America—there are no 'white' or 'coloured' signs on the foxholes or graveyards of battle.
Message to Congress on proposed Civil Rights Bill, 19 June 1963, in *New York Times* 20 June 1963

17 *Ich bin ein Berliner.*
I am a Berliner.
speech in West Berlin, 26 June 1963, in *New York Times* 27 June 1963; cf. **Cicero** 217:21

18 In free society art is not a weapon . . . Artists are not engineers of the soul.
speech at Amherst College, Mass., 26 October 1963, in *New York Times* 27 October 1963; cf. **Gorky** 347:3, **Stalin** 736:2

19 It was involuntary. They sank my boat.
on being asked how he became a war hero
Arthur M. Schlesinger Jr. *A Thousand Days* (1965) ch. 4

Joseph P. Kennedy 1888–1969

American financier and diplomat; father of J. F. **Kennedy**

20 We're going to sell Jack like soapflakes.
when his son John made his bid for the Presidency
John H. Davis *The Kennedy Clan* (1984) ch. 23

21 When the going gets tough, the tough get going.
also attributed to Knute Rockne
J. H. Cutler *Honey Fitz* (1962); cf. **Proverbs** 614:28

Robert Kennedy 1925–68

American Democratic politician, son of Joseph and Rose **Kennedy**, *brother of John Fitzgerald* **Kennedy**

22 One-fifth of the people are against everything all the time.
speech, University of Pennsylvania, 6 May 1964; in *Philadelphia Inquirer* 7 May 1964

Rose Kennedy 1890–1995

*wife of Joseph **Kennedy**, mother of John Fitzgerald and Robert **Kennedy***

1 It's our money, and we're free to spend it any way we please . . . If you have money you spend it, and win.

in response to criticism of overlavish funding of her son Robert's 1968 presidential campaign

in *Daily Telegraph* 24 January 1995 (obituary)

2 Now Teddy must run.

*to her daughter, on hearing of the assassination of Robert **Kennedy***

in *The Times* 24 January 1995 (obituary); attributed, perhaps apocryphal

Jomo Kenyatta 1891–1978

Kenyan statesman, Prime Minister of Kenya 1963 and President 1964–78

3 The African is conditioned, by the cultural and social institutions of centuries, to a freedom of which Europe has little conception, and it is not in his nature to accept serfdom forever. He realizes that he must fight unceasingly for his own emancipation; for without this he is doomed to remain the prey of rival imperialisms.

Facing Mount Kenya (1938); conclusion

Lady Caroline Keppel b. 1735

English poet

4 What's this dull town to me?
Robin's not near.
He whom I wished to see,
Wished for to hear;
Where's all the joy and mirth
Made life a heaven on earth?
O! they're all fled with thee,
Robin Adair.

'Robin Adair' (*c.*1750)

Jack Kerouac 1922–69

Amerian novelist

5 The beat generation.

phrase coined in the course of a conversation; in *Playboy* June 1959

6 It is not my fault that certain so-called bohemian elements have found in my writings something to hang their peculiar beatnik theories on.

in *New York Journal-American* 8 December 1960

Jean Kerr 1923–

American writer

7 As someone pointed out recently, if you can keep your head when all about you are losing theirs, it's just possible you haven't grasped the situation.

Please Don't Eat the Daisies (1957) introduction; cf. **Kipling** 439:2

8 I feel about airplanes the way I feel about diets. It seems to me that they are wonderful things for other people to go on.

The Snake Has All the Lines (1958)

9 I'm tired of all this nonsense about beauty being only skin-deep. That's deep enough. What do you want—an adorable pancreas?

The Snake has all the Lines (1958)

William Kethe d. 1594

Scottish Calvinist

10 All people that on earth do dwell,
Sing to the Lord with cheerful voice.

'All people that on earth do dwell' in *Fourscore and Seven Psalms of David* (Geneva, 1561; later known as the Geneva Psalter); usually sung to the tune 'Old Hundredth', and often known by that name

11 The Lord, ye know, is God indeed;
Without our aid he did us make;
We are his folk, he doth us feed,
And for his sheep he doth us take.
O enter then his gates with praise,
Approach with joy his courts unto;
Praise, laud, and bless his name always,
For it is seemly so to do.

'All people that on earth do dwell' in *Fourscore and Seven Psalms of David* (Geneva, 1561; later known as the Geneva Psalter)

Ralph Kettell 1563–1643

President of Trinity College, Oxford, from 1599

12 Here is Hey for Garsington! and Hey for Cuddesdon! and Hey Hockley! but here's nobody cries, Hey for God Almighty!

sermon at Garsington Revel, in Oliver Lawson Dick (ed.) *Aubrey's Brief Lives* (1949) 'Ralph Kettell'

Thomas Kettle 1880–1916

Irish economist and poet

13 My only programme for Ireland consists, in equal parts, of Home Rule and the Ten Commandments. My only counsel to Ireland is, that in order to become deeply Irish, she must become European.

'Apology'

14 Ireland is a small but insuppressible island half an hour nearer the sunset than Great Britain.

'On Crossing the Irish Sea'

15 Dublin Castle, if it did not know what the Irish people want, could not so infallibly have maintained its tradition of giving them the opposite.

Ulick O'Connor *The Troubles* (rev. ed., 1996)

Francis Scott Key 1779–1843

American lawyer and verse-writer

16 'Tis the star-spangled banner; O long may it wave
O'er the land of the free, and the home of the brave!

'The Star-Spangled Banner' (1814)

Marian Keyes

Irish writer

17 My biological clock is ticking so loud I'm nearly deafened by it. They search me going into planes.

'Late Opening at the Last Chance Saloon' (1997)

1 Genetics had the final say . . . If my father had married a dainty little woman, I might have had a very different life. Very different thighs, certainly.
Rachel's Holiday (1997) ch. 1

2 I hadn't meant to overdo it, I had simply overestimated the quality of the cocaine I had taken.
Rachel's Holiday (1997) ch. 1

John Maynard Keynes 1883–1946
English economist

3 I work for a Government I despise for ends I think criminal.
letter to Duncan Grant, 15 December 1917, in *British Library Add. MSS 57931* fo. 119

4 He felt about France what Pericles felt of Athens—unique value in her, nothing else mattering; but his theory of politics was Bismarck's. He had one illusion—France; and one disillusion—mankind, including Frenchmen, and his colleagues not least.
of Georges **Clemenceau**
The Economic Consequences of the Peace (1919) ch. 3

5 Like Odysseus, the President looked wiser when he was seated.
of Woodrow **Wilson**
The Economic Consequences of the Peace (1919) ch. 3

6 Lenin was right. There is no subtler, no surer means of overturning the existing basis of society than to debauch the currency. The process engages all the hidden forces of economic law on the side of destruction, and does it in a manner which not one man in a million is able to diagnose.
The Economic Consequences of the Peace (1919) ch. 6

7 I do not know which makes a man more conservative—to know nothing but the present, or nothing but the past.
The End of Laissez-Faire (1926) pt. 1

8 This extraordinary figure of our time, this syren, this goat-footed bard, this half-human visitor to our age from the hag-ridden magic and enchanted woods of Celtic antiquity.
Essays in Biography (1933) 'Mr Lloyd George'

9 If the Treasury were to fill old bottles with banknotes, bury them at suitable depths in disused coalmines which are then filled up to the surface with town rubbish, and leave it to private enterprise on well-tried principles of *laissez-faire* to dig the notes up again (the right to do so being obtained, of course, by tendering for leases of the note-bearing territory) there need be no more unemployment and, with the help of the repercussions, the real income of the community, and its capital wealth also, would probably become a good deal greater than it actually is.
General Theory (1936) bk. 3, ch. 10

10 Madmen in authority, who hear voices in the air, are distilling their frenzy from some academic scribbler of a few years back.
General Theory (1947 ed.) ch. 24

11 *In the long run* we are all dead.
A Tract on Monetary Reform (1923) ch. 3

12 We threw good housekeeping to the winds. But we saved ourselves and helped save the world.
of Britain in the Second World War
A. J. P. Taylor *English History, 1914–1945* (1965)

Ruhollah Khomeini 1900–89
Iranian Shiite Muslim leader

13 If laws are needed, Islam has established them all. There is no need . . . after establishing a government, to sit down and draw up laws.
Islam and Revolution: Writings and Declarations of Imam Khomeini (1981) 'Islamic Government'

14 I would like to inform all the intrepid Muslims in the world that the author of the book entitled *The Satanic Verses*, which has been compiled, printed and published in opposition to Islam, the Prophet and the Qur'an, as well as those publishers who were aware of its contents, have been declared *madhur el dam* [those whose blood must be shed]. I call on all zealous Muslims to execute them quickly, wherever they find them, so that no-one will dare to insult Islam again. Whoever is killed in this path will be regarded as a martyr.
fatwa against Salman **Rushdie**, issued 14 February 1989; Malise Ruthven *A Satanic Affair* (1990) ch. 5; cf. **Wesker** 810:19

Nikita Khrushchev 1894–1971
Soviet statesman; Premier, 1958–64
see also **Epstein** *301:1*

15 If anyone believes that our smiles involve abandonment of the teaching of Marx, Engels and Lenin he deceives himself. Those who wait for that must wait until a shrimp learns to whistle.
speech in Moscow, 17 September 1955, in *New York Times* 18 September 1955

16 Whether you like it or not, history is on our side. We will bury you.
speech to Western diplomats at reception in Moscow for Polish leader Mr Gomulka, 18 November 1956, in *The Times* 19 November 1956

17 If one cannot catch the bird of paradise, better take a wet hen.
in *Time* 6 January 1958

18 If you start throwing hedgehogs under me, I shall throw a couple of porcupines under you.
in *New York Times* 7 November 1963

Kitty Kiernan d. 1945
Irish fiancée of Michael **Collins**

19 I felt, if we were ever to part, it would be easier for us both, especially for me, to do it soon, because later it would be bitter for me. But I'd love you just the same.
letter to Michael Collins, 1921; L. O'Broin (ed.) *The Letters of Michael Collins and Kitty Kiernan* (1983)

Joyce Kilmer 1886–1918
American poet

20 I think that I shall never see
A poem lovely as a tree.
'Trees' (1914); cf. **Nash** 539:18

1 Poems are made by fools like me,
But only God can make a tree.
'Trees' (1914)

David Maxwell Fyfe, Lord Kilmuir 1900–67

British Conservative politician and lawyer
on Kilmuir: see **Anonymous** 17:22

2 Loyalty is the Tory's secret weapon.
Anthony Sampson *Anatomy of Britain* (1962) ch. 6

Francis Kilvert 1840–79

English clergyman and diarist

3 Of all noxious animals, too, the most noxious is a tourist. And of all tourists the most vulgar, ill-bred, offensive and loathsome is the British tourist.
W. Plomer (ed.) *Selections from the Diary of the Rev. Francis Kilvert* (1938–40) 5 April 1870

4 It is a fine thing to be out on the hills alone. A man can hardly be a beast or a fool alone on a great mountain.
W. Plomer (ed.) *Selections from the Diary . . .* 29 May 1871

Benjamin Franklin King 1857–94

American poet

5 Nothing to do but work,
Nothing to eat but food,
Nothing to wear but clothes
To keep one from going nude.
'The Pessimist'

6 Nowhere to go but out,
Nowhere to come but back.
'The Pessimist'

Henry King 1592–1669

English poet; Bishop of Chichester from 1642

7 Sleep on (my Love!) in thy cold bed
Never to be disquieted.
My last Good-night! Thou wilt not wake
Till I thy fate shall overtake:
Till age, or grief, or sickness must
Marry my body to that dust
It so much loves; and fill the room
My heart keeps empty in thy tomb.
Stay for me there: I will not fail
To meet thee in that hollow vale.
'An Exequy' (1657) l. 81 (written for his wife Anne, d. 1624)

8 But hark! My pulse, like a soft drum
Beats my approach, tells thee I come.
'An Exequy' (1657) l. 111

Martin Luther King 1929–68

American civil rights leader

9 I want to be the white man's brother, not his brother-in-law.
in *New York Journal-American* 10 September 1962

10 Judicial decrees may not change the heart; but they can restrain the heartless.
speech in Nashville, Tennessee, 27 December 1962, in James Melvin Washington (ed.) *A Testament of Hope: The Essential Writings of Martin Luther King, Jr.* (1986) ch. 22

11 Injustice anywhere is a threat to justice everywhere.
letter from Birmingham Jail, Alabama, 16 April 1963, in *Atlantic Monthly* August 1963

12 The Negro's great stumbling block in the stride toward freedom is not the White Citizens Councillor or the Ku Klux Klanner but the white moderate who is more devoted to order than to justice; who prefers a negative peace which is the absence of tension to a positive peace which is the presence of justice.
letter from Birmingham Jail, Alabama, 16 April 1963, in *Atlantic Monthly* August 1963

13 If a man hasn't discovered something he will die for, he isn't fit to live.
speech in Detroit, 23 June 1963, in James Bishop *The Days of Martin Luther King* (1971) ch. 4

14 I have a dream that one day on the red hills of Georgia the sons of former slaves and the sons of former slave owners will be able to sit down together at the table of brotherhood . . .
I have a dream that my four little children will one day live in a nation where they will not be judged by the colour of their skin but by the content of their character.
speech at Civil Rights March in Washington, 28 August 1963, in *New York Times* 29 August 1963

15 We must learn to live together as brothers or perish together as fools.
speech at St Louis, 22 March 1964, in *St Louis Post-Dispatch* 23 March 1964

16 I just want to do God's will. And he's allowed me to go up to the mountain. And I've looked over, and I've seen the promised land . . . So I'm happy tonight. I'm not worried about anything. I'm not fearing any man.
on the day before his assassination
speech in Memphis, 3 April 1968, in *New York Times* 4 April 1968

17 The means by which we live have outdistanced the ends for which we live. Our scientific power has outrun our spiritual power. We have guided missiles and misguided men.
Strength to Love (1963) ch. 7

18 A riot is at bottom the language of the unheard.
Where Do We Go From Here? (1967) ch. 4

Stoddard King 1889–1933

British songwriter

19 There's a long, long trail awinding
Into the land of my dreams.
'There's a Long, Long Trail' (1913 song)

William King 1650–1729

Irish cleric

20 The cry of the whole people is loud for bread; God knows what will be the consequence; many are starved, and I am afraid many more will be.
view of the Archbishop of Dublin in 1720
Daniel Corkery *The Hidden Ireland* (1925)

William Lyon Mackenzie King
1874–1950

Canadian Liberal statesman, Prime Minister 1921–6, 1926–30, and 1935–48

1 If some countries have too much history, we have too much geography.
speech, Canadian House of Commons, 18 June 1936

2 Not necessarily conscription, but conscription if necessary.
speech, Canadian House of Commons, 7 July 1942

Stephen King 1947–
American writer

3 Terror . . . often arises from a pervasive sense of disestablishment; that things are in the unmaking.
Danse Macabre (1981)

Charles Kingsley 1819–75
English writer and clergyman

on Kingsley: see ***Stubbs*** *745:3*

4 Be good, sweet maid, and let who will be clever;
Do noble things, not dream them, all day long.
'A Farewell' (1858)

5 Do the work that's nearest,
Though it's dull at whiles,
Helping, when we meet them,
Lame dogs over stiles.
'The Invitation. To Tom Hughes' (1856)

6 Welcome, wild North-easter!
Shame it is to see
Odes to every zephyr;
Ne'er a verse to thee.
'Ode to the North-East Wind' (1858)

7 'Tis the hard grey weather
Breeds hard English men.
'Ode to the North-East Wind' (1858)

8 Come; and strong within us
Stir the Vikings' blood;
Bracing brain and sinew;
Blow, thou wind of God!
'Ode to the North-East Wind' (1858)

9 'O Mary, go and call the cattle home,
And call the cattle home,
And call the cattle home,
Across the sands of Dee.'
The western wind was wild and dank with foam,
And all alone went she.
'The Sands of Dee' (1858)

10 And never home came she.
'The Sands of Dee' (1858)

11 Three fishers went sailing away to the west,
Away to the west as the sun went down;
Each thought on the woman who loved him the best,
And the children stood watching them out of the town.
'The Three Fishers' (1858)

12 For men must work, and women must weep,
And there's little to earn, and many to keep,
Though the harbour bar be moaning.
'The Three Fishers' (1858)

13 When all the world is young, lad,
And all the trees are green;
And every goose a swan, lad,
And every lass a queen;
Then hey for boot and horse, lad,
And round the world away:
Young blood must have its course, lad,
And every dog his day.
'Young and Old' (from *The Water Babies*, 1863)

14 We have used the Bible as if it was a constable's handbook—an opium-dose for keeping beasts of burden patient while they are being overloaded.
Letters to the Chartists no. 2; cf. **Marx** 499:13

15 Eustace is a man no longer; he is become a thing, a tool, a Jesuit.
Westward Ho! (1855) ch. 23

Hugh Kingsmill (Hugh Kingsmill Lunn)
1889–1949

English man of letters

16 What still alive at twenty-two,
A clean upstanding chap like you?
Sure, if your throat 'tis hard to slit,
Slit your girl's, and swing for it.
'Two Poems, after A. E. Housman' (1933) no. 1

17 But bacon's not the only thing
That's cured by hanging from a string.
'Two Poems, after A. E. Housman' (1933) no. 1

18 God's apology for relations.
of friends
Michael Holroyd *The Best of Hugh Kingsmill* (1970) introduction

Neil Kinnock 1942–
British Labour politician

during the Falklands War, replying to a heckler who said that Mrs ***Thatcher*** *'showed guts'*

19 It's a pity others had to leave theirs on the ground at Goose Green to prove it.
television interview, 6 June 1983

20 If Margaret Thatcher wins on Thursday, I warn you not to be ordinary, I warn you not to be young, I warn you not to fall ill, and I warn you not to grow old.
on the prospect of a Conservative re-election
speech at Bridgend, 7 June 1983

21 Why am I the first Kinnock in a thousand generations to be able to get to a university?
later plagiarized by the American politician Joe Biden
speech in party political broadcast, 21 May 1987

Alfred Kinsey 1894–1956
American zoologist and sex researcher

22 The only unnatural sex act is that which you cannot perform.
in *Time* 21 January 1966

Rudyard Kipling 1865–1936

English writer and poet
on Kipling: see **Stephen** *738:1; see also* **Epitaphs** *304:6*

1 When you've shouted 'Rule Britannia', when you've sung 'God save the Queen'—
When you've finished killing Kruger with your mouth.
'The Absent-Minded Beggar' (1899) st. 1

2 He's an absent-minded beggar and his weaknesses are great—
But we and Paul must take him as we find him—
He is out on active service, wiping something off a slate—
And he's left a lot o' little things behind him!
'The Absent-Minded Beggar' (1899) st. 1

3 England's on the anvil—hear the hammers ring—
Clanging from the Severn to the Tyne!
Never was a blacksmith like our Norman King—
England's being hammered, hammered, hammered into line!
'The Anvil' (1927)

4 Seek not to question other than
The books I leave behind.
'The Appeal' (1940)

5 Oh, East is East, and West is West, and never the twain shall meet,
Till Earth and Sky stand presently at God's great Judgement Seat;
But there is neither East nor West, Border, nor Breed, nor Birth,
When two strong men stand face to face, tho' they come from the ends of earth!
'The Ballad of East and West' (1892)

6 Four things greater than all things are,—
Women and Horses and Power and War.
'The Ballad of the King's Jest' (1892)

7 Foot—foot—foot—foot—sloggin' over Africa—
(Boots—boots—boots—boots—movin' up and down again!)
'Boots' (1903)

8 If any question why we died,
Tell them, because our fathers lied.
'Common Form' (1919)

9 The Devil whoops, as he whooped of old: 'It's clever, but is it Art?'
'The Conundrum of the Workshops' (1892)

10 For they're hangin' Danny Deever, you can hear the Dead March play,
The regiment's in 'ollow square—they're hangin' him to-day;
They've taken of his buttons off an' cut his stripes away,
An' they're hangin' Danny Deever in the mornin'.
'Danny Deever' (1892)

11 The 'eathen in 'is blindness bows down to wood an' stone;
'E don't obey no orders unless they is 'is own.
'The 'Eathen' (1896); cf. **Heber** 367:7

12 And what should they know of England who only England know?
'The English Flag' (1892)

13 I could not dig: I dared not rob:
Therefore I lied to please the mob.
Now all my lies are proved untrue
And I must face the men I slew.
What tale shall serve me here among
Mine angry and defrauded young?
'Epitaphs of the War: A Dead Statesman' (1919)

14 My son was killed while laughing at some jest. I would I knew
What it was, and it might serve me in a time when jests are few.
'Epitaphs of the War: A Son' (1919)

15 The female of the species is more deadly than the male.
'The Female of the Species' (1919); cf. **Proverbs** 600:17

16 So 'ere's *to* you, Fuzzy-Wuzzy, at your 'ome in the Soudan;
You're a pore benighted 'eathen but a first-class fightin' man.
'Fuzzy-Wuzzy' (1892)

17 We're poor little lambs who've lost our way,
Baa! Baa! Baa!
We're little black sheep who've gone astray,
Baa-aa-aa!
Gentlemen-rankers out on the spree,
Damned from here to Eternity,
God ha' mercy on such as we,
Baa! Yah! Bah!
'Gentlemen-Rankers' (1892)

18 We have done with Hope and Honour, we are lost to Love and Truth,
We are dropping down the ladder rung by rung,
And the measure of our torment is the measure of our youth.
God help us, for we knew the worst too young!
'Gentlemen-Rankers' (1892)

19 Our England is a garden, and such gardens are not made
By singing:—'Oh, how beautiful!' and sitting in the shade,
While better men than we go out and start their working lives
At grubbing weeds from gravel paths with broken dinner-knives.
'The Glory of the Garden' (1911)

20 As it will be in the future, it was at the birth of Man—
There are only four things certain since Social Progress began:—
That the Dog returns to his Vomit and the Sow returns to her Mire,
And the burnt Fool's bandaged finger goes wabbling back to the Fire.
'The Gods of the Copybook Headings' (1927)

21 Though I've belted you and flayed you,
By the livin' Gawd that made you,
You're a better man than I am, Gunga Din!
'Gunga Din' (1892)

1 What is a woman that you forsake her,
And the hearth-fire and the home-acre,
To go with the old grey Widow-maker?
'Harp Song of the Dane Women' (1906)

2 If you can keep your head when all about you
Are losing theirs and blaming it on you;
If you can trust yourself when all men doubt you,
But make allowance for their doubting too;
If you can wait and not be tired by waiting,
Or being lied about, don't deal in lies,
Or being hated, don't give way to hating,
And yet don't look too good, nor talk too wise;
If you can dream—and not make dreams your master;
If you can think—and not make thoughts your aim,
If you can meet with triumph and disaster
And treat those two impostors just the same...
'If—' (1910)

3 If you can talk with crowds and keep your virtue,
Or walk with Kings—nor lose the common touch,
If neither foes nor loving friends can hurt you,
If all men count with you, but none too much;
If you can fill the unforgiving minute
With sixty seconds' worth of distance run,
Yours is the Earth and everything that's in it,
And—which is more—you'll be a Man, my son!
'If—' (1910)

4 There are nine and sixty ways of constructing tribal lays,
And—every—single—one—of—them—is—right!
'In the Neolithic Age' (1893)

5 Old days! the wild geese are flighting,
Head to the storm as they faced it before.
'The Irish Guards'

6 Then ye returned to your trinkets; then ye contented your souls
With the flannelled fools at the wicket or the muddied oafs at the goals.
'The Islanders' (1903)

7 I've taken my fun where I've found it,
An' now I must pay for my fun,
For the more you 'ave known o' the others
The less will you settle to one.
'The Ladies' (1896)

8 When you get to a man in the case,
They're like as a row of pins—
For the Colonel's Lady an' Judy O'Grady
Are sisters under their skins!
'The Ladies' (1896)

9 And Ye take mine honour from me if Ye take away the sea!
'The Last Chantey' (1896)

10 Down to Gehenna or up to the Throne,
He travels the fastest who travels alone.
L'Envoi to *The Story of the Gadsbys* (1890), 'The Winners' cf. **Proverbs** 602:23

11 The Liner she's a lady, an' she never looks nor 'eeds—
The Man-o'-War's 'er 'usband, an' 'e gives 'er all she needs;
But, oh, the little cargo boats that sail the wet seas roun',
They're just the same as you an' me a-plyin' up and down!
'The Liner She's a Lady' (1896)

12 By the old Moulmein Pagoda, lookin' eastward to the sea,
There's a Burma girl a-settin', and I know she thinks o' me;
For the wind is in the palm-trees, an' the temple-bells they say:
'Come you back, you British soldier; come you back to Mandalay!'
'Mandalay' (1892)

13 On the road to Mandalay,
Where the flyin'-fishes play,
An' the dawn comes up like thunder outer China 'crost the Bay!
'Mandalay' (1892)

14 Ship me somewheres east of Suez, where the best is like the worst,
Where there aren't no Ten Commandments an' a man can raise a thirst.
'Mandalay' (1892)

15 They shall not return to us, the resolute, the young,
The eager and whole-hearted whom we gave:
But the men who left them thriftily to die in their own dung,
Shall they come with years and honour to the grave?
'Mesopotamia' (1917)

16 Dawn off the Foreland—the young flood making
Jumbled and short and steep—
Black in the hollows and bright where it's breaking—
Awkward water to sweep.
'Mines reported in the fairway,
'Warn all traffic and detain.
' 'Sent up *Unity*, *Claribel*, *Assyrian*, *Stormcock*, and *Golden Gain*.'
'Mine Sweepers' (1915)

17 'Have you news of my boy Jack?'
Not this tide.
'When d'you think that he'll come back?'
Not with this wind blowing, and this tide.
'My Boy Jack' (1916)

18 And the end of the fight is a tombstone white, with the name of the late deceased,
And the epitaph drear: 'A fool lies here who tried to hustle the East.'
The Naulahka (1892) ch. 5

19 A Nation spoke to a Nation,
A Throne sent word to a Throne:
'Daughter am I in my mother's house,
But mistress in my own.
The gates are mine to open,
As the gates are mine to close,
And I abide by my Mother's House.'
Said our Lady of the Snows.
'Our Lady of the Snows' (1898)

1 The toad beneath the harrow knows
Exactly where each tooth-point goes;
The butterfly upon the road
Preaches contentment to that toad.
'Pagett, MP' (1886)

2 There is sorrow enough in the natural way
From men and women to fill our day;
But when we are certain of sorrow in store,
Why do we always arrange for more?
Brothers and Sisters, I bid you beware
Of giving your heart to a dog to tear.
'The Power of the Dog' (1909)

3 The tumult and the shouting dies—
The captains and the kings depart—
Still stands Thine ancient Sacrifice,
An humble and a contrite heart.
Lord God of Hosts, be with us yet,
Lest we forget—lest we forget!
'Recessional' (1897); cf. **Knox** 442:13

4 Far-called our navies melt away—
On dune and headland sinks the fire—
Lo, all our pomp of yesterday
Is one with Nineveh, and Tyre!
'Recessional' (1897)

5 Such boasting as the Gentiles use,
Or lesser breeds without the Law.
'Recessional' (1897)

6 How far is St. Helena from the field of Austerlitz?
'A St. Helena Lullaby' (1910)

7 Who hath desired the Sea?—the sight of salt water unbounded—
The heave and the halt and the hurl and the crash of the comber wind-hounded?
The sleek-barrelled swell before storm, grey, foamless, enormous, and growing—
Stark calm on the lap of the Line or the crazy-eyed hurricane blowing.
'The Sea and the Hills' (1903)

8 Five and twenty ponies,
Trotting through the dark—
Brandy for the Parson,
'Baccy for the Clerk;
Laces for a lady, letters for a spy,
Watch the wall, my darling, while the Gentlemen go by!
'A Smuggler's Song' (1906)

9 If blood be the price of admiralty,
Lord God, we ha' paid in full!
'The Song of the Dead' (1896)

10 And here the sea-fogs lap and cling
And here, each warning each,
The sheep-bells and the ship-bells ring
Along the hidden beach.
'Sussex' (1903)

11 One man in a thousand, Solomon says,
Will stick more close than a brother.
'The Thousandth Man' (1910); cf. **Bible** 83:6

12 For the sin ye do by two and two ye must pay for one by one!
'Tomlinson' (1892)

13 Then it's Tommy this, an' Tommy that, an' 'Tommy 'ow's yer soul?'
But it's 'Thin red line of 'eroes' when the drums begin to roll.
'Tommy' (1892); cf. **Russell** 640:13

14 Of all the trees that grow so fair,
Old England to adorn,
Greater are none beneath the Sun,
Than Oak, and Ash, and Thorn.
'A Tree Song' (1906)

15 What answer from the North?
One Law, one Land, one Throne.
If England drive us forth,
We shall not fall alone.
'Ulster' (1912)

16 A fool there was and he made his prayer
(Even as you and I!)
To a rag and a bone and a hank of hair
(We called her the woman who did not care)
But the fool he called her his lady fair—
(Even as you and I!)
'The Vampire' (1897) st. 1

17 They shut the road through the woods
Seventy years ago.
Weather and rain have undone it again,
And now you would never know
There was once a road through the woods.
'The Way through the Woods' (1910)

18 It is always a temptation to a rich and lazy nation,
To puff and look important and to say:-
'Though we know we should defeat you, we have not the time to meet you,
We will therefore pay you cash to go away.'
And that is called paying the Dane-geld,
But we've proved it again and again,
That if once you have paid him the Dane-geld
You never get rid of the Dane.
'What Dane-geld means' (1911)

19 And only the Master shall praise us, and only the Master shall blame;
And no one shall work for money, and no one shall work for fame,
But each for the joy of the working, and each, in his separate star,
Shall draw the Thing as he sees It for the God of Things as They are!
'When Earth's Last Picture is Painted' (1896)

20 When 'Omer smote 'is bloomin' lyre,
He'd 'eard men sing by land an' sea;
An' what he thought 'e might require,
'E went an' took—the same as me!
'When 'Omer smote 'is bloomin' lyre' (1896)

21 Take up the White Man's burden—
Send forth the best ye breed—
Go, bind your sons to exile
To serve your captives' need.
'The White Man's Burden' (1899)

22 When you're wounded and left on Afghanistan's plains
And the women come out to cut up what remains
Just roll to your rifle and blow out your brains

An' go to your Gawd like a soldier.
'The Young British Soldier' (1892)

1 Lalun is a member of the most ancient profession in the world.
In Black and White (1888) 'On the City Wall'; cf. **Reagan** 623:3

2 They settled things by making up a saying, 'What the Bandar-log think now the Jungle will think later': and that comforted them a great deal.
The Jungle Book (1894) 'Kaa's Hunting'

3 'We be of one blood, thou and I', Mowgli answered. 'I take my life from thee to-night. My kill shall be thy kill if ever thou art hungry, O Kaa.'
The Jungle Book (1894) 'Kaa's Hunting'

4 The motto of all the mongoose family is, 'Run and find out.'
The Jungle Book (1894) 'Rikki-Tikki-Tavi'

5 Brother, thy tail hangs down behind!
The Jungle Book (1894) 'Road Song of the Bandar-Log'

6 He walked by himself, and all places were alike to him.
Just So Stories (1902) 'The Cat that Walked by Himself'

7 And he went back through the Wet Wild Woods, waving his wild tail and walking by his wild lone. But he never told anybody.
Just So Stories (1902) 'The Cat that Walked by Himself'

8 One Elephant—a new Elephant—an Elephant's Child—who was full of 'satiable curtiosity.
Just So Stories (1902) 'The Elephant's Child'

9 The great grey-green, greasy, Limpopo River, all set about with fever trees.
Just So Stories (1902) 'The Elephant's Child'

10 I keep six honest serving-men
(They taught me all I knew);
Their names are What and Why and When
And How and Where and Who.
Just So Stories (1902) 'The Elephant's Child'

11 You must *not* forget the suspenders, Best Beloved.
Just So Stories (1902) 'How the Whale got his Throat'

12 And the small 'Stute Fish said in a small 'stute voice, 'Noble and generous Cetacean, have you ever tasted Man?' 'No,' said the Whale. 'What is it like?' 'Nice,' said the small 'Stute Fish. 'Nice but nubbly.'
Just So Stories (1902) 'How the Whale got his Throat'

13 He had his Mummy's leave to paddle, or else he would never have done it, because he was a man of infinite-resource-and-sagacity.
Just So Stories (1902) 'How the Whale got his Throat'

14 Little Friend of all the World.
Kim's nickname
Kim (1901) ch. 1

15 The mad all are in God's keeping.
Kim (1901) ch. 2

16 The man who would be king.
title of short story (1888)

17 He swathed himself in quotations—as a beggar would enfold himself in the purple of Emperors.
Many Inventions (1893) 'The Finest Story in the World'

18 Take my word for it, the silliest woman can manage a clever man; but it takes a very clever woman to manage a fool.
Plain Tales from the Hills (1888) 'Three and—an Extra'

19 Now this is the Law of the Jungle—as old and as true as the sky;
And the Wolf that shall keep it may prosper, but the Wolf that shall break it must die.
The Second Jungle Book (1895) 'The Law of the Jungle'

20 One learns more from a good scholar in a rage than from a score of lucid and laborious drudges.
Something of Myself (1937)

21 My Daemon was with me in the *Jungle Books*, *Kim*, and both Puck books, and good care I took to walk delicately lest he should withdraw. I know that he did not, because when these books were finished they said so themselves with, almost, the water-hammer click of a tap turned off.
Something of Myself (1937)

22 I gloat!
Stalky & Co. (1899)

23 A Flopshus Cad, an Outrageous Stinker, a Jelly-bellied Flag-flapper.
Stalky & Co. (1899)

24 'Tisn't beauty, so to speak, nor good talk necessarily. It's just It. Some women'll stay in a man's memory if they once walked down a street.
Traffics and Discoveries (1904) 'Mrs Bathurst'

25 Power without responsibility: the prerogative of the harlot throughout the ages.
summing up Lord ***Beaverbrook****'s political standpoint* vis-à-vis *the* Daily Express, *and quoted by Stanley* ***Baldwin****, 18 March 1931*
in *Kipling Journal* vol. 38, no. 180, December 1971; cf. **Stoppard** 743:12

Henry Kissinger 1923–

American politician

26 The management of a balance of power is a permanent undertaking, not an exertion that has a foreseeable end.
White House Years (1979)

27 The conventional army loses if it does not win. The guerrilla wins if he does not lose.
in *Foreign Affairs* January 1969

28 Power is the great aphrodisiac.
in *New York Times* 19 January 1971

29 We are the President's men.
M. and B. Kalb *Kissinger* (1974) ch. 7

30 For other nations, Utopia is a blessed past never to be recovered; for Americans it is just beyond the horizon.
attributed

Lord Kitchener 1850–1916

British soldier and statesman
on Kitchener: see ***Asquith*** *31:7*

31 You are ordered abroad as a soldier of the King to help our French comrades against the invasion of a common enemy . . . In this new experience you may find temptations both in wine and women. You must entirely resist both temptations, and, while treating all women with perfect courtesy, you should avoid any intimacy. Do your duty bravely. Fear God. Honour the King.

message to soldiers of the British Expeditionary Force (1914), in *The Times* 19 August 1914

1 I don't mind your being killed, but I object to your being taken prisoner.

to the Prince of Wales during the First World War

in *Journals and Letters of Reginald Viscount Esher* (1938) vol. 3, 18 December 1914

Paul Klee 1879–1940

Swiss painter

2 Art does not reproduce the visible; rather, it makes visible.

Inward Vision (1958) 'Creative Credo' (1920)

3 An active line on a walk, moving freely without a goal. A walk for walk's sake. The agent is a point that shifts position.

Pedagogical Sketchbook (1925)

4 Colour has taken hold of me; no longer do I have to chase after it. I know that it has hold of me for ever. That is the significance of this blessed moment.

on a visit to Tunis in 1914

Herbert Read *A Concise History of Modern Painting* (1968)

Friedrich Klopstock 1724–1803

German poet

5 God and I both knew what it meant once; now God alone knows.

C. Lombroso *The Man of Genius* (1891) pt. 1, ch. 2; cf. **Browning** 158:16

Charles Knight and **Kenneth Lyle**

British songwriters

6 When there's trouble brewing,
When there's something doing,
Are we downhearted?
No! Let 'em all come!

'Here we are! Here we are again!!' (1914 song)

Frank H. Knight 1885–1973

American economist

7 Costs merely register competing attractions.

Risk, Uncertainty and Profit (1921)

L. C. Knights 1906–97

English critic and academic

8 How many children had Lady Macbeth?

satirizing an over-realistic approach to criticism

title of essay (1933)

Mary Knowles 1733–1807

English Quaker

9 He gets at the substance of a book directly; he tears out the heart of it.

*on Samuel **Johnson***

James Boswell *The Life of Samuel Johnson* (1791) 15 April 1778

John Knox *c.*1505–72

Scottish Protestant reformer

*on Knox: see **Douglas** 276:13*

10 The first blast of the trumpet against the monstrous regiment of women.

regiment = *rule*

title of pamphlet (1558)

11 *Un homme avec Dieu est toujours dans la majorité.*

A man with God is always in the majority.

inscription on the Reformation Monument, Geneva

Ronald Knox 1888–1957

English writer and Roman Catholic priest

12 When suave politeness, tempering bigot zeal,
Corrected *I believe* to *One does feel.*

'Absolute and Abitofhell' (1913)

13 The tumult and the shouting dies,
The captains and the kings depart,
And we are left with large supplies
Of cold blancmange and rhubarb tart.

'After the Party' in L. E. Eyres (ed.) *In Three Tongues* (1959); cf. **Kipling** 440:3

14 There once was a man who said, 'God
Must think it exceedingly odd
If he finds that this tree
Continues to be
When there's no one about in the Quad.'

Langford Reed *Complete Limerick Book* (1924), to which came the anonymous reply:

Dear Sir,
Your astonishment's odd:
I am always about in the Quad.
And that's why the tree
Will continue to be,
Since observed by
Yours faithfully,
God.

15 The baby doesn't understand English and the Devil knows Latin.

on being asked to perform a baptism in English

Evelyn Waugh *Ronald Knox* (1959) pt. 1, ch. 5

16 A loud noise at one end and no sense of responsibility at the other.

definition of a baby

attributed

Vicesimus Knox 1752–1821

English writer

17 All sensible people agree in thinking that large seminaries of young ladies, though managed with

all the vigilance and caution which human abilities can exert, are in danger of great corruption.
Liberal Education (1780) sect. 27 'On the literary education of women'

1 Can anything be more absurd than keeping women in a state of ignorance, and yet so vehemently to insist on their resisting temptation?
Mary Wollstonecraft *A Vindication of the Rights of Woman* (1792) ch. 7

Ted Koehler
American songwriter

2 Stormy weather,
Since my man and I ain't together.
'Stormy Weather' (1933 song)

Arthur Koestler 1905–83
Hungarian-born writer

3 One may not regard the world as a sort of metaphysical brothel for emotions.
Darkness at Noon (1940) 'The Second Hearing' pt. 7

4 God seems to have left the receiver off the hook, and time is running out.
The Ghost in the Machine (1967) ch. 18

5 A writer's ambition should be . . . to trade a hundred contemporary readers for ten readers in ten years' time and for one reader in a hundred years.
in *New York Times Book Review* 1 April 1951

Helmut Kohl 1930–
German statesman, Chancellor of West Germany (1982–90) and first postwar Chancellor of united Germany (1990–8)

6 We Germans now have the historic chance to realize the unity of our fatherland.
on the reunification of Germany
in *Guardian* 15 February 1990

7 The policy of European integration is in reality a question of war and peace in the 21st century.
speech at Louvain University, 2 February 1996

Johann Georg Kohl 1808–78
German travel writer

8 We had now entered the notorious county of Tipperary, in which more murders and assaults are committed in one year than in the whole Kingdom of Saxony in five.
Ireland, Scotland and England (1844); cf. **Trollope** 782:12

9 What the horse is to the Arab, or the dog is to the Greenlander, the pig is to the Irishman.
Ireland, Scotland and England (1844)

Käthe Kollwitz 1867–1945
German sculptor and graphic artist

10 As you, the children of my body, have been my tasks, so too are my other works.
letter to her son Hans, 21 February 1915

11 I have never done any work cold . . . I have always worked with my blood, so to speak.
letter to her son Hans, 16 April 1917

The Koran
textual translations are those of A. J. Arberry, 1964

12 In the Name of God, the Merciful, the Compassionate.
sura 1

13 Praise belongs to God, the Lord of all Being,
the All-merciful, the All-compassionate,
the Master of the Day of Doom.
sura 1

14 Thee only we serve; to Thee alone we pray for succour.
Guide us in the straight path,
the path of those whom Thou hast blessed,
not of those against whom Thou art wrathful,
nor of those who are astray.
sura 1

15 That is the Book [the Koran], wherein is no doubt,
a guidance to the godfearing
who believe in the Unseen.
sura 2

16 And if you are in doubt concerning that We have sent down on Our servant [Muhammad], then bring a sura
like it, and call your witnesses, apart from God, if you are truthful.
And if you do not—and you will not—then fear the Fire, whose fuel is men and stones,
prepared for unbelievers.
sura 2

17 True piety is this:
to believe in God, and the Last Day,
the angels, the Book, and the Prophets,
to give of one's substance, however cherished,
to kinsmen, and orphans,
the needy, the traveller, beggars,
and to ransom the slave,
to perform the prayer, to pay the alms.
sura 2

18 The month of Ramadan, wherein the Koran
was sent down to be a guidance
to the people, and as clear signs
of the Guidance and the Salvation
So let those of you, who are present
at the month, fast it.
sura 2

19 And fight in the way of God with those
who fight with you, but aggress not: God loves
not the aggressors.
sura 2

20 No compulsion is there in religion.
sura 2

21 God is the protector of the believers;
He brings them forth from the shadows
into the light.
sura 2

22 God has
permitted trafficking, and forbidden usury.
sura 2

23 Say to the unbelievers: 'You shall be
overthrown, and mustered into Gehenna—

an evil cradling!'
sura 3

1 The true religion with God is Islam.
sura 3

2 Abraham in truth was not a Jew,
neither a Christian; but he was a Muslim
and one pure of faith; certainly he was never
of the idolaters.
sura 3

3 Say: 'We believe in God, and that which has been sent
down on us, and sent down on Abraham and Ishmael,
Isaac and Jacob, and the Tribes, and in that which was
given to Moses and Jesus, and the Prophets of their
Lord; we make no division between any of them, and
to Him we surrender.'
sura 3

4 Whoso desires another religion than Islam, it shall
not be accepted of him; in the next world he shall
be among the losers.
sura 3

5 Every soul shall taste of death; you shall surely
be paid in full your wages on the Day
of Resurrection.
sura 3

6 Men are the managers of the affairs of women.
sura 4

7 Righteous women are therefore obedient,
guarding the secret for God's guarding.
And those you fear may be rebellious
admonish; banish them to their couches,
and beat them.
sura 4

8 So let them fight in the way of God who
sell the present life for the world to come;
and whosoever fights in the way of God
and is slain, or conquers, We shall bring him
a mighty wage.
sura 4

9 How is it with you, that you do not fight
in the way of God, and for the men,
women, and children who, being abased,
say, 'Our Lord, bring us forth from this city
whose people are evildoers, and appoint to us
a protector from Thee, and appoint to us
from Thee a helper?'
sura 4

10 Whatever good visits thee, it is of God;
whatever evil visits thee is of thyself.
sura 4

11 What, do they not ponder the Koran?
If it had been from other than God
surely they would have found in it much
inconsistency.
sura 4

12 God—
there is no God but He.
He will surely gather you
to the Resurrection Day,
no doubt of it.
And who is truer in tidings than God?
sura 4

13 To God belongs all that is in the heavens
and in the earth, and God encompasses
everything.
sura 4

14 Souls are very
prone to avarice. If you do good
and are godfearing, surely God is aware of the things you do.
sura 4;

Men's souls are naturally inclined to
covetousness; but if ye be kind towards women
and fear to wrong them, God is well acquainted
with what ye do.
in George Sale's translation, 1734

15 The Messiah, Jesus son of Mary,
was only the Messenger of God.
sura 4

16 Today I have perfected your religion
for you, and I have completed My blessing
upon you and I have approved Islam for
your religion.
sura 5

17 And we have sent down to thee the Book
with the truth, confirming the Book
that was before it, and assuring it.
sura 5

18 He originates
creation, then He brings it back again
that He may recompense those who believe
and do deeds of righteousness, justly.
sura 10

19 Glory be to Him, who carried His servant by night
from the Holy Mosque to the Further Mosque
the precincts of which We have blessed,
that We might show him some of Our signs.
sura 17

20 Perform the prayer
at the sinking of the sun to the darkening of the night
and the recital of dawn.
sura 17

21 Even so We have sent it down
as an Arabic Koran, and We
have turned about in it something
of threats, that haply they may be
godfearing, or it may arouse in
them remembrance.
sura 20

22 And do thou purify
My House [Kaaba] for those that shall go about it
and those that stand, for those that bow
and prostrate themselves;
and proclaim among men the Pilgrimage.
sura 22

1 He
named you Muslims
aforetime and in this, that the Messenger
might be a witness against you, and that
you might be witnesses against mankind.
sura 22

2 God is the Light of the heavens and the earth;
the likeness of His Light is as a niche
wherein is a lamp . . .
kindled from a Blessed Tree,
an olive that is neither of the East nor of the West
whose oil wellnigh would shine, even if no fire
touched it;
Light upon Light.
sura 24

3 Muhammad is not the father of any one
of your men, but the Messenger of God,
and the Seal of the Prophets
sura 33

4 God knows the Unseen in the heavens and the
earth;
He knows the thoughts within the breasts.
It is He who appointed you viceroys in the earth.
sura 35

5 The sending down of the Book is from God
the All-mighty, the All-wise.
We have sent down to thee the Book with the
truth;
so worship God, making thy religion
His sincerely.
sura 39

6 It belongs not to any mortal that
God should speak to him, except
by revelation, or from behind
a veil,
or that He should send a messenger
and he reveal whatsoever He will,
by His leave.
sura 42

7 Surely,
unto God all things come home.
sura 42

8 And those who are slain in the way of God, He
will not send their works astray,
He will guide them, and dispose their minds aright,
and He will admit them to Paradise,
that He has made known to them.
sura 47

9 It is He who has sent his Messenger with
the guidance and the religion of truth, that
He may uplift it above every religion.
sura 48

10 Muhammed is the Messenger of God,
and those who are with him are hard
against the unbelievers, merciful
one to another.
sura 48

11 Thou seest them [believers]
bowing, prostrating, seeking bounty
from God and good pleasure. Their
mark is on their faces, the trace of
prostration. That is their likeness
in the Torah, and their likeness
in the Gospel.
sura 48

12 By the glorious Koran!
sura 50

13 We indeed created man; and We know
what his soul whispers within him,
and We are nearer to him than the
jugular vein.
sura 50

14 He [God] is the First and the Last, the Outward and
the Inward.
sura 57

15 He is God
the Creator, the Maker, the Shaper,
To Him belong the Names Most Beautiful.
sura 59

16 On that day [the Day of Judgement] you shall be
exposed, not one secret
of yours concealed.
Then as for him who is given his book in his right
hand,
he shall say, 'Here, take and read my book!
Certainly
I thought that I should encounter my reckoning.'
So he
shall be in a pleasing life
in a lofty Garden,
its clusters nigh to gather.
sura 69

17 Recite: In the Name of thy Lord who created
created Man of a blood-clot.
sura 96

Karl Kraus 1874–1936

Austrian satirist

18 How is the world ruled and how do wars start?
Diplomats tell lies to journalists and then believe
what they read.
Aphorisms and More Aphorisms (1909)

19 There is no unhappier creature on earth than a
fetishist who yearns to embrace a woman's shoe
and has to embrace the whole woman.
Aphorisms and More Aphorisms (1909)

20 What good is speed if the brain has oozed out on
the way?
in *Die Fackel* September 1909 'The Discovery of the North Pole'

Jiddu Krishnamurti d. 1986

Indian spiritual philosopher

21 Religion is the frozen thought of men out of which
they build temples.
in *Observer* 22 April 1928 'Sayings of the Week'

22 Truth is a pathless land, and you cannot approach
it by any path whatsoever, by any religion, by any
sect.
speech in Holland, 3 August 1929

1 Happiness is a state of which you are unconscious, of which you are not aware. The moment you are aware that you are happy, you cease to be happy . . . You want to be consciously happy; the moment you are consciously happy, happiness is gone.

Penguin Krishnamurti Reader (1970) 'Questions and Answers'

Kris Kristofferson 1936–

American actor

2 Freedom's just another word for nothin' left to lose,
Nothin' ain't worth nothin', but it's free.

'Me and Bobby McGee' (1969 song, with Fred Foster)

Paul Kruger see **Telegrams** 758:3

Joseph Wood Krutch 1893–1970

American critic and naturalist

3 The most serious charge which can be brought against New England is not Puritanism but February.

The Twelve Seasons (1949) 'February'

Stanley Kubrick 1928–99

American film director

4 The great nations have always acted like gangsters, and the small nations like prostitutes.

in *Guardian* 5 June 1963

Satish Kumar 1937–

Indian writer

5 Lead me from death to life, from falsehood to truth.
Lead me from despair to hope, from fear to trust.
Lead me from hate to love, from war to peace.
Let peace fill our heart, our world, our universe.

'Prayer for Peace' (1981); adapted from the **Upanishads**; cf. **Upanishads** 787:19

Milan Kundera 1929–

Czech novelist

6 The unbearable lightness of being.

title of novel (1984)

7 Mankind's true moral test, its fundamental test (which lies deeply buried from view) consists of its attitudes towards those who are at its mercy: animals.

The Unbearable Lightness of Being (1984)

Thomas Kyd 1558–94

English dramatist

8 Thus must we toil in other men's extremes,
That know not how to remedy our own.

The Spanish Tragedy (1592) act 3, sc. 6, l. 1

9 My son—and what's a son? A thing begot
Within a pair of minutes, thereabout,
A lump bred up in darkness.

The Spanish Tragedy (1592) act 3, sc. 11, The Third Addition (1602 ed.) l. 5

10 It grew a gallows and did bear our son,
It bore thy fruit and mine.

The Spanish Tragedy (1592) act 3, sc. 12, The Fourth Addition (1602 ed.) l. 70

11 For what's a play without a woman in it?

The Spanish Tragedy (1592) act 4, sc. 1, l. 97

12 Hieronimo is mad again.

alternative title given to *The Spanish Tragedy* in 1615

Henry Labouchere 1831–1912

British politician

13 He [Labouchere] did not object to the old man always having a card up his sleeve, but he did object to his insinuating that the Almighty had placed it there.

on ***Gladstone****'s 'frequent appeals to a higher power'*

Earl Curzon *Modern Parliamentary Eloquence* (1913); another version is:

Who cannot refrain from perpetually bringing an ace down his sleeve, even when he has only to play fair to win the trick.

letter in A. L. Thorold *The Life of Henry Labouchere* (1913) ch. 15

Jean de la Bruyère 1645–96

French satiric moralist

14 *Le commencement et le déclin de l'amour se font sentir par l'embarras où l'on est de se trouver seuls.*

The onset and the waning of love make themselves felt in the uneasiness experienced at being alone together.

Les Caractères ou les moeurs de ce siècle (1688) 'Du Coeur'

15 *Le peuple n'a guère d'esprit et les grands n'ont point d'âme . . . faut-il opter, je ne balance pas, ne veux être peuple.*

The people have little intelligence, the great no heart . . . if I had to choose I should have no hesitation: I would be of the people.

Les Caractères ou les moeurs de ce siècle (1688) 'Des Grands'

16 *Il n'y a pour l'homme que trois événements: naître, vivre et mourir. Il ne sent pas naître, il souffre à mourir, et il oublie de vivre.*

Man has but three events in his life: to be born, to live, and to die. He is not conscious of his birth, he suffers at his death and he forgets to live.

Les Caractères ou les moeurs de ce siècle (1688) 'De l'homme'

17 *Entre le bon sens et le bon goût il y a la différence de la cause et son effet.*

Between good sense and good taste there is the same difference as between cause and effect.

Les Caractères ou les moeurs de ce siècle (1688) 'Des Jugements'

18 *Tout est dit et l'on vient trop tard depuis plus de spet mille ans qu'il y a des hommes et qui pensent.*

Everything has been said, and we are more than seven thousand years of human thought too late.

Les Caractères ou les moeurs de ce siècle (1688) 'Des Ouvrages de l'esprit'

19 *C'est un métier que de faire un livre, comme de faire une pendule: il faut plus que de l'esprit pour être auteur.*

Making a book is a craft, as is making a clock; it takes more than wit to become an author.

Les Caractères ou les moeurs de ce siècle (1688) 'Des Ouvrages de l'esprit'

Nivelle de la Chaussée 1692–1754

French dramatist

1 *Quand tout le monde a tort, tout le monde a raison.*

When everyone is wrong, everyone is right.

La Gouvernante (1747) act 1, sc. 3

James Lackington 1746–1815

English bookseller

2 At last, by singing and repeating enthusiastic amorous hymns, and ignorantly applying particular texts of scripture, I got my imagination to the proper pitch, and thus was I born again in an instant.

Memoirs (1792 ed.) Letter 6

Pierre Choderlos de Laclos 1741–1803

French soldier and writer

3 *M. de Valmont, avec un beau nom, une grande fortune, beaucoup de qualités aimables, a reconnu de bonne heure que pour avoir l'empire dans la société, il suffisoit de manier, avec une égale adresse, la louange et la ridicule.*

Monsieur de Valmont, with an illustrious name, a large fortune, and many agreeable qualities, early realized that to achieve influence in society no more is required than to practise the arts of adulation and ridicule with equal skill.

Les Liaisons Dangereuses (1782) letter 32

4 *Voilà bien les hommes! tous également scélérats dans leurs projets, ce qu'ils mettent de faiblesse dans l'exécution, ils l'appellent probité.*

Our intentions make blackguards of us all; our weakness in carrying them out we call probity.

Les Liaisons Dangereuses (1782) letter 66

5 *Il me prise donc bien peu, s'il croit valoir assez pour me fixer!*

He cannot rate me very high if he thinks he is worth my fidelity!

Les Liaisons Dangereuses (1782) letter 113

6 *L'homme jouit du bonheur qu'il ressent, et la femme de celui qu'elle procure.*

A man enjoys the happiness he feels, a woman the happiness she gives.

Les Liaisons Dangereuses (1782) letter 130

7 *Si vous permettez à mon âge une réflexion qu'on ne fait guère au vôtre, c'est que, si on étoit éclairé sur son véritable bonheur, on ne le chercherait jamais hors des bornes prescrites par les loix et la religion.*

If you will allow me, at my age, a reflection that is scarcely ever made at yours, I must say that if one only knew where one's true happiness lay one would never look for it outside the limits prescribed by the law and by religion.

Les Liaisons Dangereuses (1782) letter 171

Christian Lacroix 1951–

French couturier

8 Haute Couture should be fun, foolish and almost unwearable.

in *Observer* 27 December 1987 'Sayings of the Year'

Jean de la Fontaine 1621–95

French poet

9 *Aide-toi, le ciel t'aidera.*

Help yourself, and heaven will help you.

Fables bk. 6 (1668) 'Le Chartier Embourbé'; cf. **Proverbs** 601:12

10 *Je plie et ne romps pas.*

I bend and I break not.

Fables bk. 1 (1668) 'Le Chêne et le Roseau'

11 *C'est double plaisir de tromper le trompeur.*

It is doubly pleasing to trick the trickster.

Fables bk. 2 (1668) 'Le Coq et le Renard'

12 *Il connaît l'univers et ne se connaît pas.*

He knows the universe and does not know himself.

Fables bk. 8 (1678–9) 'Démocrite et les Abdéritains'

13 *La mort ne surprend point le sage,*
Il est toujours prêt à partir.

Death never takes the wise man by surprise; he is always ready to go.

Fables bk. 8 (1678–9) 'La Mort et le Mourant'; cf. **Montaigne** 527:7

14 *Certain renard voulut, dit-on, se faire loup. Hé! qui peu dire que pour le métier de mouton jamais aucun loup ne soupire?*

A certain fox, it is said, wanted to become a wolf. Ah! who can say why no wolf has ever craved the life of a sheep?

Fables Choisies (1693 ed.) bk. 7, no. 9

Madame de La Fayette 1634–93

French novelist

15 One reproaches a lover, but can one reproach a husband, when his only fault is that he no longer loves?

The Princess of Clèves (1678) pt. 4

Jules Laforgue 1860–87

French poet

16 *Ah! que la vie est quotidienne.*

Oh, what a day-to-day business life is.

Complainte sur certains ennuis (1885)

Fiorello La Guardia 1882–1947

American politician

17 When I make a mistake, it's a beaut!

on the appointment of Herbert O'Brien as a judge in 1936

William Manners *Patience and Fortitude* (1976)

John Lahr 1941–
American critic

1 Criticism is a life without risk.
Light Fantastic (1996)

2 Society drives people crazy with lust and calls it advertising.
in *Guardian* 2 August 1989

3 Momentum was part of the exhilaration and the exhaustion of the twentieth century which Coward decoded for the British but borrowed wholesale from the Americans.
in *New Yorker* 9 September 1996

R. D. Laing 1927–89
Scottish psychiatrist

4 The divided self.
title of book (1960) on schizophrenia

5 Madness need not be all breakdown. It may also be break-through.
The Politics of Experience (1967) ch. 6

Alphonse de Lamartine 1790–1869
French poet

6 *Un être seul vous manque, et tout est dépeuplé.*
Only one being is wanting, and your whole world is bereft of people.
'L'Isolement' (1820)

7 *Ô temps! suspend ton vol, et vous, heures propices!*
Suspendez votre cours.
O Time! arrest your flight, and you, propitious hours, stay your course.
Le Lac (1820) st. 6

Lady Caroline Lamb 1785–1828
wife of William Lamb, Lord **Melbourne**

8 Mad, bad, and dangerous to know.
of **Byron**, *after their first meeting at a ball*
diary, March 1812; in Elizabeth Jenkins *Lady Caroline Lamb* (1932) ch. 6

Charles Lamb 1775–1834
English writer
on Lamb: see **Hazlitt** *365:4*

9 If the husband be a man with whom you have lived on a friendly footing before marriage,—if you did not come in on the wife's side,—if you did not sneak into the house in her train, but were an old friend in first habits of intimacy before their courtship was so much as thought on,—look about you . . . Every long friendship, every old authentic intimacy, must be brought into their office to be new stamped with their currency, as a sovereign Prince calls in the good old money that was coined in some reign before he was born or thought of, to be new marked and minted with the stamp of his authority, before he will let it pass current in the world.
Essays of Elia (1823) 'A Bachelor's Complaint of the Behaviour of Married People'

10 Ceremony is an invention to take off the uneasy feeling which we derive from knowing ourselves to be less the object of love and esteem with a fellow-creature than some other person is. It endeavours to make up, by superior attentions in little points, for that invidious preference which it is forced to deny in the greater.
Essays of Elia (1823) 'A Bachelor's Complaint of the Behaviour of Married People'

11 Presents, I often say, endear Absents.
Essays of Elia (1823) 'A Dissertation upon Roast Pig'

12 The human species, according to the best theory I can form of it, is composed of two distinct races, *the men who borrow*, and *the men who lend*.
Essays of Elia (1823) 'The Two Races of Men'

13 Your *borrowers of books*—those mutilators of collections, spoilers of the symmetry of shelves, and creators of odd volumes.
Essays of Elia (1823) 'The Two Races of Men'

14 Not many sounds in life . . . exceed in interest a knock at the door.
Essays of Elia (1823) 'Valentine's Day'

15 Books think for me.
Last Essays of Elia (1833) 'Detached Thoughts on Books and Reading'

16 Things in books' clothing.
Last Essays of Elia (1833) 'Detached Thoughts on Books and Reading'

17 [A pun] is a pistol let off at the ear; not a feather to tickle the intellect.
Last Essays of Elia (1833) 'Popular Fallacies' no. 9

18 For thy sake, Tobacco, I
Would do any thing but die.
'A Farewell to Tobacco' l. 122

19 Gone before
To that unknown and silent shore.
'Hester' (1803) st. 7

20 I have had playmates, I have had companions,
In my days of childhood, in my joyful school-days,—
All, all are gone, the old familiar faces.
'The Old Familiar Faces'

21 A child's a plaything for an hour.
'Parental Recollections' (1809); often attributed to Lamb's sister Mary

22 I have something more to do than feel.
on the death of his mother, at his sister Mary's hands
letter to S. T. Coleridge, 27 September 1796, in E. W. Marrs (ed.) *Letters of Charles and Mary Lamb* (1975) vol. 1

23 Cultivate simplicity, Coleridge.
letter to S. T. Coleridge, 8 November 1796, in E. W. Marrs (ed.) *Letters of Charles and Mary Lamb* (1975) vol. 1

24 The man must have a rare recipe for melancholy, who can be dull in Fleet Street.
letter to Thomas Manning, 15 February 1802, in E. W. Marrs (ed.) *Letters of Charles and Mary Lamb* (1976) vol. 2

25 Nursed amid her noise, her crowds, her beloved smoke—what have I been doing all my life, if I

have not lent out my heart with usury to such scenes?
of London
letter to Thomas Manning, 15 February 1802, in E. W. Marrs (ed.) *Letters of Charles and Mary Lamb* (1976) vol. 2

1 Nothing puzzles me more than time and space; and yet nothing troubles me less, as I never think about them.
letter to Thomas Manning, 2 January 1810, in E. W. Marrs (ed.) *Letters of Charles and Mary Lamb* (1978) vol. 3

2 This very night I am going to leave off tobacco! Surely there must be some other world in which this unconquerable purpose shall be realized.
letter to Thomas Manning, 26 December 1815, in E. W. Marrs (ed.) *Letters of Charles and Mary Lamb* (1978) vol. 3

3 An Archangel a little damaged.
of **Coleridge**
letter to Wordsworth, 26 April 1816, in E. W. Marrs (ed.) *Letters of Charles and Mary Lamb* (1978) vol. 3

4 Fanny Kelly's divine plain face.
letter to Mary Wordsworth, 18 February 1818, in Henry H. Harper (ed.) *Letters of Charles Lamb* (1905) vol. 4

5 The ever-haunting importunity
Of business?
letter to Bernard Barton, 11 September 1822, in Henry H. Harper (ed.) *Letters of Charles Lamb* (1905) vol. 4

6 When my sonnet was rejected, I exclaimed, 'Damn the age; I will write for Antiquity!'
letter to B. W. Proctor, 22 January 1829, in *Works* (1912) vol. 6

7 The greatest pleasure I know, is to do a good action by stealth, and to have it found out by accident.
'Table Talk by the late Elia' in *The Athenaeum* 4 January 1834

8 I toiled after it, sir, as some men toil after virtue.
on being asked 'how he had acquired his power of smoking at such a rate'
Thomas Noon Talfourd *Memoirs of Charles Lamb* (1892)

Constant Lambert 1905–51
English composer

9 The whole trouble with a folk song is that once you have played it through there is nothing much you can do except play it over again and play it rather louder.
Music Ho! (1934) ch. 3

10 The average English critic is a don *manqué*, hopelessly parochial when not exaggeratedly teutonophile, over whose desk must surely hang the motto (presumably in Gothic lettering) 'Above all no enthusiasm'.
in *Opera* December 1950; cf. **Talleyrand** 753:5

John Lambert 1619–83
English soldier and Parliamentary supporter

11 The quarrel is now between light and darkness, not who shall rule, but whether we shall live or be preserved or no. Good words will not do with the cavaliers.
speech in the Parliament of 1656 supporting the rule of the major-generals
in *Dictionary of National Biography* (1917–)

John George Lambton see **Lord Durham**

George Lamming b. 1927
Barbados-born novelist and poet

12 In the castle of my skin.
title of novel (1953)

Norman Lamont 1942–
British Conservative politician
see also **Misquotations** *521:13*

13 Rising unemployment and the recession have been the price that we've had to pay to get inflation down. [Labour shouts] That is a price well worth paying.
speech in the House of Commons, 16 May 1991

14 We give the impression of being in office but not in power.
as a backbencher
speech in the House of Commons, 9 June 1993

Giuseppe di Lampedusa 1896–1957
Italian writer

15 If we want things to stay as they are, things will have to change.
The Leopard (1957)

16 Love. Of course, love. Flames for a year, ashes for thirty.
The Leopard (1957)

Osbert Lancaster 1908–86
English writer and cartoonist

17 Fan-vaulting . . . from an aesthetic standpoint frequently belongs to the 'Last-supper-carved-on-a-peach-stone' class of masterpiece.
Pillar to Post (1938) 'Perpendicular'

18 All over the country the latest and most scientific methods of mass-production are being utilized to turn out a stream of old oak beams, leaded window-panes and small discs of bottle-glass, all structural devices which our ancestors lost no time in abandoning as soon as an increase in wealth and knowledge enabled them to do so.
Pillar to Post (1938) 'Stockbroker's Tudor'

Letitia Elizabeth Landon (L. E. L.) 1802–38
English writer

19 Few, save the poor, feel for the poor.
'The Poor'

Walter Savage Landor 1775–1864

English poet

1 I strove with none; for none was worth my strife;
Nature I loved, and, next to Nature, Art.
'Dying Speech of an Old Philosopher' (1853)

2 Ireland never was contented . . .
Say you so? You are demented.
Ireland was contented when
All could use the sword and pen,
And when Tara rose so high
That her turrets split the sky.
'Ireland never was contented' (1853)

3 Ah, what avails the sceptred race!
Ah, what the form divine!
'Rose Aylmer' (1806)

4 George the First was always reckoned
Vile, but viler George the Second;
And what mortal ever heard
Any good of George the Third?
When from earth the Fourth descended
God be praised the Georges ended!
epigram in *The Atlas*, 28 April 1855; earlier versions are discussed in *Notes and Queries* 3 May 1902

5 There are no fields of amaranth on this side of the grave.
Imaginary Conversations 'Aesop and Rhodope' in *Works of Walter Savage Landor* (1846) vol. 2

6 Authors are like cattle going to a fair: those of the same field can never move on without butting one another.
Imaginary Conversations (1824–9) 'Archdeacon Hare and Walter Landor' in *Works of Walter Savage Landor* (1846) vol. 2

7 States, like men, have their growth, their manhood, their decrepitude, their decay.
Imaginary Conversations 'Pollio and Calvus' in *Works of Walter Savage Landor* (1876) vol. 2

8 Fleas know not whether they are upon the body of a giant or upon one of ordinary size.
Imaginary Conversations (1824) 'Southey and Porson'

Andrew Lang 1844–1912

Scottish man of letters

9 St Andrews by the Northern sea,
A haunted town it is to me!
'Almae Matres' (1884)

10 If the wild bowler thinks he bowls,
Or if the batsman thinks he's bowled,
They know not, poor misguided souls,
They too shall perish unconsoled.
I am the batsman and the bat,
I am the bowler and the ball,
The umpire, the pavilion cat,
The roller, pitch, and stumps, and all.
'Brahma'; cf. **Emerson** 299:5

11 They hear like ocean on a western beach
The surge and thunder of the Odyssey.
'The Odyssey' (1881)

12 He uses statistics as a drunken man uses lamp posts—for support rather than illumination.
Alan L. Mackay *Harvest of a Quiet Eye* (1977); attributed

Fritz Lang 1890–1976

Austrian-born film director

13 Don't forget the Western is not only the history of this country, it is what the Saga of the Nibelungen is for the European.
Peter Bogdanovich *Fritz Lang in America* (1967)

Susanne Langer 1895–1985

American philosopher

14 Art is the objectification of feeling, and the subjectification of nature.
Mind (1967) vol. 1

William Langland *c.*1330–*c.*1400

English poet

15 In a somer seson, whan softe was the sonne.
The Vision of Piers Plowman B text (ed. A. V. C. Schmidt, 1987) prologue l. 1

16 Ac on a May morwenynge on Malverne hilles
Me bifel a ferly, of Fairye me thoghte.
The Vision of Piers Plowman B text (ed. A. V. C. Schmidt, 1987) prologue l. 5

Ac on a May mornyng on Maluerne hulles
Me biful for to slepe, for werynesse of-walked.
The Vision of Piers Plowman C text (ed. D. Pearsall, 1978) prologue l. 6)

17 A faire feeld ful of folk fond I ther bitwene—
Of alle manere of men, the meene and the riche,
Werchynge and wandrynge as the world asketh.
The Vision of Piers Plowman B text (ed. A. V. C. Schmidt, 1987) prologue l. 17

18 Brewesteres and baksteres, bochiers and cokes—
For thise are men on this molde that moost harm wercheth
To the povere peple.
The Vision of Piers Plowman B text (ed. A. V. C. Schmidt, 1987) Passus 3, l. 79

As bakeres and breweres, bocheres and cokes;
For thyse men don most harm to the mene peple.
The Vision of Piers Plowman C text (ed. D. Pearsall, 1978) Passus 3, l. 80)

19 Suffraunce is a soverayn vertue, and a swift vengeaunce.
Who suffreth moore than God?
The Vision of Piers Plowman B text (ed. A. V. C. Schmidt, 1987) Passus 11, l. 378

20 Grammer, the ground of al.
The Vision of Piers Plowman B text (ed. A. V. C. Schmidt, 1987) Passus 15, l. 370

21 Innocence is next God, and nyght and day it crieth
'Vengeaunce! Vengeaunce! Forgyve be it nevere
That shente us and shedde oure blood!'
The Vision of Piers Plowman B text (ed. A. V. C. Schmidt, 1987) Passus 17, l. 289

22 'After sharpest shoures,' quath Pees 'most shene is the sonne;
Is no weder warmer than after watry cloudes.'
Pees = *Peace*
The Vision of Piers Plowman B text (ed. A. V. C. Schmidt, 1987) Passus 18, l. 411

Stephen Langton d. 1228
Archbishop of Canterbury

1 *Veni, Sancte Spiritus,*
Et emitte coelitus
Lucis tuae radium.

Come, Holy Spirit, and send out from heaven the beam of your light.

The 'Golden Sequence' for Whit Sunday (also attributed to several others, notably Pope Innocent III)

2 *Lava quod est sordidum,*
Riga quod est aridum,
Sana quod est saucium.
Flecte quod est rigidum,
Fove quod est frigidum,
Rege quod est devium.

Wash what is dirty, water what is dry, heal what is wounded. Bend what is stiff, warm what is cold, guide what goes off the road.

The 'Golden Sequence' for Whit Sunday

Emilia Lanier 1569–1645
Anglo-Italian poet

3 And since all arts at first from Nature came,
That goodly creature, mother of perfection,
Whom Jove's almighty hand at first did frame,
Taking both her and hers in his protection:
Why should not she now grace my barren muse,
And in a woman all defects excuse.

'The Dedications' (1611)

4 The walks put on their summer liveries,
And all things else did hold like similes:
The trees with leaves, with fruits, with flowers clad,
Embrac'd each other, seeming to be glad.

'The Description of Cookham' (1611)

Lao Tzu *c.*604–*c.*531 BC
Chinese philosopher; founder of Taoism
textual translations are those of Wing-Tsit Chan, 1963

5 The Tao [Way] that can be told of is not the eternal Tao;
The name that can be named is not the eternal name.
The Nameless is the origin of Heaven and Earth;
The Named is the mother of all things.

Tao-te Ching ch. 1

6 Front and back follow each other.
Therefore the sage manages affairs without action
And spreads doctrines without words.

Tao-te Ching ch. 2

7 Heaven and earth are not humane
They regard all things as straw dogs.
The sage is not humane.
He regards all people as straw dogs.

Tao-te Ching ch. 5

8 Thirty spokes are united around the hub to make a wheel,
But it is on its non-being that the utility of the carriage depends.
Clay is moulded to form a utensil,
But it is on its non-being that the utility of the utensil depends.
Doors and windows are cut out to make a room,
But it is on its non-being that the utility of the room depends.
Therefore turn being into advantage, and non-being into utility.

non-being *sometimes translated* hole

Tao-te-Ching ch. 11

9 The best [rulers] are those whose existence is [merely] known by the people.
The next best are those who are loved and praised.
The next are those who are feared.
And the next are those who are reviled . . .
[The great rulers] accomplish their task; they complete their work.
Nevertheless their people say that they simply follow Nature.

Tao-te Ching ch. 17

10 Let people hold on to these:
Manifest plainness,
Embrace simplicity,
Reduce selfishness,
Have few desires.

Tao-te Ching ch. 19

11 The thing that is called Tao is eluding and vague.
Vague and eluding, there is in it the form.
Eluding and vague, in it are things.
Deep and obscure, in it is the essence.
The essence is very real; in it are evidences.

Tao-te Ching ch. 21

12 I call it Tao.
If forced to give it a name, I shall call it Great.
Now being great means functioning everywhere.
Functioning everywhere means far-reaching.
Being far-reaching means returning to the original point.
Therefore Tao is great.

Tao-te Ching ch. 25

13 The man of superior virtue is not [conscious of] his virtue,
And in this way he really possesses virtue.
The man of inferior virtue never loses [sight of] his virtue,
And in this way he loses his virtue.

Tao-te Ching ch. 38

14 Reversion is the action of the Tao.
Weakness is the function of the Tao.
All things in the world come from being.
And being comes from non-being.

Tao-te Ching ch. 40

15 Tao produced the One.
The One produced the two.
The two produced the three.
And the three produced the ten thousand things.
The ten thousand things carry the yin and embrace the yang,
and through the blending of the material force they achieve harmony.

Tao-te Ching ch. 42

1 One may know the world without going out of doors.
One may see the Way of Heaven without looking through windows.
The further one goes, the less one knows.
Tao-te Ching ch. 47

2 The pursuit of learning is to increase day after day.
The pursuit of Tao is to decrease day after day.
It is to decrease and further decrease until one reaches the point of taking no action.
No action is undertaken, and yet nothing is left undone.
Tao-te Ching ch. 48

3 He who knows does not speak.
He who speaks does not know.
Tao-te Ching ch. 56

4 The female always overcomes the male by tranquillity,
And by tranquillity she is underneath.
Tao-te Ching ch. 61

5 A tower of nine storeys begins with a heap of earth.
The journey of a thousand *li* starts from where one stands.
Tao-te Ching ch. 64

6 Heaven's net is indeed vast.
Though its meshes are wide, it misses nothing.
Tao-te Ching ch. 73

7 There is nothing softer and weaker than water,
And yet there is nothing better for attacking hard and strong things.
For this reason there is no substitute for it.
All the world knows that the weak overcomes the strong and the soft overcomes the hard.
But none can practice it.
Tao-te Ching ch. 78

8 The sage does not accumulate for himself.
The more he uses for others, the more he has himself.
The more he gives to others, the more he possesses of his own.
The Way of Heaven is to benefit others and not to injure.
The Way of the sage is to act but not to compete.
Tao-te Ching ch. 81

Dionysius Lardner 1793–1859

Irish scientific writer

9 Men might as well project a voyage to the moon as attempt to employ steam navigation against the stormy North Atlantic Ocean.
speech to the British Association for the Advancement of Science, 1838

Ring Lardner 1885–1933

American writer

10 Are you lost daddy I arsked tenderly.
Shut up he explained.
The Young Immigrunts (1920) ch. 10

James Larkin 1867–1947

Irish labour leader

11 Hell has no terror for me. I have lived there. Thirty six years of hunger and poverty have been my portion. They cannot terrify me with hell. Better to be in hell with Dante and Davitt than to be in heaven with Carson and Murphy.
in 1913, during the 'Dublin lockout' labour dispute
Ulick O'Connor *The Troubles* (rev. ed., 1996)

Philip Larkin 1922–1985

English poet

12 Sexual intercourse began
In nineteen sixty-three
(Which was rather late for me) —
Between the end of the *Chatterley* ban
And the Beatles' first LP.
'Annus Mirabilis' (1974)

13 Time has transfigured them into
Untruth. The stone fidelity
They hardly meant has come to be
Their final blazon, and to prove
Our almost-instinct almost true:
What will survive of us is love.
'An Arundel Tomb' (1964)

14 What are days for?
Days are where we live.
'Days' (1964)

15 Life is first boredom, then fear.
Whether or not we use it, it goes,
And leaves what something hidden from us chose,
And age, and then the only end of age.
'Dockery & Son' (1964)

16 And that will be England gone,
The shadows, the meadows, the lanes,
The guildhalls, the carved choirs.
There'll be books; it will linger on
In galleries; but all that remains
For us will be concrete and tyres.
'Going, Going' (1974)

17 Rather than words comes the thought of high windows:
The sun-comprehending glass,
And beyond it, the deep blue air, that shows
Nothing, and is nowhere, and is endless.
'High Windows' (1974)

18 Nothing, like something, happens anywhere.
'I Remember, I Remember' (1955)

19 Never such innocence,
Never before or since,
As changed itself to past
Without a word—the men
Leaving the gardens tidy,
The thousands of marriages
Lasting a little while longer:
Never such innocence again.
'MCMXIV' (1964)

1 Weeds are not supposed to grow,
But by degrees
Some achieve a flower, although
No one sees.
'Modesties' (1951)

2 I listen to money singing. It's like looking down
From long french windows at a provincial town,
The slums, the canal, the churches ornate and mad
In the evening sun. It is intensely sad.
'Money' (1974)

3 Perhaps being old is having lighted rooms
Inside your head, and people in them, acting.
People you know, yet can't quite name.
'The Old Fools' (1974)

4 They fuck you up, your mum and dad.
They may not mean to, but they do.
They fill you with the faults they had
And add some extra, just for you.
'This Be The Verse' (1974)

5 Man hands on misery to man.
It deepens like a coastal shelf.
Get out as early as you can,
And don't have any kids yourself.
'This Be The Verse' (1974)

6 Why should I let the toad *work*
Squat on my life?
Can't I use my wit as a pitchfork
And drive the brute off?
'Toads' (1955)

7 Give me your arm, old toad;
Help me down Cemetery Road.
'Toads Revisited' (1964)

8 I thought of London spread out in the sun,
Its postal districts packed like squares of wheat.
'The Whitsun Weddings' (1964)

9 A beginning, a muddle, and an end.
on the 'classic formula' for a novel
in *New Fiction* no. 15, January 1978; cf. **Aristotle** 24:22

10 Deprivation is for me what daffodils were for Wordsworth.
Required Writing (1983); cf. **Wordsworth** 828:27

11 I am afraid the compulsion to write poems left me about seven years ago, since when I have written virtually nothing. Naturally this is a disappointment, but I would sooner write no poems than bad poems.
letter, 11 August 1984; Anthony Thwaite (ed.) *Selected Letters of Philip Larkin* (1992)

Duc de la Rochefoucauld 1613–80

French moralist

12 *Nous avons tous assez de force pour supporter les maux d'autrui.*
We are all strong enough to bear the misfortunes of others.
Maximes (1678) no. 19

13 *Il est plus honteux de se défier de ses amis que d'en être trompé.*
It is more shameful to doubt one's friends than to be duped by them.
Maximes (1678) no. 84

14 *Il y a de bons mariages, mais il n'y en a point de délicieux.*
There are good marriages, but no delightful ones.
Maximes (1678) no. 113

15 *L'hypocrisie est un hommage que le vice rend à la vertu.*
Hypocrisy is a tribute which vice pays to virtue.
Maximes (1678) no. 218

16 *C'est une grande habileté que de savoir cacher son habileté.*
The height of cleverness is to be able to conceal it.
Maximes (1678) no. 245

17 *Il n'y a guère d'homme assez habile pour connaître tout le mal qu'il fait.*
There is scarcely a single man sufficiently aware to know all the evil he does.
Maximes (1678) no. 269

18 *L'absence diminue les médiocres passions, et augmente les grandes, comme le vent éteint les bougies, et allume le feu.*
Absence diminishes commonplace passions and increases great ones, as the wind extinguishes candles and kindles fire.
Maximes (1678) no. 276; cf. **Bussy-Rabutin** 171:6, **Francis de Sales** 323:2

19 *La reconnaissance de la plupart des hommes n'est qu'une secrète envie de recevoir de plus grands bienfaits.*
In most of mankind gratitude is merely a secret hope for greater favours.
Maximes (1678) no. 298; cf. **Walpole** 802:7

20 *L'accent du pays où l'on est né demeure dans l'esprit et dans le coeur comme dans le langage.*
The accent of one's birthplace lingers in the mind and in the heart as it does in one's speech.
Maximes (1678) no. 342

21 *Dans l'adversité de nos meilleurs amis, nous trouvons toujours quelque chose qui ne nous deplaît pas.*
In the misfortune of our best friends, we always find something which is not displeasing to us.
Réflexions ou Maximes Morales (1665) maxim 99

22 *On n'est jamais si malheureux qu'on croit, ni si heureux qu'on espère.*
One is never as unhappy as one thinks, nor as happy as one hopes.
Sentences et Maximes de Morale (Dutch edition, 1664) maxim 128

Duc de la Rochefoucauld-Liancourt 1747–1827

French social reformer

23 LOUIS XVI: *C'est une grande révolte.*
LA ROCHEFOUCAULD-LIANCOURT: *Non, Sire, c'est une grande révolution.*
LOUIS XVI: It is a big revolt.

LA ROCHEFOUCAULD-LIANCOURT: No, Sir, it is a big revolution.
on a report reaching Versailles of the Fall of the Bastille, 1789
F. Dreyfus *La Rochefoucauld-Liancourt* (1903) ch. 2, sect. 3

Harold Laski 1893–1950
British Labour politician
see also ***Crossman*** *246:12*

1 That state of resentful coma that . . . dons dignify by the name of research.
letter to Oliver Wendell Holmes Jr., 10 October 1922

2 It was like watching someone organize her own immortality. Every phrase and gesture was studied. Now and again, when she said something a little out of the ordinary, she wrote it down herself in a notebook.
of Virginia ***Woolf***
letter to Oliver Wendell Holmes Jr., 30 November 1930

□ Last words
see box opposite

Hugh Latimer *c.*1485–1555
English Protestant martyr
see also ***Last words*** *455:4*

3 *Gutta cavat lapidem, non vi sed saepe cadendo.*
The drop of rain maketh a hole in the stone, not by violence, but by oft falling.
The Second Sermon preached before the King's Majesty (19 April 1549); cf. **Ovid** 561:11, **Proverbs** 597:36

William Laud 1573–1645
Archbishop of Canterbury from 1633; executed for treason

4 Lord I am coming as fast as I can, I know I must pass through the shadow of death, before I can come to see thee; But it is but *Umbra Mortis*, a mere shadow of death, a little darkness upon nature; but thou by thy merits and passion, hast broke through the jaws of death; the Lord receive my soul, and have mercy upon me, and bless this kingdom with peace and plenty, and with brotherly love and charity, that there may not be this effusion of Christian blood amongst them, for Jesus Christ his sake, if it be thy will.
at the scaffold, in Peter Heylin *Cyprianus Anglicus* (1668)

Harry Lauder (Hugh MacLennan) 1870–1950
Scottish music-hall entertainer
see also ***Morrison*** *533:3*

5 Keep right on to the end of the road,
Keep right on to the end.
Tho' the way be long, let your heart be strong,
Keep right on round the bend.
'The End of the Road' (1924 song)

6 I love a lassie, a bonnie, bonnie lassie,
She's as pure as the lily in the dell.
She's as sweet as the heather, the bonnie bloomin' heather—
Mary, ma Scotch Bluebell.
'I Love a Lassie' (1905 song)

7 Roamin' in the gloamin',
On the bonnie banks o' Clyde.
'Roamin' in the Gloamin'' (1911 song)

Stan Laurel (Arthur Stanley Jefferson) 1890–1965
American film comedian, born in Britain

8 Another nice mess you've gotten me into.
often 'another fine mess'
Another Fine Mess (1930 film) and many other Laurel and Hardy films; spoken by Oliver Hardy

William L. Laurence 1888–1977
American journalist

9 At first it was a giant column that soon took the shape of a supramundane mushroom.
on the first atomic explosion in New Mexico, 16 July 1945
in *New York Times* 26 September 1945

Wilfrid Laurier 1841–1919
Canadian politician

10 The nineteenth century was the century of the United States. I think we can claim that it is Canada that shall fill the twentieth century.
speech in Ottawa, 18 January 1904; cf. **Trudeau** 783:22

Johann Kaspar Lavater 1741–1801
Swiss theologian

11 Trust not him with your secrets, who, when left alone in the room, turns over your papers.
Aphorisms on Man (*c.*1788)

12 The public seldom forgive twice.
Aphorisms on Man (*c.*1788)

Emily Lawless 1845–1913
Irish poet

13 She said, 'God knows they owe me nought,
I tossed them to the foaming sea,
I tossed them to the howling wastes,
Yet still their love comes home to me.'
'After Aughrim'

14 There's famine in the land, its grip is tightening still!
There's trouble, black and bitter, on every side I glance.
'An Exile's Mother'

D. H. Lawrence 1885–1930
English novelist and poet
on Lawrence: see ***Gibbons*** *336:8,* ***Griffith-Jones*** *353:10,* ***Robinson*** *629:20*

15 To the Puritan all things are impure, as somebody says.
Etruscan Places (1932) 'Cerveteri'; cf. **Bible** 109:24

continued

Last words

1 *Adieu, mes amis. Je vais à la gloire.*

Farewell, my friends. I go to glory.

Isadora Duncan (1878–1927), before her scarf caught in a car wheel, breaking her neck

Mary Desti *Isadora Duncan's End* (1929) ch. 25

2 All my possessions for a moment of time.

Queen ***Elizabeth I*** *(1533–1603)*

attributed, but almost certainly apocryphal

3 All this buttoning and unbuttoning.

18th-century suicide note

4 Be of good comfort Master Ridley, and play the man. We shall this day light such a candle by God's grace in England, as (I trust) shall never be put out.

Hugh ***Latimer*** *(c.1485–1555), prior to being burned for heresy, 16 October 1555*

John Foxe *Actes and Monuments* (1570 ed.); cf. **Bible** 91:4

5 Bugger Bognor.

King ***George V*** *(1865–1936) on his deathbed in 1936, when someone remarked 'Cheer up, your Majesty, you will soon be at Bognor again.'; alternatively, a comment made in 1929, when it was proposed that the town be named Bognor Regis on account of the king's convalescence there after a serious illness*

probably apocryphal; Kenneth Rose *King George V* (1983) ch. 9; cf. **Last words** 455:18

6 Come closer, boys. It will be easier for you.

Erskine ***Childers*** *(1870–1922) to the firing squad at his execution*

Burke Wilkinson *The Zeal of the Convert* (1976) ch. 26

7 Crito, we owe a cock to Aesculapius; please pay it and don't forget it.

Socrates (469–399 BC)

Plato *Phaedo* 118

8 Die, my dear Doctor, that's the last thing I shall do!

Lord ***Palmerston*** *(1784–1865)*

E. Latham *Famous Sayings and their Authors* (1904)

9 *Dieu me pardonnera, c'est son métier.*

God will pardon me, it is His trade.

Heinrich ***Heine*** *(1797–1856), on his deathbed*

Alfred Meissner *Heinrich Heine. Erinnerungen* (1856) ch. 5; cf. **Catherine** 194:12

10 *Dilexi iustitiam et odi iniquitatem, propterea morior in exilio.*

I have loved justice and hated iniquity: therefore I die in exile.

Pope Gregory VII (c.1020–85) at Salerno, following his conflict with the Emperor Henry IV

J. W. Bowden *The Life and Pontificate of Gregory VII* (1840) vol. 2, bk. 3, ch. 20

11 Don't let the awkward squad fire over me.

said by Robert ***Burns*** *(1759–96) shortly before his death*

A. Cunningham *The Works of Robert Burns; with his Life* vol. 1 (1834)

12 An emperor ought to die standing.

Vespasian (AD 9–79)

Suetonius *Lives of the Caesars* 'Vespasian' sect. 24

13 For God's sake look after our people.

Robert Falcon ***Scott*** *(1868–1912)*

last diary entry, 29 March 1912, in *Scott's Last Expedition* (1913) vol. 1, ch. 20

14 For my name and memory, I leave it to men's charitable speeches, and to foreign nations, and the next ages.

will of Francis ***Bacon*** *(1561–1626), 19 December 1625*

J. Spedding (ed.) *The Letters and Life of Francis Bacon* vol. 7 (1874)

15 Give Dayrolles a chair.

Lord ***Chesterfield*** *(1694–1773) to his godson Dayrolles*

W. H. Craig *Life of Lord Chesterfield* (1907)

16 God save Ireland!

called out from the dock by the Manchester Martyrs, William Allen (d. 1867), Michael Larkin (d. 1867), and William O'Brien (d. 1867)

Robert Kee *The Bold Fenian Men* (1989); cf. **Sullivan** 746:1

17 Greetings, we win!

dying words of Pheidippides (or Philippides) (d. 490 BC), having run back to Athens from Marathon with news of victory over the Persians

Lucian bk. 3, ch. 64 'Pro Lapsu inter salutandum' para. 3

18 How's the Empire?

said by King ***George V*** *(1865–1936) to his private secretary on the morning of his death*

letter from Lord Wigram, 31 January 1936, in J. E. Wrench *Geoffrey Dawson and Our Times* (1955) ch. 28; cf. **Last words** 455:5

19 I am about to take my last voyage, a great leap in the dark.

Thomas ***Hobbes*** *(1588–1679)*

attributed (cf. **Vanbrugh** 789:7), but with no authoritative source; a contemporary version is:

On his death bed he should say that he was 91 years finding out a hole to go out of this world, and at length found it.

Anthony Wood diary, 10 December 1679, in Andrew Clark (ed.) *The Life and Times of Anthony Wood* vol. 2 (1892)

20 *Je vais quérir un grand peut-être . . . Tirez le rideau, la farce est jouée.*

I am going to seek a great perhaps . . . Bring down the curtain, the farce is played out.

François ***Rabelais*** *(c.1494–c.1553)*

attributed, but probably apocryphal; Jean Fleury *Rabelais et ses oeuvres* (1877) vol. 1, ch. 3, pt. 15

Last words *continued*

1 I am just going outside and may be some time.
Captain Lawrence Oates (1880–1912)
Robert Falcon **Scott** diary entry, 16–17 March 1912 in *Scott's Last Expedition* (1913) ch. 20; cf. **Epitaphs** 302:12, **Mahon** 490:18

2 I die happy.
Charles James **Fox** *(1749–1806)*
Lord John Russell *Life and Times of C. J. Fox* vol. 3 (1860) ch. 69

3 I find, then, I am but a bad anatomist.
Wolfe Tone (1763–98), who in trying to cut his throat in prison severed his windpipe instead of his jugular, and lingered for several days
Oliver Knox *Rebels and Informers* (1998)

4 If this is dying, then I don't think much of it.
Lytton **Strachey** *(1880–1932), on his deathbed*
Michael Holroyd *Lytton Strachey* vol. 2 (1968) pt. 2, ch. 6

5 I have a long journey to take, and must bid the company farewell.
Walter **Ralegh** *(c.1552–1618)*
E. Thompson *Sir Walter Raleigh* (1935) ch. 26

6 I'm tired, and I have to go to sleep.
Allen **Ginsberg** *(1912–97), before lapsing into a final coma*
in *Athens News* 9 April 1997

7 In this life there's nothing new in dying,
But nor, of course, is living any newer.
Sergei **Yesenin** *(1895–1925); his final poem, written in his own blood the day before he hanged himself in his Leningrad hotel room, 28 December 1925*
'Goodbye, my Friend, Goodbye' (translated by Gordon McVay)

8 I only regret that I have but one life to lose for my country.
Nathan Hale (1755–76), prior to his execution by the British for spying, 22 September 1776
Henry Phelps Johnston *Nathan Hale, 1776* (1914) ch. 7; cf. **Addison** 4:14 21

9 It's been so long since I've had champagne.
Anton **Chekhov** *(1860–1904), after which, he slowly drank the glass and died*
Henri Troyat *Chekhov* (1984)

10 I will die like a true-blue rebel. Don't waste any time in mourning—organize.
Joe **Hill** *(1879–1915) before his death by firing squad*
farewell telegram to Bill Haywood, 18 November 1915, in *Salt Lake* (Utah) *Tribune* 19 November 1915

11 Let not poor Nelly starve.
Charles II *(1630–85), referring to Nell* **Gwyn**, *his mistress*
Bishop Gilbert Burnet *History of My Own Time* (1724) vol. 1, bk. 3

12 Lord, open the King of England's eyes!
William **Tyndale** *(c.1494–1536), at the stake*
John Foxe *Actes and Monuments* (1570)

13 The love boat has crashed against the everyday. You and I, we are quits, and there is no point in listing mutual pains, sorrows, and hurts.
from an unfinished poem found among ***Mayakovsky****'s papers, a variant of which he quoted in his suicide letter*
Vladimir Mayakovsky (1893–1930) letter 12 April 1930

14 Love? What is it? Most natural painkiller. What there is . . . LOVE.
final entry in the journal of William S. **Burroughs**, *1 August 1997, the day before he died*
in *New Yorker* 18 August 1997

15 *Mehr Licht!*
More light!
Johann Wolfgang von **Goethe** *(1749–1832); abbreviated version of* 'Macht doch den zweiten Fensterladen auch auf, damit mehr Licht hereinkomme [Open the second shutter, so that more light can come in]')
K. W. Müller *Goethes letze literarische Thätigkeit* (1832)

16 My design is to make what haste I can to be gone.
Oliver **Cromwell** *(1599–1658)*
John Morley *Oliver Cromwell* (1900) bk. 5, ch. 10

17 Now God be praised, I will die in peace.
James **Wolfe** *(1727–59)*
J. Knox *Historical Journal of the Campaigns in North America* (ed. A. G. Doughty, 1914) vol. 2

18 Now I'll have eine kleine Pause.
last words of Kathleen Ferrier (1912–53)
Gerald Moore *Am I Too Loud?* (1962)

19 *Ô liberté! Ô liberté! que de crimes on commet en ton nom!*
O liberty! O liberty! what crimes are committed in thy name!
Mme **Roland** *(1754–93), before being guillotined*
A. de Lamartine *Histoire des Girondins* (1847) bk. 51, ch. 8; cf. **George** 334:10

20 Oh, my country! how I leave my country!
William **Pitt** *(1759–1806); also variously reported as* 'How I love my country'; *and* 'My country! oh, my country!'
Earl Stanhope *Life of the Rt. Hon. William Pitt* vol. 3 (1879) ch. 43; Earl Stanhope *Life of the Rt. Hon. William Pitt* (1st ed.), vol. 4 (1862) ch. 43; and G. Rose *Diaries and Correspondence* (1860) vol. 2, 23 January 1806; oral tradition reports:

I think I could eat one of Bellamy's veal pies.
attributed

21 One of us must go.
Oscar **Wilde** *(1854–1900), of the wallpaper in the room where he was dying*
attributed, probably apocryphal

Last words *continued*

1 On the contrary.
Henrik Ibsen (1828–1926), after a nurse had said that he 'seemed to be a little better'
Michael Meyer *Ibsen* (1967)

2 *Qualis artifex pereo!*
What an artist dies with me!
Nero (AD *37–68*)
Suetonius *Lives of the Caesars* 'Nero' sect. 49

3 See in what peace a Christian can die.
Joseph **Addison** *(1672–1719), dying words to his stepson Lord Warwick*
Edward Young *Conjectures on Original Composition* (1759)

4 So little done, so much to do.
Cecil **Rhodes** *(1853–1902), on the day of his death*
Lewis Michell *Life of Rhodes* (1910) vol. 2, ch. 39; cf. **Tennyson** 761:17

5 Strike the tent.
Robert E. **Lee** *(1807–70), 12 October 1870*
attributed

6 Tell them I've had a wonderful life.
Ludwig **Wittgenstein** *(1889–1951) to his doctor's wife, before losing consciousness, 28 April 1951*
Ray Monk *Ludwig Wittgenstein* (1990)

7 Tell them to stand up for Jesus.
American evangelist, Dudley Atkins Tyng (d. 1858), to George **Duffield***, inspiring him to write the hymn; cf.* **Duffield** *284:8*
Ian Bradley (ed.) *The Penguin Book of Hymns* (1989)

8 Thank God, I have done my duty.
Horatio, Lord **Nelson** *(1758–1805) at the battle of Trafalgar, 21 October 1805*
Robert Southey *Life of Nelson* (1813) ch. 9

9 They couldn't hit an elephant at this distance.
John Sedgwick (d. 1864), Union general, immediately prior to being killed by enemy fire at the battle of Spotsylvania in the American Civil War
Robert Denney *The Civil War Years* (1992)

10 This hath not offended the king.
Thomas **More** *(1478–1535), lifting his beard aside after laying his head on the block*
Francis Bacon *Apophthegms New and Old* (1625) no. 22

11 This, this is the end of earth. I am content.
John Quincy **Adams** *(1767–1848) on collapsing in the Senate, 21 February 1848 (he died two days later)*
William H. Seward *Eulogy of John Quincy Adams to Legislature of New York* 1848

12 Thomas—Jefferson—still surv—
Jefferson *died on the same day*
John **Adams** (1735–1826), on 4 July 1826

13 Turn up the lights; I don't want to go home in the dark.
O. **Henry** *(1862–1910), quoting a song*
Charles Alphonso Smith *O. Henry Biography* (1916) ch. 9

I'm afraid to come home in the dark.
Harry Williams (1874–1924) title of song (1907)

14 *Vicisti, Galilaee.*
You have won, Galilean.
supposed dying words of the Roman emperor Julian the Apostate (AD *c.332–363*)
a late embellishment of Theodoret *Ecclesiastical History* (AD c.450) bk. 3, ch. 25; cf. **Swinburne** 751:5

15 We are all going to Heaven, and Vandyke is of the company.
Thomas **Gainsborough** *(1727–88)*
attributed, in William B. Boulton *Thomas Gainsborough* (1905) ch. 9

16 Well, I've had a happy life.
William **Hazlitt** *(1778–1830)*
W. C. Hazlitt *Memoirs of William Hazlitt* (1867)

17 'What *is* the answer?' No answer came. She laughed and said, 'In that case what is the question?'
Gertrude **Stein** *(1874–1946)*
Donald Sutherland *Gertrude Stein, A Biography of her Work* (1951)

18 Why fear death? It is the most beautiful adventure in life.
Charles Frohman (1860–1915), before drowning in the Lusitania*, 7 May 1915*
I. F. Marcosson and D. Frohman *Charles Frohman* (1916) ch. 19; cf. **Barrie** 55:16

19 Why not? Why not? Why not? Yeah.
Timothy **Leary** *(1920–96)*
in *Independent* 1 June 1996

20 Would to God this wound had been for Ireland.
Patrick Sarsfield (c.1655–93) on being mortally wounded at the battle of Landen, 19 August 1693, while fighting for France
attributed

D. H. Lawrence *continued*

21 It was in 1915 the old world ended.
Kangaroo (1923)

22 John Thomas says good-night to Lady Jane, a little droopingly, but with a hopeful heart.
Lady Chatterley's Lover (1928) ch. 19

23 The English . . . are paralysed by fear. That is what thwarts and distorts the Anglo-Saxon existence . . . Nothing could be more lovely and fearless than Chaucer. But already Shakespeare is morbid with fear, fear of consequences. That is the strange phenomenon of the English Renaissance: this mystic terror of the consequences, the consequences of action.
Phoenix (1936) 'An Introduction to these Paintings'

1 If you try to nail anything down in the novel, either it kills the novel, or the novel gets up and walks away with the nail.
Phoenix (1936) 'Morality and the Novel'

2 Morality in the novel is the trembling instability of the balance. When the novelist puts his thumb in the scale, to pull down the balance to his own predilection, that is immorality.
Phoenix (1936) 'Morality and the Novel'

3 Pornography is the attempt to insult sex, to do dirt on it.
Phoenix (1936) 'Pornography and Obscenity' ch. 3

4 Never trust the artist. Trust the tale. The proper function of a critic is to save the tale from the artist who created it.
Studies in Classic American Literature (1923) ch. 1

5 Be a good animal, true to your instincts.
The White Peacock (1911) pt. 2, ch. 2

6 Don't you find it a beautiful clean thought, a world empty of people, just uninterrupted grass, and a hare sitting up?
Women in Love (1920) ch. 11

7 Is it the secret of the long-nosed Etruscans?
The long-nosed, sensitive-footed, subtly-smiling Etruscans
Who made so little noise outside the cypress groves?
'Cypresses' (1923)

8 How beastly the bourgeois is
Especially the male of the species.
'How Beastly the Bourgeois Is' (1929)

9 While we have sex in the mind, we truly have none in the body.
'Leave Sex Alone' (1929)

10 Men! The only animal in the world to fear!
'Mountain Lion' (1923)

11 I never saw a wild thing
Sorry for itself.
'Self-Pity' (1929)

12 Now it is autumn and the falling fruit
And the long journey towards oblivion . . .
Have you built your ship of death, O have you?
O build your ship of death, for you will need it.
'Ship of Death' (1932)

13 A snake came to my water-trough
On a hot, hot day, and I in pyjamas for the heat,
To drink there.
'Snake' (1923)

14 And so, I missed my chance with one of the lords
Of life.
And I have something to expiate:
A pettiness.
'Snake' (1923)

15 Not I, not I, but the wind that blows through me!
'Song of a Man who has Come Through' (1917)

16 When I read Shakespeare I am struck with wonder
That such trivial people should muse and thunder
In such lovely language.
'When I Read Shakespeare' (1929)

17 Curse the blasted, jelly-boned swines, the slimy, the belly-wriggling invertebrates, the miserable sodding rotters, the flaming sods, the snivelling, dribbling, dithering, palsied, pulse-less lot that make up England today. They've got white of egg in their veins, and their spunk is that watery it's a marvel they can breed. They *can* nothing but frog-spawn—the gibberers! God, how I hate them!
letter to Edward Garnett, 3 July 1912, in H. T. Moore (ed.) *Collected Letters of D. H. Lawrence* (1962) vol. 1

18 Tragedy ought really to be a great kick at misery.
letter to A. W. McLeod, 6 October 1912, in H. T. Moore (ed.) *Collected Letters of D. H. Lawrence* (1962) vol. 1

19 I like to write when I feel spiteful; it's like having a good sneeze.
letter to Lady Cynthia Asquith, *c.*25 November 1913, in H. T. Moore (ed.) *Collected Letters of D. H. Lawrence* (1962) vol. 1

20 Australia has a marvellous sky and air and blue clarity, and a hoary sort of land beneath it, like a Sleeping Princess on whom the dust of ages has settled.
letter to Jan Juta, 20 May 1922; *Letters and Works* (1987) vol. 4

21 The dead don't die. They look on and help.
letter to J. Middleton Murry, 2 February 1923, in H. T. Moore (ed.) *Collected Letters of D. H. Lawrence* (1962) vol. 2

22 I want to go south, where there is no autumn, where the cold doesn't crouch over one like a snow-leopard waiting to pounce. The heart of the North is dead, and the fingers of cold are corpse fingers.
letter to J. Middleton Murry, 3 October 1924, in H. T. Moore (ed.) *Collected Letters of D. H. Lawrence* (1962) vol. 2

23 My God, what a clumsy *olla putrida* James Joyce is! Nothing but old fags and cabbage-stumps of quotations from the Bible and the rest, stewed in the juice of deliberate, journalistic dirty-mindedness.
letter to Aldous and Maria Huxley, 15 August 1928, in H. T. Moore (ed.) *Collected Letters of D. H. Lawrence* (1962) vol. 2

T. E. Lawrence 1888–1935

English soldier and writer
see also ***Borrowed titles*** 144:15

24 Many men would take the death-sentence without a whimper to escape the life-sentence which fate carries in her other hand.
The Mint (1955) pt. 1, ch. 4

25 The trumpets came out brazenly with the last post . . . A man hates to be moved to folly by a noise.
The Mint (1955) pt. 3, ch. 9

26 I loved you, so I drew these tides of men into my hands and wrote my will across the sky in stars
To earn you freedom, the seven pillared worthy house, that your eyes might be shining for me
When we came.
The Seven Pillars of Wisdom (1926) dedication

1 Surely the sex business isn't worth all this damned fuss? I've met only a handful of people who cared a biscuit for it.
on reading Lady Chatterley's Lover
Christopher Hassall *Edward Marsh* (1959)

Laws of Manu

a code of Hindu religious law, dating in its present form from the 1st century BC
textual translations are those of W. Doniger with B. K. Smith, 1991

2 The very birth of a priest [brahmin] is the eternal physical form of religion; for he is born for the sake of religion and is fit to become one with ultimate reality.
ch. 1, v. 98

3 The man who gives him [the pupil] the benefit of the revealed canon . . . should be known as his guru.
ch. 1, v. 149

4 Since people in the other three stages of life are supported every day by the knowledge and the food of the householder, therefore the householder stage of life is the best.
ch. 3, v. 78

5 You can never get meat without violence to creatures with the breath of life, and the killing of creatures with the breath of life does not get you to heaven; therefore you should not eat meat.
ch. 5, v. 48

6 A girl, a young woman, or even an old woman should not do anything independently, even in [her own] house.
In childhood a woman should be under her father's control, in youth under her husband's, and when her husband is dead, under her sons'.
ch. 5, v. 147

7 There is no difference at all between the goddesses of good fortune . . . who live in houses and women . . . who are the lamps of their houses, worthy of reverence and greatly blessed because of their progeny.
ch. 9, v. 26

8 'Let there be mutual absence of infidelity until death'; this should be known as the supreme duty of a man and a woman, in a nutshell.
ch. 9, v. 101

9 All of those castes who are excluded from the world of those who were born from the mouth, arms, thighs and feet (of the primordial Man) are traditionally regarded as aliens.
ch. 10, v. 45

10 Manu has said that non-violence, truth, not stealing, purification, and the suppression of the sensory powers is the duty of the four classes, in a nutshell.
ch. 10, v. 63

Nigel Lawson 1932–

British Conservative politician

11 It represented the tip of a singularly ill-concealed iceberg, with all the destructive potential that icebergs possess.
of an article by Alan Walters, Margaret **Thatcher**'s *economic adviser, criticizing the Exchange Rate Mechanism*
in the House of Commons following his resignation as Chancellor, 31 October 1989

Emma Lazarus 1849–87

American poet

12 Give me your tired, your poor,
Your huddled masses yearning to breathe free,
The wretched refuse of your teeming shore,
Send these, the homeless, tempest-tossed, to me:
I lift my lamp beside the golden door.
inscription on the Statue of Liberty, New York
'The New Colossus' (1883)

Edmund Leach 1910–89

English anthropologist

13 Far from being the basis of the good society, the family, with its narrow privacy and tawdry secrets, is the source of all our discontents.
BBC Reith Lectures, 1967, in *Listener* 30 November 1967

Stephen Leacock 1869–1944

Canadian humorist

14 When Rutherford was done with the atom all the solidity was pretty well knocked out of it.
The Boy I Left Behind Me (1947)

15 The parent who could see his boy as he really is, would shake his head and say: 'Willie, is no good; I'll sell him.'
Essays and Literary Studies (1916) 'Lot of a Schoolmaster'

16 Advertising may be described as the science of arresting human intelligence long enough to get money from it.
Garden of Folly (1924) 'The Perfect Salesman'

17 I am what is called a *professor emeritus*—from the Latin *e*, 'out', and *meritus*, 'so he ought to be'.
Here are my Lectures (1938) ch. 14

18 A sportsman is a man who, every now and then, simply has to get out and kill something. Not that he's cruel. He wouldn't hurt a fly. It's not big enough.
My Remarkable Uncle (1942)

19 Lord Ronald said nothing; he flung himself from the room, flung himself upon his horse and rode madly off in all directions.
Nonsense Novels (1911) 'Gertrude the Governess'

20 A decision of the courts decided that the game of golf may be played on Sunday, not being a game within the view of the law, but being a form of moral effort.
Over the Footlights (1923) 'Why I Refuse to Play Golf'

Mary Leapor 1722–46

English poet

1 In spite of all romantic poets sing,
This gold, my dearest, is an useful thing.
'Mira to Octavia'

2 Woman, a pleasing but a short-lived flower,
Too soft for business and too weak for power:
A wife in bondage, or neglected maid:
Despised, if ugly; if she's fair, betrayed.
'An Essay on Woman'

Edward Lear 1812–88

English artist and writer of humorous verse

3 Who, or why, or which, or what,
Is the Akond of Swat?
'The Akond of Swat' (1888)

4 There was an Old Man with a beard,
Who said, 'It is just as I feared!—
Two Owls and a Hen,
Four Larks and a Wren,
Have all built their nests in my beard!'
A Book of Nonsense (1846)

5 On the coast of Coromandel
Where the early pumpkins blow,
In the middle of the woods,
Lived the Yonghy-Bonghy-Bó.
'The Courtship of the Yonghy-Bonghy-Bó' (1871)

6 The Dong with a luminous nose.
title of poem (1871)

7 When awful darkness and silence reign
Over the great Gromboolian plain.
'The Dong with a Luminous Nose' (1871)

8 When storm-clouds brood on the towering heights
Of the Hills of the Chankly Bore.
'The Dong with a Luminous Nose' (1871)

9 Far and few, far and few,
Are the lands where the Jumblies live;
Their heads are green, and their hands are blue,
And they went to sea in a Sieve.
'The Jumblies' (1871)

10 And they bought an Owl, and a useful Cart,
And a pound of Rice, and a Cranberry Tart,
And a hive of silvery Bees.
And they bought a Pig, and some green Jackdaws,
And a lovely Monkey with lollipop paws,
And forty bottles of Ring-Bo-Ree,
And no end of Stilton Cheese.
'The Jumblies' (1871)

11 Nasticreechia Krorluppia.
More Nonsense (1872) 'Nonsense Botany'

12 There was an old man of Thermopylae,
Who never did anything properly.
More Nonsense (1872) 'One Hundred Nonsense Pictures and Rhymes'

13 Till Mrs Discobbolos said
'Oh! W! X! Y! Z!
It has just come into my head—
Suppose we should happen to fall!!!!
Darling Mr Discobbolos?'
'Mr and Mrs Discobbolos' (1871)

14 'How pleasant to know Mr Lear!'
Who has written such volumes of stuff!
Some think him ill-tempered and queer,
But a few think him pleasant enough.
Nonsense Songs (1871) preface

15 Old Foss is the name of his cat:
His body is perfectly spherical,
He weareth a runcible hat.
Nonsense Songs (1871) preface

16 The Owl and the Pussy-Cat went to sea
In a beautiful pea-green boat.
They took some honey, and plenty of money,
Wrapped up in a five-pound note.
The Owl looked up to the Stars above
And sang to a small guitar,
'Oh lovely Pussy! O Pussy, my love,
What a beautiful Pussy you are.'
'The Owl and the Pussy-Cat' (1871)

17 Pussy said to the Owl, 'You elegant fowl!
How charmingly sweet you sing!
O let us be married! too long we have tarried:
But what shall we do for a ring?'
They sailed away for a year and a day,
To the land where the Bong-tree grows,
And there in a wood a Piggy-wig stood
With a ring at the end of his nose.
'The Owl and the Pussy-Cat' (1871)

18 'Dear Pig, are you willing to sell for one shilling
Your ring?' Said the Piggy, 'I will.'
'The Owl and the Pussy-Cat' (1871)

19 They dined on mince, and slices of quince,
Which they ate with a runcible spoon;
And hand in hand, on the edge of the sand,
They danced by the light of the moon.
'The Owl and the Pussy-Cat' (1871)

20 The Pobble who has no toes
Had once as many as we;
When they said, 'Some day you may lose them all';—
He replied,—'Fish fiddle de-dee!'
'The Pobble Who Has No Toes' (1871)

21 He has gone to fish, for his Aunt Jobiska's
Runcible Cat with crimson whiskers!
'The Pobble Who Has No Toes' (1871)

22 'But the longer I live on this Crumpetty Tree
The plainer than ever it seems to me
That very few people come this way
And that life on the whole is far from gay!'
Said the Quangle-Wangle Quee.
'The Quangle-Wangle's Hat' (1871)

Timothy Leary 1920–96

American psychologist

see also ***Epitaphs*** *304:7*, ***Last words*** *457:19*

23 If you take the game of life seriously, if you take your nervous system seriously, if you take your sense organs seriously, if you take the energy process seriously, you must turn on, tune in and drop out.
lecture, June 1966, in *The Politics of Ecstasy* (1968) ch. 21

1 The PC is the LSD of the '90s.
remark made in the early 1990s; in *Guardian* 1 June 1996

2 The key to dying well is for you to decide where, when, how and whom to invite to the last party.
to a visitor, during the last days of his final illness
in *Daily Telegraph* 3 May 1996

Mary Elizabeth Lease 1853–1933
American writer and lecturer

3 Kansas had better stop raising corn and begin raising hell.
E. J. James et al. *Notable American Women 1607–1950* (1971) vol. 2

F. R. Leavis 1895–1978
English literary critic

4 The common pursuit.
title of book (1952)

5 The few really great—the major novelists . . . are significant in terms of the human awareness they promote; awareness of the possibilities of life.
The Great Tradition (1948) ch. 1

6 He energized the Garden-Suburb ethos with a certain original talent and the vigour of a prolonged adolescence . . . rather like Keats's vulgarity with a Public School accent.
of Rupert **Brooke**
New Bearings in English Poetry (1932) ch. 2

7 Self-contempt, well-grounded.
on the foundation of T. S. **Eliot***'s work*
in *Times Literary Supplement* 21 October 1988 (quoted by Christopher Ricks in a BBC radio talk); cf. **Milton** 517:11

Fran Lebowitz 1946–
American writer

8 There is no such thing as inner peace. There is only nervousness or death.
Metropolitan Life (1978)

9 Life is something to do when you can't get to sleep.
Metropolitan Life (1978)

10 The best fame is a writer's fame: it's enough to get a table at a good restaurant, but not enough that you get interrupted when you eat.
in *Observer* 30 May 1993 'Sayings of the Week'

Stanislaw Lec 1909–66
Polish writer

11 Is it progress if a cannibal uses knife and fork?
Unkempt Thoughts (1962)

John le Carré (David John Moore Cornwell) 1931–
English thriller writer

12 The spy who came in from the cold.
title of novel (1963)

Le Corbusier (Charles-Édouard Jeanneret) 1887–1965
French architect

13 *Une maison est une machine-à-habiter.*
A house is a machine for living in.
Vers une architecture (1923); cf. **Tolstoy** 779:13

14 This frightful word [function] was born under other skies than those I have loved—those where the sun reigns supreme.
Stephen Gardiner *Le Corbusier* (1974) introduction

Alexandre Auguste Ledru-Rollin 1807–74
French politician

15 Ah well! I am their leader, I really had to follow them!
E. de Mirecourt *Les Contemporains* vol. 14 (1857) 'Ledru-Rollin'

Francis Ledwidge 1891–1917
Irish poet

16 He shall not hear the bittern cry
In the wild sky where he is lain,
Nor voices of the sweeter birds
Above the wailing of the rain.
'Lament for Thomas MacDonagh'

17 I joined the British Army because she stood between Ireland and an enemy common to our civilization and I would not have her say she defended us while we did nothing but pass resolutions.
Alice Curtayne *Francis Ledwidge* (1972)

18 If someone were to tell me now that the Germans were coming in over our back wall, I wouldn't lift up a finger to stop them. They could come!
Alice Curtayne *Francis Ledwidge* (1972)

Gypsy Rose Lee (Rose Louise Hovick) 1914–70
American striptease artiste

19 God is love, but get it in writing.
attributed

Harper Lee 1926–
American novelist

20 Shoot all the bluejays you want, if you can hit 'em, but remember it's a sin to kill a mockingbird.
To Kill a Mockingbird (1960) ch. 10

Henry Lee ('Light-Horse Harry') 1756–1818
American soldier and politician

21 A citizen, first in war, first in peace, and first in the hearts of his countrymen.
Funeral Oration on the death of General Washington (1800)

Laurie Lee 1914–97
English writer

1 I was set down from the carrier's cart at the age of three; and there with a sense of bewilderment and terror my life in the village began.
Cider with Rosie (1959)

2 Quiet incest flourished where roads were bad.
Guardian 15 May 1997; obituary

Nathaniel Lee *c.*1653–92
English dramatist

3 When the sun sets, shadows, that showed at noon
But small, appear most long and terrible.
Oedipus (with John Dryden, 1679) act 4, sc. 1

4 Then he will talk, Good Gods,
How he will talk.
The Rival Queens (1677) act 3

5 When Greeks joined Greeks, then was the tug of war!
The Rival Queens (1677) act 4, sc. 2

6 Man, false man, smiling, destructive man.
Theodosius (1680) act 3, sc. 2

7 They called me mad, and I called them mad, and damn them, they outvoted me.
R. Porter *A Social History of Madness* (1987), introduction; attributed

Robert E. Lee 1807–70
American Confederate general
see also: ***Last words*** 457:5

8 It is well that war is so terrible. We should grow too fond of it.
after the battle of Fredericksburg, December 1862
attributed

9 I have fought against the people of the North because I believed they were seeking to wrest from the South its dearest rights. But I have never cherished toward them bitter or vindictive feelings, and I have never seen the day when I did not pray for them.
Geoffrey C. Ward *The Civil War* (1991) ch. 5

refusing an offer to write his memoirs:
10 I should be trading on the blood of my men.
attributed, perhaps apocryphal

Lynda Lee-Potter
British journalist

11 Powerful men often succeed through the help of their wives. Powerful women only succeed in spite of their husbands.
in *Daily Mail* 16 May 1984

Richard Le Gallienne 1866–1947
English poet

12 The cry of the Little Peoples goes up to God in vain,
For the world is given over to the cruel sons of Cain.
'The Cry of the Little Peoples' (1899)

Ursula K. Le Guin 1929–
American writer

13 He had grown up in a country run by politicians who sent the pilots to man the bombers to kill the babies to make the world safer for children to grow up in.
The Lathe of Heaven (1971) ch. 6

14 Love doesn't just sit there, like a stone, it has to be made, like bread; remade all the time, made new.
The Lathe of Heaven (1971) ch. 10

15 We like to think we live in daylight, but half the world is always dark; and fantasy, like poetry, speaks the language of the night.
in *World Magazine* 21 November 1979

Ernest Lehman see **Film titles** 313:4

Tom Lehrer 1928–
American humorist

16 Plagiarize! Let no one else's work evade your eyes,
Remember why the good Lord made your eyes.
'Lobachevski' (1953 song)

17 Poisoning pigeons in the park.
song title, 1953

18 It is sobering to consider that when Mozart was my age he had already been dead for a year.
N. Shapiro (ed.) *An Encyclopedia of Quotations about Music* (1978)

19 In my youth there were words you couldn't say in front of a girl; now you can't say 'girl'.
in *Sunday Telegraph* 10 March 1996

Gottfried Wilhelm Leibniz 1646–1716
German philosopher

20 It is God who is the ultimate reason of things, and the knowledge of God is no less the beginning of science than his essence and will are the beginning of beings.
Letter on a General Principle Useful in Explaining the Laws of Nature (1687)

21 It is the knowledge of necessary and eternal truths which distinguishes us from mere animals, and gives us *Reason* and the sciences, raising us to knowledge of ourselves and of God. It is this in us which we call the rational soul or *Mind.*
The Monadology (1714) sect. 29 (translated by R. Latta)

22 *Nihil est sine ratione.*
There is nothing without a reason.
Studies in Physics and the Nature of Body (1671)

23 *Eadem sunt quorum unum potest substitui alteri salva veritate.*
Two things are identical if one can be substituted for the other without affecting the truth.
'Table de définitions' (1704) in L. Coutourat (ed.) *Opuscules et fragments inédits de Leibniz* (1903)

24 We should like Nature to go no further; we should like it to be finite, like our mind; but this is to

ignore the greatness and majesty of the Author of things.

letter to S. Clarke, 1715, translated by M. Morris and G. H. R. Parkinson in *Leibniz: Philosophical Writings* (1973)

Fred W. Leigh d. 1924

British songwriter

1 Can't get away to marry you today,
My wife won't let me!

'Waiting at the Church (My Wife Won't Let Me)' (1906 song)

2 Why am I always the bridesmaid,
Never the blushing bride?

'Why Am I Always the Bridesmaid?' (1917 song, with Charles Collins and Lily Morris); cf. **Proverbs** 595:7

Vivien Leigh 1913–67

English actress

3 Shaw is like a train. One just speaks the words and sits in one's place. But Shakespeare is like bathing in the sea—one swims where one wants.

letter from Harold Nicolson to Vita Sackville-West, 1 February 1956

Curtis E. LeMay 1906–90

US air-force officer

4 They've got to draw in their horns and stop their aggression, or we're going to bomb them back into the Stone Age.

on the North Vietnamese

Mission with LeMay (1965)

Ninon de Lenclos 1620–1705

French courtesan

5 How often have I told you, that love seldom dies of hunger, but frequently of satiety?

letter 41 to the Marquis de Sevigné, *The Memoirs of Ninon de L'Enclos* (1778)

Lenin (Vladimir Ilich Ulyanov) 1870–1924

Russian revolutionary

on Lenin: see ***Schlesinger*** *648:19; see also* ***Keynes*** *435:6,* ***Misquotations*** *521:5*

6 Imperialism is the monopoly stage of capitalism.

Imperialism as the Last Stage of Capitalism (1916) ch. 7 'Briefest possible definition of imperialism'

7 No, Democracy is *not* identical with majority rule. Democracy is a *State* which recognizes the subjection of the minority to the majority, that is, an organization for the systematic use of *force* by one class against the other, by one part of the population against another.

State and Revolution (1919) ch. 4

8 While the State exists, there can be no freedom. When there is freedom there will be no State.

State and Revolution (1919) ch. 5

9 What is to be done?

title of pamphlet (1902); originally the title of a novel (1863) by N. G. Chernyshevsky

10 Communism is Soviet power plus the electrification of the whole country.

Report to 8th Congress, 1920, in *Collected Works* (ed. 5) vol. 42

11 Who? Whom? [i.e. Who masters whom?]

definition of political science, meaning 'Who will outstrip whom?'

in *Polnoe Sobranie Sochinenii* vol. 44 (1970) 17 October 1921 and elsewhere

12 A good man fallen among Fabians.

of George Bernard ***Shaw***

Arthur Ransome *Six Weeks in Russia in 1919* (1919) 'Notes of Conversations with Lenin'

13 Liberty is precious—so precious that it must be rationed.

Sidney and Beatrice Webb *Soviet Communism* (1936)

John Lennon 1940–80

English pop singer and songwriter

see also ***Lennon and McCartney***

14 Happiness is a warm gun.

title of song (1968); cf. **Advertising slogans** 7:23

15 Imagine there's no heaven,
It's easy if you try,
No hell below us,
Above us only sky.

'Imagine' (1971 song)

16 Will the people in the cheaper seats clap your hands? All the rest of you, if you'll just rattle your jewellery.

at the Royal Variety Performance, 4 November 1963, in R. Colman *John Winston Lennon* (1984) pt. 1, ch. 11

17 We're more popular than Jesus now; I don't know which will go first—rock 'n' roll or Christianity.

of The Beatles

interview in *Evening Standard* 4 March 1966

John Lennon 1940–1980 and **Paul McCartney** 1942–

English pop singers and songwriters

see also ***Lennon, McCartney***

18 Back in the USSR.

title of song (1968)

19 For I don't care too much for money,
For money can't buy me love.

'Can't Buy Me Love' (1964 song)

20 Eleanor Rigby picks up the rice in the church
where a wedding has been,
Lives in a dream.
Waits at the window, wearing the face that she
keeps in a jar by the door,
Who is it for?
All the lonely people, where do they all come from?

'Eleanor Rigby' (1966 song)

21 Give peace a chance.

title of song (1969)

22 It's been a hard day's night,
And I've been working like a dog.

'A Hard Day's Night' (1964 song)

1 Strawberry fields forever.
title of song (1967)

2 She's got a ticket to ride, but she don't care.
'Ticket to Ride' (1965 song)

3 Will you still need me, will you still feed me,
When I'm sixty four?
'When I'm Sixty Four' (1967 song)

4 Oh I get by with a little help from my friends,
Mm, I get high with a little help from my friends.
'With a Little Help From My Friends' (1967 song)

Dan Leno (George Galvin) 1860–1904
English entertainer

5 Ah! what is man? Wherefore does he why?
Whence did he whence? Whither is he withering?
Dan Leno Hys Booke (1901) ch. 1

William Lenthall 1591–1662
Speaker of the House of Commons

6 I have neither eye to see, nor tongue to speak here, but as the House is pleased to direct me.
to **Charles I**, *on being asked if he had seen any of the five MPs whom the King had ordered to be arrested*, 4 *January* 1642
John Rushworth *Historical Collections. The Third Part* vol. 2 (1692); cf. **Lincoln** 469:2

Hugh Leonard 1926–
Irish writer

7 The black dog was the only intelligent member of the family. He died a few years later. He was poisoned, and no one will convince me it wasn't suicide.
Da (1973)

8 In those days people confused old age with valour; they called her a great old warrior. This had the effect of inspiring her to gasp even more distressingly by way of proving them right and herself indomitable.
Home Before Night (1979)

9 Her cooking verged on the poisonous . . . I have known no other woman who could make fried eggs taste like perished rubbber.
Home Before Night (1979)

10 Its tail was a plume of such magnificence that it almost wore the cat.
Rover and Other Cats (1992)

11 We do not squabble, fight or have rows. We collect grudges. We're in an arms race, storing up warheads for the domestic Armageddon.
Time Was (1980)

Leonardo da Vinci 1452–1519
Italian painter and designer

12 Whoever in discussion adduces authority uses not intellect but rather memory.
Edward McCurdy (ed. and trans.) *Leonardo da Vinci's Notebooks* (1906) bk. 1

13 Life well spent is long.
Edward McCurdy (ed. and trans.) *Leonardo da Vinci's Notebooks* (1906) bk. 1

14 Iron rusts from disuse; stagnant water loses its purity and in cold weather becomes frozen; even so does inaction sap the vigour of the mind.
Edward McCurdy (ed. and trans.) *Leonardo da Vinci's Notebooks* (1906) bk. 1

15 Human subtlety . . . will never devise an invention more beautiful, more simple or more direct than does Nature, because in her inventions nothing is lacking, and nothing is superfluous.
Edward McCurdy (ed. and trans.) *Leonardo da Vinci's Notebooks* (1906) bk. 1

16 Perspective is the bridle and rudder of painting.
Irma Richter (ed.) *Selections from the Notebooks of Leonardo da Vinci* (World's Classics, 1952)

17 The span of a man's outspread arms is equal to his height.
Irma Richter (ed.) *Selections from the Notebooks of Leonardo da Vinci* (World's Classics, 1952)

18 Every man at three years old is half his height.
Irma A. Richter (ed.) *Selections from the Notebooks of Leonardo da Vinci* (World's Classics, 1952)

19 The poet ranks far below the painter in the representation of visible things, and far below the musician in that of invisible things.
Irma A. Richter (ed.) *Selections from the Notebooks of Leonardo da Vinci* (World's Classics, 1952)

Mikhail Lermontov 1814–41
Russian novelist and poet

20 The love of savages isn't much better than the love of noble ladies; ignorance and simple-heartedness can be as tiresome as coquetry.
A Hero of our Time (1840) 'Bella' (translated by Philip Longworth)

21 Of two close friends, one is always the slave of the other.
A Hero of our Time (1840) 'Princess Mary' (translated by Philip Longworth)

22 Ever since I lived and entered into action, fate has somehow led me to the climax of other people's dramas, as if no one could die, no one could despair without me. I have always been the essential character of the fifth act.
A Hero of our Time (1840) 'Princess Mary' (translated by Philip Longworth)

23 I am like a man yawning at a ball; the only reason he does not go home to bed is that his carriage has not arrived yet.
A Hero of our Time (1840) 'Princess Mary' (translated by Philip Longworth)

24 No, I'm not Byron, it's my role
To be an undiscovered wonder,
Like him, a persecuted wand'rer,
But furnished with a Russian soul.
'No, I'm not Byron' (1832) (translated by Alan Myers)

Alan Jay Lerner 1918–86

American songwriter

1 Don't let it be forgot
That once there was a spot
For one brief shining moment that was known
As Camelot.
now particularly associated with the White House of John Fitzgerald **Kennedy**
'Camelot' (1960 song)

2 I'm getting married in the morning,
Ding! dong! the bells are gonna chime.
Pull out the stopper;
Let's have a whopper;
But get me to the church on time!
'Get me to the Church on Time' (1956 song) in *My Fair Lady*

3 Why can't a woman be more like a man?
Men are so honest, so thoroughly square;
Eternally noble, historically fair;
Who, when you win, will always give your back a pat.
Why can't a woman be like that?
'A Hymn to Him' (1956 song) in *My Fair Lady*

4 We met at nine.
We met at eight.
I was on time.
No, you were late.
Ah yes! I remember it well.
'I Remember it Well' (1958 song) in *Gigi*

5 I've grown accustomed to the trace
Of something in the air;
Accustomed to her face.
'I've Grown Accustomed to her Face' (1956 song) in *My Fair Lady*

6 The rain in Spain stays mainly in the plain.
'The Rain in Spain' (1956 song) in *My Fair Lady*

7 In Hertford, Hereford, and Hampshire,
Hurricanes hardly happen.
'The Rain in Spain' (1956 song) in *My Fair Lady*

8 Thank heaven for little girls!
For little girls get bigger every day.
'Thank Heaven for Little Girls' (1958 song) in *Gigi*

9 All I want is a room somewhere,
Far away from the cold night air,
With one enormous chair;
Oh, wouldn't it be loverly?
'Wouldn't it be Loverly' (1956 song) in *My Fair Lady*

10 Oozing charm from every pore,
He oiled his way around the floor.
'You Did It' (1956 song) in *My Fair Lady*

Doris Lessing 1919–

English writer

11 There's only one real sin, and that is to persuade oneself that the second-best is anything but the second-best.
The Golden Notebook (1962)

12 When old settlers say 'One has to understand the country,' what they mean is, 'You have to get used to our ideas about the native.'
The Grass is Singing (1950) ch. 1

13 What of October, that ambiguous month, the month of tension, the unendurable month?
Martha Quest (1952) pt. 4, sect. 1

14 What is charm then? The free giving of a grace, the spending of something given by nature in her role of spendthrift . . . something extra, superfluous, unnecessary, essentially a power thrown away.
Particularly Cats (1967) ch. 9

G. E. Lessing 1729–81

German dramatist and critic

15 *Gestern liebt' ich,*
Heute leid' ich,
Morgen sterb' ich:
Dennoch denk' ich
Heut und morgen
Gern an gestern.
Yesterday I loved, today I suffer, tomorrow I die: but I still think fondly, today and tomorrow, of yesterday.
'Lied aus dem Spanischen' (1780)

16 *Ein einziger dankbarer Gedanke gen Himmel ist das vollkommenste Gebet.*
One single grateful thought raised to heaven is the most perfect prayer.
Minna von Barnhelm (1767) act 2, sc. 7

17 *Wenn Gott in seiner Rechten alle Wahrheit und in seiner Linken den einzigen, immer regen Trieb nach Wahrheit, obgleich mit dem Zusatz, mich immer und ewig zu irren, verschlossen hielte and spräche zu mir: Wähle! ich fiele ihm mit Demut in seine Linke und sagte: Vater, gieb! Die reine Wahrheit ist ja doch nur für Dich allein.*
If God were to hold out enclosed in His right hand all Truth, and in His left hand just the active search for Truth, though with the condition that I should always err therein, and He should say to me: Choose! I should humbly take His left hand and say: Father! Give me this one; absolute Truth belongs to Thee alone.
Eine Duplik (1778) pt. 1

Winifred Mary Letts 1882–1972

English writer

18 I saw the spires of Oxford
As I was passing by,
The grey spires of Oxford
Against a pearl-grey sky;
My heart was with the Oxford men
Who went abroad to die.
'The Spires of Oxford' (1916)

Oscar Levant 1906–72

American pianist

19 Underneath this flabby exterior is an enormous lack of character.
Memoirs of an Amnesiac (1965)

1 Epigram: a wisecrack that played Carnegie Hall.
in *Coronet* September 1958

Lord Leverhulme 1851–1925
English industrialist and philanthropist

2 Half the money I spend on advertising is wasted, and the trouble is I don't know which half.
David Ogilvy *Confessions of an Advertising Man* (1963)

Ada Leverson 1865–1936
English novelist

3 He seemed at ease and to have the look of the last gentleman in Europe.
of Oscar ***Wilde***
Letters to the Sphinx (1930)

Denise Levertov 1923–
English-born American poet

4 Images
split the truth
in fractions.
'A Sequence' (1961)

5 two by two in the ark of
the ache of it.
'The Ache of Marriage' (1964)

Primo Levi 1919–87
Italian novelist and poet

6 Our language lacks words to express this offence, the demolition of a man.
of a year spent in Auschwitz
If This is a Man (1958)

Bernard Levin 1928–
British journalist

7 Between them, then, Walrus and Carpenter, they divided up the Sixties.
of the Harolds, ***Macmillan*** *and* ***Wilson***
The Pendulum Years (1970) ch. 12

8 The Stag at Bay with the mentality of a fox at large.
of Harold ***Macmillan***
The Pendulum Years (1970) ch. 12

9 Whom the mad would destroy, they first make gods.
of ***Mao*** *Zedong in 1967*
Levin quoting himself in *The Times* 21 September 1987; cf. **Proverbs** 615:4

Duc de Lévis 1764–1830
French soldier and writer

10 *Noblesse oblige.*
Nobility has its obligations.
Maximes et Réflexions (1812 ed.) 'Morale: Maximes et Préceptes' no. 73

11 *Gouverner, c'est choisir.*
To govern is to choose.
Maximes et Réflexions (1812 ed.) 'Politique: Maximes de Politique' no. 19

Claude Lévi-Strauss 1908–
French social anthropologist

12 Language is a form of human reason, and has its reasons which are unknown to man.
The Savage Mind (1962) ch. 9; cf. **Pascal** 568:17

13 The purpose of myth is to provide a logical model capable of overcoming a contradiction (an impossible achievement if, as it happens, the contradiction is real).
Structural Anthropology (1968) ch. 11

G. H. Lewes 1817–78
English man of letters; common-law husband of George ***Eliot***

14 Murder, like talent, seems occasionally to run in families.
The Physiology of Common Life (1859) ch. 12

15 The pen, in our age, weighs heavier in the social scale than the sword of a Norman Baron.
Ranthorpe (1847) epilogue

16 Many a genius has been slow of growth. Oaks that flourish for a thousand years do not spring up into beauty like a reed.
The Spanish Drama (1846) ch. 2

C. S. Lewis 1898–1963
English literary scholar

17 No one ever told me that grief felt so like fear.
A Grief Observed (1961)

18 We have trained them [men] to think of the Future as a promised land which favoured heroes attain—not as something which everyone reaches at the rate of sixty minutes an hour, whatever he does, whoever he is.
The Screwtape Letters (1942) no. 25

19 She's the sort of woman who lives for others—you can always tell the others by their hunted expression.
The Screwtape Letters (1942) no. 26

20 A young man who wishes to remain a sound atheist cannot be too careful of his reading.
Surprised by Joy (1955)

21 This extraordinary pride in being exempt from temptation that you have not yet risen to the level of! Eunuchs boasting of their chastity!
'Unreal Estates' in Kingsley Amis and Robert Conquest (eds.) *Spectrum IV* (1965)

22 For twenty years I've stared my level best
To see if evening—any evening—would suggest
A patient etherized upon a table;
In vain. I simply wasn't able.
on contemporary poetry
'A Confession' (1964); cf. **Eliot** 295:3

23 Often when I pray I wonder if I am not posting letters to a non-existent address.
letter to Arthur Greeves, 24 December 1930

24 Courage is not simply *one* of the virtues but the form of every virtue at the testing point.
Cyril Connolly *The Unquiet Grave* (1944) ch. 3

1 He that but looketh on a plate of ham and eggs to lust after it, hath already committed breakfast with it in his heart.
letter, 10 March 1954

Esther Lewis (later Clark) fl. 1747–89
English poet

2 Are simple women only fit
To dress, to darn, to flower, or knit,
To mind the distaff, or the spit?
Why are the needle and the pen
Thought incompatible by men?
'A Mirror for Detractors' (1754) l. 146

George Cornewall Lewis 1806–63
British Liberal politician and writer

3 Life would be tolerable but for its amusements.
in *The Times* 18 September 1872; cf. **Surtees** 747:2

Sam M. Lewis 1885–1959 and Joe Young 1889–1939
American songwriters

4 How 'ya gonna keep 'em down on the farm (after they've seen Paree)?
title of song (1919)

5 Mammy, Mammy, look at me. Don't you know me? I'm your little baby.
'My Mammy' (1918 song); sung by Al **Jolson**

Sinclair Lewis 1885–1951
American novelist

6 Our American professors like their literature clear and cold and pure and very dead.
The American Fear of Literature (Nobel Prize Address, 12 December 1930), in H. Frenz *Literature 1901–1967* (1969)

7 To George F. Babbitt, as to most prosperous citizens of Zenith, his motor car was poetry and tragedy, love and heroism. The office was his pirate ship but the car his perilous excursion ashore.
Babbitt (1922) ch. 3

8 In other countries, art and literature are left to a lot of shabby bums living in attics and feeding on booze and spaghetti, but in America the successful writer or picture-painter is indistinguishable from any other decent business man.
Babbitt (1922) ch. 14

9 She did her work with the thoroughness of a mind which reveres details and never quite understands them.
Babbitt (1922) ch. 18

10 It can't happen here.
title of novel (1935)

Willmott Lewis 1877–1950
British journalist

11 I think it well to remember that, when writing for the newspapers, we are writing for an elderly lady in Hastings who has two cats of which she is passionately fond. Unless our stuff can successfully compete for her interest with those cats, it is no good.
Claud Cockburn *In Time of Trouble* (1957)

Wyndham Lewis 1882–1957
English novelist, painter, and critic

12 Gertrude Stein's prose-song is a cold, black suet-pudding . . . Cut it at any point, it is the same thing . . . all fat, without nerve.
of Three Lives (1909)
Time and Western Man (1927)

13 Angels in jumpers.
describing the figures in Stanley ***Spencer****'s paintings*
attributed

Ludwig Lewisohn 1882–1955
German-born novelist

14 There are philosophies which are unendurable not because men are cowards, but because they are men.
The Modern Drama (1916)

George Leybourne d. 1884
English songwriter

15 He'd fly through the air with the greatest of ease,
A daring young man on the flying trapeze.
'The Flying Trapeze' (1868 song)

Liberace (Wladziu Valentino Liberace) 1919–87
American showman

16 When the reviews are bad I tell my staff that they can join me as I cry all the way to the bank.
Autobiography (1973) ch. 2; originally:

He [Liberace] begins to belabour the critics announcing that *he* doesn't mind what they say but that poor George [his brother] 'cried all the way to the bank'.
in *Collier's* 17 September 1954

Georg Christoph Lichtenberg 1742–99
German scientist and drama critic

17 The journalists have constructed for themselves a little wooden chapel, which they also call the Temple of Fame, in which they put up and take down portraits all day long and make such a hammering you can't hear yourself speak.
A. Leitzmann *Georg Christoph Lichtenberg Aphorismen* (1904)

18 There is a great deal of difference between *still* believing something, and *again* believing it.
Notebook E no. 8 1775–6 in *Aphorisms* (1990)

A. J. Liebling 1904–63
American writer

19 Freedom of the press is guaranteed only to those who own one.
'The Wayward Press: Do you belong in Journalism?' (1960)

Charles-Joseph, Prince de Ligne
1735–1814
Belgian soldier

1 *Le congrès ne marche pas, il danse.*
The Congress makes no progress; it dances.
Auguste de la Garde-Chambonas *Souvenirs du Congrès de Vienne* (1820) ch. 1

Beatrice Lillie 1894–1989
British comedienne

2 Never darken my Dior again!
to a waiter who had spilled soup down her neck
in *Every Other Inch a Lady* (1973) ch. 14

George Lillo 1693–1739
Flemish-born dramatist

3 There's sure no passion in the human soul,
But finds its food in music.
The Fatal Curiosity (1736) act 1, sc. 2

Abraham Lincoln 1809–65
16th President of the US
on Lincoln: see ***Booth*** *142:16,* ***Stanton*** *736:8*

4 To give victory to the right, not bloody bullets, but peaceful ballots only, are necessary.
speech, 18 May 1858, in R. P. Basler (ed.) *Collected Works of Abraham Lincoln* (1953) vol. 2; cf. **Misquotations** 521:3

5 'A house divided against itself cannot stand.' I believe this government cannot endure permanently, half slave and half free.
speech, 16 June 1858, in R. P. Basler (ed.) *Collected Works . . .* (1953) vol. 2; cf. **Bible** 98:2

6 What is conservatism? Is it not adherence to the old and tried, against the new and untried?
speech, 27 February 1860, in R. P. Basler (ed.) *Collected Works . . .* (1953) vol. 3

7 Let us have faith that right makes might, and in that faith, let us, to the end, dare to do our duty as we understand it.
speech, 27 February 1860, in R. P. Basler (ed.) *Collected Works . . .* (1953) vol. 3

8 I take the official oath to-day with no mental reservations, and with no purpose to construe the Constitution or laws by any hypercritical rules.
first inaugural address, 4 March 1861, in R. P. Basler (ed.) *Collected Works . . .* (1953) vol. 4

9 The mystic chords of memory, stretching from every battlefield and patriot grave to every living heart and heartstone all over this broad land, will yet swell the chorus of the Union when again touched, as surely they will be, by the better angels of our nature.
first inaugural address, 4 March 1861

10 I think the necessity of being *ready* increases. Look to it.
the whole of a letter to Governor Andrew Curtin of Pennsylvania, 8 April 1861, in R. P. Basler (ed.) *Collected Works . . .* (1953) vol. 4

11 My paramount object in this struggle is to save the Union . . . If I could save the Union without freeing any slave, I would do it; and if I could save it by freeing all the slaves, I would do it; and if I could save it by freeing some and leaving others alone, I would also do that . . . I have here stated my purpose according to my views of official duty and I intend no modification of my oft-expressed personal wish that all men everywhere could be free.
letter to Horace Greeley, 22 August 1862, in R. P. Basler (ed.) *Collected Works . . .* (1953) vol. 5

12 In giving freedom to the slave, we assure freedom to the free—honourable alike in what we give and what we preserve. We shall nobly save, or meanly lose, the last, best hope of earth.
Annual Message to Congress, 1 December 1862, in R. P. Basler (ed.) *Collected Works . . .* (1953) vol. 5

13 Fourscore and seven years ago our fathers brought forth upon this continent a new nation, conceived in liberty, and dedicated to the proposition that all men are created equal . . . In a larger sense we cannot dedicate, we cannot consecrate, we cannot hallow this ground. The brave men, living and these dead, who struggled here, have consecrated it far above our power to add or detract. The world will little note, nor long remember, what we say here, but it can never forget what they did here. It is for us, the living, rather to be dedicated here to the unfinished work which they who fought here have thus far so nobly advanced . . . we here highly resolve that the dead shall not have died in vain, that this nation, under God, shall have a new birth of freedom; and that government of the people, by the people, and for the people, shall not perish from the earth.
the Lincoln Memorial inscription reads 'by the people, for the people'
address at the dedication of the National Cemetery at Gettysburg, 19 November 1863, as reported the following day, in R. P. Basler (ed.) *Collected Works . . .* (1953) vol. 7; cf. **Webster** 807:11

14 The President tonight has a dream:—He was in a party of plain people, and, as it became known who he was, they began to comment on his appearance. One of them said:—'He is a very common-looking man.' The President replied:—'The Lord prefers common-looking people. That is the reason he makes so many of them.'
John Hay *Letters of John Hay and Extracts from Diary* (1908) vol 1, 23 December 1863

15 I claim not to have controlled events, but confess plainly that events have controlled me.
letter to A. G. Hodges, 4 April 1864, in R. P. Basler (ed.) *Collected Works . . .* (1953) vol. 7

16 It is not best to swap horses when crossing streams.
reply to National Union League, 9 June 1864, in R. P. Basler (ed.) *Collected Works . . .* (1953) vol. 7; cf. **Proverbs** 598:30

17 Fondly do we hope, fervently do we pray, that this mighty scourge of war may speedily pass away. Yet, if God wills that it continue until all the wealth piled by the bond-man's two hundred and fifty years of unrequited toil shall be sunk, and until every drop of blood drawn with the lash shall be paid by another drawn with the sword, as was said three thousand years ago, so still it must be said,

'The judgements of the Lord are true and righteous altogether.'

second inaugural address, 4 March 1865, in R. P. Basler (ed.) *Collected Works . . .* (1953) vol. 8; cf. **Book of Common Prayer** 132:17

1 With malice toward none; with charity for all; with firmness in the right, as God gives us to see the right, let us strive on to finish the work we are in: to bind up the nation's wounds; to care for him who shall have borne the battle, and for his widow and his orphan, to do all which may achieve and cherish a just and lasting peace among ourselves, and with all nations.

second inaugural address, 4 March 1865, in R. P. Basler (ed.) *Collected Works . . .* (1953) vol. 8

2 As President, I have no eyes but constitutional eyes; I cannot see you.

attributed reply to the South Carolina Commissioners; cf. **Lenthall** 464:6

3 People who like this sort of thing will find this the sort of thing they like.

judgement of a book

G. W. E. Russell *Collections and Recollections* (1898) ch. 30

4 So you're the little woman who wrote the book that made this great war!

on meeting Harriet Beecher **Stowe**, *author of* Uncle Tom's Cabin

Carl Sandburg *Abraham Lincoln: The War Years* (1936) vol. 2, ch. 39

5 You may fool all the people some of the time; you can even fool some of the people all the time; but you can't fool all of the people all the time.

also attributed to Phineas **Barnum**

Alexander K. McClure *Lincoln's Yarns and Stories* (1904)

R. M. Lindner see Film titles 313:1

J. A. Lindon

6 Points
Have no parts or joints
How then can they combine
To form a line?

M. Gardner *Wheels, Life and Other Mathematical Amusements* (1983)

Vachel Lindsay 1879–1931

American poet

7 Then I saw the Congo, creeping through the black,
Cutting through the forest with a golden track.

'The Congo' pt. 1 (1914)

8 Booth led boldly with his big bass drum—
(Are you washed in the blood of the Lamb?)

'General William Booth Enters into Heaven' (1913); cf. **Bible** 112:10

9 Booth died blind and still by faith he trod,
Eyes still dazzled by the ways of God.

'General William Booth Enters into Heaven' (1913)

Graham Linehan and Arthur Mathews

Irish writers

10 It's great being a priest, isn't it, Ted?

'Good Luck, Father Ted' (1994), episode from *Father Ted* (Channel 4 TV, 1994–8)

11 Careful now!

placard alerting Craggy Island to a banned film

'The Passion of St Tibulus' (1994), episode from *Father Ted* (Channel 4 TV, 1994–8)

12 Where are you going
With your fetlocks blowing in the . . . wind
I want to shower you with sugar lumps
And ride you over . . . fences
I want to polish your hooves every single day
And bring you to the horse . . . dentist.

'My Lovely Horse' as sung by Fathers Ted and Dougal

'A Song for Europe' (1996), episode from *Father Ted* (Channel 4 TV, 1994–8)

Gary Lineker 1960–

English footballer

13 The nice aspect about football is that, if things go wrong, it's the manager who gets the blame.

remark before his first match as captain of England

in *Independent* 12 September 1990

Eric Linklater 1899–1974

Scottish novelist

14 'There won't be any revolution in America,' said Isadore. Nikitin agreed. 'The people are all too clean. They spend all their time changing their shirts and washing themselves. You can't feel fierce and revolutionary in a bathroom.'

Juan in America (1931) bk. 5, pt. 3

Art Linkletter 1912–

American broadcaster and humorist

15 The four stages of man are infancy, childhood, adolescence and obsolescence.

A Child's Garden of Misinformation (1965) ch. 8

George Linley 1798–1865

English songwriter

16 Among our ancient mountains,
And from our lovely vales,
Oh, let the prayer re-echo:
'God bless the Prince of Wales!'

'God Bless the Prince of Wales' (1862 song); translated from the Welsh original by J. C. Hughes (1837–87)

Lin Yutang 1895–1976

Chinese writer and philologist

17 A good traveller is one who does not know where he is going to, and a perfect traveller does not know where he came from.

The Importance of Living (1938) ch. 11

18 [The traveller can] get the greatest joy of travel even without going to the mountains, by staying at home and watching and going about the field to

watch a sailing cloud, or a dog, or a hedge, or a lonely tree.
The Importance of Living (1938) ch. 11

Walter Lippmann 1889–1974
American journalist

1 Mr Coolidge's genius for inactivity is developed to a very high point. It is far from being an indolent activity. It is a grim, determined, alert inactivity which keeps Mr Coolidge occupied constantly. Nobody has ever worked harder at inactivity, with such force of character, with such unremitting attention to detail, with such conscientious devotion to the task.
Men of Destiny (1927)

2 The final test of a leader is that he leaves behind him in other men the conviction and the will to carry on.
in *New York Herald Tribune* 14 April 1945

Richard Littledale 1833–90
English clergyman

3 Come down, O Love divine,
Seek thou this soul of mine,
And visit it with thine own ardour glowing;
O Comforter, draw near,
Within my heart appear,
And kindle it, thy holy flame bestowing.
O let it freely burn,
Till earthly passion turn
To dust and ashes in its heat consuming.
'Come down, O Love divine' (1867 hymn); translation of 'Discendi, Amor santo' by Bianco da Siena (c.1350–1434)

4 Let holy charity
Mine outward vesture be,
And lowliness become mine inner clothing;
True lowliness of heart,
Which takes the humbler part,
And o'er its own shortcomings weeps with loathing.
'Come down, O Love divine' (1867 hymn)

Joan Littlewood 1914– and **Charles Chilton** 1914–

5 Oh what a lovely war.
title of stage show (1963)

Maxim Litvinov 1876–1951
Soviet diplomat

6 Peace is indivisible.
note to the Allies, 25 February 1920; A. U. Pope *Maxim Litvinoff* (1943)

Penelope Lively 1933–
English novelist

7 Language tethers us to the world; without it we spin like atoms.
Moon Tiger (1987)

8 We are walking lexicons. In a single sentence of idle chatter we preserve Latin, Anglo-Saxon, Norse; we carry a museum inside our heads, each day we commemorate peoples of whom we have never heard.
Moon Tiger (1987)

Ken Livingstone 1945–
British Labour politician

9 If voting changed anything, they'd abolish it.
title of book, 1987

Livy (Titus Livius) 59 BC–AD 17
Roman historian

10 *Vae victis.*
Down with the defeated!
cry (already proverbial) of the Gallic King, Brennus, on capturing Rome in 390 BC
Ab Urbe Condita bk. 5, ch. 48, sect. 9

11 *Pugna magna victi sumus.*
We were defeated in a great battle.
announcement of disaster for the Romans in Hannibal's ambush at Lake Trasimene in 217 BC
Ab Urbe Condita bk. 22, ch. 7, sect. 8

Richard Llewellyn (Richard Llewellyn Lloyd) 1907–83
Welsh novelist and dramatist

12 How green was my valley.
title of book (1939)

Robert Lloyd
English poet

13 Turn parson, Colman, that's the way to thrive;
Your parsons are the happiest men alive.
'The Law-Student' (1762)

14 Alone from Jargon born to rescue Law,
From precedent, grave hum, and formal saw!
To strip chicanery of its vain pretence,
And marry Common Law to Common Sense!
'The Law-Student' (1762); on Lord Mansfield, Lord Chief Justice, 1756–88

15 True Genius, like Armida's wand,
Can raise the spring from barren land.
While all the art of Imitation,
Is pilf'ring from the first creation.
'Shakespeare' (1762)

David Lloyd George 1863–1945
British Liberal statesman; Prime Minister, 1916–22
on Lloyd George: see **Asquith** *31:10*, **Clemenceau** *220:12*, **Keynes** *435:8*

16 The leal and trusty mastiff which is to watch over our interests, but which runs away at the first snarl of the trade unions . . . A mastiff? It is the right hon. Gentleman's poodle.
on the House of Lords and A. J. **Balfour** *respectively*
in the House of Commons, 26 June 1907

17 I have no nest-eggs. I am looking for someone else's hen-roost to rob next year.
in 1908, as Chancellor
Frank Owen *Tempestuous Journey* (1954) ch. 10

1 A fully-equipped duke costs as much to keep up as two Dreadnoughts; and dukes are just as great a terror and they last longer.
speech at Newcastle, 9 October 1909, in *The Times* 11 October 1909

2 The great peaks of honour we had forgotten—Duty, Patriotism, and—clad in glittering white—the great pinnacle of Sacrifice, pointing like a rugged finger to Heaven.
speech at Queen's Hall, London, 19 September 1914, in *The Times* 20 September 1914

3 At eleven o'clock this morning came to an end the cruellest and most terrible war that has ever scourged mankind. I hope we may say that thus, this fateful morning, came to an end all wars.
speech in the House of Commons, 11 November 1918; cf. **Wells** 810:16

4 What is our task? To make Britain a fit country for heroes to live in.
speech at Wolverhampton, 23 November 1918, in *The Times* 25 November 1918

5 Unless I am mistaken, by the steps we have taken [in Ireland] we have murder by the throat.
speech at the Mansion House, 9 November 1920; Frank Owen *Tempestuous Journey* (1954) ch. 28

6 The world is becoming like a lunatic asylum run by lunatics.
in *Observer* 8 January 1933; cf. **Rowland** 636:15

7 A politician was a person with whose politics you did not agree. When you did agree, he was a statesman.
speech at Central Hall, Westminster, 2 July 1935, in *The Times* 3 July 1935

8 Negotiating with de Valera . . . is like trying to pick up mercury with a fork.
to which ***de Valera*** *replied, 'Why doesn't he use a spoon?'*
M. J. MacManus *Eamon de Valera* (1944) ch. 6

9 Sufficient conscience to bother him, but not sufficient to keep him straight.
of Ramsay ***MacDonald***
A. J. Sylvester *Life with Lloyd George* (1975)

Liz Lochhead 1947–
British poet and playwright

10 I wouldn't thank you for a Valentine
I won't wake up early wondering if the postman's been.
Should 10 red-padded satin hearts arrive with a sticky sickly saccharine
Sentiments in very vulgar verses I wouldn't wonder if you meant them.
'I Wouldn't Thank You for a Valentine' (1985)

John Locke 1632–1704
English philosopher

11 New opinions are always suspected, and usually opposed, without any other reason but because they are not already common.
An Essay concerning Human Understanding (1690) 'Dedicatory Epistle'

12 The commonwealth of learning is not at this time without master-builders, whose mighty designs, in advancing the sciences, will leave lasting monuments to the admiration of posterity . . . in an age that produces such masters as the great Huygenius and the incomparable Mr Newton . . . 'tis ambition enough to be employed as an under-labourer in clearing ground a little, and removing some of the rubbish that lies in the way of knowledge.
An Essay concerning Human Understanding (1690) 'Epistle to the Reader'

13 General propositions are seldom mentioned in the huts of Indians: much less are they to be found in the thoughts of children.
An Essay concerning Human Understanding (1690) bk. 1, ch. 2, sect. 11

14 Nature never makes excellent things for mean or no uses.
An Essay concerning Human Understanding (1690) bk. 2, ch. 1, sect. 15

15 No man's knowledge here can go beyond his experience.
An Essay concerning Human Understanding (1690) bk. 2, ch. 1, sect. 19

16 It is one thing to show a man that he is in error, and another to put him in possession of truth.
An Essay concerning Human Understanding (1690) bk. 4, ch. 7, sect. 11

17 There are very few lovers of truth, for truth-sake, even among those who persuade themselves that they are so. How a man may know, whether he be so, in earnest, is worth enquiry; and I think, there is this one unerring mark of it, viz. the not entertaining any proposition with greater assurance than the proofs it is built on will warrant. Whoever goes beyond this measure of assent, it is plain, receives not truth in the love of it, loves not truth for truth-sake, but for some other by-end.
An Essay concerning Human Understanding (1690) bk. 4, ch. 19, sect. 1

18 Reason is natural revelation, whereby the eternal Father of light, and fountain of all knowledge communicates to mankind that portion of truth which he has laid within the reach of their natural faculties.
An Essay concerning Human Understanding (1690) bk. 4, ch. 19, sect. 4

19 Crooked things may be as stiff and unflexible as straight: and men may be as positive in error as in truth.
An Essay concerning Human Understanding (1690) bk. 4, ch. 19, sect. 11

20 All men are liable to error; and most men are, in many points, by passion or interest, under temptation to it.
An Essay concerning Human Understanding (1690) bk. 4, ch. 20, sect. 17

21 Whatsoever . . . [man] removes out of the state that nature hath provided and left it in, he hath mixed his labour with, and joined to it something that is his own, and thereby makes it his property.

Second Treatise of Civil Government (1690) ch. 5, sect. 27

1 [That] ill deserves the name of confinement which hedges us in only from bogs and precipices. So that, however it may be mistaken, the end of law is, not to abolish or restrain, but to preserve and enlarge freedom.

Second Treatise of Civil Government (1690) ch. 6, sect. 57

2 Man . . . hath by nature a power . . . to preserve his property—that is, his life, liberty, and estate—against the injuries and attempts of other men.

Second Treatise of Civil Government (1690) ch. 7, sect. 87

3 Man being . . . by nature all free, equal, and independent, no one can be put out of this estate, and subjected to the political power of another, without his own consent.

Second Treatise of Civil Government (1690) ch. 8, sect. 95

4 The only way by which any one divests himself of his natural liberty and puts on the bonds of civil society is by agreeing with other men to join and unite into a community.

Second Treatise of Civil Government (1690) ch. 8, sect. 95

5 The great and chief end, therefore, of men's uniting into commonwealths, and putting themselves under government, is the preservation of their property.

Second Treatise of Civil Government (1690) ch. 9, sect. 124

6 This power to act according to discretion for the public good, without the prescription of the law, and sometimes even against it, is that which is called prerogative.

Second Treatise of Civil Government (1690) ch. 14, sect. 160

7 The rod, which is the only instrument of government that tutors generally know, or ever think of, is the most unfit of any to be used in education.

Some Thoughts Concerning Education (5th ed., 1705) sect. 47

8 You would think him a very foolish fellow, that should not value a virtuous, or a wise man, infinitely before a great scholar.

Some Thoughts Concerning Education (5th ed., 1705) sect. 147

Frederick Locker-Lampson 1821–95

English writer of light verse

9 And many are afraid of God—
And more of Mrs Grundy.

'The Jester's Plea' (1868); cf. **Morton** 534:3

John Gibson Lockhart 1794–1854

Scottish writer and critic
see also **Epitaphs** 303:4

10 It is a better and a wiser thing to be a starved apothecary than a starved poet; so back to the shop Mr John, back to 'plasters, pills, and ointment boxes.'

reviewing Keats's Endymion

in *Blackwood's Edinburgh Magazine* August 1818

11 Barring drink and the girls, I ne'er heard of a sin:
Many worse, better few, than bright, broken Maginn.

'Epitaph for William Maginn (1794–1842)', in William Maginn *Miscellanies* (1885) vol. 1, p. xviii

David Lodge 1935–

English novelist

12 Literature is mostly about having sex and not much about having children. Life is the other way round.

The British Museum is Falling Down (1965) ch. 4

13 Four times, under our educational rules, the human pack is shuffled and cut—at eleven-plus, sixteen-plus, eighteen-plus and twenty-plus—and happy is he who comes top of the deck on each occasion, but especially the last. This is called Finals, the very name of which implies that nothing of importance can happen after it.

Changing Places (1975) ch. 1

14 He understood . . . Walt Whitman who laid end to end words never seen in each other's company before outside of a dictionary, and Herman Melville who split the atom of the traditional novel in the effort to make whaling a universal metaphor.

Changing Places (1975) ch. 5

15 I gave up screwing around a long time ago. I came to the conclusion that sex is a sublimation of the work instinct.

Small World (1984) pt. 1, ch. 2

16 Morris read through the letter. Was it a shade too fulsome? No, that was another law of academic life: *it is impossible to be excessive in flattery of one's peers.*

Small World (1984) pt. 3, ch. 1

Thomas Lodge 1558–1625

English man of letters

17 Love in my bosom like a bee
Doth suck his sweet;
Now with his wings he plays with me,
Now with his feet.
Within mine eyes he makes his nest,
His bed amidst my tender breast;
My kisses are his daily feast,
And yet he robs me of my rest.
Ah, wanton, will ye?

'Love in my bosom like a bee' (1590)

18 Love guards the roses of thy lips
And flies about them like a bee;
If I approach he forward skips,
And if I kiss he stingeth me.

Love in thine eyes doth build his bower,
And sleeps within their pretty shine;
And if I look the boy will lour,
And from their orbs shoots shafts divine.

'Love guards the roses of thy lips' (1593)

Frank Loesser 1910–69
American songwriter

1 See what the boys in the back room will have
And tell them I'm having the same.
'Boys in the Back Room' (1939 song)

2 Isn't it grand! Isn't it fine! Look at the cut, the style, the line!
The suit of clothes is altogether, but altogether it's altogether
The most remarkable suit of clothes that I have ever seen.
'The King's New Clothes' (1952 song); from the film *Hans Christian Andersen*

Christopher Logue 1926–
English poet

3 Come to the edge.
We might fall.
Come to the edge.
It's too high!
COME TO THE EDGE!
And they came
and he pushed
and they flew . . .
on ***Apollinaire***
'Come to the edge' (1969)

4 I, Christopher Logue, was baptized the year
Many thousands of Englishmen,
Fists clenched, their bellies empty,

Walked day and night on the capital city.
'The Song of Autobiography' (1996)

Jack London 1876–1916
American novelist

5 The call of the wild.
title of novel (1903)

Huey Long 1893–1935
American Democratic politician

6 For the present you can just call me the Kingfish.
Every Man a King (1933)

7 I can go Mr Wilson one better; I was born barefoot.
replying to the claim that an opponent had gone barefoot as a boy
T. Harry Williams *Huey Long* (1969)

8 Oh hell, say that I am *sui generis* and let it go at that.
to journalists attempting to analyse his political personality
T. Harry Williams *Huey Long* (1969)

Henry Wadsworth Longfellow 1807–82
American poet

9 I shot an arrow into the air,
It fell to earth, I knew not where.
'The Arrow and the Song' (1845)

10 Thou, too, sail on, O Ship of State!
Sail on, O Union, strong and great!
Humanity with all its fears,
With all the hopes of future years,
Is hanging breathless on thy fate!
'The Building of the Ship' (1849)

11 Between the dark and the daylight,
When the night is beginning to lower,
Comes a pause in the day's occupations,
That is known as the Children's Hour.
'The Children's Hour' (1859)

12 The cares that infest the day
Shall fold their tents, like the Arabs,
And as silently steal away.
'The Day is Done' (1844)

13 If you would hit the mark, you must aim a little above it;
Every arrow that flies feels the attraction of earth.
'Elegiac Verse' (1880)

14 This is the forest primeval.
Evangeline (1847) introduction

15 Sorrow and silence are strong, and patient endurance is godlike.
Evangeline (1847) pt. 2, l. 60

16 The shades of night were falling fast,
As through an Alpine village passed
A youth, who bore, 'mid snow and ice,
A banner with the strange device,
Excelsior!
'Excelsior' (1841)

17 A traveller, by the faithful hound,
Half-buried in the snow was found.
'Excelsior' (1841)

18 Giotto's tower,
The lily of Florence blossoming in stone.
'Giotto's Tower' (1866)

19 I like that ancient Saxon phrase, which calls
The burial-ground God's-Acre!
'God's-Acre' (1841)

20 The holiest of all holidays are those
Kept by ourselves in silence and apart;
The secret anniversaries of the heart.
'Holidays' (1877)

21 The heights by great men reached and kept
Were not attained by sudden flight,
But they, while their companions slept,
Were toiling upward in the night.
'The Ladder of Saint Augustine' (1850)

22 Standing, with reluctant feet,
Where the brook and river meet.
'Maidenhood' (1841)

23 I remember the black wharves and the slips,
And the sea-rides tossing free;
And Spanish sailors with bearded lips,
And the beauty and mystery of the ships,
And the magic of the sea.
And the voice of that wayward song
Is singing and saying still:
'A boy's will is the wind's will
And the thoughts of youth are long, long thoughts.'
'My Lost Youth' (1858)

1 *Emigravit* is the inscription on the tombstone where he lies;
Dead he is not, but departed,—for the artist never dies.
on Albrecht Dürer
'Nuremberg' (1844)

2 Not in the clamour of the crowded street,
Not in the shouts and plaudits of the throng,
But in ourselves, are triumph and defeat.
'The Poets' (1876)

3 Tell me not, in mournful numbers,
Life is but an empty dream!
For the soul is dead that slumbers,
And things are not what they seem.
Life is real! Life is earnest!
And the grave is not its goal;
Dust thou art, to dust returnest,
Was not spoken of the soul.
'A Psalm of Life' (1838); cf. **Bible** 74:7

4 Art is long, and Time is fleeting,
And our hearts, though stout and brave,
Still, like muffled drums, are beating
Funeral marches to the grave.
'A Psalm of Life' (1838); cf. **Hippocrates** 377:15

5 Trust no Future, howe'er pleasant!
Let the dead Past bury its dead!
Act,—act in the living Present!
Heart within, and God o'erhead!
'A Psalm of Life' (1838); cf. **Bible** 94:20

6 Lives of great men all remind us
We can make our lives sublime,
And, departing, leave behind us
Footprints on the sands of time.
'A Psalm of Life' (1838)

7 Let us, then, be up and doing,
With a heart for any fate;
Still achieving, still pursuing,
Learn to labour and to wait.
'A Psalm of Life' (1838)

8 Though the mills of God grind slowly, yet they grind exceeding small;
Though with patience He stands waiting, with exactness grinds He all.
'Retribution' (1870), translation of Friedrich von Logau (1604–55) *Sinnegedichte* (1654) no. 3224; cf. **Proverbs** 606:37

9 A Lady with a Lamp shall stand
In the great history of the land,
A noble type of good,
Heroic womanhood.
on Florence **Nightingale**
'Santa Filomena' (1857)

10 The forests, with their myriad tongues,
Shouted of liberty;
And the Blast of the Desert cried aloud,
With a voice so wild and free,
That he started in his sleep and smiled
At their tempestuous glee.
'The Slave's Dream' (1842)

11 By the shore of Gitche Gumee,
By the shining Big-Sea-Water,
Stood the wigwam of Nokomis,
Daughter of the Moon, Nokomis.
The Song of Hiawatha (1855) 'Hiawatha's Childhood'

12 Dark behind it rose the forest,
Rose the black and gloomy pine-trees,
Rose the firs with cones upon them;
Bright before it beat the water,
Beat the clear and sunny water,
Beat the shining Big-Sea-Water.
The Song of Hiawatha (1855) 'Hiawatha's Childhood'

13 From the waterfall he named her,
Minnehaha, Laughing Water.
The Song of Hiawatha (1855) 'Hiawatha and Mudjekeewis'

14 He is dead, the sweet musician!
He the sweetest of all singers!
He has gone from us for ever,
He has moved a little nearer
To the Master of all music,
To the Master of all singing!
O my brother, Chibiabos!
The Song of Hiawatha (1855) 'Hiawatha's Lamentation'

15 Listen, my children, and you shall hear
Of the midnight ride of Paul Revere,
On the eighteenth of April in Seventy-five.
Tales of a Wayside Inn pt. 1 (1863) 'The Landlord's Tale: Paul Revere's Ride'

16 One if by land and two if by sea;
And I on the opposite shore will be,
Ready to ride and sound the alarm.
Tales of a Wayside Inn pt. 1 (1863) 'The Landlord's Tale: Paul Revere's Ride'; cf. **Revere** 624:18

17 The fate of a nation was riding that night.
Tales of a Wayside Inn pt. 1 (1863) 'The Landlord's Tale: Paul Revere's Ride'

18 Ships that pass in the night, and speak each other in passing;
Only a signal shown and a distant voice in the darkness;
So on the ocean of life we pass and speak one another,
Only a look and a voice; then darkness again and a silence.
Tales of a Wayside Inn pt. 3 (1874) 'The Theologian's Tale: Elizabeth' pt. 4

19 Under a spreading chestnut tree
The village smithy stands;
The smith, a mighty man is he,
With large and sinewy hands;
And the muscles of his brawny arms
Are strong as iron bands.
'The Village Blacksmith' (1839)

20 Each morning sees some task begin,
Each evening sees it close;
Something attempted, something done,
Has earned a night's repose.
'The Village Blacksmith' (1839)

1 It was the schooner Hesperus,
That sailed the wintry sea;
And the skipper had taken his little daughter,
To bear him company.

'The Wreck of the Hesperus' (1839)

2 There was a little girl
Who had a little curl
Right in the middle of her forehead,
When she was good
She was very, very good,
But when she was bad she was horrid.

composed for, and sung to, his second daughter while a babe in arms, c.1850

B. R. Tucker-Macchetta *The Home Life of Henry W. Longfellow* (1882) ch. 5

3 The square root of half a number of bees, and also eight-ninths of the whole, alighted on the jasmines, and a female buzzed responsive to the hum of the male inclosed at night in a water-lily. O, beautiful damsel, tell me the number of bees.

Kavanagh (1849) ch. 4

Lord Longford 1905–
British Labour politician and philanthropist

4 In 1969 I published a small book on Humility. It was a pioneering work which has not, to my knowledge, been superseded.

in *Tablet* 22 January 1994

Longinus on the Sublime
Greek literary treatise of unknown authorship and date

5 Sublimity is the echo of a noble mind.

sect. 9

Michael Longley 1939–
Irish poet

6 Astrologers or three wise men
Who may shortly be setting out
For a small house up the Shankill
Or the Falls, should pause on their way
To buy gifts at Jim Gibson's shop,
Dates and chestnuts and tambourines.

'The Greengrocer' (1979)

7 I am travelling from one April to another.
It is the same train between the same
embankments.
Gorse fires are smoking, but primroses burn
And celandines and white may and gorse flowers.

'Gorse Fires' (1991)

Alice Roosevelt Longworth 1884–1980
daughter of Theodore ***Roosevelt***

8 If you haven't got anything good to say about anyone come and sit by me.

maxim embroidered on a cushion in her home

Michael Teague *Mrs L: Conversations with Alice Roosevelt Longworth* (1981)

Anita Loos 1893–1981
American writer

9 Gentlemen prefer blondes.

title of book (1925)

10 So this gentleman said a girl with brains ought to do something with them besides think.

Gentlemen Prefer Blondes (1925) ch. 1

11 So I really think that American gentlemen are the best after all, because kissing your hand may make you feel very very good but a diamond and safire bracelet lasts forever.

Gentlemen Prefer Blondes (1925) ch. 4; cf. **Advertising slogans** 7:13, **Robin** 629:9

12 Fun is fun but no girl wants to laugh all of the time.

Gentlemen Prefer Blondes (1925) ch. 4

13 So then Dr Froyd said that all I needed was to cultivate a few inhibitions and get some sleep.

Gentlemen Prefer Blondes (1925) ch. 5

Frederico García Lorca see **García Lorca**

Edward N. Lorenz 1917–
American meteorologist

14 Predictability: Does the flap of a butterfly's wings in Brazil set off a tornado in Texas?

title of paper given to the American Association for the Advancement of Science, Washington, 29 December 1979; James Gleick *Chaos* (1988)

Konrad Lorenz 1903–89
Austro-German zoologist

15 It is a good morning exercise for a research scientist to discard a pet hypothesis every day before breakfast. It keeps him young.

Das Sogenannte Böse (1963; translated by Marjorie Latzke as *On Aggression*, 1966) ch. 2

Louis XIV (the 'Sun King') 1638–1715
King of France from 1643

16 *L'État c'est moi.*

I am the State.

before the Parlement de Paris, 13 April 1655

probably apocryphal; J. A. Dulaure *Histoire de Paris* (1834) vol. 6

17 *J'ai failli attendre.*

I was nearly kept waiting.

attribution queried, among others, by E. Fournier in *L'Esprit dans l'Histoire* (1857) ch. 48

18 *Toutes les fois que je donne une place vacante, je fais cent mécontents et un ingrat.*

Every time I create an appointment, I create a hundred malcontents and one ingrate.

Voltaire *Siècle de Louis XIV* (1768 ed.) vol. 2, ch. 26

1 *Il n'y a plus de Pyrénées.*
The Pyrenees are no more.
on the accession of his grandson to the throne of Spain, 1700
attributed to Louis by Voltaire in *Siècle de Louis XIV* (1753) ch. 26, but to the Spanish Ambassador to France in the *Mercure Galant* (Paris) November 1700

2 It means I'm growing old when ladies declare war on me.
following the accession of Queen Anne, Britain declared war on France
Gila Curtis *The Life and Times of Queen Anne* (1972)

Louis XVI 1754–93

King of France from 1774; deposed in 1789 on the outbreak of the French Revolution and executed in 1793
see also **La Rochefoucauld-Liancourt** *453:23*

diary entry for 14 July 1789, the day of the storming of the Bastille:
3 *Rien.*
Nothing.
Simon Schama *Citizens* (1989) ch. 10

Louis XVIII 1755–1824

King of France from 1814; titular king from 1795

4 *Rappelez-vous bien qu'il n'est aucun de vous qui n'ait dans sa giberne le bâton de maréchal du duc de Reggio; c'est à vous à l'en faire sortir.*
Remember that there is not one of you who does not carry in his cartridge-pouch the marshal's baton of the duke of Reggio; it is up to you to bring it forth.
speech to Saint-Cyr cadets, 9 August 1819, in *Moniteur Universel* 10 August 1819

5 *L'exactitude est la politesse des rois.*
Punctuality is the politeness of kings.
attributed in *Souvenirs de J. Lafitte* (1844) bk. 1, ch. 3; cf. **Proverbs** 609:48

Louis Philippe 1773–1850

King of France 1830–48

6 Died, has he? Now I wonder what he meant by that?
of ***Talleyrand***
attributed, perhaps apocryphal

Joe Louis 1914–81

American boxer

7 He can run. But he can't hide.
of Billy Conn, his opponent, before a heavyweight title fight, 19 June 1946
Louis: My Life Story (1947)

Courtney Love 1965–

American rock singer, wife of Kurt ***Cobain***

8 When . . . you're first famous and you're flush with your influence and you say something whimsical, at a party or something to be cool, it gets reported for real.
interview in *Guardian* 28 February 1997

Ada Lovelace 1815–52

English mathematican, daughter of Lord ***Byron***

9 The Analytical Engine weaves algebraic patterns just as the Jacquard loom weaves flowers and leaves.
of ***Babbage****'s mechanical computer*
Luigi Menabrea *Sketch of the Analytical Engine invented by Charles Babbage* (1843), translated and annotated by Ada Lovelace, Note A

Richard Lovelace 1618–58

English poet

10 Lucasta that bright northern star.
'Amyntor from Beyond the Sea to Alexis' (1649)

11 Forbear, thou great good husband, little ant.
'The Ant' (1660)

12 When Love with unconfinèd wings
Hovers within my gates;
And my divine Althea brings
To whisper at the grates:
When I lie tangled in her hair,
And fettered to her eye;
The Gods, that wanton in the air
Know no such liberty.
'To Althea, From Prison' (1649)

13 When thirsty grief in wine we steep,
When healths and draughts go free,
Fishes, that tipple in the deep,
Know no such liberty.
'To Althea, From Prison' (1649)

14 Stone walls do not a prison make,
Nor iron bars a cage;
Minds innocent and quiet take
That for an hermitage.
If I have freedom in my love,
And in my soul am free;
Angels alone, that soar above,
Enjoy such liberty.
'To Althea, From Prison' (1649)

15 Tell me not, Sweet, I am unkind,
That from the nunnery
Of thy chaste breast, and quiet mind,
To war and arms I fly.
True; a new mistress now I chase,
The first foe in the field;
And with a stronger faith embrace
A sword, a horse, a shield.
'To Lucasta, Going to the Wars' (1649)

16 Yet this inconstancy is such,
As you too shall adore;
I could not love thee, Dear, so much,
Loved I not honour more.
'To Lucasta, Going to the Wars' (1649)

Bernard Lovell 1913–

British astronomer

17 The pursuit of the good and evil are now linked in astronomy as in almost all science . . . The fate of human civilization will depend on whether the

rockets of the future carry the astronomer's telescope or a hydrogen bomb.
The Individual and the Universe (1959)

1 Youth is vivid rather than happy, but memory always remembers the happy things.
in *The Times* 20 August 1993

James Lovell 1928–
American astronaut

2 Houston, we've had a problem.
on Apollo 13 space mission, 14 April 1970
in *The Times* 15 April 1970

Samuel Lover 1797–1868
Irish writer

3 When once the itch of literature comes over a man, nothing can cure it but the scratching of a pen.
Handy Andy (1842) ch. 36

4 Young Rory O'More courted Kathaleen bawn,
He was bold as a hawk, and she soft as the dawn.
'Rory O'More' (1837 song); cf. **Thurber** 777:2

David Low 1891–1963
British political cartoonist

5 Colonel Blimp.
Cartoon creation, proponent of reactionary establishment opinions

6 I have never met anyone who wasn't against war. Even Hitler and Mussolini were, according to themselves.
in *New York Times Magazine* 10 February 1946

Robert Lowe, Lord Sherbrooke 1811–92
British Liberal politician
on Lowe: see **Bright** *148:14*

7 I believe it will be absolutely necessary that you should prevail on our future masters to learn their letters.
on the passing of the Reform Bill, popularized as 'We must educate our masters'
speech, House of Commons, 15 July 1867

8 The Chancellor of the Exchequer is a man whose duties make him more or less of a taxing machine. He is intrusted with a certain amount of misery which it is his duty to distribute as fairly as he can.
speech, House of Commons, 11 April 1870

Amy Lowell 1874–1925
American poet

9 And the softness of my body will be guarded by embrace
By each button, hook, and lace.
For the man who should loose me is dead,
Fighting with the Duke in Flanders,
In a pattern called a war.
Christ! What are patterns for?
'Patterns' (1916)

10 All books are either dreams or swords,
You can cut, or you can drug, with words.
'Sword Blades and Poppy Seed' (1914); cf. **Farquhar** 307:19

James Russell Lowell 1819–91
American poet

11 An' you've gut to git up airly
Ef you want to take in God.
The Biglow Papers (First Series, 1848) no. 1 'A Letter'

12 We've a war, an' a debt, an' a flag; an' ef this
Ain't to be inderpendunt, why, wut on airth is?
The Biglow Papers (Second Series, 1867) no. 4 'A Message of Jeff. Davis in Secret Session'

13 There comes Poe with his raven like Barnaby Rudge,
Three-fifths of him genius, and two-fifths sheer fudge.
'A Fable for Critics' (1848) l. 1215; cf. **Poe** 579:15

14 Blessèd are the horny hands of toil!
'A Glance Behind the Curtain' (1844); cf. **Salisbury** 643:1

15 Once to every man and nation comes the moment to decide,
In the strife of Truth with Falsehood, for the good or evil side.
'The Present Crisis' (1845)

16 Truth forever on the scaffold, Wrong forever on the throne,—
Yet that scaffold sways the future, and, behind the dim unknown,
Standeth God within the shadow, keeping watch above his own.
'The Present Crisis' (1845)

17 May is a pious fraud of the almanac.
'Under the Willows' (1869) l. 21

18 There is no good in arguing with the inevitable. The only argument available with an east wind is to put on your overcoat.
Democracy and other Addresses (1887) 'Democracy'

Robert Lowell 1917–77
American poet

19 My eyes have seen what my hand did.
'Dolphin' (1973)

20 Terrible that old life of decency
without unseemly intimacy
or quarrels, when the unemancipated woman
still had her Freudian papa and maids!
'During Fever' (1959)

21 The aquarium is gone. Everywhere,
giant finned cars nose forward like fish;
a savage servility
slides by on grease.
'For the Union Dead' (1964)

22 Their monument sticks like a fishbone
in the city's throat.
'For the Union Dead' (1964)

23 These are the tranquillized *Fifties*,
and I am forty. Ought I to regret my seed-time?
'Memories of West Street and Lepke' (1956)

1 At forty-five,
What next, what next?
At every corner,
I meet my Father,
my age, still alive.
'Middle Age' (1964)

2 I saw the spiders marching through the air,
Swimming from tree to tree that mildewed day
In latter August when the hay
Came creaking to the barn.
'Mr Edwards and the Spider' (1950); cf. **Edwards** 289:9

3 This is death.
To die and know it. This is the Black Widow, death.
'Mr Edwards and the Spider' (1950)

4 The Lord survives the rainbow of His will.
'The Quaker Graveyard in Nantucket' (1950)

5 If we see light at the end of the tunnel,
It's the light of the oncoming train.
'Since 1939' (1977); cf. **Dickson** 267:1

6 But I suppose even God was born
too late to trust the old religion.
'Tenth Muse' (1964)

7 None of the wilder subtleties
of grace or art will sweeten these
stiff quatrains shovelled out four-square.
of hymns as contrasted with poetry and the Bible
'Waking Early Sunday Morning' (1967)

8 Folly comes from something—
the present, yes,
we are in it,
it's the infection
of things gone.
'We Took Our Paradise' (1977)

William Lowndes 1652–1724
English politician

9 Take care of the pence, and the pounds will take care of themselves.
Lord Chesterfield *Letters to his Son* (1774) 5 February 1750 ('*for* the pounds . . .' in an earlier letter, 6 November 1747); cf. **Carroll** 190:1, **Chesterfield** 209:12, **Proverbs** 611:38

L. S. Lowry 1887–1976
English painter

10 I'm a simple man, and I use simple materials.
Mervyn Levy *Paintings of L. S. Lowry* (1975)

Malcolm Lowry 1909–57
English novelist

11 How alike are the groans of love to those of the dying.
Under the Volcano (1947) ch. 12

Mina Loy d. 1966
American poet

12 [Be] *Brave* and deny at the outset—that pathetic clap-trap war cry *Woman is the equal of man* for She is NOT! . . . Leave off looking to men to find out what you are *not*—Seek within yourselves to find out what you *are*.
'Feminist Manifesto' (1914, unpublished) in Virginia M. Kovidis *Mina Loy* (1980)

Lucan (Marcus Annaeus Lucanus) AD 39–65
Roman poet

13 *Quis iustius induit arma*
Scire nefas, magno se iudice quisque tuetur:
Victrix causa deis placuit, sed victa Catoni.
It is not granted to know which man took up arms with more right on his side. Each pleads his cause before a great judge: the winning cause pleased the gods, but the losing one pleased Cato.
Pharsalia bk. 1, l. 128

14 *Stat magni nominis umbra.*
There stands the ghost of a great name.
of Pompey
Pharsalia bk. 1, l. 135

15 *Nil actum credens, dum quid superesset agendum.*
Thinking nothing done while anything remained to be done.
Pharsalia bk. 2, l. 657; cf. **Rogers** 631:12

16 *Coniunx*
Est mihi, sunt nati: dedimus tot pignora fatis.
I have a wife, I have sons: we have given so many hostages to the fates.
Pharsalia bk. 6, l. 661; cf. **Bacon** 43:17

17 *Jupiter est quodcumque vides, quocumque moveris.*
Jupiter is whatever you see, whichever way you move.
Pharsalia bk. 9, l. 580

George Lucas see **Film lines** 311:23, **Film titles** 312:19

Clare Booth Luce 1903–87
American diplomat, politician, and writer

18 Much of . . . his global thinking is, no matter how you slice it, still globaloney.
speech to the House of Representatives, February 1943

19 But if God had wanted us to think just with our wombs, why did He give us a brain?
in *Life* 16 October 1970

Lucilius (Gaius Lucilius) *c.*180–102 BC
Latin poet

20 *Maior erat natu; non omnia possumus omnes.*
He was greater in years; we cannot all do everything.
Macrobius *Saturnalia* bk. 6, ch. 1, sect. 35; cf. **Virgil** 796:10

Lucretius (Titus Lucretius Carus) *c.*94–55 BC
Roman poet
on Lucretius: see **Virgil** *796:18*

21 *Ergo vivida vis animi pervicit, et extra*
Processit longe flammantia moenia mundi
Atque omne immensum peragravit, mente animoque.

So the vital strength of his spirit won through, and he made his way far outside the flaming walls of the world and ranged over the measureless whole, both in mind and spirit.
De Rerum Natura bk. 1, l. 72 (on Epicurus)

1 *Tantum religio potuit suadere malorum.*

So much wrong could religion induce.
De Rerum Natura bk. 1, l. 101

2 *. . . Nil posse creari*
De nilo.

Nothing can be created out of nothing.
De Rerum Natura bk. 1, l. 155

3 *Suave, mari magno turbantibus aequora ventis,*
E terra magnum alterius spectare laborem.
Non quia vexari quemquamst iucunda voluptas,
Sed quibus ipse malis careas quia cernere suave est.
Suave etiam belli certamina magna tueri
Per campos instructa tua sine parte pericli.
Sed nil dulcius est, bene quam munita tenere
Edita doctrina sapientum templa serena,
Despicere unde queas alios passimque videre
Errare atque viam palantis quaerere vitae,
Certare ingenio, contendere nobilitate,
Noctes atque dies niti praestante labore
Ad summas emergere opes rerumque potiri.

Lovely it is, when the winds are churning up the waves on the great sea, to gaze out from the land on the great efforts of someone else; not because it's an enjoyable pleasure that somebody is in difficulties, but because it's lovely to realize what troubles you are yourself spared. Lovely also to witness great battle-plans of war, carried out across the plains, without your having any share in the danger. But nothing is sweeter than to occupy the quiet precincts that are well protected by the teachings of the wise, from where you can look down on others and see them wandering all over the place, getting lost and striving as they seek the way in life, striving by their wits, pitting their noble birth, by night and by day struggling by superior efforts to rise to power at the top and gain possession of all things.
De Rerum Natura bk. 2, l. 1

4 *Augescunt aliae gentes, aliae minuuntur,*
Inque brevi spatio mutantur saecla animantum
Et quasi cursores vitai lampada tradunt.

Some races increase, others are reduced, and in a short while the generations of living creatures are changed and like runners relay the torch of life.
De Rerum Natura bk. 2, l. 8

5 *Nil igitur mors est ad nos neque pertinet hilum,*
Quandoquidem natura animi mortalis habetur.

Death therefore is nothing to us nor does it concern us a scrap, seeing that the nature of the spirit we possess is something mortal.
De Rerum Natura bk. 3, l. 830

6 *Vitaque mancipio, nulli datur, omnibus usu.*

And life is given to none freehold, but it is leasehold for all.
De Rerum Natura bk. 3, l. 971

7 *Scire licet nobis nil esse in morte timendum*
Nec miserum fieri qui non est posse neque hilum
Differre an nullo fuerit iam tempore natus,
Mortalem vitam mors cum immortalis ademit.

We can know there is nothing to be feared in death, that one who is not cannot be made unhappy, and that it matters not a scrap whether one might ever have been born at all, when death that is immortal has taken over one's mortal life.
De Rerum Natura bk. 3, l. 866

8 *Cur non ut plenus vitae conviva recedis*
Aequo animoque capis securam, stulte, quietem?

Why not, like a banqueter fed full of life, withdraw with contentment and rest in peace, you fool?
De Rerum Natura bk. 3, l. 938

9 *Medio de fonte leporum*
Surgit amari aliquid quod in ipsis floribus angat.

From the midst of the fountain of delights rises something bitter that chokes them all amongst the flowers.
De Rerum Natura bk. 4, l. 1133

Fray Luis de León c.1527–91

Spanish poet and religious writer

10 *Que descansada vida*
la del que huye el mundanal ruido,
y sigue la escondida
senda, por donde han ido
los pocos sabios que en el mundo han sido!

What a relaxed life is that which flees the worldly clamour, and follows the hidden path down which have gone the few wise men there have been in the world!
'Vida Retirada'

11 *Dicebamus hesterno die . . .*

We were saying yesterday . . .
on resuming a lecture at Salamanca University in 1577, after five years' imprisonment
attributed, among others, by A. F. G. Bell in *Luis de León* (1925) ch. 8

Martin Luther 1483–1546

German Protestant theologian
on Luther: see ***Arnold*** *29:4*

12 *Esto peccator et pecca fortiter, sed fortius fide et gaude in Christo.*

Be a sinner and sin strongly, but more strongly have faith and rejoice in Christ.
letter to Melanchthon, 1521, in *Epistolae* (Jena, 1556) vol. 1, folio 345 verso

13 Here stand I. I can do no other. God help me. Amen.
speech at the Diet of Worms, 18 April 1521; attributed

14 If I had heard that as many devils would set on me in Worms as there are tiles on the roofs, I should none the less have ridden there.
to the Princes of Saxony, 21 August 1524, in *Sämmtliche Schriften* vol. 16 (1745) ch. 10, sect. 1, no. 763:15

1 For, where God built a church, there the devil would also build a chapel . . . In such sort is the devil always God's ape.
Colloquia Mensalia (1566) ch. 2 (translated by H. Bell as *Martin Luther's Divine Discourses*, 1652); cf. **Proverbs** 614:36

2 *Eine feste Burg ist unser Gott,*
Ein gute Wehr und Waffen.
A safe stronghold our God is still,
A trusty shield and weapon.
'Eine feste Burg ist unser Gott' (1529); translated by Thomas Carlyle

3 The confidence and faith of the heart alone make both God and an idol.
Large Catechism (1529) 'The First Commandment'

4 Whatever your heart clings to and confides in, that is really your God.
Large Catechism (1529) 'The First Commandment'

5 So our Lord God commonly gives riches to those gross asses to whom He vouchsafes nothing else.
Tischreden oder Colloquia (collected by J. Aurifaber, 1566) ch. 4

6 *Wer nicht liebt Wein, Weib und Gesang,*
Der bleibt ein Narr sein Leben lang.
Who loves not woman, wine, and song
Remains a fool his whole life long.
attributed (later inscribed in the Luther room in the Wartburg, but with no proof of authorship)

Edwin Lutyens 1869–1944
English architect

7 There will never be great architects or great architecture without great patrons.
in *Country Life* 8 May 1915

Rosa Luxemburg 1871–1919
German revolutionary

8 *Freiheit ist immer nur Freiheit des anders Denkenden.*
Freedom is always and exclusively freedom for the one who thinks differently.
Die Russische Revolution (1918) sect. 4

John Lydgate c.1370–c.1451
English poet

9 Sithe off oure language he was the lodesterre.
of ***Chaucer***
The Fall of Princes (1431–8) prologue l. 252

10 Comparisouns doon offte gret greuaunce.
The Fall of Princes (1431–8) bk. 3, l. 2188

11 Woord is but wynd; leff woord and tak the dede.
Secrets of Old Philosophers l. 1224

12 Love is mor than gold or gret richesse.
The Story of Thebes pt. 3, l. 2716

John Lyly c.1554–1606
English poet and dramatist

13 CAMPASPE: Were women never so fair, men would be false.
APELLES: Were women never so false, men would be fond.
Campaspe (1584) act 3, sc. 3

14 Cupid and my Campaspe played
At cards for kisses, Cupid paid.
Campaspe (1584) act 3, sc. 5

15 At last he set her both his eyes;
She won, and Cupid blind did rise.
O Love! has she done this to thee?
What shall, alas! become of me?
Campaspe (1584) act 3, sc. 5

16 What bird so sings, yet so does wail?
O 'tis the ravished nightingale.
Jug, jug, jug, jug, tereu, she cries,
And still her woes at midnight rise.
Campaspe (1584) act 5, sc. 1; cf. **Eliot** 296:3

17 Night hath a thousand eyes.
The Maydes Metamorphosis (1600) act 3, sc. 1

18 If all the earth were paper white
And all the sea were ink
'Twere not enough for me to write
As my poor heart doth think.
'If all the earth were paper white'

Jack Lynch 1917–
Irish statesman, Taoiseach 1966–73, 1977–9

19 I have never and never will accept the right of a minority who happen to be a majority in a small part of the country to opt out of a nation.
in *Irish Times* 14 November 1970 'This Week They Said'

Lord Lyndhurst 1772–1863
English politician and lawyer; three times Lord Chancellor

20 Campbell has added another terror to death.
on Lord Campbell's Lives of the Lord Chancellors *being written without the consent of heirs or executors*
E. Bowen-Rowlands *Seventy-Two Years At the Bar* (1924) ch. 10; cf. **Arbuthnot** 23:16, **Tree** 781:6, **Wetherell** 812:22

Jonathan Lynn 1943– and Antony Jay 1930–
English writers

21 I think it will be a clash between the political will and the administrative won't.
Yes Prime Minister (1987) vol. 2

Lysander d. 395 BC
Spartan naval commander

22 Deceive boys with toys, but men with oaths.
Plutarch *Parallel Lives* 'Lysander' ch. 8; cf. **Plutarch** 579:9

Henry Francis Lyte 1793–1847
Perpetual curate of Lower Brixham, Devon, from 1823

23 Abide with me: fast falls the eventide;
The darkness deepens; Lord, with me abide:
When other helpers fail, and comforts flee,
Help of the helpless, O abide with me.
Swift to its close ebbs out life's little day;

Earth's joys grow dim, its glories pass away;
Change and decay in all around I see;
O Thou, who changest not, abide with me.
'Abide with Me' (probably written in 1847); cf. **Bible** 100:33

1 Praise my soul, the King of heaven;
To his feet thy tribute bring.
Ransomed, healed, restored, forgiven,
Who like me his praise should sing?
'Praise, my soul, the King of heaven' (1834 hymn)

2 Father-like, he tends and spares us.
'Praise, my soul, the King of heaven' (1834 hymn)

George Lyttelton, Lord Lyttelton 1709–73
English politician and man of letters

3 Seek to be good, but aim not to be great;
A woman's noblest station is retreat.
'Advice to a Lady' (1773)

E. R. Bulwer, Lord Lytton see Owen Meredith

Mary McAleese 1951–
Irish stateswoman; President from 1997

4 Apart from the shamrock, the President should not wear emblems or symbols of any kind.
deciding not to wear a poppy at her inauguration on 11 November 1997
in *Guardian* 6 November 1997

Douglas MacArthur 1880–1964
American general

5 I came through and I shall return.
on reaching Australia, 20 March 1942, having broken through Japanese lines en route from Corregidor
in *New York Times* 21 March 1942

6 In war, indeed, there can be no substitute for victory.
in *Congressional Record* 19 April 1951, vol. 97, pt. 3

Rose Macaulay 1881–1958
English novelist
see also ***Opening lines*** *556:19*

7 Love's a disease. But curable.
Crewe Train (1926)

Thomas Babington Macaulay 1800–59
English politician and historian
on Macaulay: see ***Arnold*** *28:19,* ***Carlyle*** *188:20,* ***Smith*** *725:20*

8 In order that he might rob a neighbour whom he had promised to defend, black men fought on the coast of Coromandel, and red men scalped each other by the Great Lakes of North America.
Biographical Essays (1857) 'Frederic the Great'

9 The gallery in which the reporters sit has become a fourth estate of the realm.
Essays Contributed to the Edinburgh Review (1843) vol. 1 'Hallam'

10 He knew that the essence of war is violence, and that moderation in war is imbecility.
Essays Contributed to the Edinburgh Review (1843) vol. 1 'John Hampden'

11 Homer is not more decidedly the first of heroic poets, Shakespeare is not more decidedly the first of dramatists, Demosthenes is not more decidedly the first of orators, than Boswell is the first of biographers.
Essays Contributed to the Edinburgh Review (1843) vol. 1 'Samuel Johnson'

12 They knew luxury; they knew beggary; but they never knew comfort.
of writers struggling to make a living in ***Johnson****'s day*
Essays Contributed to the Edinburgh Review (1843) vol. 1 'Samuel Johnson'

13 The gigantic body, the huge massy face, seamed with the scars of disease, the brown coat, the black worsted stockings, the grey wig with the scorched foretop, the dirty hands, the nails bitten and pared to the quick.
Essays Contributed to the Edinburgh Review (1843) vol. 1 'Samuel Johnson'

14 Out of his surname they have coined an epithet for a knave, and out of his Christian name a synonym for the Devil.
Essays Contributed to the Edinburgh Review (1843) vol. 1 'Machiavelli'

15 As civilization advances, poetry almost necessarily declines.
Essays Contributed to the Edinburgh Review (1843) vol. 1 'Milton'

16 If men are to wait for liberty till they become wise and good in slavery, they may indeed wait for ever.
Essays Contributed to the Edinburgh Review (1843) vol. 1 'Milton'

17 They esteemed themselves rich in a more precious treasure, and eloquent in a more sublime language, nobles by the right of an earlier creation, and priests by the imposition of a mightier hand.
of the Puritans
Essays Contributed to the Edinburgh Review (1843) vol. 1 'Milton'

18 We know no spectacle so ridiculous as the British public in one of its periodical fits of morality.
Essays Contributed to the Edinburgh Review (1843) vol. 1 'Moore's *Life of Lord Byron*'

19 We have heard it said that five per cent is the natural interest of money.
Essays Contributed to the Edinburgh Review (1843) vol. 1 'Southey's Colloquies'

20 With the dead there is no rivalry. In the dead there is no change. Plato is never sullen. Cervantes is never petulant. Demosthenes never comes unseasonably. Dante never stays too long. No difference of political opinion can alienate Cicero. No heresy can excite the horror of Bossuet.
Essays Contributed to the Edinburgh Review (1843) vol. 2 'Lord Bacon'

1 An acre in Middlesex is better than a principality in Utopia.
Essays Contributed to the Edinburgh Review (1843) vol. 2 'Lord Bacon'

2 The highest intellects, like the tops of mountains, are the first to catch and to reflect the dawn.
Essays Contributed to the Edinburgh Review (1843) vol. 2 'Sir James Mackintosh'

3 The history of England is emphatically the history of progress.
Essays Contributed to the Edinburgh Review (1843) vol. 2 'Sir James Mackintosh'

4 Biographers, translators, editors, all, in short, who employ themselves in illustrating the lives or writings of others, are peculiarly exposed to the *Lues Boswelliana*, or disease of admiration.
Essays Contributed to the Edinburgh Review (1843) vol. 2 'William Pitt, Earl of Chatham'

5 On the day of the accession of George the Third, the ascendancy of the Whig party terminated; and on that day the purification of the Whig party began.
Essays Contributed to the Edinburgh Review (1843) vol. 2 'William Pitt, Earl of Chatham'

6 The conformation of his mind was such that whatever was little seemed to him great, and whatever was great seemed to him little.
Essays Contributed to the Edinburgh Review (1843) vol. 2 'Horace Walpole'

7 Every schoolboy knows who imprisoned Montezuma, and who strangled Atahualpa.
Essays Contributed to the Edinburgh Review (1843) vol. 3 'Lord Clive'; cf. **Taylor** 756:18

8 The Chief Justice was rich, quiet, and infamous.
Essays Contributed to the Edinburgh Review (1843) vol. 3 'Warren Hastings'

9 That temple of silence and reconciliation where the enmities of twenty generations lie buried.
of Westminster Abbey
Essays Contributed to the Edinburgh Review (1843) vol. 3 'Warren Hastings'

10 She [the Roman Catholic Church] may still exist in undiminished vigour when some traveller from New Zealand shall, in the midst of a vast solitude, take his stand on a broken arch of London Bridge to sketch the ruins of St Paul's.
Essays Contributed to the Edinburgh Review (1843) vol. 3 'Von Ranke'; cf. **Walpole** 801:3

11 She [the Church of Rome] thoroughly understands what no other church has ever understood, how to deal with enthusiasts.
Essays Contributed to the Edinburgh Review (1843) vol. 3 'Von Ranke'

12 Persecution produced its natural effect on them [Puritans and Calvinists]. It found them a sect; it made them a faction.
History of England vol. 1 (1849) ch. 1

13 It was a crime in a child to read by the bedside of a sick parent one of those beautiful collects which had soothed the griefs of forty generations of Christians.
History of England vol. 1 (1849) ch. 2

14 The Puritan hated bear-baiting, not because it gave pain to the bear, but because it gave pleasure to the spectators.
History of England vol. 1 (1849) ch. 2

15 The English Bible, a book which, if everything else in our language should perish, would alone suffice to show the whole extent of its beauty and power.
T. F. Ellis (ed.) *Miscellaneous Writings of Lord Macaulay* (1860) 'John Dryden' (1828)

16 His imagination resembled the wings of an ostrich. It enabled him to run, though not to soar.
T. F. Ellis (ed.) *Miscellaneous Writings of Lord Macaulay* (1860) 'John Dryden' (1828)

17 This province of literature is a debatable line. It lies on the confines of two distinct territories . . . It is sometimes fiction. It is sometimes theory.
of history
T. F. Ellis (ed.) *Miscellaneous Writings of Lord Macaulay* (1860) vol. 1 'History' (1828)

18 The rugged miners poured to war from Mendip's
sunless caves.
'The Armada' (1833)

19 Till Skiddaw saw the fire that burned on Gaunt's
embattled pile,
And the red glare on Skiddaw roused the burghers
of Carlisle.
'The Armada' (1833)

20 Obadiah Bind-their-kings-in-chains-and-their-nobles-with-links-of-iron.
'The Battle of Naseby' (1824) fictitious author's name; cf. **Book of Common Prayer** 142:2

21 Oh, wherefore come ye forth in triumph from the
north,
With your hands, and your feet, and your raiment
all red?
And wherefore doth your rout send forth a joyous
shout?
And whence be the grapes of the wine-press which
ye tread?
'The Battle of Naseby' (1824)

22 And the Man of Blood was there, with his long
essenced hair,
And Astley, and Sir Marmaduke, and Rupert of the
Rhine.
'The Battle of Naseby' (1824)

23 For him I languished in a foreign clime,
Grey-haired with sorrow in my manhood's prime;
Heard on Lavernia Scargill's whispering trees,
And pined by Arno for my lovelier Tees.
'A Jacobite's Epitaph' (1845)

24 By those white cliffs I never more must see,
By that dear language which I spake like thee,
Forget all feuds, and shed one English tear
O'er English dust. A broken heart lies here.
'A Jacobite's Epitaph' (1845)

25 Gay are the Martian Calends:
December's Nones are gay:
But the proud Ides, when the squadron rides,
Shall be Rome's whitest day!
Lays of Ancient Rome (1842) 'The Battle of Lake Regillus' st. 1

1 From where the Witch's fortress
O'er hangs the dark blue seas,
From the still glassy lake that sleeps
Beneath Aricia's trees—
Those trees in whose grim shadow
The ghastly priest doth reign,
The priest who slew the slayer,
And shall himself be slain.
Lays of Ancient Rome (1842) 'The Battle of Lake Regillus' st. 10

2 Let no man stop to plunder,
But slay, and slay, and slay;
The Gods who live for ever
Are on our side to-day.
Lays of Ancient Rome (1842) 'The Battle of Lake Regillus' st. 35

3 Lars Porsena of Clusium
By the nine gods he swore
That the great house of Tarquin
Should suffer wrong no more.
Lays of Ancient Rome (1842) 'Horatius' st. 1

4 The harvests of Arretium,
This year, old men shall reap.
This year, young boys in Umbro
Shall plunge the struggling sheep;
And in the vats of Luna,
This year, the must shall foam
Round the white feet of laughing girls
Whose sires have marched to Rome.
Lays of Ancient Rome (1842) 'Horatius' st. 8

5 And how can man die better
Than facing fearful odds,
For the ashes of his fathers,
And the temples of his Gods?
Lays of Ancient Rome (1842) 'Horatius' st. 27

6 Now who will stand on either hand,
And keep the bridge with me?
Lays of Ancient Rome (1842) 'Horatius' st. 29

7 Then none was for a party;
Then all were for the state;
Then the great man helped the poor,
And the poor man loved the great:
Then lands were fairly portioned;
Then spoils were fairly sold:
The Romans were like brothers
In the brave days of old.
Lays of Ancient Rome (1842) 'Horatius' st. 32

8 But hark! the cry is Astur
And lo! the ranks divide,
And the great Lord of Luna
Comes with his stately stride.
Lays of Ancient Rome (1842) 'Horatius' st. 42

9 Was none who would be foremost
To lead such dire attack;
But those behind cried 'Forward!'
And those before cried 'Back!'
Lays of Ancient Rome (1842) 'Horatius' st. 50

10 Oh, Tiber! father Tiber
To whom the Romans pray,
A Roman's life, a Roman's arms,
Take thou in charge this day!
Lays of Ancient Rome (1842) 'Horatius' st. 59

11 And even the ranks of Tuscany
Could scarce forbear to cheer.
Lays of Ancient Rome (1842) 'Horatius' st. 60

12 With weeping and with laughter
Still is the story told,
How well Horatius kept the bridge
In the brave days of old.
Lays of Ancient Rome (1842) 'Horatius' st. 70

13 On the left side goes Remus,
With wrists and fingers red,
And in his hand a boar-spear,
And on the point a head—
A wrinkled head and aged,
With silver beard and hair,
And holy fillets round it,
Such as the pontiffs wear—
The head of ancient Camers,
Who spoke the words of doom:
'The children to the Tiber,
The mother to the tomb.'
Lays of Ancient Rome (1842) 'The Prophecy of Capys'

14 Thank you, madam, the agony is abated.
aged four, having had hot coffee spilt over his legs
G. O. Trevelyan *Life and Letters of Lord Macaulay* (1876) ch. 1

15 We must at present do our best to form a class who may be interpreters between us and the millions whom we govern; a class of persons, Indian in blood and colour, but English in taste, in opinions, in morals, and in intellect.
minute, as Member of Supreme Council of India, 2 February 1835, in W. Nassan Lees *Indian Musalmàns* (1871)

16 How odd that people of sense should find any pleasure in being accompanied by a beast who is always spoiling conversation.
of dogs
G. O. Trevelyan *Life and Letters of Macaulay* (1876) ch. 14

Anthony McAuliffe 1898–1975
American general

17 Nuts!
replying to the German demand for surrender at Bastogne, Belgium, 22 December 1944
in *New York Times* 28 December 1944

Norman McCaig 1910–96
Scottish poet

18 Who owns this landscape?
The millionaire who bought it or
the poacher staggering downhill in the early
morning
with a deer on his back?
'A Man in Assynt' (1969)

Joseph McCarthy 1908–57
American politician and anti-Communist agitator

19 I have here in my hand a list of two hundred and five [people] that were known to the Secretary of

State as being members of the Communist Party and who nevertheless are still working and shaping the policy of the State Department.
speech at Wheeling, West Virginia, 9 February 1950

1 McCarthyism is Americanism with its sleeves rolled.
speech in Wisconsin, 1952, in Richard Rovere *Senator Joe McCarthy* (1973)

Mary McCarthy 1912–89
American novelist

2 Europe is the unfinished negative of which America is the proof.
On the Contrary (1961) 'America the Beautiful'

3 If someone tells you he is going to make a 'realistic decision', you immediately understand that he has resolved to do something bad.
On the Contrary (1961) 'American Realist Playwrights'

4 Every word she writes is a lie, including 'and' and 'the'.
on Lillian ***Hellman***
in *New York Times* 16 February 1980

Paul McCartney 1942–
English pop singer and songwriter
see also ***Lennon and McCartney***

5 Ballads and babies. That's what happened to me.
on reaching the age of fifty
in *Time* 8 June 1992

6 You cannot reheat a soufflé.
discounting rumours of a Beatles reunion
attributed; L. Botts *Loose Talk* (1980)

George B. McClellan 1826–85
American soldier and politician

7 All quiet along the Potomac.
said at the time of the American Civil War
attributed; cf. **Beers** 61:18

Ewen MacColl 1915–89
English folksinger and songwriter

8 I found my love by the gasworks crofts
Dreamed a dream by the old canal
Kissed my girl by the factory wall
Dirty old town, dirty old town.
'Dirty Old Town' (1950 song)

9 And I used to sleep standing on my feet
As we hunted for the shoals of herring.
'The Shoals of Herring' (1960 song, from the BBC Radio broadcast *Singing the Fishing*)

David McCord 1897–

10 By and by
God caught his eye.
'Remainders' (1935); epitaph for a waiter

Horace McCoy 1897–1955
American novelist

11 They shoot horses don't they.
title of novel (1935)

John McCrae 1872–1918
Canadian poet and military physician

12 In Flanders fields the poppies blow
Between the crosses, row on row,
That mark our place; and in the sky
The larks, still bravely singing, fly
Scarce heard amid the guns below.
'In Flanders Fields' (1915)

13 To you from failing hands we throw
The torch; be yours to hold it high.
If ye break faith with us who die
We shall not sleep, though poppies grow.
In Flanders fields.
'In Flanders Fields' (1915)

Hugh MacDiarmid (Christopher Murray Grieve) 1892–1978
Scottish poet and nationalist

14 Scotland small? Our multiform, our infinite
Scotland *small*?
Only as a patch of hillside may be a cliché corner
To a fool who cries 'Nothing but heather!' . . .
Direadh 1 (1974)

15 I'll ha'e nae hauf-way hoose, but aye be whaur
Extremes meet—it's the only way I ken
To dodge the curst conceit o' bein' richt
That damns the vast majority o' men.
A Drunk Man Looks at the Thistle (1926)

16 He's no a man ava',
And lacks a proper pride,
Gin less than a' the world
Can ser' him for a bride!
A Drunk Man Looks at the Thistle (1926)

17 Hold a glass of pure water to the eye of the sun!
. . . This is the nearest analogy to the essence of human life
Which is even more difficult to see.
Dismiss anything you can see more easily;
It is not alive—it is not worth seeing.
'The Glass of Pure Water' (1962)

18 The rose of all the world is not for me.
I want for my part
Only the little white rose of Scotland
That smells sharp and sweet—and breaks the heart.
'The Little White Rose' (1934)

Dwight Macdonald 1906–82
American writer and film critic

19 Götterdämmerung without the gods.
of the use of atomic bombs against the Japanese
in *Politics* September 1945 'The Bomb'

George MacDonald 1824–1905
Scottish writer and poet
see also ***Epitaphs*** *302:13*

20 Where did you come from, baby dear?
Out of the everywhere into here.
At the Back of the North Wind (1871) ch. 33 'Song'

Ramsay MacDonald 1866–1937

British Labour statesman; Prime Minister, 1924, 1931–5

on MacDonald: see **Churchill** 215:2, **Lloyd George** 471:9, **Nicolson** 545:1

1 We hear war called murder. It is not: it is suicide.
in *Observer* 4 May 1930

2 Tomorrow every Duchess in London will be wanting to kiss me!
after forming the National Government, 25 August 1931
Viscount Snowden *An Autobiography* (1934) vol. 2

Trevor McDonald 1939–

West Indian-born broadcaster

3 I am a West Indian peasant who has drifted into this business and who has survived. If I knew the secret, I would bottle it and sell it.
in *Independent* 20 April 1996 'Quote Unquote'

A. G. MacDonell 1889–1941

Scottish writer

4 England, their England.
title of novel (1933); cf. **Henley** 370:1

Neil McElroy

American businessman; pioneer of soap operas

5 The problem of improving literary taste is one for the schools. Soap operas sell lots of soap.
attributed; Katie Hafner and Matthew Lyon *Where Wizards Stay Up Late: the Origins of the Internet* (1996)

Ian McEwan 1948–

English novelist

6 Shakespeare would have grasped wave functions, Donne would have understood complementarity and relative time. They would have been excited. What richness! They would have plundered this new science for their imagery. And they would have educated their audiences too. But you 'arts' people, you're not only ignorant of these magnificent things, you're rather proud of knowing nothing.
The Child in Time (1987) ch. 2

William McGonagall *c.*1825–1902

Scottish writer of doggerel

7 Beautiful Railway Bridge of the Silv'ry Tay!
Alas, I am very sorry to say
That ninety lives have been taken away
On the last Sabbath day of 1879,
Which will be remembered for a very long time.
'The Tay Bridge Disaster'

Patrick McGoohan 1928–

American actor,

George Markstein, and David Tomblin

8 I am not a number, I am a free man!
Number Six, in *The Prisoner* (TV series 1967–68); additional title sequence from the second episode onwards

Roger McGough 1937–

English poet

9 You will put on a dress of guilt
and shoes with broken high ideals.
'Comeclose and Sleepnow' (1967)

10 Let me die a youngman's death
Not a clean & in-between-
The-sheets, holy-water death,
Not a famous-last-words
Peaceful out-of-breath death.
'Let Me Die a Youngman's Death' (1967)

11 And though poets I admire have published poems
Whose imperfections reflect our own decay,
I could never begin a poem; 'When I am dead'
In case it tempted Fate, and Fate gave way.
'When I am Dead' (1982)

Jimmie McGregor 1932–

Scottish singer and songwriter

12 Oh, he's football crazy, he's football mad
And the football it has robbed him o' the wee bit sense he had.
And it would take a dozen skivvies, his clothes to wash and scrub,
Since our Jock became a member of that terrible football club.
'Football Crazy' (1960 song)

Niccolò Machiavelli 1469–1527

Florentine statesman and political philosopher

on Machiavelli: see **Macaulay** 481:14

13 *E seppure qualche volta è necessario nascondere con le parole una cosa, bisogna farlo in modo o che non appaia, o apparendo, sia parata e prestala difesa.*
If . . . sometimes you need to conceal a fact with words, do it in such a way that it does not become known, or, if it does become known, that you have a ready and quick defence.
'Advice to Raffaello Girolami when he went as Ambassador to the Emperor' (October 1522) in *Machiavelli: The Chief Works and Others* (translated by Allan Gilbert, 1965)

14 *È necessario a chi dispone una republica, ed ordina leggi in quella, prassuppoie tutti gli nomini rei, e che li abbiano sempre a usare la malignità dello animo loro, qualunque volta ne abbiano libera occasione.*
It is necessary for him who lays out a state and arranges laws for it to presuppose that all men are evil and that they are always going to act according to the wickedness of their spirits whenever they have free scope.
Discourse upon the First Ten Books of Livy (written 1513–17) bk. 1, ch. 3 (translated by Allan Gilbert)

15 *Gli nomini si debbano o vezzeggiate o peguere; perchè si vendiciano delle leggieri offese, delle gravi non possono.*
Men should be either treated generously or destroyed, because they take revenge for slight injuries—for heavy ones they cannot.
The Prince (written 1513) ch. 3 (translated by Allan Gilbert)

16 *Nasce da questo una disputa: s'egli è meglio essere amato che temuto, o è converso. Rispondesi che si*

voiebbe essere l'uno e l'altro; ma perche egli è difficile accozzarli insieme, è molto più sicuro essere temuto che amato, quando si abbia a mancare dell'uno de'due.

This leads to a debate: is it better to be loved than feared, or the reverse? The answer is that it is desirable to be both, but because it is difficult to join them together, it is much safer for a prince to be feared than loved, if he is to fail in one of the two.

The Prince (written 1513) ch. 8 (translated by Allan Gilbert)

1 *E non sia alcuno che repugni a questa mia opinione con quello proverbio trito, che chi fonda in sul popolo, fonda in sul fango.*

Let no one oppose this belief of mine with that well-worn proverb: 'He who builds on the people builds on mud.'

The Prince (written 1513) ch. 9 (translated by Allan Gilbert)

2 *Uno principe necessitato sapere bene usare la bestia, debbe di quelle pigliare la golpe e il lione; perchè il lione non si defende da' lupi. Bisogna, adunque, essere golpe a conoscere e' lacci, e lione a sbigottire e' lupi.*

Since, then, a prince is necessitated to play the animal well, he chooses among the beasts the fox and the lion, because the lion does not protect himself from traps; the fox does not protect himself from wolves. The prince must be a fox, therefore, to recognize the traps and a lion to frighten the wolves.

The Prince (written 1513) ch. 18 (translated by Allan Gilbert)

3 *Qualunque volta alle universalità degli nomini non si toglie nè roba nè onore, vivono contenti.*

So long as the great majority of men are not deprived of either property or honour, they are satisfied.

The Prince (written 1513) ch. 19 (translated by Allan Gilbert)

4 *Non ci è altro modo a guardarsi dalle adulazioni, se non che gli nomini intendino che non ti offendino a dirti el vero; ma quando ciascuno può dirti el vero, ti manca la reverenzia.*

There is no other way for securing yourself against flatteries except that men understand that they do not offend you by telling you the truth; but when everybody can tell you the truth, you fail to get respect.

The Prince (written 1513) ch. 23 (translated by Allan Gilbert)

Jay McInerney 1955–

American writer

5 A party is like a marriage . . . making itself up while seeming to follow precedent, running on steel rails into uncharted wilderness while the promises shiver and wobble on the armrests like crystal stemware.

Brightness Falls (1992) ch.1

Claude McKay 1890–1948

American poet and novelist

6 If we must die, let it not be like hogs
Hunted and penned in an inglorious spot,
While round us bark the mad and hungry dogs,
Making their mock at our accursed lot.

'If We Must Die' (1953)

Compton Mackenzie 1883–1972

English novelist

7 Prostitution. Selling one's body to keep one's soul: this is the meaning of the sins that were forgiven to the woman because she loved much: one might say of most marriages that they were selling one's soul to keep one's body.

The Adventures of Sylvia Scarlett (1918) bk. 2, ch. 5

8 Women do not find it difficult nowadays to behave like men, but they often find it extremely difficult to behave like gentlemen.

Literature in My Time (1933) ch. 22

9 You are offered a piece of bread and butter that feels like a damp handkerchief and sometimes, when cucumber is added to it, like a wet one.

Vestal Fire (1927) bk. 1, ch. 3

Kelvin Mackenzie 1946–

British journalist and media executive

10 We are surfing food.

of cable television

in *Trouble at the Top* (BBC2) 12 February 1997, a documentary on the launch of Live TV, originally run by Janet **Street-Porter**

James Mackintosh 1765–1832

Scottish philosopher and historian

11 Men are never so good or so bad as their opinions.

Dissertation on the Progress of Ethical Philosophy (1830) sect. 6 'Jeremy Bentham'

12 The Commons, faithful to their system, remained in a wise and masterly inactivity.

Vindiciae Gallicae (1791) sect. 1

Alexander Maclaren 1826–1910

Scottish divine

13 'The Church is an anvil which has worn out many hammers', and the story of the first collision is, in essentials, the story of all.

Expositions of Holy Scripture: Acts of the Apostles (1907) ch. 4

Don McLean 1945–

American songwriter

14 Something touched me deep inside
The day the music died.

on the death of Buddy Holly

'American Pie' (1972 song)

15 So, bye, bye, Miss American Pie,
Drove my Chevy to the levee
But the levee was dry.
Them good old boys was drinkin' whiskey and rye
Singin' 'This'll be the day that I die.'

'American Pie' (1972 song)

Archibald MacLeish 1892–1982

American poet and public official

1 A Poem should be palpable and mute
As a globed fruit.
'Ars Poetica' (1926)

2 A poem should be wordless
As the flight of birds.
'Ars Poetica' (1926)

3 A poem should not mean
But be.
'Ars Poetica' (1926)

Iain Macleod 1913–70

British Conservative politician
on Macleod: see **Salisbury** *643:6*

4 It is some measure of the tightness of the magic circle on this occasion that neither the Chancellor of the Exchequer nor the Leader of the House of Commons had any inkling of what was happening.
*of the 'evolvement' of Alec Douglas-***Home** *as Conservative leader after the resignation of Harold* ***Macmillan***
in *The Spectator* 17 January 1964

5 The Conservative Party always in time forgives those who were wrong. Indeed often, in time, they forgive those who were right.
in *The Spectator* 21 February 1964

Murdoch McLennan fl. 1715

Scottish poet

6 There's some say that we wan, some say that they wan,
Some say that nane wan at a', man;
But one thing I'm sure, that at Sheriffmuir
A battle there was which I saw, man:
And we ran, and they ran, and they ran, and we ran,
And we ran; and they ran awa', man!
'Sheriffmuir' in J. Woodfall Ebsworth (ed.) *Roxburghe Ballads* vol. 6 (1889)

Marshall McLuhan 1911–80

Canadian communications scholar

7 The new electronic interdependence recreates the world in the image of a global village.
The Gutenberg Galaxy (1962)

8 The medium is the message.
Understanding Media (1964) ch. 1 (title)

9 The name of a man is a numbing blow from which he never recovers.
Understanding Media (1964) ch. 2

10 The car has become an article of dress without which we feel uncertain, unclad and incomplete in the urban compound.
Understanding Media (1964) ch. 22

11 Television brought the brutality of war into the comfort of the living room. Vietnam was lost in the living rooms of America—not the battlefields of Vietnam.
in *Montreal Gazette* 16 May 1975

12 Gutenberg made everybody a reader. Xerox makes everybody a publisher.
in *Guardian Weekly* 12 June 1977

Comte de MacMahon 1808–93

French soldier and statesman; President of the Third Republic, 1873–9

13 *J'y suis, j'y reste.*
Here I am, and here I stay.
at the taking of the Malakoff fortress during the Crimean War, 8 September 1855
G. Hanotaux *Histoire de la France Contemporaine* (1903–8) vol. 2, ch. 1, sect. 1; MacMahon later denied that he had expressed himself in such 'lapidary form'

Harold Macmillan 1894–1986

British Conservative statesman; Prime Minister, 1957–63
on Macmillan: see **Levin** *466:7, 466:8,* **Thorpe** *776:21; see also* **Hitler** *378:5*

14 We . . . are Greeks in this American empire . . . We must run the Allied Forces HQ as the Greeks ran the operations of the Emperor Claudius.
to Richard **Crossman** *in 1944*
in *Sunday Telegraph* 9 February 1964

15 There ain't gonna be no war.
at a London press conference, 24 July 1955, following the Geneva summit; in *News Chronicle* 25 July 1955

16 Forever poised between a cliché and an indiscretion.
on the life of a Foreign Secretary
in *Newsweek* 30 April 1956

17 Let us be frank about it: most of our people have never had it so good.
'You Never Had It So Good' was the Democratic Party slogan during the 1952 US election campaign
speech at Bedford, 20 July 1957, in *The Times* 22 July 1957

18 I thought the best thing to do was to settle up these little local difficulties, and then turn to the wider vision of the Commonwealth.
on leaving for a Commonwealth tour, following the resignation of the Chancellor of the Exchequer and others
statement at London airport, 7 January 1958; in *The Times* 8 January 1958

19 The wind of change is blowing through this continent, and, whether we like it or not, this growth of [African] national consciousness is a political fact.
speech at Cape Town, 3 February 1960, in *Pointing the Way* (1972)

20 I was determined that no British government should be brought down by the action of two tarts.
comment on the Profumo affair, July 1963
Anthony Sampson *Macmillan* (1967)

21 There are three bodies no sensible man directly challenges: the Roman Catholic Church, the Brigade of Guards and the National Union of Mineworkers.
in *Observer* 22 February 1981; cf. **Baldwin** 49:12

1 First of all the Georgian silver goes, and then all that nice furniture that used to be in the saloon. Then the Canalettos go.
on privatization
speech to the Tory Reform Group, 8 November 1985, in *The Times* 9 November 1985; cf. **Misquotations** 522:7

2 Events, dear boy. Events.
when asked what his biggest problem was
attributed

Robert McNamara 1916–
American Democratic politician, Secretary of Defense during the Vietnam War

3 I don't object to it's being called 'McNamara's War' . . . It is a very important war and I am pleased to be identified with it and do whatever I can to win it.
in *New York Times* 25 April 1964

4 We . . . acted according to what we thought were the principles and traditions of this nation. We were wrong. We were terribly wrong.
of the conduct of the Vietnam War by the ***Kennedy*** *and* ***Johnson*** *administrations*
speaking in Washington, just before the twentieth anniversary of the American withdrawal from Vietnam; in *Daily Telegraph* (electronic edition) 10 April 1995

5 Military force—especially when wielded by an outside power—cannot bring order in a country that cannot govern itself.
in *Daily Telegraph* (electronic edition) 10 April 1995

Louis MacNeice 1907–63
British poet, born in Belfast

6 Better authentic mammon than a bogus god.
Autumn Journal (1939)

7 It's no go the merrygoround, it's no go the rickshaw,
All we want is a limousine and a ticket for the peepshow.
'Bagpipe Music' (1938)

8 It's no go the picture palace, it's no go the stadium,
It's no go the country cot with a pot of pink geraniums,
It's no go the Government grants, it's no go the elections,
Sit on your arse for fifty years and hang your hat on a pension.
'Bagpipe Music' (1938)

9 The glass is falling hour by hour, the glass will fall for ever,
But if you break the bloody glass you won't hold up the weather.
'Bagpipe Music' (1938)

10 Crumbling between the fingers, under the feet,
Crumbling behind the eyes,
Their world gives way and dies
And something twangs and breaks at the end of the street.
'Débâcle' (1941)

11 So they were married—to be the more together—
And found they were never again so much together,
Divided by the morning tea,
By the evening paper,
By children and tradesmen's bills.
'Les Sylphides' (1941)

12 Time was away and somewhere else,
There were two glasses and two chairs
And two people with the one pulse
(Somebody stopped the moving stairs):
Time was away and somewhere else.
'Meeting Point' (1941)

13 I am not yet born; O fill me
With strength against those who would freeze my humanity.
'Prayer Before Birth' (1944)

14 Let them not make me a stone and let them not spill me,
Otherwise kill me.
'Prayer Before Birth' (1944)

15 Down the road someone is practising scales,
The notes like little fishes vanish with a wink of tails,
Man's heart expands to tinker with his car
For this is Sunday morning, Fate's great bazaar.
'Sunday Morning' (1935)

16 The sunlight on the garden
Hardens and grows cold,
We cannot cage the minute
Within its net of gold.
'Sunlight on the Garden' (1938)

17 By a high star our course is set,
Our end is Life. Put out to sea.
'Thalassa' (1964)

18 I would have a poet able-bodied, fond of talking, a reader of the newspapers, capable of pity and laughter, informed in economics, appreciative of women, involved in personal relationships, actively interested in politics, susceptible to physical impressions.
Modern Poetry (1938)

Geoffrey Madan 1895–1947
English bibliophile

19 The great tragedy of the classical languages is to have been born twins.
Geoffrey Madan's Notebooks (1981)

20 Conservative ideal of freedom and progress: everyone to have an unfettered opportunity of remaining exactly where they are.
Geoffrey Madan's Notebooks (1981)

21 The dust of exploded beliefs may make a fine sunset.
Livre sans nom: Twelve Reflections (privately printed 1934) no. 12

Salvador de Madariaga 1886–1978
Spanish writer and diplomat

22 Since, in the main, it is not armaments that cause wars but wars (or the fears thereof) that cause

armaments, it follows that every nation will at every moment strive to keep its armament in an efficient state as required by its fear, otherwise styled security.

Morning Without Noon (1974) pt. 1, ch. 9

Samuel Madden 1686–1765

Irish poet

1 Words are men's daughters, but God's sons are things.

Boulter's Monument (1745) l. 377; cf. **Johnson** 409:4

James Madison 1751–1836

American Democratic Republican statesman; 4th President of the US, 1809–17

2 Liberty is to faction what air is to fire, an ailment without which it instantly expires. But it could not be less folly to abolish liberty, which is essential to political life, because it nourishes faction than it would be to wish the annihilation of air, which is essential to animal life, because it imparts to fire its destructive agency.

The Federalist (1787) no. 10

3 The diversity in the faculties of men, from which the rights of property originate, is not less an insuperable obstacle to a uniformity of interests. The protection of these faculties is the first object of government. From the protection of different and unequal faculties of acquiring property, the possession of different degrees and kinds of property immediately results.

The Federalist (1787) no. 10

Madonna 1958–

American pop singer and actress

4 Being blonde is definitely a different state of mind. I can't really put my finger on it, but the artifice of being blonde has some incredible sort of sexual connotation.

in *Rolling Stone* 23 March 1989

5 Many people see Eva Perón as either a saint or the incarnation of Satan. That means I can definitely identify with her.

on playing the starring role in the film Evita

in *Newsweek* 5 February 1996

Gaeus Cilnius Maecenas d. 8 BC

Roman statesman

6 Never allow any innovation in religion, because the peace of the state depends on it.

attributed; M. F. Wiles *Archetypal Heresy* (1996)

Maurice Maeterlinck 1862–1949

Belgian poet, dramatist, and essayist

7 *Il n'y a pas de morts.*

There are no dead.

L'Oiseau bleu (1909) act 4

John Gillespie Magee 1922–41

American airman, member of the Royal Canadian Airforce

8 Oh! I have slipped the surly bonds of earth
And danced the skies on laughter-silvered wings.

'High Flight' (1943); cf. **Reagan** 623:7

9 And, while with silent lifting mind I've trod
The high, untrespassed sanctity of space,
Put out my hand and touched the face of God.

'High Flight' (1943); cf. **Reagan** 623:7

William Connor Magee 1821–91

English clergyman, Bishop of Peterborough and Archbishop of York

10 It would be better that England should be free than that England should be compulsorily sober.

speech on the Intoxicating Liquor Bill, House of Lords, 2 May 1872

Magna Carta

Political charter signed by King John at Runnymede, 1215

11 *Quod Anglicana ecclesia libera sit.*

That the English Church shall be free.

Clause 1

12 *Nullius liber homo capiatur, vel imprisonetur, aut dissaisiatur, aut utlagetur, aut exuletur, aut aliquo modo destruator, nec super eum ibimus, nec super eum mittemus, nisi per legale judicium parium suorum vel per legem terrae.*

No free man shall be taken or imprisoned or dispossessed, or outlawed or exiled, or in any way destroyed, nor will we go upon him, nor will we send against him except by the lawful judgement of his peers or by the law of the land.

Clause 39

13 *Nulli vendemus, nulli negabimus aut differemus, rectum aut justitiam.*

To no man will we sell, or deny, or delay, right or justice.

Clause 40

Mahāyāna Buddhist texts

a tradition which emerged in India around the 1st century AD, *which later spread to China, Japan, and elsewhere*

14 This all-knowledge of the Tathagata has come forth from the perfection of wisdom. The physical personality of the Tathagata, on the other hand, is the result of the skill in means of the perfection of wisdom.

Perfect Wisdom in 8,000 Lines (*c.*100 BC–100 AD) ch. 3, v. 58

15 Where there is no perception, appellation, conception, or conventional expression, there one speaks of 'perfect wisdom'.

Perfect Wisdom in 8,000 Lines (*c.*100 BC–100 AD) ch. 7, v. 177

16 A Bodhisattva who is full of pity and concerned with the welfare of all beings, who dwells in

friendliness, compassion, sympathetic joy and even mindedness.

Perfect Wisdom in 8,000 Lines (*c*.100 BC–100 AD) ch. 20, v. 373

1 A glow-worm, or some other luminous animal, does not think that its light could illuminate the Continent of Jambudvipa [India], or radiate over it. Just so the Disciples and Pratyekabuddhas do not think that they should, after winning full enlightenment lead all beings to Nirvana. But the sun, when it has arisen, radiates its light over the whole of Jambudvipa. Just so a Bodhisattva, after he has accomplished the practices which lead to the full enlightenment of Buddhahood, leads countless beings to Nirvana.

Large Sutra on Perfect Wisdom (in 25,000 lines) (*c*.50–200 AD) v. 41

2 Form is emptiness and the very emptiness is form; emptiness does not differ from form, nor does form differ from emptiness; whatever is form, that is emptiness, whatever is emptiness, that is form.

Heart Sutra (4th century AD) v. 3

3 One should know the Prajnaparamita as the great spell, the spell of great knowledge, the utmost spell, the unequalled spell, allayer of all suffering, in truth,—for what could go wrong? By the Prajnaparamita has this spell been delivered. It runs like this: gone, gone, gone beyond, gone altogether beyond, O what an awakening, all hail!

Heart Sutra (4th century AD) v. 8

4 This saying has been taught by the Tathagata in a hidden sense: 'Those who know the discourse on dharma as a raft should forsake dharmas, and how much more so non-dharmas.'

Diamond Sutra (4th century AD) v. 6

5 Those who by my form did see me,
And those who followed me by my voice,
Wrong are the efforts they engaged in,
Me those people will not see.

Diamond Sutra (4th century AD) v. 26a

6 As stars, a fault of vision, as a lamp,
A mock show, dew drops, or a bubble,
A dream, a lightning flash, or cloud,
So we should view what is conditioned.

Diamond Sutra (4th century AD) v. 32a

7 Foolish common people do not understand that what is seen is merely their own mind.

Lankāvatāra Sutra (*c*.4th century AD) p. 90

8 The road to Buddhahood is open to all.
At all times have all living beings the Germ of Buddhahood in them.

Ratnagotravibhāga (*c*.3th century AD) v. 28

9 When I rain down the rain of Dharma,
Then all this world is well refreshed . . .
And then, refreshed, just like the plants,
The world will burst forth into blossoms.

Lotus Sutra pt. 5, v. 36

10 In the world deluded by ignorance, the supreme all-knowing one,
The Tathagata, the great physician, appears, full of compassion.

Lotus Sutra pt. 5, v. 60

11 There is no triad of vehicles, but here there is only one vehicle.

Lotus Sutra pt. 5, v. 82

12 [The Happy Land] which is the world system of the Lord Amitabha [Buddha of Infinite Light], is rich and prosperous, comfortable, fertile, delightful and crowded with many gods and men.

Pure Land Sutra ch. 15

13 All beings are irreversible from the supreme enlightenment if they hear the name of the Lord Amitabha, and, on hearing it, with one single thought only raise their hearts to him with a resolve connected with serene faith.

Larger Pure Land Sutra ch. 26

14 Sons or daughters of good family, who may desire to see that Tathagata Amitabha in this very life . . . should dedicate their store of merit to being reborn therein [Sukhāvatī].

Larger Pure Land Sutra ch. 27

15 Universally Good is present in all lands
Sitting on a jewelled lotus throne, beheld by all;
He manifests all psychic powers
And is able to enter infinite meditations.

Flower Garland Sutra (*c*.2nd century AD) bk. 3

Gustav Mahler 1860–1911

Austrian composer

16 Fortissimo at last!
on seeing Niagara Falls

K. Blaukopf *Gustav Mahler* (1973) ch. 8

17 The symphony must be like the world. It must embrace everything.

remark to Sibelius, Helsinki, 1907; K. and H. Blaukopf (eds.) *Mahler: his life, work and world* (1976)

Derek Mahon 1941–

Irish poet

18 'I am just going outside and may be some time.'
The others nod, pretending not to know.
At the heart of the ridiculous, the sublime.

Antarctica (1985) title poem; cf. **Last words** 456:1

19 Somewhere beyond the scorched gable end and the burnt-out buses
there is a poet indulging
his wretched rage for order.

'Rage for Order' (1978)

20 Even now there are places where a thought might grow—
Peruvian mines, worked out and abandoned
To a slow clock of condensation,
An echo trapped for ever, and a flutter
Of wildflowers in the lift-shaft . . .
And in a disused shed in Co. Wexford.

'A Disused Shed in Co. Wexford' (1978)

Norman Mailer 1923–
American novelist and essayist

1 The horror of the Twentieth Century was the size of each event, and the paucity of its reverberation.
A Fire on the Moon (1970) pt. 1, ch. 2

2 So we think of Marilyn who was every man's love affair with America, Marilyn Monroe who was blonde and beautiful and had a sweet little rinky-dink of a voice and all the cleanliness of all the clean American backyards.
Marilyn (1973)

3 Society is built on many people hurting many people, it is just who does the hurting, which is forever in dispute.
Miami and the Siege of Chicago (1968)

4 All the security around the American president is just to make sure the man who shoots him gets caught.
in *Sunday Telegraph* 4 March 1990

Maimonides (Moses ben Maimon) 1135–1204
Jewish philosopher and Rabbinic scholar, born in Spain
see also ***Epitaphs*** *302:8*

5 The basic tenets of our Torah and its fundamental principles are thirteen in number: *The first fundamental principle* is the existence of the Creator. There is a being who exists in the most perfect mode of existence, and he is the cause of the existence of all other beings.
Commentary on the Mishnah Sanhedrin 10 (Heleq)

6 When I find the road narrow, and can see no other way of teaching a well established truth except by pleasing one intelligent man and displeasing ten thousand fools—I prefer to address myself to the man.
The Guide for the Perplexed, introduction

7 Know that for the human mind there are certain objects of perception which are within the scope of its nature and capacity; on the other hand, there are, amongst things which actually exist, certain objects which the mind can in no way and by no means grasp: the gates of perception are closed against it.
The Guide for the Perplexed ch. 31

8 Man's love of God is identical with his knowledge of Him.
The Guide for the Perplexed ch. 51

9 Astrology is a disease, not a science.
Laws of Repentance

Henry Maine 1822–88
English jurist

10 The movement of the progressive societies has hitherto been a movement *from Status to Contract.*
Ancient Law (1861) ch. 5

11 So great is the ascendancy of the Law of Actions in the infancy of Courts of Justice, that substantive law has at first the look of being gradually secreted in the interstices of procedure; and the early lawyer can only see the law through the envelope of its technical forms.
Dissertations on Early Law and Custom (1883) ch. 11

12 Except the blind forces of Nature, nothing moves in this world which is not Greek in its origin.
Village Communities (3rd ed., 1876)

Joseph de Maistre 1753–1821
French writer and diplomat

13 *Toute nation a le gouvernement qu'elle mérite.*
Every country has the government it deserves.
Lettres et Opuscules Inédits (1851) vol. 1, letter 53 (15 August 1811)

John Major 1943–
British Conservative statesman; Prime Minister, 1990–7

14 If the policy isn't hurting, it isn't working.
on controlling inflation
speech in Northampton, 27 October 1989; cf. **Political slogans** 582:9

15 Society needs to condemn a little more and understand a little less.
interview with *Mail on Sunday* 21 February 1993

16 Fifty years on from now, Britain will still be the country of long shadows on county [cricket] grounds, warm beer, invincible green suburbs, dog lovers, and—as George Orwell said—old maids bicycling to Holy Communion through the morning mist.
speech to the Conservative Group for Europe, 22 April 1993; cf. **Orwell** 558:17

17 It is time to get back to basics: to self-discipline and respect for the law, to consideration for others, to accepting responsibility for yourself and your family, and not shuffling it off on the state.
speech to the Conservative Party Conference, 8 October 1993

18 So right. OK. We lost.
on election night
in *Guardian* 3 May 1997

19 When the final curtain comes down, it's time to get off the stage.
outside 10 Downing Street on 2 May, leaving office as Prime Minister and announcing that he would resign as Party Leader
in *Guardian* 3 May 1997

Bernard Malamud 1914–86
American novelist and short-story writer

20 There's no such thing as an unpolitical man, especially a Jew.
The Fixer (1966) ch. 9

Malcolm X 1925–65
American civil rights campaigner

21 If you're born in America with a black skin, you're born in prison.
in an interview, June 1963

1 You can't separate peace from freedom because no one can be at peace unless he has his freedom.
speech in New York, 7 January 1965, *Malcolm X Speaks* (1965)

Stéphane Mallarmé 1842–98
French poet

2 *La chair est triste, hélas! et j'ai lu tous les livres.*
The flesh, alas, is wearied; and I have read all the books there are.
'Brise Marin' (1887)

3 *Prélude à l'après-midi d'un faune.*
Prelude to the afternoon of a faun.
title of poem (*c.*1865)

4 *Un coup de dés jamais n'abolira le hasard.*
A throw of the dice will never eliminate chance.
title of poem (1897)

David Mallet (or Malloch) *c.*1705–65
Scottish poet

5 O grant me, Heaven, a middle state,
Neither too humble nor too great;
More than enough, for nature's ends,
With something left to treat my friends.
'Imitation of Horace'; cf. **Horace** 389:24

George Leigh Mallory 1886–1924
British mountaineer

6 Because it's there.
on being asked why he wanted to climb Mount Everest (Mallory was lost on Everest in the following year)
in *New York Times* 18 March 1923

Thomas Malory d. 1471
English writer
see also ***Caxton*** *199:1*

7 Whoso pulleth out this sword of this stone and anvil is rightwise King born of all England.
Le Morte D'Arthur (finished 1470, printed by Caxton 1485) bk. 1, ch. 4

8 Me repenteth, said Merlin; because of the death of that lady thou shalt strike a stroke most dolorous that ever man struck, except the stroke of our Lord, for thou shalt hurt the truest knight and the man of most worship that now liveth, and through that stroke three kingdoms shall be in great poverty, misery and wretchedness twelve years, and the knight shall not be whole of that wound for many years.
Le Morte D'Arthur (1485) bk. 2, ch. 8

9 Ah, my little son, thou hast murdered thy mother! And therefore I suppose thou that art a murderer so young, thou art full likely to be a manly man in thine age . . . When he is christened let call him Tristram, that is as much to say as a sorrowful birth.
Le Morte D'Arthur (1485) bk. 8, ch. 1

10 The questing beast . . . had in shape like a serpent's head and a body like a leopard, buttocked like a lion and footed like a hart. And in his body there was such a noise as it had been twenty couple of hounds questing, and such noise that beast made wheresomever he went.
questing = *yelping*
Le Morte D'Arthur (1485) bk. 9, ch. 12

11 God defend me, said Dinadan, for the joy of love is too short, and the sorrow thereof, and what cometh thereof, dureth over long.
Le Morte D'Arthur (1485) bk. 10, ch. 56

12 Thus endeth the story of the Sangreal, that was briefly drawn out of French into English, the which is a story chronicled for one of the truest and the holiest that is in this world.
Le Morte D'Arthur (1485) bk. 17, ch. 23

13 Therefore all ye that be lovers call unto your remembrance the month of May, like as did Queen Guenevere, for whom I make here a little mention, that while she lived she was a true lover, and therefore she had a good end.
Le Morte D'Arthur (1485) bk. 18, ch. 25

14 Wherefore, madam, I pray you kiss me and never no more. Nay, said the queen, that shall I never do, but abstain you from such works: and they departed. But there was never so hard an hearted man but he would have wept to see the dolour that they made.
Le Morte D'Arthur (1485) bk. 21, ch. 10

15 Thou wert never matched of earthly knight's hand; and thou wert the courteoust knight that ever bare shield; and thou wert the truest friend to thy lover that ever bestrad horse; and thou wert the truest lover of a sinful man that ever loved woman; and thou wert the kindest man that ever struck with sword; and thou wert the goodliest person that ever came among press of knights; and thou wert the meekest man and the gentlest that ever ate in hall among ladies; and thou wert the sternest knight to thy mortal foe that ever put spear in the rest.
to Sir Launcelot
Le Morte D'Arthur (1485) bk. 21, ch. 13

16 And many men say that there is written upon his tomb this verse: *Hic iacet Arthurus, rex quondam rexque futurus* [Here lies Arthur, the once and future king].
Le Morte d'Arthur (1485) bk. 31, ch. 7

André Malraux 1901–76
French novelist, essayist, and art critic

17 *La condition humaine.*
The human condition.
title of book (1933)

18 *Il n'y a pas cinquante manières de combattre, il n'y en a qu'une, c'est d'être vainqueur. Ni la révolution ni la guerre ne consistent à se plaire à soi-même.*
There are not fifty ways of fighting, there's only one, and that's to win. Neither revolution nor war consists in doing what one pleases.
L'Espoir (1937) pt. 2, sect. 2, ch. 12

1 *L'homme sait que le monde n'est pas à l'échelle humaine; et il voudrait qu'il le fût.*

Man knows that the world is not made on a human scale; and he wishes that it were.

Les Noyers d'Altenburg (1945) pt. 2, ch. 3

2 *L'art est un anti-destin.*

Art is a revolt against fate.

Les Voix du silence (1951) pt. 4, ch. 7

Thomas Robert Malthus 1766–1834

English political economist

3 Population, when unchecked, increases in a geometrical ratio. Subsistence only increases in an arithmetical ratio.

Essay on the Principle of Population (1798) ch. 1

4 The perpetual struggle for room and food.

Essay on the Principle of Population (1798) ch. 3

Lord Mancroft 1914–87

British Conservative politician

5 Cricket—a game which the English, not being a spiritual people, have invented in order to give themselves some conception of eternity.

Bees in Some Bonnets (1979)

W. R. Mandale

6 Up and down the City Road,
In and out the Eagle,
That's the way the money goes—
Pop goes the weasel!

'Pop Goes the Weasel' (1853 song); also attributed to Charles Twiggs

Nelson Mandela 1918–

South African statesman

7 I have dedicated my life to this struggle of the African people. I have fought against white domination, and I have fought against black domination. I have cherished the ideal of a democratic and free society in which all persons live together in harmony with equal opportunities. It is an ideal which I hope to live for, and to see realized. But my lord, if needs be, it is an ideal for which I am prepared to die.

speech in Johannesburg, 20 April 1964, which he quoted on his release in Cape Town, 11 February 1990

8 I stand here before you not as a prophet but as a humble servant of you, the people. Your tireless and heroic sacrifices have made it possible for me to be here today. I therefore place the remaining years of my life in your hands.

speech in Cape Town, 11 February 1990

9 No one is born hating another person because of the colour of his skin, or his background, or his religion. People must learn to hate, and if they can learn to hate, they can be taught to love, for love comes more naturally to the human heart than its opposite.

Long Walk to Freedom (1994)

10 True reconciliation does not consist in merely forgetting the past.

speech, 7 January 1996

Winnie Mandela 1934–

South African political activist; former wife of Nelson ***Mandela***

11 With that stick of matches, with our necklace, we shall liberate this country.

speech in black townships, 14 April 1986, in *Guardian* 15 April 1986

12 Maybe there is no rainbow nation after all because it does not have the colour black.

at the funeral of a black child reportedly shot dead by a white farmer

in *Irish Times* 25 April 1998 'Quotes of the Week'

Osip Mandelstam 1892–1938

Russian poet

13 The age is rocking the wave
with human grief
to a golden beat, and an adder
is breathing in time with it in the grass.

'The Age' (1923) (translated by C. M. Bowra)

14 Cruel and feeble, you'll look back
with the smile of a half-wit:
an animal that could run once,
staring at its own tracks.

'The Age' (1923) (translated by C. M. Bowra)

15 Only in war our fate has consummation,
And divination too will perish then.

'Tristia' (1919) (translated by C. M. Bowra)

Manilius (Marcus Manilius)

1st-century Latin poet

16 *Eripuitque Jovi fulmen viresque tonandi,*
et sonitum ventis concessit, nubibus ignem.

And snatched from Jove the lightning shaft and power to thunder, and attributed the noise to the winds, the flame to the clouds.

of human intelligence

Astronomica bk. 1, l. 104; cf. **Turgot** 785:9

Mrs Manley 1663–1724

English novelist and dramatist

17 No time like the present.

The Lost Lover (1696) act 4, sc. 1

Horace Mann 1796–1859

American educationist

18 The object of punishment is, prevention from evil; it never can be made impulsive to good.

Lectures and Reports on Education (1867 ed.) lecture 7

19 Lost, yesterday, somewhere between Sunrise and Sunset, two golden hours, each set with sixty diamond minutes. No reward is offered, for they are gone forever.

'Lost, Two Golden Hours'

Thomas Mann 1875–1955

German novelist

1 *Unsere Fähigkeit zum Ekel ist, wie ich anmerken möchte, desto grösser, je lebhafter unsere Begierde ist, das heisst: je inbrünstiger wir eigentlich der Welt und ihren Darbietungen anhangen.*

Our capacity for disgust, let me observe, is in proportion to our desires; that is in proportion to the intensity of our attachment to the things of this world.

The Confessions of Felix Krull (1954) pt. 1, ch. 5 (translated by Denver Lindley)

2 *Die Zeit hat in Wirklichkeit keine Einschnitte, es gibt kein Gewitter oder Drommetengetön beim Beginn eines neuen Monats oder Jahres, und selbst bei dem eines neuen Säkulums sind es nur wir Menschen, die schiessen und läuten.*

Time has no divisions to mark its passage, there is never a thunderstorm or blare of trumpets to announce the beginning of a new month or year. Even when a new century begins it is only we mortals who ring bells and fire off pistols.

The Magic Mountain (1924) ch. 4, sect. 4 (translated by H. T. Lowe-Porter)

3 *Warten heisst: Voraneilen, heisst: Zeit und Gegenwart nicht als Geschenk, sondern nur als Hindernis empfinden, ihren Eigenwert verneinen und vernichten und sie im Geist überspringen. Warten, sagt man, sei langweilig. Es ist jedoch ebensowohl oder sogar eigentlich kurzweilig, indem es Zeitmengen verschlingt, ohne sie um ihrer selbst willen zu leben und auszunutzen.*

And waiting means hurrying on ahead, it means regarding time and the present moment not as a boon, but an obstruction; it means making their actual content null and void, by mentally overleaping them. Waiting we say is long. We might just as well—or more accurately—say it is short, since it consumes whole spaces of time without our living them or making any use of them as such.

The Magic Mountain (1924) ch. 5, sect. 5 (translated by H. T. Lowe-Porter)

4 *Wir kommen aus dem Dunkel und gehen ins Dunkel, dazwischen liegen Erlebnisse; aber Anfang und Ende, Geburt und Tod, werden von uns nicht erlebt, sie haben keinen subjektiven Charakter, sie fallen als Vorgänge ganz ins Gebiet des Objektiven, so ist es damit.*

We come out of the dark and go into the dark again, and in between lie the experiences of our life. But the beginning and end, birth and death, we do not experience; they have no subjective character, they fall entirely in the category of objective events, and that's that.

The Magic Mountain (1924) ch. 6, sect. 8 (translated by H. T. Lowe-Porter)

5 *Unser Sterben ist mehr eine Angelegenheit der Weiterlebenden als unserer selbst.*

A man's dying is more the survivors' affair than his own.

The Magic Mountain (1924) ch. 6, sect. 8 (translated by H. T. Lowe-Porter)

6 *Die Zeit ist das Element der Erzählung, wie sie das Element des Lebens ist,—unlösbar damit verbunden, wie mit den Körpern im Raum. Sie ist auch das Element der Musik, als welche die Zeit misst und gliedert, sie kurzweilig und kostbar auf einmal macht.*

For time is the medium of narration, as it is the medium of life. Both are inextricably bound up with it, as are bodies in space. Similarly, time is the medium of music; music divides, measures, articulates time, and can shorten it, yet enhance its value, both at once.

The Magic Mountain (1924) ch. 7, sect. 1 (translated by H. T. Lowe-Porter)

John Manners, Duke of Rutland 1818–1906

English Tory politician and writer

7 Let wealth and commerce, laws and learning die,
But leave us still our old nobility!

England's Trust (1841) pt. 3, l. 227

Katherine Mansfield (Kathleen Mansfield Beauchamp) 1888–1923

New Zealand-born short-story writer

8 E. M. Forster never gets any further than warming the teapot. He's a rare fine hand at that. Feel this teapot. Is it not beautifully warm? Yes, but there ain't going to be no tea.

Journal (1927) May 1917

9 Whenever I prepare for a journey I prepare as though for death. Should I never return, all is in order.

Journal (1927) 29 January 1922

William Murray, Lord Mansfield 1705–93

Scottish lawyer and politician

10 The constitution does not allow reasons of state to influence our judgements: God forbid it should! We must not regard political consequences; however formidable soever they might be: if rebellion was the certain consequence, we are bound to say '*fiat justitia, ruat caelum*'.

Rex v. Wilkes, 8 June 1768, in *The English Reports* (1909) vol. 98; cf. **Adams** 3:17, **Watson** 805:1

11 Consider what you think justice requires, and decide accordingly. But never give your reasons; for your judgement will probably be right, but your reasons will certainly be wrong.

advice to a newly appointed colonial governor ignorant in the law

John Lord Campbell *The Lives of the Chief Justices of England* (1849) vol. 2, ch. 40

Richard Mant 1776–1848

Irish divine and ecclesiastical historian

12 Bright the vision that delighted
Once the sight of Judah's seer;
Sweet the countless tongues united
To entrance the prophet's ear.

'Bright the vision that delighted' (1837 hymn)

Mao Zedong 1893–1976
Chinese statesman; de facto leader of the Communist Party

1 Politics is war without bloodshed while war is politics with bloodshed.
lecture, 1938, in *Selected Works* (1965) vol. 2

2 Every Communist must grasp the truth, 'Political power grows out of the barrel of a gun'.
speech, 6 November 1938, in *Selected Works* (1965) vol. 2

3 The atom bomb is a paper tiger which the United States reactionaries use to scare people. It looks terrible, but in fact it isn't . . . All reactionaries are paper tigers.
interview, 1946, in *Selected Works* (1961) vol. 4

4 Letting a hundred flowers blossom and a hundred schools of thought contend is the policy for promoting progress in the arts and the sciences and a flourishing socialist culture in our land.
speech in Peking, 27 February 1957, in *Quotations of Chairman Mao* (1966)

Diego Maradona 1960–
Argentine football player

5 The goal was scored a little bit by the hand of God, another bit by head of Maradona.
on his controversial goal against England in the 1986 World Cup
in *Guardian* 1 July 1986

John Marchi 1948–
American Republican politician

6 We ought not to permit a cottage industry in the God business.
on hearing that British scientists had successfully cloned a lamb (Dolly)
in *Guardian* 28 February 1997

William Learned Marcy 1786–1857
American politician

7 The politicians of New York . . . see nothing wrong in the rule, that to the victor belong the spoils of the enemy.
speech to the Senate, 25 January 1832, in James Parton *Life of Andrew Jackson* (1860) vol. 3, ch. 29

Miriam Margolyes 1941–
English actress

8 Life, if you're fat, is a minefield—you have to pick your way, otherwise you blow up.
in *Observer* 9 June 1991

Marguerite of Angoulême 1492–1549
French writer, sister of **Francis I** *and Queen of Navarre*

9 Though jealousy be produced by love, as ashes are by fire, yet jealousy extinguishes love as ashes smother the flame.
Heptameron (1558) 'Novel 48, the Fifth Day'

Lynn Margulis 1938–
American biologist

10 Gaia is a tough bitch. People think the earth is going to die and they have to save it, that's ridiculous . . . There's no doubt that Gaia can compensate for our output of greenhouse gases, but the environment that's left will not be happy for any people.
in *New York Times Biographical Service* January 1996

Marie-Antoinette 1755–93
Queen consort of **Louis XVI**

11 *Qu'ils mangent de la brioche.*
Let them eat cake.
on being told that her people had no bread
attributed, but much older; in his *Confessions* (1740) Rousseau refers to a similar remark being a well-known saying; another version is:
Que ne mangent-ils de la croûte de pâté?
Why don't they eat pastry?
attributed to Marie-Thérèse (1638–83), wife of Louis XIV, in Louis XVIII *Relation d'un Voyage à Bruxelles et à Coblentz en 1791* (1823)

Edwin Markham 1852–1940
American poet

12 A thing that grieves not and that never hopes,
Stolid and stunned, a brother to the ox?
'The Man with the Hoe' (1899)

Johnny Marks 1909–85
American songwriter

13 Rudolph, the Red-Nosed Reindeer
Had a very shiny nose,
And if you ever saw it,
You would even say it glows.
'Rudolph, the Red-Nosed Reindeer' (1949 song)

Sarah, Duchess of Marlborough 1660–1744

14 The Duke returned from the wars today and did pleasure me in his top-boots.
oral tradition, attributed in various forms; I. Butler *Rule of Three* (1967) ch. 7

15 If I were young and handsome as I was, instead of old and faded as I am, and you could lay the empire of the world at my feet, you should never share the heart and hand that once belonged to John, Duke of Marlborough.
refusing an offer of marriage from the Duke of Somerset
W. S. Churchill *Marlborough: His Life and Times* vol. 4 (1938) ch. 39

Bob Marley 1945–81
Jamaican reggae musician and songwriter

16 Get up, stand up
Stand up for your rights
Get up, stand up
Never give up the fight.
'Get up, Stand up' (1973 song)

1 I shot the sheriff
But I swear it was in self-defence
I shot the sheriff
And they say it is a capital offence.
'I Shot the Sheriff' (1974 song)

Christopher Marlowe 1564–93

English dramatist and poet
on Marlowe: see **Drayton** *279:6,* **Jonson** *420:23; see also* **Anonymous** *17:1*

2 I'll have them fly to India for gold,
Ransack the ocean for orient pearl.
Doctor Faustus (1604) act 1, sc. 1

3 Why, this is hell, nor am I out of it.
Doctor Faustus (1604) act 1, sc. 3

4 Hell hath no limits nor is circumscribed
In one self place, where we are is Hell,
And to be short, when all the world dissolves,
And every creature shall be purified,
All places shall be hell that are not heaven.
Doctor Faustus (1604) act 2, sc. 1

5 Was this the face that launched a thousand ships,
And burnt the topless towers of Ilium?
Sweet Helen, make me immortal with a kiss!
Doctor Faustus (1604) act 5, sc. 1

6 Now hast thou but one bare hour to live,
And then thou must be damned perpetually.
Stand still, you ever-moving spheres of heaven,
That time may cease, and midnight never come.
Doctor Faustus (1604) act 5, sc. 2

7 *O lente lente currite noctis equi.*
The stars move still, time runs, the clock will strike,
The devil will come, and Faustus must be damned.
O I'll leap up to my God: who pulls me down?
See, see, where Christ's blood streams in the firmament.
One drop would save my soul, half a drop, ah my Christ.
Doctor Faustus (1604) act 5, sc. 2; cf. **Ovid** 561:2

8 Cut is the branch that might have grown full straight,
And burnèd is Apollo's laurel bough,
That sometime grew within this learned man.
Doctor Faustus (1604) epilogue

9 My men, like satyrs grazing on the lawns,
Shall with their goat feet dance an antic hay.
Edward II (1593) act 1, sc. 1

10 Tell Isabel the Queen, I looked not thus,
When for her sake I ran at tilt in France.
Edward II (1593) act 5, sc. 5

11 Base Fortune, now I see, that in thy wheel
There is a point, to which when men aspire,
They tumble headlong down.
Edward II (1593) act 5, sc. 6

12 It lies not in our power to love, or hate,
For will in us is over-ruled by fate.
Hero and Leander (1598) First Sestiad, l. 167

13 Where both deliberate, the love is slight;
Who ever loved that loved not at first sight?
Hero and Leander (1598) First Sestiad, l. 175; cf. **Shakespeare** 659:17

14 And as she wept, her tears to pearl he turned,
And wound them on his arm, and for her mourned.
Hero and Leander (1598) First Sestiad, l. 375

15 I count religion but a childish toy,
And hold there is no sin but ignorance.
The Jew of Malta (*c.*1592) prologue

16 Thus methinks should men of judgement frame
Their means of traffic from the vulgar trade,
And, as their wealth increaseth, so enclose
Infinite riches in a little room.
The Jew of Malta (*c.*1592) act 1, sc. 1

17 As for myself, I walk abroad o' nights
And kill sick people groaning under walls:
Sometimes I go about and poison wells.
The Jew of Malta (*c.*1592) act 2, sc. 3

18 BARNARDINE: Thou hast committed—
BARABAS: Fornication? But that was in another country: and besides, the wench is dead.
The Jew of Malta (*c.*1592) act 4, sc. 1

19 Come live with me, and be my love,
And we will all the pleasures prove,
That valleys, groves, hills and fields,
Woods or steepy mountain yields.
'The Passionate Shepherd to his Love'; cf. **Donne** 273:19, **Ralegh** 620:9

20 From jigging veins of rhyming mother-wits,
And such conceits as clownage keeps in pay,
We'll lead you to the stately tents of war.
Tamburlaine the Great (1590) pt. 1, prologue

21 With milk-white harts upon an ivory sled
Thou shalt be drawn amidst the frozen pools,
And scale the icy mountains' lofty tops,
Which with thy beauty will be soon resolved.
Tamburlaine the Great (1590) pt. 1, act 1, sc. 2

22 Our swords shall play the orators for us.
Tamburlaine the Great (1590) pt. 1, act 1, sc. 2

23 His looks do menace heaven and dare the Gods.
His fiery eyes are fixed upon the earth.
Tamburlaine the Great (1590) pt. 1, act 1, sc. 2

24 Accurst be he that first invented war.
Tamburlaine the Great (1590) pt. 1, act 2, sc. 4

25 Is it not passing brave to be a king,
And ride in triumph through Persepolis?
Tamburlaine the Great (1590) pt. 1, act 2, sc. 5

26 The ripest fruit of all,
That perfect bliss and sole felicity,
The sweet fruition of an earthly crown.
Tamburlaine the Great (1590) pt. 1, act 2, sc. 7

27 Virtue is the fount whence honour springs.
Tamburlaine the Great (1590) pt. 1, act 4, sc. 4

28 Ah fair Zenocrate, divine Zenocrate,
Fair is too foul an epithet for thee.
Tamburlaine the Great (1590) pt. 1, act 5, sc. 5

29 Now walk the angels on the walls of heaven,
As sentinels to warn th' immortal souls,

To entertain divine Zenocrate.
Tamburlaine the Great (1590) pt. 2, act 2, sc. 4

1 Yet let me kiss my Lord before I die,
And let me die with kissing of my Lord.
Tamburlaine the Great (1590) pt. 2, act 2, sc. 4

2 More childish valorous than manly wise.
Tamburlaine the Great (1590) pt. 2, act 4, sc. 1

3 Holla, ye pampered jades of Asia!
What, can ye draw but twenty miles a day . . . ?
Tamburlaine the Great (1590) pt. 2, act 4, sc. 3; cf. **Shakespeare** 669:32

Don Marquis 1878–1937
American poet and journalist

4 procrastination is the
art of keeping
up with yesterday.
archy and mehitabel (1927) 'certain maxims of archy'

5 an optimist is a guy
that has never had
much experience.
archy and mehitabel (1927) 'certain maxims of archy'

6 it s cheerio
my deario that
pulls a lady through.
archy and mehitabel (1927) 'cheerio, my deario'

7 I have got you out here
in the great open spaces
where cats are cats.
archy and mehitabel (1927) 'mehitabel has an adventure'

8 but wotthehell archy wotthehell
jamais triste archy jamais triste
that is my motto.
archy and mehitabel (1927) 'mehitabel sees paris'

9 boss there is always
a comforting thought
in time of trouble when
it is not our trouble.
archy does his part (1935) 'comforting thoughts'

10 did you ever
notice that when
a politician
does get an idea
he usually
gets it all wrong.
archys life of mehitabel (1933) 'archygrams'

11 Writing a book of poetry is like dropping a rose petal down the Grand Canyon and waiting for the echo.
E. Anthony *O Rare Don Marquis* (1962)

12 The art of newspaper paragraphing is to stroke a platitude until it purrs like an epigram.
E. Anthony *O Rare Don Marquis* (1962)

John Marriot 1780–1825
English clergyman

13 Thou, whose eternal Word
Chaos and darkness heard,
And took their flight,
Hear us, we humbly pray,
And, where the Gospel-day
Sheds not its glorious ray,
Let there be light!
'almighty' substituted for 'eternal' from 1861
'Thou, whose eternal Word' (hymn written *c.*1813)

Frederick Marryat 1792–1848
English naval captain and novelist

14 There's no getting blood out of a turnip.
Japhet, in Search of a Father (1836) ch. 4

15 As savage as a bear with a sore head.
The King's Own (1830) vol. 2, ch. 6

16 If you please, ma'am, it was a very little one.
the nurse, excusing her illegitimate baby
Mr Midshipman Easy (1836) ch. 3

17 All zeal . . . all zeal, Mr Easy.
Mr Midshipman Easy (1836) ch. 9

Arthur Marshall 1910–89
British journalist and former schoolmaster

18 What, knocked a tooth out? Never mind, dear, laugh it off, laugh it off; it's all part of life's rich pageant.
The Games Mistress (recorded monologue, 1937)

John Marshall 1755–1835
American jurist

19 The power to tax involves the power to destroy.
in *McCulloch v. Maryland* (1819)

20 The people made the Constitution, and the people can unmake it. It is the creature of their own will, and lives only by their will.
in *Cohens v. Virginia* (1821)

Thomas R. Marshall 1854–1925
American politician

21 What this country needs is a really good 5-cent cigar.
in *New York Tribune* 4 January 1920, pt. 7

Martial AD *c.*40–*c.*104
Spanish-born Latin epigrammatist

22 *Non est, crede mihi, sapientis dicere 'Vivam':*
Sera nimis vita est crastina: vive hodie.
Believe me, wise men don't say 'I shall live to do that', tomorrow's life's too late; live today.
Epigrammata bk. 1, no. 15

23 *Non amo te, Sabidi, nec possum dicere quare:*
Hoc tantum possum dicere, non amo te.
I don't love you, Sabidius, and I can't tell you why;
all I can tell you is this, that I don't love you.
Epigrammata bk. 1, no. 32; cf. **Brown** 152:7, **Watkyns** 804:14

24 *Laudant illa sed ista legunt.*
They praise those works, but read these.
Epigrammata bk. 4, no. 49

1 *Bonosque*
Soles effugere atque abire sentit,
Qui nobis pereunt et imputantur.

Each of us feels the good days speed and depart,
and they're lost to us and counted against us.

Epigrammata bk. 5, no. 20

2 *Non est vivere, sed valere vita est.*

Life's not just being alive, but being well.

Epigrammata bk. 6, no. 70

3 *Vitam quae faciant beatiorem,*
Iucundissime Martialis, haec sunt:
Res non parta labore sed relicta;
non ingratus ager, focus perennis.

Of what does the happy life consist,
My dear friend, Julius? Here's a list:
Inherited wealth, no need to earn
Fires that continually burn,
And fields that give a fair return.

Epigrammata bk. 10, no. 47; cf. **Surrey** 746:8

4 *Difficilis facilis, iucundus acerbus es idem:*
Nec tecum possum vivere nec sine te.

Difficult or easy, pleasant or bitter, you are the
same you: I cannot live with you—or without you.

Epigrammata bk. 12, no. 46(47); cf. **Addison** 5:1

5 *Rus in urbe.*

Country in the town.

Epigrammata bk. 12, no. 57

Andrew Marvell 1621–78

English poet

6 Where the remote Bermudas ride
In the ocean's bosom unespied.

'Bermudas' (*c.*1653)

7 He hangs in shades the orange bright,
Like golden lamps in a green night.

'Bermudas' (*c.*1653)

8 And makes the hollow seas, that roar,
Proclaim the ambergris on shore.

'Bermudas' (*c.*1653)

9 Echo beyond the Mexique Bay.

'Bermudas' (*c.*1653)

10 My love is of a birth as rare
As 'tis for object strange and high:
It was begotten by Despair
Upon Impossibility.
Magnanimous Despair alone
Could show me so divine a thing,
Where feeble Hope could ne'er have flown
But vainly flapped its tinsel wing.

'The Definition of Love' (1681)

11 As lines (so loves) oblique may well
Themselves in every angle greet:
But ours so truly parallel,
Though infinite, can never meet.
Therefore the love which us doth bind,
But Fate so enviously debars,
Is the conjunction of the mind,
And opposition of the stars.

'The Definition of Love' (1681)

12 Choosing each stone, and poising every weight,
Trying the measures of the breadth and height;
Here pulling down, and there erecting new,
Founding a firm state by proportions true.

'The First Anniversary of the Government under His Highness the Lord Protector, 1655' l. 245

13 How vainly men themselves amaze
To win the palm, the oak, or bays.

'The Garden' (1681) st. 1

14 The gods, that mortal beauty chase,
Still in a tree did end their race.
Apollo hunted Daphne so,
Only that she might laurel grow.
And Pan did after Syrinx speed,
Not as a nymph, but for a reed.

'The Garden' (1681) st. 4

15 What wondrous life is this I lead!
Ripe apples drop about my head;
The luscious clusters of the vine
Upon my mouth do crush their wine;
The nectarine, and curious peach,
Into my hands themselves do reach;
Stumbling on melons, as I pass,
Ensnared with flowers, I fall on grass.

'The Garden' (1681) st. 5

16 Annihilating all that's made
To a green thought in a green shade.

'The Garden' (1681) st. 6

17 Here at the fountain's sliding foot,
Or at some fruit-tree's mossy root,
Casting the body's vest aside,
My soul into the boughs does glide.

'The Garden' (1681) st. 7

18 Two paradises 'twere in one
To live in paradise alone.

'The Garden' (1681) st. 8

19 *He* nothing common did or mean
Upon that memorable scene:
But with his keener eye
The axe's edge did try.

on the execution of ***Charles I***

'An Horatian Ode upon Cromwell's Return from Ireland' (written 1650) l. 57

20 So much one man can do,
That does both act and know.

'An Horatian Ode upon Cromwell's Return from Ireland' (written 1650) l. 75

21 Ye country comets, that portend
No war, nor prince's funeral.

'The Mower to the Glow-worms' (1681)

22 Had it lived long, it would have been
Lilies without, roses within.

'The Nymph Complaining for the Death of her Fawn' (1681) l. 91

23 Had we but world enough, and time,
This coyness, lady, were no crime.

'To His coy Mistress' (1681) l. 1

1 I would
Love you ten years before the flood:
And you should, if you please, refuse
Till the conversion of the Jews.
My vegetable love should grow
Vaster than empires, and more slow.

'To His coy Mistress' (1681) l. 7

2 But at my back I always hear
Time's wingèd chariot hurrying near:
And yonder all before us lie
Deserts of vast eternity.

'To His Coy Mistress' (1681) l. 21; cf. **Eliot** 296:7

3 Then worms shall try
That long preserved virginity:
And your quaint honour turn to dust;
And into ashes all my lust.
The grave's a fine and private place,
But none, I think, do there embrace.

'To His Coy Mistress' (1681) l. 27

4 Let us roll all our strength, and all
Our sweetness, up into one ball:
And tear our pleasures with rough strife,
Thorough the iron gates of life.
Thus, though we cannot make our sun
Stand still, yet we will make him run.

'To His Coy Mistress' (1681) l. 41

5 He is translation's thief that addeth more,
As much as he that taketh from the store
Of the first author.

'To His Worthy Friend Dr Witty' (1651)

6 Oh thou, that dear and happy isle
The garden of the world ere while,
Thou paradise of four seas,
Which heaven planted us to please,
But, to exclude the world, did guard
With watery if not flaming sword;
What luckless apple did we taste,
To make us mortal, and thee waste?

'Upon Appleton House' (1681) st. 41

7 'Tis not what once it was, the world,
But a rude heap together hurled.

'Upon Appleton House' (1681) st. 96

8 But now the salmon-fishers moist
Their leathern boats begin to hoist;
And, like Antipodes in shoes,
Have shod their heads in their canoes.
How tortoise-like, but not so slow,
These rational amphibii go!

'Upon Appleton House' (1681) st. 97

Holt Marvell

English songwriter

9 A cigarette that bears a lipstick's traces,
An airline ticket to romantic places;
And still my heart has wings
These foolish things
Remind me of you.

'These Foolish Things Remind Me of You' (1935 song)

Chico Marx 1891–1961

American film comedian
see also **Film lines** *311:18*

10 I wasn't kissing her, I was just whispering in her mouth.

on being discovered by his wife with a chorus girl

Groucho Marx and Richard J. Anobile *Marx Brothers Scrapbook* (1973) ch. 24

Groucho Marx 1895–1977

American film comedian
on Marx: see **Sayings** *647:27; see also* **Epitaphs** *303:2,* **Film lines** *311:4, 311:13, 311:18, 312:7, 312:11*

11 PLEASE ACCEPT MY RESIGNATION. I DON'T WANT TO BELONG TO ANY CLUB THAT WILL ACCEPT ME AS A MEMBER.

Groucho and Me (1959) ch. 26

12 I never forget a face, but in your case I'll be glad to make an exception.

Leo Rosten *People I have Loved, Known or Admired* (1970) 'Groucho'

Karl Marx 1818–83

German political philosopher; founder of modern Communism
on Marx: see **Benn** *65:7,* **Sayings** *647:27*

13 Religion is the sigh of the oppressed creature, the heart of a heartless world . . . It is the opium of the people.

A Contribution to the Critique of Hegel's Philosophy of Right (1843–4) introduction; cf. **Kingsley** 437:14

14 Mankind always sets itself only such problems as it can solve; since, looking at the matter more closely, it will always be found that the task itself arises only when the material conditions for its solution already exist or are at least in the process of formation.

A Contribution to the Critique of Political Economy (1859) preface (translated by D. McLellan)

15 From each according to his abilities, to each according to his needs.

Critique of the Gotha Programme (written 1875, but of earlier origin); cf. **Blanc** 121:16, **Morelly** 531:17, and:

The formula of Communism, as propounded by Cabet, may be expressed thus:—'the duty of each is according to his faculties; his right according to his wants'.

in *North British Review* (1849) vol 10

16 And even when a society has got upon the right track for the discovery of the natural laws of its movement—and it is the ultimate aim of this work, to lay bare the economic law of motion of modern society—it can neither clear by bold leaps, nor remove by legal enactments, the obstacles offered by the successive phases of its normal development. But it can shorten and lessen the birth-pangs.

Das Kapital (1st German ed., 1867) preface (25 July 1865)

17 Centralization of the means of production, and socialization of labour at last reach a point where they become incompatible with their capitalist integument. This integument is burst asunder. The

knell of capitalist private property sounds. The expropriators are expropriated.
Das Kapital (1867) ch. 32

1 Hegel says somewhere that all great events and personalities in world history reappear in one fashion or another. He forgot to add: the first time as tragedy, the second as farce.
The Eighteenth Brumaire of Louis Bonaparte (1852) sect. 1; the origin of the Hegel reference is uncertain, but cf. **Hegel** 367:10

2 The philosophers have only interpreted the world in various ways; the point is to change it.
Theses on Feuerbach (written 1845, published 1888) no. 11

3 What I did that was new was to prove . . . that the class struggle necessarily leads to the dictatorship of the proletariat.
the phrase 'dictatorship of the proletariat' had been used earlier in the Constitution of the World Society of Revolutionary Communists (1850), signed by Marx and others
letter to Georg Weydemeyer 5 March 1852; Marx claimed that the phrase had been coined by Auguste Blanqui (1805–81), but it has not been found in this form in Blanqui's work

4 All I know is that I am not a Marxist.
attributed in a letter from Friedrich Engels to Conrad Schmidt, 5 August 1890; in Karl Marx and Friedrich Engels *Correspondence* (1934)

Karl Marx 1818–83 and Friedrich Engels 1820–95

Co-founders of modern Communism

5 A spectre is haunting Europe—the spectre of Communism.
The Communist Manifesto (1848) opening words

6 The history of all hitherto existing society is the history of class struggles.
The Communist Manifesto (1848) pt. 1

7 The proletarians have nothing to lose but their chains. They have a world to win. WORKING MEN OF ALL COUNTRIES, UNITE!
commonly rendered as 'Workers of the world, unite!'
The Communist Manifesto (1848) closing words (from the 1888 translation by Samuel Moore, edited by Engels)

Queen Mary 1867–1953

*Queen Consort of **George V***

8 All *this* thrown away for *that*.
*on returning home to Marlborough House, London after the abdication of her son, King **Edward VIII**, December 1936*
David Duff *George and Elizabeth* (1983) ch. 10

9 I do not think you have ever realised the shock, which the attitude you took up caused your family and the whole nation. It seemed inconceivable to those who had made such sacrifices during the war that you, as their King, refused a lesser sacrifice.
letter to the Duke of Windsor (formerly **Edward VIII**), July 1938, in J. Pope-Hennessy *Queen Mary* (1959) ch. 7

Mary, Queen of Scots 1542–87

Queen of Scotland, 1542–67
*on Mary: see **Elizabeth I** 296:23, **Gray** 350:1, **James V** 402:20*

10 Look to your consciences and remember that the theatre of the world is wider than the realm of England.
to the commissioners appointed to try her at Fotheringhay, 13 October 1586
Antonia Fraser *Mary Queen of Scots* (1969) ch. 25

11 *En ma fin git mon commencement.*
In my end is my beginning.
motto embroidered with an emblem of her mother, Mary of Guise, and quoted in a letter from William Drummond of Hawthornden to Ben Jonson in 1619; cf. **Eliot** 294:6

Mary Tudor (Mary I) 1516–58

Queen of England from 1553

12 When I am dead and opened, you shall find 'Calais' lying in my heart.
Holinshed's Chronicles vol. 4 (1808); cf. **Sellar and Yeatman** 654:8

John Masefield 1878–1967

English poet

13 Quinquireme of Nineveh from distant Ophir
Rowing home to haven in sunny Palestine,
With a cargo of ivory,
And apes and peacocks,
Sandalwood, cedarwood, and sweet white wine.
'Cargoes' (1903); cf. **Bible** 79:19

14 Dirty British coaster with a salt-caked smoke stack,
Butting through the Channel in the mad March days,
With a cargo of Tyne coal,
Road-rails, pig lead,
Firewood, ironware, and cheap tin trays.
'Cargoes' (1903)

15 The corn that makes the holy bread
By which the soul of man is fed,
The holy bread, the food unpriced,
Thy everlasting mercy, Christ.
'The Everlasting Mercy' (1911) st. 86

16 I must go down to the sea again, to the lonely sea and the sky,
And all I ask is a tall ship and a star to steer her by,
And the wheel's kick and the wind's song and the white sail's shaking,
And a grey mist on the sea's face and a grey dawn breaking.
'I must down to the seas' in the original of 1902, possibly a misprint
'Sea Fever' (1902)

17 I must go down to the sea again, for the call of the running tide
Is a wild call and a clear call that may not be denied.
'Sea Fever' (1902)

18 I must go down to the sea again, to the vagrant gypsy life,

To the gull's way and the whale's way where the wind's like a whetted knife;
And all I ask is a merry yarn from a laughing fellow-rover,
And quiet sleep and a sweet dream when the long trick's over.
'Sea Fever' (1902)

Donald Mason 1913–
American naval officer

1 Sighted sub, sank same.
on sinking a Japanese submarine in the Atlantic region (the first US naval success in the war)
radio message, 28 January 1942; in *New York Times* 27 February 1942

Philip Massinger 1583–1640
English dramatist

2 Ambition, in a private man a vice,
Is in a prince the virtue.
The Bashful Lover (licensed 1636, published 1655) act 1, sc. 2

3 Pray enter
You are learned Europeans and we worse
Than ignorant Americans.
The City Madam (licensed 1632, published 1658) act 3, sc. 3

4 Greatness, with private men
Esteemed a blessing, is to me a curse;
And we, whom, for our high births, they conclude
The only freemen, are the only slaves.
Happy the golden mean!
The Great Duke of Florence (licensed 1627, printed 1635) act 1, sc. 1

5 Oh that thou hadst like others been all words,
And no performance.
The Parliament of Love (1624) act 4, sc. 2

6 Death has a thousand doors to let out life:
I shall find one.
A Very Woman (licensed 1634, published 1655) act 5, sc. 4; cf. **Fletcher** 318:4, **Seneca** 654:20, **Webster** 808:1

Cotton Mather 1662–1728
New England puritan preacher and divine, son of Increase ***Mather***

7 I write the wonders of the Christian religion, flying from the depravations of Europe, to the American strand: and, assisted by the Holy Author of that religion, I do, with all conscience of truth, required therein by Him, who is the Truth itself, report the wonderful displays of His infinite power, wisdom, goodness, and faithfulness, wherewith His Divine Providence hath irradiated an Indian wildnerness.
introduction to *Magnalia Christi Americana* (1702), opening line

8 Every man will have his own style which will distinguish him as much as his gait.
Manuductio ad Ministerium (1726) 'Of Style'

9 That there is a Devil is a thing doubted by none but such as are under the influences of the Devil. For any to deny the being of a Devil must be from an ignorance or profaneness worse than diabolical.
The Wonders of the Invisible World (1693)

Increase Mather 1639–1723
New England puritan divine and writer, father of Cotton ***Mather***

10 Now as usually providence so ordereth that they who have been speaking all their lives long shall not say much when they come to die.
The Life and Death of . . . Mr Richard Mather (1670)

11 Thunder is the voice of God, and, therefore, to be dreaded.
Remarkable Providences (1684)

James Mathew 1830–1908
Irish judge

12 In England, justice is open to all—like the Ritz Hotel.
R. E. Megarry *Miscellany-at-Law* (1955); cf. **Anonymous** 16:10

Henri Matisse 1869–1954
French painter

13 What I dream of is an art of balance, of purity and serenity devoid of troubling or depressing subject matter . . . a soothing, calming influence on the mind, rather like a good armchair which provides relaxation from physical fatigue.
Notes d'un peintre (1908)

Leonard Matlovich d. 1988
American Air Force Sergeant

14 When I was in the military, they gave me a medal for killing two men and a discharge for loving one.
attributed

W. Somerset Maugham 1874–1965
English novelist

15 From the earliest times the old have rubbed it into the young that they are wiser than they, and before the young had discovered what nonsense this was they were old too, and it profited them to carry on the imposture.
Cakes and Ale (1930) ch. 11

16 Poor Henry, he's spending eternity wandering round and round a stately park and the fence is just too high for him to peep over and they're having tea just too far away for him to hear what the countess is saying.
of Henry ***James***
Cakes and Ale (1930) ch. 11

17 The most useful thing about a principle is that it can always be sacrificed to expediency.
The Circle (1921) act 3

18 Impropriety is the soul of wit.
The Moon and Sixpence (1919) ch. 4

19 It is not true that suffering ennobles the character; happiness does that sometimes, but suffering, for the most part, makes men petty and vindictive.
The Moon and Sixpence (1919) ch. 17

1 A woman can forgive a man for the harm he does her, but she can never forgive him for the sacrifices he makes on her account.
The Moon and Sixpence (1919) ch. 41

2 Like all weak men he laid an exaggerated stress on not changing one's mind.
Of Human Bondage (1915) ch. 39

3 People ask you for criticism, but they only want praise.
Of Human Bondage (1915) ch. 50

4 Money is like a sixth sense without which you cannot make a complete use of the other five.
Of Human Bondage (1915) ch. 51

5 I [Death] was astonished to see him in Baghdad, for I had an appointment with him tonight in Samarra.
Sheppey (1933) act 3

6 Few misfortunes can befall a boy which bring worse consequences than to have a really affectionate mother.
A Writer's Notebook (1949), written in 1896

7 Dying is a very dull, dreary affair. And my advice to you is to have nothing whatever to do with it.
to his nephew Robin, in 1965
Robin Maugham *Conversations with Willie* (1978)

Bill Mauldin 1921–
American cartoonist

8 I feel like a fugitive from th' law of averages.
cartoon caption in *Up Front* (1945)

André Maurois 1885–1967
French writer

9 Growing old is no more than a bad habit which a busy man has no time to form.
The Art of Living (1940) ch. 8

10 Wells, in part of Europe and in the United States, will for some years have wielded an intellectual dominion comparable to that won and held by Voltaire in the eighteenth century.
André Maurois *Poets and Prophets* (1936)

James Maxton 1885–1946
British Labour politician

11 All I say is, if you cannot ride two horses you have no right in the circus.
opposing disaffiliation of the Scottish Independent Labour Party from the Labour Party; usually quoted as, '. . . no right in the bloody circus'
in *Daily Herald* 12 January 1931; cf. **Proverbs** 603:28

Glyn Maxwell 1962–
English poet

12 May his anorak grow big with jotters,
Noting the numbers of trains he saw.
'Curse on a Child' (1995)

James Clerk Maxwell 1831–79
Scottish physicist

13 Scientific truth should be presented in different forms, and should be regarded as equally scientific whether it appears in the robust form and the vivid colouring of a physical illustration, or in the tenuity and paleness of a symbolic expression.
attributed; in *Physics Teacher* December 1969

Vladimir Mayakovsky 1893–1930
Russian poet
see also **Last words** 456:13

14 If you wish—
. . . I'll be irreproachably tender;
not a man, but—a cloud in trousers!
'The Cloud in Trousers' (1915) (translated by Samuel Charteris)

15 Not a sound. The universe sleeps, resting a huge ear on its paw with mites of stars.
'The Cloud in Trousers' (1915) (translated by Samuel Charteris)

16 In our language rhyme is a barrel. A barrel of dynamite. The line is a fuse. The line smoulders to the end and explodes; and the town is blown sky-high in a stanza.
'Conversation with an Inspector of Taxes about Poetry' (1926) (translated by Dmitri Obolensky)

17 Oh for just
one
more conference
regarding the eradication of all conferences!
'In Re Conferences'; Herbert Marshall (ed.) *Mayakovsky* (1965)

18 To us love says humming that the heart's stalled motor has begun working again.
'Letter from Paris to Comrade Kostorov on the Nature of Love' (1928) (translated by Samuel Charteris)

19 Ours is the land.
The air—ours.
Ours the diamond mines of stars.
And we will never,
never!
Allow anyone,
anyone!
To ravage our land with shells,
to tear our air with sharpened spear points.
'Revolution: a Poet's Chronicle' (1917) (translated by C. M. Bowra)

Jonathan Mayhew 1720–66
American divine

20 Rulers have no authority from God to do mischief.
A Discourse Concerning Unlimited Submission and Non-Resistance to the Higher Powers (1750)

21 As soon as the prince sets himself up above the law, he loses the king in the tyrant; he does to all intents and purpose unking himself.
A Discourse Concerning Unlimited Submission and Non-Resistance to the Higher Powers (1750)

Margaret Mead 1901–78
American anthropologist

1 The knowledge that the personalities of the two sexes are socially produced is congenial to every programme that looks forward towards a planned order of society. It is a two-edged sword.
Sex and Temperament in Three Primitive Societies (1935) pt. 4 'Conclusion'

Shepherd Mead 1914–
American advertising executive

2 How to succeed in business without really trying.
title of book (1952)

Hughes Mearns 1875–1965
American writer

3 As I was walking up the stair
I met a man who wasn't there.
He wasn't there again today.
I wish, I wish he'd stay away.
lines written for *The Psycho-ed*, an amateur play, in Philadelphia, 1910 (set to music in 1939 as 'The Little Man Who Wasn't There')

Peter Medawar 1915–87
English immunologist and author

4 A bishop wrote gravely to the *Times* inviting all nations to destroy 'the formula' of the atomic bomb. There is no simple remedy for ignorance so abysmal.
The Hope of Progress (1972)

5 If a scientist were to cut his ear off, no one would take it as evidence of a heightened sensibility.
'J. B. S.' (1968)

6 If politics is the art of the possible, research is surely the art of the soluble. Both are immensely practical-minded affairs.
in *New Statesman* 19 June 1964; cf. **Bismarck** 116:6

7 During the 1950s, the first great age of molecular biology, the English Schools of Oxford and particularly of Cambridge produced more than a score of graduates of quite outstanding ability—much more brilliant, inventive, articulate and dialectically skilful than most young scientists; right up in the Watson class. But Watson had one towering advantage over all of them: in addition to being extremely clever he had something important to be clever *about*.
review of James D. **Watson**'s *The Double Helix* in *New York Review of Books* 28 March 1968

Catherine de' Medici 1518–89
Italian-born queen consort of Henri II of France

8 A false report, if believed during three days, may be of great service to a government.
Isaac D'Israeli *Curiosities of Literature* 2nd series (1849) vol. 2; perhaps apocryphal

Cosimo de' Medici 1389–1464
Italian statesman and patron of the arts

9 We read that we ought to forgive our enemies; but we do not read that we ought to forgive our friends.
speaking of what **Bacon** *refers to as 'perfidious friends'*
Francis Bacon *Apophthegms* (1625) no. 206

Lorenzo de' Medici 1449–92
Italian statesman and poet

10 *Quanto è bella giovinezza*
Che si fugge tuttavia!
Chi vuol esser lieto sia:
Di doman non ci è certezza.
How beautiful is youth, that is always slipping away! Whoever wants to be happy, let him be so: of tomorrow there's no knowing.
'Trionfo di Bacco e di Arianna'

Golda Meir 1898–1978
Israeli stateswoman, Prime Minister 1969–74

11 Those that perished in Hitler's gas chambers were the last Jews to die without standing up to defend themselves.
speech to United Jewish Appeal Rally, New York, 11 June 1967

12 Women's Liberation is just a lot of foolishness. It's the men who are discriminated against. They can't bear children. And no-one's likely to do anything about that.
in *Newsweek* 23 October 1972

Nellie Melba (Helen Porter Mitchell) 1861–1931
Australian operatic soprano

13 Sing 'em muck! It's all they can understand!
advice to Dame Clara Butt, prior to her departure for Australia
W. H. Ponder *Clara Butt* (1928) ch. 12

William Lamb, Lord Melbourne 1779–1848
British Whig statesman, and husband of Lady Caroline **Lamb**; *Prime Minister 1834, 1835–41*
see also **Anonymous** *16:14*

14 Damn it! Another Bishop dead! I believe they die to vex me.
attributed; Lord David Cecil *Lord M* (1954) ch. 4

15 God help the Minister that meddles with art!
Lord David Cecil *Lord M* (1954) ch. 3

16 If left out he would be dangerous, but if taken in, he would be simply destructive.
when forming his second administration, Melbourne omitted the former Lord Chancellor, **Brougham**
Lord David Cecil *Lord M* (1954) ch. 4

17 I wish I was as cocksure of anything as Tom Macaulay is of everything.
Lord Cowper's preface to *Lord Melbourne's Papers* (1889)

1 Now, is it to lower the price of corn, or isn't it? It is not much matter which we say, but mind, we must all say *the same.*

attributed; Walter Bagehot *The English Constitution* (1867) ch. 1

2 Things have come to a pretty pass when religion is allowed to invade the sphere of private life.

on hearing an evangelical sermon

G. W. E. Russell *Collections and Recollections* (1898) ch. 6

3 What all the wise men promised has not happened, and what all the d—d fools said would happen has come to pass.

of the Catholic Emancipation Act (1829)

H. Dunckley *Lord Melbourne* (1890) ch. 9

4 What I want is men who will support me when I am in the wrong.

replying to a politician who said 'I will support you as long as you are in the right'

Lord David Cecil *Lord M* (1954) ch. 4

5 When in doubt what should be done, do nothing.

Lord David Cecil *Lord M* (1954) ch. 1

David Mellor 1949–

British Conservative politician

6 I do believe the popular press is drinking in the last chance saloon.

interview on *Hard News* (Channel 4), 21 December 1989

Herman Melville 1819–91

American novelist and poet

see also **Opening lines** 555:10

7 That Calvinistic sense of innate depravity and original sin from whose visitations, in some shape or other, no deeply thinking mind is always and wholly free.

Hawthorne and His Mosses (1850)

8 A whaleship was my Yale College and my Harvard.

Moby Dick (1851) ch. 24

9 Aye, toil as we may, we all sleep at last on the field. Sleep? Aye, and rust amid greenness; as last year's scythes flung down, and left in the half-cut swaths.

Moby Dick (1851) ch. 132

10 Towards thee I roll, thou all-destroying but unconquering whale . . . from hell's heart I stab at thee.

Moby Dick (1851) ch. 135

Gilles Ménage 1613–92

French scholar

11 *Comme nous nous entretenions de ce qui pouvait rendre heureux, je lui dis;* Sanitas sanitatum, et omnia sanitas.

While we were discussing what could make one happy, I said to him: *Sanitas sanitatum et omnia sanitas* [Health of healths and everything is health].

from a conversation with Jean-Louis Guez de Balzac (1594–1654), in *Ménagiana* (1693); cf. **Bible** 113:26

Menander 342–c.292 BC

Greek comic dramatist

12 Whom the gods love dies young.

Dis Exapaton fragment 4, in F. H. Sandbach (ed.) *Menandri Reliquiae Selectae* (1990); cf. **Byron** 177:5, **Proverbs** 615:3

13 We live, not as we wish to, but as we can.

The Lady of Andros in *Menander: the Principal Fragments* (translated by F. G. Allinson, 1951)

Mencius see Meng-tzu

H. L. Mencken 1880–1956

American journalist and literary critic

14 Love is the delusion that one woman differs from another.

Chrestomathy (1949) ch. 30; cf. **Shaw** 707:29

15 Puritanism. The haunting fear that someone, somewhere, may be happy.

Chrestomathy (1949) ch. 30

16 Democracy is the theory that the common people know what they want, and deserve to get it good and hard.

A Little Book in C major (1916)

17 Conscience: the inner voice which warns us that someone may be looking.

A Little Book in C major (1916)

18 It is now quite lawful for a Catholic woman to avoid pregnancy by a resort to mathematics, though she is still forbidden to resort to physics and chemistry.

Notebooks (1956) 'Minority Report'

Moses Mendelssohn 1729–86

German-born Jewish philosopher

19 To put it in one word: I believe that Judaism knows nothing of revealed religion, in the sense in which this is understood by Christians. The Israelites possess divine legislation.

Jerusalem (1783) pt. 2

Meng-tzu (Mencius) 371–289 BC

Chinese philosopher

20 All men have the mind which cannot bear [to see the suffering of] others.

The Book of Mencius bk. 2, pt. A, v. 6

21 It is useless to talk to those who do violence to their own nature, and it is useless to do anything with those who throw themselves away. To speak what is against propriety and righteousness is to do violence to oneself. To say that one cannot abide by humanity and follow righteousness is to throw oneself away.

The Book of Mencius bk. 4, pt. A, v. 10

22 The great man is the one who does not lose his [originally good] child's heart.

The Book of Mencius bk. 4, pt. B, v. 12

23 If you let people follow their feelings [original nature], they will be able to do good. This is what is meant by saying that human nature is good.

The Book of Mencius bk. 6, pt. A, v. 6

1 Moral principles please our minds as beef and mutton and pork please our mouths.
The Book of Mencius bk. 6, pt. A, v. 7

2 All things are already complete in oneself. There is no greater joy than to examine oneself and be sincere. When in ones's conduct one vigorously exercises altruism, humanity is not far to seek, but right by him.
The Book of Mencius bk. 7, pt. A, v. 4

Robert Gordon Menzies 1894–1978

Australian Liberal statesman, Prime Minister 1939–41 and 1949–66

3 What Great Britain calls the Far East is to us the near north.
in *Sydney Morning Herald* 27 April 1939

David Mercer 1928–80

English dramatist

4 A suitable case for treatment.
title of television play (1962); later filmed as *Morgan—A Suitable Case for Treatment* (1966)

Johnny Mercer 1909–76

American songwriter

5 You've got to ac-cent-tchu-ate the positive
Elim-my-nate the negative
Latch on to the affirmative
Don't mess with Mister In-between.
'Ac-cent-tchu-ate the Positive' (1944 song)

6 Jeepers Creepers—where you get them peepers?
'Jeepers Creepers' (1938 song)

7 Make it one for my baby
And one more for the road.
'One For My Baby' (1943 song)

8 That old black magic.
title of song (1942)

George Meredith 1828–1909

English novelist and poet
on Meredith: see **Wilde** *817:26, 818:7*

9 A witty woman is a treasure; a witty beauty is a power.
Diana of the Crossways (1885) ch. 1

10 'Tis Ireland gives England her soldiers, her generals too.
Diana of the Crossways (1885) ch. 2

11 She was a lady of incisive features bound in stale parchment.
Diana of the Crossways (1885) ch. 14

12 A Phoebus Apollo turned fasting friar.
The Egoist (1879) ch. 2

13 A dainty rogue in porcelain.
The Egoist (1879) ch. 5

14 Cynicism is intellectual dandyism without the coxcomb's feathers.
The Egoist (1879) ch. 7

15 I expect that Woman will be the last thing civilized by Man.
The Ordeal of Richard Feverel (1859) ch. 1

16 Kissing don't last: cookery do!
The Ordeal of Richard Feverel (1859) ch. 28

17 Speech is the small change of silence.
The Ordeal of Richard Feverel (1859) ch. 34

18 The lark ascending.
title of poem (1881)

19 She whom I love is hard to catch and conquer,
Hard, but O the glory of the winning were she won!
'Love in the Valley' st. 2

20 On a starred night Prince Lucifer uprose.
Tired of his dark dominion swung the fiend . . .
He reached a middle height, and at the stars,
Which are the brain of heaven, he looked, and sank.
Around the ancient track marched, rank on rank,
The army of unalterable law.
'Lucifer in Starlight' (1883)

21 Ah, what a dusty answer gets the soul
When hot for certainties in this our life!
Modern Love (1862) st. 50

22 Enter these enchanted woods,
You who dare.
'The Woods of Westermain' (1883)

Owen Meredith (Edward Robert Bulwer Lytton, Lord Lytton) 1831–91

English poet and statesman; Viceroy of India, 1876–80

23 Genius does what it must, and Talent does what it can.
'Last Words of a Sensitive Second-Rate Poet' (1868)

Bob Merrill 1921–98

American songwriter and composer

24 How much is that doggie in the window?
title of song (1953)

25 People who need people are the luckiest people in the world.
'People who Need People' (1964 song)

James Merrill 1926–95

American poet

26 Each thirteenth year he married. When he died
There were already several chilled wives
In sable orbit—rings, cars, permanent waves.
We'd felt him warming up for a green bride.

He could afford it. He was 'in his prime'
And three score ten. But money was not time.
'The Broken Home' (1966)

27 Always that same old story—
Father Time and Mother Earth,
a marriage on the rocks.
'The Broken Home' (1966)

Dixon Lanier Merritt 1879–1972

1 Oh, a wondrous bird is the pelican!
His beak holds more than his belican.
He takes in his beak
Food enough for a week.
But I'll be darned if I know how the helican.

in *Nashville Banner* 22 April 1913

W. S. Merwin 1927–

American poet

2 Sometimes it is inconceivable that I should be the age I am.

'The Child' (1968)

3 This is the black sea-brute bulling through wave-wrack,
Ancient as ocean's shifting hills.

'Leviathan' (1956)

4 The sea curling
Star-climbed, wind-combed, cumbered with itself still
As at first it was, is the hand not yet contented
Of the Creator. And he waits for the world to begin.

'Leviathan' (1956)

Jean Meslier *c.*1664–1733

French priest

5 I remember, on this matter, the wish made once by an ignorant, uneducated man . . . He said he wished . . . that all the great men in the world and all the nobility could be hanged, and strangled with the guts of priests. For myself . . . I wish I could have the strength of Hercules to purge the world of all vice and sin, and to have the pleasure of destroying all those monsters of error and sin [priests] who make all the peoples of the world groan so pitiably.

often quoted 'I should like . . . the last of the kings to be strangled with the guts of the last priest'

Testament (ed. R. Charles, 1864) vol. 1, ch. 2; cf. **Diderot** 267:2

Methodist Service Book 1975

6 I am no longer my own, but yours. Put me to what you will, rank me with whom you will; put me to doing, put me to suffering; let me be employed for you or laid aside for you, exalted for you or brought low for you; let me be full, let me be empty; let me have all things, let me have nothing.

The Covenant Prayer (based on the words of Richard Alleine in the First Covenant Service, 1782)

Prince Metternich 1773–1859

Austrian statesman

7 The greatest gift of any statesman rests not in knowing what concessions to make, but recognising when to make them.

Concessionen und Nichtconcessionen (1852)

8 The word 'freedom' means for me not a point of departure but a genuine point of arrival. The point of departure is defined by the word 'order'. Freedom cannot exist without the concept of order.

Mein Politisches Testament in *Aus Metternich's Nachgelassenen Papieren* (ed. A. von Klinkowström, 1880) vol. 7

9 Italy is a geographical expression.

discussing the Italian question with **Palmerston** *in 1847*

Mémoires, Documents, etc. de Metternich publiés par son fils (1883) vol. 7

10 I feel obliged to call to the supporters of the social uprising: Citizens of a dream-world, nothing is altered. On 14 March 1848, there was merely one man fewer.

of his own downfall

Aus Metternich's Nachgelassenen Papieren (ed. A. von Klinkowström, 1880) vol. 8

11 The Emperor is everything, Vienna is nothing.

letter to Count Bombelles, 5 June 1848, in *Aus Metternich's Nachgelassenen Papieren* (ed. A. von Klinkowström, 1880) vol. 8

12 *L'erreur n'a jamais approché de mon esprit.*

Error has never approached my spirit.

addressed to Guizot in 1848, in François Pierre G. Guizot *Mémoires* (1858–67) vol. 4

Charlotte Mew 1869–1928

English poet

13 She sleeps up in the attic there
Alone, poor maid. 'Tis but a stair
Betwixt us. Oh! my God! the down,
The soft young down of her, the brown,
The brown of her—her eyes, her hair, her hair!

'The Farmer's Bride' (1916)

Anthony Meyer 1920–

British Conservative politician

14 I question the right of that great Moloch, national sovereignty, to burn its children to save its pride.

speaking against the Falklands War, 1982

in *Listener* 27 September 1990

Michelangelo 1475–1564

Italian sculptor, painter, architect, and poet

15 I've finished that chapel I was painting. The Pope is quite satisfied.

on completing the ceiling of the Sistine chapel

letter to his father, October 1512; E. H. Ramsden (ed.) *The Letters of Michelangelo* (1963)

Jules Michelet 1798–1874

French historian

16 What is the first part of politics? Education. The second? Education. And the third? Education.

Le Peuple (1846); cf. **Blair** 117:11

1 England is an empire, Germany is a nation, a race, France is a person.
Histoire de France (1833–1867)

William Julius Mickle 1735–88
Scottish poet

2 For there's nae luck about the house,
There's nae luck at a',
There's little pleasure in the house
When our gudeman's awa.
'The Mariner's Wife' (1769)

Thomas Middleton *c.*1580–1627
English dramatist

3 Anything for a quiet life.
title of play (written *c.*1620, possibly with John Webster); cf. **Dickens** 265:18

4 I could not get the ring without the finger.
The Changeling (with William Rowley, *c.*1622) act 3, sc. 4

5 Y'are the deed's creature.
The Changeling (with William Rowley, *c.*1622) act 3, sc. 4

6 My study's ornament, thou shell of death,
Once the bright face of my betrothèd lady.
The Revenger's Tragedy (1607) act 1, sc. 1 (previously attributed to Cyril Tourneur, *c.*1575–1626)

7 Nine coaches waiting—hurry, hurry, hurry.
The Revenger's Tragedy (1607) act 2, sc. 1

8 Does the silk-worm expend her yellow labours
For thee? for thee does she undo herself?
The Revenger's Tragedy (1607) act 3, sc. 5

Bette Midler 1945–
American actress

9 When it's three o'clock in New York, it's still 1938 in London.
attributed

Midrash
ancient commentary on the Hebrew scriptures, dating from the 2nd century AD

10 The Holy One, blessed be He, makes ladders by which He makes one go up, and another go down.
Leviticus Rabbah 8:1

11 The Holy One, blessed be He, waits for the nations of the world in the hope that they will repent, and be brought beneath His wings.
Numbers Rabbah 10:1

12 Whatever you think of your friend, he thinks the same of you.
Sifre Deuteronomy, piska 24

13 The words of Torah are likened to fire. Just as fire was given from heaven, so were the words of Torah given from heaven . . . just as fire lives forever, so do the words of Torah live forever.
Sifre Deuteronomy, piska 343

14 Should a person tell you there is wisdom among the nations, believe it . . . if he tells you that there is Torah among the nations, do not believe it.
Lamentations Rabbah 2:13

15 When a person enters the world his hands are clenched as though to say, 'The whole world is mine, I shall inherit it'; but when he takes leave of it his hands are spread open as though to say, 'I have inherited nothing from the world.'
Ecclesiastes Rabbah 5:14

16 A man cannot say to the Angel of Death, 'Wait for me until I make up my accounts.'
Ecclesiastes Rabbah 8:8

17 While God's face is above, His heart is below.
Song of Songs Rabbah 4:4

George Mikes 1912–
Hungarian-born writer

18 On the Continent people have good food; in England people have good table manners.
How to be an Alien (1946)

19 Continental people have sex life; the English have hot-water bottles.
How to be an Alien (1946) p. 25

20 An Englishman, even if he is alone, forms an orderly queue of one.
How to be an Alien (1946) p. 44

William Porcher Miles 1822–96

21 'Vote early and vote often,' the advice openly displayed on the election banners in one of our northern cities.
in the House of Representatives, 31 March 1858

□ Military sayings, slogans, and songs
see box overleaf

John Stuart Mill 1806–73
English philosopher and economist
on Mill: see **Bentley** *67:5; see also* ***Epitaphs*** *304:11*

22 Ask yourself whether you are happy, and you cease to be so.
Autobiography (1873) ch. 5

23 No great improvements in the lot of mankind are possible, until a great change takes place in the fundamental constitution of their modes of thought.
Autobiography (1873) ch. 7

24 The Conservatives . . . being by the law of their existence the stupidest party.
Considerations on Representative Government (1861) ch. 7 n.

25 I will call no being good, who is not what I mean when I apply that epithet to my fellow-creatures; and if such a being can sentence me to hell for not so calling him, to hell I will go.
Examination of Sir William Hamilton's Philosophy (1865) ch. 7

continued

Military sayings, slogans, and songs

1 Action this day.
annotation as used by Winston Churchill at the Admiralty in 1940

2 All present and correct.
King's Regulations (Army) Report of the Orderly Sergeant to the Officer of the Day

3 Any officer who shall behave in a scandalous manner, unbecoming the character of an officer and a gentleman shall . . . be CASHIERED.
Articles of War (1872) 'Disgraceful Conduct' Article 79; the Naval Discipline Act, 10 August 1860, Article 24, uses the words 'conduct unbecoming the character of an Officer'

4 Are we downhearted? No!
expression much taken up by British soldiers during the First World War; cf. **Chamberlain** 200:15

5 Conduct . . . to the prejudice of good order and military discipline.
Army Discipline and Regulation Act (1879) Section 40

6 The difficult we do immediately; the impossible takes a little longer.
US Armed Forces' slogan; cf. **Calonne** 182:1, **Nansen** 538:7, **Proverbs** 598:15

7 Fifty million Frenchmen can't be wrong.
saying popular with American servicemen during the First World War; later associated with Mae **West** and Texas Guinan (1884–1933), it was also the title of a 1927 song by Billy Rose and Willie Raskin

8 From the halls of Montezuma,
To the shores of Tripoli,
We fight our country's battles,
On the land as on the sea.
'The Marines' Hymn' (1847)

9 If it moves, salute it; if it doesn't move, pick it up; and if you can't pick it up, paint it.
1940s saying, in Paul Dickson *The Official Rules* (1978)

10 *Ils ne passeront pas.*
They shall not pass.
slogan used by the French army at the defence of Verdun in 1916; variously attributed to Marshal **Pétain** and to General Robert Nivelle, and taken up by the Republicans in the Spanish Civil War in the form '*No pasarán!*'; cf. **Ibarruri** 398:4

11 Lions led by donkeys.
associated with British soldiers during the First World War
attributed to Max Hoffman (1869–1927) in Alan Clark *The Donkeys* (1961); this attribution has not been traced elsewhere, and the phrase is of much earlier origin:

Unceasingly they had drummed into them the utterance of *The Times*: 'You are lions led by packasses.'
of French troops defeated by Prussians
Francisque Sarcey *Paris during the Siege* (1871)

12 Mademoiselle from Armenteers,
Hasn't been kissed for forty years,
Hinky, dinky, parley-voo.
song of the First World War, variously attributed to Edward Rowland and to Harry Carlton

13 O Death, where is thy sting-a-ling-a-ling,
O grave, thy victory?
The bells of Hell go ting-a-ling-a-ling
For you but not for me.
'For You But Not For Me', in S. Louis Guiraud (ed.) *Songs That Won the War* (1930); cf. **Bible** 107:4

14 She was poor but she was honest
Victim of a rich man's game.
First he loved her, then he left her,
And she lost her maiden name . . .
It's the same the whole world over,
It's the poor wot gets the blame,
It's the rich wot gets the gravy.
Ain't it all a bleedin' shame?
'She was Poor but she was Honest' (sung by British soldiers in the First World War)

15 We're here
Because
We're here.
sung to the tune of 'Auld Lang Syne', in John Brophy and Eric Partridge *Songs and Slang of the British Soldier 1914–18* (1930)

16 What's the use of worrying?
It never was worth while,
So, pack up your troubles in your old kit-bag,
And smile, smile, smile.
'Pack up your Troubles' (1915 song), written by George Asaf (1880–1951)

17 Your King and Country need you.
recruitment slogan for First World War, coined by Eric Field, July 1914; *Advertising* (1959); cf. **Rubens** 637:3

John Stuart Mill *continued*

18 The only purpose for which power can be rightfully exercised over any member of a civilized community, against his will, is to prevent harm to others. His own good, either physical or moral, is not a sufficient warrant.
On Liberty (1859) ch. 1

19 If all mankind minus one were of one opinion, and only one person were of the contrary opinion, mankind would be no more justified in silencing that one person, than he, if he had the power, would be justified in silencing mankind.
On Liberty (1859) ch. 2

20 A party of order or stability, and a party of progress or reform, are both necessary elements of a healthy state of political life.
On Liberty (1859) ch. 2

21 The liberty of the individual must be thus far limited; he must not make himself a nuisance to other people.
On Liberty (1859) ch. 3

1 Liberty consists in doing what one desires.
On Liberty (1859) ch. 5

2 A State which dwarfs its men, in order that they may be more docile instruments in its hands even for beneficial purposes, will find that with small men no great thing can really be accomplished.
On Liberty (1859) ch. 5

3 The principle which regulates the existing social relations between the two sexes—the legal subordination of one sex to the other—is wrong in itself, and now one of the chief hindrances to human improvement.
The Subjection of Women (1869) ch. 1

4 What is now called the nature of women is an eminently artificial thing—the result of forced repression in some directions, unnatural stimulation in others.
The Subjection of Women (1869) ch. 1

5 No slave is a slave to the same lengths, and in so full a sense of the word, as a wife is.
The Subjection of Women (1869) ch. 2

6 The laws of most countries are far worse than the people who execute them, and many of them are only able to remain laws by being seldom or never carried into effect. If married life were all that it might be expected to be, looking to the laws alone, society would be a hell upon earth.
The Subjection of Women (1869) ch. 2

7 The true virtue of human beings is fitness to live together as equals; claiming nothing for themselves but what they as freely concede to everyone else; regarding command of any kind as an exceptional necessity, and in all cases a temporary one.
The Subjection of Women (1869) ch. 2

8 The most important thing women have to do is to stir up the zeal of women themselves.
letter to Alexander Bain, 14 July 1869, in Hugh S. R. Elliot (ed.) *Letters of John Stuart Mill* vol. 2 (1910)

Edna St Vincent Millay 1892–1950

American poet

9 Childhood is the kingdom where nobody dies.
Nobody that matters, that is.
'Childhood is the Kingdom where Nobody dies' (1934)

10 Down, down, down into the darkness of the grave
Gently they go, the beautiful, the tender, the kind;
Quietly they go, the intelligent, the witty, the brave.
I know. But I do not approve. And I am not resigned.
'Dirge Without Music' (1928)

11 My candle burns at both ends;
It will not last the night;
But ah, my foes, and oh, my friends—
It gives a lovely light.
A Few Figs From Thistles (1920) 'First Fig'

12 Euclid alone
Has looked on Beauty bare. Fortunate they
Who, though once only and then but far away,
Have heard her massive sandal set on stone.
The Harp-Weaver and Other Poems (1923) sonnet 22

13 Justice denied in Massachusetts.
relating to the trial of Sacco and **Vanzetti** *and their execution on 22 August 1927*
title of poem (1928)

14 The sun that warmed our stooping backs and withered the weeds uprooted—
We shall not feel it again.
We shall die in darkness, and be buried in the rain.
'Justice Denied in Massachusetts' (1928)

15 Death devours all lovely things;
Lesbia with her sparrow
Shares the darkness—presently
Every bed is narrow.
'Passer Mortuus Est' (1921); cf. **Catullus** 194:22

16 After all, my erstwhile dear,
My no longer cherished,
Need we say it was not love,
Now that love is perished?
'Passer Mortuus Est' (1921)

Alice Duer Miller 1874–1942

American writer

17 I am American bred,
I have seen much to hate here—much to forgive,
But in a world where England is finished and dead,
I do not wish to live.
The White Cliffs (1940)

Arthur Miller 1915–

American dramatist
on Miller: see **Newspaper headlines** 544:4

18 A suicide kills two people, Maggie, that's what it's for!
After the Fall (1964) act 2

19 Death of a salesman.
title of play (1949)

20 The world is an oyster, but you don't crack it open on a mattress.
Death of a Salesman (1949) act 1

21 Willy Loman never made a lot of money. His name was never in the paper. He's not the finest character that ever lived. But he's a human being, and a terrible thing is happening to him. So attention must be paid.
Death of a Salesman (1949) act 1

22 He's a man way out there in the blue, riding on a smile and a shoeshine. And when they start not smiling back—that's an earthquake . . . A salesman is got to dream, boy. It comes with the territory.
Death of a Salesman (1949) 'Requiem'

23 The car, the furniture, the wife, the children—everything has to be disposable. Because you see the main thing today is—shopping.
The Price (1968) act 1

24 I love her too, but our neuroses just don't match.
The Ride Down Mount Morgan (1991) act 1

1 This is Red Hook, not Sicily . . . This is the gullet of New York swallowing the tonnage of the world.
A View from the Bridge (1955) act 1

2 The structure of a play is always the story of how the birds came home to roost.
'Shadows of the Gods' in *Harper's Magazine* August 1958

3 A good newspaper, I suppose, is a nation talking to itself.
in *Observer* 26 November 1961

Henry Miller 1891–1980
American novelist

4 Every man with a bellyful of the classics is an enemy to the human race.
Tropic of Cancer (1934)

Jonathan Miller 1934–
English writer and director

5 In fact, I'm not really a *Jew*. Just Jew-*ish*. Not the whole hog, you know.
Beyond the Fringe (1960 review) 'Real Class'

6 I successfully don't think about it for most of my life because I'm in that sunlit part of the landscape where I don't hear the cries of the tormented. It's the way things are.
when asked how he dealt with the atrocities of this century
in *Observer* 10 March 1996

Spike Milligan (Terence Alan Milligan) 1918–
Irish comedian
see also **Catchphrases** 195:25, 196:32, 196:34

7 Money couldn't buy friends but you got a better class of enemy.
Puckoon (1963) ch. 6

A. J. Mills, Fred Godfrey, and Bennett Scott
British songwriters

8 Take me back to dear old Blighty.
title of song (1916)

Irving Mills 1894–1985

9 It don't mean a thing
If it ain't got that swing.
'It Don't Mean a Thing' (1932 song; music by Duke **Ellington**)

Henry Hart Milman 1791–1868
English clergyman

10 Ride on! ride on in majesty!
The wingèd squadrons of the sky
Look down with sad and wond'ring eyes
To see the approaching sacrifice.
'Ride on! ride on in majesty!' (1827 hymn)

A. A. Milne 1882–1956
English writer for children

11 The more he looked inside the more Piglet wasn't there.
The House at Pooh Corner (1928) ch. 1

12 'I don't *want* him,' said Rabbit. 'But it's always useful to know where a friend-and-relation *is*, whether you want him or whether you don't.'
The House at Pooh Corner (1928) ch. 3

13 He respects Owl, because you can't help respecting anybody who can spell TUESDAY, even if he doesn't spell it right; but spelling isn't everything. There are days when spelling Tuesday simply doesn't count.
The House at Pooh Corner (1928) ch. 5

14 When you are a Bear of Very Little Brain, and you Think of Things, you find sometimes that a Thing which seemed very Thingish inside you is quite different when it gets out into the open and has other people looking at it.
The House at Pooh Corner (1928) ch. 6

15 They're changing guard at Buckingham Palace—
Christopher Robin went down with Alice.
Alice is marrying one of the guard.
'A soldier's life is terrible hard,'
Says Alice.
When We Were Very Young (1924) 'Buckingham Palace'

16 James James
Morrison Morrison
Weatherby George Dupree
Took great
Care of his Mother,
Though he was only three.
James James
Said to his Mother,
'Mother,' he said, said he;
'You must never go down to the end of the town, if you don't go down with me.'
When We Were Very Young (1924) 'Disobedience'

17 There once was a Dormouse who lived in a bed
Of delphiniums (blue) and geraniums (red),
And all the day long he'd a wonderful view
Of geraniums (red) and delphiniums (blue).
When We Were Very Young (1924) 'The Dormouse and the Doctor'

18 The King asked
The Queen, and
The Queen asked
The Dairymaid:
'Could we have some butter for
The Royal slice of bread?'
When We Were Very Young (1924) 'The King's Breakfast'

19 And some of the bigger bears try to pretend
That they came round the corner to look for a friend;
And they try to pretend that nobody cares
Whether you walk on the lines or squares.
When We Were Very Young (1924) 'Lines and Squares'

20 *What* is the matter with Mary Jane?
She's perfectly well and she hasn't a pain,

And it's lovely rice pudding for dinner again!
What *is* the matter with Mary Jane?
When We Were Very Young (1924) 'Rice Pudding'

1 Little Boy kneels at the foot of the bed,
Droops on the little hands little gold head.
Hush! Hush! Whisper who dares!
Christopher Robin is saying his prayers.
When We Were Very Young (1924) 'Vespers'; cf. **Morton** 533:1

2 Isn't it funny
How a bear likes honey?
Buzz! Buzz! Buzz!
I wonder why he does?
Winnie-the-Pooh (1926) ch. 1

3 How sweet to be a Cloud
Floating in the Blue!
It makes him very proud
To be a little cloud.
Winnie-the-Pooh (1926) ch. 1

4 Time for a little something.
Winnie-the-Pooh (1926) ch. 6

5 My spelling is Wobbly. It's good spelling but it Wobbles, and the letters get in the wrong places.
Winnie-the-Pooh (1926) ch. 6

6 Owl hasn't exactly got Brain, but he Knows Things.
Winnie-the-Pooh (1926) ch. 9

7 Eeyore was saying to himself, 'This writing business. Pencils and what-not. Over-rated, if you ask me. Silly stuff. Nothing in it.'
Winnie-the-Pooh (1926) ch. 10

Lord Milner 1854–1925

British colonial administrator

8 If we believe a thing to be bad, and if we have a right to prevent it, it is our duty to try to prevent it and to damn the consequences.
speech in Glasgow, 26 November 1909, in *The Times* 27 November 1909

John Milton 1608–74

English poet
on Milton: see ***Aubrey*** *32:16, 32:17, 32:18,* ***Blake*** *119:11,* ***Byron*** *176:29,* ***Gray*** *351:2,* ***Johnson*** *410:7, 417:12,* ***Tennyson*** *764:20,* ***Wordsworth*** *829:8*

9 Such sweet compulsion doth in music lie.
'Arcades' (1645) l. 68

10 Blest pair of Sirens, pledges of heaven's joy,
Sphere-born harmonious sisters, Voice, and Verse.
'At a Solemn Music' (1645)

11 Where the bright seraphim in burning row
Their loud uplifted angel trumpets blow.
'At a Solemn Music' (1645)

12 Before the starry threshold of Jove's Court
My mansion is.
Comus (1637) l. 1

13 Above the smoke and stir of this dim spot,
Which men call earth.
Comus (1637) l. 5

14 Yet some there be that by due steps aspire
To lay their just hands on that golden key
That opes the palace of eternity.
Comus (1637) l. 12

15 An old and haughty nation proud in arms.
Comus (1637) l. 33

16 And the gilded car of day
His glowing axle doth allay
In the steep Atlantic stream.
Comus (1637) l. 95

17 What hath night to do with sleep?
Comus (1637) l. 122

18 Come, knit hands, and beat the ground,
In a light fantastic round.
Comus (1637) l. 143

19 Sweet Echo, sweetest nymph that liv'st unseen
Within thy airy shell
By slow Meander's margent green,
And in the violet-embroidered vale.
Comus (1637) l. 230

20 Virtue could see to do what Virtue would
By her own radiant light, though sun and moon
Were in the flat sea sunk.
Comus (1637) l. 373

21 He that has light within his own clear breast
May sit i' the centre, and enjoy bright day,
But he that hides a dark soul, and foul thoughts
Benighted walks under the midday sun;
Himself is his own dungeon.
Comus (1637) l. 381

22 Yet where an equal poise of hope and fear
Does arbitrate the event, my nature is
That I incline to hope, rather than fear,
And gladly banish squint suspicion.
Comus (1637) l. 410

23 'Tis chastity, my brother, chastity:
She that has that, is clad in complete steel.
Comus (1637) l. 420

24 How charming is divine philosophy!
Not harsh and crabbèd, as dull fools suppose,
But musical as is Apollo's lute.
Comus (1637) l. 475

25 Storied of old in high immortal verse
Of dire chimeras and enchanted isles,
And rifted rocks whose entrance leads to hell.
Comus (1637) l. 516

26 And filled the air with barbarous dissonance.
Comus (1637) l. 550

27 Against the threats
Of malice or of sorcery, or that power
Which erring men call chance, this I hold firm,
Virtue may be assailed, but never hurt,
Surprised by unjust force, but not enthralled.
Comus (1637) l. 586

28 Those budge doctors of the Stoic fur.
Comus (1637) l. 707

29 Beauty is Nature's brag, and must be shown
In courts, at feasts, and high solemnities

Where most may wonder at the workmanship.
Comus (1637) l. 745

1 Sabrina fair,
Listen where thou art sitting
Under the glassy, cool, translucent wave,
In twisted braids of lilies knitting
The loose train of thy amber-dropping hair.
Comus (1637) l. 859 'Song'

2 Thus I set my printless feet
O'er the cowslip's velvet head,
That bends not as I tread.
Comus (1637) l. 897

3 Hence, vain deluding joys,
The brood of folly without father bred.
'Il Penseroso' (1645) l. 1

4 As thick and numberless
As the gay motes that people the sunbeams.
'Il Penseroso' (1645) l. 7

5 Come, pensive nun, devout and pure,
Sober, steadfast, and demure.
'Il Penseroso' (1645) l. 31

6 Sweet bird that shunn'st the noise of folly,
Most musical, most melancholy!
'Il Penseroso' (1645) l. 61

7 Where glowing embers through the room
Teach light to counterfeit a gloom,
Far from all resort of mirth,
Save the cricket on the hearth.
'Il Penseroso' (1645) l. 79

8 Or bid the soul of Orpheus sing
Such notes as warbled to the string,
Drew iron tears down Pluto's cheek.
'Il Penseroso' (1645) l. 105

9 Where more is meant than meets the ear.
'Il Penseroso' (1645) l. 120

10 Hide me from day's garish eye.
'Il Penseroso' (1645) l. 141; cf. **Newman** 542:20

11 And storied windows richly dight,
Casting a dim religious light.
'Il Penseroso' (1645) l. 159

12 Hence, loathèd Melancholy,
Of Cerberus, and blackest Midnight born,
In Stygian cave forlorn
'Mongst horrid shapes, and shrieks, and sights unholy.
'L'Allegro' (1645) l. 1

13 So buxom, blithe, and debonair.
of Euphrosyne [Mirth], one of the three Graces
'L'Allegro' (1645) l. 24

14 Haste thee nymph, and bring with thee
Jest and youthful jollity,
Quips and cranks, and wanton wiles,
Nods, and becks, and wreathèd smiles.
'L'Allegro' (1645) l. 25

15 Sport that wrinkled Care derides,
And Laughter holding both his sides.
Come, and trip it as ye go
On the light fantastic toe.
'L'Allegro' (1645) l. 31

16 While the cock with lively din
Scatters the rear of darkness thin,
And to the stack, or the barn door,
Stoutly struts his dames before.
'L'Allegro' (1645) l. 49

17 Right against the eastern gate,
Where the great sun begins his state.
'L'Allegro' (1645) l. 59

18 And the milkmaid singeth blithe,
And the mower whets his scythe,
And every shepherd tells his tale
Under the hawthorn in the dale.
'L'Allegro' (1645) l. 65

19 Meadows trim with daisies pied,
Shallow brooks, and rivers wide.
'L'Allegro' (1645) l. 75

20 Where perhaps some beauty lies,
The cynosure of neighbouring eyes.
'L'Allegro' (1645) l. 79

21 And the jocund rebecks sound
To many a youth, and many a maid,
Dancing in the chequered shade;
And young and old come forth to play
On a sunshine holiday.
'L'Allegro' (1645) l. 94

22 Then to the spicy nut-brown ale.
'L'Allegro' (1645) l. 100

23 Towered cities please us then,
And the busy hum of men.
'L'Allegro' (1645) l. 117

24 Such sights as youthful poets dream
On summer eves by haunted stream.
Then to the well-trod stage anon,
If Jonson's learnèd sock be on,
Or sweetest Shakespeare fancy's child,
Warble his native wood-notes wild.
'L'Allegro' (1645) l. 129

25 Let us with a gladsome mind
Praise the Lord, for he is kind,
For his mercies ay endure,
Ever faithful, ever sure.
'Let us with a gladsome mind' (1645); paraphrase of Psalm 136; cf. **Book of Common Prayer** 141:6

26 Yet once more, O ye laurels, and once more
Ye myrtles brown, with ivy never sere.
'Lycidas' (1638) l. 1

27 Bitter constraint, and sad occasion dear,
Compels me to disturb your season due;
For Lycidas is dead, dead ere his prime,
Young Lycidas, and hath not left his peer:
Who would not sing for Lycidas?
'Lycidas' (1638) l. 6

28 He must not float upon his watery bier
Unwept, and welter to the parching wind,
Without the meed of some melodious tear.
'Lycidas' (1638) l. 12

29 For we were nursed upon the self-same hill.
'Lycidas' (1638) l. 23

1 The woods, and desert caves,
With wild thyme and the gadding vine o'ergrown.
'Lycidas' (1638) l. 39

2 Were it not better done as others use,
To sport with Amaryllis in the shade,
Or with the tangles of Neaera's hair?
Fame is the spur that the clear spirit doth raise
(That last infirmity of noble mind)
To scorn delights, and live laborious days.
'Lycidas' (1638) l. 67

3 Comes the blind Fury with th' abhorrèd shears,
And slits the thin-spun life.
'Lycidas' (1638) l. 75

4 Fame is no plant that grows on mortal soil.
'Lycidas' (1638) l. 78

5 Last came, and last did go,
The pilot of the Galilean lake,
Two massy keys he bore of metals twain
(The golden opes, the iron shuts amain).
'Lycidas' (1638) l. 108

6 Their lean and flashy songs
Grate on their scrannel pipes of wretched straw,
The hungry sheep look up, and are not fed.
'Lycidas' (1638) l. 123

7 But that two-handed engine at the door
Stands ready to smite once, and smite no more.
'Lycidas' (1638) l. 130

8 Bring the rathe primrose that forsaken dies,
The tufted crow-toe, and pale jessamine.
'Lycidas' (1638) l. 142

9 Look homeward angel now, and melt with ruth.
'Lycidas' (1638) l. 163

10 So sinks the day-star in the ocean bed,
And yet anon repairs his drooping head,
And tricks his beams, and with new spangled ore,
Flames in the forehead of the morning sky.
'Lycidas' (1638) l. 168

11 Through the dear might of Him that walked the waves.
'Lycidas' (1638) l. 173

12 While the still morn went out with sandals grey.
'Lycidas' (1638) l. 187

13 At last he rose, and twitched his mantle blue:
Tomorrow to fresh woods, and pastures new.
'Lycidas' (1638) l. 192

14 What needs my Shakespeare for his honoured bones,
The labour of an age in pilèd stones.
'On Shakespeare' (1632)

15 O fairest flower no sooner blown but blasted,
Soft silken primrose fading timelessly.
'On the Death of a Fair Infant Dying of a Cough' (1673) st. 1

16 For what can war, but endless war still breed?
'On the Lord General Fairfax at the Siege of Colchester' (written 1648)

17 This is the month, and this the happy morn
Wherein the son of heaven's eternal king,
Of wedded maid, and virgin mother born,
Our great redemption from above did bring.
'On the Morning of Christ's Nativity' (1645) st. 1

18 The star-led wizards haste with odours sweet.
'On the Morning of Christ's Nativity' (1645) st. 4

19 It was the winter wild,
While the heaven-born-child
All meanly wrapped in the rude manger lies;
Nature in awe to him
Had doffed her gaudy trim,
With her great master so to sympathize.
'On the Morning of Christ's Nativity' (1645) 'The Hymn' st. 1

20 No war, or battle's sound
Was heard the world around.
'On the Morning of Christ's Nativity' (1645) 'The Hymn' st. 4

21 The stars with deep amaze
Stand fixed in steadfast gaze,
Bending one way their precious influence,
And will not take their flight
For all the morning light,
Or Lucifer that often warned them thence.
'On the Morning of Christ's Nativity' (1645) 'The Hymn' st. 6

22 The helmèd cherubim
And sworded seraphim
Are seen in glittering ranks with wings displayed.
'On the Morning of Christ's Nativity' (1645) 'The Hymn' st. 11

23 Ring out, ye crystal spheres,
Once bless our human ears
(If ye have power to touch our senses so),
And let your silver chime
Move in melodious time;
And let the base of heaven's deep organ blow,
And with your ninefold harmony
Make up full consort to the angelic symphony.
'On the Morning of Christ's Nativity' (1645) 'The Hymn' st. 13

24 Time will run back, and fetch the age of gold.
'On the Morning of Christ's Nativity' (1645) 'The Hymn' st. 14

25 And hell itself will pass away,
And leave her dolorous mansions to the peering day.
'On the Morning of Christ's Nativity' (1645) 'The Hymn' st. 14

26 Swinges the scaly horror of his folded tail.
'On the Morning of Christ's Nativity' (1645) 'The Hymn' st. 18

27 The oracles are dumb,
No voice or hideous hum
Runs through the archèd roof in words deceiving.
Apollo from his shrine
Can no more divine,
With hollow shriek the steep of Delphos leaving.
'On the Morning of Christ's Nativity' (1645) 'The Hymn' st. 19

28 So when the sun in bed,
Curtained with cloudy red,

Pillows his chin upon an orient wave.
'On the Morning of Christ's Nativity' (1645) 'The Hymn' st. 26

1 Time is our tedious song should here have ending.
'On the Morning of Christ's Nativity' (1645) 'The Hymn' st. 27

2 New *Presbyter* is but old *Priest* writ large.
'On the New Forcers of Conscience under the Long Parliament' (1646)

3 Fly envious Time, till thou run out thy race,
Call on the lazy leaden-stepping hours.
'On Time' (1645)

4 If any ask for him, it shall be said,
Hobson has supped, and's newly gone to bed.
'On the University Carrier' (1645)

5 Rhyme being . . . but the invention of a barbarous age, to set off wretched matter and lame metre.
Paradise Lost (1667) 'The Verse' (preface, added 1668)

6 The troublesome and modern bondage of rhyming.
Paradise Lost (1667) 'The Verse' (preface, added 1668)

7 Of man's first disobedience, and the fruit
Of that forbidden tree, whose mortal taste
Brought death into the world, and all our woe,
With loss of Eden.
Paradise Lost (1667) bk. 1, l. 1

8 Things unattempted yet in prose or rhyme.
Paradise Lost (1667) bk. 1, l. 16

9 What in me is dark
Illumine, what is low raise and support;
That to the height of this great argument
I may assert eternal providence,
And justify the ways of God to men.
Paradise Lost (1667) bk. 1, l. 22; cf. **Housman** 391:9, **Pope** 585:5

10 The infernal serpent; he it was, whose guile
Stirred up with envy and revenge, deceived
The mother of mankind.
Paradise Lost (1667) bk. 1, l. 34

11 Him the almighty power
Hurled headlong flaming from the ethereal sky
With hideous ruin and combustion down.
Paradise Lost (1667) bk. 1, l. 44

12 No light, but rather darkness visible
Served only to discover sights of woe.
Paradise Lost (1667) bk. 1, l. 63

13 What though the field be lost?
All is not lost; the unconquerable will,
And study of revenge, immortal hate,
And courage never to submit or yield.
Paradise Lost (1667) bk. 1, l. 105

14 Vaunting aloud, but racked with deep despair.
Paradise Lost (1667) bk. 1, l. 126

15 To do aught good never will be our task,
But ever to do ill our sole delight.
Paradise Lost (1667) bk. 1, l. 159

16 And out of good still to find means of evil.
Paradise Lost (1667) bk. 1, l. 165

17 What reinforcement we may gain from hope;
If not, what resolution from despair.
Paradise Lost (1667) bk. 1, l. 190

18 The will
And high permission of all-ruling heaven
Left him at large to his own dark designs,
That with reiterated crimes he might
Heap on himself damnation.
Paradise Lost (1667) bk. 1, l. 211

19 Is this the region, this the soil, the clime,
Said then the lost archangel, this the seat
That we must change for heaven, this mournful gloom
For that celestial light?
Paradise Lost (1667) bk. 1, l. 242

20 The mind is its own place, and in itself
Can make a heaven of hell, a hell of heaven.
Paradise Lost (1667) bk. 1, l. 254

21 Better to reign in hell, than serve in heaven.
Paradise Lost (1667) bk. 1, l. 263

22 His spear, to equal which the tallest pine
Hewn on Norwegian hills, to be the mast
Of some great admiral, were but a wand,
He walked with to support uneasy steps
Over the burning marl.
Paradise Lost (1667) bk. 1, l. 292

23 Thick as autumnal leaves that strew the brooks
In Vallombrosa, where the Etrurian shades
High overarched imbower.
Paradise Lost (1667) bk. 1, l. 302

24 First Moloch, horrid king besmeared with blood
Of human sacrifice, and parents' tears.
Paradise Lost (1667) bk. 1, l. 392

25 Astarte, queen of heaven, with crescent horns.
Paradise Lost (1667) bk. 1, l. 439

26 Thammuz came next behind,
Whose annual wound in Lebanon allured
The Syrian damsels to lament his fate
In amorous ditties all a summer's day,
While smooth Adonis from his native rock
Ran purple to the sea.
Paradise Lost (1667) bk. 1, l. 446

27 And when night
Darkens the streets, then wander forth the sons
Of Belial, flown with insolence and wine.
Paradise Lost (1667) bk. 1, l. 500

28 The imperial ensign, which full high advanced
Shone like a meteor streaming to the wind.
Paradise Lost (1667) bk. 1, l. 536; cf. **Gray** 350:3

29 A shout that tore hell's concave, and beyond
Frighted the reign of Chaos and old Night.
Paradise Lost (1667) bk. 1, l. 542

30 What resounds
In fable or romance of Uther's son
Begirt with British and Armoric knights;
And all who since, baptized or infidel,
Jousted in Aspramont or Montalban,
Damasco, or Marocco, or Trebisond,
Or whom Biserta sent from Afric shore

When Charlemain with all his peerage fell
By Fontarabia.
Paradise Lost (1667) bk. 1, l. 579

1 In dim eclipse disastrous twilight sheds
On half the nations, and with fear of change
Perplexes monarchs.
Paradise Lost (1667) bk. 1, l. 597

2 Who overcomes
By force, hath overcome but half his foe.
Paradise Lost (1667) bk. 1, l. 648

3 Mammon led them on,
Mammon, the least erected spirit that fell
From heaven, for even in heaven his looks and thoughts
Were always downward bent, admiring more
The riches of heaven's pavement, trodden gold,
Than aught divine or holy else enjoyed
In vision beatific.
Paradise Lost (1667) bk. 1, l. 678

4 Let none admire
That riches grow in hell; that soil may best
Deserve the precious bane.
Paradise Lost (1667) bk. 1, l. 690

5 From morn
To noon he fell, from noon to dewy eve,
A summer's day; and with the setting sun
Dropped from the zenith like a falling star.
Paradise Lost (1667) bk. 1, l. 742

6 Pandemonium, the high capital
Of Satan and his peers.
Paradise Lost (1667) bk. 1, l. 756

7 High on a throne of royal state, which far
Outshone the wealth of Ormuz and of Ind,
Or where the gorgeous East with richest hand
Showers on her kings barbaric pearl and gold,
Satan exalted sat, by merit raised
To that bad eminence.
Paradise Lost (1667) bk. 2, l. 1

8 His trust was with the eternal to be deemed
Equal in strength, and rather than be less
Cared not to be at all.
Paradise Lost (1667) bk. 2, l. 46

9 Belial, in act more graceful and humane;
A fairer person lost not heaven; he seemed
For dignity composed and high exploit:
But all was false and hollow; though his tongue
Dropped manna, and could make the worse appear
The better reason.
Paradise Lost (1667) bk. 2, l. 109; cf. **Aristophanes** 24:9

10 To perish rather, swallowed up and lost
In the wide womb of uncreated night,
Devoid of sense and motion?
Paradise Lost (1667) bk. 2, l. 149

11 Unrespited, unpitied, unreprieved,
Ages of hopeless end.
Paradise Lost (1667) bk. 2, l. 185

12 Thus Belial with words clothed in reason's garb
Counselled ignoble ease, and peaceful sloth,
Not peace.
Paradise Lost (1667) bk. 2, l. 226

13 Our torments also may in length of time
Become our elements.
Paradise Lost (1667) bk. 2, l. 274

14 With grave
Aspect he rose, and in his rising seemed
A pillar of state; deep on his front engraven
Deliberation sat and public care;
And princely counsel in his face yet shone,
Majestic though in ruin.
Paradise Lost (1667) bk. 2, l. 300

15 To sit in darkness here
Hatching vain empires.
Paradise Lost (1667) bk. 2, l. 377

16 And through the palpable obscure find out
His uncouth way.
Paradise Lost (1667) bk. 2, l. 406

17 Long is the way
And hard, that out of hell leads up to light.
Paradise Lost (1667) bk. 2, l. 432

18 For eloquence the soul, song charms the sense.
Paradise Lost (1667) bk. 2, l. 556

19 Of good and evil much they argued then,
Of happiness and final misery,
Passion and apathy, and glory and shame,
Vain wisdom all, and false philosophy.
Paradise Lost (1667) bk. 2, l. 562

20 The parching air
Burns frore, and cold performs the effect of fire.
Paradise Lost (1667) bk. 2, l. 594

21 O'er many a frozen, many a fiery alp,
Rocks, caves, lakes, fens, bogs, dens, and shades of death,
A universe of death, which God by curse
Created evil.
Paradise Lost (1667) bk. 2, l. 620

22 Black it stood as night,
Fierce as ten Furies, terrible as hell,
And shook a dreadful dart.
Paradise Lost (1667) bk. 2, l. 670

23 Incensed with indignation Satan stood
Unterrified, and like a comet burned
That fires the length of Ophiuchus huge
In the Arctic sky, and from his horrid hair
Shakes pestilence and war.
Paradise Lost (1667) bk. 2, l. 707

24 I fled, and cried out Death!
Hell trembled at the hideous name, and sighed
From all her caves, and back resounded Death.
Paradise Lost (1667) bk. 2, l. 787

25 Chaos umpire sits,
And by decision more embroils the fray
By which he reigns; next him high arbiter
Chance governs all.
Paradise Lost (1667) bk. 2, l. 907

26 Sable-vested Night, eldest of things.
Paradise Lost (1667) bk. 2, l. 962

27 With ruin upon ruin, rout on rout,
Confusion worse confounded.
Paradise Lost (1667) bk. 2, l. 995

1 So he with difficulty and labour hard
Moved on, with difficulty and labour he.
Paradise Lost (1667) bk. 2, l. 1021

2 Die he or justice must.
Paradise Lost (1667) bk. 3, l. 210; cf. **Andrewes** 14:13

3 Dark with excessive bright.
Paradise Lost (1667) bk. 3, l. 380

4 So on this windy sea of land, the fiend
Walked up and down alone bent on his prey.
Paradise Lost (1667) bk. 3, l. 440

5 Into a limbo large and broad, since called
The Paradise of Fools, to few unknown.
Paradise Lost (1667) bk. 3, l. 495

6 Hypocrisy, the only evil that walks
Invisible, except to God alone.
Paradise Lost (1667) bk. 3, l. 683

7 At whose sight all the stars
Hide their diminished heads.
Paradise Lost (1667) bk. 4, l. 34

8 Warring in heaven against heaven's matchless king.
Paradise Lost (1667) bk. 4, l. 41

9 Me miserable! which way shall I fly
Infinite wrath, and infinite despair?
Which way I fly is hell; myself am hell.
Paradise Lost (1667) bk. 4, l. 73

10 Farewell remorse! All good to me is lost;
Evil, be thou my good.
Paradise Lost (1667) bk. 4, l. 109

11 So clomb this first grand thief into God's fold:
So since into his church lewd hirelings climb.
Thence up he flew, and on the tree of life,
The middle tree and highest there that grew,
Sat like a cormorant.
Paradise Lost (1667) bk. 4, l. 192

12 Groves whose rich trees wept odorous gums and balm,
Others whose fruit burnished with golden rind
Hung amiable, Hesperian fables true,
If true, here only.
Paradise Lost (1667) bk. 4, l. 248

13 Flowers of all hue, and without thorn the rose.
Paradise Lost (1667) bk. 4, l. 256

14 Not that fair field
Of Enna, where Proserpine gathering flowers
Herself a fairer flower by gloomy Dis
Was gathered, which cost Ceres all that pain.
Paradise Lost (1667) bk. 4, l. 268

15 For contemplation he and valour formed,
For softness she and sweet attractive grace,
He for God only, she for God in him.
Paradise Lost (1667) bk. 4, l. 297

16 Yielded with coy submission, modest pride,
And sweet reluctant amorous delay.
Paradise Lost (1667) bk. 4, l. 310

17 Adam, the goodliest man of men since born
His sons, the fairest of her daughters Eve.
Paradise Lost (1667) bk. 4, l. 323

18 These two
Emparadised in one another's arms
The happier Eden, shall enjoy their fill
Of bliss on bliss.
Paradise Lost (1667) bk. 4, l. 505

19 Now came still evening on, and twilight grey
Had in her sober livery all things clad.
Paradise Lost (1667) bk. 4, l. 598

20 Now glowed the firmament
With living sapphires: Hesperus that led
The starry host, rode brightest, till the moon
Rising in clouded majesty, at length
Apparent queen unveiled her peerless light,
And o'er the dark her silver mantle threw.
Paradise Lost (1667) bk. 4, l. 604

21 God is thy law, thou mine: to know no more
Is woman's happiest knowledge and her praise.
With thee conversing I forget all time.
Paradise Lost (1667) bk. 4, l. 637

22 Sweet the coming on
Of grateful evening mild, then silent night
With this her solemn bird and this fair moon,
And these the gems of heaven, her starry train.
Paradise Lost (1667) bk. 4, l. 646

23 Millions of spiritual creatures walk the earth
Unseen, both when we wake, and when we sleep.
Paradise Lost (1667) bk. 4, l. 677

24 Nor turned I ween
Adam from his fair spouse, nor Eve the rites
Mysterious of connubial love refused.
Paradise Lost (1667) bk. 4, l. 741

25 Hail, wedded love, mysterious law, true source
Of human offspring, sole propriety
In Paradise of all things common else.
Paradise Lost (1667) bk. 4, l. 750

26 Sleep on
Blest pair; and O yet happiest if ye seek
No happier state, and know to know no more.
Paradise Lost (1667) bk. 4, l. 773

27 Him there they found
Squat like a toad, close at the ear of Eve.
Paradise Lost (1667) bk. 4, l. 799

28 But wherefore thou alone? Wherefore with thee
Came not all hell broke loose?
Paradise Lost (1667) bk. 4, l. 917

29 My fairest, my espoused, my latest found,
Heaven's last best gift, my ever new delight.
Paradise Lost (1667) bk. 5, l. 18

30 Best image of myself and dearer half.
Paradise Lost (1667) bk. 5, l. 95

31 On earth join all ye creatures to extol
Him first, him last, him midst, and without end.
Paradise Lost (1667) bk. 5, l. 164

32 Nor jealousy
Was understood, the injured lover's hell.
Paradise Lost (1667) bk. 5, l. 449

33 What if earth
Be but the shadow of heaven, and things therein

Each to other like, more than on earth is thought?
Paradise Lost (1667) bk. 5, l. 574

1 Hear all ye angels, progeny of light,
Thrones, dominations, princedoms, virtues, powers.
Paradise Lost (1667) bk. 5, l. 600; cf. **Bible** 109:2

2 All seemed well pleased, all seemed, but were not all.
Paradise Lost (1667) bk. 5, l. 617

3 Mystical dance, which yonder starry sphere
Of planets and of fixed in all her wheels
Resembles nearest, mazes intricate,
Eccentric intervolved, yet regular
Then most, when most irregular they seem,
And in their motions harmony divine
So smoothes her charming tones, that God's own ear
Listens delighted.
Paradise Lost (1667) bk. 5, l. 620

4 Satan, so call him now, his former name
Is heard no more in heaven.
Paradise Lost (1667) bk. 5, l. 658

5 Servant of God, well done, well hast thou fought
The better fight, who single has maintained
Against revolted multitudes the cause
Of truth, in word mightier than they in arms.
Paradise Lost (1667) bk. 6, l. 29

6 Still govern thou my song,
Urania, and fit audience find, though few.
Paradise Lost (1667) bk. 7, l. 30

7 There Leviathan
Hugest of living creatures, on the deep
Stretched like a promontory sleeps or swims,
And seems a moving land, and at his gills
Draws in, and at his trunk spouts out a sea.
Paradise Lost (1667) bk. 7, l. 412

8 The planets in their stations listening stood,
While the bright pomp ascended jubilant.
Open, ye everlasting gates, they sung,
Open, ye heavens, your living doors; let in
The great creator from his work returned
Magnificent, his six days' work, a world.
Paradise Lost (1667) bk. 7, l. 563

9 In solitude
What happiness? who can enjoy alone,
Or all enjoying, what contentment find?
Paradise Lost (1667) bk. 8, l. 364

10 So absolute she seems
And in herself complete, so well to know
Her own, that what she wills to do or say
Seems wisest, virtuousest, discreetest, best.
Paradise Lost (1667) bk. 8, l. 547

11 Oft-times nothing profits more
Than self esteem, grounded on just and right
Well managed.
Paradise Lost (1667) bk. 8, l. 571; cf. **Leavis** 461:7

12 And dictates to me slumbering, or inspires
Easy my unpremeditated verse.
Paradise Lost (1667) bk. 9, l. 23

13 The serpent subtlest beast of all the field.
Paradise Lost (1667) bk. 9, l. 86

14 As one who long in populous city pent,
Where houses thick and sewers annoy the air,
Forth issuing on a summer's morn to breathe
Among the pleasant villages and farms
Adjoined, from each thing met conceives delight.
Paradise Lost (1667) bk. 9, l. 445; cf. **Keats** 430:16

15 She fair, divinely fair, fit love for gods.
Paradise Lost (1667) bk. 9, l. 489

16 God so commanded, and left that command
Sole daughter of his voice; the rest, we live
Law to our selves, our reason is our law.
Paradise Lost (1667) bk. 9, l. 652

17 Her rash hand in evil hour
Forth reaching to the fruit, she plucked, she ate:
Earth felt the wound, and Nature from her seat
Sighing through all her works gave signs of woe
That all was lost.
Paradise Lost (1667) bk. 9, l. 780

18 O fairest of creation, last and best
Of all God's works.
Paradise Lost (1667) bk. 9, l. 896

19 Flesh of flesh,
Bone of my bone thou art, and from thy state
Mine never shall be parted, bliss or woe.
Paradise Lost (1667) bk. 9, l. 914; cf. **Bible** 73:22

20 What thou art is mine;
Our state cannot be severed, we are one,
One flesh; to lose thee were to lose my self.
Paradise Lost (1667) bk. 9, l. 957

21 . . . Yet I shall temper so
Justice with mercy.
Paradise Lost (1667) bk. 10, l. 77

22 He hears
On all sides, from innumerable tongues
A dismal universal hiss, the sound
Of public scorn.
Paradise Lost (1667) bk. 10, l. 506

23 This novelty on earth, this fair defect
Of nature?
Paradise Lost (1667) bk. 10, l. 891

24 Demoniac frenzy, moping melancholy
And moon-struck madness.
Paradise Lost (1667) bk. 11, l. 485

25 The evening star,
Love's harbinger.
Paradise Lost (1667) bk. 11, l. 588

26 For now I see
Peace to corrupt no less than war to waste.
Paradise Lost (1667) bk. 11, l. 783

27 O goodness infinite, goodness immense!
That all this good of evil shall produce,
And evil turn to good; more wonderful
Than that which by creation first brought forth
Light out of darkness!
Paradise Lost (1667) bk. 12, l. 469

28 Then wilt thou not be loath
To leave this Paradise, but shalt possess

A paradise within thee, happier far.
Paradise Lost (1667) bk. 12, l. 585

1 In me is no delay; with thee to go,
Is to stay here; without thee here to stay,
Is to go hence unwilling; thou to me
Art all things under heaven, all places thou,
Who for my wilful crime art banished hence.
Paradise Lost (1667) bk. 12, l. 615

2 They looking back, all the eastern side beheld
Of Paradise, so late their happy seat.
Paradise Lost (1667) bk. 12, l. 641

3 The world was all before them, where to choose
Their place of rest, and Providence their guide:
They hand in hand, with wandering steps and slow,
Through Eden took their solitary way.
Paradise Lost (1667) bk. 12, l. 646

4 Of whom to be dispraised were no small praise.
Paradise Regained (1671) bk. 3, l. 56

5 But on occasion's forelock watchful wait.
Paradise Regained (1671) bk. 3, l. 173

6 He who seeking asses found a kingdom.
of Saul
Paradise Regained (1671) bk. 3, l. 242; cf. **Bible** 78:20

7 The childhood shows the man,
As morning shows the day.
Paradise Regained (1671) bk. 4, l. 220; cf. **Wordsworth** 829:10

8 Athens, the eye of Greece, mother of arts
And eloquence, native to famous wits
Or hospitable, in her sweet recess,
City or suburban, studious walks and shades;
See there the olive grove of Academe,
Plato's retirement, where the Attic bird
Trills her thick-warbled notes the summer long.
Paradise Regained (1671) bk. 4, l. 240

9 The first and wisest of them all professed
To know this only, that he nothing knew.
Paradise Regained (1671) bk. 4, l. 293; cf. **Davies** 251:16, **Socrates** 726:21

10 Who reads
Incessantly, and to his reading brings not
A spirit and judgement equal or superior
(And what he brings, what needs he elsewhere seek?)
Uncertain and unsettled still remains,
Deep-versed in books and shallow in himself.
Paradise Regained (1671) bk. 4, l. 322

11 In them is plainest taught, and easiest learnt,
What makes a nation happy, and keeps it so.
of the prophets
Paradise Regained (1671) bk. 4, l. 361

12 But headlong joy is ever on the wing.
'The Passion' (1645) st. 1

13 Ask for this great deliverer now, and find him
Eyeless in Gaza at the mill with slaves.
Samson Agonistes (1671) l. 40

14 O dark, dark, dark, amid the blaze of noon,
Irrecoverably dark, total eclipse
Without all hope of day!
Samson Agonistes (1671) l. 80

15 The sun to me is dark
And silent as the moon,
When she deserts the night
Hid in her vacant interlunar cave.
Samson Agonistes (1671) l. 86

16 To live a life half dead, a living death.
Samson Agonistes (1671) l. 100

17 Just are the ways of God,
And justifiable to men;
Unless there be who think not God at all.
Samson Agonistes (1671) l. 293

18 What boots it at one gate to make defence,
And at another to let in the foe?
Samson Agonistes (1671) l. 560

19 Yet beauty, though injurious, hath strange power,
After offence returning, to regain
Love once possessed.
Samson Agonistes (1671) l. 1003

20 Love-quarrels oft in pleasing concord end.
Samson Agonistes (1671) l. 1008

21 Lords are lordliest in their wine.
Samson Agonistes (1671) l. 1418

22 Like that self-begotten bird
In the Arabian woods embossed,
That no second knows nor third,
And lay erewhile a holocaust.
Samson Agonistes (1671) l. 1699

23 And though her body die, her fame survives,
A secular bird ages of lives.
Samson Agonistes (1671) l. 1706

24 Samson hath quit himself
Like Samson, and heroically hath finished
A life heroic.
Samson Agonistes (1671) l. 1709

25 Nothing is here for tears, nothing to wail.
Samson Agonistes (1671) l. 1721

26 And calm of mind, all passion spent.
Samson Agonistes (1671) l. 1758

27 Time the subtle thief of youth.
Sonnet 7 'How soon hath time' (1645)

28 Licence they mean when they cry liberty;
For who loves that, must first be wise and good.
Sonnet 12 'I did but prompt the age' (1673)

29 When I consider how my light is spent,
E're half my days, in this dark world and wide,
And that one talent which is death to hide
Lodged with me useless.
Sonnet 16 'When I consider how my light is spent' (1673)

30 Doth God exact day-labour, light denied,
I fondly ask; but patience to prevent
That murmur, soon replies, God doth not need
Either man's work or his own gifts, who best
Bear his mild yoke, they serve him best, his state
Is kingly. Thousands at his bidding speed
And post o'er land and ocean without rest:
They also serve who only stand and wait.
Sonnet 16 'When I consider how my light is spent' (1673)

1 Methought I saw my late espousèd saint
Brought to me like Alcestis from the grave.
Sonnet 19 'Methought I saw my late espousèd saint' (1673)

2 But oh as to embrace me she inclined
I waked, she fled, and day brought back my night.
Sonnet 19 'Methought I saw my late espousèd saint' (1673)

3 Cromwell, our chief of men.
'To the Lord General Cromwell' (written 1652)

4 Peace hath her victories
No less renowned than war.
'To the Lord General Cromwell' (written 1652)

5 He who would not be frustrate of his hope to write well hereafter in laudable things, ought himself to be a true poem.
An Apology for Smectymnuus (1642) introduction

6 For this is not the liberty which we can hope, that no grievance ever should arise in the Commonwealth, that let no man in this world expect; but when complaints are freely heard, deeply considered, and speedily reformed, then is the utmost bound of civil liberty attained that wise men look for.
Areopagitica (1644)

7 Books are not absolutely dead things, but do contain a potency of life in them to be as active as that soul was whose progeny they are; nay they do preserve as in a vial the purest efficacy and extraction of that living intellect that bred them.
Areopagitica (1644)

8 As good almost kill a man as kill a good book: who kills a man kills a reasonable creature, God's image; but he who destroys a good book, kills reason itself, kills the image of God, as it were in the eye.
Areopagitica (1644)

9 A good book is the precious life-blood of a master spirit, embalmed and treasured up on purpose to a life beyond life.
Areopagitica (1644)

10 I cannot praise a fugitive and cloistered virtue, unexercised and unbreathed, that never sallies out and sees her adversary, but slinks out of the race, where that immortal garland is to be run for, not without dust and heat . . . that which purifies us is trial, and trial is by what is contrary.
Areopagitica (1644)

11 Here the great art lies, to discern in what the law is to be to restraint and punishment, and in what things persuasion only is to work.
Areopagitica (1644)

12 If we think to regulate printing, thereby to rectify manners, we must regulate all recreations and pastimes, all that is delightful to man . . . And who shall silence all the airs and madrigals, that whisper softness in chambers?
Areopagitica (1644)

13 From that time ever since, the sad friends of Truth, such as durst appear, imitating the careful search that Isis made for the mangled body of Osiris, went up and down gathering up limb by limb still as they could find them. We have not yet found them all, Lords and Commons, nor ever shall do, till her Master's second coming; He shall bring together every joint and member, and shall mould them into an immortal feature of loveliness and perfection.
Areopagitica (1644)

14 To be still searching what we know not, by what we know, still closing up truth to truth as we find it (for all her body is homogeneal and proportional), this is the golden rule in theology as well as in arithmetic, and makes up the best harmony in a church.
Areopagitica (1644)

15 God is decreeing to begin some new and great period in his Church, even to the reforming of Reformation itself. What does he then but reveal Himself to his servants, and as his manner is, first to his Englishmen?
Areopagitica (1644)

16 A city of refuge, the mansion-house of liberty.
of London
Areopagitica (1644)

17 Where there is much desire to learn, there of necessity will be much arguing, much writing, many opinions; for opinion in good men is but knowledge in the making.
Areopagitica (1644) p. 31

18 Give me the liberty to know, to utter, and to argue freely according to conscience, above all liberties.
Areopagitica (1644)

19 Though all the winds of doctrine were let loose to play upon the earth, so Truth be in the field, we do injuriously by licensing and prohibiting to misdoubt her strength. Let her and Falsehood grapple; who ever knew Truth put to the worse, in a free and open encounter?
Areopagitica (1644)

20 Let not England forget her precedence of teaching nations how to live.
The Doctrine and Discipline of Divorce (1643) 'To the Parliament of England'

21 In those vernal seasons of the year, when the air is calm and pleasant, it were an injury and sullenness against nature not to go out, and see her riches, and partake in her rejoicing with heaven and earth.
Of Education (1644) 'Their Exercise'

22 What I have spoken, is the language of that which is not called amiss *The good old Cause.*
The Ready and Easy Way to Establish a Free Commonwealth (2nd ed., 1660); cf. **Wordsworth** 830:13

23 This manner of writing [prose] wherein knowing myself inferior to myself . . . I have the use, as I may account it, but of my left hand.
The Reason of Church Government (1642) bk. 2, introduction

24 The land had once enfranchised herself from this impertinent yoke of prelaty, under whose inquisitorious and tyrannical duncery no free and splendid wit can flourish.
The Reason of Church Government (1642) bk. 2, introduction

1 Beholding the bright countenance of truth in the quiet and still air of delightful studies.
The Reason of Church Government (1642) bk. 2, introduction

2 None can love freedom heartily, but good men; the rest love not freedom, but licence.
The Tenure of Kings and Magistrates (1649)

3 No man who knows aught, can be so stupid to deny that all men naturally were born free.
The Tenure of Kings and Magistrates (1649)

Comte de Mirabeau 1749–91

French revolutionary

4 War is the national industry of Prussia.
attributed to Mirabeau by Albert Sorel (1842–1906), based on Mirabeau's introduction to *De la monarchie prussienne sous Frédéric le Grand* (1788)

Helen Mirren 1945–

English actress

5 When you do Shakespeare they think you must be intelligent because they *think* you understand what you're saying.
interviewed on *Ruby Wax Meets . . .*; in *Mail on Sunday* 16 February 1997 'Night and Day'

☐ Misquotations

see box opposite

The Missal

The Latin Eucharistic liturgy used by the Roman Catholic Church up to 1964

6 *Asperges me, Domine, hyssopo, et mundabor.*
Sprinkle me with hyssop, O Lord, and I shall be cleansed.
Anthem at Sprinkling the Holy Water; cf. **Book of Common Prayer** 135:6

7 *Dominus vobiscum.*
Et cum spiritu tuo.
The Lord be with you.
And with thy spirit.
The Ordinary of the Mass

8 *In Nomine Patris, et Filii, et Spiritus Sancti.*
In the Name of the Father, and of the Son, and of the Holy Ghost.
The Ordinary of the Mass

9 *Introibo ad altare Dei.*
I will go unto the altar of God.
The Ordinary of the Mass; cf. **Book of Common Prayer** 133:8

10 *Gloria Patri, et Filio, et Spiritui Sancto. Sicut erat in principio, et nunc, et semper, et in saecula saeculorum.*
Glory be to the Father, and to the Son, and to the Holy Ghost. As it was in the beginning, is now, and ever shall be, world without end.
The Ordinary of the Mass 'The Doxology'; cf. **Book of Common Prayer** 125:19

11 *Confiteor Deo omnipotenti . . . quia peccavi nimis cogitatione, verbo, et opere, mea culpa, mea culpa, mea maxima culpa.*
I confess to almighty God . . . that I have sinned exceedingly in thought, word, and deed, through my fault, through my fault, through my most grievous fault.
The Ordinary of the Mass

12 *Kyrie eleison . . . Christe eleison.*
Lord, have mercy upon us . . . Christ, have mercy upon us.
The Ordinary of the Mass

13 *Gloria in excelsis Deo, et in terra pax hominibus bonae voluntatis. Laudamus te, benedicimus te, adoramus te, glorificamus te.*
Glory be to God on high, and on earth peace to men of good will. We praise thee, we bless thee, we adore thee, we glorify thee.
The Ordinary of the Mass; cf. **Bible** 98:22

14 *Oremus.*
Let us pray.
The Ordinary of the Mass

15 *Deo gratias.*
Thanks be to God.
The Ordinary of the Mass

16 *Credo in unum Deum, Patrem omnipotentem, factorem coeli et terrae, visibilium omnium et invisibilium.*
I believe in one God, the Father almighty, maker of heaven and earth, and of all things visible and invisible.
The Ordinary of the Mass 'The Nicene Creed'; cf. **Book of Common Prayer** 126:10

17 *Deum de Deo, lumen de lumine, Deum verum de Deo vero.*
God of God, light of light; true God of true God.
The Ordinary of the Mass 'The Nicene Creed'

18 *Et incarnatus est de Spiritu Sancto, ex Maria Virgine;* ET HOMO FACTUS EST.
And became incarnate by the Holy Ghost, of the Virgin Mary; AND WAS MADE MAN.
The Ordinary of the Mass 'The Nicene Creed'

19 *Sursum corda.*
Lift up your hearts.
The Ordinary of the Mass; cf. **Book of Common Prayer** 129:18

20 *Dignum et justum est.*
It is right and fitting.
The Ordinary of the Mass; cf. **Book of Common Prayer** 129:20

21 *Sanctus, sanctus, sanctus, Dominus Deus Sabaoth. Pleni sunt coeli et terra gloria tua. Hosanna in excelsis. Benedictus qui venit in nomine Domini.*
Holy, holy, holy, Lord God of Hosts. Heaven and earth are full of thy glory. Hosanna in the highest. Blessed is he that cometh in the name of the Lord.
The Ordinary of the Mass; cf. **Bible** 111:32, **Book of Common Prayer** 129:20

continued

Misquotations

1 All is lost save honour.

popular summary of the words of **Francis I** of France:

Of all I had, only honour and life have been spared.

letter to his mother following his defeat at Pavia, 1525; cf. **Francis I** 323:1

2 All rowed fast, but none so fast as stroke.

popular summary of the following passage:

His blade struck the water a full second before any other: the lad had started well. Nor did he flag as the race wore on . . . as the boats began to near the winning-post, his oar was dipping into the water nearly *twice* as often as any other.

Desmond Coke (1879–1931) *Sandford of Merton* (1903) ch. 12

3 The ballot is stronger than the bullet.

popular version of a speech by **Lincoln**, 18 May 1858; cf. **Lincoln** 468:4

4 Beam me up, Scotty.

supposedly the form in which Captain Kirk habitually requested to be returned from a planet to the Starship *Enterprise*; in fact the nearest equivalent found is

Beam us up, Mr Scott.

Gene Roddenberry *Star Trek* (1966 onwards) 'Gamesters of Triskelion'

5 The capitalists will sell us the rope with which to hang them.

attributed to **Lenin**, but not found in his published works; I. U. Annenkov, in 'Remembrances of Lenin' includes a manuscript note attributed to Lenin:

They [capitalists] will furnish credits which will serve us for the support of the Communist Party in their countries and, by supplying us materials and technical equipment which we lack, will restore our military industry necessary for our future attacks against our suppliers. To put it in other words, they will work on the preparation of their own suicide.

in *Novyi Zhurnal/New Review* September 1961

6 Come with me to the Casbah.

often attributed to Charles Boyer (1898–1978) in the film Algiers *(1938), but the line does not in fact occur*

L. Swindell *Charles Boyer* (1983)

7 Crisis? What Crisis?

Sun headline, 11 January 1979, summarizing James **Callaghan**'s remark

I don't think other people in the world would share the view there is mounting chaos.

interview at London Airport, 10 January 1979

8 Dreams are the royal road to the unconscious.

popular summary of **Freud**'s *The Interpretation of Dreams* (2nd ed., 1909); cf. **Freud** 324:13

9 Elementary, my dear Watson, elementary.

remark attributed to Sherlock Holmes, but not found in this form in any book by Arthur Conan **Doyle**, *first found in P.G.* **Wodehouse** Psmith Journalist *(1915)*

attributed; cf. **Doyle** 277:16

10 England and America are two countries divided by a common language.

attributed in this and other forms to George Bernard **Shaw**, but not found in Shaw's published writings; cf. **Wilde** 817:11

11 Faith, the dark night of the soul.

St **John** of the Cross *Complete Works* (1864), translated by David Lewis, vol. 1, bk. 1, ch. 3; the phrase appears in the translator's chapter heading for the poem:

Noche oscura.

Dark night.

title of poem, St John of the Cross (1542–91) *The Ascent of Mount Carmel* (1578–80)

12 Few die and none resign.

popular summary of a letter of Thomas **Jefferson**, 1801; cf. **Jefferson** 405:15

13 The green shoots of recovery.

popular misquotation of the Chancellor's upbeat assessment of the economic situation:

The green shoots of economic spring are appearing once again.

Norman **Lamont**, speech at Conservative Party Conference, 9 October 1991

14 I disapprove of what you say, but I will defend to the death your right to say it.

to **Helvétius**, *following the burning of* De l'esprit *in 1759*

attributed to **Voltaire**, but in fact a later summary of his attitude by S. G. Tallentyre in *The Friends of Voltaire* (1907); cf. **Voltaire** 798:14

15 In trust I have found treason.

traditional concluding words of a speech by **Elizabeth I** to a Parliamentary deputation at Richmond, 12 November 1586; cf. **Elizabeth I** 296:25

16 I paint with my prick.

attributed to Pierre Auguste **Renoir**; possibly an inversion of:

It's with my brush that I make love.

A. André *Renoir* (1919)

17 It is necessary only for the good man to do nothing for evil to triumph.

attributed (in a number of forms) to **Burke**, but not found in his writings; cf. **Burke** 164:16

18 Licensed to kill.

popular description of the status of Secret Service agent James Bond, 007, in the novels of Ian **Fleming**

The licence to kill for the Secret Service, the double-o prefix, was a great honour.

Dr No (1958)

Misquotations *continued*

1 Man, if you gotta ask you'll never know.
alternative version of Louis **Armstrong**'s response when asked what jazz was; cf. **Armstrong** 25:17

2 Me Tarzan, you Jane.
Johnny Weissmuller (1904–84) summing up his role in Tarzan, the Ape Man *(1932 film)*
in *Photoplay Magazine* June 1932; the words do not occur in the film or in the original novel by Edgar Rice Burroughs

3 Mind has no sex.
summarizing the view of Mary **Wollstonecraft**; cf. **Wollstonecraft** 825:17

4 My lips are sealed.
popular version of **Baldwin**'s speech on the Abyssinian crisis, 10 December 1935; cf. **Baldwin** 49:10

5 Once aboard the lugger and the maid is mine.
popular version of the line:

I want you to assist me in forcing her on board the lugger; once there, I'll frighten her into marriage.
John Benn Johnstone (1803–91) *The Gipsy Farmer* (performed 1845)

6 Play it again, Sam.
in the film Casablanca, *written by Julius J. Epstein et al., Humphrey Bogart says, 'If she can stand it, I can. Play it!'; earlier in the film Ingrid Bergman says, 'Play it, Sam. Play* As Time Goes By.*'*
Casablanca (1942 film); cf. **Film lines** 311:12, **Hupfeld** 396:10

7 Selling off the family silver.
popular summary of Harold **Macmillan**'s attack on privatization, 8 November 1985; cf. **Macmillan** 488:1

8 The soft underbelly of Europe.
popular version of **Churchill**'s words in the House of Commons, 11 November 1942; cf. **Churchill** 215:18

9 Something must be done.
popular version of **Edward VIII**'s words at the derelict Dowlais Iron and Steel Works, 18 November 1936; cf. **Edward VIII** 289:6

10 Take away these baubles.
popular version of **Cromwell**'s words at the dismissal of the Rump Parliament, 20 April 1653; cf. **Cromwell** 245:15

11 Warts and all.
popular summary of **Cromwell**'s instructions to the court painter Lely:

Mr Lely, I desire you would use all your skill to paint my picture truly like me, and not flatter me at all; but remark all these roughnesses, pimples, warts, and everything as you see me; otherwise I will never pay a farthing for it.
Horace Walpole *Anecdotes of Painting in England* vol. 3 (1763) ch. 1

12 We are the masters now.
popular misquotation of Hartley **Shawcross**'s speech in the House of Commons, 2 April 1946; cf. **Shawcross** 709:27

13 *Was für plündern!*
What a place to plunder!
misquotation of the comment of **Blücher** on London, as seen from the Monument in June 1814; cf. **Blücher** 122:8

14 The white heat of technology.
popular version of Harold **Wilson**'s speech at the Labour Party Conference, 1 October 1963; cf. **Wilson** 821:15

15 Why don't you come up and see me sometime?
alteration of Mae **West**'s invitation in the film *She Done Him Wrong* (1933); cf. **West** 812:6

16 You dirty rat!
associated with James Cagney (1899–1986), but not used by him in any film; in a speech at the American Film Institute banquet, 13 March 1974, Cagney said, 'I never said "Mmm, you dirty rat!"'
Cagney by Cagney (1976)

The Missal *continued*

17 *Pater noster, qui es in coelis, sanctificetur nomen tuum; adveniat regnum tuum; fiat voluntas tua sicut in coelo, et in terra . . . sed libera nos a malo.*
Our Father, who art in heaven, hallowed be thy name; thy kingdom come; thy will be done on earth, as it is in heaven . . . but deliver us from evil.
The Ordinary of the Mass; cf. **Bible** 93:19

18 *Pax Domini sit semper vobiscum.*
The peace of the Lord be always with you.
The Ordinary of the Mass

19 *Agnus Dei, qui tollis peccata mundi, miserere nobis. Agnus Dei, qui tollis peccata mundi, dona nobis pacem.*
Lamb of God, who takest away the sins of the world, have mercy on us. Lamb of God, who takest away the sins of the world, give us peace.
The Ordinary of the Mass; cf. **Bible** 101:10

20 *Domine, non sum dignus ut intres sub tectum meum; sed tantum dic verbo, et sanabitur anima mea.*
Lord, I am not worthy that thou shouldst enter under my roof; but say only the word, and my soul shall be healed.
The Ordinary of the Mass; cf. **Bible** 94:15

21 *Ite missa est.*
Go, you are dismissed.
commonly interpreted as 'Go, the Mass is ended'
The Ordinary of the Mass

22 *In principio erat Verbum, et Verbum erat apud Deum, et Deus erat Verbum.*
In the beginning was the Word, and the Word was with God, and the Word was God.
The Ordinary of the Mass; cf. **Bible** 101:1

1 VERBUM CARO FACTUM EST.

THE WORD WAS MADE FLESH.

The Ordinary of the Mass; cf. **Bible** 101:7

2 *Requiem aeternam dona eis, Domine: et lux perpetua luceat eis.*

Grant them eternal rest, O Lord; and let perpetual light shine on them.

Order of Mass for the Dead

3 *Dies irae, dies illa,*
Solvet saeclum in favilla,
Teste David cum Sibylla.

That day, the day of wrath, will turn the universe to ashes, as David foretells (and the Sibyl too).

Order of Mass for the Dead 'Sequentia' l. 1; commonly known as *Dies Irae* and sometimes attributed to Thomas of Celano (*c.*1190–1260)

4 *Tuba mirum spargens sonum*
Per sepulcra regionum,
Coget omnes ante thronum.

Mors stupebit et natura,
Cum resurget creatura
Iudicanti responsura.

Liber scriptus proferetur,
In quo totum continetur
Unde mundus iudicetur.

The trumpet will fling out a wonderful sound through the tombs of all regions, it will drive everyone before the throne. Death will be aghast and so will nature, when creation rises again to make answer to the judge. The written book will be brought forth, in which everything is included whereby the world will be judged.

Order of Mass for the Dead 'Sequentia' l. 7

5 *Rex tremendae maiestatis,*
Qui salvandos salvas gratis,
Salva me, fons pietatis!

O King of tremendous majesty, who freely saves those who should be saved, save me, O source of pity!

Order of Mass for the Dead 'Sequentia' l. 22

6 *Inter oves locum praesta*
Et ab haedis me sequestra
Statuens in parte dextra.

Among the sheep set me a place and separate me from the goats, standing me on the right-hand side.

Order of Mass for the Dead 'Sequentia' l. 43

7 *Requiescant in pace.*

May they rest in peace.

Order of Mass for the Dead

8 *O felix culpa, quae talem ac tantum meruit habere Redemptorem.*

O happy fault, which has earned such a mighty Redeemer.

'Exsultet' on Holy Saturday

Mistinguette 1875–1956

French actress

9 A kiss can be a comma, a question mark or an exclamation point. That's basic spelling that every woman ought to know.

in *Theatre Arts* December 1955

Adrian Mitchell 1932–

English poet, novelist, and dramatist

10 When I am sad and weary,
When I think all hope has gone,
When I walk along High Holborn
I think of you with nothing on.

'Celia, Celia'

11 Most people ignore most poetry
because
most poetry ignores most people.

Poems (1964)

George Mitchell 1933–

American politician, chairman of the Northern Ireland peace talks

12 Nobody ever said it would be easy—and that was an understatement.

on the peace talks

in *Times* 19 February 1998

13 I am pleased to announce that the two governments and the political parties in Northern Ireland have reached agreement.

announcing the Good Friday agreement

in *Times* 11 April 1998

John Mitchell 1785–1859

English soldier

14 The most important political question on which modern times have to decide is the policy that must now be pursued, in order to maintain the security of Western Europe against the overgrown power of Russia.

Thoughts on Tactics (1838)

Joni Mitchell (Roberta Joan Anderson) 1945–

Canadian singer and songwriter

15 They paved paradise
And put up a parking lot,
With a pink hotel,
A boutique, and a swinging hot spot.

'Big Yellow Taxi' (1970 song)

16 I've looked at life from both sides now,
From win and lose and still somehow
It's life's illusions I recall;
I really don't know life at all.

'Both Sides Now' (1967 song)

17 We are stardust,
We are golden,
And we got to get ourselves
Back to the garden.

'Woodstock' (1969 song)

Margaret Mitchell 1900–49

American novelist

1 Death and taxes and childbirth! There's never any convenient time for any of them.
Gone with the Wind (1936) ch. 38

2 I wish I could care what you do or where you go but I can't . . . My dear, I don't give a damn.
Gone with the Wind (1936) ch. 57; cf. **Film lines** 311:7

3 After all, tomorrow is another day.
Gone with the Wind (1936), closing words; cf. **Proverbs** 613:10

Mary Russell Mitford 1787–1855

English novelist and dramatist

4 Till *Pride and Prejudice* showed what a precious gem was hidden in that unbending case, she was no more regarded in society than a poker or a fire-screen, or any other thin upright piece of wood or iron that fills its corner in peace and quietness. The case is very different now; she is still a poker—but a poker of whom every one is afraid.
of Jane ***Austen***
letter to Sir William Elford, 3 April 1815, in R. Brimley Johnson (ed.) *The Letters of Mary Russell Mitford* (1925)

Nancy Mitford 1904–73

English writer

5 Love in a cold climate.
title of book (1949); cf. **Southey** 731:7

6 'Always be civil to the girls, you never know who they may marry' is an aphorism which has saved many an English spinster from being treated like an Indian widow.
Love in a Cold Climate (1949) pt. 1, ch. 2; cf. **Ailesbury** 9:1

7 An aristocracy in a republic is like a chicken whose head has been cut off: it may run about in a lively way, but in fact it is dead.
Noblesse Oblige (1956) 'The English Aristocracy'

8 Wooing, so tiring.
The Pursuit of Love (1945) ch. 4

9 Frogs . . . are slightly better than Huns or Wops, but abroad is unutterably bloody and foreigners are fiends.
The Pursuit of Love (1945) ch. 15; cf. **George VI** 334:8

François Mitterrand 1916–96

French socialist statesman; President of France 1981–95

10 She has the eyes of Caligula, but the mouth of Marilyn Monroe.
of Margaret ***Thatcher****, briefing his new European Minister Roland Dumas*
in *Observer* 25 November 1990

Wilson Mizner 1876–1933

American dramatist

11 Be nice to people on your way up because you'll meet 'em on your way down.
Alva Johnston *The Legendary Mizners* (1953) ch. 4

12 If you steal from one author, it's plagiarism; if you steal from many, it's research.
Alva Johnston *The Legendary Mizners* (1953) ch. 4

13 A trip through a sewer in a glass-bottomed boat.
of Hollywood; reworked by Mayor Jimmy Walker into 'A reformer is a guy who rides through a sewer in a glass-bottomed boat'
Alva Johnston *The Legendary Mizners* (1953) ch. 4

Ariane Mnouchkine 1934–

French theatre director

14 A cultural Chernobyl.
of Euro Disney
in *Harper's Magazine* July 1992; cf. **Ballard** 52:13

Emilio Mola 1887–1937

Spanish nationalist general

15 Fifth column.
an extra body of supporters claimed by General Mola in a broadcast as being within Madrid when he besieged the city with four columns of Nationalist forces
in *New York Times* 16 and 17 October 1936

Molière (Jean-Baptiste Poquelin) 1622–73

French comic dramatist

16 *Présentez toujours le devant au monde.*
Always present your front to the world.
L'Avare (1669) act 3, sc. 1

17 *Il faut manger pour vivre et non pas vivre pour manger.*
One should eat to live, and not live to eat.
L'Avare (1669) act 3, sc. 1

18 *Tout ce qui n'est point prose est vers; et tout ce qui n'est point vers est prose.*
All that is not prose is verse; and all that is not verse is prose.
Le Bourgeois Gentilhomme (1671) act 2, sc. 4

19 M. JOURDAIN: *Quoi? quand je dis: 'Nicole, apportez-moi mes pantoufles, et me donnez mon bonnet de nuit', c'est de la prose?*
MAÎTRE DE PHILOSOPHIE: *Oui, Monsieur.*
M. JOURDAIN: Par ma foi! il y a plus de quarante ans que je dis de la prose sans que j'en susse rien.
M. JOURDAIN: What? when I say: 'Nicole, bring me my slippers, and give me my night-cap,' is that prose?
PHILOSOPHY TEACHER: Yes, Sir.
M. JOURDAIN: Good heavens! For more than forty years I have been speaking prose without knowing it.
Le Bourgeois Gentilhomme (1671) act 2, sc. 4

20 *Ah, la belle chose que de savoir quelque chose.*
Ah, it's a lovely thing, to know a thing or two.
Le Bourgeois Gentilhomme (1671) act 2, sc. 4

21 *C'est une étrange entreprise que celle de faire rire les honnêtes gens.*
It's an odd job, making decent people laugh.
La Critique de l'école des femmes (1663) sc. 6

22 *Je voudrais bien savoir si la grande règle de toutes les règles n'est pas de plaire.*

I shouldn't be surprised if the greatest rule of all weren't to give pleasure.
La Critique de l'école des femmes (1663) sc. 6

1 *On ne meurt qu'une fois, et c'est pour si longtemps!*
One dies only once, and it's for such a long time!
Le Dépit amoureux (performed 1656, published 1662) act 5, sc. 3

2 *Qui vit sans tabac n'est pas digne de vivre.*
He who lives without tobacco is not worthy to live.
Don Juan (performed 1665) act 1, sc. 1

3 *Je vis de bonne soupe et non de beau langage.*
It's good food and not fine words that keeps me alive.
Les Femmes savantes (1672) act 2, sc. 7

4 *Guenille, si l'on veut: ma guenille m'est chère.*
Rags and tatters, if you like: I am fond of my rags and tatters.
Les Femmes savantes (1672) act 2, sc. 7

5 *Un sot savant est sot plus qu'un sot ignorant.*
A knowledgeable fool is a greater fool than an ignorant fool.
Les Femmes savantes (1672) act 4, sc. 3

6 *Les livres cadrent mal avec le mariage.*
Reading and marriage don't go well together.
Les Femmes savantes (1672) act 5, sc. 3

7 *Que diable allait-il faire dans cette galère?*
What the devil was he doing in that galley?
Les Fourberies de Scapin (1671) act 2, sc. 11

8 *Vous l'avez voulu, Georges Dandin, vous l'avez voulu.*
You've asked for it, Georges Dandin, you've asked for it.
Georges Dandin (1668) act 1, sc. 9

9 GÉRONTE: *Il me semble que vous les placez autrement qu'ils ne sont: que le coeur est du côté gauche, et le foie du côté droit.*
SGANARELLE: *Oui, cela était autrefois ainsi, mais nous avons changé tout cela, et nous faisons maintenant la médecine d'une méthode toute nouvelle.*
GÉRONTE: It seems to me you are locating them wrongly: the heart is on the left and the liver is on the right.
SGANARELLE: Yes, in the old days that was so, but we have changed all that, and we now practise medicine by a completely new method.
Le Médecin malgré lui (1667) act 2, sc. 4

10 *Il faut, parmi le monde, une vertu traitable.*
What's needed in this world is an accommodating sort of virtue.
Le Misanthrope (1666) act 1, sc. 1

11 *Et c'est une folie à nulle autre seconde,*
De vouloir se mêler de corriger le monde.
Of all human follies there's none could be greater
Than trying to render our fellow-men better.
Le Misanthrope (1666) act 1, sc. 1

12 *On doit se regarder soi-même, un fort long temps,*
Avant que de songer à condamner les gens.
One should look long and carefully at oneself before one considers judging others.
Le Misanthrope (1666) act 3, sc. 4

13 *C'est un homme expéditif, qui aime à dépêcher ses malades; et quand on a à mourir, cela se fait avec lui le plus vite du monde.*
He's an expeditious man, who likes to hurry his patients along; and when you have to die, he sees to that quicker than anyone.
Monsieur de Pourceaugnac (1670) act 1, sc. 5

14 *Ils commencent ici par faire pendre un homme et puis ils lui font son procès.*
Here [in Paris] they hang a man first, and try him afterwards.
Monsieur de Pourceaugnac (1670) act 1, sc. 5

15 *Les gens de qualité savent tout sans avoir jamais rien appris.*
People of quality know everything without ever having been taught anything.
Les Précieuses ridicules (1660) sc. 9

16 *Assassiner c'est le plus court chemin.*
Assassination is the quickest way.
Le Sicilien (1668) sc. 12

17 *Ah, pour être dévot, je n'en suis pas moins homme.*
I am not the less human for being devout.
Le Tartuffe (performed 1664, published 1669) act 3, sc. 3

18 *Le ciel défend, de vrai, certains contentements,*
Mais on trouve avec lui des accommodements.
God, it is true, does some delights condemn,
But 'tis not hard to come to terms with Him.
Le Tartuffe (1669) act 4, sc. 5

19 *Le scandale du monde est ce qui fait l'offense,*
Et ce n'est pas pécher que pécher en silence.
It is public scandal that constitutes offence, and to sin in secret is not to sin at all.
Le Tartuffe (1669) act 4, sc. 5

20 *L'homme est, je vous l'avoue, un méchant animal.*
Man, I can assure you, is a nasty creature.
Le Tartuffe (1669) act 5, sc. 6

21 *Il m'est permis de reprendre mon bien où je le trouve.*
It is permitted me to take good fortune where I find it.
in J. L. Le Gallois *La Vie de Molière* (1704) p. 14

Mary Mollineux (née Southworth) 1651–95
English Quaker and poet

22 How sweet is harmless solitude!
What can its joys control?
Tumults and noise may not intrude,
To interrupt the soul.
'Solitude' (1670)

Helmuth von Moltke 1800–91
Prussian military commander
on Moltke: see ***Bagehot*** *46:14*

23 Everlasting peace is a dream, and not even a pleasant one; and war is a necessary part of God's

arrangement of the world . . . Without war the world would deteriorate into materialism.
letter to Dr J. K. Bluntschli, 11 December 1880 (translated by Mary Herms), in *Helmuth von Moltke as a Correspondent* (1893)

Walter Mondale 1928–
American Democratic politician

1 When I hear your new ideas I'm reminded of that ad, 'Where's the beef?'
in a televised debate with Gary Hart, 11 March 1984; cf. **Advertising slogans** 8:20

Piet Mondrian 1872–1944
Dutch painter

2 The essence of painting has actually always been to make it [the universal] plastically perceptible through colour and line.
'Natural Reality and Abstract Reality' (written 1919)

3 In order to approach the spiritual in art, one employs reality as little as possible . . . This explains logically why primary forms are employed. Since these forms are abstract, an abstract art comes into being.
Sketchbook II (1914)

James, Duke of Monmouth 1649–85
Illegitimate son of Charles II; leader of the failed Monmouth rebellion against James II

4 Do not hack me as you did my Lord Russell.
to his executioner
T. B. Macaulay *History of England* vol. 1 (1849) ch. 5

Jean Monnet 1888–1979
French economist and diplomat; founder of the European Community

5 Europe has never existed. It is not the addition of national sovereignties in a conclave which creates an entity. One must genuinely *create* Europe.
Anthony Sampson *The New Europeans* (1968)

6 We should not create a nation Europe instead of a nation France.
François Duchêne *Jean Monnet* (1994)

Marilyn Monroe 1926–62
American actress
on Monroe: see ***John*** *407:17,* ***Mailer*** *491:2,* ***Newspaper headlines*** *544:4*

when asked if she really had nothing on in a calendar photograph:
7 I had the radio on.
in *Time* 11 August 1952

on being asked what she wore in bed:
8 Chanel No. 5.
Pete Martin *Marilyn Monroe* (1956)

James Monroe 1758–1831
American Democratic Republican statesman, 5th President of the US 1817–25

9 We owe it . . . to the amicable relations existing between the United States and those [European] powers to declare that we should consider any attempt on their part to extend their system to any portion of this hemisphere as dangerous to our peace and safety.
principle that became known as the 'Monroe Doctrine'
annual message to Congress, 2 December 1823

John Samuel Bewley Monsell 1811–75
Irish-born clergyman

10 Fight the good fight with all thy might.
'The Fight for Faith' (1863 hymn); cf. **Bible** 109:19

11 Run the straight race through God's good grace,
Lift up thine eyes and seek his face;
Life with its way before us lies,
Christ is the path and Christ the prize.
'The Fight for Faith' (1863 hymn)

12 O worship the Lord in the beauty of holiness,
Bow down before him, his glory proclaim;
With gold of obedience and incense of lowliness,
Kneel and adore him: the Lord is his name.
'O Worship the Lord' (1863 hymn)

Lady Mary Wortley Montagu 1689–1762
English writer

13 But the fruit that can fall without shaking,
Indeed is too mellow for me.
'Answered, for Lord William Hamilton' in J. Dodsley (ed.) *A Collection of Poems* vol. 6 (1758)

14 Let this great maxim be my virtue's guide:
In part she is to blame, who has been tried,
He comes too near, that comes to be denied.
The Plain Dealer (27 April 1724) 'The Resolve'

15 And we meet with champagne and a chicken at last.
Six Town Eclogues (1747) 'The Lover' l. 25

16 As Ovid has sweetly in parable told,
We harden like trees, and like rivers grow cold.
Six Town Eclogues (1747) 'The Lover' l. 47

17 In chains and darkness, wherefore should I stay,
And mourn in prison, while I keep the key?
'Verses on Self-Murder' in *The London Magazine* (1749)

18 This world consists of men, women, and Herveys.
'Herveys' being a reference to Lord ***Hervey***
attributed by Lord Wharncliffe in *Letters and Works of Lady Mary Wortley Montagu* (1837) vol. 1

19 General notions are generally wrong.
letter to her husband Edward Wortley Montagu, 28 March 1710, in Robert Halsband (ed.) *Complete Letters of Lady Mary Wortley Montagu* (1965) vol. 1

20 Men are vile inconstant toads.
letter to Anne Justice, *c.*12 June 1710, in *Selected Letters* (1997)

21 I have too much indulged my sedentary humour and have been a rake in reading.
letter to her daughter Lady Bute, 11 April 1759, in Robert Halsband (ed.) *Complete Letters of Lady Mary Wortley Montagu* (1967) vol. 3

1 Civility costs nothing and buys everything.
letter to her daughter Lady Bute, 30 May 1756, in Robert Halsband (ed.) *Complete Letters of Lady Mary Wortley Montagu* (1967) vol. 3

2 People wish their enemies dead—but I do not; I say give them the gout, give them the stone!
W. S. Lewis et al. (eds.) *Horace Walpole's Correspondence* (1973) vol. 35

C. E. Montague 1867–1928

British writer

3 War hath no fury like a non-combatant.
Disenchantment (1922) ch. 16

John Montague 1929–

Irish poet and writer

4 To grow
a second tongue, as
harsh a humiliation
as twice to be born.
'A Grafted Tongue' (1972)

5 Like dolmens round my childhood, the old people.
'Like Dolmens Round my Childhood' (1972)

Montaigne (Michel Eyquem de Montaigne) 1533–92

French moralist and essayist

6 *Pour juger des choses grandes et hautes, il faut une âme de même, autrement nous leur attribuons le vice qui est le nôtre.*
To make judgements about great and lofty things, a soul of the same stature is needed; otherwise we ascribe to them that vice which is our own.
Essais (1580, ed. M. Rat, 1958) bk. 1, ch. 14

7 *Il faut être toujours botté et prêt à partir.*
One should always have one's boots on, and be ready to leave.
Essais (1580, ed. M. Rat, 1958) bk. 1, ch. 20; cf. **La Fontaine** 447:13

8 *Je veux . . . que la mort me trouve plantant mes choux, mais nonchalant d'elle, et encore plus de mon jardin imparfait.*
I want death to find me planting my cabbages, but caring little for it, and even less about the imperfections of my garden.
Essais (1580, ed. M. Rat, 1958) bk. 1, ch. 20

9 *Le continuel ouvrage de votre vie, c'est bâtir la mort.*
The ceaseless labour of your life is to build the house of death.
Essais (1580, ed. M. Rat, 1958) bk. 1, ch. 20

10 *L'utilité du vivre n'est pas en l'espace, elle est en l'usage; tel a vécu longtemps qui a peu vécu . . . Il gît en votre volonté, non au nombre des ans, que vous ayez assez vécu.*
The value of life lies not in the length of days but in the use you make of them; he has lived for a long time who has little lived. Whether you have lived enough depends not on the number of your years but on your will.
Essais (1580, ed. M. Rat, 1958) bk. 1, ch. 20

11 *Il faut noter, que les jeux d'enfants ne sont pas jeux, et les faut juger en eux comme leurs plus sérieuses actions.*
It should be noted that children at play are not playing about; their games should be seen as their most serious-minded activity.
Essais (1580, ed. M. Rat, 1958) bk. 1, ch. 23

12 *Si on me presse de dire pourquoi je l'aimais, je sens que cela ne se peut s'exprimer, qu'en répondant: 'Parce que c'était lui; parce que c'était moi.'*
of his friend Étienne de la Boétie
If I am pressed to say why I loved him, I feel it can only be explained by replying: 'Because it was he; because it was me.'
Essais (1580, ed. M. Rat, 1958) bk. 1, ch. 28

13 *Il n'y a guère moins de tourment au gouvernement d'une famille que d'un état entier . . . et, pour être les occupations domestiques moins importantes, elles n'en sont pas moins importunes.*
There is scarcely any less bother in the running of a family than in that of an entire state. And domestic business is no less importunate for being less important.
Essais (1580, ed. M. Rat, 1958) bk. 1, ch. 39

14 *Il se faut réserver une arrière boutique toute nôtre, toute franche, en laquelle nous établissons nôtre vraie liberté et principale retraite et solitude.*
A man should keep for himself a little back shop, all his own, quite unadulterated, in which he establishes his true freedom and chief place of seclusion and solitude.
Essais (1580, ed. M. Rat, 1958) bk. 1, ch. 39

15 *La plus grande chose du monde, c'est de savoir être à soi.*
The greatest thing in the world is to know how to be oneself.
Essais (1580, ed. M. Rat, 1958) bk. 1, ch. 39

16 *La gloire et le repos sont choses qui ne peuvent loger en même gîte.*
Fame and tranquillity can never be bedfellows.
Essais (1580, ed. M. Rat, 1958) bk. 1, ch. 39

17 *Mon métier et mon art c'est vivre.*
Living is my job and my art.
Essais (1580, ed. M. Rat, 1958) bk. 2, ch. 6

18 *La vertu refuse la facilité pour compagne . . . Elle demande un chemin âpre et épineux.*
Virtue shuns ease as a companion . . . It demands a rough and thorny path.
Essais (1580, ed. M. Rat, 1958) bk. 2, ch. 11

19 *Notre religion est faite pour extirper les vices; elle les couvre, les nourrit, les incite.*
Our religion is made so as to wipe out vices; it covers them up, nourishes them, incites them.
Essais (1580, ed. M. Rat, 1958) bk. 2, ch. 12

20 *Quand je me joue à ma chatte, qui sait si elle passe son temps de moi plus que je ne fais d'elle?*

When I play with my cat, who knows whether she isn't amusing herself with me more than I am with her?
Essais (1580, ed. M. Rat, 1958) bk. 2, ch. 12

1 *Que sais-je?*
What do I know?
on the position of the sceptic
Essais (1580, ed. M. Rat, 1958) bk. 2, ch. 12

2 *L'homme est bien insensé. Il ne saurait forger un ciron, et forge des dieux à douzaines.*
Man is quite insane. He wouldn't know how to create a maggot, and he creates gods by the dozen.
Essais (1580, ed. M. Rat, 1958) bk. 2, ch. 12

3 *Ceux qui ont apparié notre vie à un songe, ont eu de la raison, à l'aventure plus qu'ils ne pensaient . . . Nous veillons dormants, et veillants dormons.*
Those who have likened our life to a dream were more right, by chance, than they realised. We are awake while sleeping, and waking sleep.
Essais (1580, ed. M. Rat, 1958) bk. 2, ch. 12

4 *Il n'est si homme de bien, qu'il mette à l'examen des lois toutes ses actions et pensées, qui ne soit pendable dix fois en sa vie.*
There is no man, good as he may be, who, if all his thoughts and actions were submitted to the scrutiny of the laws, would not deserve hanging ten times in his life.
Essais (1580, ed. M. Rat, 1958) bk. 3, ch. 9

5 *Quelqu'un pourrait dire de moi que j'ai seulement fait ici un amas de fleurs étrangères, n'y ayant fourni du mien que le filet à les lier.*
It could be said of me that in this book I have only made up a bunch of other men's flowers, providing of my own only the string that ties them together.
Essais (1580, ed. M. Rat, 1958) bk. 3, ch. 12

Eugenio Montale 1896–1981
Italian poet

6 *Felicità raggiunta, si cammina*
per te sul fil de lama.
Agli occhi sei barlume che vacilla
al piede, teso ghiaccio che s'incrina;
e dunque non ti tocchi chi piu t'ama.

Happiness, for you we walk on a knife edge. To the eyes you are a flickering light, to the feet, thin ice that cracks; and so may no one touch you who loves you.
'Felicità raggiunta' (1925)

Montesquieu (Charles-Louis de Secondat) 1689–1755
French political philosopher

7 *Il faut pleurer les hommes à leur naissance, et non pas à leur mort.*
Men should be bewailed at their birth, and not at their death.
Lettres Persanes (1721) no. 40 (translated by J. Ozell, 1722)

8 *Si les triangles faisoient un Dieu, ils lui donneroient trois côtés.*
If the triangles were to make a God they would give him three sides.
Lettres Persanes (1721) no. 59 (translated by J. Ozell, 1722)

9 *Les grands seigneurs ont des plaisirs, le peuple a de la joie.*
Great lords have their pleasures, but the people have fun.
Pensées et fragments inédits . . . vol. 2 (1901) no. 992

10 *Les Anglais sont occupés; ils n'ont pas le temps d'être polis.*
The English are busy; they don't have time to be polite.
Pensées et fragments inédits . . . vol. 2 (1901) no. 1428

11 Happy the people whose annals are blank in history-books!
attributed to Montesquieu by Thomas Carlyle in *History of Frederick the Great* bk. 16, ch. 1; cf. **Eliot** 293:5, **Proverbs** 601:49

Lord Montgomery of Alamein 1887–1976
British field marshal
on Montgomery: see **Churchill** *216:10*

12 *Here* we will stand and fight; there will be no further withdrawal. I have ordered that all plans and instructions dealing with further withdrawal are to be burnt, and at once. We will stand and fight *here*. If we can't stay here alive, then let us stay here dead.
speech in Cairo, 13 August 1942

13 Rule 1, on page 1 of the book of war, is: 'Do not march on Moscow' . . . [Rule 2] is: 'Do not go fighting with your land armies in China.'
speech in the House of Lords, 30 May 1962

14 I have heard some say . . . [homosexual] practices are allowed in France and in other NATO countries. We are not French, and we are not other nationals. We are British, thank God!
on the 2nd reading of the Sexual Offences Bill
speech in the House of Lords, 24 May 1965

Robert Montgomery 1807–55
English clergyman and poet

15 The solitary monk who shook the world.
Luther: a Poem (1842) ch. 3 'Man's Need and God's Supply'

16 And thou, vast ocean! on whose awful face
Time's iron feet can print no ruin-trace.
The Omnipresence of the Deity (1830 ed.) pt. 1, l. 105

Casimir, Comte de Montrond 1768–1843
French diplomat

17 Have no truck with first impulses for they are always generous ones.
attributed, in Comte J. d'Estourmel *Derniers Souvenirs* (1860), where the alternative attribution to Talleyrand is denied; cf. **Corneille** 236:17

18 If something pleasant happens to you, don't forget to tell it to your friends, to make them feel bad.
attributed, in Comte J. d'Estourmel *Derniers Souvenirs* (1860) p. 319

James Graham, Marquess of Montrose 1612–50

Scottish royalist general and poet

1 Let them bestow on every airth a limb.
'Lines written on the Window of his Jail the Night before his Execution'

2 He either fears his fate too much,
Or his deserts are small,
That puts it not unto the touch
To win or lose it all.
'My Dear and Only Love' (written *c.*1642)

3 But if thou wilt be constant then,
And faithful of thy word,
I'll make thee glorious by my pen,
And famous by my sword.
'My Dear and Only Love' (written *c.*1642)

Percy Montrose

American songwriter

4 In a cavern, in a canyon,
Excavating for a mine,
Dwelt a miner, Forty-niner,
And his daughter, Clementine.
Oh, my darling, oh my darling, oh my darling
Clementine!
Thou art lost and gone for ever, dreadful sorry,
Clementine.
'Clementine' (1884 song)

Monty Python's Flying Circus 1969–74

BBC TV programme, written by Graham Chapman (1941–89), John Cleese (1939–), Terry Gilliam (1940–), Eric Idle (1943–), Terry Jones (1942–), and Michael Palin (1943–)
see also **Catchphrases** 195:2

5 Your wife interested in . . . *photographs*? Eh? Know what I mean—*photographs*? He asked him knowingly . . . nudge nudge, snap snap, grin grin, wink wink, say no more.
Monty Python's Flying Circus (1969)

6 It's *not* pining—it's passed on! This parrot is no more! It has ceased to be! It's expired and gone to meet its maker! This is a late parrot! It's a stiff! Bereft of life it rests in peace—if you hadn't nailed it to the perch it would be pushing up the daisies! It's rung down the curtain and joined the choir invisible! THIS IS AN EX-PARROT!
Monty Python's Flying Circus (1969)

7 Nobody expects the Spanish Inquisition!
Monty Python's Flying Circus (1970)

Clement C. Moore 1779–1863

American writer

8 'Twas the night before Christmas, when all
through the house
Not a creature was stirring, not even a mouse;
The stockings were hung by the chimney with
care,
In hopes that St Nicholas soon would be there.
'A Visit from St Nicholas' (December 1823)

Edward Moore 1712–57

English dramatist

9 This is adding insult to injuries.
The Foundling (1748) act 5, sc. 5

10 I am rich beyond the dreams of avarice.
The Gamester (1753) act 2, sc. 2; cf. **Johnson** 416:20

George Moore 1852–1933

Anglo-Irish novelist

11 All reformers are bachelors.
The Bending of the Bough (1900) act 1

12 A man travels the world in search of what he needs and returns home to find it.
The Brook Kerith (1916) ch. 11

Henry Moore 1898–1986

English sculptor and draughtsman

13 Sculpture in stone should look honestly like stone . . . to make it look like flesh and blood, hair and dimples is coming down to the level of the stage conjuror.
in *Architectural Association Journal* May 1930

14 The first hole made through a piece of stone is a revelation.
in *Listener* 18 August 1937

Marianne Moore 1887–1972

American poet

15 She says 'Men are monopolists
of "stars, garters, buttons
and other shining baubles"—
unfit to be the guardians
of another person's happiness.'
'Marriage' (1935); see below

Men practically reserve for themselves stately funerals, splendid monuments, memorial statues, titles, honorary degrees, stars, garters, ribbons, buttons and other shining baubles, so valueless in themselves and yet so infinitely desirable because they are symbols of recognition by their fellow-craftsmen of difficult work well done.
Miss M. Carey Thomas, Founder's address, Mount Holyoke, 1921

16 O to be a dragon,
a symbol of the power of Heaven—of silkworm
size or immense; at times invisible.
Felicitous phenomenon!
'O To Be a Dragon' (1959)

17 I, too, dislike it: there are things that are important
beyond all this fiddle.
Reading it, however, with a perfect contempt for it,
one discovers in it, after all, a place for the
genuine.
'Poetry' (1935)

18 Imaginary gardens with real toads in them.
'Poetry' (1935)

19 My father used to say,
'Superior people never make long visits,

have to be shown Longfellow's grave
or the glass flowers at Harvard.'
'Silence' (1935)

1 Nor was he insincere in saying, 'Make my house your inn.'
Inns are not residences.
'Silence' (1935)

2 The passion for setting people right is in itself an afflictive disease.
Distaste which takes no credit to itself is best.
'Snakes, Mongooses. Snake-Charmers, and the Like' (1935)

3 I am troubled, I'm dissatisfied, I'm Irish.
'Spenser's Ireland' (1941)

4 I never knew anyone who had a passion for words who had as much difficulty in saying things as I do. I very seldom say them in a manner I like. If I do it's because I don't know I'm trying.
George Plimpton (ed.) *The Writer's Chapbook* (1989)

5 READER: Miss Moore, your poetry is very difficult to read.
MARIANNE MOORE: It is very difficult to write.
George Plimpton (ed.) *The Writer's Chapbook* (1989)

Sturge Moore 1870–1944

English poet and engraver
on Moore: see **Gosse** 347:7

6 Then, cleaving the grass, gazelles appear
(The gentler dolphins of kindlier waves)
With sensitive heads alert of ear;
Frail crowds that a delicate hearing saves.
'The Gazelles' (1904)

Thomas Moore 1779–1852

Irish musician and songwriter

7 Yet, who can help loving the land that has taught us
Six hundred and eighty-five ways to dress eggs?
The Fudge Family in Paris (1818) Letter 8, l. 64

8 Though an angel should write, still 'tis *devils* must print.
The Fudges in England (1835) Letter 3, l. 65

9 Believe me, if all those endearing young charms,
Which I gaze on so fondly today,
Were to change by tomorrow, and fleet in my arms,
Like fairy gifts fading away!
Irish Melodies (1807) 'Believe me, if all those endearing young charms'

10 'Twas from Kathleen's eyes he flew,
Eyes of most unholy blue!
Irish Melodies (1807) 'By that Lake'

11 You may break, you may shatter the vase, if you will,
But the scent of the roses will hang round it still.
Irish Melodies (1807) 'Farewell!—but whenever'

12 The harp that once through Tara's halls
The soul of music shed,
Now hangs as mute on Tara's walls
As if that soul were fled.
Irish Melodies (1807) 'The harp that once through Tara's halls'

13 No, there's nothing half so sweet in life
As love's young dream.
Irish Melodies (1807) 'Love's Young Dream'

14 The Minstrel Boy to the war is gone,
In the ranks of death you'll find him;
His father's sword he has girded on,
And his wild harp slung behind him.
Irish Melodies (1807) 'The Minstrel Boy'

15 Oh! breathe not his name, let it sleep in the shade,
Where cold and unhonoured his relics are laid.
Irish Melodies (1807) 'Oh! breathe not his name'

16 Rich and rare were the gems she wore,
And a bright gold ring on her wand she bore.
Irish Melodies (1807) 'Rich and rare were the gems she wore'

17 'Tis the last rose of summer
Left blooming alone;
All her lovely companions
Are faded and gone.
Irish Melodies (1807) ''Tis the last rose of summer'

18 I never nursed a dear gazelle,
To glad me with its soft black eye,
But when it came to know me well,
And love me, it was sure to die!
Lalla Rookh (1817) 'The Fire-Worshippers' pt. 1, l. 283; cf. **Carroll** 191:27, **Dickens** 264:11, **Payn** 570:12

19 Like Dead Sea fruits, that tempt the eye,
But turn to ashes on the lips!
Lalla Rookh (1817) 'The Fire-Worshippers' pt. 2, l. 484

20 Oft, in the stilly night,
Ere Slumber's chain has bound me,
Fond Memory brings the light
Of other days around me.
National Airs (1815) 'Oft in the Stilly Night'

Thomas Osbert Mordaunt 1730–1809

British soldier

21 One crowded hour of glorious life
Is worth an age without a name.
'A Poem, said to be written by Major Mordaunt during the last German War', in *The Bee, or Literary Weekly Intelligencer* 12 October 1791

Hannah More 1745–1833

English writer of tracts

22 For you'll ne'er mend your fortunes, nor help the just cause,
By breaking of windows, or breaking of laws.
'An Address to the Meeting in Spa Fields' (1817) in H. Thompson *Life of Hannah More* (1838) appendix, no. 7; cf. **Pankhurst** 566:16

23 He liked those literary cooks
Who skim the cream of others' books;
And ruin half an author's graces
By plucking bon-mots from their places.
Florio (1786) pt. 1, l. 123

24 Did not God
Sometimes withhold in mercy what we ask,

We should be ruined at our own request.
Moses in the Bulrushes (1782) pt. 1, l. 35

1 Whether we consider the manual industry of the poor, or the intellectual exertions of the superior classes, we shall find that diligent occupation, if not criminally perverted from its purposes, is at once the instrument of virtue and the secret of happiness. Man cannot be safely trusted with a life of leisure.
Christian Morals (1813) vol. 2, ch. 23

2 The prevailing manners of an age depend more than we are aware, or are willing to allow, on the conduct of the women; this is one of the principal hinges on which the great machine of human society turns.
Essays on Various Subjects . . . for Young Ladies (1777) 'On Dissipation'

3 How much it is to be regretted, that the British ladies should ever sit down contented to polish, when they are able to reform; to entertain, when they might instruct; and to dazzle for an hour, when they are candidates for eternity!
Essays on Various Subjects . . . for Young Ladies (1777) 'On Dissipation'

4 It is humbling to reflect, that in those countries in which the fondness for the mere persons of women is carried to the highest excess, they are slaves; and that their moral and intellectual degradation increases in direct proportion to the adoration which is paid to mere external charms.
Strictures on the Modern System of Female Education (1799) vol. 1, ch. 1

Thomas More 1478–1535

English scholar and saint; Lord Chancellor of England, 1529–32

on More: see **Whittington** *816:9; see also* **Last words** *457:10*

5 *Oves inquam vestrae, quae tam mites esse, tamque exiguo solent ali, nunc (uti fertur) tam edaces atque indomitae esse coeperunt ut homines devorent ipsos.*
Your sheep, that were wont to be so meek and tame, and so small eaters, now, as I hear say, be become so great devourers, and so wild, that they eat up and swallow down the very men themselves.
Utopia (1516) bk. 1

6 Son Roper, I may tell thee I have no cause to be proud thereof [the King having entertained him at Chelsea], for if my head could wish him a castle in France it should not fail to go.
of **Henry VIII**
William Roper *Life of Sir Thomas More*

7 We may not look at our pleasure to go to heaven in feather-beds; it is not the way.
William Roper *Life of Sir Thomas More*

8 If the parties will at my hands call for justice, then, all were it my father stood on the one side, and the Devil on the other, his cause being good, the Devil should have right.
William Roper *Life of Sir Thomas More*

9 In good faith, I rejoiced, son, that I had given the devil a foul fall, and that with those Lords I had gone so far, as without great shame I could never go back again.
William Roper *Life of Sir Thomas More*

10 'By god's body, master More, *Indignatio principis mors est* [The anger of the sovereign is death].' 'Is that all, my Lord?' quoth he [to the Duke of Norfolk]. 'Then in good faith is there no more difference between your grace and me, but that I shall die to-day, and you to-morrow.'
William Roper *Life of Sir Thomas More*

11 Son Roper, I thank our Lord the field is won.
William Roper *Life of Sir Thomas More*

12 Is not this house as nigh heaven as my own?
of the Tower of London
William Roper *Life of Sir Thomas More*

13 I cumber you good Margaret much, but I would be sorry, if it should be any longer than tomorrow, for it is S. Thomas even and the vtas of Saint Peter and therefore tomorrow long I to go to God, it were a day very meet and convenient for me. I never liked your manner toward me better than when you kissed me last for I love when daughterly love and dear charity hath no leisure to look to worldly courtesy. Fare well my dear child and pray for me, and I shall for you and all your friends that we may merrily meet in heaven.
last letter to his daughter Margaret Roper, 5 July 1535, on the eve of his execution, in E. F. Rogers (ed.) *Correspondence of Sir Thomas More* (1947)

14 I pray you, master Lieutenant, see me safe up, and my coming down let me shift for my self.
of mounting the scaffold
William Roper *Life of Sir Thomas More*

15 Pluck up thy spirits, man, and be not afraid to do thine office; my neck is very short; take heed therefore thou strike not awry, for saving of thine honesty.
words addressed to the executioner; William Roper *Life of Sir Thomas More*

Thomas Morell 1703–84

English librettist

16 See, the conquering hero comes!
Sound the trumpets, beat the drums!
Judas Maccabeus (1747) 'A chorus of youths' and *Joshua* (1748) pt. 3 (to music by Handel)

Morelly

French writer

17 *Tout Citoyen contribuera pour sa part à l'utilité publique selon ses forces, ses talens et son âge; c'est sur cela que seront réglés ses devoirs, conformément aux loix distributives.*
Every citizen will make his own contribution to the activities of the community according to his strength, his talent, and his age: it is on this basis that his duties will be determined, conforming with the distributive laws.
Code de la Nature (1755) pt. 4; cf. **Blanc** 121:16, **Marx** 499:15

Robin Morgan 1941–
American feminist

1 Sisterhood is powerful.
title of book (1970)

Christopher Morley 1890–1957
American writer

2 Life is a foreign language: all men mispronounce it.
Thunder on the Left (1925) ch. 14; cf. **Hartley** 363:13

Lord Morley 1838–1923
British Liberal politician and writer

3 The golden Gospel of Silence is effectively compressed in thirty fine volumes.
on ***Carlyle****'s* History of Frederick the Great *(1858–65), Carlyle having written of his subject as 'that strong, silent man'*
Critical Miscellanies (1886) 'Carlyle'

4 You have not converted a man, because you have silenced him.
On Compromise (1874) ch. 5

Countess Morphy (Marcelle Azra Forbes) fl. 1930–50

5 The tragedy of English cooking is that 'plain' cooking cannot be entrusted to 'plain' cooks.
English Recipes (1935)

Charles Morris 1745–1838
English songwriter

6 But a house is much more to my mind than a tree,
And for groves, O! a good grove of chimneys for me.
'Country and Town' (1840)

Desmond Morris 1928–
English anthropologist

7 The city is not a concrete jungle, it is a human zoo.
The Human Zoo (1969) introduction

8 There are one hundred and ninety-three living species of monkeys and apes. One hundred and ninety-two of them are covered with hair. The exception is a naked ape self-named *Homo sapiens*.
The Naked Ape (1967) introduction

George Pope Morris 1802–64
American poet
see also ***Political slogans*** *581:17*

9 Woodman, spare that tree!
Touch not a single bough!
In youth it sheltered me,
And I'll protect it now.
'Woodman, Spare That Tree' (1830); cf. **Campbell** 183:5

William Morris 1834–96
English writer, artist, and designer

10 What is this, the sound and rumour? What is this that all men hear,
Like the wind in hollow valleys when the storm is drawing near,
Like the rolling on of ocean in the eventide of fear?
'Tis the people marching on.
Chants for Socialists (1885) 'The March of the Workers'

11 The idle singer of an empty day.
The Earthly Paradise (1868–70) 'An Apology'

12 Dreamer of dreams, born out of my due time,
Why should I strive to set the crooked straight?
The Earthly Paradise (1868–70) 'An Apology'

13 Forget six counties overhung with smoke,
Forget the snorting steam and piston stroke,
Forget the spreading of the hideous town;
Think rather of the pack-horse on the down,
And dream of London, small and white and clean,
The clear Thames bordered by its gardens green.
The Earthly Paradise (1868–70) 'Prologue: The Wanderers' l. 1

14 Had she come all the way for this,
To part at last without a kiss?
Yea, had she borne the dirt and rain
That her own eyes might see him slain
Beside the haystack in the floods?
'The Haystack in the Floods' (1858) l. 1

15 And ever she sung from noon to noon,
'Two red roses across the moon.'
'Two Red Roses across the Moon' (1858)

16 Fellowship is heaven, and lack of fellowship is hell.
A Dream of John Ball (1888) ch. 4

17 Have nothing in your houses that you do not know to be useful, or believe to be beautiful.
Hopes and Fears for Art (1882) 'Making the Best of It'

18 The reward of labour is life.
News from Nowhere (1891) ch. 15

19 I spend my life ministering to the swinish luxury of the rich.
reported by Sir Lowthian Bell to Alfred Powell, *c.*1877; W.R. Lethaby *Philip Webb* (1935)

Herbert Morrison 1888–1965
British Labour politician

20 Work is the call. Work at war speed. Good-night—and go to it.
broadcast as Minister of Supply, 22 May 1940, in *Daily Herald* 23 May 1940

Jim Morrison 1943–71
American rock singer and songwriter

21 Five to one, baby, one in five,
No one here gets out alive . . .
They got the guns but we got the numbers
Gonna win, yeah, we're taking over.
'Five to One' (1968 song)

22 C'mon, baby, light my fire.
'Light My Fire' (1967 song, with Robby Krieger)

23 What have they done to the earth?
What have they done to our fair sister?
Ravaged and plundered and ripped her and did her,
Stuck her with knives in the side of the dawn,

And tied her with fences and dragged her down.
I hear a very gentle sound,
With your ear down to the ground:
WE WANT THE WORLD AND WE WANT IT NOW!
'When the Music's Over' (1967 song)

1 I'm interested in anything about revolt, disorder, chaos, especially activity that appears to have no meaning. It seems to me to be the road toward freedom.
in *Time* 24 January 1968

2 When you make your peace with authority, you become an authority.
Andrew Doe and John Tobler *In Their Own Words: The Doors* (1988)

R. F. Morrison

3 Just a wee deoch-an-doris,
Just a wee yin, that's a'.
Just a wee deoch-an-doris,
Before we gang awa'.
There's a wee wifie waitin',
In a wee but-an-ben;
If you can say
'It's a braw bricht moonlicht nicht',
Ye're a' richt, ye ken.
'Just a Wee Deoch-an-Doris' (1911 song); popularized by Harry Lauder

Toni Morrison 1931–
American novelist

4 Grab this land! Take it, hold it, my brothers, make it, my brothers, shake it, squeeze it, turn it, twist it, beat it, kick it, whip it, stomp it, dig it, plough it, seed it, reap it, rent it, buy it, sell it, own it, build it, multiply it, and pass it on—Can you hear me? Pass it on!
Song of Solomon 1977 ch. 10

Van Morrison 1945–
Irish singer, songwriter, and musician

5 Music is spiritual. The music business is not.
in *The Times* 6 July 1990

Dwight Morrow 1873–1931
American lawyer, banker, and diplomat

6 The world is divided into people who do things and people who get the credit. Try, if you can, to belong to the first class. There's far less competition.
letter to his son, in Harold Nicolson *Dwight Morrow* (1935) ch. 3

Owen Morshead b. 1893
English librarian

7 The House of Hanover, like ducks, produce bad parents—they trample on their young.
as Royal Librarian, in conversation with Harold **Nicolson**, *biographer of* **George V**
Harold Nicolson, letter to Vita Sackville-West, 7 January 1949

John Mortimer 1923–
English novelist, barrister, and dramatist

8 The law seems like a sort of maze through which a client must be led to safety, a collection of reefs, rocks, and underwater hazards through which he or she must be piloted.
Clinging to the Wreckage (1982) ch. 7

9 They do you a decent death on the hunting-field.
Paradise Postponed (1985) ch. 18

10 At school I never minded the lessons. I just resented having to work terribly hard at playing.
A Voyage Round My Father (1971) act 1

11 No brilliance is needed in the law. Nothing but common sense, and relatively clean fingernails.
A Voyage Round My Father (1971) act 1

12 The worst fault of the working classes is telling their children they're not going to succeed, saying: 'There is life, but it's not for you.'
in *Daily Mail* 31 May 1988

J. B. Morton ('Beachcomber') 1893–1975
British journalist

13 One disadvantage of being a hog is that at any moment some blundering fool may try to make a silk purse out of your wife's ear.
By the Way (1931)

14 Hush, hush,
Nobody cares!
Christopher Robin
Has
Fallen
Down-
Stairs.
By the Way (1931); cf. **Milne** 511:1

15 The man with the false nose had gone to that bourne from which no hollingsworth returns.
Gallimaufry (1936) 'Another True Story'; cf. **Shakespeare** 664:4

16 Dr Strabismus (Whom God Preserve) of Utrecht has patented a new invention. It is an illuminated trouser-clip for bicyclists who are using main roads at night.
Morton's Folly (1933)

Jelly Roll Morton 1885–1941
American jazz pianist, composer, and bandleader

17 Jazz music is to be played sweet, soft, plenty rhythm.
Mister Jelly Roll (1950)

Rogers Morton 1914–79
American public relations officer

18 I'm not going to rearrange the furniture on the deck of the Titanic.
having lost five of the last six primaries as President **Ford**'s *campaign manager*
in *Washington Post* 16 May 1976

Thomas Morton c.1764–1838

English dramatist

1 Approbation from Sir Hubert Stanley is praise indeed.

A Cure for the Heartache (1797) act 5, sc. 2

2 I eat well, and I drink well, and I sleep well—but that's all.

A Roland for an Oliver (1819) act 1, sc. 1

3 Always ding, dinging Dame Grundy into my ears—what will Mrs Grundy zay? What will Mrs Grundy think?

Speed the Plough (1798) act 1, sc. 1; cf. **Locker-Lampson** 472:9

Edwin Moses 1955–

American athlete

4 I don't really see the hurdles. I sense them like a memory.

attributed

Andrew Motion 1952–

English poet

5 Each sudden gust of light explains itself
as flames, but neither they, nor even
bombs redoubled on the hills tonight
can quite include me in their fear.
What does remains invisible, is lost
in curt societies whose deaths become
revenge by morning, and whose homes
are nothing more than all they pity most.

'Leaving Belfast' (1978)

6 Beside the river, swerving under ground.
your future tracked you, snapping at your heels:
Diana, breathless, hunted by your own quick
hounds.

'Mythology' (1997)

John Lothrop Motley 1814–77

American historian

7 As long as he lived, he was the guiding-star of a whole brave nation, and when he died the little children cried in the streets.

of William of Orange (1533–84)

The Rise of the Dutch Republic (1856) pt. 6, ch. 7; cf. **Auden** 33:26

8 Give us the luxuries of life, and we will dispense with its necessities.

Oliver Wendell Holmes *Autocrat of the Breakfast-Table* (1857–8) ch. 6

□ Mottoes

see box opposite

Lord Mountbatten 1900–79

British sailor, soldier, and statesman

on Mountbatten: see **Ziegler** *840:3*

9 Right, now I understand people think you're the Forgotten Army on the Forgotten Front. I've come here to tell you you're quite wrong. You're not the Forgotten Army on the Forgotten Front. No, make no mistake about it. Nobody's ever *heard* of you.

encouragement to troops when taking over as Supreme Allied Commander South-East Asia in late 1943

R. Hough *Mountbatten* (1980)

Marjorie ('Mo') Mowlam 1949–

British Labour politician, Secretary of State for Northern Ireland since 1997

10 It takes courage to push things forward.

on her decision to visit Loyalist prisoners in The Maze

in *Guardian* 8 January 1998

Daniel P. Moynihan 1927–

American Democratic politician

11 Welfare became a term of opprobrium—a contentious, often vindictive area of political conflict in which liberals and conservatives clashed and children were lost sight of.

in *The Washington Post* 25 November 1994

Wolfgang Amadeus Mozart 1756–91

Austrian composer

on Mozart: see ***Baring*** *54:12,* ***Barth*** *56:6,* ***Joseph II*** *421:7,* ***Lehrer*** *462:18,* ***Schnabel*** *648:23*

12 Melody is the essence of music. I compare a good melodist to a fine racer, and counterpoints to hack post-horses.

remark to Michael Kelly, 1786; Michael Kelly *Reminiscences* (1826)

Robert Mugabe 1924–

African statesman; Prime Minister of Zimbabwe, 1980–7

13 Cricket civilizes people and creates good gentlemen. I want everyone to play cricket in Zimbabwe; I want ours to be a nation of gentlemen.

in *Sunday Times* 26 February 1984

Malcolm Muggeridge 1903–90

British journalist

14 An orgy looks particularly alluring seen through the mists of righteous indignation.

The Most of Malcolm Muggeridge (1966) 'Dolce Vita in a Cold Climate'

15 Something beautiful for God.

title of book (1971); see **Teresa** 768:7

16 The orgasm has replaced the Cross as the focus of longing and the image of fulfilment.

Tread Softly (1966)

17 He was not only a bore; he bored for England.

of Anthony ***Eden***

Tread Softly (1966)

18 Good taste and humour . . . are a contradiction in terms, like a chaste whore.

in *Time* 14 September 1953

continued

Mottoes

1 *Ad majorem Dei gloriam.*
To the greater glory of God.
motto of the Society of Jesus

2 *Aut Caesar, aut nihil.*
Caesar or nothing.
motto inscribed on the sword of Cesare Borgia (1476–1507)

3 Be happy while y'er leevin,
For y'er a lang time deid.
Scottish motto for a house
in *Notes and Queries* 9th series, vol. 8, 7 December 1901

4 Be prepared.
motto of the Scout Association, based on the ititials of the founder, Lord Baden-Powell
Robert Baden-Powell *Scouting for Boys* (1908) pt. 1

5 *Cor ad cor loquitur.*
Heart speaks to heart.
motto of John Henry **Newman**; cf. **Francis** 323:3

6 Defence, not defiance.
motto of the Volunteers Movement (1859)

7 *Dominus illuminatio mea.*
The Lord is my light.
motto of the University of Oxford; cf. **Bible** 113:17

8 *Fiat justitia et pereat mundus.*
Let justice be done, though the world perish.
motto of Ferdinand I (1503–64), Holy Roman Emperor; Johannes Manlius *Locorum Communium Collectanea* (1563) vol. 2 'De Lege: Octatum Praeceptum'; cf. **Watson** 805:1

9 *Honi soit qui mal y pense.*
Evil be to him who evil thinks.
motto of the Order of the Garter, originated by **Edward III**, probably on 23 April of 1348 or 1349; cf. **Sellar and Yeatman** 654:6

10 *Nemo me impune lacessit.*
No one provokes me with impunity.
motto of the Crown of Scotland and of all Scottish regiments

11 *Nisi Dominus frustra.*
In vain without the Lord.
motto of the city of Edinburgh; see **Bible** 113:24

12 *Nullius in verba.*
In the word of none.
emphasizing reliance on experiment rather than authority
motto of the Royal Society; cf. **Horace** 386:8

13 *Palmam qui meruit, ferat.*
Let him who has won it bear the palm.
adopted by Lord **Nelson** as his motto, from John Jortin (1698–1770) *Lusus Poetici* (3rd ed., 1748) 'Ad Ventos'

14 *Per ardua ad astra.*
Through struggle to the stars.
motto of the Mulvany family, quoted and translated by Rider **Haggard** in *The People of the Mist* (1894) ch. 1; still in use as motto of the R.A.F., having been proposed by J. S. Yule in 1912 and approved by King **George V** in 1913

15 Rebellion to tyrants is obedience to God.
motto of Thomas **Jefferson**, from John **Bradshaw**; cf. **Bradshaw** 146:12

16 *Semper eadem.*
Ever the same.
motto of **Elizabeth I**

17 *Sic semper tyrannis.*
Thus always to tyrants.
motto of the State of Virginia; cf. **Booth** 142:16

18 *Similia similibus curantur.*
Like cures like.
motto of homeopathic medicine, although not found in this form in the writings of C. F. S. Hahnemann (1755–1843); the Latin appears as an anonymous side-note in Paracelsus *Opera Omnia* (*c.*1490–1541, ed. 1658) vol. 1

19 They haif said: Quhat say they? Lat thame say.
motto of the Earls Marischal of Scotland, inscribed at Marischal College, Aberdeen, 1593; a similarly defiant motto in Greek has been found engraved in remains from classical antiquity

20 Who dares wins.
motto of the British Special Air Service regiment, from 1942

Malcolm Muggeridge *continued*

21 On television I feel like a man playing a piano in a brothel; every now and again he solaces himself by playing 'Abide with Me' in the hope of edifying both the clients and the inmates.
interview on *Parkinson*, BBC1 TV, 23 September 1972

Edwin Muir 1887–1959
Scottish poet

22 And without fear the lawless roads
Ran wrong through all the land.
'Hölderlin's Journey' (1937)

23 Barely a twelvemonth after
The seven days war that put the world to sleep,
Late in the evening the strange horses came.
'The Horses' (1956)

Frank Muir 1920–98
English writer and broadcaster

24 The thinking man's crumpet.
of Joan ***Bakewell***
attributed

Paul Muldoon 1951–
Irish poet

25 I thought of you tonight, *a leanbh*, lying there in your long barrow,

colder and dumber than a fish by Francisco de Herrera.
'Incantata' (1994)

1 The Volkswagen parked in the gap,
But gently ticking over.
You wonder if it's lovers
And not men hurrying back
Across two fields and a river.
'Ireland' (1980)

H. J. Muller 1890–1967
American geneticist

2 To say, for example, that a man is made up of certain chemical elements is a satisfactory description only for those who intend to use him as a fertilizer.
Science and Criticism (1943)

Herbert J. Muller 1905–

3 Few have heard of Fra Luca Pacioli, the inventor of double-entry bookkeeping; but he has probably had much more influence on human life than has Dante or Michelangelo.
Uses of the Past (1957) ch. 8

Wilhelm Müller 1794–1827
German poet

4 *Vom Abendrot zum Morgenlicht*
Ward mancher Kopf zum Greise.
Wer glaubt's? Und meiner ward es nicht
Auf dieser ganzen Reise.

Between dusk and dawn many a head has turned white. Who can believe it? And mine has not changed on all this long journey.
Die Winterreise (1823) bk. 2 'Der greise Kopf'

Ethel Watts Mumford et al. 1878–1940
American writer and humorist

5 In the midst of life we are in debt.
Altogether New Cynic's Calendar (1907); cf. **Book of Common Prayer** 131:13

Lewis Mumford 1895–1990
American sociologist

6 Every generation revolts against its fathers and makes friends with its grandfathers.
The Brown Decades (1931)

7 Our national flower is the concrete cloverleaf.
in *Quote Magazine* 8 October 1961

Mumonkan *c.*1228
a Japanese Zen textbook

8 A monk once asked Jōshū, 'Has a dog the Buddha-Nature?'
Jōshū answered, 'Mu!'
case 1

9 He [Buddha] held up a flower before the congregation of monks. At this time all were silent but the Venerable Kasyapa only smiled. The World-Honoured One said . . . 'Without relying upon words and letters, beyond all teaching as a special transmission, I pass this all on to Mahakasyapa.'
case 6

10 A monk asked Tōzan, 'What is the Buddha?' He replied 'Three pounds of flax.'
case 18

11 A monk asked Ummon, 'What is the Buddha?' 'It is a shit-wiping stick,' replied Ummon.
case 21

12 A monk asked Jōshū, 'What did Daruma [Bodhidharma] come to China for?' Jōshū answered, 'The oak tree in the [temple] front garden.'
case 37

Edvard Munch 1863–1944
Norwegian painter and engraver

13 You should not paint the chair, but only what someone has felt about it.
written *c.*1891; R. Heller *Munch* (1984) ch. 4

Murasaki Shikibu *c.*978–*c.*1031
Japanese writer and courtier

14 Anything whatsoever may become the subject of a novel, provided only that it happens in this mundane life and not in some fairyland beyond our human ken.
The Tale of Genji

15 People who have become so precious that they go out of their way to try and be sensitive in the most unpromising situations, trying to capture every moment of interest, are bound to look ridiculous and superficial.
The Diary of Lady Murasaki (translated by Richard Bowring, 1996)

Iris Murdoch 1919–99
English novelist

16 Dora Greenfield left her husband because she was afraid of him. She decided six months later to return to him for the same reason.
The Bell (1958) ch. 1

17 All our failures are ultimately failures in love.
The Bell (1958) ch. 19

18 One doesn't have to get anywhere in a marriage. It's not a public conveyance.
A Severed Head (1961) ch. 3

19 Love is the extremely difficult realisation that something other than oneself is real. Love, and so art and morals, is the discovery of reality.
'The Sublime and the Good' in *Chicago Review* 13 (1959)

20 Anything that consoles is fake.
R. Harries *Prayer and the Pursuit of Happiness* (1985)

21 We live in a fantasy world, a world of illusion. The great task in life is to find reality.
in *The Times* 15 April 1983 'Profile'

1 I'm just wandering, I think of things and then they go away for ever.
in September 1996 on her inability to write; the following February it was announced that she was suffering from Alzheimer's disease
in *Times* 5 February 1997

Rupert Murdoch 1931–
Australian-born American publisher and media entrepreneur

asked why he had allowed Page 3 to develop:
2 I don't know. The editor did it when I was away.
in *Guardian* 25 February 1994

C. W. Murphy and Will Letters

3 Has anybody here seen Kelly?
Kelly from the Isle of Man?
'Has Anybody Here Seen Kelly?' (1909 song)

Fred Murray
American songwriter

4 Ginger, you're balmy!
title of song (1910)

James Augustus Henry Murray 1837–1915
Scottish lexicographer, first Editor of the Oxford English Dictionary

5 I feel that in many respects I and my assistants are simply pioneers, pushing our way experimentally through an untrodden forest, where no white man's axe has been before us.
'Report on the Philological Society's Dictionary' (1884) in *Transactions of the Philological Society* 1882–4

Les A. Murray 1938–
Australian poet

6 The trouble
with being best man is, you don't get a chance to
prove it.
The Boys Who Stole the Funeral (1989)

Ed Murrow 1908–65
American broadcaster and journalist

7 No one can terrorize a whole nation, unless we are all his accomplices.
of Joseph **McCarthy**
'See It Now', broadcast, 7 March 1954

8 He mobilized the English language and sent it into battle to steady his fellow countrymen and hearten those Europeans upon whom the long dark night of tyranny had descended.
of Winston **Churchill**
broadcast, 30 November 1954, in *In Search of Light* (1967)

9 Anyone who isn't confused doesn't really understand the situation.
on the Vietnam War
Walter Bryan *The Improbable Irish* (1969) ch. 1

Alfred de Musset 1810–57
French poet and dramatist

10 *Je haïs comme la mort l'état de plagiaire;*
Mon verre n'est pas grand mais je bois dans mon verre.
I hate like death the situation of the plagiarist; the glass I drink from is not large, but at least it is my own.
La Coupe et les lèvres (1832)

11 *Malgré moi l'infini me tourmente.*
I can't help it, the idea of the infinite torments me.
'L'Espoir en Dieu' (1838)

12 *Le seul bien qui me reste au monde*
Est d'avoir quelquefois pleuré.
The only good thing left to me is that I have sometimes wept.
'Tristesse' (1841)

13 *Je suis venu trop tard dans un monde trop vieux.*
I have come too late into a world too old.
Rollo (1833)

Benito Mussolini 1883–1945
Italian Fascist dictator

14 We must leave exactly on time . . . From now on everything must function to perfection.
to a station-master
Giorgio Pini *Mussolini* (1939) vol. 2, ch. 6; an early report was:
The first benefit of Benito Mussolini's direction in Italy begins to be felt when one crosses the Italian Frontier and hears '*Il treno arriva all'orario* [The train is arriving on time]'.
Infanta Eulalia of Spain *Courts and Countries after the War* (1925)

A. J. Muste 1885–1967
American pacifist

15 If I can't love Hitler, I can't love at all.
at a Quaker meeting 1940; in *New York Times* 12 February 1967

16 There is no way to peace. Peace is the way.
in *New York Times* 16 November 1967

Vladimir Nabokov 1899–1977
Russian novelist

17 Lolita, light of my life, fire of my loins. My sin, my soul. Lo-lee-ta: the tip of the tongue taking a trip of three steps down the palate to tap, at three, on the teeth. Lo. Lee. Ta.
Lolita (1955) ch. 1

18 You can always count on a murderer for a fancy prose style.
Lolita (1955) ch. 1

19 Life is a great surprise. I do not see why death should not be an even greater one.
Pale Fire (1962)

20 The cradle rocks above an abyss, and common sense tells us that our existence is but a brief crack of light between two eternities of darkness.
Speak, Memory (1951) ch. 1

1 That life-quickening atmosphere of a big railway station where everything is something trembling on the brink of something else.
Spring in Fialta and other stories (1956) 'Spring in Fialta'

Ralph Nader 1934–
American consumer protectionist

2 Unsafe at any speed.
title of book (1965)

Nagarjuna *c.*2nd century AD
Indian philosopher

3 The doctrine of the Buddha is taught with reference to two truths—conventional truth and ultimate truth.
Those who do not understand the difference between these two truths do not understand the profound essence of the doctrine of the Buddha.
Root Verses of the Middle Way ch. 24, v. 8

Sarojini Naidu 1879–1949
Indian politician

4 If only Bapu knew the cost of setting him up in poverty!
of Mahatma ***Gandhi***
A. Campbell-Johnson *Mission with Mountbatten* (1951) ch. 12

Ian Nairn 1930–
British architect

5 If what is called development is allowed to multiply at the present rate, then by the end of the century Great Britain will consist of isolated oases of preserved monuments in a desert of wire, concrete roads, cosy plots and bungalows . . . Upon this new Britain the *Review* bestows a name in the hope that it will stick—SUBTOPIA.
in *Architectural Review* June 1955

Lewis Namier 1888–1960
Polish-born British historian

6 No number of atrocities however horrible can deprive a nation of its right to independence, nor justify its being put under the heel of its worst enemies and persecutors.
in 1919; Julia Namier *Lewis Namier* (1971)

Fridtjof Nansen 1861–1930
Norwegian polar explorer

7 Never stop because you are afraid—you are never so likely to be wrong. Never keep a line of retreat: it is a wretched invention. The difficult is what takes a little time; the impossible is what takes a little longer.
in *Listener* 14 December 1939; cf. **Calonne** 182:1, **Military sayings** 508:6

Napoleon I 1769–1821
Emperor of France, 1804–15
on Napoleon: see ***Byron*** *178:18,* ***Wellington*** *809:19; see also* ***Dumouriez*** *285:1*

8 Think of it, soldiers; from the summit of these pyramids, forty centuries look down upon you.
speech to the Army of Egypt on 21 July 1798, before the Battle of the Pyramids
Gaspard Gourgaud *Mémoires* (1823) vol. 2 'Égypte—Bataille des Pyramides'

9 It [the Channel] is a mere ditch, and will be crossed as soon as someone has the courage to attempt it.
letter to Consul Cambacérès, 16 November 1803, in *Correspondance de Napoléon Ier* (1858–69) vol. 9

10 A prince who gets a reputation for good nature in the first year of his reign, is laughed at in the second.
letter to his brother Louis, King of Holland, 4 April 1807, in *Correspondance de Napoléon Ier* (1858–69) vol. 15

11 It is easier to put up with unpleasantness from a man of one's own way of thinking than from one who takes an entirely different point of view.
letter to J. Finckenstein, 14 April 1807, in *Mémoires et Correspondance politique et militaire du Roi Joseph* (1854) vol. 3

12 I want the whole of Europe to have one currency; it will make trading much easier.
letter to his brother Louis, 6 May 1807; Alistair Horne *How Far from Austerlitz?* (1996)

13 Religion is an all-important matter in a public school for girls. Whatever people say, it is the mother's safeguard, and the husband's. What we ask of education is not that girls should think, but that they should believe.
'Note sur L'Établissement D'Écouen' 15 May 1807, in *Correspondance de Napoléon Ier* (1858–69) vol. 15

14 In war, three-quarters turns on personal character and relations; the balance of manpower and materials counts only for the remaining quarter.
'Observations sur les affaires d'Espagne, Saint-Cloud, 27 août 1808' in *Correspondance de Napoléon Ier* (1858–69) vol. 17

15 It is a matter of great interest what sovereigns are doing; but as to what Grand Duchesses are doing—Who cares?
letter, 17 December 1811, in *Lettres inédits de Napoléon I* (1897) vol. 2

16 There is only one step from the sublime to the ridiculous.
to De Pradt, Polish ambassador, after the retreat from Moscow in 1812
D. G. De Pradt *Histoire de l'Ambassade dans le grand-duché de Varsovie en 1812* (1815); cf. **Paine** 563:10, **Proverbs** 600:14

17 As to moral courage, I have very rarely met with two o'clock in the morning courage: I mean instantaneous courage.
E. A. de Las Cases *Mémorial de Ste-Hélène* (1823) vol. 1, pt. 2, 4–5 December 1815; cf. **Thoreau** 776:9

18 Nothing is more contrary to the organization of the mind, of the memory, and of the imagination . . . The new system of weights and measures will be a

stumbling block and the source of difficulties for several generations . . . It's just tormenting the people with trivia!!!
on the introduction of the metric system
Mémoires . . . écrits à Ste-Hélène (1823–5) bk. 4, ch. 21, pt. 4

1 An army marches on its stomach.
attributed, but probably condensed from a long passage in E. A. de Las Cases *Mémorial de Ste-Hélène* (1823) vol. 4, 14 November 1816; also attributed to **Frederick the Great**, in *Notes and Queries* 10 March 1866; cf. **Proverbs** 595:16, **Sellar and Yeatman** 654:13

2 As though he had 200,000 men.
when asked how to deal with the Pope
J. M. Robinson *Cardinal Consalvi* (1987); cf. **Stalin** 736:3

3 *La carrière ouverte aux talents.*
The career open to the talents.
Barry E. O'Meara *Napoleon in Exile* (1822) vol. 1

4 England is a nation of shopkeepers.
Barry E. O'Meara *Napoleon in Exile* (1822) vol. 2; cf. **Adams** 3:19, **Proverbs** 599:15, **Smith** 723:10

5 Not tonight, Josephine.
attributed, but probably apocryphal; the phrase does not appear in contemporary sources, but was current by the early twentieth century

of **Talleyrand**:
6 A pile of shit in a silk stocking.
attributed

Ogden Nash 1902–71
American humorist

7 The turtle lives 'twixt plated decks
Which practically conceal its sex.
I think it clever of the turtle
In such a fix to be so fertile.
'Autres Bêtes, Autres Moeurs' (1931)

8 The camel has a single hump;
The dromedary, two;
Or else the other way around,
I'm never sure. Are you?
'The Camel' (1936)

9 The cow is of the bovine ilk;
One end is moo, the other, milk.
'The Cow' (1931)

10 One would be in less danger
From the wiles of the stranger
If one's own kin and kith
Were more fun to be with.
'Family Court' (1931)

11 Professional men, they have no cares;
Whatever happens, they get theirs.
'I Yield to My Learned Brother' (1935)

12 Beneath this slab
John Brown is stowed.
He watched the ads,
And not the road.
'Lather as You Go' (1942)

13 Do you think my mind is maturing late,
Or simply rotted early?
'Lines on Facing Forty' (1942)

14 Good wine needs no bush,
And perhaps products that people really want need no hard-sell or soft-sell TV push.
Why not?
Look at pot.
'Most Doctors Recommend or yours For Fast, Fast, Fast Relief' (1972)

15 Any kiddie in school can love like a fool,
But hating, my boy, is an art.
'Plea for Less Malice Toward None' (1933)

16 Candy
Is dandy
But liquor
Is quicker.
'Reflections on Ice-breaking' (1931)

17 I test my bath before I sit,
And I'm always moved to wonderment
That what chills the finger not a bit
Is so frigid upon the fundament.
'Samson Agonistes' (1942)

18 I think that I shall never see
A billboard lovely as a tree.
Perhaps, unless the billboards fall,
I'll never see a tree at all.
'Song of the Open Road' (1933); cf. **Kilmer** 435:14

19 Sure, deck your lower limbs in pants;
Yours are the limbs, my sweeting.
You look divine as you advance—
Have you seen yourself retreating?
'What's the Use?' (1940)

Thomas Nashe 1567–1601
English pamphleteer and dramatist

20 O, tis a precious apothegmatical Pedant, who will find matter enough to dilate a whole day of the first invention of *Fy, fa, fum*, I smell the blood of an English-man.
Have with you to Saffron-walden (1596); cf. **Shakespeare** 679:9

21 Beauty is but a flower
Which wrinkles will devour.
Summer's Last Will and Testament (1600) l. 1588

22 Brightness falls from the air;
Queens have died young and fair;
Dust hath closed Helen's eye.
I am sick, I must die.
Lord have mercy on us.
Summer's Last Will and Testament (1600) l. 1590

23 From winter, plague and pestilence, good lord, deliver us!
Summer's Last Will and Testament (1600) l. 1878

James Ball Naylor 1860–1945

24 King David and King Solomon
Led merry, merry lives,
With many, many lady friends,
And many, many wives;
But when old age crept over them—
With many, many qualms!—
King Solomon wrote the Proverbs

And King David wrote the Psalms.
'King David and King Solomon' (1935)

John Mason Neale 1818–66
English clergyman

1 All glory, laud, and honour
To thee, Redeemer, King,
To whom the lips of children
Made sweet hosannas ring.
'All glory, laud, and honour' (1851 hymn)

2 Good King Wenceslas looked out,
On the feast of Stephen;
When the snow lay round about,
Deep and crisp and even.
'Good King Wenceslas'

3 Jerusalem the golden,
With milk and honey blessed,
Beneath thy contemplation
Sink heart and voice oppressed.
'Jerusalem the golden' (1858 hymn); translated from the Latin of St Bernard of Cluny (b. *c.*1100)

Jawaharlal Nehru 1889–1964
Indian statesman

4 At the stroke of the midnight hour, while the world sleeps, India will awake to life and freedom.
immediately prior to Independence
speech to the Indian Constituent Assembly, 14 August 1947

5 The light has gone out of our lives and there is darkness everywhere.
following **Gandhi**'s *assassination*
broadcast, 30 January 1948; Richard J. Walsh *Nehru on Gandhi* (1948) ch. 6

6 I may lose many things including my temper, but I do not lose my nerve.
at a press conference in Delhi, 4 June 1958

7 Democracy and socialism are means to an end, not the end itself.
'Basic Approach'; written for private circulation and reprinted in Vincent Shean *Nehru: the Years of Power* (1960)

8 There is no easy walk-over to freedom anywhere, and many of us will have to pass through the valley of the shadow again and again before we reach the mountain-tops of our desire.
'From Lucknow to Tripuri' (1939)

9 After every other Viceroy has been forgotten, Curzon will be remembered because he restored all that was beautiful in India.
in conversation with Lord Swinton
Kenneth Rose *Superior Person* (1969)

10 I shall be the last Englishman to rule in India.
J. K. Galbraith *A Life in Our Times* (1981)

A. S. Neill 1883–1973
Scottish teacher and educationist

11 If we have to have an exam at 11, let us make it one for humour, sincerity, imagination, character—and where is the examiner who could test such qualities.
letter to *Daily Telegraph* 1957; in *Daily Telegraph* 25 September 1973

Horatio, Lord Nelson 1758–1805
British admiral
on Nelson: see **Southey** *731:6; see also* **Last words** *457:8,* **Mottoes** *535:13*

12 It is my turn now; and if I come back, it is yours.
exercising his privilege, as second lieutenant, to board a prize ship before the Master
Robert Southey *Life of Nelson* (1813) ch. 1

13 You must consider every man your enemy who speaks ill of your king: and . . . you must hate a Frenchman as you hate the devil.
Robert Southey *Life of Nelson* (1813) ch. 3

14 Before this time to-morrow I shall have gained a peerage, or Westminster Abbey.
before the battle of the Nile, 1798
Robert Southey *Life of Nelson* (1813) ch. 5

15 I have only one eye,—I have a right to be blind sometimes . . . I really do not see the signal!
at the battle of Copenhagen, 1801
Robert Southey *Life of Nelson* (1813) ch. 7

16 In honour I gained them, and in honour I will die with them.
when asked to cover the stars on his uniform
Robert Southey *Life of Nelson* (1813) ch. 9

17 I believe my arrival was most welcome, not only to the Commander of the Fleet but almost to every individual in it.
letter to Lady Hamilton, 1 October 1805, in Robert Southey *Life of Nelson* (1813) ch. 9

18 When I came to explain to them the '*Nelson touch*', it was like an electric shock. Some shed tears, all approved—'It was new—it was singular—it was simple!'
letter to Lady Hamilton, 1 October 1805, in Robert Southey *Life of Nelson* (1813) ch. 9

19 May the Great God, whom I worship, grant to my Country and for the benefit of Europe in general a great and glorious victory; and may no misconduct in anyone tarnish it; and may humanity after Victory be the predominant feature of the British Fleet. For myself, individually, I commit my life to Him who made me, and may His blessing light upon my endeavours for serving my Country faithfully. To Him I resign myself and the just cause which is entrusted to me to defend. Amen. Amen. Amen.
diary entry, on the eve of the battle of Trafalgar, 21 October 1805
Nicholas Harris Nicolas (ed.) *Dispatches and Letters of . . . Nelson* (1846) vol. 7, p. 139

20 England expects that every man will do his duty.
at the battle of Trafalgar, 21 October 1805
Robert Southey *Life of Nelson* (1813) ch. 9

1 This is too warm work, Hardy, to last long.
at the battle of Trafalgar, 21 October 1805
Robert Southey *Life of Nelson* (1813) ch. 9

2 Kiss me, Hardy.
at the battle of Trafalgar, 21 October 1805
Robert Southey *Life of Nelson* (1813) ch. 9

Howard Nemerov 1920–91
American poet and novelist

3 praise without end the go-ahead zeal
of whoever it was invented the wheel;
but never a word for the poor soul's sake
that thought ahead, and invented the brake.
'To the Congress of the United States, Entering Its Third Century' 26 February 1989

Pablo Neruda 1904–73
Chilean poet

4 I have gone marking the blank atlas of your body
with crosses of fire.
My mouth went across: a spider, trying to hide.
In you, behind you, timid, driven by thirst.
'I Have Gone Marking' (1924), translated 1969 by W. S. Merwin

5 The typewriter separated me from a deeper intimacy with poetry, and my hand brought me closer to that intimacy again.
in *Writers at Work* (5th series, 1981)

Gérard de Nerval 1808–55
French poet

6 *Dieu est mort! le ciel est vide—*
Pleurez! enfants, vous n'avez plus de père.

God is dead! Heaven is empty—Weep, children, you no longer have a father.
Les Chimères (1854) 'Le Christ aux Oliviers' epigraph (summarizing a passage in Jean Paul's *Blumen-Frucht-und Dornstücke* (1796–7) in which God's children are referred to as 'orphans')

7 *Je suis le ténébreux,—le veuf,—l'inconsolé,*
Le prince d'Aquitaine à la tour abolie:
Ma seule étoile est morte, et mon luth constellé
Porte le soleil *noir de la* mélancolie.

I am the darkly shaded, the bereaved, the inconsolate, the prince of Aquitaine, with the blasted tower. My only *star* is dead, and my star-strewn lute carries on it the black *sun* of *melancholy*.
Les Chimères (1854) 'El Desdichado'

8 Why should a lobster be any more ridiculous than a dog . . . or any other animal that one chooses to take for a walk? I have a liking for lobsters. They are peaceful, serious creatures. They know the secrets of the sea, they don't bark, and they don't gnaw upon one's monadic privacy like dogs do. And Goethe had an aversion to dogs, and he wasn't mad.
justifying his walking a lobster on a lead in the gardens of the Palais Royal
T. Gautier *Portraits et Souvenirs Littéraires* (1875), translated by Richard Holmes

Edith Nesbit 1858–1924
English writer

9 It is a curious thing that people only ask if you are enjoying yourself when you aren't.
Five of Us, and Madeline (1925)

10 The affection you get back from children is sixpence given as change for a sovereign.
Julia Briggs *A Woman of Passion* (1987)

John von Neumann 1903–57
Hungarian-born American mathematician and computer pioneer

11 In mathematics you don't understand things. You just get used to them.
Gary Zukav *The Dancing Wu Li Masters* (1979)

Otto Neurath 1882–1945
German philosopher

12 We are like sailors who must rebuild their ship on the open sea, never able to dismantle it in dry-dock and to reconstruct it there out of the best materials.
'Protocol Sentences', in A. J. Ayer (ed.) *Logical Positivism* (1959)

Allan Nevins 1890–1971
American historian

13 The former Allies had blundered in the past by offering Germany too little, and offering even that too late, until finally Nazi Germany had become a menace to all mankind.
in *Current History* (New York) May 1935

Henry Newbolt 1862–1938
English lawyer, poet, and man of letters

14 'Take my drum to England, hang et by the shore,
Strike et when your powder's runnin' low;
If the Dons sight Devon, I'll quit the port o' Heaven,
An' drum them up the Channel as we drummed them long ago.'
'Drake's Drum' (1897)

15 Drake he's in his hammock till the great Armadas come.
(Capten, art tha sleepin' there below?)
Slung atween the round shot, listenin' for the drum,
An' dreamin' arl the time o' Plymouth Hoe.
'Drake's Drum' (1897)

16 Now the sunset breezes shiver,
And she's fading down the river,
But in England's song for ever
She's the Fighting Téméraire.
'The Fighting Téméraire' (1897)

17 'Qui procul hinc', the legend's writ,—
The frontier-grave is far away—
'Qui ante diem periit:
Sed miles, sed pro patria.'
The Island Race (1898) 'Clifton Chapel'

18 There's a breathless hush in the Close to-night—
Ten to make and the match to win—

A bumping pitch and a blinding light,
An hour to play and the last man in.
And it's not for the sake of a ribboned coat,
Or the selfish hope of a season's fame,
But his Captain's hand on his shoulder smote—
'Play up! play up! and play the game!'
'Vitaï Lampada' (1897)

Anthony Newley 1931– and Leslie Bricusse 1931–

1 Stop the world, I want to get off.
title of musical (1961)

John Henry Newman 1801–90

English theologian and leader of the Oxford Movement; later Cardinal
see also ***Epitaphs*** *302:5,* ***Mottoes*** *535:5,* ***Toasts*** *778:3*

2 It is very difficult to get up resentment towards persons whom one has never seen.
Apologia pro Vita Sua (1864) 'Mr Kingsley's Method of Disputation'

3 There is such a thing as legitimate warfare: war has its laws; there are things which may fairly be done, and things which may not be done . . . He has attempted (as I may call it) to *poison the wells.*
Apologia pro Vita Sua (1864) 'Mr Kingsley's Method of Disputation'

4 I will vanquish, not my Accuser, but my judges.
Apologia pro Vita Sua (1864) 'True Mode of meeting Mr Kingsley'

5 Two and two only supreme and luminously self-evident beings, myself and my Creator.
Apologia pro Vita Sua (1864) 'History of My Religious Opinions to the Year 1833'

6 It would be a gain to the country were it vastly more superstitious, more bigoted, more gloomy, more fierce in its religion than at present it shows itself to be.
Apologia pro Vita Sua (1864) 'History of My Religious Opinions from 1833 to 1839'

7 From the age of fifteen, dogma has been the fundamental principle of my religion: I know no other religion; I cannot enter into the idea of any other sort of religion; religion, as a mere sentiment, is to me a dream and a mockery.
Apologia pro Vita Sua (1864) 'History of My Religious Opinions from 1833 to 1839'

8 This is what the Church is said to want, not party men, but sensible, temperate, sober, well-judging persons, to guide it through the channel of no-meaning, between the Scylla and Charybdis of Aye and No.
Apologia pro Vita Sua (1864) 'History of My Religious Opinions from 1833 to 1839'

9 Ten thousand difficulties do not make one doubt.
Apologia pro Vita Sua (1864) 'Position of my Mind since 1845'

10 The all-corroding, all-dissolving scepticism of the intellect in religious enquiries.
Apologia pro Vita Sua (1864) 'Position of my Mind since 1845'

11 It is almost a definition of a gentleman to say that he is one who never inflicts pain.
The Idea of a University (1852) 'Knowledge and Religious Duty'

12 She [the Catholic Church] holds that it were better for sun and moon to drop from heaven, for the earth to fail, and for all the many millions who are upon it to die of starvation in extremest agony, as far as temporal affliction goes, than that one soul, I will not say, should be lost, but should commit one single venial sin, should tell one wilful untruth . . . or steal one poor farthing without excuse.
Lectures on Anglican Difficulties (1852) Lecture 8

13 It is as absurd to argue men, as to torture them, into believing.
'The Usurpations of Reason' (1831) in *Oxford University Sermons* (1843) no. 4

14 And this is all that is known, and more than all—yet nothing to what the angels know—of the life of a servant of God, who sinned and repented, and did penance and washed out his sins, and became a Saint, and reigns with Christ in heaven.
Lives of the English Saints (1844–5) 'The Legend of Saint Bettelin'; though attributed to Newman, 'and more than all' may have been added by J. A. Froude (1818–94)

15 When men understand what each other mean, they see, for the most part, that controversy is either superfluous or hopeless.
'Faith and Reason, contrasted as Habits of Mind' (Epiphany, 1839) in *Oxford University Sermons* (1843) no. 10

16 May He support us all the day long, till the shades lengthen, and the evening comes, and the busy world is hushed, and the fever of life is over, and our work is done! Then in His mercy may He give us a safe lodging, and a holy rest, and peace at the last.
'Wisdom and Innocence' (19 February 1843) in *Sermons Bearing on Subjects of the Day* (1843) no. 20

17 Firmly I believe and truly
God is Three, and God is One;
And I next acknowledge duly
Manhood taken by the Son.
The Dream of Gerontius (1865)

18 Praise to the Holiest in the height,
And in the depth be praise;
In all his words most wonderful,
Most sure in all His ways.
The Dream of Gerontius (1865)

19 Lead, kindly Light, amid the encircling gloom,
Lead thou me on;
The night is dark, and I am far from home,
Lead thou me on.
Keep Thou my feet; I do not ask to see
The distant scene; one step enough for me.
'Lead, kindly Light' (1834)

20 I loved the garish day, and spite of fears,
Pride ruled my will: remember not past years.
'Lead, kindly Light' (1834); cf. **Milton** 512:10

1 *We can believe what we choose.* We are answerable for what we choose to believe.

letter to Mrs William Froude, 27 June 1848, in C. S. Dessain (ed.) *Letters and Diaries of John Henry Newman* vol. 12 (1962)

☐ Newspaper headlines and leaders

see box overleaf

Huey Newton 1942–

American political activist

2 I suggested [in 1966] that we use the panther as our symbol and call our political vehicle the Black Panther Party. The panther is a fierce animal, but he will not attack until he is backed into a corner; then he will strike out.

Revolutionary Suicide (1973) ch. 16; cf. **Political slogans** 581:28

Isaac Newton 1642–1727

English mathematician and physicist

on Newton: see ***Auden*** *34:14,* ***Blake*** *119:7,* ***Brereton*** *148:1,* ***Cowper*** *241:27,* ***Pope*** *584:9,* ***Thomson*** *775:18,* ***Wordsworth*** *831:3*

3 Whence is it that Nature does nothing in vain: and whence arises all that order and beauty which we see in the world? . . . does it not appear from phenomena that there is a Being incorporeal, living, intelligent, omnipresent, who in infinite space, as it were in his Sensory, sees the things themselves intimately, and thoroughly perceives them, and comprehends them wholly.

Opticks (1730 ed.) bk. 3, pt. 1, question 28

4 The changing of bodies into light, and light into bodies, is very conformable to the course of Nature, which seems delighted with transmutations.

Opticks (1730 ed.) bk. 3, pt. 1, question 30

5 *Corpus omne perseverare in statu suo quiescendi vel movendi uniformiter in directum, nisi quatenus illud a viribus impressis cogitur statum suum mutare.*

Every body continues in its state of rest, or of uniform motion in a right line, unless it is compelled to change that state by forces impressed upon it.

Principia Mathematica (1687) Laws of Motion 1 (translated by Andrew Motte, 1729)

6 *Mutationem motus proportionalem esse vi motrici impressae et fieri secundum lineam rectam qua vis illa imprimitur.*

The alteration of motion is ever proportional to the motive force impressed; and is made in the direction of the right line in which that force is impressed.

Principia Mathematica (1687) Laws of Motion 2 (translated by Andrew Motte, 1729)

7 *Actioni contrarium semper et aequalem esse reactionem: sive corporum duorum actiones in se mutuo semper esse aequales et in partes contrarias dirigi.*

To every action there is always opposed an equal reaction: or, the mutual actions of two bodies upon each other are always equal, and directed to contrary parts.

Principia Mathematica (1687) Laws of Motion 3 (translated by Andrew Motte, 1729)

8 *Hypotheses non fingo.*

I do not feign hypotheses.

Principia Mathematica (1713 ed.) 'Scholium Generale'

9 If I have seen further it is by standing on the shoulders of giants.

letter to Robert Hooke, 5 February 1676, in H. W. Turnbull (ed.) *Correspondence of Isaac Newton* vol. 1 (1959); cf. **Bernard** 68:22, **Coleridge** 227:14

10 Philosophy is such an impertinently litigious lady that a man has as good be engaged in law suits as have to do with her.

letter to Edmond Halley, 20 June 1686, in H. W. Turnbull (ed.) *Correspondence of Isaac Newton* vol. 2 (1960)

11 I don't know what I may seem to the world, but as to myself, I seem to have been only like a boy playing on the sea-shore and diverting myself in now and then finding a smoother pebble or a prettier shell than ordinary, whilst the great ocean of truth lay all undiscovered before me.

Joseph Spence *Anecdotes* (ed. J. Osborn, 1966) no. 1259

12 O Diamond! Diamond! thou little knowest the mischief done!

to a dog, who knocked over a candle which set fire to some papers and thereby 'destroyed the almost finished labours of some years'

Thomas Maude *Wensley-Dale . . . a Poem* (1772) st. 23 n.; probably apocryphal

John Newton 1725–1807

English clergyman

13 Amazing grace! how sweet the sound
That saved a wretch like me!
I once was lost, but now am found,
Was blind, but now I see.

Olney Hymns (1779) 'Amazing grace'

14 Glorious things of thee are spoken,
Zion, city of our God!

Olney Hymns (1779) 'Glorious things of thee are spoken'

15 How sweet the name of Jesus sounds
In a believer's ear!
It soothes his sorrows, heals his wounds,
And drives away his fear.

Olney Hymns (1779) 'How sweet the name of Jesus sounds'

Nicholas I 1796–1855

Russian emperor from 1825

16 Turkey is a dying man. We may endeavour to keep him alive, but we shall not succeed. He will, he must die.

F. Max Müller (ed.) *Memoirs of Baron Stockmar* (translated by G. A. M. Müller, 1873) vol. 2

17 Russia has two generals in whom she can confide—Generals Janvier [January] and Février [February].

attributed; in *Punch* 10 March 1855

continued

Newspaper headlines and leaders

1 Believe it or not.
title of syndicated newspaper feature (from 1918), written by Robert L. Ripley (1893–1949)

2 Crisis? What crisis?
summarizing an interview with James **Callaghan**
headline in *Sun*, 11 January 1979; cf. **Misquotations** 521:7

3 Dewey defeats Truman.
anticipating the result of the Presidential election, which **Truman** *won against expectation*
in *Chicago Tribune* 3 November 1948

4 Egghead weds hourglass.
on the marriage of Arthur **Miller** *and Marilyn* **Monroe**
headline in *Variety* 1956; attributed

5 Freddie Starr ate my hamster.
headline in *Sun* 13 March 1986

6 GOTCHA!
on the sinking of the General Belgrano
headline in *Sun* 4 May 1982

7 Go West, young man, go West!
editorial in *Terre Haute* [Indiana] *Express* (1851), by John L. B. Soule (1815–91); cf. **Greeley** 351:10

8 Is THIS the most dangerous man in Britain?
headline beside a picture of Tony **Blair**, *attacking his perceived sympathy for the euro*
in *The Sun* 25 June 1998

9 It is a moral issue.
leader following the resignation of **Profumo**
in *The Times* 11 June 1963; cf. **Hailsham** 356:11, **Macmillan** 487:20

10 It's that man again . . . ! At the head of a cavalcade of seven black motor cars Hitler swept out of his Berlin Chancellery last night on a mystery journey.
headline in *Daily Express* 2 May 1939; the acronym ITMA became the title of a BBC radio show, from September 1939

11 It's The Sun wot won it.
following the 1992 general election
headline in *Sun* 11 April 1992

12 King's Moll Reno'd in Wolsey's home town.
US newspaper headline on the divorce proceedings of Wallis Simpson (later Duchess of **Windsor**) *in Ipswich*
Frances Donaldson *Edward VIII* (1974) ch. 7

13 Splendid isolation.
headline in *The Times* 22 January 1896, referring to

In these somewhat troublesome days when the great Mother Empire stands splendidly isolated in Europe.
speech by George Foster (1847–1931) 16 January 1896, in *Official Report of the Debates of the House of Commons of the Dominion of Canada* (1896) vol. 41

14 Sticks nix hick pix.
front-page headline on the lack of enthusiasm for farm dramas among rural populations
in *Variety* 17 July 1935

15 Unless the people—the people everywhere—come forward and petition, ay, thunder for reform.
leader on the Reform Bill, possibly written by Edward Sterling (1773–1847), resulting in the nickname 'The Thunderer'
in *The Times* 29 January 1831; the phrase 'we thundered out' had been used earlier, 11 February 1829

16 Wall St. lays an egg.
crash headline, *Variety* 30 October 1929

17 We shall not pretend that there is nothing in his long career which those who respect and admire him would wish otherwise.
on **Edward VII***'s accession to the throne*
in *The Times* 23 January 1901, leading article

18 Who breaks a butterfly on a wheel?
defending Mick **Jagger** *after his arrest for cannabis possession*
leader in *The Times* 1 June 1967, written by William Rees-Mogg; cf. **Pope** 583:9

19 Whose finger do you want on the trigger?
referring to the atom bomb
headline in *Daily Mirror* 21 September 1951

20 Winter of discontent.
headline in *Sun* 30 April 1979; cf. **Callaghan** 181:11, **Shakespeare** 696:7

Nicias c.470–413 BC
Athenian politician and general

21 For a city consists in men, and not in walls nor in ships empty of men.
speech to the defeated Athenian army at Syracuse, 413 BC
Thucydides *History of the Peloponnesian Wars* bk. 7, sect. 77

Harold Nicolson 1886–1968
English diplomat, politician, and writer; husband of Vita **Sackville-West**

22 Ponderous and uncertain is that relation between pressure and resistance which constitutes the balance of power. The arch of peace is morticed by no iron tendons . . . One night a handful of dust will patter from the vaulting: the bats will squeak and wheel in sudden panic: nor can the fragile fingers of man then stay the rush and rumble of destruction.
Public Faces (1932) ch. 6

23 We shall have to walk and live a Woolworth life hereafter.
anticipating the aftermath of the Second World War
diary, 4 June 1941, in *Diaries and Letters 1939–45* (1967)

1 I am haunted by mental decay such as I saw creeping over Ramsay MacDonald. A gradual dimming of the lights.
diary, 28 April 1947, in *Diaries and Letters 1945–62* (1968)

2 To be a good diarist one must have a little snouty, sneaky mind.
of Samuel **Pepys**
diary, 9 November 1947, in *Diaries and Letters 1945–62* (1968)

3 For seventeen years he did nothing at all but kill animals and stick in stamps.
of King **George V**
diary, 17 August 1949 in *Diaries and Letters 1945–62* (1968)

4 Suez—a smash and grab raid that was all smash and no grab.
in conversation with Antony Jay, November 1956; see also letter to Vita Sackville-West, 8 November 1956, 'Our smash-and-grab raid got stuck at the smash'

Reinhold Niebuhr 1892–1971
American theologian

5 Man's capacity for justice makes democracy possible, but man's inclination to injustice makes democracy necessary.
Children of Light and Children of Darkness (1944) foreword

6 Our gadget-filled paradise suspended in a hell of international insecurity.
Pious and Secular America (1957)

Martin Niemöller 1892–1984
German theologian

7 Ask the first man you meet what he means by defending freedom, and he'll tell you privately he means defending the standard of living.
address at Augsburg, January 1958; James Bentley *Martin Niemöller* (1984)

8 When Hitler attacked the Jews I was not a Jew, therefore, I was not concerned. And when Hitler attacked the Catholics, I was not a Catholic, and therefore, I was not concerned. And when Hitler attacked the unions and the industrialists, I was not a member of the unions and I was not concerned. Then, Hitler attacked me and the Protestant church—and there was nobody left to be concerned.
often quoted in the form 'In Germany they came first for the Communists, and I didn't speak up because I wasn't a Communist . . . ' and so on
in *Congressional Record* 14 October 1968

Friedrich Nietzsche 1844–1900
German philosopher and writer

9 *Ich lehre euch den Übermenschen. Der Mensch ist Etwas, das überwunden werden soll.*
I teach you the superman. Man is something to be surpassed.
Also Sprach Zarathustra (1883) prologue, sect. 3

10 You are going to women? Do not forget the whip!
Also Sprach Zarathustra (1883) bk. 1 'Von Alten und jungen Weiblein'

11 God's first blunder: Man didn't find the animals amusing,—he dominated them, and didn't even want to be an 'animal'.
Der Antichrist (1888) aphorism 48

12 Woman was God's second blunder.
Der Antichrist (1888) aphorism 48; cf. **Cowley** 239:26

13 What I understand by 'philosopher': a terrible explosive in the presence of which everything is in danger.
Ecce Homo (1908) 'Die Unzeitgemässen' sect. 3

14 God is dead: but considering the state the species Man is in, there will perhaps be caves, for ages yet, in which his shadow will be shown.
Die fröhliche Wissenschaft (1882) bk. 3, sect. 108; cf. **Plato** 578:8

15 Morality is the herd-instinct in the individual.
Die fröhliche Wissenschaft (1882) bk. 3, sect. 116

16 The secret of reaping the greatest fruitfulness and the greatest enjoyment from life is *to live dangerously*!
Die fröhliche Wissenschaft (1882) bk. 4, sect. 283

17 He who fights with monsters might take care lest he thereby become a monster. And if you gaze for long into an abyss, the abyss gazes also into you.
Jenseits von Gut und Böse (1886) ch. 4, no. 146

18 The thought of suicide is a great source of comfort: with it a calm passage is to be made across many a bad night.
Jenseits von Gut und Böse (1886) ch. 4, no. 157

19 Master-morality and slave-morality.
Jenseits von Gut und Böse (1886) ch. 9, no. 260

20 Wit is the epitaph of an emotion.
Menschliches, Allzumenschliches (1867–80) vol. 2, sect. 1, no. 202

21 At the base of all these aristocratic races the predator is not to be mistaken, the splendorous *blond beast*, avidly rampant for plunder and victory.
Zur Genealogie der Moral (1887) 1st treatise, no. 11

Florence Nightingale 1820–1910
English nurse
on Nightingale: see **Longfellow** *474:9,* **Strachey** *744:8*

22 It may seem a strange principle to enunciate as the very first requirement in a Hospital that it should do the sick no harm.
Notes on Hospitals (1863 ed.) preface

23 I would earnestly ask my sisters to keep clear of both the jargons now current everywhere . . . of the jargon, namely about the 'rights' of women, which urges women to do all that men do . . . merely because men do it, and without regard to whether this *is* the best that women can do; and of the jargon which urges women to do nothing that men do, merely because they are women . . . Woman should bring the best she has, *whatever* that is . . . without attending to either of these cries.
Notes on Nursing (1860)

24 No *man*, not even a doctor, ever gives any other definition of what a nurse should be than this—

'devoted and obedient.' This definition would do just as well for a porter. It might even do for a horse. It would not do for a policeman.
Notes on Nursing (1860)

1 Too kind, too kind.
on the Order of Merit being brought to her at her home, 5 December 1907
E. Cook *Life of Florence Nightingale* (1913) vol. 2, pt. 7, ch. 9

Anaïs Nin 1903–77

French-born American writer

2 The very touch of the letter was as if you had taken me all into your arms.
letter to Henry Miller, 6 August 1932

3 Anxiety is love's greatest killer. It creates the failures. It makes others feel as you might when a drowning man holds on to you. You want to save him, but you know he will strangle you with his panic.
diary, February 1947; *The Diary of Anais Nin* vol. 4 (1944–7)

Richard Milhous Nixon 1913–94

American Republican statesman, 37th President of the US
see also **Anonymous** *16:5*

4 The great silent majority.
broadcast, 3 November 1969 in *New York Times* 4 November 1969

5 There can be no whitewash at the White House.
on Watergate
television speech, 30 April 1973, in *New York Times* 1 May 1973

6 I made my mistakes, but in all my years of public life, I have never profited, never profited from public service. I've earned every cent. And in all of my years in public life I have never obstructed justice . . . I welcome this kind of examination because people have got to know whether or not their President is a crook. Well, I'm not a crook.
speech at press conference, 17 November 1973, in *New York Times* 18 November 1973

7 This country needs good farmers, good businessmen, good plumbers, good carpenters.
farewell address at White House, 9 August 1974, in *New York Times* 10 August 1974

8 When the President does it, that means that it is not illegal.
David Frost *I Gave Them a Sword* (1978) ch. 8

9 I brought myself down. I gave them a sword. And they stuck it in.
television interview, 19 May 1977, in David Frost *I Gave Them a Sword* (1978) ch. 10

Kwame Nkrumah 1900–72

Ghanaian statesman, Prime Minister 1957–60, President 1960–6

10 Freedom is not something that one people can bestow on another as a gift. They claim it as their own and none can keep it from them.
speech in Accra, 10 July 1953

11 We face neither East nor West: we face forward.
conference speech, Accra, 7 April 1960; *Axioms of Kwame Nkrumah* (1967)

Caroline Maria Noel 1817–77

English hymn-writer

12 At the name of Jesus
Every knee shall bow,
Every tongue confess him
King of glory now.
'At the name of Jesus' (1861 hymn); cf. **Bible** 108:17

Thomas Noel 1799–1861

English poet

13 Rattle his bones over the stones;
He's only a pauper, whom nobody owns!
'The Pauper's Drive' (1841)

Charles Howard, Duke of Norfolk 1746–1815

14 I cannot be a good Catholic; I cannot go to heaven; and if a man is to go to the devil, he may as well go thither from the House of Lords as from any other place on earth.
Henry Best *Personal and Literary Memorials* (1829) ch. 18

Christopher North (John Wilson) 1785–1854

Scottish literary critic

15 Minds like ours, my dear James, must always be above national prejudices, and in all companies it gives me true pleasure to declare, that, as a people, the English are very little indeed inferior to the Scotch.
Blackwood's Magazine (October 1826) 'Noctes Ambrosianae' no. 20

16 His Majesty's dominions, on which the sun never sets.
Blackwood's Magazine (April 1829) 'Noctes Ambrosianae' no. 42; cf. **Schiller** 648:11

17 Laws were made to be broken.
Blackwood's Magazine (May 1830) 'Noctes Ambrosianae' no. 49

18 I cannot sit still, James, and hear you abuse the shopocracy.
Blackwood's Magazine (February 1835) 'Noctes Ambrosianae' no. 71

Alfred Harmsworth, Lord Northcliffe 1865–1922

British newspaper proprietor
on Northcliffe: see **Anonymous** *16:13*

19 The power of the press is very great, but not so great as the power of suppress.
office message, *Daily Mail* 1918; Reginald Rose and Geoffrey Harmsworth *Northcliffe* (1959) ch. 22

20 When I want a peerage, I shall buy it like an honest man.
Tom Driberg *Swaff* (1974) ch. 2

Caroline Norton (née Sheridan) 1808–77

English poet and songwriter

1 And all our calm is in that balm—
Not lost but gone before.

'Not Lost but Gone Before'; cf. **Cyprian** 248:11, **Rogers** 631:13

Jack Norworth 1879–1959

American songwriter

2 Oh, shine on, shine on, harvest moon
Up in the sky.
I ain't had no lovin'
Since April, January, June, or July.

'Shine On, Harvest Moon' (1908 song)

Novalis (Friedrich von Hardenberg) 1772–1801

German poet and novelist

3 I often feel, and ever more deeply I realize, that Fate and character are the same conception.

often quoted as 'Character is destiny' or 'Character is fate'

Heinrich von Ofterdingen (1802) bk. 2; cf. **Eliot** 293:7, **Heraclitus** 371:9

4 A God-intoxicated man.

of ***Spinoza***

attributed

Alfred Noyes 1880–1958

English poet

5 Go down to Kew in lilac-time, in lilac-time, in lilac-time,
Go down to Kew in lilac-time (it isn't far from London!).

'The Barrel-Organ' (1904)

6 The wind was a torrent of darkness among the gusty trees,
The moon was a ghostly galleon tossed upon cloudy seas,
The road was a ribbon of moonlight over the purple moor,
And the highwayman came riding—
Riding—riding—
The highwayman came riding, up to the old inn-door.

'The Highwayman' (1907)

7 Look for me by moonlight;
Watch for me by moonlight;
I'll come to thee by moonlight, though hell should bar the way!

'The Highwayman' (1907)

Lord Nuffield 1877–1963

British motor manufacturer and philanthropist

on seeing the Morris Minor prototype in 1945:

8 It looks like a poached egg—we can't make that.

attributed

Sam Nunn 1938–

American Democratic politician

9 Don't ask, don't tell.

summary of the **Clinton** administration's compromise policy on homosexuals serving in the armed forces, in *New York Times* 12 May 1993

Nursery rhymes

Citations given are generally for the first appearance of the rhyme. For detailed bibliographical descriptions and variants, see The Oxford Dictionary of Nursery Rhymes

10 A was an apple-pie;
B bit it;
C cut it.

John Eachard *Some Observations* (1671)

11 As I was going to St Ives
I met a man with seven wives.

Harley MS mid 18th century

12 Baa, baa, black sheep,
Have you any wool?
Yes, sir, yes, sir
Three bags full:
One for the master,
And one for the dame,
And one for the little boy
Who lives down the lane.

Tommy Thumb's Pretty Song Book (c.1744)

13 Boys and girls come out to play,
The moon doth shine as bright as day.

William King *Useful Transactions in Philosophy* (1708–9)

14 Bye, baby bunting,
Daddy's gone a hunting,
Gone to get a rabbit skin
To wrap the baby bunting in.

Gammer Gurton's Garland (1784)

15 The children in Holland take pleasure in making
What the children in England take pleasure in breaking.

traditional

16 Cock a doodle doo!
My dame has lost her shoe,
My master's lost his fiddlestick,
And knows not what to do.

The Most Cruel and Bloody Murder Committed by an Innkeeper's Wife (1606)

17 Cross-patch,
Draw the latch,
Sit by the fire and spin;
Take a cup,
And drink it up,
Then call your neighbours in.

Mother Goose's Melody (c.1765)

18 Curly locks, Curly locks,
Wilt thou be mine?
Thou shalt not wash dishes
Nor yet feed the swine.
But sit on a cushion
And sew a fine seam,
And feed upon strawberries,
Sugar and cream.

Infant Institutes (1797)

1 Dance to your daddy,
My little babby,
Dance to your daddy, my little lamb;
You shall have a fishy
In a little dishy,
You shall have a fishy when the boat comes in.
Vocal Harmony (*c.*1806)

2 Daffy-down-dilly is new come to town,
With a yellow petticoat, and a green gown.
Songs for the Nursery (1805)

3 Diddle, diddle, dumpling, my son John,
Went to bed with his trousers on.
Newest Christmas Box (*c.*1797)

4 Ding, dong, bell,
Pussy's in the well.
Mother Goose's Melody (*c.*1765)

5 Fiddle-de-dee, Fiddle-de-dee,
The fly shall marry the humble-bee.
'Fiddle-de-dee' (*c.*1803)

6 A frog he would a-wooing go,
'Heigh-ho!' says Rowley . . .

. . . while they were all a-merry-making,
'Heigh-ho!' says Rowley,
A cat and her kittens came tumbling in.
Thomas Ravenscroft *Melismata* (1611)

7 Georgie Porgie, pudding and pie,
Kissed the girls and made them cry;
When the girls came out to play,
Georgie Porgie ran away.
J. O. Halliwell (ed.) *Nursery Rhymes* (1844)

8 Goosey, goosey gander,
Whither shall I wander?
Upstairs and downstairs,
And in my lady's chamber.
There I met an old man
Who would not say his prayers.
I took him by the left leg
And threw him down the stairs.
Gammer Gurton's Garland (1784)

9 Grey goose and gander,
Waft your wings together,
And carry the good king's daughter
Over the one-strand river.
J. O. Halliwell (ed.) *Nursery Rhymes* (1844)

10 He began to bark,
And she began to cry,
Lawk a mercy on me,
This is none of I!
'There was a little woman', Mansfield MS, *c.*1775; Iona and Peter Opie (eds.) *Oxford Dictionary of Nursery Rhymes* (new edn. 1997)

11 Here am I,
Little Jumping Joan;
When nobody's with me
I'm all alone.
T. Hughes *Adventures of Jumping Joan* (advertised 1808)

12 Hey diddle diddle,
The cat and the fiddle,
The cow jumped over the moon;
The little dog laughed
To see such sport,
And the dish ran away with the spoon.
Mother Goose's Melody (*c.*1765)

13 Hickety, pickety, my black hen,
She lays eggs for gentlemen.
J. O. Halliwell (ed.) *Nursery Rhymes* (1853)

14 Hickory, dickory, dock,
The mouse ran up the clock.
The clock struck one,
The mouse ran down,
Hickory, dickory, dock.
Tommy Thumb's Pretty Song Book (*c.*1744)

15 How many miles to Babylon?
Threescore miles and ten.
Can I get there by candle-light?
Yes, and back again.
Songs for the Nursery (1805)

16 Humpty Dumpty sat on a wall,
Humpty Dumpty had a great fall;
All the king's horses,
And all the king's men,
Couldn't put Humpty together again.
MS addition to a copy of *Mother Goose's Melody* (*c.*1803)

17 I had a little nut tree
Nothing would it bear
But a silver nutmeg
And a golden pear;

The King of Spain's daughter
Came to visit me,
And all for the sake
Of my little nut tree.
Newest Christmas Box (*c.*1797)

18 I'll tell you a story
About Jack a Nory.
Nurse Lovechild *Jacky Nory's Story Book for all Little Masters and Misses* (advertised December 1745)

19 I love little pussy,
Her coat is so warm,
And if I don't hurt her
She'll do me no harm.
Hints for the Formation of Infant Schools (1829)

20 I'm the king of the castle,
Get down you dirty rascal.
W. C. Hazlitt (ed.) *Brand's Popular Antiquities* (1870)

21 Jack and Jill went up the hill
To fetch a pail of water;
Jack fell down and broke his crown,
And Jill came tumbling after.
Mother Goose's Melody (*c.*1765)

22 Jack be nimble,
Jack be quick,
Jack jump over
The candle stick.
Douce MS, *c.*1815; J. O. Halliwell (ed.) *Nursery Rhymes* (1844)

23 Jack Sprat could eat no fat,
His wife could eat no lean,
And so between them both, you see,
They licked the platter clean.
John Clarke *Paroemiologia Anglo-Latina* (1639)

1 Ladybird, ladybird,
Fly away home,
Your house is on fire
And your children all gone;
All except one
And that's little Ann
And she has crept under
The warming pan.
Tommy Thumb's Pretty Song Book (*c.*1744)

2 Lavender's blue, diddle, diddle,
Lavender's green;
When I am king, diddle, diddle,
You shall be queen.
J. Wright etc. *Diddle Diddle* (*c.*1680)

3 The lion and the unicorn
Were fighting for the crown;
The lion beat the unicorn
All round the town.
Some gave them white bread,
And some gave them brown;
Some gave them plum cake,
And sent them out of town.
MS inscription (*c.*1691) beside a woodcut of the royal arms in a bible in the Opie Collection; William King *Useful Transactions in Philosophy* (1708–9)

4 Little Bo-Peep has lost her sheep,
And can't tell where to find them;
Leave them alone, and they'll come home,
And bring their tails behind them.
Douce MS, *c.*1805; *Gammer Gurton's Garland* (1810)

5 Little Boy Blue,
Come blow your horn,
The sheep's in the meadow,
The cow's in the corn;
But where is the boy
Who looks after the sheep?
He's under a haycock,
Fast asleep.
The Famous Tommy Thumb's Little Story Book (*c.*1760)

6 Little Jack Horner
Sat in the corner,
Eating a Christmas pie;
He put in his thumb,
And pulled out a plum,
And said, what a good boy am I!
Henry Carey *Namby Pamby* (1725)

7 Little Miss Muffet
Sat on a tuffet
Eating her curds and whey;
There came a big spider,
Who sat down beside her
And frightened Miss Muffet away.
Songs for the Nursery (1805)

8 Little Polly Flinders
Sat among the cinders,
Warming her pretty little toes;
Her mother came and caught her,
And whipped her little daughter
For spoiling her nice new clothes.
J. Harris *Original Ditties for the Nursery* (*c.*1805)

9 Little Tommy Tucker
Sings for his supper;
What shall we give him?
White bread and butter.
Tommy Thumb's Pretty Song Book (*c.*1744)

10 London Bridge is broken down
My fair lady.
Henry Carey *Namby Pamby* (1725)

11 Lucy Locket lost her pocket
Kitty Fisher found it.
J. O. Halliwell (ed.) *Nursery Rhymes* (1842)

12 A man in the wilderness asked me,
How many strawberries grow in the sea?
I answered him, as I thought good,
As many red herrings as grow in the wood.
Bodleian MS; Iona and Peter Opie (eds.) *The Oxford Dictionary of Nursery Rhymes* (new edn., 1997)

13 Mary, Mary, quite contrary,
How does your garden grow?
With silver bells and cockle shells
And pretty maids all in a row.
Tommy Thumb's Pretty Song Book (*c.*1744)

14 Monday's child is fair of face,
Tuesday's child is full of grace,
Wednesday's child is full of woe,
Thursday's child has far to go,
Friday's child is loving and giving,
Saturday's child works hard for his living,
And the child that is born of the Sabbath day,
Is bonny, and blithe, and good and gay.
A. E. Bray *Traditions of Devonshire* (1838)

15 My mother said that I never should
Play with the gypsies in the wood.
Robert Graves *Less Familiar Nursery Rhymes* (1927)

16 The north wind doth blow,
And we shall have snow,
And what will poor robin do then?
Poor thing.
He'll sit in a barn,
To keep himself warm,
And hide his head under his wing.
Poor thing.
Songs for the Nursery (1805)

17 Old King Cole
Was a merry old soul,
And a merry old soul was he;
He called for his pipe,
And he called for his bowl,
And he called for his fiddlers three.
William King *Useful Transactions in Philosophy* (1708–9)

18 Old Mother Hubbard
Went to the cupboard
To fetch her poor dog a bone;
But when she came there
The cupboard was bare
And so the poor dog had none.
Sarah Catherine Martin *The Comic Adventures of Old Mother Hubbard* (1805), based on a traditional rhyme

19 Old Mother Slipper Slopper jumped out of bed,
And out of the window she popped her head:
Oh! John, John, John, the grey goose is gone,
And the fox is off to his den O! . . .

... And the little ones picked the bones O!
'A fox jumped up one winter's night' in *Gammer Gurton's Garland* (1810)

1 One a penny, two a penny,
Hot cross buns!
If your daughters do not like them,
Give them to your sons.
Christmas Box (1797)

2 One flew east and one flew west,
And one flew over the cuckoo's nest.
traditional American version of counting-out rhyme 'Intry mintry cutry corn'; Roger D. Abrahams *Jump-Rope Rhymes* (1969)

3 One, two
Buckle my shoe;
Three, four,
Knock at the door;
Five, six,
Pick up sticks.
Seven, eight,
Lay them straight;
Nine, ten
A big fat hen.
Songs for the Nursery (1805)

4 Oranges and lemons
Say the bells of St. Clements ...

... When will you pay me?
Say the bells of Old Bailey.

When I grow rich,
Say the bells of Shoreditch ...

... Here comes a candle to light you to bed,
Here comes a chopper to chop off your head.
Tommy Thumb's Pretty Song Book (c.1744)

5 Pat-a-cake, pat-a-cake, baker's man,
Bake me a cake as fast as you can;
Pat it and prick it, and mark it with B,
Put it in the oven for baby and me.
Tom D'Urfey *The Campaigners* (1698)

6 Pease porridge hot,
Pease porridge cold,
Pease porridge in the pot
Nine days old.
Newest Christmas Box (c.1797)

7 Peter Piper picked a peck of pickled pepper.
Peter Piper's Practical Principles of Plain and Perfect Pronunciation (1813)

8 Polly put the kettle on,
We'll all have tea.
Charles Dickens *Barnaby Rudge* (1841)

9 Pussy cat, pussy cat, where have you been?
I've been to London to look at the queen.
Songs for the Nursery (1805)

10 The Queen of Hearts
She made some tarts,
All on a summer's day;
The Knave of Hearts
He stole the tarts,
And took them clean away.
'The Hive, A Collection of Scraps' in *The European Magazine* April 1782

11 Rain, rain, go away,
Come again another day.
James Howell *Proverbs* (1659)

12 Ride a cock-horse to Banbury Cross,
To see a fine lady upon a white horse;
Rings on her fingers and bells on her toes,
And she shall have music wherever she goes.
Gammer Gurton's Garland (1784)

13 Ring-a-ring o'roses,
A pocket full of posies,
A-tishoo! A-tishoo!
We all fall down.
Kate Greenaway *Mother Goose* (1881)

14 Round and round the garden
Like a teddy bear.
orally collected, 1946–50; Iona and Peter Opie (eds.) *The Oxford Dictionary of Nursery Rhymes* (new edn., 1997)

15 Rub-a-dub-dub,
Three men in a tub
And how do you think they got there?
The butcher, the baker,
The candlestick-maker,
They all jumped out of a rotten potato
'Twas enough to make a man stare.
Christmas Box vol. 2 (1798)

16 See-saw, Margery Daw,
Jacky shall have a new master;
Jacky shall have but a penny a day,
Because he can't work any faster.
Mother Goose's Melody (c.1765)

17 Simple Simon met a pieman,
Going to the fair;
Says Simple Simon to the pieman,
Let me taste your ware.
Simple Simon, chapbook advertisement, 1764

18 Sing a song of sixpence,
A pocket full of rye;
Four and twenty blackbirds,
Baked in a pie.

When the pie was opened,
The birds began to sing;
Was not that a dainty dish,
To set before the king?

The king was in his counting-house,
Counting out his money;
The queen was in the parlour,
Eating bread and honey.

The maid was in the garden,
Hanging out the clothes,
There came a little blackbird,
And snapped off her nose.
Tommy Thumb's Pretty Song Book (c.1744)

19 Solomon Grundy,
Born on a Monday,
Christened on Tuesday,
Married on Wednesday,
Took ill on Thursday,
Worse on Friday,
Died on Saturday,
Buried on Sunday:
This is the end

Of Solomon Grundy.
J. O. Halliwell *Nursery Rhymes* (1842)

1 Taffy was a Welshman, Taffy was a thief,
Taffy came to my house and stole a piece of beef.
Nancy Cock's Pretty Song Book (*c.*1780)

2 Tell tale tit,
Your tongue shall be slit.
Mother Goose's Melody (1780)

3 There was a crooked man, and he walked a crooked mile,
He found a crooked sixpence against a crooked stile;
He bought a crooked cat, which caught a crooked mouse,
And they all lived together in a little crooked house.
J. O. Halliwell (ed.) *Nursery Rhymes* (1842)

4 There was a lady loved a swine,
Honey, quoth she,
Pig-hog wilt thou be mine?
Hoogh, quoth he.
Bodley MS, *c.*1620; Iona and Peter Opie (eds.) *The Oxford Dictionary of Nursery Rhymes* (new edn, 1997)

5 There was a little man, and he had a little gun.
Tommy Thumb's Pretty Song Book (*c.*1744)

6 There was an old woman who lived in a shoe,
She had so many children she didn't know what to do.
Gammer Gurton's Garland (1784)

7 This is the house that Jack built . . .
. . . This is the farmer sowing his corn,
That kept the cock that crowed in the morn,
That waked the priest all shaven and shorn,
That married the man all tattered and torn,
That kissed the maiden all forlorn,
That milked the cow with the crumpled horn,
That tossed the dog,
That worried the cat,
That killed the rat,
That ate the malt
That lay in the house that Jack built.
Nurse Truelove's New-Year's-Gift (1755)

8 This is the way the ladies ride.
Robert Chambers *The Popular Rhymes of Scotland* (1842)

9 This little pig went to market,
This little pig stayed at home,
This little pig had roast beef,
This little pig had none,
And this little pig cried, Wee-wee-wee-wee-wee, I can't find my way home.
The Famous Tommy Thumb's Little Story Book (*c.*1760)

10 Three blind mice, see how they run!
They all ran after the farmer's wife,
Who cut off their tails with a carving knife,
Did you ever see such a thing in your life,
As three blind mice?
Thomas Ravenscroft *Deuteromelia* (1609)

11 Three little kittens they lost their mittens.
Eliza Follen *New Nursery Songs* (1853)

12 Three wise men of Gotham
Went to sea in a bowl:
And if the bowl had been stronger,
My song would have been longer.
Mother Goose's Melody (*c.*1765)

13 Tinker,
Tailor,
Soldier,
Sailor,
Rich man,
Poor man,
Beggarman,
Thief.
traditional fortune-telling rhyme for counting out objects such as cherry stones or daisy petals; Iona and Peter Opie (eds.) *The Oxford Dictionary of Nursery Rhymes* (new edn, 1997)

14 To market, to market,
To buy a plum bun:
Home again, home again,
Market is done.
John Florio *Worlde of Wordes* (1611 edn.), *Songs for the Nursery* (1805)

15 Tom he was a piper's son,
He learned to play when he was young,
But all the tune that he could play,
Was 'Over the hills and far away.'
Tom, the Piper's Son (chapbooks, from *c.*1795)

16 Tom, Tom, the piper's son,
Stole a pig and away he run;
The pig was eat
And Tom was beat
And Tom went howling down the street.
Tom, the Piper's Son (chapbooks, from *c.*1795)

17 Twist about, turn about, jump Jim Crow.
Humorous Adventures of Jump Jim Crow (*c.*1836)

18 Wee Willie Winkie runs through the town,
Upstairs and downstairs in his night-gown,
Rapping at the window, crying through the lock,
Are the children all in bed, for now it's eight o'clock.
Cries of Banbury and London (*c.*1840); this traditional rhyme formed the basis for a longer poem by William Miller (1810–72) in *Whistle-Binkie; A Collection of Songs for the Social Circle* (1841)

19 What are little boys made of?
What are little boys made of?
Frogs and snails
And puppy-dogs' tails,
That's what little boys are made of.
What are little girls made of?
What are little girls made of?
Sugar and spice
And all that's nice,
That's what little girls are made of.
J. O. Halliwell *Nursery Rhymes* (1844)

20 Where are you going to, my pretty maid? . . .
. . . My face is my fortune, sir, she said.
Then I can't marry you, my pretty maid.
Nobody asked you, sir, she said.
William Pryce *Archaeologica Cornu-Britannica* (1790)

1 Who killed Cock Robin?
I, said the Sparrow,
With my bow and arrow,
I killed Cock Robin.

Who saw him die?
I, said the Fly,
With my little eye,
I saw him die . . .

. . . All the birds of the air
Fell a-sighing and a-sobbing,
When they heard the bell toll
For poor Cock Robin.

Tommy Thumb's Pretty Song Book (c.1744)

Bill Nye (Edgar Wilson Nye) 1850–96

American humorist

2 I have been told that Wagner's music is better than it sounds.

Mark Twain *Autobiography* (1924) vol. 1

Julius Nyerere 1922–

Tanzanian statesman, President of Tanganyika 1962–4 and of Tanzania 1964–85

3 Should we really let our people starve so we can pay our debts?

in *Guardian* 21 March 1985

4 We are a poor country and we opted for socialist policies, but to build a socialist society you have to have a developed society.

in *Observer* 28 July 1985 'Sayings of the Week'

Charles Edward Oakley 1832–65

English clergyman

5 Hills of the North, rejoice:
Rivers and mountain-spring,
Hark to the advent voice!
Valley and lowland, sing!

'Hills of the North, rejoice' (1870 hymn)

Lawrence Oates see **Epitaphs** 302:12, **Last words** 456:1

Conor Cruise O'Brien 1917–

Irish politician, writer, and journalist
see also **Haughey** 364:1

6 The strength of these men was that each of them could look a Pearsean ghost in the eye . . . Each of them, in their youth, had done the thing the ghost asked them to do, in 1916 or 1919—21 or both. That was it; from now on they would do what seemed reasonable to themselves in the interests of the actual people inhabiting the island of Ireland and not of a personified abstraction, or of a disembodied voice, or of a ghost.

of Sean Lemass (1899–1971) and other senior Irish politicians in the 1960s; cf. **Pearse** 571:8

Ancestral Voices (1994)

7 If I saw Mr Haughey buried at midnight at a crossroads, with a stake driven through his heart—politically speaking—I should continue to wear a clove of garlic round my neck, just in case.

in *Observer* 10 October 1982

Edna O'Brien 1932–

Irish novelist and short-story writer

8 August is a wicked month.

title of novel (1965)

Flann O'Brien (Brian O'Nolan or O Nuallain) 1911–66

Irish novelist and journalist

9 The conclusion of your syllogism, I said lightly, is fallacious, being based upon licensed premises.

At Swim-Two-Birds (1939) ch. 1

10 A pint of plain is your only man.

At Swim-Two-Birds (1939) 'The Workman's Friend'

Sean O'Casey 1880–1964

Irish dramatist

11 I killin' meself workin', an' he shtruttin' about from mornin' till night like a paycock!

Juno and the Paycock (1925) act 1

12 He's an oul' butty o' mine—oh, he's a darlin' man, a daarlin' man.

Juno and the Paycock (1925) act 1

13 The whole worl's in a state o' chassis!

Juno and the Paycock (1925) act 1

14 English literature's performing flea.

of P. G. **Wodehouse**

P. G. Wodehouse *Performing Flea* (1953)

William of Occam c.1285–1349

English Franciscan friar and philosopher

15 *Entia non sunt multiplicanda praeter necessitatem.*

No more things should be presumed to exist than are absolutely necessary.

'Occam's Razor', an ancient philosophical principle often attributed to Occam but earlier in origin

not found in this form in his writings, although he frequently used similar expressions, such as:

Pluralitas non est ponenda sine necessitate.

Plurality should not be assumed unnecessarily.

Quodlibeta (c.1324) no. 5, question 1, art. 2

Daniel O'Connell 1775–1847

Irish nationalist leader and social reformer, elected to Parliament in 1828

16 I have given my advice to my countrymen, and whenever I feel it necessary I shall continue to do

so, careless whether it pleases or displeases this
House or any mad person out of it.
in *Dictionary of National Biography* (1917–)

Bernard O'Donoghue 1945–
Irish poet and academic

1 We were terribly lucky to catch
The Ceauşescus' execution, being
By sheer chance that Christmas Day
In the only house for twenty miles
With satellite TV. We sat,
Cradling brandies, by the fire
Watching those two small, cranky autocrats
Lying in snow against a blood-spattered wall,
Hardly able to believe our good fortune.
'Carolling' (1995)

☐ Official advice
see box overleaf

David Ogilvy 1911–
British-born advertising executive

2 The consumer isn't a moron; she is your wife.
Confessions of an Advertising Man (1963) ch. 5

James Ogilvy, Lord Seafield 1664–1730
Lord Chancellor of Scotland

3 Now there's ane end of ane old song.
as he signed the engrossed exemplification of the Act of Union, 1706
in *The Lockhart Papers* (1817) vol. 1

John O'Hara 1905–70
American writer

4 An artist is his own fault.
The Portable F. Scott Fitzgerald (1945) introduction

Theodore O'Hara 1820–67
American poet

5 The bivouac of the dead.
title of poem (1847)

6 Sons of the dark and bloody ground.
'The Bivouac of the Dead' (1847) st. 1

John O'Keeffe 1747–1833
Irish dramatist

7 Amo, amas, I love a lass,
As a cedar tall and slender;
Sweet cowslip's grace
Is her nom'native case,
And she's of the feminine gender.
The Agreeable Surprise (1781) act 2, sc. 2

8 Fat, fair and forty were all the toasts of the young men.
The Irish Mimic (1795) sc. 2

Dennis O'Kelly c.1720–87
Irish racehorse-owner

9 Eclipse first, the rest nowhere.
comment at Epsom on the occasion of the horse Eclipse's first race, 3 May 1769; the Dictionary of National Biography *gives the occasion as the Queen's Plate at Winchester, 1769*
in *Annals of Sporting* vol. 2 (1822)

Abraham Okpik
Canadian Inuit spokesman

10 I am proud to be an Eskimo, but I think we can improve on the igloo as a permanent dwelling.
in *Northern Affairs Bulletin* March 1960

11 There are very few Eskimos, but millions of Whites, just like mosquitoes. It is something very special and wonderful to be an Eskimo—they are like the snow geese. If an Eskimo forgets his language and Eskimo ways, he will be nothing but just another mosquito.
attributed, 1966

Bruce Oldfield 1950–
English fashion designer

12 Fashion is more usually a gentle progression of revisited ideas.
in *Independent* 9 September 1989

William Oldys 1696–1761
English antiquary

13 Busy, curious, thirsty fly,
Gently drink, and drink as I;
Freely welcome to my cup.
'The Fly' (1732)

Frederick Scott Oliver 1864–1934
Scottish writer

14 A wise politician will never grudge a genuflexion or a rapture if it is expected of him by prevalent opinion.
The Endless Adventure (1930) vol. 1, pt. 1, ch. 20

Laurence Olivier 1907–89
English actor and director

15 The tragedy of a man who could not make up his mind.
introduction to his 1948 screen adaptation of *Hamlet*

16 Shakespeare—the nearest thing in incarnation to the eye of God.
in *Kenneth Harris Talking To* (1971) 'Sir Laurence Olivier'

17 Acting is a masochistic form of exhibitionism. It is not quite the occupation of an adult.
in *Time* 3 July 1978

18 Can a muse of fire exist under a ceiling of commerce?
appealing on behalf of the Rose Theatre remains
in *The Times* 12 July 1989; cf. **Shakespeare** 670:26

Official advice

1 Careless talk costs lives.
Second World War security slogan (popularly inverted as 'careless lives cost talk')

2 Clunk, click, every trip.
road safety campaign promoting the use of seat-belts, 1971

3 Coughs and sneezes spread diseases. Trap the germs in your handkerchief.
Second World War health slogan (1942)

4 Dig for Victory.
Second World War slogan; see below:

Let 'Dig for Victory' be the motto of every one with a garden and of every able-bodied man and woman capable of digging an allotment in their spare time.
Reginald Dorman-Smith (1899–1977) radio broadcast, 3 October 1939, in *The Times* 4 October 1939

5 Don't ask a man to drink and drive.
UK road safety slogan, from 1964

6 Don't die of ignorance.
Aids publicity campaign, 1987

7 Is your journey *really* necessary?
slogan coined to discourage Civil Servants from going home for Christmas, 1939

8 Keep Britain tidy.
issued by the Central Office of Information, 1950s

9 Make do and mend.
wartime slogan, 1940s

10 Slip, slop, slap.
sun protection slogan, meaning slip *on a T-shirt,* slop *on some suncream,* slap *on a hat*
Australian health education programme, 1980s

11 Smoking can seriously damage your health.
government health warning now required by British law to be printed on cigarette packets
from early 1970s, in form 'Smoking can damage your health'

12 Stop-look-and-listen.
road safety slogan, current in the US from 1912

13 *Taisez-vous! Méfiez-vous! Les oreilles ennemies vous écoutent.*
Keep your mouth shut! Be on your guard! Enemy ears are listening to you.
official notice in France, 1915

14 Tradition dictates that we have a lawn—but do we really need one? Why not increase the size of your borders or replace lawned areas with paving stones or gravel?
Severn Trent Water 'The Gardener's Water Code' (1996)

Frank Ward O'Malley see Elbert Hubbard

Omar c.581–644
Muslim caliph, conqueror of Syria, Palestine, and Egypt

15 If these writings of the Greeks agree with the book of God, they are useless and need not be preserved; if they disagree, they are pernicious and ought to be destroyed.
on burning the library of Alexandria, AD *c.*641
Edward Gibbon *The Decline and Fall of the Roman Empire* (1776–88) ch. 51

Jacqueline Kennedy Onassis 1929–94
wife of John Fitzgerald **Kennedy***, First Lady of the US 1961–3*

16 If you bungle raising your children I don't think whatever else you do well matters very much.
Theodore C. Sorenson *Kennedy* (1965)

17 The one thing I do not want to be called is First Lady. It sounds like a saddle horse.
Peter Colier and David Horowitz *The Kennedys* (1984)

Eugene O'Neill 1888–1953
American dramatist

18 For de little stealin' dey gits you in jail soon or late. For de big stealin' dey makes you Emperor and puts you in de Hall o' Fame when you croaks.
The Emperor Jones (1921) sc. 1

19 The iceman cometh.
title of play (1946)

20 A long day's journey into night.
title of play (written 1940–1)

21 Life is perhaps most wisely regarded as a bad dream between two awakenings, and every day is a life in miniature.
Marco Millions (1928) act 2, sc. 2

22 Mourning becomes Electra
title of play (1931)

23 The sea hates a coward!
Mourning becomes Electra (1931) pt. 2, act 4

24 The only living life is in the past and future . . . the present is an interlude . . . strange interlude in which we call on past and future to bear witness we are living.
Strange Interlude (1928) pt. 2, act 8

Yoko Ono 1933–
Japanese poet and songwriter

25 Woman is the nigger of the world.
remark made in a 1968 interview for *Nova* magazine and adopted by her husband John **Lennon** as the title of a song (1972); J. Robertson *Art and Music of John Lennon* (1990) ch. 11

Brian O'Nolan see Flann O'Brien

□ Opening lines
see box opposite

Opening lines

1 Achilles' cursed anger sing, O goddess, that son of Peleus, which started a myriad sufferings for the Achaeans.
Homer *The Iliad*

2 Achilles' wrath, to Greece the direful spring
Of woes unnumbered, heavenly goddess, sing!
Alexander **Pope** translation of *The Iliad* (1715)

3 *Arma virumque cano.*
I sing of arms and the man.
Virgil *Aeneid*

4 Arms, and the man I sing, who, forced by fate,
And haughty Juno's unrelenting hate,
Expelled and exiled, left the Trojan shore.
John **Dryden** translation of Virgil *Aeneid* (*Aeneis*, 1697)

5 Mom and Pop were just a couple of kids when they got married. He was eighteen, she was sixteen, and I was three.
Billie **Holiday** *Lady Sings the Blues* (1956)

6 As I walked through the wilderness of this world.
John **Bunyan** *The Pilgrim's Progress* (1678) pt. 1

7 At the age of fifteen my grandmother became the concubine of a warlord general.
Jung Chang *Wild Swans* (1991)

8 *Aujourd'hui, maman est morte. Ou peut-être hier, je ne sais pas.*
Mother died today. Or perhaps it was yesterday, I don't know.
Albert **Camus** *L'Étranger* (1944)

9 The boy stood on the burning deck
Whence all but he had fled.
Felicia **Hemans** 'Casabianca' (1849)

10 Call me Ishmael.
Herman **Melville** *Moby Dick* (1851)

11 'Christmas won't be Christmas without any presents,' grumbled Jo, lying on the rug.
Louisa May **Alcott** *Little Women* (1868–9)

12 *Gallia est omnis divisa in partes tres.*
Gaul as a whole is divided into three parts.
Julius **Caesar** *De Bello Gallico*

13 If I am out of my mind, it's all right with me, thought Moses Herzog.
Saul **Bellow** *Herzog* (1961)

14 If I should die, think only this of me:
That there's some corner of a foreign field
That is for ever England.
Rupert **Brooke** 'The Soldier' (1914)

15 If music be the food of love, play on.
William **Shakespeare** *Twelfth Night* (1601)

16 In a hole in the ground there lived a hobbit.
J. R. R. **Tolkien** *The Hobbit* (1937)

17 In my beginning is my end.
T. S. **Eliot** *Four Quartets* 'East Coker' (1940)

18 In the beginning God created the heaven and the earth. And the earth was without form, and void; and darkness was upon the face of the deep. And the Spirit of God moved upon the face of the waters.
And God said, Let there be light: and there was light.
Bible Genesis

19 In the beginning was the Word, and the Word was with God, and the Word was God.
Bible St John

20 I shall not say why and how I became, at the age of fifteen, the mistress of the Earl of Craven.
Harriett **Wilson** *Memoirs* (1825)

21 'Is there anybody there?' said the Traveller,
Knocking on the moonlit door.
Walter **de la Mare** 'The Listener' (1912)

22 It is a truth universally acknowledged, that a single man in possession of a good fortune, must be in want of a wife.
Jane **Austen** *Pride and Prejudice* (1813)

23 It is Christmas Day in the Workhouse.
George R. **Sims** 'In the Workhouse—Christmas Day' (1879)

24 It was a bright cold day in April, and the clocks were striking thirteen.
George **Orwell** *Nineteen Eighty-Four* (1949)

25 It was a dark and stormy night.
Edward George **Bulwer-Lytton** *Paul Clifford* (1830)

26 It was not until several weeks after he had decided to murder his wife that Dr Bickleigh took any active steps in the matter. Murder is a serious business.
Francis Iles *Malice Aforethought* (1931)

27 It was the afternoon of my eighty-first birthday, and I was in bed with my catamite when Ali announced that the archbishop had come to see me.
Anthony **Burgess** *Earthly Powers* (1980)

28 It was the best of times, it was the worst of times.
Charles **Dickens** *A Tale of Two Cities* (1859)

29 The king sits in Dunfermline town
Drinking the blude-red wine.
Ballads 'Sir Patrick Spens'

30 Last night I dreamt I went to Manderley again.
Daphne **Du Maurier** *Rebecca* (1938)

Opening lines *continued*

1 Lolita, light of my life, fire of my loins. My sin, my soul. Lo-lee-ta: the tip of the tongue taking a trip of three steps down the palate to tap, at three, on the teeth. Lo. Lee. Ta.
Vladimir **Nabokov** *Lolita* (1955)

2 Much have I travelled in the realms of gold,
And many goodly states and kingdoms seen.
John **Keats** 'On First Looking into Chapman's Homer' (1817)

3 My heart aches, and a drowsy numbness pains
My sense.
John **Keats** 'Ode to a Nightingale' (1820)

4 *Nel mezzo del cammin di nostra vita.*
Midway along the path of our life.
Dante *Divina Commedia* 'Inferno'

5 Of man's first disobedience, and the fruit
Of that forbidden tree, whose mortal taste
Brought death into the world, and all our woe,
With loss of Eden.
John **Milton** *Paradise Lost* (1667)

6 O! for a Muse of fire, that would ascend
The brightest heaven of invention.
William **Shakespeare** *Henry V* (1599)

7 Oh, what can ail thee knight at arms
Alone and palely loitering?
John **Keats** 'La belle dame sans merci' (1820)

8 Once upon a time . . .
traditional opening to a story, especially a fairy story
Anonymous, recorded from 1595

9 Once upon a time and a very good time it was there was a moocow coming down along the road and this moocow that was down along the road met a nicens little boy named baby tuckoo.
James **Joyce** *A Portrait of the Artist as a Young Man* (1916)

10 The opening was barred by a black bank of clouds, and the tranquil waterway leading to the uttermost ends of the earth flowed sombre under an overcast sky—seemed to lead into the heart of an immense darkness.
Joseph **Conrad** *Heart of Darkness* (1902)

11 The past is a foreign country: they do things differently there.
L. P. **Hartley** *The Go-Between* (1953)

12 riverrun, past Eve and Adam's, from swerve of shore to bend of bay, brings us by a commodious vicus of recirculation back to Howth Castle and Environs.
James **Joyce** *Finnegans Wake* (1939)

13 St Agnes' Eve—Ah, bitter chill it was!
The owl, for all his feathers, was a-cold.
John **Keats** 'The Eve of St Agnes' (1820)

14 Season of mists and mellow fruitfulness,
Close bosom-friend of the maturing sun.
John **Keats** 'To Autumn' (1820)

15 Should auld acquaintance be forgot
And never brought to mind?
Robert **Burns** 'Auld Lang Syne' (1796)

16 Sir Walter Elliot, of Kellynch-hall, in Somersetshire, was a man who, for his own amusement, never took up any book but the Baronetage; there he found occupation for an idle hour, and consolation in a distressed one.
Jane **Austen** *Persuasion* (1818)

17 Someone must have traduced Joseph K., for without having done anything wrong he was arrested one fine morning.
Franz **Kafka** *The Trial* (1925)

18 Stately, plump Buck Mulligan came from the stairhead, bearing a bowl of lather on which a mirror and a razor lay crossed.
James **Joyce** *Ulysses* (1922)

19 'Take my camel, dear,' said my aunt Dot, as she climbed down from this animal on her return from High Mass.
Rose **Macaulay** *The Towers of Trebizond* (1956)

20 Tell me, Muse, of the man of many devices, who wandered far and wide after he had sacked Troy's sacred city, and saw the towns of many men and knew their mind.
Homer *The Odyssey*

21 There was no possibility of taking a walk that day.
Charlotte **Brontë** *Jane Eyre* (1847)

22 A thing of beauty is a joy for ever
John **Keats** *Endymion* (1818)

23 Thou still unravished bride of quietness,
Thou foster-child of silence and slow time.
John **Keats** 'Ode on a Grecian Urn' (1820)

24 To begin at the beginning: It is spring, moonless night in the small town, starless and bible-black.
Dylan **Thomas** *Under Milk Wood* (1954)

25 Whan that Aprill with his shoures soote
The droghte of March hath perced to the roote.
Geoffrey **Chaucer** *The Canterbury Tales* 'General Prologue'

26 When Gregor Samsa awoke one morning from uneasy dreams he found himself transformed in his bed into a gigantic insect.
Franz **Kafka** *The Metamorphosis* (1915)

27 When Mary Lennox was sent to Misselthwaite Manor to live with her uncle, everybody said she was the most disagreeable-looking child ever seen.
Frances Hodgson Burnett *The Secret Garden* (1911)

28 Yet once more, O ye laurels, and once more
Ye myrtles brown, with ivy never sere.
John **Milton** 'Lycidas' (1638)

John Opie 1761–1807
English painter

1 I mix them with my brains, sir.
on being asked with what he mixed his colours
Samuel Smiles *Self-Help* (1859) ch. 4

J. Robert Oppenheimer 1904–67
American physicist

2 I remembered the line from the Hindu scripture, the *Bhagavad Gita* . . . 'I am become death, the destroyer of worlds.'
on the explosion of the first atomic bomb near Alamogordo, New Mexico, 16 July 1945
Len Giovannitti and Fred Freed *The Decision to Drop the Bomb* (1965); cf. **Bhagavadgita** 73:2

3 The physicists have known sin; and this is a knowledge which they cannot lose.
lecture at Massachusetts Institute of Technology, 25 November 1947, in *Open Mind* (1955) ch. 5

4 When you see something that is technically sweet, you go ahead and do it and you argue about what to do about it only after you have had your technical success. That is the way it was with the atomic bomb.
in *In the Matter of J. Robert Oppenheimer, USAEC Transcript of Hearing Before Personnel Security Board* (1954)

Susie Orbach 1946–
American psychotherapist

5 Fat is a feminist issue.
title of book (1978)

Roy Orbison 1936–88
American singer and songwriter

and Joe Melsom

6 Only the lonely (know the way I feel).
title of song (1960)

Orchoth Zadikkim
Jewish ethical work [The Ways of the Righteous] *of c.15th century*

7 The thread on which the different good qualities of human beings are strung as pearls, is the fear of God. When the fastenings of this fear are unloosed, the pearls roll in all directions, and are lost one by one.
Orchoth Zaddikim

8 Be not blind, but open-eyed, to the great wonders of Nature, familiar, everyday objects though they be to thee. But men are more wont to be astonished at the sun's eclipse than at his unfailing rise.
Orchoth Zaddikim

9 Be grateful for, not blind to the many, many sufferings which thou art spared; thou art no better than those who have been searched out and racked by them.
Orchoth Zaddikim

Baroness Orczy (Mrs Montague Barstow) 1865–1947
Hungarian-born novelist

10 We seek him here, we seek him there,
Those Frenchies seek him everywhere.
Is he in heaven?—Is he in hell?
That demmed, elusive Pimpernel?
The Scarlet Pimpernel (1905) ch. 12

Orderic Vitalis 1075–c.1142
Anglo-Norman monk and chronicler

11 For the mangled bodies that had been the flower of the English nobility and youth covered the ground as far as the eye could see.
of the battlefield at Hastings after the Norman victory in 1066
Ecclesiastical History

12 For the fortifications called castles by the French were scarcely known in the English provinces.
explaining the weakness of the English resistance, despite their fighting prowess
Ecclesiastical History

Tony O'Reilly 1936–
Irish newspaper entrepreneur

13 You grab a paper and there is a rush, there is adrenalin. Good God—look what we said today! It's more than you can get out of baked beans.
in *Guardian* 7 September 1998

Meta Orred
19th-century writer and poet

14 In the gloaming, Oh my darling!
When the lights are dim and low,
And the quiet shadows falling
Softly come and softly go.
'In the Gloaming' (1877 song)

José Ortega y Gasset 1883–1955
Spanish writer and philosopher

15 *Yo soy yo y mi circunstancia, y si no la salvo a ella no me salvo yo.*
I am I plus my surroundings, and if I do not preserve the latter I do not preserve myself.
Meditaciones del Quijote (1914)

16 *La civilización no es otra cosa que el ensayo de reducir la fuerza a ultima ratio.*
Civilization is nothing more than the effort to reduce the use of force to the last resort.
La Rebelión de las Masas (1930)

Joe Orton 1933–67
English dramatist

17 I'd the upbringing a nun would envy . . . Until I was fifteen I was more familiar with Africa than my own body.
Entertaining Mr Sloane (1964) act 1

1 It's all any reasonable child can expect if the dad is present at the conception.
Entertaining Mr Sloane (1964) act 3

2 Policemen, like red squirrels, must be protected.
Loot (1967) act 1

3 Reading isn't an occupation we encourage among police officers. We try to keep the paper work down to a minimum.
Loot (1967) act 2

4 You were born with your legs apart. They'll send you to the grave in a Y-shaped coffin.
What the Butler Saw (1969) act 1

George Orwell (Eric Blair) 1903–50

English novelist

5 Man is the only creature that consumes without producing.
Animal Farm (1945) ch. 1

6 Four legs good, two legs bad.
Animal Farm (1945) ch. 3

7 All animals are equal but some animals are more equal than others.
Animal Farm (1945) ch. 10

8 Good prose is like a window-pane.
Collected Essays (1968) vol. 1 'Why I Write'

9 I'm fat, but I'm thin inside. Has it ever struck you that there's a thin man inside every fat man, just as they say there's a statue inside every block of stone?
Coming up For Air (1939) pt. 1, ch. 3; cf. **Connolly** 234:1

10 Roast beef and Yorkshire, or roast pork and apple sauce, followed up by suet pudding and driven home, as it were, by a cup of mahogany-brown tea, have put you in just the right mood . . . In these blissful circumstances, what is it that you want to read about?
Naturally, about a murder.
Decline of the English Murder and other essays (1965) title essay, written 1946

11 Down and out in Paris and London.
title of book (1933)

12 He was an embittered atheist (the sort of atheist who does not so much disbelieve in God as personally dislike Him), and took a sort of pleasure in thinking that human affairs would never improve.
Down and Out in Paris and London (1933) ch. 30

13 Down here it was still the England I had known in my childhood: the railway cuttings smothered in wild flowers . . . the red buses, the blue policemen—all sleeping the deep, deep sleep of England, from which I sometimes fear that we shall never wake till we are jerked out of it by the roar of bombs.
Homage to Catalonia (1938) ch. 14

14 Most revolutionaries are potential Tories, because they imagine that everything can be put right by altering the *shape* of society; once that change is effected, as it sometimes is, they see no need for any other.
Inside the Whale (1940) 'Charles Dickens'

15 Keep the aspidistra flying.
title of novel (1936)

16 England is not the jewelled isle of Shakespeare's much-quoted passage, nor is it the inferno depicted by Dr Goebbels. More than either it resembles a family, a rather stuffy Victorian family, with not many black sheep in it but with all its cupboards bursting with skeletons . . . A family with the wrong members in control.
The Lion and the Unicorn (1941) pt. 1 'England Your England'

17 Old maids biking to Holy Communion through the mists of the autumn mornings . . . these are not only fragments, but *characteristic* fragments, of the English scene.
The Lion and the Unicorn (1941) pt. 1 'England Your England'; cf. **Major** 491:16

18 Probably the battle of Waterloo *was* won on the playing-fields of Eton, but the opening battles of all subsequent wars have been lost there.
The Lion and the Unicorn (1941) pt. 1 'England Your England'; cf. **Wellington** 810:1

19 It was a bright cold day in April, and the clocks were striking thirteen.
Nineteen Eighty-Four (1949) pt. 1, ch. 1

20 BIG BROTHER IS WATCHING YOU.
Nineteen Eighty-Four (1949) pt. 1, ch. 1

21 War is peace. Freedom is slavery. Ignorance is strength.
Nineteen Eighty-Four (1949) pt. 1, ch. 1

22 Who controls the past controls the future: who controls the present controls the past.
Nineteen Eighty-Four (1949) pt. 1, ch. 3

23 Don't you see that the whole aim of Newspeak is to narrow the range of thought? In the end we shall make thoughtcrime literally impossible, because there will be no words in which to express it.
Nineteen Eighty-Four (1949) pt. 1, ch. 5

24 Freedom is the freedom to say that two plus two make four. If that is granted, all else follows.
Nineteen Eighty-Four (1949) pt. 1, ch. 7

25 The Lottery, with its weekly pay-out of enormous prizes, was the one public event to which the proles paid serious attention . . . It was their delight, their folly, their anodyne, their intellectual stimulant . . . the prizes were largely imaginary. Only small sums were actually paid out, the winners of the big prizes being non-existent persons.
Nineteen Eighty-Four (1949) pt. 1, ch. 8

26 Syme was not only dead, he was abolished, an un-person.
Nineteen Eighty-Four (1949) pt. 2, ch. 5

27 *Doublethink* means the power of holding two contradictory beliefs in one's mind simultaneously, and accepting both of them.
Nineteen Eighty-Four (1949) pt. 2, ch. 9

1 Power is not a means, it is an end. One does not establish a dictatorship in order to safeguard a revolution; one makes the revolution in order to establish the dictatorship.
Nineteen Eighty-Four (1949) pt. 3, ch. 3

2 If you want a picture of the future, imagine a boot stamping on a human face—for ever.
Nineteen Eighty-Four (1949) pt. 3, ch. 3

3 In a Lancashire cotton-town you could probably go for months on end without once hearing an 'educated' accent, whereas there can hardly be a town in the South of England where you could throw a brick without hitting the niece of a bishop.
The Road to Wigan Pier (1937) ch. 7

4 The typical Socialist is . . . a prim little man with a white-collar job, usually a secret teetotaller and often with vegetarian leanings, with a history of Nonconformity behind him, and, above all, with a social position which he has no intention of forfeiting.
The Road to Wigan Pier (1937) ch. 11

5 To the ordinary working man, the sort you would meet in any pub on Saturday night, Socialism does not mean much more than better wages and shorter hours and nobody bossing you about.
The Road to Wigan Pier (1937) ch. 11

6 The high-water mark, so to speak, of Socialist literature is W. H. Auden, a sort of gutless Kipling.
The Road to Wigan Pier (1937) ch. 11

7 We of the sinking middle class . . . may sink without further struggles into the working class where we belong, and probably when we get there it will not be so dreadful as we feared, for, after all, we have nothing to lose but our aitches.
The Road to Wigan Pier (1937) ch. 13

8 Serious sport has nothing to do with fair play. It is bound up with hatred, jealousy, boastfulness, and disregard of all the rules.
Shooting an Elephant (1950) 'I Write as I Please'

9 The great enemy of clear language is insincerity. When there is a gap between one's real and one's declared aims, one turns as it were instinctively to long words and exhausted idioms, like a cuttlefish squirting out ink.
Shooting an Elephant (1950) 'Politics and the English Language'

10 In our time, political speech and writing are largely the defence of the indefensible.
Shooting an Elephant (1950) 'Politics and the English Language'

11 Political language . . . is designed to make lies sound truthful and murder respectable, and to give an appearance of solidity to pure wind.
Shooting an Elephant (1950) 'Politics and the English Language'

12 Saints should always be judged guilty until they are proved innocent.
Shooting an Elephant (1950) 'Reflections on Gandhi'

13 Whatever is funny is subversive, every joke is ultimately a custard pie . . . A dirty joke is a sort of mental rebellion.
in *Horizon* September 1941 'The Art of Donald McGill'

14 The quickest way of ending a war is to lose it.
in *Polemic* May 1946 'Second Thoughts on James Burnham'

15 At 50, everyone has the face he deserves.
last words in his notebook, 17 April 1949, in *Collected Essays, Journalism and Letters . . .* (1968) vol. 4

16 Advertising is the rattling of a stick inside a swill bucket.
attributed

Dorothy Osborne 1627–95
wife of William Temple from 1654

17 About six or seven o'clock, I walk out into a common that lies hard by the house, where a great many young wenches keep sheep and cows and sit in the shade singing of ballads . . . I talk to them, and find they want nothing to make them the happiest people in the world, but the knowledge that they are so.
Letters of Dorothy Osborne to William Temple (ed. G. C. Moore Smith, 1928) 2 June 1653

18 All letters, methinks, should be free and easy as one's discourse, not studied as an oration, nor made up of hard words like a charm.
letter to William Temple, September 1653

19 'Tis much easier sure to get a good fortune than a good husband, but whosoever marries without any consideration of fortune shall never be allowed to do it out of so reasonable an apprehension.
letter to William Temple, 4 February 1654

20 I do not see that it puts any value upon men when women marry them for love (as they term it); 'tis not their merit but our folly that is always presumed to cause it, and would it be any advantage to you to have your wife thought an indiscreet person?
letter to William Temple, 4 February 1654

21 Dr Taylor . . . says there is a great advantage to be gained in resigning up one's will to the command of another, because the same action which in itself is wholly indifferent if done upon our own choice, becomes an act of duty and religion if done in obedience to the command of any person whom nature, the laws, or our selves have given a power over us.
letter to William Temple, 19 February 1654

John Osborne 1929–94
English dramatist

22 Don't clap too hard—it's a very old building.
The Entertainer (1957) no. 7

23 Thank God we're normal,
Yes, this is our finest shower!
The Entertainer (1957) no. 7; cf. **Churchill** 215:11

24 But I have a go, lady, don't I? I 'ave a go. I do.
The Entertainer (1957) no. 7

1 Look back in anger.
title of play (1956); cf. **Paul** 570:5

2 Oh heavens, how I long for a little ordinary human enthusiasm. Just enthusiasm—that's all. I want to hear a warm, thrilling voice cry out Hallelujah! Hallelujah! I'm alive!
Look Back in Anger (1956) act 1

3 His knowledge of life and ordinary human beings is so hazy, he really deserves some sort of decoration for it—a medal inscribed 'For Vaguery in the Field'.
Look Back in Anger (1956) act 1

4 Slamming their doors, stamping their high heels, banging their irons and saucepans—the eternal flaming racket of the female.
Look Back in Anger (1956) act 1

5 I don't think one 'comes down' from Jimmy's university. According to him, it's not even red brick, but white tile.
Look Back in Anger (1956) act 2, sc. 1

6 Reason and Progress, the old firm, is selling out! Everyone get out while the going's good. Those forgotten shares you had in the old traditions, the old beliefs are going up—up and up and up.
Look Back in Anger (1956) act 2, sc. 1

7 They spend their time mostly looking forward to the past.
Look Back in Anger (1956) act 2, sc. 1

8 There aren't any good, brave causes left. If the big bang does come, and we all get killed off, it won't be in aid of the old-fashioned, grand design. It'll just be for the Brave New-nothing-very-much-thank-you. About as pointless and inglorious as stepping in front of a bus.
Look Back in Anger (1956) act 3, sc. 1

9 Royalty is the gold filling in a mouthful of decay.
'They call it cricket' in T. Maschler (ed.) *Declaration* (1957)

10 This is a letter of hate. It is for you my countrymen, I mean those men of my country who have defiled it. The men with manic fingers leading the sightless, feeble, betrayed body of my country to its death . . . damn you England.
in *Tribune* 18 August 1961

Arthur O'Shaughnessy 1844–81
English poet

11 We are the music makers,
We are the dreamers of dreams . . .
We are the movers and shakers
Of the world for ever, it seems.
'Ode' (1874)

12 For each age is a dream that is dying,
Or one that is coming to birth.
'Ode' (1874)

Peter Osgood
British footballer

13 Women are around all the time but World Cups come only every four years.
in *The Times* 9 May 1998

William Osler 1849–1919
Canadian-born physician

14 That man can interrogate as well as observe nature, was a lesson slowly learned in his evolution.
Aphorisms from his Bedside Teachings (1961)

15 One finger in the throat and one in the rectum makes a good diagnostician.
Aphorisms from his Bedside Teachings (1961)

16 The natural man has only two primal passions, to get and beget.
Science and Immortality (1904) ch. 2

17 The desire to take medicine is perhaps the greatest feature which distinguishes man from animals.
H. Cushing *Life of Sir William Osler* (1925) vol. 1, ch. 14

John L. O'Sullivan 1813–95
American journalist and diplomat

18 Understood as a central consolidated power, managing and directing the various general interests of the society, all government is evil, and the parent of evil . . . The best government is that which governs least.
in *United States Magazine and Democratic Review* (1837) introduction; cf. **Thoreau** 775:25

19 A spirit of hostile interference against us . . . checking the fulfilment of our manifest destiny to overspread the continent allotted by Providence for the free development of our yearly multiplying millions.
on opposition to the annexation of Texas
in *United States Magazine and Democratic Review* (1845) vol. 17

20 A torchlight procession marching down your throat.
describing certain kinds of whisky
G. W. E. Russell *Collections and Recollections* (1898) ch. 19

James Otis 1725–83
American politician

21 Taxation without representation is tyranny.
associated with his attack on writs of assistance, 1761, and later a watchword of the American Revolution, in *Dictionary of American Biography* vol. 14; cf. **Camden** 182:12

Thomas Otway 1652–85
English dramatist

22 And for an apple damn'd mankind.
The Orphan (1680) act 3

23 No praying, it spoils business.
Venice Preserved (1682) act 2, sc. 1

24 Give but an Englishman his whore and ease,
Beef and a sea-coal fire, he's yours for ever.
Venice Preserved (1682) act 2, sc. 3

Peter Demianovich Ouspensky 1878–1947
Russian-born journalist and philosopher

25 Truths that become old become decrepit and unreliable; sometimes they may be kept going

artificially for a certain time, but there is no life in them.

A New Model of the Universe (2nd ed., 1934) preface

Thomas Overbury 1581–1613

English poet and courtier

1 He disdains all things above his reach, and preferreth all countries before his own.

Miscellaneous Works (1632) 'An Affected Traveller'; cf. **Canning** 185:1, **Disraeli** 269:17, **Gilbert** 338:2

Ovid (Publius Ovidius Naso) 43 BC–AD c.17

Roman poet

on Ovid: see **Dryden** *281:33*

2 *Lente currite noctis equi.*

Run slowly, horses of the night.

Amores bk. 1, no. 13, l. 40; cf. **Marlowe** 496:7

3 *Procul omen abesto!*

Far be that fate from us!

Amores bk. 1, no. 14, l. 41

4 *Procul hinc, procul este, severae!*

Far hence, keep far from me, you grim women!

Amores bk. 2, no. 1, l. 3

5 *Spectatum veniunt, veniunt spectentur ut ipsae.*

The women come to see the show, they come to make a show themselves.

Ars Amatoria bk. 1, l. 99

6 *Iuppiter ex alto periuria ridet amantum.*

Jupiter from on high laughs at lovers' perjuries.

Ars Amatoria bk. 1, l. 633; cf. **Dryden** 282:8, **Proverbs** 604:45

7 *Expedit esse deos, et, ut expedit, esse putemus.*

It is convenient that there be gods, and, as it is convenient, let us believe that there are.

Ars Amatoria bk. 1, l. 637; cf. **Voltaire** 797:16

8 *Forsitan et nostrum nomen miscebitur istis.*

Perhaps my name too will be linked with theirs.

on the names of famous poets

Ars Amatoria bk. 3, l. 339

9 *Adde quod ingenuas didicisse fideliter artes*
Emollit mores nec sinit esse feros.

Add the fact that to have conscientiously studied the liberal arts refines behaviour and does not allow it to be savage.

Epistulae Ex Ponto bk. 2, no. 9, l. 47

10 *Ut desint vires, tamen est laudanda voluntas.*

Though the strength is lacking, yet the willingness is commendable.

Epistulae Ex Ponto bk. 3, no. 4, l. 79

11 *Gutta cavat lapidem, consumitur anulus usu.*

Dripping water hollows out a stone, a ring is worn away by use.

Epistulae Ex Ponto bk. 4, no. 10, l. 5; cf. **Latimer** 454:3, **Proverbs** 597:36

12 *Chaos, rudis indigestaque moles.*

Chaos, a rough and unordered mass.

Metamorphoses bk. 1, l. 7

13 *Materiam superabat opus.*

The workmanship surpasses the material.

of the bronze doors made by Vulcan for the palace of Apollo

Metamorphoses bk 2, l. 5

14 *Medio tutissimus ibis.*

You will go most safely by the middle way.

Metamorphoses bk. 2, l. 137

15 *Inopem me copia fecit.*

Plenty has made me poor.

Metamorphoses bk. 3, l. 466

16 *Ipse docet quid agam; fas est et ab hoste doceri.*

He himself teaches what I should do; it is right to be taught by the enemy.

Metamorphoses bk. 4, l. 428

17 *Video meliora, proboque;*
Deteriora sequor.

I see the better things, and approve; I follow the worse.

Metamorphoses bk. 7, l. 20; cf. **Bible** 105:4

18 *Tempus edax rerum.*

Time the devourer of everything.

Metamorphoses bk. 15, l. 234

19 *Iamque opus exegi, quod nec Iovis ira, nec ignis,*
Nec poterit ferrum, nec edax abolere vetustas.

And now I have finished the work, which neither the wrath of Jove, nor fire, nor the sword, nor devouring age shall be able to destroy.

Metamorphoses bk. 15, l. 871

20 *Principiis obsta; sero medicina paratur*
Cum mala per longas convaluere moras.

Stop it at the start, it's late for medicine to be prepared when disease has grown strong through long delays.

Remedia Amoris l. 91; cf. **Persius** 574:5

21 *Qui finem quaeris amoris,*
Cedet amor rebus; res age, tutus eris.

You who seek an end of love, love will yield to business: be busy, and you will be safe.

Remedia Amoris l. 143

22 *Teque, rebellatrix, tandem, Germania, magni*
Triste caput pedibus supposuisse ducis!

How you, rebellious Germany, laid your wretched head beneath the feet of the great general.

Tristia bk. 3, no. 12, l. 47

23 *Sponte sua carmen numeros veniebat ad aptos,*
Et quod temptabam dicere versus erat.

Of its own accord my song would come in the right rhythms, and what I was trying to say was poetry.

Tristia bk. 4, no. 10, l. 25; cf. **Pope** 583:3

24 *Vergilium vidi tantum.*

I have just seen Virgil.

Tristia bk. 4, no. 10, l. 51

John Owen c.1563–1622
Epigrammatist

1 God and the doctor we alike adore
But only when in danger, not before;
The danger o'er, both are alike requited,
God is forgotten, and the Doctor slighted.
Epigrams; cf. **Quarles** 618:12

Robert Owen 1771–1858
Welsh-born socialist and philanthropist

2 All the world is queer save thee and me, and even thou art a little queer.
to his partner W. Allen, on severing business relations at New Lanark, 1828
attributed

Wilfred Owen 1893–1918
English poet

3 My subject is War, and the pity of War.
The Poetry is in the pity.
Preface (written 1918) in *Poems* (1963)

4 All a poet can do today is warn.
Preface (written 1918) in *Poems* (1963)

5 What passing-bells for these who die as cattle?
Only the monstrous anger of the guns.
'Anthem for Doomed Youth' (written 1917)

6 The shrill, demented choirs of wailing shells;
And bugles calling for them from sad shires.
'Anthem for Doomed Youth' (written 1917)

7 The pallor of girls' brows shall be their pall;
Their flowers the tenderness of patient minds,
And each slow dusk a drawing-down of blinds.
'Anthem for Doomed Youth' (written 1917)

8 If you could hear, at every jolt, the blood
Come gargling from the froth-corrupted lungs,
Obscene as cancer, bitter as the cud
Of vile, incurable sores on innocent tongues,—
My friend, you would not tell with such high zest
To children ardent for some desperate glory,
The old Lie: Dulce et decorum est
Pro patria mori.
'Dulce et Decorum Est' (1963 ed.); cf. **Horace** 388:14

9 Was it for this the clay grew tall?
'Futility' (written 1918)

10 So secretly, like wrongs hushed-up, they went.
They were not ours:
We never heard to which front these were sent.
'The Send-Off' (written 1918)

11 It seemed that out of battle I escaped
Down some profound dull tunnel, long since
scooped
Through granites which titanic wars had groined.
'Strange Meeting' (written 1918)

12 'Strange friend,' I said, 'here is no cause to mourn.'
'None,' said that other, 'save the undone years,
The hopelessness. Whatever hope is yours,
Was my life also.'
'Strange Meeting' (written 1918)

13 I am the enemy you killed, my friend.
I knew you in this dark: for you so frowned
Yesterday through me as you jabbed and killed . . .
Let us sleep now.
'Strange Meeting' (written 1918)

Count Oxenstierna 1583–1654
Swedish statesman

14 Dost thou not know, my son, with how little wisdom the world is governed?
letter to his son, 1648, in J. F. af Lundblad *Svensk Plutark* (1826) pt. 2; an alternative attribution quotes 'a certain Pope' (possibly Julius III, 1487–1555) saying:

Thou little thinkest what *a little foolery governs the whole world!*.
John Selden *Table Talk* (1689) 'Pope' no. 2

Edward de Vere, Earl of Oxford 1550–1604
English poet
see also ***Elizabeth I*** *297:12*

15 The labouring man, that tills the fertile soil,
And reaps the harvest fruit, hath not in deed
The gain, but pain; and if for all his toil
He gets the straw, the lord will have the seed.
'The labouring man, that tills the fertile soil' (1573) st. 1

16 So he that takes the pain to pen the book
Reaps not the gifts of goodly golden Muse,
But those gain that who on the work shall look,
And from the sour the sweet by skill doth choose.
For he that beats the bush the bird not gets,
But who sits still and holdeth fast the nets.
'The labouring man, that tills the fertile soil' (1573) st. 6

Vance Packard 1914–97
American writer and journalist

17 The hidden persuaders.
title of a study of the advertising industry (1957)

William Tyler Page 1868–1942

18 I believe in the United States of America as a government of the people, by the people, for the people, whose just powers are derived from the consent of the governed; a democracy in a republic; a sovereign Nation of many sovereign States; a perfect Union, one and inseparable, established upon those principles of freedom, equality, justice, and humanity for which American patriots sacrificed their lives and fortunes. I therefore believe it is my duty to my country to love it, to support its Constitution, to obey its laws, to respect its flag, and to defend it against all enemies.
American's Creed (prize-winning competition entry, 1918) in *Congressional Record* vol. 56; cf. **Lincoln** 468:13

Lord George Paget 1818–80
English soldier

1 As far as it engendered excitement the finest run in Leicestershire could hardly bear comparison.
the second-in-command's view of the charge of the Light Brigade
The Light Cavalry Brigade in the Crimea (1881) ch. 5

Camille Paglia 1947–
American author and critic

2 Television is actually closer to reality than anything in books. The madness of TV is the madness of human life.
in *Harper's Magazine* March 1991

3 There is no female Mozart because there is no female Jack the Ripper.
in *International Herald Tribune* 26 April 1991

4 Gay men may seek sex without emotion; lesbians often end up in emotion without sex.
in *Esquire* October 1991

5 He tried to lecture *me* on how women felt when they were raped.
having walked out of a recorded interview with Jonathan Dimbleby, 23 June 1998
in *Daily Telegraph* 25 June 1998

Marcel Pagnol 1895–1974
French dramatist and film-maker

6 Honour is like a match, you can only use it once.
Marius (1946) act 4, sc. 5

7 It's better to choose the culprits than to seek them out.
Topaze (1930) act 1

Thomas Paine 1737–1809
English political theorist

8 It is necessary to the happiness of man that he be mentally faithful to himself. Infidelity does not consist in believing, or in disbelieving, it consists in professing to believe what one does not believe.
The Age of Reason pt. 1 (1794)

9 Any system of religion that has any thing in it that shocks the mind of a child cannot be a true system.
The Age of Reason pt. 1 (1794)

10 The sublime and the ridiculous are often so nearly related, that it is difficult to class them separately. One step above the sublime, makes the ridiculous; and one step above the ridiculous, makes the sublime again.
The Age of Reason pt. 2 (1795); cf. **Napoleon** 538:16, **Proverbs** 600:49

11 Government, even in its best state, is but a necessary evil; in its worst state, an intolerable one. Government, like dress, is the badge of lost innocence; the palaces of kings are built upon the ruins of the bowers of paradise.
Common Sense (1776) ch. 1

12 Though we have been wise enough to shut and lock a door against absolute Monarchy, we at the same time have been foolish enough to put the crown in possession of the key.
Common Sense (1776) ch. 1

13 Monarchy and succession have laid . . . the world in blood and ashes.
Common Sense (1776) ch. 2

14 Freedom hath been hunted round the globe. Asia and Africa have long expelled her. Europe regards her like a stranger, and England hath given her warning to depart. O! receive the fugitive, and prepare in time an asylum for mankind.
to America
Common Sense (1776) ch. 3

15 As to religion, I hold it to be the indispensable duty of government to protect all conscientious professors thereof, and I know of no other business which government hath to do therewith.
Common Sense (1776) ch. 4

16 These are the times that try men's souls. The summer soldier and the sunshine patriot will, in this crisis, shrink from the service of their country; but he that stands it *now*, deserves the love and thanks of men and women.
The Crisis (December 1776) introduction

17 The religion of humanity.
The Crisis (November 1778)

18 As he rose like a rocket, he fell like the stick.
on Edmund **Burke**'*s losing the debate on the French Revolution to Charles James* **Fox**, *in the House of Commons*
Letter to the Addressers on the late Proclamation (1792)

19 [He] is not affected by the reality of distress touching his heart, but by the showy resemblance of it striking his imagination. He pities the plumage, but forgets the dying bird.
on Edmund **Burke**'*s* Reflections on the Revolution in France, *1790*
The Rights of Man (1791)

20 Lay then the axe to the root, and teach governments humanity. It is their sanguinary punishments which corrupt mankind.
The Rights of Man (1791)

21 [In France] All that class of equivocal generation, which in some countries is called *aristocracy*, and in others *nobility*, is done away, and the peer is exalted into MAN.
The Rights of Man (1791)

22 Titles are but nick-names, and every nick-name is a title.
The Rights of Man (1791)

23 The idea of hereditary legislators is as inconsistent as that of hereditary judges, or hereditary juries; and as absurd as an hereditary mathematician, or an hereditary wise man; and as ridiculous as an hereditary poet laureate.
The Rights of Man (1791)

24 Persecution is not an original feature of *any* religion; but it is always the strongly marked

feature of all law-religions, or religions established by law.
The Rights of Man (1791)

1 All hereditary government is in its nature tyranny . . . To inherit a government, is to inherit the people, as if they were flocks and herds.
The Rights of Man pt. 2 (1792)

2 I compare it to something kept behind a curtain, about which there is a great deal of bustle and fuss, and a wonderful air of seeming solemnity; but when, by any accident, the curtain happens to be open, and the company see what it is, they burst into laughter.
of monarchy
The Rights of Man pt. 2 (1792)

3 The Minister, whoever he at any time may be, touches it as with an opium wand, and it sleeps obedience.
of Parliament
The Rights of Man pt. 2 (1792)

4 When, in countries that are called civilized, we see age going to the workhouse and youth to the gallows, something must be wrong in the system of government.
The Rights of Man pt. 2 (1792)

5 My country is the world, and my religion is to do good.
The Rights of Man pt. 2 (1792)

6 I do not believe that any two men, on what are called doctrinal points, think alike who think at all. It is only those who have not thought that appear to agree.
The Rights of Man pt. 2 (1792)

7 A share in two revolutions is living to some purpose.
Eric Foner *Tom Paine and Revolutionary America* (1976) ch. 7

Ian Paisley 1926–

Northern Irish politician and Presbyterian minister

8 The mother of all treachery.
on the Good Friday agreement
in *Times* 16 April 1998

9 She has become a parrot.
on the perceived readiness of the Queen to repeat the views of her Prime Minister
in *Daily Telegraph* 27 May 1998

José de Palafox 1780–1847

Spanish general

10 *Guerra a cuchillo.*
War to the knife.
on 4 August 1808, at the siege of Saragossa, the French general Verdier sent a one-word suggestion: 'Capitulation'. Palafox replied 'Guerra y cuchillo [War and the knife]', *later reported as above; it subsequently appeared, at the behest of Palafox himself, on survivors' medals*
José Gòmez de Arteche y Moro *Guerra de la Independencia* (1875) vol. 2, ch. 4

William Paley 1743–1805

English theologian and philosopher

11 Suppose I had found a *watch* upon the ground, and it should be enquired how the watch happened to be in that place . . . the inference, we think, is inevitable; that the watch must have had a maker, that there must have existed, at some time and at some place or other, an artificer or artificers, who formed it for the purpose which we find it actually to answer; who comprehended its construction, and designed its use.
Natural Theology (1802) ch. 1; cf. **Dawkins** 253:1

12 Who can refute a sneer?
Principles of Moral and Political Philosophy (1785) bk. 5, ch. 9

Pali Tripitaka

the earliest collection of Buddhist sacred texts, c.2nd century BC

13 Is it fitting to consider what is impermanent, painful, and subject to change as, 'This is mine, this am I, this is my self'?
Vinaya, Mahāv. [Book of Discipline] 1, 6

14 I go, reverend one, to the Lord and to the doctrine and the Order of monks. May the Lord take me as a lay disciple from this day forth while life lasts, who have gone to him as a refuge.
He [Yasa] was the first layman in the world received by the triple utterance.
Vinaya, Mahāv. [Book of Discipline] 1, 7

15 1) Refraining from taking life. 2) Refraining from taking what is not given. 3) Refraining from incontinence. 4) Refraining from falsehood. 5) Refraining from strong drink, intoxicants, and liquor, which are occasions of carelessness.
The Five Precepts
Vinaya, Mahāv. [Book of Discipline] 1, 56

16 I [Buddha] directed my mind to the knowledge of the extinction of the outflows. I understood it as it really is: This is suffering, this its arising, this its stopping, this the course leading to its stopping.
Vinaya [Book of Discipline] 3, 6

17 Dhamma has been taught by me without making a distinction between esoteric and exoteric. For the Tathagata has not the closed fist of a teacher in respect of mental states.
Dīgha-nikāya [Longer Collection] pt. 2, p. 100

18 You [monks] should live as islands, unto yourselves, being your own refuge, with no one else as your refuge, with the Dhamma as an island, with the Dhamma as your refuge, with no other refuge.
some translations prefer 'lamps' to 'islands'
Dīgha-nikāya [Longer Collection] pt. 2, p. 100

19 'Now, monks, I declare to you: all conditioned things are of a nature to decay—strive on untiringly.' These were the Tathagata's last words.
Dīgha-nikāya [Longer Collection] pt. 2, p. 156

20 In regard to things that are past, future and present the Tathagata is a speaker at a suitable

time, a speaker of fact, on what has bearing, of Dhamma, of Discipline. Therefore is he called Tathagata.
Dīgha-nikāya [Longer Collection] pt. 3, p. 135

1 Monks, I will teach you Dhamma—the Parable of the Raft—for crossing over, not for retaining.
Majjhima-nikāya [Medium Collection] pt. 1, p. 134

2 Precisely this do I teach, now as formerly: ill and the stopping of ill.
Majjhima-nikāya [Medium Collection] pt. 1, p. 140

3 Who sees Conditioned Genesis sees Dhamma; who sees Dhamma sees Conditioned Genesis.
Majjhima-nikāya [Medium Collection] pt. 1, p. 190; cf. **Pali Tripitaka** 565:8

4 It is called Nirvana because of the getting rid of craving.
Samyutta-nikāya [Kindred Sayings] pt. 1, p. 39

5 In the Sakyan clan there was born
A Buddha, peerless among men,
Conqueror of all, repelling Mara—
The Visioned One sees all.
Samyutta-nikāya [Kindred Sayings] pt. 1, p. 134

6 The instructed disciple of the Aryans well and wisely reflects on Conditioned Genesis itself: If this is that comes to be; from the arising of this that arises; if this is not that does not come to be; from the stopping of this that is stopped.
Samyutta-nikāya [Kindred Sayings] pt. 2, p. 64

7 If one does not behold any self or anything of the nature of self in the five groups of grasping (material shape, feeling, perception, the impulses, consciousness), one is an Arahant, the outflows extinguished.
Samyutta-nikāya [Kindred Sayings] pt. 3, p. 127

8 Whoso sees Dhamma sees me; whoso sees me sees Dhamma.
Samyutta-nikāya [Kindred Sayings] pt. 3, p. 120

9 To what extent is the world called 'empty' Lord? Because it is empty of self or what belongs to self, it is therefore said: 'The world is empty.'
Samyutta-nikāya [Kindred Sayings] pt. 4, p. 54

10 I teach Dhamma that is lovely at the beginning, lovely in the middle and lovely at the ending, with the spirit and the letter.
Samyutta-nikāya [Kindred Sayings] pt. 4, p. 315

11 Avoiding both these extremes, [indulgence of sense pleasures, devotion to self-mortification] the Tathagata has realized the Middle Path: it gives vision, it gives knowledge, and it leads to calm, to insight, to enlightenment, to Nirvana.
First Sermon of the Buddha
Samyutta-nikāya [Kindred Sayings] pt. 56, p. 11

12 The Noble Truth of Suffering is this: Birth is suffering, ageing is suffering; sickness is suffering; death is suffering; sorrow and lamentation, pain, grief and despair are suffering; association with the unpleasant is suffering; dissociation from the pleasant is suffering; not to get what one wants is suffering—in brief, the five aggregates of attachment are suffering.
First Sermon of the Buddha
Samyutta-nikāya [Kindred Sayings] pt. 56, p. 11

13 The Noble Truth of the Path leading to the Cessation of suffering is this: It is simply the Noble Eightfold Path, namely right view; right thought; right speech; right action; right livelihood; right effort; right mindfulness; right concentration.
First Sermon of the Buddha
Samyutta-nikāya [Kindred Sayings] pt. 56, p. 11

14 Bhikkhus [monks], all is burning.
Fire Sermon
Samyutta-nikāya [Kindred Sayings] pt. 35, p. 28

15 As the great ocean has but one taste, that of salt, so has this Dharma and Discipline but one taste, the taste of Freedom.
Anguttara-nikāya [Gradual Sayings] pt. 4, p. 203

16 What we are today comes from our thoughts of yesterday, and our present thoughts build our life of tomorrow: our life is the creation of our mind.
Dhammapada v. 1

17 For hate is not conquered by hate: hate is conquered by love. This is a law eternal.
Dhammapada v. 5

18 Even as rain breaks not through a well-thatched house, passions break not through a well-guarded mind.
Dhammapada v. 14

19 Who can trace the invisible path of the man who soars in the sky of liberation, the infinite Void without beginning, whose passions are peace and over whom pleasures have no power? His path is as difficult to trace as that of the birds in the air.
Dhammapada v. 93

20 If a man should conquer in battle a thousand and a thousand more, and another man should conquer himself, his would be the greater victory, because the greatest of victories is the victory over oneself.
Dhammapada v. 103

21 Because there is, monks, an unborn, not become, not made, uncompounded, therefore an escape can be shown for what is born, has become, is made, is compounded.
Udāna [Solemn Utterances] p. 81

22 I see no other single hindrance such as this hindrance of ignorance, obstructed by which mankind for a long long time runs on and circles on.
Itivuttaka [Thus Was Said] p. 8

23 The person who is searching for his own happiness should pull out the dart that he has stuck in himself, the arrow-head of grieving, of desiring, of despair.
Sutta-Nipāta [Woven Cadences] v. 592

24 Of all beings this one is perfect, this man is the pinnacle, the ultimate, the hero of creatures! This is the man who, from the forest of the Masters, will set the Wheel of Teaching turning—the roar of the lion, King of Beasts!

Sutta-Nipāta [Woven Cadences] v. 684

1 There are no waves in the depths of the sea: it is still, unbroken. It is the same with the monk. He is still, without any quiver of desire, without a remnant on which to build pride and desire.

Sutta-Nipāta [Woven Cadences] v. 920

Henry John Temple, Lord Palmerston 1784–1865

British statesman; Prime Minister, 1855–8, 1859–65
see also ***Last words*** *455:8*

2 We have no eternal allies and we have no perpetual enemies. Our interests are eternal and perpetual, and those interests it is our duty to follow.

speech, House of Commons, 1 March 1848

3 I therefore fearlessly challenge the verdict which this House . . . is to give . . . whether, as the Roman, in days of old, held himself free from indignity, when he could say *Civis Romanus sum*; so also a British subject, in whatever land he may be, shall feel confident that the watchful eye and the strong arm of England will protect him against injustice and wrong.

in the debate on the protection afforded to the Greek trader David Pacifico (1784–1854) who had been born a British subject at Gibraltar

speech, House of Commons, 25 June 1850; cf. **Cicero** 217:21

4 You may call it combination, you may call it the accidental and fortuitous concurrence of atoms.

on a projected Palmerston–Disraeli coalition

speech, House of Commons, 5 March 1857

5 We do not want Egypt any more than any rational man with an estate in the north of England and a residence in the south, would have wished to possess the inns on the north road. All he could want would have been that the inns should be well kept, always accessible, and furnishing him, when he came, with mutton chops and post horses.

letter to Earl Cowley, 25 November 1859, in Hon. Evelyn Ashley *Life of . . . Viscount Palmerston 1846–65* (1876) vol. 2, ch. 4

6 The function of a government is to calm, rather than to excite agitation.

P. Guedalla *Gladstone and Palmerston* (1928)

7 How d'ye do, and how is the old complaint?

reputed to be his greeting to all those he did not know

A. West *Recollections* (1899) vol. 1, ch. 2

8 Lord Palmerston, with characteristic levity had once said that only three men in Europe had ever understood [the Schleswig-Holstein question], and of these the Prince Consort was dead, a Danish statesman (unnamed) was in an asylum, and he himself had forgotten it.

R. W. Seton-Watson *Britain in Europe 1789–1914* (1937) ch. 11

9 What is merit? The opinion one man entertains of another.

T. Carlyle *Shooting Niagara: and After?* (1867) ch. 8

10 Yes we have. Humbug.

on being told there was no English word equivalent to sensibilité

attributed

Christabel Pankhurst 1880–1958

English suffragette; daughter of Emmeline Pankhurst

11 Never lose your temper with the Press or the public is a major rule of political life.

Unshackled (1959) ch. 5

12 We are here to claim our right as women, not only to be free, but to fight for freedom. That it is our right as well as our duty.

in *Votes for Women* 31 March 1911

Emmeline Pankhurst 1858–1928

English suffragette leader; founder of the Women's Social and Political Union, 1903

13 There is something that Governments care far more for than human life, and that is the security of property, and so it is through property that we shall strike the enemy . . . I say to the Government: You have not dared to take the leaders of Ulster for their incitement to rebellion. Take me if you dare.

speech at Albert Hall, 17 October 1912, in *My Own Story* (1914)

14 The argument of the broken window pane is the most valuable argument in modern politics.

George Dangerfield *The Strange Death of Liberal England* (1936) pt. 2, ch. 3, sect. 4; cf. **More** 530:22

Anna Paquin 1982–

New Zealand actress

15 Acting is pretending to be someone else.

in *Guardian* 24 January 1997

Mitchell Parish

16 When the deep purple falls over sleepy garden walls,
And the stars begin to flicker in the sky,
Thru' the mist of a memory you wander back to me,
Breathing my name with a sigh.

'Deep Purple' (1939); words added to music (1934) by Peter de Rose

Charlie Parker 1920–55

American jazz saxophonist

17 Music is your own experience, your thoughts, your wisdom. If you don't live it, it won't come out of your horn.

Nat Shapiro and Nat Hentoff *Hear Me Talkin' to Ya* (1955)

Dorothy Parker 1893–1967

American critic and humorist

on Parker: see **Woollcott** *827:7; see also* **Epitaphs** *302:4,* **Telegrams** *758:5*

1 Oh, life is a glorious cycle of song,
A medley of extemporanea;
And love is a thing that can never go wrong;
And I am Marie of Roumania.
'Comment' (1937)

2 Four be the things I'd been better without:
Love, curiosity, freckles, and doubt.
'Inventory' (1937)

3 Men seldom make passes
At girls who wear glasses.
'News Item' (1937)

4 Why is it no one ever sent me yet
One perfect limousine, do you suppose?
Ah no, it's always just my luck to get
One perfect rose.
'One Perfect Rose' (1937)

5 If, with the literate, I am
Impelled to try an epigram,
I never seek to take the credit;
We all assume that Oscar said it.
'A Pig's-Eye View of Literature' (1937)

6 Guns aren't lawful;
Nooses give;
Gas smells awful;
You might as well live.
'Résumé' (1937)

7 Where's the man could ease a heart like a satin gown?
'The Satin Dress' (1937)

8 By the time you say you're his,
Shivering and sighing
And he vows his passion is
Infinite, undying—
Lady, make a note of this:
One of you is lying.
'Unfortunate Coincidence' (1937)

9 Sorrow is tranquillity remembered in emotion.
Here Lies (1939) 'Sentiment'; cf. **Wordsworth** 832:20

10 *House Beautiful* is play lousy.
review in *New Yorker*, 1933, in Phyllis Hartnoll *Plays and Players* (1984)

11 She ran the whole gamut of the emotions from A to B.
of Katharine Hepburn at a Broadway first night, 1933
attributed

12 There's a hell of a distance between wise-cracking and wit. Wit has truth in it; wise-cracking is simply callisthenics with words.
in *Paris Review* Summer 1956

13 How do they know?
on being told that Calvin **Coolidge** *had died*
Malcolm Cowley *Writers at Work* 1st Series (1958)

14 Hollywood money isn't money. It's congealed snow, melts in your hand, and there you are.
Malcolm Cowley *Writers at Work* 1st Series (1958)

15 You can lead a horticulture, but you can't make her think.
John Keats *You Might as well Live* (1970)

16 It serves me right for putting all my eggs in one bastard.
on her abortion
John Keats *You Might as well Live* (1970) pt. 2, ch. 3

Martin Parker d. *c.*1656

English balladmonger

17 You gentlemen of England
Who live at home at ease,
How little do you think
On the dangers of the seas.
'The Valiant Sailors'; J. O. Halliwell (ed.) *Early Naval Ballads* (Percy Society, 1841)

18 The times will not mend
Till the King enjoys his own again.
'Upon Defacing of Whitehall' (1671)

Ross Parker 1914–74 and Hugh Charles 1907–

British songwriters

19 There'll always be an England
While there's a country lane.
'There'll always be an England' (1939 song)

Henry Parkes 1815–95

English-born Australian statesman

20 The crimson thread of kinship runs through us all.
on Australian federation
speech at banquet in Melbourne 6 February 1890; *The Federal Government of Australasia* (1890)

C. Northcote Parkinson 1909–93

English writer

21 Expenditure rises to meet income.
The Law and the Profits (1960) ch. 1

22 Work expands so as to fill the time available for its completion.
Parkinson's Law (1958) ch. 1

23 Time spent on any item of the agenda will be in inverse proportion to the sum involved.
Parkinson's Law (1958) ch. 3

24 The man who is denied the opportunity of taking decisions of importance begins to regard as important the decisions he is allowed to take.
Parkinson's Law (1958) ch. 10

Charles Stewart Parnell 1846–91

Irish nationalist leader

25 Why should Ireland be treated as a geographical fragment of England . . . Ireland is not a geographical fragment, but a nation.
in the House of Commons, 26 April 1875

26 My policy is not a policy of conciliation, but a policy of retaliation.
in 1877, on his parliamentary tactics in the House of Commons as leader of the Irish party
in *Dictionary of National Biography* (1917–)

1 No man has a right to fix the boundary of the march of a nation; no man has a right to say to his country—thus far shalt thou go and no further.
speech at Cork, 21 January 1885, in *The Times* 22 January 1885

2 Get the advice of everybody whose advice is worth having—they are very few—and then do what you think best yourself.
Conor Cruise O'Brien *Parnell* (1957)

Matthew Parris 1949–
British journalist and former politician

of Lady **Thatcher** *in the House of Lords:*
3 A big cat detained briefly in a poodle parlour, sharpening her claws on the velvet.
Look Behind You! (1993)

4 Being an MP feeds your vanity and starves your self-respect.
in *The Times* 9 February 1994

Tony Parsons 1953–
English critic and writer

5 I never saw a beggar yet who would recognise guilt if it bit him on his unwashed ass.
Dispatches from the Front Line of Popular Culture (1994)

Blaise Pascal 1623–62
French mathematician, physicist, and moralist

6 *Je n'ai fait celle-ci plus longue que parce que je n'ai pas eu le loisir de la faire plus courte.*
I have made this [letter] longer than usual, only because I have not had the time to make it shorter.
Lettres Provinciales (1657) no. 16; cf. **Thoreau** 775:29

7 *La dernière chose qu'on trouve en faisant un ouvrage, est de savoir celle qu'il faut mettre la première.*
The last thing one knows in constructing a work is what to put first.
Pensées (1670, ed. L. Brunschvicg, 1909) sect. 1, no. 19

8 *Quand on voit le style naturel, on est tout étonné et ravi, car on s'attendait de voir un auteur, et on trouve un homme.*
When we see a natural style, we are quite surprised and delighted, for we expected to see an author and we find a man.
Pensées (1670, ed. L. Brunschvicg, 1909) sect. 1, no. 29

9 *Car enfin, qu'est-ce que l'homme dans la nature? Un néant à l'égard de l'infini, un tout à l'égard du néant, un milieu entre rien et tout.*
For after all, what is man in nature? A nothing in respect of that which is infinite, an all in respect of nothing, a middle betwixt nothing and all.
Pensées (1670, ed. L. Brunschvicg, 1909) sect. 2, no. 72

10 *Quelle vanité que la peinture, qui attire l'admiration par la ressemblance des choses dont on n'admire point les originaux.*
How vain painting is, exciting admiration by its resemblance to things of which we do not admire the originals.
Pensées (1670, ed. L. Brunschvicg, 1909) sect. 2, no. 134

11 *Tout le malheur des hommes vient d'une seule chose, qui est de ne savoir pas demeurer en repos dans une chambre.*
All the misfortunes of men derive from one single thing, which is their inability to be at ease in a room.
Pensées (1670, ed. L. Brunschvicg, 1909) sect. 2, no. 139

12 *Le nez de Cléopâtre: s'il eût été plus court, toute la face de la terre aurait changé.*
Had Cleopatra's nose been shorter, the whole face of the world would have changed.
Pensées (1670, ed. L. Brunschvicg, 1909) sect. 2, no. 162

13 *Le silence éternel de ces espaces infinis m'effraie.*
The eternal silence of these infinite spaces [the heavens] terrifies me.
Pensées (1670, ed. L. Brunschvicg, 1909) sect. 2, no. 206

14 *Le dernier acte est sanglant, quelque belle que soit la comédie en tout le reste; on jette enfin de la terre sur la tête, et en voilà pour jamais.*
The last act is bloody, however charming the rest of the play may be; they throw earth over your head, and it is finished forever.
Pensées (1670, ed. L. Brunschvicg, 1909) sect. 3, no. 210

15 *On mourra seul.*
We shall die alone.
Pensées (1670, ed. L. Brunschvicg, 1909) sect. 3, no. 211

16 *'Dieu est, ou il n'est pas.' Mais de quel côté pencherons-nous? . . . Pesons le gain et la perte, en prenant croix que Dieu est. Estimons ces deux cas: si vous gagnez, vous gagnez tout; si vous perdez, vous ne perdez rien. Gagez donc qu'il est, sans hésiter.*
'God is or he is not.' But to which side shall we incline? . . . Let us weigh the gain and the loss in wagering that God is. Let us estimate the two chances. If you gain, you gain all; if you lose, you lose nothing. Wager then without hesitation that he is.
known as Pascal's wager
Pensées (1670, ed. L. Brunschvicg, 1909) sect. 3, no. 233

17 *Le coeur a ses raisons que la raison ne connaît point.*
The heart has its reasons which reason knows nothing of.
Pensées (1670, ed. L. Brunschvicg, 1909) sect. 4, no. 277

18 *L'homme n'est qu'un roseau, le plus faible de la nature; mais c'est un roseau pensant.*
Man is only a reed, the weakest thing in nature; but he is a thinking reed.
Pensées (1670, ed. L. Brunschvicg, 1909) sect. 6, no. 347

19 *L'éloquence continue ennuie.*
Continual eloquence is tedious.
Pensées (1670, ed. L. Brunschvicg, 1909) sect. 6, no. 355

20 *Le moi est haïssable.*
The self is hateful.
Pensées (1670, ed. L. Brunschvicg, 1909) sect. 7, no. 455

21 *Console-toi, tu ne me chercherais pas si tu ne m'avais trouvé.*

Comfort yourself, you would not seek me if you had not found me.

Pensées (1670, ed. L. Brunschvicg, 1909) sect. 7, no. 553

1 FEU. *Dieu d'Abraham, Dieu d'Isaac, Dieu de Jacob, non des philosophes et savants. Certitude. Certitude. Sentiment. Joie. Paix.*

FIRE. God of Abraham, God of Isaac, God of Jacob, not of the philosophers and scholars. Certainty. Certainty. Feeling. Joy. Peace.

on a paper, dated 23 November 1654, stitched into the lining of his coat and found after his death

Boris Pasternak 1890–1960

Russian novelist and poet

2 Man is born to live, not to prepare for life.

Doctor Zhivago (1958) pt. 2, ch. 9, sect. 14 (translated by Max Hayward and Manya Harari)

3 Most people experience love, without noticing that there is anything remarkable about it.

Doctor Zhivago (1958) pt. 2, ch. 13, sect. 10

4 I don't like people who have never fallen or stumbled. Their virtue is lifeless and it isn't of much value. Life hasn't revealed its beauty to them.

Doctor Zhivago (1958) pt. 2, ch. 13, sect. 12

5 Art always serves beauty, and beauty is the joy of possessing form, and form is the key to organic life since no living thing can exist without it.

Doctor Zhivago (1958) pt. 2, ch. 14, sect. 14

6 One day Lara went out and did not come back . . . She died or vanished somewhere, forgotten as a nameless number on a list which was afterwards mislaid.

Doctor Zhivago (1958) pt. 2, ch. 15, sect. 17

7 Yet the order of the acts is planned
And the end of the way inescapable.
I am alone; all drowns in the Pharisees' hypocrisy.
To live your life is not as simple as to cross a field.

Doctor Zhivago (1958) 'Zhivago's Poems: Hamlet'

8 As after a storm
The surf floods over the reeds,
So in his heart
Her image is submerged.

In the years of trial,
When life was inconceivable,
From the bottom of the sea the tide of destiny
Washed her up to him.

Doctor Zhivago (1958) 'Zhivago's Poems: Parting'

9 In time to come, I tell them, we'll be equal
to any living now. If cripples, then
no matter; we shall just have been run over
by 'New Man' in the wagon of his 'Plan'.

'When I Grow Weary' (1932) (translated by J. M. Cohen)

10 The whole wide world is a cathedral;
I stand inside, the air is calm,
And from afar at times there reaches
My ear the echo of a psalm.

'When It Clears Up' (1958) (translated by Lydia Pasternak Slater)

Louis Pasteur 1822–95

French chemist and bacteriologist

11 Where observation is concerned, chance favours only the prepared mind.

address given on the inauguration of the Faculty of Science, University of Lille, 7 December 1854; in R. Vallery-Radot *La Vie de Pasteur* (1900) ch. 4

12 There are no such things as applied sciences, only applications of science.

address, 11 September 1872, in *Comptes rendus des travaux du Congrès viticole et séricicole de Lyon, 9–14 septembre 1872*

Walter Pater 1839–94

English essayist and critic

13 She is older than the rocks among which she sits; like the vampire, she has been dead many times, and learned the secrets of the grave.

of the Mona Lisa

Studies in the History of the Renaissance (1873) 'Leonardo da Vinci'

14 All art constantly aspires towards the condition of music.

Studies in the History of the Renaissance (1873) 'The School of Giorgione'

15 To burn always with this hard, gemlike flame, to maintain this ecstasy, is success in life.

Studies in the History of the Renaissance (1873) 'Conclusion'

'Banjo' Paterson (Andrew Barton Paterson) 1864–1941

Australian poet

16 Once a jolly swagman camped by a billabong,
Under the shade of a coolibah tree;
And he sang as he watched and waited till his
'Billy' boiled:
'You'll come a-waltzing, Matilda, with me.'

'Waltzing Matilda' (1903 song)

Sadashiv Kanoji Patil

Indian politician

17 The Prime Minister is like the great banyan tree. Thousands shelter beneath it, but nothing grows.

when asked in an interview who would be **Nehru***'s successor*

J. K. Galbraith *A Life in Our Times* (1981)

Coventry Patmore 1823–96

English poet

18 The angel in the house.

title of poem (1854–62)

19 'I saw you take his kiss!' ''Tis true.'
'O modesty!' ''Twas strictly kept:
He thought me asleep; at least, I knew
He thought I thought he thought I slept.'

The Angel in the House (1854–62) bk. 2, canto 8, 'The Kiss'

20 Some dish more sharply spiced than this
Milk-soup men call domestic bliss.

'Olympus' l. 15

21 He that but once too nearly hears
The music of forfended spheres

Is thenceforth lonely, and for all
His days as one who treads the Wall
Of China, and, on this hand, sees
Cities and their civilities
And, on the other, lions.
The Victories of Love bk. 1 (1860) 'From Mrs Graham'

Alan Paton 1903–88
South African writer

1 Cry, the beloved country.
title of novel (1948)

St Patrick fl. 5th cent.
patron saint and Apostle of Ireland, of Romano-British parentage

2 Today I put on
a terrible strength
invoking the Trinity,
confessing the Three
with faith in the one
as I face my Maker.
'St Patrick's Breastplate', traditionally attributed to St Patrick; cf. **Alexander** 11:11

3 Christ beside me,
Christ before me,
Christ behind me,
Christ within me,
Christ beneath me,
Christ above me.
'St Patrick's Breastplate'

Mark Pattison 1813–84
English educationist

4 In research the horizon recedes as we advance, and is no nearer at sixty than it was at twenty. As the power of endurance weakens with age, the urgency of the pursuit grows more intense . . . And research is always incomplete.
Isaac Casaubon (1875) ch. 10

Leslie Paul 1905–85
Irish writer

5 Angry young man.
the phrase was later associated with John **Osborne***'s play* Look Back in Anger *(1956)*
title of book (1951)

Wolfgang Pauli 1900–58
Austrian-born American physicist who worked chiefly in Switzerland
on Pauli: see **Weisskopf** *809:1*

6 I don't mind your thinking slowly: I mind your publishing faster than you think.
attributed

Tom Paulin 1949–
English poet and critic

7 Now dream
of that sweet
equal republic
where the juniper
talks to the oak,
the thistle,
the bandaged elm,
and the jolly jolly chestnut.
'The Book of Juniper' (1983)

8 The owl of Minerva in a hired car.
'Desertmartin' (1983)

9 That stretch of water, it's always
There for you to cross over
To the other shore, observing
The light of cities on blackness.
'States' (1977)

Jeremy Paxman 1950–
British journalist and broadcaster

10 It's like turning news into a sausage factory.
on the BBC's proposed changes to radio and television news broadcasting
in *Guardian* 18 September 1997

11 No government in history has been as obsessed with public relations as this one . . . Speaking for myself, if there is a message I want to be off it.
after criticism from Alastair Campbell of interviewing tactics in The World at One *and* Newsnight
in *Daily Telegraph* 3 July 1998

James Payn 1830–98
English writer

12 I had never had a piece of toast
Particularly long and wide,
But fell upon the sanded floor,
And always on the buttered side.
in *Chambers's Journal* 2 February 1884; cf. **Moore** 530:18

J. H. Payne 1791–1852
American actor, dramatist, and songwriter

13 Home, sweet home.
title of song, from *Clari, or, The Maid of Milan* (1823 opera); cf. **Proverbs** 602:43

14 Mid pleasures and palaces though we may roam,
Be it ever so humble, there's no place like home.
Clari, or, The Maid of Milan (1823 opera) 'Home, Sweet Home'

Thomas Love Peacock 1785–1866
English novelist and poet
on Peacock: see **Shelley** *712:2; see also* **Epitaphs** *303:13*

15 Ancient sculpture is the true school of modesty. But where the Greeks had modesty, we have cant; where they had poetry, we have cant; where they had patriotism, we have cant; where they had anything that exalts, delights, or adorns humanity, we have nothing but cant, cant, cant.
Crotchet Castle (1831) ch. 7

16 The march of mind has marched in through my back parlour shutters, and out again with my silver spoons, in the dead of night. The policeman, who was sent down to examine, says my house has been broken open on the most scientific principles.
Crotchet Castle (1831) ch. 17

1 'I distinguish the picturesque and the beautiful, and I add to them, in the laying out of grounds, a third and distinct character, which I call *unexpectedness.*'
'Pray, sir,' said Mr Milestone, 'by what name do you distinguish this character, when a person walks round the grounds for the second time?'
Headlong Hall (1816) ch. 4

2 Marriage may often be a stormy lake, but celibacy is almost always a muddy horsepond.
Melincourt (1817) ch. 7

3 Laughter is pleasant, but the exertion is too much for me.
Nightmare Abbey (1818) ch. 5

4 Sir, I have quarrelled with my wife; and a man who has quarrelled with his wife is absolved from all duty to his country.
Nightmare Abbey (1818) ch. 11

5 The mountain sheep are sweeter,
But the valley sheep are fatter;
We therefore deemed it meeter
To carry off the latter.
'The War Song of Dinas Vawr' (1823)

Norman Vincent Peale 1898–
American religious broadcaster and writer

6 The power of positive thinking.
title of book (1952)

Patrick Pearse 1879–1916
Irish nationalist leader; executed after the Easter Rising
on Pearse: see ***Yeats*** *835:21*

7 The fools, the fools, the fools, they have left us our Fenian dead, and while Ireland holds these graves Ireland unfree shall never be at peace.
oration over the grave of the Fenian Jeremiah O'Donovan Rossa, 1 August 1915

8 Here be ghosts that I have raised this Christmastide, ghosts of dead men that have bequeathed a trust to us living men. Ghosts are troublesome things in a house or in a family, as we knew even before Ibsen taught us. There is only one way to appease a ghost. You must do the thing it asks you. The ghosts of a nation sometimes ask very big things and they must be appeased, whatever the cost.
on Christmas Day, 1915; Conor Cruise O'Brien *Ancestral Voices* (1994); cf. **O'Brien** 552:6

Hesketh Pearson 1887–1964
English actor and biographer

9 Misquotation is, in fact, the pride and privilege of the learned. A widely-read man never quotes accurately, for the rather obvious reason that he has read too widely.
Common Misquotations (1934) introduction

10 There is no stronger craving in the world than that of the rich for titles, except perhaps that of the titled for riches.
The Pilgrim Daughters (1961) ch. 6

Lester Pearson 1897–1972
Canadian diplomat and Liberal statesman, Prime Minister 1963–8

11 The grim fact is that we prepare for war like precocious giants and for peace like retarded pygmies.
speech in Toronto, 14 March 1955

Pedro I (Pedro IV of Portugal) 1798–1834
first Emperor of Brazil, 1822–31

12 As it is for the good of all and the general happiness of the nation, I am ready and willing. Tell the people I'm staying.
in response to a popular delegation, and in defiance of a decree from Lisbon requiring his return; commonly rendered 'Fico [I'm staying]'
letter to D. João VI, 9 January 1822; R. J. Barman *Brazil* (1988)

Robert Peel 1788–1850
British Conservative statesman; Prime Minister, 1834–5, 1841–6
on Peel: see ***Curran*** *248:3,* ***Disraeli*** *268:10*

13 There is not a single law connected with my name which has not had as its object some mitigation of the severity of the criminal law; some prevention of abuse in the exercise of it; or some security for its impartial administration.
speech, House of Commons, 1 May 1827

14 As minister of the Crown . . . I reserve to myself, distinctly and unequivocally, the right of adapting my conduct to the exigency of the moment, and to the wants of the country.
in the House of Commons, 30 March 1829

15 All my experience in public life is in favour of the employment of what the world would call young men instead of old ones.
to Wellington in 1829; Norman Gash *Sir Robert Peel* (ed. 2, 1986)

16 The hasty inordinate demand for peace might be just as dangerous as the clamour for war.
in the House of Commons, 1832

17 I see no dignity in persevering in error.
in the House of Commons, 1833

18 Of all vulgar arts of government, that of solving every difficulty which might arise by thrusting the hand into the public purse is the most delusory and contemptible.
in the House of Commons, 1834

George Peele *c.*1556–96
English dramatist and poet
see also ***Closing lines*** *222:11*

19 What thing is love for (well I wot) love is a thing.
It is a prick, it is a sting,
It is a pretty, pretty thing;
It is a fire, it is a coal
Whose flame creeps in at every hole.
The Hunting of Cupid (*c.*1591)

20 When as the rye reach to the chin,
And chopcherry, chopcherry ripe within,

Strawberries swimming in the cream,
And schoolboys playing in the stream,
Then O, then O, then O, my true love said,
Till that time come again,
She could not live a maid.

The Old Wive's Tale (1595) l. 75 'Song'

1 His golden locks time hath to silver turned;
O time too swift, O swiftness never ceasing!

Polyhymnia (1590) 'Sonnet'

2 His helmet now shall make a hive for bees,
And, lovers' sonnets turned to holy psalms,
A man-at-arms must now serve on his knees,
And feed on prayers, which are age his alms.

Polyhymnia (1590) 'Sonnet'

Charles Péguy 1873–1914

French poet and essayist

3 He who does not bellow the truth when he knows the truth makes himself the accomplice of liars and forgers.

Basic Verities (1943) 'Lettre du Provincial' 21 December 1899

4 Tyranny is always better organised than freedom.

Basic Verities (1943) 'War and Peace'; cf. **Baez** 45:20

5 The sinner is at the heart of Christianity . . . No one is as competent as the sinner in matters of Christianity. No one, except a saint.

Basic Verities (1943) 'Un Nouveau théologien . . . ' (1911)

Pelé 1940–

Brazilian footballer

6 Football? It's the beautiful game.

attributed

Mary Herbert, Countess of Pembroke 1561–1621

English poet and translator, sister of Philip ***Sidney***

7 Men drawn by worth a woman to obey.

'Even now that Care which on thy Crown attends' (poem addressed to Queen Elizabeth)

8 Sing what God doth, and do what men may sing.

'Even now that Care which on thy Crown attends' (poem addressed to Queen Elizabeth)

William Herbert, Lord Pembroke c.1501–70

9 Out ye whores, to work, to work, ye whores, go spin.

Andrew Clark (ed.) *'Brief Lives' . . . by John Aubrey* (1898) vol. 1 'William Herbert, 1st Earl of Pembroke'; see **Scott** 652:11

Henry Herbert, Lord Pembroke c.1534–1601

10 A parliament can do any thing but make a man a woman, and a woman a man.

quoted by his son, the 4th Earl, in a speech on 11 April 1648, proving himself Chancellor of Oxford

in *Harleian Miscellany* (1745) vol. 5

Henry Herbert, Lord Pembroke 1734–94

11 Dr Johnson's sayings would not appear so extraordinary, were it not for his bow-wow way.

James Boswell *Life of Samuel Johnson* (1791) 27 March 1775; cf. **Scott** 652:12

Vladimir Peniakoff 1897–1951

Belgian soldier and writer

12 A message came on the wireless for me. It said: 'SPREAD ALARM AND DESPONDENCY'. So the time had come, I thought, Eighth Army was taking the offensive. The date was, I think, May 18th, 1942.

Private Army (1950) pt. 2, ch. 5; see below

Every person subject to military law who . . . spreads reports calculated to create unnecessary alarm or despondency . . . shall . . . be liable to suffer penal servitude.

Army Act (1879)

William Penn 1644–1718

English Quaker; founder of Pennsylvania

13 No pain, no palm; no thorns, no throne; no gall, no glory; no cross, no crown.

No Cross, No Crown (1669 pamphlet)

14 It is a reproach to religion and government to suffer so much poverty and excess.

Some Fruits of Solitude (1693) pt. 1, no. 52

15 Men are generally more careful of the breed of their horses and dogs than of their children.

Some Fruits of Solitude (1693) pt. 1, no. 85

16 The taking of a bribe or gratuity, should be punished with as severe penalties as the defrauding of the State.

Some Fruits of Solitude (1693) pt. 1, no. 384

Roger Penrose 1931–

British mathematician and theoretical physicist

17 Consciousness . . . is the phenomenon whereby the universe's very existence is made known.

The Emperor's New Mind (1989) ch. 10 'Conclusion'

Samuel Pepys 1633–1703

English diarist

18 And so to bed.

Diary 20 April 1660

19 I went out to Charing Cross, to see Major-general Harrison hanged, drawn, and quartered; which was done there, he looking as cheerful as any man could do in that condition.

Diary 13 October 1660

20 A good honest and painful sermon.

Diary 17 March 1661

21 If ever I was foxed it was now.

Diary 23 April 1661

22 It lessened my esteem of a king, that he should not be able to command the rain.

Diary 19 July 1662

1 I see it is impossible for the King to have things done as cheap as other men.
Diary 21 July 1662

2 But Lord! to see the absurd nature of Englishmen, that cannot forbear laughing and jeering at everything that looks strange.
Diary 27 November 1662

3 My wife, who, poor wretch, is troubled with her lonely life.
Diary 19 December 1662

4 A woman sober, and no high flyer, as he calls it.
Diary 27 May 1663

5 Most of their discourse was about hunting, in a dialect I understand very little.
Diary 22 November 1663

6 While we were talking came by several poor creatures carried by, by constables, for being at a conventicle . . . I would to God they would either conform, or be more wise, and not be catched!
Diary 7 August 1664

7 Pretty witty Nell.
of Nell ***Gwyn***
Diary 3 April 1665

8 I saw a dead corpse in a coffin lie in the close unburied—and a watch is constantly kept there, night and day, to keep the people in—the plague making us cruel as dogs one to another.
Diary 4 September 1665

9 Strange to see how a good dinner and feasting reconciles everybody.
Diary 9 November 1665

10 Strange to say what delight we married people have to see these poor fools decoyed into our condition.
Diary 25 December 1665

11 In the heighth of it [the plague] . . . bold people there were to go in sport to one another's burials. And in spite to well people, would breathe in the faces . . . of well people going by.
Diary 12 February 1666

12 Music and women I cannot but give way to, whatever my business is.
Diary 9 March 1666

13 But it is pretty to see what money will do.
Diary 21 March 1667

14 This day my wife made it appear to me that my late entertainment this week cost me above £12, an expense which I am almost ashamed of, though it is but once in a great while, and is the end for which, in the most part, we live, to have such a merry day once or twice in a man's life.
Diary 6 March 1669

15 And so I betake myself to that course, which is almost as much as to see myself go into my grave—for which, and all the discomforts that will accompany my being blind, the good God prepare me!
Diary 31 May 1669 closing lines

16 Memoirs are true and useful stars, whilst studied histories are those stars joined in constellations, according to the fancy of the poet.
J. R. Tanner (ed.) *Samuel Pepys's Naval Minutes* (1926)

S. J. Perelman 1904–79
American humorist

17 Crazy like a fox.
title of book (1944)

Shimon Peres 1923–
Israeli statesman

18 Television has made dictatorship impossible, but democracy unbearable.
at a Davos meeting, in *Financial Times* 31 January 1995

Pericles *c*.495–429 BC
Athenian statesman

19 Our love of what is beautiful does not lead to extravagance; our love of the things of the mind does not make us soft.
Funeral Oration, Athens, 430 BC, in Thucydides *History of the Peloponnesian War* bk. 2, ch. 40, sect. 1 (translated by Rex Warner)

20 For famous men have the whole earth as their memorial.
Thucydides *History of the Peloponnesian War* bk. 2, ch. 43, sect. 3

21 Your great glory is not to be inferior to what God has made you, and the greatest glory of a woman is to be least talked about by men, whether they are praising you or criticizing you.
Thucydides *History of the Peloponnesian War* bk. 2, ch. 45, sect. 2

Anthony Perkins 1932–92
American actor

22 I have learned more about love, selflessness and human understanding in this great adventure in the world of Aids than I ever did in the cut-throat, competitive world in which I spent my life.
posthumous statement, in *Independent on Sunday* 20 September 1992

Eva Perón 1919–52
wife of Juan Perón
on Perón: see **Epitaphs** *303:10,* **Madonna** *489:5*

23 Keeping books on charity is capitalist nonsense! I just use the money for the poor. I can't stop to count it.
Fleur Cowles *Bloody Precedent: the Peron Story* (1952)

Charles Perrault 1628–1703
French poet and critic

24 *'Anne, ma sœur Anne, ne vois-tu rien venir?' Et la sœur Anne lui répondit, 'Je ne vois rien que le soleil qui poudroye, et l'herbe qui verdoye.'*
'Anne, sister Anne, do you see nothing coming?' And her sister Anne replied, 'I see nothing but the sun showing up the dust, and the grass looking green.'
Histoires et contes du temps passé (1697) 'La barbe bleue'

Edward Perronet 1726–92
English clergyman

1 All hail the power of Jesus' Name;
Let Angels prostrate fall;
Bring forth the royal diadem
To crown Him Lord of all.
'All hail the power of Jesus' Name' (1780 hymn)

Jimmy Perry
British songwriter

2 Who do you think you are kidding, Mister Hitler?
If you think we're on the run?
We are the boys who will stop your little game
We are the boys who will make you think again.
'Who do you think you are kidding, Mister Hitler' (theme song of *Dad's Army*, BBC television, 1968–77)

Persius (Aulus Persius Flaccus) AD 34–62
Roman poet

3 *Nec te quaesiveris extra.*
And don't consult anyone's opinions but your own.
Satires no. 1, l. 7

4 *Virtutem videant intabescantque relicta.*
Let them recognize virtue and rot for having lost it.
Satires no. 3, l. 38

5 *Venienti occurrite morbo.*
Confront disease at its onset.
Satires no. 3, l. 64; cf. **Ovid** 561:20

6 *Tecum habita: noris quam sit tibi curta supellex.*
Live with yourself: get to know how poorly furnished you are.
Satires no. 4, l. 52

Ted Persons

7 Things ain't what they used to be.
title of song (1941)

Max Perutz 1914–
Austrian-born scientist

8 The priest persuades humble people to endure their hard lot; the politician urges them to rebel against it; and the scientist thinks of a method that does away with the hard lot altogether.
Is Science Necessary (1989)

Henri Philippe Pétain 1856–1951
French soldier and statesman
see also ***Military sayings*** *508:10*

9 To write one's memoirs is to speak ill of everybody except oneself.
in *Observer* 26 May 1946

Laurence J. Peter 1919–90
Canadian writer

10 In a hierarchy every employee tends to rise to his level of incompetence.
The Peter Principle (1969) ch. 1

Mike Peters
American cartoonist

11 When I go into the voting booth, do I vote for the person who is the best President? Or the slime bucket who will make my life as a cartoonist wonderful?
in *Wall Street Journal* 20 January 1993

Petrarch (Francesco Petrarca) 1304–74
Italian poet
on Petrarch: see **Byron** *176:20*

12 *E del mio vaneggiar vergogna è 'l frutto*
e 'l pentersi, e 'l conoscer chiaramente
che quanto piace al mondo è breve sogno.
And the fruit of my vanity is shame, and repentance, and the clear knowledge that whatever the world finds pleasing, is but a brief dream.
'Voi ch'ascoltate in rime sparse il suono' (*c.*1352)

13 *Continue morimur, ego dum hec scribo, tu dum leges, alii dum audient, dumque non audient, ego quoque dum hec leges moriar, tu moreris dum hec scribo, ambo morimur, omnes morimur, semper morimur.*
We are continually dying; I while I am writing these words, you while you are reading them, others when they hear them or fail to hear them. I shall be dying when you read this, you die while I write, we both are dying, we all are dying, we are dying forever.
letter to Philippe de Cabassoles *c.*1360; *Letters on Familiar Matters* bk. 14

Petronius (Petronius Arbiter) d. AD 65
Roman satirist
on Petronius: see **Tacitus** *752:13*

14 *Canis ingens, catena vinctus, in pariete erat pictus superque quadrata littera scriptum 'Cave canem.'*
A huge dog, tied by a chain, was painted on the wall and over it was written in capital letters 'Beware of the dog.'
Satyricon 'Cena Trimalchionis' ch. 29, sect. 1

15 *Abiit ad plures.*
He's gone to join the majority.
meaning the dead
Satyricon 'Cena Trimalchionis' ch. 42, sect. 5; cf. **Young** 839:15

16 *Nam Sibyllam quidem Cumis ego ipse oculis meis vidi in ampulla pendere, et cum illi pueri dicerent: Σίβυλλα, τί θέλεις; respondebat illa: ἀποθανεῖν θέλω.*
I myself with my own eyes saw the Sibyl at Cumae hanging in a flask; and when the boys cried at her: ' Sibyl, Sibyl, what do you want?' 'I would that I were dead,' she used to answer.
Satyricon 'Cena Trimalchionis' ch. 48, sect. 8; cf. **Rossetti** 635:19

17 *Horatii curiosa felicitas.*
Horace's careful felicity.
Satyricon ch. 118, sect. 5

18 *Foeda est in coitu et brevis voluptas*
Et taedet Veneris statim peractae.

Delight of lust is gross and brief
And weariness treads on desire.

A. Baehrens *Poetae Latini Minores* (1882) vol. 4, no. 101 (translated by Helen Waddell)

Michelle Pfeiffer 1959–

American actress

1 You can have it all, but you can't do it all.

attributed; in *Guardian* 4 January 1996

Pheidippides see **Last words** 455:17

Edward John Phelps 1822–1900

American lawyer and diplomat

2 The man who makes no mistakes does not usually make anything.

speech at the Mansion House, London, 24 January 1889; in *The Times* 25 January 1889; cf. **Proverbs** 603:30

Kim Philby (Harold Adrian Russell Philby) 1912–88

British intelligence officer and Soviet spy

3 To betray, you must first belong.

in *Sunday Times* 17 December 1967

Prince Philip, Duke of Edinburgh 1921–

husband of ***Elizabeth II***

4 Gentlemen, I think it is about time we 'pulled our fingers out' . . . If we want to be more prosperous we've simply got to get down to it and work for it. The rest of the world does not owe us a living.

speech in London, 17 October 1961

5 If you stay here much longer you'll all be slitty-eyed.

remark to Edinburgh University students in Peking, 16 October 1986

6 Tolerance is the one essential ingredient . . . You can take it from me that the Queen has the quality of tolerance in abundance.

his recipe for a successful marriage, during celebrations for their golden wedding anniversary

in *The Times* 20 November 1997

John Woodward ('Jack') Philip 1840–1900

American naval captain in the Spanish–American war

7 Don't cheer, men; those poor devils are dying.

at the Battle of Santiago, 4 July 1898

in *Dictionary of American Biography* vol. 14 (1934) 'John Woodward Philip'

Ambrose Philips c.1675–1749

English poet

8 The flowers anew, returning seasons bring;
But beauty faded has no second spring.

The First Pastoral (1708) 'Lobbin' l. 47

9 There solid billows of enormous size,
Alps of green ice, in wild disorder rise.

'A Winter-Piece' in *The Tatler* 7 May 1709

10 The stag in limpid currents with surprise,
Sees crystal branches on his forehead rise.

'A Winter-Piece' in *The Tatler* (7 May 1709)

Katherine Philips 1632–64

English poet

11 I did but see him, and he disappeared,
I did but touch the rosebud, and it fell;
A sorrow unforeseen and scarcely feared,
So ill can mortals their afflictions spell.

'On the Death of my First and Dearest Child, Hector Philips' (1655)

Arthur Angell Phillips 1900–85

Australian critic and editor

12 Above our writers—and other artists—looms the intimidating mass of Anglo-Saxon culture. Such a situation almost inevitably produces the characteristic Australian Cultural Cringe—appearing either as the Cringe Direct, or as the Cringe Inverted, in the attitude of the Blatant Blatherskite, the God's-Own-Country and I'm-a-better-man-than-you-are Australian bore.

Meanjin (1950) 'The Cultural Cringe'; cf. **Keating** 426:12

Morgan Phillips 1902–63

British Labour politician

13 The Labour Party owes more to Methodism than to Marxism.

James Callaghan *Time and Chance* (1987) ch. 1

Pablo Picasso 1881–1973

Spanish painter

14 The fact that for a long time Cubism has not been understood and that even today there are people who cannot see anything in it, means nothing. I do not read English, an English book is a blank book to me. This does not mean that the English language does not exist.

interview with Marius de Zayas, 1923; Herschel B. Chipp *Theories of Modern Art* (1968)

15 There is nothing more dangerous than justice in the hands of judges, and a paintbrush in the hands of a painter. Just think of the danger to society! But today we haven't the heart to expel the painters and poets from society because we refuse to admit to ourselves that there is any danger in keeping them in our midst.

conversation, 1935; Herschel B. Chipp *Theories of Modern Art* (1968)

16 No, painting is not made to decorate apartments. It's an offensive and defensive weapon against the enemy.

interview with Simone Téry, 24 March 1945, in Alfred H. Barr *Picasso* (1946)

17 The artist is a receptacle for emotions that come from all over the place: from the sky, from the earth, from a scrap of paper, from a passing shape, from a spider's web.

Alfred H. Barr Jr. *Picasso: Fifty Years of his Art* (1946)

1 When I was the age of these children I could draw like Raphael: it took me many years to learn how to draw like these children.
*to Herbert **Read**, when visiting an exhibition of childen's drawings*
quoted in letter from Read to *The Times* 27 October 1956

2 I paint objects as I think them, not as I see them.
John Golding *Cubism* (1959)

3 God is really only another artist. He invented the giraffe, the elephant, and the cat. He has no real style. He just goes on trying other things.
F. Gilot and C. Lake *Life With Picasso* (1964) pt. 1

4 Every positive value has its price in negative terms . . . The genius of Einstein leads to Hiroshima.
F. Gilot and C. Lake *Life With Picasso* (1964) pt. 2

5 We all know that Art is not truth. Art is a lie that makes us realize truth.
Dore Ashton *Picasso on Art* (1972) 'Two statements by Picasso'

John Pilger 1939–
Australian journalist

6 I used to see Vietnam as a war, rather than a country.
in *Sunday Times* 1 December 1996

Ben Pimlott 1945–
English historian and royal biographer

7 If you have a Royal Family you have to make the best of whatever personalities the genetic lottery comes up with.
in *Independent* 13 September 1997 'Quote Unquote'

Pindar 518–438 BC
Greek lyric poet

8 Water is best. But gold shines like fire blazing in the night, supreme of lordly wealth.
Olympian Odes bk. 1, l. 1

9 I have many swift arrows in my quiver which speak to the wise, but for the crowd they need interpreters. The skilled poet is one who knows much through natural gift, but those who have learned their art chatter turbulently, like ravens, vainly, against the divine bird of Zeus.
Olympian Odes bk. 2, l. 83

10 My soul, do not seek immortal life, but exhaust the realm of the possible.
Pythian Odes bk. 3, l. 109

11 Creatures of a day, what is a man? What is he not? Mankind is a dream of a shadow. But when a god-given brightness comes, a radiant light rests on men, and a gentle life.
Pythian Odes bk. 8, l. 135

Harold Pinter 1930–
English dramatist

12 If only I could get down to Sidcup! I've been waiting for the weather to break. He's got my papers, this man I left them with, it's got it all down there, I could prove everything.
The Caretaker (1960) act 1

13 Apart from the known and the unknown, what else is there?
The Homecoming (1965) act 2, sc. 1

14 The weasel under the cocktail cabinet.
on being asked what his plays were about
J. Russell Taylor *Anger and After* (1962)

Luigi Pirandello 1867–1936
Italian dramatist and novelist

15 *Sei personaggi in cerca d'autore.*
Six characters in search of an author.
title of play (1921)

Robert M. Pirsig 1928–
American writer

16 Zen and the art of motorcycle maintenance.
title of book (1974)

17 That's the classical mind at work, runs fine inside but looks dingy on the surface.
Zen and the Art of Motorcycle Maintenance (1974) pt. 3, ch. 26

Walter B. Pitkin 1878–1953

18 Life begins at forty.
title of book (1932); cf. **Proverbs** 605:25

William Pitt, Earl of Chatham 1708–78
British Whig statesman; Prime Minister, 1766–8
*on Pitt: see **Walpole** 802:6*

19 The atrocious crime of being a young man . . . I shall neither attempt to palliate nor deny.
speech, House of Commons, 2 March 1741

20 The poorest man may in his cottage bid defiance to all the forces of the Crown. It may be frail—its roof may shake—the wind may blow through it—the storm may enter—the rain may enter—but the King of England cannot enter!
speech, *c.*March 1763, in Lord Brougham *Historical Sketches of Statesmen in the Time of George III* First Series (1845) vol. 1

21 Confidence is a plant of slow growth in an aged bosom: youth is the season of credulity.
speech, House of Commons, 14 January 1766

22 Unlimited power is apt to corrupt the minds of those who possess it.
speech, House of Lords, 9 January 1770; cf. **Acton** 1:16

23 There is something behind the throne greater than the King himself.
speech, House of Lords, 2 March 1770

24 We have a Calvinistic creed, a Popish liturgy, and an Arminian clergy.
speech, House of Lords, 19 May 1772; Basil Williams *Life of William Pitt Earl of Chatham* (1913) vol. 2, ch. 24

25 You cannot conquer America.
speech, House of Lords, 18 November 1777

26 I invoke the genius of the Constitution!
speech, House of Lords, 18 November 1777

1 Our watchword is security.

attributed

2 The parks are the lungs of London.

quoted by William Windham in the House of Commons, 30 June 1808

William Pitt 1759–1806

British Tory statesman; Prime Minister, 1783–1801, 1804–6

on Pitt: see **Burke** *165:2,* **Canning** *185:4,* **Fox** *322:4; see also* **Last words** *456:20*

3 Necessity is the plea for every infringement of human freedom: it is the argument of tyrants; it is the creed of slaves.

speech, House of Commons, 18 November 1783

4 We must anew commence the salvation of Europe.

in 1795; in *Dictionary of National Biography* (1917–)

5 We must recollect . . . what it is we have at stake, what it is we have to contend for. It is for our property, it is for our liberty, it is for our independence, nay, for our existence as a nation; it is for our character, it is for our very name as Englishmen, it is for everything dear and valuable to man on this side of the grave.

on the rupture of the Peace of Amiens and the resumption of war with Napoleon

speech, 22 July 1803, in *Speeches of the Rt. Hon. William Pitt* (1806) vol. 4

6 England has saved herself by her exertions, and will, as I trust, save Europe by her example.

replying to a toast in which he had been described as the saviour of his country in the wars with France

R. Coupland *War Speeches of William Pitt* (1915)

7 Roll up that map; it will not be wanted these ten years.

of a map of Europe, on hearing of Napoleon's victory at Austerlitz, December 1805

Earl Stanhope *Life of the Rt. Hon. William Pitt* vol. 4 (1862) ch. 43

Pius VII 1742–1823

Pope from 1800

8 We are prepared to go to the gates of Hell—but no further.

attempting to reach an agreement with **Napoleon***, c.1800–1*

J. M. Robinson *Cardinal Consalvi* (1987)

Pius XII 1876–1958

Italian cleric; Pope from 1939

9 One Galileo in two thousand years is enough.

on being asked to proscribe the works of **Teilhard de Chardin**

attributed; Stafford Beer *Platform for Change* (1975)

Max Planck 1858–1947

German physicist

10 A new scientific truth does not triumph by convincing its opponents and making them see the light, but rather because its opponents eventually die, and a new generation grows up that is familiar with it.

A Scientific Autobiography (1949, translated by F. Gaynor)

Sylvia Plath 1932–63

American poet

11 A living doll, everywhere you look.
It can sew, it can cook,
It can talk, talk, talk.

It works, there is nothing wrong with it.
You have a hole, it's a poultice.
You have an eye, it's an image.
My boy, it's your last resort.
Will you marry it, marry it, marry it.

'The Applicant' (1966)

12 Is there no way out of the mind?

'Apprehensions' (1971)

13 I have always been scared of *you*,
With your Luftwaffe, your gobbledygoo.
And your neat moustache
And your Aryan eye, bright blue.
Panzer-man, panzer-man, O You—

'Daddy' (1963)

14 Every woman adores a Fascist,
The boot in the face, the brute
Brute heart of a brute like you.

'Daddy' (1963)

15 The woman is perfected
Her dead
Body wears the smile of accomplishment.

opening lines of her last poem, written a week before her suicide

'Edge'

16 I am the ghost of an infamous suicide,
My own blue razor rusting in my throat.
O pardon the one who knocks for pardon at
Your gate, father—your hound-bitch, daughter, friend.
It was my love that did us both to death.

'Electra on Azalea Path' (1959)

17 Dying,
Is an art, like everything else.

'Lady Lazarus' (1963)

18 Out of the ash
I rise with my red hair
And I eat men like air.

'Lady Lazarus' (1963)

19 Love set you going like a fat gold watch.
The midwife slapped your footsoles, and your bald cry
Took its place among the elements.

'Morning Song' (1965)

20 Widow. The word consumes itself.

'Widow' (1971)

Plato 429–347 BC
Greek philosopher
see also **Anonymous** *21:3*

1 Socrates, he says, breaks the law by corrupting young men and not recognizing the gods that the city recognizes, but some other new deities.
Apologia 24b

2 Is that which is holy loved by the gods because it is holy, or is it holy because it is loved by the gods?
Euthyphro 10

3 Socrates, I shall not accuse you as I accuse others, of getting angry and cursing me when I tell them to drink the poison imposed by the authorities. I know you on the contrary in your time here to be the noblest and gentlest and best man of all who ever came here; and now I am sure you are not angry with me, for you know who are responsible, but with them.
spoken by Socrates' jailor
Phaedo 116c

4 This was the end, Echekrates, of our friend; a man of whom we may say that of all whom we met at that time he was the wisest and justest and best.
on the death of ***Socrates***
Phaedo 118a

5 What I say is that 'just' or 'right' means nothing but what is in the interest of the stronger party.
spoken by Thrasymachus
The Republic bk. 1, 338c (translated by F. M. Cornford)

6 For our discussion is about no ordinary matter, but on the right way to conduct our lives.
The Republic bk. 1, 352d

7 And so with the objects of knowledge: these derive from the Good not only their power of being known, but their very being and reality; and Goodness is not the same thing as being, but even beyond being, surpassing it in dignity and power.
The Republic bk. 6, 509b (translated by F. M. Cornford)

8 Behold! human beings living in a underground den . . . Like ourselves . . . they see only their own shadows, or the shadows of one another, which the fire throws on the opposite wall of the cave.
The Republic bk. 7, 515b; cf. **Nietzsche** 545:14

9 The blame is his who chooses: God is blameless.
The Republic bk. 10, 617e

10 But if we are guided by me we shall believe that the soul is immortal and capable of enduring all extremes of good and evil, and so we shall hold ever to the upward way and pursue righteousness with wisdom always and ever, that we may be dear to ourselves and to the gods both during our sojourn here and when we receive our reward.
The Republic bk. 10, 621c

11 Evils, Theodorus, can never pass away, for there must always remain something which is antagonistic to good. Having no place among the gods in heaven, of necessity they hover around the mortal nature and this earthly sphere. Wherefore we ought to fly away from earth to heaven as quickly as we can; and to fly away is to become like God, as far as this is possible; and to become like him is to become holy, just, and wise.
Theaetetus 176a (translated by Benjamin Jowett)

Plautus c.250–184 BC
Roman comic dramatist

12 *Lupus est homo homini, non homo, quom qualis sit non novit.*
A man is a wolf rather than a man to another man, when he hasn't yet found out what he's like.
often quoted as 'Homo homini lupus [A man is a wolf to another man]'
Asinaria l. 495; cf. **Vanzetti** 789:19

13 *Dictum sapienti sat est.*
A sentence is enough for a sensible man.
proverbially: 'Verbum sapienti sat est [A word is enough for the wise]', *and abbreviated to* 'verb. sap.'
Persa l. 729; cf. **Proverbs** 615:18

14 LABRAX: *Immo edepol una littera plus sum quam medicus.*
GRIPUS: *Tum tu*
Mendicus es?
LABRAX: *Tetigisti acu.*
LABRAX: One letter more than a medical man, that's what I am.
GRIPUS: Then you're a mendicant?
LABRAX: You've hit the point.
Rudens l. 1305

Pliny the Elder AD 23–79
Roman statesman and scholar, uncle of ***Pliny*** *the Younger*

15 *Scito enim conferentum auctores me deprehendisse a iuratissimis et proximis veteres transcriptos ad verbum neque nominatos.*
When collating authorities I have found that the most professedly reliable and modern writers have copied the old authors word for word, without acknowledgement.
preface to *Historia Naturalis*

16 *Bruta fulmina.*
Harmless thunderbolts.
Historia Naturalis bk. 2, sect. 113

17 *Semper aliquid novi Africam adferre.*
Africa always brings [us] something new.
often quoted as 'Ex Africa semper aliquid novi [Always something new out of Africa]'
Historia Naturalis bk. 8, sect. 42

18 *Optimumque est, ut volgo dixere, aliena insania frui.*
And the best plan is, as the popular saying was, to profit by the folly of others.
Historia Naturalis bk. 18, sect. 31

19 *Addito salis grano.*
With the addition of a grain of salt.
commonly quoted as 'Cum grano salis [With a grain of salt]'
Historia Naturalis bk. 23, sect. 149

Pliny the Younger AD c.61–c.112

Roman senator and writer, nephew of **Pliny** *the Elder*

1 *Nihil est, inquis, quod scribam. At hoc ipsum scribe, nihil esse quod scribas, vel solum illud unde incipere priores solebant: 'Si vales, bene est; ego valeo.' Hoc mihi sufficit; est enim maximum.*

You say you have nothing to write about. Well, you can at least write about *that*—or else simply the phrase our elders used to start a letter with: 'If you are well, well and good; I am well.' That will do for me—it is all that matters.

letter to Fabius Justus, in *Letters* (Loeb ed., 1969) bk. 1, sect. 11

William Plomer 1903–73

British poet

2 Out of that bungled, unwise war
An alp of unforgiveness grew.

'The Boer War' (1960)

3 With first-rate sherry flowing into second-rate whores,
And third-rate conversation without one single pause:
Just like a young couple
Between the wars.

'Father and Son: 1939' (1945)

4 On a sofa upholstered in panther skin
Mona did researches in original sin.

'Mews Flat Mona' (1960)

5 A rose-red sissy half as old as time.

'Playboy of the Demi-World: 1938' (1945); cf. **Burgon** 162:4

Plutarch AD c.46–c.120

Greek philosopher and biographer

6 I am writing biography, not history, and the truth is that the most brilliant exploits often tell us nothing of the virtues or vices of the men who performed them, while on the other hand a chance remark or a joke may reveal far more of a man's character than the mere feat of winning battles in which thousands fall, or of marshalling great armies, or laying siege to cities.

Parallel Lives 'Alexander' ch. 7

7 For we are told that when a certain man was accusing both of them to him, he [Caesar] said that he had no fear of those fat and long-haired fellows, but rather of those pale and thin ones.

Parallel Lives 'Anthony' sect. 11; cf. **Shakespeare** 674:16

8 The man who is thought to have been the first to see beneath the surface of Caesar's public policy and to fear it, as one might fear the smiling surface of the sea.

of ***Cicero***

Parallel Lives 'Julius Caesar' sect. 4

9 He who cheats with an oath acknowledges that he is afraid of his enemy, but that he thinks little of God.

Parallel Lives 'Lysander' ch. 8; cf. **Lysander** 480:22

Edgar Allan Poe 1809–49

American writer

on Poe: see **Lowell** 477:13

10 I was a child and she was a child,
In this kingdom by the sea;
But we loved with a love which was more than love—
I and my Annabel Lee.

'Annabel Lee' (1849)

11 And so, all the night-tide, I lie down by the side
Of my darling, my darling, my life and my bride
In her sepulchre there by the sea,
In her tomb by the side of the sea.

'Annabel Lee' (1849)

12 Keeping time, time, time,
In a sort of Runic rhyme,
To the tintinnabulation that so musically wells
From the bells, bells, bells, bells.

'The Bells' (1849) st. 1

13 All that we see or seem
Is but a dream within a dream.

'A Dream within a Dream' (1849)

14 The fever called 'Living'
Is conquered at last.

'For Annie' (1849)

15 Once upon a midnight dreary, while I pondered, weak and weary,
Over many a quaint and curious volume of forgotten lore,
While I nodded, nearly napping, suddenly there came a tapping,
As of some one gently rapping, rapping at my chamber door.

'The Raven' (1845) st. 1

16 Eagerly I wished the morrow,—vainly had I sought to borrow
From my books surcease of sorrow—sorrow for the lost Lenore—
For the rare and radiant maiden whom the angels name Lenore—
Nameless here for evermore.

'The Raven' (1845) st. 2

17 Ghastly, grim and ancient raven wandering from the Nightly shore—
Tell me what thy lordly name is on the Night's Plutonian shore!

'The Raven' (1845) st. 8

18 Take thy beak from out my heart, and take thy form from off my door!
Quoth the Raven, 'Nevermore'.

'The Raven' (1845) st. 17

19 And his eyes have all the seeming of a demon's that is dreaming.

'The Raven' (1845) st. 18

20 Helen, thy beauty is to me
Like those Nicean barks of yore.

'To Helen' (1831)

21 Thy Naiad airs have brought me home,
To the glory that was Greece

And the grandeur that was Rome.
'To Helen' (1831)

1 To be *thoroughly* conversant with a man's heart, is to take our final lesson in the iron-clasped volume of despair.
'Marginalia'; in *Southern Literary Messenger* (Richmond, Virginia) June 1849

Henri Poincaré 1854–1912

French mathematician and philosopher of science

2 Science is built up of facts, as a house is built of stones; but an accumulation of facts is no more a science than a heap of stones is a house.
Science and Hypothesis (1905) ch. 9

□ Political slogans and songs

see box opposite
see also **Connell** 233:22, **Marx and Engels** 500:7, **Pottier** 589:5

Jackson Pollock 1912–56

American painter

3 There was a reviewer a while back who wrote that my pictures didn't have any beginning or any end. He didn't mean it as a compliment, but it was. It was a fine compliment.
Francis V. O'Connor *Jackson Pollock* (1967)

Polybius *c.*200–*c.*118 BC

Greek historian

4 Those who know how to win are much more numerous than those who know how to make proper use of their victories.
History bk 10

John Pomfret 1667–1702

English clergyman

5 We live and learn, but not the wiser grow.
'Reason' (1700) l. 112

Madame de Pompadour (Antoinette Poisson, Marquise de Pompadour) 1721–64

favourite of Louis XV of France

6 *Après nous le déluge.*
After us the deluge.
Madame du Hausset *Mémoires* (1824)

Georges Pompidou 1911–74

French statesman; President of France from 1969

7 A statesman is a politician who places himself at the service of the nation. A politician is a statesman who places the nation at his service.
in *Observer* 30 December 1973 'Sayings of the Year'

Alexander Pope 1688–1744

English poet
on Pope: see **Arnold** 28:23, 29:5, **Bentley** 67:10, **Brereton** 148:1

8 Poetic Justice, with her lifted scale,
Where, in nice balance, truth with gold she weighs,
And solid pudding against empty praise.
The Dunciad (1742) bk. 1, l. 52

9 While pensive poets painful vigils keep,
Sleepless themselves, to give their readers sleep.
The Dunciad (1742) bk. 1, l. 93

10 Or where the pictures for the page atone,
And Quarles is saved by beauties not his own.
The Dunciad (1742) bk. 1, l. 139

11 Gentle Dullness ever loves a joke.
The Dunciad (1742) bk. 2, l. 34

12 A brain of feathers, and a heart of lead.
The Dunciad (1742) bk. 2, l. 44

13 How little, mark! that portion of the ball,
Where, faint at best, the beams of science fall.
The Dunciad (1742) bk. 3, l. 83

14 All crowd, who foremost shall be damned to Fame.
The Dunciad (1742) bk. 3, l. 158

15 Flow Welsted, flow! like thine inspirer, Beer,
Tho' stale, not ripe; tho' thin, yet never clear;
So sweetly mawkish, and so smoothly dull;
Heady, not strong; o'erflowing tho' not full.
The Dunciad (1742) bk. 3, l. 169

16 'Till Isis' elders reel, their pupils' sport,
And Alma mater lie dissolved in port!
The Dunciad (1742) bk. 3, l. 337

17 None need a guide, by sure attraction led,
And strong impulsive gravity of head.
The Dunciad (1742) bk. 4, l. 75

18 A wit with dunces, and a dunce with wits.
The Dunciad (1742) bk. 4, l. 90

19 Whate'er the talents, or howe'er designed,
We hang one jingling padlock on the mind.
The Dunciad (1742) bk. 4, l. 161

20 The Right Divine of Kings to govern wrong.
The Dunciad (1742) bk. 4, l. 187

21 For thee explain a thing till all men doubt it,
And write about it, Goddess, and about it.
The Dunciad (1742) bk. 4, l. 251

22 With the same cement, ever sure to bind,
We bring to one dead level ev'ry mind.
Then take him to develop, if you can,
And hew the block off, and get out the man.
The Dunciad (1742) bk. 4, l. 267

23 Isles of fragrance, lily-silver'd vales.
The Dunciad (1742) bk. 4, l. 303

24 Love-whisp'ring woods, and lute-resounding waves.
The Dunciad (1742) bk. 4, l. 306

25 She marked thee there,
Stretched on the rack of a too easy chair,
And heard thy everlasting yawn confess
The pains and penalties of idleness.
The Dunciad (1742) bk. 4, l. 342

continued

Political slogans and songs

1 All power to the Soviets.
workers in Petrograd, 1917

2 All the way with LBJ.
US Democratic Party campaign slogan, 1960

3 Ban the bomb.
US anti-nuclear slogan, adopted by the Campaign for Nuclear Disarmament, 1953 onwards

4 A bayonet is a weapon with a worker at each end.
British pacifist slogan (1940)

5 As Maine goes, so goes the nation.
American political saying, *c.*1840; cf. **Farley** 307:1

6 Better red than dead.
slogan of nuclear disarmament campaigners, late 1950s

7 A bigger bang for a buck.
Charles E. **Wilson**'s defence policy, in *Newsweek* 22 March 1954

8 Black is beautiful.
slogan of American civil rights campaigners, mid-1960s

9 Burn, baby, burn.
Black extremist slogan in use during the Los Angeles riots, August 1965

10 Can't pay, won't pay.
anti-Poll Tax slogan, *c.*1990; cf. **Fo** 318:21

11 *Ein Reich, ein Volk, ein Führer.*
One realm, one people, one leader.
Nazi Party slogan, early 1930s

12 Fair shares for all, is Labour's call.
slogan for the North Battersea by-election, 1946, coined by Douglas ***Jay***
Douglas Jay *Change and Fortune* (1980) ch. 7

13 Fifty-four forty, or fight!
slogan of expansionist Democrats in the US presidential campaign of 1844, in which the Oregon boundary definition was an issue (in 1846 the new Democratic president, James K. Polk, compromised on the 49th parallel with Great Britain)

14 Hey, hey, LBJ, how many kids did you kill today?
anti-Vietnam marching slogan, 1960s

15 I like Ike.
used when General ***Eisenhower*** *was first seen as a potential presidential nominee*
US button badge, 1947; coined by Henry D. Spalding (d. 1990)

16 I met wid Napper Tandy, and he took me by the hand,
And he said, 'How's poor ould Ireland, and how does she stand?'
She's the most disthressful country that iver yet was seen,
For they're hangin' men an' women for the wearin' o' the Green.
'The Wearin' o' the Green' (*c.*1795 ballad)

17 The iron-armed soldier, the true-hearted soldier,
The gallant old soldier of Tippecanoe.
presidential campaign song for William Henry Harrison, 1840; cf. ***Political slogans*** *582:2 below*
attributed to George Pope Morris (1802–64)

18 It'll play in Peoria.
catchphrase of the **Nixon** administration (early 1970s) meaning 'it will be acceptable to middle America', but originating in a standard music hall joke of the 1930s

19 It's morning again in America.
slogan for Ronald **Reagan**'s election campaign, 1984; coined by Hal Riney (1932–); in *Newsweek* 6 August 1984

20 It's the economy, stupid.
on a sign put up at the 1992 **Clinton** presidential campaign headquarters by campaign manager James Carville

21 *Kraft durch Freude.*
Strength through joy.
German Labour Front slogan, from 1933; coined by Robert Ley (1890–1945)

22 Labour isn't working.
on poster showing a long queue outside an unemployment office
Conservative Party slogan 1978–9

23 Labour's double whammy.
Conservative Party election slogan 1992

24 *Liberté! Égalité! Fraternité!*
Freedom! Equality! Brotherhood!
motto of the French Revolution, but of earlier origin
the Club des Cordeliers passed a motion, 30 June 1793, 'that owners should be urged to paint on the front of their houses, in large letters, the words: Unity, indivisibility of the Republic, Liberty, Equality, Fraternity or death'; in *Journal de Paris* no. 182 (from 1795 the words 'or death' were dropped); cf. **Chamfort** 201:10

25 Life's better with the Conservatives. Don't let Labour ruin it.
Conservative Party election slogan, 1959

26 New Labour, new danger.
Conservative slogan, 1996

27 No surrender!
the defenders of the besieged city of Derry to the Jacobite army of James II, April 1689, adopted as a slogan of Protestant Ulster
Jonathan Bardon *A History of Ulster* (1992)

28 Power to the people.
slogan of the Black Panther movement, from *c.*1968 onwards; cf. **Newton** 543:2

29 So on the Twelfth I proudly wear the sash my father wore.
'The Sash My Father Wore', traditional Orange song

30 Thirteen years of Tory misrule.
unofficial Labour party election slogan, also in the form 'Thirteen wasted years', 1964

Political slogans and songs *continued*

1 Three acres and a cow.
regarded as the requirement for self-sufficiency; associated with the radical politician Jesse Collings (1831–1920) and his land reform campaign begun in 1885
Jesse Collings in the House of Commons, 26 January 1886, although used earlier by Joseph **Chamberlain** in a speech at Evesham (in *The Times* 17 November 1885), by which time it was already proverbial

2 Tippecanoe and Tyler, too.
presidential campaign song for William Henry Harrison, 1840
attributed to A. C. Ross (fl. 1840); cf. **Political slogans** 581:17 above

3 'Tis bad enough in man or woman
To steal a goose from off a common;
But surely he's without excuse
Who steals the common from the goose.
'On Inclosures'; in *The Oxford Book of Light Verse* (1938)

4 Votes for women.
adopted when it proved impossible to use a banner with the longer slogan 'Will the Liberal Party Give Votes for Women?' made by Emmeline ***Pankhurst*** *(1858–1928), Christabel* ***Pankhurst*** *(1880–1958), and Annie Kenney (1879–1953)*
slogan of the women's suffrage movement, from 13 October 1905; Emmeline Pankhurst *My Own Story* (1914)

5 War will cease when men refuse to fight.
pacifist slogan, from *c.*1936 (often quoted as, 'Wars will cease . . . ')

6 We shall not be moved.
title of labour and civil rights song (1931) adapted from an earlier gospel hymn

7 We shall overcome.
title of song, originating from before the American Civil War, adapted as a Baptist hymn ('I'll Overcome Some Day', 1901) by C. Albert Tindley; revived in 1946 as a protest song by black tobacco workers, and in 1963 during the black Civil Rights Campaign

8 Would you buy a used car from this man?
campaign slogan directed against Richard **Nixon**, 1968

9 Yes it hurt, yes it worked.
Conservative Party slogan, 1996; cf. **Major** 491:14

10 Yesterday's men (they failed before!).
Labour Party slogan, referring to the Conservatives, 1970; coined by David Kingsley, Dennis Lyons, and Peter Lovell-Davis

Alexander Pope *continued*

11 Thy truffles, Perigord! thy hams, Bayonne!
The Dunciad (1742) bk. 4, l. 558

12 See skulking Truth to her old cavern fled,
Mountains of casuistry heaped o'er her head!
Philosophy, that leaned on Heav'n before,
Shrinks to her second cause, and is no more.
Physic of Metaphysic begs defence,
And Metaphysic calls for aid on Sense!
The Dunciad (1742) bk. 4, l. 641

13 Religion blushing veils her sacred fires,
And unawares Morality expires.
The Dunciad (1742) bk. 4, l. 649

14 Lo! thy dread empire, Chaos! is restored;
Light dies before thy uncreating word:
Thy hand, great Anarch! lets the curtain fall;
And universal darkness buries all.
The Dunciad (1742) bk. 4, l. 653

15 Vital spark of heav'nly flame!
Quit, oh quit this mortal frame:
Trembling, hoping, ling'ring, flying,
Oh the pain, the bliss of dying!
'The Dying Christian to his Soul' (1730); cf. **Hadrian** 355:11

16 What beck'ning ghost, along the moonlight shade
Invites my step, and points to yonder glade?
'Elegy to the Memory of an Unfortunate Lady' (1717) l. 1

17 Is it, in heav'n, a crime to love too well?
'Elegy to the Memory of an Unfortunate Lady' (1717) l. 6

18 Is there no bright reversion in the sky,
For those who greatly think, or bravely die?
'Elegy to the Memory of an Unfortunate Lady' (1717) l. 9

19 Ambition first sprung from your blest abodes;
The glorious fault of angels and of gods.
'Elegy to the Memory of an Unfortunate Lady' (1717) l. 13

20 On all the line a sudden vengeance waits,
And frequent hearses shall besiege your gates.
'Elegy to the Memory of an Unfortunate Lady' (1717) l. 37

21 Oh happy state! when souls each other draw,
When love is liberty, and nature, law:
All then is full, possessing, and possessed,
No craving void left aching in the breast.
'Eloisa to Abelard' (1717) l. 91

22 Of all affliction taught a lover yet,
'Tis sure the hardest science to forget!
'Eloisa to Abelard' (1717) l. 189

23 How shall I lose the sin, yet keep the sense,
And love th'offender, yet detest th'offence?
'Eloisa to Abelard' (1717) l. 191; cf. **Augustine** 36:11

24 How happy is the blameless Vestal's lot!
The world forgetting, by the world forgot.
'Eloisa to Abelard' (1717) l. 207

25 You beat your pate, and fancy wit will come:
Knock as you please, there's nobody at home.
'Epigram: You beat your pate' (1732)

26 I am his Highness' dog at Kew;
Pray, tell me sir, whose dog are you?
'Epigram Engraved on the Collar of a Dog which I gave to his Royal Highness' (1738)

27 Sir, I admit your gen'ral rule
That every poet is a fool:
But you yourself may serve to show it,

That every fool is not a poet.
'Epigram from the French' (1732)

1 Shut, shut the door, good John! fatigued I said,
Tie up the knocker, say I'm sick, I'm dead,
The dog-star rages!
'An Epistle to Dr Arbuthnot' (1735) l. 1

2 You think this cruel? take it for a rule,
No creature smarts so little as a fool.
Let peals of laughter, Codrus! round thee break,
Thou unconcerned canst hear the mighty crack.
Pit, box, and gall'ry in convulsions hurled,
Thou stand'st unshook amidst a bursting world.
'An Epistle to Dr Arbuthnot' (1735) l. 83; cf. **Addison** 4:23, **Horace** 388:16

3 As yet a child, nor yet a fool to fame,
I lisped in numbers, for the numbers came.
'An Epistle to Dr Arbuthnot' (1735) l. 127; cf. **Ovid** 561:23

4 The Muse but served to ease some friend, not wife,
To help me through this long disease, my life.
'An Epistle to Dr Arbuthnot' (1735) l. 131

5 Pretty! in amber to observe the forms
Of hairs, or straws, or dirt, or grubs, or worms;
The things, we know, are neither rich nor rare,
But wonder how the devil they got there?
'An Epistle to Dr Arbuthnot' (1735) l. 169

6 And he, whose fustian's so sublimely bad,
It is not poetry, but prose run mad.
'An Epistle to Dr Arbuthnot' (1735) l. 187

7 Damn with faint praise, assent with civil leer,
And without sneering, teach the rest to sneer;
Willing to wound, and yet afraid to strike,
Just hint a fault, and hesitate dislike.
of ***Addison***
'An Epistle to Dr Arbuthnot' (1735) l. 201; cf. **Wycherley** 834:13

8 But still the great have kindness in reserve,
He helped to bury whom he helped to starve.
of a noble patron
'An Epistle to Dr Arbuthnot' (1735) l. 247

9 'Satire or sense, alas! can Sporus feel?
Who breaks a butterfly upon a wheel?'
Yet let me flap this bug with gilded wings,
This painted child of dirt that stinks and stings.
of Lord ***Hervey***
'An Epistle to Dr Arbuthnot' (1735) l. 307; cf. **Newspaper headlines** 544:18

10 A cherub's face, a reptile all the rest.
of Lord ***Hervey***
'An Epistle to Dr Arbuthnot' (1735) l. 331

11 Unlearn'd, he knew no schoolman's subtle art,
No language, but the language of the heart.
of his own father
'An Epistle to Dr Arbuthnot' (1735) l. 398

12 A very heathen in the carnal part,
Yet still a sad, good Christian at her heart.
Epistles to Several Persons 'To a Lady' (1735) l. 67

13 Chaste to her husband, frank to all beside,
A teeming mistress, but a barren bride.
Epistles to Several Persons 'To a Lady' (1735) l. 71

14 Virtue she finds too painful an endeavour,
Content to dwell in decencies for ever.
Epistles to Several Persons 'To a Lady' (1735) l. 163

15 Still round and round the ghosts of Beauty glide,
And haunt the places where their honour died.
See how the world its veterans rewards!
A youth of frolics, an old age of cards.
Epistles to Several Persons 'To a Lady' (1735) l. 241

16 And mistress of herself, though china fall.
Epistles to Several Persons 'To a Lady' (1735) l. 268

17 Woman's at best a contradiction still.
Epistles to Several Persons 'To a Lady' (1735) l. 270

18 Who shall decide, when doctors disagree?
Epistles to Several Persons 'To Lord Bathurst' (1733) l. 1

19 But thousands die, without or this or that,
Die, and endow a college, or a cat.
Epistles to Several Persons 'To Lord Bathurst' (1733) l. 97

20 The ruling passion, be it what it will,
The ruling passion conquers reason still.
Epistles to Several Persons 'To Lord Bathurst' (1733) l. 155; cf. **Pope** 584:2

21 Who sees pale Mammon pine amidst his store,
Sees but a backward steward for the poor;
This year a reservoir, to keep and spare,
The next a fountain, spouting through his heir,
In lavish streams to quench a country's thirst,
And men and dogs shall drink him 'till they burst.
Epistles to Several Persons 'To Lord Bathurst' (1733) l. 173

22 In the worst inn's worst room, with mat half-hung,
The floors of plaister, and the walls of dung,
On once a flock-bed, but repaired with straw,
With tape-tied curtains, never meant to draw,
The George and Garter dangling from that bed
Where tawdry yellow strove with dirty red,
Great Villiers lies.
Epistles to Several Persons 'To Lord Bathurst' (1733) l. 299

23 Consult the genius of the place in all.
Epistles to Several Persons 'To Lord Burlington' (1731) l. 57; cf. **Virgil** 795:4

24 To rest, the cushion and soft Dean invite,
Who never mentions Hell to ears polite.
Epistles to Several Persons 'To Lord Burlington' (1731) l. 149

25 Another age shall see the golden ear
Imbrown the slope, and nod on the parterre,
Deep harvests bury all his pride has planned,
And laughing Ceres re-assume the land.
Epistles to Several Persons 'To Lord Burlington' (1731) l. 173

26 'Tis use alone that sanctifies expense,
And splendour borrows all her rays from sense.
Epistles to Several Persons 'To Lord Burlington' (1731) l. 179

27 To observations which ourselves we make,
We grow more partial for th'observer's sake.
Epistles to Several Persons 'To Lord Cobham' (1734) l. 11

28 Like following life thro' creatures you dissect,
You lose it in the moment you detect.
Epistles to Several Persons 'To Lord Cobham' (1734) l. 39

29 'Tis from high life high characters are drawn;
A saint in crape is twice a saint in lawn.
Epistles to Several Persons 'To Lord Cobham' (1734) l. 87

1 'Tis education forms the common mind,
Just as the twig is bent, the tree's inclined.
Epistles to Several Persons 'To Lord Cobham' (1734) l. 101; cf. **Proverbs** 595:21

2 Search then the Ruling Passion: There, alone,
The wild are constant, and the cunning known;
The fool consistent, and the false sincere.
Epistles to Several Persons 'To Lord Cobham' (1734) l. 174; cf. **Pope** 583:20

3 Odious! in woollen! 'twould a saint provoke!
Epistles to Several Persons 'To Lord Cobham' (1734) l. 242

4 One would not, sure, be frightful when one's dead—
And—Betty—give this cheek a little red.
Epistles to Several Persons 'To Lord Cobham' (1734) l. 246

5 Old politicians chew on wisdom past,
And totter on in business to the last.
Epistles to Several Persons 'To Lord Cobham' (1734) l. 248

6 Statesman, yet friend to Truth! of soul sincere,
In action faithful, and in honour clear;
Who broke no promise, served no private end,
Who gained no title, and who lost no friend.
Epistles to Several Persons 'To Mr Addison' (1720) l. 67

7 She went, to plain-work, and to purling brooks,
Old-fashioned halls, dull aunts, and croaking rooks.
She went from op'ra, park, assembly, play,
To morning-walks, and prayers three hours a day;
To pass her time 'twixt reading and Bohea,
To muse, and spill her solitary tea,
'Epistle to Miss Blount, on her leaving the Town, after the Coronation [of King George I, 1715]' (1717)

8 Or o'er cold coffee trifle with the spoon,
Court the slow clock, and dine exact at noon.
'Epistle to Miss Blount, on her leaving the Town, after the Coronation [of King George I, 1715]' (1717)

9 Nature, and Nature's laws lay hid in night.
God said, *Let Newton be!* and all was light.
'Epitaph: Intended for Sir Isaac Newton' (1730); cf. **Squire** 735:16

10 Of manners gentle, of affections mild;
In wit, a man; simplicity, a child;
With native humour temp'ring virtuous rage,
Formed to delight at once and lash the age.
'Epitaph: On Mr Gay in Westminster Abbey' (1733)

11 Some are bewildered in the maze of schools,
And some made coxcombs Nature meant but fools.
An Essay on Criticism (1711) l. 26

12 Some have at first for wits, then poets passed,
Turned critics next, and proved plain fools at last.
An Essay on Criticism (1711) l. 36

13 First follow Nature, and your judgement frame
By her just standard, which is still the same:
Unerring Nature, still divinely bright,
One clear, unchanged, and universal light,
Life, force and beauty must to all impart,
At once the source and end and test of art.
An Essay on Criticism (1711) l. 68

14 Great wits may sometimes gloriously offend,
And rise to faults true critics dare not mend.
From vulgar bounds with brave disorder part
And snatch a grace beyond the reach of art.
An Essay on Criticism (1711) l. 152; cf. **Addison** 5:18

15 A little learning is a dangerous thing;
Drink deep, or taste not the Pierian spring:
There shallow draughts intoxicate the brain,
And drinking largely sobers us again.
An Essay on Criticism (1711) l. 215; cf. **Drayton** 279:7, **Proverbs** 605:38

16 Hills peep o'er hills, and Alps on Alps arise!
An Essay on Criticism (1711) l. 232

17 Whoever thinks a faultless piece to see,
Thinks what ne'er was, nor is, nor e'er shall be.
An Essay on Criticism (1711) l. 253

18 Poets like painters, thus unskilled to trace
The naked nature and the living grace,
With gold and jewels cover ev'ry part,
And hide with ornaments their want of art.
True wit is Nature to advantage dressed,
What oft was thought, but ne'er so well expressed.
An Essay on Criticism (1711) l. 293

19 Expression is the dress of thought.
An Essay on Criticism (1711) l. 318; cf. **Johnson** 410:1, **Wesley** 821:1

20 As some to church repair,
Not for the doctrine, but the music there.
An Essay on Criticism (1711) l. 342

21 Then, at the last and only couplet fraught
With some unmeaning thing they call a thought,
A needless Alexandrine ends the song,
That, like a wounded snake, drags its slow length along.
An Essay on Criticism (1711) l. 354

22 True ease in writing comes from art, not chance,
As those move easiest who have learned to dance.
'Tis not enough no harshness gives offence,
The sound must seem an echo to the sense.
An Essay on Criticism (1711) l. 362

23 But when loud surges lash the sounding shore,
The hoarse, rough verse should like the torrent roar.
When Ajax strives, some rock's vast weight to throw,
The line too labours, and the words move slow.
An Essay on Criticism (1711) l. 368

24 Yet let not each gay turn thy rapture move,
For fools admire, but men of sense approve.
An Essay on Criticism (1711) l. 390

25 What woeful stuff this madrigal would be,
In some starved hackney sonneteer, or me?
But let a Lord once own the happy lines,
How the wit brightens! how the style refines!
An Essay on Criticism (1711) l. 418

26 Some praise at morning what they blame at night;
But always think the last opinion right.
An Essay on Criticism (1711) l. 430

27 To err is human; to forgive, divine.
An Essay on Criticism (1711) l. 525; cf. **Proverbs** 613:8

28 All seems infected that th'infected spy,
As all looks yellow to the jaundiced eye.
An Essay on Criticism (1711) l. 558

1 Men must be taught as if you taught them not,
And things unknown proposed as things forgot.
An Essay on Criticism (1711) l. 574

2 The bookful blockhead, ignorantly read,
With loads of learned lumber in his head.
An Essay on Criticism (1711) l. 612

3 For fools rush in where angels fear to tread.
An Essay on Criticism (1711) l. 625; cf. **Proverbs** 600:40

4 Awake, my St John! leave all meaner things
To low ambition, and the pride of kings.
Let us (since Life can little more supply
Than just to look about us and to die)
Expatiate free o'er all this scene of man;
A mighty maze! but not without a plan.
An Essay on Man Epistle 1 (1733) l. 1

5 Eye Nature's walks, shoot Folly as it flies,
And catch the Manners living as they rise.
Laugh where we must, be candid where we can;
But vindicate the ways of God to man.
An Essay on Man Epistle 1 (1733) l. 13; cf. **Milton** 514:9

6 Observe how system into system runs,
What other planets circle other suns.
An Essay on Man Epistle 1 (1733) l. 25

7 Pleased to the last, he crops the flowery food,
And licks the hand just raised to shed his blood.
An Essay on Man Epistle 1 (1733) l. 83

8 Who sees with equal eye, as God of all,
A hero perish, or a sparrow fall,
Atoms or systems into ruin hurled,
And now a bubble burst, and now a world.
An Essay on Man Epistle 1 (1733) l. 87

9 Hope springs eternal in the human breast:
Man never Is, but always To be blest.
An Essay on Man Epistle 1 (1733) l. 95; cf. **Proverbs** 603:1

10 Lo! the poor Indian, whose untutored mind
Sees God in clouds, or hears him in the wind.
His soul proud Science never taught to stray
Far as the solar walk, or milky way;
Yet simple Nature to his hope has giv'n,
Behind the cloud-topped hill, an humbler heav'n.
An Essay on Man Epistle 1 (1733) l. 99; cf. **Crabbe** 242:26

11 But thinks, admitted to that equal sky,
His faithful dog shall bear him company.
An Essay on Man Epistle 1 (1733) l. 111

12 Pride still is aiming at the blest abodes,
Men would be angels, angels would be gods.
An Essay on Man Epistle 1 (1733) l. 125

13 Why has not man a microscopic eye?
For this plain reason, man is not a fly.
An Essay on Man Epistle 1 (1733) l. 193

14 Die of a rose in aromatic pain?
An Essay on Man Epistle 1 (1733) l. 200; cf. **Winchilsea** 823:1

15 The spider's touch, how exquisitely fine!
Feels at each thread, and lives along the line.
An Essay on Man Epistle 1 (1733) l. 217

16 All are but parts of one stupendous whole,
Whose body, Nature is, and God the soul.
An Essay on Man Epistle 1 (1733) l. 267

17 All nature is but art, unknown to thee;
All chance, direction, which thou canst not see;
All discord, harmony, not understood;
All partial evil, universal good.
An Essay on Man Epistle 1 (1733) l. 289

18 And, spite of Pride, in erring Reason's spite,
One truth is clear, 'Whatever IS, is RIGHT.'
An Essay on Man Epistle 1 (1733) l. 293

19 Know then thyself, presume not God to scan;
The proper study of mankind is man.
Placed on this isthmus of a middle state,
A being darkly wise, and rudely great.
With too much knowledge for the sceptic side,
With too much weakness for the stoic's pride,
He hangs between; in doubt to act or rest,
In doubt to deem himself a god, or beast;
In doubt his mind or body to prefer,
Born but to die, and reas'ning but to err;
Alike in ignorance, his reason such,
Whether he thinks too little, or too much.
An Essay on Man Epistle 2 (1733) l. 1; cf. **Charron** 204:2, **Huxley** 396:18

20 Created half to rise, and half to fall;
Great lord of all things, yet a prey to all;
Sole judge of truth, in endless error hurled;
The glory, jest, and riddle of the world!
An Essay on Man Epistle 2 (1733) l. 15

21 Go, teach Eternal Wisdom how to rule—
Then drop into thyself, and be a fool!
An Essay on Man Epistle 2 (1733) l. 29

22 Vice is a monster of so frightful mien,
As, to be hated, needs but to be seen;
Yet seen too oft, familiar with her face,
We first endure, then pity, then embrace.
An Essay on Man Epistle 2 (1733) l. 217

23 The learn'd is happy nature to explore,
The fool is happy that he knows no more.
An Essay on Man Epistle 2 (1733) l. 263

24 Behold the child, by Nature's kindly law
Pleased with a rattle, tickled with a straw.
An Essay on Man Epistle 2 (1733) l. 275

25 Scarfs, garters, gold, amuse his riper stage;
And beads and pray'r-books are the toys of age:
Pleased with this bauble still, as that before;
Till tired he sleeps, and life's poor play is o'er!
An Essay on Man Epistle 2 (1733) l. 279

26 For forms of government let fools contest;
Whate'er is best administered is best.
An Essay on Man Epistle 3 (1733) l. 303

27 Thus God and nature linked the gen'ral frame,
And bade self-love and social be the same.
An Essay on Man Epistle 3 (1733) l. 317; *An Essay on Man* Epistle 4 (1734) l. 396 is similar

28 Oh Happiness! our being's end and aim!
Good, pleasure, ease, content! whate'er thy name:
That something still which prompts th' eternal sigh,
For which we bear to live, or dare to die.
An Essay on Man Epistle 4 (1734) l. 1

1 A wit's a feather, and a chief a rod;
An honest man's the noblest work of God.
An Essay on Man Epistle 4 (1734) l. 247; cf. **Burns** 166:26, **Ingersoll** 399:13

2 And more true joy Marcellus exil'd feels
Than Caesar with a senate at his heels.
An Essay on Man Epistle 4 (1734) l. 258

3 If parts allure thee, think how Bacon shined,
The wisest, brightest, meanest of mankind:
Or ravished with the whistling of a name,
See Cromwell, damned to everlasting fame!
An Essay on Man Epistle 4 (1734) l. 281

4 Slave to no sect, who takes no private road,
But looks thro' Nature, up to Nature's God.
An Essay on Man Epistle 4 (1734) l. 331

5 All our knowledge is, ourselves to know.
An Essay on Man Epistle 4 (1734) l. 398

6 Achilles' wrath, to Greece the direful spring
Of woes unnumbered, heavenly goddess, sing!
translation of *The Iliad* (1715) bk. 1, l. 1; cf. **Bentley** 67:10, **Homer** 381:20

7 For I, who hold sage Homer's rule the best,
Welcome the coming, speed the going guest.
Imitations of Horace Horace bk. 2, Satire 2 (1734) l. 159; see below

Speed the parting guest
Pope's translation of *The Odyssey* (1725–6) bk. 15, l. 84

8 Our Gen'rals now, retired to their estates,
Hang their old trophies o'er the garden gates,
In life's cool ev'ning satiate of applause.
Imitations of Horace Horace bk. 1, Epistle 1 (1738) l. 7

9 Not to go back, is somewhat to advance,
And men must walk at least before they dance.
Imitations of Horace Horace bk. 1, Epistle 1 (1738) l. 53

10 Get place and wealth, if possible, with grace;
If not, by any means get wealth and place.
Imitations of Horace Horace bk. 1, Epistle 1 (1738) l. 103; cf. **Horace** 386:11

11 Not to admire, is all the art I know,
To make men happy, and to keep them so.
Imitations of Horace Horace bk. 1, Epistle 6 (1738) l. 1; cf. **Horace** 386:18

12 The worst of madmen is a saint run mad.
Imitations of Horace Horace bk. 1, Epistle 6 (1738) l. 27

13 Shakespeare (whom you and ev'ry play-house bill
Style the divine, the matchless, what you will)
For gain, not glory, winged his roving flight,
And grew immortal in his own despite.
Imitations of Horace Horace bk. 2, Epistle 1 (1737) l. 69

14 Who now reads Cowley? if he pleases yet,
His moral pleases, not his pointed wit.
Imitations of Horace Horace bk. 2, Epistle 1 (1737) l. 75

15 The people's voice is odd,
It is, and it is not, the voice of God.
Imitations of Horace Horace bk. 2, Epistle 1 (1737) l. 89; cf. **Alcuin** 10:10

16 But those who cannot write, and those who can,
All rhyme, and scrawl, and scribble, to a man.
Imitations of Horace Horace bk. 2, Epistle 1 (1737) l. 187; cf. **Horace** 387:6

17 Waller was smooth; but Dryden taught to join
The varying verse, the full-resounding line,
The long majestic march, and energy divine.
Imitations of Horace Horace bk. 2, Epistle 1 (1737) l. 267

18 Ev'n copious Dryden, wanted, or forgot,
The last and greatest art, the art to blot.
Imitations of Horace Horace bk. 2, Epistle 1 (1737) l. 280; cf. **Heming** 369:8, **Jonson** 421:2

19 There still remains, to mortify a wit,
The many-headed monster of the pit.
Imitations of Horace Horace bk. 2, Epistle 1 (1737) l. 304

20 Let humble Allen, with an awkward shame,
Do good by stealth, and blush to find it fame.
Imitations of Horace Epilogue to the Satires (1738) Dialogue 1, l. 135

21 Ask you what provocation I have had?
The strong antipathy of good to bad.
Imitations of Horace Epilogue to the Satires (1738) Dialogue 2, l. 197

22 Yes, I am proud; I must be proud to see
Men not afraid of God, afraid of me.
Imitations of Horace Epilogue to the Satires (1738) Dialogue 2, l. 208

23 Ye gods! annihilate but space and time,
And make two lovers happy.
Martinus Scriblerus . . . or The Art of Sinking in Poetry ch. 11 (Miscellanies, 1727); possibly quoting another poet

24 Happy the man, whose wish and care
A few paternal acres bound,
Content to breathe his native air,
In his own ground.
'Ode on Solitude' (written *c.*1700, aged about twelve)

25 Thus let me live, unseen, unknown;
Thus unlamented let me die;
Steal from the world, and not a stone
Tell where I lie.
'Ode on Solitude' (written *c.*1700)

26 Where'er you walk, cool gales shall fan the glade,
Trees, where you sit, shall crowd into a shade:
Where'er you tread, the blushing flow'rs shall rise,
And all things flourish where you turn your eyes.
Pastorals (1709) 'Summer' l. 73

27 To wake the soul by tender strokes of art,
To raise the genius, and to mend the heart;
To make mankind, in conscious virtue bold,
Live o'er each scene, and be what they behold:
For this the Tragic Muse first trod the stage.
Prologue to Addison's *Cato* (1713) l. 1

28 What dire offence from am'rous causes springs,
What mighty contests rise from trivial things.
The Rape of the Lock (1714) canto 1, l. 1

29 Now lap-dogs give themselves the rousing shake,
And sleepless lovers, just at twelve, awake.
The Rape of the Lock (1714) canto 1, l. 15

30 With varying vanities, from ev'ry part,
They shift the moving toyshop of their heart.
The Rape of the Lock (1714) canto 1, l. 100

31 Here files of pins extend their shining rows,
Puffs, powders, patches, bibles, billet-doux.
The Rape of the Lock (1714) canto 1, l. 137

1 If to her share some female errors fall,
Look on her face, and you'll forget 'em all.
The Rape of the Lock (1714) canto 2, l. 17

2 Fair tresses man's imperial race insnare,
And beauty draws us with a single hair.
The Rape of the Lock (1714) canto 2, l. 27

3 Belinda smiled, and all the world was gay.
The Rape of the Lock (1714) canto 2, l. 52

4 Whether the nymph shall break Diana's law,
Or some frail china jar receive a flaw,
Or stain her honour, or her new brocade,
Forget her pray'rs, or miss a masquerade.
The Rape of the Lock (1714) canto 2, l. 105

5 Here thou, great Anna! whom three realms obey,
Dost sometimes counsel take—and sometimes tea.
The Rape of the Lock (1714) canto 3, l. 7

6 At ev'ry word a reputation dies.
The Rape of the Lock (1714) canto 3, l. 16; cf. **Sheridan** 716:12

7 The hungry judges soon the sentence sign,
And wretches hang that jury-men may dine.
The Rape of the Lock (1714) canto 3, l. 21

8 Let spades be trumps! she said, and trumps they were.
The Rape of the Lock (1714) canto 3, l. 46

9 Coffee, (which makes the politician wise,
And see thro' all things with his half-shut eyes).
The Rape of the Lock (1714) canto 3, l. 117

10 Not louder shrieks to pitying heav'n are cast,
When husbands or when lapdogs breathe their last.
The Rape of the Lock (1714) canto 3, l. 157

11 Sir Plume, of amber snuff-box justly vain,
And the nice conduct of a clouded cane.
The Rape of the Lock (1714) canto 4, l. 123

12 Beauties in vain their pretty eyes may roll;
Charms strike the sight, but merit wins the soul.
The Rape of the Lock (1714) canto 5, l. 33

13 Teach me to feel another's woe;
To hide the fault I see;
That mercy I to others show,
That mercy show to me.
'The Universal Prayer' (1738)

14 Here hills and vales, the woodland and the plain,
Here earth and water seem to strive again;
Not chaos-like together crushed and bruised,
But, as the world, harmoniously confused:
Where order in variety we see,
And where, though all things differ, all agree.
'Windsor Forest' (1711) l. 11

15 Party-spirit, which at best is but the madness of many for the gain of a few.
letter to Edward Blount, 27 August 1714, in G. Sherburn (ed.) *Correspondence of Alexander Pope* (1956) vol. 1

16 How often are we to die before we go quite off this stage? In every friend we lose a part of ourselves, and the best part.
letter to Jonathan Swift, 5 December 1732, in G. Sherburn (ed.) *Correspondence of Alexander Pope* (1956) vol. 3

17 To endeavour to work upon the vulgar with fine sense, is like attempting to hew blocks with a razor.
Miscellanies (1727) vol. 2 'Thoughts on Various Subjects'

18 A man should never be ashamed to own he has been in the wrong, which is but saying, in other words, that he is wiser to-day than he was yesterday.
Miscellanies (1727) vol. 2 'Thoughts on Various Subjects'

19 It is with narrow-souled people as with narrow-necked bottles: the less they have in them, the more noise they make in pouring it out.
Miscellanies (1727) vol. 2 'Thoughts on Various Subjects'

20 When men grow virtuous in their old age, they only make a sacrifice to God of the devil's leavings.
Miscellanies (1727) vol. 2 'Thoughts on Various Subjects'

21 The most positive men are the most credulous.
Miscellanies (1727) vol. 2 'Thoughts on Various Subjects'

22 All gardening is landscape-painting.
Joseph Spence *Anecdotes* (ed. J. Osborn, 1966) no. 606

23 Here am I, dying of a hundred good symptoms.
to George, Lord Lyttelton, 15 May 1744, in Joseph Spence *Anecdotes* (ed. J. Osborn, 1966) no. 637

Karl Popper 1902–94
Austrian-born philosopher

24 I shall certainly admit a system as empirical or scientific only if it is capable of being *tested* by experience. These considerations suggest that not the *verifiability* but the *falsifiability* of a system is to be taken as a criterion of demarcation . . . *It must be possible for an empirical scientific system to be refuted by experience.*
The Logic of Scientific Discovery (1934) ch. 1, sect. 6

25 We may become the makers of our fate when we have ceased to pose as its prophets.
The Open Society and its Enemies (1945) introduction

26 We should therefore claim, in the name of tolerance, the right not to tolerate the intolerant.
The Open Society and Its Enemies (1945) ch. 7

27 We must plan for freedom, and not only for security, if for no other reason than that only freedom can make security secure.
The Open Society and its Enemies (1945) vol. 2, ch. 21

28 There is no history of mankind, there are only many histories of all kinds of aspects of human life. And one of these is the history of political power. This is elevated into the history of the world.
The Open Society and its Enemies (1945) vol. 2, ch. 25

29 Science must begin with myths, and with the criticism of myths.
'The Philosophy of Science' in C. A. Mace (ed.) *British Philosophy in the Mid-Century* (1957)

30 On the pre-scientific level we hate the very idea that we may be mistaken. So we cling dogmatically to our conjectures, as long as possible. On the scientific level, we systematically search for our mistakes . . . Thus on the pre-scientific level, we are often ourselves destroyed, eliminated, with our false theories; we perish with our false theories. On the scientific level, we systematically try to eliminate our false theories—we try to let our false theories die in our stead.

B. Magee (ed.) *Modern British Philosophy* (1971) 'Conversation with Karl Popper'

Cole Porter 1891–1964

American songwriter

1 But I'm always true to you, darlin', in my fashion.
Yes I'm always true to you, darlin', in my way.

'Always True to You in my Fashion' (1949 song)

2 In olden days a glimpse of stocking
Was looked on as something shocking
Now, heaven knows,
Anything goes.

'Anything Goes' (1934 song)

3 When they begin the Beguine
It brings back the sound of music so tender,
It brings back a night of tropical splendour,
It brings back a memory ever green.

'Begin the Beguine' (1935 song)

4 But how strange the change from major to minor
Every time we say goodbye.

'Every Time We Say Goodbye' (1944 song)

5 I get no kick from champagne,
Mere alcohol doesn't thrill me at all,
So tell me why should it be true
That I get a kick out of you?

'I Get a Kick Out of You' (1934 song) in *Anything Goes*

6 It was great fun,
But it was just one of those things.

'Just One of Those Things' (1935 song)

7 Birds do it, bees do it,
Even educated fleas do it.
Let's do it, let's fall in love.

'Let's Do It' (1954 song; words added to the 1928 original)

8 Miss Otis regrets (she's unable to lunch today).

title of song (1934)

9 My heart belongs to Daddy.

title of song (1938)

10 Night and day, you are the one,
Only you beneath the moon and under the sun.

'Night and Day' (1932 song) in *Gay Divorce*

11 Have you heard it's in the stars,
Next July we collide with Mars?
WELL, DID YOU EVAH! What a swell party this is.

'Well, Did You Evah?' (1940 song; revived for the film *High Society*, 1956)

12 You're the top! You're the Coliseum,
You're the top! You're the Louvre Museum,
You're a melody
From a symphony by Strauss,
You're a Bendel bonnet,
A Shakespeare sonnet,
You're Mickey Mouse!

'You're the Top' (1934 song) in *Anything Goes*

Beilby Porteus 1731–1808

English poet and prelate

13 . . . One murder made a villain,
Millions a hero.

Death (1759) l. 154; cf. **Rostand** 635:16, **Young** 838:20

14 War its thousands slays, Peace its ten thousands.

Death (1759) l. 179; cf. **Bible** 78:34

15 Teach him how to live,
And, oh! still harder lesson! how to die.

Death (1759) l. 319

Francis Pott 1832–1909

English clergyman

16 The strife is o'er, the battle done;
Now is the Victor's triumph won;
O let the song of praise be sung:
Alleluia!

'The strife is o'er, the battle done' (1861 hymn); translation of 'Finita iam sunt praelia' (*c.*1695)

Beatrix Potter 1866–1943

English writer for children

17 In the time of swords and periwigs and full-skirted coats with flowered lappets—when gentlemen wore ruffles, and gold-laced waistcoats of paduasoy and taffeta—there lived a tailor in Gloucester.

The Tailor of Gloucester (1903) p. 9

18 I am worn to a ravelling . . . I am undone and worn to a thread-paper, for I have NO MORE TWIST.

The Tailor of Gloucester (1903)

19 It is said that the effect of eating too much lettuce is 'soporific'.

The Tale of the Flopsy Bunnies (1909)

20 Don't go into Mr McGregor's garden: your father had an accident there, he was put into a pie by Mrs McGregor.

The Tale of Peter Rabbit (1902)

Dennis Potter 1935–94

English television dramatist

21 Below my window . . . the blossom is out in full now . . . I *see* it is the whitest, frothiest, blossomiest blossom that there ever could be, and I can see it. Things are both more trivial than they ever were, and more important than they ever were, and the difference between the trivial and the important doesn't seem to matter. But the nowness of everything is absolutely wondrous.

on his heightened awareness of things, in the face of his imminent death

interview with Melvyn Bragg on Channel 4, March 1994, in *Seeing the Blossom* (1994)

22 Religion to me has always been the wound, not the bandage.

interview with Melvyn Bragg on Channel 4, March 1994, in *Seeing the Blossom* (1994)

23 But the cigarette, well, I love stroking this lovely tube of delight.

interview with Melvyn Bragg on Channel 4, March 1994, in *Seeing the Blossom* (1994)

Stephen Potter 1900–69

British writer

1 A good general rule is to state that the bouquet is better than the taste, and vice versa.
on wine-tasting
One-Upmanship (1952) ch. 14

2 *How to be one up*—how to make the other man feel that something has gone wrong, however slightly.
Lifemanship (1950)

3 'Yes, but not in the South', with slight adjustments, will do for any argument about any place, if not about any person.
Lifemanship (1950) p. 43

4 The theory and practice of gamesmanship or The art of winning games without actually cheating.
title of book (1947)

Eugène Pottier 1816–87

French politician

5 *Debout! les damnés de la terre!*
Debout! les forçats de la faim!
La raison tonne en son cratère,
C'est l'éruption de la fin . . .
Nous ne sommes rien, soyons tout!
C'est la lutte finale
Groupons-nous, et, demain,
L'Internationale
Sera le genre humain.
On your feet, you damned souls of the earth! On your feet, inmates of hunger's prison! Reason is rumbling in its crater, and its final eruption is on its way . . . We are nothing, let us be everything! This is the final conflict: let us form up and, tomorrow, the International will encompass the human race.
'L'Internationale' (1871); in H. E. Piggot *Songs that made History* (1937) ch. 8

Ezra Pound 1885–1972

American poet

6 Winter is icummen in,
Lhude sing Goddamm,
Raineth drop and staineth slop,
And how the wind doth ramm!
Sing: Goddamm.
'Ancient Music' (1917); cf. **Anonymous** 18:22

7 With usura hath no man a house of good stone
each block cut smooth and well fitting.
Cantos (1954) no. 45

8 Tching prayed on the mountain and
wrote MAKE IT NEW
on his bath tub.
Cantos (1954) no. 53; cf. **Bible** 113:8

9 Bah! I have sung women in three cities,
But it is all the same;
And I will sing of the sun.
'Cino' (1908)

10 Hang it all, Robert Browning,
There can be but the one 'Sordello'.
Draft of XXX Cantos (1930) no. 2

11 And even I can remember
A day when the historians left blanks in their
writings,
I mean for things they didn't know.
Draft of XXX Cantos (1930) no. 13

12 For three years, out of key with his time,
He strove to resuscitate the dead art
Of poetry; to maintain 'the sublime'
In the old sense. Wrong from the start.
Hugh Selwyn Mauberley (1920) 'E. P. *Ode pour l'élection de son sépulcre*' pt. 1

13 His true Penelope was Flaubert,
He fished by obstinate isles;
Observed the elegance of Circe's hair
Rather than the mottoes on sundials.
Hugh Selwyn Mauberley (1920) 'E. P. *Ode* . . . ' pt. 1

14 The age demanded an image
Of its accelerated grimace,
Something for the modern stage,
Not, at any rate, an Attic grace.
Hugh Selwyn Mauberley (1920) 'E. P. *Ode* . . . ' pt. 2

15 Christ follows Dionysus,
Phallic and ambrosial
Made way for macerations;
Caliban casts out Ariel.
Hugh Selwyn Mauberley (1920) 'E. P. *Ode* . . . ' pt. 3

16 Died some, pro patria,
non 'dulce' non 'et decor' . . .
walked eye-deep in hell
believing in old men's lies, the unbelieving
came home, home to a lie.
Hugh Selwyn Mauberley (1920) 'E. P. *Ode* . . . ' pt. 4; cf. **Horace** 388:14

17 There died a myriad,
And of the best, among them,
For an old bitch gone in the teeth,
For a botched civilization.
Hugh Selwyn Mauberley (1920) 'E. P. *Ode* . . . ' pt. 5

18 The apparition of these faces in the crowd;
Petals on a wet, black bough.
'In a Station of the Metro' (1916)

19 O woe, woe,
People are born and die,
We also shall be dead pretty soon
Therefore let us act as if we were dead already.
Mr Housman's Message (1911)

20 The ant's a centaur in his dragon world.
Pisan Cantos (1948) no. 81

21 Pull down thy vanity,
Paquin pull down!
The green casque has outdone your elegance.
Pisan Cantos (1948) no. 81

22 Pull down thy VANITY
Thou art a beaten dog beneath the hail,
A swollen magpie in a fitful sun,
Half black half white
Nor knowst'ou wing from tail.
Pisan Cantos (1948) no. 81

23 The leaves fall early this autumn, in wind.
The paired butterflies are already yellow with
August

Over the grass in the West garden;
They hurt me. I grow older.
If you are coming down through the narrows of
the river Kiang,
Please let me know beforehand,
And I will come out to meet you
As far as Cho-fu-Sa.

'The River Merchant's Wife' (1915); from the Chinese of Rihaku

1 He hath not heart for harping, nor in ring-having
Nor winsomeness to wife, nor world's delight
Nor any whit else save the wave's slash,
Yet longing comes upon him to fare forth on the
water.
Bosque takes blossom, cometh beauty of berries.

'The Seafarer' (1912); from the Anglo-Saxon original

2 Music begins to atrophy when it departs too far from the dance; that poetry begins to atrophy when it gets too far from music.

The ABC of Reading (1934) 'Warning'

3 Literature is news that STAYS news.

The ABC of Reading (1934) ch. 2

4 Real education must ultimately be limited to one who INSISTS on knowing, the rest is mere sheep-herding.

The ABC of Reading (1934) ch. 8

5 Great literature is simply language charged with meaning to the utmost possible degree.

How To Read (1931) pt. 2

6 Poetry must be *as well written as prose.*

letter to Harriet Monroe, January 1915, in D. D. Paige (ed.) *Selected Letters of Ezra Pound* (1950)

Nicolas Poussin 1594–1665

French painter

7 An imitation in lines and colours on any surface of all that is to be found under the sun.

of painting

letter to M. de Chambray, 1665; C. Jouamy (ed.) *Correspondance de Nicolas Poussin* (1911)

Anthony Powell 1905–2000

English novelist

8 Books do furnish a room.

title of novel (1971); cf. **Smith** 725:15

9 A dance to the music of time.

title of novel sequence (1951–75), after

Le 4 stagioni che ballano al suono del tempo.

The four seasons dancing to the sound of time.

title given by Giovanni Pietro Bellori to a painting by Nicolas **Poussin**

10 He's so wet you could shoot snipe off him.

A Question of Upbringing (1951) ch. 1

11 Growing old is like being increasingly penalized for a crime you haven't committed.

Temporary Kings (1973) ch. 1

Colin Powell 1937–

American general

12 First, we are going to cut it off, and then, we are going to kill it.

strategy for dealing with the Iraqi Army in the Gulf War

at a press conference, 23 January 1991

Dilys Powell 1902–95

English critic and writer

13 You come out of *Gone With the Wind* feeling that history isn't so disturbing after all. One can always make a dress out of a curtain.

in *Independent on Sunday* 29 April 1990

Enoch Powell 1912–98

British Conservative politician

14 History is littered with the wars which everybody knew would never happen.

speech to the Conservative Party Conference, 19 October 1967, in *The Times* 20 October 1967

15 As I look ahead, I am filled with foreboding. Like the Roman, I seem to see 'the River Tiber foaming with much blood'.

speech at the Annual Meeting of the West Midlands Area Conservative Political Centre, Birmingham, 20 April 1968, in *Observer* 21 April 1968; cf. **Virgil** 794:16

16 Judas was paid! I am sacrificing my whole political life.

response to a heckler's call of 'Judas', having advised Conservatives to vote Labour at the coming general election

speech at Bull Ring, Birmingham, 23 February 1974

17 To write a diary every day is like returning to one's own vomit.

interview in *Sunday Times* 6 November 1977

18 For a politician to complain about the press is like a ship's captain complaining about the sea.

in *Guardian* 3 December 1984

19 ANNE BROWN: How would you like to be remembered?
ENOCH POWELL: I should like to have been killed in the war.

in a radio interview, 13 April 1986

20 To be and to remain a member of the House of Commons was the overriding and undiscussable motivation of my life as a politician.

'Theory and Practice' 1990

21 All political lives, unless they are cut off in midstream at a happy juncture, end in failure, because that is the nature of politics and of human affairs.

Joseph Chamberlain (1977)

John Powell 1645–1713

English judge

22 Nothing is law that is not reason.

Lord Raymond's *Reports* (1765) vol. 2

John O'Connor Power 1848–1919
Irish lawyer and politician

1 The mules of politics: without pride of ancestry, or hope of posterity.
of the Liberal Unionists
H. H. Asquith *Memories and Reflections* (1928) vol. 1, ch. 16; cf. **Disraeli** 270:4

Terry Pratchett 1948–
English science fiction writer

2 Personal isn't the same as important.
Men at Arms (1993)

3 Most modern fantasy just rearranges the furniture in Tolkien's attic.
Stan Nicholls (ed.) *Wordsmiths of Wonder* (1993)

□ Prayers
see box overleaf

John Prescott 1938–
British Labour politician

4 People like me were branded, pigeon-holed, a ceiling put on our ambitions.
on failing his 11-plus
speech at Ruskin College, Oxford, 13 June 1996; in *Guardian* 14 June 1996

5 We did it! Let's wallow in our victory!
on Tony ***Blair****'s warning that the Labour Party should not be triumphalist in victory*
speech to the Labour Party Conference, 29 September 1997

Keith Preston 1884–1927
American poet

6 Of all the literary scenes
Saddest this sight to me:
The graves of little magazines
Who died to make verse free.
'The Liberators'

Jacques Prévert 1900–77
French poet and screenwriter

7 *C'est tellement simple, l'amour.*
Love is so simple.
Les Enfants du Paradis (1945 film)

Anthony Price 1928–
English thriller writer and editor

8 The Devil himself had probably redesigned Hell in the light of information he had gained from observing airport layouts.
The Memory Trap (1989)

Richard Price 1723–91
English nonconformist minister

9 Now, methinks, I see the ardour for liberty catching and spreading; a general amendment beginning in human affairs; the dominion of kings changed for the dominion of laws, and the dominion of priests giving way to the dominion of reason and conscience.
A Discourse on the Love of our Country (1790)

Gerald Priestland 1927–91
English writer and journalist

10 Journalists belong in the gutter because that is where the ruling classes throw their guilty secrets.
on Radio London 19 May 1988; in *Observer* 22 May 1988

J. B. Priestley 1894–1984
English novelist, dramatist, and critic

11 I never read the life of any important person without discovering that he knew more and could do more than I could ever hope to know or to do in half a dozen lifetimes.
Apes and Angels (1928)

12 The first fall of snow is not only an event, but it is a magical event. You go to bed in one kind of world and wake up to find yourself in another quite different, and if this is not enchantment, then where is it to be found?
Apes and Angels (1928) 'First Snow'

13 To say that these men paid their shillings to watch twenty-two hirelings kick a ball is merely to say that a violin is wood and catgut, that *Hamlet* is so much paper and ink. For a shilling the Bruddersford United AFC offered you Conflict and Art.
Good Companions (1929) bk. 1, ch. 1

14 I can't help feeling wary when I hear anything said about the masses. First you take their faces from 'em by calling 'em the masses and then you accuse 'em of not having any faces.
Saturn Over the Water (1961) ch. 2

15 This little steamer, like all her brave and battered sisters, is immortal. She'll go sailing proudly down the years in the epic of Dunkirk. And our great-grand-children, when they learn how we began this war by snatching glory out of defeat, and then swept on to victory, may also learn how the little holiday steamers made an excursion to hell and came back glorious.
radio broadcast, 5 June 1940, in *Listener* 13 June 1940

16 The weakness of American civilization, and perhaps the chief reason why it creates so much discontent, is that it is so curiously abstract. It is a bloodless extrapolation of a satisfying life . . . You dine off the advertiser's 'sizzling' and not the meat of the steak.
in *New Statesman* 10 December 1971

on being awarded the Order of Merit in 1977:
17 I've only two things to say about it. First I deserve it. Second, they've been too long about giving me it. There'll be another vacancy very soon.
in a radio interview, October 1977; John Braine *J. B. Priestley* (1978)

Prayers

1 *Ave Maria, gratia plena, Dominus tecum: Benedicta tu in mulieribus, et benedictus fructus ventris tui, Jesus.*

Hail Mary, full of grace, the Lord is with thee: Blessed art thou among women, and blessed is the fruit of thy womb, Jesus.

'Ave Maria' or 'Hail Mary', also known as 'The Angelic Salutation', dating from the 11th century; cf. **Bible** 98:15

2 From ghoulies and ghosties and long-leggety beasties
And things that go bump in the night,
Good Lord, deliver us!

'The Cornish or West Country Litany', in Francis T. Nettleinghame *Polperro Proverbs and Others* (1926) 'Pokerwork Panels'

3 God be in my head,
And in my understanding;
God be in my eyes,
And in my looking;
God be in my mouth,
And in my speaking;
God be in my heart,
And in my thinking;
God be at my end,
And at my departing.

Sarum Missal (11th century)

4 Matthew, Mark, Luke, and John,
The bed be blest that I lie on.
Four angels to my bed,
Four angels round my head,
One to watch, and one to pray,
And two to bear my soul away.

traditional (the first two lines in Thomas Ady *A Candle in the Dark*, 1656)

5 Now I lay me down to sleep;
I pray the Lord my soul to keep.
If I should die before I wake,
I pray the Lord my soul to take.

first printed in a late edition of the *New England Primer* (1781)

6 *Salve, regina, mater misericordiae,*
Vita, dulcedo et spes nostra, salve!
Ad te clamamus exsules filii Evae,
Ad te suspiramus gementes et flentes
In hac lacrimarum valle.
Eia ergo, advocata nostra,
Illos tuos misericordes oculos ad nos converte.
Et Iesum, benedictum fructum ventris tui,
Nobis post hoc exsilium ostende,
O clemens, o pia,
O dulcis virgo Maria.

Hail holy queen, mother of mercy, hail our life, our sweetness, and our hope! To thee do we cry, poor banished children of Eve; to thee do we send up our sighs, mourning and weeping in this vale of tears. Turn then, most gracious advocate, thine eyes of mercy towards us; and after this our exile show unto us the blessed fruit of thy womb, Jesus, O clement, O loving, O sweet virgin Mary.

attributed to various 11th century authors; *Analecta Hymnica* vol. 50 (1907) p. 318

7 *Te Deum laudamus: Te Dominum confitemur.*

We praise thee, God: we own thee Lord.

'Te Deum'; hymn traditionally attributed to St **Ambrose** and St **Augustine** in AD 387, though more recently to St Niceta (d. *c.*414); cf. **Book of Common Prayer** 125:20, **Prayers** 592:8

8 *In te Domine, speravi: non confundar in aeternum.*

Lord, I have set my hopes in thee, I shall not be destroyed for ever.

'Te Deum'; cf. **Book of Common Prayer** 126:2, **Prayers** 592:7

Joseph Priestley 1733–1804

English nonconformist minister
see also **Bentham** *66:18*

9 Every man, when he comes to be sensible of his natural rights, and to feel his own importance, will consider himself as fully equal to any other person whatever.

An Essay on the First Principles of Government (1768) pt. 1

Matthew Prior 1664–1721

English poet

10 I court others in verse: but I love thee in prose:
And they have my whimsies, but thou hast my heart.

'A Better Answer' (1718)

11 Be to her virtues very kind;
Be to her faults a little blind;
Let all her ways be unconfined;
And clap your padlock—on her mind.

'An English Padlock' (1705) l. 79

12 Nobles and heralds, by your leave,
Here lies what once was Matthew Prior,
The son of Adam and of Eve,
Can Stuart or Nassau go higher?

'Epitaph' (1702)

13 For the idiom of words very little she heeded,
Provided the matter she drove at succeeded,
She took and gave languages just as she needed.

'Jinny the Just' (after 1700)

14 Venus, take my votive glass;
Since I am not what I was,
What from this day I shall be,
Venus, let me never see.

'The Lady who Offers her Looking-Glass to Venus' (1718)

15 The merchant, to secure his treasure,
Conveys it in a borrowed name:
Euphelia serves to grace my measure;

But Chloe is my real flame.
'An Ode' (1709)

1 He ranged his tropes, and preached up patience;
Backed his opinion with quotations.
'Paulo Purganti and his Wife' (1709) l. 138

2 Cured yesterday of my disease,
I died last night of my physician.
'The Remedy Worse than the Disease' (1727)

3 What is a King?—a man condemned to bear
The public burden of the nation's care.
Solomon (1718) bk. 3, l. 275

4 For, as our different ages move,
'Tis so ordained (would Fate but mend it!)
That I shall be past making love,
When she begins to comprehend it.
'To a Child of Quality of Five Years Old' (1704)

5 From ignorance our comfort flows,
The only wretched are the wise.
'To the Hon. Charles Montague' (1692) st. 9; cf. **Gray** 350:18

6 No, no; for my virginity,
When I lose that, says Rose, I'll die:
Behind the elms last night, cried Dick,
Rose, were you not extremely sick?
'A True Maid' (1718)

7 They never taste who always drink;
They always talk, who never think.
'Upon this Passage in Scaligerana' (1740)

V. S. Pritchett 1900–97

English writer and critic

8 The principle of procrastinated rape is said to be the ruling one in all the great best-sellers.
The Living Novel (1946) 'Clarissa'

9 The detective novel is the art-for-art's-sake of our yawning Philistinism, the classic example of a specialized form of art removed from contact with the life it pretends to build on.
in *New Statesman* 16 June 1951 'Books in General'

Procopius AD *c.*499—565

Byzantine administrator and historian

10 So the church has become a spectacle of marvellous beauty, overwhelming to those who see it, but to those who know it by hearsay altogether incredible. For it soars on high to match the sky, and as if surging up from amongst the other buildings it stands on high and looks down on the remainder of the city.
of the church of the Hagia Sophia; cf. ***Justinian*** *424:2*
Buildings

Adelaide Ann Procter 1825–64

English writer of popular verse

11 A lost chord.
title of poem (1858)

12 Seated one day at the organ,
I was weary and ill at ease,
And my fingers wandered idly
Over the noisy keys.
'A Lost Chord' (1858)

13 But I struck one chord of music,
Like the sound of a great Amen.
'A Lost Chord' (1858)

14 It may be that Death's bright Angel
Will speak in that chord again
It may be that only in Heaven
I shall hear that grand Amen.
'A Lost Chord' (1858)

Propertius *c.*50–after 16 BC

Roman poet

15 *Navita de ventis, de tauris narrat arator,*
Enumerat miles vulnera, pastor oves.
The seaman tells stories of winds, the ploughman of bulls; the soldier details his wounds, the shepherd his sheep.
Elegies bk. 2, no. 1, l. 43

16 *Quod si deficiant vires, audacia certe*
Laus erit: in magnis et voluisse sat est.
Even if strength fail, boldness at least will deserve praise: in great endeavours even to have had the will is enough.
Elegies bk. 2, no. 10, l. 5

17 *Cedite Romani scriptores, cedite Grai!*
Nescioquid maius nascitur Iliade.
Make way, you Roman writers, make way, Greeks! Something greater than the Iliad is born.
of ***Virgil****'s* Aeneid
Elegies bk. 2, no. 34, l. 65

Protagoras b. *c.*485 BC

Greek sophist

18 That man is the measure of all things.
Plato *Theaetetus* 160d; cf. **Proverbs** 606:16

Pierre-Joseph Proudhon 1809–65

French social reformer

19 *La propriété c'est le vol.*
Property is theft.
Qu'est-ce que la propriété? (1840) ch. 1

Marcel Proust 1871–1922

French novelist
see also **Borrowed titles** *144:13*
Textual translations are those of C. K. Scott-Moncrieff and S. Hudson, revised by T. Kilmartin, 1981

20 *Longtemps, je me suis couché de bonne heure.*
For a long time I used to go to bed early.
Du côté de chez Swann (Swann's Way, 1913) vol. 1, p. 1

21 *Et tout d'un coup le souvenir m'est apparu. Ce goût c'était celui du petit morceau de madeleine que le dimanche matin à Combray . . . ma tante Léonie m'offrait après l'avoir trempé dans son infusion de thé ou de tilleul.*
And suddenly the memory revealed itself. The taste was that of the little piece of madeleine which on

Sunday mornings at Combray . . . my aunt Léonie used to give me, dipping it first in her own cup of tea or tisane.

Du côté de chez Swann (Swann's Way, 1913) vol. 1

1 *Et il ne fut plus question de Swann chez les Verdurin.*

After which there was no more talk of Swann at the Verdurins'.

Du côté de chez Swann (Swann's Way, 1913) vol. 2

2 *Dire que j'ai gâché des années de ma vie, que j'ai voulu mourir, que j'ai eu mon plus grand amour, pour une femme qui ne me plaisait pas, qui n'était pas mon genre!*

To think that I've wasted years of my life, that I've longed to die, that I've experienced my greatest love for a woman who didn't appeal to me, who wasn't even my type!

Du côté de chez Swann (Swann's Way, 1913) vol. 2

3 *On devient moral dès qu'on est malheureux.*

One becomes moral as soon as one is unhappy.

A l'ombre des jeunes filles en fleurs (Within a Budding Grove, 1918) vol. 1

4 *Tout ce que nous connaissons de grand nous vient des nerveux. Ce sont eux et non pas d'autres qui ont fondé les religions et composé les chefs-d'œuvre. Jamais le monde ne saura tout ce qu'il leur doit et surtout ce qu'eux ont souffert pour le lui donner.*

Everything we think of as great has come to us from neurotics. It is they and they alone who found religions and create great works of art. The world will never realise how much it owes to them and what they have suffered in order to bestow their gifts on it.

Le Côté de Guermantes (Guermantes Way, 1921) vol. 1

5 *Il n'y a rien comme le désir pour empêcher les choses qu'on dit d'avoir aucune ressemblance avec ce qu'on a dans la pensée.*

There is nothing like desire for preventing the things one says from bearing any resemblance to what one has in one's mind.

Le Côté de Guermantes (Guermantes Way, 1921) vol. 2

6 *Un artiste n'a pas besoin d'exprimer directement sa pensée dans son ouvrage pour que celui-ci en reflète la qualité; on a même pu dire que la louange la plus haute de Dieu est dans la négation de l'athée qui trouve la Création assez parfaite pour se passer d'un créateur.*

An artist has no need to express his thought directly in his work for the latter to reflect its quality; it has even been said that the highest praise of God consists in the denial of Him by the atheist who finds creation so perfect that it can dispense with a creator.

Le Côté de Guermantes (Guermantes Way, 1921) vol. 2

7 *J'ai horreur des couchers de soleil, c'est romantique, c'est opéra.*

I have a horror of sunsets, they're so romantic, so operatic.

Sodome et Gomorrhe (Cities of the Plain, 1922) vol. 1

8 *On ne guérit d'une souffrance qu'à condition de l'éprouver pleinement.*

We are healed of a suffering only by experiencing it to the full.

Albertine disparue (The Sweet Cheat Gone, 1925) ch. 1

9 *Une de ces dépêches dont M. de Guermantes avait spirituellement fixé le modèle: 'Impossible venir, mensonge suit'.*

One of those telegrams of which M. de Guermantes had wittily fixed the formula: 'Cannot come, lie follows'.

Le Temps retrouvé (Time Regained, 1926) ch. 1; cf. **Telegrams** 758:11

10 *Les vrais paradis sont les paradis qu'on a perdus.*

The true paradises are the paradises that we have lost.

Le Temps retrouvé (Time Regained, 1926) ch. 3

11 *Le bonheur seul est salutaire pour le corps, mais c'est le chagrin qui développe les forces de l'esprit.*

For if unhappiness develops the forces of the mind, happiness alone is salutary to the body.

Le Temps retrouvé (Time Regained, 1926) ch. 3, p. 259

Proverbs

see also ***Sayings and slogans***

Dates given are generally for the first written appearance of a form of the proverb in English; the proverb may well have been in spoken use much earlier, and in many cases is cited as 'an old saying' at that time. For more detailed information, see The Concise Oxford Dictionary of Proverbs

12 Absence makes the heart grow fonder.

mid 19th century; 1st century BC in Latin

13 Accidents will happen (in the best-regulated families).

mid 19th century; cf. **Dickens** 262:2

14 Actions speak louder than words.

early 17th century

15 Adventures are to the adventurous.

mid 19th century

16 Adversity makes strange bedfellows.

mid 19th century; cf. **Shakespeare** 698:33

17 After a storm comes a calm.

late 14th century

18 After dinner rest awhile, after supper walk a mile.

late 16th century

19 The age of miracles is past.

late sixteenth century

20 All cats are grey in the dark.

mid 16th century

21 All good things must come to an end.

mid 15th century

22 All is fish that comes to the net.

early 16th century

23 All is grist that comes to the mill.

grist = *corn which is to be ground*

mid 17th century

24 All roads lead to Rome.

late 14th century; earlier in Latin

25 All's fair in love and war.

early 17th century

1 All's for the best in the best of all possible worlds.
early 20th century, from **Voltaire**; see **Voltaire** 797:5

2 All's well that ends well.
late 14th century

3 All that glitters is not gold.
early 13th century

4 All things are possible with God.
late 17th century; see **Bible** 96:16

5 All things come to those who wait.
early 16th century

6 All work and no play makes Jack a dull boy.
mid 17th century

7 Always a bridesmaid, never a bride.
early 20th century; cf. **Leigh** 463:2

8 Any port in a storm.
mid 18th century

9 Any publicity is good publicity.
early 20th century; cf. **Behan** 62:5

10 An ape's an ape, a varlet's a varlet, though they be clad in silk or scarlet.
mid 16th century; 2nd century AD in Greek

11 Appearances are deceptive.
mid 17th century

12 Appetite comes with eating.
mid 17th century, from **Rabelais**; see **Rabelais** 619:9

13 An apple a day keeps the doctor away.
mid 19th century

14 The apple never falls far from the tree.
mid nineteenth century

15 April showers bring forth May flowers.
mid 16th century

16 An army marches on its stomach.
mid 19th century, variously attributed to **Frederick** the Great and **Napoleon**; see **Napoleon** 539:1

17 Art is long and life is short.
late 14th century, from **Hippocrates**; see **Chaucer** 206:28, **Hippocrates** 377:15

18 As a tree falls, so shall it lie.
mid 16th century; see **Bible** 84:28

19 As good be an addled egg as an idle bird.
late 16th century

20 As the day lengthens, so the cold strengthens.
early 17th century

21 As the twig is bent, so is the tree inclined.
early 18th century, from **Pope**; see **Pope** 584:1

22 As you bake so shall you brew.
late 16th century

23 As you brew, so shall you bake.
late 16th century

24 As you make your bed, so you must lie upon it.
late 16th century, late 15th century in French

25 As you sow, so you reap.
late 15th century; see **Bible** 107:22

26 Ask a silly question and you get a silly answer.
early 14th century

27 Ask no questions and hear no lies.
late 18th century

28 Attack is the best form of defence.
usually quoted as 'the best defence is a good offence' in the US
late 18th century

29 A bad excuse is better than none.
mid 16th century

30 Bad money drives out good.
known as Gresham's Law, after Sir Thomas Gresham (c.1519–79), who formulated the principle, though not the proverb, in 1558
early twentieth century

31 Bad news travels fast.
late 16th century

32 A bad penny always turns up.
mid 18th century

33 A bad workman blames his tools.
early 17th century; late 13th century in French

34 A barking dog never bites.
mid 16th century; 13th century in French

35 Barnaby bright, Barnaby bright, the longest day and the shortest night.
St Barnabas' Day, 11 June, in Old Style reckoned the longest day of the year
mid 17th century

36 Bear and forbear.
late 16th century

37 Beauty draws with a single hair.
late 16th century; cf. **Howell** 391:17, **Pope** 587:2

38 Beauty is in the eye of the beholder.
mid 18th century; 3rd century BC in Greek

39 Beauty is only skin deep.
early 17th century

40 Beggars can't be choosers.
mid 16th century

41 Be just before you're generous.
mid eighteenth century

42 Believe nothing of what you hear, and only half of what you see.
mid 19th century

43 A bellowing cow soon forgets her calf.
late 19th century

44 The best doctors are Dr Diet, Dr Quiet, and Dr Merryman.
mid sixteenth century

45 The best is the enemy of the good.
mid nineteenth century; cf. **Voltaire** 797:11

46 The best of friends must part.
early seventeenth century

47 The best of men are but men at best.
late seventeenth century

48 The best things come in small packages.
late nineteenth century

49 The best things in life are free.
early twentieth century, from **De Sylva**; cf. **De Sylva** 259:3

1 The best-laid schemes of mice and men gang aft agley.
late eighteenth century, from **Burns**; cf. **Burns** 168:24

2 Be the day weary or be the day long, at last it ringeth to evensong.
early 16th century

3 Better a dinner of herbs than a stalled ox where hate is.
mid 16th century; see **Bible** 82:36

4 Better a good cow than a cow of a good kind.
early 20th century

5 Better be an old man's darling than a young man's slave.
mid 16th century

6 Better be envied than pitied.
mid 16th century; 5th century BC in Greek

7 Better be out of the world than out of the fashion.
mid 17th century

8 Better be safe than sorry.
mid 19th century

9 Better late than never.
early 14th century; 1st century BC in Greek

10 Better one house spoiled than two.
of two wicked or foolish people joined in marriage
late 16th century

11 The better the day, the better the deed.
early seventeenth century

12 Better the devil you know than the devil you don't know.
mid 19th century

13 Better to wear out than to rust out.
early 18th century; cf. **Cumberland** 247:2, **Shakespeare** 669:27

14 Better wed over the mixen than over the moor.
mixen = *midden; better to marry a neighbour than a stranger*
early 17th century

15 Between two stools one falls to the ground.
late 14th century

16 Beware of an oak, it draws the stroke; avoid an ash, it counts the flash; creep under the thorn, it can save you from harm.
on where to shelter from lightning
late 19th century

17 Be what you would seem to be.
late 14th century

18 Big fish eat little fish.
early 13th century

19 Big fleas have little fleas upon their backs to bite them, and little fleas have lesser fleas, and so *ad infinitum.*
early 18th century, from **Swift**; see **Swift** 749:19

20 The bigger they are, the harder they fall.
early twentieth century; cf. **Fitzsimmons** 315:20

21 A bird in the hand is worth two in the bush.
mid 15th century; 13th century in Latin

22 A bird never flew on one wing.
early 18th century

23 Birds in their little nests agree.
early 18th century, from **Watts**; see **Watts** 805:10

24 Birds of a feather flock together.
mid 16th century

25 A bleating sheep loses a bite.
late 16th century

26 Blessed are the dead that the rain rains on.
early 17th century

27 Blessed is he who expects nothing, for he shall never be disappointed.
early 18th century

28 Blessings brighten as they take their flight.
mid 18th century

29 A blind man's wife needs no paint.
mid 17th century

30 Blood is thicker than water.
early 19th century

31 The blood of the martyrs is the seed of the Church.
mid sixteenth century; cf. **Tertullian** 768:15

32 Blood will have blood.
mid 15th century; cf. **Shakespeare** 684:14

33 Blood will tell.
mid 19th century

34 Blue are the hills that are far away.
late 19th century, northern in origin

35 Boys will be boys.
occasionally 'girls will be girls'
early 17th century

36 Brag is a good dog, but Holdfast is better.
early 18th century

37 Brave men lived before Agamemnon.
early 19th century; cf. **Horace** 389:9

38 The bread never falls but on its buttered side.
mid nineteenth century

39 Brevity is the soul of wit.
early 17th century, from **Shakespeare**; see **Shakespeare** 663:9

40 A bully is always a coward.
early 19th century

41 A burnt child dreads the fire.
mid 13th century

42 The busiest men have the most leisure.
late nineteenth century

43 Business before pleasure.
mid 19th century

44 The buyer has need of a hundred eyes, the seller of but one.
mid seventeenth century

45 Buy in the cheapest market and sell in the dearest.
late 16th century

46 Caesar's wife must be above suspicion.
late 18th century; see **Caesar** 180:17

1 Call no man happy till he dies.
mid 16th century; cf. **Solon** 727:9

2 Candlemas day, put beans in the clay; put candles and candlesticks away.
late 17th century

3 Care killed the cat.
late 16th century; cf. **Shakespeare** 691:21

4 A carpenter is known by his chips.
early 16th century

5 Catching's before hanging.
early 19th century

6 A cat in gloves catches no mice.
late 16th century; 14th century in French

7 A cat may look at a king.
mid 16th century

8 The cat would eat fish, but would not wet her feet.
early thirteenth century

9 A chain is no stronger than its weakest link.
mid 19th century

10 A change is as good as a rest.
late 19th century

11 Charity begins at home.
late 14th century

12 Charity covers a multitude of sins.
early 17th century; see **Bible** 111:6

13 Cheats never prosper.
early 19th century

14 A cherry year, a merry year; a plum year, a dumb year.
late 17th century

15 The child is the father of the man.
early nineteenth century, from **Wordsworth**; cf. **Wordsworth** 829:10

16 Children and fools tell the truth.
mid 16th century; late 14th century in French

17 Children are certain cares, but uncertain comforts.
mid 17th century

18 Children should be seen and not heard.
originally applied specifically to (young) women
early 15th century

19 The church is an anvil which has worn out many hammers.
early twentieth century; cf. **Maclaren** 486:13

20 Circumstances alter cases.
late 17th century

21 Civility costs nothing.
early 18th century; late 15th century in French

22 A civil question deserves a civil answer.
mid 19th century

23 Cleanliness is next to godliness.
late 18th century; cf. **Wesley** 811:12

24 Clergymen's sons always turn out badly.
late 19th century

25 Clothes make the man.
early 15th century

26 The cobbler to his last and the gunner to his linstock.
mid eighteenth century

27 Cold hands, warm heart.
early 20th century

28 Come live with me and you'll know me.
early 20th century

29 Coming events cast their shadow before.
early 19th century

30 Common fame is seldom to blame.
mid 17th century

31 The company makes the feast.
mid seventeenth century

32 Comparisons are odious.
mid 15th century; cf. **Shakespeare** 691:14

33 Confess and be hanged.
late 16th century

34 Confession is good for the soul.
mid 17th century

35 Conscience makes cowards of us all.
early 17th century, from **Shakespeare**; cf. **Shakespeare** 664:4

36 Constant dropping wears away a stone.
mid 13th century, earlier in Greek; cf. **Latimer** 454:3

37 Corporations have neither bodies to be punished nor souls to be damned.
mid 17th century; cf. **Coke** 224:12, **Thurlow** 777:4

38 Councils of war never fight.
mid 19th century

39 The course of true love never did run smooth.
late sixteenth century, from **Shakespeare**; cf. **Shakespeare** 689:4

40 Cowards may die many times before their death.
late 16th century, from **Shakespeare**; see **Shakespeare** 675:10

41 The cowl does not make the monk.
late fourteenth century

42 A creaking door hangs longest.
late 18th century

43 Crosses are ladders that lead to heaven.
early 17th century

44 Curiosity killed the cat.
early 20th century

45 Curses, like chickens, come home to roost.
late 14th century

46 The customer is always right.
early twentieth century; cf. **Ritz** 628:14

47 Cut your coat according to your cloth.
mid 16th century

48 The darkest hour is just before dawn.
mid seventeenth century

49 Dead men don't bite.
mid 16th century; 1st century AD in Greek

50 Dead men tell no tales.
mid 17th century

1 A deaf husband and a blind wife are always a happy couple.
late 16th century

2 Death is the great leveller.
early 18th century

3 Death pays all debts.
early 17th century; cf. **Shakespeare** 699:4

4 Delays are dangerous.
late 16th century

5 Desperate diseases must have desperate remedies.
mid 16th century; cf. **Fawkes** 308:3, **Shakespeare** 665:26

6 The devil can quote Scripture for his own ends.
late sixteenth century

7 The devil finds work for idle hands to do.
early eighteenth century; cf. **Watts** 805:6

8 The devil is not so black as he is painted.
mid sixteenth century

9 The devil looks after his own.
early eighteenth century

10 The devil makes his Christmas pies of lawyers' tongues and clerks' fingers.
late sixteenth century

11 The devil's children have the devil's luck.
late seventeenth century

12 Devil take the hindmost.
early 17th century

13 The devil was sick, the Devil a saint would be; the Devil was well, the devil a saint was he.
'saint' is sometimes replaced by 'monk'
early seventeenth century, variant of a medieval Latin proverb

14 Diamond cuts diamond.
early 17th century

15 The difficult is done at once, the impossible takes a little longer.
late nineteenth century; cf. **Military sayings** 508:6

16 Diligence is the mother of good luck.
late 16th century

17 Dirty water will quench fire.
mid 16th century

18 Discretion is the better part of valour.
late 16th century, from **Shakespeare**; cf. **Shakespeare** 669:16

19 Distance lends enchantment to the view.
late 18th century, from **Campbell**; see **Campbell** 183:13

20 Divide and rule.
early 17th century

21 Do as I say, not as I do.
mid 16th century

22 Do as you would be done by.
late 16th century

23 Dog does not eat dog.
mid 16th century

24 The dog returns to its vomit.
late fourteenth century; see **Bible** 83:24

25 Dogs bark, but the caravan goes on.
late 19th century

26 A dog that will fetch a bone will carry a bone.
early 19th century

27 Do not meet troubles half-way.
late 19th century

28 Do not spoil the ship for a ha'porth of tar.
ship = *a dialectal pronunciation of sheep, and the original literal sense was 'do not allow sheep to die for the lack of a trifling amount of tar', tar being used to protect sores and wounds on sheep from flies*
early 17th century

29 Do not throw pearls to swine.
mid 14th century; see **Bible** 94:2

30 Don't change horses in mid stream.
mid 19th century; cf. **Lincoln** 468:16

31 Don't count your chickens before they are hatched.
late 16th century

32 Don't cross the bridge till you come to it.
mid 19th century

33 Don't cry before you're hurt.
mid 16th century; early 14th century in French

34 Don't cut off your nose to spite your face.
mid 16th century; mid 14th century in French

35 Don't go near the water until you learn how to swim.
mid 19th century

36 Don't halloo till you are out of the wood.
late 18th century

37 Don't put all your eggs in one basket.
mid 17th century

38 Don't teach your grandmother to suck eggs.
early 18th century

39 Don't throw out your dirty water until you get in fresh.
late 15th century

40 Don't throw the baby out with the bathwater.
mid 19th century; early 17th century in German

41 A door must be either shut or open.
mid 18th century

42 Do right and fear no man.
mid 15th century

43 Do unto others as you would they should do unto you.
late 15th century

44 Dream of a funeral and you hear of a marriage.
mid 17th century

45 Dreams go by contraries.
early 15th century

46 A dripping June sets all in tune.
mid 18th century

47 Drive gently over the stones.
early 18th century

48 A drowning man will clutch at a straw.
mid 16th century

1 Eagles don't catch flies.
mid 16th century

2 The early bird catches the worm.
mid seventeenth century

3 The early man never borrows from the late man.
mid seventeenth century

4 Early to bed and early to rise, makes a man healthy, wealthy, and wise.
late 15th century

5 East, west, home's best.
mid 19th century

6 Easy come, easy go.
mid 17th century

7 Easy does it.
mid 19th century

8 Eat to live, not live to eat.
late 14th century; cf. **Socrates** 726:22

9 Empty sacks will never stand upright.
mid 17th century

10 Empty vessels make the most sound.
early 15th century

11 The end crowns the work.
early sixteenth century

12 The end justifies the means.
late sixteenth century

13 England is the paradise of women, the hell of horses, and the purgatory of servants.
late 16th century; a similar proverb in French is found applied to Paris in the mid 16th century

14 England's difficulty is Ireland's opportunity.
mid 19th century

15 The English are a nation of shopkeepers.
early nineteenth century; cf. **Napoleon** 539:4

16 An Englishman's home is his castle.
late 16th century; cf. **Coke** 224:10

17 An Englishman's word is his bond.
early 16th century

18 Enough is as good as a feast.
late 14th century

19 Even a worm will turn.
mid 16th century

20 Every bullet has its billet.
late 16th century; cf. **William III** 820:2

21 Every cloud has a silver lining.
mid 19th century; cf. **Coward** 238:20, **Ford** 320:6, **Weston** 812:21

22 Every cock will crow upon his own dunghill.
mid 13th century; 1st century AD in Latin

23 Every dog has his day.
mid 16th century

24 Every dog is allowed one bite.
based on the common law rule (dating at least from the 17th century) by which the keeper of a domestic animal was not liable for harm done by it unless he knew of its vicious propensities
early 20th century

25 Every elm has its man.
early 20th century

26 Every herring must hang by its own gill.
early 17th century

27 Every Jack has his Jill.
early 17th century

28 Every land has its own law.
early 17th century

29 Every little helps.
early 17th century

30 Every man for himself.
late 14th century

31 Every man for himself and God for us all.
mid 16th century

32 Every man for himself, and the Devil take the hindmost.
early 16th century

33 Every man has his price.
mid 18th century; cf. **Walpole** 802:4

34 Every man is the architect of his own fortune.
early 16th century; cf. **Claudius** 219:18

35 Every man to his taste.
late 16th century

36 Every man to his trade.
late 16th century

37 Every picture tells a story.
early 20th century; see **Advertising slogans** 7:19

38 Every tub must stand on its own bottom.
mid 16th century

39 Everybody loves a lord.
late 19th century

40 Everybody's business is nobody's business.
early 17th century

41 Everyone speaks well of the bridge which carries him over.
late 17th century

42 Everyone stretches his legs according to the length of his coverlet.
early 14th century

43 Everything has an end.
late 14th century

44 Evil communications corrupt good manners.
early 15th century; see **Bible** 106:25

45 Evil doers are evil dreaders.
late 16th century

46 Example is better than precept.
early 15th century

47 The exception proves the rule.
mid seventeenth century

48 Experience is the best teacher.
late 16th century; cf. **Tacitus** 752:18

49 Experience is the father of wisdom.
mid 16th century

50 Experience keeps a dear school.
mid 18th century

1 Extremes meet.
mid 18th century; mid 17th century in French

2 The eye of a master does more work than both his hands.
mid eighteenth century

3 The eyes are the window of the soul.
mid sixteenth century

4 Fact is stranger than fiction.
mid 19th century

5 Facts are stubborn things.
early 18th century

6 Faint heart never won fair lady.
mid 16th century

7 Fair and softly goes far in a day.
mid 14th century

8 A fair exchange is no robbery.
mid 16th century

9 Fair play's a jewel.
early 19th century

10 Faith will move mountains.
late 19th century; cf. **Bible** 96:6

11 Familiarity breeds contempt.
late 14th century; 5th century AD in Latin

12 Far-fetched and dear-bought is good for ladies.
mid 14th century

13 A fault confessed is half redressed.
mid 16th century

14 Fear the Greeks bearing gifts.
late 19th century, from **Virgil**; see **Virgil** 793:18

15 February fill dyke, be it black or be it white.
mid 16th century

16 Feed a cold and starve a fever.
probably intended as two separate admonitions, but sometimes interpreted to mean that if you feed a cold you will have to starve a fever later
mid 19th century

17 The female of the species is more deadly than the male.
early twentieth century, from **Kipling**; cf. **Kipling** 438:14

18 Fields have eyes and woods have ears.
early 13th century

19 Fight fire with fire.
mid 19th century

20 Finders keepers (losers weepers).
early 19th century

21 Findings keepings.
mid 19th century

22 Fine feathers make fine birds.
late 16th century

23 Fine words butter no parsnips.
mid 17th century

24 Fingers were made before forks.
the form 'God made hands before knives' is found in the mid 16th century
mid 18th century

25 Fire is a good servant but a bad master.
early 17th century

26 First catch your hare.
early 19th century, early 14th century in Latin; cf. **Glasse** 341:18

27 First come, first served.
late 14th century, late 13th century in French

28 The first duty of a soldier is obedience.
mid nineteenth century

29 First impressions are the most lasting.
early 18th century

30 First things first.
late 19th century

31 The fish always stinks from the head downwards.
late sixteenth century

32 Fish and guests stink after three days.
late 16th century

33 A fool and his money are soon parted.
late 16th century

34 A fool at forty is a fool indeed.
early 18th century, from **Young**; see **Young** 838:18

35 A fool may give a wise man counsel.
mid 14th century

36 Fools and bairns should never see half-done work.
early 18th century

37 Fools ask questions that wise men cannot answer.
mid 17th century

38 Fools build houses and wise men live in them.
late 17th century

39 Fools for luck.
mid 19th century

40 Fools rush in where angels fear to tread.
from **Pope**, early 18th century; see **Pope** 585:3

41 For want of a nail the shoe was lost; for want of a shoe the horse was lost; and for want of a horse the man was lost.
early 17th century; late 15th century in French

42 Forewarned is forearmed.
early 16th century

43 Fortune favours fools.
mid 16th century

44 Fortune favours the brave.
late 14th century; cf. **Terence** 768:4, **Virgil** 795:9

45 Four eyes see more than two.
late 16th century

46 A friend in need is a friend indeed.
mid 11th century; 5th century BC in Greek

47 From clogs to clogs is only three generations.
late 19th century

48 From shirtsleeves to shirtsleeves in three generations.
early 20th century; often attributed to Andrew **Carnegie** but not found in his writings

49 From the sublime to the ridiculous is only one step.
late 19th century; cf. **Napoleon** 538:16, **Paine** 563:10

1 From the sweetest wine, the tartest vinegar.
late 16th century

2 Full cup, steady hand.
early 11th century

3 Genius is an infinite capacity for taking pains.
late 19th century; cf. **Carlyle** 187:20

4 Give a dog a bad name and hang him.
early 18th century

5 Give a man rope enough and he will hang himself.
mid 17th century

6 Give a thing, and take a thing, to wear the devil's gold ring.
late 16th century

7 Give and take is fair play.
late 18th century

8 Give credit where credit is due.
late 18th century

9 Give the Devil his due.
late 16th century

10 Go abroad and you'll hear news of home.
late 17th century

11 Go further and fare worse.
mid 16th century

12 God helps them that help themselves.
mid 16th century; early 15th century in French

13 God made the country and man made the town.
mid 17th century; cf. **Cowley** 239:12, **Cowper** 241:19

14 God makes the back to the burden.
early 19th century

15 God never sends mouths but He sends meat.
late 14th century

16 God's in his heaven; all's right with the world.
from early 16th century in the form 'God is where he was'; now largely replaced by **Browning**; see **Browning** 157:12

17 God sends meat, but the Devil sends cooks.
mid 16th century

18 The gods send nuts to those who have no teeth.
early twentieth century

19 God tempers the wind to the shorn lamb.
mid 17th century

20 Gold may be bought too dear.
mid 16th century

21 A golden key can open any door.
late 16th century

22 Good Americans when they die go to Paris.
mid 19th century, from Thomas Gold **Appleton**; see **Appleton** 23:4

23 A good beginning makes a good ending.
early 14th century

24 The good die young.
late seventeenth century

25 Good fences make good neighbours.
mid 17th century

26 A good horse cannot be of a bad colour.
early 17th century

27 The good is the enemy of the best.
early twentieth century; cf. **Voltaire** 797:11

28 A good Jack makes a good Jill.
early 17th century

29 Good men are scarce.
early 17th century

30 Good seed makes a good crop.
late 16th century

31 Good wine needs no bush.
early 15th century

32 The grass is always greener on the other side of the fence.
mid twentieth century

33 A great book is a great evil.
early 17th century; cf. **Callimachus** 181:17

34 The greater the sinner, the greater the saint.
late eighteenth century

35 The greater the truth, the greater the libel.
late eighteenth century

36 Great minds think alike.
early 17th century

37 Great oaks from little acorns grow.
late 14th century

38 A green Yule makes a fat churchyard.
meaning a mild winter
mid 17th century

39 The grey mare is the better horse.
mid sixteenth century

40 A guilty conscience needs no accuser.
late 14th century; earlier in Latin

41 Half a loaf is better than no bread.
mid 16th century

42 The half is better than the whole.
mid sixteenth century

43 Half the truth is often a whole lie.
mid 18th century

44 Handsome is as handsome does.
late 16th century

45 The hand that rocks the cradle rules the world.
mid nineteenth century, from **Wallace**; cf. **Wallace** 799:16

46 Hang a thief when he's young, and he'll no' steal when he's old.
early 19th century

47 Hanging and wiving go by destiny.
mid 16th century

48 Happy is the bride that the sun shines on.
mid 17th century

49 Happy is the country which has no history.
early 19th century; cf. **Montesquieu** 528:11

50 Happy's the wooing that is not long a-doing.
late 16th century

51 Hard cases make bad law.
mid 19th century

52 Hard words break no bones.
late 17th century

1 Haste is from the Devil.
mid 17th century

2 Haste makes waste.
late 14th century

3 Hasty climbers have sudden falls.
mid 15th century

4 Hawks will not pick out hawks' eyes.
late 16th century

5 He gives twice who gives quickly.
mid 16th century; cf. **Publilius Syrus** 616:11

6 He is a good dog who goes to church.
early 19th century

7 He laughs best who laughs last.
early seventeenth century

8 He lives long who lives well.
mid sixteenth century

9 He that cannot obey cannot command.
early sixteenth century

10 He that cannot pay, let him pray.
early seventeenth century

11 He that complies against his will is of his own opinion still.
late seventeenth century, from Samuel **Butler**; see **Butler** 172:12

12 He that drinks beer, thinks beer.
early nineteenth century

13 He that follows freits, freits will follow him.
freits = *omens*
early eighteenth century

14 He that goes a-borrowing, goes a-sorrowing.
late fifteenth century

15 He that has an ill name is half hanged.
early fifteenth century

16 He that lives in hope dances to an ill tune.
late sixteenth century

17 He that touches pitch shall be defiled.
early fourteenth century; see **Bible** 91:27

18 He that will not when he may, when he will he shall have nay.
early eleventh century

19 He that will thrive must first ask his wife.
early sixteenth century

20 He that will to Cupar maun to Cupar.
early eighteenth century

21 He that would eat the fruit must climb the tree.
early eighteenth century

22 He that would go to sea for pleasure would go to hell for a pastime.
late nineteenth century

23 He travels fastest who travels alone.
late nineteenth century; cf. **Kipling** 439:10

24 He who can does, he who cannot, teaches.
early twentieth century, from **Shaw**; see **Shaw** 708:18

25 He who excuses, accuses himself.
early seventeenth century

26 He who fights and runs away, may live to fight another day.
mid sixteenth century

27 He who hesitates is lost.
early eighteenth century; cf. **Addison** 4:12

28 He who is absent is always in the wrong.
mid seventeenth century

29 He who laughs last, laughs longest.
early twentieth century

30 He who lives by the sword dies by the sword.
mid seventeenth century; see **Bible** 97:25

31 He who pays the piper calls the tune.
late nineteenth century

32 He who rides a tiger is afraid to dismount.
late nineteenth century

33 He who sups with the Devil should have a long spoon.
late fourteenth century

34 He who wills the end, wills the means.
late seventeenth century

35 Hear all, see all, say nowt, tak'all, keep all, gie nowt, and if tha ever does owt for nowt do it for thysen.
early fifteenth century

36 Heaven protects children, sailors, and drunken men.
mid nineteenth century

37 Hell hath no fury like a woman scorned.
late seventeenth century, from **Congreve**; see **Congreve** 232:26

38 Help you to salt, help you to sorrow.
mid seventeenth century

39 The higher the monkey climbs the more he shows his tail.
late fourteenth century

40 History repeats itself.
mid nineteenth century

41 Home is home, as the Devil said when he found himself in the Court of Session.
early nineteenth century

42 Home is home though it's never so homely.
mid sixteenth century

43 Home is where the heart is.
late nineteenth century

44 Homer sometimes nods.
late fourteenth century, from **Horace**; see **Horace** 386:5

45 Honesty is the best policy.
early seventeenth century

46 Honey catches more flies than vinegar.
mid seventeenth century

47 Hope deferred makes the heart sick.
early sixteenth century; see **Bible** 82:27

48 Hope for the best and prepare for the worst.
mid sixteenth century

49 Hope is a good breakfast but a bad supper.
mid seventeenth century; cf. **Bacon** 45:8

1 Hope springs eternal.
early eighteenth century, from **Pope**; see **Pope** 585:9

2 Horses for courses.
late nineteenth century

3 A house divided cannot stand.
mid 11th century; cf. **Bible** 98:2

4 Hunger drives the wolf out of the wood.
late fifteenth century

5 Hunger is the best sauce.
early sixteenth century

6 A hungry man is an angry man.
mid 17th century

7 Hurry no man's cattle.
early nineteenth century

8 The husband is always the last to know.
early seventeenth century

9 An idle brain is the devil's workshop.
early 17th century

10 Idle people have the least leisure.
late seventeenth century

11 Idleness is the root of all evil.
early fifteenth century; cf. **Proverbs** 606:45

12 If a thing's worth doing, it's worth doing well.
mid eighteenth century

13 If at first you don't succeed, try, try, try again.
mid nineteenth century

14 If Candlemas day be sunny and bright, winter will have another flight; if Candlemas day be cloudy with rain, winter is gone and won't come again.
Candlemas Day = *2 February*
late seventeenth century

15 If every man would sweep his own door-step the city would soon be clean.
early seventeenth century

16 If ifs and ands were pots and pans, there'd be no work for tinkers' hands.
mid nineteenth century

17 If in February there be no rain, 'tis neither good for hay nor grain.
early eighteenth century

18 If it were not for hope, the heart would break.
mid thirteenth century

19 If Saint Paul's day be fair and clear, it will betide a happy year.
late sixteenth century

20 If the cap fits, wear it.
early eighteenth century

21 If the mountain will not come to Mahomet, Mahomet must go to the mountain.
early seventeenth century

22 If the shoe fits, wear it.
late eighteenth century

23 If the sky falls we shall catch larks.
mid fifteenth century

24 If there were no receivers, there would be no thieves.
late fourteenth century

25 If two ride on a horse, one must ride behind.
late sixteenth century

26 If wishes were horses, beggars would ride.
early seventeenth century

27 If you can't be good, be careful.
early twentieth century; the Latin form *Si non caste tamen caute* is found from the mid eleventh century

28 If you can't ride two horses at once, you shouldn't be in the circus.
early twentieth century, from **Maxton**; cf. **Maxton** 502:11

29 If you don't like the heat, get out of the kitchen.
mid twentieth century; cf. **Truman** 784:3

30 If you don't make mistakes you don't make anything.
late nineteenth century; cf. **Phelps** 575:2

31 If you don't speculate, you can't accumulate.
mid twentieth century

32 If you don't work you shan't eat.
mid sixteenth century; see **Bible** 109:12

33 If you gently touch a nettle it'll sting you for your pains; grasp it like a lad of mettle, an' as soft as silk remains.
late sixteenth century; cf. **Hill** 376:11

34 If you lie down with dogs, you will get up with fleas.
late sixteenth century

35 If you play with fire you get burnt.
late nineteenth century

36 If you're born to be hanged then you'll never be drowned.
late sixteenth century

37 If you run after two hares you will catch neither.
early sixteenth century

38 If you want a thing done well, do it yourself.
mid sixteenth century

39 If you want peace, you must prepare for war.
mid sixteenth century; cf. **Vegetius** 791:4

40 If you want to live and thrive, let the spider run alive.
mid nineteenth century

41 If you would be happy for a week take a wife; if you would be happy for a month kill a pig; but if you would be happy all your life plant a garden.
mid seventeenth century

42 If you would be well served, serve yourself.
mid seventeenth century

43 Ignorance of the law is no excuse for breaking it.
early fifteenth century; cf. **Selden** 653:16

44 Ill gotten goods never thrive.
early sixteenth century

45 Ill weeds grow apace.
late fifteenth century

46 Imitation is the sincerest form of flattery.
early nineteenth century

47 In for a penny, in for a pound.
late seventeenth century

1 In the country of the blind the one eyed man is king.
early sixteenth century; cf. **Erasmus** 301:4

2 In vain the net is spread in the sight of the bird.
late fourteenth century; see **Bible** 82:6

3 It is a long lane that has no turning.
early seventeenth century

4 It is a poor dog that's not worth whistling for.
mid sixteenth century

5 It is a poor heart that never rejoices.
mid nineteenth century

6 It is a wise child that knows its own father.
late sixteenth century

7 It is as cheap sitting as standing.
mid seventeenth century

8 It is best to be off with the old love before you are on with the new.
early nineteenth century

9 It is best to be on the safe side.
late seventeenth century

10 It is better to be born lucky than rich.
mid seventeenth century

11 It is better to give than to receive.
late fourteenth century; see **Bible** 104:14

12 It is better to travel hopefully than to arrive.
late nineteenth century, from **Stevenson**; see **Stevenson** 741:25

13 It is easier to pull down than to build up.
late sixteenth century

14 It is easier to raise the Devil than to lay him.
mid seventeenth century

15 It is easy to be wise after the event.
early seventeenth century

16 It is easy to find a stick to beat a dog.
mid sixteenth century

17 It is good to make a bridge of gold to a flying enemy.
late sixteenth century

18 It is idle to swallow the cow and choke on the tail.
mid seventeenth century

19 It is ill sitting at Rome and striving with the Pope.
early seventeenth century

20 It is merry in hall when beards wag all.
early fourteenth century

21 It is never too late to learn.
late seventeenth century

22 It is never too late to mend.
late sixteenth century

23 It is no use crying over spilt milk.
mid seventeenth century

24 It is not spring until you can plant your foot upon twelve daisies.
mid nineteenth century

25 It is not work that kills, but worry.
late nineteenth century

26 It is the first step that is difficult.
late sixteenth century; cf. **Du Deffand** 284:6

27 It is the last straw that breaks the camel's back.
mid seventeenth century

28 It is the pace that kills.
mid nineteenth century

29 It never rains but it pours.
early eighteenth century

30 It's a sin to steal a pin.
late nineteenth century

31 It's an ill bird that fouls its own nest.
mid thirteenth century

32 It's an ill wind that blows nobody any good.
mid sixteenth century

33 It's dogged as does it.
mid nineteenth century; cf. **Trollope** 782:17

34 It's ill speaking between a full man and a fasting.
mid seventeenth century

35 It's ill waiting for dead men's shoes.
early sixteenth century

36 It's too late to shut the stable-door after the horse has bolted.
mid fourteenth century

37 It takes all sorts to make a world.
early seventeenth century

38 It takes three generations to make a gentleman.
early nineteenth century

39 It takes two to make a bargain.
late sixteenth century

40 It takes two to make a quarrel.
early eighteenth century

41 It takes two to tango.
mid twentieth century, from **Hoffman**; cf. **Hoffman** 379:15

42 Jack is as good as his master.
early eighteenth century

43 Jam tomorrow and jam yesterday, but never jam today.
late nineteenth century, from **Carroll**; cf. **Carroll** 190:23

44 Jouk and let the jaw go by.
jouk = *stoop*, jaw = *a rush of water*
early eighteenth century

45 Jove but laughs at lovers' perjury.
mid sixteenth century; cf. **Dryden** 282:8, **Tibullus** 777:9

46 Judge not, that ye be not judged.
late fifteenth century; see **Bible** 93:28

47 Keep a thing seven years and you'll always find a use for it.
early seventeenth century

48 Keep no more cats than will catch mice.
late seventeenth century

49 Keep your shop and your shop will keep you.
early seventeenth century

50 Keep your own fish-guts for your own sea-maws.
early eighteenth century

1 Killing no murder.
mid seventeenth century, from **Sexby**; cf. **Sexby** 655:3

2 The king can do no wrong.
mid seventeenth century

3 A king's chaff is worth more than other men's corn.
early 17th century

4 Kings have long arms.
mid sixteenth century

5 Kissing goes by favour.
early seventeenth century

6 Know thyself.
inscribed on the temple of Apollo at Delphi, in the form γνῶθι σεαυτόν.; Plato, in Protagoras *343 b, ascribes the saying to the Seven Wise Men*
late fourteenth century; cf. **Goethe** 343:18

7 Knowledge is power.
late sixteenth century; cf. **Bacon** 44:30

8 The labourer is worthy of his hire.
late fourteenth century; see **Bible** 99:8

9 The last drop makes the cup run over.
mid seventeenth century

10 Laugh and the world laughs with you, weep and you weep alone.
late nineteenth century, from **Wilcox**; cf. **Wilcox** 817:9

11 Lay-overs for meddlers.
late eighteenth century

12 Learning is better than house and land.
late eighteenth century

13 Least said, soonest mended.
mid fifteenth century

14 Lend your money and lose your friend.
late fifteenth century

15 Length begets loathing.
mid eighteenth century

16 The leopard does not change his spots.
mid sixteenth century; see **Bible** 89:17

17 Less is more.
mid nineteenth century, often associated with Mies van der **Rohe**

18 Let sleeping dogs lie.
late fourteenth century

19 Let the buyer beware.
early sixteenth century

20 Let the cobbler stick to his last
mid sixteenth century

21 Let the dead bury the dead.
early nineteenth century; see **Bible** 94:20

22 Let them laugh that win.
mid sixteenth century

23 Let well alone.
late sixteenth century

24 A liar ought to have a good memory.
mid 16th century; 1st century AD in Latin

25 Life begins at forty.
early twentieth century, from **Pitkin**; cf. **Pitkin** 576:18

26 Life isn't all beer and skittles.
mid nineteenth century

27 Light come, light go.
late fourteenth century

28 Lightning never strikes the same place twice.
mid nineteenth century

29 Like breeds like.
mid sixteenth century

30 Like father, like son.
mid fourteenth century

31 Like master, like man.
early sixteenth century

32 Like mother, like daughter.
early fourteenth century; see **Bible** 89:28

33 Like people, like priest.
late sixteenth century; see **Bible** 90:9

34 Like will to like.
early fifteenth century

35 Listeners never hear any good of themselves.
mid seventeenth century

36 Little birds that can sing and won't sing must be made to sing.
late seventeenth century

37 Little fish are sweet.
early nineteenth century

38 A little knowledge is a dangerous thing.
from **Pope**, early 18th century; see **Pope** 584:15

39 Little leaks sink the ship.
early seventeenth century

40 Little pitchers have large ears.
mid sixteenth century

41 A little pot is soon hot.
mid 16th century

42 Little strokes fell great oaks.
early fifteenth century

43 Little thieves are hanged, but great ones escape.
mid seventeenth century

44 Little things please little minds.
late sixteenth century

45 Live and learn.
early seventeenth century

46 Live and let live.
early seventeenth century

47 A live dog is better than a dead lion.
late 14th century; cf. **Bible** 84:20

48 Long and lazy, little and loud; fat and fulsome, pretty and proud.
late sixteenth century

49 The longest way round is the shortest way home.
mid seventeenth century

50 Long foretold, long last; short notice, soon past.
mid nineteenth century

51 Look before you leap.
mid fourteenth century

1 Lookers-on see most of the game.
early sixteenth century

2 Love and a cough cannot be hid.
early sixteenth century

3 Love begets love.
mid seventeenth century

4 Love is blind.
late fourteenth century; cf. **Anonymous** 20:8

5 Love laughs at locksmiths.
early nineteenth century; cf. **Colman** 229:16

6 Love makes the world go round.
mid nineteenth century, from a traditional French song

7 Love me little, love me long.
early sixteenth century

8 Love me, love my dog.
early sixteenth century

9 Love will find a way.
early seventeenth century

10 Lucky at cards, unlucky in love.
mid eighteenth century

11 Make haste slowly.
late sixteenth century; cf. **Augustus** 36:16

12 Make hay while the sun shines.
mid sixteenth century

13 Man cannot live by bread alone.
late nineteenth century; see **Bible** 92:32

14 A man is as old as he feels, and a woman as old as she looks.
late 19th century

15 A man is known by the company he keeps.
mid 16th century

16 Man is the measure of all things.
mid sixteenth century; cf. **Protagoras** 593:18

17 Manners maketh man.
mid fourteenth century; motto of William of Wykeham (1324–1404)

18 Man proposes, God disposes.
mid fifteenth century; cf. **Thomas à Kempis** 771:1

19 Man's extremity is God's opportunity.
early seventeenth century

20 The man who is born in a stable is not a horse.
early nineteenth century

21 A man who is his own lawyer has a fool for his client.
early 19th century

22 Many a little makes a mickle.
mid thirteenth century

23 Many a mickle makes a muckle.
a popular corruption of 'Many a little makes a mickle'
late eighteenth century

24 Many a true word is spoken in jest.
late fourteenth century

25 Many are called but few are chosen.
late nineteenth century; see **Bible** 96:21

26 Many go out for wool and come home shorn.
late sixteenth century

27 Many hands make light work.
early fourteenth century

28 March comes in like a lion, and goes out like a lamb.
early seventeenth century

29 Marriage is a lottery.
mid seventeenth century

30 Marriages are made in heaven.
mid sixteenth century

31 Marry in haste repent at leisure.
late sixteenth century; cf. **Congreve** 232:34

32 Marry in May, rue for aye.
late seventeenth century

33 May chickens come cheeping.
late nineteenth century

34 Meat and mass never hindered man.
early seventeenth century

35 Might is right.
early fourteenth century

36 The mill cannot grind with the water that is past.
early seventeenth century

37 The mills of God grind slowly, yet they grind exceeding small.
mid seventeenth century; translation of an anonymous verse in Sextus Empiricus *Adversus Mathematicos* bk. 1, sect. 287; cf. **Longfellow** 474:8

38 Misery loves company.
late sixteenth century

39 Misfortunes never come singly.
early fourteenth century

40 A miss is as good as a mile.
the syntax has been distorted by abridgement: the original form was ' an inch in a miss is as good as an ell'
early 17th century

41 Moderation in all things.
mid nineteenth century; cf. **Horace** 389:15

42 Monday's child is fair of face,
Tuesday's child is full of grace,
Wednesday's child is full of woe,
Thursday's child has far to go,
Friday's child is loving and giving,
Saturday's child works hard for its living,
And a child that's born on the Sabbath day
Is fair and wise and good and gay.
mid nineteenth century

43 Money has no smell.
early twentieth century; cf. **Vespasian** 791:14

44 Money is power.
mid eighteenth century

45 Money is the root of all evil.
mid fifteenth century; see **Bible** 109:18

46 Money isn't everything.
early twentieth century

1 A moneyless man goes fast through the market.
early 18th century; late 14th century in French

2 Money makes a man.
early sixteenth century

3 Money makes money.
late sixteenth century

4 Money makes the mare to go.
early sixteenth century

5 Money talks.
mid seventeenth century

6 More haste, less speed.
mid fourteenth century

7 More people know Tom Fool than Tom Fool knows.
mid seventeenth century

8 The more the merrier.
late fourteenth century

9 The more you get the more you want.
mid fourteenth century

10 The more you stir it the worse it stinks.
mid sixteenth century

11 Morning dreams come true.
mid sixteenth century

12 The mother of mischief is no bigger than a midge's wing.
early seventeenth century

13 A mouse may help a lion.
alluding to Aesop's fable of the lion and the rat
mid 16th century

14 Much cry and little wool.
late fifteenth century

15 Much would have more.
mid fourteenth century

16 Murder will out.
early fourteenth century; cf. **Chaucer** 206:3

17 My son is my son till he gets him a wife, but my daughter's my daughter all the days of her life.
late seventeenth century

18 Nature abhors a vacuum.
mid sixteenth century; cf. **Rabelais** 619:10

19 The nearer the bone, the sweeter the meat.
late fourteenth century

20 The nearer the church, the farther from God.
early fourteenth century

21 Near is my kirtle, but nearer is my smock.
mid fifteenth century

22 Near is my shirt, but nearer is my skin.
late sixteenth century

23 Necessity is the mother of invention.
mid sixteenth century

24 Necessity knows no law.
late fourteenth century; cf. **Publilius Syrus** 616:13

25 Ne'er cast a clout till May be out.
early eighteenth century

26 Needs must when the devil drives.
mid fifteenth century

27 Never choose your women or linen by candlelight.
late sixteenth century

28 Never do evil that good may come of it.
late sixteenth century

29 Never give a sucker an even break.
early twentieth century; cf. **Fields** 310:18

30 Never is a long time.
late fourteenth century

31 Never let the sun go down on your anger.
mid seventeenth century; see **Bible** 108:5

32 Never look a gift horse in the mouth.
early sixteenth century

33 Never marry for money, but marry where money is.
late nineteenth century; cf. **Tennyson** 764:23

34 Never mention rope in the house of a man who has been hanged.
late sixteenth century

35 Never put off till tomorrow what you can do today.
late fourteenth century

36 Never send a boy to do a man's job.
early twentieth century

37 Never speak ill of the dead.
mid sixteenth century; 6th century BC in Greek

38 Never tell tales out of school.
early sixteenth century

39 Never too old to learn.
early sixteenth century

40 Never trouble trouble till trouble troubles you.
late nineteenth century

41 New brooms sweep clean.
mid sixteenth century

42 New lords, new laws.
mid sixteenth century

43 Night brings counsel.
late sixteenth century

44 Nine tailors make a man.
the literal meaning is that a gentleman must select his attire from various sources; it is now also associated with bell-ringing: tailors = tellers = *strokes, the number of strokes on the passing bell indicating the sex of the deceased*
early seventeenth century

45 No cure, no pay.
expression used on Lloyd's of London's Standard Form of Salvage Agreement
late nineteenth century

46 A nod's as good as a wink to a blind horse.
late 18th century

47 No man can serve two masters.
early fourteenth century; see **Bible** 93:22

48 No man is a hero to his valet.
mid eighteenth century; cf. **Cornuel** 237:7

49 No money, no Swiss.
the Swiss were particularly noted as mercenaries
late sixteenth century; cf. **Racine** 620:1

1 No moon, no man.
late nineteenth century

2 No names, no pack-drill.
early twentieth century

3 No news is good news.
early seventeenth century

4 No one should be judge in his own cause.
mid fifteenth century

5 No pain, no gain.
late sixteenth century

6 No penny, no paternoster.
early sixteenth century

7 No smoke without fire.
late fourteenth century

8 No time like the present.
mid sixteenth century

9 None but the brave deserve the fair.
late seventeenth century, from **Dryden**; see **Dryden** 280:17

10 Nothing comes of nothing.
late fourteenth century

11 Nothing for nothing.
early eighteenth century

12 Nothing is certain but death and taxes.
early eighteenth century; cf. **Defoe** 254:15, **Franklin** 323:15

13 Nothing is certain but the unforeseen.
late nineteenth century

14 Nothing should be done in haste but gripping a flea.
mid seventeenth century

15 Nothing so bad but it might have been worse.
late nineteenth century

16 Nothing so bold as a blind mare.
early seventeenth century

17 Nothing succeeds like success.
mid nineteenth century

18 Nothing venture, nothing gain.
early seventeenth century

19 Nothing venture, nothing have.
late fourteenth century

20 Obey orders, if you break owners.
late eighteenth century

21 Of two evils choose the less.
late fourteenth century; similar sentiments are found in **Aristotle** and **Cicero**

22 Offenders never pardon.
mid seventeenth century

23 Old habits die hard.
mid eighteenth century

24 An old poacher makes the best gamekeeper.
late 14th century

25 Old sins cast long shadows.
early twentieth century

26 Old soldiers never die.
early twentieth century; cf. **Foley** 318:24

27 The only good Indian is a dead Indian.
mid nineteenth century; cf. **Sheridan** 715:12

28 On Saint Thomas the Divine kill all turkeys, geese and swine.
St Thomas the Apostle's feast is on 21 December
mid eighteenth century

29 On the first of March, the crows begin to search.
mid nineteenth century

30 Once a—, always a—
the formula is found from the early seventeenth century

31 Once a priest, always a priest.
mid nineteenth century

32 Once a whore, always a whore.
early seventeenth century

33 Once bitten, twice shy.
mid nineteenth century

34 One cannot love and be wise.
early sixteenth century

35 One does not wash one's dirty linen in public.
early nineteenth century

36 One Englishman can beat three Frenchmen.
late sixteenth century

37 One for sorrow; two for mirth; three for a wedding, four for a birth.
referring to the number of magpies seen
mid nineteenth century

38 One for the mouse, one for the crow, one to rot, one to grow.
referring to sowing seed
mid nineteenth century

39 One funeral makes many.
late nineteenth century

40 One good turn deserves another.
early fifteenth century

41 One half of the world does not know how the other half lives.
early seventeenth century

42 One hand for oneself and one for the ship.
late eighteenth century

43 One hand washes the other.
late sixteenth century

44 One hour's sleep before midnight is worth two after.
mid seventeenth century

45 One law for the rich and another for the poor.
early nineteenth century

46 One man may steal a horse, while another may not look over a hedge.
mid sixteenth century

47 One man's loss is another man's gain.
early sixteenth century

48 One man's meat is another man's poison.
late sixteenth century

49 One might as well be hanged for a sheep as a lamb.
late seventeenth century

1 One nail drives out another.
mid thirteenth century; also found in **Aristotle**

2 One picture is worth ten thousand words.
early twentieth century; cf. **Barnard** 54:16

3 One step at a time.
mid nineteenth century

4 One story is good till another is told.
late sixteenth century

5 One swallow does not make a summer.
mid sixteenth century

6 One volunteer is worth two pressed men.
early eighteenth century

7 One wedding brings another.
mid seventeenth century

8 One white foot, buy him; two white feet, try him; three white feet, look well about him; four white feet, go without him.
on horse-dealing
late nineteenth century

9 One year's seeding makes seven years weeding.
late nineteenth century

10 Opportunity makes a thief.
early thirteenth century

11 Opportunity never knocks twice at any man's door.
mid sixteenth century

12 Other times, other manners.
late sixteenth century

13 An ounce of practice is worth a pound of precept.
late 16th century

14 Out of debt, out of danger.
mid seventeenth century

15 Out of sight, out of mind.
mid thirteenth century; cf. **Thomas à Kempis** 771:4

16 Out of the fullness of the heart the mouth speaks.
late fourteenth century; see **Bible** 95:13

17 Out of the mouths of babes—.
late nineteenth century; see **Book of Common Prayer** 131:26

18 Parsley seed goes nine times to the Devil.
mid seventeenth century

19 Patience is a virtue.
late fourteenth century

20 Pay beforehand was never well served.
late sixteenth century

21 A peck of March dust is worth a king's ransom.
early 16th century

22 The pen is mightier than the sword.
late sixteenth century; cf. **Bulwer-Lytton** 160:7

23 A penny saved is a penny earned.
mid 17th century

24 Penny wise and pound foolish.
early seventeenth century

25 Physician, heal thyself.
early fifteenth century; see **Bible** 98:29

26 The pitcher will go to the well once too often.
mid fourteenth century

27 Pity is akin to love.
early seventeenth century

28 A place for everything, and everything in its place.
mid 17th century; often associated with Samuel **Smiles** and Mrs Beeton

29 Please your eye and plague your heart.
early seventeenth century

30 Politics makes strange bedfellows.
mid nineteenth century

31 Possession is nine points of the law.
early seventeenth century

32 A postern door makes a thief.
mid 15th century

33 The post of honour is the post of danger.
early sixteenth century

34 Poverty is no disgrace, but it's a great inconvenience.
late sixteenth century

35 Poverty is not a crime.
late sixteenth century

36 Power corrupts.
late nineteenth century, now commonly used in allusion to **Acton**; cf. **Acton** 1:16

37 Practice makes perfect.
mid sixteenth century

38 Practise what you preach.
late fourteenth century

39 Praise the child, and you make love to the mother.
early nineteenth century

40 Prevention is better than cure.
early seventeenth century

41 Pride feels no pain.
early seventeenth century

42 Pride goes before a fall.
late fourteenth century; see **Bible** 82:38

43 Procrastination is the thief of time.
mid eighteenth century, from **Young**; cf. **Young** 839:6

44 Promises, like pie-crust, are made to be broken.
late seventeenth century

45 The proof of the pudding is in the eating.
early fourteenth century

46 A prophet is not without honour save in his own country.
late 15th century; see **Bible** 95:24

47 Providence is always on the side of the big battalions.
early nineteenth century; cf. **Bussy-Rabutin** 171:5, **Voltaire** 798:4

48 Punctuality is the politeness of princes.
mid nineteenth century; cf. **Louis XVIII** 476:5

49 Punctuality is the soul of business.
mid nineteenth century

50 Put a stout heart to a stey brae.
stey = *steep*
late sixteenth century

1 Put your trust in God, and keep your powder dry.
attributed to Oliver **Cromwell**
mid nineteenth century; cf. **Blacker** 116:21

2 The quarrel of lovers is the renewal of love.
early sixteenth century; cf. **Edwards** 289:13

3 Quickly come, quickly go.
late sixteenth century

4 The race is not to the swift, nor the battle to the strong.
early seventeenth century; see **Bible** 84:23

5 Rain before seven, fine before eleven.
mid nineteenth century

6 Red sky at night, shepherd's delight; red sky in the morning, shepherd's warning.
late fourteenth century

7 A reed before the wind lives on, while mighty oaks do fall.
late 14th century

8 Revenge is a dish that can be eaten cold.
late nineteenth century

9 Revenge is sweet.
mid sixteenth century

10 Revolutions are not made with rose-water.
early nineteenth century

11 The rich man has his ice in the summer and the poor man gets his in the winter.
early twentieth century

12 A rising tide lifts all boats.
principally known in the United States; associated with the **Kennedy** *family*
mid 20th century

13 The road to hell is paved with good intentions.
late sixteenth century

14 The robin and the wren are God's cock and hen; the martin and the swallow are God's mate and marrow.
late eighteenth century

15 Robin Hood could brave all weathers but a thaw wind.
mid nineteenth century

16 A rolling stone gathers no moss.
mid 14th century

17 Rome was not built in a day.
mid sixteenth century

18 The rotten apple injures its neighbour.
mid fourteenth century

19 Safe bind, safe find.
mid sixteenth century

20 Saint Swithun's day, if thou be fair, for forty days it will remain; Saint Swithun's day, if thou bring rain, for forty days it will remain.
Saint Swithun's day is 15 July
early seventeenth century

21 Save us from our friends.
late fifteenth century

22 Scratch a Russian and you find a Tartar.
early nineteenth century

23 The sea refuses no river.
early seventeenth century

24 Second thoughts are best.
late sixteenth century

25 See a pin and pick it up, all the day you'll have good luck; see a pin and let it lie, bad luck you'll have all day.
mid nineteenth century

26 See no evil, hear no evil, speak no evil.
conventionally represented by the monkeys ('the three wise monkeys') covering their eyes, ears, and mouth respectively with their hands
early twentieth century

27 Seeing is believing.
early seventeenth century

28 Seek and ye shall find.
early sixteenth century; see **Bible** 94:3

29 Self-praise is no recommendation.
early nineteenth century

30 Self-preservation is the first law of nature.
early seventeenth century

31 September blow soft till the fruit's in the loft.
late sixteenth century

32 Set a beggar on horseback, and he'll ride to the Devil.
late sixteenth century

33 Set a thief to catch a thief.
mid seventeenth century

34 The sharper the storm, the sooner it's over.
late nineteenth century

35 The shoemaker's son always goes barefoot.
mid sixteenth century

36 A short horse is soon curried.
mid 14th century

37 Short reckonings make long friends.
early sixteenth century

38 Shrouds have no pockets.
mid nineteenth century

39 A shut mouth catches no flies.
late 16th century

40 Silence is a woman's best garment.
mid sixteenth century

41 Silence is golden.
mid nineteenth century

42 Silence means consent.
late fourteenth century

43 Sing before breakfast, cry before night.
early seventeenth century

44 Six hours sleep for a man, seven for a woman, and eight for a fool.
early seventeenth century

45 A slice off a cut loaf isn't missed.
late 16th century

1 Slow but sure.
late seventeenth century

2 Small choice in rotten apples.
late sixteenth century

3 Small is beautiful.
late twentieth century, from **Schumacher**; cf. **Schumacher** 649:7

4 A soft answer turneth away wrath.
late 14th century; see **Bible** 82:34

5 Softly, softly, catchee monkey.
early twentieth century

6 So many men, so many opinions.
late fourteenth century; cf. **Terence** 768:5

7 So many mists in March, so many frosts in May.
early seventeenth century

8 Something is better than nothing.
mid sixteenth century

9 The sooner begun, the sooner done.
late sixteenth century

10 Soon ripe, soon rotten.
late fourteenth century

11 Sow dry and set wet.
mid seventeenth century

12 A sow may whistle, though it has an ill mouth for it.
early 19th century

13 Spare at the spigot, and let out the bung-hole.
mid seventeenth century

14 Spare the rod and spoil the child.
early eleventh century; see **Bible** 82:30

15 Spare well and have to spend.
mid sixteenth century

16 Speak not of my debts unless you mean to pay them.
mid seventeenth century

17 Speech is silver, but silence is golden.
mid nineteenth century

18 The squeaking wheel gets the grease.
mid twentieth century

19 A stern chase is a long chase.
stern chase = *a chase in which the pursuing ship follows directly in the wake of the pursued*
early 19th century

20 Sticks and stones may break my bones, but words will never hurt me.
late nineteenth century

21 A still tongue makes a wise head.
mid 16th century

22 Still waters run deep.
early fifteenth century

23 A stitch in time saves nine.
early 18th century

24 Stolen fruit is sweet.
early seventeenth century

25 Stolen waters are sweet.
late fourteenth century; see **Bible** 82:19

26 Stone-dead hath no fellow.
mid seventeenth century

27 Straws tell which way the wind blows.
mid seventeenth century

28 A stream cannot rise above its source.
mid 17th century

29 Stretch your arm no further than your sleeve will reach.
mid sixteenth century

30 Strike while the iron is hot.
late fourteenth century

31 The style is the man.
early twentieth century, from **Buffon**; cf. **Buffon** 159:19

32 Success has many fathers, while failure is an orphan.
mid twentieth century; cf. **Ciano** 217:3

33 Sue a beggar and catch a louse.
mid seventeenth century

34 Sufficient unto the day is the evil thereof.
mid eighteenth century; see **Bible** 93:27

35 The sun loses nothing by shining into a puddle.
early fourteenth century, of Classical origin

36 Sussex won't be druv.
early twentieth century

37 A swarm in May is worth a load of hay; a swarm in June is worth a silver spoon; but a swarm in July is not worth a fly.
beekeepers' saying
mid 17th century

38 Take care of the pence and the pounds will take care of themselves.
mid eighteenth century; cf. **Lowndes** 478:9

39 Take the goods the gods provide.
late seventeenth century

40 A tale never loses in the telling.
mid 16th century

41 Talk is cheap.
mid nineteenth century

42 Talk of the Devil, and he is bound to appear.
mid seventeenth century

43 Tastes differ.
early nineteenth century

44 Tell the truth and shame the Devil.
mid sixteenth century

45 There are as good fish in the sea as ever came out of it.
late sixteenth century

46 There are more ways of killing a cat than choking it with cream.
mid nineteenth century

47 There are more ways of killing a dog than choking it with butter.
mid nineteenth century

48 There are more ways of killing a dog than hanging it.
late seventeenth century

1 There are no birds in last year's nest.
early seventeenth century

2 There are tricks in every trade.
early seventeenth century

3 There are two sides to every question.
early nineteenth century

4 There goes more to marriage than four bare legs in a bed.
mid sixteenth century

5 There is a remedy for everything except death.
early fifteenth century

6 There is a time for everything.
late fourteenth century; see **Bible** 84:7

7 There is always a first time.
late eighteenth century

8 There is always room at the top.
early twentieth century; cf. **Webster** 807:18

9 There is an exception to every rule.
late sixteenth century

10 There is a time and place for everything.
early sixteenth century

11 There is honour among thieves.
early nineteenth century

12 There is luck in leisure.
late seventeenth century

13 There is luck in odd numbers.
late sixteenth century

14 There is measure in all things.
late fourteenth century; cf. **Horace** 389:15

15 There is no accounting for tastes.
late eighteenth century

16 There is no little enemy.
mid seventeenth century

17 There is no royal road to learning.
early nineteenth century; cf. **Euclid** 301:17

18 There is nothing like leather.
late seventeenth century

19 There is nothing lost by civility.
late nineteenth century

20 There is nothing new under the sun.
late sixteenth century; see **Bible** 84:3

21 There is nothing so good for the inside of a man as the outside of a horse.
early twentieth century

22 There is reason in the roasting of eggs.
mid seventeenth century

23 There is safety in numbers.
late seventeenth century

24 There is truth in wine.
mid sixteenth century

25 There's many a good cock come out of a tattered bag.
late nineteenth century

26 There's many a good tune played on an old fiddle.
early twentieth century

27 There's many a slip 'twixt cup and lip.
mid sixteenth century

28 There's no fool like an old fool.
mid sixteenth century

29 There's no great loss without some gain.
mid seventeenth century

30 There's no place like home.
late sixteenth century; cf. **Payne** 570:14

31 There's none so blind as those who will not see.
mid sixteenth century

32 There's none so deaf as those who will not hear.
mid sixteenth century

33 There's nowt so queer as folk.
early twentieth century

34 They that dance must pay the fiddler.
mid seventeenth century

35 They that live longest, see most.
early seventeenth century

36 They that sow the wind, shall reap the whirlwind.
late sixteenth century; see **Bible** 90:10

37 Things past cannot be recalled.
late fifteenth century

38 Think first and speak afterwards.
mid sixteenth century

39 Third time lucky.
mid nineteenth century

40 The third time pays for all.
late sixteenth century

41 Those who hide can find.
early fifteenth century

42 Those who live in glass houses shouldn't throw stones.
mid seventeenth century

43 Those who play at bowls must look out for rubbers.
mid eighteenth century

44 Thought is free.
late fourteenth century

45 Threatened men live long.
mid sixteenth century

46 Three may keep a secret, if two of them are dead.
mid sixteenth century

47 Three removals are as bad as a fire.
mid eighteenth century

48 Three things are not to be trusted; a cow's horn, a dog's tooth, and a horse's hoof.
late fourteenth century

49 Thrift is a great revenue.
mid seventeenth century

50 Throw dirt enough, and some will stick.
mid seventeenth century

51 Time and tide wait for no man.
late fourteenth century

52 Time flies.
late fourteenth century; cf. **Virgil** 797:1

1 Time is a great healer.
late fourteenth century

2 Time is money.
late sixteenth century

3 Time will tell.
mid sixteenth century

4 Time works wonders.
late sixteenth century

5 Times change and we with time.
attributed to the Emperor Lothar I (795–855) in the form 'Omnia mutantur, nos et mutamur in illis [All things change, and we change with them]'
late sixteenth century

6 'Tis better to have loved and lost, than never to have loved at all.
early eighteenth century; cf. **Congreve** 233:6, **Tennyson** 761:4

7 Today you; tomorrow me.
early seventeenth century

8 To err is human (to forgive divine).
late sixteenth century; cf. **Pope** 584:27

9 To know all is to forgive all.
mid twentieth century; cf. **Staël** 735:17

10 Tomorrow is another day.
early sixteenth century; cf. **Mitchell** 524:3

11 Tomorrow never comes.
early sixteenth century

12 The tongue always returns to the sore tooth.
late sixteenth century

13 Too many cooks spoil the broth.
late sixteenth century

14 To the pure all things are pure.
mid nineteenth century; see **Bible** 109:24

15 Trade follows the flag.
late nineteenth century

16 Travel broadens the mind.
early twentieth century

17 The tree is known by its fruit.
early sixteenth century; see **Bible** 95:12

18 A trouble shared is a trouble halved.
early 20th century

19 Truth is stranger than fiction.
early nineteenth century, from **Byron**; cf. **Byron** 177:26

20 Truth lies at the bottom of a well.
mid sixteenth century

21 Truth will out.
mid fifteenth century

22 Turkey, heresy, hops, and beer came into England all in one year.
late sixteenth century

23 Turn about is fair play.
mid eighteenth century

24 Two blacks don't make a white.
early eighteenth century

25 Two boys are half a boy, and three boys are no boy at all.
early twentieth century

26 Two heads are better than one.
late fourteenth century

27 Two is company, but three is none.
often used with the alternative ending 'three's a crowd'
early eighteenth century

28 Two of a trade never agree.
early seventeenth century

29 Two wrongs don't make a right.
late eighteenth century

30 The unexpected always happens.
late nineteenth century

31 Union is strength.
mid seventeenth century

32 United we stand, divided we fall.
late eighteenth century, from **Dickinson**; cf. **Dickinson** 266:23

33 Variety is the spice of life.
late eighteenth century, from **Cowper**; cf. **Cowper** 241:23

34 Virtue is its own reward.
early sixteenth century

35 The voice of the people is the voice of God.
early fifteenth century; cf. **Alcuin** 10:10

36 Walls have ears.
late sixteenth century

37 Walnuts and pears you plant for your heirs.
mid seventeenth century

38 Wanton kittens make sober cats.
early eighteenth century

39 Waste not, want not.
late eighteenth century

40 A watched pot never boils.
mid 19th century

41 The way to a man's heart is through his stomach.
early nineteenth century

42 The weakest go to the wall.
early sixteenth century

43 Wedlock is a padlock.
late seventeenth century

44 Well begun is half done.
early fifteenth century

45 We must eat a peck of dirt before we die.
mid eighteenth century

46 We must learn to walk before we can run.
mid fourteenth century

47 What a neighbour gets is not lost.
mid sixteenth century

48 What can't be cured must be endured.
late sixteenth century

49 What can you expect from a pig but a grunt.
early eighteenth century

50 Whatever man has done, man may do.
mid nineteenth century

51 What everybody says must be true.
early fifteenth century

1 What goes up must come down.
early twentieth century

2 What is got over the Devil's back is spent under his belly.
late sixteenth century

3 What is new cannot be true.
mid seventeenth century

4 What Manchester says today, the rest of England says tomorrow.
late nineteenth century

5 What must be, must be.
late fourteenth century

6 What's bred in the bone will come out in the flesh.
late fifteenth century

7 What's done cannot be undone.
mid fifteenth century

8 What's sauce for the goose is sauce for the gander.
late seventeenth century

9 What the eye doesn't see, the heart doesn't grieve over.
mid sixteenth century; earlier in Latin

10 What the soldier said isn't evidence.
mid nineteenth century; cf. **Dickens** 265:14

11 What you don't know can't hurt you.
late sixteenth century

12 What you have, hold.
mid fifteenth century

13 What you lose on the swings you gain on the roundabouts.
early twentieth century

14 What you spend, you have.
early fourteenth century

15 What you've never had you never miss.
early twentieth century

16 When Adam delved and Eve span, who was then the gentleman?
traditionally taken by John Ball as the text of his revolutionary sermon on the outbreak of the Peasants' Revolt, 1381
late fourteenth century; cf. **Rolle** 632:6

17 When all fruit fails, welcome haws.
early eighteenth century

18 When all you have is a hammer, everything looks like a nail.
late twentieth century, mainly North American

19 When Greek meets Greek, then comes the tug of war.
late seventeenth century

20 When house and land are gone and spent, then learning is most excellent.
mid eighteenth century

21 When in doubt, do nowt.
late nineteenth century

22 When in Rome, do as the Romans do.
mid sixteenth century; cf. **Ambrose** 13:4

23 When one door shuts, another opens.
late sixteenth century

24 When poverty comes in at the door, love flies out of the window.
early seventeenth century

25 When the blind lead the blind, both shall fall into the ditch.
late ninth century; see **Bible** 95:29

26 When the cat's away, the mice will play.
early seventeenth century

27 When the furze is in bloom, my love's in tune.
mid eighteenth century

28 When the going gets tough, the tough get going.
mid twentieth century; cf. **Kennedy** 433:21

29 When the gorse is out of bloom, kissing's out of fashion.
mid nineteenth century

30 When the oak is before the ash, then you will only get a splash; when the ash is before the oak, then you may expect a soak.
mid nineteenth century

31 When the wind is in the east, 'tis neither good for man nor beast.
early seventeenth century

32 When the wine is in, the wit is out.
late fourteenth century

33 When thieves fall out, honest men come by their own.
mid sixteenth century

34 When things are at the worst they begin to mend.
late sixteenth century

35 Where bees are, there is honey.
early seventeenth century

36 Where God builds a church, the Devil will build a chapel.
mid sixteenth century; cf. **Luther** 480:1

37 Where ignorance is bliss, 'tis folly to be wise.
mid eighteenth century, from **Gray**; cf. **Gray** 350:18

38 Where MacGregor sits at the head of the table.
mid nineteenth century

39 Where the carcase is, there shall the eagles be gathered together.
mid sixteenth century; see **Bible** 97:3

40 Where there's a will there's a way.
mid seventeenth century

41 Where there's muck there's brass.
late seventeenth century

42 While the grass grows, the steed starves.
mid fourteenth century

43 While there's life there's hope.
mid sixteenth century

44 While two dogs are fighting for a bone, a third runs away with it.
late fourteenth century

45 A whistling woman and a crowing hen are neither fit for God nor men.
early 18th century

1 Who says A must say B.
mid nineteenth century, usually North American

2 Who won't be ruled by the rudder must be ruled by the rock.
mid seventeenth century

3 Whom the Gods love die young.
mid sixteenth century; cf. **Menander** 504:12

4 Whom the gods would destroy, they first make mad.
early seventeenth century, earlier in Greek; cf. **Anonymous** 21:2

5 Whosoever draws his sword against the prince must throw the scabbard away.
early seventeenth century

6 Why buy a cow when milk is so cheap?
mid seventeenth century

7 Why keep a dog and bark yourself?
late sixteenth century

8 Why should the devil have all the best tunes?
mid nineteenth century; cf. **Hill** 377:3

9 A wilful man must have his way.
early 19th century

10 Wilful waste makes woeful want.
early eighteenth century

11 Winter never rots in the sky.
early seventeenth century

12 The wish is father to the thought.
late sixteenth century, from **Shakespeare**; cf. **Shakespeare** 670:16

13 A woman, a dog, and a walnut tree, the more you beat them the better they be.
late 16th century

14 A woman and a ship ever want mending.
late 16th century; 2nd century BC in Latin

15 A woman's place is in the home.
mid 19th century

16 A woman's work is never done.
late 16th century

17 Wonders will never cease.
late eighteenth century

18 A word to the wise is enough.
early 16th century; cf. **Plautus** 578:13

19 Work expands so as to fill the time available.
mid twentieth century, from **Parkinson**; cf. **Parkinson** 567:22

20 The worth of a thing is what it will bring.
late sixteenth century

21 Yorkshire born and Yorkshire bred, strong in the arm and weak in the head.
the names of other (chiefly northern) English counties and towns are also used instead of Yorkshire
mid nineteenth century

22 You are what you eat.
mid twentieth century; cf. **Feuerbach** 309:4

23 You buy land, you buy stones; you buy meat, you buy bones.
late seventeenth century

24 You can drive out nature with a pitchfork but she keeps on coming back.
mid sixteenth century; cf. **Horace** 386:19

25 You can have too much of a good thing.
late fifteenth century

26 You can only die once.
mid fifteenth century

27 You can't make a silk purse out of a sow's ear.
early sixteenth century

28 You can't please everyone.
late fifteenth century

29 You can't put new wine in old bottles.
early twentieth century; see **Bible** 94:26

30 You can't teach an old dog new tricks.
early sixteenth century

31 You can't tell a book by its cover.
early twentieth century

32 You can't win them all.
mid twentieth century

33 You can take a horse to the water, but you can't make him drink.
late twelfth century

34 You can take the boy out of the country but you can't take the country out of the boy.
mid twentieth century, usually North American

35 You cannot catch old birds with chaff.
late fifteenth century

36 You cannot get a quart into a pint pot.
late nineteenth century

37 You cannot get blood from a stone.
mid seventeenth century

38 You cannot have your cake and eat it.
mid sixteenth century

39 You cannot lose what you never had.
late sixteenth century

40 You cannot make an omelette without breaking eggs.
mid nineteenth century

41 You cannot make bricks without straw.
mid seventeenth century

42 You cannot put an old head on young shoulders.
late sixteenth century

43 You cannot run with the hare and hunt with the hounds.
mid fifteenth century

44 You cannot serve God and Mammon.
early sixteenth century; see **Bible** 93:22

45 You cannot shift an old tree without it dying.
early sixteenth century

46 You don't get something for nothing.
late nineteenth century

47 You never know what you can do till you try.
early nineteenth century

48 You never miss the water till the well runs dry.
early seventeenth century

1 Young folks think old folks to be fools, but old folks know young folks to be fools.
late sixteenth century

2 A young man married is a young man marred.
late 16th century; cf. **Shakespeare** 656:3

3 Young men may die, but old men must die.
mid sixteenth century

4 Young saint, old devil.
early fifteenth century

5 You pays your money and you takes your choice.
mid nineteenth century

6 You should know a man seven years before you stir his fire.
early nineteenth century

7 Youth must be served.
early nineteenth century

8 You win a few, you lose a few.
mid twentieth century

Pu Yi 1906–67

Emperor of China 1908–12; Japan's puppet emperor of Manchuria 1934–45

9 For the past 40 years I had never folded my own quilt, made my own bed, or poured out my own washing. I had never even washed my own feet or tied my shoes.
From Emperor to Citizen (1964)

Publilius Syrus

writer of Latin mimes in the 1st century BC

10 *Formosa facies muta commendatio est.*
A beautiful face is a mute recommendation.
Sententiae no. 199, in J. and A. Duff *Minor Latin Poets* (Loeb ed., 1934); translated by Thomas Tenison in *Baconiana* (1679) 'Ornamenta Rationalia' no. 12

11 *Inopi beneficium bis dat qui dat celeriter.*
He gives the poor man twice as much good who gives quickly.
proverbially 'Bis dat qui cito dat [He gives twice who gives soon]'
Sententiae no. 274, in J. and A. Duff *Minor Latin Poets*; cf. **Proverbs** 602:5

12 *Iudex damnatur ubi nocens absolvitur.*
The judge is condemned when the guilty party is acquitted.
Sententiae no. 296, in J. and A. Duff *Minor Latin Poets*

13 *Necessitas dat legem non ipsa accipit.*
Necessity gives the law without itself acknowledging one.
proverbially 'Necessitas non habet legem [Necessity has no law]'
Sententiae no. 444, in J. and A. Duff *Minor Latin Poets*; cf. **Cromwell** 245:17, **Proverbs** 607:24

John Pudney 1909–77

English poet and writer

14 Do not despair
For Johnny-head-in-air;
He sleeps as sound
As Johnny underground.

Fetch out no shroud
For Johnny-in-the-cloud;
And keep your tears
For him in after years.

Better by far
For Johnny-the-bright-star,
To keep your head,
And see his children fed.
'For Johnny' (1942); cf. **Hoffmann** 380:2

Augustus Welby Pugin 1812–52

English architect and designer

15 The two great rules for design are these: 1*st, that there should be no features about a building which are not necessary for convenience, construction or propriety;* 2*nd, that all ornament should consist of the essential construction of the building.* The neglect of these two rules is the cause of all the bad architecture of the present time.
True Principles (1841)

16 A man who remains any length of time in a modern Gothic room, and escapes without being wounded by some of its minutiae, may consider himself extremely fortunate.
True Principles (1841)

17 There is nothing worth living for but Christian Architecture and a boat.
in *The Builder* 1852 vol. 10

18 How can you expect to convert England if you use a cope like that?
to an unidentified Catholic priest
Bernard England *The Sequel to Catholic Emancipation* (1915)

19 Nothing can be more dangerous than looking at prints of buildings, and trying to imitate bits of them. These architectural books are as bad as the Scriptures in the hands of the Protestants.
J. Mordaunt Crook *Dilemma of Style* (1987)

20 Yet notwithstanding the palpable impracticability of adapting Greek temples to our climate, habits and religion, we see the attempt and failure continuously made and repeated; post office, theatre, church, bath, reading-room, hotel, methodist chapel and turnpike gate, all the present the eternal sameness of a Grecian temple outraged in all its proportions and character.
J. Mordaunt Crook *The Greek Revival* (1995)

Joseph Pulitzer 1847–1911

Hungarian-born American newspaper proprietor and editor

21 A cynical, mercenary, demagogic, corrupt press will produce in time a people as base as itself.
inscribed on the gateway to the Columbia School of Journalism in New York
W. J. Granberg *The World of Joseph Pulitzer* (1965)

William Pulteney, Earl of Bath
1684–1764
English peer

1 For Sir Ph—p well knows
That innuendos
Will serve him no longer in verse or in prose,
Since twelve honest men have decided the cause,
And were judges of fact, tho' not judges of laws.
on the unsuccessful prosecution of The Craftsman, *1729 by Philip Yorke, later Lord* **Hardwicke**
'The Honest Jury' (1729) st. 3

Punch 1841–1992
English humorous weekly periodical

2 Advice to persons about to marry.—'Don't.'
4 January 1845; cf. **Bacon** 43:20

3 You pays your money and you takes your choice.
3 January 1846

4 The Half-Way House to Rome, Oxford.
27 January 1849

5 Never do to-day what you can put off till to-morrow.
22 December 1849

6 Who's 'im, Bill?
A stranger!
'Eave 'arf a brick at 'im.
25 February 1854

7 What is Matter?—Never mind.
What is Mind?—No matter.
14 July 1855

8 It ain't the 'unting as 'urts 'im, it's the 'ammer, 'ammer, 'ammer along the 'ard 'igh road.
31 May 1856

9 Mun, a had na' been the-erre abune two hours when—*bang*—went saxpence!!!
5 December 1868

10 Cats is 'dogs' and rabbits is 'dogs' and so's Parrats, but this 'ere 'Tortis' is a insect, and there ain't no charge for it.
6 March 1869

11 Nothink for nothink 'ere, and precious little for sixpence.
16 October 1869

12 Go directly—see what she's doing, and tell her she mustn't.
16 November 1872

13 There was one poor tiger that hadn't *got* a Christian.
3 April 1875

14 It's worse than wicked, my dear, it's vulgar.
Almanac (1876)

15 I never read books—I *write* them.
11 May 1878; cf. **Disraeli** 271:10

16 I am not hungry; but thank goodness, I am greedy.
28 December 1878

17 BISHOP: Who is it that sees and hears all we do, and before whom even I am but as a crushed worm?
PAGE: The Missus, my Lord.
14 August 1880

18 Ah whiles hae ma doobts aboot the meenister.
11 December 1880

19 WIFE OF TWO YEARS' STANDING: Oh yes! I'm sure he's not so fond of me as at first. He's away so much, neglects me dreadfully, and he's so cross when he comes home. What *shall* I do?
WIDOW: Feed the brute!
31 October 1885

20 Nearly all our best men are dead! Carlyle, Tennyson, Browning, George Eliot!—I'm not feeling very well myself.
6 May 1893

21 Botticelli isn't a wine, you Juggins! Botticelli's a *cheese*!
6 June 1894

22 I'm afraid you've got a bad egg, Mr Jones.
Oh no, my Lord, I assure you! Parts of it are excellent!
11 May 1895

23 Look here, Steward, if this is coffee, I want tea; but if this is tea, then I wish for coffee.
23 July 1902

24 Sometimes I sits and thinks, and then again I just sits.
24 October 1906

Al Purdy 1918–
Canadian poet and writer

25 Look here
You've never seen this country
it's not the way you thought it was
Look again.
of Canada
'The Country of the Young' (1976)

Alexander Pushkin 1799–1837
Russian poet

26 Storm-clouds whirl and storm-clouds scurry;
From behind them pale moonlight
Flickers where the snowflakes hurry.
Dark the sky and dark the night.
'Devils' (1830) (translated by C. M. Bowra)

27 From early youth his dedication
Was to a single occupation . . .
The science of the tender passion.
Eugene Onegin (1833) ch. 1, st. 8 (translated by Babette Deutsch)

28 A woman's love for us increases
The less we love her, sooth to say—
She stoops, she falls, her struggling ceases;
Caught fast, she cannot get away.
Eugene Onegin (1833) ch. 4, st. 1 (translated by Babette Deutsch)

29 A tedious season they await
Who hear November at the gate.
Eugene Onegin (1833) ch. 4, st. 40 (translated by Babette Deutsch)

1 Moscow: those syllables can start
A tumult in the Russian heart.
Eugene Onegin (1833) ch. 7, st. 36 (translated by Babette Deutsch)

2 A green oak grows by a curving shore;
And round that oak hangs a golden chain.
Ruslan and Lyudmila (1820) 'Prologue' (translated by Elisaveta Fen)

3 When trade and traffic and all the noise of town
Is dimmed, and on the streets and squares
The filmy curtain of the night sinks down
With sleep, the recompense of cares,
To me the darkness brings not sleep nor rest.
'Remembrances' (1828) (translated by R. M. Hewitt)

Israel Putnam 1718–90

American general

4 Men, you are all marksmen—don't one of you fire until you see the white of their eyes.
also attributed to William Prescott (1726–95)
at Bunker Hill, 1775, in R. Frothingham *History of the Siege of Boston* (1873) ch. 5

Mario Puzo 1920–

American novelist

5 I'll make him an offer he can't refuse.
The Godfather (1969) ch. 1

6 A lawyer with his briefcase can steal more than a hundred men with guns.
The Godfather (1969) ch. 1

Barbara Pym 1913–80

English novelist

7 She experienced all the cosiness and irritation which can come from living with thoroughly nice people with whom one has nothing in common.
Less than Angels (1955) ch. 23

John Pym 1584–1643

English Parliamentary leader

8 To have granted liberties, and not to have liberties in truth and realities, is but to mock the kingdom.
pointing out the illusory nature of **Charles I**'*s promises*
in *Dictionary of National Biography* (1917–)

Pyrrhus 319–272 BC

King of Epirus from 306 BC

9 One more such victory and we are lost.
on defeating the Romans at Asculum, 279 BC
Plutarch *Parallel Lives* 'Pyrrhus' ch. 21, sect. 9

Mary Quant 1934–

English fashion designer

10 Having money is rather like being a blonde. It is more fun but not vital.
in *Observer* 2 November 1986 'Sayings of the Week'

11 Being young is greatly overestimated . . . Any failure seems so total. Later on you realize you can have another go.
interview in *Observer* 5 May 1996

Francis Quarles 1592–1644

English poet

12 Our God and soldiers we alike adore
Ev'n at the brink of danger; not before:
After deliverance, both alike requited,
Our God's forgotten, and our soldiers slighted.
Divine Fancies (1632) 'Of Common Devotion'; cf. **Owen** 562:1

13 I wish thee as much pleasure in the reading, as I had in the writing.
Emblems (1635) 'To the Reader'

14 The heart is a small thing, but desireth great matters. It is not sufficient for a kite's dinner, yet the whole world is not sufficient for it.
Emblems (1635) bk. 1, no. 12 'Hugo *de Anima*'

15 My soul, sit thou a patient looker-on;
Judge not the play before the play is done:
Her plot hath many changes; every day
Speaks a new scene; the last act crowns the play.
Emblems (1635) bk. 1, no. 15 'Respice Finem'

16 We spend our midday sweat, our midnight oil;
We tire the night in thought, the day in toil.
Emblems (1635) bk. 2, no. 2, l. 33; cf. **Gay** 332:6

17 Be wisely worldly, be not worldly wise.
Emblems (1635) bk. 2, no. 2, l. 46

18 Thou art my way; I wander, if thou fly;
Thou art my light; if hid, how blind am I!
Thou art my life; if thou withdraw, I die.
Emblems (1643) bk. 3, no. 7

19 He teaches to deny that faintly prays.
A Feast for Worms (1620) sect. 7, Meditation 7, l. 2

20 Man is man's A.B.C. There is none that can
Read God aright, unless he first spell Man.
Hieroglyphics of the Life of Man (1638) no. 1, l. 1

21 Physicians of all men are most happy; what good success soever they have, the world proclaimeth, and what faults they commit, the earth covereth.
Hieroglyphics of the Life of Man (1638) no. 4; cf. **Wright** 833:10

22 We'll cry both arts and learning down,
And hey! then up go we!
The Shepherd's Oracles (1646) Eclogue 11 'Song of Anarchus'

François Quesnay 1694–1774

French political economist

23 *Vous ne connaissez qu'une seule règle du commerce; c'est (pour me servir de vos propres termes) de laisser passer et de laisser faire tous les acheteurs et tous les vendeurs quelconques.*

You recognize but one rule of commerce; that is (to avail myself of your own terms) to allow free passage and freedom of action to all buyers and sellers whoever they may be.

letter from M. Alpha to Quesnay, 1767, in L. Salleron *François Quesnay et la Physiocratie* (1958) vol. 2; not found in Quesnay's own writings; cf. **Anonymous** 20:7, **Argenson** 24:5

Arthur Quiller-Couch ('Q') 1863–1944

English writer and critic

1 The best is the best, though a hundred judges have declared it so.

Oxford Book of English Verse (1900) preface

2 All the old statues of Victory have wings: but Grief has no wings. She is the unwelcome lodger that squats on the hearthstone between us and the fire and will not move or be dislodged.

Armistice Day anniversary sermon, Cambridge, November 1923

Josiah Quincy 1772–1864

American Federalist politician

3 As it will be the right of all, so it will be the duty of some, definitely to prepare for a separation, amicably if they can, violently if they must.

speech, 14 January 1811, in *Abridgement of Debates of Congress* vol. 4; cf. **Clay** 220:2

W. V. O. Quine 1908–

American philosopher

4 On the doctrinal side, I do not see that we are farther along today than where [David] Hume left us. The Humean predicament is the human predicament.

Ontological Relativity and Other Essays (1969) ch. 3

5 It is the tension between the scientist's laws and his own attempted breaches of them that powers the engines of science and makes it forge ahead.

Quiddities (1987) p. 8 'Anomaly'

6 Students of the heavens are separable into astronomers and astrologers as readily as are the minor domestic ruminants into sheep and goats, but the separation of philosophers into sages and cranks seems to be more sensitive to frames of reference.

Theories and Things (1981) ch. 23

7 Different persons growing up in the same language are like different bushes trimmed and trained to take the shape of identical elephants. The anatomical details of twigs and branches will fulfill the elephantine shape differently from bush to bush, but the overall outward results are alike.

Word and Object (1960)

Quintilian AD c.35–c.96

Roman rhetorician

8 *Satura quidem tota nostra est.*

Verse satire indeed is entirely our own.

meaning Roman as opposed to Greek

Institutio Oratoria bk. 10, ch. 1, sect. 93

The Qur'an see The Koran

François Rabelais c.1494–c.1553

French humanist, satirist, and physician

see also ***Last words*** *455:20*

9 *L'appétit vient en mangeant.*

The appetite grows by eating.

Gargantua (1534) bk. 1, ch. 5; cf. **Proverbs** 595:12

10 *Natura vacuum abhorret.*

Nature abhors a vacuum.

quoting, in Latin, an article of ancient wisdom

Gargantua (1534) bk. 1, ch. 5; cf. **Proverbs** 607:18

11 *Fay ce que vouldras.*

Do what you like.

Gargantua (1534) bk. 1, ch. 57; cf. **Crowley** 246:17

12 *Quaestio subtilissima, utrum chimera in vacuo bombinans possit comedere secundas intentiones.*

A most subtle question: whether a chimera buzzing in a vacuum can devour second intentions.

Pantagruel bk. 2, ch. 7

13 A child is not a vase to be filled, but a fire to be lit.

attributed

Yitzhak Rabin 1922–95

Israeli statesman and military leader, Prime Minister 1974–7 and 1992–5

14 We say to you today in a loud and a clear voice: enough of blood and tears. Enough.

to the Palestinians, at the signing of the Israel–Palestine Declaration

in Washington, 13 September, 1993

Jean Racine 1639–99

French tragedian

15 *Je l'ai trop aimé pour ne le point haïr!*

I have loved him too much not to feel any hatred for him.

Andromaque (1667) act 2, sc. 1

16 *C'était pendant l'horreur d'une profonde nuit.*

It was during the horror of a deep night.

Athalie (1691) act 2, sc. 5

17 *Elle flotte, elle hésite; en un mot, elle est femme.*

She floats, she hesitates; in a word, she's a woman.

Athalie (1691) act 3, sc. 3

18 *Ce n'est plus une ardeur dans mes veines cachée:*
C'est Vénus tout entière à sa proie attachée.

It's no longer a burning within my veins: it's Venus entire latched onto her prey.

Phèdre (1677) act 1, sc. 3

19 *Dans le fond des forêts votre image me suit.*

Deep in the forest glade your picture chases me.

Phèdre (1677) act 2, sc. 2

20 *Tous les jours se levaient clairs et sereins pour eux.*

Every day dawned clear and untroubled for them.

Phèdre (1677) act 4, sc. 6

1 *Point d'argent, point de Suisse, et ma porte était close.*

No money, no service, and my door stayed shut.
Les Plaideurs (1668) act 1, sc. 1; cf. **Proverbs** 607:49

2 *Sans argent l'honneur n'est qu'une maladie.*

Honour, without money, is just a disease.
Les Plaideurs (1668) act 1, sc. 1

Lord Radcliffe 1899–1977
British lawyer and public servant

3 Governments always tend to want not really a free press but a managed or well-conducted one.
in 1967; Peter Hennessy *What the Papers Never Said* (1985)

James Rado 1939– and Gerome Ragni 1942–
American songwriters

4 When the moon is in the seventh house,
And Jupiter aligns with Mars,
Then peace will guide the planets,
And love will steer the stars;
This is the dawning of the age of Aquarius.
'Aquarius' (1967 song) in *Hair*

John Rae 1931–
English writer

5 War is, after all, the universal perversion . . . war stories, the pornography of war.
The Custard Boys (1960) ch. 13

Thomas Rainborowe d. 1648
English soldier and parliamentarian

6 The poorest he that is in England hath a life to live as the greatest he.
during the Army debates at Putney, 29 October 1647, in C. H. Firth (ed.) *The Clarke Papers* vol. 1, Camden Society, New Series 49 (1891)

Craig Raine 1944–
English poet

7 In homes, a haunted apparatus sleeps,
that snores when you pick it up.
If the ghost cries, they carry it
to their lips and soothe it to sleep
with sounds. And yet, they wake it up
deliberately, but tickling it with a finger.
'A Martian sends a Postcard Home' (1979)

Kathleen Raine 1908–
British poet

8 He has married me with a ring, a ring of bright water
Whose ripples spread from the heart of the sea,
He has married me with a ring of light, the glitter
Broadcast on the swift river.
'The Marriage of Psyche' (1952)

Walter Ralegh c.1552–1618
English explorer and courtier
see also ***Last words*** 456:5

9 If all the world and love were young,
And truth in every shepherd's tongue,
These pretty pleasures might me move
To live with thee, and be thy love.
'Answer to Marlow'; cf. **Donne** 273:19, **Marlowe** 496:19

10 Now what is love? I pray thee, tell.
It is that fountain and that well,
Where pleasure and repentance dwell.
It is perhaps that sauncing bell,
That tolls all in to heaven or hell:
And this is love, as I hear tell.
'A Description of Love'

11 A maze wherein affection finds no end,
A ranging cloud that runs before the wind,
A substance like the shadow of the sun,
A goal of grief for which the wisest run.
'Farewell false love' (1588)

12 Go, Soul, the body's guest,
Upon a thankless arrant:
Fear not to touch the best;
The truth shall be thy warrant:
Go, since I needs must die,
And give the world the lie.
Say to the court, it glows
And shines like rotten wood;
Say to the church, it shows
What's good, and doth no good:
If church and court reply,
Then give them both the lie.
'The Lie' (1608)

13 Tell zeal it wants devotion;
Tell love it is but lust;
Tell time it metes but motion;
Tell flesh it is but dust:
And wish them not reply,
For thou must give the lie.
'The Lie' (1608)

14 Only we die in earnest, that's no jest.
'On the Life of Man'

15 Give me my scallop-shell of quiet,
My staff of faith to walk upon,
My scrip of joy, immortal diet,
My bottle of salvation,
My gown of glory, hope's true gage,
And thus I'll take my pilgrimage.
'The Passionate Man's Pilgrimage' (1604)

16 Our passions are most like to floods and streams;
The shallow murmur, but the deep are dumb.
'Sir Walter Ralegh to the Queen' (1655)

17 Three things there be that prosper all apace,
And flourish while they are asunder far;
But on a day, they meet all in a place,
And when they meet, they one another mar.
And they be these: the Wood, the Weed, the Wag:
The Wood is that that makes the gallows tree;
The Weed is that that strings the hangman's bag;

The Wag, my pretty knave, betokens thee.
'Sir Walter Ralegh to his Son'

1 As you came from the holy land
Of Walsinghame,
Met you not with my true love
By the way as you came?
How shall I know your true love,
That have met many one
As I went to the holy land,
That have come, that have gone?
'Walsinghame'

2 But true love is a durable fire,
In the mind ever burning,
Never sick, never old, never dead,
From itself never turning.
'Walsinghame'

3 Fain would I climb, yet fear I to fall.
line written on a window-pane, in Thomas Fuller *History of the Worthies of England* (1662) 'Devonshire'; cf. **Elizabeth I** 297:7

4 Even such is Time, which takes in trust
Our youth, our joys, and all we have,
And pays us but with age and dust;
Who in the dark and silent grave,
When we have wandered all our ways,
Shuts up the story of our days:
And from which earth, and grave, and dust,
The Lord shall raise me up, I trust.
written the night before his death, and found in his Bible in the Gate-house at Westminster

5 [History] hath triumphed over time, which besides it, nothing but eternity hath triumphed over.
The History of the World (1614) preface

6 Whosoever, in writing a modern history, shall follow truth too near the heels, it may happily strike out his teeth.
The History of the World (1614) preface

7 O eloquent, just, and mighty Death! . . . thou hast drawn together all the farstretched greatness, all the pride, cruelty, and ambition of man, and covered it all over with these two narrow words, *Hic jacet* [Here lies].
The History of the World (1614) bk. 5, ch. 6

8 'Tis a sharp remedy, but a sure one for all ills.
on feeling the edge of the axe prior to his execution
D. Hume *History of Great Britain* (1754) vol. 1, ch. 4

9 So the heart be right, it is no matter which way the head lies.
at his execution, on being asked which way he preferred to lay his head
W. Stebbing *Sir Walter Raleigh* (1891) ch. 30

Walter Raleigh 1861–1922

English lecturer and critic

10 In examinations those who do not wish to know ask questions of those who cannot tell.
Laughter from a Cloud (1923) 'Some Thoughts on Examinations'

11 I wish I loved the Human Race;
I wish I loved its silly face;
I wish I liked the way it walks;
I wish I liked the way it talks;
And when I'm introduced to one
I wish I thought *What Jolly Fun!*
'Wishes of an Elderly Man' (1923)

12 An anthology is like all the plums and orange peel picked out of a cake.
letter to Mrs Robert Bridges, 15 January 1915

Srinivasa Ramanujan 1887–1920

Indian mathematician

replying to G. H. **Hardy***'s suggestion that the number of a taxi-cab (1729) was 'dull':*

13 No, it is a very interesting number; it is the smallest number expressible as a sum of two cubes in two different ways.
the two ways being 1^3+12^3 *and* 9^3+10^3
in *Proceedings of the London Mathematical Society* 26 May 1921

Ayn Rand 1905–82

American writer

14 Civilization is the progress toward a society of privacy. The savage's noble existence is public, ruled by the laws of his tribe. Civilization is the process of setting man free from men.
The Fountainhead (1947)

John Randolph 1773–1833

American politician

15 God has given us Missouri, and the devil shall not take it from us.
in the debate in the US Senate in 1820 on the admission of Missouri to the Union as a slave state
Robert V. Remini *Henry Clay* (1991) ch. 11

16 Never were abilities so much below mediocrity so well rewarded; no, not when Caligula's horse was made Consul.
on John Quincy **Adams***'s appointment of Richard Rush as Secretary of the Treasury*
speech, 1 February 1828

17 He is a man of splendid abilities but utterly corrupt. He shines and stinks like rotten mackerel by moonlight.
of Edward Livingston
W. Cabell Bruce *John Randolph of Roanoke* (1923) vol. 2

18 That most delicious of all privileges—spending other people's money.
William Cabell Bruce *John Randolph of Roanoke* (1923) vol. 2

John Crowe Ransom 1888–1974

American poet and critic

19 The lazy geese, like a snow cloud
Dripping their snow on the green grass,
Tricking and stopping, sleepy and proud,
Who cried in goose, alas.
'Bells for John Whiteside's Daughter' (1924)

20 Here lies a lady of beauty and high degree.
Of chills and fever she died, of fever and chills,

The delight of her husband, her aunts, an infant of three,
And of medicos marvelling sweetly on her ills.
'Here Lies a Lady' (1924)

1 Two evils, monstrous either one apart,
Possessed me, and were long and loath at going:
A cry of Absence, Absence, in the heart,
And in the wood the furious winter blowing.
'Winter Remembered' (1945)

Raoul Glabar c.985–c.1046
Cluniac monk and chronicler

2 After the above-mentioned millennium which is now about three years past, there occurred throughout the whole world . . . a rebuilding of church basilicas . . . It was as if the whole earth, having cast off the old by shaking itself, were clothing itself everywhere in a white robe of churches.
of the rebuilding of churches in the 11th century
Histories bk 3, ch. 4

Frederic Raphael 1931–
British novelist and screenwriter
see also **Borrowed titles** 144:7

3 Your idea of fidelity is not having more than one man in bed at the same time.
Darling (1965) ch. 18

4 City of perspiring dreams.
of Cambridge
The Glittering Prizes (1976) ch. 3; cf. **Arnold** 27:25

Gerald Ratner 1949–
English businessman

5 We even sell a pair of earrings for under £1, which is cheaper than a prawn sandwich from Marks & Spencers. But I have to say the earrings probably won't last as long.
speech to the Institute of Directors, Albert Hall, 23 April 1991

Terence Rattigan 1911–77
English dramatist

6 Do you know what 'le vice Anglais'—the English vice—really is? Not flagellation, not pederasty—whatever the French believe it to be. It's our refusal to admit our emotions. We think they demean us, I suppose.
In Praise of Love (1973) act 2

7 You can be in the Horseguards and still be common, dear.
Separate Tables (1954) 'Table Number Seven' sc. 1

Gwen Raverat 1885–1957
English wood-engraver

8 Ladies were ladies in those days; they did not do things themselves.
Period Piece (1952) ch. 5

Derek Raymond 1931–94
English thriller writer

9 The psychopath is the furnace that gives no heat.
The Hidden Files (1992)

Herbert Read 1893–1968
English art historian

10 Do not judge this movement kindly. It is not just another amusing stunt. It is defiant—the desperate act of men too profoundly convinced of the rottenness of our civilization to want to save a shred of its respectability.
International Surrealist Exhibition Catalogue, New Burlington Galleries, London, 11 June–4 July 1936, introduction

11 Art is . . . pattern informed by sensibility.
The Meaning of Art (1955) ch. 1

12 Lorca was killed, singing,
and Fox who was my friend.
The rhythm returns: the song
which has no end.
'The Heart Conscripted' (1938)

13 I saw him stab
And stab again
A well-killed Boche.
This is the happy warrior,
This is he . . .
Naked Warriors (1919) 'The Scene of War, 4. The Happy Warrior'; cf. **Wordsworth** 827:18

Piers Paul Read 1941–
English novelist

14 Sins become more subtle as you grow older. You commit sins of despair rather than lust.
in *Daily Telegraph* 3 October 1990

Charles Reade 1814–84
English novelist and dramatist

15 *Courage, mon ami, le diable est mort!*
Take courage, my friend, the devil is dead!
The Cloister and the Hearth (1861) ch. 24, and *passim*

16 Sow an act, and you reap a habit. Sow a habit and you reap a character. Sow a character, and you reap a destiny.
attributed; in *Notes and Queries* (9th Series) vol. 12, 17 October 1903

Peter Reading 1946–
British poet

17 Midnight,
a hotel bedroom, open window,
sibilant tyres on rain-washed asphalt streets
whispering a repetitious *finish, finish.*
You stroke your lover comprehensively,
who purrs contentment, clings to your neck and sobs.
'Midnight' (1994)

Nancy Reagan 1923–

American actress and wife of Ronald **Reagan**, *First Lady of the US, 1981–9*

1 A woman is like a teabag—only in hot water do you realize how strong she is.

in *Observer* 29 March 1981

2 If the President has a bully pulpit, then the First Lady has a white glove pulpit . . . more refined, restricted, ceremonial, but it's a pulpit all the same.

in *New York Times* 10 March 1988; cf. **Roosevelt** 633:13

Ronald Reagan 1911–

American Republican statesman; 40th President of the US, 1981–9

on Reagan: see **Vidal** *792:11; see also* **Dempsey** *257:5,* **Gipp** *340:2*

3 Politics is supposed to be the second oldest profession. I have come to realize that it bears a very close resemblance to the first.

at a conference in Los Angeles, 2 March 1977; in Bill Adler *Reagan Wit* (1981) ch. 5; cf. **Kipling** 441:1

4 You can tell a lot about a fellow's character by his way of eating jellybeans.

in *New York Times* 15 January 1981

5 An evil empire.

of the Soviet Union

speech to the National Association of Evangelicals, 8 March 1983; in *New York Times* 9 March 1983

6 We are especially not going to tolerate these attacks from outlaw states run by the strangest collection of misfits, Looney Tunes, and squalid criminals since the advent of the Third Reich.

speech following the hijack of a US plane, 8 July 1985, in *New York Times* 9 July 1985

7 We will never forget them, nor the last time we saw them this morning, as they prepared for the journey and waved goodbye and 'slipped the surly bonds of earth' to 'touch the face of God.'

after the loss of the space shuttle Challenger *with all its crew*

broadcast from the Oval Office, 28 January 1986; cf. **Magee** 489:8

8 I now begin the journey that will lead me into the sunset of my life.

statement to the American people revealing that he had Alzheimer's disease

in *Daily Telegraph* 5 January 1995

Erell Reaves

9 Lady of Spain, I adore you.
Right from the night I first saw you,
My heart has been yearning for you,
What else could any heart do?

'Lady of Spain' (1913 song)

Red Cloud (Mahpiua Luta) 1822–1909

Oglala Sioux leader

10 You have heard the sound of the white soldier's axe upon the Little Piney. His presence here is . . . an insult to the spirits of our ancestors. Are we then to give up their sacred graves to be ploughed for corn? Dakotas, I am for war!

speech at council at Fort Laramie, 1866; Charles A. Eastman *Indian Heroes and Great Chieftains* (1918)

John Redmond 1856–1918

Irish politician and nationalist leader

in the spring of 1914, having been asked if anything could now prevent Home Rule:

11 A European war might do it.

in *Dictionary of National Biography* (1917–)

Henry Reed 1914–86

English poet and dramatist

12 As we get older we do not get any younger.
Seasons return, and today I am fifty-five,
And this time last year I was fifty-four,
And this time next year I shall be sixty-two.

'Chard Whitlow (Mr Eliot's Sunday Evening Postscript)' (1946)

13 Today we have naming of parts. Yesterday,
We had daily cleaning. And tomorrow morning,
We shall have what to do after firing. But today,
Today we have naming of parts. Japonica
Glistens like coral in all of the neighbour gardens,
And today we have naming of parts.

'Lessons of the War: 1, Naming of Parts' (1946)

14 They call it easing the Spring: it is perfectly easy
If you have any strength in your thumb: like the bolt,
And the breech, and the cocking-piece, and the point of balance,
Which in our case we have not got; and the almond blossom
Silent in all of the gardens and the bees going backwards and forwards,
For today we have naming of parts.

'Lessons of the War: 1, Naming of Parts' (1946)

15 And as for war, my wars
Were global from the start.

'Lessons of the War: 3, Unarmed Combat' (1946)

16 In a civil war, a general must know—and I'm afraid it's a thing rather of instinct than of practice—he must know exactly when to move over to the other side.

Not a Drum was Heard: The War Memoirs of General Gland (unpublished radio play, 1959)

17 And the sooner the tea's out of the way, the sooner we can get out the gin, eh?

Private Life of Hilda Tablet (1954 radio play) in *Hilda Tablet and Others* (1971)

18 Of course we've all *dreamed* of reviving the *castrati*; but it's needed Hilda to take the first practical steps towards making them a reality . . . She's drawn up a list of well-known singers who she thinks would benefit . . . It's only a question of getting them to agree.

Private Life of Hilda Tablet (1954 radio play) in *Hilda Tablet and Others* (1971)

1 Modest? My word, no . . . He was an all-the-lights-on man.
A Very Great Man Indeed (1953 radio play) in *Hilda Tablet and Others* (1971)

2 I have known her pass the whole evening without mentioning a single book, or *in fact anything unpleasant*, at all.
A Very Great Man Indeed (1953 radio play) in *Hilda Tablet and Others* (1971)

John Reed 1887–1920
American journalist and revolutionary

3 Ten days that shook the world.
title of book (1919)

Joseph Reed 1741–85
American Revolutionary politician

4 I am not worth purchasing, but such as I am, the King of Great Britain is not rich enough to do it.
replying to an offer from Governor George Johnstone of £10,000, and any office in the Colonies in the King's gift, if he were able successfully to promote a Union between the UK and the US
reply as recorded in a declaration of Congress, 11 August 1778; the earliest version is:

My influence is but small, but were it as great as Governor Johnstone would insinuate, the King of Great Britain has nothing within his gift that would tempt me.
reply to Mrs Elizabeth Ferguson, 21 June 1778; W. B. Read *Life and Correspondence of Joseph Reed* (1847) vol. 1, ch. 18

Max Reger 1873–1916
German composer

5 I am sitting in the smallest room of my house. I have your review before me. In a moment it will be behind me.
responding to a savage review by Rudolph Louis in Münchener Neueste Nachrichten, *7 February 1906*
Nicolas Slonimsky *Lexicon of Musical Invective* (1953)

Charles A. Reich 1928–
American jurist

6 The greening of America.
title of book (1970)

Keith Reid 1946–
English pop singer and songwriter

7 Her face, at first . . . just ghostly
Turned a whiter shade of pale.
'A Whiter Shade of Pale' (1967 song)

Lord Reith 1889–1971
British administrator and politician, first general manager (1922–7) and first director-general (1927–8) of the BBC

8 By the time the civil service has finished drafting a document to give effect to a principle, there may be little of the principle left.
Into the Wind (1949)

9 When people feel deeply, impartiality is bias.
Into the Wind (1949)

Erich Maria Remarque 1898–1970
German novelist

10 All quiet on the western front.
English title of *Im Westen nichts Neues* (1929 novel); cf. **Beers** 61:18, **McClellan** 484:7

Ernest Renan 1823–92
French philologist and historian

11 Before French culture, German culture, Italian culture, there is human culture.
'Qu'est-ce qu'une nation', address given in 1882

Jules Renard 1864–1910
French novelist and dramatist

12 *Les bourgeois, ce sont les autres.*
The bourgeois are other people.
diary, 28 January 1890, in *Oeuvres Complètes* (1925–7) vol. 5

Montague John Rendall 1862–1950
member of the first BBC Board of Governors

13 Nation shall speak peace unto nation.
motto of the BBC; cf. **Bible** 86:13

Jean Renoir 1894–1979
French film director

14 Is it possible to succeed without any act of betrayal?
My Life and My Films (1974) 'Nana'

15 Don't think that this is a letter. It is only a small eruption of a disease called friendship.
letter to Janine Bazin, 12 June 1974; D. Thompson and L. LoBianco (eds.) *Letters* (1994)

Pierre Auguste Renoir 1841–1919
French painter
see also ***Misquotations*** *521:16*

16 *C'étaient des fous, mais ils avaient cette petite flamme qui ne s'éteint pas.*
They were madmen; but they had in them that little flame which is not to be snuffed out.
on the men of the French Commune
Jean Renoir *Renoir, My Father* (translated by R. and D. Weaver, 1962) ch. 12

Walter Reuther 1907–70
American labour leader

17 If it looks like a duck, walks like a duck and quacks like a duck, then it just may be a duck.
as a test, during the **McCarthy** *era, of Communist affiliations*
attributed

Paul Revere 1735–1818
American patriot
on Revere: see **Longfellow** *474:15*

18 [We agreed] that if the British went out by water, we would show two lanterns in the North Church

steeple; and if by land, one as a signal; for we were apprehensive it would be difficult to cross the Charles River or get over Boston Neck.

signals to be used if the British troops moved out of Boston; cf. ***Longfellow*** *474:16*

arrangements agreed with the Charlestown Committee of Safety on 16 April, 1775

Charles Revson 1906–75

American businessman

1 In the factory we make cosmetics; in the store we sell hope.

A. Tobias *Fire and Ice* (1976)

Frederic Reynolds 1764–1841

English dramatist

2 It is better to have written a damned play, than no play at all—it snatches a man from obscurity.

The Dramatist (1789) act 1, sc. 1

Joshua Reynolds 1723–92

English painter

on Reynolds: see ***Goldsmith*** *345:5,* ***Walpole*** *801:12*

3 Few have been taught to any purpose who have not been their own teachers.

Discourses on Art (ed. R. Wark, 1975) no. 2 (11 December 1769)

4 If you have great talents, industry will improve them: if you have but moderate abilities, industry will supply their deficiency.

Discourses on Art (ed. R. Wark, 1975) no. 2 (11 December 1769)

5 A mere copier of nature can never produce anything great.

Discourses on Art (ed. R. Wark, 1975) no. 3 (14 December 1770)

6 Could we teach taste or genius by rules, they would be no longer taste and genius.

Discourses on Art (ed. R. Wark, 1975) no. 3 (14 December 1770)

7 The whole beauty and grandeur of the art consists . . . in being able to get above all singular forms, local customs, particularities, and details of every kind.

Discourses on Art (ed. R. Wark, 1975) no. 3 (14 December 1770)

8 The value and rank of every art is in proportion to the mental labour employed in it, or the mental pleasure produced by it.

Discourses on Art (ed. R. Wark, 1975) no. 4 (10 December 1771)

9 Genius . . . is the child of imitation.

Discourses on Art (ed. R. Wark, 1975) no. 6 (10 December 1774)

10 The mind is but a barren soil; a soil which is soon exhausted, and will produce no crop, or only one, unless it be continually fertilized and enriched with foreign matter.

Discourses on Art (ed. R. Wark, 1975) no. 6 (10 December 1774)

11 Art in its perfection is not ostentatious; it lies hid, and works its effect, itself unseen.

Discourses on Art (ed. R. Wark, 1975) no. 6 (10 December 1774)

12 It is the very same taste which relishes a demonstration in geometry, that is pleased with the resemblance of a picture to an original, and touched with the harmony of music.

Discourses on Art (ed. R. Wark, 1975) no. 7 (10 December 1776)

13 I should desire that the last words which I should pronounce in this Academy, and from this place, might be the name of—Michael Angelo.

Discourses on Art (ed. R. Wark, 1975) no. 15 (10 December 1790)

Malvina Reynolds 1900–78

American songwriter

14 Little boxes on the hillside . . .
And they're all made out of ticky-tacky
And they all look just the same.

on the tract houses in the hills to the south of San Francisco

'Little Boxes' (1962 song)

Cecil Rhodes 1853–1902

South African statesman

see also ***Last words*** *457:4*

15 Ask any man what nationality he would prefer to be, and ninety-nine out of a hundred will tell you that they would prefer to be Englishmen.

Gordon Le Sueur *Cecil Rhodes* (1913)

Jean Rhys (Ella Gwendolen Rees Williams) c.1890–1979

British novelist and short-story writer

16 We can't all be happy, we can't all be rich, we can't all be lucky—and it would be so much less fun if we were . . . Some must cry so that others may be able to laugh the more heartily.

Good Morning, Midnight (1939) pt. 1

17 The perpetual hunger to be beautiful and that thirst to be loved which is the real curse of Eve.

The Left Bank (1927) 'Illusion'

18 Only the hopeless are starkly sincere and . . . only the unhappy can either give or take sympathy.

The Left Bank (1927) 'In the Rue de l'Arrivée'

19 Love was a terrible thing. You poisoned it and stabbed at it and knocked it down into the mud—well down—and it got up and staggered on, bleeding and muddy and awful. Like—like Rasputin.

Quartet (1928)

20 The feeling of Sunday is the same everywhere, heavy, melancholy, standing still. Like when they

say 'As it was in the beginning, is now, and ever shall be, world without end.'
Voyage in the Dark (1934) ch. 4, pt. 1

1 A doormat in a world of boots.
describing herself
in *Guardian* 6 December 1990

David Ricardo 1772–1823
British economist

2 Rent is that portion of the earth, which is paid to the landlord for the use of the original and indestructible powers of the soil.
On the Principles of Political Economy and Taxation (1817) ch. 2

Grantland Rice 1880–1954
American sports writer

3 For when the One Great Scorer comes to mark
against your name,
He writes—not that you won or lost—but how you
played the Game.
'Alumnus Football' (1941)

4 All wars are planned by old men
In council rooms apart.
'The Two Sides of War' (1955)

5 Outlined against a blue-grey October sky, the Four Horsemen rode again. In dramatic lore they were known as Famine, Pestilence, Destruction, and Death. These are only aliases. Their real names are Stuhldreher, Miller, Crowley, and Layden. They formed the crest of the South Bend cyclone before which another fighting Army football team was swept over the precipice.
report of football match between US Military Academy at West Point NY and University of Notre Dame
in *New York Tribune* 19 October 1924

Stephen Rice 1637–1715
Irish lawyer

6 I will drive a coach and six horses through the Act of Settlement.
W. King *State of the Protestants of Ireland* (1672) ch. 3, sect. 8

Alice Caldwell Rice 1870–1942
American humorist

7 Life is made up of desires that seem big and vital one minute and little and absurd the next. I guess we get what's best for us in the end.
A Romance of Billy-Goat Hill (1912) ch. 2

Tim Rice 1944–
English songwriter

8 Prove to me that you're no fool
Walk across my swimming pool.
Jesus Christ Superstar (1970) 'Herod's Song'; music by Andrew Lloyd Webber

Mandy Rice-Davies 1944–
English model and showgirl

9 He would, wouldn't he?
on hearing that Lord Astor denied her allegations, concerning himself and his house parties at Cliveden
at the trial of Stephen Ward, 29 June 1963; in *Guardian* 1 July 1963

Adrienne Rich 1923–
American poet and critic

10 The thing I came for:
the wreck and not the story of the wreck
the thing itself and not the myth.
'Diving into the Wreck' (1973)'

11 Memory says: Want to do right? Don't count on
me.
'Eastern War Time' (1991)

12 I'm accused of child-death of drinking blood . . .
there is spit on my sleeve there are phonecalls in
the night . . .
'Eastern War Time' (1991)

13 Our friends were not unearthly beautiful.
Nor spoke with tongues of gold; our lovers
blundered
Now and again when most we sought perfection,
Or hid in cupboards when the heavens thundered.
The human rose to haunt us everywhere,
Raw, flawed, and asking more than we could bear.
'Ideal Landscape' (1955)

Ann Richards 1933–
American Democratic politician

14 Poor George, he can't help it—he was born with a silver foot in his mouth.
of George ***Bush***
keynote speech at the Democratic convention, 1988; in *Independent* 20 July 1988

Frank Richards (Charles Hamilton) 1876–1961
English writer for boys

15 The fat greedy owl of the Remove.
'Billy Bunter' in the *Magnet* (1909) vol. 3, no. 72 'The Greyfriars Photographer'

I. A. Richards 1893–1979
English literary critic

16 It [poetry] is capable of saving us; it is a perfectly possible means of overcoming chaos.
Science and Poetry (1926) ch. 7

Justin Richardson 1900–75
British poet

17 People who have three daughters try once more
And then it's fifty-fifty they'll have four.
Those with a son or sons will let things be.
Hence all these surplus women. Q.E.D.
'Note for the Scientist' (1959)

18 For years a secret shame destroyed my peace—
I'd not read Eliot, Auden or MacNeice.

But then I had a thought that brought me hope—
Neither had Chaucer, Shakespeare, Milton, Pope.
'Take Heart, Illiterates' (1966)

Samuel Richardson 1689–1761
English novelist
on Richardson: see **Diderot** *267:8*, **Johnson** *414:17*

1 I have known a bird actually starve itself, and die with grief, at its being caught and caged—But never did I meet with a lady who was so silly . . . And yet we must all own that it is more difficult to catch a bird than a lady.
Clarissa (1747–8) vol. 3, letter 75

2 Mine is the most plotting heart in the world.
Clarissa (1747–8) vol. 3, letter 76

3 I love to write to the moment.
Clarissa (1747–8) vol. 4, letter 49

4 The affair is over. Clarissa lives.
announcement by Lovelace of his successful seduction of Clarissa
Clarissa (1747–8) vol. 5, letter 22

5 What, my Lord, is ancestry? I live to my own heart.
History of Sir Charles Grandison (1754) vol. 3, letter 26

6 A feeling heart is a blessing that no one, who has it, would be without; and it is a moral security of innocence; since the heart that is able to partake of the distress of another, cannot wilfully give it.
History of Sir Charles Grandison (1754) vol. 3, letter 32

7 I often compare myself to a poor old woman, who, having no bellows, lays herself down on her heart, and with her mouth endeavours to blow up into a faint blaze a little handful of sticks, half green, half dry, in order to warm a mess of pottage, that, after all her pains, hardly keeps life and soul together.
letter to Lady Bradshaigh, spring 1751, in J. Carroll (ed.) *Selected Letters* (1964)

8 His spurious brat, Tom Jones.
of **Fielding**
letter to Thomas Edwards, 21 February 1752

9 Instruction, Madam, is the pill; amusement is the gilding.
letter to Lady Echlin, 22 September 1755

Duc de Richelieu 1585–1642
French cardinal and statesman

10 If you give me six lines written by the hand of the most honest of men, I will find something in them which will hang him.
attributed

Hans Richter 1843–1916
German conductor

11 Up with your damned nonsense will I put twice, or perhaps once, but sometimes always, by God, never.
attributed

Johann Paul Friedrich Richter ('Jean Paul') 1763–1825
German novelist

12 Providence has given to the French the empire of the land, to the English that of the sea, and to the Germans that of—the air!
Thomas Carlyle 'Jean Paul Friedrich Richter' in *Edinburgh Review* no. 91 (1827)

George Ridding 1828–1904
Bishop of Southwell from 1884

13 I feel a feeling which I feel you all feel.
sermon in the London Mission, 1885; in G. W. E. Russell *Collections and Recollections* (1898) ch. 29

Laura Riding 1901–91
American poet and novelist

14 Without dressmakers to connect
The good-will of the body
With the purpose of the head,
We should be two worlds
Instead of a world and its shadow
The flesh.
'Because of Clothes' (1938)

Nicholas Ridley 1929–93
British Conservative politician

of the European community:
15 This is all a German racket, designed to take over the whole of Europe.
in *Spectator* 14 July 1990

Rig Veda
a collection of hymns in early Sanskrit, composed in the 2nd millenium BC

16 We meditate on the lovely light of the god, Savitri:
May it stimulate our thoughts!
The Gāyatrī bk. 3, hymn 62, v. 10

17 Whence this creation has arisen—perhaps it formed itself, or perhaps it did not—the one who looks down on it, in the highest heaven, only he knows—or perhaps he does not know.
Creation Hymn bk. 10, hymn 129, v. 7

18 When they divided the Man, into how many parts did they apportion him? What did they call his mouth, his two arms and thighs and feet?
His mouth became the Brahman; his arms were made into the Warrior, his thighs the People, and from his feet the Servants were born.
Hymn of Man bk. 10, hymn 190, v. 11

Rainer Maria Rilke 1875–1926
German poet

19 Works of art are of an infinite solitariness, and nothing is less likely to bring us near to them than criticism. Only love can apprehend and hold them, and can be just towards them.
Briefe an einen jungen Dichter (1929) 23 April 1903 (translated by Reginald Snell)

1 *Wer hat uns also umgedreht, dass wir,*
was wir auch tun, in jener Haltung sind
von einem, welcher fortgeht? Wie er auf
dem letzten Hügel, der ihm ganz sein Tal
noch einmal zeigt, sich wendet, anhält, weilt—,
So leben wir und nehmen immer Abschied.

Who's turned us around like this, so that we always,
do what we may, retain the attitude
of someone who's departing? Just as he,
on the last hill, that shows him all his valley
for the last time, will turn and stop and linger,
We live our lives, for ever taking leave.

Duineser Elegien (translated by J. B. Leishman and Stephen Spender, 1948) no. 8

2 *Wir haben, wo wir lieben, ja nur dies:*
einander lassen; denn dass wir uns halten,
das fällt uns leicht und ist nicht erst zu lernen.

We need in love to practise only this:
letting each other go. For holding on
comes easily; we do not need to learn it.

Requiem für eine Freundin ('Requiem for a Friend')

3 *Er ist einer der bleibenden Boten,*
der noch weit in die Türen der Toten
Schalen mit rühmlichen Früchten halt.

He is one of the staying messengers
Who still holds far into the doors of the dead
bowls of fruit worthy of praise.

'Sonnets to Orpheus', first part (*c.*1922)

4 I hold this to be the highest task for a bond between two people: that each protects the solitude of the other.

letter to Paula Modersohn-Becker, 12 February 1902, in *Gesammelte Briefe* (1904) vol. 1

5 I don't think of work, only of gradually regaining my health through reading, rereading, reflecting.

letter, *c.*1911; Donald Prater *A Ringing Glass* (1986)

Arthur Rimbaud 1854–91

French poet

6 *Plus douce qu'aux enfants la chair des pommes surettes,*
L'eau verte pénétra ma coque de sapin.

Sweeter than the flesh of tart apples to children,
the green water penetrates my wooden hull.

'Le Bâteau ivre' (1883)

7 *. . . Je me suis baigné dans le Poème*
De la Mer, infusé d'astres, et lactescent,
Dévorant les azurs verts.

I have bathed in the Poem of the Sea, steeped in stars, and milky, devouring the green azures.

'Le Bâteau ivre' (1883)

8 *J'ai vu le soleil bas, taché d'horreurs mystiques*
Illuminant de longs figements violets,
Pareils à des acteurs de drames très-antiques.

I have seen the sun set, stained with mystic horrors, illuminating the long violet [blood-] clots, just like actors in very ancient plays.

'Le Bâteau ivre' (1883)

9 *Je regrette l'Europe aux anciens parapets!*

I pine for Europe of the ancient parapets!

'Le Bâteau ivre' (1883)

10 *Je m'en allais, les poings dans mes poches crevées;*
Mon paletot aussi devenait idéal.

I was walking along, hands in holey pockets; my overcoat also was entering the realms of the ideal.

'Ma Bohème' (1870)

11 *A l'aurore, armés d'une ardente patience, nous entrerons aux splendides villes.*

At dawn, armed with a burning patience, we shall enter the splendid cities.

'Une Saison en enfer' (1873)

12 *Ô saisons, ô châteaux!*
Quelle âme est sans défauts?
O saisons, ô châteaux,
J'ai fait la magique étude
Du bonheur, que nul n'élude.

O seasons, O castles! What soul is without fault? I have made the magic study of good fortune which not one eludes.

'Ô saisons, ô châteaux' (1872)

13 *A noir, E blanc, I rouge, U vert, O bleu: voyelles,*
Je dirais quelque jour vos naissances latentes . . .
I, pourpres, sang craché, rire des lèvres belles
Dans la colère ou les ivresses pénitentes.

A black, E white, I red, U green, O blue: vowels, some day I will tell of the births that may be yours. I, purples, coughed-up blood, laughter of beautiful lips in anger or penitent drunkennesses.

'Voyelles' (1870)

César Ritz 1850–1918

Swiss hotel proprietor

14 *Le client n'a jamais tort.*

The customer is never wrong.

R. Nevill and C. E. Jerningham *Piccadilly to Pall Mall* (1908); cf. **Proverbs** 597:46

Antoine de Rivarol 1753–1801

French man of letters

15 *Ce qui n'est pas clair n'est pas français.*

What is not clear is not French.

Discours sur l'Universalité de la Langue Française (1784)

Joan Riviere b. 1883

16 Civilization and its discontents.

title given to her translation of Sigmund **Freud**'s *Das Unbehagen in der Kultur* (1930)

Lord Robbins 1898–1984

British economist

17 Economics is the science which studies human behaviour as a relationship between ends and scarce means which have alternative uses.

Essay on the Nature and Significance of Economic Science (1932) ch. 1, sect. 3

Robin Robertson

1 then bite out the tongue by the root . . .
and chew, never swallow.
This is not sex, remember;
you are eating the sea.
'Oyster' (1997)

Maximilien Robespierre 1758–94

French revolutionary
on Robespierre: see **Carlyle** *187:24,* **Heine** *368:10*

2 I am no courtesan, nor moderator, nor Tribune, nor defender of the people: I am myself the people.
speech at the Jacobin Club, 27 April 1792; in G. Laurent (ed.) *Le Defénseur de la Constitution* (1939)

3 The general will rules in society as the private will governs each separate individual.
Lettres à ses commettans (2nd series) 5 January 1793

4 Any law which violates the inalienable rights of man is essentially unjust and tyrannical; it is not a law at all.
Déclaration des droits de l'homme 24 April 1793, article 6; this article, in slightly different form, is recorded as having figured in Robespierre's *Projet* of 21 April 1793

5 Any institution which does not suppose the people good, and the magistrate corruptible, is evil.
Déclaration des droits de l'homme 24 April 1793, article 25

6 Wickedness is the root of despotism as virtue is the essence of the Republic.
in the Convention, 7 May 1794; in C. Vellay (ed.) *Discours et Rapports de Robespierre* (1908)

7 One single will is necessary.
private note, in S. A. Berville and J. F. Barrière *Papiers inédits trouvés chez Robespierre* vol. 2 (1828) no. 44

8 Intimidation without virtue is disastrous; virtue without intimidation is powerless.
J. M. Thompson *The French Revolution* (1943); attributed

Leo Robin 1900–84

American songwriter

9 A kiss on the hand may be quite continental,
But diamonds are a girl's best friend.
'Diamonds are a Girl's Best Friend' (1949 song) from the film *Gentlemen Prefer Blondes*; cf. **Loos** 475:11

10 Thanks for the memory.
title of song (with Ralph Rainger, 1937)

Elizabeth Robins 1862–1952

American writer

11 To say in print what she thinks is the last thing the woman novelist or journalist is so rash as to attempt . . . Her publishers are not women.
in 1908, as first president of the Women Writers' Suffrage League

Edwin Arlington Robinson 1869–1935

American poet

12 I shall have more to say when I am dead.
'John Brown' (1920)

13 Go to the western gate, Luke Havergal,
There where the vines cling crimson on the wall,
And in the twilight wait for what will come.
'Luke Havergal' (1896)

14 Miniver loved the Medici,
Albeit he had never seen one;
He would have sinned incessantly
Could he have been one.
'Miniver Cheevy' (1910)

15 So on we worked, and waited for the light,
And went without meat, and cursed the bread;
And Richard Cory, one calm summer night,
Went home and put a bullet through his head.
'Richard Cory' (1897)

16 The world is not a 'prison house', but a kind of kindergarten, where millions of bewildered infants are trying to spell God with the wrong blocks.
Literature in the Making (1917)

John Robinson ?1576–1625

English pastor to the Pilgrim Fathers

17 The Lord has more truth yet to break forth out of his holy word.
alleged address to the departing pilgrims, 1620
in *Dictionary of National Biography* (1917–)

18 The Lutherans refuse to advance beyond what Luther saw, while the Calvinists stick fast where they were left by that great man of God, who saw not all things.
regretting the current state of the reformed churches, in the alleged address to the departing pilgrims, 1620
in *Dictionary of National Biography* (1917–)

John Robinson 1919–83

English theologian; Bishop of Woolwich, 1959–69

19 Honest to God.
title of book (1963)

20 I think Lawrence tried to portray this [sex] relation as in a real sense an act of holy communion. For him flesh was sacramental of the spirit.
as defence witness in the case against Penguin Books for publishing Lady Chatterley's Lover
in *The Times* 28 October 1960

Mary Robinson 1758–1800

English poet

21 Pavement slippery, people sneezing,
Lords in ermine, beggars freezing;
Titled gluttons dainties carving,
Genius in a garret starving.
'January, 1795'

Mary Robinson 1944–

Irish Labour stateswoman; President 1990–97

22 Instead of rocking the cradle, they rocked the system.
in her victory speech, paying tribute to the women of Ireland
in *The Times* 10 November 1990; cf. **Wallace** 799:16

Boyle Roche 1743–1807
Irish politician

1 The best way to avoid danger is to meet it plump.
Jonah Barrington *Personal Sketches and Recollections of his own Times* (1827)

2 A disorderly set of people whom no king can govern and no God can please.
of the Ulster Protestants
attributed

3 Mr Speaker, I smell a rat; I see him forming in the air and darkening the sky; but I'll nip him in the bud.
attributed

John Wilmot, Lord Rochester 1647–80
English poet
see also **Epitaphs** 302:14

4 Tell me no more of constancy,
that frivolous pretence,
Of cold age, narrow jealousy,
disease and want of sense.
'Against Constancy' (1676)

5 Kindness only can persuade;
It gilds the lover's servile chain
And makes the slave grow pleased and vain.
'Give me leave to rail at you' (1680)

6 'Is there then no more?'
She cries. 'All this to love and rapture's due;
Must we not pay a debt to pleasure too?'
'The Imperfect Enjoyment' (1680)

7 May'st thou ne'er piss, who didst refuse to spend
When all my joys did on false thee depend.
'The Imperfect Enjoyment' (1680)

8 Love . . .
That cordial drop heaven in our cup has thrown
To make the nauseous draught of life go down.
'A Letter from Artemisia in the Town to Chloe in the Country' (1679)

9 All my past life is mine no more:
The flying hours are gone
Like transitory dreams given o'er,
Whose images are kept in store
By memory alone.
'Love and Life' (1680)

10 An age in her embraces passed
Would seem a winter's day,
Where life and light with envious haste
Are torn and snatched away.
'The Mistress: A Song' (1691)

11 Kind jealous doubts, tormenting fears,
And anxious cares, when past,
Prove our hearts' treasure fixed and dear,
And make us blest at last.
'The Mistress: A Song' (1691)

12 Natural freedoms are but just:
There's something generous in mere lust.
'A Ramble in St James' Park' (1680)

13 Reason, an *ignis fatuus* of the mind,
Which leaves the light of nature, sense, behind.
'A Satire against Mankind' (1679) l. 11

14 Then Old Age, and Experience, hand in hand,
Lead him to Death, and make him understand,
After a search so painful, and so long
That all his life he has been in the wrong.
Huddled in dirt the reasoning engine lies,
Who was so proud, so witty and so wise.
'A Satire against Mankind' (1679) l. 25

15 Wretched *Man* is still in arms for fear;
For fear he arms, and is of arms afraid,
By fear, to fear, successively betrayed
Base fear.
'A Satire against Mankind' (1679) l. 141

16 For all men would be cowards if they durst.
'A Satire against Mankind' (1679) l. 158

17 A merry monarch, scandalous and poor.
'A Satire on King Charles II' (1697)

18 Love a woman? You're an ass!
'Tis a most insipid passion
To choose out for your happiness
The silliest part of God's creation.
'Song' (1680)

19 Ancient person, for whom I
All the flattering youth defy,
Long be it ere thou grow old,
Aching, shaking, crazy, cold;
But still continue as thou art,
Ancient person of my heart.
'A Song of a Young Lady to her Ancient Lover' (1691)

20 Nothing, thou elder brother even to shade!
Thou hadst a being ere the world was made,
And, well fixed, art alone of ending not afraid.
'Upon Nothing' (1680)

21 Ere time and place were, time and place were not;
Where primitive nothing something straight begot;
Then all proceeded from the great united what.
'Upon Nothing' (1680)

22 Matter, the wickedest offspring of thy race,
By form assisted, flew from thy embrace,
And rebel light obscured thy reverend dusky face.

With form and matter, time and place did join;
Body, thy foe, with these did leagues combine,
To spoil thy peaceful realm, and ruin all thy line.
'Upon Nothing' (1680)

John D. Rockefeller 1839–1937
American industrialist and philanthropist

23 The growth of a large business is merely a survival of the fittest . . . The American beauty rose can be produced in the splendour and fragrance which bring cheer to its beholder only by sacrificing the early buds which grow up around it.
W. J. Ghent *Our Benevolent Feudalism* (1902); 'American Beauty Rose' became the title of a 1950 song by Hal David and others; cf. **Darwin** 250:20, **Spencer** 732:5

Gene Roddenberry 1921–91
American film producer
see also **Misquotations** 521:4

1 These are the voyages of the starship *Enterprise*. Its five-year mission . . . to boldly go where no man has gone before.
Star Trek (television series, from 1966)

Anita Roddick 1942–
English businesswoman

2 I think that business practices would improve immeasurably if they were guided by 'feminine' principles—qualities like love and care and intuition.
Body and Soul (1991)

3 Running a company on market research is like driving while looking in the rear view mirror.
in *Independent* 22 August 1997

Richard Rodgers 1902–79
American composer and songwriter

4 The sweetest sounds I'll ever hear
Are still inside my head.
The kindest words I'll ever know
Are waiting to be said.
The most entrancing sight of all
Is yet for me to see.
And the dearest love in all the world
Is waiting somewhere for me.
'The Sweetest Sounds' (1962 song) in *No Strings*

Theodore Roethke 1908–63
American poet

5 Thought does not crush to stone.
The great sledge drops in vain.
Truth never is undone;
Its shafts remain.
'The Adamant' (1941)

6 I can hear, underground, that sucking and sobbing,
In my veins, in my bones I feel it,—
The small waters seeping upward,
The tight grains parting at last.
'Cuttings Later' (1948)

7 I have known the inexorable sadness of pencils,
Neat in their boxes, dolour of pad and paper-weight,
All the misery of manilla folders and mucilage,
Desolation in immaculate public places.
'Dolour' (1948)

8 I remember the neckcurls, limp and damp, as tendrils;
And her quick look, a sidelong pickerel smile;
And how, once startled into talk, the light syllables leaped for her,
And she balanced in the delight of her thought.
'Elegy for Jane' (1953)

9 In a dark wood I saw—
I saw my several selves
Come running from the leaves,
Lewd, tiny, careless lives
That scuttled under stones,
Or broke, but would not go.
'The Exorcism' (1958)

10 The body and the soul know how to play
In that dark world where gods have lost thir way.
'Four for Sir John Davies' (1953) no. 2

11 O who can be
Both moth and flame? The weak moth blundering by.
Whom do we love? I thought I knew the truth;
Of grief I died, but no one knew my death.
'The Sequel' (1964)

Samuel Rogers 1763–1855
English poet

12 Think nothing done while aught remains to do.
'Human Life' (1819) l. 49; cf. **Lucan** 478:15

13 But there are moments which he calls his own,
Then, never less alone than when alone,
Those whom he loved so long and sees no more,
Loved and still loves—not dead—but gone before,
He gathers round him.
'Human Life' (1819) l. 755; cf. **Cyprian** 248:11, **Norton** 547:1

14 By many a temple half as old as Time.
Italy (1838 ed.) epilogue; cf. **Burgon** 162:4

15 Go—you may call it madness, folly;
You shall not chase my gloom away.
There's such a charm in melancholy,
I would not, if I could, be gay.
'To —, 1814'

16 It doesn't much signify whom one marries, for one is sure to find next morning that it was someone else.
Alexander Dyce (ed.) *Table Talk of Samuel Rogers* (1860)

Thorold Rogers 1823–90
English economic historian

17 See, ladling butter from alternate tubs
Stubbs butters Freeman, Freeman butters Stubbs.
***Stubbs** and **Freeman** both being historians*
W. H. Hutton (ed.) *Letters of William Stubbs* (1904)

Will Rogers 1879–1935
American actor and humorist

18 There is only one thing that can kill the movies, and that is education.
Autobiography of Will Rogers (1949) ch. 6

19 Income Tax has made more Liars out of the American people than Golf.
The Illiterate Digest (1924) 'Helping the Girls with their Income Taxes'

20 Everything is funny as long as it is happening to Somebody Else.
The Illiterate Digest (1924) 'Warning to Jokers: lay off the prince'

21 Well, all I know is what I read in the papers.
in *New York Times* 30 September 1923

1 You can't say civilization don't advance, however, for in every war they kill you in a new way.
in *New York Times* 23 December 1929

2 Half our life is spent trying to find something to do with the time we have rushed through life trying to save.
letter in *New York Times* 29 April 1930

Mies van der Rohe 1886–1969
German-born architect and designer
see also ***Proverbs*** *605:17*

3 God is in the details.
in *New York Times* 19 August 1969

Mme Roland (Marie-Jeanne Philipon) 1754–93
French revolutionary
see also ***Last words*** *456:19*

4 The more I see of men, the more I like dogs.
attributed, in *Notes and Queries* 5 September 1908; cf. **Toussenel** 780:2

Frederick William Rolfe ('Baron Corvo') 1860–1913
English novelist

5 Pray for the repose of His soul. He was so tired.
Hadrian VII (1904) ch. 24

Richard Rolle de Hampole *c.*1290–1349
English mystic

6 When Adam dalfe and Eve spane
Go spire if thou may spede,
Where was than the pride of man
That now merres his mede?
G. G. Perry *Religious Pieces* (Early English Text Society, Original Series no. 26, revised ed. 1914); cf. **Proverbs** 614:16

Pierre de Ronsard 1524–85
French poet

7 *Mignonne, allons voir si la rose,*
Qui, ce matin, avait déclose
Sa robe de pourpre au soleil,
A point perdu, cette vêprée,
Les plis de sa robe pourprée
Et son teint au vôtre pareil.

See, Mignonne, hath not the rose
That this morning did unclose
Her purple mantle to the light,
Lost, before the day be dead,
The glory of her raiment red,
Her colour, bright as yours is bright?
Odes, à Cassandre (1555) bk. 1, no. 17 (translated by Andrew Lang)

8 *Quand vous serez bien vieille, au soir, à la chandelle,*
Assise auprès du feu, dévidant et filant,
Direz, chantant mes vers, en vous émerveillant,
Ronsard me célébrait du temps que j'étais belle.

When you are very old, and sit in the candle-light
at evening spinning by the fire, you will say, as you
murmur my verses, a wonder in your eyes,
'Ronsard sang of me in the days when I was fair.'
Sonnets pour Hélène (1578) bk. 2, no. 42

Eleanor Roosevelt 1884–1962
American humanitarian and diplomat
on Roosevelt: see ***Stevenson*** *740:15*

9 No one can make you feel inferior without your consent.
in *Catholic Digest* August 1960

Franklin D. Roosevelt 1882–1945
American Democratic statesman, 32nd President of the US

10 These unhappy times call for the building of plans that . . . build from the bottom up and not from the top down, that put their faith once more in the forgotten man at the bottom of the economic pyramid.
radio address, 7 April 1932, in *Public Papers* (1938) vol. 1

11 I pledge you, I pledge myself, to a new deal for the American people.
speech to the Democratic Convention in Chicago, 2 July 1932, accepting the presidential nomination; in *Public Papers* (1938) vol. 1

12 The only thing we have to fear is fear itself.
inaugural address, 4 March 1933, in *Public Papers* (1938) vol. 2

13 In the field of world policy I would dedicate this Nation to the policy of the good neighbour.
inaugural address, 4 March 1933, in *Public Papers* (1938) vol. 2

14 I have seen war . . . I hate war.
speech at Chautauqua, NY, 14 August 1936, in *Public Papers* (1938) vol. 5

15 I see one-third of a nation ill-housed, ill-clad, ill-nourished.
second inaugural address, 20 January 1937, in *Public Papers* (1941) vol. 6

16 Your boys are not going to be sent into any foreign wars.
speech in Boston, 30 October 1940, in *Public Papers* (1941) vol. 9; cf. **Johnson** 408:17

17 We must be the great arsenal of democracy.
'Fireside Chat' radio broadcast, 29 December 1940, in *Public Papers* (1941) vol. 9

18 We look forward to a world founded upon four essential human freedoms. The first is freedom of speech and expression—everywhere in the world. The second is freedom of every person to worship God in his own way—everywhere in the world. The third is freedom from want . . . everywhere in the world. The fourth is freedom from fear . . . anywhere in the world.
message to Congress, 6 January 1941, in *Public Papers* (1941) vol. 9

19 Yesterday, December 7, 1941—a date which will live in infamy—the United States of America was suddenly and deliberately attacked by naval and air forces of the Empire of Japan.
address to Congress, 8 December 1941, in *Public Papers* (1950) vol. 10

1 Books can not be killed by fire. People die, but books never die. No man and no force can abolish memory . . . In this war, we know, books are weapons. And it is a part of your dedication always to make them weapons for man's freedom.
'Message to the Booksellers of America' 6 May 1942, in *Publisher's Weekly* 9 May 1942

2 It is fun to be in the same decade with you.
acknowledging congratulations on his 60th birthday
cabled reply to Winston **Churchill**, in W. S. Churchill *The Hinge of Fate* (1950) ch. 4

3 The work, my friend, is peace. More than an end of this war—an end to the beginnings of all wars.
undelivered address for Jefferson Day, 13 April 1945 (the day after Roosevelt died) in *Public Papers* (1950) vol. 13

Theodore Roosevelt 1858–1919

26th President of the US

4 I wish to preach, not the doctrine of ignoble ease, but the doctrine of the strenuous life.
speech to the Hamilton Club, Chicago, 10 April 1899, in *Works* (Memorial edition, 1923–6) vol. 15

5 There is a homely old adage which runs: 'Speak softly and carry a big stick; you will go far.' If the American nation will speak softly, and yet build and keep at a pitch of the highest training a thoroughly efficient navy, the Monroe Doctrine will go far.
speech in Chicago, 3 April 1903, in *New York Times* 4 April 1903

6 A man who is good enough to shed his blood for the country is good enough to be given a square deal afterwards. More than that no man is entitled to, and less than that no man shall have.
speech at the Lincoln Monument, Springfield, Illinois, 4 June 1903, in *Addresses and Presidential Messages 1902–4* (1904)

7 The men with the muck-rakes are often indispensable to the well-being of society; but only if they know when to stop raking the muck.
speech in Washington, 14 April 1906, in *Works* (Memorial edition, 1923–6) vol. 18; cf. **Bunyan** 161:10

8 It is not the critic who counts; not the man who points out how the strong man stumbles, or where the doer of deeds could have done better. The credit belongs to the man who is actually in the arena.
'Citizenship in a Republic', speech at the Sorbonne, Paris, 23 April 1910

9 We stand at Armageddon, and we battle for the Lord.
speech at the Republican National Convention, 18 June 1912

10 There is no room in this country for hyphenated Americanism . . . The one absolutely certain way of bringing this nation to ruin, of preventing all possibility of its continuing to be a nation at all, would be to permit it to become a tangle of squabbling nationalities.
speech in New York, 12 October 1915, in *Works* (Memorial edition, 1923–6) vol. 20

11 One of our defects as a nation is a tendency to use what have been called 'weasel words'. When a weasel sucks eggs the meat is sucked out of the egg. If you use a 'weasel word' after another, there is nothing left of the other.
speech in St Louis, 31 May 1916

12 I am as strong as a bull moose and you can use me to the limit.
'Bull Moose' subsequently became the popular name of the Progressive Party
letter to Mark Hanna, 27 June 1900, in *Works* (Memorial edition, 1923–6) vol. 23

13 I have got such a bully pulpit!
his personal view of the presidency
in *Outlook* (New York) 27 February 1909; cf. **Reagan** 623:2

Lord Rootes 1894–1964

English motor-car manufacturer

14 No other man-made device since the shields and lances of ancient knights fulfils a man's ego like an automobile.
attributed, 1958

Lord Rosebery 1847–1929

British Liberal statesman; Prime Minister, 1894–5

15 I have never known the sweets of place with power, but of place without power, of place with the minimum of power—that is a purgatory, and if not a purgatory it is a hell.
in *Spectator* 6 July 1895

16 Imperialism, sane Imperialism, as distinguished from what I may call wild-cat Imperialism, is nothing but this—a larger patriotism.
speech, City of London Liberal Club, 5 May 1899, in *Daily News* 6 May 1899

17 It is beginning to be hinted that we are a nation of amateurs.
Rectorial Address at Glasgow University, 16 November 1900, in *The Times* 17 November 1900

18 I must plough my furrow alone.
on remaining outside the Liberal Party leadership
speech, 19 July 1901, in *The Times* 20 July 1901

19 There are two supreme pleasures in life. One is ideal, the other real. The ideal is when a man receives the seals of office from his Sovereign. The real pleasure comes when he hands them back.
Sir Robert Peel (1899)

Ethel Rosenberg 1916–53 and Julius Rosenberg 1918–53

husband and wife; convicted of spying for the Russians

20 We are innocent . . . To forsake this truth is to pay too high a price even for the priceless gift of life.
petition for executive clemency, filed 9 January 1953, in Ethel Rosenberg *Death House Letters* (1953)

21 We are the first victims of American Fascism.
letter from Julius to Emanuel Bloch before the Rosenbergs' execution, 19 June 1953; in *Testament of Ethel and Julius Rosenberg* (1954)

A. C. Ross see **Political slogans**

Christina Rossetti 1830–94

English poet; sister of Dante Gabriel **Rossetti**

1 My heart is like a singing bird
Whose nest is in a watered shoot.
'A Birthday' (1862)

2 Because the birthday of my life
Is come, my love is come to me.
'A Birthday' (1862)

3 Come to me in the silence of the night;
Come in the speaking silence of a dream;
Come with soft rounded cheeks and eyes as bright
As sunlight on a stream;
Come back in tears,
O memory, hope, love of finished years.
'Echo' (1862)

4 For there is no friend like a sister
In calm or stormy weather;
To cheer one on the tedious way,
To fetch one if one goes astray,
To lift one if one totters down,
To strengthen while one stands.
'Goblin Market' (1862)

5 In the bleak mid-winter
Frosty wind made moan,
Earth stood hard as iron,
Water like a stone;
Snow had fallen, snow on snow,
Snow on snow,
In the bleak mid-winter,
Long ago.
'Mid-Winter' (1875)

6 The hope I dreamed of was a dream,
Was but a dream; and now I wake,
Exceeding comfortless, and worn, and old,
For a dream's sake.
'Mirage' (1862)

7 Oh roses for the flush of youth,
And laurel for the perfect prime;
But pluck an ivy branch for me
Grown old before my time.
'Oh roses for the flush of youth' (1862)

8 Remember me when I am gone away,
Gone far away into the silent land.
'Remember' (1862)

9 Better by far you should forget and smile
Than that you should remember and be sad.
'Remember' (1862)

10 O Earth, lie heavily upon her eyes;
Seal her sweet eyes weary of watching, Earth.
'Rest' (1862)

11 Silence more musical than any song.
'Rest' (1862)

12 Does the road wind up-hill all the way?
Yes, to the very end.
Will the day's journey take the whole long day?
From morn to night, my friend.
'Up-Hill' (1862)

13 When I am dead, my dearest,
Sing no sad songs for me;
Plant thou no roses at my head,
Nor shady cypress tree:
Be the green grass above me
With showers and dewdrops wet;
And if thou wilt, remember,
And if thou wilt, forget.
'When I am dead' (1862)

14 Our Indian Crown is in great measure the trapping of a splendid misery.
letter to Amelia Heimann, 29 July 1880

Dante Gabriel Rossetti 1828–82

English poet and painter, brother of Christina **Rossetti**

15 Like the sweet apple which reddens upon the
topmost bough,
A-top on the topmost twig,—which the pluckers
forgot, somehow,—
Forgot it not, nay, but got it not, for none could get
it till now.
'Beauty: A Combination from Sappho' (1861); cf. **Sappho** 644:15

16 The blessed damozel leaned out
From the gold bar of Heaven;
Her eyes were deeper than the depth
Of waters stilled at even;
She had three lilies in her hand,
And the stars in her hair were seven.
'The Blessed Damozel' (1870) st. 1

17 Her hair that lay along her back
Was yellow like ripe corn.
'The Blessed Damozel' (1870) st. 2

18 As low as where this earth
Spins like a fretful midge.
'The Blessed Damozel' (1870) st. 6

19 And the souls mounting up to God
Went by her like thin flames.
'The Blessed Damozel' (1870) st. 7

20 'We two,' she said, 'will seek the groves
Where the lady Mary is,
With her five handmaidens, whose names
Are five sweet symphonies,
Cecily, Gertrude, Magdalen,
Margaret and Rosalys.'
'The Blessed Damozel' (1870) st. 18

21 A sonnet is a moment's monument,—
Memorial from the Soul's eternity
To one dead deathless hour.
The House of Life (1881) pt. 1, introduction

22 'Tis visible silence, still as the hour-glass.
The House of Life (1881) pt. 1 'Silent Noon'

23 Deep in the sun-searched growths the dragon-fly
Hangs like a blue thread loosened from the sky:—
So this winged hour is dropt to us from above.
Oh! clasp we to our hearts, for deathless dower,
This close-companioned inarticulate hour
When twofold silence was the song of love.
The House of Life (1881) pt. 1 'Silent Noon'

1 They die not,—for their life was death,—but cease;
And round their narrow lips the mould falls close.
The House of Life (1881) pt. 2 'The Choice' pt. 1

2 I do not see them here; but after death
God knows I know the faces I shall see,
Each one a murdered self, with low last breath.
'I am thyself,—what hast thou done to me?'
'And I—and I—thyself,' (lo! each one saith,)
'And thou thyself to all eternity!'
The House of Life (1881) pt. 2 'Lost Days'

3 Give honour unto Luke Evangelist;
For he it was (the aged legends say)
Who first taught Art to fold her hands and pray.
The House of Life (1881) pt. 2 'Old and New Art'

4 When vain desire at last and vain regret
Go hand in hand to death, and all is vain,
What shall assuage the unforgotten pain
And teach the unforgetful to forget?
The House of Life (1881) pt. 2 'The One Hope'

5 Look in my face; my name is Might-have-been;
I am also called No-more, Too-late, Farewell.
The House of Life (1881) pt. 2 'A Superscription'; cf. **Traill** 780:19

6 Sleepless with cold commemorative eyes.
The House of Life (1881) pt. 2 'A Superscription'

7 Unto the man of yearning thought
And aspiration, to do nought
Is in itself almost an act.
'Soothsay' (1881) st. 10

8 I have been here before,
But when or how I cannot tell:
I know the grass beyond the door,
The sweet keen smell,
The sighing sound, the lights around the shore.
'Sudden Light' (1870)

9 'I saw the Sibyl at Cumae'
(One said) 'with mine own eye.
She hung in a cage, and read her rune
To all the passers-by.
Said the boys, "What wouldst thou, Sibyl?"
She answered, "I would die." '
translation of Petronius *Satyricon* 'Cena Trimalchionis' ch. 48, sect. 8; cf. **Petronius** 574:16

Gioacchino Rossini 1792–1868
Italian composer

10 Wagner has lovely moments but awful quarters of an hour.
to Emile Naumann, April 1867, in E. Naumann *Italienische Tondichter* (1883) vol. 4

Edmond Rostand 1868–1918
French dramatist

11 *. . . Un grand nez est proprement l'indice*
D'un homme affable, bon, courtois, spirituel,
Libéral, courageux, tel que je suis.
A large nose is in fact the sign of an affable man, good, courteous, witty, liberal, courageous, such as I am.
Cyrano de Bergerac (1897) act 1, sc. 1

12 *Il y a malgré vous quelque chose*
Que j'emporte, et ce soir, quand j'entrerai chez Dieu,
Mon salut balaiera largement le seuil bleu,
Quelque chose que sans un pli, sans une tache,
J'emporte malgré vous . . . et c'est . . . Mon panache!
There is, in spite of you, something which I shall take with me. And tonight, when I go into God's house, my bow will make a wide sweep across the blue threshold. Something which, with not a crease, not a mark, I'm taking away in spite of you . . . and it's . . . My panache!
Cyrano de Bergerac (1897) act 5, sc. 4

13 *Le seul rêve intéresse,*
Vivre sans rêve, qu'est-ce?
The dream, alone, is of interest. What is life, without a dream?
La Princesse Lointaine (1895) act 1, sc. 4

Jean Rostand 1894–1977
French biologist

14 The biologist passes, the frog remains.
sometimes quoted as 'Theories pass. The frog remains'
Inquiétudes d'un biologiste (1967)

15 To be adult is to be alone.
Pensées d'un biologiste (1954)

16 Kill a man, and you are an assassin. Kill millions of men, and you are a conqueror. Kill everyone, and you are a god.
Pensées d'un biologiste (1939) p. 116; cf. **Porteus** 588:13, **Young** 838:20

Leo Rosten 1908–97
American writer and social scientist

17 Any man who hates dogs and babies can't be all bad.
of W. C. ***Fields****, and often attributed to him*
speech at Masquers' Club dinner, 16 February 1939; letter in *Times Literary Supplement* 24 January 1975

Philip Roth 1933–
American novelist

18 A Jewish man with parents alive is a fifteen-year-old boy, and will remain a fifteen-year-old boy until *they die*!
Portnoy's Complaint (1967)

19 Doctor, my doctor, what do you say, LET'S PUT THE ID BACK IN YID!
Portnoy's Complaint (1967)

Lord Rothschild 1910–90
British administrator and scientist

20 Politicians often believe that their world is the real one. Officials sometimes take a different view.
in *The Times* 13 October 1974

21 The promises and panaceas that gleam like false teeth in the party manifestoes.
Meditations of a Broomstick (1977)

Claude-Joseph Rouget de Lisle
1760–1836
French soldier

1 *Allons, enfants de la patrie,*
Le jour de gloire est arrivé . . .
Aux armes, citoyens!
Formez vos battaillons!
Come, children of our country, the day of glory has arrived . . . To arms, citizens! Form your battalions!
'La Marseillaise' (25 April 1792)

Charles Roupell
Official referee of the British High Court of Justice

2 To play billiards well is a sign of an ill-spent youth.
attributed, in D. Duncan *Life of Herbert Spencer* (1908) ch. 20

Jean-Jacques Rousseau 1712–78
French philosopher and novelist
on Rousseau: see **Berlin** *68:18,* **Blake** *120:2,* **Heine** *368:10*

3 I am commencing an undertaking, hitherto without precedent, and which will never find an imitator. I desire to set before my fellows the likeness of a man in all the truth of nature, and that man myself.
Myself alone! I know the feeling of my heart, and I know men. I am not made like any of those I have seen; I venture to believe that I am not made like any of those in existence.
Confessions (1782)

4 *Du contrat social.*
The social contract.
title of book, *Du contrat social* (1762)

5 *L'homme est né libre, et partout il est dans les fers.*
Man was born free, and everywhere he is in chains.
Du Contrat social (1762) ch. 1

6 *Laisse, mon ami, ces vains moralistes et rentre au fond de ton âme: c'est là que tu retrouveras toujours la source de ce feu sacré qui nous embrasa tant de fois de l'amour des sublimes vertus; c'est là que tu verras ce simulacre éternel du vrai beau dont la contemplation nous anime d'un saint enthousiasme.*
Leave those vain moralists, my friend, and return to the depth of your soul: that is where you will always rediscover the source of the sacred fire which so often inflamed us with love of the sublime virtues; that is where you will see the eternal image of true beauty, the contemplation of which inspires us with a holy enthusiasm.
La Nouvelle Héloïse (1761, ed. M. Launay, 1967) pt. 2, letter 11

Martin Joseph Routh 1755–1854
English classicist

7 You will find it a very good practice always to verify your references, sir!
John William Burgon *Lives of Twelve Good Men* (1888 ed.) vol. 1

Matthew Rowbottom, Richard Stannard, and The Spice Girls
(Melanie Brown, Victoria Adams, Geri Halliwell, Emma Bunton, and Melanie Chisholm)
English songwriters and English pop singers

8 Yo I'll tell you what I want, what I really really want
so tell me what you want, what you really really want.
'Wannabe' (1996 song)

Nicholas Rowe 1674–1718
English dramatist

9 Is this that haughty, gallant, gay Lothario?
The Fair Penitent (1703) act 5, sc. 1

10 Like Helen, in the night when Troy was sacked,
Spectatress of the mischief which she made.
The Fair Penitent (1703) act 5, sc. 1

11 Death is the privilege of human nature,
And life without it were not worth our taking.
The Fair Penitent (1703) act 5, sc. 1

Helen Rowland 1875–1950
American writer

12 A husband is what is left of a lover, after the nerve has been extracted.
A Guide to Men (1922)

13 Somehow a bachelor never quite gets over the idea that he is a thing of beauty and a boy forever.
A Guide to Men (1922); cf. **Keats** 426:16

14 The follies which a man regrets most, in his life, are those which he didn't commit when he had the opportunity.
A Guide to Men (1922)

Richard Rowland *c.*1881–1947
American film producer

15 The lunatics have taken charge of the asylum.
on the take-over of United Artists by Charles **Chaplin** *and others*
Terry Ramsaye *A Million and One Nights* (1926) vol. 2, ch. 79; cf. **Lloyd George** 471:6

Maude Royden 1876–1956
English religious writer

16 The Church should go forward along the path of progress and be no longer satisfied only to represent the Conservative Party at prayer.
address at Queen's Hall, London, 16 July 1917, in *The Times* 17 July 1917

Naomi Royde-Smith *c.*1875–1964
English novelist and dramatist

17 I know two things about the horse
And one of them is rather coarse.
Weekend Book (1928)

Matthew Roydon fl. 1580–1622
English poet

1 A sweet attractive kind of grace,
A full assurance given by looks,
Continual comfort in a face,
The lineaments of Gospel books;
I trow that countenance cannot lie,
Whose thoughts are legible in the eye.
'An Elegy . . . for his Astrophill [Sir Philip Sidney]' (1593) st. 18

2 Was never eye, did see that face,
Was never ear, did hear that tongue,
Was never mind, did mind his grace,
That ever thought the travel long—
But eyes, and ears, and ev'ry thought,
Were with his sweet perfections caught.
'An Elegy . . . for his Astrophill' (1593) st. 19

Paul Alfred Rubens 1875–1917
English songwriter

3 Oh! we don't want to lose you but we think you ought to go
For your King and your Country both need you so.
'Your King and Country Want You' (1914 song); cf. **Military sayings** 508:17

Richard Rumbold *c.*1622–85
English republican conspirator

4 I never could believe that Providence had sent a few men into the world, ready booted and spurred to ride, and millions ready saddled and bridled to be ridden.
on the scaffold
T. B. Macaulay *History of England* vol. 1 (1849) ch. 1

Carol Rumens 1944–
British poet

5 A slow psalm of two nations
Mourning a common pain
—Hebrew and Arabic mingling
Their silver-rooted vine;
Olives and roses falling
To sweeten Palestine.
'A New Song' (1993)

6 It's simple, isn't it?
Never say the yes
you don't mean, but the no
you always meant, say that,
even if it's too late,
even if it kills you.
'A Woman of a Certain Age' (1993)

Robert Runcie 1921–
English Protestant clergyman; Archbishop of Canterbury
on Runcie: see **Field** *309:11*

7 People are mourning on both sides of this conflict. In our prayers we shall quite rightly remember those who are bereaved in our own country and the relations of the young Argentinian soldiers who were killed. Common sorrow could do something to reunite those who were engaged in this struggle. A shared anguish can be a bridge of reconciliation. Our neighbours are indeed like us.
service of thanksgiving at the end of the Falklands war, St. Paul's Cathedral, London, 26 July 1982

8 In the middle ages people were tourists because of their religion, whereas now they are tourists because tourism is their religion.
speech in London, 6 December 1988

9 I have done my best to die before this book is published. It now seems possible that I may not succeed.
letter to Humphrey Carpenter, July 1996, in H. Carpenter *Robert Runcie* (1996)

Damon Runyon 1884–1946
American writer

10 Guys and dolls.
title of book (1931)

11 'My boy,' he says, 'always try to rub up against money, for if you rub up against money long enough, some of it may rub off on you.'
in *Cosmopolitan* August 1929, 'A Very Honourable Guy'

12 I do see her in tough joints more than somewhat.
in *Collier's* 22 May 1930, 'Social Error'

13 'You are snatching a hard guy when you snatch Bookie Bob. A very hard guy, indeed. In fact,' I say, 'I hear the softest thing about him is his front teeth.'
in *Collier's* 26 September 1931, 'The Snatching of Bookie Bob'

14 I always claim the mission workers came out too early to catch any sinners on this part of Broadway. At such an hour the sinners are still in bed resting up from their sinning of the night before, so they will be in good shape for more sinning a little later on.
in *Collier's* 28 January 1933, 'The Idyll of Miss Sarah Brown'

15 I long ago come to the conclusion that all life is 6 to 5 against.
in *Collier's* 8 September 1934, 'A Nice Price'

16 You can keep the things of bronze and stone, and give me one man to remember me just once a year.
note to his friends shortly before he died
Ed Weiner *The Damon Runyon Story* (1948)

Salman Rushdie 1947–
Indian-born British novelist
on Rushdie: see **Khomeini** *435:14*

17 No story comes from nowhere; new stories are born from old—it is the new combinations that make them new.
Haroun and the Sea of Stories (1990)

18 What is freedom of expression? Without the freedom to offend, it ceases to exist.
in *Weekend Guardian* 10 February 1990

1 One of the things a writer is for is to say the unsayable, speak the unspeakable and ask difficult questions.

in *Independent on Sunday* 10 September 1995 'Quotes of the Week'

2 It means everything—it means freedom.

on the news that the fatwa had effectively been lifted

in *Mail on Sunday* 27 September 1998

Dean Rusk 1909–94

US politician; Secretary of State, 1961–9

3 We're eyeball to eyeball, and I think the other fellow just blinked.

on the Cuban missile crisis, 24 October 1962

in *Saturday Evening Post* 8 December 1962

John Ruskin 1819–1900

English art and social critic

4 You hear of me, among others, as a respectable architectural man-milliner; and you send for me, that I may tell you the leading fashion.

The Crown of Wild Olive (1866) Lecture 2 'Traffic'

5 Thackeray settled like a meat-fly on whatever one had got for dinner, and made one sick of it.

Fors Clavigera (1871–84) Letter 31, 1 July 1873

6 I have seen, and heard, much of Cockney impudence before now; but never expected to hear a coxcomb ask two hundred guineas for flinging a pot of paint in the public's face.

*on **Whistler**'s* Nocturne in Black and Gold

Fors Clavigera (1871–84) Letter 79, 18 June 1877; cf. **Whistler** 81:[illegible]

7 No person who is not a great sculptor or painter can be an architect. If he is not a sculptor or painter, he can only be a *builder*.

Lectures on Architecture and Painting (1854) Lectures 1 and 2 (addenda)

8 Life without industry is guilt, and industry without art is brutality.

Lectures on Art (1870) Lecture 3 'The Relation of Art to Morals' sect. 95

9 What is poetry? . . . The suggestion, by the imagination, of noble grounds for the noble emotions.

Modern Painters (1856) vol. 3, pt. 4, ch. 1

10 All violent feelings . . . produce in us a falseness in all our impressions of external things, which I would generally characterize as the 'Pathetic Fallacy'.

Modern Painters (1856) vol. 3, pt. 4, ch. 12

11 To see clearly is poetry, prophecy, and religion—all in one.

Modern Painters (1856) vol. 3, pt. 4 'Of Modern Landscape'

12 Mountains are the beginning and the end of all natural scenery.

Modern Painters (1856) vol. 4, pt. 5, ch. 20

13 There was a rocky valley between Buxton and Bakewell . . . You enterprised a railroad . . . you blasted its rocks away . . . And now, every fool in Buxton can be at Bakewell in half-an-hour, and every fool in Bakewell at Buxton.

Praeterita vol. 3 (1889) 'Joanna's Cave'

14 All books are divisible into two classes, the books of the hour, and the books of all time.

Sesame and Lilies (1865) 'Of Kings' Treasuries'

15 Be sure that you go to the author to get at his meaning, not to find yours.

Sesame and Lilies (1865) 'Of Kings' Treasuries'

16 Which of us . . . is to do the hard and dirty work for the rest, and for what pay? Who is to do the pleasant and clean work, and for what pay?

Sesame and Lilies (1865) 'Of Kings' Treasuries'

17 How long most people would look at the best book before they would give the price of a large turbot for it.

Sesame and Lilies (1865) 'Of Kings' Treasuries'

18 We call ourselves a rich nation, and we are filthy and foolish enough to thumb each other's books out of circulating libraries!

Sesame and Lilies (1865) 'Of Kings' Treasuries'

19 I believe the right question to ask, respecting all ornament, is simply this: Was it done with enjoyment—was the carver happy while he was about it?

Seven Lamps of Architecture (1849) 'The Lamp of Life' sect. 24

20 Better the rudest work that tells a story or records a fact, than the richest without meaning.

Seven Lamps of Architecture (1849) 'The Lamp of Memory' sect. 7

21 When we build, let us think that we build for ever.

Seven Lamps of Architecture (1849) 'The Lamp of Memory' sect. 10

22 Remember that the most beautiful things in the world are the most useless; peacocks and lilies for instance.

Stones of Venice vol. 1 (1851) ch. 2, sect. 17

23 Labour without joy is base. Labour without sorrow is base. Sorrow without labour is base. Joy without labour is base.

Time and Tide (1867) Letter 5

24 Your honesty is *not* to be based either on religion or policy. Both your religion and policy must be based on *it*.

Time and Tide (1867) Letter 8

25 The first duty of a State is to see that every child born therein shall be well housed, clothed, fed and educated, till it attain years of discretion.

Time and Tide (1867) Letter 13

26 Fine art is that in which the hand, the head, and the heart of man go together.

The Two Paths (1859) Lecture 2

27 Not only is there but one way of *doing* things rightly, but there is only one way of *seeing* them, and that is, seeing the whole of them.

The Two Paths (1859) Lecture 2

28 Nobody cares much at heart about Titian; only there is a strange undercurrent of everlasting

murmur about his name, which means the deep consent of all great men that he is greater than they.
The Two Paths (1859) Lecture 2

1 It ought to be quite as natural and straightforward a matter for a labourer to take his pension from his parish, because he has deserved well of his parish, as for a man in higher rank to take his pension from his country, because he has deserved well of his country.
Unto this Last (1862) preface, p. xviii

2 The force of the guinea you have in your pocket depends wholly on the default of a guinea in your neighbour's pocket. If he did not want it, it would be of no use to you.
Unto this Last (1862) Essay 2

3 Soldiers of the ploughshare as well as soldiers of the sword.
Unto this Last (1862) Essay 3, p. 102

4 Government and cooperation are in all things the laws of life; anarchy and competition the laws of death.
Unto this Last (1862) Essay 3, p. 102

5 Whereas it has long been known and declared that the poor have no right to the property of the rich, I wish it also to be known and declared that the rich have no right to the property of the poor.
Unto this Last (1862) Essay 3, p. 103

6 There is no wealth but life.
Unto this Last (1862) Essay 4, p. 156

7 If only the geologists would let me alone, I could do very well, but those dreadful hammers! I hear the clink of them at the end of every cadence of the Bible verses.
letter to Henry Acland, 24 May 1851

8 I knew exactly what I had got to say, put the words firmly in their places like so many stitches, hemmed the edges of chapters round with what seemed to me the graceful flourishes, touched them finally with my cunningest points of colour, and read the work to papa and mamma at breakfast next morning, as a girl shows her sampler.
in *Dictionary of National Biography* (1917–)

9 Remember that it is the glory of Gothic architecture that it can do *anything*.
J. Mordaunt Crook *Dilemma of Style* (1987)

Bertrand Russell 1872–1970

British philosopher and mathematician

10 Men who are unhappy, like men who sleep badly, are always proud of the fact.
The Conquest of Happiness (1930) ch. 1

11 Boredom is . . . a vital problem for the moralist, since half the sins of mankind are caused by the fear of it.
The Conquest of Happiness (1930) ch. 4

12 One of the symptoms of approaching nervous breakdown is the belief that one's work is terribly important, and that to take a holiday would bring all kinds of disaster.
The Conquest of Happiness (1930) ch. 5

13 One should as a rule respect public opinion in so far as is necessary to avoid starvation and to keep out of prison, but anything that goes beyond this is voluntary submission to an unnecessary tyranny.
The Conquest of Happiness (1930) ch. 9

14 A sense of duty is useful in work, but offensive in personal relations. People wish to be liked, not to be endured with patient resignation.
The Conquest of Happiness (1930) ch. 10

15 Of all forms of caution, caution in love is perhaps the most fatal to true happiness.
The Conquest of Happiness (1930) ch. 12

16 To be able to fill leisure intelligently is the last product of civilization.
The Conquest of Happiness (1930) ch. 14

17 Work is of two kinds: first, altering the position of matter at or near the earth's surface relatively to other such matter; second, telling other people to do so. The first kind is unpleasant and ill paid; the second is pleasant and highly paid.
In Praise of Idleness and Other Essays (1986) title essay (1932)

18 To fear love is to fear life, and those who fear life are already three parts dead.
Marriage and Morals (1929) ch. 19

19 Mathematics may be defined as the subject in which we never know what we are talking about, nor whether what we are saying is true.
Mysticism and Logic (1918) ch. 4

20 The law of causality, I believe, like much that passes muster among philosophers, is a relic of a bygone age, surviving, like the monarchy, only because it is erroneously supposed to do no harm.
Mysticism and Logic (1918) ch. 9

21 Only on the firm foundation of unyielding despair, can the soul's habitation henceforth be safely built.
Philosophical Essays (1910) no. 2

22 Mathematics, rightly viewed, possesses not only truth, but supreme beauty—a beauty cold and austere, like that of sculpture.
Philosophical Essays (1910) no. 4

23 The man who has fed the chicken every day throughout its life at last wrings its neck instead, showing that a more refined view as to the uniformity of nature would have been useful to the chicken.
The Problems of Philosophy (1912)

24 The recrudescence of Puritanism.
title of essay, 1928

25 Every man, wherever he goes, is encompassed by a cloud of comforting convictions, which move with him like flies on a summer day.
Sceptical Essays (1928) 'Dreams and Facts'

26 The infliction of cruelty with a good conscience is a delight to moralists. That is why they invented Hell.
Sceptical Essays (1928) 'On the Value of Scepticism'

1 It is obvious that 'obscenity' is not a term capable of exact legal definition; in the practice of the Courts, it means 'anything that shocks the magistrate'.
Sceptical Essays (1928) 'The Recrudescence of Puritanism'

2 Next to enjoying ourselves, the next greatest pleasure consists in preventing others from enjoying themselves, or, more generally, in the acquisition of power.
Sceptical Essays (1928) 'The Recrudescence of Puritanism'

3 Man is a credulous animal, and must believe *something*; in the absence of good grounds for belief, he will be satisfied with bad ones.
Unpopular Essays (1950) 'An Outline of Intellectual Rubbish'

4 Fear is the main source of superstition, and one of the main sources of cruelty.
Unpopular Essays (1950) 'An Outline of Intellectual Rubbish'

5 'Change' is scientific, 'progress' is ethical; change is indubitable, whereas progress is a matter of controversy.
Unpopular Essays (1950) 'Philosophy and Politics'

6 The linguistic philosophy, which cares only about language, and not about the world, is like the boy who preferred the clock without the pendulum because, although it no longer told the time, it went more easily than before and at a more exhilarating pace.
foreword to Ernest Gellner *Words and Things* (1959)

Bob Russell and **Bobby Scott**

7 He ain't heavy . . . he's my brother.
title of song (1969)

Dora Russell 1894–1986

English feminist

8 We want better reasons for having children than not knowing how to prevent them.
Hypatia (1925) ch. 4

George William Russell see **Æ**

Lord John Russell 1792–1878

British Whig statesman; Prime Minister 1846–52, 1865–6

on Russell: see **Derby** *258:14*

9 It is impossible that the whisper of a faction should prevail against the voice of a nation.
reply to an Address from a meeting of 150,000 persons at Birmingham on the defeat of the second Reform Bill, October 1831
S. Walpole *Life of Lord John Russell* (1889) vol. 1, ch. 7

10 If peace cannot be maintained with honour, it is no longer peace.
speech at Greenock, 19 September 1853, in *The Times* 21 September 1853; cf. **Chamberlain** 200:18, **Disraeli** 269:18

11 Among the defects of the Bill, which were numerous, one provision was conspicuous by its presence and another by its absence.
speech to the electors of the City of London, April 1859, in *The Times* 9 April 1859

12 A proverb is one man's wit and all men's wisdom.
R. J. Mackintosh *Sir James Mackintosh* (1835) vol. 2, ch. 7

William Howard Russell 1820–1907

British journalist; war correspondent of The Times

13 They dashed on towards that thin red line tipped with steel.
of the Russians charging the British at the battle of Balaclava, 1854
The British Expedition to the Crimea (1877); Russell's original dispatch read:

That thin red streak topped with a line of steel.
in *The Times* 14 November 1854; cf. **Kipling** 440:13

Ernest Rutherford 1871–1937

British physicist

on Rutherford: see **Bullard** *159:21*

14 All science is either physics or stamp collecting.
J. B. Birks *Rutherford at Manchester* (1962)

15 If your experiment needs statistics, you ought to have done a better experiment.
Norman T. J. Bailey *The Mathematical Approach to Biology and Medicine* (1967)

16 It was quite the most incredible event that has ever happened to me in my life. It was almost as incredible as if you fired a 15-inch shell at a piece of tissue paper and it came back and hit you.
on the back-scattering effect of metal foil on alpha-particles
E. N. da C. Andrade *Rutherford and the Nature of the Atom* (1964)

17 We haven't got the money, so we've got to think!
in *Bulletin of the Institute of Physics* (1962) vol. 13 (as recalled by R. V. Jones)

Gilbert Ryle 1900–76

English philosopher

18 A myth is, of course, not a fairy story. It is the presentation of facts belonging to one category in the idioms appropriate to another. To explode a myth is accordingly not to deny the facts but to re-allocate them.
The Concept of Mind (1949) introduction

19 Philosophy is the replacement of category-habits by category-disciplines.
The Concept of Mind (1949) introduction

20 The dogma of the Ghost in the Machine.
on the mental-conduct concepts of **Descartes**
The Concept of Mind (1949) ch. 1

Sa'adiah ben Joseph Gaon 882–942

Jewish philosopher

21 We enquire into and speculate on the teachings of our religion for two reasons: first, to find out for ourselves what we have learned as imparted knowledge from the prophets of God; and secondly, to be able to refute anyone who argues against us concerning anything to do with our religion.
The Book of Beliefs and Opinions introduction, sect. 6

1 Even women and children and those with no aptitude for speculation can attain to a complete religion, for all men are on an equal footing as far as knowledge derived from the senses is concerned. Praised be God who in his wisdom ordered things thus.

The Book of Beliefs and Opinions introduction, sect. 6

Rafael Sabatini 1875–1950

Italian novelist

2 He was born with a gift of laughter and a sense that the world was mad. And that was all his patrimony.

Scaramouche (1921) bk. 1, ch. 1

Thomas Sackville, Lord Dorset 1536–1608

English poet and dramatist

3 The wrathful winter, 'proaching on apace,
With blustering blasts had all ybared the treen,
And old Saturnus, with his frosty face,
With chilling cold had pierced the tender green . . .

And sorrowing I to see the summer flowers,
The lively green, the lusty leas, forlorn,
The sturdy trees so shattered with the showers,
The fields so fade that flourished so beforn,
It taught me well all earthly things be born
To die the death, for nought long time may last;
The summer's beauty yields to winter's blast.

The Mirror for Magistrates (1563) st. 1

4 Crookbacked he was, tooth-shaken, and blear-eyed,
Went on three feet, and sometime crept on four,
With old lame bones that rattled by his side,
His scalp all pilled and he will eld forlore;
His withered fist still knocking at Death's door,
Fumbling and drivelling as he draws his breath;
For brief, the shape and messenger of Death.

of Old Age

The Mirror for Magistrates (1563) st. 48

Victoria ('Vita') Sackville-West 1892–1962

English writer and gardener; wife of Harold **Nicolson**

5 The greater cats with golden eyes
Stare out between the bars.
Deserts are there, and different skies,
And night with different stars.

The King's Daughter (1929) pt. 2, no. 1

6 The country habit has me by the heart,
For he's bewitched for ever who has seen,
Not with his eyes but with his vision, Spring
Flow down the woods and stipple leaves with sun.

The Land (1926) 'Winter'

Anwar al-Sadat 1918–81

Egyptian statesman, President 1970–81

7 Peace is much more precious than a piece of land.

speech in Cairo, 8 March 1978

Marquis de Sade 1740–1814

French writer and soldier

8 Do not breed. Nothing gives less pleasure than childbearing. Pregnancies are damaging to health, spoil the figure, wither the charms, and it's the cloud of uncertainty forever hanging over these events that darkens a husband's mood.

Juliette (1797) pt. 1

Françoise Sagan 1935–

French novelist

9 To jealousy, nothing is more frightful than laughter.

La Chamade (1965) ch. 9

Charles-Augustin Sainte-Beuve 1804–69

French critic

10 *Et Vigny plus secret,*
Comme en sa tour d'ivoire, avant midi rentrait.

And Vigny more discreet, as if in his ivory tower, returned before noon.

Les Pensées d'Août, à M. Villemain (1837)

Antoine de Saint-Exupéry 1900–44

French novelist

11 Grown-ups never understand anything for themselves, and it is tiresome for children to be always and forever explaining things to them.

Le Petit Prince (1943) ch. 1

12 It is only with the heart that one can see rightly; what is essential is invisible to the eye.

Le Petit Prince (1943) ch. 21

13 Experience shows us that love does not consist in gazing at each other but in looking together in the same direction.

Terre des Hommes (translated as 'Wind, Sand and Stars', 1939) ch. 8

Yves Saint Laurent 1936–

French couturier

14 I don't really like knees.

in *Observer* 3 August 1958

Andrei Sakharov 1921–89

Russian nuclear physicist

15 Every day I saw the huge material, intellectual and nervous resources of thousands of people being poured into the creation of a means of total destruction, something capable of annihilating all human civilization. I noticed that the control levers were in the hands of people who, though talented in their own ways, were cynical.

Sakharov Speaks (1974)

Saki (Hector Hugh Munro) 1870–1916

Scottish writer

1 Waldo is one of those people who would be enormously improved by death.

Beasts and Super-Beasts (1914) 'The Feast of Nemesis'

2 The people of Crete unfortunately make more history than they can consume locally.

Chronicles of Clovis (1911) 'The Jesting of Arlington Stringham'

3 All decent people live beyond their incomes nowadays, and those who aren't respectable live beyond other peoples'.

Chronicles of Clovis (1911) 'The Match-Maker'

4 The cook was a good cook, as cooks go; and as cooks go, she went.

Reginald (1904) 'Reginald on Besetting Sins'

5 I always say beauty is only sin deep.

Reginald (1904) 'Reginald's Choir Treat'

6 Good gracious, you've got to educate him first. You can't expect a boy to be vicious till he's been to a good school.

Reginald in Russia (1910) 'The Baker's Dozen'

7 A little inaccuracy sometimes saves tons of explanation.

The Square Egg (1924) 'Clovis on the Alleged Romance of Business'

8 Children with Hyacinth's temperament don't know better as they grow older; they merely know more.

Toys of Peace and Other Papers (1919) 'Hyacinth'

9 We all know that Prime Ministers are wedded to the truth, but like other married couples they sometimes live apart.

The Unbearable Bassington (1912) ch. 13

J. D. Salinger 1919–

American novelist and short-story writer
see also ***Borrowed titles*** *144:3*

10 Sex is something I really don't understand too hot. You never know *where* the hell you are. I keep making up these sex rules for myself, and then I break them right away.

The Catcher in the Rye (1951) ch. 9

11 Take most people, they're crazy about cars. They worry if they get a little scratch on them, and they're always talking about how many miles they get to a gallon . . . I don't even like *old* cars. I mean they don't even interest me. I'd rather have a goddam horse. A horse is at least *human*, for God's sake.

The Catcher in the Rye (1951) ch. 17

12 I keep picturing all these little kids playing some game in this big field of rye and all . . . I mean if they're running and they don't look where they're going I have to come out from somewhere and catch them. That's all I'd do all day. I'd just be the catcher in the rye.

The Catcher in the Rye (1951) ch. 22

Lord Salisbury (3rd Marquess of Salisbury) 1830–1903

British Conservative statesman; Prime Minister 1855–6, 1886–92, 1895–1902
on Salisbury: see ***Bismarck*** *116:16,* ***Disraeli*** *269:18*

13 Too clever by half.

of ***Disraeli****'s amendment on Disestablishment*

speech, House of Commons, 30 March 1868; cf. **Salisbury** 643:6

14 English policy is to float lazily downstream, occasionally putting out a diplomatic boathook to avoid collisions.

letter to Lord Lytton, 9 March 1877; in Lady Gwendolen Cecil *Life of Robert, Marquis of Salisbury* (1921–32) vol. 2

15 A great deal of misapprehension arises from the popular use of maps on a small scale. As with such maps you are able to put a thumb on India and a finger on Russia, some persons at once think that the political situation is alarming and that India must be looked to. If the noble Lord would use a larger map—say one on the scale of the Ordnance Map of England—he would find that the distance between Russia and British India is not to be measured by the finger and thumb, but by a rule.

speech, House of Commons, 11 June 1877

16 No lesson seems to be so deeply inculcated by the experience of life as that you never should trust experts. If you believe the doctors, nothing is wholesome: if you believe the theologians, nothing is innocent: if you believe the soldiers, nothing is safe. They all require to have their strong wine diluted by a very large admixture of insipid common sense.

letter to Lord Lytton, 15 June 1877; in Lady Gwendolen Cecil *Life of Robert, Marquis of Salisbury* (1921–32) vol. 2

17 The agonies of a man who has to finish a difficult negotiation, and at the same time to entertain four royalties at a country house can be better imagined than described.

letter to Lord Lyons, 5 June 1878

18 What with deafness, ignorance of French, and Bismarck's extraordinary mode of speech, Beaconsfield has the dimmest idea of what is going on—understands everything crossways—and imagines a perpetual conspiracy.

letter to Lady Salisbury from the Congress of Berlin, 23 June 1878

19 We are part of the community of Europe and we must do our duty as such.

speech at Caernarvon, 10 April 1888, in *The Times* 11 April 1888

20 Where property is in question I am guilty . . . of erecting individual liberty as an idol, and of resenting all attempts to destroy or fetter it; but when you pass from liberty to life, in no well-governed State, in no State governed according to the principles of common humanity, are the claims of mere liberty allowed to endanger the lives of the citizens.

speech in the House of Lords, 29 July 1897

1 Horny-handed sons of toil.
in *Quarterly Review* October 1873; later popularized in the US by Denis Kearney (1847–1907); cf. **Lowell** 477:14

2 By office boys for office boys.
of the Daily Mail
H. Hamilton Fyfe *Northcliffe, an Intimate Biography* (1930) ch. 4

3 If these gentlemen had their way, they would soon be asking me to defend the moon against a possible attack from Mars.
of his senior military advisers, and their tendency to see threats which did not exist
Robert Taylor *Lord Salisbury* (1975)

4 I rank myself no higher in the scheme of things than a policeman—whose utility would disappear if there were no criminals.
comparing his role in the Conservative Party with that of ***Gladstone***
Lady Gwendolen Cecil *Biographical Studies . . . of Robert, Third Marquess of Salisbury* (1962)

5 To defend a bad policy as an 'error of judgement' does not excuse it—the right functioning of a man's judgement is his most fundamental responsibility.
Lady Gwendolen Cecil *Life of Robert, Marquis of Salisbury* (1921–32) vol. 3

Lord Salisbury (5th Marquess of Salisbury) 1893–1972
British Conservative politician

6 Too clever by half.
of Iain Macleod, Colonial Secretary 'in his relationship to the white communities of Africa'
in the House of Lords, 7 March 1961; cf. **Salisbury** 642:13

Sallust (Gaius Sallustius Crispus) 86–35 BC
Roman historian

7 *Alieni appetens, sui profusus.*
Greedy for the property of others, extravagant with his own.
Catiline ch. 5

8 *Quieta movere magna merces videbatur.*
To stir up undisputed matters seemed a great reward in itself.
Catiline ch. 21

9 *Esse quam videri bonus malebat.*
He preferred to be rather than to seem good.
of Cato
Catiline ch. 54

10 *Urbem venalem et mature perituram, si emptorem invenerit.*
A venal city ripe to perish, if a buyer can be found.
of Rome
Jugurtha ch. 35

11 *Punica fide.*
With Carthaginian trustworthiness.
meaning treachery
Jugurtha ch. 108, sect. 3

Lord Samuel 1870–1963
British Liberal politician

12 A library is thought in cold storage.
A Book of Quotations (1947)

Paul A. Samuelson 1915–
American economist

13 The consumer, so it is said, is the king . . . each is a voter who uses his money as votes to get the things done that he wants done.
Economics (8th ed., 1970)

George Sand (Amandine-Aurore Lucille Dupin, Baronne Dudevant) 1804–76
French novelist

14 *Nous ne pouvons arracher une seule page de notre vie, mais nous pouvons jeter le livre au feu.*
We cannot tear out a single page of our life, but we can throw the book in the fire.
Mauprat (1837)

15 There is only one happiness in life, to love and be loved.
letter to Lina Calamatta, 31 March 1862

16 Faith is an excitement and an enthusiasm; it is a condition of intellectual magnificence to which we must cling as to a treasure, and not squander on our way through life in the small coin of empty words, or in exact and priggish argument.
letter to Des Planches, 25 May 1866

17 Art for art's sake is an empty phrase. Art for the sake of the true, art for the sake of the good and the beautiful, that is the faith I am searching for.
letter to Alexandre Saint-Jean, 1872

Carl Sandburg 1878–1967
American poet

18 Hog Butcher for the World,
Tool Maker, Stacker of Wheat,
Player with Railroads and the Nation's Freight
Handler;
Stormy, husky, brawling,
City of the Big Shoulders.
'Chicago' (1916)

19 When Abraham Lincoln was shovelled into the
tombs,
he forgot the copperheads and the assassin . . .
in the dust, in the cool tombs.
'Cool Tombs' (1918)

20 The fog comes
on little cat feet.
It sits looking
over harbour and city
on silent haunches
and then moves on.
'Fog' (1916)

21 Pile the bodies high at Austerlitz and Waterloo.
Shovel them under and let me work—
I am the grass; I cover all.
'Grass' (1918)

1 I tell you the past is a bucket of ashes.
'Prairie' (1918)

2 Little girl . . . Sometime they'll give a war and nobody will come.
The People, Yes (1936); cf. **Film titles** 313:3, **Ginsberg** 339:19

3 Poetry is the achievement of the synthesis of hyacinths and biscuits.
in *Atlantic Monthly* March 1923 'Poetry Considered'

4 Slang is a language that rolls up its sleeves, spits on its hands and goes to work.
in *New York Times* 13 February 1959

Henry 'Red' Sanders

5 Sure, winning isn't everything. It's the only thing.
in *Sports Illustrated* 26 December 1955; often attributed to Vince Lombardi

Lord Sandwich 1718–92

British politician and diplomat; First Lord of the Admiralty

6 If any man will draw up his case, and put his name at the foot of the first page, I will give him an immediate reply. Where he compels me to turn over the sheet, he must wait my leisure.
N. W. Wraxall *Memoirs* (1884) vol. 1

Martha Sansom 1690–1736

English poet

7 Foolish eyes, thy streams give over,
Wine, not water, binds the lover.
At the table then be shining,
Gay coquette, and all designing.
'Song' (written *c.*1726)

George Santayana 1863–1952

Spanish-born philosopher and critic

8 Fanaticism consists in redoubling your effort when you have forgotten your aim.
The Life of Reason (1905) vol. 1, introduction

9 Those who cannot remember the past are condemned to repeat it.
The Life of Reason (1905) vol. 1, ch. 12

10 It takes patience to appreciate domestic bliss; volatile spirits prefer unhappiness.
The Life of Reason (1905) vol. 2, ch. 2

11 Fashion is something barbarous, for it produces innovation without reason and imitation without benefit.
The Life of Reason (1905) vol. 3, ch. 7

12 Music is essentially useless, as life is: but both have an ideal extension which lends utility to its conditions.
The Life of Reason (1905) vol. 4, ch. 4

13 There is no cure for birth and death save to enjoy the interval.
Soliloquies in England (1922) 'War Shrines'

Sappho

Greek lyric poet of the late 7th century BC
on Sappho: see **Byron** *174:4*

14 That man seems to me on a par with the gods who sits in your company and listens to you so close to him speaking sweetly and laughing sexily, such a thing makes my heart flutter in my breast, for when I see you even for a moment, then power to speak another word fails me, instead my tongue freezes into silence, and at once a gentle fire has caught throughout my flesh, and I see nothing with my eyes, and there's a drumming in my ears, and sweat pours down me, and trembling seizes all of me, and I become paler than grass, and I seem to fail almost to the point of death in my very self.
D. L. Page (ed.) *Lyrica Graeca Selecta* (1968) no. 199; cf. **Catullus** 197:9

15 Just as the sweet-apple reddens on the high branch, high on the highest, and the apple-pickers missed it, or rather did not miss it out, but could not reach it.
describing a girl before her marriage
D. L. Page (ed.) *Lyrica Graeca Selecta* (1968) no. 224; cf. **Rossetti** 634:15

16 For in a house that serves the Muses
there must be no lamentation: such a thing
does not befit it.
sometimes described as her dying words
A. Weighall *Sappho of Lesbos* (1932)

John Singer Sargent 1856–1925

American painter
on Sargent: see **Anonymous** *17:5*

17 Every time I paint a portrait I lose a friend.
N. Bentley and E. Esar *Treasury of Humorous Quotations* (1951)

Leslie Sarony 1897–1985

British songwriter

18 Ain't it grand to be blooming well dead?
title of song (1932)

Nathalie Sarraute 1902–

French novelist

19 Radio and television . . . have succeeded in lifting the manufacture of banality out of the sphere of handicraft and placed it in that of a major industry.
in *Times Literary Supplement* 10 June 1960

Jean-Paul Sartre 1905–80

French philosopher, novelist, dramatist, and critic
on Sartre: see **de Gaulle** *256:2*

20 *Quand les riches se font la guerre ce sont les pauvres qui meurent.*
When the rich wage war it's the poor who die.
Le Diable et le bon Dieu (1951) act 1, tableau 1

21 Nothingness haunts being.
L'Être et le néant (1943)

1 *L'existence précède et commande l'essence.*

Existence precedes and rules essence.

L'Être et le néant (1943) pt. 4, ch. 1

2 *Je suis condamné à être libre.*

I am condemned to be free.

L'Être et le néant (1943) pt. 4, ch. 1

3 *L'homme est une passion inutile.*

Man is a useless passion.

L'Être et le néant (1943) pt. 4, ch. 2

4 *Alors, c'est ça l'Enfer. Je n'aurais jamais cru . . . Vous vous rappelez: le soufre, le bûcher, le gril . . . Ah! quelle plaisanterie. Pas besoin de gril, L'Enfer, c'est les Autres.*

So that's what Hell is: I'd never have believed it . . . Do you remember, brimstone, the stake, the gridiron? . . . What a joke! No need of a gridiron, Hell is other people.

Huis Clos (1944) sc. 5; cf. **Eliot** 293:23

5 *Comme tous les songe-creux, je confondis le désenchantement avec la vérité.*

Like all dreamers, I mistook disenchantment for truth.

Les Mots (1964) 'Écrire'

6 *Je confondis les choses avec leurs noms: c'est croire.*

I confused things with their names: that is belief.

Les Mots (1964) 'Écrire'

7 *Il n'y a pas de bon père, c'est la règle; qu'on n'en tienne pas grief aux hommes mais au lien de paternité qui est pourri. Faire des enfants, rien de mieux; en* avoir, *quelle iniquité!*

There is no good father, that's the rule. Don't lay the blame on men but on the bond of paternity, which is rotten. To beget children, nothing better; to *have* them, what iniquity!

Les Mots (1964) 'Lire'

8 *Les bons pauvres ne savent pas que leur office est d'exercer notre générosité.*

The poor don't know that their function in life is to exercise our generosity.

Les Mots (1964) 'Lire'

9 *Elle ne croyait à rien; seul, son scepticisme l'empêchait d'être athée.*

She believed in nothing; only her scepticism kept her from being an atheist.

Les Mots (1964) 'Lire'

10 *La vie humaine commence de l'autre côté du désespoir.*

Human life begins on the far side of despair.

Les Mouches (1943) act 3, sc. 2

11 *Ma pensée, c'est* moi: *voilà pourquoi je ne peux pas m'arrêter. J'existe par ce que je pense . . . et je ne peux pas m'empêcher de penser.*

My thought is *me*: that's why I can't stop. I exist by what I think . . . and I can't prevent myself from thinking.

La Nausée (1938) 'Lundi'

12 *Je me méfie des incommunicables, c'est la source de toute violence.*

I distrust the incommunicable: it is the source of all violence.

'Qu'est-ce que la littérature?' in *Les Temps Modernes* July 1947, p. 106

13 *Je déteste les victimes quand elles respectent leurs bourreaux.*

I hate victims who respect their executioners.

Les Séquestrés d'Altona (1960) act 1, sc. 1

14 *L'écrivain doit donc refuser de se laisser transformer en institution.*

A writer must refuse, therefore, to allow himself to be transformed into an institution.

refusing the Nobel Prize at Stockholm, 22 October 1964; in M. Contat and M. Rybalka (eds.) *Les Écrits de Sartre* (1970)

Siegfried Sassoon 1886–1967

English poet

15 If I were fierce, and bald, and short of breath,
I'd live with scarlet Majors at the Base,
And speed glum heroes up the line to death.

'Base Details' (1918)

16 I'd like to see a Tank come down the stalls,
Lurching to rag-time tunes, or 'Home, sweet Home',—
And there'd be no more jokes in Music-halls
To mock the riddled corpses round Bapaume.

'Blighters' (1917)

17 Does it matter?—losing your sight? . . .
There's such splendid work for the blind;
And people will always be kind,
As you sit on the terrace remembering
And turning your face to the light.

'Does it Matter?' (1918)

18 Soldiers are citizens of death's grey land,
Drawing no dividend from time's tomorrows.

'Dreamers' (1918)

19 You are too young to fall asleep for ever;
And when you sleep you remind me of the dead.

'The Dug-Out' (1919)

20 Everyone suddenly burst out singing;
And I was filled with such delight
As prisoned birds must find in freedom.

'Everyone Sang' (1919)

21 The song was wordless; the singing will never be done.

'Everyone Sang' (1919)

22 'Good-morning; good morning!' the General said
When we met him last week on our way to the line.
Now the soldiers he smiled at are most of 'em dead,
And we're cursing his staff for incompetent swine.
'He's a cheery old card,' grunted Harry to Jack
As they slogged up to Arras with rifle and pack.

But he did for them both by his plan of attack.

'The General' (1918)

23 Here was the world's worst wound. And here with pride
'Their name liveth for ever' the Gateway claims.
Was ever an immolation so belied

As these intolerably nameless names?
'On Passing the New Menin Gate' (1928); cf. **Epitaphs** 304:6

Cicely Saunders 1916–
English founder of St Christopher's Hospice, London

1 Deception is not as creative as truth. We do best in life if we look at it with clear eyes, and I think that applies to coming up to death as well.
of the Hospice movement
in *Time* 5 September 1988

Ferdinand de Saussure 1857–1913
Swiss linguistics scholar

2 In language there are only differences.
Course in General Linguistics (1916)

3 Language can . . . be compared with a sheet of paper: thought is the front and sound the back; one cannot cut the front without cutting the back at the same time.
Course in General Linguistics (1916)

George Savile see **Lord Halifax**

Dorothy L. Sayers 1893–1957
English writer of detective fiction

4 A society in which consumption has to be artificially stimulated in order to keep production going is a society founded on trash and waste, and such a society is a house built upon sand.
Creed or Chaos? (1947) ch. 6

5 I admit it is better fun to punt than to be punted, and that a desire to have all the fun is nine-tenths of the law of chivalry.
Gaudy Night (1935) ch. 14

6 I always have a quotation for everything—it saves original thinking.
Have His Carcase (1932)

7 Perhaps it is no wonder that women were first at the Cradle and the Cross. They had never known a man like this man—there has never been such another . . . who never made jokes about them, never treated them either as 'The women, God help us', or 'The ladies, God bless them!'
J. Morley and H. Ward (eds.) *Celebrating Women* (1986); attributed

☐ Sayings and slogans
see box opposite

Gerald Scarfe 1936–
English caricaturist

8 I find a particular delight in taking the caricature as far as I can. It satisfies me to stretch the human frame about and recreate it and yet keep a likeness.
Scarfe by Scarfe (1986)

Arthur Scargill 1938–
British trades-union leader

9 Parliament itself would not exist in its present form had people not defied the law.
evidence to House of Commons Select Committee on Employment, 2 April 1980, in *House of Commons Paper no. 462 of Session 1979–80*

Lord Scarman 1911–
British judge

10 The people as a source of sovereign power are in truth only occasional partners in the constitutional minuet danced for most of the time by Parliament and the political party in power.
The Shape of Things to Come (1989) ch. 1

11 A government above the law is a menace to be defeated.
Why Britain Needs a Written Constitution (1992)

Barry Scheck
American lawyer

12 It is not a question of how skilfully we played our cards but of whether we were given a fair deck.
appealing against the conviction of Louise Woodward for second-degree murder, asserting that photographic evidence had not been made available to the defence at an early enough stage
in Cambridge, Massachusetts, 4 November 1997

Friedrich von Schelling 1775–1854
German philosopher

13 Architecture in general is frozen music.
Philosophie der Kunst (1809)

Friedrich von Schiller 1759–1805
German dramatist and poet

14 *Freude, schöner Götterfunken,*
Wir betreten feuertrunken,
Himmlische, dein Heiligtum.
Deine Zauber binden wieder,
Was die Mode streng geteilt,
Tochter aus Elysium,

Joy, beautiful radiance of the gods, daughter of Elysium, we set foot in your heavenly shrine dazzled by your brilliance. Your charms re-unite what common use has harshly divided
'An die Freude' (1785)

15 *Alle Menschen werden Brüder*
Wo dein sanfter Flügel weilt.

All men become brothers under your tender wing.
'An die Freude' (1785)

16 *Ein Augenblick, gelebt im Paradiese,*
Wird nicht zu teuer mit dem Tod gebüsst.

One moment spent in Paradise
Is not too dearly paid for with one's life.
Don Carlos (1787) act 1, sc. 5

continued

Sayings and slogans

1 Been there, done that, got the T-shirt.
'been there, done that' recorded from 1980s, expanded form from 1990s

2 Burn your bra.
feminist slogan, 1970s

3 Business is like a car: it will not run by itself except downhill.
American saying

4 Children: one is one, two is fun, three is a houseful.
American

5 Close your eyes and think of England.
said to derive from a 1912 entry in the journal of Lady Hillingdon (1857–1940), but the journal has never been traced

6 A committee is a group of the unwilling, chosen from the unfit, to do the unnecessary.
various attributions (origin unknown)

7 Crime doesn't pay.
a slogan of the FBI and the cartoon detective Dick Tracy

8 Daddy, what did you do in the Great War?
daughter to father in First World War recruiting poster

9 [Death is] nature's way of telling you to slow down.
life insurance proverb; in *Newsweek* 25 April 1960

10 Different strokes for different folks.
strokes = *comforting gestures of approval or congratulation*
of US origin, late twentieth century saying

11 A dog is for life, and not just for Christmas.
slogan of the National Canine Defence League

12 Do not fold, spindle or mutilate.
instruction on punched cards (1950s, and in differing forms from the 1930s)

13 Don't get mad, get even.
late twentieth century saying

14 The family that prays together stays together.
motto devised by Al Scalpone for the Roman Catholic Family Rosary Crusade, 1947

15 Garbage in, garbage out.
in computing, incorrect or faulty input will always cause poor output; origin of the acronym GIGO

16 Give me a child for the first seven years, and you may do what you like with him afterwards.
attributed as a Jesuit maxim, in *Lean's Collectanea* vol. 3 (1903); cf. **Spark** 731:18

17 Go to jail. Go directly to jail. Do not pass go. Do not collect £200.
instructions on 'Community Chest' card in the game 'Monopoly'; invented by Charles Brace Darrow (1889–1967) in 1931

18 If anything can go wrong, it will.
commonly known as Murphy's Law
mid twentieth century saying; said to have been invented by George Nichols in 1949, based on a remark by his colleague Captain E. Murphy

19 If it ain't broke, don't fix it.
Bert Lance (1931–) in *Nation's Business* May 1977

20 If you can't beat them, join them.
beat *is usually replaced by* lick *in the US*
mid twentieth century saying

21 If you pay peanuts, you get monkeys.
mid twentieth century saying

22 If you're not part of the solution, you're part of the problem.
late twentieth century saying; cf. **Cleaver** 220:7

23 *Il ne faut pas être plus royaliste que le roi.*
You mustn't be more of a royalist than the king.
saying from the time of Louis XVI; François René, Vicomte de Chateaubriand *De la monarchie selon la charte* (1816) ch. 81

24 I married my husband for life, not for lunch.
origin unknown

25 I'm backing Britain.
slogan coined by workers at the Colt factory, Surbiton, Surrey and subsequently used in a national campaign, in *The Times* 1 January 1968

26 It takes 40 dumb animals to make a fur coat, but only one to wear it.
slogan of an anti-fur campaign poster, 1980s; sometimes attributed to David **Bailey**

27 *Je suis Marxiste—tendance Groucho.*
I am a Marxist—of the Groucho tendency.
slogan used at Nanterre in Paris, 1968

28 Let's run it up the flagpole and see if anyone salutes it.
Reginald Rose *Twelve Angry Men* (1955); recorded as an established advertising expression in the 1960s

29 Life is a sexually transmitted disease.
graffito found on the London Underground, in D. J. Enright (ed.) *The Faber Book of Fevers and Frets* (1989)

30 Lousy but loyal.
London East End slogan at George V's Jubilee (1935)

31 Make love not war.
student slogan, 1960s

32 Members [of civil service orders] rise from CMG (known sometimes in Whitehall as 'Call Me God') to the KCMG ('Kindly Call Me God') to—for a select few governors and super-ambassadors—the GCMG ('God Calls Me God').
Anthony Sampson *Anatomy of Britain* (1962) ch. 18

33 *Nil carborundum illegitimi.*
Don't let the bastards grind you down.
cod Latin saying in circulation during the Second World War, though possibly of earlier origin; often quoted as '*nil carborundum*' or '*illegitimi non carborundum*'

34 Nostalgia isn't what it used to be.
graffito; taken as title of book by Simone Signoret, 1978

35 The opera ain't over 'til the fat lady sings.
Dan Cook, in *Washington Post* 3 June 1978

Sayings and slogans *continued*

1 Pile it high, sell it cheap.
slogan coined by John Cohen (1898–1979), founder of Tesco

2 *Post coitum omne animal triste.*
After coition every animal is sad.
post-classical saying

3 *Se non è vero, è molto ben trovato.*
If it is not true, it is a happy invention.
common saying from the 16th century

4 There's no such thing as a free lunch.
colloquial axiom in US economics from the 1960s, much associated with Milton **Friedman**; recorded in form 'there ain't no such thing as a free lunch' from 1938, which gave rise to the acronym TANSTAAFL in Robert Heinlein's *The Moon is a Harsh Mistress* (1966) ch. 11

5 Think globally, act locally.
Friends of the Earth slogan, *c.*1985

6 Thirty days hath September,
April, June, and November;
All the rest have thirty-one,
Excepting February alone,
And that has twenty-eight days clear
And twenty-nine in each leap year.
Stevins MS (*c.*1555)

7 To err is human but to really foul things up requires a computer.
Farmers' Almanac for 1978 'Capsules of Wisdom'; cf. **Pope** 584:27

8 What goes around comes around.
late twentieth century saying

9 What you see is what you get.
a computing expression, from which the acronym wysiwig *derives*
late twentieth century saying

10 When war is declared, Truth is the first casualty.
attributed to Hiram Johnson, speaking in the US Senate, 1918, but not recorded in his speech; the first recorded use is as epigraph to Arthur Ponsonby's *Falsehood in Wartime* (1928); see **Johnson** 409:17

Friedrich von Schiller *continued*

11 *Die Sonne geht in meinem Staat nicht unter.*
The sun does not set in my dominions.
Philip II
Don Carlos (1787) act 1, sc. 6; cf. **North** 546:16

12 *Dreiundzwanzig Jahre,*
Und nichts für die Unsterblichkeit getan!
Twenty-three years old,
and I've done nothing for my immortality!
Don Carlos (1787) act 2, sc. 2

13 *Mit der Dummheit kämpfen Götter selbst vergebens.*
With stupidity the gods themselves struggle in vain.
The Maid of Orleans (1801) act 3, sc. 6

14 *Was ist der langen Rede kurzer Sinn?*
What is the brief meaning of the lengthy speech?
Die Piccolomini (1800) act 1, sc. 2

15 *Die Weltgeschichte ist das Weltgericht.*
The world's history is the world's judgement.
'Resignation' (1786) st. 19

16 *Der Mohr hat seine Arbeit getan, der Mohr kann gehen.*
The Moor has done his work, the Moor can go.
usually misquoted as 'Der Mohr hat seine Schuldigkeit getan [The Moor has done his duty]'
Die Verschwörung des Fiesco (1782) act 3, sc. 4

17 *Wir wollen sein ein einzig Volk von Brüdem*
In keiner Not uns trennen und Gefahr.
We would be a single nation of brothers
Standing together in any hour of need or danger.
Wilhelm Tell (1804) act 2, sc. 2

Arthur M. Schlesinger Jr. 1917–
American historian

18 The answer to the runaway Presidency is not the messenger-boy Presidency. The American democracy must discover a middle way between making the President a czar and making him a puppet.
The Imperial Presidency (1973) preface

19 Suppose . . . that Lenin had died of typhus in Siberia in 1895 and Hitler had been killed on the western front in 1916. What would the twentieth century have looked like now?
The Cycles of American History (1986)

Moritz Schlick 1882–1936
German philosopher

20 The meaning of a proposition is the method of its verification.
Philosophical Review (1936) vol. 45

Artur Schnabel 1882–1951
Austrian-born pianist

21 I know two kinds of audiences only—one coughing, and one not coughing.
My Life and Music (1961) pt. 2, ch. 10

22 The notes I handle no better than many pianists. But the pauses between the notes—ah, that is where the art resides!
in *Chicago Daily News* 11 June 1958

23 Too easy for children, and too difficult for artists.
of Mozart's sonatas
Nat Shapiro (ed.) *Encyclopaedia of Quotations about Music* (1978); see below:

Children are given Mozart because of the small *quantity* of the notes; grown-ups avoid Mozart because of the great *quality* of the notes.
My Life and Music (1961)

Arnold Schoenberg 1874–1951
Austrian-born American composer and musical theorist

1 If it is art, it is not for the masses. 'If it is for the masses it is not art' is a topic which is rather similar to a word of yourself.
letter to W. S. Schlamm, 1 July 1945

2 I am delighted to add another unplayable work to the repertoire. I want the Concerto to be difficult and I want the little finger to become longer. I can wait.
of his Violin Concerto
Joseph Machlis *Introduction to Contemporary Music* (1963)

Arthur Schopenhauer 1788–1860
German philosopher

3 The ordinary man has no sense for general truths . . . the genius on the contrary, overlooks and neglects what is individual.
Parerga and Paralipomena (1851)

Patricia Schroeder 1940–
American Democratic politician

4 Ronald Reagan . . . is attempting a great breakthrough in political technology—he has been perfecting the Teflon-coated Presidency. He sees to it that nothing sticks to him.
speech in the US House of Representatives, 2 August 1983

Budd Schulberg 1914–
American writer
see also **Film lines** 311:11

5 What makes Sammy run?
title of book (1941)

E. F. Schumacher 1911–77
German-born economist

6 It was not the power of the Spaniards that destroyed the Aztec Empire but the disbelief of the Aztecs in themselves.
Roots of Economic Growth (1962)

7 Small is beautiful. A study of economics as if people mattered.
title of book (1973); cf. **Proverbs** 611:3

8 Call a thing immoral or ugly, soul-destroying or a degradation of man, a peril to the peace of the world or to the well-being of future generations: as long as you have not shown it to be 'uneconomic' you have not really questioned its right to exist, grow, and prosper.
Small is Beautiful (1973) pt. 1, ch. 3

9 The most striking thing about modern industry is that it requires so much and accomplishes so little. Modern industry seems to be inefficient to a degree that surpasses one's ordinary powers of imagination. Its inefficiency therefore remains unnoticed.
Small is Beautiful (1973) pt. 2, ch. 3

10 It is of little use trying to suppress terrorism if the production of deadly devices continues to be deemed a legitimate employment of man's creative powers.
Small is Beautiful (1973) epilogue

Robert Schumann 1810–56
German composer

11 Hats off, gentlemen—a genius!
of Chopin
'An Opus 2' (1831); H. Pleasants (ed.) *Schumann on Music* (1965)

J. A. Schumpeter 1883–1950
American economist

12 The cold metal of economic theory is in Marx's pages immersed in such a wealth of steaming phrases as to acquire a temperature not naturally its own.
Capitalism, Socialism and Democracy (1942)

13 One servant is worth a thousand gadgets.
J. K. Galbraith *A Life in our Times* (1981) ch. 6

Carl Schurz 1829–1906
American soldier and politician

14 My country, right or wrong; if right, to be kept right; and if wrong, to be set right!
speech, US Senate, 29 February 1872, in *Congressional Globe* vol. 45; cf. **Decatur** 254:10

Delmore Schwartz 1913–66
American poet

15 Dogs are Shakespearean, children are strangers.
Let Freud and Wordsworth discuss the child,
Angels and Platonists shall judge the dog.
'Dogs are Shakespearean, Children are Strangers' (1938)

16 The heavy bear who goes with me,
A manifold honey to smear his face,
Clumsy and lumbering here and there,
The central ton of every place,
The hungry beating brutish one
In love with candy, anger, and sleep,
Crazy factotum, dishevelling all,
Climbs the building, kicks the football,
Boxes his brother in the hate-ridden city.
'The Heavy Bear Who Goes With Me' (1958)

Albert Schweitzer 1875–1965
Franco-German missionary

17 Late on the third day, at the very moment when, at sunset, we were making our way through a herd of hippopotamuses, there flashed upon my mind, unforeseen and unsought, the phrase, 'Reverence for Life'.
Aus meinem Leben und Denken (1933) ch. 13

1 Truth has no special time of its own. Its hour is now—always, and indeed then most truly when it seems most unsuitable to actual circumstances.

Zwischen Wasser und Urwald (On the Edge of the Primeval Forest, 1922) ch. 11

Kurt Schwitters 1887–1948

German painter

2 I am a painter and I nail my pictures together.

R. Hausmann *Am Anfang war Dada* (1972)

Alexander Scott *c.*1525–*c.*1584

Scottish poet

3 Love is ane fervent fire,
Kindled without desire,
Short pleasure, long displeasure;
Repentance is the hire;
And pure treasure without measure.
Love is ane fervent fire.

'Lo, What it is to Love' (*c.*1568)

C. P. Scott 1846–1932

British journalist; editor of the Manchester Guardian, *1872–1929*

4 Comment is free, but facts are sacred.

in *Manchester Guardian* 5 May 1921; cf. **Stoppard** 743:15

5 *Television?* The word is half Greek, half Latin. No good can come of it.

Asa Briggs *The BBC: the First Fifty Years* (1985)

Paul Scott 1920–78

English novelist

6 For a writer, going back home means back to the pen, pencil, and typewriter—and the blank, implacable sheet of white paper.

Hilary Spurling *Paul Scott* (1990)

Robert Falcon Scott 1868–1912

English polar explorer
see also ***Last words*** *455:13*

7 Great God! this is an awful place.

of the South Pole

diary, 17 January 1912, in *Scott's Last Expedition* (1913) vol. 1, ch. 18

8 Make the boy interested in natural history if you can; it is better than games.

last letter to his wife, in *Scott's Last Expedition* (1913) vol. 1, ch. 20

9 Had we lived, I should have had a tale to tell of the hardihood, endurance, and courage of my companions which would have stirred the heart of every Englishman. These rough notes and our dead bodies must tell the tale.

'Message to the Public' in late editions of *The Times* 11 February 1913, and those of the following day; in *Scott's Last Expedition* (1913) vol. 1, ch. 20

Sir Walter Scott 1771–1832

Scottish novelist and poet
on Scott: see ***Anonymous*** *18:6,* ***Hazlitt*** *365:17*

10 The valiant Knight of Triermain
Rung forth his challenge-blast again,
But answer came there none.

The Bridal of Triermain (1813) canto 3, st. 10; cf. **Carroll** 190:21

11 To the Lords of Convention 'twas Claver'se who spoke,
'Ere the King's crown shall fall there are crowns to be broke;
So let each cavalier who loves honour and me,
Come follow the bonnet of Bonny Dundee.
Come fill up my cup, come fill up my can,
Come saddle your horses, and call up your men;
Come open the West Port, and let me gang free,
And it's room for the bonnets of Bonny Dundee!'

The Doom of Devorgoil (1830) act 2, sc. 2 'Bonny Dundee'; cf. **Scott** 652:6

12 His ready speech flowed fair and free,
In phrase of gentlest courtesy;
Yet seemed that tone, and gesture bland,
Less used to sue than to command.

The Lady of the Lake (1810) canto 1, st. 21; cf. **Shakespeare** 694:10

13 He is gone on the mountain,
He is lost to the forest,
Like a summer-dried fountain,
When our need was the sorest.

The Lady of the Lake (1810) canto 3, st. 16

14 Respect was mingled with surprise,
And the stern joy which warriors feel
In foemen worthy of their steel.

The Lady of the Lake (1810) canto 5, st. 10

15 Vengeance, deep-brooding o'er the slain,
Had locked the source of softer woe;
And burning pride and high disdain
Forbade the rising tear to flow.

The Lay of the Last Minstrel (1805) canto 1, st. 9

16 If thou would'st view fair Melrose aright,
Go visit it by the pale moonlight;
For the gay beams of lightsome day
Gild, but to flout, the ruins grey.

The Lay of the Last Minstrel (1805) canto 2, st. 1

17 For ne'er
Was flattery lost on poet's ear:
A simple race! they waste their toil
For the vain tribute of a smile.

The Lay of the Last Minstrel (1805) canto 4, closing words

18 It is the secret sympathy,
The silver link, the silken tie,
Which heart to heart, and mind to mind,
In body and in soul can bind.

The Lay of the Last Minstrel (1805) canto 5, st. 13

19 Breathes there the man, with soul so dead,
Who never to himself hath said,
This is my own, my native land!
Whose heart hath ne'er within him burned,
As home his footsteps he hath turned

From wandering on a foreign strand!
The Lay of the Last Minstrel (1805) canto 6, st. 1

1 Despite those titles, power, and pelf,
The wretch, concentred all in self,
Living, shall forfeit fair renown,
And, doubly dying, shall go down
To the vile dust, from whence he sprung,
Unwept, unhonoured, and unsung.
The Lay of the Last Minstrel (1805) canto 6, st. 1

2 O Caledonia! stern and wild,
Meet nurse for a poetic child!
Land of brown heath and shaggy wood,
Land of the mountain and the flood,
Land of my sires! what mortal hand
Can e'er untie the filial band
That knits me to thy rugged strand!
The Lay of the Last Minstrel (1805) canto 6, st. 2

3 O! many a shaft, at random sent,
Finds mark the archer little meant!
And many a word, at random spoken,
May soothe or wound a heart that's broken.
The Lord of the Isles (1813) canto 5, st. 18

4 Had'st thou but lived, though stripped of power,
A watchman on the lonely tower.
Marmion (1808) introduction to canto 1, st. 8

5 Now is the stately column broke,
The beacon-light is quenched in smoke,
The trumpet's silver sound is still,
The warder silent on the hill!
Marmion (1808) introduction to canto 1, st. 8

6 And come he slow, or come he fast,
It is but Death who comes at last.
Marmion (1808) canto 2, st. 30

7 O, young Lochinvar is come out of the west,
Through all the wide Border his steed was the best.
Marmion (1808) canto 5, st. 12 ('Lochinvar' st. 1)

8 So faithful in love, and so dauntless in war,
There never was knight like the young Lochinvar.
Marmion (1808) canto 5, st. 12 ('Lochinvar' st. 1)

9 For a laggard in love, and a dastard in war,
Was to wed the fair Ellen of brave Lochinvar.
Marmion (1808) canto 5, st. 12 ('Lochinvar' st. 2)

10 O come ye in peace here, or come ye in war,
Or to dance at our bridal, young Lord Lochinvar?
Marmion (1808) canto 5, st. 12 ('Lochinvar' st. 3)

11 And now I am come, with this lost love of mine,
To lead but one measure, drink one cup of wine.
Marmion (1808) canto 5, st. 12 ('Lochinvar' st. 4)

12 O what a tangled web we weave,
When first we practise to deceive!
Marmion (1808) canto 6, st. 17

13 O Woman! in our hours of ease,
Uncertain, coy, and hard to please,
And variable as the shade
By the light quivering aspen made;
When pain and anguish wring the brow,
A ministering angel thou!
Marmion (1808) canto 6, st. 30; cf. **Shakespeare** 666:26

14 The stubborn spear-men still made good
Their dark impenetrable wood,
Each stepping where his comrade stood,
The instant that he fell.
Marmion (1808) canto 6, st. 34

15 Still from the sire the son shall hear
Of the stern strife, and carnage drear,
Of Flodden's fatal field,
Where shivered was fair Scotland's spear,
And broken was her shield!
Marmion (1808) canto 6, st. 34

16 O, Brignal banks are wild and fair,
And Greta woods are green,
And you may gather garlands there
Would grace a summer queen.
Rokeby (1813) canto 3, st. 16

17 It's no fish ye're buying—it's men's lives.
The Antiquary (1816) ch. 11

18 Widowed wife, and married maid,
Betrothed, betrayer, and betrayed!
The Betrothed (1825) ch. 15

19 Vacant heart and hand, and eye,—
Easy live and quiet die.
The Bride of Lammermoor (1819) ch. 2

20 I live by twa trades . . . fiddle, sir, and spade; filling the world, and emptying of it.
The Bride of Lammermoor (1819) ch. 24

21 Touch not the cat but a glove.
but = *without*
The Fair Maid of Perth (1828) ch. 34

22 It's ill taking the breeks aff a wild Highlandman.
The Fortunes of Nigel (1822) ch. 5

23 Gin by pailfuls, wine in rivers,
Dash the window-glass to shivers!
For three wild lads were we, brave boys,
And three wild lads were we;
Thou on the land, and I on the sand,
And Jack on the gallows-tree!
Guy Mannering (1815) ch. 34

24 The hour is come, but not the man.
The Heart of Midlothian (1818) ch. 4, title

25 The passive resistance of the Tolbooth-gate.
The Heart of Midlothian (1818) ch. 6

26 Proud Maisie is in the wood,
Walking so early,
Sweet Robin sits in the bush,
Singing so rarely.
The Heart of Midlothian (1818) ch. 40

27 'Pax vobiscum [Peace be with you]' will answer all queries.
Ivanhoe (1819) ch. 26

28 His morning walk was beneath the elms in the churchyard; 'for death,' he said, 'had been his next-door neighbour for so many years, that he had no apology for dropping the acquaintance.'
A Legend of Montrose (1819) introduction

29 March, march, Ettrick and Teviotdale,
Why the deil dinna ye march forward in order?
March, march, Eskdale and Liddesdale,
All the Blue Bonnets are bound for the Border.
The Monastery (1820) ch. 25

1 It is fortunate for tale-tellers that they are not tied down like theatrical writers to the unities of time and place.
'Old Mortality' (*Tales of My Landlord* 1st series, 1816)

2 Ah! County Guy, the hour is nigh,
The sun has left the lea,
The orange flower perfumes the bower,
The breeze is on the sea.
Quentin Durward (1823) ch. 4

3 And it's ill speaking between a fou man and a fasting.
Redgauntlet (1824) letter 11 'Wandering Willie's Tale'

4 The ae half of the warld thinks the tither daft.
Redgauntlet (1824) 'Journal of Darsie Latimer' ch. 7

5 But with the morning cool repentance came.
Rob Roy (1817) ch. 12

6 Come fill up my cup, come fill up my cann,
Come saddle my horses, and call up my man;
Come open your gates, and let me gae free,
I daurna stay langer in bonny Dundee.
Rob Roy (1817) ch. 23; cf. **Scott** 650:11

7 There's a gude time coming.
Rob Roy (1817) ch. 32

8 The play-bill, which is said to have announced the tragedy of Hamlet, the character of the Prince of Denmark being left out.
commonly alluded to as 'Hamlet without the Prince'
The Talisman (1825) introduction; W. J. Parke *Musical Memories* (1830) vol. 1 gives a similar anecdote from 1787

9 Rouse the lion from his lair.
The Talisman (1825) ch. 6

10 Turner's palm is as itchy as his fingers are ingenious.
letter to James Skene, 30 April 1823; *Letters* (1934)

11 But I must say to the Muse of fiction, as the Earl of Pembroke said to the ejected nun of Wilton, 'Go spin, you jade, go spin'.
diary, 9 February 1826; cf. **Pembroke** 572:9

12 The Big Bow-Wow strain I can do myself like any now going; but the exquisite touch, which renders ordinary commonplace things and characters interesting, from the truth of the description and the sentiment, is denied to me.
*on Jane **Austen***
W. E. K. Anderson (ed.) *Journals of Sir Walter Scott* (1972) 14 March 1826; cf. **Pembroke** 572:11

13 I would like to be there, were it but to see how the cat jumps.
W. E. K. Anderson (ed.) *Journals of Sir Walter Scott* (1972) 7 October 1826

14 The blockheads talk of my being like Shakespeare—not fit to tie his brogues.
W. E. K. Anderson (ed.) *Journals of Sir Walter Scott* (1972) 11 December 1826

15 Were I my own man . . . I would refuse this offer (with all gratitude); but as I am situated, L.300 or L.400 a-year is not to be sneezed at.
on being offered the Laureateship
letter to James Ballantyne, 24 August 1813; John Gibson Lockhart *Memoirs of the Life of Sir Walter Scott* (1837–8)

16 Too many flowers . . . too little fruit.
*describing the work of Felicia **Hemans***
letter to Joanna Baillie, 18 July 1823, in *Letters* (Centenary ed.) vol. 8

17 We shall never learn to feel and respect our real calling and destiny, unless we have taught ourselves to consider every thing as moonshine, compared with the education of the heart.
to J. G. Lockhart, August 1825, in Lockhart's *Life of Sir Walter Scott* vol. 6 (1837) ch. 2

18 Their factions have been so long envenomed and having so little ground to fight their battle in that they [the Irish] are like people fighting with daggers in a hogshead.
letter to Joanna Baillie, 12 October 1825, in H. J. C. Grierson (ed.) *Letters of Sir Walter Scott* vol. 9 (1935)

19 All men who have turned out worth anything have had the chief hand in their own education.
letter to J. G. Lockhart, *c.*16 June 1830, in H. J. C. Grierson (ed.) *Letters of Sir Walter Scott* vol. 11 (1936)

Scottish Metrical Psalms 1650

20 The Lord's my shepherd, I'll not want.
He makes me down to lie
In pastures green: he leadeth me
the quiet waters by.
My soul he doth restore again;
and me to walk doth make
Within the paths of righteousness,
ev'n for his own name's sake.
Yea, though I walk in death's dark vale,
yet will I fear none ill:
For thou art with me; and thy rod
and staff me comfort still.
My table thou hast furnished
in presence of my foes;
My head thou dost with oil anoint,
and my cup overflows.
Psalm 23, v. 1; cf. **Book of Common Prayer** 132:26

21 How lovely is thy dwelling-place,
O Lord of hosts, to me!
The tabernacles of thy grace
how pleasant, Lord, they be!
Psalm 84, v. 1; cf. **Book of Common Prayer** 137:13

22 I to the hills will lift mine eyes
from whence doth come mine aid.
My safety cometh from the Lord,
who heav'n and earth hath made.
Psalm 121, v. 1; cf. **Book of Common Prayer** 140:12

23 The race that long in darkness pined
have seen a glorious light.
Paraphrase 19; cf. **Bible** 86:28

Edmund Hamilton Sears 1810–76

American minister

24 It came upon the midnight clear,
That glorious song of old,
From Angels bending near the earth
To touch their harps of gold;
'Peace on the earth, good will to man
From Heaven's all gracious King.'

The world in solemn stillness lay
To hear the angels sing.
The Christian Register (1850) 'That Glorious Song of Old'

Charles Sedley c.1639–1701
English dramatist and poet

1 Ah, Chloris! that I now could sit
As unconcerned as when
Your infant beauty could beget
No pleasure, nor no pain!
'Child and Maiden' (1668)

2 Love still has something of the sea
From whence his mother rose.
'Love still has something'

3 Phyllis, without frown or smile,
Sat and knotted all the while.
'Phyllis Knotting' (1694)

4 Phyllis is my only joy,
Faithless as the winds or seas;
Sometimes coming, sometimes coy,
Yet she never fails to please.
'Song'

Alan Seeger 1888–1916
American poet

5 I have a rendezvous with Death
At some disputed barricade.
'I Have a Rendezvous with Death' (1916)

Pete Seeger 1919–
American folk singer and songwriter

6 Where have all the flowers gone?
title of song (1961)

7 Education is when you read the fine print; experience is what you get when you don't.
L. Botts *Loose Talk* (1980)

John Seeley 1834–95
English historian

8 We [the English] seem, as it were, to have conquered and peopled half the world in a fit of absence of mind.
The Expansion of England (1883) Lecture 1

Sefer Yezirah
Hebrew esoteric text on cosmology, 3rd–6th century AD

9 Thirty-two wondrous paths were engraved by Yah, the Lord of hosts, the God of Israel, the living God, God Almighty . . . who . . . created his world by three principles: by limit, by letter and by number. There are ten primordial numbers and twenty-two fundamental letters.
1:1

Erich Segal 1937–
American novelist

10 Love means not ever having to say you're sorry.
Love Story (1970)

Sei Shōnagon c.966–c.1013
Japanese diarist and writer

11 There is nothing in the whole world so painful as feeling that one is not liked. It always seems to me that people who hate me must be suffering from some strange form of lunacy.
The Pillow Book of Sei Shonagōn

12 If writing did not exist, what terrible depressions we should suffer from.
The Pillow Book of Sei Shonagōn

John Selden 1584–1654
English historian and antiquary

13 *Scrutamini scripturas* [Let us look at the scriptures]. These two words have undone the world.
Table Talk (1689) 'Bible Scripture'; cf. **Bible** 101:24

14 Old friends are best. King James used to call for his old shoes; they were easiest for his feet.
Table Talk (1689) 'Friends'

15 'Tis not the drinking that is to be blamed, but the excess.
Table Talk (1689) 'Humility'

16 Ignorance of the law excuses no man; not that all men know the law, but because 'tis an excuse every man will plead, and no man can tell how to confute him.
Table Talk (1689) 'Law'; cf. **Proverbs** 603:43

17 Take a straw and throw it up into the air, you shall see by that which way the wind is.
Table Talk (1689) 'Libels'

18 Marriage is nothing but a civil contract.
Table Talk (1689) 'Marriage'

19 A king is a thing men have made for their own sakes, for quietness' sake. Just as in a family one man is appointed to buy the meat.
Table Talk (1689) 'Of a King'

20 There never was a merry world since the fairies left off dancing, and the Parson left conjuring.
Table Talk (1689) 'Parson'

21 There is not anything in the world so much abused as this sentence, *Salus populi suprema lex esto.*
Table Talk (1689) 'People'; cf. **Cicero** 217:12

22 Pleasure is nothing else but the intermission of pain.
Table Talk (1689) 'Pleasure'

23 Syllables govern the world.
Table Talk (1689) 'Power: State'

24 Preachers say, Do as I say, not as I do.
Table Talk (1689) 'Preaching'

Arthur Seldon 1916–
British economist

25 Government of the busy by the bossy for the bully.
on over-government
Capitalism (1990)

Will Self 1961–

English novelist and journalist

1 So I was smacked out on the Prime Minister's jet, big deal.
having been dismissed as a columnist by the Observer *after taking heroin on John* **Major**'*s plane during the election campaign*
in *Independent on Sunday* 20 April 1997

W. C. Sellar 1898–1951 and R. J. Yeatman 1898–1968

British writers

2 For every person who wants to teach there are approximately thirty who don't want to learn—much.
And Now All This (1932) introduction

3 1066 and all That
title of book (1930)

4 History is not what you thought. *It is what you can remember.*
1066 and All That (1930) 'Compulsory Preface'

5 The Roman Conquest was, however, a *Good Thing*, since the Britons were only natives at the time.
1066 and All That (1930) ch. 1

6 Edward III had very good manners . . . and made the memorable epitaph: 'Honi soie qui mal y pense' ('Honey, your silk stocking's hanging down').
1066 and All That (1930) ch. 24; cf. **Mottoes** 535:9

7 Are you Edmund Mortimer? If not, have you got him?
1066 and All That (1930) ch. 28

8 The cruel Queen died and a post-mortem examination revealed the word 'CALLOUS' engraved on her heart.
1066 and All That (1930) ch. 32; cf. **Mary** 500:12

9 The Cavaliers (Wrong but Wromantic) and the Roundheads (Right but Repulsive).
1066 and All That (1930) ch. 35

10 The Rump Parliament—so called because it had been sitting for such a long time.
1066 and All That (1930) ch. 35

11 Charles II was always very merry and was therefore not so much a king as a Monarch.
1066 and All That (1930) ch. 36; cf. **Rochester** 630:17

12 The National Debt is a very Good Thing and it would be dangerous to pay it off, for fear of Political Economy.
1066 and All That (1930) ch. 38

13 Napoleon's armies always used to march on their stomachs shouting: 'Vive l'Intérieur!'
1066 and All That (1930) ch. 48; cf. **Napoleon** 539:1

14 Most memorable . . . was the discovery (made by all the rich men in England at once) that women and children could work twenty-five hours a day in factories without many of them dying or becoming excessively deformed. This was known as the Industrial Revelation.
1066 and All That (1930) ch. 49

15 Gladstone . . . spent his declining years trying to guess the answer to the Irish Question; unfortunately whenever he was getting warm, the Irish secretly changed the Question.
1066 and All That (1930) ch. 57

16 AMERICA was thus clearly top nation, and History came to a .
1066 and All That (1930) ch. 62

Seneca ('the Younger') *c.*4 BC–AD 65

Roman philosopher and poet

17 *Ignoranti, quem portum petat, nullus suus ventus est.*
If one does not know to which port one is sailing, no wind is favourable.
Epistulae ad Lucilium no. 71, sect. 3

18 *Homines dum docent discunt.*
Even while they teach, men learn.
Epistulae Morales no. 7, sect. 8

19 *Nil melius aeterna lex fecit, quam quod unum introitum nobis ad vitam dedit, exitus multos.*
Eternal law has arranged nothing better than this, that it has given us one way in to life, but many ways out.
Epistulae Morales no. 70, sect. 14

20 *Eripere vitam nemo non homini potest,*
At nemo mortem; mille ad hanc aditus patent.
Anyone can stop a man's life, but no one his death; a thousand doors open on to it.
Phoenissae l. 152; cf. **Massinger** 318:4, **Webster** 808:1

21 *Illi mors gravis incubat*
Qui notus nimis omnibus
Ignotus moritur sibi.
On him does death lie heavily who, but too well known to all, dies to himself unknown.
Thyestes chorus 2 (translated by F. J. Miller)

Gitta Sereny 1923–

Hungarian-born British writer and journalist

to Albert Speer, who having always denied knowledge of the Holocaust had said that he was at fault in having 'looked away':

22 You cannot look away from something you don't know. If you looked away, then you knew.
recalled on BBC2 *Reputations*, 2 May 1996

Robert W. Service 1874–1958

Canadian poet

23 A promise made is a debt unpaid, and the trail has its own stern code.
'The Cremation of Sam McGee' (1907)

24 Ah! the clock is always slow;
It is later than you think.
'It Is Later Than You Think' (1921)

25 This is the law of the Yukon, that only the Strong shall thrive;
That surely the Weak shall perish, and only the Fit survive.
'The Law of the Yukon' (1907)

1 When we, the Workers, all demand: 'What are WE fighting for?' . . .
Then, then we'll end that stupid crime, that devil's madness—War.
'Michael' (1921)

2 Back of the bar, in a solo game, sat Dangerous Dan McGrew,
And watching his luck was his light-o'-love, the lady that's known as Lou.
'The Shooting of Dan McGrew' (1907)

William Seward 1801–72
American politician

3 I know, and all the world knows, that revolutions never go backward.
speech at Rochester, 25 October 1858, in *The Irrepressible Conflict* (1858)

Edward Sexby d. 1658
English conspirator

4 Killing no murder briefly discourst in three questions.
an apology for tyrannicide
title of pamphlet (1657)

Anne Sexton 1928–74
American poet

5 I was tired of being a woman,
tired of the spoons and the pots,
tired of my mouth and my breasts
tired of the cosmetics and silks . . .
I was tired of the gender of things.
'Consorting with angels' (1967)

6 God owns heaven
but He craves the earth.
'The Earth' (1975)

7 My sleeping pill is white.
It is a splendid pearl;
it floats me out of myself,
my stung skin as alien
as a loose bolt of cloth.
'Lullaby' (1960)

8 In a dream you are never eighty.
'Old' (1962)

9 But suicides have a special language.
Like carpenters they want to know *which tools*.
They never ask *why build*.
'Wanting to Die' (1966)

Thomas Shadwell c.1642–92
English dramatist
on Shadwell: see **Dryden** *281:36*

10 Words may be false and full of art,
Sighs are the natural language of the heart.
Psyche (1675) act 3

11 And wit's the noblest frailty of the mind.
A True Widow (1679) act 2, sc. 1; cf. **Dryden** 281:27

12 Every man loves what he is good at.
A True Widow (1679) act 5, sc. 1

13 Instantly, in the twinkling of a bed-staff.
The Virtuoso (1676) act 1, sc. 1

Peter Shaffer 1926–
English dramatist

14 All my wife has ever taken from the Mediterranean—from that whole vast intuitive culture—are four bottles of Chianti to make into lamps.
Equus (1973) act 1, sc. 18

Anthony Ashley Cooper, 1st Earl of Shaftesbury 1621–83
English statesman
on Shaftesbury: see **Cromwell** *246:3*

15 Admit lords, and you admit all.
refusing the claims of Cromwell's House of Lords
in *Dictionary of National Biography* (1917–)

16 'People differ in their discourse and profession about these matters, but men of sense are really but of one religion.' . . . 'Pray, my lord, what religion is that which men of sense agree in?' 'Madam,' says the earl immediately, 'men of sense never tell it.'
Bishop Gilbert Burnet *History of My Own Time* vol. 1 (1724) bk. 2, ch. 1 n.; cf. **Disraeli** 270:12

Anthony Ashley Cooper, 3rd Earl of Shaftesbury 1671–1713
English statesman and philosopher

17 How comes it to pass, then, that we appear such cowards in reasoning, and are so afraid to stand the test of ridicule?
A Letter Concerning Enthusiasm (1708) sect. 2

18 Truth, 'tis supposed, may bear all lights: and one of those in which things are to be viewed, in order to [attain] a thorough recognition is that by which we discern whatever is liable to ridicule in any subject.
Sensus Communis: an essay on the freedom of wit and humour (1709) pt. 1, sect. 1; cf. **Chesterfield** 209:21

William Shakespeare 1564–1616
English dramatist
on Shakespeare: see **Arnold** *27:13,* **Aubrey** *32:22,* **Basse** *156:6,* **Browning** *57:1,* **Coleridge** *227:13,* **Dryden** *283:6, 283:9,* **George III** *333:14,* **Gray** *351:1,* **Greene** *352:5,* **Johnson** *410:12, 410:14, 410:15, 410:16,* **Jonson** *420:18, 420:22, 420:23, 420:25, 420:26,* **Lawrence** *457:23,* **Milton** *512:24, 513:14,* **Olivier** *553:16,* **Pope** *586:13,* **Scott** *652:14,* **Walpole** *800:19,* **Wordsworth** *831:18; see also* **Epitaphs** *302:10,* **Fletcher** *318:8*

The line number is given without brackets where the scene is all verse up to the quotation and the line number is certain, and in square brackets where prose makes it variable. All references are to the Oxford Standard Authors edition in one volume

ALL'S WELL THAT ENDS WELL

19 It were all one
That I should love a bright particular star
And think to wed it, he is so above me.
All's Well that Ends Well (1603–4) act 1, sc. 1, l. [97]

1 Our remedies oft in ourselves do lie
Which we ascribe to heaven.
All's Well that Ends Well (1603–4) act 1, sc. 1, l. [232]

2 It is like a barber's chair that fits all buttocks.
All's Well that Ends Well (1603–4) act 2, sc. 2, l. [18]

3 A young man married is a man that's marred.
All's Well that Ends Well (1603–4) act 2, sc. 3, l. [315]; cf. **Proverbs** 616:2

4 I know a man that had this trick of melancholy sold a goodly manor for a song.
All's Well that Ends Well (1603–4) act 3, sc. 2, l. [8]

5 The flowery way that leads to the broad gate and the great fire.
All's Well that Ends Well (1603–4) act 4, sc. 5, l. [58]; cf. **Shakespeare** 683:14

ANTONY AND CLEOPATRA

6 The triple pillar of the world transformed
Into a strumpet's fool.
Antony and Cleopatra (1606–7) act 1, sc. 1, l. 12

7 CLEOPATRA: If it be love indeed, tell me how much.
ANTONY: There's beggary in the love that can be reckoned.
CLEOPATRA: I'll set a bourn how far to be beloved.
ANTONY: Then must thou needs find out new heaven, new earth.
Antony and Cleopatra (1606–7) act 1, sc. 1, l. 14

8 Let Rome in Tiber melt, and the wide arch
Of the ranged empire fall. Here is my space.
Kingdoms are clay.
Antony and Cleopatra (1606–7) act 1, sc. 1, l. 33

9 I love long life better than figs.
Antony and Cleopatra (1606–7) act 1, sc. 2, l. [34]

10 On the sudden
A Roman thought hath struck him.
Antony and Cleopatra (1606–7) act 1, sc. 2, l. [90]

11 The nature of bad news infects the teller.
Antony and Cleopatra (1606–7) act 1, sc. 2, l. [103]

12 There's a great spirit gone!
Antony and Cleopatra (1606–7) act 1, sc. 2, l. [131]

13 Indeed the tears live in an onion that should water this sorrow.
Antony and Cleopatra (1606–7) act 1, sc. 2, l. [181]

14 CHARMIAN: In each thing give him way, cross him in nothing.
CLEOPATRA: Thou teachest like a fool; the way to lose him.
Antony and Cleopatra (1606–7) act 1, sc. 3, l. 9

15 In time we hate that which we often fear.
Antony and Cleopatra (1606–7) act 1, sc. 3, l. 12

16 Eternity was in our lips and eyes,
Bliss in our brows bent.
Antony and Cleopatra (1606–7) act 1, sc. 3, l. 35

17 O! my oblivion is a very Antony,
And I am all forgotten.
Antony and Cleopatra (1606–7) act 1, sc. 3, l. 90

18 Give me to drink mandragora . . .
That I might sleep out this great gap of time
My Antony is away.
Antony and Cleopatra (1606–7) act 1, sc. 5, l. 4

19 O happy horse, to bear the weight of Antony!
Antony and Cleopatra (1606–7) act 1, sc. 5, l. 21

20 He's speaking now,
Or murmuring, 'Where's my serpent of old Nile?
Antony and Cleopatra (1606–7) act 1, sc. 5, l. 24

21 My salad days,
When I was green in judgment, cold in blood,
To say as I said then!
Antony and Cleopatra (1606–7) act 1, sc. 5, l. 73

22 I do not much dislike the matter, but
The manner of his speech.
Antony and Cleopatra (1606–7) act 2, sc. 2, l. 117

23 The barge she sat in, like a burnished throne,
Burned on the water; the poop was beaten gold,
Purple the sails, and so perfumed, that
The winds were love-sick with them, the oars were silver,
Which to the tune of flutes kept stroke, and made
The water which they beat to follow faster,
As amorous of their strokes. For her own person,
It beggared all description.
Antony and Cleopatra (1606–7) act 2, sc. 2, l. [199]; cf. **Eliot** 296:2

24 Her gentlewomen, like the Nereides,
So many mermaids, tended her i' the eyes,
And made their bends adornings.
Antony and Cleopatra (1606–7) act 2, sc. 2, l. [214]

25 Antony,
Enthroned i' the market-place, did sit alone,
Whistling to the air; which, but for vacancy,
Had gone to gaze on Cleopatra too
And made a gap in nature.
Antony and Cleopatra (1606–7) act 2, sc. 2, l. [222]

26 I saw her once
Hop forty paces through the public street;
And having lost her breath, she spoke, and panted
That she did make defect perfection,
And, breathless, power breathe forth.
Antony and Cleopatra (1606–7) act 2, sc. 2, l. [236]

27 Age cannot wither her, nor custom stale
Her infinite variety; other women cloy
The appetites they feed, but she makes hungry
Where most she satisfies; for vilest things
Become themselves in her, that the holy priests
Bless her when she is riggish.
Antony and Cleopatra (1606–7) act 2, sc. 2, l. [243]

28 I have not kept the square, but that to come
Shall all be done by the rule.
Antony and Cleopatra (1606–7) act 2, sc. 3, l. 6

29 I' the east my pleasure lies.
Antony and Cleopatra (1606–7) act 2, sc. 3, l. 40

30 Give me some music—music, moody food
Of us that trade in love.
Antony and Cleopatra (1606–7) act 2, sc. 5, l. 1

31 Give me mine angle; we'll to the river: there—
My music playing far off—I will betray
Tawny-finned fishes; my bended hook shall pierce

Their slimy jaws; and, as I draw them up,
I'll think them every one an Antony,
And say, 'Ah, ha!' you're caught.
Antony and Cleopatra (1606–7) act 2, sc. 5, l. 10

1 I laughed him out of patience; and that night
I laughed him into patience: and next morn,
Ere the ninth hour, I drunk him to his bed.
Antony and Cleopatra (1606–7) act 2, sc. 5, l. 19

2 LEPIDUS: What manner o' thing is your crocodile?
ANTONY: It is shaped, sir, like itself, and it is as broad as it hath breadth; it is just so high as it is, and moves with its own organs; it lives by that which nourisheth it; and the elements once out of it, it transmigrates.
Antony and Cleopatra (1606–7) act 2, sc. 7, l. [47]

3 Egypt, thou knew'st too well
My heart was to thy rudder tied by th' strings,
And thou shouldst tow me after.
Antony and Cleopatra (1606–7) act 3, sc. 9, l. 56

4 He wears the rose
Of youth upon him.
Antony and Cleopatra (1606–7) act 3, sc. 11, l. 20

5 I found you as a morsel, cold upon
Dead Caesar's trencher.
Antony and Cleopatra (1606–7) act 3, sc. 11, l. 116

6 Let's have one other gaudy night: call to me
All my sad captains; fill our bowls once more;
Let's mock the midnight bell.
Antony and Cleopatra (1606–7) act 3, sc. 11, l. 182

7 To business that we love we rise betime,
And go to 't with delight.
Antony and Cleopatra (1606–7) act 4, sc. 4, l. 20

8 O! my fortunes have
Corrupted honest men.
Antony and Cleopatra (1606–7) act 4, sc. 5, l. 16

9 O infinite virtue! com'st thou smiling from
The world's great snare uncaught?
Antony and Cleopatra (1606–7) act 4, sc. 8, l. 17

10 The hearts
That spanieled me at heels, to whom I gave
Their wishes, do discandy, melt their sweets
On blossoming Caesar.
Antony and Cleopatra (1606–7) act 4, sc. 10, l. 33

11 The soul and body rive not more in parting
Than greatness going off.
Antony and Cleopatra (1606–7) act 4, sc. 11, l. 5

12 Sometimes we see a cloud that's dragonish;
A vapour sometime like a bear or lion,
A towered citadel, a pendant rock,
A forked mountain, or blue promontory
With trees upon 't, that nod unto the world
And mock our eyes with air.
Antony and Cleopatra (1606–7) act 4, sc. 12, l. 2

13 Unarm, Eros; the long day's task is done,
And we must sleep.
Antony and Cleopatra (1606–7) act 4, sc. 12, l. 35

14 Stay for me:
Where souls do couch on flowers, we'll hand in hand,
And with our sprightly port make the ghosts gaze;
Dido and her Aeneas shall want troops,
And all the haunt be ours.
Antony and Cleopatra (1606–7) act 4, sc. 12, l. 50

15 I will be
A bridegroom in my death, and run into 't
As to a lover's bed.
Antony and Cleopatra (1606–7) act 4, sc. 12, l. 99

16 None but Antony
Should conquer Antony.
Antony and Cleopatra (1606–7) act 4, sc. 13, l. 16

17 I am dying, Egypt, dying.
Antony and Cleopatra (1606–7) act 4, sc. 13, l. 18

18 A Roman by a Roman
Valiantly vanquished.
Antony and Cleopatra (1606–7) act 4, sc. 13, l. 57

19 O! withered is the garland of the war,
The soldier's pole is fall'n; young boys and girls
Are level now with men; the odds is gone,
And there is nothing left remarkable
Beneath the visiting moon.
Antony and Cleopatra (1606–7) act 4, sc. 13, l. 64

20 What's brave, what's noble,
Let's do it after the high Roman fashion,
And make death proud to take us.
Antony and Cleopatra (1606–7) act 4, sc. 13, l. 86

21 My desolation does begin to make
A better life. 'Tis paltry to be Caesar;
Not being Fortune, he's but Fortune's knave,
A minister of her will; and it is great
To do that thing that ends all other deeds,
Which shackles accidents, and bolts up change,
Which sleeps, and never palates more the dug,
The beggar's nurse and Caesar's.
Antony and Cleopatra (1606–7) act 5, sc. 2, l. 1

22 He words me, girls, he words me, that I should not
Be noble to myself.
Antony and Cleopatra (1606–7) act 5, sc. 2, l. 190

23 Finish, good lady; the bright day is done,
And we are for the dark.
Antony and Cleopatra (1606–7) act 5, sc. 2, l. 192

24 Antony
Shall be brought drunken forth, and I shall see
Some squeaking Cleopatra boy my greatness
I' the posture of a whore.
Antony and Cleopatra (1606–7) act 5, sc. 2, l. 217

25 My resolution's placed, and I have nothing
Of woman in me; now from head to foot
I am marble-constant, now the fleeting moon
No planet is of mine.
Antony and Cleopatra (1606–7) act 5, sc. 2, l. 237

26 His biting is immortal; those that do die of it do seldom or never recover.
Antony and Cleopatra (1606–7) act 5, sc. 2, l. [246]

27 I wish you all joy of the worm.
Antony and Cleopatra (1606–7) act 5, sc. 2, l. [260]

28 Give me my robe, put on my crown; I have
Immortal longings in me.
Antony and Cleopatra (1606–7) act 5, sc. 2, l. [282]

1 I am fire and air; my other elements
I give to baser life.
Antony and Cleopatra (1606–7) act 5, sc. 2, l. [291]

2 Come, thou mortal wretch,
With thy sharp teeth this knot intrinsicate
Of life at once untie; poor venomous fool,
Be angry, and dispatch. O! couldst thou speak,
That I might hear thee call great Caesar ass
Unpolicied.
Antony and Cleopatra (1606–7) act 5, sc. 2, l. [305]

3 CHARMIAN: O eastern star!
CLEOPATRA: Peace! peace!
Dost thou not see my baby at my breast,
That sucks the nurse asleep?
Antony and Cleopatra (1606–7) act 5, sc. 2, l. [309]

4 Now boast thee, death, in thy possession lies
A lass unparalleled.
Antony and Cleopatra (1606–7) act 5, sc. 2, l. [317]

5 She looks like sleep,
As she would catch a second Antony
In her strong toil of grace.
Antony and Cleopatra (1606–7) act 5, sc. 2, l. [347]

6 She hath pursued conclusions infinite
Of easy ways to die.
Antony and Cleopatra (1606–7) act 5, sc. 2, l. [356]

AS YOU LIKE IT

7 Fleet the time carelessly, as they did in the golden world.
As You Like It (1599) act 1, sc. 1, l. [126]

8 Let us sit and mock the good housewife Fortune from her wheel, that her gifts may henceforth be bestowed equally.
As You Like It (1599) act 1, sc. 2, l. [35]

9 Hereafter, in a better world than this,
I shall desire more love and knowledge of you.
As You Like It (1599) act 1, sc. 2, l. [301]

10 Thus must I from the smoke into the smother;
From tyrant duke unto a tyrant brother.
As You Like It (1599) act 1, sc. 2, l. [304]

11 O, how full of briers is this working-day world!
As You Like It (1599) act 1, sc. 3, l. [12]

12 We'll have a swashing and a martial outside,
As many other mannish cowards have
That do outface it with their semblances.
As You Like It (1599) act 1, sc. 3, l. [123]

13 Are not these woods
More free from peril than the envious court?
Here feel we but the penalty of Adam,
The seasons' difference; as, the icy fang
And churlish chiding of the winter's wind,
Which, when it bites and blows upon my body,
Even till I shrink with cold, I smile and say,
'This is no flattery.'
As You Like It (1599) act 2, sc. 1, l. 3

14 Sweet are the uses of adversity,
Which like the toad, ugly and venomous,
Wears yet a precious jewel in his head;
And this our life, exempt from public haunt,
Finds tongues in trees, books in the running brooks,
Sermons in stones, and good in everything.
As You Like It (1599) act 2, sc. 1, l. 12; cf. **Bernard** 69:1

15 Unregarded age in corners thrown.
As You Like It (1599) act 2, sc. 3, l. 42

16 Therefore my age is as a lusty winter,
Frosty, but kindly.
As You Like It (1599) act 2, sc. 3, l. 52

17 O good old man! how well in thee appears
The constant service of the antique world,
When service sweat for duty, not for meed!
Thou art not for the fashion of these times,
Where none will sweat but for promotion.
As You Like It (1599) act 2, sc. 3, l. 56

18 Ay, now am I in Arden; the more fool I. When I was at home I was in a better place; but travellers must be content.
As You Like It (1599) act 2, sc. 4, l. [16]

19 In thy youth thou wast as true a lover
As ever sighed upon a midnight pillow.
As You Like It (1599) act 2, sc. 4, l. [26]

20 Under the greenwood tree
Who loves to lie with me,
And turn his merry note
Unto the sweet bird's throat,
Come hither, come hither, come hither:
Here shall he see
No enemy
But winter and rough weather.
As You Like It (1599) act 2, sc. 5, l. 1

21 I can suck melancholy out of a song as a weasel sucks eggs.
As You Like It (1599) act 2, sc. 5, l. [12]

22 Who doth ambition shun
And loves to live i' the sun,
Seeking the food he eats,
And pleased with what he gets.
As You Like It (1599) act 2, sc. 5, l. [38]

23 And so, from hour to hour, we ripe and ripe,
And then from hour to hour, we rot and rot:
And thereby hangs a tale.
As You Like It (1599) act 2, sc. 7, l. 26

24 My lungs began to crow like chanticleer,
That fools should be so deep-contemplative,
And I did laugh sans intermission
An hour by his dial. O noble fool!
A worthy fool! Motley's the only wear.
As You Like It (1599) act 2, sc. 7, l. 30

25 All the world's a stage,
And all the men and women merely players:
They have their exits and their entrances;
And one man in his time plays many parts,
His acts being seven ages.
As You Like It (1599) act 2, sc. 7, l. 139

26 At first the infant,
Mewling and puking in the nurse's arms.
And then the whining schoolboy, with his satchel,
And shining morning face, creeping like snail
Unwillingly to school.
As You Like It (1599) act 2, sc. 7, l. 143

1 Then a soldier,
Full of strange oaths, and bearded like the pard,
Jealous in honour, sudden and quick in quarrel,
Seeking the bubble reputation
Even in the cannon's mouth. And then the justice,
In fair round belly with good capon lined.
As You Like It (1599) act 2, sc. 7, l. 149

2 The sixth age shifts
Into the lean and slippered pantaloon,
With spectacles on nose and pouch on side,
His youthful hose well saved a world too wide
For his shrunk shank.
As You Like It (1599) act 2, sc. 7, l. 157

3 Last scene of all,
That ends this strange eventful history,
Is second childishness, and mere oblivion,
Sans teeth, sans eyes, sans taste, sans everything.
As You Like It (1599) act 2, sc. 7, l. 163

4 Blow, blow, thou winter wind,
Thou art not so unkind
As man's ingratitude.
As You Like It (1599) act 2, sc. 7, l. 174

5 Heigh-ho! sing, heigh-ho! unto the green holly:
Most friendship is feigning, most loving mere folly.
Then heigh-ho! the holly!
This life is most jolly.
As You Like It (1599) act 2, sc. 7, l. 180

6 Run, run, Orlando: carve on every tree
The fair, the chaste, and unexpressive she.
As You Like It (1599) act 3, sc. 2, l. 9

7 From the east to western Ind,
No jewel is like Rosalind.
As You Like It (1599) act 3, sc. 2, l. [94]

8 Let us make an honourable retreat; though not with bag and baggage, yet with scrip and scrippage.
As You Like It (1599) act 3, sc. 2, l. [170]

9 O wonderful, wonderful, and most wonderful wonderful! and yet again wonderful, and after that, out of all whooping!
As You Like It (1599) act 3, sc. 2, l. [202]

10 Do you not know I am a woman? when I think, I must speak.
As You Like It (1599) act 3, sc. 2, l. [265]

11 I do desire we may be better strangers.
As You Like It (1599) act 3, sc. 2, l. [276]

12 JAQUES: I do not like her name.
ORLANDO: There was no thought of pleasing you when she was christened.
As You Like It (1599) act 3, sc. 2, l. [283]

13 ROSALIND: Time travels in divers paces with divers persons. I'll tell you who Time ambles withal, who Time trots withal, who Time gallops withal, and who Time stands still withal . . .
ORLANDO: Who stays it still withal?
ROSALIND: With lawyers in the vacation; for they sleep between term and term.
As You Like It (1599) act 3, sc. 2, l. [328]

14 I am not a slut, though I thank the gods I am foul.
As You Like It (1599) act 3, sc. 3, l. [40]

15 Down on your knees,
And thank heaven, fasting, for a good man's love.
As You Like It (1599) act 3, sc. 5, l. 57

16 I pray you, do not fall in love with me,
For I am falser than vows made in wine.
As You Like It (1599) act 3, sc. 5, l. [72]

17 Dead shepherd, now I find thy saw of might:
'Who ever loved that loved not at first sight?'
As You Like It (1599) act 3, sc. 5, l. [81]; cf. **Marlowe** 496:13

18 Come, woo me, woo me; for now I am in a holiday humour, and like enough to consent.
As You Like It (1599) act 4, sc. 1, l. [70]

19 You were better speak first, and when you were gravelled for lack of matter, you might take occasion to kiss.
As You Like It (1599) act 4, sc. 1, l. [75]

20 Men are April when they woo, December when they wed: maids are May when they are maids, but the sky changes when they are wives.
As You Like It (1599) act 4, sc. 1, l. [153]

21 The horn, the horn, the lusty horn
Is not a thing to laugh to scorn.
As You Like It (1599) act 4, sc. 2, l. [17]

22 Oh! how bitter a thing it is to look into happiness through another man's eyes.
As You Like It (1599) act 5, sc. 2, l. [48]

23 'Tis like the howling of Irish wolves against the moon.
As You Like It (1599) act 5, sc. 2, l. [120]

24 It was a lover and his lass,
With a hey, and a ho, and a hey nonino,
That o'er the green cornfield did pass,
In the spring time, the only pretty ring time,
When birds do sing, hey ding a ding, ding;
Sweet lovers love the spring.
As You Like It (1599) act 5, sc. 3, l. [18]

25 A poor virgin, sir, an ill-favoured thing, sir, but mine own.
As You Like It (1599) act 5, sc. 4, l. [60]

26 The retort courteous . . . the quip modest . . . the reply churlish . . . the reproof valiant . . . the countercheck quarrelsome . . . the lie circumstantial . . . the lie direct.
of the degrees of a lie
As You Like It (1599) act 5, sc. 4, l. [96]

27 Your 'if' is the only peace-maker; much virtue in 'if'.
As You Like It (1599) act 5, sc. 4, l. [108]

28 He uses his folly like a stalking-horse, and under the presentation of that he shoots his wit.
As You Like It (1599) act 5, sc. 4, l. [112]

29 If it be true that 'good wine needs no bush', 'tis true that a good play needs no epilogue.
As You Like It (1599) act 5, sc. 4, epilogue l. [3]; cf. **Proverbs** 601:31

THE COMEDY OF ERRORS

30 They brought one Pinch, a hungry, lean-faced villain,

A mere anatomy, a mountebank,
A threadbare juggler, and a fortune-teller,
A needy, hollow-eyed, sharp-looking wretch,
A living-dead man.
The Comedy of Errors (1594) act 5, sc. 1, l. 238

CORIOLANUS

1 He's a very dog to the commonalty.
Coriolanus (1608) act 1, sc. 1, l. [29]

2 What's the matter, you dissentious rogues,
That, rubbing the poor itch of your opinion,
Make yourselves scabs?
Coriolanus (1608) act 1, sc. 1, l. [170]

3 He that depends
Upon your favours swims with fins of lead,
And hews down oaks with rushes.
Coriolanus (1608) act 1, sc. 1, l. 179

4 Bid them wash their faces,
And keep their teeth clean.
Coriolanus (1608) act 2, sc. 1, l. [65]

5 My gracious silence, hail!
Coriolanus (1608) act 2, sc. 1, l. [194]

6 Hear you this Triton of the minnows? mark you
His absolute 'shall'?
Coriolanus (1608) act 3, sc. 1, l. 88

7 What is the city but the people?
Coriolanus (1608) act 3, sc. 1, l. 198

8 You common cry of curs! whose breath I hate
As reek o' the rotten fens, whose loves I prize
As the dead carcases of unburied men
That do corrupt my air,—I banish you.
Coriolanus (1608) act 3, sc. 3, l. 118

9 Despising,
For you, the city, thus I turn my back:
There is a world elsewhere.
Coriolanus (1608) act 3, sc. 3, l. 131

10 The beast
With many heads butts me away.
Coriolanus (1608) act 4, sc. 1, l. 1

11 Let me have war, say I; it exceeds peace as far as day does night; it's spritely, waking, audible, and full of vent. Peace is a very apoplexy, lethargy: mulled, deaf, sleepy, insensible; a getter of more bastard children than war's a destroyer of men.
Coriolanus (1608) act 4, sc. 5, l. [237]

12 I think he'll be to Rome
As is the osprey to the fish, who takes it
By sovereignty of nature.
Coriolanus (1608) act 4, sc. 7, l. 33

13 Like a dull actor now,
I have forgot my part, and I am out,
Even to a full disgrace.
Coriolanus (1608) act 5, sc. 3, l. 40

14 O! a kiss
Long as my exile, sweet as my revenge!
Now, by the jealous queen of heaven, that kiss
I carried from thee, dear, and my true lip
Hath virgined it e'er since.
Coriolanus (1608) act 5, sc. 3, l. 44

15 Chaste as the icicle
That's curdied by the frost from purest snow,
And hangs on Dian's temple.
Coriolanus (1608) act 5, sc. 3, l. 65

16 O mother, mother!
What have you done? Behold, the heavens do ope,
The gods look down, and this unnatural scene
They laugh at.
Coriolanus (1608) act 5, sc. 3, l. 182

17 If you have writ your annals true, 'tis there,
That, like an eagle in a dove-cote, I
Fluttered your Volscians in Corioli:
Alone I did it.
Coriolanus (1608) act 5, sc. 5, l. 114

CYMBELINE

18 If she be furnished with a mind so rare,
She is alone the Arabian bird, and I
Have lost the wager. Boldness be my friend!
Arm me, audacity.
Cymbeline (1609–10) act 1, sc. 6, l. 16

19 But kiss: one kiss! Rubies unparagoned,
How dearly they do't!
Cymbeline (1609–10) act 2, sc. 2, l. 17

20 On her left breast
A mole cinque-spotted, like the crimson drops
I' the bottom of a cowslip.
Cymbeline (1609–10) act 2, sc. 2, l. 37

21 Hark! hark! the lark at heaven's gate sings,
And Phoebus 'gins arise,
His steeds to water at those springs
On chaliced flowers that lies;
And winking Mary-buds begin
To ope their golden eyes:
With everything that pretty is,
My lady sweet, arise!
Cymbeline (1609–10) act 2, sc. 3, l. [22]

22 I thought her
As chaste as unsunned snow.
Cymbeline (1609–10) act 2, sc. 5, l. 12

23 The natural bravery of your isle, which stands
As Neptune's park, ribbed and paled in
With rocks unscalable, and roaring waters.
Cymbeline (1609–10) act 3, sc. 1, l. 18

24 O, for a horse with wings!
Cymbeline (1609–10) act 3, sc. 2, l. [49]

25 How hard it is to hide the sparks of nature!
Cymbeline (1609–10) act 3, sc. 3, l. 79

26 Hath Britain all the sun that shines?
Cymbeline (1609–10) act 3, sc. 4, l. [139]

27 Weariness
Can snore upon the flint when resty sloth
Finds the down pillow hard.
Cymbeline (1609–10) act 3, sc. 6, l. 33

28 Great griefs, I see, medicine the less.
Cymbeline (1609–10) act 4, sc. 2, l. 243

29 Thersites' body is as good as Ajax'
When neither are alive.
Cymbeline (1609–10) act 4, sc. 2, l. 252

1 Fear no more the heat o' the sun,
Nor the furious winter's rages;
Thou thy worldly task hast done,
Home art gone and ta'en thy wages:
Golden lads and girls all must,
As chimney-sweepers, come to dust.
Cymbeline (1609–10) act 4, sc. 2, l. 258

2 No exorciser harm thee!
Nor no witchcraft charm thee!
Ghost unlaid forbear thee!
Nothing ill come near thee!
Quiet consummation have:
And renowned be thy grave!
Cymbeline (1609–10) act 4, sc. 2, l. 276

3 Hang there like fruit, my soul,
Till the tree die.
Cymbeline (1609–10) act 5, sc. 5, l. 263

HAMLET

4 You come most carefully upon your hour.
Hamlet (1601) act 1, sc. 1, l. 6

5 For this relief much thanks; 'tis bitter cold
And I am sick at heart.
Hamlet (1601) act 1, sc. 1, l. 8

6 Not a mouse stirring.
Hamlet (1601) act 1, sc. 1, l. 10

7 Look, where it comes again!
Hamlet (1601) act 1, sc. 1, l. 40

8 This bodes some strange eruption to our state.
Hamlet (1601) act 1, sc. 1, l. 69

9 In the most high and palmy state of Rome,
A little ere the mightiest Julius fell,
The graves stood tenantless and the sheeted dead
Did squeak and gibber in the Roman streets.
Hamlet (1601) act 1, sc. 1, l. 113

10 And then it started like a guilty thing
Upon a fearful summons.
Hamlet (1601) act 1, sc. 1, l. 148

11 It faded on the crowing of the cock.
Some say that ever 'gainst that season comes
Wherein our Saviour's birth is celebrated,
The bird of dawning singeth all night long;
And then, they say, no spirit can walk abroad.
The nights are wholesome; then no planets strike,
No fairy takes, nor witch hath power to charm,
So hallowed and so gracious is the time.
Hamlet (1601) act 1, sc. 1, l. 157

12 But, look, the morn, in russet mantle clad,
Walks o'er the dew of yon high eastern hill.
Hamlet (1601) act 1, sc. 1, l. 166

13 Though yet of Hamlet our dear brother's death
The memory be green.
Hamlet (1601) act 1, sc. 2, l. 1

14 Therefore our sometime sister, now our queen . . .
Have we, as 'twere with a defeated joy,
With one auspicious and one dropping eye,
With mirth in funeral and with dirge in marriage,
In equal scale weighing delight and dole,
Taken to wife.
Hamlet (1601) act 1, sc. 2, l. 8

15 The head is not more native to the heart,
The hand more instrumental to the brain,
Than is the throne of Denmark to thy father.
Hamlet (1601) act 1, sc. 2, l. 47

16 A little more than kin, and less than kind.
Hamlet (1601) act 1, sc. 2, l. 65

17 Not so, my lord; I am too much i' the sun.
Hamlet (1601) act 1, sc. 2, l. 67

18 Good Hamlet, cast thy nighted colour off,
And let thine eye look like a friend on Denmark.
Hamlet (1601) act 1, sc. 2, l. 68

19 QUEEN: Thou know'st 'tis common; all that live must die,
Passing through nature to eternity.
HAMLET: Ay, madam, it is common.
Hamlet (1601) act 1, sc. 2, l. 72

20 Seems, madam! Nay, it is; I know not 'seems'.
'Tis not alone my inky cloak, good mother,
Nor customary suits of solemn black,
Nor windy suspiration of forced breath,
No, nor the fruitful river in the eye,
Nor the dejected 'haviour of the visage,
Together with all forms, modes, shows of grief,
That can denote me truly.
Hamlet (1601) act 1, sc. 2, l. 76

21 But I have that within which passeth show;
These but the trappings and the suits of woe.
Hamlet (1601) act 1, sc. 2, l. 85

22 O! that this too too solid flesh would melt,
Thaw, and resolve itself into a dew;
Or that the Everlasting had not fixed
His canon 'gainst self-slaughter!
Hamlet (1601) act 1, sc. 2, l. 129

23 How weary, stale, flat, and unprofitable
Seem to me all the uses of this world.
Hamlet (1601) act 1, sc. 2, l. 133

24 Things rank and gross in nature
Possess it merely. That it should come to this!
Hamlet (1601) act 1, sc. 2, l. 136

25 So excellent a king; that was, to this,
Hyperion to a satyr: so loving to my mother,
That he might not beteem the winds of heaven
Visit her face too roughly.
Hamlet (1601) act 1, sc. 2, l. 139

26 Frailty, thy name is woman!
A little month; or ere those shoes were old
With which she followed my poor father's body,
Like Niobe, all tears; why she, even she,—
O God! a beast, that wants discourse of reason,
Would have mourned longer.
Hamlet (1601) act 1, sc. 2, l. 146

27 My father's brother, but no more like my father
Than I to Hercules.
Hamlet (1601) act 1, sc. 2, l. 152

28 It is not, nor it cannot come to good;
But break, my heart, for I must hold my tongue!
Hamlet (1601) act 1, sc. 2, l. 158

29 A truant disposition, good my lord.
Hamlet (1601) act 1, sc. 2, l. 169

1 Thrift, thrift, Horatio! the funeral baked meats
Did coldly furnish forth the marriage tables.
Hamlet (1601) act 1, sc. 2, l. 180

2 In my mind's eye, Horatio.
Hamlet (1601) act 1, sc. 2, l. 185

3 He was a man, take him for all in all,
I shall not look upon his like again.
Hamlet (1601) act 1, sc. 2, l. 187

4 But answer made it none.
Hamlet (1601) act 1, sc. 2, l. 215

5 A countenance more in sorrow than in anger.
Hamlet (1601) act 1, sc. 2, l. 231

6 All is not well;
I doubt some foul play.
Hamlet (1601) act 1, sc. 2, l. 254

7 Foul deeds will rise,
Though all the earth o'erwhelm them, to men's eyes.
Hamlet (1601) act 1, sc. 2, l. 256

8 And keep you in the rear of your affection,
Out of the shot and danger of desire.
The chariest maid is prodigal enough
If she unmask her beauty to the moon.
Hamlet (1601) act 1, sc. 3, l. 34

9 Do not, as some ungracious pastors do,
Show me the steep and thorny way to heaven,
Whiles, like a puffed and reckless libertine,
Himself the primrose path of dalliance treads,
And recks not his own rede.
Hamlet (1601) act 1, sc. 3, l. 47

10 The friends thou hast, and their adoption tried,
Grapple them to thy soul with hoops of steel.
Hamlet (1601) act 1, sc. 3, l. 62

11 Costly thy habit as thy purse can buy,
But not expressed in fancy; rich, not gaudy;
For the apparel oft proclaims the man.
Hamlet (1601) act 1, sc. 3, l. 70

12 Neither a borrower, nor a lender be;
For loan oft loses both itself and friend.
Hamlet (1601) act 1, sc. 3, l. 75

13 This above all: to thine own self be true,
And it must follow, as the night the day,
Thou canst not then be false to any man.
Hamlet (1601) act 1, sc. 3, l. 78; cf. **Bacon** 44:22

14 You speak like a green girl,
Unsifted in such perilous circumstance.
Hamlet (1601) act 1, sc. 3, l. 101

15 Ay, springes to catch woodcocks.
Hamlet (1601) act 1, sc. 3, l. 115

16 It is a nipping and an eager air.
Hamlet (1601) act 1, sc. 4, l. 2

17 But to my mind,—though I am native here,
And to the manner born,—it is a custom
More honoured in the breach than the observance.
Hamlet (1601) act 1, sc. 4, l. 14

18 Angels and ministers of grace defend us!
Be thou a spirit of health or goblin damned,
Bring with thee airs from heaven or blasts from hell,
Be thy intents wicked or charitable,
Thou com'st in such a questionable shape
That I will speak to thee: I'll call thee Hamlet,
King, father; royal Dane, O! answer me.
Hamlet (1601) act 1, sc. 4, l. 39

19 What may this mean,
That thou, dead corse again in complete steel
Revisit'st thus the glimpses of the moon,
Making night hideous.
Hamlet (1601) act 1, sc. 4, l. 51

20 I do not set my life at a pin's fee;
And for my soul, what can it do to that,
Being a thing immortal as itself?
Hamlet (1601) act 1, sc. 4, l. 65

21 Unhand me, gentlemen,
By heaven! I'll make a ghost of him that lets me.
Hamlet (1601) act 1, sc. 4, l. 84

22 Something is rotten in the state of Denmark.
Hamlet (1601) act 1, sc. 4, l. 90

23 I am thy father's spirit;
Doomed for a certain term to walk the night.
Hamlet (1601) act 1, sc. 5, l. 9

24 List, list, O, list!
Hamlet (1601) act 1, sc. 5, l. 13

25 I could a tale unfold whose lightest word
Would harrow up thy soul, freeze thy young blood,
Make thy two eyes, like stars, start from their spheres,
Thy knotted and combinèd locks to part,
And each particular hair to stand on end,
Like quills upon the fretful porpentine.
Hamlet (1601) act 1, sc. 5, l. 15

26 Revenge his foul and most unnatural murder.
Hamlet (1601) act 1, sc. 5, l. 25

27 Murder most foul, as in the best it is;
But this most foul, strange, and unnatural.
Hamlet (1601) act 1, sc. 5, l. 27

28 And duller shouldst thou be than the fat weed
That rots itself in ease on Lethe wharf,
Wouldst thou not stir in this.
Hamlet (1601) act 1, sc. 5, l. 32

29 O my prophetic soul!
My uncle!
Hamlet (1601) act 1, sc. 5, l. 40

30 But, soft! methinks I scent the morning air.
Hamlet (1601) act 1, sc. 5, l. 58

31 Thus was I, sleeping, by a brother's hand,
Of life, of crown, of queen, at once dispatched;
Cut off even in the blossoms of my sin,
Unhouseled, disappointed, unaneled,
No reckoning made, but sent to my account
With all my imperfections on my head:
O, horrible! O, horrible! most horrible!
Hamlet (1601) act 1, sc. 5, l. 74

32 Remember thee!
Ay, thou poor ghost, while memory holds a seat
In this distracted globe.
Hamlet (1601) act 1, sc. 5, l. 95

1 O most pernicious woman!
O villain, villain, smiling, damnèd villain!
My tables,—meet it is I set it down,
That one may smile, and smile, and be a villain;
At least I'm sure it may be so in Denmark.
Hamlet (1601) act 1, sc. 5, l. 105

2 These are but wild and whirling words, my lord.
Hamlet (1601) act 1, sc. 5, l. 133

3 Well said, old mole! canst work i' the earth so fast?
Hamlet (1601) act 1, sc. 5, l. 162

4 There are more things in heaven and earth, Horatio,
Than are dreamt of in your philosophy.
Hamlet (1601) act 1, sc. 5, l. 166; cf. **Haldane** 356:15

5 To put an antic disposition on.
Hamlet (1601) act 1, sc. 5, l. 172

6 Rest, rest, perturbèd spirit.
Hamlet (1601) act 1, sc. 5, l. 182

7 The time is out of joint; O cursèd spite,
That ever I was born to set it right!
Hamlet (1601) act 1, sc. 5, l. 188

8 By indirections find directions out.
Hamlet (1601) act 2, sc. 1, l. 66

9 Brevity is the soul of wit.
Hamlet (1601) act 2, sc. 2, l. 90; cf. **Proverbs** 596:39

10 To define true madness,
What is't but to be nothing else but mad?
Hamlet (1601) act 2, sc. 2, l. 93

11 More matter with less art.
Hamlet (1601) act 2, sc. 2, l. 95

12 POLONIUS: What do you read, my lord?
HAMLET: Words, words, words.
Hamlet (1601) act 2, sc. 2, l. [195]

13 Though this be madness, yet there is method in't.
Hamlet (1601) act 2, sc. 2, l. [211]

14 POLONIUS: My honourable lord, I will most humbly take my leave of you.
HAMLET: You cannot, sir, take from me any thing that I will more willingly part withal; except my life, except my life, except my life.
Hamlet (1601) act 2, sc. 2, l. [221]

15 HAMLET: Then you live about her waist, or in the middle of her favours?
GUILDENSTERN: Faith, her privates, we.
HAMLET: In the secret parts of Fortune? O! most true; she is a strumpet.
Hamlet (1601) act 2, sc. 2, l. [240]

16 There is nothing either good or bad, but thinking makes it so.
Hamlet (1601) act 2, sc. 2, l. [259]

17 O God! I could be bounded in a nut-shell, and count myself a king of infinite space, were it not that I have bad dreams.
Hamlet (1601) act 2, sc. 2, l. [263]

18 It goes so heavily with my disposition that this goodly frame, the earth, seems to me a sterile promontory; this most excellent canopy, the air, look you, this brave o'erhanging firmament, this majestical roof fretted with golden fire, why, it appears no other thing to me but a foul and pestilent congregation of vapours. What a piece of work is a man! How noble in reason! how infinite in faculty! in form, in moving, how express and admirable! in action how like an angel! in apprehension how like a god! the beauty of the world! the paragon of animals! And yet, to me, what is this quintessence of dust? man delights not me; no, nor woman neither, though, by your smiling, you seem to say so.
Hamlet (1601) act 2, sc. 2, l. [316]

19 He that plays the king shall be welcome; his majesty shall have tribute of me.
Hamlet (1601) act 2, sc. 2, l. [341]

20 There is something in this more than natural, if philosophy could find it out.
Hamlet (1601) act 2, sc. 2, l. [392]

21 I am but mad north-north-west; when the wind is southerly, I know a hawk from a handsaw.
Hamlet (1601) act 2, sc. 2, l. [405]

22 The best actors in the world, either for tragedy, comedy, history, pastoral, pastoral-comical, historical-pastoral, tragical-historical, tragical-comical-historical-pastoral, scene individable, or poem unlimited.
Hamlet (1601) act 2, sc. 2, l. [424]

23 The play, I remember, pleased not the million; 'twas caviare to the general.
Hamlet (1601) act 2, sc. 2, l. [465]

24 Good my lord, will you see the players well bestowed? Do you hear, let them be well used; for they are the abstracts and brief chronicles of the time: after your death you were better have a bad epitaph than their ill report while you live.
Hamlet (1601) act 2, sc. 2, l. [553]

25 Use every man after his desert, and who should 'scape whipping?
Hamlet (1601) act 2, sc. 2, l. [561]

26 O, what a rogue and peasant slave am I.
Hamlet (1601) act 2, sc. 2, l. [584]

27 For Hecuba!
What's Hecuba to him or he to Hecuba
That he should weep for her?
Hamlet (1601) act 2, sc. 2, l. [592]

28 He would drown the stage with tears,
And cleave the general ear with horrid speech,
Make mad the guilty, and appal the free,
Confound the ignorant, and amaze, indeed,
The very faculties of eyes and ears.
Hamlet (1601) act 2, sc. 2, l. [596]

29 But I am pigeon-livered, and lack gall
To make oppression bitter.
Hamlet (1601) act 2, sc. 2, l. [613]

30 Bloody, bawdy villain!
Remorseless, treacherous, lecherous, kindless villain!
Hamlet (1601) act 2, sc. 2, l. [616]

1 I have heard,
That guilty creatures sitting at a play
Have by the very cunning of the scene
Been struck so to the soul that presently
They have proclaimed their malefactions;
For murder, though it have no tongue, will speak
With most miraculous organ.
Hamlet (1601) act 2, sc. 2, l. [625]

2 The play's the thing
Wherein I'll catch the conscience of the king.
Hamlet (1601) act 2, sc. 2, l. [641]

3 To be, or not to be: that is the question:
Whether 'tis nobler in the mind to suffer
The slings and arrows of outrageous fortune,
Or to take arms against a sea of troubles,
And by opposing end them? To die: to sleep;
No more; and, by a sleep to say we end
The heart-ache and the thousand natural shocks
That flesh is heir to, 'tis a consummation
Devoutly to be wished. To die, to sleep;
To sleep: perchance to dream: ay, there's the rub;
For in that sleep of death what dreams may come
When we have shuffled off this mortal coil,
Must give us pause.
Hamlet (1601) act 3, sc. 1, l. 56

4 For who would bear the whips and scorns of time,
The oppressor's wrong, the proud man's contumely,
The pangs of disprized love, the law's delay,
The insolence of office, and the spurns
That patient merit of the unworthy takes,
When he himself might his quietus make
With a bare bodkin? Who would fardels bear,
To grunt and sweat under a weary life,
But that the dread of something after death,
The undiscovered country from whose bourn
No traveller returns, puzzles the will,
And makes us rather bear those ills we have,
Than fly to others that we know not of?
Thus conscience doth make cowards of us all;
And thus the native hue of resolution
Is sicklied o'er with the pale cast of thought,
And enterprises of great pith and moment
With this regard their currents turn awry,
And lose the name of action.
Hamlet (1601) act 3, sc. 1, l. 70; cf. **Morton** 533:15, **Proverbs** 597:35

5 Nymph, in thy orisons
Be all my sins remembered.
Hamlet (1601) act 3, sc. 1, l. 89

6 Get thee to a nunnery: why wouldst thou be a breeder of sinners?
Hamlet (1601) act 3, sc. 1, l. [124]

7 Be thou as chaste as ice, as pure as snow, thou shalt not escape calumny. Get thee to a nunnery, go; farewell.
Hamlet (1601) act 3, sc. 1, l. [142]

8 I have heard of your paintings too, well enough. God hath given you one face and you make yourselves another.
Hamlet (1601) act 3, sc. 1, l. [150]

9 I say, we will have no more marriages.
Hamlet (1601) act 3, sc. 1, l. [156]

10 O! what a noble mind is here o'erthrown:
The courtier's, soldier's, scholar's, eye, tongue, sword;
The expectancy and rose of the fair state,
The glass of fashion, and the mould of form,
The observèd of all observers, quite, quite, down!
Hamlet (1601) act 3, sc. 1, l. [159]

11 Now see that noble and most sovereign reason,
Like sweet bells jangled, out of tune and harsh.
Hamlet (1601) act 3, sc. 1, l. [166]

12 O! woe is me,
To have seen what I have seen, see what I see!
Hamlet (1601) act 3, sc. 1, l. [169]

13 Speak the speech, I pray you, as I pronounced it to you, trippingly on the tongue; but if you mouth it, as many of your players do, I had as lief the town-crier spoke my lines. Nor do not saw the air too much with your hand, thus; but use all gently.
Hamlet (1601) act 3, sc. 2, l. 1

14 I would have such a fellow whipped for o'erdoing Termagant; it out-herods Herod.
Hamlet (1601) act 3, sc. 2, l. 14

15 Suit the action to the word, the word to the action.
Hamlet (1601) act 3, sc. 2, l. [20]

16 To hold, as 'twere, the mirror up to nature.
Hamlet (1601) act 3, sc. 2, l. [25]

17 I have thought some of nature's journeymen had made men and not made them well, they imitated humanity so abominably.
Hamlet (1601) act 3, sc. 2, l. [38]

18 Give me that man
That is not passion's slave, and I will wear him
In my heart's core, ay, in my heart of heart,
As I do thee.
Hamlet (1601) act 3, sc. 2, l. [76]

19 The chameleon's dish: I eat the air, promise-crammed; you cannot feed capons so.
Hamlet (1601) act 3, sc. 2, l. [98]

20 Here's metal more attractive.
Hamlet (1601) act 3, sc. 2, l. [117]

21 For, O! for, O! the hobby-horse is forgot.
Hamlet (1601) act 3, sc. 2, l. [145]

22 Marry, this is miching mallecho; it means mischief.
Hamlet (1601) act 3, sc. 2, l. [148]

23 The lady doth protest too much, methinks.
Hamlet (1601) act 3, sc. 2, l. [242]

24 HAMLET: No, no, they do but jest, poison in jest; no offence i' the world.
KING: What do you call the play?
HAMLET: The Mouse-trap.
Hamlet (1601) act 3, sc. 2, l. [247]

25 Let the galled jade wince, our withers are unwrung.
Hamlet (1601) act 3, sc. 2, l. [256]

26 What! frighted with false fire?
Hamlet (1601) act 3, sc. 2, l. [282]

1 Why, let the stricken deer go weep,
The hart ungallèd play;
For some must watch, while some must sleep:
So runs the world away.
Hamlet (1601) act 3, sc. 2, l. [287]; cf. **Cowper** 241:24

2 You would play upon me; you would seem to know my stops; you would pluck out the heart of my mystery; you would sound me from my lowest note to the top of my compass.
Hamlet (1601) act 3, sc. 2, l. [387]

3 Very like a whale.
Hamlet (1601) act 3, sc. 2, l. [406]

4 They fool me to the top of my bent.
Hamlet (1601) act 3, sc. 2, l. [408]

5 'Tis now the very witching time of night,
When churchyards yawn and hell itself breathes out
Contagion to this world: now could I drink hot blood,
And do such bitter business as the day
Would quake to look on.
Hamlet (1601) act 3, sc. 2, l. [413]

6 Let me be cruel, not unnatural;
I will speak daggers to her, but use none.
Hamlet (1601) act 3, sc. 2, l. [420]

7 O! my offence is rank, it smells to heaven.
Hamlet (1601) act 3, sc. 3, l. 36

8 Now might I do it pat, now he is praying.
Hamlet (1601) act 3, sc. 3, l. 73

9 He took my father grossly, full of bread,
With all his crimes broad blown, as flush as May;
And how his audit stands who knows save heaven?
Hamlet (1601) act 3, sc. 3, l. 80

10 My words fly up, my thoughts remain below:
Words without thoughts never to heaven go.
Hamlet (1601) act 3, sc. 3, l. 97

11 You go not, till I set you up a glass
Where you may see the inmost part of you.
Hamlet (1601) act 3, sc. 4, l. 19

12 How now! a rat? Dead, for a ducat, dead!
Hamlet (1601) act 3, sc. 4, l. 23

13 A bloody deed! almost as bad, good mother,
As kill a king, and marry with his brother.
Hamlet (1601) act 3, sc. 4, l. 28

14 Thou wretched, rash, intruding fool, farewell!
I took thee for thy better.
Hamlet (1601) act 3, sc. 4, l. 31

15 You cannot call it love, for at your age
The hey-day in the blood is tame, it's humble,
And waits upon the judgment.
Hamlet (1601) act 3, sc. 4, l. 68

16 Speak no more;
Thou turn'st mine eyes into my very soul.
Hamlet (1601) act 3, sc. 4, l. 88

17 Nay, but to live
In the rank sweat of an enseamèd bed,
Stewed in corruption, honeying and making love
Over the nasty sty.
Hamlet (1601) act 3, sc. 4, l. 91

18 A cut-purse of the empire and the rule,
That from a shelf the precious diadem stole,
And put it in his pocket!
Hamlet (1601) act 3, sc. 4, l. 99

19 A king of shreds and patches.
Hamlet (1601) act 3, sc. 4, l. 102; cf. **Gilbert** 337:21

20 Mother, for love of grace,
Lay not that flattering unction to your soul.
Hamlet (1601) act 3, sc. 4, l. 142

21 For in the fatness of these pursy times,
Virtue itself of vice must pardon beg.
Hamlet (1601) act 3, sc. 4, l. 153

22 Assume a virtue, if you have it not.
That monster, custom, who all sense doth eat,
Of habits devil, is angel yet in this.
Hamlet (1601) act 3, sc. 4, l. 160

23 I must be cruel only to be kind.
Hamlet (1601) act 3, sc. 4, l. 178

24 For 'tis the sport to have the enginer
Hoist with his own petar.
Hamlet (1601) act 3, sc. 4, l. 206

25 I'll lug the guts into the neighbour room.
Hamlet (1601) act 3, sc. 4, l. 212

26 Diseases desperate grown,
By desperate appliances are relieved,
Or not at all.
Hamlet (1601) act 4, sc. 2, l. 9; cf. **Fawkes** 308:3, **Proverbs** 598:5

27 A certain convocation of politic worms are e'en at him. Your worm is your only emperor for diet.
Hamlet (1601) act 4, sc. 2, l. [21]

28 A man may fish with the worm that hath eat of a king, and eat of the fish that hath fed of that worm.
Hamlet (1601) act 4, sc. 2, l. [29]

29 We go to gain a little patch of ground,
That hath in it no profit but the name.
Hamlet (1601) act 4, sc. 4, l. 18

30 How all occasions do inform against me,
And spur my dull revenge!
Hamlet (1601) act 4, sc. 4, l. 32

31 Sure he that made us with such large discourse,
Looking before and after, gave us not
That capability and god-like reason
To fust in us unused.
Hamlet (1601) act 4, sc. 4, l. 36

32 Some craven scruple
Of thinking too precisely on the event.
Hamlet (1601) act 4, sc. 4, l. 40

33 Rightly to be great
Is not to stir without great argument,
But greatly to find quarrel in a straw
When honour's at the stake.
Hamlet (1601) act 4, sc. 4, l. 53

34 How should I your true love know
From another one?

By his cockle hat and staff,
And his sandal shoon.
Hamlet (1601) act 4, sc. 5, l. [23]

1 He is dead and gone, lady,
He is dead and gone,
At his head a grass-green turf;
At his heels a stone.
Hamlet (1601) act 4, sc. 5, l. [29]

2 Lord! we know what we are, but know not what we may be.
Hamlet (1601) act 4, sc. 5, l. [43]

3 Come, my coach! Good-night, ladies; good-night, sweet ladies; good-night, good-night.
Hamlet (1601) act 4, sc. 5, l. [72]

4 When sorrows come, they come not single spies,
But in battalions.
Hamlet (1601) act 4, sc. 5, l. [78]

5 We have done but greenly
In hugger-mugger to inter him.
Hamlet (1601) act 4, sc. 5, l. [83]

6 There's such divinity doth hedge a king,
That treason can but peep to what it would.
Hamlet (1601) act 4, sc. 5, l. [123]

7 There's rosemary, that's for remembrance; pray, love, remember: and there is pansies, that's for thoughts.
Hamlet (1601) act 4, sc. 5, l. [174]

8 There's fennel for you, and columbines; there's rue for you; and here's some for me; we may call it herb of grace o' Sundays. O! you must wear your rue with a difference. There's a daisy; I would give you some violets, but they withered all when my father died. They say he made a good end,— For bonny sweet Robin is all my joy.
Hamlet (1601) act 4, sc. 5, l. [179]

9 His means of death, his obscure burial,
No trophy, sword, nor hatchment o'er his bones,
No noble rite nor formal ostentation.
Hamlet (1601) act 4, sc. 5, l. [213]

10 And where the offence is let the great axe fall.
Hamlet (1601) act 4, sc. 5, l. [218]

11 A very riband in the cap of youth.
Hamlet (1601) act 4, sc. 7, l. 77

12 There is a willow grows aslant a brook,
That shows his hoar leaves in the glassy stream.
Hamlet (1601) act 4, sc. 7, l. 167

13 There with fantastic garlands did she come,
Of crow-flowers, nettles, daisies, and long purples,
That liberal shepherds give a grosser name,
But our cold maids do dead men's fingers call them.
Hamlet (1601) act 4, sc. 7, l. 169

14 There, on the pendent boughs her coronet weeds
Clambering to hang, an envious sliver broke,
When down her weedy trophies and herself
Fell in the weeping brook. Her clothes spread wide,
And, mermaid-like, awhile they bore her up;
Which time she chanted snatches of old tunes,
As one incapable of her own distress.
Hamlet (1601) act 4, sc. 7, l. 173

15 Too much of water hast thou, poor Ophelia,
And therefore I forbid my tears; but yet
It is our trick, nature her custom holds,
Let shame say what it will.
Hamlet (1601) act 4, sc. 7, l. 186

16 Is she to be buried in Christian burial that wilfully seeks her own salvation?
Hamlet (1601) act 5, sc. 1, l. 1

17 There is no ancient gentlemen but gardeners, ditchers and grave-makers; they hold up Adam's profession.
Hamlet (1601) act 5, sc. 1, l. [32]

18 FIRST CLOWN: What is he that builds stronger than either the mason, the shipwright, or the carpenter?
SECOND CLOWN: The gallows-maker; for that frame outlives a thousand tenants.
Hamlet (1601) act 5, sc. 1, l. [44]

19 Cudgel thy brains no more about it, for your dull ass will not mend his pace with beating.
Hamlet (1601) act 5, sc. 1, l. [61]

20 But age, with his stealing steps
Hath clawed me in his clutch,
And hath shipped me intil the land,
As if I had never been such.
Hamlet (1601) act 5, sc. 1, l. [77]; cf. **Vaux** 790:19

21 This might be the pate of a politician . . . one that would circumvent God, might it not?
Hamlet (1601) act 5, sc. 1, l. [84]

22 The age is grown so picked that the toe of the peasant comes so near the heel of the courtier, he galls his kibe.
Hamlet (1601) act 5, sc. 1, l. [150]

23 Alas, poor Yorick. I knew him, Horatio; a fellow of infinite jest, of most excellent fancy.
Hamlet (1601) act 5, sc. 1, l. [201]

24 To what base uses we may return, Horatio!
Hamlet (1601) act 5, sc. 1, l. [222]

25 Imperious Caesar, dead, and turned to clay,
Might stop a hole to keep the wind away.
Hamlet (1601) act 5, sc. 1, l. [235]

26 Lay her i' the earth;
And from her fair and unpolluted flesh
May violets spring! I tell thee, churlish priest,
A ministering angel shall my sister be,
When thou liest howling.
Hamlet (1601) act 5, sc. 1, l. [260]; cf. **Scott** 651:13

27 Sweets to the sweet: farewell!
Hamlet (1601) act 5, sc. 1, l. [265]

28 I thought thy bride-bed to have decked, sweet maid,
And not have strewed thy grave.
Hamlet (1601) act 5, sc. 1, l. [267]

29 I loved Ophelia: forty thousand brothers
Could not, with all their quantity of love,
Make up my sum.
Hamlet (1601) act 5, sc. 1, l. [291]

1 There's a divinity that shapes our ends,
Rough-hew them how we will.
Hamlet (1601) act 5, sc. 2, l. 10

2 I once did hold it, as our statists do,
A baseness to write fair, and laboured much
How to forget that learning; but, sir, now
It did me yeoman's service.
Hamlet (1601) act 5, sc. 2, l. 33

3 Not a whit, we defy augury; there's a special providence in the fall of a sparrow. If it be now, 'tis not to come; if it be not to come, it will be now; if it be not now, yet it will come: the readiness is all.
Hamlet (1601) act 5, sc. 2, l. [232]

4 I have shot mine arrow o'er the house,
And hurt my brother.
Hamlet (1601) act 5, sc. 2, l. [257]

5 A hit, a very palpable hit.
Hamlet (1601) act 5, sc. 2, l. [295]

6 Why, as a woodcock to mine own springe, Osric;
I am justly killed with my own treachery.
Hamlet (1601) act 5, sc. 2, l. [320]

7 This fell sergeant, death,
Is swift in his arrest.
Hamlet (1601) act 5, sc. 2, l. [350]

8 Report me and my cause aright
To the unsatisfied.
Hamlet (1601) act 5, sc. 2, l. [353]

9 I am more an antique Roman than a Dane.
Hamlet (1601) act 5, sc. 2, l. [355]

10 If thou didst ever hold me in thy heart,
Absent thee from felicity awhile,
And in this harsh world draw thy breath in pain,
To tell my story.
Hamlet (1601) act 5, sc. 2, l. [360]

11 The rest is silence.
Hamlet (1601) act 5, sc. 2, l. [372]

12 Now cracks a noble heart. Good-night, sweet prince,
And flights of angels sing thee to thy rest!
Hamlet (1601) act 5, sc. 2, l. [373]

13 That Rosencrantz and Guildenstern are dead.
Hamlet (1601) act 5, sc. 2, l. [385]

14 Let four captains
Bear Hamlet, like a soldier, to the stage;
For he was likely, had he been put on,
To have proved most royally.
Hamlet (1601) act 5, sc. 2, l. [409]

HENRY IV, PART I

15 Let us be Diana's foresters, gentlemen of the shade, minions of the moon.
Henry IV, Part 1 (1597) act 1, sc. 2, l. [28]

16 FALSTAFF: And is not my hostess of the tavern a most sweet wench?
PRINCE: As the honey of Hybla, my old lad of the castle.
Henry IV, Part 1 (1597) act 1, sc. 2, l. [44]

17 What, in thy quips and thy quiddities?
Henry IV, Part 1 (1597) act 1, sc. 2, l. [50]

18 Shall there be gallows standing in England when thou art king, and resolution thus fobbed as it is with the rusty curb of old father antick, the law.
Henry IV, Part 1 (1597) act 1, sc. 2, l. [66]

19 I would to God thou and I knew where a commodity of good names were to be bought.
Henry IV, Part 1 (1597) act 1, sc. 2, l. [92]

20 O! thou hast damnable iteration, and art, indeed, able to corrupt a saint.
Henry IV, Part 1 (1597) act 1, sc. 2, l. [101]

21 Why, Hal, 'tis my vocation, Hal; 'tis no sin for a man to labour in his vocation.
referring to stealing
Henry IV, Part 1 (1597) act 1, sc. 2, l. [116]

22 If all the year were playing holidays,
To sport would be as tedious as to work;
But when they seldom come, they wished for come.
Henry IV, Part 1 (1597) act 1, sc. 2, l. [226]

23 So pestered with a popinjay.
Henry IV, Part 1 (1597) act 1, sc. 3, l. 50

24 To put down Richard, that sweet lovely rose,
And plant this thorn, this canker, Bolingbroke.
Henry IV, Part 1 (1597) act 1, sc. 3, l. 175

25 O! the blood more stirs
To rouse a lion than to start a hare.
Henry IV, Part 1 (1597) act 1, sc. 3, l. 197

26 By heaven methinks it were an easy leap
To pluck bright honour from the pale-faced moon,
Or dive into the bottom of the deep,
Where fathom-line could never touch the ground,
And pluck up drownèd honour by the locks.
Henry IV, Part 1 (1597) act 1, sc. 3, l. 201

27 Why, what a candy deal of courtesy
This fawning greyhound then did proffer me!
Henry IV, Part 1 (1597) act 1, sc. 3, l. 251

28 I know a trick worth two of that.
Henry IV, Part 1 (1597) act 2, sc. 1, l. [40]

29 We have the receipt of fern-seed, we walk invisible.
Henry IV, Part 1 (1597) act 2, sc. 1, l. [95]

30 I am bewitched with the rogue's company. If the rascal have not given me medicines to make me love him, I'll be hanged.
Henry IV, Part 1 (1597) act 2, sc. 2, l. [19]

31 Go hang thyself in thine own heir-apparent garters!
Henry IV, Part 1 (1597) act 2, sc. 2, l. [49]

32 On, bacons, on!
Henry IV, Part 1 (1597) act 2, sc. 2, l. [99]

33 It would be argument for a week, laughter for a month, and a good jest for ever.
Henry IV, Part 1 (1597) act 2, sc. 2, l. [104]

34 Falstaff sweats to death
And lards the lean earth as he walks along.
Henry IV, Part 1 (1597) act 2, sc. 2, l. [119]

35 Out of this nettle, danger, we pluck this flower, safety.
Henry IV, Part 1 (1597) act 2, sc. 3, l. [11]

1 Away, you trifler! Love! I love thee not,
I care not for thee, Kate: this is no world
To play with mammets and to tilt with lips:
We must have bloody noses and cracked crowns.
Henry IV, Part 1 (1597) act 2, sc. 3, l. [95]

2 I am not yet of Percy's mind, the Hotspur of the North; he that kills me some six or seven dozen of Scots at a breakfast, washes his hands, and says to his wife, 'Fie upon this quiet life! I want work.'
Henry IV, Part 1 (1597) act 2, sc. 4, l. [116]

3 There live not three good men unhanged in England, and one of them is fat and grows old.
Henry IV, Part 1 (1597) act 2, sc. 4, l. [146]

4 Call you that backing of your friends? A plague upon such backing! give me them that will face me.
Henry IV, Part 1 (1597) act 2, sc. 4, l. [168]

5 Nay that's past praying for: I have peppered two of them: two I am sure I have paid, two rogues in buckram suits. I tell thee what, Hal, if I tell thee a lie, spit in my face, call me horse. Thou knowest my old ward; here I lay, and thus I bore my point. Four rogues in buckram let drive at me,—
Henry IV, Part 1 (1597) act 2, sc. 4, l. [214]

6 O monstrous! eleven buckram men grown out of two.
Henry IV, Part 1 (1597) act 2, sc. 4, l. [247]

7 These lies are like the father that begets them; gross as a mountain, open, palpable.
Henry IV, Part 1 (1597) act 2, sc. 4, l. [253]

8 Give you a reason on compulsion! if reasons were as plentiful as blackberries I would give no man a reason upon compulsion, I.
Henry IV, Part 1 (1597) act 2, sc. 4, l. [267]

9 Mark now, how a plain tale shall put you down.
Henry IV, Part 1 (1597) act 2, sc. 4, l. [285]

10 Instinct is a great matter, I was a coward on instinct.
Henry IV, Part 1 (1597) act 2, sc. 4, l. [304]

11 I will do it in King Cambyses' vein.
Henry IV, Part 1 (1597) act 2, sc. 4, l. [430]

12 Shall the blessed sun of heaven prove a micher and eat blackberries? a question not to be asked.
Henry IV, Part 1 (1597) act 2, sc. 4, l. [454]

13 There is a devil haunts thee in the likeness of a fat old man; a tun of man is thy companion.
Henry IV, Part 1 (1597) act 2, sc. 4, l. [498]

14 That roasted Manningtree ox with the pudding in his belly, that reverend vice, that grey iniquity, that father ruffian, that vanity in years.
Henry IV, Part 1 (1597) act 2, sc. 4, l. [504]

15 If sack and sugar be a fault, God help the wicked!
Henry IV, Part 1 (1597) act 2, sc. 4, l. [524]

16 No, my good lord; banish Peto, banish Bardolph, banish Poins; but for sweet Jack Falstaff, kind Jack Falstaff, true Jack Falstaff, valiant Jack Falstaff, and therefore more valiant, being, as he is, old Jack Falstaff, banish not him thy Harry's company, banish not him thy Harry's company: banish plump Jack and banish all the world.
Henry IV, Part 1 (1597) act 2, sc. 4, l. [528]

17 O monstrous! but one half-pennyworth of bread to this intolerable deal of sack!
Henry IV, Part 1 (1597) act 2, sc. 4, l. [598]

18 GLENDOWER: At my nativity
The front of heaven was full of fiery shapes,
Of burning cressets; and at my birth
The frame and huge foundation of the earth
Shaked like a coward.
HOTSPUR: Why, so it would have done at the same season, if your mother's cat had but kittened.
Henry IV, Part 1 (1597) act 3, sc. 1, l. 13

19 GLENDOWER: I can call spirits from the vasty deep.
HOTSPUR: Why, so can I, or so can any man;
But will they come when you do call for them?
Henry IV, Part 1 (1597) act 3, sc. 1, l. [53]

20 I had rather be a kitten and cry mew
Than one of these same metre ballad-mongers.
Henry IV, Part 1 (1597) act 3, sc. 1, l. [128]

21 That would set my teeth nothing on edge,
Nothing so much as mincing poetry:
'Tis like the forced gait of a shuffling nag.
Henry IV, Part 1 (1597) act 3, sc. 1, l. [132]

22 Thy tongue
Makes Welsh as sweet as ditties highly penned,
Sung by a fair queen in a summer's bower,
With ravishing division, to her lute.
Henry IV, Part 1 (1597) act 3, sc. 1, l. [207]

23 Now I perceive the devil understands Welsh.
Henry IV, Part 1 (1597) act 3, sc. 1, l. [233]

24 You swear like a comfit-maker's wife.
Henry IV, Part 1 (1597) act 3, sc. 1, l. [252]

25 Swear me, Kate, like a lady as thou art,
A good mouth-filling oath.
Henry IV, Part 1 (1597) act 3, sc. 1, l. [257]

26 He was but as the cuckoo is in June,
Heard, not regarded.
Henry IV, Part 1 (1597) act 3, sc. 2, l. 75

27 My near'st and dearest enemy.
Henry IV, Part 1 (1597) act 3, sc. 2, l. 123

28 Company, villanous company, hath been the spoil of me.
Henry IV, Part 1 (1597) act 3, sc. 3, l. [10]

29 Thou knowest in the state of innocency Adam fell; and what should poor Jack Falstaff do in the days of villainy. Thou seest I have more flesh than another man, and therefore more frailty.
Henry IV, Part 1 (1597) act 3, sc. 3, l. [184]

30 I saw young Harry, with his beaver on,
His cushes on his thighs, gallantly armed,
Rise from the ground like feathered Mercury,
And vaulted with such ease into his seat,
As if an angel dropped down from the clouds,
To turn and wind a fiery Pegasus,
And witch the world with noble horsemanship.
Henry IV, Part 1 (1597) act 4, sc. 1, l. 104

1 Doomsday is near; die all, die merrily.
Henry IV, Part 1 (1597) act 4, sc. 1, l. 134

2 Tut, tut; good enough to toss; food for powder, food for powder; they'll fill a pit as well as better: tush, man, mortal men, mortal men.
Henry IV, Part 1 (1597) act 4, sc. 2, l. [72]

3 Greatness knows itself.
Henry IV, Part 1 (1597) act 4, sc. 3, l. 74

4 I could be well content
To entertain the lag-end of my life
With quiet hours.
Henry IV, Part 1 (1597) act 5, sc. 1, l. 23

5 Rebellion lay in his way, and he found it.
Henry IV, Part 1 (1597) act 5, sc. 1, l. 28

6 I would it were bed-time, Hal, and all well.
Henry IV, Part 1 (1597) act 5, sc. 1, l. [125]

7 Thou owest God a death.
Henry IV, Part 1 (1597) act 5, sc. 1, l. [126]; cf. **Shakespeare** 670:8

8 Honour pricks me on. Yea, but how if honour prick me off when I come on? how then?
Henry IV, Part 1 (1597) act 5, sc. 1, l. [131]

9 What is honour? A word. What is that word, honour? Air. A trim reckoning! Who hath it? He that died o' Wednesday.
Henry IV, Part 1 (1597) act 5, sc. 1, l. [136]

10 Now, *Esperance*! Percy! and set on.
Henry IV, Part 1 (1597) act 5, sc. 2, l. 96

11 Two stars keep not their motion in one sphere.
Henry IV, Part 1 (1597) act 5, sc. 4, l. 65

12 But thought's the slave of life, and life time's fool;
And time, that takes survey of all the world,
Must have a stop.
Henry IV, Part 1 (1597) act 5, sc. 4, l. [81]

13 When that this body did contain a spirit,
A kingdom for it was too small a bound;
But now two paces of the vilest earth
Is room enough: this earth, that bears thee dead,
Bears not alive so stout a gentleman.
Henry IV, Part 1 (1597) act 5, sc. 4, l. [89]

14 Thy ignominy sleep with thee in the grave,
But not remembered in thy epitaph!
Henry IV, Part 1 (1597) act 5, sc. 4, l. [100]

15 Poor Jack, farewell!
I could have better spared a better man.
Henry IV, Part 1 (1597) act 5, sc. 4, l. [103]

16 The better part of valour is discretion; in the which better part, I have saved my life.
Henry IV, Part I (1597) act 5, sc. 4, l. [121]; cf. **Proverbs** 598:18

17 Lord, Lord, how this world is given to lying! I grant you I was down and out of breath; and so was he; but we rose both at an instant, and fought a long hour by Shrewsbury clock.
Henry IV, Part 1 (1597) act 5, sc. 4, l. [148]

18 For my part, if a lie may do thee grace,
I'll gild it with the happiest terms I have.
Henry IV, Part 1 (1597) act 5, sc. 4, l. [161]

19 I'll purge, and leave sack, and live cleanly, as a nobleman should do.
Henry IV, Part 1 (1597) act 5, sc. 4, l. [168]

HENRY IV, PART 2

20 Rumour is a pipe
Blown by surmises, jealousies, conjectures,
And of so easy and so plain a stop
That the blunt monster with uncounted heads,
The still-discordant wavering multitude,
Can play upon it.
Henry IV, Part 2 (1597) induction, l. 15

21 Yet the first bringer of unwelcome news
Hath but a losing office, and his tongue
Sounds ever after as a sullen bell,
Remembered knolling a departed friend.
Henry IV, Part 2 (1597) act 1, sc. 1, l. 100

22 I am not only witty in myself, but the cause that wit is in other men.
Henry IV, Part 2 (1597) act 1, sc. 2, l. [10]; cf. **Foote** 319:7

23 It is the disease of not listening, the malady of not marking, that I am troubled withal.
Henry IV, Part 2 (1597) act 1, sc. 2, l. [139]

24 I am as poor as Job, my lord, but not so patient.
Henry IV, Part 2 (1597) act 1, sc. 2, l. [145]

25 CHIEF JUSTICE: God send the prince a better companion!
FALSTAFF: God send the companion a better prince! I cannot rid my hands of him.
Henry IV, Part 2 (1597) act 1, sc. 2, l. [227]

26 It was always yet the trick of our English nation, if they have a good thing, to make it too common.
Henry IV, Part 2 (1597) act 1, sc. 2, l. [244]

27 I would to God my name were not so terrible to the enemy as it is: I were better to be eaten to death with rust than to be scoured to nothing with perpetual motion.
Henry IV, Part 2 (1597) act 1, sc. 2, l. [247]; cf. **Proverbs** 596:13

28 I can get no remedy against this consumption of the purse: borrowing only lingers and lingers it out, but the disease is incurable.
Henry IV, Part 2 (1597) act 1, sc. 2, l. [268]

29 Away, you scullion! you rampallion! you fustilarian! I'll tickle your catastrophe.
Henry IV, Part 2 (1597) act 2, sc. 1, l. [67]

30 Doth it not show vilely in me to desire small beer?
Henry IV, Part 2 (1597) act 2, sc. 2, l. [7]

31 He was indeed the glass
Wherein the noble youth did dress themselves.
Henry IV, Part 2 (1597) act 2, sc. 3, l. 21

32 Shall pack-horses,
And hollow pampered jades of Asia,
Which cannot go but thirty miles a day,
Compare with Caesars, and with Cannibals,
And Trojan Greeks? nay, rather damn them with
King Cerberus; and let the welkin roar.
Henry IV, Part 2 (1597) act 2, sc. 4, l. [176]; cf. **Marlowe** 497:3

33 Thou whoreson little tidy Bartholomew boar-pig.
Henry IV, Part 2 (1597) act 2, sc. 4, l. [249]

1 Is it not strange that desire should so many years outlive performance?
Henry IV, Part 2 (1597) act 2, sc. 4, l. [283]

2 Uneasy lies the head that wears a crown.
Henry IV, Part 2 (1597) act 3, sc. 1, l. 31

3 O God! that one might read the book of fate,
And see the revolution of the times
Make mountains level, and the continent,—
Weary of solid firmness,—melt itself
Into the sea!
Henry IV, Part 2 (1597) act 3, sc. 1, l. 45

4 There is a history in all men's lives,
Figuring the nature of the times deceased,
The which observed, a man may prophesy,
With a near aim, of the main chance of things
As yet not come to life, which in their seeds
And weak beginnings lie intreasurèd.
Henry IV, Part 2 (1597) act 3, sc. 1, l. 80

5 A soldier is better accommodated than with a wife.
Henry IV, Part 2 (1597) act 3, sc. 2, l. [73]

6 Most forcible Feeble.
Henry IV, Part 2 (1597) act 3, sc. 2, l. [181]

7 We have heard the chimes at midnight.
Henry IV, Part 2 (1597) act 3, sc. 2, l. [231]

8 I care not; a man can die but once; we owe God a death.
Henry IV, Part 2 (1597) act 3, sc. 2, l. [253]; cf. **Shakespeare** 669:7

9 He that dies this year is quit for the next.
Henry IV, Part 2 (1597) act 3, sc. 2, l. [257]

10 When a' was naked, he was, for all the world, like a forked radish, with a head fantastically carved upon it with a knife.
Henry IV, Part 2 (1597) act 3, sc. 2, l. [335]

11 Against ill chances men are ever merry,
But heaviness foreruns the good event.
Henry IV, Part 2 (1597) act 4, sc. 2, l. 81

12 That I may justly say with the hook-nosed fellow of Rome, 'I came, saw, and overcame.'
Henry IV, Part 2 (1597) act 4, sc. 3, l. [44]; cf. **Caesar** 180:21

13 A man cannot make him laugh; but that's no marvel; he drinks no wine.
Henry IV, Part 2 (1597) act 4, sc. 3, l. [95]

14 O polished perturbation! golden care!
Henry IV, Part 2 (1597) act 4, sc. 5, l. 22

15 This sleep is sound indeed; this is a sleep
That from this golden rigol hath divorced
So many English kings.
Henry IV, Part 2 (1597) act 4, sc. 5, l. 34

16 Thy wish was father, Harry, to that thought.
Henry IV, Part 2 (1597) act 4, sc. 5, l. 91; cf. **Proverbs** 615:12

17 Commit
The oldest sins the newest kind of ways.
Henry IV, Part 2 (1597) act 4, sc. 5, l. 124

18 It hath been prophesied to me many years
I should not die but in Jerusalem,
Which vainly I supposed the Holy Land.
But bear me to that chamber; there I'll lie:
In that Jerusalem shall Harry die.
Henry IV, Part 2 (1597) act 4, sc. 5, l. 235

19 This is the English, not the Turkish court;
Not Amurath an Amurath succeeds,
But Harry, Harry.
Henry IV, Part 2 (1597) act 5, sc. 2, l. 47

20 My father is gone wild into his grave.
Henry IV, Part 2 (1597) act 5, sc. 2, l. 123

21 I speak of Africa and golden joys.
Henry IV, Part 2 (1597) act 5, sc. 3, l. [101]

22 I know thee not, old man: fall to thy prayers;
How ill white hairs become a fool and jester!
Henry IV, Part 2 (1597) act 5, sc. 5, l. [52]

23 Presume not that I am the thing I was.
Henry IV, Part 2 (1597) act 5, sc. 5, l. [61]

24 Falstaff shall die of a sweat, unless already a' be killed with your hard opinions.
Henry IV, Part 2 (1597) act 5, sc. 5, epilogue, l. [32]

HENRY V

25 O! for a Muse of fire, that would ascend
The brightest heaven of invention;
A kingdom for a stage, princes to act
And monarchs to behold the swelling scene.
Henry V (1599) chorus, l. 1; cf. **Olivier** 553:18

26 Can this cockpit hold
The vasty fields of France? or may we cram
Within this wooden O the very casques
That did affright the air at Agincourt?
Henry V (1599) chorus, l. 11

27 Consideration like an angel came,
And whipped the offending Adam out of him.
Henry V (1599) act 1, sc. 1, l. 20

28 For so work the honey-bees,
Creatures that by a rule in nature teach
The act of order to a peopled kingdom.
They have a king and officers of sorts;
Where some, like magistrates, correct at home,
Others, like merchants, venture trade abroad,
Others, like soldiers, armèd in their stings,
Make boot upon the summer's velvet buds;
Which pillage they with merry march bring home
To the tent-royal of their emperor:
Who, busied in his majesty, surveys
The singing masons building roofs of gold.
Henry V (1599) act 1, sc. 2, l. 187

29 When we have matched our rackets to these balls,
We will in France, by God's grace, play a set
Shall strike his father's crown into the hazard.
Henry V (1599) act 1, sc. 2, l. 261

30 Now all the youth of England are on fire,
And silken dalliance in the wardrobe lies.
Henry V (1599) act 2, chorus, l. 1

31 For now sits Expectation in the air
And hides a sword from hilts unto the point
With crowns imperial, crowns and coronets,
Promised to Harry and his followers.
Henry V (1599) act 2, chorus, l. 8

1 O England! model to thy inward greatness,
Like little body with a mighty heart,
What might'st thou do, that honour would thee do,
Were all thy children kind and natural!
But see thy fault!
Henry V (1599) act 2, chorus, l. 16

2 He's in Arthur's bosom, if ever man went to Arthur's bosom.
Henry V (1599) act 2, sc. 3, l. [9]

3 His nose was as sharp as a pen, and a' babbled of green fields.
Henry V (1599) act 2, sc. 3, l. [17]

4 Trust none;
For oaths are straws, men's faiths are wafer-cakes,
And hold-fast is the only dog, my duck.
Henry V (1599) act 2, sc. 3, l. [53]

5 Once more unto the breach, dear friends, once more;
Or close the wall up with our English dead!
In peace there's nothing so becomes a man
As modest stillness and humility:
But when the blast of war blows in our ears,
Then imitate the action of the tiger;
Stiffen the sinews, summon up the blood,
Disguise fair nature with hard-favoured rage;
Then lend the eye a terrible aspect.
Henry V (1599) act 3, sc. 1, l. 1

6 I see you stand like greyhounds in the slips,
Straining upon the start. The game's afoot:
Follow your spirit; and, upon this charge
Cry 'God for Harry! England and Saint George!'
Henry V (1599) act 3, sc. 1, l. 31

7 Give them great meals of beef and iron and steel, they will eat like wolves and fight like devils.
Henry V (1599) act 3, sc. 7, l. [166]

8 Now entertain conjecture of a time
When creeping murmur and the poring dark
Fills the wide vessel of the universe.
Henry V (1599) act 4, chorus, l. 1

9 The royal captain of this ruined band.
Henry V (1599) act 4, chorus, l. 29

10 A little touch of Harry in the night.
Henry V (1599) act 4, chorus, l. 47

11 Thus may we gather honey from the weed,
And make a moral of the devil himself.
Henry V (1599) act 4, sc. 1, l. 11

12 The king's a bawcock, and a heart of gold,
A lad of life, an imp of fame,
Of parents good, of fist most valiant:
I kiss his dirty shoe, and from my heart-string
I love the lovely bully.
Henry V (1599) act 4, sc. 1, l. 44

13 If you would take the pains but to examine the wars of Pompey the Great, you shall find, I warrant you, that there is no tiddle-taddle nor pibble-pabble in Pompey's camp.
Henry V (1599) act 4, sc. 1, l. [69]

14 Though it appear a little out of fashion,
There is much care and valour in this Welshman.
Henry V (1599) act 4, sc. 1, l. [86]

15 I think the king is but a man, as I am: the violet smells to him as it doth to me.
Henry V (1599) act 4, sc. 1, l. [106]

16 I am afeard there are few die well that die in a battle; for how can they charitably dispose of any thing when blood is their argument?
Henry V (1599) act 4, sc. 1, l. [149]

17 Every subject's duty is the king's; but every subject's soul is his own.
Henry V (1599) act 4, sc. 1, l. [189]

18 Upon the king! let us our lives, our souls,
Our debts, our careful wives,
Our children, and our sins lay on the king!
Henry V (1599) act 4, sc. 1, l. [250]

19 What infinite heart's ease
Must kings neglect, that private men enjoy!
And what have kings that privates have not too,
Save ceremony, save general ceremony?
Henry V (1599) act 4, sc. 1, l. [256]

20 'Tis not the balm, the sceptre and the ball,
The sword, the mace, the crown imperial,
The intertissued robe of gold and pearl,
The farcèd title running 'fore the king,
The throne he sits on, nor the tide of pomp
That beats upon the high shore of this world,
No, not all these, thrice-gorgeous ceremony,
Not all these, laid in bed majestical,
Can sleep so soundly as the wretched slave,
Who with a body filled and vacant mind
Gets him to rest, crammed with distressful bread.
Henry V (1599) act 4, sc. 1, l. [280]

21 O God of battles! steel my soldiers' hearts;
Possess them not with fear; take from them now
The sense of reckoning, if the opposèd numbers
Pluck their hearts from them.
Henry V (1599) act 4, sc. 1, l. [309]

22 If we are marked to die, we are enow
To do our country loss; and if to live,
The fewer men, the greater share of honour.
Henry V (1599) act 4, sc. 3, l. 20

23 He which hath no stomach to this fight,
Let him depart; his passport shall be made,
And crowns for convoy put into his purse:
We would not die in that man's company
That fears his fellowship to die with us.
This day is called the feast of Crispian:
He that outlives this day and comes safe home,
Will stand a tip-toe when this day is named,
And rouse him at the name of Crispian.
Henry V (1599) act 4, sc. 3, l. 35

24 Then will he strip his sleeve and show his scars,
And say, 'These wounds I had on Crispin's day.'
Old men forget: yet all shall be forgot,
But he'll remember with advantages
What feats he did that day.
Henry V (1599) act 4, sc. 3, l. 47

25 And Crispin Crispian shall ne'er go by,
From this day to the ending of the world,

But we in it shall be rememberèd;
We few, we happy few, we band of brothers;
For he to-day that sheds his blood with me
Shall be my brother; be he ne'er so vile
This day shall gentle his condition:
And gentlemen in England, now a-bed
Shall think themselves accursed they were not here,
And hold their manhoods cheap whiles any speaks
That fought with us upon Saint Crispin's day.
Henry V (1599) act 4, sc. 3, l. 57

1 But now behold,
In the quick forge and working-house of thought,
How London doth pour out her citizens.
Henry V (1599) act 5, chorus, l. 22

2 Not for Cadwallader and all his goats.
Henry V (1599) act 5, sc. 1, l. [29]

3 By this leek, I will most horribly revenge.
Henry V (1599) act 5, sc. 1, l. [49]

4 The naked, poor, and manglèd Peace,
Dear nurse of arts, plenties, and joyful births.
Henry V (1599) act 5, sc. 2, l. 34

5 For these fellows of infinite tongue, that can rhyme themselves into ladies' favours, they do always reason themselves out again.
Henry V (1599) act 5, sc. 2, l. [162]

HENRY VI, PART 1

6 Hung be the heavens with black, yield day to night!
Henry VI, Part 1 (1592) act 1, sc. 1, l. 1

7 Expect Saint Martin's summer, halcyon days.
Henry VI, Part 1 (1592) act 1, sc. 2, l. 131

8 Unbidden guests
Are often welcomest when they are gone.
Henry VI, Part 1 (1592) act 2, sc. 2, l. 55

9 But in these nice sharp quillets of the law,
Good faith, I am no wiser than a daw.
Henry VI, Part 1 (1592) act 2, sc. 4, l. 17

10 From off this brier pluck a white rose with me.
Plantagenet
Henry VI, Part 1 (1592) act 2, sc. 4, l. 30

11 Pluck a red rose from off this thorn with me.
Somerset
Henry VI, Part 1 (1592) act 2, sc. 4, l. 33

12 I owe him little duty and less love.
Henry VI, Part 1 (1592) act 4, sc. 4, l. 34

13 She's beautiful and therefore to be wooed;
She is a woman, therefore to be won.
Henry VI, Part 1 (1592) act 5, sc. 3, l. 78; cf. **Shakespeare** 699:26

HENRY VI, PART 2

14 Put forth thy hand, reach at the glorious gold.
Henry VI, Part 2 (1592) act 1, sc. 2, l. 11

15 Is this the government of Britain's isle,
And this the royalty of Albion's king?
Henry VI, Part 2 (1592) act 1, sc. 3, l. [47]

16 She bears a duke's revenues on her back,
And in her heart she scorns our poverty.
Henry VI, Part 2 (1592) act 1, sc. 3, l. [83]

17 What stronger breastplate than a heart untainted!
Thrice is he armed that hath his quarrel just,
And he but naked, though locked up in steel,
Whose conscience with injustice is corrupted.
Henry VI, Part 2 (1592) act 3, sc. 2, l. 232

18 The gaudy, blabbing, and remorseful day
Is crept into the bosom of the sea.
Henry VI, Part 2 (1592) act 4, sc. 1, l. 1

19 More can I bear than you dare execute.
Henry VI, Part 2 (1592) act 4, sc. 1, l. 130

20 I say it was never merry world in England since gentlemen came up.
Henry VI, Part 2 (1592) act 4, sc. 2, l. [10]

21 CADE: There shall be in England seven halfpenny loaves sold for a penny; the three-hooped pot shall have ten hoops; and I will make it felony to drink small beer. All the realm shall be in common, and in Cheapside shall my palfrey go to grass. And when I am king,—as king I will be,— . . . there shall be no money; all shall eat and drink on my score; and I will apparel them all in one livery, that they may agree like brothers, and worship me their lord.
DICK: The first thing we do, let's kill all the lawyers.
Henry VI, Part 2 (1592) act 4, sc. 2, l. [73]

22 Is not this a lamentable thing, that of the skin of an innocent lamb should be made parchment? that parchment, being scribbled o'er, should undo a man?
Henry VI, Part 2 (1592) act 4, sc. 2, l. [88]

23 And Adam was a gardener.
Henry VI, Part 2 (1592) act 4, sc. 2, l. [146]

24 Thou hast most traitorously corrupted the youth of the realm in erecting a grammar school: and whereas, before, our forefathers had no other books but the score and the tally, thou hast caused printing to be used; and, contrary to the king, his crown and dignity, thou hast built a paper-mill.
Henry VI, Part 2 (1592) act 4, sc. 7, l. [35]

25 Away with him! away with him! he speaks Latin.
Henry VI, Part 2 (1592) act 4, sc. 7, l. [62]

HENRY VI, PART 3

26 O tiger's heart wrapped in a woman's hide!
Henry VI, Part 3 (1592) act 1, sc. 4, l. 137

27 This battle fares like to the morning's war,
When dying clouds contend with growing light,
What time the shepherd, blowing of his nails,
Can neither call it perfect day nor night.
Henry VI, Part 3 (1592) act 2, sc. 5, l. 1

28 Gives not the hawthorn bush a sweeter shade
To shepherds, looking on their silly sheep,
Than doth a rich embroidered canopy
To kings that fear their subjects' treachery?
Henry VI, Part 3 (1592) act 2, sc. 5, l. 42

29 Why, I can smile, and murder whiles I smile.
Henry VI, Part 3 (1592) act 3, sc. 2, l. 182

30 I'll drown more sailors than the mermaid shall;
I'll slay more gazers than the basilisk;
I'll play the orator as well as Nestor,

Deceive more slyly than Ulysses could,
And, like a Sinon, take another Troy.
I can add colours to the chameleon,
Change shapes with Proteus for advantages,
And set the murderous Machiavel to school.
Can I do this, and cannot get a crown?
Tut, were it farther off, I'll pluck it down.
Henry VI, Part 3 (1592) act 3, sc. 2, l. 186

1 Peace! impudent and shameless Warwick, peace;
Proud setter up and puller down of kings.
Henry VI, Part 3 (1592) act 3, sc. 3, l. 156

2 A little fire is quickly trodden out,
Which, being suffered, rivers cannot quench.
Henry VI, Part 3 (1592) act 4, sc. 8, l. 7

3 Lo! now my glory smeared in dust and blood;
My parks, my walks, my manors that I had,
Even now forsake me; and, of all my lands
Is nothing left me but my body's length.
Why, what is pomp, rule, reign, but earth and dust?
And, live we how we can, yet die we must.
Henry VI, Part 3 (1592) act 5, sc. 2, l. 23

4 Suspicion always haunts the guilty mind;
The thief doth fear each bush an officer.
Henry VI, Part 3 (1592) act 5, sc. 6, l. 11

5 Down, down to hell; and say I sent thee thither.
Henry VI, Part 3 (1592) act 5, sc. 6, l. 67

HENRY VIII

6 Heat not a furnace for your foe so hot
That it do singe yourself.
Henry VIII (1613) act 1, sc. 1, l. 140; play written with John **Fletcher**

7 Go with me, like good angels, to my end;
And, as the long divorce of steel falls on me,
Make of your prayers one sweet sacrifice,
And lift my soul to heaven.
Henry VIII (1613) act 2, sc. 1, l. 75

8 Heaven will one day open
The king's eyes, that so long have slept upon
This bold bad man.
Henry VIII (1613) act 2, sc. 2, l. [42]; cf. **Spenser** 733:15

9 Orpheus with his lute made trees,
And the mountain-tops that freeze,
Bow themselves when he did sing.
Henry VIII (1613) act 3, sc. 1, l. 3

10 In sweet music is such art,
Killing care and grief of heart
Fall asleep, or hearing die.
Henry VIII (1613) act 3, sc. 1, l. 12

11 I shall fall
Like a bright exhalation in the evening,
And no man see me more.
Henry VIII (1613) act 3, sc. 2, l. 226

12 Farewell! a long farewell, to all my greatness!
This is the state of man: to-day he puts forth
The tender leaves of hope; to-morrow blossoms,
And bears his blushing honours thick upon him;
The third day comes a frost, a killing frost;
And, when he thinks, good easy man, full surely
His greatness is a-ripening, nips his root,
And then he falls, as I do. I have ventured,
Like little wanton boys that swim on bladders,
This many summers in a sea of glory,
But far beyond my depth.
Henry VIII (1613) act 3, sc. 2, l. 352

13 O how wretched
Is that poor man that hangs on princes' favours!
There is, betwixt that smile we would aspire to,
That sweet aspect of princes, and their ruin,
More pangs and fears than wars or women have;
And when he falls, he falls like Lucifer,
Never to hope again.
Henry VIII (1613) act 3, sc. 2, l. 367

14 A peace above all earthly dignities,
A still and quiet conscience.
Henry VIII (1613) act 3, sc. 2, l. 380

15 Cromwell, I charge thee, fling away ambition:
By that sin fell the angels.
Henry VIII (1613) act 3, sc. 2, l. 441

16 Love thyself last: cherish those hearts that hate thee;
Corruption wins not more than honesty.
Henry VIII (1613) act 3, sc. 2, l. 444

17 Had I but served my God with half the zeal
I served my king, he would not in mine age
Have left me naked to mine enemies.
Henry VIII (1613) act 3, sc. 2, l. 456; cf. **Wolsey** 826:5

18 An old man, broken with the storms of state
Is come to lay his weary bones among ye;
Give him a little earth for charity.
Henry VIII (1613) act 4, sc. 2, l. 21; cf. **Wolsey** 826:4

19 He gave his honours to the world again,
His blessed part to Heaven, and slept in peace.
Henry VIII (1613) act 4, sc. 2, l. 29

20 So may he rest; his faults lie gently on him!
Henry VIII (1613) act 4, sc. 2, l. 31

21 His promises were, as he then was, mighty;
But his performance, as he is now, nothing.
Henry VIII (1613) act 4, sc. 2, l. 41

22 Men's evil manners live in brass; their virtues
We write in water.
Henry VIII (1613) act 4, sc. 2, l. 45; cf. **Epitaphs** 303:3

23 He was a scholar, and a ripe and good one;
Exceeding wise, fair-spoken, and persuading:
Lofty and sour to them that loved him not;
But, to those men that sought him, sweet as summer.
Henry VIII (1613) act 4, sc. 2, l. 51

24 Those twins of learning that he raised in you,
Ipswich and Oxford!
Henry VIII (1613) act 4, sc. 2, l. 58

25 'Tis a cruelty
To load a falling man.
Henry VIII (1613) act 5, sc. 3, l. 76

26 In her days every man shall eat in safety
Under his own vine what he plants; and sing
The merry songs of peace to all his neighbours.
Henry VIII (1613) act 5, sc. 5, l. 34

27 Nor shall this peace sleep with her; but as when
The bird of wonder dies, the maiden phoenix,

Her ashes new-create another heir
As great in admiration as herself.
Henry VIII (1613) act 5, sc. 5, l. 40

1 Some come to take their ease
And sleep an act or two.
Henry VIII (1613) act 5, epilogue, l. 2

JULIUS CAESAR

2 Hence! home, you idle creatures, get you home:
Is this a holiday?
Julius Caesar (1599) act 1, sc. 1, l. 1

3 You blocks, you stones, you worse than senseless things!
O you hard hearts, you cruel men of Rome,
Knew you not Pompey?
Julius Caesar (1599) act 1, sc. 1, l. [39]

4 CAESAR: Who is it in the press that calls on me?
I hear a tongue, shriller than all the music,
Cry 'Caesar'. Speak; Caesar is turned to hear.
Beware the ides of March.
Julius Caesar (1599) act 1, sc. 2, l. 15

5 I do lack some part
Of that quick spirit that is in Antony.
Julius Caesar (1599) act 1, sc. 2, l. 28

6 Brutus, I do observe you now of late:
I have not from your eyes that gentleness
And show of love as I was wont to have:
You bear too stubborn and too strange a hand
Over your friend that loves you.
Julius Caesar (1599) act 1, sc. 2, l. 32

7 Poor Brutus, with himself at war,
Forgets the shows of love to other men.
Julius Caesar (1599) act 1, sc. 2, l. 46

8 Set honour in one eye and death i' the other,
And I will look on both indifferently.
Julius Caesar (1599) act 1, sc. 2, l. 86

9 Well, honour is the subject of my story.
I cannot tell what you and other men
Think of this life: but, for my single self,
I had as lief not be as live to be
In awe of such a thing as I myself.
Julius Caesar (1599) act 1, sc. 2, l. 92

10 I was born free as Caesar; so were you:
We both have fed as well, and we can both
Endure the winter's cold as well as he.
Julius Caesar (1599) act 1, sc. 2, l. 97

11 He had a fever when he was in Spain,
And when the fit was on him, I did mark
How he did shake; 'tis true, this god did shake.
Julius Caesar (1599) act 1, sc. 2, l. 119

12 Ye gods, it doth amaze me,
A man of such a feeble temper should
So get the start of the majestic world,
And bear the palm alone.
Julius Caesar (1599) act 1, sc. 2, l. 128

13 Why, man, he doth bestride the narrow world
Like a Colossus; and we petty men
Walk under his huge legs, and peep about
To find ourselves dishonourable graves.
Men at some time are masters of their fates:
The fault, dear Brutus, is not in our stars,
But in ourselves, that we are underlings.
Julius Caesar (1599) act 1, sc. 2, l. 134

14 'Brutus' will start a spirit as soon as 'Caesar'.
Now in the names of all the gods at once,
Upon what meat doth this our Caesar feed,
That he is grown so great?
Julius Caesar (1599) act 1, sc. 2, l. 146

15 When could they say, till now, that talked of Rome,
That her wide walls encompassed but one man?
Now is it Rome indeed and room enough,
When there is in it but one only man.
Julius Caesar (1599) act 1, sc. 2, l. 153

16 Let me have men about me that are fat;
Sleek-headed men and such as sleep o' nights;
Yond' Cassius has a lean and hungry look;
He thinks too much: such men are dangerous.
Julius Caesar (1599) act 1, sc. 2, l. 191; cf. **Plutarch** 579:7

17 Would he were fatter! but I fear him not:
Yet if my name were liable to fear,
I do not know the man I should avoid
So soon as that spare Cassius. He reads much;
He is a great observer.
Julius Caesar (1599) act 1, sc. 2, l. 197

18 He loves no plays,
As thou dost, Antony.
Julius Caesar (1599) act 1, sc. 2, l. 202

19 Such men as he be never at heart's ease,
Whiles they behold a greater than themselves,
And therefore are they very dangerous.
I rather tell thee what is to be feared
Than what I fear, for always I am Caesar.
Julius Caesar (1599) act 1, sc. 2, l. 207

20 'Tis very like: he hath the falling sickness.
Julius Caesar (1599) act 1, sc. 2, l. [255]

21 CASSIUS: Did Cicero say any thing?
CASCA: Ay, he spoke Greek.
CASSIUS: To what effect?
CASCA: Nay, an I tell you that, I'll ne'er look you i' the face again; but those that understood him smiled at one another and shook their heads; but, for mine own part, it was Greek to me.
Julius Caesar (1599) act 1, sc. 2, l. [288]

22 Yesterday the bird of night did sit,
Even at noon-day, upon the market-place,
Hooting and shrieking.
Julius Caesar (1599) act 1, sc. 3, l. 26

23 Cassius from bondage will deliver Cassius.
Julius Caesar (1599) act 1, sc. 3, l. 90

24 Nor stony tower, nor walls of beaten brass,
Nor airless dungeon, nor strong links of iron,
Can be retentive to the strength of spirit;
But life, being weary of these worldly bars,
Never lacks power to dismiss itself.
Julius Caesar (1599) act 1, sc. 3, l. 93

25 It is the bright day that brings forth the adder;
And that craves wary walking.
Julius Caesar (1599) act 2, sc. 1, l. 14

1 Between the acting of a dreadful thing
And the first motion, all the interim is
Like a phantasma, or a hideous dream.
Julius Caesar (1599) act 2, sc. 1, l. 63

2 Let us be sacrificers, but not butchers, Caius.
Julius Caesar (1599) act 2, sc. 1, l. 166

3 Let's carve him as a dish fit for the gods,
Not hew him as a carcass fit for hounds.
Julius Caesar (1599) act 2, sc. 1, l. 173

4 For he is superstitious grown of late,
Quite from the main opinion he held once
Of fantasy, of dreams, and ceremonies.
Julius Caesar (1599) act 2, sc. 1, l. 195

5 But when I tell him he hates flatterers,
He says he does, being then most flattered.
Julius Caesar (1599) act 2, sc. 1, l. 207

6 What! is Brutus sick,
And will he steal out of his wholesome bed
To dare the vile contagion of the night?
Julius Caesar (1599) act 2, sc. 1, l. 263

7 PORTIA: Dwell I but in the suburbs
Of your good pleasure? If it be no more,
Portia is Brutus' harlot, not his wife.
BRUTUS: You are my true and honourable wife,
As dear to me as are the ruddy drops
That visit my sad heart.
Julius Caesar (1599) act 2, sc. 1, l. 285

8 I grant I am a woman, but, withal,
A woman that Lord Brutus took to wife;
I grant I am a woman, but, withal,
A woman well-reputed, Cato's daughter.
Think you I am no stronger than my sex,
Being so fathered and so husbanded?
Julius Caesar (1599) act 2, sc. 1, l. 292

9 When beggars die, there are no comets seen;
The heavens themselves blaze forth the death of princes.
Julius Caesar (1599) act 2, sc. 2, l. 30

10 Cowards die many times before their deaths;
The valiant never taste of death but once.
Of all the wonders that I yet have heard,
It seems to me most strange that men should fear;
Seeing that death, a necessary end,
Will come when it will come.
Julius Caesar (1599) act 2, sc. 2, l. 32

11 Danger knows full well
That Caesar is more dangerous than he:
We are two lions littered in one day,
And I the elder and more terrible.
Julius Caesar (1599) act 2, sc. 2, l. 44

12 The cause is in my will: I will not come.
Julius Caesar (1599) act 2, sc. 2, l. 71

13 See! Antony, that revels long o' nights,
Is notwithstanding up.
Julius Caesar (1599) act 2, sc. 2, l. 116

14 CAESAR: The ides of March are come.
SOOTHSAYER: Ay, Caesar; but not gone.
Julius Caesar (1599) act 3, sc. 1, l. 1

15 But I am constant as the northern star,
Of whose true-fixed and resting quality
There is no fellow in the firmament.
Julius Caesar (1599) act 3, sc. 1, l. 60

16 *Et tu, Brute?* Then fall, Caesar!
Julius Caesar (1599) act 3, sc. 1, l. 77; cf. **Caesar** 180:22

17 Ambition's debt is paid.
Julius Caesar (1599) act 3, sc. 1, l. 83

18 How many ages hence
Shall this our lofty scene be acted o'er,
In states unborn, and accents yet unknown!
Julius Caesar (1599) act 3, sc. 1, l. 111

19 O mighty Caesar! dost thou lie so low?
Are all thy conquests, glories, triumphs, spoils,
Shrunk to this little measure?
Julius Caesar (1599) act 3, sc. 1, l. 148

20 Live a thousand years,
I shall not find myself so apt to die:
No place will please me so, no mean of death,
As here by Caesar, and by you cut off,
The choice and master spirits of this age.
Julius Caesar (1599) act 3, sc. 1, l. 159

21 O! pardon me, thou bleeding piece of earth,
That I am meek and gentle with these butchers;
Thou art the ruins of the noblest man
That ever livèd in the tide of times.
Julius Caesar (1599) act 3, sc. 1, l. 254

22 Caesar's spirit, ranging for revenge,
With Ate by his side, come hot from hell,
Shall in these confines, with a monarch's voice
Cry, 'Havoc!' and let slip the dogs of war.
Julius Caesar (1599) act 3, sc. 1, l. 270

23 Passion, I see, is catching.
Julius Caesar (1599) act 3, sc. 1, l. 283

24 Not that I loved Caesar less, but that I loved Rome more.
Julius Caesar (1599) act 3, sc. 2, l. [22]

25 As he was valiant, I honour him: but, as he was ambitious, I slew him.
Julius Caesar (1599) act 3, sc. 2, l. [27]

26 Who is here so base that would be a bondman? If any, speak; for him have I offended. Who is here so rude that would not be a Roman? If any, speak; for him have I offended. Who is here so vile that will not love his country? If any, speak; for him have I offended. I pause for a reply.
Julius Caesar (1599) act 3, sc. 2, l. [31]

27 Friends, Romans, countrymen, lend me your ears;
I come to bury Caesar, not to praise him.
The evil that men do lives after them,
The good is oft interrèd with their bones.
Julius Caesar (1599) act 3, sc. 2, l. [79]

28 The noble Brutus
Hath told you Caesar was ambitious;
If it were so, it was a grievous fault;
And grievously hath Caesar answered it.
Julius Caesar (1599) act 3, sc. 2, l. [83]

29 For Brutus is an honourable man;
So are they all, all honourable men.
Julius Caesar (1599) act 3, sc. 2, l. [88]

30 He was my friend, faithful and just to me:
But Brutus says he was ambitious;

And Brutus is an honourable man.
Julius Caesar (1599) act 3, sc. 2, l. [91]

1 When that the poor have cried, Caesar hath wept;
Ambition should be made of sterner stuff.
Julius Caesar (1599) act 3, sc. 2, l. [97]

2 On the Lupercal
I thrice presented him a kingly crown
Which he did thrice refuse: was this ambition?
Julius Caesar (1599) act 3, sc. 2, l. [101]

3 You all did love him once, not without cause.
Julius Caesar (1599) act 3, sc. 2, l. [108]

4 But yesterday the word of Caesar might
Have stood against the world; now lies he there,
And none so poor to do him reverence.
Julius Caesar (1599) act 3, sc. 2, l. [124]

5 You are not wood, you are not stones, but men;
And, being men, hearing the will of Caesar,
It will inflame you, it will make you mad.
Julius Caesar (1599) act 3, sc. 2, l. [148]

6 If you have tears, prepare to shed them now.
Julius Caesar (1599) act 3, sc. 2, l. [174]

7 This was the most unkindest cut of all.
Julius Caesar (1599) act 3, sc. 2, l. [188]

8 O! what a fall was there, my countrymen;
Then I, and you, and all of us fell down,
Whilst bloody treason flourished over us.
Julius Caesar (1599) act 3, sc. 2, l. [195]

9 I am no orator, as Brutus is;
But, as you know me all, a plain, blunt man,
That love my friend.
Julius Caesar (1599) act 3, sc. 2, l. [221]

10 For I have neither wit, nor words, nor worth,
Action, nor utterance, nor power of speech,
To stir men's blood; I only speak right on;
I tell you that which you yourselves do know.
Julius Caesar (1599) act 3, sc. 2, l. [225]

11 But were I Brutus,
And Brutus Antony, there were an Antony
Would ruffle up your spirits, and put a tongue
In every wound of Caesar, that should move
The stones of Rome to rise and mutiny.
Julius Caesar (1599) act 3, sc. 2, l. [230]

12 He hath left you all his walks,
His private arbours, and new-planted orchards,
On this side Tiber; he hath left them you,
And to your heirs for ever; common pleasures,
To walk abroad, and recreate yourselves.
Julius Caesar (1599) act 3, sc. 2, l. [252]

13 Here was a Caesar! when comes such another?
Julius Caesar (1599) act 3, sc. 2, l. [257]

14 Now let it work; mischief, thou art afoot,
Take thou what course thou wilt!
Julius Caesar (1599) act 3, sc. 2, l. [265]

15 Tear him for his bad verses, tear him for his bad verses.
Julius Caesar (1599) act 3, sc. 3, l. [34]

16 He shall not live; look, with a spot I damn him.
Julius Caesar (1599) act 4, sc. 1, l. 6

17 This is a slight unmeritable man,
Meet to be sent on errands.
Julius Caesar (1599) act 4, sc. 1, l. 12

18 Let me tell you, Cassius, you yourself
Are much condemned to have an itching palm.
Julius Caesar (1599) act 4, sc. 3, l. 7

19 I had rather be a dog, and bay the moon,
Than such a Roman.
Julius Caesar (1599) act 4, sc. 3, l. 27

20 Away, slight man!
Julius Caesar (1599) act 4, sc. 3, l. 37

21 You wrong me every way; you wrong me, Brutus;
I said an elder soldier, not a better:
Did I say 'better'?
Julius Caesar (1599) act 4, sc. 3, l. 55

22 Do not presume too much upon my love;
I may do that I shall be sorry for.
Julius Caesar (1599) act 4, sc. 3, l. 63

23 There is no terror, Cassius, in your threats;
For I am armed so strong in honesty
That they pass by me as the idle wind,
Which I respect not.
Julius Caesar (1599) act 4, sc. 3, l. 66

24 A friend should bear his friend's infirmities,
But Brutus makes mine greater than they are.
Julius Caesar (1599) act 4, sc. 3, l. 85

25 Cassius is aweary of the world;
Hated by one he loves; braved by his brother;
Checked like a bondman; all his faults observed,
Set in a note-book, learned, and conned by rote,
To cast into my teeth.
Julius Caesar (1599) act 4, sc. 3, l. 94

26 O Cassius! you are yokèd with a lamb
That carries anger as the flint bears fire;
Who, much enforcèd, shows a hasty spark,
And straight is cold again.
Julius Caesar (1599) act 4, sc. 3, l. 109

27 Good reasons must, of force, give place to better.
Julius Caesar (1599) act 4, sc. 3, l. 202

28 There is a tide in the affairs of men,
Which, taken at the flood, leads on to fortune;
Omitted, all the voyage of their life
Is bound in shallows and in miseries.
Julius Caesar (1599) act 4, sc. 3, l. 217; cf. **Byron** 177:11

29 But for your words, they rob the Hybla bees,
And leave them honeyless.
Julius Caesar (1599) act 5, sc. 1, l. 34

30 Forever, and forever, farewell, Cassius!
If we do meet again, why, we shall smile!
If not, why then, this parting was well made.
Julius Caesar (1599) act 5, sc. 1, l. 118

31 O! that a man might know
The end of this day's business, ere it come;
But it sufficeth that the day will end,
And then the end is known.
Julius Caesar (1599) act 5, sc. 1, l. 123

32 O hateful error, melancholy's child!
Why dost thou show, to the apt thoughts of men,

The things that are not?
Julius Caesar (1599) act 5, sc. 3, l. 67

1 O Julius Caesar! thou art mighty yet!
Thy spirit walks abroad, and turns our swords
In our own proper entrails.
Julius Caesar (1599) act 5, sc. 3, l. 94

2 Thou seest the world, Volumnius, how it goes;
Our enemies have beat us to the pit:
It is more worthy to leap in ourselves,
Than tarry till they push us.
Julius Caesar (1599) act 5, sc. 5, l. 22

3 Thy life hath had some smatch of honour in it.
Julius Caesar (1599) act 5, sc. 5, l. 46

4 This was the noblest Roman of them all;
All the conspirators save only he
Did that they did in envy of great Caesar;
He only in a general honest thought
And common good to all, made one of them.
His life was gentle, and the elements
So mixed in him that Nature might stand up
And say to all the world, 'This was a man!'
Julius Caesar (1599) act 5, sc. 5, l. 68

KING JOHN

5 Hadst thou rather be a Faulconbridge
And like thy brother, to enjoy thy land,
Or the reputed son of Coeur-de-Lion,
Lord of thy presence and no land beside.
King John (1591–8) act 1, sc. 1, l. 134

6 And if his name be George, I'll call him Peter;
For new-made honour doth forget men's names.
King John (1591–8) act 1, sc. 1, l. 186

7 Mad world! mad kings! mad composition!
King John (1591–8) act 2, sc. 1, l. 561

8 Well, whiles I am a beggar, I will rail,
And say there is no sin, but to be rich;
And, being rich, my virtue then shall be,
To say there is no vice, but beggary.
King John (1591–8) act 2, sc. 1, l. 593

9 Old Time the clock-setter, that bald sexton, Time.
King John (1591–8) act 3, sc. 1, l. 324

10 Bell, book, and candle shall not drive me back,
When gold and silver becks me to come on.
King John (1591–8) act 3, sc. 3, l. 12

11 Grief fills the room up of my absent child,
Lies in his bed, walks up and down with me,
Puts on his pretty looks, repeats his words,
Remembers me of all his gracious parts,
Stuffs out his vacant garments with his form:
Then have I reason to be fond of grief.
King John (1591–8) act 3, sc. 4, l. 93

12 Life is as tedious as a twice-told tale,
Vexing the dull ear of a drowsy man.
King John (1591–8) act 3, sc. 4, l. 108

13 Heat me these irons hot.
King John (1591–8) act 4, sc. 1, l. 1

14 Will you put out mine eyes?
These eyes that never did nor never shall
So much as frown on you?
King John (1591–8) act 4, sc. 1, l. 56

15 To gild refinèd gold, to paint the lily,
To throw a perfume on the violet,
To smooth the ice, or add another hue
Unto the rainbow, or with taper light
To seek the beauteous eye of heaven to garnish,
Is wasteful and ridiculous excess.
King John (1591–8) act 4, sc. 2, l. 11; cf. **Byron** 176:24

16 Another lean unwashed artificer
Cuts off his tale and talks of Arthur's death.
King John (1591–8) act 4, sc. 2, l. 201

17 How oft the sight of means to do ill deeds
Makes ill deeds done!
King John (1591–8) act 4, sc. 2, l. 219

18 Heaven take my soul, and England keep my bones!
King John (1591–8) act 4, sc. 3, l. 10

19 Whate'er you think, good words, I think, were best.
King John (1591–8) act 4, sc. 3, l. 28

20 I do not ask you much:
I beg cold comfort.
King John (1591–8) act 5, sc. 7, l. 41

21 This England never did, nor never shall,
Lie at the proud foot of a conqueror,
But when it first did help to wound itself.
Now these her princes are come home again,
Come the three corners of the world in arms,
And we shall shock them: nought shall make us rue,
If England to itself do rest but true.
King John (1591–8) act 5, sc. 7, l. 112

KING LEAR

22 Nothing will come of nothing: speak again.
King Lear (1605–6) act 1, sc. 1, l. [92]

23 LEAR: So young, and so untender?
CORDELIA: So young, my lord, and true.
LEAR: Let it be so; thy truth then be thy dower:
For, by the sacred radiance of the sun,
The mysteries of Hecate and the night,
By all the operation of the orbs
From whom we do exist and cease to be,
Here I disclaim all my paternal care,
Propinquity and property of blood,
And as a stranger to my heart and me
Hold thee from this for ever.
King Lear (1605–6) act 1, sc. 1, l. [108]

24 Come not between the dragon and his wrath.
King Lear (1605–6) act 1, sc. 1, l. [124]

25 I want that glib and oily art
To speak and purpose not; since what I well intend,
I'll do't before I speak.
King Lear (1605–6) act 1, sc. 1, l. [227]

26 It is no vicious blot nor other foulness,
No unchaste action, or dishonoured step,
That hath deprived me of your grace and favour,
But even for want of that for which I am richer,
A still-soliciting eye, and such a tongue
That I am glad I have not, though not to have it
Hath lost me in your liking.
King Lear (1605–6) act 1, sc. 1, l. [230]

1 Love is not love
When it is minglèd with regards that stand
Aloof from the entire point.
King Lear (1605–6) act 1, sc. 1, l. [241]

2 'Tis the infirmity of his age; yet he hath ever but slenderly known himself.
King Lear (1605–6) act 1, sc. 1, l. 293

3 Why bastard? wherefore base?
When my dimensions are as well compact,
My mind as generous, and my shape as true,
As honest madam's issue?
King Lear (1605–6) act 1, sc. 2, l. 6

4 I grow, I prosper;
Now, gods, stand up for bastards!
King Lear (1605–6) act 1, sc. 2, l. 21

5 This is the excellent foppery of the world, that, when we are sick in fortune,—often the surfeit of our own behaviour,— we make guilty of our own disasters the sun, the moon, and the stars; as if we were villains by necessity, fools by heavenly compulsion, knaves, thieves, and treachers by spherical predominance, drunkards, liars, and adulterers by an enforced obedience of planetary influence.
King Lear (1605–6) act 1, sc. 2, l. [132]

6 My father compounded with my mother under the dragon's tail, and my nativity was under *ursa major*; so that it follows I am rough and lecherous. 'Sfoot! I should have been that I am had the maidenliest star in the firmament twinkled on my bastardizing.
King Lear (1605–6) act 1, sc. 2, l. [144]

7 My cue is villanous melancholy, with a sigh like Tom o' Bedlam.
King Lear (1605–6) act 1, sc. 2, l. [151]

8 LEAR: Dost thou call me fool, boy?
FOOL: All thy other titles thou hast given away; that thou wast born with.
King Lear (1605–6) act 1, sc. 4, l. [163]

9 Who is it that can tell me who I am?
King Lear (1605–6) act 1, sc. 4, l. 230

10 Ingratitude, thou marble-hearted fiend,
More hideous, when thou show'st thee in a child,
Than the sea-monster.
King Lear (1605–6) act 1, sc. 4, l. [283]

11 How sharper than a serpent's tooth it is
To have a thankless child!
King Lear (1605–6) act 1, sc. 4, l. [312]

12 O! let me not be mad, not mad, sweet heaven;
Keep me in temper; I would not be mad!
King Lear (1605–6) act 1, sc. 5, l. [51]

13 Thou whoreson zed! thou unnecessary letter!
King Lear (1605–6) act 2, sc. 2, l. [68]

14 Goose, if I had you upon Sarum plain,
I'd drive ye cackling home to Camelot.
King Lear (1605–6) act 2, sc. 2, l. [88]

15 Down, thou climbing sorrow!
Thy element's below.
King Lear (1605–6) act 2, sc. 4, l. [57]

16 O, sir! you are old;
Nature in you stands on the very verge
Of her confine.
King Lear (1605–6) act 2, sc. 4, l. [148]

17 O reason not the need! Our basest beggars
Are in the poorest thing superfluous.
Allow not nature more than nature needs,
Man's life is cheap as beast's.
King Lear (1605–6) act 2, sc. 4, l. 264

18 I will do such things,—
What they are yet I know not,—but they shall be
The terrors of the earth.
King Lear (1605–6) act 2, sc. 4, l. [283]

19 No, I'll not weep:
I have full cause of weeping, but this heart
Shall break into a hundred thousand flaws
Or ere I'll weep. O fool! I shall go mad.
King Lear (1605–6) act 2, sc. 4, l. [286]

20 Contending with the fretful elements;
Bids the wind blow the earth into the sea,
Or swell the curlèd waters 'bove the main,
That things might change or cease.
King Lear (1605–6) act 3, sc. 1, l. 4

21 Blow, winds, and crack your cheeks! rage! blow!
You cataracts and hurricanoes, spout
Till you have drenched our steeples, drowned the cocks!
You sulphurous and thought-executing fires,
Vaunt-couriers to oak-cleaving thunderbolts,
Singe my white head! And thou, all-shaking thunder,
Strike flat the thick rotundity o' the world!
Crack nature's moulds, all germens spill at once
That make ingrateful man!
King Lear (1605–6) act 3, sc. 2, l. 1

22 Rumble thy bellyful! Spit, fire! Spout, rain!
Nor rain, wind, thunder, fire, are my daughters:
I tax not you, you elements, with unkindness.
King Lear (1605–6) act 3, sc. 2, l. 14

23 There was never yet fair woman but she made mouths in a glass.
King Lear (1605–6) act 3, sc. 2, l. [35]

24 No, I will be the pattern of all patience; I will say nothing.
King Lear (1605–6) act 3, sc. 2, l. [37]

25 I am a man
More sinned against than sinning.
King Lear (1605–6) act 3, sc. 2, l. [59]; cf. **Bowra** 146:2

26 He that has a little tiny wit,
With hey, ho, the wind and the rain,
Must make content with his fortunes fit,
Though the rain it raineth every day.
King Lear (1605–6) act 3, sc. 2, l. [74]

27 O! that way madness lies; let me shun that.
King Lear (1605–6) act 3, sc. 4, l. 21

28 Poor naked wretches, wheresoe'er you are,
That bide the pelting of this pitiless storm,
How shall your houseless heads and unfed sides,
Your loopèd and windowed raggedness, defend you

From seasons such as these?
King Lear (1605–6) act 3, sc. 4, l. 28

1 Take physic, pomp;
Expose thyself to feel what wretches feel.
King Lear (1605–6) act 3, sc. 4, l. 33

2 Pillicock sat on Pillicock-hill:
Halloo, halloo, loo, loo!
King Lear (1605–6) act 3, sc. 4, l. [75]

3 Keep thy foot out of brothels, thy hand out of plackets, thy pen from lenders' books, and defy the foul fiend.
King Lear (1605–6) act 3, sc. 4, l. [96]

4 Thou art the thing itself; unaccommodated man is no more but such a poor, bare, forked animal as thou art. Off, off, you lendings! Come; unbutton here.
King Lear (1605–6) act 3, sc. 4, l. [109]

5 This is the foul fiend Flibbertigibbet: he begins at curfew, and walks till the first cock; he gives the web and the pin, squints the eye, and makes the harelip; mildews the white wheat, and hurts the poor creatures of earth.
King Lear (1605–6) act 3, sc. 4, l. [118]

6 The green mantle of the standing pool.
King Lear (1605–6) act 3, sc. 4, l. [136]

7 The prince of darkness is a gentleman.
King Lear (1605–6) act 3, sc. 4, l. [148]

8 Poor Tom's a-cold.
King Lear (1605–6) act 3, sc. 4, l. [151]

9 Child Roland to the dark tower came,
His word was still, Fie, foh, and fum,
I smell the blood of a British man.
King Lear (1605–6) act 3, sc. 4, l. [185]; cf. **Browning** 155:21, **Nashe** 539:20

10 The little dogs and all,
Tray, Blanch, and Sweet-heart, see, they bark at me.
King Lear (1605–6) act 3, sc. 6, l. [65]

11 I am tied to the stake, and I must stand the course.
King Lear (1605–6) act 3, sc. 7, l. [54]

12 Out, vile jelly!
Where is thy lustre now?
King Lear (1605–6) act 3, sc. 7, l. [83]

13 The lowest and most dejected thing of fortune,
Stands still in esperance, lives not in fear:
The lamentable change is from the best;
The worst returns to laughter.
King Lear (1605–6) act 4, sc. 1, l. 3

14 The worst is not,
So long as we can say, 'This is the worst.'
King Lear (1605–6) act 4, sc. 1, l. 27

15 As flies to wanton boys, are we to the gods;
They kill us for their sport.
King Lear (1605–6) act 4, sc. 1, l. 36

16 You are not worth the dust which the rude wind
Blows in your face.
King Lear (1605–6) act 4, sc. 2, l. 30

17 It is the stars,
The stars above us, govern our conditions.
King Lear (1605–6) act 4, sc. 3, l. [34]

18 Crowned with rank fumitor and furrow weeds,
With burdocks, hemlock, nettles, cuckoo-flowers,
Darnel, and all the idle weeds that grow
In our sustaining corn.
King Lear (1605–6) act 4, sc. 4, l. 3

19 How fearful
And dizzy 'tis to cast one's eyes so low!
The crows and choughs that wing the midway air
Show scarce so gross as beetles; half-way down
Hangs one that gathers samphire, dreadful trade!
Methinks he seems no bigger than his head.
The fishermen that walk upon the beach
Appear like mice.
King Lear (1605–6) act 4, sc. 6, l. 12

20 GLOUCESTER: Is't not the king?
LEAR: Ay, every inch a king.
King Lear (1605–6) act 4, sc. 6, l. [110]

21 Die: die for adultery! No:
The wren goes to't, and the small gilded fly
Does lecher in my sight.
Let copulation thrive.
King Lear (1605–6) act 4, sc. 6, l. [115]

22 LEAR: The fitchew nor the soiled horse goes to't
With a more riotous appetite.
Down from the waist they are Centaurs,
Though women all above:
But to the girdle do the Gods inherit,
Beneath is all the fiends':
There's hell, there's darkness, there is the sulphurous pit,
Burning, scalding, stench, consumption; fie, fie, fie! pah, pah! Give me an ounce of civet, good apothecary, to sweeten my imagination; there's money for thee.
GLOUCESTER: O! let me kiss that hand!
LEAR: Let me wipe it first; it smells of mortality.
GLOUCESTER: O ruined piece of nature! This great world
Should so wear out to nought.
King Lear (1605–6) act 4, sc. 6, l. [125]

23 A man may see how this world goes with no eyes. Look with thine ears: see how yond justice rails upon yond simple thief. Hark, in thine ear: change places; and, handy-dandy, which is the justice, which is the thief?
King Lear (1605–6) act 4, sc. 6, l. [154]

24 Thou rascal beadle, hold thy bloody hand!
Why dost thou lash that whore? Strip thine own back;
Thou hotly lust'st to use her in that kind
For which thou whipp'st her.
King Lear (1605–6) act 4, sc. 6, l. 158

25 Get thee glass eyes;
And, like a scurvy politician, seem
To see the things thou dost not.
King Lear (1605–6) act 4, sc. 6, l. [175]

1 When we are born we cry that we are come
To this great stage of fools.
King Lear (1605–6) act 4, sc. 6, l. [187]

2 Mine enemy's dog,
Though he had bit me, should have stood that night
Against my fire.
King Lear (1605–6) act 4, sc. 7, l. 36

3 Thou art a soul in bliss; but I am bound
Upon a wheel of fire.
King Lear (1605–6) act 4, sc. 7, l. 46

4 I am a very foolish, fond old man,
Fourscore and upward, not an hour more or less;
And, to deal plainly,
I fear I am not in my perfect mind.
King Lear (1605–6) act 4, sc. 7, l. 60

5 Men must endure
Their going hence, even as their coming hither:
Ripeness is all.
King Lear (1605–6) act 5, sc. 2, l. 9

6 Come, let's away to prison;
We two alone will sing like birds i' the cage:
When thou dost ask me blessing, I'll kneel down,
And ask of thee forgiveness: and we'll live
And pray, and sing, and tell old tales, and laugh
At gilded butterflies.
King Lear (1605–6) act 5, sc. 3, l. 8; cf. **Webster** 808:15

7 Talk of court news; and we'll talk with them too,
Who loses, and who wins; who's in, who's out;
And take upon 's the mystery of things,
As if we were God's spies; and we'll wear out,
In a walled prison, packs and sets of great ones
That ebb and flow by the moon.
King Lear (1605–6) act 5, sc. 3, l. 14

8 Upon such sacrifices, my Cordelia,
The gods themselves throw incense.
King Lear (1605–6) act 5, sc. 3, l. 20

9 The gods are just, and of our pleasant vices
Make instruments to plague us.
King Lear (1605–6) act 5, sc. 3, l. [172]

10 The wheel is come full circle.
King Lear (1605–6) act 5, sc. 3, l. [176]

11 Howl, howl, howl, howl! O! you are men of stones:
Had I your tongue and eyes, I'd use them so
That heaven's vaults should crack. She's gone for ever!
King Lear (1605–6) act 5, sc. 3, l. [259]

12 KENT: Is this the promised end?
EDGAR: Or image of that horror?
ALBION: Fall and cease?
King Lear (1605–6) act 5, sc. 3, l. [265]

13 Her voice was ever soft,
Gentle and low, an excellent thing in woman.
King Lear (1605–6) act 5, sc. 3, l. [274]

14 And my poor fool is hanged! No, no, no life!
Why should a dog, a horse, a rat, have life,
And thou no breath at all? Thou'lt come no more,
Never, never, never, never, never!
Pray you, undo this button.
King Lear (1605–6) act 5, sc. 3, l. [307]

15 Vex not his ghost: O! let him pass; he hates him
That would upon the rack of this tough world
Stretch him out longer.
King Lear (1605–6) act 5, sc. 3, l. [314]

16 The oldest hath borne most: we that are young,
Shall never see so much, nor live so long.
King Lear (1605–6) act 5, sc. 3, l. [327]

LOVE'S LABOUR'S LOST

17 Cormorant devouring Time.
Love's Labour's Lost (1595) act 1, sc. 1, l. 4

18 Study is like the heaven's glorious sun,
That will not be deep-searched with saucy looks.
Love's Labour's Lost (1595) act 1, sc. 1, l. 84

19 At Christmas I no more desire a rose
Than wish a snow in May's new-fangled mirth;
But like of each thing that in season grows.
Love's Labour's Lost (1595) act 1, sc. 1, l. 105

20 Assist me some extemporal god of rime, for I am sure I shall turn sonneter. Devise, wit; write, pen; for I am for whole volumes in folio.
Love's Labour's Lost (1595) act 1, sc. 2, l. [192]

21 Warble, child; make passionate my sense of hearing.
Love's Labour's Lost (1595) act 3, sc. 1, l. 1

22 This wimpled, whining, purblind, wayward boy,
This senior-junior, giant-dwarf, Dan Cupid.
Love's Labour's Lost (1595) act 3, sc. 1, l. [189]

23 A wightly wanton with a velvet brow,
With two pitch balls stuck in her face for eyes;
Ay, and, by heaven, one that will do the deed
Though Argus were her eunuch and her guard:
And I to sigh for her! to watch for her!
To pray for her!
Love's Labour's Lost (1595) act 3, sc. 1, l. [206]

24 He hath not fed of the dainties that are bred in a book; he hath not eat paper, as it were; he hath not drunk ink.
Love's Labour's Lost (1595) act 4, sc. 2, l. [25]

25 Old Mantuan! old Mantuan! Who understandeth thee not, loves thee not.
Love's Labour's Lost (1595) act 4, sc. 2, l. [102]

26 From women's eyes this doctrine I derive:
They are the ground, the books, the academes,
From whence doth spring the true Promethean fire.
Love's Labour's Lost (1595) act 4, sc. 3, l. [302]; cf. **Shakespeare** 680:28

27 For valour, is not love a Hercules,
Still climbing trees in the Hesperides?
Love's Labour's Lost (1595) act 4, sc. 3, l. [340]

28 From women's eyes this doctrine I derive:
They sparkle still the right Promethean fire;
They are the books, the arts, the academes,
That show, contain, and nourish all the world.
Love's Labour's Lost (1595) act 4, sc. 3, l. [350]; cf. **Shakespeare** 680:26

29 They have been at a great feast of languages, and stolen the scraps.
Love's Labour's Lost (1595) act 5, sc. 1, l. [39]

30 Taffeta phrases, silken terms precise.
Love's Labour's Lost (1595) act 5, sc. 2, l. 407

1 Henceforth my wooing mind shall be expressed
In russet yeas and honest kersey noes.
Love's Labour's Lost (1595) act 5, sc. 2, l. 413

2 A jest's prosperity lies in the ear
Of him that hears it, never in the tongue
Of him that makes it.
Love's Labour's Lost (1595) act 5, sc. 2, l. [869]

3 When daisies pied and violets blue
And lady-smocks all silver-white
And cuckoo-buds of yellow hue
Do paint the meadows with delight,
The cuckoo then, on every tree,
Mocks married men.
Love's Labour's Lost (1595) act 5, sc. 2, l. [902]

4 When icicles hang by the wall,
And Dick the shepherd, blows his nail,
And Tom bears logs into the hall,
And milk comes frozen home in pail,
When blood is nipped and ways be foul,
Then nightly sings the staring owl,
Tu-who;
Tu-whit, tu-who—a merry note,
While greasy Joan doth keel the pot.
Love's Labour's Lost (1595) act 5, sc. 2, l. [920]

5 The words of Mercury are harsh after the songs of Apollo. You, that way: we, this way.
Love's Labour's Lost (1595) act 5, sc. 2, l. [938]

MACBETH

6 FIRST WITCH: When shall we three meet again
In thunder, lightning, or in rain?
SECOND WITCH: When the hurly-burly's done,
When the battle's lost and won.
THIRD WITCH: That will be ere the set of sun.
FIRST WITCH: Where the place?
SECOND WITCH: Upon the heath.
THIRD WITCH: There to meet with Macbeth.
FIRST WITCH: I come, Graymalkin!
SECOND WITCH: Paddock calls.
THIRD WITCH: Anon!
Macbeth (1606) act 1, sc. 1, l. 1

7 Fair is foul, and foul is fair:
Hover through the fog and filthy air.
Macbeth (1606) act 1, sc. 1, l. 11

8 What bloody man is that?
Macbeth (1606) act 1, sc. 2, l. 1

9 Till he unseamed him from the nave to the chaps,
And fixed his head upon our battlements.
Macbeth (1606) act 1, sc. 2, l. 22

10 Bellona's bridegroom, lapped in proof,
Confronted him with self-comparisons,
Point against point, rebellious arm 'gainst arm,
Curbing his lavish spirit.
Macbeth (1606) act 1, sc. 2, l. 55

11 A sailor's wife had chestnuts in her lap,
And munched, and munched, and munched: 'Give me,' quoth I:
'Aroint thee, witch!' the rump-fed ronyon cries.
Her husband's to Aleppo gone, master o' the Tiger:
But in a sieve I'll thither sail,
And, like a rat without a tail,
I'll do, I'll do, and I'll do.
Macbeth (1606) act 1, sc. 3, l. 4

12 Sleep shall neither night nor day
Hang upon his pent-house lid.
He shall live a man forbid.
Weary se'nnights nine times nine
Shall he dwindle, peak, and pine:
Though his bark cannot be lost,
Yet it shall be tempest-tost.
Macbeth (1606) act 1, sc. 3, l. 19

13 The weird sisters, hand in hand,
Posters of the sea and land,
Thus do go about, about.
Macbeth (1606) act 1, sc. 3, l. 32

14 So foul and fair a day I have not seen.
Macbeth (1606) act 1, sc. 3, l. 38

15 What are these,
So withered, and so wild in their attire,
That look not like th' inhabitants o' the earth,
And yet are on 't?
Macbeth (1606) act 1, sc. 3, l. 39

16 If you can look into the seeds of time,
And say which grain will grow and which will not,
Speak then to me, who neither beg nor fear
Your favours nor your hate.
Macbeth (1606) act 1, sc. 3, l. 58

17 Say, from whence
You owe this strange intelligence? or why
Upon this blasted heath you stop our way
With such prophetic greeting?
Macbeth (1606) act 1, sc. 3, l. 72

18 Or have we eaten on the insane root
That takes the reason prisoner?
Macbeth (1606) act 1, sc. 3, l. 84

19 What! can the devil speak true?
Macbeth (1606) act 1, sc. 3, l. 107

20 Two truths are told,
As happy prologues to the swelling act
Of the imperial theme.
Macbeth (1606) act 1, sc. 3, l. 127

21 Present fears
Are less than horrible imaginings;
My thought, whose murder yet is but fantastical,
Shakes so my single state of man that function
Is smothered in surmise, and nothing is
But what is not.
Macbeth (1606) act 1, sc. 3, l. 137

22 Come what come may,
Time and the hour runs through the roughest day.
Macbeth (1606) act 1, sc. 3, l. 146

23 MALCOLM: Nothing in his life
Became him like the leaving it: he died
As one that had been studied in his death
To throw away the dearest thing he owed
As 'twere a careless trifle.
DUNCAN: There's no art
To find the mind's construction in the face;
He was a gentleman on whom I built
An absolute trust.
Macbeth (1606) act 1, sc. 4, l. 7

1 Glamis thou art, and Cawdor; and shalt be
What thou art promised. Yet I do fear thy nature;
It is too full o' the milk of human kindness
To catch the nearest way; thou wouldst be great,
Art not without ambition; but without
The illness should attend it; what thou wouldst
highly,
That thou wouldst holily; wouldst not play false,
And yet wouldst wrongly win.
Macbeth (1606) act 1, sc. 5, l. [16]

2 The raven himself is hoarse
That croaks the fatal entrance of Duncan
Under my battlements. Come, you spirits
That tend on mortal thoughts! unsex me here,
And fill me from the crown to the toe top full
Of direst cruelty; make thick my blood,
Stop up the access and passage to remorse,
That no compunctious visitings of nature
Shake my fell purpose.
Macbeth (1606) act 1, sc. 5, l. [38]

3 Come to my woman's breasts,
And take my milk for gall, you murdering
ministers.
Macbeth (1606) act 1, sc. 5, l. [47]

4 Come, thick night,
And pall thee in the dunnest smoke of hell,
That my keen knife see not the wound it makes,
Nor heaven peep through the blanket of the dark,
To cry 'Hold, hold!'
Macbeth (1606) act 1, sc. 5, l. [50]

5 Your face, my thane, is as a book where men
May read strange matters. To beguile the time,
Look like the time; bear welcome in your eye,
Your hand, your tongue: look like the innocent
flower,
But be the serpent under't.
Macbeth (1606) act 1, sc. 5, l. [63]

6 This castle hath a pleasant seat; the air
Nimbly and sweetly recommends itself
Unto our gentle senses.
Macbeth (1606) act 1, sc. 6, l. 1

7 This guest of summer,
The temple-haunting martlet, does approve
By his loved mansionry that the heaven's breath
Smells wooingly here: no jutty, frieze,
Buttress, nor coign of vantage, but this bird
Hath made his pendent bed and procreant cradle:
Where they most breed and haunt, I have
observed,
The air is delicate.
Macbeth (1606) act 1, sc. 6, l. 3

8 If it were done when 'tis done, then 'twere well
It were done quickly: if the assassination
Could trammel up the consequence, and catch
With his surcease success; that but this blow
Might be the be-all and the end-all here,
But here, upon this bank and shoal of time,
We'd jump the life to come.
Macbeth (1606) act 1, sc. 7, l. 1

9 We but teach
Bloody instructions, which, being taught, return,
To plague the inventor.
Macbeth (1606) act 1, sc. 7, l. 8

10 Besides, this Duncan
Hath borne his faculties so meek, hath been
So clear in his great office, that his virtues
Will plead like angels trumpet-tongued, against
The deep damnation of his taking-off.
Macbeth (1606) act 1, sc. 7, l. 16

11 And pity, like a naked new-born babe,
Striding the blast, or heaven's cherubim, horsed
Upon the sightless couriers of the air,
Shall blow the horrid deed in every eye,
That tears shall drown the wind.
Macbeth (1606) act 1, sc. 7, l. 21

12 I have no spur
To prick the sides of my intent, but only
Vaulting ambition, which o'erleaps itself,
And falls on the other.
Macbeth (1606) act 1, sc. 7, l. 25

13 We will proceed no further in this business:
He hath honoured me of late; and I have bought
Golden opinions from all sorts of people.
Macbeth (1606) act 1, sc. 7, l. 31

14 Was the hope drunk,
Wherein you dressed yourself? hath it slept since,
And wakes it now, to look so green and pale
At what it did so freely? From this time
Such I account thy love.
Macbeth (1606) act 1, sc. 7, l. 35

15 Letting 'I dare not' wait upon 'I would,'
Like the poor cat i' the adage?
Macbeth (1606) act 1, sc. 7, l. 44

16 I dare do all that may become a man;
Who dares do more is none.
Macbeth (1606) act 1, sc. 7, l. 46

17 LADY MACBETH: I have given suck, and know
How tender 'tis to love the babe that milks me:
I would, while it was smiling in my face,
Have plucked my nipple from his boneless gums,
And dash'd the brains out, had I so sworn as you
Have done to this.
MACBETH: If we should fail,—
LADY MACBETH: We fail!
But screw your courage to the sticking-place,
And we'll not fail.
Macbeth (1606) act 1, sc. 7, l. 54

18 Bring forth men-children only;
For thy undaunted mettle should compose
Nothing but males.
Macbeth (1606) act 1, sc. 7, l. 72

19 False face must hide what the false heart doth
know.
Macbeth (1606) act 1, sc. 7, l. 82

20 There's husbandry in heaven;
Their candles are all out.
Macbeth (1606) act 2, sc. 1, l. 4

21 Is this a dagger which I see before me,
The handle toward my hand? Come, let me clutch
thee:
I have thee not, and yet I see thee still.

Art thou not, fatal vision, sensible
To feeling as to sight? or art thou but
A dagger of the mind, a false creation,
Proceeding from the heat-oppressed brain?
Macbeth (1606) act 2, sc. 1, l. 33

1 Witchcraft celebrates
Pale Hecate's offerings; and withered murder,
Alarumed by his sentinel, the wolf,
Whose howl's his watch, thus with his stealthy pace,
With Tarquin's ravishing strides, toward his design
Moves like a ghost.
Macbeth (1606) act 2, sc. 1, l. 49

2 The bell invites me.
Hear it not, Duncan; for it is a knell
That summons thee to heaven or to hell.
Macbeth (1606) act 2, sc. 1, l. 62

3 That which hath made them drunk hath made me bold,
What hath quenched them hath given me fire.
Macbeth (1606) act 2, sc. 2, l. 1

4 It was the owl that shrieked, the fatal bellman,
Which gives the stern'st good-night.
Macbeth (1606) act 2, sc. 2, l. 4

5 The attempt and not the deed,
Confounds us.
Macbeth (1606) act 2, sc. 2, l. 12

6 Had he not resembled
My father as he slept I had done't.
Macbeth (1606) act 2, sc. 2, l. 14

7 . . . Wherefore could not I pronounce 'Amen'?
I had most need of blessing, and 'Amen'
Stuck in my throat.
Macbeth (1606) act 2, sc. 2, l. 32

8 Methought I heard a voice cry, 'Sleep no more!
Macbeth does murder sleep,' the innocent sleep,
Sleep that knits up the ravelled sleave of care,
The death of each day's life, sore labour's bath,
Balm of hurt minds, great nature's second course,
Chief nourisher in life's feast.
Macbeth (1606) act 2, sc. 2, l. 36

9 Glamis hath murdered sleep, and therefore Cawdor
Shall sleep no more, Macbeth shall sleep no more!
Macbeth (1606) act 2, sc. 2, l. 43

10 MACBETH: I am afraid to think what I have done;
Look on't again I dare not.
LADY MACBETH: Infirm of purpose!
Give me the daggers. The sleeping and the dead
Are but as pictures; 'tis the eye of childhood
That fears a painted devil.
If he do bleed
I'll gild the faces of the grooms withal;
For it must seem their guilt.
Macbeth (1606) act 2, sc. 2, l. 53

11 Will all great Neptune's ocean wash this blood
Clean from my hand? No, this my hand will rather
The multitudinous seas incarnadine,
Making the green one red.
Macbeth (1606) act 2, sc. 2, l. 61

12 A little water clears us of this deed.
Macbeth (1606) act 2, sc. 2, l. 68

13 Here's a knocking, indeed! If a man were porter of hell-gate he should have old turning the key. Knock, knock, knock! Who's there i' the name of Beelzebub? Here's a farmer that hanged himself on the expectation of plenty.
Macbeth (1606) act 2, sc. 3, l. 1

14 This place is too cold for hell. I'll devil-porter it no further: I had thought to have let in some of all professions, that go the primrose way to the everlasting bonfire.
Macbeth (1606) act 2, sc. 3, l. [19]; cf. **Shakespeare** 656:5

15 PORTER: Drink, sir, is a great provoker of three things.
MACDUFF: What three things does drink especially provoke?
PORTER: Marry, sir, nose-painting, sleep, and urine. Lechery, sir, it provokes, and unprovokes; it provokes the desire, but it takes away the performance.
Macbeth (1606) act 2, sc. 3, l. [28]

16 The labour we delight in physics pain.
Macbeth (1606) act 2, sc. 3, l. [56]

17 The night has been unruly: where we lay
Our chimneys were blown down; and, as they say,
Lamentings heard i' the air; strange screams of death,
And prophesying with accents terrible
Of dire combustion and confused events
New-hatched to the woeful time. The obscure bird
Clamoured the live-long night: some say the earth
Was feverous and did shake.
Macbeth (1606) act 2, sc. 3, l. [60]

18 Confusion now hath made his masterpiece!
Most sacrilegious murder hath broke ope
The Lord's anointed temple, and stole thence
The life o' the building!
Macbeth (1606) act 2, sc. 3, l. [72]

19 Shake off this downy sleep, death's counterfeit,
And look on death itself! up, up, and see
The great doom's image!
Macbeth (1606) act 2, sc. 3, l. [83]

20 MACDUFF: Our royal master's murdered!
LADY MACBETH: Woe, alas!
What! in our house?
Macbeth (1606) act 2, sc. 3, l. [95]

21 Had I but died an hour before this chance,
I had lived a blessed time.
Macbeth (1606) act 2, sc. 3, l. [98]

22 Where we are,
There's daggers in men's smiles: the near in blood,
The nearer bloody.
Macbeth (1606) act 2, sc. 3, l. [146]

23 A falcon, towering in her pride of place,
Was by a mousing owl hawked at and killed.
Macbeth (1606) act 2, sc. 4, l. 12

24 Thou hast it now: King, Cawdor, Glamis, all,
As the weird women promised; and, I fear,

Thou play'dst most foully for't.
Macbeth (1606) act 3, sc. 1, l. 1

1 BANQUO: Go not my horse the better,
I must become a borrower of the night
For a dark hour or twain.
MACBETH: Fail not our feast.
Macbeth (1606) act 3, sc. 1, l. 26

2 FIRST MURDERER: We are men, my liege.
MACBETH: Ay, in the catalogue ye go for men,
As hounds and greyhounds, mongrels, spaniels, curs,
Shoughs, water-rugs, and demi-wolves are clipt
All by the name of dogs.
Macbeth (1606) act 3, sc. 1, l. 90

3 Leave no rubs nor botches in the work.
Macbeth (1606) act 3, sc. 1, l. 134

4 LADY MACBETH: Things without all remedy
Should be without regard: what's done is done.
MACBETH: We have scotched the snake, not killed it:
She'll close and be herself, whilst our poor malice
Remains in danger of her former tooth.
Macbeth (1606) act 3, sc. 2, l. 11

5 Duncan is in his grave;
After life's fitful fever he sleeps well;
Treason has done his worst: nor steel, nor poison,
Malice domestic, foreign levy, nothing,
Can touch him further.
Macbeth (1606) act 3, sc. 2, l. 22

6 Ere the bat hath flown
His cloistered flight, ere, to black Hecate's summons
The shard-borne beetle with his drowsy hums
Hath rung night's yawning peal, there shall be done
A deed of dreadful note.
Macbeth (1606) act 3, sc. 2, l. 40

7 Come, seeling night,
Scarf up the tender eye of pitiful day,
And with thy bloody and invisible hand,
Cancel and tear to pieces that great bond
Which keeps me pale! Light thickens, and the crow
Makes wing to the rooky wood;
Good things of day begin to droop and drowse,
Whiles night's black agents to their preys do rouse.
Macbeth (1606) act 3, sc. 2, l. 46

8 The west yet glimmers with some streaks of day:
Now spurs the lated traveller apace
To gain the timely inn.
Macbeth (1606) act 3, sc. 3, l. 5

9 But now I am cabined, cribbed, confined, bound in
To saucy doubts and fears.
Macbeth (1606) act 3, sc. 4, l. 24

10 Now good digestion wait on appetite,
And health on both!
Macbeth (1606) act 3, sc. 4, l. 38

11 Thou canst not say I did it: never shake
Thy gory locks at me.
Macbeth (1606) act 3, sc. 4, l. 50

12 What man dare, I dare;
Approach thou like the rugged Russian bear,
The armed rhinoceros or the Hyrcan tiger,
Take any shape but that, and my firm nerves
Shall never tremble.
Macbeth (1606) act 3, sc. 4, l. 99

13 Stand not upon the order of your going.
Macbeth (1606) act 3, sc. 4, l. 119

14 It will have blood, they say; blood will have blood:
Stones have been known to move and trees to speak;
Augurs and understood relations have
By maggot-pies and choughs and rooks brought forth
The secret'st man of blood.
Macbeth (1606) act 3, sc. 4, l. 122; cf. **Proverbs** 596:32

15 I am in blood
Stepped in so far that, should I wade no more,
Returning were as tedious as go o'er.
Macbeth (1606) act 3, sc. 4, l. 136

16 You lack the season of all natures, sleep.
Macbeth (1606) act 3, sc. 4, l. 141

17 Round about the cauldron go;
In the poisoned entrails throw.
Toad, that under cold stone
Days and nights hast thirty-one
Sweltered venom sleeping got,
Boil thou first i' the charmèd pot.
Double, double toil and trouble;
Fire burn and cauldron bubble.
Macbeth (1606) act 4, sc. 1, l. 4

18 Eye of newt, and toe of frog,
Wool of bat, and tongue of dog,
Adder's fork, and blind-worm's sting,
Lizard's leg, and howlet's wing,
For a charm of powerful trouble,
Like a hell-broth boil and bubble.
Macbeth (1606) act 4, sc. 1, l. 14

19 Liver of blaspheming Jew,
Gall of goat, and slips of yew
Slivered in the moon's eclipse,
Nose of Turk, and Tartar's lips,
Finger of birth-strangled babe
Ditch-delivered by a drab,
Make the gruel thick and slab.
Macbeth (1606) act 4, sc. 1, l. 26

20 By the pricking of my thumbs,
Something wicked this way comes.
Macbeth (1606) act 4, sc. 1, l. 44

21 MACBETH: How now, you secret, black, and midnight hags!
What is't you do?
WITCHES: A deed without a name.
Macbeth (1606) act 4, sc. 1, l. 48

22 Be bloody, bold, and resolute; laugh to scorn
The power of man, for none of woman born
Shall harm Macbeth.
Macbeth (1606) act 4, sc. 1, l. 79

1 But yet, I'll make assurance double sure,
And take a bond of fate.
Macbeth (1606) act 4, sc. 1, l. 83

2 Macbeth shall never vanquished be until
Great Birnam wood to high Dunsinane hill
Shall come against him.
Macbeth (1606) act 4, sc. 1, l. 92

3 His flight was madness: when our actions do not,
Our fears do make us traitors.
Macbeth (1606) act 4, sc. 2, l. 3

4 He loves us not;
He wants the natural touch.
Macbeth (1606) act 4, sc. 2, l. 8

5 SON: And must they all be hanged that swear and lie?
LADY MACDUFF: Every one.
SON: Who must hang them?
LADY MACDUFF: Why, the honest men.
SON: Then the liars and swearers are fools, for there are liars and swearers enow to beat the honest men and hang up them.
Macbeth (1606) act 4, sc. 2, l. [51]

6 Stands Scotland where it did?
Macbeth (1606) act 4, sc. 3, l. 164

7 Give sorrow words: the grief that does not speak
Whispers the o'er-fraught heart, and bids it break.
Macbeth (1606) act 4, sc. 3, l. 209

8 He has no children. All my pretty ones?
Did you say all? O hell-kite! All?
What! all my pretty chickens and their dam,
At one fell swoop?
Macbeth (1606) act 4, sc. 3, l. 216

9 Out, damned spot! out, I say! One; two: why then, 'tis time to do't. Hell is murky! Fie, my lord, fie! a soldier, and afeard? What need we fear who knows it, when none can call our power to account? Yet who would have thought the old man to have had so much blood in him?
Macbeth (1606) act 5, sc. 1, l. [38]

10 The Thane of Fife had a wife: where is she now?
Macbeth (1606) act 5, sc. 1, l. [46]

11 All the perfumes of Arabia will not sweeten this little hand.
Macbeth (1606) act 5, sc. 1, l. [56]

12 What's done cannot be undone.
Macbeth (1606) act 5, sc. 1, l. [74]

13 Foul whisperings are abroad. Unnatural deeds
Do breed unnatural troubles; infected minds
To their deaf pillows will discharge their secrets;
More needs she the divine than the physician.
Macbeth (1606) act 5, sc. 1, l. [78]

14 Now does he feel his title
Hang loose about him, like a giant's robe
Upon a dwarfish thief.
Macbeth (1606) act 5, sc. 2, l. 20

15 Bring me no more reports; let them fly all:
Till Birnam wood remove to Dunsinane
I cannot taint with fear.
Macbeth (1606) act 5, sc. 3, l. 1

16 The devil damn thee black, thou cream-faced loon!
Where gott'st thou that goose look?
Macbeth (1606) act 5, sc. 3, l. 11

17 I have lived long enough: my way of life
Is fall'n into the sear, the yellow leaf;
And that which should accompany old age,
As honour, love, obedience, troops of friends,
I must not look to have; but, in their stead,
Curses, not loud but deep, mouth-honour, breath,
Which the poor heart would fain deny, and dare not.
Macbeth (1606) act 5, sc. 3, l. 22; cf. **Byron** 177:3, 178:22

18 Canst thou not minister to a mind diseased?
Pluck from the memory a rooted sorrow,
Raze out the written troubles of the brain,
And with some sweet oblivious antidote
Cleanse the stuffed bosom of that perilous stuff
Which weighs upon the heart?
Macbeth (1606) act 5, sc. 3, l. 37

19 Throw physic to the dogs; I'll none of it.
Macbeth (1606) act 5, sc. 3, l. 47

20 The cry is still, 'They come'.
Macbeth (1606) act 5, sc. 5, l. 2

21 I have almost forgot the taste of fears.
The time has been my senses would have cooled
To hear a night-shriek, and my fell of hair
Would at a dismal treatise rouse and stir
As life were in't. I have supped full with horrors;
Direness, familiar to my slaughterous thoughts,
Cannot once start me.
Macbeth (1606) act 5, sc. 5, l. 9

22 She should have died hereafter;
There would have been a time for such a word,
To-morrow, and to-morrow, and to-morrow,
Creeps in this petty pace from day to day,
To the last syllable of recorded time;
And all our yesterdays have lighted fools
The way to dusty death. Out, out, brief candle!
Life's but a walking shadow, a poor player,
That struts and frets his hour upon the stage,
And then is heard no more; it is a tale
Told by an idiot, full of sound and fury,
Signifying nothing.
Macbeth (1606) act 5, sc. 5, l. 16

23 I 'gin to be aweary of the sun,
And wish the estate o' the world were now undone.
Ring the alarum-bell! Blow, wind! come, wrack!
At least we'll die with harness on our back.
Macbeth (1606) act 5, sc. 5, l. 49

24 I bear a charmèd life, which must not yield
To one of woman born.
Macbeth (1606) act 5, sc. 7, l. 41

25 Macduff was from his mother's womb
Untimely ripped.
Macbeth (1606) act 5, sc. 7, l. 44

26 Lay on, Macduff;
And damned be him that first cries, 'Hold, enough!'
Macbeth (1606) act 5, sc. 7, l. 62

MEASURE FOR MEASURE

1 Now, as fond fathers,
Having bound up the threat'ning twigs of birch,
Only to stick it in their children's sight
For terror, not to use, in time the rod
Becomes more mocked than feared; so our decrees,
Dead to infliction, to themselves are dead,
And liberty plucks justice by the nose;
The baby beats the nurse, and quite athwart
Goes all decorum.
Measure for Measure (1604) act 1, sc. 3, l. 23

2 I hold you as a thing enskyed and sainted;
By your renouncement an immortal spirit,
And to be talked with in sincerity,
As with a saint.
Measure for Measure (1604) act 1, sc. 4, l. 34

3 A man whose blood
Is very snow-broth; one who never feels
The wanton stings and motions of the sense.
Measure for Measure (1604) act 1, sc. 4, l. 57

4 We must not make a scarecrow of the law,
Setting it up to fear the birds of prey,
And let it keep one shape, till custom make it
Their perch and not their terror.
Measure for Measure (1604) act 2, sc. 1, l. 1

5 'Tis one thing to be tempted, Escalus,
Another thing to fall. I not deny,
The jury, passing on the prisoner's life,
May in the sworn twelve have a thief or two
Guiltier than him they try.
Measure for Measure (1604) act 2, sc. 1, l. 17

6 This will last out a night in Russia,
When nights are longest there.
Measure for Measure (1604) act 2, sc. 1, l. [144]

7 Condemn the fault and not the actor of it?
Measure for Measure (1604) act 2, sc. 2, l. 37

8 No ceremony that to great ones 'longs,
Not the king's crown, nor the deputed sword,
The marshal's truncheon, nor the judge's robe,
Become them with one half so good a grace
As mercy does.
Measure for Measure (1604) act 2, sc. 2, l. 59

9 O! it is excellent
To have a giant's strength, but it is tyrannous
To use it like a giant.
Measure for Measure (1604) act 2, sc. 2, l. 107

10 Man, proud man,
Drest in a little brief authority,
Most ignorant of what he's most assured,
His glassy essence, like an angry ape,
Plays such fantastic tricks before high heaven,
As make the angels weep.
Measure for Measure (1604) act 2, sc. 2, l. 117

11 That in the captain's but a choleric word,
Which in the soldier is flat blasphemy.
Measure for Measure (1604) act 2, sc. 2, l. 130

12 Is this her fault or mine?
The tempter or the tempted, who sins most?
Measure for Measure (1604) act 2, sc. 2, l. 162

13 O cunning enemy, that, to catch a saint,
With saints dost bait thy hook! Most dangerous
Is that temptation that doth goad us on
To sin in loving virtue; never could the strumpet,
With all her double vigour, art and nature,
Once stir my temper; but this virtuous maid
Subdues me quite. Ever till now
When men were fond, I smiled and wondered how.
Measure for Measure (1604) act 2, sc. 2, l. 186

14 Might there not be a charity in sin
To save this brother's life?
Measure for Measure (1604) act 2, sc. 4, l. 64

15 The miserable have no other medicine
But only hope.
Measure for Measure (1604) act 3, sc. 1, l. 2

16 Be absolute for death; either death or life
Shall thereby be the sweeter. Reason thus with life:
If I do lose thee, I do lose a thing
That none but fools would keep: a breath thou art.
Measure for Measure (1604) act 3, sc. 1, l. 5

17 If I must die,
I will encounter darkness as a bride,
And hug it in mine arms.
Measure for Measure (1604) act 3, sc. 1, l. 81

18 CLAUDIO: Death is a fearful thing.
ISABELLA: And shamed life a hateful.
CLAUDIO: Ay, but to die, and go we know not where;
To lie in cold obstruction and to rot;
This sensible warm motion to become
A kneaded clod; and the delighted spirit
To bathe in fiery floods or to reside
In thrilling region of thick-ribbèd ice.
Measure for Measure (1604) act 3, sc. 1, l. 114

19 There, at the moated grange, resides this dejected Mariana.
Measure for Measure (1604) act 3, sc. 1, l. [279]; cf. **Tennyson** 763:19

20 When he makes water his urine is congealed ice.
Measure for Measure (1604) act 3, sc. 2, l. [119]

21 Take, O take those lips away,
That so sweetly were forsworn;
And those eyes, the break of day,
Lights that do mislead the morn.
Measure for Measure (1604) act 4, sc. 1, l. 1

22 Music oft hath such a charm
To make bad good, and good provoke to harm.
Measure for Measure (1604) act 4, sc. 1, l. 16

23 The old fantastical Duke of dark corners.
Measure for Measure (1604) act 4, sc. 3, l. 156

24 I am a kind of burr; I shall stick.
Measure for Measure (1604) act 4, sc. 3, l. [193]

25 Haste still pays haste, and leisure answers leisure;
Like doth quit like, and Measure still for Measure.
Measure for Measure (1604) act 5, sc. 1, l. [411]

26 They say best men are moulded out of faults,
And, for the most, become much more the better
For being a little bad: so may my husband.
Measure for Measure (1604) act 5, sc. 1, l. [440]

THE MERCHANT OF VENICE

1 In sooth I know not why I am so sad:
It wearies me; you say it wearies you.
The Merchant of Venice (1596–8) act 1, sc. 1, l. 1

2 I hold the world but as the world, Gratiano;
A stage where every man must play a part,
And mine a sad one.
The Merchant of Venice (1596–8) act 1, sc. 1, l. 77

3 I am Sir Oracle,
And when I ope my lips let no dog bark!
The Merchant of Venice (1596–8) act 1, sc. 1, l. 93

4 Fish not, with this melancholy bait,
For this fool gudgeon, this opinion.
The Merchant of Venice (1596–8) act 1, sc. 1, l. 101

5 In Belmont is a lady richly left,
And she is fair, and fairer than the word,
Of wondrous virtues.
The Merchant of Venice (1596–8) act 1, sc. 1, l. [162]

6 They are as sick that surfeit with too much, as they that starve with nothing.
The Merchant of Venice (1596–8) act 1, sc. 2, l. [5]

7 If to do were as easy as to know what were good to do, chapels had been churches, and poor men's cottages princes' palaces. It is a good divine that follows his own instructions; I can easier teach twenty what were good to be done, than be one of the twenty to follow mine own teaching.
The Merchant of Venice (1596–8) act 1, sc. 2, l. [13]

8 God made him, and therefore let him pass for a man.
The Merchant of Venice (1596–8) act 1, sc. 2, l. [59]

9 I think he bought his doublet in Italy, his round hose in France, his bonnet in Germany, and his behaviour everywhere.
The Merchant of Venice (1596–8) act 1, sc. 2, l. [78]

10 Ships are but boards, sailors but men; there be land-rats and water-rats, land-thieves and water-thieves.
The Merchant of Venice (1596–8) act 1, sc. 3, l. [22]

11 I will buy with you, sell with you, talk with you, walk with you, and so following; but I will not eat with you, drink with you, nor pray with you.
What news on the Rialto?
The Merchant of Venice (1596–8) act 1, sc. 3, l. [36]

12 How like a fawning publican he looks!
I hate him for he is a Christian;
But more for that in low simplicity
He lends out money gratis, and brings down
The rate of usance here with us in Venice.
The Merchant of Venice (1596–8) act 1, sc. 3, l. [42]

13 If I can catch him once upon the hip,
I will feed fat the ancient grudge I bear him.
He hates our sacred nation, and he rails,
Even there where merchants most do congregate,
On me, my bargains, and my well-won thrift,
Which he calls interest.
The Merchant of Venice (1596–8) act 1, sc. 3, l. [47]

14 The devil can cite Scripture for his purpose.
The Merchant of Venice (1596–8) act 1, sc. 3, l. [99]

15 Still have I borne it with a patient shrug,
For sufferance is the badge of all our tribe.
You call me misbeliever, cut-throat dog,
And spit upon my Jewish gabardine,
And all for use of that which is mine own.
The Merchant of Venice (1596–8) act 1, sc. 3, l. [110]

16 Mislike me not for my complexion,
The shadowed livery of the burnished sun,
To whom I am a neighbour and near bred.
The Merchant of Venice (1596–8) act 2, sc. 1, l. 1

17 My conscience says, 'Launcelot, budge not.'
'Budge,' says the fiend. 'Budge not,' says my conscience. 'Conscience,' say I, 'you counsel well;' 'fiend,' say I, 'you counsel well.'
The Merchant of Venice (1596–8) act 2, sc. 2, l. [19]

18 It is a wise father that knows his own child.
The Merchant of Venice (1596–8) act 2, sc. 2, l. [83]; cf. **Proverbs** 604:6

19 Truth will come to light; murder cannot be hid long.
The Merchant of Venice (1596–8) act 2, sc. 2, l. [86]

20 There is some ill a-brewing towards my rest.
For I did dream of money-bags to-night.
The Merchant of Venice (1596–8) act 2, sc. 5, l. 17

21 Let not the sound of shallow foppery enter
My sober house.
The Merchant of Venice (1596–8) act 2, sc. 5, l. [35]

22 What! must I hold a candle to my shames?
The Merchant of Venice (1596–8) act 2, sc. 6, l. 41

23 My daughter! O my ducats! O my daughter!
Fled with a Christian! O my Christian ducats!
Justice! the law! my ducats, and my daughter!
The Merchant of Venice (1596–8) act 2, sc. 8, l. 15

24 Like the martlet,
Builds in the weather on the outward wall,
Even in the force and road of casualty.
The Merchant of Venice (1596–8) act 2, sc. 9, l. 28

25 The portrait of a blinking idiot.
The Merchant of Venice (1596–8) act 2, sc. 9, l. 54

26 Thus hath the candle singed the moth.
O, these deliberate fools!
The Merchant of Venice (1596–8) act 2, sc. 9, l. 79

27 The Goodwins, I think they call the place; a very dangerous flat, and fatal, where the carcasses of many a tall ship lie buried, as they say, if my gossip Report be an honest woman of her word.
The Merchant of Venice (1596–8) act 3, sc. 1, l. [4]

28 Let him look to his bond.
The Merchant of Venice (1596–8) act 3, sc. 1, l. [51]

29 Hath not a Jew eyes? hath not a Jew hands, organs, dimensions, senses, affections, passions?
The Merchant of Venice (1596–8) act 3, sc. 1, l. [63]

30 If you prick us, do we not bleed? if you tickle us, do we not laugh? if you poison us, do we not die? and if you wrong us, shall we not revenge?
The Merchant of Venice (1596–8) act 3, sc. 1, l. [69]

31 The villainy you teach me I will execute, and it shall go hard but I will better the instruction.
The Merchant of Venice (1596–8) act 3, sc. 1, l. [76]

1 He makes a swan-like end,
Fading in music.
The Merchant of Venice (1596–8) act 3, sc. 2, l. 44

2 Tell me where is fancy bred.
Or in the heart or in the head?
The Merchant of Venice (1596–8) act 3, sc. 2, l. 63

3 So may the outward shows be least themselves:
The world is still deceived with ornament.
The Merchant of Venice (1596–8) act 3, sc. 2, l. 73

4 . . . An unlessoned girl, unschooled, unpractised;
Happy in this, she is not yet so old
But she may learn; happier than this,
She is not bred so dull but she can learn.
The Merchant of Venice (1596–8) act 3, sc. 2, l. 160

5 I will have my bond.
The Merchant of Venice (1596–8) act 3, sc. 3, l. 17

6 I pray thee, understand a plain man in his plain meaning.
The Merchant of Venice (1596–8) act 3, sc. 5, l. [63]

7 I am not bound to please thee with my answer.
The Merchant of Venice (1596–8) act 4, sc. 1, l. 65

8 I am a tainted wether of the flock,
Meetest for death: the weakest kind of fruit
Drops earliest to the ground.
The Merchant of Venice (1596–8) act 4, sc. 1, l. 114

9 I never knew so young a body with so old a head.
The Merchant of Venice (1596–8) act 4, sc. 1, l. [163]

10 The quality of mercy is not strained,
It droppeth as the gentle rain from heaven
Upon the place beneath: it is twice blessed;
It blesseth him that gives and him that takes:
'Tis mightiest in the mightiest: it becomes
The thronèd monarch better than his crown.
The Merchant of Venice (1596–8) act 4, sc. 1, l. [182]

11 Though justice be thy plea, consider this,
That in the course of justice none of us
Should see salvation: we do pray for mercy,
And that same prayer doth teach us all to render
The deeds of mercy.
The Merchant of Venice (1596–8) act 4, sc. 1, l. [197]

12 My deeds upon my head! I crave the law.
The Merchant of Venice (1596–8) act 4, sc. 1, l. [206]

13 Wrest once the law to your authority:
To do a great right, do a little wrong.
The Merchant of Venice (1596–8) act 4, sc. 1, l. [215]

14 A Daniel come to judgement! yea, a Daniel!
The Merchant of Venice (1596–8) act 4, sc. 1, l. [223]

15 The court awards it, and the law doth give it.
The Merchant of Venice (1596–8) act 4, sc. 1, l. [301]

16 Nay, take my life and all; pardon not that:
You take my house when you do take the prop
That doth sustain my house; you take my life
When you do take the means whereby I live.
The Merchant of Venice (1596–8) act 4, sc. 1, l. [375]

17 He is well paid that is well satisfied.
The Merchant of Venice (1596–8) act 4, sc. 1, l. [416]

18 You taught me first to beg, and now methinks
You teach me how a beggar should be answered.
The Merchant of Venice (1596–8) act 4, sc. 1, l. [440]

19 The moon shines bright: in such a night as this . . .
Troilus methinks mounted the Troyan walls,
And sighed his soul toward the Grecian tents,
Where Cressid lay that night.
The Merchant of Venice (1596–8) act 5, sc. 1, l. 1

20 In such a night
Stood Dido with a willow in her hand
Upon the wild sea-banks, and waft her love
To come again to Carthage.
The Merchant of Venice (1596–8) act 5, sc. 1, l. 9

21 How sweet the moonlight sleeps upon this bank!
Here will we sit, and let the sounds of music
Creep in our ears; soft stillness and the night
Become the touches of sweet harmony.
The Merchant of Venice (1596–8) act 5, sc. 1, l. 54

22 Look, how the floor of heaven
Is thick inlaid with patines of bright gold.
The Merchant of Venice (1596–8) act 5, sc. 1, l. 58

23 But in this motion like an angel sings
Still quiring to the young-eyed cherubins.
The Merchant of Venice (1596–8) act 5, sc. 1, l. 61

24 I am never merry when I hear sweet music.
The Merchant of Venice (1596–8) act 5, sc. 1, l. 69

25 The man that hath no music in himself,
Nor is not moved with concord of sweet sounds,
Is fit for treasons, stratagems, and spoils.
The Merchant of Venice (1596–8) act 5, sc. 1, l. 79

26 How far that little candle throws his beams!
So shines a good deed in a naughty world.
The Merchant of Venice (1596–8) act 5, sc. 1, l. 90

27 The nightingale, if she should sing by day,
When every goose is cackling, would be thought
No better a musician than the wren.
How many things by season seasoned are
To their right praise and true perfection!
The Merchant of Venice (1596–8) act 5, sc. 1, l. 104

28 This night methinks is but the daylight sick.
The Merchant of Venice (1596–8) act 5, sc. 1, l. 124

29 These blessed candles of the night.
The Merchant of Venice (1596–8) act 5, sc. 1, l. 220

THE MERRY WIVES OF WINDSOR

30 I will make a Star-Chamber matter of it.
The Merry Wives of Windsor (1597) act 1, sc. 1, l. 1

31 She has brown hair, and speaks small like a woman.
The Merry Wives of Windsor (1597) act 1, sc. 1, l. [48]

32 Here will be an old abusing of God's patience, and the king's English.
The Merry Wives of Windsor (1597) act 1, sc. 4, l. [5]

33 We burn daylight.
The Merry Wives of Windsor (1597) act 2, sc. 1, l. [54]

34 Why, then the world's mine oyster,
Which I with sword will open.
The Merry Wives of Windsor (1597) act 2, sc. 2, l. 2

35 O, what a world of vile ill-favoured faults
Looks handsome in three hundred pounds a year!
The Merry Wives of Windsor (1597) act 3, sc. 4, l. [32]

1 There is divinity in odd numbers, either in nativity, chance or death.
The Merry Wives of Windsor (1597) act 5, sc. 1, l. 3

A MIDSUMMER NIGHT'S DREAM

2 To live a barren sister all your life,
Chanting faint hymns to the cold fruitless moon.
A Midsummer Night's Dream (1595–6) act 1, sc. 1, l. 72

3 But earthlier happy is the rose distilled,
Than that which withering on the virgin thorn
Grows, lives, and dies, in single blessedness.
A Midsummer Night's Dream (1595–6) act 1, sc. 1, l. 76

4 The course of true love never did run smooth.
A Midsummer Night's Dream (1595–6) act 1, sc. 1, l. 134

5 Swift as a shadow, short as any dream,
Brief as the lightning in the collied night.
A Midsummer Night's Dream (1595–6) act 1, sc. 1, l. 144

6 So quick bright things come to confusion.
A Midsummer Night's Dream (1595–6) act 1, sc. 1, l. 149

7 Things base and vile, holding no quantity,
Love can transpose to form and dignity.
Love looks not with the eyes, but with the mind,
And therefore is winged Cupid painted blind.
A Midsummer Night's Dream (1595–6) act 1, sc. 1, l. 232

8 The most lamentable comedy, and most cruel death of Pyramus and Thisby.
A Midsummer Night's Dream (1595–6) act 1, sc. 2, l. [11]

9 Masters, spread yourselves.
A Midsummer Night's Dream (1595–6) act 1, sc. 2, l. [16]

10 I could play Ercles rarely, or a part to tear a cat in, to make all split.
A Midsummer Night's Dream (1595–6) act 1, sc. 2, l. [31]

11 This is Ercles' vein, a tyrant's vein.
A Midsummer Night's Dream (1595–6) act 1, sc. 2, l. [43]

12 Nay, faith, let me not play a woman; I have a beard coming.
A Midsummer Night's Dream (1595–6) act 1, sc. 2, l. [50]

13 I will roar you as gently as any sucking dove; I will roar you as 'twere any nightingale.
A Midsummer Night's Dream (1595–6) act 1, sc. 2, l. [85]

14 Pyramus is a sweet-faced man; a proper man, as one shall see in a summer's day.
A Midsummer Night's Dream (1595–6) act 1, sc. 2, l. [89]

15 Hold, or cut bow-strings.
A Midsummer Night's Dream (1595–6) act 1, sc. 2, l. [115]

16 PUCK: How now, spirit! whither wander you?
FAIRY: Over hill, over dale,
Thorough bush, thorough brier,
Over park, over pale,
Thorough flood, thorough fire,
I do wander everywhere,
Swifter than the moone's sphere;
And I serve the fairy queen.
A Midsummer Night's Dream (1595–6) act 2, sc. 1, l. 1

17 The cowslips tall her pensioners be;
In their gold coats spots you see;
Those be rubies, fairy favours,
In those freckles live their savours:
I must go seek some dew-drops here,
And hang a pearl in every cowslip's ear.
A Midsummer Night's Dream (1595–6) act 2, sc. 1, l. 10

18 The wisest aunt, telling the saddest tale.
A Midsummer Night's Dream (1595–6) act 2, sc. 1, l. 51

19 Ill met by moonlight, proud Titania.
A Midsummer Night's Dream (1595–6) act 2, sc. 1, l. 60

20 The fold stands empty in the drownèd field,
And crows are fatted with the murrion flock;
The nine men's morris is filled up with mud.
A Midsummer Night's Dream (1595–6) act 2, sc. 1, l. 96

21 Therefore the moon, the governess of floods,
Pale in her anger, washes all the air,
That rheumatic diseases do abound:
And thorough this distemperature we see
The seasons alter: hoary-headed frosts
Fall in the fresh lap of the crimson rose.
A Midsummer Night's Dream (1595–6) act 2, sc. 1, l. 103

22 Since once I sat upon a promontory,
And heard a mermaid on a dolphin's back
Uttering such dulcet and harmonious breath,
That the rude sea grew civil at her song,
And certain stars shot madly from their spheres,
To hear the sea-maid's music.
A Midsummer Night's Dream (1595–6) act 2, sc. 1, l. 149

23 And the imperial votaress passed on,
In maiden meditation, fancy-free.
Yet marked I where the bolt of Cupid fell:
It fell upon a little western flower,
Before milk-white, now purple with love's wound,
And maidens call it, Love-in-idleness.
A Midsummer Night's Dream (1595–6) act 2, sc. 1, l. 163

24 I'll put a girdle round about the earth
In forty minutes.
A Midsummer Night's Dream (1595–6) act 2, sc. 1, l. 175

25 I know a bank whereon the wild thyme blows,
Where oxlips and the nodding violet grows
Quite over-canopied with luscious woodbine,
With sweet musk-roses, and with eglantine.
A Midsummer Night's Dream (1595–6) act 2, sc. 1, l. 249

26 And there the snake throws her enamelled skin,
Weed wide enough to wrap a fairy in.
A Midsummer Night's Dream (1595–6) act 2, sc. 1, l. 255

27 You spotted snakes with double tongue,
Thorny hedge-hogs, be not seen;
Newts, and blind-worms, do no wrong;
Come not near our fairy queen.
A Midsummer Night's Dream (1595–6) act 2, sc. 2, l. 9

28 Weaving spiders come not here;
Hence you long-legged spinners, hence!
Beetles black, approach not near;
Worm nor snail, do no offence.
A Midsummer Night's Dream (1595–6) act 2, sc. 2, l. 20

29 God shield us!—a lion among ladies, is a most dreadful thing; for there is not a more fearful wild-fowl than your lion living.
A Midsummer Night's Dream (1595–6) act 3, sc. 1, l. [32]

30 Look in the almanack; find out moonshine, find out moonshine.
A Midsummer Night's Dream (1595–6) act 3, sc. 1, l. [55]

1 What hempen home-spuns have we swaggering here,
So near the cradle of the fairy queen?
A Midsummer Night's Dream (1595–6) act 3, sc. 1, l. [82]

2 Bless thee, Bottom! bless thee! thou art translated.
A Midsummer Night's Dream (1595–6) act 3, sc. 1, l. [124]

3 What angel wakes me from my flowery bed?
A Midsummer Night's Dream (1595–6) act 3, sc. 1, l. [135]

4 Out of this wood do not desire to go.
A Midsummer Night's Dream (1595–6) act 3, sc. 1, l. [159]

5 Lord, what fools these mortals be!
A Midsummer Night's Dream (1595–6) act 3, sc. 2, l. 115

6 Two lovely berries moulded on one stem;
So, with two seeming bodies, but one heart.
A Midsummer Night's Dream (1595–6) act 3, sc. 2, l. 211

7 O! when she's angry she is keen and shrewd.
She was a vixen when she went to school:
And though she be but little, she is fierce.
A Midsummer Night's Dream (1595–6) act 3, sc. 2, l. 323

8 . . . Night's swift dragons cut the clouds full fast,
And yonder shines Aurora's harbinger;
At whose approach, ghosts, wandering here and there,
Troop home to churchyards.
A Midsummer Night's Dream (1595–6) act 3, sc. 2, l. 379

9 Cupid is a knavish lad,
Thus to make poor females mad.
A Midsummer Night's Dream (1595–6) act 3, sc. 2, l. 440

10 Jack shall have Jill;
Nought shall go ill;
The man shall have his mare again,
And all shall be well.
A Midsummer Night's Dream (1595–6) act 3, sc. 2, l. 461

11 Let us have the tongs and the bones.
A Midsummer Night's Dream (1595–6) act 4, sc. 1, l. [33]

12 Methinks I have a great desire to a bottle of hay: good hay, sweet hay, hath no fellow.
A Midsummer Night's Dream (1595–6) act 4, sc. 1, l. [37]

13 I have an exposition of sleep come upon me.
A Midsummer Night's Dream (1595–6) act 4, sc. 1, l. [43]

14 My Oberon! what visions have I seen!
Methought I was enamoured of an ass.
A Midsummer Night's Dream (1595–6) act 4, sc. 1, l. [82]

15 I was with Hercules and Cadmus once,
When in a wood of Crete they bayed the bear
With hounds of Sparta: never did I hear . . .
So musical a discord, such sweet thunder.
A Midsummer Night's Dream (1595–6) act 4, sc. 1, l. [118]

16 I have had a dream, past the wit of man to say what dream it was.
A Midsummer Night's Dream (1595–6) act 4, sc. 1, l. [211]

17 The eye of man hath not heard, the ear of man hath not seen, man's hand is not able to taste, his tongue to conceive, nor his heart to report, what my dream was.
A Midsummer Night's Dream (1595–6) act 4, sc. 1, l. [218]

18 The lunatic, the lover, and the poet,
Are of imagination all compact.
A Midsummer Night's Dream (1595–6) act 5, sc. 1, l. 7

19 The lover, all as frantic,
Sees Helen's beauty in a brow of Egypt:
The poet's eye, in a fine frenzy rolling,
Doth glance from heaven to earth, from earth to heaven;
And, as imagination bodies forth
The forms of things unknown, the poet's pen
Turns them to shapes, and gives to airy nothing
A local habitation and a name.
A Midsummer Night's Dream (1595–6) act 5, sc. 1, l. 10

20 Or in the night, imagining some fear,
How easy is a bush supposed a bear!
A Midsummer Night's Dream (1595–6) act 5, sc. 1, l. 21

21 What revels are in hand? Is there no play,
To ease the anguish of a torturing hour?
A Midsummer Night's Dream (1595–6) act 5, sc. 1, l. 36

22 Merry and tragical! tedious and brief!
That is, hot ice and wondrous strange snow.
A Midsummer Night's Dream (1595–6) act 5, sc. 1, l. 58

23 To show our simple skill,
That is the true beginning of our end.
A Midsummer Night's Dream (1595–6) act 5, sc. 1, l. [110]

24 Whereat, with blade, with bloody blameful blade,
He bravely broached his boiling bloody breast.
A Midsummer Night's Dream (1595–6) act 5, sc. 1, l. [148]

25 I see a voice: now will I to the chink,
To spy an I can hear my Thisby's face.
A Midsummer Night's Dream (1595–6) act 5, sc. 1, l. [195]

26 The best in this kind are but shadows, and the worst are no worse, if imagination amend them.
A Midsummer Night's Dream (1595–6) act 5, sc. 1, l. [215]

27 The iron tongue of midnight hath told twelve;
Lovers, to bed; 'tis almost fairy time.
A Midsummer Night's Dream (1595–6) act 5, sc. 1, l. [372]

28 Now the hungry lion roars,
And the wolf behowls the moon;
Whilst the heavy ploughman snores,
All with weary task fordone.
A Midsummer Night's Dream (1595–6) act 5, sc. 2, l. 1

29 Not a mouse
Shall disturb this hallowed house:
I am sent with broom before,
To sweep the dust behind the door.
A Midsummer Night's Dream (1595–6) act 5, sc. 2, l. 17

30 If we shadows have offended,
Think but this, and all is mended,
That you have but slumbered here
While these visions did appear.
A Midsummer Night's Dream (1595–6) act 5, sc. 2, l. 54

MUCH ADO ABOUT NOTHING

31 He hath indeed better bettered expectation than you must expect of me to tell you how.
Much Ado About Nothing (1598–9) act 1, sc. 1, l. [15]

32 He is a very valiant trencher-man.
Much Ado About Nothing (1598–9) act 1, sc. 1, l. [52]

33 I see, lady, the gentleman is not in your books.
Much Ado About Nothing (1598–9) act 1, sc. 1, l. [79]

34 BEATRICE: I wonder that you will still be talking, Signior Benedick: nobody marks you.

BENEDICK: What! my dear Lady Disdain, are you yet living?
Much Ado About Nothing (1598–9) act 1, sc. 1, l. [121]

1 In time the savage bull doth bear the yoke.
Much Ado About Nothing (1598–9) act 1, sc. 1, l. [271]

2 Lord! I could not endure a husband with a beard on his face: I had rather lie in the woollen.
Much Ado About Nothing (1598–9) act 2, sc. 1, l. [31]

3 Speak low, if you speak love.
Much Ado About Nothing (1598–9) act 2, sc. 1, l. [104]

4 Friendship is constant in all other things
Save in the office and affairs of love.
Much Ado About Nothing (1598–9) act 2, sc. 1, l. [184]

5 There was a star danced, and under that was I born.
Much Ado About Nothing (1598–9) act 2, sc. 1, l. [351]

6 Is it not strange, that sheeps' guts should hale souls out of men's bodies?
Much Ado About Nothing (1598–9) act 2, sc. 3, l. [62]

7 Sigh no more, ladies, sigh no more,
Men were deceivers ever;
One foot in sea, and one on shore,
To one thing constant never.
Much Ado About Nothing (1598–9) act 2, sc. 3, l. [65]

8 Sits the wind in that corner?
Much Ado About Nothing (1598–9) act 2, sc. 3, l. [108]

9 For look where Beatrice, like a lapwing, runs
Close by the ground, to hear our counsel.
Much Ado About Nothing (1598–9) act 3, sc. 1, l. 24

10 Disdain and scorn ride sparkling in her eyes.
Much Ado About Nothing (1598–9) act 3, sc. 1, l. 51

11 Contempt, farewell! and maiden pride, adieu!
No glory lives behind the back of such.
And, Benedick, love on; I will requite thee,
Taming my wild heart to thy loving hand.
Much Ado About Nothing (1598–9) act 3, sc. 1, l. 109

12 He hath a heart as sound as a bell, and his tongue is the clapper; for what his heart thinks his tongue speaks.
Much Ado About Nothing (1598–9) act 3, sc. 2, l. [12]

13 Well, every one can master a grief but he that has it.
Much Ado About Nothing (1598–9) act 3, sc. 2, l. [28]

14 Comparisons are odorous.
Much Ado About Nothing (1598–9) act 3, sc. 5, l. [18]; cf. **Proverbs** 597:32

15 A good old man, sir; he will be talking: as they say, 'when the age is in, the wit is out.'
Much Ado About Nothing (1598–9) act 3, sc. 5, l. [36]

16 O! what men dare do! what men may do! what men daily do, not knowing what they do!
Much Ado About Nothing (1598–9) act 4, sc. 1, l. [19]

17 You have stayed me in a happy hour.
Much Ado About Nothing (1598–9) act 4, sc. 1, l. [283]

18 O God, that I were a man! I would eat his heart in the market-place.
Much Ado About Nothing (1598–9) act 4, sc. 1, l. [311]

19 Patch grief with proverbs.
Much Ado About Nothing (1598–9) act 5, sc. 1, l. 17

20 There was never yet philosopher
That could endure the toothache patiently.
Much Ado About Nothing (1598–9) act 5, sc. 1, l. 35

21 What though care killed a cat, thou hast mettle enough in thee to kill care.
Much Ado About Nothing (1598–9) act 5, sc. 1, l. [135]; cf. **Proverbs** 597:3

22 No, I was not born under a rhyming planet.
Much Ado About Nothing (1598–9) act 5, sc. 2, l. [40]

23 Look, the gentle day,
Before the wheels of Phoebus, round about
Dapples the drowsy east with spots of grey.
Much Ado About Nothing (1598–9) act 5, sc. 3, l. 25

OTHELLO

24 But I will wear my heart upon my sleeve
For daws to peck at: I am not what I am.
Othello (1602–4) act 1, sc. 1, l. 64

25 Even now, now, very now, an old black ram
Is tupping your white ewe.
Othello (1602–4) act 1, sc. 1, l. 88

26 Your daughter and the Moor are now making the beast with two backs.
Othello (1602–4) act 1, sc. 1, l. [117]

27 Though I do hate him as I do hell-pains,
Yet, for necessity of present life,
I must show out a flag and sign of love,
Which is indeed but sign.
Othello (1602–4) act 1, sc. 1, l. [155]

28 Though in the trade of war I have slain men,
Yet do I hold it very stuff o' the conscience
To do no contrived murder: I lack iniquity
Sometimes to do me service.
Othello (1602–4) act 1, sc. 2, l. 1

29 Keep up your bright swords, for the dew will rust them.
Othello (1602–4) act 1, sc. 2, l. 59

30 The wealthy curlèd darlings of our nation.
Othello (1602–4) act 1, sc. 2, l. 67

31 Rude am I in my speech,
And little blessed with the soft phrase of peace.
Othello (1602–4) act 1, sc. 3, l. 81

32 I will a round unvarnished tale deliver
Of my whole course of love; what drugs, what charms,
What conjuration, and what mighty magic,
For such proceeding I am charged withal,
I won his daughter.
Othello (1602–4) act 1, sc. 3, l. 90

33 Wherein I spake of most disastrous chances,
Of moving accidents by flood and field,
Of hair-breadth 'scapes i' the imminent deadly breach,
Of being taken by the insolent foe
And sold to slavery, of my redemption thence
And portance in my travel's history.
Othello (1602–4) act 1, sc. 3, l. 134

34 And of the Cannibals that each other eat,
The Anthropophagi, and men whose heads

Do grow beneath their shoulders.
Othello (1602–4) act 1, sc. 3, l. 143

1 My story being done,
She gave me for my pains a world of sighs:
She swore, in faith, 'twas strange, 'twas passing strange;
'Twas pitiful, 'twas wondrous pitiful.
Othello (1602–4) act 1, sc. 3, l. 158

2 She loved me for the dangers I had passed,
And I loved her that she did pity them.
Othello (1602–4) act 1, sc. 3, l. 167

3 I do perceive here a divided duty.
Othello (1602–4) act 1, sc. 3, l. 181

4 The robbed that smiles steals something from the thief.
Othello (1602–4) act 1, sc. 3, l. 208

5 But words are words; I never yet did hear
That the bruised heart was piercèd through the ear.
Othello (1602–4) act 1, sc. 3, l. 218

6 The tyrant custom, most grave senators,
Hath made the flinty and steel couch of war
My thrice-driven bed of down.
Othello (1602–4) act 1, sc. 3, l. [230]

7 If I be left behind,
A moth of peace, and he go to the war,
The rites for which I love him are bereft me.
Othello (1602–4) act 1, sc. 3, l. [257]

8 Hell and night
Must bring this monstrous birth to the world's light.
Othello (1602–4) act 1, sc. 3, l. [409]

9 Our great captain's captain.
Othello (1602–4) act 2, sc. 1, l. 74

10 I am not merry, but I do beguile
The thing I am by seeming otherwise.
Othello (1602–4) act 2, sc. 1, l. 122

11 To suckle fools and chronicle small beer.
Othello (1602–4) act 2, sc. 1, l. 163

12 If it were now to die,
'Twere now to be most happy.
Othello (1602–4) act 2, sc. 1, l. [192]

13 A slipper and subtle knave.
Othello (1602–4) act 2, sc. 1, l. [247]

14 Make the Moor thank me, love me, and reward me
For making him egregiously an ass
And practising upon his peace and quiet
Even to madness.
Othello (1602–4) act 2, sc. 1, l. [320]

15 Silence that dreadful bell! it frights the isle
From her propriety.
Othello (1602–4) act 2, sc. 3, l. [177]

16 O! I have lost my reputation. I have lost the immortal part of myself, and what remains is bestial.
Othello (1602–4) act 2, sc. 3, l. [264]

17 Come, come; good wine is a good familiar creature if it be well used; exclaim no more against it.
Othello (1602–4) act 2, sc. 3, l. [315]

18 O! thereby hangs a tail.
Othello (1602–4) act 3, sc. 1, l. [8]

19 Excellent wretch! Perdition catch my soul
But I do love thee! and when I love thee not,
Chaos is come again.
Othello (1602–4) act 3, sc. 3, l. 90

20 Good name in man and woman, dear my lord,
Is the immediate jewel of their souls;
Who steals my purse steals trash; 'tis something, nothing;
'Twas mine, 'tis his, and has been slave to thousands;
But he that filches from me my good name
Robs me of that which not enriches him,
And makes me poor indeed.
Othello (1602–4) act 3, sc. 3, l. 155

21 O! beware, my lord, of jealousy;
It is the green-eyed monster which doth mock
The meat it feeds on.
Othello (1602–4) act 3, sc. 3, l. 165

22 Foh! one may smell in such, a will most rank,
Foul disposition, thoughts unnatural.
Othello (1602–4) act 3, sc. 3, l. 232

23 If I do prove her haggard,
Though that her jesses were my dear heart-strings,
I'd whistle her off and let her down the wind,
To prey at fortune.
Othello (1602–4) act 3, sc. 3, l. 260

24 I am black,
And have not those soft parts of conversation
That chamberers have.
Othello (1602–4) act 3, sc. 3, l. 263

25 I am declined
Into the vale of years.
Othello (1602–4) act 3, sc. 3, l. 265

26 I had rather be a toad,
And live upon the vapour of a dungeon,
Than keep a corner in the thing I love
For others' uses.
Othello (1602–4) act 3, sc. 3, l. 270

27 If she be false, O! then heaven mocks itself.
I'll not believe it.
Othello (1602–4) act 3, sc. 3, l. 278

28 Trifles light as air
Are to the jealous confirmations strong
As proofs of holy writ.
Othello (1602–4) act 3, sc. 3, l. 323

29 Not poppy, nor mandragora,
Nor all the drowsy syrups of the world,
Shall ever medicine thee to that sweet sleep
Which thou owedst yesterday.
Othello (1602–4) act 3, sc. 3, l. 331

30 Farewell the tranquil mind; farewell content!
Farewell the plumèd troop and the big wars
That make ambition virtue! O, farewell!
Farewell the neighing steed and the shrill trump,
The spirit-stirring drum, the ear-piercing fife,
The royal banner, and all quality,
Pride, pomp, and circumstance of glorious war!
Othello (1602–4) act 3, sc. 3, l. 349

1 Othello's occupation's gone!
Othello (1602–4) act 3, sc. 3, l. 358

2 This denoted a foregone conclusion.
Othello (1602–4) act 3, sc. 3, l. 429

3 Like to the Pontick sea,
Whose icy current and compulsive course
Ne'er feels retiring ebb, but keeps due on
To the Propontic and the Hellespont,
Even so my bloody thoughts, with violent pace,
Shall ne'er look back.
Othello (1602–4) act 3, sc. 3, l. 454

4 For here's a young and sweating devil here,
That commonly rebels. 'Tis a good hand,
A frank one.
Othello (1602–4) act 3, sc. 4, l. 43

5 That handkerchief
Did an Egyptian to my mother give.
Othello (1602–4) act 3, sc. 4, l. 56

6 'Tis true; there's magic in the web of it;
A sibyl, that had numbered in the world
The sun to course two hundred compasses,
In her prophetic fury sewed the work;
The worms were hallowed that did breed the silk,
And it was dyed in mummy which the skilful
Conserved of maidens' hearts.
Othello (1602–4) act 3, sc. 4, l. 70

7 Jealous souls will not be answered so;
They are not ever jealous for the cause,
But jealous for they are jealous.
Othello (1602–4) act 3, sc. 4, l. 158

8 O! it comes o'er my memory,
As doth the raven o'er the infected house,
Boding to all.
Othello (1602–4) act 4, sc. 1, l. 20

9 But yet the pity of it, Iago! O! Iago, the pity of it, Iago!
Othello (1602–4) act 4, sc. 1, l. [205]

10 O well-painted passion!
Othello (1602–4) act 4, sc. 1, l. [268]

11 Is this the noble nature
Whom passion could not shake? whose solid virtue
The shot of accident nor dart of chance
Could neither graze nor pierce?
Othello (1602–4) act 4, sc. 1, l. [277]

12 Your mystery, your mystery; nay, dispatch.
Othello (1602–4) act 4, sc. 2, l. 29

13 But, alas! to make me
The fixèd figure for the time of scorn
To point his slow and moving finger at.
Othello (1602–4) act 4, sc. 2, l. 52

14 Heaven stops the nose at it and the moon winks.
Othello (1602–4) act 4, sc. 2, l. 76

15 I took you for that cunning whore of Venice
That married with Othello.
Othello (1602–4) act 4, sc. 2, l. 88

16 Those that do teach young babes
Do it with gentle means and easy tasks;
He might have chid me so; for, in good faith,
I am a child to chiding.
Othello (1602–4) act 4, sc. 2, l. 111

17 Unkindness may do much;
And his unkindness may defeat my life,
But never taint my love.
Othello (1602–4) act 4, sc. 2, l. 159

18 The poor soul sat sighing by a sycamore tree,
Sing all a green willow;
Her hand on her bosom, her head on her knee,
Sing willow, willow, willow.
Othello (1602–4) act 4, sc. 3, l. [41]

19 Sing all a green willow must be my garland.
Othello (1602–4) act 4, sc. 3, l. [49]; cf. **Heywood** 376:6

20 Who would not make her husband a cuckold to make him a monarch?
Othello (1602–4) act 4, sc. 3, l. [76]

21 This is the night
That either makes me or fordoes me quite.
Othello (1602–4) act 5, sc. 1, l. 128

22 It is the cause, it is the cause, my soul;
Let me not name it to you, you chaste stars!
It is the cause. Yet I'll not shed her blood,
Nor scar that whiter skin of hers than snow,
And smooth as monumental alabaster.
Yet she must die, else she'll betray more men.
Put out the light, and then put out the light.
Othello (1602–4) act 5, sc. 2, l. 1

23 One more, and this the last:
So sweet was ne'er so fatal.
Othello (1602–4) act 5, sc. 2, l. 19

24 Kill me to-morrow; let me live to-night!
Othello (1602–4) act 5, sc. 2, l. 80

25 It is the very error of the moon;
She comes more near the earth than she was wont,
And makes men mad.
Othello (1602–4) act 5, sc. 2, l. 107

26 Murder's out of tune,
And sweet revenge grows harsh.
Othello (1602–4) act 5, sc. 2, l. 113

27 OTHELLO: She's like a liar gone to burning hell;
'Twas I that killed her.
EMILIA: O! the more angel she,
And you the blacker devil.
Othello (1602–4) act 5, sc. 2, l. 127

28 May his pernicious soul
Rot half a grain a day!
Othello (1602–4) act 5, sc. 2, l. 153

29 I will play the swan,
And die in music.
Othello (1602–4) act 5, sc. 2, l. 245

30 Here is my journey's end, here is my butt,
And very sea-mark of my utmost sail.
Othello (1602–4) act 5, sc. 2, l. 266

31 O ill-starred wench!
Pale as thy smock! when we shall meet at compt,
This look of thine will hurl my soul from heaven,
And fiends will snatch at it. Cold, cold, my girl!
Even like thy chastity.
Othello (1602–4) act 5, sc. 2, l. 271

1 Blow me about in winds! roast me in sulphur!
Wash me in steep-down gulfs of liquid fire!
O Desdemona! Desdemona! dead!
Othello (1602–4) act 5, sc. 2, l. 278

2 An honourable murderer, if you will;
For nought did I in hate, but all in honour.
Othello (1602–4) act 5, sc. 2, l. 293

3 I have done the state some service, and they know 't;
No more of that. I pray you, in your letters,
When you shall these unlucky deeds relate,
Speak of me as I am; nothing extenuate,
Nor set down aught in malice: then, must you speak
Of one that loved not wisely but too well;
Of one not easily jealous, but, being wrought,
Perplexed in the extreme; of one whose hand,
Like the base Indian, threw a pearl away
Richer than all his tribe.
Othello (1602–4) act 5, sc. 2, l. 338

4 And say besides, that in Aleppo once,
Where a malignant and a turbaned Turk
Beat a Venetian and traduced the state,
I took by the throat the circumcised dog,
And smote him thus.
Othello (1602–4) act 5, sc. 2, l. 351

5 I kissed thee ere I killed thee, no way but this,
Killing myself to die upon a kiss.
Othello (1602–4) act 5, sc. 2, l. 357

PERICLES

6 See where she comes apparelled like the spring.
Pericles (1606–8) act 1, sc. 1, l. 12

7 THIRD FISHERMAN: Master, I marvel how the fishes live in the sea.
FIRST FISHERMAN: Why, as men do a-land: the great ones eat up the little ones.
Pericles (1606–8) act 2, sc. 1, l. 26; cf. **Sidney** 718:3

RICHARD II

8 Old John of Gaunt, time-honoured Lancaster.
Richard II (1595) act 1, sc. 1, l. 1

9 The purest treasure mortal times afford
Is spotless reputation; that away,
Men are but gilded loam or painted clay.
A jewel in a ten-times-barred-up chest
Is a bold spirit in a loyal breast.
Mine honour is my life; both grow in one;
Take honour from me, and my life is done.
Richard II (1595) act 1, sc. 1, l. 177

10 We were not born to sue, but to command.
Richard II (1595) act 1, sc. 1, l. 196; cf. **Scott** 650:12

11 The language I have learned these forty years,
My native English, now I must forego;
And now my tongue's use is to me no more
Than an unstringèd viol or a harp.
Richard II (1595) act 1, sc. 3, l. 159

12 How long a time lies in one little word!
Four lagging winters and four wanton springs
End in a word; such is the breath of kings.
Richard II (1595) act 1, sc. 3, l. 213

13 Things sweet to taste prove in digestion sour.
Richard II (1595) act 1, sc. 3, l. 236

14 Must I not serve a long apprenticehood
To foreign passages, and in the end,
Having my freedom, boast of nothing else
But that I was a journeyman to grief?
Richard II (1595) act 1, sc. 3, l. 271

15 All places that the eye of heaven visits
Are to a wise man ports and happy havens.
Teach thy necessity to reason thus;
There is no virtue like necessity.
Richard II (1595) act 1, sc. 3, l. 275

16 O! who can hold a fire in his hand
By thinking on the frosty Caucasus?
Or cloy the hungry edge of appetite,
By bare imagination of a feast?
Or wallow naked in December snow
By thinking on fantastic summer's heat?
O, no! the apprehension of the good
Gives but the greater feeling to the worse.
Richard II (1595) act 1, sc. 3, l. 294

17 They say the tongues of dying men
Enforce attention, like deep harmony.
Richard II (1595) act 2, sc. 1, l. 5

18 More are men's ends marked than their lives before:
The setting sun, and music at the close,
As the last taste of sweets, is sweetest last,
Writ in remembrance more than things long past.
Richard II (1595) act 2, sc. 1, l. 11

19 This royal throne of kings, this sceptered isle,
This earth of majesty, this seat of Mars,
This other Eden, demi-paradise,
This fortress built by Nature for herself
Against infection and the hand of war,
This happy breed of men, this little world,
This precious stone set in the silver sea,
Which serves it in the office of a wall,
Or as a moat defensive to a house,
Against the envy of less happier lands,
This blessèd plot, this earth, this realm, this England,
This nurse, this teeming womb of royal kings,
Feared by their breed and famous by their birth,
Renownèd for their deeds as far from home,—
For Christian service and true chivalry,—
As is the sepulchre in stubborn Jewry
Of the world's ransom, blessèd Mary's Son:
This land of such dear souls, this dear, dear land,
Dear for her reputation through the world,
Is now leased out,—I die pronouncing it,—
Like to a tenement or pelting farm:
England, bound in with the triumphant sea,
Whose rocky shore beats back the envious siege
Of watery Neptune, is now bound in with shame,
With inky blots, and rotten parchment bonds:
That England, that was wont to conquer others,
Hath made a shameful conquest of itself.
Richard II (1595) act 2, sc. 1, l. 40

20 I am a stranger here in Gloucestershire:
These high wild hills and rough uneven ways

Draw out our miles and make them wearisome.
Richard II (1595) act 2, sc. 3, l. 2

1 Grace me no grace, nor uncle me no uncle.
Richard II (1595) act 2, sc. 3, l. 87

2 The caterpillars of the commonwealth.
Richard II (1595) act 2, sc. 3, l. 166

3 Things past redress are now with me past care.
Richard II (1595) act 2, sc. 3, l. 171

4 Eating the bitter bread of banishment.
Richard II (1595) act 3, sc. 1, l. 21

5 Not all the water in the rough rude sea
Can wash the balm from an anointed king;
The breath of worldly men cannot depose
The deputy elected by the Lord.
For every man that Bolingbroke hath pressed
To lift shrewd steel against our golden crown,
God for his Richard hath in heavenly pay
A glorious angel; then, if angels fight,
Weak men must fall, for heaven still guards the right.
Richard II (1595) act 3, sc. 2, l. 54

6 O! call back yesterday, bid time return.
Richard II (1595) act 3, sc. 2, l. 69

7 The worst is death, and death will have his day.
Richard II (1595) act 3, sc. 2, l. 103

8 Let's talk of graves, of worms, and epitaphs;
Make dust our paper, and with rainy eyes
Write sorrow on the bosom of the earth.
Let's choose executors, and talk of wills.
Richard II (1595) act 3, sc. 2, l. 145

9 For God's sake, let us sit upon the ground
And tell sad stories of the death of kings:
How some have been deposed, some slain in war,
Some haunted by the ghosts they have deposed,
Some poisoned by their wives, some sleeping killed;
All murdered.
Richard II (1595) act 3, sc. 2, l. 155

10 Within the hollow crown
That rounds the mortal temples of a king
Keeps Death his court, and there the antick sits,
Scoffing his state and grinning at his pomp;
Richard II (1595) act 3, sc. 2, l. 160

11 Comes at the last, and with a little pin
Bores through his castle wall, and farewell king!
Richard II (1595) act 3, sc. 2, l. 169

12 See, see, King Richard doth himself appear,
As doth the blushing discontented sun
From out the fiery portal of the east.
Richard II (1595) act 3, sc. 3, l. 62

13 The purple testament of bleeding war.
Richard II (1595) act 3, sc. 3, l. 94

14 What must the king do now? Must he submit?
The king shall do it: must he be deposed?
The king shall be contented: must he lose
The name of king? o' God's name, let it go.
I'll give my jewels for a set of beads,
My gorgeous palace for a hermitage,
My gay apparel for an almsman's gown,
My figured goblets for a dish of wood,
My sceptre for a palmer's walking staff,
My subjects for a pair of carved saints,
And my large kingdom for a little grave,
A little little grave, an obscure grave.
Richard II (1595) act 3, sc. 3, l. 143

15 Shall we play the wantons with our woes,
And make some pretty match with shedding tears?
Richard II (1595) act 3, sc. 3, l. 164

16 Go, bind thou up yon dangling apricocks,
Which, like unruly children, make their sire
Stoop with oppression of their prodigal weight.
Richard II (1595) act 3, sc. 4, l. 29

17 Old Adam's likeness, set to dress this garden.
Richard II (1595) act 3, sc. 4, l. 73

18 Here did she fall a tear; here, in this place,
I'll set a bank of rue, sour herb of grace;
Rue, even for ruth, here shortly shall be seen,
In the remembrance of a weeping queen.
Richard II (1595) act 3, sc. 4, l. 104

19 Disorder, horror, fear and mutiny
Shall here inhabit, and this land be called
The field of Golgotha and dead men's skulls.
Richard II (1595) act 4, sc. 1, l. 142

20 God save the king! Will no man say, amen?
Am I both priest and clerk? Well then, amen.
Richard II (1595) act 4, sc. 1, l. 172

21 Give me the crown. Here, cousin, seize the crown;
Here cousin,
On this side my hand and on that side thine.
Now is this golden crown like a deep well
That owes two buckets filling one another;
The emptier ever dancing in the air,
The other down, unseen, and full of water:
That bucket down and full of tears am I,
Drinking my griefs, whilst you mount up on high.
Richard II (1595) act 4, sc. 1, l. 181

22 You may my glories and my state depose,
But not my griefs; still am I king of those.
Richard II (1595) act 4, sc. 1, l. 192

23 With mine own tears I wash away my balm,
With mine own hands I give away my crown.
Richard II (1595) act 4, sc. 1, l. 207

24 This is the way
To Julius Caesar's ill-erected tower.
Richard II (1595) act 5, sc. 1, l. 1

25 I am sworn brother, sweet,
To grim Necessity, and he and I
Will keep a league till death.
Richard II (1595) act 5, sc. 1, l. 20

26 That were some love but little policy.
Richard II (1595) act 5, sc. 1, l. 84

27 As in a theatre, the eyes of men,
After a well-graced actor leaves the stage,
Are idly bent on him that enters next,
Thinking his prattle to be tedious;
Even so, or with much more contempt, men's eyes
Did scowl on Richard.
Richard II (1595) act 5, sc. 2, l. 23

1 Who are the violets now
That strew the green lap of the new come spring?
Richard II (1595) act 5, sc. 2, l. 46

2 He prays but faintly and would be denied.
Richard II (1595) act 5, sc. 3, l. 103

3 I have been studying how I may compare
This prison where I live unto the world.
Richard II (1595) act 5, sc. 5, l. 1

4 How sour sweet music is,
When time is broke, and no proportion kept!
So is it in the music of men's lives.
Richard II (1595) act 5, sc. 5, l. 42

5 I wasted time, and now doth time waste me.
Richard II (1595) act 5, sc. 5, l. 49

6 Mount, mount, my soul! thy seat is up on high,
Whilst my gross flesh sinks downwards here to die.
Richard II (1595) act 5, sc. 5, l. 112

RICHARD III

7 Now is the winter of our discontent
Made glorious summer by this sun of York.
Richard III (1591) act 1, sc. 1, l. 1; cf. **Newspaper headlines** 544:20

8 Grim-visaged war hath smoothed his wrinkled front;
And now, instead of mounting barbèd steeds,
To fright the souls of fearful adversaries,—
He capers nimbly in a lady's chamber
To the lascivious pleasing of a lute.
Richard III (1591) act 1, sc. 1, l. 9

9 But I, that am not shaped for sportive tricks,
Nor made to court an amorous looking-glass;
I, that am rudely stamped, and want love's majesty
To strut before a wanton ambling nymph;
I, that am curtailed of this fair proportion,
Cheated of feature by dissembling nature,
Deformed, unfinished, sent before my time
Into this breathing world, scarce half made up,
And that so lamely and unfashionable
That dogs bark at me, as I halt by them.
Richard III (1591) act 1, sc. 1, l. 14

10 This weak piping time of peace.
Richard III (1591) act 1, sc. 1, l. 24

11 And therefore, since I cannot prove a lover,
To entertain these fair well-spoken days,
I am determinèd to prove a villain,
And hate the idle pleasures of these days.
Richard III (1591) act 1, sc. 1, l. 28

12 No beast so fierce but knows some touch of pity.
Richard III (1591) act 1, sc. 2, l. 71

13 Was ever woman in this humour wooed?
Was ever woman in this humour won?
I'll have her, but I will not keep her long.
Richard III (1591) act 1, sc. 2, l. 229

14 Cannot a plain man live and think no harm,
But that his simple truth must be abused
By silken, sly, insinuating Jacks?
Richard III (1591) act 1, sc. 3, l. 51

15 Since every Jack became a gentleman
There's many a gentle person made a Jack.
Richard III (1591) act 1, sc. 3, l. 72

16 And thus I clothe my naked villainy
With odd old ends stol'n forth of holy writ,
And seem a saint when most I play the devil.
Richard III (1591) act 1, sc. 3, l. 336

17 Methought I saw a thousand fearful wracks;
A thousand men that fishes gnawed upon;
Wedges of gold, great anchors, heaps of pearl,
Inestimable stones, unvalued jewels,
All scattered in the bottom of the sea.
Some lay in dead men's skulls; and in those holes
Where eyes did once inhabit, there were crept
As 'twere in scorn of eyes, reflecting gems,
That wooed the slimy bottom of the deep,
And mocked the dead bones that lay scattered by.
Richard III (1591) act 1, sc. 4, l. 24

18 Clarence is come,—false, fleeting, perjured Clarence.
Richard III (1591) act 1, sc. 4, l. 55

19 Woe to the land that's governed by a child!
Richard III (1591) act 2, sc. 3, l. 11; cf. **Bible** 84:25

20 So wise so young, they say, do never live long.
Richard III (1591) act 3, sc. 1, l. 79

21 Talk'st thou to me of 'ifs'? Thou art a traitor:
Off with his head!
Richard III (1591) act 3, sc. 4, l. 74; cf. **Cibber** 217:5

22 I am not in the giving vein to-day.
Richard III (1591) act 4, sc. 2, l. 115

23 The sons of Edward sleep in Abraham's bosom.
Richard III (1591) act 4, sc. 3, l. 38

24 Thou cam'st on earth to make the earth my hell.
Richard III (1591) act 4, sc. 4, l. 167

25 An honest tale speeds best being plainly told.
Richard III (1591) act 4, sc. 4, l. 359

26 Harp not on that string.
Richard III (1591) act 4, sc. 4, l. 365

27 True hope is swift, and flies with swallow's wings;
Kings it makes gods, and meaner creatures kings.
Richard III (1591) act 5, sc. 2, l. 23

28 The king's name is a tower of strength.
Richard III (1591) act 5, sc. 3, l. 12

29 Give me another horse! bind up my wounds!
Have mercy, Jesu! Soft! I did but dream.
O coward conscience, how dost thou afflict me!
Richard III (1591) act 5, sc. 3, l. 178

30 I shall despair. There is no creature loves me;
And if I die, no soul will pity me:
Nay, wherefore should they, since that I myself
Find in myself no pity to myself?
Richard III (1591) act 5, sc. 3, l. 201

31 By the apostle Paul, shadows to-night
Have struck more terror to the soul of Richard
Than can the substance of ten thousand soldiers.
Richard III (1591) act 5, sc. 3, l. 217

32 Conscience is but a word that cowards use,
Devised at first to keep the strong in awe.
Richard III (1591) act 5, sc. 3, l. 310

33 A horse! a horse! my kingdom for a horse!
Richard III (1591) act 5, sc. 4, l. 7

1 Slave! I have set my life upon a cast,
And I will stand the hazard of the die.
Richard III (1591) act 5, sc. 4, l. 9

ROMEO AND JULIET

2 A pair of star-crossed lovers.
Romeo and Juliet (1595) prologue

3 The two hours' traffick of our stage.
Romeo and Juliet (1595) prologue

4 Younger than she are happy mothers made.
Romeo and Juliet (1595) act 1, sc. 2, l. 12

5 O! then, I see, Queen Mab hath been with you . . .
She is the fairies' midwife, and she comes
In shape no bigger than an agate-stone
On the forefinger of an alderman,
Drawn with a team of little atomies
Athwart men's noses as they lie asleep.
Romeo and Juliet (1595) act 1, sc. 4, l. 53

6 You and I are past our dancing days.
Romeo and Juliet (1595) act 1, sc. 5, l. [35]

7 O! she doth teach the torches to burn bright.
It seems she hangs upon the cheek of night
Like a rich jewel in an Ethiop's ear;
Beauty too rich for use, for earth too dear.
Romeo and Juliet (1595) act 1, sc. 5, l. [48]

8 My only love sprung from my only hate!
Too early seen unknown, and known too late!
Romeo and Juliet (1595) act 1, sc. 5, l. [142]

9 He jests at scars, that never felt a wound.
But, soft! what light through yonder window breaks?
It is the east, and Juliet is the sun.
Romeo and Juliet (1595) act 2, sc. 2, l. 1

10 See! how she leans her cheek upon her hand:
O! that I were a glove upon that hand,
That I might touch that cheek.
Romeo and Juliet (1595) act 2, sc. 2, l. 23

11 O Romeo, Romeo! wherefore art thou Romeo?
Romeo and Juliet (1595) act 2, sc. 2, l. 33

12 What's in a name? that which we call a rose
By any other name would smell as sweet.
Romeo and Juliet (1595) act 2, sc. 2, l. 43

13 For stony limits cannot hold love out,
And what love can do that dares love attempt.
Romeo and Juliet (1595) act 2, sc. 2, l. 67

14 O! swear not by the moon, the inconstant moon,
That monthly changes in her circled orb,
Lest that thy love prove likewise variable.
Romeo and Juliet (1595) act 2, sc. 2, l. 109

15 It is too rash, too unadvised, too sudden.
Romeo and Juliet (1595) act 2, sc. 2, l. 118

16 Love goes toward love, as schoolboys from their books;
But love from love, toward school with heavy looks.
Romeo and Juliet (1595) act 2, sc. 2, l. 156

17 O! for a falconer's voice,
To lure this tassel-gentle back again.
Romeo and Juliet (1595) act 2, sc. 2, l. 158

18 How silver-sweet sound lovers' tongues by night,
Like softest music to attending ears!
Romeo and Juliet (1595) act 2, sc. 2, l. 165

19 Good-night, good-night! parting is such sweet sorrow
That I shall say good-night till it be morrow.
Romeo and Juliet (1595) act 2, sc. 2, l. 184

20 O flesh, flesh, how art thou fishified!
Romeo and Juliet (1595) act 2, sc. 4, l. [41]

21 I am the very pink of courtesy.
Romeo and Juliet (1595) act 2, sc. 4, l. [63]

22 No, 'tis not so deep as a well, nor so wide as a church door; but 'tis enough, 'twill serve.
Romeo and Juliet (1595) act 3, sc. 1, l. [100]

23 A plague o' both your houses!
Romeo and Juliet (1595) act 3, sc. 1, l. [112]

24 O! I am Fortune's fool.
Romeo and Juliet (1595) act 3, sc. 1, l. [142]

25 Gallop apace, you fiery-footed steeds,
Towards Phoebus' lodging.
Romeo and Juliet (1595) act 3, sc. 2, l. 1

26 Spread thy close curtain, love-performing night!
Romeo and Juliet (1595) act 3, sc. 2, l. 5

27 Come, civil night,
Thou sober-suited matron, all in black.
Romeo and Juliet (1595) act 3, sc. 2, l. 10

28 Come, night! come, Romeo! come, thou day in night!
Romeo and Juliet (1595) act 3, sc. 2, l. 17

29 Give me my Romeo: and, when he shall die,
Take him and cut him out in little stars,
And he will make the face of heaven so fine
That all the world will be in love with night,
And pay no worship to the garish sun.
Romeo and Juliet (1595) act 3, sc. 2, l. 21

30 Affliction is enamoured of thy parts,
And thou art wedded to calamity.
Romeo and Juliet (1595) act 3, sc. 3, l. 2

31 Adversity's sweet milk, philosophy.
Romeo and Juliet (1595) act 3, sc. 3, l. 54

32 Wilt thou be gone? it is not yet near day:
It was the nightingale, and not the lark,
That pierced the fearful hollow of thine ear.
Romeo and Juliet (1595) act 3, sc. 5, l. 1

33 Night's candles are burnt out, and jocund day
Stands tiptoe on the misty mountain tops.
Romeo and Juliet (1595) act 3, sc. 5, l. 9

34 I have more care to stay than will to go.
Romeo and Juliet (1595) act 3, sc. 5, l. 23

35 Thank me no thankings, nor proud me no prouds.
Romeo and Juliet (1595) act 3, sc. 5, l. 153

36 Romeo's a dishclout to him.
Romeo and Juliet (1595) act 3, sc. 5, l. 221

37 Death lies on her like an untimely frost
Upon the sweetest flower of all the field.
Romeo and Juliet (1595) act 4, sc. 5, l. 28

1 Tempt not a desperate man.
Romeo and Juliet (1595) act 5, sc. 3, l. 59

2 How oft when men are at the point of death
Have they been merry! which their keepers call
A lightning before death.
Romeo and Juliet (1595) act 5, sc. 3, l. 88

3 Beauty's ensign yet
Is crimson in thy lips and in thy cheeks,
And death's pale flag is not advancèd there.
Romeo and Juliet (1595) act 5, sc. 3, l. 94

4 Seal with a righteous kiss
A dateless bargain to engrossing death!
Romeo and Juliet (1595) act 5, sc. 3, l. 114

5 Seal up the mouth of outrage for a while,
Till we can clear these ambiguities.
Romeo and Juliet (1595) act 5, sc. 3, l. 216

THE TAMING OF THE SHREW

6 I must dance bare-foot on her wedding day,
And, for your love to her, lead apes in hell.
The Taming of the Shrew (1592) act 2, sc. 1, l. 33

7 You are called plain Kate,
And bonny Kate, and sometimes Kate the curst;
But, Kate, the prettiest Kate in Christendom;
Kate of Kate-Hall, my super-dainty Kate,
For dainties are all cates: and therefore, Kate,
Take this of me, Kate of my consolation.
The Taming of the Shrew (1592) act 2, sc. 1, l. 186

8 Kiss me Kate, we will be married o' Sunday.
The Taming of the Shrew (1592) act 2, sc. 1, l. 318

9 This is the way to kill a wife with kindness.
The Taming of the Shrew (1592) act 4, sc. 1, l. [211]

10 What say you to a piece of beef and mustard?
The Taming of the Shrew (1592) act 4, sc. 3, l. [23]

11 O vile,
Intolerable, not to be endured!
The Taming of the Shrew (1592) act 5, sc. 2, l. 93

12 Fie, fie! unknit that threatening unkind brow,
And dart not scornful glances from those eyes,
To wound thy lord, thy king, thy governor.
The Taming of the Shrew (1592) act 5, sc. 2, l. 137

13 A woman moved is like a fountain troubled,
Muddy, ill-seeming, thick, bereft of beauty.
The Taming of the Shrew (1592) act 5, sc. 2, l. 143

14 Such duty as the subject owes the prince,
Even such a woman oweth to her husband.
The Taming of the Shrew (1592) act 5, sc. 2, l. 156

15 I am ashamed that women are so simple
To offer war where they should kneel for peace.
The Taming of the Shrew (1592) act 5, sc. 2, l. 162

THE TEMPEST

16 He hath no drowning mark upon him; his complexion is perfect gallows.
The Tempest (1611) act 1, sc. 1, l. [33]

17 Now would I give a thousand furlongs of sea for an acre of barren ground.
The Tempest (1611) act 1, sc. 1, l. [70]

18 I would fain die a dry death.
The Tempest (1611) act 1, sc. 1, l. [73]

19 What seest thou else
In the dark backward and abysm of time?
The Tempest (1611) act 1, sc. 2, l. 49

20 Your tale, sir, would cure deafness.
The Tempest (1611) act 1, sc. 2, l. 106

21 My library
Was dukedom large enough.
The Tempest (1611) act 1, sc. 2, l. 109

22 The still-vexed Bermoothes.
The Tempest (1611) act 1, sc. 2, l. 229

23 As wicked dew as e'er my mother brushed
With raven's feather from unwholesome fen
Drop on you both! A southwest blow on ye,
And blister you all o'er!
The Tempest (1611) act 1, sc. 2, l. 321

24 You taught me language; and my profit on't
Is, I know how to curse: the red plague rid you,
For learning me your language!
The Tempest (1611) act 1, sc. 2, l. 363

25 I must obey; his art is of such power,
It would control my dam's god, Setebos,
And make a vassal of him.
The Tempest (1611) act 1, sc. 2, l. 372

26 Come unto these yellow sands,
And then take hands.
The Tempest (1611) act 1, sc. 2, l. 375

27 Full fathom five thy father lies;
Of his bones are coral made:
Those are pearls that were his eyes:
Nothing of him that doth fade,
But doth suffer a sea-change
Into something rich and strange.
Sea-nymphs hourly ring his knell:
Ding-dong.
Hark! now I hear them,—ding-dong, bell.
The Tempest (1611) act 1, sc. 2, l. 394

28 The fringèd curtains of thine eye advance,
And say what thou seest yond.
The Tempest (1611) act 1, sc. 2, l. 405

29 He receives comfort like cold porridge.
The Tempest (1611) act 2, sc. 1, l. 10

30 What's past is prologue.
The Tempest (1611) act 2, sc. 1, l. [261]

31 A very ancient and fish-like smell.
The Tempest (1611) act 2, sc. 2, l. [27]

32 When they will not give a doit to relieve a lame beggar, they will lay out ten to see a dead Indian.
The Tempest (1611) act 2, sc. 2, l. [33]

33 Misery acquaints a man with strange bedfellows.
The Tempest (1611) act 2, sc. 2, l. [42]

34 The master, the swabber, the boatswain and I,
The gunner and his mate,
Loved Mall, Meg, and Marian and Margery,
But none of us cared for Kate;
For she had a tongue with a tang,
Would cry to a sailor, 'Go hang!'
The Tempest (1611) act 2, sc. 2, l. [48]

1 'Ban, 'Ban, Ca-Caliban,
Has a new master—Get a new man.
The Tempest (1611) act 2, sc. 2, l. [197]

2 Thou deboshed fish thou.
The Tempest (1611) act 3, sc. 2, l. [30]

3 Flout 'em, and scout 'em; and scout 'em, and flout 'em;
Thought is free.
The Tempest (1611) act 3, sc. 2, l. [133]

4 He that dies pays all debts.
The Tempest (1611) act 3, sc. 2, l. [143]; cf. **Proverbs** 598:3

5 Be not afeard: the isle is full of noises,
Sounds and sweet airs, that give delight, and hurt not.
Sometimes a thousand twangling instruments
Will hum about mine ears, and sometime voices
That if I then had waked after long sleep
Will make me sleep again; and then in dreaming,
The clouds methought would open and show riches
Ready to drop upon me; that, when I waked
I cried to dream again.
The Tempest (1611) act 3, sc. 2, l. [135]

6 Our revels now are ended. These our actors,
As I foretold you, were all spirits and
Are melted into air, into thin air:
And, like the baseless fabric of this vision,
The cloud-capped towers, the gorgeous palaces,
The solemn temples, the great globe itself,
Yea, all which it inherit, shall dissolve
And, like this insubstantial pageant faded,
Leave not a rack behind. We are such stuff
As dreams are made on, and our little life
Is rounded with a sleep.
The Tempest (1611) act 4, sc. 1, l. 148

7 I do begin to have bloody thoughts.
The Tempest (1611) act 4, sc. 1, l. [221]

8 Ye elves of hills, brooks, standing lakes, and groves;
And ye, that on the sands with printless foot
Do chase the ebbing Neptune and do fly him
When he comes back.
The Tempest (1611) act 5, sc. 1, l. 33

9 To the dread rattling thunder
Have I given fire, and rifted Jove's stout oak
With his own bolt; the strong-based promontory
Have I made shake, and by the spurs plucked up
The pine and cedar; graves at my command
Have waked their sleepers, oped, and let 'em forth
By my so potent art. But this rough magic
I here abjure.
The Tempest (1611) act 5, sc. 1, l. 44

10 I'll break my staff,
Bury it certain fathoms in the earth,
And, deeper than did ever plummet sound,
I'll drown my book.
The Tempest (1611) act 5, sc. 1, l. 54

11 Where the bee sucks, there suck I
In a cowslip's bell I lie;
There I couch when owls do cry.
On the bat's back I do fly
After summer merrily:
Merrily, merrily shall I live now
Under the blossom that hangs on the bough.
The Tempest (1611) act 5, sc. 1, l. 88

12 How many goodly creatures are there here!
How beauteous mankind is! O brave new world,
That has such people in't.
The Tempest (1611) act 5, sc. 1, l. 182

TIMON OF ATHENS

13 'Tis not enough to help the feeble up,
But to support him after.
Timon of Athens (c.1607) act 1, sc. 1, l. 108

14 The strain of man's bred out
Into baboon and monkey.
Timon of Athens (c.1607) act 1, sc. 1, l. [260]

15 I wonder men dare trust themselves with men.
Timon of Athens (c.1607) act 1, sc. 2, l. [45]

16 Like madness is the glory of this life.
Timon of Athens (c.1607) act 1, sc. 2, l. [141]

17 Men shut their doors against a setting sun.
Timon of Athens (c.1607) act 1, sc. 2, l. [152]

18 You fools of fortune, trencher-friends, time's flies.
Timon of Athens (c.1607) act 3, sc. 6, l. [107]

19 We have seen better days.
Timon of Athens (c.1607) act 4, sc. 2, l. 27

20 O! the fierce wretchedness that glory brings us.
Timon of Athens (c.1607) act 4, sc. 2, l. 30

21 Never learned
The icy precepts of respect, but followed
The sugared game before thee. But myself,
Who had the world as my confectionary,
The mouths, the tongues, the eyes, and hearts of men
At duty, more than I could frame employment;
That numberless upon me stuck as leaves
Do on the oak, have with one winter's brush
Fell from their boughs, and left me open, bare,
For every storm that blows.
Timon of Athens (c.1607) act 4, sc. 3, l. 257

22 The moon's an arrant thief,
And her pale fire she snatches from the sun.
Timon of Athens (c.1607) act 4, sc. 3, l. 437

23 He has almost charmed me from my profession, by persuading me to it.
Timon of Athens (c.1607) act 4, sc. 3, l. [457]

24 My long sickness
Of health and living now begins to mend,
And nothing brings me all things.
Timon of Athens (c.1607) act 5, sc. 1, l. [191]

25 Timon hath made his everlasting mansion
Upon the beachèd verge of the salt flood;
Who once a day with his embossèd froth
The turbulent surge shall cover.
Timon of Athens (c.1607) act 5, sc. 1, l. [220]

TITUS ANDRONICUS

26 She is a woman, therefore may be wooed;
She is a woman, therefore may be won;

She is Lavinia, therefore must be loved.
Titus Andronicus (1590) act 2, sc. 1, l. 82; cf. **Shakespeare** 672:13

1 Come, and take choice of all my library,
And so beguile thy sorrow.
Titus Andronicus (1590) act 4, sc. 1, l. 34

2 Both bakèd in this pie
Whereof their mother daintily hath fed,
Eating the flesh that she herself hath bred.
Titus Andronicus (1590) act 5, sc. 3, l. 59

3 If one good deed in all my life I did,
I do repent it from my very soul.
Titus Andronicus (1590) act 5, sc. 3, l. [189]

TROILUS AND CRESSIDA

4 I have had my labour for my travail.
Troilus and Cressida (1602) act 1, sc. 1, l. [73]

5 Things won are done; joy's soul lies in the doing.
Troilus and Cressida (1602) act 1, sc. 2, l. [311]

6 Take but degree away, untune that string,
And, hark! what discord follows.
Troilus and Cressida (1602) act 1, sc. 3, l. 109

7 An envious fever
Of pale and bloodless emulation.
Troilus and Cressida (1602) act 1, sc. 3, l. 133

8 We are soldiers;
And may that soldier a mere recreant prove,
That means not, hath not, or is not in love!
Troilus and Cressida (1602) act 1, sc. 3, l. 286

9 The baby figure of the giant mass
Of things to come at large.
Troilus and Cressida (1602) act 1, sc. 3, l. 345

10 You have both said well;
And on the cause and question now in hand
Have glozed but superficially; not much
Unlike young men, whom Aristotle thought
Unfit to hear moral philosophy.
Troilus and Cressida (1602) act 2, sc. 2, l. 163

11 Thus to persist
In doing wrong extenuates not wrong,
But makes it much more heavy.
Troilus and Cressida (1602) act 2, sc. 2, l. 186

12 I am giddy, expectation whirls me round.
The imaginary relish is so sweet
That it enchants my sense.
Troilus and Cressida (1602) act 3, sc. 2, l. [17]

13 To be wise, and love,
Exceeds man's might.
Troilus and Cressida (1602) act 3, sc. 2, l. [163]

14 Time hath, my lord, a wallet at his back,
Wherein he puts alms for oblivion,
A great-sized monster of ingratitudes:
Those scraps are good deeds past; which are devoured
As fast as they are made, forgot as soon
As done.
Troilus and Cressida (1602) act 3, sc. 3, l. 145

15 Perseverance, dear my lord,
Keeps honour bright.
Troilus and Cressida (1602) act 3, sc. 3, l. 150

16 Time is like a fashionable host
That slightly shakes his parting guest by the hand,
And with his arms outstretched, as he would fly,
Grasps in the comer: welcome ever smiles,
And farewell goes out sighing.
Troilus and Cressida (1602) act 3, sc. 3, l. 165

17 Beauty, wit,
High birth, vigour of bone, desert in service,
Love, friendship, charity, are subjects all
To envious and calumniating time.
One touch of nature makes the whole world kin.
Troilus and Cressida (1602) act 3, sc. 3, l. 171

18 A plague of opinion! a man may wear it on both sides, like a leather jerkin.
Troilus and Cressida (1602) act 3, sc. 3, l. [267]

19 What a pair of spectacles is here!
Pandarus, of the lovers
Troilus and Cressida (1602) act 4, sc. 4, l. [13]

20 Fie, fie upon her!
There's language in her eye, her cheek, her lip,
Nay, her foot speaks; her wanton spirits look out
At every joint and motive of her body.
Troilus and Cressida (1602) act 4, sc. 5, l. 54

21 What's past, and what's to come is strewed with husks
And formless ruin of oblivion.
Troilus and Cressida (1602) act 4, sc. 5, l. 165

22 The end crowns all,
And that old common arbitrator, Time,
Will one day end it.
Troilus and Cressida (1602) act 4, sc. 5, l. 223

23 Lechery, lechery; still, wars and lechery: nothing else holds fashion.
Troilus and Cressida (1602) act 5, sc. 2, l. 192

24 Words, words, mere words, no matter from the heart.
Troilus and Cressida (1602) act 5, sc. 3, l. [109]

25 Hector is dead; there is no more to say.
Troilus and Cressida (1602) act 5, sc. 10, l. 22

TWELFTH NIGHT

26 If music be the food of love, play on;
Give me excess of it, that, surfeiting,
The appetite may sicken, and so die.
That strain again! it had a dying fall:
O! it came o'er my ear like the sweet sound
That breathes upon a bank of violets,
Stealing and giving odour! Enough! no more:
'Tis not so sweet now as it was before.
Twelfth Night (1601) act 1, sc. 1, l. 1

27 O! when mine eyes did see Olivia first,
Methought she purged the air of pestilence.
Twelfth Night (1601) act 1, sc. 1, l. 19

28 And what should I do in Illyria?
My brother he is in Elysium.
Twelfth Night (1601) act 1, sc. 2, l. 2

29 I am a great eater of beef, and I believe that does harm to my wit.
Twelfth Night (1601) act 1, sc. 3, l. [92]

1 I would I had bestowed that time in the tongues that I have in fencing, dancing, and bear-baiting. O! had I but followed the arts!
Twelfth Night (1601) act 1, sc. 3, l. [99]

2 Is it a world to hide virtues in?
Twelfth Night (1601) act 1, sc. 3, l. [142]

3 Thy small pipe
Is as the maiden's organ, shrill and sound;
And all is semblative a woman's part.
Twelfth Night (1601) act 1, sc. 4, l. 32

4 Many a good hanging prevents a bad marriage.
Twelfth Night (1601) act 1, sc. 5, l. [20]

5 A plague o' these pickle herring!
Twelfth Night (1601) act 1, sc. 5, l. [127]

6 He is very well-favoured, and he speaks very shrewishly: one would think his mother's milk were scarce out of him.
Twelfth Night (1601) act 1, sc. 5, l. [170]

7 Make me a willow cabin at your gate,
And call upon my soul within the house;
Write loyal cantons of contemnèd love,
And sing them loud even in the dead of night;
Halloo your name to the reverberate hills,
And make the babbling gossip of the air
Cry out, 'Olivia!' O! you should not rest
Between the elements of air and earth,
But you should pity me!
Twelfth Night (1601) act 1, sc. 5, l. [289]

8 Not to be a-bed after midnight is to be up betimes.
Twelfth Night (1601) act 2, sc. 3, l. 1

9 O mistress mine! where are you roaming?
O! stay and hear; your true love's coming,
That can sing both high and low.
Trip no further, pretty sweeting;
Journeys end in lovers meeting,
Every wise man's son doth know.
Twelfth Night (1601) act 2, sc. 3, l. [42]

10 What is love? 'tis not hereafter;
Present mirth hath present laughter;
What's to come is still unsure:
In delay there lies no plenty;
Then come kiss me, sweet and twenty,
Youth's a stuff will not endure.
Twelfth Night (1601) act 2, sc. 3, l. [50]

11 Am not I consanguineous? am I not of her blood?
Twelfth Night (1601) act 2, sc. 3, l. [85]

12 He does it with a better grace, but I do it more natural.
Twelfth Night (1601) act 2, sc. 3, l. [91]

13 Is there no respect of place, persons, nor time, in you?
Twelfth Night (1601) act 2, sc. 3, l. [100]

14 Dost thou think, because thou art virtuous, there shall be no more cakes and ale?
Twelfth Night (1601) act 2, sc. 3, l. [124]

15 My purpose is, indeed, a horse of that colour.
Twelfth Night (1601) act 2, sc. 3, l. [184]

16 I was adored once too.
Twelfth Night (1601) act 2, sc. 3, l. [200]

17 Now, good Cesario, but that piece of song,
That old and antique song we heard last night;
Methought it did relieve my passion much,
More than light airs and recollected terms
Of these most brisk and giddy-pacèd times.
Twelfth Night (1601) act 2, sc. 4, l. 2

18 Let still the woman take
An elder than herself, so wears she to him,
So sways she level in her husband's heart:
For, boy, however we do praise ourselves,
Our fancies are more giddy and unfirm,
More longing, wavering, sooner lost and worn,
Than women's are.
Twelfth Night (1601) act 2, sc. 4, l. 29

19 Then let thy love be younger than thyself,
Or thy affection cannot hold the bent.
Twelfth Night (1601) act 2, sc. 4, l. 36

20 The spinsters and the knitters in the sun.
Twelfth Night (1601) act 2, sc. 4, l. 44

21 Come away, come away, death,
And in sad cypress let me be laid;
Fly away, fly away, breath:
I am slain by a fair cruel maid.
Twelfth Night (1601) act 2, sc. 4, l. 51

22 Now, the melancholy god protect thee, and the tailor make thy doublet of changeable taffeta, for thy mind is a very opal.
Twelfth Night (1601) act 2, sc. 4, l. [74]

23 My father had a daughter loved a man,
As it might be, perhaps, were I a woman,
I should your lordship.
Twelfth Night (1601) act 2, sc. 4, l. [108]

24 DUKE: And what's her history?
VIOLA: A blank, my lord. She never told her love,
But let concealment, like a worm i' the bud,
Feed on her damask cheek: she pined in thought;
And with a green and yellow melancholy,
She sat like patience on a monument,
Smiling at grief. Was not this love indeed?
Twelfth Night (1601) act 2, sc. 4, l. [111]

25 I am all the daughters of my father's house,
And all the brothers too.
Twelfth Night (1601) act 2, sc. 4, l. [122]

26 Now is the woodcock near the gin.
Twelfth Night (1601) act 2, sc. 5, l. [93]

27 I may command where I adore.
Twelfth Night (1601) act 2, sc. 5, l. [117]

28 But be not afraid of greatness: some men are born great, some achieve greatness, and some have greatness thrust upon them.
Twelfth Night (1601) act 2, sc. 5, l. [158]; cf. **Heller** 368:14

29 Remember who commended thy yellow stockings, and wished to see thee ever cross-gartered.
Twelfth Night (1601) act 2, sc. 5, l. [168]

30 Jove and my stars be praised! Here is yet a postscript.
Twelfth Night (1601) act 2, sc. 5, l. [190]

31 This fellow's wise enough to play the fool,
And to do that well craves a kind of wit.
Twelfth Night (1601) act 3, sc. 1, l. [68]

1 O world! how apt the poor are to be proud.
Twelfth Night (1601) act 3, sc. 1, l. [141]

2 O! what a deal of scorn looks beautiful
In the contempt and anger of his lip.
Twelfth Night (1601) act 3, sc. 1, l. [159]

3 Love sought is good, but giv'n unsought is better.
Twelfth Night (1601) act 3, sc. 1, l. [170]

4 You are now sailed into the north of my lady's opinion; where you will hang like an icicle on a Dutchman's beard.
Twelfth Night (1601) act 3, sc. 2, l. [29]

5 As many lies as will lie in thy sheet of paper, although the sheet were big enough for the bed of Ware in England, set 'em down.
Twelfth Night (1601) act 3, sc. 2, l. [51]

6 Look, where the youngest wren of nine comes.
Twelfth Night (1601) act 3, sc. 2, l. [73]

7 He does smile his face into more lines than are in the new map with the augmentation of the Indies.
Twelfth Night (1601) act 3, sc. 2, l. [85]

8 In the south suburbs, at the Elephant,
Is best to lodge.
Twelfth Night (1601) act 3, sc. 3, l. 39

9 I think we do know the sweet Roman hand.
Twelfth Night (1601) act 3, sc. 4, l. [31]

10 Why, this is very midsummer madness.
Twelfth Night (1601) act 3, sc. 4, l. [62]

11 Go, hang yourselves all! you are idle shallow things: I am not of your element.
Twelfth Night (1601) act 3, sc. 4, l. [138]

12 If this were played upon a stage now, I could condemn it as an improbable fiction.
Twelfth Night (1601) act 3, sc. 4, l. [142]

13 More matter for a May morning.
Twelfth Night (1601) act 3, sc. 4, l. [158]

14 Still you keep o' the windy side of the law.
Twelfth Night (1601) act 3, sc. 4, l. [183]

15 Nay, let me alone for swearing.
Twelfth Night (1601) act 3, sc. 4, l. [204]

16 I hate ingratitude more in a man
Than lying, vainness, babbling drunkenness,
Or any taint of vice whose strong corruption
Inhabits our frail blood.
Twelfth Night (1601) act 3, sc. 4, l. [390]

17 In nature there's no blemish but the mind;
None can be called deformed but the unkind.
Twelfth Night (1601) act 3, sc. 4, l. [403]

18 Leave thy vain bibble-babble.
Twelfth Night (1601) act 4, sc. 2, l. [106]

19 Why have you suffered me to be imprisoned,
Kept in a dark house, visited by the priest,
And made the most notorious geck and gull
That e'er invention played on? Tell me why.
Twelfth Night (1601) act 5, sc. 1, l. [353]

20 Thus the whirligig of time brings in his revenges.
Twelfth Night (1601) act 5, sc. 1, l. [388]

21 I'll be revenged on the whole pack of you.
Twelfth Night (1601) act 5, sc. 1, l. [390]

22 When that I was and a little tiny boy,
With hey, ho, the wind and the rain;
A foolish thing was but a toy,
For the rain it raineth every day.
But when I came to man's estate,
With hey, ho, the wind and the rain;
'Gainst knaves and thieves men shut their gates,
For the rain it raineth every day.
Twelfth Night (1601) act 5, sc. 1, l. [401]

THE TWO GENTLEMEN OF VERONA

23 Home-keeping youth have ever homely wits.
The Two Gentlemen of Verona (1592–3) act 1, sc. 1, l. 2

24 I have no other but a woman's reason:
I think him so, because I think him so.
The Two Gentlemen of Verona (1592–3) act 1, sc. 2, l. 23

25 Fie, fie! how wayward is this foolish love
That, like a testy babe, will scratch the nurse
And presently all humbled kiss the rod!
The Two Gentlemen of Verona (1592–3) act 1, sc. 2, l. 55

26 O! how this spring of love resembleth
The uncertain glory of an April day,
Which now shows all the beauty of the sun,
And by and by a cloud takes all away!
The Two Gentlemen of Verona (1592–3) act 1, sc. 3, l. 84

27 Except I be by Silvia in the night,
There is no music in the nightingale;
Unless I look on Silvia in the day,
There is no day for me to look upon.
The Two Gentlemen of Verona (1592–3) act 3, sc. 1, l. 178

28 Much is the force of heaven-bred poesy.
The Two Gentlemen of Verona (1592–3) act 3, sc. 2, l. 71

29 Who is Silvia? what is she,
That all our swains commend her?
Holy, fair, and wise is she;
The heaven such grace did lend her,
That she might admirèd be.
Is she kind as she is fair?
For beauty lives with kindness:
Love doth to her eyes repair,
To help him of his blindness;
And, being helped, inhabits there.
The Two Gentlemen of Verona (1592–3) act 4, sc. 2, l. 40

30 O heaven! were man
But constant, he were perfect.
The Two Gentlemen of Verona (1592–3) act 5, sc. 4, l. 110

THE WINTER'S TALE

31 Two lads that thought there was no more behind
But such a day to-morrow as to-day,
And to be boy eternal.
The Winter's Tale (1610–11) act 1, sc. 2, l. 63

32 We were as twinned lambs that did frisk i' the sun,
And bleat the one at the other: what we changed
Was innocence for innocence; we knew not
The doctrine of ill-doing, no, nor dreamed
That any did.
The Winter's Tale (1610–11) act 1, sc. 2, l. 67

33 But to be paddling palms and pinching fingers,
As now they are, and making practised smiles,

As in a looking-glass.
The Winter's Tale (1610–11) act 1, sc. 2, l. 116

1 How like, methought, I then was to this kernel,
This squash, this gentleman.
The Winter's Tale (1610–11) act 1, sc. 2, l. 160

2 A sad tale's best for winter.
I have one of sprites and goblins.
The Winter's Tale (1610–11) act 2, sc. 1, l. 24

3 There may be in the cup
A spider steeped, and one may drink, depart,
And yet partake no venom, for his knowledge
Is not infected; but if one present
Th' abhorred ingredient to his eye, make known
How he hath drunk, he cracks his gorge, his sides,
With violent hefts. I have drunk, and seen the spider.
The Winter's Tale (1610–11) act 2, sc. 1, l. 39

4 It is a heretic that makes the fire,
Not she which burns in 't.
The Winter's Tale (1610–11) act 2, sc. 3, l. 114

5 I am a feather for each wind that blows.
The Winter's Tale (1610–11) act 2, sc. 3, l. 153

6 HERMIONE: My life stands in the level of your dreams,
Which I'll lay down.
LEONTES: Your actions are my dreams.
The Winter's Tale (1610–11) act 3, sc. 2, l. 81

7 What's gone and what's past help
Should be past grief.
The Winter's Tale (1610–11) act 3, sc. 2, l. [223]

8 Exit, pursued by a bear.
stage direction
The Winter's Tale (1610–11) act 3, sc. 3

9 When daffodils begin to peer,
With heigh! the doxy, over the dale,
Why, then comes in the sweet o' the year;
For the red blood reigns in the winter's pale.
The Winter's Tale (1610–11) act 4, sc. 2, l. 1

10 While we lie tumbling in the hay.
The Winter's Tale (1610–11) act 4, sc. 2, l. 12

11 My father named me Autolycus; who being, as I am, littered under Mercury, was likewise a snapper-up of unconsidered trifles.
The Winter's Tale (1610–11) act 4, sc. 2, l. [24]

12 Jog on, jog on the foot-path way,
And merrily hent the stile-a:
A merry heart goes all the day,
Your sad tires in a mile-a.
The Winter's Tale (1610–11) act 4, sc. 2, l. [133]

13 For you there's rosemary and rue; these keep
Seeming and savour all the winter long.
The Winter's Tale (1610–11) act 4, sc. 3, l. 74

14 The fairest flowers o' the season
Are our carnations and streaked gillyvors,
Which some call nature's bastards.
The Winter's Tale (1610–11) act 4, sc. 3, l. 81

15 I'll not put
The dibble in earth to set one slip of them.
The Winter's Tale (1610–11) act 4, sc. 3, l. 99

16 Here's flowers for you;
Hot lavender, mints, savory, marjoram;
The marigold, that goes to bed wi' the sun,
And with him rises weeping.
The Winter's Tale (1610–11) act 4, sc. 3, l. 103

17 O Proserpina!
For the flowers now that frighted thou let'st fall
From Dis's waggon! daffodils,
That come before the swallow dares, and take
The winds of March with beauty.
The Winter's Tale (1610–11) act 4, sc. 3, l. 118

18 Pale prime-roses,
That die unmarried, ere they can behold
Bright Phoebus in his strength,—a malady
Most incident to maids; bold oxlips and
The crown imperial; lilies of all kinds,
The flower-de-luce being one.
The Winter's Tale (1610–11) act 4, sc. 3, l. 122

19 Each your doing,
So singular in each particular,
Crowns what you are doing in the present deed,
That all your acts are queens.
The Winter's Tale (1610–11) act 4, sc. 3, l. 144

20 The queen of curds and cream.
The Winter's Tale (1610–11) act 4, sc. 3, l. 161

21 I love a ballad in print, a-life, for then we are sure they are true.
The Winter's Tale (1610–11) act 4, sc. 3, l. [262]

22 The self-same sun that shines upon his court
Hides not his visage from our cottage, but
Looks on alike.
The Winter's Tale (1610–11) act 4, sc. 3, l. [457]

23 Being now awake, I'll queen it no inch further,
But milk my ewes and weep.
The Winter's Tale (1610–11) act 4, sc. 3, l. [463]

24 Though I am not naturally honest, I am so sometimes by chance.
The Winter's Tale (1610–11) act 4, sc. 3, l. [734]

25 Stars, stars!
And all eyes else dead coals.
The Winter's Tale (1610–11) act 5, sc. 1, l. 67

26 O! she's warm.
If this be magic, let it be an art
Lawful as eating.
The Winter's Tale (1610–11) act 5, sc. 3, l. 109

THE PASSIONATE PILGRIM (ATTRIBUTION DOUBTFUL)

27 Crabbed age and youth cannot live together:
Youth is full of pleasance, age is full of care.
The Passionate Pilgrim (1599) no. 12

28 Age, I do abhor thee, youth, I do adore thee.
The Passionate Pilgrim (1599) no. 12

THE RAPE OF LUCRECE

29 What I have done is yours; what I have to do is yours; being part in all I have, devoted yours.
The Rape of Lucrece (1594) dedication

30 Beauty itself doth of itself persuade
The eyes of men without an orator.
The Rape of Lucrece (1594) l. 29

1 Who buys a minute's mirth to wail a week?
Or sells eternity to get a toy?
For one sweet grape who will the vine destroy?
The Rape of Lucrece (1594) l. 213

2 Time's glory is to calm contending kings,
To unmask falsehood, and bring truth to light.
The Rape of Lucrece (1594) l. 939

3 And now this pale swan in her watery nest
Begins the sad dirge of her certain ending.
The Rape of Lucrece (1594) l. 1611

SONNETS

4 To the onlie begetter of these insuing sonnets, Mr. W. H.
also attributed to Thomas Thorpe, the publisher
Sonnets (1609) dedication

5 From fairest creatures we desire increase,
That thereby beauty's rose might never die.
Sonnet 1

6 When forty winters shall besiege thy brow,
And dig deep trenches in thy beauty's field.
Sonnet 2

7 Thou art thy mother's glass, and she in thee
Calls back the lovely April of her prime.
Sonnet 3

8 When lofty trees I see barren of leaves,
Which erst from heat did canopy the herd,
And summer's green all girded up in sheaves,
Borne on the bier with white and bristly beard.
Sonnet 12

9 Shall I compare thee to a summer's day?
Thou art more lovely and more temperate:
Rough winds do shake the darling buds of May,
And summer's lease hath all too short a date.
Sonnet 18

10 But thy eternal summer shall not fade,
Nor lose possession of that fair thou ow'st,
Nor shall death brag thou wander'st in his shade,
When in eternal lines to time thou grow'st;
So long as men can breathe, or eyes can see,
So long lives this, and this gives life to thee.
Sonnet 18

11 As an unperfect actor on the stage,
Who with his fear is put beside his part,
Or some fierce thing replete with too much rage,
Whose strength's abundance weakens his own heart;
So I, for fear of trust, forget to say
The perfect ceremony of love's rite.
Sonnet 23

12 O! let my books be then the eloquence
And dumb presagers of my speaking breast.
Sonnet 23

13 When in disgrace with fortune and men's eyes
I all alone beweep my outcast state.
Sonnet 29

14 Desiring this man's art, and that man's scope,
With what I most enjoy contented least.
Sonnet 29

15 Haply I think on thee,—and then my state,
Like to the lark at break of day arising
From sullen earth, sings hymns at heaven's gate;
For thy sweet love remembered such wealth brings
That then I scorn to change my state with kings.
Sonnet 29

16 When to the sessions of sweet silent thought
I summon up remembrance of things past,
I sigh the lack of many a thing I sought,
And with old woes new wail my dear times' waste.
Sonnet 30; cf. **Borrowed titles** 144:13

17 Full many a glorious morning have I seen
Flatter the mountain-tops with sovereign eye,
Kissing with golden face the meadows green,
Gilding pale streams with heavenly alchemy.
Sonnet 33

18 Roses have thorns, and silver fountains mud;
Clouds and eclipses stain both moon and sun,
And loathsome canker lives in sweetest bud.
Sonnet 35

19 What is your substance, whereof are you made,
That millions of strange shadows on you tend?
Sonnet 53

20 O! how much more doth beauty beauteous seem
By that sweet ornament which truth doth give!
Sonnet 54

21 Not marble, nor the gilded monuments
Of princes, shall outlive this powerful rhyme.
Sonnet 55

22 So true a fool is love that in your will,
Though you do anything, he thinks no ill.
Sonnet 57

23 Like as the waves make towards the pebbled shore,
So do our minutes hasten to their end.
Sonnet 60

24 Time doth transfix the flourish set on youth
And delves the parallels in beauty's brow.
Sonnet 60

25 When I have seen by Time's fell hand defaced
The rich-proud cost of outworn buried age.
Sonnet 64

26 When I have seen the hungry ocean gain
Advantage on the kingdom of the shore.
Sonnet 64

27 Since brass, nor stone, nor earth, nor boundless sea,
But sad mortality o'ersways their power,
How with this rage shall beauty hold a plea,
Whose action is no stronger than a flower?
Sonnet 65

28 No longer mourn for me when I am dead
Than you shall hear the surly sullen bell
Give warning to the world that I am fled
From this vile world, with vilest worms to dwell.
Sonnet 71

29 That time of year thou mayst in me behold
When yellow leaves, or none, or few, do hang
Upon those boughs which shake against the cold,
Bare ruined choirs, where late the sweet birds sang.
Sonnet 73

1 So all my best is dressing old words new,
Spending again what is already spent.
Sonnet 76

2 Time's thievish progress to eternity.
Sonnet 77

3 Was it the proud full sail of his great verse,
Bound for the prize of all too precious you,
That did my ripe thoughts in my brain inhearse,
Making their tomb the womb wherein they grew?
Sonnet 86

4 Farewell! thou art too dear for my possessing.
Sonnet 87

5 Thus have I had thee, as a dream doth flatter,
In sleep a king, but, waking, no such matter.
Sonnet 87

6 They that have power to hurt and will do none,
That do not do the thing they most do show,
Who, moving others, are themselves as stone,
Unmovèd, cold, and to temptation slow;
They rightly do inherit heaven's graces,
And husband nature's riches from expense.
Sonnet 94

7 For sweetest things turn sourest by their deeds;
Lilies that fester smell far worse than weeds.
Sonnet 94

8 How like a winter hath my absence been
From thee, the pleasure of the fleeting year!
What freezings have I felt, what dark days seen!
What old December's bareness everywhere!
Sonnet 97

9 When in the chronicle of wasted time
I see descriptions of the fairest wights,
And beauty making beautiful old rime,
In praise of ladies dead and lovely knights.
Sonnet 106

10 For we, which now behold these present days,
Have eyes to wonder, but lack tongues to praise.
Sonnet 106

11 Not mine own fears, nor the prophetic soul
Of the wide world dreaming on things to come.
Sonnet 107

12 And thou in this shalt find thy monument,
When tyrants' crests and tombs of brass are spent.
Sonnet 107

13 Alas! 'tis true I have gone here and there,
And made myself a motley to the view,
Gored mine own thoughts, sold cheap what is most dear,
Made old offences of affections new.
Sonnet 110

14 My nature is subdued
To what it works in, like the dyer's hand.
Sonnet 111

15 Let me not to the marriage of true minds
Admit impediments. Love is not love
Which alters when it alteration finds,
Or bends with the remover to remove:
O, no! it is an ever-fixèd mark,
That looks on tempests and is never shaken.
Sonnet 116

16 Love's not Time's fool.
Sonnet 116

17 Love alters not with his brief hours and weeks,
But bears it out even to the edge of doom.
If this be error, and upon me proved,
I never writ, nor no man ever loved.
Sonnet 116

18 What potions have I drunk of Siren tears,
Distilled from limbecks foul as hell within.
Sonnet 119

19 The expense of spirit in a waste of shame
Is lust in action; and till action, lust
Is perjured, murderous, bloody, full of blame,
Savage, extreme, rude, cruel, not to trust;
Enjoyed no sooner but despisèd straight.
Sonnet 129

20 My mistress' eyes are nothing like the sun;
Coral is far more red than her lips' red:
If snow be white, why then her breasts are dun;
If hairs be wires, black wires grow on her head.
Sonnet 130

21 And yet, by heaven, I think my love as rare
As any she belied with false compare.
Sonnet 130

22 Whoever hath her wish, thou hast thy *Will*,
And *Will* to boot, and *Will* in over-plus.
Sonnet 135

23 When my love swears that she is made of truth,
I do believe her, though I know she lies.
Sonnet 138

24 Two loves I have of comfort and despair,
Which like two spirits do suggest me still:
The better angel is a man right fair,
The worser spirit a woman, coloured ill.
Sonnet 144

25 So shalt thou feed on Death, that feeds on men,
And Death once dead, there's no more dying then.
Sonnet 146

26 Past cure I am, now Reason is past care,
And frantic-mad with evermore unrest;
My thoughts and my discourse as madmen's are,
At random from the truth vainly expressed;
For I have sworn thee fair, and thought thee bright,
Who art as black as hell, as dark as night.
Sonnet 147

VENUS AND ADONIS

27 If the first heir of my invention prove deformed, I shall be sorry it had so noble a godfather.
Venus and Adonis (1593) dedication

28 Hunting he loved, but love he laughed to scorn.
Venus and Adonis (1593) l. 4

29 Bid me discourse, I will enchant thine ear,
Or like a fairy trip upon the green,
Or, like a nymph, with long dishevelled hair,
Dance on the sands, and yet no footing seen:
Love is a spirit all compact of fire,
Not gross to sink, but light, and will aspire.
Venus and Adonis (1593) l. 145

1 Love comforteth like sunshine after rain.
Venus and Adonis (1593) l. 799

2 For he being dead, with him is beauty slain,
And, beauty dead, black chaos comes again.
Venus and Adonis (1593) l. 1019

3 Item, I give unto my wife my second best bed, with the furniture.
will, 1616; E. Chambers *William Shakespeare* (1930) vol. 2

Shammai *c.*1st century BC–1st century AD
Jewish scholar and teacher

4 Say little and do much. Receive all men with a cheerful countenance.
in *Talmud* Mishnah 'Pirqei Avot' 1:15

Eileen Shanahan

5 The length of a meeting rises with the square of the number of people present.
in *New York Magazine* 17 March 1968

Bill Shankly 1914–81
Scottish footballer

6 Some people think football is a matter of life and death . . . I can assure them it is much more serious than that.
in *Sunday Times* 4 October 1981

Shantideva *c.*685–763
Indian scholar, monk, and poet

7 May I allay all the suffering of every living being. I am the medicine for the sick. May I be both the doctor and their nurse, until the sickness does not recur.
Bodhicaryāvatāra ch. 3, v. 6

8 Whoever longs to rescue quickly both himself and others should practise the supreme mystery: exchange of self and other.
Bodhicaryāvatāra ch. 8, v. 120

9 All those who suffer in the world do so because of their desire for their own happiness. All those happy in the world are so because of their desire for the happiness of others.
Bodhicaryāvatāra ch. 8, v. 129

10 Whatever suffering is in store for the world, may it all ripen in me. May the world find happiness through all the pure deeds of the Bodhisattvas.
Bodhicaryāvatāra ch. 10, v. 56

Robert Shapiro 1942–
American lawyer

11 Not only did we play the race card, we played it from the bottom of the deck.
on the defence team's change of strategy at the trial of O. J. Simpson
in *The Times* 5 October 1995; cf. **Churchill** 214:13

George Bernard Shaw 1856–1950
Irish dramatist
on Shaw: see **Lenin** *463:12,* **Wilde** *819:11; see also* ***Misquotations*** *521:10*

12 All great truths begin as blasphemies.
Annajanska (1919)

13 One man that has a mind and knows it can always beat ten men who haven't and don't.
The Apple Cart (1930) act 1

14 What Englishman will give his mind to politics as long as he can afford to keep a motor car?
The Apple Cart (1930) act 1

15 You can always tell an old soldier by the inside of his holsters and cartridge boxes. The young ones carry pistols and cartridges; the old ones, grub.
Arms and the Man (1898) act 1

16 Oh, you are a very poor soldier—a chocolate cream soldier!
Arms and the Man (1898) act 1

17 I enjoy convalescence. It is the part that makes illness worth while.
Back to Methuselah (1921) pt. 2

18 He [the Briton] is a barbarian, and thinks that the customs of his tribe and island are the laws of nature.
Caesar and Cleopatra (1901) act 2

19 When a stupid man is doing something he is ashamed of, he always declares that it is his duty.
Caesar and Cleopatra (1901) act 3

20 A man of great common sense and good taste, meaning thereby a man without originality or moral courage.
Notes to Caesar and Cleopatra (1901) 'Julius Caesar'

21 We have no more right to consume happiness without producing it than to consume wealth without producing it.
Candida (1898) act 1

22 Do you think that the things people make fools of themselves about are any less real and true than the things they behave sensibly about? They are more true: they are the only things that are true.
Candida (1898) act 1

23 It is easy—terribly easy— to shake a man's faith in himself. To take advantage of that to break a man's spirit is devil's work.
Candida (1898) act 1

24 I'm only a beer teetotaller, not a champagne teetotaller.
Candida (1898) act 3

25 The worst sin towards our fellow creatures is not to hate them, but to be indifferent to them: that's the essence of inhumanity.
The Devil's Disciple (1901) act 2

26 Martyrdom . . . the only way in which a man can become famous without ability.
The Devil's Disciple (1901) act 3

27 I never expect a soldier to think.
The Devil's Disciple (1901) act 3

1 SWINDON: What will history say?
BURGOYNE: History, sir, will tell lies as usual.
The Devil's Disciple (1901) act 3

2 The British soldier can stand up to anything except the British War Office.
The Devil's Disciple (1901) act 3

3 There is at bottom only one genuinely scientific treatment for all diseases, and that is to stimulate the phagocytes.
The Doctor's Dilemma (1911) act 1

4 All professions are conspiracies against the laity.
The Doctor's Dilemma (1911) act 1

5 A government which robs Peter to pay Paul can always depend on the support of Paul.
Everybody's Political What's What? (1944) ch. 30

6 It's all that the young can do for the old, to shock them and keep them up to date.
Fanny's First Play (1914) 'Induction'

7 Home life as we understand it is no more natural to us than a cage is natural to a cockatoo.
Getting Married (1911) preface 'Hearth and Home'

8 The one point on which all women are in furious secret rebellion against the existing law is the saddling of the right to a child with the obligation to become the servant of a man.
Getting Married (1911) preface 'The Right to Motherhood'

9 Physically there is nothing to distinguish human society from the farm-yard except that children are more troublesome and costly than chickens and calves, and that men and women are not so completely enslaved as farm stock.
Getting Married (1911) preface 'The Personal Sentimental Basis of Monogamy'

10 What God hath joined together no man ever shall put asunder: God will take care of that.
Getting Married (1911) p. 216; cf. **Book of Common Prayer** 131:7

11 I am a woman of the world, Hector; and I can assure you that if you will only take the trouble always to do the perfectly correct thing, and to say the perfectly correct thing, you can do just what you like.
Heartbreak House (1919) act 1

12 Go anywhere in England where there are natural, wholesome, contented, and really nice English people; and what do you always find? That the stables are the real centre of the household.
Heartbreak House (1919) act 3

13 The captain is in his bunk, drinking bottled ditch-water; and the crew is gambling in the forecastle. She will strike and sink and split. Do you think the laws of God will be suspended in favour of England because you were born in it?
Heartbreak House (1919) act 3

14 Money is indeed the most important thing in the world; and all sound and successful personal and national morality should have this fact for its basis.
The Irrational Knot (1905) preface

15 Reminiscences make one feel so deliciously aged and sad.
The Irrational Knot (1905) ch. 14

16 A man who has no office to go to—I don't care who he is—is a trial of which you can have no conception.
The Irrational Knot (1905) ch. 18

17 John Bull's other island.
title of play (1907)

18 An Irishman's heart is nothing but his imagination.
John Bull's Other Island (1907) act 1

19 What really flatters a man is that you think him worth flattering.
John Bull's Other Island (1907) act 4

20 There are only two qualities in the world: efficiency and inefficiency, and only two sorts of people: the efficient and the inefficient.
John Bull's Other Island (1907) act 4

21 The greatest of evils and the worst of crimes is poverty . . . our first duty—a duty to which every other consideration should be sacrificed—is not to be poor.
Major Barbara (1907) preface

22 Nobody can say a word against Greek: it stamps a man at once as an educated gentleman.
Major Barbara (1907) act 1

23 I am a Millionaire. That is my religion.
Major Barbara (1907) act 2

24 I can't talk religion to a man with bodily hunger in his eyes.
Major Barbara (1907) act 2

25 Wot prawce Selvytion nah?
Major Barbara (1907) act 2

26 Alcohol is a very necessary article . . . It enables Parliament to do things at eleven at night that no sane person would do at eleven in the morning.
Major Barbara (1907) act 2

27 He knows nothing; and he thinks he knows everything. That points clearly to a political career.
Major Barbara (1907) act 3

28 Nothing is ever done in this world until men are prepared to kill one another if it is not done.
Major Barbara (1907) act 3

29 Like all young men, you greatly exaggerate the difference between one young woman and another.
Major Barbara (1907) act 3; cf. **Mencken** 504:14

30 But a lifetime of happiness! No man alive could bear it: it would be hell on earth.
Man and Superman (1903) act 1

31 The more things a man is ashamed of, the more respectable he is.
Man and Superman (1903) act 1

32 Vitality in a woman is a blind fury of creation.
Man and Superman (1903) act 1

1 Of all human struggles there is none so treacherous and remorseless as the struggle between the artist man and the mother woman.
Man and Superman (1903) act 1

2 You think that you are Ann's suitor; that you are the pursuer and she the pursued . . . Fool: it is you who are the pursued, the marked down quarry, the destined prey.
Man and Superman (1903) act 2

3 MENDOZA: I am a brigand: I live by robbing the rich.
TANNER: I am a gentleman: I live by robbing the poor.
Man and Superman (1903) act 3

4 Hell is full of musical amateurs: music is the brandy of the damned.
Man and Superman (1903) act 3

5 Englishmen never will be slaves: they are free to do whatever the Government and public opinion allow them to do.
Man and Superman (1903) act 3

6 An Englishman thinks he is moral when he is only uncomfortable.
Man and Superman (1903) act 3

7 In the arts of life man invents nothing; but in the arts of death he outdoes Nature herself, and produces by chemistry and machinery all the slaughter of plague, pestilence and famine.
Man and Superman (1903) act 3

8 In the arts of peace Man is a bungler.
Man and Superman (1903) act 3

9 As an old soldier I admit the cowardice: it's as universal as sea sickness, and matters just as little.
Man and Superman (1903) act 3

10 When the military man approaches, the world locks up its spoons and packs off its womankind.
Man and Superman (1903) act 3; cf. **Emerson** 299:15

11 What is virtue but the Trade Unionism of the married?
Man and Superman (1903) act 3

12 Those who talk most about the blessings of marriage and the constancy of its vows are the very people who declare that if the chain were broken and the prisoners were left free to choose, the whole social fabric would fly asunder. You can't have the argument both ways. If the prisoner is happy, why lock him in? If he is not, why pretend that he is?
Man and Superman (1903) act 3

13 Beauty is all very well at first sight; but who ever looks at it when it has been in the house three days?
Man and Superman (1903) act 4

14 Revolutions have never lightened the burden of tyranny: they have only shifted it to another shoulder.
Man and Superman (1903) 'The Revolutionist's Handbook' foreword

15 The art of government is the organization of idolatry.
Man and Superman (1903) 'Maxims: Idolatry'

16 Democracy substitutes election by the incompetent many for appointment by the corrupt few.
Man and Superman (1903) 'Maxims: Democracy'

17 Liberty means responsibility. That is why most men dread it.
Man and Superman (1903) 'Maxims: Liberty and Equality'

18 He who can, does. He who cannot, teaches.
Man and Superman (1903) 'Maxims: Education'

19 Marriage is popular because it combines the maximum of temptation with the maximum of opportunity.
Man and Superman (1903) 'Maxims: Marriage'

20 Titles distinguish the mediocre, embarrass the superior, and are disgraced by the inferior.
Man and Superman (1903) 'Maxims: Titles'

21 If you strike a child take care that you strike it in anger, even at the risk of maiming it for life. A blow in cold blood neither can nor should be forgiven.
Man and Superman (1903) 'Maxims: How to Beat Children'

22 Beware of the man whose god is in the skies.
Man and Superman (1903) 'Maxims: Religion'

23 Self-denial is not a virtue: it is only the effect of prudence on rascality.
Man and Superman (1903) 'Maxims: Virtues and Vice'

24 The reasonable man adapts himself to the world: the unreasonable one persists in trying to adapt the world to himself. Therefore all progress depends on the unreasonable man.
Man and Superman (1903) 'Maxims: Reason'

25 The man who listens to Reason is lost: Reason enslaves all whose minds are not strong enough to master her.
Man and Superman (1903) 'Maxims: Reason'

26 Decency is Indecency's conspiracy of silence.
Man and Superman (1903) 'Maxims: Decency'

27 Life levels all men: death reveals the eminent.
Man and Superman (1903) 'Maxims: Fame'

28 Home is the girl's prison and the woman's workhouse.
Man and Superman (1903) 'Maxims: Women in the Home'

29 Every man over forty is a scoundrel.
Man and Superman (1903) 'Maxims: Stray Sayings'

30 Youth, which is forgiven everything, forgives itself nothing: age, which forgives itself everything, is forgiven nothing.
Man and Superman (1903) 'Maxims: Stray Sayings'

31 Take care to get what you like or you will be forced to like what you get.
Man and Superman (1903) 'Maxims: Stray Sayings'

32 Beware of the man who does not return your blow: he neither forgives you nor allows you to forgive yourself.
Man and Superman (1903) 'Maxims: Stray Sayings'

1 Self-sacrifice enables us to sacrifice other people without blushing.
Man and Superman (1903) 'Maxims: Self-Sacrifice'

2 There is nothing so bad or so good that you will not find Englishmen doing it; but you will never find an Englishman in the wrong. He does everything on principle. He fights you on patriotic principles; he robs you on business principles; he enslaves you on imperial principles; he bullies you on manly principles; he supports his king on loyal principles and cuts off his king's head on republican principles.
The Man of Destiny (1898)

3 Anarchism is a game at which the police can beat you.
Misalliance (1914)

4 The only way for a woman to provide for herself decently is for her to be good to some man that can afford to be good to her.
Mrs Warren's Profession (1898) act 2

5 A great devotee of the Gospel of Getting On.
Mrs Warren's Profession (1898) act 4

6 You'll never have a quiet world till you knock the patriotism out of the human race.
O'Flaherty V.C. (1919)

7 The secret of being miserable is to have leisure to bother about whether you are happy or not. The cure for it is occupation.
Parents and Children (1914) 'Children's Happiness'

8 A perpetual holiday is a good working definition of hell.
Parents and Children (1914) 'Children's Happiness'

9 There is only one religion, though there are a hundred versions of it.
Plays Pleasant and Unpleasant (1898) vol. 2, preface

10 It is impossible for an Englishman to open his mouth without making some other Englishman hate or despise him.
Pygmalion (1916) preface

11 I don't want to talk grammar, I want to talk like a lady.
Pygmalion (1916) act 2

12 PICKERING: Have you no morals, man?
DOOLITTLE: Can't afford them, Governor.
Pygmalion (1916) act 2

13 I'm one of the undeserving poor . . . up agen middle-class morality all the time . . . What is middle-class morality? Just an excuse for never giving me anything.
Pygmalion (1916) act 2

14 Gin was mother's milk to her.
Pygmalion (1916) act 3

15 Walk! Not bloody likely.
Pygmalion (1916) act 3

16 No Englishman is ever fairly beaten.
Saint Joan (1924) sc. 4

17 How can what an Englishman believes be heresy? It is a contradiction in terms.
Saint Joan (1924) sc. 4

18 Must then a Christ perish in torment in every age to save those that have no imagination?
Saint Joan (1924) epilogue

19 Assassination is the extreme form of censorship.
The Showing-Up of Blanco Posnet (1911) 'Limits to Toleration'

20 'Do you know what a pessimist is?' 'A man who thinks everybody is as nasty as himself, and hates them for it.'
An Unsocial Socialist (1887) ch. 5

21 You never can tell.
title of play (1898)

22 The great advantage of a hotel is that it's a refuge from home life.
You Never Can Tell (1898) act 2

23 The younger generation is knocking at the door, and as I open it there steps spritely in the incomparable Max.
on handing over the theatre review column to Max **Beerbohm**
in *Saturday Review* 21 May 1898 'Valedictory'

24 The photographer is like the cod which produces a million eggs in order that one may reach maturity.
introduction to the catalogue for Alvin Langdon Coburn's exhibition at the Royal Photographic Society, 1906; Bill Jay and Margaret Moore *Bernard Shaw and Photography* (1989)

25 The trouble, Mr Goldwyn, is that you are only interested in art and I am only interested in money.
telegraphed version of the outcome of a conversation between Shaw and Sam **Goldwyn**
Alva Johnson *The Great Goldwyn* (1937) ch. 3

26 [Dancing is] a perpendicular expression of a horizontal desire.
in *New Statesman* 23 March 1962

Hartley Shawcross 1902–
British Labour politician

27 'But,' said Alice, 'the question is whether you can make a word mean different things.' 'Not so,' said Humpty-Dumpty, 'the question is which is to be the master. That's all.' We are the masters at the moment, and not only at the moment, but for a very long time to come.
speech in the House of Commons, 2 April 1946; cf. **Carroll** 191:3, **Misquotations** 522:12

Charles Shaw-Lefevre, Lord Eversley 1794–1888

28 What is that fat gentleman in such a passion about?
as a child, on hearing Charles James **Fox** *speak in Parliament*
G. W. E. Russell *Collections and Recollections* (1898) ch. 11

Patrick Shaw-Stewart 1888–1917

29 I saw a man this morning
Who did not wish to die;
I ask and cannot answer
If otherwise wish I.
poem (1916); M. Baring *Have You Anything to Declare?* (1936)

1 Stand in the trench, Achilles,
Flame-capped, and shout for me.
poem (1916); M. Baring *Have You Anything to Declare?* (1936)

2 I continue to believe that the luck of my generation must change . . . nowadays we who are alive have the sense of being old, old survivors.
letter from Gallipoli, where he was killed; Brian Gardner (ed.) *Up the Line to Death* (rev. ed., 1976)

Lord Shelburne 1737–1805

British Whig politician; Prime Minister

3 The country will neither be united at home nor respected abroad, till the reins of government are lodged with men who have some little pretensions to common sense and common honesty.
in the House of Lords, 22 November 1770

4 The sun of Great Britain will set whenever she acknowledges the independence of America . . . the independence of America would end in the ruin of England.
in the House of Lords, October 1782

Mary Shelley (née Godwin) 1797–1851

English novelist; daughter of William **Godwin** *and Mary* **Wollstonecraft**, *wife of Percy Bysshe* **Shelley**

5 'We will each write a ghost story,' said Lord Byron; and his proposition was acceded to. There were four of us . . . *Have you thought of a story?* I was asked each morning, and each morning I was forced to reply with a mortifying negative . . . On the morrow I announced that I had *thought of a story* . . . At first I thought but of a few pages—of a short tale; but Shelley urged me to develop the idea at greater length.
on beginning Frankenstein
introduction to *Frankenstein* (ed. 3, 1831)

6 You seek for knowledge and wisdom as I once did; and I ardently hope that the gratification of your wishes may not be a serpent to sting you, as mine has been.
Frankenstein (1818) Letter 4

7 It was the secrets of heaven and earth that I desired to learn.
Frankenstein (1818) ch. 4

8 I beheld the wretch—the miserable monster whom I had created.
Frankenstein (1818) ch. 5

9 All men hate the wretched; how, then, must I be hated, who am miserable beyond all living things! Yet you, my creator, detest and spurn me, thy creature, to whom thou art bound by ties only dissoluble by the annihilation of one of us.
Frankenstein (1818) ch. 10

10 Everywhere I see bliss, from which I alone am irrevocably excluded.
Frankenstein (1818) ch. 10

11 Teach him to think for himself? Oh, my God, teach him rather to think like other people!
on her son's education
Matthew Arnold *Essays in Criticism* Second Series (1888) 'Shelley'

Percy Bysshe Shelley 1792–1822

English poet; husband of Mary **Shelley**
on Shelley: see **Arnold** 28:21, **Browning** 156:23

12 The cemetery is an open space among the ruins, covered in winter with violets and daisies. It might make one in love with death, to think that one should be buried in so sweet a place.
Adonais (1821) preface

13 I weep for Adonais—he is dead!
O, weep for Adonais! though our tears
Thaw not the frost which binds so dear a head!
Adonais (1821) st. 1

14 He died,
Who was the Sire of an immortal strain,
Blind, old and lonely.
Adonais (1821) st. 4

15 To that high Capital, where kingly Death
Keeps his pale court in beauty and decay,
He came.
Adonais (1821) st. 7

16 The quick Dreams,
The passion-wingèd Ministers of thought.
Adonais (1821) st. 9

17 Lost Angel of a ruined Paradise!
She knew not 'twas her own; as with no stain
She faded, like a cloud which had outwept its rain.
Adonais (1821) st. 10

18 Winter is come and gone,
But grief returns with the revolving year.
Adonais (1821) st. 18

19 From the great morning of the world when first
God dawned on Chaos.
Adonais (1821) st. 19

20 Alas! that all we loved of him should be,
But for our grief, as if it had not been,
And grief itself be mortal!
Adonais (1821) st. 21

21 A pardlike Spirit, beautiful and swift—
A Love in desolation masked;—a Power
Girt round with weakness;—it can scarce uplift
The weight of the superincumbent hour;
It is a dying lamp, a falling shower,
A breaking billow;—even whilst we speak
Is it not broken?
Adonais (1821) st. 32

22 He wakes or sleeps with the enduring dead;
Thou canst not soar where he is sitting now—
Dust to the dust! but the pure spirit shall flow
Back to the burning fountain whence it came,
A portion of the Eternal.
Adonais (1821) st. 38

23 He hath awakened from the dream of life—
'Tis we, who lost in stormy visions, keep

With phantoms an unprofitable strife,
And in mad trance, strike with our spirit's knife
Invulnerable nothings.
Adonais (1821) st. 39

1 He has out-soared the shadow of our night;
Envy and calumny and hate and pain,
And that unrest which men miscall delight,
Can touch him not and torture not again;
From the contagion of the world's slow stain
He is secure, and now can never mourn
A heart grown cold, a head grown grey in vain.
Adonais (1821) st. 40

2 He lives, he wakes,—'tis Death is dead, not he.
Adonais (1821) st. 41

3 He is a portion of the loveliness
Which once he made more lovely.
Adonais (1821) st. 43

4 The One remains, the many change and pass;
Heaven's light forever shines, Earth's shadows fly;
Life, like a dome of many-coloured glass,
Stains the white radiance of Eternity.
Adonais (1821) st. 52

5 A widow bird sat mourning for her love
Upon a wintry bough;
The frozen wind crept on above,
The freezing stream below.
Charles the First (1822) sc. 5, l. 9

6 That orbèd maiden, with white fire laden,
Whom mortals call the Moon.
'The Cloud' (1819)

7 I am the daughter of Earth and Water,
And the nursling of the Sky.
I pass through the pores of the ocean and shores;
I change, but I cannot die,
For after the rain when with never a stain
The pavilion of Heaven is bare,
And the winds and sunbeams with their convex gleams
Build up the blue dome of air,
I silently laugh at my own cenotaph,
And out of the caverns of rain,
Like a child from the womb, like a ghost from the tomb,
I arise and unbuild it again.
'The Cloud' (1819)

8 I never was attached to that great sect,
Whose doctrine is that each one should select
Out of the crowd a mistress or a friend,
And all the rest, though fair and wise, commend
To cold oblivion.
'Epipsychidion' (1821) l. 149

9 The beaten road
Which those poor slaves with weary footsteps tread,
Who travel to their home among the dead
By the broad highway of the world, and so
With one chained friend, perhaps a jealous foe,
The dreariest and the longest journey go.
'Epipsychidion' (1821) l. 154

10 Chameleons feed on light and air:
Poets' food is love and fame.
'An Exhortation' (1820)

11 Let there be light! said Liberty,
And like sunrise from the sea,
Athens arose!
Hellas (1822) l. 682

12 The world's great age begins anew,
The golden years return,
The earth doth like a snake renew
Her winter weeds outworn.
Hellas (1822) l. 1060

13 O cease! must hate and death return?
Cease! must men kill and die?
Hellas (1822) l. 1096

14 The world is weary of the past,
Oh, might it die or rest at last!
Hellas (1822) l. 1100

15 I pursued a maiden and clasped a reed.
Gods and men, we are all deluded thus!
It breaks in our bosom and then we bleed.
'Hymn of Pan' (1824)

16 The awful shadow of some unseen Power
Floats though unseen among us,—visiting
This various world with as inconstant wing
As summer winds that creep from flower to flower.
'Hymn to Intellectual Beauty' (1816)

17 The day becomes more solemn and serene
When noon is past—there is a harmony
In autumn, and a lustre in its sky,
Which through the summer is not heard or seen,
As if it could not be, as if it had not been!
'Hymn to Intellectual Beauty' (1816)

18 I love all waste
And solitary places.
'Julian and Maddalo' (1818) l. 14

19 Thou Paradise of exiles, Italy!
'Julian and Maddalo' (1818) l. 57

20 *Me*—who am as a nerve o'er which do creep
The else unfelt oppressions of this earth.
'Julian and Maddalo' (1818) l. 449

21 Most wretched men
Are cradled into poetry by wrong:
They learn in suffering what they teach in song.
'Julian and Maddalo' (1818) l. 544

22 . . . London, that great sea, whose ebb and flow
At once is deaf and loud, and on the shore
Vomits its wrecks, and still howls on for more.
'Letter to Maria Gisborne' (1820) l. 193

23 You will see Coleridge—he who sits obscure
In the exceeding lustre and the pure
Intense irradiation of a mind,
Which, with its own internal lightning blind,
Flags wearily through darkness and despair—
A cloud-encircled meteor of the air,
A hooded eagle among blinking owls.
of Samuel Taylor **Coleridge**
'Letter to Maria Gisborne' (1820) l. 202

24 You will see Hunt—one of those happy souls
Which are the salt of the earth, and without whom

This world would smell like what it is—a tomb.
of Leigh **Hunt**
'Letter to Maria Gisborne' (1820) l. 209

1 Have you not heard
When a man marries, dies, or turns Hindoo,
His best friends hear no more of him?
'Letter to Maria Gisborne' (1820) l. 235

2 His fine wit
Makes such a wound, the knife is lost in it.
of Thomas Love **Peacock**
'Letter to Maria Gisborne' (1820) l. 240

3 When the lamp is shattered
The light in the dust lies dead—
When the cloud is scattered
The rainbow's glory is shed.
When the lute is broken,
Sweet tones are remembered not;
When the lips have spoken,
Loved accents are soon forgot.
'Lines: When the lamp' (1824)

4 Beneath is spread like a green sea
The waveless plain of Lombardy.
'Lines written amongst the Euganean Hills' (1818) l. 90

5 Underneath Day's azure eyes
Ocean's nursling, Venice lies,
A peopled labyrinth of walls,
Amphitrite's destined halls.
'Lines written amongst the Euganean Hills' (1818) l. 94

6 Sun-girt city, thou hast been
Ocean's child, and then his queen;
Now is come a darker day,
And thou soon must be his prey.
of Venice
'Lines written amongst the Euganean Hills' (1818) l. 115

7 The fountains mingle with the river,
And the rivers with the ocean;
The winds of heaven mix for ever
With a sweet emotion;
Nothing in the world is single;
All things, by a law divine,
In one spirit meet and mingle.
Why not I with thine?
'Love's Philosophy' (written 1819)

8 I met Murder on the way—
He had a mask like Castlereagh—
Very smooth he looked, yet grim,
Seven bloodhounds followed him.
'The Mask of Anarchy' (1819) st. 2

9 His big tears, for he wept well,
Turned to mill-stones as they fell.
And the little children, who
Round his feet played to and fro,
Thinking every tear a gem,
Had their brains knocked out by them.
of 'Fraud' [Lord Eldon]
'The Mask of Anarchy' (1819) st. 4

10 Nought may endure but Mutability.
'Mutability' (1816)

11 I stood within the City disinterred;
And heard the autumnal leaves like light footfalls
Of spirits passing through the streets; and heard
The Mountain's slumberous voice at intervals
Thrill through those roofless halls.
'Ode to Naples' (1820) l. 1

12 O wild West Wind, thou breath of Autumn's being,
Thou, from whose unseen presence the leaves dead
Are driven, like ghosts from an enchanter fleeing,
Yellow, and black, and pale, and hectic red,
Pestilence-stricken multitudes: O thou,
Who chariotest to their dark wintry bed
The wingèd seeds, where they lie cold and low,
Each like a corpse within its grave, until
Thine azure sister of the spring shall blow
Her clarion o'er the dreaming earth, and fill
(Driving sweet buds like flocks to feed in air)
With living hues and odours plain and hill:
Wild Spirit, which art moving everywhere;
Destroyer and preserver; hear, oh, hear!
'Ode to the West Wind' (1819) l. 1

13 There are spread
On the blue surface of thine aëry surge,
Like the bright hair uplifted from the head
Of some fierce Maenad.
'Ode to the West Wind' (1819) l. 18

14 Thou who didst waken from his summer dreams
The blue Mediterranean, where he lay,
Lulled by the coil of his crystàlline streams
Beside a pumice isle in Baiae's bay,
And saw in sleep old palaces and towers
Quivering within the wave's intenser day.
'Ode to the West Wind' (1819) l. 29

15 The sea-blooms and the oozy woods which wear
The sapless foliage of the ocean.
'Ode to the West Wind' (1819) l. 39

16 Oh, lift me as a wave, a leaf, a cloud!
I fall upon the thorns of life! I bleed!
'Ode to the West Wind' (1819) l. 53

17 Make me thy lyre, even as the forest is:
What if my leaves are falling like its own!
The tumult of thy mighty harmonies
Will take from both a deep, autumnal tone,
Sweet though in sadness.
'Ode to the West Wind' (1819) l. 57

18 And, by the incantation of this verse,
Scatter, as from an unextinguished hearth
Ashes and sparks, my words among mankind!
'Ode to the West Wind' (1819) l. 65

19 O, Wind,
If Winter comes, can Spring be far behind?
'Ode to the West Wind' (1819) l. 69

20 Its horror and its beauty are divine.
'On the Medusa of Leonardo da Vinci' (1824)

21 I met a traveller from an antique land
Who said: Two vast and trunkless legs of stone
Stand in the desert.
'Ozymandias' (1819)

22 The hand that mocked them and the heart that fed.
'Ozymandias' (1819)

1 'My name is Ozymandias, king of kings:
Look on my works, ye Mighty, and despair!'
Nothing beside remains. Round the decay
Of that colossal wreck, boundless and bare
The lone and level sands stretch far away.
'Ozymandias' (1819)

2 Hell is a city much like London—
A populous and smoky city.
'Peter Bell the Third' (1819) pt. 3, st. 1

3 But from the first 'twas Peter's drift
To be a kind of moral eunuch,
He touched the hem of Nature's shift,
Felt faint—and never dared uplift
The closest, all-concealing tunic.
'Peter Bell the Third' (1819) pt. 4, st. 11

4 Ere Babylon was dust,
The Magus Zoroaster, my dead child,
Met his own image walking in the garden,
That apparition, sole of men, he saw.
Prometheus Unbound (1819) act 1, l. 191

5 Cruel he looks, but calm and strong,
Like one who does, not suffers wrong.
Prometheus Unbound (1819) act 1, l. 238

6 Grief for awhile is blind, and so was mine.
Prometheus Unbound (1820) act 1, l. 304

7 Kingly conclaves stern and cold
Where blood with guilt is bought and sold.
Prometheus Unbound (1820) act 1, l. 530

8 The good want power, but to weep barren tears.
The powerful goodness want: worse need for them.
The wise want love; and those who love want wisdom.
Prometheus Unbound (1820) act 1, l. 625

9 Peace is in the grave.
The grave hides all things beautiful and good:
I am a God and cannot find it there.
Prometheus Unbound (1820) act 1, l. 638

10 The dust of creeds outworn.
Prometheus Unbound (1820) act 1, l. 697

11 To be
Omnipotent but friendless is to reign.
Prometheus Unbound (1820) act 2, sc. 4, l. 47

12 He gave man speech, and speech created thought,
Which is the measure of the universe.
Prometheus Unbound (1820) act 2, sc. 4, l. 72

13 My soul is an enchanted boat,
Which, like a sleeping swan, doth float
Upon the silver waves of thy sweet singing.
Prometheus Unbound (1820) act 2, sc. 5, l. 72

14 The loathsome mask has fallen, the man remains
Sceptreless, free, uncircumscribed, but man
Equal, unclassed, tribeless, and nationless,
Exempt from awe, worship, degree, the king
Over himself; just, gentle, wise: but man
Passionless?—no, yet free from guilt or pain,
Which were, for his will made or suffered them,
Nor yet exempt, though ruling them like slaves,
From chance, and death, and mutability,
The clogs of that which else might oversoar
The loftiest star of unascended heaven,
Pinnacled dim in the intense inane.
Prometheus Unbound (1820) act 3, sc. 4, l. 193

15 A traveller from the cradle to the grave
Through the dim night of this immortal day.
Prometheus Unbound (1820) act 4, l. 551

16 To suffer woes which Hope thinks infinite;
To forgive wrongs darker than death or night;
To defy Power, which seems omnipotent;
To love, and bear; to hope till Hope creates
From its own wreck the thing it contemplates;
Neither to change, nor falter, nor repent;
This, like thy glory, Titan, is to be
Good, great and joyous, beautiful and free;
This is alone Life, Joy, Empire and Victory.
Prometheus Unbound (1820) act 4, l. 570

17 How wonderful is Death,
Death and his brother Sleep!
Queen Mab (1813) canto 1, l. 1; cf. **Daniel** 249:1, **Fletcher** 318:9

18 That sweet bondage which is freedom's self.
Queen Mab (1813) canto 9, l. 76

19 I dreamed that, as I wandered by the way,
Bare Winter suddenly was changed to Spring.
'The Question' (1822)

20 Daisies, those pearled Arcturi of the earth,
The constellated flower that never sets.
'The Question' (1822)

21 And in the warm hedge grew lush eglantine,
Green cowbind and the moonlight-coloured may.
'The Question' (1822)

22 A Sensitive Plant in a garden grew.
'The Sensitive Plant' (1820) pt. 1, l. 1

23 And the jessamine faint, and the sweet tuberose,
The sweetest flower for scent that blows.
'The Sensitive Plant' (1820) pt. 1, l. 37

24 Rarely, rarely, comest thou,
Spirit of Delight!
'Song' (1824); epigraph to **Elgar**'s Second Symphony

25 Men of England, wherefore plough
For the lords who lay ye low?
'Song to the Men of England' (written 1819)

26 The seed ye sow, another reaps;
The wealth ye find, another keeps;
The robes ye weave, another wears;
The arms ye forge, another bears.
'Song to the Men of England' (written 1819)

27 Lift not the painted veil which those who live
Call Life.
'Sonnet' (1824)

28 An old, mad, blind, despised, and dying king.
of ***George III***
'Sonnet: England in 1819' (written 1819)

29 I see the waves upon the shore,
Like light dissolved in star-showers, thrown.
'Stanzas Written in Dejection, near Naples' (1818)

30 Alas! I have nor hope nor health,
Nor peace within nor calm around,

Nor that content surpassing wealth
The sage in meditation found.
'Stanzas Written in Dejection, near Naples' (1818)

1 Music, when soft voices die,
Vibrates in the memory—
Odours, when sweet violets sicken,
Live within the sense they quicken.
'To—: Music, when soft voices die' (1824)

2 The desire of the moth for the star,
Of the night for the morrow,
The devotion to something afar
From the sphere of our sorrow.
'To—: One word is too often profaned' (1824)

3 Hail to thee, blithe Spirit!
Bird thou never wert,
That from Heaven, or near it,
Pourest thy full heart
In profuse strains of unpremeditated art.
'To a Skylark' (1819)

4 And singing still dost soar, and soaring ever
singest.
'To a Skylark' (1819)

5 Thou art unseen, but yet I hear thy shrill delight.
'To a Skylark' (1819)

6 Like a Poet hidden
In the light of thought,
Singing hymns unbidden,
Till the world is wrought
To sympathy with hopes and fears it heeded not.
'To a Skylark' (1819)

7 With thy clear keen joyance
Languor cannot be:
Shadow of annoyance
Never came near thee:
Thou lovest—but ne'er knew love's sad satiety.
'To a Skylark' (1819)

8 We look before and after,
And pine for what is not:
Our sincerest laughter
With some pain is fraught;
Our sweetest songs are those that tell of saddest
thought.
'To a Skylark' (1819)

9 Teach me half the gladness
That thy brain must know,
Such harmonious madness
From my lips would flow
The world should listen then—as I am listening
now.
'To a Skylark' (1819)

10 Less oft is peace in Shelley's mind,
Than calm in waters, seen.
'To Jane: The Recollection' (written 1822)

11 Swiftly walk o'er the western wave,
Spirit of Night!
Out of the misty eastern cave,
Where, all the long and lone daylight,
Thou wovest dreams of joy and fear,
Which make thee terrible and dear,—
Swift be thy flight!
'To Night' (1824)

12 Death will come when thou art dead,
Soon, too soon.
'To Night' (1824)

13 Art thou pale for weariness
Of climbing heaven, and gazing on the earth,
Wandering companionless
Among the stars that have a different birth,—
And ever changing, like a joyless eye
That finds no object worth its constancy?
'To the Moon' (1824)

14 In honoured poverty thy voice did weave
Songs consecrate to truth and liberty,—
Deserting these, thou leavest me to grieve,
Thus having been, that thou shouldst cease to be.
'To Wordsworth' (1816)

15 And like a dying lady, lean and pale,
Who totters forth, wrapped in a gauzy veil.
'The Waning Moon' (1824)

16 A lovely lady, garmented in light
From her own beauty.
'The Witch of Atlas' (written 1820) st. 5

17 For she was beautiful—her beauty made
The bright world dim, and everything beside
Seemed like the fleeting image of a shade.
'The Witch of Atlas' (written 1820) st. 12

18 The discussion of any subject is a right that you have brought into the world with your heart and tongue. Resign your heart's blood before you part with this inestimable privilege of man
An Address to the Irish People (1812)

19 Titles are tinsel, power a corrupter, glory a bubble, and excessive wealth a libel on its possessor.
Declaration of Rights (1812) article 27

20 The vanity of translation; it were as wise to cast a violet into a crucible that you might discover the formal principle of its colour and odour, as seek to transfuse from one language to another the creations of a poet. The plant must spring again from its seed, or it will bear no flower.
A Defence of Poetry (written 1821)

21 The great instrument of moral good is the imagination; and poetry administers to the effect by acting on the cause.
A Defence of Poetry (written 1821)

22 A single word even may be a spark of inextinguishable thought.
A Defence of Poetry (written 1821)

23 Poetry is the record of the best and happiest moments of the happiest and best minds.
A Defence of Poetry (written 1821)

24 Poets are the hierophants of an unapprehended inspiration; the mirrors of the gigantic shadows which futurity casts upon the present; the words which express what they understand not; the trumpets which sing to battle, and feel not what they inspire; the influence which is moved not, but moves. Poets are the unacknowledged legislators of the world.

A Defence of Poetry (written 1821); cf. **Johnson** 410:25

1 What is Love? It is that powerful attraction towards all that we conceive, or fear, or hope beyond ourselves.

'On Love' (notebook essay, *c.*1815), in D. L. Clark (ed.) *Shelley's Prose* (1966)

2 Tyranny entrenches itself within the existing interests of the most refined citizens of a nation and says 'If you dare trample upon these, be free.'

A Philosophical View of Reform (written 1819–20) ch. 1

3 Monarchy is only the string that ties the robber's bundle.

A Philosophical View of Reform (written 1819–20) ch. 2

4 Thought can with difficulty visit the intricate and winding chambers which it inhabits. It is like a river whose rapid and perpetual stream flows outwards—like one in dread who speeds through the recesses of some haunted pile and dares not look behind.

'Speculations on Metaphysics [On the Science of Mind]' (written 1815), in D. L. Clark (ed.) *Shelley's Prose* (1966)

William Shenstone 1714–63

English poet and essayist

5 The charm dissolves; th' aerial music's past;
The banquet ceases, and the vision flies.

'Elegy 11. He complains how soon the pleasing novelty of life is over' (1764)

6 Whoe'er has travelled life's dull round,
Where'er his stages may have been,
May sigh to think he still has found
The warmest welcome, at an inn.

'Written at an Inn at Henley' (1758); cf. **Johnson** 415:10

7 Laws are generally found to be nets of such a texture, as the little creep through, the great break through, and the middle-sized are alone entangled in.

Works in Verse and Prose (1764) vol. 2 'On Politics'; cf. **Anacharsis** 14:6

8 A fool and his words are soon parted.

Works . . . (1764) vol. 2 'On Reserve'

9 The world may be divided into people that read, people that write, people that think, and fox-hunters.

Works . . . (1764) vol. 2 'On Writing and Books'

10 Every good poet includes a critic; the reverse will not hold.

Works . . . (1764) vol. 2 'On Writing and Books'

11 To endeavour, all one's days, to fortify our minds with learning and philosophy, is to spend so much in armour that one has nothing left to defend.

Works . . . (1764) vol. 2 'On Writing and Books'

Philip Henry Sheridan 1831–88

American Union cavalry commander in the Civil War

12 The only good Indians I ever saw were dead.

in response to the Comanche chief Toch-a-way, who described himself as a 'good Indian'

at Fort Cobb, January 1869; attributed but denied by Sheridan; a similar remark had been made by J. M. Cavanaugh in Congress on 28 May 1868; cf. **Proverbs** 608:27

Richard Brinsley Sheridan 1751–1816

Anglo-Irish dramatist

on Sheridan: see **Anonymous** *16:11*, **Byron** *180:7*, **Walpole** *801:13*

13 The newspapers! Sir, they are the most villainous—licentious—abominable—infernal—Not that I ever read them—No—I make it a rule never to look into a newspaper.

The Critic (1779) act 1, sc. 1

14 If it is abuse,—why one is always sure to hear of it from one damned goodnatured friend or another!

The Critic (1779) act 1, sc. 1

15 Egad I think the interpreter is the hardest to be understood of the two!

The Critic (1779) act 1, sc. 2

16 I wish sir, you would practise this without me. I can't stay dying here all night.

The Critic (1779) act 3, sc. 1

17 O Lord, Sir—when a heroine goes mad she always goes into white satin.

The Critic (1779) act 3, sc. 1

18 Enter Tilburina stark mad in white satin, and her confidante stark mad in white linen.

The Critic (1779) act 3, sc. 1

19 An oyster may be crossed in love!

The Critic (1779) act 3, sc. 1

20 I was struck all of a heap.

The Duenna (1775) act 2, sc. 2

21 Conscience has no more to do with gallantry than it has with politics.

The Duenna (1775) act 2, sc. 4

22 The throne *we* honour is the *people's choice.*

Pizarro (1799) act 2, sc. 2

23 Illiterate him, I say, quite from your memory.

The Rivals (1775) act 1, sc. 2

24 'Tis safest in matrimony to begin with a little aversion.

The Rivals (1775) act 1, sc. 2

25 Madam, a circulating library in a town is as an evergreen tree of diabolical knowledge; it blossoms throughout the year. And depend on it . . . that they who are so fond of handling the leaves, will long for the fruit at last.

The Rivals (1775) act 1, sc. 2

26 He is the very pineapple of politeness!

The Rivals (1775) act 3, sc. 3

27 An aspersion upon my parts of speech!

The Rivals (1775) act 3, sc. 3

1 If I reprehend any thing in this world, it is the use of my oracular tongue, and a nice derangement of epitaphs!
The Rivals (1775) act 3, sc. 3

2 She's as headstrong as an allegory on the banks of the Nile.
The Rivals (1775) act 3, sc. 3

3 Too civil by half.
The Rivals (1775) act 3, sc. 4

4 Our ancestors are very good kind of folks; but they are the last people I should choose to have a visiting acquaintance with.
The Rivals (1775) act 4, sc. 1

5 No caparisons, Miss, if you please!—Caparisons don't become a young woman.
The Rivals (1775) act 4, sc. 2

6 You are not like Cerberus, three gentlemen at once, are you?
The Rivals (1775) act 4, sc. 2

7 The quarrel is a very pretty quarrel as it stands—we should only spoil it by trying to explain it.
The Rivals (1775) act 4, sc. 3

8 My valour is certainly going!—it is sneaking off!—I feel it oozing out as it were at the palms of my hands!
The Rivals (1775) act 5, sc. 3

9 You shall see them on a beautiful quarto page where a neat rivulet of text shall meander through a meadow of margin.
The School for Scandal (1777) act 1, sc. 1

10 You had no taste when you married me.
The School for Scandal (1777) act 2, sc. 1

11 MRS CANDOUR: I'll swear her colour is natural—I have seen it come and go—
LADY TEAZLE: I dare swear you have, ma'am; it goes of a night and comes again in the morning.
The School for Scandal (1777) act 2, sc. 2

12 Here is the whole set! a character dead at every word.
The School for Scandal (1777) act 2, sc. 2; cf. **Pope** 587:6

13 I'm called away by particular business—but I leave my character behind me.
The School for Scandal (1777) act 2, sc. 2

14 Here's to the maiden of bashful fifteen
Here's to the widow of fifty
Here's to the flaunting, extravagant quean;
And here's to the housewife that's thrifty.
Let the toast pass—
Drink to the lass—
I'll warrant she'll prove an excuse for the glass!
The School for Scandal (1777) act 3, sc. 3

15 An unforgiving eye, and a damned disinheriting countenance!
The School for Scandal (1777) act 4, sc. 1

16 ROWLEY: I believe there is no sentiment he has more faith in as that 'Charity begins at home'.
SIR OLIVER SURFACE: And his I presume is of that domestic sort which never stirs abroad at all.
The School for Scandal (1777) act 5, sc. 1

17 There is no trusting appearances.
The School for Scandal (1777) act 5, sc. 2

18 You write with ease, to show your breeding,
But easy writing's vile hard reading.
'Clio's Protest' (written 1771, published 1819)

19 A man may surely be allowed to take a glass of wine by his own fireside.
on being encountered drinking a glass of wine in the street, while watching his theatre, the Drury Lane, burn down
T. Moore *Life of Sheridan* (1825) vol. 2

20 The Right Honourable gentleman is indebted to his memory for his jests, and to his imagination for his facts.
speech in reply to Mr Dundas, in T. Moore *Life of Sheridan* (1825) vol. 2

21 They talk of avarice, lust, ambition, as great passions. It is a mistake; they are little passions. Vanity is the great commanding passion of all.
to Lord Holland
Thomas Moore *Journal* (1984) 5 August 1824

22 To her! To that magnificent and appalling creature! I should as soon have thought of making love to the Archbishop of Canterbury!
responding to Samuel Rogers's suggestion that Sheridan might 'make open love' to Mrs Siddons
Henry Colborn (ed.) *Sheridaniana* (1826)

23 Won't you come into the garden? I would like my roses to see you.
to a young lady; attributed

Hugh Sherlock 1905–

24 Lord, thy church on earth is seeking
Thy renewal from above;
Teach us all the art of speaking
With the accent of thy love.
'Lord, thy church on earth is seeking' (hymn)

Sidney Sherman 1805–73

American soldier

25 Remember the Alamo!
battle cry at San Jacinto, 21 April 1836, traditionally attributed to General Sherman

William Tecumsah Sherman 1820–91

American Union general

26 *Vox populi, vox humbug.*
letter to his wife Jane, 2 June 1863; see **Alcuin** 10:10, **Proverbs** 613:35

27 Hold out. Relief is coming.
usually quoted as 'Hold the fort! I am coming!'
flag signal from Kennesaw Mountain to General John Murray Corse at Allatoona Pass, 5 October 1864; cf. **Bliss** 122:2

28 [Grant] stood by me when I was crazy, and I stood by him when he was drunk; and now we stand by each other always.
of his relationship with his fellow Union commander, Ulysses S. ***Grant***
in 1864; Geoffrey C. Ward *The Civil War* (1991)

1 War is the remedy our *enemies* have chosen, and I say let us give them all they want.
in 1864; Geoffrey C. Ward *The Civil War* (1991)

2 There is many a boy here to-day who looks on war as all glory, but, boys, it is all hell.
speech at Columbus, Ohio, 11 August 1880, in Lloyd Lewis *Sherman, Fighting Prophet* (1932)

3 I will not accept if nominated, and will not serve if elected.
telegram to General Henderson, on being urged to stand as Republican candidate in the 1884 US presidential election
Memoirs (4th ed., 1891) ch. 27

Emanuel Shinwell 1884–1986
British Labour politician

4 We know that the organised workers of the country are our friends. As for the rest, they don't matter a tinker's cuss.
speech to the Electrical Trades Union conference at Margate, 7 May 1947; in *Manchester Guardian* 8 May 1947

Arthur Shipley 1861–1927
English zoologist

5 When we were a soft amoeba, in ages past and gone,
Ere you were Queen of Sheba, or I King Solomon,
Alone and undivided, we lived a life of sloth,
Whatever you did, I did; one dinner served for both.
Anon came separation, by fission and divorce,
A lonely pseudopodium I wandered on my course.
Life (1923) ch. 13 'Ere you were Queen of Sheba'

Jonathan Shipley 1714–88
English clergyman, Bishop of St Asaph

6 I look upon North America as the only great nursery of freemen left on the face of the earth.
in 1774, after voting against the alteration of the constitution of Massachusetts, proposed as a punishment for the tea-ship riots at Boston
in *Dictionary of National Biography* (1917–)

William Shippen 1673–1743
English Jacobite politician

7 Robin and I are two honest men: he is for King George and I for King James, but those men in long cravats [Sandys, Rushout, Pulteney, and their following] only desire places under one or the other.
view of his relationship with his political opponent Robert **Walpole**
in *Dictionary of National Biography* (1917–)

James Shirley 1596–1666
English dramatist

8 The glories of our blood and state
Are shadows, not substantial things;
There is no armour against fate;
Death lays his icy hand on kings:
Sceptre and crown
Must tumble down,
And in the dust be equal made
With the poor crooked scythe and spade.
The Contention of Ajax and Ulysses (1659) act 1, sc. 3

9 Only the actions of the just
Smell sweet, and blossom in their dust.
The Contention of Ajax and Ulysses (1659) act 1, sc. 3

10 I presume you're mortal, and may err.
The Lady of Pleasure (1637) act 2, sc. 2

11 How little room
Do we take up in death, that, living know
No bounds?
The Wedding (1629) act 4, sc. 4

Mikhail Sholokhov 1905–84
Russian novelist

12 And quiet flows the Don.
title of novel (1934)

Clare Short 1946–
British Labour politician

contrasting political advisers with elected politicians:
13 I sometimes call them the people who live in the dark. Everything they do is in hiding . . . Everything we do is in the light. They live in the dark.
in *New Statesman* 9 August 1996

14 It will be golden elephants next.
suggesting that the government of Montserrat was 'talking mad money' in claiming assistance for evacuating the island
in *Observer* 24 August 1997

The Shorter Catechism (1647)

15 'What is the chief end of man?'
'To glorify God and to enjoy him for ever'.

Walter Sickert 1860–1942
English painter

16 Nothing knits man to man, the Manchester School wisely taught, like the frequent passage from hand to hand of cash.
'The Language of Art' in *New Age* 28 July 1910

The Siddur
Jewish prayer book

17 Hear, O Israel: the Lord our God, the Lord is One.
The Shema; cf. **Bible** 77:6

18 Blessed are you, O Lord our God and God of our fathers, God of Abraham, God of Isaac, God of Jacob, the great, mighty, and revered God, God most high, generous and kind, owner of all things. You remember the pious deeds of the patriarchs, and in love will bring a redeemer to their children's children, for your name's sake, O King, Helper, Saviour and Shield. Blessed are you, O Lord, the Shield of Abraham.
The Amidah Benediction 1

1 Blessed are you, O Lord our God, King of the universe, who has made a distinction between the holy and the profane, between light and darkness, between Israel and the nations, between the seventh day and the six working days.
The Havdalah

Algernon Sidney 1622–83

English conspirator, executed for his alleged part in the Rye House Plot, 1683

2 Liars ought to have good memories.
Discourses concerning Government (1698) ch. 2, sect. 15

3 Men lived like fishes; the great ones devoured the small.
Discourses concerning Government (1698) ch. 2, sect. 18; cf. **Shakespeare** 694:7

4 'Tis not necessary to light a candle to the sun.
Discourses concerning Government (1698) ch. 2, sect. 23; cf. **Burton** 170:18, **Young** 839:1

5 The law is established, which no passion can disturb. 'Tis void of desire and fear, lust and anger . . . 'Tis deaf, inexorable, inflexible.
Discourses concerning Government (1698) ch. 3, sect. 15

Philip Sidney 1554–86

English soldier, poet, and courtier
on Sidney: see ***Browning*** *158:1,* ***Carew*** *186:4,* ***Cokayne*** *224:5,* ***Dyer*** *286:12*

6 Shallow brooks murmur most, deep silent slide away.
Arcadia ('Old Arcadia', completed 1581) bk. 1 'First Eclogues: Lalus and Dorus'

7 Who shoots at the mid-day sun, though he be sure he shall never hit the mark; yet as sure he is he shall shoot higher than who aims but at a bush.
Arcadia ('New Arcadia', 1590) bk. 2

8 My true love hath my heart and I have his,
By just exchange one for the other giv'n;
I hold his dear, and mine he cannot miss,
There never was a better bargain driv'n.
Arcadia ('Old Arcadia', completed 1581) bk. 3

9 Biting my truant pen, beating myself for spite,
'Fool,' said my Muse to me; 'look in thy heart and write.'
Astrophil and Stella (1591) sonnet 1

10 With how sad steps, O Moon, thou climb'st the skies;
How silently, and with how wan a face.
What, may it be that even in heavenly place
That busy archer his sharp arrows tries?
Astrophil and Stella (1591) sonnet 31

11 O moon, tell me,
Is constant love deemed there but want of wit?
Are beauties there as proud as here they be?
Do they above love to be loved, and yet
These lovers scorn whom that love doth possess?
Do they call virtue there ungratefulness?
Astrophil and Stella (1591) sonnet 31

12 Come, sleep, O sleep, the certain knot of peace,
The baiting place of wit, the balm of woe.
Astrophil and Stella (1591) sonnet 39

13 That sweet enemy, France.
Astrophil and Stella (1591) sonnet 41

14 Dumb swans, not chattering pies, do lovers prove;
They love indeed who quake to say they love.
Astrophil and Stella (1591) sonnet 54

15 Doubt you to whom my Muse these songs intendeth,
Which now my breast, o'ercharged, to music lendeth?
To you, to you, all song of praise is due;
Only in you my song begins and endeth.
Astrophil and Stella (1591) first song

16 I never drank of Aganippe well,
Nor ever did in shade of Tempe sit.
Astrophil and Stella (1591) sonnet 74

17 I am no pick-purse of another's wit.
Astrophil and Stella (1591) sonnet 74

18 Highway, since you my chief Parnassus be.
Astrophil and Stella (1591) sonnet 84

19 Stella, think not that I by verse seek fame;
Who seek, who hope, who love, who live, but thee:
Thine eyes my pride, thy lips my history;
If thou praise not, all other praise is shame.
Astrophil and Stella (1591) sonnet 90

20 Leave me, O Love which reachest but to dust,
And thou, my mind, aspire to higher things;
Grow rich in that which never taketh rust;
Whatever fades, but fading pleasure brings.
Certain Sonnets (written 1577–81) no. 32

21 O fair! O sweet! When I do look on thee,
In whom all joys so well agree,
Heart and soul do sing in me,
Just accord all music makes.
'To the Tune of a Spanish Song' (written *c.*1581)

22 Nature never set forth the earth in so rich tapestry as diverse poets have done . . . her world is brazen, the poets only deliver a golden.
The Defence of Poetry (1595)

23 Poetry therefore, is an art of *imitation* . . . that is to say, a representing, counterfeiting, or figuring forth to speak metaphorically. A speaking picture, with this end: to teach and delight.
The Defence of Poetry (1595)

24 With a tale forsooth he [the poet] cometh unto you, with a tale which holdeth children from play, and old men from the chimney corner.
The Defence of Poetry (1595)

25 Comedy is an imitation of the common errors of our life.
The Defence of Poetry (1595)

26 Certainly I must confess mine own barbarousness, I never heard the old song of Percy and Douglas, that I found not my heart moved more than with a trumpet.
The Defence of Poetry (1595)

27 Laughter almost ever cometh of things most disproportioned to our selves, and nature. Delight hath a joy in it either permanent or present. Laughter hath only a scornful tickling.
The Defence of Poetry (1595)

1 Thy necessity is yet greater than mine.
on giving his water-bottle to a dying soldier on the battle-field of Zutphen, 1586; commonly quoted as 'thy need is greater than mine'
Fulke Greville *Life of Sir Philip Sidney* (1652) ch. 12

Emmanuel Joseph Sieyès 1748–1836
French abbot and statesman

2 *La mort, sans phrases.*
Death, without rhetoric.
on voting in the French Convention for the death of Louis XVI, 16 January 1793
attributed to Sieyès, but afterwards repudiated by him; *Le Moniteur* 20 January 1793 records his vote as 'La mort'

3 *J'ai vécu.*
I survived.
when asked what he had done during the French Revolution
F. A. M. Mignet *Notice historique sur la vie et les travaux de M. le Comte de Sieyès* (1836)

Maurice Sigler 1901–61 and Al Hoffman 1902–60
American songwriters

4 Little man, you've had a busy day.
title of song (1934)

Simone Signoret 1921–85
French actress

5 Chains do not hold a marriage together. It is threads, hundreds of tiny threads which sew people together through the years. That is what makes a marriage last—more than passion or even sex!
in *Daily Mail* 4 July 1978

Sikh Scriptures
a monotheistic religion founded in the Punjab in the 15th century by Guru Nanak
translated by W. H. McLeod, 1984

6 There is one Supreme Being, the Eternal Reality. He is the Creator, without fear and devoid of enmity. He is immortal, never incarnated, self-existent, known by grace through the Guru.
Adi Granth: Guru Nanak *Japji* mul mantra

7 If as the lord of powerful armies, if as a king enthroned,
Though my commands bring prompt obedience, yet would my strength be vain.
Grant that your name remain, O Master, in my thoughts and in my heart.
Adi Granth: Guru Nanak *Siri Raga I*

8 When the Guru comes, O mother, joyous bliss is mine;
Boundless blessing, mystic rapture, rise within my soul.
Surging music, strains of glory, fill my heart with joy;
Breaking forth in songs of gladness, praise to God within.
Comes the Guru, I have found him; joyous bliss is mine.
Adi Granth: Guru Amar Das *Ramkali Anand*

9 The Name of God is sweet ambrosia, source of all inner peace and joy.
The Name of God brings blissful peace to the hearts of the truly devout.
Adi Granth: Guru Arjan *Sukhmani*

10 Better by far than any other way is the act of repeating the perfect Name of God.
Better by far than any other rite is the cleansing of one's heart in the company of the devout.
Better by far than any other skill is endlessly to utter the wondrous Name of God.
Better by far than any sacred text is hearing and repeating the praises of the Lord.
Better by far than any other place is the heart wherein abides that most precious Name of God.
Adi Granth: Guru Arjan *Sukhmani*

11 Grant me protection, merciful Lord, prostrate here at your door;
Guard me and keep me, Friend of the humble, weary from wandering far.
You love the devout and recover the sinful; to you alone I address this prayer:
Take me and hold me, merciful Lord, carry me safely to joy.
Adi Granth: Guru Arjan *Var Jaitasari*

12 Strengthen me, O Lord, that I shrink not from righteous deeds,
That freed from the fear of my enemies I may fight with faith and win.
The wisdom which I crave is the grace to sing your praises.
When this life's allotted course has run may I meet my death in battle.
Dasam Granth: Guru Gobind Singh *Chandi Charitra*

13 Around us lies God's dwelling place, his joyous presence on every side.
Self-existent and supremely beautiful, he dwells as a presence immanent in all creation.
Birth and death are abolished by his power, by the grace made manifest in his being.
Eternally present within all humanity he reigns in glory for ever.
Dasam Granth: Guru Gobind Singh *Jap*

14 Some worship stones, borne on their heads; some hang lingams from their necks.
Some claim that God dwells in the south, whilst others bow to the West.
Some worship idols, foolishly ignorant; others put trust in the tombs of the dead.
All are astray, seduced by false ritual; none knows the secret of God.
Dasam Granth: Guru Gobind Singh *Ten Savayyas*

15 A Sikh should rise as night draws near to dawn
and begin each day with an early-morning bathe.
Devoutly reading the Guru's words he goes to the
dharamsala to hear eternal truth.
Joining the sangat there assembled he hears with
deepest reverence the Guru's sacred songs.
Bhai Gurdas (d. 1633) var 40, v. 11

1 The light which shone from each of the ten Masters shines now from the sacred pages of the Guru Granth Sahib. Turn your thoughts to its message and call on God, saying, *Vahiguru!*
Ardas

2 Grant to your Sikhs a true knowledge of their faith, the blessing of uncut hair, guidance in conduct, spiritual perception, patient trust, abiding faith, and the supreme gift of the divine Name.
Ardas

3 You must always wear the Five Ks. These are uncut hair [*kes*], a sword or dagger [*kirpan*], a pair of shorts [*kachh*], a comb [*kangha*], and a steel bangle [*kara*].
Sikh Rahit Maryada

4 After three days and three nights had passed he [Guru Nanak] emerged from the stream, and having done so he declared: 'There is neither Hindu nor Muslim'
Mahima Prakas Varatak

5 The Guru [Ram Das] then pronounced his blessing on the sacred pool [Amritsar]. 'He who bathes here with a heart filled with devotion to God shall thereby receive the deliverance which I confer. This will assuredly happen. Even a bird which flies over this pool shall attain to the same sure deliverance without any effort on its part. They who obtain this salvation will find blissful peace in mystical union with God.
Mahima Prakas Kavita

Alan Sillitoe 1928–
English writer

6 The loneliness of the long-distance runner.
title of novel (1959)

Georges Simenon 1903–89
Belgian novelist

7 Writing is not a profession but a vocation of unhappiness.
interview in *Paris Review* Summer 1955

Paul Simon 1942–
American singer and songwriter

8 Like a bridge over troubled water
I will lay me down.
'Bridge over Troubled Water' (1970 song)

9 And here's to you, Mrs Robinson
Jesus loves you more than you will know.
'Mrs Robinson' (1967 song, from the film *The Graduate*)

10 People talking without speaking
People hearing without listening . . .
'Fools,' said I, 'You do not know
Silence like a cancer grows.'
'Sound of Silence' (1964 song)

11 Still crazy after all these years.
title of song (1975)

12 Improvisation is too good to leave to chance.
in *International Herald Tribune* 12 October 1990

Simonides *c.*556–468 BC
Greek poet
see also **Epitaphs** *302:11*

13 Painting is silent poetry, poetry is eloquent painting.
Plutarch *Moralia* 'De Gloria Atheniensium' sect. 3

Harold Simpson

14 Down in the forest something stirred:
It was only the note of a bird.
'Down in the Forest' (1906 song)

John Simpson 1944–
British journalist

15 I'm sick to death of the 'I'm going to tell you everything about me and what I think' school of journalism. You don't watch the BBC for polemic.
interview in *Radio Times* 9 August 1997

Kirke Simpson 1881–1972
American journalist

16 [Warren] Harding of Ohio was chosen by a group of men in a smoke-filled room early today as Republican candidate for President.
often attributed to Harry Daugherty, one of Harding's supporters, who appears merely to have concurred with this version of events, when pressed for comment by Simpson
news report, filed 12 June 1920; William Safire *New Language of Politics* (1968)

George R. Sims see **Opening lines** 555:23

C. H. Sisson 1914–
English poet

17 Here lies a civil servant. He was civil
To everyone, and servant to the devil.
The London Zoo (1961)

Sitting Bull (Tatanka Iyotake) *c.*1831–90
Hunkpapa Sioux leader

18 What law have I broken? Is it wrong for me to love my own? Is it wicked for me because my skin is red, because I am Sioux, because I was born where my fathers lived, because I would die for my people and my country?
to Major Brotherton, recorded July 1881; Gary C. Anderson *Sitting Bull* (1996)

19 The Black Hills belong to me. If the whites try to take them, I will fight.
Dee Brown *Bury My Heart at Wounded Knee* (1970) ch. 12

20 The life of white men is slavery. They are prisoners in towns or farms.
Robert M. Utely *The Lance and the Shield* (1993)

Edith Sitwell 1887–1964
English poet and critic
on Sitwell: see **Bowen** *145:17*

21 Jane, Jane,
Tall as a crane,

The morning light creaks down again.
Façade (1923) 'Aubade'

1 The fire was furry as a bear.
Façade (1923) 'Dark Song'

2 Still falls the Rain—
Dark as the world of man, black as our loss—
Blind as the nineteen hundred and forty nails
Upon the Cross.
'Still Falls the Rain' (1942)

3 I feel as if all my blood had been sucked, and my brains eaten by clothes moths. What I would give to be able to work uninterrupted!
letter to Allen Tanner, 15 August 1933, in Richard Green (ed.) *Selected Letters of Edith Sitwell* (1997)

4 Calling a spade a spade never made the spade interesting yet. Take my advice, leave spades alone.
letter to Charles Henri Ford, 23 August 1933, in Richard Green (ed.) *Selected Letters of Edith Sitwell* (1997)

5 I enjoyed talking to her, but thought *nothing* of her writing. I considered her 'a beautiful little knitter'.
of Virginia **Woolf**
letter to Geoffrey Singleton, 11 July 1955, in John Lehmann and Derek Palmer (eds.) *Selected Letters* (1970)

Osbert Sitwell 1892–1969
English writer

6 The British Bourgeoise
Is not born,
And does not die,
But, if it is ill,
It has a frightened look in its eyes.
At the House of Mrs Kinfoot (1921) p. 8

7 In reality, killing time
Is only the name for another of the multifarious ways
By which Time kills us.
'Milordo Inglese' (1958); cf. **Boucicault** 144:24

8 On the coast of Coromandel
Dance they to the tunes of Handel.
'On the Coast of Coromandel' (1943)

John Skelton c.1460–1529
English poet

9 The sovereign'st thing that any man may have
Is little to say, and much to hear and see.
The Bouge of Court (1499) l. 211

10 With solace and gladness,
Much mirth and no madness,
All good and no badness;
So joyously,
So maidenly,
So womanly,
Her demeaning.
The Garland of Laurel (1523) 'To Mistress Margaret Hussey'

11 Far may be sought
Erst that ye can find
So courteous, so kind,
As Merry Margaret,
This midsummer flower,
Gentle as falcon
Or hawk of the tower.
The Garland of Laurel (1523) 'To Mistress Margaret Hussey'

12 With margerain gentle,
The flower of goodlihead,
Embroidered the mantle
Is of your maidenhead.
The Garland of Laurel (1523) 'To Mistress Margery Wentworth'

13 I blunder, I bluster, I blow, and I blother,
I make on the one day, and I mar on the other.
Busy, busy, and ever busy,
I dance up and down till I am dizzy.
I can find fantasies where none is:
I will not have it so, I will have it this!
Magnificence (1530) l. 1037

14 So many vagabonds, so many beggars bold;
So much decay of monasteries and of religious places;
So hot hatred against the Church, and charity so cold;
So much of 'my Lord's Grace,' and in him no grace is;
So much hollow hearts, and so double faces;
So much sanctuary-breaking, and privilege-barred—
Since Deucalion's flood was never seen nor lered.
'Speak, Parrot' (written *c.*1520) l. 498

Noel Skelton 1880–1935
British Conservative politician

15 To state as clearly as may be what means lie ready to develop a property-owning democracy, to bring the industrial and economic status of the wage-earner abreast of his political and educational, to make democracy stable and four-square.
in *The Spectator* 19 May 1923

B. F. Skinner 1904–90
American psychologist

16 The real question is not whether machines think but whether men do.
Contingencies of Reinforcement (1969) ch. 9

17 Education is what survives when what has been learned has been forgotten.
New Scientist 21 May 1964

Gillian Slovo 1952–
South African writer

18 In most families it is the children who leave home. In mine it was the parents.
of her anti-apartheid activist parents, Joe Slovo and Ruth First
Every Secret Thing (1997)

Christopher Smart 1722–71
English poet
on Smart: see **Johnson** 413:2

19 Now the winds are all composure,
But the breath upon the bloom,
Blowing sweet o'er each enclosure,

Grateful off'rings of perfume.
Tansy, calaminth and daisies
On the river's margin thrive;
And accompany the mazes
Of the stream that leaps alive.
Hymns and Spiritual Songs (1765) 'St Mark'

1 Nature's decorations glisten
Far above their usual trim;
Birds on box and laurels listen,
As so near the cherubs hymn.
Hymns and Spiritual Songs (1765) 'The Nativity of Our Lord and Saviour Jesus Christ'

2 God all-bounteous, all-creative,
Whom no ills from good dissuade,
Is incarnate, and a native
Of the very world he made.
Hymns and Spiritual Songs (1765) 'The Nativity of Our Lord and Saviour Jesus Christ'

3 For in my nature I quested for beauty, but God,
God hath sent me to sea for pearls.
Jubilate Agno (c.1758–63) Fragment B, l. 30

4 For Charity is cold in the multitude of possessions, and the rich are covetous of their crumbs.
Jubilate Agno (c.1758–63) Fragment B, l. 154

5 For I will consider my Cat Jeoffrey.
For he is the servant of the Living God duly and daily serving him.
For at the first glance of the glory of God in the East he worships in his way.
For this is done by wreathing his body seven times round with elegant quickness.
Jubilate Agno (c.1758–63) Fragment B, l. 695

6 For when his day's work is done his business more properly begins.
For he keeps the Lord's watch in the night against the adversary.
For he counteracts the powers of darkness by his electrical skin and glaring eyes.
For he counteracts the Devil, who is death, by brisking about the life.
Jubilate Agno (c.1758–63) Fragment B, l. 719

7 Ye beauties! O how great the sum
Of sweetness that ye bring;
On what a charity ye come
To bless the latter spring!
How kind the visit that ye pay,
Like strangers on a rainy day.
'On a Bed of Guernsey Lilies' (1764)

8 Lo, through her works gay nature grieves
How brief she is and frail,
As ever o'er the falling leaves
Autumnal winds prevail.
Yet still the philosophic mind
Consolatory food can find,
And hope her anchorage maintain:
We never are deserted quite;
'Tis by succession of delight
That love supports his reign.
'On a Bed of Guernsey Lilies' (1764)

9 He sung of God—the mighty source
Of all things—the stupendous force
On which all strength depends;
From whose right arm, beneath whose eyes,
All period, pow'r, and enterprise
Commences, reigns, and ends.
A Song to David (1763) st. 18

10 Strong is the lion—like a coal
His eye-ball—like a bastion's mole
His chest against his foes.
Strong, the gier-eagle on his sail,
Strong against tide, th' enormous whale
Emerges as he goes.
A Song to David (1763) st. 76

11 But stronger still, in earth and air,
And in the sea, the man of pray'r;
And far beneath the tide;
And in the seat to faith assigned,
Where ask is have, where seek is find,
Where knock is open wide.
A Song to David (1763) st. 77

12 Beauteous the fleet before the gale;
Beauteous the multitudes in mail,
Ranked arms and crested heads;
Beauteous the garden's umbrage mild,
Walk, water, meditated wild,
And all the bloomy beds.
A Song to David (1763) st. 78

13 Glorious the northern lights astream;
Glorious the song, when God's the theme;
Glorious the thunder's roar:
Glorious hosanna from the den;
Glorious the catholic amen;
Glorious the martyr's gore.

Glorious—more glorious is the crown
Of Him that brought salvation down
By meekness, called thy Son;
Thou that stupendous truth believed,
And now the matchless deed's achieved,
Determined, dared, and done.
A Song to David (1763) st. 85

14 Ah! Posthumus, the years, the years
Glide swiftly on, nor can our tears
Or piety the wrinkled age forefend,
Or for one hour retard th' inevitable end.
translation of Horace *Odes* bk. 2, no. 14; cf. **Horace** 388:8

Samuel Smiles 1812–1904

English writer

15 We each day dig our graves with our teeth.
Duty (1880) ch. 16

16 This extraordinary metal, the soul of every manufacture, and the mainspring perhaps of civilised society.
of iron
Men of Invention and Industry (1884) ch. 4

17 The spirit of self-help is the root of all genuine growth in the individual.
Self-Help (1859) ch. 1

18 The shortest way to do many things is to do only one thing at once.
Self-Help (1859) ch. 9

1 Middle class people are apt to live up to their incomes, if not beyond them.
Self-Help (1859) ch. 9

2 Cheerfulness gives elasticity to the spirit. Spectres fly before it.
Self-Help (1859) ch. 12

Adam Smith 1723–90
Scottish philosopher and economist

3 Wonder . . . and not any expectation of advantage from its discoveries, is the first principle which prompts mankind to the study of Philosophy, of that science which pretends to lay open the concealed connections that unite the various appearances of nature.
Essays on Philosophical Subjects (1795) 'The History of Astronomy' sect. 3, para. 3

4 And thus, *Place*, that great object which divides the wives of aldermen, is the end of half the labours of human life; and is the cause of all the tumult and bustle, all the rapine and injustice, which avarice and ambition have introduced into this world.
Theory of Moral Sentiments (1759) pt. 1, sect. 3, ch. 2

5 Though our brother is on the rack, as long as we ourselves are at our ease, our senses will never inform us of what he suffers . . . It is by imagination that we can form any conception of what are his sensations.
Theory of Moral Sentiments (2nd ed., 1762) p. 2

6 It is not from the benevolence of the butcher, the brewer, or the baker, that we expect our dinner, but from their regard to their own interest. We address ourselves not to their humanity but their self love.
Wealth of Nations (1776) bk. 1, ch. 2

7 People of the same trade seldom meet together, even for merriment and diversion, but the conversation ends in a conspiracy against the public, or in some contrivance to raise prices.
Wealth of Nations (1776) bk. 1, ch. 10, pt. 2

8 The chief enjoyment of riches consists in the parade of riches.
Wealth of Nations (1776) bk. 1, ch. 11

9 Every individual necessarily labours to render the annual revenue of society as great as he can. He generally neither intends to promote the public interest, nor knows how much he is promoting it. He intends only his own gain, and he is, in this, as in many other cases, led by an invisible hand to promote an end which was no part of his intention.
Wealth of Nations (1776) bk. 4, ch. 3

10 To found a great empire for the sole purpose of raising up a people of customers, may at first sight appear a project fit only for a nation of shopkeepers. It is, however, a project altogether unfit for a nation of shopkeepers; but extremely fit for a nation whose government is influenced by shopkeepers.
Wealth of Nations (1776) bk. 4, ch. 7, pt. 3; cf. **Adams** 3:19, **Napoleon** 539:4

11 Consumption is the sole end and purpose of production; and the interest of the producer ought to be attended to only so far as it may be necessary for promoting that of the consumer.
Wealth of Nations (1776) bk. 4, ch. 8

12 The discipline of colleges and universities is in general contrived, not for the benefit of the students, but for the interest, or more properly speaking, for the ease of the masters.
Wealth of Nations (1776) bk. 5, ch. 1, pt. 3

13 There is no art which one government sooner learns of another than that of draining money from the pockets of the people.
Wealth of Nations (1776) bk. 5, ch. 2

14 If any of the provinces of the British empire cannot be made to contribute towards the support of the whole empire, it is surely time that Great Britain should free herself from the expense of defending those provinces in time of war, and of supporting any part of their civil or military establishments in time of peace, and endeavour to accommodate her future views and designs to the real mediocrity of her circumstances.
Wealth of Nations (1776) bk. 5, ch. 3

Alfred Emanuel Smith 1873–1944
American politician

15 All the ills of democracy can be cured by more democracy.
speech in Albany, 27 June 1933, in *New York Times* 28 June 1933

Delia Smith
English cookery expert

16 Football and cookery are the two most important subjects in the country.
having been appointed a director of Norwich City football club
in *Observer* 23 February 1997 'Said and Done'

Dodie Smith 1896–1990
English novelist and dramatist

17 The family—that dear octopus from whose tentacles we never quite escape.
Dear Octopus (1938)

Edgar Smith 1857–1938
American songwriter

18 You may tempt the upper classes
With your villainous demi-tasses,
But; Heaven will protect a working-girl!
'Heaven Will Protect the Working-Girl' (1909 song)

F. E. Smith, Lord Birkenhead 1872–1930
British Conservative politician and lawyer
on Smith: see ***Asquith*** *31:9*

19 The world continues to offer glittering prizes to those who have stout hearts and sharp swords.
rectorial address, Glasgow University, 7 November 1923, in *The Times* 8 November 1923; cf. **Borrowed titles** 144:7

1 We have the highest authority for believing that the meek shall inherit the earth; though I have never found any particular corroboration of this aphorism in the records of Somerset House.
Contemporary Personalities (1924) 'Marquess Curzon'; cf. **Bible** 93:3

2 Nature has no cure for this sort of madness, though I have known a legacy from a rich relative work wonders.
of Bolshevism
Law, Life and Letters (1927) vol. 2, ch. 19

3 JUDGE DARLING: And who is George Robey?
SMITH: Mr George Robey is the Darling of the music halls, m'lud.
A. E. Wilson *The Prime Minister of Mirth* (1956) ch. 1

4 JUDGE: What do you suppose I am on the Bench for, Mr Smith?
SMITH: It is not for me, Your Honour, to attempt to fathom the inscrutable workings of Providence.
2nd Earl of Birkenhead *F. E.* (1959 ed.) ch. 9

5 JUDGE: You are extremely offensive, young man.
SMITH: As a matter of fact, we both are, and the only difference between us is that I am trying to be, and you can't help it.
2nd Earl of Birkenhead *Earl of Birkenhead* (1933) vol. 1, ch. 9

Godfrey Smith 1926–
English journalist and columnist

6 In a world full of audio visual marvels, may words matter to you and be full of magic.
letter to a new grandchild, in *Sunday Times* 5 July 1987

Ian Smith 1919–
Rhodesian statesman; Prime Minister, 1964–79

7 I don't believe in black majority rule in Rhodesia—not in a thousand years.
broadcast speech, 20 March 1976, in *Sunday Times* 21 March 1976

Langdon Smith 1858–1908

8 When you were a tadpole, and I was a fish,
In the Palaeozoic time,
And side by side in the ebbing tide
We sprawled through the ooze and slime.
'A Toast to a Lady' in *The Scrap-Book* April 1906

Logan Pearsall Smith 1865–1946
American-born man of letters

9 There is more felicity on the far side of baldness than young men can possibly imagine.
Afterthoughts (1931) 'Age and Death'

10 The test of a vocation is the love of the drudgery it involves.
Afterthoughts (1931) 'Art and Letters'

11 A best-seller is the gilded tomb of a mediocre talent.
Afterthoughts (1931) 'Art and Letters'

12 People say that life is the thing, but I prefer reading.
Afterthoughts (1931) 'Myself'

13 Thank heavens, the sun has gone in, and I don't have to go out and enjoy it.
Afterthoughts (1931) 'Myself'

14 Most people sell their souls, and live with a good conscience on the proceeds.
Afterthoughts (1931) 'Other People'

15 What I like in a good author is not what he says, but what he whispers.
All Trivia (1933) 'Afterthoughts' pt. 5

Samuel Francis Smith 1808–95
American poet and divine
on Smith: see ***Holmes*** *381:7*

16 My country, 'tis of thee,
Sweet land of liberty,
Of thee I sing:
Land where my fathers died,
Land of the pilgrims' pride,
From every mountain-side
Let freedom ring.
'America' (1831)

Stevie Smith (Florence Margaret Smith) 1902–71
English poet and novelist

17 Oh I am a cat that likes to
Gallop about doing good.
'The Galloping Cat' (1972)

18 A good time was had by all.
title of book (1937)

19 Marriage I think
For women
Is the best of opiates.
It kills the thoughts
That think about the thoughts,
It is the best of opiates.
'Marriage I Think'

20 Why does my Muse only speak when she is unhappy?
She does not, I only listen when I am unhappy.
'My Muse' (1964)

21 I was much too far out all my life
And not waving but drowning.
'Not Waving but Drowning' (1957)

22 People who are always praising the past
And especially the times of faith as best
Ought to go and live in the Middle Ages
And be burnt at the stake as witches and sages.
'The Past' (1957)

23 Private Means is dead
God rest his soul, officers and fellow-rankers said.
'Private Means is Dead' (1962)

24 This Englishwoman is so refined
She has no bosom and no behind.
'This Englishwoman' (1937)

25 I long for the Person from Porlock
To bring my thoughts to an end,
I am growing impatient to see him

I think of him as a friend.
'Thoughts about the "Person from Porlock" ' (1962); cf. **Coleridge** 225:19

1 If you cannot have your dear husband for a comfort and a delight, for a breadwinner and a crosspatch, for a sofa, chair or a hot-water bottle, one can use him as a Cross to be Borne.
Novel on Yellow Paper (1936) p. 24

2 If there wasn't death, I think you couldn't go on.
in *Observer* 9 November 1969

Sydney Smith 1771–1845

English clergyman and essayist

3 The moment the very name of Ireland is mentioned, the English seem to bid adieu to common feeling, common prudence, and common sense, and to act with the barbarity of tyrants, and the fatuity of idiots.
Letters of Peter Plymley (1807) letter 2

4 A Curate—there is something which excites compassion in the very name of a Curate!!!
'Persecuting Bishops' in *Edinburgh Review* (1822)

5 Bishop Berkeley destroyed this world in one volume octavo; and nothing remained, after his time, but mind; which experienced a similar fate from the hand of Mr Hume in 1739.
Sketches of Moral Philosophy (1849) introduction

6 We shall generally find that the triangular person has got into the square hole, the oblong into the triangular, and a square person has squeezed himself into the round hole. The officer and the office, the doer and the thing done, seldom fit so exactly that we can say they were almost made for each other.
Sketches of Moral Philosophy (1849) Lecture 9

7 I look upon Switzerland as an inferior sort of Scotland.
letter to Lord Holland, 1815, in N. C. Smith (ed.) *Letters of Sydney Smith* (1953)

8 Tory and Whig in turns shall be my host,
I taste no politics in boiled and roast.
letter to John Murray, November 1834, in *Letters of Sidney Smith* (1953)

9 I have no relish for the country; it is a kind of healthy grave.
letter to Miss G. Harcourt, 1838, in *Letters of Sidney Smith* (1953)

10 I have seen nobody since I saw you, but persons in orders. My only varieties are vicars, rectors, curates, and every now and then (by way of turbot) an archdeacon.
letter to Miss Berry, 28 January 1843, in *Letters of Sidney Smith* (1953)

11 If there is a pure and elevated pleasure in this world it is a roast pheasant with bread sauce. Barn-door fowls for dissenters, but for the real Churchman, the thiry-nine-times articled clerk—the pheasant, the pheasant.
letter to R. H. Barham, 15 November 1841, in *Letters of Sidney Smith* (1953)

12 It requires a surgical operation to get a joke well into a Scotch understanding. Their only idea of wit . . . is laughing immoderately at stated intervals.
Lady Holland *Memoir* (1855) vol. 1, ch. 2

13 That knuckle-end of England—that land of Calvin, oat-cakes, and sulphur.
of Scotland
Lady Holland *Memoir* (1855) vol. 1, ch. 2

14 Take short views, hope for the best, and trust in God.
Lady Holland *Memoir* (1855) vol. 1, ch. 6

15 No furniture so charming as books.
Lady Holland *Memoir* (1855) vol. 1, ch. 9; cf. **Powell** 590:8

16 How can a bishop marry? How can he flirt? The most he can say is, 'I will see you in the vestry after service.'
Lady Holland *Memoir* (1855) vol. 1, ch. 9

17 As the French say, there are three sexes—men, women, and clergymen.
Lady Holland *Memoir* (1855) vol. 1, ch. 9

18 Daniel Webster struck me much like a steam-engine in trousers.
Lady Holland *Memoir* (1855) vol. 1, ch. 9

19 My definition of marriage . . . it resembles a pair of shears, so joined that they cannot be separated; often moving in opposite directions, yet always punishing anyone who comes between them.
Lady Holland *Memoir* (1855) vol. 1, ch. 11

20 He has occasional flashes of silence, that make his conversation perfectly delightful.
of ***Macaulay***
Lady Holland *Memoir* (1855) vol. 1, ch. 11

21 Let onion atoms lurk within the bowl,
And, scarce-suspected, animate the whole.
Lady Holland *Memoir* (1855) vol. 1, ch. 11 'Receipt for a Salad'

22 Serenely full, the epicure would say,
Fate cannot harm me, I have dined to-day.
Lady Holland *Memoir* (1855) vol. 1, ch. 11 'Receipt for a Salad'; cf. **Dryden** 282:32

23 Deserves to be preached to death by wild curates.
Lady Holland *Memoir* (1855) vol. 1, ch. 11

24 Brighton Pavilion looks as if St Paul's had slipped down to Brighton and pupped.
attributed; Alan Bell (ed.) *The Sayings of Sydney Smith* (1993)

25 Correspondences are like small-clothes before the invention of suspenders; it is impossible to keep them up.
Peter Virgin *Sydney Smith* (1994)

26 Death must be distinguished from dying, with which it is often confused.
H. Pearson *The Smith of Smiths* (1934) ch. 11

1 I am just going to pray for you at St Paul's, but with no very lively hope of success.
H. Pearson *The Smith of Smiths* (1934) ch. 13

2 I never read a book before reviewing it; it prejudices a man so.
H. Pearson *The Smith of Smiths* (1934) ch. 3

3 Minorities . . . are almost always in the right.
H. Pearson *The Smith of Smiths* (1934) ch. 9

4 My idea of heaven is, eating *pâté de foie gras* to the sound of trumpets.
view ascribed by Smith to his friend Henry Luttrell
H. Pearson *The Smith of Smiths* (1934) ch. 10; cf. **Disraeli** 270:34

5 Science is his forte, and omniscience his foible.
on ***Whewell***
Isaac Todhunter *William Whewell* (1876) vol. 1

6 What a pity it is that we have no amusements in England but vice and religion!
H. Pearson *The Smith of Smiths* (1934) ch. 10

7 What two ideas are more inseparable than Beer and Britannia?
H. Pearson *The Smith of Smiths* (1934) ch. 11

Walter Chalmers Smith 1824–1908
Scottish clergyman

8 Immortal, invisible, God only wise.
'God, All in All' (1867 hymn)

9 Unresting, unhasting, and silent as light,
Nor wanting, nor wasting, thou rulest in might.
'God, All in All' (1867 hymn)

10 We blossom and flourish as leaves on the tree,
And wither and perish; but naught changeth thee.
'God, All in All' (1867 hymn)

Tobias Smollett 1721–71
Scottish novelist

11 I think for my part one half of the nation is mad—and the other not very sound.
The Adventures of Sir Launcelot Greaves (1762) ch. 6

12 The capital [London] is become an overgrown monster; which, like a dropsical head, will in time leave the body and extremities without nourishment and support.
Humphry Clinker (1771) vol. 1 (letter from Matthew Bramble, 29 May)

13 I am pent up in frowzy lodgings, where there is not room enough to swing a cat.
Humphry Clinker (1771) vol. 1 (letter from Matthew Bramble, 8 June)

14 'Begging your honour's pardon, (replied Clinker) may not the new light of God's grace shine upon the poor and the ignorant in their humility, as well as upon the wealthy, and the philosopher in all his pride of human learning?' What you imagine to be the new light of grace, (said his master) I take to be a deceitful vapour, glimmering through a crack in your upper storey.
Humphry Clinker (1771) vol. 2 (letter from Jery Melford, 10 June)

15 Mourn, hapless Caledonia, mourn
Thy banished peace, thy laurels torn.
'The Tears of Scotland' (1746)

16 That great Cham of literature, Samuel Johnson.
letter to John Wilkes, 16 March 1759, in James Boswell *Life of Samuel Johnson* (1934 ed.) vol. 1

Jan Christiaan Smuts 1870–1950
South African soldier and statesman, Prime Minister 1919–24 and 1939–48

17 Mankind is once more on the move. The very foundations have been shaken and loosened, and things are again fluid. The tents have been struck, and the great caravan of humanity is once more on the march.
on the setting up of the League of Nations, in the wake of the First World War
W. K. Hancock *Smuts* (1968)

C. P. Snow 1905–80
English novelist and scientist

18 The official world, the corridors of power.
Homecomings (1956) ch. 22

19 The two cultures and the scientific revolution.
title of The Rede Lecture (1959)

Socrates 469–399 BC
Greek philosopher
on Socrates: see **Plato** 570:41; *see also* **Burton** 170:11, **Last words** 455:7

20 How many things I can do without!
on looking at a multitude of goods exposed for sale
Diogenes Laertius *Lives of the Philosophers* bk. 2, ch. 25

21 I know nothing except the fact of my ignorance.
Diogenes Laertius *Lives of the Philosophers* bk. 2, sect. 32; cf. **Davies** 251:16, **Milton** 518:9

22 The rest of the world lives to eat, while I eat to live.
Diogenes Laertius *Lives of the Philosophers* bk. 2, sect. 34; cf. **Proverbs** 599:8

23 Most excellent man, are you who are a citizen of Athens, the greatest of cities and the most famous for wisdom and power, not ashamed to care for the acquisition of wealth and for reputation and honour, when you neither care nor take thought for wisdom and truth and the perfection of your soul?
Plato *Apology* 29d

24 Virtue does not come from money, but from virtue comes money and all other good things to man, both to the individual and to the state.
Plato *Apology* 30b

25 Then I, however, showed again, by action, not in word only, that I did not care a whit for death . . . -

but that I did care with all my might not to do anything unjust or unholy.
on being ordered by the Thirty Commissioners to take part in the liquidation of Leon of Salamis
Plato *Apology* 32d

1 The unexamined life is not worth living.
Plato *Apology* 38a

2 But already it is time to depart, for me to die, for you to go on living; which of us takes the better course, is not known to anyone except God.
Plato *Apology* 42a

3 It is never right to do wrong or to requite wrong with wrong, or when we suffer evil to defend ourselves by doing evil in return.
Plato *Crito* 49d

4 It is perfectly certain that the soul is immortal and imperishable, and our souls will actually exist in another world.
Plato *Phaedo* 107a

5 A man should feel confident concerning his soul, who has renounced those pleasures and fineries that go with the body, as being alien to him, and considering them to result more in harm than in good, but has pursued the pleasures that go with learning and made the soul fine with no alien but rather its own proper refinements, moderation and justice and courage and freedom and truth; thus he is ready for the journey to the world below, ready to go when Fate calls him.
Plato *Phaedo* 114d

6 'What do you say about pouring a libation to some god from this cup? Is it allowed or not?' 'We only prepare just the right amount to drink, Socrates,' he [the jailer] said. 'I understand,' he went on; 'but it is allowed and necessary to pray to the gods, that my moving from hence to there may be blessed; thus I pray, and so be it.'
Plato *Phaedo* 117b

7 But, my dearest Agathon, it is truth which you cannot contradict; you can without any difficulty contradict Socrates.
Plato *Symposium* 201d

Solon *c*.640–after 556 BC
Athenian statesman and poet

8 I grow old ever learning many things.
Theodor Bergk (ed.) *Poetae Lyrici Graeci* (1843) no. 18

9 Call no man happy before he dies, he is at best but fortunate.
Herodotus *Histories* bk. 1, ch. 32; cf. **Bible** 91:26, **Proverbs** 597:3

Alexander Solzhenitsyn 1918–
Russian novelist

10 You only have power over people as long as you don't take *everything* away from them. But when you've robbed a man of *everything* he's no longer in your power — he's free again.
The First Circle (1968) ch. 17

11 The Gulag archipelago.
title of book (1973–5)

12 How can you expect a man who's warm to understand one who's cold?
One Day in the Life of Ivan Denisovich (1962) p. 22 (translated by Ralph Parker)

13 The thoughts of a prisoner—they're not free either. They keep returning to the same things.
One Day in the Life of Ivan Denisovich (1962) p. 34 (translated by Ralph Parker)

14 After the suffering of decades of violence and oppression, the human soul longs for higher things, warmer and purer than those offered by today's mass living habits, introduced as by a calling card by the revolting invasion of commercial advertising, by TV stupor and by intolerable music.
speech in Cambridge, Massachusetts, 8 June 1978

15 The clock of communism has stopped striking. But its concrete building has not yet come crashing down. For that reason, instead of freeing ourselves, we must try to save ourselves being crushed by the rubble.
in *Komsomolskaya Pravda* 18 September 1990

16 The Iron Curtain did not reach the ground and under it flowed liquid manure from the West.
speaking at Far Eastern Technical University, Vladivostok, 30 May 1994; cf. **Churchill** 216:1

William Somerville 1675–1742
English country gentleman

17 My hoarse-sounding horn
Invites thee to the chase, the sport of kings;
Image of war, without its guilt.
The Chase (1735) bk. 1, l. 13; cf. **D'Avenant** 251:10, **Surtees** 746:16

18 Hail, happy Britain! highly favoured isle,
And Heaven's peculiar care!
The Chase (1735) bk. 1, l. 84

Anastasio Somoza 1925–80
Nicaraguan dictator

19 You won the elections, but I won the count.
replying to an accusation of ballot-rigging
in *Guardian* 17 June 1977; cf. **Stoppard** 743:11

Stephen Sondheim 1930–
American songwriter

20 I like to be in America!
O.K. by me in America!
Ev'rything free in America
For a small fee in America!
'America' (1957 song) in *West Side Story*

21 Every day a little death
title of song (1973) in *A Little Night Music*

22 Ev'ry day a little death
On the lips and in the eyes,
In the murmurs, in the pauses,

In the gestures, in the sighs.
Ev'ry day a little dies.

'Every Day a Little Death' (1973 song) in *A Little Night Music*

1 Everything's coming up roses.

title of song (1959) in *Gypsy*

2 Isn't it rich?
Are we a pair?
Me here at last on the ground, you in mid-air.

'Send in the Clowns' (1973 song) in *A Little Night Music*

3 Where are the clowns?
Send in the clowns.

'Send in the Clowns' (1973 song) in *A Little Night Music*

□ Songs, spirituals, and shanties

see box opposite
see also ***Ballads, Political slogans and songs***

Susan Sontag 1933–

American writer

4 Societies need to have one illness which becomes identified with evil, and attaches blame to its 'victims'.

AIDS and its Metaphors (1989)

5 Interpretation is the revenge of the intellect upon art.

in *Evergreen Review* December 1964

6 What pornography is really about, ultimately, isn't sex but death.

in *Partisan Review* Spring 1967

7 The white race *is* the cancer of human history, it is the white race, and it alone—its ideologies and inventions—which eradicates autonomous civilizations wherever it spreads, which has upset the ecological balance of the planet, which now threatens the very existence of life itself.

in *Partisan Review* Winter 1967

8 The camera makes everyone a tourist in other people's reality, and eventually in one's own.

in *New York Review of Books* 18 April 1974

9 Illness is the night-side of life, a more onerous citizenship. Everyone who is born holds dual citizenship, in the kingdom of the well and in the kingdom of the sick.

in *New York Review of Books* 26 January 1978

Donald Soper 1903–98

British Methodist minister

10 It is, I think, good evidence of life after death.

on the quality of debate in the House of Lords

in *Listener* 17 August 1978

Sophocles *c.*496–406 BC

Greek dramatist

on Sophocles: see ***Aristophanes*** *24:11,* ***Arnold*** *27:30; see also* ***Anonymous*** *21:2*

11 My son, may you be happier than your father.

Ajax l. 550

12 Enemies' gifts are no gifts and do no good.

Ajax l. 665

13 His death concerns the gods, not those men, no!

of Ajax's enemies, the Greek leaders

Ajax l. 970

14 There are many wonderful things, and nothing is more wonderful than man.

Antigone l. 333

15 Not to be born is, past all prizing, best.

Oedipus Coloneus l. 1225 (translation by R. C. Jebb); cf. **Auden** 33:23, **Yeats** 836:3

16 Someone asked Sophocles, 'How is your sex-life now? Are you still able to have a woman?' He replied, 'Hush, man; most gladly indeed am I rid of it all, as though I had escaped from a mad and savage master.'

Plato *Republic* bk. 1, 329b

Charles Hamilton Sorley 1895–1915

English poet

17 We swing ungirded hips,
And lightened are our eyes,
The rain is on our lips,
We do not run for prize.

'Song of the Ungirt Runners' (1916)

18 When you see millions of the mouthless dead
Across your dreams in pale battalions go,
Say not soft things as other men have said,
That you'll remember. For you need not so.
Give them not praise. For, deaf, how should they know
It is not curses heaped on each gashed head?

'A Sonnet' (1916)

19 If Goethe really died saying 'more light', it was very silly of him: what *he* wanted was more warmth.

letter, July 1914; *The Letters of Charles Sorley* (1919); cf. **Last words** 456:15

20 I do wish people would not deceive themselves by talk of a just war. There is no such thing as a just war. What we are doing is casting out Satan by Satan.

letter to his mother from Aldershot, March 1915; *The Letters of Charles Sorley* (1919); cf. **Bible** 98:1

Robert South 1634–1716

English court preacher

21 An Aristotle was but the rubbish of an Adam, and Athens but the rudiments of Paradise.

Twelve Sermons . . . (1692) vol. 1, no. 2

Thomas Southerne 1660–1746

Irish dramatist

22 When we're worn,
Hacked hewn with constant service, thrown aside
To rust in peace, or rot in hospitals.

The Loyal Brother (1682) act 1

continued

Songs, spirituals, and shanties

1 A-roving! A-roving!
Since roving's been my ru-i-n
I'll go no more a-roving
With you fair maid.
'A-roving' (traditional song)

2 Come, landlord, fill the flowing bowl
Until it doth run over . . .
For to-night we'll merry be,
To-morrow we'll be sober.
'Come, Landlord, Fill the Flowing Bowl' (traditional song)

3 Come lasses and lads, get leave of your dads,
And away to the Maypole hie,
For every he has got him a she,
And the fiddler's standing by.
For Willie shall dance with Jane,
And Johnny has got his Joan,
To trip it, trip it, trip it, trip it, trip it up and down.
'Come Lasses and Lads' (traditional song, *c.*1670)

4 Early one morning, just as the sun was rising,
I heard a maid sing in the valley below:
'Oh, don't deceive me; Oh, never leave me!
How could you use a poor maiden so?'
'Early One Morning' (traditional song)

5 Frankie and Albert were lovers, O Lordy, how they could love.
Swore to be true to each other, true as the stars above;
He was her man, but he done her wrong.
'Frankie and Albert', in John Huston *Frankie and Johnny* (1930) (St Louis ballad later better known as 'Frankie and Johnny')

6 God gave Noah the rainbow sign,
No more water, the fire next time.
Home in that Rock (Negro spiritual)

7 God save our gracious king!
Long live our noble king!
God save the king!
Send him victorious,
Happy, and glorious,
Long to reign over us:
God save the king!
'God save the King', attributed to various authors of the mid eighteenth century, including Henry **Carey**; Jacobite variants, such as James Hogg 'The King's Anthem' in *Jacobite Relics of Scotland* Second Series (1821) also exist

8 Confound their politics,
Frustrate their knavish tricks.
'God save the King'

9 Greensleeves was all my joy,
Greensleeves was my delight,
Greensleeves was my heart of gold,
And who but Lady Greensleeves?
'A new Courtly Sonnet of the Lady Greensleeves, to the new tune of "Greensleeves" ', in *A Handful of Pleasant Delights* (1584)

10 The holly and the ivy,
When they are both full grown,
Of all the trees that are in the wood,
The holly bears the crown:
The rising of the sun
And the running of the deer,
The playing of the merry organ,
Sweet singing in the choir.
'The Holly and the Ivy' (traditional carol)

11 I'll sing you twelve O.
Green grow the rushes O.
What is your twelve O?
Twelve for the twelve apostles,
Eleven for the eleven who went to heaven,
Ten for the ten commandments,
Nine for the nine bright shiners,
Eight for the eight bold rangers,
Seven for the seven stars in the sky,
Six for the six proud walkers,
Five for the symbol at your door,
Four for the Gospel makers,
Three for the rivals,
Two, two, the lily-white boys,
Clothed all in green O,
One is one and all alone
And ever more shall be so.
'The Dilly Song', in G. Grigson (ed.) *The Faber Book of Popular Verse* (1971); cf. **Burns** 167:8

12 In good King Charles's golden days,
When loyalty no harm meant;
A furious High-Churchman I was,
And so I gained preferment.
Unto my flock I daily preached,
Kings are by God appointed,
And damned are those who dare resist,
Or touch the Lord's Anointed.
And this is law, I will maintain,
Unto my dying day, Sir,
That whatsoever King shall reign,
I will be the Vicar of Bray, sir!
'The Vicar of Bray' in *British Musical Miscellany* (1734) vol. 1

13 John Brown's body lies a mould'ring in the grave,
His soul is marching on.
inspired by the execution of the abolitionist John **Brown**, *after the raid on Harper's Ferry, on 2 December 1859*
song (1861), variously attributed to Charles Sprague Hall, Henry Howard Brownell, and Thomas Brigham Bishop

14 Like a fine old English gentleman,
All of the olden time.
'The Fine Old English Gentleman' (traditional song)

15 One Friday morn when we set sail,
And our ship not far from land,
We there did espy a fair pretty maid,
With a comb and a glass in her hand.
While the raging seas did roar,
And the stormy winds did blow,
And we jolly sailor-boys were all up aloft
And the land-lubbers lying down below.
'The Mermaid' (traditional song)

Songs, spirituals, and shanties *continued*

1 O ye'll tak' the high road, and I'll tak' the low road,
And I'll be in Scotland afore ye,
But me and my true love will never meet again,
On the bonnie, bonnie banks o' Loch Lomon'.

‘The Bonnie Banks of Loch Lomon’’ (traditional song)

2 A ship I have got in the North Country
And she goes by the name of the *Golden Vanity*,
O I fear she will be taken by a Spanish Ga-la-lee,
As she sails by the Low-lands low.

‘The Golden Vanity’ (traditional song)

3 Some talk of Alexander, and some of Hercules;
Of Hector and Lysander, and such great names as these;
But of all the world's brave heroes, there's none that can compare
With a tow, row, row, row, row, row, for the British Grenadier.

‘The British Grenadiers’ (traditional song)

4 Swing low, sweet chariot—
Comin' for to carry me home;
I looked over Jordan and what did I see?
A band of angels comin' after me—
Comin' for to carry me home.

Negro spiritual (*c.*1850)

5 There is a tavern in the town,
And there my dear love sits him down,
And drinks his wine 'mid laughter free,
And never, never thinks of me.
Fare thee well, for I must leave thee,
Do not let this parting grieve thee,
And remember that the best of friends must part.
Adieu, adieu, kind friends, adieu, adieu, adieu,
I can no longer stay with you,
I'll hang my harp on a weeping willow-tree,
And may the world go well with thee.

‘There is a Tavern in the Town’ (traditional song)

6 This lass so neat, with smiles so sweet,
Has won my right good-will,
I'd crowns resign to call thee mine,
Sweet lass of Richmond Hill.

Leonard MacNally (1752–1820) ‘The Lass of Richmond Hill’; also attributed to W. Upton in *The Oxford Song Book* (1916), and to W. Hudson in S. Baring-Gould *English Minstrelsie* (1895) vol. 3

7 Were you there when they crucified my Lord?

title of Negro spiritual (1865)

8 When Israel was in Egypt land,
Let my people go,
Oppressed so hard they could not stand,
Let my people go.
Go down, Moses,
Way-down in Egypt land,
Tell old Pharaoh
To let my people go.

‘Go Down, Moses’ (Negro spiritual); cf. **Bible** 75:35

9 Yankee Doodle came to town
Riding on a pony;
Stuck a feather in his cap
And called it Macaroni.

‘Yankee Doodle’ (song, 1755 or earlier); Nicholas Smith *Stories of Great National Songs* (1899) ch. 2; cf. **Cohan** 224:1

Thomas Southerne *continued*

10 Be wise, be wise, and do not try
How he can court, or you be won;
For love is but discovery:
When that is made, the pleasure's done.

Sir Anthony Love (1690) act 2 ‘Song’

Robert Southey 1774–1843

English poet and writer

11 It was a summer evening,
Old Kaspar's work was done,
And he before his cottage door
Was sitting in the sun,
And by him sported on the green
His little grandchild Wilhelmine.

‘The Battle of Blenheim’ (1800)

12 Now tell us all about the war,
And what they fought each other for.

‘The Battle of Blenheim’ (1800)

13 ‘And everybody praised the Duke,
Who this great fight did win.’
‘But what good came of it at last?’
Quoth little Peterkin.
‘Why that I cannot tell,’ said he,
‘But 'twas a famous victory.’

‘The Battle of Blenheim’ (1800)

14 Curses are like young chickens, they always come home to roost.

The Curse of Kehama (1810) motto

15 No stir in the air, no stir in the sea,
The ship was still as she could be.

‘The Inchcape Rock’ (1802)

16 And then they knew the perilous rock,
And blessed the Abbot of Aberbrothock.

‘The Inchcape Rock’ (1802)

17 Oh Christ! It is the Inchcape Rock!

‘The Inchcape Rock’ (1802)

18 My name is Death: the last best friend am I.

‘The Lay of the Laureate’ (1816) st. 87

19 Blue, darkly, deeply, beautifully blue.

Madoc (1805) pt. 1, canto 5 ‘Lincoya’ l. 102

20 We wage no war with women nor with priests.

Madoc (1805) pt. 1, canto 15 ‘The Excommunication’ l. 65

21 You are old, Father William, the young man cried,
The few locks which are left you are grey;
You are hale, Father William, a hearty old man,
Now tell me the reason, I pray.

‘The Old Man's Comforts’ (1799); cf. **Carroll** 189:12

1 The arts babblative and scribblative.
Colloquies on the Progress and Prospects of Society (1829) no. 10, pt. 2

2 The march of intellect.
Colloquies on the Progress and Prospects of Society (1829) no. 14

3 Your true lover of literature is never fastidious.
The Doctor (1812) ch. 17

4 Show me a man who cares no more for one place than another, and I will show you in that same person one who loves nothing but himself. Beware of those who are homeless by choice.
The Doctor (1812) ch. 34

5 Live as long as you may, the first twenty years are the longest half of your life.
The Doctor (1812) ch. 130

6 Men started at the intelligence, and turned pale, as if they had heard of the loss of a dear friend.
on the death of **Nelson**
The Life of Nelson (1813) ch. 9

7 She has made me in love with a cold climate, and frost and snow, with a northern moonlight.
on Mary **Wollstonecraft***'s letters from Sweden and Norway*
letter to his brother Thomas, 28 April 1797, in Charles Southey *Life and Correspondence of Robert Southey* vol. 1 (1849); cf. **Mitford** 524:5

8 Literature cannot be the business of a woman's life: and it ought not to be.
letter to Charlotte Brontë, 12 March 1837, in Margaret Smith (ed.) *The Letters of Charlotte Brontë* (1995)

Robert Southwell *c.*1561–95
English poet and Roman Catholic martyr

9 As I in hoary winter night stood shivering in the snow,
Surprised was I with sudden heat which made my heart to glow;
And lifting up a fearful eye to view what fire was near
A pretty Babe all burning bright did in the air appear.
'The Burning Babe' (*c.*1590)

10 My faultless breast the furnace is,
The fuel wounding thorns;
Love is the fire, and sighs the smoke,
The ashes, shame and scorns;

The fuel Justice layeth on,
And Mercy blows the coals;
The metal in this furnace wrought
Are men's defiled souls.
'The Burning Babe' (*c.*1590)

11 To rise by other's fall
I deem a losing gain;
All states with others' ruins built
To ruin run amain.
'Content and Rich' (1595)

12 Man's mind a mirror is of heavenly sights,
A brief wherein all marvels summèd lie.
'Look Home' (1595)

13 Times go by turns, and chances change by course,
From foul to fair, from better hap to worse.
'Times go by Turns' (1595)

14 Before my face the picture hangs,
That daily should put me in mind
Of those cold qualms, and bitter pangs,
That shortly I am like to find:
But yet alas full little I
Do think hereon that I must die.
'Upon the Image of Death' (attributed)

Muriel Spark 1918–
British novelist

15 From my experience of life I believe my personal motto should be 'Beware of men bearing flowers.'
Curriculum Vitae (1992)

16 I am a hoarder of two things: documents and trusted friends.
Curriculum Vitae (1992)

17 I am putting old heads on your young shoulders . . . all my pupils are the crème de la crème.
The Prime of Miss Jean Brodie (1961) ch. 1

18 Give me a girl at an impressionable age, and she is mine for life.
The Prime of Miss Jean Brodie (1961) ch. 1; cf. **Sayings** 647:16

19 One's prime is elusive. You little girls, when you grow up, must be on the alert to recognise your prime at whatever time of your life it may occur.
The Prime of Miss Jean Brodie (1961) ch. 1

20 To me education is a leading out of what is already there in the pupil's soul. To Miss Mackay it is a putting in of something that is not there, and that is not what I call education, I call it intrusion.
The Prime of Miss Jean Brodie (1961) ch. 2

21 If you're going to do a thing, you should do it thoroughly. If you're going to be a Christian, you may as well be a Catholic.
in *Independent* 2 August 1989

John Sparrow 1906–92
Warden of All Souls College, Oxford, 1952–77
see also **Epitaphs** 304:15

22 That indefatigable and unsavoury engine of pollution, the dog.
letter to *The Times* 30 September 1975

Rachel Speght fl. 1621
English poet

23 God's image man doth bear
Without it he is but a human shape,
Worse than the Devil.
'Mortality's Memorandum' (1621)

Herbert Spencer 1820–1903

English philosopher

1 Science is organized knowledge.
Education (1861) ch. 2

2 People are beginning to see that the first requisite to success in life is to be a good animal.
Education (1861) ch. 2

3 Absolute morality is the regulation of conduct in such a way that pain shall not be inflicted.
Essays (1891) vol. 3 'Prison Ethics'

4 Evolution . . . is—a change from an indefinite, incoherent homogeneity, to a definite coherent heterogeneity.
First Principles (1862) ch. 16

5 This survival of the fittest which I have here sought to express in mechanical terms, is that which Mr Darwin has called 'natural selection, or the preservation of favoured races in the struggle for life.
Principles of Biology (1865) pt. 3, ch. 12; cf. **Darwin** 250:20

6 How often misused words generate misleading thoughts.
Principles of Ethics (1879) bk. 1, pt. 2, ch. 8, sect. 152

7 Progress, therefore, is not an accident, but a necessity . . . It is a part of nature.
Social Statics (1850) pt. 1, ch. 2, sect. 4

8 A clever theft was praiseworthy amongst the Spartans; and it is equally so amongst Christians, provided it be on a sufficiently large scale.
Social Statics (1850) pt. 2, ch. 16, sect. 3

9 Hero-worship is strongest where there is least regard for human freedom.
Social Statics (1850) pt. 4, ch. 30, sect. 6

10 No one can be perfectly free till all are free; no one can be perfectly moral till all are moral; no one can be perfectly happy till all are happy.
Social Statics (1850) pt. 4, ch. 30, sect. 16

Lord Spencer 1964–

English peer

11 I always believed the press would kill her in the end. But not even I could believe they would take such a direct hand in her death as seems to be the case . . . Every proprietor and editor of every publication that has paid for intrusive and exploitative photographs of her . . . has blood on their hands today.
on the death of his sister, ***Diana****, Princess of Wales, in a car crash while being pursued by photographers, 31 August 1997*
in *Daily Telegraph* 1 September 1997

12 She needed no royal title to continue to generate her particular brand of magic.
tribute at the funeral of his sister, ***Diana****, Princess of Wales, 7 September 1997*
in *Guardian* 8 September 1997

13 A girl given the name of the ancient goddess of hunting was, in the end, the most hunted person of the modern age.
funeral tribute, 7 September 1997
in *Guardian* 8 September 1997

14 We, your blood family, will do all we can to continue the imaginative way in which you were steering these two exceptional young men so that their souls are not simply immersed by duty and tradition but can sing openly as you planned.
referring to his nephews, Prince William and Prince Harry; funeral tribute, 7 September 1997
in *Guardian* 8 September 1997

Raine, Countess Spencer 1929–

15 Alas, for our towns and cities. Monstrous carbuncles of concrete have erupted in gentle Georgian Squares.
The Spencers on Spas (1983) p. 14; cf. **Charles** 203:18

Stanley Spencer 1891–1959

English painter
on Spencer: see ***Lewis*** *467:13*

16 Painting is saying 'Ta' to God.
letter from Spencer's daughter Shirin, in *Observer* 7 February 1988

Stephen Spender 1909–95

English poet

17 After the first powerful plain manifesto
The black statement of pistons, without more fuss
But gliding like a queen, she leaves the station.
'The Express' (1933)

18 I think continually of those who were truly great
'I think continually of those who were truly great' (1933)

19 Born of the sun they travelled a short while
towards the sun,
And left the vivid air signed with their honour.
'I think continually of those who were truly great' (1933)

20 My parents kept me from children who were rough
And who threw words like stones and who wore
torn clothes.
'My parents kept me from children who were rough' (1933)

21 Never being, but always at the edge of Being.
title of poem (1933)

22 Their collected
Hearts wound up with love, like little watch
springs.
'The Past Values' (1939)

23 Pylons, those pillars
Bare like nude, giant girls that have no secret.
'The Pylons' (1933)

24 What I had not foreseen
Was the gradual day
Weakening the will
Leaking the brightness away.
'What I expected, was' (1933)

25 Who live under the shadow of a war,
What can I do that matters?
'Who live under the shadow of a war' (1933)

1 The nineties is a good time to die.
Joseph Brodsky *On Grief and Reason* (1996)

Edmund Spenser *c.*1552–99

English poet
on Spenser: see **Cecil** 199:7

2 The merry cuckoo, messenger of Spring,
His trumpet shrill hath thrice already sounded.
Amoretti (1595) sonnet 19

3 Most glorious Lord of life, that on this day
Didst make thy triumph over death and sin:
And, having harrowed hell, didst bring away
Captivity thence captive, us to win.
Amoretti (1595) sonnet 68

4 One day I wrote her name upon the strand,
But came the waves and washèd it away:
Again I wrote it with a second hand,
But came the tide, and made my pains his prey.
Vain man, said she, that dost in vain assay,
A mortal thing so to immortalize,
For I myself shall like to this decay,
And eke my name be wipèd out likewise.
Not so, quoth I, let baser things devise
To die in dust, but you shall live by fame:
My verse your virtues rare shall eternize,
And in the heavens write your glorious name,
Where when as death shall all the world subdue,
Our love shall live, and later life renew.
Amoretti (1595) sonnet 75

5 So love is Lord of all the world by right.
Colin Clout's Come Home Again (1595) l. 883

6 So you great Lord, that with your counsel sway
The burden of this kingdom mightily,
With like delights sometimes may eke delay,
The rugged brow of careful Policy.
'Dedicatory Sonnet to Sir Christopher Hatton' (1590)

7 Wake now, my love, awake; for it is time.
The rosy morn long since left Tithones bed,
All ready to her silver coach to climb,
And Phoebus gins to shew his glorious head.
Hark how the cheerful birds do chant their lays
And carol of love's praise.
The merry lark her matins sings aloft,
The thrush replies, the mavis descant plays,
The ouzel shrills, the ruddock warbles soft,
So goodly all agree with sweet consent,
To this day's merriment.
'Epithalamion' (1595) l. 74

8 Open the temple gates unto my love,
Open them wide that she may enter in.
'Epithalamion' (1595) l. 204

9 Ah! when will this long weary day have end,
And lend me leave to come unto my love?
How slowly do the hours their numbers spend!
How slowly does sad Time his feathers move!
'Epithalamion' (1595) l. 278

10 Song made in lieu of many ornaments,
With which my love should duly have been decked.
'Epithalamion' (1595) l. 427

11 The general end therefore of all the book is to fashion a gentleman or noble person in virtuous and gentle discipline.
The Faerie Queen (1596) preface

12 A gentle knight was pricking on the plain.
The Faerie Queen (1596) bk. 1, canto 1, st. 1

13 But on his breast a bloody cross he bore,
The dear remembrance of his dying Lord.
The Faerie Queen (1596) bk. 1, canto 1, st. 2

14 But of his cheer did seem too solemn sad;
Yet nothing did he dread, but ever was ydrad.
The Faerie Queen (1596) bk. 1, canto 1, st. 2

15 A bold bad man, that dared to call by name
Great Gorgon, Prince of darkness and dead night.
The Faerie Queen (1596) bk. 1, canto 1, st. 37; cf. **Shakespeare** 673:8

16 Her angel's face
As the great eye of heaven shinèd bright,
And made a sunshine in the shady place;
Did never mortal eye behold such heavenly grace.
The Faerie Queen (1596) bk. 1, canto 3, st. 4

17 And all the hinder parts, that few could spy,
Were ruinous and old, but painted cunningly.
The Faerie Queen (1596) bk. 1, canto 4, st. 5

18 The noble heart, that harbours virtuous thought,
And is with child of glorious great intent,
Can never rest, until it forth have brought
Th' eternal brood of glory excellent.
The Faerie Queen (1596) bk. 1, canto 5, st. 1

19 A cruel crafty crocodile,
Which in false grief hiding his harmful guile,
Doth weep full sore, and sheddeth tender tears.
The Faerie Queen (1596) bk. 1, canto 5, st. 18

20 Still as he fled, his eye was backward cast,
As if his fear still followed him behind.
The Faerie Queen (1596) bk. 1, canto 9, st. 21

21 That darksome cave they enter, where they find
That cursèd man, low sitting on the ground,
Musing full sadly in his sullen mind.
The Faerie Queen (1596) bk. 1, canto 9, st. 35

22 Sleep after toil, port after stormy seas,
Ease after war, death after life does greatly please.
The Faerie Queen (1596) bk. 1, canto 9, st. 40

23 So double was his pains, so double be his praise.
The Faerie Queen (1596) bk. 2, canto 2, st. 25

24 Upon her eyelids many Graces sate,
Under the shadow of her even brows.
The Faerie Queen (1596) bk. 2, canto 3, st. 25

25 And with rich metal loaded every rift.
The Faerie Queen (1596) bk. 2, canto 7, st. 28; cf. **Keats** 431:23

26 And all for love, and nothing for reward.
The Faerie Queen (1596) bk. 2, canto 8, st. 2

27 So passeth, in the passing of a day,
Of mortal life the leaf, the bud, the flower,
No more doth flourish after first decay,
That erst was sought to deck both bed and bower.
The Faerie Queen (1596) bk. 2, canto 12, st. 75

1 Gather therefore the rose, whilst yet is prime,
For soon comes age, that will her pride deflower:
Gather the rose of love, whilst yet is time,
Whilst loving thou mayst lovèd be with equal crime.
The Faerie Queen (1596) bk. 2, canto 12, st. 75

2 The dunghill kind
Delights in filth and foul incontinence:
Let Grill be Grill, and have his hoggish mind.
The Faerie Queen (1596) bk. 2, canto 12, st. 87

3 Whether it divine tobacco were,
Or panachaea, or polygony.
The Faerie Queen (1596) bk. 3, canto 5, st. 32

4 And painful pleasure turns to pleasing pain.
The Faerie Queen (1596) bk. 3, canto 10, st. 60

5 And as she looked about, she did behold,
How over that same door was likewise writ,
Be bold, be bold, and everywhere Be bold . . .
At last she spied at that room's upper end
Another iron door, on which was writ
Be not too bold.
The Faerie Queen (1596) bk. 3, canto 11, st. 54

6 Dan Chaucer, well of English undefiled,
On Fame's eternal beadroll worthy to be filed.
The Faerie Queen (1596) bk. 4, canto 2, st. 32

7 For all that nature by her mother wit
Could frame in earth.
The Faerie Queen (1596) bk. 4, canto 10, st. 21

8 Ill can he rule the great, that cannot reach the small.
The Faerie Queen (1596) bk. 5, canto 2, st. 43

9 O sacred hunger of ambitious minds.
The Faerie Queen (1596) bk. 5, canto 12, st. 1

10 A monster, which the Blatant beast men call,
A dreadful fiend of gods and men ydrad.
The Faerie Queen (1596) bk. 5, canto 12, st. 37

11 The gentle mind by gentle deeds is known.
For a man by nothing is so well bewrayed,
As by his manners.
The Faerie Queen (1596) bk. 6, canto 3, st. 1

12 What man that sees the ever-whirling wheel
Of Change, the which all mortal things doth sway,
But that thereby doth find, and plainly feel,
How Mutability in them doth play
Her cruel sports, to many men's decay?
The Faerie Queen (1596) bk. 7, canto 6, st. 1

13 For all that moveth doth in Change delight:
But thenceforth all shall rest eternally
With Him that is the God of Sabbaoth hight:
O that great Sabbaoth God, grant me that Sabbaoth's sight.
The Faerie Queen (1596) bk. 7, canto 8, st. 2

14 That beauty is not, as fond men misdeem,
An outward show of things, that only seem.
'An Hymn in Honour of Beauty' (1596) l. 90

15 For of the soul the body form doth take;
For soul is form, and doth the body make.
'An Hymn in Honour of Beauty' (1596) l. 132

16 What more felicity can fall to creature,
Than to enjoy delight with liberty.
'Muiopotmos' (1591) l. 209

17 Of such deep learning little had he need,
Ne yet of Latin, ne of Greek that breed
Doubts 'mongst Divines, and difference of texts,
From whence arise diversity of sects,
And hateful heresies.
'Prosopopoia or Mother Hubbard's Tale' (1591) l. 385

18 Calm was the day, and through the trembling air,
Sweet breathing Zephyrus did softly play.
Prothalamion (1596) l. 1

19 With that, I saw two swans of goodly hue,
Come softly swimming down along the Lee . . .
So purely white they were,
That even the gentle stream, the which them bare,
Seemed foul to them, and bade his billows spare
To wet their silken feathers, lest they might
Soil their fair plumes with water not so fair
And mar their beauties bright,
That shone as Heaven's light,
Against their bridal day, which was not long:
Sweet Thames, run softly, till I end my song.
Prothalamion (1596) l. 37

20 To be wise and eke to love,
Is granted scarce to God above.
The Shepherd's Calendar (1579) 'March. Willy's Emblem'

21 Bring hither the pink and purple columbine,
With gillyflowers:
Bring coronation, and sops in wine,
Worn of paramours.
Strew me the ground with daffadowndillies,
And cowslips, and kingcups, and loved lilies.
The Shepherd's Calendar (1579) 'April' l. 136

22 And he that strives to touch the stars,
Oft stumbles at a straw.
The Shepherd's Calendar (1579) 'July' l. 99

23 Uncouth unkist, said the old famous poet Chaucer.
The Shepherd's Calendar (1579) 'Letter to Gabriel Harvey'

24 So now they have made our English tongue a gallimaufry or hodgepodge of all other speeches.
The Shepherd's Calendar (1579) 'Letter to Gabriel Harvey'

Baruch Spinoza 1632–77

Dutch philosopher
on Spinoza: see **Novalis** *547:4*

25 *Deus, sive Natura.*
God, or in other words, Nature.
Ethics (1677) pt. 1, para. 6

26 There is no hope without fear, and no fear without hope.
Ethics (1677) pt. 2, para. 178

27 I have striven not to laugh at human actions, not to weep at them, nor to hate them, but to understand them.
Tractatus Politicus (1677) ch. 1, sect. 4

Benjamin Spock 1903–98
American paediatrician

1 You know more than you think you do.
Common Sense Book of Baby and Child Care (1946) [later *Baby and Child Care*], opening words

2 To win in Vietnam, we will have to exterminate a nation.
Dr Spock on Vietnam (1968) ch. 7

William Archibald Spooner 1844–1930
English clergyman; Warden of New College, Oxford, 1903–24

3 You will find as you grow older that the weight of rages will press harder and harder upon the employer.
William Hayter *Spooner* (1977) ch. 6

4 Her late husband, you know, a very sad death—eaten by missionaries—poor soul!
William Hayter *Spooner* (1977) ch. 6

Thomas Sprat 1635–1713
English clergyman and writer

5 A most venomous thing in the making of sciences; for whoever has fixed on his cause, before he has experimented, can hardly avoid fitting his experiment to his own cause ... rather than the cause to the truth of the experiment itself.
on 'Aristotelian experiments, intended to illustrate a preconceived truth and convince people of its validity'
History of the Royal Society (1667)

Cecil Spring-Rice 1859–1918
British diplomat; Ambassador to Washington from 1912

6 I vow to thee, my country—all earthly things above—
Entire and whole and perfect, the service of my love,
The love that asks no question: the love that stands the test,
That lays upon the altar the dearest and the best:
The love that never falters, the love that pays the price,
The love that makes undaunted the final sacrifice.
'I Vow to Thee, My Country' (written on the eve of his departure from Washington, 12 January 1918)

7 And there's another country, I've heard of long ago—
Most dear to them that love her, most great to them that know.
'I Vow to Thee, My Country' (written 1918)

8 Her ways are ways of gentleness and all her paths are Peace.
'I Vow to Thee, My Country' (written 1918); cf. **Bible** 82:9

9 I am the Dean of Christ Church, Sir:
There's my wife; look well at her.
She's the Broad and I'm the High;
We are the University.
The Masque of Balliol (composed by and current among members of Balliol College, Oxford, in the 1870s) in W. G. Hiscock (ed.) *The Balliol Rhymes* (1939); the first couplet was unofficially altered to:
I am the Dean, and this is Mrs Liddell;
She the first, and I the second fiddle.
cf. **Anonymous** 17:20, **Beeching** 61:9

Bruce Springsteen 1949–
American rock singer and songwriter

10 Born in the USA.
title of song (1984)

11 Born down in a dead man's town
The first kick I took was when I hit the ground.
'Born in the USA' (1984 song)

12 We gotta get out while we're young,
'Cause tramps like us, baby, we were born to run.
'Born to Run' (1974 song)

13 Is a dream a lie if it don't come true,
Or is it something worse?
'The River' (1980 song)

C. H. Spurgeon 1834–92
English nonconformist preacher

14 If you want truth to go round the world you must hire an express train to pull it; but if you want a lie to go round the world, it will fly: it is as light as a feather, and a breath will carry it. It is well said in the old proverb, 'a lie will go round the world while truth is pulling its boots on'.
Gems from Spurgeon (1859)

J. C. Squire 1884–1958
English man of letters

15 But I'm not so think as you drunk I am.
'Ballade of Soporific Absorption' (1931)

16 It did not last: the Devil howling 'Ho!
Let Einstein be!' restored the status quo.
'In continuation of Pope on Newton' (1926); see **Pope** 584:9

Mme de Staël (Anne-Louise-Germaine Necker) 1766–1817
French writer

17 *Tout comprendre rend très indulgent.*
To be totally understanding makes one very indulgent.
Corinne (1807) bk. 18, ch. 5; cf. **Proverbs** 613:9

18 *Un homme peut braver l'opinion; une femme doit s'y soumettre.*
A man can brave opinion, a woman must submit to it.
Delphine (1802) epigraph

19 Speech happens not to be his language.
on being asked what she found to talk about with her new lover, a hussar
attributed

Joseph Stalin (Iosif Vissarionovich Dzhugashvili) 1879–1953

Soviet dictator

1 The State is an instrument in the hands of the ruling class, used to break the resistance of the adversaries of that class.

Foundations of Leninism (1924) section 4/6

2 There are various forms of production: artillery, automobiles, lorries. You also produce 'commodities', 'works', 'products'. Such things are highly necessary. Engineering things. For people's souls. 'Products' are highly necessary too. 'Products' are very important for people's souls. You are engineers of human souls.

speech to writers at **Gorky**'s house, 26 October 1932; A. Kemp-Welch *Stalin and the Literary Intelligentsia, 1928–39* (1991); cf. **Gorky** 347:3

3 The Pope! How many divisions has *he* got?

on being asked to encourage Catholicism in Russia by way of conciliating the Pope, 13 May 1935

W. S. Churchill *The Gathering Storm* (1948) ch. 8; cf. **Napoleon** 539:2

4 There is one eternally true legend—that of Judas.

at the trial of Radek in 1937

Robert Payne *The Rise and Fall of Stalin* (1966)

5 One death is a tragedy, a million deaths a statistic.

attributed

Henry Morton Stanley 1841–1904

British explorer

6 Dr Livingstone, I presume?

How I found Livingstone (1872) ch. 11

Charles E. Stanton 1859–1933

American soldier

7 *Lafayette, nous voilà!*

Lafayette, we are here.

at the tomb of Lafayette in Paris, 4 July 1917; in *New York Tribune* 6 September 1917

Edwin Mcmasters Stanton 1814–69

American lawyer

8 Now he belongs to the ages.

of Abraham **Lincoln**, *following his assassination, 15 April 1865*

I. M. Tarbell *Life of Abraham Lincoln* (1900) vol. 2

Elizabeth Cady Stanton 1815–1902

American suffragist

9 The Bible teaches that woman brought sin and death into the world, that she precipitated the fall of the race . . . marriage for her was to be a condition of bondage, maternity a period of suffering and anguish, and in silence and subjection, she was to play the role of a dependant on man's bounty for all her material wants.

The Woman's Bible (1895) pt. 1, introduction

10 Woman's degradation is in man's idea of his sexual rights. Our religion, laws, customs, are all founded on the belief that woman was made for man.

letter to Susan B. Anthony, 14 June 1860, in T. Stanton and H. Stanton Blatch (eds.) *Elizabeth Cady Stanton* (1922) vol. 2

Frank L. Stanton 1857–1927

American journalist and poet

11 Sweetes' li'l' feller,
Everybody knows;
Dunno what to call him,
But he's mighty lak' a rose!

'Mighty Lak' a Rose' (1901 song)

John Stark 1728–1822

American Revolutionary officer

12 We beat them to-day or Molly Stark's a widow.

before the Battle of Bennington, 16 August 1777, in *Cyclopaedia of American Biography* vol. 5

Christina Stead 1902–83

Australian novelist

13 A self-made man is one who believes in luck and sends his son to Oxford.

House of All Nations (1938) 'Credo'

David Steel 1938–

British Liberal politician; Leader of the Liberal Party 1976–88

14 I have the good fortune to be the first Liberal leader for over half a century who is able to say to you at the end of our annual assembly: go back to your constituencies and prepare for government.

speech to the Liberal Party Assembly, 18 September 1981

Richard Steele 1672–1729

Irish-born essayist and dramatist

15 The insupportable labour of doing nothing.

in *The Spectator* no. 54 (2 May 1711)

16 A woman seldom writes her mind but in her postscript.

in *The Spectator* no. 79 (31 May 1711); cf. **Bacon** 42:20

17 We were in some little time fixed in our seats, and sat with that dislike which people not too good-natured usually conceive of each other at first sight.

in *The Spectator* no. 132 (1 August 1711)

18 There are so few who can grow old with a good grace.

in *The Spectator* no. 263 (1 January 1712)

19 Will Honeycomb calls these over-offended ladies the outrageously virtuous.

in *The Spectator* no. 266 (4 January 1712)

20 It is to be noted that when any part of this paper appears dull there is a design in it.

in *The Tatler* no. 38 (7 July 1709)

21 To love her is a liberal education.

of Lady Elizabeth Hastings

in *The Tatler* no. 49 (2 August 1709)

1 Reading is to the mind what exercise is to the body.
in *The Tatler* no. 147 (18 March 1710)

2 It was very prettily said, that we may learn the little value of fortune by the persons on whom heaven is pleased to bestow it.
in *The Tatler* no. 203 (27 July 1710); cf. **Luther** 480:5, **Swift** 748:9

Lincoln Steffens 1866–1936
American journalist

3 I have seen the future; and it works.
following a visit to the Soviet Union in 1919
letter to Marie Howe, 3 April 1919, in *Letters* (1938) vol. 1; in J. M. Thompson *Russia, Bolshevism and the Versailles Treaty* (1954) it is recalled that Steffens had composed the expression before he had even arrived in Russia

Edward Steichen 1879–1973
Luxembourg-born American photographer

4 The mission of photography is to explain man to man and each man to himself.
Cornell Capa (ed.) *The Concerned Photographer* (1972)

Gertrude Stein 1874–1946
American writer
on Stein: see **Anonymous** *16:20*, **Fadiman** *306:2*, **Lewis** *467:12; see also* **Last words** *457:17*

5 Remarks are not literature.
Autobiography of Alice B. Toklas (1933) ch. 7

6 Pigeons on the grass alas.
Four Saints in Three Acts (1934) act 3, sc. 2

7 In the United States there is more space where nobody is than where anybody is. That is what makes America what it is.
The Geographical History of America (1936)

8 Rose is a rose is a rose is a rose, is a rose.
Sacred Emily (1913)

9 You are all a lost generation.
of the young who served in the First World War
the phrase having been borrowed (in translation) from a French garage mechanic, whom Stein heard address it disparagingly to an incompetent apprentice; Ernest **Hemingway** subsequently took it as his epigraph to *The Sun Also Rises* (1926)

John Steinbeck 1902–68
American novelist
see also **Borrowed titles** *144:9*

10 Man, unlike any other thing organic or inorganic in the universe, grows beyond his work, walks up the stairs of his concepts, emerges ahead of his accomplishments.
The Grapes of Wrath (1939) ch. 14

11 Okie use' ta mean you was from Oklahoma. Now it means you're a dirty son-of-a-bitch. Okie means you're scum. Don't mean nothing itself, it's the way they say it.
The Grapes of Wrath (1939) ch. 18

Gloria Steinem 1934–
American journalist

12 We are becoming the men we wanted to marry.
in *Ms* July/August 1982

13 Outrageous acts and everyday rebellions.
title of book (1983)

14 A woman without a man is like a fish without a bicycle.
attributed

Stendhal (Henri Beyle) 1783–1842
French novelist
on Stendhal: see **Gide** *336:18*

15 For those who have tasted the profound activity of writing, reading is no more than a secondary pleasure.
De l'Amour (1822)

16 *Un roman est un miroir qui se promène sur une grande route. Tantôt il reflète à vos yeux l'azur des cieux, tantôt la fange des bourbiers de la route.*
A novel is a mirror which passes over a highway. Sometimes it reflects to your eyes the blue of the skies, at others the churned-up mud of the road.
Le Rouge et le noir (1830) bk. 2, ch. 19

17 *La politique au milieu des intérêts d'imagination, c'est un coup de pistolet au milieu d'un concert.*
Politics in the middle of things that concern the imagination are like a pistol-shot in the middle of a concert.
Le Rouge et le noir (1830) bk. 2, ch. 22

18 *J'aimais, et j'aime encore, les mathématiques pour elles-mêmes comme n'admettant pas* l'hypocrisie *et le* vague, *mes deux bêtes d'aversion.*
I used to love mathematics for its own sake, and I still do, because it allows for no hypocrisy and no vagueness, my two *bêtes noires*.
La Vie d'Henri Brulard (1890) ch. 10

19 I know of only one rule: style cannot be too *clear*, too *simple*.
letter to Balzac, 30 October 1840

J. K. Stephen 1859–92
English journalist and writer of light verse

20 Ah! Matt.: old age has brought to me
Thy wisdom, less thy certainty:
The world's a jest, and joy's a trinket:
I knew that once: but now—I think it.
'Senex to Matt. Prior' (1891); cf. **Epitaphs** 303:12

21 Two voices are there: one is of the deep;
It learns the storm-cloud's thunderous melody,
Now roars, now murmurs with the changing sea,
Now bird-like pipes, now closes soft in sleep:
And one is of an old half-witted sheep
Which bleats articulate monotony,
And indicates that two and one are three,
That grass is green, lakes damp, and mountains steep
And, Wordsworth, both are thine.
'A Sonnet' (1891); cf. **Wordsworth** 832:8

1 When the Rudyards cease from kipling
And the Haggards ride no more.
'To R.K.' (1891)

Leslie Stephen 1832–1904

English scholar and philosopher, first editor of the Dictionary of National Biography

2 The editor of such a work must, by the necessity of the case, be autocratic. He will do his best to be a considerate autocrat.

of the compilation of a dictionary of national biography
in *Athenaeum* 23 December 1882

James Stephens 1882–1950

Irish poet and writer

3 Finality is death. Perfection is finality. Nothing is perfect. There are lumps in it.
The Crock of Gold (1912) bk. 1, ch. 4

4 I hear a sudden cry of pain!
There is a rabbit in a snare:
Now I hear the cry again,
But I cannot tell from where . . .
Little one! Oh, little one!
I am searching everywhere.
'The Snare' (1915)

Laurence Sterne 1713–68

English novelist
on Sterne: see **Johnson** *416:22*

5 They order, said I, this matter better in France.
A Sentimental Journey (1768) opening words

6 As an Englishman does not travel to see Englishmen, I retired to my room.
A Sentimental Journey (1768) 'Preface. In the Desobligeant'

7 I pity the man who can travel from Dan to Beersheba, and cry, 'tis all barren.
A Sentimental Journey (1768) 'In the Street. Calais'

8 If ever I do a mean action, it must be in some interval betwixt one passion and another.
A Sentimental Journey (1768) 'Montriul'

9 Vive l'amour! et vive la bagatelle!
A Sentimental Journey (1768) 'The letter'

10 There are worse occupations in this world than feeling a woman's pulse.
A Sentimental Journey (1768) 'The Pulse. Paris'

11 God tempers the wind, said Maria, to the shorn lamb.
derived from a French proverb, but familiar in this form of words
A Sentimental Journey (1768) 'Maria'

12 Dear sensibility! source inexhausted of all that's precious in our joys, or costly in our sorrows!
A Sentimental Journey (1768) 'The Bourbonnois'

13 I wish either my father or my mother, or indeed both of them, as they were in duty both equally bound to it, had minded what they were about when they begot me.
Tristram Shandy (1759–67) bk. 1, ch. 1

14 'Pray, my dear,' quoth my mother, 'have you not forgot to wind up the clock?'—'Good G—!' cried my father, making an exclamation, but taking care to moderate his voice at the same time,—'Did ever woman, since the creation of the world, interrupt a man with such a silly question?'
Tristram Shandy (1759–67) bk. 1, ch. 1

15 As we jog on, either laugh with me, or at me, or in short do anything,—only keep your temper.
Tristram Shandy (1759–67) bk. 1, ch. 6

16 So long as a man rides his Hobby-Horse peaceably and quietly along the King's highway, and neither compels you or me to get up behind him,—pray, Sir, what have either you or I to do with it?
Tristram Shandy (1759–67) bk. 1, ch. 7

17 He was in a few hours of giving his enemies the slip for ever.
Tristram Shandy (1759–67) bk. 1, ch. 12

18 'Tis known by the name of perseverance in a good cause,—and of obstinacy in a bad one.
Tristram Shandy (1759–67) bk. 1, ch. 17

19 What is the character of a family to an hypothesis? my father would reply.
Tristram Shandy (1759–67) bk. 1, ch. 21

20 My uncle Toby would never offer to answer this by any other kind of argument, than that of whistling half a dozen bars of Lillabullero.
Tristram Shandy (1759–67) bk. 1, ch. 21; cf. **Wharton** 813:4

21 Digressions, incontestably, are the sunshine;—they are the life, the soul of reading;—take them out of this book for instance,—you might as well take the book along with them
Tristram Shandy (1759–67) bk. 1, ch. 22

22 I should have no objection to this method, but that I think it must smell too strong of the lamp.
Tristram Shandy (1759–67) bk. 1, ch. 23

23 Writing, when properly managed (as you may be sure I think mine is) is but a different name for conversation.
Tristram Shandy (1759–67) bk. 2, ch. 11

24 'I'll not hurt thee,' says my uncle Toby, rising from his chair, and going across the room, with the fly in his hand,—'I'll not hurt a hair of thy head:—Go,' says he, lifting up the sash, and opening his hand as he spoke, to let it escape;—'go, poor devil, get thee gone, why should I hurt thee?—This world surely is wide enough to hold both thee and me.'
Tristram Shandy (1759–67) bk. 2, ch. 12

25 Whenever a man talks loudly against religion,—always suspect that it is not his reason, but his passions which have got the better of his creed.
Tristram Shandy (1759–67) bk. 2, ch. 17

26 It is the nature of an hypothesis, when once a man has conceived it, that it assimilates every thing to itself, as proper nourishment; and, from the first moment of your begetting it, it generally grows the

stronger by every thing you see, hear, read, or understand.
Tristram Shandy (1759–67) bk. 2, ch. 19

1 'Our armies swore terribly in Flanders,' cried my uncle Toby,—'but nothing to this.'
Tristram Shandy (1759–67) bk. 3, ch. 11

2 The corregiescity of Corregio.
Tristram Shandy (1759–67) bk. 3, ch. 12

3 Of all the cants which are canted in this canting world,—though the cant of hypocrites may be the worst,—the cant of criticism is the most tormenting!
Tristram Shandy (1759–67) bk. 3, ch. 12

4 Is this a fit time, said my father to himself, to talk of Pensions and Grenadiers?
Tristram Shandy (1759–67) bk. 4, ch. 5

5 True *Shandeism*, think what you will against it, opens the heart and lungs, and like all those affections which partake of its nature, it forces the blood and other vital fluids of the body to run freely through its channels, and makes the wheel of life run long and cheerfully round.
Tristram Shandy (1759–67) bk. 4, ch. 32

6 'There is no terror, brother Toby, in its [death's] looks, but what it borrows from groans and convulsions—and the blowing of noses, and the wiping away of tears with the bottoms of curtains, in a dying man's room—Strip it of these, what is it?'—''Tis better in battle than in bed', said my uncle Toby.
Tristram Shandy (1759–67) bk. 5, ch. 3

7 There is a North-west passage to the intellectual World.
Tristram Shandy (1759–67) bk. 5, ch. 42

8 'The poor soul will die:—' 'He shall not die, by G—', cried my uncle Toby.—The Accusing Spirit, which flew up to heaven's chancery with the oath, blushed as he gave it in;—and the Recording Angel, as he wrote it down, dropped a tear upon the word, and blotted it out for ever.
Tristram Shandy (1759–67) bk. 6, ch. 8

9 To say a man is fallen in love,—or that he is deeply in love,—or up to the ears in love,—and sometimes even over head and ears in it,—carries an idiomatical kind of implication, that love is a thing below a man:—this is recurring again to Plato's opinion, which, with all his divinityship,—I hold to be damnable and heretical:—and so much for that.

Let love therefore be what it will,—my uncle Toby fell into it.
Tristram Shandy (1759–67) bk. 6, ch. 37

10 My brother Toby, quoth she, is going to be married to Mrs Wadman.

Then he will never, quoth my father, lie *diagonally* in his bed again as long as he lives.
Tristram Shandy (1759–67) bk. 6, ch. 39

11 Now hang it! quoth I, as I look'd towards the French coast—A man should know something of his own country too, before he goes abroad.
Tristram Shandy (1759–67) bk. 7, ch. 2

12 And who are you? said he.—Don't puzzle me, said I.
Tristram Shandy (1759–67) bk. 7, ch. 33

13 'A soldier,' cried my Uncle Toby, interrupting the corporal, 'is no more exempt from saying a foolish thing, Trim, than a man of letters.'—'But not so often, an' please your honour,' replied the corporal.
Tristram Shandy (1759–67) bk. 8, ch. 19

14 Everything presses on—whilst thou art twisting that lock,—see! it grows grey; and every time I kiss thy hand to bid adieu, and every absence which follows it, are preludes to that eternal separation which we are shortly to make.
Tristram Shandy (1759–67) bk. 9, ch. 10

15 —d! said my mother, 'what is all this story about?'— 'A Cock and a Bull,' said Yorick.
Tristram Shandy (1759–67) bk. 9, ch. 33

16 This sad vicissitude of things.
Sermons (1767) no. 16 'The character of Shimei'

Brooks Stevens 1911–
American industrial designer

17 Our whole economy is based on planned obsolescence.
Vance Packard *The Waste Makers* (1960) ch. 6

Wallace Stevens 1879–1955
American poet

18 The poet is the priest of the invisible.
'Adagia' (1957)

19 Chieftain Iffucan of Azcan in caftan
Of tan with henna hackles, halt!
'Bantams in Pine Woods' (1923)

20 Call the roller of big cigars,
The muscular one, and bid him whip
In kitchen cups concupiscent curds.
'The Emperor of Ice-Cream' (1923)

21 Let be be finale of seem.
The only emperor is the emperor of ice-cream.
'The Emperor of Ice-Cream' (1923)

22 Frogs Eat Butterflies. Snakes Eat Frogs. Hogs Eat Snakes. Men Eat Hogs.
title of poem (1923)

23 Poetry is the supreme fiction, madame.
'A High-Toned old Christian Woman' (1923)

24 They said, 'You have a blue guitar,
You do not play things as they are.'

The man replied, 'Things as they are
Are changed upon the blue guitar.'
'The Man with the Blue Guitar' (1937)

25 They will get it straight one day at the Sorbonne.
We shall return at twilight from the lecture
Pleased that the irrational is rational.
Notes Toward a Supreme Fiction (1947) 'It Must Give Pleasure' no. 10

26 The palm at the end of the mind,
Beyond the last thought, rises . . .
A gold-feathered bird

Sings in the palm.
'Of Mere Being' (1957)

1 Music is feeling, then, not sound.
'Peter Quince at the Clavier' (1923) pt. 1

2 Beauty is momentary in the mind—
The fitful tracing of a portal;
But in the flesh it is immortal.
The body dies; the body's beauty lives.
'Peter Quince at the Clavier' (1923) pt. 4

3 Susanna's music touched the bawdy strings
Of those white elders.
'Peter Quince at the Clavier' (1923) pt. 4

4 One must have a mind of winter
To regard the frost and the boughs
Of the pine trees crusted with snow;
And have been cold a long time
To behold the junipers shagged with ice,
The spruces rough in the distant glitter
Of the January sun; and not to think
Of any misery in the sound of the wind,
In the sound of a few leaves,
Which is the sound of the land
Full of the same wind
That is blowing in the same bare place
For the listener, who listens in the snow,
And nothing himself, beholds
Nothing that is not there and nothing that is.
'The Snow Man' (1921)

5 Complacencies of the peignoir, and late
Coffee and oranges in a sunny chair,
And the green freedom of a cockatoo
Upon a rug mingle to dissipate
The holy hush of ancient sacrifice.
'Sunday Morning' (1923) st. 1

6 Deer walk upon our mountains, and the quail
Whistle about us their spontaneous cries;
Sweet berries ripen in the wilderness;
And, in the isolation of the sky,
At evening, casual flocks of pigeons make
Ambiguous undulations as they sink,
Downward to darkness, on extended wings.
'Sunday Morning' (1923) st. 8

7 I do not know which to prefer,
The beauty of inflections
Or the beauty of innuendoes,
The blackbird whistling
Or just after.
'Thirteen Ways of Looking at a Blackbird' (1923)

Adlai Stevenson 1900–65

American Democratic politician
see also **Anonymous** 15:4

8 I suppose flattery hurts no one, that is, if he doesn't inhale.
television broadcast, 30 March 1952, in N. F. Busch *Adlai E. Stevenson* (1952) ch. 5

9 If they [the Republicans] will stop telling lies about the Democrats, we will stop telling the truth about them.
speech during 1952 Presidential campaign; in J. B. Martin *Adlai Stevenson and Illinois* (1976) ch. 8

10 Let's talk sense to the American people. Let's tell them the truth, that there are no gains without pains.
speech of acceptance at the Democratic National Convention, Chicago, Illinois, 26 July 1952; in *Speeches* (1952)

11 In America any boy may become President and I suppose it's just one of the risks he takes!
speech in Indianapolis, 26 September 1952; in *Major Campaign Speeches . . .* 1952 (1953)

12 A free society is a society where it is safe to be unpopular.
speech in Detroit, 7 October 1952; in *Major Campaign Speeches . . .* 1952 (1953)

13 The young man who asks you to set him one heart-beat from the Presidency of the United States.
of Richard **Nixon** *as Vice-Presidential nominee*
speech at Cleveland, Ohio, 23 October 1952, in *New York Times* 24 October 1952

14 We hear the Secretary of State boasting of his brinkmanship—the art of bringing us to the edge of the abyss.
speech in Hartford, Connecticut, 25 February 1956; in *New York Times* 26 February 1956; see **Dulles** 284:13

15 She would rather light a candle than curse the darkness, and her glow has warmed the world.
of Eleanor **Roosevelt**
in *New York Times* 8 November 1962

16 Do you remember that in classical times when Cicero had finished speaking, the people said, 'How well he spoke', but when Demosthenes had finished speaking, they said, 'Let us march.'
introducing John Fitzgerald **Kennedy** *in 1960*
Bert Cochran *Adlai Stevenson* (1969) ch. 3

17 The kind of politician who would cut down a redwood tree, and then mount the stump and make a speech on conservation.
of Richard **Nixon**
Fawn M. Brodie *Richard Nixon* (1983)

Anne Stevenson 1933–

English poet

18 Blackbirds are the cellos of the deep farms.
'Green Mountain, Black Mountain' (1982)

19 At fifty, menopausal, nervous, thin,
She joined a women's group and studied Zen.
Her latest book, *The Happy Lesbian*,
Is recommended reading for gay men.
'A Quest' (1993)

Robert Louis Stevenson 1850–94

Scottish novelist

20 Every one lives by selling something.
Across the Plains (1892) 'Beggars' pt. 3

21 The harmless art of knucklebones has seen the fall of the Roman empire and the rise of the United States.
Across the Plains (1892) 'The Lantern-Bearers' pt. 1

22 The bright face of danger.
Across the Plains (1892) 'The Lantern-Bearers' pt. 4

1 Here lies one who meant well, tried a little, failed much:—surely that may be his epitaph, of which he need not be ashamed.
Across the Plains (1892) 'A Christmas Sermon' pt. 4

2 The web, then, or the pattern; a web at once sensuous and logical, an elegant and pregnant texture: that is style, that is the foundation of the art of literature.
The Art of Writing (1905) 'On some technical Elements of Style in Literature' (written 1885)

3 There are two duties incumbent upon any man who enters on the business of writing: truth to the fact and a good spirit in the treatment.
Essays Literary and Critical (1923) 'Morality of the Profession of Letters'

4 Politics is perhaps the only profession for which no preparation is thought necessary.
Familiar Studies of Men and Books (1882) 'Yoshida-Torajiro'

5 Am I no a bonny fighter?
Kidnapped (1886) ch. 10

6 I've a grand memory for forgetting, David.
Kidnapped (1886) ch. 18

7 I have thus played the sedulous ape to Hazlitt, to Lamb, to Wordsworth, to Sir Thomas Browne, to Defoe, to Hawthorne, to Montaigne, to Baudelaire and to Obermann.
Memories and Portraits (1887) ch. 4 'A College Magazine'

8 These are my politics: to change what we can; to better what we can; but still to bear in mind that man is but a devil weakly fettered by some generous beliefs and impositions; and for no word however sounding, and no cause however just and pious, to relax the stricture of these bonds.
More New Arabian Nights: The Dynamiter (1885) 'Epilogue of the Cigar Divan'

9 He who was prepared to help the escaping murderer or to embrace the impenitent thief, found, to the overthrow of all his logic, that he objected to the use of dynamite.
More New Arabian Nights: The Dynamiter (1885) 'The Superfluous Mansion'

10 I regard you with an indifference closely bordering on aversion.
New Arabian Nights (1882) 'The Rajah's Diamond: Story of the Bandbox'

11 The devil, depend upon it, can sometimes do a very gentlemanly thing.
New Arabian Nights (1882) 'The Suicide Club: Story of the Young Man with the Cream Tarts'

12 The strange case of Dr Jekyll and Mr Hyde.
title of novel, 1886

13 With every day, and from both sides of my intelligence, the moral and the intellectual, I thus drew steadily nearer to that truth, by whose partial discovery I have been doomed to such a dreadful shipwreck: that man is not truly one, but truly two.
The Strange Case of Dr Jekyll and Mr Hyde (1886)

14 Every book is, in an intimate sense, a circular letter to the friends of him who writes it. They alone take his meaning; they find private messages, assurances of love, and expressions of gratitude, dropped at every corner. The public is but a generous patron who defrays the postage.
dedicatory letter to *Travels with a Donkey* (1879)

15 A faddling hedonist.
Travels with a Donkey (1879) 'The Boarders'

16 For my part, I travel not to go anywhere, but to go. I travel for travel's sake. The great affair is to move.
Travels with a Donkey (1879) 'Cheylard and Luc'

17 I own I like definite form in what my eyes are to rest upon; and if landscapes were sold, like the sheets of characters of my boyhood, one penny plain and twopence coloured, I should go the length of twopence every day of my life.
Travels with a Donkey (1879) 'Father Apollinaris'

18 Fifteen men on the dead man's chest
Yo-ho-ho, and a bottle of rum!
Drink and the devil had done for the rest—
Yo-ho-ho, and a bottle of rum!
Treasure Island (1883) ch. 1

19 Tip me the black spot.
Treasure Island (1883) ch. 3

20 Pieces of eight, pieces of eight, pieces of eight!
Treasure Island (1883) ch. 10

21 Many's the long night I've dreamed of cheese—toasted, mostly.
Treasure Island (1883) ch. 15

22 Even if the doctor does not give you a year, even if he hesitates about a month, make one brave push and see what can be accomplished in a week.
Virginibus Puerisque (1881) 'Aes Triplex'

23 There is no duty we so much underrate as the duty of being happy.
Virginibus Puerisque (1881) 'An Apology for Idlers'

24 Old and young, we are all on our last cruise.
Virginibus Puerisque (1881) 'Crabbed Age and Youth'

25 To travel hopefully is a better thing than to arrive, and the true success is to labour.
Virginibus Puerisque (1881) 'El Dorado'; cf. **Proverbs** 604:12

26 In marriage, a man becomes slack and selfish, and undergoes a fatty degeneration of his moral being.
Virginibus Puerisque (1881) title essay, pt. 1

27 Even if we take matrimony at its lowest, even if we regard it as no more than a sort of friendship recognised by the police.
Virginibus Puerisque (1881) title essay, pt. 1

28 A little amateur painting in water-colour shows the innocent and quiet mind.
Virginibus Puerisque (1881) title essay, pt. 1

29 Lastly (and this is, perhaps, the golden rule), no woman should marry a teetotaller, or a man who does not smoke.
Virginibus Puerisque (1881) title essay, pt. 1

30 Marriage is a step so grave and decisive that it attracts light-headed, variable men by its very awfulness.
Virginibus Puerisque (1881) title essay, pt. 1

1 Marriage is like life in this—that it is a field of battle, and not a bed of roses.
Virginibus Puerisque (1881) title essay, pt. 1

2 To marry is to domesticate the Recording Angel. Once you are married, there is nothing left for you, not even suicide, but to be good.
Virginibus Puerisque (1881) title essay, pt. 2

3 Man is a creature who lives not upon bread alone, but principally by catchwords.
Virginibus Puerisque (1881) title essay, pt. 2

4 The cruellest lies are often told in silence.
Virginibus Puerisque (1881) title essay, pt. 4

5 What hangs people . . . is the unfortunate circumstance of guilt.
The Wrong Box (with Lloyd Osbourne, 1889) ch. 7

6 Nothing like a little judicious levity.
The Wrong Box (with Lloyd Osbourne, 1889) ch. 7

7 Between the possibility of being hanged in all innocence, and the certainty of a public and merited disgrace, no gentleman of spirit could long hesitate.
The Wrong Box (with Lloyd Osbourne, 1889) ch. 10

8 If you are going to make a book end badly, it must end badly from the beginning.
letter to J. M. Barrie, November 1892, in Sidney Colvin (ed.) *Letters of Robert Louis Stevenson* (1911) vol. 4

9 I am an Epick writer with a k to it, but without the necessary genius.
letter to Henry James, 5 December 1892, in Sidney Colvin (ed.) *Letters of Robert Louis Stevenson* (1911) vol. 4

10 I believe in an ultimate decency of things.
letter to Sidney Colvin, 23 August 1893, in Sidney Colvin (ed.) *Letters of Robert Louis Stevenson* (1911) vol. 4

11 In winter I get up at night
And dress by yellow candle-light.
In summer, quite the other way,—
I have to go to bed by day.
A Child's Garden of Verses (1885) 'Bed in Summer'

12 The world is so full of a number of things,
I'm sure we should all be as happy as kings.
A Child's Garden of Verses (1885) 'Happy Thought'

13 I was the giant great and still
That sits upon the pillow-hill,
And sees before him, dale and plain,
The pleasant land of counterpane.
A Child's Garden of Verses (1885) 'The Land of Counterpane'

14 I have a little shadow that goes in and out with me,
And what can be the use of him is more than I can see.
He is very, very like me from the heels up to the head;
And I see him jump before me, when I jump into my bed.
A Child's Garden of Verses (1885) 'My Shadow'

15 Let us arise and go like men,
And face with an undaunted tread
The long black passage up to bed.
A Child's Garden of Verses (1885) 'North-West Passage. Good-Night'

16 A child should always say what's true,
And speak when he is spoken to,
And behave mannerly at table:
At least as far as he is able.
A Child's Garden of Verses (1885) 'Whole Duty of Children'

17 Whenever the moon and stars are set,
Whenever the wind is high,
All night long in the dark and wet,
A man goes riding by.
Late in the night when the fires are out,
Why does he gallop and gallop about?
A Child's Garden of Verses (1885) 'Windy Nights'

18 But all that I could think of, in the darkness and the cold,
Was that I was leaving home and my folks were growing old.
Ballads (1890) 'Christmas at Sea'

19 In the highlands, in the country places,
Where the old plain men have rosy faces,
And the young fair maidens
Quiet eyes.
Songs of Travel (1896) 'In the highlands, in the country places'

20 I will make you brooches and toys for your delight
Of bird-song at morning and star-shine at night.
Songs of Travel (1896) 'I will make you brooches and toys for your delight'

21 I will make my kitchen, and you shall keep your room,
Where white flows the river and bright blows the broom,
And you shall wash your linen and keep your body white
In rainfall at morning and dewfall at night.
Songs of Travel (1896) 'I will make you brooches and toys for your delight'

22 Trusty, dusky, vivid, true,
With eyes of gold and bramble-dew,
Steel-true and blade-straight,
The great artificer
Made my mate.
Songs of Travel (1896) 'My Wife'

23 Sing me a song of a lad that is gone,
Say, could that lad be I?
Merry of soul he sailed on a day
Over the sea to Skye.
Songs of Travel (1896) 'Sing me a song of a lad that is gone'

24 Be it granted to me to behold you again in dying,
Hills of home! and to hear again the call;
Hear about the graves of the martyrs the peewees crying,
And hear no more at all.
Songs of Travel (1896) 'To S. R. Crockett'

25 Give to me the life I love,
Let the lave go by me,
Give the jolly heaven above
And the byway nigh me.
Bed in the bush with stars to see,
Bread I dip in the river—
There's the life for a man like me,

There's the life for ever.
Songs of Travel (1896) 'The Vagabond'

1 Let the blow fall soon or late,
Let what will be o'er me;
Give the face of earth around
And the road before me.
Wealth I seek not, hope nor love,
Nor a friend to know me;
All I seek, the heaven above
And the road below me.
Songs of Travel (1896) 'The Vagabond'

2 Of all my verse, like not a single line;
But like my title, for it is not mine.
That title from a better man I stole;
Ah, how much better, had I stol'n the whole!
Underwoods (1887) foreword

3 Go, little book, and wish to all
Flowers in the garden, meat in the hall,
A bin of wine, a spice of wit,
A house with lawns enclosing it,
A living river by the door,
A nightingale in the sycamore!
Underwoods (1887) 'Envoy'; cf. **Chaucer** 207:18

4 Under the wide and starry sky
Dig the grave and let me lie.
Glad did I live and gladly die,
And I laid me down with a will.
This be the verse you grave for me:
'Here he lies where he longed to be;
Home is the sailor, home from sea,
And the hunter home from the hill.'
Underwoods (1887) 'Requiem'

5 And what should Master Gauger play
But 'Over the hills and far away'?
Underwoods (1887) 'A Song of the Road'

Ian Stewart 1945–
British mathematician

6 Genes are not like engineering blueprints; they are more like recipes in a cookbook. They tell us what ingredients to use, in what quantities, and in what order—but they do not provide a complete, accurate plan of the final result.
Life's Other Secret (1998) preface

Sting (Gordon Sumner) 1951–
English rock singer, songwriter, and actor

7 If I were a Brazilian without land or money or the means to feed my children, I would be burning the rain forest too.
in *International Herald Tribune* 14 April 1989

Caskie Stinnett 1911–
American writer

8 A diplomat . . . is a person who can tell you to go to hell in such a way that you actually look forward to the trip.
Out of the Red (1960) ch. 4

Samuel John Stone 1839–1900
English clergyman

9 The Church's one foundation
Is Jesus Christ, her Lord;
She is his new creation
By water and the word:
From heaven he came and sought her
To be his holy bride,
With his own blood he bought her,
And for her life he died.
Lyra Fidelium (1866) 'The Church's one foundation'

Marie Stopes 1880–1958
Scottish pioneer of birth-control clinics

10 An impersonal and scientific knowledge of the structure of our bodies is the surest safeguard against prurient curiosity and lascivious gloating.
Married Love (1918) ch. 5

Tom Stoppard 1937–
British dramatist

11 It's not the voting that's democracy, it's the counting.
Jumpers (1972) act 1; cf. **Somoza** 727:19

12 The House of Lords, an illusion to which I have never been able to subscribe—responsibility without power, the prerogative of the eunuch throughout the ages.
Lord Malquist and Mr Moon (1966) pt. 6; cf. **Kipling** 441:25

13 The media. It sounds like a convention of spiritualists.
Night and Day (1978) act 1

14 I'm with you on the free press. It's the newspapers I can't stand.
Night and Day (1978) act 1

15 Comment is free but facts are on expenses.
Night and Day (1978) act 2; cf. **Scott** 650:4

16 You're familiar with the tragedies of antiquity, are you? The great homicidal classics?
Rosencrantz and Guildenstern are Dead (1967) act 1

17 I can do you blood and love without the rhetoric, and I can do you blood and rhetoric without the love, and I can do you all three concurrent or consecutive, but I can't do you love and rhetoric without the blood. Blood is compulsory—they're all blood, you see.
Rosencrantz and Guildenstern are Dead (1967) act 1

18 Eternity's a terrible thought. I mean, where's it all going to end?
Rosencrantz and Guildenstern are Dead (1967) act 2

19 The bad end unhappily, the good unluckily. That is what tragedy means.
Rosencrantz and Guildenstern are Dead (1967) act 2; cf. **Wilde** 817:19

20 Life is a gamble at terrible odds—if it was a bet, you wouldn't take it.
Rosencrantz and Guildenstern are Dead (1967) act 3

1 War is capitalism with the gloves off and many who go to war know it but they go to war because they don't want to be a hero.
Travesties (1975) act 1

William Stoughton 1631–1701
American clergyman

2 God hath sifted a nation that he might send choice grain into this wilderness.
sermon in Boston, 29 April 1669

Harriet Beecher Stowe 1811–96
American novelist
on Stowe: see **Lincoln** 469:4

3 I s'pect I growed. Don't think nobody never made me.
Topsy
Uncle Tom's Cabin (1852) ch. 20

William Scott, Lord Stowell 1745–1836
English jurist

4 The elegant simplicity of the three per cents.
Lord Campbell *Lives of the Lord Chancellors* (1857) vol. 10, ch. 212; cf. **Disraeli** 270:13

5 A precedent embalms a principle.
an opinion, while Advocate-General, 1788, quoted by Disraeli in House of Commons, 22 February 1848

Lytton Strachey 1880–1932
English biographer
see also: **Last words** 456:4

6 Francis Bacon has been described more than once with the crude vigour of antithesis . . . He was no striped frieze; he was shot silk.
Elizabeth and Essex (1928) ch. 5

7 The time was out of joint, and he was only too delighted to have been born to set it right.
of Hurrell Froude
Eminent Victorians (1918) 'Cardinal Manning' pt. 2; cf. **Shakespeare** 663:7

8 Her conception of God was certainly not orthodox. She felt towards Him as she might have felt towards a glorified sanitary engineer; and in some of her speculations she seems hardly to distinguish between the Deity and the Drains.
Eminent Victorians (1918) 'Florence Nightingale' pt. 4

9 CHAIRMAN OF MILITARY TRIBUNAL: What would you do if you saw a German soldier trying to violate your sister?
STRACHEY: I would try to get between them.
otherwise rendered as, 'I should interpose my body'
Robert Graves *Good-bye to All That* (1929) ch. 23

10 Discretion is not the better part of biography.
Michael Holroyd *Lytton Strachey* vol. 1 (1967) preface

Thomas Wentworth, Lord Strafford 1593–1641
English statesman

11 The authority of a King is the keystone which closeth up the arch of order and government which, once shaken, all the frame falls together in a confused heap of foundation and battlement.
Hugh Trevor-Roper *Historical Essays* (1952) 'The Outbreak of the Great Rebellion'

William L. Strauss and A. J. E. Cave

12 Notwithstanding, if he could be reincarnated and placed in a New York subway—provided that he were bathed, shaved, and dressed in modern clothing—it is doubtful whether he would attract any more attention than some of its other denizens.
of Neanderthal man
in *Quarterly Review of Biology* Winter 1957

Igor Stravinsky 1882–1971
Russian composer

13 Tradition is entirely different from habit, even from an excellent habit, since habit is by definition an unconscious acquisition and tends to become mechanical, whereas tradition results from a conscious and deliberate acceptance . . . Tradition presupposes the reality of what endures.
Poetics of Music (1947) ch. 3 (translated by A. Knodel and I. Dahl)

14 Conductors' careers are made for the most part with 'romantic' music. 'Classic' music eliminates the conductor; we do not remember him in it.
Robert Craft *Conversations with Stravinsky* (1958) ch. 4

15 My music is best understood by children and animals.
in *Observer* 8 October 1961

16 Academism results when the reasons for the rule change, but not the rule.
attributed

John Whitaker ('Jack') Straw 1946–
British Labour politician

17 It's not because ageing wrinklies have tried to stop people having fun. It's because . . . these so-called soft drugs are potentially very dangerous.
asserting his opposition to the legalization of cannabis
on *Breakfast with Frost*, BBC1 TV, 4 January 1998

Janet Street-Porter 1946–
English broadcaster and programme-maker

18 A terminal blight has hit the TV industry nipping fun in the bud and stunting our growth. This blight is management—the dreaded Four M's: male, middle class, middle-aged and mediocre.
MacTaggart Lecture, Edinburgh Television Festival, 25 August 1995

August Strindberg 1849–1912
Swedish dramatist and novelist

19 Family! . . . the home of all social evil, a charitable institution for comfortable women, an anchorage for house-fathers, and a hell for children.
The Son of a Servant (1886)

Randall E. Stross

1 American anti-intellectualism will never again be the same because of Bill Gates. Gates embodies what was supposed to be impossible—the practical intellectual.

The Microsoft Way (1996)

Jan Struther (Joyce Placzek) 1901–53

English-born novelist and hymn-writer

2 Lord of all hopefulness, Lord of all joy,
Whose trust, ever childlike, no cares could destroy,
Be there at our waking, and give us, we pray,
Your bliss in our hearts, Lord, at the break of the day.

'All Day Hymn' (1931 hymn)

William Stubbs 1825–1901

English historian and prelate
on Stubbs: see **Rogers** *631:17*

3 Froude informs the Scottish youth
That parsons do not care for truth.
The Reverend Canon Kingsley cries
History is a pack of lies.
What cause for judgements so malign?
A brief reflection solves the mystery—
Froude believes Kingsley a divine,
And Kingsley goes to Froude for history.

letter to J. R. Green, 17 December 1871, in *Letters* (1904)

G. A. Studdert Kennedy 1883–1929

British poet

4 Waste of Blood, and waste of Tears,
Waste of youth's most precious years,
Waste of ways the saints have trod,
Waste of Glory, waste of God,
War!

More Rough Rhymes of a Padre by 'Woodbine Willie' (1919) 'Waste'

5 When Jesus came to Birmingham they simply passed Him by,
They never hurt a hair of Him, they only let Him die.

Peace Rhymes of a Padre (1921) 'Indifference'

John Suckling 1609–42

English poet and dramatist

6 Women enjoyed (whatsoe'er before they've been)
Are like romances read, or sights once seen:
Fruition's dull, and spoils the play much more
Than if one read or knew the plot before.

'Against Fruition' (1646)

7 Why so pale and wan, fond lover?
Prithee, why so pale?
Will, when looking well can't move her,
Looking ill prevail?
Prithee, why so pale?

Aglaura (1637) act 4, sc. 1 'Song'

8 Her feet beneath her petticoat,
Like little mice, stole in and out.

'A Ballad upon a Wedding' (1646) st. 8

9 Love is the fart
Of every heart:
It pains a man when 'tis kept close,
And others doth offend, when 'tis let loose.

'Love's Offence' (1646)

10 Out upon it, I have loved
Three whole days together;
And am like to love three more,
If it prove fair weather.

'A Poem with the Answer' (1659)

11 Sure beauty's empires, like to greater states,
Have certain periods set, and hidden fates.

'Sonnet' (1646)

Suger 1081–1151

French monk and statesman, abbot of Saint-Denis, and regent of France during the Second Crusade

12 Thus, when—out of my delight in the beauty of the house of God—the loveliness of the many-coloured gems has called me away from external cares, and worthy meditation has induced me to reflect, transferring that which is material to that which is immaterial, on the diversity of the sacred virtues; then it seems to me that I see myself dwelling, as it were, in some strange region of the universe which neither exists entirely in the slime of the earth nor entirely in the purity of Heaven; and that, by the grace of God, I can be transported from this inferior to that higher world in an anagogical manner.

De Consecratione

13 No one among the countless thousands of people because of their very density could move a foot; that no one, because of their very congestion could do anything but stand like a marble statue, stay benumbed or, as a last resort, scream.

description of the church of St-Denis on a feast day

De Consecratione

Annie Sullivan 1866–1936

American educator; tutor of Helen **Keller**

14 Language grows out of life, out of its needs and experiences . . . *Language* and *knowledge* are indissolubly connected; they are interdependent. Good work in language presupposes and depends on a real knowledge of things

speech to the American Association to Promote the Teaching of Speech to the Deaf, July 1894; Helen Keller *The Story of My Life* (1902)

Louis Henri Sullivan 1856–1924

American architect

15 Form follows function.

The Tall Office Building Artistically Considered (1896)

Terry Sullivan

see also Harry **Bedford** *and Terry* **Sullivan**

16 She sells sea-shells on the sea-shore,
The shells she sells are sea-shells, I'm sure,
For if she sells sea-shells on the sea-shore,
Then I'm sure she sells sea-shore shells.

'She Sells Sea-Shells' (1908 song)

Timothy Daniel Sullivan 1827–1914

Irish writer and politician

1 'God save Ireland!' said the heroes;
'God save Ireland', say they all:
Whether on the scaffold high
Or the battlefield we die,
Oh, what matter when for Erin dear we fall.

'God Save Ireland' (1867); cf. **Last words** 455:16

Maximilien de Béthune, Duc de Sully 1559–1641

French statesman

see also **Henri IV** 370:7

2 Tilling and grazing are the two breasts by which France is fed.

Mémoires (1638) pt. 1, ch. 15

3 The English take their pleasures sadly after the fashion of their country.

attributed

Arthur Hays Sulzberger 1891–1968

American newspaper proprietor

4 We tell the public which way the cat is jumping. The public will take care of the cat.

on journalism

in *Time* 8 May 1950

Edith Summerskill 1901–80

British Labour politician

5 Nagging is the repetition of unpalatable truths.

speech to the Married Women's Association, House of Commons, 14 July 1960; in *The Times* 15 July 1960

Charles Sumner 1811–74

American politician and orator

6 Where Slavery is, there Liberty cannot be; and where Liberty is, there Slavery cannot be.

'Slavery and the Rebellion'; speech at Cooper Institute 5 November 1864

7 There is the national flag. He must be cold, indeed, who can look upon its folds rippling in the breeze without pride of country.

Are We a Nation? 19 November 1867

Henry Howard, Earl of Surrey c.1517–47

English poet

8 Martial, the things for to attain
The happy life be these, I find:
The riches left, not got with pain;
The fruitful ground, the quiet mind.

'The Happy Life' (1547); translation of Martial *Epigrams* bk. 10, no. 47; cf. **Martial** 498:3

9 Love, that doth reign and live within my thought,
And built his seat within my captive breast,
Clad in the arms wherein with me he fought,
Oft in my face he doth his banner rest.

'Love, that doth reign' (1557)

10 Set me whereas the sun doth parch the green,
Or where his beams may not dissolve the ice,
In temperate heat, where he is felt and seen,
With proud people, in presence sad and wise;
Set me in base, or yet in high degree,
In the long night, or in the shortest day,
In clear weather, or where mists thickest be,
In lusty youth, or when my hairs be grey . . .
Yours will I be, and with that only thought
Comfort myself when that my hap is nought.

'Set me whereas the sun doth parch the green' (1557)

11 So cruel prison how could betide, alas,
As proud Windsor? Where I in lust and joy
With a king's son my childish years did pass
In greater feast than Priam's sons of Troy.

'So cruel prison' (1557)

12 Wyatt resteth here, that quick could never rest;
Whose heavenly gifts increased by disdain,
And virtue sank the deeper in his breast;
Such profit he of envy could obtain.

'Wyatt resteth here' (1557)

R. S. Surtees 1805–64

English sporting journalist and novelist

13 More people are flattered into virtue than bullied out of vice.

The Analysis of the Hunting Field (1846) ch. 1

14 The only infallible rule we know is, that the man who is always talking about being a gentleman never is one.

Ask Mamma (1858) ch. 1

15 Major Yammerton was rather a peculiar man, inasmuch as he was an ass, without being a fool.

Ask Mamma (1858) ch. 25

16 'Unting is all that's worth living for—all time is lost wot is not spent in 'unting—it is like the hair we breathe—if we have it not we die—it's the sport of kings, the image of war without its guilt, and only five-and-twenty per cent of its danger.

Handley Cross (1843) ch. 7; cf. **D'Avenant** 251:10, **Somerville** 727:17

17 Many a good run I have in my sleep. Many a dig in the ribs I gives Mrs J when I think they're running into the warmint . . . No man is fit to be called a sportsman wot doesn't kick his wife out of bed on a haverage once in three weeks!

Handley Cross (1843) ch. 11

18 I'll fill hup the chinks wi' cheese.

Handley Cross (1843) ch. 15

19 It ar'n't that I loves the fox less, but that I loves the 'ound more.

Handley Cross (1843) ch. 16

20 Three things I never lends—my 'oss, my wife, and my name.

Hillingdon Hall (1845) ch. 33

21 Champagne certainly gives one werry gentlemanly ideas, but for a continuance, I don't know but I should prefer mild hale.

Jorrocks's Jaunts and Jollities (1838) 'Mr Jorrocks in Paris'

22 Jorrocks, who is not afraid of 'the pace' so long as there is no leaping.

Jorrocks's Jaunts and Jollities (1838) 'Swell and the Surrey'

1 Better be killed than frightened to death.
Mr Facey Romford's Hounds (1865) ch. 32

2 Life would be very pleasant if it were not for its enjoyments.
Mr Facey Romford's Hounds (1865) ch. 32; cf. **Lewis** 467:3

3 Everyone knows that the real business of a ball is either to look out for a wife, to look after a wife, or to look after somebody else's wife.
Mr Facey Romford's Hounds (1865) ch. 56

4 The young ladies entered the drawing-room in the full fervour of sisterly animosity.
Mr Sponge's Sporting Tour (1853) ch. 17

5 Women never look so well as when one comes in wet and dirty from hunting.
Mr Sponge's Sporting Tour (1853) ch. 21

6 He was a gentleman who was generally spoken of as having nothing a-year, paid quarterly.
Mr Sponge's Sporting Tour (1853) ch. 24

7 There is no secret so close as that between a rider and his horse.
Mr Sponge's Sporting Tour (1853) ch. 31

David Sutton 1944–
English poet

8 Sorrow in all lands, and grievous omens.
Great anger in the dragon of the hills,
And silent now the earth's green oracles
That will not speak again of innocence.
'Geomancies' (1991)

Hannen Swaffer 1879–1962
British journalist

9 Freedom of the press in Britain means freedom to print such of the proprietor's prejudices as the advertisers don't object to.
Tom Driberg *Swaff* (1974) ch. 2

Jonathan Swift 1667–1745
Anglo-Irish poet and satirist
on Swift: see **Coleridge** *227:23*, **Dryden** *283:18*, **Johnson** *410:9; see also* **Epitaphs** *304:8*

10 I conceive some scattered notions about a superior power to be of singular use for the common people, as furnishing excellent materials to keep children quiet when they grow peevish, and providing topics of amusement in a tedious winter-night.
An Argument Against Abolishing Christianity (1708)

11 Satire is a sort of glass, wherein beholders do generally discover everybody's face but their own.
The Battle of the Books (1704) preface

12 Instead of dirt and poison we have rather chosen to fill our hives with honey and wax; thus furnishing mankind with the two noblest of things, which are sweetness and light.
The Battle of the Books (1704); cf. **Arnold** 28:8, **Forster** 320:13

13 It is the folly of too many, to mistake the echo of a London coffee-house for the voice of the kingdom.
The Conduct of the Allies (1711)

14 Laws are like cobwebs, which may catch small flies, but let wasps and hornets break through.
A Critical Essay upon the Faculties of the Mind (1709); cf. **Anacharsis** 14:6

15 There is nothing in this world constant, but inconstancy.
A Critical Essay upon the Faculties of the Mind (1709)

16 I have heard of a man who had a mind to sell his house, and therefore carried a piece of brick in his pocket, which he shewed as a pattern to encourage purchasers.
The Drapier's Letters (1724) no. 2

17 He [the emperor] is taller by almost the breadth of my nail than any of his court, which alone is enough to strike an awe into the beholders.
Gulliver's Travels (1726) 'A Voyage to Lilliput' ch. 2

18 He put this engine to our ears, which made an incessant noise like that of a water-mill; and we conjecture it is either some unknown animal, or the god that he worships; but we are more inclined to the latter opinion.
a watch
Gulliver's Travels (1726) 'A Voyage to Lilliput' ch. 2

19 It is alleged indeed, that the high heels are most agreeable to our ancient constitution: but however this be, his Majesty hath determined to make use of only low heels in the administration of the government.
Gulliver's Travels (1726) 'A Voyage to Lilliput' ch. 4

20 It is computed, that eleven thousand persons have, at several times. suffered death, rather than submit to break their eggs at the smaller end. Many large volumes have been published upon this controversy: but the books of the Big-Endians have been long forbidden, and the whole party rendered incapable by law of holding employments.
Gulliver's Travels (1726) 'A Voyage to Lilliput' ch. 4

21 I cannot but conclude the bulk of your natives to be the most pernicious race of little odious vermin that nature ever suffered to crawl upon the surface of the earth.
Gulliver's Travels (1726) 'A Voyage to Brobdingnag' ch. 6

22 And he gave it for his opinion, that whoever could make two ears of corn or two blades of grass to grow upon a spot of ground where only one grew before, would deserve better of mankind, and do more essential service to his country than the whole race of politicians put together.
Gulliver's Travels (1726) 'A Voyage to Brobdingnag' ch. 7

23 He had been eight years upon a project for extracting sun-beams out of cucumbers, which were to be put into vials hermetically sealed, and let out to warm the air in raw inclement summers.
Gulliver's Travels (1726) 'A Voyage to Laputa, etc.' ch. 5

24 These unhappy people were proposing schemes for persuading monarchs to choose favourites upon the score of their wisdom, capacity and virtue; of teaching ministers to consult the public good; of rewarding merit, great abilities and eminent services; of instructing princes to know their true

interest by placing it on the same foundation with that of their people: of choosing for employment persons qualified to exercise them; with many other wild impossible chimeras, that never entered before into the heart of man to conceive, and confirmed in me the old observation, that there is nothing so extravagant and irrational which some philosophers have not maintained for truth.
Gulliver's Travels (1726) 'A Voyage to Laputa, etc.' ch. 6; cf. **Cicero** 217:10

1 He replied that I must needs be mistaken, or that I *said the thing which was not*. (For they have no word in their language to express lying or falsehood.)
Gulliver's Travels (1726) 'A Voyage to the Houyhnhnms' ch. 3

2 I told him . . . that we ate when we were not hungry, and drank without the provocation of thirst.
Gulliver's Travels (1726) 'A Voyage to the Houyhnhnms' ch. 6

3 We are so fond of one another, because our ailments are the same.
Journal to Stella (in *Works*, 1768) 1 February 1711

4 Will she pass in a crowd? Will she make a figure in a country church?
Journal to Stella (in *Works*, 1768) 9 February 1711

5 I love good creditable acquaintance; I love to be the worst of the company.
Journal to Stella (in *Works*, 1768) 17 May 1711

6 I value not your bill of fare, give me your bill of company.
Journal to Stella (in *Works*, 1768) 2 September 1711

7 We were to do more business after dinner; but after dinner is after dinner—an old saying and a true, 'much drinking, little thinking'.
Journal to Stella (in *Works*, 1768) 26 February 1712

8 Proper words in proper places, make the true definition of a style.
Letter to a Young Gentleman lately entered into Holy Orders (9 January 1720)

9 If Heaven had looked upon riches to be a valuable thing, it would not have given them to such a scoundrel.
letter to Miss Vanhomrigh, 12–13 August 1720, in H. Williams (ed.) *Correspondence of Jonathan Swift* (1963) vol. 2; cf. **Steele** 737:2

10 I have ever hated all nations, professions and communities, and all my love is towards individuals . . . But principally I hate and detest that animal called man; although I heartily love John, Peter, Thomas, and so forth.
letter to Pope, 29 September 1725, in H. Williams (ed.) *Correspondence of Jonathan Swift* (1963) vol. 3

11 Not die here in a rage, like a poisoned rat in a hole.
letter to Bolingbroke, 21 March 1730, in H. Williams (ed.) *Correspondence of Jonathan Swift* (1963) vol. 3

12 Surely mortal man is a broomstick!
A Meditation upon a Broomstick (1710)

13 I have been assured by a very knowing American of my acquaintance in London, that a young healthy child well nursed is at a year old a most delicious, nourishing, and wholesome food, whether stewed, roasted, baked, or boiled, and I make no doubt that it will equally serve in a fricassee, or a ragout.
A Modest Proposal for Preventing the Children of Ireland from being a Burden to their Parents or Country (1729)

14 I mean, you lie—under a mistake.
Polite Conversation (1738) Dialogue 1

15 She wears her clothes, as if they were thrown on her with a pitchfork.
Polite Conversation (1738) Dialogue 1

16 He was a bold man that first eat an oyster.
Polite Conversation (1738) Dialogue 2

17 Faith, that's as well said, as if I had said it myself.
Polite Conversation (1738) Dialogue 2

18 I always love to begin a journey on Sundays, because I shall have the prayers of the church, to preserve all that travel by land, or by water.
Polite Conversation (1738) Dialogue 2; cf. **Book of Common Prayer** 127:11

19 Books, like men their authors, have no more than one way of coming into the world, but there are ten thousand to go out of it, and return no more.
A Tale of a Tub (1704) 'Epistle Dedicatory'; cf. **Seneca** 654:20

20 Satire, being levelled at all, is never resented for an offence by any.
A Tale of a Tub (1704) 'Author's Preface'

21 What though his head be empty, provided his commonplace book be full.
A Tale of a Tub (1704) ch. 7 'Digression in Praise of Digressions'

22 Last week I saw a woman flayed, and you will hardly believe, how much it altered her person for the worse.
A Tale of a Tub (1704) ch. 9

23 I never saw, heard, nor read, that the clergy were beloved in any nation where Christianity was the religion of the country. Nothing can render them popular, but some degree of persecution.
Thoughts on Religion (1765)

24 We have just enough religion to make us hate, but not enough to make us love one another.
Thoughts on Various Subjects (1711)

25 When a true genius appears in the world, you may know him by this sign, that the dunces are all in confederacy against him.
Thoughts on Various Subjects (1711)

26 What they do in heaven we are ignorant of; what they do *not* we are told expressly, that they neither marry, nor are given in marriage.
Thoughts on Various Subjects (1711); cf. **Bible** 96:23

27 The stoical scheme of supplying our wants, by lopping off our desires, is like cutting off our feet when we want shoes.
Thoughts on Various Subjects (1711)

28 The reasons why so few marriages are happy, is, because young ladies spend their time in making nets, not in making cages.
Thoughts on Various Subjects (1711)

1 Few are qualified to shine in company; but it is in most men's power to be agreeable.
Thoughts on Various Subjects (1727 ed.)

2 Every man desires to live long; but no man would be old.
Thoughts on Various Subjects (1727 ed.)

3 A nice man is a man of nasty ideas.
Thoughts on Various Subjects (1727 ed.)

4 Old men and comets have been reverenced for the same reason; their long beards, and pretences to foretell events.
Thoughts on Various Subjects (1727 ed.)

5 A coming shower your shooting corns presage.
'A Description of a City Shower' (1710) l. 9

6 They never would hear,
But turn the deaf ear,
As a matter they had no concern in.
'Dingley and Brent' (written 1724)

7 I often wished that I had clear,
For life, six hundred pounds a-year,
A handsome house to lodge a friend,
A river at my garden's end,
A terrace walk, and half a rood
Of land, set out to plant a wood.
'Imitation of Horace' (written 1714); cf. **Horace** 389:24

8 How haughtily he lifts his nose,
To tell what every schoolboy knows.
'The Journal' (1727) l. 81

9 Nor do they trust their tongue alone,
But speak a language of their own;
Can read a nod, a shrug, a look,
Far better than a printed book;
Convey a libel in a frown,
And wink a reputation down.
'The Journal of a Modern Lady' (1729) l. 188

10 Hail, fellow, well met,
All dirty and wet:
Find out, if you can,
Who's master, who's man.
'My Lady's Lamentation' (written 1728) l. 165

11 Th' artillery of words.
'Ode to Dr William Sancroft' (written 1692)

12 Philosophy! the lumber of the schools.
'Ode to Sir W. Temple' (written 1692)

13 Say, Britain, could you ever boast,—
Three poets in an age at most?
Our chilling climate hardly bears
A sprig of bays in fifty years.
'On Poetry' (1733) l. 5

14 Then, rising with Aurora's light,
The Muse invoked, sit down to write;
Blot out, correct, insert, refine,
Enlarge, diminish, interline.
'On Poetry' (1733) l. 85

15 As learned commentators view
In Homer more than Homer knew.
'On Poetry' (1733) l. 103

16 So geographers, in Afric-maps,
With savage-pictures fill their gaps;
And o'er unhabitable downs
Place elephants for want of towns.
'On Poetry' (1733) l. 177

17 He gives directions to the town,
To cry it up, or run it down.
'On Poetry' (1733) l. 269

18 Hobbes clearly proves, that every creature
Lives in a state of war by nature.
'On Poetry' (1733) l. 319

19 So, naturalists observe, a flea
Hath smaller fleas that on him prey;
And these have smaller fleas to bite 'em,
And so proceed *ad infinitum*.
Thus every poet, in his kind,
Is bit by him that comes behind.
'On Poetry' (1733) l. 337; cf. **Proverbs** 596:19

20 Walls have tongues, and hedges ears.
'A Pastoral Dialogue between Richmond Lodge and Marble Hill' (written 1727) l. 8

21 Humour is odd, grotesque, and wild,
Only by affectation spoiled;
'Tis never by invention got,
Men have it when they know it not.
'To Mr Delany' (written 1718) l. 25

22 Hated by fools, and fools to hate,
Be that my motto and my fate.
'To Mr Delany' (written 1718) l. 171

23 In all distresses of our friends,
We first consult our private ends;
While nature, kindly bent to ease us,
Points out some circumstance to please us.
'Verses on the Death of Dr Swift' (1731) l. 7

24 Poor Pope will grieve a month, and Gay
A week, and Arbuthnot a day.
St John himself will scarce forbear
To bite his pen, and drop a tear.
The rest will give a shrug, and cry,
'I'm sorry—but we all must die!'
'Verses on the Death of Dr Swift' (1731) l. 207

25 Yet malice never was his aim;
He lashed the vice, but spared the name;
No individual could resent,
Where thousands equally were meant.
'Verses on the Death of Dr Swift' (1731) l. 512

26 He gave the little wealth he had
To build a house for fools and mad;
And showed, by one satiric touch,
No nation wanted it so much.
'Verses on the Death of Dr Swift' (1731) l. 538

27 In Church your grandsire cut his throat;
To do the job too long he tarried,
He should have had my hearty vote,
To cut his throat before he married.
'Verses on the Upright Judge' (written 1724)

28 'Libertas et natale solum':
Fine words! I wonder where you stole 'em.
Libertas . . . = *Freedom and my native skies*
'Whitshed's Motto on his Coach' (written 1724)

1 Good God! what a genius I had when I wrote that book.
of A Tale of a Tub
Sir Walter Scott (ed.) *Works of Swift* (1814) vol. 1

2 I shall be like that tree, I shall die at the top.
Sir Walter Scott (ed.) *Works of Swift* (1814) vol. 1

3 A stick and a string, with a fly at one end and a fool at the other.
description of angling; the remark has also been attributed to Samuel **Johnson**, *in the form 'Fly fishing may be a very pleasant amusement; but angling or float fishing I can only compare to a stick and a string, with a worm at one end and a fool at the other'*
in *The Indicator* 27 October 1819

Algernon Charles Swinburne

1837–1909
English poet

4 Maiden, and mistress of the months and stars
Now folded in the flowerless fields of heaven.
Atalanta in Calydon (1865) l. 1

5 When the hounds of spring are on winter's traces,
The mother of months in meadow or plain
Fills the shadows and windy places
With lisp of leaves and ripple of rain;
And the brown bright nightingale amorous
Is half assuaged for Itylus,
For the Thracian ships and the foreign faces,
The tongueless vigil and all the pain.
Atalanta in Calydon (1865) chorus 'When the hounds of spring'

6 For winter's rains and ruins are over,
And all the season of snows and sins;
The days dividing lover and lover,
The light that loses, the night that wins;
And time remembered is grief forgotten,
And frosts are slain and flowers begotten,
And in green underwood and cover
Blossom by blossom the spring begins.
Atalanta in Calydon (1865) chorus 'When the hounds of spring'

7 And soft as lips that laugh and hide
The laughing leaves of the tree divide,
And screen from seeing and leave in sight
The god pursuing, the maiden hid.
Atalanta in Calydon (1865) chorus 'When the hounds of spring'

8 Before the beginning of years
There came to the making of man
Time with a gift of tears,
Grief with a glass that ran.
Atalanta in Calydon (1865) chorus 'Before the beginning of years'

9 Strength without hands to smite,
Love that endures for a breath;
Night, the shadow of light,
And Life, the shadow of death.
Atalanta in Calydon (1865) chorus 'Before the beginning of years'

10 For words divide and rend;
But silence is most noble till the end.
Atalanta in Calydon (1865) chorus 'Who hath given man speech'

11 Sleep; and if life was bitter to thee, pardon,
If sweet, give thanks; thou hast no more to live;
And to give thanks is good, and to forgive.
'Ave atque Vale' (1878) st. 17

12 Villon, our sad bad glad mad brother's name.
'Ballad of François Villon' (1878)

13 O slain and spent and sacrificed
People, the grey-grown speechless Christ.
'Before a Crucifix' (1871)

14 We shift and bedeck and bedrape us,
Thou art noble and nude and antique.
'Dolores' (1866) st. 7

15 Change in a trice
The lilies and languors of virtue
For the raptures and roses of vice.
'Dolores' (1866) st. 9

16 O splendid and sterile Dolores,
Our Lady of Pain.
'Dolores' (1866) st. 9

17 For the crown of our life as it closes
Is darkness, the fruit thereof dust;
No thorns go as deep as a rose's,
And love is more cruel than lust.
'Dolores' (1866) st. 20

18 In a coign of the cliff between lowland and highland,
At the sea-down's edge between windward and lee,
Walled round with rocks as an inland island,
The ghost of a garden fronts the sea.
'A Forsaken Garden' (1878)

19 As a god self-slain on his own strange altar,
Death lies dead.
'A Forsaken Garden' (1878)

20 Pale, beyond porch and portal,
Crowned with calm leaves, she stands
Who gathers all things mortal
With cold immortal hands.
'The Garden of Proserpine' (1866)

21 We are not sure of sorrow,
And joy was never sure.
'The Garden of Proserpine' (1866)

22 From too much love of living,
From hope and fear set free,
We thank with brief thanksgiving
Whatever gods may be
That no man lives forever,
That dead men rise up never;
That even the weariest river
Winds somewhere safe to sea.
'The Garden of Proserpine' (1866)

23 Fiddle, we know, is diddle: and diddle, we take it, is dee.
The Heptalogia (1880) 'The Higher Pantheism in a Nutshell'; cf. **Tennyson** 759:10

1 Even love, the beloved Republic, that feeds upon freedom lives.
'Hertha' (1871); cf. **Forster** 321:5

2 But God, if a God there be, is the substance of men which is man.
'Hymn of Man' (1871)

3 Glory to Man in the highest! for Man is the master of things.
'Hymn of Man' (1871); cf. **Bible** 98:22

4 Yea, is not even Apollo, with hair and harpstring of gold,
A bitter God to follow, a beautiful God to behold?
'Hymn to Proserpine' (1866)

5 Thou hast conquered, O pale Galilean; the world has grown grey from Thy breath;
We have drunken of things Lethean, and fed on the fullness of death.
'Hymn to Proserpine' (1866); cf. **Last words** 457:14

6 Though these that were Gods are dead, and thou being dead art a God,
Though before thee the throned Cytherean be fallen, and hidden her head,
Yet thy kingdom shall pass, Galilean, thy dead shall go down to thee dead.
'Hymn to Proserpine' (1866)

7 I remember the way we parted,
The day and the way we met;
You hoped we were both broken-hearted,
And knew we should both forget.
'An Interlude' (1866)

8 And the best and the worst of this is
That neither is most to blame,
If you have forgotten my kisses
And I have forgotten your name.
'An Interlude' (1866)

9 Swallow, my sister, O sister swallow,
How can thine heart be full of the spring?
A thousand summers are over and dead.
What hast thou found in the spring to follow?
What hast thou found in thine heart to sing?
What wilt thou do when the summer is shed?
'Itylus' (1864)

10 Till life forget and death remember,
Till thou remember and I forget.
'Itylus' (1864)

11 The small slain body, the flowerlike face,
Can I remember if thou forget?
O sister, sister, thy first-begotten!
The hands that cling and the feet that follow,
The voice of the child's blood crying yet
Who hath remembered me? Who hath forgotten?
Thou hast forgotten, O summer swallow,
But the world shall end when I forget.
'Itylus' (1864)

12 Apples of gold for the king's daughter.
'The King's Daughter'

13 Ah, yet would God this flesh of mine might be
Where air might wash and long leaves cover me;
Where tides of grass break into foam of flowers,
Or where the wind's feet shine along the sea.
'Laus Veneris' (1866)

14 If love were what the rose is,
And I were like the leaf,
Our lives would grow together
In sad or singing weather,
Blown fields or flowerful closes,
Green pleasure or grey grief.
'A Match' (1866)

15 There was a poor poet named Clough,
Whom his friends all united to puff,
But the public, though dull,
Had not such a skull
As belonged to believers in Clough.
Essays and Studies (1875) 'Matthew Arnold'

16 I will go back to the great sweet mother,
Mother and lover of men, the sea.
I will go down to her, I and no other,
Close with her, kiss her and mix her with me.
'The Triumph of Time' (1866)

17 I shall sleep, and move with the moving ships,
Change as the winds change, veer in the tide.
'The Triumph of Time' (1866)

18 There lived a singer in France of old
By the tideless dolorous midland sea.
In a land of sand and ruin and gold
There shone one woman, and none but she.
'The Triumph of Time' (1866)

Thomas Sydenham 1624–89
English physician

19 Almighty God hath not bestowed on mankind a remedy of so universal an extent and so efficacious in curing divers maladies as opiates.
manuscript version of published text, *Observationes Medicae* (1676, G. G. Meynell (ed.) 1991)

John Millington Synge 1871–1909
Irish dramatist

20 'A man who is not afraid of the sea will soon be drownded,' he said 'for he will be going out on a day he shouldn't. But we do be afraid of the sea, and we do only be drownded now and again.'
The Aran Islands (1907) pt. 2

21 'A translation is no translation,' he said, 'unless it will give you the music of a poem along with the words of it.'
The Aran Islands (1907) pt. 3

22 Oh my grief, I've lost him surely. I've lost the only Playboy of the Western World.
The Playboy of the Western World (1907) act 3

Thomas Szasz 1920–
Hungarian-born psychiatrist

23 A teacher should have maximal authority and minimal power.
The Second Sin (1973) 'Education'

24 Happiness is an imaginary condition, formerly often attributed by the living to the dead, now

usually attributed by adults to children, and by children to adults.
The Second Sin (1973) 'Emotions'

1 The stupid neither forgive nor forget; the naïve forgive and forget; the wise forgive but do not forget.
The Second Sin (1973) 'Personal Conduct'

2 If you talk to God, you are praying; if God talks to you, you have schizophrenia. If the dead talk to you, you are a spiritualist; if God talks to you, you are a schizophrenic.
The Second Sin (1973) 'Schizophrenia'

3 Formerly, when religion was strong and science weak, men mistook magic for medicine; now, when science is strong and religion weak, men mistake medicine for magic.
The Second Sin (1973) 'Science and Scientism'

4 Two wrongs don't make a right, but they make a good excuse.
The Second Sin (1973) 'Social Relations'

Albert von Szent-Györgyi 1893–1986
Hungarian-born biochemist

5 Discovery consists of seeing what everybody has seen and thinking what nobody has thought.
Irving Good (ed.) *The Scientist Speculates* (1962)

Tacitus (Cornelius Tacitus) AD *c.*56–after 117
Roman senator and historian

6 *Res olim dissociabiles miscuerit, principatum ac libertatem.*
He [Nerva] has united things long incompatible, the principate and liberty.
Agricola ch. 3; cf. **Disraeli** 269:22

7 *Haud semper errat fama.*
Rumour is not always wrong.
Agricola ch. 9

8 *Nunc terminus Britanniae patet, atque omne ignotum pro magnifico est.*
Now the boundary of Britain is revealed, and everything unknown is held to be glorious.
reporting the speech of a British leader, Calgacus
Agricola ch. 30

9 *Solitudinem faciunt pacem appellant.*
They make a wilderness and call it peace.
Agricola ch. 30

10 *Proprium humani ingenii est odisse quem laeseris.*
It is part of human nature to hate the man you have hurt.
Agricola ch. 42

11 *Tu vero felix, Agricola, non vitae tantum claritate, sed etiam opportunitate mortis.*
You were indeed fortunate, Agricola, not only in the distinction of your life, but also in the lucky timing of your death.
Agricola ch. 45

12 *Sine ira et studio.*
With neither anger nor partiality.
Annals bk. 1, ch. 1

13 *Elegantiae arbiter.*
The arbiter of taste.
of ***Petronius***
Annals bk. 16, ch. 18

14 *Rara temporum felicitate ubi sentire quae velis et quae sentias dicere licet.*
These times having the rare good fortune that you may think what you like and say what you think.
Histories bk. 1, ch. 1

15 *Maior privato visus dum privatus fuit, et omnium consensu capax imperii nisi imperasset.*
He seemed much greater than a private citizen while he still was a private citizen, and by everyone's consent capable of reigning if only he had not reigned.
of the Emperor Galba
Histories bk. 1, ch. 49

16 *Cupido gloriae novissima exuitur.*
Love of fame is the last thing to be given up.
Histories bk. 4, ch. 6

17 *Deos fortioribus adesse.*
The gods are on the side of the stronger.
Histories bk. 4, ch. 17; cf. **Bussy-Rabutin** 171:7, **Proverbs** 609:47

18 *Experientia docuit.*
Experience has taught.
commonly quoted as 'Experientia docet [experience teaches]'
The Histories bk. 5, ch. 6; cf. **Dickens** 261:17, **Proverbs** 599:48

William Howard Taft 1857–1930
American Republican statesman, 27th President of the US, 1909–13

19 Next to the right of liberty, the right of property is the most important individual right guaranteed by the Constitution and the one which, united with that of personal liberty, has contributed more to the growth of civilization than any other institution established by the human race.
Popular Government (1913) ch. 3

Rabindranath Tagore 1861–1941
Bengali poet and philosopher

20 Bigotry tries to keep truth safe in its hand
With a grip that kills it.
Fireflies (1928)

21 Touch my life with the magic of thy fire.
sung at the funeral of Mother ***Teresa*** *in Calcutta, 13 September 1997*
'The Magic of thy Fire'

1 Man goes into the noisy crowd to drown his own clamour of silence.
'Stray Birds' (1916)

Nellie Talbot

2 Jesus wants me for a sunbeam.
title of hymn (1921) in *CSSM Choruses* No. 1

Charles-Maurice de Talleyrand

1754–1838
French statesman
on Talleyrand: see **Louis Philippe** 476:6

3 *Voilà le commencement de la fin.*
This is the beginning of the end.
on the announcement of Napoleon's Pyrrhic victory at Borodino, 1812
attributed; Sainte-Beuve *M. de Talleyrand* (1870) ch. 3

4 It is not an event, it is an item of news.
on hearing of the death of ***Napoleon*** *in 1821*
Philip Henry Stanhope *Notes of Conversations with the Duke of Wellington* (1888) 1 November 1831

5 *Surtout, Messieurs, point de zèle.*
Above all, gentlemen, not the slightest zeal.
P. Chasles *Voyages d'un critique à travers la vie et les livres* (1868) vol. 2; cf. **Lambert** 449:10

6 *Qui n'a pas vécu dans les années voisines de 1789 ne sait pas ce que c'est que le plaisir de vivre.*
He who has not lived during the years around 1789 can not know what is meant by the pleasure of life.
M. Guizot *Mémoires pour servir à l'histoire de mon temps* (1858) vol. 1, ch. 6

7 *Ils n'ont rien appris, ni rien oublié.*
They have learnt nothing, and forgotten nothing.
of the Bourbons in exile
oral tradition, attributed to Talleyrand by the Chevalier de Panat, see below; cf. **Dumouriez** 285:1
Personne n'est corrigé, personne n'a su ni rien oublier ni rien apprendre.
Nobody has improved, nobody has known how to forget or to learn.
letter from the Chevalier de Panat to Mallet du Pan, January 1796); A. Sayons (ed.) *Mémoires et correspondance de Mallet du Pan* (1851) vol. 2

8 That, Sire, is a question of dates.
often quoted as, 'treason is a matter of dates'; replying to the Tsar's criticism of those who 'betrayed the cause of Europe'
Duff Cooper *Talleyrand* (1932)

9 *Quelle triste vieillesse vous vous préparez.*
What a sad old age you are preparing for yourself.
to a young diplomat who boasted of his ignorance of whist
J. Amédée Pichot *Souvenirs Intimes sur M. de Talleyrand* (1870) 'Le Pour et le Contre'

The Talmud

compilation of Jewish civil and ceremonial law and legend, dating from the 5th century AD, *and comprising the Mishnah and the Gemara. There are two versions of the Talmud, the Babylonian Talmud and the earlier Palestinian or Jerusalem Talmud*
see also ***Hillel***, ***Shammai***

MISHNAH

10 A single man was created in the world, to teach that if any man caused a single soul to perish from Israel, Scripture imputes it to him as though he had caused a whole world to perish; and if any man saves alive a single soul from Israel Scripture imputes it to him as though he had saved alive a whole world.
Mishnah Sanhedrin 4:5

11 Moses received the Law from Sinai and committed it to Joshua, and Joshua to the elders, and the elders to the Prophets; and the Prophets committed it to the men of the Great Synagogue. They said three things: Be deliberate in judgement, raise up many disciples, and make a fence around the Law.
Mishnah Pirqei Avot 1:1

12 By three things is the world sustained: by the Law, by the [Temple-]service, and by deeds of loving-kindness.
Mishnah Pirqei Avot 1:2

13 Love labour and hate mastery and seek not acquaintance with the ruling power.
Mishnah Pirqei Avot 1:10

14 By three things is the world sustained: by truth, by judgement, and by peace.
Mishnah Pirqei Avot 1:18

15 Let the property of thy fellow be dear to thee as thine own.
Mishnah Pirqei Avot 2:12

16 The day is short and the task is great and the labourers are idle and the wage is abundant and the master of the house is urgent.
Mishnah Pirqei Avot 2:15

17 The tradition is a fence around the Law.
Mishnah Pirqei Avot 3:14

18 Beloved is man, for he was created in the image [of God]; still greater was the love in that it was made known to him that he was created in the image of God.
Mishnah Pirqei Avot 3:15

19 All is foreseen, but freedom of choice is given; and the world is judged by grace, yet all is according to the excess of works [that be good or evil].
Mishnah Pirqei Avot 3:16

20 He that neglects the Law in wealth shall in the end neglect it in poverty.
Mishnah Pirqei Avot 4:9

21 He that performs one precept gets for himself one advocate . . . Repentance and good works are as a shield against retribution.
Mishnah Pirqei Avot 4:11

1 Turn it [Torah] and turn it again, for everything is in it.
Mishnah Pirqei Avot 5:22

GEMARA

2 Let thy tongue acquire the habit of saying, 'I know not', lest thou be led to falsehoods.
Babylonian Talmud Berakhot 4a

3 The seal of the Holy One, blessed be He, is *emeth* [truth].
Babylonian Talmud Shabbat 55a

4 If circumcision . . . supersedes the Sabbath, the saving of life, *a minori*, must supersede the Sabbath.
Babylonian Talmud Shabbat 132a

5 As to every man who becomes angry, if he is a sage, his wisdom departs from him; if he is a prophet, his prophecy departs from him.
Babylonian Talmud Pesahim 66b

6 Even an iron partition cannot interpose between Israel and their Father in Heaven.
Babylonian Talmud Pesahim 85b

7 *He shall live by them* [the laws of the Torah], but he shall not die because of them.
Babylonian Talmud Yoma 85b; cf. **Bible** 76:22

8 Repentance is so great that premeditated sins are accounted as though they were merits.
Babylonian Talmud Yoma 86b

9 The talk of the child in the market-place is either that of his father or of his mother.
Babylonian Talmud Sukkah 56b

10 A man's prayer is only answered if he takes his heart into his hand.
Babylonian Talmud Taanit 8a

11 A man . . . loves his wife as himself . . . honours her more than himself.
Babylonian Talmud Yevamot 62b

12 This nation [Israel] is distinguished by three characteristics; They are merciful, bashful, and benevolent.
Babylonian Talmud Yevamot 79a

13 Great is labour, for it honours the worker.
Babylonian Talmud Nedarim 49b

14 Unfaithfulness in the house is like a worm in a sesame plant.
Babylonian Talmud Sotah 3b

15 As to someone who started to do something which someone else came along and finished, Scripture regards the one who completed the task as if he had done [the whole of it].
Babylonian Talmud Sotah 13b

16 The father loves the son, and the son loves his sons.
Babylonian Talmud Sotah 49a

17 If a man divorces his first wife, even the altar sheds tears.
Babylonian Talmud Gittin 90b

18 He who does not teach his son a craft, teaches him brigandage.
Babylonian Talmud Qiddushin 29a

19 A man who gives charity in secret is greater than Moses.
Babylonian Talmud Bava Bathra 9b

20 It is the penalty of a liar, that should he even tell the truth, he is not listened to.
Babylonian Talmud Sanhedrin 89b

21 One is allowed to follow the road he wishes to pursue.
Babylonian Talmud Makkot 10b

22 If the soft [water] can wear away the hard [stone], how much more can the words of the Torah, which are hard like iron, carve a way into my heart which is of flesh and blood!
Babylonian Talmud Avot de Rabbi Nathan 20b

23 All that the Holy One, blessed be He, created in the world, He also created in man.
Babylonian Talmud Avot de Rabbi Nathan 29a

24 No man bruises his finger here on earth unless it was so decreed against him in heaven.
Babylonian Talmud Hullin 7b

25 Why [does Yohanan say that one may pray all day long]? Because prayer never loses its value.
Jerusalem Talmud Berakhot 1:1

26 One should not [recite one's prayers] as if he were reading a letter.
Jerusalem Talmud Berakhot 4:4

27 The Holy Spirit rests only on someone whose heart is happy.
Jerusalem Talmud Sukkah 5:1

28 [If] a man keeps himself from transgression one time, then a second and a third time, the Holy One, blessed be He, keeps him from transgressing further.
Jerusalem Talmud Qiddushin 1:9

Tantric Buddhist texts

ritualist form of Buddhism, dating from the 7th century or earlier

29 Just as water that has entered the ear may be removed by water and just as a thorn may be removed by a thorn, so those who know how, remove passion by means of passion itself.
Just as a washerman removes the grime from a garment by means of grime, so the wise man renders himself free of impurity by means of impurity itself.
Citta Vishuddhiprakarana v. 37

30 By the enjoyment of all desires, to which one devotes oneself just as one pleases, it is by such practice as this that one may speedily gain Buddhahood.
With the enjoyment of all desires, to which one

devotes oneself just as one pleases, in union with one's chosen divinity, one worships oneself, the Supreme One.

Guhyasamāja Tantra v. 7

1 Mantras and tantras, meditation and concentration
They are all a cause of self-deception.
Do not defile in contemplation thought that is pure in its own nature,
But abide in the bliss of yourself and cease those torments.

Saraha *Dohākosha* (*c.*9th century) v. 23

2 Enjoying the world of sense, one is undefiled by the world of sense,
One plucks the lotus without touching the water.
So the yogi who has gone to the root of things,
Is not enslaved by the senses although he enjoys them.

Saraha *Dohākosha* (*c.*9th century) v. 64

Booth Tarkington 1869–1946

American novelist

3 There are two things that will be believed of any man whatsoever, and one of them is that he has taken to drink.

Penrod (1914) ch. 10

Allen Tate 1899–1979

American poet

4 Alice grown lazy, mammoth but not fat,
Declines upon her lost and twilight age;
Above in the dozing leaves the grinning cat
Quivers forever with his abstract rage.

Whatever light swayed on the perilous gate
Forever sways, nor will the arching grass,
Caught when the world clattered, undulate
In the deep suspension of the looking-glass.

'Last Days of Alice' (1932)

5 Row after row with strict impunity
The headstones yield their names to the element,
The wind whirrs without recollection;
In the riven troughs the splayed leaves
Pile up, of nature the casual sacrament
To the seasonal eternity of death.

'Ode to the Confederate Dead (1928)

6 The shut gate and the decomposing wall:
The gentle serpent, green in the mulberry bush,
Riots with his tongue through the hush—
Sentinel of the grave who counts us all!

'Ode to the Confederate Dead (1928)

Nahum Tate 1652–1715

English dramatist

7 When I am laid in earth my wrongs create.
No trouble in thy breast,
Remember me, but ah! forget my fate.

Dido and Aeneas (1689) act 3 ('Dido's Lament')

8 As pants the hart for cooling streams
When heated in the chase.

New Version of the Psalms (1696) Psalm 42 (with Nicholas Brady); cf. **Book of Common Prayer** 134:5

9 Through all the changing scenes of life,
In trouble and in joy,
The praises of my God shall still
My heart and tongue employ.

New Version of the Psalms (1696) Psalm 34 (with Nicholas Brady)

10 While shepherds watched their flocks by night,
All seated on the ground,
The angel of the Lord came down,
And glory shone around.

Supplement to the New Version of the Psalms (1700) 'While Shepherds Watched'

R. H. Tawney 1880–1962

British economic historian

11 Militarism . . . is fetish worship. It is the prostration of men's souls and the laceration of their bodies to appease an idol.

The Acquisitive Society (1921) ch. 4

12 That seductive border region where politics grease the wheels of business and polite society smiles hopefully on both.

Business and Politics under James I (1958)

13 Those who dread a dead-level of income or wealth . . . do not dread, it seems, a dead-level of law and order, and of security for life and property.

Equality (4th ed., 1931) ch. 3, sect. 3

14 Freedom for the pike is death for the minnows.

Equality (ed. 4, rev. ed., 1938) ch. 5, sect. 2

15 Private property is a necessary institution, at least in a fallen world; men work more and dispute less when goods are private than when they are common. But it is to be tolerated as a concession to human frailty, not applauded as desirable in itself.

Religion and the Rise of Capitalism (1926) ch. 1, sect. 1

16 To take usury is contrary to Scripture; it is contrary to Aristotle; it is contrary to nature, for it is to live without labour; it is to sell time, which belongs to God, for the advantage of wicked men; it is to rob those who use the money lent, and to whom, since they make it profitable, the profits should belong.

Religion and the Rise of Capitalism (1926) ch. 1, sect. 2

17 Both the existing economic order, and too many of the projects advanced for reconstructing it, break down through their neglect of the truism that, since even quite common men have souls, no increase in material wealth will compensate them for arrangements which insult their self-respect and impair their freedom. A reasonable estimate of economic organisation must allow for the fact that, unless industry is to be paralysed by recurrent revolts on the part of outraged human nature, it must satisfy criteria which are not purely economic.

Religion and the Rise of Capitalism (1926) conclusion

1 Never be afraid of throwing away what you have, if you *can* throw it away, it is not really yours.

diary, 1912, in *Dictionary of National Biography* (1917–)

2 What harm have I ever done to the Labour Party?

declining the offer of a peerage

in *Evening Standard* 18 January 1962

A. J. P. Taylor 1906–90

British historian

3 German history reached its turning-point and failed to turn. This was the fateful essence of 1848.

The Course of German History (1945) ch. 4

4 He aroused every feeling except trust.

of **Lloyd George**

English History 1914–1945 (1965) ch. 5

5 History gets thicker as it approaches recent times.

English History 1914–45 (1965); bibliography

6 The First World War had begun—imposed on the statesmen of Europe by railway timetables. It was an unexpected climax to the railway age.

The First World War (1963) ch. 1

7 Human blunders, usually, do more to shape history than human wickedness.

The Origins of the Second World War (1961) ch. 10

8 Crimea: The war that would not boil.

Rumours of Wars (1952) ch. 6; originally the title of an essay in *History Today* 2 February 1951

9 Bismarck was a political genius of the highest rank, but he lacked one essential quality of the constructive statesman: he had no faith in the future.

in *Encyclopedia Britannica* (1954)

Ann Taylor 1782–1866 and Jane Taylor 1783–1824

English writers of books for children

10 I thank the goodness and the grace
Which on my birth have smiled,
And made me, in these Christian days,
A happy English child.

Hymns for Infant Minds (1810) 'A Child's Hymn of Praise'

11 'Tis a *credit* to any good girl to be neat,
But quite a *disgrace* to be fine.

Hymns for Sunday Schools (1810) 'The Folly of Finery'

12 Who ran to help me when I fell,
And would some pretty story tell,
Or kiss the place to make it well?
My Mother.

Original Poems for Infant Minds (1804) 'My Mother'

13 Twinkle, twinkle, little star,
How I wonder what you are!
Up above the world so high,
Like a diamond in the sky!

Rhymes for the Nursery (1806) 'The Star'; cf. **Carroll** 189:18

14 How pleasant it is, at the end of the day,
No follies to have to repent;
But reflect on the past, and be able to say,
That my time has been properly spent.

Rhymes for the Nursery (1806) 'The Way to be Happy'

Bayard Taylor 1825–78

American traveller and writer

15 Till the sun grows cold,
And the stars are old,
And the leaves of the Judgement Book unfold.

'Bedouin Song'

Edward Taylor ?1645–1729

New England puritan divine and poet

16 Who laced and filleted the earth so fine
With rivers like green ribbons smaragdine?
Who made the seas its selvage, and its locks
Like a quilt ball within a silver box?
Who spread its canopy? Or curtains spun?
Who in this bowling alley bowled the sun?

'God's Determination Touching His Elect'; Perry Miller *The American Puritans* (1956)

Henry Taylor 1800–86

British writer

17 Good nature and kindness towards those with whom they come in personal contact, at the expense of public interests, that is of those whom they never see, is the besetting sin of public men.

The Statesman (1836)

Jeremy Taylor 1613–67

English divine

18 This thing . . . that can be understood and not expressed, may take a neuter gender;—and every schoolboy knows it.

The Real Presence . . . (1654) sect. 5, subsect. 1; cf. **Macaulay** 482:7

19 As our life is very short, so it is very miserable, and therefore it is well it is short.

The Rule and Exercise of Holy Dying (1651) ch. 1, sect. 4

20 How many people there are that weep with want, or are mad with oppression, or are desperate by too quick a sense of a constant infelicity.

The Rule and Exercise of Holy Dying (1651) ch. 1, sect. 5

21 The union of hands and hearts.

XXV Sermons Preached at Golden Grove (1653) 'The Marriage Ring' pt. 1

Tom Taylor 1817–80

English dramatist; editor of Punch from 1874

22 Hawkshaw, the detective.

usually quoted as 'I am Hawkshaw, the detective'

The Ticket-of-leave Man (1863) act 4, sc. 1

Norman Tebbit 1931–

British Conservative politician

on Tebbit: see **Foot** *00:00*

1 I grew up in the Thirties with our unemployed father. He did not riot, he got on his bike and looked for work.

speech at Conservative Party Conference, 15 October 1981, in *Daily Telegraph* 16 October 1981

2 The cricket test—which side do they cheer for? . . . Are you still looking back to where you came from or where you are?

on the loyalties of Britain's immigrant population

interview in *Los Angeles Times*, reported in *Daily Telegraph* 20 April 1990

Tecumseh 1768–1813

Shawnee leader

3 Where today are the Pequot? Where are the Narragansett, the Mohican, the Pokanoket, and many other once powerful tribes of our people? They have vanished before the avarice and oppression of the white man, as snow before the summer sun.

Dee Brown *Bury My Heart at Wounded Knee* (1970) ch. 1

Pierre Teilhard de Chardin 1881–1955

French Jesuit philosopher and palaeontologist

on Teilhard de Chardin: see **Pius XII** *577:9*

4 The history of the living world can be summarised as the elaboration of ever more perfect eyes within a cosmos in which there is always something more to be seen.

The Phenomenon of Man (1959)

□ Telegrams

see next page

William Temple 1628–99

English diplomat and essayist

5 When all is done, human life is, at the greatest and the best, but like a froward child, that must be played with and humoured a little to keep it quiet till it falls asleep, and then the care is over.

Miscellanea. The Second Part (1690) 'Of Poetry'

William Temple 1881–1944

English theologian; Archbishop of Canterbury from 1942

6 Human status ought not to depend upon the changing demands of the economic process.

in *The Life of the Church and the Order of Society* (Malvern, 1941) p. 221

7 It is a mistake to suppose that God is only, or even chiefly, concerned with religion.

R. V. C. Bodley *In Search of Serenity* (1955) ch. 12

8 Personally, I have always looked on cricket as organized loafing.

attributed

John Tenniel 1820–1914

English draughtsman

9 Dropping the pilot.

on **Bismarck***'s departure from office*

cartoon caption, and title of poem, in *Punch* 29 March 1890

Alfred, Lord Tennyson 1809–92

English poet

on Tennyson: see **Bagehot** *47:24,* **Bulwer-Lytton** *160:6,* **Chesterton** *211:16; see also* **Closing lines** *222:4*

10 For nothing worthy proving can be proven,
Nor yet disproven: wherefore thou be wise,
Cleave ever to the sunnier side of doubt.

'The Ancient Sage' (1885) l. 66

11 Break, break, break,
On thy cold grey stones, O Sea!
And I would that my tongue could utter
The thoughts that arise in me.

'Break, Break, Break' (1842)

12 And the stately ships go on
To their haven under the hill;
But O for the touch of a vanished hand,
And the sound of a voice that is still!

'Break, Break, Break' (1842)

13 I come from haunts of coot and hern,
I make a sudden sally
And sparkle out among the fern,
To bicker down a valley.

'The Brook' (1855) l. 23

14 For men may come and men may go,
But I go on for ever.

'The Brook' (1855) l. 33

15 Half a league, half a league,
Half a league onward,
All in the valley of Death
Rode the six hundred.

'The Charge of the Light Brigade' (1854)

16 'Forward, the Light Brigade!'
Was there a man dismayed?
Not though the soldier knew
Some one had blundered:
Their's not to make reply,
Their's not to reason why,
Their's but to do and die:
Into the valley of Death
Rode the six hundred.
Cannon to right of them,
Cannon to left of them,
Cannon in front of them
Volleyed and thundered.

'The Charge of the Light Brigade' (1854)

17 Into the jaws of Death,
Into the mouth of Hell.

'The Charge of the Light Brigade' (1854)

18 Sunset and evening star,
And one clear call for me!
And may there be no moaning of the bar,
When I put out to sea.

'Crossing the Bar' (1889)

continued

Telegrams

1 AM IN MARKET HARBOROUGH. WHERE OUGHT I TO BE?
sent by G. K. **Chesterton** *to his wife in London*
G. K. Chesterton *Autobiography* (1936)

2 BETTER DROWNED THAN DUFFERS IF NOT DUFFERS WONT DROWN.
Arthur Ransome *Swallows and Amazons* (1930) ch. 1

3 A bill of indemnity . . . for raid by Dr Jameson and the British South Africa Company's troops. The amount falls under two heads—first, material damage, total of claim, £677,938 3*s*. 3*d*.—second, moral or intellectual damage, total of claim, £1,000,000.
from Paul Kruger (1825–1904) representing the South African Republic
communicated to the House of Commons by Joseph Chamberlain, 18 February 1897

4 DEEPLY REGRET INFORM YOUR GRACE LAST NIGHT TWO BLACK OWLS CAME AND PERCHED ON BATTLEMENTS REMAINED THERE THROUGH NIGHT HOOTING AT DAWN FLEW AWAY NONE KNOWS WHITHER AWAITING INSTRUCTIONS JELLINGS.
Max Beerbohm *Zuleika Dobson* (1911) ch. 14; cf. **Telegrams** 758:9

5 GOOD WORK, MARY. WE ALL KNEW YOU HAD IT IN YOU.
from Dorothy **Parker** *to Mrs Sherwood on the arrival of her baby*
Alexander Woollcott *While Rome Burns* (1934) 'Our Mrs Parker'

6 HOW DARE YOU BECOME PRIME MINISTER WHEN I'M AWAY GREAT LOVE CONSTANT THOUGHT VIOLET.
from Violet Bonham Carter (1887–1969) to her father, H. H. **Asquith**, *7 April 1908*
Mark Bonham Carter and Mark Pottle (eds.) *Lantern Slides* (1996)

7 QUESTION: HOW OLD CARY GRANT?
ANSWER: OLD CARY GRANT FINE. HOW YOU?
from Cary Grant (1904–86)
R. Schickel *Cary Grant* (1983)

8 PLEASE FENCE ME IN BABY THE WORLD'S TOO BIG OUT HERE AND I DON'T LIKE IT WITHOUT YOU.
from Humphrey Bogart (1899–1957) to Lauren **Bacall**
Lauren Bacall *By Myself* (1978)

9 PREPARE VAULT FOR FUNERAL MONDAY DORSET.
Max Beerbohm *Zuleika Dobson* (1911) ch. 14; cf. **Telegrams** 758:4

10 STREETS FLOODED. PLEASE ADVISE.
message sent by Robert **Benchley** *on arriving in Venice*
R. E. Drennan (ed.) *Wits End* (1973) 'Robert Benchley'

11 VERY SORRY CAN'T COME. LIE FOLLOWS BY POST.
message from Lord Charles Beresford (1846–1919) to the Prince of Wales, on being summoned to dine at the eleventh hour
Ralph Nevill *The World of Fashion 1837–1922* (1923) ch. 5; cf. **Proust** 594:9

12 What hath God wrought.
Samuel Morse, in the first electric telegraph message, 24 May 1844; cf. **Bible** 77:1

Alfred, Lord Tennyson *continued*

13 Twilight and evening bell,
And after that the dark!
And may there be no sadness of farewell,
When I embark;
For though from out our bourne of time and place
The flood may bear me far,
I hope to see my pilot face to face
When I have crossed the bar.
'Crossing the Bar' (1889)

14 O Love, what hours were thine and mine,
In lands of palm and southern pine;
In lands of palm, of orange-blossom,
Of olive, aloe, and maize and vine.
'The Daisy' (1855) st. 1

15 A dream of fair women.
title of poem (1832)

16 A daughter of the gods, divinely tall,
And most divinely fair.
'A Dream of Fair Women' (1832) l. 87

17 He clasps the crag with crookèd hands;
Close to the sun in lonely lands,
Ringed with the azure world, he stands.
The wrinkled sea beneath him crawls;
He watches from his mountain walls,
And like a thunderbolt he falls.
'The Eagle' (1851)

18 The mellow lin-lan-lone of evening bells.
'Far-Far-Away' (1889)

19 O Love, O fire! once he drew
With one long kiss my whole soul through
My lips, as sunlight drinketh dew.
'Fatima' (1832) st. 3

20 There beneath the Roman ruin where the purple flowers grow,
Came that 'Ave atque Vale' of the Poet's hopeless woe,
Tenderest of Roman poets nineteen-hundred years ago,
'Frater Ave atque Vale'—as we wander'd to and fro
Gazing at the Lydian laughter of the Garda Lake below
Sweet Catullus's all-but-island, olive-silvery Sirmio!
'Frater Ave atque Vale' (1885); cf. **Catullus** 197:5, 198:1

21 More black than ashbuds in the front of March.
'The Gardener's Daughter' (1842) l. 28

22 A sight to make an old man young.
'The Gardener's Daughter' (1842) l. 140

1 I waited for the train at Coventry.
'Godiva' (1842) l. 1

2 Then she rode forth, clothed on with chastity.
'Godiva' (1842) l. 53

3 With twelve great shocks of sound, the shameless noon
Was clashed and hammered from a hundred towers.
'Godiva' (1842) l. 74

4 Ah! when shall all men's good
Be each man's rule, and universal peace
Lie like a shaft of light across the land?
'The Golden Year' (1846) l. 47

5 Through all the circle of the golden year.
'The Golden Year' (1846) l. 51

6 That a lie which is all a lie may be met and fought with outright,
But a lie which is part a truth is a harder matter to fight.
'The Grandmother' (1859) st. 8

7 That man's the true Conservative
Who lops the mouldered branch away.
'Hands all Round' (1882) l. 7

8 Pray God our greatness may not fail
Through craven fears of being great.
'Hands all Round' (1882) l. 31

9 Gigantic daughter of the West,
We drink to thee across the flood,
We know thee most, we love thee best,
For art thou not of British blood?
'Hands all Round' (1852) st. 4

10 Speak to Him thou for He hears, and Spirit with Spirit can meet—
Closer is He than breathing, and nearer than hands and feet.
'The Higher Pantheism' (1869); cf. **Swinburne** 750:23

11 Wearing the white flower of a blameless life,
Before a thousand peering littlenesses,
In that fierce light which beats upon a throne,
And blackens every blot.
of Prince ***Albert***
Idylls of the King (1862 ed.) dedication l. 24

12 Man's word is God in man.
Idylls of the King 'The Coming of Arthur' (1869) l. 132

13 Clothed in white samite, mystic, wonderful.
Idylls of the King 'The Coming of Arthur' (1869) l. 284; 'The Passing of Arthur' (1869) l. 199

14 Rain, rain, and sun! a rainbow in the sky!
A young man will be wiser by and by;
An old man's wit may wander ere he die.
Idylls of the King 'The Coming of Arthur' (1869) l. 402

15 From the great deep to the great deep he goes.
Idylls of the King 'The Coming of Arthur' (1869) l. 410

16 Blow trumpet, for the world is white with May.
Idylls of the King 'The Coming of Arthur' (1869) l. 481

17 Live pure, speak true, right wrong, follow the King—
Else, wherefore born?
Idylls of the King 'Gareth and Lynette' (1872) l. 117

18 The city is built
To music, therefore never built at all,
And therefore built for ever.
Idylls of the King 'Gareth and Lynette' (1872) l. 272

19 To reverence the King, as if he were
Their conscience, and their conscience as their King,
To break the heathen and uphold the Christ,
To ride abroad redressing human wrongs,
To speak no slander, no, nor listen to it,
To honour his own word as if his God's.
Idylls of the King 'Guinevere' (1859) l. 465

20 To love one maiden only, cleave to her,
And worship her by years of noble deeds,
Until they won her; for indeed I knew
Of no more subtle master under heaven
Than is the maiden passion for a maid,
Not only to keep down the base in man,
But teach high thought, and amiable words
And courtliness, and the desire of fame,
And love of truth, and all that makes a man.
Idylls of the King 'Guinevere' (1859) l. 472

21 I thought I could not breathe in that fine air
That pure severity of perfect light—
I yearned for warmth and colour which I found
In Lancelot.
Idylls of the King 'Guinevere' (1859) l. 640

22 We needs must love the highest when we see it.
Idylls of the King 'Guinevere' (1859) l. 655

23 For good ye are and bad, and like to coins,
Some true, some light, but every one of you
Stamped with the image of the King.
Idylls of the King 'The Holy Grail' (1869) l. 25

24 I will be deafer than the blue-eyed cat,
And thrice as blind as any noonday owl,
To holy virgins in their ecstasies,
Henceforward.
Idylls of the King 'The Holy Grail' (1869) l. 862

25 Elaine the fair, Elaine the loveable,
Elaine, the lily maid of Astolat.
Idylls of the King 'Lancelot and Elaine' (1859) l. 1

26 He is all fault who hath no fault at all:
For who loves me must have a touch of earth.
Idylls of the King 'Lancelot and Elaine' (1859) l. 132

27 In me there dwells
No greatness, save it be some far-off touch
Of greatness to know well I am not great.
Idylls of the King 'Lancelot and Elaine' (1859) l. 447

28 I know not if I know what true love is,
But if I know, then, if I love not him,
I know there is none other I can love.
Idylls of the King 'Lancelot and Elaine' (1859) l. 672

29 His honour rooted in dishonour stood,
And faith unfaithful kept him falsely true.
Idylls of the King 'Lancelot and Elaine' (1859) l. 871

30 He makes no friend who never made a foe.
Idylls of the King 'Lancelot and Elaine' (1859) l. 1082

31 The greater man, the greater courtesy.
Idylls of the King 'The Last Tournament' (1871) l. 628

1 For man is man and master of his fate.
Idylls of the King 'The Marriage of Geraint' (1859) l. 355

2 They take the rustic murmur of their bourg
For the great wave that echoes round the world.
Idylls of the King 'The Marriage of Geraint' (1859) l. 419

3 It is the little rift within the lute,
That by and by will make the music mute,
And ever widening slowly silence all.
Idylls of the King 'Merlin and Vivien' (1859) l. 388

4 And trust me not at all or all in all.
Idylls of the King 'Merlin and Vivien' (1859) l. 396

5 Man dreams of fame while woman wakes to love.
Idylls of the King 'Merlin and Vivien' (1859) l. 458

6 Where blind and naked Ignorance
Delivers brawling judgements, unashamed,
On all things all day long.
Idylls of the King 'Merlin and Vivien' (1859) l. 662

7 But every page having an ample marge,
And every marge enclosing in the midst
A square of text that looks a little blot.
Idylls of the King 'Merlin and Vivien' (1859) l. 667

8 And none can read the text, not even I;
And none can read the comment but myself.
Idylls of the King 'Merlin and Vivien' (1859) l. 679

9 I found Him in the shining of the stars,
I marked Him in the flowering of His fields,
But in His ways with men I find Him not.
Idylls of the King 'The Passing of Arthur' (1869) l. 9

10 So all day long the noise of battle rolled
Among the mountains by the winter sea.
Idylls of the King 'The Passing of Arthur' (1869) l. 170

11 On one side lay the Ocean, and on one
Lay a great water, and the moon was full.
Idylls of the King 'The Passing of Arthur' (1869) l. 179

12 Authority forgets a dying king.
Idylls of the King 'The Passing of Arthur' (1869) l. 289

13 Clothed with his breath, and looking, as he walked,
Larger than human on the frozen hills.
He heard the deep behind him, and a cry
Before.
Idylls of the King 'The Passing of Arthur' (1869) l. 350

14 And the days darken round me, and the years,
Among new men, strange faces, other minds.
Idylls of the King 'The Passing of Arthur' (1869) l. 405

15 The old order changeth, yielding place to new,
And God fulfils himself in many ways,
Lest one good custom should corrupt the world.
Idylls of the King 'The Passing of Arthur' (1869) l. 408

16 If thou shouldst never see my face again,
Pray for my soul. More things are wrought by prayer
Than this world dreams of.
Idylls of the King 'The Passing of Arthur' (1869) l. 414

17 I am going a long way
With these thou seëst—if indeed I go
(For all my mind is clouded with a doubt)—
To the island-valley of Avilion;
Where falls not hail, or rain, or any snow,
Nor ever wind blows loudly; but it lies
Deep-meadowed, happy, fair with orchard lawns
And bowery hollows crowned with summer sea,
Where I will heal me of my grievous wound.
Idylls of the King 'The Passing of Arthur' (1869) l. 424

18 Like some full-breasted swan
That, fluting a wild carol ere her death,
Ruffles her pure cold plume, and takes the flood
With swarthy webs.
Idylls of the King 'The Passing of Arthur' (1869) l. 434

19 Thou madest man, he knows not why,
He thinks he was not made to die;
And thou hast made him: thou art just.
In Memoriam A. H. H. (1850) Prologue

20 Our little systems have their day;
They have their day and cease to be:
They are but broken lights of thee,
And thou, O Lord, art more than they.
In Memoriam A. H. H. (1850) Prologue

21 Let knowledge grow from more to more,
But more of reverence in us dwell;
That mind and soul, according well,
May make one music as before.
In Memoriam A. H. H. (1850) Prologue

22 I held it truth, with him who sings
To one clear harp in divers tones,
That men may rise on stepping-stones
Of their dead selves to higher things.
In Memoriam A. H. H. (1850) canto 1

23 For words, like Nature, half reveal
And half conceal the Soul within.
In Memoriam A. H. H. (1850) canto 5

24 But, for the unquiet heart and brain,
A use in measured language lies;
The sad mechanic exercise,
Like dull narcotics, numbing pain.
In Memoriam A. H. H. (1850) canto 5

25 And common is the commonplace,
And vacant chaff well meant for grain.
In Memoriam A. H. H. (1850) canto 6

26 Never morning wore
To evening, but some heart did break.
In Memoriam A. H. H. (1850) canto 6

27 His heavy-shotted hammock-shroud
Drops in his vast and wandering grave.
In Memoriam A. H. H. (1850) canto 6

28 Dark house, by which once more I stand
Here in the long unlovely street,
Doors, where my heart was used to beat
So quickly, waiting for a hand.
In Memoriam A. H. H. (1850) canto 7

29 And ghastly through the drizzling rain
On the bald street breaks the blank day.
In Memoriam A. H. H. (1850) canto 7

30 The last red leaf is whirled away,
The rooks are blown about the skies.
In Memoriam A. H. H. (1850) canto 15

31 There twice a day the Severn fills;
The salt sea-water passes by,

And hushes half the babbling Wye,
And makes a silence in the hills.
In Memoriam A. H. H. (1850) canto 19

1 The Shadow cloaked from head to foot,
Who keeps the keys of all the creeds.
In Memoriam A. H. H. (1850) canto 23

2 And Thought leapt out to wed with Thought
Ere Thought could wed itself with Speech.
In Memoriam A. H. H. (1850) canto 23

3 I envy not in any moods
The captive void of noble rage,
The linnet born within the cage,
That never knew the summer woods.
In Memoriam A. H. H. (1850) canto 27

4 'Tis better to have loved and lost
Than never to have loved at all.
In Memoriam A. H. H. (1850) canto 27; cf. **Butler** 172:21, **Clough** 223:1, **Congreve** 233:6, **Proverbs** 613:6

5 A solemn gladness even crowned
The purple brows of Olivet.
In Memoriam A. H. H. (1850) canto 31

6 Her eyes are homes of silent prayer.
In Memoriam A. H. H. (1850) canto 32

7 Short swallow-flights of song, that dip
Their wings in tears, and skim away.
In Memoriam A. H. H. (1850) canto 48

8 Be near me when my light is low,
When the blood creeps, and the nerves prick
And tingle; and the heart is sick,
And all the wheels of Being slow.
Be near me when the sensuous frame
Is racked with pains that conquer trust;
And Time, a maniac scattering dust,
And Life, a Fury slinging flame.
In Memoriam A. H. H. (1850) canto 50

9 Oh yet we trust that somehow good
Will be the final goal of ill.
In Memoriam A. H. H. (1850) canto 54

10 That nothing walks with aimless feet;
That not one life shall be destroyed,
Or cast as rubbish to the void,
When God hath made the pile complete.
In Memoriam A. H. H. (1850) canto 54

11 But what am I?
An infant crying in the night:
An infant crying for the light:
And with no language but a cry.
In Memoriam A. H. H. (1850) canto 54

12 So careful of the type she seems,
So careless of the single life.
of Nature
In Memoriam A. H. H. (1850) canto 55

13 The great world's altar-stairs
That slope through darkness up to God.
In Memoriam A. H. H. (1850) canto 55

14 Man . . .
Who trusted God was love indeed
And love Creation's final law—
Though Nature, red in tooth and claw
With ravine, shrieked against his creed.
In Memoriam A. H. H. (1850) canto 56

15 Peace; come away: the song of woe
Is after all an earthly song:
Peace; come away: we do him wrong
To sing so wildly: let us go.
In Memoriam A. H. H. (1850) canto 57

16 O Sorrow, wilt thou live with me
No casual mistress, but a wife.
In Memoriam A. H. H. (1850) canto 59

17 So many worlds, so much to do,
So little done, such things to be.
In Memoriam A. H. H. (1850) canto 73; cf. **Last words** 457:4

18 Death has made
His darkness beautiful with thee.
In Memoriam A. H. H. (1850) canto 74

19 And round thee with the breeze of song
To stir a little dust of praise.
In Memoriam A. H. H. (1850) canto 75

20 O last regret, regret can die!
In Memoriam A. H. H. (1850) canto 78

21 Laburnums, dropping-wells of fire.
In Memoriam A. H. H. (1850) canto 83

22 God's finger touched him, and he slept.
In Memoriam A. H. H. (1850) canto 85

23 Fresh from brawling courts
And dusty purlieus of the law.
In Memoriam A. H. H. (1850) canto 89; cf. **Etherege** 301:11

24 You tell me, doubt is Devil-born.
In Memoriam A. H. H. (1850) canto 96

25 There lives more faith in honest doubt,
Believe me, than in half the creeds.
In Memoriam A. H. H. (1850) canto 96

26 Their meetings made December June,
Their every parting was to die.
In Memoriam A. H. H. (1850) canto 97

27 He seems so near and yet so far.
In Memoriam A. H. H. (1850) canto 97

28 Ring out, wild bells, to the wild sky,
The flying cloud, the frosty light:
The year is dying in the night;
Ring out, wild bells, and let him die.
Ring out the old, ring in the new,
Ring, happy bells, across the snow:
The year is going, let him go;
Ring out the false, ring in the true.
In Memoriam A. H. H. (1850) canto 106

29 Ring out the want, the care, the sin,
The faithless coldness of the times;
Ring out, ring out my mournful rhymes,
But ring the fuller minstrel in.
Ring out false pride in place and blood,
The civic slander and the spite;
Ring in the love of truth and right,
Ring in the common love of good.
Ring out old shapes of foul disease;

Ring out the narrowing lust of gold;
Ring out the thousand wars of old,
Ring in the thousand years of peace.

Ring in the valiant man and free,
The larger heart, the kindlier hand;
Ring out the darkness of the land;
Ring in the Christ that is to be.
In Memoriam A. H. H. (1850) canto 106

1 Not the schoolboy heat,
The blind hysterics of the Celt.
In Memoriam A. H. H. (1850) canto 109

2 Now fades the last long streak of snow,
Now burgeons every maze of quick
About the flowering squares, and thick
By ashen roots the violets blow.
In Memoriam A. H. H. (1850) canto 115

3 And drowned in yonder living blue
The lark becomes a sightless song.
In Memoriam A. H. H. (1850) canto 115

4 There, where the long street roars, hath been
The stillness of the central sea.
In Memoriam A. H. H. (1850) canto 123

5 Wearing all that weight
Of learning lightly like a flower.
In Memoriam A. H. H. (1850) canto 131

6 One God, one law, one element,
And one far-off divine event,
To which the whole creation moves.
In Memoriam A. H. H. (1850) canto 131

7 The voice of the dead was a living voice to me.
'In the Valley of Cauteretz' (1864)

8 Below the thunders of the upper deep,
Far, far beneath in the abysmal sea,
His ancient, dreamless, uninvaded sleep
The Kraken sleepeth.
'The Kraken' (1830)

9 There hath he lain for ages and will lie
Battening upon huge seaworms in his sleep,
Until the latter fire shall heat the deep.
'The Kraken' (1830)

10 At me you smiled, but unbeguiled
I saw the snare, and I retired:
The daughter of a hundred Earls,
You are not one to be desired.
'Lady Clara Vere de Vere' (1842) st. 1

11 Kind hearts are more than coronets,
And simple faith than Norman blood.
'Lady Clara Vere de Vere' (1842) st. 7

12 On either side the river lie
Long fields of barley and of rye,
That clothe the wold and meet the sky;
And through the field the road runs by
To many-towered Camelot.
'The Lady of Shalott' (1832, revised 1842) pt. 1

13 Willows whiten, aspens quiver,
Little breezes dusk and shiver.
'The Lady of Shalott' (1832, revised 1842) pt. 1

14 Only reapers, reaping early
In among the bearded barley,
Hear a song that echoes cheerly
From the river winding clearly,
Down to towered Camelot.
'The Lady of Shalott' (1832, revised 1842) pt. 1

15 Or when the moon was overhead,
Came two young lovers lately wed;
'I am half sick of shadows,' said
The Lady of Shalott.
'The Lady of Shalott' (1832, revised 1842) pt. 2

16 A bow-shot from her bower-eaves,
He rode between the barley-sheaves,
The sun came dazzling through the leaves,
And flamed upon the brazen greaves
Of bold Sir Lancelot.
A red-cross knight for ever kneeled
To a lady in his shield,
That sparkled on the yellow field,
Beside remote Shalott.
'The Lady of Shalott' (1832, revised 1842) pt. 3

17 All in the blue unclouded weather
Thick-jewelled shone the saddle-leather,
The helmet and the helmet-feather
Burned like one burning flame together,
As he rode down to Camelot.
'The Lady of Shalott' (1832, revised 1842) pt. 3

18 'Tirra lirra,' by the river
Sang Sir Lancelot.
'The Lady of Shalott' (1832, revised 1842) pt. 3

19 She left the web, she left the loom,
She made three paces through the room,
She saw the water-lily bloom,
She saw the helmet and the plume,
She looked down to Camelot.
Out flew the web and floated wide;
The mirror cracked from side to side;
'The curse is come upon me,' cried
The Lady of Shalott.
'The Lady of Shalott' (1832, revised 1842) pt. 3

20 But Lancelot mused a little space;
He said 'She has a lovely face;
God in his mercy lend her grace,
The Lady of Shalott.'
'The Lady of Shalott' (1832, revised 1842) pt. 4

21 Airy, fairy Lilian.
'Lilian' (1830)

22 In the spring a livelier iris changes on the burnished dove;
In the spring a young man's fancy lightly turns to thoughts of love.
'Locksley Hall' (1842) l. 19

23 He will hold thee, when his passion shall have spent its novel force,
Something better than his dog, a little dearer than his horse.
'Locksley Hall' (1842) l. 49

24 This is truth the poet sings,
That a sorrow's crown of sorrow is remembering happier things.
'Locksley Hall' (1842) l. 75; cf. **Boethius** 123:11, **Dante** 249:12

1 But the jingling of the guinea helps the hurt that Honour feels.
'Locksley Hall' (1842) l. 105

2 Men, my brothers, men the workers, ever reaping something new:
That which they have done but earnest of the things that they shall do:
'Locksley Hall' (1842) l. 117

3 For I dipped into the future, far as human eye could see,
Saw the vision of the world, and all the wonder that would be;
Saw the heavens fill with commerce, argosies of magic sails,
Pilots of the purple twilight, dropping down with costly bales;
Heard the heavens fill with shouting, and there rained a ghastly dew
From the nations' airy navies grappling in the central blue;
Far along the world-wide whisper of the south-wind rushing warm,
With the standards of the peoples plunging through the thunder-storm;
Till the war-drum throbbed no longer, and the battle-flags were furled
In the Parliament of man, the Federation of the world.
'Locksley Hall' (1842) l. 119

4 Science moves, but slowly slowly, creeping on from point to point.
'Locksley Hall' (1842) l. 134

5 Yet I doubt not through the ages one increasing purpose runs,
And the thoughts of men are widened with the process of the suns.
'Locksley Hall' (1842) l. 137

6 Knowledge comes, but wisdom lingers.
'Locksley Hall' (1842) l. 141

7 I will take some savage woman, she shall rear my dusky race.
'Locksley Hall' (1842) l. 168

8 I the heir of all the ages, in the foremost files of time.
'Locksley Hall' (1842) l. 178

9 Forward, forward let us range,
Let the great world spin for ever down the ringing grooves of change.
'Locksley Hall' (1842) l. 181

10 Better fifty years of Europe than a cycle of Cathay.
'Locksley Hall' (1842) l. 184

11 Music that gentlier on the spirit lies,
Than tired eyelids upon tired eyes.
'The Lotos-Eaters' (1832) Choric Song, st. 1

12 There is no joy but calm!
'The Lotos-Eaters' (1832) Choric Song, st. 2

13 Death is the end of life; ah, why
Should life all labour be?
'The Lotos-Eaters' (1832) Choric Song, st. 4

14 Live and lie reclined
On the hills like Gods together, careless of mankind.
For they lie beside their nectar, and the bolts are hurled
Far below them in the valleys, and the clouds are lightly curled
Round their golden houses, girdled with the gleaming world.
'The Lotos-Eaters' (1832) Choric Song, st. 8 (1842 revision)

15 Surely, surely, slumber is more sweet than toil, the shore
Than labour in the deep mid-ocean, wind and wave and oar;
Oh rest ye, brother mariners, we will not wander more.
'The Lotos-Eaters' (1832) Choric Song, st. 8

16 I saw the flaring atom-streams
And torrents of her myriad universe,
Ruining along the illimitable inane.
'Lucretius' (1868) l. 38

17 Nor at all can tell
Whether I mean this day to end myself,
Or lend an ear to Plato where he says,
That men like soldiers may not quit the post
Allotted by the Gods.
'Lucretius' (1868) l. 145

18 Passionless bride, divine Tranquillity,
Yearned after by the wisest of the wise,
Who fail to find thee, being as thou art
Without one pleasure and without one pain.
'Lucretius' (1868) l. 265

19 Weeded and worn the ancient thatch
Upon the lonely moated grange.
She only said, 'My life is dreary,
He cometh not,' she said;
She said, 'I am aweary, aweary,
I would that I were dead!'
Her tears fell with the dews at even;
Her tears fell ere the dews were dried.
'Mariana' (1830) st. 1; cf. **Shakespeare** 686:19

20 I hate that dreadful hollow behind the little wood.
Maud (1855) pt. 1, sect. 1

21 Faultily faultless, icily regular, splendidly null,
Dead perfection, no more.
Maud (1855) pt. 1, sect. 2

22 The passionate heart of the poet is whirled into folly and vice.
Maud (1855) pt. 1, sect. 4, st. 7

23 And most of all would I flee from the cruel madness of love,
The honey of poison-flowers and all the measureless ill.
Maud (1855) pt. 1, sect. 4, st. 10

24 That jewelled mass of millinery,
That oiled and curled Assyrian Bull.
Maud (1855) pt. 1, sect. 6, st. 6

25 She came to the village church,
And sat by a pillar alone;
An angel watching an urn

Wept over her, carved in stone.
Maud (1855) pt. 1, sect. 8

1 I heard no longer
The snowy-banded, dilettante,
Delicate-handed priest intone.
Maud (1855) pt. 1, sect. 8

2 Ah God, for a man with heart, head, hand,
Like some of the simple great ones gone
For ever and ever by,
One still strong man in a blatant land,
Whatever they call him, what care I,
Aristocrat, democrat, autocrat—one
Who can rule and dare not lie.
Maud (1855) pt. 1, sect. 10, st. 5

3 I kissed her slender hand,
She took the kiss sedately;
Maud is not seventeen,
But she is tall and stately.
Maud (1855) pt. 1, sect. 12, st. 4

4 Gorgonised me from head to foot
With a stony British stare.
Maud (1855) pt. 1, sect. 13, st. 2

5 A livelier emerald twinkles in the grass,
A purer sapphire melts into the sea.
Maud (1855) pt. 1, sect. 18, st. 6

6 Come into the garden, Maud,
For the black bat, night, has flown,
Come into the garden, Maud,
I am here at the gate alone.
And the woodbine spices are wafted abroad,
And the musk of the rose is blown.
For a breeze of morning moves,
And the planet of Love is on high,
Beginning to faint in the light that she loves
On a bed of daffodil sky.
Maud (1855) pt. 1, sect. 22, st. 1

7 All night has the casement jessamine stirred
To the dancers dancing in tune;
Till a silence fell with the waking bird,
And a hush with the setting moon.
Maud (1855) pt. 1, sect. 22, st. 3

8 Queen rose of the rosebud garden of girls.
Maud (1855) pt. 1, sect. 22, st. 9

9 There has fallen a splendid tear
From the passion-flower at the gate.
She is coming, my dove, my dear;
She is coming, my life, my fate;
The red rose cries, 'She is near, she is near;'
And the white rose weeps, 'She is late.'
The larkspur listens, 'I hear, I hear;'
And the lily whispers, 'I wait.'
Maud (1855) pt. 1, sect. 22, st. 10

10 She is coming, my own, my sweet;
Were it ever so airy a tread,
My heart would hear her and beat,
Were it earth in an earthy bed;
My dust would hear her and beat;
Had I lain for a century dead;
Would start and tremble under her feet,
And blossom in purple and red.
Maud (1855) pt. 1, sect. 22, st. 11

11 O that 'twere possible
After long grief and pain
To find the arms of my true love
Round me once again!
Maud (1855) pt. 2, sect. 4, st. 1

12 But the churchmen fain would kill their church,
As the churches have killed their Christ.
Maud (1855) pt. 2, sect. 5, st. 2

13 O me, why have they not buried me deep enough?
Is it kind to have made me a grave so rough,
Me, that was never a quiet sleeper?
Maud (1855) pt. 2, sect. 5, st. 11

14 My life has crept so long on a broken wing
Through cells of madness, haunts of horror and fear,
That I come to be grateful at last for a little thing.
Maud (1855) pt. 3, sect. 6, st. 1

15 When the face of night is fair on the dewy downs,
And the shining daffodil dies.
Maud (1855) pt. 3, sect. 6, st. 1

16 The blood-red blossom of war with a heart of fire.
Maud (1855) pt. 3, sect. 6, st. 4

17 It is better to fight for the good, than to rail at the ill;
I have felt with my native land, I am one with my kind,
I embrace the purpose of God, and the doom assigned.
Maud (1855) pt. 3, sect. 6, st. 5

18 You must wake and call me early, call me early, mother dear;
Tomorrow 'ill be the happiest time of all the glad New-year;
Of all the glad New-year, mother, the maddest merriest day;
For I'm to be Queen o' the May, mother, I'm to be Queen o' the May.
'The May Queen' (1832)

19 Launch your vessel,
And crowd your canvas,
And, ere it vanishes
Over the margin,
After it, follow it,
Follow The Gleam.
'Merlin and The Gleam' (1889) st. 9

20 O mighty-mouthed inventor of harmonies,
O skilled to sing of time or eternity,
God-gifted organ-voice of England,
Milton, a name to resound for ages.
'Milton: Alcaics' (1863)

21 All that bowery loneliness,
The brooks of Eden mazily murmuring.
'Milton: Alcaics' (1863)

22 O you chorus of indolent reviewers.
'Milton: Hendecasyllabics' (1863)

23 Doänt thou marry for munny, but goä wheer munny is!
'Northern Farmer. New Style' (1869) st. 5; cf. **Proverbs** 607:33

1 The poor in a loomp is bad.
'Northern Farmer. New Style' (1869) st. 12

2 The last great Englishman is low.
'Ode on the Death of the Duke of Wellington' (1852) st. 3

3 O good grey head which all men knew!
'Ode on the Death of the Duke of Wellington' (1852) st. 4

4 O fall'n at length that tower of strength
Which stood four-square to all the winds that blew!
'Ode on the Death of the Duke of Wellington' (1852) st. 4

5 That world-earthquake, Waterloo!
'Ode on the Death of the Duke of Wellington' (1852) st. 6

6 Who never sold the truth to serve the hour,
Nor paltered with Eternal God for power.
'Ode on the Death of the Duke of Wellington' (1852) st. 7

7 Naked they came to that smooth-swarded bower,
And at their feet the crocus brake like fire,
Violet, amaracus, and asphodel,
Lotos and lilies.
'Oenone' (1832, revised 1842) l. 93

8 I built my soul a lordly pleasure-house,
Wherein at ease for aye to dwell.
'The Palace of Art' (1832) st. 1

9 Still as, while Saturn whirls, his steadfast shade
Sleeps on his luminous ring.
'The Palace of Art' (1832) st. 4

10 An English home—grey twilight poured
On dewy pasture, dewy trees,
Softer than sleep—all things in order stored,
A haunt of ancient Peace.
'The Palace of Art' (1832) st. 22

11 Vex not thou the poet's mind
With thy shallow wit:
Vex not thou the poet's mind;
For thou canst not fathom it.
'The Poet's Mind' (1830)

12 With prudes for proctors, dowagers for deans,
And sweet girl-graduates in their golden hair.
The Princess (1847) 'Prologue' l. 141

13 And blessings on the falling out
That all the more endears,
When we fall out with those we love
And kiss again with tears!
The Princess (1847) pt. 2, song (added 1850)

14 A classic lecture, rich in sentiment,
With scraps of thundrous epic lilted out
By violet-hooded Doctors, elegies
And quoted odes, and jewels five-words-long,
That on the stretched forefinger of all Time
Sparkle for ever.
The Princess (1847) pt. 2, l. 352

15 Sweet and low, sweet and low,
Wind of the western sea,
Low, low, breathe and blow,
Wind of the western sea!
Over the rolling waters go,
Come from the dying moon, and blow,
Blow him again to me;
While my little one, while my pretty one, sleeps.
The Princess (1847) pt. 3, song (added 1850)

16 The splendour falls on castle walls
And snowy summits old in story:
The long light shakes across the lakes,
And the wild cataract leaps in glory.
Blow, bugle, blow, set the wild echoes flying,
Blow, bugle; answer, echoes, dying, dying, dying.
The Princess (1847) pt. 4, song (added 1850)

17 O sweet and far from cliff and scar
The horns of Elfland faintly blowing!
The Princess (1847) pt. 4, song (added 1850)

18 O love, they die in yon rich sky,
They faint on hill or field or river:
Our echoes roll from soul to soul,
And grow for ever and for ever.
The Princess (1847) pt. 4, song (added 1850)

19 Tears, idle tears, I know not what they mean,
Tears from the depth of some divine despair
Rise in the heart, and gather to the eyes,
In looking on the happy autumn-fields,
And thinking of the days that are no more.
The Princess (1847) pt. 4, l. 21, song (added 1850)

20 So sad, so fresh, the days that are no more.
The Princess (1847) pt. 4, l. 30, song (added 1850)

21 Ah, sad and strange as in dark summer dawns
The earliest pipe of half-awakened birds
To dying ears, when unto dying eyes
The casement slowly grows a glimmering square;
So sad, so strange, the days that are no more.

Dear as remembered kisses after death,
And sweet as those by hopeless fancy feigned
On lips that are for others; deep as love,
Deep as first love, and wild with all regret;
O Death in Life, the days that are no more.
The Princess (1847) pt. 4, l. 31, song (added 1850)

22 O Swallow, Swallow, flying, flying South,
Fly to her, and fall upon her gilded eaves,
And tell her, tell her, what I tell to thee.

O tell her, Swallow, thou that knowest each,
That bright and fierce and fickle is the South,
And dark and true and tender is the North.
The Princess (1847) pt. 4, l. 75, song (added 1850)

23 O tell her, Swallow, that thy brood is flown:
Say to her, I do but wanton in the South,
But in the North long since my nest is made.
The Princess (1847) pt. 4, l. 90, song (added 1850)

24 Man is the hunter; woman is his game:
The sleek and shining creatures of the chase,
We hunt them for the beauty of their skins;
They love us for it, and we ride them down.
The Princess (1847) pt. 5, l. 147

25 Home they brought her warrior dead.
She nor swooned, nor uttered cry:
All her maidens, watching said,
'She must weep or she will die.'
The Princess (1847) pt. 6, song (added 1850)

26 Rose a nurse of ninety years,
Set his child upon her knee—
Like summer tempest came her tears—
'Sweet my child, I live for thee.'
The Princess (1847) pt. 6, song (added 1850)

1 The woman is so hard
Upon the woman.
The Princess (1847) pt. 6, l. 205

2 Ask me no more: what answer should I give?
I love not hollow cheek or faded eye:
Yet, O my friend, I will not have thee die!
Ask me no more, lest I should bid thee live.
The Princess (1847) pt. 7, song (added 1850)

3 Now sleeps the crimson petal, now the white;
Nor waves the cypress in the palace walk;
Nor winks the gold fin in the porphyry font:
The fire-fly wakens: waken thou with me.
Now droops the milkwhite peacock like a ghost,
And like a ghost she glimmers on to me.
Now lies the Earth all Danaë to the stars,
And all thy heart lies open unto me.
Now slides the silent meteor on, and leaves
A shining furrow, as thy thoughts in me.
Now folds the lily all her sweetness up,
And slips into the bosom of the lake:
So fold thyself, my dearest, thou, and slip
Into my bosom and be lost in me.
The Princess (1847) pt. 7, l. 161, song (added 1850)

4 Come down, O maid, from yonder mountain height:
What pleasure lives in height?
The Princess (1847) pt. 7, l. 177, song (added 1850)

5 For Love is of the valley, come thou down
And find him; by the happy threshold, he,
Or hand in hand with Plenty in the maize,
Or red with spirted purple of the vats,
Or foxlike in the vine.
The Princess (1847) pt. 7, l. 194, song (added 1850)

6 Sweet is every sound,
Sweeter thy voice, but every sound is sweet;
Myriads of rivulets hurrying through the lawn,
The moan of doves in immemorial elms,
And murmuring of innumerable bees.
The Princess (1847) pt. 7, l. 203, song (added 1850)

7 No little lily-handed baronet he,
A great broad-shouldered genial Englishman,
A lord of fat prize-oxen and of sheep,
A raiser of huge melons and of pine,
A patron of some thirty charities,
A pamphleteer on guano and on grain.
The Princess (1847) 'Conclusion' l. 84

8 At Flores in the Azores Sir Richard Grenville lay,
And a pinnace, like a fluttered bird, came flying from far away:
'Spanish ships of war at sea! we have sighted fifty-three!'
Then sware Lord Thomas Howard: ''Fore God I am no coward;
But I cannot meet them here, for my ships are out of gear,
And the half my men are sick. I must fly, but follow quick.
We are six ships of the line; can we fight with fifty-three?'
Then spake Sir Richard Grenville: 'I know you are no coward;
You fly them for a moment to fight with them again.
But I've ninety men and more that are lying sick ashore.
I should count myself the coward if I left them, my Lord Howard,
To these Inquisition dogs and the devildoms of Spain.'
So Lord Howard passed away with five ships of war that day,
Till he melted like a cloud in the silent summer heaven.
'The Revenge' (1878) st. 1

9 And Sir Richard said again: 'We be all good English men.
Let us bang these dogs of Seville, the children of the devil,
For I never turned my back upon Don or devil yet.'
'The Revenge' (1878) st. 4

10 And the sun went down, and the stars came out far over the summer sea,
But never a moment ceased the fight of the one and the fifty-three.
'The Revenge' (1878) st. 9

11 Sink me the ship, Master Gunner—sink her, split her in twain!
Fall into the hands of God, not into the hands of Spain!
And the gunner said 'Ay, ay,' but the seamen made reply:
'We have children we have wives,
And the Lord hath spared our lives.'
'The Revenge' (1878) st. 11

12 And they praised him to his face with their courtly foreign grace;
But he rose upon their decks, and he cried:
'I have fought for Queen and Faith like a valiant man and true;
I have only done my duty as a man is bound to do:
With a joyful spirit I Sir Richard Grenville die!'
And he fell upon their decks, and he died.
'The Revenge' (1878) st. 13

13 And the little Revenge herself went down by the island crags
To be lost evermore in the main.
'The Revenge' (1878) st. 14

14 My strength is as the strength of ten,
Because my heart is pure.
'Sir Galahad' (1842)

15 Alone and warming his five wits,
The white owl in the belfry sits.
'Song—The Owl' (1830)

16 The woods decay, the woods decay and fall,
The vapours weep their burthen to the ground,
Man comes and tills the field and lies beneath,
And after many a summer dies the swan.
Me only cruel immortality
Consumes: I wither slowly in thine arms,
Here at the quiet limit of the world.
'Tithonus' (1860, revised 1864) l. 1

1 Why wilt thou ever scare me with thy tears,
And make me tremble lest a saying learnt,
In days far-off, on that dark earth, be true?
The gods themselves cannot recall their gifts.
'Tithonus' (1860, revised 1864) l. 49

2 Of happy men that have the power to die,
And grassy barrows of the happier dead.
'Tithonus' (1860, revised 1864) l. 70

3 You'll have no scandal while you dine,
But honest talk and wholesome wine.
'To the Revd F. D. Maurice' (1855) st. 5

4 All the charm of all the Muses
often flowering in a lonely word.
'To Virgil' (1882) st. 3

5 I salute thee, Mantovano,
I that loved thee since my day began,
Wielder of the stateliest measure
ever moulded by the lips of man.
'To Virgil' (1882) st. 10

6 This truth within thy mind rehearse,
That in a boundless universe
Is boundless better, boundless worse.
'The Two Voices' (1842) st. 9

7 No life that breathes with human breath
Has ever truly longed for death.
'The Two Voices' (1842) st. 132

8 It little profits that an idle king,
By this still hearth, among these barren crags,
Matched with an agèd wife, I mete and dole
Unequal laws unto a savage race.
'Ulysses' (1842) l. 1

9 I will drink
Life to the lees: all times I have enjoyed
Greatly, have suffered greatly, both with those
That loved me, and alone; on shore, and when
Through scudding drifts the rainy Hyades
Vext the dim sea: I am become a name;
For always roaming with a hungry heart
Much have I seen and known; cities of men
And manners, climates, councils, governments,
Myself not least, but honoured of them all;
And drunk delight of battle with my peers,
Far on the ringing plains of windy Troy.
I am a part of all that I have met;
Yet all experience is an arch wherethrough
Gleams that untravelled world, whose margin fades
For ever and for ever when I move.
How dull it is to pause, to make an end,
To rust unburnished, not to shine in use!
As though to breathe were life.
'Ulysses' (1842) l. 11

10 This grey spirit yearning in desire
To follow knowledge like a sinking star,
Beyond the utmost bound of human thought.
'Ulysses' (1842) l. 30

11 This is my son, mine own Telemachus.
'Ulysses' (1842) l. 33

12 There lies the port; the vessel puffs her sail:
There gloom the dark broad seas. My mariners,
Souls that have toiled, and wrought, and thought with me—
That ever with a frolic welcome took
The thunder and the sunshine, and opposed
Free hearts, free foreheads—you and I are old;
Old age hath yet his honour and his toil;
Death closes all: but something ere the end,
Some work of noble note, may yet be done,
Not unbecoming men that strove with gods.
The lights begin to twinkle from the rocks:
The long day wanes: the slow moon climbs: the deep
Moans round with many voices. Come, my friends,
'Tis not too late to seek a newer world.
Push off, and sitting well in order smite
The sounding furrows; For my purpose holds
To sail beyond the sunset, and the baths
Of all the western stars, until I die.
It may be that the gulfs will wash us down:
It may be we shall touch the Happy Isles,
And see the great Achilles, whom we knew.
Though much is taken, much abides; and though
We are not now that strength which in old days
Moved earth and heaven; That which we are, we are;
One equal temper of heroic hearts,
Made weak by time and fate, but strong in will
To strive, to seek, to find, and not to yield.
'Ulysses' (1842) l. 51

13 Every moment dies a man,
Every moment one is born.
'The Vision of Sin' (1842) pt. 4, st. 9; cf. **Babbage** 40:14

14 I grow in worth, and wit, and sense,
Unboding critic-pen,
Or that eternal want of pence,
Which vexes public men.
'Will Waterproof's Lyrical Monologue' (1842) st. 6

15 A land of settled government,
A land of just and old renown,
Where Freedom slowly broadens down
From precedent to precedent.
'You ask me, why, though ill at ease' (1842) st. 3

16 In the end I accepted the honour, because during dinner Venables told me, that, if I became Poet Laureate, I should always when I dined out be offered the liver-wing of a fowl.
on being made Poet Laureate in 1850
in *Alfred Lord Tennyson: A Memoir by his Son* (1897) vol. 1

17 I see land! Mr Kendal is just going to be confirmed.
in Charlotte Yonge's novel The Young Stepmother, *the happiness of the Kendal family depends on their being full members of the Anglican church*
Alethea Hayter *Charlotte Yonge* (1996)

18 It is the height of luxury to sit in a hot bath and read about little birds.
having had running hot water installed in his new house at Aldworth
Hallam Tennyson *Tennyson and his Friends* (1911)

19 A louse in the locks of literature.
of Churton Collins
Evan Charteris *Life and Letters of Sir Edmund Gosse* (1931) ch. 14

Terence (Publius Terentius Afer) c.190–159 BC
Roman comic dramatist

1 *Hinc illae lacrimae.*

Hence those tears.

Andria l. 126

2 *Nullumst iam dictum quod non dictum sit prius.*

Nothing has yet been said that's not been said before.

Eunuchus prologue l. 41

3 *Homo sum; humani nil a me alienum puto.*

I am a man, I count nothing human foreign to me.

Heauton Timorumenos l. 77

4 *Fortis fortuna adiuvat.*

Fortune assists the brave.

Phormio l. 203; cf. **Proverbs** 600:44, **Virgil** 795:9

5 *Quot homines tot sententiae: suus cuique mos.*

There are as many opinions as there are people: each has his own correct way.

Phormio l. 454; cf. **Proverbs** 611:6

Mother Teresa 1910–97
Roman Catholic nun and missionary, born in what is now Macedonia of Albanian parentage

6 We ourselves feel that what we are doing is just a drop in the ocean. But if that drop was not in the ocean, I think the ocean would be less because of that missing drop. I do not agree with the big way of doing things.

A Gift for God (1975)

7 Now let us do something beautiful for God.

letter to Malcolm Muggeridge before making a BBC TV programme about the Missionaries of Charity, 1971; cf. **Muggeridge** 534:15

8 The biggest disease today is not leprosy or tuberculosis, but rather the feeling of being unwanted, uncared for and deserted by everybody.

in *The Observer* 3 October 1971

9 I see God in every human being. When I wash the leper's wounds I feel I am nursing the Lord himself.

in 1977; in obituary, *Guardian* 6 September 1997

10 By blood and origin I am Albanian. My citizenship is Indian. I am a Catholic nun. As to my calling, I belong to the whole world. As to my heart, I belong entirely to the heart of Jesus.

in *Independent* 6 September 1997; obituary

St Teresa of Ávila 1512–82
Spanish Carmelite nun and mystic
see also **John** 407:15

11 Alas, O Lord, to what a state dost Thou bring those who love Thee!

Interior Castle Mansion 6, ch. 11, para. 6 (translated by the Benedictines of Stanbrook, 1921)

St Teresa of Lisieux 1873–97
French Carmelite nun

12 I will spend my heaven doing good on earth.

T. N. Taylor (ed.) *Soeur Thérèse of Lisieux* (1912) epilogue

13 After my death I will let fall a shower of roses.

T. N. Taylor (ed.) *Soeur Thérèse of Lisieux* (1912) epilogue

Tertullian (Quintus Septimius Florens Tertullianus) AD c.160–c.225
Latin Church father from Carthage

14 *O testimonium animae naturaliter Christianae.*

O evidence of a naturally Christian soul!

Apologeticus ch. 17, sect. 6

15 *Plures efficimus quoties metimur a vobis, semen est sanguis Christianorum.*

As often as we are mown down by you, the more we grow in numbers; the blood of Christians is the seed.

traditionally 'The blood of the martyrs is the seed of the Church'

Apologeticus ch. 50, sect. 13; cf. **Proverbs** 596:31

16 *Certum est quia impossibile est.*

It is certain because it is impossible.

often quoted as 'Credo quia impossibile'

De Carne Christi ch. 5

A. S. J. Tessimond 1902–62

17 Cats, no less liquid than their shadows,
Offer no angles to the wind.
They slip, diminished, neat, through loopholes
Less than themselves.

Cats (1934) p. 20

William Makepeace Thackeray 1811–63
English novelist
on Thackeray: see **Ruskin** 638:5

18 He who meanly admires mean things is a Snob.

The Book of Snobs (1848) ch. 2

19 'Tis not the dying for a faith that's so hard, Master Harry—every man of every nation has done that—'tis the living up to it that is difficult.

The History of Henry Esmond (1852) bk. 1, ch. 6

20 'Tis strange what a man may do, and a woman yet think him an angel.

The History of Henry Esmond (1852) bk. 1, ch. 7

21 What money is better bestowed than that of a school-boy's tip?

The Newcomes (1853–5) vol. 1, ch. 16

22 He lifted up his head a little, and quickly said, 'Adsum!' and fell back . . . he, whose heart was as that of a little child, had answered to his name, and stood in the presence of The Master.

The Newcomes (1853–5) vol. 1, ch. 80

23 Yes, I am a fatal man, Madame Fribsbi. To inspire hopeless passion is my destiny.

Mirobolant

Pendennis (1848–50) ch. 23

1 Remember, it is as easy to marry a rich woman as a poor woman.
Pendennis (1848–50) ch. 28

2 For a slashing article, sir, there's nobody like the Capting.
Mr Bungay
Pendennis (1848–50) ch. 32

3 The *Pall Mall Gazette* is written by gentlemen for gentlemen.
Pendennis (1848–50) ch. 32

4 Business first; pleasure afterwards.
The Rose and the Ring (1855) ch. 1

5 A woman with fair opportunities and without a positive hump, may marry whom she likes.
Vanity Fair (1847–8) ch. 4

6 Whenever he met a great man he grovelled before him, and my-lorded him as only a free-born Briton can do.
Vanity Fair (1847–8) ch. 13

7 If a man's character is to be abused, say what you will, there's nobody like a relation to do the business.
Vanity Fair (1847–8) ch. 19

8 Them's my sentiments!
Fred Bullock
Vanity Fair (1847–8) ch. 21

9 Darkness came down on the field and city: and Amelia was praying for George, who was lying on his face, dead, with a bullet through his heart.
Vanity Fair (1847–8) ch. 32

10 Nothing like blood, sir, in hosses, dawgs, and men.
James Crawley
Vanity Fair (1847–8) ch. 35

11 How to live well on nothing a year.
Vanity Fair (1847–8) ch. 36 (title)

12 I think I could be a good woman if I had five thousand a year.
Vanity Fair (1847–8) ch. 36

13 As she had never thought or done anything mortally guilty herself, she had not that abhorrence for wickedness which distinguishes moralists much more knowing.
Vanity Fair (1847–8) ch. 65

14 Ah! *Vanitas Vanitatum!* Which of us is happy in this world? Which of us has his desire? or, having it, is satisfied?—Come, children, let us shut up the box and the puppets, for our play is played out.
Vanity Fair (1847–8) ch. 67

15 Werther had a love for Charlotte
Such as words could never utter;
Would you know how first he met her?
She was cutting bread and butter.
'Sorrows of Werther' (1855)

16 Charlotte, having seen his body
Borne before her on a shutter,
Like a well-conducted person
Went on cutting bread and butter.
'Sorrows of Werther' (1855)

17 Oh, Vanity of vanities!
How wayward the decrees of Fate are;
How very weak the very wise,
How very small the very great are!
'Vanitas Vanitatum'

18 Mind, no biography!
injunction to his daughters
John Sutherland *Is Heathcliff a Murderer?* (1996)

Margaret Thatcher 1925–

British Conservative stateswoman; Prime Minister, 1979–90

on Thatcher: see **Callaghan** *181:13*, **Healey** *366:4*, **Jenkins** *406:8*, **Kinnock** *437:20*, **Mitterrand** *524:10*, **Parris** *568:3*

19 No woman in my time will be Prime Minister or Chancellor or Foreign Secretary—not the top jobs. Anyway I wouldn't want to be Prime Minister. You have to give yourself 100%.
on her appointment as Shadow Education Spokesman
in *Sunday Telegraph* 26 October 1969

20 In politics if you want anything said, ask a man. If you want anything done, ask a woman.
in *People* (New York) 15 September 1975

21 I stand before you tonight in my red chiffon evening gown, my face softly made up, my fair hair gently waved . . . the Iron Lady of the Western World! Me? A cold war warrior? Well, yes—if that is how they wish to interpret my defence of values and freedoms fundamental to our way of life.
speech at Finchley, 31 January 1976; see below:

The iron lady.
name given to Thatcher by the Soviet defence ministry newspaper Red Star, *which accused her of trying to revive the cold war*
in *Sunday Times* 25 January 1976

22 Pennies don't fall from heaven. They have to be earned on earth.
in *Observer* 18 November 1979 'Sayings of the Week'; cf. **Burke** 165:16

23 No one would remember the Good Samaritan if he'd only had good intentions. He had money as well.
television interview, 6 January 1980, in *The Times* 12 January 1980

24 To those waiting with bated breath for that favourite media catchphrase, the U-turn, I have only this to say. 'You turn if you want; the lady's not for turning.'
speech at Conservative Party Conference in Brighton, 10 October 1980; cf. **Fry** 326:21

25 Just rejoice at that news and congratulate our armed forces and the Marines. Rejoice!
on the recapture of South Georgia, usually quoted as, 'Rejoice, rejoice!'
to newsmen outside 10 Downing Street, 25 April 1982

1 It is exciting to have a real crisis on your hands, when you have spent half your political life dealing with humdrum issues like the environment.
on the Falklands campaign, 1982
speech to Scottish Conservative Party conference, 14 May 1982, in Hugo Young *One of Us* (1990) ch. 13

2 We have to see that the spirit of the South Atlantic—the real spirit of Britain—is kindled not only by war but can now be fired by peace. We have the first prerequisite. We know that we can do it—we haven't lost the ability. That is the Falklands Factor.
speech in Cheltenham, 3 July 1982

3 I was asked whether I was trying to restore Victorian values. I said straight out I was. And I am.
speech to the British Jewish Community, 21 July 1983, referring to an interview with Brian Walden on 17 January 1983

4 Now it must be business as usual.
on the steps of Brighton police station a few hours after the bombing of the Grand Hotel, Brighton; often quoted as 'We shall carry on as usual'
in *The Times* 13 October 1984

5 We can do business together.
of Mikhail **Gorbachev**
in *The Times* 18 December 1984

6 We must try to find ways to starve the terrorist and the hijacker of the oxygen of publicity on which they depend.
speech to American Bar Association in London, 15 July 1985, in *The Times* 16 July 1985

7 There is no such thing as Society. There are individual men and women, and there are families.
in *Woman's Own* 31 October 1987

8 We have become a grandmother.
in *The Times* 4 March 1989

9 Advisers advise and ministers decide.
on the respective roles of her personal economic adviser, Alan Walters, and her Chancellor, Nigel **Lawson** *(who resigned the following day)*
in the House of Commons, 26 October 1989

10 I am naturally very sorry to see you go, but understand . . . your wish to be able to spend more time with your family.
reply to Norman **Fowler***'s resignation letter*
in *Guardian* 4 January 1990; cf. **Fowler** 322:2

11 No! No! No!
making clear her opposition to a single European currency, and more centralized controls from Brussels
in the House of Commons, 30 October 1990

12 I fight on, I fight to win.
having failed to win outright in the first ballot for party leader
comment, 21 November 1990

13 It's a funny old world.
on withdrawing from the contest for leadership of the Conservative party
comment, 22 November 1990; cf. **Film lines** 311:17

14 Home is where you come to when you have nothing better to do.
in *Vanity Fair* May 1991

William Roscoe Thayer 1859–1923
American biographer and historian

15 Log-cabin to White House.
title of biography (1910) of James **Garfield**

Themistocles *c.*528–*c.*462 BC
Athenian statesman

16 The wooden wall is your ships.
interpreting the words of the Delphic oracle to the Athenians, before the battle of Salamis in 480 BC
Plutarch *Parallel Lives* 'Themistocles' bk. 2, ch. 1; see below

Yet Zeus the all-seeing grants to Athene's prayer
That the wooden wall only shall not fall, but help
you and your children.
words of the prophetess at Delphi; Herodotus *Histories* bk. 7, sect. 141

Theocritus *c.*300–260 BC
Hellenistic poet

17 Something sweet is the whisper of the pine, O goatherd, that makes her music by yonder springs.
Idylls no. 1

Louis Adolphe Thiers 1797–1877
French statesman and historian

18 [Le roi] *règne et le peuple se gouverne.*
The king reigns, and the people govern themselves.
unsigned article in *Le National*, 20 January 1830; see below:

Le roi n'administre pas, ne gouverne pas, il règne.
The king neither administers nor governs, he reigns.
signed article in *Le National*, 4 February 1830

Thomas à Kempis *c.*1380–1471
German ascetical writer

19 *Opto magis sentire compunctionem: quam scire eius definitionem.*
I would far rather feel remorse than know how to define it.
De Imitatione Christi bk. 1, ch. 1, sect. 3

20 *O quam cito transit gloria mundi.*
Oh how quickly the glory of the world passes away!
De Imitatione Christi bk. 1, ch. 3, sect. 6; cf. **Anonymous** 21:13

21 *Non quaeras quis hoc dixerit: sed, quid diciatur attende.*
Seek not to know who said this or that, but take note of what has been said.
De Imitatione Christi bk. 1, ch. 5, sect. 1

22 *Multo tutius est stare in subiectione: quam in praelatura.*
It is much safer to be in a subordinate position than in authority.
De Imitatione Christi bk. 1, ch. 9, sect. 1

1 *Nam homo proponit, sed Deus disponit.*
For man proposes, but God disposes.
De Imitatione Christi bk. 1, ch. 19, sect. 2; cf. **Proverbs** 606:18

2 *Numquam sis ex toto otiosus, sed aut legens, aut scribens, aut orans, aut meditans, aut aliquid utilitatis pro communi laborans.*
Never be completely idle, but either reading, or writing, or praying, or meditating, or at some useful work for the common good.
De Imitatione Christi bk. 1, ch. 19, sect. 4

3 *Nemo secure praecipit, nisi qui bene obedire didicit.*
Nobody rules safely but he who has learned well how to obey.
De Imitatione Christi bk. 1, ch. 20, sect. 2

4 *Hodie homo est: et cras non comparet. Cum autem sublatus fuerit ab oculis: etiam cito transit a mente.*
Today the man is here; tomorrow he is gone. And when he is 'out of sight', quickly also is he out of mind.
De Imitatione Christi bk. 1, ch. 23, sect. 1; cf. **Proverbs** 609:15

5 *Utinam per unam diem bene essemus conversati in hoc mundo.*
Would that we had spent one whole day well in this world!
De Imitatione Christi bk. 1, ch. 23, sect. 2

6 *Multi annos computant conversionis: sed saepe parvus et fructus emendationis. Si formidolosum est mori: forsitan periculosius erit diutius vivere. Beatus qui horam mortis suae semper ante oculos habet: et ad moriendum cotidiae se disponsit.*
Many count the years since their conversion, but their lives often show little sign of improvement. If it is dreadful to die, it is perhaps more dangerous to live long. Happy is the man who keeps the hour of death always in mind, and daily prepares himself to die.
De Imitatione Christi bk. 1, ch. 23, sect. 2

7 *Passione interdum movemur: et zelum putamus.*
We are sometimes stirred by emotion and take it for zeal.
De Imitatione Christi bk. 2, ch. 5, sect. 1

8 *Si libenter crucem portas portabit te.*
If you bear the cross gladly, it will bear you.
De Imitatione Christi bk. 2, ch. 12, sect. 5

9 *De duobus malis minus est semper eligendum.*
Of the two evils the lesser is always to be chosen.
De Imitatione Christi bk. 3, ch. 12, sect. 2

St Thomas Aquinas c.1225–74

Italian Dominican friar and Doctor of the Church

10 *Pange, lingua, gloriosi*
Corporis mysterium,
Sanguinisque pretiosi,
Quem in mundi pretium
Fructus ventris generosi
Rex effudit gentium.
Now, my tongue, the mystery telling
Of the glorious Body sing,
And the Blood, all price excelling,
Which the Gentiles' Lord and King,
In a Virgin's womb once dwelling,
Shed for this world's ransoming.
'Pange Lingua Gloriosi' (Corpus Christi hymn, translated by J. M. Neale, E. Caswall, and others); cf. **Fortunatus** 321:6

11 *Tantum ergo sacramentum*
Veneremur cernui;
Et antiquum documentum
Novo cedat ritui.
Therefore we, before him bending,
This great Sacrament revere;
Types and shadows have their ending,
For the newer rite is here.
'Pange Lingua Gloriosi' (Corpus Christi hymn, translated by J. M. Neale, E. Caswall, and others)

12 *Multo ergo magis ad moralem pertinet considerare de amicitia quam de justitia.*
Moral science is better occupied when treating of friendship than of justice.
Exposition of Aristotle's Ethics (c.1271) bk. 8, lecture 1

13 *Finis autem nostri desiderii Deus est; unde actus quo ei primo coniungimur, est originaliter et substantialiter nostra beatitudo. Primo autem Deo coniungimur per actum* intellectus*; et ideo ipsa Dei visio, quae est actus intellectus, est substantialiter et originaliter nostra beatitudo.*
Now, the end of our desires is God; hence, the act whereby we are primarily joined to Him is basically and substantially our happiness. But we are primarily united with God by an act of understanding; and therefore, the very seeing of God, which is an act of the intellect, is substantially and basically our happiness.
Quodlibetal Questions (c.1256) vol. 8, bk. 9, pt. 19 (translated by Bourke)

14 *Ergo necesse est devenire ad aliquod primum movens, quod a nullo movetur; et hoc omnes intelligunt Deum.*
Therefore it is necessary to arrive at a prime mover, put in motion by no other; and this everyone understands to be God.
Summa Theologicae (c.1265) pt. 1, qu. 2, art. 3 (translated by English Dominican Fathers)

15 *Si enim omnia mala impedirentur, multa bona deessent universo: non enim esset vita lionis, si non esset occisio animalium; nec esset patientia martyrum, si non esset persecutio tyrannorum.*
If all evil were prevented, much good would be absent from the universe. A lion would cease to live, if there were no slaying of animals; and there would be no patience of martyrs if there were no tyrannical persecution.
Summa Theologicae (c.1265) pt. 1, qu. 22, art. 2 (translated by English Dominican Fathers)

Brandon Thomas 1856–1914

English dramatist

16 I'm Charley's aunt from Brazil—where the nuts come from.
Charley's Aunt (1892) act 1

Dylan Thomas 1914–53

Welsh poet
see also **Opening lines** *556:24*

1 Though they go mad they shall be sane,
Though they sink through the sea they shall rise again;
Though lovers be lost love shall not;
And death shall have no dominion.
'And death shall have no dominion' (1936); cf. **Bible** 105:1

2 Do not go gentle into that good night,
Old age should burn and rave at close of day;
Rage, rage against the dying of the light.
'Do Not Go Gentle into that Good Night' (1952)

3 Now as I was young and easy under the apple boughs
About the lilting house and happy as the grass was green.
'Fern Hill' (1946)

4 Oh as I was young and easy in the mercy of his means,
Time held me green and dying
Though I sang in my chains like the sea.
'Fern Hill' (1946)

5 The force that through the green fuse drives the flower
Drives my green age; that blasts the roots of trees
Is my destroyer.
And I am dumb to tell the crooked rose
My youth is bent by the same wintry fever.
'The force that through the green fuse drives the flower' (1934)

6 And I am dumb to tell the lover's tomb
How at my sheet goes the same crooked worm.
'The force that through the green fuse drives the flower' (1934)

7 The hand that signed the paper felled a city;
Five sovereign fingers taxed the breath,
Doubled the globe of dead and halved a country;
These five kings did a king to death.
'The hand that signed the paper felled a city' (1936)

8 The hand that signed the treaty bred a fever,
And famine grew, and locusts came;
Great is the hand that holds dominion over
Man by a scribbled name.
'The hand that signed the paper felled a city' (1936)

9 Light breaks where no sun shines;
Where no sea runs, the waters of the heart
Push in their tides.
'Light breaks where no sun shines' (1934)

10 It was my thirtieth year to heaven
Woke to my hearing from harbour and neighbour wood
And the mussel pooled and the heron
Priested shore
The morning beckon.
'Poem in October' (1946)

11 Pale rain over the dwindling harbour
And over the sea wet church the size of a snail
With its horns through mist and the castle
Brown as owls
But all the gardens
Of spring and summer were blooming in the tall vales
Beyond the border and under the lark full cloud.
There could I marvel
My birthday
Away but the weather turned around.
'Poem in October' (1946)

12 Deep with the first dead lies London's daughter,
Robed in the long friends,
The grains beyond age, the dark veins of her mother,
Secret by the unmourning water
Of the riding Thames.
After the first death, there is no other.
'A Refusal to Mourn the Death, by Fire, of a Child in London' (1946)

13 I can never remember whether it snowed for six days and six nights when I was twelve or whether it snowed for twelve days and twelve nights when I was six.
A Child's Christmas in Wales (1954)

14 Books that told me everything about the wasp, except why.
A Child's Christmas in Wales (1954)

15 There is only one position for an artist anywhere: and that is, upright.
on the position of the artists of Wales
Quite Early One Morning (1954) pt. 2 'Wales and the Artist'

16 Chasing the naughty couples down the grassgreen gooseberried double bed of the wood.
Under Milk Wood (1954)

17 Before you let the sun in, mind it wipes its shoes.
Under Milk Wood (1954)

18 Oh, isn't life a terrible thing, thank God?
Under Milk Wood (1954) p. 30

19 I want, above all, to work like a fiend, a *good* fiend.
letter to Edith **Sitwell**, 11 April 1947; *Collected Letters* (1987)

20 The land of my fathers. My fathers can have it.
of Wales
in *Adam* December 1953; cf. **James** 402:21

21 A man you don't like who drinks as much as you do.
definition of an alcoholic
Constantine Fitzgibbon *Life of Dylan Thomas* (1965) ch. 6

22 Poetry is not the most important thing in life . . . I'd much rather lie in a hot bath reading Agatha Christie and sucking sweets.
Joan Wyndham *Love is Blue* (1986) 6 July 1943

Edward Thomas 1878–1917

English poet

23 Yes; I remember Adlestrop—
The name, because one afternoon
Of heat the express-train drew up there
Unwontedly. It was late June.
'Adlestrop' (1917)

24 The past is the only dead thing that smells sweet.
'Early one morning in May I set out' (1917)

1 If I should ever by chance grow rich
I'll buy Codham, Cockridden, and Childerditch,
Roses, Pyrgo, and Lapwater,
And let them all to my elder daughter.
'Household Poems: Bronwen' (1917)

2 I have come to the borders of sleep,
The unfathomable deep
Forest where all must lose
Their way, however straight
Or winding, soon or late;
They can not choose.
'Lights Out' (1917)

3 As for myself,
Where first I met the bitter scent is lost.
I, too, often shrivel the grey shreds,
Sniff them and think and sniff again and try
Once more to think what it is I am remembering,
Always in vain. I cannot like the scent,
Yet I would gather up others more sweet,
With no meaning, than this bitter one.

I have mislaid the key. I sniff the spray
And think of nothing; I see and hear nothing;
Yet seem, too, to be listening, lying in wait
For what I should, yet never can, remember.
No garden appears, no path, no hoar-green bush
Of Lad's-love, or Old Man, no child beside,
Neither father nor mother, nor any playmate;
Only an avenue, dark, nameless, without end.
'Old Man' (1917)

4 Out in the dark over the snow
The fallow fawns invisible go
With the fallow doe;
And the winds blow
Fast as the stars are slow.
'Out in the dark' (1917)

5 As well as any bloom upon a flower
I like the dust on the nettles, never lost
Except to prove the sweetness of a shower.
'Tall Nettles' (1917)

Elizabeth Thomas 1675–1731
English poet

6 From marrying in haste, and repenting at leisure;
Not liking the person, yet liking his treasure:
Libera nos.
'A New Litany, occasioned by an invitation to a wedding' (1722); cf. **Proverbs** 606:31

Gwyn Thomas 1913–81
Welsh novelist and dramatist

7 I wanted a play that would paint the full face of sensuality, rebellion and revivalism. In South Wales these three phenomena have played second fiddle only to Rugby Union which is a distillation of all three.
introduction to *Jackie the Jumper* (1962)

8 There are still parts of Wales where the only concession to gaiety is a striped shroud.
in *Punch* 18 June 1958

Irene Thomas
British writer and broadcaster

9 Protestant women may take the pill. Roman Catholic women must keep taking The Tablet.
in *Guardian* 28 December 1990

R. S. Thomas 1913–
Welsh poet and clergyman

10 The ousel singing in the woods of Cilgwri,
Tirelessly as a stream over the mossed stones,
Is not so old as the toad of Cors Fochno
Who feels the cold skin sagging round his bones.
'The Ancients of the World' (1952)

11 Or the dry whisper of unseen wings,
Bats not angels, in the high roof.
'In a Country Church' (1955)

12 Doctors in verse
Being scarce now, most poets
Are their own patients, compelled to treat
Themselves first, their complaint being
Peculiar always.
'The Cure' (1958)

13 There is no love
For such, only a willed
gentleness.
'They' (1968)

14 Hate takes a long time
To grow in, and mine
Has increased from birth;
Not for the brute earth . . .
. . . I find
This hate's for my own kind . . .
'Those Others' (1961)

15 God is that great absence
In our lives, the empty silence
Within, the place where we go
Seeking, not in hope to
Arrive or find.
'Via Negativa' (1972)

16 There is no present in Wales,
And no future;
There is only the past,
Brittle with relics . . .
And an impotent people,
Sick with inbreeding,
Worrying the carcase of an old song.
'Welsh Landscape' (1955)

Emma Thompson 1959–
British actress

17 Marriages stop. Marriages change. People are always saying a marriage 'failed'. It's such a negative way of putting it . . . Failure is terribly important. Perhaps that's why I'm saying: the notion that failure is a negative thing is wrong.
in *Vanity Fair* February 1996

Francis Thompson 1859–1907

English poet

1 As the run-stealers flicker to and fro,
To and fro:—
O my Hornby and my Barlow long ago!
'At Lord's' (1913)

2 The fairest things have fleetest end,
Their scent survives their close:
But the rose's scent is bitterness
To him that loved the rose!
'Daisy' (1913)

3 Nothing begins, and nothing ends,
That is not paid with moan;
For we are born in other's pain,
And perish in our own.
'Daisy' (1913)

4 I fled Him, down the nights and down the days;
I fled Him, down the arches of the years;
I fled Him, down the labyrinthine ways
Of my own mind; and in the mist of tears
I hid from Him, and under running laughter.
'The Hound of Heaven' (1913) pt. 1

5 But with unhurrying chase,
And unperturbèd pace,
Deliberate speed, majestic instancy,
They beat—and a Voice beat
More instant than the Feet—
All things betray thee, who betrayest Me.
'The Hound of Heaven' (1913) pt. 1

6 I said to Dawn: Be sudden—to Eve:
Be soon.
'The Hound of Heaven' (1913) pt. 2

7 Such is: what is to be?
The pulp so bitter, how shall taste the rind?
'The Hound of Heaven' (1913) pt. 4

8 Yet ever and anon a trumpet sounds
From the hid battlements of Eternity;
Those shaken mists a space unsettle, then
Round the half-glimpsèd turrets slowly wash again.
'The Hound of Heaven' (1913) pt. 4

9 Now of that long pursuit
Comes on at hand the bruit;
That Voice is round me like a bursting sea:
'And is thy earth so marred,
Shattered in shard on shard?
Lo, all things fly thee, for thou fliest Me!'
'The Hound of Heaven' (1913) pt. 5

10 There is no expeditious road
To pack and label men for God,
And save them by the barrel-load.
Some may perchance, with strange surprise,
Have blundered into Paradise.
'A Judgement in Heaven' (1913) epilogue

11 O world invisible, we view thee,
O world intangible, we touch thee,
O world unknowable, we know thee,
Inapprehensible, we clutch thee!
'The Kingdom of God' (1913)

12 The angels keep their ancient places;—
Turn but a stone, and start a wing!
'Tis ye, 'tis your estrangèd faces,
That miss the many-splendoured thing.
'The Kingdom of God' (1913)

13 Upon thy so sore loss
Shall shine the traffic of Jacob's ladder
Pitched betwixt Heaven and Charing Cross.
'The Kingdom of God' (1913)

14 And lo, Christ walking on the water
Not of Gennesareth, but Thames!
'The Kingdom of God' (1913)

15 Look for me in the nurseries of heaven.
'To My Godchild Francis M.W.M.' (1913)

16 What heart could have thought you?—
Past our devisal
(O filigree petal!)
Fashioned so purely,
Fragilely, surely,
From what Paradisal
Imagineless metal,
Too costly for cost?
'To a Snowflake' (1913)

17 Insculped and embossed,
With His hammer of wind,
And His graver of frost.
'To a Snowflake' (1913)

Julian Thompson 1934–

British soldier, second-in-command of the land forces during the Falklands campaign.

18 You don't mind dying for Queen and country, but you certainly don't want to die for politicians.
'The Falklands War—the Untold Story' (Yorkshire Television) 1 April 1987; cf. **France** 322:19, **Graham** 348:1

William Hepworth Thompson 1810–86

English classicist; Master of Trinity College, Cambridge, from 1866

19 What time he can spare from the adornment of his person he devotes to the neglect of his duties.
of Sir Richard Jebb, later Professor of Greek at Cambridge University, in M. R. Bobbit *With Dearest Love to All* (1960) ch. 7

James Thomson 1700–48

Scottish poet

20 When Britain first, at heaven's command,
Arose from out the azure main,
This was the charter of the land,
And guardian angels sung this strain:
'Rule, Britannia, rule the waves;
Britons never will be slaves.'
Alfred: a Masque (1740) act 2

21 Soft quilts on quilts, on carpets carpets spread,
And couches stretch around in seemly band;
And endless pillows rise to prop the head.
The Castle of Indolence (1748) canto 1, st. 33

22 A bard here dwelt, more fat than bard beseems.
The Castle of Indolence (1748) canto 1, st. 68 (of himself)

23 A little round, fat, oily man of God,
Was one I chiefly marked among the fry:

He had a roguish twinkle in his eye.
The Castle of Indolence (1748) canto 1, st. 69

1 Here lies a man who never lived,
Yet still from death was flying;
Who, if not sick, was never well;
And died—for fear of dying!
'Epitaph on Solomon Mendez' (published 1782)

2 Still as I gazed new beauties met my sight.
letter to Elizabeth Young, 19 April 1743

3 But now those white unblemished minutes, whence
The fabling poets took their golden age,
Are found no more amid these iron times,
These dregs of life!
The Seasons (1746) 'Spring' l. 272

4 The daisy, primrose, violet, darkly blue,
And polyanthus of unnumbered dyes;
The yellow wall-flower, stained with iron brown;
And lavish stock that scents the garden round.
The Seasons (1746) 'Spring' l. 531

5 Delightful task! to rear the tender thought,
To teach the young idea how to shoot.
The Seasons (1746) 'Spring' l. 1152

6 An elegant sufficiency, content,
Retirement, rural quiet, friendship, books.
The Seasons (1746) 'Spring' l. 1161

7 O'er heaven and earth, far as the ranging eye
Can sweep, a dazzling deluge reigns; and all
From pole to pole is undistinguished blaze.
The Seasons (1746) 'Summer' l. 434

8 Ships, dim-discovered, dropping from the clouds.
The Seasons (1746) 'Summer' l. 946

9 Sighed and looked unutterable things.
The Seasons (1746) 'Summer' l. 1188

10 While listening senates hang upon thy tongue.
The Seasons (1746) 'Autumn' l. 15

11 For loveliness
Needs not the foreign aid of ornament,
But is when unadorned adorned the most.
The Seasons (1746) 'Autumn' l. 204

12 Find other lands beneath another sun.
The Seasons (1746) 'Autumn' l. 1286

13 Poor is the triumph o'er the timid hare!
The Seasons (1746) 'Autumn' l. 401

14 See, Winter comes to rule the varied year,
Sullen and sad.
The Seasons (1746) 'Winter' l. 1

15 Welcome, kindred glooms!
Congenial horrors, hail!
The Seasons (1746) 'Winter' l. 5

16 Studious let me sit,
And hold high converse with the mighty dead.
The Seasons (1746) 'Winter' l. 431

17 For ever, Fortune, wilt thou prove
An unrelenting foe to Love;
And, when we meet a mutual heart,
Come in between and bid us part?
'Song' (1732)

18 Even Light itself, which every thing displays,
Shone undiscovered, till his brighter mind
Untwisted all the shining robe of day.
on **Newton**'*s* Opticks
'To the Memory of Sir Isaac Newton' (1727) l. 96

19 Did ever poet image aught so fair,
Dreaming in whispering groves, by the hoarse brook!
Or prophet, to whose rapture heaven descends!
on **Newton**'*s explanation of the rainbow in terms of refraction*
'To the Memory of Sir Isaac Newton' (1727) l. 96

James Thomson 1834–82

Scottish poet

20 The city of dreadful night.
title of poem, written 1870–3

21 The City is of Night; perchance of Death,
But certainly of Night.
'The City of Dreadful Night' (written 1870–3)

22 As we rush, as we rush in the train,
The trees and the houses go wheeling back,
But the starry heavens above that plain
Come flying on our track.
'Sunday at Hampstead' (written 1863–5) st. 10

23 Give a man a horse he can ride,
Give a man a boat he can sail.
'Sunday up the River' (written 1865) st. 15

Roy Thomson 1894–1976

Canadian-born British newspaper proprietor

24 Like having your own licence to print money.
on the profitability of commercial television in Britain
R. Braddon *Roy Thomson* (1965) ch. 32

Henry David Thoreau 1817–62

American writer
on Thoreau: see **James** 403:5

25 I heartily accept the motto, 'That government is best which governs least' . . . Carried out, it finally amounts to this, which I also believe,— 'That government is best which governs not at all.'
Civil Disobedience (1849); cf. **O'Sullivan** 560:18

26 Under a government which imprisons any unjustly, the true place for a just man is also a prison.
Civil Disobedience (1849)

27 Some circumstantial evidence is very strong, as when you find a trout in the milk.
Journal 11 November 1850

28 We do not enjoy poetry unless we know it to be poetry.
Journal 1 October 1856

29 Not that the story need be long, but it will take a long while to make it short.
letter to Harrison Blake, 16 November 1857, in *Writings* (1906 ed.) vol. 6; cf. **Pascal** 568:6

1 By avarice and selfishness, and a grovelling habit, from which none of us is free, of regarding the soil as property . . . the landscape is deformed.
Walden (1854) 'The Bean Field'

2 I have travelled a good deal in Concord.
Walden (1854) 'Economy'

3 As if you could kill time without injuring eternity.
Walden (1854) 'Economy'

4 The mass of men lead lives of quiet desperation.
Walden (1854) 'Economy'; in *Histoire de ma vie* vol. 4 (1854), George Sand described Chopin as being in a state of '*désespérance tranquille*'

5 In any weather, at any hour of the day or night, I have been anxious to improve the nick of time, and notch it on my stick too; to stand on the meeting of two eternities, the past and the future, which is precisely the present moment; to toe that line.
Walden (1854) 'Economy'

6 Beware of all enterprises that require new clothes.
Walden (1854) 'Economy'

7 For more than five years I maintained myself thus solely by the labour of my hands, and I found, that by working about six weeks in a year, I could meet all the expenses of living.
Walden (1854) 'Economy'

8 As for Doing-good, that is one of the professions which are full.
Walden (1854) 'Economy'

9 The three-o'-clock in the morning courage, which Bonaparte thought was the rarest.
Walden (1854) 'Sounds'; cf. **Napoleon** 538:17

10 Wherever a man goes, men will pursue him and paw him with their dirty institutions, and, if they can, constrain him to belong to their desperate oddfellow society.
Walden (1854) 'The Village'

11 I had three chairs in my house; one for solitude, two for friendship, three for society.
Walden (1854) 'Visitors'

12 I wanted to live deep and suck out all the marrow of life . . . to drive life into a corner, and reduce it to its lowest terms, and, if it proved to be mean, why then to get the whole and genuine meanness of it, and publish its meanness to the world; or if it were sublime, to know it by experience.
Walden (1854) 'Where I lived, and what I lived for'

13 Our life is frittered away by detail . . . Simplify, simplify.
Walden (1854) 'Where I lived, and what I lived for'

14 I once had a sparrow alight upon my shoulder for a moment while I was hoeing in a village garden, and I felt that I was more distinguished by that circumstance than I should have been by any epaulette I could have worn.
Walden (1854) 'Winter Animals'

15 It is not worthwhile to go around the world to count the cats in Zanzibar.
Walden (1854) 'Conclusion'

16 If a man does not keep pace with his companions, perhaps it is because he hears a different drummer. Let him step to the music which he hears, however measured or far away.
Walden (1854) 'Conclusion'

17 The government of the world I live in was not framed, like that of Britain, in after-dinner conversations over the wine.
Walden (1854) 'Conclusion'

18 It takes two to speak the truth,—one to speak, and another to hear.
A Week on the Concord and Merrimack Rivers (1849) 'Wednesday'

19 It were treason to our love
And a sin to God above
One iota to abate
Of a pure impartial hate.
'Indeed, Indeed I Cannot Tell' (1852)

Robert Thorne d. 1527
English merchant and geographical writer

20 There is no land unhabitable nor sea innavigable.
Richard Hakluyt *The Principal Navigations, Voyages, and Discoveries of the English Nation* (1589)

Jeremy Thorpe 1929–
British Liberal politician

21 Greater love hath no man than this, that he lay down his friends for his life.
on Harold ***Macmillan***'*s sacking seven of his Cabinet on 13 July 1962*
D. E. Butler and Anthony King *The General Election of 1964* (1965) ch. 1; cf. **Bible** 102:22

Thucydides *c.*455–*c.*400 BC
Greek historian

22 Happiness depends on being free, and freedom depends on being courageous.
Thucydides *History of the Peloponnesian War* bk. 2, ch. 4, sect. 43 (translated by Rex Warner)

James Thurber 1894–1961
American humorist

23 Her own mother lived the latter years of her life in the horrible suspicion that electricity was dripping invisibly all over the house.
My Life and Hard Times (1933) ch. 2

24 You might as well fall flat on your face as lean over too far backward.
'The Bear Who Let It Alone' in *New Yorker* 29 April 1939

25 The war between men and women.
cartoon series title in *New Yorker* 20 January–28 April 1934

26 It's a naïve domestic Burgundy without any breeding, but I think you'll be amused by its presumption.
cartoon caption in *New Yorker* 27 March 1937

27 Well, if I called the wrong number, why did you answer the phone?
cartoon caption in *New Yorker* 5 June 1937

1 Early to rise and early to bed makes a male healthy and wealthy and dead.

'The Shrike and the Chipmunks' in *New Yorker* 18 February 1939; cf. **Proverbs** 599:4

2 It's our *own* story *exactly*! He bold as a hawk, she soft as the dawn.

cartoon caption in *New Yorker* 25 February 1939; cf. **Lover** 477:4

3 Humour is emotional chaos remembered in tranquillity.

in *New York Post* 29 February 1960; cf. **Wordsworth** 832:20

Edward, Lord Thurlow 1731–1806

English jurist; Lord Chancellor, 1778–83, 1783–92

4 Corporations have neither bodies to be punished, nor souls to be condemned, they therefore do as they like.

usually quoted as 'Did you ever expect a corporation to have a conscience, when it has no soul to be damned, and no body to be kicked?'

John Poynder *Literary Extracts* (1844) vol. 1; cf. **Coke** 224:12, **Proverbs** 597:37

Edward, Lord Thurlow 1781–1829

English poet

5 Nature is always wise in every part.

'To a Bird, that haunted the Waters of Lacken, in the Winter'

Anthony Thwaite 1930–

English writer

6 The name is history.
The thick Miljacka flows
Under its bridges through a canyon's breadth
Fretted with minarets and plump with domes,
Cupped in its mountains, caught on a drawn breath.

'Sarajevo: I' (1973)

Tibullus (Albius Tibullus) *c.*50–19 BC

Roman poet

7 *Te spectem, suprema mihi cum venerit hora,*
Et teneam moriens deficiente manu.

May I be looking at you when my last hour has come, and dying may I hold you with my weakening hand.

Elegies bk. 1, no. 1, l. 59

8 *Te propter nullos tellus tua postulat imbres,*
Arida nec pluvio supplicat herba Iovi.

Because of you your land never pleads for showers, nor does its parched grass pray to Jupiter the Rain-giver.

of the River Nile in Egypt

Elegies bk. 1, no. 7, l. 25

9 *Periuria ridet amantum Iuppiter*

Jupiter laughs at lovers' perjuries.

Elegies bk. 3, no. 6, l. 49; cf. **Proverbs** 604:45

Chidiock Tichborne *c.*1558–86

English Roman Catholic conspirator

10 My prime of youth is but a frost of cares;
My feast of joy is but a dish of pain;
My crop of corn is but a field of tares;
And all my good is but vain hope of gain.
The day is past, and yet I saw no sun;
And now I live, and now my life is done.

'Elegy' (composed in the Tower of London prior to his execution)

Thomas Tickell 1686–1740

English poet

11 There taught us how to live; and (oh! too high
The price for knowledge) taught us how to die.

'To the Earl of Warwick. On the Death of Mr Addison' (1721) l. 76

Lionel Tiger 1937–

American anthropologist

12 Male bonding.

Men in Groups (1969)

Paul Tillich 1886–1965

German-born Protestant theologian

13 Neurosis is the way of avoiding non-being by avoiding being.

The Courage To Be (1952) pt. 2, ch. 3

14 Faith is the state of being ultimately concerned.

Dynamics of Faith (1957) ch. 1

Tipu Sultan *c.*1750–99

15 In this world I would rather live two days like a tiger, than two hundred years like a sheep.

Alexander Beatson *A View of the Origin and Conduct of the War with Tippoo Sultan* (1800) ch. 10

Titus (Titus Flavius Vespasianus) AD 39–81

Roman emperor from AD 79

16 *Amici, diem perdidi.*

Friends, I have lost a day.

on reflecting that he had done nothing to help anybody all day

Suetonius *Lives of the Caesars* 'Titus' ch. 8, sect. 1

□ Toasts

see box overleaf

see also ***Bossidy*** *143:15,* ***Decatur*** *254:10,* ***Jackson*** *400:13*

Alexis de Tocqueville 1805–59

French historian and politician

17 Freedom alone substitutes from time to time for the love of material comfort more powerful and more lofty passions; it alone supplies ambition with greater objectives than the acquisition of riches, and creates the light that makes it possible to see and to judge the vices and virtues of mankind.

L'Ancien régime (1856, ed. J. P. Mayer, 1951; translated by M. W. Patterson, 1933)

continued

Toasts

1 George Washington, Commander of the American Armies, who, like Joshua of old, commanded the sun and the moon to stand still, and they obeyed him.

proposed by Benjamin **Franklin** *(1706–90) at a dinner at Versailles, supposedly after the British minister had proposed a toast to* **George III**, *likening him to the sun, and the French minister had likened* **Louis XVI** *to the moon*

attributed, perhaps apocryphal

2 Here's tae us; wha's like us?
Gey few, and they're a' deid.

Scottish toast, probably of 19th-century origin; the first line appears in T. W. H. Crosland *The Unspeakable Scot* (1902), and various versions of the second line are current

3 If I am obliged to bring religion into after-dinner toasts (which indeed does not seem quite the thing) I shall drink—to the Pope, if you please—still, to Conscience first, and to the Pope afterwards.

John Henry Newman *A Letter Addressed to the Duke of Norfolk . . .* (1875) sect. 5

4 The King over the Water.

Jacobite toast (18th-century)

5 A willing foe and sea room.

naval toast in the time of **Nelson**

W. N. T. Beckett *A Few Naval Customs, Expressions, Traditions, and Superstitions* (1931) 'Customs'

Alexis de Tocqueville *continued*

6 Where is the man of soul so base that he would prefer to depend on the caprices of one of his fellow men rather than obey the laws which he has himself contributed to establish?

L'Ancien régime (1856)

7 Despots themselves do not deny that freedom is excellent; only they desire it for themselves alone, and they maintain that everyone else is altogether unworthy of it.

L'Ancien régime (1856)

8 The French Revolution operated in reference to this world in exactly the same manner as religious revolutions acted in view of the other world. It considered the citizen as an abstract proposition apart from any particular society, in the same way as religions considered man as man, independent of country and time.

L'Ancien régime (1856)

9 History is a gallery of pictures in which there are few originals and many copies.

L'Ancien régime (1856)

10 He who desires in liberty anything other than itself is born to be a servant.

L'Ancien régime (1856)

11 It is not always by going from bad to worse that a society falls into revolution . . . The social order destroyed by a revolution is almost always better than that which immediately preceded it, and experience shows that the most dangerous moment for a bad government is generally that in which it sets about reform.

L'Ancien régime (1856)

12 Providence has not created mankind entirely independent or entirely free. It is true that around every man a fatal circle is traced, beyond which he cannot pass; but within the wide verge of that circle he is powerful and free.

De la Démocratie en Amérique (1835–40, translated by H. Reeve, 1841, ed. J. P. Mayer, 1951) vol. 1

13 Of all nations, those submit to civilization with the most difficulty which habitually live by the chase.

De la Démocratie en Amérique (1835–40) vol. 1

14 What is understood by republican government in the United States is the slow and quiet action of society upon itself.

De la Démocratie en Amérique (1835–40) vol. 1

15 There are, at the present time, two great nations in the world, which seem to tend towards the same end, although they started from different points; I allude to the Russians and the Americans . . . Their starting point is different, and their courses are not the same; yet each of them seems to be marked out by the will of Heaven to sway the destinies of half the globe.

De la Démocratie en Amérique (1835–40) vol. 1

16 Unable to judge at once of the social position of those he meets, an Englishman prudently avoids all contact with them. Men are afraid less some slight service rendered should draw them into an unsuitable acquaintance; they dread civilities, and they avoid the obtrusive gratitude of a stranger quite as much as his hatred.

De la Démocratie en Amérique (1835–40)

17 The French want no-one to be their *superior*. The English want *inferiors*. The Frenchman constantly raises his eyes above him with anxiety. The Englishman lowers his beneath him with satisfaction. On either side it is pride, but understood in a different way.

Voyage en Angleterre et en Irlande de 1835 (ed. J. P. Mayer, 1958) 8 May 1835

18 It is from the midst of this putrid sewer that the greatest river of human industry springs up and carries fertility to the whole world. From this foul drain pure gold flows forth. Here it is that humanity achieves for itself both perfection and brutalization, that civilization produces its

wonders, and that civilized man becomes again almost a savage.
of Manchester

Voyage en Angleterre et en Irlande de 1835 (ed. J. P. Mayer, 1958) 2 July 1835

Alvin Toffler 1928–

American writer

1 Culture shock is relatively mild in comparison with a much more serious malady that might be called 'future shock'. Future shock is the dizzying disorientation brought on by the premature arrival of the future.

in *Horizon* Summer 1965; the book *Future Shock* was published 1970

J. R. R. Tolkien 1892–1973

British philologist and writer

on Tolkien: see **Pratchett** 591:3; *see also* **Opening lines** 555:16

2 Never laugh at live dragons.

The Hobbit (1937) ch. 12

3 One Ring to rule them all, One Ring to find them
One Ring to bring them all and in the darkness
bind them.

The Fellowship of the Ring (1954) epigraph

4 Do not meddle in the affairs of Wizards, for they are subtle and quick to anger.

The Lord of the Rings pt. 1 *The Fellowship of the Ring* (1954) bk. 1, ch. 3

5 A real taste for fairy-stories was wakened by philology on the threshold of manhood, and quickened to full life by war.

Tree and Leaf (1964) 'On Fairy-Stories'

Leo Tolstoy 1828–1910

Russian novelist

6 All happy families resemble one another, but each unhappy family is unhappy in its own way.

Anna Karenina (1875–7) pt. 1, ch. 1 (translated by A. and L. Maude)

7 A desire for desires—boredom.

Anna Karenina (1875–7) pt. 5, ch. 8 (translated by A. and L. Maude)

8 There are no conditions of life to which a man cannot get accustomed, especially if he sees them accepted by everyone about him.

Anna Karenina (1875–7) pt. 7, ch. 13 (translated by Rosemary Edmonds)

9 The candle by which she had been reading the book filled with trouble and deceit, sorrow and evil, flared up with a brighter light, illuminating for her everything that before had been enshrouded in darkness, flickered, grew dim, and went out for ever.

Anna Karenina (1875–7) pt. 7, ch. 31 (translated by Rosemary Edmonds)

10 The hero of my tale—whom I love with all the power of my soul, whom I have tried to portray in all his beauty, who has been, is, and will be beautiful—is Truth.

Sevastopol in May (1855) ch. 16 (translated by A. and L. Maude)

11 In historical events great men—so-called—are but labels serving to give a name to the event, and like labels they have the least possible connexion with the event itself.

War and Peace (1868–9) bk. 3, pt. 1, ch. 1 (translated by Rosemary Edmonds)

12 The cudgel of the people's war was lifted with all its menacing and majestic might, and caring nothing for good taste and procedure, with dull-witted simplicity but sound judgement it rose and fell, making no distinctions.

War and Peace (1868–9) bk. 4, pt. 3, ch. 1 (translated by Rosemary Edmonds)

13 Our body is a machine for living. It is organized for that, it is its nature. Let life go on in it unhindered and let it defend itself, it will do more than if you paralyse it by encumbering it with remedies.

War and Peace (1865–9) bk. 10, ch. 29 (translated by A. and L. Maude); cf. **Le Corbusier** 461:13

14 I sit on a man's back, choking him and making him carry me, and yet assure myself and others that I am very sorry for him and wish to ease his lot by all possible means—except by getting off his back.

What Then Must We Do? (1886) ch. 16 (translated by A. Maude)

15 All newspaper and journalistic activity is an intellectual brothel from which there is no retreat.

letter to Prince V. P. Meshchersky, 22 August 1871, in *Letters* (ed. R. F. Christian, 1978) vol. 1

Augustus Montague Toplady 1740–78

English clergyman

16 Rock of Ages, cleft for me,
Let me hide myself in Thee.
Let the water and the blood,
From Thy riven side which flowed,
Be of sin the double cure,
Cleanse me from its guilt and power.

'Rock of Ages, cleft for me' (1776 hymn)

Michael Torke 1961–

American composer

17 Why waste money on psychotherapy when you can listen to the B Minor Mass?

in *Observer* 23 September 1990 'Sayings of the Week'

Robert Torrens 1780–1864

British economist

18 In the first stone which he [the savage] flings at the wild animals he pursues, in the first stick that he seizes to strike down the fruit which hangs above his reach, we see the appropriation of one article for the purpose of aiding in the acquisition of another, and thus discover the origin of capital.

An Essay on the Production of Wealth (1821) ch. 2

Arturo Toscanini 1867–1957
Italian conductor

1 I smoked my first cigarette and kissed my first woman on the same day. I have never had time for tobacco since.
in *Observer* 30 June 1946

Cyril Tourneur see **Thomas Middleton**

A. Toussenel 1803–85
French writer

2 *Plus on apprend à connaître l'homme, plus on apprend à estimer le chien.*
The more one gets to know of men, the more one values dogs.
L'Esprit des bêtes (1847) ch. 3; cf. **Roland** 632:4

Pete Townshend 1945–
British rock musician and songwriter

3 Hope I die before I get old.
'My Generation' (1965 song)

Arnold Toynbee 1889–1975
English historian

4 Civilization is a movement and not a condition, a voyage and not a harbour.
in *Readers Digest* October 1958

5 The twentieth century will be remembered chiefly, not as an age of political conflicts and technical inventions, but as an age in which human society dared to think of the health of the whole human race as a practical objective.
attributed

Polly Toynbee 1946–
English journalist

6 Feminism is the most revolutionary idea there has ever been. Equality for women demands a change in the human psyche more profound than anything Marx dreamed of. It means valuing parenthood as much as we value banking.
in *Guardian* 19 January 1987

7 It is Stupidvision—where most of the presenters look like they have to pretend to be stupid because they think their audience is . . . It patronises. It talks to the vacuum cleaner and the washing machine and the microwave without much contact with the human brain.
of daytime television
in *Radio Times* 11 May 1996

Thomas Traherne *c.*1637–74
English mystic

8 An empty book is like an infant's soul, in which anything may be written. It is capable of all things, but containeth nothing.
Centuries of Meditations 'First Century' opening line

9 You never enjoy the world aright, till the sea itself floweth in your veins, till you are clothed with the heavens, and crowned with the stars: and perceive yourself to be the sole heir of the whole world.
Centuries of Meditations 'First Century' sect. 29

10 Will you see the infancy of this sublime and celestial greatness?
Centuries of Meditations 'Third Century' sect. 1

11 All appeared new, and strange at first, inexpressibly rare and delightful and beautiful. I was a little stranger, which at my entrance into the world was saluted and surrounded with innumerable joys. My knowledge was divine.
Centuries of Meditations 'Third Century' sect. 2

12 All things were spotless and pure and glorious . . . I knew not that there were any sins or complaints or laws. I dreamed not of poverties, contentions or vices. All tears and quarrels were hidden from my eyes. Everything was at rest, free and immortal.
Centuries of Meditations 'Third Century' sect. 2

13 The corn was orient and immortal wheat, which never should be reaped, nor was ever sown. I thought it had stood from everlasting to everlasting.
Centuries of Meditations 'Third Century' sect. 3

14 The green trees when I saw them first . . . transported and ravished me, their sweetness and unusual beauty made my heart to leap and almost mad with ecstasy, they were such strange and wonderful things.
Centuries of Meditations 'Third Century' sect. 3

15 O what venerable creatures did the aged seem! Immortal cherubims! And young men glittering and sparkling angels, and maids strange seraphic pieces of life and beauty! Boys and girls tumbling in the street, and playing, were moving jewels. I knew not that they were born or should die; but all things abided eternally.
Centuries of Meditations 'Third Century' sect. 3

16 The hands are a sort of feet, which serve us in our passage towards Heaven, curiously distinguished into joints and fingers, and fit to be applied to any thing which reason can imagine or desire.
Meditations on the Six Days of Creation (1717) 'Sixth Day'

17 Contentment is a sleepy thing
If it in death alone must die;
A quiet mind is worse than poverty,
Unless it from enjoyment spring!
That's blessedness alone that makes a King!
'Of Contentment'

18 I within did flow
With seas of life, like wine.
I nothing in this world did know,
But 'twas divine!
'Wonder'

Henry Duff Traill 1842–1900
British journalist

19 Look in my face. My name is Used-to-was;
I am also called Played-out and Done-to-death,
And It-will-wash-no-more.
'After Dilettante Concetti' (i.e. Dante Gabriel Rossetti) st. 8; cf. **Rossetti** 635:5

Joseph Trapp 1679–1747
English poet and pamphleteer

1 The King, observing with judicious eyes
The state of both his universities,
To Oxford sent a troop of horse, and why?
That learned body wanted loyalty;
To Cambridge books, as very well discerning
How much that loyal body wanted learning.
lines written on **George I**'s *donation of the Bishop of Ely's Library to Cambridge University*
John Nichols *Literary Anecdotes* (1812–16) vol. 3; cf. **Browne** 154:7

Merle Travis 1917–83
American country singer

2 Sixteen tons, what do you get?
Another day older and deeper in debt.
Say brother, don't you call me 'cause I can't go
I owe my soul to the company store.
'Sixteen Tons' (1947 song)

Herbert Beerbohm Tree 1852–1917
English actor-manager

3 He is an old bore. Even the grave yawns for him.
of Israel **Zangwill**
Max Beerbohm *Herbert Beerbohm Tree* (1920) appendix 4

4 Ladies, just a little more virginity, if you don't mind.
to a motley collection of females, assembled to play ladies-in-waiting to a queen
Alexander Woollcott *Shouts and Murmurs* (1923) 'Capsule Criticism'

5 My poor fellow, why not carry a watch?
to a man in the street, carrying a grandfather clock
Hesketh Pearson *Beerbohm Tree* (1956) ch. 12

6 Sirs, I have tested your machine. It adds a new terror to life and makes death a long-felt want.
when pressed by a gramophone company for a written testimonial
Hesketh Pearson *Beerbohm Tree* (1956) ch. 19; cf. **Wetherell** 812:22

G. M. Trevelyan 1876–1962
English historian

7 Disinterested intellectual curiosity is the life-blood of real civilization.
English Social History (1942) introduction

8 If the French noblesse had been capable of playing cricket with their peasants, their chateaux would never have been burnt.
English Social History (1942) ch. 8

9 [Education] has produced a vast population able to read but unable to distinguish what is worth reading, an easy prey to sensations and cheap appeals.
English Social History (1942) ch. 18

10 In a world of voluble hates, he plotted to make men like, or at least tolerate one another.
of Stanley **Baldwin**
in *Dictionary of National Biography 1941–50* (1959)

William Trevor (William Trevor Cox) 1928–
Anglo-Irish novelist and short story writer

11 A disease in the family that is never mentioned.
of the troubles in Northern Ireland
in *Observer* 18 November 1990

Calvin Trillin 1935–
American journalist and writer

12 The shelf life of the modern hardback writer is somewhere between the milk and the yoghurt.
in *Sunday Times* 9 June 1991; attributed

David Trimble 1944–
Northern Irish politician, leader of the Ulster Unionists

13 We are not here to negotiate with them, but to confront them.
on entering the Mitchell talks on Northern Ireland with Sinn Feinn
in *Guardian* 18 September 1997

14 The fundamental Act of Union is there, intact.
of the Northern Ireland settlement
in *Daily Telegraph* 11 April 1998

15 Once we are agreed our only weapons will be our words, then there is nothing that cannot be said, there is nothing that cannot be achieved.
in *Guardian* 4 September 1998

Tommy Trinder 1909–89
British comedian

16 Overpaid, overfed, oversexed, and over here.
of American troops in Britain during the Second World War
associated with Trinder, but probably not his invention

Anthony Trollope 1815–82
English novelist

17 He must have known me had he seen me as he was wont to see me, for he was in the habit of flogging me constantly. Perhaps he did not recognize me by my face.
Autobiography (1883) ch. 1

18 Take away from English authors their copyrights, and you would very soon take away from England her authors.
Autobiography (1883) ch. 6

19 A novel can hardly be made interesting or successful without love . . . It is necessary because the passion is one which interests or has interested all. Everyone feels it, has felt it, or expects to feel it.
Autobiography (1883) ch. 12

20 Three hours a day will produce as much as a man ought to write.
Autobiography (1883) ch. 15

21 A man who entertains in his mind any political doctrine, except as a means of improving the condition of his fellows, I regard as a political intriguer, a charlatan, and a conjuror.
Autobiography (1883) ch. 16

1 I think that Plantagenet Palliser, Duke of Omnium, is a perfect gentleman. If he be not, then I am unable to describe a gentleman.
Autobiography (1883) ch. 20

2 A man's mind will very generally refuse to make itself up until it be driven and compelled by emergency.
Ayala's Angel (1881) ch. 41

3 She was rich in apparel, but not bedizened with finery . . . she well knew the great architectural secret of decorating her constructions, and never descended to construct a decoration.
Barchester Towers (1857) ch. 9

4 The end of a novel, like the end of a children's dinner-party, must be made up of sweetmeats and sugar-plums.
Barchester Towers (1857) ch. 53

5 When taken in the refreshing waters of office any . . . pill can be swallowed.
The Bertrams (1859) ch. 16

6 Those who have courage to love should have courage to suffer.
The Bertrams (1859) ch. 27

7 Oh, indelicate! How I do hate that word. If any word in the language reminds me of a whited sepulchre it is that:—all clean and polished outside with filth and rottenness within. Are your thoughts delicate? That's the thing.
Can You Forgive Her? (1864) ch. 6

8 Mr Palliser was one of those politicians in possessing whom England has perhaps more reason to be proud than of any other of her resources, and who, as a body, give to her that requisite combination of conservatism and progress which is her present strength and best security for the future.
Can You Forgive Her? (1864) ch. 24

9 How I did respect you when you dared to speak the truth to me! Men don't know women, or they would be harder to them.
The Claverings (1867) ch. 15

10 There is no road to wealth so easy and respectable as that of matrimony.
Doctor Thorne (1858) ch. 16

11 Let no man boast himself that he has got through the perils of winter till at least the seventh of May.
Doctor Thorne (1858) ch. 47

12 'It's in Tipperary—not at all a desirable country to live in.'
'Oh, dear, no! Don't they murder the people?'
The Eustace Diamonds (1872) ch. 8; cf. **Kohl** 443:8

13 We cannot have heroes to dine with us. There are none. And were those heroes to be had, we should not like them . . . the persons whom you cannot care for in a novel, because they are so bad, are the very same that you so dearly love in your life, because they are so good.
The Eustace Diamonds (1873) ch. 35

14 For the most of us, if we do not talk of ourselves, or at any rate of the individual circles of which we are the centres, we can talk of nothing. I cannot hold with those who wish to put down the insignificant chatter of the world.
Framley Parsonage (1860) ch. 10

15 They who do not understand that a man may be brought to hope that which of all things is the most grievous to him, have not observed with sufficient closeness the perversity of the human mind.
He Knew He Was Right (1869) ch. 38

16 She understood how much louder a cock can crow in its own farmyard than elsewhere.
The Last Chronicle of Barset (1867) ch. 17

17 It's dogged as does it. It ain't thinking about it.
Giles Hoggett
The Last Chronicle of Barset (1867) ch. 61

18 With many women I doubt whether there be any more effectual way of touching their hearts than ill-using them and then confessing it. If you wish to get the sweetest fragrance from the herb at your feet, tread on it and bruise it.
Miss Mackenzie (1865) ch. 10

19 There is nothing more tyrannical than a strong popular feeling among a democratic people.
North America (1862) vol. 1, ch. 11

20 I have sometimes thought that there is no being so venomous, so bloodthirsty as a professed philanthropist.
North America (1862) vol. 1, ch. 16

21 We cannot bring ourselves to believe it possible that a foreigner should in any respect be wiser than ourselves. If any such point out to us our follies, we at once claim those follies as the special evidences of our wisdom.
Orley Farm (1862) ch. 18

22 It is because we put up with bad things that hotel-keepers continue to give them to us.
Orley Farm (1862) ch. 18

23 As for conceit, what man will do any good who is not conceited? Nobody holds a good opinion of a man who has a low opinion of himself.
Orley Farm (1862) ch. 22

24 A fainéant government is not the worst government that England can have. It has been the great fault of our politicians that they have all wanted to do something.
Phineas Finn (1869) ch. 13

25 The first necessity for good speaking is a large audience.
Phineas Finn (1869) ch. 18

26 Mr Turnbull had predicted evil consequences . . . and was now doing the best in his power to bring about the verification of his own prophecies.
Phineas Finn (1869) ch. 25

27 A man destined to sit conspicuously on our Treasury Bench, or on the seat opposite to it, should ask the Gods for a thick skin as a first gift.
Phineas Finn (1869) ch. 33

28 Perhaps there is no position more perilous to a man's honesty than that . . . of knowing himself to

be quite loved by a girl whom he almost loves himself.
Phineas Finn (1869) ch. 50

1 She knew how to allure by denying, and to make the gift rich by delaying it.
Phineas Finn (1869) ch. 57

2 What man thinks of changing himself so as to suit his wife? And yet men expect that women shall put on altogether new characters when they are married, and girls think that they can do so.
Phineas Redux (1874) ch. 3

3 It is the necessary nature of a political party in this country to avoid, as long as it can be avoided, the consideration of any question which involves a great change . . . The best carriage horses are those which can most steadily hold back against the coach as it trundles down the hill.
Phineas Redux (1874) ch. 4

4 Newspaper editors sport daily with the names of men of whom they do not hesitate to publish almost the severest words that can be uttered; but let an editor be himself attacked, even without his name, and he thinks that the thunderbolt of heaven should fall upon the offender.
Phineas Redux (1874) ch. 27

5 Equality would be a heaven, if we could attain it.
The Prime Minister (1876) ch. 68

6 To think of one's absent love is very sweet; but it becomes monotonous . . . I doubt whether any girl would be satisfied with her lover's mind if she knew the whole of it.
The Small House at Allington (1864) ch. 4

7 Why is it that girls so constantly do this,—so frequently ask men who have loved them to be present at their marriages with other men? There is no triumph in it. It is done in sheer kindness and affection. They intend to offer something which shall soften and not aggravate the sorrow that they have caused . . . I fully appreciate the intention, but in honest truth, I doubt the eligibility of the proffered entertainment.
The Small House at Allington (1864) ch. 9

8 It may almost be a question whether such wisdom as many of us have in our mature years has not come from the dying out of the power of temptation, rather than as the results of thought and resolution.
The Small House at Allington (1864) ch. 14

9 Never think that you're not good enough yourself. A man should never think that. My belief is that in life people will take you very much at your own reckoning.
The Small House at Allington (1864) ch. 32

10 The tenth Muse, who now governs the periodical press.
The Warden (1855) ch. 14

11 Is it not singular how some men continue to obtain the reputation of popular authorship without adding a word to the literature of their country worthy of note? . . . To puff and to get one's self puffed have become different branches of a new profession.
The Way We Live Now (1875) ch. 1

12 Nothing perhaps is so efficacious in preventing men from marrying as the tone in which married women speak of the struggles made in that direction by their unmarried friends.
The Way We Live Now (1875) ch. 32

13 Love is like any other luxury. You have no right to it unless you can afford it.
The Way We Live Now (1875) ch. 84

Frances Trollope 1780–1863

English writer, mother of Anthony **Trollope**

14 I draw from life—but I always pulp my acquaintance before serving them up. You would never recognize a pig in a sausage.
remark, *c.*1848; S. Baring-Gould *Early Reminiscences 1834-1864* (1923)

Leon Trotsky (Lev Davidovich Bronstein) 1879–1940

Russian revolutionary

15 Old age is the most unexpected of all things that happen to a man.
Diary in Exile (1959) 8 May 1935

16 Civilization has made the peasantry its pack animal. The bourgeoisie in the long run only changed the form of the pack.
History of the Russian Revolution (1933) vol. 3, ch. 1

17 You [the Mensheviks] are pitiful isolated individuals; you are bankrupts; your role is played out. Go where you belong from now on — into the dustbin of history!
History of the Russian Revolution (1933) vol. 3, ch. 10; cf. **Birrell** 115:13

18 It was the supreme expression of the mediocrity of the apparatus that Stalin himself rose to his position.
My Life (1930) ch. 40

19 Where force is necessary, there it must be applied boldly, decisively and completely. But one must know the limitations of force; one must know when to blend force with a manoeuvre, a blow with an agreement.
What Next? (1932) ch. 14

20 Not believing in force is the same thing as not believing in gravitation.
G. Maximov *The Guillotine at Work* (1940)

Pierre Trudeau 1919–

Canandian Liberal statesman, Prime Minister, 1968–79 and 1980–4

21 The state has no place in the nation's bedrooms.
interview, Ottawa, 22 December 1967

22 The twentieth century really belongs to those who will build it. The future can be promised to no one.
in 1968; cf. **Laurier** 454:10

23 Living next to you is in some ways like sleeping with an elephant. No matter how friendly and

even-tempered the beast, one is affected by every twitch and grunt.
on relations between Canada and the US
speech at National Press Club, Washington D. C., 25 March 1969

François Truffaut 1932–84
French film director

1 I've always had the impression that real militants are like cleaning women, doing a thankless, daily but necessary job.
letter to Jean-Luc Godard, May-June 1973

Harry S. Truman 1884–1972
American Democratic statesman, 33rd President of the US
see also **Newspaper headlines** 544:3

2 All the President is, is a glorified public relations man who spends his time flattering, kissing and kicking people to get them to do what they are supposed to do anyway.
letter to his sister, 14 November 1947, in *Off the Record* (1980)

3 If you can't stand the heat, get out of the kitchen.
associated with Truman, but attributed by him to Harry Vaughan, his 'military jester'; in *Time* 28 April 1952; cf. **Proverbs** 603:29

4 I never give them [the public] hell. I just tell the truth, and they think it is hell.
in *Look* 3 April 1956

5 A politician is a man who understands government, and it takes a politician to run a government. A statesman is a politician who's been dead 10 or 15 years.
in *New York World Telegram and Sun* 12 April 1958

6 It's a recession when your neighbour loses his job; it's a depression when you lose yours.
in *Observer* 13 April 1958

7 Wherever you have an efficient government you have a dictatorship.
lecture at Columbia University, 28 April 1959, in *Truman Speaks* (1960)

8 I didn't fire him [General MacArthur] because he was a dumb son of a bitch, although he was, but that's not against the law for generals. If it was, half to three-quarters of them would be in jail.
Merle Miller *Plain Speaking* (1974) ch. 24

9 Always be sincere, even if you don't mean it.
attributed

10 The buck stops here.
unattributed motto on Truman's desk

Donald Trump 1946–
American businessman

11 Deals are my art form. Other people paint beautifully on canvas or write wonderful poetry. I like making deals, preferably big deals. That's how I get my kicks.
Donald Trump and Tony Schwartz *The Art of the Deal* (1987)

Sojourner Truth c.1797–1883
American evangelist and reformer

12 That man . . . says that women need to be helped into carriages, and lifted over ditches, and to have the best place everywhere. Nobody ever helps me into carriages, or over mud puddles, or gives me any best place, and aren't I a woman? . . . I have ploughed, and planted, and gathered into barns, and no man could head me—and aren't I a woman? I could work as much and eat as much as a man (when I could get it), and bear the lash as well—and aren't I a woman? I have borne thirteen children and seen them most all sold off into slavery, and when I cried out with a mother's grief, none but Jesus heard—and aren't I a woman?
speech at Women's Rights Convention, Akron, Ohio, 1851

13 That little man . . . he says women can't have as much rights as men, cause Christ wasn't a woman. Where did your Christ come from? From God and a woman. Man had nothing to do with Him.
speech at Women's Rights Convention, Akron, Ohio, 1851

14 There is a great stir about coloured men getting their rights, but not a word about the coloured women; and if coloured men get their rights, and not coloured women theirs, you see the coloured men will be masters over the women, and it will be just as bad as it was before. So I am for keeping the thing going while things are stirring; because if we wait till it is still, it will take a great while to get it going again.
speech, Equal Rights Convention, New York, 9 May 1867

Barbara W. Tuchman 1912–89
American writer

15 Dead battles, like dead generals, hold the military mind in their dead grip and Germans, no less than other peoples, prepare for the last war.
August 1914 (1962) ch. 2

16 For one August in its history Paris was French—and silent.
August 1914 (1962) ch. 20

Sophie Tucker (Sophia Abuza) 1884–1966
Russian-born American vaudeville artiste

17 From birth to 18 a girl needs good parents. From 18 to 35, she needs good looks. From 35 to 55, good personality. From 55 on, she needs good cash.
Michael Freedland *Sophie* (1978)

Martin Tupper 1810–89
English writer

18 A good book is the best of friends, the same to-day and for ever.
Proverbial Philosophy Series I (1838) 'Of Reading'

Ivan Turgenev 1818–83
Russian novelist

19 Superfluous, superfluous . . . A supernumerary—that's all. Nature, obviously, hadn't counted on my

showing up and consequently treated me as an unexpected and uninvited guest.
Diary of a Superfluous Man (1850) 23 March (translated by Franklin Reeve)

1 Nature is not a temple, but a workshop, and man's the workman in it.
Fathers and Sons (1862) ch. 9 (translated by Rosemary Edmonds)

2 I share no one's ideas. I have my own.
Fathers and Sons (1862) ch. 13 (translated by Rosemary Edmonds)

3 Your sort, the gentry, can never go farther than well-bred resignation or well-bred indignation.
Fathers and Sons (1862) ch. 26 (translated by Rosemary Edmonds)

4 Just try and set death aside. It sets you aside, and that's the end of it!
Fathers and Sons (1862) ch. 27 (translated by Rosemary Edmonds)

5 No matter how often you knock at nature's door, she won't answer in words you can understand—for Nature is dumb. She'll vibrate and moan like a violin, but you mustn't expect a song.
On the Eve (1860) ch. 1 (translated by Gilbert Gardiner)

6 Death is like a fisherman, who, having caught a fish in his net, leaves it in the water for a time; the fish continues to swim about, but all the while the net is round it, and the fisherman will snatch it out in his own good time.
On the Eve (1860) ch. 35 (translated by Gilbert Gardiner)

7 Whatever a man prays for, he prays for a miracle. Every prayer reduces itself to this: Great God, grant that twice two be not four.
Poems in Prose (1881) 'Prayer'

8 The only people who remain misunderstood are those who either do not know what they want or are not worth understanding.
Rudin (1856) ch. 5 (translated by Richard Freeborn)

A. R. J. Turgot 1727–81
French economist and statesman

9 *Eripuit coelo fulmen, sceptrumque tyrannis.*
He snatched the lightning shaft from heaven, and the sceptre from tyrants.
inscription for a bust of Benjamin **Franklin**, inventor of the lightning conductor; cf. **Manilius** 493:16

Alan Turing 1912–54
English mathematician and codebreaker

10 We are not interested in the fact that the brain has the consistency of cold porridge.
A. P. Hodges *Alan Turing: the Enigma* (1983)

Sherry Turkle 1948–
American sociologist

11 Like the anthropologist returning home from a foreign culture, the voyager in virtuality can return home to a real world better equipped to understand its artifices.
Life on the Screen: Identity in the Age of the Internet (1995)

Charles Tennyson Turner 1808–79
English poet

12 Bright over Europe fell her golden hair.
'Letty's Globe' (1880)

J. M. W. Turner 1775–1851
English landscape painter
on Turner: see **Scott** *652:10*

13 It will all wash off, and Lawrence was so unhappy.
in 1826, having treated his picture 'Cologne' with a wash of lampblack to prevent the brilliant colour detracting from the effect of adjacent portraits by Lawrence
in *Dictionary of National Biography* (1917–)

14 It is something to feel that gifted talent can be acknowledged by the many who yesterday waded up to their knees in snow and muck to see the funeral pomp swelled up by carriages of the great *without the persons themselves.*
after the funeral of Lawrence
letter, January 1830; in *Dictionary of National Biography* (1917–)

15 He *sees* more in my pictures than I ever painted!
of John **Ruskin**
Mary Lloyd *Sunny Memories* (1879) vol. 1

16 If I could find anything blacker than black, I'd use it.
when a friend complained of the blackness of the sails in 'Peace—Burial at Sea' (1844)
in *Dictionary of National Biography* (1917–)

17 I did not expect to escape, but I felt bound to record it if I did.
of watching a storm at sea, while on board a Margate steamer
in *Dictionary of National Biography* (1917–)

Thomas Turner 1729–93
English diarist

18 Our diversion was dancing (or jumping about) without a violin or any music, singing of foolish and bawdy healths and more such-like stupidity, and drinking all the time as fast as could be poured down; and the parson of the parish was one amongst the mixed multitude, all the time.
Diary (ed. D. Vaisey, 1984) 22 February 1758

Walter James Redfern Turner 1889–1946
British writer and critic

19 When I was but thirteen or so
I went into a golden land,
Chimborazo, Cotopaxi
Took me by the hand.
'Romance' (1916)

John Tusa 1936–
British broadcaster and radio journalist

1 Management that wants to change an institution must first show it loves that institution.
in *Observer* 27 February 1994 'Sayings of the Week'; cf. **Arnold** 29:17

Mark Twain (Samuel Langhorne Clemens) 1835–1910
American writer
see also ***Anonymous*** *16:1*

2 There was things which he stretched, but mainly he told the truth.
The Adventures of Huckleberry Finn (1884) ch. 1

3 'Pilgrim's Progress', about a man that left his family it didn't say why . . . The statements was interesting, but tough.
The Adventures of Huckleberry Finn (1884) ch. 17

4 All kings is mostly rapscallions.
The Adventures of Huckleberry Finn (1884) ch. 23

5 Hain't we got all the fools in town on our side? and ain't that a big enough majority in any town?
The Adventures of Huckleberry Finn (1884) ch. 26

6 Soap and education are not as sudden as a massacre, but they are more deadly in the long run.
A Curious Dream (1872) 'Facts concerning the Recent Resignation'

7 Truth is the most valuable thing we have. Let us economize it.
Following the Equator (1897) ch. 7; cf. **Armstrong** 25:20

8 It is by the goodness of God that in our country we have those three unspeakably precious things: freedom of speech, freedom of conscience, and the prudence never to practise either of them.
Following the Equator (1897) ch. 20

9 Man is the Only Animal that Blushes. Or needs to.
Following the Equator (1897) ch. 27

10 There are several good protections against temptations, but the surest is cowardice.
Following the Equator (1897) ch. 36

11 It takes your enemy and your friend, working together, to hurt you to the heart: the one to slander you and the other to get the news to you.
Following the Equator (1897) ch. 45

12 The innocents abroad.
title of book (1869)

13 They spell it Vinci and pronounce it Vinchy; foreigners always spell better than they pronounce.
The Innocents Abroad (1869) ch. 19

14 Lump the whole thing! say that the Creator made Italy from designs by Michael Angelo!
The Innocents Abroad (1869) ch. 27

15 If you've got a nice *fresh* corpse, fetch him out!
The Innocents Abroad (1869) ch. 27

16 There are laws to protect the freedom of the press's speech, but none that are worth anything to protect the people from the press;
'License of the Press' (1873)

17 What a good thing Adam had. When he said a good thing he knew nobody had said it before.
Notebooks (1935)

18 Familiarity breeds contempt—and children.
Notebooks (1935)

19 Good breeding consists in concealing how much we think of ourselves and how little we think of the other person.
Notebooks (1935)

20 Adam was but human—this explains it all. He did not want the apple for the apple's sake; he wanted it only because it was forbidden.
Pudd'nhead Wilson (1894) ch. 2

21 Whoever has lived long enough to find out what life is, knows how deep a debt of gratitude we owe to Adam, the first great benefactor of our race. He brought death into the world.
Pudd'nhead Wilson (1894) ch. 3

22 Cauliflower is nothing but cabbage with a college education.
Pudd'nhead Wilson (1894) ch. 5

23 When angry, count four; when very angry, swear.
Pudd'nhead Wilson (1894) ch. 10

24 As to the Adjective: when in doubt, strike it out.
Pudd'nhead Wilson (1894) ch. 11

25 Few things are harder to put up with than the annoyance of a good example.
Pudd'nhead Wilson (1894) ch. 19

26 There is a sumptuous variety about the New England weather that compels the stranger's admiration—and regret. The weather is always doing something there; always attending strictly to business; always getting up new designs and trying them on the people to see how they will go.
speech to New England Society, 22 December 1876, in *Speeches* (1910)

27 All you need in this life is ignorance and confidence; then success is sure.
letter to Mrs Foote, 2 December 1887, in B. DeCasseres *When Huck Finn Went Highbrow* (1934)

28 The report of my death was an exaggeration.
usually quoted as 'Reports of my death have been greatly exaggerated'
in *New York Journal* 2 June 1897

29 At bottom he was probably fond of them [Americans], but he was always able to conceal it.
of Thomas ***Carlyle***
in *New York World* 10 December 1899 'Mark Twain's Christmas Book'

30 Get your facts first, and then you can distort them as much as you please.
Rudyard Kipling *From Sea to Sea* (1899) letter 37

Kenneth Tynan 1927–80
English theatre critic

31 A good drama critic is one who perceives what is happening in the theatre of his time. A great drama critic also perceives what is *not* happening.
Tynan Right and Left (1967)

1 A critic is a man who knows the way but can't drive the car.
in *New York Times Magazine* 9 January 1966

2 'Sergeant Pepper'—a decisive moment in the history of Western Civilization.
in 1967; Howard Elson *McCartney* (1986)

3 A neurosis is a secret you don't know you're keeping.
Kathleen Tynan *Life of Kenneth Tynan* (1987) ch. 19

William Tyndale c.1494–1536

English translator of the **Bible** *and Protestant martyr*
see also **Last words** 456:12

4 If God spare my life, ere many years I will cause a boy that driveth the plough shall know more of the scripture than thou doest!
to an opponent
in *Dictionary of National Biography* (1917–)

Ulpian (Domitius Ulpianus) d. 228

Roman jurist

5 *Nulla iniuria est, quae in volentem fiat.*
No injustice is done to someone who wants that thing done.
usually quoted as 'Volenti non fit iniuria'
Corpus Iuris Civilis Digests bk. 47, ch. 10, sect. 1, subsect. 5 (usually quoted '*Volenti non fit iniuria*')

Miguel de Unamuno 1864–1937

Spanish philosopher and writer

6 *La vida es duda,*
y la fe sin la duda es sólo muerte.
Life is doubt,
And faith without doubt is nothing but death.
Poesías (1907) 'Salmo II'

7 An idea does not pass from one language to another without change.
The Tragic Sense of Life (1913)

8 Cure yourself of the condition of bothering about how you look to other people. Concern yourself only with how you appear to God, with the idea that God has of you.
Vida de Don Quixote y Sancho (1905) pt. 1

The Upanishads

Hindu sacred treatises written in Sanskrit c.800–200 BC

9 From delusion lead me to Truth.
From darkness lead me to Light.
from death lead me to immortality.
Brihadāranyaka Upanishad ch. 1, pt. 3, v. 28; cf. **Kumar** 446:5

10 Even as airy threads come from a spider, or small sparks come from a fire, so from Atman, the Spirit in man, come all the powers of life, all the worlds, all the gods: all beings. To know the Atman is to know the mystery of the *Upanishads*: the Truth of truth.
Brihadāranyaka Upanishad ch. 2, pt. 1, v. 20

11 Then spoke Yajñavalkya:
In truth it is not for the love of a husband that a husband is dear; but for the love of Soul in the husband that a husband is dear.
It is not for love of a wife that a wife is dear; but for the love of the Soul in the wife that a wife is dear.
to his wife Maitreyi
Brihadāranyaka Upanishad ch. 2, pt. 4, v. 5

12 How can the Knower be known?
Brihadāranyaka Upanishad ch. 2, pt. 4, v. 14

13 He who, dwelling in all things, yet is other than all things, whom all things do not know, whose body all things are, who controls all things from within—He is your Soul, the Inner Controller, the Immortal.
Brihadāranyaka Upanishad ch. 3, pt. 7, v. 15

14 Even as a caterpillar, when coming to the end of a blade of grass, reaches out to another blade of grass and draws itself over to it, in the same way the Soul, leaving the body and unwisdom behind, reaches out to another body and draws itself over to it.
Brihadāranyaka Upanishad ch. 4, pt. 4, v. 3

15 That Soul [*Atman*] is not this, it is not that [*neti, neti*]. It is unseizable, for it cannot be seized; it is indestructible, for it cannot be destroyed; unattached, for it does not attach itself; is unbound, does not tremble, is not injured.
Brihadāranyaka Upanishad ch. 4, pt. 5, v. 15

16 This same thing does the divine voice hear, thunder, repeat: *Da*! *Da*! *Da*! that is, restrain yourselves, give, be compassionate. One should practise this same triad: self-restraint, giving, compassion.
Brihadāranyaka Upanishad ch. 5, pt. 2, v. 3

17 We should consider that in the inner world Brahman is consciousness; and we should consider that in the outer world Brahman is space. These are the two meditations.
Chāndogya Upanishad ch. 3, pt. 18, v. 1

18 This invisible and subtle essence is the Spirit of the whole universe. That is Reality. That is Truth. THOU ART THAT.
Chāndogya Upanishad ch. 6, pt. 14

19 *Shantih, shantih, shantih.*
Peace! Peace! Peace!
Taittirīya Upanishad ch. 1, pt. 1, mantra; cf. **Eliot** 296:15

20 Abiding in the midst of ignorance, thinking themselves wise and learned, fools go aimlessly hither and thither, like blind led by the blind.
Katha Upanishad ch. 2, v. 5; cf. **Bible** 95:29

21 If any man thinks he slays, and if another thinks he is slain, neither knows the ways of truth. The Eternal in man cannot kill: the Eternal in man cannot die.
Katha Upanishad ch. 2, v. 19; cf. **Bhagavadgita** 72:15, **Emerson** 299:5

22 Concealed in the hearts of all beings is the Atman, the Spirit, the Self; smaller than the smallest atom, greater than the vast spaces.
Katha Upanishad ch. 2, v. 20

1 Know the Atman as Lord of a chariot; and the body as the chariot itself. Know that reason is the charioteer; and the mind indeed is the reins. The horses they say are the senses; and their paths are the objects of sense.
Katha Upanishad ch. 3, v. 3

2 Sages say the path is narrow and difficult to tread, narrow as the edge of a razor.
Katha Upanishad ch. 3, v. 15

3 The Tree of Eternity has its roots in heaven above and its branches reach down to earth. It is Brahman, pure Spirit, who in truth is called the Immortal.
Katha Upanishad ch. 6, v. 1

4 There is ONE in whose hands is the net of Maya, who rules with his power, who rules all the worlds with his power. He is the same at the time of creation and at the time of dissolution.
Shvetāshvatara Upanishad ch. 3, v. 1

5 Two birds, close-linked companions,
Cling to the selfsame tree:
Of these the one eats of the sweet fruit,
The other, eating nothing, looks on intent.
Mundaka Upanishad ch. 3, pt. 2, v. 1

6 Whoever really knows that all-highest Brahman, really becomes Brahman.
Mundaka Upanishad ch. 3, pt. 2, v. 9

7 Let the spirit of life surrender itself into what is called *turya*, the fourth condition of consciousness. For it has been said:
There is something beyond our mind which abides in silence within our mind. It is the supreme mystery beyond thought.
Maitri Upanishad ch. 6, v. 19

8 The sound of Brahman is OM. At the end of OM is silence. It is a silence of joy.
Maitri Upanishad ch. 6, v. 23

John Updike 1932–
American novelist and short-story writer

9 A healthy male adult bore consumes *each year* one and a half times his own weight in other people's patience.
Assorted Prose (1965) 'Confessions of a Wild Bore'

10 Writing criticism is to writing fiction and poetry as hugging the shore is to sailing in the open sea.
foreword to *Hugging the Shore* (1983)

11 A soggy little island huffing and puffing to keep up with Western Europe.
of England
Picked Up Pieces (1976) 'London Life' (written 1969)

12 America is a land whose centre is nowhere;
England one whose centre is everywhere.
Picked Up Pieces (1976) 'London Life' (written 1969)

13 America is a vast conspiracy to make you happy.
Problems (1980) 'How to love America and Leave it at the Same Time'

14 Celebrity is a mask that eats into the face.
Self-Consciousness: Memoirs (1989)

15 Neutrinos, they are very small
They have no charge and have no mass
And do not interact at all.
'Cosmic Gall' (1964)

16 The artist brings something into the world that didn't exist before, and . . . he does it without destroying something else.
George Plimpton (ed.) *Writers at Work* (4th series, 1977) ch. 16

17 Some sense of religious mission is part of being American.
interview in *New York Review of Books* 29 February 1996

Urban II (Odo of Lagery) *c.*1035–99
French cleric, Pope from 1088

18 Let such as are going to fight for Christianity put the form of the cross upon their garments, that they might outwardly demonstrate their devotion to their inward faith.
launching the First Crusade
at the Council of Clermont in 1095; William of Malmesbury *De Gestis Regum Anglorum*

19 Let no attachment to your native soil be an impediment, because . . . all the world is exile to the Christian, and all the world his country: thus exile is his country, and his country exile.
launching the First Crusade
at the Council of Clermont in 1095; William of Malmesbury *De Gestis Regum Anglorum*

James Ussher 1581–1656
Irish prelate and scholar

20 Which beginning of time according to our Chronology, fell upon the entrance of the night preceding the twenty third day of *Octob.* in the year of the Julian Calendar, 710.
giving the date of the Creation as 4004 BC
The Annals of the World (1658)

Peter Ustinov 1921–
Russian-born actor, director, and writer

21 Laughter . . . the most civilized music in the world.
Dear Me (1977) ch. 3

22 I do not believe that friends are necessarily the people you like best, they are merely the people who got there first.
Dear Me (1977) ch. 5; cf. **Adams** 2:14

23 I sometimes wished he would realize that he was poor instead of being that most nerve-racking of phenomena, a rich man without money.
Dear Me (1977) ch. 6

24 At the age of four with paper hats and wooden swords we're all Generals. Only some of us never grow out of it.
Romanoff and Juliet (1956) act 1

25 Laughter would be bereaved if snobbery died.
in *Observer* 13 March 1955

Paul Valéry 1871–1945

French poet, critic, and man of letters

1 Science means simply the aggregate of all the recipes that are always successful. The rest is literature.

Moralités (1932) p. 41; cf. **Verlaine** 791:7

2 God created man and, finding him not sufficiently alone, gave him a companion to make him feel his solitude more keenly.

Tel Quel 1 (1941) 'Moralités'

3 Politics is the art of preventing people from taking part in affairs which properly concern them.

Tel Quel 2 (1943) 'Rhumbs'

John Vanbrugh 1664–1726

English architect and dramatist

on Vanbrugh: see ***Epitaphs*** *304:10*

4 Much of a muchness.

The Provoked Husband (1728) act 1, sc. 1

5 BELINDA: Ay, but you know we must return good for evil.
LADY BRUTE: That may be a mistake in the translation.

The Provoked Wife (1697) act 1, sc. 1

6 LADY BRUTE: 'Tis a hard fate I should not be believed.
SIR JOHN: 'Tis a damned atheistical age, wife.

The Provoked Wife (1697) act 5, sc. 2

7 So, now I am in for Hobbes's voyage, a great leap in the dark.

'Heartfree' on marriage

The Provoked Wife (1697) act 5, sc. 5; cf. **Last words** 455:19

8 Thinking is to me the greatest fatigue in the world.

The Relapse (1696) act 2, sc. 1

9 When once a woman has given you her heart, you can never get rid of the rest of her body.

The Relapse (1696) act 3, sc. 1

10 In matters of love men's eyes are always bigger than their bellies. They have violent appetites, 'tis true; but they have soon dined.

The Relapse (1696) act 5, sc. 2

Vivian van Damm c.1889–1960

British theatre manager

11 We never closed.

of the Windmill Theatre, London, during the Second World War

Tonight and Every Night (1952) ch. 18

William Henry Vanderbilt 1821–85

American railway magnate

12 The public be damned!

on whether the public should be consulted about luxury trains

letter from A. W. Cole to *New York Times* 25 August 1918

Laurens van der Post 1906–96

South African explorer and writer

13 Human beings are perhaps never more frightening than when they are convinced beyond doubt that they are right.

Lost World of the Kalahari (1958)

14 I don't think a man who has watched the sun going down could walk away and commit a murder.

in *Daily Telegraph* 17 December 1996; obituary

Henry Van Dyke 1852–1933

American Presbyterian minister and writer

15 Time is
Too slow for those who wait,
Too swift for those who fear,
Too long for those who grieve,
Too short for those who rejoice;
But for those who love,
Time is eternity.

'Time is too slow for those who wait' (1905), read at the funeral of **Diana**, Princess of Wales; Nigel Rees in 'Quote . . . Unquote' October 1997 notes that the original form of the last line is 'Time is not'

Raoul Vaneigem 1934–

Belgian philosopher

16 Never before has a civilization reached such a degree of a contempt for life; never before has a generation, drowned in mortification, felt such a rage to live.

of the 1960s

The Revolution of Everyday Life (1967) ch. 5

17 Work to survive, survive by consuming, survive to consume: the hellish cycle is complete.

The Revolution of Everyday Life (1967)

Vincent Van Gogh 1853–90

Dutch painter

18 I cannot help it that my pictures do not sell. Nevertheless the time will come when people will see that they are worth more than the price of the paint.

letter to his brother Theo, 20 October 1888; *Further Letters of Vincent Van Gogh to his Brother* (1929)

Bartolomeo Vanzetti 1888–1927

American anarchist, born in Italy

19 Sacco's name will live in the hearts of the people and in their gratitude when Katzmann's and yours bones will be dispersed by time, when your name, his name, your laws, institutions, and your false god are but a deem rememoring of a cursed past in which man was wolf to the man.

statement disallowed at his trial, with Nicola Sacco, for murder and robbery; both were sentenced to death on 9 April 1927, and executed on 23 August 1927

M. D. Frankfurter and G. Jackson *Letters of Sacco and Vanzetti* (1928); cf. **Plautus** 578:12

20 If it had not been for these thing, I might have live out my life talking at street corners to scorning men. I might have die, unmarked, unknown, a failure. Now we are not a failure. This is our career and our triumph. Never in our full life could we hope to do such work for tolerance, for joostice, for man's onderstanding of man as now we do by accident.

statement after being sentenced to death, in M. D. Frankfurter and G. Jackson *Letters of Sacco and Vanzetti* (1928) preface

Michel Vaucaire

French songwriter

1 *Non! rien de rien,*
Non! je ne regrette rien,
Ni le bien, qu'on m'a fait,
Ni le mal—tout ça m'est bien égal!

No, no regrets,
No, we will have no regrets,
As you leave, I can say—
Love was king, tho' for only a day.

'*Non, je ne regrette rien*' (1960 song); sung by Edith Piaf

Henry Vaughan 1622–95

English poet

2 Man is the shuttle, to whose winding quest
And passage through these looms
God ordered motion, but ordained no rest.

Silex Scintillans (1650–5) 'Man'

3 Wise Nicodemus saw such light
As made him know his God by night.

Silex Scintillans (1650–5) 'The Night'

4 Most blest believer he!
Who in that land of darkness and blind eyes
Thy long expected healing wings could see
When Thou didst rise!
And, what can never more be done,
Did at midnight speak with the Sun!

Silex Scintillans (1650–5) 'The Night'

5 Dear Night! this world's defeat;
The stop to busy fools; care's check and curb.

Silex Scintillans (1650–5) 'The Night'

6 My soul, there is a country
Far beyond the stars,
Where stands a wingèd sentry
All skilful in the wars;
There, above noise and danger,
Sweet Peace is crowned with smiles,
And One born in a manger
Commands the beauteous files.

Silex Scintillans (1650–5) 'Peace'

7 Happy those early days, when I
Shined in my angel-infancy.
Before I understood this place
Appointed for my second race,
Or taught my soul to fancy aught
But a white, celestial thought.

Silex Scintillans (1650–5) 'The Retreat'

8 And in those weaker glories spy
Some shadows of eternity.

Silex Scintillans (1650–5) 'The Retreat'

9 But felt through all this fleshly dress
Bright shoots of everlastingness.

Silex Scintillans (1650–5) 'The Retreat'

10 Some men a forward motion love,
But I by backward steps would move,
And when this dust falls to the urn,
In that state I came, return.

Silex Scintillans (1650–5) 'The Retreat'

11 They are all gone into the world of light,
And I alone sit lingering here.

Silex Scintillans (1650–5) 'They are all gone'

12 I see them walking in an air of glory,
Whose light doth trample on my days:
My days, which are at best but dull and hoary,
Mere glimmering and decays.

Silex Scintillans (1650–5) 'They are all gone'

13 Dear, beauteous death! the jewel of the just,
Shining nowhere but in the dark;
What mysteries do lie beyond thy dust,
Could man outlook that mark!

Silex Scintillans (1650–5) 'They are all gone'

14 And yet, as angels in some brighter dreams
Call to the soul when man doth sleep,
So some strange thoughts transcend our wonted themes,
And into glory peep.

Silex Scintillans (1650–5) 'They are all gone'

15 If a star were confined into a tomb
Her captive flames must needs burn there;
But when the hand that locked her up gives room,
She'll shine through all the sphere.

Silex Scintillans (1650–5) 'They are all gone'

16 Sure thou didst flourish once! and many springs,
Many bright mornings, much dew, many showers
Passed o'er thy head; many light hearts and wings
Which now are dead, lodged in thy living bowers.

Silex Scintillans (1650–5) 'The Timber'

17 I saw Eternity the other night,
Like a great ring of pure and endless light,
All calm, as it was bright;
And round beneath it, Time in hours, days, years,
Driv'n by the spheres
Like a vast shadow moved; in which the world
And all her train were hurled.

Silex Scintillans (1650–5) 'The World'

Janet-Maria Vaughan 1899–1993

English scientist

18 I am here—trying to do science in hell.
working as a doctor in Belsen at the end of the war

letter to a friend, 12 May 1945; P. A. Adams (ed.) *Janet-Maria Vaughan* (1993)

Thomas, Lord Vaux 1510–56

English writer and courtier

19 My lusts they do me leave,
My fancies all be fled,
And tract of time begins to weave
Grey hairs upon my head.

For age with stealing steps

Hath clawed me with his clutch,
And lusty life away she leaps,
As there had been none such.
'The Aged Lover Renounceth Love' (1557); a garbled version is sung by the gravedigger in *Hamlet*; cf. **Shakespeare** 666:20

1 When all is done and said, in the end thus shall you find,
He most of all doth bathe in bliss that hath a quiet mind;
And, clear from worldly cares, to deem can be content
The sweetest time in all his life in thinking to be spent.
'The Pleasures of Thinking' (1576)

Thorstein Veblen 1857–1929
American economist and social scientist

2 Conspicuous consumption of valuable goods is a means of reputability to the gentleman of leisure.
Theory of the Leisure Class (1899) ch. 4

3 From the foregoing survey of conspicuous leisure and consumption, it appears that the utility of both alike for the purposes of reputability lies in the element of waste that is common to both. In the one case it is a waste of time and effort, in the other it is a waste of goods.
Theory of the Leisure Class (1899) ch. 4

Vegetius (Flavius Vegetius Renatus) AD 379–95
Roman military writer

4 *Qui desiderat pacem, praeparet bellum.*
Let him who desires peace, prepare for war.
usually quoted as 'Si vis pacem, para bellum [If you want peace, prepare for war]'
Epitoma Rei Militaris bk. 3, prologue; cf. **Aristotle** 24:19, **Proverbs** 603:39

Robert Venturi 1925–
American architect

5 Less is a bore.
Complexity and Contradiction in Architecture (1966) ch. 2; cf. **Proverbs** 605:17

Pierre Vergniaud 1753–93
French revolutionary; executed with other Girondists

6 There was reason to fear that the Revolution, like Saturn, might devour in turn each one of her children.
Alphonse de Lamartine *Histoire des Girondins* (1847) bk. 38, ch. 20

Paul Verlaine 1844–96
French poet

7 *Et tout le reste est littérature.*
All the rest is mere fine writing.
'Art poétique' (1882); cf. **Valéry** 789:1

8 *Les sanglots longs*
Des violons
De l'automne
Blessent mon cœur
D'une langueur
Monotone.
The drawn-out sobs of autumn's violins wound my heart with a monotonous languor.
'Chanson d'Automne' (1866)

9 *Prends l'éloquence et tords-lui le cou.*
Take eloquence and break its neck.
Jadis et naguère (1884)

10 *Et, Ô ces voix d'enfants chantants dans la coupole!*
And oh those children's voices, singing beneath the dome!
'Parsifal' A Jules Tellier (1886)

11 *Il pleure dans mon coeur*
Comme il pleut sur la ville.
Tears are shed in my heart like the rain on the town.
Romances sans paroles (1874) 'Ariettes oubliées' no. 3

René Aubert, Abbé de Vertot 1655–1735
French historian

12 *Mon siège est fait.*
My siege is over.
on receiving long-awaited documents for his history of the siege of Rhodes when it had already been completed
J. Le Rond d'Alembert *Œuvres* (1821 ed.) vol. 2, pt. 1

Hendrik Frensch Verwoerd 1901–66
South African statesman; Prime Minister from 1958

13 Up till now he [the Bantu] has been subjected to a school system which drew him away from his own community and practically misled him by showing him the green pastures of the European but still did not allow him to graze there . . . It is abundantly clear that unplanned education creates many problems, disrupts the communal life of the Bantu and endangers the communal life of the European.
speech in South African Senate, 7 June 1954

Vespasian (Titus Flavius Vespasianus) AD 9–79
Roman emperor from AD *69*
see also ***Last words*** *455:12*

14 *Pecunia non olet.*
Money has no smell.
upon ***Titus****'s objecting to his tax on public lavatories, Vespasian held a coin to Titus's nose; on being told it didn't smell, he replied,* 'Atque e lotio est [Yes, that's made from urine]'
traditional summary of Suetonius *Lives of the Caesars* 'Vespasian' sect. 23, subsect. 3; cf. **Proverbs** 606:43

15 *Vae, puto deus fio.*
Woe is me, I think I am becoming a god.
when fatally ill
Suetonius *Lives of the Caesars* 'Vespasian' sect. 23, subsect. 4

Queen Victoria 1819–1901

Queen of the United Kingdom from 1837
on Victoria: see **Disraeli** *269:25*

1 I will be good.
on being shown a chart of the line of succession, 11 March 1830
Theodore Martin *The Prince Consort* (1875) vol. 1, ch. 2

2 It was with some emotion . . . that I beheld Albert—who is beautiful.
of her first meeting with Prince **Albert**, *c.1838*
attributed; Stanley Weintraub *Albert: Uncrowned King* (1997)

3 What you say of the pride of giving life to an immortal soul is very fine, dear, but I own I can not enter into that; I think much more of our being like a cow or a dog at such moments; when our poor nature becomes so very animal and unecstatic.
letter to the Princess Royal, 15 June 1858; Roger Fulford *Dearest Child* (1964)

4 Dirty, dark, and undevotional.
of St Paul's Cathedral, where a service of Thanksgiving had been held, following the recovery of the Prince of Wales from typhoid fever
attributed in this form, but recorded in her Journal, 27 February 1872, as 'so cold, dreary and dingy. It so badly lacks decoration and colour.'; G. E. Buckle (ed.) *Letters of Queen Victoria: 2nd Series* vol. 2 (1870–78)

5 The danger to the country, to Europe, to her vast Empire, which is involved in having all these great interests entrusted to the shaking hand of an old, wild, and incomprehensible man of 82, is very great!
on **Gladstone**'s *last appointment as Prime Minister*
letter to Lord Lansdowne, 12 August 1892, in T. Wodehouse Legh *Lord Lansdowne* (1929)

6 The future Vice Roy must . . . not be guided by the *snobbish* and vulgar, over-bearing and offensive behaviour of our Civil and Political Agents, if we are to go on peaceably and happily in India . . . not trying to trample on the people and continuously reminding them and making them feel they are a conquered people.
letter to Lord Salisbury, 27 May 1898, in Kenneth Rose *Superior Person* (1969) ch. 23

7 He speaks to Me as if I was a public meeting.
of **Gladstone**
G. W. E. Russell *Collections and Recollections* (1898) ch. 14

8 We are not interested in the possibilities of defeat; they do not exist.
on the Boer War during 'Black Week', December 1899
Lady Gwendolen Cecil *Life of Robert, Marquis of Salisbury* (1931) vol. 3, ch. 6

9 We are not amused.
attributed, in Caroline Holland *Notebooks of a Spinster Lady* (1919) ch. 21, 2 January 1900

Gore Vidal 1925–

American novelist and critic

10 Whenever a friend succeeds, a little something in me dies.
in *Sunday Times Magazine* 16 September 1973

11 A triumph of the embalmer's art.
of Ronald **Reagan**
in *Observer* 26 April 1981

12 He will lie even when it is inconvenient: the sign of the true artist.
attributed

José Antonio Viera Gallo 1943–

Chilean politician

13 Socialism can only arrive by bicycle.
Ivan Illich *Energy and Equity* (1974) epigraph

Alfred de Vigny 1797–1863

French poet

14 *J'aime le son du cor, le soir, au fond des bois.*
I love the sound of the horn, at night, in the depth of the woods.
'Le Cor' (1826)

15 *J'aime la majesté des souffrances humaines.*
I love the majesty of human suffering.
La Maison du Berger (1844)

16 *Seul le silence est grand; tout le reste est faiblesse . . .*
Fais énergiquement ta longue et lourde tâche . . .
Puis, après, comme moi, souffre et meurs sans parler.
Silence alone is great; all else is feebleness.
'La mort du loup' (1843) pt. 3

Matteo Villani d. *c.*1363

Florentine chronicler

17 My mind is stupefied as it approaches the task of recording the sentence that divine justice mercifully delivered upon men, who deserve, because they have been corrupted by sin, a last judgement.
of the outbreak of the Black Death in the mid 14th century
Chronicle of Matteo Villani bk 1; M. Meiss *Painting in Florence and Siena after the Black Death* (1951)

Philippe-Auguste Villiers de L'Isle-Adam 1838–89

French writer

18 *Vivre? les serviteurs feront cela pour nous.*
Living? The servants will do that for us.
Axël (1890) pt. 4, sect. 2

François Villon b. 1431

French poet
on Villon: see **Swinburne** *750:12*

19 *Frères humains qui après nous vivez,*
N'ayez les cœurs contre nous endurcis,
Car, si pitié de nous pauvres avez,

Dieu en aura plus tôt de vous mercis . . .
Mais priez Dieu que tous nous veuille absoudre!

Brothers in humanity who live after us, let not your hearts be hardened against us, for, if you take pity on us poor ones, God will be more likely to have mercy on you. But pray God that he may be willing to absolve us all.

'Ballade des pendus'

1 *Mais où sont les neiges d'antan?*

But where are the snows of yesteryear?

Le Grand Testament (1461) 'Ballade des dames du temps jadis' (translated by D. G. Rossetti)

2 *En cette foi je veux vivre et mourir.*

In this faith I wish to live and to die.

Le Grand Testament (1461) 'Ballade pour prier Nostre Dame'

St Vincent of Lerins d. AD *c.*450

3 *Quod ubique, quod semper, quod ab omnibus creditum est.*

What is everywhere, what is always, what is by all people believed.

Commonitorium Primum sect. 2

Virgil (Publius Vergilius Maro) 70–19 BC

Roman poet

on Virgil: see **Arnold** *29:5,* **Horace** *387:14,* **Propertius** *593:17,* **Tennyson** *767:5; see also* **Borrowed titles** *144:8*

4 *Arma virumque cano, Troiae qui primus ab oris*
Italiam fato profugus Laviniaque venit
Litora, multum ille et terris iactatus et alto
Vi superum, saevae memorem Iunonis ob iram.

I sing of arms and the man who first from the shores of Troy came destined an exile to Italy and the Lavinian beaches, a man much buffeted on land and on the deep by force of the gods because of fierce Juno's never-forgetting anger.

Aeneid bk. 1, l. 1; cf. **Dryden** 283:1

5 *Tantaene animis caelestibus irae?*

Why such great anger in those heavenly minds?

Aeneid bk. 1, l. 11

6 *Tantae molis erat Romanam condere gentem.*

So massive was the effort to found the Roman nation.

Aeneid bk. 1, l. 33

7 *Apparent rari nantes in gurgite vasto.*

Odd figures swimming were glimpsed in the waste of waters.

Aeneid bk. 1, l. 118

8 *Constitit hic arcumque manu celerisque sagittas*
Corripuit fidus quae tela gerebat Achates.

Hereupon he stopped and snatched up in his hand a bow and swift arrows, the weapons that trusty Achates carried.

Aeneid bk. 1, l. 187

9 *O passi graviora, dabit deus his quoque finem.*

O you who have borne even heavier things, God will grant an end to these too.

Aeneid bk. 1, l. 199

10 *Forsan et haec olim meminisse iuvabit.*

Maybe one day it will be cheering to remember even these things.

Aeneid bk. 1, l. 203

11 *Dux femina facti.*

The leader of the enterprise a woman.

Aeneid bk. 1, l. 364

12 *Dixit et avertens rosea cervice refulsit,*
Ambrosiaeque comae divinum vertice odorem
Spiravere; pedes vestis defluxit ad imos,
Et vera incessu patuit dea.

Thus she spoke and turned away with a flash of her rosy neck, and her ambrosial hair exhaled a divine fragrance; her dress flowed right down to her feet and her true godhead was evident from her walk.

Aeneid bk. 1, l. 405

13 *Sunt lacrimae rerum et mentem mortalia tangunt.*

'Look, there's Priam! Even here prowess has its due rewards, there are tears shed for things even here and mortality touches the heart. Abandon your fears; I tell you, this fame will stand us somehow in good stead.' So he spoke, and fed his thoughts on the unreal painting.

Aeneid bk. 1, l. 462

14 *Di tibi, si qua pios respectant numina, si quid*
Usquam iustitia est et mens sibi conscia recti,
Praemia digna ferant.

If the divine powers take note of the dutiful in any way, if there is any justice anywhere and a mind recognizing in itself what is right, may the gods bring you your earned rewards.

Aeneid bk. 1, l. 603

15 *Non ignara mali miseris succurrere disco.*

No stranger to trouble myself I am learning to care for the unhappy.

Aeneid bk. 1, l. 630

16 *Infandum, regina, iubes renovare dolorem.*

A grief too much to be told, O queen, you bid me renew.

Aeneid bk. 2, l. 3

17 *Quaeque ipse miserrima vidi*
Et quorum pars magna fui.

And the most miserable things which I myself saw and of which I was a major part.

Aeneid bk. 2, l. 5

18 *Equo ne credite, Teucri.*
Quidquid id est, timeo Danaos et dona ferentes.

Do not trust the horse, Trojans. Whatever it is, I fear the Greeks even when they bring gifts.

Aeneid bk. 2, l. 48; cf. **Proverbs** 600:14

19 *. . . Crimine ab uno*
Disce omnis.

From the one crime recognize them all as culprits.

Aeneid bk. 2, l. 65

20 *Tacitae per amica silentia lunae.*

Through the friendly silence of the soundless moonlight.

Aeneid bk. 2, l. 255

1 *Tempus erat quo prima quies mortalibus aegris*
Incipit et dono divum gratissima serpit.

It was the time when first sleep begins for weary mortals and by the gift of the gods creeps over them most welcomely.

Aeneid bk. 2, l. 268

2 *Quantum mutatus ab illo*
Hectore qui redit exuvias indutus Achilli.

How greatly changed from that Hector who came back arrayed in the armour of Achilles!

Aeneid bk. 2, l. 274

3 *Iam proximus ardet*
Ucalegon.

Ucalegon burns very near.

Aeneid bk. 2, l. 311

4 *Fuimus Troes, fuit Ilium et ingens*
Gloria Teucrorum.

We Trojans are at an end, Ilium has ended and the vast glory of the Trojans.

Aeneid bk. 2, l. 325

5 *Moriamur et in media arma ruamus.*
Una salus victis nullam sperare salutem.

Let us die even as we rush into the midst of the battle. The only safe course for the defeated is to expect no safety.

Aeneid bk. 2, l. 354

6 *Dis aliter visum.*

The gods thought otherwise.

Aeneid bk. 2, l. 428

7 *Non tali auxilio nec defensoribus istis*
Tempus eget.

Neither the hour requires such help, nor those defenders.

Aeneid bk. 2, l. 521

8 *Quid non mortalia pectora cogis,*
Auri sacra fames!

To what do you not drive human hearts, cursed craving for gold!

Aeneid bk. 3, l. 56

9 *Monstrum horrendum, informe, ingens, cui lumen ademptum.*

A monster horrendous, hideous and vast, deprived of sight.

Aeneid bk. 3, l. 658

10 *Agnosco veteris vestigia flammae.*

I feel again a spark of that ancient flame.

Aeneid bk. 4, l. 23; cf. **Dante** 250:1

11 *Quis fallere possit amantem?*

Who could deceive a lover?

Aeneid bk. 4, l. 296

12 *Nec me meminisse pigebit Elissae*
Dum memor ipse mei, dum spiritus hos regit artus.

Nor will it ever upset me to remember Elissa so long as I can remember who I am, so long as the breath of life controls these limbs.

Aeneid bk. 4, l. 335

13 *Varium et mutabile semper*
Femina.

Fickle and changeable always is woman.

Aeneid bk. 4, l. 569; see below

A windfane changabil huf puffe
Always is a woomman.

Richard Stanyhurst's translation, 1582

14 *Exoriare aliquis nostris ex ossibus ultor.*

Rise up from my dead bones, avenger!

Aeneid bk. 4, l. 625 (translation by C. Day-Lewis)

15 *Hos successus alit: possunt, quia posse videntur.*

These success encourages: they can because they think they can.

Aeneid bk. 5, l. 231

16 *Bella, horrida bella,*
Et Thybrim multo spumantem sanguine cerno.

I see wars, horrible wars, and the Tiber foaming with much blood.

Aeneid bk. 6, l. 86; cf. **Powell** 590:15

17 *Facilis descensus Averno:*
Noctes atque dies patet atri ianua Ditis;
Sed revocare gradum superasque evadere ad auras,
Hoc opus, hic labor est.

Easy is the way down to the Underworld: by night and by day dark Hades' door stands open; but to retrace one's steps and to make a way out to the upper air, that's the task, that is the labour.

Aeneid bk. 6, l. 126

18 *Procul, o procul este, profani.*

Far off, Oh keep far off, you uninitiated ones.

Aeneid bk. 6, l. 258

19 *Ibant obscuri sola sub nocte per umbram*
Perque domos Ditis vacuas et inania regna.

Darkling they went under the lonely night through the shadow and through the empty dwellings and unsubstantial realms of Hades.

Aeneid bk. 6, l. 268

20 *Vestibulum ante ipsum primisque in faucibus Orci*
Luctus et ultrices posuere cubilia Curae,
Pallentesque habitant Morbi tristisque Senectus,
Et Metus et malesuada Fames ac turpis Egestas,
Terribiles visu formae, Letumque Labosque.

Before the very forecourt and in the opening of the jaws of hell Grief and avenging Cares have placed their beds, and wan Diseases and sad Old Age live there, and Fear and Hunger that urges to wrongdoing, and shaming Destitution, figures terrible to see, and Death and Toil.

Aeneid bk. 6, l. 273

21 *Stabant orantes primi transmittere cursum*
Tendebantque manus ripae ulterioris amore.

They stood begging to be the first to make the voyage over and they reached out their hands in longing for the further shore.

Aeneid bk. 6, l. 313

22 *Spiritus intus alit, totamque infusa per artus*
Mens agitat molem et magno se corpore miscet.

The spirit within nourishes, and mind instilled throughout the living parts activates the whole mass and mingles with the vast frame.

Aeneid bk. 6, l. 726

1 *Excudent alii spirantia mollius aera*
(Credo equidem), vivos ducent de marmore vultus,
Orabunt causas melius, caelique meatus
Describent radio et surgentia sidera dicent:
Tu regere imperio populos, Romane, memento
(Hae tibi erunt artes), pacique imponere morem,
Parcere subiectis et debellare superbos.

Others shall shape bronzes more smoothly so that they seem alive (yes, I believe it), shall mould from marble living faces, shall better plead their cases in court, and shall demonstrate with a pointer the motions of the heavenly bodies and tell the stars as they rise: you, Roman, make your task to rule nations by your government (these shall be your skills), to impose ordered ways upon a state of peace, to spare those who have submitted and to subdue the arrogant.

Aeneid bk. 6, l. 847

2 *Heu, miserande puer, si qua fata aspera rumpas,*
Tu Marcellus eris. Manibus date lilia plenis.

Alas, pitiable boy—if only you might break your cruel fate!—you are to be Marcellus. [People,] give me lilies in armfuls.

Aeneid bk. 6, l. 883

3 *Sunt geminae Somni portae, quarum altera fertur*
Cornea, qua veris facilis datur exitus umbris,
Altera candenti perfecta nitens elephanto,
Sed falsa ad caelum mittunt insomnia Manes.

There are two gates of Sleep, one of which it is held is made of horn and by it easy egress is given to real ghosts; the other shining, fashioned of gleaming white ivory, but the shades send deceptive visions that way to the light.

Aeneid bk. 6, l. 893

4 *Geniumque loci primamque deorum*
Tellurem Nymphasque et adhuc ignota precatur
Flumina.

He prays to the spirit of the place and to Earth, the first of the gods, and to the Nymphs and as yet unknown rivers.

Aeneid bk. 7, l. 136; cf. **Pope** 583:23

5 *Flectere si nequeo superos, Acheronta movebo.*

If I am unable to make the gods above relent, I shall move Hell.

Aeneid bk. 7, l. 312

6 *O mihi praeteritos referat si Iuppiter annos.*

Oh if only Jupiter would give me back my past years.

Aeneid bk. 8, l. 560

7 *Quadripedante putrem sonitu quatit ungula campum.*

The hoof with a galloping sound is shaking the powdery plain.

Aeneid bk. 8, l. 596

8 *Macte nova virtute, puer, sic itur ad astra.*

Blessings on your young courage, boy; that's the way to the stars.

Aeneid bk. 9, l. 641

9 *Audentis Fortuna iuvat.*

Fortune assists the bold.

often quoted as 'Fortune favours the brave'

Aeneid bk. 10, l. 284; cf. **Proverbs** 600:44, **Terence** 768:4

10 *Et dulcis moriens reminiscitur Argos.*

And dying remembers his sweet Argos.

Aeneid bk. 10, l. 782

11 *Experto credite.*

Trust one who has gone through it.

Aeneid bk. 11, l. 283

12 *Pereat, qui crastina curat!*
Mors aurem vellens 'vivite' ait, 'venio.'

Away with him who heeds the morrow! Death, plucking the ear, cries: 'Live; I come!'

Copa l. 37 (translated by H. Rushton Fairclough)

13 *Tityre, tu patulae recubans sub tegmine fagi*
Silvestrem tenui Musam meditaris avena.

Tityrus, you who lie under cover of the spreading beech-tree, you are practising your pastoral music on a thin stalk.

Eclogues no. 1, l. 1

14 *O Meliboee, deus nobis haec otia fecit.*

O Meliboeus, it is a god that has made this peaceful life for us.

Eclogues no. 1, l. 6

15 *At nos hinc alii sitientis ibimus Afros,*
Pars Scythiam et rapidum cretae veniemus Oaxen
Et penitus toto divisos orbe Britannos.

But we from here are to go some to the parched Africans, another group to Scythia and others of us shall come to the Oaxes swirling with clay, and amongst the Britons who are kept far away from the whole world.

Eclogues no. 1, l. 64

16 *Formosum pastor Corydon ardebat Alexin,*
Delicias domini, nec quid speraret habebat.

The Shepherd, Corydon, burned with love for handsome Alexis, his master's favourite, but he was not getting what he hoped for.

Eclogues no. 2, l. 1

17 *O formose puer, nimium ne crede colori.*

Don't bank too much on your complexion, lovely boy.

Eclogues no. 2, l. 17

18 *Quem fugis, a! demens? Habitarunt di quoque silvas.*

Who are you running from, you crazy man? . . . Even gods have lived in the woods like me.

Eclogues no. 2, l. 60

19 *Trahit sua quemque voluptas.*

Everyone is dragged on by their favourite pleasure.

Eclogues no. 2, l. 65

20 *Malo me Galatea petit, lasciva puella,*
Et fugit ad salices et se cupit ante videri.

Galatea aims at me with an apple, sexy girl, and runs away into the willows and wants to have been spotted.

Eclogues no. 3, l. 64

1 *Latet anguis in herba.*

There's a snake hidden in the grass.

Eclogues no. 3, l. 93

2 *Non nostrum inter vos tantas componere lites.*

It's not in my power to decide such a great dispute between you.

Eclogues no. 3, l. 108

3 *Claudite iam rivos, pueri; sat prata biberunt.*

Close the sluices now, lads; the fields have drunk enough.

Eclogues no. 3, l. 111

4 *Sicelides Musae, paulo maiora canamus!*
Non omnis arbusta iuvant humilesque myricae;
Si canimus silvas, silvae sint consule dignae.
Ultima Cumaei venit iam carminis aetas;
Magnus ab integro saeclorum nascitur ordo.
Iam redit et virgo, redeunt Saturnia regna,
Iam nova progenies caelo demittitur alto.

Sicilian Muses, let us sing of rather greater things. Bushes and low tamarisks do not please everyone; if we sing of the woods, let them be woods of consular dignity. Now has come the last age according to the oracle at Cumae; the great series of lifetimes starts anew. Now too the virgin goddess returns, the golden days of Saturn's reign return, now a new race is sent down from high heaven.

Eclogues no. 4, l. 1

5 *Incipe, parve puer, risu cognoscere matrem.*

Begin, baby boy, to recognize your mother with a smile.

Eclogues no. 4, l. 60

6 *Incipe, parve puer: qui non risere parenti,*
Nec deus hunc mensa, dea nec dignata cubili est.

Begin, baby boy: if you haven't had a smile for your parent, then neither will a god think you worth inviting to dinner, nor a goddess to bed.

Eclogues no. 4, l. 62

7 *Ambo florentes aetatibus, Arcades ambo,*
Et cantare pares et respondere parati.

Both in the flower of their youth, Arcadians both, and matched and ready alike to start a song and to respond.

Eclogues no. 7, l. 4

8 *Saepibus in nostris parvam te roscida mala*
(Dux ego vester eram) vidi cum matre legentem.
Alter ab undecimo tum me iam acceperat annus,
Iam fragilis poteram a terra contingere ramos:
Ut vidi, ut perii, ut me malus abstulit error!

In our orchard I saw you as a child picking dewy apples with your mother (I was showing you the way). I had just turned twelve years old, I could reach the brittle branches even from the ground: how I saw you! how I perished [for love of you]! how an awful madness swept me away!

Eclogues no. 8, l. 37

9 *Nunc scio quid sit Amor.*

Now I know what Love is.

Eclogues no. 8, l. 43

10 *Non omnia possumus omnes.*

We can't all do everything.

Eclogues no. 8, l. 63; cf. **Lucilius** 478:20

11 *Et me fecere poetam*
Pierides, sunt et mihi carmina, me quoque dicunt
Vatem pastores; sed non ego credulus illis.
Nam neque adhuc Vario videor nec dicere Cinna
Digna, sed argutos inter strepere anser olores.

Me too the Muses made write verse. I have songs of my own, the shepherds call me also a poet; but I'm not inclined to trust them. For I don't seem yet to write things as good either as Varius or as Cinna, but to be a goose honking amongst tuneful swans.

Eclogues no. 9, l. 32

12 *Omnia vincit Amor: et nos cedamus Amori.*

Love conquers all things: let us too give in to Love.

Eclogues no. 10, l. 69; cf. **Chaucer** 204:15

13 *Ite domum saturae, venit Hesperus, ite capellae.*

Go on home, you have fed full, the evening star is coming, go on, my she-goats.

Eclogues no. 10, l. 77

14 *Ultima Thule.*

Farthest Thule.

Georgics no. 1, l. 30

15 *Nosque ubi primus equis Oriens adflavit anhelis*
Illic sera rubens accendit lumina Vesper.

And when the rising sun has first breathed on us with his panting horses, over there the red evening-star is lighting his late lamps.

Georgics no. 1, l. 250

16 *Ter sunt conati imponere Pelio Ossam*
Scilicet atque Ossae frondosum involvere Olympum;
Ter pater exstructos disiecit fulmine montis.

Three times they endeavoured to pile Ossa on Pelion, no less, and to roll leafy Olympus on top of Ossa; three times our Father broke up the towering mountains with a thunderbolt.

Georgics no. 1, l. 281

17 *O fortunatos nimium, sua si bona norint,*
Agricolas!

O farmers excessively fortunate if only they recognized their blessings!

Georgics no. 2, l. 458

18 *Felix qui potuit rerum cognoscere causas.*

Lucky is he who has been able to understand the causes of things.

of **Lucretius**

Georgics no. 2, l. 490

19 *Fortunatus et ille deos qui novit agrestis.*

Fortunate too is the man who has come to know the gods of the countryside.

Georgics no. 2, l. 493

20 *Optima quaeque dies miseris mortalibus aevi*
Prima fugit; subeunt morbi tristisque senectus
Et labor, et durae rapit inclementia mortis.

All the best days of life slip away from us poor mortals first; illnesses and dreary old age and pain

sneak up, and the fierceness of harsh death snatches away.
Georgics no. 3, l. 66

1 *Sed fugit interea, fugit inreparabile tempus.*
But meanwhile it is flying, irretrievable time is flying.
usually quoted as 'tempus fugit [time flies]'
Georgics no. 3, l. 284; cf. **Proverbs** 612:52

2 *Hi motus animorum atque haec certamina tanta*
Pulveris exigui iactu compressa quiescent.
These movements of souls and these contests, however great, having been contained by the throwing of a little dust, will be quiet.
Georgics no. 4, l. 86 (of the battle of the bees)

3 *Non aliter, si parva licet componere magnis,*
Cecropias innatus apes amor urget habendi
Munere quamque suo.
Just so, if one may compare small things with great, an innate love of getting drives these Attic bees each with his own function.
Georgics no. 4, l. 176

4 *Sic vos non vobis mellificatis apes.*
Sic vos non vobis nidificatis aves.
Sic vos non vobis vellera fertis oves.
Thus you bees make honey not for yourselves. Thus you birds build nests not for yourselves. Thus you sheep bear fleeces not for yourselves.
on Bathyllus claiming authorship of certain lines by Virgil
attributed

Voltaire (François-Marie Arouet) 1694–1778

French writer and philosopher
on Voltaire: see ***Blake*** *120:2,* ***Hugo*** *394:1,* ***Maurois*** *502:10,* ***Wordsworth*** *828:10; see also* ***Misquotations*** *521:14*

5 *Dans ce meilleur des mondes possibles . . . tout est au mieux.*
In this best of possible worlds . . . all is for the best.
usually quoted 'All is for the best in the best of all possible worlds'
Candide (1759) ch. 1; cf. **Proverbs** 595:1

6 *Si nous ne trouvons pas des choses agréables, nous trouverons du moins des choses nouvelles.*
If we do not find anything pleasant, at least we shall find something new.
Candide (1759) ch. 17

7 *Vous savez que ces deux nations sont en guerre pour quelques arpens de neiges vers le Canada, et qu'elles dépensent pour cette belle guerre beaucoup plus que tout le Canada ne vaut.*
These two nations have been at war over a few acres of snow near Canada, and . . . they are spending on this fine struggle more than Canada itself is worth.
of the struggle between the French and the British for the control of colonial north Canada
Candide (1759) ch. 23

8 *Dans ce pays-ci il est bon de tuer de temps en temps un amiral pour encourager les autres.*
In this country [England] it is thought well to kill an admiral from time to time to encourage the others.
referring to the contentious execution of Admiral Byng (1704–57) for neglect of duty in failing to relieve Minorca
Candide (1759) ch. 23; cf. **Walpole** 801:18

9 *Il faut cultiver notre jardin.*
We must cultivate our garden.
Candide (1759) ch. 30

10 *Ils ne se servent de la pensée que pour autoriser leurs injustices, et n'emploient les paroles que pour déguiser leurs pensées.*
[Men] use thought only to justify their injustices, and speech only to conceal their thoughts.
Dialogues (1763) 'Le Chapon et la poularde'

11 *Le mieux est l'ennemi du bien.*
The best is the enemy of the good.
Contes (1772) 'La Begueule' l. 2; though often attributed to Voltaire, the notion in fact derives from an Italian proverb quoted in his *Dictionnaire philosophique* (1770 ed.) 'Art Dramatique': '*Le meglio è l'inimico del bene*'; cf. **Proverbs** 595:45

12 *Le sens commun est fort rare.*
Common sense is not so common.
Dictionnaire philosophique (1765) 'Sens Commun'

13 *La superstition met le monde entier en flammes; la philosophie les éteint.*
Superstition sets the whole world in flames; philosophy quenches them.
Dictionnaire philosophique (1764) 'Superstition'

14 *Le secret d'ennuyer est . . . de tout dire.*
The secret of being a bore . . . is to tell everything.
Discours en vers sur l'homme (1737) 'De la nature de l'homme' l. 172

15 *Tous les genres sont bons hors le genre ennuyeux.*
All styles are good except the tiresome kind.
L'Enfant prodigue (1736) preface

16 *Si Dieu n'existait pas, il faudrait l'inventer.*
If God did not exist, it would be necessary to invent him.
Épîtres no. 96 'A l'Auteur du livre des trois imposteurs'; cf. **Ovid** 561:7

17 *Ce corps qui s'appelait et qui s'appelle encore le saint empire romain n'était en aucune manière ni saint, ni romain, ni empire.*
This agglomeration which was called and which still calls itself the Holy Roman Empire was neither holy, nor Roman, nor an empire.
Essai sur l'histoire générale et sur les moeurs et l'esprit des nations (1756) ch. 70

18 *En effet, l'histoire n'est que le tableau des crimes et des malheurs.*
Indeed, history is nothing more than a tableau of crimes and misfortunes.
L'Ingénu (1767) ch. 10; cf. **Gibbon** 335:6

19 *C'est une des superstitions de l'esprit humain d'avoir imaginé que la virginité pouvait être une vertu.*

It is one of the superstitions of the human mind to have imagined that virginity could be a virtue.

'The Leningrad Notebooks' (*c.*1735–50) in T. Besterman (ed.) *Voltaire's Notebooks* (2nd ed., 1968) vol. 2, p. 455

1 *Le superflu, chose très nécessaire.*

The superfluous, a very necessary thing.

Le Mondain (1736) l. 22

2 *Il faut qu'il y ait des moments tranquilles dans les grands ouvrages, comme dans la vie après les instants de passions, mais non pas des moments de dégoût.*

There ought to be moments of tranquillity in great works, as in life after the experience of passions, but not moments of disgust.

'The Piccini Notebooks' (*c.*1735–50) in T. Besterman (ed.) *Voltaire's Notebooks* (2nd ed., 1968) vol. 2

3 *Il faut, dans le gouvernement, des bergers et des bouchers.*

Governments need both shepherds and butchers.

'The Piccini Notebooks' (*c.*1735–50) in T. Besterman (ed.) *Voltaire's Notebooks* (2nd ed., 1968) vol. 2

4 *Dieu n'est pas pour les gros bataillons, mais pour ceux qui tirent le mieux.*

God is on the side not of the heavy battalions, but of the best shots.

'The Piccini Notebooks' (*c.*1735–50) in T. Besterman (ed.) *Voltaire's Notebooks* (2nd ed., 1968) vol. 2; cf. **Anouilh** 22:7, **Bussy-Rabutin** 171:7, **Proverbs** 609:47

5 *On doit des égards aux vivants; on ne doit aux morts que la vérité.*

We owe respect to the living; to the dead we owe only truth.

'Première Lettre sur Oedipe' in *Oeuvres* (1785) vol. 1

6 *Quoi que vous fassiez, écrasez l'infâme, et aimez qui vous aime.*

Whatever you do, stamp out abuses [superstition], and love those who love you.

letter to M. d'Alembert, 28 November 1762, in Voltaire Foundation (ed.) *Complete Works* vol. 25 (1973)

7 *Il est plaisant qu'on fait une vertu du vice de chasteté; et voilà encore une drôle de chasteté que celle qui mène tout droit les hommes au péché d'Onan, et les filles aux pâles couleurs!*

It is amusing that a virtue is made of the vice of chastity; and it's a pretty odd sort of chastity at that, which leads men straight into the sin of Onan, and girls to the waning of their colour.

letter to M. Mariott, 28 March 1766, in Voltaire Foundation (ed.) *Complete Works* vol. 30 (1973)

8 *Quand la populace se mêle de raisonner, tout est perdu.*

When the masses get involved in reasoning, everything is lost.

letter to Etienne Noël Darnilaville, 1 April 1766; Theodore Besterman et al. (eds.) *The Complete Works of Voltaire* (1973) vol. 114

9 *Je ne suis pas comme une dame de la cour de Versailles, qui disait: c'est bien dommage que l'aventure de la tour de Babel ait produit la confusion des langues; sans cela tout le monde aurait toujours parlé français.*

I am not like a lady at the court of Versailles, who said: 'What a dreadful pity that the bother at the tower of Babel should have got language all mixed up; but for that, everyone would always have spoken French.'

letter to Catherine the Great, 26 May 1767, in Voltaire Foundation (ed.) *Complete Works* vol. 32 (1974)

10 The art of government is to make two-thirds of a nation pay all it possibly can pay for the benefit of the other third.

attributed; Walter Bagehot *The English Constitution* (1867) ch. 5

11 The composition of a tragedy requires *testicles*.

on being asked why no woman had ever written 'a tolerable tragedy'

letter from Byron to John Murray, 2 April 1817, in L. A. Marchand (ed.) *Byron's Letters and Journals* vol. 5 (1976)

12 The English plays are like their English puddings: nobody has any taste for them but themselves.

Joseph Spence *Anecdotes* (ed. J. M. Osborn, 1966) no. 1033

13 *Habacuc était capable de tout.*

Habakkuk was capable of anything.

attributed; in *Notes and Queries* 26 July 1941

14 What a fuss about an omelette!

what Voltaire apparently said on the burning of De l'esprit

James Parton *Life of Voltaire* (1881) vol. 2, ch. 25; cf. **Misquotations** 521:14

15 This is no time for making new enemies.

on being asked to renounce the Devil, on his deathbed

attributed

Andrei Voznesensky 1933–

Russian poet

16 I am Goya
of the bare field, by the enemy's beak gouged
till the craters of my eyes gape,
I am grief,
I am the tongue
of war, the embers of cities
on the snows of the year 1941
I am hunger.

'Goya' (published 1960) (translated by Stanley Kunitz)

Peter Vyazemsky 1792–1878

Russian poet

17 God of frostbite, God of famine,
beggars, cripples by the yard,
farms with no crops to examine—
that's him, that's your Russian God.

'The Russian God' (1828) (translated by Alan Myers)

Richard Wagner 1813–83

German composer

18 *Frisch weht der Wind*
der Heimat zu:—
mein irisch Kind,
wo weilest du?

Freshly blows the wind homewards: my Irish child, where are you dwelling?

Tristan und Isolde (1865) act 1, sc. 1

Derek Walcott 1930–
West Indian poet and dramatist

1 I who have cursed
The drunken officer of British rule, how choose
Between this Africa and the English tongue I love?
'A Far Cry From Africa' (1962)

2 Famine sighs like scythe
across the field of statistics and the desert
is a moving mouth.
'The Fortunate Traveller' (1981)

3 I come from a backward place: your duty is supplied by life around you. One guy plants bananas; another plants cocoa; I'm a writer, I plant lines. There's the same clarity of occupation, and the sense of devotion.
in *Guardian* 12 July 1997

Lech Wałęsa 1943–
Polish trade unionist and statesman, President since 1990

4 You have riches and freedom here but I feel no sense of faith or direction. You have so many computers, why don't you use them in the search for love?
in Paris, on his first journey outside the Soviet area, in *Daily Telegraph* 14 December 1988

Alice Walker 1944–
American poet

5 Did this happen to your mother? Did your sister throw up a lot?
title of poem (1979)

6 I thought love would adapt itself
to my needs.
But needs grow too fast;
they come up like weeds.
Through cracks in the conversation.
Through silences in the dark.
Through everything you thought was concrete.
'Did This Happen to Your Mother? Did Your Sister Throw Up a Lot?' (1979)

7 Expect nothing. Live frugally
on surprise.
'Expect nothing' (1973)

8 The quietly pacifist peaceful
always die
to make room for men
who shout. Who tell lies to
children, and crush the corners
off of old men's dreams.
'The QPP' (1973)

9 We have a beautiful
mother
Her green lap
immense
Her brown embrace
eternal
Her blue body
everything
we know.
'We Have a Beautiful Mother' (1991)

10 a woman is not
a potted plant
her leaves trimmed
to the contours
of her sex.
'A woman is not a potted plant'

11 I think it pisses God off if you walk by the colour purple in a field somewhere and don't notice it.
The Colour Purple (1982)

Felix Walker fl. 1820
American politician

12 I'm talking to Buncombe ['bunkum'].
excusing a long, dull, irrelevant speech in the House of Representatives, c.1820 (Buncombe being his constituency)
W. Safire *New Language of Politics* (2nd ed., 1972); cf. **Carlyle** 188:4

Edgar Wallace 1875–1932
English thriller writer

13 Dreamin' of thee! Dreamin' of thee!
'T. A. in Love' (1900); popularized by Cyril Fletcher in 1930s radio shows

George Wallace 1919–98
American Democratic politician

14 Segregation now, segregation tomorrow and segregation forever!
inaugural speech as Governor of Alabama, January 1963, in *Birmingham World* 19 January 1963

Henry Wallace 1888–1965
American Democratic politician

15 The century on which we are entering—the century which will come out of this war—can be and must be the century of the common man.
speech, 8 May 1942, in *Vital Speeches* (1942) vol. 8

William Ross Wallace d. 1881
American poet

16 For the hand that rocks the cradle
Is the hand that rules the world.
'What rules the world' (1865); cf. **Proverbs** 601:45, **Robinson** 629:22

Graham Wallas 1858–1932
British political scientist

17 The little girl had the making of a poet in her who, being told to be sure of her meaning before she spoke, said, 'How can I know what I think till I see what I say?'
The Art of Thought (1926) ch. 4

Edmund Waller 1606–87

English poet

1 So was the huntsman by the bear oppressed,
Whose hide he sold—before he caught the beast!
'The Battle of the Summer Islands' (1645) canto 2

2 Go, lovely rose!
Tell her, that wastes her time and me,
That now she knows,
When I resemble her to thee,
How sweet and fair she seems to be.
'Go, lovely rose!' (1645)

3 Others may use the ocean as their road,
Only the English make it their abode.
'Of a War with Spain' (1658) l. 25

4 Poets that lasting marble seek
Must carve in Latin or in Greek.
'Of English Verse' (1645)

5 The soul's dark cottage, battered and decayed
Lets in new light through chinks that time has made;
Stronger by weakness, wiser men become,
As they draw near to their eternal home.
Leaving the old, both worlds at once they view,
That stand upon the threshold of the new.
'Of the Last Verses in the Book' (1685) l. 18

6 That which her slender waist confined
Shall now my joyful temples bind;
No monarch but would give his crown
His arms might do what this has done.
'On a Girdle' (1645)

7 Rome, though her eagle through the world had flown,
Could never make this island all her own.
'Panegyric to My Lord Protector' (1655) st. 17

8 Illustrious acts high raptures do infuse,
And every conqueror creates a Muse.
'Panegyric to My Lord Protector' (1655) st. 46

9 It is not that I love you less
Than when before your feet I lay:
But, to prevent the sad increase
Of hopeless love, I keep away.
In vain, alas! for every thing
Which I have known belong to you,
Your form does to my fancy bring
And makes my old wounds bleed anew.
'The Self-Banished' (1645)

10 Why came I so untimely forth
Into a world which, wanting thee,
Could entertain us with no worth,
Or shadow of felicity?
'To My Young Lady Lucy Sidney' (1645)

11 So all we know
Of what they do above,
Is that they happy are, and that they love.
'Upon the Death of My Lady Rich' (1645) l. 75

12 Under the tropic is our language spoke,
And part of Flanders hath received our yoke.
'Upon the Late Storm, and of the Death of His Highness Ensuing the Same' (1659) l. 21

Horace Walpole, Lord Orford 1717–97

English writer and connoisseur
on Walpole: see ***Macaulay*** *482:6*

13 Our supreme governors, the mob.
letter to Horace Mann, 7 September 1743, in *Correspondence* (Yale ed. 1937–83) vol. 18

14 [Lovat] was beheaded yesterday, and died extremely well, without passion, affectation, buffoonery or timidity: his behaviour was natural and intrepid.
letter to Horace Mann, 10 April 1747, in *Correspondence* (Yale ed.) vol. 19

15 [Strawberry Hill] is a little plaything-house that I got out of Mrs Chenevix's shop, and is the prettiest bauble you ever saw. It is set in enamelled meadows, with filigree hedges.
letter to Hon. Henry Conway, 8 June 1747, in *Correspondence* (Yale ed.) vol. 37

16 But, thank God! the Thames is between me and the Duchess of Queensberry.
letter to Hon. Henry Conway, 8 June 1747, in *Correspondence* (Yale ed.) vol. 37

17 Every drop of ink in my pen ran cold.
letter to George Montagu, 30 July 1752, in *Correspondence* (Yale ed.) vol. 9

18 At present, nothing is talked of, nothing admired, but what I cannot help calling a very insipid and tedious performance: it is a kind of novel, called *The Life and Opinions of Tristram Shandy*; the great humour of which consists in the whole narration always going backwards.
letter to David Dalrymple, 4 April 1760, in *Correspondence* (Yale ed.) vol. 15

19 One of the greatest geniuses that ever existed, Shakespeare, undoubtedly wanted taste.
letter to Christopher Wren, 9 August 1764, in *Correspondence* (Yale ed.) vol. 40

20 What has one to do, when one grows tired of the world, as we both do, but to draw nearer and nearer, and gently waste the remains of life with friends with whom one began it?
letter to George Montagu, 21 November 1765, in *Correspondence* (Yale ed.) vol. 10

21 It is charming to totter into vogue.
letter to George Selwyn, 2 December 1765, in *Correspondence* (Yale ed.) vol. 30

22 The best sun we have is made of Newcastle coal.
letter to George Montagu, 15 June 1768, in *Correspondence* (Yale ed.) vol. 10

23 Everybody talks of the constitution, but all sides forget that the constitution is extremely well, and would do very well, if they would but let it alone.
letter to Horace Mann, 18–19 January 1770, in *Correspondence* (Yale ed.) vol. 23

24 One's mind suffers only when one is young and while one is ignorant of the world. When one has lived for some time, one learns that the young think too little and the old too much, and one grows careless about both.
letter to Horace Mann, 14 January 1772, in *Correspondence* (Yale ed.) vol. 23

1 It was easier to conquer it [the East] than to know what to do with it.
letter to Horace Mann, 27 March 1772, in *Correspondence* (Yale ed.) vol. 23

2 The way to ensure summer in England is to have it framed and glazed in a comfortable room.
letter to Revd William Cole, 28 May 1774, in *Correspondence* (Yale ed.) vol. 1

3 The next Augustan age will dawn on the other side of the Atlantic. There will, perhaps, be a Thucydides at Boston, a Xenophon at New York, and, in time, a Virgil at Mexico, and a Newton at Peru. At last, some curious traveller from Lima will visit England and give a description of the ruins of St Paul's, like the editions of Balbec and Palmyra.
letter to Horace Mann, 24 November 1774, in *Correspondence* (Yale ed.) vol. 24; cf. **Macaulay** 482:10

4 By the waters of Babylon we sit down and weep, when we think of thee, O America!
letter to Revd William Mason, 12 June 1775, in *Correspondence* (Yale ed.) vol. 28; cf. **Book of Common Prayer** 141:7

5 This world is a comedy to those that think, a tragedy to those that feel.
letter to Anne, Countess of Upper Ossory, 16 August 1776, in *Correspondence* (Yale ed.) vol. 32

6 Tell me, ye divines, which is the most virtuous man, he who begets twenty bastards, or he who sacrifices an hundred thousand lives?
letter to Horace Mann, 7 July 1778, in *Correspondence* (Yale ed.) vol. 24

7 When will the world know that peace and propagation are the two most delightful things in it?
letter to Horace Mann, 7 July 1778, in *Correspondence* (Yale ed.) vol. 24

8 When men write for profit, they are not very delicate.
letter to Revd William Cole, 1 September 1778, in *Correspondence* (Yale ed.) vol. 2

9 When people will not weed their own minds, they are apt to be overrun with nettles.
letter to Caroline, Countess of Ailesbury, 10 July 1779, in *Correspondence* (Yale ed.) vol. 39

10 Prognostics do not always prove prophecies,—at least the wisest prophets make sure of the event first.
letter to Thomas Walpole, 19 February 1785, in *Correspondence* (Yale ed.) vol. 36

11 It is the story of a mountebank and his zany.
of **Boswell**'*s* Tour of the Hebrides
letter to Hon. Henry Conway, 6 October 1785, in *Correspondence* (Yale ed.) vol. 39

12 All his own geese are swans, as the swans of others are geese.
of Joshua **Reynolds**
letter to Anne, Countess of Upper Ossory, 1 December 1786, in *Correspondence* (Yale ed.) vol. 33

13 How should such a fellow as Sheridan, who has no diamonds to bestow, fascinate all the world?—yet witchcraft, no doubt there has been, for when did simple eloquence ever convince a majority?
letter to Lady Ossory, 9 February 1787, in *Correspondence* (Yale ed.) vol. 33

14 That hyena in petticoats, Mrs Wollstonecraft.
letter to Hannah More, 26 January 1795, in *Correspondence* (Yale ed.) vol. 31

15 His speeches were fine, but as much laboured as his extempore sayings.
of Lord **Chesterfield**
Memoirs of the Reign of King George II (ed. Lord Holland, 1846) vol. 1, 1751

16 Whoever knows the interior of affairs, must be sensible to how many more events the faults of statesmen give birth, than are produced by their good intentions.
Memoirs of the Reign of King George II (ed. Lord Holland, 1846) vol. 1, 1754

17 The keenness of his sabre was blunted by the difficulty with which he drew it from the scabbard; I mean, the hesitation and ungracefulness of his delivery took off from the force of his arguments.
of Henry Fox, Lord **Holland**
Memoirs of the Reign of King George II (ed. Lord Holland, 1846) vol. 2, 1755

18 While he felt like a victim, he acted like a hero.
of Admiral Byng, on the day of his execution
Memoirs of the Reign of King George II (ed. Lord Holland, 1846) vol. 2, 1757; cf. **Voltaire** 797:8

19 Perhaps those, who, trembling most, maintain a dignity in their fate, are the bravest: resolution on reflection is real courage.
Memoirs of the Reign of King George II (ed. Lord Holland, 1846) vol. 2, 1757

20 They seem to know no medium between a mitre and a crown of martyrdom. If the clergy are not called to the latter, they never deviate from the pursuit of the former. One would think their motto was, *Canterbury or Smithfield.*
Memoirs of the Reign of King George II (ed. Lord Holland, 1846) vol. 3, 1758

21 All his passions were expressed by one livid smile.
of George Grenville
Memoirs of the Reign of King George III (ed. D. Le Marchant, 1845) vol. 1, 1763

22 His courage and his tenderness were never disunited. He was dauntless on every occasion, but when it was necessary to surmount his bashfulness.
of Lord Granby in 1770
Memoirs of the Reign of King George III (ed. D. Le Marchant, 1845) vol. 4

23 He lost his dominions in America, his authority over Ireland, and all influence in Europe, by aiming at despotism in England; and exposed himself to more mortifications and humiliations than can happen to a quiet Doge of Venice.
of King **George III**
Memoirs of the Reign of King George III (ed. D. Le Marchant, 1845) vol. 4, 1770

1 Pieces of land and sea so natural that one steps back for fear of being splashed.
*of two landscapes by Thomas **Gainsborough**, exhibited in 1781*
in *Dictionary of National Biography* (1917–)

2 Virtue knows to a farthing what it has lost by not having been vice.
L. Kronenberger *The Extraordinary Mr Wilkes* (1974) pt. 3, ch. 2

Robert Walpole, Lord Orford 1676–1745

English Whig statesman; first British Prime Minister, 1721–42

3 They now *ring* the bells, but they will soon *wring* their hands.
on the declaration of war with Spain, 1739
W. Coxe *Memoirs of Sir Robert Walpole* (1798) vol. 1

4 All those men have their price.
of fellow parliamentarians
W. Coxe *Memoirs of Sir Robert Walpole* (1798) vol. 1; cf. **Proverbs** 599:33

5 Madam, there are fifty thousand men slain this year in Europe, and not one Englishman.
*to Queen **Caroline**, 1734, on the war of the Polish succession, in which the English had refused to participate*
John Hervey *Memoirs* (written 1734–43, published 1848) vol. 1

6 We must muzzle this terrible young cornet of horse.
*of the elder William **Pitt**, who had held a cornetcy before his election to Parliament, c.1736*
in *Dictionary of National Biography* (1917–)

7 [Gratitude of place-expectants] is a lively sense of future favours.
W. Hazlitt *Lectures on the English Comic Writers* (1819) 'On Wit and Humour'; cf. **La Rochefoucauld** 453:19

8 You can read. It is a great happiness. I totally neglected it while I was in business, which has been the whole of my life, and to such a degree that I cannot now read a page—a warning to all Ministers.
*on seeing Henry Fox (Lord **Holland**) reading in the library at Houghton*
Edmund Fitzmaurice *Life of Shelburne* (1875) vol. 1

William Walsh 1663–1708

English poet

9 A lover forsaken
A new love may get,
But a neck when once broken
Can never be set.
'The Despairing Lover' l. 17

10 By partners, in each other kind,
Afflictions easier grow;
In love alone we hate to find
Companions of our woe.
'Song: Of All the Torments'

11 I can endure my own despair,
But not another's hope.
'Song: Of All the Torments'

Izaak Walton 1593–1683

English writer

12 Angling may be said to be so like the mathematics, that it can never be fully learnt.
The Compleat Angler (1653) 'Epistle to the Reader'

13 And for winter fly-fishing it is as useful as an almanac out of date.
The Compleat Angler (1653) 'Epistle to the Reader'

14 As no man is born an artist, so no man is born an angler.
The Compleat Angler (1653) 'Epistle to the Reader'

15 I shall stay him no longer than to wish him a rainy evening to read this following discourse; and that if he be an honest angler, the east wind may never blow when he goes a-fishing.
The Compleat Angler (1653) 'Epistle to the Reader'

16 I am, Sir, a Brother of the Angle.
The Compleat Angler (1653) pt. 1, ch. 1

17 Sir Henry Wotton . . . was also a most dear lover, and a frequent practiser of the art of angling; of which he would say, 'it was an employment for his idle time, which was then not idly spent . . . a rest to his mind, a cheerer of his spirits, a diverter of sadness, a calmer of unquiet thoughts, a moderator of passions, a procurer of contentedness; and that it begat habits of peace and patience in those that professed and practised it.'
The Compleat Angler (1653) pt. 1, ch. 1

18 Good company and good discourse are the very sinews of virtue.
The Compleat Angler (1653) pt. 1, ch. 2

19 An excellent angler, and now with God.
The Compleat Angler (1653) pt. 1, ch. 4

20 I love such mirth as does not make friends ashamed to look upon one another next morning.
The Compleat Angler (1653) pt. 1, ch. 5

21 A good, honest, wholesome, hungry breakfast.
The Compleat Angler (1653) pt. 1, ch. 5

22 No man can lose what he never had.
The Compleat Angler (1653) pt. 1, ch. 5

23 In so doing, use him as though you loved him.
on baiting a hook with a live frog
The Compleat Angler (1653) pt. 1, ch. 8

24 This dish of meat is too good for any but anglers, or very honest men.
The Compleat Angler (1653) pt. 1, ch. 8

25 I love any discourse of rivers, and fish and fishing.
The Compleat Angler (1653) pt. 1, ch. 18

26 Look to your health; and if you have it, praise God, and value it next to a good conscience; for health is the second blessing that we mortals are capable of; a blessing that money cannot buy.
The Compleat Angler (1653) pt. 1, ch. 21

27 Let the blessing of St Peter's Master be . . . upon all that are lovers of virtue; and dare trust in His providence; and be quiet; and go a-Angling.
The Compleat Angler (1653) pt. 1, ch. 21

1 The great Secretary of Nature and all learning, Sir Francis Bacon.

Life of Herbert (1670 ed.)

2 But God, who is able to prevail, wrestled with him, as the Angel did with Jacob, and marked him; marked him for his own.

Life of Donne (1670 ed.)

3 Of this blest man, let his just praise be given,
Heaven was in him, before he was in heaven.

written in a copy of Dr Richard Sibbes's *The Returning Backslider*, now preserved in Salisbury Cathedral Library.

William Warburton 1698–1779

English theologian; Bishop of Gloucester from 1759

4 Orthodoxy is my doxy; heterodoxy is another man's doxy.

to Lord Sandwich, in Joseph Priestley *Memoirs* (1807) vol. 1; cf. **Carlyle** 187:23

Artemus Ward (Charles Farrar Browne) 1834–67

American humorist

5 It is a pity that Chawcer, who had geneyus, was so unedicated. He's the wuss speller I know of.

Artemus Ward in London (1867) ch. 4

6 Let us all be happy, and live within our means, even if we have to borrer the money to do it with.

Artemus Ward in London (1867) ch. 7

7 I am happiest when I am idle. I could live for months without performing any kind of labour, and at the expiration of that time I should feel fresh and vigorous enough to go right on in the same way for numerous more months.

Artemus Ward in London (1867) ch. 9

8 He is dreadfully married. He's the most married man I ever saw in my life.

Artemus Ward's Lecture (1869) 'Brigham Young's Palace'

9 Why is this thus? What is the reason of this thusness?

Artemus Ward's Lecture (1869) 'Heber C. Kimball's Harem'

Barbara Ward 1914–81

British author and educator

10 We cannot cheat on DNA. We cannot get round photosynthesis. We cannot say I am not going to give a damn about phytoplankton. All these tiny mechanisms provide the preconditions of our planetary life. To say we do not care is to say in the most literal sense that 'we choose death'.

Only One Earth (1972)

Nathaniel Ward 1578–1652

English clergyman

11 The world is full of care, much like unto a bubble;
Woman and care, and care and women, and
women and care and trouble.

epigram, attributed by Ward to a lady at the Court of the Queen of Bohemia, in *The Simple Cobbler of Aggawam in America* (1647)

Andy Warhol 1927–87

American artist

12 In the future everybody will be world famous for fifteen minutes.

Andy Warhol (1968) (volume released to mark his exhibition in Stockholm, February–March, 1968)

13 Being good in business is the most fascinating kind of art.

Philosophy of Andy Warhol (From A to B and Back Again) (1975)

14 An artist is someone who produces things that people don't need to have but that he—for *some reason*—thinks it would be a good idea to give them.

Philosophy of Andy Warhol (From A to B and Back Again) (1975)

15 Isn't life a series of images that change as they repeat themselves?

Victor Bokris *Andy Warhol* (1989)

16 The things I want to show are mechanical. Machines have less problems.

Mike Wrenn *Andy Warhol: In His Own Words* (1991)

Sylvia Townsend Warner 1893–1978

English writer

17 I discovered that dinners follow the order of creation—fish first, then entrées, then joints, lastly the apple as dessert. The soup is chaos.

diary, 26 May 1929; Claire Harman (ed.) *The Diaries of Sylvia Townsend Warner* (1994)

18 One need not write in a diary what one is to remember for ever.

diary, 22 October 1930

19 One cannot overestimate the power of a good rancorous hatred on the part of the *stupid*. The stupid have so much more industry and energy to expend on hating. They build it up like coral insects.

diary, 26 September 1954

20 Total grief is like a minefield. No knowing when one will touch the tripwire.

diary, 11 December 1969

Earl Warren 1891–1974

American Chief Justice

21 In civilized life, law floats in a sea of ethics.

in *New York Times* 12 November 1962

Robert Penn Warren 1905–1989

American poet, novelist, and critic

22 Long ago in Kentucky, I, a boy, stood
By a dirt road, in first dark, and heard
The great geese hoot northward.

Audubon (1969) 'Tell Me a Story'

23 Ages to our construction went,
Dim architecture, hour by hour:
And violence, forgot now, lent
The present stillness all its power.

'Bearded Oaks' (1942)

1 They were human, they suffered, wore long black coat and gold watch chain.
They stare from daguerrotype with severe reprehension,
Or from genuine oil, and you'd never guess any pain
In those merciless eyes that now remark our own time's sad declension.
'Promises' (1957)

Booker T. Washington 1856–1915
American educationist and emancipated slave

2 No race can prosper till it learns that there is as much dignity in tilling a field as in writing a poem.
Up from Slavery (1901)

3 You can't hold a man down without staying down with him.
attributed

George Washington 1732–99
1st President of the US
on Washington: see **Byron** *178:20*, **Lee** *461:21*

4 The time is now near at hand which must probably determine whether Americans are to be freemen or slaves; whether they are to have any property they can call their own . . . The fate of unborn millions will now depend, under God, on the courage and conduct of this army. Our cruel and unrelenting enemy leaves us only the choice of brave resistance, or the most abject submission. We have, therefore, to resolve to conquer or die.
General orders, 2 July 1776, in J. C. Fitzpatrick (ed.) *Writings of George Washington* vol. 5 (1932)

5 Few men have virtue to withstand the highest bidder.
letter, 17 August 1779

6 'Tis our true policy to steer clear of permanent alliances, with any portion of the foreign world.
President's Address . . . retiring from Public Life 17 September 1796

7 Let me . . . warn you in the most solemn manner against the baneful effects of the spirit of party.
President's Address . . . 17 September 1796

8 The nation which indulges toward another an habitual hatred or an habitual fondness is in some degree a slave. It is a slave to its animosity or to its affection, either of which is sufficient to lead it astray from its duty and its interest.
President's Address . . . 17 September 1796

9 I can't tell a lie, Pa; you know I can't tell a lie. I did cut it with my hatchet.
M. L. Weems *Life of George Washington* (10th ed., 1810) ch. 2

10 Liberty, when it begins to take root, is a plant of rapid growth.
attributed

Ned Washington 1901–76
American songwriter

11 Hi diddle dee dee (an actor's life for me).
title of song (1940) from the film *Pinocchio*

12 The night is like a lovely tune,
Beware my foolish heart!
How white the ever-constant moon,
Take care, my foolish heart!
'My Foolish Heart' (1949 song)

Edward Waterfield

13 Two men wrote a lexicon, Liddell and Scott;
Some parts were clever, but some parts were not.
Hear, all ye learned, and read me this riddle,
How the wrong part wrote Scott, and the right part wrote Liddell.
of Henry Liddell (1811–98) and Robert Scott (1811–87) co-authors of the Greek Lexicon *(1843), Liddell being in the habit of ascribing to his co-author usages which he criticised in his pupils, and which they said that they had culled from the* Lexicon
L. E. Tanner *Westminster School: A History* (1934) ch. 9

Rowland Watkyns *c.*1616–64

14 I love him not, but show no reason can
Wherefore, but this, *I do not love* the man.
'Antipathy'; cf. **Brown** 152:7, **Martial** 497:23

15 For every marriage then is best in tune,
When that the wife is May, the husband June.
'To the most Courteous and Fair Gentlewoman, Mrs Elinor Williams'

James Dewey Watson 1928–
American biologist
see also **Crick and Watson** *245:3*

16 No *good* model ever accounted for *all* the facts, since some data was bound to be misleading if not plain wrong.
Francis Crick *Some Mad Pursuit* (1988)

17 Some day a child is going to sue its parents for being born. They will say, my life is so awful with these terrible genetic defects and you just callously didn't find out.
on the question of genetic screening of foetuses
interview in *Sunday Telegraph* 16 February 1997

Thomas Watson Snr. 1874–1956
American businessman; Chairman of IBM 1914–52

18 Clothes don't make the man . . . but they go a long way toward making a businessman.
Robert Sobel *IBM: Colossus in Transition* (1981)

19 You cannot be a success in any business without believing that it is the greatest business in the world . . . You have to put your heart in the business and the business in your heart.
Robert Sobel *IBM: Colossus in Transition* (1981)

William Watson c.1559–1603

English Roman Catholic conspirator

1 *Fiat justitia et ruant coeli.*
Let justice be done though the heavens fall.
A Decacordon of Ten Quodlibeticall Questions Concerning Religion and State (1602), being the first citation in an English work of a famous maxim; cf. **Mansfield** 494:10, **Mottoes** 538:8

William Watson 1858–1936

English poet

2 April, April,
Laugh thy girlish laughter.
Then, the moment after,
Weep thy girlish tears!
'April'

3 His friends he loved. His direst earthly foes—
Cats—I believe he did but feign to hate.
My hand will miss the insinuated nose,
Mine eyes the tail that wagged contempt at Fate.
'An Epitaph'

Isaac Watts 1674–1748

English hymn-writer

4 One sickly sheep infects the flock,
And poisons all the rest.
Divine Songs for Children (1715) 'Against Evil Company'

5 How doth the little busy bee
Improve each shining hour,
And gather honey all the day
From every opening flower!
Divine Songs for Children (1715) 'Against Idleness and Mischief'; cf. **Carroll** 189:9

6 For Satan finds some mischief still
For idle hands to do.
Divine Songs for Children (1715) 'Against Idleness and Mischief'; cf. **Proverbs** 598:7

7 Let me be dressed fine as I will,
Flies, worms, and flowers, exceed me still.
Divine Songs for Children (1715) 'Against Pride in Clothes'

8 Let dogs delight to bark and bite,
For God hath made them so.
Divine Songs for Children (1715) 'Against Quarrelling'

9 But, children, you should never let
Such angry passions rise;
Your little hands were never made
To tear each other's eyes.
Divine Songs for Children (1715) 'Against Quarrelling'

10 Birds in their little nests agree
And 'tis a shameful sight,
When children of one family
Fall out, and chide, and fight.
Divine Songs for Children (1715) 'Love between Brothers and Sisters'; cf. **Proverbs** 596:23

11 'Tis the voice of the sluggard; I heard him complain,
'You have waked me too soon, I must slumber again'.
As the door on its hinges, so he on his bed,
Turns his sides and his shoulders and his heavy head.
Divine Songs for Children (1715) 'The Sluggard'; cf. **Carroll** 190:6

12 Come, let us join our cheerful songs
With angels round the throne;
Ten thousand thousand are their tongues,
But all their joys are one.

'Worthy the Lamb that died,' they cry,
'To be exalted thus;'
'Worthy the Lamb,' our lips reply,
'For he was slain for us.'
Hymns and Spiritual Songs (1707) 'Come, let us join our cheerful songs'

13 We are a garden walled around,
Chosen and made peculiar ground;
A little spot enclosed by grace,
Out of the world's wide wilderness.
Hymns and Spiritual Songs (1707) 'The Church the Garden of Christ'

14 When I survey the wondrous cross
On which the prince of glory died,
My richest gain I count but loss,
And pour contempt on all my pride.
Hymns and Spiritual Songs (1707) 'Crucifixion to the World, by the Cross of Christ'

15 Hark! from the tombs a doleful sound.
Hymns and Spiritual Songs (1707) 'Hark! from the Tombs'

16 There is a land of pure delight,
Where saints immortal reign.
Hymns and Spiritual Songs (1707) 'A Prospect of Heaven makes Death easy'

17 Death like a narrow sea divides
This heavenly land from ours.
Hymns and Spiritual Songs (1707) 'A Prospect of Heaven makes Death easy'

18 Jesus shall reign where'er the sun
Does his successive journeys run;
His kingdom stretch from shore to shore,
Till moons shall wax and wane no more.
The Psalms of David Imitated (1719) Psalm 72

19 Our God, our help in ages past
Our hope for years to come,
Our shelter from the stormy blast,
And our eternal home.

Beneath the shadow of Thy Throne
Thy saints have dwelt secure;
Sufficient is Thine Arm alone,
And our defence is sure.

Before the hills in order stood,
Or earth received her frame,
From everlasting Thou art God,
To endless years the same.

A thousand ages in Thy sight
Are like an evening gone;
Short as the watch that ends the night
Before the rising sun.

Time, like an ever-rolling stream,
Bears all its sons away;
They fly forgotten, as a dream

Dies at the opening day.
'Our God' altered to 'O God' by John **Wesley**, *1738*
The Psalms of David Imitated (1719) Psalm 90

Evelyn Waugh 1903–66
English novelist

1 I am not I: thou art not he or she: they are not they.
Brideshead Revisited (1945) 'Author's Note'

2 Charm is the great English blight. It does not exist outside these damp islands. It spots and kills anything it touches. It kills love, it kills art.
Brideshead Revisited (1945) bk. 3, ch. 2

3 Any who have heard that sound will shrink at the recollection of it; it is the sound of English county families baying for broken glass.
Decline and Fall (1928) 'Prelude'; cf. **Belloc** 63:24

4 I expect you'll be becoming a schoolmaster, sir. That's what most of the gentlemen does, sir, that gets sent down for indecent behaviour.
Decline and Fall (1928) 'Prelude'

5 Any one who has been to an English public school will always feel comparatively at home in prison. It is the people brought up in the gay intimacy of the slums, Paul learned, who find prison so soul-destroying.
Decline and Fall (1928) pt. 3, ch. 4

6 Only when one has lost all curiosity about the future has one reached the age to write an autobiography.
A Little Learning (1964)

7 You never find an Englishman among the under-dogs—except in England, of course.
The Loved One (1948) ch. 1

8 His strongest tastes were negative. He abhorred plastics, Picasso, sunbathing and jazz—everything in fact that had happened in his own lifetime.
The Ordeal of Gilbert Pinfold (1957) ch. 1

9 *The Beast* stands for strong mutually antagonistic governments everywhere . . . Self-sufficiency at home, self-assertion abroad.
Scoop (1938) bk. 1, ch. 1

10 Up to a point, Lord Copper.
Scoop (1938) bk. 1, ch. 1

11 'Feather-footed through the plashy fen passes the questing vole' . . . 'Yes,' said the Managing Editor. 'That must be good style.'
Scoop (1938) bk. 1, ch. 1

12 Remember that the Patriots are in the right and are going to win . . . But they must win quickly. The British public has no interest in a war that drags on indecisively. A few sharp victories, some conspicuous acts of personal bravery on the Patriot side and a colourful entry into the capital. That is *The Beast* Policy for the war.
Scoop (1938) bk. 1, ch. 3

13 News is what a chap who doesn't care much about anything wants to read. And it's only news until he's read it. After that it's dead.
Scoop (1938) bk. 1, ch. 5

14 I will not stand for being called a woman in my own house.
Scoop (1938) bk. 2, ch. 1

15 Other nations use 'force'; we Britons alone use 'Might'.
Scoop (1938) bk. 2, ch. 5

16 Is there any place that is free from evil? It is too simple to say that only the Nazis wanted war . . . Even good men thought that their private honour would be satisfied by war. They could assert their manhood by killing and being killed. They would accept hardship in recompense for having been selfish and lazy. Danger justified privilege.
Unconditional Surrender (1961) bk. 3, sect. 4

17 All this fuss about sleeping together. For physical pleasure I'd sooner go to my dentist any day.
Vile Bodies (1930) ch. 6

18 To see him fumbling with our rich and delicate language is to experience all the horror of seeing a Sèvres vase in the hands of a chimpanzee.
of Stephen ***Spender***
in *The Tablet* 5 May 1951

19 Punctuality is the virtue of the bored.
Michael Davie (ed.) *Diaries of Evelyn Waugh* (1976) 'Irregular Notes 1960–65', 26 March 1962

20 A typical triumph of modern science to find the only part of Randolph that was not malignant and remove it.
on hearing that Randolph Churchill's lung, when removed, proved non-malignant
Michael Davie (ed.) *Diaries of Evelyn Waugh* (1976) 'Irregular Notes 1960–65', March 1964

21 I drink for it.
when asked, while at Oxford, what he did for his college
attributed

22 I wouldn't give up writing about God at this stage, if I was you. It would be like P. G. Wodehouse dropping Jeeves half way through the Wooster series.
to Graham Greene
Christopher Sykes *Evelyn Waugh* (1975)

23 You have no idea how much nastier I would be if I was not a Catholic. Without supernatural aid I would hardly be a human being.
Noel Annan *Our Age* (1990)

Frederick Weatherly 1848–1929
English songwriter

24 Where are the boys of the old Brigade,
Who fought with us side by side?
'The Old Brigade' (1886 song)

25 Roses are flowering in Picardy,
But there's never a rose like you.
'Roses of Picardy' (1916 song)

Beatrice Webb 1858–1943
English socialist

26 I never visualised labour as separate men and women of different sorts and kinds . . . labour was

an abstraction, which seemed to denote an arithmetically calculable mass of human beings, each individual a repetition of the other.
My Apprenticeship (1926) ch. 1

Sidney Webb 1859–1947

English socialist

1 The inevitability of gradualness.
Presidential address to the annual conference of the Labour Party, 26 June 1923, in *The Labour Party on the Threshold* (Fabian Tract no. 207, 1923)

2 Marriage is the waste-paper basket of the emotions.
Bertrand Russell *Autobiography* (1967) vol. 1, ch. 4

Max Weber 1864–1920

German sociologist

3 The protestant ethic and the spirit of capitalism.
Archiv für Sozialwissenschaft Sozialpolitik vol. 20 (1904–5) (title of article)

4 In Baxter's view the care for external goods should only lie on the shoulders of the saint like 'a light cloak, which can be thrown aside at any moment.' But fate decreed that the cloak should become an iron cage.
Gesammelte Aufsätze zur Religionssoziologie (1920) vol. 1 (translated by T. Parsons, 1930)

5 The State is a relation of men dominating men, a relation supported by means of legitimate (i.e. considered to be legitimate) violence.
'Politik als Beruf' (1919) (translated by H. Gerth and C. Wright Mills, 1948)

6 The authority of the 'eternal yesterday'.
'Politik als Beruf' (1919)

7 The experience of the irrationality of the world has been the driving force of all religious revolution.
'Politik als Beruf' (1919)

8 The concept of the 'official secret' is its [bureaucracy's] specific invention.
'Politik als Beruf' (1919)

Daniel Webster 1782–1852

American politician
on Webster: see **Smith** *725:18*

9 It is, Sir, as I have said, a small college. And yet *there are those who love it*!
argument in the case of the Trustees of Dartmouth College v. Woodward, 10 March 1818

10 The past, at least, is secure.
second speech in the Senate on Foote's Resolution, 26 January 1830; *Writings and Speeches* (1903) vol. 6

11 The people's government, made for the people, made by the people, and answerable to the people.
second speech in the Senate on Foote's Resolution, 26 January 1830; *Writings and Speeches* (1903) vol. 6; cf. **Lincoln** 468:13

12 Liberty *and* Union, now and forever, one and inseparable!
second speech in the Senate on Foote's Resolution, 26 January 1830; *Writings and Speeches* (1903) vol. 6

13 On this question of principle, while actual suffering was yet afar off, they [the Colonies] raised their flag against a power, to which, for purposes of foreign conquest and subjugation, Rome, in the height of her glory, is not to be compared; a power which has dotted over the surface of the whole globe with her possessions and military posts, whose morning drum-beat, following the sun, and keeping company with the hours, circles the earth with one continuous and unbroken strain of the martial airs of England.
speech in the Senate on the President's Protest, 7 May 1834; *Writings and Speeches* (1903) vol. 7

14 Whatever government is not a government of laws, is a despotism, let it be called what it may.
at a reception in Bangor, Maine, 25 August 1835; *Writings and Speeches* (1903) vol. 2

15 Thank God, I—I also—am an American!
speech on the completion of Bunker Hill Monument, 17 June 1843; *Writings and Speeches* (1903) vol. 1

16 The Law: It has honoured us, may we honour it.
speech at the Charleston Bar Dinner, 10 May 1847; *Writings and Speeches* (1903) vol. 4

17 I was born an American; I will live an American; I shall die an American.
speech in the Senate on 'The Compromise Bill', 17 July 1850; *Writings and Speeches* (1903) vol. 10

18 There is always room at the top.
on being advised against joining the overcrowded legal profession
attributed; cf. **Proverbs** 612:8

John Webster *c.*1580–*c.*1625

English dramatist
on Webster: see **Brooke** *150:18*, **Eliot** *296:16*

19 Vain the ambition of kings
Who seek by trophies and dead things,
To leave a living name behind,
And weave but nets to catch the wind.
The Devil's Law-Case (1623) act 5, sc. 4

20 What cannot a neat knave with a smooth tale
Make a woman believe?
The Duchess of Malfi (1623) act 1, sc. 1

21 Why should only I . . .
Be cased up, like a holy relic? I have youth
And a little beauty.
The Duchess of Malfi (1623) act 3, sc. 2

22 Raised by that curious engine, your white hand.
The Duchess of Malfi (1623) act 3, sc. 2

23 O, that it were possible,
We might but hold some two days' conference
With the dead!
The Duchess of Malfi (1623) act 4, sc. 2

24 I have made a soap-boiler costive.
The Duchess of Malfi (1623) act 4, sc. 2

25 I am Duchess of Malfi still.
The Duchess of Malfi (1623) act 4, sc. 2

26 Glories, like glow-worms, afar off shine bright,
But looked to near, have neither heat nor light.
The Duchess of Malfi (1623) act 4, sc. 2

1 I know death hath ten thousand several doors
For men to take their exits.
The Duchess of Malfi (1623) act 4, sc. 2; cf. **Fletcher** 318:4, **Massinger** 501:6, **Seneca** 654:20

2 Cover her face; mine eyes dazzle: she died young.
The Duchess of Malfi (1623) act 4, sc. 2

3 Physicians are like kings,—they brook no contradiction.
The Duchess of Malfi (1623) act 5, sc. 2

4 Strangling is a very quiet death.
The Duchess of Malfi (1623) act 5, sc. 4

5 We are merely the stars' tennis-balls, struck and bandied
Which way please them.
The Duchess of Malfi (1623) act 5, sc. 4

6 Is not old wine wholesomest, old pippins toothsomest, old wood burn brightest, old linen wash whitest? Old soldiers, sweethearts, are surest, and old lovers are soundest.
Westward Hoe (1607) act 2, sc. 2

7 Fortune's a right whore:
If she give aught, she deals it in small parcels,
That she may take away all at one swoop.
The White Devil (1612) act 1, sc. 1

8 'Tis just like a summer birdcage in a garden; the birds that are without despair to get in, and the birds that are within despair, and are in a consumption, for fear they shall never get out.
The White Devil (1612) act 1, sc. 2

9 A mere tale of a tub, my words are idle.
The White Devil (1612) act 2, sc. 1

10 Only the deep sense of some deathless shame.
The White Devil (1612) act 2, sc. 1

11 Cowardly dogs bark loudest.
The White Devil (1612) act 3, sc. 2

12 A rape! a rape! . . .
Yes, you have ravished justice;
Forced her to do your pleasure.
The White Devil (1612) act 3, sc. 2

13 Call for the robin-red-breast and the wren,
Since o'er shady groves they hover,
And with leaves and flowers do cover
The friendless bodies of unburied men.
The White Devil (1612) act 5, sc. 4

14 But keep the wolf far thence that's foe to men,
For with his nails he'll dig them up again.
The White Devil (1612) act 5, sc. 4

15 We think caged birds sing, when indeed they cry.
The White Devil (1612) act 5, sc. 4; cf. **Dunbar** 285:2, **Shakespeare** 680:6

16 And of all axioms this shall win the prize,—
'Tis better to be fortunate than wise.
The White Devil (1612) act 5, sc. 6

17 There's nothing of so infinite vexation
As man's own thoughts.
The White Devil (1612) act 5, sc. 6

18 My soul, like to a ship in a black storm,
Is driven, I know not whither.
The White Devil (1612) act 5, sc. 6

19 Prosperity doth bewitch men, seeming clear;
But seas do laugh, show white, when rocks are near.
The White Devil (1612) act 5, sc. 6

20 I have caught
An everlasting cold; I have lost my voice
Most irrecoverably.
The White Devil (1612) act 5, sc. 6

Josiah Wedgwood 1730–95
English potter

21 Am I not a man and a brother.
legend on Wedgwood cameo, depicting a kneeling Negro slave in chains
reproduced in facsimile in E. Darwin *The Botanic Garden* pt. 1 (1791)

Simone Weil 1909–43
French essayist and philosopher

22 I would suggest that barbarism be considered as a permanent and universal human characteristic which becomes more or less pronounced according to the play of circumstances.
Écrits Historiques et politiques (1960) 'Réflexions sur la barbarie' (written *c.*1939)

23 An obligation which goes unrecognized by anybody loses none of the full force of its existence. A right which goes unrecognized by anybody is not worth very much.
L'Enracinement (1949) 'Les Besoins de l'âme' (translated by A. F. Wills)

24 All sins are attempts to fill voids.
La Pesanteur et la grâce (1948)

25 The authentic and pure values—truth, beauty, and goodness—in the activity of a human being are the result of one and the same act, a certain application of the full attention to the object.
La Pesanteur et la grâce (1948)

26 A work of art has an author and yet, when it is perfect, it has something which is essentially anonymous about it.
La Pesanteur et la grâce (1948)

27 What a country calls its vital economic interests are not the things which enable its citizens to live, but the things which enable it to make war.
W. H. Auden *A Certain World* (1971)

Arabella Weir
British actress

28 Does my bum look big in this?
title of book (1997)

29 No matter how much of a gargoyle someone is, if they are in love they have that spring in their step, accompanied by that infuriating I'm-in-an-exclusive-secret-special-club-and-you-don't-know-the-password smugness.
Does My Bum Look Big in This? (1997)

Victor Weisskopf 1908–
American physicist

1 It was absolutely marvellous working for Pauli. You could ask him anything. There was no worry that he would think a particular question was stupid, since he thought *all* questions were stupid.
in *American Journal of Physics* 1977

Johnny Weissmuller see **Misquotations** 522:2

Chaim Weizmann 1874–1952
Russian-born Israeli statesman, President 1949–52

2 Something had been done for us which, after two thousand years of hope and yearning, would at last give us a resting-place in this terrible world.
of the Balfour declaration
speech in Jerusalem, 25 November 1936; cf. **Balfour** 49:16

Thomas Earle Welby 1881–1933
British writer

3 'Turbot, Sir,' said the waiter, placing before me two fishbones, two eyeballs, and a bit of black mackintosh.
The Dinner Knell (1932) 'Birmingham or Crewe?'

Raquel Welch 1940–
American actress

4 Being a sex symbol is rather like being a convict.
in *Observer* 25 February 1979

Fay Weldon 1931–
British novelist and scriptwriter
see also ***Advertising slogans*** *7:21*

5 She was the kind of wife who looks out of her front door in the morning and, if it's raining, apologizes.
Heart of the Country (1987)

6 The life and loves of a she-devil.
title of novel (1984)

7 Men are so romantic, don't you think? They look for a perfect partner when what they should be looking for is perfect love.
in *Sunday Times* 6 September 1987

8 Reading about sex in yesterday's novels is like watching people smoke in old films.
in *Guardian* 1 December 1989

9 Every time you open your wardrobe, you look at your clothes and you wonder what you are going to wear. What you are really saying is 'Who am I going to be today?'
in *New Yorker* 26 June 1995

10 It's very unfashionable to say this, but rape actually isn't the worst thing that can happen to a woman if you're safe, alive and unmarked after the event.
in *Radio Times* 4 July 1998

Orson Welles 1915–85
American actor and film director
see also ***Film lines*** *311:16, 312:1*

11 I hate television. I hate it as much as peanuts. But I can't stop eating peanuts.
in *New York Herald Tribune* 12 October 1956

12 The biggest electric train set any boy ever had!
of the RKO studios
Peter Noble *The Fabulous Orson Welles* (1956) ch. 7

13 There are only two emotions in a plane: boredom and terror.
interview to celebrate his 70th birthday, in *The Times* 6 May 1985

Duke of Wellington 1769–1852
British soldier and statesman
on Wellington: see ***Bagehot*** *46:14,* ***Byron*** *173:11,* ***Tennyson*** *765:2*

14 As Lord Chesterfield said of the generals of his day, 'I only hope that when the enemy reads the list of their names, he trembles as I do.'
usually quoted as, 'I don't know what effect these men will have upon the enemy, but, by God, they frighten me'
letter, 29 August 1810, in *Supplementary Despatches . . .* (1860) vol. 6

15 Up Guards and at them!
letter from an officer in the Guards, 22 June 1815, in *The Battle of Waterloo* by a Near Observer [J. Booth] (1815); later denied by Wellington

16 Hard pounding this, gentlemen; let's see who will pound longest.
at the Battle of Waterloo, 1815
Sir Walter Scott *Paul's Letters* (1816) Letter 8

17 Next to a battle lost, the greatest misery is a battle gained.
in *Diary of Frances, Lady Shelley 1787–1817* (ed. R. Edgcumbe, 1912) vol. 1, ch. 9; Wellington made a similar remark many times

18 Publish and be damned.
replying to a blackmail threat prior to the publication of Harriette ***Wilson****'s* Memoirs *(1825)*
attributed; Elizabeth Longford *Wellington: The Years of the Sword* (1969) ch. 10

19 I used to say of him that his presence on the field made the difference of forty thousand men.
of ***Napoleon***
Philip Henry Stanhope *Notes of Conversations with the Duke of Wellington* (1888) 2 November 1831

20 Ours is composed of the scum of the earth—the mere scum of the earth.
of the army
Philip Henry Stanhope *Notes of Conversations with the Duke of Wellington* (1888) 4 November 1831

21 I never saw so many shocking bad hats in my life.
on seeing the first Reformed Parliament, 1832
William Fraser *Words on Wellington* (1889)

22 All the business of war, and indeed all the business of life, is to endeavour to find out what you don't

know by what you do; that's what I called 'guessing what was at the other side of the hill'.
in *The Croker Papers* (1885) vol. 3 ch. 28

1 The battle of Waterloo was won on the playing fields of Eton.
oral tradition, but probably apocryphal; the earliest reference is a remark said to have been made when revisiting Eton, below; cf. **Orwell** 558:18

It is here that the battle of Waterloo was won!
C. F. R. Montalembert *De l'avenir politique de l'Angleterre* (1856) ch. 10

2 A conquerer, like a cannonball, must go on; if he rebounds, his career is over.
attributed; Alistair Horne *How Far from Austerlitz?* (1996)

3 An extraordinary affair. I gave them their orders and they wanted to stay and discuss them.
of his first Cabinet meeting as Prime Minister
attributed; Peter Hennessy *Whitehall* (1990)

4 If you believe that, you'll believe anything.
to a gentleman who had accosted him in the street saying, 'Mr Jones, I believe?'; George Jones RA (1786–1869), painter of military subjects, bore a striking resemblance to Wellington
Elizabeth Longford *Pillar of State* (1972) ch. 10

5 You must build your House of Parliament upon the river . . . the populace cannot exact their demands by sitting down round you.
William Fraser *Words on Wellington* (1889)

H. G. Wells 1866–1946

English novelist
on Wells: see ***Maurois*** *502:10*

6 It is leviathan retrieving pebbles. It is a magnificent but painful hippopotamus resolved at any cost, even at the cost of its dignity, upon picking up a pea which has got into a corner of its den.
of Henry ***James***
Boon (1915) ch. 4

7 He had read Shakespeare and found him weak in chemistry.
Complete Short Stories (1927) 'Lord of the Dynamos'

8 'Sesquippledan,' he would say. 'Sesquippledan verboojuice.'
The History of Mr Polly (1909) ch. 1, pt. 5; cf. **Horace** 385:17

9 A drink that tasted, she thought, like weak vinegar mixed with a packet of pins.
of champagne
Joan and Peter (1918) ch. 12

10 'I'm a Norfan, both sides,' he would explain, with the air of one who had seen trouble.
Kipps (1905) bk. 1, ch. 6, pt. 1

11 I was thinking jest what a Rum Go everything is.
Kipps (1905) bk. 3, ch. 3, pt. 8

12 The Social Contract is nothing more or less than a vast conspiracy of human beings to lie to and humbug themselves and one another for the general Good. Lies are the mortar that bind the savage individual man into the social masonry.
Love and Mr Lewisham (1900) ch. 23

13 Human history becomes more and more a race between education and catastrophe.
The Outline of History (1920) vol. 2, ch. 41, pt. 4

14 Bah! the thing is not a nose at all, but a bit of primordial chaos clapped on to my face.
Select Conversations with an Uncle (1895) 'The Man with a Nose'

15 The shape of things to come.
title of book (1933)

16 The war that will end war.
title of book (1914); cf. **Lloyd George** 471:3

17 Moral indignation is jealousy with a halo.
The Wife of Sir Isaac Harman (1914) ch. 9, sect. 2

Arnold Wesker 1932–

English dramatist

18 Chips with every damn thing. You breed babies and you eat chips with everything.
Chips with Everything (1962) act 1, sc. 2

19 The Khomeini cry for the execution of Rushdie is an infantile cry. From the beginning of time we have seen that. To murder the thinker does not murder the thought.
in *Weekend Guardian* 3 June 1989; cf. **Khomeini** 435:14

Charles Wesley 1707–88

English Methodist preacher and hymn-writer

20 Amazing love! How can it be
That thou, my God, shouldst die for me?
'And can it be' (1738 hymn)

21 My chains fell off, my heart was free,
I rose, went forth, and followed thee.
'And can it be' (1738 hymn)

22 Hark! how all the welkin rings,
Glory to the King of kings.
Peace on earth and mercy mild,
God and sinners reconciled.
Hymns and Sacred Poems (1739) 'Hymn for Christmas'; the first two lines altered to:

Hark! the herald-angels sing
Glory to the new born king.
George Whitefield *Hymns for Social Worship* (1753)

23 Hail, the heaven-born Prince of Peace!
Hail, the Sun of Righteousness!
Hymns and Sacred Poems (1739) 'Hymn for Christmas'; cf. **Bible** 90:25

24 O for a thousand tongues to sing.
Hymns and Sacred Poems (1740) 'For the Anniversary Day of one's Conversion'

25 Jesu, lover of my soul,
Let me to thy bosom fly.
Hymns and Sacred Poems (1740) 'In Temptation'

26 Gentle Jesus, meek and mild,
Look upon a little child;
Pity my simplicity,
Suffer me to come to thee.
Hymns and Sacred Poems (1742) 'Gentle Jesus, Meek and Mild'

1 Come, O thou Traveller unknown,
Whom still I hold, but cannot see.
Hymns and Sacred Poems (1742) 'Wrestling Jacob'

2 Wrestling, I will not let thee go,
Till I thy name, thy nature know.
Hymns and Sacred Poems (1742) 'Wrestling Jacob'

3 Forth in thy name, O Lord, I go,
My daily labour to pursue;
Thee, only thee, resolved to know,
In all I think or speak or do.
Hymns and Sacred Poems (1749) 'Forth in thy name, O Lord, I go'

4 Soldiers of Christ, arise,
And put your armour on.
Hymns and Sacred Poems (1749) 'The Whole Armour of God'

5 God is gone up on high
With a triumphant noise.
Hymns for our Lord's Resurrection (1746) 'God is gone up'

6 Rejoice, the Lord is King!
Your Lord and King adore;
Mortals, give thanks and sing,
And triumph evermore:
Lift up your heart, lift up your voice;
Rejoice, again, I say rejoice.
Hymns for our Lord's Resurrection (1746) 'Rejoice, the Lord is King!'

7 Love divine, all loves excelling,
Joy of heav'n, to earth come down,
Fix in us thy humble dwelling,
All thy faithful mercies crown.
Jesu, thou art all compassion,
Pure unbounded love thou art;
Visit us with thy salvation,
Enter every trembling heart.
Hymns for those that seek . . . Redemption (1747) 'Love divine', based on Dryden; cf. **Dryden** 281:32

8 Lo! He comes with clouds descending,
Once for favoured sinners slain;
Thousand thousand Saints attending
Swell the triumph of His train.
Hymns of Intercession for all Mankind (1758) 'Lo! He comes'

John Wesley 1703–91

English preacher; founder of Methodism
on Wesley: see ***Johnson*** *415:26*

9 Thou hidden love of God, whose height,
Whose depth unfathomed no man knows,
I see from far thy beauteous light,
Inly I sigh for thy repose.
A Collection of Psalms and Hymns (1738) 'Divine Love' (a translation of G. Tersteegen's 'Verborgen Gottesliebe du', 1729)

10 The Gospel of Christ knows of no religion but social; no holiness but social holiness.
Hymns and Sacred Poems (1739) Preface

11 I design plain truth for plain people.
Sermons on Several Occasions (1746)

12 Slovenliness is no part of religion; that neither this, nor any text of Scripture, condemns neatness of apparel. Certainly this is a duty, not a sin. 'Cleanliness is, indeed, next to godliness.'
Sermons on Several Occasions (1788) Sermon 88; cf. **Proverbs** 597:23

13 No circumstances can make it necessary for a man to burst in sunder all the ties of humanity.
Thoughts upon Slavery (1774) in *Works* (Centenary ed.) vol. 11, p. 72

14 I went to America to convert the Indians; but oh, who shall convert me?
Journal (ed. N. Curnock) 24 January 1738

15 I felt my heart strangely warmed. I felt I did trust in Christ, Christ alone for salvation; and an assurance was given me that He had taken away *my* sins, even *mine*, and saved *me* from the law of sin and death.
on his conversion
Journal (ed. N. Curnock) 24 May 1738

16 I look upon all the world as my parish.
Journal (ed. N. Curnock) 11 June 1739

17 Either I or you mistake the whole meaning of Christianity from the beginning to the end.
letter to John Taylor, who rejected the accepted orthodoxy on the subject of original sin
Journal (ed. N. Curnock) 3 July 1759

18 I let you loose, George, on the great continent of America. Publish your message in the open face of the sun, and do all the good you can.
letter to a preacher, George Shadford, March 1773 in *Letters* (ed. J. Telford, 1931) vol. 6

19 Though I am always in haste, I am never in a hurry.
letter to Miss March, 10 December 1777, in *Letters* (ed. J. Telford, 1931) vol. 6

20 I have this day lived fourscore years . . . God grant that I may never live to be useless!
Journal (ed. N. Curnock) 28 June 1783

21 Time has shaken me by the hand and death is not far behind.
letter to Ezekiel Cooper, 1 February 1791, in *Letters* (ed. J. Telford, 1931) vol. 8

22 Men may call me a knave or a fool, a rascal, a scoundrel, and I am content; but they shall never by my consent call me a Bishop!
Betty M. Jarboe *Wesley Quotations* (1990)

Mary Wesley 1912–

English novelist

23 When people discussed tonics, pick-me-ups after a severe illness, she kept to herself the prescription of a quick dip in bed with someone you liked but were not in love with. A shock of sexual astonishment which could make you feel astonishingly well and high spirited.
Not That Sort of Girl (1987)

24 In my day, I would only have sex with a man if I found him extremely attractive. These days, girls seem to choose them in much the same way as they might choose to suck on a boiled sweet.
in *Independent* 18 October 1997 'Quote Unquote'

Samuel Wesley 1662–1735
English clergyman and poet

1 Style is the dress of thought; a modest dress,
Neat, but not gaudy, will true critics please.
'An Epistle to a Friend concerning Poetry' (1700); cf. **Johnson** 410:1, **Pope** 584:19

Mae West 1892–1980
American film actress
see also ***Film lines*** *311:19*

2 I always say, keep a diary and some day it'll keep you.
Every Day's a Holiday (1937 film)

3 Beulah, peel me a grape.
I'm No Angel (1933 film)

4 It's not the men in my life that counts—it's the life in my men.
I'm No Angel (1933 film)

5 'Goodness, what beautiful diamonds!'
'Goodness had nothing to do with it.'
Night After Night (1932 film)

6 Why don't you come up sometime, and see me?
She Done Him Wrong (1933 film); cf. **Misquotations** 522:15

7 Is that a gun in your pocket, or are you just glad to see me?
usually quoted as 'Is that a pistol in your pocket . . . '
Joseph Weintraub *Peel Me a Grape* (1975)

8 I used to be Snow White . . . but I drifted.
Joseph Weintraub *Peel Me a Grape* (1975)

Rebecca West (Cicily Isabel Fairfield) 1892–1983
English novelist and journalist

9 Having watched the form of our traitors for a number of years, I cannot think that espionage can be recommended as a technique for building an impressive civilization. It's a lout's game.
The Meaning of Treason (1982 ed.), introduction

10 She was not so much a person as an implication of dreary poverty, like an open door in a mean house that lets out the smell of cooking cabbage and the screams of children.
The Return of the Soldier (1918)

11 The point is that nobody likes having salt rubbed into their wounds, even if it is the salt of the earth.
The Salt of the Earth (1935) ch. 2

12 It is always one's virtues and not one's vices that precipitate one into disaster.
There is No Conversation (1935) ch. 1

13 There is no such thing as conversation. It is an illusion. There are intersecting monologues, that is all.
There is No Conversation (1935) 'The Harsh Voice' sect. 1

14 I myself have never been able to find out precisely what feminism is: I only know that people call me a feminist whenever I express sentiments that differentiate me from a doormat or a prostitute.
in *The Clarion* 14 November 1913

15 It was in dealing with the early feminist that the Government acquired the tact and skilfulness with which it is now handling Ireland.
in *Daily News* 7 August 1916

16 Just how difficult it is to write biography can be reckoned by anybody who sits down and considers just how many people know the truth about his or her love affairs.
in *Vogue* 1 November 1952

17 Journalism—an ability to meet the challenge of filling the space.
in *New York Herald Tribune* 22 April 1956

18 Whatever happens, never forget that people would rather be led to *perdition* by a man, than to *victory* by a woman.
in conversation in 1979, just before Margaret ***Thatcher****'s first election victory*
in *Sunday Telegraph* 17 January 1988

19 Every other inch a gentleman.
of Michael Arlen; the phrase is also attributed to Arlen himself
Victoria Glendinning *Rebecca West* (1987) pt. 3, ch. 5

John Fane, Lord Westmorland 1759–1841

20 *Merit*, indeed! . . . We are come to a pretty pass if they talk of *merit* for a bishopric.
noted in Lady Salisbury's diary, 9 December 1835; C. Oman *The Gascoyne Heiress* (1968) pt. 5

R. P. Weston 1878–1936 and **Bert Lee** 1880–1947
British songwriters

21 Good-bye-ee!—Good-bye-ee!
Wipe the tear, baby dear, from your eye-ee.
Tho' it's hard to part, I know,
I'll be tickled to death to go.
Don't cry-ee—don't sigh-ee!
There's a silver lining in the sky-ee!
Bonsoir, old thing! cheerio! chin-chin!
Nahpoo! Toodle-oo! Good-bye-ee!
'Good-bye-ee!' (*c.*1915 song)

Charles Wetherell 1770–1846
English lawyer and politician

22 Then there is my noble and biographical friend who has added a new terror to death.
of Lord Campbell
Lord St Leonards *Misrepresentations in Campbell's Lives of Lyndhurst and Brougham* (1869); cf. **Arbuthnot** 23:16, **Lyndhurst** 480:20

Adelheid Wette 1858–1916
German librettist; sister of Engelbert Humperdinck

23 When at night I go to sleep,
Fourteen angels watch do keep.
Two stand here beside me,
Two stand there to guide me . . .
Two more light the path to heaven!
Hansel and Gretel (1893); music by Engelbert Humperdinck

Edith Wharton 1862–1937

American novelist

1 An unalterable and unquestioned law of the musical world required that the German text of French operas sung by Swedish artists should be translated into Italian for the clearer understanding of English-speaking audiences.

The Age of Innocence (1920) bk. 1, ch. 1

2 My last page is always latent in my first; but the intervening windings of the way become clear only as I write.

A Backward Glance (1934)

3 Mrs Ballinger is one of the ladies who pursue Culture in bands, as though it were dangerous to meet it alone.

Xingu and Other Stories (1916) 'Xingu'

Thomas, Lord Wharton 1648–1715

4 Ho, Brother Teague, dost hear de decree?
Lilli burlero bullen a la.
Dat we shall have a new Debity,
Lilli burlero bullen a la.

debity = *deputy; the refrain parodies the Irish language*

'A New Song' (written 1687), in *Poems on Affairs of State* (1704) vol. 3

5 Ara! but why does King James stay behind?
Lilli burlero bullen a la
Ho! by my shoul 'tis a Protestant wind

'A New Song' (written 1687)

6 I sang a king out of three kingdoms.

said to have been Wharton's boast after 'A New Song' *became an propaganda weapon against James II*

in *Dictionary of National Biography* (1917–)

Richard Whately 1787–1863

English philosopher and theologian; Archbishop of Dublin from 1831

7 Preach not because you have to say something, but because you have something to say.

Apophthegms (1854)

8 Happiness is no laughing matter.

Apophthegms (1854)

9 It is a folly to expect men to do all that they may reasonably be expected to do.

Apophthegms (1854)

10 Honesty is the best policy; but he who is governed by that maxim is not an honest man.

Apophthegms (1854)

11 It is not that pearls fetch a high price *because* men have dived for them; but on the contrary, men dive for them because they fetch a high price.

Introductory Lectures on Political Economy (1832) p. 253

12 'Never forget, gentlemen,' he [Whateley] said, to his astonished hearers, as he held up a copy of the 'Authorized Version' of the Bible, 'never forget that this is *not* the Bible,' then, after a moment's pause, he continued, 'This, gentlemen, is only a *translation* of the Bible.'

to a meeting of his diocesan clergy, in H. Solly *These Eighty Years* (1893) vol. 2, ch. 2

William Whewell 1794–1866

English philosopher and scientist

on Whewell: see **Smith** 726:5

13 Nature, so far as it is the object of scientific research, is a collection of facts governed by *laws*: our knowledge of nature is our knowledge of laws.

Astronomy and General Physics considered with reference to Natural Theology (1834) ch. 1

14 Hence no force however great can stretch a cord however fine into an horizontal line which is accurately straight: there will always be a bending downwards.

often cited as an example of accidental metre and rhyme, and changed in later editions

Elementary Treatise on Mechanics (1819) ch. 4, problem 2

15 Man is the interpreter of nature, science the right interpretation.

Philosophy of the Inductive Sciences (1840) Aphorism 17

James McNeill Whistler 1834–1903

American-born painter

on Whistler: see **Ruskin** 638:6

16 I am not arguing with you—I am telling you.

The Gentle Art of Making Enemies (1890)

17 Art is upon the Town!

Mr Whistler's 'Ten O'Clock' (1885) p. 7

18 Listen! There never was an artistic period. There never was an Art-loving nation.

Mr Whistler's 'Ten O'Clock' (1885)

19 Nature is usually wrong.

Mr Whistler's 'Ten O'Clock' (1885)

20 I maintain that two and two would continue to make four, in spite of the whine of the amateur for three, or the cry of the critic for five.

Whistler v. Ruskin. Art and Art Critics (1878)

21 No, I ask it for the knowledge of a lifetime.

in his case against **Ruskin**, *replying to the question: 'For two days' labour, you ask two hundred guineas?'*

D. C. Seitz *Whistler Stories* (1913)

22 OSCAR WILDE: How I wish I had said that.
WHISTLER: You will, Oscar, you will.

R. Ellman *Oscar Wilde* (1987) pt. 2, ch. 5

23 Yes madam, Nature is creeping up.

to a lady who had been reminded of his work by an 'exquisite haze in the atmosphere'

D. C. Seitz *Whistler Stories* (1913)

E. B. White 1899–1985

American humorist

24 Commuter—one who spends his life
In riding to and from his wife;
A man who shaves and takes a train,
And then rides back to shave again.

'The Commuter' (1982)

1 MOTHER: It's broccoli, dear.
CHILD: I say it's spinach, and I say the hell with it.
cartoon caption in *New Yorker* 8 December 1928

2 Democracy is the recurrent suspicion that more than half of the people are right more than half of the time.
in *New Yorker* 3 July 1944

Edmund White 1940–
American writer and critic

3 The Aids epidemic has rolled back a big rotting log and revealed all the squirming life underneath it, since it involves, all at once, the main themes of our existence: sex, death, power, money, love, hate, disease and panic. No American phenomenon has been so compelling since the Vietnam War.
States of Desire: Travels in Gay America (afterword to 1986 edition)

H. Kirke White 1785–1806
English poet

4 Oft in danger, oft in woe,
Onward, Christians, onward go.
'Oft in danger, oft in woe' (1812 hymn)

Patrick White 1912–90
Australian novelist
see also ***Closing lines*** 222:21

5 Conversation is imperative if gaps are to be filled, and old age, it is the last gap but one.
The Tree of Man (1955) ch. 22

6 In all directions stretched the great Australian Emptiness, in which the mind is the least of possessions.
The Vital Decade (1968) 'The Prodigal Son'

Theodore H. White 1915–86
American writer and journalist

7 America is a nation created by all the hopeful wanderers of Europe, not out of geography and genetics, but out of purpose.
The Making of the President (1960)

8 Johnson's instinct for power is as primordial as a salmon's going upstream to spawn.
of Lyndon ***Johnson***
The Making of the President (1964)

9 The flood of money that gushes into politics today is a pollution of democracy.
in *Time* 19 November 1984

Alfred North Whitehead 1861–1947
English philosopher and mathematician

10 Life is an offensive, directed against the repetitious mechanism of the Universe.
Adventures of Ideas (1933) pt. 1, ch. 5

11 It is more important that a proposition be interesting than that it be true. This statement is almost a tautology. For the energy of operation of a proposition in an occasion of experience is its interest, and is its importance. But of course a true proposition is more apt to be interesting than a false one.
Adventures of Ideas (1933) pt. 4, ch. 16

12 There are no whole truths; all truths are half-truths. It is trying to treat them as whole truths that plays the devil.
Dialogues (1954) prologue

13 *Ideas won't keep*. Something must be done about them.
Dialogues (1954) 28 April 1938

14 Intelligence is quickness to apprehend as distinct from ability, which is capacity to act wisely on the thing apprehended.
Dialogues (1954) 15 December 1939

15 What is morality in any given time or place? It is what the majority then and there happen to like, and immorality is what they dislike.
Dialogues (1954) 30 August 1941

16 Art is the imposing of a pattern on experience, and our aesthetic enjoyment is recognition of the pattern.
Dialogues (1954) 10 June 1943

17 Civilization advances by extending the number of important operations which we can perform without thinking about them.
Introduction to Mathematics (1911) ch. 5

18 The safest general characterization of the European philosophical tradition is that it consists of a series of footnotes to Plato.
Process and Reality (1929) pt. 2, ch. 1

19 Since a babe was born in a manger, it may be doubted whether so great a thing has happened with so little stir.
on the scientific revolution in the sixteenth century
Science and the Modern World (1925) ch. 1

Katharine Whitehorn 1928–
English journalist

20 An office party is not, as is sometimes supposed, the Managing Director's chance to kiss the tea-girl. It is the tea-girl's chance to kiss the Managing Director.
Roundabout (1962) 'The Office Party'

21 I wouldn't say when you've seen one Western you've seen the lot; but when you've seen the lot you get the feeling you've seen one.
Sunday Best (1976) 'Decoding the West'

George Whiting
American songwriter

22 My blue heaven.
title of song (1927)

23 When you're all dressed up and have no place to go.
title of song (1912)

William Whiting 1825–78

English teacher; master of the Quiristers of Winchester College from 1842

1 Eternal Father, strong to save,
Whose arm doth bind the restless wave,
Who bidd'st the mighty ocean deep
Its own appointed limits keep:
O hear us when we cry to thee,
For those in peril on the sea.
'Eternal Father, Strong to Save' (1869 hymn)

Walt Whitman 1819–92

American poet

2 I dreamed in a dream I saw a city invincible to the attacks of the whole of the rest of the earth,
I dreamed that was the new city of Friends.
'I dreamed in a dream' (1867)

3 I sing the body electric.
title of poem (1855)

4 O Captain! my Captain! our fearful trip is done,
The ship has weathered every rack, the prize we sought is won,
The port is near, the bells I hear, the people all exulting.
'O Captain! My Captain!' (1871)

5 The ship is anchored safe and sound, its voyage closed and done.
From fearful trip the victor ship comes in with object won;
Exult O shores, and ring O bells! But I with mournful tread
Walk the deck my Captain lies, Fallen cold and dead.
'O Captain! My Captain!' (1871)

6 Out of the cradle endlessly rocking,
Out of the mocking-bird's throat, the musical shuttle . . .
A reminiscence sing.
'Out of the cradle endlessly rocking' (1881)

7 Have you your pistols? have you your sharp-edged axes?
Pioneers! O pioneers!
'Pioneers! O Pioneers!' (1881)

8 Camerado, this is no book,
Who touches this touches a man.
'So Long!' (1881)

9 Where the populace rise at once against the never-ending audacity of elected persons.
'Song of the Broad Axe' (1881) pt. 5, l. 12

10 I celebrate myself, and sing myself.
'Song of Myself' (written 1855) pt. 1

11 Urge and urge and urge,
Always the procreant urge of the world.
'Song of Myself' (written 1855) pt. 3

12 Has any one supposed it lucky to be born?
I hasten to inform him or her, it is just as lucky to die and I know it.
'Song of Myself' (written 1855) pt. 7

13 I also say it is good to fall, battles are lost in the same spirit in which they are won.
'Song of Myself' (written 1855) pt. 18

14 I believe a leaf of grass is no less than the journey-work of the stars,
And the pismire is equally perfect, and a grain of sand, and the egg of the wren,
And the tree toad is a chef-d'oeuvre for the highest,
And the running blackberry would adorn the parlours of heaven.
'Song of Myself' (written 1855) pt. 31

15 I think I could turn and live with animals, they are so placid and self-contained,
I stand and look at them long and long.
They do not sweat and whine about their condition,
They do not lie awake in the dark and weep for their sins,
They do not make me sick discussing their duty to God,
Not one is dissatisfied, not one is demented with the mania of owning things,
Not one kneels to another, nor to his kind that lived thousands of years ago,
Not one is respectable or unhappy over the whole earth.
'Song of Myself' (written 1855) pt. 32

16 Behold, I do not give lectures or a little charity,
When I give I give myself.
'Song of Myself' (written 1855) pt. 40

17 My rendezvous is appointed, it is certain,
The Lord will be there and wait till I come on perfect terms.
'Song of Myself' (written 1855) pt. 45

18 Do I contradict myself?
Very well then I contradict myself,
(I am large, I contain multitudes.)
'Song of Myself' (written 1855) pt. 51

19 I sound my barbaric yawp over the roofs of the world.
'Song of Myself' (written 1855) pt. 52

20 Afoot and light-hearted I take to the open road,
Healthy, free, the world before me,
The long brown path before me leading wherever I choose.
'Song of the Open Road' (1871) pt. 1, l. 1

21 The earth does not argue,
Is not pathetic, has no arrangements.
'A Song of the Rolling Earth' (1881) pt. 1

22 This dust was once the man,
Gentle, plain, just and resolute, under whose cautious hand,
Against the foulest crime in history known in any land or age,
Was saved the Union of these States.
'This dust was once the man' (1881)

23 When lilacs last in the dooryard bloomed,
And the great star early drooped in the western sky in the night,

I mourned, and yet shall mourn with ever-returning spring.
'When lilacs last in the dooryard bloomed' (1881) st. 1

1 The United States themselves are essentially the greatest poem.
Leaves of Grass (1855) preface

Isabella Whitney fl. 1573
English poet

2 Had I a husband or a house, and all that longs thereto
Myself could frame about to rouse as other women do,
But til some household cares me tie
My books and pen I will apply.
A Sweet Nosegay (1573)

Ben Whittaker 1934–

3 We can no more hope to end drug abuse by eliminating heroin and cocaine than we could alter the suicide rate by outlawing high buildings or the sale of rope.
The Global Fix (1987)

John Greenleaf Whittier 1807–92
American poet

4 'Shoot, if you must, this old grey head,
But spare your country's flag,' she said.
'Barbara Frietchie' (1863)

5 Dear Lord and Father of mankind,
Forgive our foolish ways!
Re-clothe us in our rightful mind,
In purer lives thy service find,
In deeper reverence praise.
'The Brewing of Soma' (1872)

6 For of all sad words of tongue or pen,
The saddest are these: 'It might have been!'
'Maud Muller' (1854); cf. **Harte** 363:10

7 The Indian Summer of the heart!
'Memories' (1841)

8 O brother man! fold to thy heart thy brother.
'Worship' (1848)

Robert Whittington
English grammarian

9 As time requireth, a man of marvellous mirth and pastimes, and sometime of as sad gravity, as who say: a man for all seasons.
of Sir Thomas **More**
Vulgaria (1521) pt. 2 'De constructione nominum'; Erasmus had applied the idea earlier, saying that More played:
Omnium horarum hominem.
A man of all hours.
Erasmus *In Praise of Folly* (1509) prefatory letter

Charlotte Whitton 1896–1975
Canadian writer and politician

10 Whatever women do they must do twice as well as men to be thought half as good.
in *Canada Month* June 1963

Cornelius Whur

11 While lasting joys the man attend
Who has a faithful female friend.
'The Female Friend' (1837)

William H. Whyte 1917–
American writer

12 This book is about the organization man . . . I can think of no other way to describe the people I am talking about. They are not the workers, nor are they the white-collar people in the usual, clerk sense of the word. These people only work for the Organization. The ones I am talking about *belong* to it as well.
The Organization Man (1956) ch. 1

George John Whyte-Melville 1821–78
Scottish-born novelist, killed in the hunting-field

13 But I freely admit that the best of my fun
I owe it to horse and hound.
'The Good Grey Mare' (1933)

Ann Widdecombe 1947–
British Conservative politician

14 He has something of the night in him.
of Michael Howard as a contender for the Conservative leadership
in *Sunday Times* 11 May 1997 (electronic edition)

Elie Wiesel 1928–
Romanian-born American writer and Nobel Prize winner; Auschwitz survivor

15 The opposite of love is not hate, it's indifference.
The opposite of art is not ugliness, it's indifference.
The opposite of faith is not heresy, it's indifference.
And the opposite of life is not death, it's indifference.
in *U.S. News and World Report* 27 October 1986

16 Take sides. Neutrality helps the oppressor, never the victim. Silence encourages the tormentor, never the tormented.
accepting the Nobel Peace Prize
in *New York Times* 11 December 1986

17 God of forgiveness, do not forgive those murderers of Jewish children here.
at Auschwitz
in *The Times* 27 January 1995

Michael Wigglesworth 1631–1705
New England puritan preacher and writer

18 By the power of eloquence old truth receives a new habit; though its essence be the same, yet its visage is so altered that it may currently pass and be accepted as a novelty.
oration, 1650; Perry Miller *The American Puritans* (1956)

Samuel Wilberforce 1805–73

English prelate
on Wilberforce: see **Huxley** *397:20*

1 If I were a cassowary
On the plains of Timbuctoo,
I would eat a missionary,
Cassock, band, and hymn-book too.
impromptu verse (attributed)

2 Was it through his grandfather or his grandmother that he claimed his descent from a monkey?
addressed to T. H. Huxley at a meeting of the British Association for the Advancement of Science, Oxford, June 1860; in *Macmillan's Magazine* vol. 78 (October 1898); cf. **Huxley** 397:20

Richard Wilbur 1921–

American poet

3 Spare us all word of the weapons, their force and range,
The long numbers that rocket the mind.
'Advice to a Prophet' (1961)

4 There is a poignancy in all things clear,
In the stare of the deer, in the ring of a hammer in the morning.
'Clearness' (1950)

5 We milk the cow of the world, and as we do
We whisper in her ear, 'You are not true.'
'Epistemology' (1950)

6 Mind in its purest play is like some bat
That beats about in caverns all alone,
Contriving by a kind of senseless wit
Not to conclude against a wall of stone.
'Mind' (1956)

7 The good grey guardians of art
Patrol the halls on spongy shoes,
Impartially protective, though
Perhaps suspicious of Toulouse.
Here dozes one against the wall,
Disposed upon a funeral chair.
A Degas dancer pirouettes
Upon the parting of his hair.
'Museum Piece' (1950)

8 Love is the greatest mercy,
A volley of the sun
That lashes all with shade,
That the first day be mended.
'Someone Talking to Himself' (1961)

Ella Wheeler Wilcox 1855–1919

American poet

9 Laugh and the world laughs with you;
Weep, and you weep alone;
For the sad old earth must borrow its mirth,
But has trouble enough of its own.
'Solitude'

10 So many gods, so many creeds,
So many paths that wind and wind,
While just the art of being kind
Is all the sad world needs.
'The World's Need'

Oscar Wilde 1854–1900

Anglo-Irish dramatist and poet
on Wilde: see **Betjeman** *70:4,* **Housman** *390:4,* **Leverson** *466:3,* **Parker** *567:5,* **Whistler** *813:22*

11 We have really everything in common with America nowadays except, of course, language.
The Canterville Ghost (1887); cf. **Misquotations** 521:10

12 Really, if the lower orders don't set us a good example, what on earth is the use of them?
The Importance of Being Earnest (1895) act 1

13 The truth is rarely pure, and never simple.
The Importance of Being Earnest (1895) act 1

14 In married life three is company and two none.
The Importance of Being Earnest (1895) act 1

15 Ignorance is like a delicate exotic fruit; touch it and the bloom is gone. The whole theory of modern education is radically unsound. Fortunately, in England, at any rate, education produces no effect whatsoever.
The Importance of Being Earnest (1895) act 1

16 To lose one parent, Mr Worthing, may be regarded as a misfortune; to lose both looks like carelessness.
The Importance of Being Earnest (1895) act 1

17 LADY BRACKNELL: A handbag?
The Importance of Being Earnest (1895) act 1

18 All women become like their mothers. That is their tragedy. No man does. That's his.
The Importance of Being Earnest (1895) act 1; the same words occur in dialogue form in *A Woman of No Importance* (1893) act 2

19 The good ended happily, and the bad unhappily. That is what fiction means.
The Importance of Being Earnest (1895) act 2; cf. **Stoppard** 743:19

20 I hope you have not been leading a double life, pretending to be wicked and being really good all the time. That would be hypocrisy.
The Importance of Being Earnest (1895) act 2

21 Charity, dear Miss Prism, charity! None of us are perfect. I myself am peculiarly susceptible to draughts.
The Importance of Being Earnest (1895) act 2

22 I never travel without my diary. One should always have something sensational to read in the train.
The Importance of Being Earnest (1895) act 2

23 CECILY: When I see a spade I call it a spade.
GWENDOLEN: I am glad to say that I have never seen a spade.
The Importance of Being Earnest (1895) act 3

24 Thirty-five is a very attractive age. London society is full of women of the very highest birth who have, of their own free choice, remained thirty-five for years.
The Importance of Being Earnest (1895) act 3

25 Every great man nowadays has his disciples, and it is always Judas who writes the biography.
Intentions (1891) 'The Critic as Artist' pt. 1

26 Meredith's a prose Browning, and so is Browning.
Intentions (1891) 'The Critic as Artist' pt. 1

1 Anybody can make history. Only a great man can write it.
Intentions (1891) 'The Critic as Artist' pt. 1

2 The one duty we owe to history is to rewrite it.
Intentions (1891) 'The Critic as Artist' pt. 1

3 It is through Art, and through Art only, that we can realise our perfection; through Art, and through Art only, that we can shield ourselves from the sordid perils of actual existence.
Intentions (1891) 'The Critic as Artist' pt. 2

4 All art is immoral.
Intentions (1891) 'The Critic as Artist' pt. 2

5 A little sincerity is a dangerous thing, and a great deal of it is absolutely fatal.
Intentions (1891) 'The Critic as Artist' pt. 2

6 Life imitates Art far more than Art imitates Life.
Intentions (1891) 'The Decay of Lying'

7 Meredith! Who can define him? His style is chaos illuminated by flashes of lightning.
Intentions (1891) 'The Decay of Lying'; Ada Leverson *Letters to the Sphinx* (1930) attributes to Wilde a similar remark about **Browning**

8 I can resist everything except temptation.
Lady Windermere's Fan (1892) act 1; cf. **Graham** 347:17

9 Many a woman has a past, but I am told that she has at least a dozen, and that they all fit.
Lady Windermere's Fan (1892) act 1

10 We are all in the gutter, but some of us are looking at the stars.
Lady Windermere's Fan (1892) act 3

11 There is nothing in the whole world so unbecoming to a woman as a Nonconformist conscience.
Lady Windermere's Fan (1892) act 3

12 A man who knows the price of everything and the value of nothing.
definition of a cynic
Lady Windermere's Fan (1892) act 3

13 Experience is the name every one gives to their mistakes.
Lady Windermere's Fan (1892) act 3

14 There is no such thing as a moral or an immoral book. Books are well written, or badly written.
The Picture of Dorian Gray (1891) preface

15 The nineteenth century dislike of Realism is the rage of Caliban seeing his own face in the glass.
The Picture of Dorian Gray (1891) preface

16 The moral life of man forms part of the subject matter of the artist, but the morality of art consists in the perfect use of an imperfect medium.
The Picture of Dorian Gray (1891) preface

17 There is only one thing in the world worse than being talked about, and that is not being talked about.
The Picture of Dorian Gray (1891) ch. 1

18 A man cannot be too careful in the choice of his enemies.
The Picture of Dorian Gray (1891) ch. 1

19 A cigarette is the perfect type of a perfect pleasure. It is exquisite, and it leaves one unsatisfied.
The Picture of Dorian Gray (1891) ch. 6

20 Anybody can be good in the country.
The Picture of Dorian Gray (1891) ch. 19

21 It is better to be beautiful than to be good. But . . . it is better to be good than to be ugly.
The Picture of Dorian Gray (1891) ch. 17

22 A thing is not necessarily true because a man dies for it.
The Portrait of Mr W. H. (1901)

23 MRS ALLONBY: They say, Lady Hunstanton, that when good Americans die they go to Paris.
LADY HUNSTANTON: Indeed? And when bad Americans die, where do they go to?
LORD ILLINGWORTH: Oh, they go to America.
A Woman of No Importance (1893) act 1; cf. **Appleton** 23:5

24 The English country gentleman galloping after a fox—the unspeakable in full pursuit of the uneatable.
A Woman of No Importance (1893) act 1

25 One should never trust a woman who tells one her real age. A woman who would tell one that, would tell one anything.
A Woman of No Importance (1893) act 1

26 LORD ILLINGWORTH: The Book of Life begins with a man and a woman in a garden.
MRS ALLONBY: It ends with Revelations.
A Woman of No Importance (1893) act 1

27 Children begin by loving their parents; after a time they judge them; rarely, if ever, do they forgive them.
A Woman of No Importance (1893) act 2

28 GERALD: I suppose society is wonderfully delightful!
LORD ILLINGWORTH: To be in it is merely a bore. But to be out of it simply a tragedy.
A Woman of No Importance (1893) act 3

29 You should study the Peerage, Gerald . . . It is the best thing in fiction the English have ever done.
A Woman of No Importance (1893) act 3

30 He did not wear his scarlet coat,
For blood and wine are red,
And blood and wine were on his hands
When they found him with the dead.
The Ballad of Reading Gaol (1898) pt. 1, st. 1

31 I never saw a man who looked
With such a wistful eye
Upon that little tent of blue
Which prisoners call the sky.
The Ballad of Reading Gaol (1898) pt. 1, st. 3

32 Yet each man kills the thing he loves,
By each let this be heard,
Some do it with a bitter look,
Some with a flattering word.
The coward does it with a kiss,
The brave man with a sword!
The Ballad of Reading Gaol (1898) pt. 1, st. 7

33 The Governor was strong upon
The Regulations Act:

The Doctor said that Death was but
A scientific fact:
And twice a day the Chaplain called,
And left a little tract.
The Ballad of Reading Gaol (1898) pt. 3, st. 3

1 Something was dead in each of us,
And what was dead was Hope.
The Ballad of Reading Gaol (1898) pt. 3, st. 31

2 And the wild regrets, and the bloody sweats,
None knew so well as I:
For he who lives more lives than one
More deaths than one must die.
The Ballad of Reading Gaol (1898) pt. 3, st. 37

3 And alien tears will fill for him
Pity's long-broken urn,
For his mourners will be outcast men,
And outcasts always mourn.
inscribed on Wilde's tomb in Père Lachaise cemetery
The Ballad of Reading Gaol (1898) pt. 4, st. 23

4 How else but through a broken heart
May Lord Christ enter in?
The Ballad of Reading Gaol (1898) pt. 5, st. 14

5 All her bright golden hair
Tarnished with rust,
She that was young and fair
Fallen to dust.
'Requiescat' (1881)

6 Democracy means simply the bludgeoning of the people by the people for the people.
in *Fortnightly Review* February 1891 'The Soul of Man under Socialism'; cf. **Lincoln** 468:13

7 When I ask for a watercress sandwich, I do not mean a loaf with a field in the middle of it.
to a waiter
Max Beerbohm, letter to Reggie Turner, 15 April 1893

8 Ah, well, then, I suppose that I shall have to die beyond my means.
at the mention of a huge fee for a surgical operation
R. H. Sherard *Life of Oscar Wilde* (1906) ch. 18

9 Do you want to know the great drama of my life? It's that I have put my genius into my life; all I've put into my works is my talent.
André Gide *Oscar Wilde* (1910) 'In Memoriam'

10 He has fought a good fight and has had to face every difficulty except popularity.
of W. E. **Henley**
unpublished character sketch, written for Rothenstein's *English Portraits*; W. Rothenstein *Men and Memories* vol. 1 (1931) ch. 25

11 Shaw has not an enemy in the world; and none of his friends like him.
letter from Bernard Shaw to Archibald Henderson, 22 February 1911; Bernard Shaw *Collected Letters, 1911–1925* (1985)

12 I have nothing to declare except my genius.
at the New York Custom House
Frank Harris *Oscar Wilde* (1918)

13 Work is the curse of the drinking classes.
H. Pearson *Life of Oscar Wilde* (1946) ch. 12

Billy Wilder (Samuel Wilder) 1906–

American screenwriter and director
see also: **Film lines** *312:9, 312:12, 312:15*

14 Hindsight is always twenty-twenty.
J. R. Columbo *Wit and Wisdom of the Moviemakers* (1979) ch. 7

Thornton Wilder 1897–1975

American novelist and dramatist

15 Marriage is a bribe to make a housekeeper think she's a householder.
The Merchant of Yonkers (1939) act 1

16 Literature is the orchestration of platitudes.
in *Time* 12 January 1953

Robert Wilensky 1951–

American academic

17 We've all heard that a million monkeys banging on a million typewriters will eventually reproduce the entire works of Shakespeare. Now, thanks to the Internet, we know this is not true.
in *Mail on Sunday* 16 February 1997 'Quotes of the Week'; cf. **Eddington** 287:22

Wilhelm II ('Kaiser Bill') 1859–1941

German emperor and King of Prussia, 1888–1918

18 We have . . . fought for our place in the sun and have won it. It will be my business to see that we retain this place in the sun unchallenged, so that the rays of that sun may exert a fructifying influence upon our foreign trade and traffic.
speech in Hamburg, 18 June 1901; in *The Times* 20 June 1901; cf. **Bülow** 160:4

John Wilkes 1727–97

English parliamentary reformer

19 EARL OF SANDWICH: 'Pon my soul, Wilkes, I don't know whether you'll die upon the gallows or of the pox.
WILKES: That depends, my Lord, whether I first embrace your Lordship's principles, or your Lordship's mistresses.
Charles Petrie *The Four Georges* (1935); probably apocryphal

Emma Hart Willard 1787–1870

American pioneer of women's education

20 Rocked in the cradle of the deep.
title of song (1840), inspired by a prospect of the Bristol Channel

William I (William the Conqueror) 1027–87

Duke of Normandy; from 1066 King of England

21 If the Normans are disciplined under a just and firm rule they are men of great valour, who . . . fight resolutely to overcome all enemies. But without such rule they tear each other to pieces and destroy themselves, for they hanker after rebellion, cherish sedition, and are ready for any treachery.
attributed deathbed speech
Orderic Vitalis *Ecclesiastical History*

William III (William of Orange) 1650–1702
King of Great Britain and Ireland from 1688

1 'Do you not see your country is lost?' asked the Duke of Buckingham. 'There is one way never to see it lost' replied William, 'and that is to die in the last ditch.'
Bishop Gilbert Burnet *History of My Own Time* (1838 ed.)

2 Every bullet has its billet.
John Wesley *Journal* (1827) 6 June 1765; cf. **Proverbs** 599:20

William le Breton fl. 13th century
French priest, chaplain to King Philip Augustus of France

3 You could well ask whether the king loved his people more than the people their king. It was as if each tried to outdo the other in their love.
Philippide; G. Duby *France in the Middle Ages* (1991)

William of Malmesbury *c.*1090–*c.*1143
English monastic chronicler

4 The English at that time wore short garments, reaching to the mid-knee; they had their hair cropped, their beards shaven, their arms laden with golden bracelets, their skin adorned with punctured designs; they were accustomed to eat until they became surfeited, and to drink till they were sick. These latter qualities they imparted to their conquerors.
De Gestis Regum Anglorum (A History of the Norman Kings)

5 The Normans are a race inured to war, and can hardly live without it, fierce in rushing against the enemy, and, where force fails of success, ready to use stratagem, or corrupt by bribery.
De Gestis Regum Anglorum (A History of the Norman Kings)

Heathcote Williams 1941–
British dramatist and poet

6 Whales play, in an amniotic paradise.
Their light minds shaped by buoyancy, unrestricted by gravity,
Somersaulting.
Like angels, or birds;
Like our own lives, in the womb.
Whale Nation (1988)

Isaac Williams 1802–65
English clergyman

7 Be thou my Guardian and my Guide.
title of hymn (1842)

Peter Williams

8 Guide me, O thou great Jehovah,
Pilgrim through this barren land;
I am weak, but thou art mighty;
Hold me with thy powerful hand;
Bread of heaven, bread of heaven,
Feed me till I want no more.
first line frequently in the form 'O thou great Redeemer'
'Praying for Strength' (1771); translation of 'Arglwydd, arwain trwy'r anialwch' (1745) by William Williams (1717–91)

9 When I tread the verge of Jordan,
Bid my anxious fears subside.
'Praying for Strength' (1771)

R. J. P. Williams 1926–
British chemist

10 Biology is the search for the chemistry that works.
lecture in Oxford, June 1996

Shirley Williams 1930–
British Labour and Social Democrat politician

11 No test tube can breed love and affection. No frozen packet of semen ever read a story to a sleepy child.
in *Daily Mirror* 2 March 1978

12 The Catholic Church has never really come to terms with women. What I object to is being treated either as Madonnas or Mary Magdalenes.
in *Observer* 22 March 1981

Tennessee Williams (Thomas Lanier Williams) 1911–83
American dramatist

13 We have to distrust each other. It's our only defence against betrayal.
Camino Real (1953) block 10

14 We're all of us guinea pigs in the laboratory of God. Humanity is just a work in progress.
Camino Real (1953) block 12

15 What is the victory of a cat on a hot tin roof?—I wish I knew . . . Just staying on it, I guess, as long as she can.
Cat on a Hot Tin Roof (1955) act 1

16 BRICK: Well, they say nature hates a vacuum, Big Daddy.
BIG DADDY: That's what they say, but sometimes I think that a vacuum is a hell of a lot better than some of the stuff that nature replaces it with.
Cat on a Hot Tin Roof (1955) act 2

17 I didn't go to the moon, I went much further—for time is the longest distance between two places.
The Glass Menagerie (1945)

18 We're all of us sentenced to solitary confinement inside our own skins, for life!
Orpheus Descending (1958) act 2, sc. 1

19 Turn that off! I won't be looked at in this merciless glare!
A Streetcar Named Desire (1947) sc. 1

20 BLANCHE: I don't want realism.
MITCH: Naw, I guess not.
BLANCHE:I'll tell you what I want. Magic!
A Streetcar Named Desire (1947) sc. 9

21 I have always depended on the kindness of strangers.
A Streetcar Named Desire (1947) sc. 11

William Carlos Williams 1883–1963

American poet

1 Minds like beds always made up,
(more stony than a shore)
unwilling or unable.
Paterson (1946) bk. 1, preface

2 so much depends
upon
a red wheel
barrow
glazed with rain
water
beside the white
chickens.
'The Red Wheelbarrow' (1923)

3 Is it any better in Heaven, my friend Ford,
Than you found it in Provence?
'To Ford Madox Ford in Heaven' (1944)

Marianne Williamson 1953–

American writer and philanthropist

4 Our deepest fear is not that we are inadequate. Our deepest fear is that we are powerful beyond measure. It is our light, not our darkness, that most frightens us.
A Return to Love (1992) ch. 7

Roy Williamson 1936–90

Scottish folksinger and musician

5 O flower of Scotland, when will we see your like
again,
that fought and died for your bit hill and glen
and stood against him, proud Edward's army,
and sent him homeward tae think again.
unofficial Scottish Nationalist anthem
'O Flower of Scotland' (1968)

Love Maria Willis (née Whitcomb) 1824–1908

American doctor's wife

6 Father, hear the prayer we offer:
Not for ease that prayer shall be,
But for strength that we may ever
Live our lives courageously.

Not for ever in green pastures
Do we ask our way to be,
But the steep and rugged pathway
May we tread rejoicingly.
'Father, hear the prayer we offer' (1864 hymn)

Wendell Willkie 1892–1944

American lawyer and politician

7 The constitution does not provide for first and second class citizens.
An American Programme (1944) ch. 2

8 Freedom is an indivisible word. If we want to enjoy it, and fight for it, we must be prepared to extend it to everyone, whether they are rich or poor, whether they agree with us or not, no matter what their race or the colour of their skin.
One World (1943) ch. 13

Angus Wilson 1913–91

English novelist and short-story writer

9 Once a Catholic always a Catholic.
The Wrong Set (1949) p. 168

Charles E. Wilson 1890–1961

American industrialist; President of General Motors, 1941–53

10 For years I thought what was good for our country was good for General Motors and vice versa. The difference did not exist. Our company is too big. It goes with the welfare of the country.
testimony to the Senate Armed Services Committee on his proposed nomination for Secretary of Defence, 15 January 1953, in *New York Times* 24 February 1953

Edward O. Wilson 1929–

sociobiologist

11 Every human brain is born not as a blank tablet (a *tabula rasa*) waiting to be filled in by experience but as 'an exposed negative waiting to be slipped into developer fluid'.
on the nature v. nurture debate
attributed; Tom Wolfe in *Independent on Sunday* 2 February 1997

Harold Wilson 1916–95

British Labour statesman; Prime Minister, 1964–70, 1974–6

on Wilson: see **Bulmer-Thomas** *160:3*, **Home** *381:19*, **Junor** *423:18*, **Levin** *466:7*

12 All these financiers, all the little gnomes in Zurich.
speech in the House of Commons 12 November 1956

13 This party is a moral crusade or it is nothing.
speech at the Labour Party Conference, 1 October 1962; in *The Times* 2 October 1962

14 The university of the air.
an early term for the Open University
in *Glasgow Herald* 9 September 1963

15 The Britain that is going to be forged in the white heat of this revolution will be no place for restrictive practices or for outdated methods on either side of industry.
speech at the Labour Party Conference, 1 October 1963; cf. **Misquotations** 522:14

16 A week is a long time in politics.
probably first said at the time of the 1964 sterling crisis
Nigel Rees *Sayings of the Century* (1984) ; cf. **Chamberlain** 200:12

17 [Labour is] the natural party of government.
in 1965; Anthony Sampson *The Changing Anatomy of Britain* (1982)

18 From now the pound abroad is worth 14 per cent or so less in terms of other currencies. It does not mean, of course, that the pound here in Britain, in

your pocket or purse or in your bank, has been devalued.
often quoted as 'the pound in your pocket'
ministerial broadcast, 19 November 1967, in *The Times* 20 November 1967

1 Get your tanks off my lawn, Hughie.
to the trade union leader Hugh Scanlon, at Chequers in June 1969
Peter Jenkins *The Battle of Downing Street* (1970)

2 If I had the choice between smoked salmon and tinned salmon, I'd have it tinned. With vinegar.
in *Observer* 11 November 1962

3 This party is a bit like an old stagecoach. If you drive along at a rapid rate, everyone aboard is either so exhilarated or so seasick that you don't have a lot of difficulty.
of the Labour Party, c.1974
Anthony Sampson *The Changing Anatomy of Britain* (1982)

4 Whichever party is in office, the Treasury is in power.
while in opposition, c.1974
Anthony Sampson *The Changing Anatomy of Britain* (1982)

5 The Monarchy is a labour-intensive industry.
in *Observer* 13 February 1977

Harriette Wilson (née Dubochet) 1789–1846

English courtesan
see also **Wellington** *809:18*

6 I shall not say why and how I became, at the age of fifteen, the mistress of the Earl of Craven.
Memoirs (1825) opening words

John Wilson see **Christopher North**

Sandy Wilson 1924–

English songwriter

7 We've got to have
We plot to have
For it's so dreary not to have
That certain thing called the Boy Friend.
The Boyfriend (1954) title song

Woodrow Wilson 1856–1924

28th President of the US
on Wilson: see **Clemenceau** *220:12,* **Keynes** *435:5*

8 The future is not for parties 'playing politics', but for measures conceived in the largest spirit, pushed by parties whose leaders are statesmen, not demagogues, who love, not their offices, but their duty and their opportunity for service
speech at Trenton, New Jersey, 5 September 1910

9 It is like writing history with lightning. And my only regret is that it is all so terribly true.
on seeing D. W. Griffith's film The Birth of a Nation
at the White House, 18 February 1915

10 No nation is fit to sit in judgement upon any other nation.
speech in New York, 20 April 1915; in *Selected Addresses* (1918)

11 There is such a thing as a man being too proud to fight.
speech in Philadelphia, 10 May 1915; in *Selected Addresses* (1918) p. 88

12 We have stood apart, studiously neutral.
speech to Congress, 7 December 1915, in *New York Times* 8 December 1915

13 It must be a peace without victory . . . Only a peace between equals can last.
speech to US Senate, 22 January 1917, in *Messages and Papers* (1924) vol. 1

14 Armed neutrality is ineffectual enough at best.
speech to Congress, 2 April 1917, in *Selected Addresses* (1918)

15 The world must be made safe for democracy.
speech to Congress, 2 April 1917, in *Selected Addresses* (1918); cf. **Wolfe** 825:10

16 Once lead this people into war and they will forget there ever was such a thing as tolerance.
John Dos Passos *Mr Wilson's War* (1917) pt. 3, ch. 12

17 Open covenants of peace, openly arrived at.
the first of the 'Fourteen Points'
speech to Congress, 8 January 1918, in *Selected Addresses* (1918)

18 America is the only idealistic nation in the world.
speech at Sioux Falls, South Dakota, 8 September 1919; in *Messages and Papers* (1924) vol. 2

Anne Finch, Lady Winchilsea 1661–1720

English poet

19 Thirst of wealth no quiet knows,
But near the death-bed fiercer grows.
'Enquiry after Peace' (1713) l. 30

20 Love (if such a thing there be)
Is all despair, or ecstasy.
Poetry's the feverish fit,
Th' o'erflowing of unbounded wit.
'Enquiry after Peace' (1713) l. 40

21 Alas! a woman that attempts the pen
Such an intruder on the rights of men,
Such presumptuous creature is esteemed
The fault can by no virtue be redeemed.
'The Introduction' (1713) l. 9

22 To write, or read, or think, or to enquire
Would cloud our beauty, and exhaust our time,
And interrupt the conquests of our prime;
While the dull manage of a servile house
Is held by some our utmost art and use.
'The Introduction' (1713) l. 17

23 How are we fallen! Fallen by mistaken rules,
And education's, more than nature's, fools;
Debarred from all improvements of the mind,
And to be dull, expected and designed.
'The Introduction' (1713) l. 51

24 Give me yet before I die
A sweet, yet absolute retreat,
'Mongst paths so lost and trees so high
That the world may ne'er invade
Through such windings and such shade.
'The Petition for an Absolute Retreat' (1713) l. 2

1 Now the jonquil o'ercomes the feeble brain;
We faint beneath the aromatic pain.
'The Spleen' (1701); cf. **Pope** 585:14

2 My hand delights to trace unusual things,
And deviates from the known and common way;
Nor will in fading silks compose
Faintly the inimitable rose.
'The Spleen' (1701) l. 82

William Windham 1750–1810
English politician

3 No one would select the hurricane season in which to begin repairing his house.
speech opposing Flood's reform bill in 1790; *Dictionary of National Biography* (1917–)

4 Those entrusted with arms . . . should be persons of some substance and stake in the country.
speech in the House of Commons, 22 July 1807

Duchess of Windsor (Wallis Simpson) 1896–1986
wife of the former ***Edward VIII***
on Windsor: see ***Newspaper headlines*** *544:12*

5 You can never be too rich or too thin.
attributed

Duke of Windsor see Edward VIII

Catherine Winkworth 1827–78
English translator of German hymns

6 Now thank we all our God,
With heart and hands and voices,
Who wondrous things hath done,
In whom his world rejoices;
Who from our mother's arms
Hath blessed us on our way
With countless gifts of love,
And still is ours to-day.

O may this bounteous God
Through all our life be near us,
With ever joyful hearts
And blessèd peace to cheer us;
And keep us in his grace,
And guide us when perplexed,
And free us from all ills
In this world and the next.
Lyra Germanica (1858) 'Now thank we all our God' (translation of Martin Rinkart's 'Nun danket alle Gott', *c.*1636)

7 Praise to the Lord! the Almighty, the King of creation!
title of hymn (1863); translated from the German of Joachim Neander (1650–80)

8 Hast thou not seen?
All that is needful hath been
Granted in what he ordaineth.
'Praise to the Lord! the Almighty . . . ' (1863 hymn)

9 Ponder anew
What the Almighty can do
If with his love he befriend thee.
'Praise to the Lord! the Almighty . . . ' (1863 hymn)

10 *Peccavi*—I have Sindh.
of Sir Charles Napier's conquest of Sindh, 1843, supposedly sent by Napier to Lord Ellenborough; peccavi = *I have sinned*
in *Punch* 18 May 1844; attributed in *Notes and Queries* May 1954

Yvor Winters 1900–68
American poet and critic

11 The young are quick of speech.
Grown middle-aged, I teach
Corrosion and distrust,
Exacting what I must.
'On Teaching the Young' (1934)

Jeanette Winterson 1959–
English novelist and critic

12 [Roger Fry] gave us the term 'Post-Impressionist', without realising that the late twentieth century would soon be entirely fenced in with posts.
Art Objects (1995)

13 No one working in the English language now comes close to my exuberance, my passion, my fidelity to words.
on being asked to name the best living author writing in English
in *Sunday Times* 13 March 1994

John Winthrop 1588–1649
American settler

14 We must consider that we shall be a city upon a hill, the eyes of all people are on us; so that if we shall deal falsely with our God in this work we have undertaken, and so cause Him to withdraw His present help from us, we shall be made a story and a byword through the world.
Christian Charity, A Model Hereof (sermon, 1630) in Massachusetts Historical Society *Winthrop Papers* (1929–47) vol. 2

Robert Charles Winthrop 1809–94
American politician

15 A Star for every State, and a State for every Star.
speech on Boston Common, 27 August 1862, in *Addresses and Speeches* vol. 2 (1867)

Nicholas Wiseman 1802–65
English Catholic priest, Cardinal-archbishop of Westminster

16 Full in the panting heart of Rome,
Beneath the apostle's crowning dome,
From pilgrims' lips that kiss the ground,
Breathes in all tongues one only sound:
God bless our Pope, the great, the good.
'Full in the panting heart of Rome'

Owen Wister 1860–1938
American novelist

17 When you call me that, *smile!*
'that' being 'you son-of-a—'
The Virginian (1902) ch. 2

George Wither 1588–1667

English poet and pamphleteer

1 When I behold the havoc and the spoil
Which, even within the compass of my days,
Is made through every quarter of this isle,
In woods and groves, which were this kingdom's praise;
And when I mind with how much greediness
We seek the present gain in everything,
Not caring (so our lust we may possess)
What damage to posterity we bring . . .
What our forefathers planted, we destroy:
Nay, all men's labours, living heretofore,
And all our own, we lavishly employ
To serve our present lusts, and for no more.
A Collection of Emblems (1635) bk. 1, no. 35

2 I loved a lass, a fair one,
As fair as e'er was seen;
She was indeed a rare one,
Another Sheba queen.
A Description of Love (1620) 'I loved a lass, a fair one'

Ludwig Wittgenstein 1889–1951

Austrian-born philosopher
see also **Last words** 457:6

3 Philosophy is a battle against the bewitchment of our intelligence by means of language.
Philosophische Untersuchungen (1953) pt. 1, sect. 109

4 The philosopher's treatment of a question is like the treatment of an illness.
Philosophische Untersuchungen (1953) pt. 1, sect. 255

5 What is your aim in philosophy?—To show the fly the way out of the fly-bottle.
Philosophische Untersuchungen (1953) pt. 1, sect. 309

6 What can be said at all can be said clearly; and whereof one cannot speak thereof one must be silent.
Tractatus Logico-Philosophicus (1922) preface

7 The world is everything that is the case.
Tractatus Logico-Philosophicus (1922)

8 The limits of my language mean the limits of my world.
Tractatus Logico-Philosophicus (1922)

9 The world of the happy is quite different from that of the unhappy.
Tractatus Logico-Philosophicus (1922)

P. G. Wodehouse 1881–1975

English writer; an American citizen from 1955
on Wodehouse: see **O'Casey** 552:14; *see also* **Misquotations** 521:9

10 Chumps always make the best husbands . . . All the unhappy marriages come from the husbands having brains.
The Adventures of Sally (1920) ch. 10

11 There was another ring at the front door. Jeeves shimmered out and came back with a telegram.
Carry On, Jeeves! (1925) 'Jeeves Takes Charge'

12 He spoke with a certain what-is-it in his voice, and I could see that, if not actually disgruntled, he was far from being gruntled.
The Code of the Woosters (1938) ch. 1

13 Slice him where you like, a hellhound is always a hellhound.
The Code of the Woosters (1938) ch. 1

14 It is no use telling me that there are bad aunts and good aunts. At the core, they are all alike. Sooner or later, out pops the cloven hoof.
The Code of the Woosters (1938) ch. 2

15 Roderick Spode? Big chap with a small moustache and the sort of eye that can open an oyster at sixty paces?
The Code of the Woosters (1938) ch. 2

16 To my daughter Leonora without whose never-failing sympathy and encouragement this book would have been finished in half the time.
The Heart of a Goof (1926) dedication

17 I turned to Aunt Agatha, whose demeanour was now rather like that of one who, picking daisies on the railway, has just caught the down express in the small of the back.
The Inimitable Jeeves (1923) ch. 4

18 Sir Roderick Glossop . . . is always called a nerve specialist, because it sounds better, but everybody knows that he's really a sort of janitor to the looney-bin.
The Inimitable Jeeves (1923) ch. 7

19 When Aunt is calling to Aunt like mastodons bellowing across primeval swamps.
The Inimitable Jeeves (1923) ch. 16

20 It was my Uncle George who discovered that alcohol was a food well in advance of medical thought.
The Inimitable Jeeves (1923) ch. 16

21 It is a good rule in life never to apologize. The right sort of people do not want apologies, and the wrong sort take a mean advantage of them.
The Man Upstairs (1914) title story; cf. **Hubbard** 392:10

22 She fitted into my biggest armchair as if it had been built round her by someone who knew they were wearing armchairs tight about the hips that season.
My Man Jeeves (1919) 'Jeeves and the Unbidden Guest'

23 What with excellent browsing and sluicing and cheery conversation and what-not, the afternoon passed quite happily.
My Man Jeeves (1919) 'Jeeves and the Unbidden Guest'

24 Ice formed on the butler's upper slopes.
Pigs Have Wings (1952) ch. 5

25 The Right Hon. was a tubby little chap who looked as if he had been poured into his clothes and had forgotten to say 'When!'
Very Good, Jeeves (1930) 'Jeeves and the Impending Doom'

Terry Wogan 1938–
Irish broadcaster

1 Television contracts the imagination and radio expands it.
in *Observer* 30 December 1984 'Sayings of the Year'

Naomi Wolf 1962–
American writer

2 To ask women to become unnaturally thin is to ask them to relinquish their sexuality.
The Beauty Myth (1990)

Charles Wolfe 1791–1823
Irish poet

3 Not a drum was heard, not a funeral note,
As his corse to the rampart we hurried.
'The Burial of Sir John Moore at Corunna' (1817)

4 We buried him darkly at dead of night,
The sods with our bayonets turning.
'The Burial of Sir John Moore at Corunna' (1817)

5 We carved not a line, and we raised not a stone—
But we left him alone with his glory.
'The Burial of Sir John Moore at Corunna' (1817)

Humbert Wolfe 1886–1940
British poet

6 You cannot hope
to bribe or twist,
thank God! the
British journalist.
But, seeing what
the man will do
unbribed, there's
no occasion to.
'Over the Fire' (1930)

James Wolfe 1727–59
British general; captor of Quebec
on Wolfe: see **George II** *333:12; see also* **Last words** *456:17*

7 The General . . . repeated nearly the whole of Gray's Elegy . . . adding, as he concluded, that he would prefer being the author of that poem to the glory of beating the French to-morrow.
J. Playfair *Biographical Account of J. Robinson* in *Transactions of the Royal Society of Edinburgh* vol. 7 (1815)

Thomas Wolfe 1900–38
American novelist

8 Which of us has not remained forever prison-pent? Which of us is not forever a stranger and alone?
foreword to *Look Homeward, Angel* (1929)

9 Most of the time we think we're sick, it's all in the mind.
Look Homeward, Angel (1929) pt. 1, ch. 1

10 'Where they got you stationed now, Luke?' said Harry Tugman peering up snoutily from a mug of coffee. 'At the p-p-p-present time in Norfolk at the Navy base,' Luke answered, 'm-m-making the world safe for hypocrisy.'
Look Homeward, Angel (1929) pt. 3, ch. 36; cf. **Wilson** 822:15

11 You can't go home again.
title of book, 1940

Tom Wolfe 1931–
American writer

12 The bonfire of the vanities.
title of novel (1987); deriving from Savonarola's 'burning of the vanities' in Florence, 1497

13 A liberal is a conservative who has been arrested.
The Bonfire of the Vanities (1987) ch. 24

14 Electric Kool-Aid Acid test.
title of novel on hippy culture (1968)

15 We are now in the Me Decade.
Mauve Gloves and Madmen (1976) 'The Me Decade'

16 Radical Chic . . . is only radical in Style; in its heart it is part of Society and its tradition—Politics, like Rock, Pop, and Camp, has its uses.
in *New York* 8 June 1970

Mary Wollstonecraft 1759–97
English feminist; mother of Mary **Shelley**
on Wollstonecraft: see **Southey** *731:7,* **Walpole** *801:14*

17 To give a sex to mind was not very consistent with the principles of a man [Rousseau] who argued so warmly, and so well, for the immortality of the soul.
A Vindication of the Rights of Woman (1792) ch. 3; cf. **Misquotations** 522:3

18 The mind will ever be unstable that has only prejudices to rest on, and the current will run with destructive fury when there are no barriers to break its force.
A Vindication of the Rights of Woman (1792) ch. 4

19 She [woman] was created to be the toy of man, his rattle, and it must jingle in his ears whenever, dismissing reason, he chooses to be amused.
A Vindication of the Rights of Woman (1792) ch. 4

20 A king is always a king—and a woman always a woman: his authority and her sex ever stand between them and rational converse.
A Vindication of the Rights of Woman (1792) ch. 4

21 I do not wish them [women] to have power over men; but over themselves.
A Vindication of the Rights of Woman (1792) ch. 4

22 When a man seduces a woman, it should, I think, be termed a *left-handed* marriage.
A Vindication of the Rights of Woman (1792) ch. 4

23 Taught from infancy that beauty is woman's sceptre, the mind shapes itself to the body, and roaming round its gilt cage, only seeks to adorn its prison.
A Vindication of the Rights of Woman (1792) ch. 5

24 The pure animal spirits which make both mind and body shoot out, and unfold the tender blossoms of

hope, are turned sour and vented in vain wishes, or pert repinings, that contract the faculties and spoil the temper; else they mount to the brain, and sharpening the understanding before it gains proportional strength, produce that pitiful cunning which disgracefully characterizes the female mind and I fear will characterize it whilst women remain the slaves of power.

A Vindication of the Rights of Woman (1792) ch. 9

1 A slavish bondage to parents cramps every faculty of the mind.

A Vindication of the Rights of Woman (1792) ch. 11

2 Was not the world a vast prison, and women born slaves?

The Wrongs of Woman: or, Maria (1798)

3 Minute attention to propriety stops the growth of virtue.

Collected Letters (ed. R. Wardle, 1979) p. 141

Thomas Wolsey c.1475–1530

English cardinal; Lord Chancellor, 1515–29

4 Father Abbot, I am come to lay my bones amongst you.

George Cavendish *Negotiations of Thomas Wolsey* (1641); cf. **Shakespeare** 673:18

5 Had I but served God as diligently as I have served the King, he would not have given me over in my grey hairs.

George Cavendish *Negotiations of Thomas Wolsey* (1641); cf. **Shakespeare** 673:17

Kenneth Wolstenholme

English sports commentator

6 They think it's all over—it is now.

television commentary in closing moments of the World Cup Final, 30 July 1966

Mrs Henry Wood (née Ellen Price) 1814–87

English novelist

7 Dead! and . . . never called me mother.

East Lynne (dramatized by T. A. Palmer, 1874, the words do not occur in the novel of 1861)

Woodbine Willie see G. A. Studdert Kennedy

George Woodcock 1912–95

Canadian writer

8 Canadians do not like heroes, and so they do not have them.

Canada and the Canadians (1970)

Thomas Woodrooffe 1899–1978

British naval officer

9 At the present moment, the whole Fleet's lit up. When I say 'lit up', I mean lit up by fairy lamps.

live outside broadcast, Spithead Review, 20 May 1937

Asa Briggs *History of Broadcasting in the UK* (1965) vol. 2

Harry Woods

10 Oh we ain't got a barrel of money,
Maybe we're ragged and funny,
But we'll travel along
Singin' a song,
Side by side.

'Side by Side' (1927 song)

Tiger Woods 1975–

American golfer

11 Growing up, I came up with this name: I'm a Cablinasian.

explaining his rejection of 'African-American' as the term to describe his Caucasian, Afro-American, Native American, Thai, and Chinese ancestry

interviewed by Oprah Winfrey, 21 April 1997

Virginia Woolf 1882–1941

English novelist

on Woolf: see **Sitwell** *721:5*

12 Trivial personalities decomposing in the eternity of print.

The Common Reader (1925) 'The Modern Essay'

13 Examine for a moment an ordinary mind on an ordinary day.

The Common Reader (1925) 'Modern Fiction'

14 Life is not a series of gig lamps symmetrically arranged; life is a luminous halo, a semi-transparent envelope surrounding us from the beginning of consciousness to the end.

The Common Reader (1925) 'Modern Fiction'

15 Let us record the atoms as they fall upon the mind in the order in which they fall, let us trace the pattern, however disconnected and incoherent in appearance, which each sight or incident scores upon the consciousness. Let us not take it for granted that life exists more fully in what is commonly thought big than in what is commonly thought small.

The Common Reader (1925) 'Modern Fiction'

16 On or about December 1910 human nature changed . . . All human relations have shifted—those between masters and servants, husbands and wives, parents and children. And when human relations change there is at the same time a change in religion, conduct, politics, and literature.

'Mr Bennett and Mrs Brown' (1924)

17 A woman must have money and a room of her own if she is to write fiction.

A Room of One's Own (1929) ch. 1

18 Women have served all these centuries as looking-glasses possessing the magic and delicious power of reflecting the figure of a man at twice its natural size.

A Room of One's Own (1929) ch. 2

19 This is an important book, the critic assumes, because it deals with war. This is an insignificant

book because it deals with the feelings of women in a drawing-room.
A Room of One's Own (1929) ch. 4

1 So that is marriage, Lily thought, a man and a woman looking at a girl throwing a ball.
To the Lighthouse (1927) pt. 1, ch. 13

2 Things have dropped from me. I have outlived certain desires; I have lost friends, some by death . . . others through sheer inability to cross the street.
The Waves (1931)

3 The scratching of pimples on the body of the bootboy at Claridges.
of James **Joyce***'s* Ulysses
letter to Lytton Strachey, 24 April 1922, in *Letters* (ed. N. Nicolson and J. Trautmann, 1976) vol. 2

4 I read the book of Job last night. I don't think God comes well out of it.
letter to Lady Robert Cecil, 12 November 1922, in *Letters* (ed. N. Nicolson and J. Trautmann, 1976) vol. 2

5 As an experience, madness is terrific . . . and in its lava I still find most of the things I write about.
letter to Ethel Smyth, 22 June 1930, in *Letters* (ed. N. Nicolson and J. Trautmann, 1976) vol. 2

Alexander Woollcott 1887–1943
American writer

6 She was like a sinking ship firing on the rescuers.
of Mrs Patrick **Campbell**
While Rome Burns (1944) 'The First Mrs Tanqueray'

7 She is so odd a blend of Little Nell and Lady Macbeth. It is not so much the familiar phenomenon of a hand of steel in a velvet glove as a lacy sleeve with a bottle of vitriol concealed in its folds.
of Dorothy **Parker**
While Rome Burns (1934) 'Our Mrs Parker'

8 All the things I really like to do are either illegal, immoral, or fattening.
R. E. Drennan *Wit's End* (1973)

Dorothy Wordsworth 1771–1855
English writer; sister of William **Wordsworth**

9 One only leaf upon the top of a tree—the sole remaining leaf—danced round and round like a rag blown by the wind.
'Alfoxden Journal' 7 March 1798, in *Journals* (ed. E. de Selincourt, 1941)

10 Coleridge dined with us. He brought his ballad [*The Ancient Mariner*] finished. A beautiful evening, very starry, the horned moon.
'Alfoxden Journal' 23 March 1798, in *Journals* (ed. E. de Selincourt, 1941); cf. **Coleridge** 226:15

11 We saw a raven very high above us. It called out, and the dome of the sky seemed to echo the sound. It called again and again as it flew onwards, and the mountains gave back the sound, seeming as if from their centre; a musical bell-like answering to the bird's hoarse voice.
'Grasmere Journal' 27 July 1800, in *Journals* (ed. E. de Selincourt, 1941)

12 I never saw daffodils so beautiful. They grew among the mossy stones about and about them; some rested their heads upon these stones as on a pillow for weariness; and the rest tossed and reeled and danced, and seemed as if they verily laughed with the wind that blew upon them over the lake.
'Grasmere Journal' 15 April 1802, in *Journals* (ed. E. de Selincourt, 1941); cf. **Wordsworth** 828:26

13 We walked up to the house and stood some minutes watching the swallows that flew about restlessly, and flung their shadows upon the sunbright walls of the old building; the shadows glanced and twinkled, interchanged and crossed each other, expanded and shrunk up, appeared and disappeared every instant.
'Recollections of a Tour made in Scotland' 16 August 1803, in *Journals* (ed. E. de Selincourt, 1941)

Elizabeth Wordsworth 1840–1932
English educationist; first Principal of Lady Margaret Hall, Oxford

14 If all the good people were clever,
And all clever people were good,
The world would be nicer than ever
We thought that it possibly could.
But somehow, 'tis seldom or never
The two hit it off as they should;
The good are so harsh to the clever,
The clever so rude to the good!
'Good and Clever'

William Wordsworth 1770–1850
English poet; brother of Dorothy **Wordsworth**
on Wordsworth: see **Arnold** *26:16, 28:25,* **Bagehot** *47:24,* **Browning** *156:17,* **Bulwer-Lytton** *160:6,* **Byron** *176:30, 177:1, 178:3, 178:7, 180:4,* **Hazlitt** *365:19,* **Jeffrey** *406:5,* **Keats** *430:26,* **Shelley** *714:14,* **Stephen** *737:21; see also* **Arnold** *29:5*

15 My apprehensions come in crowds;
I dread the rustling of the grass;
The very shadows of the clouds
Have power to shake me as they pass.
'The Affliction of Margaret —' (1807)

16 And five times did I say to him
'Why, Edward, tell me why?'
'Anecdote for Fathers' (1798)

17 Action is transitory,—a step, a blow,
The motion of a muscle—this way or that—
'Tis done, and in the after vacancy
We wonder at ourselves like men betrayed:
Suffering is permanent, obscure and dark,
And shares the nature of infinity.
The Borderers (1842) act 3, l. 1539

18 Who is the happy Warrior? Who is he
Whom every man in arms should wish to be?
'Character of the Happy Warrior' (1807); cf. **Read** 622:13

19 Earth has not anything to show more fair:
Dull would he be of soul who could pass by
A sight so touching in its majesty:
This City now doth like a garment wear
The beauty of the morning; silent, bare,

Ships, towers, domes, theatres, and temples lie
Open unto the fields, and to the sky;
All bright and glittering in the smokeless air.
'Composed upon Westminster Bridge' (1807)

1 Dear God! the very houses seem asleep;
And all that mighty heart is lying still!
'Composed upon Westminster Bridge' (1807)

2 The light that never was, on sea or land,
The consecration, and the Poet's dream.
on a picture of Peele Castle in a storm
'Elegiac Stanzas' (1807)

3 Not in the lucid intervals of life
That come but as a curse to party-strife . . .
Is Nature felt, or can be.
'Evening Voluntaries' (1835) no. 4

4 By grace divine,
Not otherwise, O Nature! we are thine.
'Evening Voluntaries' (1835) no. 4

5 On Man, on Nature, and on Human Life,
Musing in solitude.
The Excursion (1814) Preface, l. 1

6 The Mind of Man—
My haunt, and the main region of my song.
The Excursion (1814) Preface, l. 40

7 Oh! many are the Poets that are sown
By Nature; men endowed with highest gifts,
The vision and the faculty divine;
Yet wanting the accomplishment of verse.
The Excursion (1814) bk. 1, l. 77

8 What soul was his, when from the naked top
Of some bold headland, he beheld the sun
Rise up, and bathe the world in light!
The Excursion (1827 ed.) bk. 1, l. 198

9 The good die first,
And they whose hearts are dry as summer dust
Burn to the socket.
The Excursion (1814) bk. 1, l. 500

10 This dull product of a scoffer's pen.
of **Voltaire**'s Candide
The Excursion (1814) bk. 2, l. 484

11 The intellectual power, through words and things,
Went sounding on, a dim and perilous way!
The Excursion (1814) bk. 3, l. 700

12 Society became my glittering bride,
And airy hopes my children.
The Excursion (1814) bk. 3, l. 735

13 'Tis a thing impossible, to frame
Conceptions equal to the soul's desires;
And the most difficult of tasks to keep
Heights which the soul is competent to gain.
The Excursion (1814) bk. 4, l. 136

14 'To every Form of being is assigned,'
Thus calmly spoke the venerable Sage,
'An *active* Principle.'
The Excursion (1814) bk. 9, l. 1

15 How fast has brother followed brother,
From sunshine to the sunless land!
'Extempore Effusion upon the Death of James Hogg' (1835)

16 Bliss was it in that dawn to be alive,
But to be young was very heaven!
'The French Revolution, as it Appeared to Enthusiasts' (1809); also *The Prelude* (1850) bk. 9, l. 108

17 A genial hearth, a hospitable board,
And a refined rusticity.
'A genial hearth, a hospitable board' (1822)

18 Not choice
But habit rules the unreflecting herd.
'Grant that by this unsparing hurricane' (1822)

19 The moving accident is not my trade;
To freeze the blood I have no ready arts:
'Tis my delight, alone in summer shade,
To pipe a simple song for thinking hearts.
'Hart-Leap Well' (1800) pt. 2, l. 1

20 All shod with steel
We hissed along the polished ice, in games
Confederate.
'Influence of Natural Objects' (1809); also *The Prelude* (1850) bk. 1, l. 414

21 Leaving the tumultuous throng,
To cut across the reflex of a star;
Image, that, flying still before me, gleamed
Upon the glassy plain.
'Influence of Natural Objects' (1809)

22 Yet still the solitary cliffs
Wheeled by me—even as if the earth had rolled
With visible motion her diurnal round!
'Influence of Natural Objects' (1809); also *The Prelude* (1850) bk. 1, l. 458

23 It is a beauteous evening, calm and free;
The holy time is quiet as a nun
Breathless with adoration.
'It is a beauteous evening, calm and free' (1807)

24 We must be free or die, who speak the tongue
That Shakespeare spake; the faith and morals hold
Which Milton held.
'It is not to be thought of that the Flood' (1807)

25 I travelled among unknown men,
In lands beyond the sea;
Nor England! did I know till then
What love I bore to thee.
'I travelled among unknown men' (1807)

26 I wandered lonely as a cloud
That floats on high o'er vales and hills,
When all at once I saw a crowd,
A host, of golden daffodils;
Beside the lake, beneath the trees,
Fluttering and dancing in the breeze.
'I wandered lonely as a cloud' (1815 ed.); cf. **Wordsworth** 827:12

27 For oft, when on my couch I lie
In vacant or in pensive mood,
They flash upon that inward eye
Which is the bliss of solitude;
And then my heart with pleasure fills,
And dances with the daffodils.
'I wandered lonely as a cloud' (1815 ed.)

28 The gods approve
The depth, and not the tumult, of the soul.
'Laodamia' (1815) l. 74

1 More pellucid streams,
An ampler ether, a diviner air,
And fields invested with purpureal gleams.
'Laodamia' (1815) l. 103

2 I have owed to them
In hours of weariness, sensations sweet,
Felt in the blood, and felt along the heart;
And passing even into my purer mind,
With tranquil restoration:—feelings too
Of unremembered pleasure: such, perhaps,
As may have had no trivial influence
On that best portion of a good man's life,
His little, nameless, unremembered, acts
Of kindness and of love.
'Lines composed a few miles above Tintern Abbey' (1798) l. 33

3 That blessed mood
In which the burthen of the mystery,
In which the heavy and the weary weight
Of all this unintelligible world,
Is lightened.
'Lines composed . . . above Tintern Abbey' (1798) l. 37

4 The sounding cataract
Haunted me like a passion: the tall rock,
The mountain, and the deep and gloomy wood,
Their colours and their forms, were then to me
An appetite.
'Lines composed . . . above Tintern Abbey' (1798) l. 72

5 I have learned
To look on nature, not as in the hour
Of thoughtless youth; but hearing oftentimes
The still, sad music of humanity,
Nor harsh nor grating, though of ample power
To chasten and subdue. And I have felt
A presence that disturbs me with the joy
Of elevated thoughts; a sense sublime
Of something far more deeply interfused,
Whose dwelling is the light of setting suns,
And the round ocean and the living air,
And the blue sky, and in the mind of man.
'Lines composed . . . above Tintern Abbey' (1798) l. 88

6 All the mighty world
Of eye and ear, both what they half-create,
And what perceive.
'Lines composed . . . above Tintern Abbey' (1798) l. 106; cf. **Young** 839:10

7 And much it grieved my heart to think
What man has made of man.
'Lines Written in Early Spring' (1798)

8 Milton! thou shouldst be living at this hour:
England hath need of thee: she is a fen
Of stagnant waters: altar, sword, and pen,
Fireside, the heroic wealth of hall and bower,
Have forfeited their ancient English dower
Of inward happiness.
'Milton! thou shouldst be living at this hour' (1807)

9 Some happy tone
Of meditation, slipping in between
The beauty coming and the beauty gone.
'Most sweet it is' (1835)

10 My heart leaps up when I behold
A rainbow in the sky:
So was it when my life began;
So is it now I am a man;
So be it when I shall grow old,
Or let me die!
The Child is father of the Man;
And I could wish my days to be
Bound each to each by natural piety.
'My heart leaps up when I behold' (1807); cf. **Milton** 518:7, **Proverbs** 597:15

11 Nuns fret not at their convent's narrow room;
And hermits are contented with their cells.
'Nuns fret not at their convent's narrow room' (1807)

12 Bound
Within the Sonnet's scanty plot of ground.
'Nuns fret not at their convent's narrow room' (1807)

13 With gentle hand
Touch—for there is a spirit in the woods.
'Nutting' (1800)

14 There was a time when meadow, grove, and stream,
The earth, and every common sight,
To me did seem
Apparelled in celestial light,
The glory and the freshness of a dream.
'Ode. Intimations of Immortality' (1807) st. 1

15 The rainbow comes and goes,
And lovely is the rose,
The moon doth with delight
Look round her when the heavens are bare;
Waters on a starry night
Are beautiful and fair;
The sunshine is a glorious birth;
But yet I know, where'er I go,
That there hath passed away a glory from the earth.
'Ode. Intimations of Immortality' (1807) st. 2

16 A timely utterance gave that thought relief,
And I again am strong.
'Ode. Intimations of Immortality' (1807) st. 3

17 The winds come to me from the fields of sleep.
'Ode. Intimations of Immortality' (1807) st. 3

18 Shout round me, let me hear thy shouts, thou happy Shepherd Boy!
'Ode. Intimations of Immortality' (1807) st. 3

19 Both of them speak of something that is gone:
The pansy at my feet
Doth the same tale repeat:
Whither is fled the visionary gleam?
Where is it now, the glory and the dream?
'Ode. Intimations of Immortality' (1807) st. 4

20 Our birth is but a sleep and a forgetting:
The Soul that rises with us, our life's Star,
Hath had elsewhere its setting,
And cometh from afar:
Not in entire forgetfulness,
And not in utter nakedness,
But trailing clouds of glory do we come
From God, who is our home:
Heaven lies about us in our infancy!
Shades of the prison-house begin to close

Upon the growing boy.
'Ode. Intimations of Immortality' (1807) st. 5

1 And by the vision splendid
Is on his way attended;
At length the man perceives it die away,
And fade into the light of common day.
'Ode. Intimations of Immortality' (1807) st. 5

2 As if his whole vocation
Were endless imitation.
'Ode. Intimations of Immortality' (1807) st. 7

3 Thou Eye among the blind,
That, deaf and silent, read'st the eternal deep,
Haunted for ever by the eternal mind.
'Ode. Intimations of Immortality' (1807) st. 8

4 Full soon thy Soul shall have her earthly freight,
And custom lie upon thee with a weight,
Heavy as frost, and deep almost as life!
'Ode. Intimations of Immortality' (1807) st. 8

5 O joy! that in our embers
Is something that doth live,
That nature yet remembers
What was so fugitive!
The thought of our past years in me doth breed
Perpetual benediction.
'Ode. Intimations of Immortality' (1832 ed.) st. 9

6 Not for these I raise
The song of thanks and praise;
But for those obstinate questionings
Of sense and outward things,
Fallings from us, vanishings;
Blank misgivings of a creature
Moving about in worlds not realised,
High instincts before which our mortal nature
Did tremble like a guilty thing surprised.
'Ode. Intimations of Immortality' (1807) st. 9

7 Our noisy years seem moments in the being
Of the eternal Silence: truths that wake,
To perish never.
'Ode. Intimations of Immortality' (1807) st. 9

8 Hence, in a season of calm weather,
Though inland far we be,
Our souls have sight of that immortal sea
Which brought us hither,
Can in a moment travel thither,
And see the children sport upon the shore,
And hear the mighty waters rolling evermore.
'Ode. Intimations of Immortality' (1807) st. 9

9 Though nothing can bring back the hour
Of splendour in the grass, of glory in the flower;
We will grieve not, rather find
Strength in what remains behind . . .
In the faith that looks through death,
In years that bring the philosophic mind.
'Ode. Intimations of Immortality' (1807) st. 10

10 Another race hath been, and other palms are won.
Thanks to the human heart by which we live,
Thanks to its tenderness, its joys, and fears,
To me the meanest flower that blows can give
Thoughts that do often lie too deep for tears.
'Ode. Intimations of Immortality' (1807) st. 11

11 But Thy most dreaded instrument,
In working out a pure intent,
Is man—arrayed for mutual slaughter,—
Yea, Carnage is thy daughter!
'Ode. The Morning of the Day Appointed for a General Thanksgiving' (1816)

12 Stern daughter of the voice of God!
O Duty! if that name thou love
Who art a light to guide, a rod
To check the erring, and reprove.
'Ode to Duty' (1807)

13 Plain living and high thinking are no more:
The homely beauty of the good old cause
Is gone.
'O friend! I know not which way I must look' (1807); cf. **Milton** 519:22

14 Once did she hold the gorgeous East in fee,
And was the safeguard of the West.
'On the Extinction of the Venetian Republic' (1807)

15 There's something in a flying horse,
There's something in a huge balloon;
But through the clouds I'll never float
Until I have a little Boat,
Shaped like the crescent-moon.
Peter Bell (1819) prologue, l. 1

16 Is it some party in a parlour,
Crammed just as they on earth were crammed—
Some sipping punch, some sipping tea,
But as you by their faces see
All silent, and all damned?
Peter Bell pt. 1, l. 541 in 1819 MS (subsequently deleted so as 'not to offend the pious')

17 Physician art thou?—one, all eyes,
Philosopher!—a fingering slave,
One that would peep and botanize
Upon his mother's grave?
'A Poet's Epitaph' (1800)

18 A reasoning, self-sufficing thing,
An intellectual All-in-all!
'A Poet's Epitaph' (1800)

19 In common things that round us lie
Some random truths he can impart,—
The harvest of a quiet eye
That broods and sleeps on his own heart.
'A Poet's Epitaph' (1800)

20 Escaped
From the vast city, where I long had pined
A discontented sojourner.
The Prelude (1850) bk. 1, l. 6

21 I recoil and droop, and seek repose
In listlessness from vain perplexity;
Unprofitably travelling toward the grave.
The Prelude (1850) bk. 1, l. 267

22 Made one long bathing of a summer's day.
The Prelude (1850) bk. 1, l. 290

23 Fair seed-time had my soul, and I grew up
Fostered alike by beauty and by fear.
The Prelude (1850) bk. 1, l. 301

24 Dust as we are, the immortal spirit grows
Like harmony in music; there is a dark

Inscrutable workmanship that reconciles
Discordant elements, makes them cling together
In one society.
The Prelude (1850) bk. 1, l. 340

1 And I was taught to feel, perhaps too much,
The self-sufficing power of Solitude.
The Prelude (1850) bk. 2, l. 76

2 To thee
Science appears but what in truth she is,
Not as our glory and our absolute boast,
But as a succedaneum, and a prop
To our infirmity.
The Prelude (1850) bk. 2, l. 211

3 The statue stood
Of Newton, with his prism, and silent face:
The marble index of a mind for ever
Voyaging through strange seas of Thought, alone.
The Prelude (1850) bk. 3, l. 60

4 Spirits overwrought
Were making night do penance for a day
Spent in a round of strenuous idleness.
The Prelude (1850) bk. 4, l. 376

5 And, through the turnings intricate of verse,
Present themselves as objects recognised,
In flashes, and with glory not their own.
The Prelude (1850) bk. 5, l. 605

6 We were brothers all
In honour, as in one community,
Scholars and gentlemen.
The Prelude (1850) bk. 9, l. 227

7 All things have second birth;
The earthquake is not satisfied at once.
The Prelude (1850) bk. 10, l. 83

8 Not in Utopia,—subterranean fields,—
Or some secreted island, Heaven knows where!
But in the very world, which is the world
Of all of us,—the place where in the end
We find our happiness, or not at all!
The Prelude (1850) bk. 11, l. 140

9 There is
One great society alone on earth,
The noble Living, and the noble Dead.
The Prelude (1850) bk. 11, l. 393

10 I shook the habit off
Entirely and for ever, and again
In Nature's presence stood, as now I stand,
A sensitive being, a *creative* soul.
The Prelude (1850) bk. 12, l. 204

11 Imagination, which in truth,
Is but another name for absolute power
And clearest insight, amplitude of mind,
And Reason, in her most exalted mood.
The Prelude (1850) bk. 14, l. 190

12 I thought of Chatterton, the marvellous boy,
The sleepless soul that perished in its pride;
Of him who walked in glory and in joy
Behind his plough, upon the mountain side:
By our own spirits are we deified;
We poets in our youth begin in gladness;
But thereof comes in the end despondency and
madness.
'Resolution and Independence' (1807) st. 7

13 His words came feebly, from a feeble chest,
Yet each in solemn order followed each,
With something of a lofty utterance drest;
Choice words, and measured phrase; above the
reach
Of ordinary men; a stately speech!
Such as grave Livers do in Scotland use.
'Resolution and Independence' (1807) st. 15

14 Cold, pain, and labour, and all fleshly ills;
And mighty Poets in their misery dead.
'Resolution and Independence' (1820 ed.) st. 17

15 Still glides the Stream, and shall for ever glide;
The Form remains, the Function never dies.
'The River Duddon' (1820) no. 34 'After-Thought'

16 Enough, if something from our hands have power
To live, and act, and serve the future hour;
And if, as toward the silent tomb we go,
Through love, through hope, and faith's
transcendent dower,
We feel that we are greater than we know.
'The River Duddon' (1820) no. 34 'After-Thought'

17 The good old rule
Sufficeth them, the simple plan,
That they should take who have the power,
And they should keep who can.
'Rob Roy's Grave' (1807) l. 37

18 Scorn not the Sonnet; Critic, you have frowned,
Mindless of its just honours; with this key
Shakespeare unlocked his heart.
'Scorn not the Sonnet' (1827); cf. **Browning** 156:6

19 She dwelt among the untrodden ways
Beside the springs of Dove,
A maid whom there were none to praise
And very few to love.
'She dwelt among the untrodden ways' (1800)

20 A violet by a mossy stone
Half hidden from the eye!
'She dwelt among the untrodden ways' (1800)

21 She lived unknown, and few could know
When Lucy ceased to be;
But she is in her grave, and, oh,
The difference to me!
'She dwelt among the untrodden ways' (1800)

22 She was a phantom of delight.
title of poem (1807)

23 And now I see with eye serene
The very pulse of the machine;
A being breathing thoughtful breath;
A traveller betwixt life and death.
'She was a phantom of delight' (1807)

24 A perfect woman; nobly planned,
To warn, to comfort, and command.
'She was a phantom of delight' (1807)

25 A slumber did my spirit seal;
I had no human fears:
She seemed a thing that could not feel

The touch of earthly years.
No motion has she now, no force;
She neither hears nor sees;
Rolled round in earth's diurnal course,
With rocks, and stones, and trees.
'A slumber did my spirit seal' (1800)

1 O Man! that from thy fair and shining youth
Age might but take the things Youth needed not!
'The Small Celandine' (1807)

2 Behold her, single in the field,
Yon solitary Highland lass!
'The Solitary Reaper' (1807)

3 Will no one tell me what she sings?
Perhaps the plaintive numbers flow
For old, unhappy, far-off things,
And battles long ago.
'The Solitary Reaper' (1807)

4 What, you are stepping westward?
'Stepping Westward' (1807)

5 Surprised by joy—impatient as the wind
I wished to share the transport—Oh! with whom
But thee, long buried in the silent tomb.
'Surprised by joy—impatient as the wind' (1815)

6 One impulse from a vernal wood
May teach you more of man,
Of moral evil and of good,
Than all the sages can.
'The Tables Turned' (1798); cf. **Bernard** 69:1

7 Our meddling intellect
Mis-shapes the beauteous forms of things:—
We murder to dissect.
Enough of science and of art;
Close up these barren leaves.
'The Tables Turned' (1798)

8 Two Voices are there; one is of the sea,
One of the mountains; each a mighty Voice:
In both from age to age thou didst rejoice,
They were thy chosen music, Liberty!
'Thought of a Briton on the Subjugation of Switzerland' (1807); cf. **Stephen** 737:21

9 O blithe new-comer! I have heard,
I hear thee and rejoice:
O Cuckoo! Shall I call thee bird,
Or but a wandering voice?
'To the Cuckoo' (1807)

10 Oft on the dappled turf at ease
I sit, and play with similes,
Loose types of things through all degrees.
'To the Daisy' ('With little here to do or see', 1820 ed.)

11 Type of the wise who soar, but never roam;
True to the kindred points of heaven and home!
'To a Skylark' ('Ethereal minstrel! pilgrim of the sky', 1827)

12 Though fallen thyself, never to rise again,
Live, and take comfort. Thou hast left behind
Powers that will work for thee; air, earth, and skies;
There's not a breathing of the common wind
That will forget thee; thou hast great allies;
Thy friends are exultations, agonies,
And love, and man's unconquerable mind.
'To Toussaint L'Ouverture' (1807)

13 We are seven.
title of poem (1798)

14 A simple child, dear brother Jim,
That lightly draws its breath,
And feels its life in every limb,
What should it know of death?
'We are Seven' (1798)

15 The world is too much with us; late and soon,
Getting and spending, we lay waste our powers.
'The world is too much with us' (1807)

16 Great God! I'd rather be
A Pagan suckled in a creed outworn;
So might I, standing on this pleasant lea,
Have glimpses that would make me less forlorn;
Have sight of Proteus rising from the sea;
Or hear old Triton blow his wreathèd horn.
'The world is too much with us' (1807)

17 I propose to myself to imitate, and as far as possible, to adopt the very language of men . . . I wish to keep my reader in the company of flesh and blood.
Lyrical Ballads (1800) preface

18 It may be safely affirmed, that there neither is, nor can be, any *essential* difference between the language of prose and metrical composition.
Lyrical Ballads (1800) preface

19 The Poet writes under one restriction only, namely, the necessity of giving immediate pleasure to a human Being possessed of that information which may be expected from him, not as a lawyer, a physician, a mariner, an astronomer or a natural philosopher, but as a Man.
Lyrical Ballads (2nd ed., 1802) preface

20 Poetry is the spontaneous overflow of powerful feelings: it takes its origin from emotion recollected in tranquillity.
Lyrical Ballads (2nd ed., 1802) preface; cf. **Parker** 567:9, **Thurber** 777:3

21 Poetry is the breath and finer spirit of all knowledge; it is the impassioned expression which is in the countenance of all science.
Lyrical Ballads (2nd ed., 1802) Preface

22 Never forget what I believe was observed to you by Coleridge, that every great and original writer, in proportion as he is great and original, must himself create the taste by which he is to be relished.
letter to Lady Beaumont, 21 May 1807, in E. de Selincourt (ed.) *Letters of William and Dorothy Wordsworth* vol. 2 (revised by M. Moorman, 1969)

Henry Wotton 1568–1639
English poet and diplomat

23 And entertains the harmless day
With a religious book, or friend.
'The Character of a Happy Life' (1614)

24 This man is freed from servile bands,
Of hope to rise, or fear to fall:—
Lord of himself, though not of lands,

And having nothing, yet hath all.
'The Character of a Happy Life' (1614)

1 You meaner beauties of the night,
That poorly satisfy our eyes,
More by your number, than your light;
You common people of the skies,
What are you when the moon shall rise?
'On His Mistress, the Queen of Bohemia' (1624)

2 Untrue she was; yet I believed her eyes,
Instructed spies,
Till I was taught, that love was but a school
To breed a fool.
'Poem written in his youth' (1602)

3 He first deceased; she for a little tried
To live without him: liked it not, and died.
'Upon the Death of Sir Albertus Moreton's Wife' (1651)

4 Dazzled thus with height of place,
Whilst our hopes our wits beguile,
No man marks the narrow space
'Twixt a prison and a smile.
'Upon the sudden restraint of the Earl of Somerset' (1651)

5 In architecture as in all other operative arts, the end must direct the operation. The end is to build well. Well building hath three conditions. Commodity, firmness, and delight.
Elements of Architecture (1624) pt. 1

6 An ambassador is an honest man sent to lie abroad for the good of his country.
written in the album of Christopher Fleckmore in 1604; Izaak Walton *Reliquiae Wottonianae* (1651) 'The Life of Sir Henry Wotton'

7 Critics are like brushers of noblemen's clothes.
Francis Bacon *Apophthegms New and Old* (1625) no. 64

8 Take heed of thinking, *The farther you go from the church of Rome, the nearer you are to God.*
Izaak Walton *Reliquiae Wottonianae* (1651) 'The Life of Sir Henry Wotton'

Frank Lloyd Wright 1867–1959
American architect

9 The necessities were going by default to save the luxuries until I hardly knew which were necessities and which luxuries.
Autobiography (1945) bk. 2

10 The physician can bury his mistakes, but the architect can only advise his client to plant vines—so they should go as far as possible from home to build their first buildings.
in *New York Times* 4 October 1953, sect. 6; cf. **Quarles** 618:21

11 The modern city is a place for banking and prostitution and very little else.
Robert C. Twombly *Frank Lloyd Wright* (1973) ch. 9

James Wright 1927–80
American poet

12 Suddenly I realize
That if I stepped out of my body I would break
Into blossom.
'A Blessing' (1963)

13 Between two cold white shadows,
But I dreamed they would rise
Together,
My black Ohioan swan.
'Three Sentences for a Dead Swan' (1968)

Mehetabel ('Hetty') Wright (née Wesley) 1697–1750
English poet

14 Transient lustre, beauteous clay,
Smiling wonder of a day.
'To an Infant Expiring the Second Day of its Birth' (1733)

15 Thou tyrant whom I will not name,
Whom heaven and hell alike disclaim;
Abhorred and shunned, for different ends,
By angels, Jesuits, beasts and fiends!
What terms to curse thee shall I find,
Thou plague peculiar to mankind? . . .
That wretch, if such a wretch there be,
Who hopes for happiness from thee,
May search successfully as well
For truth in whores and ease in hell.
'Wedlock' (*c.*1730)

Lady Mary Wroth *c.*1586–*c.*1652
English poet

16 Love, a child, is ever crying:
Please him and he straight is flying,
Give him, he the more is craving,
Never satisfied with having.
'Love, a child, is ever crying' (1621)

Harry Wu 1937–
Chinese-born American political activist

17 I want to see the word laogai in every dictionary in every language in the world. I want to see the laogai ended. Before 1974, the word 'gulag' did not appear in any dictionary. Today, this single word conveys the meaning of Soviet political violence and its labour camp system. 'Laogai' also deserves a place in our dictionaries.
the laogai *are Chinese labour camps*
in *Washington Post* 26 May 1996

St Wulfstan *c.*1009–1095
English monk and prelate, bishop of Worcester from 1062

18 We miserable people have destroyed the work of saints, that we may provide praise for ourselves. The age of that most happy man did not know how to build pompous buildings, but knew how to offer themselves to God under any sort of roof, and to attract to their example subordinates. We on the contrary strive that, neglecting our souls, we may pile up stones.
on the demolition of St Oswald's Anglo-Saxon cathedral at Worcester, the new Romanesque choir having been recently completed
William of Malmesbury *Gesta Pontificum* (Rolls series (1870) vol. 52)

Thomas Wyatt c.1503–42
English poet

1 Farewell, Love, and all thy laws forever.
Thy baited hooks shall tangle me no more.
'Farewell, Love' (1557)

2 Go trouble younger hearts
And in me claim no more authority.
With idle youth go use thy property
And thereon spend thy many brittle darts:
For hitherto though I have lost all my time,
Me lusteth no longer rotten boughs to climb.
'Farewell, Love' (1557)

3 With serving still
This have I won:
For my good will
To be undone.

And for redress
Of all my pain
Disdainfulness
I have again.
'With serving still'

4 *Quondam* was I. She said, 'for ever'.
That 'ever' lasted but a short while,
A promise made not to dissever;
I thought she laughed, she did but smile.
Then *quondam* was I.
'Quondam was I'

5 They flee from me, that sometime did me seek
With naked foot, stalking in my chamber.
'They flee from me' (1557)

6 When her loose gown from her shoulders did fall,
And she me caught in her arms long and small;
Therewith all sweetly did me kiss,
And softly said, 'Dear heart, how like you this?'
'They flee from me' (1557)

7 Throughout the world, if it were sought,
Fair words enough a man shall find.
They be good cheap; they cost right naught;
Their substance is but only wind.
But well to say and so to mean—
That sweet accord is seldom seen.
'Throughout the world, if it were sought' (1557)

William Wycherley c.1640–1716
English dramatist

8 A mistress should be like a little country retreat near the town, not to dwell in constantly, but only for a night and away.
The Country Wife (1675) act 1, sc. 1

9 Go to your business, I say, pleasure, whilst I go to my pleasure, business.
The Country Wife (1675) act 2

10 Women and fortune are truest still to those that trust 'em.
The Country Wife (1675) act 5, sc. 4

11 Nay, you had both felt his desperate deadly daunting dagger:—there are your d's for you!
The Gentleman Dancing-Master (1672) act 5

12 Fy! madam, do you think me so ill bred as to love a husband?
Love in a Wood (1672) act 3, sc. 4

13 You who scribble, yet hate all who write . . .
And with faint praises one another damn.
of drama critics
The Plain Dealer (1677) prologue; cf. **Pope** 583:7

14 A man without money needs no more fear a crowd of lawyers than a crowd of pickpockets.
The Plain Dealer (1677) act 3, sc. 1

Tammy Wynette 1942–98 and Billy Sherrill c.1938–

15 Stand by your man.
title of song (1968); cf. *Clinton* 220:18

Andrew of Wyntoun c.1350–c.1420
Scottish churchman

16 Quhen Alysander oure kyng wes dede,
That Scotland led in luve and le,
Away wes sons of ale and brede,
Of wyne and wax, of gamyn and gle;
Oure gold wes changyd into lede,
Cryst, borne into virgynyte,
Succour Scotland, and remede,
That stad is in perplexyte.
The Orygynale Cronykil (1795 ed.) vol. 1, bk. 7, ch. 10, l. 527

Xenophon c.428–c.354 BC
Greek historian

17 *θάλαττα θάλαττα*
The sea! the sea!
Anabasis bk. 4, ch. 7, sect. 24

Augustin, Marquis de Ximénèz 1726–1817
French poet

18 *Attaquons dans ses eaux*
La perfide Albion!
Let us attack in her own waters perfidious Albion!
'L'Ère des Français' (October 1793) in *Poésies Révolutionnaires et contre-révolutionnaires* (1821) vol. 1; cf. **Bossuet** 143:16

William Yancey 1814–63
American Confederate politician

19 The man and the hour have met.
of Jefferson ***Davis****, President-elect of the Confederacy, in 1861*
Shelby Foote *The Civil War: Fort Sumter to Perryville* (1991)

Thomas Russell Ybarra b. 1880

20 A Christian is a man who feels
Repentance on a Sunday
For what he did on Saturday
And is going to do on Monday.
'The Christian' (1909)

W. F. Yeames 1835–1918

British painter

1 And when did you last see your father?
a Roundhead officer addressing the child of a Cavalier family
title of painting (1878), now in the Walker Art Gallery, Liverpool

W. B. Yeats 1865–1939

Irish poet
on Yeats: see **Auden** *33:31, 34:2*

2 I said 'a line will take us hours maybe;
Yet if it does not seem a moment's thought,
Our stitching and unstitching has been naught.'
'Adam's Curse' (1904)

3 O body swayed to music, O brightening glance,
How can we know the dancer from the dance?
'Among School Children' (1928)

4 A young man when the old men are done talking
Will say to an old man, 'Tell me of that lady
The poet stubborn with his passion sang us
When age might well have chilled his blood.'
'Broken Dreams' (1914)

5 The unpurged images of day recede;
The Emperor's drunken soldiery are abed.
'Byzantium' (1933)

6 A starlit or a moonlit dome disdains
All that man is,
All mere complexities,
The fury and the mire of human veins.
'Byzantium' (1933)

7 Those images that yet
Fresh images beget,
That dolphin-torn, that gong-tormented sea.
'Byzantium' (1933)

8 The intellect of man is forced to choose
Perfection of the life, or of the work,
And if it take the second must refuse
A heavenly mansion, raging in the dark.
'The Choice' (1933)

9 Now that my ladder's gone
I must lie down where all the ladders start,
In the foul rag-and-bone shop of the heart.
'The Circus Animals' Desertion' (1939) pt. 3

10 I made my song a coat
Covered with embroideries
Out of old mythologies
From heel to throat;
But the fools caught it,
Wore it in the world's eye
As though they'd wrought it.
Song, let them take it,
For there's more enterprise
In walking naked.
'A Coat' (1914)

11 We were the last romantics — chose for theme
Traditional sanctity and loveliness.
'Coole Park and Ballylee, 1931' (1933)

12 The years like great black oxen tread the world,
And God the herdsman goads them on behind,
And I am broken by their passing feet.
The Countess Cathleen (1895) act 4

13 A woman can be proud and stiff
When on love intent;
But Love has pitched his mansion in
The place of excrement;
For nothing can be sole or whole
That has not been rent.
'Crazy Jane Talks with the Bishop' (1932)

14 Nor dread nor hope attend
A dying animal;
A man awaits his end
Dreading and hoping all.
'Death' (1933)

15 He knows death to the bone—
Man has created death.
'Death' (1933)

16 Down by the salley gardens my love and I did meet;
She passed the salley gardens with little snow-white feet.
She bid me take love easy, as the leaves grow on the tree;
But I, being young and foolish, with her would not agree.
'Down by the Salley Gardens' (1889)

17 She bid me take life easy, as the grass grows on the weirs;
But I was young and foolish, and now am full of tears.
'Down by the Salley Gardens' (1889)

18 I have met them at close of day
Coming with vivid faces
From counter or desk among grey
Eighteenth-century houses.
I have passed with a nod of the head
Or polite meaningless words.
'Easter, 1916' (1921)

19 All changed, changed utterly:
A terrible beauty is born.
'Easter, 1916' (1921)

20 Too long a sacrifice
Can make a stone of the heart.
O when may it suffice?
'Easter, 1916' (1921)

21 I write it out in a verse—
MacDonagh and MacBride
And Connolly and Pearse
Now and in time to be,
Wherever green is worn,
Are changed, changed utterly:
A terrible beauty is born.
'Easter, 1916' (1921)

22 The rhetorician would deceive his neighbours,
The sentimentalist himself; while art
Is but a vision of reality.
'Ego Dominus Tuus' (1917)

1 I see a schoolboy when I think of him
With face and nose pressed to a sweet-shop window.
of ***Keats***
'Ego Dominus Tuus' (1917)

2 The fascination of what's difficult
Has dried the sap of my veins, and rent
Spontaneous joy and natural content
Out of my heart.
'The Fascination of What's Difficult' (1910)

3 Never to have lived is best, ancient writers say;
Never to have drawn the breath of life, never to have looked into the eye of day;
The second best's a gay goodnight and quickly turn away.
'From *Oedipus at Colonus*' (1928); cf. **Sophocles** 728:15

4 The ghost of Roger Casement
Is beating on the door.
'The Ghost of Roger Casement' (1939)

5 Had I the heavens' embroidered cloths,
Enwrought with golden and silver light,
The blue and the dim and the dark cloths
Of night and light and the half-light,
I would spread the cloths under your feet:
But I, being poor, have only my dreams;
I have spread my dreams under your feet;
Tread softly because you tread on my dreams.
'He Wishes for the Cloths of Heaven' (1899)

6 The light of evening, Lissadell,
Great windows open to the south,
Two girls in silk kimonos, both
Beautiful, one a gazelle.
'In Memory of Eva Gore Booth and Con Markiewicz' (1933)

7 The innocent and the beautiful
Have no enemy but time.
'In Memory of Eva Gore Booth and Con Markiewicz' (1933)

8 Soldier, scholar, horseman, he,
As 'twere all life's epitome.
What made us dream that he could comb grey hair?
'In Memory of Major Robert Gregory' (1919)

9 My country is Kiltartan Cross;
My countrymen Kiltartan's poor.
'An Irish Airman Foresees his Death' (1919)

10 Nor law, nor duty bade me fight,
Nor public men, nor cheering crowds,
A lonely impulse of delight
Drove to this tumult in the clouds;
I balanced all, brought all to mind,
The years to come seemed waste of breath,
A waste of breath the years behind
In balance with this life, this death.
'An Irish Airman Foresees his Death' (1919)

11 I will arise and go now, and go to Innisfree,
And a small cabin build there, of clay and wattles made;
Nine bean rows will I have there, a hive for the honey-bee,
And live alone in the bee-loud glade.
'The Lake Isle of Innisfree' (1893)

12 I hear lake water lapping with low sounds by the shore . . .
I hear it in the deep heart's core.
'The Lake Isle of Innisfree' (1893)

13 Land of Heart's Desire,
Where beauty has no ebb, decay no flood,
But joy is wisdom, Time an endless song.
The Land of Heart's Desire (1894) p. 36

14 A sudden blow: the great wings beating still
Above the staggering girl, her thighs caressed
By the dark webs, her nape caught in his bill,
He holds her helpless breast upon his breast.

How can those terrified vague fingers push
The feathered glory from her loosening thighs?
'Leda and the Swan' (1928)

15 A shudder in the loins engenders there
The broken wall, the burning roof and tower
And Agamemnon dead.
'Leda and the Swan' (1928)

16 Like a long-legged fly upon the stream
His mind moves upon silence.
'Long-Legged Fly' (1939)

17 Did that play of mine send out
Certain men the English shot?
'The Man and the Echo' (1939)

18 We had fed the heart on fantasies,
The heart's grown brutal from the fare;
More substance in our enmities
Than in our love; O, honey-bees
Come build in the empty house of the stare.
'Meditations in Time of Civil War' no. 6 'The Stare's Nest by my Window' (1928)

19 Think where man's glory most begins and ends,
And say my glory was I had such friends.
'The Municipal Gallery Re-visited' (1939)

20 Why, what could she have done, being what she is?
Was there another Troy for her to burn?
'No Second Troy' (1910)

21 I think it better that at times like these
A poet's mouth be silent, for in truth
We have no gift to set a statesman right;
He has had enough of meddling who can please
A young girl in the indolence of her youth
Or an old man upon a winter's night.
'On being asked for a War Poem' (1919)

22 Where, where but here have Pride and Truth,
That long to give themselves for wage,
To shake their wicked sides at youth
Restraining reckless middle-age?
'On hearing that the Students of our New University have joined the Agitation against Immoral Literature' (1910)

23 A pity beyond all telling,
Is hid in the heart of love.
'The Pity of Love' (1893)

24 Out of Ireland have we come.
Great hatred, little room,
Maimed us at the start.
I carry from my mother's womb

A fanatic heart.
'Remorse for Intemperate Speech' (1933)

1 That is no country for old men. The young
In one another's arms, birds in the trees
—Those dying generations—at their song,
The salmon-falls, the mackerel-crowded seas.
'Sailing to Byzantium' (1928)

2 An aged man is but a paltry thing,
A tattered coat upon a stick, unless
Soul clap its hands and sing, and louder sing
For every tatter in its mortal dress.
'Sailing to Byzantium' (1928)

3 And therefore I have sailed the seas and come
To the holy city of Byzantium.
'Sailing to Byzantium' (1928)

4 All shuffle there; all cough in ink;
All wear the carpet with their shoes;
All think what other people think;
All know the man their neighbour knows.
Lord, what would they say
Did their Catullus walk that way?
'The Scholars' (1919)

5 Turning and turning in the widening gyre
The falcon cannot hear the falconer;
Things fall apart; the centre cannot hold;
Mere anarchy is loosed upon the world,
The blood-dimmed tide is loosed, and everywhere
The ceremony of innocence is drowned;
The best lack all conviction, while the worst
Are full of passionate intensity.
'The Second Coming' (1921)

6 The darkness drops again; but now I know
That twenty centuries of stony sleep
Were vexed to nightmare by a rocking cradle,
And what rough beast, its hour come round at last,
Slouches towards Bethlehem to be born?
'The Second Coming' (1921)

7 Far-off, most secret and inviolate Rose.
'The Secret Rose' (1899)

8 A woman of so shining loveliness
That men threshed corn at midnight by a tress,
A little stolen tress.
'The Secret Rose' (1899)

9 Romantic Ireland's dead and gone,
It's with O'Leary in the grave.
'September, 1913' (1914)

10 O, who could have foretold
That the heart grows old?
'A Song' (1919)

11 The woods of Arcady are dead,
And over is their antique joy;
Of old the world on dreaming fed;
Grey Truth is now her painted toy.
'The Song of the Happy Shepherd' (1889)

12 And pluck till time and times are done
The silver apples of the moon,
The golden apples of the sun.
'Song of Wandering Aengus' (1899)

13 You think it horrible that lust and rage
Should dance attendance upon my old age;
They were not such a plague when I was young;
What else have I to spur me into song?
'The Spur' (1939)

14 We Irish, born into that ancient sect
But thrown upon this filthy modern tide
And by its formless spawning fury wrecked,
Climb to our proper dark, that we may trace
The lineaments of a plummet-measured face.
'The Statues' (1939)

15 Swift has sailed into his rest;
Savage indignation there
Cannot lacerate his breast.
Imitate him if you dare,
World-besotted traveller; he
Served human liberty.
'Swift's Epitaph' (1933); cf. **Epitaphs** 304:8

16 But was there ever dog that praised his fleas?
'To a Poet, Who would have Me Praise certain bad Poets, Imitators of His and of Mine' (1910)

17 Red Rose, proud Rose, sad Rose of all my days!
Come near me, while I sing the ancient ways.
'To the Rose upon the Rood of Time' (1893)

18 What shall I do with this absurdity—
O heart, O troubled heart—this caricature,
Decrepit age that has been tied to me
As to a dog's tail?
'The Tower' (1928) pt. 1

19 Michael Angelo left a proof
On the Sistine Chapel roof,
Where but half-awakened Adam
Can disturb globe-trotting Madam.
'Under Ben Bulben' (1939) pt. 4

20 Irish poets, learn your trade,
Sing whatever is well made.
'Under Ben Bulben' (1939) pt. 5

21 Cast your mind on other days
That we in coming days may be
Still the indomitable Irishry.
'Under Ben Bulben' (1939) pt. 5

22 On limestone quarried near the spot
By his command these words are cut:
Cast a cold eye
On life, on death.
Horseman, pass by!
'Under Ben Bulben' (1939) pt. 6

23 When you are old and grey and full of sleep,
And nodding by the fire, take down this book,
And slowly read, and dream of the soft look
Your eyes had once, and of their shadows deep.
'When You Are Old' (1893)

24 Unwearied still, lover by lover,
They paddle in the cold
Companionable streams or climb the air;
Their hearts have not grown old.
'The Wild Swans at Coole' (1919)

25 We make out of the quarrel with others, rhetoric, but of the quarrel with ourselves, poetry.
Essays (1924) 'Anima Hominis' sect. 5

26 Even when the poet seems most himself . . . he is never the bundle of accident and incoherence that

sits down to breakfast; he has been reborn as an idea, something intended, complete.
Essays and Introductions (1961) 'A General Introduction for my Work'

1 In dreams begins responsibility.
Responsibilities (1914) epigraph

of the Anglo-Irish:
2 We . . . are no petty people. We are one of the great stocks of Europe. We are the people of Burke; we are the people of Swift, the people of Emmet, the people of Parnell. We have created most of the modern literature of this country. We have created the best of its political intelligence.
speech in the Irish Senate, 11 June 1925

3 Think like a wise man but express yourself like the common people.
Letters on Poetry from W. B. Yeats to Dorothy Wellesley (1940) 21 December 1935; cf. **Ascham** 30:9

Boris Yeltsin 1931–
Russian statesman, President of the Russian Federation since 1991

4 You can make a throne of bayonets, but you can't sit on it for long.
from the top of a tank, during the attempted military coup against ***Gorbachev***
in *Independent* 24 August 1991; cf. **Inge** 399:9

5 Europe is in danger of plunging into a cold peace.
at the summit meeting of the Conference on Security and Co-operation in Europe
in *Newsweek* 19 December 1994; cf. **Baruch** 56:9

6 Today is the last day of an era past
at a Berlin ceremony to end the Soviet military presence
in *Guardian* 1 September 1994

Sergei Yesenin 1895–1925
Russian poet
see also ***Last words*** 456:7

7 The poet's gift is to soothe and harass,
He bears the stamp of fate.
On earth I wanted to marry
A white rose to a pitch-black toad.
'I Have One Remaining Pastime' (1923) (translated by Gordon McVay)

8 It's always the good feel rotten.
Pleasure's for those who are bad.
'Pleasure's for the Bad' (1923) (translated by Gordon McVay)

Yevgeny Yevtushenko 1933–
Russian poet

9 Over Babiy Yar
There are no memorials.
The steep hillside like a rough inscription.
'Babiy Yar' (1961) (translated by Robin Milner-Gulland)

10 So on and on
we walked without thinking of rest
passing craters, passing fire,
under the rocking sky of '41
tottering crazy on its smoking columns.
'The Companion' (1954) (translated by Robin Milner-Gulland)

11 No people are uninteresting.
Their fate is like the chronicle of planets.
Nothing in them is not particular,
and planet is dissimilar from planet.
'No People are Uninteresting' (1961) (translated by Robin Milner-Gulland)

12 Life is a rainbow which also includes black.
in *Guardian* 11 August 1987

Shoichi Yokoi 1915–97
Japanese soldier

13 It is a terrible shame for me—I came back, still alive, without having won the war.
on returning to Japan after surviving for 28 years in the jungles of Guam before surrendering to the Americans in 1972
in *Independent* 26 September 1997

Charlotte Yonge 1823–1901
English novelist and writer for children

14 I have had a dreadful day; I have killed the Bishop and Felix.
while working simultaneously on her biography of the missionary Bishop Patteson, killed in Melanesia, and her novel Pillars of the House, *in which the death of Felix Underwood is a tragic climax.*
Margaret Mare and Alicia C. Percival *Victorian Best-Seller* (1947)

Andrew Young 1932–
American clergyman and diplomat

15 Nothing is illegal if one hundred well-placed business men decide to do it.
Morris K. Udall *Too Funny to be President* (1988)

Edward Young 1683–1765
English poet and dramatist

16 Some for renown on scraps of learning dote,
And think they grow immortal as they quote.
The Love of Fame (1725–8) Satire 1, l. 89

17 None think the great unhappy, but the great.
The Love of Fame (1725–8) Satire 1, l. 238

18 Be wise with speed;
A fool at forty is a fool indeed.
The Love of Fame (1725–8) Satire 2, l. 282; cf. **Proverbs** 600:34

19 Hot, envious, noisy, proud, the scribbling fry
Burn, hiss, and bounce, waste paper, stink, and die.
The Love of Fame (1725–8) Satire 3, l. 65

20 One to destroy, is murder by the law;
And gibbets keep the lifted hand in awe;
To murder thousands, takes a specious name,
'War's glorious art', and gives immortal fame.
The Love of Fame (1725–8) Satire 7, l. 55; cf. **Porteous** 588:13, **Rostand** 635:16

1 How science dwindles, and how volumes swell,
How commentators each dark passage shun,
And hold their farthing candle to the sun.
The Love of Fame (1725–8) Satire 7, l. 96; cf. **Burton** 170:18, **Johnson** 413:16, **Sidney** 718:4

2 Tired Nature's sweet restorer, balmy sleep!
Night Thoughts (1742–5) 'Night 1' l. 1

3 We take no note of Time
But from its loss.
Night Thoughts (1742–5) 'Night 1' l. 55

4 Death! Great proprietor of all! 'Tis thine
To tread out empire, and to quench the stars.
Night Thoughts (1742–5) 'Night 1' l. 204

5 Be wise to-day; 'tis madness to defer.
Night Thoughts (1742–5) 'Night 1' l. 390

6 Procrastination is the thief of time.
Night Thoughts (1742–5) 'Night 1' l. 393; cf. **Proverbs** 609:43

7 At thirty a man suspects himself a fool;
Knows it at forty, and reforms his plan;
At fifty chides his infamous delay,
Pushes his prudent purpose to resolve;
In all the magnanimity of thought
Resolves; and re-resolves; then dies the same.
Night Thoughts (1742–5) 'Night 1' l. 417

8 All men think all men mortal, but themselves.
Night Thoughts (1742–5) 'Night 1' l. 424

9 By night an atheist half believes a God.
Night Thoughts (1742–5) 'Night 5' l. 176

10 [The senses] Take in at once the landscape of the world,
At a small inlet, which a grain might close,
And half create the wondrous world they see.
Night Thoughts (1742–5) 'Night 6' l. 425; cf. **Wordsworth** 829:6

11 To know the world, not love her, is thy point,
She gives but little, nor that little, long.
Night Thoughts (1742–5) 'Night 8' l. 1276; cf. **Goldsmith** 344:20

12 Devotion! daughter of astronomy!
An undevout astronomer is mad.
Night Thoughts (1742–5) 'Night 9' l. 769

13 How glorious, then, appears the mind of man,
When in it all the stars, and planets, roll.
And what it seems, it is: great objects make
Great minds.
Night Thoughts (1742–5) 'Night 9' l. 1062

14 The course of Nature is the art of God.
Night Thoughts (1742–5) 'Night 9' l. 1267

15 Life is the desert, life the solitude;
Death joins us to the great majority.
The Revenge (1721) act 4; cf. **Petronius** 574:15

George W. Young 1846–1919

16 The lips that touch liquor must never touch mine.
title of poem (*c.*.1870); also attributed, in a different form, to Harriet A. Glazebrook, 1874

Neil Young 1945– and Jeff Blackburn

Canadian singer and songwriter

17 It's better to burn out
Than to fade away.
quoted by Kurt **Cobain** *in his suicide note, 8 April 1994*
'My My, Hey Hey (Out of the Blue)' (1978 song)

Yevgeny Zamyatin 1884–1937

Russian writer

18 Heretics are the only bitter remedy against the entropy of human thought.
'Literature, Revolution and Entropy' quoted in *The Dragon and other Stories* (1967, translated by M. Ginsberg) introduction

19 Yesterday there was a tsar and there were slaves; today there is no tsar, but the slaves remain; tomorrow there will be only tsars . . . We have lived through the epoch of suppression of the masses; we are living in an epoch of suppression of the individual in the name of the masses; tomorrow will bring the liberation of the individual—in the name of man.
'Tomorrow' (1919) in *A Soviet Heretic* (1970)

Israel Zangwill 1864–1926

Jewish spokesman and writer

20 Scratch the Christian and you find the pagan—spoiled.
Children of the Ghetto (1892) bk. 2, ch. 6

21 America is God's Crucible, the great Melting-Pot where all the races of Europe are melting and re-forming!
The Melting Pot (1908) act 1

Emiliano Zapata 1879–1919

Mexican revolutionary
see also **Ibarruri** *398:4*

22 Many of them, so as to curry favour with tyrants, for a fistful of coins, or through bribery or corruption, are shedding the blood of their brothers.
on the maderistas *who, in Zapata's view, had betrayed the revolutionary cause*
Plan de Ayala 28 November 1911, para. 10

Frank Zappa 1940–93

American rock musician and songwriter

23 A drug is neither moral or immoral—it's a chemical compound. The compound itself is not a menace to society until a human being treats it as if consumption bestowed a temporary licence to act like an asshole.
The Real Frank Zappa Book (1989)

24 Rock journalism is people who can't write interviewing people who can't talk for people who can't read.
Linda Botts *Loose Talk* (1980); cf. **Capp** 185:16

Zeno of Citium *c.*335–*c.*263 BC
Greek philosopher, founder of Stoicism

1 The reason why we have two ears and only one mouth is that we may listen the more and talk the less.
to a youth who was talking nonsense
Diogenes Laertius *Lives of the Philosophers* 'Zeno' ch. 7

Mikhail Zhvanetsky 1934–
Russian writer

2 We enjoyed . . . his slyness. He mastered the art of walking backward into the future. He would say 'After me'. And some people went ahead, and some went behind, and he would go backward.
of Mikhail ***Gorbachev***
in *Time* 12 September 1994; attributed

Zhuangzi see **Chuang Tzu**

Philip Ziegler 1929–
British historian

3 Remember. In Spite of Everything, He Was A Great Man.
notice kept on his desk while working on his biography of ***Mountbatten*** *(published 1985)*
Andrew Roberts *Eminent Churchillians* (1994)

Ronald L. Ziegler 1939–
American government spokesman

4 [Mr Nixon's latest statement] is the Operative White House Position . . . and all previous statements are inoperative.
in *Boston Globe* 18 April 1973

Grigori Zinoviev 1883–1936
Soviet politician

5 Armed warfare must be preceded by a struggle against the inclinations to compromise which are embedded among the majority of British workmen, against the ideas of evolution and peaceful extermination of capitalism. Only then will it be possible to count upon complete success of an armed insurrection.
letter to the British Communist Party, 15 September 1924, in *The Times* 25 October 1924; the 'Zinoviev Letter', said by some to be a forgery

Hiller B. Zobel
American judge

6 Asking the ignorant to use the incomprehensible to decide the unknowable.
'The Jury on Trial' in *American Heritage* July–August 1995

7 Judges must follow their oaths and do their duty, heedless of editorials, letters, telegrams, threats, petitions, panellists and talk shows.
In this country, we do not administer justice by plebiscite. A judge . . . is a public servant who must follow his conscience, whether or not he counters the manifest wishes of those he serves; whether or not his decision seems a surrender to prevalent demands.
judicial ruling reducing the conviction of Louise Woodward from murder to manslaughter, 10 November 1997

Zohar
chief text of the Jewish Kabbalah, dating from the 13th century, presented as an allegorical or mystical interpretation of the Pentateuch

8 The Holy One, blessed be He, said to the world, when he had made it, and created man: O world, world, you and your laws can be sustained only through the Torah. That is why I created man [to live] in you, so that he might study it. But if he does not do so, I will return you to chaos.
bk. 1, 134b

9 Come and see . . . whatever is in the earth has its parallel in the world above. There is not a single thing, however small, in the world that does not depend on something that is higher . . . for everything is interdependent.
bk. 1, 156b

10 He made this world to match the world above, and whatever exists above has its counterpart below . . . and all is one.
bk. 2, 20a

11 We have taught that every man who talks of the Exodus from Egypt and rejoices fully in its narration will eventually rejoice in the *Shekinah* in the world to come, and this is the greatest joy of all.
bk. 2, 40b

12 After he had fashioned the image of the Chariot of Supernal Man, he descended into it and was known under the image of YHVH, so that man might apprehend him through his attributes, through each of them severally, and he was called El, Elohim, Shaddai, Zeva'ot, and YHVH, so that man might apprehend him through each of his attributes and perceive how the world is governed by kindness and by justice in accordance with men's deeds.
bk. 2, 42b

13 The narratives of the Torah are the garments of the Torah. If a man thinks that the garment is the actual Torah itself, and not something quite other, may his spirit depart, and may he have no portion in the world to come.
bk. 3, 152a

Émile Zola 1840–1902
French novelist

14 Don't go on looking at me like that, because you'll wear your eyes out.
La Bête humaine (1889–90) ch. 5

15 One forges one's style on the terrible anvil of daily deadlines.
Le Figaro 1881

1 Smut detected in it by moral men is theirs rather than mine. Scientific truth was my touchstone for every scene, even the most febrile.
Thérèse Raquin, preface to 2nd edition (1868)

2 What a man! . . . He crushes the entire century.
of ***Balzac***
letter to Anthony Valabrègue, 29 May 1867; *Correspondance* (1978) vol. 1

3 *J'accuse.*
I accuse.
title of an open letter to the President of the French Republic, in connection with the Dreyfus affair
in *L'Aurore* 13 January 1898

Zoroastrian Scriptures

a religion of ancient Persia founded by Zoroaster in the 6th century BC*; texts compiled in the 4th century*
translations by M. Boyce, 1984

4 We worship Mithra of wide pastures, possessing a thousand ears, possessing ten thousand eyes, the divinity worshipped with spoken name.
The Yashts yasht 10: Avestan Hymn to Mithra, v.1

5 Never break a covenant, whether you make it with a false man or a just man of good conscience. The covenant holds for both, the false and the just.
The Yashts yasht 10: Avestan Hymn to Mithra, v. 2

6 O Green One [Haoma], I call down your intoxication, your strength, victory, health, healing, furtherance, increase, power for the whole body, ecstasy of all kinds.
The Gathas yasna 9, v. 17

7 I profess myself a Mazda-worshipper, a follower of Zarathustra, opposing the Daevas, accepting the Ahuric doctrine; one who praises the Amesha Spentas, who worships the Amesha Spentas.
The Gathas The Creed (Fravarane) yasna 12, v. 1

8 This one, Zarathustra Spitama, has been found here by me, who alone has hearkened to our teachings. He wishes, O Mazda, to chant hymns of praise for Us and for Truth. So let us give him sweetness of utterance.
The Gathas yasna 29, v. 8

9 Truly there are two primal Spirits, twins renowned to be in conflict. In thought and word, in act they are two: the better and the bad. And those who act well have chosen rightly between these two, not so the evildoers.
The Gathas yasna 30, v. 3

10 I am Zarathustra, Were I able, I should be a true foe to the Deceiver, but a strong support to the Just One.
The Gathas yasna 43, v. 8

11 May truth be embodied, strong with life.
The Gathas yasna 43, v. 16

12 This I ask Thee, tell me truly, Lord. Who in the beginning, at creation, was Father of Order [Asha]? Who established the course of sun and stars? Through whom does the moon wax, then wane? This and yet more, O Mazda, I seek to know.
The Gathas yasna 44, v. 3

13 Him shall I seek to glorify for us with sacrifices of devotion, Him who is known in the soul as Lord Mazda; for he has promised by his truth and good purpose that there shall be wholeness and immortality within His kingdom, strength and perpetuity within His house.
The Gathas yasna 45, v. 10

14 They truly shall be 'saoshyants' [saviours] of the lands who follow knowledge of Thy teaching, Mazda, with good purpose, with acts inspired by truth. They indeed have been appointed opponents of Fury.
The Gathas yasna 48, v. 12

15 But the wicked, of bad power, bad act, bad word, bad Inner Self, bad purpose . . . they shall be rightful guests in the House of the Lie.
The Gathas yasna 49, v. 11

16 As the Master, so is the Judge to be chosen in accord with truth. Establish the power of acts arising from a life lived with good purpose, for Mazda and for the lord whom they made pastor for the poor.
The Gathas 'Ahuna Vairyo'

17 It is thus revealed in the Good Religion that Ohrmazd was on high in omniscience and goodness. For boundless time He was ever in the light. That light is the space and place of Ohrmazd. Some call it Endless Light . . . Ahriman was abased in slowness of knowledge and the lust to smite. The lust to smite was his sheath and darkness his place. Some call it Endless Darkness. And between them was emptiness.
Greater Bundahishn ch. 1

18 For the sake of freedom in the end from the enmity of the Adversary, and restoration, whole and immortal, in the future body for ever and ever, they [the *fravahrs* or souls of men] agreed to go into the world.
Greater Bundahishn ch. 3

19 He [the Evil Spirit] defiled the whole creation . . . So the things of the material world appeared in duality, turning, opposites, fights, up and down, and mixture.
Greater Bundahishn ch. 4

Selective Thematic Index

Administration

care more for routine than results BAGE 47:7
concept of the 'official secret' WEBE 807:8
every human relationship suffers FORS 321:1
finished drafting a document REIT 624:8
gentleman in Whitehall JAY 404:14
mothers-in-law and Wigan Pier BRID 148:6
name at the foot of the first page SAND 644:6
No grand idea ever born in a conference FITZ 315:9
Only an organizing genius BEVA 71:12
opinion of the virtue of paper government BURK 162:21
perceiving—HOW NOT TO DO IT DICK 262:25
political will and administrative won't LYNN 480:21
rise to his level of incompetence PETE 574:10
subservience to the desk FRAN 323:18
unwilling chosen from the unfit SAYI 647:6
When in trouble, delegate BORE 143:2
work of an eyeless computer BETJ 71:1

Age

afternoon of human life JUNG 423:10
best is yet to be BROW 157:18
Considering the alternative CHEV 211:23
don't know the language AMIS 14:5
evening of life GIBB 336:3
fading power to feel the sudden shock BLIS 122:1
fifteen years older than I am BARU 56:10
If I'd known I was gonna live this long BLAK 117:15
in one autumnal face DONN 272:10
I shall wear purple JOSE 421:10
keep your face, and stay sitting down CART 193:2
learn how to be aged BLYT 123:4
most unexpected of all things TROT 783:15
my brain is 30 years old EISE 291:12
nineties is a good time to die SPEN 733:1
no man would be old SWIF 749:2
no more than a bad habit MAUR 502:9
past sixty it's the young AUDE 35:4
recently turned ALLE 12:18
seventy years young HOLM 381:11
Time has shaken me by the hand WESL 811:21
To live beyond eighty is an exaggeration CALL 181:8
two more years in a geriatric home AMIS 14:3
Will you still need me LENN 464:3

America

billion dollar country FOST 321:10
Black Hills belong to me SITT 720:19
city upon a hill WINT 823:14
conspiracy to make you happy UPDI 788:13
do all for the Union CLAY 220:4
essentially the greatest poem WHIT 816:1
Ev'rything free SOND 727:20
From sea to shining sea BATE 57:4
God's crucible ZANG 839:21
huddled masses yearning LAZA 459:12
Star for every State WINT 823:15
Utopia is a blessed past KISS 441:30
worse Than ignorant Americans MASS 501:3

Art

active line on a walk KLEE 442:3
Angels in jumpers LEWI 467:13
cylinder, the sphere, the cone CÉZA 200:8
Every time I paint a portrait SARG 644:17
Good painters imitate nature CERV 200:6
imitation in lines and colours POUS 590:7
I, too, am a painter CORR 237:9
meant to disturb, science reassures BRAQ 147:2
not made to decorate apartments PICA 575:16
Painting is saying 'Ta' to God SPEN 732:16
Picasso is a genius. I am too DALI 248:13
product of the untalented, sold CAPP 185:16
serious and the smirk DICK 263:23
stretch the human frame about SCAR 646:8
what someone has felt about it MUNC 536:13
why don't they stick to murder EPST 301:1
You don't marry it, you rape it DEGA 255:17

Books

have been a rake in reading MONT 526:21
like a conversation with the best men DESC 258:16
Lo here a little volume CRAS 244:9
none are undeservedly remembered AUDE 35:15
some few to be chewed and digested BACO 44:6
there is no end; and much study BIBL 85:4
to every cow her calf COLU 230:6
Twenty bookes, clad in blak or reed CHAU 204:19
where things are explained to you BARN 55:1
will never keep down a single petticoat BYRO 180:9

Britain

country of long shadows MAJO 491:16
Graces do not seem to be natives CHES 209:18
greatness of the British Nation ADDI 5:8
land of embarrassment and breakfast BARN 54:17
national dish no longer fish and chips JEAN 404:16
not yet found a role ACHE 1:12
old people dying of hypothermia BENN 65:13
Rule Britannia THOM 774:20
soggy little island UPDI 788:11

Business

cheaper than a prawn sandwich RATN 622:5
customer is never wrong RITZ 628:14
Deals are my art form TRUM 784:11
Do other men, for they would do you DICK 263:5
Do you sincerely want to be rich? CORN 236:19
good for General Motors WILS 821:10
Greed is all right BOES 123:10
guided by 'feminine' principles RODD 631:2
in the store we sell hope REVS 625:1
main thing today is—shopping MILL 509:23
Nothing is illegal YOUN 838:15
nothing more requisite than dispatch ADDI 4:18
not run by itself except downhill SAYI 647:3
Only the paranoid survive GROV 354:8
People of the same trade SMIT 723:7
put your heart in the business WATS 804:19
really want to make a million ANON 16:22
sleeping under the desk GATE 331:2
Virgin is the possibility BRAN 147:1

Computing

between obsolescent and nonexistent BREN 147:25
count everything and understand nothing CORN 236:18
Internet is an élite organization CHOM 212:13
logic gates stretched out to the horizon AUGA 35:20
talking about surfing the Net ELIZ 297:20
to really foul things up SAYI 648:7
use them in the search for love WAŁĘ 799:4
voyager in virtuality can return TURK 785:11
weaves algebraic patterns LOVE 476:9

Drinks

bouquet is better than the taste POTT 589:1
can't bear iced drinks DEAN 253:17
cheer but not inebriate COWP 241:31
Cocoa is a cad and coward CHES 210:20
he who aspires to be a hero JOHN 416:8
It would be port if it could BENT 67:11
makes the politician wise POPE 587:9
malt does more than Milton can HOUS 391:9
naïve domestic Burgundy THUR 776:26
only a beer SHAW 706:24
Shaken and not stirred FLEM 317:9
took the cork out of my lunch FIEL 310:19
union of gin and vermouth DEV 259:10

Education

dawn of legibility in his handwriting HAY 364:17
destroy every grammar school CROS 246:6
dread of games BETJ 71:8
education, education, and education BLAI 117:11
Example is the school of mankind BURK 164:24
gained in the university of life BOTT 144:23
gladly wolde he lerne CHAU 204:20
Ignorance is an evil weed BEVE 72:5
I have been at my book JONS 420:7
impossible to enslave BROU 151:14
More will mean worse AMIS 13:20
no matter what you teach them first JOHN 413:14
rattle for young people when older ARIS 25:8
read Shakespeare and shoot dice BANK 53:8
Studies serve for delight BACO 44:2
Technology is just a tool GATE 331:3
while they teach, men learn SENE 654:18

Environment

Greenpeace said ecology and antiwar HUNT 396:8
I would be burning the rain forest STIN 743:7
keep disappearing CHEK 208:11
Little boxes on the hillside REYN 625:14
Make it a *green* peace DARN 250:10
parks are the lungs of London PITT 577:2
regarding the soil as property THOR 776:1
remains will be concrete and tyres LARK 452:16
replace lawns with paving stones OFFI 554:14
spring now comes unheralded CARS 192:7
They paved paradise MITC 523:15
Think globally, act locally SAYI 648:5
weeds and the wilderness HOPK 384:10
what they knocked down FENT 308:8

Europe

cockpit of Christendom HOWE 392:1
continent of energetic mongrels FISH 313:12
Europe des patries DE G 255:24
geographical concept BISM 116:10
instead of a nation France MONN 526:6
open that Pandora's box BEVI 72:11
part of the community of Europe SALI 642:19

Roll up that map PITT 577:7
thousand years of history GAIT 328:2
war and peace in the 21st century KOHL 443:7
You are learned Europeans MASS 501:3

Family

father was frightened of his mother GEOR 334:6
happy families resemble one another TOLS 779:6
having two children you are a referee FROS 325:12
home of all social evil STRI 744:19
If you bungle raising your children ONAS 554:16
little more than kin SHAK 661:16
no cold relation is a zealous citizen BURK 164:5
one's own kin and kith NASH 539:10
out pops the cloven hoof WODE 824:14
source of all our discontents LEAC 459:13
that dear octopus SMIT 723:17
two is fun, three is a houseful SAYI 647:4

Fashion

Amusing little seams and witty pleats BAIL 48:4
charming to totter into vogue WALP 800:21
Clothes are our weapons CART 192:8
Clothes by a man who doesn't know CHAN 202:1
ease a heart like a satin gown PARK 567:7
Folly's child CRAB 243:1
fun, foolish and almost unwearable LACR 447:8
gentle progression of revisited ideas OLDF 553:12
I don't really like knees SAIN 641:14
innovation without reason SANT 644:11
No perfumes, but very fine linen BRUM 158:23
sense of being well-dressed FORB 319:9
trick of wearing mink BALM 52:16
well dressed in cheap shoes AMIE 13:9
Who am I going to be today WELD 809:9
women come to see the show OVID 561:5

Film

Anything except that damned Mouse GEOR 334:4
biggest electric train set WELL 809:12
cinema is truth 24 times per second GODA 341:20
images of life and death BERG 67:15
invention of a mouse DISN 268:5
Kiss Kiss Bang Bang KAEL 425:6
lie down in clean postures FOWL 321:20
lunatics have taken charge ROWL 636:15
messages should be delivered by Western Union GOLD 346:6
Mickey Mouse could direct a movie HYTN 398:2
park, a policeman and a pretty girl CHAP 202:9
pictures that got small FILM 312:15
shoot me through linoleum BANK 53:9
when you've seen one Western WHIT 814:21
writing history with lightning WILS 822:9

Food

cabbage with a college education TWAI 786:22
Candy is dandy NASH 539:16
cucumber should be well sliced JOHN 412:3
egg boiled very soft AUST 37:13
God could have made a better berry BUTL 173:4
Great chieftain o' the puddin'-race BURN 168:20
Irish ortolans are famous good eating EDGE 288:12
it has no theme CHUR 217:2
It's broccoli, dear WHIT 814:1
loaf with a field in the middle WILD 819:7
love British beef BAKE 48:15
Milk's leap toward immortality FADI 306:1
national dish no longer fish and chips JEAN 404:16
Roast Beef, Medium FERB 308:14
roast pheasant with bread sauce SMIT 725:11
sharks' fins navigating in the Burgundy FLEM 317:20

Future

ain't what it used to be BERR 69:10
Away with him who heeds the morrow VIRG 795:12
bad times just around the corner COWA 238:20
belongs to those who will build it TRUD 783:22
boot stamping on a human face ORWE 559:2
cannot fight against the future GLAD 340:16
For your tomorrow EPIT 304:14
Future as a promised land LEWI 466:18
It comes soon enough EINS 290:13
neither nirvana nor Armageddon HEWI 375:18
pie in the sky HILL 377:1
Posterity do something for us ADDI 5:17
question of what tomorrow may bring HORA 387:20
ruins of St Paul's WALP 801:3
tomorrow is another day MITC 524:3
Tomorrow to fresh woods MILT 513:13
world is changing almost too fast ELIZ 297:18

Gardening

All gardening is landscape-painting POPE 587:22
come and talk to the plants CHAR 203:19
eastward in Eden BIBL 73:17
green grass finely shorn BACO 43:5
I am but a young gardener JEFF 405:17
laying out of grounds PEAC 571:1
not beauty because it is not nature CONS 235:7
plant whose virtues have not been discovered EMER 299:28
Sowe Carrets GARD 329:14

Health and Fitness

Any man who goes to a psychiatrist GOLD 346:5
blessing that money cannot buy WALT 802:26
diets . . . wonderful for other people KERR 434:8
Exercise is bunk FORD 319:17
Fat is a feminist issue ORBA 557:5
I am getting better and better COUÉ 238:4
listen to the B Minor Mass TORK 779:17
Mens sana in corpore sano JUVE 425:2
not just being alive MART 498:2
Some, hilly walks; all, exercise GREE 351:12
to become unnaturally thin WOLF 825:2
yuppie version of bulimia EHRE 290:1

Law

believed the gentleman was an *attorney* JOHN 414:9
Be ye never so high DENN 257:17
boa constrictor as a tape-measure GOGA 343:21
deaf as an adder to the clamours ADAM 3:3
if it be against reason COKE 224:6
ignorant to use the incomprehensible ZOBE 840:6
is a bottomless pit ARBU 23:15
isn't worth the paper it is written on GOLD 346:3
law is a ass DICK 264:19
like houses, lean on one another BURK 164:20
made to be broken NORT 546:17
no kind of fault or flaw GILB 337:12
that jury-men may dine POPE 587:7
Written laws are like spiders' webs ANAC 14:6

Literature

always a good card to play for honours BENN 66:10
bad review may spoil your breakfast AMIS 14:2
ideal reader of my novels BURG 161:26
If a writer has to rob his mother FAUL 308:1
novel tells a story FORS 320:11
poetry makes nothing happen AUDE 34:1
school of Snobbery with Violence BENN 65:20
way of taking life by the throat FROS 326:16
What was the message of your play BEHA 62:4

Love

comforteth like sunshine after rain SHAK 706:1
Flames for a year LAMP 449:16
For God's sake hold your tongue DONN 273:21
friends in the garrison HALI 357:7
Games people play BERN 69:8
If you could see my legs DICK 262:16
in the spring a young man's fancy TENN 762:22
Let me count the ways BROW 154:21
like a red, red rose BURN 168:6
most natural painkiller LAST 456:14
moves the sun and the other stars DANT 250:5
my North, my South, my East and West AUDE 33:28
neither can the floods drown it BIBL 86:8
noblest frailty of the mind DRYD 281:27
Nor cord nor cable can so forcibly draw BURT 170:19
not ever having to say you're sorry SEGA 653:10
nothing half so sweet MOOR 530:13
outer life of telegrams and anger FORS 320:17
pour nous, c'est l'amour BOUS 145:6
someone to call you darling after sex BARN 55:4
Two souls with but a single thought CLOS 222:23
Vénus tout entière à sa proie attachée. RACI 619:18
what a ravishing thing BEHN 62:6
whatever that may mean CHAR 203:17
worse when it comes late in life JERR 407:6

Marriage

Being a husband is a whole-time job BENN 66:8
celibacy has no pleasures JOHN 410:27
comfortable estate of widowhood GAY 331:15
companions for middle age BACO 43:19
deep peace of the double-bed CAMP 182:15
ennui of a solitary existence BONA 125:1
If *Miss* means respectably unmarried CART 192:10
I married beneath me, all women do ASTO 31:19
isn't a word . . . it's a sentence FILM 311:24
it is a field of battle STEV 742:1
it was a bit crowded DIAN 260:5
never again so much together MACN 488:11
Never marry a man who hates his mother BENN 66:11
not a public conveyance MURD 536:18
nothing but a civil contract SELD 653:18
not that adults produce children DEV 259:13
old maid like death by drowning FERB 308:12
one essential ingredient PHIL 575:6
put an end to a woman's liberty BURN 166:4
qualities as would wear well GOLD 345:26
resembles a pair of shears SMIT 725:19
small circle of a wedding-ring CIBB 217:4
so is a bicyle repair kit CONN 233:24
truth universally acknowledged AUST 38:14
waste-paper basket of the emotions WEBB 807:2
wedlock's the devil BYRO 179:9

Men and Women

all men are rapists FREN 324:6
cares and pleasures of domestic life GIBB 335:7
Every woman adores a Fascist PLAT 577:14
fish without a bicycle STEI 737:14
food, sports and last, relationships FISH 313:10
He for God only MILT 516:15
If men had to have babies DIAN 260:3

juggle work, love, home and children FRIE 324:24
little idea of how much men hate them GREE 352:7
Making contact with this Wild Man BLY 123:2
Man is the hunter TENN 765:24
man's desire is for the woman COLE 227:21
Men are vile inconstant toads MONT 526:20
not merely tolerated but valued AUNG 36:20
takes a very clever woman KIPL 441:18
they don't have to sew buttons BROU 151:15
Toughness not in a pinstripe suit FEIN 308:6
wanted us to think with our wombs LUCE 478:19
who does the dishes FREN 324:7
Why can't a woman LERN 465:3
woman has only the right to spring FOND 318:25
woman's whole existence BYRO 176:7
Women have no wilderness in them BOGA 123:12

Music

brandy of the damned SHAW 708:4
cannot be expressed otherwise DELI 256:23
charms to soothe a savage breast CONG 232:25
departs too far from the dance POUN 590:2
en famille angels play Mozart BART 56:6
hills are alive with the sound HAMM 359:1
how potent cheap music is COWA 239:3
If you don't live it PARK 566:17
jazz the sound of surprise BALL 52:15
Let's face the music and dance BERL 68:8
lets the ears lie back in an easy chair IVES 400:11
like scrabble with the vowels missing ELLI 298:7
little finger to become longer SCHO 649:2
much too many notes JOSE 421:7
pauses between the notes SCHN 648:22
sensual pleasure without vice JOHN 418:12
start together and finish together BEEC 61:5
sweet, soft, plenty rhythm MORT 533:17

Past

Antiquities are history defaced BACO 41:10
blue remembered hills HOUS 391:5
fairies left off dancing SELD 653:20
forty centuries look down NAPO 538:8
glory that was Greece POE 579:21
go and live in the Middle Ages SMIT 724:22
god cannot change the past AGAT 6:20
Hindsight is always twenty-twenty WILD 819:14
Middle Ages ended suddenly in the 1950s HOBS 379:7
moving finger writes FITZ 314:17
Old mortality BROW 152:18
only dead thing that smells sweet THOM 772:24
où sont les neiges d'antan VILL 793:1
past is a bucket of ashes SAND 644:1
past is a foreign country HART 363:13
Stands the Church clock at ten to three BROO 150:15

Photography

camera makes everyone a tourist SONT 728:8
cod which produces a million eggs SHAW 709:24
in a fraction of a second CART 193:1
learn to see the ordinary BAIL 48:3
more important to click with people EISE 291:13
point of view of a paralysed cyclops HOCK 379:10
secret about a secret ARBU 23:13
you aren't close enough CAPA 185:13

Politics

argument of the broken window pane PANK 566:14
art of the possible BISM 116:6
Art of the Possible BUTL 171:16
disastrous and the unpalatable GALB 328:11
done very well out of the war BALD 49:5
executive expression of human immaturity BRIT 149:1
Finality is not the language DISR 268:19
government by discussion ATTL 32:5
Great Britain has lost an empire ACHE 1:12
Instead of rocking the cradle ROBI 629:22
It's a *way* of seeing KEEN 432:9
job all working-class parents want ABBO 1:1
middle way is none at all ADAM 3:6
most people vote against somebody ADAM 2:8
no preparation thought necessary STEV 741:4
no use looking beyond the next fortnight CHAM 200:12
only safe pleasure CRIT 245:6
Safe is spelled D-U-L-L CLAR 219:5
second oldest profession REAG 623:3
socialism would not lose its human face DUBČ 283:20
State business is a cruel trade HALI 358:2
systematic organization of hatreds ADAM 2:13
too serious to be left to politicians DE G 255:23
Tudor monarchy with telephones BURG 162:1
turkeys vote for an early Christmas CALL 181:12
Vote for the man who promises least BARU 56:11
war without bloodshed MAO 495:1
week is a long time WILS 821:16
Women, and Champagne, and Bridge BELL 64:2

Present

discern signs of the times BIBL 96:3
dwarfs on the shoulders of giants BERN 68:22
Everything is becoming science fiction BALL 52:11
Exhaust the little moment BROO 151:5
for I have lived today DRYD 282:32
It was the best of times DICK 265:21
never jam today CARR 190:23
nowness of everything POTT 588:21
O tempora, O mores CICE 217:19
Ours is the age of substitutes BENT 67:8
plastics, Picasso, jazz WAUG 806:8

present is the funeral of the past CLAR 218:17
strange interlude O'NE 554:24
Suppose that Lenin had died SCHL 648:19
this age best pleaseth me HERR 374:19
times they are a-changin' DYLA 287:15
We are now in the Me Decade WOLF 825:15
What we are today PALI 565:16

Press

By office boys for office boys SALI 643:2
Comment is free, but facts are sacred SCOT 650:4
editor did it when I was away MURD 537:2
elderly lady in Hastings who has two cats LEWI 467:11
forgives nothing, only hunts for mistakes DIAN 260:7
Go to where the silence is GOOD 346:12
if a man bites a dog, that is news BOGA 123:13
I'll furnish the war HEAR 367:2
intellectual brothel TOLS 779:15
master passion is the love of news CRAB 243:4
men with the muck-rakes ROOS 633:7
more than you can get out of baked beans O'RE 557:13
my one form of continuous fiction BEVA 72:2
nation talking to itself MILL 510:3
not so great as the power of suppress NORT 546:19
paparazzi nothing but dogs of war DENE 257:8
protect the people from the press TWAI 786:16
ran the paper purely for propaganda BEAV 59:4
say a thing that they know isn't true BENN 66:9
saying 'Lord Jones Dead' CHES 211:20
When seagulls follow a trawler CANT 185:12

Quotations

achieve unexpected felicities HOLM 381:16
cream of others' books MORE 530:23
enfold himself in the purple KIPL 441:17
for an uneducated man to read CHUR 216:15
grow immortal as they quote YOUN 838:16
make a monkey out of a man BENC 64:19
make quite a fair show of knowledge DOUG 276:21
plums and orange peel picked out RALE 621:12
privilege of the learned PEAR 571:9
Tell me what you know EMER 300:1
Windbags can be right FENT 308:11
You will, Oscar, you will WHIS 813:22

Religion

but a childish toy MARL 496:15
Disneyfication of Christianity CUPI 248:1
elderly lady, who mutters away CARE 186:17
frozen thought of men KRIS 445:21
good enough to be a JOHN 414:16
I do not pretend to know DARR 250:11
kept alive by heresies BREN 147:23
Men have lost their reason BROW 153:1
morality touched by emotion ARNO 29:1
much wrong could religion induce LUCR 479:1
not enough to make us love SWIF 748:24
opium of the people MARX 499:13
pretending to extraordinary revelations BUTL 171:12
shocks the mind of a child PAIN 563:9
superstition to enslave a philosophy INGE 399:5
Thanks to God, I am still an atheist BUÑU 160:13
There are no atheists in the foxholes CUMM 247:14
they cannot even get My gender right ARNO 29:11
those in the pulpit and those in the pews AUST 39:16
throw open the windows of the Church JOHN 407:12
to be a collateral security CHES 209:20
walks in his golden slippers BUNY 161:4
wholesome pills for the sick HOBB 379:3
who shall convert me WESL 811:14
wish for prayer is a prayer itself BERN 68:20
women were first at the Cradle SAYE 646:7
wound, not the bandage POTT 588:22

Royalty

boy will ruin himself GEOR 334:3
corpulent man of fifty HUNT 396:5
damned if I'm an alien GEOR 334:5
devoted to your service ELIZ 297:14
done as cheap as other men PEPY 573:1
fountain of honour BACO [illegible]
glad we've been bombed ELIZ 298:1
gold filling in a mouthful of decay OSBO 560:9
Harris, I am not well GEOR 333:15
heart and stomach of a king ELIZ 296:27
help and support of the woman I love EDWA 289:7
I will be good VICT 792:1
kill animals and stick in stamps NICO 545:3
labour-intensive industry WILS 822:5
lay it on with a trowel DISR 270:37
leave the Englishwoman at home BISM 116:4
let in daylight upon magic BAGE 47:4
looking like the Jungfrau CHAN 202:7
make someone that height look regal AMIE 13:10
My firstborn is the greatest ass CARO 189:3
My husband and I ELIZ 297:15
needed no royal title SPEN 732:12
only five Kings left FARO 307:3
Princess of Wales's letter AUST 39:8
queen in people's hearts DIAN 260:4
retired widow and an unemployed youth BAGE 46:22
Right Divine of Kings POPE 580:20
She was the People's Princess BLAI 117:13
string that ties the robber's bundle SHEL 715:3
subject and a sovereign CHAR 203:4
The family firm GEOR 334:9
To be Prince of Wales BENN 65:22

Uneasy lies the head SHAK 670:2
Whoso pulleth out this sword MALO 492:7

Science

art of the soluble MEDA 503:6
ask an impertinent question BRON 149:9
blind watchmaker DAWK 253:1
Books must follow sciences BACO 45:6
built up of facts POIN 580:2
chance favours the prepared mind PAST 569:11
does not triumph by convincing PLAN 577:10
edged tool, with which men play EDDI 288:3
frog remains ROST 635:14
Genes not like engineering blueprints STEW 743:6
grand aim of all science EINS 291:2
If you cannot measure it KELV 432:17
man who convinces the world DARW 251:6
most incomprehensible fact EINS 290:14
not be content to manufacture life BERN 68:19
one small step for a man ARMS 25:19
physics or stamp collecting RUTH 640:14
redefined the task of science HAWK 364:9
scientist states that something is possible CLAR 219:8
search for the chemistry that works WILL 820:10
set a limit to infinite error BREC 147:9
shocked by this subject BOHR 124:1
There is no democracy in physics ALVA 13:2
trained and organized common sense HUXL 397:12
understand the causes of things VIRG 796:18
when I don't know what I'm doing BRAU 147:7

Seasons

April is the cruellest month ELIO 295:26
Aprill with his shoures soote CHAU 204:6
Blossom by blossom the spring SWIN 750:6
cloudy days of autumn and winter CLAR 218:18
Early autumn—rice field BASH 56:14
ending in July, To recommence in August BYRO 177:23
first hour of spring strikes BOWE 145:11
June is bustin' out all over HAMM 358:19
not Puritanism but February KRUT 446:3
October, that ambiguous month LESS 465:13
Season of mists KEAT 430:8
something about winter CANN 185:11
Wearing white for Eastertide HOUS 390:14
winter is past BIBL 85:10

Sex

after wyn on Venus moste I thynke CHAU 206:17
by a timely compliance FIEL 309:18
composer and *not* homosexual DIAG 260:2
did pleasure me in his top-boots MARL 495:14
expense of spirit in a waste of shame SHAK 705:19
foolishest act a wise man commits BROW 153:29
Give me chastity and continency AUGU 36:3
He said it was artificial respiration BURG 161:25
in the street and frighten the horses CAMP 182:16
License my roving hands DONN 272:16
mad and savage master SOPH 728:16
most fun I ever had without laughing ALLE 12:8
only unnatural sex act KINS 437:22
pleasure is momentary CHES 209:26
rapist bothers to buy a bottle of wine DWOR 286:11
silk stockings and white bosoms JOHN 412:10

Sport

by the hand of God MARA 495:5
Chaos umpire sits MILT 515:25
don't really see the hurdles MOSE 534:4
Football? It's the beautiful game PELÉ 572:6
game is about glory BLAN 121:18
harmless art of knucklebones STEV 740:21
manager who gets the blame LINE 469:13
matched our rackets to these balls SHAK 670:29
Nice guys finish last DURO 286:7
not as fast as the world record COLE 224:15
nothing to do with fair play ORWE 559:8
play up! and play the game NEWB 541:18
show business with blood BRUN 159:1
Spill your guts at Wimbledon CONN 234:7
Swing, swing together CORY 237:11
time to win this game DRAK 278:20
Winning is everything HILL 376:14

Technology

impossible—the practical intellectual STRO 745:1
make a machine that would walk APOL 23:1
need not experience the world FRIS 325:8
project a voyage to the moon LARD 452:9
reality must take precedence FEYN 309:6
something that is technically sweet OPPE 557:4
spark-gap mightier than the pen HOGB 380:10
technology indistinguishable from magic CLAR 219:9
white heat of technology MISQ 522:14
you always end up using scissors HOCK 379:12

Television

contracts the imagination WOGA 825:1
for appearing on, not looking at COWA 239:7
It is Stupidvision TOYN 780:7
madness of human life PAGL 563:2
male, middle class, middle-aged STRE 744:18
manufacture of banality SARR 644:19
No good can come of it SCOT 650:5

no plain women on television FORD 319:10
own licence to print money THOM 775:24
playing a piano in a brothel MUGG 535:21
so much chewing gum for the eyes ANON 18:21
thrives on unreason DAY 253:9
ultimate sanction of switching off EYRE 305:13
We are surfing food MACK 486:10

Transport

any colour so long as it is black FORD 319:14
be at Bakewell in half-an-hour RUSK 638:13
boredom and terror WELL 809:13
car crash as a sexual event BALL 52:12
equivalent of the great Gothic cathedrals BART 56:8
gondola of London DISR 270:20
he got on his bike TEBB 757:1
lances of ancient knights ROOT 633:14
looks like a poached egg NUFF 547:8
messing about in boats GRAH 348:7
Night Mail crossing the Border AUDE 34:12
poetry of motion GRAH 348:8
Quinquireme of Nineveh MASE 500:13
steel canisters hurtling about CASS 193:11
Take my camel, dear OPEN 556:19
Walk! Not bloody likely SHAW 709:15
What else is like the gondola CLOU 221:19

Travel

'abroad' to be Catholic and sensual CHAN 202:5
Been there, done that SAYI 647:1
begin a journey on Sundays SWIF 748:18
count the cats in Zanzibar THOR 776:15
first class, and with children BENC 64:20
great affair is to move STEV 741:16
is a part of education BACO 44:14
most noxious is a tourist KILV 436:3
no sea innavigable THOR 776:20
not worth going to see JOHN 416:10
preferreth all countries before his own OVER 561:1
redesigned Hell from airport layouts PRIC 591:8
ruin of all happiness BURN 165:25
São Paulo is like Reading FLEM 317:19
See one promontory BURT 170:11
tourism is their religion RUNC 637:8
travel broadens the mind; but CHES 211:13

War

all are losers CHAM 200:16
always finds a way BREC 147:14
blood, toil, tears and sweat CHUR 215:7
bomber will always get through BALD 49:8
boys, it is all hell SHER 717:2
continuation of politics CLAU 219:19
destroy the town in order to save it ANON 17:4
diminution of the love of truth JOHN 409:17
endless war still breed MILT 513:16
essence of war is violence MACA 481:10
everlasting peace is a dream MOLT 525:23
Götterdämmerung without the gods MACD 484:19
greatest misery a battle gained WELL 809:17
grow too fond of it LEE 462:8
guerrilla wins if he does not lose KISS 441:27
has a good deal to recommend it HAY 364:15
just for a scrap of paper BETH 70:3
Laws are silent CICE 217:24
lost in the living rooms of America MCLU 487:11
national industry of Prussia MIRA 520:4
Patriotism is not enough CAVE 198:10
smell of napalm in the morning FILM 311:15
Somme is like the Holocaust BARK 54:15
so much owed by so many to so few CHUR 215:12
that we may live in peace ARIS 24:19
There never was a good war FRAN 323:14
This was their finest hour CHUR 215:11
two cardinal virtues HOBB 378:22
way to win an atomic war BRAD 146:9
Who has matched us with His hour BROO 150:16

Weather

bleak wind of March HOOD 382:15
comes on little cat feet SAND 643:20
compels the stranger's admiration TWAI 786:26
frolic architecture of the snow EMER 299:10
frost performs its secret ministry COLE 225:12
hurricane on the way FISH 313:9
I am the gentle autumn's rain ANON 15:24
Ice and Snow, bless ye the Lord BOOK 126:6
it is a magical event PRIE 591:12
It isn't this time of year at all GOGA 343:20
rain is destroying his grain HERB 371:12
Rain! Rain! Rain! KEAT 431:4
Rainy days—silkworms droop BASH 56:18
soft refreshing rain CAMP 182:14
sound of abundance of rain BIBL 79:29
This is a London particular DICK 260:19
When two Englishmen meet JOHN 409:16

Youth

Any failure seems so total QUAN 618:11
At eighteen our convictions are hills FITZ 315:8
fitter to invent than to judge BACO 44:25
have more virtue than old men JOHN 413:11
ideal state if it came later in life ASQU 31:3
longest half of your life SOUT 731:5
more of an influence to your son ICE 398:14

neither attempt to palliate or deny PITT 576:19
Shades of the prison-house WORD 829:20
sweet and twenty SHAK 701:10
times they are a-changin' DYLA 287:16
trustees of Posterity DISR 270:26
twenty years ago no one mentioned it CHAN 202:4
vivid rather than happy LOVE 477:1
when Mozart was my age LEHR 462:18
Whom the gods love MENA 504:12
Youth on the prow GRAY 350:5

Keyword Index

A *A noir, E blanc, I rouge* RIMB 628:13
A was an apple-pie NURS 547:10
from A to B PARK 567:11
Who says A must say B PROV 615:1
Aaron A.'s rod BIBL 75:34
abandon A. all hope DANT 249:7
a. his mind JOHN 417:3
abased shall be a. BIBL 99:26
abated agony is a. MACA 483:14
Abba cry, A., Father BIBL 105:7
abbeys with the beautiful a. JOIN 418:19
abbot blessed the A. SOUT 730:16
abbreviation a. of time GIBB 336:3
A.B.C. Droop in a hundred A.'s ELIO 293:24
Man is man's A. QUAR 618:20
a-bed a. after midnight SHAK 701:8
Abednego Shadrach, Meshach, and A. BIBL 90:2
Abendrot *Vom A. zum Morgenlicht* MÜLL 536:4
Aberbrothock Abbot of A. SOUT 730:16
Aberdour half-owre to A. BALL 51:17
Aberglaube *A. ist die Poesie des Lebens* GOET 343:7
abgeschafft *Der Staat wird nicht 'a.'* ENGE 300:11
abhorrence a. for wickedness THAC 769:13
my heart's a. BROW 157:28
abhors Trick that everyone a. BELL 63:11
abibis *tu missus a.* HORA 389:22
abide a. his frost BOOK 141:26
a. in honour BOOK 135:1
A. with me LYTE 480:23
a. with my Creator God CLAR 218:16
A. with us BIBL 100:33
Lord, who may a. it BOOK 141:1
Others a. our question ARNO 27:13
abides much a. TENN 767:12
abiding there is none a. BIBL 80:29
abiit *A. at plures* PETR 574:15
A., excessit CICE 217:20
abilities according to his a. MARX 499:15
God has given you good a. ARAB 23:9
Great a. are not requisite JOHN 413:5
instincts and a. BALZ 52:17
uncommon a. BAGE 46:1
ability a. for doing things GONC 346:8
according to his a. BLAN 121:16
as distinct from a. WHIT 814:14
famous without a. SHAW 706:26
furnished with a. BIBL 92:15
abire *Tempus a. tibi est* HORA 387:10
abject So a.—yet alive BYRO 178:18
abjure rough magic I here a. SHAK 699:9
able have a poet a.-bodied MACN 488:18
ablution pure a. KEAT 426:14
abnormal Living is a. IONE 399:20
aboard Once a. the lugger MISQ 522:5
abode English make it their a. WALL 800:3
live in a numble a. DICK 261:21
abolish a. or restrain LOCK 472:1
a. serfdom ALEX 11:7
a. the death penalty KARR 425:20
abolished State is not 'a.' ENGE 300:11
abolishing a. Religious Houses AUST 37:21
abominable altogether become a. BOOK 132:6
abomination a. of desolation BIBL 97:2
a. unto the Lord ANON 15:4
incense is an a. BIBL 86:11
Lying lips are a. BIBL 82:26
abominations A. OF THE EARTH BIBL 112:31
abortion a. would be a sacrament KENN 433:5
contraception and a. BURC 161:22
abortions A. will not let BROO 151:6
Abou Ben Adhem A. (may his tribe increase!) HUNT 395:11
abound that grace may a. BIBL 104:37
about a. must go DONN 273:14
minded what they were a. STER 738:13
not *a.* something BECK 59:18
above a., between, below DONN 272:16
affection on things a. BIBL 109:3
parallel in the world a. ZOHA 840:9
think yourself a. BAGE 47:23
This a. all SHAK 662:13
what they do a. WALL 800:11
Abraham A. in truth was not a Jew KORA 444:2
God of A. BIBL 75:30
God of A. HA-L 357:6
into A.'s bosom BIBL 100:10
Shield of A. SIDD 717:18
sleep in A.'s bosom SHAK 696:23
abridgement a. of all that was pleasant GOLD 345:2
abroad A. is bloody GEOR 334:8
A. is unutterably bloody MITF 524:9
'A.', that large home ELIO 292:14
'a.' to be Catholic CHAN 202:5
before he goes a. STER 739:11
Go a. and you'll hear news PROV 601:10
go a. no more CHAR 203:12
I will a. HERB 372:6
I will a. HERB 372:7
never stirs a. SHER 716:16
sent to lie a. WOTT 833:6
suicide to be a. BECK 59:9
Thy spirit walks a. SHAK 677:1
whoever seeks a. KEAT 430:9
You are ordered a. KITC 441:31
Absalom O A., my son, my son BIBL 79:11
absence A. diminishes commonplace passions LA R 453:18
a., in this country ARNO 28:20
A. is to love BUSS 171:6
A. makes heart grow fonder PROV 594:12
a. of mind SEEL 653:8
another by its a. RUSS 640:11
cry of A. RANS 622:1
God is that great a. THOM 773:15
hath my a. been From thee SHAK 705:8
shoot me in my a. BEHA 62:1
absent a. always in the wrong PROV 602:28
a. are always in the wrong DEST 259:2
A. in body BIBL 105:33
a.-minded beggar KIPL 438:2
a. one from another BIBL 75:5
A. thee from felicity SHAK 667:10
fit of a.-mindedness HAIL 356:13
love the a. BEHN 62:9
my a. child SHAK 677:11
absentee a. aristocracy DISR 268:8
confirm him an a. EDGE 288:11
absents endear A. LAMB 448:11
absolute a. power corrupts ACTO 1:16
a. Truth belongs to Thee LESS 465:17
Be a. for death SHAK 686:16
So a. she seems MILT 517:10
absolutism a. moderated by assassination ANON 16:3
absolve a. us all VILL 792:19
History will a. me CAST 193:14
abstain A. from fleshly lusts BIBL 110:29
a. you from such works MALO 492:14
abstinence A. is as easy to me JOHN 417:23
sin of a. DRYD 281:4
total a. AUGU 36:10
abstract a. and premeditated city DOST 276:7
a. art comes into being MOND 526:3
a. reasoning HUME 394:7
all painting is a. HOCK 379:11
abstracted a. meditation JOHN 409:26
abstraction labour was an a. WEBB 806:26
abstracts a. and brief chronicles SHAK 663:24
abstulit *ut me malus a. error* VIRG 796:8
absurd nothing so a. but CICE 217:10
thing becomes a. HOPE 383:15
absurdities errors and a. BURN 165:20
absurdity this a.—O heart YEAT 837:18
abundance a. of rain BIBL 79:29
a. of the heart BIBL 95:13
a. of thy mercy BOOK 128:15
he shall have a. BIBL 97:10
abundantly laboured more a. BIBL 106:20
abuse a. our patience CICE 217:18
dangerous the a. BURK 164:25
If it is a. SHER 715:14
no more hope to end drug a. WHIT 816:3
prevention of a. PEEL 571:13
abused a. as this sentence SELD 653:21
character is to be a. THAC 769:7
abuses attended with considerable a. BURK 162:18
carry away their a. GLAD 340:19
conceal its own a. CLAY 220:3
stamp out a. VOLT 798:6
abusing a. of God's patience SHAK 688:32
abysm a. of time SHAK 698:19
abyss a. gazes into you NIET 545:17
Abyssinia A. or Zanzibar GLAD 341:3
Abyssinian It was an A. maid COLE 225:24
academe groves of A. HORA 387:8
olive grove of A. MILT 518:8
academes books, the a. SHAK 680:26
academia a. in Oxford AUNG 36:19
academic law of a. life LODG 472:16
some a. scribbler KEYN 435:10
academism A. results when STRA 744:16
accent a. of a coming Foot DICK 266:8
a. of one's birthplace LA R 453:20
a. of thy love SHER 716:24
'educated' a. ORWE 559:3
for not keeping of a. JONS 421:1
accents a. that are ours DANI 249:3
A. uncertain BROW 155:32
a. yet unknown SHAK 675:18
caught his clear a. BROW 156:18
follow with a. sweet CAMP 183:23
In a. clear and still BODE 123:9
Loved a. are soon forgot SHEL 712:3
accentuate a. the positive MERC 505:5
accept will not a. if nominated SHER 717:3
acceptable a. in thy sight BOOK 132:18
a. unto God BIBL 105:14
a. with God BIBL 110:31
a. year of the Lord BIBL 89:5
accepted comfortable and the a. GALB 328:6
now is the a. time BIBL 107:8
access A.—flexible friend ADVE 7:1

accident A. counts for much ADAM 2:14
chance and a. BACO 45:15
found out by a. LAMB 449:7
moving a. is not my trade WORD 828:19
never the bundle of a. YEAT 837:26
shot of a. SHAK 693:11
There's been an a. GRAH 348:14
accidents A. will happen PROV 594:13
A. will occur DICK 262:2
chapter of a. CHES 209:23
Of moving a. SHAK 691:33
shackles a. SHAK 657:21
accommodating a. sort of virtue MOLI 525:10
accompany a. me with a pure heart BOOK 125:14
accomplice a. of liars PÉGU 572:3
accomplices we are all his a. MURR 537:7
accomplished a. in a week STEV 741:22
a. man HORA 389:19
desire a. BIBL 82:29
accomplishments a. give lustre CHES 209:22
emerges ahead of his a. STEI 737:10
accord a. all music makes SIDN 718:21
sweet a. is seldom seen WYAT 834:7
with one a. BOOK 126:18
according a. to his abilities MARX 499:15
a. to his strength MORE 531:17
account give a. thereof BIBL 95:14
sent to my a. SHAK 662:31
accountable To whom are you a. BENN 65:9
accounting a. for the moral sense CARL 187:15
accounts make up my a. MIDR 507:16
accumulate you can't a. PROV 603:31
accuracy a. must be sacrificed JOHN 409:1
accurately not thinking a. HOLM 381:15
accursed think themselves a. SHAK 671:25
accuse *J'a.* ZOLA 841:3
accused a. of child death RICH 626:12
a. of deficiency JOHN 415:20
before you be a. CHAR 202:25
accuser conscience needs no a. PROV 601:40
not my A. NEWM 542:4
accuses excuses, a. himself PROV 602:25
accusing a. the rest of the human race CAMU 184:6
accustomed A. to her face LERN 465:5
cannot get a. TOLS 779:8
ace about to play the a. FIEL 309:10
a. caff with a nice museum ADVE 7:2
a. down his sleeve LABO 446:13
Achaeans sufferings for the A. HOME 381:20
sufferings for the A. OPEN 555:1
well-greaved A. have suffered HOME 381:23
Achates *fidus quae tela gerebat A.* VIRG 793:8
ache ark of the a. LEVE 466:5
Acheronta *A. movebo* VIRG 795:5
achieve a. of, the mastery of HOPK 385:2
I shall a. in time GILB 338:9
some a. greatness SHAK 701:28
achieved that cannot be a. TRIM 781:15
achievement Great a. is assured HEGE 367:16
achieving Still a. LONG 474:7
Achilles A.' cursed anger OPEN 555:1
A.' cursed anger sing HOME 381:20
A. his armour BROW 152:13
A.'s wrath OPEN 555:2
A.' wrath POPE 586:6
armour of A. VIRG 794:2
in the trench, A. SHAW 710:1
I've stood upon A.' tomb BYRO 177:6
name A. assumed BROW 153:4
see the great A. TENN 767:12
aching A., shaking, crazy ROCH 630:19
O a. time KEAT 427:26
Achitophel false A. was first DRYD 279:21
Achivi *plectuntur A.* HORA 386:13
acid Electric Kool-Aid A. test WOLF 825:14
acknowledge a. my faults BOOK 135:4
a. thee to be the Lord BOOK 125:20
acknowledgement a. passes for current payment BURN 165:23
acorns oaks from little a. PROV 601:37
acquaintance A. I would have COWL 239:15
apology for dropping the a. SCOT 651:28
auld a. be forgot BURN 166:11
auld a. be forgot OPEN 556:15
creditable a. SWIF 748:5
make a new a. JOHN 417:19
make new a. JOHN 412:21
visiting a. SHER 716:4
acquainted a. with grief BIBL 88:16
a. with the night FROS 325:13
what I am not a. with FLEM 317:16
acquisition not a personal a. JUNG 423:5
acquitted guilty party is a. PUBL 616:12
acre a. in Middlesex MACA 482:1
a. of barren ground SHAK 698:17
acres a. o' charms BURN 167:10
few a. of snow VOLT 797:7
few paternal a. POPE 586:24
Three a. and a cow POLI 582:1
Two wise a. and a cow COWA 239:9
acrimonious a. and surly republican JOHN 410:7
acrostic province in A. Land DRYD 282:1
act a. but not to compete LAO 452:8
a. of dying JOHN 414:5
A. of Union is there TRIM 781:14
Between the motion And the a. ELIO 294:25
both a. and know MARV 498:20
character of the fifth a. LERM 464:22
easier to a. than to think AREN 24:4
fire in the last a. CHEK 208:21
in any A. of Parliament HERB 371:18
in itself almost an a. ROSS 635:7
sleep an a. or two SHAK 674:1
swelling a. SHAK 681:20
To see him a. COLE 227:19
wants to get inta the a. CATC 195:14
within the meaning of the A. ANON 18:7
acted I a. so tragic MARG 367:6
lofty scene be a. o'er SHAK 675:18
acting A. a masochistic form OLIV 553:17
A. is pretending to be PAQU 566:15
a. of a dreadful thing SHAK 675:1
when he was off he was a. GOLD 345:3
action a. Is a most dangerous thing CLOU 221:13
A. is consolatory CONR 234:18
A. is transitory WORD 827:17
a. of the tiger SHAK 671:5
a.'s dizzying eddy ARNO 27:1
A. this day MILI 508:1
a. to the word SHAK 664:15
affairs without a. LAO 451:6
again third, 'a.' DEMO 257:4
end of man is an a. CARL 188:13
honourable a. AGES 8:23
in a. how like an angel SHAK 663:18
lose the name of a. SHAK 664:4
lust in a. SHAK 705:19
Makes that and th' a. fine HERB 372:14
man of a. GALS 328:18
Place, and A. DRYD 283:4
point of taking no a. LAO 452:2
single completed a. BOIL 124:6
talents of a. BYRO 180:1
Thought is the child of A. DISR 270:32
world only grasped by a. BRON 149:8
actions a. are what they are BUTL 171:11
a. of the just SHIR 717:9
a. of two bodies NEWT 543:7
A. receive their tincture DEFO 255:6
a. speak louder than words PROV 594:14
Great a. are not always BUTL 172:4
laugh at human a. SPIN 734:27
my a. are my ministers' CHAR 203:14
Your a. are my dreams SHAK 703:6
active a. line on a walk KLEE 442:3
a. Principle WORD 828:14
to seem a. BONA 125:3
activity just a new a. DYSO 287:19
actor a.'s life for me WASH 804:11
Like a dull a. SHAK 660:13
unperfect a. on the stage SHAK 704:11
well-graced a. SHAK 695:27
actors A. are cattle HITC 378:1
best a. in the world SHAK 663:22
actress a. to be a success BARR 56:3
acts a. being seven ages SHAK 658:25
all your a. are queens SHAK 703:19
desires but a. not BLAK 119:14
first four a. BERK 68:4
no second a. in American lives FITZ 315:16
Our a. our angels are FLET 318:5
actual for the a. object BOCC 123:7
What is rational is a. HEGE 367:14
actualité economical with the *a.* CLAR 219:3
actum *Nil a. credens* LUCA 478:15
ad reminded of that a. MOND 526:1
adage poor cat i' the a. SHAK 682:15
Adam A. ate the apple HUGH 393:7
A. from his fair spouse MILT 516:24
A. Had 'em ANON 15:5
A., the goodliest man MILT 516:17
A. was a gardener SHAK 672:23
A. was born hungry BRIL 148:19
A. was but human TWAI 786:20
good thing A. had TWAI 786:17
gratitude we owe to A. TWAI 786:21
half-awakened A. YEAT 837:19
hold up A.'s profession SHAK 666:17
in A. all die BIBL 106:22
old A. in this Child BOOK 130:8
Old A.'s likeness SHAK 695:17
penalty of A. SHAK 658:13
riverrun, past Eve and A.'s JOYC 421:17
riverrun, past Eve and A.'s OPEN 556:12
rubbish of an A. SOUT 728:21
sleep to fall upon A. BIBL 73:21
When A. dalfe ROLL 632:6
When A. delved and Eve span PROV 614:16
Whilst A. slept ANON 18:16
whipped the offending A. SHAK 670:27
adamant a. for drift CHUR 215:3
frame of a. JOHN 411:15
adapting right of a. my conduct PEEL 571:14
adazzle sweet, sour; a., dim HOPK 384:15
added all these things shall be a. BIBL 93:26
adder a. is breathing in time with it MAND 493:13
A.'s fork SHAK 684:18
brings forth the a. SHAK 674:25
deaf as an a. ADAM 3:3
like the deaf a. BOOK 135:18
lion and a. BOOK 137:23
stingeth like an a. BIBL 83:16
addeth that a. more MARV 499:5
addicted a. to prayers ASHF 30:12
addiction a. is bad JUNG 423:8
prisoners of a. ILLI 398:20
addictive sin tends to be a. AUDE 35:12
Addison Cato did, and A. approved EPIT 304:12
addled a. delusion ELIO 292:11
address non-existent a. LEWI 466:23
adeste *A., fideles* ANON 21:4
ad-hoc a. 'chat shows' AHER 8:27
adieu A., she cries GAY 332:22
Bidding a. KEAT 429:5
ad infinitum proceed *a.* SWIF 749:19
adire *a. Corinthum* HORA 386:22
adjective As to the A. TWAI 786:24
than an a. GREE 351:25
adjectives a. are the sugar JAME 403:20
Adlestrop Yes; I remember A. THOM 772:23
administered Whate'er is best a. POPE 585:26

administration a. of the government SWIF 747:19
criticism of a. BAGE 46:9
administrative a. won't LYNN 480:21
admiral kill an a. from time to time VOLT 797:8
mast Of some great a. MILT 514:22
admirals A. extolled COWP 241:13
admiralty price of a. KIPL 440:9
admirari *Nil a.* HORA 386:18
admiration disease of a. MACA 482:4
exciting a. PASC 568:10
exercise our a. DONN 275:10
great in a. SHAK 673:27
admire a., we should not understand CONG 232:21
Not to a., is all the art POPE 586:11
scarce begun to a. the one DRYD 283:9
admired she might a. be SHAK 702:29
admires a. mean things THAC 768:18
admiring a. the House of Lords BAGE 46:19
admit A. lords SHAF 655:15
admittance No a. till CARR 191:16
ado heathen make much a. BOOK 134:19
adolescence a. and obsolescence LINK 469:15
Adonais I weep for A. SHEL 710:13
Adonis A. in loveliness HUNT 396:5
smooth A. from his native rock MILT 514:26
adopted By roads not a. BETJ 71:7
adoption Spirit of a. BIBL 105:7
adoration a. which is paid MORE 531:4
Breathless with a. WORD 828:23
adore come, let us a. him ANON 21:4
command where I a. SHAK 701:27
Pam, I a. you BETJ 71:2
adored I was a. once SHAK 701:16
adorings soft a. KEAT 427:6
adorn a. a tale JOHN 411:16
touched none that he did not a. EPIT 303:17
adorned Christ a. and beautified BOOK 131:1
unadorned a. the most THOM 775:11
adornings made their bends a. SHAK 656:24
adornment a. of his person THOM 774:19
adorns a. my legs HOUS 390:5
ads watched the a. NASH 539:12
adsuitur *Purpureus A. pannus* HORA 385:12
adsum quickly said, 'A.' THAC 768:22
adulation a. and ridicule LACL 447:3
Adullam cave A. BIBL 78:35
political Cave of A. BRIG 148:14
adult a. is to be alone ROST 635:15
not the occupation of an a. OLIV 553:17
adulteration adultery, but a. BYRO 177:20
adulteries a. of art JONS 419:20
adulterous evil and a. generation BIBL 95:15
found in a. bed BLAK 118:15
adultery as common as a. GRIG 353:13
call gallantry, and gods a. BYRO 175:30
commit a. at one end CARY 193:6
committed a. in my heart CART 192:14
die for a. SHAK 679:21
Do not a. commit CLOU 222:25
Not quite a. BYRO 177:20
rather be taken in a. HUXL 396:16
Thou shalt not commit a. BIBL 76:13
woman taken in a. BIBL 101:32
adults by a. to children SZAS 751:24
children produce a. DEV 259:13
advance retrograde if it does not a. GIBB 335:15
somewhat to a. POPE 586:9
When we our sails a. DRAY 279:9
advantage a. of doing one's praising BUTL 172:19
A. rarely comes of it CLOU 222:25
expectation of a. SMIT 723:3
Japan's a. HIRO 377:18
take a mean a. of them WODE 824:21
undertaking of Great A. ANON 15:21
with equal a. content CANN 184:19
advent A. What was there to say BINC 115:6
Hark to the a. voice OAKL 552:5
adventure a. in the world of Aids PERK 573:22
a. is ended ALAI 10:2
a. is only an inconvenience CHES 211:2
awfully big a. BARR 55:16
most beautiful a. in life LAST 457:18
pass out into a. FORS 320:15
adventurer a. pure and simple FOOT 319:2
adventures a. are to the adventurous PROV 594:15
a. of his soul FRAN 322:17
a. were by the fire-side GOLD 345:27
bold and hard a. FITZ 314:6
adverb beastly a. GREE 351:25
adverbs a. the salt JAME 403:20
adversary No, sir! I am his a. GLAS 341:17
adversities defended from all a. BOOK 128:4
adversity a. doth best BACO 42:5
A. makes strange bedfellows PROV 594:16
A.'s sweet milk SHAK 697:31
bread of a. BIBL 87:17
brother is born for a. BIBL 83:3
contending with a. BURT 170:13
day of a. BIBL 84:16
fortunes sharpe a. CHAU 207:12
Sweet are the uses of a. SHAK 658:14
that will stand a. CARL 188:2
advertisement soul of an a. JOHN 409:18
advertisements ideals by its a. DOUG 276:18
knew a column of a. HOLM 381:16
advertiser a.'s 'sizzling' PRIE 591:16
advertisers a. don't object to SWAF 747:9
advertising A. may be described LEAC 459:16
A. the rattling of a stick ORWE 559:16
invasion of a. SOLZ 727:14
lust and calls it a. LAHR 448:2
money I spend on a. LEVE 466:2
advice a. is good or bad AUST 38:13
A. is seldom welcome CHES 209:13
a. to my countrymen O'CO 552:16
controlled by a. GAY 331:12
never give any a. CHES 209:3
seldom asks a. ADDI 5:14
took tea and comfortable a. KEAT 431:9
whose a. is worth having PARN 568:2
advise a. no man to marry JOHN 418:13
Advisers a. THAT 770:9
A. the prince ELIO 295:9
STREETS FLOODED. PLEASE A. TELE 758:10
advisers political a. SHOR 717:13
advises my old girl that a. DICK 261:3
advocate gets one a. TALM 753:21
intellect of an a. BAGE 46:2
Mediator and A. BOOK 127:15
advocates of a. the best CATU 197:8
aequam *A. memento* HORA 388:6
aequor *Cras ingens iterabimus a.* HORA 387:19
aequus *animus si te non deficit a.* HORA 386:20
aere *Exegi monumentum a. perennius* HORA 388:24
aeroplanes it wasn't the a. FILM 312:5
aes *a. triplex* HORA 387:15
Aesculapius owe a cock to A. LAST 455:7
aesthetic a. enjoyment recognition of the pattern WHIT 814:16
degree of my a. emotion BELL 62:20
high a. line GILB 338:17
aetas *A. parentum* HORA 388:19
fugerit invida A. HORA 387:22
afar you which were a. off BIBL 107:25
afeared Be not a. SHAK 699:5
affable sign of an a. man ROST 635:11
affair a. is over RICH 627:4
affairs his or her love a. WEST 812:16
knows the interior of a. WALP 801:16
taking part in a. VALÉ 789:3
tide in the a. SHAK 676:28
tide in the a. of women BYRO 177:11
affectation by a. spoiled SWIF 749:21
sophistry and a. BACO 44:29
affection A. beaming in one eye DICK 263:3
a. cannot hold the bent SHAK 701:19
a. on things above BIBL 109:3
a. you get back NESB 541:10
one a. left CARS 192:4
rear of your a. SHAK 662:8
affections a. run to waste BYRO 174:28
holiness of the heart's a. KEAT 430:21
old offences of a. new SHAK 705:13
souls descend T'a. DONN 273:26
unruly wills and a. BOOK 128:7
affinities Elective a. GOET 343:9
afflicted oppressed, and he was a. BIBL 88:17
affliction A. is enamoured SHAK 697:30
a. taught a lover POPE 582:22
bread of a. BIBL 80:10
furnace of a. BIBL 88:8
mine a. and my misery BIBL 89:24
saveth in time of a. BIBL 91:16
waters of a. BIBL 87:17
afflictions A. easier grow WALS 802:10
a. of Job BACO 42:4
all their a. BOOK 127:18
affluent a. society GALB 328:5
afford a. it or no GAY 332:17
a. to be good to her SHAW 709:4
any way a. it EDGE 288:14
Can't a. them SHAW 709:12
unless you can a. it TROL 783:13
Afghanistan left on A.'s plains KIPL 440:22
afloat A. We move: Delicious CLOU 221:19
afraid a. of his enemy PLUT 579:9
a. of me POPE 586:22
a. of the sea SYNG 751:20
a. of Virginia Woolf ALBE 10:5
a. to look upon God BIBL 75:27
because she was a. of him MURD 536:16
conscience is a. BOOK 128:15
feel somewhat a. DEV 259:8
he is a. to feel FORS 320:10
I, a stranger and a. HOUS 390:7
in short, I was a. ELIO 295:8
many are a. of God LOCK 472:9
not a. to speak evil BIBL 111:9
not so much a. BROW 153:24
not that I'm a. to die ALLE 12:14
of whom then shall I be a. BOOK 133:10
poker of whom every one is a. MITF 524:4
sore a. BIBL 98:20
taught to be a. HAMM 359:5
what you are a. to do EMER 299:19
Afric A.'s sunny fountains HEBE 367:6
in A.-maps SWIF 749:16
Africa A. and her prodigies BROW 153:19
A. than my own body ORTO 557:17
choose between this A. WALC 799:1
deported A. GENE 333:5
I speak of A. SHAK 670:21
new out of A. PLIN 578:17
shape of A. FANO 306:8
silent over A. BROW 156:5
sloggin' over A. KIPL 438:7
Till China and A. meet AUDE 33:18
African A. is conditioned KENY 434:3
[A.] national consciousness MACM 487:19
I'm not an A. GOLD 344:4
struggle of the A. people MAND 493:7
Africans A. experience people KAUN 426:7
A. were a low, filthy nation HEAD 365:24
some to the parched A. VIRG 795:15
after A. many a summer TENN 766:16
a.-silence on the shore BYRO 178:21
A. the first death THOM 772:12
A. you, Claude CATC 195:1
happily ever a. ANON 15:9
one damned thing a. another HUBB 392:11
Or just a. STEV 740:7
tell them that come a. BOOK 134:26
afternoon a. of human life JUNG 423:10
At five in the a. GARC 329:10

afternoon (*cont.*):
hot summer a. ANON 19:6
lose the war in an a. CHUR 216:20
summer a. JAME 403:23
willing every a. AUDE 34:5
afternoons Winter A. DICK 266:16
aftersight a. and foresight ELIO 294:16
Afton Flow gently, sweet A. BURN 166:10
again believing it a. LICH 467:18
hang the man over a. BARH 54:2
I'll see you a. COWA 238:13
against a. anything CONF 231:9
a. every man BIBL 74:27
a. everything KENN 433:22
A. thee only have I sinned BOOK 135:4
always vote *a.* FIEL 310:22
He was a. it COOL 236:3
life is 6 to 5 a. RUNY 637:15
never met anyone who wasn't a. war LOW 477:6
not with me is a. me BIBL 95:10
somewhat a. thee BIBL 111:24
those that work a. them HALI 357:9
vote a. somebody ADAM 2:8
who can be a. us BIBL 105:11
Agamemnon And A. dead YEAT 836:15
lived before A. PROV 596:37
When A. cried aloud ELIO 295:25
Agamemnona *ante A.* HORA 389:9
agate bigger than an a.-stone SHAK 697:5
age A. cannot wither her SHAK 656:27
a. demanded an image POUN 589:14
a., Disease, or sorrows CLOU 221:23
a. fatal to Revolutionists DESM 259:1
a. going to the workhouse PAIN 564:4
A., I do abhor thee SHAK 703:28
a. in her embraces ROCH 630:10
a. is a dream that is dying O'SH 560:12
A. is deformed BAST 57:2
a. is in, the wit is out SHAK 691:15
a. is rocking the wave MAND 493:13
A. might but take the things WORD 832:1
a. might well have chilled YEAT 835:4
a. of chivalry BURK 163:21
a. of ease GOLD 344:9
A. of Machinery CARL 187:16
a. shall not weary them BINY 115:8
a. we live in BURK 164:11
a., which forgives itself SHAW 708:30
A. will not be defied BACO 43:27
a., with his stealing steps SHAK 666:20
a. with stealing steps VAUX 790:19
be the a. I am MERW 506:2
caricature, Decrepit a. YEAT 837:18
cold a., narrow jealousy ROCH 630:4
commendation of old a. BACO 41:20
confused old a. with valour LEON 464:8
Crabbed a. and youth SHAK 703:27
dawning of the a. of Aquarius RADO 620:4
days of our a. BOOK 137:19
died in a good old a. BIBL 80:30
die in the flower of their a. BIBL 78:13
Diseases and sad Old A. VIRG 794:20
dreary old a. VIRG 796:20
Every a. DRYD 283:3
fetch the a. of gold MILT 513:24
for at your a. SHAK 665:15
good old a. BIBL 74:26
harsh a. changed my course AKHM 9:7
He was not of an a. JONS 420:25
if a. could ESTI 301:10
I meet my Father, my a. LOWE 478:1
infirmity of his a. SHAK 678:2
in the time of a. BOOK 136:16
invention of a barbarous a. MILT 514:5
labour of an a. MILT 513:14
language of the a. GRAY 351:6
my a. is as a lusty winter SHAK 658:16
nor devouring a. OVID 561:19
now in a. I bud again HERB 372:17
of a. BIBL 102:3
old a. always fifteen years older BARU 56:10
Old A., and Experience ROCH 630:14
Old-a., a second child CHUR 213:23
Old a. hath yet his honour TENN 767:12
Old a. is the most unexpected TROT 783:15
Old a. should burn THOM 772:2
only end of a. LARK 452:15
outworn buried a. SHAK 704:25
serene, That men call a. BROO 150:7
son of his old a. BIBL 75:8
soon comes a. SPEN 734:1
Soul of the A. JONS 420:22
Spirit of the A. HAZL 365:19
Stretch a.'s truth JONS 419:10
tells her real a. WILD 818:25
Their a., not Charlemagne's BROW 154:10
this a. best pleaseth me HERR 374:19
To youth and a. in common ARNO 28:6
very attractive a. WILD 817:24
virtuous in their old a. POPE 587:20
wealth a well-spent a. CAMP 183:24
well an old a. is out DRYD 282:18
well stricken in a. BIBL 74:28
when Mozart was my a. LEHR 462:18
with a. and dust RALE 621:4
With leaden a. o'ercargoed FLEC 317:5
worth an a. without a name MORD 530:21
wrinkled a. forefend SMAR 722:14
aged a. man is but a paltry thing YEAT 837:2
a. thrush HARD 361:11
allow this a. man his right CLOS 222:11
deliciously a. and sad SHAW 707:15
did the a. seem TRAH 780:15
I saw an a., aged man CARR 191:13
learn how to be a. BLYT 123:4
means Certainly a. BYRO 177:12
agenda any item of the a. PARK 567:23
agendum *quid superessit a.* LUCA 478:15
agents Civil and Political A. VICT 792:6
night's black a. SHAK 684:7
ages acts being seven a. SHAK 658:25
A. of hopeless end MILT 515:11
a. of imagination BLAK 119:27
A. to our construction went WARR 803:23
belongs to the a. STAN 736:8
different a. move PRIO 583:4
God, our help in a. past WATT 805:19
heir of all the a. TENN 763:8
Rock of A. TOPL 779:16
aggressors God loves not the a. KORA 443:19
Agincourt affright the air at A. SHAK 670:26
agitation hope and a. BARA 53:14
than to excite a. PALM 566:6
Agnes St A.' Eve KEAT 427:3
St A.' Eve OPEN 556:13
agnostic title of 'a.' HUXL 397:10
agnosticism all a. means DARR 250:11
agnus *A. Dei* MISS 522:19
agog All a. at the plasterer HEAN 366:8
agonies exultations, a. WORD 832:12
agony a. is abated MACA 483:14
am in a. CATU 197:19
Beyond is a. GREV 353:2
By thine A. BOOK 127:7
intense the a. BRON 150:1
it was a., Ivy CATC 195:12
most extreme a. BETT 71:11
My soul in a. COLE 226:17
agree a. in the truth BOOK 129:11
a. with the book of God OMAR 554:15
all things differ, all a. POPE 587:14
appear to a. PAIN 564:6
both a. is wrong CECI 199:3
colours will a. BACO 44:19
how a. the kettle BIBL 91:28
in which they a. BAGE 47:16
Two of a trade never a. PROV 613:28
agreeable power to be a. SWIF 749:1
agreed except they be a. BIBL 90:16
agreement a. between two men CECI 199:3
a. with hell GARR 330:11
blow with an a. TROT 783:19
have reached a. MITC 523:13
with hell are we at a. BIBL 87:14
agrestis *ille deos qui novit a.* VIRG 796:19
agri *modus a.* HORA 389:24
agriculture taxes must fall upon a. GIBB 335:9
Ahab ran before A. BIBL 80:1
ahead get a., get a hat ADVE 7:28
Ahriman A. was abased ZORO 841:17
a-hunting a. we will go FIEL 309:16
We daren't go a. ALLI 12:21
aids adventure in the world of A. PERK 573:22
A. epidemic has rolled WHIT 814:3
[A. was] an illness in stages GUIB 354:16
seventeen-year-olds dying of A. GING 339:18
ail Oh, what can a. thee KEAT 428:7
what can a. thee OPEN 556:7
ailes *a. de géant* BAUD 57:5
ailments our a. are the same SWIF 748:3
aim a. a little above it LONG 473:13
That at which all things a. ARIS 24:15
when you have forgotten your a. SANT 644:8
aimez *a. qui vous aime* VOLT 798:6
aiming a. at a million BROW 156:1
aimless nothing walks with a. feet TENN 761:10
aims divided a. ARNO 27:10
ain hame to my a. countree CUNN 247:16
ain't a. necessarily so HEYW 376:3
Say it a. so ANON 18:14
air A. and angels DONN 273:15
a. a solemn stillness holds GRAY 350:6
a. broke into a mist BROW 157:8
a. Nimbly and sweetly SHAK 682:6
a. of delightful studies MILT 520:1
a. that kills HOUS 391:5
along the dusky a. COLE 227:4
conscience-stricken a. HOUS 390:4
death of a. ELIO 294:15
deep blue a. LARK 452:17
England was too pure an A. ANON 18:5
excellent canopy, the a. SHAK 663:18
fly through the a. LEYB 467:15
fowl of the a. BIBL 73:14
fowls of the a. BIBL 93:23
I am fire and a. SHAK 658:1
In the clear a. FERG 308:18
into thin a. SHAK 699:6
lands hatless from the a. BETJ 70:8
music in the a. ELGA 291:19
nipping and an eager a. SHAK 662:16
Now a. is hushed COLL 229:8
Of a.-balloons BYRO 176:2
one that beateth the a. BIBL 106:11
or climb the a. YEAT 837:24
parching a. Burns frore MILT 515:20
that word, honour? A. SHAK 669:9
through the trembling a. SPEN 734:18
to the Germans that of—the a. RICH 627:12
'twixt a. and angels' purity DONN 273:17
university of the a. WILS 821:14
Where a. might wash SWIN 751:13
with pinions skim the a. FRER 324:10
airconditioning respectability and a. BARA 53:13
airline a. ticket to romantic places MARV 499:9
airplanes feel about a. KERR 434:8
airport observing a. layouts PRIC 591:8
airs a. and madrigals MILT 519:12
don't give yourself a. CARR 189:13
Sounds and sweet a. SHAK 699:5
airy A., fairy Lilian TENN 762:21
A. nothing, as they deemed COLE 224:18
cuts the a. way BLAK 119:26
nations' a. navies TENN 763:3
aitches nothing to lose but our a. ORWE 559:7
Ajalon Moon, in the valley of A. BIBL 77:22
Ajax A. strives POPE 584:23
as good as A.' SHAK 660:29

Akond A. of Swat LEAR 460:3
alabaster a. box BIBL 97:14
Alamo Remember the A. SHER 716:25
alarm little a. now and then BURN 165:18
SPREAD A. AND DESPONDENCY PENI 572:12
viewed the morning with a. GERS 334:12
alarms a. of struggle and flight ARNO 26:5
alas A. but cannot pardon AUDE 35:8
A., poor Yorick SHAK 666:23
Hugo—a. GIDE 336:19
on the grass a. STEI 737:6
albatross I shot the A. COLE 226:8
Albert A. is beautiful VICT 792:2
message to A. DISR 269:25
Went there with young A. EDGA 288:9
Albion perfidious A. XIMÉ 834:18
alchemy happy a. of mind GREE 351:14
with heavenly a. SHAK 704:17
alcohol A. a very necessary article SHAW 707:26
a. doesn't thrill me PORT 588:5
a. or morphine JUNG 423:8
a. was a food WODE 824:20
taken more out of a. CHUR 216:9
aldermen divides the wives of a. SMIT 723:4
Aldershot burnish'd by A. sun BETJ 71:5
ale a.'s the stuff to drink HOUS 391:9
bliss in a. CRAB 242:26
fed purely upon a. FARQ 307:5
good a. enough ANON 15:12
no more cakes and a. SHAK 701:14
prefer mild a. SURT 746:21
spicy nut-brown a. MILT 512:22
Aleppo husband's to A. gone SHAK 681:11
in A. once SHAK 694:4
Alexander A. oure kyng wes dede WYNT 834:16
gane, like A. BURN 166:19
not A. ALEX 11:5
Some talk of A. SONG 730:3
Alexandria A.'s library burned HUGH 393:5
Alexandrine needless A. POPE 584:21
Alexin *pastor Corydon ardebat A.* VIRG 795:16
algebraic weaves a. patterns LOVE 476:9
alget *Probitas laudatur et a.* JUVE 424:4
alibi always has an a. ELIO 295:18
Alice A. grown lazy TATE 755:4
Christopher Robin went down with A. MILN 510:15
Pass the sick bag, A. CATC 196:18
remember sweet A. ENGL 300:13
alien a. people clutching their gods ELIO 295:2
a. tears will fill for him WILD 819:3
amid the a. corn KEAT 429:14
blame the a. AESC 6:12
damned if I'm an a. GEOR 334:5
alienated any measure which a. GRIF 353:7
alieni *A. appetens* SALL 643:7
alienum *humani nil a me a.* TERE 768:3
alike all places were a. to him KIPL 441:6
By nature men are a. CONF 232:4
aliter *Dis a. visum* VIRG 794:6
alive a. and well ANON 17:6
a. I shall be delighted HOLL 381:1
all be made a. BIBL 106:22
Bears not a. SHAK 669:13
came back, still a. YOKO 838:13
gets out a. MORR 532:21
gets out of it a. FILM 311:17
Half dead and half a. BETJ 70:6
hallelujah! I'm a. OSBO 560:2
I am a. for evermore BIBL 111:23
If we can't stay here a. MONT 528:12
man fully a. IREN 399:23
noise and tumult when a. EDWA 289:10
no longer a. BENT 67:3
not just being a. MART 498:2
Not while I'm a. BEVI 72:13
Officiously to keep a. CLOU 222:24
show that one's a. BURN 165:27
still a. at twenty-two KING 437:16
was dead, and is a. BIBL 100:6
ways of being a. DAWK 253:2
what keeps you a. CAST 193:12
all 1066 and a. that SELL 654:3
A. by my own-alone HARR 362:15
a. for love SPEN 733:26
A. for one, one for all DUMA 284:15
a. gone out of the way BOOK 132:6
a. hell broke loose MILT 516:28
a. in respect of nothing PASC 568:9
a. men are evil MACH 485:14
A.-merciful KORA 443:13
A. my pretty ones SHAK 685:8
a. our yesterdays SHAK 685:22
a. shall be well ELIO 294:20
a. shall be well JULI 423:3
A. that a man hath BIBL 80:37
A. that I am I give BOOK 131:6
a. the silent manliness GOLD 344:17
a. the world is young KING 437:13
A. things are lawful for me BIBL 106:12
a. things to all men ANON 17:8
a. things to all men BIBL 106:9
A. things were made by him BIBL 101:2
a. this for a song CECI 199:7
a. to Heaven JONE 419:5
Christ is a. BIBL 109:4
Evening, a. CATC 195:13
Fair shares for a. POLI 581:12
given Her a. on earth BYRO 175:18
have a. in all CARE 186:4
have his a. neglected JOHN 412:15
Hear a., see all PROV 602:35
it's a. right DYLA 287:5
Jack — I'm a. right BONE 125:7
Lord upholdeth a. BOOK 141:19
man for a. seasons WHIT 816:9
or a. in all TENN 760:4
we should at a. times BOOK 129:20
You can have it a. PFEI 575:1
you were a. to me BROW 158:12
allegiance a. to the flag BELL 62:24
religious a. BAGE 46:4
to which you have pledged a. BALD 49:3
allegory headstrong as an a. SHER 716:2
things are an a. BIBL 107:19
Alleluia A.! sing to Jesus DIX 271:12
Allen love of Barbara A. BALL 50:5
alley lives in our a. CARE 186:21
rats' a. ELIO 296:4
alleys vilest a. in London DOYL 277:9
alleyways in the a. CATU 197:10
alliance A., *n.* In international politics BIER 114:17
morganatic a. HARD 360:2
alliances clear of permanent a. WASH 804:6
entangling a. with none JEFF 405:13
allies no a. to be polite to GEOR 334:7
no eternal a. PALM 566:2
alliteration A.'s artful aid CHUR 214:5
allons *A., enfants de la patrie* ROUG 636:1
allow Government and public opinion a. SHAW 708:5
Allsopp Guinness, A., Bass CALV 182:3
allure a. by denying TROL 783:1
alluring more a. than a levee CONG 233:11
Almack go to Carlisle's, and to a.'s too ANST 22:15
alma mater A. lie dissolved in port POPE 580:16
almanac as an a. out of date WALT 802:13
pious fraud of the a. LOWE 477:17
almanack Look in the a. SHAK 689:30
almighty a. dollar IRVI 400:4
A. had placed it there LABO 446:13
A.'s orders to perform ADDI 4:7
A., the King of Creation WINK 823:7
almond a. tree shall flourish BIBL 85:2
almost A. thou persuadest me BIBL 104:22
alms a. and oblations BOOK 129:11
a. may be in secret BIBL 93:17
puts a. for oblivion SHAK 700:14
alone adult is to be a. ROST 635:15
all a. went she KING 437:9
a. against smiling enemies BOWE 145:14
A., alone, all, all alone COLE 226:17
a. and completely unsuspecting DANT 249:13
A. and palely loitering KEAT 428:7
A. and palely loitering OPEN 556:7
A. I did it SHAK 660:17
A., poor maid MEW 506:13
a. upon the house-top BOOK 138:14
be a. on earth BYRO 174:7
Being a. and liking it HASK 363:15
being a. together LA B 446:14
dangerous to meet it a. WHAR 813:3
I'm all a. NURS 548:11
I want to be a. GARB 329:9
Let me a. BIBL 81:12
Let well a. PROV 605:23
live a. and smash his mirror ANON 20:9
live, as we dream — a. CONR 234:11
Lives not a. BLAK 118:9
more a. while living CARR 189:5
never a. with a Strand ADVE 8:22
never less a. ROGE 631:13
never walk a. HAMM 359:4
not sufficiently a. VALÉ 789:2
One is always a. ELIO 293:23
One is one and all a. SONG 729:11
plough my furrow a. ROSE 633:18
stranger and a. WOLF 825:8
that the man should be a. BIBL 73:20
travels a. PROV 602:23
We were a. JAME 403:16
when wholly a. CICE 217:16
who travels a. KIPL 439:10
would but let it a. WALP 800:23
along All a., down along BALL 52:10
aloof a. from the congregation HILL 377:10
regards that stand A. SHAK 678:1
aloud Angels cry a. BOOK 125:20
Prayed a. AUBR 32:20
alp a. of unforgiveness PLOM 579:2
many a fiery a. MILT 515:21
Alpes *saevas curre per A.* JUVE 424:23
Alph A., the sacred river, ran COLE 225:20
Alpha A. and Omega BIBL 111:18
alpine through an A. village LONG 473:16
alps a. and archipelagoes ALDR 11:3
A. of green ice PHIL 575:9
A. on Alps arise POPE 584:16
O'er the white A. DONN 272:14
passages through the A. COLM 229:18
altar a. of God BOOK 134:10
a. with this inscription BIBL 104:8
even the a. sheds tears TALM 754:17
great world's a.-stairs TENN 761:13
high a. on the move BOWE 145:17
lays upon the a. SPRI 735:6
on his own strange a. SWIN 750:19
so will I go to thine a. BOOK 133:8
To what green a. KEAT 428:27
altars a. to the ground JORD 421:6
thy a., O Lord BOOK 137:11
alter tastes greatly a. JOHN 413:23
alteram *Audi partem a.* AUGU 36:8
alteration A. though it be HOOK 383:7
alters when it a. finds SHAK 705:15
altered a. her person for the worse SWIF 748:22
alternative Considering the a. CHEV 211:23
alternatives a. that are not their own BONH 125:9
exhausted all other a. EBAN 287:20
ignorance of a. ANGE 14:17
Althea divine A. brings LOVE 476:12
altitudo to an *O a.* BROW 153:16
altogether A. elsewhere, vast herds AUDE 33:27
righteous a. BOOK 132:17
altruism conscientiousness and a. CONF 231:10
vigorously exercises a. MENG 505:2

alway a. must be with us KEAT 426:17
I am with you a. BIBL 97:30
always a. be an England PARK 567:19
a. in the majority KNOX 442:11
not a. be chiding BOOK 138:18
Once a—, a. a— PROV 608:30
sometimes a. RICH 627:11
Alzheimer from A.'s disease BAYL 58:1
he had A.'s disease REAG 623:8
on A.'s disease MURD 537:1
am a.—yet what I am CLAR 218:15
I A. THAT I AM BIBL 75:29
I think, therefore I a. DESC 258:18
Ama *A. et fac quod vis* AUGU 36:9
amantem *Quis fallere possit a.* VIRG 794:11
amaranth no fields of a. LAND 450:5
amare *amans a.* AUGU 35:23
amari *Surgit a.* LUCR 479:9
Amaryllis sport with A. MILT 513:2
amateur a. is a man who can't AGAT 6:18
a. sport DOYL 277:21
whine of the a. for three WHIS 813:20
amateurs Hell full of musical a. SHAW 708:4
nation of a. ROSE 633:17
amavi *Sero te a.* AUGU 36:5
amaze vainly men themselves a. MARV 498:13
amazing A. grace NEWT 543:13
A. love WESL 810:20
ambassador a. is an honest man WOTT 833:6
ambassadors A. cropped up like hay GILB 337:9
amber gold and a. JONS 420:11
in a. to observe the forms POPE 583:5
lutes of a. HERR 375:5
ambergris a. on shore MARV 498:8
ambiguities clear these a. SHAK 698:5
ambiguity Seven types of a. EMPS 300:9
ambition a. can creep BURK 164:9
A. first sprung POPE 582:19
A., in a private man a vice MASS 501:2
A.'s debt is paid SHAK 675:17
A. should be made SHAK 676:1
a. to be a wag JOHN 418:3
a. with greater objectives TOCQ 777:17
Art not without a. SHAK 682:1
by a. hewn DRAY 279:5
fling away a. SHAK 673:15
Let not a. mock GRAY 350:9
make a. virtue SHAK 692:30
never yet exerted a. BOSW 144:19
To low a. POPE 585:4
Vain the a. of kings WEBS 807:19
Vaulting a. SHAK 682:12
Who doth a. shun SHAK 658:22
ambitions ceiling put on our a. PRES 591:4
ambitious as he was a., I slew him SHAK 675:25
Brutus says he was a. SHAK 675:30
Caesar was a. SHAK 675:28
of a. minds SPEN 734:9
ambles who Time a. withal SHAK 659:13
ambo *Arcades a.* VIRG 796:7
Amboss *A. oder Hammer sein* GOET 343:5
Ambree Mary A. BALL 51:5
ambrosia God is sweet a. SIKH 719:9
ambrosial a. hair VIRG 793:12
Phallic and a. POUN 589:15
âme *â. est sans défauts* RIMB 628:12
amemus *atque a.* CATU 197:2
amen 'A.' Stuck in my throat SHAK 683:7
Glorious the catholic a. SMAR 722:13
sound of a great A. PROC 593:13
Will no man say, a. SHAK 695:20
amenities wanted to say 'a.' CATU 197:18
amens few mumbled a. HUNT 396:2
America America! A. BATE 57:4
A. is now given over HAWT 364:14
A. is a country EMER 299:32
A. is a land whose UPDI 788:12
A. is a nation WHIT 814:7
A. is a vast conspiracy UPDI 788:13
A. is God's Crucible ZANG 839:21
A. is just ourselves ARNO 28:7
A. is the only idealistic WILS 822:18
A. is the proof MCCA 484:2
A.'s present need HARD 360:5
A., thou half-brother BAIL 48:7
A. thus top nation SELL 654:16
born in A. MALC 491:21
cannot conquer A. PITT 576:25
come back to A. JAME 403:18
continent of A. WESL 811:18
debated in A. ADAM 3:8
England and A. divided MISQ 521:10
every man's love affair with A. MAIL 491:2
glorious morning for A. ADAM 3:18
God bless A. BERL 68:7
huntsmen are up in A. BROW 152:17
I like to be in A. SOND 727:20
I look upon North A. SHIP 717:6
impresses me most about A. EDWA 289:8
in A. the successful writer LEWI 467:8
in common with A. WILD 817:11
independence of A. SHEL 710:4
in the living rooms of A. MCLU 487:11
I, too, sing A. HUGH 392:17
loss of A. FREE 324:4
lost his dominions in A. WALP 801:23
makes A. what it is STEI 737:7
morning again in A. POLI 581:19
next to god a. CUMM 247:4
O my A. DONN 272:16
think of thee, O A. WALP 801:4
to A. to convert the Indians WESL 811:14
United States of A. PAGE 562:18
what A. did you have GINS 339:23
whole A. BURK 162:25
American A. as cherry pie BROW 151:20
A. beauty rose ROCK 630:23
A. culture COLO 230:1
A. daydream BROD 149:4
A. Express ADVE 7:5
A.-outward-bound HOPK 385:4
A., this new man CEÈV 244:21
A. women shoot FORS 320:8
bad news to the A. people KEIL 432:11
chief business of the A. people COOL 236:2
free man, an A. JOHN 408:10
Greeks in this A. empire MACM 487:14
I also—am an A. WEBS 807:15
I am A. bred MILL 509:17
I'm an A. GOLD 344:4
in love with A. names BENÉ 64:23
I shall die an A. WEBS 807:17
Miss A. Pie MCLE 486:15
no second acts in A. lives FITZ 315:16
not a Virginian, but an A. HENR 371:2
oil controlling A. soil DYLA 287:14
part of being A. UPDI 788:17
send A. boys JOHN 408:17
tenth A. muse BRON 149:11
texture of A. life JAME 403:4
truth, justice and the A. way ANON 16:7
vacant lands in A. JEFF 405:8
weakness of A. civilization PRIE 591:16
Americanism A. with its sleeves rolled MCCA 484:1
hyphenated A. ROOS 633:10
Americans A. are to be freemen WASH 804:4
A. when they die PROV 601:22
borrowed from the A. LAHR 448:3
for A. it is just beyond KISS 441:30
Good A., when they die APPL 23:4
ignorant A. MASS 501:3
my fellow A. KENN 433:14
passed to new generation of A. KENN 433:9
Russians and the A. TOCQ 778:15
when bad A. die WILD 818:23
Americas off for the A. BARR 56:1
amiable a. are thy dwellings BOOK 137:11
amicably a. if they can QUIN 619:3
amicus *A. Plato* ARIS 25:9
Amis cocoa for Kingsley A. COPE 236:8
amiss all is a. BARN 55:9
mark what is done a. BOOK 141:1
amitti *non a. sed praemitti* CYPR 248:11
ammunition pass the a. FORG 320:7
amniotic in an a. paradise WILL 820:6
amo A., amas O'KE 553:7
Non a. te MART 497:23
Odi et a. CATU 197:19
amoeba When we were a soft a. SHIP 717:5
among A. them, but not of them BYRO 174:23
amongst be a. you BOOK 130:3
amor *a. che muove il sole* DANT 250:5
A. vincit omnia CHAU 204:15
L'a. che muove CLOS 222:2
Nunc scio quid sit A. VIRG 796:9
Omnia vincit A. VIRG 796:12
Suprema citius solvet a. die HORA 387:23
amorem *subito deponere a.* CATU 197:15
Amorites king of the A. BOOK 141:5
amorous a. ditties MILT 514:26
a. of their strokes SHAK 656:23
be a., but be chaste BYRO 178:4
from a. causes springs POPE 586:28
my a. propensities JOHN 412:10
reluctant a. delay MILT 516:16
amour beginning of an A. BEHN 62:6
c'est l'a. BOUS 145:6
Vive l'a. STER 738:9
amphibi rational a. go MARV 499:8
ample cabined a. Spirit ARNO 26:23
ampullas *Proicit a.* HORA 385:17
Amurath Not A. an Amurath succeeds SHAK 670:19
amuse talent to a. COWA 238:12
amused a. by its presumption THUR 776:26
People mutht be a. DICK 262:24
We are not a. VICT 792:9
amusements but for its a. LEWI 467:3
amusing not an a. occupation FERB 308:13
Anabaptist a. is a thing I am not FLEM 317:15
Anabaptists certain A. BOOK 142:14
anagram mild a. DRYD 282:1
analogies A. decide nothing FREU 324:15
analytical A. Engine weaves LOVE 476:9
anarch Thy hand, great A POPE 582:14
anarchism A. is a game SHAW 709:3
A. stands for the liberation GOLD 344:5
anarchist small a. community BENN 65:21
anarchy a. and competition RUSK 639:4
democracy, call it *a.* HOBB 379:1
Mere a. is loosed YEAT 837:5
anatomist am but a bad a. LAST 456:3
anatomy A. is destiny FREU 324:12
mere a., a mountebank SHAK 659:30
ancestor If there were an a. HUXL 397:20
ancestors a. are very good SHER 716:4
a. lost no time in abandoning LANC 449:18
look backward to their a. BURK 163:16
ancestral A. voices prophesying war COLE 225:23
ancestry pride of a. POWE 591:1
trace my a. GILB 337:22
What, my Lord, is a. RICH 627:5
anchor a. to let fall ASKE 30:20
become our a. HARR 363:2
anchorage hope her a. maintain SMAR 722:8
anchored a. safe and sound WHIT 815:5
ancient a. and fish-like smell SHAK 698:31
a. nobility BACO 43:22
A. of days BIBL 90:6
A. of Days GRAN 348:15
A. person of my heart ROCH 630:19
A. times BACO 41:22
Beauty so a. AUGU 36:5
feet in a. time BLAK 120:1
It is an a. Mariner COLE 226:3
most a. profession KIPL 441:1
rivers a. as the world HUGH 392:18
signals of the a. flame DANT 250:1

sing the a. ways YEAT 837:17
spark of that a. flame VIRG 794:10
With the a. is wisdom BIBL 81:16
ancients a. dreaded death HARE 362:3
a. without idolatry CHES 209:15
architecture, the a. CHAM 201:4
love the a. CONF 231:15
and including 'a.' MCCA 484:4
Andromache kissed his sad A. CORN 237:1
anecdotage fell into his a. DISR 270:21
anecdote a. dehumanizing EPHR 300:19
anfractuosities a. of the human mind JOHN 416:12
angel a. from your door BLAK 120:16
a. in the house PATM 569:18
A. o'er a new inn door BYRO 173:18
a. of death BRIG 148:9
A. of Death BYRO 175:24
a. of the Lord came down TATE 755:10
a. of the Lord came upon them BIBL 98:20
a. should write MOOR 530:8
a. watching an urn TENN 763:25
ape or an a. DISR 269:2
as the A. did with Jacob WALT 803:2
beautiful and ineffectual a. ARNO 28:21
better a. is a man SHAK 705:24
clip an A.'s wings KEAT 428:19
Death's bright a. PROC 593:14
domesticate the Recording A. STEV 742:2
drew an a. down DRYD 280:23
for an a. to pass FIRB 313:6
Her a.'s face SPEN 733:16
in action how like an a. SHAK 663:18
Like a.-visits, few CAMP 183:16
Look homeward a. MILT 513:9
Lost A. SHEL 710:17
mighty a. took up a stone BIBL 113:1
ministering a. SHAK 666:26
ministering a. thou SCOT 651:13
O! the more a. she SHAK 693:27
Recording A., as he wrote it down STER 739:8
say to the A. of Death MIDR 507:16
Shined in my a.-infancy VAUG 790:7
What a. wakes me SHAK 690:3
White as an a. BLAK 120:18
woman think him an a. THAC 768:20
wrote like an a. GARR 330:4
angelheaded a. hipsters burning GINS 339:20
angeli *Non Angli sed A.* GREG 352:13
angels Air and a. DONN 273:15
all the a. stood BIBL 112:8
A. affect us DONN 273:16
a. all were singing BYRO 179:11
A. and Archangels BOOK 129:20
A. and ministers of grace SHAK 662:18
A. bending near the earth SEAR 652:24
A. came and ministered BIBL 93:1
A. cry aloud BOOK 125:20
a. fear to tread POPE 585:3
a. fear to tread PROV 600:40
a. go about their task BART 56:6
A. in jumpers LEWI 467:13
a. in some brighter dreams VAUG 790:14
a. keep their ancient places THOM 774:12
a., nor principalities BIBL 105:12
a. on the walls MARL 496:29
a. would be gods POPE 585:12
band of a. comin' after me SONG 730:4
behold the a. of God BIBL 75:1
better a. of our nature LINC 468:9
By that sin fell the a. SHAK 673:15
entertained a. unawares BIBL 110:6
flights of a. SHAK 667:12
Four a. round my head PRAY 592:4
Fourteen a. watch WETT 812:23
give his a. charge over thee BOOK 137:23
glorious fault of a. POPE 582:19
God and a. BACO 41:16
Hear all ye a. MILT 517:1
if a. fight SHAK 695:5
lower than the a. BOOK 131:27
make the a. weep SHAK 686:10
maketh his a. spirits BOOK 139:1
man did eat a.' food BOOK 137:6
Michael and his a. BIBL 112:19
neglect God and his A. DONN 275:8
Not Angles but A. GREG 352:13
Our acts our a. are FLET 318:5
plead like a. SHAK 682:10
saw a treefull of a. BENÉ 65:3
sparkling a. TRAH 780:15
tongues of men and of a. BIBL 106:16
'twixt air and a.' purity DONN 273:17
what the a. know NEWM 542:14
Where a. tremble GRAY 351:2
With a. round the throne WATT 805:12
women are a. BYRO 179:9
Ye holy a. bright GURN 355:5
anger Achilles' cursed a. OPEN 555:1
Achilles' cursed a. sing HOME 381:20
A. and jealousy ELIO 293:2
A. is a short madness HORA 386:16
A. is never without an argument HALI 357:11
a. is not turned away BIBL 86:20
A. is one of the sinews FULL 327:9
A. makes dull men BACO 45:9
a. of his lip SHAK 702:2
a. of men who have no opinions CHES 211:5
a. of the sovereign MORE 531:10
Frozen a. FREU 324:19
Great a. in the dragon SUTT 747:8
Juno's never-forgetting a. VIRG 793:4
lamb That carries a. SHAK 676:26
life of telegrams and a. FORS 320:17
Look back in a. OSBO 560:1
monstrous a. of the guns OWEN 562:5
more in sorrow than in a. SHAK 662:5
neither a. nor partiality TACI 752:12
neither keepeth he his a. BOOK 138:18
prone to a. and revenge GIRA 340:5
slow to a. BIBL 83:1
strike it in a. SHAW 708:21
such great a. VIRG 793:5
sun go down on your a. PROV 607:31
angle a.-faced, Dreary mouthed HUNT 395:13
Brother of the A. WALT 802:16
Give me mine a. SHAK 656:31
in every a. greet MARV 498:11
angler excellent a. WALT 802:19
if he be an honest a. WALT 802:15
no man is born an a. WALT 802:14
anglers too good for any but a. WALT 802:24
angles Bats not a. THOM 773:11
Not A. but Angels GREG 352:13
Offer no a. TESS 768:17
Angli *Non A. sed Angeli* GREG 352:13
angling A. may be said to be WALT 802:12
be quiet and go a-A. WALT 802:27
Anglo-Irish A. might consider themselves BINC 115:3
Anglo-Irishman He was an A. BEHA 61:22
Anglo-Saxon A. attitudes CARR 191:7
idol of the A. BAGE 46:16
angry a. at a slander JONS 419:15
a. nearly every day ALCO 10:9
a. with my friend BLAK 121:5
A. young man PAUL 570:5
Be ye a. BIBL 108:5
hungry man is an a. man PROV 603:6
man who becomes a. TALM 754:5
O! when she's a. SHAK 690:7
When he was a. BECK 60:11
when very a., swear TWAI 786:23
anguis *Latet a. in herba* VIRG 796:1
anguish a. of a torturing hour SHAK 690:21
howls of a. HEAL 366:2
With a. moist KEAT 428:8
angusta *Res a. domi* JUVE 424:12
anima Swift was *a. Rabelaisii* COLE 227:23
animae *A. dimidium meae* HORA 387:14
animal a. he studied less GOSS 347:6
attend a dying a. YEAT 835:14
Be a good a. LAWR 458:5
be a good a. SPEN 732:2
every a. is sad SAYI 648:2
Man is a noble a. BROW 153:10
Man is the Only A. TWAI 786:9
only a. in the world to fear LAWR 458:10
political a. ARIS 25:2
pure a. spirits WOLL 825:24
religious a. BURK 163:27
so very a. and unecstatic VICT 792:3
vegetable, a., and mineral GILB 339:3
animalculous beings a. GILB 339:3
animals All a. are equal ORWE 558:7
a. are divided BORG 143:4
A., whom we have DARW 251:2
at its mercy: a. KUND 446:7
distinguishes us from mere a. LEIB 462:21
distinguish us from other a. BEAU 58:10
find the a. amusing NIET 545:11
man from a. OSLE 560:17
minutely small a. JAIN 402:8
not over-fond of a. ATTE 31:21
production of the higher a. DARW 250:21
soft little a. pottering CASS 193:11
takes 40 dumb a. SAYI 647:26
turn and live with a. WHIT 815:15
animam *Liberavi a. meam* BERN 69:3
animate a. the whole SMIT 725:21
animated all a. nature COLE 225:8
animi *natura a.* LUCR 479:5
vivida vis a. LUCR 478:21
animosity sisterly a. SURT 747:4
animula *A. vagula blandula* HADR 355:11
animum *Caelum non a. mutant* HORA 386:20
Anjou sweetness of A. DU B 283:23
Ann that's little A. NURS 549:1
Anna Here thou, great A. POPE 587:5
Annabel Lee I and my A. POE 579:10
annals a. are blank MONT 528:11
a. of the poor GRAY 350:9
War's a. will cloud HARD 361:17
Anne of A. of Cleves HENR 370:11
sister A., do you see nothing PERR 573:24
annihilate a. but space and time POPE 586:23
annihilated illimitable was a. DISR 268:20
annihilating a. all civilization SAKH 641:15
A. all that's made MARV 498:16
annihilation a. of one of us SHEL 710:9
my own a. GUNN 354:20
anniversaries secret a. LONG 473:20
Anno Domini only a. HILT 377:12
taste my A. FARQ 307:4
annoy a. with what you write AMIS 14:1
only does it to a. CARR 189:15
annoyance a. of a good example TWAI 786:25
Shadow of a. SHEL 714:7
source of a. BAED 45:18
annuity a. is a very serious business AUST 38:26
annus a. horribilis ELIZ 297:16
motet a. et almum HORA 389:7
anointed a. my head with oil BOOK 133:1
balm from an a. king SHAK 695:5
anointing Thou the a. Spirit art BOOK 142:7
anonymous essentially a. WEIL 808:26
anorak a. grow big with jotters MAXW 502:12
another always a. one walking ELIO 296:13
a. fine mess LAUR 454:8
a. shall gird thee BIBL 103:11
in a. country MARL 496:18
members one of a. BIBL 108:4
not a. thing BUTL 171:10
when comes such a. SHAK 676:13
anser *inter strepere a. olores* VIRG 796:11
answer A. a fool BIBL 83:23
a. came there none CARR 190:21
a. came there none SCOT 650:10
a. is blowin' in the wind DYLA 287:3

answer (*cont.*):
a. is 'himself' IBSE 398:11
a. made it none SHAK 662:4
a. the phone THUR 776:27
a. to 'Hi!' CARR 191:20
a. to the Irish Question SELL 654:15
on the way to a pertinent a. BRON 149:9
please thee with my a. SHAK 688:7
sent an a. back to me CARR 191:6
soft a. BIBL 82:34
soft a. turneth PROV 611:4
stay for an a. BACO 44:15
what a dusty a. MERE 505:21
what a. should I give TENN 766:2
What *is* the a. LAST 457:17
wise men cannot a. PROV 600:37
wisest man can a. COLT 230:3
answerable a. for what we choose NEWM 543:1
answerably a. to your Christian calling BOOK 130:9
answered hath Caesar a. it SHAK 675:28
no one a. DE L 256:16
prayer is only a. TALM 754:10
answering a. that of God FOX 322:10
bell-like a. WORD 827:11
answers Kind are her a. CAMP 184:2
Science offers best a. DAWK 253:5
ant a. Appears a monstrous elephant COTT 237:16
a.'s a centaur POUN 589:20
a. which has foreseen BART 56:5
good husband, little a. LOVE 476:11
Go to the a. BIBL 82:13
antagonist Our a. is our helper BURK 164:2
antediluvian a. families CONG 232:22
anthology a. is like all RALE 621:12
Anthropophagi A., and men SHAK 691:34
anti savage a.-everythings HOLM 381:8
antic a. disposition SHAK 663:5
dance an a. hay MARL 496:9
Antichrist against the a. of Communism BUCH 159:10
anticipation only in the a. of it HITC 378:3
antick old father a., the law SHAK 667:18
anti-destin *L'art est un a.* MALR 493:2
antipathy a. of good to bad POPE 586:21
antipodes act our A. BROW 152:17
like A. in shoes MARV 499:8
sheer opposite, a. KEAT 427:19
antique group that's quite a. BYRO 176:16
noble and nude and a. SWIN 750:14
old and a. song SHAK 701:17
over is their a. joy YEAT 837:11
traveller from an a. land SHEL 712:21
antiquities A. are history defaced BACO 41:10
antiquity write for A. LAMB 449:6
antiwar ecology and a. HUNT 396:8
Antony A., Enthroned SHAK 656:25
A. Shall be brought SHAK 657:24
A. Would ruffle up SHAK 676:11
catch a second A. SHAK 658:5
conquer A. SHAK 657:16
O! my oblivion is a very A. SHAK 656:17
spirit that is in A. SHAK 674:5
anvil a. of daily deadlines ZOLA 840:15
be the a. or the hammer GOET 343:5
Church is an a. MACL 486:13
church is an a. PROV 597:19
England's on the a. KIPL 438:3
My sledge and a. EPIT 303:16
anxiety a. like fishbones HILL 377:4
A. love's greatest killer NIN 546:3
taboo'd by a. GILB 337:18
any A. old iron COLL 228:12
anybody Is there a. there DE L 256:15
Is there a. there OPEN 555:21
no one's a. GILB 337:10
anything A. for a quiet life MIDD 507:3
A. goes PORT 588:2
believe in a. CHES 211:22
If a. can go wrong SAYI 647:18
anywhere get a. in a marriage MURD 536:18
apart have stood a. WILS 822:12
of man's life a thing a. BYRO 176:7
ape a. for his grandfather HUXL 397:20
a.'s an ape PROV 595:10
gorgeous buttocks of the a. HUXL 397:8
Is man an a. DISR 269:2
naked a. MORR 532:8
played the sedulous a. STEV 741:7
apes a. and peacocks MASE 500:13
a. are apes JONS 420:1
dogs and a. BROW 155:33
ivory, and a. BIBL 79:19
lead a. in hell SHAK 698:6
people his a. CHAU 205:6
aphorists A. can be wrong FENT 308:11
aphrodisiac Power is the great a. KISS 441:28
apocalypse write a new a. HEIN 368:7
Apollo A. from his shrine MILT 513:27
A. hunted Daphne MARV 498:14
Phoebus A. MERE 505:12
songs of A. SHAK 681:5
Yea, is not even A. SWIN 751:4
young A., golden-haired CORN 237:3
Apollos A. watered BIBL 105:30
Apollyon his name is A. BUNY 160:18
apologies do not want a. WODE 824:21
apologize good rule never to a. WODE 824:21
Never a. FISH 313:15
apologizes if it's raining, a. WELD 809:5
apology a. for the Devil BUTL 172:25
defence or a. CHAR 202:25
God's a. for relations KING 437:18
apostle great a. of the Philistines ARNO 28:19
apostles a. of equality ARNO 28:9
A.: praise thee BOOK 125:20
A. would have done BYRO 176:1
He gave some, a. BIBL 108:3
I am the least of the a. BIBL 106:19
Twelve for the twelve a. SONG 729:11
apostolic Catholick and A. Church BOOK 129:3
apothecary starved a. LOCK 472:10
apparatus haunted a. sleeps RAIN 620:7
mediocrity of the a. TROT 783:18
Persicos odi, puer, a. HORA 388:4
apparel a. oft proclaims the man SHAK 662:11
put on glorious a. BOOK 138:2
rich in a. TROL 782:3
apparelled a. like the spring SHAK 694:6
apparition Anno 1670, was an a. AUBR 33:1
appeal a. against something CAMU 184:6
a. open from criticism JOHN 410:14
a. unto Caesar BIBL 104:18
appear a. considerable JOHN 414:11
how you a. to God UNAM 787:8
appearance a. always stately EINH 290:7
a. of Your Majesty BIBL 73:8
outward a. BIBL 78:27
reality than in a. HUME 394:17
appearances a. are deceptive PROV 595:11
Keep up a. CHUR 214:1
no trusting a. SHER 716:17
appearing Television is for a. on COWA 239:7
appetite A. comes with eating PROV 595:12
a. grows by eating RABE 619:9
a. may sicken SHAK 700:26
good digestion wait on a. SHAK 684:10
hungry edge of a. SHAK 694:16
more riotous a. SHAK 679:22
voracious a. FIEL 310:9
were then to me An a. WORD 829:4
appetites carnal lusts and a. BOOK 131:1
have violent a. VANB 789:10
Our a. as apt to change DRYD 280:27
Subdue your a. DICK 263:20
wrecched worldes a. CHAU 207:21
applause A., *n.* The echo BIER 114:18
in the sunshine and with a. BUNY 161:4
apple aims at me with an a. VIRG 795:20
a. a day PROV 595:13
a. falling towards England AUDE 34:14
a. never falls far PROV 595:14
a. of his eye BIBL 77:11
a. on its bough CRAN 243:22
a. on the tree DICK 266:12
a. pie and cheese FIEL 309:8
a. which reddens ROSS 634:15
A was an a.-pie NURS 547:10
cabbage-leaf to make an a.-pie FOOT 319:8
for an a. damn'd mankind OTWA 560:22
rotten a. injures PROV 610:18
sweet-a. reddens SAPP 644:15
under the a. boughs THOM 772:3
vor me the a. tree BARN 55:6
want the a. for the apple's sake TWAI 786:20
apples a., cherries, hops DICK 265:3
a. of gold BIBL 83:18
A. of gold SWIN 751:12
a. on the Dead Sea's shore BYRO 174:16
choice in rotten a. PROV 611:2
flesh of tart a. RIMB 628:6
golden a. of the sun YEAT 837:12
moon-washed a. of wonder DRIN 279:11
picking dewy a. VIRG 796:8
Ripe a. drop MARV 498:15
stolen, be your a. HUNT 395:16
applications a. for situations AUDE 34:13
applied no such things as a. sciences PAST 569:12
apply a. our hearts unto wisdom BOOK 137:20
appointed a. for all living BIBL 81:27
even in the time a. BOOK 137:9
to th'a. place we tend DRYD 282:11
appointment a. at the end of the world DINE 267:18
a. by the corrupt few SHAW 708:16
a. with him in Samarra MAUG 502:5
create an a. LOUI 475:18
have kept our a. BECK 60:1
apprehension a. of the good SHAK 694:16
apprehensions a. come in crowds WORD 827:15
apprenticeship a. for freedom BARA 53:12
approbation A. from Sir Hubert MORT 534:1
a. of all their actions HOBB 378:24
appropriate that was not a. CLIN 221:8
to each what is a. AUCT 33:7
approve I do not a. MILL 509:10
après *A. nous le déluge* POMP 580:6
apricocks dangling a. SHAK 695:16
apricot blushing a. JONS 420:28
April A., April, Laugh WATS 805:2
A. is the cruellest month ELIO 295:26
A. of her prime SHAK 704:7
A. of your youth HERB 371:22
A. showers bring forth PROV 595:15
A. shroud KEAT 429:4
A. with his shoures OPEN 556:25
bright cold day in A. OPEN 555:24
bright cold day in A. ORWE 558:19
from one A. to another LONG 475:7
glory of an A. day SHAK 702:26
Men are A. when they woo SHAK 659:20
Now that A.'s there BROW 156:2
Whan that A. CHAU 204:6
aprons made themselves a. BIBL 73:26
apt A. Alliteration CHUR 214:5
a. to die SHAK 675:20
aquae *scribuntur a. potoribus* HORA 387:4
aquarium a. is gone LOWE 477:21
Aquarius dawning of the age of A. RADO 620:4
Aquitaine prince of A. NERV 541:7
Arabia gold of A. BOOK 136:19
kings of A. and Saba BOOK 136:18

perfumes of A. SHAK 685:11
spell of far A. DE L 256:10
Arabian alone the A. bird SHAK 660:18
in the A. woods MILT 518:22
Arabians Cretes and A. BIBL 103:16
Arabic as an A. Koran KORA 444:21
Hebrew and A. mingling RUME 637:5
Arabs hundred thousand A. BALF 49:18
like the A. LONG 473:12
Araby burns in glorious A. DARL 250:9
Aram Eugene A. walked between HOOD 382:17
Arbeit *A. macht frei* ANON 20:16
arbiter a. of others' fate BYRO 178:19
Elegantiae a. TACI 752:13
high a. Chance governs all MILT 515:25
arbitrary given way to an a. way CHAR 203:5
supreme power must be a. HALI 357:14
arbitrate a. the even MILT 511:22
arbitrator old common a., Time SHAK 700:22
arboreal a. in its habits DARW 250:16
arbours His private a. SHAK 676:12
Arcades *A. ambo* VIRG 796:7
Arcadia *Et in A. ego* EPIT 302:3
Arcadians A. both VIRG 796:7
Arcady woods of A. are dead YEAT 837:11
arceo *profanum vulgus et a.* HORA 388:11
arch a.-flatterer is a man's self BACO 43:16
a. of order STRA 744:11
a. Of the ranged empire SHAK 656:8
experience is an a. ADAM 2:16
like a triumphal a. DUNN 285:14
triumphant a. COMM 230:9
archangel A. a little damaged LAMB 449:3
Said then the lost a. MILT 514:19
archangels Angels and A. BOOK 129:20
archbishop a. had come to see me OPEN 555:27
love to the A. SHER 716:22
My Lord A. BULL 160:2
archdeacon (by way of turbot) an a. SMIT 725:10
archer a. his sharp arrows SIDN 718:10
mark the a. little meant SCOT 651:3
arches down the a. of the years THOM 774:4
Underneath the A. FLAN 315:21
archetypes known as *a.* JUNG 423:5
archipelago Gulag a. SOLZ 727:11
archipelagoes alps and a. ALDR 11:3
architect a. can only advise WRIG 833:10
a. of own fortune PROV 599:34
A. of the Universe JEAN 405:1
can be an a. RUSK 638:7
consent to be the a. DOST 276:1
architects great a. LUTY 480:7
architectural a. books PUGI 616:19
a. man-milliner RUSK 638:4
great a. secret TROL 782:3
architecture A. acts the most slowly DIMN 267:17
A. at the head BLOM 122:7
A. in general SCHE 646:13
A. is the art JOHN 408:22
a., the ancients CHAM 201:4
Christian A. PUGI 616:17
Dim a. WARR 803:23
frolic a. of the snow EMER 299:10
Gothic a. RUSK 639:9
great a. LUTY 480:7
In a. as in all other WOTT 833:5
rise and fall of English a. BETJ 71:10
archwives Ye a., stondeth CHAU 205:9
Arcturi Daisies, those pearled A. SHEL 713:20
Arden Ay, now am I in A. SHAK 658:18
ardet *paries cum proximus a.* HORA 387:2
ardeur *a. dans mes veines* RACI 619:18
ardour thine own a. glowing LITT 470:3
ardua *a. ad astra* MOTT 535:14
arduis *rebus in a.* HORA 388:6
are be as they a. CLEM 220:13
we know what we a. SHAK 666:2
arena actually in the a. ROOS 633:8
Argentinian young A. soldiers RUNC 637:7
Argos remembers his sweet A. VIRG 795:10
argosies a. of magic sails TENN 763:3
argue absurd to a. men NEWM 542:13
a. freely MILT 519:18
cannot a. with AUCT 33:3
earth does not a. WHIT 815:21
arguing no good in a. LOWE 477:18
not a. with you WHIS 813:16
will be much a. MILT 519:17
argument All a. is against it JOHN 415:25
a. for a week SHAK 667:33
a. of the broken window PANK 566:14
a. of tyrants PITT 577:3
exact and priggish a. SAND 643:16
height of this great a. MILT 514:9
I have found you an a. JOHN 417:14
impression, not an a. HARD 360:18
never without an a. HALI 357:11
nice knock-down a. CARR 191:2
no a. but force BROW 154:7
no force but a. BROW 154:7
rotten a. ANON 19:6
stir without great a. SHAK 665:33
argumentative then talky, then a. BYRO 180:3
arguments attract the worst a. FISH 314:1
force of his a. WALP 801:17
Argus A. were her eunuch SHAK 680:23
argutos *a. inter strepere* VIRG 796:11
Ariel Caliban casts out A. POUN 589:15
deal of A. HENL 369:19
aright sought the Lord a. BURN 166:23
arise a. and go like men STEV 742:15
a. and unbuild it again SHEL 711:7
A., shine BIBL 89:4
My lady sweet, a. SHAK 660:21
will a. and go now YEAT 836:11
arising from the a. of this PALI 565:6
aristocracy a. in a republic MITF 524:7
a. means government by CHES 211:21
a. of Great Britain BRIG 148:11
A. of the moneybag CARL 187:26
called a. PAIN 563:21
displeased with *a.* HOBB 379:1
natural a. among men JEFF 405:18
aristocrat A., democrat TENN 764:2
aristocratic a. class ARNO 28:10
Aristotle A. and his philosophie CHAU 204:19
A. was but the rubbish SOUT 728:21
God of A. HA-L 357:6
arithmetic theology as in a. MILT 519:14
arithmetical a. ratio MALT 493:3
ark a. of bulrushes BIBL 75:22
entered into the a. BIBL 97:5
into the A. BIBL 74:16
two by two in the a. LEVE 466:5
arm a. of the Lord BIBL 88:14
auld moon in her a. BALL 51:15
by a stretched out a. BIBL 77:5
crowns my a. DONN 274:1
did not put your a. around it BLAC 116:20
long a. of coincidence CHAM 201:3
pearls upon an Ethiop's a. DYER 286:17
strength with his a. BIBL 98:17
Stretch your a. no further PROV 611:29
with his holy a. BOOK 138:9
wound them on his a. MARL 496:14
arma *A. virumque cano* OPEN 555:3
A. virumque cano VIRG 793:4
Cedant a. togae CICE 217:15
leges inter a. CICE 217:24
Moriamur et in media a. ruamus VIRG 794:5
armadas till the great A. come NEWB 541:15
Armageddon called in the Hebrew tongue A. BIBL 112:29
domestic A. LEON 464:11
Lincoln County Road or A. DYLA 287:13
We stand at A. ROOS 633:9
armaments not a. that cause wars MADA 488:22
armchair like a good a. MATI 501:13
armchairs a. tight about the hips WODE 824:22
armed a. conflict EDEN 288:6
A. neutrality is ineffectual WILS 822:14
a. so strong in honesty SHAK 676:23
A. warfare must be preceded ZINO 840:5
a. with more than complete steel ANON 17:1
Armenteers Mademoiselle from A. MILI 508:12
armes *Aux a., citoyens* ROUG 636:1
armful very nearly an a. GALT 328:20
armies a. clash by night ARNO 26:5
a. swore terribly STER 739:1
commander of three a. CONF 231:19
disbanding hired a. CARL 188:9
Kings with their a. BOOK 136:7
money and large a. ANOU 22:7
stronger than all the a. ANON 19:3
Arminian A. clergy PITT 576:24
armistice It is an a. for twenty years FOCH 318:23
armonies tumult of thy mighty a. SHEL 712:17
armour Achilles his a. BROW 152:13
a. of Achilles VIRG 794:2
a. of God BIBL 108:12
a. of light BIBL 105:21
a. of light BOOK 127:21
put your a. on WESL 811:4
spend so much in a. SHEN 715:11
armoured a. cars of dreams BISH 115:18
arms a. against a sea of troubles SHAK 664:3
a. and the man OPEN 555:3
a. and the man VIRG 793:4
A., and the man I sing DRYD 283:1
A. and the man I sing OPEN 555:4
a. do flourish BACO 44:21
a. of a chambermaid JOHN 416:6
a. were made the Warrior RIG 627:18
a. ye forge SHEL 713:26
caught in her a. WYAT 834:6
Emparadised in one another's a. MILT 516:18
everlasting a. BIBL 77:14
For fear, he a. ROCH 630:15
he laid down his a. HOOD 382:18
His a. might do WALL 800:6
if my love were in my a. ANON 19:13
in an a. race LEON 464:11
in my a. BALL 50:18
it hath very long a. HALI 357:18
keep and bear a. CONS 235:13
Kings have long a. PROV 605:4
man's outspread a. LEON 464:17
mightier than they in a. MILT 517:5
proud in a. MILT 511:15
This world in a. EISE 291:8
Those entrusted with a. WIND 823:4
To war and a. LOVE 476:15
world in a. SHAK 677:21
army a. marches on its stomach NAPO 539:1
a. marches on its stomach PROV 595:16
a. of Martyrs BOOK 125:20
a. of unalterable law MERE 505:20
a. would be a base rabble BURK 163:7
contemptible little a. ANON 16:6
Forgotten A. MOUN 534:9
formation of an Irish a. GRIF 353:9
invasion by an a. HUGO 393:18
joined the British A. LEDW 461:17
little ships brought the A. home GUED 354:10
terrible as an a. BIBL 86:1
Your poor a. CROM 245:18
Arno pined by A. MACA 482:23
aroint A. thee, witch SHAK 681:11
aroma a. of performing seals HART 363:5
aromatic beneath the a. pain WINC 823:1
rose in a. pain POPE 585:14

arose a. and followed him BIBL 94:22
around goes a. comes around SAYI 648:8
aroused a. every feeling TAYL 756:4
a-roving go no more a. SONG 729:1
arrange French a. CATH 194:6
arrangements has no a. WHIT 815:21
arrears pay glad life's a. BROW 157:17
arrest a. all beauty CAME 182:13
swift in his a. SHAK 667:7
arrested a. one fine morning OPEN 556:17
conservative been a. WOLF 825:13
arrival a. was most welcome NELS 540:17
arrive A. or find THOM 773:15
a. where I am BUNY 161:18
a. where we started ELIO 294:17
barbarians are to a. CAVA 198:7
better thing than to a. STEV 741:25
arrived a. and to prove it CATC 196:6
arrogant subdue the a. VIRG 795:1
arrow a. from the Almighty's bow BLAK 119:1
a.-head of grieving PALI 565:23
a. that flieth by day BOOK 137:22
Every a. that flies LONG 473:13
shot an a. LONG 473:9
shot mine a. SHAK 667:4
time's a. EDDI 287:21
arrows archer his sharp a. SIDN 718:10
a. of desire BLAK 120:1
Like as the a. BOOK 140:22
mine a. upon them BIBL 77:13
slings and a. SHAK 664:3
swift a. in my quiver PIND 576:9
ars *A. longa, vita brevis* HIPP 377:15
arse politician is an a. upon CUMM 247:7
Sit on your a. for fifty years MACN 488:8
arsenal a. of old Europe HEGE 367:12
great a. of democracy ROOS 632:17
arsenic like a. FIEL 310:11
art adulteries of a. JONS 419:20
all the rules of a. ADDI 5:18
almost lost in A. COLL 229:13
A. alone Enduring stays DOBS 271:14
A. always serves beauty PAST 569:5
A. and Religion are two roads BELL 62:19
A. a revolt against fate MALR 493:2
a. can wash her guilt away GOLD 345:30
a. constantly aspires PATE 569:14
A. does not reproduce the visible KLEE 442:2
A. for art's sake CONS 235:10
a. for art's sake COUS 238:6
A. for art's sake DIET 267:11
a. for the sake SAND 643:17
a. has an author WEIL 808:26
a. has no other end FLAU 316:20
A. has something to do BELL 64:14
A. in its perfection REYN 625:11
A. is a jealous mistress EMER 299:14
A. is an abstraction GAUG 331:4
A. is born of humiliation AUDE 35:16
a. is but a vision of reality YEAT 835:22
a. is immoral WILD 818:4
A. is long LONG 474:4
A. is long PROV 595:17
A. is meant to disturb BRAQ 147:2
A. is not a *brassière* BARN 54:18
a. is not a weapon KENN 433:18
A. is not truth PICA 576:5
A. is only Nature HOLB 380:16
A. is pattern informed by sensibility READ 622:11
A. is significant deformity FRY 326:27
A. is the imposing of a pattern WHIT 814:16
A. is the objectification LANG 450:14
A. is upon the Town WHIS 813:17
A. is vice DEGA 255:17
A. most cherishes BROW 157:2
a. of balance MATI 501:13
a. of being wise JAME 404:2
a. of getting drunk JOHN 416:9
a. of the possible BISM 116:6
a. of the possible GALB 328:11
a. of the soluble MEDA 503:6
a.'s hid causes JONS 419:19
a. which one government sooner SMIT 723:13
beyond the reach of a. POPE 584:14
clever, but is it A. KIPL 438:9
dead a. Of poetry POUN 589:12
Deals are my a. form TRUM 784:11
Desiring this man's a. SHAK 704:14
detective novel is a.-for-art's-sake PRIT 593:9
Dying is an a. PLAT 577:17
E in A-level a. HIRS 377:19
end and test of a. POPE 584:13
enemy of good a. CONN 233:26
example of modern a. CHUR 216:24
fascinating kind of a. WARH 803:13
Fine a. is that RUSK 638:26
first taught A. ROSS 635:3
Football is an a. GREE 352:12
from a., not chance POPE 584:22
genius and a. HAZL 365:14
glib and oily a. SHAK 677:25
good grey guardians of a. WILB 817:7
grandeur of the a. REYN 625:7
great design of a. DENN 258:2
great religious a. of the world CLAR 219:7
have learned their a. PIND 576:9
Here the great a. lies MILT 519:11
history of a. BUTL 172:24
If a. does not enlarge ELIO 293:14
In a. the best is good enough GOET 343:6
industry without a. RUSK 638:8
in Jonson, A. DENH 257:13
is the a. of God YOUN 839:14
it is not a. SCHO 649:1
last and greatest a. GOET 343:16
last and greatest a. POPE 586:18
Life imitates A. WILD 818:6
Life is short, the a. long HIPP 377:15
madness of a. JAME 403:8
Minister that meddles with a. MELB 503:15
morality of a. WILD 818:16
More matter with less a. SHAK 663:11
my job and my a. MONT 527:17
nature is the a. of God BROW 153:20
nature's handmaid a. DRYD 200:28
Nature that is above all a. DANI 240:17
necessary a. DULL 284:13
never was an A.-loving nation WHIS 813:18
next to Nature, A. LAND 450:1
noblest point of a. EPIT 302:6
offered you Conflict and A. PRIE 591:13
only interested in a. SHAW 709:25
people start on all this A. HERB 371:13
probité de l'a. INGR 399:19
rank of every a. REYN 625:8
responsibility is to his a. FAUL 308:1
revenge of the intellect upon a. SONT 728:5
Robust a. alone is eternal GAUT 331:6
Shakespeare wanted a. JONS 421:1
stick to murder and leave a. EPST 301:1
Story the spoiled child of a. JAME 402:24
supreme master of a. CONR 234:22
symbol of Irish a. JOYC 422:8
through A., and through Art only WILD 818:3
true test of a. INGR 399:19
War's glorious a. YOUN 838:20
what great a. removes BOLA 124:9
when A. Is too precise HERR 374:8
where the a. resides SCHN 648:22
works of a. ALBE 10:6
Works of a. RILK 627:19
artful a. Dodger DICK 264:14
Arthur in A.'s bosom SHAK 671:2
talks of A.'s death SHAK 677:16
article excellent a. BAGE 47:21
first a. of my faith GAND 329:6
snuffed out by an a. BYRO 177:18
articles These a. subscribed CONG 233:13
articulate made a. all that I saw BROW 151:19
When they call you a. ICE- 398:16
artifact Death's a. ABSE 1:7
artificer great a. Made my mate STEV 742:22
lean unwashed a. SHAK 677:16
artificial All things are a. BROW 153:20
but an a. man HOBB 378:12
said it was a. respiration BURG 161:25
sort of a. inlet FOST 321:12
artillery a. of words SWIF 749:11
love's great a. CRAS 244:10
terrible a. FLAT 316:6
artisan employment to the a. BELL 63:23
artist a. a receptacle PICA 575:17
a. brings something into UPDI 788:16
a. has no need to express PROU 594:6
a. is his own fault O'HA 553:4
a. is someone who WARH 803:14
a. man and the mother woman SHAW 708:1
a. must be in his work FLAU 316:17
a. never dies LONG 474:1
a. remains within or behind JOYC 422:4
a. will be judged CONN 234:4
enemies to a real a. GAIN 327:17
God only another a. PICA 576:3
Industry, Which dignifies the a. DYER 286:15
Never trust the a. LAWR 458:4
No a. should ever marry DELI 256:24
no man is born an a. WALT 802:14
one position for an a. THOM 772:15
portrait of the a. JOYC 421:22
sign of a true a. VIDA 792:12
task of the a. BECK 59:19
What an a. dies LAST 457:2
artistic a. verisimilitude GILB 338:13
never was an a. period WHIS 813:18
artists A. not engineers of the soul KENN 433:18
arts a. at first from Nature came LANI 451:3
a. babblative and scribblative SOUT 731:1
cry both a. and learning QUAR 618:22
Dear nurse of a. SHAK 672:4
followed the a. SHAK 701:1
France, famed in all great a. ARNO 28:1
France, mother of a. DU B 283:21
head of the a. BLOM 122:7
interested in the a. AYCK 40:2
In the a. of life BLUM 708:7
mother of a. MILT 518:8
No a.; no letters HOBB 378:21
one of the fine a. DE Q 258:10
recreation in the a. CONF 231:16
studied the liberal a. OVID 561:9
virtues were his a. BURK 165:15
you 'a.' people MCEW 485:6
artus *totamque infusa per a.* VIRG 794:22
Aryan your A. eye PLAT 577:13
ascend that would a. OPEN 556:6
ascendancy a. of the Whig party MACA 482:5
ascended a. into heaven BOOK 126:10
ascendeth a. up for ever and ever BIBL 112:25
ascending angels of God a. BIBL 75:1
lark a. MERE 505:18
ascribe A. unto the Lord BOOK 138:7
ash a. on an old man's sleeve ELIO 294:14
avoid an a. PROV 596:16
empty a. can CRAN 243:21
Oak, and A., and Thorn KIPL 440:14
oak is before the a. PROV 614:30
Out of the a. PLAT 577:18
ashamed a. and confounded BOOK 136:14
a. thereof BROW 153:24
a. to look upon one another WALT 802:20
feel a. of home DICK 262:21
men are a. of GAY 332:18
more things a man is a. of SHAW 707:31
something he is a. of SHAW 706:19
ashbuds a. in the front of March TENN 758:21

ashen in oure a. olde CHAU 206:9
Your a. hair Shulamith CELA 199:8
ashes a. for thirty LAMP 449:16
a. new-create SHAK 673:27
a. of an Oak DONN 275:5
a. of his fathers MACA 483:5
a. on the lips MOOR 530:19
a. taken to Australia ANON 17:2
a. to ashes BOOK 131:14
a. to the taste BYRO 174:16
a. under Uricon HOUS 391:3
beauty for a. BIBL 89:6
burnt to a. GRAH 348:5
Dust and a. BROW 158:9
I am a. BYRO 179:8
into a. all my lust MARV 499:3
past is a bucket of a. SAND 644:1
sour grapes and a. ASHF 30:15
universe to a. MISS 523:3
Asia churches which are in A. BIBL 111:17
churches which are in A. BIBL 111:20
not in A. ARDR 23:20
pampered jades of A. MARL 497:3
Will end up in A. BLY 122:15
Asian A. boys ought to be JOHN 408:17
Asians A. could still smile HEAD 365:24
aside set death a. TURG 785:4
ask all that we do a. BIBL 108:1
a. and cannot answer SHAW 709:29
A., and it shall be given BIBL 94:3
a. faithfully BOOK 128:19
a. if you are enjoying NESB 541:9
a. is have SMAR 722:11
A. me no more CARE 186:13
A. me no more TENN 766:2
a. nothing ELGA 291:18
a. not what your country KENN 433:14
could a. him anything WEIS 809:1
Don't a., don't tell NUNN 547:9
Don't a. me, ask the horse FREU 324:16
Don't let's a. for the moon FILM 311:3
for our blindness we cannot a. BOOK 130:6
if you gotta a. ARMS 25:17
if you gotta a. MISQ 522:1
To a. the hard question AUDE 35:9
Would this man a. why AUDE 33:25
askance looking a., other nations GOGO 344:2
asked Nobody a. you NURS 551:20
You've a. for it MOLI 525:8
asketh Every one that a. receiveth BIBL 94:4
asking a. too much CANN 184:19
mere a. of a question FORS 320:22
time of a. BOOK 130:21
aslant grows a. a brook SHAK 666:12
asleep Fall a., or hearing die SHAK 673:10
Half a. as they stalk HARD 361:16
men were all a. BRID 148:8
sucks the nurse a. SHAK 658:3
those that are a. BIBL 86:6
till it falls a. TEMP 757:5
very houses seem a. WORD 828:1
asp hole of the a. BIBL 87:5
asparagus Grew like a. in May GILB 337:9
aspens Willows whiten, a. quiver TENN 762:13
asperges *A. me, Domine* MISS 520:6
A. me hyssopo BIBL 113:18
aspersion a. upon my parts of speech SHER 715:27
aspes as an a. leef CHAU 207:10
asphalt only monument the a. road ELIO 295:22
aspidistra biggest a. in the world HARP 362:12
Keep the a. flying ORWE 558:15
thick leaf of the a. GREE 352:1
aspiration a., to do nought ROSS 635:7
aspire by due steps a. MILT 511:14
gaze, and there a. ARNO 27:20
light, and will a. SHAK 705:29
when men a. MARL 496:11
aspirin a. for a brain tumour CHAN 201:15
ass a., without being a fool SURT 746:15
call great Caesar a. SHAK 658:2
crowned a. HENR 370:8
dull a. will not mend SHAK 666:19
enamoured of an a. SHAK 690:14
firstborn the greatest a. CARO 189:3
kiss my a. in Macy's window JOHN 408:18
law is a a. DICK 264:19
law is such an a. CHAP 202:20
making him egregiously an a. SHAK 692:14
not covet his a. BIBL 76:13
on his unwashed a. PARS 568:5
with the jaw of an a. BIBL 78:4
You're an a. ROCH 630:18
assailed A., fight, taken DONN 272:14
assassin copperheads and the a. SAND 643:19
you are an a. ROST 635:16
assassination absolutism moderated by a. ANON 16:3
a. Could trammel up SHAK 682:8
A. has never changed DISR 269:3
A. is the extreme form SHAW 709:19
A. is the quickest MOLI 525:16
assault a. and hurt the soul BOOK 128:4
assaults a. of our enemies BOOK 126:12
a. of the devil BOOK 127:3
assay a. so hard CHAU 206:28
assemblies calling of a. BIBL 86:11
asserted boldly a. BURR 169:13
asses Death hath a.' ears BEDD 60:17
go seek the a. BIBL 78:20
seeking a. found MILT 518:6
to those great a. LUTH 480:5
assigned doom a. TENN 764:17
assume A. a virtue SHAK 665:22
assurance a. given by looks ROYD 637:1
a. of incorruption BIBL 91:14
low on whom a. sits ELIO 296:10
make a. double sure SHAK 685:1
Assyrian A. came down BYRO 175:23
curled A. Bull TENN 763:24
Astarte A., queen of heaven MILT 514:25
Astolat lily maid of A. TENN 759:25
astonish A. me DIAG 260:1
a. the bourgeois BAUD 57:13
astonished a. at eclipse ORCH 557:8
a. at my own moderation CLIV 221:9
rightly a. by events BART 56:5
astonishment Your a.'s odd KNOX 442:14
astounded a. by them ATTE 31:21
astra *ardua ad a.* MOTT 535:14
sic itur ad a. VIRG 795:8
astray as sheep going a. BIBL 111:1
like sheep have gone a. BIBL 88:17
not send their works a. KORA 445:8
astrologers A. or three wise men LONG 475:6
astronomers and a. QUIN 619:6
astrology A. is a disease MAIM 491:9
astronomer undevout a. is mad YOUN 839:12
astronomers a. and astrologers QUIN 619:6
astronomy daughter of a. YOUN 839:12
linked in a. LOVE 476:17
Astur cry is A. MACA 483:8
asunder bones are smitten a. BOOK 134:8
let no man put a. BOOK 131:7
let not man put a. BIBL 96:12
asylum lunatic a. run by lunatics LLOY 471:6
taken charge of the a. ROWL 636:15
was in an a. PALM 566:8
ate a. when we were not hungry SWIF 748:2
Freddie Starr a. my hamster NEWS 544:5
With A. by his side SHAK 675:22
atheism inclineth man's mind to a. BACO 42:7
owlet A. COLE 225:11
atheist a. half believes a God YOUN 839:9
a. is a man BUCH 159:9
a.-laugh's a poor exchange BURN 167:3
denial of Him by the a. PROU 594:6
female a. JOHN 411:9
from being an a. SART 645:9
I am still an a. BUÑU 160:13
remain a sound a. LEWI 466:20
sort of a. ORWE 558:12
superstitious a. BROW 155:9
village a. brooding CHES 211:15
was no a. CHAR 203:8
atheistical damned a. age VANB 789:6
atheists far from a. CUDW 247:1
no a. in the foxholes CUMM 247:14
Athenians A. and strangers BIBL 104:7
Athens A. arose SHEL 711:11
A., the eye of Greece MILT 518:8
citizen of A. SOCR 726:23
Ye men of A. BIBL 104:8
athirst give unto him that is a. BIBL 113:9
Atlanta A. is gone CHES 208:23
Atlantic steep A. stream MILT 511:16
stormy North A. Ocean LARD 452:9
Atlas A. of the state COWP 241:9
atlas blank a. of your body NERU 541:4
atman A., the Spirit in man UPAN 787:10
A., the Spirit, the Self UPAN 787:22
That [*A.*] is not this UPAN 787:15
atmosphere shove against an a. EDDI 288:1
atom a. has changed everything EINS 290:16
carbon a. JEAN 404:19
defence against the a. bomb ANON 15:14
done with the a. LEAC 459:14
flaring a.-streams TENN 763:16
grasped the mystery of the a. BRAD 146:10
leads through the a. EDDI 288:2
atomic primordial a. globule GILB 337:22
win an a. war BRAD 146:9
atoms a. and space DEMO 257:2
a. of Democritus BLAK 120:3
A. or systems POPE 585:8
concurrence of a. PALM 566:4
motions of a. in my brain HALD 356:16
record the a. WOOL 826:15
atone a. for our past CHEK 208:3
atrocities a. however horrible NAMI 538:6
attach wish to a. AUST 38:4
attachment free from a. BHAG 73:3
attack a. from Mars SALI 643:3
A. is best form of defence PROV 595:28
by his plan of a. SASS 645:22
lead such dire a. MACA 483:9
Problems worthy of a. HEIN 368:2
attacked when a. it defends itself ANON 20:3
attacking I am a. FOCH 318:22
attain I cannot a. unto it BOOK 141:10
attainable We look at the a. GLAD 341:4
attempt a. and not the deed SHAK 683:5
that dares love a. SHAK 697:13
attempted Something a. LONG 474:20
attendant a. lord, one that will do ELIO 295:9
attention a. must be paid MILL 509:21
a. to the object WEIL 808:25
Enforce a. SHAK 694:17
attentive a. and favourable hearers HOOK 383:5
attic A. grace POUN 589:14
Beauty crieth in an a. BUTL 173:3
brain a. stocked DOYL 277:10
furniture in Tolkien's a. PRAT 591:3
glory of the A. stage ARNO 27:30
O A. shape KEAT 428:28
sleeps up in the a. there MEW 506:13
Where the A. bird MILT 518:8
attire bride forget her a. BIBL 89:10
Her rich a. KEAT 427:10
attitude Fair a. KEAT 428:28
attitudes Anglo-Saxon a. CARR 191:7
attorney a.'s Elderly ugly daughter GILB 339:11
gentleman was an *a.* JOHN 414:9
attracted a. by God INGE 399:6
attraction A. and repulsion BLAK 119:9
feels the a. of earth LONG 473:13

attraction (*cont.*):
put a. on BEHN 62:9
sure a. led POPE 580:17
that powerful a. SHEL 715:1
attractions Costs register competing a. KNIG 442:7
attributes through each of his a. ZOHA 840:12
auburn Sweet A., loveliest village GOLD 344:7
audace *toujours de l'a.* DANT 250:6
audacity Arm me, a. SHAK 660:18
a. of elected persons WHIT 815:9
tactful in a. COCT 223:19
aude *sapere a.* HORA 386:15
audendi *a. semper fuit aequa potestas* HORA 385:11
audi *A. partem alteram* AUGU 36:8
audience fit a. find MILT 517:6
is a large a. TROL 782:25
whisks his a. HORA 386:1
audiences English-speaking a. WHAR 813:1
two kinds of a. SCHN 648:21
audio-visual full of a. marvels SMIT 724:6
audit how his a. stands SHAK 665:9
auditorem *notas a. rapit* HORA 386:1
augmentation a. of the Indies SHAK 702:7
augury we defy a. SHAK 667:3
august A. for the people AUDE 33:22
A. is a wicked month O'BR 552:8
corny as Kansas in A. HAMM 359:3
recommence in A. BYRO 177:23
Augustan next A. age WALP 801:3
Augustus A. was a chubby lad HOFF 379:17
auld do wi' an a. man BURN 169:9
For a. lang syne BURN 166:12
aunt A. is calling to Aunt WODE 824:19
Charley's a. from Brazil THOM 771:16
aunts bad a. and good aunts WODE 824:14
dull a., and croaking rooks POPE 584:7
his cousins and his a. GILB 338:26
auream *A. quisquis mediocritatem* HORA 388:7
auri *A. sacra fames* VIRG 794:8
Auschwitz [illegible] Jew from A. AUDE 35:19
write a poem after A. ADOR 6:7
year spent in A. LEVI 466:6
austere beauty cold and a. RUSS 639:22
austerities monk destroys by a. JAIN 402:5
Austerlitz A. and Waterloo SAND 643:21
field of A. KIPL 440:6
Australia A. has a marvellous sky LAWR 458:20
take A. right back KEAT 426:12
Australian great A. Emptiness WHIT 814:6
Australians A. wouldn't give ADVE 7:7
Austria Don John of A. is going CHES 210:11
author amended By its A. EPIT 302:1
art has an a. WEIL 808:26
a. and finisher of our faith BIBL 110:2
a. and giver BOOK 128:14
a. of his own disgrace COWP 240:9
a. of peace BOOK 126:12
a. ought to write FITZ 315:17
a. who speaks DISR 269:12
Choose an a. DILL 267:13
expected to see an a. PASC 568:8
go to the a. RUSK 638:15
half an a.'s graces MORE 530:23
in search of an a. PIRA 576:15
like in a good a. SMIT 724:15
majesty of the A. of things LEIB 462:24
more than wit to become an a. LA B 446:19
No a. ever spared a brother GAY 332:7
shrimp of an a. GRAY 351:8
store Of the first a. MARV 499:5
to be an a. HAZL 365:18
authoress dared to be an a. AUST 39:10
authorities imposed by the a. PLAT 578:3
authority adduces a. LEON 464:12
A. forgets a dying king TENN 760:12
a. of the eternal yesterday WEBE 807:6
Experience, though noon a. CHAU 206:15
in a. under her BOOK 129:12
little brief a. SHAK 686:10
make your peace with a. MORR 533:2
man under a. BIBL 94:16
maximal a. and minimal power SZAS 751:23
no a. from God to do mischief MAYH 502:20
taught them as one having a. BIBL 94:14
than in a. THOM 770:22
authorized copy of the A. Version WHAT 813:12
authors A. are like cattle LAND 450:6
a. their copyrights TROL 781:18
damn those a. CHUR 213:12
great a. have their due BACO 41:7
invades a. like a monarch DRYD 283:7
praise of ancient a. HOBB 379:5
'Till a. hear at length COWP 241:12
women-a. COOP 236:7
authorship popular a. TROL 783:11
autobiography age to write an a. WAUG 806:6
a. is an obituary CRIS 245:5
A. is now as common GRIG 353:13
autocrat a.: that's my trade CATH 194:12
considerate a. STEP 738:2
automatic smoothes her hair with a. hand ELIO 296:11
automobile fix up his a. CLAR 219:14
like an a. ROOT 633:14
autres *encourager les a.* VOLT 797:8
autumn a. arrives BOWE 145:11
a. evening ARNO 27:2
cloudy days of a. CLAR 218:18
Early a. BASH 56:14
happy a. fields TENN 765:19
harmony In a. SHEL 711:17
I saw old A. HOOD 382:26
mists of the a. mornings ORWE 558:17
Now it is a. LAWR 458:12
autumnal A. winds prevail SMAR 722:8
deep a. tone SHEL 712:17
one a. face DONN 272:10
availeth struggle naught a. CLOU 223:2
avalanche [illegible] of a mighty a. HOUS 391:12
avarice a. begin AUST 38:21
a., lust, ambition SHER 716:21
A., the spur HUME 394:10
By a. and selfishness THOR 776:1
dreams of a. JOHN 416:20
dreams of a. MOOR 529:10
must take up with a. BYRO 176:10
punishment Is a. JONS 420:6
very prone to a. KORA 444:14
ave *a. atque vale* CATU 198:1
A. Maria PRAY 592:1
A. verum corpus ANON 21:6
songs were A. Marys CORB 236:13
avenge a. even a look BURK 163:20
avenger from my dead bones, a. VIRG 794:14
Time, the a. BYRO 175:1
average a. guy who could carry EPIT 303:8
averages fugitive from th' law of a. MAUL 502:8
Averno *Facilis descensus A.* VIRG 794:17
aversion begin with a little a. SHER 715:24
bordering on a. STEV 741:10
manner which is my a. BYRO 176:30
avertant *di omen a.* CICE 217:22
Avilion island-valley of A. TENN 760:17
avis *Rara a.* JUVE 424:14
avocados Wives in the a. GINS 339:22
Avogadro bigness of A.'s number BENT 66:15
avoid wise man should a. wrath JAIN 401:15
avoiding a. being TILL 777:13
a. superstition BACO 44:9
Avon Sweet Swan of A. JONS 420:26
awake A., my soul KEN 432:18
A., O north wind BIBL 85:17
a. right early BOOK 135:17
a. while sleeping MONT 528:3
Being now a. SHAK 703:23
England! a. BLAK 119:4
West's a. DAVI 252:17
When you're lying a. GILB 337:18
awaked must be a. BIBL 79:28
So the Lord a. BOOK 137:7
awakenings dream between two a. O'NE 554:21
aware a. of all the evil LA R 453:17
a. that you are happy KRIS 446:1
insignificant and is a. of it BECK 59:8
surely God is a. KORA 444:14
away a.! for I will fly KEAT 429:11
A. from me BOOK 131:25
go a. for ever MURD 537:1
Over the hills and far a. STEV 743:5
Rain, rain, go a. NURS 550:11
WHEN I'M A. TELE 758:6
awe a. into the beholders SWIF 747:17
In a. of such a thing SHAK 674:9
keep the strong in a. SHAK 696:32
Stand in a., and sin not BOOK 131:19
wonder and a. KANT 425:12
aweary a. of the sun SHAK 685:23
Cassius is a. SHAK 676:25
I am a., aweary TENN 763:19
awful bleeding and muddy and a. RHYS 625:19
this is an a. place SCOT 650:7
awfully a. big adventure BARR 55:16
awkward a. squad fire over me LAST 455:11
awoke a. one morning BYRO 180:11
a. one morning OPEN 556:26
So I a., and behold BUNY 161:9
When Gregor Samsa a. one morning KAFK 425:9
awry leaning all a. FITZ 314:19
axe a. is laid unto the root BIBL 92:30
a.'s edge did try MARV 498:19
a. to the root PAIN 563:20
let the great a. fall SHAK 666:10
Lizzie Borden took an a. ANON 17:10
axes have you your sharp-edged a. WHIT 815:7
no a. being ground BROU 151:17
axis a. of the earth HOLM 381:5
sword the a. of the world DE G 255:29
axle fly sat upon the a.-tree BACO 44:20
Azores Flores in the A. TENN 766:8
Aztec destroyed the A. Empire SCHU 649:6
azure a. sister of the spring SHEL 712:12
a., white, and red DRUM 279:14
out of the a. main THOM 774:20
slept an a.-lidded sleep KEAT 427:13

baa B., baa, black sheep NURS 547:12
babblative b. and scribblative SOUT 731:1
babble Coffee house b. DISR 269:16
babbled b. of green fields SHAK 671:3
babbler this b. BIBL 104:6
babe b. was born in a manger WHIT 814:19
birth-strangled b. SHAK 684:19
Come little b. BRET 148:4
love the b. SHAK 682:17
naked new-born b. SHAK 682:11
pretty B. all burning SOUT 731:9
young b. were born BALL 52:9
Babel bother at the tower of B. VOLT 798:9
stir Of the great B. COWP 241:32
babes As newborn b. BIBL 110:27
b. and sucklings BOOK 131:26
mouths of b. PROV 609:17
babies b. in the tomatoes GINS 339:22
Ballads and b. MCCA 484:5
hates dogs and b. ROST 635:17
If men had to have b. DIAN 260:3
Other people's b. HERB 371:14
putting milk into b. CHUR 215:20
twelve-year-olds having b. GING 339:18

Babiy Yar Over B. there are no memorials YEVT 838:9
Bab-lock-hithe Thames at B. ARNO 27:6
baboon b. and monkey SHAK 699:14
he who understands b. DARW 251:3
baby b. beats the nurse SHAK 686:1
b. doesn't understand English KNOX 442:15
b. figure of the giant SHAK 700:9
B. in an ox's stall BETJ 70:5
b. out with the bathwater PROV 598:40
Begin, b. boy VIRG 796:5
Burn, b., burn POLI 581:9
come from, b. dear MACD 484:20
first b. laughed BARR 55:14
I'm your little b. LEWI 467:5
my b. at my breast SHAK 658:3
one for my b. MERC 505:7
Who loves ya, b. CATC 196:28
Babylon B. be thrown down BIBL 113:1
B. in all its desolation DAVI 252:4
B. is fallen BIBL 112:24
By the waters of B. BOOK 141:7
By the waters of B. WALP 801:4
Ere B. was dust SHEL 713:4
How many miles to B. NURS 548:15
King in B. HENL 370:2
modern b. DISR 270:30
MYSTERY, B. THE GREAT BIBL 112:31
Bacchus charioted by B. KEAT 429:11
baccy B. for the Clerk KIPL 440:8
Bach B. almost persuades me FRY 326:28
of J. S. B. BEEC 61:6
they play only B. BART 56:6
bachelor b. never quite gets over ROWL 636:13
bachelors b. to go out ELIO 293:6
reformers are b. MOOR 529:11
back at my b. from time to time I hear ELIO 296:7
at my b. I always hear MARV 499:2
b. in the closet lays FITZ 314:15
B. in the USSR LENN 463:18
b. in the water ADVE 7:37
b. to common earth again FITZ 314:21
B. to the future FILM 312:16
boys in the b. room LOES 473:1
boys in the b. rooms BEAV 59:3
counted them all b. HANR 359:11
Empire strikes b. FILM 312:19
got over the Devil's b. PROV 614:2
in the small of the b. WODE 824:17
looking b. BIBL 99:7
makes b. to the burden PROV 601:14
never turned his b. BROW 155:4
Not to go b. POPE 586:9
plowers plowed upon my b. BOOK 140:25
sit on a man's b. TOLS 779:14
steps b. for fear WALP 802:1
those before cried 'B.!' MACA 483:9
time to get b. to basics MAJO 491:17
wouldn't want them b. BECK 59:14
backhand wonderful b. drive BETJ 71:2
backing I'm b. Britain SAYI 647:25
plague upon such b. SHAK 668:4
backs beast with two b. SHAK 691:26
With our b. to the wall HAIG 356:9
backward B. ran sentences GIBB 336:9
by b. steps would move VAUG 790:10
let them be turned b. BOOK 136:14
look b. to their ancestors BURK 163:16
never go b. SEWA 655:3
walking b. into future ZHVA 840:2
backwards memory that only works b. CARR 190:24
backyards clean American b. MAIL 491:2
bacon b.'s not the only thing KING 437:17
bacons On, b., on SHAK 667:32
bad always b. men ACTO 1:17
and the b. unhappily WILD 817:19
b. as bad can be JOHN 417:10
b. at heart BELL 63:12
b. aunts and good aunts WODE 824:14
b. die late DEFO 255:4
b. end unhappily STOP 743:19
b. in the best of us ANON 19:4
B. laws BURK 164:28
B. money drives out good PROV 595:30
b. news for you ATWO 32:9
b. news infects SHAK 656:11
B. news travels fast PROV 595:31
b. penny always turns up PROV 595:32
b. publicity BEHA 62:5
b. taste HOPK 385:7
b. times just around COWA 238:20
B. women never take the blame BROO 150:19
better For being a little b. SHAK 686:26
bold b. man SPEN 733:15
brave b. man CLAR 218:23
brave b. man CLOS 222:12
cannot be of a b. colour PROV 601:26
come to a b. end BEER 61:14
Defend the b. against the worse DAY- 253:14
either good or b. SHAK 663:16
everything is b. BRAD 146:8
for one b. man HESI 375:12
for those who are b. YESE 838:8
from b. to worse TOCQ 778:11
good, the b., and the ugly FILM 312:21
good ye are and b. TENN 759:23
How sad and b. BROW 155:22
Mad, b., and dangerous LAMB 448:8
make b. good SHAK 686:22
make them feel b. MONT 528:18
neither good nor b. BALZ 52:17
Nothing so b. but PROV 608:15
put up with b. things TROL 782:22
sad b. glad mad SWIN 750:12
shocking b. hats WELL 809:21
This bold b. man SHAK 673:8
When b. men combine BURK 164:16
when she was b. LONG 475:2
where roads were b. LEE 462:2
badge b. of all our tribe SHAK 687:15
red b. of courage CRAN 243:27
badgers When b. fight CLAR 218:6
badly end b. STEV 742:8
worth doing b. CHES 211:18
badness good and no b. SKEL 721:10
bag b. and baggage GLAD 340:19
b. with holes BIBL 90:24
Lays eggs inside a paper b. ISHE 400:7
old b. lady HEAL 366:4
out of a tattered b. PROV 612:25
with b. and baggage SHAK 659:8
bagatelle vive la b. STER 738:9
baggage bag and b. GLAD 340:19
b. loves me CONG 232:28
bagman Cobden is an inspired b. CARL 188:21
bags carry other people's b. FILM 312:12
bah 'B.,' said Scrooge DICK 261:8
Bailey come home Bill B. CANN 185:9
bailiff b.'s daughter BALL 50:4
Bainters hate all Boets and B. GEOR 333:9
bairns Fools and b. PROV 600:36
baits b. do fleetest fish entice GASC 330:16
bake b. so shall you brew PROV 595:22
brew, so shall you b. PROV 595:23
baked b. cookies and had teas CLIN 221:1
b. in this pie SHAK 700:2
get out of b. beans O'RE 557:13
baker b. rhymes for his pursuit BROW 157:27
b.'s man NURS 550:5
butcher, the b. NURS 550:15
bakers b. and breweres LANG 450:18
Baker Street B. irregulars DOYL 278:3
Bakewell B. in half-an-hour RUSK 638:13
balance art of b. MATI 501:13
b. and weight that equalizes CERV 200:5
b. of power KISS 441:26
b. of power NICO 544:22
b. of the Old CANN 185:6
small dust of the b. BIBL 88:3
uncertain b. of proud time GREE 352:2
words in a b. BIBL 92:4
balances weighed in the b. BIBL 90:4
bald b., and short of breath SASS 645:15
b. and unconvincing GILB 338:13
b. as the bare mountain ARNO 28:25
fight between two b. men BORG 143:7
found him b. too BROW 155:32
Go up, thou b. head BIBL 80:14
baldness far side of b. SMIT 724:9
Balfour of the B. declaration WEIZ 809:2
Balkans damned silly thing in the B. BISM 116:15
ball b. no question makes FITZ 314:16
b. rolled out of reach AGAT 6:16
girl throwing a b. WOOL 827:1
real business of a b. SURT 747:3
that portion of the b. POPE 580:13
wind it into a b. BLAK 119:3
yawning at a b. LERM 464:23
ballad love a b. in print SHAK 703:21
metre b.-mongers SHAK 668:20
met with a b. CALV 182:2
ballads B. and babies MCCA 484:5
b., songs and snatches GILB 337:21
permitted to make all the b. FLET 317:22
ballet b. in the evening HACK 355:10
Ballinderry B. in the springtime FERG 308:17
Balliol God be with you, B. men BELL 64:9
balloon b. of experience JAME 402:26
something in a huge b. WORD 830:15
balloons Of air-b. BYRO 176:2
ballot b. is stronger than MISQ 521:3
rap at the b. box CHIL 211:25
ballots peaceful b. LINC 468:4
balls B. will be lost always BERR 69:17
elliptical billiard b. GILB 338:10
rackets to these b. SHAK 670:29
With two pitch b. SHAK 680:23
Ballyjamesduff to B. FREN 324:8
balm B. of hurt minds SHAK 683:8
b. upon the world KEAT 427:19
general b. DONN 274:9
no b. in Gilead BIBL 89:16
wash the b. SHAK 695:5
balmy Ginger, you're b. MURR 537:4
Baltimore then you're in B. GORD 347:1
ban B. the bomb POLI 581:3
banal b. Eldorado BAUD 57:9
banality b. of evil AREN 24:1
manufacture of b. SARR 644:19
Banbury to B. Cross NURS 550:12
band heaven-born b. HOPK 385:9
of this ruined b. SHAK 671:9
we b. of brothers SHAK 671:25
when the wearied B. HUXL 397:7
bandage wound, not the b. POTT 588:22
bandaged death b. my eyes BROW 157:17
Bandar-log What the B. think KIPL 441:2
bandied struck and b. WEBS 808:5
bands b. of love BIBL 90:11
b. of Orion BIBL 81:34
b. of wickedness BIBL 89:1
Most people get into b. GELD 332:27
bandy b. civilities JOHN 413:24
bane Deserve the precious b. MILT 515:4
baneful b. effects WASH 804:7
bang B.! Now the animal Is dead DE L 256:13
b.-up chariot DICK 264:26
b.—went saxpence PUNC 617:9
bigger b. for a buck POLI 581:7
If the big b. does come OSBO 560:8
Kiss Kiss B. Bang KAEL 425:6
no terror in a b. HITC 378:3
Not with a b. but a whimper ELIO 294:26
bangs b. one about ELIZ 298:3
banish b. not him SHAK 668:16
b. them to their couches KORA 444:7
I b. you SHAK 660:8
banished Alone, a b. man BALL 51:7
art b. hence MILT 518:1

banishment bitter bread of b. SHAK 695:4
bank b. and shoal of time SHAK 682:8
b. will lend you money HOPE 383:17
cry all the way to the b. LIBE 467:16
deposit at a Swiss b. ALLE 12:15
I know a b. SHAK 689:25
pregnant b. swelled up DONN 273:24
robbing a b. BREC 147:19
sleeps upon this b. SHAK 688:21
waly, up the b. BALL 52:7
banker as a Scotch b. DAVI 252:2
banking as much as we value b. TOYN 780:6
b. and prostitution WRIG 833:11
banknotes fill old bottles with b. KEYN 435:9
bankrupt B. of life DRYD 280:3
bankruptcy intellectual b. HOLM 381:12
banks bonnie, bonnie b. SONG 730:1
Letters from b. AUDE 34:13
Ye b. and braes BURN 166:16
banner b. with the strange device LONG 473:16
Freedom's b. DRAK 278:21
star-spangled b. KEY 434:16
banners army with b. BIBL 86:1
b. of the king advance FORT 321:7
Confusion on thy b. wait GRAY 350:2
royal b. forward go FORT 321:7
banquet b. ceases SHEN 715:5
Church's b. HERB 373:4
banqueter b. fed full LUCR 479:8
banqueting b. upon borrowing BIBL 91:31
banter how does fortune b. us BOLI 124:17
Bantu [B.] has been subjected VERW 791:13
banyan like the great b. tree PATI 569:17
baptism B., and the Supper BOOK 130:17
b., a regeneration ELIO 291:22
B. be administered BOOK 130:7
in my B. BOOK 130:10
baptize I b. with water BIBL 101:9
bar no moaning of the b. TENN 757:18
treat if met where any b. is HARD 361:18
When I have crossed the b. TENN 758:13
Barabbas B. was a publisher CAMP 183:20
B. was a robber BIBL 102:31
crowd will always save B. COCT 223:20
Barbara love of B. Allen BALL 50:5
barbarian He is a b. SHAW 706:18
barbarians b. are to arrive CAVA 198:7
B., Philistines, and Populace ARNO 28:7
Greeks, and to the B. BIBL 104:25
in my own mind *the B.* ARNO 28:10
without the b. CAVA 198:8
young b. all at play BYRO 175:3
barbaric sound my b. yawp WHIT 815:19
barbarism b. be considered WEIL 808:22
barbarisms colloquial b. JOHN 410:22
barbarity b. of tyrants SMIT 725:3
barbarous b. ages BAGE 47:14
b. dissonance MILT 511:26
b., savage DIDE 267:3
b. to write a poem ADOR 6:7
invention of a b. age MILT 514:5
barbarousness confess mine own b. SIDN 718:26
barber like a b.'s chair SHAK 656:2
bard goat-footed b. KEYN 435:8
more fat than b. beseems THOM 774:22
voice of the B. BLAK 120:21
Bardot read into B.'s face DE B 254:2
bards as b. will not CRAB 243:14
worst of b. confessed CATU 197:8
bare Back and side go b. ANON 15:12
B. like nude, giant girls SPEN 732:23
b. mountain tops ARNO 28:25
B. ruined choirs SHAK 704:29
barefoot always goes b. PROV 610:35
b. friars GIBB 335:25
I was born b. LONG 473:7
bareness old December's b. SHAK 705:8
bargain dateless b. SHAK 698:4
made a good b. FRAN 323:10
never was a better b. SIDN 718:8
two to make a b. PROV 604:39
bargains rule for b. DICK 263:5
barge b. she sat in SHAK 656:23
Baring Rothschild and B. GILB 337:20
bark come out, and *b.* JOHN 416:26
dogs b. at me SHAK 696:9
He began to b. NURS 548:10
his b. cannot be lost SHAK 681:12
keep a dog and b. yourself PROV 615:7
see, they b. at me SHAK 679:10
barking b. dog never bites PROV 595:34
Barkis B. is willin' DICK 261:15
barks Nicean b. of yore POE 579:20
barley among the bearded b. TENN 762:14
Corn rigs, an' b. rigs BURN 167:16
fields of b. and of rye TENN 762:12
barleycorn bold John B. BURN 168:15
Barlow Hornby and my B. THOM 774:1
barn b. and the forge HOUS 391:1
b.-cocks say Night is growing HARD 361:19
Barnaby B. bright PROV 595:35
like B. Rudge LOWE 477:13
Barney Give him the money, B. CATC 195:16
barns nor gather into b. BIBL 93:23
baronet No little lily-handed b. TENN 766:7
baronetage any book but the B. AUST 38:7
any book but the B. OPEN 556:16
barrel ain't got a b. of money WOOD 826:10
drowned in a b. of Malmesey FABY 305:23
grows out of the b. of a gun MAO 495:2
meal in a b. BIBL 79:26
barren b. and dry land BOOK 135:24
b. strand JOHN 411:16
b. superfluity of words GART 330:13
b. woman to keep house BOOK 139:20
cry, 'tis all b. STER 738:7
I am but a b. stock ELIZ 296:23
live a b. sister SHAK 689:2
none is b. BIBL 85:14
barricade some disputed b. SEEG 653:5
barrier b. of your teeth HOME 382:1
barriers b. of our prison EDGE 288:16
there are no b. WOLL 825:18
barrow there in your long b. MULD 535:25
barrows grassy b. of the happier dead TENN 767:2
bars weary of these worldly b. SHAK 674:24
Basan fat bulls of B. BOOK 132:23
Og the king of B. BOOK 141:5
base Labour without joy is b. RUSK 638:23
man of soul so b. TOCQ 778:6
people as b. as itself PULI 616:21
Things b. and vile SHAK 689:7
To what b. uses may we SHAK 666:24
Why bastard? wherefore b. SHAK 678:3
baseless b. fabric SHAK 699:6
baseness b.' varlet JONS 420:1
baser fellows of the b. sort BIBL 104:4
bashfulness particular b. ADDI 5:11
surmount his b. WALP 801:22
basia *Da mi b. mille* CATU 197:3
basics time to get back to b. MAJO 491:17
basil Hung over her sweet B. KEAT 428:3
steal my B.-pot KEAT 428:4
Basingstoke hidden meaning—like B. GILB 339:8
basket come from the same b. CONR 234:21
eggs in one b. PROV 598:37
Basle At B. I founded HERZ 375:9
Basques say of the B. CHAM 201:8
Bass Guinness, Allsopp, B. CALV 182:3
bassoon heard the loud b. COLE 226:6
bastard all my eggs in one b. PARK 567:16
b. who gets the mail KEAT 426:13
God . . . the b. BECK 59:13
more b. children SHAK 660:11
we knocked the b. off HILL 377:5
Why b.? wherefore base SHAK 678:3
bastardizing twinkled on my b. SHAK 678:6
bastards begets twenty b. WALP 801:6
Don't let the b. SAYI 647:33
some call nature's b. SHAK 703:14
stand up for b. SHAK 678:4
Bastille Voltaire in the B. DE G 256:2
bat b. that beats about in caverns WILB 817:6
beetle and the b. JOHN 414:3
black b., night, has flown TENN 764:6
couldn't b. for the time COMP 230:10
Ere the b. hath flown SHAK 684:6
On the b.'s back SHAK 699:11
Twinkle, twinkle, little b. CARR 189:18
weak-eyed b. COLL 229:8
Wool of b. SHAK 684:18
bath rather lie in a hot b. THOM 772:22
sit in a hot b. TENN 767:18
sore labour's b. SHAK 683:8
test my b. before I sit NASH 539:17
tired of B. AUST 38:3
bathe b. in his tears DONN 274:26
b. those beauteous feet FLET 318:13
early-morning b. SIKH 719:15
bathes He who b. here SIKH 720:5
bathing caught the Whigs b. DISR 268:10
large b. machine GILB 337:19
one long b. of a summer's day WORD 830:22
bathroom can't feel revolutionary in a b. LINK 469:14
baths Two walking b. CRAS 244:12
bathwater baby out with the b. PROV 598:40
baton marshal's b. LOUI 476:4
bâton *dans sa giberne le b.* LOUI 476:4
bats b. amongst birds BACO 44:10
b. have been broken HOWE 391:13
B. not angels THOM 773:11
b. will squeak and wheel NICO 544:22
batsman *I* am the b. LANG 450:10
batsmen opening b. to the crease HOWE 391:13
battalions big b. PROV 609:47
in pale b. go SORL 728:18
not of the heavy b. VOLT 798:4
battening B. upon huge seaworms TENN 762:9
batter B. my heart DONN 272:24
battle at Sheriffmuir A b. MCLE 487:6
b. and murder BOOK 127:6
b. done POTT 588:16
b. flags were furled TENN 763:3
b. fought of late HARI 362:7
B., *n.* A method BIER 114:19
b.'s lost and won SHAK 681:6
b. to the strong BIBL 84:23
b. to the strong DAVI 251:13
b. to the strong PROV 610:4
better in b. than in bed STER 739:6
defeated in a great b. LIVY 470:11
die in a b. SHAK 671:16
die in the b. CLOU 221:15
foremost in b. BALL 51:5
France has lost a b. DE G 255:18
glorious b. FORT 321:6
half the b. GOLD 345:23
happen to one in a b. CARR 190:22
into the midst of the b. VIRG 794:5
Ireland's b. CONN 234:6
it is a field of b. STEV 742:1
Lord mighty in b. BOOK 133:3
make them ready to b. BOOK 140:11
meet my death in b. SIKH 719:12
Next to a b. lost WELL 809:17
noise of b. rolled TENN 760:10
No war, or b.'s sound MILT 513:20
out of b. I escaped OWEN 562:11
prepare himself to the b. BIBL 106:17
See the front o' b. BURN 168:7
smelleth the b. afar off BIBL 81:37
This b.fares SHAK 672:27
we b. for the Lord ROOS 633:9
battledore B. and shuttlecock DICK 265:6
battlefield b. is the heart DOST 275:16
battlements down from the white b. HEAT 367:4

his head upon our b. SHAK 681:9
PERCHED ON B. TELE 758:4
battles b. are lost WHIT 815:13
b. long ago WORD 832:3
Dead b., like dead generals TUCH 784:15
forced marches, b. and death GARI 329:17
mother of all b. HUSS 396:13
O God of b. SHAK 671:21
opening b. of subsequent wars ORWE 558:18
bauble Pleased with this b. POPE 585:25
baubles Take away these b. MISQ 522:10
Baum *Lebens goldner B.* GOET 342:20
bawcock king's a b. SHAK 671:12
bawdy Bloody, b. villain SHAK 663:30
touched the b. strings STEV 740:3
bay b. the moon SHAK 676:19
flourishing like a green b.-tree BOOK 133:27
steamer breaking from the b. AUDE 34:5
bayonet b. is a weapon POLI 581:4
bayonets throne of b. INGE 399:9
throne of b. YELT 838:4
with our b. turning WOLF 825:4
Bayonne hams, B. POPE 582:11
bays Have I no b. HERB 372:6
oak, or b. MARV 498:13
sprig of b. in fifty years SWIF 749:13
bazaar Fate's great b. MACN 488:15
BBC don't watch B. for polemic SIMP 720:15
be b.-all and the end-all SHAK 682:8
b. as they are CLEM 220:13
better to b. AUCT 33:6
B. what you would seem PROV 596:17
How less what we may b. BYRO 177:30
Let b. be finale of seem STEV 739:21
poem should not mean but b. MACL 487:3
that which shall b. BIBL 84:3
To b., or not to be SHAK 664:3
beach Along the hidden b. KIPL 440:10
On the b. CHES 211:6
beachèd Upon the b. verge SHAK 699:25
beaches fight on the b. CHUR 215:10
beacon b.-light is quenched SCOT 651:5
beacons b. of wise men HUXL 397:19
beaded With b. bubbles KEAT 429:8
beadsman be your b. CLOS 222:11
beak b. from out my heart POE 579:18
in his b. Food enough MERR 506:1
beaker O for a b. full KEAT 429:8
Beale Miss Buss and Miss B. ANON 17:17
beam B. me up, Scotty MISQ 521:4
b. that is in thine own eye BIBL 94:1
beamish But oh, b. nephew CARR 191:24
my b. boy CARR 190:13
beams b. of his chambers BOOK 139:1
bean b. and the cod BOSS 143:15
Nine b. rows YEAT 836:11
not too French French b. GILB 338:19
beans B. meanz Heinz ADVE 7:8
get out of baked b. O'RE 557:13
put b. in the clay PROV 597:2
bear asking more than we could b. RICH 626:13
B. and forbear PROV 595:36
B. of Very Little Brain MILN 510:14
b. thee in their hands BOOK 137:23
b. the yoke in his youth BIBL 89:25
b. those ills we have SHAK 664:4
B. up—trust to time FORS 320:20
b. very much reality ELIO 294:3
b. with a sore head MARR 497:15
bush supposed a b. SHAK 690:20
cannot b. them BIBL 102:25
Exit, pursued by a b. SHAK 703:8
fire was furry as a b. SITW 721:1
fitted by nature to b. AURE 37:3
Grizzly B. is huge and wild HOUS 390:6
heavy b. who goes with me SCHW 649:16
How a b. likes honey MILN 511:2
huntsman by the b. oppressed WALL 800:1
More can I b. SHAK 672:19
No dancing b. was so genteel COWP 240:15
Puritan hated b.-baiting MACA 482:14
rugged Russian b. SHAK 684:12
so b. ourselves that CHUR 215:11
still less the b. FRER 324:10
who can b. BIBL 83:5
beard By thy long grey b. COLE 226:3
husband with a b. SHAK 691:2
I have a b. coming SHAK 689:12
King of Spain's B. DRAK 278:18
Loose his b. GRAY 350:3
Old Man with a b. LEAR 460:4
on a Dutchman's b. SHAK 702:4
white and bristly b. SHAK 704:8
womman hath no b. CHAU 205:27
bearded all scroungy and b. CORS 237:10
b. like the pard SHAK 659:1
beards long b., and pretences SWIF 749:4
when b. wag all PROV 604:20
beareth B. all things BIBL 106:16
b. up things light BACO 43:26
bears b. might come with buns ISHE 400:7
b. the marks of the last person HAIG 356:8
bigger b. try to pretend MILN 510:19
dancing dogs and b. HODG 379:13
rhythms for b. to dance FLAU 316:7
Teddy B. have their Picnic BRAT 147:5
beast above a b. BIBL 84:8
b. hath devoured him BIBL 75:11
b. or a fool KILV 436:4
b. or a god ARIS 25:3
b., or a god BACO 42:34
b. who is always spoiling MACA 483:16
b. With many heads SHAK 660:10
b. with two backs SHAK 691:26
Beauty killed the B. FILM 312:5
before he caught the b. WALL 800:1
Blatant b. men call SPEN 734:10
blond b. NIET 545:21
but a just b. ANON 15:13
fit night out for man or b. FIEL 310:20
life of his b. BIBL 82:25
Man's life is cheap as b.'s SHAK 678:17
mark, or the name of the b. BIBL 112:21
marks of the b. HARD 360:13
more subtil than any b. BIBL 73:24
No b. so fierce SHAK 696:12
number of the b. BIBL 112:22
questing b. MALO 492:10
serpent subtlest b. MILT 517:13
whan a b. is deed CHAU 205:16
What rough b. YEAT 837:6
Who is like unto the b. BIBL 112:20
who worship the b. BIBL 112:25
beastie cow'rin', tim'rous b. BURN 168:22
beasties long-leggety b. PRAY 592:2
beastly b. the bourgeois is LAWR 458:8
b. to the Germans COWA 238:10
beasts b. at Ephesus BIBL 106:24
b. of the earth BIBL 103:28
b. of the field BOOK 139:2
b. of the forest BOOK 135:2
b. of the forest BOOK 139:5
compared unto the b. BOOK 135:1
elders and the four b. BIBL 112:8
four b. BIBL 112:3
four b. full of eyes BIBL 111:31
invent new b. HEIN 368:7
kin to the b. BACO 42:8
like brute b. BOOK 131:1
beat b. down Satan BOOK 127:10
b. generation KERO 434:5
b. him when he sneezes CARR 189:15
b. their swords BIBL 86:13
can't b. them, join them SAYI 647:20
dread b. JOHN 408:7
enemies have b. us SHAK 677:2
he b. them all BYRO 180:7
We b. them today STAR 736:12
beaten b. path to his door EMER 300:3
b. road SHEL 711:9
No Englishman is ever fairly b. SHAW 709:16
Thrice was I b. BIBL 107:13
beateth one that b. the air BIBL 106:11
beating Charity and b. FLET 318:12
driven by b. ASCH 30:1
glory of b. the French WOLF 825:7
Greeks take the b. HORA 386:13
hearts b. BROW 156:22
mend his pace with b. SHAK 666:19
beatings dread of b. BETJ 71:8
Beatles B.' first LP LARK 452:12
beatnik peculiar b. theories KERO 434:6
beats b. as it sweeps ADVE 7:30
Beattock Pulling up B. AUDE 34:12
beatum *ab omni Parte b.* HORA 388:9
vocaveris Recte b. HORA 389:10
beatus *B. ille, qui procul negotiis* HORA 387:11
B. vir qui timet Dominum BIBL 113:21
beaut it's a b. LA G 447:17
beauteous b. and sublime AKEN 9:4
B. the garden's umbrage SMAR 722:12
How b. mankind is SHAK 699:12
It is a b. evening WORD 828:23
beauties B. in vain their pretty eyes POPE 587:12
b.! O how great the sum SMAR 722:7
many b. grace a poem HORA 386:4
meaner b. of the night WOTT 833:1
new b. met my sight THOM 775:2
pale, unripened b. ADDI 4:11
saved by b. not his own POPE 580:10
beautified b. with his presence BOOK 131:1
beautiful Albert is b. VICT 792:2
All things bright and b. ALEX 11:8
b. and damned FITZ 315:7
b. and death-struck year HOUS 391:6
b. and ineffectual angel ARNO 28:21
b. and simple HENR 370:17
b. and the clever GREE 351:17
b. are thy feet BIBL 86:3
b. cannot be the way COUS 238:6
B. dreamer FOST 321:14
b. face is a mute PUBL 616:10
b. game PELÉ 572:6
b. God to behold SWIN 751:4
b. upon the mountains BIBL 88:12
believe to be b. MORR 532:17
better to be b. WILD 818:21
Black is b. POLI 581:8
comes up more b. HORA 389:4
how b. they are COLE 225:2
hunger to be b. RHYS 625:17
innocent and the b. YEAT 836:7
love of what is b. PERI 573:19
most b. things RUSK 638:22
Names Most B. KORA 445:15
scorn looks b. SHAK 702:2
She's b. SHAK 672:13
singing:—'Oh, how b.!' KIPL 438:19
slaying of a b. hypothesis HUXL 397:11
Small is b. PROV 611:3
Small is b. SCHU 649:7
Something b. for God MUGG 534:15
something b. for God TERE 768:7
When a woman isn't b. CHEK 208:12
beauty all that b., all that wealth GRAY 350:9
American b. rose ROCK 630:23
arrest all b. CAME 182:13
b. all very well at first sight SHAW 708:13
b. being only skin-deep KERR 434:9
b. coming and the beauty gone WORD 829:9
B. crieth in an attic BUTL 173:3
b. draws us POPE 587:2
B. draws with single PROV 595:37
b. faded PHIL 575:8
b. for ashes BIBL 89:6
B. for some provides escape HUXL 397:8
B. in music IVES 400:11
B. is but a flower NASH 539:21
B. is in the eye PROV 595:38
B. is momentary in the mind STEV 740:2
B. is mysterious DOST 275:16
B. is Nature's brag MILT 511:29
B. is no quality HUME 395:1
b. is not, as fond men misdeem SPEN 734:14

beauty (*cont.*):
b. is only sin deep SAKI 642:5
b. is past change HOPK 384:15
B. is the first test HARD 360:7
B. is the lover's gift CONG 233:9
B. is truth KEAT 429:1
b. is woman's sceptre WOLL 825:23
B. itself doth of itself SHAK 703:30
B. killed the Beast FILM 312:5
b. lives though lilies die FLEC 317:3
b. lives with kindness SHAK 702:29
b. made The bright world dim SHEL 714:17
b. making beautiful old rime SHAK 705:9
b. of a rare kind DIMN 267:16
b. of holiness BOOK 138:7
b. of holiness MONS 526:12
b. of inflections STEV 740:7
b. of Israel BIBL 79:1
b. of the house of God SUGE 745:12
B. only skin deep PROV 595:39
b.'s empires SUCK 745:11
B.'s ensign SHAK 698:3
B. so ancient AUGU 36:5
b.'s rose SHAK 704:5
b.'s self she is ANON 17:23
b.'s Silent music CAMP 184:1
B. that must die KEAT 429:5
b. the joy of possessing form PAST 569:5
b., though injurious MILT 518:19
B. too rich for use SHAK 697:7
b. unadorned BEHN 62:16
B. vanishes DE L 256:11
b. will be soon resolved MARL 496:21
b. without vanity BYRO 179:20
befriended us with b. CAVE 198:13
body's b. lives STEV 740:2
cloud our b. WINC 822:22
do not spring into b. LEWE 466:16
doth b. beauteous seem SHAK 704:20
dreamed that life was b. HOOP 383:8
England, home and b. ARNO 29:12
Exuberance is b. BLAK 119:23
fatal gift of b. BYRO 174:26
Fostered alike by b. WORD 830:23
ghosts of B. glide POPE 583:15
Helen's b. SHAK 690:19
horror and its b. SHEL 712:20
If you get simple b. BROW 155:29
image of true b. ROUS 636:6
imagination seizes as b. KEAT 430:21
infant b. could beget SEDL 653:1
in thy b.'s field SHAK 704:6
I quested for b. SMAR 722:3
issuing forth into b. HUNT 395:20
looked on B. bare MILL 509:12
Love built on b. DONN 272:9
no excellent b. BACO 42:10
No woman can be a b. FARQ 307:9
Of its own b. BYRO 174:29
order and b. BAUD 57:8
parallels in b.'s brow SHAK 704:24
principal b. in building FULL 327:10
She walks in b. BYRO 178:24
some b. lies MILT 512:20
stone to b. grew EMER 299:9
struggle for superhuman b. GREE 352:8
supreme b. RUSS 639:22
terrible b. is born YEAT 835:19
there is no b. BIBL 88:15
thick, bereft of b. SHAK 698:13
thing of b. KEAT 426:16
thing of b. OPEN 556:22
thing of b. ROWL 636:13
thy b. is to me POE 579:20
unmask her b. SHAK 662:8
we just b. see JONS 420:21
Where B. was GALS 328:17
winds of March with b. SHAK 703:17
with him is b. slain SHAK 706:2
witty b. is a power MERE 505:9
your b.'s orient deep CARE 186:13

beaver Cock up your b. HOGG 380:12
Harry, with his b. on SHAK 668:30
because B. I do not hope to turn ELIO 293:19
b. I think him so SHAK 702:24
B. it's there MALL 492:6
B. it was he MONT 527:12
B. We're here MILI 508:15
cannot do it, Sir, b. CARR 191:6
beck upon the peple I b. CHAU 206:6
beckoning What b. ghost POPE 582:16
becks Nods, and b. MILT 512:14
become all that may b. a man SHAK 682:16
unborn, not b. PALI 565:21
becomes nothing so b. a man SHAK 671:5
that which *is not* b. GALE 328:12
becometh b. thine house BOOK 138:3
bed And so to b. PEPY 572:18
as little as my b. KEN 433:3
As to a lover's b. SHAK 657:15
b. be blest that I lie on PRAY 592:4
b. is the cold grave BALL 50:11
better in battle than in b. STER 739:6
blue b. to the brown GOLD 345:27
boys go first to b. HERB 373:3
By night on my b. BIBL 85:13
deck both b. and bower SPEN 733:27
Early to b. PROV 599:4
for the b. of Ware SHAK 702:5
found out thy b. BLAK 121:7
four bare legs in a b. PROV 612:4
gooseberried double b. THOM 772:16
go to b. by day STEV 742:11
go to b. early PROU 593:20
go to b. in another world HENS 371:5
go to b. with me ALLE 12:13
home to b. BARH 54:2
in b. with my catamite OPEN 555:27
in my b. again ANON 19:13
kick his wife out of b. SURT 746:17
Lying in b. would be CHES 211:14
make your b., so you must lie PROV 595:24
mind is not a b. AGAT 6:17
mother, make my b. BALL 50:6
mother, make my b. BALL 51:1
(my Love!) in thy cold b. KING 436:7
my second best b. SHAK 700:3
never made my own b. PUY 616:9
newly gone to b. MILT 514:4
no need to get out of b. AMIS 13:19
nor a goddess to b. VIRG 796:6
not having more than one man in b. RAPH 622:3
on the lawn I lie in b. AUDE 34:16
out of b. two hours sooner JOHN 414:6
passage up to b. STEV 742:15
prescription of a quick dip in b. WESL 811:23
Rode their horses Up to b. DE L 256:14
should of stood in b. JACO 401:2
sweat of an enseamèd b. SHAK 665:17
take up thy b., and walk BIBL 101:22
This b. thy centre is DONN 274:16
thy bride-b. to have decked SHAK 666:28
wore in b. MONR 526:8
bedfellows Adversity makes strange b. PROV 594:16
strange b. PROV 609:30
strange b. SHAK 698:33
Bedlam sigh like Tom o' B. SHAK 678:7
bedlam B. vision BYRO 180:10
bedroom French widow in every b. HOFF 380:9
unless with b. eyes AUDE 34:19
what you do in the b. CAMP 182:16
bedrooms in the nation's b. TRUD 783:21
beds Minds like b. always made up WILL 821:1
not only the b. you lay on CAVA 198:4
rejoice in their b. BOOK 142:2
bedstaff twinkling of a b. SHAD 655:13
bedytime I would it were b., Hal SHAK 669:6
bee b.-loud glade YEAT 836:11
b. of sorrow BABE 40:19

brisk as a b. JOHN 412:9
How doth the little busy b. WATT 805:5
I am the b. FITZ 314:5
in my bosom like a b. LODG 472:17
sting like a b. ALI 12:4
Where the b. sucks SHAK 699:11
while the b.-mouth sips KEAT 429:5
beech spreading b.-tree VIRG 795:13
beechen plot Of b. green KEAT 429:6
beef B. and a sea-coal fire OTWA 560:24
great eater of b. SHAK 700:29
great meals of b. SHAK 671:7
love British b. BAKE 48:15
piece of b. and mustard SHAK 698:10
Roast B., Medium FERB 308:14
roast b. of England FIEL 309:17
roast b. of old England BURK 164:15
Where's the b. ADVE 8:20
Where's the b. MOND 526:1
beefsteak as English as a b. HAWT 364:12
been as if it had not b. SHEL 710:20
B. there, done that SAYI 647:1
beer B. and Britannia SMIT 726:7
b. and skittles CALV 182:4
b. and skittles PROV 605:26
b. of a man in Klondike CHES 210:21
chronicle small b. SHAK 692:11
desire small b. SHAK 669:30
drinks b., thinks beer PROV 602:12
here for the b. ADVE 7:29
heresy, hops, and b. PROV 613:22
muddy ecstasies of b. CRAB 242:26
O B.! O Hodgson CALV 182:3
only a b. teetotaller SHAW 706:24
thine inspirer, B. POPE 580:15
warm b., invincible suburbs MAJO 491:16
beers other b. cannot reach ADVE 7:25
Beersheba Dan even to B. BIBL 78:10
from Dan to B. STER 738:7
bees b. do it PORT 588:7
b. make honey VIRG 797:4
from these Attic b. VIRG 797:3
half a number of b. LONG 475:3
industrious b. do hourly COLL 228:7
innumberable b. TENN 766:6
of b. [illegible] COND 231:2
rob the Hybla b. SHAK 676:29
so work the honey-b. SHAK 670:28
was it his b.-winged eyes BETJ 70:4
Where b. are PROV 614:35
beetle b. and the bat JOHN 414:3
b., nor the death-moth KEAT 429:3
b. wheels his droning flight GRAY 350:6
black water b. BLY 123:1
shard-borne b. SHAK 684:6
beetles B. black, approach not SHAK 689:28
special preference for b. HALD 356:18
befalleth b. the sons of men BIBL 84:8
before B. we were her people FROS 326:1
Christ is gone b. BOOK 128:8
days b. the flood BIBL 97:5
my thoughts long b. BOOK 141:9
Not lost but gone b. NORT 547:1
not lost but sent b. CYPR 248:11
sent b. my time SHAK 696:9
things which are b. BIBL 108:21
beforehand Pay b. PROV 609:20
befriend with his love he b. thee WINK 823:9
beg b. in the streets FRAN 322:15
taught me first to b. SHAK 688:18
began b. in order BROW 152:15
when my life b. WORD 829:10
beget get and b. OSLE 560:16
never to b. HOPK 385:8
begetter To the onlie b. SHAK 704:4
beggar absent-minded b. KIPL 438:2
b. amidst great riches HORA 388:21
b. on horseback PROV 610:32
b. should be answered SHAK 688:18
b. would enfold himself KIPL 441:17
b. would recognise guilt PARS 568:5
Be not made a b. BIBL 91:31

relieve a lame b. SHAK 698:32
Sue a b. PROV 611:33
whiles I am a b. SHAK 677:8
beggared b. all description SHAK 656:23
beggarman B., Thief NURS 551:13
beggars B. can't be choosers PROV 595:40
b. freezing ROBI 629:21
b. would ride PROV 603:26
Our basest b. SHAK 678:17
so many b. bold SKEL 721:14
When b. die SHAK 675:9
beggary no vice, but b. SHAK 677:8
There's b. in the love SHAK 656:7
they knew b. MACA 481:12
begged living HOMER b. his bread ANON 18:18
begging his seed b. their bread BOOK 133:26
begin B. at the beginning CARR 190:8
b. at the beginning OPEN 556:24
b. the Beguine PORT 588:3
b. with certainties BACO 41:8
b. with the beginning BYRO 175:27
But let us b. KENN 433:13
Then I'll b. CATC 195:4
warily to b. charges BACO 42:30
beginning As it was in the b. BOOK 125:19
badly from the b. STEV 742:8
begin at the b. OPEN 556:24
b., a middle ARIS 24:22
b., a muddle LARK 453:9
b. is often the end ELIO 294:18
b. of an Amour BEHN 62:6
b. of any great matter DRAK 278:17
b. of science LEIB 462:20
b. of the end TALL 753:3
b. of time USSH 788:20
b. of wisdom BOOK 139:18
b. of years SWIN 750:8
b. thereof BIBL 84:14
end of the b. CHUR 215:17
good b. makes PROV 601:23
In my b. is my end ELIO 294:6
In my b. is my end OPEN 555:17
In my end is my b. MARY 500:11
In the b. BIBL 73:10
In the b. OPEN 555:18
In the b. was the Word BIBL 101:1
In the b. was the Word OPEN 555:19
lovely at the b. PALI 565:10
Movies should have a b. GODA 342:1
new b., a raid on the inarticulate ELIO 294:11
no difficulty in b. JAME 403:17
pictures didn't have b. POLL 580:3
Thou, Lord, in the b. BOOK 138:15
told you from the b. BIBL 88:4
true b. SHAK 690:23
unnatural b. AUST 38:8
beginnings B. are always troublesome ELIO 293:15
ends by our b. know DENH 257:12
from small b. grow DRYD 280:28
begins glory most b. and ends YEAT 836:19
tower of nine storeys b. LAO 452:5
begot thing b. KYD 446:9
when they b. me STER 738:13
begotten b. by Despair MARV 498:10
B., not made BOOK 129:8
only b. of the Father BIBL 101:7
beguile b. thy sorrow SHAK 700:1
b. your pilgrimage FLEC 317:3
beguiled serpent b. me BIBL 74:3
Beguine begin the B. PORT 588:3
begun b., continued, and ended BOOK 130:5
b. to fight JONE 419:1
sooner b. PROV 611:9
To have b. is half the job HORA 386:15
Well b. is half done PROV 613:44
behave all b. quite differently COWA 239:1
difficult to b. like gentlemen MACK 486:8
behaving language and ways of b. JUVE 424:9
behaviour refines b. OVID 561:9
studies human b. ROBB 628:17
beheaded b. priests HENR 370:12
[Lovat] was b. WALP 800:14
behemoth Behold now b. BIBL 81:38
behind b. the throne PITT 576:23
b. your scenes JOHN 412:10
Get thee b. me, Satan BIBL 96:5
it will be b. me REGE 624:5
let them go, B., before DONN 272:16
no bosom and no b. SMIT 724:24
one must ride b. PROV 603:25
things which are b. BIBL 108:21
those b. cried 'Forward!' MACA 483:9
turn thee b. me BIBL 80:22
with a light b. her GILB 339:12
behold B. an Israelite BIBL 101:12
B. my mother BIBL 95:19
B. the man BIBL 114:8
beholder eye of the b. PROV 595:38
being at the edge of B. SPEN 732:21
avoiding b. TILL 777:13
b. comes from non-being LAO 451:14
darkness of mere b. JUNG 423:7
have our b. BIBL 104:10
may not be worried into b. FROS 326:15
misery of b. DRAB 278:15
Nothingness haunts b. SART 644:21
not the same thing as b. PLAT 578:7
one Supreme B. SIKH 719:6
unbearable lightness of b. KUND 446:6
beings beginning of b. LEIB 462:20
Belbroughton B. Road is bonny BETJ 70:16
Belfast be kind to B. CRAI 243:18
belfry while owl in the b. TENN 766:15
Belgians idlers and B. BAUD 57:12
Belgium B. put the kibosh on the Kaiser ELLE 298:5
B. recovers ASQU 31:2
B.'s capital had gathered BYRO 174:13
Belgrave Square May beat in B. GILB 337:13
Belial B., in act more graceful MILT 515:9
B. with words MILT 515:12
sons Of B., flown with insolence MILT 514:27
thou man of B. BIBL 79:9
belied b. with false compare SHAK 705:21
belief all b. is for it JOHN 415:25
b. of truth BACO 44:18
It is my b., Watson DOYL 277:9
loved each other beyond b. HEIN 368:8
that is b. SART 645:6
beliefs dust of exploded b. MADA 488:21
my b. are true HALD 356:16
some generous b. STEV 741:8
believe being born to b. DISR 269:1
b. in life DU B 284:1
b. in the life to come BECK 59:12
b. is not necessarily true BELL 62:21
B. it or not NEWS 544:1
B. me, you who come after HORA 388:10
B. nothing of what you hear PROV 595:42
b. what isn't happening COLE 224:14
b. what they wish CAES 180:16
b. what we choose NEWM 543:1
Corrected *I b.* KNOX 442:12
determination to b. HUME 394:9
don't b. in fairies BARR 55:15
fight for what I b. in CAST 193:12
Firmly I b. NEWM 542:17
he couldn't b. it CUMM 247:8
I b. in God the Father BOOK 126:10
I do b. her SHAK 705:23
I don't *b.* it CATC 196:16
If you b., clap your hands BARR 55:17
I will not b. BIBL 103:3
Lord, I b. BIBL 98:9
must b. *something* RUSS 640:3
professing to b. PAIN 563:8
recompense those who b. KORA 444:18
save them that b. BIBL 105:26
that they should b. NAPO 538:13
Though ye b. not me BIBL 102:9
We b. in God KORA 444:3
ye will not b. BIBL 101:21
you'll b. anything WELL 810:4
believed all that b. were together BIBL 103:17
b. in hope BIBL 104:34
b. of any man TARK 755:3
b. our report BIBL 88:14
by all people b. VINC 793:3
if b. during three days MEDI 503:8
I should not be b. VANB 789:6
not seen, and yet have b. BIBL 103:6
believer In a b.'s ear NEWT 543:15
Most blest b. VAUG 790:4
believers all b. BOOK 126:1
b. in Clough SWIN 751:15
Light half-b. in our casual creeds ARNO 27:9
protector of the b. KORA 443:21
believes more readily b. BACO 45:2
politician never b. what he says DE G 255:26
believeth b. all things BIBL 106:16
He that b. on me BIBL 101:30
whosoever b. in him BIBL 101:18
believing b. something LICH 467:18
b. their own lies ARBU 23:14
but b. BIBL 103:4
Not b. in force TROT 783:20
Seeing is b. PROV 610:27
stop b. in God CHES 211:22
torture them, into b. NEWM 542:13
Belinda B. smiled POPE 587:3
bell B., book, and candle SHAK 677:10
b. invites me SHAK 683:2
Cuckoo-echoing, b.-swarmèd HOPK 384:4
Ding, dong, b. NURS 548:4
dinner b. BYRO 177:9
For whom the b. tolls BORR 144:6
for whom the b. tolls DONN 275:3
heart as sound as a b. SHAK 691:12
hear the little b. tinkle HEIN 368:9
Let's mock the midnight b. SHAK 657:6
little b. tinkle CLOS 222:13
perhaps that sauncing b. RALE 620:10
sexton tolled the b. HOOD 382:20
Silence that dreadful b. SHAK 692:15
surly sullen b. SHAK 704:28
Twilight and evening b. TENN 758:13
word is like a b. KEAT 429:15
bella B., *horrida bella* VIRG 794:16
Bellamy B.'s veal pies LAST 456:20
belle b. *chose que de savoir* MOLI 524:20
b. dame sans mercy KEAT 427:14
b. folie BANV 53:10
j'étais b. RONS 632:8
bellies bigger than their b. VANB 789:10
their b. empty LOGU 473:4
bellman B., perplexed and distressed CARR 191:23
fatal b. SHAK 683:4
Bellona B.'s bridegroom SHAK 681:10
bellowing b. cow soon forgets PROV 595:43
bellows b. too have lost their wind EPIT 303:16
bells b. are gonna chime LERN 465:2
b. I hear WHIT 815:4
b. of Hell MILI 508:13
b. on her toes NURS 550:12
b. ringeth to evensong HAWE 364:5
daze with little b. HUGO 393:21
floating many b. down CUMM 247:3
From the b., bells, bells POE 579:12
into a mist with b. BROW 157:8
Like sweet b. jangled SHAK 664:11
lin-lan-lone of evening b. TENN 758:18
now ring the b. WALP 802:3
Ring out, wild b. TENN 761:28
ring the b. of Ecstasy GINS 339:19
ring the b. of Heaven HODG 379:13
Say the b. NURS 550:4
sheep-b. and ship-bells KIPL 440:10
silver b. and cockle shells NURS 549:13
with a tower and b. CRAB 242:20

belly b. God send thee ANON 15:12
b. is as bright ivory BIBL 85:21
b. like an heap of wheat BIBL 86:4
dark, dull, bitter b.-tension GIBB 336:8
filled his b. BIBL 100:3
God is their b. BIBL 108:22
in Jonadge's b. DICK 263:11
my b. was bitter BIBL 112:17
O wombe! O b. CHAU 206:7
Pee, po, b., bum, drawers FLAN 316:3
bellyful Rumble thy b. SHAK 678:22
Belmont In B. is a lady SHAK 687:5
belong b. not to you GIBR 336:11
b. to it as well WHYT 816:12
don't want to b. to any club MARX 499:11
man doesn't b. out there BRAU 147:6
To betray, you must first b. PHIL 575:3
where we really b. GREE 351:19
beloved B. is man TALM 753:18
Cry, the b. country PATO 570:1
Dearly b. BOOK 130:22
how far to be b. SHAK 656:7
Let my b. come BIBL 85:17
man greatly b. BIBL 90:7
My b. is mine BIBL 85:12
My b. is white and ruddy BIBL 85:20
never be b. BLAK 117:20
This is my b. BIBL 85:21
This is my b. Son BIBL 92:31
voice of my b. BIBL 85:18
below above, between, b. DONN 272:16
its counterpart b. ZOHA 840:10
journey to the world b. SOCR 727:5
love is a thing b. a man STER 739:9
belt b. without hitting below it ASQU 31:10
belted b. you and flayed you KIPL 438:21
Ben Bolt remember sweet Alice, B. ENGL 300:13
bend b. and I break not LA F 447:10
b. to favour ev'ry client GAY 332:11
B. what is stiff LANG 451:2
right on round the b. LAUD 454:5
sidelong would she b. KEAT 428:11
bending always be a b. downwards WHEW 813:14
bends made their b. adornings SHAK 656:24
beneath B. is all the fiends' SHAK 679:22
married b. me ASTO 31:19
benedicite *B., omnia opera Domini* BIBL 114:2
benediction breed Perpetual b. WORD 830:5
benedictus *B. qui venit* MISS 520:21
benefacta *recordanti b. priora* CATU 197:14
benefactor become the b. of someone DOST 276:4
b. of our race TWAI 786:21
benefits forget not all his b. BOOK 138:16
benevolence b. of mankind BAGE 47:13
b. of the butcher SMIT 723:6
enticed by b. BAGE 46:3
benevolent bashful, and b. TALM 754:12
B. Knowledge BORG 143:4
benighted B. walks under the midday sun MILT 511:21
poor b. 'eathen KIPL 438:16
benison For a b. to fall HERR 374:2
Benjamin of the tribe of B. BIBL 108:19
bent top of my b. SHAK 665:4
bereaved b. if snobbery died USTI 788:25
bereft b. Of wet HOPK 384:10
Berliner *Ich bin ein B.* KENN 433:17
Bermoothes still-vexed B. SHAK 698:22
Bermudas remote B. ride MARV 498:6
berries Sweet b. ripen STEV 740:6
Two lovely b. SHAK 690:6
berry made a better b. BUTL 173:4
sweeter than the b. GAY 331:8
Bertie Burlington B. HARG 362:5
beryl rings set with the b. BIBL 85:21
beseech pray and b. you BOOK 125:14
beside b. thyself BIBL 104:20
Christ b. me PATR 570:3
fall b. thee BOOK 137:22
besiege b. thy brow SHAK 704:6
best All's for the b. PROV 595:1
all the great b.-sellers PRIT 593:8
Always to be b. HOME 382:3
any other person's b. HAZL 365:17
bad in the b. of us ANON 19:4
being b. man is MURR 537:6
b. and the worst of this SWIN 751:8
b. chosen language AUST 38:2
b. days of life VIRG 796:20
b. in this kind SHAK 690:26
b. is enemy of good PROV 595:45
b. is like the worst KIPL 439:14
b. is the best QUIL 619:1
b. is the enemy of the good VOLT 797:11
b. is yet to be BROW 157:18
b. lack all conviction YEAT 837:5
b.-laid schemes PROV 596:1
b. men are dead PUNC 617:20
b. of all possible worlds BRAD 146:7
b. of all possible worlds CABE 180:13
b. of all possible worlds PROV 595:1
b. of all possible worlds VOLT 797:5
b. of men PROV 595:47
b. of times OPEN 555:28
b. Prime Minister we have BUTL 171:14
b. rulers LAO 451:9
b.-seller is the gilded tomb SMIT 724:11
b. thing God invents BROW 155:29
b. things in life PROV 595:49
b. things in life are free DE S 259:3
b. years are gone BECK 59:14
discreetest, b. MILT 517:10
enemy of the b. PROV 601:27
get what's b. for us RICE 626:7
In art the b. is good enough GOET 343:6
It was the b. of times DICK 265:21
justest and b. PLAT 578:4
past all prizing, b. SOPH 728:15
poetry = the *b.* words COLE 227:20
propagate the b. that is known ARNO 28:17
pursuing of the b. ends HUTC 396:14
record of the b. SHEL 714:23
Send forth the b. KIPL 440:21
that is the b. AUST 38:10
we two, one another's b. DONN 273:24
Whate'er is b. administered POPE 585:26
Beste *das B. gut genug* GOET 343:6
bestow b. on every airth a limb MONT 529:1
bestride b. the narrow world SHAK 674:13
bet You b. your sweet bippy CATC 196:29
betake b. myself to that course PEPY 573:15
Bethel O God of B. DODD 271:20
Bethlehem But thou, B. BIBL 90:19
little town of B. BROO 151:9
Slouches towards B. YEAT 837:6
Betjemanless We are now B. EWAR 305:8
betray All things b. thee THOM 774:5
b. me to a lingering book HERB 371:23
b. me to your mirth or hate FORD 320:3
guts to b. my country FORS 321:4
those who b. their friends GAY 331:23
To b., you must first belong PHIL 575:3
betrayal any act of b. RENO 624:14
ecstasy of b. GENE 333:6
only defence against b. WILL 820:13
betrayed betrayer, and b. SCOT 651:18
by ourselves, b. CONG 232:29
If she's fair, b. LEAP 460:2
night that he was b. BOOK 129:22
one of them b. me BEAV 59:7
betrayer b., and betrayed SCOT 651:18
betrayeth he that b. thee BIBL 103:12
betrothed B., betrayer SCOT 651:18
of my b. lady MIDD 507:6
better appear the b. reason MILT 515:9
b. angels of our nature LINC 468:9
B. be courted and jilted CAMP 183:9
B. by far than any SIKH 719:10
B. by far you should forget ROSS 634:9
b. day, the worse deed HENR 370:14
b. hap to worse SOUT 731:13
B. is the end BIBL 84:14
b. man than I am KIPL 438:21
B. red than dead POLI 581:6
better spared a b. man SHAK 669:15
B. than a play CHAR 203:7
b. than a thousand BOOK 137:13
b. than it sounds NYE 552:2
b. than ourselves CAMU 184:7
b. the day PROV 596:11
b. the instruction SHAK 687:31
b. to be AUCT 33:6
b. to have fought and lost CLOU 223:1
b. to have loved and lost TENN 761:4
b. what we can STEV 741:8
desires what is b. AUCT 33:8
don't know b. SAKI 642:8
Every day, I am getting b. COUÉ 238:4
Fail b. BECK 60:5
far, far b. thing DICK 266:3
for b. for worse BOOK 131:5
from worse to b. HOOK 383:7
from worse to b. JOHN 409:3
Gad! she'd b. CARL 188:19
give place to b. SHAK 676:27
go b. with Coke ADVE 8:14
go the b. things CATH 194:7
He is not b. ANON 15:8
Hereafter, in a b. world SHAK 658:9
If way to the B. there be HARD 361:13
I took thee for thy b. SHAK 665:14
I was in a b. place SHAK 658:18
made b. by their presence ELIO 293:11
make a b. mouse-trap EMER 300:3
much b. than likely BRON 150:4
nae b. than he shou'd be BURN 166:28
nothing *b.* CARR 191:9
nothing b. to do THAT 770:14
see b. days BEHN 62:12
seemed a little b. LAST 457:1
see the b. things OVID 561:17
takes the b. course SOCR 727:2
We have seen b. days SHAK 699:19
You could do b. DUFF 284:9
bettered b. expectation SHAK 690:31
between B. the idea And the reality ELIO 294:25
'ouses in b. BATE 57:3
try to get b. them STRA 744:9
betwixt B. the stirrup and the ground EPIT 303:15
bewailed b. at their birth MONT 528:7
beware B., lest in the worm BARR 53:16
B., madam GRAV 349:11
B. my foolish heart WASH 804:12
B. of desperate steps COWP 240:14
B. of men bearing flowers SPAR 731:15
B. of rudely crossing it AUDE 34:19
B. of the dog PETR 574:14
B. the ides of March SHAK 674:4
bid you b. KIPL 440:2
cry, B.! Beware COLE 225:25
beweep b. my outcast state SHAK 704:13
bewildered Bewitched, bothered, and b. HART 363:4
to the utterly b. CAPP 185:16
bewitch Do more b. me HERR 374:8
bewitched B., bothered, and bewildered HART 363:4
I am b. SHAK 667:30
bewrapt B. past knowing HARD 361:20
bewrayeth speech b. thee BIBL 97:26
beyond But is there anything b. BROO 150:9
loved each other b. belief HEIN 368:8
bias impartiality is b. REIT 624:9
mind's wrong b. GREE 351:12
biases critic is a bundle of b. BALL 52:14
bibble vain b.-babble SHAK 702:18
bibendum *Nunc est b.* HORA 388:3
bibisti *edisti satis atque b.* HORA 387:10
Bible B. and the Bible only CHIL 212:3
B.-Society . . . is found CARL 187:17
B. teaches that woman STAN 736:9

big ha'-B. BURN 166:25
Both read the B. BLAK 118:11
cadence of the B. verses RUSK 639:7
English B. MACA 482:15
have used the B. KING 437:14
knows even his B. ARNO 28:13
read in de B. HEYW 376:3
starless and b.-black OPEN 556:24
that book is the B. ARNO 29:7
translation of the B. WHAT 813:12
Bibles B. laid open HERB 373:11
bicker b. down a valley TENN 757:13
bicycle arrive by b. VIER 792:13
b.-pump the human heart AMIS 13:16
fish without a b. STEI 737:14
so is a b. repair kit CONN 233:24
bicycling old maids b. MAJO 491:16
bicyclists illuminated trouser-clip for b. MORT 533:16
bidder withstand the highest b. WASH 804:5
bien *mieux est l'ennemi du b.* VOLT 797:11
bier upon his watery b. MILT 512:28
big b. enough to take away everything FORD 319:11
B. fish eat little fish PROV 596:18
B. fleas have little fleas PROV 596:19
b. squadrons against the small BUSS 171:7
b. way of doing things TERE 768:6
b. words for little matters JOHN 413:19
books of the B.-Endians SWIF 747:20
commonly thought b. WOOL 826:15
Does my bum look b. WEIR 808:28
fall victim to a b. lie HITL 378:4
I am b. FILM 312:15
shining B.-Sea-Water LONG 474:11
too b. for them BULM 160:3
bigamy B. is having ANON 15:15
bigger b. bang for a buck POLI 581:7
b. they are FITZ 315:20
b. they are PROV 596:20
biggest b. aspidistra in the world HARP 362:12
b. electric train set WELL 809:12
bigness b. of Avogadro's number BENT 66:15
bigoted more superstitious, more b. NEWM 542:6
bigotry B. the anger of men who CHES 211:5
B. tries to keep truth TAGO 752:20
bike got on his b. TEBB 757:1
Mind my b. CATC 196:13
Bilbo B.'s the word CONG 232:30
bill b. of my divorce DONN 273:3
called upon to pay the b. HARD 360:2
give me your b. of company SWIF 748:6
nape caught in his b. YEAT 836:14
billabong swagman camped by a b. PATE 569:16
billboard b. lovely as a tree NASH 539:18
billet bullet has its b. PROV 599:20
bullet has its b. WILL 820:2
billets-doux bibles, b. POPE 586:31
billiard elliptical b. balls GILB 338:10
billiards play b. well ROUP 636:2
billion b. dollar country FOST 321:10
billow breaking b. SHEL 710:21
Fierce was the wild b. ANAT 14:7
billows b. of enormous size PHIL 575:9
bills By children and tradesmen's b. MACN 488:11
inflammation of his weekly b. BYRO 176:22
Receipted b. AUDE 34:13
billy B., in one of his sashes GRAH 348:5
That's the way for B. HOGG 380:11
till his 'B.' boiled PATE 569:16
bind B. me, or set me free GODO 342:3
b. my hair HUNT 396:7
b. their kings in chains BOOK 142:2
b. the sweet influences BIBL 81:34
b. unto myself today ALEX 11:11
b. your sons to exile KIPL 440:21
Obadiah B.-their-kings MACA 482:20
Safe b., safe find PROV 610:19
binds b. to himself a joy BLAK 120:8
Binnorie B., *O Binnorie* BALL 50:8
binomial b. theorem GILB 339:4
biographers B., translators MACA 482:4
first of b. MACA 481:11
Grubstreet b. ADDI 4:19
muck-raking b. BENN 66:3
picklocks of b. BENÉ 65:1
biographical noble and b. friend WETH 812:22
biographies essence of innumerable b. CARL 187:9
biography better part of b. STRA 744:10
B. is about Chaps BENT 67:2
Judas who writes the b. WILD 817:25
no b. THAC 769:18
no history; only b. EMER 299:20
nothing but b. DISR 270:7
to write b. WEST 812:16
write a b. GASK 330:22
biological b. clock is ticking KEYE 434:17
biologist b. passes ROST 635:14
biology B. is the search for WILL 820:10
bippy You bet your sweet b. CATC 196:29
bird addled egg as an idle b. PROV 595:19
b.-haunted English lawn ARNO 26:19
b. in the hand PROV 596:21
b. never flew on one PROV 596:22
b. not gets OXFO 562:16
b. of dawning SHAK 661:11
b. of night SHAK 674:22
b. of Paradise HERB 373:5
B. of the wilderness HOGG 380:14
b. of wonder dies SHAK 673:27
b. on the wing BOUL 145:2
b. that cuts the airy way BLAK 119:26
B. thou never wert SHEL 714:3
Both man and b. COLE 226:27
cannot catch the b. of paradise KHRU 435:17
catch a b. RICH 627:1
divine b. of Zeus PIND 576:9
early b. catches worm PROV 599:2
escaped even as a b. BOOK 140:17
forgets the dying b. PAIN 563:19
gold-feathered b. STEV 739:26
household b. DONN 272:18
immortal b. KEAT 429:14
It's a b. ANON 16:7
like a singing b. ROSS 634:1
obscure b. clamoured SHAK 683:17
only the note of a b. SIMP 720:14
rare b. on this earth JUVE 424:14
secular b. MILT 518:23
self-begotten b. MILT 518:22
Shall I call thee b. WORD 832:9
sight of any b. BIBL 82:6
sight of the b. PROV 604:2
silence fell with the waking b. TENN 764:7
some b. would trust HERB 371:24
Stirred for a b. HOPK 385:2
sweet b.'s throat SHAK 658:20
Sweet b. that shunn'st MILT 512:6
this her solemn b. MILT 516:22
What b. so sings LYLY 480:16
why the caged b. sings DUNB 285:2
birdcage And a b., sir DICK 265:16
like a summer b. WEBS 808:8
birds All the b. of the air NURS 552:1
As the flight of b. MACL 487:2
b., and Prime Ministers BALD 49:7
b. are faint KEAT 429:23
b. are flown CHAR 203:1
B. build HOPK 384:24
b. build nests VIRG 797:4
b. do chant their lays SPEN 733:7
b. fly through it HEIS 368:12
b. got to fly HAMM 358:16
B. in their little nests PROV 596:23
B. in their little nests agree WATT 805:10
B. of a feather PROV 596:24
b. of the air BIBL 95:22
b. of the air have nests BIBL 94:19
B. on box and laurels SMAR 722:1
b. that are without despair WEBS 808:8
b. trying to communicate AUDE 35:17
catch old b. with chaff PROV 615:35
half-awakened b. TENN 765:21
If b. confabulate or no COWP 240:28
late the sweet b. sang SHAK 704:29
like small b. DISR 269:15
Little b. that can sing PROV 605:36
nest of singing b. JOHN 412:6
no b. sing KEAT 428:7
prisoned b. must find SASS 645:20
read about little b. TENN 767:18
singing of b. BIBL 85:10
sing like b. i' the cage SHAK 680:6
these unobservant b. ISHE 400:7
think caged b. sing WEBS 808:15
Two b., close-linked UPAN 788:5
voices of the sweeter b. LEDW 461:16
birdsong b. at morning STEV 742:20
Birmingham B. by way of Beachy Head CHES 210:14
B. Six released DENN 257:19
no great hopes from B. AUST 37:19
When Jesus came to B. STUD 745:5
Birnam Great B. wood SHAK 685:2
Till B. wood remove SHAK 685:15
birth bewailed at their b. MONT 528:7
B., and copulation, and death ELIO 295:23
b. is but a sleep WORD 829:20
b.-strangled babe SHAK 684:19
disqualified by the accident of b. CHES 211:10
flummery of a b. place KEAT 431:6
give b. astride of a grave BECK 60:3
grace, new b. ARNO 28:27
Invisible before b. BHAG 72:17
lessen the b.-pangs MARX 499:16
my b. and spirit HERB 371:23
Nobility of b. BACO 43:23
no cure for b. and death SANT 644:13
not conscious of his b. LA B 446:16
one that is coming to b. O'SH 560:12
on my b. have smiled TAYL 756:10
present at the b. ORTO 558:1
Rainbow gave thee b. DAVI 252:7
Saviour's b. is celebrated SHAK 661:11
seen b. and death ELIO 295:1
sorrowful b. MALO 492:9
this monstrous b. SHAK 692:8
birthday b. of my life ROSS 634:2
eighty-first b. OPEN 555:27
Happy b. to you HILL 377:2
marvel my b. away THOM 772:11
birthplace accent of one's b. LA R 453:20
birthright Esau selleth his b. BIBL 74:34
sold his b. BIBL 74:36
births b. of time BACO 43:13
plenties, and joyful b. SHAK 672:4
tell of the b. RIMB 628:13
bis *B. dat qui cito dat* PUBL 616:11
biscuit b., or confectionary plum COWP 240:26
cared a b. for it LAWR 459:1
biscuits hyacinths and b. SAND 644:3
bisexuality b. doubles your chances ALLE 12:16
bishop Another B. dead MELB 503:14
b. must be blameless BIBL 109:14
B. of Rome BOOK 142:12
B. of your souls BIBL 111:1
call me a B. WESL 811:22
hitting the niece of a b. ORWE 559:3
How can a b. marry SMIT 725:16
illustrious b. of Cambrai GODW 342:5
killed the B. YONG 838:14
make a b. kick a hole CHAN 201:12
No b., no King JAME 402:13
There lies the B. AUBR 32:11
bishopric *merit* for a b. WEST 812:20
bishops B., and Curates BOOK 126:17
B. and Curates BOOK 129:13

bishops (*cont.*):
B., Priests, and Deacons BOOK 127:9
much against the B. AUBR 32:20
bit b. by him that comes behind SWIF 749:19
b. the babies BROW 157:10
for requital b. CHIL 212:4
Though he had b. me SHAK 680:2
bitch b.-goddess success JAME 404:5
called John a Impudent B. FLEM 317:12
Gaia is a tough b. MARG 495:10
old b. gone in the teeth POUN 589:17
bite b. his pen SWIF 749:24
b. some of my other generals GEOR 333:12
b. the hand that fed them BURK 164:10
bleating sheep loses b. PROV 596:25
Dead men don't b. PROV 597:49
dog is allowed one b. PROV 599:24
man recovered of the b. GOLD 344:22
bites barking dog never b. PROV 595:34
dead woman b. not GRAY 350:1
biteth b. like a serpent BIBL 83:16
biting b. is immortal SHAK 657:26
b. the hand that lays GOLD 346:2
bitten Once b., twice shy PROV 608:33
bitter be not b. against them BIBL 109:5
b. as wormwood BIBL 82:12
b. bread of banishment SHAK 695:4
b. God to follow SWIN 751:4
b. herbs BIBL 75:39
b. tears to shed CORY 237:13
life unto the b. in soul BIBL 81:6
make oppression b. SHAK 663:29
my belly was b. BIBL 112:17
rises something b. LUCR 479:9
sweet water and b. BIBL 110:20
bittern hear the b. cry LEDW 461:16
bitterness b. of his soul BIBL 91:21
b. of life CARR 191:28
b. of my soul BIBL 87:26
rose's scent is b. THOM 774:2
bivouac b. of the dead O'HA 553:5
bizarre b. happening HAUG 364:1
Bizet Chopin and B. FISH 313:17
blabbing b., and remorseful day SHAK 672:18
black art as b. as hell SHAK [illegible]
Baa, baa, b. sheep NURS 547:12
b. against may BUNT 160:12
b. and merciless things JAME 403:6
b. as he is painted PROV 598:8
b. as if bereaved of light BLAK 120:18
b. as our loss SITW 721:2
b. as they might be BALL 52:3
b. black oxen YEAT 835:12
b., but comely BIBL 85:7
b. chaos comes again SHAK 706:2
b. dog JOHN 417:7
blacker than b. TURN 785:16
B. Hills belong to me SITT 720:19
B. is beautiful POLI 581:8
B. it stood as night MILT 515:22
b. majority rule SMIT 724:7
b. man or a fair man ADDI 4:24
b. men fought MACA 481:8
B. Panther Party NEWT 543:2
B. Power CARM 188:24
b., purgatorial rails KEAT 427:4
B.'s not so black CANN 185:2
b. water beetle BLY 123:1
B. Widow, death LOWE 478:3
bread is b. BARC 53:22
devil damn thee b. SHAK 685:16
drop of b. blood HUGH 393:1
during the B. Death BOCC 123:5
growth of b. consciousness BIKO 115:1
Hung be the heavens with b. SHAK 672:6
I am b. SHAK 692:24
I found some b. people EQUI 301:3
Just call me b. GOLD 344:4
little b. sheep KIPL 438:17
looking for a b. hat BOWE 145:19
matron, all in b. SHAK 697:27
More b. than ashbuds TENN 758:21
neutralize the b. BROW 157:26
night's b. agents SHAK 684:7
not b. and white BOY 146:4
not have the colour b. MAND 493:12
old b. magic MERC 505:8
old b. ram SHAK 691:25
rainbow which includes b. YEVT 838:12
sad, b. isle BAUD 57:9
so long as it is b. FORD 319:14
talks good for a b. guy ICE- 398:16
thou read'st b. BLAK 118:11
Tip me the b. spot STEV 741:19
wearing a b. gown CHES 209:6
Why do you wear b. CHEK 208:4
with a b. skin MALC 491:21
young, gifted and b. HANS 359:12
Young, gifted and b. IRVI 400:1
blackberries as plentiful as b. SHAK 668:8
micher and eat b. SHAK 668:12
blackbird B. has spoken FARJ 306:15
b. whistling STEV 740:7
blackbirds B. are the cellos STEV 740:18
Four and twenty b. NURS 550:18
blackened b. by charcoal EDGE 288:19
blackens b. all the water ADDI 5:15
blacker b. than black TURN 785:16
blackguard Sesquipedalian b. CLOU 221:16
blackguards intentions make b. LACL 447:4
Blackpool famous seaside place called B. EDGA 288:9
blacks poor are Europe's b. CHAM 201:9
Two b. don't make a white PROV 613:24
blacksmith Never was a b. KIPL 438:3
bladders boys that swim on b. SHAK 673:12
blade bloody blameful b. SHAK 690:24
Steel-true and b.-straight STEV 742:22
trenchant b. BUTL 172:2
vorpal b. went snicker-snack CARR 190:13
blains breaking forth with b. BIBL 75:36
Blair Atholl B.'s mine BALL 50:19
blame Bad women never take the b. BROO 150:19
b. at night POPE 584:26
b. is his who chooses PLAT 578:9
b. Marx for what was done BENN 65:7
b. the alien AESC 6:12
grief as is the b. AYTO 40:9
manager who gets the b. LINE 469:13
neither is most to b. SWIN 751:8
poor wot gets the b. MILI 508:14
she is to b. MONT 526:14
blamed never had been b. D'AV 251:9
blameless bishop must be b. BIBL 109:14
Fearless, b. knight ANON 20:4
flower of a b. life TENN 759:11
blames bad workman b. his tools PROV 595:33
blaming b. it on you KIPL 439:2
b. on his boots BECK 59:22
blanch B., and Sweet-heart SHAK 679:10
when counsellors b. BACO 42:17
blancmange cold b. and rhubarb tart KNOX 442:13
bland bland lead the b. GALB 328:6
composed and b. ARNO 26:22
liquid lines mellifluously b. BYRO 177:7
blandula *Animula vagula b.* HADR 355:11
blank B. cheques HOLM 381:12
b. implacable sheet SCOT 650:6
b., my lord SHAK 701:24
political b. cheque GOSC 347:5
blanket b. of the dark SHAK 682:4
with the b. over his head BABE 41:2
blankets rough male kiss of b. BROO 150:8
blasphemies truths begin as b. SHAW 706:12
blaspheming Liver of b. Jew SHAK 684:19
blasphemous b. fables BOOK 142:11
blasphemy b. against the Holy Ghost BIBL 95:11
flat b. SHAK 686:11
blast b.-beruffled plume HARD 361:11
B. from the Desert LONG 474:10
b. of vain doctrine BOOK 128:21
b. of war SHAK 671:5
blasted b. with excess GRAY 351:2
Kindled he was, and b. BYRO 174:20
no sooner blown but b. MILT 513:15
Upon this b. heath SHAK 681:17
blasts With blustering b. SACK 641:3
blatant B. beast men call SPEN 734:10
in a b. land TENN 764:2
blatherskite Blatant B. PHIL 575:12
blaze b. of living light BYRO 175:20
blow up into a faint b. RICH 627:7
heavens themselves b. forth SHAK 675:9
undistinguished b. THOM 775:7
blazer make them wear a b. BAIL 48:5
bleak In the b. mid-winter ROSS 634:5
bleat b. the one at the other SHAK 702:32
bleating b. sheep loses bite PROV 596:25
bleed b. a while BALL 51:12
b., fall, and die DONN 272:14
do we not b. SHAK 687:30
fat, and then they b. JONS 420:15
old wounds b. anew WALL 800:9
thorns of life! I b. SHEL 712:16
bleeding Ain't it all a b. shame MILI 508:14
b., beating fire JOHN 408:8
b. piece of earth SHAK 675:21
b. war SHAK 695:13
instead of b., he sings GARD 329:15
pageant of his b. heart ARNO 27:22
blemish lamb shall be without b. BIBL 75:38
no b. but the mind SHAK 702:17
Blenheim still fighting B. BEVA 71:16
bless B. 'em all HUGH 392:16
b. me, With apple pie FIEL 309:8
B. relaxes BLAK 119:22
B. the Lord BIBL 114:2
b. ye the Lord BOOK 126:3
dying, b. the hand DRYD 282:25
except thou b. me BIBL 75:6
God b. us every one DICK 261:10
holy priests B. her SHAK 656:27
load and b. With fruit KEAT 430:8
blessed B. are the dead BIBL 112:26
B. are the eyes BIBL 99:10
B. are the poor BIBL 93:3
B. are the pure in heart KEBL 432:3
B. are you, O Lord SIDD 717:18
b. art thou among women BIBL [illegible]
B. art thou among women PRAY 592:1
B. be he that cometh BOOK 140:7
b. be the name of the Lord BIBL 80:36
b. damozel ROSS 634:16
b. is the man BOOK 133:20
B. is the man BOOK 137:12
b. part to Heaven SHAK 673:19
b. them unaware COLE 226:19
blessest is b. BIBL 76:28
from hence to there may be b. SOCR 727:6
generations shall call me b. BIBL 98:16
Judge none b. BIBL 91:26
Lord b. the latter end BIBL 82:5
more b. to give BIBL 104:14
That b. mood WORD 829:3
This b. plot SHAK 694:19
thou hast b. them BIBL 77:2
you should call b. HORA 389:10
blessedness b. alone that makes a King TRAH 780:17
dies, in single b. SHAK 689:3
blesseth b. him that gives SHAK 688:10
blessing b. cannot pass through JOHN 407:13
b. of a rainbow ABSE 1:7
b. of God Almighty BOOK 130:3
b. that money cannot buy WALT 802:26
b. to the country BISM 116:4
boon and a b. ADVE 8:13
continual dew of thy b. BOOK 126:17
contrariwise b. BIBL 111:4
give us his b. BOOK 136:4
national b. HAMI 358:13
Prosperity is the b. BACO 42:3

taken away thy b. BIBL 74:39
unmixed b. HORA 388:9
When thou dost ask me b. SHAK 680:6
Yet possessing every b. EDME 289:3
blessings B. brighten PROV 596:28
b. of the light KEN 433:2
b. on the falling out TENN 765:13
b. on your head COWP 240:17
glass of b. HERB 373:6
blest always to be b. ARMS 25:15
always To be b. POPE 585:9
B. pair of Sirens MILT 511:10
b. that I lie on PRAY 592:4
Kings may be b. BURN 168:12
make us b. at last ROCH 630:11
Of this b. man WALT 803:3
O Mother b. ALPH 12:22
promotion to the b. DRYD 282:29
blight b. man was born for HOPK 384:19
great English b. WAUG 806:2
Blighty back to dear old B. MILL 510:8
blimp Colonel B. LOW 477:5
blind accompany my being b. PEPY 573:15
b. as any noonday owl TENN 759:24
b., but now I see NEWT 543:13
b. guides BIBL 96:27
b. lead the blind BIBL 95:29
b. led by the blind UPAN 787:20
b. man in a dark room BOWE 145:19
b. man's wife needs PROV 596:29
B., old and lonely SHEL 710:14
b. side of the heart CHES 210:3
b. watchmaker DAWK 253:1
b. wife PROV 598:1
bold as a b. mare PROV 608:16
Booth died b. LIND 469:9
country of the b. ERAS 301:4
country of the b. PROV 604:1
Cupid b. did rise LYLY 480:15
Cupid painted b. SHAK 689:7
darkness and b. eyes VAUG 790:4
Eye among the b. WORD 830:3
eyes to the b. BIBL 81:26
giveth sight to the b. BOOK 141:22
Grief for awhile is b. SHEL 713:6
halt, and the b. BIBL 99:29
I was b., now I see BIBL 102:4
Justice, though she's painted b. BUTL 172:13
Love is b. ANON 20:8
Love is b. PROV 606:4
my being b. CLOS 222:3
none so b. as those PROV 612:31
O b. entencioun CHAU 206:30
old, mad, b. SHEL 713:28
religion without science is b. EINS 290:8
right to be b. sometimes NELS 540:15
splendid work for the b. SASS 645:17
though she be b. BACO 42:33
Three b. mice NURS 551:10
When the b. lead the blind PROV 614:25
blindness 'eathen in 'is b. KIPL 438:11
for our b. we cannot ask BOOK 130:6
heathen in his b. HEBE 367:7
help him of his b. SHAK 702:29
Love comes from b. BUSS 171:5
triple sight in b. KEAT 430:14
blinds drawing-down of b. OWEN 562:7
Truth, like the light, b. CAMU 184:15
blindworm b.'s sting SHAK 684:18
blindworms Newts, and b. SHAK 689:27
blinked other fellow just b. RUSK 638:3
blinking portrait of a b. idiot SHAK 687:25
bliss appreciate domestic b. SANT 644:10
B. goes but to a certain bound GREV 353:2
b. in ale CRAB 242:26
B. in our brows bent SHAK 656:16
b. or woe MILT 517:19
B. was it in that dawn WORD 828:16
body is in the b. AKHM 9:8
doth bathe in b. VAUX 791:1
Everywhere I see b. SHEL 710:10
joyous b. is mine SIKH 719:8
men call domestic b. PATM 569:20
Of b. on bliss MILT 516:18
soul in b. SHAK 680:3
source of all my b. GOLD 344:19
Where ignorance is b. GRAY 350:18
wingèd hours of b. CAMP 183:16
Your b. in our hearts STRU 745:2
blissful b. old times BLAM 121:15
blister b. you all o'er SHAK 698:23
blithe b. Spirit SHEL 714:3
buxom, b., and debonair MILT 512:13
blithesome B. and cumberless HOGG 380:14
blitz b. of a boy is Timothy Winters CAUS 198:3
blizzard walked to his death in a b. EPIT 302:12
block each b. cut smooth POUN 589:7
hew the b. off POPE 580:22
old b. itself BURK 165:2
blockhead b.'s insult JOHN 411:10
bookful b. POPE 585:2
diversion in a talking b. FARQ 307:8
No man but a b. JOHN 415:17
very great b. CHAR 203:10
blocks hew b. with a razor POPE 587:17
You b., you stones SHAK 674:3
blond b. beast NIET 545:21
B. comme un soleil BANV 53:10
blonde Being b. is definitely MADO 489:4
b. to make a bishop kick CHAN 201:12
having money like being b. QUAN 618:10
blondes Gentlemen prefer b. LOOS 475:9
blood am I not of her b. SHAK 701:11
ancient troughs of b. HILL 376:17
b. and ashes PAIN 563:13
b. and iron BISM 116:12
b. and love without STOP 743:17
b. and wine WILD 818:30
b. be the price KIPL 440:9
b. come gargling OWEN 562:8
b.-dimmed tide is loosed YEAT 837:5
b. drawn with the lash LINC 468:17
b. his blood YEAT 835:4
b. is their argument SHAK 671:16
b. Is very snow-broth SHAK 686:3
b. more stirs SHAK 667:25
b. of Christians is the seed TERT 768:15
b. Of human sacrifice MILT 514:24
b. of patriots JEFF 405:7
b. of the martyrs PROV 596:31
b. on their hands SPEN 732:11
b. out of a turnip MARR 497:14
b.-red flag BLOK 122:6
b.'s a rover HOUS 390:16
B. sport brought INGH 399:15
B., sweat, and tear-wrung BYRO 173:13
B. thicker than water PROV 596:30
b., toil, tears and sweat CHUR 215:7
b. was on their horn BYRO 178:10
B. will have blood PROV 596:32
b. will have blood SHAK 684:14
B. will tell PROV 596:33
b. with guilt is bought SHEL 713:7
but with b. BROW 152:3
by b. Albanian TERE 768:10
Christ's b. streams MARL 496:7
coughed-up b. RIMB 628:13
created Man of a b.-clot KORA 445:17
Deliver me from b.-guiltiness BOOK 135:8
Dread Beat an B. JOHN 408:7
drink the b. of goats BOOK 135:3
drop of Negro b. HUGH 393:1
effusion of Christian b. LAUD 454:4
enough of b. and tears RABI 619:14
flesh and b. BIBL 108:13
flesh and b. so cheap HOOD 383:1
flow of human b. HUGH 392:18
foaming with much b. POWE 590:15
for cooling the b. FLAN 316:2
fountain filled with b. COWP 240:20
get b. from a stone PROV 615:37
give me B. DICK 261:27
glories of our b. and state SHIR 717:8
guiltless of his country's b. GRAY 350:11
hawser of the b.-tie HARR 363:2
heart within b.-tinctured BROW 154:18
Here lies b. EPIT 303:6
in b. Stepped in SHAK 684:15
innocent of the b. BIBL 97:27
I smell the b. NASH 539:20
I smell the b. SHAK 679:9
is this b., then, formed BYRO 177:8
Let there be b. BYRO 177:13
make thick my b. SHAK 682:2
Man of B. was there MACA 482:22
mingle my b. BROW 152:2
my God feels as b. HERB 372:2
near in b. SHAK 683:22
Nothing like b., sir THAC 769:10
one glorious b.-red BROW 156:4
on the b. of my men LEE 462:10
Propinquity and property of b. SHAK 677:23
pure and eloquent b. DONN 273:9
raised to shed his b. POPE 585:7
rather have b. on my hands GREE 351:15
red b. reigns SHAK 703:9
redeemed us by his b. DIX 271:12
rivers of b. JEFF 406:1
seas of b. COBB 223:7
shall his b. be shed BIBL 74:21
shedde oure b. LANG 450:21
shed innocent b. BIBL 89:3
sheds his b. with me SHAK 671:25
show business with b. BRUN 159:1
so much b. in him SHAK 685:9
summon up the b. SHAK 671:5
thicks man's b. with cold COLE 226:13
this is my B. BOOK 129:22
Thy b. was shed for me ELLI 298:10
Tiber foaming with much b. VIRG 794:16
tincture in the b. DEFO 255:8
voice of the child's b. SWIN 751:11
voice of thy brother's b. BIBL 74:9
waded thro' red b. BALL 52:2
washed in the b. of the Lamb LIND 469:8
wash this b. Clean SHAK 683:11
We be of one b. KIPL 441:3
We, your b. family SPEN 732:14
When b. is nipped SHAK 681:4
When the b. creeps TENN 761:8
white in the b. of the Lamb BIBL 112:10
With his own b. he bought her STON 743:9
Without shedding of b. BIBL 109:26
worked with my b. KOLL 443:11
Young b. must have its course KING 437:13
bloodhounds Seven b. followed SHEL 712:8
bloodless b. emulation SHAK 700:7
b. lay the untrodden snow CAMP 183:8
bloodshed war without b. MAO 495:1
bloodthirsty so venomous, so b. TROL 782:20
bloody Abroad is b. GEOR 334:8
b. blameful blade SHAK 690:24
b., bold, and resolute SHAK 684:22
b., but unbowed HENL 369:20
b. cross he bore SPEN 733:13
b. noses and cracked crowns SHAK 668:1
b. principles and practices FOX 322:12
come out, thou b. man BIBL 79:9
dark and b. ground O'HA 553:6
have b. thoughts SHAK 699:7
last act is b. PASC 568:14

bloody (*cont.*):
my b. thoughts SHAK 693:3
no right in the b. circus MAXT 502:11
Not b. likely SHAW 709:15
sang within the b. wood ELIO 295:25
Sunday, b. Sunday FILM 313:2
teach B. instructions SHAK 682:9
under the b. past AHER 8:28
What b. man SHAK 681:8
wipe a b. nose GAY 332:9
Woe to the b. city BIBL 90:21
bloom b. in the spring GILB 338:14
b. is gone WILD 817:15
How can ye b. sae fresh BURN 166:16
hung with b. HOUS 390:14
Leopold B. ate with relish JOYC 422:12
lilac is in b. BROO 150:10
look at things in b. HOUS 390:15
sort of b. on a woman BARR 55:19
with the b. go I ARNO 27:26
blooming grand to be b. well dead SARO 644:18
bloomy all the b. beds SMAR 722:12
blossom blood-red b. of war TENN 764:16
b. about me BOSW 143:17
b. and flourish SMIT 726:10
b. as the rose BIBL 87:21
B. by blossom SWIN 750:6
b. in purple and red TENN 764:10
b. in the dust SHIR 717:9
b. into a Duchess AILE 9:1
b. on the tomb CRAB 242:21
b. soup BASH 56:19
b. that hangs on the bough SHAK 699:11
break Into b. WRIG 833:12
frothiest, blossomiest b. POTT 588:21
hundred flowers b. MAO 495:4
blossoms b., birds, and bowers HERR 374:3
to-morrow b. SHAK 673:12
blot art to b. POPE 586:18
b. on the escutcheon GRAY 349:24
B. out, correct SWIF 749:14
b. out his name BIBL 111:26
looks a little b. TENN 760:7
scarce received from him a b. HEMI 368:6
This world's no b. BROW 155:30
blotted b. a thousand JONS 421:2
b. from life's page BYRO 174:7
b. it out for ever STER 739:8
blow Blow, b., thou winter wind SHAK 659:4
B., bugle, blow TENN 765:16
b. fall soon or late STEV 743:1
B. him again to me TENN 765:15
B. out, you bugles BROO 150:7
B., thou wind of God KING 437:8
b. upon my garden BIBL 85:17
B. up the trumpet BOOK 137:9
B., winds, and crack SHAK 678:21
b. with an agreement TROT 783:19
first b. is half GOLD 345:23
great winds shorewards b. ARNO 26:11
hand that gave the b. DRYD 282:25
knock-down b. HUNT 396:3
not return your b. SHAW 708:32
strike the b. BYRO 174:6
sudden b.: the great wings YEAT 836:14
when will thou b. ANON 19:13
bloweth wind b. where it listeth BIBL 101:17
blowing answer is b. in the wind DYLA 287:3
B. sweet o'er each SMAR 721:19
I'm forever b. bubbles KENB 433:4
blown flower that once hath b. FITZ 314:13
no sooner b. but blasted MILT 513:15
pipe B. by surmises SHAK 669:20
rooks are b. TENN 760:30
blows B. out his brains BROW 157:27
b. so red The rose FITZ 314:11
It b. so hard HOUS 391:3
blubbering b. Cabinet GLAD 341:9
bludgeoning b. of the people WILD 819:6
bludgeonings b. of chance HENL 369:20
blue across the b. threshold ROST 635:12
b. above the trees KEAT 428:3
B. are the hills PROV 596:34
b. bed to the brown GOLD 345:27
B. Bonnets are bound SCOT 651:29
b. guitar STEV 739:24
b. is all in a rush HOPK 384:16
b. of the night CROS 246:4
b. remembered hills HOUS 391:5
B., silver-white KEAT 429:17
deeply, beautifully b. SOUT 730:19
Eyes of most unholy b. MOOR 530:10
floating in the B. MILN 511:3
Her b. body WALK 799:9
Lavender's b. NURS 549:2
Little Boy B. NURS 549:5
little tent of b. WILD 818:31
My b. heaven WHIT 814:22
Space is b. HEIS 368:12
yonder living b. TENN 762:3
bluebell mary, ma Scotch B. LAUD 454:6
bluebirds b. over the white cliffs BURT 169:19
blueprints Genes not like b. STEW 743:6
blues got the Weary B. HUGH 393:2
blunder frae mony a b. free us BURN 168:21
God's first b. NIET 545:11
I b., I bluster SKEL 721:13
it is a b. BOUL 144:25
so grotesque a b. BENT 67:7
Youth is a b. DISR 270:3
blundered b. on some virtue unawares CHUR 214:8
Some one had b. TENN 757:16
blunders Human b. TAYL 756:7
Nature's agreeable b. COWL 239:26
blunt plain, b. man SHAK 676:9
blush b. into the cheek DICK 264:24
born to b. unseen GRAY 350:11
blushed saw its God, and b. CRAS 244:3
blushes Only Animal that B. TWAI 786:9
blushful b. Hippocrene KEAT 429:8
blushing bears his b. honours SHAK 673:12
b. apricot JONS 420:28
b. discontented sun SHAK 695:12
b. either for a sigh CONG 233:5
other people without b. SHAW 709:1
boa b. constrictor as a tape-measure GOGA 343:21
boar tidy Bartholomew b.-pig SHAK 669:33
board carried on b. HUME 394:14
hospitable b. WORD 828:17
I struck the b. HERB 372:6
There wasn't any B. HERB 371:15
boards Ships are but b. SHAK 687:10
boast B. not thyself of to morrow BIBL 83:27
b. of heraldry GRAY 350:9
do falsely b. BOOK 142:14
Such is the patriot's b. GOLD 345:7
boasteth then he b. BIBL 83:11
boat Architecture and a b. PUGI 616:17
b. he can sail THOM 775:23
first launched his frail b. HORA 387:15
if men are together in a b. HALI 357:8
love b. has crashed LAST 456:13
sank my b. KENN 433:19
sewer in a glass-bottomed b. MIZN 524:13
soul is an enchanted b. SHEL 713:13
Speed, bonnie b. BOUL 145:2
Until I have a little b. WORD 830:15
When the b. comes in NURS 548:1
boathook diplomatic b. SALI 642:14
boating Jolly b. weather CORY 237:11
boatman B., do not tarry CAMP 183:11
boats leathern b. MARV 499:8
messing about in b. GRAH 348:7
seek happiness in b. HORA 386:20
bobtail money on de b. nag FOST 321:15
Boche well-killed B. READ 622:13
bodes b. some strange eruption SHAK 661:8
Bodhidharma [B.] come to China MUMO 536:12
Bodhisattva B. who is full of pity MAHĀ 489:16
Bodhisattvas pure deeds of the B. SHAN 706:10
bodice lace my b. blue HUNT 396:7
bodies b. are buried in peace BIBL 92:17
b. but not their souls GIBR 336:11
b. into light NEWT 543:4
B. never lie DE M 257:1
b. of those EDWA 289:10
b. of unburied men WEBS 808:13
contact of two b. CHAM 201:7
men's poor b. JUVE 425:1
One soul inhabiting two b. ARIS 25:10
Our b. why do we forbear DONN 273:25
our dead b. SCOT 650:9
outwardly in our b. BOOK 128:4
Pile the b. high SAND 643:21
present your b. BIBL 105:14
scorn their b. BAST 57:2
souls out of men's b. SHAK 691:6
structure of our b. STOP 743:10
well-developed b. FORS 320:9
with two seeming b. SHAK 690:6
bodkin With a bare b. SHAK 664:4
body Absent in b. BIBL 105:33
Africa than my own b. ORTO 557:17
b. and the soul know ROET 631:10
b. as the chariot UPAN 788:1
b. between your knees CORY 237:11
b. Borne before her THAC 769:16
b. continues in its state of rest NEWT 543:5
b. did contain a spirit SHAK 669:13
b. form doth take SPEN 734:15
b. is a machine TOLS 779:13
b. is in the bliss AKHM 9:8
b. is the temple BIBL 106:3
b., Nature is POPE 585:16
b. of a weak and feeble woman ELIZ 296:27
b. of Benjamin Franklin EPIT 302:1
b. of this death BIBL 105:5
b., of thought CARL 188:12
B., remember not only CAVA 198:4
b.'s beauty lives STEV 740:2
b.'s vest aside MARV 498:17
b. swayed to music YEAT 835:3
b. than raiment BIBL 93:23
change our vile b. BOOK 131:14
commit his b. to the deep BOOK 142:6
commit his b. to the ground BOOK 131:14
every interstice of my b. EDDI 288:1
exercise is to the b. STEE 737:1
Fretted the pigmy b. DRYD 279:21
future b. for ever ZORO 841:18
gigantic b. MACA 481:13
Gin a body meet a b. BURN 166:20
give my b. to be burned BIBL 106:16
good-will of the b. RIDI 627:14
her b. thought DONN 273:9
I keep under my b. BIBL 106:11
i like my b. CUMM 247:12
in a sound b. JUVE 425:2
in mind, b., or estate BOOK 127:18
interpose my b. STRA 744:9
in the midst of my b. BOOK 132:24
John Brown's b. SONG 729:13
keep your b. white STEV 742:21
left me but my b.'s length SHAK 673:3
liberation of the human b. GOLD 344:5
Marry my b. to that dust KING 436:7
my useless b. BROW 151:19
no b. to be kicked THUR 777:4
none in the b. LAWR 458:9
Of the glorious B. sing THOM 771:10
out of my b. HAND 359:8
out of the b. BIBL 107:15
renouncing his b. JAIN 402:4
Resurrection of the b. BOOK 126:10
rid of the rest of her b. VANB 789:9
salutary to the b. PROU 594:11

shapes itself to the b. WOLL 825:23
sing the b. electric WHIT 815:3
Soul, leaving the b. UPAN 787:14
so young a b. SHAK 688:9
spirit leaves his mortal b. BHAG 72:16
stepped out of my b. WRIG 833:12
Thersites' b. SHAK 660:29
this is my b. BIBL 97:18
though her b. die MILT 518:23
to keep one's b. MACK 486:7
use of my b. BECK 59:16
wanders on to a new b. BHAG 72:14
with my b. I thee worship BOOK 131:6
woman watches her b. uneasily COHE 224:3
wreathing his b. SMAR 722:5
Boets hate all B. and Bainters GEOR 333:9
boggy dark, b., dirty GOLD 345:21
Bognor Bugger B. LAST 455:5
bogs from b. and precipices LOCK 472:1
bogus than a b. god MACN 488:6
bohemian so-called b. elements KERO 434:6
boil b. at different degrees EMER 299:31
b. breaking forth BIBL 75:36
war that would not b. TAYL 756:8
boiled in b. and roast SMIT 725:8
boiler centrally-heated b.-room HILL 377:4
boilers b. and vats JOHN 416:20
boiling b. bloody breast SHAK 690:24
boils watched pot never b. PROV 613:40
bois *au fond des b.* VIGN 792:14
Nous n'irons plus aux b. ANON 20:11
bold be b. and be sensible HORA 386:15
Be b., be bold SPEN 734:5
b. as a blind mare PROV 608:16
b. as a hawk LOVE 477:4
b. as a hawk THUR 777:2
b. as a lion BIBL 83:31
b. bad man SPEN 733:15
b. man that first SWIF 748:16
Fortune assists the b. VIRG 795:9
made me b. SHAK 683:3
This b. bad man SHAK 673:8
boldest b. held his breath CAMP 183:3
boldly to b. go RODD 631:1
boldness B., and again boldness DANT 250:6
b. at least will deserve PROP 593:16
B. be my friend SHAK 660:18
B. is an ill keeper BACO 42:13
what first? b. BACO 42:12
Bolingbroke this canker, B. SHAK 667:24
bolt b., and the breech REED 623:14
b. is shot back somewhere ARNO 26:3
bolts b. are hurled TENN 763:14
bomb atom b. is a paper tiger MAO 495:3
Ban the b. POLI 581:3
b. them back into the Stone Age LEMA 463:4
defence against the atom b. ANON 15:14
'formula' of the atomic b. MEDA 503:4
ones we intended to b. BLY 122:15
bombazine B. would have shown GASK 330:19
bombed glad we've been b. ELIZ 298:1
protect him from being b. BALD 49:8
bomber b. will always get through BALD 49:8
bombers b. named for girls JARR 404:10
bombinans *chimera in vacuo b.* RABE 619:12
bombs b. redoubled on the hills MOTI 534:5
Come, friendly b. BETJ 71:4
bond b. between two people RILK 628:4
b. nor free BIBL 109:4
break that sole b. BURK 163:6
great b. SHAK 684:7
I will have my b. SHAK 688:5
look to his b. SHAK 687:28
take a b. of fate SHAK 685:1
word is his b. PROV 599:17
bondage b. of rhyming MILT 514:6
b. to parents WOLL 826:1
b. which is freedom's self SHEL 713:18
Cassius from b. will deliver SHAK 674:23
condition of b. STAN 736:9
house of b. BIBL 76:8
spirit of b. BIBL 105:7
bonding male b. TIGE 777:12
bondman b.'s two hundred and fifty years LINC 468:17
Checked like a b. SHAK 676:25
so base that would be a b. SHAK 675:26
bonds b. of civil society LOCK 472:4
except these b. BIBL 104:23
surly b. of earth MAGE 489:8
surly b. of earth REAG 623:7
bondsmen Hereditary b. BYRO 174:6
bondwoman of the b. BIBL 107:19
bone B. of my bone MILT 517:19
b. of my bones BIBL 73:22
commend the b. DICK 266:20
dog that will fetch a b. PROV 598:26
fighting for a b. PROV 614:44
hair about the b. DONN 274:10
knows death to the b. YEAT 835:15
nearer the b. PROV 607:19
poor dog a b. NURS 549:18
rag and a b. KIPL 440:16
What's bred in the b. PROV 614:6
boneless b. wonder CHUR 215:2
bones b. are out of joint BOOK 132:24
b. are smitten asunder BOOK 134:8
b. of a person COMP 230:18
b. of a single Pomeranian BISM 116:9
b. of one British Grenadier HARR 362:13
b. which thou hast broken BOOK 135:6
Can these b. live BIBL 89:33
come to lay his weary b. SHAK 673:18
conjuring trick with b. JENK 406:6
dead men lost their b. ELIO 296:4
dead men's b. BIBL 96:28
England keep my b. SHAK 677:18
for his honoured b. MILT 513:14
from my dead b., avenger VIRG 794:14
hadde pigges b. CHAU 205:6
Hard words break no b. PROV 601:52
hatchment o'er his b. SHAK 666:9
he that moves my b. EPIT 302:10
his b. are coral SHAK 698:27
I may tell all my b. BOOK 132:25
In my veins, in my b. ROET 631:6
lay my b. amongst you WOLS 826:4
little ones picked the b. O! NURS 549:19
mocked the dead b. SHAK 696:17
my b. consumed away BOOK 133:17
O ye dry b. BIBL 89:34
Rattle his b. NOEL 546:13
subsist in b. BROW 153:5
tongs and the b. SHAK 690:11
valley full of b. BIBL 89:32
you buy meat, you buy b. PROV 615:23
bonfire b. of the vanities WOLF 825:12
to the everlasting b. SHAK 683:14
Bong-tree where the B. grows LEAR 460:17
bonheur *b. seul est salutaire* PROU 594:11
bonhomie natural *b.* BENT 67:5
bonjour *B. tristesse* ÉLUA 299:2
bon-mots b. from their places MORE 530:23
bonnets Blue B. are bound SCOT 651:29
b. of Bonny Dundee SCOT 650:11
bonny Am I no a b. fighter STEV 741:5
Belbroughton Road is b. BETJ 70:16
bonnets of B. Dundee SCOT 650:11
b., bonnie banks SONG 730:1
longer in b. Dundee SCOT 652:6
saw ye b. Lesley BURN 166:19
bono *Cui b.* CICE 217:25
bonum *Summum b.* CICE 217:14
bonus *b. homo* AUCT 33:9
videri b. malebat SALL 643:9
Boojum Snark *was* a B. CARR 191:26
book agree with the b. of God OMAR 554:15
any b. but the Baronetage AUST 38:7
any b. but the Baronetage OPEN 556:16
before this b. is published RUNC 637:9
Bell, b., and candle SHAK 677:10
b. a devil's chaplain DARW 251:1
B., and the Prophets KORA 443:17
b. cannot take the place ANON 19:5
b. is the precious life-blood MILT 519:9
b. is the purest essence CARL 188:18
b. of life BIBL 111:26
B. of Life begins WILD 818:26
b. of nature GALI 328:13
b. of the living BOOK 136:13
b. of verse—and Thou FITZ 314:9
b. that ever took him out of bed JOHN 414:6
B. wherein is no doubt KORA 443:15
b., who runs may read KEBL 432:6
b. would have been finished WODE 824:16
bred in a b. SHAK 680:24
but his b. JONS 420:18
Camerado, this is no b. WHIT 815:8
damned, thick, square b. GLOU 341:19
destroys a good b. MILT 519:8
doth best commend a b. HEMI 369:7
Each country B.-club BYRO 178:2
empty b. is like an infant's TRAH 780:8
Farewel my b. CHAU 206:24
Galeotto was the b. DANT 249:14
Go, litel b. CHAU 207:18
Go, little b. STEV 743:3
good b. is the best of friends TUPP 784:18
great b. CALL 181:17
great b. is a great evil PROV 601:33
had been reading the b. TOLS 779:9
I'll drown my b. SHAK 699:10
insignificant b. because WOOL 826:19
In the volume of the b. BOOK 134:1
Kiss the b.'s outside COWP 240:4
knows this out of the b. DICK 263:21
leaves of the Judgement B. unfold TAYL 756:15
little volume, but large b. CRAS 244:9
look at the best b. RUSK 638:17
make one b. JOHN 415:2
Making a b. is a craft LA B 446:19
my little b. JUVE 424:6
nice new little b. CATU 194:19
noble grand b. GASK 330:23
no Frigate like a B. DICK 266:10
non-reading a b. BYRO 180:9
noted in thy b. BOOK 135:13
oldest rule in the b. CARR 190:9
only half the b. CONR 234:26
pain to pen the b. OXFO 562:16
peruses a b. ADDI 4:24
print My b. HERR 375:1
read a b. before reviewing it SMIT 726:2
Reading one b. DUAN 283:19
read the b. BEVA 71:15
sending down of the B. KORA 445:5
sent down to thee the B. KORA 444:17
substance of a b. directly KNOW 442:9
take the b. along STER 738:21
tell a b. by its cover PROV 615:31
this b. I directe To the CHAU 207:22
throw the b. in the fire SAND 643:14
throw this b. about BELL 63:2
to every b. its copy COLU 230:6
use of a b. CARR 189:7
valuable b. by chance GRAY 351:9
when I wrote that b. SWIF 750:1
where's the b. CHUR 213:19
with a religious b. WOTT 832:23
without mentioning a single b. REED 624:2
worthy to open the b. BIBL 112:2
write in a b. BIBL 111:20
writing a b. BRON 150:4
written a b. JOWE 421:14
written b. MISS 523:4
wrote the b. LINC 469:4
Your face, my thane, is as a b. SHAK 682:5
bookful b. blockhead POPE 585:2
bookkeeping inventor of double-entry b. MULL 536:3
books b. are divisible RUSK 638:14
b. are either dreams or swords LOWE 477:10
B. are made FLAU 316:18

books (*cont.*):
B. are not absolutely dead MILT 519:7
b. are to be tasted BACO 44:6
b. are weapons ROOS 633:1
B. are well written WILD 818:14
b. be then the eloquence SHAK 704:12
b., clad in blak or reed CHAU 204:19
B. do furnish a room POWE 590:8
B. from Boots' and country lanes BETJ 70:13
b. I leave behind KIPL 438:4
B.,in Mallow BOWE 145:8
b. in the running brooks SHAK 658:14
B., like men their authors SWIF 748:19
B. must follow sciences BACO 45:6
b. of law JOHN 408:13
b. of travel ELIO 293:3
B. say: she did this because BARN 55:1
b., the academes SHAK 680:26
B. think for me LAMB 448:15
b. to gather facts from CARL 188:17
b. undeservedly forgotten AUDE 35:15
b. were opened BIBL 90:6
B. will speak plain BACO 42:17
borrowers of b. LAMB 448:13
collection of b. CARL 188:1
cream of others' b. MORE 530:23
Deep-versed in b. MILT 518:10
gentleman is not in your b. SHAK 690:33
God has written all the b. BUTL 172:25
his b. were read BELL 64:4
If my b. had been any worse CHAN 201:17
in b.' clothing LAMB 448:16
In b. lies the *soul* CARL 187:29
I never read b. PUNC 617:15
Keeping b. on charity PERÓ 573:23
lard their lean b. BURT 170:3
learn men from b. DISR 270:32
made the b. and he died FAUL 307:26
making many b. BIBL 85:4
more in woods than b. BERN 69:1
new French b. BROW 155:9
proper study of mankind is b. HUXL 396:18
quiet, friendship, b. THOM 775:6
read all the b. MALL 492:2
read any good b. lately CATC 195:20
read b. *through* JOHN 414:21
reading of good b. DESC 258:16
so charming as b. SMIT 725:15
speaks about his own b. DISR 269:12
spectacles of b. DRYD 283:6
studied b. than men BACO 44:27
thumb each other's b. RUSK 638:18
thy toil O'er b. GAY 332:6
to Cambridge b. he sent BROW 154:7
Wherever b. will be burned HEIN 368:3
You remember b. CROS 246:8
booksellers nor men, nor even b. HORA 386:7
boon b. and a blessing ADVE 8:13
boot b. in the face PLAT 577:14
B., saddle, to horse BROW 155:15
b. stamping on a human face ORWE 559:2
bootboy body of the b. at Claridges WOOL 827:3
booted b. and spurred RUMB 637:4
boots blaming on his b. BECK 59:22
Books from B.' and country lanes BETJ 70:13
boots—b.—movin' KIPL 438:7
doormat in a world of b. RHYS 626:1
have one's b. on MONT 527:7
in his top-b. MARL 495:14
truth is pulling its b. on SPUR 735:14
went to school without any b. BULM 160:3
when I take my b. off DICK 262:16
booze fool with b. FAUL 308:2
boozes tell a man who "b." BURT 169:17
bop Playing 'B.' ELLI 298:7
Bo-Peep Little B. NURS 549:4
Borden Lizzie B. took an axe ANON 17:10
border B., nor Breed KIPL 438:5
bound for the B. SCOT 651:29
crossing the B. AUDE 34:12
gaed o'er the b. BURN 166:19
seductive b. TAWN 755:12
We'll over the B. HOGG 380:12
borders b. of sleep THOM 773:2
bore healthy male adult b. UPDI 788:9
hero becomes a b. EMER 299:29
Less is a b. VENT 791:5
old b. TREE 781:3
secret of being a b. VOLT 797:14
To be in it is merely a b. WILD 818:28
bored b. for England MUGG 534:17
b.; the great things are done BISM 116:13
Bores and *B.* BYRO 177:24
Ever to confess you're b. BERR 69:19
I'd get b. and fall over COMP 230:10
boredom b. and terror WELL 809:13
B. a problem for the moralist RUSS 639:11
b. on a large scale INGE 399:4
b. stays CHAN 202:2
desire for desires—b. TOLS 779:7
Life is first b., then fear LARK 452:15
perish of despair and b. FRAN 322:16
bores *B.* and *Bored* BYRO 177:24
B. have succeeded to dragons DISR 270:35
virtue of b. WAUG 806:19
Borgias In Italy under the B. FILM 311:16
boring Life, friends, is b. BERR 69:19
born as soon as we were b. BIBL 91:12
because you were b. in it SHAW 707:13
blight man was b. for HOPK 384:19
b. after the flesh BIBL 107:19
b. again BIBL 101:16
b. for death KEAT 429:14
b. for the sake of religion LAWS 459:2
b. free ANON 15:6
b. free as Caesar SHAK 674:10
b. in a cellar CONG 232:18
B. in a cellar FOOT 319:5
b. in a house JEAN 404:17
b. in a stable PROV 606:20
b. in one another's pain THOM 774:3
B. in the garret BYRO 179:2
B. in the USA SPRI 735:10
b. into the world alive GILB 337:14
b. King of the Jews BIBL [illegible]
b. of a woman BIBL 81:18
B. of the sun SPEN 732:19
B. of the very sigh KEAT 428:5
B. of the Virgin Mary BOOK 126:10
B. on Monday NURS 550:19
B. on the fourth of July COHA 224:1
b. out of due time BIBL 106:19
b. out of my due time MORR 532:12
b. three thousand years old DELA 256:22
b. to be hanged PROV 603:36
b. to run SPRI 735:12
b. to set it right SHAK 663:7
b. to set it right STRA 744:7
b. under a rhyming planet SHAK 691:22
b. where my fathers lived SITT 720:18
b. with a different face BLAK 119:8
b. with a gift of laughter SABA 641:2
b. with uprightness CONF 231:12
b. with your legs apart ORTO 558:4
British Bourgeoise is not b. SITW 721:6
Christians are not b. JERO 406:17
die as to be b. BACO 42:24
Else, wherefore b. TENN 759:17
Every moment one is b. TENN 767:13
for being b. WATS 804:17
had not been b. BIBL 97:17
house where I was b. HOOD 382:21
I am not yet b. MACN 488:13
I was b. barefoot LONG 473:7
I was b. sneering GILB 337:22
I was free b. BIBL 104:16
less than to be b. BEAU 58:16
lucky to be b. WHIT 815:12
Man is b. to live PAST 569:2
Man is b. unto trouble BIBL 81:9
man that is b. CONR 234:15
Man that is b. of a woman BOOK 131:12
Man was b. free ROUS 636:5
naturally were b. free MILT 520:3
Not to be b. BACO 45:13
Not to be b. SOPH 728:15
not to be b. is best AUDE 33:23
One is not b. a woman DE B 254:4
one of woman b. SHAK 685:24
powerless to be b. ARNO 27:21
some men are b. great SHAK 701:28
sucker b. every minute BARN 55:11
that thou was b. with SHAK 678:8
Then surely I was b. CHES 210:4
those who are to be b. BURK 163:29
thus was I b. again LACK 447:2
time to be b. BIBL 84:7
took the trouble to be b. BEAU 58:11
to the manner b. SHAK 662:17
under that was I b. SHAK 691:5
unto us a child is b. BIBL 87:1
virgin mother b. MILT 513:17
We all are b. mad BECK 60:2
were b. or should die TRAH 780:15
We were not b. to sue SHAK 694:10
When we are b. SHAK 680:1
wherein I was b. BIBL 81:3
women are b. slaves ASTE 31:15
Yorkshire b. PROV 615:21
borne b. even heavier things VIRG 793:9
It is b. in upon me HARE 362:4
Still have I b. it SHAK 687:15
borogoves mimsy were the b. CARR 190:12
boroughs bright b. HOPK 384:20
borrow have to b. the money WARD 803:6
men who b. LAMB 448:12
borrower b., nor a lender be SHAK 662:12
b. of the night SHAK 684:1
borrowers b. of books LAMB 448:13
borrowing banqueting upon b. BIBL 91:31
b., goes a sorrowing PROV 602:14
b. only lingers SHAK 669:28
borrows early man never b. PROV 599:3
bosom b. and half her side COLE 224:20
b. of a single state DURH 286:6
carry them in his b. BIBL 88:2
Close b.-friend KEAT 430:8
in Arthur's b. SHAK 671:2
in my b. like a bee LODG 472:17
into Abraham's b. BIBL 100:10
into his b. creeps FLET 318:16
in your fragrant b. CARE 186:15
in your white b. CRAS 244:10
no b. and no behind SMIT 724:24
seat is the b. of God HOOK 383:6
sleep in Abraham's b. SHAK 696:23
slip Into my b. TENN 766:3
take fire in his b. BIBL 82:15
bosoms Quiet to quick b. BYRO 174:17
white b. JOHN 412:10
boss b. there is always MARQ 497:9
bossing nobody b. you ORWE 559:5
bossy by the b. for the bully SELD 653:25
Boston B. man is the east wind APPL 23:5
good old B. BOSS 143:15
Boswelliana *Lues B.* MACA 482:4
botanist I am not a b. JOHN 412:23
I'd be a b. FERM 309:2
botanize b. Upon his mother's grave WORD 830:17
Botany Bay New colonies seek for at B. FREE 324:4
botch make a b. BELL 64:3
botches Leave no rubs nor b. SHAK 684:3
both long as ye b. shall live BOOK 131:4
wear it on b. sides SHAK 700:18
bother 'B. it' I may GILB 338:25
Sufficient conscience to b. him LLOY 471:9
young whom I hope to b. AUDE 35:4
bothered Bewitched, b., and bewildered HART 363:4
botté *toujours b.* MONT 527:7
Botticelli B.'s a cheese PUNC 617:21

bottle bothers to buy a b. DWOR 286:11
b. and a bag GASC 330:14
b. has just been opened HESI 375:14
b. it and sell it MCDO 485:3
b. of hay SHAK 690:12
b. on the chimley-piece DICK 263:6
b. to give him DICK 262:13
little for the b. DIBD 260:10
tears into thy b. BOOK 135:13
way out of the b.-bottle WITT 824:5
bottles fill old b. with banknotes KEYN 435:9
narrow-necked b. POPE 587:19
new wine in old b. PROV 615:29
new wine into old b. BIBL 94:26
bottom Bless thee, B. SHAK 690:2
fairies at the b. of our garden FYLE 327:16
forgotten man at the b. ROOS 632:10
from the b. of the deck SHAP 706:11
reach the b. first GRAH 348:3
sit down on my b. FLEM 317:17
bottomless Law is a b. pit ARBU 23:15
pit that is b. JAME 402:12
boue *nostalgie de la b.* AUGI 35:21
bough bloom along the b. HOUS 390:14
blossom that hangs on the b. SHAK 699:11
bread beneath the b. FITZ 314:9
golden b. BORR 144:8
Petals on a wet, black b. POUN 589:18
boughs hang Upon those b. SHAK 704:29
I got me b. off many a tree HERB 372:11
rotten b. to climb WYAT 834:2
bought Gold be b. too dear PROV 601:20
with guilt is b. and sold SHEL 713:7
bound b. for the same bourn HOUS 391:6
b. him a thousand years BIBL 113:4
b. in misery and iron BOOK 139:12
b. in the spirit BIBL 104:13
tied and b. BOOK 127:15
to another b. GREV 353:4
boundary b. of Britain TACI 752:8
right to fix the b. PARN 568:1
bounded b. in a nut-shell SHAK 663:17
bounden b. duty BOOK 129:20
b. duty and service BOOK 130:1
boundless b. better, boundless worse TENN 767:6
b., endless, and sublime BYRO 175:11
bounds shall thy b. be set BENS 66:13
bounteous may this b. God WINK 823:6
bounties morning b. COWP 240:26
bountiful My Lady b. FARQ 307:6
bouquet b. is better than the taste POTT 589:1
bouquets broken Anne of gathering b. FROS 326:11
bourg rustic murmur of their b. TENN 760:2
bourgeois astonish the b. BAUD 57:13
beastly the b. is LAWR 458:8
b., ce sont les autres RENA 624:12
b. climb up on them FLAU 316:18
b. prefers comfort HESS 375:16
bourgeoise British B. is not born SITW 721:6
bourgeoisie b. in the long run TROT 783:16
discreet charm of the b. FILM 312:18
bourn bound for the same b. HOUS 391:6
country from whose b. SHAK 664:4
see beyond our b. KEAT 430:15
set a b. how far SHAK 656:7
bourne b. from which no hollingsworth MORT 533:15
b. of time and place TENN 758:13
Bovril B. prevents ADVE 7:9
bow B. down before him MONS 526:12
b. myself BIBL 80:19
b. of burning gold BLAK 120:1
b. was made in England DOYL 278:9
b., ye tradesmen GILB 337:11
breaketh the b. BOOK 134:20
drew a b. at a venture BIBL 80:11
every knee should b. BIBL 108:17
from the Almighty's b. BLAK 119:1
I b. my knees BIBL 107:27
Lord of the unerring b. BYRO 175:6
set my b. in the cloud BIBL 74:22
bowed At her feet he b. BIBL 77:29
bowels b. of compassion BIBL 111:12
b. of the earth DRAY 279:5
in the b. of Christ CROM 245:12
bower b. we shrined to Tennyson HARD 361:7
deck both bed and b. SPEN 733:27
doth build his b. LODG 472:18
lime-tree b. my prison COLE 227:3
smooth-swarded b. TENN 765:7
St Johnston's b. BALL 50:19
bowers green and pleasant b. BLAK 119:5
lodged in thy living b. VAUG 790:16
bowl b. we call The Sky FITZ 314:18
fill the flowing b. SONG 729:2
golden b. be broken BIBL 85:2
lurk within the b. SMIT 725:21
Morning in the b. of night FITZ 314:7
bowlder wild b. things he bowls LANG 450:10
bowled b. the sun TAYL 756:16
bowling lies poor Tom B. DIBD 260:14
recommend the b.-green GREE 351:12
bowls play at b. must look out PROV 612:43
bows B. down to wood and stone HEBE 367:7
bowstrings Hold, or cut b. SHAK 689:15
bow windows putting b. to the house DICK 261:18
bow-wow Big B. strain SCOT 652:12
his b. way PEMB 572:11
bow-wows to the demnition b. DICK 264:9
box B. about AUBR 32:21
b. where sweets lie HERB 373:17
life like a b. of chocolates FILM 312:2
twelve good men into a b. BROU 151:12
Worth a guinea a b. ADVE 8:21
boxes Little b. on the hillside REYN 625:14
boxing B.'s just showbusiness BRUN 159:1
boy Alas, pitiable b. VIRG 795:2
and a b. forever ROWL 636:13
any b. may become President STEV 740:11
befall a b. MAUG 502:6
Being read to by a b. ELIO 294:21
b. brought in the white sheet GARC 329:10
b. eternal SHAK 702:31
b. my greatness SHAK 657:24
b. on the sea-shore NEWT 543:11
b. out of the country PROV 615:34
b. stood on the burning deck HEMA 369:5
b. stood on the burning deck OPEN 555:9
b.'s will is the wind's LONG 473:23
b. to do a man's job PROV 607:36
b. will ruin himself GEOR 334:3
Chatterton, the marvellous b. WORD 831:12
Let the b. win EDWA 289:4
Little B. Blue NURS 549:5
little tiny b. SHAK 702:22
Mad about the b. COWA 238:14
Minstrel B. to the war MOOR 530:14
plaything of the b. BAGE 47:19
remain a fifteen-year-old b. ROTH 635:18
sat the journeying b. HARD 361:20
schoolrooms for 'the b.' COOK 235:16
silly twisted b. CATC 196:34
soaring human b. DICK 260:24
thanks of a b. BEEC 61:8
Two boys are half a b. PROV 613:25
Upon the growing b. WORD 829:20
When I was a little b. ANON 19:14
whining, purblind, wayward b. SHAK 680:22
your little b. CARR 189:15
boyfriend best way to obtain b. FIEL 309:12
certain thing called the B. WILS 822:7
boyhood b. of Judas Æ 6:8
boys As flies to wanton b. SHAK 679:15
B. and girls NURS 547:13
b. get at one end JOHN 415:8
b. go first to bed HERB 373:3
b. in the back room LOES 473:1
b. in the back rooms BEAV 59:3
b. late at their play ARNO 27:2
b. not going to be sent ROOS 632:16
b. of the old Brigade WEAT 806:24
B. will be boys PROV 596:35
b. with breeches BARB 53:18
Christian b. ARNO 29:13
Deceive b. with toys LYSA 480:22
for office b. SALI 643:2
if the b. are still there BARU 56:12
lightfoot b. are laid HOUS 391:8
Like little wanton b. SHAK 673:12
little b. made of NURS 551:19
loaded guns with b. CRAB 243:11
send American b. JOHN 408:17
three merry b. are we FLET 318:3
Till the b. come home FORD 320:6
two sorts of b. DICK 264:16
virgin girls and b. HORA 388:11
bra Burn your b. SAYI 647:2
I want a b. BLUM 122:9
bracelet b. of bright hair DONN 274:10
braces Damn b. BLAK 119:22
bracing B. brain and sinew KING 437:8
bracket date slides into the b. EWAR 305:8
Bradford silk hat on a B. millionaire ELIO 296:10
Bradshaw vocabulary of 'B.' DOYL 278:7
brae stout heart to stey b. PROV 609:50
braes among thy green b. BURN 166:10
Ye banks and b. BURN 166:16
brag Beauty is Nature's b. MILT 511:29
B. is a good dog PROV 596:36
Brahman B. is consciousness UPAN 787:17
knows that all-highest B. UPAN 788:6
braid b., braid road BALL 52:1
braided b. her yellow hair BALL 51:18
braids b. of lilies knitting MILT 512:1
brain Bear of Very Little B. MILN 510:14
b. attic stocked DOYL 277:10
b. has the consistency TURI 785:10
b. is 30 years old EISE 291:12
b.? my second favourite organ ALLE 12:12
b. of feathers POPE 580:12
b. to think again BRON 150:1
dry b. in a dry season ELIO 294:23
dull b. perplexes KEAT 429:11
fibre from the b. does tear BLAK 117:19
fingerprints across his b. HEND 369:17
gleaned my teeming b. KEAT 430:17
good b. may do JONS 419:10
harmful to the b. JAME 402:12
hasn't exactly got B. MILN 511:6
heat-oppressed b. SHAK 682:21
idle b. is devil's workshop PROV 603:9
if the b. has oozed out KRAU 445:20
instrumental to the b. SHAK 661:15
leave that b. outside GILB 337:15
motions of atoms in my b. HALD 356:16
petrifactions of a plodding b. BYRO 178:5
possess a poet's b. DRAY 279:6
schoolmasters puzzle their b. GOLD 345:17
tares of mine own b. BROW 153:23
thus concern His b. BYRO 176:3
why did He give us a b. LUCE 478:19
brained large-b. woman BROW 154:23
brains blow out your b. KIPL 440:22
Blows out his b. BROW 157:27
b. eaten by moths SITW 721:3
b. go to his head ASQU 31:9
b. of a Minerva BARR 56:3
busy b. must beat on tickle toys GASC 330:16
Cudgel thy b. no more SHAK 666:19
dash'd the b. out SHAK 682:17
girl with b. ought to LOOS 475:10
Had their b. knocked out SHEL 712:9
mix them with my b. OPIE 557:1
brainwashing it is called b. GREE 352:10
brake invented the b. NEME 541:3

brambles b. in the fortresses BIBL 87:20
b. like tall cedars show COTT 237:16
branch b. shall grow BIBL 87:3
Cut is the b. MARL 496:8
lops the mouldered b. TENN 759:7
on the high b. SAPP 644:15
branches lodge in the b. BIBL 95:22
branchy b. between towers HOPK 384:4
brandy B. for the parson KIPL 440:8
b. of the damned SHAW 708:4
drink b. JOHN 416:8
fou o' b. BURN 167:12
get me a glass of b. GEOR 333:15
brass b., nor stone, nor earth SHAK 704:27
evil manners live in b. SHAK 673:22
I am become as sounding b. BIBL 106:16
muck there's b. PROV 614:41
brassière Art is not a *b.* BARN 54:18
brat rambling b. (in print) BRAD 146:13
spurious b., Tom Jones RICH 627:8
brave b. bad man CLAR 218:23
b. bad man CLOS 222:12
b. deserve the fair PROV 608:9
b. man with a sword WILD 818:32
B. men lived before PROV 596:37
B. new world BORR 144:1
b. world, Sir BEHN 62:12
cry, 'you are b.!' GRAH 348:6
Fears of the b. JOHN 411:18
Fortune assists the b. TERE 768:4
Fortune favours the b. PROV 600:44
Fortune favours the b. VIRG 795:9
home of the b. KEY 434:16
How sleep the b. COLL 229:9
Many b. men lived HORA 389:9
None but the b. DRYD 280:17
O b. new world SHAK 699:12
Oh, the b. music FITZ 314:10
one b. push STEV 741:22
one half of mankind b. JOHN 416:5
souls of the b. CLOU 221:15
Toll for the b. COWP 240:23
to-morrow to be b. ARMS 25:16
What's b., what's noble SHAK 657:20
braver done one b. thing DONN 274:18
bravery acts of personal b. WAUG 806:12
natural b. of your isle SHAK 660:23
braw b. bricht moonlicht MORR 533:3
b. gallant BALL 50:10
brawler not a b. BIBL 109:14
brawling b. woman BIBL 83:12
bray Vicar of B. SONG 729:12
brazen her world is b. SIDN 718:22
Brazil Charley's aunt from B. THOM 771:16
Brazilian If I were a B. STIN 743:7
breach goaded to the b. of order GODW 342:8
More honoured in the b. SHAK 662:17
Once more unto the b. SHAK 671:5
bread ate his b. in sorrow GOET 343:11
better than no b. PROV 601:41
bitter b. of banishment SHAK 695:4
b. and circuses JUVE 424:21
b. beneath the bough FITZ 314:9
b. eaten in secret BIBL 82:19
b. eaten up CERV 199:17
b. is black BARC 53:22
b. never falls but PROV 596:38
b. of adversity BIBL 87:17
b. of affliction BIBL 80:10
b. of God BIBL 101:27
B. of heaven WILL 820:8
b. of poverty HAGG 355:13
b.-sauce of the happy ending JAME 403:14
b. should be so dear HOOD 383:1
b. to strengthen man's heart BOOK 139:3
b. with joy BIBL 84:21
breaking of b. BIBL 100:35
Cast thy b. upon the waters BIBL 84:27
crammed with distressful b. SHAK 671:20
cutting b. and butter THAC 769:15
eat dusty b. BOGA 123:12
holy b., the food unpriced MASE 500:15
I am the b. of life BIBL 101:28
if his son ask b. BIBL 94:5
live by b. alone BIBL 92:32
live by b. alone PROV 606:13
looked to government for b. BURK 164:10
loud for b. KING 436:20
made, like b. LE G 462:14
not by b. alone STEV 742:3
offered a piece of b. and butter MACK 486:9
one half-pennyworth of b. SHAK 668:17
our daily b. BIBL 93:19
ravens brought him b. BIBL 79:25
Royal slice of b. MILN 510:18
shalt thou eat b. BIBL 74:6
taste of another man's b. DANT 250:4
that which is not b. BIBL 88:20
took B. BOOK 129:22
took b., and blessed it BIBL 97:18
took the b. and brake it ELIZ 297:13
unleavened b. BIBL 75:39
unleavened b. of sincerity BIBL 106:2
we did eat b. BIBL 76:7
breadth length and b. BALL 50:14
break at the b. of the day STRU 745:2
bend and I b. not LA F 447:10
b. a man's spirit SHAW 706:23
B., break, break TENN 757:11
b. every yoke BIBL 89:1
b. Into blossom WRIG 833:12
b. the ice BACO 42:19
b. them at pleasure EDGE 288:17
But b., my heart SHAK 661:28
Have a b. ADVE 7:24
if you b. the bloody glass MACN 488:9
I'll b. my staff SHAK 699:10
lark at b. of day SHAK 704:15
Never give a sucker an even b. FIEL 310:18
shall he not b. BIBL 88:6
sucker an even b. PROV 607:29
thyself must b. at last ARNO 26:14
breakdown approaching nervous b. RUSS 639:12
Madness need not be all b. LAIN 448:5
breaketh b. the bow BOOK 134:20
b. the cedar-trees BOOK 133:13
breakfast bad review may spoil b. AMIS 14:2
committed b. with it LEWI 467:1
critical period is b.-time HERB 371:19
embarrassment and b. BARN 54:17
Hope is a good b. BACO 45:8
Hope is a good b. PROV 602:49
impossible things before b. CARR 190:25
One doth but b. here HENS 371:5
our b. take BALL 52:3
Sing before b. PROV 610:43
that sits down to b. YEAT 837:26
wholesome, hungry b. WALT 802:21
breakfasted b. with you BRUC 158:19
breaking b. of bread BIBL 100:35
b. of windows MORE 530:22
take pleasure in b. NURS 547:15
without b. eggs PROV 615:40
breaks something twangs and b. MACN 488:10
breast aching in the b. POPE 582:21
boiling bloody b. SHAK 690:24
b. high amid the corn HOOD 382:27
broods with warm b. HOPK 384:6
dwell, alas! in my b. GOET 342:17
faultless b. the furnace is SOUT 731:10
leaned on his b. at supper BIBL 103:12
now my b., o'ercharged SIDN 718:15
Oak was round his b. HORA 387:15
parts of the b. BYRD 173:6
sooth a savage b. CONG 232:25
weariness May toss him to My b. HERB 373:8
with dauntless b. GRAY 350:11
breastie panic's in thy b. BURN 168:22
breastplate b. of faith BIBL 109:9
b. of judgement BIBL 76:15
b. of righteousness BIBL 108:13
breasts betwixt my b. BIBL 85:8
b. are like two young roes BIBL 85:14
b. by which France is fed SULL 746:2
her b. are dun SHAK 705:20
Sestos and Abydos of her b. DONN 272:12
breath boldest held his b. CAMP 183:3
b. can make them GOLD 344:8
Breathe on me, B. of God HATC 363:17
breathes with human b. TENN 767:7
breathing thoughtful b. WORD 831:23
b. of life BIBL 73:17
b. of worldly men SHAK 695:5
B.'s a ware HOUS 390:16
b. thou art SHAK 686:16
call the fleeting b. GRAY 350:10
Clothed with his b. TENN 760:13
down and out of b. SHAK 669:17
drawn the b. of life YEAT 836:3
draw thy b. in pain SHAK 667:10
every thing that hath b. BOOK 142:3
fly away, b. SHAK 701:21
having lost her b., she spoke SHAK 656:26
healthy b. of morn KEAT 427:22
last b. of Julius Caesar JEAN 404:18
lighter than b. BERR 69:16
lightly draws its b. WORD 832:14
love thee with the b. BROW 154:22
sweeter woman ne'er drew b. INGE 399:12
taxed the b. THOM 772:7
thou no b. at all SHAK 680:14
toil of b. COLE 225:10
waste of b. YEAT 836:10
while you have it use your b. FLET 318:1
breathe As though to b. were life TENN 767:9
b. by a sort of artificial inlet FOST 321:12
b. in that fine air TENN 759:21
b. in the faces PEPY 573:11
b. not his name MOOR 530:15
B. on me, Breath of God HATC 363:17
b. when I expire BYRO 175:2
let me b. or move FEAV 308:4
privilege to b. ELEA 291:16
So long as men can b. SHAK 704:10
summer's morn to b. MILT 517:14
yearning to b. free LAZA 451:11
breathes B. there the man SCOT 650:19
breathing Closer is He than b. TENN 759:10
breathless b. hush in the Close NEWB 541:18
b. on thy fate LONG 473:10
B. with adoration WORD 828:23
bred B. en bawn in a brier-patch HARR 362:17
What's b. in the bone PROV 614:6
Bredon In summertime on B. HOUS 390:19
bree little abune her b. BALL 51:18
breeches boys with b. BARB 53:18
breed Border, nor B. KIPL 438:5
b. of their horses PENN 572:15
b. one work that wakes HOPK 384:24
Feared by their b. SHAK 694:19
happy b. of men SHAK 694:19
wife for b. GAY 332:23
breeding b. consists in concealing TWAI 786:19
show your b. SHER 716:18
without any b. THUR 776:26
breeks b. aff a wild Highlandman SCOT 651:22
breeze b. from foggy mount BYRO 175:22
b. is on the sea SCOT 652:2
b. of morning moves TENN 764:6
dancing in the b. WORD 828:26
wander like a b. COLE 225:15
with the b. of song TENN 761:19
breezes b. dusk and shiver TENN 762:13
breezy B., Sneezy, Freezy ELLI 298:14
Breffny little waves of B. GORE 347:2
brekekekex B. koax koax ARIS 24:12
brethren b., to dwell together BOOK 141:4
Dearly beloved b. BOOK 125:13
least of these my b. BIBL 97:13

my mother and my b. BIBL 95:19
we be b. BIBL 74:24
brevis *Ars longa, vita b.* HIPP 377:15
B. esse laboro HORA 385:13
Vitae summa b. HORA 387:17
brevity B. is the sister CHEK 208:15
B. is the soul of wit PROV 596:39
B. is the soul of wit SHAK 663:9
Its body b. COLE 225:9
brew bake so shall you b. PROV 595:22
b., so shall you bake PROV 595:23
b. that is true FILM 312:6
brewers bakeres and b. LANG 450:18
brewery take me to a b. ANON 16:21
bribe b. or gratuity PENN 572:16
cannot hope to b. or twist WOLF 825:6
done without a b. CENT 199:14
Marriage is a b. WILD 819:15
Too poor for a b. GRAY 351:5
bribery corrupt by b. WILL 820:5
bribes open to b. GREE 351:18
bricht braw b. moonlicht MORR 533:3
brick b. in his pocket JOHN 410:12
carried a piece of b. SWIF 747:16
'Eave arf a b. at 'im PUNC 617:6
Follow the yellow b. road HARB 359:19
Goodbye yellow b. road JOHN 408:4
hardly throw a b. ORWE 559:3
inherited it b. AUGU 36:17
paved with yellow b. BAUM 57:15
threw it a b. at a time HARG 362:6
bricks b. to Lewley BETJ 71:3
make b. without straw PROV 615:41
bridal Against their b. day SPEN 734:19
b. of the earth and sky HERB 373:17
dance at our b. SCOT 651:10
bride as a b. adorned for her husband BIBL 113:7
barren b. POPE 583:13
became my glittering b. WORD 828:12
b. forget her attire BIBL 89:10
b. of a ducal coronet DICK 263:15
b. of quietness OPEN 556:23
b. that sun shines on PROV 601:48
encounter darkness as a b. SHAK 686:17
jealousy to the b. BARR 55:18
mourning b. DRYD 282:12
my life and my b. POE 579:11
never a b. PROV 595:7
Never the blushing b. LEIG 463:2
Passionless b. TENN 763:18
ser' him for a b. MACD 484:16
thy b.-bed to have decked SHAK 666:28
To be his holy b. STON 743:9
unravished b. of quietness KEAT 428:21
virgin, yet a b. CARE 186:10
bridegroom Bellona's b. SHAK 681:10
b. in my death SHAK 657:15
cometh forth as a b. BOOK 132:15
Like a b. AYTO 40:10
bridegrooms Of b., brides HERR 374:3
brides B. of Enderby INGE 399:10
Of bride-grooms, b. HERR 374:3
bridesmaid Always a b. PROV 595:7
always the b. LEIG 463:2
bridge Beautiful Railway B. MCGO 485:7
b. of gold PROV 604:17
b. over troubled water SIMO 720:8
cross the b. PROV 598:32
Every good poem is a b. DAY- 253:15
going a b. too far BROW 154:24
Horatius kept the b. MACA 483:12
keep the b. with me MACA 483:6
London B. is broken down NURS 549:10
On the B. of Toome CARB 186:2
speaks well of the b. PROV 599:41
Women, and Champagne, and B. BELL 64:2
brief B. as the lightning SHAK 689:5
b. wherein all marvels SOUT 731:12
little b. authority SHAK 686:10
strive to be b. HORA 385:13
tedious and b. SHAK 690:22
brier bawn in a b.-patch HARR 362:17
instead of the b. BIBL 88:23
Thorough bush, thorough b. SHAK 689:16
briers O, how full of b. SHAK 658:11
brig From B. o' Dread BALL 51:3
brigade boys of the old B. WEAT 806:24
Viva la the New B. DAVI 252:14
brigand I am a b. SHAW 708:3
brigandage teaches him b. TALM 754:18
bright All things b. and beautiful ALEX 11:8
Behold the b. original GAY 332:15
b. and fierce and fickle TENN 765:22
B. as the day GRAN 349:4
b. day is done SHAK 657:23
b. day that brings forth SHAK 674:25
b. face of danger STEV 740:22
b. northern star LOVE 476:10
b. particular star SHAK 655:19
B. the vision MANT 494:12
dark and b. BYRO 178:24
Death's b. angel PROC 593:14
excessive b. MILT 516:3
eyes are b. KEAT 431:13
Goddess, excellently b. JONS 419:17
Keep up your b. swords SHAK 691:29
look, the land is b. CLOU 223:4
obscurely b. BYRO 175:20
quick b. things SHAK 689:6
thought thee b. SHAK 705:26
torches to burn b. SHAK 697:7
Tyger, burning b. BLAK 121:8
young lady named B. BULL 160:1
brighten Blessings b. PROV 596:28
brightest B. and best HEBE 367:5
brightness B. falls from the air NASH 539:22
b. of his presence BOOK 132:12
his Darkness and his B. BYRO 179:15
leaking the b. away SPEN 732:24
Brighton B. Pavilion looks as if SMIT 725:24
Brignal B. banks are wild SCOT 651:16
brilliance Renew your b. GRAC 347:15
brilliant dullard's envy of b. men BEER 61:14
brillig 'Twas b. CARR 190:12
brim sparkles near the b. BYRO 174:10
winking at the b. KEAT 429:8
brimstone fire and b. BOOK 132:3
smouldering b. ALAB 9:14
bring b. home knowledge JOHN 416:1
B. me my arrows of desire BLAK 120:1
B. out number BLAK 119:17
day may b. forth BIBL 83:27
what it will b. PROV 615:20
bringer b. of unwelcome news SHAK 669:21
bringing b. me up by hand DICK 262:20
brink trembling on the b. NABO 538:1
walked to the b. DULL 284:13
brinkmanship boasting of his b. STEV 740:14
brioche *mangent de la b.* MARI 495:11
brisk b. as a bee JOHN 412:9
b. little somebody BROW 155:6
brisking b. about the life SMAR 722:6
Britain boundary of B. TACI 752:8
B. a fit country LLOY 471:4
B., could you ever boast SWIF 749:13
B.'s stand alone DEV 259:7
B. will be honoured by historians HARL 362:10
B. will still be MAJO 491:16
dangerous man in B. NEWS 544:8
government of B.'s isle SHAK 672:15
hail, happy B. SOME 727:18
Hath B. all the sun SHAK 660:26
I'm backing B. SAYI 647:25
Keep B. tidy OFFI 554:8
should belong to B. GIRA 340:4
speak for B. BOOT 142:20
When B. first THOM 774:20
Without B., Europe ERHA 301:5
Britannia Beer and B. SMIT 726:7
Rule, B. THOM 774:20
shouted 'Rule B.' KIPL 438:1
think of Cool B. BENN 65:13
British as the B. public MACA 481:18
blood of a B. man SHAK 679:9
bones of one B. Grenadier HARR 362:13
B. and Armoric knights MILT 514:30
B. female CLOU 221:12
B. Grenadier SONG 730:3
B. Museum had lost its charm GERS 334:12
B. Nation ADDI 5:8
Come you back, you B. soldier KIPL 439:12
destinies of the B. Empire DISR 268:21
drunken officer of B. rule WALC 799:1
joined the B. Army LEDW 461:17
less known by the B. BORR 143:8
of B. blood TENN 759:9
removed By B. hands BYRO 174:2
so also a B. subject PALM 566:3
stony B. stare TENN 764:4
thank God! the B. journalist WOLF 825:6
We are B., thank God MONT 528:14
west from the B. coast BOWE 145:15
Briton free-born B. can THAC 769:6
glory in the name of B. GEOR 333:13
No good man is a B. AUSO 37:11
Britons B. alone use 'Might' WAUG 806:15
B. never will be slaves THOM 774:20
B. who are kept far away VIRG 795:15
broad b. is the way BIBL 94:7
B. of Church BETJ 71:9
how b. and far JOHN 418:16
make b. their phylacteries BIBL 96:25
She's the B. SPRI 735:9
too b. for leaping HOUS 391:8
broadens travel b. the mind; but CHES 211:13
broadminded superior man is b. CONF 231:8
Broadway sinners on this part of B. RUNY 637:14
broccoli b., dear WHIT 814:1
brogues not fit to tie his b. SCOT 652:14
broke If it ain't b. SAYI 647:19
broken bats have been b. HOWE 391:13
bones which thou hast b. BOOK 135:6
both b.-hearted SWIN 751:7
b. and contrite heart BOOK 135:9
b. Anne of gathering bouquets FROS 326:11
b. by their passing feet YEAT 835:12
b.-hearted woman HAYE 365:2
b. the lock AUDE 34:18
Can it be b. JENK 406:7
healeth those that are b. BOOK 141:24
house has been b. open PEAC 570:16
Is it not b. SHEL 710:21
London Bridge is b. down NURS 549:10
made to be b. NORT 546:17
made to be b. PROV 609:44
Morning has b. FARJ 306:15
neck once b. WALS 802:9
not quickly b. BIBL 84:10
old man, b. SHAK 673:18
taken up the b. blade DE G 255:20
through a b. heart WILD 819:4
brokenhearted bind up the b. BIBL 89:5
broker honest b. BISM 116:11
bronze b. and stone RUNY 637:16
monument more lasting than b. HORA 388:24
noontide was b. CHUR 216:12
bronzes Others shall shape b. VIRG 795:1
brooches b. and toys STEV 742:20
brood b. of folly MILT 512:3
b. of glory SPEN 733:18
thy b. is flown TENN 765:23
broods b. with warm breast HOPK 384:6
brook b. and river meet LONG 473:22
dwelt by the b. Cherith BIBL 79:25
grows aslant a b. SHAK 666:12
noise like a hidden b. COLE 226:23
salad from the b. COWP 242:9
willows of the b. BIBL 82:2
brooks b. of Eden TENN 764:21
By b. too broad HOUS 391:8

broom sent with b. before SHAK 690:29
brooms New b. sweep clean PROV 607:41
broomstick mortal man is a b. SWIF 748:12
broth spoil the b. PROV 613:13
brothel intellectual b. TOLS 779:15
metaphysical b. for the emotions KOES 443:3
playing a piano in a b. MUGG 535:21
brothels b. with bricks of religion BLAK 119:19
Keep thy foot out of b. SHAK 679:3
brother Be my b. CHAM 201:10
BIG B. IS WATCHING YOU ORWE 558:20
b. came with subtilty BIBL 74:39
B. can you spare a dime HARB 359:15
b. followed brother WORD 828:15
b., hail, and farewell CATU 198:1
b. he is in Elysium SHAK 700:28
b. in God BELL 63:17
b. is born for adversity BIBL 83:3
b. is on the rack SMIT 723:5
B. of the Angle WALT 802:16
b. sin against me BIBL 96:11
b.'s soul BARB 53:16
B., thy tail hangs down KIPL 441:5
B. to Death DANI 249:1
b. to dragons BIBL 81:28
closer than a b. BIBL 83:6
dear b. here departed BOOK 131:14
Death and his b. SHEL 713:17
especially Sir B. Sun FRAN 323:4
every man's b. BIBL 74:20
fold to thy heart thy b. WHIT 816:8
glad mad b.'s name SWIN 750:12
Had it been his b. EPIT 303:1
hateth his b. BIBL 111:15
he's my b. RUSS 640:7
hurt my b. SHAK 667:4
lo'ed him like a vera b. BURN 168:11
man and a b. WEDG 808:21
marry with his b. SHAK 665:13
my b. is a hairy man BIBL 74:37
my b. Jonathan BIBL 79:3
my b.'s keeper BIBL 74:8
my likeness, my b. BAUD 57:6
O b. man WHIT [illegible]
stick more close than a b. KIPL 440:11
to my b. turns GOLD 345:6
unto a tyrant b. SHAK 658:10
voice of thy b.'s blood BIBL 74:9
want to be the white man's b. KING 436:9
what my b. will do CHAR 203:12
brotherhood broadened into a b. JOHN 408:14
crown thy good with b. BATE 57:4
Love the b. BIBL 110:30
sit down at the table of b. KING 436:14
brotherly b. love continue BIBL 110:5
brothers All men become b. SCHI 646:15
all the b. too SHAK 701:25
B. and sisters rocking JOHN 408:7
B. in humanity VILL 792:19
B. of the Great GERS 334:20
feel they are b. GODW 342:7
forty thousand b. SHAK 666:29
live together as b. KING 436:15
noble pair of b. HORA 389:23
single nation of b. SCHI 648:17
So the two b. KEAT 428:2
we band of b. SHAK 671:25
We were b. all WORD 831:6
brought b. forth her firstborn son BIBL 98:20
safely b. KEBL 432:4
brow b. of Egypt SHAK 690:19
b. of labour BRYA 159:3
rugged b. of careful Policy SPEN 733:6
with a velvet b. SHAK 680:23
Your bonny b. was brent BURN 167:17
brown b. coat MACA 481:13
b. of her MEW 506:13
b. study CONG 232:15
Brünnhilde had b. braids JARR 404:8
falling on the city b. BRID 148:8
Her b. embrace WALK 799:9
Jeanie with the light b. hair FOST 321:16
John B.'s body SONG 729:13
river Is a strong b. god ELIO 294:12
She has b. hair SHAK 688:31
browner tinge with a b. shade GIBB 336:3
Browning God and Robert B. BROW 158:16
Hang it all, Robert B. POUN 589:10
safety-catch of my B. JOHS 418:17
brows Bliss in our b. bent SHAK 656:16
nodded with his darkish b. HOME 381:22
pallor of girls' b. OWEN 562:7
shadow of her even b. SPEN 733:24
browsing b. and sluicing WODE 824:23
bruise b. them with a rod of iron BOOK 131:17
It shall b. thy head BIBL 74:4
tread on it and b. it TROL 782:18
bruised b. for our iniquities BIBL 88:17
b. in a new place IRVI 400:3
b. reed BIBL 80:28
b. reed BIBL 88:6
bruisers b. of England BORR 143:10
bruises No man b. his finger TALM 754:24
Brünnhilde B. had brown braids JARR 404:8
brunt Bear the b. BROW 157:17
brush so fine a b. AUST 39:11
with my b. I make love MISQ 521:16
brushers b. of noblemen's clothes WOTT 833:7
Brust *in meiner B.* GOET 342:17
bruta *B. fulmina* PLIN 578:16
brutal heart's grown b. from the fare YEAT 836:18
brutality without art is b. RUSK 638:8
brute b. vote BAGE 46:15
Et tu, B.? SHAK 675:16
Feed the b. PUNC 617:19
heart of a b. like you PLAT 577:14
like b. beasts BOOK 131:1
brutes Exterminate all the b. CONR 234:12
made to live as b. DANT 249:17
brutish hungry beating b. one SCHW 649:16
nasty, b., and short HOBB 378:21
Brutus B. is an honourable man SHAK 675:29
B. makes mine greater SHAK [illegible]
B. took to wife SHAK 675:8
'B.' will start a spirit SHAK 674:14
is B. sick SHAK 675:6
noble B. Hath told you SHAK 675:28
Portia is B.' harlot SHAK 675:7
You too, B. CAES 180:22
BSE B. holds no terror BAKE 48:15
bubble dew drops, or a b. MAHĀ 490:6
empty b. GRAI 348:11
Honour but an empty b. DRYD 280:20
light-blown b. BOLT 124:22
like unto a b. WARD 803:11
mostly froth and b. GORD 346:19
now a b. burst POPE 585:8
Seeking the b. reputation SHAK 659:1
world's a b. BACO 45:10
bubbles frill of b. DUNM 285:8
I'm forever blowing b. KENB 433:4
With beaded b. KEAT 429:8
bubus *b. exercet suis* HORA 387:11
Bücher *wo man B. Verbrennt* HEIN 368:3
buck bigger bang for a b. POLI 581:7
b. stops here TRUM 784:10
bucket as a drop of a b. BIBL 88:3
b. down and full of tears SHAK 695:21
past is a b. of ashes SAND 644:1
stick inside a swill b. ORWE 559:16
buckets b. into empty wells COWP 241:26
Buckingham so much for B. CIBB 217:5
Buckingham Palace changing guard at B. MILN 510:15
buckle B. my shoe NURS 550:3
b. which fastens BAGE 46:8
buckram eleven b. men SHAK 668:6
Four rogues in b. SHAK 668:5
bud be a b. again KEAT 427:12
b., and yet a rose HERR 375:6
leaf, the b., the flower SPEN 733:27
nip him in the b. ROCH 630:3
now in age I b. again HERB 372:17
Buddha B., peerless among men PALI 565:5
Has a dog the B.-Nature MUMO 536:8
Kill the B. I-HS 398:19
real B. is to be found HUI- 394:5
What is the B. MUMO 536:10
What is the B. MUMO 536:11
Buddhahood Germ of B. MAHĀ 490:8
speedily gain B. TANT 754:30
budding b. morrow in midnight KEAT 430:14
budge b. doctors of the Stoic fur MILT 511:28
'B.,' says the fiend SHAK 687:17
buds darling b. of May SHAK 704:9
sweet b. like flocks SHEL 712:12
buffalo breath of a b. CROW 246:16
buffeted b. for your faults BIBL 110:31
bug b. with gilded wings POPE 583:9
snug As a b. In a rug EPIT 303:7
bugger B. Bognor LAST 455:5
bugle Blow, b., blow TENN 765:16
bugles Blow out, you b. BROO 150:7
b. calling from sad shires OWEN 562:6
build Birds b. HOPK 384:24
b. a tower BIBL 99:31
b. the house of death MONT 527:9
easy to b. IBSE 398:10
end is to b. well WOTT 833:5
Lord b. the house BOOK 140:21
never ask *why b.* SEXT 655:9
than to b. up PROV 604:13
think we b. for ever RUSK 638:21
those who will b. it TRUD 783:22
builded b. better than he knew EMER 299:9
builder can only be a *b.* RUSK 638:7
maker and b. is God BIBL 109:29
builders stone which the b. refused BOOK 140:6
building principal beauty in b. FULL 327:10
very old b. OSBO 559:22
buildings pompous b. WULF 833:18
builds b. on mud MACH 486:1
he that b. stronger SHAK 666:18
Office b. up a man BENN 65:6
built All we have b. [illegible]
b. in a day PROV 610:17
not what they b. FENT 308:8
therefore b. for ever TENN 759:18
Till we have b. Jerusalem BLAK 120:1
Who b. Thebes BREC 147:20
bulimia yuppie version of b. EHRE 290:1
bull b. doth bear the yoke SHAK 691:1
Cock and a B. STER 739:15
curled Assyrian B. TENN 763:24
Dance tiptoe, b. BUNT 160:12
milk the b. JOHN 413:10
strong as a b. moose ROOS 633:12
bullet b. has its billet PROV 599:20
b. has its billet WILL 820:2
b. through his head ROBI 629:15
b. through his heart THAC 769:9
Faster than a speeding b. ANON 16:7
stronger than the b. MISQ 521:3
bullets bloody b. LINC 468:4
b. made of platinum BELL 63:3
bullfighters b. of Spain BORR 143:10
bullied b. into a certain philosophy KEAT 430:26
b. out of vice SURT 746:13
bulling b. through wave-wrack MERW 506:3
bullocks talk is of b. BIBL 92:12
bulls eat b.' flesh BOOK 135:3
fat b. of Basan BOOK 132:23
bully b. is always a coward PROV 596:40
by the bossy for the b. SELD 653:25
love the lovely b. SHAK 671:12
such a b. pulpit ROOS 633:13
bulrushes ark of b. BIBL 75:22
bulwark floating b. of the island BLAC 117:3

bulwarks Mark well her b. BOOK 134:26
bum Does my b. look big WEIR 808:28
Indicat Motorem B. GODL 342:2
Pee, po, belly, b., drawers FLAN 316:3
bump go b. in the night PRAY 592:2
bumpy going to be a b. night FILM 311:6
Buncombe talking to B. WALK 799:12
through reporters to B. CARL 188:4
bundle never the b. of accident YEAT 837:26
bungler good nature is a b. HALI 358:2
Man is a b. SHAW 708:8
bunk Exercise is b. FORD 319:17
History more or less b. FORD 319:15
bunkers gloomy b. were built ESHE 301:8
buns bears might come with b. ISHE 400:7
hot cross b. NURS 550:1
bunting Bye, baby b. NURS 547:14
burbled b. as it came CARR 190:13
burd b. Helen dropt BALL 50:18
burden bear any b. KENN 433:10
bear the b. and the heat ARNO 26:18
borne the b. BIBL 96:18
b. of them is intolerable BOOK 129:16
b. of the nation's care PRIO 593:3
impossible to carry the heavy b. EDWA 289:7
makes back to the b. PROV 601:14
my b. is light BIBL 95:9
White Man's B. KIPL 440:21
burdens undo the heavy b. BIBL 89:1
bureaucracy [b.'s] specific invention WEBE 807:8
bureaucrats b. will care more BAGE 47:7
Guidelines for b. BORE 143:2
Burg *Eine feste B.* LUTH 480:2
burghers b. of Carlisle MACA 482:19
burgundy naive domestic B. THUR 776:26
burial b.-ground God's-Acre LONG 473:19
buried in Christian b. SHAK 666:16
his obscure b. SHAK 666:9
thought they had only one b. BOCC 123:5
buried all b. here BRON 149:19
bodies are b. in peace BIBL 92:17
b. at midnight O'BR 552:7
b. him darkly WOLF 825:4
b. in a good old age BIBL 74:26
b. in so sweet a place SHEL 710:12
b. in the rain MILL 509:14
This living b. man DONN 273:12
when they b. him CLOS 222:4
where some b. Caesar bled FITZ 314:11
why have they not b. me deep TENN 764:13
burlesque once romantic to b. BYRO 177:3
Burlington B. Bertie HARG 362:5
Burma B. girl a-settin' KIPL 439:12
burn another Troy for her to b. YEAT 836:20
better to b. out YOUN 839:17
better to marry than to b. BIBL 106:4
b. always with this hard, gemlike PATE 569:15
B., baby, burn POLI 581:9
b. inwardly BRON 149:14
b. its children to save MEYE 506:14
B. to the socket WORD 828:9
B. your bra SAYI 647:2
b. your letters ADAM 3:7
Did not our heart b. BIBL 100:34
let it freely b. LITT 470:3
Old age should b. THOM 772:2
sun shall not b. thee BOOK 140:12
We b. daylight SHAK 688:33
burned Alexandria's library b. HUGH 393:5
B. on the water SHAK 656:23
B. women BRAN 146:19
bush b. with fire BIBL 75:25
clothes not be b. BIBL 82:15
give my body to be b. BIBL 106:16
men also, in the end, are b. HEIN 368:3
wanted the Aeneid b. FLAU 316:14
burning all is b. PALI 565:14
boy stood on the b. deck HEMA 369:5
b. and a shining light BIBL 101:23
b. fiery furnace BIBL 90:1
B. for burning BIBL 76:14
b. of the leaves BINY 115:9
b. patience RIMB 628:11
b. roof and tower YEAT 836:15
b. the rain forest STIN 743:7
by b. him CEAU 199:2
Is Paris b. HITL 378:9
Keep the Home-fires b. FORD 320:6
lady's not for b. FRY 326:21
out of the b. BIBL 90:18
pretty Babe all b. SOUT 731:9
smell of b. BELL 64:1
stood on the b. deck OPEN 555:9
Tyger, b. bright BLAK 121:8
burnished Furnish'd and b. BETJ 71:5
like a b. throne ELIO 296:2
burns B., Shelley, were with us BROW 156:18
candle b. at both ends MILL 509:11
Not she which b. in 't SHAK 703:4
Ucalegon b. very near VIRG 794:3
burnt b. at the stake as witches SMIT 724:22
b. child dreads the fire PROV 596:41
b. each other BYRO 176:1
b.-out ends of smoky days ELIO 295:19
b., tortured, fined JEFF 406:2
delightest not in b.-offerings BOOK 135:9
burps History just b. BARN 55:3
burr I am a kind of b. SHAK 686:24
Burren Stony outcrop of the B. BETJ 70:14
burst Words, words or I shall b. FARQ 307:15
burthen b. of the mystery WORD 829:3
Burton B. built on Trent HOUS 391:9
bury B. it certain fathoms SHAK 699:10
B. my heart at Wounded Knee BENÉ 64:24
dead b. the dead PROV 605:21
dead b. their dead BIBL 94:20
helped to b. POPE 583:8
I come to b. Caesar SHAK 675:27
physician can b. his mistakes WRIG 833:10
We will b. you KHRU 435:16
bus Can it be a Motor B. GODL 342:2
missed the b. CHAM 201:2
not even a b., I'm a tram HARE 362:4
stepping in front of a b. OSBO 560:8
bush beats the b. OXFO 562:16
Behold, the b. burned BIBL 75:25
b. afire with God BROW 154:13
b. supposed a bear SHAK 690:20
fear each b. an officer SHAK 673:4
Good wine needs no b. PROV 601:31
Thorough b., thorough brier SHAK 689:16
worth two in the b. PROV 596:21
bushel neither under a b. BIBL 99:18
bushes B. and low tamarisks VIRG 796:4
b. trimmed and trained QUIN 619:7
bushmen they were not b. HEAD 365:24
busier semed b. than he was CHAU 204:21
busiest b. have most leisure PROV 596:42
business about my Father's b. BIBL 98:27
attended b. college ADE 6:1
Being good in b. WARH 803:13
b. as usual THAT 770:4
B. before pleasure PROV 596:43
B. carried on as usual CHUR 214:20
B. first THAC 769:4
B. is like a car SAYI 647:3
b. like show business BERL 68:11
b. of consequence BARH 54:11
b. of the day DRYD 281:11
b. practices improve RODD 631:2
b. that we love SHAK 657:7
B. was his aversion EDGE 288:15
conduct of b. CORN 237:5
do b. together THAT 770:5
do your own b. BIBL 109:8
Everybody's b. PROV 599:40
far away from b. HORA 387:11
go to my pleasure, b. WYCH 834:9
growth of a large b. ROCK 630:23
heart in the b. WATS 804:19
How to succeed in b. MEAD 503:2
importunity Of b. LAMB 449:5
In civil b. BACO 42:12
it is your b. HORA 387:2
it spoils b. OTWA 560:23
Liberty is unfinished b. ANON 17:7
little b. BIBL 92:11
make b. for itself DICK 261:4
minded their own b. CARR 189:14
Murder is a serious b. OPEN 555:26
music b. is not MORR 533:5
occupy their b. BOOK 139:14
of the American people is b. COOL 236:2
principal b. of life BUTL 172:18
requisite in b. ADDI 4:18
serious b. AUST 38:26
servants of b. BACO 43:8
settled b. BACO 44:25
soul of b. PROV 609:49
spring of b. BAGE 46:7
That's no b. FILM 312:12
thief to b. DEFO 254:12
Too soft for b. LEAP 460:2
totter on in b. POPE 584:5
true b. precept DICK 263:5
wheels of b. TAWN 755:12
businessman any other decent b. LEWI 467:8
toward making a b. WATS 804:18
businessmen well-placed b. decide YOUN 838:15
Buss Miss B. and Miss Beale ANON 17:17
bust animated b. GRAY 350:10
b. survives the city GAUT 331:6
dance it b. to bust GREN 352:15
buste *Le B. Survit à la cité* GAUT 331:6
busting June is b. out HAMM 358:19
bustle B. in a House DICK 266:11
busy be b. OVID 561:21
B., busy, and ever busy SKEL 721:13
B., curious OLDY 553:13
b. man has no time MAUR 502:9
B. old fool DONN 274:14
Government of the b. SELD 653:25
had a b. day SIGL 719:4
how b. I must be ASTL 31:18
Nowher so b. a man CHAU 204:21
butcher benevolence of the b. SMIT 723:6
b., the baker NURS 550:15
Hog B. for the World SAND 643:18
Prime Minister has to be a b. BUTL 171:15
right have they to b. me DICK 264:20
want to know a b. paints BROW 157:27
When a b. tells you JOHN 412:25
butchered B. to make a Roman holiday BYRO 175:3
butchers gentle with these b. SHAK 675:21
sacrificers, but not b. SHAK 675:2
shepherds and b. VOLT 798:3
butler b. did it CATC 195:5
b.'s upper slopes WODE 824:24
butt here is my b. SHAK 693:30
knocks you down with the b. GOLD 345:31
butter *B. and eggs* CALV 182:2
B. and honey BIBL 86:26
b. for the Royal slice of bread MILN 510:18
b. from alternate tubs ROGE 631:17
b. made of dolphins' milk JONS 419:9
b. no parsnips PROV 600:23
choking it with b. PROV 611:47
cutting bread and b. THAC 769:15
manage without b. GOEB 342:9
no money for b. JOSE 421:10
rather have b. or guns GOER 342:11
she brought forth b. BIBL 77:28
softer than b. BOOK 135:12
Stork from b. ADVE 7:11
buttercup I'm called Little B. GILB 338:23
buttercups B. and daisies HOWI 392:4
buttered always on the b. side PAYN 570:12
on its b. side PROV 596:38

butterflies b. of vertigo BECK 59:11
Frogs eat B. STEV 739:22
I look for b. CARR 191:14
butterfly breaks a b. POPE 583:9
breaks a b. on a wheel NEWS 544:18
b. dreaming that CHUA 213:2
b. upon the road KIPL 440:1
flap of a b.'s wings LORE 475:14
Float like a b. ALI 12:4
You, the b. BASH 56:20
butting B. through the Channel MASE 500:14
buttock boiling his b. AUBR 32:19
buttocks chair that fits all b. SHAK 656:2
gorgeous b. of the ape HUXL 397:8
button each b., hook, and lace LOWE 477:9
job of sewing on a b. BROU 151:15
little round b. at top FOOT 319:8
undo this b. SHAK 680:14
buttoning b. and unbuttoning LAST 455:3
buttons soul above b. COLM 229:17
stars, garters, b. MOOR 529:15
buttresses [the Church's] b. ANON 16:14
butts b. me away SHAK 660:10
butty oul' b. o' mine O'CA 552:12
buxom b., blithe, and debonair MILT 512:13
Buxton every fool in B. RUSK 638:13
buy b. a used car POLI 582:8
b. Codham, Cockridden THOM 773:1
B. in the cheapest market PROV 596:45
b. it first HEMI 369:7
b. it like an honest man NORT 546:20
b. wine and milk BIBL 88:20
client will beg to b. BURR 169:14
Don't b. a single vote more KENN 433:7
I will b. with you SHAK 687:11
money can't b. me love LENN 463:19
no man might b. or sell BIBL 112:21
Stop me and b. one ADVE 8:11
You b. land, you buy stones PROV 615:23
buyer b. can be found SALL 643:10
b. needs hundred eyes PROV 596:44
Let the b. beware PROV 605:19
naught, saith the b. BIBL 83:11
buying no fish ye're b. SCOT 651:17
buys b. everything MONT 527:1
Who b. a minute's mirth SHAK 704:1
buzz B.! Buzz! Buzz! MILN 511:2
stings, The crowd, and b. COWL 239:19
stumbling B. DICK 266:9
by B. and by MCCO 484:10
bymatter been a b. BACO 42:20
Byron I'm not B. LERM 464:24
Byronic think all poets were B. COPE 236:9
byway And the b. nigh me STEV 742:25
his own b. to heaven DEFO 255:10
byword b. among all people BIBL 79:16
story and a b. WINT 823:14
Byzantium holy city of B. YEAT 837:3
Soldan of B. CHES 210:9

C C Major BROW 155:1
ça *Ç. ira* ANON 20:2
cabbage c.-leaf to make an apple-pie FOOT 319:8
c. with a college education TWAI 786:22
smell of cooking c. WEST 812:10
cabbages Of c.—and kings CARR 190:20
planting my c. MONT 527:8
cabin c. left still standing DUFF 284:7
Make me a willow c. SHAK 701:7
cabined c. ample Spirit ARNO 26:23
c., cribbed, confined SHAK 684:9
cabinet another to mislead the C. ASQU 31:6
blubbering C. GLAD 341:10
c. is a combining BAGE 46:8
c. of pleasure HERB 373:2
group of C. Ministers CURZ 248:5
cable little c. cars climb CROS 246:10
No cord nor c. BURT 170:19
of c. television MACK 486:10
Cablinasian I'm a C. WOOD 826:11
Cabots Lowells talk to the C. BOSS 143:15
cacoethes *Scribendi c.* JUVE 424:17
cad Cocoa is a c. and coward CHES 210:20
Flopshus C. KIPL 441:23
cadence *dans les vers une juste c.* BOIL 124:4
harsh c. of a rugged line DRYD 282:28
Cadiz reeking into C. Bay BROW 156:4
Cadwallader C. and all his goats SHAK 672:2
caelum *C. non animum mutant* HORA 386:20
Caesar always I am C. SHAK 674:19
appeal unto C. BIBL 104:18
Aut C., aut nihil MOTT 535:2
Ave C., morituri te salutant ANON 21:5
blossoming C. SHAK 657:10
C. and his fortune CAES 180:19
C. hath wept SHAK 676:1
C. is more dangerous SHAK 675:11
C.'s laurel crown BLAK 118:3
C.'s public policy PLUT 579:8
C.'s self is God's CRAS 244:13
C.'s wife CAES 180:17
C.'s wife PROV 596:46
C. with the senate POPE 586:2
call great C. ass SHAK 658:2
decree from C. Augustus BIBL 98:19
decrees of C. BIBL 104:5
doth this our C. feed SHAK 674:14
Hail C. ANON 21:5
Here was a C. SHAK 676:13
I come to bury C. SHAK 675:27
Imperious C., dead SHAK 666:25
in envy of great C. SHAK 677:4
Like C.'s wife ANON 17:8
loved C. less SHAK 675:24
O mighty C. SHAK 675:19
Render unto C. BIBL 96:22
that C. might be great CAMP 183:15
Then fall, C. SHAK 675:16
unto C. shalt thou go BIBL 104:19
upon Dead C.'s trencher SHAK 657:5
where some buried C. bled FITZ 314:11
word of C. SHAK 676:4
your boy, your C. DRYD 280:26
Caesars C. and Napoleons HUXL 397:3
Compare with C. SHAK 669:32
cafe in ev'ry street c. HAMM 358:20
caff ace c. with a nice museum ADVE 7:2
caftan Iffucan of Azcan in c. STEV 739:19
cage become an iron c. WEBE 807:4
born within the c. TENN 761:3
c. upon the wall BISH 115:19
cannot c. the minute MACN 488:16
lady in a c. CHES 210:19
no more natural to us than a c. SHAW 707:7
Nor iron bars a c. LOVE 476:14
red breast in a c. BLAK 117:18
roaming round its gilt c. WOLL 825:23
sing like birds i' the c. SHAK 680:6
caged think c. birds sing WEBS 808:15
why the c. bird sings DUNB 285:2
cages not in making c. SWIF 748:28
Cain cruel sons of C. LE G 462:12
first city C. COWL 239:12
Had C. been Scot CLEV 220:17
land God gave to C. CART 192:18
mark upon C. BIBL 74:11
cake Bake me a c. NURS 550:5
child looks at a c. GASK 331:1
have your c. and eat it PROV 615:38
Let them eat c. MARI 495:11
picked out of a c. RALE 621:12
cakes no more c. and ale SHAK 701:14
Calais 'C.' lying in my heart MARY 500:12
shew light at C. JOHN 413:16
calamities C. are of two kinds BIER 114:20
perturbations and c. BACO 44:26
calamity Oh, c. CATC 196:15
power of no c. BROW 153:26
wedded to c. SHAK 697:30
calamus *quam sit c. saevior ense* BURT 170:10
calculating desiccated c. machine BEVA 71:21
calculation c. shining out DICK 263:3
calculus integral and differential c. GILB 339:3
Caledonia Mourn, hapless C. SMOL 726:15
O C.! stern and wild SCOT 651:2
calends Gay are the Martian C. MACA 482:25
calf c. and the young lion BIBL 87:4
fatted c. BIBL 100:5
golden-c. of self-love CARL 187:5
skip like a c. BOOK 133:13
Caliban C. casts out Ariel POUN 589:15
C., Has a new master SHAK 699:1
rage of C. WILD 818:15
calico c. millennium CARL 188:21
California C. to the New York Island GUTH 355:7
Caligula C.'s horse was made Consul RAND 621:16
eyes of C. MITT 524:10
call c. it a day COMD 230:8
c. me early, mother dear TENN 764:18
C. me Ishmael OPEN 555:10
c. of the running tide MASE 500:17
c. of the wild LOND 473:5
c. the cattle home KING 437:9
c. themselves Christians BOOK 127:17
c. ye upon him BIBL 88:21
come when you do c. SHAK 668:19
Go, for they c. you ARNO 27:3
how you c. to me HARD 361:21
Labour's c. POLI 581:12
May I c. you 338 COWA 239:5
Now c. on Christ GILB 337:2
O! c. back yesterday SHAK 695:6
one clear c. for me TENN 757:18
please God to c. me BOOK 130:16
When you c. me that WIST 823:17
called c. unto thee, O Lord BOOK 141:1
many are c. BIBL 96:21
Many are c. PROV 606:25
calleth c. them all by their names BOOK 141:24
One deep c. another BOOK 134:7
calling answerably to your Christian c. BOOK 130:9
dignity of this high c. BURK 163:9
Germany c. JOYC 422:20
heard my c. BOOK 133:31
mercenary c. HOUS 390:9
callisthenics c. with words PARK 567:12
callous 'c.' engraved SELL 654:8
calls If anybody c. BENT 67:6
calm After a storm comes a c. PROV 594:17
c., as it was bright VAUG 790:17
c. on the lap of the Line KIPL 440:7
c., rather than to excite PALM 566:6
C. soul of all things ARNO 26:15
c. the troubled mind CONG 233:16
C. was the day SPEN 734:18
famous c. and dead BROW 155:31
hopelessness and c. BARA 53:14
more than usual c. FLEM 317:10
no joy but c. TENN 763:12
remember to keep c. HORA 388:6
season of c. weather WORD 830:8
still c. of life ADAM 2:1
Than c. in waters SHEL 714:10
calumnies C. are answered best JONS 420:8
calumny thou shalt not escape c. SHAK 664:7
Calvinism C. [in Switzerland] BANC 53:4
Calvinist Papist, yet a C. EPIT 303:6
Calvinistic C. creed PITT 576:24
C. sense of innate depravity MELV 504:7
Calvinists C. stick fast ROBI 629:18
Cambridge C. ladies in furnished souls CUMM 247:13
C. people rarely smile BROO 150:14
fields of C. COWL 239:22
more attractive than C. BAED 45:17
To C. books TRAP 781:1
to C. books he sent BROW 154:7
Cambyses in King C.' vein SHAK 668:11

came c. first for the Communists NIEM 545:8
c. unto his own BIBL 101:6
I c., I saw, I conquered CAES 180:21
I c., saw, and overcame SHAK 670:12
I c. through MACA 481:5
nobody c. FILM 313:3
Tell them I c. DE L 256:16
camel breaks the c.'s back PROV 604:27
c. has a single hump NASH 539:8
c. is a horse ISSI 400:10
easier for a c. BIBL 96:15
raiment of c.'s hair BIBL 92:28
swallow a c. BIBL 96:27
Take my c., dear OPEN 556:19
Camelot cackling home to C. SHAK 678:14
C. to minstrels seemed BROW 154:11
known as C. LERN 465:1
many-towered C. TENN 762:12
rode down to C. TENN 762:17
camera c. makes everyone a tourist SONT 728:8
I am a c. ISHE 400:8
camerado C., this is no book WHIT 815:8
cammin *c. del nostra vita* OPEN 556:4
c. di nostra vita DANT 249:6
campaign c. in poetry CUOM 247:18
camps Courts and c. CHES 209:9
can but as we c. MENA 504:13
C. something, hope HOPK 384:2
He who c. does PROV 602:24
He who c., does SHAW 708:18
know a man who c. ADVE 7:10
talent does what it c. BARI 54:12
they c. because they think they can VIRG 794:15
They *c.* nothing but frog-spawn LAWR 458:17
think you c. INGE 399:2
youth replies, *I c.* EMER 299:11
Canada C. could have enjoyed COLO 230:1
C. that shall fill LAUR 454:10
I see C. DAVI 252:2
more than C. itself is worth VOLT 797:7
Canadians C. do not like heroes WOOD 826:8
canary mine host's C. wine KEAT 428:20
cancel back to c. half a line FITZ 314:17
C. and tear to pieces SHAK 684:7
cancer c. close to the Presidency DEAN 253:16
Obscene as c. OWEN 562:8
Silence like a c. grows SIMO 720:10
white race *is* the c. SONT 728:7
candelabrum c. of gold BERN 69:6
candid be c. where we can POPE 585:5
c. friend CANN 185:3
candied c. apple, quince KEAT 427:13
candle Bell, book, and c. SHAK 677:10
blew out the c. ALAI 9:16
called him 'C.-ends' CARR 191:21
c. burns at both ends MILL 509:11
c. by which she TOLS 779:9
c. in that great turnip CHUR 216:5
c. in the wind JOHN 407:17
c. in the wind JOHN 408:3
c. of understanding BIBL 91:4
c. singed the moth SHAK 687:26
c. to the sun SIDN 718:4
c. to the sun YOUN 839:1
farthing c. at Dover JOHN 413:16
Fire and fleet and c.-lighte BALL 51:2
hold a c. to my shames SHAK 687:22
lighted a c. BIBL 99:18
light such a c. LAST 455:4
little c. throws his beams SHAK 688:26
Out, out, brief c. SHAK 685:22
rather light a c. STEV 740:15
scarcely fit to hold a c. BYRO 173:9
set a c. in the sun BURT 170:18
candlelight Colours seen by c. BROW 154:19
dress by yellow c. STEV 742:11
get there by c. NURS 548:15
linen by c. PROV 607:27
Candlemas C. day be sunny and bright PROV 603:14
C. day, put beans PROV 597:2
candles c. are all out SHAK 682:20
c. burn their sockets HOUS 390:8
carry c. and set chairs HERV 375:8
Night's c. SHAK 697:33
These blessed c. SHAK 688:29
wind extinguishes c. LA R 453:18
candlestick baker, The c.-maker NURS 550:15
C.-maker much acquaints BROW 157:27
wrote over against the c. BIBL 90:3
candlesticks seven golden c. BIBL 111:21
candour combines force with c. CHUR 216:24
candy C. is dandy NASH 539:16
cane conduct of a clouded c. POPE 587:11
canem *Cave c.* PETR 574:14
canisters steel c. hurtling about CASS 193:11
canker loathsome c. lives SHAK 704:18
this c., Bolingbroke SHAK 667:24
cankerworm c., and the caterpillar BIBL 90:13
cannibal c. uses knife and fork LEC 461:11
cannibals Caesars, and with C. SHAK 669:32
C. that each other eat SHAK 691:34
cannon C. to right of them TENN 757:16
in the c.'s mouth SHAK 659:1
pulse like a c. EMER 299:16
shaking scythes at c. HEAN 366:16
cannonball c. took off his legs HOOD 382:18
like a c. WELL 810:2
cano *Arma virumque c.* VIRG 793:4
canoe coffin clapt in a c. BYRO 173:14
canoes heads in their c. MARV 499:8
canonization sort of natural c. HAZL 365:15
canopy excellent c., the air SHAK 663:18
rich embroidered c. SHAK 672:28
Canossa not go to C. BISM 116:8
cant c. about DECORUM BURN 167:21
can't c. go on BECK 59:20
cant c. of criticism STER 739:3
c. of *Not men* BURK 164:17
Clear your mind of c. JOHN 417:6
we have nothing but c. PEAC 570:15
cantate *C. Domino canticum novum* BIBL 113:19
Canterbury C. or Smithfield WALP 801:20
to the Archbishop of C. SHER 716:22
canting in this c. world STER 739:3
cantons Write loyal c. SHAK 701:7
cantos c. of unvanquished space CRAN 243:19
Cantuar how full of C. BULL 160:2
canvas crowd your c. TENN 764:19
canvasses c. and factions BACO 42:18
cap If the c. fits, wear it PROV 603:20
riband in the c. SHAK 666:11
capability c. and god-like reason SHAK 665:31
Negative C. KEAT 430:24
capable *c. de tout* VOLT 798:13
c. of all things TRAH 780:8
c. of reigning TACI 752:15
caparisons No c., Miss SHER 716:5
cape Nobly, nobly C. Saint Vincent BROW 156:4
Round the c. BROW 157:6
capers He c. nimbly SHAK 696:8
Cape Town Natal and C. GLAD 341:3
capital C. must be propelled BAGE 46:3
Does c. punishment tend FRY 326:25
high c. Of Satan MILT 515:6
high C., where kingly Death SHEL 710:15
origin of c. TORR 779:18
capitalism C. is using its money CAST 193:15
c. with the gloves off STOP 744:1
extermination of c. ZINO 840:5
monopoly stage of c. LENI 463:6
spirit of c. WEBE 807:3
unacceptable face of c. HEAT 367:3
capitalist slave of the c. society CONN 234:5
capitalists c. will sell us MISQ 521:5
Capitol strangers in the C. HEWI 375:19
capitulate I will not c. JOHN 417:20
capons cannot feed c. so SHAK 664:19
Capri letter came from C. JUVE 424:20
caprices depend on the c. TOCQ 778:6
caps C. tilted BLOK 122:5
captain broken by the team c. HOWE 391:13
c. is in his bunk SHAW 707:13
c. of my soul HENL 369:21
c. of the Hampshire grenadiers GIBB 335:24
c. of twenty-four soldiers ANON 20:6
Fighting in the c.'s tower DYLA 287:4
my C. lies, Fallen WHIT 815:5
nobody like the C. THAC 769:2
O C.! my Captain WHIT 815:4
Our great captain's c. SHAK 692:9
plain russet-coated c. CROM 245:9
royal c. of this ruined SHAK 671:9
ship's c. complaining POWE 590:18
spruce sea-c. BARN 55:2
That in the c. SHAK 686:11
train-band c. eke was he COWP 240:11
captains All my sad c. SHAK 657:6
c. and the kings KIPL 440:3
c. and the kings depart KNOX 442:13
c. courageous BALL 51:5
C. of industry CARL 188:8
Star c. glow FLEC 317:1
thunder of the c. BIBL 81:37
captive led captivity c. BOOK 136:9
within my c. breast SURR 746:9
captives all prisoners and c. BOOK 127:11
proclaim liberty to the c. BIBL 89:5
captivity c. of Sion BOOK 140:19
prisoners out of c. BOOK 136:6
Turn our c., O Lord BOOK 140:20
car afford to keep a motor c. SHAW 706:14
Business is like a c. SAYI 647:3
buy a used c. POLI 582:8
can't drive the c. TYNA 787:1
c. could go straight upwards HOYL 392:7
c. crash as a sexual event BALL 52:12
c. has become an article of dress MCLU 487:10
c. in every garage HOOV 383:11
commodious c. JAME 402:26
gilded c. of day MILT 511:16
motor c. was poetry and tragedy LEWI 467:7
owl of Minerva in a hired c. PAUL 570:8
to tinker with his c. MACN 488:15
caravan c. goes on PROV 598:25
great c. of humanity SMUT 726:17
Put up your c. HODG 379:14
carbon c. atom JEAN 404:19
carborundum *Nil c.* SAYI 647:33
carbuncle monstrous c. CHAR 203:18
carbuncles Monstrous c. SPEN 732:15
carcase c. of an old song THOM 773:16
Wheresoever the c. is BIBL 97:3
Where the c. is PROV 614:39
carcases c. of unburied men SHAK 660:8
carcass hew him as a c. SHAK 675:3
carcinoma sing of rectal c. HALD 356:17
card c. up his sleeve LABO 446:13
memories are c.-indexes CONN 234:2
Orange c. CHUR 214:13
play the race c. SHAP 706:11
cardboard C. Iron. Their hardships BOLA 124:8
over a c. sea HARB 359:16
cardinal on the C.'s chair BARH 54:3
cards buy a pack of c. COLE 228:4
c. with a man called Doc ALGR 12:1
learned to play at c. JOHN 412:4
Lucky at c. PROV 606:10
old age of c. POPE 583:15
pack the c. BACO 42:18
played At c. for kisses LYLY 480:14
played our c. SCHE 646:12
shuffle the c. CERV 200:3
wicked pack of c. ELIO 295:29

care age is full of c. SHAK 703:27
better c. of myself BLAK 117:15
Black C. sits behind HORA 388:13
c. for nobody BICK 114:15
c. for the unhappy VIRG 793:15
C. killed the cat PROV 597:3
c. of all the churches BIBL 107:13
c.'s check and curb VAUG 790:5
c. whether Mr John Keats KEAT 431:7
closed our anxious c. EPIT 303:13
disclaim all my paternal c. SHAK 677:23
don't c. too much for money LENN 463:19
feeling her c. HOOK 383:6
Heaven's peculiar c. SOME 727:18
Hippocleides doesn't c. HIPP 377:14
if, full of c. DAVI 252:8
kill c. SHAK 691:21
Killing c. SHAK 673:10
more c. to stay SHAK 697:34
much c. and valour SHAK 671:14
Nor c. beyond to-day GRAY 350:16
ravelled sleave of c. SHAK 683:8
she don't c. LENN 464:2
Sorrow and C. BURN 166:21
take c. of minutes CHES 209:12
Teach us to c. ELIO 293:20
Took great C. of his Mother MILN 510:16
To say we do not c. WARD 803:10
wish I could c. what you do MITC 524:2
with artful c. Affecting CONG 233:15
with me past c. SHAK 695:3
women and c. and trouble WARD 803:11
wrinkled C. derides MILT 512:15
cared C. not to be at all MILT 515:8
career c. is over WELL 810:2
C. open to the talents CARL 187:13
c. open to the talents NAPO 539:3
East is a c. DISR 270:29
loyal to his own c. DALT 248:14
nothing in his long c. NEWS 544:17
our c. and our triumph VANZ 789:20
careful be c. out there CATC 196:11
cannot be too c. WILD 818:18
can't be good, be c. PROV 603:27
c. felicity PETR 574:17
C. now LINE 469:11
c. of the type TENN 761:12
carefully got to be c. taught HAMM 359:5
You come most c. SHAK 661:4
careless c. of the single life TENN 761:12
C. she is with artful care CONG 233:15
C. talk costs lives OFFI 554:1
c. trifle SHAK 681:23
first fine c. rapture BROW 156:3
impudently c. CENT 191:12
They were c. people FITZ 315:13
carelessness both looks like c. WILD 817:16
carefullest c. BETJ 71:6
cares anxious c., when past ROCH 630:11
c. and pleasures GIBB 335:7
c. can make the sweetest love GREE 352:4
c. that infest the day LONG 473:12
Children are certain c. PROV 597:17
Grief and avenging C. VIRG 794:20
Nobody c. MORT 533:14
none c. or knows CLAR 218:15
one c. for none of them AUST 39:7
Professional men, they have no c. NASH 539:11
Carew grave of Mad C. HAYE 365:2
carf c. biforn his fader CHAU 204:11
cargo little c. boats KIPL 439:11
caricature c. as far as I can SCAR 646:8
c., Decrepit age YEAT 837:18
carlines made the c. ladies JAME 402:18
Carlisle burghers of C. MACA 482:19
carmina *Nulla placere diu c. possunt* HORA 387:4
sunt et mihi c. VIRG 796:11
carmine *Verum ubi plura nitent in c.* HORA 386:4
carnage C. is thy daughter WORD 830:11
strife, and c. drear SCOT 651:15
carnal c. lusts and appetites BOOK 131:1
heathen in the c. part POPE 583:12
carnally to be c. minded is death BIBL 105:6
carnations c. and streaked gillyvors SHAK 703:14
morn Of bright c. DRUM 279:15
carnivorous sheep born c. FAGU 306:3
caro VERBUM C. FACTUM EST MISS 523:1
carol fluting a wild c. TENN 760:18
Carolina ham'n eggs in C. GORD 347:1
carollings little cause for c. HARD 361:12
carpe *c. diem* HORA 387:22
carpenter Between them, Walrus and C. LEVI 466:7
c. known by his chips PROV 597:4
I said to the c. CART 192:15
Walrus and the C. CARR 190:19
You may scold a c. JOHN 413:3
carpenters special language like c. SEXT 655:9
carpet figure in the c. JAME 403:3
wear the c. with their shoes YEAT 837:4
carpets long c. rose KEAT 427:15
carping each c. tongue BRAD 146:14
carriage C. held but just Ourselves DICK 266:6
small second class c. GILB 337:19
carriages c. of the great TURN 785:14
carried ought to be c. EPIC 300:20
carrier down from the c.'s cart LEE 462:1
carrion c. comfort, Despair HOPK 384:2
graced his c. with BROW 155:12
carrots Sowe C. in your Gardens GARD 329:14
carry c. a big stick ROOS 633:5
c. knowledge with him JOHN 416:1
c. nothing out BIBL 109:17
c. them in his bosom BIBL 88:2
making him c. me TOLS 779:14
cars c. the great Gothic cathedrals BART 56:8
crazy about c. SALI 642:11
cart and a useful C. LEAR 460:10
Carthage C. must be destroyed CATO 194:13
Carthaginian C. trustworthiness SALL 643:11
cartoonist life as a c. wonderful PETE 574:11
carve c. heads upon cherry-stones JOHN 417:12
c. my epitaph BROW 155:13
c. on every tree SHAK 659:6
Let's c. him SHAK 675:3
must c. in Latin WALL 800:4
carved c. not a line WOLF 825:5
carver was the c. happy RUSK 638:19
carving C. is interrelated HEPW 371:6
tails with a c. knife NURS 551:10
casbah Come with me to the C. MISQ 521:6
case c. is concluded AUGU 36:12
corpse in the c. BARH 54:8
everything that is the c. WITT 824:7
in our c. we have not got REED 623:14
lady's in the c. GAY 332:8
nothing to do with the c. GILB 338:14
this c. is that case ARAB 23:8
would have passed in any c. BECK 59:28
cased c. up, like a holy relic WEBS 807:21
casement c. ope at night KEAT 429:19
casements magic c. KEAT 429:14
cases Circumstances alter c. PROV 597:20
Hard c. make bad law PROV 601:51
plead their c. in court VIRG 795:1
cash C. before conscience HORA 386:10
c. payment CARL 187:4
from hand to hand of c. SICK 717:16
needfu' c. BURN 169:1
needs good c. TUCK 784:17
pay you c. to go away KIPL 440:18
takes your c. CHUR 213:19
take the c. in hand FITZ 314:10
casket seal the hushèd c. KEAT 430:7
Cassidy C.'s hanging hill KAVA 426:8
Cassiopeia C. was over KAVA 426:8
Cassius C. from bondage will deliver SHAK 674:23
C. is aweary SHAK 676:25
cassock C., band, and hymn-book WILB 817:1
cassocked c. huntsman COWP 241:2
cassowary If I were a c. WILB 817:1
cast C. a cold eye YEAT 837:22
c. me in the teeth BOOK 134:8
C. me not away BOOK 135:7
c. off the works of darkness BIBL 105:21
C. thy bread BIBL 84:27
C. your mind on other days YEAT 837:21
die is c. CAES 180:20
for the most part c. up HOBB 379:3
in no wise c. out BIBL 101:29
let him first c. a stone BIBL 101:33
more he c. away BUNY 161:14
my life upon a c. SHAK 697:1
Ne'er c. a clout PROV 607:25
never be c. down BOOK 132:2
Satan c. out Satan BIBL 98:1
suddenly c. down BOOK 134:24
castaway c. wine-pots CLOU 221:11
I myself should be a c. BIBL 106:11
castaways tales of c., colonial museums GENE 333:5
castes c. who are excluded LAWS 459:9
casteth casteth out devils BIBL 94:29
Castilian old C. Poor noble BYRO 179:16
castle c. hath a pleasant seat SHAK 682:6
c. in France MORE 531:6
c. of my skin LAMM 449:12
Dublin C. KETT 434:15
falls on c. walls TENN 765:16
home is his c. PROV 599:16
house is his c. COKE 224:10
king of the c. NURS 548:20
old lad of the c. SHAK 667:16
owre the C. Downe BALL 50:10
rich man in his c. ALEX 11:9
Castlereagh had a mask like C. SHEL 712:8
intellectual eunuch C. BYRO 179:26
castles C. in the air IBSE 398:10
fortifications called c. ORDE 557:12
Thou shalt make c. CHAU 206:29
castrati reviving the *c.* REED 623:18
casualties c. were low JARR 404:10
casualty is the first c. SAYI 648:10
road of c. SHAK 687:24
casuistry Mountains of c. POPE 582:12
cat big c. in a poodle parlour PARR 568:3
Care killed the c. PROV 597:3
c. and her kittens NURS 548:6
c. and the fiddle NURS 548:12
c. in gloves PROV 597:6
c. may look at a king PROV 597:7
c. on a hot tin roof WILL 820:15
c. that likes to gallop SMIT 724:17
C., the Rat, and Lovell COLL 228:9
C. with crimson whiskers LEAR 460:21
c. would eat fish PROV 597:8
consider my C. Jeoffrey SMAR 722:5
cosmic Cheshire c. HUXL 397:9
Curiosity killed the c. PROV 597:44
endow a college, or a c. POPE 583:19
Foss is the name of his c. LEAR 460:15
grinning c. Quivers TATE 755:4
Had Tiberius been a c. ARNO 26:22
Hanging of his c. BRAT 147:4
if a c. is black or white DENG 257:9
it almost wore the c. LEON 464:10
killed the c. NURS 551:7
Lat take a c. CHAU 205:23
Like a powerful graceful c. CHUR 216:11
part to tear a c. in SHAK 689:10
pavilion c. LANG 450:10
play with my c. MONT 527:20
poor c. i' the adage SHAK 682:15

room to swing a c. SMOL 726:13
see how the c. jumps SCOT 652:13
Touch not the c. SCOT 651:21
very fine c. JOHN 417:5
want to swing a c. DICK 262:5
ways of killing a c. PROV 611:46
What c.'s averse to fish GRAY 350:20
When the c.'s away PROV 614:26
which way the c. is jumping SULZ 746:4
wildest of all wild animals was the C. KIPL 441:6
catalogue c. of human crime CHUR 215:8
find a husband in a c. EHRE 290:2
in the c. ye go for men SHAK 684:2
catalyst c. that sparks the revolution DURY 286:10
catamite in bed with my c. OPEN 555:27
cataract wild c. leaps TENN 765:16
cataracts You c. and hurricanoes SHAK 678:21
catastrophe between education and c. WELL 810:13
drift toward unparalleled c. EINS 290:16
tickle your c. SHAK 669:29
catch catch as c. can FOOT 319:8
First c. your hare PROV 600:26
hard to c. and conquer MERE 505:19
If I can c. him once SHAK 687:13
thief to c. a thief PROV 610:33
Catch-22 anything as good as C. HELL 368:15
only one catch and that was C. HELL 368:13
catched and not be c. PEPY 573:6
catcher c. in the rye BORR 144:3
c. in the rye SALI 642:12
catches c. no mice PROV 597:6
catching C.'s before hanging PROV 597:5
Passion, I see, is c. SHAK 675:23
poverty's c. BEHN 62:14
catchwords principally by c. STEV 742:3
catechist Shorter-C. HENL 369:19
categorical imperative is C. KANT 425:15
category replacement of c.-habits RYLE 640:19
caterpillar cankerworm, and the c. BIBL 90:13
c. on the leaf BLAK 117:21
c., when coming to UPAN 787:14
caterpillars c. of the commonwealth SHAK 695:2
cates dainties are all c. SHAK 698:7
Cathay cycle of C. TENN 763:10
cathedral C. time ANON 15:16
Heft Of C. Tunes DICK 266:16
world is a c. PAST 569:10
cathedrals cars the great Gothic c. BART 56:8
Catherine child of Karl Marx and C. ATTL 32:4
catholic cannot be a good C. NORF 546:14
C. and Apostolick Church BOOK 129:9
C. and sensual CHAN 202:5
C. Church has never come WILL 820:12
C. Faith BOOK 126:21
Gentlemen, I am a C. BELL 64:12
holy C. Church BOOK 126:10
if I was not a C. WAUG 806:23
lawful for a C. woman MENC 504:18
may as well be a C. SPAR 731:21
Once a C. WILS 821:9
Roman C. Church MACM 487:21
Roman C. women must THOM 773:9
She [the C. Church] NEWM 542:12
was C. AMIS 13:15
Catholicism accessories of C. HOPK 385:7
Catholics C. and Communists GREE 351:15
When Hitler attacked the C. NIEM 545:8
Catiline our patience, C. CICE 217:18
Cato C.'s daughter SHAK 675:8
losing one pleased C. LUCA 478:13
Voice of C. JONS 419:14
What C. did EPIT 304:12
catract sounding c. Haunted me WORD 829:4
cats All c. are grey in the dark PROV 594:20
C. and monkeys JAME 403:7
c. are cats MARQ 497:7
c. is 'dogs' PUNC 617:10
C. look down on us CHUR 216:22
C., no less liquid TESS 768:17
count the c. in Zanzibar THOR 776:15
direst earthly foes—C. WATS 805:3
elderly lady who has two c. LEWI 467:11
greater c. with golden eyes SACK 641:5
Keep no more c. PROV 604:48
killed the c. BROW 157:10
make sober c. PROV 613:38
Naming of C. ELIO 295:17
cattle Actors are c. HITC 378:1
Authors are like c. LAND 450:6
call the c. home KING 437:9
C. die ANON 22:4
c. upon a thousand hills BOOK 135:2
dominion over the c. BIBL 73:14
grass for the c. BOOK 139:3
Hurry no man's c. PROV 603:7
thousands of great c. BURK 163:26
Catullus Did their C. walk that way YEAT 837:4
Poor C. CATU 197:4
caught man who shoots him gets c. MAIL 491:4
cauldron Fire burn and c. bubble SHAK 684:17
cauliflower C. is nothing but cabbage TWAI 786:22
causality law of c. RUSS 639:20
causas *rerum cognoscere c.* VIRG 796:18
vitam vivende perdere c. JUVE 424:18
cause already in the c. BERG 67:16
between c. and effect LA B 446:17
c. is in my will SHAK 675:12
c. may be inconvenient BENN 66:7
c. of dullness in others FOOT 319:7
c. of the human nose COLE 227:18
c. of the widows BOOK 136:6
c., or just impediment BOOK 130:21
c. that perishes with them CLOU 221:15
c. that wit is SHAK 669:22
defend my c. BOOK 134:9
experiment to his own c. SPRA 735:5
full c. of weeping SHAK 678:19
good old C. MILT 519:22
good old c. WORD 830:13
great c. of cheering BENN 66:5
his c. being good MORE 531:8
it is the c., my soul SHAK 693:22
judge in his own c. PROV 608:4
judge thou my c. BIBL 89:27
little c. for carollings HARD 361:12
Our c. is just DICK 266:22
perseverance in a good c. STER 738:18
Rebel without a c. FILM 313:1
Report me and my c. SHAK 667:8
shew any just c. BOOK 131:3
Whose c. is God COWP 242:8
winning c. pleased the gods LUCA 478:13
causes aren't any good, brave c. OSBO 560:8
best c. tend to attract FISH 314:1
declare the c. JEFF 405:2
Home of lost c. ARNO 28:15
in its c. just DRYD 282:6
knowledge of c. BACO 45:1
malice, to breed c. JONS 420:14
thread of c. AURE 37:9
Tough on the c. of crime BLAI 117:7
caution c. in love RUSS 639:15
cautiously do c., and look to the end ANON 21:12
cavaliero perfect c. BYRO 173:15
cavaliers C. (Wrong but Wromantic) SELL 654:9
will not do with the c. LAMB 449:11
cave burst stomach like a c. DOUG 276:16
C. canem PETR 574:14
darksome c. they enter SPEN 733:21
political C. of Adullam BRIG 148:14
vacant interlunar c. MILT 518:15
wall of the c. PLAT 578:8
cavern c. sparkling BYRO 178:9
caverns bat that beats about in c. WILB 817:6
c. measureless to man COLE 225:20
Sand-strewn c. ARNO 26:12
ten thousand C. KEAT 430:1
caves c. in which we hide FITZ 315:8
c. of ice COLE 225:22
dark unfathomed c. of ocean GRAY 350:11
Mendip's sunless c. MACA 482:18
there will be c. NIET 545:14
caviare c. to the general SHAK 663:23
Cawdor Glamis thou art, and C. SHAK 682:1
cease c. from exploration ELIO 294:17
c. from mental fight BLAK 120:1
C.! must men kill SHEL 711:13
c. to live ARNO 28:5
c. upon the midnight KEAT 429:13
Fall and c. SHAK 680:12
fears that I may c. to be KEAT 430:17
maketh wars to c. BOOK 134:20
that thou shouldst c. SHEL 714:14
Wonders will never c. PROV 615:17
ceased c. to be with Sarah BIBL 74:28
ceasing Remembering without c. BIBL 109:7
Ceauşescus C.' execution O'DO 553:1
Cecilia Blessed C., appear AUDE 33:17
cedar breaketh the c.-trees BOOK 133:13
moonlit c. ARNO 26:20
cedars c. of Lebanon BIBL 77:36
c. of Libanus BOOK 139:3
excellent as the c. BIBL 85:21
cedite *C. Romani scriptores* PROP 593:17
ceiling draw on the c. CHES 211:14
lines of the c. ÉLUA 299:2
celebrity C. is a mask UPDI 788:14
of mathematical c. DOYL 277:17
celestial Apparelled in c. light WORD 829:14
C. Emporium BORG 143:4
c. greatness TRAH 780:10
For that c. light MILT 514:19
lighten with c. fire BOOK 142:7
Celia Come, my C. JONS 420:12
celibacy c. has no pleasures JOHN 410:27
c. is almost always PEAC 571:2
cell Each in his narrow c. GRAY 350:8
hot c. of their hearts BOGA 123:12
cellar born in a c. CONG 232:18
Born in a c. FOOT 319:5
cellos c. of the deep farms STEV 740:18
cells c. and gibbets COOK 235:16
little grey c. CHRI 212:15
vast assembly of nerve c. CRIC 245:1
Celt hysterics of the C. TENN 762:1
Celtic woods of C. antiquity KEYN 435:8
cement grass can grow through c. CHER 208:22
With the same c. POPE 580:22
cemetery c. is an open space SHEL 710:12
Help me down C. Road LARK 453:7
cenotaph laugh at my own c. SHEL 711:7
censor c. of the young HORA 386:2
censorship extreme form of c. SHAW 709:19
censure c. of a man's self JOHN 416:3
c. this mysterious writ DRYD 281:22
read, and c. HEMI 369:7
centaur ant's a c. POUN 589:20
moral c., man and wife BYRO 177:10
centaurs from the waist they are C. SHAK 679:22
centre c. cannot hold YEAT 837:5
c. is everywhere ANON 17:21
c. is everywhere UPDI 788:12
earth is the c. DONN 275:11
My c. is giving way FOCH 318:22
This bed thy c. is DONN 274:16

cents simplicity of the three per c. DISR 270:13
centuries All c. but this GILB 338:2
forty c. look down NAPO 538:8
lie through c. BROW 155:14
Through what wild c. DE L 256:9
century c. of light BAHA 47:25
c. of the common man WALL 799:15
c.'s cool nursery AKHM 9:12
crushes the entire c. ZOLA 841:2
last for more than a c. CATU 194:21
sad, glittering c. BURC 161:23
So the 20th C. CRAN 243:24
when a new c. begins MANN 494:2
Cerberus C., and blackest Midnight MILT 512:12
damn them with King C. SHAK 669:32
You are not like C. SHER 716:6
cerebellum If they've a brain and c. GILB 337:15
ceremonies dreams, and c. SHAK 675:4
ceremony C. is an invention LAMB 448:10
c. of innocence is drowned YEAT 837:5
c. that to great ones 'longs SHAK 686:8
general c. SHAK 671:19
thrice-gorgeous c. SHAK 671:20
Ceres C. re-assume the land POPE 583:25
certain c. because it is impossible TERT 768:16
c. of nothing KEAT 430:21
c. thing called the Boy Friend WILS 822:7
four things c. KIPL 438:20
her c. ending SHAK 704:3
lady of a 'c. age' BYRO 177:12
Nothing is c. but PROV 608:12
Nothing is c. but PROV 608:13
sure and c. hope BOOK 131:14
certainties begin with c. BACO 41:8
hot for c. MERE 505:21
most people's c. HARD 360:6
certainty C. Feeling PASC 569:1
not the test of c. HOLM 381:13
certamina *atque haec c. tanta* VIRG 797:2
certezza *Di doman non ci è c.* MEDI 503:10
certified that I may be c. BOOK [illegible]
cesspool London, that great c. DOYL 278:4
cetacean generous C. KIPL 441:12
Ceylon soft o'er C.'s isle HEBE 367:7
chaff catch old birds with c. PROV 615:35
king's c. is worth PROV 605:3
tastes like c. KEAT 431:22
vacant c. well meant TENN 760:25
wheat from the c. HUBB 392:12
chaffinch While the c. sings BROW 156:2
chagrin *c'est le c. qui développe C. d'amour* PROU 594:11
C. d'amour FLOR 318:20
chain c. is no stronger PROV 597:9
c. of our sins BOOK 127:15
flesh to feel the c. BRON 150:1
hangs a golden c. PUSH 618:2
lengthening c. GOLD 345:6
lover's servile c. ROCH 630:5
sever The c. CORY 237:12
winds th'exhausted c. BURN 168:10
chained With one c. friend SHEL 711:9
chainless spirit of the c. mind BYRO 179:3
chains bandage might be c. BYRO 178:10
better to be in c. KAFK 425:8
bind their kings in c. BOOK 142:2
c. and darkness MONT 526:17
C. and slaverie BURN 168:7
C. do not hold a marriage SIGN 719:5
c. Of heart-debasing slavery GRAI 348:12
deliverance from c. DOUG 277:1
everywhere he is in c. ROUS 636:5
lose but their c. CLOS 222:19
lose but their c. MARX 500:7
My c. fell off WESL 810:21
sang in my c. THOM 772:4
slightest c. EDGE 288:17
woman must wear c. FARQ 307:8
chainsaw imagination and a c. HIRS 377:19
chair *c. est triste* MALL 492:2
C. she sat in ELIO 296:2
Give Dayrolles a c. LAST 455:15
like a barber's c. SHAK 656:2
on the Cardinal's c. BARH 54:3
Seated in thy silver c. JONS 419:17
should not paint the c. MUNC 536:13
speaks of a c. BISH 116:1
With one enormous c. LERN 465:9
chairs carry candles and set c. HERV 375:8
empty c. in my drawing-room BURN 165:21
next suggested elbow-c. COWP 241:17
three c. in my house THOR 776:11
chaise longue hurly-burly of the c. CAMP 182:15
chalice c. from the palace FILM 312:6
chalices golden c. JEWE 407:8
Cham great C. of literature SMOL 726:16
chamber bridegroom out of his c. BOOK 132:15
in my lady's c. NURS 548:8
in your c. BOOK 131:19
stalking in my c. WYAT 834:5
chambermaid arms of a c. JOHN 416:6
more worth than his c. GODW 342:5
chambers beams of his c. BOOK 139:1
intricate and winding c. SHEL 715:4
Steel c. HARD 361:9
chameleon add colours to the c. SHAK 672:30
c.'s dish SHAK 664:19
chameleons C. feed on light and air SHEL 711:10
champagne c. and a chicken MONT 526:15
C. certainly gives one SURT 746:21
c. or high heels BENN 66:7
get no kick from c. PORT 588:5
not a c. teetotaller SHAW 706:24
since I've had c. LAST 456:9
some c. DEAN 253:17
Women, and C. BELL 64:2
chance All c., direction POPE 585:17
bludgeonings of c. HENL 369:20
c. and accident BACO 45:15
c., and death SHEL 713:11
c. favours only the prepared PAST 569:11
C. governs all MILT 515:25
C. has appointed her BUNT 160:11
C. herself DAVI 251:20
dart of c. SHAK 693:11
erring men call c. MILT 511:27
Give peace a c. LENN 463:21
I missed my c. LAWR 458:14
in the last c. saloon MELL 504:6
it was by c. BRAD 146:14
law, c., hath slain DONN 272:21
never eliminate c. MALL 492:4
no gifts from c. ARNO 26:25
too good to leave to c. SIMO 720:12
Chancellor C. of the Exchequer LOWE 477:8
chances c. change SOUT 731:13
changes and c. BOOK 130:4
Chanel C. No. 5 MONR 526:8
change bolts up c. SHAK 657:21
C. and decay LYTE 480:23
C. as the winds change SWIN 751:17
c., but I cannot die SHEL 711:7
c. from Jane to Elizabeth AUST 38:17
c. his spots PROV 605:16
c. horses in mid stream PROV 598:30
c. is as good as a rest PROV 597:10
C. is constant DISR 269:5
'C.' is scientific RUSS 640:5
c. my state SHAK 704:15
c. our vile body BOOK 131:14
c. partners BERL 68:5
C. the name HORA 389:14
c. the past AGAT 6:20
c. the people who teach BYAT 173:5
c. we think we see FROS 325:16
c. what we can STEV 741:8
C. without inconvenience JOHN 409:3
c. your mind AURE 37:7
compelled to c. that state NEWT 543:5
doth in C. delight SPEN 734:13
fear of c. Perplexes monarchs MILT 515:1
in all c. BAUD 57:11
involves a great c. TROL 783:3
it's bound to c. HART 363:12
lamentable c. SHAK 679:13
Management that wants to c. TUSA 786:1
means of some c. BURK 163:14
more things c. KARR 426:1
most stupid do not c. CONF 232:5
necessary not to c. FALK 306:6
Neither to c., nor falter SHEL 713:16
point is to c. it MARX 500:2
relief in c. IRVI 400:3
religion, knavery, and c. BEHN 62:12
see c. in the things ARIS 24:18
shalt thou c. them BOOK 138:15
subject to c. PALI 564:13
things will have to c. LAMP 449:15
Times c. PROV 613:5
torrent of c. CHES 211:11
try to c. things BOLD 124:12
wheel Of C. SPEN 734:12
wind of c. is blowing MACM 487:19
wish to c. in the child JUNG 423:11
without c. UNAM 787:7
changeable c. always is woman VIRG 794:13
changed all things are c. BACO 41:21
changed, c. utterly YEAT 835:19
changed, c. utterly YEAT 835:21
c. from that Hector VIRG 794:2
c. upon the blue guitar STEV 739:24
human nature c. WOOL 826:16
If voting c. anything LIVI 470:9
its name c. DANT 249:22
we shall all be c. BIBL 107:3
changes c. and chances BOOK 130:4
c. we fear be thus irresistible JOHN 409:7
sundry and manifold c. BOOK 128:7
changing c. scenes of life TATE 755:9
ever c., like a joyless eye SHEL 714:13
everything within them was c. DIDE 267:5
fixed point in a c. age DOYL 277:15
stress on not c. one's mind [illegible]
thinks of c. himself TROL 783:2
times they are a-c. DYLA 287:15
world is c. ELIZ 297:18
Chankly Hills of the C. Bore LEAR 460:8
channel C. forbidding Union GRAT 349:7
[C.] is a mere ditch NAPO 538:9
crossing the C. GILB 337:19
Fog in C. BROC 149:2
in a different c. AKHM 9:7
chanting C. faint hymns SHAK 689:2
chaos bit of primordial c. WELL 810:14
black c. comes again SHAK 706:2
C. and darkness MARR 497:13
C. and old Night MILT 514:29
c. illuminated by lightning WILD 818:7
C. is come again SHAK 692:19
C. often breeds life ADAM 2:19
C., rough and unordered mass OVID 561:12
C. umpire sits MILT 515:25
dread empire, C. POPE 582:14
God dawned on C. SHEL 710:19
Humour is emotional c. THUR 777:3
means of overcoming c. RICH 626:16
Not c.-like together crushed POPE 587:14
return you to c. ZOHA 840:8
stillness in the midst of c. BELL 64:14
chapel also build a c. LUTH 480:1
c. I was painting MICH 506:15
Devil will build a c. PROV 614:36
chapels nice in c. HUNT 395:16
chaplain twice a day the C. called WILD 818:33
chaps Biography is about C. BENT 67:2
kills a lot more c. HALD 356:17
nave to the c. SHAK 681:9

chapter c. of accidents CHES 209:23
repeat a complete c. JOHN 415:29
write the next c. JOHN 408:13
character about a fellow's c. REAG 623:4
by the content of their c. KING 436:14
c. dead at every word SHER 716:12
c. in the full current GOET 343:8
c. is destiny ELIO 293:7
c. is his fate HERA 371:9
c. is to be abused THAC 769:7
c. of a family STER 738:19
c. of the fifth act LERM 464:22
discover their real c. EDGE 288:13
enormous lack of c. LEVA 465:19
Fate and c. NOVA 547:3
leave my c. behind me SHER 716:13
reap a c. READ 622:16
reganing my c. FLEM 317:14
reveal more of a man's c. PLUT 579:6
turns on personal c. NAPO 538:14
What is c. JAME 403:10
wise about his c. ELIO 291:20
characteristics c. of the human species GODW 342:4
characters c. and conduct of their rulers ADAM 3:12
c. of hell to trace GRAY 350:4
c. to lose BURN 167:21
high c. are drawn POPE 583:29
Six c. in search PIRA 576:15
charcoal blackened by c. EDGE 288:19
charge give his angels c. over thee BOOK 137:23
I'm in c. CATC 196:2
Take thou in c. MACA 483:10
charged c. the troops BROW 153:13
thought c. with emotion GIDE 336:18
charges die to save c. BURT 170:8
warily to begin c. BACO 42:30
charging marching, c. feet JAGG 401:7
chariest c. maid is prodigal SHAK 662:8
Charing Cross existence is at C. JOHN 414:27
Heaven and C. THOM 774:13
chariot axle-tree of the c.-wheel BACO 44:20
body as the c. UPAN 788:1
c. of fire BLAK 120:1
C. of Supernal Man ZOHA 840:12
clouds his c. BOOK 139:1
Swing low, sweet c. SONG 730:4
Time's wingèd c. MARV 499:2
charioted c. by Bacchus KEAT 429:11
chariots burneth the c. BOOK 134:20
trust in c. BOOK 132:19
wheels of his c. BIBL 77:30
charitably c. dispose of any thing SHAK 671:16
charities cold c. CRAB 243:16
Defer not c. BACO 43:30
patron of some thirty c. TENN 766:7
charity C. and beating FLET 318:12
C. and Mercy DICK 263:4
C. begins at home PROV 597:11
C. begins at home SHER 716:16
C. covers a multitude PROV 597:12
C., dear Miss Prism WILD 817:21
c. edifieth BIBL 106:7
c. for all LINC 469:1
c. in sin SHAK 686:14
c. is cold SMAR 722:4
C. never faileth BIBL 106:16
C. shall cover BIBL 111:6
c. so cold SKEL 721:14
C. suffereth long BIBL 106:16
c. will hardly water BACO 43:18
gives c. in secret TALM 754:19
give with c. a stone BLAK 118:13
have not c. BIBL 106:16
in love and c. BOOK 129:15
Keeping books on c. PERÓ 573:23
lectures or a little c. WHIT 815:16
Let holy c. LITT 470:4
little earth for c. SHAK 673:18
living need c. ARNO 26:1
love and dear c. MORE 531:13
On what a c. ye come SMAR 722:7
charlatan c., and a conjuror TROL 781:21
Charlemagne C. with all his peerage MILT 514:30
Charles C. II was always very merry SELL 654:11
gentle-hearted C. COLE 227:5
keep King C. the First out DICK 261:20
King C.'s golden days SONG 729:12
King C.'s head DICK 261:22
Charley C.'s aunt from Brazil THOM 771:16
Charlie o'er the water to C. HOGG 380:13
Charlotte C. has been writing BRON 150:4
charm British Museum had lost its c. GERS 334:12
C. a sort of bloom on a woman BARR 55:19
c. dissolves SHEN 715:5
c. he never so wisely BOOK 135:18
c. in melancholy ROGE 631:15
c. of all the Muses TENN 767:4
c. of powerful trouble SHAK 684:18
C. the great English blight WAUG 806:2
Completing the c. ELIO 293:26
discreet c. of the bourgeoisie FILM 312:18
double c. DYER 286:17
hard words like a c. OSBO 559:18
Oozing c. from every pore LERN 465:10
What c. can soothe GOLD 345:30
what c. is CAMU 184:5
What is c. LESS 465:14
charmed c. it with smiles CARR 191:25
c. me from my profession SHAK 699:23
I bear a c. life SHAK 685:24
charmer voice of the c. BOOK 135:18
Were t'other dear c. away GAY 332:1
charms acres o' c. BURN 167:10
C. strike the sight POPE 587:12
Do not all c. fly KEAT 428:18
endearing young c. MOOR 530:9
fields and flocks have c. CRAB 243:13
hath a thousand c. COWP 241:14
mere external c. MORE 531:4
Music has c. CONG 232:25
nameless c. unmarked BYRO 173:20
Charon C. quit poling GINS 339:23
charter c. of the land THOM 774:20
chase have to c. after it KLEE 442:4
live by the c. TOCQ 778:13
stern c. a long chase PROV 611:19
with unhurrying c. THOM 774:5
chases your picture c. me RACI 619:19
chassis worl's in a state o' c. O'CA 552:13
chaste as c. as ice SHAK 664:7
c. and fair JONS 419:17
C. as the icicle SHAK 660:15
c. as unsunned snow SHAK 660:22
c. polygamy CARE 186:10
C. to her husband POPE 583:13
Married, charming, c. BYRO 175:29
My English text is c. GIBB 336:2
Nor ever c. DONN 272:25
Was Jesus c. BLAK 118:15
chasten c. and subdue WORD 829:5
chasteneth he c. BIBL 110:3
chastised c. you with whips BIBL 79:22
chastisement c. of our peace BIBL 88:17
chastity boasting of their c. LEWI 466:21
c. and continency AUGU 36:3
c. shines out GIRA 340:6
C.—the most unnatural HUXL 397:4
clothed on with c. TENN 759:2
Even like thy c. SHAK 693:31
'Tis c., my brother MILT 511:23
vice of c. VOLT 798:7
chat ad-hoc 'c. shows' AHER 8:27
chateaux *ô c.* RIMB 628:12
Chatham Great C. ANON 16:12
chats spoiled the women's c. BROW 157:10
Chattanooga C. Choo-choo GORD 347:1
chatter c. of the world TROL 782:14
hare-brained c. DISR 269:21
only idle c. GILB 338:18
chattering not c. pies SIDN 718:14
Chatterley Between the end of the C. ban LARK 452:12
Chatterton C., the marvellous boy WORD 831:12
cheap c. but wholesome salad COWP 242:9
c. sitting as standing PROV 604:7
done as c. as other men PEPY 573:1
flesh and blood so c. HOOD 383:1
hold their manhoods c. SHAK 671:25
how potent c. music is COWA 239:3
in c. shoes AMIE 13:9
maketh himself c. BACO 42:16
Man's life is c. as beast's SHAK 678:17
milk is so c. PROV 615:6
sell it c. SAYI 648:1
sold c. what is most dear SHAK 705:13
Talk is c. PROV 611:41
They be good c. WYAT 834:7
Words are c. CHAP 202:10
cheaper c. than a prawn sandwich RATN 622:5
c. to do this BUTL 172:28
in the c. seats LENN 463:16
cheapest Buy in the c. market PROV 596:45
cheat cannot c. on DNA WARD 803:10
c. at cards genteelly BOSW 144:21
detecting what I think a c. JOHN 414:23
so lucrative to c. CLOU 222:26
To c. a man is nothing GAY 331:21
cheated be exceedingly c. EVEL 305:5
c. than not to trust JOHN 410:19
Of being c. BUTL 172:10
Old men who never c. BETJ 70:8
cheating c. of our friends CHUR 213:19
period of c. BIER 114:23
cheats C. never prosper PROV 597:13
c. with an oath PLUT 579:9
checked C. like a bondman SHAK 676:25
cheek blush into the c. DICK 264:24
c. of night SHAK 697:7
dancing c.-to-cheek BERL 68:6
Feed on her damask c. SHAK 701:24
giveth his c. BIBL 89:26
give this c. a little red POPE 584:4
how she leans her c. SHAK 697:10
iron tears down C.'s cheek MILT 512:8
iron tears down Pluto's c. MILT 512:8
loves a rosy cheek CARE 186:5
smite thee on thy right c. BIBL 93:12
cheeks blood Spoke in her c. DONN 273:9
crack your c.! rage! blow SHAK 678:21
on thy c. KEAT 428:8
ruddy c. Augustus had HOFF 379:17
cheer Be ay of c. CHAU 205:10
Be of good c. BIBL 95:26
be of good c. BIBL 102:27
c. but not inebriate BERK 67:19
c. but not inebriate COWP 241:31
Don't c., men PHIL 575:7
let thy heart c. thee BIBL 85:1
scarce forbear to c. MACA 483:11
So c. up, my lads HUGH 392:16
which side do they c. for TEBB 757:2
with a c. BROW 155:5
cheerer c. of his spirits WALT 802:17
cheerful as c. as any man could PEPY 572:19
c. countenance BIBL 82:35
c. countenance BOOK 139:3
c. giver BIBL 107:10
It's being so c. CATC 196:5
join our c. songs WATT 805:12
make a c. noise BOOK 137:9
with a c. countenance SHAM 706:4
cheerfulness C. gives elasticity SMIL 723:2
c. keeps up ADDI 5:7
c. was always breaking in EDWA 289:11
cheeriness Chintzy, Chintzy c. BETJ 70:6
cheering c. us all up BENN 66:5

cheerio c. my deario MARQ 497:6
cheers Two c. for Democracy FORS 321:5
cheese apple pie and c. FIEL 309:8
Botticelli's a c. PUNC 617:21
chinks wi' c. SURT 746:18
I've dreamed of c. STEV 741:21
like some valley c. AUDE 35:5
of c. FADI 306:1
pound of c. CALV 182:2
varieties of c. DE G 255:25
chemical made up of c. elements MULL 536:2
two c. substances JUNG 423:9
chemically They may be sound c. HALD 356:16
chemist as objective as a c. CHEK 208:13
c., fiddler, statesman DRYD 280:9
chemistry c. that works WILL 820:10
found him weak in c. WELL 810:7
produces by c. SHAW 708:7
cheque political blank c. GOSC 347:5
chequerboard c. of nights and days FITZ 314:15
cheques Blank c. HOLM 381:12
cherchez C. la femme DUMA 284:14
cherish c. those hearts SHAK 673:16
love, c., and to obey BOOK 131:5
cherished lay aside long-c. love CATU 197:15
My no longer c. MILL 509:16
Chernobyl cultural C. MNOU 524:14
cherries apples, c., hops DICK 265:3
Life is just a bowl of c. BROW 152:5
cherry American as c. pie BROW 151:20
carve heads upon c.-stones JOHN 417:12
c. hung with snow HOUS 390:15
c. now HOUS 390:14
C. ripe CAMP 183:25
C.-ripe, ripe, ripe HERR 374:5
c. year, a merry year PROV 597:14
ruddier than the c. GAY 331:8
Under the c. BASH 56:19
cherub c.'s face POPE 583:10
cherubim C. and Seraphim HEBE 367:8
c. does cease to sing BLAK 117:19
helmèd c. MILT 513:22
cherubims Immortal c. TRAH 780:15
rode upon the c. BOOK 132:11
sitteth between the c. BOOK 138:12
cherubin C., and Seraphin BOOK 125:20
cherubins quiring to the young-eyed c. SHAK 688:23
cherubs so near the c. hymn SMAR 722:1
Cheshire cosmic C. cat HUXL 397:9
chess First of the c. CHAU 204:5
chessboard c. is the world HUXL 397:15
chest on the dead man's c. STEV 741:18
Chesterton dared attack my C. BELL 63:18
chestnut spreading c. tree LONG 474:19
chestnuts pop like c. FLAU 316:11
chevalier *c. sans peur et sans reproche* ANON 20:4
Chevy Drove my C. to the levee MCLE 486:15
chew can't fart and c. gum JOHN 408:20
chewed c., are cast up HOBB 379:3
cheweth c. not the cud BIBL 76:20
chewing gum c. for the eyes ANON 18:21
Chianti bottles of C. SHAF 655:14
Chibiabos my brother, C. LONG 474:14
chic Radical C. . . . only radical in Style WOLF 825:16
chicken champagne and a c. MONT 526:15
c. in every pot HOOV 383:11
c. in his pot HENR 370:4
c. shit JOHN 408:9
c. whose head has been cut off MITF 524:7
fed the c. every day RUSS 639:23
over the frozen c. BINC 115:5
Some c.! Some neck CHUR 215:15
chickens all my pretty c. SHAK 685:8
as a hen gathereth her c. BIBL 96:29
beside the white c. WILL 821:2
costly than c. SHAW 707:9
count your c. PROV 598:31
Curses are like young c. SOUT 730:14
Curses, like c. PROV 597:45
May c. come cheeping PROV 606:33
chiding c. of the winter's wind SHAK 658:13
I am a child to c. SHAK 693:16
not alway be c. BOOK 138:18
chief c. end of man SHOR 717:15
C. Justice was rich MACA 482:8
c. of the ways BIBL 82:1
Cromwell, our c. of men MILT 519:3
Sinners; of whom I am c. BIBL 109:13
chieftain C. Iffucan of Azcan STEV 739:19
c. o' the puddin'-race BURN 168:20
child accused of c. death RICH 626:12
As yet a c. POPE 583:3
cherished c. ELIO 292:1
C.! do not throw BELL 63:2
c. for the first seven SAYI 647:16
c. imposes on the man DRYD 281:24
c. in a forest BART 56:5
c. in the street CLOU 221:12
C. is father WORD 829:10
c. is father of the man PROV 597:15
c. is known by his doings BIBL 83:9
c.is not a vase RABE 619:13
c. is owed the greatest JUVE 425:5
c. looks at a cake GASK 331:1
c. of God BOOK 130:10
c. of law BENT 66:16
c. of Time HALL 358:6
c. ought to be of the party AUST 38:27
c.'s a plaything LAMB 448:21
c. shall lead them BIBL 87:4
c. should always say what's true STEV 742:16
c.'s rattle JOHN 413:23
devoured the infant c. HOUS 390:6
disagreeable-looking c. OPEN 556:27
English c. BLAK 120:18
every c. born therein RUSK 638:25
every c. may reach JONS 420:28
Get with c. a mandrake DONN 274:11
God bless the c. HOLI 380:19
governed by a c. SHAK 696:19
happy English c. TAYL 756:10
hare's own c. HOFF 380:7
have a thankless c. SHAK 678:11
healthy c. well nursed SIME 748:13
I am a c. to chiding SHAK 693:16
I am to have his c. BURG 161:25
If you strike a c. SHAW 708:21
I heard one calling, 'C.' HERB 372:8
Is it well with the c. BIBL 80:15
I was a c. POE 579:10
knows his own c. SHAK 687:18
leave a c. alone BROW 157:23
like a froward c. TEMP 757:5
little c., a limber elf COLE 225:1
little c. I stand HERR 374:2
lose his c.'s heart MENG 504:22
Love, a c. WROT 833:16
Magus Zoroaster, my dead c. SHEL 713:4
man c. conceived BIBL 81:3
mid-May's eldest c. KEAT 429:12
Monday's c. is fair PROV 606:42
mother for the c. COLE 227:2
my absent c. SHAK 677:11
not fair to the c. FROS 326:11
On a cloud I saw a c. BLAK 120:12
one c. makes you a parent FROS 325:12
Praise the c. PROV 609:39
receive one such little c. BIBL 96:8
right to a c. SHAW 707:8
shocks the mind of a c. PAIN 563:9
show'st thee in a c. SHAK 678:10
simple c., dear brother WORD 832:14
spare the rod, and spoil the c. BUTL 172:8
sucking c. shall play BIBL 87:5
talk of the c. TALM 754:9
that of a little c. THAC 768:22
this thy C. BOOK 130:20
thy king is a c. BIBL 84:25
Train up a c. BIBL 83:14
unto us a c. is born BIBL 87:1
use of a new-born c. FRAN 323:17
voice of the c.'s blood SWIN 751:11
When I was a c. BIBL 106:16
While the c. was yet alive BIBL 79:7
wise c. that knows its own PROV 604:6
wish to change in the c. JUNG 423:11
with c. of glorious great intent SPEN 733:18
woman forget her sucking c. BIBL 88:11
childbirth Death and taxes and c. MITC 524:1
childhood C. is the kingdom MILL 509:9
c. shows the man MILT 518:7
dolmens round my c. MONT 527:5
eye of c. SHAK 683:10
From his c. onward HARD 360:2
have you seen my c. JACK 400:18
lost your ability in c. GONC 346:8
moment in c. GREE 351:23
wove a web in c. BRON 149:12
childish c. pleasures ALAI 9:16
c. valorous MARL 497:2
chime his c. verse BYRO 178:7
put away c. things BIBL 106:16
childishness second c. SHAK 659:3
children airy hopes my c. WORD 828:12
as c. fear BACO 42:22
become as little c. BIBL 96:7
bring forth c. BIBL 74:5
burn its c. to save MEYE 506:14
By c. and tradesmen's bills MACN 488:11
by c. to adults SZAS 751:24
c. all gone NURS 549:1
C. and fools tell PROV 597:16
C. are certain cares PROV 597:17
C. are given Mozart SCHN 648:23
c. are more troublesome SHAW 707:9
c. are not your children GIBR 336:11
c. are strangers SCHW 649:15
c. at play MONT 527:11
C. begin by loving WILD 818:27
c. died in the streets AUDE 33:26
C. have never been very good BALD 48:18
c. in Holland NURS 547:15
c. inter their parents HERO 373:22
c. in whom is no faith BIBL 77:12
c. like the olive-branches BOOK 140:23
c. love their parents AUCT 33:12
c. of a larger growth CHIL [illegible]:17
c. of a larger growth DRYD 280:27
c. of God BIBL 93:3
c. of God BIBL 105:8
c. of light BIBL 100:7
c. of light BOOK 130:9
c. of my body KOLL 443:10
C. of the future age BLAK 121:4
C.: one is one SAYI 647:4
c. only scream BYRO 179:23
c. produce adults DEV 259:13
c., sailors, and drunken men PROV 602:36
c.'s birthplace taken DUFF 284:7
C. should be seen PROV 597:18
c. sooner allured by love ASCH 30:1
c. sport upon the shore WORD 830:8
C.'s talent to endure ANGE 14:17
c. stood watching KING 437:11
c. sweeten labours BACO 43:25
c. were lost sight of MOYN 534:11
c. who leave home SLOV 721:18
c. who were rough SPEN 732:20
C. with Hyacinth's temperament SAKI 642:8
c. with their play COWP 240:8
c., you should never let WATT 805:9
Come, dear c. ARNO 26:10
committed by c. on children BOWE 145:12
contempt—and c. TWAI 786:18
draw like these c. PICA 576:1
each one of her c. VERG 791:6
efforts to shield c. ADDA 4:4
first class, and with c. BENC 64:20
fortunate in his c. EURI 305:2
get back from c. NESB 541:10

Goodnight, c. CATC 195:19
had so many c. NURS 551:6
hear the c. weeping BROW 154:15
He has no c. SHAK 685:8
hell for c. STRI 744:19
holdeth c. from play SIDN 718:24
How many c. KNIG 442:8
idea that all c. ANNE 15:3
in the hands of young c. DYLA 287:6
in the thoughts of c. LOCK 471:13
keep c. quiet SWIF 747:10
kept from c. and from fools DRYD 282:19
kitchen and their c. FITZ 315:4
known as the C.'s Hour LONG 473:11
little c. cried MOTL 534:7
made c. laugh AWDR 39:20
many women, and many c. JOHN 413:1
more than all his c. BIBL 75:8
music understood by c. STRA 744:15
my c. are frightened of me GEOR 334:6
Myself and c. three COWP 240:12
my work and my c. HILL 376:17
not much about having c. LODG 472:12
Nourish thy c. BIBL 91:2
oh those c.'s voices VERL 791:10
old men and c. BOOK 142:1
other people's c. CLIN 221:2
parents obey their c. EDWA 289:8
pitieth his own c. BOOK 138:19
poor get c. KAHN 425:10
procreation of c. BOOK 131:2
provoke not your c. to wrath BIBL 108:10
raising your c. ONAS 554:16
reasons for having c. RUSS 640:8
remember the c. you got BROO 151:6
screams of c. WEST 812:10
see his c. fed PUDN 616:14
sleepless c.'s hearts are glad BETJ 70:5
so are the young c. BOOK 140:22
stars are my c. KEAT 431:11
Suffer the little c. BIBL 98:10
teach them [c.] first JOHN 413:14
than of their c. PENN 572:15
their unborn c. DURC 286:2
They were privileged c. BROO 151:3
thou shalt have c. BOOK 134:17
tiresome for c. SAIN 641:11
To beget c. SART 645:7
upon the c. BIBL 76:9
voices of c. BLAK 120:19
Weep, c. NERV 541:6
weeping for her c. BIBL 92:25
wife and c. BACO 43:17
women and c. could work SELL 654:14
world safer for c. LE G 462:13
wrong name of innocent c. BINC 115:4
child-wife only my c. DICK 262:6
Chile Small earthquake in C. COCK 223:15
chill bitter c. it was KEAT 427:3
bitter c. it was OPEN 556:13
chills Of c. and fever RANS 621:20
chilly By c. fingered spring KEAT 427:2
c. and grown old BROW 158:11
our c. women BYRO 173:17
room grows c. GRAH 348:5
chimaera c. of my age BERN 69:2
Chimborazo C., Cotopaxi TURN 785:19
chime let your silver c. MILT 513:23
some soft c. JONS 420:16
chimera c. buzzing in a vacuum RABE 619:12
c. in my brains DONN 275:9
chimeras dire c. and enchanted isles MILT 511:25
wild impossible c. SWIF 747:24
chimes c. at midnight SHAK 670:7
chimney c.-sweepers, come to dust SHAK 661:1
old men from the c. corner SIDN 718:24
chimneys c. were blown down SHAK 683:17
grove of c. MORR 532:6
your c. I sweep BLAK 120:13
chimpanzee vase in the hands of a c. WAUG 806:18
china C. to Peru JOHN 411:13
frail c. jar POPE 587:4
Hong Kong's return to C. DENG 257:10
land armies in C. MONT 528:13
outer C. 'crost the Bay KIPL 439:13
though c. fall POPE 583:16
Till C. and Africa meet AUDE 33:18
wall of C. was finished BREC 147:20
Chinese went to a C. dinner FLEM 317:20
chinks c. wi' cheese SURT 746:18
chintzy Chintzy, C. cheeriness BETJ 70:6
chip c. of the old 'block' BURK 165:2
chips carpenter known by his c. PROV 597:4
c. with everything WESK 810:18
chivalry age of c. BURK 163:21
age of c. is past DISR 270:35
Christian service and true c. SHAK 694:19
He loved c. CHAU 204:8
nine-tenths of the law of c. SAYE 646:5
noble acts of c. CAXT 199:1
smiled Spain's c. away BYRO 177:22
Chloris C.! that I now could sit SEDL 653:1
chloroform c. of the Irish GOGA 343:19
chocolate c. cream soldier SHAW 706:16
chocolates life like a box of c. FILM 312:2
choice c. and master spirits SHAK 675:20
c. in rotten apples PROV 611:2
c. of all my library SHAK 700:1
c. of working or starving JOHN 409:2
C. words WORD 831:13
freedom of c. is given TALM 753:19
is the *people's c.* SHER 715:22
just the terrible c. BROW 157:26
measure and the c. JOHN 411:20
Not c. But habit WORD 828:18
parties having any c. JOHN 415:11
perpetual potential c. BAGE 46:17
simply *independent* c. DOST 276:9
these the c. dishes GARR 330:6
when c. was any more DIDI 267:9
you takes your c. PROV 616:5
you takes your c. PUNC 617:3
choir in a wailful c. KEAT 430:11
in the folk mass c. DOYL 278:11
join the c. invisible ELIO 293:11
singing in the c. SONG 729:10
virgin-c. KEAT 429:18
choirs Bare ruined c. SHAK 704:29
C. and Places BOOK 126:14
c. of wailing shells OWEN 562:6
choisir *Gouverner, c'est c.* LÉVI 466:11
choke c. on the tail PROV 604:18
c. the word BIBL 95:21
choked sprang up and c. them BIBL 95:20
choking on a man's back, c. him TOLS 779:14
choleric but a c. word SHAK 686:11
chommoda *C. dicebat* CATU 197:18
choo-choo Chattanooga C. GORD 347:1
choose *believe what we c.* NEWM 543:1
better to c. the culprits PAGN 563:7
cannot c. but hear COLE 226:5
C. an author DILL 267:13
c. time BACO 42:28
c. your women or linen PROV 607:27
He should say to me: 'C.' LESS 465:17
intellect of man is forced to c. YEAT 835:8
Let's c. executors SHAK 695:8
not c. not to be HOPK 384:2
Of two evils c. PROV 608:21
ones we c. to love HARR 363:2
people c. for friends GILM 339:17
therefore c. life BIBL 77:10
to govern is to c. LÉVI 466:11
woman can hardly ever c. ELIO 292:12
choosers Beggars can't be c. PROV 595:40
choosing C. each stone MARV 498:12
just c. so BROW 155:20
chopcherry c. ripe within PEEL 571:20
Chopin C. and Bizet FISH 313:17
chopper cheap and chippy c. GILB 338:6
Here comes a c. NURS 550:4
chord common c. again BROW 155:1
lost c. PROC 593:11
struck one c. of music PROC 593:13
chords c. in the human mind DICK 261:1
chortled c. in his joy CARR 190:13
chorus c.-ending from Euripides BROW 155:7
c. of indolent reviewers TENN 764:22
chose c. him five smooth stones BIBL 78:32
chosen best c. language AUST 38:2
c. generation BIBL 110:28
few are c. BIBL 96:21
few are c. PROV 606:25
I have c. thee BIBL 88:8
Mary hath c. BIBL 99:16
Ye have not c. me BIBL 102:23
choughs crows and c. that wing SHAK 679:19
Christ all at once what C. is HOPK 384:22
all things through C. BIBL 109:1
C. adorned and beautified BOOK 131:1
C. and his mother HOPK 384:21
C. and His saints ANON 22:3
C. being raised from the dead BIBL 105:1
C. beside me PATR 570:3
[C.] came and preached peace BIBL 107:25
C. cannot find ANON 19:19
C. follows Dionysus POUN 589:15
C. is all BIBL 109:4
C. is the path MONS 526:11
C. our passover BIBL 106:2
C. perish in torment SHAW 709:18
C. risen from the dead BIBL 106:22
C. sailing to me BLOK 122:3
C.'s blood streams MARL 496:7
C.'s particular love's sake BROW 157:23
C. that is to be TENN 761:29
C. walking on the water THOM 774:14
C. wasn't a woman TRUT 784:13
churches have killed their C. TENN 764:12
counted loss for C. BIBL 108:20
hope in C. BIBL 106:21
I did trust in C. WESL 811:15
If Jesus C. were to come CARL 188:22
in C. Church hall ARNO 27:8
in C. shall all be made alive BIBL 106:22
Jesus C. BIBL 110:7
Jesus C. his only Son BOOK 126:10
joint-heirs with C. BIBL 105:8
lady of C.'s College AUBR 32:17
Lord C. enter in WILD 819:4
love of C. BIBL 107:28
ministers of C. BIBL 107:12
Now call on C. GILB 337:2
Priest did offer C. BOOK 142:11
rejoice in C. LUTH 479:12
speechless C. SWIN 750:13
to live is C. BIBL 108:14
uphold the C. TENN 759:19
Vision of C. BLAK 118:10
We preach C. crucified BIBL 105:28
Christabel softely tread, said C. COLE 224:19
Christe *C. eleison* MISS 520:12
C. receive thy saule BALL 51:2
christened when she was c. SHAK 659:12
Christian buried in C. burial SHAK 666:16
C. Architecture PUGI 616:17
C. boys ARNO 29:13
C. can die LAST 457:3
C. can only fear dying HARE 362:3
C. ideal has not been tried CHES 211:17
C. is a man who feels YBAR 834:20
C. religion HUME 394:9
C. service and true chivalry SHAK 694:19
die a C. CHAR 203:6
effusion of C. blood LAUD 454:4
exile to the C. URBA 788:19
forgive them as a C. AUST 38:24
gentleman, and a C. HUGH 393:13
going to be a C. SPAR 731:21
hadn't *got* a C. PUNC 617:13
I mean the C. religion FIEL 310:7

Christian (*cont.*):
made me, in these C. days TAYL 756:10
naturally C. soul TERT 768:14
Onward, C. soldiers BARI 54:13
persuades me to be a C. FRY 326:28
persuadest me to be a C. BIBL 104:22
sad, good C. POPE 583:12
Scratch the C. ZANG 839:20
three C. men CAXT 198:17
wonders of the c. religion MATH 501:7
you were a C. slave HENL 370:2
Christianity at the heart of C. PÉGU 572:5
C. better than Truth COLE 227:7
C. deposes Nature HUGH 393:11
C. is not so much BUTL 171:8
C. is part of the laws HALE 357:3
C., of course BALF 50:1
C. was the religion SWIF 748:23
Disneyfication of C. CUPI 248:1
Evidences of C. COLE 227:8
fight for C. URBA 788:18
His C. was muscular DISR 270:9
local thing called C. HARD 360:8
meaning of C. WESL 811:17
rock 'n' roll or C. LENN 463:17
whole effect of C. GIDE 336:16
Christians blood of C. is the seed TERT 768:15
call themselves C. BOOK 127:17
C. are not born JERO 406:17
C., awake BYRO 173:8
C. have burnt each other BYRO 176:1
generations of C. MACA 482:13
Jews are not unlike C. JUDA 422:23
Christmas At C. I no more desire SHAK 680:19
call off C. FILM 311:2
child on C. Eve BART 56:5
C. Day in the Workhouse OPEN 555:23
C. is the Disneyfication CUPI 248:1
C.-morning bells say 'Come!' BETJ 70:5
C. stories tortured BYRO 178:3
C. won't be Christmas OPEN 555:11
Do they know it's C. GELD 332:28
Ghost of C. Past DICK 261:9
insulting C. card [illegible]
night before C. MOOR 529:8
not just for C. SAYI 647:11
turkeys vote for C. CALL 181:12
well that C. should fall ADDI 5:4
white C. BERL 68:12
Christopher Robin C. has fallen MORT 533:14
C. is saying his prayers MILN 511:1
chronicle c. of the planets YEVT 838:11
c. of wasted time SHAK 705:9
c. small beer SHAK 692:11
chronicles abstracts and brief c. SHAK 663:24
Chuang Tzu C.'s dreaming heart BASH 56:20
chuck C. it, Smith CHES 209:28
chuckles c. of the waves AESC 6:11
chumps C. make the best husbands WODE 824:10
church beset the C. of England CECI 199:5
best harmony in a c. MILT 519:14
Broad of C. BETJ 71:9
came to the village c. TENN 763:25
Catholick and Apostolick C. BOOK 129:9
Catholick C. BOOK 127:17
Christ's C. militant BOOK 129:10
c. for his mother CYPR 248:10
c. furniture at best COWP 242:13
c. has become a spectacle PROC 593:10
c. he currently did not attend AMIS 13:15
C. is an anvil MACL 486:13
c. is an anvil PROV 597:19
C. is 'one generation' CARE 186:18
C. is said to want NEWM 542:8
C. of England CHAR 203:6
C. of [England] should ROYD 636:16
C. of England were to fail KEBL 432:8
[C. of Rome] thoroughly MACA 482:11
C.'s banquet HERB 373:4
C. shall be free MAGN 489:11
C.'s one foundation STON 743:9
C.'s Restoration BETJ 70:12
except in the C. CYPR 248:12
free c. CAVO 198:15
Get me to the church LERN 465:2
glory in the c. BIBL 108:1
God built a c. LUTH 480:1
good dog goes to c. PROV 602:6
hatred against the C. SKEL 721:14
Housbondes at c. dore CHAU 204:23
household and the C. BOOK 128:18
in a country c. SWIF 748:4
into his c. lewd hirelings MILT 516:11
I will build my c. BIBL 96:4
nearer the c. PROV 607:20
never passes a c. JOHN 413:4
no salvation outside the c. AUGU 36:7
open the windows of the C. JOHN 407:12
publick Prayer in the C. BOOK 142:10
religion the C. of England FIEL 310:7
satisfied in C. of England HOPK 385:7
Say to the c., it shows RALE 620:12
seed of the C. PROV 596:31
She [the Catholic C.] NEWM 542:12
some to c. repair POPE 584:20
Stands the C. clock BROO 150:15
[the c.'s] buttresses ANON 16:14
there must be the C. AMBR 13:3
thy c. on earth is seeking SHER 716:24
What is a c. CRAB 242:20
Where God builds a c. PROV 614:36
wisdom of the C. of England BOOK 125:11
churches care of all the c. BIBL 107:13
C. built to please BURN 167:20
c. have killed their Christ TENN 764:12
c. which are in Asia BIBL 111:20
John to the seven c. BIBL 111:17
white robe of c. RAOU 622:2
Churchill never was a C. GLAD 341:2
churchman for the real C. SMIT 725:11
churchmen c. fain would kill TENN 764:12
doth well with c. BACO 43:18
churchyard dust of the C. DONN 275:6
lone c. at night BLAI 117:6
makes a fat c. PROV 601:38
palsy-stricken, c. thing KEAT 427:7
worse taste, than in a c. JOWE 421:13
churchyards Troop home to c. SHAK 690:8
When c. yawn SHAK 665:5
ciel *montez au c.* FIRM 313:8
cigar c. called Hamlet ADVE 7:23
really good 5-cent c. MARS 497:21
cigarette But the c., well POTT 588:23
c. is the perfect type WILD 818:19
c. that bears a lipstick's traces MARV 499:9
smoked my first c. TOSC 780:1
throw your c. into the lake GIDE 336:17
cigars roller of big c. STEV 739:20
Cinara C. was my queen HORA 389:2
Cinarae *bonae Sub regno C.* HORA 389:2
Cincinnatus C. of the West BYRO 178:20
cinco *c. en punto de la tarde* GARC 329:10
cinder how dry a c. this world DONN 272:8
cinders c., ashes, dust KEAT 428:15
Sat among the c. NURS 549:8
cinema c. is truth 24 times per second GODA 341:20
cinnamon tinct with c. KEAT 427:13
Circe elegance of C.'s hair POUN 589:13
circenses *Panem et c.* JUVE 424:21
circle c. of the golden year TENN 759:5
fatal c. is traced TOCQ 778:12
God is a c. ANON 17:21
Love is a c. HERR 374:13
makes by c. just DONN 274:20
Round and round the c. ELIO 293:26
tightness of the magic c. MACL 487:4
Weave a c. round him COLE 225:25
wheel is come full c. SHAK 680:10
circles individual c. TROL 782:14
circumcised c. dog SHAK 694:4
circumcision c. nor uncircumcision BIBL 109:4
circumference c. is nowhere ANON 17:21
circumlocution C. Office DICK 262:25
circumnavigation c. of our globe DISR 268:20
circumspectly walk c. BIBL 108:8
circumspice *Si monumentum requiris, c.* EPIT 304:4
circumstance fell clutch of c. HENL 369:20
force of c. DIDE 267:4
Pride, pomp, and c. SHAK 692:30
circumstances C. alter cases PROV 597:20
C. beyond my control DICK 262:7
play of c. WEIL 808:22
circumstantial c. evidence THOR 775:27
lie c. SHAK 659:26
circumvent c. God SHAK 666:21
circunstancia *Yo soy yo y mi c.* ORTE 557:15
circus no right in the c. MAXT 502:11
shouldn't be in the c. PROV 603:28
circuses bread and c. JUVE 424:21
cistern loud the c. BENN 66:2
citadel peaceful c. KEAT 428:27
citadels circle-c. there HOPK 384:20
cities C. and their civilities PATM 569:21
c. we had learned about JARR 404:10
flower of c. ANON 17:13
hell to c. AESC 6:9
hum Of human c. BYRO 174:19
lousy skin scabbed by c. BUNT 160:11
not look in great c. AUST 37:25
Seven c. warred HEYW 376:8
streets of a hundred c. HOOV 383:12
Towered c. please us MILT 512:23
citizen c. as an abstract proposition TOCQ 778:8
c., first in war LEE 461:21
c. in this world AURE 37:10
c. of no mean city BIBL 104:15
c. of the world BACO 43:6
c. of the world BOSW 143:18
c. or the police AUDE 35:2
Every c. will make MORE 531:17
good man and a good c. AUCT 33:9
greater than a private c. [illegible]
I am a Roman c. CICE 217:21
John Gilpin was a c. COWP 240:11
zealous c. BURK 164:5
citizens c. of death's grey land SASS 645:18
first and second class c. WILL 821:7
refined c. SHEL 715:2
citizenship c. Indian TERE 768:10
cito *Bis dat qui c. dat* PUBL 616:11
città C. DOLENTE DANT 249:7
city abstract and premeditated c. DOST 276:7
as of a c. BROW 153:14
big hard-boiled c. CHAN 201:13
bring us forth from this c. KORA 444:9
buildings of a c. KEAT 431:13
citizen of no mean c. BIBL 104:15
c. consists in men NICI 544:21
c. housekeeping has failed ADDA 4:3
c. is built TENN 759:18
c. is not a concrete jungle MORR 532:7
C. now doth like a garment wear WORD 827:19
c. of dreadful night THOM 775:20
c. of God AURE 36:22
c. of God BOOK 137:16
C. of God JOHN 418:16
c. of perspiring dreams RAPH 622:4
c. of refuge MILT 519:16
C. of the Big Shoulders SAND 643:18
c. that is set on an hill BIBL 93:5
c. upon a hill WINT 823:14
c., where I long had pined WORD 830:20
c. which hath foundations BIBL 109:29
c. will follow you CAVA 198:9
Despising, For you, the c. SHAK 660:9
down the C. Road MAND 493:6
every town or c. HOLM 381:5

evil in a c. BIBL 90:17
feel, amid the c.'s jar ARNO 26:15
first c. Cain COWL 239:12
Hell is a c. SHEL 713:2
holy c., new Jerusalem BIBL 113:7
How doth the c. sit solitary BIBL 89:22
in populous c. pent MILT 517:14
In the great c., pent COLE 225:15
Jerusalem is built as a c. BOOK 140:14
live in a c. COLT 230:4
long in c. pent KEAT 430:16
Lord keep the c. BOOK 140:21
modern c. is a place WRIG 833:11
nation, not a c. DISR 270:19
new c. of Friends WHIT 815:2
no continuing c. BIBL 110:8
oppressing c. BIBL 90:23
people went up into the c. BIBL 77:20
peper felled a c. THOM 772:7
rose-red c. BURG 162:4
set all the c. on an uproar BIBL 104:4
splendid C. RIMB 628:11
stood within the C. disinterred SHEL 712:11
street of the c. was gold BIBL 113:10
streets and lanes of the c. BIBL 99:29
Sun-girt c. SHEL 712:6
that great c. BIBL 112:24
this great hive, the c. COWL 239:19
What is the c. but the people SHAK 660:7
whole c. is paid HESI 375:12
Without a c. wall ALEX 11:12
Woe to the bloody c. BIBL 90:21
civet Give me an ounce of c. SHAK 679:22
civil Always be c. to the girls MITF 524:6
c. discord CLOS 222:9
c. question deserves PROV 597:22
c. to everyone SISS 720:17
In a c. war REED 623:16
In c. business BACO 42:12
never lost our c. war BIRN 115:12
nothing but a c. contract SELD 653:18
Pray, good people, be c. GWYN 355:8
rude sea grew c. SHAK 689:22
Too c. by half SHER 716:3
utmost bound of c. liberty MILT 519:6
civilian mushroom rich c. BYRO 179:16
civilisation sweetness of present c. HUGO 394:1
civilities bandy c. JOHN 413:24
dread c. TOCQ 778:16
civility C. costs nothing MONT 527:1
C. costs nothing PROV 597:21
c. of my knee BROW 153:12
I see a wild c. HERR 374:8
nothing lost by c. PROV 612:19
civilization annihilating all c. SAKH 641:15
can't say c. don't advance ROGE 632:1
c. advances MACA 481:15
C. advances by extending WHIT 814:17
C. a movement TOYN 780:4
C. and its discontents RIVI 628:16
C. and profits COOL 236:1
c. has from time to time ELLI 298:16
C. has made the peasantry TROT 783:16
C. nothing more than ORTE 557:16
c. of the Fabians INGE 399:4
C. the progress RAND 621:14
elements of modern c. CARL 187:19
For a botched c. POUN 589:17
history of Western C. TYNA 787:2
in a state of c. JEFF 405:19
items of high c. JAME 403:4
last product of c. RUSS 639:16
life-blood of real c. TREV 781:7
rottenness of our c. READ 622:10
submit to c. TOCQ 778:13
thought of modern c. GAND 329:8
civilizations eradicates autonomous c. SONT 728:7
civilized c. circumstances BAGE 47:14
C. people must get off FINK 310:24
c. suffice CASS 193:10
last thing c. by Man MERE 505:15
of c. society SMIL 722:16
that are called c. PAIN 564:4
civilizers two c. of man DISR 269:10
civilizes Cricket c. people MUGA 534:13
civil servant c. doesn't make jokes IONE 399:22
Here lies a c. SISS 720:17
civil servants conviction c. BANC 53:5
of c. BRID 148:6
Civil Service business of the C. ARMS 25:21
c. has finished REIT 624:8
C. is deferential CROS 246:13
civis *C. Romanus sum* CICE 217:21
C. Romanus sum PALM 566:3
claes some upo' their c. BURN 167:11
claim last territorial c. HITL 378:7
clair *n'est pas c.* RIVA 628:15
clairvoyante famous c. ELIO 295:29
clamour c. for war PEEL 571:16
c. of silence TAGO 753:1
c. of the crowded street LONG 474:2
clap C. her broad wings FRER 324:11
Don't c. too hard OSBO 559:22
If you believe, c. your hands BARR 55:17
in the cheaper seats c. your hands LENN 463:16
O c. your hands together BOOK 134:21
Clapham man on the C. omnibus BOWE 145:18
clapped-out c., post-imperial DRAB 278:14
claps If someone c. his hand HAKU 356:14
Clarence perjured C. SHAK 696:18
claret c. is the liquor for boys JOHN 416:8
Claridges body of the bootboy at C. WOOL 827:3
clarion c. o'er the dreaming earth SHEL 712:12
Clarissa C. lives RICH 627:4
clasped C. by the golden light HOOD 382:27
clasps c. the crag TENN 758:17
class c. struggle MARX 500:3
first and second c. citizens WILL 821:7
hands of the ruling c. STAL 736:1
history of c. struggles MARX 500:6
I could have had c. FILM 311:11
In education no c. distinction CONF 232:3
solvent of c. distinction BENN 65:15
use of *force* by one c. LENI 463:7
whatever his c. CHEK 208:8
While there is a lower c. DEBS 254:9
classes All c. of society JEVO 407:7
But the two c. FOST 321:11
lower c. had such white CURZ 248:7
masses against the c. GLAD 341:8
two c. of travel BENC 64:20
classic 'c.' music eliminates STRA 744:14
C. music is th'kind HUBB 392:13
tread on c. ground ADDI 4:20
classical c. mind at work PIRS 576:17
C. quotation JOHN 416:21
tragedy of the c. languages MADA 488:19
classicism C. is health GOET 343:17
classics bellyful of the c. MILL 510:4
classify Germans c. CATH 194:6
Claudel pardon Paul C. AUDE 34:3
claudite *C. iam rivos* VIRG 796:3
Claus ain't no Sanity C. FILM 311:18
claw red in tooth and c. TENN 761:14
clawed c. me with his clutch VAUX 790:19
claws neatly spreads his c. CARR 189:10
pair of ragged c. ELIO 295:7
clay associate of this c. HADR 355:11
beauteous c. WRIG 833:14
C. is moulded LAO 451:8
C. is the word KAVA 426:9
C. lies still HOUS 390:16
for this the c. grew tall OWEN 562:9
grey stone and grassy c. EPIT 303:13
Kingdoms are c. SHAK 656:8
mire and c. BOOK 133:31
potter and c. endure BROW 157:20
potter power over the c. BIBL 105:13
Shall the c. say BIBL 88:7
clean All c. and comfortable KEAT 431:18
c. American backyards MAIL 491:2
c. place to die KAVA 426:10
c. the sky ELIO 295:16
c., verb active DICK 263:21
did not love c. linen JOHN 413:2
I shall be c. BOOK 135:6
keep their teeth c. SHAK 660:4
let other people c. up FITZ 315:13
lie down in c. postures FOWL 321:20
Make me a c. heart BOOK 135:7
New brooms sweep c. PROV 607:41
nice c. faces BARH 54:4
Not a c. & in-between-the-sheets MCGO 485:10
thing to keep c. FRY 326:22
tragedy is c. ANOU 22:9
cleaned I c. the windows GILB 338:27
cleaning militants like c. women TRUF 784:1
cleanliness C. is, indeed, next WESL 811:12
C. is next to PROV 597:23
of late for c. CORB 236:12
What C. everywhere GIDE 336:17
cleanness swimmers into c. leaping BROO 150:16
cleans sweeps as it c. ADVE 7:30
cleanse c. me from my sin BOOK 135:4
C. the thoughts of our hearts BOOK 129:4
cleansed doors of perception were c. BLAK 119:28
What God hath c. BIBL 103:29
clear c. in his great office SHAK 682:10
C. your mind of cant JOHN 417:6
In the c. air FERG 308:18
poignancy in all things c. WILB 817:4
too c., too simple STEN 737:19
What is not c. RIVA 628:15
clearing c. up the obscure corners HUXL 397:16
clearing-house c. of the world CHAM 200:13
clearly ideas too c. GRAC 347:16
clears little water c. us SHAK 683:12
cleave c. the general ear SHAK 663:28
c. the wood ANON 18:13
c. unto his wife BIBL 73:23
cleaveth spirit c. not stedfastly BOOK 137:4
cleaving c. the grass MOOR 530:6
cleft c. for me TOPL 779:16
clementine his daughter, C. MONT 529:4
clenched hands are c. MIDR 507:15
Cleopatra C.'s nose been shorter PASC 568:12
gone to gaze on C. too SHAK 656:25
in the bed of C. BROW 152:16
squeaking C. SHAK 657:24
with less than C. DRYD 280:26
clercs *trahison des c.* BEND 64:22
clergy Arminian c. PITT 576:24
benefit o' the C. CONG 232:17
c. are not called WALP 801:20
c. of this country GIRA 340:6
c. were beloved SWIF 748:23
Established C. GLAD 341:1
clergyman good enough to be a c. JOHN 414:16
clergymen C.'s sons always PROV 597:24
men, women, and c. SMIT 725:17
cleric C. before, and Lay behind BUTL 172:5
neither c. nor layman BERN 69:2
clerk C. there was of Oxenford CHAU 204:18
'twixt the Priest and C. HERR 374:15
clerks gretteste c. been noght wisest CHAU 206:10
statesmen or of c. DISR 269:28
treason of all c. AUDE 33:21
clever beautiful and the c. GREE 351:17
c., but is it Art KIPL 438:9
c. enough to get all that CHES 211:19
c. men at Oxford GRAH 348:10
c. theft was praiseworthy SPEN 732:8

clever (*cont.*):
c. to a fault BROW 155:10
good people were c. WORD 827:14
important to be c. *about* MEDA 503:7
let who will be c. KING 437:4
manage a c. man KIPL 441:18
Too c. by half SALI 642:13
Too c. by half SALI 643:6
cleverness height of c. LA R 453:16
cliché c. and an indiscretion MACM 487:16
click c. with people EISE 291:13
Clunk, c., every trip OFFI 554:2
client bend to favour ev'ry c. GAY 332:11
c. n'a jamais tort RITZ 628:14
c. will crawl through BURR 169:14
fool for his c. PROV 606:21
cliff coign of the c. SWIN 750:18
cliffs bluebirds over the white c. BURT 169:19
chalk c. of Dover BALD 49:9
c. of fall HOPK 384:12
glittering c. on cliffs BEAT 58:4
still the solitary c. WORD 828:22
white c. I never more must see MACA 482:24
climate adapting to our c. PUGI 616:21
chilling c. hardly bears SWIF 749:13
c.'s ruined CHEK 208:11
in love with a cold c. SOUT 731:7
lived in a warm, sunny c. COWA 239:1
Love in a cold c. MITF 524:5
Our cloudy c. BYRO 173:17
whole c. of opinion AUDE 33:29
climax c. of all human ills BYRO 176:22
climb C. ev'ry mountain HAMM 358:17
c. not at all ELIZ 297:7
c. up into the heaven BOOK 141:11
Fain would I c. RALE 621:3
climbers Hasty c. PROV 602:3
climbing c. clear up to the sky HAMM 358:21
c., shakes his dewy wings D'AV 251:11
clime mottie, misty c. BURN 169:8
They change their c. HORA 386:20
clinging c. to life ARNO 28:14
c. to their crosses CHES 209:27
cloak c. become an iron cage WEBE 807:4
knyf under the c. CHAU 206:19
clock as is making a c. LA B 446:19
biological c. is ticking KEYE 434:17
by Shrewsbury c. SHAK 669:17
c. is always slow SERV 654:24
c. of communism has stopped SOLZ 727:15
c. will strike MARL 496:7
c. without the pendulum RUSS 640:6
Court the slow c. POPE 584:8
forgot to wind up the c. STER 738:14
mouse ran up the c. NURS 548:14
Old Time the c.-setter SHAK 677:9
Stands the Church c. BROO 150:15
turned into a sort of c. HUXL 397:13
clocks c. were striking thirteen OPEN 555:24
c. were striking thirteen ORWE 558:19
morning c. will ring HOUS 390:17
clockwork c. orange BURG 161:24
clods harrowing c. HARD 361:16
clog c. of his body FULL 327:11
clogs From c. to clogs PROV 600:47
cloistered fugitive and c. virtue MILT 519:10
cloisters quiet collegiate c. CLOU 221:14
cloned successfully c. a lamb MARC 495:6
Clonmacnoise monks at C. HEAN 366:13
close breathless hush in the C. NEWB 541:18
C. encounters FILM 312:17
c. the wall up SHAK 671:5
c. your eyes before AYCK 40:1
Doth c. behind him tread COLE 226:24
hasten to a c. COWP 239:30
not c. enough CAPA 185:13
peacefully towards its c. DAWS 253:8
Swift to its c. LYTE 480:23
closed We never c. VAN 789:11
closer C. is He than breathing TENN 759:10
c. walk with God COWP 240:21
Come c., boys LAST 455:6
friend that sticketh c. BIBL 83:6
closest c. friends won't tell you ADVE 7:18
closet back in the c. lays FITZ 314:15
from forth the c. KEAT 427:13
not in a c. CHES 209:7
put me in the c. DICK 266:17
closing c. time in the gardens CONN 234:4
cloth according to your c. PROV 597:47
fair white linen c. BOOK 129:3
On a c. untrue GILB 338:10
trick of wearing a c. coat BALM 52:16
clothe c. my naked villainy SHAK 696:16
clothed c., fed, and educated RUSK 638:25
C. in white samite TENN 759:13
c. on with chastity TENN 759:2
C. with his breath TENN 760:13
man c. in soft raiment BIBL 95:6
Naked, and ye c. me BIBL 97:12
woman c. with the sun BIBL 112:18
clothes brushers of noblemen's c. WOTT 833:7
C. are our weapons CART 192:8
C. by a man CHAN 202:1
C. don't make the man WATS 804:18
C. make the man PROV 597:25
c. not be burned BIBL 82:15
Emperor's new c. ANDE 14:8
Fine c. are good JOHN 415:14
in c. a wantonness HERR 374:8
liquefaction of her c. HERR 375:4
poured into his c. WODE 824:25
remarkable suit of c. LOES 473:2
require new c. THOR 776:6
wears her c. SWIF 748:15
Who touched my c. BIBL 98:6
witnesses laid down their c. BIBL 103:21
wore torn c. SPEN 732:20
clothing c. is of wrought gold BOOK 134:16
c. itself in a robe RAOU 622:2
go in long c. BIBL 98:11
in books' c. LAMB 448:16
in sheep's c. BIBL 94:9
sheep in sheep's c. CHUR 217:1
sheep in sheep's c. GOSS 347:7
cloths heavens' embroidered c. YEAT 836:5
clotted lump of c. nonsense DRYD 283:14
cloud by a c. takes all away SHAK 702:26
c.-continents ALDR 11:3
c. has a silver lining PROV 599:21
c. in the west GLAD 340:12
c. in trousers MAYA 502:14
c. of comforting convictions RUSS 639:25
c. of unknowing ANON 15:17
c. of witnesses BIBL 110:2
c. that runs before the wind RALE 620:11
c. that's dragonish SHAK 657:12
each c. contains pennies BURK 165:16
faded, like a c. SHEL 710:17
fair luminous c. COLE 225:4
fiend hid in a c. BLAK 121:3
Get off my c. JAGG 401:4
lonely as a c. WORD 828:26
On a c. I saw a child BLAK 120:12
pillar of a c. BIBL 76:5
set my bow in the c. BIBL 74:22
sweet to be a C. MILN 511:3
There ariseth a little c. BIBL 79:30
watch a sailing c. LIN 469:18
wat'ry c. AKEN 9:5
cloudcuckooland How about 'C.' ARIS 24:8
clouded upon our c. hills BLAK 120:1
cloudiness dead-pan c. HEAN 366:20
clouds C. and eclipses SHAK 704:18
c. and wind without rain BIBL 83:19
c. his chariot BOOK 139:1
c. rain down righteousness BIBL 114:1
c. return after the rain BIBL 85:2
c. would break BROW 155:4
c. ye so much dread COWP 240:17
comes with c. descending WESL 811:8
cometh with c. BIBL 111:18
dropping from the c. THOM 775:8
dying c. contend SHAK 672:27
his c. removed BOOK 132:12
O c., unfold! BLAK 120:1
prince of the c. BAUD 57:5
through the c. I'll never float WORD 830:15
thy c. drop fatness BOOK 136:2
trailing c. of glory WORD 829:20
clout Ne'er cast a c. PROV 607:25
clouts stones and c. make martyrs BROW 153:1
cloven out pops the c. hoof WODE 824:14
though he be c.-footed BIBL 76:20
cloverleaf concrete c. MUMF 536:7
clownage c. keeps in pay MARL 496:20
clowns Send in the c. SOND 728:3
club best c. in London DICK 264:25
don't want to belong to any c. MARX 499:11
exclusive-secret-special-c. WEIR 808:29
savage wields his c. HUXL 397:12
that terrible football c. MCGR 485:12
clue almost invariably a c. DOYL 277:8
Clun Clungunford and C. HOUS 391:7
Clunbury Clunton and C. HOUS 391:7
Clungunford C. and Clun HOUS 391:7
clunk C., click, every trip OFFI 554:2
Clunton C. and Clunbury HOUS 391:7
clutch clawed me with his c. VAUX 790:19
fell c. of circumstance HENL 369:20
clutching alien people c. their gods ELIO 295:2
c. the inviolable shade ARNO 27:11
Clyde poems should be C.-built DUNN 285:10
CMG C. (Call Me God) SAYI 647:32
coach c. and six horses RICE 626:6
indifference and a c. and six COLM 229:14
rattling of a c. DONN 275:8
to her silver c. SPEN 733:7
coaches Nine c. waiting MIDD 507:7
coal island made mainly of c. BEVA 71:12
like a c. His eye-ball SMAR 722:10
like miners' c. dust BOOT 143:1
live c. in his hand BIBL 86:23
made of Newcastle c. WALP 800:22
coalition rainbow c. JACK 400:17
coalitions England does not love c. DISR 268:18
coals all eyes else dead c. SHAK 703:25
c. of fire BIBL 83:21
c. of fire BOOK 132:12
My c. are spent EPIT 303:16
sleep on the c. DICK 261:16
coarse one of them is rather c. ROYD 636:17
coast c. of Coromandel SITW 721:8
On the c. of Coromandel LEAR 460:5
coaster Dirty British c. MASE 500:14
coat c. is so warm NURS 548:19
c. of many colours BIBL 75:8
Cut your c. PROV 597:47
eternal Footman hold my c. ELIO 295:8
long black c. WARR 804:1
made my song a c. YEAT 835:10
off like a heavy c. FEAV 308:4
stick in his c. BROW 156:17
tattered c. upon a stick YEAT 837:2
cobble On c.-stones I lay FLAN 315:21
Cobbleigh Uncle Tom C. BALL 52:10
cobbler c. stick to his last PROV 605:20
c. to his last PROV 597:26
Cobden C. is an inspired bagman CARL 188:21
cobweb c. of the brain BUTL 172:6
cobwebs Laws are like c. SWIF 747:14
tickles with the c. FROS 325:14
Coca-Cola blue jeans and C. GREE 352:9
cocaine C. habit-forming BANK 53:6
c. I had taken KEYE 435:2
cock before the c. crow BIBL 97:19
C. a doodle doo! NURS 547:16
C. and a Bull STER 739:15
c. crowing on its own dunghill ALDI 10:11

c. had in his governaunce CHAU 206:2
C. up your beaver HOGG 380:12
c. who thought the sun ELIO 291:21
c. with lively din MILT 512:16
crowing of the c. SHAK 661:11
Every c. will crow PROV 599:22
good c. come out of PROV 612:25
immediately the c. crew BIBL 97:26
Lion and the C. GOGA 343:23
louder a c. can crow TROL 782:16
Our c. won't fight BEAV 59:6
owe a c. to Aesculapius LAST 455:7
Ride a c.-horse NURS 550:12
walks till the first c. SHAK 679:5
Who killed C. Robin NURS 552:1
cockatoo cage is natural to a c. SHAW 707:7
green freedom of a c. STEV 740:5
cockatrice hand on the c.' den BIBL 87:5
cockle c. hat and staff SHAK 665:34
cockles c. boiled in silver shells JONS 419:9
cockleshells silver bells and c. NURS 549:13
Cockney C. impudence RUSK 638:6
cockpit Can this c. hold SHAK 670:26
c. of Christendom HOWE 392:1
cocks drowned the c. SHAK 678:21
cocksure c. of anything MELB 503:17
c. of many things HOLM 381:13
cocktail weasel under the c. cabinet PINT 576:14
cocoa c. for Kingsley Amis COPE 236:8
C. is a cad and coward CHES 210:20
cod bean and the c. BOSS 143:15
O stynkyng c. CHAU 206:7
photographer is like the c. SHAW 709:24
code trail has its own stern c. SERV 654:23
Codlin C.'s the friend DICK 264:10
coeli *Rorate, c.* BIBL 114:1
coercion effect of c. JEFF 406:2
coeur *Il pleure dans mon c.* VERL 791:11
Coeur-de-Lion reputed son of C. SHAK 677:5
coffee C. and oranges STEV 740:5
c. and other slop-kettle COBB 223:8
c.-house SWIF 747:13
C. house babble DISR 269:16
C., (which makes the politician wise) POPE 587:9
if this is c. PUNC 617:23
measured out my life with c. spoons ELIO 295:6
o'er cold c. POPE 584:8
put poison in your c. CHUR 216:23
to some c.-house I stray GREE 351:13
coffin c. clapt in a canoe BYRO 173:14
in a Y-shaped c. ORTO 558:4
silver plate on a c. CURR 248:3
cogito *C., ergo sum* DESC 258:18
cognoscere *rerum c. causas* VIRG 796:18
cohorts his c. were gleaming BYRO 175:23
coign c. of the cliff SWIN 750:18
coil Lulled by the c. SHEL 712:14
coin C., Tiberius DOBS 271:14
coincidence long arm of c. CHAM 201:3
coiner c. of sweet words ARNO 27:15
coins for a fistful of c. ZAPA 839:22
like to c. TENN 759:23
coition way of c. BROW 153:29
coitu *Foeda est in c.* PETR 574:18
coitum *Post c.* SAYI 648:2
coke go better with C. ADVE 8:14
cold can be eaten c. PROV 610:8
Cast a c. eye YEAT 837:22
caught An everlasting c. WEBS 808:20
chilling c. had pierced SACK 641:3
c. a long time STEV 740:4
c. charities CRAB 243:16
Cold, c., my girl SHAK 693:31
c. coming they had of it ANDR 14:15
c. coming we had of it ELIO 294:27
c. grave BALL 52:6
C. hands, warm heart PROV 597:27
c. in blood SHAK 656:21
C. in the earth BRON 150:2
C. lights hurting JOHN 408:8
c. metal of economic theory SCHU 649:12
C. Pastoral KEAT 428:29
c. performs the effect of fire MILT 515:20
c. relation BURK 164:5
C. the seat BENN 66:2
c. war BARU 56:9
c. war warrior THAT 769:21
come with your c. music BROW 158:8
Fallen c. and dead WHIT 815:5
Feed a c. PROV 600:16
fingers of c. are corpse fingers LAWR 458:22
I beg c. comfort SHAK 677:20
ink in my pen ran c. WALP 800:17
in love with a c. climate SOUT 731:7
in the darkness and the c. STEV 742:18
i' the c. o' the moon BROW 155:19
lie in c. obstruction SHAK 686:18
like c. porridge SHAK 698:29
like rivers grow c. MONT 526:16
Love in a c. climate MITF 524:5
neither c. nor hot BIBL 111:28
offspring of c. hearts BURK 163:22
O ye Frost and C. BOOK 126:6
past the common c. AYRE 40:8
plunging into a c. peace YELT 838:5
Poor Tom's a-c. SHAK 679:8
so the c. strengthens PROV 595:20
spy who came in from the c. LE C 461:12
straight is c. again SHAK 676:26
till I shrink with c. SHAK 658:13
'tis bitter c. SHAK 661:5
To c. oblivion SHEL 711:8
too c. for hell SHAK 683:14
understand one who's c. SOLZ 727:12
waxeth c. BALL 52:8
colder c. and dumber than a fish MULD 535:25
coldly C., sadly descends ARNO 27:2
Cole Old King C. NURS 549:17
Coliseum While stands the C. BYRO 175:5
You're the C. PORT 588:12
collapse c. in deepest humiliation EDDI 287:23
C. of Stout Party ANON 15:18
collar braw brass c. BURN 169:5
collateral c. security CHES 209:20
colleague c.-free day DALT 248:15
collections mutilators of c. LAMB 448:13
collective *c. unconscious* JUNG 423:5
collects beautiful c. MACA 482:13
college cabbage with a c. education TWAI 786:22
endow a c. POPE 583:19
Master of this c. BEEC 61:9
small c. WEBS 807:9
colleges discipline of c. SMIT 723:12
collied in the c. night SHAK 689:5
Collins marry Mr C. AUST 38:19
collision avoid foreign c. CLAY 220:1
colonel C. Blimp LOW 477:5
C.'s Lady KIPL 439:8
colonial tales of castaways, c. museums GENE 333:5
colonies commerce with our c. BURK 162:23
New c. seek FREE 324:4
These wretched c. DISR 268:16
colonnade sound of the cool c. COWP 241:1
Colonus Singer of sweet C. ARNO 27:30
colony fuzzy wuzzy c. CAIR 181:3
colori *nimium ne crede c.* VIRG 795:17
colossus C. from a rock JOHN 417:12
Like a C. SHAK 674:13
colour any c. that he wants FORD 319:14
By convention there is c. DEMO 257:2
by the c. of their skin KING 436:14
cannot be of a bad c. PROV 601:26
cast thy nighted c. off SHAK 661:18
C. has taken hold of me KLEE 442:4
c. of his hair HOUS 390:4
c. purple WALK 799:11
Her c. comes and goes DOBS 271:16
her c. is natural SHER 716:11
horse of that c. SHAK 701:15
I know the c. rose ABSE 1:6
Life is C. GREN 352:17
or the c. of their skin WILL 821:8
perceptible through c. MOND 526:2
problem of the c. line DU B 284:2
sense of c. BLUN 122:14
waning of their c. VOLT 798:7
yearned for warmth and c. TENN 759:21
coloured about the c. women TRUT 784:14
best c. man JOHN 408:11
makes a man c. HUGH 393:1
no 'white' or 'c.' signs KENN 433:16
penny plain and twopence c. STEV 741:17
see the c. counties HOUS 390:19
colourless C. green ideas CHOM 212:10
colours add c. to the chameleon SHAK 672:30
coat of many c. BIBL 75:8
c. and their forms WORD 829:4
c. laid so thick DRYD 281:12
C. seen by candle-light BROW 154:19
c. will agree BACO 44:19
lines and c. POUS 590:7
map-makers' c. BISH 115:17
nailing his c. FIEL 309:11
Who put the c. BOOT 142:17
Columbia Hail, C.! happy land HOPK 385:9
columbine pink and purple c. SPEN 734:21
Columbus laughed at C. GERS 334:18
column Fifth c. MOLA 524:15
like a black c. BABE 40:18
stately c. broke SCOT 651:5
columnae *non concessere c.* HORA 386:7
columns crazy on its smoking c. YEVT 838:10
coma state of resentful c. LASK 454:1
comae *Arboribusque c.* HORA 389:6
comb c. and a glass in her hand SONG 729:15
c. was redder than the fyn coral CHAU 206:2
siller c. BALL 50:21
two bald men over a c. BORG 143:7
combat c. may be glorious COWP 241:30
comber crash of the c. KIPL 440:7
combination call it c. PALM 566:4
combinations irregular c. JOHN 410:22
metrical c. FLAU 316:12
combine When bad men c. BURK 164:16
combining c. committee BAGE 46:8
combs gowd c. in their hair BALL 51:16
combustion hideous ruin and c. MILT 514:11
come All things c. to those who wait PROV 595:5
behold, I c. quickly BIBL 113:14
believe in the life to c. BECK 59:12
better not c. at all KEAT 431:2
But will they c. SHAK 668:19
cannot c. again HOUS 391:5
c. all the way for this MORR 532:14
C., and he cometh BIBL 94:16
C. away, come away, death SHAK 701:21
C., come, dear Night CHAP 202:17
C., dear children ARNO 26:10
C. down, O Love divine LITT 470:3
c. for your good GEOR 333:10
C., Holy Spirit LANG 451:1
C. in the speaking silence ROSS 634:3
C. into the garden TENN 764:6
C., let us join our cheerful songs WATT 805:12
c., let us sing BOOK 138:5
c., Lord Jesus BIBL 113:16
C. mothers and fathers DYLA 287:16
C., my Celia JONS 420:12
C. not between the dragon SHAK 677:24
c. out, thou bloody man BIBL 79:9
C. over into Macedonia BIBL 104:2
C. to me in my dreams ARNO 26:9
c. to my father AUBR 32:21
c. to my heart ELLI 298:8
C. to the edge LOGU 473:3

come (*cont.*):
C. unto me BIBL 95:9
c. unto my love SPEN 733:9
C. unto these yellow sands SHAK 698:26
C. what come may SHAK 681:22
c. without warning DAVI 252:16
don't want to c. out BERR 69:11
dreaming on things to c. SHAK 705:11
Easy c., easy go PROV 599:6
First c. PROV 600:27
he that should c. BIBL 95:5
I go—I c. back CATC 195:27
it needn't c. to that CARR 191:5
I will not c. SHAK 675:12
jump the life to c. SHAK 682:8
King of glory shall c. in BOOK 133:3
let him c. out JOHN 416:26
Light c., light go PROV 605:27
men may c. TENN 757:14
mine hour is not yet c. BIBL 101:13
Mr Watson, c. here BELL 62:18
nobody will c. SAND 644:2
O c., all ye faithful ANON 21:4
One to c., and one to go CARR 191:8
Quickly c., quickly go PROV 610:3
shape of things to c. WELL 810:15
Sumer is c. in ANON 18:22
That it should c. to this SHAK 661:24
therefore I cannot c. BIBL 99:28
things to c. at large SHAK 700:9
'tis not to c. SHAK 667:3
What's past, and what's to c. SHAK 700:21
What's to c. is still unsure SHAK 701:10
wheel is c. full circle SHAK 680:10
when death is c., we are not EPIC 300:21
where do they all c. from LENN 463:20
wherefore art thou c. BIBL 97:24
which is to c. BIBL 111:17
whistle, an' I'll c. BURN 168:5
Why don't you c. up WEST 812:6
comeback c. kid CLIN 221:5
comedies All c. are ended BYRO 176:21
comedy All I need to make a c. CHAP 202:9
C. is an imitation SIDN 718:25
C. is tragedy that happens CART 192:9
c. to those that think WALP 801:5
C. wears itself out HAZL 365:10
most lamentable c. SHAK 689:8
tragedy, c., history SHAK 663:22
comeliness no form nor c. BIBL 88:15
comely black, but c. BIBL 85:7
comer Grasps in the c. SHAK 700:16
comes c. again in the morning SHER 716:11
conquering hero c. MORE 531:16
Look, where it c. again SHAK 661:7
nobody c. BECK 59:25
Tomorrow never c. PROV 613:11
comest c. into thy kingdom BIBL 100:27
cometh Blessed be he that c. BOOK 140:7
c. unto the Father BIBL 102:18
c. with clouds BIBL 111:18
He c. not TENN 763:19
Him that c. to me BIBL 101:29
master of the house c. BIBL 98:13
comets country c. MARV 498:21
no c. seen SHAK 675:9
Old men and c. SWIF 749:4
comfit like a c.-maker's wife SHAK 668:24
comfort a' the c. we're to get BURN 169:4
bourgeois prefers c. HESS 375:16
carrion c., Despair HOPK 384:2
c. all that mourn BIBL 89:5
c. and despair SHAK 705:24
c. and help the weak-hearted BOOK 127:10
c. and relieve them BOOK 127:18
c. cruel men CHES 210:8
c. in my people's happiness ELIZ 297:3
c. of thy help BOOK 135:7
C.'s a cripple DRAY 278:22
c. ye my people BIBL 87:27
found I any to c. me BOOK 136:11
good c., Master Ridley LAST 455:4
great source of c. NIET 545:18
I beg cold c. SHAK 677:20
love her, c. her BOOK 131:4
love of material c. TOCQ 777:17
naught for your c. CHES 210:1
our c. flows PRIO 593:5
receives c. SHAK 698:29
Sacrament to your c. BOOK 129:15
take c. a little BIBL 81:12
they never knew c. MACA 481:12
to c., and command WORD 831:24
waters of c. BOOK 132:26
What a c. CARR 190:11
comfortable All clean and c. KEAT 431:18
c. and the accepted GALB 328:6
c. estate of widowhood GAY 331:15
c. words BOOK 129:17
comfortably lived c. so long together GAY 331:11
sitting c. CATC 195:4
Speak ye c. BIBL 87:27
comforted c. his people BIBL 88:13
they shall be c. BIBL 93:3
would not be c. BIBL 92:25
comforter C. will not come BIBL 102:24
Guide, a C. AUBE 32:10
O C., draw near LITT 470:3
comforters Miserable c. BIBL 81:19
comforting always a c. thought MARQ 497:9
cloud of c. convictions RUSS 639:25
where is your c. HOPK 384:11
comfortless Exceeding c. ROSS 634:6
leave us not c. BOOK 128:8
comforts c. flee LYTE 480:23
recapture the c. BRYS 159:5
uncertain c. PROV 597:17
comic business of a c. poet CONG 232:8
comical Beautiful c. things HARV 363:14
I often think it's c. GILB 337:14
coming cold c. we had of it ELIO 294:27
c. as fast as I can LAUD 454:4
C. events cast PROV 597:29
c. events cast their shadows CAMP 183:10
c. for us that night BALD 49:4
C. in on a wing and a pray'r ADAM 4:1
c. of the King of Heaven ANON 19:19
c. of the Son of Man BIBL 97:5
C. thro' the rye BURN 166:20
c. to that holy room DONN 273:5
Everything's c. up roses SOND 728:1
good time c. SCOT 652:7
He is c. AYTO 40:10
my c. down MORE 531:14
She is c., my dove TENN 764:9
their c. hither SHAK 680:5
Yanks are c. COHA 223:22
comma c.-hunting CORN 237:5
kiss can be a c. MIST 523:9
command cannot obey cannot c. PROV 602:9
c. of any kind as an exceptional MILL 509:7
c. success ADDI 4:9
c. the rain PEPY 572:22
c. where I adore SHAK 701:27
give what you c. AUGU 36:6
left that c. MILT 517:16
not born to sue, but to c. SHAK 694:10
sue than to c. SCOT 650:12
to comfort, and c. WORD 831:24
to the c. of another OSBO 559:21
commander c. of three armies CONF 231:19
commandest thing which thou c. BOOK 128:7
commandment c. of the Lord BOOK 132:16
first and great c. BIBL 96:24
commandments hearkened to my c. BIBL 88:9
keep his c. BIBL 85:5
learn by these C. BOOK 130:12
Ten for the ten c. SONG 729:11
commencement *c. de la fin* TALL 753:3
commend c. my spirit BIBL 100:29
c. my spirit BOOK 133:16
c. the bone DICK 266:20
virtue to c. CONG 233:18
virtue to c. CONG 233:19
commendatio *Formosafacies muta c.* PUBL 616:10
commendeth obliquely c. himself BROW 152:10
comment C. is free SCOT 650:4
C. is free STOP 743:15
couldn't possibly c. CATC 196:30
none can read the c. TENN 760:8
commentators c. each dark passage YOUN 839:1
learned c. view SWIF 749:15
commerce c. between equals GOLD 345:13
c. with our colonies BURK 162:23
In matters of c. CANN 184:19
Peace, c. JEFF 405:13
under a ceiling of c. OLIV 553:18
where c. long prevails GOLD 345:8
commissary Destiny the c. of God DONN 273:11
commissions royal c. FRAN 323:19
commit c. his body to the deep BOOK 142:6
c. his body to the ground BOOK 131:14
committed c. breakfast with it LEWI 467:1
committee combining c. BAGE 46:8
C.—a group of men ALLE 12:7
c. a group of unwilling SAYI 647:6
c. is a group of the unwilling ANON 15:19
horse designed by a c. ISSI 400:10
commodious c. car JAME 402:26
commodity C., firmness, and delight WOTT 833:5
c. of good names SHAK 667:19
common according to the c. weal JAME 402:16
all things held in c. CALL 181:16
and still be c. RATT 622:7
Ay, madam, it is c. SHAK 661:19
back to c. earth again FITZ 314:21
call not thou c. BIBL 103:29
century of the c. man WALL 799:15
C. as the air GRAN 349:4
c. chord again BROW 155:1
C. fame is seldom PROV 597:30
c. law itself COKE 224:7
C. Law of England HERB 371:21
c. man BEVI 72:9
c. pursuit LEAV 461:4
c. reader JOHN 410:4
Common sense is not so c. VOLT 797:12
c. things that round us WORD 830:19
had all things c. BIBL 103:17
light of c. day WORD 830:1
like the c. people YEAT 838:3
make it too c. SHAK 669:26
nor lose the c. touch KIPL 439:3
not already c. LOCK 471:11
not c. BOOK 142:14
nothing c. did or mean MARV 498:19
of a c. law JEFF 405:10
of all things c. else MILT 516:25
prefers c.-looking people LINC 468:14
speak as the c. people do ASCH 30:9
steals a c. ANON 16:8
steals the c. POLI 582:3
trivial round, the c. task KEBL 432:5
utter c. notions HORA 385:19
with whom one has nothing in c. PYM 618:7
commonalty very dog to the c. SHAK 660:1
commoner persistent c. BENN 65:4
common law marry C. LLOY 470:14
commonplace common is the c. TENN 760:25
c. book be full SWIF 748:21
featureless and c. DOYL 277:8
ordinary c. things SCOT 652:12
Common Prayer they hated C. JORD 421:6

commons C., faithful to their system MACK 486:12
C. lives in a state BAGE 46:17
House of C., Regiment COBB 223:10
libraries of the C. CHAN 202:8
member of the House of C. POWE 590:20
on the House of C. DICK 264:25
common sense back to c. BERK 68:1
c. and common honesty SHEL 710:3
c., and observation BROW 153:23
C. is nothing more EINS 291:1
C. is the best distributed DESC 258:17
Defend me, therefore, c. COWP 241:26
insipid c. SALI 642:16
man of great c. SHAW 706:20
marry Common Law to C. LLOY 470:14
Nothing but c. MORT 533:11
organized c. HUXL 397:12
commonwealth arise in the C. MILT 519:6
caterpillars of the c. SHAK 695:2
c. is fixed and stable BURK 164:29
c. of learning LOCK 471:12
conduct of the c. BURK 164:18
fatal to the C. DRUM 279:16
commonwealths raise up c. DRYD 279:20
uniting into c. LOCK 472:5
commune c. with your own heart BOOK 131:19
communia *proprie c. dicere* HORA 385:19
communicate birds trying to c. AUDE 35:17
to c. forget not BIBL 110:9
communicated C. monthly BETJ 70:8
communication c. Of the dead ELIO 294:13
communications Evil c. BIBL 106:25
Evil c. PROV 599:44
communion C. of Saints BOOK 126:10
plucked c. tables JORD 421:6
Table, at the C.-time BOOK 129:3
communism against the anti-Christ of C. BUCH 159:10
caused the fall of c. JOHN 408:6
clock of c. has stopped SOLZ 727:15
C. is Soviet power LENI 463:10
Russian C. the illegitimate child ATTL 32:4
spectre of C. MARX 500:5
communist call me a c. CAMA 182:10
I wasn't a C. NIEM 545:8
members of the C. Party MCCA 483:19
Picasso is a C. DALI 248:13
What is a c. ELLI 298:12
communists Catholics and C. GREE 351:15
community part of the c. of Europe SALI 642:19
rest of the c. KALD 425:11
small anarchist c. BENN 65:21
unite into a c. LOCK 472:4
commuter C.—one who spends WHIT 813:24
compact c. which exists GARR 330:11
made a c. them between BALL 50:15
of imagination all c. SHAK 690:18
compacted sweets c. lie HERB 373:17
companion c. to owls BIBL 81:28
even thou, my c. BOOK 135:11
gave him a c. VALÉ 789:2
old and agreeable c. GIBB 336:1
send the prince a better c. SHAK 669:25
companionless c. Among the stars SHEL 714:13
companions c. for middle age BACO 43:19
C. of our woe WALS 802:10
company before God and this c. BOOK 131:8
c. and good discourse WALT 802:18
C. for carrying on ANON 15:21
c. he chooses BURT 169:17
c. makes the feast PROV 597:31
c. of all faithful people BOOK 130:2
c. of men CHEK 208:19
c. of the preachers BOOK 136:7
Company, villanous c. SHAK 668:28
crowd is not c. BACO 43:1
give me your bill of c. SWIF 748:6
good c. AUBR 32:22
in whose c. I delight BUNY 161:20
known by c. he keeps PROV 606:15
Misery loves c. PROV 606:38
not good c. AUST 38:10
owe my soul to the c. store TRAV 781:2
shine in c. SWIF 749:1
three is c. WILD 817:14
tone of the c. CHES 209:10
to the best c. BOSW 144:19
Two is c. PROV 613:27
up breaks the c. CERV 199:17
worse c. AUST 37:16
worst of the c. SWIF 748:5
compare belied with false c. SHAK 705:21
c. small things with great VIRG 797:3
c. This prison SHAK 696:3
not reason and c. BLAK 118:20
Shall I c. thee SHAK 704:9
compared c. unto the beasts BOOK 135:1
comparison in c. of the earth BOOK 138:19
comparisons C. are odious PROV 597:32
C. are odorous SHAK 691:14
C. doon offte LYDG 480:10
compass c. lost COWP 240:27
c. of the world BOOK 133:2
fire did c. him GILB 337:2
mariner's needle [c.] BACO 45:4
top of my c. SHAK 665:2
compassed c. me round BOOK 140:1
we also are compassed about BIBL 110:2
compassion bowels of c. BIBL 111:12
c. and mercy BIBL 91:16
c. and mercy BOOK 138:18
c. on the son of her womb BIBL 88:11
feel c. for fellow men ANNA 15:2
friendliness, c. MAHĀ 489:16
sharp c. of the healer's art ELIO 294:10
something which excites c. SMIT 725:4
thou art all c. WESL 811:7
compassionate Merciful, the C. KORA 443:12
compel c. thee to go a mile BIBL 93:13
compete act but not to c. LAO 452:8
competing Costs register c. attractions KNIG 442:7
competition anarchy and c. RUSK 639:4
Approves all forms of c. CLOU 222:27
c., and mutual envy HOBB 379:5
rigour of c. ANON 15:20
competitive Sex was a c. event GELD 332:26
complacencies C. of the peignoir STEV 740:5
complacency peace Built on c. GAUN 331:5
complain c. of the age BURK 164:11
c. we cannot see BERK 68:2
flourish and c. CRAB 243:5
how is the old c. PALM 566:7
knows to whom to c. FIRB 313:7
Never c. and never explain DISR 271:4
complainers c. for the public BURK 162:17
complaining daily c. BOOK 133:17
complaint most fatal c. of all HILT 377:12
voice of my c. BOOK 141:1
words of my c. BOOK 132:21
complaints c. are freely heard MILT 519:6
complementarity understood c. MCEW 485:6
complete become c. yourself FRIE 324:23
clad in c. steel MILT 511:23
c. and great CATH 194:8
completed c. labours are pleasant CICE 217:11
c. the task TALM 754:15
complex ugly, heavy and c. FLAU 316:20
complexes *feeling-toned c.* JUNG 423:5
complexion bank too much on your c. VIRG 795:17
have a different c. CONR 234:10
Mislike me not for my c. SHAK 687:16
schoolgirl c. ADVE 7:38
complexities All mere c. YEAT 835:6
compliance c. with my wishes after reasonable discussion CHUR 216:19
timely c. FIEL 309:18
complicity Our tribe's c. HEAN 366:10
complies c. against his will BUTL 172:12
componere *inter vos tantas c. lites* VIRG 796:2
parva licet c. magnis VIRG 797:3
composed Cruel, but c. ARNO 26:22
composer c. and *not* homosexual DIAG 260:2
requirement for a c. HONE 382:12
composing C.'s not voluntary BIRT 115:14
composition in one c. JOHN 410:14
mad kings! mad c. SHAK 677:7
compound it's a chemical c. ZAPP 839:23
comprehend she begins to c. it PRIO 593:4
comprehended darkness c. it not BIBL 101:3
comprehensible universe is c. EINS 290:14
comprendre *Tout c. rend très indulgent* STAË 735:17
compris *Je vous ai c.* DE G 255:21
compromise Give me the Brown c. HUGH 393:14
iota of c. DAY- 253:13
compulsion c. to write LARK 453:11
fools by heavenly c. SHAK 678:5
No c. in religion KORA 443:20
reason on c. SHAK 668:8
Such sweet c. MILT 511:9
compulsive c. course SHAK 693:3
compunctious c. visitings of nature SHAK 682:2
computer modern c. hovers BREN 147:25
requires a c. SAYI 648:7
work of an eyeless c. BETJ 71:1
computers C. are anti-Faraday CORN 236:18
C. are composed of AUGA 35:20
so many c. WALĘ 799:4
conceal able to c. it LA R 453:16
able to c. it TWAI 786:29
c. a fact with words MACH 485:13
c. our wants GOLD 345:12
Fate tried to c. him HOLM 381:7
should c. it AUST 38:4
concealing hazard of c. BURN 167:2
concealment c., like a worm SHAK 701:24
conceit curst c. o' bein' richt MACD 484:15
folly and c. AUST 38:18
man wise in his own c. BIBL 83:25
never forgive any c. DRYD 283:13
wise in his own c. BIBL 83:23
wiser in his own c. BIBL 83:26
conceited who is not c. TROL 782:23
conceits accepted for c. BACO 41:14
c. do prove the greatest liars DRAY 279:1
wise in your own c. BIBL 105:16
conceive virgin shall c. BIBL 86:26
conceived c. by the Holy Ghost BOOK 126:10
man child c. BIBL 81:3
my mother c. me BOOK 135:5
concentrated c. in you KEAT 431:22
concentrates c. his mind JOHN 415:23
conception present at the c. ORTO 558:1
conceptions C. equal to the soul's WORD 828:13
concepts walks up the stairs of his c. STEI 737:10
concern had no c. in SWIF 749:6
concerned being ultimately c. TILL 777:14
nobody left to be c. NIEM 545:8
concert middle of a c. STEN 737:17
concerto C. to be difficult SCHO 649:2
concessions c. of the weak BURK 162:22
what c. to make METT 506:7
conciliation not a policy of c. PARN 567:26
conciseness sacrificed to c. JOHN 409:1
conclaves Kingly c. stern SHEL 713:7
concluded case is c. AUGU 36:12
conclusion c., shewing from various causes JOHN 412:18
denoted a foregone c. SHAK 693:2

conclusions pursued c. infinite SHAK 658:6
concord c. of sweet sounds SHAK 688:25
in pleasing c. end MILT 518:20
lover of c. BOOK 126:12
travelled a good deal in C. THOR 776:2
truth, unity, and c. BOOK 129:11
concordia C. *discors* HORA 386:21
concrete city is not a c. jungle MORR 532:7
c. and tyres LARK 452:16
c. cloverleaf MUMF 536:7
everything you thought was c. WALK 799:6
concubine c. of a warlord OPEN 555:7
concupiscent c. curds STEV 739:20
concupiscite *sine dolo lac c.* BIBL 114:11
concurrence sweet c. of the heart HERR 374:10
condamner *c. les gens* MOLI 525:12
condemn c. a little more MAJO 491:15
C. the fault SHAK 686:7
Neither do I c. thee BIBL 101:34
some delights c. MOLI 525:18
condemned c. to be free SART 645:2
you yourself Are much c. SHAK 676:18
condemns c. whatever he disapproves BURN 166:1
condition c. upon which God CURR 248:2
could do in that c. PEPY 572:19
wearisome c. of humanity GREV 353:4
conditioned all c. things PALI 564:19
C. Genesis PALI 565:3
conditions c. of men BOOK 127:16
govern our c. SHAK 679:17
no c. of life TOLS 779:8
conduct C. is three-fourths ARNO 29:2
c. of a clouded cane POPE 587:11
c. of a losing party BURK 162:6
c. of their rulers ADAM 3:12
c. of the women MORE 531:2
C. . . . to the prejudice MILI 508:5
c. unbecoming MILI 508:3
regulation of c. SPEN 732:3
rottenness begins in his c. JEFF 405:9
conductor music eliminates the c. STRA 744:14
conductors third-rate foreign c. BEEC 61:7
cone inverted c. JOHN 415:30
sphere, the c. CÉZA 200:8
cones eat the c. under his pines FROS 326:5
confabulate If birds c. or no COWP 240:28
confederacy dunces are all in c. SWIF 748:25
if the C. fails DAVI 252:11
confederate in games C. WORD 828:20
conference c. a ready man BACO 44:7
ever born in a c. FITZ 315:9
hold some two days' c. WEBS 807:23
naked into the c. chamber BEVA 71:20
conferences eradication of c. MAYA 502:17
confess C. and be hanged PROV 597:33
c. them BOOK 125:13
c. to almighty God MISS 520:11
Never c.! Never, never CONR 234:8
confessed fault c. PROV 600:13
confessing then c. it TROL 782:18
confession be there at the C. DONN 275:4
C. good for soul PROV 597:34
make your humble c. BOOK 129:15
confessions c. of a justified sinner HOGG 380:15
confidante c. stark mad SHER 715:18
confide seldom c. CAMU 184:7
confidence C. is a plant PITT 576:21
c. of a passed-over FIEL 309:13
c. of the people CONF 231:22
ignorance and c. TWAI 786:27
In quietness and in c. BIBL 87:16
too great c. JOHN 411:3
confident c. in each other ARIS 25:7
glad c. morning BROW 156:19
confine verge Of her c. SHAK 678:16
confined cabined, cribbed, c. SHAK 684:9
c. him home CLEV 220:17
confinement ill deserves the name of c. LOCK 472:1
solitary c. inside our own skins WILL 820:18
confirmed to be c. TENN 767:17
confiscation legalized c. DISR 269:7
Confiteor *C. Deo omnipotenti* MISS 520:11
conflict armed c. EDEN 288:6
end of the c. of centuries GRIF 353:8
Never in the field of human c. CHUR 215:12
offered you C. and Art PRIE 591:13
tragic c. of loyalties HOWE 391:14
conflicts all disputes or c. BRIA 148:5
conform c., or be more wise PEPY 573:6
conforms man c. ANON 18:16
confound C. their politics SONG 729:8
c. the wise BIBL 105:29
confounded Confusion worse c. MILT 515:27
let me never be c. BOOK 126:2
confounding c. the Persons BOOK 126:22
confront to c. them TRIM 781:13
confundar *non c. in aeternam* PRAY 592:8
confused anyone who isn't c. MURR 537:9
casts aside whatever is c. CHUA 213:1
confusion come to c. SHAK 689:6
C. now hath made SHAK 683:18
C. on thy banners wait GRAY 350:2
C. worse confounded MILT 515:27
couch in some c. CONG 233:11
in our sea of c. GAMO 329:2
confute tell how to c. him SELD 653:16
congeals When love c. HART 363:5
Congo C., creeping through the black LIND 469:7
congratulatory c. regrets DISR 269:19
congregation aloof from the c. HILL 377:10
c. of the poor BOOK 136:21
c. of vapours SHAK 663:18
face of this c. BOOK 130:22
largest c. DEFO 255:9
praise the Lord in the c. BOOK 133:9
whole c. ADDI 5:2
congregations all c. BOOK 126:17
congress C. makes no progress LIGN 468:1
conies rocks for the c. BOOK 139:4
conjunx *C. Est mihi* LUCA 478:16
conjecture not beyond all c. BROW 153:4
Now entertain c. SHAK 671:8
conjectures dogmatically to our c. POPP 587:30
conjuring c. trick with bones JENK 406:6
Parson left off c. SELD 653:20
conjuror charlatan, and a c. TROL 781:21
level of the stage c. MOOR 529:13
conked c. out on November 15th EPIT 303:11
connaît *ne se c. pas* LA F 447:12
Connaught Hell or C. CROM 246:2
connect Only c. FORS 320:18
connection without c. BYRO 180:7
connections concealed c. SMIT 723:3
conned c. by rote SHAK 676:25
connive c. in civilised outrage HEAN 366:15
connubial of c. love MILT 516:24
conquer c. Antony SHAK 657:16
c. or die WASH 804:4
easier to c. it WALP 801:1
hard to catch and c. MERE 505:19
Like Douglas c. HOME 381:18
man should c. himself PALI 565:20
must c. them anew GOET 343:2
shalt thou c. CONS 235:11
we will c. BEE 61:1
wont to c. others SHAK 694:19
conquered c. and peopled SEEL 653:8
I came, I saw, I c. CAES 180:21
I will be c. JOHN 417:20
perpetually to be c. BURK 162:24
they are a c. people VICT 792:6
They c. continents DUNN 285:11
Thou has c. SWIN 751:5
conquering c. hero comes MORE 531:16
C. kings CHAN 201:11
c. one's enemies GENG 333:7
He went forth c. BIBL 112:4
conqueror c. must go on WELL 810:2
every c. creates a Muse WALL 800:8
Every other c. BURK 165:3
proud foot of a c. SHAK 677:21
you are a c. ROST 635:16
conquerors to their c. WILL 820:4
conquest c. and subjugation WEBS 807:13
c. of the earth CONR 234:10
fanned by C.'s crimson wing GRAY 350:2
shameful c. of itself SHAK 694:19
urge for c. ADLE 6:5
conquests c., glories, triumphs SHAK 675:19
spread her c. BURN 166:19
consanguineous Am I not c. SHAK 701:11
Conscience C.: the inner voice MENC 504:17
conscience according to c. MILT 519:18
Cash before c. HORA 386:10
c. as their King TENN 759:19
C. avaunt CIBB 217:7
c. doth make cowards SHAK 664:4
C. has no more to do SHER 715:21
c. is afraid BOOK 128:15
C. is but a word SHAK 696:32
C. is thoroughly well-bred BUTL 173:1
C. makes cowards PROV 597:35
c. of the king SHAK 664:2
c. says, 'Launcelot, budge not.' SHAK 687:17
c.-stricken air HOUS 390:4
c. void of offence BIBL 104:17
corporation to have a c. THUR 777:4
cruelty with a good c. RUSS 639:26
cut my c. HELL 368:16
ease your c. ALAI 10:1
freedom of c. TWAI 786:8
guilty c. needs PROV 601:40
live with a good c. SMIT 724:14
no c. in intrusion AUST 39:1
Nonconformist c. WILD 818:11
O coward c. SHAK 696:29
pure and noble c. DANT 249:19
reason and c. PRIC 591:9
still and quiet c. SHAK 673:14
Sufficient c. to bother him LLOY 471:9
taking your c. round BEVI 72:8
to C. first TOAS 778:3
value next a good c. WALL 802:26
consciences binding on the c. JOHN 407:9
Look to your c. MARY 500:10
conscientiousness c. and altruism CONF 231:10
conscious c. stone EMER 299:9
consciousness agreeable c. JOHN 413:22
Brahman is c. UPAN 787:17
c.-expanding drug CLAR 219:11
C. . . . is the phenomenon PENR 572:17
fourth condition of c. UPAN 788:7
from the beginning of c. WOOL 826:14
tragic c. FUEN 326:29
conscription Not necessarily c. KING 437:2
consecrated c. by the experience of mankind GIBB 335:16
c. obstruction BAGE 47:1
consecration c., and the Poet's WORD 828:2
consent all with one c. BIBL 99:27
c. of heaven JONS 419:14
demand not his free c. CHAR 203:3
like enough to c. SHAK 659:18
shalt not c. BIBL 77:8
Silence means c. PROV 610:42
whispering 'I will ne'er c.' BYRO 176:4
without his c. CAMD 182:12
without your c. ROOS 632:9
consented c. together BOOK 131:8
consenting c. unto his death BIBL 103:22
consequence business of c. BARH 54:11
trammel up the c. SHAK 682:8
consequences c. of them will be BUTL 171:11
damn the c. MILN 511:8
political c. MANS 494:10

terror of the c. LAWR 457:23
there are c. INGE 399:14
conservation make a speech on c. STEV 740:17
means of its c. BURK 163:14
conservatism c. and progress TROL 782:8
C. discards Prescription DISR 270:1
c. is based upon the idea CHES 211:11
What is c. LINC 468:6
conservative become a c. AREN 24:3
c. been arrested WOLF 825:13
C. Government DISR 268:12
C. ideal of freedom MADA 488:20
C., *n.* A statesman BIER 114:21
C. Party always MACL 487:5
C. Party at prayer ROYD 636:16
make me c. when old FROS 326:7
makes a man more c. KEYN 435:7
most c. man in this world BEVI 72:7
Or else a little C. GILB 337:14
sound C. government DISR 270:2
That man's the true C. TENN 759:7
conservatives better with the C. POLI 581:25
C. . . . being by the law MILL 507:24
C. do not believe HAIL 356:10
more formalistic than c. CALV 182:9
consider c. her ways, and be wise BIBL 82:13
c. how my light is spent MILT 518:29
let thine ears c. BOOK 141:1
weigh and c. BACO 44:5
considerable appear c. JOHN 414:11
considerate c. autocrat STEP 738:2
C. la vostra semenza DANT 249:17
consideration C. like an angel came SHAK 670:27
considered c. the days of old BOOK 137:2
consiliis *Misce stultitiam c.* HORA 389:11
consistency foolish c. EMER 299:23
consistent completely c. are the dead HUXL 397:1
c. with the laws of nature FARA 306:12
consolation Kate of my c. SHAK 698:7
console be consoled as to c. FRAN 323:5
C.-toi PASC 568:21
consoles Anything that c. is fake MURD 536:20
conspicuous c. by its presence RUSS 640:11
C. consumption VEBL 791:2
Vega c. overhead AUDE 34:16
conspiracies c. against the laity SHAW 707:4
conspiracy c. against the public SMIT 723:7
c. of silence COMT 230:20
c. to make you happy UPDI 788:13
Indecency's c. of silence SHAW 708:26
party is but a kind of c. HALI 357:19
perpetual c. SALI 642:18
conspirators All the c. save only he SHAK 677:4
conspiring C. with him KEAT 430:8
constable c.'s handbook KING 437:14
constabulary c. duty's to be done GILB 339:5
constancy c. in a good BROW 153:21
c. to a bad, ugly woman BYRO 179:13
no object worth its c. SHEL 714:13
Tell me no more of c. ROCH 630:4
witness to their c. DIDE 267:5
constant c. as the northern star SHAK 675:15
C. dropping wears away PROV 597:36
C., in Nature were inconstancy COWL 239:17
c. love deemed there SIDN 718:11
Friendship is c. SHAK 691:4
Like to a c. woman FORD 319:20
nothing in this world c. SWIF 747:15
One here will c. be BUNY 161:16
sense of a c. infelicity TAYL 756:20
To one thing c. never SHAK 691:7
were man But c. SHAK 702:30
wilt be c. then MONT 529:3
constellated c. flower SHEL 713:20
constellation bright c. JEFF 405:14
constituencies go back to your c. STEE 736:14
constitution c. does not provide WILL 821:7
C., in all its provisions CHAS 204:3
c. is extremely well WALP 800:23
construe the C. LINC 468:8
essence of the c. JUNI 423:13
establishment of C. CARD 186:3
Every country has its own c. ANON 16:3
genius of the C. PITT 576:26
people made the C. MARS 497:20
principle of the English c. BLAC 117:4
support its C. PAGE 562:18
constitutional c. eyes LINC 469:2
c. minuet SCAR 646:10
constrained by violence c. ELIZ 296:24
c. to dwell with Mesech BOOK 140:10
construction mind's c. SHAK 681:23
constructions decorating her c. TROL 782:3
constructive in the c. part CHAM 201:4
consuetudo *C. est altera natura* AUCT 33:2
consul born when I was c. CICE 218:1
horse was made C. RAND 621:16
consuls Let the c. see to it ANON 21:7
consult C. the genius POPE 583:23
consulted right to be c. BAGE 47:5
consume born to c. resources HORA 386:14
can c. locally SAKI 642:2
consumed bush was not c. BIBL 75:25
my bones c. away BOOK 133:17
consumer c. isn't a moron OGIL 553:2
c. is the king SAMU 643:13
c. society ILLI 398:20
consumere *fruges c. nati* HORA 386:14
consumes c. without producing ORWE 558:5
consuming in its heat c. LITT 470:3
survive by c. VANE 789:17
consummation c. Devoutly to be wished SHAK 664:3
Quiet c. have SHAK 661:2
consummatum *C. est* BIBL 114:9
consumption Conspicuous c. VEBL 791:2
c. artificially stimulated SAYE 646:4
C. is the sole end SMIT 723:11
c. of the purse SHAK 669:28
contact come in personal c. TAYL 756:17
c. of two bodies CHAM 201:7
c. with this Wild Man BLY 123:2
Fly hence, our c. fear ARNO 27:10
contagion c. of the world's slow stain SHEL 711:1
hell itself breathes out C. SHAK 665:5
vile c. of the night SHAK 675:6
contemned utterly be c. BIBL 86:8
contemneth c. small things BIBL 91:32
contemplation defile in c. TANT 755:1
For c. he MILT 516:15
Has left for c. BETJ 70:12
mind serene for c. GAY 332:14
contempt c. and anger SHAK 702:2
C., farewell SHAK 691:11
c. on all my pride WATT 805:14
Familiarity breeds c. PROV 600:11
Familiarity breeds c. TWAI 786:18
for c. too high COWL 239:14
moderns without c. CHES 209:15
Object of C. AUST 37:23
rags and c. BUNY 161:4
contemptible c. little army ANON 16:6
poor c. men CROM 245:18
contend Let's c. no more BROW 158:14
contender could have been a c. FILM 311:11
contending C. with the fretful SHAK 678:20
content c. surpassing wealth SHEL 713:30
c. with his fortunes fit SHAK 678:26
I am c. LAST 457:11
land of lost c. HOUS 391:5
Nothing less will c. me BURK 162:25
O sweet c. DEKK 256:5
pleasure, ease, c. POPE 585:28
Spontaneous joy and natural c. YEAT 836:2
sweet Well-c. DAVI 252:10
contented c. least SHAK 704:14
C. wi' little BURN 166:21
c. with his lot HORA 389:12
c. with their cells WORD 829:11
Ireland was c. when LAND 450:2
king shall be c. SHAK 695:14
was c. there, is contented here ARIS 24:11
contention Let the long c. cease ARNO 26:14
man of c. BIBL 89:18
contentious c. woman BIBL 83:30
contentment all enjoying, what c. MILT 517:9
C. is a sleepy thing TRAH 780:17
Preaches c. to the toad KIPL 440:1
withdraw with c. LUCR 479:8
contentus *C. vivat* HORA 389:12
contest Great c. follows COWP 241:25
not the victory but the c. COUB 238:3
contests What mighty c. POPE 586:28
continency chastity and c. AUGU 36:3
continent Africa, drifting c. GENE 333:5
brought forth upon this c. LINC 468:13
C. isolated BROC 149:2
knowest of no strange c. DAVI 252:10
overspread the c. O'SU 560:19
piece of the C. DONN 275:3
continental may be quite c. ROBI 629:9
continual c. dew of thy blessing BOOK 126:17
continually c. dying PETR 574:13
think c. of those SPEN 732:18
continuance c. in well doing BIBL 104:28
in c. of time BOOK 125:12
continuation c. of politics CLAU 219:19
continue c. thine for ever BOOK 130:20
once begun will c. BACO 42:30
runagates c. in scarceness BOOK 136:6
continued c., and ended in thee BOOK 130:5
How long soever it hath c. COKE 224:6
continuing c. unto the end DRAK 278:17
no c. city BIBL 110:8
contraception c. and abortion BURC 161:22
oral c. ALLE 12:13
contract C. into a span HERB 373:6
nothing but a civil c. SELD 653:18
social c. ROUS 636:4
Social C. is nothing more WELL 810:12
Society is indeed a c. BURK 163:29
to C. MAIN 491:10
tugging at every c. EMER 299:13
verbal c. isn't worth GOLD 346:3
contradict Do I c. myself WHIT 815:18
I never c. DISR 271:3
Never c. FISH 313:15
Read not to c. BACO 44:5
truth which you cannot c. SOCR 727:7
contradicted c. by observation EDDI 287:23
dogmatise and am c. JOHN 418:6
contradiction c. in terms SHAW 709:17
c. is real LÉVI 466:13
they brook no c. WEBS 808:3
Woman's at best a c. POPE 583:17
contradictions bundle of c. COLT 230:5
chain of c. CLAR 218:8
glaring c. HUME 394:16
contraire *Au c.* BECK 60:10
contraries c. there is no progression BLAK 119:9
Dreams go by c. PROV 598:45
contrariwise 'C.,' continued Tweedledee CARR 190:18
contrary directed to c. parts NEWT 543:7
everythink goes c. with me DICK 261:12
Mary, quite c. NURS 549:13
most c. to custom HUME 394:9
On the c. LAST 457:1
trial is by what is c. MILT 519:10
contribution make his own c. MORE 531:17
contrite broken and c. heart BOOK 135:9
broken and c. heart ELEA 291:15
sighing of a c. heart BOOK 127:14

contrive How Nature always does c. GILB 337:14
control Circumstances beyond my c. DICK 262:7
Ground c. to Major Tom BOWI 145:21
ought to c. our thoughts DARW 250:14
woman under her father's c. LAWS 459:6
wrong members in c. ORWE 558:16
controller Soul, the Inner C. UPAN 787:13
controls Who c. the past ORWE 558:22
controversies forged in c. FRAN 323:7
controversy c. is either superfluous NEWM 542:15
man of c. GALB 328:6
contumely proud man's c. SHAK 664:4
convalescence enjoy c. SHAW 706:17
convenience prefers c. to liberty HESS 375:16
'Twixt treason and c. EPIT 303:6
convenient c. that there be gods OVID 561:7
food c. for me BIBL 83:35
convent C. of the Sacred Heart ELIO 295:25
c.'s narrow room WORD 829:11
convention By c. there is colour DEMO 257:2
Lords of C. SCOT 650:11
conventional c. truth NAGA 538:3
merely c. signs CARR 191:22
conventionality C. is not morality BRON 149:13
conversation always spoiling c. MACA 483:16
bee in c. JOHN 412:9
careless c. EDGE 288:13
c. among gentlemen JOHN 415:13
C. is imperative WHIT 814:5
c. perfectly delightful SMIT 725:20
c.-scraps, Kitchen-cabals CRAB 242:22
c. with the best men DESC 258:16
different name for c. STER 738:23
no such thing as c. WEST 812:13
rhymed c. GERS 334:19
soft parts of c. SHAK 692:24
subject of c. CHES 209:4
third-rate c. PLOM 579:3
conversations after dinner c. THOR 776:17
without pictures or c. CARR 189:7
converse hold high c. THOM 775:16
rational c. WOLL 825:20
conversing With thee c. MILT 516:21
conversion c. of the Jews MARV 499:1
convert to c. England PUGI 616:18
who shall c. me WESL 811:14
converted Except ye be c. BIBL 96:7
have not c. a man MORL 532:4
converts can true c. make FARQ 307:16
convict like being a c. WELC 809:4
conviction best lack all c. YEAT 837:5
C. politicians BANC 53:5
what is called c. HUNT 396:3
convictions cloud of comforting c. RUSS 639:25
c. are hills FITZ 315:8
convince we c. ourselves JUNI 423:14
convinces man who c. the world DARW 251:6
convincing less c. than one HUXL 397:5
Oh! too c. BYRO 175:17
conviva *plenus vitae c.* LUCR 479:8
convoy crowns for c. SHAK 671:23
convulsions gall'ry in c. POPE 583:2
cookery c. do MERE 505:16
Football and c. SMIT 723:16
cookies baked c. and had teas CLIN 221:1
cooking C. is the most ancient BRIL 148:19
'plain' c. cannot be entrusted MORP 532:5
cooks as c. go SAKI 642:4
Devil sends c. GARR 330:6
Devil sends c. PROV 601:17
literary c. MORE 530:23
praise it, not the c. HARI 362:8
Synod of C. JOHN 413:18
Too many c. PROV 613:13
cool Be still and c. FOX 322:11
c. as a mountain stream ADVE 7:12
c. web of language GRAV 349:12
in the c. of the day BIBL 73:26
rather be dead than c. COBA 223:6
something to be c. LOVE 476:8
Sweet day, so c. HERB 373:17
think of C. Britannia BENN 65:13
cooled C. a long age KEAT 429:7
cooling for c. the blood FLAN 316:2
cooperation Government and c. RUSK 639:4
partnership and c. ANON 15:20
coot haunts of c. and hern TENN 757:13
cope use a c. like that PUGI 616:18
copied c. the old authors PLIN 578:15
copier mere c. of nature REYN 625:5
copies few originals and many c. TOCQ 778:9
copperheads c. and the assassin SAND 643:19
coppers like the old time 'c.' COLL 228:13
cops C. are like a doctor CHAN 201:15
copulating skeletons c. BEEC 61:3
copulation Birth, and c., and death ELIO 295:23
Let c. thrive SHAK 679:21
copy to every book its c. COLU 230:6
copyrights authors their c. TROL 781:18
coque *pénétra ma c.* RIMB 628:6
coquetry tiresome as c. LERM 464:20
coquette Gay c. SANS 644:7
cor *C. ad cor loquitur* MOTT 535:5
J'aime le son du c. VIGN 792:14
coral C. is far more red SHAK 705:20
c. lip admires CARE 186:5
his bones are c. SHAK 698:27
India's c. strand HEBE 367:6
like c. insects WARN 803:19
redder than the fyn c. CHAU 206:2
corbies twa c. BALL 52:5
cord silver c. be loosed BIBL 85:2
stretch a c. however fine WHEW 813:14
threefold c. BIBL 84:10
triple c. BURK 162:10
corda *Sursum c.* MISS 520:19
Cordelia such sacrifices, my C. SHAK 680:8
cordial Love . . . That c. drop ROCH 630:8
cords scourge of small c. BIBL 101:15
core c. of a world's culture BOLD 124:10
deep heart's c. YEAT 836:12
Corinth lucky enough to get to C. HORA 386:22
Corinthian C. capital BURK 163:30
Corinthum *adire C.* HORA 386:22
cork c. out of my lunch FIEL 310:19
corkscrew tumbler, and a c. DICK 264:6
corkscrews crooked as c. AUDE 33:23
cormorant common c. (or shag) ISHE 400:7
C. devouring Time SHAK 680:17
Sat like a c. MILT 516:11
corn amid the alien c. KEAT 429:14
breast high amid the c. HOOD 382:27
c. as high as an elephant's eye HAMM 358:21
C. King beckoning JARR 404:9
C. rigs, an' barley rigs BURN 167:16
c. that makes the holy bread MASE 500:15
c. was orient TRAH 780:13
lower the price of c. MELB 504:1
My crop of c. TICH 777:10
our sustaining c. SHAK 679:18
raise the price of c. BYRO 173:12
stop raising c. LEAS 461:3
there was c. in Egypt BIBL 75:15
thick with c. BOOK 136:2
threshed c. at midnight YEAT 837:8
two ears of c. SWIF 747:22
yellow like ripe c. ROSS 634:17
cornea *C., qua veris facilis* VIRG 795:3
corner At every c., I meet my Father LOWE 478:1
came round the c. MILN 510:19
c. in the thing I love SHAK 692:26
c. of a foreign field BROO 150:17
c. of a foreign field OPEN 555:14
draughty street c. GRIF 353:11
drive life into a c. THOR 776:12
head-stone in the c. BOOK 140:6
in a c., some untidy spot AUDE 34:10
just around the c. COWA 238:20
mutters away to herself in a c. CARE 186:17
not done in a c. BIBL 104:21
round the c. of nonsense COLE 227:26
Sat in the c. NURS 549:6
wind in that c. SHAK 691:8
corners age in c. thrown SHAK 658:15
clearing up the obscure c. HUXL 397:16
c. of the earth BOOK 138:6
Duke of dark c. SHAK 686:23
polished c. of the temple BOOK 141:18
round earth's imagined c. DONN 272:20
sheet knit at the four c. BIBL 103:28
three c. of the world SHAK 677:21
cornet young c. of horse WALP 802:6
cornfield o'er the green c. SHAK 659:24
cornfields Miles of c. HACK 355:10
Cornish twenty thousand C. men HAWK 364:6
corns shooting c. presage SWIF 749:5
corny c. as Kansas in August HAMM 359:3
Coromandel coast of C. SITW 721:8
On the coast of C. LEAR 460:5
coronation c., and sops in wine SPEN 734:21
coronet bride of a ducal c. DICK 263:15
coronets more than c. TENN 762:11
corporation c. to have a conscience THUR 777:4
corporations [c.] cannot commit treason COKE 224:12
C. have neither bodies PROV 597:37
corpore *Mens sana in c. sano* JUVE 425:2
corpse carry one's father's c. APOL 23:2
c. in a coffin PEPY 573:8
c. in the case BARH 54:8
good wishes to the c. BARR 55:18
make a lovely c. DICK 263:9
nice *fresh* c. TWAI 786:15
corpses laid the c. BOCC 123:6
mock the riddled c. SASS 645:16
corpulent c. man of fifty HUNT 396:5
corpus *Ave verum c.* ANON 21:6
corpuscula *hominum c.* JUVE 425:1
correct All present and c. MILI 508:2
Blot out, c. SWIF 749:14
c. with those men CICE 217:27
do the perfectly c. thing SHAW 707:11
corrected C. and amended EPIT 302:1
correcteth he c. BIBL 82:7
Correggios Raphaels, C., and stuff GOLD 345:5
corregiescity c. of Corregio STER 739:2
Corregio corregiescity of C. STER 739:2
correlative objective c. ELIO 296:17
correspondences C. like small-clothes SMIT 725:25
correspondent c. for posterity BAGE 47:22
corridors c. of power SNOW 726:18
corriger *c. le monde* MOLI 525:11
corroborative c. detail GILB 338:13
corrupt Among a people generally c. BURK 162:15
become the most c. government JEFF 405:10
c. good manners BIBL 106:25
c. my air SHAK 660:8
c. the heart BYRO 178:6
moth and rust doth c. BIBL 93:20
Peace to c. MILT 517:26
power is apt to c. PITT 576:22
should c. the world TENN 760:15
corrupted c. by sentiment GREE 351:18
C. honest men SHAK 657:8
c. the youth SHAK 672:24
hath not been c. BOOK 125:12
corruptible c. crown BIBL 106:11
this c. must put on BIBL 107:3

corruption C., the most infallible symptom GIBB 335:11
C. wins not more SHAK 673:16
danger of great c. KNOX 442:17
dong and of c. CHAU 206:7
see c. BOOK 132:10
sown in c. BIBL 107:1
Stewed in c. SHAK 665:17
to be turned into c. BOOK 142:6
vice whose strong c. SHAK 702:16
corrupts absolute power c. ACTO 1:16
Power c. PROV 609:36
corse c. to the rampart WOLF 825:3
c., whose monument I am CONS 235:5
thou, dead c. SHAK 662:19
Cortez like stout C. KEAT 429:21
Corydon *pastor C. ardebat Alexin* VIRG 795:16
Time, not C. ARNO 27:28
cosiness c. and irritation PYM 618:7
cosmetics tired of the c. SEXT 655:5
we make c. REVS 625:1
cost at what c. BECK 59:10
c. of setting him up in poverty NAID 538:4
counteth the c. BIBL 99:31
count the c. IGNA 398:17
independence may c. DOST 276:9
They c. right naught WYAT 834:7
costive made a soap-boiler c. WEBS 807:24
costly c. in our sorrows STER 738:12
C. thy habit SHAK 662:11
Too c. for cost THOM 774:16
costs C. register competing attractions KNIG 442:7
c. them nothing BURT 170:14
cot no go the country c. MACN 488:8
paint the c. CRAB 243:14
Cotopaxi Chimborazo, C. TURN 785:19
Cotswold As of C.: war told me GURN 355:4
cottage c. is not happy DISR 271:5
Love and a c. COLM 229:14
poorest man may in his c. PITT 576:20
soul's dark c. WALL 800:5
straw c. to a palace turns DYER 286:15
visage from our c. SHAK 703:22
cotton c. is high HEYW 376:4
C. is King CHRI 212:17
c. is king HUGO 393:20
cou *tords-lui le c.* VERL 791:9
couch c. when owls do cry SHAK 699:11
steel c. of war SHAK 692:6
water my c. with my tears BOOK 131:24
when on my c. I lie WORD 828:27
couché *Longtemps, je me suis c.* PROU 593:20
couches banish them to their c. KORA 444:7
c. stretch around THOM 774:21
cough all c. in ink YEAT 837:4
c. by them ready made CHUR 213:17
Love and a c. cannot PROV 606:2
coughing one c., and one not SCHN 648:21
coughs C. and sneezes OFFI 554:3
could It c. be you ADVE 7:31
councils C. of war never fight PROV 597:38
counsel c. and might BIBL 87:3
c. of the ungodly BOOK 131:15
c. that I once heard EMER 299:19
darkeneth c. BIBL 81:30
evil c. is most evil HESI 375:13
give good c. BURT 170:14
intention to keep my c. GLAD 341:6
Night brings c. PROV 607:43
princely c. in his face MILT 515:14
sometimes c. take POPE 587:5
took sweet c. BOOK 135:11
you c. well SHAK 687:17
counsellor Wonderful, C. BIBL 87:1
counsellors kings and c. BIBL 81:4
when c. blanch BACO 42:17
counsels all good c. BOOK 126:19
count c. everything CORN 236:18
c. the cost IGNA 398:17
c. your chickens PROV 598:31
Don't c. on me RICH 626:11
if you can c. your money GETT 335:2
I won the c. SOMO 727:19
Let me c. the ways BROW 154:21
let us c. our spoons JOHN 413:8
some did c. him mad BUNY 161:14
When angry, c. four TWAI 786:23
counted c. as the small dust BIBL 88:3
c. loss for Christ BIBL 108:20
c. our spoons EMER 299:15
c. them all out HANR 359:11
countenance cheerful c. BIBL 82:35
cheerful c. BOOK 139:3
c. cannot lie ROYD 637:1
C. Divine BLAK 120:1
c. is as Lebanon BIBL 85:21
c. of truth MILT 520:1
c. was as the sun BIBL 111:22
disinheriting c. SHER 716:15
grim grew his c. BALL 50:12
help of my c. BOOK 134:11
Knight of the Doleful C. CERV 199:16
light of his c. BOOK 136:3
light of thy c. BOOK 131:20
light of thy c. BOOK 137:8
Lord lift up his c. BIBL 76:24
of a beautiful c. BIBL 78:28
originality of your c. CLAI 218:5
counter All things c. HOPK 384:15
countercheck c. quarrelsome SHAK 659:26
counterfeit c. a gloom MILT 512:7
sleep, death's c. SHAK 683:19
counterfeited laughed with c. glee GOLD 344:13
counterpane land of c. STEV 742:13
counterpoint Too much c. BEEC 61:6
counterpoints c. to hack post-horses MOZA 534:12
counters Words are wise men's c. HOBB 378:15
counties coloured c. HOUS 390:19
Forget six c. MORR 532:13
counting it's the c. STOP 743:11
countries all c. before his own OVER 561:1
no c. in the world BORR 143:8
country all their c.'s wishes COLL 229:9
Anyone who loves his c. GARI 329:17
ask not what your c. KENN 433:14
be good in the c. WILD 818:20
betraying my c. FORS 321:4
billion dollar c. FOST 321:10
boy out of the c. PROV 615:34
Britain a fit c. LLOY 471:4
c. be always successful ADAM 3:17
c. governed by a despot JOHN 415:30
c. habit has me SACK 641:6
c. has the government MAIS 491:13
C. in the town MART 498:5
c. is lost WILL 820:1
c. is the world PAIN 564:5
c. loves such sweet desires do gain GREE 352:4
c. needs good farmes NIXO 546:7
c. of young men EMER 299:32
c. takes her place EMME 300:4
c. town is my detestation BURN 166:3
c. which has no history PROV 601:49
c. will be called upon HARD 360:2
Cry, the beloved c. PATO 570:1
departed into their own c. BIBL 92:24
died to save their c. CHES 210:6
die for one's c. HORA 388:14
dying for your c. FRAN 322:19
every c. but his own GILB 338:2
everyday story of c. folk CATC 195:15
exile is his c. URBA 788:19
fate of this c. DISR 269:13
fight for its King and C. GRAH 348:1
first, best c. GOLD 345:7
for his c.'s sake FITZ 314:6
for our c.'s good CART 192:11
friend of every c. CANN 185:1
friends of every c. DISR 269:17
from c. to country GOLD 345:24
From yon far c. HOUS 391:5
God made the c. COWP 241:19
God made the c. PROV 601:13
good news from a far c. BIBL 83:22
good of his c. WOTT 833:6
good of one's c. FARQ 307:11
grow up with the c. GREE 351:10
hame to my ain c. CUNN 247:16
How can you govern a c. DE G 255:25
how I leave my c. LAST 456:20
I love thee still— My c. COWP 241:21
importance of the c. HUXL 396:17
impossible to live in a c. KEAT 431:4
in a c. village AUST 39:9
in another c. MARL 496:18
in defence of one's c. HOME 382:6
in the c. places STEV 742:19
In this frozen whited c. HUGH 393:10
I pray for the c. HALE 357:2
journey into a far c. BIBL 100:2
King and c. need you MILI 508:17
know something of his own c. STER 739:11
leave his c. as good COBB 223:9
like a little c. retreat WYCH 834:8
likes the c. COWP 241:10
lose for my c. LAST 456:8
love his c. SHAK 675:26
Love of our c. GODW 342:6
love one's c. ANNA 15:2
Love thy c. DODI 271:21
love to serve my c. GIBR 336:10
make unto me one c. BROW 153:27
My c. is Kiltartan Cross YEAT 836:9
My c., right or wrong SCHU 649:14
my c. 'tis of centuries CUMM 247:4
My c., 'tis of thee SMIT 724:16
My soul, there is a c. VAUG 790:6
no c. for old men YEAT 837:1
no relish for the c. SMIT 725:9
Our c. is the world GARR 330:10
our c., right or wrong DECA 254:10
past is a foreign c. OPEN 556:11
past is a foreign c. HART 363:13
peace of each c. JOHN 407:10
quarrel in a far away c. CHAM 200:17
Queen and c. THOM 774:18
rather than a c. PILG 576:6
right part of the c. FROS 326:17
see much of the c. GLAD 340:18
serve our c. ADDI 4:14
service of their c. PAIN 563:16
she is my c. still CHUR 213:14
sucked on c. pleasures DONN 274:2
there's another c. SPRI 735:7
This was my c. BLUN 122:13
to all the c. dear GOLD 344:11
to be had in the c. HAZL 365:9
too long in c. towns CATH 194:9
tremble for my c. JEFF 406:3
understand the c. LESS 465:12
undone his c. ADDI 4:13
unmapped c. ELIO 292:5
vow to thee, my c. SPRI 735:6
we can do for our c. HOLM 381:10
what was good for our c. WILS 821:10
While there's a c. lane PARK 567:19
win our c. back FABE 305:15
your King and your C. RUBE 637:3
You've never seen this c. PURD 617:25
countryman c. must have praise BLYT 123:3
countrymen advice to my c. O'CO 552:16
c. are all mankind GARR 330:10
Friends, Romans, c. SHAK 675:27
hearts of his c. LEE 461:21
rebels are our c. GRAN 348:8
countryside gods of the c. VIRG 796:19
smiling and beautiful c. DOYL 277:9
county C. Guy, the hour is nigh SCOT 652:2
English c. families WAUG 806:3
countymen fellow-c. won't kill me COLL 229:5

coup *c. de dés* MALL 492:4
couple young c. between the wars PLOM 579:3
courage Be strong and of a good c. BIBL 77:17
c. and skill BUNY 161:18
C. in your own GORD 346:19
C., mon ami READ 622:15
c. never to submit MILT 514:13
C. not simply *one* of the virtues LEWI 466:24
c. the greater ANON 21:15
c. to suffer TROL 782:6
c. without ferocity BYRO 179:20
endurance and c. SCOT 650:9
fresh c. take COWP 240:17
have the c. to dare DOST 276:3
in the morning c. THOR 776:9
It takes c. MOWL 534:10
on reflection is real c. WALP 801:19
Pathos, piety, c. FORS 320:23
red badge of c. CRAN 243:27
screw your c. SHAK 682:17
two o'clock in the morning c. NAPO 538:17
with a good c. BOOK 133:19
without originality or moral c. SHAW 706:20
courageous captains c. BALL 51:5
freedom depends on being c. THUC 776:22
couriers Vaunt-c. SHAK 678:21
cours *Suspendez votre c.* LAMA 448:7
course c. of human events JEFF 405:2
c. of true love SHAK 689:4
finished my c. BIBL 109:23
I must stand the c. SHAK 679:11
myself to that c. PEPY 573:15
Of c., of course JAME 403:22
run his c. BOOK 132:15
what c. thou wilt SHAK 676:14
courses Horses for c. PROV 603:2
court bright lustre of a c. CECI 199:6
c. awards it SHAK 688:15
c. for owls BIBL 87:20
c. is obliged CHEK 208:16
C. of Session PROV 602:41
c. others in verse PRIO 592:10
envious c. SHAK [illegible]
four ways in c. ASCH 30:4
How he can c. SOUT 730:10
Keeps his pale c. SHEL 710:15
not having a C. BAGE 47:2
Say to the c., it glows RALE 620:12
she will c. you JONS 420:19
shines upon his c. SHAK 703:22
Talk of c. news SHAK 680:7
courted c. and jilted CAMP 183:9
courteous C. he was, lowely CHAU 204:11
c. to strangers BACO 43:6
courtesy candy deal of c. SHAK 667:27
Grace of God is in C. BELL 63:13
greater man, the greater c. TENN 759:31
mirour of alle c. CHAU 205:22
very pink of c. SHAK 697:21
women with perfect c. KITC 441:31
courtier heel of the c. SHAK 666:22
Here lies a noble c. EPIT 302:16
courtmartialled c. in my absence BEHA 62:1
courts Approach with joy his c. KETH 434:11
case is still before the c. HORA 385:16
C. and camps CHES 209:9
C. for cowards were erected BURN 167:20
c. of the Lord BOOK 137:11
c. of the sun CHES 210:9
Fresh from brawling c. TENN 761:23
one day in thy c. BOOK 137:13
courtship C. to marriage CONG 233:1
cousins his c. and his aunts GILB 338:26
couture Haute C. should be fun LACR 447:8
covenant c. with death BIBL 87:14
c. with death GARR 330:11
Never break a c. ZORO 841:5
token of a c. BIBL 74:22
covenanted c. with him BIBL 97:16
covenants Open c. of peace WILS 822:17
Covent Garden committee on C. KAUF 426:4
Coventry for the train at C. TENN 759:1
cover C. her face WEBS 808:2
c. of a jest HORA 389:13
I c. all SAND 643:21
tell a book by its c. PROV 615:31
covered c. his face BIBL 86:21
coverlet length of his c. PROV 599:42
covers c. a multitude of sins PROV 597:12
covet Thou shalt not c. BIBL 76:13
Thou shalt not c. CLOU 222:27
covetous not c. BIBL 109:14
covetousness inclined to c. KORA 444:14
uncleanness, or c. BIBL 108:6
cow bellowing c. soon forgets PROV 595:43
Better a good c. PROV 596:4
c. is of the bovine ilk NASH 539:9
c. jumped over NURS 548:12
c.'s horn PROV 612:48
c.'s in the corn NURS 549:5
c. with the crumpled horn NURS 551:7
grass to graze a c. BETJ 71:4
keep a c. BUTL 172:28
like a c. or a dog VICT 792:3
milk the c. of the world WILB 817:5
never saw a Purple C. BURG 162:2
swallow the c. PROV 604:18
three acres and a c. POLI 582:1
To every c. her calf COLU 230:6
Truth, Sir, is a c. JOHN 413:10
Two wise acres and a c. COWA 239:9
Was the c. crossed HERB 371:20
Why buy a c. when PROV 615:6
coward bully is always a c. PROV 596:40
c. does it with a kiss WILD 818:32
c. on instinct SHAK 668:10
c. shame BURN 167:24
c.'s weapon, poison FLET 318:19
No c. soul is mine BRON 149:21
sea hates a c. O'NE 554:23
cowardice c. keeps us in peace JOHN 416:5
I admit the c. SHAW 708:9
surest is c. TWAI 786:10
cowardly C. dogs bark loudest WEBS 808:11
cowards all men would be c. ROCH 630:16
being all c. JOHN 416:5
Conscience makes c. PROV 597:35
C. die many times SHAK 675:10
c. in reasoning SHAF 655:17
C. in scarlet GRAN 349:5
C. may die many times PROV 597:40
make c. of us all SHAK 664:4
many other mannish c. SHAK 658:12
not because men are c. LEWI 467:14
word that c. use SHAK 696:32
cowbind Green c. SHEL 713:21
cowl c. does not make monk PROV 597:41
cows contented—that's for the c. CHAN 202:3
C. are my passion DICK 262:15
cowslip C. and shad-blow CRAN 243:20
In a c.'s bell SHAK 699:11
I' the bottom of a c. SHAK 660:20
O'er the c.'s velvet head MILT 512:2
cowslips c. tall her pensioners be SHAK 689:17
coxcombs some made c. POPE 584:11
coy c. and tender to offend HERB 373:15
sometimes c. SEDL 653:4
Then be not c. HERR 375:3
coyness This c., lady MARV 498:23
cozenage greatest c. CROM 245:17
crabbed C. age and youth SHAK 703:27
crabs sidelong c. had scrawled CRAB 242:24
crack C. and sometimes break ELIO 294:5
c. in the tea-cup opens AUDE 33:19
c. in your upper storey SMOL 726:14
c. it too JONS 419:10
heaven's vaults should c. SHAK 680:11
cracked bloody noses and c. crowns SHAK 668:1
c. from side to side TENN 762:19
crackling c. of thorns BIBL 84:13
cracks c. in the conversation WALK 799:6
Now c. a noble heart SHAK 667:12
cradle c. and the grave DYER 286:16
c. endlessly rocking WHIT 815:6
c. of an infant BURK 162:14
c. of the deep WILL 819:20
c. of the fairy queen SHAK 690:1
c. rocks above an abyss NABO 537:20
c. to the grave SHEL 713:15
from the c. to the grave CHUR 215:19
hand that rocks the c. PROV 601:45
hand that rocks the c. WALL 799:16
rocking the c. ROBI 629:22
cradles babies in the c. BROW 157:10
cradling evil c. BORR 144:4
evil c. KORA 443:23
craft c. and credulity BURK 162:12
c. so long to lerne CHAU 206:28
not teach his son a c. TALM 754:18
craftier c. to pley she was CHAU 204:5
crafts c. and assaults BOOK 127:3
crag c. with crookèd hands TENN 758:17
craggy c. paths of study JONS 420:7
cramped won't lie too c. CELA 199:8
cranberry And a C. Tart LEAR 460:10
crane tall as a c. SITW 720:21
cranks into sages and c. QUIN 619:6
crankum crinkum c. AUBR 32:15
cras *C. ingens iterabimus aequor* HORA 387:19
crash car c. as a sexual event BALL 52:12
c. will come twenty years after BISM 116:14
crastina *Pereat, qui c. curat* VIRG 795:12
Sera nimis vita est c. MART 497:22
craters passing c., passing fire YEVT 838:10
crave my mind forbids to c. DYER 286:13
craven c. fears of being great TENN 759:8
craving full as c. too DRYD 280:27
getting rid of c. PALI 565:4
he the more is c. WROT 833:16
crawls sea-worm c.—grotesque HARD 361:9
crazed c. with the spell of far Arabia DE L 256:10
crazy C. like a fox [illegible]
c. to fly more missions HELL 368:13
he's football c. MCGR 485:12
Still c. after all SIMO 720:11
stood by me when I was c. SHER 716:28
two c. people together HART 363:7
creaking c. door hangs longest PROV 597:42
c. to the barn LOWE 478:2
creaks morning light c. down again SITW 720:21
cream choking it with c. PROV 611:46
c.-faced loon SHAK 685:16
queen of curds and c. SHAK 703:20
crease with not a c. ROST 635:12
create c. the taste WORD 832:22
c. the wondrous world YOUN 839:10
genuinely *c.* Europe MONN 526:5
must c. a system BLAK 118:20
new-c. another heir SHAK 673:27
transmit but do not c. CONF 231:15
What I cannot c. FEYN 309:7
what they half-c. WORD 829:6
created all men are c. equal ANON 19:11
c. all things BIBL 112:1
c. him in his own image DOST 275:17
c. in the image TALM 753:18
c. Man of a blood-clot KORA 445:17
C. sick GREV 353:4
He also c. in man TALM 754:23
just c. like mistakes EMEC 299:4
men are c. equal JEFF 405:3
monster whom I had c. SHEL 710:8
Nothing can be c. LUCR 479:2
why I c. man ZOHA 840:8
creation bless thee for our c. BOOK 127:19
blind fury of c. SHAW 707:32

c. rises again MISS 523:4
eternal act of c. COLE 227:11
finds c. so perfect PROU 594:6
follow the order of c. WARN 803:17
from the first c. LLOY 470:15
I hold C. in my foot HUGH 393:4
immanent in all c. SIKH 719:13
love C.'s final law TENN 761:14
originates c. KORA 444:18
present at the C. ALFO 11:14
this c. has arisen RIG 627:17
whole c. groaneth BIBL 105:9
whole c. moves TENN 762:6
your niche in c. HALL 358:8
creative c. hate CATH 194:11
c. soul WORD 831:10
c. urge BAKU 48:16
Deception is not as c. SAUN 646:1
man's c. powers SCHU 649:10
creator abide with my C. God CLAR 218:16
can dispense with a c. PROU 594:6
C., if He exists HALD 356:18
C. made Italy TWAI 786:14
C., without fear SIKH 719:6
creature more than the C. BIBL 104:27
existence of the C. MAIM 491:5
feel at times like the C. BELL 62:23
glory of the C. BACO 41:9
great c. from his work MILT 517:8
image of the C. BONA 125:5
myself and my C. NEWM 542:5
Of the C. MERW 506:4
Remember now thy C. BIBL 85:2
creature c. hath a purpose KEAT 431:13
c. more than the Creator BIBL 104:27
deed's c. MIDD 507:5
God's first C. BACO 44:32
lone lorn c. DICK 261:12
no lyves c. Withouten love CHAU 207:7
one tiny c. DOST 276:1
creatures c. great and small ALEX 11:8
c. set upon tables JOHN 415:6
How many goodly c. SHAK 699:12
living, sentient c. JAIN 401:16
credat *C. Iudaeus Apella* HORA 389:20
credence no c. to his word BOOK 139:10
credit citizen Of c. and renown COWP 240:11
c. to any good girl TAYL 756:11
c. where credit is due PROV 601:8
greatly to his c. GILB 338:30
In science the c. goes DARW 251:6
let the c. go FITZ 314:10
my c. in this world FITZ 315:1
people who get the c. MORR 533:6
To c. marvels HEAN 366:12
creditable c. acquaintance SWIF 748:5
credite *Experto c.* VIRG 795:11
creditor trembling at a c. JOHN 409:26
credo *C. in unum Deum* MISS 520:16
C. quia impossibile TERT 768:16
credulity craft and c. BURK 162:12
craving c. DISR 268:23
season of c. PITT 576:21
soften into a c. BURK 164:14
credulous are the most c. POPE 587:21
Man is a c. animal RUSS 640:3
creed Calvinistic c. PITT 576:24
c. of slaves PITT 577:3
got the better of his c. STER 738:25
last article of my c. GAND 329:6
my political c. ADAM 3:11
Sapping a solemn c. BYRO 174:21
suckled in a c. outworn WORD 832:16
This c. of the Nirgranthas JAIN 402:10
creeds dust of c. outworn SHEL 713:10
keys of all the c. TENN 761:1
Light half-believers in our casual c. ARNO 27:9
live their c. GUES 354:14
so many c. WILC 817:10
than in half the c. TENN 761:25
creep Ambition can c. BURK 164:9
bade me c. past BROW 157:17
c. again, leap again DE L 256:13
C. into thy narrow bed ARNO 26:14
make your flesh c. DICK 265:4
music C. in our ears SHAK 688:21
creeping c. things BIBL 103:28
every c. thing BIBL 73:14
creeps C. in this petty pace SHAK 685:22
c. rustling to her knees KEAT 427:10
crème c. de la crème SPAR 731:17
crescent with c. horns MILT 514:25
Crete people of C. SAKI 642:2
Cretes C. and Arabians BIBL 103:16
crevasse like a scream from a c. GREE 351:20
crew We were a ghastly c. COLE 226:22
crib shadow of the c. BISH 115:19
cribbed cabined, c., confined SHAK 684:9
cricket C.—a game which the English MANC 493:5
c. as organized loafing TEMP 757:8
C. civilizes people MUGA 534:13
c. on the hearth MILT 512:7
c. test TEBB 757:2
c. with their peasants TREV 781:8
everything lost but c. CARD 186:3
cried little children c. MOTL 534:7
pig c., Wee-wee-wee NURS 551:9
poor have c. SHAK 676:1
when he c. AUDE 33:26
cries on me she c. BALL 50:18
crieth c. in the wilderness BIBL 87:28
Crillon Hang yourself, brave C. HENR 370:5
crime catalogue of human c. CHUR 215:8
commonplace a c. DOYL 277:8
C. doesn't pay SAYI 647:7
c. of being a young man PITT 576:19
c. so shameful as poverty FARQ 307:7
c. to love too well POPE 582:17
c. you haven't committed POWE 590:11
foulest c. in history WHIT 815:22
From the one c. VIRG 793:19
lovèd be with equal c. SPEN 734:1
my wilful c. MILT 518:1
Napoleon of c. DOYL 277:17
never a c. CORN 236:17
No c.'s so great CHUR 213:13
Poverty is not a c. PROV 609:35
punishment fit the c. GILB 338:9
Tough on c. BLAI 117:7
was thought a c. BLAK 121:4
worse than a c. BOUL 144:25
crimes all his c. broad blown SHAK 665:9
c. are committed in thy name LAST 456:19
c., follies, and misfortunes GIBB 335:6
C., like virtues FARQ 307:17
c. of this guilty land BROW 152:3
one virtue, and a thousand c. BYRO 175:19
Successful c. alone DRYD 282:5
virtues made or c. DEFO 255:6
with reiterated c. MILT 514:18
worst of c. SHAW 707:21
criminal crime and the c. AREN 24:2
ends I think c. KEYN 435:3
severity of the c. law PEEL 571:13
while there is a c. element DEBS 254:9
criminals if there were no c. SALI 643:4
Looney Tunes, and squalid c. REAG 623:6
crimine *C. ab uno* VIRG 793:19
crimson Cat with c. whiskers LEAR 460:21
c. in thy lips SHAK 698:3
c. thread of kinship PARK 567:20
Now sleeps the c. petal TENN 766:3
cringe Australian Cultural C. PHIL 575:12
to the cultural c. KEAT 426:12
crinkum c. crankum AUBR 32:15
cripples If c., then no matter PAST 569:9
crisis C.? What Crisis? MISQ 521:7
C.? What crisis NEWS 544:2
drama out of a c. ADVE 8:19
fit for a great c. BAGE 46:11
real c. on your hands THAT 770:1
crisp Deep and c. and even NEAL 540:2
eating one c. DUAN 283:19
Crispian feast of C. SHAK 671:23
Crispin C. Crispian shall ne'er go by SHAK 671:25
crisps like eating c. BOY 146:4
criterion infallible c. of wisdom BURK 162:6
critic average English c. LAMB 449:10
C. and whippersnapper BROW 155:6
c. is a bundle of biases BALL 52:14
c. is a man who knows the way TYNA 787:1
c. spits on what is done HOOD 383:2
C., you have frowned WORD 831:18
cry of the c. for five WHIS 813:20
function of the c. BELL 62:20
good c. is he who relates FRAN 322:17
great drama c. TYNA 786:31
important book, the c. assumes WOOL 826:19
knew the c.'s part COLL 229:13
not the c. who counts ROOS 633:8
poet includes a c. SHEN 715:10
true c. ought ADDI 5:5
Unboding c.-pen TENN 767:14
critical Papa's c. indignation EDGE 288:18
criticism cant of c. STER 739:3
C. is a life without risk LAHR 448:1
c. of life ARNO 28:24
father of English c. JOHN 410:2
from c. to nature JOHN 410:14
my own definition of c. ARNO 28:17
near to them than c. RILK 627:19
People ask you for c. MAUG 502:3
wreathed the rod of c. D'IS 271:11
Writing c. UPDI 788:10
criticize c. What you can't understand DYLA 287:16
criticized to be c. is not always EDEN 288:7
critics c. all are ready made BYRO 178:1
C. are like brushers WOTT 833:7
c. of the next FITZ 315:17
know who the c. are DISR 270:22
therefore they turn c. COLE 227:17
Turned c. next POPE 584:12
croaks c. the fatal entrance SHAK 682:2
crocodile cruel crafty c. SPEN 733:19
How doth the little c. CARR 189:9
manner o' thing is your c. SHAK 657:2
these c.'s tears BURT 170:20
crocodiles wisdom of the c. BACO 44:24
crocus c. brake like fire TENN 765:7
crofts by the gasworks c. MACC 484:8
Cromwell C., I charge thee SHAK 673:15
ruin that C. knocked about BEDF 60:20
Some C. guiltless GRAY 350:11
cronies money-grabbing c. HAGU 356:7
crony rusty, drouthy c. BURN 168:11
crook President is a c. NIXO 546:6
crookbacked C. he was SACK 641:4
crooked crag with c. hands TENN 758:17
c. as corkscrews AUDE 33:23
c. be made straight ELIO 293:26
c. shall be made straight BIBL 87:28
C. things may be as stiff LOCK 471:19
c. timber of humanity KANT 425:19
set the c. straight MORR 532:12
There was a c. man NURS 551:3
croon Wanna cry, wanna c. HARB 359:17
crop c.-headed Parliament BROW 156:20
fruitful c. should bring IRWI 400:5
Good seed makes good c. PROV 601:30
croppy Hoppy, C., Droppy ELLI 298:14
crops c. the flowery food POPE 585:7
cross bear the c. gladly THOM 771:8
bloody c. he bore SPEN 733:13
by thy C. and Passion BOOK 127:7
c. him in nothing SHAK 656:14
c. of gold BRYA 159:3
c. of Jesus BARI 54:13
c. the bridge PROV 598:32
c. upon their garments URBA 788:18
death upon the c. BOOK 129:21

cross (*cont.*):
first at Cradle and the C. SAYE 646:7
hangs upon the C. DONN 274:26
mystery of the c. FORT 321:7
no c., no crown PENN 572:13
old rugged c. BENN 65:14
orgasm has replaced the C. MUGG 534:16
see thee ever c.-gartered SHAK 701:29
survey the wondrous c. WATT 805:14
There for you to c. PAUL 570:9
though it be a c. ADAM 3:21
use him as a C. SMIT 725:1
crossbow With my c. I shot COLE 226:8
crossed may be c. in love SHER 715:19
Was the cow c. HERB 371:20
crosses Between the c., row on row MCCR 484:12
clinging to their c. CHES 209:27
C. are ladders PROV 597:43
tumbled down the c. JORD 421:6
with c. of fire NERU 541:4
crossing double c. of a pair of heels HEBE 367:8
HART 363:5
crossness make c. and dirt succeed FORS 320:13
crosspatch C., Draw the latch NURS 547:17
crossways understands everything c. SALI 642:18
crow before the cock c. BIBL 97:19
carrion c., that loathsome beast GASC 330:15
c. in its own farmyard TROL 782:16
c. Makes wing SHAK 684:7
c. upon his own dunghill PROV 599:22
jump Jim C. NURS 551:17
one for the c. PROV 608:38
risen to hear him c. ELIO 291:21
thenk upon the c. CHAU 205:24
upstart c. GREE 352:5
crowd c. flowed over London Bridge ELIO 296:1
c. is not company BACO 43:1
c. will always save Barabbas COCT 223:20
Far from the madding c.'s GRAY 350:13
not feel the c. COWP 241:32
pass in a c. SWIF 748:4
try to c. out real life FORS 321:2
crowded Across a c. room HAMM 358:23
c. hour of glorious life MORD 530:21
crowds C. without company GIBB 335:23
her noise, her c. LAMB 448:25
nor cheering c. YEAT 836:10
talk with c. KIPL 439:3
crowing whistling woman and a c. hen PROV 614:45
crown abdicate the C. JUAN 422:22
better than his c. SHAK 688:10
both divide the c. DRYD 280:23
broke his c. NURS 548:21
Caesar's laurel c. BLAK 118:3
cannot get a c. SHAK 672:30
corruptible c. BIBL 106:11
c. in possession PAIN 563:12
C. is, according to the saying BAGE 46:7
c. of life BIBL 110:11
c. of life BIBL 111:25
c. of our life SWIN 750:17
c. of snowflake pearls BLOK 122:6
c. of thorns BEVA 71:18
C. of Thorns BRON 149:13
c. of thorns BRYA 159:3
c. of twelve stars BIBL 112:18
c. ourselves with rosebuds BIBL 91:6
c. the just ANON 21:11
C., the symbol of permanence JUAN 422:21
c. thy good with brotherhood BATE 57:4
c. to her husband BIBL 82:24
fighting for the c. NURS 549:3
Give me the c. SHAK 695:21
glory of my c. ELIZ 297:4
head that wears a c. SHAK 670:2
I give away my c. SHAK 695:23
Indian c. ROSS 634:14
influence of the C. DUNN 285:16
king's c. SHAK 686:8
mace, the c. imperial SHAK 671:20
no cross, no c. PENN 572:13
of an earthly c. MARL 496:26
of c., of queen SHAK 662:31
power of the c. BURK 164:13
presented him a kingly c. SHAK 676:2
put on my c. SHAK 657:28
sorrow's c. of sorrow TENN 762:24
strike his father's c. SHAK 670:29
wished to restore the c. JOHN 414:28
Within the hollow c. SHAK 695:10
worn the c. BIBL 91:25
crowned C. with rank fumitor SHAK 679:18
c. with thorns KELL 432:16
sitting c. upon the grave HOBB 379:4
crowner C.'s Quest BARH 54:8
crownest Thou c. the year BOOK 136:2
crowning c. mercy CROM 245:13
crowns Casting down their golden c. HEBE 367:8
c. and coronets, Promised SHAK 670:31
c. are empty things DEFO 255:16
c. for convoy SHAK 671:23
c. resign to call thee mine SONG 730:6
end c. the work PROV 599:11
end that c. us HERR 374:9
crows c. and choughs that wing SHAK 679:19
c. begin to search PROV 608:29
Til c. feet be growe CHAU 207:5
crucible America is God's C. ZANG 839:21
violet into a c. SHEL 714:20
crucified c., dead, and buried BOOK 126:10
when they c. my Lord SONG 730:7
crucifix on the trunk of the c. HENR 370:12
crucify c. mankind BRYA 159:3
God they ought to c. CART 192:15
not even c. him CARL 188:22
cruel comfort c. men CHES 210:8
c. and unusual punishment CONS 235:14
C., but composed ARNO 26:22
C. he looks, but calm SHEL 713:5
c. men of Rome SHAK 674:3
C. necessity CROM 245:18
c., not unnatural SHAK 665:6
c. only to be kind SHAK 665:23
c. person who commits JUDA 422:24
c. to be kind COMP 230:12
c. works of nature DARW 251:1
jealousy is c. as the grave BIBL 86:7
State business is a c. trade HALI 358:2
Such c. glasses HOWE 392:2
cruellest April is the c. month ELIO 295:26
c. lies are often told STEV 742:4
cruelty C. has a human heart BLAK 121:11
C., like every other vice ELIO 293:9
c. To load a falling man SHAK 673:25
full Of direst c. SHAK 682:2
gratification of c. FOST 321:13
infliction of c. RUSS 639:26
main sources of c. RUSS 640:4
years of c. GLAD 341:16
cruise on our last c. STEV 741:24
crumbling C. between the fingers MACN 488:10
c. to dust DIDE 267:5
crumbs bags to hold the c. ISHE 400:7
covetous of their c. SMAR 722:4
dogs eat of the c. BIBL 96:1
fed with the c. BIBL 100:10
learning's c. BROW 155:27
crumpet Muffin and C. DICK 263:16
thinking man's c. MUIR 535:24
crumpled cow with the c. horn NURS 551:7
crunch munch on, c. on BROW 157:11
crusade party is a moral c. WILS 821:13
crusaders C. have multiplied BERN 69:5
cruse my small c. HERR 374:21
oil in a c. BIBL 79:26
crush c. people to the earth CHIL 211:24
c., to annihilate a man DOST 276:6
crushes c. the entire century ZOLA 841:2
cry and a c. Before TENN 760:13
behold a c. BIBL 86:17
bubbling c. BYRO 176:12
continually do c. BOOK 125:20
c. all the way to the bank LIBE 467:16
c. before night PROV 610:43
c. before you're hurt PROV 598:33
c. come unto thee BOOK 130:19
c. in the day-time BOOK 132:21
c. is still SHAK 685:20
c. it up SWIF 749:17
C. not when his father dies JOHN 418:8
c. of gulls ELIO 296:12
c. of the Little Peoples LE G 462:12
c. of the whole people KING 436:20
c. over me, There, there BOOK 136:14
C., the beloved country PATO 570:1
cuckoo's parting c. ARNO 27:26
great c. in Egypt BIBL 76:3
his little son should c. CORN 237:1
hush, little baby, don' yo' c. HEYW 376:4
indeed they c. WEBS 808:15
Much c. and little wool PROV 607:14
Never c. over spilt milk FIEL 310:23
no language but a c. TENN 761:11
she began to c. NURS 548:10
Some must c. RHYS 625:16
Speechless still, and never c. EPIT 303:6
stones would c. out BIBL 100:18
Truth is the c. BERK 67:20
we c. that we are come SHAK 680:1
we still should c. BACO 45:13
crying child is ever c. WROT 833:16
c. in the wilderness BIBL 92:27
c. over spilt milk PROV 604:23
except those c. ABSE 1:5
not hear it c. HERB 372:9
crystal clear as c. BIBL 113:12
c. branches on his forehead PHIL 575:10
like unto c. BIBL 111:31
read the c. BEVA 71:15
crystals instants become c. BLY 122:15
cubes sum of two c. RAMA 621:13
Cubism C. has not been understood PICA 575:14
cubit add one c. BIBL 93:24
cuckold make her husband a c. SHAK 693:20
cuckoo as the c. is in June SHAK 668:26
c.-buds of yellow hue SHAK 681:3
c. clock FILM 311:16
C.-echoing, bell-swarmèd HOPK 384:4
C.! Shall I call thee bird WORD 832:9
c.'s parting cry ARNO 27:26
c. then, on every tree SHAK 681:3
hear the pleasant c. DAVI 252:5
Lhude sing c. ANON 18:22
merry c. SPEN 733:2
over the c.'s nest NURS 550:2
rainbow and a c.'s song DAVI 252:6
to the c.'s note GRAY 350:23
weather the c. likes HARD 361:22
cucumber c. should be well sliced JOHN 412:3
when c. is added to it MACK 486:9
cucumbers but c. after all JOHN 416:14
garden of c. BIBL 86:10
sun-beams out of c. SWIF 747:23
cud cheweth not the c. BIBL 76:20
Cuddesdon Hey for C. KETT 434:12
cuddled c. by a complete stranger ANNE 15:3
cudgel c. of the people's war TOLS 779:12
cue With a twisted c. GILB 338:10
cui *C. bono* CICE 217:25
cully Woman's c. made CONG 232:29
culpa *mea c.* MISS 520:11
O felix c. MISS 523:8
culpable How c. was he HEAN 366:10
culprits better to choose the c. PAGN 563:7
recognize them all as c. VIRG 793:19
cult What's a c. ALTM 13:1

cultivate c. our garden VOLT 797:9
C. simplicity LAMB 448:23
c. your friendship JOHN 416:24
cultiver *Il faut c. notre jardin* VOLT 797:9
cultural Australian C. Cringe PHIL 575:12
c. Chernobyl MNOU 524:14
c. identity serves FINK 313:4
c. Stalingrad BALL 52:13
culture Before French c. RENA 624:11
core of a world's c. BOLD 124:10
c. of poverty FRIE 325:6
hear the word 'c.' ESHE 301:7
hear the word c. JOHS 418:17
integral part of c. GOUL 347:9
man of c. rare GILB 338:17
men of c. ARNO 28:9
pursue C. in bands WHAR 813:3
stage in moral c. DARW 250:14
vast intuitive c. SHAF 655:14
cultures two c. SNOW 726:19
Cumae saw the Sibyl at C. ROSS 635:9
Cumaei *Ultima C.* VIRG 796:4
cumber c. you good Margaret MORE 531:13
cumbered c. about much serving BIBL 99:15
cumberless Blithesome and c. HOGG 380:14
cumin tithes of mint and c. BIBL 96:26
cunctando *c. restituit rem* ENNI 300:16
cunning C. is the dark sanctuary CHES 209:5
c. men pass for wise BACO 42:21
c. plan CATC 195:28
c. whore of Venice SHAK 693:15
produce that pitiful c. WOLL 825:24
right hand forget her c. BOOK 141:8
silence, exile, and c. JOYC 422:5
cunningly little world made c. DONN 272:26
cup after supper he took the C. BOOK 129:22
Ah, fill the c. FITZ 314:14
death in the c. BURN 167:14
fill up my c. SCOT 652:6
glory in a shallow c. FITZ 315:1
let this c. pass BIBL 97:21
my c. overflows SCOT 652:20
my c. shall be full BOOK 133:1
tak a c. o' kindness yet BURN 166:12
'twixt c. and lip PROV 612:27
welcome to my c. OLDY 553:13
Cupar will to C. maun to Cupar PROV 602:20
cupboard c. of food HERB 373:2
c. was bare NURS 549:18
Cupid C. and my Campaspe LYLY 480:14
C. is a knavish lad SHAK 690:9
C. painted blind SHAK 689:7
C.'s darts do not feel ANON 17:17
giant-dwarf, Dan C. SHAK 680:22
Cupidinesque *Veneres C.* CATU 196:34
cupidinibus *Responsare c.* HORA 390:2
cupidons all the little c. BURN 165:24
cups c., That cheer COWP 241:31
cur half lurcher and half c. COWP 242:4
cura *sedet atra C.* HORA 388:13
curable disease. But c. MACA 481:7
curantur *Similia similibus c.* MOTT 535:18
curate c. faced the laurels GRAH 348:6
like a shabby c. AUDE 35:14
name of a C. SMIT 725:4
pale young c. GILB 339:10
curates abundant shower of c. BRON 149:16
Bishops, and C. BOOK 126:17
Bishops and C. BOOK 129:13
C., long dust BROO 150:12
preached to death by wild c. SMIT 725:23
curb rusty c. SHAK 667:18
use the snaffle and the c. CAMP 183:2
curds queen of c. and cream SHAK 703:20
cure better than c. PROV 609:40
c. for admiring BAGE 46:19
c. of all diseases BROW 154:1
c. of a romantic first flame BURN 165:22
C. the disease BACO 43:3
c. thine heart BEDD 60:15
malady without a c. DRYD 282:7
no c. for birth and death SANT 644:13
no C. for this Disease BELL 63:6
No c., no pay PROV 607:45
palliate what we cannot c. JOHN 409:7
cured can't be c. must be endured PROV 613:48
c. by hanging from a string KING 437:17
c. by more democracy SMIT 723:15
C. yesterday of my disease PRIO 593:2
cures c. are suggested CHEK 208:1
Like c. like MOTT 535:18
curfew begins at c. SHAK 679:5
c. tolls the knell GRAY 350:6
curiosa *c. felicitas* PETR 574:17
curiosities c. would be quite forgot AUBR 32:12
curiosity c. about the future WAUG 806:6
c., freckles, and doubt PARK 567:2
C. killed the cat PROV 597:44
c. of individuals ARTS 29:20
Disinterested intellectual c. TREV 781:7
curious c. in unnecessary matters BIBL 91:18
Raised by that c. engine WEBS 807:22
curiouser C. and curiouser CARR 189:8
curl had a little c. LONG 475:2
curled C. minion ARNO 27:15
curlèd wealthy c. darlings SHAK 691:30
curls Frocks and C. DICK 266:19
curly C. locks, Wilt thou NURS 547:18
currency c. that buys all CERV 200:5
Debasing the moral c. ELIO 292:15
debauch the c. KEYN 435:6
one c. NAPO 538:12
current c. to the whole HOPK 385:5
c. will run with fury WOLL 825:18
icy c. SHAK 693:3
what a strong c. ideas are FLAU 316:10
currents their c. turn awry SHAK 664:4
curried short horse soon c. PROV 610:36
curry national dish is c. JEAN 404:16
curs You common cry of c. SHAK 660:8
curse c. be ended ELIO 293:26
C. God, and die BIBL 81:2
c. is come upon me TENN 762:19
c. mine enemies BIBL 77:2
c. of the drinking classes WILD 819:13
C. on his virtues ADDI 4:13
C. the blasted, jelly-boned swines LAWR 458:17
c. thine own inconstancy CARE 186:16
c. with their heart BOOK 135:21
I know how to c. SHAK 698:24
is to me a c. MASS 501:4
open foe may prove a c. GAY 332:10
real c. of Eve RHYS 625:17
terrible c. BARH 54:6
What terms to c. thee WRIG 833:15
cursed C. be the heart BALL 50:18
c. him in sleeping BARH 54:5
cursest is c. BIBL 76:28
That c. man SPEN 733:21
curses C. are like young chickens SOUT 730:14
c. from pole to pole BLAK 118:16
C., like chickens PROV 597:45
not c. heaped SORL 728:18
cursing blessing and c. BIBL 77:10
curst c. be he that moves my bones EPIT 302:10
to all succeeding ages c. DRYD 279:21
curtain Bring down the c. LAST 455:20
c. of the night PUSH 618:3
final c. comes down MAJO 491:19
iron c. CHUR 216:1
Iron C. did not reach SOLZ 727:16
kept behind a c. PAIN 564:2
lets the c. fall POPE 582:14
make a dress out of a c. POWE 590:13
putteth aside the c. BIBL 73:9
Up with the c. BROW 155:32
curtained C. with cloudy red MILT 513:28
curtains Damp c. glued HILL 376:16
fringèd c. of thine eye SHAK 698:28
gap between the lace c. GREE 352:1
curtiosity full of 'satiable c. KIPL 441:8
curtsey C. while you're thinking CARR 190:14
curveship of the c. lend a myth CRAN 243:25
Cusha Cusha! Cusha! C. INGE 399:11
cushion c. and soft Dean POPE 583:24
cuss don't matter a tinker's c. SHIN 717:4
custodes *quis custodiet ipsos C.* JUVE 424:16
custodiet *quis c. ipsos Custodes* JUVE 424:16
custody *Wragg is in c.* ARNO 28:16
custom c. and experience HUME 394:9
C. is the great guide HUME 394:6
c. lie upon thee WORD 830:4
c. loathsome to the eye JAME 402:12
C. reconciles us BURK 163:11
c. stale Her infinite variety SHAK 656:27
C. that is before all law DANI 248:17
C., that unwritten law D'AV 251:7
follow the c. AMBR 13:4
Lest one good c. TENN 760:15
receipt of c. BIBL 94:22
That monster, c. SHAK 665:22
unwritten c. supported CATT 194:17
customer c. is always right PROV 597:46
c. is never wrong RITZ 628:14
customers people of c. SMIT 723:10
customs ancient c. and its manhood ENNI 300:15
c. of his tribe SHAW 706:18
cut c. him out in little stars SHAK 697:29
c. his ear off MEDA 503:5
c. his throat before SWIF 749:27
c. my conscience to fit HELL 368:16
c. off BIBL 88:18
c. off my head CHAR 203:2
C. your coat PROV 597:47
etiquette to c. any one CARR 191:17
guardsman's c. and thrust HUXL 397:12
in the evening it is c. down BOOK 137:18
Look at the c. LOES 473:2
man who c. his country's BYRO 178:12
most unkindest c. of all SHAK 676:7
shall not be c. off BIBL 88:24
we are going to c. it off POWE 590:12
will I c. off Israel BIBL 79:16
cutpurse c. of the empire SHAK 665:18
cuts c. from Homer AESC 6:13
cutting hand the c. edge of the mind BRON 149:8
cuttlefish like a c. ORWE 559:9
Cutty-sark Weel done, C. BURN 168:17
cycle c. of Cathay TENN 763:10
cyclone crest of the South Bend c. RICE 626:5
Cyclops c. with one eye COLE 227:16
view of a paralysed c. HOCK 379:10
cylinder in terms of the c. CÉZA 200:8
cymbal talk but a tinkling c. BACO 43:1
tinkling c. BIBL 106:16
cymbals well-tuned c. BOOK 142:3
Cynara faithful to thee, C. DOWS 277:5
cynic definition of a c. WILD 818:12
cynicism C. is intellectual dandyism MERE 505:14
cynosure c. of neighbouring eyes MILT 512:20
cypress in sad c. SHAK 701:21
outside the c. groves LAWR 458:7
Cyprus rings black C. FLEC 317:5
Cyrene Libya about C. BIBL 103:16
Cyril Nice one, C. ADVE 8:3
Cythera C., so they say BAUD 57:9
Cytherean throned C. be fallen SWIN 751:6

D never use a big, big D GILB 338:25
there are your d's for you WYCH 834:11
da *D.! Da! Da* UPAN 787:16
dad girls in slacks remember D. BETJ 70:5
if the d. is present ORTO 558:1

dad (*cont.*):
They fuck you up, your mum and d. LARK 453:4
To meet their D. BURN 166:22
dada mama of d. FADI 306:2
daddy D.'s gone a-hunting NURS 547:14
D., what did you do SAYI 647:8
Dance to your d. NURS 548:1
heart belongs to d. PORT 588:9
Oh, yo' d.'s rich HEYW 376:4
daemon D. was with me KIPL 441:21
daemonum call poesy *vinum d.* BACO 41:17
daffadowndillies d., And cowslips SPEN 734:21
daffodil bed of d. sky TENN 764:6
shining d. dies TENN 764:15
daffodils d., That come before SHAK 703:17
dances with the d. WORD 828:27
Fair d., we weep HERR 374:25
host, of golden d. WORD 828:26
never saw d. so beautiful WORD 827:12
what d. were for Wordsworth LARK 453:10
When d. begin to peer SHAK 703:9
daffy D.-down-dilly NURS 548:2
daft thinks the tither d. SCOT 652:4
dagger d. of the mind SHAK 682:21
deadly daunting d. WYCH 834:11
Is this a d. SHAK 682:21
daggers d. in a hogshead SCOT 652:18
d. in men's smiles SHAK 683:22
Give me the d. SHAK 683:10
speak d. to her SHAK 665:6
daguerrotype stare from d. WARR 804:1
daily d. complaining BOOK 133:17
d. increase in thy holy Spirit BOOK 130:20
d. Labour to pursue WESL 811:3
our d. bread BIBL 93:19
dainties d. are all cates SHAK 698:7
fed of the d. SHAK 680:24
spiced d. KEAT 427:13
daintily I must have things d. served BETJ 70:10
dainty d. little woman KEYE 435:1
d. rogue in porcelain MERE 505:13
d. that is in that hous CHAU 205:23
Nothing's so d. sweet FLET 318:6
dairy doth nightly rob the d. JONS 419:18
dairymaid Queen asked the D. MILN 510:18
daisies Buttercups and d. HOWI 392:4
calaminth and d. SMAR 721:19
d. growing over me KEAT 432:1
d. pied and violets blue SHAK 681:3
D., those pearled Arcturi SHEL 713:20
foot upon twelve d. PROV 604:24
Meadows trim with d. pied MILT 512:19
Swiche as men callen d. CHAU 206:25
daisy 'd.,' or elles the 'ye of day' CHAU 206:26
d., primrose, violet THOM 775:4
Dakotas D., I am for war RED 623:10
dalliance d. in the wardrobe lies SHAK 670:30
primrose path of d. SHAK 662:9
dam pretty chickens and their d. SHAK 685:8
damage d. to the earth COUS 238:7
I can pay for the d. CLOU 221:21
MORAL OR INTELLECTUAL D. TELE 758:3
seriously d. your health OFFI 554:11
damaged Archangel a little d. LAMB 449:3
D. people are dangerous HART 363:3
damages d. his mind ANON 21:2
Damascus rivers of D. BIBL 80:18
damasked deep-d. wings KEAT 427:9
dame belle d. sans merci KEAT 428:12
belle d. sans mercy KEAT 427:14
My d. has lost her shoe NURS 547:16
nothin' like a d. HAMM 359:2
dames struts his d. before MILT 512:16
dammed saved by being d. HOOD 383:4
damn D. braces BLAK 119:22
D. the age LAMB 449:6
d. the consequences MILN 511:8
D. the torpedoes FARR 307:24
d. those authors CHUR 213:12
D. with faint praise POPE 583:7
d. you England OSBO 560:10
don't give a d. MITC 524:2
give a singel d. FLEM 317:10
I care not a d. CLOU 221:21
I don't give a d. FILM 311:7
old man who said, 'D.!' HARE 362:4
one another d. WYCH 834:13
with a spot I d. him SHAK 676:16
damnation d. of his taking-off SHAK 682:10
everlasting d. BOOK 127:3
From sleep and from d. CHES 210:8
Heap on himself d. MILT 514:18
damnations Twenty-nine distinct d. BROW 157:29
damned All silent, and all d. WORD 830:16
beautiful and d. FITZ 315:7
brandy of the d. SHAW 708:4
D. below Judas COWP 240:6
D. from here to Eternity KIPL 438:17
d. if you don't DOW 277:3
d. (looking dismally) JOHN 417:11
d. to everlasting fame POPE 586:3
d. to Fame POPE 580:14
d. would make no noise HERR 375:5
Faustus must be d. MARL 496:7
for an apple d. mankind OTWA 560:22
lies, d. lies and statistics DISR 271:8
public be d. VAND 789:12
Publish and be d. WELL 809:18
souls to be d. PROV 597:37
written a d. play REYN 625:2
damning d. those they have no mind to BUTL 172:1
damnosa *D. hereditas* GAIU 328:4
D. quid non imminuit dies HORA 388:19
damozel blessed d. ROSS 634:16
damp d. souls of housemaids ELIO 295:12
damsel d. with a dulcimer COLE 225:24
Dan D. even to Beer-sheba BIBL 78:10
Dangerous D. McGrew SERV 655:2
Danaë all D. to the stars TENN 766:3
Danaos *timeo D. et dona ferentes* VIRG 793:18
dance ae best d. e'er cam BURN 160:2
at least before they d. POPE 586:9
d. at our bridal SCOT 651:10
D., dance, dance, little lady COWA 238:9
d. is a measured pace BACO 41:15
d. it bust to bust GREN 352:15
d. round in a ring FROS 326:10
D. tiptoe, bull BUNT 160:12
d. to the music of time POWE 590:9
D. to your daddy NURS 548:1
d. with me BERL 68:5
d. wyt me, in irlaunde ANON 16:19
know the dancer from the d. YEAT 835:3
Learn then to d. DAVI 251:21
Let's face the music and d. BERL 68:8
Lord of the D. CART 192:16
Love makes them d. DAVI 251:19
Mystical d. MILT 517:3
On with the d. BYRO 174:14
see me d. the Polka GROS 354:2
They that d. must pay PROV 612:34
too far from the d. POUN 590:2
will you join the d. CARR 190:5
danced d. by the light of the moon LEAR 460:19
d. his did CUMM 247:3
d. in the morning CART 192:16
d. with the Prince of Wales FARJ 306:16
David d. before the Lord BIBL 79:4
reeled and d. WORD 827:12
remaining leaf—d. WORD 827:9
There was a star d. SHAK 691:5
ye have not d. BIBL 95:7
dancer know the d. from the dance YEAT 835:3
minion, d. ARNO 27:15
dancers Breaks time, as d. CAMP 184:2
d. are all gone under the hill ELIO 294:8
d. dancing in tune TENN 764:7
nation of d. EQUI 301:2
dances d. to an ill tune PROV 602:16
d. were procession CORB 236:13
d. with the daffodils WORD 828:27
it d. LIGN 468:1
truest expression in its d. DE M 257:1
danceth d. without music HERB 373:20
dancing [D.] a perpendicular expression SHAW 709:26
d. cheek-to-cheek BERL 68:6
d. dogs and bears HODG 379:13
D. in the chequered shade MILT 512:21
d. is love's proper exercise DAVI 251:18
d. not on a volcano FLAU 316:8
diversion was d. TURN 785:18
Fluttering and d. WORD 828:26
manners of a d. master JOHN 412:14
mature women, *d.* FRIE 325:5
past our d. days SHAK 697:6
dandy Yankee Doodle D. COHA 224:1
dandyism intellectual d. MERE 505:14
Dane paying the D.-geld KIPL 440:18
Roman than a D. SHAK 667:9
danger avoid d. ROCH 630:1
big with d. and mischief GIBB 335:5
bright face of d. STEV 740:22
d. from all men ADAM 3:4
d. from those that work HALI 357:9
D. justified privilege WAUG 806:16
D. knows full well SHAK 675:11
d. of her former tooth SHAK 684:4
d. of the past FROM 325:11
D., the spur CHAP 202:23
d. to the country VICT 792:5
everything is in d. NIET 545:13
in d. of hell fire BIBL 93:9
less d. from the wiles NASH 539:10
New Labour, new d. POLI 581:26
no d. to a man CHAP 202:16
Oft in d. WHIT 814:4
only when in d. OWEN 562:1
out of d. PROV 609:14
out of d. sit ASTE 31:12
Out of this nettle, d. SHAK 667:35
post of d. PROV 609:33
run into any kind of d. BOOK 126:13
share in the d. LUCR 479:3
so much as to be out of d. HUXL 397:14
dangerous Damaged people are d. HART 363:3
d. deceits BOOK 142:11
d. edge of things BROW 155:9
d. to know LAMB 448:8
d. to meet it alone WHAR 813:3
delays are d. in war DRYD 282:31
generalizations d. DUMA 284:16
knowledge is d. HUXL 397:14
left out he would be d. MELB 503:16
little knowledge is d. PROV 605:38
many a d. thing BISH 115:18
more d. than an idea ALAI 9:15
more d. than justice PICA 575:15
most d. man NEWS 544:8
most d. moment TOCQ 778:11
such men are d. SHAK 674:16
dangers D. by being despised BURK 165:10
d. of the seas PARK 567:17
d. of this night BOOK 126:20
d. thou canst make us scorn BURN 168:15
No d. fright him JOHN 411:15
She loved me for the d. SHAK 692:2
so many great d. BOOK 128:3
tomorrow's d. DONN 275:9
dangling d. apricocks SHAK 695:16
Daniel D. come to judgement SHAK 688:14
Danish fame of D. kings ANON 21:16
Danny hangin' D. Deever KIPL 438:10
dapper You look d. COLL 228:12
dapple d.-dawn-drawn Falcon HOPK 385:1
dappled d. things HOPK 384:14
dapples D. the drowsy east SHAK 691:23

dare d. to be poor GAY 332:18
for our unworthiness we d. not BOOK 130:6
have the courage to d. DOST 276:3
I d. not SHAK 682:15
licence to d. anything HORA 385:11
none d. call it treason HARI 362:9
O! what men d. do SHAK 691:16
Take me if you d. PANK 566:13
What man d., I dare SHAK 684:12
You who d. MERE 505:22
dared d., and done SMAR 722:13
dares that d. love attempt SHAK 697:13
Who d. do more is none SHAK 682:16
Who d. wins MOTT 535:20
Darien peak in D. CLOS 222:20
Silent, upon a peak in D. KEAT 429:21
daring d. pilot in extremity DRYD 280:1
d. young man LEYB 467:15
dark agree in the d. BACO 44:19
All cats are grey in the d. PROV 594:20
as good i' th' d. HERR 374:15
blanket of the d. SHAK 682:4
blind man in a d. room BOWE 145:19
come out of the d. MANN 494:4
comes the d. COLE 226:14
d. and bloody ground O'HA 553:6
d. and bright BYRO 178:24
d. and evil days INGR 399:17
d. and stormy night OPEN 555:25
d. and true and tender TENN 765:22
d. as night SHAK 705:26
D. as the world of man SITW 721:2
D. behind it rose the forest LONG 474:12
d., boggy, dirty GOLD 345:21
d. cold day AUDE 33:30
d., dark, dark MILT 518:14
d. into the life BERR 69:16
d. is light enough FRY 326:20
d. night of the soul FITZ 315:14
d. night of the soul MISQ 521:11
d. Satanic mills BLAK 120:1
d. summer dawns TENN 765:21
D. the sky PUSH 617:26
D. with excessive bright MILT 516:3
d. world of sin BICK 114:16
d. world where gods ROET 631:10
Duke of d. corners SHAK 686:23
fear to go in the d. BACO 42:22
go home in the d. LAST 457:13
great leap in the d. VANB 789:7
half the world is always d. LE G 462:15
hides a d. soul MILT 511:21
I knew you in the d. OWEN 562:13
In a d. wood I saw ROET 631:9
In the d. backward SHAK 698:19
In the nightmare of the d. AUDE 34:2
in thy d. streets BROO 151:9
Kept in a d. house SHAK 702:19
leap in the d. LAST 455:19
leap into the d. BROW 152:6
O d. dark dark ELIO 294:9
Out in the d. THOM 773:4
people who live in the d. SHOR 717:13
poring d. SHAK 671:8
raging in the d. YEAT 835:8
Tired of his d. dominion MERE 505:20
we are for the d. SHAK 657:23
We work in the d. JAME 403:8
What in me is d. MILT 514:9
darken Never d. my Dior again LILL 468:2
darkeneth d. counsel BIBL 81:30
darker I am the d. brother HUGH 392:17
darkest d. day COWP 240:14
d. hour PROV 597:48
darkies Oh! d., how my heart FOST 321:18
darkling D. I listen KEAT 429:13
d. plain ARNO 26:5
darkly through a glass, d. BIBL 106:16
darkness as it closes Is d. SWIN 750:17
cast off the works of d. BIBL 105:21
chains and d. MONT 526:17
Chaos and d. MARR 497:13
counteracts the powers of d. SMAR 722:6
curse the d. STEV 740:15
d. and silence LEAR 460:7
d. brings not sleep PUSH 618:3
d. comprehended it not BIBL 101:3
d. falls at Thy behest ELLE 298:6
d. of mere being JUNG 423:7
d. of the land TENN 761:29
d. visible MILT 514:12
d. was upon the face BIBL 73:10
d. which may be felt BIBL 75:37
Dawn on our d. HEBE 367:5
Downward to d. STEV 740:6
encounter d. as a bride SHAK 686:17
even d. and silence KELL 432:13
Go out into the d. HASK 363:16
Gorgon, Prince of d. SPEN 733:15
heart of an immense d. OPEN 556:10
his D. and his Brightness BYRO 179:15
horror of great d. BIBL 74:25
immense d. CONR 234:9
In me d. BONH 125:8
in the d. and the cold STEV 742:18
in the d. bind them TOLK 779:3
into outer d. BIBL 94:18
land of d. BIBL 81:12
leaves the world to d. GRAY 350:6
Lighten our d. BOOK 126:20
light excelleth d. BIBL 84:6
light is as d. BIBL 81:13
light to them that sit in d. BIBL 98:18
little d. LAUD 454:4
long in d. pined SCOT 652:23
lump bred up in d. KYD 446:9
made His d. beautiful TENN 761:18
make d. more visible EDGE 288:16
Men loved d. BIBL 101:19
ocean of d. FOX 322:7
on the shores of d. KEAT 430:14
people that walked in d. BIBL 86:28
pestilence that walketh in d. BOOK 137:22
prince of d. SHAK 679:7
rulers of the d. BIBL 108:13
Scatters the rear of d. MILT 512:16
sit in d. BOOK 139:12
sit in d. here MILT 515:15
struggling with the d. COLE 225:18
there is d. everywhere NEHR 540:5
Thou makest d. BOOK 139:5
through d. up to God TENN 761:13
two eternities of d. NABO 537:20
universal d. buries all POPE 582:14
works of d. BOOK 127:21
darksome d. road CATU 197:1
spent the d. hours GOET 343:11
darling call you d. after sex BARN 55:4
d. buds of May SHAK 704:9
d. in an urn CARE 186:12
d. man, a daarlin' man O'CA 552:12
D. of the music halls SMIT 724:3
my d. from the lions BOOK 133:24
Nature's d. GRAY 351:1
Of my d., my darling POE 579:11
old man's d. PROV 596:5
darlings wealthy curlèd d. SHAK 691:30
dart shook a dreadful d. MILT 515:22
Time shall throw a d. EPIT 304:9
darts fiery d. of the wicked BIBL 108:13
dastard d. in war SCOT 651:9
data some d. was bound to be WATS 804:16
date d. which will live in infamy ROOS 632:19
doubles your chances for a d. ALLE 12:16
keep them up to d. SHAW 707:6
last d. slides EWAR 305:8
Standards are always out of d. BENN 65:19
dateless d. bargain SHAK 698:4
dates Manna and d. KEAT 427:13
matter of d. TALL 753:8
daubed d. it with slime BIBL 75:22
daughter attorney's Elderly ugly d. GILB 339:11
bailiff's d. BALL 50:4
Carnage is thy d. WORD 830:11
Cato's d. SHAK 675:8
D. am I in my mother's house KIPL 439:19
d. of a hundred earls TENN 762:10
d. of debate ELIZ 297:1
d. of Earth and Water SHEL 711:7
d. of the gods TENN 758:16
d. of the West TENN 759:9
d. of Zion BIBL 86:10
d.'s my daughter PROV 607:17
d. went through the river BUNY 161:17
Don't put your d. on the stage COWA 238:16
ever rear a d. GAY 331:10
farmer's d. CALV 182:2
father had a d. SHAK 701:23
for the d.'s daughter SWIN 751:12
King's d. BOOK 134:16
lies London's d. THOM 772:12
Like mother, like d. PROV 605:32
Lord Ullin's d. CAMP 183:12
O my ducats! O my d. SHAK 687:23
so is her d. BIBL 89:28
Sole d. of his voice MILT 517:16
taken his little d. LONG 475:1
to my elder d. THOM 773:1
virgin-d. of the skies DRYD 282:29
wish his d. to see ANON 16:9
daughterly d. love MORE 531:13
daughters d. of men BIBL 74:15
d. of my father's house SHAK 701:25
d. of the Philistines BIBL 79:1
have three d. RICH 626:17
Kings' d. BOOK 134:15
that our d. may be BOOK 141:18
thunder, fire, are my d. SHAK 678:22
Words are men's d. MADD 489:1
words are the d. JOHN 409:4
dauntless d. on every occasion WALP 801:22
D. the slug-horn BROW 155:21
so d. in war SCOT 651:8
with d. breast GRAY 350:11
dauphin kingdom of daylight's d. HOPK 385:1
David D. his ten thousands BIBL 78:34
D. wrote the Psalms NAYL 539:24
royal D.'s city ALEX 11:10
Well done, D. ADAM 2:12
Davis Thomas D., is thy toil FERG 308:17
Davy Sir Humphrey D. BENT 67:4
daw no wiser than a d. SHAK 672:9
See-saw, Margery D. NURS 550:16
Dawley Webb from D. BETJ 71:3
dawn Between dusk and d. MÜLL 536:4
d. comes up like thunder KIPL 439:13
D. on our darkness HEBE 367:5
first d. of life EGER 289:14
grey d. is breaking CRAW 244:16
in that d. to be alive WORD 828:16
just before d. PROV 597:48
redemption's happy d. CASW 194:3
reflect the d. MACA 482:2
Rosy-fingered d. HOME 382:10
see by the d.'s early CUMM 247:4
dawning bird of d. SHAK 661:11
d. of the age of Aquarius RADO 620:4
dawns dark summer d. TENN 765:21
day Action this D. MILI 508:1
All d. long from 10 till 4 BELL 63:25
all in one d. BOIL 124:6
arrow that flieth by d. BOOK 137:22
at the latter d. BIBL 81:22
be the d. long PROV 596:2
better the d. PROV 596:11
breaks the blank d. TENN 760:29
bright d. is done SHAK 657:23
built in a d. PROV 610:17
burn thee by d. BOOK 140:12
d. becomes more solemn SHEL 711:17
d. brought back my night MILT 519:2
D. by day BOOK 126:2
d. is at hand BIBL 105:21

day (*cont.*):
d. is past TICH 777:10
d. is short TALM 753:16
d. joins the past eternity BYRO 174:25
d. may bring forth BIBL 83:27
d. of his death AUDE 33:30
d. of his wrath is come BIBL 112:6
d. of small nations CHAM 200:14
d. of the Lord is near BIBL 90:15
d. of vengeance BIBL 89:5
d. of wrath MISS 523:3
d. or a brief period ARIS 24:17
d.'s at the morn BROW 157:12
D.'s azure eyes SHEL 712:5
d.'s garish eye MILT 512:10
d. star arise BIBL 111:8
d. that I die MCLE 486:15
d. the music died MCLE 486:14
d. Thou gavest, Lord ELLE 298:6
d.-to-day business LAFO 447:16
d. war broke out CATC 195:8
d. when heaven was falling HOUS 390:9
d. which the Lord hath made BOOK 140:6
death of each d.'s life SHAK 683:8
dwell in realms of d. BLAK 118:7
each d. dies with sleep HOPK 384:13
each d. that has dawned HORA 386:17
end of a perfect d. BOND 125:6
end of this d.'s business SHAK 676:31
Every d. dawned clear RACI 619:20
every d. that Fate allows HORA 387:20
every d. to be lost JOHN 417:19
Every d. we die JERO 406:16
Every dog has his d. PROV 599:23
Ev'ry d. a little dies SOND 727:22
first d. BIBL 73:11
first, last, everlasting d. DONN 273:18
gold of the d. CROS 246:4
Good things of d. SHAK 684:7
heat of the d. BIBL 96:18
I have lost a d. TITU 777:16
Joy ruled the d. DRYD 282:17
knell of parting d. GRAY 350:6
lark at break of d. SHAK 704:15
Let the d. perish BIBL [illegible]
life's little d. LYTE 480:23
long d.'s journey O'NE 554:20
long d. wanes TENN 767:12
Lord went before them by d. BIBL 76:5
make my d. FILM 311:8
Mars a d. ADVE 7:43
met them at close of d. YEAT 835:18
murmur of a summer's d. ARNO 27:4
night and d., brother BORR 143:9
night succeeds thy little d. EPIT 303:13
no d. for me to look upon SHAK 702:27
not a second on the d. COOK 235:15
not yet near d. SHAK 697:32
now is the d. of salvation BIBL 107:8
Now's the d. BURN 168:7
of this immortal d. SHEL 713:15
on an ordinary d. WOOL 826:13
one d. in thy courts BOOK 137:13
on the Lord's d. BIBL 111:19
penance for a d. WORD 831:4
perfect d. nor night SHAK 672:27
robs us of the fair d. HORA 389:7
rule the d. BIBL 73:13
seize the d. HORA 387:22
sinks the d.-star MILT 513:10
So foul and fair a d. SHAK 681:14
spent one whole d. THOM 771:5
Sufficient unto the d. BIBL 93:27
Sufficient unto the d. PROV 611:34
They have their d. TENN 760:20
think each d. your own EURI 304:17
this d. as if thy last KEN 433:1
thou d. in night SHAK 697:28
through her busy d. JAGG 401:5
to a summer's d. SHAK 704:9
tomorrow is another d. CLOS 222:1
tomorrow is another d. MITC 524:3
Tomorrow is another d. PROV 613:10
Until the d. break BIBL 85:12
unto the perfect d. BIBL 82:11
wave's intenser d. SHEL 712:14
weary d. have end SPEN 733:9
welcome d. BUNY 161:17
who can say each d. HORA 388:23
Without all hope of d. MILT 518:14
write every other d. DOUG 276:20

daydream American d. BROD 149:4

daylight but the d. sick SHAK 688:28
d. in upon magic BAGE 47:4
kind of d. ADDI 5:7
kingdom of d.'s dauphin HOPK 385:1
long and lone d. SHEL 714:11
We burn d. SHAK 688:33

Dayrolles Give D. a chair LAST 455:15

days all the d. of my life BOOK 133:1
behold these present d. SHAK 705:10
best d. of life VIRG 796:20
brave d. of old MACA 483:7
burnt-out ends of smoky d. ELIO 295:19
Cast your mind on other d. YEAT 837:21
chequerboard of nights and d. FITZ 314:15
d. are evil BIBL 108:8
d. are in the yellow leaf BYRO 178:22
d. are swifter BIBL 81:10
D. are where we live LARK 452:14
d. darken round me TENN 760:14
d. grow short ANDE 14:10
d. of Methuselah BIBL 74:14
d. of wine and roses DOWS 277:7
d. on the earth are as a shadow BIBL 80:29
d. that are no more TENN 765:19
E'er half my d. MILT 518:29
fair well-spoken d. SHAK 696:11
first 1,000 d. KENN 433:13
former d. were better BIBL 84:15
forty d. it will remain PROV 610:20
good d. speed and depart MART 498:1
in length of d. BIBL 81:16
in the house three d. SHAW 708:13
in the midst of his d. BIBL 89:20
Length of d. BIBL 82:8
multitude of d. JOHN 411:17
number of my d. BOOK 133:23
number our d. BOOK 137:20
of few d. BIBL 81:18
only three d. old JEAN 404:17
O ye Nights, and D. BOOK 126:6
see better d. BEHN 62:12
seemed but a few d. BIBL 75:4
Six d. shalt thou labour BIBL 76:11
six working d. SIDD 718:1
Ten d. that shook the world REED 624:3
that thy d. may be long BIBL 76:13
Three whole d. together SUCK 745:10
two d. like a tiger TIPU 777:15
We have seen better d. SHAK 699:19

daytime cry in the d. BOOK 132:21
d. television TOYN 780:7

daze d. with little bells HUGO 393:21

dazzle d. for an hour MORE 531:3
mine eyes d. WEBS 808:2

dazzled D. thus with height WOTT 833:4
Eyes still d. LIND 469:9

dea *vera incessu patuit d.* VIRG 793:12

dead act as if we were d. POUN 589:19
already three parts d. RUSS 639:18
among the d. BIBL 100:31
and Guildenstern are d. SHAK 667:13
and the noble D. WORD 831:9
Ay, d. BROW 158:15
barrows of the happier d. TENN 767:2
being d. BENT 67:3
best men are d. PUNC 617:20
Better red than d. POLI 581:6
better than a d. lion PROV 605:47
bivouac of the d. O'HA 553:5
Blessed are the d. BIBL 112:26
character d. at every word SHER 716:12
cold and pure and very d. LEWI 467:6
completely consistent are the d. HUXL 397:1
composer is to be d. HONE 382:12
conference With the d. WEBS 807:23
converse with the mighty d. THOM 775:16
cut in half; he's d. GRAH 348:4
D.! and never called me WOOD 826:7
D. battles, like d. generals TUCH 784:15
d. Body wears PLAT 577:15
d.-born from the press. HUME 395:3
d. bury the dead PROV 605:21
d. bury their dead BIBL 94:20
d., but in the Elysian fields DISR 271:1
d. by fate BEAU 58:14
d. donkey DICK 265:19
d. don't die LAWR 458:21
D., for a ducat SHAK 665:12
d. for the duration ASQU 30:21
D. he is not LONG 474:1
d. he would like to see me HOLL 381:1
d. level ELIO 293:4
d. lion BIBL 84:20
d. man's town SPRI 735:11
D. men don't bite PROV 597:49
d. men lost their bones ELIO 296:4
d. men's shoes PROV 604:35
D. men tell no tales PROV 597:50
dead Past bury its d. LONG 474:5
d. rest well CLAR 218:11
D., Right Reverends DICK 261:5
d. shall be raised incorruptible BIBL 107:3
d. shall go down to thee SWIN 751:6
d. shall live DRYD 282:23
d. shall not have died in vain LINC 468:13
d. sinner BIER 114:25
d. that the rain rains on PROV 596:26
d. there is no rivalry MACA 481:20
d. these two years CHES 209:25
dead which are already d. BIBL 84:9
d. which he slew at his death BIBL 78:8
d. woman bites not GRAY 350:1
d. writers are remote ELIO 296:19
democracy of the d. CHES 211:9
doors of the d. RILK 628:3
Down among the d. DYER 287:2
dread a d.-level of income TAWN 755:13
Either he's d. FILM 311:4
ere I am laid out d. HERR 374:4
Evelyn Hope is d. BROW 155:28
face of the d. BEER 61:18
famous calm and d. BROW 155:31
fell at his feet as d. BIBL 111:22
food that d. men eat DOBS 271:15
fortnight d. ELIO 296:12
found, when she was d. GOLD 344:21
God is d. FROM 325:11
grand to be blooming well d. SARO 644:18
had already been d. a year LEHR 462:18
Harrow the house of the d. AUDE 35:6
healthy and wealthy and d. THUR 777:1
Hector is d. SHAK 700:25
He is d. and gone, lady SHAK 666:1
He is d., the sweet musician LONG 474:14
he is d., who will not fight GREN 352:17
home among the d. SHEL 711:9
HOMER d. ANON 18:18
if the d. rise not BIBL 106:24
If the d. talk to you SZAS 752:2
if two of them are d. PROV 612:46
immortal d. who live again ELIO 293:11
In praise of ladies d. SHAK 705:9
judge the quick and the d. BOOK 126:10
King of all these the d. HOME 382:11
know that thou wert d. CONS 235:4
lain for a century d. TENN 764:10
lang time d. MOTT 535:3
Lilacs out of the d. land ELIO 295:26
Lycidas is d. MILT 512:27
mansions of the d. CRAB 242:27
millions of the mouthless d. SORL 728:18
Mistah Kurtz—he d. CONR 234:14
more than the d. ARNO 26:1
more to say when I am d. ROBI 629:12

My d. king JOYC 422:1
No one wept for the d. AGNO 8:26
not absolutely d. things MILT 519:7
not d.—but gone ROGE 631:13
not d., but sleepeth BIBL 94:28
Not many d. COCK 223:15
Of their d. selves TENN 760:22
only the d. smiled AKHM 9:9
on the d. man's chest STEV 741:18
oure kyng wes d. WYNT 834:16
our English d. SHAK 671:5
past is the only d. thing THOM 772:24
past never d. FAUL 307:25
pay for my d. people JOSE 421:9
people will have to be d. GEOG 333:8
quick, and the d. DEWA 259:15
quite for ever d. CONG 232:27
rather be d. than cool COBA 223:6
remind me of the d. SASS 645:19
resurrection of the d. BIBL 107:1
saying 'Lord Jones D.' CHES 211:20
sculptured d. KEAT 427:4
sea gave up the d. BIBL 113:6
Sea shall give up her d. BOOK 142:6
see a d. Indian SHAK 698:32
sheeted d. Did squeak SHAK 661:9
She, she is d. DONN 272:8
simplify me when I'm d. DOUG 276:15
sleeping and the d. SHAK 683:10
speak ill of the d. PROV 607:37
Stone-d. hath no fellow PROV 611:26
Strike them all d. DICK 264:20
talks you d. JOHN 411:9
There are no d. MAET 489:7
they're a' d. TOAS 778:2
think you are d. or deported HOWE 392:3
thirteen men lay d. HEAN 366:17
those who are d. BURK 163:29
told me you were d. CORY 237:13
to the d. we owe only truth VOLT 798:5
very d. of Winter ANDR 14:15
very d. of winter ELIO 294:27
voice of the d. TENN 762:7
waken the d. GRAY 349:10
was alive and is d. EPIT 303:1
was d., and is alive BIBL 100:6
water—fire live—and we d. BYRO 177:8
ways of being d. DAWK 253:2
we are all d. KEYN 435:11
Weep me not d. DONN 274:21
wench is d. MARL 496:18
we, that are d. to sin BIBL 104:37
what was d. was Hope WILD 819:1
When I am d. MCGO 485:11
When I am d. ROSS 634:13
Where d. men meet BUTL 173:2
where there was not one d. BIBL 76:3
wife, or himself must be d. AUST 39:6
without works is d. BIBL 110:17
with the enduring d. SHEL 710:22
would that I were d. TENN 763:19
you're ten years d. HAYE 365:1
deaded told you I'd be d. CATC 196:32
deadener Habit is a great d. BECK 60:4
deadlines daily d. ZOLA 840:15
deadlock Holy d. HERB 371:17
deadly more d. in the long run TWAI 786:6
more d. than the male KIPL 438:15
more d. than the male PROV 600:17
Dead Sea apples on the D.'s shore BYRO 174:16
Like D. fruits MOOR 530:19
deaf d. as an adder ADAM 3:3
d., how should they know SORL 728:18
d. husband PROV 598:1
d., inexorable SIDN 718:5
none so d. as those PROV 612:32
prove me d. and blind BROW 158:5
turn the d. ear SWIF 749:6
deafer d. the blue-eyed cat TENN 759:24
deafness would cure d. SHAK 698:20
deal new d. for the American people ROOS 632:11
square d. afterwards ROOS 633:6
deals D. are my art form TRUM 784:11
dean cushion and soft D. POPE 583:24
I am the D. SPRI 735:9
no dogma, no D. DISR 271:6
sly shade of a Rural D. BROO 150:12
deans dowagers for d. TENN 765:12
dear bread should be so d. HOOD 383:1
dangerously d. BYRO 175:17
D. 338171 COWA 239:5
D. dead women BROW 158:11
D., dirty Dublin JOYC 421:16
d. in the sight BOOK 140:4
d. to them that love her SPRI 735:7
Far-fetched and d.-bought PROV 600:12
fault, d. Brutus SHAK 674:13
Plato is d. to me ARIS 25:9
sold cheap what is most d. SHAK 705:13
this dear, d. land SHAK 694:19
too d. for my possessing SHAK 705:4
dearer D. than self BYRO 174:3
d. unto me BOOK 140:8
d. was the mother COLE 227:2
Or was there a d. one HOOD 382:14
dearest d. thing he owed SHAK 681:23
d., you're a dunce JOHN 416:22
near'st and d. enemy SHAK 668:27
she's the d. girl DICK 262:1
dearie For thinking on my d. BURN 166:15
deario cheerio my d. MARQ 497:6
dearly D. beloved BOOK 130:22
D. beloved brethren BOOK 125:13
dearth in a year of d. BLAK 119:17
death abolish the d. penalty KARR 425:20
accused of child d. RICH 626:12
afraid of d. BROW 153:24
After the first d. THOM 772:12
All Life d. does end HOPK 384:13
ancients dreaded d. HARE 362:3
angel of d. BRIG 148:9
Angel of D. BYRO 175:24
another terror to d. LYND 480:20
any man's d. diminishes me DONN 275:3
at the point of d. SHAK 698:2
back resounded D. MILT 515:24
bargain to engrossing d. SHAK 698:4
Be absolute for d. SHAK 686:16
beautiful and d.-struck year HOUS 391:6
before his d. BIBL 91:26
betwixt life and d. WORD 831:23
Birth, and copulation, and d. ELIO 295:23
black d.'s wing AKHM 9:6
Black Widow, d. LOWE 478:3
body of this d. BIBL 105:5
born for d. KEAT 429:14
bridegroom in my d. SHAK 657:15
brooding over d. HILL 376:16
brother of d. BROW 154:5
Brother to D. DANI 249:1
Brother to D. FLET 318:9
Brought d. into the world MILT 514:7
brought d. into the world TWAI 786:21
brought sin and d. STAN 736:9
build the house of d. MONT 527:9
build your ship of d. LAWR 458:12
by man came d. BIBL 106:22
Call in thy d.'s-head there HERB 372:7
came d. into the world BIBL 91:7
caught his d. FABY 305:22
chance, and d. SHEL 713:14
citizens of d.'s grey land SASS 645:18
Come away, come away, d. SHAK 701:21
Comes d. BARN 55:10
coming up to d. SAUN 646:1
consenting unto his d. BIBL 103:22
could not stop for D. DICK 266:6
covenant with d. BIBL 87:14
covenant with d. GARR 330:11
day of his d. AUDE 33:30
day of our Jubilee is d. BROW 153:25
dead which he slew at his d. BIBL 78:8
Dear, beauteous d. VAUG 790:13
d. after life SPEN 733:22
D. alone reveals JUVE 425:1
d. a long-felt want TREE 781:6
D. and his brother SHEL 713:17
d. and taxes DEFO 254:15
d. and taxes FRAN 323:15
d. and taxes PROV 608:12
D. and taxes and childbirth MITC 524:1
D. and Toil VIRG 794:20
d. bandaged my eyes BROW 157:17
D. be not proud DONN 272:22
D. cancels everything HAZL 365:15
D. closes all TENN 767:12
[D.] comes equally DONN 275:5
d. concerns the gods SOPH 728:13
d. could not daunt BALL 51:5
D. devours all lovely things MILL 509:15
D., ere thou hast slain another EPIT 304:9
d. ever life devouring ALAB 9:14
D.! Great proprietor YOUN 839:4
d. . . . had been his next-door neighbour SCOT 651:28
d. had undone so many ELIO 296:1
D. has a thousand doors MASS 501:6
D. has got something AMIS 13:19
D. has made His darkness TENN 761:18
D. hath asses' ears BEDD 60:17
d. hath no more dominion BIBL 105:1
D. hath so many doors FLET 318:4
d. hath ten thousand WEBS 808:1
D., in itself, is nothing DRYD 281:2
d. in life ANON 17:22
D. in Life TENN 765:21
d. in the cup BURN 167:14
d. in the pot BIBL 80:16
D. is a fearful thing SHAK 686:18
D. is a master from Germany CELA 199:10
d. is but a groom DONN 273:8
D. is dead, not he SHEL 711:2
d. is in our own BROW 153:26
D. is like a fisherman TURG 785:6
[D. is] nature's way ANON 15:22
[D. is] nature's way SAYI 647:9
d. is not far behind WESL 811:21
D. is nothing at all HOLL 381:2
D. is still working HERB 372:19
d. is the cure BROW 154:1
D. is the end of life TENN 763:13
D. is the great leveller PROV 598:2
D. is the only great emotion FULL 327:6
D. is the privilege ROWE 636:11
d. i' the other SHAK 674:8
D. joins us to YOUN 839:15
D. lays his icy hand SHIR 717:8
D. lies dead SWIN 750:19
D. lies on her SHAK 697:37
D. like a narrow sea WATT 805:17
D. must be distinguished SMIT 725:26
D. never takes the wise man LA F 447:13
d., nor life BIBL 105:12
d. of a great man ADDI 4:19
d. of air ELIO 294:15
d. of a political economist BAGE 47:9
D. of a salesman MILL 509:19
d. of each day's life SHAK 683:8
d. of his saints BOOK 140:4
d. of kings SHAK 695:9
d. of princes SHAK 675:9
d. on the hunting-field MORT 533:9
D. . . . openeth the gate BACO 42:25
d. or Santa Claus BERN 69:9
d. part thee and me BIBL 78:12
D. pays all debts PROV 598:3
d. reveals the eminent SHAW 708:27
D.'s artifact ABSE 1:7
D.'s bright angel PROC 593:14
d. shall have no dominion THOM 772:1
d.-shot glowing BYRO 173:23
d.'s pale flag SHAK 698:3

death (*cont.*):
D. stepped tacitly BROW 158:7
d. that is immortal LUCR 479:7
d., the grand physician CLAR 218:11
d. the journey's end DRYD 282:11
D., the most awful of evils EPIC 300:21
D. therefore is nothing LUCR 479:5
d., The undiscovered country SHAK 664:4
D. thou shalt die DONN 272:23
d.-tick is audible CURZ 248:5
D. was but a scientific fact WILD 818:33
d., where is thy sting BIBL 107:4
D., where is thy sting-a-ling MILI 508:13
D. who comes at last SCOT 651:6
d., who had the soldier singled DOUG 276:16
D. will be aghast MISS 523:4
D. will come SHEL 714:12
d. will have his day SHAK 695:7
d. will provide the meaning ALAI 10:2
d. with one's will JAIN 401:19
D., without rhetoric SIEY 719:2
D. would summon Everyman HEAN 366:9
Defer not charities till d. BACO 43:30
did not care a whit for d. SOCR 726:25
die a dry d. SHAK 698:18
died a good d. ACHE 1:10
direful d. indeed FLEM 317:10
disqualified by the accident of d. CHES 211:10
doth d. lie heavily SENE 654:21
Do we take up in d. SHIR 717:11
dull cold ear of d. GRAY 350:10
easeful D. KEAT 429:13
eaten to d. with rust SHAK 669:27
ere her d. TENN 760:18
Even d. is unreliable BECK 60:8
everyone expected d. AGNO 8:26
everything except d. PROV 612:5
evidence of life after d. SOPE 728:10
Ev'ry day a little d. SOND 727:22
faithful unto d. BIBL 111:25
faith that looks through d. WORD 830:9
Fear d. BROW 157:16
fed on the fullness of d. SWIN 751:5
feed on D. SHAK 705:25
feet go down to d. [illegible]
fierceness of harsh d. VIRG 796:20
film of d. KEAT 430:13
Finality is d. STEP 738:3
finished by a d. BYRO 176:21
fled and cried out D. MILT 515:24
forced marches, battles and d. GARI 329:17
Found d. in life COLE 225:10
from d. lead me to UPAN 787:9
gave d. time to live GUIB 354:16
Glad to d.'s mystery HOOD 382:16
go on living even after d. FRAN 323:6
hard at d.'s door BOOK 139:13
her own d.-warrant BAGE 47:3
high Capital, where kingly D. SHEL 710:15
His means of d. SHAK 666:9
his name that sat on him was d. BIBL 112:5
hour of d. BOOK 127:8
hour of my d. KEAT 431:16
I am become d. OPPE 557:2
If there wasn't d. SMIT 725:2
image of d. ELIO 293:8
improved by d. SAKI 642:1
in d.'s dark vale SCOT 652:20
interest in d. JAME 403:26
in that sleep of d. SHAK 664:3
in their d. not divided BIBL 79:2
in the shadow of d. BIBL 98:18
in the valley of D. TENN 757:15
Into the jaws of D. TENN 757:17
I signed my d. warrant COLL 229:2
isn't sex but d. SONT 728:6
just, and mighty D. RALE 621:7
keep a league till d. SHAK 695:25
Keeps D. his court SHAK 695:10
keys of hell and of d. BIBL 111:23
laws of d. RUSK 639:4
Lead me from d. to life KUMA 446:5
liberty, or give me d. HENR 371:3
life forget and d. remember SWIN 751:10
Life, the shadow of d. SWIN 750:9
life went through with d. FORT 321:7
living d. MILT 518:16
love is strong as d. BIBL 86:7
love thee better after d. BROW 154:22
make d. proud SHAK 657:20
make one in love with d. SHEL 710:12
man after his d. CHAU 205:16
Man has created d. YEAT 835:15
matter of life and d. SHAN 706:6
Men fear d. BACO 42:22
messenger of D. SACK 641:4
Morning after D. DICK 266:11
much possessed by d. ELIO 296:16
must hate and d. return SHEL 711:13
My name is D. SOUT 730:18
new terror to d. WETH 812:22
no cure for birth and d. SANT 644:13
No d. in my lifetime HEAN 367:1
no drinking after d. FLET 318:1
no mean of d. SHAK 675:20
no one his d. SENE 654:20
no one knew my d. ROET 631:11
not at their d. MONT 528:7
not d., but dying FIEL 309:14
nothing but d. AUST 39:15
nothing but d. UNAM 787:6
Now boast thee, d. SHAK 658:4
O D. BURN 167:27
of the sovereign is d. MORE 531:10
one fear, D.'s shadow BLUN 122:10
one life and one d. BROW 156:9
only nervousness or d. LEBO 461:8
owe God a d. SHAK 670:8
owest God a d. SHAK 669:7
Pale D. breaks HORA 387:16
perchance of D. THOM 775:21
preached to d. by wild curates SMIT 725:23
prepare as though for d. MANS 494:9
put it to a violent d. ETHE 301:12
reaction to her d. ELIZ 297:17
remedy is d. CHAM 201:5
[illegible] Hazard and d. BOLA 124:9
rendezvous with D. SEEG 653:5
Reports of my d. TWAI 786:28
Revenge triumphs over d. BACO 42:23
run the race with D. JOHN 417:17
say to the Angel of D. MIDR 507:16
seasonal eternity of d. TATE 755:5
seeds of the d. of any state HOBB 378:24
seen birth and d. ELIO 295:1
set d. aside TURG 785:4
shadow of d. BIBL 81:12
shadow of d. BIBL 86:28
shadow of d. BOOK 139:12
shadow of d. BROW 152:12
shall be destroyed is d. BIBL 106:23
shall men seek d. BIBL 112:15
sharpness of d. BOOK 126:1
sin, d., and Hell BUNY 161:13
sleep, d.'s counterfeit SHAK 683:19
snares of d. BOOK 140:1
so cheap a d. DONN 273:27
some one's d. BROW 155:7
soul shall taste of d. KORA 444:5
stars of d. AKHM 9:10
still from d. was flying THOM 775:1
stroke of d. JOHN 410:8
studied in his d. SHAK 681:23
sudden d. BOOK 127:6
suffers at his d. LA B 446:16
suicide 25 years after his d. BEAV 59:5
swallow up d. in victory BIBL 87:11
Swarm over, D. BETJ 71:4
talks of Arthur's d. SHAK 677:16
Ten years after your d. HUGH 393:9
than a noble d. EURI 304:20
than frightened to d. SURT 747:1
there shall be no more d. BIBL 113:8
This fell sergeant, d. SHAK 667:7
Those by d. are few JEFF 405:15
thoughts so crowded with d. GUNN 354:20
thou shell of d. MIDD 507:6
thou wilt bring me to d. BIBL 81:27
till d. us do part BOOK 131:5
timing of your d. TACI 752:11
to be carnally minded is d. BIBL 105:6
triumph over d. and sin SPEN 733:3
true to thee till d. FABE 305:14
truly longed for d. TENN 767:7
universe of d. MILT 515:21
up the line to d. SASS 645:15
valley of the shadow of d. BOOK 133:1
vasty hall of d. ARNO 26:23
very quiet d. WEBS 808:4
wages of sin is d. BIBL 105:2
way to dusty d. SHAK 685:22
we are in d. BOOK 131:13
week of d. DONN 274:25
What life and d. is CHAP 202:16
What should it know of d. WORD 832:14
When d. approached GIBB 336:4
While there is d. CROS 246:12
Why fear d. LAST 457:18
yet afraid of d. CHUR 213:23
deathbed near the d. fiercer grows WINC 822:19
deathless sense of some d. shame WEBS 808:10
deaths After so many d. I live HERB 372:17
by feigned d. to die DONN 274:13
million d. a statistic STAL 736:5
More d. than one must die WILD 819:2
death sentence take the d. without a whimper LAWR 458:24
debasing D. the moral currency ELIO 292:15
debatable d. line MACA 482:17
debate daughter of d. ELIZ 297:1
Rupert of D. BULW 160:5
debonair blithe, and d. MILT 512:13
deboshed Thou d. fish SHAK 699:2
debout *D.! les damnés* POTT 589:5
debt Ambition's d. is paid SHAK 675:17
d. by disputation BUTL 171:18
d. of nature FABY 305:21
deeper in d. TRAV 781:2
in love, and in d. BROM 149:6
national d. HAMI 358:13
National D. is a very Good Thing SELL 654:12
Out of d. PROV 609:14
pay a d. to pleasure ROCH 630:6
promise made is a d. unpaid SERV 654:23
war, an' a d. LOWE 477:12
we are in d. MUMF 536:5
debtor d. to his profession BACO 41:26
I am d. BIBL 104:25
debts Death pays all d. PROV 598:3
forgive us our d. BIBL 93:19
pays all d. SHAK 699:4
so we can pay our d. NYER 552:3
Speak not of my d. PROV 611:16
decade fun to be in the same d. ROOS 633:2
now in the Me D. WOLF 825:15
decay Change and d. LYTE 480:23
D. with imprecision ELIO 294:5
decrepitude, their d. LAND 450:7
flourish after first d. SPEN 733:27
found its d. COCK 223:12
human things are subject to d. DRYD 281:35
of a nature to d. PALI 564:19
our love hath no d. DONN 273:18
to many men's d. SPEN 734:12
decayed sufficiently d. GILB 338:16
decays Mere glimmering and d. VAUG 790:12
restore the d. DENN 258:2
deceased He first d. WOTT 833:3
name of the late d. KIPL 439:18
decede *d. peritis* HORA 387:10
deceit used no d. in his tongue BOOK 132:7
deceitful children of d. are d. BOOK 135:22
d. and wicked man BOOK 134:9
heart is d. BIBL 89:19

deceits dangerous d. BOOK 142:11
d. of the world BOOK 127:5
prophesy d. BIBL 87:15
deceive Bred to d. IRWI 400:6
D. boys with toys LYSA 480:22
d. ourselves BIBL 111:11
Let no man d. you BIBL 108:7
Oh, don't d. me SONG 729:4
practise to d. SCOT 651:12
Who could d. a lover VIRG 794:11
deceived d. with ornament SHAK 688:3
desire to be d. BUTL 171:11
deceiver foe to the D. ZORO 841:10
gay d. COLM 229:16
deceivers Men were d. ever SHAK 691:7
deceiving d. elf KEAT 429:15
nearly d. your friends CORN 237:6
December D. when they wed SHAK 659:20
drear nighted D. KEAT 428:1
May to D. ANDE 14:10
meetings made D. June TENN 761:26
old D.'s bareness SHAK 705:8
Decembers fifteen wild D. BRON 150:2
decencies dwell in d. POPE 583:14
decency D. is Indecency's conspiracy SHAW 708:26
Terrible that old life of d. LOWE 477:20
ultimate d. of things STEV 742:10
want of d. DILL 267:14
decent d. obscurity GIBB 336:2
d. people live beyond SAKI 642:3
decently d. and in order BIBL 106:18
deception D. is not as creative SAUN 646:1
decide ministers d. THAT 770:9
moment to d. LOWE 477:15
not in my power to d. VIRG 796:2
decision losses from a delayed d. GALB 328:10
make a 'realistic d.' MCCA 484:3
monologue is not a d. ATTL 32:6
multitudes in the valley of d. BIBL 90:15
will or d. CHOM 212:12
decisions regard as important the d. PARK 567:24
deck boy stood on the burning d. HEMA 369:5
d. her mistress' head BYRO 179:2
from the bottom of the d. SHAP 706:11
given a fair d. SCHE 646:12
stood on the burning d. OPEN 555:9
Walk the d. my Captain lies WHIT 815:5
decked should have been duly d. SPEN 733:10
thy bride-bed to have d. SHAK 666:28
declaration no d. of war EDEN 288:6
declare d., if thou hast understanding BIBL 81:31
d. the glory of God BOOK 132:14
nothing to d. WILD 819:12
ye are to d. it BOOK 130:21
declared d. how much he knew GOLD 344:14
decline management of d. ARMS 25:21
weary Night's d. BLAK 118:19
writing the d. and fall GIBB 335:25
declined Carrie rightly d. GROS 354:5
decoded Coward d. for the British LAHR 448:3
decomposing personalities d. WOOL 826:12
deconstructionism what d. was ATWO 32:9
decorate painting not made to d. PICA 575:16
decorated d., and got rid of CICE 218:2
decoration construct a d. TROL 782:3
decorative to be d. and to do right FIRB 313:5
decorum athwart Goes all d. SHAK 686:1
cant about D. BURN 167:21
Dulce et d. est HORA 388:14
Dulce et d. est OWEN 562:8
hunt D. down BYRO 178:6
Regularity and D. COOP 236:7
decoyed d. into our condition PEPY 573:10
decrease d. day after day LAO 452:2
decree d. from Caesar Augustus BIBL 98:19
establish the d. BIBL 90:5
hear de D. WHAR 813:4
decrees d. may not change KING 436:10
dedicate d. your volumes CLAR 219:15
deduction d. from the smallest EINS 291:2
Dee Across the sands of D. KING 437:9
Lived on the river D. BICK 114:14
deed attempt and not the d. SHAK 683:5
better day, the worse d. HENR 370:14
better the d. PROV 596:11
bloody d. SHAK 665:13
d. is all, the glory nothing GOET 343:3
d. of dreadful note SHAK 684:6
d.'s creature MIDD 507:5
d. without a name SHAK 684:21
one good d. SHAK 700:3
right d. for the wrong reason ELIO 295:15
so I may do the d. KEAT 430:3
So shines a good d. SHAK 688:26
tak the d. LYDG 480:11
deeds d. of the past DAVI 252:19
d. were evil BIBL 101:19
Foul d. will rise SHAK 662:7
gentle mind by gentle d. SPEN 734:11
My d. upon my head SHAK 688:12
nameless in worthy d. BROW 153:7
Our d. determine us ELIO 291:20
deedy at all d. COMP 230:19
deep commit his body to the d. BOOK 142:6
coveredst it with the d. BOOK 139:1
cradle of the d. WILL 819:20
d. almost as life WORD 830:4
D. and crisp and even NEAL 540:2
d. are dumb RALE 620:16
d. as a well SHAK 697:22
D. as first love TENN 765:21
D. in the shady sadness KEAT 427:22
d. silent slide away SIDN 718:6
d. sleep of England ORWE 558:13
D.-versed in books MILT 518:10
face of the d. BIBL 73:10
From the great d. TENN 759:15
heard the d. behind him TENN 760:13
I am not d. BALZ 53:3
Not d. the Poet sees ARNO 26:24
One d. calleth another BOOK 134:7
one is of the d. STEP 737:21
Out of the d. BOOK 141:1
Plunge it into d. water HORA 389:4
slimy bottom of the d. SHAK 696:17
spirits from the vasty d. SHAK 668:19
Still waters run d. PROV 611:22
thunders of the upper d. TENN 762:8
too d. for tears WORD 830:10
wonders in the d. BOOK 139:14
deepens d. like a coastal shelf LARK 453:5
deeper d. sense of her loss GASK 330:19
d. than did ever plummet SHAK 699:10
d. than the sea BALL 51:10
In d. reverence praise WHIT 816:5
deer a-chasing the d. BURN 168:1
D. walk upon our mountains STEV 740:6
dying d. AYTO 40:11
I was a stricken d. COWP 241:24
red-d.'s herd BYRO 178:10
running of the d. SONG 729:10
stare of the d. WILB 817:4
stricken d. SHAK 665:1
Deever hangin' Danny D. KIPL 438:10
défauts *âme est sans d.* RIMB 628:12
defeat d. is an orphan CIAN 217:3
In d.; defiance CHUR 216:16
In d. unbeatable CHUR 216:10
possibilities of d. VICT 792:8
this world's d. VAUG 790:5
triumph and d. LONG 474:2
defeated d. in a great battle LIVY 470:11
Down with the d. LIVY 470:10
history to the d. AUDE 35:8
Love is never d. JOHN 408:5
safe course for the d. VIRG 794:5
defeats Dewey d. Truman NEWS 544:3
defect fair d. of nature MILT 517:23
she did make d. perfection SHAK 656:26
defence at one gate to make d. MILT 518:18
best form of d. PROV 595:28
d. against the atom bomb ANON 15:14
D., not defiance MOTT 535:6
d. of the country ARIS 24:14
d. of the indefensible ORWE 559:10
house of d. BOOK 137:23
in d. of one's country HOME 382:6
Lord is thy d. BOOK 140:12
Never make a d. CHAR 202:25
only d. against betrayal WILL 820:13
only d. is in offence BALD 49:8
our d. is sure WATT 805:19
think of the d. of England BALD 49:9
defend d. my cause BOOK 134:9
D., O Lord BOOK 130:20
d. ourselves with guns GOEB 342:9
d. to the death your right MISQ 521:14
d. us from all perils BOOK 126:20
D. us thy humble servants BOOK 126:12
nothing left to d. SHEN 715:11
defendants whole number of the d. CROM 245:11
defended God abandoned, these d. HOUS 390:9
defending d. himself GARC 329:13
d. those provinces SMIT 723:14
means by d. freedom NIEM 545:7
defends when attacked it d. itself ANON 20:3
defensoribus *tali auxilio nec d.* VIRG 794:7
defer madness to d. YOUN 839:5
deferred Hope d. PROV 602:47
defiance Defence, not d. MOTT 535:6
d. in their eye GOLD 345:9
In defeat; d. CHUR 216:16
defied Age will not be d. BACO 43:27
defiled shall be d. BIBL 91:27
touches pitch shall be d. PROV 602:17
defileth d. a man BIBL 95:28
define d. true madness SHAK 663:10
know how to d. it THOM 770:19
definition d. is the enclosing BUTL 172:26
d. of the best government HALI 357:17
working d. of hell SHAW 709:8
definitions words; which . . . they call D. HOBB 378:14
deflower will her pride d. SPEN 734:1
deformed D., unfinished SHAK 696:9
None can be called d. SHAK 702:17
prove d. SHAK 705:27
deformity Art is significant d. FRY 326:27
time's d. JONS 419:21
defrauding d. of the State PENN 572:16
defy d. the foul fiend SHAK 679:3
dégagé Or half so d. COWP 240:15
degeneration d. of his moral being STEV 741:26
degradation breath of d. BYRO 178:14
degree exalted them of low d. BIBL 98:17
degrees through all d. WORD 832:10
dehumanizing anecdote d. EPHR 300:19
dei *D. gloriam* MOTT 535:1
vox D. ALCU 10:10
deities some other new d. PLAT 578:1
deity D. and the Drains STRA 744:8
D. disowns me COWP 240:7
D. offended BURN 167:3
Half dust, half d. BYRO 178:14
déjà d. all over again BERR 69:13
delay deny, or d. MAGN 489:13
In d. there lies no plenty SHAK 701:10
In me is no d. MILT 518:1
Nothing lost by d. GREE 351:16
reluctant amorous d. MILT 516:16
delayed d. till I am indifferent JOHN 412:17
losses from a d. decision GALB 328:10

delaying One man by d. ENNI 300:16
rich by d. TROL 783:1
delays D. are dangerous PROV 598:4
d. are dangerous in war DRYD 282:31
delectable D. Mountains BUNY 161:6
delectando *d. pariterque monendo* HORA 386:3
delegate When in trouble, d. BORE 143:2
delenda *D. est Carthago* CATO 194:13
deleted Expletive d. ANON 16:5
Delia While D. is away JAGO 401:10
deliberate O, these d. fools SHAK 687:26
Where both d. MARL 496:13
deliberately d. tries to hurt BAIN 48:8
deliberates woman who d. ADDI 4:12
deliberation D. sat and public care MILT 515:14
delicate not very d. WALP 801:8
delicias *D. domini* VIRG 795:16
delicious Afloat. We move: D. CLOU 221:19
delight begins in d. FROS 326:13
born to sweet d. BLAK 118:6
by succession of d. SMAR 722:8
D. hath a joy SIDN 718:27
d. in conceiving KEAT 431:10
D. in lust PETR 574:18
d. is in lies BOOK 135:21
d. with liberty SPEN 734:16
do ill our sole d. MILT 514:15
Energy is Eternal D. BLAK 119:10
ever new d. MILT 516:29
firmness, and d. WOTT 833:5
Formed to d. POPE 584:10
give d., and hurt not SHAK 699:5
go to 't with d. SHAK 657:7
hear thy shrill d. SHEL 714:5
immense world of d. BLAK 119:26
labour we d. in SHAK 683:16
land of pure d. WATT 805:16
Let dogs d. WATT 805:8
lovely tube of d. POTT 588:23
men miscall d. SHEL 711:1
phantom of d. WORD 831:22
Spirit of D. SHEL 713:24
still my d. BURN 167:10
Studies serve for d. BACO 44:2
temple of D. KEAT 429:5
thing met conceives d. MILT 517:14
turn d. into a sacrifice HERB 372:4
delighteth king d. to honour BIBL 80:33
neither d. he BOOK 141:25
delightful no d. ones LA R 453:14
delighting d. the reader HORA 386:3
delights king of intimate d. COWP 242:1
man d. not me SHAK 663:18
some d. condemn MOLI 525:18
delinquencies indulge in a few d. ELIO 293:10
delinquent condemns a less d. BUTL 172:16
delirant *Quidquid d. reges* HORA 386:13
delitabill Storys to rede ar d. BARB 53:20
deliver D. Israel, O God BOOK 133:6
d. us from evil BIBL 93:19
d. us from evil MISS 522:17
d. us, good Lord CHES 210:8
let him d. him BOOK 132:22
Lord, d. us BOOK 127:3
O d. me from the deceitful BOOK 134:9
O d. my soul BOOK 133:24
who shall d. me BIBL 105:5
deliverance d. from chains DOUG 277:1
delivered d. my soul BOOK 140:2
d. them BIBL 77:24
God hath d. him BIBL 78:36
delivereth he d. them BOOK 139:15
delivery ungracefulness of his d. WALP 801:17
delphiniums d. (blue) and geraniums (red) MILN 510:17
Delphos steep of D. leaving MILT 513:27
deluding dear d. woman BURN 169:2
deluge *Après nous le d.* POMP 580:6
dazzling d. reigns THOM 775:7
delusion d., a mockery DENM 257:15
under some d. BURK 165:5
delusive d. seduction BURN 166:2
demands cannot exact their d. WELL 810:5
demens *Quem fugis, a! d.* VIRG 795:18
demi-paradise other Eden, d. SHAK 694:19
demitasses villainous d. SMIT 723:18
democracies d. against despots DEMO 257:3
in d. it is the only sacred FRAN 322:14
democracy cured by more d. SMIT 723:15
D. and socialism are means NEHR 540:7
D. is the current suspicion WHIT 814:2
D. is the name we give FLER 317:21
D. is the theory MENC 504:16
D. is the worst form CHUR 216:2
d. means government ATTL 32:5
D. means government by CHES 211:21
D. means simply WILD 819:6
D. *not* identical with majority rule LENI 463:7
d. of the dead CHES 211:9
d. or absolute oligarchy ARIS 25:6
D. resumed her reign BELL 64:2
D. substitutes election SHAW 708:16
d. unbearable PERE 573:18
five hundred years of d. FILM 311:16
great arsenal of d. ROOS 632:17
grieved under a *d.* HOBB 379:1
justice makes d. possible NIEB 545:5
less d. to save ATKI 31:20
made safe for d. WILS 822:15
myth of d. CROS 246:14
no d. can afford BEVE 72:5
no d. in physics ALVA 13:2
not the voting that's d. STOP 743:11
perfect d. BURK 163:28
pollution of d. WHIT 814:9
property-owning d. SKEL 721:15
Russia an empire or d. BRZE 159:6
Two cheers for D. FORS 321:5
democrat Senator, and a D. JOHN 408:10
democratic among a d. people TROL 782:19
disrupt the d. process JUAN 422:21
get on with the d. process BENN 65:12
democrats D. object to men being disqualified CHES 211:10
Democritus D. would laugh HORA 387:7
demolition d. of a man LEVI 466:6
demon d.'s that is dreaming POE 579:19
wailing for her d.-lover COLE 225:21
demonstrandum *Quod erat d.* EUCL 301:15
Demosthenes D. is not more decidedly MACA 481:11
den d. of thieves BIBL 96:20
denial d. of Him by the atheist PROU 594:6
denials needing to issue d. CHAR 204:1
denied comes to be d. MONT 526:14
Justice d. MILL 509:13
would be d. SHAK 696:2
denies spirit that always d. GOET 342:18
deniges Who d. of it DICK 263:12
denizen spider is sole d. HARD 361:7
Denmark in the state of D. SHAK 662:22
it may be so in D. SHAK 663:1
throne of D. SHAK 661:15
dens d. o' Yarrow BALL 50:15
hid themselves in the d. BIBL 112:6
dentist sooner go to my d. WAUG 806:17
deny d. a God BACO 42:8
d. me thrice BIBL 97:19
d., or delay MAGN 489:13
d. the being of a devil MATH 501:9
He teaches to d. QUAR 618:19
I never d. DISR 271:3
will I not d. thee BIBL 97:20
You must d. yourself GOET 342:19
denying allure by d. TROL 783:1
Deo *D. gratias* MISS 520:15
Jubilate D., omnis terra BIBL 113:20
deoch-an-doris Just a wee d. MORR 533:3
deorum *Parcus d. cultor* HORA 388:2
depart already time to d. SOCR 727:2
desire to d. BIBL 108:15
servant d. in peace BIBL 98:24
will not d. BIBL 83:14
departed Dead he is not, but d. LONG 474:1
dear brother here d. BOOK 131:14
d., he withdrew CICE 217:20
d. into their own country BIBL 92:24
D., never to return BURN 166:18
d. this life BOOK 129:14
glory is d. BIBL 78:19
Lord was d. BIBL 78:6
departing and at my d. PRAY 592:3
departure point of d. METT 506:8
dépêches *Une de ces d.* PROU 594:9
depend did on false thee d. ROCH 630:7
dependant d. on man's bounty STAN 736:9
depends d. on the tip FILM 312:12
d. upon a red wheel barrow WILL 821:2
d. what you mean by CATC 196:4
dépeuplé *tout est d.* LAMA 448:6
deported think you are dead or d. HOWE 392:3
deportment adapt her methods and d. CRAN 243:23
for his D. DICK 260:23
depose my state d. SHAK 695:22
depraved suddenly became d. JUVE 424:8
depravity sense of innate d. MELV 504:7
stupidity than d. JOHN 414:7
depression d. when you lose yours TRUM 784:6
depressions terrible d. SEI 653:12
deprivation D. is for me LARK 453:10
depth d. and breadth and height BROW 154:21
d., and not the tumult WORD 828:28
d. of every acre GURN 355:4
far beyond my d. SHAK 673:12
deputy d. elected by the Lord SHAK 695:5
we shall have a new D. WHAR 813:4
derangement nice d. of epitaphs SHER 716:1
Derry oak would sprout in D. HEAN 366:17
descansada *Que d. vida* LUIS 479:10
descending comes with clouds d. WESL 811:8
descensus *Facilis d. Averno* VIRG 794:17
descent d. from a monkey WILB 817:2
description beggared all d. SHAK 656:23
descriptions d. of the fairest wights SHAK 705:9
Desdemona D.! dead SHAK 694:1
desert Blast from the D. LONG 474:10
d. is a moving mouth WALC 799:2
d. shall rejoice BIBL 87:21
d. sighs in the bed AUDE 33:19
d. were my dwelling-place BYRO 175:7
in a d. land BIBL 77:11
Life is the d. YOUN 839:15
make straight in the d. BIBL 87:28
Nothing went unrewarded, but d. DRYD 280:10
on the d. air GRAY 350:11
out into the d. CLOU 223:5
owl that is in the d. BOOK 138:14
scare myself with my own d. FROS 325:20
Stand in the d. SHEL 712:21
Use every man after his d. SHAK 663:25
water but the d. BYRO 174:28
deserted D. in his utmost need DRYD 280:19
towns are d. BERN 69:5
deserts d. of the heart AUDE 34:4
D. of vast eternity MARV 499:2
his d. are small MONT 529:2
she d. the night MILT 518:15
deserve and d. to get it MENC 504:16
d. any thanks CATU 197:13
d. success ADDI 4:9
I d. it PRIE 591:17
only d. it CHUR 215:13

those who really d. them FIEL 310:5
you somehow haven't to d. FROS 325:19
deserves gets what he d. ANON 20:17
desiccated d. calculating machine BEVA 71:21
design there is a d. in it STEE 736:20
two rules for d. PUGI 616:15
designs at large to his own dark d. MILT 514:18
d. were strictly honourable FIEL 310:12
instruments of their crooked d. GODW 342:6
Official d. BETJ 71:1
desinat *D. in piscem* HORA 385:10
desipere *Dulce est d.* HORA 389:11
desire d. accomplished BIBL 82:29
d. and longing BOOK 137:11
d. for desires TOLS 779:7
d. for their own happiness SHAN 706:9
d. of power HOBB 378:17
d. of the moth SHEL 714:2
d. other men's goods BOOK 130:16
d. shall fail BIBL 85:2
d. should so many years SHAK 670:1
fond d. ADDI 4:16
gratified d. BLAK 120:9
her d.,— Shining suspension CRAN 243:22
land of d. HEGE 367:12
Land of Heart's D. YEAT 836:13
man's d. is for the woman COLE 227:21
nothing like d. PROU 594:5
provokes the d. SHAK 683:15
shot and danger of d. SHAK 662:8
vain d. at last ROSS 635:4
weariness treads on d. PETR 574:18
what I've tasted of d. FROS 325:21
when the d. cometh BIBL 82:27
Which of us has his d. THAC 769:14
without any quiver of d. PALI 566:1
desired chiefly to be d. CICE 217:26
I have d. to go HOPK 384:9
More to be d. BOOK 132:17
not one to be d. TENN 762:10
You who d. so much— CRAN 243:26
desires all d. known BOOK 129:4
all holy d. BOOK 126:19
answer back to d. HORA 390:2
d. and petitions BOOK 126:18
d. but acts not BLAK 119:14
d. of our own hearts BOOK 125:15
d. of the heart AUDE 33:23
d. of the mind BACO 41:11
d. that seem big RICE 626:7
d. which thereof did ensue DONN 272:13
doing what one d. MILL 509:1
end of our d. THOM 771:13
enjoyment of all d. TANT 754:30
fondly flatter our d. DRAY 279:1
lopping off our d. SWIF 748:27
nurse unacted d. BLAK 119:24
proportion to our d. MANN 494:1
desirest d. no sacrifice BOOK 135:9
desireth as the hart d. BOOK 134:5
desiring D. this man's art SHAK 704:14
desirous ought else on earth d. GAY 331:17
desk but a d. to write upon BUTL 172:7
man's subservience to the d. FRAN 323:18
sleeping under the d. GATE 331:2
Turn upward from the d. ELIO 296:8
desks Stick close to your d. GILB 338:29
desolate d. and oppressed BOOK 127:12
d. places BIBL 81:4
vast d. night BYRO 173:21
desolated province they have d. GLAD 340:19
desolation abomination of d. BIBL 97:2
D. in immaculate public places ROET 631:7
Love in D. SHEL 710:21
Magnificent d. ALDR 11:4
years of d. JEFF 406:1
despair begotten by D. MARV 498:10
Bid me d. HERR 374:24
black d. CONG 232:15
carrion comfort, D. HOPK 384:2
comfort and d. SHAK 705:24
D. a smilingness assume BYRO 174:12
D. had a wife BUNY 161:5
D. yawns HUGO 393:19
Do not d. PUDN 616:14
endure my own d. WALS 802:11
far side of d. SART 645:10
Heaven in Hell's d. BLAK 121:1
I d. for it FLEM 317:14
In d. there are DOST 276:8
I shall d. SHAK 696:30
needst not then d. ARNO 26:8
racked with deep d. MILT 514:14
sins of d. READ 622:14
some divine d. TENN 765:19
unyielding d. RUSS 639:21
volume of d. POE 580:1
what resolution from d. MILT 514:17
ye Mighty, and d. SHEL 713:1
despairer Too quick d. ARNO 27:27
desperandum *Nil d.* HORA 387:18
desperate Beware of d. steps COWP 240:14
D. diseases PROV 598:5
Diseases d. grown SHAK 665:26
Tempt not a d. man SHAK 698:1
desperation lives of quiet d. THOR 776:4
despise and d. him DICK 264:1
ere you d. the other DRYD 283:9
shalt thou not d. BOOK 135:9
work for a Government I d. KEYN 435:3
despised Dangers by being d. BURK 165:10
d. and rejected BIBL 88:16
d. Mr Tattle CONG 232:24
d. the world HAZL 365:7
despite Hell in Heaven's d. BLAK 121:2
despond slough was D. BUNY 160:15
despondency d. and madness WORD 831:12
last words of Mr D. BUNY 161:17
SPREAD ALARM AND D. PENI 572:12
despot country governed by a d. JOHN 415:30
despotism D. accomplishes great things BALZ 53:1
d. in England WALP 801:23
d., let it be called WEBS 807:14
d., or unlimited sovereignty ADAM 3:11
d. tempered by epigrams CARL 187:25
d. will come ARIS 25:6
root of d. ROBE 629:6
despots against d.—suspicion DEMO 257:3
D. themselves do not deny TOCQ 778:7
dessin *d. est la probité* INGR 399:19
destinies d. of half the globe TOCQ 778:15
destiny Anatomy is d. FREU 324:12
character is d. ELIO 293:7
d. obscure GRAY 350:9
D. the commissary of God DONN 273:11
D. with Men for pieces FITZ 314:15
fabric of human d. DOST 276:1
manifest d. O'SU 560:19
tide of d. PAST 569:8
wiving go by d. PROV 601:47
destitution shaming D. VIRG 794:20
destroy against us to d. us HAGG 355:14
d. the town to save it ANON 17:4
gods wish to d. CONN 233:25
man determined to d. himself CUMM 247:11
not to d., but to fulfil BIBL 93:7
One to d. YOUN 838:20
planted, we d. WITH 824:1
power to d. MARS 497:19
shall be able to d. OVID 561:19
shall not hurt nor d. BIBL 87:5
Whom the gods would d. PROV 615:4
Whom the mad would d. LEVI 466:9
winged life d. BLAK 120:8
worms d. this body BIBL 81:22
destroyed Carthage must be d. CATO 194:13
enemy that shall be d. BIBL 106:23
name d. HILL 377:8
not one life shall be d. TENN 761:10
ought to be d. OMAR 554:15
treated generously or d. MACH 485:15
destroyer D. and preserver SHEL 712:12
d. of worlds OPPE 557:2
destroyeth d. in the noon-day BOOK 137:22
destroying without d. something UPDI 788:16
destroys d. a good book MILT 519:8
Time which d. all things BHAG 73:2
destruction d. of the poor BIBL 82:21
d. of the whole world HUME 395:7
for d. ice Is also great FROS 325:21
leadeth to d. BIBL 94:7
means of total d. SAKH 641:15
Pride goeth before d. BIBL 82:38
startles at d. ADDI 4:16
to their d. draw DONN 273:18
urge for d. BAKU 48:16
whether the mad d. is wrought GAND 329:4
destructive smiling, d. man LEE 462:6
To the d. element CONR 234:16
would be simply destructive MELB 503:16
detail corroborative d. GILB 338:13
frittered away by d. THOR 776:13
occupied in trivial d. BAGE 46:14
details d. of every kind REYN 625:7
God is in the d. ROHE 632:3
mind which reveres d. LEWI 467:9
detect lose it in the moment you d. POPE 583:28
detection D. is an exact science DOYL 277:22
detective d. novel is art-for-art's-sake PRIT 593:9
d. story is about JAME 403:25
Hawkshaw, the d. TAYL 756:22
deteriora *D. sequor* OVID 561:17
determination d. of incident JAME 403:10
determine we d. our deeds ELIO 291:20
determined D., dared, and done SMAR 722:13
determinèd d. to prove a villain SHAK 696:11
detest d. at leisure BYRO 177:21
I hate and d. SWIF 748:10
detraction D. is but baseness' varlet JONS 420:1
Deum *D. de Deo* MISS 520:17
deus *d. nobis haec otia fecit* VIRG 795:14
puto d. fio VESP 791:15
Deutschland *D. über alles* HOFF 379:16
devastating d. or redeeming fires GONC 346:7
developed fairly d. minds FORS 320:9
have a d. society NYER 552:4
developer slipped into d. WILS 821:11
development what is called d. NAIR 538:5
De Vere name and dignity of D. CREW 244:22
deviates d. into sense DRYD 281:36
device imagined such a d. BOOK 132:20
with the strange d. LONG 473:16
devices d. and desires BOOK 125:15
man of many d. HOME 382:9
man of many d. OPEN 556:20
devil apology for the D. BUTL 172:25
assaults of the d. BOOK 127:3
Better the d. you know PROV 596:12
can the d. speak true SHAK 681:19
cleft the D.'s foot DONN 274:11
counteracts the D. SMAR 722:6
D. always builds a chapel DEFO 255:9
d. and all his works BOOK 130:11
d. can cite Scripture SHAK 687:14
d. can quote Scripture PROV 598:6
d. damn thee black SHAK 685:16
d., depend upon it STEV 741:11
d. doesn't exist DOST 275:17
d. finds work PROV 598:7
d. have all the best tunes PROV 615:8
D. howling 'Ho' SQUI 735:16
d. is dead READ 622:15
d. is not so black PROV 598:8

devil (*cont.*):
D. knows Latin KNOX 442:15
d. looks after his own PROV 598:9
d. makes his Christmas pies PROV 598:10
D. Moon in your eyes HARB 359:17
d. more wicked BALL 51:10
d.-porter it no further SHAK 683:14
D. said when he found himself PROV 602:41
d.'s awa wi' th'Exciseman BURN 166:29
D. sends cooks GARR 330:6
D. sends cooks PROV 601:17
d. shall not take it from us RAND 621:15
d. should have all HILL 377:3
D. should have right MORE 531:8
d.'s leavings POPE 587:20
d.'s luck PROV 598:11
d.'s madness—War SERV 655:1
d.'s most devilish BROW 154:12
d.'s walking parody CHES 210:4
D. take the hindmost PROV 598:12
D. take the hindmost PROV 599:32
d. taketh him up BIBL 92:34
d., taking him up BIBL 98:28
d. understands Welsh SHAK 668:23
d. was sick PROV 598:13
d. weakly fettered STEV 741:8
D. whoops KIPL 438:9
D. will build a chapel PROV 614:36
d. will come MARL 496:7
d. would also build LUTH 480:1
doubt is D.-born TENN 761:24
dreamed of the d. ANST 22:14
dream of the d. BARH 54:5
Drink and the d. STEV 741:18
easier to raise the D. PROV 604:14
envy of the d. BIBL 91:7
face the d. BURN 168:15
fears a painted d. SHAK 683:10
first Whig was the D. JOHN 416:4
flesh, and the d. BOOK 127:5
given the d. a foul fall MORE 531:9
Give the d. his due PROV 601:9
God and d. DOST 275:16
go to the d. JOHN 411:22
go to the d. NORF 546:14
got over the D.'s back PROV 614:2
Haste is from the D. PROV 602:1
idle brain is d.'s workshop PROV 603:9
laughing d. BYRO 175:14
moral of the d. SHAK 671:11
my back upon Don or d. TENN 766:9
of the D.'s party BLAK 119:11
of the witty d. GRAV 349:11
of your father the d. BIBL 102:1
puzzle the d. BURN 168:9
reference to the d. CHUR 216:18
serpent, which is the D. BIBL 113:4
shame the D. PROV 611:44
sups with the D. PROV 602:33
synonym for the D. MACA 481:14
Talk of the D. PROV 611:42
there is a D. MATH 501:9
wedlock's the d. BYRO 179:9
What the d. was he doing MOLI 525:7
when most I play the d. SHAK 696:16
when the d. drives PROV 607:26
young and sweating d. SHAK 693:4
Young saint, old d. PROV 616:4
your adversary the d. BIBL 111:7
you the blacker d. SHAK 693:27

devilish most d. thing FLEM 317:11
Tough, and d. sly DICK 262:9

devils casteth out devils BIBL 94:29
d. in life and condition ASCH 30:7
d. must print MOOR 530:8
d. would set on me LUTH 479:14
fight like d. SHAK 671:7
lighting d. BINC 115:4

devised so well d. BOOK 125:12

Devon glorious D. BOUL 145:1
If the Dons sight D. NEWB 541:14

devote d. themselves to what men do FITZ 315:4

devotion D.! daughter of astronomy YOUN 839:12
my bok and my d. CHAU 206:24
object of universal d. IRVI 400:4
Tell zeal it wants d. RALE 620:13

devour d. in turn each one VERG 791:6
seeking whom he may d. BIBL 111:7
when they would d. BACO 44:24

devoured beast hath d. him BIBL 75:11

devourer Time the d. OVID 561:18

devourers become so great d. MORE 531:5

devout d. in dishabilly FARQ 307:23
for being d. MOLI 525:17

dew as sunlight drinketh d. TENN 758:19
begotten the d. BIBL 81:33
continual d. of thy blessing BOOK 126:17
d. bespangling herb HERR 374:6
d. shall weep thy fall HERB 373:17
d. will rust them SHAK 691:29
drenched with d. DE L 256:19
Drop down d., heavens BIBL 114:1
fades awa' like morning d. BALL 52:8
let there be no d. BIBL 79:1
morning d. ARNO 27:29
On whom the d. of heaven drops FORD 319:19
resolve itself into a d. SHAK 661:22
Showers, and D. BOOK 126:5
smell the d. and rain HERB 372:17
soft falls the d. BEER 61:18
Walks o'er the d. SHAK 661:12
wicked d. SHAK 698:23

dewdrop Starlight and d. FOST 321:14

dewdrops seek some d. here SHAK 689:17

dewfall d. at night STEV 742:21

dews early d. were falling INGE 399:11

dewy d. pasture, dewy trees TENN 765:10
fair on the d. downs TENN 764:15
shakes his d. wings D'AV 251:11

dhamma D. has been taught PALI 564:17
sees D. sees me PALI 565:8
teach you D. PALI 565:1

dharamsala goes to the d. SIKH 719:15

dharma discourse on d. as a raft MAHĀ 490:4
rain of D. MAHĀ 490:9

di *d. omen avertant* CICE 217:22

diable *d. est mort* READ 622:15

diabolical tree of d. knowledge SHER 715:25

diadem d. of frost BLOK 122:6
precious d. stole SHAK 665:18

diagnostician makes a good d. OSLE 560:15

diagonally lie d. in his bed STER 739:10

dialect Babylonish d. BUTL 171:20
d. I understand very little PEPY 573:5
D. words HARD 360:13
purify the d. of the tribe ELIO 294:16

dial-plate looking on the d. JOHN 413:25

diamond d. and safire bracelet LOOS 475:11
D. cuts diamond PROV 598:14
d. in the sky TAYL 756:13
d. is forever ADVE 7:13
like a rough d. DEFO 254:13
matchwood, immortal d. HOPK 384:22
O D.! Diamond NEWT 543:12
polished d. CHES 209:18

diamonds d. a girl's best friend ROBI 629:9
has no d. WALP 801:13
what beautiful d. WEST 812:5

Dian hangs on D.'s temple SHAK 660:15

Diana D., breathless, hunted MOTI 534:6
D.'s foresters SHAK 667:15
Great is D. BIBL 104:12

diapason d. closing full DRYD 282:20

diaries I've kept political d. GEOG 333:8

diarist To be a good d. NICO 545:2

diary discreet d. CHAN 202:6
keep a d. and some day WEST 812:2
living for one's d. AGAT 6:19
never travel without my d. WILD 817:22
To keep such a d. ISHE 400:9
write a d. every day POWE 590:17
write in a d. WARN 803:18

diaspora for the new d. DUNN 285:15

dibble put The d. in earth SHAK 703:15

dic *sed tantum d. verbo* MISS 522:20

dice God does not play d. EINS 290:11
throw of the d. MALL 492:4

Dick D. the shepherd SHAK 681:4
Mr. D. had been for upwards of ten years DICK 261:20

dicky D.-bird, why do you sit GILB 338:15

dictate one day d. to him JOHN 411:4
suggest, never to *d.* BRON 149:20

dictates d. to me slumbering MILT 517:12
still d. to us ALLI 12:20
woman d. ELIO 292:17

dictation told at d. speed AMIS 13:13

dictator Every d. uses religion BHUT 73:6

dictators D. ride to and fro upon tigers CHUR 215:4
weed d. may cultivate BEVE 72:5

dictatorship d. impossible PERE 573:18
d. of the proletariat MARX 500:3
elective d. HAIL 356:12
establish a d. ORWE 559:1
have a d. TRUM 784:7

dictionaries D. are like watches JOHN 417:18
d. is dull work JOHN 409:8
Lexicographer. A writer of d. JOHN 409:10

dictionary but a walking d. CHAP 202:24
D. is CARR 190:11

dictum *D. sapienti* PLAU 578:13
non d. sit prius TERE 768:2

did danced his d. CUMM 247:3
d. for them both SASS 645:22

diddle D., diddle, dumpling NURS 548:3
d., we take it, is dee SWIN 750:23
Hey d. diddle NURS 548:12

Dido Stood D. with a willow SHAK 688:20

die Americans when they d. PROV 601:22
and gladly d. STEV 743:4
And shall Trelawny d. HAWK 364:6
apt to d. SHAK 675:20
Ay, but to d., and go SHAK 686:18
being born, to d. BACO 45:13
better to d. on your feet IBAR 398:3
bid me d. HERR 374:24
bleed, fall, and d. DONN 272:14
bravely d. POPE 582:18
Christian can d. LAST 457:3
clean place to d. KAVA 426:10
conquer or d. WASH 804:4
Cowards d. many times SHAK 675:10
Cowards may d. many times PROV 597:40
Curse God, and d. BIBL 81:2
day that I d. MCLE 486:15
Death thou shalt d. DONN 272:23
determine to d. here BEE 61:1
did not wish to d. SHAW 709:29
d. a Christian CHAR 203:6
d. all, die merrily SHAK 669:1
D., and endow a college POPE 583:19
d. before book is published RUNC 637:9
d. before I wake PRAY 592:5
d. beyond my means WILD 819:8
d. but do not surrender CAMB 182:11
d.—but never to live JAME 403:18
d. but once ADDI 4:14
die, dear, d. BEDD 60:15
d. eating ortolans DISR 270:34
d. for adultery SHAK 679:21
d. for him to-morrow BALL 50:6
d. for one's country HORA 388:14
d. for politicians THOM 774:18
d. for the industrialists FRAN 322:19
d. for the people BIBL 102:12
D. he or justice must MILT 516:2
d. here in a rage SWIF 748:11
d. in music SHAK 693:29
d. in my week JOPL 421:5
d. in peace LAST 456:17

d. in that man's company SHAK 671:23
d. in the flower of their age BIBL 78:13
d. in the last ditch WILL 820:1
d. is cast CAES 180:20
d. like a true-blue rebel LAST 456:10
d. like men BOOK 137:10
D., my dear Doctor LAST 455:8
d. of that roar ELIO 292:23
d. or rest at last SHEL 711:14
d. to save charges BURT 170:8
d. to vex me MELB 503:14
d. upon a kiss SHAK 694:5
d. when the body dies BHAG 72:15
d. when the trees were green CLAR 218:7
d. with harness SHAK 685:23
d. with kissing MARL 497:1
d. with thee BIBL 97:20
Don't d. of ignorance OFFI 554:6
do we not d. SHAK 687:30
Easy live and quiet d. SCOT 651:19
easy ways to d. SHAK 658:6
Every day we d. JERO 406:16
faith is something you d. for BENN 65:8
Fall asleep, or hearing d. SHAK 673:10
Few d. and none resign MISQ 521:12
few d. well SHAK 671:16
for me to d. SOCR 727:2
frogs don't d. for 'fun' BION 115:10
gave its victims time to d. GUIB 354:16
Gods love d. young PROV 615:3
Good Americans, when they d. APPL 23:4
good d. early DEFO 255:4
good d. young PROV 601:24
have the power to d. TENN 767:2
hazard of the d. SHAK 697:1
he can d. who complains BROW 153:26
he must d. NICH 543:16
He shall not d. STER 739:8
Hope I d. before TOWN 780:3
how can man d. better MACA 483:5
How can we d. like this INDI 399:1
how to d. PORT 588:15
I did not d. ANON 15:24
I die because I do not d. JOHN 407:15
I d. happy LAST 456:2
I d., if he die not ANDR 14:13
I d. pronouncing it SHAK 694:19
if he d., I die too ANDR 14:13
If I should d. BROO 150:17
If I should d. KEAT 431:21
If I should d. OPEN 555:14
If it were now to d. SHAK 692:12
If we must d. MCKA 486:6
I'll d. young BRUC 158:18
I must d. SOUT 731:14
in Adam all d. BIBL 106:22
I needs must d. RALE 620:12
I shall d. at the top SWIF 750:2
I shall d. today MORE 531:10
I shall not altogether d. HORA 389:1
I Sir Richard Grenville d. TENN 766:12
it was sure to d. MOOR 530:18
I who am about to d. JOHN 418:7
I will d. with them NELS 540:16
I would d. ROSS 635:9
just as lucky to d. WHIT 815:12
last Jews to d. MEIR 503:11
Let me d. a youngman's death MCGO 485:10
Let us d. VIRG 794:5
Let us do—or d. BURN 168:8
let us do or d. CAMP 183:6
like Douglas d. HOME 381:18
longed to d. PROU 594:2
love her till I d. ANON 19:2
love one another or d. AUDE 35:2
make a malefactor d. sweetly DRYD 283:16
man can d. but once SHAK 670:8
marked to d. SHAK 671:22
Muse forbids to d. HORA 389:8
natural to d. BACO 42:24
nineties is a good time to d. SPEN 733:1
not d. because of them TALM 754:7
not so difficult to d. BYRO 178:16
not that I'm afraid to d. ALLE 12:14
often are we to d. POPE 587:16
Old soldiers never d. FOLE 318:24
Old soldiers never d. PROV 608:26
O love, they d. TENN 765:18
only let Him d. STUD 745:5
Only we d. in earnest RALE 620:14
or dare to d. POPE 585:28
ought to d. standing LAST 455:12
People can't d. DICK 262:4
seemed to d. BIBL 91:8
seems it rich to d. KEAT 429:13
shall Harry d. SHAK 670:18
something he will d. for KING 436:13
taught us how to d. TICK 777:11
Their's but to do and d. TENN 757:16
these who d. as cattle OWEN 562:5
They d. not ROSS 635:1
They that d. by famine HENR 370:16
those who are about to d. ANON 21:5
thou must d. HERB 373:17
thou shalt surely d. BIBL 73:19
time to d. BIBL 84:7
To d. and know it LOWE 478:3
to d. is gain BIBL 108:14
To d. will be an awfully big BARR 55:16
To go away is to d. HARA 359:13
to live and to d. VILL 793:2
tomorrow we d. BIBL 106:24
to morrow we shall d. BIBL 87:9
unlamented let me d. POPE 586:25
was not made to d. TENN 760:19
we all must d. SWIF 749:24
weep or she will d. TENN 765:25
we needs must d. BIBL 79:8
went abroad to d. LETT 465:18
We shall d. alone PASC 568:15
What 'tis to d. BEAU 58:16
When beggars d. SHAK 675:9
when they come to d. MATH 501:10
when you d. HILL 377:1
when you have to d. MOLI 525:13
where myths Go when they d. FENT 308:10
Who saw him d. NURS 552:1
who would wish to d. BORR 143:9
will not have thee d. TENN 766:2
wisdom shall d. with you BIBL 81:15
with us, or we d. KEAT 426:17
wretch that dares not d. BURN 167:24
yet d. we must SHAK 673:3
You and I ought not to d. ADAM 3:10
You can only d. once PROV 615:26
Young men may d. PROV 616:3
Dieb *er war ein D.* HEIN 368:8
died could have d. contented DICK 262:12
d. an hour before SHAK 683:21
d. extremely well WALP 800:14
d.—for fear of dying THOM 775:1
D., has he LOUI 476:6
d. hereafter SHAK 685:22
d. in a good old age BIBL 80:30
d. in faith BIBL 109:30
d. last night of my physician PRIO 593:2
d. of grieving KEAT 427:31
D. some, pro patria POUN 589:16
d. to save their country CHES 210:6
d. unto sin once BIBL 105:1
dog it was that d. GOLD 344:22
He that d. o' Wednesday SHAK 669:9
'I never d.,' says he HAYE 365:1
liked it not, and d. WOTT 833:3
made the books and he d. FAUL 307:26
Mithridates, he d. old HOUS 391:10
Mother d. today OPEN 555:8
question why we d. KIPL 438:8
she d. young WEBS 808:2
Suppose Lenin had d. SCHL 648:19
What millions d. CAMP 183:15
would God I had d. for thee BIBL 79:11
Would to God we had d. BIBL 76:7
diem *carpe d.* HORA 387:22
d. perdidi TITU 777:16
d. tibi diluxisse supremum HORA 386:17
dienen *d. und verlieren* GOET 343:5
dies because a man d. for it WILD 818:22
before he d. SOLO 727:9
d. from lack of sex ATWO 32:8
D. irae MISS 523:3
d. only once MOLI 525:1
d., or turns Hindoo SHEL 712:1
d. to himself unknown SENE 654:21
d. young MENA 504:12
Every moment d. a man BABB 40:14
He that d. SHAK 699:4
He that d. this year SHAK 670:9
kingdom where nobody d. MILL 509:9
king never d. BLAC 117:2
love seldom d. of hunger LENC 463:5
man who d. . . . rich CARN 188:25
matters not how a man d. JOHN 414:5
moment d. a man TENN 767:13
no man happy till he d. PROV 597:1
once hath blown for ever d. FITZ 314:13
Optima quaeque d. miseris VIRG 796:20
something in me d. VIDA 792:10
then d. the same YOUN 839:7
diesel London Transport d.-engined FLAN 316:5
diest Where thou d., will I die BIBL 78:12
diet best doctors are Dr D. PROV 595:44
d. unparalleled DICK 263:17
dietetics first law of d. ASIM 30:19
diets feel about d. KERR 434:8
repent of my d. ALLE 12:19
Dieu *D. est mort* NERV 541:6
Si D. n'existait pas VOLT 797:16
differ all things d. POPE 587:14
d. from others BAGE 47:16
difference d. of forty thousand WELL 809:19
exaggerate the d. SHAW 707:29
made all the d. FROS 326:9
oh, The d. to me WORD 831:21
wear your rue with a d. SHAK 666:8
What d. does it make GAND 329:4
differences against small d. FREU 324:14
in language there are only d. SAUS 646:2
different boil at d. degrees EMER 299:31
convictions d. from your own EMPS 300:8
D. strokes SAYI 647:10
follow d. paths HORA 389:12
hears a d. drummer THOR 776:16
How d. from us ANON 17:17
how very d. ANON 16:18
other naturs thinks d. DICK 263:7
rich are d. from you and me FITZ 315:6
something completely d. CATC 195:2
thought they were d. ELIO 295:1
differential integral and d. calculus GILB 339:3
differently do things d. there HART 363:13
do things d. there OPEN 556:11
freedom for the one who thinks d. LUXE 480:8
difficile *D. est* JUVE 424:3
D. est longum CATU 197:15
difficult d.; and left untried CHES 211:17
D. do you call it, Sir JOHN 418:2
d. is done at once PROV 598:15
d. takes a little time NANS 538:7
d. to be a father BUSC 170:24
d. to speak BURK 165:7
d. to write MOOR 530:5
d. we do immediately MILI 508:6
fascination of what's d. YEAT 836:2
first step that is d. DU D 284:6
first step that is d. PROV 604:26
not so d. to die BYRO 178:16
Poets must be *d.* ELIO 296:21
too d. for artists SCHN 648:23
difficulties d. do not make one doubt NEWM 542:9

difficulties (*cont.*):
d. for several generations NAPO 538:18
little local d. MACM 487:18
difficulty d. in saying things MOOR 530:4
England's d. PROV 599:14
every d. except popularity WILD 819:10
no d. in beginning JAME 403:17
solving every d. PEEL 571:18
with d. and labour MILT 516:1
with great d. I am got hither BUNY 161:18
diffidence her name was D. BUNY 161:5
diffugere *D. nives* HORA 389:6
dig D. for victory OFFI 554:4
he'll d. them up again WEBS 808:14
I could not d. KIPL 438:13
I'll d. with it HEAN 366:11
digest learn, and inwardly d. BOOK 127:22
digestion good d. wait on appetite SHAK 684:10
in d. sour SHAK 694:13
diggeth He that d. a pit BIBL 84:24
dignified *d.* parts BAGE 46:5
dignitate *Cum d. otium* CICE 217:26
dignities by indignities men come to d. BACO 43:10
speak evil of d. BIBL 111:9
dignity conciliate with d. GREN 352:18
d. in tilling a field WASH 804:2
d. of history BOLI 124:14
d. of this high calling BURK 163:9
d. which His Majesty BALD 49:11
maintain a d. in their fate WALP 801:19
no d. in persevering in error PEEL 571:17
Official d. HUXL 396:17
with silent d. GROS 354:6
write trifles with d. JOHN 416:17
dignum *D. et justum* MISS 520:20
D. laude virum Musa vetat mori HORA 389:8
dignus *non sum d.* MISS 522:20
digression began a lang d. BURN 169:6
digressions D. are the sunshine STER 738:21
eloquent d. HUXL 397:20
digs d. my grave HERB 372:19
Dijon young man of D. ANON 20:5
dilettante snowy-banded d. TENN 764:1
dilige *D. et quod vis fac* AUGU 36:9
diligence D. is the mother CERV 200:4
D. is the mother PROV 598:16
dillied But I d. and dallied COLL 228:13
dilly-dally Don't d. on the way COLL 228:13
dim d. and perilous way WORD 828:11
d. religious light MILT 512:11
flickered, grew d. TOLS 779:9
made The bright world d. SHEL 714:17
Nor d. nor red COLE 226:9
dime Brother can you spare a d. HARB 359:15
dimensions my d. are as well compact SHAK 678:3
Time has three d. HOPK 385:5
dimidium *Animae d. meae* HORA 387:14
diminished ought to be d. DUNN 285:16
dimittis *Nunc d.* BIBL 114:5
dimming d. of the lights NICO 545:1
dine d. exact at noon POPE 584:8
gang and d. BALL 52:5
heroes to d. with us TROL 782:13
scandal while you d. TENN 767:3
dined I have d. today SMIT 725:22
more d. against BOWR 146:2
ding D., dong, bell NURS 548:4
dinner after d. is after dinner SWIF 748:7
After d. rest awhile PROV 594:18
ask him to d. CARL 188:22
best number for a d. party GULB 354:18
d. bell BYRO 177:9
D. in the diner GORD 347:1
d. of herbs BIBL 82:36
d. of herbs PROV 596:3
doubtful of his d. JOHN 409:26
good d. and feasting PEPY 573:9
good d. upon his table JOHN 418:11
have had a better d. JOHN 413:18
hungry for d. at eight HART 363:6
refrain from asking it to d. HALS 358:11
three hours' march to d. HAZL 365:23
we expect our d. SMIT 723:6
went to a Chinese d. FLEM 317:20
with broken d.-knives KIPL 438:19
worth inviting to d. VIRG 796:6
dinners d. follow the creation WARN 803:17
Homer's mighty d. AESC 6:13
diocese All the air is thy D. DONN 272:17
Diogenes would be D. ALEX 11:5
Dior Never darken my D. again LILL 468:2
diplomacy D. is to do and say GOLD 344:3
diplomas d. they can't read GING 339:18
diplomat d. . . . is a person STIN 743:8
diplomatic d. boathook SALI 642:14
diplomats D. tell lies KRAU 445:18
direct could d. a movie HYTN 398:2
d. and rule our hearts BOOK 128:16
lie d. SHAK 659:26
directed all d. your way HORA 386:12
direction d., which thou canst not see POPE 585:17
move in a given d. HOUS 391:12
pitch or d. HOPK 385:5
some particular d. JOHN 409:27
directions By indirections find d. out SHAK 663:8
d. to the town SWIF 749:17
rode madly off in all d. LEAC 459:19
directors way with these d. GOLD 346:2
direful d. death indeed FLEM 317:10
d. in the sound AUST 37:19
to Greece the d. spring POPE 586:6
dirge Begins the sad d. SHAK 704:3
their d. is sung COLL 229:10
dirt d. doesn't get any worse CRIS 245:4
D. is only matter GRAY 349:24
eat a peck of d. PROV 613:45
in d. the reasoning engine ROCH 630:14
In poverty, hunger, and d. HOOD 382:28
in the d. lay justice HEAN 366:17
make crossness and d. succeed FORS 320:13
painted child of d. POPE 583:9
[illegible] will be the d. GALB 328:7
Throw d. enough PROV 612:50
dirty dark, boggy, d. GOLD 345:21
Dear, d. Dublin JOYC 421:16
D., dark, and undevotional VICT 792:4
d. old town MACC 484:8
D. water will quench PROV 598:17
hard and d. work RUSK 638:16
Is sex d. ALLE 12:10
journalistic d.-mindedness LAWR 458:23
'Jug Jug' to d. ears ELIO 296:3
throw out your d. water PROV 598:39
too d. for the light CLAR 218:10
wash one's d. linen PROV 608:35
You d. rat MISQ 522:16
dis *D. aliter visum* VIRG 794:6
disagree if they d. OMAR 554:15
when doctors d. POPE 583:18
disagreeable d.-looking child OPEN 556:27
disappointed d. by that stroke JOHN 410:8
d. in human nature DONL 272:4
never be d. PROV 596:27
you have d. us BELL 63:8
disappointeth d. him not BOOK 132:8
disappointing least d. BARU 56:11
disappointment D. all I endeavour end HOPK 384:23
disapproval moral d. AYER 40:5
disapprove d. of what you say MISQ 521:14
disapproves condemns whatever he d. BURN 166:1
disaster precipitate one into d. WEST 812:12
triumph and d. KIPL 439:2
disasters d. in his morning face GOLD 344:13
guilty of our own d. SHAK 678:5
disastrous d. and the unpalatable GALB 328:11
win a war is as d. CHRI 212:14
disbelief willing suspension of d. COLE 227:12
discandy d., melt their sweets SHAK 657:10
disce *D. omnis* VIRG 793:19
discern do we d. ARNO 26:18
discerning genius a better d. GOLD 345:17
discharge d. for loving one MATL 501:14
no d. in that war BIBL 84:18
disciple d. did outrun Peter BIBL 102:39
d. is not above his master BIBL 94:35
d. whom Jesus loved BIBL 103:12
in the name of a d. BIBL 95:4
disciples great man has his d. WILD 817:25
discipline D. must be maintained DICK 261:3
d. of colleges SMIT 723:12
gentle d. SPEN 733:11
of Dhamma, of D. PALI 564:20
order and military d. MILI 508:5
wholesome d. impossible JAIN 402:1
disciplines by category-d. RYLE 640:19
disclaim d. her for a mother GIBB 335:17
disco *mali miseris succurrere d.* VIRG 793:15
Discobbolos Darling Mr D. LEAR 460:13
discomfort great d. of my soul BOOK 133:23
discomforts all the d. CLOS 222:3
discommendeth He who d. others BROW 152:10
discontent in common—d. ARNO 28:6
pale contented sort of d. KEAT 428:17
winter of d. CALL 181:11
Winter of d. NEWS 544:20
winter of our d. SHAK 696:7
discontented blushing d. sun SHAK 695:12
every one that was d. BIBL 78:35
discontents Civilization and its d. RIVI 628:16
source of all our d. LEAC 459:13
discord civil d. CLOS 222:9
d. doth sow ELIZ 297:1
hark! what d. follows SHAK 700:6
discordant D. elements WORD 830:24
still-d. wavering multitude SHAK 669:20
discors *Concordia d.* HORA 386:21
discouragement There's no d. BUNY 161:16
discourse company and good d. WALT 802:18
d. of rivers WALT 802:25
Miss not the d. BIBL 91:22
discover another can d. DOYL 277:19
in the end to d. life GUIB 354:16
discoverers ill d. BACO 41:13
discovery D. consists of seeing SZEN 752:5
d. of a new dish BRIL 148:18
love is but d. SOUT 730:10
Medicinal d. AYRE 40:8
discreet d. charm of the bourgeoisie FILM 312:18
d. diary CHAN 202:6
discretion d. end AUST 38:21
D. is better part PROV 598:18
D. is not the better part STRA 744:10
fair woman without d. BIBL 82:23
guide his words with d. BOOK 139:19
inform their d. JEFF 405:21
part of valour is d. SHAK 669:16
surety to subsequent d. BURN 165:22
their happiness in thy d. ELIZ 297:3
discriminated men who are d. MEIR 503:12
discunt *dum docent d.* SENE 654:18
discuss stay and d. them WELL 810:3
discussing d. if it existed GUNN 355:1
discussion compliance with my wishes after reasonable d. CHUR 216:19
d. of any subject SHEL 714:18
government by d. ATTL 32:5
disdain D. and scorn SHAK 691:10
little d. is not amiss CONG 233:10
my dear Lady D. SHAK 690:34
pride and high d. SCOT 650:15
disdained If now I be d. ANON 18:19

disdainfulness D. I have again WYAT 834:3
disdains d. all things OVER 561:1
disease afflictive d. MOOR 530:2
age, D., or sorrows CLOU 221:23
Astrology is a d. MAIM 491:9
biggest d. today TERE 768:8
cannot ascertain a d. KEAT 432:2
Cured yesterday of my d. PRIO 593:2
Cure the d. BACO 43:3
desperate d. FAWK 308:3
d. at its onset PERS 574:5
d. called friendship RENO 624:15
d. has grown strong OVID 561:20
D., Ignorance, and Idleness BEVE 72:6
d. in the family TREV 781:11
D. is an experience EDDY 288:5
d. is incurable CHEK 208:1
d. is incurable SHAK 669:28
d. of admiration MACA 482:4
d. of modern life ARNO 27:10
d. of not listening SHAK 669:23
incurable d. of writing JUVE 424:17
Life is an incurable d. COWL 239:23
Love's a d. MACA 481:7
no Cure for this D. BELL 63:6
Progress is a comfortable d. CUMM 247:9
remedy is worse than the d. BACO 43:34
sexually transmitted d. SAYI 647:29
suffering from the particular d. JERO 406:21
this long d., my life POPE 583:4
diseased mind d. BYRO 174:29
minister to a mind d. SHAK 685:18
diseases cure of all d. BROW 154:1
Desperate d. PROV 598:5
D. and sad Old Age VIRG 794:20
D. desperate grown SHAK 665:26
spread d. OFFI 554:3
disenchantment mistook d. for truth SART 645:5
disentangle cannot d. ANON 18:19
disestablishment sense of d. KING 437:3
disgrace author of his own d. COWP 240:9
d. to be fine TAYL 756:11
Even to a full d. SHAK 660:13
in d. with fortune SHAK 704:13
Intellectual d. Stares AUDE 34:2
no d. t'be poor HUBB 392:14
passing d. DIDE 267:4
Poverty is no d. PROV 609:34
private life is a d. ANON 18:12
public and merited d. STEV 742:7
disgraced dies . . . rich dies d. CARN 188:25
disgraceful something d. in mind JUVE 425:5
disgruntled if not actually d. WODE 824:12
disguise better go in d. BRAT 147:5
D. fair nature SHAK 671:5
men in d. ABSE 1:5
naked is the best d. CONG 232:14
this identical d. BROO 151:5
disguised England is a d. republic BAGE 46:21
disgust capacity for d. MANN 494:1
not moments of d. VOLT 798:2
play began to d. EVEL 305:7
dish discovery of a new d. BRIL 148:18
d. fit for the gods SHAK 675:3
d. ran away NURS 548:12
in a lordly d. BIBL 77:28
dishabilly devout in d. FARQ 307:23
dishclout Romeo's a d. SHAK 697:36
dishcover d. the riddle CARR 191:18
dishes these the choice d. GARR 330:6
these were the d. AUGU 36:1
washing of d. EPIT 302:15
who does the d. FREN 324:7
dishonour another unto d. BIBL 105:13
rooted in d. TENN 759:29
dishonourable d. graves SHAK 674:13
disiecti *Etiam d. membra poetae* HORA 389:18
disinheriting d. countenance SHER 716:15
disintegration d. and dismemberment GLAD 341:5
disinterested d. endeavour ARNO 28:17
D. intellectual curiosity TREV 781:7
dislike d. every thing CENT 199:15
d. the matter SHAK 656:22
hesitate d. POPE 583:7
I, too, d. it MOOR 529:17
sat with that d. STEE 736:17
dismal beset him round With d. stories BUNY 161:16
D. Science CARL 188:5
dismayed neither be thou d. BIBL 77:17
Was there a man d. TENN 757:16
dismemberment d. of the Empire GLAD 341:5
dismiss Lord, d. us BUCK 159:17
Disney of Euro D. BALL 52:13
of Euro D. MNOU 524:14
Disneyfication D. of Christianity CUPI 248:1
disobedience children of d. BIBL 108:7
man's first d. MILT 514:7
man's first d. OPEN 556:5
disorder D., horror, fear SHAK 695:19
d. in its geometry DE B 254:7
sweet d. in the dress HERR 374:8
with brave d. part POPE 584:14
dispatch in business than d. ADDI 4:18
displeasing not d. to us LA R 453:21
dispoged when I am so d. DICK 263:6
disposable everything has to be d. MILL 509:23
dispose d. of all things ANON 21:11
d. the way of thy servants BOOK 130:4
disposes God d. THOM 771:1
disposition antic d. SHAK 663:5
truant d. SHAK 661:29
dispossessed imprisoned or d. MAGN 489:12
dispraised Of whom to be d. MILT 518:4
disputants d. put me in mind ADDI 5:15
disputations Doubtful d. BIBL 105:23
dispute great d. between you VIRG 796:2
disquieted d. within me BOOK 134:6
disquieteth d. himself in vain BOOK 133:30
Disraeli D. school of Prime Ministers BLAI 117:14
disregard Atones for later d. FROS 326:8
dissatisfied I'm d. MOOR 530:3
Not one is d. WHIT 815:15
dissect creatures you d. POPE 583:28
murder to d. WORD 832:7
dissemble d. sometimes your knowledge BACO 42:26
dissent dissidence of d. BURK 162:26
dissenters Barn-door fowls for d. SMIT 725:11
dissentious you d. rogues SHAK 660:2
dissimulation one word—d. DISR 270:8
dissipation d. without pleasure GIBB 335:23
dissolution lingering d. BECK 59:9
dissolve d., and quite forget KEAT 429:9
d. the people BREC 147:21
dissolved d. into something CATH 194:8
tabernacle were d. BIBL 107:7
dissonance barbarous d. MILT 511:26
distaff mind the d. LEWI 467:2
distance d. is nothing DU D 284:6
d. lends enchantment CAMP 183:13
D. lends enchantment PROV 598:19
longest d. between two places WILL 820:17
scale of the d. SALI 642:15
distant d. from Heaven BURT 170:16
music of a *d.* drum FITZ 314:10
prospect of a d. good DRYD 281:23
relation of d. misery GIBB 335:13
distempered questions the d. part ELIO 294:10
distillation d. of rumour CARL 187:22
distinction think that there is no d. JOHN 413:8
distinctive man's d. mark BROW 155:24
distinguish style which will d. MATH 501:8
distinguished d. above the rest HOME 382:3
d. by that circumstance THOR 776:14
d. thing JAME 403:24
distort then you can d. them TWAI 786:30
distracted this d. globe SHAK 662:32
distraction thrown Into a fine d. HERR 374:8
distress d. of another RICH 627:6
every one that was in d. BIBL 78:35
Far as d. GREV 353:2
in d. Finds ways GOOG 346:14
out of their d. BOOK 139:15
pray in their d. BLAK 120:14
distressed afflicted, or d. BOOK 127:18
I am d. for thee BIBL 79:3
distresses d. of our friends SWIF 749:23
distressful most d. country POLI 581:16
distribute d. as fairly as he can LOWE 477:8
distrust have to d. each other WILL 820:13
ditch [Channel] is a mere ditch NAPO 538:9
die in the last d. WILL 820:1
D.-delivered. by a drab SHAK 684:19
dull as d. water DICK 264:27
environed with a great d. CROM 246:1
fall into the d. BIBL 95:29
ditchers gardeners, d. SHAK 666:17
ditches of Dutchmen and of d. BYRO 177:15
ditties amorous d. MILT 514:26
ditty played an ancient d. KEAT 427:14
diurnal earth's d. course WORD 831:25
her d. round WORD 828:22
dive must d. below DRYD 280:24
diver Don't forget the d. CATC 195:10
diversa *laudet d. sequentis* HORA 389:12
diversity d. of sects SPEN 734:17
some d. BARC 53:22
divide D. and rule PROV 598:20
d. the spoil BIBL 86:28
though he d. the hoof BIBL 76:20
divided d. aims ARNO 27:10
d. by a common language MISQ 521:10
D. by the morning tea MACN 488:11
d. duty SHAK 692:3
d. into three parts CAES 180:15
d. into three parts OPEN 555:12
d. self LAIN 448:4
d. the spoil BOOK 136:7
d. we fall PROV 613:32
has harshly d. SCHI 646:14
He d. the sea BOOK 137:5
house d. cannot stand PROV 603:3
If a house be d. BIBL 98:2
in their death not d. BIBL 79:2
dividend no d. from time's tomorrow SASS 645:18
dividing by d. we fall DICK 266:23
divination d. too will perish MAND 493:15
divine believes Kingsley a d. STUB 745:3
Come down, O Love d. LITT 470:3
d. Majority DICK 266:14
d. plain face LAMB 449:4
d. powers take note VIRG 793:14
d. Zenocrate MARL 496:28
faculty d. WORD 828:7
good d. that follows his own SHAK 687:7
hand that made us is d. ADDI 5:13
heavy, but no less d. BYRO 176:29
horror and its beauty are d. SHEL 712:20
human form d. BLAK 120:15
knowledge was d. TRAH 780:11
More needs she the d. SHAK 685:13
one far-off d. event TENN 762:6
possess d. legislation MEND 504:19
Right D. of Kings POPE 580:20
say that D. providence JOHN 408:6
some d. despair TENN 765:19
To forgive, d. POPE 584:27
to forgive d. PROV 613:8
what the form d. LAND 450:3
divinely most d. fair TENN 758:16
divineness participation of d. BACO 41:11
diviner d. air WORD 829:1
divines Doubts 'mongst D. SPEN 734:17
divinest two d. things HUNT 395:17
diving-bell religious d. FOST 321:12

divinity d. doth hedge a king SHAK 666:6
d. in odd numbers SHAK 689:1
d. that shapes our ends SHAK 667:1
d. that stirs within ADDI 4:16
mysteries in d. BROW 153:15
piece of d. in us BROW 154:3
division D. is as bad ANON 17:19
we make no d. between any KORA 444:3
divisions How many d. has *he* got STAL 736:3
divisos *penitus toto d. orbe* VIRG 795:15
divorce bill of my d. DONN 273:3
long d. of steel SHAK 673:7
divorces d. his first wife TALM 754:17
dixeris *D. egregie notum* HORA 385:14
dixit *Ipse d.* CICE 217:13
dizzy d. 'tis to cast one's eyes SHAK 679:19
DNA cannot cheat on D. WARD 803:10
do All one has to d. is I-HS 398:18
Can I d. you now, sir CATC 195:6
can't all d. everything VIRG 796:10
damned if you d. DOW 277:3
did not d. things themselves RAVE 622:8
D. as I say PROV 598:21
D. as I say SELD 653:24
D. as you would be done by CHES 209:11
D. as you would be done by PROV 598:22
D. IT YOURSELF BARH 54:11
Do not d. to others what CONF 232:1
d. not do to your neighbour HILL 377:7
don't d. it at all BISH 116:2
d. only one thing SMIL 722:18
D. other men DICK 263:5
D. unto others as you would PROV 598:43
d. what had to be done HAVE 364:2
d. what I please FRED 324:1
d. what is right HUXL 397:13
D. what thou wilt CROW 246:17
d. what thou wouldst do HATC 363:17
d. ye even so to them BIBL 94:6
fine pleasure is not to d. HOPK 385:8
George—don't d. that GREN 352:16
HOW NOT TO D. IT DICK 262:25
I can d. no other LUTH 479:13
If to d. were as easy SHAK 687:7
I'll do, I'll do, and I'll d. SHAK 681:11
I'll d.'t before I speak SHAK 677:25
know not what they d. BIBL 100:26
Let's d. it PORT 588:7
Let us d.—or die BURN 168:8
let us d. or die CAMP 183:6
Love and d. what you will AUGU 36:9
never know what you can d. PROV 615:47
not knowing what they d. SHAK 691:16
one that will d. the deed SHAK 680:23
people who d. things MORR 533:6
Say little and d. much SHAM 706:4
so much to d. LAST 457:4
supposed to d. anyway TRUM 784:2
to my servant, D. this BIBL 94:16
We cannot d. it, Sir CARR 191:6
what I d. in any thing HERB 372:12
What must I d. to be saved BIBL 104:3
what you are afraid to d. EMER 299:19
would they should d. unto me BOOK 130:13
doc cards with a man called D. ALGR 12:1
What's up, D. CATC 196:27
docent *dum d. discunt* SENE 654:18
doctor any other d. whatsoever HOBB 378:15
artless d. sees HERR 374:11
d. does not give you a year STEV 741:22
d. found, when she was dead GOLD 344:21
d. full of phrase ARNO 28:5
fee the d. DRYD 281:13
God and the d. OWEN 562:1
keeps the d. away PROV 595:13
doctors believe the d. SALI 642:16
best d. are Dr Diet PROV 595:44
budge d. of the stoic fur MILT 511:28
D. in verse THOM 773:12
d. know a hopeless case CUMM 247:10
might be medical doctors DICK 266:2
violet-hooded D. TENN 765:12
when d. disagree POPE 583:18
doctrinal On the d. side QUIN 619:4
doctrine all the winds of d. MILT 519:19
blast of vain d. BOOK 128:21
d. of ignoble ease ROOS 633:4
d. something you kill for BENN 65:8
every wind of d. BIBL 108:3
life and d. BOOK 129:13
loved the d. DEFO 255:5
Much d. lies under FANS 306:9
not for the d. POPE 584:20
doctrines d. without words LAO 451:6
makes all d. plain BUTL 172:11
documents d. and friends SPAR 731:16
dodger artful D. DICK 264:14
doers be ye d. of the word BIBL 110:14
Evil d. evil dreaders PROV 599:45
does d., not suffers wrong SHEL 713:5
D. she or doesn't she ADVE 7:14
He who can d. PROV 602:24
doest That thou d., do quickly BIBL 102:15
dog Am I a d. BIBL 78:33
barking d. never bites PROV 595:34
beaten d. beneath the hail POUN 589:22
better than his d. TENN 762:23
Beware of the d. PETR 574:14
black d. JOHN 417:7
call a d. *Hervey* JOHN 412:7
cut-throat d. SHAK 687:15
D. does not eat dog PROV 598:23
d. in the night-time DOYL 277:18
d. is allowed one bite PROV 599:24
d. is for life SAYI 647:11
d. is to the Greenlander KOHL 443:9
d. is turned to his own vomit BIBL 111:10
d. it was that died GOLD 344:22
d. returneth to his vomit BIBL 83:24
D. returns to his Vomit KIPL 438:20
d. returns to its vomit PROV 598:24
d. shall bear him company POPE 585:11
d.-star rages POPE 583:1
d. starved at his master's gate BLAK 117:19
d.'s tooth PROV 612:48
d.'s walking on his hinder legs JOHN 413:17
d. that will fetch a bone PROV 598:26
d. the only intelligent member LEON 464:7
engine of pollution, the d. SPAR 731:22
every d. has his day BORR 143:12
Every d. has his day PROV 599:23
every d. his day KING 437:13
Give a d. a bad name PROV 601:4
good d. goes to church PROV 602:6
Has a d. the Buddha-Nature MUMO 536:8
heart to a d. to tear KIPL 440:2
I had rather be a d. SHAK 676:19
I never heard thy d. HEYW 376:7
Is thy servant a d. BIBL 80:21
keep a d. and bark yourself PROV 615:7
lame d. over a stile CHIL 212:4
let no d. bark SHAK 687:3
limps the hungry d. BLOK 122:6
live d. is better PROV 605:47
living d. BIBL 84:20
lost d. somewhere ANOU 22:13
Lovell our d. COLL 228:9
Love me, love my d. PROV 606:8
man bites a d. BOGA 123:13
Mine enemy's d. SHAK 680:2
more ridiculous than a d. NERV 541:8
My d.! what remedy remains COWP 240:22
over the lazy d. ANON 18:11
poor d. had none NURS 549:18
poor d. that's not worth PROV 604:4
poor d. Tray CAMP 183:7
stick to beat a d. PROV 604:16
teach an old d. new tricks PROV 615:30
to a d.'s tail YEAT 837:18
tongue of d. SHAK 684:18
very d. to the commonalty SHAK 660:1
was there ever d. YEAT 837:16
ways of killing a d. PROV 611:47
ways of killing a d. PROV 611:48
whose d. are you POPE 582:26
woman, d., and walnut tree PROV 615:13
working like a d. LENN 463:22
your wife and your d. HILL 376:14
Doge quiet D. of Venice WALP 801:23
dogged d. as does it PROV 604:33
d. as does it TROL 782:17
doggie How much is that d. MERR 505:24
dogma Any stigma to beat a d. GUED 354:9
d. has been the fundamental principle NEWM 542:7
no d., no Dean DISR 271:6
dogmatize d. and am contradicted JOHN 418:6
dogs all things as straw d. LAO 451:7
Cowardly d. bark loudest WEBS 808:11
cruel as d. one to another PEPY 573:8
d. and apes BROW 155:33
D. are Shakespearean SCHW 649:15
d. bark at me SHAK 696:9
D. bark, but the caravan PROV 598:25
d. eat of the crumbs BIBL 96:1
d. go on with their doggy life AUDE 34:10
d., horses JENY 406:12
d. licked his sores BIBL 100:10
D. look up to us CHUR 216:22
d. of Europe bark AUDE 34:2
fought the d. BROW 157:10
gaze of d. CALV 182:8
go to the d. tonight HERB 371:11
hates d. and babies ROST 635:17
Lame d. over stiles KING 437:5
Let d. delight WATT 805:8
Let sleeping d. lie PROV 605:18
let slip the d. of war SHAK 675:22
lie down with d. PROV 603:34
like dancing d. JOHN 415:6
little d. and all SHAK 679:10
mad and hungry d. MCKA 486:6
Mad d. and Englishmen COWA 238:15
more I like d. ROLA 632:4
more one values d. TOUS 780:2
na men, but d. BURN 169:7
paparazzi d. of war DENE 257:8
Throw physic to the d. SHAK 685:19
two d. are fighting PROV 614:44
without are d. BIBL 113:15
doileys soiling the d. BETJ 70:11
doing As for D.-good THOR 776:8
continuance in well d. BIBL 104:28
d. in that galley MOLI 525:7
joy's soul lies in the d. SHAK 700:5
not be weary in well d. BIBL 107:23
one way of *d.* RUSK 638:27
put me to d. METH 506:6
see what she's d. PUNC 617:12
still be d. BUTL 171:24
This is the Lord's d. BOOK 140:6
doings child is known by his d. BIBL 83:9
doleful Knight of the D. Countenance CERV 199:16
dolendum *d. est Primum ipsi tibi* HORA 385:18
dolente CITTÀ D. DANT 249:7
doll d. in the doll's house DICK 265:1
living d., everywhere you look PLAT 577:11
dollar almighty d. ANON 15:7
almighty d. IRVI 400:4
billion d. country FOST 321:10
dolmens d. round my childhood MONT 527:5
dolore *Nessun maggior d.* DANT 249:12
dolorem *iubes renovare d.* VIRG 793:16
Dolores splendid and sterile D. SWIN 750:16
dolorous d. mansions MILT 513:25
stroke most d. MALO 492:8
dolour d. of pad and paper-weight ROET 631:7
d. that they made MALO 492:14

dolphin d.-torn, that gong-tormented YEAT 835:7
mermaid on a d.'s back SHAK 689:22
dolphins butter made of d.' milk JONS 419:9
gentler d. MOOR 530:6
dome blue d. of the air SHEL 711:7
d. of many-coloured glass SHEL 711:4
d. of the sky WORD 827:11
singing beneath the d. VERL 791:10
starlit or a moonlit d. YEAT 835:6
domes plump with d. THWA 777:6
domestic appreciate d. bliss SANT 644:10
d. Armageddon LEON 464:11
d. business MONT 527:13
d. sort which never stirs SHER 716:16
Malice d. SHAK 684:5
men call d. bliss PATM 569:20
pleasures of d. life GIBB 335:7
respectable d. establishment BENN 65:17
domesticate d. the Recording Angel STEV 742:2
domi *Res angusta d.* JUVE 424:12
dominant Hark, the d.'s persistence BROW 158:6
domination against white d. MAND 493:7
dominations Thrones, d. MILT 517:1
domine D., defende nos GODL 342:2
dominion death hath no more d. BIBL 105:1
death shall have no d. THOM 772:1
d. of kings changed PRIC 591:9
d. of religion GOLD 344:5
d. of the master HUME 394:14
hand that holds d. THOM 772:8
His d. shall be also BOOK 136:18
let them have d. BIBL 73:14
Man's d. BURN 168:23
dominions His Majesty's d. NORT 546:16
not set in my d. SCHI 648:11
domino 'falling d.' principle EISE 291:9
dominus *D. illuminatio mea* BIBL 113:17
D. illuminatio mea MOTT 535:7
D. vobiscum MISS 520:7
Nisi D. BIBL 113:24
domum *Ite d. saturae* VIRG 796:13
don D. John of Austria is going CHES 210:11
d. *manqué* LAMB 449:10
my back upon D. or devil TENN 766:9
quiet flows the D. SHOL 717:12
Remote and ineffectual D. BELL 63:18
dona *d. nobis pacem* MISS 522:19
Requiem aeternam d. eis MISS 523:2
timeo Danaos et d. ferentes VIRG 793:18
done Been there, d. that SAYI 647:1
decide that d. can be done ALLE 12:7
Do as you would be d. by CHES 209:11
Do as you would be d. by PROV 598:22
D. because we are too menny HARD 360:12
d. the state some service SHAK 694:3
d. very well out of the war BALD 49:5
d. when 'tis done SHAK 682:8
he d. her wrong SONG 729:5
If you want anything d. THAT 769:20
Inasmuch as ye have d. BIBL 97:13
Nay, I have d. DRAY 279:3
not a genius, I'm done for BALZ 53:2
not d. in a corner BIBL 104:21
Nothing to be d. BECK 59:21
remained to be d. LUCA 478:15
something d. LONG 474:20
Something must be d. WHIT 814:13
surprised to find it d. JOHN 413:17
that which is d. BIBL 84:3
Things won are d. SHAK 700:5
this that thou hast d. BIBL 74:2
thou hast not d. DONN 273:6
want a thing d. well PROV 603:38
we have d. those things BOOK 125:16
What could she have d. YEAT 836:20
Whatever man has d. PROV 613:50
What is to be d. LENI 463:9
What's d. cannot be undone PROV 614:7
What's d. cannot be undone SHAK 685:12
what's d. is done SHAK 684:4
what should be d. MELB 504:5
dong D. with a luminous nose LEAR 460:6
donkey dead d. DICK 265:19
donkeys Lions led by d. MILI 508:11
Donne another Newton, a new D. HUXL 397:6
John D., Anne Donne DONN 275:14
donné *Si le Roi m'avait d.* ANON 20:13
Don Quixote *D., Robinson Crusoe* JOHN 418:14
dons If the D. sight Devon NEWB 541:14
don't about to marry.—'d.' PUNC 617:2
damned if you d. DOW 277:3
D. ask me, ask the horse FREU 324:16
D. think twice DYLA 287:5
doodle Cock a d. doo! NURS 547:16
Yankee D. SONG 730:9
doom changed his d. CLEV 220:17
d. assigned TENN 764:17
great d.'s image SHAK 683:19
Master of the Day of D. KORA 443:13
regardless of their d. GRAY 350:16
scaffold and the d. AYTO 40:10
to the edge of d. SHAK 705:17
doomed D. for a certain term SHAK 662:23
d. to death DRYD 281:16
Doomsday D. is near SHAK 669:1
Doon braes o' bonny D. BURN 166:16
door angel from your d. BLAK 120:16
beating on the d. YEAT 836:4
coming in at one d. BEDE 60:19
creaking d. hangs longest PROV 597:42
Death's shadow at the d. BLUN 122:10
d. flew open HOFF 380:3
d. must be either shut PROV 598:41
d. we never opened ELIO 294:2
handle of the big front d. GILB 338:27
hard at death's d. BOOK 139:13
I am the d. BIBL 102:5
knock at the d. LAMB 448:14
knocking at Preferment's d. ARNO 27:5
knocking at the d. SHAW 709:23
lights around the d. ROSS 635:8
make a d. and bar BIBL 92:4
my d. stayed shut RACI 620:1
Never open the d. GRAC 347:14
prejudices through the d. FRED 323:21
rapping at my chamber d. POE 579:15
splintered the d. AUDE 34:18
stand at the d., and knock BIBL 111:29
Then—shuts the D. DICK 266:14
through the d. with a gun CHAN 201:19
When one d. shuts PROV 614:23
when the d. opens GREE 351:23
whining of a d. DONN 275:8
wide as a church d. SHAK 697:22
wrong side of the d. CHES 210:3
doorkeeper d. in the house of my God BOOK 137:13
doormat d. in a world of boots RHYS 626:1
d. or a prostitute WEST 812:14
doors close softly the d. JUST 423:19
Death has a thousand d. MASS 501:6
Death hath so many d. FLET 318:4
d. of perception BLAK 119:28
D., where my heart was TENN 760:28
Men shut their d. SHAK 699:17
slamming D. BELL 63:11
ten thousand several d. WEBS 808:1
thousand d. open on to it SENE 654:20
with both d. open HUGH 392:15
ye everlasting d. BOOK 133:3
your living d. MILT 517:8
doorstep do this on the d. JUNO 423:18
sweep his own d. PROV 603:15
dooryard last in the d. bloomed WHIT 815:23
Dorcas D.: this woman BIBL 103:27
dormitat *bonus d. Homerus* HORA 386:5
Dorset FUNERAL MONDAY D. TELE 758:9
dotage Pedantry is the d. JACK 400:16
streams of d. flow JOHN 411:18
dote D. on his imperfections EPHE 300:18
Dotheboys D. Hall DICK 263:17
dots damned d. meant CHUR 214:17
double Double, d. toil and trouble SHAK 684:17
d. was his praise SPEN 733:23
Labour's d. whammy POLI 581:23
leading a d. life WILD 817:20
peace of the d.-bed CAMP 182:15
doubles d. your chances for a date ALLE 12:16
doublet bought his d. in Italy SHAK 687:9
tailor make thy d. SHAK 701:22
doublethink D. means the power ORWE 558:27
doubt Book wherein is no d. KORA 443:15
curiosity, freckles, and d. PARK 567:2
do not make one d. NEWM 542:9
d. and sorrow BARI 54:14
d. is Devil-born TENN 761:24
Humility is the only d. BLAK 118:14
in d., strike it out TWAI 786:24
in d. what should be done MELB 504:5
let us never, never d. BELL 63:22
Life is d. UNAM 787:6
mind is clouded with a d. TENN 760:17
more faith in honest d. TENN 761:25
No possible d. whatever GILB 337:6
Our d. is our passion JAME 403:8
philosophy calls all in d. DONN 272:7
shameful to d. one's friends LA R 453:13
sunnier side of d. TENN 757:10
time will d. of Rome BYRO 177:6
When in d., do nowt PROV 614:21
wherefore didst thou d. BIBL 95:27
doubter d. and the doubt EMER 299:6
doubtful D. disputations BIBL 105:23
doubtless d. come again with joy BOOK 140:20
doubts Ah whiles hae ma d. PUNC 617:18
D. 'mongst Divines SPEN 734:17
end in d. BACO 41:8
His d. are better HARD 360:6
Kind jealous d. ROCH 630:11
my d. are done DRYD 281:18
saucy d. and fears SHAK 684:9
Douglas doughty D. BALL 50:7
Like D. conquer HOME 381:18
dove all the d. CRAS 244:5
at eagles with a d. HERB 373:9
d. found no rest BIBL 74:17
on the burnished d. TENN 762:22
sweet d. died KEAT 427:31
wings like a d. BOOK 135:10
wings of a d. BOOK 136:7
dovecote eagle in a d. SHAK 660:17
Dover farthing candle at D. JOHN 413:16
milestones on the D. Road DICK 262:26
white cliffs of D. BURT 169:19
doves d.' eyes BIBL 85:14
harmless as d. BIBL 94:34
moan of d. TENN 766:6
dovetailedness universal d. DICK 264:4
dowagers d. for deans TENN 765:12
dower d. of river, wood KEAT 427:1
faith's transcendent d. WORD 831:16
truth then be thy d. SHAK 677:23
dowie d. dens BALL 50:15
down born with D.'s syndrome DE G 256:1
D. among the dead DYER 287:2
D. and out in Paris ORWE 558:11
d. and out of breath SHAK 669:17
d. express in the small of the back WODE 824:17
D. in the forest SIMP 720:14
d. into the darkness MILL 509:10
D. to Gehenna KIPL 439:10
Easy is the way d. VIRG 794:17
Finds the d. pillow hard SHAK 660:27
fled Him, d. the nights THOM 774:4
go d. to the sea BOOK 139:14
Had me low and had me d. GERS 334:12

down (*cont.*):
He that is d. BUNY 161:12
kicked d. stairs HALI 358:4
knowest my d.-sitting BOOK 141:9
meet 'em on your way d. MIZN 524:11
quite, quite, d. SHAK 664:10
soft young d. of her MEW 506:13
staying d. with him WASH 804:3
What goes up must come d. PROV 614:1
downfall regress is either a d. BACO 43:10
downhearted Are we d. KNIG 442:6
Are we d. MILI 508:4
We are not d. CHAM 200:15
downhill run by itself except d. SAYI 647:3
downs in the D. the fleet was moored GAY 332:20
downstairs kick me d. BICK 114:13
downwards gross flesh sinks d. SHAK 696:6
look no way but d. BUNY 161:10
doxy Heterodoxy or Thy-d. CARL 187:23
dozens Mother to d. HERB 371:14
Whom he reckons up by d. GILB 338:26
drab Ditch-delivered by a d. SHAK 684:19
dragging naked, d. themselves GINS 339:20
dragnet swept like a d. DRYD 283:13
dragon d. and his wrath SHAK 677:24
d.-green, the luminous FLEC 317:2
d. of the hills SUTT 747:8
fought against the d. BIBL 112:19
laid hold on the d. BIBL 113:4
lion and the d. BOOK 137:23
O to be a d. MOOR 529:16
under the d.'s tail SHAK 678:6
dragonfly d. Hangs like a blue thread ROSS 634:23
dragonish cloud that's d. SHAK 657:12
dragons Bores have succeeded to d. DISR 270:35
brother to d. BIBL 81:28
d., and all deeps BOOK 141:27
d. in their pleasant palaces BIBL 87:6
habitation of d. BIBL 87:20
laugh at live d. TOLK 779:2
drain From this foul d. pure gold TOCQ 778:18
drains Deity and the D. STRA 744:8
opiate to the d. KEAT 429:8
drake D.he's in his hammock NEWB 541:15
drama d. onto the moral plane GIDE 336:16
d. out of a crisis ADVE 8:19
d.'s laws JOHN 411:11
great d. critic TYNA 786:31
dramas other people's d. LERM 464:22
dramatist d. want more liberties JAME 403:1
dramatists first of d. MACA 481:11
dramatize D. it, dramatize it JAME 402:23
Drang *Sturm und D.* KAUF 426:6
drank d. my ale FARQ 307:5
d. of Aganippe well SIDN 718:16
d. without the provocation SWIF 748:2
still my body d. COLE 226:21
drastic D. measures ANST 22:16
draughts susceptible to d. WILD 817:21
draughty d. street corner GRIF 353:11
draw d. like these children PICA 576:1
D. near with faith BOOK 129:15
D. not up seas DONN 274:21
d. to our end BIBL 91:12
d. you to her DRYD 282:36
drawers d. of water BIBL 77:21
Pee, po, belly, bum, d. FLAN 316:3
drawing D. is the true test INGR 399:19
d. on the level of an untaught child BLUN 122:14
no d. back BRON 150:5
drawing-room feelings of women in a d. WOOL 826:19
same men in the d. HALI 357:12
through my d. EDEN 288:8
dread d. beat JOHN 408:7
d. of beatings BETJ 71:8
From Brig o' D. BALL 51:3
let him be your d. BIBL 86:27
Nor d. nor hope attend YEAT 835:14
nothing did he d. SPEN 733:14
secret d. ADDI 4:16
What d. hand BLAK 121:9
dreaded most d. instrument WORD 830:11
dreadful acting of a d. thing SHAK 675:1
city of d. night THOM 775:20
deed of d. note SHAK 684:6
dreading D. and hoping all YEAT 835:14
dreadnoughts as much to keep up as two D. LLOY 471:1
dream as a d. Dies WATT 805:19
as a d. doth flatter SHAK 705:5
behold it was a d. BUNY 161:9
but a brief d. PETR 574:12
children d. not BROW 154:6
d., a lightning flash MAHĀ 490:6
d. between two awakenings O'NE 554:21
d. But of a shadow CHAP 202:13
dreamed of was a d. ROSS 634:6
d. I am dreaming COWA 238:18
d. my dreams away FLAN 315:21
D. of a funeral PROV 598:44
d. of fair women TENN 758:15
d. of money-bags SHAK 687:20
d. of peace HUNT 395:11
d. of reason GOYA 347:13
d. of the devil BARH 54:5
d. that is dying O'SH 560:12
D. the impossible DARI 250:8
d. within a dream POE 579:13
d. you are crossing GILB 337:19
falls into a d. CONR 234:15
freshness of a d. WORD 829:14
from the d. of life SHEL 710:23
glory and the d. WORD 829:19
hideous d. SHAK 675:1
if I d. I have you DONN 273:23
I have a d. KING 436:14
In a d. you are never eighty SEXT 655:8
Is a d. a lie SPRI 735:13
life to a d. MONT 528:3
like unto them that d. BOOK 140:19
love's young d. MOOR 530:13
no longer a d. CLIN 221:7
not d. them KING 437:4
old men's d. DRYD 280:5
Paradise in a d. COLE 227:1
peace is a d. MOLT 525:23
salesman is got to d. MILL 509:22
say what d. it was SHAK 690:16
short as any d. SHAK 689:5
sight to d. of COLE 224:20
silence of a d. ROSS 634:3
so d. all night KEAT 427:27
Soft! I did but d. SHAK 696:29
thou must not d. ARNO 26:8
till you find your d. HAMM 358:17
To sleep: perchance to d. SHAK 664:3
vanished like a d. CARL 187:29
waking d. KEAT 429:16
We live, as we d. CONR 234:11
what my d. was SHAK 690:17
without a d. ROST 635:13
dreamed d. in a dream WHIT 815:2
d. I saw Joe Hill HAYE 365:1
d. of, in any philosophy HALD 356:15
d. of the devil ANST 22:14
d. that I dwelt BUNN 160:10
d. that life was beauty HOOP 383:8
he d., and behold BIBL 75:1
I've d. of cheese STEV 741:21
dreamer Beautiful d. FOST 321:14
Behold, this d. cometh BIBL 75:10
d. of dreams BIBL 77:7
D. of dreams MORR 532:12
poet and the d. KEAT 427:19
dreamers d. of another existence BYRO 180:1
We are the d. of dreams O'SH 560:11
dreaming butterfly d. that CHUA 213:2
demon's that is d. POE 579:19
d. of a white Christmas BERL 68:12
D.' of thee WALL 799:13
d. on the verge of strife CORN 237:3
d. spires ARNO 27:25
world on d. fed YEAT 837:11
dreams armoured cars of d. BISH 115:18
as we see it in our d. CHEK 208:5
books are either d. or swords LOWE 477:10
city of perspiring d. RAPH 622:4
Come to me in my d. ARNO 26:9
d. are dreams CALD 181:5
D. go by contraries PROV 598:45
d. of a poet JOHN 409:6
d. of avarice JOHN 416:20
d. of avarice MOOR 529:10
d. of joy and fear SHEL 714:11
d. out of the ivory gate BROW 154:6
d. their children dreamed COLE 224:18
d. to sell BEDD 60:18
drug of d. ELIO 293:18
drunken in my d. COLE 226:21
Even in d. CALD 181:4
Fanatics have their d. KEAT 427:17
from uneasy d. KAFK 425:9
from uneasy d. OPEN 556:26
I have bad d. SHAK 663:17
Inaudible as d. COLE 225:13
In d. begins responsibility YEAT 838:1
in some brighter d. VAUG 790:14
interpretation of d. FREU 324:13
interpretation of d. MISQ 521:8
land of my d. KING 436:19
level of your d. SHAK 703:6
Like transitory d. ROCH 630:9
Morning d. come true PROV 607:11
Of fantasy, of d. SHAK 675:4
old men shall dream d. BIBL 90:14
quick D. SHEL 710:16
scream for help in d. CANE 184:18
stuff As d. are made on SHAK 699:6
tread on my d. YEAT 836:5
dreamt d. I went to Manderley DU M 284:17
d. I went to Manderley OPEN 555:30
d. of in your philosophy SHAK 663:4
dreary drags its d. length DICK 260:18
dregs d. of Romulus CICE 217:9
from the d. of life DRYD 281:3
These d. of life THOM 775:3
dress all this fleshly d. VAUG 790:9
car has become an article of d. MCLU 487:10
d. by yellow candle-light STEV 742:11
d. of thought POPE 584:19
evening d. is a must GREN 352:15
make a d. out of a curtain POWE 590:13
noble youth did d. SHAK 669:31
Peace, the human d. BLAK 120:15
put on a d. of guilt MCGO 485:9
sweet disorder in the d. HERR 374:8
why do we d. BEHN 62:9
dressed all d. up BURT 169:18
all d. up WHIT 814:23
d. fine as I will WATT 805:7
d. in modern clothing STRA 744:12
impossible to be well d. AMIE 13:9
dressing d. old words new SHAK 705:1
dressmakers Without d. RIDI 627:14
drest D. in a little brief authority SHAK 686:10
Dr Fell do not love thee, D. BROW 152:7
dried at once be d. up DOST 275:15
drift adamant for d. CHUR 215:3
drifted but I d. WEST 812:8
drink ale's the stuff to d. HOUS 391:9
but little d. below HOLM 381:9
can't make him d. PROV 615:33
d. and drive OFFI 554:5
d. and no be drunk BURN 168:19
D. and the devil STEV 741:18
d. deep HESI 375:14
D. deep, or taste not POPE 584:15
D. fair DICK 263:13

D., sir, is a great provoker SHAK 683:15
d. the blood of goats BOOK 135:3
d. till they were sick WILL 820:4
D. to me only JONS 420:20
D. ye all of this BOOK 129:22
eat and to d. BIBL 76:17
eat, d., and be merry BIBL 99:21
every creature d. but I COWL 239:11
gavest meat or d. BALL 51:4
he has taken to d. TARK 755:3
I d. for it WAUG 806:21
I d. well MORT 534:2
in debt, and in d. BROM 149:6
Let us eat and d. BIBL 87:9
never taste who always d. PRIO 593:7
Nor any drop to d. COLE 226:12
Our d. shall be prepared JONS 420:11
reasons we should d. ALDR 11:2
shall give to d. BIBL 95:4
strong d. BIBL 83:37
strong d. is raging BIBL 83:7
their portion to d. BOOK 132:3
thirsty and ye gave me d. BIBL 97:12
to buy a d. CUMM 247:5
to eat, and to d. BIBL 84:19
your husband I would d. it CHUR 216:23
drinka D. Pinta Milka Day ADVE 7:17
drinkers When d. drink BURN 167:13
drinking curse of the d. classes WILD 819:13
d. all the time TURN 785:18
D. is the soldier's pleasure DRYD 280:18
D. my griefs SHAK 695:21
D. the blude-red wine BALL 51:13
D. the blude-red wine OPEN 555:29
D. when we are not thirsty BEAU 58:10
in a tavern d. ANON 21:10
merry, dancing, d. DRYD 282:16
much d., little thinking SWIF 748:7
no d. after death FLET 318:1
Now for d. HORA 388:3
'Tis not the d. SELD 653:15
drinks d. as much as you do THOM 772:21
d. beer, thinks beer PROV 602:12
get at the d. and food CORS 237:10
dripping d. June sets all PROV 598:46
D. water hollows out OVID 561:11
electricity was d. THUR 776:23
drive can't d. the car TYNA 787:1
difficult to d. BROU 151:14
drink and d. OFFI 554:5
D. gently over the stones PROV 598:47
I d. through the street CLOU 221:21
driver in the d.'s seat BEAV 59:2
drives Who d. fat oxen JOHN 417:13
driveth d. furiously BIBL 80:23
driving d. briskly in a post-chaise JOHN 415:22
d. while looking RODD 631:3
like the d. of Jehu BIBL 80:23
drizzly every d. brain BYRO 175:22
Drogheda endeavours at D. CROM 245:11
drollery fatal d. DISR 270:27
dromedary d., two NASH 539:8
muse on d. trots COLE 226:2
droning beetle wheels his d. flight GRAY 350:6
droon d. twa ANON 18:15
droop D. in a hundred A.B.C.'s ELIO 293:24
silkworms d. BASH 56:18
droopingly d., but with a hopeful heart LAWR 457:22
drop as a d. of a bucket BIBL 88:3
Drop, d., slow tears FLET 318:13
d. in the ocean TERE 768:6
d. into thyself POPE 585:21
d. of Negro blood HUGH 393:1
last d. makes the cup PROV 605:9
like very well to d. JOHN 416:18
Nor any d. to drink COLE 226:12
thy clouds d. fatness BOOK 136:2
turn on, tune in and d. out LEAR 460:23
dropped heavens d. BOOK 136:6
Things have d. from me WOOL 827:2
wish to be d. by JOHN 416:18
dropping Constant d. wears away PROV 597:36
continual d. BIBL 83:30
d. down the ladder KIPL 438:18
D. the pilot TENN 757:9
drops D. earliest to the ground SHAK 688:8
d. on gate-bars hang HARD 361:23
Little d. of water CARN 189:2
ruddy d. SHAK 675:7
drought d. is destroying his roots HERB 371:12
d. of March CHAU 204:6
d. of March OPEN 556:25
drove d. them all out of the temple BIBL 101:15
drown D. all my faults FLET 318:14
I'll d. my book SHAK 699:10
drownded d. now and again SYNG 751:20
drowned BETTER D. THAN DUFFERS TELE 758:2
d. in the depth of the sea BIBL 96:8
d. in yonder living blue TENN 762:3
d. my glory FITZ 315:1
he was d. in GILB 337:2
Lies d. with us HERR 374:7
never be d. PROV 603:36
drowning d. man will clutch PROV 598:48
d. their speaking BROW 157:10
like death by d. FERB 308:12
no d. mark SHAK 698:16
not waving but d. SMIT 724:21
drowns d. things weighty BACO 43:26
drowsy Dapples the d. east SHAK 691:23
d. numbness OPEN 556:3
d. numbness pains KEAT 429:6
d. syrups of the world SHAK 692:29
ear of a d. man SHAK 677:12
drudge harmless d. JOHN 409:10
drudgery love of the d. SMIT 724:10
Makes d. divine HERB 372:14
drudges laborious d. KIPL 441:20
drug consciousness-expanding d. CLAR 219:11
d. neither moral nor immoral ZAPP 839:23
literature is a d. BORR 143:11
no more hope to end d. abuse WHIT 816:3
Poetry's a mere d. FARQ 307:19
you can d., with words LOWE 477:10
drugs D. is like having a cup GALL 328:15
Sex and d. and rock and roll DURY 286:9
so-called soft d. STRA 744:17
what d., what charms SHAK 691:32
drum big bass d. LIND 469:8
Dumb as a d. DICK 265:9
morning d.-beat WEBS 807:13
music of a *distant* d. FITZ 314:10
My pulse, like a soft d. KING 436:8
Not a d. was heard WOLF 825:3
Rhyme still the most effective d. GIRA 340:7
Take my d. to England NEWB 541:14
drummer hears a different d. THOR 776:16
drumming d. in my ears SAPP 644:14
in the valley d. AUDE 34:17
drums d. begin to roll KIPL 440:13
like muffled d. LONG 474:4
drunk art of getting d. JOHN 416:9
be not d. with wine BIBL 108:9
drink and no be d. BURN 168:19
d. for about a week FITZ 315:11
d. him to his bed SHAK 657:1
d. moderately BIBL 92:7
d. old wine BIBL 99:2
eaten and d. enough HORA 387:10
fields have d. enough VIRG 796:3
from Philip d. ANON 15:11
genteel when he gets d. BOSW 144:21
hasten to be d. DRYD 281:11
I have d. SHAK 703:3
inarticulate, and then d. BYRO 180:3
made them d. SHAK 683:3
must get d. BYRO 176:14
not so think as you d. SQUI 735:15
partly she was d. BURN 167:19
stood by him when he was d. SHER 716:28
this d. is drunk DICK 265:12
Was the hope d. SHAK 682:14
when men have well d. BIBL 101:14
Wordsworth d. and Porson sober HOUS 391:11
drunken brought d. forth SHAK 657:24
children, sailors, and d. men PROV 602:36
d. in my dreams COLE 226:21
d. man uses lampposts LANG 450:12
stagger like a d. man BOOK 139:15
drunkenness sin of d. JAME 402:11
druv Sussex won't be d. PROV 611:36
dry barren and d. land BOOK 135:24
But oh! I am so d. FARM 307:2
die a d. death SHAK 698:18
done in the d. BIBL 100:25
d. as summer dust WORD 828:9
d. brain in a dry season ELIO 294:23
dwelling in a d. place COLE 227:23
in a d. place BIBL 87:19
keep your powder d. BLAC 116:21
keep your powder d. PROV 610:1
oh, I am so d. ANON 16:21
old man in a d. month ELIO 294:21
on d. ground BIBL 77:19
or being d. ALDR 11:2
O ye d. bones BIBL 89:34
refresh it when it was d. BOOK 127:20
Sow d. and set wet PROV 611:11
dryad light-wingèd D. KEAT 429:6
dual holds d. citizenship SONT 728:9
duality world appeared in d. ZORO 841:19
dubious d. hand JOHN 411:16
Dublin Dear, dirty D. JOYC 421:16
D. Castle KETT 434:15
ducat Dead, for a d. SHAK 665:12
ducats O my d.! O my daughter SHAK 687:23
duce *in d. summo* JUVE 424:22
duchess blossom into a D. AILE 9:1
chambermaid as of a D. JOHN 416:6
every D. in London MACD 485:2
I am D. of Malfi still WEBS 807:25
That's my last D. BROW 156:24
duck just forgot to d. DEMP 257:5
looks like a d. REUT 624:17
ducks d., produce bad parents MORS 533:7
I turn to d. HARV 363:14
stealing d. ARAB 23:9
due Give the Devil his d. PROV 601:9
in d. time BOOK 127:13
to every one his d. JUST 424:1
dues Render to all their d. BIBL 105:20
duffers BETTER DROWNED THAN D. TELE 758:2
dugs old man with wrinkled d. ELIO 296:9
duke bears a d.'s revenues SHAK 672:16
D. of Plaza Toro GILB 337:5
everybody praised the D. SOUT 730:13
From tyrant d. SHAK 658:10
fully-equipped d. LLOY 471:1
knows enough who knows a d. COWP 242:12
dukedom d. large enough SHAK 698:21
dukes drawing room full of d. AUDE 35:14
d. were three a penny GILB 337:9
dulce *D. est desipere* HORA 389:11
D. et decorum est HORA 388:14
D. et decorum est OWEN 562:8
D. ridentem HORA 388:1
dulcet d. and harmonious breath SHAK 689:22
dulci *qui miscuit utile d.* HORA 386:3
dulcimer damsel with a d. COLE 225:24
psaltery, d. BIBL 90:1
dulcius *nil d. est* LUCR 479:3
dull at best but d. and hoary VAUG 790:12
dictionaries is d. work JOHN 409:8
d. and deep potations GIBB 335:18

dull (*cont.*):
d. as ditch water DICK 264:27
d. in a new way JOHN 414:25
d. in himself FOOT 319:7
d. it is to pause TENN 767:9
D. 'mongst the dullest CHUR 214:7
d. product of a scoffer's pen WORD 828:10
D. would he be of soul WORD 827:19
makes Jack a d. boy PROV 595:6
not bred so d. SHAK 688:4
paper appears d. STEE 736:20
Sherry is d. JOHN 413:15
smoothly d. POPE 580:15
some d. opiate KEAT 429:6
that he be d. ACHE 1:13
venerably d. CHUR 214:9
very d., dreary affair MAUG 502:7
What's this d. town to me KEPP 434:4
who can be d. in Fleet Street LAMB 448:24
dullard d.'s envy of brilliant men BEER 61:14
duller d. shouldst thou be SHAK 662:28
dullness cause of d. in others FOOT 319:7
d. and stupidity ASTE 31:13
Gentle D. POPE 580:11
dumb as a sheep is d. BIBL 88:17
D. as a drum DICK 265:9
d. presagers SHAK 704:12
d. son of a bitch TRUM 784:8
d. to tell THOM 772:6
Nature is d. TURG 785:5
otherwise I shall be d. KEAT 431:12
So d. he can't fart JOHN 408:20
takes 40 d. animals SAYI 647:26
tongue of the d. BIBL 87:23
dump What a d. FILM 312:10
dumpling Diddle, diddle, d. NURS 548:3
dun her breasts are d. SHAK 705:20
Duncan fatal entrance of D. SHAK 682:2
dunce dearest, you're a d. JOHN 416:22
d. that has been sent COWP 241:6
d. with wits POPE 580:18
Satan, thou art but a d. BLAK 118:19
duncery tyrannical d. MILT 519:24
dunces d. are all in confederacy SWIF 748:25
Dundee bonnets of Bonny D. SCOT 650:11
longer in bonny D. SCOT 652:6
Dunfermline D. town BALL 51:13
D. town OPEN 555:29
dung die in their own d. KIPL 439:15
d.-heaps CHEK 208:13
Fulfilled of d. CHAU 206:7
dungeon Himself is his own d. MILT 511:21
dungeons Brightest in d., Liberty BYRO 179:3
dungfork man with a d. HOPK 385:6
dunghill cock crowing on its own d. ALDI 10:11
crow upon his own d. PROV 599:22
d. kind Delights in filth SPEN 734:2
Dunkirk D. to Belgrade DAVI 252:13
dunnest d. smoke of hell SHAK 682:4
Dunsinane high D. hill SHAK 685:2
remove to D. SHAK 685:15
duodecimos humbler band of d. CRAB 242:28
dupe d. of friendship HAZL 365:7
duped be d. by them LA R 453:13
dupes If hopes were d. CLOU 223:3
durable true love is a d. fire RALE 621:2
duration d. of the war ASQU 30:21
fallacy in d. BROW 153:5
dusk Between d. and dawn MÜLL 536:4
each slow d. OWEN 562:7
falling of the d. HEGE 367:15
forty-three In the d. GILB 339:12
dusky along the d. air COLE 227:4
D. like night BYRO 178:9
rear my d. race TENN 763:7
dust blossom in the d. SHIR 717:9
by our mother's d. FORD 320:3
chimney-sweepers, come to d. SHAK 661:1
D. and ashes BROW 158:9
D. as we are WORD 830:24
d. falls to the urn VAUG 790:10
D. hath closed Helen's eye NASH 539:22
d. of creeds outworn SHEL 713:10
d. of exploded beliefs MADA 488:21
d. of the Churchyard DONN 275:6
d. on the nettles THOM 773:5
d. return to the earth BIBL 85:2
d. thou art BIBL 74:7
D. thou art LONG 474:3
d. to dust BOOK 131:14
D. to the dust SHEL 710:22
d. upon the paper eye DOUG 276:16
d. was once the man WHIT 815:22
d. would hear her and beat TENN 764:10
enemies shall lick the d. BOOK 136:18
Excuse my d. EPIT 302:4
Fallen to d. WILD 819:5
fear in a handful of d. ELIO 295:28
forbear To dig the d. EPIT 302:10
fruit thereof d. SWIN 750:17
give d. a tongue HERB 372:9
glory smeared in d. SHAK 673:3
Half d., half deity BYRO 178:14
handful of d. CONR 234:25
honour turn to d. MARV 499:3
Hope raises no d. ÉLUA 299:1
in the d., in the cool tombs SAND 643:19
in the d. my vice is laid EPIT 303:16
Less than the d. HOPE 383:21
little d. of praise TENN 761:19
lovers o'er the d. BYRO 174:2
Marry my body to that d. KING 436:7
much learned d. COWP 241:25
not without d. and heat MILT 519:10
not worth the d. SHAK 679:16
O'er English d. MACA 482:24
of the d. of the ground BIBL 73:17
peck of March d. PROV 609:21
provoke the silent d. GRAY 350:10
quintessence of d. SHAK 663:18
raised a d. BERK 68:2
rich earth a richer d. BROO 150:17
shake off the d. BIBL 94:33
small d. of the balance BIBL 88:3
sweep the d. SHAK 690:29
Tell flesh it is but d. RALE 620:13
This quiet D. DICK 266:12
throwing of a little d. VIRG 797:2
To d. and ashes LITT 470:3
what a d. do I raise BACO 44:20
Where can the d. alight HUI- 394:2
with age and d. RALE 621:4
without the d. of racing HORA 386:9
writes in d. BACO 45:11
dustbin d. of history TROT 783:17
dustheap d. called 'history' BIRR 115:13
dusty what a d. answer MERE 505:21
Dutch fault of the D. CANN 184:19
Dutchman on a D.'s beard SHAK 702:4
Dutchmen water-land of D. BYRO 177:15
duties d. as well as its rights DRUM 279:13
d. of the heart BAHY 48:1
d. will be determined MORE 531:17
If I had no d. JOHN 415:22
neglect of his d. THOM 774:19
spiritual d. HOBY 379:9
two d. STEV 741:3
dutiful take note of the d. VIRG 793:14
duty act of d. and religion OSBO 559:21
as much a d. as cooperation GAND 329:7
bounden d. and service BOOK 130:1
daily stage of d. KEN 432:18
dare to do our d. LINC 468:7
declares it is his d. SHAW 706:19
die in one's d. is life BHAG 73:1
divided d. SHAK 692:3
do our d. as such SALI 642:19
Do your d. CORN 236:16
d. of an Opposition DERB 258:13
d. of government PAIN 563:15
d. of the four classes LAWS 459:10
d. towards God BOOK 130:12
d. we owe to history WILD 818:2
d. we so much underrate STEV 741:23
every man's d. COBB 223:9
every man will do his d. NELS 540:20
Every subject's d. SHAK 671:17
first d. of a State RUSK 638:25
forgot that he had a d. GIBB 335:19
God, Immortality, D. ELIO 293:17
I have done my d. LAST 457:8
I've done my d. FIEL 310:15
life was d. HOOP 383:8
little d. and less love SHAK 672:12
Love is then our d. GAY 331:20
Moor has done his d. SCHI 648:16
Nor law, nor d. YEAT 836:10
of the voice of God! O D. WORD 830:12
only done my d. TENN 766:12
owe a d. BEHN 62:10
performing a public d. GRAN 349:3
picket's off d. forever BEER 61:18
sense of d. useful RUSS 639:14
Such d. as the subject owes SHAK 698:14
supreme d. of a man LAWS 459:8
terrible notions of d. CLOU 221:13
When D. whispers low EMER 299:11
whole d. of man BIBL 85:5
dux *D. femina facti* VIRG 793:11
dwarf d. sees farther COLE 227:14
my d. shall dance JONS 420:11
dwarfish d. whole COLE 225:9
dwarfs d. on the shoulders BERN 68:22
State which d. its men MILL 509:2
dwell all that d. in it BOOK 131:9
constrained to d. with Mesech BOOK 140:10
d. in a corner BIBL 83:12
d. in realms of day BLAK 118:7
d. in the house of the Lord BOOK 133:1
d. in their tents BOOK 136:12
d. in the land BIBL 86:28
d. in thy tabernacle BOOK 132:7
d. with sothfastnesse CHAU 207:23
people that on earth do d. KETH 434:10
dwelleth d. not in temples BIBL 104:9
dwelling desert were my d.-place BYRO 175:7
d. in all things UPAN 787:13
d. is the light WORD 829:5
God's d. place SIKH 719:13
lovely is thy d.-place SCOT 652:21
dwellings amiable are thy d. BOOK 137:11
dwells She d. with Beauty KEAT 429:5
dwelt d. among the untrodden ways WORD 831:19
d. among us BIBL 101:7
d. by the brook Cherith BIBL 79:25
dwindle d. into a wife CONG 233:13
dyer like the d.'s hand SHAK 705:14
dyes stains and splendid d. KEAT 427:9
dying achieve it through not d. ALLE 12:17
attend a d. animal YEAT 835:14
Autumn sunsets exquisitely d. HUXL 397:8
behold you again in d. STEV 742:24
bliss of d. POPE 582:15
can't stay d. here all night SHER 715:16
Christian can only fear d. HARE 362:3
continually d. PETR 574:13
distinguished from d. SMIT 725:26
D. and living BOOK 130:2
D. a very dull, dreary MAUG 502:7
d., bless the hand DRYD 282:25
d. breath of Socrates JEAN 404:18
d. deer AYTO 40:11
d. for a faith THAC 768:19
d., has made us gifts BROO 150:7
d. in the last dyke BURK 165:8
D. is an art PLAT 577:17
d. is nothing ANOU 22:12
d. man's room STER 739:6
d. may I hold you TIBU 777:7
d. of a hundred good symptoms POPE 587:23
d. of the light THOM 772:2
d. remembers VIRG 795:10
feel that he is d. CALI 181:7

groans of love to those of the d. LOWR 478:11
he hung, the d. Lord JACO 401:3
I am d., Egypt SHAK 657:17
If this is d. LAST 456:4
indisposeth us for d. BROW 153:3
key to d. well LEAR 461:2
like a d. lady SHEL 714:15
lips of d. men ARNO 27:17
man's d. is more the survivors' affair MANN 494:5
mouth of the d. day AUDE 33:30
My d. sight BLOK 122:3
no more d. then SHAK 705:25
not death, but d. FIEL 309:14
nothing new in d. LAST 456:7
poor devils are d. PHIL 575:7
sacraments to a d. god HEIN 368:9
Those d. generations YEAT 837:1
to a d. god CLOS 222:13
To d. ears TENN 765:21
Turkey is a d. man NICH 543:16
unconscionable time d. CHAR 203:15
dyke auld fail d. BALL 52:5
February fill d. PROV 600:15
last d. of prevarication BURK 165:8
dynamite barrel of d. MAYA 502:16
objected to the use of d. STEV 741:9
dynamo starry d. GINS 339:20

E $E = mc^2$ EINS 290:9
each beating each to e. BROW 156:22
eagle all the e. in thee CRAS 244:5
e. among blinking owls SHEL 711:23
E. has landed ARMS 25:19
e. in a dove-cote SHAK 660:17
e. in the air BIBL 83:36
e. know what is in the pit BLAK 118:8
e.'s wings, Unseen KEAT 427:28
e. through the world had flown WALL 800:7
Fate is not an e. BOWE 145:13
In and out the E. MAND 493:6
lusty as an e. BOOK 138:17
with e. eyes KEAT 429:21
eagles e. be gathered BIBL 97:3
e. be gathered together PROV 614:39
E. don't catch flies PROV 599:1
hawk at e. HERB 373:9
swifter than e. BIBL 79:2
with wings as e. BIBL 88:5
ear cleave the general e. SHAK 663:28
close at the e. of Eve MILT 516:27
cut his e. off MEDA 503:5
dull cold e. of death GRAY 350:10
e. begins to hear BRON 150:1
e., did hear that tongue ROYD 637:2
e. of jealousy BIBL 91:5
e. of man hath not seen SHAK 690:17
God's own e. Listens MILT 517:3
hath the sow by the right e. HENR 370:10
hearing e. BIBL 83:10
hearing of the e. BIBL 82:4
He that planted the e. BOOK 138:4
nor e. filled BIBL 84:2
Oon e. it herde CHAU 207:13
out of your wife's e. MORT 533:13
piercèd through the e. SHAK 692:5
Reason's e. ADDI 5:13
silk purse out of sow's e. PROV 615:27
than meets the e. MILT 512:9
upon my whorlèd e. HOPK 384:7
Vexing the dull e. SHAK 677:12
earl As far as the fourteenth e. HOME 381:19
e. and a knight of the garter ATTL 32:3
E. of Fitzdotterel's eldest BROU 151:11
earlier Here's one I made e. CATC 195:23
earls daughter of a hundred e. TENN 762:10
early awake right e. BOOK 135:17
e. bird catches worm PROV 599:2
E. in the morning HEBE 367:8
e. man never borrows PROV 599:3
E. one morning SONG 729:4
E. to bed PROV 599:4
E. to rise THUR 777:1
get up e. LOWE 477:11
go to bed e. PROU 593:20
had it been e. JOHN 412:17
rise e. JOHN 411:23
Vote e. and vote often MILE 507:21
earn little to e. KING 437:12
earned e. on earth THAT 769:22
penny e. PROV 609:23
earnest I am in e. GARR 330:9
Life is e. LONG 474:3
time to be in e. JOHN 409:21
earnestly truly and e. repent BOOK 129:15
earrings e. for under £1 RATN 622:5
ears and hedges e. SWIF 749:20
Death hath asses' e. BEDD 60:17
don thyn e. glowe CHAU 207:6
e., and hear not BOOK 139:23
e. of every one BIBL 78:16
Enemy e. are listening OFFI 554:13
hath e. to hear BIBL 98:3
heard with our e. BOOK 134:12
lend me your e. SHAK 675:27
lets the e. lie back IVES 400:11
let thine e. consider BOOK 141:1
Little pitchers have large e. PROV 605:40
Look with thine e. SHAK 679:23
music Creep in our e. SHAK 688:21
seven good e. BIBL 75:14
stoppeth her e. BOOK 135:18
That man's e. HUGH 392:15
Walls have e. PROV 613:36
we have two e. ZENO 840:1
woods have e. PROV 600:18
earth all the e. were paper LYLY 480:18
anywhere else on e. GURN 355:2
as if the e. had rolled WORD 828:22
bleeding piece of e. SHAK 675:21
call this planet E. CLAR 219:10
cold e. upon me KEAT 432:1
Cold in the e. BRON 150:2
conquest of the e. CONR 234:10
corners of the e. BOOK 138:6
creepeth upon the e. BIBL 73:14
damage to the e. COUS 238:7
daughter of E. and Water SHEL 711:7
deep-delvèd e. KEAT 429:7
done to the e. MORR 532:23
dust return to the e. BIBL 85:2
earned on e. THAT 769:22
E. all Danaë to the stars TENN 766:3
e. be moved BOOK 134:18
e. breaks up BROW 155:17
e. covereth QUAR 618:21
e. does not argue WHIT 815:21
e. doth like a snake renew SHEL 711:12
E. felt the wound MILT 517:17
E. has not anything to show WORD 827:19
e. in an earthy bed TENN 764:10
e. in fast thick pants COLE 225:21
e. is all the home I have AYTO 40:13
e. is full of his glory BIBL 86:21
e. is the centre DONN 275:11
e. is the Lord's BIBL 106:13
e. is the Lord's BOOK 133:2
E., lie heavily ROSS 634:10
e. of majesty SHAK 694:19
E., receive an honoured guest AUDE 34:2
e. received her frame WATT 805:19
e. remaineth BIBL 74:19
E.'s crammed with heaven BROW 154:13
e.'s foundations HOUS 390:13
e. shall be filled AING 9:3
e. shall be full BIBL 87:5
e. shall melt away BOOK 134:19
e. shook BOOK 136:6
e. soaks up the rain COWL 239:10
E.'s the right place for love FROS 325:15
E. stood hard as iron ROSS 634:5
E., the first of the gods VIRG 795:4
e. to earth BOOK 131:14
end of e. LAST 457:11
ends of the e. BOOK 136:1
Everything on e. GOGO 344:2
face of e. around STEV 743:1
famous men have the whole e. PERI 573:20
feel the e. move HEMI 369:10
filleted the e. so fine TAYL 756:16
flowery lap of e. ARNO 26:16
food out of the e. BOOK 139:3
foundation of the e. BOOK 138:15
foundation of the e. SHAK 668:18
foundations of the e. BIBL 81:31
frame in the e. SPEN 734:7
from e. to heaven PLAT 578:11
get away from e. awhile FROS 325:15
giants in the e. BIBL 74:15
girdle round about the e. SHAK 689:24
given Her all on e. BYRO 175:18
glory from the e. WORD 829:15
going to and fro in the e. BIBL 80:34
goodly frame, the e. SHAK 663:18
heaven and the e. BIBL 73:10
heaven and the e. OPEN 555:18
he craves the e. SEXT 655:6
hydroptic e. hath drunk DONN 274:9
I am laid in e. TATE 755:7
if e. Be but the shadow MILT 516:33
inhabitants o' the e. SHAK 681:15
inherit the e. BIBL 93:3
in the water under the e. BIBL 76:8
It fell to e. LONG 473:9
lap of E. GRAY 350:14
Lay her i' the e. SHAK 666:26
let the E. bless the Lord BOOK 126:7
Lie heavy on him, E. EPIT 304:10
little e. for charity SHAK 673:18
low as where this e. ROSS 634:18
made heaven and e. BOOK 130:18
made heaven and e. BOOK 140:17
make the e. my hell SHAK 696:24
more near the e. SHAK 693:25
more things in heaven and e. HALD 356:15
move the e. ARCH 23:19
must have a touch of e. TENN 759:26
new heaven and a new e. BIBL 113:7
new heaven, new e. SHAK 656:7
new heavens and a new e. BIBL 89:9
Nor by the e. BIBL 93:11
not for the brute e. THOM 773:14
of the e., earthy BIBL 107:2
on e. peace BIBL 98:22
On e. there is nothing great HAMI 358:15
One does not sell the e. CRAZ 244:19
paces of the vilest e. SHAK 669:13
pilgrims on the e. BIBL 109:30
poetry of e. KEAT 429:23
rich e. a richer dust BROO 150:17
round e.'s human shores KEAT 426:14
round e.'s imagined corners DONN 272:20
round e.'s shore ARNO 26:4
sad old e. must borrow WILC 817:9
salt of the e. BIBL 93:4
shall inherit the e. SMIT 724:1
sleepers in that quiet e. CLOS 222:14
slime of the e. SUGE 745:12
substance from the common e. FITZ 314:21
surly bonds of e. MAGE 489:8
surly bonds of e. REAG 623:7
terms with the e. ALAI 10:3
this e., this realm SHAK 694:19
tread on E. unguessed at ARNO 27:14
way of all the e. BIBL 77:23
Which men call e. MILT 511:13
with heaven and e. MILT 519:21
work i' the e. SHAK 663:3
Yours is the E. KIPL 439:3
earthen e. voider BARN 55:10
earthquake against an e. ADDI 5:19
e. is not satisfied WORD 831:7
Lord was not in the e. BIBL 80:3

earthquake (*cont.*):
Small e. in Chile COCK 223:15
world-e., Waterloo TENN 765:5
earthy of the earth, e. BIBL 107:2
ease age of e. GOLD 344:9
at e. for aye to dwell TENN 765:8
at e. in a room PASC 568:11
at e. with himself CHUA 212:19
Counselled ignoble e. MILT 515:12
done with so much e. DRYD 279:19
e. in hell WRIG 833:15
e. of the masters SMIT 723:12
e. the anguish SHAK 690:21
e. thine heart BEDD 60:14
e. thine heaviness GOOG 346:14
elegance and e. GAY 332:12
for another gives its e. BLAK 121:1
ignoble e. ROOS 633:4
kindly bent to e. us SWIF 749:23
never at heart's e. SHAK 674:19
Not for e. that prayer WILL 821:6
prodigal of e. DRYD 280:3
Studious of laborious e. COWP 241:29
take their e. And sleep SHAK 674:1
take thine e. BIBL 99:21
True e. in writing POPE 584:22
Virtue shuns e. MONT 527:18
we ourselves are at our e. SMIT 723:5
easeful e. Death KEAT 429:13
easer e. of all woes FLET 318:9
easier will be e. for you LAST 455:6
easing e. the Spring REED 623:14
east brims over in the E. GIRA 340:3
Britain calls the Far E. MENZ 505:3
Dapples the drowsy e. SHAK 691:23
E. is a career DISR 270:29
E. is East KIPL 438:5
E. of Suez KIPL 439:14
E., west, home's best PROV 599:5
e. wind made flesh APPL 23:5
e. wind may never blow WALT 802:15
face neither E. nor West NKRU 546:11
fiery portal of the e. SHAK 695:12
gorgeous E. in fee WORD 830:14
how wide also the e. is BOOK 138:19
I' the e. my pleasure lies SHAK 656:29
It is the e. SHAK 697:9
look the E. End in the face ELIZ 298:1
neither from the e. BOOK 136:22
neither of the E. KORA 445:2
on the e. of Eden BIBL 74:12
politics in the E. DISR 270:8
through the e.-wind BOOK 134:25
tried to hustle the E. KIPL 439:18
wind is in the e. PROV 614:31
wind's in the e. DICK 260:20
wise men from the e. BIBL 92:22
Easter E. energy about it HEAN 366:21
eastern against the e. gate MILT 512:17
E. promise ADVE 7:20
misty e. cave SHEL 714:11
Eastertide Wearing white for E. HOUS 390:14
eastward garden e. in Eden BIBL 73:17
easy E. come, easy go PROV 599:6
E. does it PROV 599:7
E. is the way down VIRG 794:17
E. live and quiet die SCOT 651:19
e. to take refuge in IBSE 398:10
e. ways to die SHAK 658:6
e. writing's vile hard reading SHER 716:18
every said it would be e. MITC 523:12
If to do were as e. SHAK 687:7
normal and e. JAME 403:12
rack of a too e. chair POPE 580:25
should be free and e. OSBO 559:18
Summer time an' the livin' is e. HEYW 376:4
Too e. for children SCHN 648:23
woman of e. virtue HAIL 356:11
eat Big fish e. little fish PROV 596:18
Dog does not e. dog PROV 598:23
don't work shan't e. PROV 603:32
e. and drunk and lived JOHN 414:13
e. a peck of dirt PROV 613:45
e. at a place called Mom's ALGR 12:1
e. bulls' flesh BOOK 135:3
e., drink, and be merry BIBL 99:21
E. my shorts CATC 195:11
e. one of Bellamy's veal pies LAST 456:20
e. the fat of the land BIBL 75:18
e. to live MOLI 524:17
E. to live PROV 599:8
e. up and swallow down MORE 531:5
great ones e. up SHAK 694:7
have meat and cannot e. BURN 167:22
have your cake and e. it PROV 615:38
I did e. BIBL 74:1
I e. well MORT 534:2
I would e. his heart SHAK 691:18
Let them e. cake MARI 495:11
Let us e. and drink BIBL 87:9
let us e. and drink BIBL 106:24
lives to e. SOCR 726:22
neither should he e. BIBL 109:12
people sat down to e. BIBL 76:17
see what I e. CARR 189:17
shalt thou e. bread BIBL 74:6
Take, e. BIBL 97:18
Take, e., this is my Body BOOK 129:22
Tell me what you e. BRIL 148:17
thou shalt not e. of it BIBL 73:19
to e., and to drink BIBL 84:19
ye e. but ye have not enough BIBL 90:24
Ye shall e. it in haste BIBL 76:1
You are what you e. PROV 615:22
eaten e. and drunk enough HORA 387:10
e. by missionaries SPOO 735:4
e. by the bear HOUS 390:6
e.of worms BIBL 103:31
e. to death with rust SHAK 669:27
God made and e. BROW 155:14
They'd e. every one CARR 190:21
we've already e. BENN 65:5
eater great e. of beef SHAK 700:29
Out of the e. BIBL 78:1
eateth e. grass as an ox BIBL 81:38
Why e. your Master BIBL 94:23
eating Appetite comes with e. PROV 595:12
appetite grows by e. RABE 619:9
e. one crisp DUAN 283:19
E. people is wrong FLAN 316:4
e. the sea ROBE 629:1
famous good e. EDGE 288:12
eats e. of the sweet fruit UPAN 788:5
Man is what he e. FEUE 309:4
eau *L'e. verte pénétra* RIMB 628:6
eave e.-drops fall COLE 225:17
ebbing e. sea FORD 320:5
Ebenezer Pale E. thought it wrong BELL 64:5
ebony his image, cut in e. FULL 327:7
ecce *E. homo* BIBL 114:8
eccentric E. intervolved MILT 517:3
eccentricities E. of genius DICK 265:10
ecclesia *Ubi Petrus, ibi ergo e.* AMBR 13:3
ecclesiam *Salus extra e.* AUGU 36:7
Ecclesiastes *Vanitas vanitatum, dixit E.* BIBL 113:26
ecclesiastic E. tyranny DEFO 255:15
ecclesiologist keen e. BETJ 71:9
echo E. beyond the Mexique Bay MARV 498:9
e. in the sense JONS 420:16
e. of a noble mind LONG 475:5
e. of a pistol-shot DURR 286:8
e. of a platitude BIER 114:18
E., sweetest nymph MILT 511:19
Footfalls e. in the memory ELIO 294:2
sound must seem an e. POPE 584:22
waiting for the e. MARQ 497:11
echoes Our e. roll TENN 765:18
stage but e. back JOHN 411:11
wild e. flying TENN 765:16
echoing e. straits between us ARNO 28:2
eclipse astonished at e. ORCH 557:8
at least an e. BACO 43:10
dim e. disastrous twilight MILT 515:1
E. first O'KE 553:9
in the moon's e. SHAK 684:19
merciful e. GILB 337:8
total e. MILT 518:14
eclipsed e. the gaiety JOHN 410:8
eclipses Clouds and e. SHAK 704:18
ecological upset the e. balance SONT 728:7
ecology e. and antiwar HUNT 396:8
economic cold metal of e. theory SCHU 649:12
demands of the e. process TEMP 757:6
e. law of motion MARX 499:16
not purely e. TAWN 755:17
vital e. interests WEIL 808:27
economical e. with the *actualité* CLAR 219:3
e. with the truth ARMS 25:20
economics E. is the science ROBB 628:17
study of e. SCHU 649:7
economist e. to prove KALD 425:11
political e. BAGE 47:9
economists e., and calculators BURK 163:21
economize Let us e. it TWAI 786:7
economy E. is going without HOPE 383:14
e. of truth BURK 164:22
E. was always 'elegant' GASK 330:18
fear of Political E. SELL 654:12
It's the e., stupid POLI 581:20
Principles of Political E. BENT 67:5
Stakeholder E. BLAI 117:10
There can be no e. DISR 269:6
ecstasies virgins in their e. TENN 759:24
ecstasy e. of being ever BROW 153:11
e. of betrayal GENE 333:6
mad with e. TRAH 780:14
ring the bells of E. GINS 339:19
seraph-wings of e. GRAY 351:2
What wild e. KEAT 428:22
ecstatic such e. sound HARD 361:12
eddy dizzying e. ARNO 27:1
Eden brooks of E. TENN 764:21
E.'s dread probationary tree COWP 241:7
garden eastward in E. BIBL 73:17
happier E. MILT 518:18
loss of E. MILT 514:7
loss of E. OPEN 556:5
on the east of E. BIBL 74:12
other E. SHAK 694:19
Through E. took CLOS 222:22
Through E. took MILT 518:3
voice that breathed o'er E. KEBL 432:7
walls of E. BYRO 173:21
edge at the e. of Being SPEN 732:21
Come to the e. LOGU 473:3
dangerous e. of things BROW 155:9
hungry e. of appetite SHAK 694:16
teeth are set on e. BIBL 89:29
teeth nothing on e. SHAK 668:21
edged Science is an e. tool EDDI 288:3
edifice found that e. DOST 276:1
edifieth charity e. BIBL 106:7
Edinburgh travels north to E. BEAV 59:1
edisti *e. satis atque bibisti* HORA 387:10
edition new And more beautiful e. EPIT 302:1
editions e. of Balbec and Palmyra WALP 801:3
editor E.: a person employed HUBB 392:12
e. did it when I was away MURD 537:2
e. himself be attacked TROL 783:4
e. of such a work STEP 738:2
Edom over E. will I cast out BOOK 135:20
wisdom in E. MIDR 507:14
educate e. our masters LOWE 477:7
e. our party DISR 269:4
educated as an e. gentleman SHAW 707:22
clothed, fed, and e. RUSK 638:25
e. and the uneducated FOST 321:11
government by the badly e. CHES 211:21
women are not e. CAVE 198:14

education ask of e. NAPO 538:13
between e. and catastrophe WELL 810:13
By e. most have been misled DRYD 281:24
cabbage with a college e. TWAI 786:22
difference of e. ADAM 1:19
discretion by e. JEFF 405:21
e., education, and education BLAI 117:11
e. forms the common mind POPE 584:1
E. has been theirs AUST 38:11
[E.] has produced TREV 781:9
e. is a little too CONG 232:23
e. is so astonishing ADAM 2:23
E. is what survives SKIN 721:17
E. is when you read SEEG 653:7
E. made us what we are HELV 369:4
E. makes a people BROU 151:14
e. of the heart SCOT 652:17
e. of the people DISR 269:13
e. produces no effect WILD 817:15
e. serves as a rattle ARIS 25:8
e.'s, more than nature's WINC 822:23
first part of politics? E. MICH 506:16
I do not call it e. SPAR 731:20
In e. no class distinction CONF 232:3
in their own e. SCOT 652:19
is a liberal e. STEE 736:21
liberal e. BANK 53:8
part of e. BACO 44:14
poor e. I have received BOTT 144:23
Real e. ultimately limited POUN 590:4
Soap and e. TWAI 786:6
thank your e. JONS 420:14
that is e. ROGE 631:18
unfit of any to be used in e. LOCK 472:7
unplanned e. creates VERW 791:13
educe e. the man BROW 156:10
eels e. boil'd in broo BALL 51:1
effect found in the e. BERG 67:16
little e. after much labour AUST 39:11
name for an e. COWP 242:8
effectually obtain e. BOOK 128:19
efficacy e. and extraction MILT 519:7
efficiency where there is no e. DISR 269:6
efficient e. and the inefficient SHAW 707:20
e. parts BAGE 46:5
have an e. government TRUM 784:7
effort e. be too great ANON 17:18
no e. is necessary I-HS 398:18
not the e. nor the failure tires EMPS 300:7
redoubling your e. SANT 644:8
written without e. JOHN 418:15
effugere *Soles e. atque abire sentit* MART 498:1
effugies *non e.* CATU 198:2
effusive don't be too e. ELIZ 297:19
Égalité *É.! Fraternité* POLI 581:24
egg addled e. as an idle bird PROV 595:19
eating a demnition e. DICK 264:2
e. boiled very soft AUST 37:13
e. by pleasure laid COWP 241:4
e. of a North African Empire GLAD 341:3
e. of the wren WHIT 815:14
From the e. HORA 389:17
got a bad e. PUNC 617:22
Go to work on an e. ADVE 7:21
hairless as an e. HERR 374:18
lays an e. NEWS 544:16
looks like a poached e. NUFF 547:8
one addled e. ELIO 292:11
radish and an e. COWP 242:2
See this e. DIDE 267:7
egghead E. weds hourglass NEWS 544:4
eggs all my e. in one bastard PARK 567:16
as a weasel sucks e. SHAK 658:21
e. at the smaller end SWIF 747:20
e. for gentlemen NURS 548:13
e. in one basket PROV 598:37
e. taste like poisoned rubber LEON 464:9
grandmother to suck e. PROV 598:38
Lays e. inside a paper bag ISHE 400:7
partridge sitteth on e. BIBL 89:20
roasting of e. PROV 612:22
roast their e. BACO 44:23
ways to dress e. MOOR 530:7
eglantine grew lush e. SHEL 713:21
with e. SHAK 689:25
ego *Et in Arcadia e.* EPIT 302:3
fulfils a man's e. ROOT 633:14
egotist whims of an e. KEAT 430:26
egotistical e. sublime KEAT 431:10
egregiously making him e. an ass SHAK 692:14
Egypt brow of E. SHAK 690:19
E.'s might COLE 224:18
firstborn in the land of E. BIBL 76:2
first site in E. GLAD 341:3
great cry in E. BIBL 76:3
Israel came out of E. BOOK 139:21
out of the land of E. BIBL 76:8
there was corn in E. BIBL 75:15
We do not want E. PALM 566:5
wonders in the land of E. BIBL 75:33
Egyptian E. to my mother SHAK 693:5
Egyptians spoiled the E. BIBL 76:4
eheu *E. fugaces Labuntur anni* HORA 388:8
eight Pieces of e. STEV 741:20
We want e. ANON 19:12
eighteen before you reach e. EINS 291:1
e.-forty-eight TAYL 756:3
eightfold E. Path PALI 565:13
eighty In a dream you are never e. SEXT 655:8
live beyond e. CALL 181:8
rottenness of e. years BYRO 179:12
Einstein Let E. be SQUI 735:16
either e. to other BOOK 131:8
happy could I be with e. GAY 332:1
Elaine E., the lily maid TENN 759:25
élan *é. vital* BERG 67:17
elasticity Cheerfulness gives e. SMIL 723:2
elbow e. has a fascination GILB 338:11
elder but five days e. BROW 153:17
e. man not at all BACO 43:20
e. soldier, not a better SHAK 676:21
I the e. SHAK 675:11
take An e. than herself SHAK 701:18
to e. statesman FOOT 319:4
elderly e. lady, who mutters away CARE 186:17
e. man of 42 ASHF 30:10
elders discourse of the e. BIBL 91:22
e. and the four beasts BIBL 112:8
four and twenty e. BIBL 112:3
Of those white e. STEV 740:3
Eldorado E. of all the old fools BAUD 57:9
elect dissolve the people and e. BREC 147:21
I was e., I was born fit GURN 355:4
knit together thine e. BOOK 128:22
elected audacity of e. persons WHIT 815:9
will not serve if e. SHER 717:3
election e. by the incompetent many SHAW 708:16
e. is coming ELIO 292:9
right of e. JUNI 423:13
elections e. are won ADAM 2:8
no go the e. MACN 488:8
You won the e. SOMO 727:19
elective E. affinities GOET 343:9
e. dictatorship HAIL 356:12
Electra Mourning becomes E. O'NE 554:22
electric biggest e. train set WELL 809:12
E. Kool-Aid Acid test WOLF 825:14
sing the body e. WHIT 815:3
tried to mend the E. Light BELL 63:23
electrical e. skin and glaring eyes SMAR 722:6
electrician E. is no longer there BELL 64:1
electricity e. was dripping THUR 776:23
usefulness of e. FARA 306:14
electrification e. of the whole country LENI 463:10
electronic new e. interdependence MCLU 487:7
elegance e. and ease GAY 332:12
elegant Economy was always 'e.' GASK 330:18
e. and pregnant texture STEV 741:2
e. but not ostentatious JOHN 409:24
e. simplicity STOW 744:4
e. sufficiency THOM 775:6
Most intelligent, very e. BUCK 159:12
so e. ELIO 296:5
with e. quickness SMAR 722:5
You e. fowl LEAR 460:17
elegy character of his e. JOHN 410:4
whole of Gray's E. WOLF 825:7
eleison *Kyrie e.* MISS 520:12
element I am not of your e. SHAK 702:11
Thy e.'s below SHAK 678:15
To the destructive e. CONR 234:16
elementary E., my dear Watson MISQ 521:9
'E.,' said he DOYL 277:16
elements Become our e. MILT 515:13
conflict of its e. BYRO 178:14
element our e. mar BYRO 177:8
e. So mixed in him SHAK 677:4
I tax not you, you e. SHAK 678:22
made cunningly Of e. DONN 272:26
with the fretful e. SHAK 678:20
elephant Appears a monstrous e. COTT 237:16
at the E. SHAK 702:8
can say is 'e.' CHAP 202:10
corn as high as an e.'s eye HAMM 358:21
couldn't hit an e. LAST 457:9
E.'s Child KIPL 441:8
English e. *Never* lies IMLA 398:21
fit the profile of an e. GAMO 329:3
herd of e. pacing DINE 267:18
masterpiece, an e. DONN 273:13
sleeping with an e. TRUD 783:23
thought he saw an E. CARR 191:28
elephanto *candenti perfecta nitens e.* VIRG 795:3
elephants e. for want of towns SWIF 749:16
golden e. next SHOR 717:14
identical e. QUIN 619:7
elevated generous and e. mind JOHN 411:7
elevates e. above the vulgar herd GAIS 327:19
eleven e. buckram men SHAK 668:6
failing his e.-plus PRES 591:4
fine before e. PROV 610:5
too long after e. GERS 334:21
elf deceiving e. KEAT 429:15
little child, a limber e. COLE 225:1
elfland horns of E. TENN 765:17
Elginbrodde Martin E. EPIT 302:13
Eli Eli, E., lama sabachthani BIBL 97:29
Elijah as E. did Elisha BURN 169:11
E. passed by him BIBL 80:4
E. went up by a whirlwind BIBL 80:12
spirit of E. BIBL 80:13
eliminated e. the impossible DOYL 278:1
Elisha rest on E. BIBL 80:13
Elizabeth my sonne's wife, E. INGE 399:12
Ellen fair E. of brave Lochinvar SCOT 651:9
elliptical e. billiard balls GILB 338:10
elm Every e. has its man PROV 599:25
Round the e.-tree bole BROW 156:2
signal-e. ARNO 27:24
vine about the e. DAVI 251:19
elms Behind the e. last night PRIO 593:6
Beneath those rugged e. GRAY 350:8
e., Fade into dimness ARNO 27:2
in immemorial e. TENN 766:6
elope e. methodically GOLD 345:16
elopement love-story or an e. DOYL 277:22
eloquence books be then the e. SHAK 704:12
e. is tedious PASC 568:19
e. the soul MILT 515:18
ornate e. in our English CAXT 198:16
parliamentary e. CARL 188:6
power of e. WIGG 816:18
simple e. ever convince WALP 801:13

eloquence (*cont.*):
Take E. and break VERL 791:9
Talking and e. JONS 421:4
eloquent e. in a more sublime language MACA 481:17
else happening to Somebody E. ROGE 631:20
elsewhere Altogether e., vast herds AUDE 33:27
There is a world e. SHAK 660:9
Elsinore stormy steep, E. CAMP 183:4
elves criticizing e. CHUR 214:10
e. also, Whose little eyes glow HERR 374:14
Ye e. of hills SHAK 699:8
Elysian in the E. fields DISR 271:1
Elysium brother he is in E. SHAK 700:28
Keep alive our lost E. BETJ 70:17
What E. have ye known KEAT 428:20
embalmer e. of the still midnight KEAT 430:6
triumph of the e.'s art VIDA 792:11
embalming For my E. (Sweetest) HERR 374:22
embarras *e. des richesses* ALLA 12:6
embarrassment annoyance and e. BAED 45:18
e. and breakfast BARN 54:17
e. of riches ALLA 12:6
keeps us in our place is e. BENN 65:15
embers glowing e. through the room MILT 512:7
joy! that in our e. WORD 830:5
emblem e. of mortality DISR 269:24
embrace do there e. MARV 499:3
e. your Lordship's principles WILK 819:19
oh as to e. me MILT 519:2
pity, then e. POPE 585:22
embraces age in her e. ROCH 630:10
embraceth mercy e. him BOOK 133:18
embroidered heavens' e. cloths YEAT 836:5
embroideries Covered with e. YEAT 835:10
embroidery little daily e. ELIO 292:10
Emelye up roos E. CHAU 205:20
emendation e. wrong JOHN 410:17
emerald green as e. COLE 226:7
like unto an e. BIBL 111:30
livelier e. twinkles TENN 764:5
men, of the E. Isle DREN 279:10
emergency compelled by e. TROL 782:2
one e. following upon another FISH 313:11
emeritus called a *professor e.* LEAC 459:17
emigration doubt but that our e. CART 192:11
emigravit *E.* is the inscription LONG 474:1
Emily E., hear CRAN 243:26
eminence raised To that bad e. MILT 515:7
eminency some e. in ourselves HOBB 378:11
eminent death reveals the e. SHAW 708:27
Emmanuel from E.'s veins COWP 240:20
emolument positions of considerable e. GAIS 327:19
emotion degree of my aesthetic e. BELL 62:20
dependable international e. ALSO 12:23
e. recollected in tranquillity WORD 832:20
epitaph of an e. NIET 545:20
masses conveying an e. HEPW 371:6
morality touched by e. ARNO 29:1
sex without e. PAGL 563:4
stirred by e. THOM 771:7
thought charged with e. GIDE 336:18
tranquillity remembered in e. PARK 567:9
emotional e. agitation ADLE 6:5
Gluttony an e. escape DEV 259:11
emotions all the human e. GOGO 344:1
e. were riveted FOOT 318:26
for the noble e. RUSK 638:9
gamut of the e. PARK 567:11
metaphysical brothel for the e. KOES 443:3
only two e. in a plane WELL 809:13
receptacle for e. PICA 575:17
refusal to admit our e. RATT 622:6
Television strikes at e. DAY 253:9
waste-paper basket of the e. WEBB 807:2
world of the e. COLE 228:2
emparadised E. in one another's arms MILT 516:18
emperice e. and flour CHAU 206:26
emperor belong to the E. BORG 143:4
dey makes you E. O'NE 554:18
E. has nothing on ANDE 14:9
e. holds the key CUST 248:9
E. is everything METT 506:11
e. of ice-cream STEV 739:21
E.'s drunken soldiery YEAT 835:5
e. to die standing LAST 455:12
sacred E. BRAM 146:17
emperors E. can do nothing BREC 147:13
empire All e. is no more DRYD 280:6
arch Of the ranged e. SHAK 656:8
course of e. BERK 68:4
cut-purse of the e. SHAK 665:18
destinies of the British E. DISR 268:21
dismemberment of the E. GLAD 341:5
E. splendidly isolated NEWS 544:13
E. strikes back FILM 312:19
e., vast as it is CUST 248:9
e. walking very slowly FITZ 315:15
evil e. REAG 623:5
found a great e. SMIT 723:10
founded the British E. HILL 376:13
glorious e. BURK 163:9
great e. and little minds BURK 163:8
Greeks in this American e. MACM 487:14
How's the E. LAST 455:18
idlers of the E. DOYL 278:4
Life, Joy, E. SHEL 713:16
lost an e. ACHE 1:12
meaning of E. Day CHES 210:21
metropolis of the e. COBB 223:11
nor Roman, nor an e. VOLT 797:17
provinces of the British e. SMIT 723:14
Russia an e. or democracy BRZE 159:6
tread out e. YOUN 839:4
unity of the e. BURK 163:6
way she disposed of an e. HARL 362:10
empires day of E. CHAM 200:14
e. of the future CHUR 215:21
Hatching vain e. MILT 515:15
Vaster than e. MARV 499:1
empirical *e. scientific system* POPP 587:24
empiricist e. view CHOM 212:11
employed innocently e. JOHN 414:24
employee In a hierarchy every e. PETE 574:10
employer harder upon the e. SPOO 735:3
employment e. for his idle time WALT 802:17
e. may be reckoned dishonest GAY 331:23
e. to the artisan BELL 63:23
seek gainful e. ACHE 1:11
emporium Celestial E. BORG 143:4
emprisoned E. in black KEAT 427:4
emptiness e. The human lack BOLD 124:10
Form is e. MAHĀ 490:2
great Australian E. WHIT 814:6
kind of e. DE B 254:2
empty Bring on the e. horses CURT 248:4
E. sacks will never PROV 599:9
e. spaces Between stars FROS 325:20
e., swept, and garnished BIBL 95:17
E. vessels make PROV 599:10
fold stands e. SHAK 689:20
house would e. be BOOT 142:19
let me be e. METH 506:6
rich he hath sent e. away BIBL 98:17
singer of an e. day MORR 532:11
turn down an e. glass FITZ 315:3
very e. heads BACO 45:7
world is e. PALI 565:9
emulation bloodless e. SHAK 700:7
enamelled e. meadows WALP 800:15
throws her e. skin SHAK 689:26
enamoured So e. on peace CLAR 218:22
enchanted e. isles MILT 511:25
Enter these e. woods MERE 505:22
holy and e. COLE 225:21
Some e. evening HAMM 358:23
enchantment distance lends e. CAMP 183:13
Distance lends e. PROV 598:19
enchantments e. of the Middle Age ARNO 28:15
e. of the Middle Age BEER 61:13
enchants e. my sense SHAK 700:12
encircling amid the e. gloom NEWM 542:19
encompassed e. but one man SHAK 674:15
encompasses God e. everything KORA 444:13
encounter e. darkness as a bride SHAK 686:17
encounters Close e. FILM 312:17
encourage e. those who betray GAY 331:23
right to e. BAGE 47:5
to e. the others VOLT 797:8
encourager *e. les autres* VOLT 797:8
Encyclopedia Britannica Behind the *E.* ELIO 293:18
end Ages of hopeless e. MILT 515:11
ane e. of ane old song OGIL 553:3
any beginning or any e. POLL 580:3
appointment at the e. of the world DINE 267:18
at the e. of the day TAYL 756:14
be-all and the e.-all SHAK 682:8
beginning of the e. TALL 753:3
Better is the e. BIBL 84:14
came to an e. all wars LLOY 471:3
commit adultery at one e. CARY 193:6
continuing unto the e. DRAK 278:17
draw to our e. BIBL 91:12
eggs at the smaller e. SWIF 747:20
e. badly STEV 742:8
e. cannot justify the means HUXL 397:2
e. crowns all SHAK 700:22
e. crowns the work PROV 599:11
e. in doubts BACO 41:8
e. is bitter as wormwood BIBL 82:12
e. is not yet BIBL 96:30
e. is where we start from ELIO 294:18
e. justifies the means BUSE 170:25
e. justifies the means PROV 599:12
e., never as means KANT 425:18
e. of all things BIBL 111:5
e. of a novel TROL 782:4
e. of a thousand years of history GAIT 328:2
e. of earth LAST 457:11
e. of history FUKU 327:1
e. of love should be HANN 359:10
e. of man is an action CARL 188:13
e. of Solomon Grundy NURS 550:19
e. of the beginning CHUR 215:17
e. of these men BOOK 136:20
e. of the way inescapable PAST 569:7
e. of this day's business SHAK 676:31
e. that crowns us HERR 374:9
e. the gods may bestow HORA 387:21
e. to be without honour BIBL 91:11
e. to the beginnings of all wars ROOS 633:3
e. where I began DONN 274:20
Everything has an e. PROV 599:43
flood unto the world's e. BOOK 136:18
God be at my e. PRAY 592:3
God will grant an e. VIRG 793:9
good things must come to an e. PROV 594:21
highest political e. ACTO 1:15
In my beginning is my e. ELIO 294:6
In my beginning is my e. OPEN 555:17
In my e. is my beginning MARY 500:11
Is this the promised e. SHAK 680:12
let me know mine e. BOOK 133:29
look to the e. ANON 21:12
Lord blessed the latter e. BIBL 82:5
made a good e. SHAK 666:8
make an e. JONS 421:3
make an e. the sooner BACO 42:27
middle, and an e. ARIS 24:22
muddle, and an e. LARK 453:9
only e. of age LARK 452:15
on to the e. of the road LAUD 454:5
Our e. is Life MACN 488:17

reserved for some e. CLIV 221:10
retard th'inevitable e. SMAR 722:14
right true e. of love DONN 272:11
sans singer, and—sans E. FITZ 314:12
she had a good e. MALO 492:13
there's an e. on't ANON 19:15
there's an e. on't JOHN 414:2
there was no e. CLOS 222:21
this day to e. myself TENN 763:17
This was the e. PLAT 578:4
till you come to the e. CARR 190:8
unto the e. of the world BIBL 97:30
Waiting for the e. EMPS 300:5
war that will e. war WELL 810:16
where's it all going to e. STOP 743:18
Whoever wills the e. KANT 425:16
wills the e. PROV 602:34
world may e. tonight BROW 156:14
world will e. in fire FROS 325:21
world without e. BOOK 125:19
endearing e. young charms MOOR 530:9
endeavours e. are unlucky explorers DOUG 276:14
ended continued, and e. in thee BOOK 130:5
Georges e. LAND 450:4
Ilium has e. VIRG 794:4
in 1915 the old world e. LAWR 457:21
Mass is e. MISS 522:21
Enderby Brides of E. INGE 399:10
ending bread-sauce of the happy e. JAME 403:14
her certain e. SHAK 704:3
makes a good e. PROV 601:23
way of e. a war ORWE 559:14
endless born to e. night BLAK 118:6
E. Light ZORO 841:17
in e. night GRAY 351:2
in e. night HERR 374:7
is e. nothing LARK 452:17
endow I thee e. BOOK 131:6
ends All's well that e. well PROV 595:2
between e. and scarce means ROBB 628:17
divinity that shapes our e. SHAK 667:1
e. all other deeds SHAK 657:21
e. by our beginnings know DENH 257:12
e. of the earth BOOK 136:1
e. of the world BOOK 132:15
More are men's e. marked SHAK 694:18
pursuing of the best e. HUTC 396:14
endue E. her plenteously BOOK 126:15
endurance e. and courage SCOT 650:9
e. is godlike LONG 473:15
endure Children's talent to e. ANGE 14:17
e. for a night BOOK 133:15
e. my own despair WALS 802:11
e. Their going hence SHAK 680:5
e. them AURE 37:8
e., then pity POPE 585:22
e. the toothache SHAK 691:20
E. the winter's cold SHAK 674:10
human hearts e. JOHN 411:12
man will not merely e. FAUL 307:27
nature itselfe cant e. FLEM 317:11
potter and clay e. BROW 157:20
props to help him e. FAUL 307:28
stuff will not e. SHAK 701:10
thou shalt e. BOOK 138:15
endured can't be cured must be e. PROV 613:48
e. with patient resignation RUSS 639:14
not to be e. SHAK 698:11
state to be e. JOHN 410:26
endureth e. all things BIBL 106:16
e. for ever BOOK 139:18
mercy e. for ever BOOK 141:6
Endymion In E., I leaped KEAT 431:9
enemies alone against smiling e. BOWE 145:14
assaults of our e. BOOK 126:12
choice of his e. WILD 818:18
conquering one's e. GENG 333:7
curse mine e. BIBL 77:2
e. be scattered BOOK 136:5
E.' gifts are no gifts SOPH 728:12
e. of Freedom do not argue INGE 399:3
e. of liberty HUME 394:15
e. of truth BROW 153:13
e. shall lick the dust BOOK 136:18
e. to a real artist GAIN 327:17
e. to laws BURK 164:27
e. will not believe HUBB 392:10
forgive e. BLAK 120:5
giving his e. STER 738:17
left me naked to mine e. SHAK 673:17
Love your e. BIBL 99:4
making new e. VOLT 798:15
no perpetual e. PALM 566:2
number of his e. FLAU 316:13
Our e. have beat us SHAK 677:2
speak with their e. BOOK 140:22
thine e. thy footstool BOOK 139:16
wish their e. dead MONT 527:2
enemy afraid of his e. PLUT 579:9
better class of e. MILL 510:7
bridge to a flying e. PROV 604:17
E. ears are listening OFFI 554:13
e. of good art CONN 233:26
e. of the best PROV 601:27
e. oppresseth me BOOK 134:8
e. that shall be destroyed BIBL 106:23
e. that will run me through BURN 165:19
e. to the human race MILL 510:4
every man your e. NELS 540:13
greatest e. is inclination BAHY 48:2
high speed toward the e. HALS 358:12
Hush! Here comes the e. COND 231:1
I am the e. you killed OWEN 562:13
If thine e. be hungry BIBL 83:21
life, its e. ANOU 22:10
Mine e.'s dog SHAK 680:2
near'st and dearest e. SHAK 668:27
no e. but time YEAT 836:7
no little e. PROV 612:16
not an e. in the world WILD 819:11
O mine e. BIBL 80:8
one e. ALI 12:2
Our friends, the e. BÉRA 67:13
potter is potter's e. HESI 375:10
quieten your e. by talking CEAU 199:2
see No e. But winter SHAK 658:20
sometimes his own worst e. BEVI 72:13
spoils of the e. MARC 495:7
sweet e., France SIDN 718:13
taught by the e. OVID 561:16
vision's greatest e. BLAK 118:10
will have upon the e. WELL 809:14
your e. and your friend TWAI 786:11
energy E. is Eternal Delight BLAK 119:10
important source of e. EINS 290:15
Symbol or e. ADAM 2:24
enfants *e. de la patrie* ROUG 636:1
Les e. terribles GAVA 331:7
enfin *E. Malherbe vint* BOIL 124:4
engine be a Really Useful E. AWDR 39:19
e. of pollution, the dog SPAR 731:22
e.-room was never installed BARN 55:2
He put this e. to our ears SWIF 747:18
human e. waits ELIO 296:8
I am An e. HARE 362:4
in dirt reasoning e. ROCH 630:14
Raised by that curious e. WEBS 807:22
two-handed e. MILT 513:7
engineers age of the e. HOGB 380:10
e. of human souls STAL 736:2
e. of the soul GORK 347:3
not e. of the soul KENN 433:18
enginer have the e. Hoist SHAK 665:24
engines e. to play a little BURK 163:13
England ah, faithless E. BOSS 143:16
always be an E. PARK 567:19
apple falling towards E. AUDE 34:14
Be E. what she will CHUR 213:14
between France and E. JERR 407:4
bored for E. MUGG 534:17
born and bred in E. GAY 332:18
children in E. NURS 547:15
Church of E. CHAR 203:6
damn you E. OSBO 560:10
deep sleep of E. ORWE 558:13
end in the ruin of E. SHEL 710:4
E.—a happy land CHUR 213:16
E. and America divided MISQ 521:10
E. and Ireland BOWE 145:9
E. and Saint George SHAK 671:6
E.! awake BLAK 119:4
E. cannot afford to go on BALF 49:15
E. expects NELS 540:20
E. has saved herself PITT 577:6
E. hath need of thee WORD 829:8
E., home and beauty ARNO 29:12
E. invented the phrase BAGE 46:9
E. is a disguised republic BAGE 46:21
E. is a garden KIPL 438:19
E. is a nation of shopkeepers NAPO 539:4
E. is an empire MICH 507:1
E. is the paradise of women PROV 599:13
E. keep my bones SHAK 677:18
E., my England HENL 370:1
E. not the jewelled isle ORWE 558:16
E. one whose centre UPDI 788:12
E.'s difficulty PROV 599:14
E.'s green and pleasant BLAK 119:5
E.'s green and pleasant land BLAK 120:1
E. shall perish ELIZ 297:8
E. should be free MAGE 489:10
E.'s native people BURN 169:12
E.'s not a bad country DRAB 278:14
E.'s on the anvil KIPL 438:3
E.'s the one land BROO 150:13
E.'s winding sheet BLAK 118:5
E., their England MACD 485:4
E. then indeed be free FABE 305:15
E. to be the workshop DISR 268:7
E. was too pure an Air ANON 18:5
E. will have her neck wrung CHUR 215:15
E., with all thy faults COWP 241:21
ensure summer in E. WALP 801:2
for ever E. OPEN 555:14
gentlemen of E. PARK 567:17
gives E. her soldiers MERE 505:10
God punish E. FUNK 327:14
Goodbye, E.'s rose JOHN 408:2
Gott strafe E. FUNK 327:14
Heart of E. DRAY 279:4
here did E. help me BROW 156:5
History is now and E. ELIO 294:19
history of E. MACA 482:3
in E. a particular bashfulness ADDI 5:11
in E. people have MIKE 507:18
in E.'s song for ever NEWB 541:16
in regard to this aged E. EMER 299:16
landscape of E. AUST 37:21
leads him to E. JOHN 413:6
Let not E. forget MILT 519:20
lot that make up E. today LAWR 458:17
no amusements in E. SMIT 726:6
Nor E.! did I know till then WORD 828:25
O E.! model SHAK 671:1
Oh, to be in E. BROW 156:2
roast beef of old E. BURK 164:15
Rule all E. COLL 228:9
Slaves cannot breathe in E. COWP 241:20
Speak for E. AMER 13:6
stately homes of E. HEMA 369:6
strong arm of E. PALM 566:3
Such is E. herself CANN 185:7
suspended in favour of E. SHAW 707:13
That is for ever E. BROO 150:17
that will be E. gone LARK 452:16
think of E. SAYI 647:5
think of the defence of E. BALD 49:9
This E. never did SHAK 677:21
this Realm of E. BOOK 142:12
this realm, this E. SHAK 694:19
to convert E. PUGI 616:18
Wake up, E. GEOR 333:16

England (*cont.*):
we are the people of E. CHES 210:16
who only E. know KIPL 438:12
world where E. is finished MILL 509:17
Ye Mariners of E. CAMP 183:18
youth of E. SHAK 670:30
Englanders Little E. ANON 17:9
English as an angel is the E. child BLAK 120:18
as E. as a beefsteak HAWT 364:12
as E. as the people who BINC 115:3
attain an E. style JOHN 409:24
baby doesn't understand E. KNOX 442:15
bird-haunted E. lawn ARNO 26:19
can't think of the E. CARR 190:16
Certain men the E. shot YEAT 836:17
Cricket—a game which the E. MANC 493:5
diversity In E. CHAU 207:18
E. a nation of PROV 599:15
E. are busy MONT 528:10
E. are foul-mouthed HAZL 365:21
E. . . . are paralysed by fear LAWR 457:23
E. are very little indeed inferior NORT 546:15
E. at that time WILL 820:4
E. Bible MACA 482:15
E. book is a blank book PICA 575:14
E. child BLAK 120:18
E. Church shall be free MAGN 489:11
E. elephant *Never* lies IMLA 398:21
E. have hot-water bottles MIKE 507:19
E. home TENN 765:10
E. in taste MACA 483:15
E. is the language BAGE 47:20
E. kept history in mind BOWE 145:16
E. know-how COLO 230:1
E. make it their abode WALL 800:3
E. manners more frightening JARR 404:11
E. never smash in a face HALS 358:11
E., not the Turkish court SHAK 670:19
E. plays are like VOLT 798:12
E. subject's sole prerogative DRYD 282:27
E. sweete upon his tonge CHAU 204:17
E. take their pleasures SULL 746:3
E. tongue I love WALC 799:1
E. unofficial rose BROO 150:11
E. up with which I will not put CHUR 216:3
E. want *inferiors* TOCQ 778:17
expression in E. ARNO 28:18
fine old E. gentleman SONG 729:14
flower of E. nobility ORDE 557:11
fragments of the E. scene ORWE 558:17
great E. blight WAUG 806:2
happy E. child TAYL 756:10
hard E. men KING 437:7
in E. the undergrowth EMPS 300:10
in the E. language JAME 403:23
king's E. SHAK 688:32
made our E. tongue SPEN 734:24
mobilized the E. language MURR 537:8
Most E. talk JAME 403:2
My native E. SHAK 694:11
our sweet E. tongue FLEC 317:7
raped and speaks E. ANON 15:10
really nice E. people SHAW 707:12
rolling E. road CHES 210:13
Saxon-Danish-Norman E. DEFO 255:12
scarcely known in E. provinces ORDE 557:12
second E. satirist HALL 358:5
seven feet of E. ground HARO 362:11
shed one E. tear MACA 482:24
talent of our E. nation DRYD 282:13
to the E. that of the sea RICH 627:12
trick of our E. nation SHAK 669:26
We be all good E. men TENN 766:9
we E. will long maintain CARL 187:28
We French, we E. BIRN 115:12
well of E. undefiled SPEN 734:6
working in E. language WINT 823:13
writing in E. JOYC 422:19
You are E. BECK 60:10
Englishman blood of an E. NASH 539:20
broad-shouldered genial E. TENN 766:7
E. among the under-dogs WAUG 806:7
E., Being flattered CHAP 202:12
E. can't feel FORS 320:10
E. does not travel STER 738:6
E., even if he is alone MIKE 507:20
E. in the wrong SHAW 709:2
E. of the strongest type DAVI 252:20
E. prudently avoids TOCQ 778:16
E.'s consitution AUST 37:27
E.'s home PROV 599:16
E.'s word PROV 599:17
E. thinks he is moral SHAW 708:6
E. to open his mouth SHAW 709:10
E. to rule in India NEHR 540:10
E. will give his mind SHAW 706:14
for E. or Jew BLAK 118:17
Give but an E. OTWA 560:24
He is an E. GILB 338:30
He remains an E. GILB 339:1
last great E. TENN 765:2
No E. is ever fairly beaten SHAW 709:16
not one E. WALP 802:5
One E. can beat PROV 608:36
one E. could beat ADDI 5:8
rights of an E. JUNI 423:12
There is in the E. DICK 264:24
thing, an E. DEFO 255:11
truth-telling E. HUGH 393:13
Englishmen absurd nature of E. PEPY 573:2
E. never will be slaves SHAW 708:5
first to his E. MILT 519:15
Mad dogs and E. COWA 238:15
prefer to be E. RHOD 625:15
very name as E. PITT 577:5
what an E. believes SHAW 709:17
When two E. meet JOHN 409:16
Englishness all the eternal E. CARD 186:3
Englishwoman E. is so refined SMIT 724:24
Princess leave the E. BISM 116:4
engrafted e. word BIBL 110:13
enigma e. of the fever chart ELIO 294:10
mystery inside an e. CHUR 215:6
enjoy business of life is to e. BUTL 172:18
do not e. poetry THOR 775:28
e. both operations at once CARY 193:6
e. convalescence SHAW 708:17
e. her while she's kind DRYD 282:34
e. him for ever SHOR 717:15
e. Paradise BECK 60:12
have to go out and e. it SMIT 724:13
inherent will to e. HARD 361:1
we may e. them BOOK 127:13
what I most e. SHAK 704:14
who can e. alone MILT 517:9
yet not to e. ELIO 292:26
enjoyed little to be e. JOHN 410:26
still to be e. KEAT 428:26
enjoying from e. themselves RUSS 640:2
if you are e. NESB 541:9
oh think, it worth e. DRYD 280:20
enjoyment chief e. of riches SMIT 723:8
complete e. HUME 394:13
e. of all desires TANT 754:30
from e. spring TRAH 780:17
was it done with e. RUSK 638:19
enjoyments Fire-side e. COWP 242:1
if it were not for its e. SURT 747:2
insufficiency of human e. JOHN 411:1
most intense e. DOST 276:8
enlarge E., diminish SWIF 749:14
enlargement stability or e. JOHN 409:5
enlightenment leads to e. PALI 565:11
supreme e. MAHĀ 490:13
winning full e. MAHĀ 490:1
enmities e. of twenty generations MACA 482:9
enmity no e. among seekers AUCT 33:11
ennuie *L'éloquence continue e.* PASC 568:19
ennuyer *secret d'e.* VOLT 797:14
ennuyeux *hors le genre e.* VOLT 797:15
Enoch E. walked with God BIBL 74:13
enormity womb and bed of e. JONS 419:11
enough eaten and drunk e. HORA 387:10
E. as good as a feast PROV 599:18
e. for everyone's need BUCH 159:11
e. of blood and tears RABI 619:14
E. that he heard it BROW 154:25
Give a man rope e. PROV 601:5
Hold, e. SHAK 685:26
not to go far e. CONF 231:21
Patriotism is not e. CAVE 198:10
'tis e., 'twill serve SHAK 697:22
two thousand years is e. PIUS 577:9
When thou hast e. BIBL 91:30
ye eat but ye have not e. BIBL 90:24
enquiries remote e. JOHN 409:26
ense *quam sit calamus saevior e.* BURT 170:10
ensign imperial e. MILT 514:28
enskyed thing e. and sainted SHAK 686:2
enslave impossible to e. BROU 151:14
enslaved should have been more e. CAVE 198:13
ensue seek peace, and e. it BOOK 133:22
entangled middle-sized are alone e. SHEN 715:7
Entbehren *E. sollst Du* GOET 342:19
enter about to e. a room EDDI 288:1
e. into the kingdom of heaven BIBL 93:8
E. not into judgement BOOK 141:17
King of England cannot e. PITT 576:20
Let no one e. ANON 21:3
rich man to e. BIBL 96:15
shall not e. BIBL 96:7
she may e. in SPEN 733:8
you who e. DANT 249:7
entered iron e. into his soul BOOK 139:8
enterprise leave it to private e. KEYN 435:9
more e. In walking naked YEAT 835:10
voyages of the starship E. RODD 631:1
enterprised not by any to be e. BOOK 131:1
enterprises e. of great pith and moment SHAK 664:4
entertain better to e. an idea JARR 404:12
e. divine Zenocrate MARL 496:29
e. four royalties SALI 642:17
e. the fag end of my life SHAK 669:4
e. this starry stranger CRAS 244:7
E., when they might instruct MORE 531:3
Tickle and e. us COWP 241:12
entertained e. angels unawares BIBL 110:6
entertainment e. this week PEPY 573:14
irrational e. JOHN 410:5
mere gossiping e. HUNT 396:2
proffered e. TROL 783:7
enthral Except you e. me DONN 272:25
enthralled but not e. MILT 511:27
enthusiasm no e. LAMB 449:10
ordinary human e. OSBO 560:2
with a holy e. ROUS 636:6
enthusiasts few e. can be trusted BALF 49:13
how to deal with e. MACA 482:11
entia *E. non sunt multiplicanda* OCCA 552:15
entice e. thee secretly BIBL 77:8
enticing with her e. parts ANON 17:3
entire E. and whole and perfect SPRI 735:6
entrails golden e. DRAY 279:5
swords In our own proper e. SHAK 677:1
entrance give back my e. ticket DOST 275:18
entrances exits and their e. SHAK 658:25
entreat e. heaven daily ELIZ 297:3
entropy e. of human thought ZAMY 839:18
nor Armageddon, but e. HEWI 375:18
entrusted Those e. with arms WIND 823:4
envelope e. of its technical forms MAIN 491:11
semi-transparent e. WOOL 826:14
envelopes backs of tattered e. HOPE 383:19
envied Better e. than pitied PROV 596:6
envious e. fever SHAK 700:7
e. siege SHAK 694:19

e. sliver broke SHAK 666:14
Hot, e., noisy YOUN 838:19
environed e. with a great ditch CROM 246:1
environment humdrum issues like the e. THAT 770:1
environmental any e. group BRUN 158:24
envy competition, and mutual e. HOBB 379:5
E. and wrath BIBL 92:5
e., hatred, and malice BOOK 127:4
e. not in any moods TENN 761:3
e. of less happier lands SHAK 694:19
e. of the devil BIBL 91:7
e. of thy happy lot KEAT 429:6
E.'s a sharper spur GAY 332:7
E.'s greener BALL 51:10
E.'s greener sea BALL 51:10
e. the pair of phoenixes HO 378:10
extinguisheth e. BACO 42:25
in e. of great Caesar SHAK 677:4
moved with e. BIBL 104:4
prisoners of e. ILLI 398:20
Toil, e., want JOHN 411:14
Too low for e. COWL 239:14
with e. and revenge MILT 514:10
épater *é. le bourgeois* BAUD 57:13
epaulette been by any e. THOR 776:14
Ephesians Diana of the E. BIBL 104:12
Ephesus beasts at E. BIBL 106:24
Ephraim grapes of E. BIBL 77:34
epic E. writer with a k STEV 742:9
name of E.'s no misnomer BYRO 176:8
scraps of thundrous e. TENN 765:12
epicure Serenely full, the e. SMIT 725:22
Epicurus E.' herd of pigs HORA 386:17
E. owene sone CHAU 204:22
epigram day of the jewelled e. ANNA 15:1
E.: a wisecrack LEVA 466:1
Impelled to try an e. PARK 567:5
purrs like an e. MARQ 497:12
What is an E. COLE 225:9
epigrams despotism tempered by e. CARL 187:25
epilogue good play needs no e. SHAK 659:29
epiphany e. a sudden spiritual JOYC 422:6
episcopal e. hat AUBR 32:11
episode but the occasional e. HARD 360:14
epistula *Verbosa et grandis e.* JUVE 424:20
epitaph better have a bad e. SHAK 663:24
carve my e. BROW 155:13
e. of an emotion NIET 545:20
e. to be my story FROS 326:3
no man write my e. EMME 300:4
not remembered in thy e. SHAK 669:14
that may be his e. STEV 741:1
epitaphs nice derangement of e. SHER 716:1
of worms, and e. SHAK 695:8
epithet e. for thee MARL 496:28
epitome all life's e. YEAT 836:8
all mankind's e. DRYD 280:9
eppur *E. si muove* GALI 328:14
equal all men are created e. LINC 468:13
consider our e. DARW 251:2
deemed E. in strength MILT 515:8
e. division of unequal earnings ELLI 298:12
e. in dignity and rights ANON 15:6
E. Pay ANTH 22:17
e. to any other person PRIE 592:9
e. with God BIBL 108:16
faith shines e. BRON 149:21
law has made him e. DARR 250:12
men are created e. JEFF 405:3
more e. than others ORWE 558:7
one e. eternity DONN 275:13
separate and e. station JEFF 405:2
talked about e. rights JOHN 408:13
to that e. sky POPE 585:11
we are all e. JUNI 423:15
we'll be e. PAST 569:9
Woman is the e. of man LOY 478:12
equality apostles of e. ARNO 28:9
E. for women demands TOYN 780:6
e. in the servants' hall BARR 55:13
e. or inequality HUGH 393:12
E. would be heaven TROL 783:5
liberty and e. ARIS 25:5
majestic e. of the law FRAN 322:15
not e. or fairness BERL 68:16
equalization natural e. CHUA 212:20
equalize never e. BURK 163:17
equally [Death] comes e. DONN 275:5
equals commerce between e. GOLD 345:13
least of all between e. BACO 42:31
live together as e. MILL 509:7
peace between e. WILS 822:13
Pigs treat us as e. CHUR 216:22
equanimity face with e. GILB 337:16
equation each e. would halve the sales HAWK 364:8
equations fire into the e. HAWK 364:10
in disagreement with Maxwell's e. EDDI 287:23
politics and e. EINS 291:6
equator join hands across the E. GLAD 341:3
equators North Poles and E. CARR 191:22
equi *currite noctis e.* MARL 496:7
currite noctis e. OVID 561:2
equinox when was the e. BROW 153:9
equity people with e. BOOK 138:11
equivocate I will not e. GARR 330:9
equo *E. ne credite* VIRG 793:18
eradication e. of conferences MAYA 502:17
erected least e. spirit MILT 515:3
eremite patient, sleepless E. KEAT 426:14
Erin for E. dear we fall SULL 746:1
fresh-stirred hearts in E. FERG 308:17
eripuit *E. coelo fulmen* TURG 785:9
eripuitque *E. Jovi* MANI 493:16
err e. is human SAYI 648:7
Man will e. GOET 342:14
mortal, and may e. SHIR 717:10
most may e. DRYD 280:12
prefer To e. ANON 19:18
To e. is human POPE 584:27
To e. is human PROV 613:8
errand thy joyous e. FITZ 315:3
errands Meet to be sent on e. SHAK 676:17
run on little e. GILB 337:7
erred e., and strayed from thy ways BOOK 125:15
e. exceedingly BIBL 78:37
erreur *L'e. n'a jamais approché* METT 506:12
error as an 'e. of judgement' SALI 643:5
E. has never approached METT 506:12
e. is immense BOLI 124:16
he is in e. LOCK 471:16
limit to infinite e. BREC 147:9
made the e. double CLAR 218:9
men are liable to e. LOCK 471:20
no dignity in persevering in e. PEEL 571:17
O hateful e. SHAK 676:32
positive in e. as in truth LOCK 471:19
stalking-horse to e. BOLI 124:13
troops of e. BROW 153:13
ut me malus abstulit e. VIRG 796:8
very e. of the moon SHAK 693:25
errors common e. of our life SIDN 718:25
e. and absurdities BURN 165:20
E., like straws DRYD 280:24
E. look so very ugly ELIO 293:10
e. of a wise man BLAK 120:6
female e. fall POPE 587:1
reasoned e. HUXL 397:18
erupit *evasit, e.* CICE 217:20
eruption bodes some strange e. SHAK 661:8
Esau E. my brother BIBL 74:37
E. selleth his birthright BIBL 74:34
E. was a cunning hunter BIBL 74:35
hands are the hands of E. BIBL 74:38
escalier *esprit de l'e.* DIDE 267:6
escape Beauty for some provides e. HUXL 397:8
can be no e. from it CHUA 213:3
did not expect to e. TURN 785:17
e. can be shown PALI 565:21
e. my iambics CATU 198:2
Gluttony an emotional e. DEV 259:11
great ones e. PROV 605:43
let me ever e. BOOK 141:16
Let no guilty man e. GRAN 349:3
many deaths do they e. BYRO 177:5
nothing to e. to ELIO 293:23
What struggle to e. KEAT 428:22
writing? A way of e. GREE 351:26
escaped e. with the skin of my teeth BIBL 81:21
Our soul is e. BOOK 140:17
through language and e. BROW 157:19
eschew E. evil BOOK 133:22
escutcheon blot on the e. GRAY 349:24
Eskdale E. and Liddesdale SCOT 651:29
Eskimo E. forgets his language OKPI 553:11
proud to be an E. OKPI 553:10
esperance Now, E.! Percy SHAK 669:10
stands still in e. SHAK 679:13
espionage e. can be recommended WEST 812:9
espoused My fairest, my e. MILT 516:29
my late e. saint MILT 519:1
esprit *e. de l'escalier* DIDE 267:6
n'a jamais approché de mon e. METT 506:12
essay e. much ELGA 291:18
esse *E. quam videri bonus* SALL 643:9
essence e. is very real LAO 451:11
e. of a human soul CARL 188:18
e. of human life MACD 484:17
e. of innumerable biographies CARL 187:9
e. of the true sublime BYRO 178:3
precedes and rules e. SART 645:1
essenced long e. hair MACA 482:22
essential e. ingredient PHIL 575:6
what is e. SAIN 641:12
established so sure e. BOOK 125:12
estate e. of the Catholick Church BOOK 127:17
e. o' the world SHAK 685:23
fourth e. of the realm MACA 481:9
holy e. BOOK 131:1
in mind, body, or e. BOOK 127:18
low e. of his handmaiden BIBL 98:16
ordered their e. ALEX 11:9
esteemed e. him not BIBL 88:16
estranging unplumbed, salt, e. sea ARNO 28:4
esuriens *Graeculus e.* JUVE 424:10
esurientes *E. implevit bonis* BIBL 114:4
état *L'É. c'est moi* LOUI 475:16
éteint *qui ne s'é.* RENO 624:16
eternal authority of the e. yesterday WEBE 807:6
boy e. SHAK 702:31
by the e. mind WORD 830:3
E. Father, strong to save WHIT 815:1
e. Footman hold my coat ELIO 295:8
E. in man cannot kill BHAG 72:15
E. in man cannot kill UPAN 787:21
E. Passion ARNO 26:21
e. rocks beneath BRON 150:3
e. silence PASC 568:13
e. triangle ANON 16:2
Grant them e. rest MISS 523:2
Hope springs e. POPE 585:9
Hope springs e. PROV 603:1
lose not the things e. BOOK 128:11
our e. home WATT 805:19
ourselves to be e. JERO 406:16
portion of the E. SHEL 710:22
Promised from e. years CASW 194:3
Robust art alone is e. GAUT 331:6
thy e. summer SHAK 704:10
way to e. suffering DANT 249:7
whose e. Word MARR 497:13
eternally things abided e. TRAH 780:15
eternities meeting of two e. THOR 776:5
eternity battlements of E. THOM 774:8
candidates for e. MORE 531:3
day joins the past e. BYRO 174:25

eternity (*cont.*):
Deserts of vast e. MARV 499:2
e. hath triumphed RALE 621:5
e. in an hour BLAK 117:17
E. is in love BLAK 119:16
e. of print WOOL 826:12
E.'s a terrible thought STOP 743:18
E. shut in a span CRAS 244:8
E.'s sunrise BLAK 120:8
E.'s too short ADDI 5:10
E.! thou pleasing, dreadful thought ADDI 4:16
E. was in our lips and eyes SHAK 656:16
E. was in that moment CONG 232:32
Heads Were toward E. DICK 266:7
image of e. BYRO 175:11
one equal e. DONN 275:13
palace of e. MILT 511:14
pinprick of e. AURE 37:5
progress to e. SHAK 705:2
same sweet e. HERR 374:13
saw E. the other night VAUG 790:17
sells e. SHAK 704:1
shadows of e. VAUG 790:8
Silence is deep as E. CARL 187:12
some conception of e. MANC 493:5
speak of e. BROW 153:17
speculations of e. ADDI 5:9
teacher affects e. ADAM 2:20
through nature to e. SHAK 661:19
Tree of E. UPAN 788:3
white radiance of E. SHEL 711:4
who love, time is e. VAN 789:15
without injuring e. THOR 776:3
ether ampler e. WORD 829:1
etherized patient e. upon a table ELIO 295:3
patient e. upon a table LEWI 466:22
ethic protestant e. WEBE 807:3
ethical nuclear giants and e. infants BRAD 146:11
ethics law floats in a sea of e. WARR 803:21
Ethiop E.'s ear SHAK 697:7
Ethiopian E. change his skin BIBL 89:17
etiquette It isn't e. CARR 191:17
Eton playing fields of E. ORWE 558:18
playing fields of E. WELL 810:1
étonne *É.-moi* DIAG 260:1
étrange *é. entreprise* MOLI 524:21
Etrurian where the E. shades MILT 514:23
Etruscans long-nosed E. LAWR 458:7
Euclid E. alone has looked MILL 509:12
fifth proposition of E. DOYL 277:22
Eugene Aram E., though a thief CALV 182:7
eunuch Argus were her e. SHAK 680:23
female e. GREE 352:6
Female E. GREE 352:9
intellectual e. Castlereagh BYRO 175:26
kills me to be time's e. HOPK 385:8
kind of moral e. SHEL 713:3
prerogative of the e. STOP 743:12
strain, Time's e. HOPK 384:24
eunuchs E. boasting LEWI 466:21
seraglio of e. FOOT 319:1
euphemism e. for the fading power BLIS 122:1
euphoric In an e. dream AUDE 35:1
Euphrates bathed in the E. HUGH 392:19
Eureka E.! [I've got it!] ARCH 23:18
Euripides chorus-ending from E. BROW 155:7
Europe another war in E. BISM 116:15
arsenal of old E. HEGE 367:12
Bright over E. TURN 785:12
corrupt as in E. JEFF 405:8
create a nation E. MONN 526:6
depravations of E. MATH 501:7
dogs of E. bark AUDE 34:2
E. a continent of energetic mongrels FISH 313:12
E. by her example PITT 577:6
E. has never existed MONN 526:5
E. in danger of plunging YELT 838:5
E. made his woe her own ARNO 27:22
E. of nations DE G 255:24
E. the unfinished negative MCCA 484:2
E. took their gold CHUR 213:21
E. will decide DE G 255:22
fifty years of E. TENN 763:10
glory of E. BURK 163:21
great stocks of E. YEAT 838:2
I pine for E. RIMB 628:9
keep up with Western E. UPDI 788:11
lamps are going out all over E. GREY 353:5
last gentleman in E. LEVE 466:3
Leave this E. FANO 306:7
madness which has taken hold of E. GONN 346:10
map of E. has been changed CHUR 214:22
nationalities of E. ASQU 31:2
part of the community of E. SALI 642:19
poor are E.'s blacks CHAM 201:9
salvation of E. PITT 577:4
security of E. MITC 523:14
spectre is haunting E. MARX 500:5
take over the whole of E. RIDL 627:15
Whoever speaks of E. BISM 116:10
whole of E. NAPO 538:12
Without Britain, E. ERHA 301:5
European become E. KETT 434:13
E. war might do it REDM 623:11
great E. race DAVI 252:18
green pastures of the E. VERW 791:13
I'm E. HEWI 376:1
not a characteristic of a E. CHAN 202:3
on E. Monetary Union CHIR 212:5
policy of E. integration KOHL 443:7
Europeans You are learned E. MASS 501:3
Euston flushpots of E. JOYC 421:19
in E. waiting-room CORN 237:1
evasit *e., erupit* CICE 217:20
eve and E. spane ROLL 632:6
E. ate Adam HUGH 393:7
E. from his side arose ANON 19:16
fairest of her daughters E. MILT 516:17
From far, from e. HOUS 391:4
nor E. the rites MILT 516:24
real curse of E. RHYS 625:17
riverrun, past E. and Adam's JOYC 421:17
riverrun, past E. and Adam's OPEN 556:12
When Adam delved and E. span PROV 614:16
Evelyn E. Hope is dead BROW 155:28
even Don't get mad, get e. SAYI 647:13
E. as you and I KIPL 440:16
E. less am I HOPE 383:21
evening along the road of e. DE L 256:19
autumn e. ARNO 27:2
came still e. on MILT 516:19
E., all CATC 195:13
e. and the morning BIBL 73:11
e.—any evening— LEWI 466:22
e. is spread out against the sky ELIO 295:3
e. of life GIBB 336:3
e. sacrifice BOOK 141:15
e. star MILT 517:25
e. star is coming VIRG 796:13
exhalation in the e. SHAK 673:11
five o'clock in an e. BOWE 145:11
grateful e. mild MILT 516:22
in the e. it is cut down BOOK 137:18
It is a beauteous e. WORD 828:23
light of e., Lissadell YEAT 836:6
like an e. gone WATT 805:19
red e.-star is lighting VIRG 796:15
Some enchanted e. HAMM 358:23
welcome peaceful e. in COWP 241:31
When e.'s come COLL 228:6
When it is e. BIBL 96:2
winter e. settles down ELIO 295:19
yet the E. listens KEAT 430:2
evensong bells ringeth to e. HAWE 364:5
ringeth to e. PROV 596:2
event as the e. decides AUST 38:13
greatest e. it is FOX 322:5
hurries to the main e. HORA 386:1
not an e. TALL 753:4
size of each e. MAIL 491:1
wise after the e. PROV 604:15
eventide fast falls the e. LYTE 480:23
events Coming e. cast PROV 597:29
e. cast their shadows CAMP 183:10
E., dear boy MACM 488:2
e. have controlled me LINC 468:15
train of e. AMER 13:5
We cannot make e. ADAM 3:20
ever e.-fixèd mark SHAK 705:15
For e. panting KEAT 428:26
Hardly e. GILB 338:24
WELL, DID YOU E. PORT 588:11
went on for e. BINC 115:6
evergreen e. tree SHER 715:25
everlasting caught An e. cold WEBS 808:20
e. arms BIBL 77:14
e. Father BIBL 87:1
e. life BIBL 101:18
e. life BIBL 101:30
e. mansion SHAK 699:25
e. mercy, Christ MASE 500:15
e. No CARL 188:14
from e. thou art God WATT 805:19
from e. time AURE 37:6
from e. to everlasting TRAH 780:13
give them an e. name BIBL 88:24
her e. rest FANS 306:10
life e. BOOK 126:10
thy e.kingdom BOOK 130:20
everlastingness shoots of e. VAUG 790:9
evermore e. shalt be HEBE 367:8
for e. BOOK 140:13
name liveth for e. BIBL 92:17
name liveth for e. EPIT 304:6
every E. day a little death SOND 727:21
E. day, I am getting better COUÉ 238:4
E. which way FILM 312:20
To e. thing BIBL 84:7
everybody E.'s business PROV 599:40
E. wants to get inta CATC 195:14
What e. says PROV 613:51
everyday against the e. LAST 456:13
e. story of country folk CATC 195:15
Everyman Death would summon E. HEAN 366:9
E., I will go with thee ANON 16:4
everyone can't please e. PROV 615:28
E. burst out singing SASS 645:20
like e. else DE G 256:1
When e. is wrong LA C 447:1
everything against e. KENN 433:22
cannot all do e. LUCI 478:20
can't all do e. VIRG 796:10
chips with e. WESK 810:18
E. has an end PROV 599:43
E. has been said LA B 446:18
e. in its place BEVA 72:4
E. is fitting AURE 36:22
e. is in it TALM 754:1
E. passes ANON 20:15
e. that is the case WITT 824:7
E. what it is BUTL 171:10
God encompasses e. KORA 444:13
Greek can do e. JUVE 424:10
knowledge of e. HERO 374:1
Life, the Universe and E. ADAM 2:4
Macaulay is of e. MELB 503:17
Money isn't e. PROV 606:46
place for e. PROV 609:28
robbed a man of *e.* SOLZ 727:10
sans taste, sans e. SHAK 659:3
smattering of e. DICK 265:20
time for e. PROV 612:6
everywhere behaviour e. SHAK 687:9
centre is e. ANON 17:21
children . . . e. CATC 195:19
Functioning e. means LAO 451:12
Out of the e. MACD 484:20
Water, water, e. COLE 226:12

evidence before you have all the e. DOYL 278:5
circumstantial e. THOR 775:27
clearer e. than this ARAB 23:8
e. against their own understanding HALI 357:13
e. of things not seen BIBL 109:28
it's not e. DICK 265:14
soldier said isn't e. PROV 614:10
evidences E. of Christianity COLE 227:8
evil all government is e. O'SU 560:18
all men are e. MACH 485:14
All partial e. POPE 585:17
all the e. he does LA R 453:17
any place that is free from e. WAUG 806:16
banality of e. AREN 24:1
call e. good BIBL 86:19
dark and e. days INGR 399:17
days are e. BIBL 108:8
deeds were e. BIBL 101:19
deliver us from e. BIBL 93:19
deliver us from e. MISS 522:17
Do e. in return AUDE 34:21
do e., that good may come BIBL 104:31
do e. that good may come PROV 607:28
doing e. in return SOCR 727:3
done e. to his neighbour BOOK 132:7
don't think that he's e. ALLE 12:11
Eschew e. BOOK 133:22
e. and adulterous generation BIBL 95:15
E., be thou my good MILT 516:10
E. be to him who evil thinks MOTT 535:9
E. communications BIBL 106:25
E. communications PROV 599:44
e. counsel is most evil HESI 375:13
e. cradling BORR 144:4
e. cradling KORA 443:23
E. doers evil dreaders PROV 599:45
e. empire REAG 623:5
e. from his youth BIBL 74:18
e. in a city BIBL 90:17
e. in thy sight BOOK 135:4
e. in young minds ARNO 29:16
e. is wrought HOOD 382:22
e. manners live in brass SHAK 673:22
e. that men do lives SHAK 675:27
e. thereof BIBL 93:27
e. thereof PROV 611:34
e. turn to good MILT 517:27
e. which I would not BIBL 105:4
expect e. of those ABEL 1:4
face of 'e.' BURR 169:15
far deeper than the e. FORS 320:19
fear nae e. BURN 168:15
Few and e. BIBL 75:20
find means of e. MILT 514:16
for e. to triumph MISQ 521:17
God by curse Created e. MILT 515:21
God prepares e. ANON 21:2
great book is a great e. PROV 601:33
he that doeth e. BIBL 111:16
Hypocrisy, the only e. MILT 516:6
Idleness is root of all e. PROV 603:11
If all e. were prevented THOM 771:15
illness identified with e. SONT 728:4
knowing good and e. BIBL 73:25
like great e. CALL 181:17
means to fight an e. DAWS 253:7
meet e.-willers ELIZ 296:25
my tongue from e.-speaking BOOK 130:15
necessary e. BRAD 146:7
necessary e. PAIN 563:11
no e. happen unto thee BOOK 137:23
non-cooperation with e. GAND 329:7
on the e. and on the good BIBL 93:14
open and notorious e. liver BOOK 129:1
overcome e. with good BIBL 105:18
perplexity of radical e. AREN 24:2
prevention from e. MANN 493:18
punishment in itself is e. BENT 66:20
rash hand in e. hour MILT 517:17
refuse the e. BIBL 86:26
rendering evil for e. BIBL 111:4
represent poverty as no e. JOHN 413:9
Resist not e. BIBL 93:12
return good for e. VANB 789:5
rewarded me e. for good BOOK 133:23
root of all e. BIBL 109:18
root of all e. PROV 606:45
See no e. PROV 610:26
speak e. of dignities BIBL 111:9
supernatural source of e. CONR 234:24
unruly e. BIBL 110:19
whatever e. visits thee KORA 444:10
What we call e. FORD 319:16
wish me e. BOOK 136:14
withstand in the e. day BIBL 108:13
evils enamoured of existing e. BIER 114:21
E., Theodorus, can never pass PLAT 578:11
expect new e. BACO 43:14
fighting e. BERL 68:14
greatest of e. SHAW 707:21
least of e. GRAC 347:14
necessary e. JOHN 410:18
Of the two e. THOM 771:9
Of two e. choose PROV 608:21
Two e., monstrous either one RANS 622:1
evoke To e. posterity GRAV 349:16
evolution E. . . . is—a change SPEN 732:4
e. is more like pushing HEAN 366:21
Some call it e. CARR 192:2
ewe one little e. lamb BIBL 79:5
tupping your white e. SHAK 691:25
ewes milk my e. and weep SHAK 703:23
my e. breed not BARN 55:9
Ewig-Weibliche *E. zieht uns hinan* GOET 343:4
exact Detection is an e. science DOYL 277:22
not to be e. BURK 162:18
writing an e. man BACO 44:7
exactitude *L'e. est la politesse* LOUI 476:5
exaggerate e. the difference SHAW 707:29
exaggerated have been greatly e. TWAI 786:28
exaggeration beyond eighty an e. CALL 181:8
e. is a truth GIBR 336:14
exalt e. us unto the same place BOOK 128:8
exalted e. among the heathen BOOK 134:20
e. them of low degree BIBL 98:17
highly e. him BIBL 108:17
Reason, in her most e. mood WORD 831:11
Sorrow proud to be e. ANON 17:3
valley shall be e. BIBL 87:28
exalteth whosoever e. himself BIBL 99:26
exam have an e. at 11 NEIL 540:11
examinations E. are formidable COLT 230:3
In e., those who do not wish RALE 621:10
examine E. for a moment WOOL 826:13
E. me, O Lord BOOK 133:7
e. my thoughts BOOK 141:14
example annoyance of a good e. TWAI 786:25
Europe by her e. PITT 577:6
E. better than precept PROV 599:46
E. is always more efficacious JOHN 410:28
E. is the school BURK 164:24
set us a good e. WILD 817:12
examples philosophy from e. DION 268:3
exceed e. his grasp BROW 155:2
excel daring to e. CHUR 213:13
thou shalt not e. BIBL 75:21
excellence in conformity with e. ARIS 24:17
ne'er will reach an e. DRYD 282:30
excellencies rather upon e. ADDI 5:5
excellent e. thing in woman SHAK 680:13
e. things for mean LOCK 471:14
his Name only is e. BOOK 142:1
too wonderful and e. BOOK 141:10
Very e. things BOOK 137:16
excellently Goddess, e. bright JONS 419:17
see them all so e. fair COLE 225:2
excelling all loves e. WESL 811:7
Excelsior strange device E. LONG 473:16
excelsis *Gloria in e.* MISS 520:13
except E. the Lord build BOOK 140:21
exception e. proves the rule PROV 599:47
e. to every rule PROV 612:9
glad to make an e. MARX 499:12
excess but the e. SELD 653:15
e. of light GRAY 351:2
e. of stupidity JOHN 413:15
Give me e. of it SHAK 700:26
Nothing in e. ANON 21:1
poverty and e. PENN 572:14
ridiculous e. SHAK 677:15
road of e. BLAK 119:12
excessit *Abiit, e.* CICE 217:20
excessive e. bright MILT 516:3
right of an e. wrong BROW 157:24
exchange By just e. one for the other SIDN 718:8
e. of self and other SHAN 706:8
fair e. no robbery PROV 600:8
excise *E.*. A hateful tax JOHN 409:9
exciseman deil's awa wi' th'E. BURN 166:29
excite e. my amorous propensities JOHN 412:10
excitement equal the e. GREE 351:22
it engendered e. PAGE 563:1
exciting films are too e. BERR 70:1
War the most e. thing DAYA 253:10
excluded castes who are e. LAWS 459:9
E. from honours ADAM 2:2
irrevocably e. SHEL 710:10
exclusion cannot be built on e. ADAM 2:11
exclusive e.-secret-special-club WEIR 808:29
excommunicate thou, poor e. CARE 186:16
excrement in the place of e. YEAT 835:13
excursion called the 'E.' BYRO 176:30
made an e. to hell PRIE 591:15
excuse bad e. better than none PROV 595:29
began to make e. BIBL 99:27
cruelty with an e. COMP 230:12
e. every man will plead SELD 653:16
E. my dust EPIT 302:4
I will not e. GARR 330:9
make a good e. SZAS 752:4
no e. for breaking it PROV 603:43
excuses e., accuses himself PROV 602:25
e. for our failures FULB 327:2
Several e. HUXL 397:5
execute people who e. them MILL 509:6
you dare e. SHAK 672:19
zealous Muslims to e. KHOM 435:14
executing thought-e. fires SHAK 678:21
execution Ceauşescus' e. O'DO 553:1
fascination of a public e. FOOT 318:26
stringent e. GRAN 349:2
executioner I am mine own E. DONN 275:2
executioners victims who respect their e. SART 645:13
executive e. expression BRIT 149:1
salary of the chief e. GALB 328:8
executives e. Would never want AUDE 34:1
executors Let's choose e. SHAK 695:8
exercise all, e. GREE 351:12
E. is bunk FORD 319:17
E. is the yuppie version EHRE 290:1
e. is to the body STEE 737:1
e. myself in great matters BOOK 141:3
e. of his soul's faculties ARIS 24:17
for cure, on e. depend DRYD 281:13
love's proper e. DAVI 251:18
sad mechanic e. TENN 760:24
exertion e. is too much for me PEAC 571:3
exertions saved herself by her e. PITT 577:6
exhalation Like a bright e. SHAK 673:11
exhaust e. the little moment BROO 151:5
exhaustion exhilaration and e. LAHR 448:3
exhibited publicly e. ALBE 10:6
exigency to the e. of the moment PEEL 571:14
exile destined as an e. VIRG 793:4
die in e. LAST 455:10
e. is his country URBA 788:19
silence, e., and cunning JOYC 422:5

exiled Marcellus e. POPE 586:2
outlawed or e. MAGN 489:12
exiles none save e. feel AYTO 40:12
Paradise of e. SHEL 711:19
exist could not possibly e. DESC 258:19
didn't e. before UPDI 788:16
e. in order to save us DEV 259:12
He doesn't e. BECK 59:13
I e. by what I think SART 645:11
presumed to e. OCCA 552:15
questioned its right to e. SCHU 649:8
existed discussing if it e. GUNN 355:1
existence e. as a nation PITT 577:5
e. is but a brief crack NABO 537:20
e. of the Creator MAIM 491:5
e. or when hope AUST 38:12
E. precedes and rules SART 645:1
paint on the face of E. BYRO 180:2
prefer mere e. JUVE 424:18
purpose of human e. JUNG 423:7
single e. is an illusion BELL 64:15
Struggle for E. DARW 250:19
threatens the e. of life SONT 728:7
woman's whole e. BYRO 176:7
your e. and this AURE 37:9
existential crude e. malpractice FENT 308:9
existing bother of e. HAWK 364:10
exists Everything e. FORS 320:23
no one e. alone AUDE 35:2
exit E., pursued by a bear SHAK 703:8
Such a graceful e. JUNO 423:18
exits e. and their entrances SHAK 658:25
men to take their exits WEBS 808:1
exitus *e. multos* SENE 654:19
exodus talks of the E. ZOHA 840:11
exorciser No e. harm thee SHAK 661:2
exoriare *E. aliquis nostris* VIRG 794:14
expands Work e. so as to fill PROV 615:19
ex-parrot THIS IS AN E. MONT 529:6
expatiate E. free o'er all this scene POPE 585:4
expect e. less of them JOHN 417:8
E. nothing WALK 799:7
people e. most AUST 37:24
expectancy e. and rose SHAK 664:10
expectation bettered e. SHAK 690:31
e. whirls me round SHAK 700:12
now sits E. SHAK 670:31
songs of e. BARI 54:14
expectations revolution of rising e. CLEV 220:16
expected reasonably be e. to do WHAT 813:9
expects England e. NELS 540:20
he who e. nothing PROV 596:27
Nobody e. MONT 529:7
expediency be sacrificed to e. MAUG 501:17
expedient all things are not e. BIBL 106:12
e. for us BIBL 102:12
e. for you BIBL 102:24
most e. for them BOOK 126:18
not a principle, but an e. DISR 268:11
expedit *E. esse deos* OVID 561:7
expedition abandoning the e. DOUG 276:14
expeditious e. man MOLI 525:13
no e. road THOM 774:10
expelles *Naturam e. furca* HORA 386:19
expende *E. Hannibalem* JUVE 424:22
expenditure annual e. nineteen DICK 261:19
E. rises to meet income PARK 567:21
expense at the e. of two CLOU 221:24
e. damnable CHES 209:26
e. of spirit SHAK 705:19
e. which I am almost ashamed of PEPY 573:14
sanctifies e. POPE 583:26
trouble and e. BELL 63:4
expenses e. run on CATO 194:15
facts are on e. STOP 743:15
meet all the e. THOR 776:7
expensive how e. it is to be poor BALD 48:19
experience balloon of e. JAME 402:26
but recorded e. CARL 187:8
can go beyond his e. LOCK 471:15
custom and e. HUME 394:9
e. and good sense DU B 283:22
E. father of wisdom PROV 599:49
E. has taught TACI 752:18
e. has taught me EDEN 288:7
e. is an arch ADAM 2:16
E. is best teacher PROV 599:48
E. is never limited JAME 403:9
E. is the child of Thought DISR 270:32
E. is the name WILD 818:13
e. is what you get SEEG 653:7
E. keeps dear school PROV 599:50
e. one thing BAGE 47:11
E., though noon auctoritee CHAU 206:15
flower of any kind of e. HUNT 395:20
founded upon my e. DOYL 277:9
I have e. CONG 233:4
know by e. ASCH 30:6
know it from e. ARAB 23:10
light which e. gives COLE 227:25
man of no e. CURZ 248:6
never had much e. MARQ 497:5
Old Age, and E. ROCH 630:14
one year's e. 30 times CARR 189:6
part of e. BACO 44:14
perfected by e. BACO 44:4
refuted by e. POPP 587:24
than e. in twenty ASCH 30:5
to be filled in by e. WILS 821:11
triumph of hope over e. JOHN 414:10
trying every e. once ANON 20:1
we need not e. it FRIS 325:8
experiences lie the e. of our life MANN 494:4
experiencing only by e. it PROU 594:8
experientia E. does it DICK 261:17
experiment best scale for an e. FISH 313:13
e. is the best test FARA 306:12
e. needs statistics RUTH 640:15
e. to his own cause SPRA 735:5
never tried an e. DARW 251:4
social and economic e. HOOV 383:9
tide of successful e. JEFF 405:12
experimental e. reasoning HUME 394:7
experimentalists e. do bungle things EDDI 287:23
expers *Vis consili e. mole* HORA 388:10
expert e. is one who knows more and more BUTL 171:13
e. is someone who knows HEIS 368:11
experto *E. credite* VIRG 795:11
experts never trust e. SALI 642:16
expiate something to e. LAWR 458:14
explain e. a thing till all men doubt POPE 580:21
e. his explanation BYRO 175:25
e. man to man STEI 737:4
e. why it didn't happen CHUR 216:21
Never complain and never e. DISR 271:4
Never e. FISH 313:15
Never e. HUBB 392:10
trying to e. it SHER 716:7
explained e. ourselves to each other ADAM 3:10
Shut up he e. LARD 452:10
when being e. BALF 50:3
explaining forever e. things SAIN 641:11
explanation saves tons of e. SAKI 642:7
expletive E. deleted ANON 16:5
explodes line smoulders and e. MAYA 502:16
exploits most brilliant e. PLUT 579:6
explore E. farthest Spain CLAU 219:17
explorers unlucky e. DOUG 276:14
exploring end of all our e. ELIO 294:17
explosive terrible e. NIET 545:13
exposes man who e. himself JOHN 416:9
exposition e. of sleep SHAK 690:13
exposure unseemly e. of the mind HAZL 365:13
express down e. in the small of the back WODE 824:17
e. our wants GOLD 345:12
e. yourself like YEAT 838:3
Never e. yourself more BOHR 124:2
expressed ne'er so well e. POPE 584:18
expressing worth e. in music DELI 256:23
expression conventional e. MAHĀ 489:15
E. is the dress POPE 584:19
impassioned e. WORD 832:21
expropriated expropriators e. MARX 499:17
expropriators e. expropriated MARX 499:17
exquisite e. touch SCOT 652:12
pleasure so e. HUNT 396:6
extant pyramidally e. BROW 153:5
extempore as his e. sayings WALP 801:15
extend attempt to e. their system MONR 526:9
extension both have an ideal e. SANT 644:12
extenuate nothing e. SHAK 694:3
extenuates e. not wrong SHAK 700:11
exterior this flabby e. LEVA 465:19
exterminate E. all the brutes CONR 234:12
e. a nation SPOC 735:2
extermination e. of capitalism ZINO 840:5
extinct wild life's become e. CHEK 208:11
extinction one generation from e. CARE 186:18
extinguished outflows e. PALI 565:7
extol e. Him first MILT 516:31
extra add some e., just for you LARK 453:4
extraction efficacy and e. MILT 519:7
extraordinary e. man JOHN 417:9
extras No e., no vacations DICK 263:17
extravagance does not lead to e. PERI 573:19
if there is e. CATO 194:14
extravagant e. with his own SALL 643:7
extreme e. part is most irritated BAGE 47:18
If thou, Lord, wilt be e. BOOK 141:1
extremes E. meet MACD 484:15
E. meet PROV 600:1
lean to wild e. DURY 286:10
mean between the two e. BOOK 125:11
other men's e. KYD 446:8
two e. CHEK 208:18
extremism e. in the defence of liberty GOLD 345:33
extremity daring pilot in e. DRYD 280:1
Man's e. PROV 606:19
exuberance E. is beauty BLAK 119:23
exultations e., agonies WORD 832:12
exulting people all e. WHIT 815:4
exuvias *redit e. indutus Achilli* VIRG 794:2
eye apple of his e. BIBL 77:11
beam that is in thine own e. BIBL 94:1
bright e. of peninsulas CATU 197:5
Cast a cold e. YEAT 837:22
cast a longing e. JEFF 405:9
close one e. DOUG 276:17
curtains of thine e. SHAK 698:28
custom loathsome to the e. JAME 402:12
day's garish e. MILT 512:10
every e. shall see him BIBL 111:18
E. among the blind WORD 830:3
e. begins to see BRON 150:1
e., did see that face ROYD 637:2
e. for eye BIBL 76:14
e. in the back of the head COLE 227:16
e. is not satisfied BIBL 84:2
e. of a master PROV 600:2
e. of a needle BIBL 96:15
e. of heaven SHAK 677:15
e. of man hath not heard SHAK 690:17
e. of the beholder PROV 595:38
e. sinks inward ARNO 26:3
e. that can open an oyster WODE 824:15
e. to the main chance CECI 199:4
e. was backward cast SPEN 733:20
fettered in her e. LOVE 476:12
great e. of heaven SPEN 733:16
Green E. HAYE 365:2
had but one e. DICK 263:18

harvest of a quiet e. WORD 830:19
he that made the e. BOOK 138:4
If thine e. offend thee BIBL 96:9
if you have the e. HOLM 381:16
In my mind's e. SHAK 662:2
in the twinkling of an e. BIBL 107:3
language in her e. SHAK 700:20
like a joyless e. SHEL 714:13
looked into the e. of day YEAT 836:3
man a microscopic e. POPE 585:13
mild and magnificent e. BROW 156:18
mine e. seeth thee BIBL 82:4
Monet is only an e. CÉZA 200:9
My tiny watching e. DE L 256:21
neither e. to see LENT 464:6
obscured that e. KEAT 430:13
Of e. and ear WORD 829:6
one e. is weeping FROS 325:14
On it may stay his e. HERB 372:13
Please your e. PROV 609:29
see e. to eye BIBL 88:13
seeing e. BIBL 83:10
soft black e. MOOR 530:18
still-soliciting e. SHAK 677:26
through the e. EPIT 302:6
to the e. of God OLIV 553:16
unforgiving e. SHER 716:15
untrusting e. on all they do GELL 333:3
What the e. doesn't see PROV 614:9
with his e. on the object ARNO 29:5
with his glittering e. COLE 226:4
With my little e. NURS 552:1
with, not through, the e. BLAK 118:14
eyeball e. to eyeball RUSK 638:3
like a coal His e. SMAR 722:10
eyebrows e. made of platinum FORS 320:8
eyed one e. man is king PROV 604:1
eyeless E. in Gaza MILT 518:13
work of an e. computer BETJ 71:1
eyelids e. heavy and red HOOD 382:28
tired e. upon tired eyes TENN 763:11
Upon her e. many Graces SPEN 733:24
eyes all e. else dead coals SHAK 703:25
And her e. were wild KEAT 428:9
bodily hunger in his e. SHAW 707:24
buyer needs hundred e. PROV 596:44
chewing gum for the e. ANON 18:21
Closed his e. GRAY 351:2
Close your e. SAYI 647:5
close your e. before AYCK 40:1
close your e. with holy dread COLE 225:25
cocking their medical e. DICK 266:2
cold commemorative e. ROSS 635:6
constitutional e. LINC 469:2
Crumbling behind the e. MACN 488:10
cynosure of neighbouring e. MILT 512:20
dark e. darting light BYRO 176:15
death bandaged my e. BROW 157:17
Donna Julia's e. BYRO 176:2
doves' e. BIBL 85:14
drew his e. along AUGU 36:2
electrical skin and glaring e. SMAR 722:6
Eternity was in our lips and e. SHAK 656:16
ever more perfect e. TEIL 757:4
e. are bright KEAT 431:13
e. are homes of silent prayer TENN 761:6
e. are oddly made HAMM 359:5
e. are window of soul PROV 600:3
e. as wide as a football-pool CAUS 198:3
e. became so terrible BECK 60:11
e. did once inhabit SHAK 696:17
e. did see Olivia SHAK 700:27
e. have all the seeming POE 579:19
e. have seen LOWE 477:19
e. have they, and see not BOOK 139:23
e. like lead BROW 155:32
e. like the fishpools BIBL 86:5
e. of Caligula MITT 524:10
E. of most unholy blue MOOR 530:10
E. still dazzled LIND 469:9
e. that looked so mild BALL 50:20
e. to behold the sun BIBL 84:31
e. to the blind BIBL 81:26
e. to wonder SHAK 705:10
e. upon his graces JOHN 410:16
e. were as a flame BIBL 111:22
e. were blacker than the sloe CARB 185:18
e. which see BIBL 99:10
Fields have e. PROV 600:18
Foolish e. SANS 644:7
four beasts full of e. BIBL 111:31
Four e. see more PROV 600:45
friendship closes its e. ANON 20:8
frightened look in its e. SITW 721:6
From women's e. SHAK 680:26
From women's e. SHAK 680:28
full of e. within BIBL 111:32
Get thee glass e. SHAK 679:25
gloom-pleased e. KEAT 430:6
God be in my e. PRAY 592:3
Hath not a Jew e. SHAK 687:29
her e., her hair MEW 506:13
Her e. the glow-worm lend HERR 374:14
hid from thine e. BIBL 100:19
I believed her e. WOTT 833:2
King of England's e. LAST 456:12
Lift up thine e. MONS 526:11
lightened are our e. SORL 728:17
Love in thine e. LODG 472:18
Love looks not with the e. SHAK 689:7
Love's tongue is in the e. FLET 318:15
maidens Quiet e. STEV 742:19
marvellous in our e. BOOK 140:6
men's e. are always bigger VANB 789:10
Mine e. have seen HOWE 391:15
mock our e. with air SHAK 657:12
My mistress' e. SHAK 705:20
night has a thousand e. BOUR 145:4
Night hath a thousand e. LYLY 480:17
one, all e. WORD 830:17
open The king's e. SHAK 673:8
optics of these e. BROW 153:25
pearls that were his e. SHAK 698:27
pick out hawks' e. PROV 602:4
Pure e. and Christian hearts KEBL 432:6
Seal her sweet e. ROSS 634:10
set her both his e. LYLY 480:15
Smoke gets in your e. HARB 359:14
soft look Your e. had once YEAT 837:23
Stars scribble on our e. CRAN 243:19
strike mine e. JONS 419:20
stuck in her face for e. SHAK 680:23
Take a pair of sparkling e. GILB 337:8
tempts your wand'ring e. GRAY 350:22
Thine e. my pride SIDN 718:19
those e., the break of day SHAK 686:21
through another man's e. SHAK 659:22
to close his e. DRYD 280:19
turn'st mine e. SHAK 665:16
unto dying e. TENN 765:21
was it his bees-winged e. BETJ 70:4
why the good Lord made your e. LEHR 462:16
will lift mine e. SCOT 652:22
Will you put out mine e. SHAK 677:14
with fortune and men's e. SHAK 704:13
with his half-shut e. POPE 587:9
Within my e. LODG 472:17
with no e. SHAK 679:23
with thine e. JONS 420:20
You have lovely e. CHEK 208:12
you'll wear your e. out ZOLA 840:14
eyeservice Not with e. BIBL 108:11

faber *F. est suae* CLAU 219:18
Fabians civilization of the F. INGE 399:4
good man fallen among F. LENI 463:12
fabill nocht bot f. BARB 53:20
fable f., song, or fleeting shade HERR 374:7
f. will not do BYRO 177:29
life's sweet f. CRAS 244:14
fables blasphemous f. BOOK 142:11
f. in the legend BACO 42:6
Hesperian f. MILT 516:12
profane and old wives' f. BIBL 109:15
fabric f. of this vision SHAK 699:6
fabula *F. narratur* HORA 389:14
fac *Dilige et quod vis f.* AUGU 36:9
face Accustomed to her f. LERN 465:5
Am I in f. to-day GOLD 345:18
beautiful f. is a mute PUBL 616:10
born with a different f. BLAK 119:8
bright f. of danger STEV 740:22
Coming with vivid f. YEAT 835:18
construction in the f. SHAK 681:23
covered his f. BIBL 86:21
Cover her f. WEBS 808:2
darkness was upon the f. BIBL 73:10
disasters in his morning f. GOLD 344:13
divine plain f. LAMB 449:4
draw a full f. DRYD 283:15
English never smash in a f. HALS 358:11
f. in a glass BIBL 110:13
f. is my fortune NURS 551:20
f. looks like a weddding-cake AUDE 35:18
f. neither East nor West NKRU 546:11
f. of a Venus BARR 56:3
f. of 'evil' BURR 169:15
f. of the dead BEER 61:18
f. of the waters BIBL 73:10
f. of this congregation BOOK 130:22
f. so pleased my mind ANON 19:2
f. the index CRAB 243:10
fall flat on your f. THUR 776:24
False f. must hide SHAK 682:19
first I saw your f. ANON 18:19
garden in her f. CAMP 183:25
garden of your f. HERB 371:22
glorifies your f. BROW 158:15
God hath given you one f. SHAK 664:8
God's f. is above MIDR 507:17
had a lonely f. HARD 360:16
harsh, distorted f. BOWE 145:9
has the f. he deserves ORWE 559:15
have a singing f. FLET 318:10
hear my Thisby's f. SHAK 690:25
hides a smiling f. COWP 240:18
hide thy f. from me BOOK 132:4
hide us from the f. BIBL 112:6
hid the f. DRYD 281:12
his prism, and silent f. WORD 831:3
honest, sonsie f. BURN 168:20
I am the family f. HARD 361:15
in the public's f. RUSK 638:6
keep your f. CART 193:2
Look in my f. ROSS 635:5
Look in my f. TRAI 780:19
Look on her f. POPE 587:1
Lord make his f. shine BIBL 76:24
lying on his f., dead THAC 769:9
mask that eats into the f. UPDI 788:14
men stand f. to face KIPL 438:5
mist in my f. BROW 157:16
Moses hid his f. BIBL 75:27
never forget a f. MARX 499:12
never see my f. again TENN 760:16
night's starred f. KEAT 430:18
not recognize me by my f. TROL 781:17
Once the bright f. MIDD 507:6
original f. HUI- 394:3
painted her f. BIBL 80:24
Pity a human f. BLAK 120:15
plain before my f. BOOK 131:22
rabbit has a charming f. ANON 18:12
rogue's f. CONG 232:17
seek his f. MONS 526:11
seen God f. to face BIBL 75:7
shining morning f. SHAK 658:26
sing in the robber's f. JUVE 424:19
smile on the f. of the tiger ANON 18:10
socialism would not lose its human f. DUBČ 283:20
spirit passed before my f. BIBL 81:7

face (*cont.*):
spite your f. PROV 598:34
stamping on a human f. ORWE 559:2
then f. to face BIBL 106:16
touched the f. of God MAGE 489:9
unacceptable f. of capitalism HEAT 367:3
View but her f. FORD 320:4
Visit her f. too roughly SHAK 661:25
Was this the f. MARL 496:5
whole life shows in your f. BACA 41:4
your f. burns and tickles FROS 325:14
your f. in your hands ANON 17:5
Your f., my thane SHAK 682:5
faces Bid them wash their f. SHAK 660:4
breathe in the f. PEPY 573:11
f. are but a gallery BACO 43:1
f. in the crowd POUN 589:18
God knows the f. I shall see ROSS 635:2
grace-proud f. BURN 169:3
grind the f. of the poor BIBL 86:14
hid as it were our f. BIBL 88:16
Mild monastic f. CLOU 221:14
nice clean f. BARH 54:4
not having any f. PRIE 591:14
old familiar f. LAMB 448:20
Private f. in public places AUDE 34:15
red f., and loose hair EQUI 301:3
slope of f. COWP 242:3
wears almost everywhere two f. DRYD 283:9
facets iceberg cuts its f. BISH 115:16
facilis *F. descensus Averno* VIRG 794:17
fact F. is stranger PROV 600:4
fatal futility of f. JAME 403:13
foundation of f. BYRO 180:6
irritable reaching after f. KEAT 430:24
judges of f. PULT 617:1
ugly f. HUXL 397:11
faction Liberty is to f. MADI 489:2
made them a f. MACA 482:12
whisper of a f. RUSS 640:9
factions canvasses and f. BACO 42:18
Old religious f. BURK 165:9
factor Falklands F. THAT 770:2
facts accounted for *all* the f. WATS 804:16
built up of f. POIN 580:2
f. are on expenses STOP 743:15
f. are sacred SCOT 650:4
F. are stubborn things PROV 600:5
f. governed by laws WHEW 813:13
f. when you come to brass tacks ELIO 295:23
Get your f. first TWAI 786:30
give you all the f. AUDE 35:3
imagination for his f. SHER 716:20
inert f. ADAM 2:23
keep to f. GASK 330:22
number of empirical f. EINS 291:2
politics consists in ignoring f. ADAM 2:22
what I want is, F. DICK 262:23
faculties borne his f. so meek SHAK 682:10
exercise of his soul's f. ARIS 24:17
f. of men MADI 489:3
T'affections, and to f. DONN 273:26
faculty f. of the mind WOLL 826:1
faddling f. hedonist STEV 741:15
fade f. as a leaf BIBL 89:7
F. far away KEAT 429:9
f. into the light WORD 830:1
Than to f. away YOUN 839:17
They simply f. away FOLE 318:24
faded It f. on the crowing SHAK 661:11
fades f. awa' like morning dew BALL 52:8
Now f. the landscape GRAY 350:6
Whatever f. SIDN 718:20
fading f. timelessly MILT 513:15
in f. silks compose WINC 823:2
faenore *Solutus omni f.* HORA 387:11
faery f. lands forlorn KEAT 429:14
f.'s child KEAT 428:9
sing A f.'s song KEAT 428:11
fag f. drooping BLOK 122:5
fail F. better BECK 60:5
F. not our feast SHAK 684:1
I will not f. thee BIBL 77:16
no man's heart f. BIBL 78:30
shall not flag or f. CHUR 215:10
we'll not f. SHAK 682:17
words f. us AUST 39:17
failed f. in literature and art DISR 270:22
f. much STEV 741:1
saying a marriage 'f.' THOM 773:17
they f. before POLI 582:10
faileth when my strength f. me BOOK 136:16
failing from f. hands MCCR 484:13
fails One sure, if another f. BROW 157:29
failure Any f. seems so total QUAN 618:11
f. is an orphan PROV 611:32
f. of hope GIBB 336:3
f.'s no success at all DYLA 287:10
not the effort nor the f. tires EMPS 300:7
Now we are not a f. VANZ 789:20
political lives end in f. POWE 590:21
tragic f. ELIO 292:16
Women can't forgive f. CHEK 208:6
failures f. in love MURD 536:17
fain F. would I climb RALE 621:3
faint eating hay when you're f. CARR 191:9
f. heart ne'er wan A lady BURN 168:25
F. heart never won PROV 600:6
f. on hill TENN 765:18
F., yet pursuing BIBL 77:35
pray, and not to f. BIBL 100:14
reap, if we f. not BIBL 107:23
walk, and not f. BIBL 88:5
with f. praises WYCH 834:13
fainted f. Alternately AUST 37:22
should utterly have f. BOOK 133:12
fair All's f. in love and war PROV 594:25
anything to show more f. WORD 827:19
brave deserve the f. PROV 608:9
chaste and f. JONS 419:17
child is f. of face PROV 606:42
deserves the f. DRYD 280:17
dream of f. women TENN 758:15
F. and softly PROV 600:7
f. as an Italian sun BANV 53:10
f. as is the rose CHAU 206:27
f. as the moon BIBL 86:1
f. defect of nature MILT 517:23
f. exchange no robbery PROV 600:8
F. is foul SHAK 681:7
F. is too foul MARL 496:28
F. play's a jewel PROV 600:9
F. shares for all POLI 581:12
F. stood the wind DRAY 279:9
f. white linen cloth BOOK 129:3
Fat, f. and forty O'KE 553:8
Give and take f. play PROV 601:7
If Saint Paul's day be f. PROV 603:19
I have sworn thee f. SHAK 705:26
kind as she is f. SHAK 702:29
make so f. BERN 69:4
never won f. lady PROV 600:6
not f. to outward view COLE 224:17
not f. to the child FROS 326:11
Outward be f. CHUR 214:1
Sabrina f. MILT 512:1
see them all so excellently f. COLE 225:2
set f. BENN 66:4
she be f. KEAT 428:24
She f., divinely fair MILT 517:15
so f. that they called him AUBR 32:17
So foul and f. a day SHAK 681:14
sweet and f. she seems WALL 800:2
Thou art all f. BIBL 85:15
thou art f., my love BIBL 85:14
Trottin' to the f. GRAV 349:8
Turn about is f. play PROV 613:23
what's right and f. HUGH 393:14
With you f. maid SONG 729:1
woman true and f. DONN 274:12
fairer f. way is not much about BACO 41:19
fairest F. Isle DRYD 281:32
f. of creation MILT 517:18
f. things have fleetest end THOM 774:2
From f. creatures SHAK 704:5
fairies beginning of f. BARR 55:14
don't believe in f. BARR 55:15
Do you believe in f. BARR 55:17
f. at the bottom of our garden FYLE 327:16
f. left off dancing SELD 653:20
f.' midwife SHAK 697:5
F. Were of the old profession CORB 236:13
rewards and F. CORB 236:11
fairy believes it was a f. AUBR 33:1
By f. hands COLL 229:10
cradle of the f. queen SHAK 690:1
f. kind of writing DRYD 281:30
f. when she's forty HENL 369:18
Like f. gifts fading MOOR 530:9
myth not a f. story RYLE 640:18
near our f. queen SHAK 689:27
No f. takes SHAK 661:11
taste for f.-stories TOLK 779:5
'tis almost f. time SHAK 690:27
fairy-tale f. of olden times HEIN 368:5
fait *un seul f. accompli* BOIL 124:6
faith author and finisher of our f. BIBL 110:2
breastplate of f. BIBL 109:9
Catholic F. BOOK 126:21
children in whom is no f. BIBL 77:12
connected with serene f. MAHĀ 490:13
died in f. BIBL 109:30
Draw near with f. BOOK 129:15
dying for a f. THAC 768:19
f. and morals hold WORD 828:24
f. as a grain of mustard seed BIBL 96:6
f. hath made thee whole BIBL 94:27
f., hope, charity, these three BIBL 106:16
f. I am searching for SAND 643:17
f. in a nation of sectaries DISR 270:5
f. in the people DICK 266:4
F. is an excitement SAND 643:16
F. is defying BARN 55:9
f. is something you die for BENN 65:8
f. is the state TILL 777:14
F. is the substance BIBL 109:28
F. of our Fathers FABE 305:14
f. of the heart LUTH 480:3
f. of those in the pulpit AUST 39:16
f. shall be my shield ASKE 30:20
f. shall wax DANI 240:[illegible]
f. shines equal BRON 149:21
f.'s transcendent dower WORD 831:16
f. that looks through death WORD 830:9
f. unfaithful TENN 759:29
F. will move mountains PROV 600:10
f. without doubt UNAM 787:6
F. without works BIBL 110:17
fight with f. and win SIKH 719:12
first article of my f. GAND 329:6
fought for Queen and F. TENN 766:12
good fight of f. BIBL 109:19
have f. LUTH 479:12
if ye break f. MCCR 484:13
In this f. I wish to live VILL 793:2
in thy f. and fear BOOK 129:14
just shall live by f. BIBL 104:26
kept the f. BIBL 109:23
left to f. BYRO 176:21
Let us have f. LINC 468:7
man's soul and f. JAGG 401:8
more f. in honest doubt TENN 761:25
of the f. AMIS 13:15
O thou of little f. BIBL 95:27
scientific f.'s absurd BROW 155:26
Sea of F. ARNO 26:4
seat to f. assigned SMAR 722:11
shake a man's f. in himself SHAW 706:23
shield of f. BIBL 108:13
so great f. BIBL 94:17
sudden explosions of f. BREN 147:23
though I have all f. BIBL 106:16
unity of the f. BIBL 108:3
What more could fright my f. DRYD 281:18
What of the f. HARD 361:19

whoever is moved by f. HUME 394:9
work of f. BIBL 109:7
World, you have kept f. HARD 361:14
faithful company of all f. people BOOK 130:2
Ever f., ever sure MILT 512:25
f. and just to me SHAK 675:30
F. and True BIBL 113:2
F. are the wounds BIBL 83:29
f. female friend WHUR 816:11
f. in that which is least BIBL 100:9
f. to thee, Cynara DOWS 277:5
f. unto death BIBL 111:25
good and f. servant BIBL 97:8
mentally f. to himself PAIN 563:8
O come, all ye f. ANON 21:4
So f. in love SCOT 651:8
faithfully ask f. BOOK 128:19
faithfulness Great is thy f. CHIS 212:7
faithless Be not f. BIBL 103:4
f. and stubborn generation BOOK 137:4
F. as the winds SEDL 653:4
f. coldness of the times TENN 761:29
Human on my f. arm AUDE 34:8
faiths men's f. are wafer-cakes SHAK 671:4
fake Anything that consoles is f. MURD 536:20
falcon dapple-dawn-drawn F. HOPK 385:1
f., towering in her pride SHAK 683:23
Gentle as f. SKEL 721:11
falconer O! for a f.'s voice SHAK 697:17
Falklands F. Factor THAT 770:2
F. thing was a fight BORG 143:7
fall all such as f. BOOK 141:19
and half to f. POPE 585:20
Another thing to f. SHAK 686:5
before a f. BIBL 82:38
by dividing we f. DICK 266:23
dew shall weep thy f. HERB 373:17
did he f. JAME 403:26
F. and cease SHAK 680:12
f. by little and little BIBL 91:32
f. flat on your face THUR 776:24
f. in love today GERS 334:13
f. into it BIBL 84:24
f. into the hands BIBL 109:27
F. into the hands of God TENN 766:11
f. into the hands of the Lord BIBL 91:17
f. like rain AUDE 35:11
f. not out by the way BIBL 75:19
F. on us BIBL 112:6
f. out with those we love TENN 765:13
f. to rise BROW 155:4
f. without shaking MONT 526:13
fear no f. BUNY 161:12
further they have to f. FITZ 315:20
great was the f. BIBL 94:13
harder they f. PROV 596:20
hard rain's a gonna f. DYLA 287:6
His f. was destined JOHN 411:16
Humpty Dumpty had a great f. NURS 548:16
it had a dying f. SHAK 700:26
it is good to f. WHIT 815:13
less likely to f. GAY 332:3
Life is a horizontal f. COCT 223:17
never f. BOOK 132:8
O! what a f. was there SHAK 676:8
Pride goes before a f. PROV 609:42
raise up them that f. BOOK 127:10
rise by other's f. SOUT 731:11
Then f., Caesar SHAK 675:16
Things f. apart YEAT 837:5
thousand shall f. BOOK 137:22
to human nature by the f. DENN 258:2
Weak men must f. SHAK 695:5
We all f. down NURS 550:13
we should happen to f. LEAR 460:13
worship and f. down BOOK 138:6
yet I fear to f. RALE 621:3
fallacy Pathetic F. RUSK 638:10
fallen Babylon is f. BIBL 112:24
Christopher Robin has f. MORT 533:14
F. by mistaken rules WINC 822:23
f. by the edge of the sword BIBL 92:3
F. cold and dead WHIT 815:5
f. from grace BIBL 107:20
f. from heaven BIBL 87:7
f. into the midst of it BOOK 135:16
good man f. among Fabians LENI 463:12
how are the mighty f. BIBL 79:1
lay great and greatly f. HOME 382:7
lot is f. unto me BOOK 132:9
people who have never f. PAST 569:4
say a man is f. in love STER 739:9
Though f. thyself WORD 832:12
throned Cytherean be f. SWIN 751:6
fallere *Quis f. possit amantem* VIRG 794:11
falleth where the tree f. BIBL 84:28
falling amidst a f. world ADDI 4:23
apple f. towards England AUDE 34:14
catch a f. star DONN 274:11
'f. domino' principle EISE 291:9
f. from stair to stair BAYL 58:1
f. sickness SHAK 674:20
load a f. man SHAK 673:25
my feet from f. BOOK 140:2
fallings F. from us, vanishings WORD 830:6
fallow like a rude f. lies IRWI 400:5
falls f. far from tree PROV 595:14
F. the Shadow ELIO 294:25
F. with the leaf FLET 318:2
sudden f. PROV 602:3
false all was f. and hollow MILT 515:9
bear f. witness BIBL 76:13
Beware of f. prophets BIBL 94:9
denials of f. stories CHAR 204:1
f. creation SHAK 682:21
F. face must hide SHAK 682:19
f., fleeting, perjured SHAK 696:18
false gift BIBL 83:19
f. report, if believed MEDI 503:8
f. sincere POPE 584:2
f. to any man SHAK 662:13
f. to others BACO 44:22
Followed f. lights DRYD 281:20
If she be f. SHAK 692:27
in f. grief hiding SPEN 733:19
in perils among f. brethren BIBL 107:14
Man, f. man LEE 462:6
one f. step AUST 38:22
perish with our f. theories POPP 587:30
philosopher, as equally f. GIBB 335:4
Ring out the f. TENN 761:28
unweaving of f. impressions ELIO 293:12
women never so f. LYLY 480:13
wouldst not play f. SHAK 682:1
falsehood cuts f. like a knife GURN 355:3
express lying or f. SWIF 748:1
F. has a perennial spring BURK 162:19
Let her and F. grapple MILT 519:19
neither Truth nor F. HOBB 378:13
strife of Truth with F. LOWE 477:15
To unmask f. SHAK 704:2
falsehoods f. which interest dictates JOHN 409:17
led to f. TALM 754:2
falsely do f. boast BOOK 142:14
prophets prophesy f. BIBL 89:13
falseness pleasure in proving their f. DARW 250:15
produce in us a f. RUSK 638:10
falser f. than vows made in wine SHAK 659:16
falsifiability *f.* of a system POPP 587:24
Falstaff F. shall die SHAK 670:24
F. sweats to death SHAK 667:34
sweet Jack F. SHAK 668:16
falters love that never f. SPRI 735:6
Famagusta F. and the hidden sun FLEC 317:5
fame best f. is a writer's fame LEBO 461:10
blush to find it f. POPE 586:20
call the Temple of F. LICH 467:17
came here for f. DISR 271:9
Common f. is seldom PROV 597:30
damned to everlasting f. POPE 586:3
damned to F. POPE 580:14
defending himself against f. GARC 329:13
establishment of my f. GIBB 336:1
F. and tranquillity MONT 527:16
F. is a food DOBS 271:15
F. is like a river BACO 43:26
F. is no plant MILT 513:4
F. is the spur MILT 513:2
food is love and f. SHEL 711:10
for his f. BARN 55:8
gate to good f. BACO 42:25
gives immortal f. YOUN 838:20
her f. survives MILT 518:23
love and f. KEAT 430:19
Love of f. is the last thing TACI 752:16
Man dreams of f. TENN 760:5
mistook it for f. GOLD 345:4
no one shall work for f. KIPL 440:19
nor yet a fool to f. POPE 583:3
Oh my f. Live CHAP 202:15
Physicians of the Utmost F. BELL 63:6
purchase f. In keen iambics DRYD 282:1
servants of f. BACO 43:8
to f. unknown GRAY 350:14
to get f. GELD 332:27
What is f. GRAI 348:11
you shall live by f. SPEN 733:4
famed France, f. in all great arts ARNO 28:1
fames *Aura sacra f.* VIRG 794:8
Metus et malesuada F. VIRG 794:20
familiar f. friend BOOK 134:4
mine own f. friend BOOK 135:11
old f. faces LAMB 448:20
familiarity F. breeds contempt PROV 600:11
F. breeds contempt TWAI 786:18
families antediluvian f. CONG 232:22
best-regulated f. DICK 262:2
best-regulated f. PROV 594:13
f. fatal to the Commonwealth DRUM 279:16
f. in a country village AUST 39:9
f. last not three oaks BROW 153:6
f. shopping at night GINS 339:22
Great f. of yesterday DEFO 255:14
happy f. resemble TOLS 779:6
mothers of large f. BELL 63:4
rooks in f. homeward go HARD 361:23
there are f. THAT 770:7
to run in f. LEWE 466:14
worst f. are those BAGE 47:8
family brought up a large f. GOLD 345:25
character of a f. STER 738:19
disease in the f. TREV 781:11
dominion [of the f.] HOBB 379:2
f. firm GEOR 334:9
f.—that dear octopus SMIT 723:17
f. that prays together SAYI 647:14
F.! . . . the home of all STRI 744:19
f., with its narrow privacy LEAC 459:13
f. with the wrong members ORWE 558:16
have a young f. FOWL 322:2
I am the f. face HARD 361:15
man that left his f. TWAI 786:3
running of a f. MONT 527:13
Selling off the f. silver MISQ 522:7
spend more time with f. THAT 770:10
We, your blood f. SPEN 732:14
famine f. in his face CHUR 214:7
f. in the land LAWL 454:14
F. Queen GONN 346:9
F. sighs like scythe WALC 799:2
feed her f. fat BYRO 177:14
God of f. VYAZ 798:17
They that die by f. HENR 370:16
famous by that time I was too f. BENC 64:21
f. by my sword MONT 529:3
f. by their birth SHAK 694:19
f. calm and dead BROW 155:31
f. for fifteen minutes WARH 803:12
f. men have the whole earth PERI 573:20
f. without ability SHAW 706:26
found myself f. BYRO 180:11

famous (*cont.*):
praise f. men BIBL 92:13
'twas a f. victory SOUT 730:13
When you're first f. LOVE 476:8
fan f. spread and streamers out CONG 233:7
F.-vaulting . . . from an aesthetic LANC 449:17
fanatic f. is a great leader BROU 151:18
fanaticism f. consists in SANT 644:8
F. is indefensible FINK 313:4
fanatics F. have their dreams KEAT 427:17
fancies drop your silly f. CATU 197:4
F. that broke BROW 157:19
heart of furious f. ANON 19:17
many f. reign GREE 352:3
fancy F. a thousand wondrous BEAT 58:4
f. is the sails KEAT 430:20
form does to my f. bring WALL 800:9
keep your f. free HOUS 390:18
let the f. roam KEAT 427:20
maiden meditation, f.-free SHAK 689:23
most excellent f. SHAK 666:23
Now my sere f. BYRO 177:3
where is f. bred SHAK 688:2
whispers of f. JOHN 410:23
young man's f. TENN 762:22
fans f. into their hand BALL 51:16
fantasies fed the heart on f. YEAT 836:18
fantastic f. summer's heat SHAK 694:16
light f. round MILT 511:18
light f. toe MILT 512:15
fantastical joys are but f. DONN 273:23
fantasy f., like poetry, speaks LE G 462:15
live in a f. world MURD 536:21
Most modern f. PRAT 591:3
much too strong for f. DONN 273:22
Of f., of dreams SHAK 675:4
far f. above the great GRAY 351:4
F. and few LEAR 460:9
F. be that fate from us OVID 561:3
f., far better thing DICK 266:3
F.-fetched and dear-bought PROV 600:12
F. from the madding BORR 144:5
F. from the madding crowd's GRAY 350:13
f. side of despair SART 645:10
f. to go PROV 606:42
going a bridge too f. BROW 154:24
good news from a f. country BIBL 83:22
hills and f. away GAY 331:16
How f. is KIPL 440:6
how f. one can go too far COCT 223:19
keep f. from me OVID 561:4
Mexico, so f. from God DIAZ 260:9
much too f. out all my life SMIT 724:21
Oh keep f. off VIRG 794:18
Over the hills and f. away NURS 551:15
quarrel in a f. away country CHAM 200:17
so near and yet so f. TENN 761:27
To go too f. CONF 231:21
unhappy, f.-off things WORD 832:3
Faraday anti-F. machines CORN 236:18
farce f. is played out LAST 455:20
second as f. MARX 500:1
second time as f. BARN 55:3
fardels Who would f. bear SHAK 664:4
fare I've got my f. GORD 347:1
value not your bill of f. SWIF 748:6
farewell Ae f., and then for ever BURN 166:9
bid the company f. LAST 456:5
F.! a long farewell SHAK 673:12
f. content SHAK 692:30
f. goes out sighing SHAK 700:16
F., great painter EPIT 302:6
f., he is gon CHAU 205:11
f. king SHAK 695:11
F., Leicester Square JUDG 423:1
F., Love WYAT 834:1
F. my bok CHAU 206:24
F., my friends LAST 455:1
F. night BUNY 161:17
F., rewards CORB 236:11
f. to the shade COWP 241:1
forever, f., Cassius SHAK 676:30
hail, and f. CATU 198:1
no sadness of f. TENN 758:13
So f. then CATC 196:21
Too-late, F. ROSS 635:5
farm down on the f. LEWI 467:4
f. is like a man CATO 194:14
farmer after the f.'s wife NURS 551:10
F. will never be happy again HERB 371:12
Here's a f. SHAK 683:13
farmers embattled f. stood EMER 299:7
f. excessively fortunate VIRG 796:17
Our f. round CRAB 243:5
farms cellos of the deep f. STEV 740:18
for him that f. CRAB 243:13
lass wi' the weel-stockit f. BURN 167:10
What spires, what f. HOUS 391:5
farmyard crow in its own f. TROL 782:16
human society from the f. SHAW 707:9
farrago *discursus nostri f. libelli* JUVE 424:6
farrow old sow that eats her f. JOYC 422:3
fart can't f. and chew gum JOHN 408:20
forgot the f. ELIZ 297:12
Love is the f. SUCK 745:9
farther *f. you go from the church* WOTT 833:8
only much f. away FLEM 317:19
farthest F. Thule VIRG 796:14
farthing f. candle to the sun YOUN 839:1
for a f. less ADDI 4:17
paid the uttermost f. BIBL 93:10
Virtue knows to a f. WALP 802:2
worth one f. CATU 197:2
farthings sold for two f. BIBL 99:20
fascinates I like work: it f. me JERO 407:1
fascination f. frantic GILB 338:16
f. of what's difficult YEAT 836:2
subject myself to his f. GLAS 341:17
Fascism victims of American F. ROSE 633:21
Fascist Every woman adores a F. PLAT 577:14
fashion f. a gentleman SPEN 733:11
f. in these things FRAN 323:19
F. is more usually OLDF 553:12
F. is something barbarous SANT 644:11
f. of these times SHAK 658:17
f. of this world BIBL 106:6
F., though Folly's child CRAB [illegible]
first style of f. AUST 39:2
glass of f. SHAK 664:10
in my f. DOWS 277:5
in my f. PORT 588:1
little out of f. SHAK 671:14
never cared for f. BAIL 48:4
nothing else holds f. SHAK 700:23
out of the f. PROV 596:7
tell you the leading f. RUSK 638:4
fashioned day by day were f. BOOK 141:13
F. so slenderly HOOD 382:13
fashions fit this year's f. HELL 368:16
fast as f. as the world record COLE 224:15
at least twice as f. CARR 190:15
come he f. SCOT 651:6
coming as f. as I can LAUD 454:4
f. that I have chosen BIBL 89:1
grew f. and furious BURN 168:16
none so f. as stroke MISQ 521:2
Snip! They go so f. HOFF 380:4
talks it so very f. FARQ 307:12
wherefore should I f. BIBL 79:7
will not f. in peace CRAB 243:3
fasten F. your seat-belts FILM 311:6
fastenings f. of this fear ORCH 557:7
faster F. than a speeding bullet ANON 16:7
good deal f. CARR 189:14
Men travel f. now CATH 194:7
fastest travels f. PROV 602:23
travels the f. KIPL 439:10
fastidious never f. SOUT 731:3
fasting die f. FRAN 323:12
fou man and a f. SCOT 652:3
full man and a f. PROV 604:34
thank heaven, f. SHAK 659:15
fat addicted to f. BAKE 48:15
Butter merely makes us f. GOER 342:11
could eat no f. NURS 548:23
f. and fulsome PROV 605:48
f. and grows old SHAK 668:3
f. and long-haired PLUT 579:7
f. bulls of Basan BOOK 132:23
F., fair and forty O'KE 553:8
f. friend BRUM 158:21
f. greedy owl RICH 626:15
F. is a feminist issue ORBA 557:5
f. lady sings SAYI 647:35
f. of others' works BURT 170:3
f. of the land BIBL 75:18
f. white woman CORN 237:2
feast of f. things BIBL 87:10
grow f. and look young DRYD 282:2
in every f. man CONN 234:1
Life, if you're f., is a minefield MARG 495:8
likeness of a f. old man SHAK 668:13
men about me that are f. SHAK 674:16
more f. than bard beseems THOM 774:22
no sex if you're f. GIOV 340:1
outside every f. man AMIS 13:14
round, f., oily man THOM 774:23
seven f. kine BIBL 75:13
should himself be f. JOHN 417:13
that f. gentleman SHAW 709:28
thin man inside every f. man ORWE 558:9
fatal deal of it is absolutely f. WILD 818:5
f. bellman SHAK 683:4
f. futility of fact JAME 403:13
f. gift of beauty BYRO 174:26
f. man, Madame Fribsbi THAC 768:23
f. to the Commonwealth DRUM 279:16
f. to true happiness RUSS 639:15
most f. complaint of all HILT 377:12
Our f. shadows FLET 318:5
So sweet was ne'er so f. SHAK 693:23
fate arbiter of others' f. BYRO 178:19
Art a revolt against f. MALR 493:2
character is his f. HERA 371:9
conquered f. ARNO 26:25
dead by f. BEAU 58:14
decide the f. of the world DE G 255:22
every day that F. allows HORA 387:20
Far be that f. from us OVID 561:3
F. and character NOVA 547:3
F. cannot harm me SMIT 725:22
f. Clasped in my fist FORD 320:5
f. has consummation MAND 493:15
f. is like the chronicle YEVT 838:11
F. is not an eagle BOWE 145:13
F. never wounds more deep JOHN 411:10
f. of a nation LONG 474:17
f. of this country DISR 269:13
F.'s great bazaar MACN 468:15
F. so enviously debars MARV 498:11
F. tried to conceal him HOLM 381:7
f. wilfully misunderstand me FROS 325:15
F. wrote her a tragedy BEER 61:17
fears his f. too much MONT 529:2
forget my f. TATE 755:7
heart for any f. LONG 474:7
limits of a vulgar f. GRAY 351:4
makers of our f. POPP 587:25
master of his f. TENN 760:1
master of my f. HENL 369:21
no f. that cannot be CAMU 184:9
over-ruled by f. MARL 496:12
read the book of f. SHAK 670:3
sealed his f. JAGG 401:8
severity of f. FORD 319:18
smile of f. DYER 286:16
suspend their f. DEFO 255:4
take a bond of f. SHAK 685:1
tempted F. MCGO 485:11
thy f. shall overtake KING 436:7
torrent of his f. JOHN 411:19
wayward the decrees of F. THAC 769:17
when F. calls him SOCR 727:5

when f. summons DRYD 281:35
would F. but mend it PRIO 593:4
fated f. not to die DRYD 281:16
fates hidden f. SUCK 745:11
masters of their f. SHAK 674:13
father about my F.'s business BIBL 98:27
ance his f.'s pride BURN 166:25
carry one's f.'s corpse APOL 23:2
child is f. of the man PROV 597:15
cometh unto the f. BIBL 102:18
come to my f. AUBR 32:21
cry, Abba, F. BIBL 105:7
cut off thy f.'s head CHAR 203:2
difficult to be a f. BUSC 170:24
Diogenes struck the f. BURT 170:21
Eternal F., strong to save WHIT 815:1
f. had a daughter SHAK 701:23
f. had an accident there POTT 588:20
F., hear the prayer WILL 821:6
F. is rather vulgar DICK 263:1
F.-like, he tends LYTE 481:2
f. loves the son TALM 754:16
f. married the ae warst BALL 50:21
f. of English criticism JOHN 410:2
F. of lights BIBL 110:12
f. of many nations BIBL 104:34
F. of our Lord BIBL 107:27
f. of the Man WORD 829:10
f.'s fortunes CORB 236:14
f.'s shame BRET 148:4
F. Time and Mother Earth MERR 505:27
f. was frightened of his mother GEOR 334:6
F. which is in heaven BIBL 93:16
from the way of his f. CONF 231:4
glad f. BIBL 82:20
Glory be to the F. BOOK 125:19
God the F. Almighty BOOK 129:8
Had it been his f. EPIT 303:1
happier than your f. SOPH 728:11
Hath the rain a f. BIBL 81:33
have God for his f. CYPR 248:10
He took my f. grossly SHAK 665:9
Honour thy f. and thy mother BIBL 76:13
I am thy f.'s spirit SHAK 662:23
I go to the F. BIBL 102:26
I meet my F., my age LOWE 478:1
In my F.'s house BIBL 102:17
knows its own f. PROV 604:6
last see your f. YEAM 835:1
like as a f. pitieth BOOK 138:19
Like f., like son PROV 605:30
limp f. of thousands JOYC 422:13
Lloyd George knew my f. ANON 17:11
Lord and F. of mankind WHIT 816:5
Muhammad is not the f. KORA 445:3
My f. feeds his flocks HOME 381:17
My f. is gone wild SHAK 670:20
my f. or my mother STER 738:13
My f. wept BLAK 121:3
no careful f. would wish ANON 16:9
no good f. SART 645:7
no longer have a f. NERV 541:6
no more like my f. SHAK 661:27
O, f. forsaken JOYC 422:18
old f. antick, the law SHAK 667:18
only begotten of the f. BIBL 101:7
Our F. BIBL 93:19
picture of his f.'s face FLET 318:16
politique f. JAME 402:15
resembled My f. as he slept SHAK 683:6
sash my f. wore POLI 581:29
shall a man leave his f. BIBL 73:23
than you are as a f. ICE 398:14
that of his f. TALM 754:9
thicker than my f.'s loins BIBL 79:21
turnip than his f. JOHN 418:8
when my f. died SHAK 666:8
will say unto him, F. BIBL 100:4
wise f. that knows SHAK 687:18
wish was f., Harry SHAK 670:16
without f. bred MILT 512:3
worshipful f. CAXT 198:16
You are old, F. William CARR 189:12
fathered so f. and so husbanded SHAK 675:8
fatherhood mirrors and f. are abominable BORG 143:6
fatherland unity of our f. KOHL 443:6
fatherless defendeth the f. BOOK 141:23
f. children, and widows BOOK 127:12
Father of the f. BOOK 136:6
visit the f. and widows BIBL 110:16
fatherly commend to thy f. goodness BOOK 127:18
fathers because our f. lied KIPL 438:8
Faith of our F. FABE 305:14
f., provoke not BIBL 108:10
four Our F. DOYL 278:12
God of our f. SIDD 717:18
He f.-forth whose beauty HOPK 384:15
I am going to my F. BUNY 161:18
Instead of thy f. BOOK 134:17
land of my f. JAME 402:21
Lord God of your f. BIBL 75:30
My f. can have it THOM 772:20
not the sins of the f. FREN 324:5
our f. have told us BOOK 134:12
our f. have told us BOOK 137:3
revolts against its f. MUMF 536:6
sins of the f. BOOK 129:5
slept with his f. BIBL 79:24
sojourners, as were all our f. BIBL 80:29
Success has many f. PROV 611:32
Victory has a hundred f. CIAN 217:3
years ago our f. brought forth LINC 468:13
your f. tempted me BOOK 138:6
Father William You are old, F. SOUT 730:21
fathom f.-line could never touch SHAK 667:26
f. the inscrutable workings SMIT 724:4
Full f. five SHAK 698:27
many a f. deep CAMP 183:4
thou canst not f. it TENN 765:11
fathoms fifty f. deep BALL 51:17
fatigue greatest f. in the world VANB 789:8
fatling lion and the f. BIBL 87:4
fatness thy clouds drop f. BOOK 136:2
fatted f. calf BIBL 100:5
fattening illegal, immoral, or f. WOOL 827:8
fatter Would he were f. SHAK 674:17
fatty f. degeneration STEV 741:26
faucibus *in f. Orci* VIRG 794:20
Faulconbridge rather be a F. SHAK 677:5
fault all f. who hath no fault TENN 759:26
artist is his own f. O'HA 553:4
clever to a f. BROW 155:10
Condemn the f. SHAK 686:7
f. confessed PROV 600:13
f., dear Brutus SHAK 674:13
glorious f. of angels POPE 582:19
hide the f. I see POPE 587:13
it was a grievous f. SHAK 675:28
Just hint a f. POPE 583:7
most grievous f. MISS 520:11
Nature's f. alone CHUR 214:11
no kind of f. or flaw GILB 337:12
O happy f. MISS 523:8
soul is without f. RIMB 628:12
sting to thee is a little f. DANT 249:19
think it is their f. BROO 150:19
faultless Faultily f. TENN 763:21
f. piece to see POPE 584:17
F. to a fault BROW 157:25
faults acknowledge my f. BOOK 135:4
acknowledge our f. BURN 165:23
all his f. observed SHAK 676:25
all, their f. confessing BUCK 159:17
buffeted for your f. BIBL 110:31
Drown all my f. FLET 318:14
England, with all thy f. COWP 241:21
f. a little blind PRIO 592:11
f. of his feet BECK 59:22
f. of statesmen WALP 801:16
fill you with the f. they had LARK 453:4
his f. lie gently SHAK 673:20
Jesus! with all thy f. BUTL 172:30
moulded out of f. SHAK 686:26
rise to f. POPE 584:14
vile ill-favoured f. SHAK 688:35
what f. they commit QUAR 618:21
With all her f. CHUR 213:14
faune *après-midi d'un f.* MALL 492:3
favilla *Solvet saeclum in f.* MISS 523:3
favour bend to f. ev'ry client GAY 332:11
Fools out of f. DEFO 255:7
in f. of the people BURK 164:12
truths being in and out of f. FROS 325:16
favourable O be f. and gracious BOOK 135:9
favoured Hail, thou that art highly f. BIBL 98:15
favourite f. has no friend GRAY 350:21
second f. organ ALLE 12:12
favourites monarchs to choose f. SWIF 747:24
favours depends Upon your f. SHAK 660:3
felt all its f. COCK 223:12
hope for greater f. LA R 453:19
in the middle of her f. SHAK 663:15
recommendation to f. FIEL 310:5
sense of future f. WALP 802:7
fawning f. publican SHAK 687:12
fawns fallow f. invisible THOM 773:4
fay *F. ce que vouldras* RABE 619:11
fear begins in f. COLE 227:24
by beauty and by f. WORD 830:23
by means of pity and f. ARIS 24:21
cannot taint with f. SHAK 685:15
concessions of f. BURK 162:22
Do right and f. no man PROV 598:42
drives away his f. NEWT 543:15
English . . . are paralysed by f. LAWR 457:23
eventide of f. MORR 532:10
F. and Hunger VIRG 794:20
f. and trembling BIBL 108:18
f. casteth out love CONN 234:3
F. God BIBL 85:5
F. God BIBL 110:30
F. God BORR 143:13
F. God. Honour the King KITC 441:31
f. in a handful of dust ELIO 295:28
F. is the foundation ADAM 3:15
F. is the main source RUSS 640:4
f. made manifest EDDY 288:5
f. my name BIBL 90:25
f. no evil BOOK 133:1
f. no fall BUNY 161:12
F. no more the heat SHAK 661:1
f. of the Law JOYC 421:20
f. of the Lord BIBL 87:3
f. of the Lord BOOK 139:18
f. still followed him SPEN 733:20
f. thee, ancient Mariner COLE 226:16
f. those big words JOYC 422:9
f., To be we know not what DRYD 281:2
f. to negotiate KENN 433:12
Fly hence, our contact f. ARNO 27:10
For f. he arms ROCH 630:15
For f. of finding something worse BELL 63:7
fourth is freedom from f. ROOS 632:18
From hope and f. set free SWIN 750:22
grief felt so like f. LEWI 466:17
hate that which we often f. SHAK 656:15
in thy faith and f. BOOK 129:14
keepet by thy f. BURN 167:13
let him be your f. BIBL 86:27
Life is first boredom, then f. LARK 452:15
Men f. death BACO 42:22
never had a f. COWP 242:15
no hope without f. SPIN 734:26
not wholly banish f. AESC 6:10
No tyrant need f. till ARIS 25:7
one f., Death's shadow BLUN 122:10
only thing we have to f. ROOS 632:12
Our deepest f. is not WILL 821:4
out of f. DONN 274:3
pearls, is the f. of God ORCH 557:7

fear (*cont.*):
Possess them not with f. SHAK 671:21
robs the mind as f. BURK 163:10
Severity breedeth f. BACO 43:11
so long as they f. ACCI 1:8
spirit of f. BIBL 109:20
There is no f. in love BIBL 111:14
those who f. life RUSS 639:18
too much joy or too much f. GRAV 349:12
travel in the direction of our f. BERR 69:18
trembled with f. ENGL 300:13
try to have no f. CHES 208:23
'Twas only f. JONS 420:2
whom then shall I f. BOOK 133:10
without f. the lawless roads MUIR 535:22
feared neither f. nor flattered DOUG 276:13
prince to be f. MACH 485:16
fearful f. symmetry BLAK 121:8
f. thing BIBL 109:27
f. trip is done WHIT 815:4
fearfully f. and wonderfully made BOOK 141:12
fearless F., blameless knight ANON 20:4
fears anxious f. subside WILL 820:9
f. dishonour more than death HORA 389:10
f. do make us traitors SHAK 685:3
f. his fate too much MONT 529:2
f. his fellowship SHAK 671:23
f. it heeded not SHEL 714:6
f. may be liars CLOU 223:3
F. of the brave JOHN 411:18
f. that I may cease to be KEAT 430:17
f. to speak of Ninety-Eight INGR 399:18
forgot the taste of f. SHAK 685:21
from sudden f. BYRO 178:23
griefs and f. BACO 43:24
hopes and f. BROO 151:9
man who f. the Lord BIBL 113:21
Not mine own f. SHAK 705:11
Present f. SHAK 681:21
saucy doubts and f. SHAK 684:9
tie up thy f. HERB 372:7
tormenting f. ROCH 630:11
feast bare imagination of a f. SHAK 694:16
Chief nourisher in life's f. SHAK [illegible]
company makes the f. PROV 597:31
comparèd to a f. BARN 55:10
Enough as good as a f. PROV 599:18
f. at ease DUCK 284:4
f. of fat things BIBL 87:10
f. of languages SHAK 680:29
going to a f. JONS 419:19
Paris is a movable f. HEMI 369:11
upon our solemn f.-day BOOK 137:9
When I make a f. HARI 362:8
feasting dinner and f. PEPY 573:9
feasts nights and f. divine HORA 390:1
feather Birds of a f. PROV 596:24
f.-footed through the plashy fen WAUG 806:11
f. for each wind SHAK 703:5
f. in his cap SONG 730:9
f. to tickle LAMB 448:17
go to heaven in f.-beds MORE 531:7
my each f. HUGH 393:4
wit's a f. POPE 586:1
feathered f. glory YEAT 836:14
f. race FRER 324:10
feathers f. like gold BOOK 136:7
Fine f. PROV 600:22
feats What f. he did that day SHAK 671:24
feature every f. works AUST 37:15
features incisive f. MERE 505:11
February F. fill dyke PROV 600:15
F. there be no rain PROV 603:17
not Puritanism but F. KRUT 446:3
fed both have f. as well SHAK 674:10
clothed, f., and educated RUSK 638:25
f. of the dainties SHAK 680:24
f. the chicken every day RUSS 639:23
you have f. full VIRG 796:13
federal Our F. Union JACK 400:13
federation F. of the world TENN 763:3
fee For a small f. in America SOND 727:20
gorgeous East in f. WORD 830:14
feeble confirm the f. knees BIBL 87:22
f. can seldom persuade GIBB 335:14
help the f. up SHAK 699:13
man of such a f. temper SHAK 674:12
Most forcible F. SHAK 670:6
o'ercomes the f. brain WINC 823:1
feebleness all else is f. VIGN 792:16
feebly His words came f. WORD 831:13
feed doth this our Caesar f. SHAK 674:14
F. a cold PROV 600:16
f. his flock BIBL 88:2
f. me in a green pasture BOOK 132:26
F. my lambs BIBL 103:8
F. my sheep BIBL 103:9
f. on Death SHAK 705:25
F. the brute PUNC 617:19
f. with the rich JOHN 414:1
will you still f. me LENN 464:3
feeding Love is mutually f. HEAD 366:1
feel be, f., live HERD 373:21
Englishman can't f. FORS 320:10
f. it happen CATU 197:19
f. that he is dying CALI 181:7
f. that you could HOPK 385:8
f. the heart-break GIBS 336:15
f. what wretches feel SHAK 679:1
I f. you all feel RIDD 627:13
learn not to f. it ALCO 10:9
more to do than f. LAMB 448:22
see and hear and f. JOYC 422:15
to *One does f.* KNOX 442:12
tragedy to those that f. WALP 801:5
would make us f. CHUR 214:10
feeling Certainty. F. PASC 569:1
depth of f. BYRO 177:31
f. is bad form FORS 320:10
f. of Sunday is the same RHYS 625:20
f. which I feel RIDD 627:13
formal f. comes DICK 266:5
generous and honest f. BURK 164:18
lost pulse of f. ARNO 26:3
mess of imprecision of f. ELIO 294:11
more true f. JOWE 421:13
Music is f., then STEV 740:1
objectification of f. LANG 450:14
other person is f. BURR 169:16
sensible To f. SHAK 682:21
without f. gay CHUR 214:3
feelings follow their f. MENG 504:23
governed more by their f. ADAM 3:20
He nursed the f. CRAB 242:25
overflow of powerful f. WORD 832:20
very f. which ought AUST 38:9
Without them [f.] CHUA 212:18
woman to define her f. HARD 360:10
feeling-toned *f. complexes* JUNG 423:5
feels Everyone f. it TROL 781:19
happiness he f. LACL 447:6
man is as old as he f. PROV 606:14
fees answered, as they took their F. BELL 63:6
but of his f. HERR 374:11
smirks accompanied by a few f. HUNT 396:2
feet aching hands and bleeding f. ARNO 26:18
at a young man's f. BIBL 103:21
At her f. he bowed BIBL 77:29
bathe those beauteous f. FLET 318:13
beautiful are thy f. BIBL 86:3
before your f. I lay WALL 800:9
better to die on your f. IBAR 398:3
cutting off our f. SWIF 748:27
dust of your f. BIBL 94:33
faults of his f. BECK 59:22
f. are always in the water AMES 13:8
f. beneath her petticoat SUCK 745:8
f. go down to death BIBL 82:12
f. have they, and walk not BOOK 139:23
f. in ancient time BLAK 120:1
f. of him that bringeth BIBL 88:12
f. shall stand BOOK 140:14
f. was I to the lame BIBL 81:26
fell at his f. as dead BIBL 111:22
fog comes on little cat f. SAND 643:20
from his f. the Servants RIG 627:18
guide our f. BIBL 98:18
hands are a sort of f. TRAH 780:16
Its f. were tied KEAT 427:31
lantern unto my f. BOOK 140:9
Lord, dost thou wash my f. BIBL 102:14
marching, charging f. JAGG 401:7
moon under her f. BIBL 112:18
more care of their f. CAVE 198:14
my f. from falling BOOK 140:2
nations under our f. BOOK 134:22
palms before my f. CHES 210:5
pierced my hands and my f. BOOK 132:25
Scots lords at his f. BALL 51:17
set my f. upon the rock BOOK 133:31
set my printless f. MILT 512:2
seven f. of English ground HARO 362:11
shoes from off thy f. BIBL 75:26
skull, and the f. BIBL 80:27
slipping underneath our f. FITZ 314:14
stablish their f. BIBL 91:2
stranger's f. may find HOUS 390:10
Til crowes f. be growe CHAU 207:5
Time's iron f. MONT 528:16
two white f. PROV 609:8
under our f. BOOK 127:10
what dread f. BLAK 121:9
Whose f. they hurt BOOK 139:8
with reluctant f. LONG 473:22
would not wet her f. PROV 597:8
feign it will not f. DE P 258:4
feigned by f. deaths to die DONN 274:13
felices *F. ter et amplius* HORA 387:23
felicities f. of Solomon BACO 42:4
felicity Absent thee from f. SHAK 667:10
behold f. BROW 153:25
careful f. PETR 574:17
Our own f. we make JOHN 411:12
shadow of f. WALL 800:10
What more f. SPEN 734:16
felix *F. qui potuit rerum* VIRG 796:18
killed the Bishop and K YONG 838:14
O f. culpa MISS 523:8
fell f. among thieves BIBL 99:11
f. at his feet as dead BIBL 111:22
f. before the throne BIBL 112:8
From morn to noon he f. MILT 515:5
help me when I f. TAYL 756:12
It f. by itself JOHN 408:6
So I f. in love GILB 339:11
touch the rosebud, and it f. PHIL 575:11
feller Sweetes' li'l' f. STAN 736:11
fellow loves his f.-men HUNT 395:12
property of thy f. TALM 753:15
testy, pleasant f. ADDI 5:1
fellow-feeling f. makes one wond'rous kind GARR 330:5
fellows f. of infinite tongue SHAK 672:5
f. we put on the spot COLL 229:6
f. whom it hurts HOUS 391:9
shoes that were not f. DEFO 254:19
fellowship F. is heaven MORR 532:16
one communion and f. BOOK 128:22
right hands of f. BIBL 107:18
felt darkness which may be f. BIBL 75:37
has f. about it MUNC 536:13
female British f. CLOU 221:12
cast on f. wits BRAD 146:14
characterizes the f. mind WOLL 825:24
faithful f. friend WHUR 816:11
f. atheist JOHN 411:9
f. errors fall POPE 587:1
f. eunuch GREE 352:6
F. Eunuch GREE 352:9
f. heart can gold despise GRAY 350:20
f. mind IRWI 400:5
f. of the species KIPL 438:15

f. of the species PROV 600:17
f. overcomes the male LAO 452:4
f. pen ALCO 10:8
f. worker slave of that slave CONN 234:5
in the f. sex ADAM 2:2
involved with the f. principle CLAR 219:7
know a f. reign EGER 289:15
Male and f. BIBL 73:15
male and the f. BIBL 74:16
no f. mind GILM 339:16
no f. Mozart PAGL 563:3
racket of the f. OSBO 560:4
uninformed f. AUST 39:10
femina *Dux f. facti* VIRG 793:11
feminine beautiful f. tissue HARD 360:19
'f.' principles RODD 631:2
Taste is the f. FITZ 315:5
feminism discussions of f. FREN 324:7
feminist call me a f. WEST 812:14
dealing with the early f. WEST 812:15
Fat is a f. issue ORBA 557:5
femme Cherchez la f. DUMA 284:14
fen f. Of stagnant waters WORD 829:8
through the plashy f. WAUG 806:11
fence colours to the f. FIEL 309:11
f. is just too high MAUG 501:16
f. leaps Sunny Jim ADVE 7:26
make a f. around the Law TALM 753:11
other side of the f. PROV 601:32
Please f. me in baby TELE 758:8
tradition is a f. TALM 753:17
fences all these f. HERB 373:12
f. make good neighbours PROV 601:25
Good f. make good neighbours FROS 326:5
tied her with f. MORR 532:23
Fenian grave of a dead F. COLL 229:1
left us our F. dead PEAR 571:7
fens reek o' the rotten f. SHAK 660:8
fercula *erant f.* AUGU 36:1
feriam *Sublimi f. sidera vertice* HORA 387:13
Fermanagh dreary steeples of F. CHUR 214:22
Fermat F.'s last theorem FERM 309:1
ferments like generous wine F. BUTL 172:15
fern receipt of f.-seed SHAK 667:29
ferocious most f. murderer DOST 276:6
press is f. DIAN 260:7
feros *nec sinit esse f.* OVID 561:9
ferry row us o'er the f. CAMP 183:11
fertile f. soil BACO 45:14
In such a fix to be so f. NASH 539:7
fertilizer use him as a f. MULL 536:2
festal line of f. light ARNO 27:8
fester Lilies that f. SHAK 705:7
limbs that f. ABSE 1:6
festina *F. lente* AUGU 36:16
fetish Militarism . . . is f. worship TAWN 755:11
fetishist f. who yearns KRAU 445:19
fetlocks f. blowing in the . . . wind LINE 469:12
fettered devil weakly f. STEV 741:8
fetters F. of gold ASTE 31:14
f. rent in twain DAVI 252:15
in love with his f. BACO 42:1
Milton wrote in f. BLAK 119:11
fever enigma of the f. chart ELIO 294:10
f. called 'Living' POE 579:14
f. of life is done NEWM 542:16
f. when he was in Spain SHAK 674:11
her f. might be it DONN 273:28
life's fitful f. SHAK 684:5
Of chills and f. RANS 621:20
starve a f. PROV 600:16
treaty bred a f. THOM 772:8
weariness, the f. KEAT 429:9
feverish f. and ghastly turmoil BROO 150:18
Février Janvier and F. NICH 543:17
few as grossly as the f. DRYD 280:12
Far and f. LEAR 460:9
F. and evil BIBL 75:20
f. and far between CAMP 183:16
f. are chosen BIBL 96:21
f. child's squalls HUNT 396:2
fit audience find, though f. MILT 517:6
Gey f. TOAS 778:2
hated the ruling f. BENT 66:22
let thy words be f. BIBL 84:11
Many worse, better f. LOCK 472:11
so much owed by so many to so f. CHUR 215:12
We few, we happy f. SHAK 671:25
fewer one man f. METT 506:10
fiancée wish his f. to see ANON 16:9
fiat F. in my soul BEDD 60:16
f. justitia MANS 494:10
F. justitia MOTT 535:8
F. justitia WATS 805:1
f. voluntas MISS 522:17
fickle f. is the South TENN 765:22
Whatever is f., freckled HOPK 384:15
fico *F.* [I'm staying] PEDR 571:12
fiction beats f. CONR 235:2
best thing in f. WILD 818:29
continuous f. BEVA 72:2
f. is a necessity CHES 211:3
f. lags after truth BURK 162:23
house of f. JAME 403:11
if she is to write f. WOOL 826:17
I hate things all *f.* BYRO 180:6
improbable f. SHAK 702:12
Poetry is the supreme f. STEV 739:23
sometimes f. MACA 482:17
Stranger than f. BYRO 177:26
stranger than f. PROV 600:4
stranger than f. PROV 613:19
That is what f. means WILD 817:19
writer of f. GASK 330:22
writing f. UPDI 788:10
fictions f. only and false hair HERB 372:20
truth to their f. HUME 395:5
fiddle cat and the f. NURS 548:12
F.-de-dee NURS 548:5
f., sir, and spade SCOT 651:20
F., we know, is diddle SWIN 750:23
important beyond all this f. MOOR 529:17
I the second f. SPRI 735:9
played on an old f. PROV 612:26
fiddler must pay the f. PROV 612:34
fiddlers his f. three NURS 549:17
fide *f. et gaude in Christo* LUTH 479:12
Punica f. SALL 643:11
Fidele fair F.'s grassy tomb COLL 229:7
fideles *Adeste, f.* ANON 21:4
fidelity stone f. they hardly meant LARK 452:13
thinks he is worth my f. LACL 447:5
Your idea of f. RAPH 622:3
fidgety f. Phil HOFF 380:1
fidus *f. quae tela gerebat Achates* VIRG 793:8
field comes and tills the f. TENN 766:16
corner of a foreign f. BROO 150:17
corner of a foreign f. OPEN 555:14
fair f. full of folk LANG 450:17
f. is won MORE 531:11
f. of Golgotha SHAK 695:19
F. Strewn ARNO 27:2
lay f. to field BIBL 86:18
lilies of the f. BIBL 93:25
man of the f. BIBL 74:35
not as simple as to cross a f. PAST 569:7
Not that fair f. Of Enna MILT 516:14
only inhabitants of the f. BURK 163:26
presence on the f. WELL 809:19
single in the f. WORD 832:2
swung the f. MERE 505:20
Vaguery in the F. OSBO 560:3
What though the f. be lost MILT 514:13
fields babbled of green f. SHAK 671:3
f. and flocks have charms CRAB 243:13
f. from Islington BLAK 118:22
F. have eyes PROV 600:18
f. invested with WORD 829:1
f. of Cambridge COWL 239:22
f. where roses fade HOUS 391:8
flowerless f. of heaven SWIN 750:4
from the f. of sleep WORD 829:17
I go among the f. KEAT 431:13
In Flanders f. MCCR 484:13
Open unto the f. WORD 827:19
plough the f. CAMP 182:14
tills his ancestral f. HORA 387:11
fiend defy the foul f. SHAK 679:3
dreadful f. SPEN 734:10
f. Flibbertigibbet SHAK 679:5
f. hid in a cloud BLAK 121:3
f. Walked up and down MILT 516:4
foul F. BUNY 160:18
frightful f. COLE 226:24
work like a f. THOM 772:19
fiends Beneath is all the f.' SHAK 679:22
fierce as I raved and grew more f. HERB 372:8
but little, she is f. SHAK 690:7
F. as ten Furies MILT 515:22
f. light which beats TENN 759:11
F. was the wild billow ANAT 14:7
fiery burning f. furnace BIBL 90:1
f. darts of the wicked BIBL 108:13
f. portal of the east SHAK 695:12
full of f. shapes SHAK 668:18
throne was like the f. flame BIBL 90:6
fife practised on a f. CARR 191:28
Thane of F. had a wife SHAK 685:10
fifteen At the age of f. OPEN 555:7
at the age of f. OPEN 555:20
at the age of f. WILS 822:6
famous for f. minutes WARH 803:12
F. men on the dead man's chest STEV 741:18
f. wild Decembers BRON 150:2
old age always f. years older BARU 56:10
fifth came f. and lost JOYC 422:14
F. column MOLA 524:15
fifties tranquillized *F.* LOWE 477:23
fifty At f. chides his infamous delay YOUN 839:7
At f., everyone ORWE 559:15
At f., menopausal STEV 740:19
corpulent man of f. HUNT 396:5
F.-four forty POLI 581:13
until he's f. FAUL 308:2
until I was nearly f. HEAN 366:12
fig f. for those by law protected BURN 167:20
sewed f. leaves together BIBL 73:26
figements *f. violets* RIMB 628:8
fight begun to f. JONE 419:1
better to f. for the good TENN 764:17
Councils of war never f. PROV 597:38
don't want to f. HUNT 395:10
end of the f. is a tombstone KIPL 439:18
Fifty-four forty, or f. POLI 581:13
f. against the future GLAD 340:16
f. and fight again GAIT 328:1
f. and no be slain BURN 168:19
f. and not to heed the wounds IGNA 398:17
F. fire with fire PROV 600:19
f. for freedom PANK 566:12
f. for freedom and truth IBSE 398:7
f. for its King and Country GRAH 348:1
f. for the living JONE 419:2
f. for what I believe in CAST 193:12
f. in defence HOME 382:6
f. in the way of God KORA 443:19
f. in the way of God KORA 444:8
f. in the way of God KORA 444:9
f. it out on this line GRAN 348:17
f. no more JOSE 421:8
F. on, my men BALL 51:12
f. on the beaches CHUR 215:10
f. on to the end HAIG 356:9
f. our country's battles MILI 508:8
F. the good fight BIBL 109:19
F. the good fight MONS 526:10
f. with faith and win SIKH 719:12
f. with them again TENN 766:8
fought a good f. BIBL 109:23
fought a good f. WILD 819:10

fight (*cont.*):
fought The better f. MILT 517:5
give the f. up BROW 157:5
go f. tomorrow BALL 50:15
Good at a f. ANON 16:11
he is dead, who will not f. GREN 352:17
I f. on THAT 770:12
I will f. SITT 720:19
like men, and f. BIBL 78:17
never a moment ceased the f. TENN 766:10
Never give up the f. MARL 495:16
nor duty bade me f. YEAT 836:10
no stomach to this f. SHAK 671:23
not the f. HERR 374:9
peril in the f. CORN 236:15
refuse to f. POLI 582:5
rise and f. againe BALL 51:12
those who bade me f. EWER 305:11
thought it wrong to f. BELL 64:5
too proud to f. WILS 822:11
Ulster will f. CHUR 214:14
When badgers f. CLAR 218:6
fighter Am I no a bonny f. STEV 741:5
I was ever a f. BROW 157:17
fighting f. for this woman's honour FILM 312:7
F. in the captain's tower DYLA 287:4
F. still DRYD 280:20
f. with daggers SCOT 652:18
first-class f. man KIPL 438:16
foremost f., fell BYRO 174:15
In f. to the death DAYA 253:10
not fifty ways of f. MALR 492:18
still f. Blenheim BEVA 71:16
street f. man JAGG 401:7
two dogs are f. PROV 614:44
What are WE f. for SERV 655:1
who dies f. has increase GREN 352:17
fights f. and runs away PROV 602:26
figs f. of thistles BIBL 94:10
love long life better than f. SHAK 656:9
figurative f., a metaphorical God DONN 275:1
figure f. a poem makes FROS 326:13
f. in the carpet JAME 403:3
f. that thou here seest JONS 420:18
losing her f. or her face CART 193:2
make a f. SWIF 748:4
figures prove anything by f. CARL 187:2
filches f. from me my good name SHAK 692:20
files foremost f. of time TENN 763:8
filial may be called f. CONF 231:4
filigree f. hedges WALP 800:15
O f. petal THOM 774:16
fill Ah, f. the cup FITZ 314:14
F. ev'ry glass GAY 331:17
F. me with life anew HATC 363:17
f. the hour EMER 299:25
O f. me MACN 488:13
take our f. of love BIBL 82:16
trying to f. them CIOR 218:4
fillest f. all things living BOOK 141:20
filling f. the space WEST 812:17
film f. of death KEAT 430:13
f., which fluttered COLE 225:14
films seldom go to f. BERR 70:1
fils *F. de Saint Louis* FIRM 313:8
filth Delights in f. SPEN 734:2
identical, and so is f. FORS 320:23
filthy are as f. rags BIBL 89:7
f. and polluted BIBL 90:23
greedy of f. lucre BIBL 109:14
fin *commencement de la f.* TALL 753:3
final f. curtain comes down MAJO 491:19
f. solution HEYD 376:2
finale Let be be f. of seem STEV 739:21
finality F. is death STEP 738:3
F. is not the language DISR 268:19
finals This is called F. LODG 472:13
finance F. is the stomach GLAD 340:14
financial with f. acumen KAUF 426:4
find do not f. anything pleasant VOLT 797:6
f. it after many days BIBL 84:27
f. out God BIBL 81:14
New places you will not f. CAVA 198:9
returns home to f. it MOOR 529:12
Run and f. out KIPL 441:4
Safe bind, safe f. PROV 610:19
Seek and ye shall f. PROV 610:28
Someday I'll f. you COWA 238:18
strive, to seek, to f. TENN 767:12
Those who hide can f. PROV 612:41
thou shalt f. me ANON 18:13
where I f. it MOLI 525:21
finders F. keepers PROV 600:20
findeth f. his life BIBL 95:3
he that seeketh f. BIBL 94:4
findings F. keepings PROV 600:21
finds he Who f. himself ARNO 27:12
fine bring in f. things BUCK 159:14
disgrace to be f. TAYL 756:11
F. art is that RUSK 638:26
F. clothes are good JOHN 415:14
F. feathers PROV 600:22
f. point of his soul KEAT 430:23
f. romance with no kisses FIEL 310:16
F. words PROV 600:23
F. writing KEAT 431:17
passage which is particularly f. JOHN 414:22
too f. a point upon it DICK 260:21
very f. cat JOHN 417:5
fine arts one of the f. STEI 737:4
finem *F. di dederint* HORA 387:21
respice f. ANON 21:12
finer nothing could be f. GORD 347:1
finery not bedizened with f. TROL 782:3
finest f. hour CHUR 215:11
our f. shower OSBO 559:23
finger bruises his f. here on earth TALM 754:24
burnt Fool's bandaged f. KIPL 438:20
by the f. and thumb SALI 642:15
chills the f. not a bit NASH 539:17
f. lickin' good ADVE 7:32
F. of birth-strangled babe SHAK 684:19
God's f. touched him TENN 761:22
little f. shall be thicker BIBL 79:21
little f. to become longer SCHO 649:2
moving f. writes FITZ 314:17
my f. and my thumb HEAN 366:11
One f. in the throat OSLE 560:15
Pressed her cold f. KEAT 427:24
ring without the f. MIDD 507:4
scratching of my f. HUME 395:7
slow and moving f. SHAK 693:13
Whose f. NEWS 544:19
fingernails indifferent, paring his f. JOYC 422:4
relatively clean f. MORT 533:11
fingerprints f. across his brain HEND 369:17
fingers Crumbling between the f. MACN 488:10
cut their own f. EDDI 288:3
dead men's f. SHAK 666:13
f. are ingenious SCOT 652:10
f. do the walking ADVE 7:41
f. of cold are corpse fingers LAWR 458:22
F. were made before PROV 600:24
Five sovereign f. THOM 772:7
pulled our f. out PHIL 575:4
Shutting, with careful f. KEAT 430:6
terrified vague f. YEAT 836:14
twisting in your yellow f. HEAT 367:4
With f. weary HOOD 382:28
fingerstalls In fitless f. GILB 338:10
fingertips to his f. HORA 389:19
finish didn't let me f. BABE 41:3
F., good lady SHAK 657:23
f. the job CHUR 215:14
Nice guys f. last DURO 286:7
repetitious *f.*, *finish* READ 622:17
started so I'll f. CATC 196:7
start together and f. BEEC 61:5
start to the f. HORA 389:17
finished books were f. KIPL 441:21
book would have been f. WODE 824:16
f. in the first 100 days KENN 433:13
f. my course BIBL 109:23
It is f. BIBL 102:37
world where England is f. MILL 509:17
finisher author and f. of our faith BIBL 110:2
finite f. quantities BERK 67:18
like it to be f. LEIB 462:24
finned giant f. cars nose forward LOWE 477:21
fins swims with f. of lead SHAK 660:3
fir f. tree BIBL 88:23
fire all compact of f. SHAK 705:29
ane fervent f. SCOT 650:3
as bad as a f. PROV 612:47
as the flint bears f. SHAK 676:26
Beef and a sea-coal f. OTWA 560:24
before you stir his f. PROV 616:6
bound Upon a wheel of f. SHAK 680:3
broad gate and the great f. SHAK 656:5
burnt child dreads the f. PROV 596:41
bush burned with f. BIBL 75:25
chariot of f. BLAK 120:1
coals of f. BIBL 83:21
dare seize the f. BLAK 121:9
don't f. until you see PUTN 618:4
dropping-wells of f. TENN 761:21
faith and f. within us HARD 361:19
Fell in the f. GRAH 348:5
Fight fire with f. PROV 600:19
f. and brimstone BOOK 132:3
F. and fleet BALL 51:2
F. and hail BOOK 141:27
f. and the rose are one ELIO 294:20
F. burn and cauldron bubble SHAK 684:17
F. burns both here ARIS 24:18
f. can burn DANI 248:19
f. come out of the bramble BIBL 77:36
f. did compass him GILB 337:2
f. in the head JOHN 408:8
f. in the last act CHEK 208:21
f. into the equations HAWK 364:10
F. is a good servant PROV 600:25
f. next time SONG 713:8
f. of my loins NABO 537:17
f. of my loins OPEN 556:1
f. of my nature BRON 149:14
F. prepared for unbelievers KORA 443:16
f. sall never BALL 51:4
f. that's in me now BECK 59:14
f. to be lit RABE 619:13
f. was furry as a bear SITW 721:1
f. when you are ready DEWE 259:16
fretted with golden f. SHAK 663:18
frighted with false f. SHAK 664:26
gentle f. has caught SAPP 644:14
glass mingled with f. BIBL 112:27
gold shines like f. PIND 576:8
gulfs of liquid f. SHAK 694:1
have kindled a f. COBB 223:7
heretic which makes the f. SHAK 703:4
hold a f. in his hand SHAK 694:16
house is on f. NURS 549:1
I am f. and air SHAK 658:1
If you play with f. PROV 603:35
in danger of hell f. BIBL 93:9
it is a f. PEEL 571:19
jewel of your f. TAGO 752:21
kindles f. LA R 453:18
latter f. shall heat the deep TENN 762:9
light my f. MORR 532:22
little f. is quickly trodden SHAK 673:2
little f. kindleth BIBL 110:18
Lord was not in the f. BIBL 80:3
Love is the f. SOUT 731:10
low-burnt f. COLE 225:14
ministers a flaming f. BOOK 139:1
Muse of f. OPEN 556:6
My f.'s extinct EPIT 303:16

neighbour's house is on f. BURK 163:13
nodding by the f. YEAT 837:23
No smoke without f. PROV 608:7
Now stir the f. COWP 241:31
O! for a Muse of f. SHAK 670:25
O look at all the f.-folk HOPK 384:20
O Love, O f. TENN 758:19
pale f. she snatches SHAK 699:22
performs the effect of f. MILT 515:20
pillar of f. BIBL 76:5
right Promethean f. SHAK 680:28
set a house on f. BACO 44:23
sheaves of sacred f. CHAP 202:17
shouted 'F.' BELL 63:10
shouting f. in a theatre HOLM 381:14
Skiddaw saw the f. MACA 482:19
soul of f. JOHN 411:15
source of the sacred f. ROUS 636:6
spark o' Nature's f. BURN 167:4
stirring the f. AUST 38:17
take a walk into the f. ENGE 300:12
take f. in his bosom BIBL 82:15
Thorough flood, thorough f. SHAK 689:16
tongued with f. ELIO 294:13
tongues like as of f. BIBL 103:15
Torah are compared to f. MIDR 507:13
torches at his f. COKA 224:5
true love is a durable f. RALE 621:2
wabbling back to the F. KIPL 438:20
wheels as burning f. BIBL 90:6
where once I was f. BYRO 179:8
wind is to f. BUSS 171:6
with a heart of f. TENN 764:16
with a lake of f. FLEC 317:5
world will end in f. FROS 325:21
youth of England are on f. SHAK 670:30
firebrand ye were as a f. BIBL 90:18
fired f. the shot BALL 50:18
firefly f. in the night CROW 246:16
firends forgive our f. MEDI 503:9
fires Big f. flare up FRAN 323:2
devastating or redeeming f. GONC 346:7
Gorse fires are f. LONG 475:7
misled by wandering f. DRYD 281:20
salamandrine f. HARD 361:9
thought-executing f. SHAK 678:21
fireside adventures were by the f. GOLD 345:27
at his own f. SHER 716:19
F. enjoyments COWP 242:1
firm family f. GEOR 334:9
old f., is selling out OSBO 560:6
firmament brave o'erhanging f. SHAK 663:18
fellow in the f. SHAK 675:15
f. sheweth his handy-work BOOK 132:14
Now glowed the f. MILT 516:20
spacious f. ADDI 5:12
streams in the f. MARL 496:7
Waters that be above the F. BOOK 126:4
firmly F. I believe NEWM 542:17
firmness f., and delight WOTT 833:5
f. makes my circle DONN 274:20
first always a f. time PROV 612:7
degrade a F. Cause HARD 360:17
Eclipse f. O'KE 553:9
F. and the Last KORA 445:14
f. article of my faith GAND 329:6
f. blow is half GOLD 345:23
F. come PROV 600:27
f. fruits of them that slept BIBL 106:22
F. impressions PROV 600:29
f. in a village CAES 180:18
f. in the hearts LEE 461:21
f. Kinnock in a thousand KINN 437:21
f. man BIBL 107:2
f. step that is difficult DU D 284:6
f. that ever burst COLE 226:10
F. things first PROV 600:30
for the f. time ELIO 294:17
if they speak f. CONG 232:16
last shall be f. BIBL 96:17
latent in my f. WHAR 813:2
men travel f. class GARC 329:12
no last nor f. BROW 157:13
nothing should be done for the f. time CORN 237:4
no truck with f. impulses MONT 528:17
people who got there f. USTI 788:22
romantic f. flame BURN 165:22
to be called F. Lady ONAS 554:17
we got in f. COLL 229:6
what to put first PASC 568:7
firstborn brought forth her f. son BIBL 98:20
f. the greatest ass CARO 189:3
smite all the f. BIBL 76:2
fish All f. that comes to net PROV 594:22
as good f. in the sea PROV 611:45
Big f. eat little fish PROV 596:18
black and ugly f. HORA 385:10
broiled f. BIBL 100:36
colder and dumber than a f. MULD 535:25
f. always stinks PROV 600:31
f. and fishing WALT 802:25
F. and guests stink PROV 600:32
F. are jumpin' HEYW 376:4
F. fiddle-de-dee LEAR 460:20
F. fuck in it FIEL 310:21
F. got to swim HAMM 358:16
F. have their stream BROO 150:9
f. of the sea BIBL 73:14
f. that *talks* DE L 256:8
f. the last Food BASS 56:21
f. without a bicycle STEI 737:14
f. with the worm SHAK 665:28
f. would have bright mail KEAT 427:1
I was a f. SMIT 724:8
Keep your own f.-guts PROV 604:50
Little f. are sweet PROV 605:37
no f. ye're buying SCOT 651:17
no longer f. and chips JEAN 404:16
nose forward like f. LOWE 477:21
Phone for the f.-knives BETJ 70:10
surrounded by f. BEVA 71:12
Thou deboshed f. SHAK 699:2
to torture f. COLM 229:19
Un-dish-cover the f. CARR 191:18
What cat's averse to f. GRAY 350:20
fishbone monument sticks like a f. LOWE 477:22
fishbones two f., two eyeballs WELB 809:3
fisher gallant f.'s life CHAL 200:10
fisherman Death is like a f. TURG 785:6
fishermen f. hold flowers DYLA 287:4
fishers Blest f. BASS 56:21
f. of men BIBL 93:2
f. went sailing away KING 437:11
fishes f. flew and forests walked CHES 210:4
f. gnawed SHAK 696:17
F., that tipple LOVE 476:13
how the f. live in the sea SHAK 694:7
little f. of the sea CARR 191:6
Men lived like f. SIDN 718:3
notes like little f. MACN 488:15
Tawny-finned f. SHAK 656:31
two small f. BIBL 101:25
welcomes little f. in CARR 189:10
fishified how art thou f. SHAK 697:20
fishing I go a f. BIBL 103:7
when he goes a-f. WALT 802:15
fishlike ancient and f. smell SHAK 698:31
fishpond great f. (the sea) DEKK 256:3
fishpools eyes like the f. BIBL 86:5
fishy You shall have a f. NURS 548:1
fist closed f. of a teacher PALI 564:17
of f. most valiant SHAK 671:12
fistful for a f. of coins ZAPA 839:22
fists F. clenched LOGU 473:4
groan and shake their f. HOUS 390:4
fit f. audience find MILT 517:6
f. for this world KEAT 430:23
I am f. for nothing HERV 375:8
only the F. survive SERV 654:25
fitchew f. nor the soiled horse SHAK 679:22
fitful life's f. fever SHAK 684:5
fitly word f. spoken BIBL 83:18
fits If the cap f., wear it PROV 603:20
If the shoe f. PROV 603:22
fittest Survival of the F. DARW 250:20
survival of the f. SPEN 732:5
fitting right and f. MISS 520:20
fittings f. of a gentleman's BOWE 145:8
five At f. in the afternoon GARC 329:10
f. minutes too late COWL 239:24
f. per cent MACA 481:19
F. to one MORR 532:21
Full fathom f. SHAK 698:27
had f. thousand a year THAC 769:12
I have wedded f. CHAU 206:16
in a f.-pound note LEAR 460:16
she hadde f. CHAU 204:23
warming his f. wits TENN 766:15
fix don't f. it SAYI 647:19
f. up his automobile CLAR 219:14
looking for an angry f. GINS 339:20
fixed f. point in a changing age DOYL 277:15
great gulf f. BIBL 100:11
flabby this f. exterior LEVA 465:19
flag allegiance to the f. BELL 62:24
blood-red f. BLOK 122:6
brought back the f. GRIF 353:9
death's pale f. SHAK 698:3
f. and sign of love SHAK 691:27
f. to which you have pledged BALD 49:3
High as a f. HAMM 359:3
Jelly-bellied F.-flapper KIPL 441:23
keep the red f. flying CONN 233:23
national f. SUMN 746:7
people's f. is deepest red CONN 233:22
raised their f. WEBS 807:13
shall not f. or fail CHUR 215:10
spare your country's f. WHIT 816:4
Trade follows the f. PROV 613:15
flagellation Not f., not pederasty RATT 622:6
flagitium *f. timet* HORA 389:10
flagpole run it up the f. SAYI 647:28
flame Both moth and f. ROET 631:11
Chloe is my real f. PRIO 592:15
eyes were as a f. BIBL 111:22
feed his sacred f. COLE 226:1
F.-capped, and shout SHAW 710:1
f. I still deplore GARR 330:8
f. out like shining HOPK 384:5
full of subtil f. BEAU 58:13
hard, gemlike f. PATE 569:15
in a shapeless f. DONN 273:16
plays about the f. GAY 331:9
romantic first f. BURN 165:22
signals of the ancient f. DANT 250:1
spark of that ancient f. VIRG 794:10
that little f. RENO 624:16
thin blue f. COLE 225:14
throne was like the fiery f. BIBL 90:6
thy holy f. bestowing LITT 470:3
tongues of f. are in-folded ELIO 294:20
tongues of living f. AUBE 32:10
When a lovely f. dies HARB 359:14
flames by her like thin f. ROSS 634:19
Commit it then to the f. HUME 394:7
f. in the forehead MILT 513:10
f. must waste away CARE 186:5
love. F. for a year LAMP 449:16
rich f. and hired tears BROW 152:19
flaming f. bounds of place and time GRAY 351:2
ministers a f. fire BOOK 139:1
flammae *veteris vestigia f.* VIRG 794:10
flamme *cette petite f.* RENO 624:16
Flanders brought him a F. mare HENR 370:11
In F. fields the poppies blow MCCR 484:12
part of F. WALL 800:12
flanks silken f. KEAT 428:27
flashes f. of silence SMIT 725:20
In f., and with glory WORD 831:5

flashing His f. eyes COLE 225:25
flask f. of wine FITZ 314:9
flat debt, an' a f. LOWE 477:12
F. and flexible truths BROW 152:13
half so f. as Walter Scott ANON 18:6
never surprises, it is f. FORS 320:12
very dangerous f. SHAK 687:27
Very f., Norfolk COWA 239:2
flats sharps and f. BROW 157:10
flatten hide is sure to f. 'em BELL 63:3
flatter before you f. a man JOHN 416:7
F. the mountain-tops SHAK 704:17
fondly f. our desires DRAY 279:1
lie, to f. ASCH 30:4
flattered being then most f. SHAK 675:5
Englishman, Being f. CHAP 202:12
f. into virtue SURT 746:13
f. its rank breath BYRO 174:22
neither feared nor f. DOUG 276:13
flatterer hypocrite and f. BLAK 119:2
flatterers petty f. BACO 43:16
sycophants and f. HARD 360:2
tell him he hates f. SHAK 675:5
within a week the same f. HALI 357:12
flatteries against f. MACH 486:4
flattering f., kissing and kicking TRUM 784:2
f. unction SHAK 665:20
think him worth f. SHAW 707:19
flattery Everyone likes f. DISR 270:37
f. hurts no one STEV 740:8
f. is worth his having JOHN 416:7
f. lost on poet's ear SCOT 650:17
f. of one's peers LODG 472:16
f. soothe the dull cold ear GRAY 350:10
ne'er was f. lost CLOS 222:8
paid with f. JOHN 409:13
sincerest form of f. PROV 603:46
This is no f. SHAK 658:13
flaunting f., extravagant quean SHER 716:14
flavour high celestial f. BYRO 176:19
flaw no kind of fault or f. GILB 337:12
flaws hundred thousand f. SHAK 678:19
flax smoking f. BIBL 88:6
Three pounds of f. MUMO 536:10
flayed saw a woman f. SWIF 748:22
flea gripping a f. PROV 608:14
literature's performing f. O'CA 552:14
louse and a f. JOHN 417:4
naturalists observe, a f. SWIF 749:19
fleas Big f. have little fleas PROV 596:19
educated f. do it PORT 588:7
F. know not whether LAND 450:8
f. that tease in the High Pyrenees BELL 64:8
get up with f. PROV 603:34
praised his f. YEAT 837:16
flectere *F. si nequeo superos* VIRG 795:5
fled f. far, far away COCK 223:12
f. From this vile world SHAK 704:28
F. is that music KEAT 429:16
I f. Him THOM 774:4
sea saw that, and f. BOOK 139:21
Still as he f. SPEN 733:20
flee death shall f. from them BIBL 112:15
f., and were discomfited BOOK 136:7
f. away, and be at rest BOOK 135:10
f. from the wrath to come BIBL 92:29
F. fro the press CHAU 207:23
f. when no man pursueth BIBL 83:31
They f. from me WYAT 834:5
fleece f. was white as snow HALE 357:4
His forest f. HOUS 391:2
won the F. and then came home DU B 283:22
fleeces sheep bear f. VIRG 797:4
fleet care of our f. ADDI 5:8
Fire and f. BALL 51:2
f. before the gale SMAR 722:12
F. in which we serve BOOK 142:4
F. the time carelessly SHAK 658:7
in the Downs the f. was moored GAY 332:20
whole F.'s lit up WOOD 826:9
fleetest have f. end THOM 774:2
fleeth My soul f. BOOK 141:2
fleeting fable, song, or f. shade HERR 374:7
fleets Ten thousand f. BYRO 175:9
Fleet Street F. to our poets BROW 154:11
who can be dull in F. LAMB 448:24
flere *Si vis me f.* HORA 385:18
flesh All f. is grass BIBL 88:1
all f. shall see it BIBL 87:28
born after the f. BIBL 107:19
bread and f. BIBL 79:25
delicate white human f. FIEL 310:9
east wind made f. APPL 23:5
eat bulls' f. BOOK 135:3
Eating the f. SHAK 700:2
fair and unpolluted f. SHAK 666:26
flattered any f. DOUG 276:13
f., alas, is wearied MALL 492:2
f. and blood BIBL 108:13
f. and blood so cheap HOOD 383:1
f., and the devil BOOK 127:5
f. is as grass BIBL 110:26
f. is weak BIBL 97:23
F. of flesh MILT 517:19
f. of my flesh BIBL 73:22
F. perishes. I live on HARD 361:15
f. to feel the chain BRON 150:1
f. was sacramental ROBI 629:20
gross f. sinks downwards SHAK 696:6
heart o' f. BALL 51:19
human f. subsisting BOOK 127:1
in my f. shall I see God BIBL 81:22
lusts of the f. BOOK 130:11
makes man and wife one f. CONG 232:11
make your f. creep DICK 265:4
more f. than another man SHAK 668:29
my heart and my f. BOOK 137:11
My Lord should take Frail f. CROS 246:15
O flesh, f. SHAK 697:20
outlive all f. BYRO 177:32
provision for the f. BIBL 105:22
shall all f. come BOOK 135:26
Tell f. it is but dust RALE 620:13
these our f. upright DONN 272:15
they shall be one f. BIBL 73:23
things of the f. BIBL 105:6
this too too solid f. SHAK 661:22
thorn in the f. BIBL 107:16
trust in the f. BIBL 108:19
we are one, One f. MILT 517:20
Word was made f. BIBL 101:7
WORD WAS MADE F. MISS 523:1
world and its shadow, The f. RIDI 627:14
would God this f. SWIN 751:13
fleshly all this f. dress VAUG 790:9
flesh pots we sat by the f. BIBL 76:7
flew and they f. LOGU 473:3
f. between me and the sun BLUN 122:13
f. over the cuckoo's nest NURS 550:2
flexible Flat and f. truths BROW 152:13
your f. friend ADVE 7:1
Flibbertigibbet fiend F. SHAK 679:5
flicker moment of my greatness f. ELIO 295:8
flies As f. to wanton boys SHAK 679:15
catch small f. SWIF 747:14
Eagles don't catch f. PROV 599:1
F., worms, and flowers WATT 805:7
full fast he f. BLAI 117:6
Honey catches more f. PROV 602:46
joy as it f. BLAK 120:8
murmurous haunt of f. KEAT 429:12
shut mouth catches no f. PROV 610:39
swart f. move DOUG 276:16
Time f. PROV 612:52
fliest for thou f. Me THOM 774:9
flight His cloistered f. SHAK 684:6
His f. was madness SHAK 685:3
not attained by sudden f. LONG 473:21
puts the stars to f. FITZ 314:7
Swift be thy f. SHEL 714:11
will not take their f. MILT 513:21
flights f. upon the banks JONS 420:26
flinders Little Polly F. NURS 549:8
fling f. the ringleaders ARNO 29:15
flint as the f. bears fire SHAK 676:26
flirtation innocent f. BYRO 177:20
flittings tellest my f. BOOK 135:13
float f. lazily downstream SALI 642:14
F. like a butterfly ALI 12:4
f. upon his watery bier MILT 512:28
floating f. bulwark of the island BLAC 117:3
his f. hair COLE 225:25
floats She f., she hesitates RACI 619:17
flock feed his f. BIBL 88:2
keeping watch over their f. BIBL 98:20
tainted wether of the f. SHAK 688:8
flocks My father feeds his f. HOME 381:17
My f. feed not BARN 55:9
shepherds watched their f. TATE 755:10
sweet buds like f. SHEL 712:12
flog f. the rank and file ARNO 29:15
flogging in the habit of f. me TROL 781:17
less f. in our great schools JOHN 415:8
flood days before the f. BIBL 97:5
f. could not wash away CONG 232:22
f. unto the world's end BOOK 136:18
just cause reaches its f.-tide CATT 194:18
return it as a f. GLAD 341:13
Since Deucalion's f. SKEL 721:14
swam the brackish f. DRAY 279:5
taken at the f. SHAK 676:28
ten years before the f. MARV 499:1
Thorough f., thorough fire SHAK 689:16
Thunder like a mighty f. DIX 271:12
verge of the salt f. SHAK 699:25
flooded STREETS F. TELE 758:10
floodgate F. of the deeper heart FLEC 317:8
floods f. are risen BOOK 138:3
f. drown it BIBL 86:8
haystack in the f. MORR 532:14
most like to f. RALE 620:16
quells the f. below CAMP 183:19
floor along the gusty f. KEAT 427:15
fell upon the sanded f. PAYN 570:12
f. of heaven SHAK 688:22
floors Scuttling across the f. of silent seas ELIO 295:7
flopping go f. yourself down DICK 265:24
flopshus F. Cad KIPL 441:23
Flora Tasting of F. KEAT 429:7
floraisons *mois des f.* ARAG 25:11
Florence lily of F. LONG 473:18
Rode past fair F. KEAT 428:2
Flores F. in the Azores TENN 766:8
flos *Ut f. in saeptis* CATU 197:11
flourish f. after first decay SPEN 733:27
f. and complain CRAB 243:5
f. set on youth SHAK 704:24
Princes and lords may f. GOLD 344:8
things f. where you turn POPE 586:26
thou didst f. once VAUG 790:16
Truth shall f. BOOK 137:15
flourisheth f. as a flower BOOK 138:20
flourishing f. like a green bay-tree BOOK 133:27
flout scout 'em, and f. 'em SHAK 699:3
flow blood must yet f. JEFF 406:1
F. gently, sweet Afton BURN 166:10
I within did f. TRAH 780:18
What need you f. so fast ANON 19:10
flower as the f. of the field BIBL 88:1
[Buddha] held up a f. MUMO 536:9
Chaucer, of makaris f. DUNB 285:5
cometh forth like a f. BIBL 81:18
constellated f. SHEL 713:20
cracks into furious f. BROO 151:7
die in the f. of their age BIBL 78:13
drives the f. THOM 772:5
every opening f. WATT 805:5
fairest f., no sooner blown MILT 513:15
flourisheth as a f. BOOK 138:20
f. fadeth BIBL 88:1
f. grows concealed CATU 197:11
f. in his hand COLE 227:9
f. of all the field SHAK 697:37
f. of any kind of experience HUNT 395:20

f. of English nobility ORDE 557:11
f. of floures alle CHAU 206:26
f. of goodlihead SKEL 721:12
f. of roses BIBL 92:18
f. of Scotland WILL 821:5
f. that once hath blown FITZ 314:13
f. thereof falleth BIBL 110:26
Full many a f. is born GRAY 350:11
heaven in a wild f. BLAK 117:17
her f., her glory pass DANI 248:18
Herself a fairer f. MILT 516:14
it will bear no f. SHEL 714:20
leaf, the bud, the f. SPEN 733:27
lightly like a f. TENN 762:5
like the innocent f. SHAK 682:5
little western f. SHAK 689:23
London, thou art the f. ANON 17:13
meanest f. that blows WORD 830:10
no stronger than a f. SHAK 704:27
pluck this f., safety SHAK 667:35
seize the f. BURN 168:13
short-lived f. LEAP 460:2
Some achieve a f. LARK 453:1
sweetest f. for scent SHEL 713:23
this same f. that smiles HERR 375:2
white f. of a blameless TENN 759:11
flowering About the f. squares TENN 762:2
f. of His fields TENN 760:9
flowerlike f. face SWIN 751:11
flowerpots your damned f. BROW 157:28
flowers among the f. LUCR 479:9
beckon to the f. HERB 372:21
Beware of men bearing f. SPAR 731:15
bring forth May f. PROV 595:15
but as a bed of f. DONN 275:7
cool-rooted f. KEAT 429:17
droop-headed f. KEAT 429:4
Ensnared with f. MARV 498:15
fairest f. o' the season SHAK 703:14
fishermen hold f. DYLA 287:4
Flies, worms, and f. WATT 805:7
f. and fruits of love BYRO 178:22
f. appear on the earth BIBL 85:10
F. in the garden STEV 743:3
f. in the mede CHAU 206:25
F. of all hue MILT 516:13
f. of the forest COCK 223:13
f. of the forest ELLI 298:9
f. that bloom in the spring GILB 338:14
f. the tenderness of patient minds OWEN 562:7
f. would bloom KEAT 427:1
foam of f. SWIN 751:13
hundred f. blossom MAO 495:4
I got me f. to strew HERB 372:11
No f., by request AING 9:2
other men's f. MONT 528:5
path is strewed with f. FARA 306:11
Say it with f. ADVE 8:8
souls do couch on f. SHAK 657:14
speckled gigantic f. DINE 267:19
Too many f. SCOT 652:16
Where have all the f. gone SEEG 653:6
wild f., and Prime Ministers BALD 49:7
won't be f. AUDE 35:11
flowery crops the f. food POPE 585:7
f. lap of earth ARNO 26:16
f. plains of honour JONS 420:7
f. way SHAK 656:5
flowing f. sea CUNN 247:15
f. with milk and honey BIBL 75:28
flown birds are f. CHAR 203:1
flows Everything f. HERA 371:7
fluidity solid for f. CHUR 215:3
flummery f. of a birth place KEAT 431:6
flung f. himself from the room LEAC 459:19
flush for the f. of youth ROSS 634:7
flushpots f. of Euston JOYC 421:19
flute f. and hautboys COLM 229:18
f., harp, sackbut BIBL 90:1
soft complaining f. DRYD 282:22
upon the f. BROW 157:27
flutter F. and bear him up BETJ 70:7
fluttering F. and dancing WORD 828:26
fly all things F. thee THOM 774:9
f. at one end SWIF 750:3
F. at your Lord's command GURN 355:5
F. away home NURS 549:1
F. envious Time MILT 514:3
f. from BYRO 174:18
F. hence, our contact fear ARNO 27:10
f. in his hand STER 738:24
f. sat upon the axletree BACO 44:20
f. shall marry NURS 548:5
f., Sir, may sting JOHN 412:12
f. them for a moment TENN 766:8
f. through the air LEYB 467:15
f. to India MARL 496:2
for I will f. to thee KEAT 429:11
I, said the F. NURS 552:1
long-legged f. upon the stream YEAT 836:16
man is not a f. POPE 585:13
noise of a f. DONN 275:8
said a spider to a f. HOWI 392:5
seen spiders f. EDWA 289:9
settled like a meat-f. RUSK 638:5
show the f. the way out WITT 824:5
small gilded f. Does lecher SHAK 679:21
There interposed a F. DICK 266:9
They f. forgotten WATT 805:19
thirsty f. OLDY 553:13
To f. is safe COWP 241:30
try to f. by those nets JOYC 422:2
which way shall I f. MILT 516:9
wings to f. away CLAR 218:10
wouldn't hurt a f. LEAC 459:18
fly-fishing for winter f. WALT 802:13
flying f. upon the wings BOOK 132:11
on the f. trapeze LEYB 467:15
time is f. VIRG 797:1
flying-fishes f. play KIPL 439:13
Flying Scotsman F. is no less BEAV 59:1
foam f. Of perilous seas KEAT 429:14
To Noroway o'er the f. BALL 51:14
wild and dank with f. KING 437:9
foaming f. with much blood POWE 590:15
foe angry with my f. BLAK 121:5
as a friend than as a f. GLAD 341:16
erect and manly f. CANN 185:3
everyone's a f. CLAR 218:6
f. outstretched BLAK 121:6
furnace for your f. SHAK 673:6
His f. was folly EPIT 303:9
never made a f. TENN 759:30
open f. may prove a curse GAY 332:10
that's f. to men WEBS 808:14
unrelenting f. THOM 775:17
Where breathes the f. DRAK 278:21
willing f. and sea room TOAS 778:5
wish my deadly f. BRET 148:3
foeda *F. est in coitu* PETR 574:18
foes man's f. BIBL 95:2
fog f. and filthy air SHAK 681:7
f. comes on little cat feet SAND 643:20
F. in Channel BROC 149:2
f. in my throat BROW 157:16
f. that rubs its back ELIO 295:5
London particular . . . A f. DICK 260:19
foggy f. day in London Town GERS 334:12
fogs f. prevail upon the day DRYD 281:36
insular country, subject to f. DISR 270:10
foi *En cette f. je veux vivre* VILL 793:2
foible omniscience his f. SMIT 726:5
foil shining from shook f. HOPK 384:5
fold Do not f. ANON 15:23
f., spindle or mutilate SAYI 647:12
f. stands empty SHAK 689:20
f. to thy heart thy brother WHIT 816:8
like the wolf on the f. BYRO 175:23
not of this f. BIBL 102:8
folded sweetest leaves yet f. BYRO 177:28
undo the f. lie AUDE 35:2
folding f. of the hands BIBL 82:14
folds f. rippling SUMN 746:7
f. shall be full of sheep BOOK 136:2
tinklings lull the distant f. GRAY 350:6
folie *belle f.* BANV 53:10
f. à nulle autre seconde MOLI 525:11
folio whole volumes in f. SHAK 680:20
folios mighty f. first CRAB 242:28
folk all music is f. music ARMS 25:18
emptied of this f. KEAT 428:27
incest and f.-dancing ANON 20:1
in the f. mass choir DOYL 278:11
nowt so queer as f. PROV 612:33
trouble with a f. song LAMB 449:9
folks for different f. SAYI 647:10
my f. were growing old STEV 742:18
O yonge, fresshe f. CHAU 207:20
where the old f. stay FOST 321:17
follies crimes, f., and misfortunes GIBB 335:6
f. a man regrets most ROWL 636:14
f. naturally grow CHUR 213:16
f. of the wise JOHN 411:18
No f. to have to repent TAYL 756:14
Of all human f. MOLI 525:11
point out to us our f. TROL 782:21
vices and f. of human kind CONG 232:8
follow allowed to f. the road TALM 754:21
F. me BIBL 93:2
f. mine own teaching SHAK 687:7
F. The Gleam TENN 764:19
F. the van COLL 228:13
f. the worse OVID 561:17
f. your Saint CAMP 183:23
F. your spirit SHAK 671:6
I really had to f. them LEDR 461:15
Pay, pack, and f. BURT 169:20
So, f. me, follow FLAN 316:2
their works do f. them BIBL 112:26
followed arose and f. him BIBL 94:22
first he f. it hymselve CHAU 205:1
follows f. freits PROV 602:13
lie f. PROU 594:9
folly according to his f. BIBL 83:23
brood of f. MILT 512:3
by the f. of others PLIN 578:18
Fashion, though F.'s child CRAB 243:1
f. and conceit AUST 38:18
f. and vice TENN 763:22
f. of people's not staying AUST 37:16
f. of the wise JOHN 418:10
F.'s at full length BRER 148:1
f. to be wise PROV 614:37
fool returneth to his f. BIBL 83:24
His foe was f. EPIT 303:9
lovely woman stoops to f. ELIO 296:11
lovely woman stoops to f. GOLD 345:30
most loving mere f. SHAK 659:5
not their merit but our f. OSBO 559:20
persist in his f. BLAK 119:18
public f. feeds COWP 242:11
shoot F. as it flies POPE 585:5
shunn'st the noise of f. MILT 512:6
'Tis f. to be wise GRAY 350:18
too presumptuous f. HART 363:9
uses his f. SHAK 659:28
usually ends in f. COLE 227:24
Wisdom excelleth f. BIBL 84:6
fond *au f. des bois* VIGN 792:14
f. of grief SHAK 677:11
grow too f. of it LEE 462:8
men would be f. LYLY 480:13
over-f. of resisting BECK 60:13
probably f. of them TWAI 786:29
so f. of one another SWIF 748:3
When men were f. SHAK 686:13
fondly F. do we hope LINC 468:17
fondness habitual f. WASH 804:8
fons *aquae f.* HORA 389:24
f. pietatis MISS 523:5
food alcohol was a f. WODE 824:20
chief of Scotia's f. BURN 166:24
Continent have good f. MIKE 507:18

food (*cont.*):
finds its f. in music LILL 468:3
F. comes first BREC 147:18
f. convenient for me BIBL 83:35
F. enough for a week MERR 506:1
f. for powder SHAK 669:2
f. from heaven BOOK 137:6
f. of love OPEN 555:15
f. out of the earth BOOK 139:3
f. that dead men eat DOBS 271:15
give f. to the poor CAMA 182:10
good f. and not fine words MOLI 525:3
homely was their f. GART 330:12
music be the f. of love SHAK 700:26
problem is f. DONL 272:5
room and f. MALT 493:4
wholesome f. SWIF 748:13
fool and be a f. POPE 585:21
Answer a f. BIBL 83:23
Any f. may write GRAY 351:9
ass, without being a f. SURT 746:15
beast or a f. KILV 436:4
become the golden f. BLAK 120:4
breed a f. WOTT 833:2
burnt F.'s bandaged finger KIPL 438:20
Busy old f. DONN 274:14
Dost thou call me f. SHAK 678:8
every f. in Buxton RUSK 638:13
every f. is not a poet POPE 582:27
f. all the people LINC 469:5
f. and his money PROV 600:33
f. and his words SHEN 715:8
f. at forty PROV 600:34
f. at forty YOUN 838:18
f. at the other SWIF 750:3
f. bolts pleasure ANTR 22:19
f. consistent POPE 584:2
f. for his client PROV 606:21
F. had stuck himself up BENT 66:19
f. hath said in his heart BOOK 132:5
f. his whole life long LUTH 480:6
f. . . . is a man who never tried DARW 251:4
f. is happy POPE 585:23
f. live here KIPL 439:18
f. may give wise man PROV 600:35
f. returneth to his folly BIBL 83:24
'F.,' said my Muse SIDN 718:9
f.'s bauble, the mace CROM 245:15
f. sees not the same tree BLAK 119:15
f. there was KIPL 440:16
f. uttereth all his mind BIBL 83:33
f. will be meddling BIBL 83:8
f. with booze FAUL 308:2
f. would persist BLAK 119:18
greater f. to admire him BOIL 124:5
greatest f. may ask COLT 230:3
He hated a f. JOHN 418:5
Into a strumpet's f. SHAK 656:6
knowledgeable f. MOLI 525:5
laughter of a f. BIBL 84:13
life time's f. SHAK 669:12
Love's not Time's f. SHAK 705:16
make a man appear a f. DRYD 283:15
more f. am I ANON 19:14
more hope of a f. BIBL 83:25
More people know Tom F. PROV 607:7
muddle-headed f. CERV 200:1
no fool like an old f. PROV 612:28
One f. at least FIEL 309:15
patriot yet, but was a f. DRYD 280:13
perfections of a f. BLAK 120:6
played the f. BIBL 78:37
Prove to me that you're no f. RICE 626:8
say, Thou f. BIBL 93:9
smarts so little as a f. POPE 583:2
So true a f. is love SHAK 704:22
stupendous genius! damned f. BYRO 180:4
suspects himself a f. YOUN 839:7
They f. me SHAK 665:4
Thou f. BIBL 99:22
to manage a f. KIPL 441:18
wise enough to play the f. SHAK 701:31
wise man or a f. BLAK 119:6
wisest f. in Christendom HENR 370:7
foolery *little f.* OXEN 562:14
foolish Beware my f. heart WASH 804:12
could be mighty f. FARQ 307:21
f., fond old man SHAK 680:4
f. son BIBL 82:20
f. thing BIBL 92:20
f. things of the world BIBL 105:29
f. thing was but a toy SHAK 702:22
f. thing well done JOHN 414:19
Forgive our f. ways WHIT 816:5
never said a f. thing EPIT 302:14
No man was more f. JOHN 416:15
pound f. PROV 609:24
saying a f. thing STER 739:13
These f. things MARV 499:9
young and f. YEAT 835:16
foolishest f. act a wise man commits BROW 153:29
foolishness Mix a little f. HORA 389:11
unto the Greeks f. BIBL 105:28
fools all the f. in town TWAI 786:5
Children and f. tell PROV 597:16
flannelled f. at the wicket KIPL 439:6
f. admire POPE 584:24
F. and bairns PROV 600:36
f. and knaves BUCK 159:13
F. are my theme BYRO 177:33
F. ask questions PROV 600:37
F. build houses PROV 600:38
f. by heavenly compulsion SHAK 678:5
F.! For I also had my hour CHES 210:5
F. for luck PROV 600:39
f. go aimlessly UPAN 787:20
F. here below for minor pleasures GRES 353:1
F. out of favour DEFO 255:7
f. rush in POPE 585:3
F. rush in PROV 600:40
f. said would happen MELB 504:3
f., the fools, the fools PEAR 571:7
f., who came to scoff GOLD 344:12
For f. to sing BURN 169:8
Fortune favours f. PROV 600:43
Hated by f. SWIF 749:22
house for f. and mad SWIF 749:20
I am two f. DONN 274:17
kept from children and from f. DRYD 282:19
leaves 'em still two f. CONG 232:11
let f. contest POPE 585:26
lighted f. The way SHAK 685:22
make f. of themselves about SHAW 706:22
millions mostly f. CARL 188:4
money of f. HOBB 378:15
Nature meant but f. POPE 584:11
one half the world f. JEFF 406:2
O, these deliberate f. SHAK 687:26
Paradise of F. MILT 516:5
perish together as f. KING 436:15
plain f. at last POPE 584:12
poor f. decoyed PEPY 573:10
scarecrows of f. HUXL 397:19
shoal of f. CONG 233:7
suffer f. gladly BIBL 107:11
term Invented to awe f. JONS 420:13
this great stage of f. SHAK 680:1
utmost industry bred f. CHUD 213:8
virtue of f. BACO 41:25
what f. these mortals be SHAK 690:5
world is full of f. ANON 20:9
foot accent of a coming F. DICK 266:8
caught my f. in the mat GROS 354:6
f. already in the stirrup CERV 200:7
f. feel, being shod HOPK 384:5
foot—f.—sloggin' KIPL 438:7
f. for foot BIBL 76:14
F.-in-the-grave young man GILB 338:22
f. less prompt ARNO 27:29
f. standeth right BOOK 133:9
Forty-second F. HOOD 382:19
her f. was light KEAT 428:9
hurt not thy f. BOOK 137:23
I hold Creation in my f. HUGH 393:4
Love is swift of f. HERB 372:10
Nay, her f. speaks SHAK 700:20
One f. in sea SHAK 691:7
One white f. PROV 609:8
print of a man's naked f. DEFO 254:20
sets f. upon a worm COWP 242:10
silver f. in his mouth RICH 626:14
sole of her f. BIBL 74:17
squeeze a right-hand f. CARR 191:15
suffer thy f. to be moved BOOK 140:12
Withdraw thy f. BIBL 83:20
with shining f. shall pass FITZ 315:3
football fighting Army f. team RICE 626:5
f. a matter of life and death SHAN 706:6
F. and cookery SMIT 723:16
F. is an art GREE 352:12
F.? the beautiful game PELÉ 572:6
he's f. crazy MCGR 485:12
owe to f. CAMU 184:16
footfalls F. echo in the memory ELIO 294:2
leaves like light f. SHEL 712:11
footman eternal F. hold my coat ELIO 295:8
footnotes series of f. to Plato WHIT 814:18
footpath jog on the f. SHAK 703:12
footprints F. on the sands LONG 474:6
those f. scare me HORA 386:12
footsteps our f. guideth BAKE 48:12
plants his f. in the sea COWP 240:16
footstool it is God's f. BIBL 93:11
thine enemies thy f. BOOK 139:16
foppery f. of the world SHAK 678:5
sound of shallow f. SHAK 687:21
for F. ever panting KEAT 428:26
not f. anything CONF 231:9
who is f. me HILL 377:9
forasmuch f. as without thee BOOK 128:16
forbear Bear and f. PROV 595:36
forbearance f. ceases to be a virtue BURK 162:16
forbid f. them not BIBL 98:10
God f. BIBL 100:20
God f. BIBL 104:37
He shall live a man f. SHAK 681:12
forbidden because it was f. TWAI 786:20
f. tree OPEN 556:5
Of that f. tree MILT 511:7
force By verray f. CHAU 206:21
combines f. with candour CHUR 216:24
driving f. of all WEBE 807:7
every living f. DOST 275:15
F., and fraud HOBB 378:22
F. is not a remedy BRIG 148:15
F. is the food ADVE 7:26
f. that through the green THOM 772:5
F., unaided by judgement HORA 388:18
f. with a manoeuvre TROT 783:19
may the f. be with you FILM 311:23
more than our f. BURK 164:3
motive f. impressed NEWT 543:6
no argument but f. BROW 154:7
no f. however great WHEW 813:14
Not believing in f. TROT 783:20
oppressive f. BARB 53:15
Other nations use 'f.' WAUG 806:15
reduce the use of f. to ORTE 557:16
spent its novel f. TENN 762:23
Surprised by unjust f. MILT 511:27
use of f. alone BURK 162:24
use of *f.* by one class LENI 463:7
Who overcomes By f. MILT 515:2
forces f. impressed upon it NEWT 543:5
two f. were at work HARD 361:1
forcible Most f. Feeble SHAK 670:6
forcibly f. if we must CLAY 220:2
ford I am a F., not a Lincoln FORD 319:12
my friend F. WILL 821:3
forearmed Forewarned is f. PROV 600:42
forefathers be as their f. BOOK 137:4
f. of the hamlet sleep GRAY 350:8
Think of your f. ADAM 3:16
forefinger f. of all Time TENN 765:12

foregone denoted a f. conclusion SHAK 693:2
forehead Flames in the f. MILT 513:10
f. was prodigious HUNT 395:18
foreign avoid f. collision CLAY 220:1
corner of a f. field BROO 150:17
corner of a f. field OPEN 555:14
courtly f. grace TENN 766:12
enriched with f. matter REYN 625:10
far, f. fields DAVI 252:13
f. country DURA 285:18
f. policy: I wage war CLEM 220:10
into any f. wars ROOS 632:16
languished in a f. clime MACA 482:23
Life is a f. language MORL 532:2
nothing human f. to me TERE 768:3
on a f. strand SCOT 650:19
past is a f. country HART 363:13
past is a f. country OPEN 556:11
portion of the f. world WASH 804:6
third-rate f. conductors BEEC 61:7
foreigner possible that a f. TROL 782:21
foreigners f. always spell better TWAI 786:13
f. are fiends MITF 524:9
more f. I saw BELL 64:17
Foreign Secretary attacking the F. BEVA 71:19
F. naked into the conference BEVA 71:20
Foreland Dawn off the F. KIPL 439:16
forelock occasion's f. watchful MILT 518:5
foremost f. in battle BALL 51:5
none who would be f. MACA 483:9
foreplay No f. BENN 65:16
foreseen All is f. TALM 753:19
What I had not f. SPEN 732:24
foresight aftersight and f. ELIO 294:16
forest beasts of the f. BOOK 135:2
beasts of the f. BOOK 139:5
behind it rose the f. LONG 474:12
burning the rain f. STIN 743:7
carry timber to the f. HORA 389:21
Cutting through the f. LIND 469:7
Deep in the f. RACI 619:19
Down in the f. SIMP 720:14
flowers of the f. COCK 223:13
flowers of the f. ELLI 298:9
f. laments CHUR 214:12
f. primeval LONG 473:14
f.'s ferny floor DE L 256:15
hedge is to a f. JOHN 418:1
In the f. CHES 211:6
lost to the f. SCOT 650:13
through an untrodden f. MURR 537:5
To the f. edge DURC 286:2
unfathomable deep f. THOM 773:2
forests fishes flew and f. walked CHES 210:4
F. keep disappearing CHEK 208:11
f. of the night BLAK 121:8
f., with their myriad tongues LONG 474:10
vast f., immense fields CHEK 208:2
foretell ability to f. CHUR 216:21
pretences to f. SWIF 749:4
foretold Long f., long last PROV 605:50
who could have f. YEAT 837:10
forever diamond is f. ADVE 7:13
F., and forever, farewell SHAK 676:30
is a joy f. OPEN 556:22
Man has F. BROW 155:33
picket's off duty f. BEER 61:18
for ever continue thine f. BOOK 130:20
f. hold his peace BOOK 131:3
joy f. KEAT 426:16
mercy endureth f. BOOK 141:6
not be destroyed f. PRAY 592:8
forewarned F. is forearmed PROV 600:42
forfended music of f. spheres PATM 569:21
forgave f. the offence DRYD 281:10
forge barn and the f. HOUS 391:1
f. and working-house SHAK 672:1
my f. decayed EPIT 303:16
forgers liars and f. PÉGU 572:3
forget Better by far you should f. ROSS 634:9
do not quite f. CHES 210:16
do not thou f. me ASTL 31:18
Don't f. the diver CATC 195:10
Don't f. the fruit gums ADVE 7:16
fact that they never f. DRAB 278:13
f. because we must ARNO 26:2
F. her pray'rs POPE 587:4
f. not all his benefits BOOK 138:16
F. six counties MORR 532:13
f. so much DAVI 251:15
f. thee, O Jerusalem BOOK 141:8
f. there ever was such a thing WILS 822:16
f. we are gentlemen BURK 164:19
f. you first ADAM 3:7
forgive but do not f. SZAS 752:1
How long wilt thou f. me BOOK 132:4
if thou wilt, f. ROSS 634:13
I sometimes f. DISR 271:3
knew we should both f. SWIN 751:7
Lest we f. KIPL 440:3
never f. a face MARX 499:12
new-made honour doth f. SHAK 677:6
nor worms f. DICK 263:14
not f. the suspenders KIPL 441:11
Old men f. SHAK 671:24
Sun himself cannot f. ANON 19:1
thou remember and I f. SWIN 751:10
to communicate f. not BIBL 110:9
unforgetful to f. ROSS 635:4
will I not f. thee BIBL 88:11
you'll f. 'em all POPE 587:1
forgets bellowing cow soon f. PROV 595:43
forgetting consist in merely f. MAND 493:10
F. those things BIBL 108:21
grand memory for f. STEV 741:6
sleep and a f. WORD 829:20
world f. POPE 582:24
forgive allows you to f. yourself SHAW 708:32
do not f. those murderers WIES 816:17
do they f. them WILD 818:27
Father, f. them BIBL 100:26
f. enemies BLAK 120:5
f. him BIBL 96:11
f. him anything COLL 229:4
F., O Lord, my little jokes FROS 325:17
F. our foolish ways WHIT 816:5
f. our friends MEDI 503:9
f. them as a Christian AUST 38:24
f. those who were right MACL 487:5
f. us our debts BIBL 93:19
f. us our trespasses BOOK 125:18
f. wrongs darker than death SHEL 713:16
lambs could not f. DICK 263:14
Lord will f. me CATH 194:12
mercy to f. DRYD 281:19
seldom f. twice LAVA 454:12
to f. a wrong ELEA 291:15
To f., divine POPE 584:27
to f. divine PROV 613:8
To know all is to f. all PROV 613:9
Wilt thou f. that sin DONN 273:6
wise f. but do not forget SZAS 752:1
woman can f. a man MAUG 502:1
Women can't f. failure CHEK 208:6
would f. you ALAI 10:1
forgiven f. everything SHAW 708:30
Her sins are f. BIBL 99:6
restored, f. LYTE 481:1
forgiveness After such knowledge, what f. ELIO 294:22
ask of thee f. SHAK 680:6
F. of each vice BLAK 118:18
F. of sins BOOK 126:10
F. to the injured DRYD 281:6
forgiveth f. sins BIBL 91:16
forgot auld acquaintance be f. BURN 166:11
auld acquaintance be f. OPEN 556:15
by the world f. POPE 582:24
curiosities would be quite f. AUBR 32:12
F. it not ROSS 634:15
f. the fart ELIZ 297:12
f. the taste of fears SHAK 685:21
I have f. my part SHAK 660:13
just f. to duck DEMP 257:5
names ignoble, born to be f. COWP 240:25
Napoleon f. Blücher CHUR 214:16
proposed as things f. POPE 585:1
she f. the stars KEAT 428:3
forgotten always a f. thing CHES 210:3
been learned has been f. SKIN 721:17
books undeservedly f. AUDE 35:15
F. Army MOUN 534:9
f. as a nameless number PAST 569:6
f. even by God BROW 157:5
f. man at the bottom ROOS 632:10
f. nothing and learnt nothing DUMO 285:1
hast thou f. CRAW 244:17
he himself had f. it PALM 566:8
I am all f. SHAK 656:17
injury is much sooner f. CHES 209:8
learnt nothing and f. nothing TALL 753:7
not one of them is f. BIBL 99:20
ruins of f. times BROW 152:18
things one has f. CANE 184:18
Thou hast f. SWIN 751:11
fork pick up mercury with a f. LLOY 471:8
forked poor, bare, f. animal SHAK 679:4
forks made before f. PROV 600:24
pursued it with f. CARR 191:25
forlorn faery lands f. KEAT 429:14
F.! the very word KEAT 429:15
maiden all f. NURS 551:7
wait f. ARNO 27:21
form earth was without f. BIBL 73:10
find a f. BECK 59:19
F. follows function SULL 745:15
f. from off my door POE 579:18
F. is emptiness MAHĀ 490:2
f. of a servant BIBL 108:16
f. of sound words BIBL 109:21
F. remains WORD 831:15
f. the key to organic life PAST 569:5
human f. divine BLAK 121:11
lick it into f. BURT 170:5
mould of f. SHAK 664:10
no action or physical f. CHUA 213:4
no f. nor comeliness BIBL 88:15
Thou, silent f. KEAT 428:29
To every F. of being WORD 828:14
formal every f. visit AUST 38:27
f. feeling comes DICK 266:5
formalistic more f. than conservatives CALV 182:9
formed him that f. it BIBL 105:13
perhaps it f. itself RIG 627:17
small, but perfectly f. COOP 236:6
former f. and the latter BOOK 127:20
f. days were better BIBL 84:15
f. things are passed away BIBL 113:8
formerly not what we were f. told BLUN 122:12
formosa *F. facies muta commendatio* PUBL 616:10
forms By f. unseen COLL 229:10
f. of government POPE 585:26
f. of things unknown SHAK 690:19
give A breath to f. BYRO 177:32
I like definite f. STEV 741:17
formula 'f.' of the atomic bomb MEDA 503:4
fornication F., and all uncleanness BIBL 108:6
fors *F. dierum cumque dabit* HORA 387:20
forsake f. me not BOOK 136:16
F. not an old friend BIBL 91:24
nor f. thee BIBL 77:16
forsaken never the righteous f. BOOK 133:26
O, father f. JOYC 422:18
primrose that f. dies MILT 513:8
utterly f. BETT 71:11
why hast thou f. me BIBL 97:29
why hast thou f. me BOOK 132:21
forsaking f. all other BOOK 131:4
forsworn so sweetly were f. SHAK 686:21
fort Hold the f. BLIS 122:2
Hold the f. SHER 716:27

fortes *Vixere f.* HORA 389:9
forth F. in thy name WESL 811:3
F., pilgrim CHAU 207:24
fortifications f. called castles ORDE 557:12
Fortissimo F. at last MAHL 490:16
fortiter *pecca f.* LUTH 479:12
fortitude f. the Soul contains DICK 266:8
fortnight beyond the next f. CHAM 200:12
f. dead ELIO 296:12
fortress f. built by Nature SHAK 694:19
petty f. JOHN 411:16
fortresses brambles in the f. BIBL 87:20
fortuna *Audentis F. iuvat* VIRG 795:9
fortunate at best but f. SOLO 727:9
better to be f. WEBS 808:16
farmers excessively f. VIRG 796:17
fortunatus *F. et ille deos qui novit* VIRG 796:19
fortune architect of own f. PROV 599:34
Base F. MARL 496:11
beauty without a f. FARQ 307:9
Blind F. still Bestows JONS 419:22
Caesar and his f. CAES 180:19
do F. what she can DRAY 278:23
face is my f. NURS 551:20
F. assists the brave TERE 768:4
F. favours fools PROV 600:43
F. favours the brave PROV 600:44
F. list to flee CHAU 205:28
F.'s a right whore WEBS 808:7
f.s sharpe adversitee CHAU 207:12
F., that favours fools JONS 419:8
F., wilt thou prove THOM 775:17
good f. than a good husband OSBO 559:19
good f. to others BIER 114:20
good housewife F. SHAK 658:8
great, ere f. made him so DRYD 281:15
he shall see F. BACO 42:33
hostages to f. BACO 43:17
how does f. banter us BOLI 124:17
I am F.'s fool SHAK 697:24
leads on to f. SHAK 676:28
leave the rest to f. EURI 304:17
little value of f. STEE 737:2
method of making a f. GRAY 351:5
mother of good f. CERV 200:4
mould of a man's f. BACO 42:32
outrageous f. SHAK 664:3
people of f. ELIO 293:10
possession of a good f. AUST 38:14
possession of a good f. OPEN 555:22
rob a lady of her f. FIEL 310:12
secret parts of F. SHAK 663:15
sick in f. SHAK 678:5
smiling of F. COCK 223:12
smith of his own f. CLAU 219:18
take good f. MOLI 525:21
to f. and to fame unknown GRAY 350:14
upon a plentiful f. JOHN 413:9
with f. and men's eyes SHAK 704:13
Women and f. WYCH 834:10
You fools of f. SHAK 699:18
fortunes content with his f. fit SHAK 678:26
my f. have SHAK 657:8
forty at f., the judgement FRAN 323:11
Every man over f. SHAW 708:29
fairy when she's f. HENL 369:18
Fat, fair and f. O'KE 553:8
fool at f. PROV 600:34
fool at f. YOUN 838:18
f. days it will remain PROV 610:20
f. stripes save one BIBL 107:13
F. years long BOOK 138:6
F. years on BOWE 145:7
In f. minutes SHAK 689:24
Knows it at f. YOUN 839:7
Life begins at f. PITK 576:18
Life begins at f. PROV 605:25
look young till f. DRYD 282:2
Men at f. JUST 423:19
miner, F.-niner MONT 529:4
When f. winters shall besiege SHAK 704:6
forty-five At f., what next LOWE 478:1
forty-three pass for f. GILB 339:12
forward F., forward let us range TENN 763:9
f. motion love VAUG 790:10
from this day f. BOOK 131:5
look f. to posterity BURK 163:16
looking f. to the past OSBO 560:7
marched breast f. BROW 155:4
nothing to look f. to FROS 325:18
those behind cried 'F.!' MACA 483:9
to push things f. MOWL 534:10
Foss F. is the name of his cat LEAR 460:15
fossil Language is f. poetry EMER 299:27
foster f.-child of silence KEAT 428:21
f.-child of silence OPEN 556:23
fostered F. alike by beauty WORD 830:23
fou f. for weeks thegither BURN 168:11
f. man and a fasting SCOT 652:3
f. o' brandy BURN 167:12
I wasna f. BURN 166:27
fought better to have f. and lost CLOU 223:1
f. against me BOOK 140:24
f. against Sisera BIBL 77:27
f. a good fight BIBL 109:23
f. a long hour SHAK 669:17
f. each other for SOUT 730:12
f. the dogs BROW 157:10
to have f. well COUB 238:3
we f. at Arques HENR 370:5
foul F. as their soil BYRO 175:22
F. deeds will rise SHAK 662:7
f. Fiend BUNY 160:18
f. is fair SHAK 681:7
f.-mouthed nation HAZL 365:21
however f. within CHUR 214:1
Murder most f. SHAK 662:27
really f. things up SAYI 648:7
So f. and fair a day SHAK 681:14
some f. play SHAK 662:6
soon be made so f. BERN 69:4
thank the gods I am f. SHAK 659:14
too f. an epithet MARL 496:28
ways be f. SHAK 681:4
foulest commonly the f. BACO 41:19
foully play'dst most f. for't SHAK 683:24
fouls f. its own nest PROV 604:31
found awoke and f. me here KEAT 428:13
f. a kingdom MILT 518:6
F. him in the shining TENN 760:9
f. my sheep which was lost BIBL 99:33
f. no more of her BIBL 80:27
f. the Roman nation VIRG 793:6
Hast thou f. me BIBL 80:8
man who has f. himself out BARR 55:21
was lost, and is f. BIBL 100:6
When f., make a note DICK 262:13
foundation Church's one f. STON 743:9
f. of all good things BURK 164:6
f. of most governments ADAM 3:15
f. of the earth BOOK 138:15
f. of unyielding despair RUSS 639:21
foundations city which hath f. BIBL 109:29
earth's f. fled HOUS 390:9
f. of the earth BIBL 81:31
f. of the earth BOOK 139:1
founded f. the Jewish state HERZ 375:9
founder f. and embellisher CAXT 198:16
founding f. a bank BREC 147:19
fount f. whence honour springs MARL 496:27
Slow, slow, fresh f. JONS 419:16
fountain Back to the burning f. SHEL 710:22
Doth a f. send forth BIBL 110:20
f. filled with blood COWP 240:20
f. momently was forced COLE 225:21
f. of all goodness BOOK 126:16
f. of delights LUCR 479:9
f. of good sense DRYD 283:12
f. of honour BACO 42:2
f. of the water of life BIBL 113:9
f. sealed BIBL 85:16
f.'s sliding foot MARV 498:17
healing f. AUDE 34:4
It is that f. RALE 620:10
like a f. troubled SHAK 698:13
Like a summer-dried f. SCOT 650:13
next a f., spouting POPE 583:21
fountains Afric's sunny f. HEBE 367:6
f. mingle with the river SHEL 712:7
living f. AKEN 9:4
sad f. ANON 19:10
silver f. mud SHAK 704:18
founts White f. falling CHES 210:9
four all f.-footed things CHES 210:4
At the age of f. USTI 788:24
fiery f.-in-hand COLE 227:26
f. beasts full of eyes BIBL 111:31
F. eyes see more PROV 600:45
f.-footed beasts BIBL 103:28
f. for a birth PROV 608:37
F. lagging winters SHAK 694:12
f.-legged friend BROO 151:8
F. legs good ORWE 558:6
f.-letter word ANNA 15:1
f.-year-old child could FILM 312:11
say that two plus two make f. ORWE 558:24
twice two be not f. TURG 785:7
fourscore come to f. years BOOK 137:19
fourteen first f. years GREE 351:22
fourteenth f. Mr Wilson HOME 381:19
fourth f. estate of the realm MACA 481:9
fous *C'étaient des f.* RENO 624:16
fowl f. of the air BIBL 73:14
liver-wing of a f. TENN 767:16
fowler snare of the f. BOOK 140:17
fowls all small f. singis DOUG 276:12
Barn-door f. for dissenters SMIT 725:11
f. of the air BIBL 93:23
f. of the air BIBL 103:28
f. of the air BOOK 139:2
smale f. maken melodye CHAU 204:7
fox beset the historical f. HUXL 397:10
certain f. wanted LA F 447:14
Crazy like a f. PERE 573:17
f. from his lair in the morning GRAV 349:10
f.-hunting—the wisest religion HAIL 356:10
f. is off to his den NURS 549:19
f. knows many things ARCH 23:17
F. who was my friend READ 622:12
galloping after a f. WILD 818:24
loves the f. less SURT 746:19
mentality of a f. at large LEVI 466:8
people that think, and f.-hunters SHEN 715:9
prince must be a f. MACH 486:2
quick brown f. ANON 18:11
sharp hot stink of f. HUGH 393:8
They've shot our f. BIRC 115:11
what the wary f. said HORA 386:12
foxed If ever I was f. PEPY 572:21
foxes f. have a sincere interest ELIO 292:9
f. have holes BIBL 94:19
f., that spoil the vines BIBL 85:11
portion for f. BOOK 135:25
second to the f. BERL 68:15
foxholes no atheists in the f. CUMM 247:14
signs on the f. KENN 433:16
foxlike f. in the vine TENN 766:5
frabjous O f. day CARR 190:13
fraction wretched f. CARL 187:7
fragment not a geographical f. PARN 567:25
fragments f. that remain BIBL 101:26
These f. I have shored ELIO 296:14
fragrance Isles of f. POPE 580:23
frail F. crowds MOOR 530:6
frailty concession to human f. TAWN 755:15
f. of our nature BOOK 128:3
f. of the mind SHAD 655:11
F., thy name is woman SHAK 661:26
love's the noblest f. DRYD 281:27
therefore more f. SHAK 668:29
frame f. in the earth SPEN 734:7
f. of adamant JOHN 411:15
f. of nature ADDI 4:23
f. of the world BERK 68:3
my f. perish BYRO 175:2
universal f. BACO 42:6

framed f. and glazed WALP 801:2
français *n'est pas f.* RIVA 628:15
France better in F. STER 738:5
between F. and England JERR 407:4
by which F. is fed SULL 746:2
F., famed in all great arts ARNO 28:1
F. has lost a battle DE G 255:18
F. is a person MICH 507:1
F., mother of arts DU B 283:21
F. wants you to take part CHIR 212:5
F. was long a despotism CARL 187:25
F. will say that I am a German EINS 290:12
I now speak for F. DE G 255:19
lived a singer in F. SWIN 751:18
one illusion—F. KEYN 435:4
Political thought, in F. ARON 29:18
round hose in F. SHAK 687:9
safeguard against F. ADEN 6:3
stood the wind for F. DRAY 279:9
sweet enemy, F. SIDN 718:13
vasty fields of F. SHAK 670:26
wield the sword of F. DE G 255:20
Francesca di Rimini F., miminy GILB 338:21
Frankie F. and Albert SONG 729:5
frankincense f., and myrrh BIBL 92:23
frankly F., my dear FILM 311:7
frantic fascination f. GILB 338:16
frater *f., ave atque vale* CATU 198:1
Fraternité *Égalité F.* POLI 581:24
fraternize beckon you to f. AUDE 34:19
fratrum *Par nobile f.* HORA 389:23
fraud Force, and f. HOBB 378:22
May is a pious f. LOWE 477:17
frauds all great men are f. BONA 125:4
frays f. at every touch FLAU 316:19
freak grotesque composite f. HENN 370:3
freaks F. born with their trauma ARBU 23:12
freckled f. like a pard KEAT 428:14
Whatever is fickle, f. HOPK 384:15
freckles curiosity, f., and doubt PARK 567:2
In those f. SHAK 689:17
Fred Here lies F. EPIT 303:1
Frederick death of F. the Great BISM 116:14
free as any spirit f. CHAU 205:11
as soon write f. verse FROS 326:18
be f. SHEL 715:2
be perfectly f. SPEN 732:10
best things are f. PROV 595:49
best things in life are f. DE S 259:3
Bind me, or set me f. GODO 342:3
bond nor f. BIBL 109:4
born f. ANON 15:6
born f. as Caesar SHAK 674:10
but it's f. KRIS 446:2
Church shall be f. MAGN 489:11
Comment is f. SCOT 650:4
condemned to be f. SART 645:2
England should be f. MAGE 489:10
Ev'rything f. in America SOND 727:20
favours f. speech BROU 151:17
f. again SOLZ 727:10
f. agent AURE 37:7
f. and immortal TRAH 780:12
f. as nature first made man DRYD 281:5
F. at last EPIT 302:7
f. church CAVO 198:15
freedom the the f. LINC 468:12
f. man, an American JOHN 408:10
f. society is a society where STEV 740:12
Greece might still be f. BYRO 176:26
half f. LINC 468:5
I am a f. man MCGO 485:8
I am not f. DEBS 254:9
ignorant and f. JEFF 405:19
in a f. country BURK 163:4
in chains than to be f. KAFK 425:8
I was f. born BIBL 104:16
know our will is f. JOHN 414:2
land of the f. KEY 434:16
let him go f. BOOK 139:9
Man was born f. ROUS 636:5
men everywhere could be f. LINC 468:11
Mother of the F. BENS 66:13
naturally were born f. MILT 520:3
No f. man shall be taken MAGN 489:12
no such thing as a f. lunch SAYI 648:4
not a f. press but a managed RADC 620:3
not f. either SOLZ 727:13
not only to be f. PANK 566:12
protection of f. speech HOLM 381:14
set f. in our remembering BERR 69:16
should themselves be f. BROO 150:6
so far kept us f. JEFF 405:12
Teach the f. man AUDE 34:4
that moment they are f. COWP 241:20
Thou art f. ARNO 27:13
Thought is f. PROV 612:44
Thought is f. SHAK 699:3
truth makes men f. AGAR 6:14
truth shall make you f. BIBL 101:35
Was he f. AUDE 35:10
We must be f. or die WORD 828:24
wholly slaves or wholly f. DRYD 281:21
Who would be f. BYRO 174:6
free-born f. mouse BARB 53:15
freed f. my soul BERN 69:3
freedom abridging the f. of speech CONS 235:12
apprenticeship for f. BARA 53:12
better organised than f. PÉGU 572:4
bondage which is f.'s self SHEL 713:18
But what is F. COLE 224:16
cause of F. BOWL 146:1
conditioned to a f. KENY 434:3
Conservative ideal of f. MADA 488:20
destroy the f. ADAM 3:13
enemies of f. do not argue INGE 399:3
fight for f. and truth IBSE 398:7
first is f. of speech ROOS 632:18
for f. freedom SPEN 732:9
For the sake of f. ZORO 841:18
F. alone he earns GOET 343:2
F. alone substitutes TOCQ 777:17
F. and not servitude BURK 163:2
F. and slavery are mental states GAND 329:5
F. and Whisky BURN 166:14
F. an English subject's DRYD 282:27
F. cannot exist METT 506:8
f. depends on being courageous THUC 776:22
f. for the one who thinks differently LUXE 480:8
f. for the pike TAWN 755:14
F. has a thousand charms COWP 241:14
F. hunted PAIN 563:14
F. is an indivisible word WILL 821:8
f. is a noble thing BARB 53:21
f. is but a light GUMI 354:19
f. is excellent TOCQ 778:7
F. is not a gift NKRU 546:10
F. is slavery ORWE 558:21
f. is something BALD 49:1
F. is the freedom to say ORWE 558:24
f. of person JEFF 405:14
f. of speech TWAI 786:8
F. of the press guaranteed LIEB 467:19
F. of the press in Britain SWAF 747:9
f. of the press's speech TWAI 786:16
F.'s banner DRAK 278:21
F. shrieked—as Kosciuszko fell CAMP 183:14
F.'s just another word KRIS 446:2
F. slowly broadens down TENN 767:15
f. to offend RUSH 637:18
f. to the slave LINC 468:12
f. women were supposed BURC 161:22
from slavery to f. HAGG 356:2
gave my life for f. EWER 305:11
give to man F. GRAI 348:12
green f. of a cockatoo STEV 740:5
I gave them f. GORB 346:18
it means f. RUSH 638:2
Let f. ring SMIT 724:16
love not f., but licence MILT 520:2
means by defending f. NIEM 545:7
no easy walk-over to f. NEHR 540:8
obtained I this f. BIBL 104:16
O F., what liberties are taken GEOR 334:10
own true f. MONT 527:14
participation of f. BURK 163:6
peace from f. MALC 492:1
Perfect f. is reserved COLL 228:11
plan for f. POPP 587:27
preserve and enlarge f. LOCK 472:1
riches and f. WAŁĘ 799:4
rights of f. JUNI 423:15
road toward f. MORR 533:1
service is perfect f. BOOK 126:12
taste of F. PALI 565:15
there can be no f. LENI 463:8
unless f. is universal HILL 376:12
freedoms four essential human f. ROOS 632:18
F. you'll not to me allow BEHN 62:11
freehold given to none f. LUCR 479:6
freeing f. some LINC 468:11
freely F. ye have received BIBL 94:32
Freeman F. butters Stubbs ROGE 631:17
freemasonry bitter f. BEER 61:15
freemen Americans are to be f. WASH 804:4
great nursery of f. SHIP 717:6
only f., are the only slaves MASS 501:4
rule o'er f. BROO 150:6
freewoman he of the f. BIBL 107:19
freeze f. my humanity MACN 488:13
f. thy young blood SHAK 662:25
freezes Yours till Hell f. FISH 313:16
freezings What f. have I felt SHAK 705:8
frei *Arbeit macht f.* ANON 20:16
freight literature goes as f. GARC 329:12
shall have her earthly f. WORD 830:4
Freiheit *F. is immer nur* LUXE 480:8
freits follows f. PROV 602:13
French always have spoken F. VOLT 798:9
Before F. culture RENA 624:11
drawn out of F. MALO 492:12
F. are wiser BACO 44:1
F. are with equal advantage CANN 184:19
F. arrange CATH 194:6
F. dinner at nine FLEM 317:20
F. government COLO 230:1
F. is the *patois* BAGE 47:20
F. of Parys CHAU 204:13
F., or Turk GILB 339:1
F. Revolution operated TOCQ 778:8
F. want no-one to be TOCQ 778:17
F. widow in every bedroom HOFF 380:9
glory of beating the F. WOLF 825:7
how it's improved her F. GRAH 348:2
If the F. noblesse TREV 781:8
Learning F. is some trouble EMPS 300:10
new F. books BROW 155:9
no more F. ANON 18:2
not clear is not F. RIVA 628:15
not too French F. bean GILB 338:19
Paris was F.—and silent TUCH 784:16
professor of F. letters JOYC 422:16
Speak in F. CARR 190:16
to men F. CHAR 203:16
to the F. the empire of the land RICH 627:12
We are not F. MONT 528:14
We F., we English BIRN 115:12
Frenchman must hate a F. NELS 540:13
Frenchmen beat three F. ADDI 5:8
beat three F. PROV 608:36
Fifty million F. MILI 508:7
frenzy Demoniac f. MILT 517:24
poet's eye, in a fine f. SHAK 690:19
What is life? a f. CALD 181:5
frequency very fact of f. ELIO 292:24
frequent f. hearses POPE 582:20
frère *Sois mon f.* CHAM 201:10
frères *f. humains après nous* VILL 792:19
fresh ancient and so f. AUGU 36:5
f. air and fun EDGA 288:9
f. as is the month of May CHAU 204:10
F. as the Angel BYRO 173:18
f. lap of the crimson rose SHAK 689:21

fresh (*cont.*):
F. shalt thou see in me DANI 248:19
It's tingling f. ADVE 7:35
nice *f.* corpse TWAI 786:15
O yonge, f. folkes CHAU 207:20
So sad, so f. TENN 765:20
fret fever, and the f. KEAT 429:9
f. a passage through FULL 327:11
F. not thyself BOOK 133:25
O f. not after knowledge KEAT 430:2
frets struts and f. his hour SHAK 685:22
fretted F. the pigmy body DRYD 279:21
Freud trouble with F. DODD 271:18
Freude F., *schöner Götterfunken* SCHI 646:14
Freudian still had her F. papa LOWE 477:20
friar turned fasting f. MERE 505:12
friars cannot all be f. CERV 199:18
f. were singing vespers GIBB 335:25
fricassee f., or a ragout SWIF 748:13
Friday F.'s child NURS 549:14
My man F. DEFO 254:21
on a F. fil al this meschaunce CHAU 206:5
one F. morn SONG 729:15
friend angry with my f. BLAK 121:5
as you choose a f. DILL 267:13
betraying my f. FORS 321:4
Boldness be my f. SHAK 660:18
candid f. CANN 185:3
Codlin's the f. DICK 264:10
countervail a f. GRIM 353:14
damned goodnatured f. SHER 715:14
diamonds a girl's best f. ROBI 629:9
ease some f. POPE 583:4
faithful female f. WHUR 816:11
familiar f. BOOK 134:4
fat f. BRUM 158:21
favourite has no f. GRAY 350:21
forgave a f. BLAK 120:5
Forsake not an old f. BIBL 91:24
four-legged f. BROO 151:8
F. and associate of this clay HADR 355:11
f.-and-relation MILN 510:12
f. friend BIBL 91:20
F., go up higher BIBL 99:25
f. in need PROV 600:48
f. in power ADAM 2:17
f. loveth at all times BIBL 83:3
f. of every country CANN 185:1
F. of my better days HALL 358:10
F. of the humble SIKH 719:11
f. should bear SHAK 676:24
f. sincere enough BULW 160:9
f. that sticketh closer BIBL 83:6
f. that will go to jail BURN 165:19
F., wherefore BIBL 97:24
He was my f. SHAK 675:30
homes without a f. CLAR 218:13
house to lodge a f. SWIF 749:7
I finds a f. DIBD 260:12
I lose a f. SARG 644:17
In every f. we lose a part POPE 587:16
Is such a f. COWP 240:5
I would not use a f. HERB 373:15
last best f. am I SOUT 730:18
lay down his wife for his f. JOYC 422:16
Little F. of all the World KIPL 441:14
look like a f. SHAK 661:18
lose her as a f. GLAD 341:16
lose your f. PROV 605:14
loss of a dear f. SOUT 731:6
lost no f. POPE 584:6
Lover for a f. ETHE 301:14
makes not f. TENN 759:30
man, That love my f. SHAK 676:9
mine own familiar f. BOOK 135:11
mistress or a f. SHEL 711:8
My f. may spit HERB 373:16
no f. like a sister ROSS 634:4
Nor a f. to know me STEV 743:1
not a f. to close his eyes DRYD 280:19
O f. unseen FLEC 317:7
only way to have a f. EMER 299:17
poor man's dearest f. BURN 167:27
pretended f. is worse GAY 332:10
religious book, or f. WOTT 832:23
'Strange f.,' I said OWEN 562:12
think of him as a f. SMIT 724:25
To find a f. DOUG 276:17
want a f. in need DICK 262:13
Whatever you think of your f. MIDR 507:12
What is a f. ARIS 25:10
Whenever a f. succeeds VIDA 792:10
wounds of a f. BIBL 83:29
your enemy and your f. TWAI 786:11
your f. that loves you SHAK 674:6
friendless f. bodies of unburied men WEBS 808:13
Omnipotent but f. SHEL 713:11
friends All her family and her f. CORS 237:10
best f. hear no more SHEL 712:1
best of f. TUPP 784:18
best of f. must part SONG 730:5
by their unmarried f. TROL 783:12
choice of f. COWL 239:15
closest f. won't tell you ADVE 7:18
comes to meet one's f. BURN 165:27
distresses of our f. SWIF 749:23
documents and f. SPAR 731:16
doubt one's f. LA R 453:13
Fair face show f. GOOG 346:13
falling out of faithful f. EDWA 289:13
f. are necessarily USTI 788:22
f. do not need it HUBB 392:10
f.' houses JOHN 417:1
f. in the garrison HALI 357:7
f. must part PROV 595:46
f. of every country DISR 269:17
F. part forever BASH 56:15
F., Romans, countrymen SHAK 675:27
f. thou hast SHAK 662:10
f. were not unearthly beautiful RICH 626:13
His f. he loved WATS 805:3
his only f. CAMP 183:24
I had such f. YEAT 836:19
I have lost f. WOOL 827:2
in the house of God as f. BOOK 135:11
I wish thee f. CORB 236:14
lay down his f. for his life THOR 778:21
letter to the f. STEV 741:14
life for his f. BIBL 102:22
love of f. BELL 64:10
Make to yourselves f. BIBL 100:8
misfortune of our best f. LA R 453:21
Money couldn't buy f. MILL 510:7
my f. pictured within ELGA 291:17
my list of f. COWP 242:10
nearly deceiving your f. CORN 237:6
new city of F. WHIT 815:2
none of his f. like him WILD 819:11
no true f. in politics CLAR 219:2
Old f. are best SELD 653:14
old f. to trust BACO 41:20
Our f., the enemy BÉRA 67:13
Save us from our f. PROV 610:21
separateth very f. BIBL 83:2
Some of my best f. are white DURE 286:3
tavern for his f. DOUG 276:19
tell it to your f. MONT 528:18
thousand f. ALI 12:2
to all thy f. BIBL 89:21
treat my f. MALL 492:5
two close f. LERM 464:21
want of f. BRET 148:3
we are f. BREC 147:12
win f. and influence people CARN 189:1
with a little help from my f. LENN 464:4
friendship cultivate your f. JOHN 416:24
disease called f. RENO 624:15
dupe of f. HAZL 365:7
Every long f. LAMB 448:9
f. closes its eyes ANON 20:8
f. ever ends in love GAY 332:5
F. from knowledge BUSS 171:5
f. in constant repair JOHN 412:21
F. is a disinterested commerce GOLD 345:13
F. is constant SHAK 691:4
F. is Love BYRO 178:11
F. not always the sequel JOHN 410:10
f. recognised by the police STEV 741:27
f. with all nations JEFF 405:13
In f. false DRYD 280:4
little f. in the world BACO 42:31
Most f. is feigning SHAK 659:5
to f. clear CARE 186:9
treating of f. THOM 771:12
two for f. THOR 776:11
friendships F. begin with liking ELIO 292:6
frieze no striped f. STRA 744:6
frigate no F. like a Book DICK 266:10
fright f. and a hiss DEAN 253:18
wake in a f. BARH 54:5
frighted f. with false fire SHAK 664:26
frighten by God, they f. me WELL 809:14
f. the horses CAMP 182:16
f. those who might hate her AUST 37:12
frightened children are f. of me GEOR 334:6
than f. to death SURT 747:1
frightening never more f. VAN 789:13
frightful f.'s when one's dead POPE 584:4
frigid f. as their snows BYRO 175:22
fringèd f. curtains of thine eye SHAK 698:28
frisch *F. weht der Wind* WAGN 798:18
fritter 'Fry me!' or 'F.-my-wig!' CARR 191:20
Friuli blue F.'s mountains BYRO 174:25
frocks F. and Curls DICK 266:19
frog f. he would a-wooing go NURS 548:6
f. remains ROST 635:14
leap-splash—a f. BASH 56:17
toe of f. SHAK 684:18
frogs F. and snails NURS 551:19
F. are slightly better MITF 524:9
f. don't die for 'fun' BION 115:10
F. eat Butterflies STEV 739:22
from F. far, from eve HOUS 391:4
front F. and back follow LAO 451:6
present your f. to the world MOLI 524:16
to which f. OWEN 562:10
frontier f.-grave is far away NEWB 541:17
f. of my Person AUDE 34:19
how f. KENN 433:8
frontiers old f. are gone BALD 49:9
frost abide his f. BOOK 141:26
but a f. of cares TICH 777:10
diadem of f. BLOK 122:6
f. performs its secret ministry COLE 225:12
Heavy as f. WORD 830:4
His graver of f. THOM 774:17
like an untimely f. SHAK 697:37
lovely Morning, rich in f. DAVI 252:9
secret ministry of f. COLE 225:17
Thaw not the f. SHEL 710:13
third day comes a f. SHAK 673:12
frostbite God of f. VYAZ 798:17
frosts Dews, and F. BOOK 126:6
f. are slain SWIN 750:6
hoary-headed f. SHAK 689:21
so many f. in May PROV 611:7
frosty F., but kindly SHAK 658:16
f. starlight ARNO 27:18
froth mostly f. and bubble GORD 346:19
Froude goes to F. for history STUB 745:3
froward f. generation BIBL 77:12
like a f. child TEMP 757:5
frown fear at your f. ENGL 300:13
libel in a f. SWIF 749:9
make the sweetest love to f. GREE 352:4
So much as f. on you SHAK 677:14
without f. or smile SEDL 653:3
frowning Behind a f. providence COWP 240:18
frozen F. anger FREU 324:19
f. in an out-of-date mould JENK 406:7
f. music SCHE 646:13
indifference or f. stare ELIO 292:21
locked and f. in each eye AUDE 34:2
milk comes f. home SHAK 681:4

on the f. hills TENN 760:13
over the f. chicken BINC 115:5
sends the f.-ground-swell FROS 326:4
through the f. grass KEAT 427:3
torrid or the f. zone CARE 186:11
Your tiny hand is f. GIAC 335:3
fructify [Money should] f. GLAD 341:15
frugal She had a f. mind COWP 240:13
fruges *f. consumere nati* HORA 386:14
fruit bore thy f. and mine KYD 446:10
bring forth f. BOOK 127:20
brought forth f. BIBL 95:20
delicate exotic f. WILD 817:15
eateth not of the f. BIBL 106:8
eats of the sweet f. UPAN 788:5
everything is f. AURE 36:22
f. fails, welcome haws PROV 614:17
f. of good works BOOK 128:20
f. Of that forbidden tree MILT 514:7
f. Of that forbidden tree OPEN 556:5
f. of the Spirit BIBL 107:21
f. of thy womb PRAY 592:1
f., she plucked MILT 517:17
f.'s in the loft PROV 610:31
f. that can fall MONT 526:13
green f. would swell KEAT 427:1
Hang there like f. SHAK 661:3
Man stole the f. HERB 373:10
Some f. for him HERB 372:15
Stolen f. is sweet PROV 611:24
too little f. SCOT 652:16
tree is known by his f. BIBL 95:12
tree is known by its f. PROV 613:17
trees bear strange f. HOLI 380:20
weakest kind of f. SHAK 688:8
would eat the f. PROV 602:21
fruitful as the f. vine BOOK 140:23
Be f., and multiply BIBL 73:16
f. ground SURR 746:8
f. hill BIBL 86:15
fruitfulness mellow f. KEAT 430:8
mellow f. OPEN 556:14
fruition f. of an earthly crown MARL 496:26
F.'s dull SUCK 745:6
fruits By their f. BIBL 94:11
eat his pleasant f. BIBL 85:17
first f. of them that slept BIBL 106:22
flowers and f. of love BYRO 178:22
f., and foliage, not my own COLE 225:5
kindly f. of the earth BOOK 127:13
Like Dead Sea f. MOOR 530:19
frustra *Nisi Dominus f.* MOTT 535:11
frustrate each f. ghost BROW 158:4
F. their knavish tricks SONG 729:8
fry scribbling f. YOUN 838:19
Such as 'F. me!' CARR 191:20
frying-pan frizzled in my f. ENGE 300:12
f. of your words FLAU 316:11
talks In the f. DE L 256:8
fuck Fish f. in it FIEL 310:21
f. all in between BENN 65:16
They f. you up, your mum and dad LARK 453:4
zipless f. JONG 419:6
fudge two-fifths sheer f. LOWE 477:13
fugaces *Eheu f. Labuntur anni* HORA 388:8
fugit *f. inreparabile tempus* VIRG 797:1
fugitive f. and cloistered virtue MILT 519:10
f. from th' law of averages MAUL 502:8
Führer *ein F.* POLI 581:11
fuimus *F. Troes* VIRG 794:4
Fuji F. through mist BASH 56:16
fulfil F. now, O Lord BOOK 126:18
not to destroy, but to f. BIBL 93:7
fulfilled f. a long time BIBL 91:10
fulfilling f. his word BOOK 141:27
full commonplace book be f. SWIF 748:21
F. cup, steady hand PROV 601:2
F. fathom five SHAK 698:27
f. man and a fasting PROV 604:34
F. speed ahead FARR 307:24
f. tide of human existence JOHN 414:27
in f.-throated ease KEAT 429:6
let me be f. METH 506:6
Serenely f., the epicure SMIT 725:22
fuller f.'s earth for reputations GAY 331:14
fullness f. of the heart PROV 609:16
fulmen *Eripuit coelo f.* TURG 785:9
fulmina *Bruta f.* PLIN 578:16
fulness f. thereof BIBL 106:13
fum *Fy, fa, f.* NASH 539:20
fume black, stinking f. JAME 402:12
fumitor Crowned with rank f. SHAK 679:18
fumo *ex f. dare lucem* HORA 385:21
fumum *F. et opes* HORA 388:22
fun Ain't we got f. KAHN 425:10
desire to have all the f. SAYE 646:5
frogs don't die for 'f.' BION 115:10
F. is fun LOOS 475:12
f. to be in the same decade ROOS 633:2
f. you *think* they had JONG 419:7
Gladstone read Homer for f. CHUR 216:14
Haute Couture should be f. LACR 447:8
I rhyme for f. BURN 169:1
more f. to be with NASH 539:10
most f. I ever had ALLE 12:8
no reference to f. HERB 371:18
noted for fresh air and f. EDGA 288:9
Oh, what f. DE L 256:13
people have f. MONT 528:9
Politics has got to be f. CLAR 219:5
stop people having f. STRA 744:17
taken my f. where I've found it KIPL 439:7
two is f. SAYI 647:4
wish I thought *What Jolly F.* RALE 621:11
function each with his own f. VIRG 797:3
Form follows f. SULL 745:15
frightful word [f.] LE C 461:14
f. Is smothered SHAK 681:21
F. never dies WORD 831:15
fundament frigid on the f. NASH 539:17
fundamental f. things apply HUPF 396:10
funeral costlier f. CLOS 222:4
Dream of a f. PROV 598:44
f. baked meats SHAK 662:1
F. marches to the grave LONG 474:4
f. of the past CLAR 218:17
not a f. note WOLF 825:3
One f. makes many PROV 608:39
PREPARE VAULT FOR F. TELE 758:9
funk in a blue f. CRAN 243:23
funny Everything is f. ROGE 631:20
f. old world FILM 311:17
f. old world THAT 770:13
f.-ha-ha HAY 364:16
F.-peculiar HAY 364:16
Isn't it f. MILN 511:2
Whatever is f. is subversive ORWE 559:13
fur On some other f. ANON 19:18
to make a f. coat SAYI 647:26
furca *Naturam expelles f.* HORA 386:19
furies Fierce as ten F. MILT 515:22
furious grew fast and f. BURN 168:16
time cracks into f. flower BROO 151:7
furiously driveth f. BIBL 80:23
green ideas sleep f. CHOM 212:10
heathen so f. rage BOOK 131:16
furled bright girdle f. ARNO 26:4
furnace as a greet f. CHAU 205:2
burning fiery f. BIBL 90:1
faultless breast the f. is SOUT 731:10
f. of affliction BIBL 88:8
Heat not a f. SHAK 673:6
furnish Books do f. a room POWE 590:8
f. all we ought to ask KEBL 432:5
f. the war HEAR 367:2
furnished Cambridge ladies in f. souls CUMM 247:13
F. and burnish'd BETJ 71:5
how poorly f. you are PERS 574:6
furniture church f. at best COWP 242:13
don't trip over the f. COWA 239:6
f. on the deck of the Titanic MORT 533:18
No f. so charming SMIT 725:15
rearranges the f. PRAT 591:3
stocked with all the f. DOYL 277:10
furor *Ira f. brevis est* HORA 386:16
furrow on a half-reaped f. KEAT 430:9
plough my f. alone ROSE 633:18
furrows made long f. BOOK 140:25
furry fire was f. as a bear SITW 721:1
further but no f. PIUS 577:8
f. one goes LAO 452:1
f. they have to fall FITZ 315:20
f. us BOOK 130:5
Go f. and fare worse PROV 601:11
fury blind f. of creation SHAW 707:32
Comes the blind F. MILT 513:3
f. and the mire of human veins YEAT 835:6
f., like a woman scorned CONG 232:26
f. of a patient man DRYD 280:14
Hell hath no f. PROV 602:37
In her prophetic f. SHAK 693:6
opponents of F. ZORO 841:14
sound and f. SHAK 685:22
War hath no f. MONT 527:3
furze When the f. is in bloom PROV 614:27
fuse line is a f. MAYA 502:16
through the green f. THOM 772:5
fuss f. about an omelette VOLT 798:14
fustian f.'s so sublimely bad POPE 583:6
futility fatal f. of fact JAME 403:13
future Back to the f. FILM 312:16
call on past and f. O'NE 554:24
Children of the f. age BLAK 121:4
controls the f. ORWE 558:22
curiosity about the f. WAUG 806:6
danger of the f. FROM 325:11
dipped into the f. TENN 763:3
empires of the f. CHUR 215:21
fight against the f. GLAD 340:16
f. ain't what it used to be BERR 69:10
f. and the past BOLA 124:9
F. as a promised land LEWI 466:18
f. can be promised to no one TRUD 783:22
F. not for parties WILS 822:8
f. of the human race JEAN 404:17
F. shock TOFF 779:1
f. states of both BYRO 176:21
hopes of the f. BURK 164:11
lets the f. in GREE 351:23
never think of the f. EINS 290:13
no faith in the f. TAYL 756:9
no preparation for the f. DISR 270:1
no trust in the f. HORA 387:22
once and f. king MALO 492:16
past, present and f. EINS 291:4
perhaps present in time f. ELIO 294:1
picture of the f. ORWE 559:2
plan the f. by the past BURK 162:9
promise of a bright f. AHER 8:28
scaffold sways the f. LOWE 477:16
seen the f. and it works STEF 737:3
sense of f. favours WALP 802:7
serve the f. hour WORD 831:16
Trust no F. LONG 474:5
walking backward into f. ZHVA 840:2
futurum *Quid sit f.* HORA 387:20
fuzzy-wuzzy 'ere's *to* you, F. KIPL 438:16
f. colony CAIR 181:3
Fyfe David Patrick Maxwell F. ANON 17:22
fyr is f. yreke CHAU 206:9

gabardine my Jewish g. SHAK 687:15
gable Skimming our g. HEAN 366:8
gad liberty to g. abroad BIBL 92:1
gadget g.-filled paradise NIEB 545:6
gadgets One servant worth a thousand g. SCHU 649:13
Gaels great G. of Ireland CHES 210:2
gag tight g. of place HEAN 366:19
Gaia G. is a tough bitch MARG 495:10

gaiety eclipsed the g. JOHN 410:8
only concession to g. THOM 773:8
Our own g. BLY 122:15
gaily G. into Ruislip gardens BETJ 70:17
gain another man's g. PROV 608:47
deem a losing g. SOUT 731:11
g., not glory POPE 586:13
g., not pain OXFO 562:15
g. of a few POPE 587:15
g. the whole world BIBL 98:8
g. to me BIBL 108:20
loss without some g. PROV 612:29
No pain, no g. PROV 608:5
So might I g. BROW 156:15
to die is g. BIBL 108:14
gained misery is a battle g. WELL 809:17
gainful seek g. employment ACHE 1:11
gains Light g. make heavy purses BACO 42:15
no g. without pains STEV 740:10
gait as much as his g. MATH 501:8
gaiters gas and g. DICK 264:7
Galatea *Malo me G. petit* VIRG 795:20
Galatians great text in G. BROW 157:29
gale g., it plies the saplings HOUS 391:3
Galen as G. says GOGA 343:23
Galeotto G. was the book DANT 249:14
galère *dans cette g.* MOLI 525:7
gales cool g. shall fan the glade POPE 586:26
Galilean O pale G. SWIN 751:5
pilot of the G. lake MILT 513:5
You have won, G. LAST 457:14
Galilee nightly on deep G. BYRO 175:23
Galileo G. in two thousand years PIUS 577:9
status of G. GOUL 347:8
gall gave me g. to eat BOOK 136:11
take my milk for g. SHAK 682:3
wormwood and the g. BIBL 89:24
gallant braw g. BALL 50:10
died a very g. gentleman EPIT 302:12
gallantry no more to do with g. SHER 715:21
What men call g. BYRO 175:30
galleon Stately as a g. GREN 352:15
gallery g. of pictures BACO 43:1
galley doing in that g. MOLI 525:7
Gallia *G. est omnis divisa* CAES 180:15
G. est omnis divisa OPEN 555:12
gallimaufry g. or hodgepodge SPEN 734:24
gallop G. about doing good SMIT 724:17
G. apace SHAK 697:25
Why does he g. STEV 742:17
galloped we g. all three BROW 156:8
galloping hoof with a g. sound VIRG 795:7
gallops who Time g. withal SHAK 659:13
gallow grew a g. KYD 446:10
gallows die upon the g. WILK 819:19
g. in every one CARL 188:17
g. in my garden CHES 209:29
g.-maker; for that frame SHAK 666:18
Jack on the g.-tree SCOT 651:23
nothing but the g. BURK 163:23
perfect g. SHAK 698:16
Under the G.-Tree FLET 318:3
galumphing went g. back CARR 190:13
gamble Life is a g. STOP 743:20
whore and the g. BLAK 118:5
game Anarchism is a g. SHAW 709:3
beautiful g. PELÉ 572:6
don't like this g. CATC 195:25
g. at which two can play BEER 61:16
g. is about glory BLAN 121:18
g. of the few BERK 67:20
g. on these lone heaths HAZL 365:23
g.'s afoot SHAK 671:6
giving over of a g. BEAU 58:16
how you played the G. RICE 626:3
nature of my g. JAGG 401:8
not being a g. LEAC 459:20
play the g. NEWB 541:18
see most of the g. PROV 606:1
'The g.,' said he CRAB 243:9
time to win this g. DRAK 278:20
war's a g. COWP 242:5
woman is his g. TENN 765:24
gamecocks Wits are g. GAY 332:7
gamekeeper life of an English g. ANON 19:5
makes the best g. PROV 608:24
games better than g. SCOT 650:8
dread of g. BETJ 71:8
G. people play BERN 69:8
g. should be seen MONT 527:11
gamesmanship theory and practice of g. POTT 589:4
gammon world of g. and spinnage DICK 261:26
gamut g. of the emotions PARK 567:11
gander goosey g. NURS 548:8
Grey goose and g. NURS 548:9
sauce for the g. PROV 614:8
gangsters great nations acted like g. KUBR 446:4
gaol world's thy g. DONN 274:23
gap g. between the lace curtains GREE 352:1
last g. but one WHIT 814:5
made a g. in nature SHAK 656:25
this great g. of time SHAK 656:18
gaping g. wretches HUNT 395:13
garage to the full g. HOOV 383:11
garbage G. in, garbage out SAYI 647:15
Garbo G.'s visage had a kind of DE B 254:2
Garcia Lorca —and you, G. GINS 339:22
Garde *La G. meurt* CAMB 182:11
garden all your life plant a g. PROV 603:41
as a lodge in a g. BIBL 86:10
Back to the g. MITC 523:17
blow upon my g. BIBL 85:17
Come into the g. TENN 764:6
enclosed g. CATU 197:11
England is a g. KIPL 438:19
fairies at the bottom of our g. FYLE 327:16
gallows in my g. CHES 209:29
g. eastward in Eden BIBL 73:17
g. inclosed BIBL 85:16
g. in her face CAMP 183:25
g. is a lovesome thing BROW 152:8
g. of the world MARV 499:6
g. of your face HERB 371:22
g.'s umbrage mild SMAR 722:12
g. with pedantic weeds CARE 186:6
ghost of a g. SWIN 750:18
God the first g. made COWL 239:12
imperfections of my g. MONT 527:8
in a lofty G. KORA 445:16
Lord God walking in the g. BIBL 73:26
man and a woman in a g. WILD 818:26
nearer God's Heart in a g. GURN 355:2
planted a g. BACO 43:4
rosebud g. of girls TENN 764:8
Round and round the g. NURS 550:14
set to dress this g. SHAK 695:17
sunlight on the g. MACN 488:16
too much time in the g. HOBY 379:9
We are a g. walled around WATT 805:13
where a g. should be HORA 389:24
Gārdena *Hwæt! wē G.* ANON 21:16
gardener Adam was a g. SHAK 672:23
I am but a young g. JEFF 405:17
supposing him to be the g. BIBL 103:1
gardeners g., ditchers SHAK 666:17
gardenias g. in your hair HOLI 380:21
gardening g. is but landscape-painting POPE 587:22
gardens Sowe Carrets in your G. GARD 329:14
sweetest delight of g. BROW 152:16
garish day's g. eye MILT 512:10
loved the g. day NEWM 542:20
no worship to the g. sun SHAK 697:29
garland green willow is my g. HEYW 376:6
O! withered is the g. SHAK 657:19
willow must be my g. SHAK 693:19
garlands may gather g. SCOT 651:16
they are g. BENN 65:18
with g. dressed KEAT 428:27
garlic clove of g. round my neck O'BR 552:7
Wel loved he g. CHAU 205:4
garment g. of thought CARL 188:12
g. was white as snow BIBL 90:6
grasp the hem of his g. BISM 116:18
leaves an old g. BHAG 72:16
left his g. in her hand BIBL 75:12
like as with a g. BOOK 139:1
not know the g. from the man BLAK 118:19
wax old as doth a g. BOOK 138:15
garmented g. in light SHEL 714:16
garments cross upon their g. URBA 788:18
g. of the Torah ZOHA 840:13
part my g. BOOK 132:25
Reasons are not like g. ESSE 301:9
Stuffs out his vacant g. SHAK 677:11
garnished empty, swept, and g. BIBL 95:17
garret Born in the g. BYRO 179:2
Genius in a g. ROBI 629:21
living in a g. FOOT 319:5
garrison friends in the g. HALI 357:7
Garsington Hey for G. KETT 434:12
garter knight of the g. ATTL 32:3
garters own heir-apparent g. SHAK 667:31
gas g. and gaiters DICK 264:7
G. smells awful PARK 567:6
g. was on BETJ 71:3
got as far as poison-g. HARD 361:8
gash be it g. or gold BROO 151:5
gasp last g. BIBL 92:21
gasworks by the g. crofts MACC 484:8
gate A-sitting on a g. CARR 191:13
at one g. to make defence MILT 518:18
cabin at your g. SHAK 701:7
Death . . . openeth the g. BACO 42:25
drops on g.-bars hang HARD 361:23
enemies in the g. BOOK 140:22
g. of glory BOOK 130:2
g. of heaven BIBL 75:3
how strait the g. HENL 369:21
laid at his g. BIBL 100:10
leads to the broad g. SHAK 656:5
lead you to Heaven's g. BLAK 119:3
man at the g. of the year HASK 363:16
November at the g. PUSH 617:29
out of the ivory g. BROW 154:6
watchful at his g. DODD 271:19
Wide is the g. BIBL 94:7
gates besiege your g. POPE 582:20
enter then his g. KETH 434:11
g. are mind to open KIPL 439:19
g. of hell BIBL 96:4
g. of it shall not be shut BIBL 113:11
g. of perception MAIM 491:7
g. to the glorious and unknown FORS 320:15
Open the temple g. SPEN 733:8
O ye g. BOOK 133:3
Sprouting despondently at area g. ELIO 295:12
stand in thy g. BOOK 140:14
to the g. of Hell PIUS 577:8
two g. of Sleep VIRG 795:3
Gath Tell it not in G. BIBL 79:1
gather G. ye rosebuds HERR 375:2
He will surely g. you KORA 444:12
who shall g. them BOOK 133:30
gathered cannot be g. up again BIBL 79:8
eagles be g. together PROV 614:39
g. together in my name BIBL 96:10
two or three are g. BOOK 126:18
gathering g. where thou hast not strawed BIBL 97:9
gat-tothed G. I was CHAU 206:20
gaude *g. in Christo* LUTH 479:12
gaudeamus *G. igitur, Juvenes dum sumus* ANON 21:9
gaudia *ira voluptas G.* JUVE 424:6
gaudy g., blabbing, and remorseful day SHAK 672:18
Neat, but not g. WESL 812:1
one other g. night SHAK 657:6
rich, not g. SHAK 662:11

gauger what should Master G. play STEV 743:5
Gaul G. as a whole OPEN 555:12
G. as a whole is divided CAES 180:15
Gaunt G.'s embattled pile MACA 482:19
Old John of G. SHAK 694:8
gauze shoot her through g. BANK 53:9
gauzy wrapped in a g. veil SHEL 714:15
gave Lord g., and the Lord BIBL 80:36
she g. me of the tree BIBL 74:1
What wee g., wee have EPIT 304:13
gay g. deceiver COLM 229:16
g. Lothario ROWE 636:9
g. man trapped BOY 146:3
G. men may seek sex PAGL 563:4
good and g. PROV 606:42
heart was warm and g. HAMM 358:20
if I could, be g. ROGE 631:15
impiously g. CRAB 243:2
making Gay *rich*, and Rich *g.* JOHN 410:3
reading for g. men STEV 740:19
second best's a g. goodnight YEAT 836:3
So g. the band GREN 352:15
without feeling g. CHUR 214:3
Gaza Eyeless in G. MILT 518:13
gaze bade me g. ARNO 27:20
fixed in steadfast g. MILT 513:21
gazelle never loved a dear G. CARR 191:27
nursed a dear G. DICK 264:11
nursed a dear g. MOOR 530:18
one a g. YEAT 836:6
gazelles g. appear MOOR 530:6
gazer g. wipe his eye HERB 373:17
gazette *Pall Mall G.* is written THAC 769:3
gazing g. at each other SAIN 641:13
g. up into heaven BIBL 103:14
géant *ailes de g.* BAUD 57:5
geese G. are swans ARNO 26:14
g., like a snow cloud RANS 621:19
great g. honk northward WARR 803:22
kill all turkeys, g. PROV 608:28
Like g. about the sky AUDE 33:18
swans of others are g. WALP 801:12
wild g. are flighting KIPL 439:5
wild g. lost BASH 56:15
Gehazi Whence comest thou, G. BIBL 80:20
Gehenna Down to G. KIPL 439:10
Geist *Ich bin der G.* GOET 342:18
gem g. of purest ray serene GRAY 350:11
precious g. was hidden MITF 524:4
Thinking every tear a g. SHEL 712:9
geminae *g. Somni portae* VIRG 795:3
gemlike hard, g. flame PATE 569:15
gems rare were the g. she wore MOOR 530:16
these the g. of heaven MILT 516:22
gender get My g. right ARNO 29:11
of the feminine g. O'KE 553:7
tired of the g. SEXT 655:5
general caviare to the g. SHAK 663:23
feet of the great g. OVID 561:22
find in that great g. JUVE 424:22
G. notions MONT 526:19
generalities glittering and sounding g. CHOA 212:8
Glittering g. EMER 300:2
generalizations g. dangerous DUMA 284:16
generally g. necessary to salvation BOOK 130:17
General Motors good for G. WILS 821:10
generals against the law for g. TRUM 784:8
bite some of my other g. GEOR 333:12
Dead battles, like dead g. TUCH 784:15
g. than in particulars HUME 394:17
Our G. now, retired POPE 586:8
Russia has two g. NICH 543:17
we're all G. USTI 788:24
generation beat g. KERO 434:5
best minds of my g. GINS 339:20
chosen g. BIBL 110:28
Every g. revolts MUMF 536:6
evil and adulterous g. BIBL 95:15
faithless and stubborn g. BOOK 137:4
froward g. BIBL 77:12
g. of men HOME 382:2
g. passeth away BIBL 83:39
G. X COUP 238:5
grieved with this g. BOOK 138:6
Had it been the whole g. EPIT 303:1
in their g. wiser BIBL 100:7
lost g. STEI 737:9
luck of my g. SHAW 710:2
never before has a g. VANE 789:16
O g. of vipers BIBL 92:29
one g. from extinction CARE 186:18
third and fourth g. BIBL 76:9
generations g. have trod HOPK 384:5
G. pass BROW 153:6
g. shall call me blessed BIBL 98:16
hungry g. KEAT 429:14
in three g. PROV 600:48
manners of future g. JOHN 410:25
only three g. PROV 600:47
Those dying g. YEAT 837:1
three g. to make PROV 604:38
generosity exercise our g. SART 645:8
generous always g. ones MONT 528:17
g. and elevated mind JOHN 411:7
g. and honest feeling BURK 164:18
just before you're g. PROV 595:41
more g. sentiments JOHN 413:11
My mind as g. SHAK 678:3
generously treated g. or destroyed MACH 485:15
genes G. not like blueprints STEW 743:6
go by the name of g. DAWK 253:4
singing in your g. BARR 56:2
what males do to g. JONE 419:3
Genesis Conditioned G. PALI 565:3
genetic g. lottery comes up with PIML 576:7
mechanism for g. material CRIC 245:3
terrible g. defects WATS 804:17
genetics G. had the final say KEYE 435:1
geography and g. WHIT 814:7
Geneva grim G. ministers AYTO 40:11
genitals make my g. to quiver JOHN 412:10
geniumque *G. loci* VIRG 795:4
genius Eccentricities of g. DICK 265:10
except my g. WILD 819:12
feminine of g. FITZ 315:5
g. a better discerning GOLD 345:17
g. and art HAZL 365:14
g. and regularity GAIN 327:18
g. and virtue HAZL 365:15
G. capacity for taking pains PROV 601:3
g. does what it must BARI 54:12
G. does what it must MERE 505:23
G. from the throne BYRO 178:2
g. has been slow of growth LEWE 466:16
G. in a garret ROBI 629:21
g. in religion ARNO 29:4
g. into my life WILD 819:9
G. is one per cent inspiration EDIS 289:2
G. is only a greater aptitude BUFF 159:20
G. is the child REYN 625:9
G., like Armida's wand LLOY 470:15
g. of Einstein leads to Hiroshima PICA 576:4
g. of its scientists EISE 291:8
g. of the Constitution PITT 576:26
g. of the place POPE 583:23
g. overlooks individual SCHO 649:3
'G.' which means CARL 187:20
g. would wish to live ADAM 2:1
gentlemen—a g. SCHU 649:11
great g. BEAU 58:11
If I'm not a g. BALZ 53:2
kind of universal g. DRYD 283:3
lively g. GERV 335:1
Milton, Madam, was a g. JOHN 417:12
Mr Wordsworth's g. HAZL 365:19
Picasso is a g. DALI 248:13
Poetic G. of my country BURN 169:11
Ramp up my g. JONS 419:23
singular g. DIDE 267:8
stupendous g.! damned fool BYRO 180:4
talent instantly recognizes g. DOYL 278:8
taste or g. REYN 625:6
Three-fifths of him g. LOWE 477:13
true g. JOHN 409:27
true g. appears SWIF 748:25
what a g. I had SWIF 750:1
Whence g. wildly flashed KEAT 430:13
works of a great g. ADDI 5:18
geniuses One of the greatest g. WALP 800:19
genres *Tous les g. sont bons* VOLT 797:15
gent indeed a valiant G. EVEL 305:4
genteel g. when he gets drunk BOSW 144:21
No dancing bear was so g. COWP 240:15
to the truly g. HARD 360:13
gentes *Laudate Dominum, omnes g.* BIBL 113:23
gentil verray, parfit g. knyght CHAU 204:9
Gentiles boasting as the G. use KIPL 440:5
light to lighten the G. BIBL 98:25
preach among the G. BIBL 107:26
gentility marks of g. BLAK 118:12
gentle Do not go g. THOM 772:2
G. as falcon SKEL 721:11
G. Child of gentle Mother DEAR 254:1
g.-hearted Charles COLE 227:5
g. his condition SHAK 671:25
G. Jesus WESL 810:26
g. mind by gentle deeds SPEN 734:11
g. rain from heaven SHAK 688:10
His life was g. SHAK 677:4
gentleman as an educated g. SHAW 707:22
cannot make a g. BURK 165:14
definition of a g. NEWM 542:11
describe a g. TROL 782:1
died a very gallant g. EPIT 302:12
Every other inch a g. WEST 812:19
fashion a g. SPEN 733:11
fine old English g. SONG 729:14
first true g. DEKK 256:4
g. and scholar BURN 169:5
g. in Whitehall JAY 404:14
g. is not in your books SHAK 690:33
g. should never go beyond ETHE 301:13
g.'s park CONS 235:7
g. who was generally spoken SURT 747:6
God send every g. BALL 52:4
I am a g. SHAW 708:3
in linen like a g. JOHN 409:19
Jack became a g. SHAK 696:15
last g. in Europe LEVE 466:3
make a g. PROV 604:38
mariner with the g. DRAK 278:19
not quite a g. ASHF 30:11
of a g.'s house BOWE 145:8
officer and a g. MILI 508:3
Once a g. DICK 263:2
prince of darkness is a g. SHAK 679:7
so stout a g. SHAK 669:13
talking about being a g. SURT 746:14
This squash, this g. SHAK 703:1
too pedantic for a g. CONG 232:23
what a g. should be DEFO 254:11
who was then the g. PROV 614:16
gentlemanly g. conduct ARNO 29:14
very g. thing STEV 741:11
werry g. ideas SURT 746:21
gentlemen Damn g. GAIN 327:17
difficult to behave like g. MACK 486:8
eggs for g. NURS 548:13
forget we are g. BURK 164:19
G. and Ladies DICK 266:19
g. both CARL 188:16
G. do not take soup at luncheon CURZ 248:8
G. go by KIPL 440:8
g. in England SHAK 671:25
g. of England PARK 567:17
G. prefer blondes LOOS 475:9
G.-rankers KIPL 438:17
Great-hearted g. BROW 156:21
nation of g. MUGA 534:13
religion for g. CHAR 203:9
Scholars and g. WORD 831:6

gentlemen (*cont.*):
since g. came up SHAK 672:20
Three jolly g. DE L 256:14
written by gentlemen for g. THAC 769:3
gentleness g. And show of love SHAK 674:6
only a willed g. THOM 773:13
ways are ways of g. SPRI 735:8
gently his faults lie g. SHAK 673:20
roar you as g. SHAK 689:13
genuflexion never grudge a g. OLIV 553:14
genuine g. poetry is conceived ARNO 28:23
place for the g. MOOR 529:17
genus *Hoc g. omne* HORA 389:16
geographers g., in Afric-maps SWIF 749:16
geographical g. concept BISM 116:10
g. expression METT 506:9
not a g. fragment PARN 567:25
geography g. and genetics WHIT 814:7
G. is about Maps BENT 67:2
too much g. KING 437:1
geologists g. would let me alone RUSK 639:7
geometrical g. ratio MALT 493:3
geometricians g. only by chance JOHN 410:6
geometry as precise as g. FLAU 316:15
demonstration in g. REYN 625:12
disorder in its g. DE B 254:7
does not know g. ANON 21:3
G. (which is the only science HOBB 378:14
'royal road' to g. EUCL 301:17
George accession of G. the Third MACA 482:5
England and Saint G. SHAK 671:6
G.—don't do that GREN 352:16
if his name be G. SHAK 677:6
Georges G. ended LAND 450:4
Georgia G. on my mind GORR 347:4
red hills of G. KING 436:14
Georgie G. Porgie, pudding and pie NURS 548:7
geranium madman shakes a dead g. ELIO 295:20
geraniums delphiniums (blue) and g. (red) MILN 510:17
pot of pink g. MACN 488:8
geriatric years in a g. home AMIS 14:3
germ G. of Buddhahood MAHĀ 490:8
German all a G. racket RIDL 627:15
G. history reached TAYL 756:3
G. *Reich* is made BISM 116:13
language of poems is G. CELA 199:11
to my horse—G. CHAR 203:16
Germans beastly to the G. COWA 238:10
G. . . . are going to be squeezed GEDD 332:25
G. classify CATH 194:6
G. have historic chance KOHL 443:6
G. were coming in LEDW 461:18
to the G. that of—the air RICH 627:12
Germany at war with G. CHAM 201:1
bonnet in G. SHAK 687:9
Death is a master from G. CELA 199:10
G. above all HOFF 379:16
G. calling JOYC 422:20
G. in the saddle BISM 116:7
G. is a nation MICH 507:1
G. will declare that I am a Jew EINS 290:12
offering G. too little NEVI 541:13
rebellious G. OVID 561:22
remaining cities of G. HARR 362:13
germs Kills all known g. ADVE 7:39
Gershwin G. songs FISH 313:17
Gesang *Das ist der ewige G.* GOET 342:19
Weib und G. LUTH 480:6
Gestern *G. liebt' ich* LESS 465:15
gestures In the g. SOND 727:22
get G. me to the church LERN 465:2
G. out as early as you can LARK 453:5
g. out of these wet clothes FILM 311:19
G. thee behind me, Satan BIBL 96:5
g. up airly LOWE 477:11
g. what you like SHAW 708:31
g. where I am today without CATC 195:24
What you see is what you g. SAYI 648:9
getting G. and spending WORD 832:15
Gospel of G. On SHAW 709:5
gewgaw This g. world DRYD 280:26
ghastly G. good taste BETJ 71:10
G., grim and ancient POE 579:17
g. through the drizzling rain TENN 760:29
We were a g. crew COLE 226:22
ghost but a kind of g. DONN 273:20
each frustrate g. BROW 158:4
each write a g. story SHEL 710:5
gave up the g. BIBL 103:31
g. asked them to do O'BR 552:6
G. in the Machine RYLE 640:20
g. of a garden SWIN 750:18
g. of a great name LUCA 478:14
g. of a rose BROW 152:16
g. of Roger Casement YEAT 836:4
g. of the deceased HOBB 379:4
g. stories written for ghosts ALDI 11:1
G. unlaid forbear thee SHAK 661:2
I am the g. PLAT 577:16
If the g. cries RAIN 620:7
I'll make a g. of him SHAK 662:21
Moves like a g. SHAK 683:1
some old lover's g. DONN 274:7
Vex not his g. SHAK 680:15
What beck'ning g. POPE 582:16
with London's g. GALV 329:1
ghosties ghoulies and g. PRAY 592:2
ghosts allowed to us moderns, are g. FIEL 310:11
egress is given to real g. VIRG 795:3
g. from an old enchanter SHEL 712:12
g. of a nation PEAR 571:8
g. of Beauty glide POPE 583:15
g. of departed quantities BERK 67:18
g. outnumber us DUNN 285:9
G., wandering here and there SHAK 690:8
lack of g. BIRN 115:12
make the g. gaze SHAK 657:14
ghoul dug them up like a G. DICK 262:11
living on another like a g. HEAD 366:1
ghoulies g. and ghosties PRAY 592:2
giant baby figure of the g. SHAK 700:9
G. Despair BUNY 161:5
g. great and still STEV 742:13
G. on the mountain stands BYRO 173:23
g.'s strength SHAK 686:9
g.'s wings BAUD 57:5
hand of the g. BOOK 140:22
like a g. BOOK 137:7
like a g.'s robe SHAK 685:14
rejoiceth as a g. BOOK 132:15
sees farther than the g. COLE 227:14
upon the body of a g. LAND 450:8
giants for war like precocious g. PEAR 571:11
g. in the earth BIBL 74:15
nuclear g. and ethical infants BRAD 146:11
on the shoulders of g. NEWT 543:9
shoulders of g. BERN 68:22
there we saw the g. BIBL 76:26
Want one only of five g. BEVE 72:6
we ought to be g. CHEK 208:2
gibber squeak and g. SHAK 661:9
gibbets cells and g. COOK 235:16
g. keep the lifted hand in awe YOUN 838:20
Gibbon Eh! Mr G. GLOU 341:19
Gibeon stand thou still upon G. BIBL 77:22
giberne *dans sa g. le bâton* LOUI 476:4
gibes great master of g. DISR 269:14
giblet liked thick g. soup JOYC 422:12
Gibraltar G. may tumble GERS 334:15
giddy I am g. SHAK 700:12
So g. the sight GREN 352:15
Gideon Lord came upon G. BIBL 77:32
gift Beauty is the lover's g. CONG 233:9
every perfect gift BIBL 110:12
Freedom is not a g. NKRU 546:10
g. horse in the mouth PROV 607:32
g. of God BIBL 103:23
g. of the divine Name SIKH 720:2
last best g. MILT 516:29
love is the g. of oneself ANOU 22:11
make the g. rich TROL 783:1
You have a g. JONS 420:14
your g. survived it all AUDE 33:31
gifted vividly g. in love DUFF 284:10
young, g. and black HANS 359:12
Young, g. and black IRVI 400:1
giftie g. gie us BURN 168:21
gifts Bestows her g. JONS 419:22
bring g. BOOK 136:18
buy g. at Jim Gibson's LONG 475:6
cannot recall their g. TENN 767:1
countless g. of love WINK 823:6
diversities of g. BIBL 106:15
Enemies' g. are no gifts SOPH 728:12
even when they bring g. VIRG 793:18
g. of God are strown HEBE 367:7
Greeks bearing g. PROV 600:14
He would adore my g. HERB 373:7
no g. from chance ARNO 26:25
Of all the heavenly g. GRIM 353:14
presented unto him g. BIBL 92:23
received g. for men BOOK 136:9
gigantic g. body MACA 481:13
gild g. refinèd gold BYRO 176:24
g. refinèd gold SHAK 677:15
I'll g. it SHAK 669:18
gilded g. car of day MILT 511:16
g. loam SHAK 694:9
gilding amusement is the g. RICH 627:9
G. pale streams SHAK 704:17
Gilead G. is mine BOOK 135:19
no balm in G. BIBL 89:16
gill hang by its own g. PROV 599:26
Gilpin John G. was a citizen COWP 240:11
gin get out the g. REED 623:17
g. and vermouth DEV 259:10
G. by pailfuls SCOT 651:23
G. was mother's milk SHAW 709:14
Of all the g. joints FILM 312:4
woodcock near the g. SHAK 701:26
ginger G., you're balmy MURR 537:4
ginless wished on a g. tonic COPE 236:9
Gioconda one isn't the real G. CRAN 243:23
Giotto G. has the palm DANT 249:21
G.'s tower LONG 473:18
giovinezza *Quanto è bella g.* MEDI 503:10
Gipfeln *Über allen G. Ist Ruh'* GOET 343:10
Gipper Win just one for the G. GIPP 340:2
gipsy Time, you old g. man HODG 379:14
giraffe g., in their gracefulness DINE 267:19
giraffes G.!—a People Who live CAMP 183:1
girded g. himself with strength BOOK 138:2
g. up his loins BIBL 80:1
g. with praise GRAN 348:15
girdeth g. on his harness BIBL 80:5
girdle bright g. furled ARNO 26:4
g. round about the earth SHAK 689:24
to the g. SHAK 679:22
girdled g. with the gleaming world TENN 763:14
girl Above the staggering g. YEAT 836:14
can't get no g. reaction JAGG 401:6
credit to any good g. TAYL 756:11
danced with a g. FARJ 306:16
diamonds a g.'s best friend ROBI 629:9
g. at an impressionable age SPAR 731:18
g. in the indolence of youth YEAT 836:21
g. needs good parents TUCK 784:17
g. throwing a ball WOOL 827:1
g. with brains ought to LOOS 475:10
loved by a g. TROL 782:28
no g. wants to laugh LOOS 475:12
Poor little rich g. COWA 238:17
pretty g. is like a melody BERL 68:9
say in front of a g. LEHR 462:19
speak like a green g. SHAK 662:14
sweetest g. I know JUDG 423:1

unlessoned g. SHAK 688:4
was a little g. LONG 475:2
girlish g. glee GILB 338:3
Laugh thy g. laughter WATS 805:2
girls abhors In Little G. BELL 63:11
Always be civil to the g. MITF 524:6
bombers named for g. JARR 404:10
Boys and girls NURS 547:13
G. aren't like that AMIS 13:16
g. in slacks remember Dad BETJ 70:5
g. that are so smart CARE 186:21
g. who wear glasses PARK 567:3
It was the g. I liked BAIL 48:4
lads for the g. HOUS 391:1
little g. made of NURS 551:19
not that g. should think NAPO 538:13
nude, giant g. SPEN 732:23
rosebud garden of g. TENN 764:8
rose-lipt g. are sleeping HOUS 391:8
Secrets with g. CRAB 243:11
Thank heaven for little g. LERN 465:8
Treaties like g. and roses DE G 255:27
white feet of laughing g. MACA 483:4
Gitche Gumee By the shore of G. LONG 474:11
give All that I am I g. BOOK 131:6
better to g. than to receive PROV 604:11
freely g. BIBL 94:32
G., and it shall be given BIBL 99:5
g. and not to count IGNA 398:17
G. and take fair play PROV 601:7
g. a singel dam FLEM 317:10
G. a thing PROV 601:6
G. crowns and pounds HOUS 390:18
g. me back my legions AUGU 36:15
G. me my Romeo SHAK 697:29
G. me yet before I die WINC 822:24
G. to me the life I love STEV 742:25
g. to the poor BIBL 96:13
g. what you command AUGU 36:6
more blessed to g. BIBL 104:14
not as the world giveth, g. I BIBL 102:21
peace which the world cannot g. BOOK 126:19
receive but what we g. COLE 225:3
such as I have g. I thee BIBL 103:18
given g. away by a novel KEAT 431:15
I would have g. gladly JOHN 408:12
shall be g. BIBL 97:10
taking what is not g. PALI 564:15
To whom nothing is g. FIEL 309:19
giver author and g. BOOK 128:14
cheerful g. BIBL 107:10
Lord and g. of life BOOK 129:9
gives g. twice who gives quickly PROV 602:5
happiness she g. LACL 447:6
who g. soon PUBL 616:11
giving g. and receiving of a Ring BOOK 131:8
Godlike in g. ANON 16:11
not in the g. vein SHAK 696:22
glacier g. knocks in the cupboard AUDE 33:19
glad g. confident morning BROW 156:19
G. did I live STEV 743:4
g. father BIBL 82:20
g. when they said unto me BOOK 140:14
just g. to see me WEST 812:7
maketh g. the heart BOOK 139:3
rejoice and be g. BOOK 140:6
shew ourselves g. in him BOOK 138:5
too soon made g. BROW 156:25
glade bee-loud g. YEAT 836:11
crown the wat'ry g. GRAY 350:15
gladiators g. of Rome BORR 143:10
gladly bear the cross g. THOM 771:8
g. wolde he lerne CHAU 204:20
I would have given g. JOHN 408:12
gladness As with g. men of old DIX 271:13
obtain joy and g. BIBL 87:24
oil of g. BOOK 134:14
serve the Lord with g. BOOK 138:13
solemn g. even crowned TENN 761:5
Teach me half the g. SHEL 714:9
gladsome g. light COKE 224:9
g. light of jurisprudence CLOS 222:10
Let us with a g. mind MILT 512:25
Glamis G. hath murdered sleep SHAK 683:9
G. thou art, and Cawdor SHAK 682:1
glance g. from heaven to earth SHAK 690:19
O brightening g. YEAT 835:3
glare looked at in this merciless g. WILL 820:19
red g. on Skiddaw MACA 482:19
Glasgow G. Empire on a Saturday night DODD 271:18
glass baying for broken g. WAUG 806:3
comb and a g. in her hand SONG 729:15
dome of many-coloured g. SHEL 711:4
excuse for the g. SHER 716:14
face in a g. BIBL 110:13
Get thee g. eyes SHAK 679:25
g. I drink from MUSS 537:10
g. of blessings HERB 373:6
g. o' the inwariable DICK 265:11
g. the opulent HARD 361:9
Grief with a g. SWIN 750:8
He was indeed the g. SHAK 669:31
if you break the bloody g. MACN 488:9
liked the Sound of Broken G. BELL 63:24
live in g. houses PROV 612:42
made mouths in a g. SHAK 678:23
man that looks on g. HERB 372:13
No g. of ours was raised HEAN 366:14
own face in the g. WILD 818:15
Satire is a sort of g. SWIF 747:11
sea of g. BIBL 111:31
sea of g. BIBL 112:27
set you up a g. SHAK 665:11
sun-comprehending g. LARK 452:17
take a g. of wine SHER 716:19
through a g., darkly BIBL 106:16
turn down an empty g. FITZ 315:3
glasses broke our painted g. JORD 421:6
brown braids and g. JARR 404:8
Fill all the g. there COWL 239:11
girls who wear g. PARK 567:3
ladder and some g. BATE 57:3
Such cruel g. HOWE 392:2
glassy around the g. sea HEBE 367:8
g., cool, translucent MILT 512:1
in the g. stream SHAK 666:12
Upon the g. plain WORD 828:21
gleam Follow The G. TENN 764:19
gleaning g. of the grapes BIBL 77:34
glee At their tempestuous g. LONG 474:10
girlish g. GILB 338:3
glen Down the rushy g. ALLI 12:21
glib g. and oily art SHAK 677:25
gliding g. like a queen SPEN 732:17
glimmering fades the g. landscape GRAY 350:6
Mere g. and decays VAUG 790:12
glimpses g. of the moon SHAK 662:19
g. that would make me WORD 832:16
glittering g. and sounding generalities CHOA 212:8
g. in the smokeless air WORD 827:19
g. prizes BORR 144:7
g. prizes SMIT 723:19
how that g. taketh me HERR 375:4
with his g. eye COLE 226:4
glitters All that g. is not gold PROV 595:3
medal g. CHUR 215:16
gloaming In the g. ORRE 557:14
Roamin' in the g. LAUD 454:7
gloat I g. KIPL 441:22
global g. thinking LUCE 478:18
image of a g. village MCLU 487:7
my wars Were g. REED 623:15
globally Think g. SAYI 648:5
globaloney still g. LUCE 478:18
globe g.-trotting Madam YEAT 837:19
great g. itself SHAK 699:6
hunted round the g. PAIN 563:14
rattle of a g. DRYD 280:26
this distracted g. SHAK 662:32
globèd wealth of g. peonies KEAT 429:4
globule primordial atomic g. GILB 337:22
Glöckchen *das G. klingeln* HEIN 368:9
G. klingeln CLOS 222:13
gloire *g. et le repos* MONT 527:16
gloom counterfeit a g. MILT 512:7
inspissated g. JOHN 414:3
this mournful g. MILT 514:19
glooms kindred g. THOM 775:15
gloomy by g. Dis Was gathered MILT 516:14
gloria *G. in excelsis* MISS 520:13
G. Patri MISS 520:10
Sic transit g. mundi ANON 21:13
gloriam *Dei g.* MOTT 535:1
glories G., like glow-worms WEBS 807:26
g. of our blood and state SHIR 717:8
in those weaker g. spy VAUG 790:8
my g. and my state SHAK 695:22
glorious all-g. above GRAN 348:15
all g. within BOOK 134:16
By the g. Koran KORA 445:12
g. by my pen MONT 529:3
g. Devon BOUL 145:1
G. things of thee NEWT 543:14
Mud! G. mud FLAN 316:2
reach at the g. gold SHAK 672:14
Tam was g. BURN 168:12
What a g. morning ADAM 3:18
glory all things give him g. HOPK 385:6
alone with his g. WOLF 825:5
brood of g. SPEN 733:18
crowned with g. now KELL 432:16
day of g. has arrived ROUG 636:1
days of our g. BYRO 179:6
declare the g. of God BOOK 132:14
deed is all, the g. nothing GOET 343:3
drowned my g. FITZ 315:1
earth is full of his g. BIBL 86:21
from another star in g. BIBL 106:26
full of thy g. BOOK 129:20
game is about g. BLAN 121:18
g. a bubble SHEL 714:19
g. and shame MILT 515:19
g. and the dream WORD 829:19
g. and the freshness WORD 829:14
g. and the nothing BYRO 175:12
g. as of the only begotten BIBL 101:7
G. be to God HOPK 384:14
G. be to the Father BOOK 125:19
g. from the earth WORD 829:15
g. in the church BIBL 108:1
g. in the name of Briton GEOR 333:13
g. in the triumph CORN 236:15
g. is departed BIBL 78:19
g. is in their shame BIBL 108:22
g., laud, and honour NEAL 540:1
g., like the phoenix BYRO 178:8
g. never dies ANON 22:4
g. not their own WORD 831:5
g. of Europe BURK 163:21
g. of God BLAK 119:20
g. of God is a man IREN 399:23
g. of Gothic RUSK 639:9
g. of man as the flower BIBL 110:26
g. of my crown ELIZ 297:4
g. of the Attic stage ARNO 27:30
g. of the coming HOWE 391:15
g. of the Creator BACO 41:9
g. of the Lord BIBL 87:28
g. of the Lord BIBL 89:4
g. of the Lord shone BIBL 98:20
g. of them BIBL 92:34
g. of the Trojans VIRG 794:4
g. of the winning MERE 505:19
g. of the world ANON 21:13
g. of this life SHAK 699:16
g. of this world passes THOM 770:20
g. shone around TATE 755:10
g. smeared in dust SHAK 673:3

glory (*cont.*):
g. that was Greece POE 579:21
G. to God in the highest BIBL 98:22
g. to her BIBL 106:14
G. to Man in the highest SWIN 751:3
greater g. of God MOTT 535:1
greatest g. of a woman PERI 573:21
her g. pass DANI 248:18
hope of g. BOOK 127:19
I felt it was g. BYRO 179:7
I go to g. LAST 455:1
joy and g. ABEL 1:3
King of g. BOOK 133:3
Land of Hope and G. BENS 66:13
looks on war as all g. SHER 717:2
Majesty: of thy G. BOOK 125:20
name thee Old G. DRIV 279:12
Not as our g. WORD 831:2
paths of g. GRAY 350:9
power, and the g. BIBL 93:19
say my g. was YEAT 836:19
sea Of g. streams along BYRO 174:25
short of the g. of God BIBL 104:32
Solomon in all his g. BIBL 93:25
some desperate g. OWEN 562:8
There's g. for you CARR 191:2
Thy g. is upon my tongue JUDA 422:25
trailing clouds of g. WORD 829:20
uncertain g. SHAK 702:26
walking in an air of g. VAUG 790:12
what g. is it BIBL 110:31
What price g. ANDE 14:11
wretchedness that g. brings SHAK 699:20
yields the true g. DRAK 278:17
gloss gain is g. CUNN 247:17
Glossop Roderick G. WODE 824:18
Gloucester tailor in G. POTT 588:17
Gloucestershire here in G. SHAK 694:20
glove O! that I were a g. SHAK 697:10
played at the g. BALL 50:10
white g. pulpit REAG 623:2
gloves brandy and summer g. JOSE 421:10
capitalism with the g. off STOP 744:1
cat in g. PROV 597:6
people in g. and such [illegible]
through the fields in g. CORN 237:2
with my g. on my hand HARG 362:5
glow don thyn eris g. CHAU 207:6
g. has warmed the world STEV 740:15
made my heart to g. SOUT 731:9
glowers sits there and g. BARH 54:9
glowing g. kiss had won HOOD 382:27
glow-worm g., or some other MAHĀ 490:1
g. that shines HAGG 356:4
Her eyes the g. lend HERR 374:14
glow-worms Glories, like g. WEBS 807:26
glut g. thy sorrow KEAT 429:4
glutton Of praise a mere g. GOLD 345:4
gluttony G. an emotional escape DEV 259:11
Glyn With Elinor G. ANON 19:18
gnashing g. of teeth BIBL 94:18
gnat strain at a g. BIBL 96:27
gnats small g. mourn KEAT 430:11
gnomes g. in Zurich WILS 821:12
go can't g. on BECK 59:20
G. ahead, make my day FILM 311:8
G., and catch DONN 274:11
G., and do thou likewise BIBL 99:14
g., and sin no more BIBL 101:34
G., and the Lord be with thee BIBL 78:31
g. anywhere I damn well please BEVI 72:10
g. away at any rate ANON 17:18
G. down, Moses SONG 730:8
G., for they call you ARNO 27:3
G. further and fare worse PROV 601:11
g. into the house BOOK 140:14
G., litel bok CHAU 207:18
G., little book STEV 743:3
G., lovely rose WALL 800:2
g. no more a-roving BYRO 179:4
G. to jail SAYI 647:17
G. to the ant BIBL 82:13
g. to the devil JOHN 411:22
g. unto the altar of God BOOK 134:10
g. we know not where SHAK 686:18
G. West, young man GREE 351:10
G. ye into all the world BIBL 98:14
I g.—I come back CATC 195:27
I g. on for ever TENN 757:14
I g. to the Father BIBL 102:26
I have a g. OSBO 559:24
In the name of God, g. AMER 13:7
In the name of God, g. CROM 245:14
I say to this man, G. BIBL 94:16
I shall g. to him BIBL 79:7
I will not let thee g. WESL 811:2
Let my people g. BIBL 75:35
neither g. nor hang BIGO 114:26
never g. back again MORE 531:9
no g. to go WHIT 814:23
no place to g. BURT 169:18
not fail to g. MORE 531:6
not g. to Canossa BISM 116:8
not let thee g. BIBL 75:6
Nowhere to g. but out KING 436:6
One of us must g. LAST 456:21
One to come, and one to g. CARR 191:8
Quickly come, quickly g. PROV 610:3
Rain, rain, g. away NURS 550:11
that I g. away BIBL 102:24
thus far shalt thou g. PARN 568:1
to boldly g. RODD 631:1
To g. away is to die HARA 359:13
to hell I will g. MILL 507:25
unto Caesar shalt thou g. BIBL 104:19
wherever he wants to g. BRAU 147:6
with thee to g. MILT 518:1
you can have another g. QUAN 618:11
goads words are as g. BIBL 85:3
goal final g. of ill TENN 761:9
g. of grief RALE 620:11
moving freely, without a g. KLEE 442:3
goals muddied oafs at the g. KIPL 439:6
positive g. BERL 68:14
goat fleecy hairy g. BELL 63:20
Gall of g. SHAK 684:19
lust of the g. BLAK 119:20
with their g. feet MARL 496:9
goats Cadwallader and all his g. SHAK 672:2
drink the blood of g. BOOK 135:3
from the g. MISS 523:6
g. on the left BIBL 97:11
go on, my she-g. VIRG 796:13
hair is as a flock of g. BIBL 85:14
refuge for the wild g. BOOK 139:4
gobbledygoo your g. PLAT 577:13
goblet navel like a round g. BIBL 86:4
goblin or g. damned SHAK 662:18
goblins sprites and g. SHAK 703:2
God acceptable unto G. BIBL 105:14
afraid to look upon G. BIBL 75:27
All things are possible with G. PROV 595:4
and now with G. WALT 802:19
armour of G. BIBL 108:12
As a g. self-slain SWIN 750:19
attracted by G. INGE 399:6
beast or a g. ARIS 25:3
beast, or a g. BACO 42:34
beauty of the house of G. SUGE 745:12
becoming a g. VESP 791:15
before the g. of love DONN 274:7
being of a g. HUME 395:8
best thing G. invents BROW 155:29
bitter G. to follow SWIN 751:4
brother in G. BELL 63:17
burial-ground G.'s-acre LONG 473:19
bush afire with G. BROW 154:13
But for the grace of G. BRAD 146:5
by the hand of G. MARA 495:5
Cabots talk only to G. BOSS 143:15
cause of G. BOWL 146:1
children of G. BIBL 91:11
children of G. BIBL 93:3
children of G. BIBL 105:8
choose a Jewish G. BROW 152:9
circumvent G. SHAK 666:21
city of G. BOOK 137:16
closer walk with G. COWP 240:21
CMG (Call Me G.) SAYI 647:32
conception of G. STRA 744:8
conscious water saw its G. CRAS 244:3
could not think G. would CHAR 203:8
daughter of the voice of G. WORD 830:12
deny a G. BACO 42:8
discussing their duty to G. WHIT 815:15
don't think G. comes well out of it WOOL 827:4
Doth G. exact day-labour MILT 518:30
Doth Job fear G. BIBL 80:35
duty towards G. BOOK 130:12
end of our desires is G. THOM 771:13
Enoch walked with G. BIBL 74:13
equal with G. BIBL 108:16
even G. was born too late LOWE 478:6
farther from G. PROV 607:20
Fear G. BIBL 85:5
Fear G. BIBL 110:30
Fear G. BORR 143:13
feel the principle of G. FOX 322:11
Fellow-citizens: G. reigns GARF 329:16
find out G. BIBL 81:14
For G.'s sake let's go DONN 275:4
For G.'s sake, look after our people LAST 455:13
forgotten before G. BIBL 99:20
forgotten even by G. BROW 157:5
from the love of G. BIBL 105:12
gift from G. ADEN 6:2
gift of G. BIBL 103:23
give thanks to G. BIBL 109:7
glory of G. BLAK 119:20
G. all-bounteous SMAR 722:2
G. Almighty first planted BACO 43:4
G. and angels BACO 41:16
G. and an idol LUTH 480:3
G. and devil DOST 275:16
G. and I both knew KLOP 442:5
G. and mammon BIBL 93:22
G. and nature AUCT 33:4
G. and Robert Browning BROW 158:16
G. and the doctor OWEN 562:1
G. beginning to resemble HUXL 397:9
G. be in my head PRAY 592:3
G. be merciful ANON 21:10
G. be merciful BIBL 100:16
G. be praised LAST 456:17
G. be thanked BROO 150:16
G. bless America BERL 68:7
G. bless the child HOLI 380:19
G. bless the Prince LINL 469:16
G. bless us every one DICK 261:10
G. cannot alter the past BUTL 172:17
g. cannot change the past AGAT 6:20
G. caught his eye MCCO 484:10
G. commonly gives riches LUTH 480:5
G. dawned on Chaos SHEL 710:19
G. disposes PROV 606:18
G. disposes THOM 771:1
G. does not play dice EINS 290:11
G. dwells in thy heart BHAG 73:4
G. erects a house DEFO 255:9
G. exists CHEK 208:18
G. forbid BIBL 100:20
G. forbid BIBL 104:37
G. for us all PROV 599:31
G. fulfils himself TENN 760:15
G. gave Noah SONG 729:6
G. has been replaced BARA 53:13
G. has given you good abilities ARAB 23:9
G. has more right JOHN 407:9
G. has written all the books BUTL 172:25
G. hath joined together BIBL 96:12
G. hath made them so WATT 805:8
G. hath numbered thy kingdom BIBL 90:4
G. hath sent me to sea SMAR 722:3
G. helps them that help PROV 601:12

G. help the Minister MELB 503:15
G. in His mercy CRAI 243:18
G. in Three Persons HEBE 367:8
G.-intoxicated man NOVA 547:4
G. is blameless PLAT 578:9
G. is dead FROM 325:11
G. is dead NERV 541:6
G. is dead NIET 545:14
G. Is distant, difficult HILL 376:17
G. is gone up on high WESL 811:5
G. is in the details ROHE 632:3
G. is just JEFF 406:3
G. is Light BLAK 118:7
G. is love BIBL 111:13
G. is love, but LEE 461:19
G. is no respecter BIBL 103:30
G. is not a man BIBL 76:29
G. is not mocked BIBL 107:22
G. is on everyone's side ANOU 22:7
G. is on the side VOLT 798:4
G. is our hope BOOK 134:18
G. is subtle but not malicious EINS 290:10
G. is that great absence THOM 773:15
G. is their belly BIBL 108:22
G. is Three NEWM 542:17
G. is thy law MILT 516:21
G. is usually on the side BUSS 171:7
G. is working his purpose out AING 9:3
G. loveth CHAU 207:7
G. made all BOOT 142:17
G. made and eaten BROW 155:14
G. made me CATE 194:5
G. made the country COWP 241:19
G. made the country PROV 601:13
G. made the wicked Grocer CHES 210:18
G. moves in a mysterious COWP 240:16
G. must think it exceedingly odd KNOX 442:14
G. never sends mouths PROV 601:15
G. now accepteth BIBL 84:21
G. o'erhead LONG 474:5
G. of Abraham HA-L 357:6
G. of Abraham PASC 569:1
G. of frostbite VYAZ 798:17
G. of Jacob BOOK 134:19
G. of life, and poesy BYRO 175:6
G. of love HERB 373:14
G. of Nature HERB 373:7
G. of our fathers SIDD 717:18
G. of Things as They are KIPL 440:19
G. only another artist PICA 576:3
G., or in other words, Nature SPIN 734:25
G., our help in ages past WATT 805:19
G. owns heaven SEXT 655:6
G. paints the scenery HART 363:7
G. prepares evil ANON 21:2
G. proved them BIBL 91:8
G. punish England FUNK 327:14
g. pursuing, the maiden hid SWIN 750:7
G. reigned from the wood FORT 321:8
G. save Ireland LAST 455:16
G. save king Solomon BIBL 79:15
G. save our gracious king SONG 729:7
G. save the king BIBL 78:22
G. save the king SHAK 695:20
G. save the king SONG 729:7
G. saw that it was good BIBL 73:12
G. seems to have left the receiver KOES 443:4
G. send every gentleman BALL 52:4
G.'s face is above MIDR 507:17
G.'s finger touched him TENN 761:22
G.'s first blunder NIET 545:11
G.'s first Creature BACO 44:32
G. shall wipe away BIBL 112:12
G. shall wipe away BIBL 113:8
G. si Love FORS 321:3
G.'s image man doth bear SPEG 731:23
G.'s in his heaven BROW 157:12
G.'s in his heaven PROV 601:16
G. so commanded MILT 517:16
G. so loved the world BIBL 101:18
G. Sometimes withhold MORE 530:24
G.'s opportunity PROV 606:19
G.'s revenge FOOT 319:6
G.-sustaining University GLAD 341:12
G. takes a text HERB 372:5
G. the Father Almighty BOOK 126:10
G. the first garden made COWL 239:12
G. their severance ARNO 28:3
G. the soul POPE 585:16
G. they ought to crucify CART 192:15
G. to be his guide BUNY 161:12
G., to me, it seems FULL 327:4
G. took him BIBL 74:13
G., who is our home WORD 829:20
G. who is the ultimate reason LEIB 462:20
G. who made thee mighty BENS 66:13
G. whom he hath not seen BIBL 111:15
G., whom I worship NELS 540:19
G. will grant an end VIRG 793:9
G. will know the truth EPIT 304:2
G. will pardon me LAST 455:9
G. will provide BIBL 74:32
G. will recognize ARNA 25:22
G. will wipe away tears BIBL 87:11
G. within the shadow LOWE 477:16
G. won't, and we can't CLOU 221:20
grandeur of G. HOPK 384:5
greater glory of G. MOTT 535:1
great g. Pan BROW 154:20
great man of G. ROBI 629:18
Had G. on his side DYLA 287:17
Had I but served G. WOLS 826:5
Had I but served my G. SHAK 673:17
half believes a G. YOUN 839:9
hands of the living G. BIBL 109:27
Has G. played Knebworth GALL 328:16
hath not seen G. BIBL 111:16
have G. for his father CYPR 248:10
hears the steps of G. BISM 116:18
He for G. only MILT 516:15
here is G.'s plenty DRYD 283:11
He sung of G. SMAR 722:9
He trusted in G. BOOK 132:22
Hey for G. Almighty KETT 434:12
honest G. INGE 399:13
Honest to G. ROBI 629:19
house of G. BIBL 75:3
house of my G. BOOK 137:13
How odd Of G. EWER 305:12
how you appear to G. UNAM 787:8
I am a G. SHEL 713:9
idea of G. ELIO 293:16
if a G. there be SWIN 751:2
If G. be for us BIBL 105:11
if G. did not exist VOLT 797:16
if G. talks to you SZAS 752:2
If Oasis are bigger than G. CHIS 212:6
If only G. would give some sign ALLE 12:15
if there be a G. ANON 18:4
I go to G. MORE 531:13
I have seen G. BIBL 75:7
image of G. TALM 753:18
image of his G. GRAI 348:12
immortal g. of harmony BEET 61:20
in apprehension how like a g. SHAK 663:18
industry in the G. business MARC 495:6
in thanking G. BROW 154:8
In the name of G., go AMER 13:7
In the name of G., go CROM 245:14
in the sight of G. BOOK 130:22
into the Hand of G. HASK 363:16
is the art of G. YOUN 839:14
it is not, the voice of G. POPE 586:15
Just are the ways of G. MILT 518:17
justify G.'s ways HOUS 391:9
justify the ways of G. MILT 514:9
kills the image of G. MILT 519:8
kingdom of G. BIBL 93:26
kingdom of G. BIBL 96:15
kingdom of G. BIBL 101:16
kingdom of G. is within you BIBL 100:12
know his G. by night VAUG 790:3
known unto G. EPIT 304:5
knows the secret of G. SIKH 719:14
know the mind of G. HAWK 364:11
know you're . . . G. BARN 55:5
label men for G. THOM 774:10
land G. gave to Cain CART 192:18
leads—G. knows where BYRO 177:11
leave the word of G. BIBL 103:20
Let G. be true BIBL 104:30
Let us pray to G. BECK 59:13
Like a g. he seems CATU 197:9
like kissing G. BRUC 158:18
liveth unto G. BIBL 105:1
Lord G. made them all ALEX 11:8
Lord G. of your fathers BIBL 75:30
Lord thy G. BIBL 76:8
love of G. is shed abroad BIBL 104:35
love the Lord thy G. BIBL 96:24
maker and builder is G. BIBL 109:29
makes a g. of me KEAT 427:30
man sent from G. BIBL 101:4
Man's love of G. MAIM 491:8
man whose g. is in the skies SHAW 708:22
man with G. is always KNOX 442:11
Man's word is G. in man TENN 759:12
many are afraid of G. LOCK 472:9
Men not afraid of G. POPE 586:22
Messenger of G. KORA 445:10
mills of G. grind slowly LONG 474:8
mills of G. grind slowly PROV 606:37
more just than G. BIBL 81:8
My G., I love Thee CASW 194:2
My God, my G. BIBL 97:29
My God, my G. BOOK 132:21
my King and my G. BOOK 137:11
My Lord and my G. BIBL 103:5
Name of G. is sweet SIKH 719:9
Name of G., the Merciful KORA 443:12
nature is the art of G. BROW 153:20
nature of G. ANON 17:21
Nearer, my G., to thee ADAM 3:21
nearer you are to G. WOTT 833:8
negation of G. GLAD 340:13
neglect G. and his Angels DONN 275:8
neither doth G. respect BIBL 79:8
next to g. america CUMM 247:4
noblest work of G. BURN 166:26
no G. can please ROCH 630:2
No man hath seen G. BIBL 101:8
not known to anyone except G. SOCR 727:2
Now thank we all our G. WINK 823:6
observing G.'s laws ELEA 291:14
Of all G.'s works MILT 517:18
of such is the kingdom of G. BIBL 98:10
of the ways of G. BIBL 82:1
O G. of Bethel DODD 271:20
oily man of G. THOM 774:23
one G. in Trinity BOOK 126:22
One G., one law TENN 762:6
one G. only CLOU 221:24
only G. can make a tree KILM 436:1
only the Messenger of G. KORA 444:15
ordained of G. BIBL 105:19
others call it G. CARR 192:2
our G. is still LUTH 480:2
Our G.'s forgotten QUAR 618:12
out of the mouth of G. BIBL 92:32
owe G. a death SHAK 670:8
paltered with Eternal G. TENN 765:6
peace of G. JAME 402:17
Perfect G. BOOK 127:1
power belongeth unto G. BOOK 135:23
praise of G. AUGU 36:14
praise to thee, my G. KEN 433:2
praising G. BIBL 103:19
presume not G. to scan POPE 585:19
put thy trust in G. BOOK 134:11
put your trust in G. BLAC 116:21
ranks the same with G. BROW 157:13
reader of the works of G. COWP 241:27
Read G. aright QUAR 618:20
really is a G. DESC 258:19

God (*cont.*):
respect for the idea of G. DUHA 284:12
Riches, the dumb g. JONS 420:3
river Is a strong brown g. ELIO 294:12
sacraments to a dying g. HEIN 368:9
saying 'Ta' to G. SPEN 732:16
scarce to G. above SPEN 734:20
see G. in every human TERE 768:9
see G. in the ordinary things AWDR 39:20
seek their meat from G. BOOK 139:5
Sees G. in clouds POPE 585:10
Servant of G., well done MILT 517:5
serve G. and Mammon PROV 615:44
shadow of G. BROW 152:12
shall I see G. BIBL 81:22
short of the glory of G. BIBL 104:32
sing My G. and King HERB 372:3
Sing what G. doth PEMB 572:8
Something beautiful for G. MUGG 534:15
something beautiful for G. TERE 768:7
sons of G. BIBL 74:15
spend and G. will send GASC 330:14
Spirit of the Lord G. BIBL 89:5
spirit shall return unto G. BIBL 85:2
Stamps G.'s own name COWP 241:15
stop believing in G. CHES 211:22
sufficiency is of G. BIBL 107:5
sung 'G. the Queen' KIPL 438:1
suppose that G. is only TEMP 757:7
task of praising G. BART 56:6
Teach me, my G. and King HERB 372:12
than a bogus g. MACN 488:6
Thanks to G. BUÑU 160:13
that is really your G. LUTH 480:4
that of G. in every one FOX 322:10
the G. that he worships SWIF 747:18
them that love G. BIBL 105:10
there is a G. ALLE 12:11
There is no G. BOOK 132:5
they shall see G. BIBL 93:3
thinks little of G. PLUT 579:9
think there is a G. CLOU 221:23
this g. did shake SHAK 674:11
thou art a direct G. DONN 275:1
thou being dead art a G. SWIN 751:6
Thou, my G., art in't HERR 375:1
three-personed G. DONN 272:24
through darkness up to G. TENN 761:13
Thunder is the voice of G. MATH 501:11
thy God my G. BIBL 78:12
Thy G. reigneth BIBL 88:12
to a dying g. CLOS 222:13
To glorify G. SHOR 717:15
To G. belongs all that is KORA 444:13
To G. I speak Spanish CHAR 203:16
To see G. only DONN 273:4
to the eye of G. OLIV 553:16
to the unknown g. BIBL 104:8
touched the face of G. MAGE 489:9
touch the face of G. REAG 623:7
transcendent g. AYER 40:6
triangles were to make a G. MONT 528:8
trying to spell G. ROBI 629:16
understands to the G. THOM 771:14
unto G. BIBL 96:22
unto G. all things come home KORA 445:7
up to Nature's G. POPE 586:4
Verb is G. HUGO 393:16
Very God of very G. BOOK 129:8
voice of G. ALCU 10:10
voice of G. PROV 613:35
wagering that G. is PASC 568:16
want to take in G. LOWE 477:11
ways of G. to man POPE 585:5
were I Lord G. EPIT 302:13
whan G. first maked man CHAU 206:4
What G. abandoned HOUS 390:9
What G. has joined together SHAW 707:10
What G. hath cleansed BIBL 103:29
What hath G. wrought BIBL 77:1
What hath G. wrought TELE 758:12
When G. at first made man HERB 373:6
when G.'s the theme SMAR 722:13
Where G. builds a church PROV 614:36
Where is now thy G. BOOK 134:8
whom G. hath joined BOOK 131:7
Whose cause is G. COWP 242:8
with G. all things are possible BIBL 96:16
women, G. help us SAYE 646:7
Word was with G. BIBL 101:1
Word was with G. OPEN 555:19
would G. this flesh SWIN 751:13
wrestling with (my God!) my G. HOPK 384:3
writing about G. WAUG 806:22
you are a g. ROST 635:16

godamm Lhude sing G. POUN 589:6

goddess bitch-g. success JAME 404:5
G., excellently bright JONS 419:17
g. of hunting SPEN 732:13

goddesses g. of good fortune LAWS 459:7
like the immortal g. HOME 381:23

godfather so noble a g. SHAK 705:27

godfathers G. and Godmothers BOOK 130:10

godhead touching his G. BOOK 127:1
true g. was evident VIRG 793:12

godless decent g. people ELIO 295:22

godliness continual g. BOOK 128:18
next to g. PROV 597:23
next to g. WESL 811:12

godly g., righteous, and sober life BOOK 125:17
unity, and g. love BOOK 129:11

godmothers Godfathers and G. BOOK 130:10

Godot waiting for G. BECK 59:24

gods alien people clutching their g. ELIO 295:2
angels would be g. POPE 585:12
By the nine g. MACA 483:3
convenient that there be g. OVID 561:7
creates g. MONT 528:2
dare the G. MARL 496:23
dark world where g. ROET 631:10
daughter of the g. TENN 758:16
death concerns the g. SOPH 728:13
dish fit for the g. SHAK 675:3
do the G. inherit SHAK 679:22
fit love for g. MILT 517:13
gave birth to the G. HOLB 380:17
g. are come down to us BIBL 103:32
g. are on the side of the stronger TACI 752:17
g. avert this omen CICE 217:22
g. have lived in the woods VIRG 795:18
g. of the countryside VIRG 796:19
g. send nuts PROV 601:18
g., that mortal beauty chase MARV 498:14
G., that wanton in the air LOVE 476:12
g. themselves cannot recall TENN 767:1
g. themselves struggle SCHI 648:13
g. thought otherwise VIRG 794:6
G. who live for ever MACA 483:2
g. wish to destroy CONN 233:25
Götterdämmerung without the g. MACD 484:19
Greeks were g. FUSE 327:15
I have said, Ye are g. BOOK 137:10
in the lap of the g. HOME 382:8
in the world made g. JONS 420:2
irregular worshipper of the g. HORA 388:2
Kings it makes g. SHAK 696:27
loved by the g. PLAT 578:2
make the g. above relent VIRG 795:5
not recognizing the g. PLAT 578:1
on a par with the g. SAPP 644:14
outcome to the G. CORN 236:16
So many g. WILC 817:10
These be thy g., O Israel BIBL 76:16
they are called g. JAME 402:14
they first make g. LEVI 466:9
Thou shalt have no other g. BIBL 76:8
use the g.' gifts wisely HORA 389:10
utterance of the early g. KEAT 427:25
Whatever g. may be SWIN 750:22
What men or g. KEAT 428:22
Whom the g. love MENA 504:12
Whom the G. love PROV 615:3
Whom the g. would destroy PROV 615:4
Ye shall be as g. BIBL 73:25
you g., Give to your boy DRYD 280:26

goes g. around comes around SAYI 648:8
g. of a night SHER 716:11

goest whithersoever thou g. BIBL 77:17
whither thou g., I will go BIBL 78:12

going At the g. down of the sun BINY 115:8
country wears their g. DUNN 285:15
endure Their g. hence SHAK 680:5
g. gets tough KENN 433:21
g. the way of all the earth BIBL 77:23
g. to a feast JONS 419:19
g. to and fro in the earth BIBL 80:34
not know where he is g. LIN 469:17
order of your g. SHAK 684:13
to what he was g. HARD 361:20
we are g. JOHN 415:12
When the g. gets tough PROV 614:28

goings numberless g.-on of life COLE 225:13
ordered my g. BOOK 133:31

gold all done up in g. ASHF 30:13
All that glitters is not g. PROV 595:3
apples of g. BIBL 83:18
Apples of g. SWIN 751:12
be it gash or g. BROO 151:5
bridge of g. PROV 604:17
bringing g., and silver BIBL 79:19
building roofs of g. SHAK 670:28
candelabrum of g. BERN 69:6
clothing is of wrought g. BOOK 134:16
cross of g. BRYA 159:3
cursed craving for g. VIRG 794:8
eighty years in g. BYRO 179:12
feathers like g. BOOK 136:7
fetch the age of g. MILT 513:24
fetters, though of g. BACO 42:1
get much g. BIBL 92:19
gild refinèd g. SHAK 677:15
g. and amber JONS 420:11
g., and frankincense BIBL 92:23
g. and silver becks me SHAK 677:10
G.? a transient, shining trouble GRAI 348:11
G. he bought too dear PROV 601:20
g. filling in a mouthful of decay OSBO 560:3
g. kames in their hair BALL 51:16
g. medal for poetry GRAV 349:19
G. never starts aside GOOG 346:14
gold of G. BOOK 136:19
g. of the day CROS 246:4
g. shines like fire PIND 576:8
g. wes changyd into lede WYNT 834:16
g., yea, than much fine gold BOOK 132:17
harpstring of g. SWIN 751:4
If g. ruste, what shall iren do CHAU 204:25
in purple and g. BYRO 175:23
Love is mor than g. LYDG 480:12
Nor all, that glisters, g. GRAY 350:22
pale—is yet of g. CRAB 243:6
path of g. BROW 157:6
patines of bright g. SHAK 688:22
poop was beaten g. SHAK 656:23
pure g. flows forth TOCQ 778:18
queen in a vesture of g. BOOK 134:15
rarer gifts than g. BROO 150:7
reach at the glorious g. SHAK 672:14
realms of g. KEAT 429:20
realms of g. OPEN 556:2
religion of g. BAGE 46:16
sand and ruin and g. SWIN 751:18
Scarfs, garters, g. POPE 585:25
street of the city was g. BIBL 113:10
streets are paved with g. COLM 229:15
stuffed their mouths with g. BEVA 72:3
This g., my dearest LEAP 460:1
thousands of g. and silver BOOK 140:8
to India for g. MARL 496:2
trodden g. MILT 515:3
what's become of all the g. BROW 158:11
Within its net of g. MACN 488:16

Would he have g. HERB 373:16
your glistering g. BRAD 146:16
golden add to g. numbers DEKK 256:5
beside the g. door LAZA 459:12
burnished with g. rind MILT 516:12
Casting down their g. crowns HEBE 367:8
circle of the g. year TENN 759:5
Clasped by the g. light HOOD 382:27
end of a g. string BLAK 119:3
fell her g. hair TURN 785:12
g. bough BORR 144:8
g. bowl be broken BIBL 85:2
g.-calf of self-love CARL 187:5
g. days of Saturn's reign VIRG 796:4
g. elephants next SHOR 717:14
g. entrails DRAY 279:5
g. key can open PROV 601:21
G. lads and girls SHAK 661:1
g. lamps in a green night MARV 498:7
g. moments of our history GLAD 341:7
G. opinions SHAK 682:13
g. pillars high BLAK 118:23
g. priests JEWE 407:8
G. Road to Samarkand FLEC 317:4
G. slumbers kiss your eyes DEKK 256:6
G. stockings GOGA 343:22
g. years return SHEL 711:12
hand that lays the g. egg GOLD 346:2
hangs a g. chain PUSH 618:2
Happy the g. mean MASS 501:4
His g. locks PEEL 572:1
in the g. world SHAK 658:7
in their g. hair TENN 765:12
Jerusalem the g. NEAL 540:3
King Charles's g. days SONG 729:12
love in a g. bowl BLAK 118:8
loves the g. mean HORA 388:7
morning had been g. CHUR 216:12
name of the G. *Vanity* SONG 730:2
observed the g. rule BLAK 120:4
poets only deliver a g. SIDN 718:22
Roll down their g. sand HEBE 367:6
seven g. candlesticks BIBL 111:21
Silence is g. PROV 610:41
took their g. age THOM 775:3
We are g. MITC 523:17
went into a g. land TURN 785:19
your g. hair Margareta CELA 199:8
Goldengrove G. unleaving HOPK 384:17
goldsmith To Oliver G., A Poet EPIT 303:17
golf g. may be played on Sunday LEAC 459:20
made more Liars than G. ROGE 631:19
thousand lost g. balls ELIO 295:22
too young to take up g. ADAM 2:7
Golgotha field of G. SHAK 695:19
in the Hebrew G. BIBL 102:32
gondola Did'st ever see a g. BYRO 173:14
g. of London DISR 270:20
What else is like the g. CLOU 221:19
gone All, all are g. LAMB 448:20
And they are g. KEAT 427:16
come out of *G. with the Wind* POWE 590:13
g. altogether beyond MAHĀ 490:3
G. before LAMB 448:19
g. from original righteousness BOOK 142:9
g. into the world of light VAUG 790:11
g. with the wind DOWS 277:5
great spirit g. SHAK 656:12
He is g. JOHN 415:12
not dead—but g. ROGE 631:13
She's g. for ever SHAK 680:11
something that is g. WORD 829:19
they are g. forever MANN 493:19
welcomest when they are g. SHAK 672:8
what haste I can to be g. LAST 456:16
What's g. SHAK 703:7
when I am g. ROSS 634:8
Wilt thou be g. SHAK 697:32
gong that g.-tormented sea YEAT 835:7
gongs Strong g. groaning CHES 210:11
struck regularly like g. COWA 239:4
good Address to the unco g. BURN 166:7
and doth no g. RALE 620:12
And now g. morrow DONN 274:3
annoyance of a g. example TWAI 786:25
antipathy of g. to bad POPE 586:21
Any g. of George the Thirds LAND 450:4
any g. thing BIBL 101:11
anything g. to say LONG 475:8
apprehension of the g. SHAK 694:16
As for Doing-g. THOR 776:8
as g. as he found it COBB 223:9
be a g. animal SPEN 732:2
be g. in the country WILD 818:20
Be g., sweet maid KING 437:4
be g. to some man SHAW 709:4
being really g. WILD 817:20
Beneath the g. how far GRAY 351:4
best is enemy of g. PROV 595:45
best is the enemy of the g. VOLT 797:11
Better a g. cow PROV 596:4
better than the G. Old Days BINC 115:7
better to be g. WILD 818:21
better to fight for the g. TENN 764:17
call a man *a g. man* JOHN 417:8
call g. evil BIBL 86:19
call no being g. MILL 507:25
can't be g., be careful PROV 603:27
choose the g. BIBL 86:26
common g. to all SHAK 677:4
could be a g. woman THAC 769:12
does most g. or harm BAGE 47:13
do evil, that g. may come BIBL 104:31
do evil that g. may come PROV 607:28
do g. and to communicate BIBL 110:9
Do g. by stealth POPE 586:20
do g. to them BIBL 99:4
either g. or bad SHAK 663:16
Evil, be thou my g. MILT 516:10
evil turn to g. MILT 517:27
few Know their own g. DRYD 282:35
for our country's g. CART 192:11
for the public g. LOCK 472:6
for your g., for all your goods GEOR 333:10
future apparent g. HOBB 378:16
Gallop about doing g. SMIT 724:17
giver of all g. things BOOK 128:14
go about doing g. CREI 244:20
God saw that it was g. BIBL 73:12
g. action by stealth LAMB 449:7
g. and faithful servant BIBL 97:8
g. and immoral CHUR 214:21
g. as he may be MONT 528:4
G. at which all things aim ARIS 24:15
g. becomes indistinguishable DAWS 253:7
g. beginning makes PROV 601:23
G., but not religious-good HARD 361:3
g. Compensate bad BROW 157:26
g. die early DEFO 255:4
g. die first WORD 828:9
g. die young PROV 601:24
g. ended happily WILD 817:19
g. enough to be a clergyman JOHN 414:16
g. fences make good neighbours FROS 326:5
g. for inside of a man PROV 612:21
g. for the people of England GLAD 341:4
g. in the worst of us ANON 19:4
g. is oft interrèd SHAK 675:27
g. is the enemy PROV 601:27
g. Jack makes a good Jill PROV 601:28
g. man and a good citizen AUCT 33:9
g. man, and a just BIBL 100:30
g. man is merciful BOOK 139:19
g. man to do nothing MISQ 521:17
G. men are scarce PROV 601:29
g. minute goes BROW 158:13
g. name BIBL 83:13
g. news from Ghent to Aix BROW 156:7
g. of human nature BACO 44:18
g. of man ARIS 24:16
G. of man ARIS 24:17
g. of one's country FARQ 307:11
g. of subjects DEFO 255:16
g. of the people CICE 217:12
g. old Cause MILT 519:22
g. old cause WORD 830:13
g. people were clever WORD 827:14
g. provoke to harm SHAK 686:22
G. seed makes good crop PROV 601:30
g. sense and good taste LA B 446:17
g. that I would I do not BIBL 105:4
g., the bad, and the ugly FILM 312:21
g. things must come to an end PROV 594:21
G. things of day SHAK 684:7
g. time coming SCOT 652:7
g. time was had by all SMIT 724:18
g. to feel rotten YESE 838:8
g. to listen ADVE 7:33
g. to talk ADVE 7:34
g. unluckily STOP 743:19
g. want power SHEL 713:8
g. when they do as others do FRAN 322:13
g. Will be the final goal TENN 761:9
g. will never be our task MILT 514:15
g. will toward men BIBL 98:22
G. wine needs no bush PROV 601:31
g. without qualification KANT 425:13
G. women always think BROO 150:19
G. words do not last long JOSE 421:9
g. words, I think, were best SHAK 677:19
g. works are not wasted CALD 181:4
g. ye are and bad TENN 759:23
Greed is g. FILM 311:9
Guinness is g. for you ADVE 7:22
had been g. for that man BIBL 97:17
Hanging is too g. for him BUNY 161:2
have a g. thing SHAK 669:26
heaven doing g. on earth TERE 768:12
He wos wery g. to me DICK 260:22
highest g. CICE 217:14
His own g. MILL 508:18
hold fast that which is g. BIBL 109:11
human nature is g. MENG 504:23
impulsive to g. MANN 493:18
In art the best is g. enough GOET 343:6
it cannot come to g. SHAK 661:28
I will be g. VICT 792:1
kept the g. wine BIBL 101:14
knowing g. and evil BIBL 73:25
leave assurèd g. DRAY 279:5
like a *g.* fiend THOM 772:19
loves what he is g. at SHAD 655:12
luxury of doing g. CRAB 243:8
luxury was doing g. GART 330:12
Men have never been g. BART 56:4
much g. would be absent THOM 771:15
neither g. nor bad BALZ 52:17
never had it so g. MACM 487:17
never so g. or so bad MACK 486:11
No g. man is a Briton AUSO 37:11
no ills from g. dissuade SMAR 722:2
none that doeth g. BOOK 132:5
not g. company AUST 38:10
nothing g. to be had HAZL 365:9
obscurely g. ADDI 4:15
Of g. and evil much they argued MILT 515:19
of g. report BIBL 108:25
one g. deed SHAK 700:3
One g. turn deserves PROV 608:40
only g. Indian PROV 608:27
only g. Indians SHER 715:12
only g. thing left MUSS 537:12
on the evil and on the g. BIBL 93:14
or be thought half as g. WHIT 816:10
out of g. still to find MILT 514:16
overcome evil with g. BIBL 105:18
policy of the g. neighbour ROOS 632:13
possibility of g. times BRAN 147:1
prospect of a distant g. DRYD 281:23
return g. for evil VANB 789:5
rewarded me evil for g. BOOK 133:23
Roman Conquest was a *G. Thing* SELL 654:5
said a g. thing TWAI 786:17
Seek to be g. LYTT 481:3
So shines a g. deed SHAK 688:26

good (*cont.*):
temptation to be g. BREC 147:8
than to seem g. SALL 643:9
that you're not g. enough TROL 783:9
thy g. with brotherhood BATE 57:4
too much of a g. thing PROV 615:25
truly great who are truly g. CHAP 202:21
universal licence to be g. COLE 224:16
Universally G. MAHĀ 490:15
Whatever g. visits thee KORA 444:10
what g. came of it SOUT 730:13
what was g. for our country WILS 821:10
when shall all men's g. TENN 759:4
When she was g. LONG 475:2
with g. things BOOK 138:17
woman was full of g. works BIBL 103:27
work together for g. BIBL 105:10
would be a g. idea GAND 329:8
would do g. to another BLAK 119:2
your g. works BIBL 93:6
goodbye Every time we say g. PORT 588:4
G.!—Good-bye-ee WEST 812:21
G., moralitee HERB 371:13
G., Piccadilly JUDG 423:1
G. to all that GRAV 349:17
goodlihead flower of g. SKEL 721:12
goodly g. to look to BIBL 78:28
I have a g. heritage BOOK 132:9
sold a g. manor for a song SHAK 656:4
goodman our g.'s awa MICK 507:2
goodness fountain of all g. BOOK 126:16
g. entirely human ELIO 293:16
g. faileth never BAKE 48:13
G. had nothing to do with it WEST 812:5
g. infinite MILT 517:27
G. is not the same thing PLAT 578:7
g. of the Lord BOOK 133:12
If g. lead him not HERB 373:8
inclination to g. BACO 43:7
long-suffering, and of great g. BOOK 138:18
My G., My Guinness ADVE 8:1
goodnight bid the world G. HERR 374:12
gives the stern'st g. SHAK 683:4
G., children CATC 195:19
G.. Ensured release HOUS 390:13
g., sweet ladies SHAK 666:3
G., sweet prince SHAK 667:12
I shall say g. SHAK 697:19
John Thomas says g. LAWR 457:22
My last G. KING 436:7
second best's a gay g. YEAT 836:3
goods all my worldly g. BOOK 131:6
care for external g. WEBE 807:4
desire other men's g. BOOK 130:16
for your good, for all your g. GEOR 333:10
g. are in peace BIBL 99:17
g. the gods provide PROV 611:39
Ill gotten g. never thrive PROV 603:44
Riches and G. BOOK 142:14
when g. are private TAWN 755:15
goodwill In peace; g. CHUR 216:16
name was Great G. HARI 362:7
goose cried in g., alas RANS 621:19
every g. a swan KING 437:13
g. honking amongst tuneful swans VIRG 796:11
G., if I had you SHAK 678:14
Grey g. and gander NURS 548:9
grey g. is gone NURS 549:19
on the ground at G. Green KINN 437:19
sauce for the g. PROV 614:8
steal a g. POLI 582:3
steals a g. ANON 16:8
that g. look SHAK 685:16
gooseberried g. double bed THOM 772:16
gooseberries planty of g. FLEM 317:13
goosey G., goosey gander NURS 548:8
gordian She was a g. shape KEAT 428:14
gore hope it mayn't be human g. DICK 260:16
gored G. mine own thoughts SHAK 705:13
you tossed and g. BOSW 144:20
gorgeous g. East in fee WORD 830:14
g. East with richest hand MILT 515:7
gorgon G., Prince of darkness SPEN 733:15
gorgonized G. me from head to foot TENN 764:4
gormed I'm G.—and I can't say DICK 262:8
gorse G. fires are smoking LONG 475:7
g. is out of bloom PROV 614:29
gory never shake Thy g. locks SHAK 684:11
Welcome to your g. bed BURN 168:7
Goschen forgot G. CHUR 214:16
gosh by gee by g. by gum CUMM 247:4
goshawk gay g. BALL 50:16
gospel Four for the G. makers SONG 729:11
G. of Christ WESL 811:10
G. of Getting On SHAW 709:5
likeness in the G. KORA 445:11
music of the G. FABE 305:17
preach the g. BIBL 98:14
truth of thy holy G. BOOK 128:21
gossip babbling g. of the air SHAK 701:7
g. achieves significance ISHE 400:9
g. from all the nations AUDE 34:13
G. is a sort of smoke ELIO 292:3
I admit there is g. DISR 269:21
in the g. columns INGH 399:15
Like all g. FORS 321:2
my g. Report SHAK 687:27
got If not, have you g. him SELL 654:7
I g. rhythm GERS 334:14
in our case we have not g. REED 623:14
gotcha G. NEWS 544:6
Gotham Three wise men of G. NURS 551:12
Gothic cars the great G. cathedrals BART 56:8
glory of G. RUSK 639:9
modern G. room PUGI 616:16
more than G. ignorance FIEL 310:10
Gott *ist unser G.* LUTH 480:2
gotta g. use words when I talk to you ELIO 295:24
Gotte *einem sterbenden G.* HEIN 368:9
gotten g. himself the victory BOOK 138:9
Götterdämmerung G. without the gods MACD 484:19
gout give them the g. MONT 527:2
gouverner *G. c'est choisir* LÉVI 466:11
govern cannot g. itself MCNA 488:5
easy to g. BROU 151:14
g. according to the common JAME 402:16
g. in prose CUOM 247:18
g. New South Wales BELL 63:8
g. our conditions SHAK 679:17
of Kings to g. wrong POPE 580:20
people g. themselves THIE 770:18
to g. is to choose LÉVI 466:11
governance by thy g. BOOK 128:12
governed faith in The People g. DICK 266:4
g. by thy good Spirit BOOK 127:17
nation is not g. BURK 162:24
not so well g. HOOK 383:5
governer G. was strong upon WILD 818:33
governess Be a g. BRON 149:17
governing incapable of g. CHES 209:24
right of g. FOX 322:4
government abandon a g. JEFF 405:12
administration of the g. SWIF 747:19
all g. is evil O'SU 560:18
art of g. VOLT 798:10
art of g. is SHAW 708:15
asks you to form a G. ATTL 32:7
at g. expense ARTS 29:20
become the most corrupt g. JEFF 405:10
definition of the best g. HALI 357:17
duty of g. PAIN 563:15
end of g. ADAM 3:14
every form of g. JOHN 414:15
for a bad g. TOCQ 778:11
forms of g. POPE 585:26
function of a g. PALM 566:6
g. above the law SCAR 646:11
G. acquired the tact WEST 812:15
G. and co-operation RUSK 639:4
G. and public opinion SHAW 708:5
g. as an adversary BRUN 158:24
G. at Washington lives GARF 329:16
g. by discussion ATTL 32:5
g. by the uneducated CHES 211:21
G., even in its best state PAIN 563:11
G. is a contrivance BURK 163:19
g. is best THOR 775:25
g. is influenced by SMIT 723:10
g. it deserves MAIS 491:13
g. of Britain's isle SHAK 672:15
g. of laws ADAM 3:5
G. of laws and not of men FORD 319:13
g. of statesmen DISR 269:28
G. of the busy SELD 653:25
g. of the people LINC 468:13
g. of the people PAGE 562:18
g. of the world DISR 269:21
g. of the world THOR 776:17
g. shall be upon his shoulder BIBL 87:1
g. which imprisons THOR 775:26
g. which robs Peter SHAW 707:5
g. without a king BANC 53:4
great service to a g. MEDI 503:8
have an efficient g. TRUM 784:7
If the G. is big enough FORD 319:11
in a disorderly g. HALI 357:16
increase of his g. BIBL 87:1
inherit a g. PAIN 564:1
land of settled g. TENN 767:15
least g. was the best FEIN 308:7
natural party of g. WILS 821:17
no British g. should be brought down MACM 487:20
no go the G. grants MACN 488:8
No G. can be long secure DISR 269:27
not a g. of laws WEBS 807:14
not get all of the g. FRIE 325:3
not the worst g. TROL 782:24
one form of g. JOHN 414:14
one g. sooner learns SMIT 723:13
only instrument of g. LOCK 472:7
Parliamentary g. is impossible DISR 269:8
people's g. WEBS 807:11
pillars of g. BACO 43:31
prepare for g. STEE 736:14
reins of g. are lodged SHEL 710:3
representative g. DISR 270:27
restraints of g. GOLD 344:5
rule nations by your g. VIRG 795:1
signifies the want of g. HOBB 379:1
sister is given to g. DICK 262:17
structure of g. HAVE 364:4
support their g. CLEV 220:15
system of G. GLAD 340:13
to run a g. TRUM 784:5
understood by republican g. TOCQ 778:14
virtue of paper g. BURK 162:21
vulgar arts of g. PEEL 571:18
well-ordered g. HALI 357:10
work for a G. I despise KEYN 435:3
worst form of G. CHUR 216:2
governments corrupted g. HALI 357:15
foundation of most g. ADAM 3:15
G. always want RADC 620:3
g. had better get out of the way EISE 291:10
g. need both shepherds VOLT 798:3
g. of Europe JEFF 405:4
Never believe g. GELL 333:3
that the two g. MITC 523:13
governors g., teachers BOOK 130:14
supreme g., the mob WALP 800:13
governs g. his state by virtue CONF 231:5
g. the passions HUME 394:13
that which g. least O'SU 560:18
which g. not at all THOR 775:25
gowd man's the g. BURN 167:6
Gower O moral G. CHAU 207:22
gown wearing a black g. CHES 209:6
wrap me in a g. HERB 371:23
Goya I am G. VOZN 798:16

grab all smash and no g. NICO 545:4
G. this land MORR 533:4
Gracchos Quis tulerit G. JUVE 424:7
grace Amazing g. NEWT 543:13
Angels and ministers of g. SHAK 662:18
attractive kind of g. ROYD 637:1
But for the g. of God BRAD 146:5
by special g. BOOK 128:5
by the g. of God BIBL 106:19
courtly foreign g. TENN 766:12
fallen from g. BIBL 107:20
free giving of a g. LESS 465:14
full of g. PRAY 592:1
full of g. PROV 606:42
G. be unto you BIBL 111:17
g. did much more abound BIBL 104:36
G. is given of God CLOU 221:18
G. me no grace SHAK 695:1
g., new birth ARNO 28:27
g. of a boy BETJ 71:6
G. of God is in Courtesy BELL 63:13
g. of God which was with me BIBL 106:20
g.-proud faces BURN 169:3
G. under pressure HEMI 369:13
grow old with a good g. STEE 736:18
inward and spiritual g. BOOK 130:17
lend her g. TENN 762:20
means of g. BOOK 127:19
new light of g. SMOL 726:14
REGRET INFORM YOUR G. TELE 758:4
snatch a g. POPE 584:14
speech be alway with g. BIBL 109:6
strong toil of g. SHAK 658:5
such g. did lend her SHAK 702:29
such heavenly g. SPEN 733:16
sweet attractive g. MILT 516:15
that g. may abound BIBL 104:37
throne of the heavenly g. BOOK 125:14
with a better g. SHAK 701:12
wordy o' a g. BURN 168:20
world is judged by g. TALM 753:19
graceful g. air and heavenly mug FLEM 317:18
Such a g. exit JUNO 423:18
graces deficiency in *the g.* JOHN 415:20
G. do not seem to be natives CHES 209:18
g. slighted CRAB 242:21
inherit heaven's g. SHAK 705:6
sacrifice to the g. BURK 164:7
Upon her eyelids many G. SPEN 733:24
gracing either other Sweetly g. CAMP 184:1
gracious all his g. parts SHAK 677:11
he is g. BOOK 141:6
how g. the Lord is BOOK 133:20
Lord is g. BIBL 110:27
O be favourable and g. BOOK 135:9
So hallowed and so g. SHAK 661:11
gradient g.'s against her AUDE 34:12
gradual g. day weakening SPEN 732:24
gradualness inevitability of g. WEBB 807:1
graduates sweet girl-g. TENN 765:12
Graeculus G. *esuriens* JUVE 424:10
graffiti g. in the urinals GIDE 336:17
graft G. in our hearts BOOK 128:14
grail g. of laughter CRAN 243:21
grain choice g. STOU 744:2
g. of salt PLIN 578:19
on guano and on g. TENN 766:7
rain is destroying his g. HERB 371:12
well meant for g. TENN 760:25
world in a g. of sand BLAK 117:17
grains tight g. parting ROET 631:6
gramina *g. campis* HORA 389:6
grammar attention to g. CHAM 200:11
destroy every g. school CROS 246:6
don't want to talk g. SHAW 709:11
erecting a g. school SHAK 672:24
g., and nonsense GOLD 345:17
G., the ground of al LANG 450:20
Heedless of g. BARH 54:7
talking bad g. DISR 269:26
grammatical g. purity JOHN 410:22
grammatici G. *certant* HORA 385:16
grammaticus G., *rhetor*, *geometres* JUVE 424:10
gramophone g. company TREE 781:6
puts a record on the g. ELIO 296:11
granary on a g. floor KEAT 430:9
grand down the G. Canyon MARQ 497:11
G. Duchesses are doing NAPO 538:15
g. Perhaps BROW 155:8
g. style ARNO 29:8
g. to be blooming well dead SARO 644:18
grandeur certain spiritual g. ELIO 292:16
charged with the g. HOPK 384:5
g. hear with a disdainful smile GRAY 350:9
g. in this view DARW 250:22
g. that was Rome POE 579:21
g. underlying the sorriest things HARD 361:5
old Scotia's g. BURN 166:26
grandfather ape for his g. HUXL 397:20
carrying a g. clock TREE 781:5
g. or his grandfather WILB 817:2
grandfathers makes friends with its g. MUMF 536:6
grandmother grandfather or his g. WILB 817:2
teach your g. PROV 598:38
We have become a g. THAT 770:8
grandsire g. cut his throat SWIF 749:27
grange at the moated g. SHAK 686:19
lonely moated g. TENN 763:19
granites Through g. which titanic wars OWEN 562:11
grant g. me this in return CATU 197:17
half g. what I wish FROS 325:15
OLD CARY G. FINE TELE 758:7
granted g. scarce to God SPEN 734:20
Granth Guru G. Sahib SIKH 720:1
grape burst Joy's g. KEAT 429:5
For one sweet g. SHAK 704:1
G. is my mulatto mother HUGH 393:10
peel me a g. WEST 812:3
grapes brought forth wild g. BIBL 86:16
gleaning of the g. BIBL 77:34
g. of the wine-press MACA 482:21
g. of thorns BIBL 94:10
g. of wrath BORR 144:9
g. of wrath HOWE 391:15
sour g. BIBL 89:29
sour g. and ashes ASHF 30:15
grapeshot whiff of g. CARL 187:21
grapple G. them to thy soul SHAK 662:10
grasp exceed his g. BROW 155:2
G. it like a man of mettle HILL 376:11
G. not at much HERB 373:13
grasped haven't g. the situation KERR 434:7
grasps G. in the comer SHAK 700:16
grass All flesh is g. BIBL 88:1
bringeth forth g. BOOK 139:3
but as g. BOOK 138:20
eateth g. as an ox BIBL 81:38
everywhere nibble g. FAGU 306:3
flesh is as g. BIBL 110:26
g. below CLAR 218:16
g. beyond the door ROSS 635:8
g. can grow through cement CHER 208:22
g. cannot dissolve BLY 122:15
g. grows on the weirs YEAT 835:17
g. is always greener PROV 601:32
g. looking green PERR 573:24
g. returns to the fields HORA 389:6
g. to graze a cow BETJ 71:4
g. will grow in the streets HOOV 383:12
greener than the g. BALL 51:10
green g. growing over me BALL 52:9
green g. shorn BACO 43:5
happy as the g. was green THOM 772:3
hearing the g. grow ELIO 292:23
I am the g. SAND 643:21
I fall on g. MARV 498:15
leaf of g. is no less WHIT 815:14
like the g. BOOK 137:18
parched g. pray TIBU 777:8
Pigeons on the g. STEI 737:6
snake hidden in the g. VIRG 796:1
splendour in the g. WORD 830:9
star-scattered on the g. FITZ 315:3
tides of g. SWIN 751:13
twinkles in the g. TENN 764:5
two blades of g. SWIF 747:22
While the g. grows PROV 614:42
grasshopper g. shall be a burden BIBL 85:2
grasshoppers half a dozen g. BURK 163:26
we were as g. BIBL 76:26
grassy fair Fidele's g. tomb COLL 229:7
grate fluttered on the g. COLE 225:14
grateful anybody can be g. CATU 197:13
single g. thought LESS 465:16
gratefully O g. sing GRAN 348:15
gratias *Deo g.* MISS 520:15
gratification g. of cruelty FOST 321:13
gratified g. desire BLAK 120:9
gratissima *g. serpit* VIRG 794:1
gratitude g. is a species of revenge JOHN 410:20
g. is merely a secret hope LA R 453:19
G., like love ALSO 12:23
g. of a stranger TOCQ 778:16
g. we owe to Adam TWAI 786:21
liking or g. ELIO 292:6
gratuity bribe or g. PENN 572:16
grau *G. ist alle Theorie* GOET 342:20
grave And on that g. HART 363:9
at her g. BALL 52:6
bed is the cold g. BALL 50:11
cold g. BALL 52:6
come to seek a g. DONN 274:24
cradle and the g. DYER 286:16
cradle to the g. SHEL 713:15
digs my g. HERB 372:19
Dig the g. and let me lie STEV 743:4
ditchers and g.-makers SHAK 666:17
dread The g. as little KEN 433:3
Even the g. yawns TREE 781:3
from the cradle to the g. CHUR 215:19
frontier-g. is far away NEWB 541:17
Funeral marches to the g. LONG 474:4
give birth astride of a g. BECK 60:3
go into my g. CLOS 222:3
go into my g. PEPY 573:15
gone wild into his g. SHAK 670:20
g., and not taunting BACO 43:11
g. hides all things SHEL 713:9
g. is not its goal LONG 474:3
g. of a dead Fenian COLL 229:1
g. of Mad Carew HAYE 365:2
g.'s a fine and private MARV 499:3
g., where is thy victory BIBL 107:4
g., whither thou goest BIBL 84:22
G. without thought CHUR 214:3
In every g. make room D'AV 251:8
in peace in his g. DONN 274:26
into the darkness of the g. MILL 509:10
Is that ayont the g. BURN 169:4
jealousy is cruel as the g. BIBL 86:7
kind of healthy g. SMIT 725:9
kingdom for a little g. SHAK 695:14
lead but to the g. GRAY 350:9
letters in the g. JOHN 417:22
made me a g. so rough TENN 764:13
Marriage is the g. CAVE 198:12
now in his colde g. CHAU 205:21
pompous in the g. BROW 153:10
renowned be thy g. SHAK 661:2
requires g. statesmen DISR 270:10
root is ever in its g. HERB 373:17
send you to the g. ORTO 558:4
Sentinel of the g. TATE 755:6
she is in her g. WORD 831:21
shovel a g. in the air CELA 199:8
shown Longfellow's g. MOOR 529:19
sinks me to the g. FORD 319:21
sitting crowned upon the g. HOBB 379:4
stand at my g. and cry ANON 15:24
thank God for the quiet g. KEAT 432:1

grave (*cont.*):
this side of the g. LAND 450:5
travelling toward the g. WORD 830:21
vast and wandering g. TENN 760:27
When my g. is broke up DONN 274:10
Without a g. BYRO 175:10
with sorrow to the g. BIBL 75:17
years and honour to the g. KIPL 439:15
graved G. inside of it BROW 155:25
gravelled g. for lack of matter SHAK 659:19
graven g. image BIBL 76:8
graves dig our g. with our teeth SMIL 722:15
dishonourable g. SHAK 674:13
g. of deceased languages DICK 262:11
g. of little magazines PRES 591:6
g. of their neighbours EDWA 289:10
g. of the martyrs STEV 742:24
g. stood tenantless SHAK 661:9
Let's talk of g. SHAK 695:8
voluntary g. HERB 373:3
watch from their g. BROW 156:18
graveyard for each g. BOCC 123:6
healthiest g. BEHA 61:21
gravitation not believing in g. TROT 783:20
gravity impulsive g. of head POPE 580:17
gravy Abominated g. BENT 67:4
grazing Tilling and g. SULL 746:2
grease gets the g. PROV 611:18
slides by on g. LOWE 477:21
greasy grey-green, g., Limpopo KIPL 441:9
top of the g. pole DISR 271:2
great aim not to be g. LYTT 481:3
all g. men are frauds BONA 125:4
between the small and g. COWP 242:14
both g. and small COLE 226:27
Brothers of the G. GERS 334:20
craven fears of being g. TENN 759:8
desireth g. matters QUAR 618:14
far above the g. GRAY 351:4
From the g. deep TENN 759:15
g. and lofty things MONT 527:6
g. book CALL 181:17
g. book is a great evil PROV 601:33
g. break through SHEN 715:7
g., ere fortune made him so DRYD 281:13
g. gulf fixed BIBL 100:11
g. have kindness POPE 583:8
g. have no heart LA B 446:15
G.-hearted gentlemen BROW 156:21
g. illusion ANGE 14:16
G. is Diana BIBL 104:12
G. is the hand THOM 772:8
g. is truth BROO 151:10
g. life if you don't weaken BUCH 159:8
g. man has his disciples WILD 817:25
g. man helped the poor MACA 483:7
G. men BIBL 81:29
G. men almost always ACTO 1:17
g. men contending BURT 170:13
g. men make mistakes CHUR 214:16
g. men—so-called TOLS 779:11
G. minds think alike PROV 601:36
g. objects make Great minds YOUN 839:13
g. ones devoured the small SIDN 718:3
g. seemed to him little MACA 482:6
G. Society JOHN 408:15
g.—the major novelists LEAV 461:5
g. things from the valley CHES 211:7
g. To do that thing SHAK 657:21
g. to them that know SPRI 735:7
g. was the fall BIBL 94:13
grown so g. SHAK 674:14
he is always g. DRYD 283:6
He Was A G. Man ZIEG 840:3
How g. a matter BIBL 110:18
Ill can he rule the g. SPEN 734:8
know well I am not g. TENN 759:27
lay g. and greatly fallen HOME 382:7
Lives of g. men LONG 474:6
make the Way g. CONF 232:2
many people think him *g.* JOHN 414:25
name made g. HILL 377:8
nothing g. but man HAMI 358:15
only truly g. DISR 270:6
Rightly to be g. SHAK 665:33
simple g. ones gone TENN 764:2
small things with g. VIRG 797:3
so g. a thing happened WHIT 814:19
some men are born g. SHAK 701:28
think the g. unhappy YOUN 838:17
those who were truly g. SPEN 732:18
though fallen, g. BYRO 174:5
thou wouldst be g. SHAK 682:1
To be g. is to be misunderstood EMER 299:24
truly g. who are truly good CHAP 202:21
very small the very g. THAC 769:17
with small men no g. thing MILL 509:2
Great Britain G. has lost an empire ACHE 1:12
G. should free herself SMIT 723:14
natives of G. CHES 209:18
greater G. love hath no man BIBL 102:22
g. man, the greater courtesy TENN 759:31
g. prey upon the less GREE 351:11
g. than a private citizen TACI 752:15
g. than Solomon BIBL 95:16
g. than the whole HESI 375:11
g. than vast spaces UPAN 787:22
g. than we know WORD 831:16
g. the sinner PROV 601:34
he is g. than they RUSK 638:28
they behold a g. SHAK 674:19
thy need is g. SIDN 719:1
greatest firstborn the g. ass CARO 189:3
g. event it is FOX 322:5
g. happiness HUTC 396:15
g. thing in the world MONT 527:15
happiness of the g. number BENT 66:18
I'm the g. ALI 12:3
life to live as the g. he RAIN 620:6
greatly g. to his credit GILB 338:30
would g. win BYRO 178:17
greatness celestial g. TRAH 780:10
dispense with g. GUIZ 354:17
farewell, to all my g. SHAK 673:12
g. going off SHAK 657:11
G. knows itself SHAK 669:3
g. may not fail TENN 759:8
g. of the Lord BIBL 98:16
g., save it be some far-off TENN 759:27
g. thrust upon them SHAK 701:28
G., with private men MASS 501:4
intended g. for men ELIO 292:27
moment of my g. flicker ELIO 295:8
nature of all g. BURK 162:18
Greece Cold is the heart, fair G. BYRO 174:2
Fair G.! sad relic BYRO 174:5
for G. a tear BYRO 176:27
glory that was G. POE 579:21
G. is fallen and Troy COLE 224:18
G. might still be free BYRO 176:26
isles of G. BYRO 176:25
To Gaul, to G. COWP 241:11
to G. the direful spring OPEN 555:2
greed G. is all right BOES 123:10
G. is good FILM 311:9
not enough for everyone's g. BUCH 159:11
greediness how much g. WITH 824:1
greedy G. for the property SALL 643:7
I am g. PUNC 617:16
Greek adapting G. temples PUGI 616:20
G. can do everything JUVE 424:10
G. in its origin MAIN 491:12
G. particles HUGH 393:13
half G., half Latin SCOT 650:5
in Latin or in G. WALL 800:4
it was G. to me SHAK 674:21
loving, natural, and G. BYRO 176:16
neither G. nor Jew BIBL 109:4
pay at the G. Kalends AUGU 36:18
questioned him in G. CARR 192:1
say a word against G. SHAW 707:22
small Latin, and less G. JONS 420:24
study of G. literature GAIS 327:19
When G. meets Greek PROV 614:19
wife talks G. JOHN 418:11
Greeks For G. a blush BYRO 176:27
G., and to the Barbarians BIBL 104:25
G. bearing gifts PROV 600:14
G. had a word AKIN 9:13
G. had modesty PEAC 570:15
G. in this American empire MACM 487:14
G. joined Greeks LEE 462:5
G. seek after wisdom BIBL 105:27
G. take the beating HORA 386:13
G. were gods FUSE 327:15
I fear the G. VIRG 793:18
Let G. be Greeks BRAD 146:15
make way, G. PROP 593:17
unto the G. foolishness BIBL 105:28
writings of the G. OMAR 554:15
green and a g. gown NURS 548:2
bordered by its gardens g. MORR 532:13
Colourless g. ideas CHOM 212:10
die when the trees were g. CLAR 218:7
drives my g. age THOM 772:5
feed me in a g. pasture BOOK 132:26
Flora and the country g. KEAT 429:7
g. and pleasant bowers BLAK 119:5
g. and pleasant land BLAK 120:1
g. as emerald COLE 226:7
g. banks of Shannon CAMP 183:7
G. Eye HAYE 365:2
g.-eyed monster SHAK 692:21
g. grass shorn BACO 43:5
G. grow the rashes, O BURN 167:8
G. grow the rushes O SONG 729:11
g. herb BOOK 139:3
g. hill far away ALEX 11:12
G. how I love you GARC 329:11
g. in judgment SHAK 656:21
g. pastures of the European VERW 791:13
G. pleasure or grey grief SWIN 751:14
g. shoots of recovery MISQ 521:13
g. trees when I saw them TRAH 780:14
g. Yule makes PROV 601:38
heard of the g. BLAK 120:19
Her g. lap WALK 799:9
How g. was my valley LLEW 470:12
in a g. tree BIBL 100:[illegible]
in g. pastures WILL 821:6
In the morning it is g. BOOK 137:18
In thy g. lap GRAY 351:1
laid him on the g. BALL 50:9
lamps in a g. night MARV 498:7
laughs to see the g. man HOFF 380:5
life springs ever g. GOET 342:20
Make it a *g.* peace DARN 250:10
Making the g. one red SHAK 683:11
memory be g. SHAK 661:13
My passport's g. HEAN 366:14
O all ye G. Things BOOK 126:8
O G. One [Haoma] ZORO 841:6
one g. BASH 56:14
Praise the g. earth BUNT 160:11
shoot the sleepy, g.-coat man HOFF 380:6
strew the g. lap SHAK 696:1
summer's g. all girded up SHAK 704:8
sun doth parch the g. SURR 746:10
Their g. felicity KEAT 428:1
To a g. thought MARV 498:16
wearin' o' the G. POLI 581:16
Wherever g. is worn YEAT 835:21
greener grass is always g. PROV 601:32
g. than the grass BALL 51:10
greenery g. of the trees DANT 249:21
In a mountain g. HART 363:7
greenery-yallery g., Grosvenor Gallery GILB 338:22
greenfly weren't any g. AYCK 40:3
greenhouse g. gases MARG 495:10
greening g. of America REIC 624:6
Greenland From G.'s icy mountains HEBE 367:6
greenly We have done but g. SHAK 666:5

greenness recovered g. HERB 372:16
rust amid g. MELV 504:9
Greenpeace *G.* had a ring to it HUNT 396:8
greens healing g. ABSE 1:6
Greensleeves G. was all my joy SONG 729:9
greenwood to the g. go BALL 51:7
Under the g. tree SHAK 658:20
greet G. the unseen BROW 155:5
How should I g. thee BYRO 179:19
Greise *Kopf zum G.* MÜLL 536:4
grenadier British G. SONG 730:3
Pomeranian g. BISM 116:9
grenadiers Pensions and G. STER 739:4
Grenville Richard G. lay TENN 766:8
grey All cats are g. in the dark PROV 594:20
bring down my g. hairs BIBL 75:17
could comb g. hair YEAT 836:8
good g. head TENN 765:3
Green pleasure or g. grief SWIN 751:14
g.-green, greasy, Limpopo KIPL 441:9
G. hairs upon my head VAUX 790:19
G. silent fragments HUGH 393:6
hair is g. BYRO 178:23
in my g. hairs WOLS 826:5
lend me your g. mare BALL 52:10
little g. cells CHRI 212:15
philosophy paints its g. HEGE 367:15
this old g. head WHIT 816:4
world has grown g. SWIN 751:5
you are old and g. YEAT 837:23
greyhound This fawning g. SHAK 667:27
greyhounds g. in the slips SHAK 671:6
grief acquainted with g. BIBL 88:16
But g. returns SHEL 710:18
first feel g. yourself HORA 385:18
forethought of g. BERR 69:14
goal of g. RALE 620:11
Green pleasure or grey g. SWIN 751:14
G. and avenging Cares VIRG 794:20
g. felt so like fear LEWI 466:17
G. fills the room up SHAK 677:11
g. flieth to it BACO 42:23
G. for awhile is blind SHEL 713:6
g. forgotten SWIN 750:6
G. has no wings QUIL 619:2
g. I did sustain CONS 235:4
G. is a species of idleness JOHN 414:18
G. is itself a med'cine COWP 239:28
g. is like a minefield WARN 803:20
g. itself be mortall SHEL 710:20
g. just collected DEAN 253:19
g. of heart SHAK 673:10
g. that does not speak SHAK 685:7
g. too much to be told VIRG 793:16
G. with a glass SWIN 750:8
hopeless g. is passionless BROW 154:17
I am g. VOZN 798:16
in false g. hiding SPEN 733:19
journeyman to g. SHAK 694:14
long g. and pain TENN 764:11
master a g. SHAK 691:13
Of g. I died ROET 631:11
pain and g. BOOK 133:28
Patch g. with proverbs SHAK 691:19
pitch of g. HOPK 384:11
see another's g. BLAK 120:20
Should be past g. SHAK 703:7
shows of g. SHAK 661:20
Silence augmenteth g. DYER 286:12
silent manliness of g. GOLD 344:17
Smiling at g. SHAK 701:24
Thine be the g. AYTO 40:9
thirsty g. in wine we steep LOVE 476:13
griefs borne our g. BIBL 88:16
But not my g. SHAK 695:22
cutteth g. in halves BACO 43:2
Drinking my g. SHAK 695:21
Great g. SHAK 660:28
g. and fears BACO 43:24
g. that harrass JOHN 411:10
soothed the g. MACA 482:13
grievance doon offte gret g. LYDG 480:10
grieve g. or triumph GOET 343:5
heart doesn't g. over PROV 614:9
Pope will g. a day SWIF 749:24
what could it g. for KEAT 427:31
grieved g. my heart to think WORD 829:7
g. with this generation BOOK 138:6
grieves thing that g. not MARK 495:12
grieving áre you g. HOPK 384:17
grievous most g. fault MISS 520:11
most g. to him TROL 782:15
remembrance of them is g. BOOK 129:16
grill Let G. be Grill SPEN 734:2
grim g. grew his countenance BALL 50:12
grimace accelerated g. POUN 589:14
grin cheerfully he seems to g. CARR 189:10
ending with the g. CARR 189:16
one universal g. FIEL 310:14
Relaxed into a universal g. COWP 242:3
grind bastards g. you down SAYI 647:33
g. in the prison house BIBL 78:7
g. the faces of the poor BIBL 86:14
Laws g. the poor GOLD 345:10
mill cannot g. with PROV 606:36
mills of God g. slowly LONG 474:8
mills of God g. slowly PROV 606:37
one demd horrid g. DICK 264:8
grinders g. cease BIBL 85:2
incisors and g. BAGE 47:10
Grisilde G. is deed CHAU 205:8
grist g. that comes to the mill PROV 594:23
groan Condemned alike to g. GRAY 350:17
g. and shake their fists HOUS 390:4
groaneth whole creation g. BIBL 105:9
groaning g. under walls MARL 496:17
weary of my g. BOOK 131:24
groans g. of love to those of the dying LOWR 478:11
grocer made the wicked G. CHES 210:18
groined titanic wars had g. OWEN 562:11
Gromboolian G. plain LEAR 460:7
groom death is but a g. DONN 273:8
grooves moves In determinate g. HARE 362:4
ringing g. of time TENN 763:9
gross g. as a mountain SHAK 668:7
Not g. to sink SHAK 705:29
Things rank and g. SHAK 661:24
grosser g. name SHAK 666:13
Grosvenor Gallery greenery-yallery, G. GILB 338:22
grotesque g. situation HAUG 364:1
ornate, and g. BAGE 47:24
Groucho of the G. tendency SAYI 647:27
ground acre of barren g. SHAK 698:17
as water spilt on the g. BIBL 79:8
Chosen and made peculiar g. WATT 805:13
commit his body to the g. BOOK 131:14
crieth from the g. BIBL 74:9
fell into good g. BIBL 95:20
gain a little patch of g. SHAK 665:29
Grammar, the g. of al LANG 450:20
G. control to Major Tom BOWI 145:21
g. of my heart BOOK 141:14
g. won to-day ARNO 27:9
here at last on the g. SOND 728:2
holy g. BIBL 75:26
in a fair g. BOOK 132:9
In his own g. POPE 586:24
let us sit upon the g. SHAK 695:9
see me cover the g. GROS 354:2
seven feet of English g. HARO 362:11
stirrup and the g. EPIT 303:15
swalloweth the g. BIBL 81:36
They are the g. SHAK 680:26
tread on classic g. ADDI 4:20
upon the g. I se thee stare CHAU 206:12
when I hit the g. SPRI 735:11
grounds laying out of g. PEAC 571:1
grove g. of chimneys MORR 532:6
olive g. of Academe MILT 518:8
windings of the g. BEAT 58:5
grovelled g. before him THAC 769:6
groves g. of Academe HORA 387:8
g. of *their* academy BURK 163:23
G. whose rich trees MILT 516:12
whispering g. THOM 775:19
grow g. in worth TENN 767:14
g. To fruit or shade HERB 371:24
g. up with the country GREE 351:10
one to g. PROV 608:38
Please help me g. God BLUM 122:9
They shall g. not old BINY 115:8
growed I s'pect I g. STOW 744:3
growl sit and *g.* JOHN 416:26
grows That which *is* g. GALE 328:12
growth children of a larger g. CHES 209:17
children of a larger g. DRYD 280:27
new g. in the plant ADDA 4:2
root of all genuine g. SMIL 722:17
States, like men, have their g. LAND 450:7
grub old ones, g. SHAW 706:15
Grubstreet G. biographers ADDI 4:19
grudge ancient g. I bear him SHAK 687:13
grudges We collect g. LEON 464:11
gruel g. thick and slab SHAK 684:19
grumbling rhythmical g. ELIO 296:22
Grundy more of Mrs G. LOCK 472:9
Solomon G. NURS 550:19
What will Mrs G. think MORT 534:3
grunt expect from a pig but a g. PROV 613:49
gruntled far from being g. WODE 824:12
guard Be on your g. OFFI 554:13
G. us, guide us EDME 289:3
guarded requires to be ever g. GOLD 345:28
well-g. mind PALI 565:18
guardian G. and my Guide WILL 820:7
guardians good grey g. of art WILB 817:7
guards Brigade of G. MACM 487:21
G. die CAMB 182:11
Up G. and at them WELL 809:15
who is to guard the g. JUVE 424:16
guardsman g.'s cut and thrust HUXL 397:12
gubu *acronym* G. HAUG 364:1
gude g. time coming SCOT 652:7
gudgeon this fool g. SHAK 687:4
gué *au g.* ANON 20:13
guenille *ma g. m'est chère* MOLI 525:4
guerre *ce n'est pas la g.* BOSQ 143:14
guerrilla g. wins if he does not KISS 441:27
guess Medical Men g. KEAT 432:2
guessing G. so much and so much CHES 210:7
g. what was at the other side WELL 809:22
guest be your g. tomorrow night ANON 19:19
Earth, receive an honoured g. AUDE 34:2
g. that tarrieth but a day BIBL 91:13
second g. to entertain DONN 274:10
shakes his parting g. SHAK 700:16
Soul, the body's g. RALE 620:12
speed the going g. POPE 586:7
Speed the parting g. POPE 586:7
uninvited g. TURG 784:19
Wedding-G. here beat COLE 226:6
guests Fish and g. stink PROV 600:32
G. can be delightful ELIZ 298:4
g. should praise it HARI 362:8
g. star-scattered FITZ 315:3
hosts and g. BEER 61:10
Unbidden g. SHAK 672:8
guidance Messenger with the g. KORA 445:9
sent down to be a g. KORA 443:18
guide God to be his g. BUNY 161:12
Guardian and my G. WILL 820:7
G., a Comforter AUBE 32:10
G. me, O thou great Jehovah WILL 820:8
g. our feet BIBL 98:18
g. what goes off the road LANG 451:2
G. where our infant Redeemer HEBE 367:5
None need a g. POPE 580:17
ruler and g. BOOK 128:11
very g. of life BUTL 171:9
guided g. missiles KING 436:17
guides blind g. BIBL 96:27

guiding g.-star of a whole brave nation MOTL 534:7
Guildenstern Rosencrantz and G. SHAK 667:13
guile hiding his harmful g. SPEN 733:19
in whom is no g. BIBL 101:12
lips, that they speak no g. BOOK 133:22
there is no g. BOOK 133:17
urban, squat, and packed with g. BROO 150:14
guilt assumption of g. CROS 246:9
beggar would recognise g. PARS 568:5
blood with g. is bought SHEL 713:7
dwell on g. AUST 38:1
for a sign of g. CONG 233:5
free from g. or pain SHEL 713:14
G. in his heart CHUR 214:7
g. of Stalin GORB 346:16
Life without industry is g. RUSK 638:8
put on a dress of g. MCGO 485:9
unfortunate circumstance of g. STEV 742:5
war without its g. SURT 746:16
wash her g. away GOLD 345:30
without its g. SOME 727:17
guilty crimes of this g. land BROW 152:3
g. conscience needs PROV 601:40
g. man is acquitted JUVE 425:3
G. of dust and sin HERB 372:22
g. of our own disasters SHAK 678:5
g. party is acquitted PUBL 616:12
g. thing surprised WORD 830:6
haunts the g. mind SHAK 673:4
Let no g. man escape GRAN 349:3
Make mad the g. SHAK 663:28
Saints should be judged g. ORWE 559:12
started like a g. thing SHAK 661:10
ten g. persons escape BLAC 117:5
guinea but the g.'s stamp BURN 167:6
disc of fire like a g. BLAK 121:13
g. pigs in the laboratory of God WILL 820:14
g. you have in your pocket RUSK 639:2
jingling of the g. TENN 763:1
to one g. JOHN 418:4
Worth a g. a box ADVE 8:21
Guinness G., Allsopp, Bass CALV 168:8
G. is good for you ADVE 7:22
My Goodness, My G. ADVE 8:1
guitar blue g. STEV 739:24
sang to a small g. LEAR 460:16
Gulag G. archipelago SOLZ 727:11
gulag word 'g.' did not appear WU 833:17
gulf great g. fixed BIBL 100:11
redwood forest to the G. Stream GUTH 355:7
gulfs g. of liquid fire SHAK 694:1
g. will wash us down TENN 767:12
whelmed in deeper g. COWP 239:27
gullet g. of New York MILL 510:1
gulls cry of g. ELIO 296:12
gum can't fart and chew g. JOHN 408:20
gums Don't forget the fruit g. ADVE 7:16
wept odorous g. MILT 516:12
gun Fire your little g. DE L 256:13
grows out of the barrel of a g. MAO 495:2
had a little g. NURS 551:5
Happiness is a warm g. LENN 463:14
Maxim G. BELL 63:19
no g., but I can spit AUDE 34:19
through the door with a g. CHAN 201:19
gunboat send a g. BEVA 71:16
gunfire towards the sound of g. GRIM 353:15
Gunga Din than I am, G. KIPL 438:21
gunner g. to his linstock PROV 597:26
Sink me the ship, Master G. TENN 766:11
gunpowder G., Printing CARL 187:19
g. ran out FOOT 319:8
G. Treason and Plot ANON 18:9
Printing, g. BACO 45:4
guns g. and sharp swords DYLA 287:6
G. aren't lawful PARK 567:6
hundred men with g. PUZO 618:6
loaded g. with boys CRAB 243:11
monstrous anger of the g. OWEN 562:5
rather have butter or g. GOER 342:11
They got the g. MORR 532:21
with g. not with butter GOEB 342:9
gurgite *rari nantes in g. vasto* VIRG 793:7
gurly g. grew the sea BALL 50:12
guru by grace through the G. SIKH 719:6
G. Granth Sahib SIKH 720:1
known as his g. LAWS 459:3
reading the G.'s words SIKH 719:15
When the G. comes SIKH 719:8
gusts our g. and storms ELIO 292:5
Gutenberg G. made everybody MCLU 487:12
gutless sort of g. Kipling ORWE 559:6
guts g. of the last priest DIDE 267:2
lug the g. SHAK 665:25
Mrs Thatcher 'showed g.' KINN 437:19
sheeps' g. SHAK 691:6
Spill your g. at Wimbledon CONN 234:7
strangled with the g. MESL 506:5
gutta *G. cavat lapidem* OVID 561:11
gutter Journalists belong in g. PRIE 591:10
We are all in the g. WILD 818:10
guys G. and dolls RUNY 637:10
Nice g. finish last DURO 286:7
gypsies play with the g. NURS 549:15
gypsy vagrant g. life MASE 500:18
gyre Did g. and gimble CARR 190:12
gyves With g. upon his wrist HOOD 382:17

ha H., ha BIBL 81:37
habeas corpus protection of *h.* JEFF 405:14
habit Cocaine h.-forming BANK 53:6
entirely different from h. STRA 744:13
Growing old a bad h. MAUR 502:9
H. is a great deadener BECK 60:4
h. is hell HOLI 380:22
H. is second nature AUCT 33:2
H. with him was all CRAB 242:23
long h. of living BROW 153:3
Not choice But h. WORD 828:18
order breeds h. ADAM 2:19
shook the h. off WORD 831:10
Sow a h. READ 622:16
habitarunt *H. di quoque silvas* VIRG 793:10
habitation God in his holy h. BOOK 136:6
h. among the tents of Kedar BOOK 140:10
h. be void BOOK 136:12
h. of dragons BIBL 87:20
local h. and a name SHAK 690:19
soul's h. henceforth RUSS 639:21
habitations everlasting h. BIBL 100:8
habits Old h. die hard PROV 608:23
prejudices and h. GIBB 335:16
habitual h. hatred WASH 804:8
nothing is h. but indecision JAME 404:1
hack Do not h. me MONM 526:4
hacked H. with constant service SOUT 728:22
Hackney Marshes You could see to H. BATE 57:3
had What I ne'er h. ASTE 31:12
Hades dark H.' door VIRG 794:17
gates of H. HOME 382:5
unsubstantial realms of H. VIRG 794:19
haedis *ab h. me sequestra* MISS 523:6
hag h. obscene BEAT 58:5
haggard prove her h. SHAK 692:23
Haggards H. ride no more STEP 738:1
hags black, and midnight h. SHAK 684:21
Haig ask for H. ADVE 7:15
hail beaten dog beneath the h. POUN 589:22
Fire and h. BOOK 141:27
h., and farewell CATU 198:1
H., fellow, well met SWIF 749:10
H. holy queen PRAY 592:6
H. Mary PRAY 592:1
h. the power PERR 574:1
H., thou that art highly favoured BIBL 98:15
H. to thee, blithe Spirit SHEL 714:3
one H. Mary DOYL 278:12
sharp and sided h. HOPK 384:9
hair All her h. BROW 157:15
amber-dropping h. MILT 512:1
bind my h. HUNT 396:7
bracelet of bright h. DONN 274:10
braided her yellow h. BALL 51:18
bright golden h. WILD 819:5
colour of his h. HOUS 390:4
draws with a single h. PROV 595:37
fell her golden h. TURN 785:12
h. has become very white CARR 189:12
h. is as a flock of goats BIBL 85:14
h. is grey BYRO 178:23
h. of a woman HOWE 391:17
h. of his head BIBL 90:6
h. of my flesh stood up BIBL 81:7
h. that lay upon her back ROSS 634:17
h. to stand on end SHAK 662:25
h. turns white BERR 69:15
her eyes, her h. MEW 506:13
Her h. was long KEAT 428:9
if a woman have long h. BIBL 106:14
Like the bright h. uplifted SHEL 712:13
long essenced h. MACA 482:22
part my h. behind ELIO 295:11
pin up my h. with prose CONG 233:8
raiment of camel's h. BIBL 92:28
red faces, and loose h. EQUI 301:3
right outa my h. HAMM 358:18
smoothes her h. with automatic hand ELIO 296:11
soft brown h. CALV 182:2
subtle wreath of h. DONN 274:1
tangled in her h. LOVE 476:12
Thy h. soft-lifted KEAT 430:9
with a single h. DRYD 282:36
with a single h. POPE 587:2
with such h. BROW 158:11
you have lovely h. CHEK 208:12
your golden h. Margareta CELA 199:8
hairless white and h. HERR 374:18
hairs bring down my grey h. BIBL 75:17
h. of your head BIBL 94:36
h. were white like wool BIBL 111:22
If h. be wires SHAK 705:20
They set our h. DONN 272:15
when my h. be grey CURR 746:10
white h. SHAK 670:22
hairy my brother is a h. man BIBL 74:37
halcyon h. days SHAK 672:7
hale You are h., Father William SOUT 730:21
half ae h. of the warld SCOT 652:4
content with h. knowledge KEAT 430:24
finished in h. the time WODE 824:16
H. a loaf PROV 601:41
h.-angel and half-bird BROW 157:21
h. as old as Time BURG 162:4
h. as old as Time ROGE 631:14
h.-brother of the world BAIL 48:7
h. but h. his foe MILT 515:2
H. dead and half alive BETJ 70:6
h. in love KEAT 429:13
h. is better than PROV 601:42
h. is greater HESI 375:11
H. my own soul HORA 387:14
H. our days we pass BROW 154:5
H.-owre to Aberdour BALL 51:17
h. slave LINC 468:5
h. that's got my keys GRAH 348:4
H. the truth PROV 601:43
h. was not told me BIBL 79:18
H.-way House to Rome PUNC 617:4
help to h.-a-crown HARD 361:18
how the other h. lives PROV 608:41
image of myself and dearer h. MILT 516:30
is h. his height LEON 464:18
longest h. of your life SOUT 731:5
One h. of the world AUST 37:14
one of those h.-alive things FORS 321:2
Too clever by h. SALI 642:13
Too clever by h. SALI 643:6
Two boys are h. a boy PROV 613:25

hall fly swiftly into the h. BEDE 60:19
hiring of a h. HANN 359:10
vasty h. of death ARNO 26:23
hallelujah H. Chorus HAND 359:8
H.! I'm alive OSBO 560:2
halloo Don't h. till PROV 598:36
H. your name SHAK 701:7
hallow cannot h. this ground LINC 468:13
hallowed H. be thy name BIBL 93:19
So h. and so gracious SHAK 661:11
halls dwelt in marble h. BUNN 160:10
h. of Montezuma MILI 508:8
halo jealousy with a h. WELL 810:17
life is a luminous h. WOOL 826:14
What after all Is a h. FRY 326:22
halt h., and the blind BIBL 99:29
h. ye between two opinions BIBL 79:27
tan with henna hackles, h. STEV 739:19
halved trouble h. PROV 613:18
ham h.'n eggs in Carolina GORD 347:1
when there's h. DICK 264:23
Hamilton young H. Tighe BARH 54:10
Hamlet cigar called H. ADVE 7:23
H. so much paper and ink PRIE 591:13
H. without the Prince SCOT 652:8
not Prince H. ELIO 295:9
saw H. Prince of Denmark EVEL 305:7
hammer all you have is a h. PROV 614:18
Amboss oder H. sein GOET 343:5
be the anvil or the h. GOET 343:5
h., 'ammer, 'ammer PUNC 617:8
ring of a h. WILB 817:4
hammered h. into line KIPL 438:3
hammering make such a h. LICH 467:17
hammers those dreadful h. RUSK 639:7
worn out many h. MACL 486:13
worn out many h. PROV 597:19
hammock Drake he's in his h. NEWB 541:15
heavy-shotted h.-shroud TENN 760:27
Hampshire Hereford, and H. LERN 465:7
hams h., Bayonne POPE 582:11
hamster Freddie Starr ate my h. NEWS 544:5
hand bird in the h. PROV 596:21
bite the h. that fed them BURK 164:10
bloody and invisible h. SHAK 684:7
bringing me up by h. DICK 262:20
by the h. of God MARA 495:5
by the h. of the Lord BIBL 76:7
Clean from my h. SHAK 683:11
glove upon that h. SHAK 697:10
go into his h. BIBL 80:28
h. delights to trace WINC 823:2
h. for hand BIBL 76:14
h. in hand CLOS 222:22
h. into the Hand of God HASK 363:16
h. is stretched out BIBL 86:20
h. more instrumental SHAK 661:15
h. not yet contented MERW 506:4
h. of every man's brother BIBL 74:20
h. of Jean Jacques Rousseau HEIN 368:10
h. of Nature GIBB 336:6
h. of the physician BIBL 92:10
h. on her bosom SHAK 693:18
h. on the cockatrice' den BIBL 87:5
h. that fired BALL 50:18
h. that lays the golden egg GOLD 346:2
h. that made us ADDI 5:13
h. that mocked them SHEL 712:22
h. that rocks the cradle PROV 601:45
h. that rocks the cradle WALL 799:16
h. that signed the paper THOM 772:7
h. that signed the treaty THOM 772:8
h. that wrote it CRAN 244:1
h. the cutting edge of the mind BRON 149:8
h., the head RUSK 638:26
h. then of the potter FITZ 314:19
h. to execute CLAR 218:20
h. to execute GIBB 335:12
Have still the upper h. COWA 238:19
Heaving up my either h. HERR 374:2
His [Ishmael's] h. BIBL 74:27
his own right h. BOOK 138:9
If someone claps his h. HAKU 356:14
in her right h. BIBL 82:8
In his h. BOOK 138:6
in his right h. seven stars BIBL 111:22
into mine h. BIBL 78:36
invisible h. in politics FRIE 325:1
kingdom of heaven is at h. BIBL 92:26
kissed her slender h. TENN 764:3
led by an invisible h. SMIT 723:9
Left h. down a bit CATC 196:10
left his garment in her h. BIBL 75:12
let me kiss that h. SHAK 679:22
let not thy left h. know BIBL 93:17
licks the h. just raised POPE 585:7
like a man's h. BIBL 79:30
like the dyer's h. SHAK 705:14
man's h. is not able to taste SHAK 690:17
mind and h. went together HEMI 369:8
my h. into his side BIBL 103:3
my knee, my hat, and h. BROW 153:12
One h. for oneself PROV 608:42
One h. washes the other PROV 608:43
On this side my h. SHAK 695:21
passage from h. to hand SICK 717:16
put his h. to the plough BIBL 99:7
Put out my h. and touched MAGE 489:9
right h. forget her cunning BOOK 141:8
seen what my h. did LOWE 477:19
sheep of his h. BOOK 138:6
Stretch out thine h. BIBL 75:37
sweeten this little h. SHAK 685:11
sweet Roman h. SHAK 702:9
sword sleep in my h. BLAK 120:1
ten thousand at thy right h. BOOK 137:22
They h. in hand MILT 518:3
through a mighty h. BIBL 77:5
Thy h., great Anarch POPE 582:14
Time's fell h. SHAK 704:25
'Tis a good h. SHAK 693:4
Took me by the h. TURN 785:19
touch of a vanished h. TENN 757:12
waved her lily h. GAY 332:22
Whatsoever thy h. findeth BIBL 84:22
What the h. BLAK 121:9
with mine own h. BIBL 107:24
with my weakening h. TIBU 777:7
Wouldst hold my h. HART 363:8
your white h. WEBS 807:22
handbag LADY BRACKNELL: A h. WILD 817:17
handbook constable's h. KING 437:14
handclasp h.'s a little stronger CHAP 202:11
handcuffs h. on his wrists HOUS 390:4
Handel Compared to H. BYRO 173:9
tunes of H. SITW 721:8
handful fear in a h. of dust ELIO 295:28
h. of dust CONR 234:25
h. of meal BIBL 79:26
handicraft sphere of h. SARR 644:19
handiwork firmament sheweth his h. BOOK 132:14
in God's h. BROW 155:27
handkerchief feels like a damp h. MACK 486:9
That h. SHAK 693:5
handle h. of the big front door GILB 338:27
handles Everything has two h. EPIC 300:20
handmaid nature's h. art DRYD 280:28
Riches are a good h. BACO 41:23
handmaiden low estate of his h. BIBL 98:16
handmaidens With her five h. ROSS 634:20
hands aching h. and bleeding feet ARNO 26:18
blood on their h. SPEN 732:11
Cold h., warm heart PROV 597:27
Father, into thy h. BIBL 100:29
folding of the h. BIBL 82:14
h., and handle not BOOK 139:23
h. are as gold rings BIBL 85:21
h. are a sort of feet TRAH 780:16
h. are spread open MIDR 507:15
h. are the hands of Esau BIBL 74:38
h. of men BIBL 91:17
h. of spoilers BIBL 77:24
h. of the living God BIBL 109:27
h. so deeply inserted BIER 114:17
hath not a Jew h. SHAK 687:29
Holding h. at midnight GERS 334:16
horny h. of toil LOWE 477:14
house not made with h. BIBL 107:7
house not made with h. BROW 155:17
in his own h. BACO 42:32
Into thy h. BOOK 133:16
joining of h. BOOK 131:8
keep my h. from picking BOOK 130:15
knit h., and beat the ground MILT 511:18
laid violent h. upon themselves BOOK 131:11
License my roving h. DONN 272:16
lifting up of my h. BOOK 141:15
little h. were never made WATT 805:9
Many h. make light work PROV 606:27
more work than h. PROV 600:2
not into the h. of Spain TENN 766:11
Pale h. I loved HOPE 383:20
pierced my h. and my feet BOOK 132:25
Pilate Washed his h. JAGG 401:8
reached out their h. in longing VIRG 794:21
right h. of fellowship BIBL 107:18
Shake h. for ever DRAY 279:3
shook h. with time FORD 320:1
Soul clap its h. and sing YEAT 837:2
spits on its h. SAND 644:4
Strengthen ye the weak h. BIBL 87:22
temples made with h. BIBL 104:9
union of h. and hearts TAYL 756:21
washed his h. BIBL 97:27
wash my h. in innocency BOOK 133:8
With mine own h. SHAK 695:23
with one of his h. BIBL 80:31
world's great h. HUNT 395:14
your face in your h. ANON 17:5
handsaw know a hawk from a h. SHAK 663:21
handsome H. is as handsome does PROV 601:44
ill-favoured faults Looks h. SHAK 688:35
handwriting legibility in his h. HAY 364:17
hang all h. together FRAN 323:13
Go h. thyself SHAK 667:31
h. a man first MOLI 525:14
h. a pearl SHAK 689:17
H. a thief when he's young PROV 601:46
H. it all, Robert Browning POUN 589:10
h. my hat JERO 407:2
h. the man over again BARH 54:2
h. upon him DONN 274:26
H. yourself, brave Crillon HENR 370:5
in them which will h. him RICH 627:10
let him h. there EHRL 290:4
neither go nor h. BIGO 114:26
will not h. myself today CHES 209:29
with which to h. them MISQ 521:5
wretches h. POPE 587:7
you would h. yourself JOHN 414:17
hanged born to be h. PROV 603:36
Confess and be h. PROV 597:33
farmer that h. himself SHAK 683:13
h., drawn, and quartered PEPY 572:19
h. for a sheep PROV 608:49
h. for stealing horses HALI 357:22
h. himself BIBL 79:10
h. in a fortnight JOHN 415:23
h. in all innocence STEV 742:7
if they'd been h. DENN 257:19
ill name is half h. PROV 602:15
Little thieves are h. PROV 605:43
man who has been h. PROV 607:34
must they all be h. SHAK 685:5
my poor fool is h. SHAK 680:14
our harps, we h. them up BOOK 141:7
see him h. BELL 63:14
hanging bare h. DRYD 283:16
Catching's before h. PROV 597:5
cured by h. from a string KING 437:17
deserve h. MONT 528:4

hanging (*cont.*):
dog than h. it PROV 611:48
H. and marriage FARQ 307:20
H. and wiving PROV 601:47
h. Danny Deever KIPL 438:10
h. garments of Marylebone JOYC 421:19
H. is too good for him BUNY 161:2
h.-look to me CONG 232:17
h. men an' women POLI 581:16
H. of his cat BRAT 147:4
Many a good h. SHAK 701:4
hangman h.'s thrusting The final nail BLOK 122:3
naked to the h.'s noose HOUS 390:17
hangs H. in the uncertain balance GREE 352:2
thereby h. a tale SHAK 658:23
What h. people STEV 742:5
hank bone and a h. of hair KIPL 440:16
Hannibalem *Expende H.* JUVE 424:22
hante *h. la tempête* BAUD 57:5
Haoma O Green One [H.] ZORO 841:6
happen can't h. here LEWI 467:10
fools said would h. MELB 504:3
h. to your mother WALK 799:5
no evil h. unto thee BOOK 137:23
poetry makes nothing h. AUDE 34:1
happened after they have h. IONE 399:21
happening believe what isn't h. COLE 224:14
what is *not* h. TYNA 786:31
happens be there when it h. ALLE 12:14
Nothing h. BECK 59:25
Nothing, like something, h. anywhere LARK 452:18
what h. to her ELIO 292:12
happier h. than your father SOPH 728:11
remembering h. things TENN 762:24
seek No h. state MILT 516:26
happiest h. and best minds SHEL 714:23
h. men alive LLOY 470:13
h. people in the world OSBO 559:17
h. women ELIO 293:5
happily h. ever after ANON 15:9
happiness another person's h. MOOR 529:15
basically our h. THOM 771:13
brief period of h. ARIS 24:17
consume h. without producing SHAW 706:21
desire for their own h. SHAN 706:9
enemy to human h. JOHN 416:27
fatal to true h. RUSS 639:15
flaw In h. KEAT 430:15
greatest h. HUTC 396:15
H. a cigar ADVE 7:23
h. alone is salutary PROU 594:11
h. and final misery MILT 515:19
H. depends on being free THUC 776:22
H., for you MONT 528:6
h. he feels LACL 447:6
H. is an imaginary SZAS 751:24
H. is a warm gun LENN 463:14
H. is no laughing matter WHAT 813:8
H. is not an ideal KANT 425:17
h. is produced JOHN 415:10
H. lies in conquering GENG 333:7
h. makes up in height FROS 326:2
h. mankind can gain DRYD 281:29
h. of an individual JOHN 414:14
h. of society ADAM 3:14
h. of the greatest number BENT 66:18
h. of the human race BURK 163:9
h. of the next world BROW 153:2
H.! our being's end POPE 585:28
h. that went on CHEK 208:17
h. was but the occasional HARD 360:14
home-born h. COWP 242:1
hopes for h. from thee WRIG 833:15
In solitude What h. MILT 517:9
lifetime of h. SHAW 707:30
look into h. SHAK 659:22
more for human h. BRIL 148:18
my people's h. ELIZ 297:3
no greatest h. principle CARL 187:15
one's true h. LACL 447:7
only one h. in life SAND 643:15
only thing for h. EDGE 288:14
or justice or human h. BERL 68:16
politics of h. HUMP 395:9
prayer to h. ALAI 10:4
pursuit of h. ANON 19:11
pursuit of h. JEFF 405:3
recipe for h. AUST 37:26
result h. DICK 261:19
ruin of all h. BURN 165:25
rush of h. CONL 233:20
searching for his own h. PALI 565:23
secret of h. MORE 531:1
seek h. in boats HORA 386:20
short-lived h. BEHN 62:9
suited to human h. DEFO 254:18
take away his h. IBSE 398:12
that is h. CATH 194:8
that is h. EMER 299:25
too happy in thine h. KEAT 429:6
We find our h. WORD 831:8
happy all be as h. as kings STEV 742:12
all who are h. JOHN 413:22
ask if they were h. CHAN 202:3
attain The h. life SURR 746:8
aware that you are h. KRIS 446:1
bread-sauce of the h. ending JAME 403:14
Call no man h. SOLO 727:9
conspiracy to make you h. UPDI 788:13
duty of being h. STEV 741:23
earthlier h. SHAK 689:3
had a h. life LAST 457:16
h. as one hopes LA R 453:22
h. as the grass was green THOM 772:3
H. birthday to you HILL 377:2
h. breed of men SHAK 694:19
h. could I be with either GAY 332:1
h. families resemble TOLS 779:6
H. field or mossy cavern KEAT 428:20
h. for a week PROV 603:41
h. he who crowns in shades GOLD 344:9
H. he who like Ulysses DU B 283:22
h. highways where I went HOUS 391:5
H. in this SHAK 688:4
h. issue BOOK 127:18
H. is the country PROV 601:49
H. is the man BOOK 140:22
H. is the man who fears BIBL 113:21
H. Land MAHĀ 490:12
h. life consist MART 498:3
h. men that have the power TENN 767:2
h. noise to hear HOUS 390:19
h. Rome, born when I CICE 218:1
H. the hare at morning AUDE 33:24
H. the man DRYD 282:32
H. the man HORA 387:11
H. the man POPE 586:24
H. the people MONT 528:11
H. those early days VAUG 790:7
h. while y'er leevin MOTT 535:3
I die h. LAST 456:2
in general be as h. JOHN 415:11
make a man h. HORA 386:18
make men h. POPE 586:11
man would be as h. JOHN 416:6
no man h. till he dies PROV 597:1
object of making men h. DOST 276:1
one of those h. souls SHEL 711:24
one thing to make me h. HAZL 365:6
one who has been h. BOET 123:11
policeman's lot is not a h. one GILB 339:5
prevent from being h. ANOU 22:13
remember a h. time DANT 249:12
remembers the h. things LOVE 477:1
remote from the h. AUDE 33:16
so late their h. seat MILT 518:2
soul that loves is h. GOET 342:13
splendid and a h. land GOLD 344:16
stayed me in a h. hour SHAK 691:17
that they h. are WALL 800:11
This is the h. warrior READ 622:13
till all are h. SPEN 732:10
too h. in thine happiness KEAT 429:6
touch the H. Isles TENN 767:12
'Twere now to be most h. SHAK 692:12
Was he h. AUDE 35:10
was the carver h. RUSK 638:19
What makes a nation h. MILT 518:11
whether you are h. MILL 507:22
whether you are h. SHAW 709:7
Whoever wants to be h. MEDI 503:10
Who is the h. Warrior WORD 827:18
whose heart is h. TALM 754:27
world of the h. WITT 824:9
harbinger Love's h. MILT 517:25
harbour h. bar be moaning KING 437:12
voyage not a h. TOYN 780:4
hard h. day's night LENN 463:22
h. day's work CHIL 212:2
h. English men KING 437:7
h.-faced men BALD 49:5
h. rain's a gonna fall DYLA 287:6
h.-sell or soft-sell TV push NASH 539:14
h. sentences of old BOOK 137:3
H. was their lodging GART 330:12
Long is the way, And h. MILT 515:17
made up of h. words OSBO 559:18
never think I have hit h. JOHN 414:26
soft can wear away the h. TALM 754:22
thine own h. case CARE 186:12
thou art an h. man BIBL 97:9
To ask the h. question AUDE 35:9
too h. for me BOOK 136:20
very h. guy indeed RUNY 637:13
woman is so h. TENN 766:1
harden h. not your hearts BOOK 138:6
h. Pharaoh's heart BIBL 75:33
harder h. they fall PROV 596:20
would be h. to them TROL 782:9
hardly Johnny, I h. knew ye BALL 50:20
hardships h. parcelled within them BOLA 124:8
Hardy Kiss me, H. NELS 541:2
hare First catch your h. PROV 600:26
Happy the h. at morning AUDE 33:24
h. limped trembling KEAT 427:3
h. sits snug in leaves HOFF 380:5
h. sitting up LAWR 458:6
h.'s own child HOFF 380:7
h. when it is cased GLAS 341:18
Hound that Caught the Pubic H. BEHA 61:23
outcry of the hunted h. BLAK 117:19
run with the h. PROV 615:43
than to start a h. SHAK 667:25
thou woldest fynde an h. CHAU 206:12
triumph o'er the timid h. THOM 775:13
hares little hunted h. HODG 379:13
run after two h. PROV 603:37
hark H., my soul COWP 240:19
H., the dominant's persistence BROW 158:6
H.! the herald-angels WESL 810:22
harlot Every h. was a virgin once BLAK 118:19
h.'s cry BLAK 118:5
hollow-cheeked h. BYRO 180:2
Portia is Brutus' h. SHAK 675:7
prerogative of the h. KIPL 441:25
harlotries synne and h. CHAU 205:2
harlots MOTHER OF H. BIBL 112:31
Harlow silent, as in *H.* ASQU 31:8
harm does h. to my wit SHAK 700:29
does most good or h. BAGE 47:13
do so much h. CREI 244:20
do the sick no h. NIGH 545:22
False views do little h. DARW 250:15
fear we'll come to h. BALL 51:15
h. Macbeth SHAK 684:22
h. that is spoken of it FLAU 316:13
meaning no h. GREE 351:24
men don most h. LANG 450:18
no h. come to the state ANON 21:7
supposed to do no h. RUSS 639:20

to prevent h. MILL 508:18
What h. have I ever done TAWN 756:2
harmless h. as doves BIBL 94:34
only h. great thing DONN 273:13
harmonical h. and ingenious soul AUBR 32:16
harmonies inventor of h. TENN 764:20
harmonious dulcet and h. breath SHAK 689:22
h. madness SHEL 714:9
harmonizes sage h. the right CHUA 212:20
harmony All discord, h. POPE 585:17
best h. in a church MILT 519:14
Discordant h. HORA 386:21
from heavenly h. DRYD 282:20
h. In autumn SHEL 711:17
h. of music REYN 625:12
h. of spring GRAY 350:23
h. of the world HOOK 383:6
h., order or proportion BROW 153:30
herkenyng h. CHAU 207:19
immortal god of h. BEET 61:20
in their motions h. divine MILT 517:3
like deep h. SHAK 694:17
ninefold h. MILT 513:23
price is asked for h. DOST 275:18
touches of sweet h. SHAK 688:21
harness girdeth on his h. BIBL 80:5
h. on our back SHAK 685:23
joints of the h. BIBL 80:11
Harold King H. was killed ANON 22:1
harp flute, h., sackbut BIBL 90:1
H. not on that string SHAK 696:26
h. that once through Tara's halls MOOR 530:12
h. with the lute BOOK 137:9
lute and h. BOOK 135:17
No h. like my own CAMP 183:7
sing to the h. BOOK 138:10
sweet h., the story BAKE 48:14
upon the h. BOOK 134:10
wild h. slung behind him MOOR 530:14
Harpic As I read the H. tin BENN 66:2
harping hath not heart for h. POUN 590:1
harps Be but organic h. COLE 225:8
h., and golden vials BIBL 112:3
our h., we hanged them up BOOK 141:7
touch their h. of gold SEAR 652:24
harpsichord describing the h. BEEC 61:3
harrass h. the distressed JOHN 411:10
harrow H. the house of the dead AUDE 35:6
h. up thy soul SHAK 662:25
toad beneath the h. KIPL 440:1
harrowing h. clods HARD 361:16
Harry God for H. SHAK 671:6
little touch of H. SHAK 671:10
Promised to H. SHAK 670:31
shall H. die SHAK 670:18
thy H.'s company SHAK 668:16
harsh h. and embittered manhood GOGO 344:1
Not h. nor grating WORD 829:5
so h. to the clever WORD 827:14
hart As pants the h. TATE 755:8
as the h. desireth BOOK 134:5
footed like a h. MALO 492:10
h. ungallèd SHAK 665:1
leap as an h. BIBL 87:23
young h. BIBL 86:9
harts milk-white h. MARL 496:21
Harvard glass flowers at H. MOOR 529:19
Yale College and my H. MELV 504:8
harvest h. is past BIBL 89:15
h. of a quiet eye WORD 830:19
h. truly is plenteous BIBL 94:30
joy in h. BIBL 86:28
laughs with a h. JERR 407:5
seedtime and h. BIBL 74:19
shine on, h. moon NORW 547:2
harvests Deep h. bury all POPE 583:25
h. of Arretium MACA 483:4
Harwich steamer from H. GILB 337:19
has washed-up h.-been DYLA 287:18
Hasdrubale *Nominis H. interempto* HORA 389:5
Hast *Ohne H., aber ohne Rast* GOET 343:15
haste always in h. WESL 811:19
done in h. PROV 608:14
H. is from the Devil PROV 602:1
H. makes waste PROV 602:2
H. still pays haste SHAK 686:25
Make h. slowly AUGU 36:16
Make h. slowly PROV 606:11
maketh h. to be rich BIBL 83:32
Marry in h. PROV 606:31
Men love in h. BYRO 177:21
More h., less speed PROV 607:6
repent in h. CONG 232:34
said in my h. BOOK 140:3
what h. I can to be gone LAST 456:16
Without h., but without rest GOET 343:15
Ye shall eat it in h. BIBL 76:1
hasten minutes h. to their end SHAK 704:23
hasty H. climbers PROV 602:3
hat get ahead, get a h. ADVE 7:28
hang my h. JERO 407:2
hang your h. on a pension MACN 488:8
h. upon my head JOHN 417:24
looking for a black h. BOWE 145:19
my knee, my h., and hand BROW 153:12
pulling off his h. JOHN 413:4
think without his h. BECK 59:26
hatches continually under h. KEAT 431:4
hatchet cut it with my h. WASH 804:9
hatcheth h. them not BIBL 89:20
hatching H. vain empires MILT 515:15
hate betray me to your mirth or h. FORD 320:3
creative h. CATH 194:11
h. a fellow whom pride JOHN 416:26
h. all Boets and Bainters GEOR 333:9
h. all that don't love me FARQ 307:14
h. a song that has sold BERL 68:13
h. is conquered by love PALI 565:17
h., mankind BYRO 174:18
H. takes a long time THOM 773:14
h. that which we often fear SHAK 656:15
h. the idle pleasures SHAK 696:11
h. the man you have hurt TACI 752:10
h. ye all COWL 239:13
hearts that h. thee SHAK 673:16
how much men h. them GREE 352:7
If h. killed men BROW 157:28
I h. and detest SWIF 748:10
I h. and I love CATU 197:19
I h. the common herd HORA 388:11
I h. war ROOS 632:14
immortal h. MILT 514:13
know enough of h. FROS 325:21
letter of h. OSBO 560:10
Let them h. ACCI 1:8
make us h. SWIF 748:24
man you love to h. ADVE 7:42
man you love to h. FILM 311:22
must h. a Frenchman NELS 540:13
must h. and death return SHEL 711:13
never bother with people I h. HART 363:6
not to h. them SHAW 706:25
nought did I in h. SHAK 694:2
of love is not h. WIES 816:15
People must learn to h. MAND 493:9
people who h. me SEI 653:11
pure impartial h. THOR 776:19
roughness breedeth h. BACO 43:11
seen much to h. here MILL 509:17
sprung from my only h. SHAK 697:8
supernatural h. BYRO 179:14
them also that h. him BOOK 136:5
them which h. you BIBL 99:4
time to h. BIBL 84:7
We can scarcely h. HAZL 365:22
Yet I do h. him SHAK 691:27
you h. something in him HESS 375:15
hated H. by fools SWIF 749:22
h. the ruling few BENT 66:22
how, then, must I be h. SHEL 710:9
loved well because he h. BROW 157:3
Make hatred h. FRAN 322:18
She might have h. BROW 156:15
hateful shamed life a h. SHAK 686:18
What is h. to you HILL 377:7
hater very good h. JOHN 418:5
hates h. dogs and babies ROST 635:17
h. them for it SHAW 709:20
just heaven now h. EPIT 302:16
marry a man who h. his mother BENN 66:11
world of voluble h. TREV 781:10
hateth h. his brother BIBL 111:15
hath Unto every one that h. BIBL 97:10
hating By h. vices too much BURK 164:4
h. all other nations GASK 330:21
h., my boy, is an art NASH 539:15
hatless lands h. from the air BETJ 70:8
hatred common h. for something CHEK 208:20
envy, h., and malice BOOK 127:4
good rancorous h. WARN 803:19
Great h., little room YEAT 836:24
habitual h. WASH 804:8
h. against the Church SKEL 721:14
H. is a tonic BALZ 52:18
h. is by far the longest BYRO 177:21
h., jealousy, boastfulness ORWE 559:8
h. therewith BIBL 82:36
love to h. turned CONG 232:26
Make h. hated FRAN 322:18
most deadly h. HUME 394:12
perpetual h. GODW 342:7
public h. CLAY 220:3
Regulated h. HARD 360:4
What we need is h. GENE 333:4
hatreds organization of h. ADAM 2:13
hats H. off, gentlemen SCHU 649:11
inside men's Sunday h. BROW 157:10
shocking bad h. WELL 809:21
Haughey H. buried at midnight O'BR 552:7
haughty h. spirit BIBL 82:38
haunted h. town it is to me LANG 450:9
haunts h. of coot and hern TENN 757:13
hause-bane white h. BALL 52:5
have h.-his-carcase, next to the perpetual DICK 265:17
h. it when they know it not SWIF 749:21
haves and the h.-nots CERV 200:2
h. to take you in FROS 325:19
I h. thee not SHAK 682:21
I'll h. her SHAK 696:13
to h. and to hold BOOK 131:5
What you h., hold PROV 614:12
What you spend, you h. PROV 614:14
will not let you h. it HAZL 365:9
You can h. it all PFEI 575:1
haven h. under the hill TENN 757:12
havens ports and happy h. SHAK 694:15
Havergal Luke H. ROBI 629:13
haves h. and the have-nots CERV 200:2
having have what she's h. FILM 311:14
Never satisfied with h. WROT 833:16
havoc Cry, 'H.!' and let slip SHAK 675:22
Strokes of h. HOPK 384:1
hawk h. at eagles HERB 373:9
h. is in the air DISR 269:15
h. of the tower SKEL 721:11
his h., his hound BALL 52:5
know a h. from a handsaw SHAK 663:21
hawking h. his conscience round BEVI 72:8
hawks pick out h.' eyes PROV 602:4
Such hounds, such h. BALL 52:4
Hawkshaw H., the detective TAYL 756:22
haws fruit fails, welcome h. PROV 614:17
hawthorn h. bush SHAK 672:28
h. in the dale MILT 512:18
hay bottle of h. SHAK 690:12
eating h. when you're faint CARR 191:9
lie tumbling in the h. SHAK 703:10

hay (*cont.*):
live on h. HILL 377:1
Make h. PROV 606:12
sheets with h. over JOHN 409:19
When the h. came creaking LOWE 478:2
haycock under a h. NURS 549:5
Hays Will H. is my shepherd FOWL 321:20
haystack h. in the floods MORR 532:14
hazard h. of the die SHAK 697:1
hazards h. whence no tears HARD 361:19
haze Purple h. is in my brain HEND 369:16
hazelnut no bigger than a h. JULI 423:2
he Art thou h. BIBL 95:5
H. would, wouldn't he RICE 626:9
While H. is mine, and I am His HERB 373:14
head at the h. of the table PROV 614:38
bear with a sore h. MARR 497:15
brains go to his h. ASQU 31:9
cut off his h. JOHN 414:15
dark hole of the h. HUGH 393:8
eye in the back of the h. COLE 227:16
feet than their h. CAVE 198:14
from the h. downwards PROV 600:31
get one's h. cut off CARR 190:22
God be in my h. PRAY 592:3
good grey h. TENN 765:3
Go up, thou bald h. BIBL 80:14
hairs of your h. BIBL 94:36
hand, the h. RUSK 638:26
hat upon my h. JOHN 417:24
h. beneath the feet OVID 561:22
h. could wish him MORE 531:6
h. grown grey SHEL 711:1
h. is not more native SHAK 661:15
h. on her knee SHAK 693:18
h. on his knee BARH 54:9
h. that once was crowned KELL 432:16
h. that wears a crown SHAK 670:2
h. to contrive CLAR 218:20
h. to contrive GIBB 335:12
his h. with his legs BIBL 75:39
hold my h. so high HORA 387:13
ideas of its "h." DISR 268:12
if S-E-X rears its h. ALLI 10:1
if you can keep your h. KERR 434:7
If you can keep your h. KIPL 439:2
imperfections on my h. SHAK 662:31
It shall bruise thy h. BIBL 74:4
jerked its h. HUGH 393:6
Johnny-h.-in-air PUDN 616:14
keep your h. PUDN 616:14
King Charles's h. DICK 261:22
learned lumber in his h. POPE 585:2
Many a h. has turned white MÜLL 536:4
maugree his h. CHAU 206:21
My deeds upon my h. SHAK 688:12
my h. is a map FIEL 310:6
My h. is bloody, but unbowed HENL 369:20
Off with her h. CARR 189:20
Off with his h. CIBB 217:5
old h. on young shoulders PROV 615:42
on each gashed h. SORL 728:18
one small h. could carry GOLD 344:15
Or in the heart or in the h. SHAK 688:2
purpose of the h. RIDI 627:14
room at your h. BALL 50:11
shew his glorious h. SPEN 733:7
shorter by the h. ELIZ 296:26
should have his h. examined GOLD 346:5
show my h. to the people DANT 250:7
so old a h. SHAK 688:9
stand on your h. CARR 189:12
takes my laily h. BALL 50:21
under my h. BALL 50:14
What though his h. be empty SWIF 748:21
where to lay his h. BIBL 94:19
which way the h. lies RALE 621:9
your good h. ELIZ 297:2
headache with a dismal h. GILB 337:18
headin do you know where we're h.' DYLA 287:13
headland Be like a h. AURE 37:2
some bold h. WORD 828:8
headlong Hurled h. flaming MILT 514:11
headmasters H. have powers CHUR 216:13
headpiece H. filled with straw ELIO 294:24
heads h. Do grow beneath SHAK 691:34
h. replete with thoughts COWP 242:6
H. Were toward Eternity DICK 266:7
Hide their diminished h. MILT 516:7
hold our h. erect JERO 406:15
Lift up your h. BOOK 133:3
Two h. are better than one PROV 613:26
very empty h. BACO 45:7
headstone h. in the corner BOOK 140:6
headstones h. yield their names TATE 755:5
headstrong h. as an allegory SHER 716:2
heady H., not strong POPE 580:15
heal h. me of my grievous wound TENN 760:17
h. what is wounded LANG 451:2
Physician, h. thyself BIBL 98:29
Physician, h. thyself PROV 609:25
time to h. BIBL 84:7
healed h. also the hurt BIBL 89:14
h. of a suffering PROU 594:8
my soul shall be h. MISS 522:20
ransomed, h. LYTE 481:1
with his stripes we are h. BIBL 88:17
healer sharp compassion of the h.'s art ELIO 294:10
Time is a great h. PROV 613:1
Time not a great h. COMP 230:11
healeth h. those that are broken BOOK 141:24
healing h. fountain AUDE 34:4
h. in his wings BIBL 90:25
H. is a matter of time HIPP 377:17
h. of the nations BIBL 113:13
h. wings could see VAUG 790:4
not heroics, but h. HARD 360:5
health damaging to h. SADE 641:8
h. and wealth HUNT 395:15
h. of the whole human race TOYN 780:5
h. shall spring forth BIBL 89:2
h. unbought DRYD 281:13
in h. and wealth BOOK 126:15
in sickness and in h. BOOK 131:5
Look to your h. WALT 802:26
no h. in us BOOK 125:16
Of h. and living SHAK 699:24
regaining my h. RILK 628:5
seriously damage your h. OFFI 554:11
so far from my h. BOOK 132:21
thy saving h. BOOK 136:3
When you have both, it's h. DONL 272:5
healthful h. Spirit of thy grace BOOK 126:17
healthiest h. graveyard BEHA 61:21
healths h. and draughts go free LOVE 476:13
healthy cuts away h. tissue FORS 320:19
h. and wealthy and dead THUR 777:1
h. bones of a single Pomeranian BISM 116:9
h. state of political life MILL 508:20
h., wealthy, and wise PROV 599:4
heap rude h., together hurled MARV 499:7
struck all of a h. SHER 715:20
waters to stand on an h. BOOK 137:5
heapeth h. up riches BOOK 133:30
hear another to h. THOR 776:18
Believe nothing of what you h. PROV 595:42
Be swift to h. BIBL 110:13
cannot choose but h. COLE 226:5
Can you h. me, mother CATC 195:7
do not wish to h. BUTL 173:1
don't h. the cries MILL 510:6
hath ears to h. BIBL 98:3
H. all, see all PROV 602:35
h. a smile CROS 246:11
h. more good things HAZL 365:20
H. my law BOOK 137:3
h. my Thisby's face SHAK 690:25
h. no evil PROV 610:26
h. no more at all STEV 742:24
h., oh, hear SHEL 712:12
H., O Israel BIBL 77:6
h. our prayers BOOK 130:19
h. the larks HOUS 390:19
H. the other side AUGU 36:8
h. the word of the Lord BIBL 89:34
h. thy shrill delight SHEL 714:5
in such wise h. them BOOK 127:22
let me h. thee speaking BODE 123:9
Listeners never h. any good PROV 605:35
make you h. CONR 234:17
never would h. SWIF 749:6
Plenty to see and h. JOYC 422:15
prefer not to h. AGAR 6:14
shall he not h. BOOK 138:4
shall not h. the bittern LEDW 461:16
those who will not h. PROV 612:32
we shall h. it by-and-by BROW 154:25
you will h. me DISR 268:6
heard have not h. them BIBL 99:10
have ye not h. BIBL 88:4
h. and known BOOK 137:3
h. for their much speaking BIBL 93:18
h. it's in the stars PORT 588:11
H., not regarded SHAK 668:26
I have h. of thee BIBL 82:4
I never h. thy fire HEYW 376:7
I will be h. GARR 330:9
Oon ere it h. CHAU 207:13
seen and not h. PROV 597:18
then is h. no more SHAK 685:22
twice I have also h. BOOK 135:23
You ain't h. nuttin' yet JOLS 418:20
hearers attentive and favourable h. HOOK 383:5
not h. only BIBL 110:14
heareth thy servant h. BIBL 78:15
hearing delicate h. saves MOOR 530:6
Fall asleep, or h. die SHAK 673:10
my sense of h. SHAK 680:21
People h. without listening SIMO 720:10
hearken to h. than the fat BIBL 78:25
hearkened h. not unto the voice BOOK 139:10
h. to my commandments BIBL 88:9
hearsay formerly lived by h. BUNY 161:20
hearse Underneath this sable h. EPIT 304:9
walk before the h. GARR 330:7
hearses frequent h. POPE 582:20
heart Absence makes h. grow fonder PROV 594:12
abundance of the h. BIBL 95:13
accompany me with a pure h. BOOK 125:14
Ancient person of my h. ROCH 630:19
And I am sick at h. SHAK 661:5
anniversaries of the h. LONG 473:20
As my poor h. doth think LYLY 480:18
ás the h. grows older HOPK 384:18
Batter my h. DONN 272:24
beak form out my h. POE 579:18
Beware my foolish h. WASH 804:12
bicycle-pump the human h. AMIS 13:16
blind side of the h. CHES 210:3
broken h. lies here MACA 482:24
bruised h. was piercèd SHAK 692:5
Bury my h. at Wounded Knee BENÉ 64:24
But break, my h. SHAK 661:28
Chuang Tzu's dreaming h. BASH 56:20
Cold hands, warm h. PROV 597:27
committed adultery in my h. CART 192:14
conversant with a man's h. POE 580:1
correct the h. EPIT 302:6
corrupt the h. BYRO 178:6
curse with their h. BOOK 135:21
deceiveth his own h. BIBL 110:15
deep h.'s core YEAT 836:12
deserts of the h. AUDE 34:4
desires of the h. AUDE 33:23
Did not our h. burn BIBL 100:34
duties of the h. BAHY 48:1
ease a h. like a satin gown PARK 567:7
ease thine h. BEDD 60:14

education of the h. SCOT 652:17
engraved on her h. SELL 654:8
examine my own h. DEV 259:4
eyes, but not my h. JONS 419:20
faint h. ne'er wan A lady BURN 168:25
faith of the h. LUTH 480:3
fed the h. on fantasies YEAT 836:18
feeling h. is a blessing RICH 627:6
found not my h. moved more SIDN 718:26
Fourteen h. attacks JOPL 421:5
from hell's h. MELV 504:10
from the h. of joy BEEC 61:8
fullness of the h. PROV 609:16
gentil h. CHAU 205:18
give A loving h. to thee HERR 374:23
given you her h. VANB 789:9
God be in my h. PRAY 592:3
God dwells in thy h. BHAG 73:4
great havė no h. LA B 446:15
grieved my h. to think WORD 829:7
harden Pharaoh's h. BIBL 75:33
hath not h. for harping POUN 590:1
h. amidst the organs HA-L 357:5
h. and hands and voices WINK 823:6
H. and soul do sing SIDN 718:21
h. and stomach of a king ELIZ 296:27
h. and tongue employ TATE 755:9
h. as sound as a bell SHAK 691:12
h. belongs to Daddy PORT 588:9
h. be troubled BIBL 102:16
h. bleeds for his country JOHN 412:25
heart-break in the h. of things GIBS 336:15
h. clings to LUTH 480:4
h. doesn't grieve over PROV 614:9
h. for any fate LONG 474:7
h. grown cold SHEL 711:1
h. grows old YEAT 837:10
h. had never known ye ANON 18:19
h. has its reasons PASC 568:17
h.—how shall I say? BROW 156:25
h. in the business WATS 804:19
h. into his hand TALM 754:10
h. is a lonely hunter BORR 144:10
h. is a small thing QUAR 618:14
h. is deceitful BIBL 89:19
h. is Highland GALT 328:19
h. is inditing BOOK 134:13
h. is like a singing bird ROSS 634:1
h. is on the left MOLI 525:9
h. is restless AUGU 35:22
h. is sick TENN 761:8
h. is sorrowful BIBL 82:31
h. leaps up WORD 829:10
h. less bounding ARNO 27:29
h. likes a little disorder DE B 254:7
h. of a man GAY 331:18
h. of an immense darkness OPEN 556:10
H. of England DRAY 279:4
h. of furious fancies ANON 19:17
h. of kings BIBL 83:17
h. of lead POPE 580:12
h. o' flesh BALL 51:19
h. of man DOST 275:16
h. of man HUME 394:16
H. of oak GARR 330:3
h. responsive swells BYRO 175:15
h. speaks to heart FRAN 323:3
H. speaks to heart MOTT 535:5
H.'s renying BARN 55:9
h.'s stalled motor MAYA 502:18
h. strangely warmed WESL 811:15
h. that fed SHEL 712:22
h. the keener ANON 21:15
h. to a dog to tear KIPL 440:2
h. to heart SCOT 650:18
h. to poke poor Billy GRAH 348:5
h. to report SHAK 690:17
h. to resolve GIBB 335:12
h. upon my sleeve SHAK 691:24
h. was not in me HÉLO 369:2
h. was to thy rudder tied SHAK 657:3
h. was warm and gay HAMM 358:20
h. was with the Oxford men LETT 465:18
h. within blood-tinctured BROW 154:18
h. would hear her and beat TENN 764:10
h. you first beguiled BALL 50:20
hides one thing in his h. HOME 382:5
His h. is below MIDR 507:17
his little h. JAME 403:16
holiness of the h.'s affections KEAT 430:21
Home is where the h. is PROV 602:43
human h. is strong BAGE 46:24
If thy h. fails thee ELIZ 297:7
imagination of man's h. BIBL 74:18
In my h.'s core SHAK 664:18
Into my h. an air HOUS 391:5
Irishman's h. SHAW 707:18
I sleep, but my h. waketh BIBL 85:18
Is your h. at rest FLET 318:7
I would eat his h. SHAK 691:18
key of my h. CLAY 220:4
Land of H.'s Desire YEAT 836:13
language of the h. POPE 583:11
language of the h. SHAD 655:10
lead into the h. CONR 234:9
left my h. in San Francisco CROS 246:10
lent out my h. LAMB 448:25
let thy h. cheer thee BIBL 85:1
let your h. be strong LAUD 454:5
Lift up your h. WESL 811:6
live to my own h. RICH 627:5
locked my h. BALL 52:9
look in thy h. and write SIDN 718:9
loosed our h. in tears ARNO 26:16
lose his child's h. MENG 504:22
lying in my h. MARY 500:12
make a stone of the h. YEAT 835:20
Make me a clean h. BOOK 135:7
maketh glad the h. BOOK 139:3
maketh the h. sick BIBL 82:27
man after his own h. BIBL 78:23
Man's h. expands MACN 488:15
man with h., head, hand TENN 764:2
may not change the h. KING 436:10
Mercy has a human h. BLAK 120:15
merry h. BIBL 82:35
merry h. doeth good BIBL 83:4
more native to the h. SHAK 661:15
most h.-easing things KEAT 430:5
most plotting h. RICH 627:2
My h. aches KEAT 429:6
My h. aches OPEN 556:3
my h. also BOOK 132:24
my h. and my flesh BOOK 137:11
my h. beats BERL 68:6
My h. did do it EPIT 303:14
My h. in hiding HOPK 385:2
My h. is heavy GOET 343:1
my h. is pure TENN 766:14
My h.'s in the Highlands BURN 168:1
my h.'s right there JUDG 423:1
My h. untravelled GOLD 345:6
my h. was free WESL 810:21
my reins and my h. BOOK 133:7
my shrivelled h. HERB 372:16
naked thinking h. DONN 273:20
never share the h. MARL 495:15
no longer tear his h. EPIT 304:8
no man layeth it to h. BIBL 88:26
no man's h. fail BIBL 78:30
no matter from the h. SHAK 700:24
None but the lonely h. GOET 343:14
not for hope, h. would break PROV 603:18
not your h. away HOUS 390:18
of the deeper h. FLEC 317:8
of thine h. BIBL 78:29
only with the h. SAIN 641:12
Open my h. BROW 155:25
Open not thine h. BIBL 91:23
opens the h. and lungs STER 739:5
Or in the h. or in the head SHAK 688:2
O tiger's h. SHAK 672:26
panting h. of Rome WISE 823:16
passionate h. of the poet TENN 763:22
plague your h. PROV 609:29
pondered them in her h. BIBL 98:23
poor h. that never rejoices PROV 604:5
rag-and-bone shop of the h. YEAT 835:9
rebellious h. BIBL 89:12
rebuke hath broken my h. BOOK 136:11
Religion's in the h. JERR 407:3
room in my h. for thee ELLI 298:8
seal upon thine h. BIBL 86:7
Shakespeare unlocked his h. BROW 156:6
sighing of a contrite h. BOOK 127:14
softer pillow than my h. BYRO 180:12
some h. did break TENN 760:26
So the h. be right RALE 621:9
squirrel's h. beat ELIO 292:23
sunshine of the h. CONS 235:8
Sweeping up the H. DICK 266:11
sweet concurrence of the h. HERR 374:10
Taming my wild h. SHAK 691:11
tears out the h. of it KNOW 442:9
there will your h. be BIBL 93:21
this h. Shall break SHAK 678:19
thou hast my h. PRIO 592:10
time by h.-throbs BAIL 48:6
true love hath my h. SIDN 718:8
visit my sad h. SHAK 675:7
want of h. HOOD 382:22
war in his h. BOOK 135:12
warmth about my h. KEAT 431:8
waters of the h. THOM 772:9
way to a man's h. PROV 613:41
weakens his own h. SHAK 704:11
where my h. is turning ever FOST 321:17
Whispers the o'er-fraught h. SHAK 685:7
whose h. is happy TALM 754:27
with all thy h. BIBL 96:24
with a mighty h. SHAK 671:1
with a well-tuned h. Sing GURN 355:6
Within my h. appear LITT 470:3
wounding h. CRAS 244:4
heartache say we end The h. SHAK 664:3
heartbeat h. from the Presidency STEV 740:13
heartbreak h. in the heart of things GIBS 336:15
hearth By this still h. TENN 767:8
cricket on the h. MILT 512:7
from an unextinguished h. SHEL 712:18
genial h. WORD 828:17
h.-fire and the home-acre KIPL 439:1
hearthstone squats on the h. QUIL 619:2
heartily let us h. rejoice BOOK 138:5
heartless h., witless nature HOUS 390:10
restrain the h. KING 436:10
hearts all h. be open BOOK 129:4
all that human h. endure GOLD 345:11
arise in your h. BIBL 111:8
cold and glittery h. HILL 377:4
Go trouble younger h. WYAT 834:2
harden not your h. BOOK 138:6
h. and house-keepings DICK 264:17
h. and intellects EPIT 304:11
h. and minds BIBL 108:24
h. are dry WORD 828:9
h. are in the right place DISR 270:16
h. beating BROW 156:22
h. have not grown old YEAT 837:24
H. just as pure GILB 337:13
h. of his countrymen LEE 461:21
h. That spanieled me SHAK 657:10
H. wound up with love SPEN 732:22
heedless h. GRAY 350:22
imagination of their h. BIBL 98:17
Incline our h. BOOK 129:6
Kind h. are more than coronets TENN 762:11
let not your h. be hardened VILL 792:19
Lift up your h. BOOK 129:18
men with Splendid H. BROO 150:13
offspring of cold h. BURK 163:22
O you hard h. SHAK 674:3
Pluck their h. from them SHAK 671:21
Pure eyes and Christian h. KEBL 432:6

hearts (*cont.*):
queen in people's h. DIAN 260:4
Queen of H. she made NURS 550:10
Two h. that beat as one CLOS 222:23
undeveloped h. FORS 320:9
union of hands and h. TAYL 756:21
heartstrings jesses were my dear h. SHAK 692:23
heat bear the burden and the h. ARNO 26:18
can't stand the h. TRUM 784:3
don't like the h. PROV 603:29
furnace that gives no h. RAYM 622:9
H. me these irons SHAK 677:13
H. not a furnace SHAK 673:6
h. of the day BIBL 96:18
h.-oppressed. brain SHAK 682:21
h. o' the sun SHAK 661:1
neither h. nor light WEBS 807:26
not without dust and h. MILT 519:10
one h., all know CHAP 202:19
white h. of revolution WILS 821:15
white h. of technology MISQ 522:14
heath Upon this blasted h. SHAK 681:17
heathen any h. author JAME 402:19
as the h. do BIBL 93:18
be avenged of the h. BOOK 142:2
break the h. TENN 759:19
converting the H. CARL 187:17
exalted among the h. BOOK 134:20
h. in his blindness HEBE 367:7
h. in 'is blindness KIPL 438:11
h. in the carnal part POPE 583:12
h. make much ado BOOK 134:19
h. so furiously rage BOOK 131:16
heather bonnie bloomin' h. LAUD 454:6
cries 'Nothing but h.' MACD 484:14
heaths game on these lone h. HAZL 365:23
heave h. and the halt KIPL 440:7
H. arf a brick at 'im. PUNC 617:6
heaven all going the H. LAST 457:15
All this, and h. too HENR 371:4
all to H. JONE 419:5
all we know of h. DICK 266:13
any better in H. WILL 821:3
ascend to h. [illegible]
become the hoped-for h. EPIT 304:11
Bread of h. WILL 820:8
by a whirlwind into h. BIBL 80:12
cannot go to h. NORF 546:14
climbing h., and gazing SHEL 714:13
climb up into the h. BOOK 141:11
consent of h. JONS 419:14
day when h. was falling HOUS 390:9
decreed against him in h. TALM 754:24
die and go to h. CONL 233:20
distant from H. BURT 170:16
Does H. say anything CONF 232:6
Earth's crammed with h. BROW 154:13
eleven who went to h. SONG 729:11
enter into the kingdom of h. BIBL 93:8
Equality would be h. TROL 783:5
eye of h. SHAK 677:15
face of h. so fine SHAK 697:29
fallen from h. BIBL 87:7
Fellowship is h. MORR 532:16
floor of h. SHAK 688:22
flowerless fields of h. SWIN 750:4
food from h. BOOK 137:6
from earth to h. PLAT 578:11
gate of h. BIBL 75:3
gazing up into h. BIBL 103:14
given from h. MIDR 507:13
Give the jolly h. above STEV 742:25
God owns h. SEXT 655:6
God's in his h. BROW 157:12
God's in his h. PROV 601:16
gold bar of H. ROSS 634:16
go to h. in feather-beds MORE 531:7
great wonder in h. BIBL 112:18
hand toward h. BIBL 75:37
H. and Charing Cross THOM 774:13
h. and earth shall pass BIBL 97:4
h. and the earth BIBL 73:10
h. and the earth OPEN 555:18
h. descends THOM 775:19
h. doing good on earth TERE 768:12
h. endures HOUS 390:13
h. expands BROW 155:17
H. has no rage CONG 232:26
H.—I'm in Heaven BERL 68:6
H. in a rage BLAK 117:18
h. in a wild flower BLAK 117:17
H. in Hell's despair BLAK 121:1
H. in ordinary HERB 373:5
H. lies about us WORD 829:20
h. mocks itself SHAK 692:27
h. peep SHAK 682:4
h. planted us to please MARV 499:6
H. sends us good meat GARR 330:6
H.'s great lamps CAMP 183:21
h.'s matchless king MILT 516:8
H.'s peculiar care SOME 727:18
h. still guards the right SHAK 695:5
H. stops the nose SHAK 693:14
h.'s vaults should crack SHAK 680:11
H. take my soul SHAK 677:18
H. was in him WALT 803:3
H. what I cannot DICK 266:12
h. will help you LA F 447:9
H. will protect SMIT 723:18
h. with their tears BLAK 121:10
H. would be too dull EPIT 304:15
Hell in H.'s despite BLAK 121:2
hills o' H. BALL 50:13
his own by-way to h. DEFO 255:10
hope for h. thereby CASW 194:2
house as nigh h. MORE 531:12
how high the h. is BOOK 138:19
hurl my soul from h. SHAK 693:31
hymns at h.'s gate SHAK 704:15
idea of h. SMIT 726:4
Imagine there's no h. LENN 463:15
inheritor of the kingdom of h. BOOK 130:10
into the kingdom of h. BIBL 96:7
I saw h. opened BIBL 113:2
jealous queen of h. SHAK 660:14
just h. now hates EPIT 302:16
kingdom of h. BIBL [illegible]
kingdom of h. BIBL 95:22
kingdom of h. is at hand BIBL 92:26
King of h. LYTE 481:1
lead you to H.'s gate BLAK 119:3
leave to h. the measure JOHN 411:20
leaving mercy to h. FIEL 310:8
lightning fall from h. BIBL 99:9
looketh this way to H. CECI 199:6
looks do menace h. MARL 496:23
made h. and earth BOOK 130:18
made h. and earth BOOK 140:17
make a h. of hell MILT 514:20
Mandate of H. CONF 231:6
Marriages are made in h. PROV 606:30
merrily meet in h. MORE 531:13
more than all in h. BYRO 175:18
more things in h. and earth HALD 356:15
My blue h. WHIT 814:22
near to h. by sea GILB 337:3
neither by h. BIBL 93:11
new h. and a new earth BIBL 113:7
new h., new earth SHAK 656:7
Not H. itself DRYD 282:33
nurseries of h. THOM 774:15
O'er h. and earth THOM 775:7
of h. we have below ADDI 4:22
One h., one hell BROW 156:9
On whom the dew of h. drops FORD 319:19
open face of h. KEAT 430:16
open the Kingdom of H. BOOK 126:1
passage toward H. TRAH 780:16
Pennies don't fall from h. THAT 769:22
pennies from h. BURK 165:16
permission of all-ruling h. MILT 514:18
points of h. and home WORD 832:11
quincunx of h. BROW 152:14
riches of h.'s pavement MILT 515:3
ring the bells of H. HODG 379:13
Road to H. BALL 52:1
saw h. opened BIBL 103:28
secrets of h. and earth SHEL 710:7
send him to—h. JUVE 424:10
silence in h. BIBL 112:13
sinned against h. BIBL 100:4
spark from h. ARNO 27:7
starry h. above me KANT 425:12
strayed into H. ALAI 10:3
summons thee to h. SHAK 683:2
Thank h. for little girls LERN 465:8
that are not h. MARL 496:4
that serve in h. MILT 514:21
then the h. espy HERB 372:13
things are the sons of h. JOHN 409:4
things in h. and earth SHAK 663:4
third h. BIBL 107:15
thirtieth year to h. THOM 772:10
thorny way to h. SHAK 662:9
top of it reached to h. BIBL 75:1
unextinguishable laugh in h. BROW 152:11
voice from h. BIBL 112:23
waitest for the spark from h. ARNO 27:9
war in h. BIBL 112:19
we know the way to h. ELST 298:17
we must change for h. MILT 514:19
what's a h. for BROW 155:2
What they do in h. SWIF 748:26
which art in h. BIBL 93:19
Which we ascribe to h. SHAK 656:1
with h. and earth MILT 519:21
young was very h. WORD 828:16
heavenly ancient h. connection GINS 339:20
fools by h. compulsion SHAK 678:5
h. mansion, raging in the dark YEAT 835:8
in those h. minds VIRG 793:5
with h. alchemy SHAK 704:17
heavens behold, I create new h. BIBL 89:9
H., and all the Powers therein BOOK 125:20
h. are the work of thy hands BOOK 138:15
h. declare the glory BOOK 132:14
h. dropped BOOK 136:6
h.' embroidered cloths YEAT 836:5
h. fill with commerce TENN 763:3
h. my wide roof-tree [illegible]
h. themselves blaze forth SHAK 675:9
rideth upon the h. BOOK 136:6
starry h. above THOM 775:22
heaventree h. of stars JOYC 422:17
heavily why go I thus h. BOOK 134:8
heaviness full of h., O my soul BOOK 134:6
H. may endure BOOK 133:15
h. of his mother BIBL 82:20
I am full of h. BOOK 136:11
their own h. ASTE 31:13
heavy He ain't h. RUSS 640:7
H. as frost WORD 830:4
h. bear who goes with me SCHW 649:16
h., but no less divine BYRO 176:29
makes it much more h. SHAK 700:11
Sob, h. world AUDE 33:16
ugly, h. and complex FLAU 316:20
wine unto those of h. hearts BIBL 83:37
hebdomada is but *h. mortium* DONN 274:25
Hebraism H. and Hellenism ARNO 28:12
Hebrew H. and Arabic mingling RUME 637:5
H. of the Hebrews BIBL 108:19
in the H. Golgotha BIBL 102:32
Hebrews Are they H. BIBL 107:12
Hebrides in dreams behold the H. GALT 328:19
seas colder than the H. FLEC 317:1
Hecate H. and the night SHAK 677:23
Pale H.'s offerings SHAK 683:1
to black H.'s summons SHAK 684:6
hectic pale, and h. red SHEL 712:12
Hector changed from that H. VIRG 794:2
H. is dead SHAK 700:25
H. took off his plume CORN 237:1
Tyrant and H. BARB 53:19

Hecuba What's H. to him SHAK 663:27
hedge black h. CANN 185:11
divinity doth h. a king SHAK 666:6
From h. to hedge KEAT 429:23
h. is to a forest JOHN 418:1
not look over a h. PROV 608:46
hedgehog h. knows one *big* one ARCH 23:17
hedgehogs personality belongs to the h. BERL 68:15
Thorny h., be not seen SHAK 689:27
throwing h. under me KHRU 435:18
hedges and h. ears SWIF 749:20
few surviving h. BETJ 70:17
into the highways and h. BIBL 99:30
hedonist faddling h. STEV 741:15
heedless H. of grammar BARH 54:7
heel lifted up his h. BOOK 134:4
thou shalt bruise his h. BIBL 74:4
heels champagne or high h. BENN 66:7
double crossing of a pair of h. HART 363:5
high h. are most agreeable SWIF 747:19
purring at his h. BLAI 117:6
heifer h. lowing at the skies KEAT 428:27
ploughed with my h. BIBL 78:2
height depth and breadth and h. BROW 154:21
equal to his h. LEON 464:17
Happiness makes up in h. FROS 326:2
h., nor depth BIBL 105:12
is half his h. LEON 464:18
Measure your mind's h. BROW 157:4
pleasure lives in h. TENN 766:4
someone that h. look regal AMIE 13:10
heights h. by great men reached LONG 473:21
let's suffer on the h. HUGO 393:17
Heinz Beanz meanz H. ADVE 7:8
heir h. of all the ages TENN 763:8
h. of my invention SHAK 705:27
h. of the whole world TRAH 780:9
new-create another h. SHAK 673:27
own h.-apparent garters SHAK 667:31
Pietro craved an h. BROW 157:22
spouting through his h. POPE 583:21
That flesh is h. to SHAK 664:3
heirs h. of God BIBL 105:8
h. through hope BOOK 130:2
plant for your h. PROV 613:37
Helen H., in the night ROWE 636:10
H.'s beauty SHAK 690:19
where H. lies BALL 50:18
Helena far is St. H. KIPL 440:6
Helicon watered our houses in H. CHAP 202:18
hell agreement with h. GARR 330:11
all h. broke loose MILT 516:28
all we need of h. DICK 266:13
bells of H. MILI 508:13
Better to reign in h. MILT 514:21
characters of h. to trace GRAY 350:4
come hot from h. SHAK 675:22
descended into h. BOOK 126:10
do science in h. VAUG 790:18
Down, down to h. SHAK 673:5
dunnest smoke of h. SHAK 682:4
ease in h. WRIG 833:15
from h.'s heart MELV 504:10
gates of h. BIBL 96:4
go to h. for a pastime PROV 602:22
go to h. like lambs CHES 210:12
Heaven in H.'s despair BLAK 121:1
h. for those you love HOLI 380:22
H. full of musical amateurs SHAW 708:4
H. has no terror for me LARK 452:11
H. hath no fury PROV 602:37
H. in Heaven's despite BLAK 121:2
H. is a city SHEL 713:2
H. is oneself ELIO 293:23
H. is other people SART 645:4
H. is to love no more BERN 68:21
h. itself will pass away MILT 513:25
h. of heaven MILT 514:20
h. of horses PROV 599:13
h. of this world BECK 60:12
H. or Connaught CROM 246:2
H. to ships AESC 6:9
H. trembled at the hideous name MILT 515:24
H. would not be Hell EPIT 304:15
If Hitler invaded h. CHUR 216:18
if I go down to h. BOOK 141:11
in danger of h. fire BIBL 93:9
In h. they'll roast thee BURN 168:18
injured lover's h. MILT 516:32
Into the mouth of H. TENN 757:17
I say the h. with it WHIT 814:1
I shall move H. VIRG 795:5
I that in h. wes DUNB 285:4
it is all h. SHER 717:2
jaws of h. VIRG 794:20
keys of h. and of death BIBL 111:23
lack of fellowship is h. MORR 532:16
lead apes in h. SHAK 698:6
leave my soul in h. BOOK 132:10
Like a h.-broth boil SHAK 684:18
made an excursion to h. PRIE 591:15
make the earth my h. SHAK 696:24
myself am h. MILT 516:9
never mentions H. POPE 583:24
Nor H. a fury CONG 232:26
O h.-kite! All SHAK 685:8
out of h. leads up to light MILT 515:17
pains of h. BOOK 140:1
panoramic view of h. BYRO 176:8
porter of h.-gate SHAK 683:13
printing house in H. BLAK 119:29
probably redesigned H. PRIC 591:8
riches grow in h. MILT 515:4
road to h. is paved PROV 610:13
rocks whose entrance leads to h. MILT 511:25
Sent to H., Sir JOHN 417:11
shout that tore h.'s concave MILT 514:29
sin, death, and H. BUNY 161:13
society would be a h. upon earth MILL 509:6
start raising h. LEAS 461:3
steps take hold on h. BIBL 82:12
tell you to go to h. STIN 743:8
that's his h. BURT 170:12
There's h., there's darkness SHAK 679:22
there was a way to H. BUNY 161:8
they think it is h. TRUM 784:4
this is h. MARL 496:3
though h. should bar the way NOYE 547:7
to heaven or to h. SHAK 683:2
to h. I will go MILL 507:25
too cold for h. SHAK 683:14
to quick bosoms is a h. BYRO 174:17
to the gates of H. PIUS 577:8
walked eye-deep in h. POUN 589:16
War is h., and all that HAY 364:15
where we are is H. MARL 496:4
why they invented H. RUSS 639:26
with h. are we at agreement BIBL 87:14
working definition of h. SHAW 709:8
would be h. on earth SHAW 707:30
Yours till H. freezes FISH 313:16
Hellenism Hebraism and H. ARNO 28:12
Hellespont straight H. between DONN 272:12
hellhound h. is always a hellhound WODE 824:13
hello H., good evening CATC 195:21
helluva h. town COMD 230:7
helmet h. and the helmet-feather TENN 762:17
h. now shall make PEEL 572:2
h., the hope of salvation BIBL 109:9
helmsman change the h. BAGE 46:12
help Can't h. lovin' dat man HAMM 358:16
comfort of thy h. BOOK 135:7
God h. me LUTH 479:13
h. and support of the woman EDWA 289:7
h. in time of trouble ANON 15:4
h. of the helpless LYTE 480:23
h. ourselves BOOK 128:4
h. standeth in the Name BOOK 140:17
h. the feeble up SHAK 699:13
H. yourself LA F 447:9
here did England h. me BROW 156:5
hour requires such h. VIRG 794:7
look on and h. LAWR 458:21
make him an h. meet BIBL 73:20
no h. but Thee EDME 289:3
no h. in them BOOK 141:21
O! h. me, heaven FIRB 313:5
Our h. is in the name BOOK 130:18
place where h. wasn't hired EPIT 302:15
scream for h. in dreams CANE 184:18
Since there's no h. DRAY 279:3
very present h. in trouble BOOK 134:18
whence cometh my h. BOOK 140:12
Who ran to h. me TAYL 756:12
with a little h. from my friends LENN 464:4
you can't h. it SMIT 724:5
your countrymen cannot h. JOHN 412:24
helped shall have h. it DICK 266:1
helper h. and redeemer BOOK 134:2
mother's little h. JAGG 401:5
Our antagonist is our h. BURK 164:2
helpers other h. fail LYTE 480:23
helpless H., naked, piping loud BLAK 121:3
help of the h. LYTE 480:23
helps Every little h. PROV 599:29
God h. them that help PROV 601:12
Nobody ever h. me TRUT 784:12
hemisphere portion of this h. MONR 526:9
hemlock of h. I had drunk KEAT 429:6
hempen sing in a h. string FLET 318:3
What h. home-spuns SHAK 690:1
hen as a h. gathereth her chickens BIBL 96:29
better take a wet h. KHRU 435:17
h.-roost to rob LLOY 470:17
my black h. NURS 548:13
of that text a pullet h. CHAU 204:16
hence H., loathèd Melancholy MILT 512:12
H., vain deluding joys MILT 512:3
henceforth from h. in his holy ways BOOK 129:15
henna tan with h. hackles STEV 739:19
henpecked h. you all BYRO 175:28
hens in his governaunce Sevene h. CHAU 206:2
Heraclitus They told me, H. CORY 237:13
herald Hark! the h.-angels WESL 810:22
heraldry boast of h. GRAY 350:9
herb bespangling h. and tree HERR 374:6
call it h. of grace SHAK 666:8
fragrance from the h. TROL 782:18
green h. BOOK 139:3
rue, sour h. of grace SHAK 695:18
herbs bitter h. BIBL 75:39
bitter h. HAGG 356:1
dinner of h. BIBL 82:36
for a garden of h. BIBL 80:7
Hercules is not love a H. SHAK 680:27
I to H. SHAK 661:27
some of H. SONG 730:3
herd elevates above the vulgar h. GAIS 327:19
h. wind slowly o'er the lea GRAY 350:6
Morality is the h.-instinct NIET 545:15
unreflecting h. WORD 828:18
herdsman God the h. goads YEAT 835:12
here Are *you* h. DANT 249:15
can't happen h. LEWI 467:10
he answered, H. am I BIBL 78:14
H. am I BIBL 86:24
h. because we're queer BEHA 62:2
h. for the beer ADVE 7:29
H. I am MACM 487:13
H.'s a how-de-doo GILB 338:7
H.'s looking at you FILM 311:10
H.'s tae us TOAS 778:2
H.'s to thee, Corbet AUBR 32:11
h.'s to you, Mrs Robinson SIMO 720:9
H. today—in next week tomorrow GRAH 348:8

here (*cont.*):
H. were decent godless people ELIO 295:22
If we can't stay h. alive MONT 528:12
I have been h. before ROSS 635:8
I'm still h. HOPE 383:18
Mr Watson, come h. BELL 62:18
We're h. MILI 508:15
What you seek is h. HORA 386:20
hereafter died h. SHAK 685:22
h. for ever BOOK 131:3
points out an h. ADDI 4:16
world may talk of h. COLL 228:10
hereditary H. bondsmen BYRO 174:6
h. government PAIN 564:1
h. monarch was insane BAGE 46:13
idea of h. legislators PAIN 563:23
hereditas *Damnosa h.* GAIU 328:4
Hereford H., and Hampshire LERN 465:7
heresies begin as h. HUXL 397:17
hateful h. SPEN 734:17
kept alive by h. BREN 147:23
heresy believes be h. SHAW 709:17
h. signifies no more HOBB 378:18
Turkey, h., hops PROV 613:22
heretic h. which makes the fire SHAK 703:4
oppressor or a h. CAMU 184:13
heretics H. the only bitter remedy ZAMY 839:18
heritage h. unto Israel BOOK 141:5
I have a goodly h. BOOK 132:9
Hermes H. in the wax ARIS 25:11
hermit h.'s fast KEAT 428:15
hermitage for an h. LOVE 476:14
palace for a h. SHAK 695:14
hermits h. are contented WORD 829:11
hern haunts of coot and h. TENN 757:13
hero acted like a h. WALP 801:18
aspires to be a h. JOHN 416:8
conquering h. comes MORE 531:16
don't want to be a h. STOP 744:1
h. becomes a bore EMER 299:29
h. from his prison AYTO 40:10
h. of my tale TOLS 779:10
h. perish POPE 585:8
h. to his valet CORN 237:7
h. to his valet PROV 607:48
H.-worship strongest SPEN 732:9
Millions a h. PORT 588:13
seemed a h. BYRO 173:15
Show me a h. FITZ 315:10
Herod for an hour of H. HOPE 383:16
out-herods H. SHAK 664:14
heroes Canadians do not like h. WOOD 826:11
feats worked by those h. ANON 21:16
fit country for h. LLOY 471:4
greatest h. COLL 228:8
h. of old BROW 157:17
h. to dine with us TROL 782:13
of all the worlds brave h. SONG 730:3
speed glum h. SASS 645:15
Thin red line of h. KIPL 440:13
Unhappy the land that needs h. BREC 147:10
heroic finished A life h. MILT 518:24
first of the h. poets MACA 481:11
h. for earth too hard BROW 154:25
h. poem of its sort CARL 187:11
H. womanhood LONG 474:9
heroically h. mad DRYD 280:15
heroics not h., but healing HARD 360:5
heroine take a h. AUST 39:14
when a h. goes mad SHER 715:17
herring Every h. must hang PROV 599:26
plague o' these pickle h. SHAK 701:5
roast thee like a h. BURN 168:18
shoals of h. MACC 484:9
herrings As many red h. NURS 549:12
herrschen *h. und gewinnen* GOET 343:5
Hertford H., Hereford, and Hampshire LERN 465:7
Hervey call a dog *H.* JOHN 412:7
Herveys men, women, and H. MONT 526:18
Herz *Mein H. ist schwer* GOET 343:1
hesitate could long h. STEV 742:7
hesitates h. is lost PROV 602:27
She floats, she h. RACI 619:17
Hesperides climbing trees in the H. SHAK 680:27
Hesperus H. entreats thy light JONS 419:17
It was the schooner H. LONG 475:1
venit H. VIRG 796:13
heterodoxy h. is another man's doxy WARB 803:4
H. or Thy-doxy CARL 187:23
heterogeneity coherent h. SPEN 732:4
heterosexual h. love no solution DURA 285:19
heu *H., miserande puer* VIRG 795:2
heures *h. propices* LAMA 448:7
Heute *H. leid' ich* LESS 465:15
hew h. him as a carcass SHAK 675:3
hewers h. of wood BIBL 77:21
hewn h. out her seven pillars BIBL 82:18
Hey H. for God Almighty KETT 434:12
hey h. for boot and horse KING 437:13
'H.-ho!' says Rowley NURS 548:6
heyday h. in the blood SHAK 665:15
hi answer to 'H.!' CARR 191:20
hic *H. jacet* RALE 621:7
Quod petis h. est HORA 386:20
hick Sticks nix h. pix NEWS 544:14
hickety H., pickety NURS 548:13
hickory H., dickory, dock NURS 548:14
hid cannot be h. BIBL 93:5
h. as it were our faces BIBL 88:16
h. from thine eyes BIBL 100:19
h. themselves in the dens BIBL 112:6
I h. from Him THOM 774:4
Which is, to keep that h. DONN 274:18
hidden follows the h. path LUIS 479:10
h. from the eye WORD 831:20
h. love of God WESL 811:9
h. persuaders PACK 562:17
teems with h. meaning GILB 339:8
hide chose from man to h. CRAB 242:24
he can't h. LOUI 476:7
h. in cooling [illegible] KEAT 429:23
h. is sure to flatten 'em BELL 63:3
h. of a rhinoceros BARR 56:3
h. thy face from me BOOK 132:4
h. us from the face BIBL 112:6
in a woman's h. SHAK 672:26
Let me h. myself TOPL 779:16
Those who h. can find PROV 612:41
Whose h. he sold WALL 800:1
wise man h. a pebble CHES 211:6
world to h. virtues in SHAK 701:2
wrapped in a player's h. GREE 352:5
hideous Making night h. SHAK 662:19
hides H. from himself his state JOHN 411:17
h. one thing in his heart HOME 382:5
hiding bloody good h. GRAN 348:14
My heart in h. HOPK 385:2
Hieronimo H. is mad again KYD 446:12
Hierusalem H., my happy home ANON 16:17
high Be ye never so h. DENN 257:17
cannot rate me very h. LACL 447:5
corn as h. as an elephant's eye HAMM 358:21
from h. life POPE 583:29
get h. with a little help LENN 464:4
h. heels are most agreeable SWIF 747:19
h.-minded. descendants CATU 197:10
h. road JOHN 413:6
h. that proved too high BROW 154:25
h.-water mark of Socialist literature ORWE 559:6
house of defence very h. BOOK 137:23
how h. the heaven is BOOK 138:19
I'm the H. SPRI 735:9
Lord, I am not h.-minded BOOK 141:3
Lord most H. BOOK 129:20
no h. flier PEPY 573:4
Pile it h. SAYI 648:1
slain upon thy h. places BIBL 79:1
thing with h.-tech HOCK 379:12
This h. man BROW 156:1
too h. for me BOOK 141:3
upon the h. horse BROW 152:1
wickedness in h. places BIBL 108:13
ye'll tak' the h. road SONG 730:1
higher Friend, go up h. BIBL 99:25
he shall shoot h. SIDN 718:7
h. the monkey climbs PROV 602:39
production of the h. animals DARW 250:21
Stuart or Nassau go h. PRIO 592:12
subject unto the h. powers BIBL 105:19
highest children of the most H. BOOK 137:10
h. good CICE 217:14
in the h. room BIBL 99:24
needs must love the h. TENN 759:22
Highland heart is H. GALT 328:19
solitary H. lass! WORD 832:2
Highlandman breeks aff a wild H. SCOT 651:22
highlands H. and ye Lawlands BALL 50:9
In the h. STEV 742:19
My heart's in the H. BURN 168:1
highly what thou wouldst h. SHAK 682:1
highness his H.' dog at Kew POPE 582:26
highway broad h. of the world SHEL 711:9
h. for our God BIBL 87:28
H., since you my chief SIDN 718:18
passes over a h. STEN 737:16
highwayman h. came riding NOYE 547:6
highways happy h. where I went HOUS 391:5
into the h. and hedges BIBL 99:30
hilarity h. like a scream GREE 351:20
hill Cassidy's hanging h. KAVA 426:8
city that is set on an h. BIBL 93:5
city upon a h. WINT 823:14
dancers are all gone under the h. ELIO 294:8
green h. far away ALEX 11:12
haven under the h. TENN 757:12
heard on the h. BLAK 120:19
hides the green h. KEAT 429:4
h. that holds his peace BERR 69:16
hunter home from h. STEV 743:4
mountain and h. BIBL 87:28
On a huge h. DONN 273:14
On the cold h.'s side KEAT 428:13
rest upon thy holy h. BOOK 132:7
self-same h. MILT 512:29
unto thy holy h. BOOK 134:10
hills and the little h. BOOK 136:17
Black H. belong to me SITT 720:19
Blue are the h. PROV 596:34
blue remembered h. HOUS 391:5
cattle upon a thousand h. BOOK 135:2
convictions are h. FITZ 315:8
h. are alive HAMM 359:1
h. are a refuge BOOK 139:4
h. be carried BOOK 134:18
h. in order stood WATT 805:19
h. like young sheep BOOK 139:21
H. of home STEV 742:24
H. of the Chankly Bore LEAR 460:8
H. of the North OAKL 552:5
h. of the South Country BELL 64:6
h. o' Heaven BALL 50:13
H. peep o'er hills POPE 584:16
h. shall rejoice BOOK 136:2
h. stand about Jerusalem BOOK 140:18
I to the h. will lift SCOT 652:22
mine eyes unto the h. BOOK 140:12
On the h. like Gods TENN 763:14
out on the h. alone KILV 436:4
Over the h. GAY 331:16
Over the h. and far away NURS 551:15
Over the h. and far away STEV 743:5
red h. of Georgia KING 436:14
strength of the h. BOOK 138:6
to the reverberate h. SHAK 701:7
touch the h. BOOK 139:7
ye high h. BOOK 136:8
hillside h.'s dew-pearled BROW 157:12

him cried, 'That's h.!' BARH 54:7
extol H. first MILT 516:31
himself answer is 'h.' IBSE 398:11
Each man for h. CHAU 205:15
Every man for h. PROV 599:30
He h. said CICE 217:13
speak for h. BIBL 102:3
subdue all things to h. BOOK 131:14
with h. at war SHAK 674:7
hinan *Ewig-Weibliche zieht uns h.* GOET 343:4
zieht uns h. CLOS 222:7
hinder all the h. parts SPEN 733:17
hindered let and h. BOOK 128:1
hinders wickedness that h. loving BROW 157:3
hindmost Devil take the h. PROV 598:12
hindrance to his own h. BOOK 132:8
hindsight H. is always twenty-twenty WILD 819:14
Hindu dies, or turns H. SHEL 712:1
neither H. nor Muslim SIKH 720:4
hinky H., dinky, parley-voo MILI 508:12
hinterland She has no h. HEAL 366:5
hip once upon the h. SHAK 687:13
smote them h. and thigh BIBL 78:3
Hippocrene blushful H. KEAT 429:8
hippopotamus h. resolved at any cost WELL 810:6
shoot the H. BELL 63:3
shoot the h. FORS 320:8
hips armchairs tight about the h. WODE 824:22
Or Mae West's h. EWAR 305:10
swing out ungirded h. SORL 728:17
hipsters angelheaded h. burning GINS 339:20
hire labourer is worthy of his h. BIBL 99:8
labourer worthy of h. PROV 605:8
hired rich flames and h. tears BROW 152:19
They h. the money COOL 236:4
hireling h. fleeth BIBL 102:7
Pay given to a state h. JOHN 409:14
hirelings lewd h. climb MILT 516:11
Hiroshima After H. BOLD 124:12
genius of Einstein leads to H. PICA 576:4
his we are h. people BOOK 138:13
hiss dismal universal h. MILT 517:22
fright and a h. DEAN 253:18
hissed h. along the polished ice WORD 828:20
historian h. of the Roman empire GIBB 335:24
h. wants more documents JAME 403:1
life of the h. must be short GIBB 336:1
requisite for an h. JOHN 413:5
historians alter the past, h. can BUTL 172:17
h. left blanks in their writings POUN 589:11
H. repeat each other GUED 354:13
historical any h. romance CLAR 219:15
histories H. make men wise BACO 44:8
studied H. PEPY 573:16
history Antiquities are h. defaced BACO 41:10
Anybody can make h. WILD 818:1
blank in h.-books MONT 528:11
by writing h. BREN 147:24
cancer of human h. SONT 728:7
country which has no h. PROV 601:49
dignity of h. BOLI 124:14
discerned in h. a plot FISH 313:11
Does h. repeat itself BARN 55:3
dustbin of h. TROT 783:17
dust-heap called 'h.' BIRR 115:13
duty we owe to h. WILD 818:2
end of h. FUKU 327:1
fair summary of h. FRAN 323:7
happiest nations, have no h. ELIO 293:5
H. a distillation CARL 187:22
H. came to a . SELL 654:16
H. gets thicker TAYL 756:5
[H.] hath triumphed RALE 621:5
h. in all men's lives SHAK 670:4
H. is a combination COCT 223:16
H. is a gallery of pictures TOCQ 778:9
H. is a nightmare JOYC 422:10
H. is a pack of lies STUB 745:3
H. . . . is, indeed, little more GIBB 335:6
h. is nothing more VOLT 797:18
H. is not what you thought SELL 654:4
h. is now and England ELIO 294:19
h. is on our side KHRU 435:16
H. is past politics FREE 324:3
H. is philosophy DION 268:3
H. is the essence CARL 187:9
H. littered with the wars POWE 590:14
h.-making creature AUDE 35:13
H. more or less bunk FORD 319:15
H., *n.* An account BIER 114:22
h. of art BUTL 172:24
h. of class struggles MARX 500:6
h. of progress MACA 482:3
h. of the world DISR 269:3
H. repeats itself GUED 354:13
H. repeats itself PROV 602:40
H. teaches us EBAN 287:20
H. to the defeated AUDE 35:8
H. will absolve me CAST 193:14
Human h. becomes more WELL 810:13
In h., we are concerned HEGE 367:13
kept h. in mind more BOWE 145:16
learned anything from h. HEGE 367:10
lips my h. SIDN 718:19
Living in h. FITZ 315:19
make more h. SAKI 642:2
men could learn from h. COLE 227:25
more to shape h. TAYL 756:7
more worthy than h. ARIS 24:23
name is h. THWA 777:6
No h. much DURR 286:8
no h. of mankind POPP 587:28
no h.; only biography EMER 299:20
not learning from h. BLAI 117:9
product of h. CARL 187:8
Read no h. DISR 270:7
Thames is liquid h. BURN 166:5
thousand years of h. GAIT 328:2
too much h. KING 437:1
tragedy, comedy, h. SHAK 663:22
War makes good h. HARD 360:9
what's her h. SHAK 701:24
What will h. say SHAW 707:1
world's h. SCHI 648:15
writing a modern h. RALE 621:6
writing h. with lightning WILS 822:9
hit can h. from far HERB 372:10
never think I have h. hard JOHN 414:26
very palpable h. SHAK 667:5
hitch H. your wagon to a star EMER 299:30
hither come hither, come h. SHAK 658:20
Hitler H. swept out NEWS 544:10
H. thought he might CHAM 201:2
If H. invaded hell CHUR 216:18
If I can't love H. MUST 537:15
kidding, Mister H. PERR 574:2
When H. attacked the Jews NIEM 545:8
hitting prove their worth by h. back HEIN 368:2
without h. below it ASQU 31:10
hive h. for the honey-bee YEAT 836:11
make a h. for bees PEEL 572:2
murmurings Of this great h. COWL 239:19
hoar shows his h. leaves SHAK 666:12
hoarder h. of two things SPAR 731:16
hoarfrost scattereth the h. BOOK 141:26
hoarse bird's h. voice WORD 827:11
raven himself is h. SHAK 682:2
hoary h. sort of land LAWR 458:20
Hobbes in for H.'s voyage VANB 789:7
hobbit there lived a h. OPEN 555:16
hobby h.-horse is forgot SHAK 664:21
rides his H. horse STER 738:16
hobgoblin h. of little minds EMER 299:23
Hobson H. has supped MILT 514:4
hoc *H. erat in votis* HORA 389:24
hock weak h. and seltzer BETJ 70:4
Hockley Hey for H. KETT 434:12
hodgepodge gallimaufry or h. SPEN 734:24
Hodgitts 'O Mr H.!' I heard her cry GRAH 348:6
hoe tickle her with a h. JERR 407:5
hog all England under a h. COLL 228:9
disadvantage of being a h. MORT 533:13
Not the whole h. MILL 510:5
hogamus H., higamous JAME 404:6
Hogarth epitaph on William H. EPIT 302:6
hoggish have his h. mind SPEN 734:2
hogs let it not be like h. MCKA 486:6
Men eat H. STEV 739:22
hogshead daggers in a h. SCOT 652:18
hoi polloi multitude, the *h.* DRYD 283:8
hoist H. with his own petar SHAK 665:24
Holborn walk along High H. MITC 523:10
hold can neither h. him JEFF 405:20
can't h. a man down WASH 804:3
cry 'H., hold!' SHAK 682:4
gat h. upon me BOOK 140:1
h., but cannot see WESL 811:1
H., enough SHAK 685:26
h. fast that which is good BIBL 109:11
H., or cut bow-strings SHAK 689:15
H. the fort BLIS 122:2
H. the fort SHER 716:27
to have and to h. BOOK 131:5
What you have, h. PROV 614:12
holder what its h. chooses ASQU 31:4
holdfast H. is better PROV 596:36
h. is the only dog SHAK 671:4
holding h. on comes easily RILK 628:2
hole dark h. of the head HUGH 393:8
first h. made through MOOR 529:14
h. in a sock EINS 291:7
h. to go out of this world LAST 455:19
if you knows of a better h. BAIR 48:11
In a h. in the ground OPEN 555:16
maketh a h. in the stone LATI 454:3
mint with the h. ADVE 7:45
poisoned rat in a h. SWIF 748:11
holes bag with h. BIBL 90:24
foxes have h. BIBL 94:19
small and full of h. BAIN 48:10
holiday Butchered to make a Roman h. BYRO 175:3
I am in a h. humour SHAK 659:18
Is this a h. SHAK 674:2
On a sunshine h. MILT 512:21
perpetual h. SHAW 709:8
to take a h. RUSS 639:12
holidays holiest of all h. LONG 473:20
playing h. SHAK 667:22
holier h. than thou BIBL 89:8
holiest Praise to the H. NEWM 542:18
holiness beauty of h. BOOK 138:7
beauty of h. MONS 526:12
h. becometh thine house BOOK 138:3
holiness but social h. WESL 811:10
h. of the heart's affections KEAT 430:21
put off h. BLAK 119:6
Holland children in H. NURS 547:15
H. . . . lies so low HOOD 383:4
hollingsworth bourne from which no h. MORT 533:15
hollow Down to the h. FLAN 316:2
hate the dreadful h. TENN 763:20
regiment's in h. square KIPL 438:10
We are the h. men ELIO 294:24
Within the h. crown SHAK 695:10
holly English oak and h. HART 363:9
heigh-ho! the h. SHAK 659:5
h. and the ivy SONG 729:10
Hollywood H. money isn't money PARK 567:14
not have been invited to H. CHAN 201:17
holocaust erewhile a h. MILT 518:22
Somme is like the H. BARK 54:15
holy and to the H. Ghost BOOK 125:19
coming to that h. room DONN 273:5
from the h. land RALE 621:1
h. and the profane SIDD 718:1

holy (*cont.*):
h. city, new Jerusalem BIBL 113:7
H. deadlock HERB 371:17
H., fair, and wise SHAK 702:29
h. ground BIBL 75:26
H., Holy, Holy HEBE 367:8
H., holy, holy, Lord BIBL 111:32
H., holy, holy, Lord BOOK 129:20
Holy, H., Holy: Lord God BOOK 125:20
h., is the Lord of hosts BIBL 86:21
h. kiss BIBL 105:25
h. nation BIBL 110:28
h. simplicity JERO 406:14
H. Spirit rests only TALM 754:27
h.-water death MCGO 485:10
h. writ SHAK 696:16
in h. wedlock BOOK 131:8
light of thy H. Spirit BOOK 128:9
neither h., nor Roman VOLT 797:17
nothing is h. BOOK 128:11
sabbath day, keep it h. BIBL 76:11
stand in the h. place BIBL 97:2
suffer thy H. One BOOK 132:10
that which is h. PLAT 578:2
unto thy h. hill BOOK 134:10
Holy Ghost be any H. BIBL 104:11
blasphemy against the h. BIBL 95:11
Come, H. BOOK 142:7
gifts of the H. BUTL 171:12
H. over the bent World HOPK 384:6
H. which is given BIBL 104:35
pencil of the h. BACO 42:4
temple of the H. BIBL 106:3
homage do her h. HOOK 383:6
h. of a tear BYRO 174:3
home all the comforts of h. BRYS 159:5
all the h. I have AYTO 40:13
beating begins at h. FLET 318:12
by staying at h. LIN 469:18
came h. to roost MILL 510:2
can't find your way h. COLL 228:13
can't go h. again WOLF 825:11
Charity begins at h. PROV 597:11
children who leave h. SLOV 721:18
come h. Bill Bailey [illegible]
comes safe h. SHAK 671:23
comfortably at h. AUST 37:16
drive one from h. HOOD 382:23
East, west, h.'s best PROV 599:5
England, h. and beauty ARNO 29:12
Englishman's h. PROV 599:16
E.T. phone h. FILM 311:5
feel ashamed of h. DICK 262:21
for to carry me h. SONG 730:4
go h. in the dark LAST 457:13
going back h. SCOT 650:6
goodman is not at h. BIBL 82:16
Go on h. VIRG 796:13
hear news of h. PROV 601:10
hearth-fire and the h.-acre KIPL 439:1
Hierusalem, my happy h. ANON 16:17
H. again, home again NURS 551:14
H. art gone SHAK 661:1
H. is home PROV 602:42
H. is home, as the Devil said PROV 602:41
H. is the girl's prison SHAW 708:28
H. is the place FROS 325:19
H. is the sailor STEV 743:4
h. is the Sule Skerry BALL 50:17
H. is where the heart is PROV 602:43
H. is where you come to THAT 770:14
H. James HILL 377:6
H.-keeping youth SHAK 702:23
H. life as we understand it SHAW 707:7
h. life of our own dear Queen ANON 16:18
H. of lost causes ARNO 28:15
h. of the brave KEY 434:16
h., rejoicing, brought me BAKE 48:13
h. sweet home JERO 407:2
H., sweet home PAYN 570:13
H. they brought her warrior TENN 765:25
h., you idle creatures SHAK 674:2
house is not a h. ADLE 6:6
hunter h. from hill STEV 743:4
in h. cosmography HABI 355:9
I was leaving h. STEV 742:18
Keep the H.-fires burning FORD 320:6
kept at h. COWP 241:6
leaves h. to mend himself GOLD 345:24
Look as much like h. FRY 326:24
man goeth to his long h. BIBL 85:2
murder into the h. HITC 378:2
never h. came she KING 437:10
never is at h. COWP 240:3
no place like h. PAYN 570:14
no place like h. PROV 612:30
O, h., hame CUNN 247:16
points of heaven and h. WORD 832:11
princes are come h. again SHAK 677:21
refuge from h. life SHAW 709:22
shortest way h. PROV 605:49
Sweet Stay-at-h. DAVI 252:10
there's nobody at h. POPE 582:25
thinks to found a h. DOUG 276:19
Till the boys come h. FORD 320:6
unto God all things come h. KORA 445:7
what is it to be at h. BECK 59:9
What's the good of a h. GROS 354:3
White House or h. DOLE 272:1
woman's place in the h. PROV 615:15
won't go h. till morning BUCK 159:18
won the Fleece and then came h. DU B 283:22
years in a geriatric h. AMIS 14:3
homeland loved my h. BELL 64:17
homeless h. by choice SOUT 731:4
h., tempest-tossed LAZA 459:12
homely h. was their food GART 330:12
h. wits SHAK 702:23
never so h. PROV 602:42
home-made H. dishes HOOD 382:23
Homer excellent H. nods HORA 386:5
Gladstone read H. for fun CHUR 216:14
had the voice of H. HALD 356:17
H. dead ANON 18:18
H. is not more decidedly MACA 481:11
H.'s mighty dinners AESC 6:13
H. smote 'is bloomin' lyre [illegible]
H. sometimes nods PROV 602:44
H. sometimes sleeps BYRO 177:1
more than H. knew SWIF 749:15
must not call it H. BENT 67:10
warred for H., being dead HEYW 376:8
Home Rule morning H. passes CARS 192:3
separation as well as H. BALF 49:15
homes h. without a friend CLAR 218:13
In h., a haunted apparatus RAIN 620:7
Stately H. of England COWA 238:19
stately h. of England HEMA 369:6
homespuns What hempen h. SHAK 690:1
homeward h. take your way COLL 228:6
Look h. angel MILT 513:9
ploughman h. plods GRAY 350:6
homicidal h. classics STOP 743:16
homo *Ecce h.* BIBL 114:8
ET H. FACTUS EST MISS 520:18
homogeneity incoherent h. SPEN 732:4
homosexual composer and *not* h. DIAG 260:2
h. sex you know exactly BURR 169:16
honest beat the h. men SHAK 685:5
buy it like an h. man NORT 546:20
Corrupted h. men SHAK 657:8
few h. men CROM 245:8
general h. thought SHAK 677:4
h. broker BISM 116:11
h. God INGE 399:13
h. madam's issue SHAK 678:3
h. man is laughed at HALI 358:1
h. man's the noblest work BURN 166:26
h. man's the noblest work POPE 586:1
h. men come by their own PROV 614:33
h., sonsie face BURN 168:20
h. tale SHAK 696:25
H. to God ROBI 629:19
h. woman of her word SHAK 687:27
I am not naturally h. SHAK 703:24
is not an h. man WHAT 813:10
least h. with themselves AUST 37:24
most h. of men RICH 627:10
poor but she was h. MILI 508:14
Robin and I are two h. men SHIP 717:7
whatsoever things are h. BIBL 108:25
while the nation is h. DOUG 277:2
honestly If possible h. HORA 386:11
honesty armed so strong in h. SHAK 676:23
common sense and common h. SHEL 710:3
h. is *not* to be based RUSK 638:24
H. is praised JUVE 424:4
H. is the best policy PROV 602:45
H. is the best policy WHAT 813:10
perilous to a man's h. TROL 782:28
saving of thine h. MORE 531:15
honey bees make h. VIRG 797:4
Eating bread and h. NURS 550:18
flowing with milk and h. BIBL 75:28
gather h. all the day WATT 805:5
hive for the h.-bee YEAT 836:11
hives with h. and wax SWIF 747:12
H. catches more flies PROV 602:46
h. from the weed SHAK 671:11
h. of Hybla SHAK 667:16
h. of poison-flowers TENN 763:23
H. of roses HERB 372:18
H., quoth she NURS 551:4
h. shall he eat BIBL 86:26
h. still for tea BROO 150:15
h. to smear his face SCHW 649:16
H., your silk stocking SELL 654:6
How a bear likes h. MILN 511:2
I did but taste a little h. BIBL 78:24
in my mouth sweet as h. BIBL 112:17
locusts and wild h. BIBL 92:28
sweeter also than h. BOOK 132:17
there is h. PROV 614:35
took some h. LEAR 460:16
With milk and h. blessed NEAL 540:3
honeycomb drop as an h. BIBL 82:12
honey, and the h. BOOK 132:17
of an h. BIBL 100:36
honeydew he on h. hath fed COLE [illegible]
honeyed h. middle of the night KEAT 427:6
honeysuckle You are my honey, h. FITZ 314:5
Hong Kong H.'s return to China DENG 257:10
honi H. soie qui mal y pense SELL 654:6
H. soit qui mal y pense MOTT 535:9
honking goose h. amongst tuneful swans VIRG 796:11
honores *contemnere h.* HORA 390:2
honour abide in h. BOOK 135:1
all in h. SHAK 694:2
All is lost save h. MISQ 521:1
As he was valiant, I h. him SHAK 675:25
cannot be maintained with h. RUSS 640:10
existence JUVE 424:18
Fear God. H. the King KITC 441:31
flowery plains of h. JONS 420:7
for this woman's h. FILM 312:7
fountain of h. BACO 42:2
greater share of h. SHAK 671:22
great peaks of h. LLOY 471:2
H. all men BIBL 110:30
h. among thieves PROV 612:11
H., and all things else JONS 420:3
h., and keep her BOOK 131:4
h. and life FRAN 323:1
h. and renown ye ANON 18:19
H. a physician BIBL 92:9
h. aspireth to it BACO 42:23
H. but an empty bubble DRYD 280:20
h. due unto his Name BOOK 138:7
h. in one eye SHAK 674:8
H. is like a match PAGN 563:6
h. is the subject SHAK 674:9

H. pricks me on SHAK 669:8
h. rooted in dishonour TENN 759:29
h. sinks where commerce GOLD 345:8
h.'s voice GRAY 350:10
H. the greatest poet DANT 249:10
h. therof EDWA 289:4
h. those whom they have slain DOST 276:2
H. thy father and thy mother BIBL 76:13
h. turn to dust MARV 499:3
H.! tut, a breath JONS 420:13
h. unto Luke Evangelist ROSS 635:3
h. unto the wife BIBL 111:3
H., without money RACI 620:2
h. would thee do SHAK 671:1
hurt that H. feels TENN 763:1
in h. clear POPE 584:6
In h. I gained them NELS 540:16
Keeps h. bright SHAK 700:15
king delighteth to h. BIBL 80:33
Leisure with h. CICE 217:26
loss of h. was a wrench GRAH 348:2
louder he talked of his h. EMER 299:15
Loved I not h. more LOVE 476:16
may we h. it WEBS 807:16
Mine h. is my life SHAK 694:9
new-made h. doth forget SHAK 677:6
one vessel unto h. BIBL 105:13
peace I hope with h. DISR 269:18
peace with h. CHAM 200:18
pluck bright h. SHAK 667:26
pluck up drownèd h. SHAK 667:26
post of h. ADDI 4:15
post of h. PROV 609:33
property or h. MACH 486:3
prophet is not without h. BIBL 95:24
prophet not without h. PROV 609:46
ready her to h. BEST 70:2
reputation and h. SOCR 726:23
riches and h. BIBL 82:8
right of h. GURN 355:3
roll of h. CLEV 220:14
safety, h., and welfare CHAR 203:13
signed with their h. SPEN 732:19
some smatch of h. SHAK 677:3
stain in thine h. BIBL 92:8
state of temporary h. JOHN 411:4
take mine h. from me KIPL 439:9
throne *we* h. SHER 715:22
Trouthe and h. CHAU 204:8
What is h. SHAK 669:9
whence h. springs MARL 496:27
When h.'s at the stake SHAK 665:33
where their h. died POPE 583:15
without h. BIBL 91:11
years and h. to the grave KIPL 439:15
honourable Brutus is an h. man SHAK 675:29
designs were strictly h. FIEL 310:12
h. alike in what we give LINC 468:12
h. among all men BOOK 131:1
humble as h. CHUA 213:1
make an h. retreat SHAK 659:8
more h. man BIBL 99:24
only h. provision AUST 38:20
thy h. women BOOK 134:15
honoured h. me of late SHAK 682:13
More h. in the breach SHAK 662:17
honours bears his blushing h. SHAK 673:12
despise h. HORA 390:2
good card to play for H. BENN 66:10
h. her more than himself TALM 754:11
h. the worker TALM 754:13
h. to the world again SHAK 673:19
neither h. nor wages GARI 329:17
hood bold Robin H. BALL 50:14
hoof though he divide the h. BIBL 76:20
hoofs h. of a swinish multitude BURK 163:25
plunging h. were gone DE L 256:17
hook bended h. shall pierce SHAK 656:31
h.-nosed fellow of Rome SHAK 670:12
That nose, the h. BYRO 173:11
thy h. Spares the next swath KEAT 430:9
with an h. BIBL 82:3
hooks Thy baited h. WYAT 834:1
hooter because the h. hoots CHES 210:12
hooting H. and shrieking SHAK 674:22
h. at the glorious sun COLE 225:11
Hoover onto the board of H. GREE 352:11
hop for what were h.-yards meant HOUS 391:9
H. forty paces SHAK 656:26
Why h. ye so BOOK 136:8
hope Abandon all h. DANT 249:7
All my h. on God BRID 148:7
All our h. is fallen HORA 389:5
believed in h. BIBL 104:34
Can something, h. HOPK 384:2
Evelyn H. is dead BROW 155:28
failure of h. GIBB 336:3
From h. and fear set free SWIN 750:22
from rising h. FOOT 319:4
God is our h. BOOK 134:18
have not h. nor health SHEL 713:30
He has no h. COWP 242:15
heirs through h. BOOK 130:2
He that lives in h. HERB 373:20
He that lives upon h. FRAN 323:12
h. and agitation BARA 53:14
h. beyond ourselves SHEL 715:1
H. deferred BIBL 82:27
H. deferred PROV 602:47
h., fear, rage, pleasure JUVE 424:6
H., for a season CAMP 183:14
h. for the best SMIT 725:14
H. for the best PROV 602:48
h. for years to come WATT 805:19
h. grew ground me COLE 225:5
h. I dreamed of ROSS 634:6
h. in Christ BIBL 106:21
H. is a good breakfast BACO 45:8
H. is a good breakfast PROV 602:49
h. is gone AUST 38:12
h. is perished BIBL 89:24
h. I will be religious again FLEM 317:14
Hopeless h. hopes on CLAR 218:13
h. little ELGA 291:18
H. maketh not ashamed BIBL 104:35
h. of all the ends BOOK 136:1
h. of glory BOOK 127:19
h. of the ungodly BIBL 91:13
h. once crushed ARNO 27:29
H. raises no dust ÉLUA 299:1
H. springs eternal POPE 585:9
H. springs eternal PROV 603:1
h. till Hope creates SHEL 713:16
I can give you no h. EDDI 287:23
in the store we sell h. REVS 625:1
Land of H. and Glory BENS 66:13
last best h. LINC 468:12
life there's h. PROV 614:43
lives in h. PROV 602:16
look forward to with h. FROS 325:18
more h. of a fool BIBL 83:25
Never to h. again SHAK 673:13
no h. without fear SPIN 734:26
Nor dread nor h. attend YEAT 835:14
not another's h. WALS 802:11
not for h., heart would break PROV 603:18
nursing the unconquerable h. ARNO 27:11
only h. that keeps up GAY 331:15
phantoms of h. JOHN 410:23
pleasing h. ADDI 4:16
poise of h. and fear MILT 511:22
Some blessed H. HARD 361:12
sure and certain h. BOOK 131:14
tender leaves of h. SHAK 673:12
there is h. CROS 246:12
There is no h. CHES 208:23
Through love, through h. WORD 831:16
triumph of h. over experience JOHN 414:10
True h. is swift SHAK 696:27
two thousand years of h. WEIZ 809:2
warns us not to h. HORA 389:7
Was the h. drunk SHAK 682:14
we may gain from h. MILT 514:17
Whatever h. is yours OWEN 562:12
What is h. BYRO 180:2
what was dead was H. WILD 819:1
Where there is despair, h. FRAN 323:5
Work without h. COLE 227:6
Youth and H. COLE 227:28
hoped things h. for BIBL 109:28
hoped-for become the h. heaven EPIT 304:11
hopeful droopingly, but with a h. heart LAWR 457:22
hopefully travel h. PROV 604:12
travel h. is a better thing STEV 741:25
hopefulness Lord of all h. STRU 745:2
hopeless Ages of h. end MILT 515:11
doctors know a h. case CUMM 247:10
h. are starkly sincere RHYS 625:18
h. grief is passionless BROW 154:17
H. hope hopes on CLAR 218:13
inspire h. passion THAC 768:23
perennially h. DICK 260:18
hopelessness h. and calm BARA 53:14
h. of one's position DOST 276:8
hopes airy h. my children WORD 828:12
enter on far-reaching h. HORA 387:17
happy as one h. LA R 453:22
h. and fears BROO 151:9
h. and fears it heeded not SHEL 714:6
h. of its children EISE 291:8
h. our wits beguile WOTT 833:4
If h. were dupes CLOU 223:3
no great h. from Birmingham AUST 37:19
no h. but from power BURK 164:27
scribbled lines like fallen h. HOPE 383:19
set my h. in thee PRAY 592:8
vanity of human h. JOHN 410:21
wholly h. to be BROW 155:24
hopeth h. all things BIBL 106:16
hoping Dreading and h. all YEAT 835:14
hops apples, cherries, h. DICK 265:3
heresy, h., and beer PROV 613:22
Horatius H. kept the bridge MACA 483:12
horizon always somebody else's h. GRAH 348:8
h. adorning HEBE 367:5
In research the h. recedes PATT 570:4
just beyond the h. KISS 441:30
rode across The h. KAVA 426:8
horizons immense fields, wide h. CHEK 208:2
horizontal h. desire SHAW 709:26
Life is a h. fall COCT 223:17
horn blow his wreathèd h. WORD 832:16
h. of the hunter CRAW 244:16
horn, the lusty h. SHAK 659:21
one of which is made of h. VIRG 795:3
sound of the h. VIGN 792:14
through the mellow h. COLL 229:11
won't come out of your h. PARK 566:17
Hornby H. and my Barlow THOM 774:1
horned h. moon WORD 827:10
Horner Little Jack H. NURS 549:6
Hornie Auld H., Satan BURN 166:6
hornpipes h. and strathspeys BURN 166:29
horns h. of Elfland TENN 765:17
memories are hunting h. APOL 22:20
horny H.-handed sons of toil SALI 643:1
h. hands of toil LOWE 477:14
horribilis annus h. ELIZ 297:16
horrible h. imaginings SHAK 681:21
O, horrible! O, h. SHAK 662:31
out of the h. pit BOOK 133:31
horrid she was h. LONG 475:2
very h. thing BUTL 171:12
With h. warning KEAT 428:13
horror haunts of h. and fear TENN 764:14
h. its beauty SHEL 712:20
h. of a deep night RACI 619:16
h. of great darkness BIBL 74:25
h. of sunsets PROU 594:7
h.! The horror CONR 234:13
image of that h. SHAK 680:12

horror *(cont.)*:
scaly h. of his folded tail MILT 513:26
there is no h. DOYL 278:6
horrors Congenial h. THOM 775:15
stained with ancient h. RIMB 628:8
supped full with h. SHAK 685:21
horse behold a pale h. BIBL 112:5
behold a white h. BIBL 113:2
Boot, saddle, to h. BROW 155:15
dearer than his h. TENN 762:23
Do not trust the h. VIRG 793:18
Don't ask me, ask the h. FREU 324:16
feeds the h. enough oats GALB 328:9
fitchew nor the soiled h. SHAK 679:22
gift h. in the mouth PROV 607:32
good h. cannot be PROV 601:26
h. designed by a committee ISSI 400:10
h. has bolted PROV 604:36
h. he can ride THOM 775:23
h. is at least *human* SALI 642:11
h. is to the Arab KOHL 443:9
h.-laugh in the reader FIEL 310:11
h. misused upon the road BLAK 117:19
h. of air ANON 19:17
h. of that colour SHAK 701:15
h. on the mountain GARC 329:11
h.'s cry ARNO 27:16
h.'s hoof PROV 612:48
h. was made Consul RAND 621:16
mare is the better h. PROV 601:39
might even do for a h. NIGH 545:24
my h., my wife, and my name SURT 746:20
my kingdom for a h. SHAK 696:33
My Lovely H. LINE 469:12
never heard no h. sing ARMS 25:18
Ninety-seven h. power FLAN 316:5
not a h. PROV 606:20
O, for a h. with wings SHAK 660:24
O happy h. SHAK 656:19
old h. that stumbles HARD 361:16
One man may steal a h. PROV 608:46
outside of a h. PROV 612:21
owe it to h. and hound WHYT 816:13
rider and his h. SURT 747:7
short h. soon curried PROV 611:21
sick h. nosing around KAVA 426:10
something in a flying h. WORD 830:15
sounds like a saddle h. ONAS 554:17
sting a stately h. JOHN 412:12
strength of an h. BOOK 141:25
take a h. to the water PROV 615:33
to my h.—German CHAR 203:16
torturer's h. scratches AUDE 34:10
two ride on a h. PROV 603:25
two things about the h. ROYD 636:17
upon the high h. BROW 152:1
want of a h. PROV 600:41
where's the bloody h. CAMP 183:2
young cornet of h. WALP 802:6
horseback beggar on h. PROV 610:32
ride On h. COWP 240:12
Horseguards be in the H. RATT 622:7
horseman *H., pass by* YEAT 837:22
sits behind the h. HORA 388:13
horsemanship forgetful of his h. HOME 382:7
horsemen Four H. rode again RICE 626:5
horses All the king's h. NURS 548:16
breed of their h. PENN 572:15
Bring on the empty h. CURT 248:4
change h. in mid stream PROV 598:30
dogs, h. JENY 406:12
don't spare the h. HILL 377:6
frighten the h. CAMP 182:16
generally given to h. JOHN 409:12
hell of h. PROV 599:13
h. are the senses UPAN 788:1
H. for courses PROV 603:2
h. in the morning BIBL 89:11
h. of instruction BLAK 119:21
h. of the night OVID 561:2
If wishes were h. PROV 603:26
if you cannot ride two h. MAXT 502:11
in h., dawgs, and men THAC 769:10
I saw the h. HUGH 393:6
ride two h. at once PROV 603:28
Rode their h. Up to bed DE L 256:14
some in h. BOOK 132:19
surmised the H. Heads DICK 266:7
swap h. when crossing LINC 468:16
that h. may not be stolen HALI 357:22
They shoot h. don't they MCCO 484:11
watered our h. in Helicon CHAP 202:18
wild white h. play ARNO 26:11
with his panting h. VIRG 796:15
Women and H. KIPL 438:6
horticulture lead a h. PARK 567:15
hortis *nascitur h.* CATU 197:11
hortus *H. ubi et tecto vicinus iugis* HORA 389:24
hosanna Glorious h. SMAR 722:13
H. in excelsis MISS 520:21
hosannas sweet h. ring NEAL 540:1
hose out of the turret with a h. JARR 404:7
youthful h. well saved SHAK 659:2
hospes *deferor h.* HORA 386:8
hospital first requirement in a H. NIGH 545:22
not an inn, but an h. BROW 154:2
hospitals rot in h. SOUT 728:22
host find such a h. ANST 22:15
h., of golden daffodils WORD 828:26
h. of Midian BIBL 77:33
like a fashionable h. SHAK 700:16
hostages h. to fortune BACO 43:17
h. to the fates LUCA 478:16
hostile universe is not h. HOLM 381:4
hosts h. and guests BEER 61:10
Lord God of h. BOOK 129:20
Lord of h. BOOK 133:4
Lord of h. is with us BOOK 134:19
hot beat the iron while it is h. DRYD 283:2
English have h.-water bottles MIKE 507:19
h. cross buns NURS 550:1
h. for certainties MERE 505:21
little pot is soon h. PROV 605:41
long h. summer FILM 312:22
neither cold nor h. BIBL 111:28
On a h., hot day LAWR 458:13
only in h. water REAG 623:1
That is, h. ice SHAK 690:22
while the iron is h. PROV 611:30
hotel great advantage of a h. SHAW 709:22
h.-keepers continue TROL 782:22
Midnight, a h. bedroom READ 622:17
Hotspur H. of the North SHAK 668:2
Houlihan Kathaleen Ní H. CARB 186:1
hound his hawk, his h. BALL 52:5
H. that Caught the Pubic Hare BEHA 61:23
loves the h. more SURT 746:19
owe it to horse and h. WHYT 816:13
slepyng h. to wake CHAU 207:8
traveller, by the faithful h. LONG 473:17
hounds by your own quick h. MOTI 534:6
carcass fit for h. SHAK 675:3
h. all join in glorious cry FIEL 309:16
h. and his horn in the morning GRAV 349:9
h. of Sparta SHAK 690:15
h. of spring SWIN 750:5
smale h. hadde she CHAU 204:14
Such h., such hawks BALL 52:4
hour accompany us one short h. FARA 306:11
anguish of a torturing h. SHAK 690:21
Awaits alike th' inevitable h. GRAY 350:9
books of the h. RUSK 638:14
but an h. or two to spend BELL 63:25
close-companioned inarticulate h. ROSS 634:23
darkest h. PROV 597:48
Ere the parting h. go by ARNO 26:17
fill the h. EMER 299:25
finest h. CHUR 215:11
for an h. of Herod HOPE 383:16
for one h. retard SMAR 722:14
h. is come SCOT 651:24
h. of death BOOK 127:8
h. of glorious life MORD 530:21
h. requires such help VIRG 794:7
I also had my h. CHES 210:5
I have had my h. DRYD 282:33
Improve each shining h. WATT 805:5
its h. come round at last YEAT 837:6
Its h. is now SCHW 650:1
known as the Children's H. LONG 473:11
know not what h. BIBL 97:7
man and the h. YANC 834:19
matched us with His h. BROO 150:16
mine h. is not yet come BIBL 101:13
most carefully upon your h. SHAK 661:4
now's the h. BURN 168:7
stayed me in a happy h. SHAK 691:17
struts and frets his h. SHAK 685:22
tell the h. JOHN 413:25
Time and the h. SHAK 681:22
'tis the h. of prayer BYRO 177:2
to serve the h. TENN 765:6
watch with me one hour BIBL 97:22
hourglass Egghead weds h. NEWS 544:4
still as the h. ROSS 634:22
hours better wages and shorter h. ORWE 559:5
flying h. are gone ROCH 630:9
h. were thine and mine TENN 758:14
h. will take care of themselves CHES 209:12
leaden-stepping h. MILT 514:3
see the h. pass CIOR 218:4
Seven h. to law JONE 419:5
Six h. in sleep COKE 224:11
Six h. sleep for a man PROV 610:44
two golden h. MANN 493:19
two h.' traffick SHAK 697:3
house angel in the h. PATM 569:18
another man's h. AUST 37:16
barren woman to keep h. BOOK 139:20
beat upon that h. BIBL 94:12
Better one h. spoiled PROV 596:10
build a h. for fools SWIF 749:26
called a woman in my own h. WAUG 806:14
Carrying his own h. DONN 274:23
Dark h., by which I once more TENN 760:28
displeases this H. O'CO 552:16
doll in the doll's h. DICK 265:1
dull manage of a servile h. WINC 822:22
dwell in the h. of the Lord BOOK 133:1
Harrow the h. of the dead AUDE 35:6
heap of stones is a h. POIN 580:2
h. and land are gone PROV 614:20
h. appointed for all living BIBL 81:27
h. as nigh heaven MORE 531:12
H. Beautiful is play lousy PARK 567:10
h. built upon sand SAYE 646:4
h. divided LINC 468:5
h. divided cannot stand PROV 603:3
h. is a machine for living in LE C 461:13
h. is his castle COKE 224:10
h. is much more MORR 532:6
h. is not a home ADLE 6:6
h. not made with hands BIBL 107:7
h. not made with hands BROW 155:17
h. of defence BOOK 137:23
h. of God BIBL 75:3
H. of Peers GILB 337:17
h. of prayer BIBL 88:25
h. of prayer BIBL 96:20
h. of the Lord BOOK 140:7
h. of the Lord BOOK 140:14
h. of the planter CLAR 219:12
h. rose like magic HARG 362:6
h. seventy years old JEAN 404:17
h. that has got over JERO 406:20
h. that Jack built NURS 551:7
h. that serves the Muses SAPP 644:16
h. to lodge a friend SWIF 749:7
h. upon the sand BIBL 94:13
h. where I was born HOOD 382:21
If a h. be divided BIBL 98:2

in a little crooked h. NURS 551:3
in a wide h. BIBL 83:12
In my Father's h. BIBL 102:17
in the h. of Rimmon BIBL 80:19
into the h. in her train LAMB 448:9
join house to h. BIBL 86:18
labour of women in the h. GILM 339:15
Learning is better than h. PROV 605:12
little plaything-h. WALP 800:15
Lord build the h. BOOK 140:21
make a H. CANN 185:8
Make my h. your inn MOOR 530:1
mind to sell his h. SWIF 747:16
My sober h. SHAK 687:21
palace is more than a h. COLE 227:22
Peace be to this h. BOOK 131:9
purify My H. KORA 444:22
return no more to his h. BIBL 81:11
see to thine own h., David BIBL 79:23
set a h. on fire BACO 44:23
Set thine h. in order BIBL 87:25
so in the way in the h. GASK 330:17
sparrow hath found her an h. BOOK 137:11
substance of his h. BIBL 86:8
there was not a h. BIBL 76:3
This H. today is a theatre BALD 49:11
What! in our h. SHAK 683:20
When in that H. MPs divide GILB 337:15
With usura hath no man a h. POUN 589:7
You take my h. SHAK 688:16
zeal of thine h. BOOK 136:10
housed h., clothed, fed RUSK 638:25
houseful three is a h. SAYI 647:4
household centre of the h. SHAW 707:12
homely h. savour BYRO 176:19
h. and the Church BOOK 128:18
h. bird DONN 272:18
h. cares me tie WHIT 816:2
h. virtue, most uncommon BYRO 179:13
put his h. in order BIBL 79:10
they of his own h. BIBL 95:2
they of the h. BOOK 136:7
trust Her h. to me HERB 371:24
householder h. stage of life LAWS 459:4
think she's a h. WILD 819:15
housekeeper make a h. think WILD 819:15
housekeeping city h. has failed ADDA 4:3
good h. to the winds KEYN 435:12
housekeepings hearts and h. DICK 264:17
houseless h. heads and unfed sides SHAK 678:28
housemaids damp souls of h. ELIO 295:12
houses falling h. thunder JOHN 411:9
Fools build h. PROV 600:38
friends' h. JOHN 417:1
h. are all gone under the sea ELIO 294:8
H. are built to live in BACO 42:14
h. go wheeling back THOM 775:22
h. in between BATE 57:3
h. thick and sewers MILT 517:14
live in glass h. PROV 612:42
nothing in your h. MORR 532:17
plague o' both your h. SHAK 697:23
Round their golden h. TENN 763:14
spaces between the h. FENT 308:8
very h. seem asleep WORD 828:1
watered our h. in Helicon CHAP 202:18
housetop alone upon the h. BOOK 138:14
corner of the h. BIBL 83:12
housewife good h. Fortune SHAK 658:8
housewives Good h. now may say CORB 236:11
housework h., with its repetition DE B 254:5
no need to do any h. CRIS 245:4
Houston H., we've had a problem LOVE 477:2
hovel *prefer* in fact a h. CALV 182:6
hover H. through the fog SHAK 681:7
how Here's a h.-de-doo GILB 338:7
H. and Where and Who KIPL 441:10
H. do I love thee BROW 154:21
H. do they know PARK 567:13
H. NOT TO DO IT DICK 262:25
not say why and h. WILS 822:6
howl H., howl, howl, howl SHAK 680:11
howlet h.'s wing SHAK 684:18
howling h. of Irish wolves SHAK 659:23
howls h. of anguish HEAL 366:2
Howth H. Castle and Environs JOYC 421:17
H. Castle and Environs OPEN 556:12
Hubbard Old Mother H. NURS 549:18
huddled h. masses yearning LAZA 459:12
hues all her lovely h. DAVI 252:7
living h. and odours SHEL 712:12
huff leave in a h. FILM 311:13
windvane changabil h. puffe VIRG 794:13
hugger h.-mugger to inter him SHAK 666:5
Hugo H.—alas GIDE 336:19
H. was a madman COCT 223:18
hulk Here, a sheer h. DIBD 260:14
hum busy h. of men MILT 512:23
human all h. life is there ADVE 7:3
all h. life is there JAME 403:7
calculable mass of h. beings WEBB 806:26
characteristics of the h. species GODW 342:4
course of h. events JEFF 405:2
disappointed in h. nature DONL 272:4
emptiness. The h. lack BOLD 124:10
err is h. SAYI 648:7
extirpated from h. nature HUME 394:8
full tide of h. existence JOHN 414:27
future of the h. race JEAN 404:17
goodness entirely h. ELIO 293:16
good of h. nature BACO 44:18
guide of h. life HUME 394:6
happiness of the h. race BURK 163:9
health of the whole h. race TOYN 780:5
horse is at least *h.* SALI 642:11
H. beings HARD 360:17
H. beings have an inalienable right GREE 352:10
H. blunders TAYL 756:7
h. characteristic WEIL 808:22
h. condition MALR 492:17
h. form display BLAK 118:7
h. hearts endure JOHN 411:12
H. kind Cannot bear ELIO 294:3
H. life is a sad show FLAU 316:20
h. life is, at the greatest TEMP 757:5
h. nature changed WOOL 826:16
h. nature is finer KEAT 431:3
H. on my faithless arm AUDE 34:8
h. race began BURN 167:5
h. rose to haunt us RICH 626:13
h. shape, Worse than the Devil SPEG 731:23
H. speech FLAU 316:7
h., they suffered WARR 804:1
h. things are subject to decay DRYD 281:35
h. zoo MORR 532:7
knowledge of h. nature AUST 38:2
Larger than h. TENN 760:13
laugh at h. actions SPIN 734:27
milk of h. kindness SHAK 682:1
nothing h. foreign to me TERE 768:3
not made on a h. scale MALR 493:1
not the less h. MOLI 525:17
Peace, the h. dress BLAK 120:15
people are only h. COMP 230:13
privilege of h. nature ROWE 636:11
robot may not injure a h. ASIM 30:16
see God in every h. TERE 768:9
soaring h. boy DICK 260:24
socialism would not lose its h. face DUBČ 283:20
there is h. culture RENA 624:11
To err is h. POPE 584:27
To err is h. PROV 613:8
To step aside is h. BURN 166:8
true virtue of h. beings MILL 509:7
wish I loved the H. Race RALE 621:11
humane Heaven and earth not h. LAO 451:7
humanitarian h. with an eye CECI 199:4
humanity all the ties of h. WESL 811:13
crooked timber of h. KANT 425:19
freeze my h. MACN 488:13
h. after Victory NELS 540:19
H. a work in progress WILL 820:14
H. cannot long dispense GUIZ 354:17
H. i love you CUMM 247:5
h. is only three days old JEAN 404:17
h., reason BURK 163:1
H. with all its fears LONG 473:10
imitated h. SHAK 664:17
law of h. BURK 165:11
man of h. CONF 231:13
not to their h. SMIT 723:6
popular h. is treason ADDI 4:13
religion of h. PAIN 563:17
sad music of h. WORD 829:5
So act as to treat h. KANT 425:18
teach governments h. PAIN 563:20
truth, justice, and h. GLAD 341:8
unremitting h. BENN 66:1
wearisome condition of h. GREV 353:4
humankind lords of h. GOLD 345:9
humans isn't fit for h. now BETJ 71:4
humble Be it ever so h. PAYN 570:14
Friend of the h. SIKH 719:11
He that is h. BUNY 161:12
h., lowly, penitent BOOK 125:13
marry the h.-bee NURS 548:5
Neither too h. MALL 492:5
Was Jesus h. BLAK 118:13
humbleth he that h. himself BIBL 99:26
humbly walk h. with thy God BIBL 90:20
humbug 'Bah,' said Scrooge. 'H.!' DICK 261:8
h. in a Pickwickian point DICK 265:2
H. or Humdrum DISR 269:28
vox h. SHER 716:26
Yes we have. H. PALM 566:10
humdrum Humbug or H. DISR 269:28
Humean H. predicament QUIN 619:4
humiliation Art is born of h. AUDE 35:16
collapse in deepest h. EDDI 287:23
valley of H. BUNY 160:17
humiliations mortifications and h. WALP 801:23
humility H. is the only doubt BLAK 118:14
modest stillness and h. SHAK 671:5
pride that apes h. COLE 225:7
proofs of h. BLAK 118:13
small book on H. LONG 475:4
such royalty as h. ELEA 291:14
visit us in great h. BOOK 127:21
humming hear the virus h. DOTY 276:10
humour Good taste and h. MUGG 534:18
H. is emotional chaos THUR 777:3
H. is odd SWIF 749:21
in this h. won SHAK 696:13
native h. POPE 584:10
one for h., sincerity NEIL 540:11
humours In all thy h. ADDI 5:1
hump camel has a single h. NASH 539:8
without a positive h. THAC 769:5
Humpty Dumpty heard H. JAME 403:26
H. had a great fall NURS 548:16
hundred His h.'s soon hit BROW 156:1
h. flowers blossom MAO 495:4
h. years hence DICK 263:22
Six h. threescore and six BIBL 112:22
three h. pounds SHAK 688:35
hung H. be the heavens SHAK 672:6
h. with bloom HOUS 390:14
hunger bodily h. in his eyes SHAW 707:24
Fear and H. VIRG 794:20
H. allows no choice AUDE 35:2
h. and poverty LARK 452:11
h. and thirst BIBL 93:3
H. drives the wolf PROV 603:4
H. is the best sauce PROV 603:5
h. to be beautiful RHYS 625:17
I am h. VOZN 798:16
In poverty, h., and dirt HOOD 382:28
lack, and suffer h. BOOK 133:21

hunger (*cont.*):
love seldom dies of h. LENC 463:5
offer you h., thirst GARI 329:17
sacred h. SPEN 734:9
shall h. no more BIBL 112:11
shall never h. BIBL 101:28
time of h. BIBL 91:30
hungered h., and ye gave me meat BIBL 97:12
hungry Adam was born h. BRIL 148:19
ate when we were not h. SWIF 748:2
filled the h. BIBL 98:17
filled the h. BIBL 114:4
h. for dinner at eight HART 363:6
h. man is an angry man PROV 603:6
h. sheep look up MILT 513:6
I am not h. PUNC 617:16
If thine enemy be h. BIBL 83:21
lean and h. look SHAK 674:16
Let all who are h. HAGG 355:13
makes h. Where most she satisfies SHAK 656:27
seen the h. ocean SHAK 704:26
Huns H. or Wops MITF 524:9
hunt Better to h. in fields DRYD 281:13
h. with the hounds PROV 615:43
hunted H. and penned MCKA 486:6
h. round the globe PAIN 563:14
hunter Esau was a cunning h. BIBL 74:35
heart is a lonely h. BORR 144:10
h. home from hill STEV 743:4
H. of the East FITZ 314:7
h.'s javelin ARNO 27:16
H.'s waking thoughts AUDE 33:24
Man is the h. TENN 765:24
Nimrod the mighty h. BIBL 74:23
snare of the h. BOOK 137:21
Hunter Dunn Miss J. H. BETJ 71:5
hunters h. ben nat hooly men CHAU 204:16
hunting ain't the h. PUNC 617:8
call h. one of them JOHN 418:9
Daddy's gone a-h. NURS 547:14
death on the h.-field MORT 533:9
discourse was about h. PEPY 573:5
goddess of h. SPEN 732:13
handsome h. man DE L 256:13
H. he loved SHAK 705:28
H. is all that's worth SURT 746:16
passion for h. DICK 264:15
preserved as h.-grounds ELIO 292:18
weary wi' h. BALL 51:1
wet and dirty from h. SURT 747:5
Huntingtower bower, and H. BALL 50:19
huntress Queen and h. JONS 419:17
huntsman cassocked h. COWP 241:2
h. by the bear oppressed WALL 800:1
huntsmen h. are up in America BROW 152:17
hurdles don't really see the h. MOSE 534:4
hurl h. my soul from heaven SHAK 693:31
hurled rude heap, together h. MARV 499:7
Swift to be h. HOOD 382:16
hurly-burly When the h.'s done SHAK 681:6
hurricane h. on the way FISH 313:9
select the h. season WIND 823:3
hurricanes H. hardly happen LERN 465:7
hurricanoes You cataracts and h. SHAK 678:21
hurry h., hurry, hurry MIDD 507:7
H. no man's cattle PROV 603:7
H. up please it's time ELIO 296:6
never in a h. WESL 811:19
old man in a h. CHUR 214:15
sick h. ARNO 27:10
hurrying waiting means h. on MANN 494:3
hurt assault and h. the soul BOOK 128:4
cry before you're h. PROV 598:33
deliberately tries to h. BAIN 48:8
don't know can't h. you PROV 614:11
hate the man you have h. TACI 752:10
have power to h. SHAK 705:6
healed also the h. BIBL 89:14
h. but I am not slain BALL 51:12
h. not thy foot BOOK 137:23
h. of my soul BOOK 135:25
h. you to the heart TWAI 786:11
if I don't h. her NURS 548:19
I'll not h. thee STER 738:24
never h. a hair STUD 745:5
no one was to be h. BROO 151:1
power to h. us BEAU 58:15
shall not h. nor destroy BIBL 87:5
wish to h. BRON 149:10
words will never h. me PROV 611:20
Yes it h. POLI 582:9
hurting Cold lights h. JOHN 408:8
If the policy isn't h. MAJO 491:14
people h. people MAIL 491:3
hurts h. to think HOUS 391:9
husband as a bride adorned for her h. BIBL 113:7
as to love a h. WYCH 834:12
Chaste to her h. POPE 583:13
crown to her h. BIBL 82:24
darkens a h.'s mood SADE 641:8
deaf h. PROV 598:1
don't need a h. COLL 228:14
find a h. in a catalogue EHRE 290:2
good fortune than a good h. OSBO 559:19
great good h. LOVE 476:11
his being my h. CONG 232:24
h. and wife FIEL 310:13
h. be a man with whom you have lived LAMB 448:9
h. is always the last PROV 603:8
h. is a whole-time job BENN 66:8
h. is fro the world ygon CHAU 206:16
h. June WATK 804:15
h. of one wife BIBL 109:14
h. or a house WHIT 816:2
h.'s first praise BARB 53:19
h. what is left of a lover ROWL 636:12
h. with a beard SHAK 691:2
in her h.'s heart SHAK 701:18
left her h. because MURD 536:16
life her h. makes for her ELIO 292:25
love of Soul in the h. UPAN 787:11
make her h. a cuckold SHAK 693:20
Man-o'-War's 'er h. KIPL 439:11
married my h. for life SAYI 647:24
My h. and I ELIZ 297:15
one h. too many ANON 15:15
over hir h. as hir love CHAU 206:22
picked out for a h. HAYW 365:3
quarrels with one's h. BONA 125:1
reproach a h. LA F 447:15
safeguard, and the h.'s NAPO 538:13
splendid h. CHEK 208:17
unbelieving h. BIBL 106:5
woman oweth to her h. SHAK 698:14
your dear h. for a comfort SMIT 725:1
husbanded so fathered and so h. SHAK 675:8
husbandry h. in heaven SHAK 682:20
husbands Aisles full of h. GINS 339:22
Chumps make the best h. WODE 824:10
hands of the h. ADAM 1:18
H. at chirche dore CHAU 204:23
H., love your wives BIBL 109:5
h. to stay at home ELIO 293:6
in spite of their h. LEE- 462:11
When h. or when lapdogs POPE 587:10
hush breathless h. in the Close NEWB 541:18
holy h. of ancient sacrifice STEV 740:5
H., hush MORT 533:14
H.! Hush! Whisper who dares MILN 511:1
h., little baby, don' yo' cry HEYW 376:4
h. with the setting moon TENN 764:7
hushing H. the latest traffic BRID 148:8
husks h. that the swine did eat BIBL 100:3
strewed with h. SHAK 700:21
hustle tried to h. the East KIPL 439:18
hut Love in a h. KEAT 428:15
huts in the h. of Indians LOCK 471:13
Hwæt *H.! wē Gārdena* ANON 21:16
hyacinths h. and biscuits SAND 644:3
Hybla rob the H. bees SHAK 676:29
Hyde Dr Jekyll and Mr H. STEV 741:12
hydrogen telescope or h. bomb LOVE 476:17
hydroptic h. earth hath drunk DONN 274:9
hyena h. in petticoats WALP 801:14
hymns Chanting faint h. SHAK 689:2
enthusiastic amorous h. LACK 447:2
h. at heaven's gate SHAK 704:15
Singing h. unbidden SHEL 714:6
Sweet h. shall be my chant JUDA 422:25
hyperbole perpetual h. BACO 43:15
hypercritical by any h. rules LINC 468:8
Hyperion H. to a satyr SHAK 661:25
hyphen *h.* which joins BAGE 46:8
hyphenated h. Americanism ROOS 633:10
hypocrisy allows for no h. STEN 737:18
H. is a tribute LA R 453:15
H., the only evil MILT 516:6
organized h. DISR 268:12
That would be h. WILD 817:20
world safe for h. WOLF 825:10
hypocrite h. and flatterer BLAK 119:2
h. in his pleasures JOHN 417:15
h. is really rotten AREN 24:2
H. lecteur,—mon semblable BAUD 57:6
hypocrites cant of h. STER 739:3
other half h. JEFF 406:2
scribes and Pharisees, h. BIBL 96:26
hypotenuse square on the h. GILB 339:4
hypothermia dying of h. BENN 65:13
hypotheses do not feign h. NEWT 543:8
smallest number of h. EINS 291:2
hypothesis construct a h. HARD 360:17
discard a pet h. LORE 475:15
nature of an h. STER 738:26
slaying of a beautiful h. HUXL 397:11
to an h. STER 738:19
hyssop purge me with h. BOOK 135:6
Sprinkle me with h. MISS 520:6
hysteria thin whine of h. DIDI 267:10
hysterical starving h. naked GINS 339:20
hysterics h. of the Celt TENN 762:1

I I am a camera ISHE 400:8
I am not I WAUG 806:1
I AM THAT I AM BIBL 75:29
I am the State LOUI 475:16
in the infinite I AM COLE 227:11
I plus my surroundings ORTE 557:15
I shall never be BOOK 132:2
My husband and I ELIZ 297:15
person becomes I BUBE 159:7
such as I am BIBL 104:23
tell me who I am SHAK 678:9
Through which we go Is I DE L 256:18
Iago I. as an Imogen KEAT 431:10
I.'s soliloquy COLE 227:15
iambics escape my i. CATU 198:2
purchase fame In keen i. DRYD 282:1
ibant *I. obscuri sola sub nocte* VIRG 794:19
ibit *in caelum iusseris i.* JUVE 424:10
IBM for buying I. ADVE 8:4
ice along the polished i. WORD 828:20
Alps of green i. PHIL 575:9
break the i. BACO 42:19
caves of i. COLE 225:22
emperor of i.-cream STEV 739:21
I. and Snow BOOK 126:6
i.-cream out of the container BRYS 159:4
I. formed WODE 824:24
i. in the summer PROV 610:11
i. like morsels BOOK 141:26
i., mast-high COLE 226:7
It's fresh as i. ADVE 7:35
Like a piece of i. on a hot stove FROS 326:15
region of thick-ribbèd i. SHAK 686:18
skating over thin i. EMER 299:21
smooth the i. SHAK 677:15
Some say in i. FROS 325:21
That is, hot i. SHAK 690:22

thin i. that cracks MONT 528:6
urine is congealed i. SHAK 686:20
iceberg i. cuts its facets BISH 115:16
i., you know DEAN 253:17
ill-concealed i. LAWS 459:11
iced three parts i. over ARNO 28:26
Iceland Natural History of I. JOHN 415:29
iceman i. cometh O'NE 554:19
Ichabod named the child I. BIBL 78:19
icicle Chaste as the i. SHAK 660:15
hang like an i. SHAK 702:4
icicles hang them up in silent i. COLE 225:17
When i. hang by the wall SHAK 681:4
icon described as an 'i.' DYLA 287:18
icy i. precepts of respect SHAK 699:21
lays his i. hand on kings SHIR 717:8
id PUT THE I. BACK IN YID ROTH 635:19
idea better to entertain an i. JARR 404:12
Between the i. And the reality ELIO 294:25
does get an i. MARQ 497:10
endowed with the i. of God DESC 258:19
good i.—son CATC 195:17
i. does not pass UNAM 787:7
i. first occurs DARW 251:6
i. whose time has come ANON 19:3
invasion by an i. HUGO 393:18
landed with an i. BIRT 115:14
more dangerous than an i. ALAI 9:15
no grand i. was ever born FITZ 315:9
only one i. DISR 270:24
pain of a new i. BAGE 47:12
possess but one i. JOHN 414:8
teach the young i. THOM 775:5
wilderness of i. BUTL 172:26
would be a good i. GAND 329:8
ideal i. for which I am prepared MAND 493:7
i. of reason KANT 425:17
i. reader suffering from JOYC 421:18
idealism morphine or i. JUNG 423:8
idealistic only i. nation WILS 822:18
ideals i. of a nation DOUG 276:18
men without i. CAMU 184:4
shoes with broken high i. MCGO 485:9
ideas Colourless green i. CHOM 212:10
express your i. GRAC 347:16
From it our i. are born GENE 333:4
genuine i., Bright Ideas BENT 67:8
i. to literature BOUR 145:5
I. won't keep WHIT 814:13
Prose is for i. IBSE 398:13
share no one's i. TURG 785:2
signs of i. JOHN 409:4
still have the i. CHUR 216:8
identical they exist, but are i. FORS 320:23
Two things are i. LEIB 462:23
identify I can i. with her MADO 489:5
ides Beware the i. of March SHAK 674:4
i. of March are come SHAK 675:14
proud I., when the squadron rides MACA 482:25
idiom i. of words PRIO 592:13
idioms i. appropriate to another RYLE 640:18
licentious i. JOHN 410:22
idiot i. who praises GILB 338:2
portrait of a blinking i. SHAK 687:25
tale Told by an i. SHAK 685:22
idiots fatuity of i. SMIT 725:3
idle addled egg as an i. bird PROV 595:19
be not i. CLOS 222:5
employment for his i. time WALT 802:17
Every i. word BIBL 95:14
For i. hands to do WATT 805:6
happiest when I am i. WARD 803:7
home, you i. creatures SHAK 674:2
i. as a painted ship COLE 226:11
i. brain is devil's workshop PROV 603:9
i. have the least leisure PROV 603:10
i. if hunger didn't pinch ELIO 292:13
i., shivering creatures AUST 37:16
i. singer of an empty day MORR 532:11
i. smoke of praise DANI 249:2
i. tales BIBL 100:32
little profits that an i. king TENN 767:8
mock the air with i. state GRAY 350:2
most i. and unprofitable GIBB 335:17
Never be completely i. THOM 771:2
occupation for an i. hour AUST 38:7
occupation for an i. hour OPEN 556:16
only i. chatter GILB 338:18
solitary, be not i. JOHN 416:11
Tears, i. tears TENN 765:19
vivacity of an i. man BAGE 47:17
We would all be i. JOHN 415:16
when wholly i. CICE 217:16
work for i. hands PROV 598:7
you are i. SHAK 702:11
idleness Grief is a species of i. JOHN 414:18
I. is only the refuge CHES 209:19
I. is root of all evil PROV 603:11
penalties of i. POPE 580:25
round of strenuous i. WORD 831:4
idlers i. and Belgians BAUD 57:12
i. of the Empire DOYL 278:4
idling impossible to enjoy i. JERO 406:18
idol God and an i. LUTH 480:3
i. of its own BYRO 178:2
i. of the Anglo-Saxon BAGE 46:16
one-eyed yellow i. HAYE 365:2
idolaters murderers, and i. BIBL 113:15
never of the i. KORA 444:2
idolatries bowed To its i. BYRO 174:22
idolatry ancients without i. CHES 209:15
god of our i. COWP 241:7
organization of i. SHAW 708:15
idols i. I have loved FITZ 315:1
if I. it moves, salute it MILI 508:9
i. you can keep your head KERR 434:7
I. you can keep your head KIPL 439:2
much virtue in 'i.' SHAK 659:27
ifs If i. and ands were pots and pans PROV 603:16
Talk'st thou to me of 'i.' SHAK 696:21
igloo improve on the i. OKPI 553:10
ignara *Non i. mali* VIRG 793:15
ignis fatuus Reason, an *i.* ROCH 630:13
ignoble i. ease ROOS 633:4
names i., born to be forgot COWP 240:25
ignominy i. sleep with thee SHAK 669:14
ignorance blind and naked I. TENN 760:6
Disease, I., and Idleness BEVE 72:6
Don't die of i. OFFI 554:6
evil is simply i. FORD 319:16
fact of my i. SOCR 726:21
From i. our comfort flows PRIO 593:5
from i. the Western World JOHN 411:8
hindrance of i. PALI 565:22
i. and confidence TWAI 786:27
i. and simple-heartedness LERM 464:20
I. excuses from sin AUCT 33:5
I. is an evil weed BEVE 72:5
i. is bliss PROV 614:37
I. is like a delicate WILD 817:15
i. is never better FERM 309:3
I. is not innocence BROW 156:12
I. is strength ORWE 558:21
i. it accumulates ADAM 2:23
i. of nature HOLB 380:17
I. of the law PROV 603:43
I. of the law SELD 653:16
i. or profaneness MATH 501:9
i. so abysmal MEDA 503:4
in i. sedate JOHN 411:19
more than Gothic i. FIEL 310:10
no sin but i. MARL 496:15
pity his i. DICK 264:1
pure i. JOHN 412:19
smallest allowance for i. HUXL 397:15
understand a writer's i. COLE 227:10
Where i. is bliss GRAY 350:18
With a knowing i. JOHN 407:16
women in a state of i. KNOX 443:1
ignorant always be i. AUST 38:4
Asking the i. ZOBE 840:6
Be not i. of any thing BIBL 91:19
Confound the i. SHAK 663:28
i. and free JEFF 405:19
i. armies clash ARNO 26:5
i. of these magnificent things MCEW 485:6
In language, the i. DUPP 285:17
many i. men are sure DARR 250:11
right of the i. man CARL 187:3
ignorantly i. worship BIBL 104:8
ignores most poetry i. most people MITC 523:11
Ignotus *I. moritur sibi* SENE 654:21
Ike I like I. POLI 581:15
Iliad greater than the I. PROP 593:17
Ilium *fuit I.* VIRG 794:4
topless towers of I. MARL 496:5
ill Against i. chances SHAK 670:11
doctrine of i.-doing SHAK 702:32
ever to do i. MILT 514:15
final goal of i. TENN 761:9
For certain i. DRAY 279:5
he thinks no i. SHAK 704:22
i. and the stopping of ill PALI 565:2
ill-clad, i.-nourished ROOS 632:15
I. fares the land GOLD 344:8
i.-favoured thing, sir SHAK 659:25
i.-fed, ill-killed JOHN 417:10
I. gotten goods never thrive PROV 603:44
i. he cannot cure ARNO 28:5
I. met by moonlight SHAK 689:19
I. news hath wings DRAY 278:22
i. wind that blows PROV 604:32
Looking i. prevail SUCK 745:7
means to do i. deeds SHAK 677:17
Nothing i. come near thee SHAK 661:2
one-third of a nation i.-housed ROOS 632:15
or of i. breeding CONG 233:5
she's not really i. JAGG 401:5
so illiberal and so i.-bred CHES 209:16
Some think him i.-tempered LEAR 460:14
speak i. of the dead PROV 607:37
suppressed i.-feeling BAGE 47:8
think me so i. bred WYCH 834:12
vain, i.-natured DEFO 255:11
warn you not to fall i. KINN 437:20
illacrimabiles *omnes i.* HORA 389:9
illegal i., immoral, or fattening WOOL 827:8
means that it is not i. NIXO 546:8
Nothing is i. if YOUN 838:15
illegally accomplishes great things i. BALZ 53:1
illegitimate i. child of Karl Marx ATTL 32:4
no i. children GLAD 340:11
illegitimi *Nil carborundum i.* SAYI 647:33
illiberal so i. and so ill-bred CHES 209:16
illimitable i. was annihilated DISR 268:20
illiterate I. him, I say SHER 715:23
i. king HENR 370:8
illness i. identified with evil SONT 728:4
I. is the night-side SONT 728:9
i. should attend it SHAK 682:1
Living is an i. CHAM 201:5
makes i. worthwhile SHAW 706:17
treatment of an i. WITT 824:4
ills climax of all human i. BYRO 176:22
free us from all i. WINK 823:6
i. of democracy SMIT 723:15
i. to come GRAY 350:16
mark what i. JOHN 411:14
O'er a' the i. o' life BURN 168:12
illuminated i. his kingdom JOIN 418:19
i. trouser-clip for bicyclists MORT 533:16
illuminating i. for her everything TOLS 779:9
illuminatio *Dominus i. mea* BIBL 113:17
Dominus i. mea MOTT 535:7
illumine What in me is dark, I. MILT 514:9
illusion great i. ANGE 14:16
one i.—France KEYN 435:4
only an i. EINS 291:4
sophistry and i. HUME 394:7
universe was an i. BORG 143:6

illusions friend of flattering i. CONR 234:18
life's i. I recall MITC 523:16
specious i. GODW 342:6
illustration i. of character JAME 403:10
illustrious I. acts high raptures WALL 800:8
Illyria what should I do in I. SHAK 700:28
ilnesses i. and dreary old age VIRG 796:20
image age demanded an i. POUN 589:14
Best i. of myself MILT 516:30
created him in his own i. DOST 275:17
God's i. man doth bear SPEG 731:23
graven i. BIBL 76:8
his i., cut in ebony FULL 327:7
his Maker's i. DRYD 279:18
i. of a shade SHEL 714:17
i. of death ELIO 293:8
i. of eternity BYRO 175:11
i. of God TALM 753:18
i. of his God GRAI 348:12
i. of his person BIBL 109:25
i. of passion BART 56:7
i. of the Creator BONA 125:5
I., that, flying WORD 828:21
just an i. GODA 341:21
kills the i. of God MILT 519:8
kindly paternal i. DANT 249:16
make man in our i. BIBL 73:14
Met his own i. SHEL 713:4
Stamped with the i. TENN 759:23
votre i. me suit RACI 619:19
worship the golden i. BIBL 90:1
imagery for their i. MCEW 485:6
images Bygone i. COLE 227:28
Fresh i. beget YEAT 835:7
i. change as they repeat WARH 803:15
i. of life BERG 67:15
I. split the truth LEVE 466:4
reflects i. ADAM 2:18
unpurged i. of day YEAT 835:5
imaginary i. relish SHAK 700:12
i. rights BENT 66:16
imagination ages of i. BLAK 119:27
blow [dealt] to all i. DISR 268:20
cut of the i. JAME 402:26
exercising the i. GIRA 340:8
f—gg—g his *i.* BYRO 180:10
force of i. DRYD 281:30
hunting-grounds for the poetic i. ELIO 292:18
ideal of i. KANT 425:17
i. amend them SHAK 690:26
i. bodies forth SHAK 690:19
i. cold and barren BURK 162:23
i. droops her pinion BYRO 177:3
i. for his facts SHER 716:20
i. is not required JOHN 413:5
I., not invention CONR 234:22
i. of a boy KEAT 426:15
i. of man's heart BIBL 74:18
i. of their hearts BIBL 98:17
i. resembled MACA 482:16
i. sleeps CAMU 184:14
i. the rudder KEAT 430:20
i. to the proper pitch LACK 447:2
I., which in truth WORD 831:11
It is by i. SMIT 723:5
lava of the i. BYRO 179:25
nothing but his i. SHAW 707:18
of i. all compact SHAK 690:18
of moral good is the i. SHEL 714:21
primary i. COLE 227:11
save those that have no i. SHAW 709:18
shaping spirit of i. COLE 225:6
sweeten my i. SHAK 679:22
takes a lot of i. BAIL 48:3
Television contracts i. WOGA 825:1
truth of i. KEAT 430:21
Vision or I. BLAK 121:12
Where there is no i. DOYL 278:6
imaginations their own i. BOOK 131:23
imaginative function of i. literature EMPS 300:8
I. readers GRAV 349:18
imagine *buona i. paterna* DANT 249:16
I. there's no heaven LENN 463:15
people i. a vain thing BOOK 131:16
imagined i. such a device BOOK 132:20
imaginibus *Ex umbris et i.* EPIT 302:5
imaginings horrible i. SHAK 681:21
imitate i. the action SHAK 671:5
i. what is before him BAGE 47:15
Immature poets i. ELIO 296:18
never failed to i. them BALD 48:18
imitated can be i. by none CHAT 204:4
i. humanity SHAK 664:17
imitation art of I. LLOY 470:15
art of *i.* SIDN 718:23
child of i. REYN 625:9
i. in lines and colours POUS 590:7
I. is the sincerest form PROV 603:46
I. lies at the root FRAN 322:13
i. without benefit SANT 644:11
Were endless i. WORD 830:2
imitator never find an i. ROUS 636:3
imitatores *O i., servum pecus* HORA 387:5
immanent I. Will HARD 361:10
Immanuel call his name I. BIBL 86:26
immaturity expression of human i. BRIT 149:1
immemorial in i. elms TENN 766:6
immense error is i. BOLI 124:16
immensity I. cloistered DONN 273:7
immolation i. so belied SASS 645:23
immoral art is i. WILD 818:4
good and i. CHUR 214:21
illegal, i., or fattening WOOL 827:8
moral or an i. book WILD 818:14
immorality i. is what they dislike WHIT 814:15
immortal death that is i. LUCR 479:7
do not seek i. life PIND 576:10
free and i. TRAH 780:12
I have I. longings SHAK 657:28
i. as they quote YOUN 838:16
i. hand or eye BLAK 121:8
i. in his own despite POPE 586:13
I., invisible SMIT 726:8
i. part of myself SHAK 697:16
i. spirit grows WORD 830:24
i. with a kiss MARL 496:5
sight of that i. sea WORD 830:8
Sire of an i. strain SHEL 710:14
soul is i. PLAT 578:10
soul is i. SOCR 727:4
With cold i. hands SWIN 750:20
immortalia *I. ne speres* HORA 389:7
immortality belief in i. DOST 275:15
cruel i. Consumes TENN 766:16
God, I., Duty ELIO 293:17
i. through my work ALLE 12:17
i. within His kingdom ZORO 841:13
just Ourselves— And I. DICK 266:6
lead me to i. UPAN 787:9
load of i. KEAT 431:8
Milk's leap toward i. FADI 306:1
Millions long for i. ERTZ 301:6
nothing for my i. SCHI 648:12
organize her own i. LASK 454:2
put on i. BIBL 107:3
they gave, their i. BROO 150:7
Imogen Iago as an I. KEAT 431:10
imp i. of fame SHAK 671:12
impaling I. worms COLM 229:19
impartial i. administration PEEL 571:13
neutrality of an i. judge BURK 165:12
pure i. hate THOR 776:19
impartiality i. is bias REIT 624:9
impatience i. would be so much fretted JOHN 414:17
impatient growing i. to see him SMIT 724:25
never so i. BOOK 138:12
impavidum *I. ferient ruinae* HORA 388:16
impediment cause, or just i. BOOK 130:21
impenetrable dark i. wood SCOT 651:14
imperative i. is Categorical KANT 425:15
imperatur *non i.* BACO 45:5
imperfect use of an i. medium WILD 818:16
yet being i. BOOK 141:13
imperfections Dote on his i. EPHE 300:18
i. on my head SHAK 662:31
than i. ADDI 5:5
imperial act Of the i. theme SHAK 681:20
our great I. family ELIZ 297:14
imperialism I. is the monopoly stage LENI 463:6
I.'s face AUDE 35:1
wild-cat I. ROSE 633:16
imperialisms prey of rival i. KENY 434:3
imperium *I. et Libertas* DISR 269:22
impermanent consider what is i. PALI 564:13
impertinent ask an i. question BRON 149:9
ask i. questions DARW 251:5
privileged to be very i. FARQ 307:22
impious lift an i. hand BRON 149:13
implacable i. in hate DRYD 280:4
importance i. of a work of art FLAU 316:13
i. of the country HUXL 396:17
taking decisions of i. PARK 567:24
important being less i. MONT 527:13
i. book, the critic assumes WOOL 826:19
i. to be clever *about* MEDA 503:7
same as i. PRAT 591:2
trivial and the i. POTT 588:21
imports i. and exports ARIS 24:14
importunate no less i. MONT 527:13
importunes *sont pas moins i.* MONT 527:13
importunity ever-haunting i. LAMB 449:5
impossibilities i. enough in religion BROW 153:15
Probable i. ARIS 25:1
impossibility Upon I. MARV 498:10
impossible certain because it is i. TERT 768:16
Dream the i. DARI 250:8
eliminated the i. DOYL 278:1
i. shore ARNO 27:23
i. takes a little longer MILI 508:6
i. takes a little longer NANS 538:7
i. takes a little longer PROV [illegible]
i.? that will be done CALO 182:1
i. to be silent BURK 165:7
i. to carry the heavy burden EDWA 289:7
i. to enjoy idling JERO 406:18
six i. things CARR 190:25
something is i. CLAR 219:8
That not i. she CRAS 244:15
'Tis a thing i. WORD 828:13
wish it were i. JOHN 418:2
impostors invented by i. GODW 342:6
treat those two i. KIPL 439:2
impotent i. people, sick THOM 773:16
imprecision Decay with i. ELIO 294:5
mess of i. of feeling ELIO 294:11
impresses i. me most about America EDWA 289:8
impression novel is an i. HARD 360:18
impressionable at an i. age SPAR 731:18
impressions First i. PROV 600:29
unweaving of false i. ELIO 293:12
imprint set it in i. CAXT 199:1
imprison Take me to you, i. me DONN 272:25
imprisoned suffered me to be i. SHAK 702:19
taken or i. MAGN 489:12
imprisonment leaves his well-beloved i. DONN 273:7
improbability high degree of i. FISH 314:2
life is statistical i. DAWK 253:3
improbable i. possibilities ARIS 25:1
whatever remains, *however i.* DOYL 278:1
improper noun, proper or i. FULL 327:4
impropriety I. is the soul of wit MAUG 501:18
without i. GILB 337:18

improve I. each shining hour WATT 805:5
i. the nick of time THOR 776:5
improved i. by death SAKI 642:1
improvement Each thing called i. BLAM 121:15
lives show little i. THOM 771:6
schemes of political i. JOHN 414:4
improvements no great i. MILL 507:23
improvisation I. is too good SIMO 720:12
impudence starve for want of i. DRYD 281:8
impudent called John a I. Bitch FLEM 317:12
impulse first i. CORN 236:17
i. from a vernal wood WORD 832:6
i. of the moment AUST 38:16
impulses no truck with first i. MONT 528:17
impune *Nemo me i. lacessit* MOTT 535:10
impunity provokes me with i. MOTT 535:10
impure to the Puritan all things are i. LAWR 454:15
imputantur *pereunt et i.* MART 498:1
imputeth Lord i. no sin BOOK 133:17
in going out, and thy coming i. BOOK 140:13
KNEW YOU HAD IT I. YOU TELE 758:5
who's i., who's out SHAK 680:7
inability i. to cross the street WOOL 827:2
i. to live GONC 346:8
inaccuracy i. sometimes saves SAKI 642:7
inaction i. sap the vigour LEON 464:14
inactivity genius for i. LIPP 470:1
masterly i. MACK 486:12
inadequate not that we are i. WILL 821:4
inadvertence by chance or i. HAIL 356:13
inane in the intense i. SHEL 713:14
inapprehensible I., we clutch THOM 774:11
inarticulate raid on the i. ELIO 294:11
inaudible I. as dreams COLE 225:13
inborn is i. JUNG 423:5
inbreeding sick with i. THOM 773:16
incantation i. of this verse SHEL 712:18
incapable i. of governing CHES 209:24
incapacity courted by I. BLAK 119:13
sanctuary of i. CHES 209:5
incarnadine multitudinous seas i. SHAK 683:11
incarnate Is i. SMAR 722:2
incarnatus *i. est* MISS 520:18
incense gods themselves throw i. SHAK 680:8
i. is an abomination BIBL 86:11
stupefying i.-smoke BROW 155:14
unfabled I. Tree DARL 250:9
incensed I. with indignation MILT 515:23
incest i. and folk-dancing ANON 20:1
i. flourished LEE 462:2
inch every i. a king SHAK 679:20
Every other i. a gentleman WEST 812:19
Inchcape It is the I. Rock SOUT 730:17
inches die by i. HENR 370:16
thirty i. from my nose AUDE 34:19
incident curious i. of the dog DOYL 277:18
determination of i. JAME 403:10
incipe *I., parve puer* VIRG 796:5
incisive i. features MERE 505:11
incisors i. and grinders BAGE 47:10
incivility i. and procrastination DE Q 258:11
inclementia *durae rapit i. mortis* VIRG 796:20
inclination door of i. DEFO 254:16
greatest enemy is i. BAHY 48:2
i. to goodness BACO 43:7
just as i. leads him JOHN 413:7
incline I. our hearts BOOK 129:6
i. your ears BOOK 137:3
inclined he i. unto me BOOK 133:31
sins, they are i. to BUTL 172:1
include i. me out GOLD 346:1
incognito preserving my i. ELIO 293:13
income Annual i. twenty pounds DICK 261:19
dread a dead-level of i. TAWN 755:13
Expenditure rises to meet i. PARK 567:21
however great the i. CATO 194:14
large i. the best recipe AUST 37:26
live beyond its i. BUTL 172:23
moderate i. DURH 286:5
incomes apt to live up to their i. SMIL 723:1
live beyond their i. SAKI 642:3
income tax I. made more liars ROGE 631:19
incommunicable burden of the i. DE Q 258:5
distrust the i. SART 645:12
incomparable i. Max SHAW 709:23
incompatible Thought i. by men LEWI 467:2
united things long i. TACI 752:6
incompetence rise to his level of i. PETE 574:10
incomprehensible most i. fact EINS 290:14
use the i. ZOBE 840:6
incomprehensibles three i. BOOK 126:23
inconceivable i. that I should be the age MERW 506:2
something i. GILB 337:22
inconnu *Au fond de l'i.* BAUD 57:10
inconsistency found in it much i. KORA 444:11
inconstancy constant, but i. SWIF 747:15
Constant, in Nature were i. COWL 239:17
thine own i. CARE 186:16
this i. is such LOVE 476:16
inconstant i. toads MONT 526:20
i. woman GAY 332:19
incontinence filth and foul i. SPEN 734:2
inconvenience Change without i. JOHN 409:3
great i. PROV 609:34
i. is often considerable AUST 37:18
i. is only an adventure CHES 211:2
inconveniences i., and those weighty HOOK 383:7
i. there must be HALI 357:17
inconvenient cause may be i. BENN 66:7
even when it is i. VIDA 792:12
i. to be poor COWP 239:29
incorporate very members i. BOOK 130:2
incorporeal there is a Being i. NEWT 543:3
incorruptible dead shall be raised i. BIBL 107:3
seagreen I. CARL 187:24
incorruption assurance of i. BIBL 91:14
put on i. BIBL 107:3
raised in i. BIBL 107:1
increase bring forth her i. BOOK 136:4
God gave the i. BIBL 105:30
I. and multiply BOOK 128:11
i. in thy holy Spirit BOOK 130:20
i. of his government BIBL 87:1
Some races i. LUCR 479:4
we desire i. SHAK 704:5
who dies fighting has i. GREN 352:17
increasing has increased, is i. DUNN 285:16
incredible i. as if you fired RUTH 640:16
incurable Life is an i. disease COWL 239:23
indecency I.'s conspiracy of silence SHAW 708:26
indecent sent down for i. behaviour WAUG 806:4
indecision nothing is habitual but i. JAME 404:1
indefensible defence of the i. ORWE 559:10
indelicate i.! How I hate that word TROL 782:7
indemnity BILL OF I. . . . FOR RAID TELE 758:3
independence i. of America SHEL 710:4
i. of judges DENN 257:18
right to i. NAMI 538:6
independent colonies will all be i. DISR 268:16
entirely i. TOCQ 778:12
simply *i.* choice DOST 276:9
to be i. LOWE 477:12
indestructible i. Union CHAS 204:3
it is i. UPAN 787:15
index i. of a feeling mind CRAB 243:10
indexes memories are card-i. CONN 234:2
India beautiful in I. NEHR 540:9
driven out of I. BURK 165:3
Englishman to rule in I. NEHR 540:10
final message of I. FORS 321:3
I.'s coral strand HEBE 367:6
I. will awake to life NEHR 540:4
key of I. DISR 269:23
Nothing in I. is identifiable FORS 320:22
peaceably and happily in I. VICT 792:6
Indian I. Crown ROSS 634:14
I. in blood and colour MACA 483:15
I. Summer of the heart WHIT 816:7
I. wilderness MATH 501:7
Like the base I. SHAK 694:3
Lo! the poor I. POPE 585:10
only good I. PROV 608:27
see a dead I. SHAK 698:32
Indians I. are you BALD 49:3
only good I. SHER 715:12
to convert the I. WESL 811:14
indictment i. against an whole people BURK 162:27
Indies augmentation of the I. SHAK 702:7
indifference ill at ease under i. ELIO 292:2
i. and a coach and six COLM 229:14
i. closely bordering on STEV 741:10
i. or frozen stare ELIO 292:21
it's i. WIES 816:15
indifferent delayed till I am i. JOHN 412:17
It is simply i. HOLM 381:4
to be i. to them SHAW 706:25
indifferently i. minister justice BOOK 129:12
look on both i. SHAK 674:8
indigenous i. variety FINK 310:24
indigestion moral i. ANTR 22:19
indignant this i. page BLAK 121:4
indignatio *facit i. versum* JUVE 424:5
I. principis mors est MORE 531:10
indignation fierce i. EPIT 304:8
i. makes me write verse JUVE 424:5
Moral i. is jealousy WELL 810:17
righteous i. MUGG 534:14
Savage i. there YEAT 837:15
well-bred i. TURG 785:3
indignities by i. men come to dignities BACO 43:10
indignity i. of being your representative BELL 64:12
indirections By i. find directions out SHAK 663:8
indiscretion cliché and an i. MACM 487:16
lover without i. HARD 360:11
inditing i. of a good matter BOOK 134:13
individual each separate i. ROBE 629:3
genius overlooks i. SCHO 649:3
in an i. way HORA 385:19
i. men and women THAT 770:7
injustice done to an i. JUNI 423:16
liberty of the i. MILL 508:21
No i. could resent SWIF 749:25
not an i. FIEL 310:1
not the i., but the species JOHN 410:24
individualism system of rugged i. HOOV 383:10
individuals I. pass like shadows BURK 164:29
love is towards i. SWIF 748:10
indivisible Freedom is an i. word WILL 821:8
Peace is i. LITV 470:6
indocilis *I. pauperiem pati* HORA 387:12
indolence girl in the i. of youth YEAT 836:21
indolent i. expression BELL 63:20
indomitable i. Irishry YEAT 837:21
indulgent makes one very i. STAË 735:17
industrial I. Revelation SELL 654:14
i. worker would sooner BLYT 123:3
industrialists die for the i. FRAN 322:19
industry Captains of i. CARL 188:8
commonly abateth i. BACO 43:23
i. applies ANON 18:16
i. is to be paralysed TAWN 755:17
i. seems inefficient SCHU 649:9
I., Which dignifies the artist DYER 286:15

industry (*cont.*):
i. will improve them REYN 625:4
i. without art RUSK 638:8
national i. of Prussia MIRA 520:4
not his i. only BURK 164:26
permit a cottage i. MARC 495:6
river of human i. TOCQ 778:18
spur of i. HUME 394:10
that of a major i. SARR 644:19
indutus *redit exuvias i. Achilli* VIRG 794:2
inebriate cheer but not i. BERK 67:19
cheer but not i. COWP 241:31
ineffectual beautiful and i. angel ARNO 28:21
Remote and i. Don BELL 63:18
inefficient efficient and the i. SHAW 707:20
industry seems i. SCHU 649:9
inertia *Strenua nos exercet i.* HORA 386:20
inestimable thine i. love BOOK 127:19
inevitability i. of gradualness WEBB 807:1
inevitable arguing with the i. LOWE 477:18
foresee the i. ASIM 30:17
i. the Titanic HAGU 356:6
inexactitude terminological i. CHUR 214:18
inexcusable done something i. ALAI 10:1
inexorable deaf, i. SIDN 718:5
inexperienced i. house JERO 406:20
inextinguishable i. thought SHEL 714:22
infallible only i. rule SURT 746:14
infâme *écrasez l'i.* VOLT 798:6
infamous rich, quiet, and i. MACA 482:8
infamy date which will live in i. ROOS 632:19
infancy about us in our i. WORD 829:20
like men, have their i. BOLI 124:15
see the i. TRAH 780:10
infandum *I., regina* VIRG 793:16
infant i. beauty could beget SEDL 653:1
i. crying in the night TENN 761:11
i., Mewling and puking SHAK 658:26
i. phenomenon DICK 264:3
Sooner murder an i. BLAK 119:24
infantile second i. ARIS 24:10
infants terrors i. go through DRAB 278:13
infected All seems i. POPE [illegible]
infection Against i. SHAK 694:19
i. of things gone LOWE 478:8
infects bad news i. SHAK 656:11
i. the world ARNO 27:1
infelicity sense of a constant i. TAYL 756:20
inferior disgraced by the i. SHAW 708:20
i. man is partisan CONF 231:8
make you feel i. ROOS 632:9
myself i. to myself MILT 519:23
inferiority conscious of an i. JOHN 415:18
feeling of i. ADLE 6:5
impatient of i. JOHN 410:20
inferiors English want *i.* TOCQ 778:17
inferno i. of his passions JUNG 423:6
infidelity absence of i. LAWS 459:8
I. does not consist PAIN 563:8
infini *l'i. me tourmente* MUSS 537:11
infinite door to i. wisdom BREC 147:9
i. in faculty SHAK 663:18
i.-resource-and-sagacity KIPL 441:13
I. riches MARL 496:16
i. spaces PASC 568:13
i. torments MUSS 537:11
i. Void PALI 565:19
I. wrath MILT 516:9
in the i. I AM COLE 227:11
number of worlds is i. ALEX 11:6
realize the i. CHUA 213:6
Though i. MARV 498:11
infinities numberless i. DONN 272:20
infinitive care what a split i. FOWL 321:21
when I split an i. CHAN 201:18
infinity Hold i. BLAK 117:17
shares the nature of i. WORD 827:17
infirmi *i. est animi* JUVE 425:4
infirmities bear his friend's i. SHAK 676:24
i. were not noxious JOHN 413:2
infirmity feblit with i. DUNB 285:4
i. of his age SHAK 678:2
i. of noble mind MILT 513:2
i. of others HOBB 378:11
prop To our i. WORD 831:2
inflame It will i. you SHAK 676:5
inflammation i. of his weekly bills BYRO 176:22
inflation I. one form of taxation FRIE 325:2
pay to get i. down LAMO 449:13
inflections beauty of i. STEV 740:7
inflicted pain shall not be i. SPEN 732:3
influence i. and not authority ACTO 1:17
i. in society LACL 447:3
i. of the Crown DUNN 285:16
i. on human life MULL 536:3
i. to your son ICE 398:14
no trivial i. WORD 829:2
planetary i. SHAK 678:5
under the name of I. BURK 164:13
where his i. stops ADAM 2:20
win friends and i. people CARN 189:1
influences bind the sweet i. BIBL 81:34
in-folded tongues of flame are i. ELIO 294:20
inform i. his princes BOOK 139:9
not to i. the reader ACHE 1:14
occasions do i. against me SHAK 665:30
information find i. upon it JOHN 415:4
I only ask for i. DICK 261:24
knowledge we have lost in i. ELIO 295:21
little i. AUST 38:15
informed i. by the light of nature BACO 41:12
infrequens *cultor et i.* HORA 388:2
ingeminate i. the word *Peace* CLAR 218:21
ingenious harmonical and i. soul AUBR 32:16
Inglese *I. Italianato* ASCH 30:7
ingots don't take i. to market CHAM 201:6
ingratitude I hate i. SHAK 702:16
I. is the blackest JUDA 422:24
I., thou marble-hearted fiend SHAK 678:10
so unkind As man's i. SHAK 659:4
inhabitants i. o' the earth SHAK 681:15
inhale didn't i. CLIN 221:4
if he doesn't i. [illegible]
inherit i. the earth BIBL 93:3
i. the people PAIN 564:1
inheritance Ruinous i. GAIU 328:4
inherited I have i. nothing MIDR 507:15
i. from your fathers GOET 342:16
i. it brick AUGU 36:17
inheritor i. of the kingdom BOOK 130:10
inhibitions cultivate a few i. LOOS 475:13
inhumanity essence of i. SHAW 706:25
i. meant cruelty FROM 325:11
Man's i. to man BURN 167:26
inimitable i. rose WINC 823:2
iniquities bruised for our i. BIBL 88:17
iniquity grey i. SHAK 668:14
hated i. BOOK 134:14
hated i. LAST 455:10
I lack i. SHAK 691:28
i. of oblivion BROW 153:8
right hand of i. BOOK 141:18
initiation i. into a new state ELIO 291:22
injured Forgiveness to the i. DRYD 281:6
i. lover's hell MILT 516:32
i. Woman BARB 53:17
injuries i. and attempts of other men LOCK 472:2
insult to i. MOOR 529:9
revenge for slight i. MACH 485:15
injury i. is much sooner forgotten CHES 209:8
[i.] to be the bondage JAIN 401:12
tone of i. HELV 369:3
injustice I. anywhere a threat KING 436:11
i. done to an individual JUNI 423:16
i. makes democracy necessary NIEB 545:5
justice or i. JOHN 411:21
No i. is done ULPI 787:5
protect him against i. PALM 566:3
so finely felt, as i. DICK 262:19
That's social i. FILM 312:12
injustices justify their i. VOLT 797:10
ink all cough in i. YEAT 837:4
all the sea were i. LYLY 480:18
he hath not drunk i. SHAK 680:24
i. in my pen ran cold WALP 800:17
inky not alone my i. cloak SHAK 661:20
inlaid thick i. with patines SHAK 688:22
inland i. far we be WORD 830:8
inlet At a small i. YOUN 839:10
inmost i. part of you SHAK 665:11
inn chamber in the i. ANON 19:19
Do you remember an I., Miranda BELL 64:7
earth his sober i. CAMP 183:24
gain the timely i. SHAK 684:8
i.'s worst room POPE 583:22
no room for them in the i. BIBL 98:20
not an i., but an hospital BROW 154:2
tavern or i. JOHN 415:10
this soul's second i. DONN 273:12
warmest welcome, at an i. SHEN 715:6
world's an i. DRYD 282:11
innavigable nor sea i. THOR 776:20
inner have no I. Resources BERR 69:19
in the i. man BIBL 107:27
innings get me this i. JOYC 422:15
Innisfree go to I. YEAT 836:11
innocence assumption of i. easy CROS 246:9
badge of lost i. PAIN 563:11
ceremony of i. is drowned YEAT 837:5
hanged in all i. STEV 742:7
Ignorance is not i. BROW 156:12
innocence for i. SHAK 702:32
i. is like a dumb leper GREE 351:24
I. is next God LANG 450:21
I. no earthly weapon HILL 376:17
insists on his i. CAMU 184:6
moral security of i. RICH 627:6
Never such i. again LARK 452:19
not in i. ARDR 23:20
not to know we sin is i. D'AV 251:9
speak again of i. SUTT 747:8
innocency wash my hands in i. BOOK 133:8
innocent heart whose love is i. BYRO 179:1
i. and quiet mind STEV 741:20
i. and the beautiful YEAT 836:7
i. are so few BOWE 145:10
i. men, women, and children JEFF 406:2
i. of the blood BIBL 97:27
one i. suffer BLAC 117:5
shall not be i. BIBL 83:32
shed i. blood BIBL 89:3
taken reward against the i. BOOK 132:8
We are i. ROSE 633:20
innocents i. abroad TWAI 786:12
innovation i. in religion MAEC 489:6
i. without reason SANT 644:11
innovations ill-shapen, so are all i. BACO 43:13
innovator time is the greatest i. BACO 43:14
inns go to i. to dine CHES 210:18
I. are not residences MOOR 530:1
i. should be well kept PALM 566:5
innuendoes beauty of i. STEV 740:7
innuendos i. Will serve him no longer PULT 617:1
inopem *I. me copia fecit* OVID 561:15
inoperative all previous statements i. ZIEG 840:4
inquiry subject of i. BUTL 171:8
inquisition Spanish I. MONT 529:7
To these I. dogs TENN 766:8
insane eaten on the i. root SHAK 681:18
hereditary monarch was i. BAGE 46:13
Man is quite i. MONT 528:2
insanius *ligna feras i.* HORA 389:21
inscription altar with this i. BIBL 104:8
like a rough i. YEVT 838:9
inscriptions In lapidary i. JOHN 415:7
inscrutable I. workmanship WORD 830:24

insculped I. and embossed THOM 774:17
insect gigantic i. OPEN 556:26
one is but an i. JOHN 412:12
'Tortis' is a i. PUNC 617:10
transformed into a gigantic i. KAFK 425:9
insecurity international i. NIEB 545:6
insensibility stark i. JOHN 412:5
inseparable one and i. WEBS 807:12
inside i. the tent pissing out JOHN 408:19
I've lived i. myself DAVI 252:3
insight i. and the stretch BROW 155:3
insignificance of the utmost i. CURZ 248:6
sterling i. AUST 39:2
insignificant i. and is aware of it BECK 59:8
i. office ADAM 3:9
insincerity enemy of clear language i. ORWE 559:9
mark of i. of purpose BRAM 146:17
insinuating sly, i. Jacks SHAK 696:14
insolence flown with i. and wine MILT 514:27
i. is not invective DISR 268:17
i. of wealth JOHN 416:2
supports with i. JOHN 409:13
insomnia *mittunt i. Manes* VIRG 795:3
suffering from ideal i. JOYC 421:18
inspiration Genius is one per cent i. EDIS 289:2
inspire our souls i. BOOK 142:7
inspired i. by divine revelation BACO 41:12
inspissated i. gloom JOHN 414:3
instability mark of i. GALB 328:6
instant i. in season BIBL 109:22
instantaneous i. courage NAPO 538:17
instinct believe upon i. BRAD 146:6
coward on i. SHAK 668:10
healthy i. for it BUTL 172:27
intimate with by i. AUST 37:27
instincts i. and abilities BALZ 52:17
panders to i. BENN 65:17
true to your i. LAWR 458:5
institute on in the I. BETJ 71:3
institution change an i. TUSA 786:1
in a long term i. DURY 286:10
i. which does not suppose ROBE 629:5
It's an i. HUGH 393:15
place, person, or i. ARNO 29:17
transformed into an i. SART 645:14
institutions acquiring their i. by chance HAIL 356:13
amending her own i. GODW 342:8
with their dirty i. THOR 776:10
instruct i. them AURE 37:8
when they might i. MORE 531:3
instructing same time as i. him HORA 386:3
instruction benefits of i. DEFO 254:14
better the i. SHAK 687:31
horses of i. BLAK 119:21
i. in the Law JAIN 401:18
I. is the pill RICH 627:9
needs no i. JAIN 401:13
no i. book came with it FULL 327:5
instructions AWAITING I. TELE 758:4
instrument i. of science JOHN 409:4
i. of Your peace FRAN 323:5
I tune the i. DONN 273:5
State is an i. STAL 736:1
instrumental i. to the brain SHAK 661:15
original or i. HOBB 378:16
instruments i. of their crooked designs GODW 342:6
with the aid of the i. HOLB 380:16
insubstantial this i. pageant SHAK 699:6
insufferable Oxford has made me i. BEER 61:11
insular i. country, subject to fogs DISR 270:10
insularum *Paene i.* CATU 197:5
insult blockhead's i. JOHN 411:10
i. to injuries MOOR 529:9
sooner forgotten than an i. CHES 209:8
threatened her with i. BURK 163:20
insulted never *hope* to get i. DAVI 252:12
insulting i. Christmas card GROS 354:7
insults our visible i. CART 192:8
insupportable i. labour STEE 736:15
insuppressible i. island KETT 434:14
insurance carry i. on those CHAN 201:14
form of moral i. BROD 149:5
National compulsory i. CHUR 215:19
intact is there, i. TRIM 781:14
intangible world i., we touch THOM 774:11
integer *I. vitae* HORA 387:24
integral i. and differential calculus GILB 339:3
integration policy of European i. KOHL 443:7
integrity i. of my intellect FARA 306:13
i. without knowledge JOHN 411:2
virgin white i. DONN 272:19
intellect highest i. MACA 482:2
integrity of my i. FARA 306:13
i. of man is forced to choose YEAT 835:8
march of i. SOUT 731:2
not i. but rather memory LEON 464:12
of that living i. MILT 519:7
Our meddling i. WORD 832:7
put on I. BLAK 119:6
restless and versatile i. HUXL 397:20
revenge of the i. upon art SONT 728:5
scepticism of the i. NEWM 542:10
strengthening one's i. KEAT 431:19
tickle the i. LAMB 448:17
intellects hearts and i. EPIT 304:11
intellectual i. ability ARNO 29:14
i. All-in-all WORD 830:18
i., amongst the noblest CALV 182:7
i. bankruptcy HOLM 381:12
i. degradation MORE 531:4
I. disgrace Stares AUDE 34:2
i. dominion MAUR 502:10
i. eunuch Castlereagh BYRO 175:26
i. improvement JOHN 414:20
i. is someone whose mind CAMU 184:3
i. nature JOHN 410:6
i. power, through words WORD 828:11
'I.' suggests AUDE 34:11
ladies i. BYRO 175:28
no i. superiority AUST 37:12
practical i. STRO 745:1
tear is an i. thing BLAK 119:1
to the i. world STER 739:7
intellectuals treachery of the i. BEND 64:22
intelligence arresting human i. LEAC 459:16
bewitchment of our i. WITT 824:3
endowed with i. DOST 276:5
I. is quickness to apprehend WHIT 814:14
people have little i. LA B 446:15
started at the i. SOUT 731:6
you pawn your i. CUMM 247:5
intelligencies we are The i. DONN 273:25
intelligent Every i. voter ADAM 2:6
i. member of the family LEON 464:7
most i. and most stupid CONF 232:5
Most i., very elegant BUCK 159:12
pleasing one i. man MAIM 491:6
rule of i. tinkering EHRL 290:3
so i. ELIO 296:5
think you must be i. MIRR 520:5
intemperance brisk i. of youth GIBB 335:18
intend what I well i. SHAK 677:25
intensity full of passionate i. YEAT 837:5
intent first avowed i. BUNY 161:16
glorious great i. SPEN 733:18
i. is al CHAU 207:17
sides of my i. SHAK 682:12
told with bad i. BLAK 118:1
intention i. to keep my counsel GLAD 341:6
intentions devour second i. RABE 619:12
i. make blackguards LACL 447:4
only had good i. THAT 769:23
paved with good i. PROV 610:13
produced by their good i. WALP 801:16
inter children i. their parents HERO 373:22
hugger-mugger to i. him SHAK 666:5
interact do not i. at all UPDI 788:15
intercession made i. BIBL 88:19
interdependence closely knit i. HARD 361:4
interdependent everything is i. ZOHA 840:9
interest compete for her i. LEWI 467:11
i.'s on the dangerous edge BROW 155:9
i. that keeps peace CROM 245:16
its duty and its i. WASH 804:8
language of i. HELV 369:3
natural i. of money MACA 481:19
passion or i. LOCK 471:20
regard to their own i. SMIT 723:6
unbound by any i. HORA 387:11
interested i. him no more HART 363:11
i. in the arts AYCK 40:2
i. in things CURI 247:19
only i. in art SHAW 709:25
interesting i. actions BAGE 46:24
i., but tough TWAI 786:3
proposition be i. WHIT 814:11
things and characters i. SCOT 652:12
Very i. . . . but CATC 196:24
interests Our i. are eternal PALM 566:2
pursue their respective i. JEVO 407:7
interjection is but an I. BYRO 177:27
interline diminish, i. SWIF 749:14
interlude present is an i. O'NE 554:24
intermission i. of pain SELD 653:22
internal i. attrition AURE 37:4
international dependable i. emotion ALSO 12:23
i. wrong AUDE 35:1
Internationale *L'I.* POTT 589:5
internationals Cambridge, Blackheath, and five I. DOYL 277:20
Internet I. is an élite CHOM 212:13
thanks to the I. WILE 819:17
interpose i. my body STRA 744:9
interpretation I. is the revenge SONT 728:5
lost in i. FROS 326:19
interpreted i. the world MARX 500:2
interpreter i. is the hardest SHER 715:15
i. of nature WHEW 813:15
interpreters i. between us and the millions MACA 483:15
interrèd good is oft i. SHAK 675:27
intersecting i. monologues WEST 812:13
interstellar vacant i. spaces ELIO 294:9
interstice every i. of my body EDDI 288:1
interstices i. between the intersections JOHN 409:11
intervals lucid i. BACO 44:26
lucid intervals of i. WORD 828:3
intervening i. windings WHAR 813:2
interview strange and fatal i. DONN 272:13
interviewer i. allows you to say BENN 65:11
intestine This is the dark i. HUGH 393:7
intestines product of the smaller i. CARL 187:18
intimacy avoid any i. KITC 441:31
determine i. AUST 39:3
every old i. LAMB 448:9
intimate i. with by instinct AUST 37:27
intimidation without i. ROBE 629:8
intolerable burden of them is i. BOOK 129:16
O vile, I. SHAK 698:11
intolerance I. of groups FREU 324:14
intolerant not to tolerate the i. POPP 587:26
intoxicated God-i. man NOVA 547:4
i. with power BURK 162:7
when he is i. JOHN 416:9
intoxication best of life is but i. BYRO 176:14
intreat I. me not to leave thee BIBL 78:12
intrepid natural and i. WALP 800:14
intricated Poor i. soul DONN 275:12
intrigues I. half-gathered CRAB 242:22
intrinsicate knot i. Of life SHAK 658:2
introduce allow me to i. myself JAGG 401:8
introduced been i. to CARR 191:17
introduction i. to any literary work JOHN 412:18
pages of I. ELIO 293:15
introibo *I. at altare Dei* MISS 520:9
introitum *i. nobis ad vitam dedit* SENE 654:19

intruding rash, i. fool SHAK 665:14
intrusion I call it i. SPAR 731:20
invades first i. the ear DRYD 281:1
i. authors like a monarch DRYD 283:7
invasion i. by an idea HUGO 393:18
invective insolence is not i. DISR 268:17
invent fitter to i. BACO 44:25
necessary to i. him VOLT 797:16
one man can i. DOYL 277:19
right to i. themselves GREE 352:10
invented England i. the phrase BAGE 46:9
i. the brake NEME 541:3
Truth exists, lies are i. BRAQ 147:3
invention Beggars i. COWP 241:12
brightest heaven of i. SHAK 670:25
[bureaucracy's] specific i. WEBE 807:8
by i. got SWIF 749:21
heaven of i. OPEN 556:6
heir of my i. SHAK 705:27
Imagination, not i. CONR 234:22
I. flags CONG 232:15
i. is unfruitful BURK 162:23
i. of a barbarous age MILT 514:5
i. of a mouse DISN 268:5
is a happy i. SAYI 648:3
It's my own i. CARR 191:12
Marriage a wonderful i. CONN 233:24
mother of i. PROV 607:23
pure i. BYRO 180:6
rash i. breeds a new device GASC 330:16
use of a new i. FRAN 323:17
inventions sought out many i. BIBL 84:17
with their own i. BOOK 139:11
inventor plague the i. SHAK 682:9
invents man i. nothing SHAW 708:7
inverse i. proportion to the sum PARK 567:23
inverted That i. bowl FITZ 314:18
invida *fugerit i. Aetas* HORA 387:22
invincible saw a city i. WHIT 815:2
inviolable clutching the i. shade ARNO 27:11
inviolate secret and i. Rose YEAT 837:7
invisible all things visible and i. BOOK 129:8
almost i. literature BALL 52:11
bloody and i. hand SHAK 684:7
Immortal, i. SMIT 728:8
i. and all-powerful FLAU 316:17
I. before birth BHAG 72:17
I., except to God MILT 516:6
i. hand in politics FRIE 325:1
i., refined out of existence JOYC 422:4
i. to the eye SAIN 641:12
join the choir i. ELIO 293:11
led by an i. hand SMIT 723:9
no i. means of support BUCH 159:9
priest of the i. STEV 739:18
representation of i. things LEON 464:19
she is not i. BACO 42:33
we walk i. SHAK 667:29
invisibly Silently, i. BLAK 120:11
invites I. my step POPE 582:16
inviting worth i. to dinner VIRG 796:6
invoking i. the Trinity PATR 570:2
invulnerable I. nothings SHEL 710:23
inward i. and spiritual grace BOOK 130:17
Outward and the I. KORA 445:14
inwardly i. in our souls BOOK 128:4
inwariable glass o' the i. DICK 265:11
ipse *I. dixit* CICE 217:13
I. docet quid agam OVID 561:16
Ipswich I. and Oxford SHAK 673:24
ira *Ça i.* ANON 20:2
I. furor brevis est HORA 386:16
Sine i. et studio TACI 752:12
irae *animis caelestibus i.* VIRG 793:5
Dies i. MISS 523:3
Iraq creating I. BELL 62:23
Ireland between I. and an enemy LEDW 461:17
bound to lose I. GLAD 341:16
coming to I. today GEOR 334:1
daunce wyt me, in i. ANON 16:19
England and I. BOWE 145:9
evacuation of I. GRIF 353:9
God save I. LAST 455:16
God save I. SULL 746:1
great Gaels of I. CHES 210:2
healthiest graveyard in I. BEHA 61:21
history of I. proves it JOHN 408:5
how's poor ould I. POLI 581:16
inhabiting island of I. O'BR 552:6
I. gives England her soldiers MERE 505:10
I. hurt you into poetry AUDE 33:31
I., Ireland! GLAD 340:12
I., Ireland, Ireland GLAD 341:9
I. is a small KETT 434:14
I. is mentioned SMIT 725:3
I. is not a geographical PARN 567:25
I. is the old sow JOYC 422:3
I., long a province DAVI 252:15
I. never was contented LAND 450:2
I.'s battle CONN 234:6
I. should be a province GOOL 346:15
I.'s opportunity PROV 599:14
I.'s present story BYRO 177:14
I. unfree shall never be at peace PEAR 571:7
I. we dreamed of DEV 259:6
jurisdiction in I. ADAM 2:10
love for I. CARS 192:4
now handling I. WEST 812:15
Out of I. have we come YEAT 836:24
pacify I. GLAD 340:17
parties in Northern I. MITC 523:13
programme for I. KETT 434:13
Romantic I.'s dead and gone YEAT 837:9
split I. BRUG 158:20
square inch of the soil of I. GRIF 353:7
what I have got for I. COLL 229:2
would had been for I. LAST 457:20
iris livelier i. changes TENN 762:22
Melted to one vast I. BYRO 174:25
irisch *mein i. Kind* WAGN 798:18
Irish answer to the I. Question SELL 654:15
become deeply I. KETT 434:13
chloroform of the I. GOGA 343:19
consider themselves I. BINC 115:3
for an I. purpose DAVI 252:20
howling of I. wolves SHAK 659:23
I'm I. MOOR 550:3
I. and Ireland ridiculous EDGE 288:11
I. and the Jews BEHA 62:3
I. Brigade DAVI 252:13
I. child, where are you WAGN 798:18
I. kept it in mind less BOWE 145:16
I. leader who would connive GRIF 353:7
I. ortolans EDGE 288:12
I. poets, learn your trade YEAT 837:20
I. Question DISR 268:8
Let the I. vessel lie AUDE 34:2
my I. subjects EDGE 289:1
river of I. mind DAVI 252:18
still an I. rebel DUFF 284:11
symbol of I. art JOYC 422:8
We I., born YEAT 837:14
what the I. people want KETT 434:15
what the I. people wanted DEV 259:4
Irishman I.'s heart SHAW 707:18
pig is to the I. KOHL 443:9
secondarily, I'm an I. HEWI 376:1
Irishmen appeal to all I. GEOR 334:1
I. in her Parliament BALF 49:15
Irishry indomitable I. YEAT 837:21
iron Any old i. COLL 228:12
beat the i. while it is hot DRYD 283:2
become an i. cage WEBE 807:4
blood and i. BISM 116:12
bound in misery and i. BOOK 139:12
bruise them with a rod of i. BOOK 131:17
Even an i. partition TALM 754:6
he's got i. teeth GROM 354:1
If gold ruste, what shall i. do CHAU 204:25
i. curtain CHUR 216:1
I. Curtain did not reach SOLZ 727:16
i. entered into his soul BOOK 139:8
i. gates of life MARV 499:4
I. Lady THAT 769:21
i. shuts amain MILT 513:5
i. tears down Pluto's cheek MILT 512:8
my i.'s gone EPIT 303:16
nobles with links of i. BOOK 142:2
Nor i. bars a cage LOVE 476:14
On i., wood and glass DAVI 252:9
painted to look like i. BISM 116:16
sound of i. on stone DE L 256:17
Time's i. feet MONT 528:16
Torah, hard like i. TALM 754:22
while the i. is hot PROV 611:30
iron-armed i. soldier POLI 581:17
iron-clasped i. volume POE 580:1
irons Heat me these i. SHAK 677:13
irrational i. is rational STEV 739:25
irrationality i. of the world WEBE 807:7
irrationally I. held truths HUXL 397:18
irreconcilable Man and woman are i. DURA 285:19
irregular most i. they seem MILT 517:3
irregulars Baker Street i. DOYL 278:3
irrevocabile *volat i. verbum* HORA 387:1
irrigation numerical i. system AUGA 35:20
irritabile *genus i. vatum* HORA 387:9
irritation cosiness and i. PYM 618:7
irrt *Es i. der Mensch* GOET 342:14
is If this i. that comes PALI 565:6
i., both now and eternally HEGE 367:13
That which *i.* grows GALE 328:12
Whatever IS, is RIGHT POPE 585:18
Isaac God of I. BIBL 75:30
thine only son I. BIBL 74:31
Iscariot not I. BIBL 102:20
Iser I., rolling rapidly CAMP 183:8
Ishmael Call me I. OPEN 555:10
Isis I.' elders reel POPE 580:16
Islam another religion than I. KORA 444:4
I. has established them KHOM 435:13
true religion is I. KORA 444:1
island as an inland i. SWIN 750:18
everyone on this i. AHER 8:29
insuppressible i. KETT 434:14
i. is moored only lightly BARR 56:1
i. made mainly of coal BEVA 71:12
i.-valley of Avilion TENN 760:17
John Bull's other i. SHAW 707:17
my lot in an i. DICK 265:23
never make this i. all her own WALL 800:7
No man is an I. DONN 275:3
oblique frayed i. BOWE 145:15
overlook your i. FRIE 325:7
snug little I. DIBD 260:15
soggy little i. UPDI 788:11
some secreted i. WORD 831:8
islands favourite i. AUDE 33:22
[monks] should live as i. PALI 564:18
peninsulas and i. CATU 197:5
isle dear and happy i. MARV 499:6
Fairest I. DRYD 281:32
i., a sickle moon FLEC 317:6
i. is full of noises SHAK 699:5
men, of the Emerald I. DREN 279:10
natural bravery of your i. SHAK 660:23
sad, black i. BAUD 57:9
sceptered i. SHAK 694:19
isles I. of fragrance POPE 580:23
i. of Greece BYRO 176:25
multitude of the i. BOOK 138:8
of Tharsis and of the i. BOOK 136:18
taketh up the isles BIBL 88:3
Islington fields from I. BLAK 118:22
lived in I. BALL 50:4
isolate limit and i. oneself GOET 343:16
love someone is to i. BAUD 57:14
isolated Continent i. BROC 149:2
fine i. verisimilitude KEAT 430:24
isolation Splendid i. NEWS 544:13
Israel between I. and their Father TALM 754:6
between I. and the nations SIDD 718:1

Deliver I., O God BOOK 133:6
Hear, O I. SIDD 717:17
heritage unto I. BOOK 141:5
he that keepeth I. BOOK 140:12
I. amidst the nations HA-L 357:5
I. came out of Egypt BOOK 139:21
[I.] is distinguished TALM 754:12
I. shall be a proverb BIBL 79:16
I.'s monarch DRYD 279:18
I. smote him BIBL 76:27
I. was in Egypt land SONG 730:8
may I. now say BOOK 140:24
mother in I. BIBL 77:26
Name is great in I. BOOK 137:1
neither will I let I. go BIBL 75:32
Now I. loved Joseph BIBL 75:8
now may I. say BOOK 140:16
of the stock of I. BIBL 108:19
out-casts of I. BOOK 141:24
prophet in I. BIBL 80:17
sweet psalmist of I. BIBL 79:13
These be thy gods, O I. BIBL 76:16
waters of I. BIBL 80:18
Israelite Behold an I. BIBL 101:12
Israelites I. passed over BIBL 77:19
isst *Der Mensch ist, was er i.* FEUE 309:4
issue happy i. BOOK 127:18
honest madam's i. SHAK 678:3
ist *Der Mensch i., was er isst* FEUE 309:4
isthmus i. of a middle state POPE 585:19
it It's just I. KIPL 441:24
Italia I.! oh Italia BYRO 174:26
Italian fair as an I. sun BANV 53:10
Proosian, Or perhaps I. GILB 339:1
to women I. CHAR 203:16
Italianato *Inglese I.* ASCH 30:7
Italie *soleil d'I.* BANV 53:10
Italy after seeing I. BURN 165:25
bought his doublet in I. SHAK 687:9
has not been in I. JOHN 415:18
In I. under the Borgias FILM 311:16
inside of it, 'I.' BROW 155:25
I. is a geographical expression METT 506:9
made I. from designs TWAI 786:14
Paradise of exiles, I. SHEL 711:19
itch i. of literature LOVE 477:3
poor i. of your opinion SHAK 660:2
itching have an i. palm SHAK 676:18
ite *I. domum saturae* VIRG 796:13
I. missa est MISS 522:21
iteration damnable i. SHAK 667:20
i. of the nuptials CONG 233:14
itself Forever be I. again GINS 339:19
itur *sic i. ad astra* VIRG 795:8
Itylus half assuaged for I. SWIN 750:5
iubeo *sic i.* JUVE 424:15
iubes *i. renovare dolorem* VIRG 793:16
Iudaeus *Credat I. Apella* HORA 389:20
iudice *se i.* JUVE 425:3
iudice *sub i. lis est* HORA 385:16
iunctura *Reddiderit i. novum* HORA 385:14
iurare *i. in verba magistri* HORA 386:8
ivory as if done in i. FULL 327:7
belly is as bright i. BIBL 85:21
cargo of i. MASE 500:13
gleaming white i. VIRG 795:3
in his i. tower SAIN 641:10
i., and apes BIBL 79:19
i. on which I work AUST 39:11
neck is as a tower of i. BIBL 86:5
out of the i. gate BROW 154:6
upon an i. sled MARL 496:21
ivy As creeping i. clings COWP 241:5
holly and the i. SONG 729:10
it was agony, I. CATC 195:12
pluck an i. branch for me ROSS 634:7
yonder i.-mantled tow'r GRAY 350:7

Jabberwock Beware the J., my son CARR 190:12
jack about J. a Nory NURS 548:18
Damn you, J. BONE 125:7
Every J. has his Jill PROV 599:27
good J. makes a good Jill PROV 601:28
house that J. built NURS 551:7
J. and Jill NURS 548:21
J. as good as his master PROV 604:42
J. became a gentleman SHAK 696:15
J. be nimble NURS 548:22
J. shall have Jill SHAK 690:10
J. Sprat could eat no fat NURS 548:23
Little J. Horner NURS 549:6
makes J. a dull boy PROV 595:6
news of my boy J. KIPL 439:17
put there by J. Nastys HUGH 393:12
This J., joke HOPK 384:22
jackals J. piss at their foot FLAU 316:18
jackdaw J. sat on the Cardinal's chair BARH 54:3
jacket *short* j. EDWA 289:5
thresh his old j. COWP 242:18
jackknife j. has Macheath BREC 147:17
jacks calls the knaves, J. DICK 262:18
Jackson J. with his Virginians BEE 61:1
Jacob as the Angel did with J. WALT 803:2
God of J. BIBL 75:30
God of J. BOOK 134:19
house of J. BOOK 139:21
J. served seven years BIBL 75:4
J. was a plain man BIBL 74:35
sold his birthright unto J. BIBL 74:36
traffic of J.'s ladder THOM 774:13
voice is J.'s voice BIBL 74:38
jade Go spin, you j. SCOT 652:11
Let the galled j. wince SHAK 664:25
jades pampered j. MARL 497:3
pampered j. of Asia SHAK 669:32
Jael J. Heber's wife BIBL 77:25
JAH his name J. BOOK 136:6
jail being in a j. JOHN 412:22
dey gits you in j. O'NE 554:18
Go to j. SAYI 647:17
patron, and the j. JOHN 411:14
jailbird looks like a j. BLOK 122:5
jails emptied the British j. DAY- 253:13
jam j. to-morrow CARR 190:23
J. tomorrow PROV 604:43
j. we thought was for BENN 65:5
jamais j. triste archy MARQ 497:8
James Home J. HILL 377:6
J. I, James II, and the Old Pretender GUED 354:12
J. James Morrison Morrison MILN 510:16
King J. stay behind WHAR 813:5
Jameson RAID BY DR J. TELE 758:3
Jane J., Jane, tall as a crane SITW 720:21
you J. MISQ 522:2
Janus very J. of poets DRYD 283:9
Janvier J. and Février NICH 543:17
Japan J.'s advantage HIRO 377:18
jar does so j. GASK 330:23
jargon from J. born to rescue Law LLOY 470:14
j. of languages DEFO 254:11
jargons clear of the j. NIGH 545:23
Jarndyce J. and Jarndyce DICK 260:18
Wards in J. DICK 261:6
Jason J. hath received BIBL 104:5
jasper j. and a sardine stone BIBL 111:30
jaundiced yellow to the j. eye POPE 584:28
javelin hunter's j. ARNO 27:16
jaw j.-jaw is always better CHUR 216:6
let the j. go by PROV 604:44
with the j. of an ass BIBL 78:4
jaws gently smiling j. CARR 189:10
Into the j. of Death TENN 757:17
j. of hell VIRG 794:20
j. of power ADAM 3:13
through the j. of death LAUD 454:4
jay-bird j. say ter der squinch-owl HARR 362:16
jazz J. music is to be played MORT 533:17
sunbathing and j. WAUG 806:8
jealous am a j. God BIBL 76:9
Art is a j. mistress EMER 299:14
As thou Art j., Lord DONN 273:2
jealous for they are j. SHAK 693:7
J. in honour SHAK 659:1
one not easily j. SHAK 694:3
to the j. SHAK 692:28
tramp is j. of tramp HESI 375:10
jealousy Anger and j. ELIO 293:2
beware, my lord, of j. SHAK 692:21
cold age, narrow j. ROCH 630:4
ear of j. BIBL 91:5
J. a human face BLAK 121:11
j. extinguishes love MARG 495:9
J. is all the fun JONG 419:7
j. is cruel as the grave BIBL 86:7
J. is feeling alone BOWE 145:14
j. of rivals ADAM 1:19
j. to the bride BARR 55:18
j. with a halo WELL 810:17
No j. Was understood MILT 516:32
resting from all j. BEAU 58:16
To j. nothing is more frighful SAGA 641:9
tyrant, tyrant J. DRYD 281:34
Jeanie J. with the light brown hair FOST 321:16
jeans blue j. and Coca-Cola GREE 352:9
jeepers J. Creepers MERC 505:6
jeering laughing and j. PEPY 573:2
jeers flouts and j. DISR 269:14
Jeeves J. shimmered out WODE 824:11
like Wodehouse dropping J. WAUG 806:22
Jefferson J.—still surv— LAST 457:12
Jehovah O thou great J. WILL 820:8
Jehu J., the son of Nimshi BIBL 80:23
Jekyll Dr J. and Mr Hyde STEV 741:12
Jellicoe J. was the only man on either side CHUR 216:20
jellies With j. soother KEAT 427:13
jelly blasted, j.-boned swines LAWR 458:17
J.-bellied Flag-flapper KIPL 441:23
Meaty j., too DICK 264:23
Out, vile j. SHAK 679:12
jellybeans way of eating j. REAG 623:4
Jena J. came twenty years after BISM 116:14
je-ne-sais-quoi *J.* young man GILB 338:21
Jenny J. kissed me HUNT 395:15
jeopardy in j. of their lives BIBL 79:14
jerks bring me up by j. DICK 262:20
Jerusalem hills stand about J. BOOK 140:18
holy city, new J. BIBL 113:7
In that J. SHAK 670:18
J. is built as a city BOOK 140:14
J. the golden NEAL 540:3
J. thy sister calls BLAK 119:4
Next year in J. HAGG 356:3
O Jerusalem, J. BIBL 96:29
peace of J. BOOK 140:15
performed in J. BOOK 135:26
Till we have built J. BLAK 120:1
unto J. BIBL 104:13
waste places of J. BIBL 88:13
jessamine casement j. stirred TENN 764:7
j. faint SHEL 713:23
pale j. MILT 513:8
Jesse stem of J. BIBL 87:3
jesses j. were my dear heart-strings SHAK 692:23
jest bitter is a scornful j. JOHN 411:10
cover of a j. HORA 389:13
fellow of infinite j. SHAK 666:23
good j. for ever SHAK 667:33
J. and youthful jollity MILT 512:14
j.'s prosperity SHAK 681:2
laughing at some j. KIPL 438:14
Life is a j. EPIT 303:12
poison in j. SHAK 664:24
that's no j. RALE 620:14
true word spoken in j. PROV 606:24
world's a j. STEP 737:20

jesting talking, nor j. BIBL 108:6
jests He j. at scars SHAK 697:9
to his memory for his j. SHER 716:20
Jesu J., good above all other DEAR 254:1
J., lover of my soul WESL 810:25
J., the very thought CASW 194:1
Jesuit thing, a tool, a J. KING 437:15
Jesus another king, one J. BIBL 104:5
at the name of J. BIBL 108:17
At the name of J. NOEL 546:12
blame J. for what was done BENN 65:7
bon Sansculotte J. DESM 259:1
come, Lord J. BIBL 113:16
cross of J. BARI 54:13
disciple whom J. loved BIBL 103:12
Gentle J. WESL 810:26
If J. Christ were to come CARL 188:22
J. Christ BIBL 110:7
J. Christ Had his moments JAGG 401:8
J. Christ, her Lord STON 743:9
J. Christ his only Son BOOK 126:10
J. is there only for others BONH 125:10
J. loves you more SIMO 720:9
J. OF NAZARETH BIBL 102:33
J. shall reign WATT 805:18
J. the author BIBL 110:2
J. the most scientific EDDY 288:4
j. told him; he wouldn't CUMM 247:8
J. wants me for a sunbeam TALB 753:2
J. wept BIBL 102:11
J. wept HUGO 394:1
J.! with all thy faults BUTL 172:30
Messiah, J. son of Mary KORA 444:15
more popular than J. now LENN 463:17
O J., I have promised BODE 123:8
power of J.' Name PERR 574:1
Socrates, and J., and Luther EMER 299:24
stand up for J. DUFF 284:8
stand up for J. LAST 457:7
sweet the name of J. NEWT 543:15
thinks he is J. Christ CLEM 220:12
this J. will not do BLAK 118:17
to the heart of J. TERE 768:10
Was J. chaste BLAK 118:15
Was J. gentle BLAK 118:12
Was J. humble BLAK 118:13
When J. came to Birmingham STUD 745:5
jeunesse *Si j. savait* ESTI 301:10
Jew especially a J. MALA 491:20
for Englishman or J. BLAK 118:17
Germany will declare that I am a J. EINS 290:12
Hath not a J. eyes SHAK 687:29
J. and the language CELA 199:11
Just J.-*ish* MILL 510:5
Let Apella the J. believe it HORA 389:20
Liver of blaspheming J. SHAK 684:19
neither Greek nor J. BIBL 109:4
saved one J. from Auschwitz AUDE 35:19
The old J. BISM 116:17
jewel As a j. of gold BIBL 82:23
j. in the crown GRAY 349:24
j. of their souls SHAK 692:20
j. of the just VAUG 790:13
Like a rich j. SHAK 697:7
No j. is like Rosalind SHAK 659:7
Wears yet a precious j. SHAK 658:14
jewelled day of the j. epigram ANNA 15:1
j. mass of millinery TENN 763:24
jewellery just rattle your j. LENN 463:16
jewels moving j. TRAH 780:15
precious j. BACO 45:7
Jewish founded the J. state HERZ 375:9
J. man with parents alive ROTH 635:18
murderers of J. children WIES 816:17
my J. gabardine SHAK 687:15
national home for the J. people BALF 49:16
total solution of J. question GOER 342:12
Jewry In J. is God known BOOK 137:1
Jews born King of the J. BIBL 92:22
But spurn the J. BROW 152:9
choose The J. EWER 305:12
conversion of the J. MARV 499:1
Irish and the J. BEHA 62:3
J. are not unlike Christians JUDA 422:23
J. require a sign BIBL 105:27
J. which believed not BIBL 104:4
KING OF THE J. BIBL 102:33
last J. to die MEIR 503:11
three paynims, three J. CAXT 198:17
unto the J. a stumbling-block BIBL 105:28
When Hitler attacked the J. NIEM 545:8
jigsaw piece in a j. puzzle FILM 312:1
Jill Every Jack has his J. PROV 599:27
good Jack makes a good J. PROV 601:28
Jack and J. NURS 548:21
jilted courted and j. CAMP 183:9
Jim dear brother J. WORD 832:14
jump J. Crow NURS 551:17
worried about J. CATC 196:3
Jinas adoration of twenty-four J. JAIN 402:3
jingle Little j., little chimes CARE 186:20
jingo by j. if we do HUNT 395:10
jo John Anderson my j. BURN 167:17
Joan J. as my Lady HERR 374:15
J. doth keel the pot SHAK 681:4
Little Jumping J. NURS 548:11
job afflictions of J. BACO 42:4
boy to do a man's j. PROV 607:36
do his j. when he doesn't feel AGAT 6:18
Doth J. fear God BIBL 80:35
finish the j. CHUR 215:14
get on with the j. DALT 248:15
he's doing a grand j. CATC 196:19
husband is a whole-time j. BENN 66:8
I am as poor as J. SHAK 669:24
j. working-class parents ABBO 1:1
Living is my j. MONT 527:17
lost the j. JOYC 422:14
neighbour loses his j. TRUM 784:6
patience of J. BIBL 110:22
read the book of J. WOOL 827:4
jog as a man *might j. on with* DURH 286:5
j. on the foot-path SHAK 703:12
jogging alternative to j. FITT 314:3
John christen him J. KEAT 431:20
D'ye ken J. Peel GRAV 349:9
J. Anderson my jo BURN 167:17
J. Bull's other island SHAW 707:17
my son J. NURS 548:3
Old J. of Gaunt SHAK 694:8
Johnny Frankie and J. SONG 729:5
J.-head-in-air PUDN 616:14
J., I hardly knew ye BALL 50:20
Little J. Head-In-Air HOFF 380:2
joie *j. venait toujours après la peine* APOL 22:21
join can't beat them, j. them SAYI 647:20
j. the choir invisible ELIO 293:11
joined God hath j. together BIBL 96:12
j. together in holy Matrimony BOOK 130:21
whom God hath j. BOOK 131:7
joint bones are out of j. BOOK 132:24
every j. and member MILT 519:13
j.-heirs with Christ BIBL 105:8
Remove the j. CARR 191:17
time is out of j. SHAK 663:7
time was out of j. STRA 744:7
joints know the j. BUTL 171:15
Of all the gin j. FILM 312:4
joke chance remark or a j. PLUT 579:6
ever loves a j. POPE 580:11
every j. a custard pie ORWE 559:13
get a j. well into a Scotch SMIT 725:12
j.'s a very serious thing CHUR 213:20
many a j. had he GOLD 344:13
This Jack, j. HOPK 384:22
jokes civil servant doesn't make j. IONE 399:22
difference of taste in j. ELIO 292:4
Forgive, O Lord, my little j. FROS 325:17
hackneyed j. from Miller BYRO 178:1
jollity Jest and youthful j. MILT 512:14
yowthe, and on my j. CHAU 206:18
jolly J. boating weather CORY 237:11
j. miller BICK 114:14
j. red nose BEAU 58:12
This life is most j. SHAK 659:5
Jonadge in J.'s belly DICK 263:11
Jonathan Saul and J. BIBL 79:2
jonquil j. o'ercomes the feeble brain WINC 823:1
Jonson Ben J. his best piece JONS 420:17
J. knew the critic's part COLL 229:13
J.'s learnèd sock MILT 512:24
learn'd J. DRAY 279:7
Jordan I looked over J. SONG 730:4
J. was driven back BOOK 139:21
tread the verge of J. WILL 820:9
Joseph Now Israel loved J. BIBL 75:8
Josephine Not tonight, J. NAPO 539:5
Joshua like J. of old TOAS 778:1
jostling j. in the street BLAK 120:7
jot one j. of former love DRAY 279:3
jouk J. and let the jaw PROV 604:44
journal page of my J. BOSW 144:18
page of your j. HUGH 393:9
journalism but why j. BALF 50:1
J.—an ability to WEST 812:17
J. largely consists CHES 211:20
journalist thank God! the British j. WOLF 825:6
journalistic j. activity TOLS 779:15
j. dirty-mindedness LAWR 458:23
journalists J. belong in gutter PRIE 591:10
j. have constructed LICH 467:17
J. say a thing BENN 66:9
tell lies to j. KRAU 445:18
journey begin a j. on Sundays SWIF 748:18
day's j. take the whole day ROSS 634:12
death the j.'s end DRYD 282:11
gave you the splendid j. CAVA 198:6
gone on a j. BIBL 82:16
he is in a j. BIBL 79:28
Here is my j.'s end SHAK 693:30
I woll this j. be his EDWA 289:4
j. into a far country BIBL 100:2
j. of a thousand *li* LAO 452:5
j. *really* necessary OFFI 554:7
j. to the world below SOCR 727:5
j. towards oblivion LAWR 458:12
j.-work of the stars WHIT 815:14
long day's j. O'NE 554:20
longest j. SHEL 711:9
long j. to take LAST 456:5
more of a J. CLAU 219:17
now begin the j. REAG 623:8
prepare for a j. MANS 494:9
such a long j. ELIO 294:27
take a j. ANDR 14:15
take with you on your j. GOGO 344:1
when the j.'s over HOUS 390:16
journeying sat the j. boy HARD 361:20
journeyman j. to grief SHAK 694:14
journeymen nature's j. SHAK 664:17
journeys J. end in lovers meeting SHAK 701:9
jousted J. in Aspramont MILT 514:30
Jove from J. the lightning MANI 493:16
J.'s planet BROW 156:5
J.'s stout oak SHAK 699:9
Of J., Appollo, of Mars CHAU 207:21
joy bed Of crimson j. BLAK 121:7
binds to himself a j. BLAK 120:8
Break forth into j. BIBL 88:13
burst J.'s grape KEAT 429:5
dreme of j. CHAU 206:29
each for the j. of working KIPL 440:19
from too much j. GRAV 349:12
good tidings of great j. BIBL 98:21
greatest j. of all ZOHA 840:11
is a j. for ever OPEN 556:22
J. always came after pain APOL 22:21
j. and glory ABEL 1:3
j. as it flies BLAK 120:8
J., beautiful radiance SCHI 646:14
j. cometh in the morning BOOK 133:15

j. for ever KEAT 426:16
j. is ever on the wing MILT 518:12
j. is wisdom YEAT 836:13
J. of heav'n WESL 811:7
j. of love is too short MALO 492:11
j. of the worm SHAK 657:27
J. Peace PASC 569:1
J. ruled the day DRYD 282:17
J. shall be in heaven BIBL 100:1
j.'s soul lies in the doing SHAK 700:5
j.! that in our embers WORD 830:5
j. unspeakable BIBL 110:25
j. was never sure SWIN 750:21
J., whose hand KEAT 429:5
Labour without j. is base RUSK 638:23
let j. be unconfined BYRO 174:14
Life, J., Empire SHEL 713:16
Lord of all J. STRU 745:2
no j. but calm TENN 763:12
not a j. the world BYRO 179:5
obtain j. and gladness BIBL 87:24
perfect j. therein I find DYER 286:13
politics of j. HUMP 395:9
reap in j. BOOK 140:20
shock of your j. HUGH 393:9
shouted for j. BIBL 81:32
Strength through j. POLI 581:21
surge of j. CONL 233:20
Surprised by j. WORD 832:5
Where's all the j. KEPP 434:4
Where there is sadness, j. FRAN 323:5
joyance clear keen j. SHEL 714:7
joyful be j. in the Lord BOOK 138:13
how good and j. BOOK 141:4
j. mother BOOK 139:20
j. rain BOOK 127:20
Let the saints be j. BOOK 142:2
joys Africa and golden j. SHAK 670:21
all j. so well agree SIDN 718:21
all my j. ROCH 630:7
All my j. to this are folly BURT 170:1
innumerable j. TRAH 780:11
j. are but fantastical DONN 273:23
j. of marriage FORD 319:20
j. of parents BACO 43:24
lasting j. the man attend WHUR 816:11
lived for j. in vain CLAR 218:11
o' departed j. BURN 166:18
precious in our j. STER 738:12
present j. are more DRYD 281:23
redoubleth j. BACO 43:2
season made for j. GAY 331:20
Their homely j. GRAY 350:9
vain deluding j. MILT 512:3
jubilant Each j. chord BAKE 48:14
jubilate *J. Deo, omnis terra* BIBL 113:20
jubilee first day of our J. BROW 153:25
Judah J. is my law-giver BOOK 135:19
J.'s seer MANT 494:12
J. was his sanctuary BOOK 139:21
Judaism J. knows nothing of MEND 504:19
Judas boyhood of J. Æ 6:8
Damned below J. COWP 240:6
J. saith unto him BIBL 102:20
J. was paid POWE 590:16
J. who writes the biography WILD 817:25
that of J. STAL 736:4
Whether J. Iscariot DYLA 287:17
judge after a time they j. them WILD 818:27
Before you j. me JACK 400:18
decided by the j. JOHN 411:21
Do not j. this movement kindly READ 622:10
Here come de j. CATC 195:22
I j. and punish ANON 21:11
I'll be j. CARR 189:11
invent than to j. BACO 44:25
j. in his own cause PROV 608:4
j. is condemned PUBL 616:12
J. none blessed BIBL 91:26
J. not BIBL 93:28
J. not PROV 604:46
J. not the preacher HERB 372:5
J. of all the earth BIBL 74:29
j.'s robe SHAK 686:8
j. the quick and the dead BOOK 126:10
j. the world BOOK 138:11
j. thou my cause BIBL 89:27
J. to be chosen ZORO 841:16
Justly to j. BROO 150:6
neutrality of an impartial j. BURK 165:12
prince and a j. BIBL 75:23
will I j. thee BIBL 100:17
wise men can j. ASCH 30:8
judged if j. by himself JUVE 425:3
they were j. every man BIBL 113:6
judgement at forty, the j. FRAN 323:11
biases the j. DOYL 278:5
breastplate of j. BIBL 76:15
by truth, by j. TALM 753:14
Daniel come to j. SHAK 688:14
day of j. BOOK 127:8
Don't wait for the last j. CAMU 184:8
Enter not into j. BOOK 141:17
fit to sit in j. WILS 822:10
Force, unaided by j. HORA 388:18
functioning of a man's j. SALI 643:5
in the day of j. BIBL 95:14
j. fouk woud hae a doubt on FERG 308:15
j. is a mere lottery DRYD 283:8
j. of his peers MAGN 489:12
j. of the great whore BIBL 112:30
j. was set BIBL 90:6
j. will probably MANS 494:11
last j. VILL 792:17
Last J. draweth nigh BLAK 117:21
leaves of the J. Book unfold TAYL 756:15
looked for j. BIBL 86:17
not give his j. rashly ADDI 5:3
owes you his j. BURK 164:26
people's j. DRYD 280:12
replace reasoned j. JUVE 424:15
right j. in all things BOOK 128:9
What j. I had DRYD 283:10
world's j. SCHI 648:15
judgements Delivers brawling j. TENN 760:6
differing j. serve COWP 240:10
j. of the Lord BOOK 132:17
To make j. MONT 527:6
judges but my J. NEWM 542:4
hundred j. have declared it QUIL 619:1
independence of j. DENN 257:18
J. must follow their oaths ZOBE 840:7
j. of fact PULT 617:1
j. soon the sentence sign POPE 587:7
justice in the hands of j. PICA 575:15
judging j. others MOLI 525:12
judicious little j. levity STEV 742:6
Judy J. O'Grady KIPL 439:8
jug j., jug, jug LYLY 480:16
'J. Jug' to dirty ears ELIO 296:3
juggle how to j. work, love, home FRIE 324:24
juggler perceive a j.'s sleight BUTL 172:10
threadbare j. SHAK 659:30
jugular than the j. vein KORA 445:13
juices sucking the living j. DOST 276:4
Julia in silks my J. goes HERR 375:4
missed the point completely, J. ELIO 293:22
my J.'s dainty leg HERR 374:18
my J.'s lips do smile HERR 374:5
Julius Caesar J.'s ill-erected tower SHAK 695:24
July Born on the fourth of J. COHA 224:1
on the Fourth of J. HAMM 359:3
winter—ending in J. BYRO 177:23
Jumblies where the J. live LEAR 460:9
jump j. Jim Crow NURS 551:17
j. the life to come SHAK 682:8
see him j. before me STEV 742:14
jumpers Angels in j. LEWI 467:13
jumping Little J. Joan NURS 548:11
jumps see how the cat j. SCOT 652:13
June as the cuckoo is in J. SHAK 668:26
dripping J. sets all PROV 598:46
J. is bustin' out HAMM 358:19
leafy month of J. COLE 226:23
meetings made December J. TENN 761:26
newly sprung in J. BURN 168:6
When J. is past CARE 186:13
Jungfrau looking like the J. CHAN 202:7
jungle city is not a concrete j. MORR 532:7
J. will think KIPL 441:2
Law of the J. KIPL 441:19
juniper j. talks to the oak PAUL 570:7
sat down under a j. tree BIBL 80:2
under a j.-tree ELIO 293:21
junk flung up old j. CANN 185:10
J. is the ideal product BURR 169:14
Juno J.'s never-forgetting anger VIRG 793:4
Jupiter *J. est quodcumque vides* LUCA 478:17
J. from on high laughs OVID 561:6
J. the Rain-giver TIBU 777:8
jurisdiction j. in Ireland ADAM 2:10
j. in this Realm BOOK 142:12
jurisprudence light of j. CLOS 222:10
light of J. COKE 224:9
jury I'll be j. CARR 189:11
j. do the deciding CHEK 208:16
j.-men may dine POPE 587:7
Trial by j. itself DENM 257:15
just actions of the j. SHIR 717:9
all j. works BOOK 126:19
Be j., my lovely swain BEHN 62:11
faithful and j. to me SHAK 675:30
false and the j. ZORO 841:5
God is j. JEFF 406:3
gods are j. SHAK 680:9
good man, and a j. BIBL 100:30
hath his quarrel j. SHAK 672:17
in its causes j. DRYD 282:6
jewel of the j. VAUG 790:13
j. and old renown TENN 767:15
j. an image GODA 341:21
J. are the ways of God MILT 518:17
J. as I am ELLI 298:10
j. before you're generous PROV 595:41
j. cause reaches its flood-tide CATT 194:18
J. like that CATC 196:8
j. man having a firm grasp HORA 388:15
j. one of those things PORT 588:6
'j.' or 'right' PLAT 578:5
j. shall live by faith BIBL 104:26
J. when you thought ADVE 7:37
may not be a j. peace IZET 400:12
more j. than God BIBL 81:8
ninety and nine j. persons BIBL 100:1
on the j. and on the unjust BIBL 93:14
Our cause is j. DICK 266:22
path of the j. BIBL 82:11
place for a j. man THOR 775:26
rain, it raineth on the j. BOWE 145:20
spirits of j. men BIBL 110:4
support to the J. One ZORO 841:10
talk of a j. war SORL 728:20
Thou art indeed j., Lord HOPK 384:23
thou art j. TENN 760:19
whatsoever things are j. BIBL 108:25
will still be j. AESC 6:10
justest wisest and j. PLAT 578:4
justice ain't the shop for j. DICK 264:18
call for j. MORE 531:8
Die he or j. must MILT 516:2
friendship than of j. THOM 771:12
if there is j. anywhere VIRG 793:14
indifferently minister j. BOOK 129:12
in the dirt lay j. HEAN 366:17
J. denied MILL 509:13
j., In fair round belly SHAK 659:1
J. is in one scale JEFF 405:20
j. is of this sort ARIS 24:18
j. is open to all MATH 501:12
J. is the constant wish JUST 424:1
J. is truth DISR 268:14
j. makes democracy possible NIEB 545:5
j. of my quarrel ANON 17:1
j. or injustice JOHN 411:21
J. should not only be done HEWA 375:17

justice (*cont.*):
J., though she's painted blind BUTL 172:13
'J.' was done CLOS 222:15
'J.' was done HARD 361:2
J. with mercy MILT 517:21
Let j. be done MOTT 535:8
Let j. be done WATS 805:1
liberty plucks j. SHAK 686:1
loved j. LAST 455:10
moderation in the pursuit of j. GOLD 345:33
moral good and of j. JOHN 407:11
more devoted to order than j. KING 436:12
Poetic J. POPE 580:8
price of j. BENN 66:6
reason, and j. BURK 163:1
Revenge is a kind of wild j. BACO 43:28
right or j. MAGN 489:13
think j. requires MANS 494:11
Though j. be thy plea SHAK 688:11
Thwackum was for doing j. FIEL 310:8
truth, j., and humanity GLAD 341:8
truth, j. and the American way ANON 16:7
What use of J. ANDR 14:13
which is the j. SHAK 679:23
you have ravished j. WEBS 808:12
justifiable j. act of war BELL 62:22
j. to men MILT 518:17
justification j. . . . terms ARNO 28:27
justified confessions of a j. sinner HOGG 380:15
no man living be j. BOOK 141:17
Wisdom is j. BIBL 95:8
justifies end j. the means BUSE 170:25
end j. the means PROV 599:12
justify j. God's ways HOUS 391:9
j. the ways of God MILT 514:9
men j. him BIBL 91:29
justitia *Fiat j.* MOTT 535:8
justly do j. BIBL 90:20
justum *Dignum et j.* MISS 520:20
juvenes *Gaudeamus igitur, J. dum sumus* ANON 21:9

K wear the Five Ks SIKH 720:3
Kaaba My House [K.] KORA 444:22
kaim siller k. BALL 50:21
Kaiser put the kibosh on the K. ELLE 298:5
Kalends pay at the Greek K. AUGU 36:18
Kansas corny as K. in August HAMM 359:3
K. had better stop raising corn LEAS 461:3
Karajan Herbert von K. BEEC 61:2
karma bad k. which he had JAIN 402:5
Karshish K., the picker-up BROW 155:27
Kaspar Old K.'s work was done SOUT 730:11
Kate cared for K. SHAK 698:34
K. of my consolation SHAK 698:7
Kiss me K. SHAK 698:8
Kathleen K. Ní Houlihan CARB 186:1
Kathleen Mavourneen K.! the grey dawn CRAW 244:16
Keats K.'s vulgarity LEAV 461:6
Kedar habitation among the tents of K. BOOK 140:10
keel Joan doth k. the pot SHAK 681:4
keener edged tool that grows k. IRVI 400:2
with his k. eye MARV 498:19
keep honour, and k. her BOOK 131:4
Ideas won't k. WHIT 814:13
If you can k. your head KIPL 439:2
I k. away WALL 800:9
intention to k. my counsel GLAD 341:6
K. a thing seven years PROV 604:47
k. me, King of Kings KEN 433:2
k. the bridge with me MACA 483:6
k. thee in all thy ways BOOK 137:23
k. who can WORD 831:17
many to k. KING 437:12
shop will k. you PROV 604:49
some day it'll k. you WEST 812:2
ware that will not k. HOUS 390:16
will not k. her long SHAK 696:13
keeper Lord himself is thy k. BOOK 140:12
my brother's k. BIBL 74:8
keepers Finders k. PROV 600:20
k. of the walls BIBL 85:19
keepeth he that k. thee BOOK 140:12
keepings Findings k. PROV 600:21
keeps gave it us for k. AYRE 40:8
Kelly K. from the Isle of Man MURP 537:3
Kempenfeld When K. went down COWP 240:24
ken D'ye k. John Peel GRAV 349:9
Kendal Mr K. is going to be confirmed TENN 767:17
kenne *k. mich auch nicht* GOET 343:18
Kennedy you're no Jack K. BENT 67:12
Kennedys Who killed the K. JAGG 401:9
kennst *K. du das Land* GOET 343:12
Kensal Green Paradise by way of K. CHES 210:15
Kent everybody knows K. DICK 265:3
Kentish K. Sir Byng BROW 156:20
Kentucky Long ago in K. WARR 803:22
kept k. the faith BIBL 109:23
k. them in thy name BIBL 102:28
What wee k., wee lost EPIT 304:13
kernel this k., This squash SHAK 703:1
kersey honest k. noes SHAK 681:1
Ketch as Jack K.'s wife said DRYD 283:16
kettle back to the tea-k. DISR 268:13
filled with the k.'s breath HILL 376:16
k. and the earthen pot BIBL 91:28
Polly put the k. NURS 550:8
speech is like a cracked k. FLAU 316:7
Kew Go down to K. NOYE 547:5
his Highness' dog at K. POPE 582:26
key golden k. can open PROV 601:21
I keep the k. MONT 526:17
just hands on that golden k. MILT 511:14
k. of India DISR 269:23
k. of knowledge BIBL 99:19
k. of the Union CLAY 220:4
out of k. with his time POUN 589:12
possession of the k. PAIN 563:12
Turn the k. KEAT 430:7
With this k. Shakespeare WORD 831:18
keys half that's got my k. GRAH 348:4
k. of all the creeds TENN 761:1
k. of hell and of death BIBL 111:23
massy k. he bore MILT 513:5
pattered with his k. BYRO 179:14
keystone k. which closeth STRA 744:11
Khatmandu to the north of K. HAYE 365:2
kibosh put the k. on the Kaiser ELLE 298:5
kick first k. I took SPRI 735:11
get no k. from champagne PORT 588:5
great k. at misery LAWR 458:18
k. against the pricks BIBL 103:25
k. his wife out of bed SURT 746:17
k. me downstairs BICK 114:13
k. to come to the top KEAT 431:5
k. you downstairs CARR 189:13
kicked k. it away AGAT 6:16
k. up stairs HALI 358:4
no body to be k. THUR 777:4
kicking flattering, kissing and k. TRUM 784:2
K. you seems the common lot BROW 158:15
kid comeback k. CLIN 221:5
Here's looking at you, k. FILM 311:10
lie down with the k. BIBL 87:4
kiddies k. have crumpled the serviettes BETJ 70:10
kidding k., Mister Hitler PERR 574:2
kidneys k. on a plate HILL 377:4
liked grilled mutton k. JOYC 422:12
kids don't have any k. yourself LARK 453:5
how many k. did you kill POLI 581:14
just a couple of k. OPEN 555:5
kill as k. a good book MILT 519:8
bombers to k. the babies LE G 462:13
half-kisses k. me quite DRAY 279:8
how many kids did you k. POLI 581:14
in every war they k. you in a new way ROGE 632:1
k. a king SHAK 665:13
k. all the lawyers SHAK 672:21
k. a mockingbird LEE 461:20
k. animals and stick in stamps NICO 545:3
k. a wife with kindness SHAK 698:9
k. care SHAK 691:21
K. me to-morrow SHAK 693:24
K. millions of men ROST 635:16
K. not the moth BLAK 117:21
k. sick people MARL 496:17
K. them all ARNA 25:22
k. the patient BACO 43:3
k. us for their sport SHAK 679:15
k. you if you quote it BURG 162:3
K. your parents or relatives I-HS 398:19
Licensed to k. MISQ 521:18
My k. shall be thy kill KIPL 441:3
not to k. anything JAIN 402:7
or I k. you CHAM 201:10
Otherwise k. me MACN 488:14
prepared to k. one another SHAW 707:28
right to k. ADAM 2:9
something you k. for BENN 65:8
Thou shalt not k. BIBL 76:13
Thou shalt not k. CLOU 222:24
time to k. BIBL 84:7
we are going to k. it POWE 590:12
won't k. me COLL 229:5
would k. their church TENN 764:12
killed Better be k. SURT 747:1
Care k. the cat PROV 597:3
Curiosity k. the cat PROV 597:44
don't mind your being k. KITC 442:1
I am the enemy you k. OWEN 562:13
If hate k. men BROW 157:28
I'm k., Sire BROW 156:11
k. in the war POWE 590:19
k. the Bishop YONG 838:14
k. with my own treachery SHAK 667:6
King Harold was k. ANON 22:1
kissed thee ere I k. thee SHAK 694:5
so many people k. AUST 39:7
Suppose Hitler had been k. SCHL 648:19
(who k. him) thought BELL 64:5
killer lover and k. are mingled DOUG 276:16
killeth letter k. BIBL 107:5
killing assert their manhood by k. WAUG 806:16
K. myself SHAK 694:5
K. no murder PROV 605:1
K. no murder SEXB 655:4
k. time Is only the name SITW 721:7
medal for k. two men MATL 501:14
talk of k. time BOUC 144:24
ways of k. a cat PROV 611:46
ways of k. a dog PROV 611:47
ways of k. a dog PROV 611:48
kills grip that k. it TAGO 752:20
K.. all known germs ADVE 7:39
k. the thing he loves WILD 818:32
pace that k. PROV 604:28
pity k. BALZ 52:18
suicide k. two people MILL 509:18
that which k. DE B 254:3
waking that k. us BROW 154:4
Kiltartan My country is K. Cross YEAT 836:9
kilted k. her green kirtle BALL 51:18
kimonos girls in silk k. YEAT 836:6
kin little more than k. SHAK 661:16
makes the whole world k. SHAK 700:17
one's own k. and kith NASH 539:10
kind cruel only to be k. SHAK 665:23
cruel to be k. COMP 230:12
enjoy her while she's k. DRYD 282:34
fordon the lawe of k. CHAU 207:1
for my own k. THOM 773:14
had been k. JOHN 412:17
if ye be k. towards women KORA 444:14
K. are her answers CAMP 184:2
k. as she is fair SHAK 702:29

K. hearts are more than coronets TENN 762:11
k. things I say COWA 239:8
less than k. SHAK 661:16
makes one wond'rous k. GARR 330:5
People will always be k. SASS 645:17
Too k., too kind NIGH 546:1
kindergarten kind of k. ROBI 629:16
kindest k. and the best BURN 167:27
k. man MALO 492:15
k. words I'll ever know RODG 631:4
kindle And k. it LITT 470:3
kindled K. he was, and blasted BYRO 174:20
kindliness cool k. of sheets BROO 150:8
kindly k. fruits of the earth BOOK 127:13
kindness generates k. JOHN 412:4
kill a wife with k. SHAK 698:9
K. in another's trouble GORD 346:19
k. in reserve POPE 583:8
K. only can persuade ROCH 630:5
k. to his Majesty HALL 358:9
milk of human k. GUED 354:11
milk of human k. SHAK 682:1
Of k. and of love WORD 829:2
on the k. of strangers WILL 820:21
spontaneous k. JOHN 416:24
tak a cup o' k. yet BURN 166:12
kindnesses thought of k. done CATU 197:14
kine seven fat k. BIBL 75:13
king a' for our rightfu' K. BURN 167:15
all the k.'s men NURS 548:16
another k., one Jesus BIBL 104:5
As to the K. CHAR 203:4
authority forgets a dying k. TENN 760:12
authority of a K. STRA 744:11
banners of the k. advance FORT 321:7
blessedness alone that makes a K. TRAH 780:17
born K. of the Jews BIBL 92:22
but yesterday a K. BYRO 178:18
cat may look at a k. PROV 597:7
coming of the K. of Heaven ANON 19:19
Conscience as their K. TENN 759:19
constitutional k. BAGE 47:6
Cotton is K. CHRI 212:17
cotton is k. HUGO 393:20
cuts off his k.'s head SHAW 709:2
despised and dying k. SHEL 713:28
divinity doth hedge a k. SHAK 666:6
duty is the k.'s SHAK 671:17
every inch a k. SHAK 679:20
fight for its K. and Country GRAH 348:1
five kings did a k. to death THOM 772:7
follow the K. TENN 759:17
God bless the K. BYRO 173:10
God for K. Charles BROW 156:21
God save k. Solomon BIBL 79:15
God save our gracious k. SONG 729:7
God save the k. BIBL 78:22
God save the k. SHAK 695:20
God save the k. SONG 729:7
government without a k. BANC 53:4
great and mighty k. EPIT 302:14
greater than the K. PITT 576:23
hath eat of a k. SHAK 665:28
have served the K. WOLS 826:5
heaven's matchless k. MILT 516:8
He played the K. FIEL 309:10
He that plays the k. SHAK 663:19
Honour the k. BIBL 110:30
If the K. asks you ATTL 32:7
illiterate k. HENR 370:8
image of the K. TENN 759:23
in the K.'s throne BENT 66:19
kill a k. SHAK 665:13
K. and country need you MILI 508:17
K. asked the Queen MILN 510:18
k. can do no wrong BLAC 117:4
k. can do no wrong PROV 605:2
K. Charles's head DICK 261:22
K. David and King Solomon NAYL 539:24
k. delighteth to honour BIBL 80:33
K. enjoys his own again PARK 567:18
k. had given me Paris ANON 20:13
K. Harold was killed ANON 22:1
K. in Babylon HENL 370:2
k. indeed CHAP 202:14
k. is always a king WOLL 825:20
k. is a thing men have made SELD 653:19
k. is but a man SHAK 671:15
k. is strongest BIBL 90:26
k. is truly *parens patriae* JAME 402:15
k. loved his people WILL 820:3
k. never dies BLAC 117:2
K., observing with judicious TRAP 781:1
K. of all these the dead HOME 382:11
k. of banks and stones KAVA 426:11
K. of England cannot enter PITT 576:20
K. of England's eyes LAST 456:12
K. of glory BOOK 133:3
K. of glory now NOEL 546:12
K. of Great Britain REED 624:4
K. of heaven LYTE 481:1
k. of infinite space SHAK 663:17
k. of intimate delights COWP 242:1
k. of kings BIBL 113:3
K. of love BAKE 48:13
k. of shreds and patches SHAK 665:19
k. of the castle NURS 548:20
K. OF THE JEWS BIBL 102:33
K. of tremendous majesty MISS 523:5
K. of Yvetot BÉRA 67:14
k. over himself SHEL 713:14
K. over the Water TOAS 778:4
K. refused a lesser sacrifice MARY 500:9
k. reigns THIE 770:18
k.'s a bawcock SHAK 671:12
King's a K. DRAY 278:23
k.'s chaff is worth PROV 605:3
k.'s daugher o' Noroway BALL 51:14
K.'s daughter BOOK 134:16
k.'s English SHAK 688:32
k. sits in Dunfermline BALL 51:13
k. sits in Dunfermline OPEN 555:29
K.'s life moving peacefully DAWS 253:8
K.'s Moll Reno'd NEWS 544:12
k.'s name SHAK 696:28
K. thought mair o' Marie BALL 51:8
K. to have things done as cheap PEPY 573:1
K. to Oxford sent BROW 154:7
k. was in his counting-house NURS 550:18
k. was much moved BIBL 79:11
K. was much pleased EDGE 289:1
lay on the k. SHAK 671:18
leave without the k. ELIZ 298:2
lessened my esteem of a k. PEPY 572:22
Lord is K. BOOK 138:2
loses the k. in the tyrant MAYH 502:21
man who would be k. KIPL 441:16
Moloch, horrid k. MILT 514:24
My dead k. JOYC 422:1
my K. and my God BOOK 137:11
my life to make you K. CHAR 203:11
neck of the last k. DIDE 267:2
No bishop, no K. JAME 402:13
no k. can govern ROCH 630:2
no k. in Israel BIBL 78:9
Northcliffe has sent for the K. ANON 16:13
not offended the k. LAST 457:10
not so much a k. SELL 654:11
Og the k. of Basan BOOK 141:5
once and future k. MALO 492:16
one eyed man is k. PROV 604:1
open The k.'s eyes SHAK 673:8
oure k. wes dede WYNT 834:16
Ozymandias, k. of kings SHEL 713:1
passing brave to be a k. MARL 496:25
rightwise K. MALO 492:7
Ruin seize thee, ruthless K. GRAY 350:2
sang a k. out of three kingdoms WHAR 813:6
shake hands with a k. HALL 358:9
smote the k. of Israel BIBL 80:11
speaks ill of your k. NELS 540:13
still am I k. of those SHAK 695:22
stomach of a k. ELIZ 296:27
stood for his K. BROW 156:20
thy k. is a child BIBL 84:25
To be a Pirate K. GILB 339:2
What is a K. PRIO 593:3
What must the k. do SHAK 695:14
whatsoever K. shall reign SONG 729:12
When I am k. NURS 549:2
With a k.'s son SURR 746:11
you must not be a k. CHAR 203:2
your K. and your Country RUBE 637:3
zeal I served my k. SHAK 673:17
kingdom but to mock the k. PYM 618:8
comest into thy k. BIBL 100:27
enter into the k. of heaven BIBL 93:8
found a k. MILT 518:6
His mind his k. COWP 242:16
into the k. of heaven BIBL 96:7
k. against kingdom BIBL 97:1
k. by the sea POE 579:10
k. for a little grave SHAK 695:14
k. for it was too small SHAK 669:13
k. of God BIBL 93:26
k. of God BIBL 96:15
k. of God BIBL 101:16
k. of God is within you BIBL 100:12
k. of heaven BIBL 93:3
k. of heaven BIBL 95:22
k. of heaven is at hand BIBL 92:26
k. of the shore SHAK 704:26
k. of the well SONT 728:9
k. shall pass SWIN 751:6
k. stretch from shore to shore WATT 805:18
mind to me a k. is DYER 286:13
my k. for a horse SHAK 696:33
My k., safeliest DONN 272:16
of such is the k. of God BIBL 98:10
thine is the k. BIBL 93:19
Thy k. come BIBL 93:19
voice of the k. SWIF 747:13
kingdoms all the k. of the world BIBL 92:34
all the k. of the world BIBL 98:28
goodly states and k. KEAT 429:20
K. are clay SHAK 656:8
out of three k. WHAR 813:6
kingfish call me the K. LONG 473:6
kingly K. conclaves stern SHEL 713:7
k. crop DAVI 251:12
kings all be as happy as k. STEV 742:12
All k. shall fall down BOOK 136:18
bind their k. in chains BOOK 142:2
captains and the k. KIPL 440:3
castles of k. HORA 387:16
Conquering k. CHAN 201:11
death of k. SHAK 695:9
dominion of k. changed PRIC 591:9
end of k. DEFO 255:16
five K. left FARO 307:3
heart of k. BIBL 83:17
keep even k. in awe D'AV 251:7
k. and counsellors BIBL 81:4
k. are not only God's lieutenants JAME 402:14
k. crept out again BROW 154:14
K.' daughters BOOK 134:15
k. haul up the lumps BREC 147:20
k. have cares GREE 352:4
K. have long arms PROV 605:4
k. have sat down BIBL 91:25
k. is mostly rapscallions TWAI 786:4
K. may be blest BURN 168:12
k. of the earth BIBL 112:6
k. of the earth BOOK 134:24
k. that fear SHAK 672:28
K. will be tyrants BURK 163:24
K. with their armies BOOK 136:7
K. would not play at COWP 242:5
last of the k. strangled MESL 506:5
laws or k. JOHN 411:12
laws or k. can cause GOLD 345:11
lays his icy hand on k. SHIR 717:8
madness their k. commit HORA 386:13
Mad world! mad k. SHAK 677:7

kings (*cont.*):
meaner creatures k. SHAK 696:27
Of cabbages—and k. CARR 190:20
Physicians are like k. WEBS 808:3
poet k. KEAT 430:5
politeness of k. LOUI 476:5
prophets and k. have desired BIBL 99:10
puller down of k. SHAK 673:1
Right Divine of K. POPE 580:20
ruined sides of k. BEAU 58:14
ruin k. DRYD 279:20
Showers on her k. MILT 515:7
So many English k. SHAK 670:15
sport of k. D'AV 251:10
sport of k. SOME 727:17
sport of k. SURT 746:16
Vain the ambition of k. WEBS 807:19
walk with K. KIPL 439:3
War is the trade of k. DRYD 281:31
kinship crimson thread of k. PARK 567:20
kinsmen k. die ANON 22:4
Kipling K. and his views AUDE 34:3
Rudyards cease from k. STEP 738:1
kirtle kilted her green k. BALL 51:18
Near is my k. PROV 607:21
kiss Ae fond k. BURN 166:9
But k.: one kiss SHAK 660:19
Close with her, k. her SWIN 751:16
clung into a k. BYRO 176:15
Colder thy k. BYRO 179:18
coward does it with a k. WILD 818:32
die upon a k. SHAK 694:5
Fain would I k. HERR 374:18
holy k. BIBL 105:25
I k. his dirty shoe SHAK 671:12
immortal with a k. MARL 496:5
k. a bonnie lass BURN 168:19
k. again with tears TENN 765:13
k., a sigh CRAS 244:14
k. but in the cup JONS 420:20
k. can be a comma MIST 523:9
k. is still a kiss HUPF 396:10
Kiss K. Bang Bang KAEL 425:6
k. me and never no more MALO 492:14
K. me, Hardy NELS 541:2
K. me Kate SHAK 698:8
k. my ass in Macy's window JOHN 408:18
k. of the sun for pardon GURN 355:2
k. on the hand ROBI 629:9
K. the book's outside COWP 240:4
k. the Managing Director WHIT 814:20
k. the place to make it well TAYL 756:12
k. the rod SHAK 702:25
last lamenting k. DONN 273:27
let me k. that hand SHAK 679:22
let us k. and part DRAY 279:3
O! a k. Long as my exile SHAK 660:14
rough male k. of blankets BROO 150:8
saw you take his k. PATM 569:19
she took the k. sedately TENN 764:3
souls did never k. KEAT 427:1
sweetly did me k. WYAT 834:6
take occasion to k. SHAK 659:19
Then come k. me SHAK 701:10
wanting to k. me MACD 485:2
With one long k. TENN 758:19
Wouldst k. me pretty HART 363:8
kissed hasn't been k. MILI 508:12
k. each other BOOK 137:15
k. his sad Andromache CORN 237:1
k. my first woman TOSC 780:1
k. thee ere I killed thee SHAK 694:5
k. the fiddler's wife BURN 168:3
K. the girls NURS 548:7
never k. an ugly girl EPIT 303:2
wist, before I k. BALL 52:9
kisses fine romance with no k. FIEL 310:16
forgotten my k. SWIN 751:8
Give me a thousand k. CATU 197:3
k. are his daily feast LODG 472:17
k. of his mouth BIBL 85:6
Love's mart of k. CHAP 202:17
more than k. DONN 274:22
played At cards for k. LYLY 480:14
Stolen k. HUNT 395:16
sweet k., pigeon-wise DIAN 260:8
These poor half-k. DRAY 279:8
kissing die with k. MARL 497:1
I wasn't k. her MARX 499:10
K. don't last MERE 505:16
K. goes by favour PROV 605:5
k. had to stop BROW 158:10
k.'s out of fashion PROV 614:29
K. with golden face SHAK 704:17
k. your hand LOOS 475:11
like k. God BRUC 158:18
wonder who's k. her ADAM 2:5
kit have a K.-Kat ADVE 7:24
old k.-bag MILI 508:16
kitchen better mind the k. FITZ 315:4
get out of the k. PROV 603:29
get out of the k. TRUM 784:3
ghastly k. BERN 69:7
in the k. bred BYRO 179:2
K.-cabals, and nursery-mishaps CRAB 242:22
send me to eat in the k. HUGH 392:17
whip in k. cups STEV 739:20
kite not sufficient for a k.'s dinner QUAR 618:14
kitten I had rather be a k. SHAK 668:20
kittens Three little k. NURS 551:11
Wanton k. make sober PROV 613:38
kitty K., a fair, but frozen maid GARR 330:8
Kjartan killed K. ANON 22:5
kleine eine k. Pause LAST 456:18
Klondike beer of a man in K. CHES 210:21
knappeth k. the spear in sunder BOOK 134:20
knave epithet for a k. MACA 481:14
k. is not punished HALI 358:1
K. of Hearts he stole NURS 550:10
makes an honest man a k. DEFO 255:3
man must be supposed a k. HUME 395:4
slipper and subtle k. SHAK 692:13
To feed the titled k. BURN 169:4
knaves calls the k., Jacks DICK 262:18
fools and k. BUCK 159:13
k. and thieves SHAK 702:22
k. in place DEFO 255:7
Knebworth Has God played K. GALL 328:16
knee blude to the k. BALL 52:2
civility of my k. BROW 153:12
down on one k. CALL 181:14
Every k. shall bow NOEL 546:12
every k. should bow BIBL 108:17
head on his k. BARH 54:9
little abune her k. BALL 51:18
kneel k. and adore him MONS 526:12
k. before him BOOK 136:18
k. before the Lord our Maker BOOK 138:6
k. for peace SHAK 698:15
kneeling meekly k. BOOK 129:15
knees body between your k. CORY 237:11
confirm the feeble k. BIBL 87:22
creeps rustling to her k. KEAT 427:10
heart, not in the k. JERR 407:3
I bow my k. BIBL 107:27
I don't really like k. SAIN 641:14
live on your k. IBAR 398:3
knell hourly ring his k. SHAK 698:27
it is a k. SHAK 683:2
k. of parting day GRAY 350:6
like a rising k. BYRO 174:13
their k. is rung COLL 229:10
knew If you looked away, you k. SERE 654:22
I k. almost as much JOHN 413:12
I k. that once STEP 737:20
Johnny, I hardly k. ye BALL 50:20
k. it best BACO 42:11
K. YOU HAD IT IN YOU TELE 758:5
told what he k. AMIS 13:13
world k. him not BIBL 101:6
knife cannibal uses k. and fork LEC 461:11
deadly k. Long aimed FANS 306:9
k. is lost in it SHEL 712:2
k. see not the wound SHAK 682:4
k. that probes far deeper FORS 320:19
my oyster k. HURS 396:11
smylere with the k. CHAU 205:19
walk on a k. edge MONT 528:6
War to the k. PALA 564:10
knight as the armèd k. ASKE 30:20
courteoust k. MALO 492:15
Fearless, blameless k. ANON 20:4
gentle k. was pricking SPEN 733:12
k. at arms KEAT 428:7
k.-errantry *is* religion CERV 199:18
k. like the young Lochinvar SCOT 651:8
K. of the Doleful Countenance CERV 199:16
k. shall not be whole MALO 492:8
k. was indeed a valiant Gent EVEL 305:4
monk and a k. HENR 370:13
new-slain k. BALL 52:5
red-cross k. for ever kneeled TENN 762:16
that was your k. CLOS 222:11
verray, parfit gentil k. CHAU 204:9
knighthoods MBEs and your k. KEAT 426:12
knights ladies dead and lovely k. SHAK 705:9
lances of ancient k. ROOT 633:14
knit k. together thine elect BOOK 128:22
life to k. me HOUS 391:4
knits k. man to man SICK 717:16
Sleep that k. up SHAK 683:8
knitter beautiful little k. SITW 721:5
knitters k. in the sun SHAK 701:20
knives night of the long k. HITL 378:5
knock k., and it shall be opened BIBL 94:3
K. as you please POPE 582:25
K. at a star HERR 374:4
k. at the door LAMB 448:14
k., breathe, shine DONN 272:24
k. him down first JOHN 415:15
k. is open wide SMAR 722:11
nice k.-down argument CARR 191:2
right to k. him down JOHN 416:13
stand at the door, and k. BIBL 111:29
when you k. COWP 240:3
knocked ruin that Cromwell k. about BEDF 60:20
we k. the bastard off HILL 377:5
what they k. down FENT 308:8
knocker Tie up the k. POPE 583:1
knocking Here's a k., indeed SHAK 683:13
k. at Preferment's door ARNO 27:5
K. on the moonlit door DE L 256:15
K. on the moonlit door OPEN 555:21
knocks k. you down with the butt GOLD 345:31
never k. twice PROV 609:11
knot crowned k. of fire ELIO 294:20
k. intrinsicate Of life SHAK 658:2
political k. BIER 114:19
So the k. be unknotted ELIO 293:26
knots pokers into true-love k. COLE 226:2
knotted Sat and k. SEDL 653:3
knotty moorish, and wild, and k. BRON 149:18
know all I k. is what I read ROGE 631:21
all we k. WALL 800:11
all ye need to k. KEAT 429:1
Better the devil you k. PROV 596:12
does not k. himself LA F 447:12
do not pretend to k. DARR 250:11
don't k. can't hurt you PROV 614:11
don't k. what I'm doing BRAU 147:7
fear, To be we k. not what DRYD 281:2
find out what you don't k. WELL 809:22
go we k. not where SHAK 686:18
hate any one that we k. HAZL 365:22
He must k. sumpin' HAMM 358:22
his place k. him BIBL 81:11
How do they k. PARK 567:13
How little do we k. BYRO 177:30
I do not k. myself GOET 343:18
I k. nothing SOCR 726:21
I k. not the Lord BIBL 75:32

I k. not the man BIBL 97:26
I k. thee not, old man SHAK 670:22
k. a man seven years PROV 616:6
k. a man who can ADVE 7:10
k., and not be known COLT 230:4
k. a thing or two MOLI 524:20
k. better what is good for people JAY 404:14
k. enough of hate FROS 325:21
k. everything MOLI 525:15
k. Him, love him CATE 194:5
k. it to be poetry THOR 775:28
k. more of mankind JOHN 417:8
k. not what they do BIBL 100:26
k. our will is free JOHN 414:2
k. that I am God BOOK 134:20
k. that my redeemer liveth BIBL 81:22
k. that you know not BACO 42:26
K. then thyself POPE 585:19
k. the place ELIO 294:17
k. the world YOUN 839:11
K. this to be thus JAIN 402:9
K. thyself PROV 605:6
k. to know no more MILT 516:26
K. what I mean, Harry BRUN 159:2
k. what I think WALL 799:17
k. what we are talking about RUSS 639:19
k. you're . . . God BARN 55:5
K. you the land GOET 343:12
let me k. mine end BOOK 133:29
master of those who k. DANT 249:11
men naturally desire to k. AUCT 33:10
merely k. more SAKI 642:8
More people k. Tom Fool PROV 607:7
never k. what you can do PROV 615:47
no one to k. ANON 15:21
not k. what they have said CHUR 214:19
not k. where he is going LIN 469:17
nought did k. DAVI 251:16
others that we k. not of SHAK 664:4
say, 'I k. not' TALM 754:2
Tell me what you k. EMER 300:1
that kan hymselven k. CHAU 205:29
things they didn't k. POUN 589:11
those who do not wish to k. RALE 621:10
thought so once; but now I k. it EPIT 303:12
to k. a little BACO 44:11
To k. all is to forgive all PROV 613:9
To k. this only MILT 518:9
What do I k. MONT 528:1
what should they k. of England KIPL 438:12
what we would, we k. ARNO 26:3
You k. more than you think SPOC 735:1
you k. who ADVE 8:9
you'll never k. ARMS 25:17
you'll never k. MISQ 522:1
you yourselves do k. SHAK 676:10
knowed all that there is to be k. GRAH 348:10
knower How can the K. be known UPAN 787:12
knowest k. all things BIBL 103:10
k. my down-sitting BOOK 141:9
thou k. not BIBL 83:27
knoweth k. not God BIBL 111:13
knowing Bewrapt past k. HARD 361:20
lust of k. FLEC 317:4
misfortune of k. anything AUST 38:4
one who INSISTS on k. POUN 590:4
With a k. ignorance JOHN 407:16
knowingly Never k. undersold ADVE 8:2
knowledge After such k., what forgiveness ELIO 294:22
all k. BIBL 106:16
all k. to be my province BACO 44:28
All our k. is POPE 586:5
bars To perfect k. BYRO 176:2
Benevolent K. BORG 143:4
bring home k. JOHN 416:1
communicate k. DE Q 258:9
Debarred from k. CHUD 213:8
desire more love and k. SHAK 658:9
dissemble sometimes your k. BACO 42:26
dotage of k. JACK 400:16
envied kind of k. ADAM 3:12
five ports of k. BROW 152:14
follow k. like a sinking star TENN 767:10
follow virtue and k. DANT 249:17
Friendship from k. BUSS 171:5
identical with his k. MAIM 491:8
increaseth k. BIBL 84:5
in the way of k. LOCK 471:12
key of k. BIBL 99:19
k. and wonder BACO 41:6
K. comes TENN 763:6
k. denied from senses SA'A 641:1
K. dwells In heads COWP 242:6
K. enormous KEAT 427:30
k. in mathematics BACO 45:16
k. in the making MILT 519:17
k. is bought CLOU 221:18
k. is dangerous HUXL 397:14
K. is of two kinds JOHN 415:4
K. is power PROV 605:7
K. is proud COWP 242:7
k. is transmitted BLAK 119:29
k. itself is power BACO 44:30
k., it shall vanish away BIBL 106:16
K. may give weight CHES 209:22
k. of a lifetime WHIS 813:21
k. of causes BACO 45:1
k. of God LEIB 462:20
k. of good and evil BIBL 73:18
K. of good and evil COWP 241:7
k. of human nature AUST 38:2
k. of man is as the waters BACO 41:12
k. of nature HOLB 380:17
k. of nature WHEW 813:13
k. of nothing DICK 265:20
k. of the extinction PALI 564:16
k. of the Lord BIBL 87:5
k. of the world CHES 209:7
k. of truth BACO 44:18
k. puffeth up BIBL 106:7
k. shall be increased BIBL 90:8
k. that they are so OSBO 559:17
k. was divine TRAH 780:11
k. we have lost in information ELIO 295:21
k. when the day was done KEAT 428:3
k. which they cannot lose OPPE 557:3
k. without integrity JOHN 411:2
Language and *k.* SULL 745:14
Let k. grow TENN 760:21
literature of *k.* DE Q 258:12
little k. is dangerous PROV 605:38
make k. available BLAC 116:20
never better than k. FERM 309:3
no k. but I know it BEEC 61:9
No man's k. LOCK 471:15
objects of k. PLAT 578:7
O fret not after k. KEAT 430:2
organized k. SPEN 732:1
Out-topping k. ARNO 27:13
passeth k. BIBL 107:28
price for k. TICK 777:11
province of k. to speak HOLM 381:6
raising us to k. LEIB 462:21
show of k. DOUG 276:21
Sorrow is k. BYRO 178:13
spirit of k. BIBL 87:3
Such k. is too wonderful BOOK 141:10
touchstone of k. AUCT 33:13
tree of diabolical k. SHER 715:25
tree of the k. BIBL 73:19
Unto this k. DONN 273:28
What is all k. CARL 187:8
words without k. BIBL 81:30
You seek for k. SHEL 710:6
known all that is k. NEWM 542:14
child is k. by his doings BIBL 83:9
devil where he is k. JOHN 411:22
don't choose to have it k. CHES 209:25
even as also I am k. BIBL 106:16
hast thou not k. me BIBL 102:19
Have ye not k. BIBL 88:4
heard and k. BOOK 137:3
How can the Knower be k. UPAN 787:12
If you would be k. COLT 230:4
k. and the unknown PINT 576:13
k. by company he keeps PROV 606:15
k. no more than other men AUBR 32:13
k. too late SHAK 697:8
k. unto God EPIT 304:5
more you 'ave k. o' the others KIPL 439:7
safer than a k. way HASK 363:16
then the end is k. SHAK 676:31
thy way may be k. BOOK 136:3
till I am k. JOHN 412:17
tree is k. by its fruit PROV 613:17
knows Every schoolboy k. MACA 482:7
has a mind and k. it SHAW 706:13
He k. nothing SHAW 707:27
if you k. of a better 'ole BAIR 48:11
knows about it all—HE k. FITZ 314:16
k. even his Bible ARNO 28:13
k. that all-highest Brahman UPAN 788:6
K. Things MILN 511:6
k. what he fights for CROM 245:9
less one k. LAO 452:1
sits in the middle and k. FROS 326:10
who k. does not speak LAO 452:3
knuckle k.-end of England SMIT 725:13
knucklebones harmless art of k. STEV 740:21
koompartoo make a K. BURN 169:12
Kopf *K. zum Greise* MÜLL 536:4
Koran By the glorious K. KORA 445:12
K. was sent down KORA 443:18
not ponder the K. KORA 444:11
Kosciuszko Freedom shrieked—as K. fell CAMP 183:14
Kraken K. sleepeth TENN 762:8
Krorluppia Nasticreechia K. LEAR 460:11
Kruger killing K. with your mouth KIPL 438:1
Kubla In Xanadu did K. Khan COLE 225:20
Kunst *In der K.* GOET 343:6
Kurtz Mistah K.—he dead CONR 234:14
Kyrie *K. eleison* MISS 520:12

label without a rag of a l. HUXL 397:10
labels l. serving to give a name TOLS 779:11
labor *hic l. est* VIRG 794:17
laboratory guinea pigs in the l. of God WILL 820:14
laborem *spectare l.* LUCR 479:3
laborious Studious of l. ease COWP 241:29
labour all his l. BIBL 83:39
all ye that l. BIBL 95:9
brow of l. BRYA 159:3
daily L. to pursue WESL 811:3
done to the L. Party TAWN 756:2
Don't let L. ruin it POLI 581:25
full of l. BIBL 84:2
Great is l. TALM 754:13
I l. for peace BOOK 140:11
In l. there is profit BIBL 82:32
insupportable l. STEE 736:15
l. against our own cure BROW 154:1
l. and not to ask IGNA 398:17
l. and sorrow BOOK 137:19
l. bears a lovely face DEKK 256:5
l. for my travail SHAK 700:4
l. in his vocation SHAK 667:21
l.-intensive industry WILS 822:5
L. isn't working POLI 581:22
l. of love BIBL 109:7
l. of my hands THOR 776:7
l. of women in the house GILM 339:15
l. of your life MONT 527:9
L. Party owes more to Methodism PHIL 575:13
L.'s call POLI 581:12
L.'s double whammy POLI 581:23
[L.] the natural party WILS 821:17
l. we delight in SHAK 683:16
L. without joy is base RUSK 638:23
life all l. be TENN 763:13

labour (*cont.*):
Love l. and hate mastery TALM 753:13
many still must l. BYRO 175:13
mental l. employed REYN 625:8
never visualised l. WEBB 806:26
New L., new danger POLI 581:26
reward of l. is life MORR 532:18
right leader for the L. Party BEVA 71:21
Six days shalt thou l. BIBL 76:11
sore l.'s bath SHAK 683:8
spend your l. BIBL 88:20
their l. is but lost BOOK 140:21
to live without l. TAWN 755:16
true success is to l. STEV 741:25
We l. soon BURN 169:4
with difficulty and l. MILT 516:1
youth of l. GOLD 344:9
laboured fine, but as much l. WALP 801:15
l. more abundantly BIBL 106:20
labourer l. is worthy of his hire BIBL 99:8
l. to take his pension RUSK 639:1
l. worthy of hire PROV 605:8
labourers l. are few BIBL 94:30
l. are idle TALM 753:16
labouring l. man, that tills OXFO 562:15
sleep of a l. man BIBL 84:12
to the l. man BUNY 161:7
women l. of child BOOK 127:11
labours Children sweeten l. BACO 43:25
completed l. are pleasant CICE 217:11
line too l. POPE 584:23
no l. tire JOHN 411:15
rest from their l. BIBL 112:26
laburnums L., dropping-wells of fire TENN 761:21
labyrinth peopled l. of walls SHEL 712:5
labyrinthical perplexed, l. soul DONN 275:12
labyrinthine down the l. ways THOM 774:4
l. buds the rose BROW 158:2
lac *sine dolo l. concupiscite* BIBL 114:11
lace l. my bodice blue HUNT 396:7
Nottingham l. of the curtains BETJ 70:4
lacessit *Nemo me impune l.* MOTT 535:10
lack can I l. nothing BOOK 132:26
l. of many a thing SHAK 704:16
lions do l. BOOK 133:21
lacked questioning, If I l. any thing HERB 372:22
lacking nothing is l. LEON 464:15
lacrimae *Hinc illae l.* TERE 768:1
Sunt l. rerum VIRG 793:13
lacy l. sleeve with vitriol WOOL 827:7
lad l. does not care JOHN 413:23
l. that is gone STEV 742:23
ladder behold a l. BIBL 75:1
dropping down the l. KIPL 438:18
l. of our vices AUGU 36:13
path of the celestial l. HEIK 368:1
traffic of Jacob's l. THOM 774:13
Wiv a l. BATE 57:3
ladders Crosses are l. PROV 597:43
Holy One makes l. MIDR 507:10
where all the l. start YEAT 835:9
laden heavy l. BIBL 95:9
ladies from a l.' seminary GILB 338:4
Gentlemen and L. DICK 266:19
good for l. PROV 600:12
In praise of l. dead SHAK 705:9
l. declare war on me LOUI 476:2
l.' favours SHAK 672:5
l., God bless them SAYE 646:7
l. intellectual BYRO 175:28
L., just a little TREE 781:4
l. of St James's DOBS 271:16
l. should ever sit down MORE 531:3
l. to please AUST 37:15
Ladies were l. RAVE 622:8
lion among l. SHAK 689:29
made the carlines l. JAME 402:18
may the l. sit BALL 51:16
remember the l. ADAM 1:18
seminaries of young l. KNOX 442:17
way the l. ride NURS 551:8
worth any number of old l. FAUL 308:1
young l. entered SURT 747:4
ladles from the cooks' own l. BROW 157:10
lads Come lasses and l. SONG 729:3
Golden l. and girls SHAK 661:1
l. in their hundreds HOUS 391:1
l. that will never be old HOUS 391:1
lady bird than a l. RICH 627:1
called her his l. fair KIPL 440:16
elderly l., who mutters away CARE 186:17
full-blown l. CLOU 221:12
Here lies a l. RANS 621:20
I met a l. KEAT 428:9
Joan as my L. HERR 374:15
l. doth protest too much SHAK 664:23
l. fair BALL 52:5
l. in a cage CHES 210:19
L. Look owre BALL 50:10
l. loved a swine NURS 551:4
l. loves Milk Tray ADVE 7:6
l. of a 'certain age' BYRO 177:12
l. of Christ's College AUBR 32:17
L. of Shalott TENN 762:15
L. of Spain REAV 623:9
l.'s in the case GAY 332:8
l.-smocks all silver-white SHAK 681:3
l.'s not for burning FRY 326:21
l.'s not for turning THAT 769:24
l. sweet and kind ANON 19:2
l. that's known as Lou SERV 655:2
L. with a Lamp LONG 474:9
Liner she's a l. KIPL 439:11
little l. comes by GAY 332:24
lovely l., garmented SHEL 714:16
My L. Bountiful FARQ 307:6
ne'er wan A l. BURN 168:25
Our L. of Pain SWIN 750:16
our L. of the Snows KIPL 439:19
saw my l. weep ANON 17:3
talk like a l. SHAW 709:11
to be called First L. ONAS 554:17
To see a fine l. NURS 550:12
What l. would not love GREE 352:4
why the l. is a tramp HART 363:6
ladybird L., ladybird NURS 549:1
Lafayette *L., nous voilà* STAN 736:7
lag l.-end of my life SHAK 669:4
laggard l. in love SCOT 651:9
laid I am l. in earth TATE 755:7
to get l. GELD 332:27
when I'm l. by thee HERR 374:22
where they have l. him BIBL 102:40
laily l. worm BALL 50:21
lain There hath he l. for ages TENN 762:9
laisser-faire *de l.* QUES 618:23
L. ARGE 24:5
laissez-faire *L.* ANON 20:7
laity conspiracies against the l. SHAW 707:4
tell the l. our love DONN 274:19
lake l. water lapping YEAT 836:12
slips into the l. of the lake TENN 766:3
with a l. of fire FLEC 317:5
lama Eli, Eli, l. sabachthani BIBL 97:29
lamb Behold the L. of God BIBL 101:10
fell down before the L. BIBL 112:3
for a sheep as a l. PROV 608:49
goes out like a l. PROV 606:28
he who made the L. BLAK 121:10
holy L. of God BLAK 120:1
holy sacrificial L. CONS 235:5
l. shall be without blemish BIBL 75:38
l. to the slaughter BIBL 88:17
leads me to the L. COWP 240:21
Little L. who made thee BLAK 120:17
Mary had a little l. HALE 357:4
O L. of God, I come ELLI 298:10
one little ewe l. BIBL 79:5
Pipe a song about a L. BLAK 120:12
provide himself a l. BIBL 74:32
skin of an innocent l. SHAK 672:22
tempers wind to shorn l. PROV 601:19
to the shorn l. STER 738:11
white in the blood of the L. BIBL 112:10
wolf shall dwell with the l. BIBL 87:4
Worthy the L. that died WATT 805:12
wrath of the L. BIBL 112:6
yokèd with a l. SHAK 676:26
lambs as twinned l. SHAK 702:32
Feed my l. BIBL 103:8
gather the l. BIBL 88:2
l. who've lost our way KIPL 438:17
lame feet was I to the l. BIBL 81:26
L. dogs over stiles KING 437:5
l. man BIBL 87:23
relieve a l. beggar SHAK 698:32
Science without religion is l. EINS 290:8
lamentation l., and weeping BIBL 92:25
must be no l. SAPP 644:16
lamented ye have not l. BIBL 95:7
laments forest l. CHUR 214:12
Lammastide fell about the L. BALL 50:7
lamp Lady with a L. LONG 474:9
l. is shattered SHEL 712:3
l. of day DOUG 276:12
lift my l. LAZA 459:12
Slaves of the L. ARNO 25:23
too strong of the l. STER 738:22
unlit l. BROW 158:4
lampada *vitai l.* LUCR 479:4
lamp post leaning on a l. GAY 332:24
lamp posts drunken man uses l. LANG 450:12
lamprey surfeit by eating of a l. FABY 305:22
lamps Heav'n's great l. CAMP 183:21
l. are going out all over Europe GREY 353:5
Life not a series of gig l. WOOL 826:14
[monks] should live as l. PALI 564:18
old l. for new ARAB 23:6
women . . . who are the l. LAWS 459:7
Lancashire L. merchants CHES 210:21
Lancaster time-honoured L. SHAK 694:8
Lancelot reading for pleasure about L. DANT 249:13
land by sea as by l. GILB 337:3
Ceres re-assume the l. POPE 583:25
empire of the l. RICH 627:12
Every l. has its own law PROV 599:28
fat of the l. BIBL 75:18
from l. to land COLE 226:26
Grab this l. MORR 533:4
heavenly l. from ours WATT 805:17
house and l. are gone PROV 614:20
if by l., one REVE 624:18
Ill fares the l. GOLD 344:8
I see l. TENN 767:17
l. flowing with milk BIBL 75:28
l. God gave to Cain CART 192:18
l. of counterpane STEV 742:13
l. of darkness BIBL 81:12
L. of Heart's Desire YEAT 836:13
L. of Hope and Glory BENS 66:13
l. of lost content HOUS 391:5
l. of my fathers JAME 402:21
l. of my fathers THOM 772:20
l. of pure delight WATT 805:16
l. of such dear souls SHAK 694:19
l. of the free KEY 434:16
l. of the living BIBL 88:18
l. of vainglory BUNY 160:16
L. that I love BERL 68:7
l. was ours before FROS 326:1
L. where my fathers died SMIT 724:16
l. . . . where the light BIBL 81:13
l. you no longer recognize AMIS 14:5
lane to the l. of the dead AUDE 33:19
more precious than l. SADA 641:7
nakedness of the l. BIBL 75:16
no l. unhabitable THOR 776:20
no yard of l. ANON 22:2
one if by l. LONG 474:16
One Law, one L. KIPL 440:15
Ours is the l. MAYA 502:19

piece of l. HORA 389:24
possessed his l. BIBL 76:27
prepared the dry l. BOOK 138:6
ready by water as by l. ELST 298:17
seems a moving l. MILT 517:7
seen the promised l. KING 436:16
splendid and a happy l. GOLD 344:16
spy out the l. BIBL 76:25
that pleasant l. BOOK 139:10
There's the l., or cherry-isle HERR 374:5
They love their l. HALL 358:9
think there is no l. BACO 41:13
This l. is your land GUTH 355:7
to enjoy thy l. SHAK 677:5
travel by l. or by water BOOK 127:11
Unhappy the l. that needs heroes BREC 147:10
windy sea of l. MILT 516:4
Woe to the l. SHAK 696:19
landed l. with an idea BIRT 115:14
landing fight on the l. grounds CHUR 215:10
landlord l., fill the flowing bowl SONG 729:2
paid to the l. RICA 626:2
Sir Roger is l. ADDI 5:2
landlubbers l. lying down below SONG 729:15
landmark Remove not the ancient l. BIBL 83:15
lands envy of less happier l. SHAK 694:19
Find other l. THOM 775:12
sound is gone out into all l. BOOK 132:15
take us l. away DICK 266:10
though not of l. WOTT 832:24
landscape gardening is but l.-painting POPE 587:22
In Claude's l. CONS 235:8
l. is deformed THOR 776:1
l. of England AUST 37:21
l. of the world YOUN 839:10
part in a l. CHEK 208:13
Who owns this l. MCCA 483:18
landscapes abstract of several l. BOWE 145:15
landslide pay for a l. KENN 433:7
lane l. to the land of the dead AUDE 33:19
long l. that has no turning PROV 604:3
lanes streets and l. of the city BIBL 99:29
lang For auld l. syne BURN 166:12
How L., O Lord BULL 160:2
language any l. you choose GILB 337:18
best chosen l. AUST 38:2
broke through l. BROW 157:19
by means of l. WITT 824:3
clear and beautiful l. EMPS 300:10
cool web of l. GRAV 349:12
dear l. that I spake MACA 482:24
divided by a common l. MISQ 521:10
don't know the l. AMIS 14:5
enemy of clear l. ORWE 559:9
enlargement of the l. JOHN 409:5
entrance into the l. BACO 44:14
everything else in our l. MACA 482:15
except, of course, l. WILD 817:11
from one l. to another SHEL 714:20
from one l. to another UNAM 787:7
In l., the ignorant DUPP 285:17
in l. there are only differences SAUS 646:2
In such lovely l. LAWR 458:16
in the same l. QUIN 619:7
l. all nations understand BEHN 62:15
l. and ways of behaving JUVE 424:9
l. an opera is sung in APPL 23:3
l., by your skill made pliant GAY 332:11
l. can be compared SAUS 646:3
l. charged with meaning POUN 590:5
l. chiefly made by men HARD 360:10
L. grows out of life SULL 745:14
l. I have learned SHAK 694:11
l. in her eye SHAK 700:20
L. is a form of human reason LÉVI 466:12
L. is called the garment CARL 188:12
L. is fossil poetry EMER 299:27
L. is only the instrument JOHN 409:4
L. is the dress JOHN 410:1
l. of another world BYRO 178:15
l. of priorities BEVA 71:14
l. of prose WORD 832:18
l. of the age GRAY 351:6
l. of the heart POPE 583:11
l. of the heart SHAD 655:10
l. of their own SWIF 749:9
l. of the living ELIO 294:13
l. of the unheard KING 436:18
l. plain COWP 239:30
L. tethers us LIVE 470:7
l. that is worn FLAU 316:19
L. was not powerful enough DICK 264:3
laogai in every l. WU 833:17
laughter in a l. GOLD 344:6
Life is a foreign l. MORL 532:2
limits of my l. WITT 824:8
Lovely enchanting l. HERB 372:18
mathematical l. GALI 328:13
mobilized the English l. MURR 537:8
mystery of l. KELL 432:12
no l. but a cry TENN 761:11
not to be his l. STAË 735:19
obscurity of a learned l. GIBB 336:2
Political l. . . . is designed ORWE 559:11
refine our l. JOHN 410:22
rich and delicate l. WAUG 806:18
Sithe off oure l. LYDG 480:9
speech nor l. BOOK 132:15
spoken in their own l. BIBL 91:15
suicides have a special l. SEXT 655:9
Under the tropic is our l. WALL 800:12
very l. of men WORD 832:17
working in English l. WINT 823:13
world understands my l. HAYD 364:18
You taught me l. SHAK 698:24
languages between and across l. CRAW 244:18
feast of l. SHAK 680:29
knowledge of the ancient l. BRIG 148:16
l. are the pedigree JOHN 412:1
None of your live l. DICK 262:11
silent in seven l. BAGE 46:14
took and gave l. PRIO 592:13
wit in all l. DRYD 283:5
languor L. cannot be SHEL 714:7
languors lilies and l. SWIN 750:15
lantern l. on the stern COLE 227:25
l. whereof tales are told JONS 420:27
word is a l. BOOK 140:9
lanterns show two l. REVE 624:18
laogai want to see l. ended WU 833:17
lap asked Carrie to sit on his l. GROS 354:5
flowery l. of earth ARNO 26:16
fresh l. of the crimson rose SHAK 689:21
in the l. of the gods HOME 382:8
l. of Earth GRAY 350:14
l. of the Line KIPL 440:7
strew the green l. SHAK 696:1
lapdogs l. breathe their last POPE 587:10
l. give themselves POPE 586:29
lapidary In l. inscriptions JOHN 415:7
lapping lake water l. YEAT 836:12
lapwing Beatrice, like a l. SHAK 691:9
lard l. their lean books BURT 170:3
lards l. the lean earth SHAK 667:34
large as l. as life CARR 191:11
how l. a letter BIBL 107:24
l.-brained woman BROW 154:23
l.-hearted man BROW 154:23
little volume, but l. book CRAS 244:9
too l. to hang ANON 19:8
we are at l. JAME 402:26
larger L. than human TENN 760:13
lark bell-swarmèd, l.-charmèd HOPK 384:4
bisy l., messager of day CHAU 205:17
l. ascending MERE 505:18
l. at break of day SHAK 704:15
l. at heaven's gate sings SHAK 660:21
l. becomes a sightless song TENN 762:3
l. now leaves his wat'ry nest D'AV 251:11
l.'s on the wing BROW 157:12
merry l. her matins SPEN 733:7
rise with the l. BRET 148:2
sweet l. sing FERG 308:18
larks catch l. PROV 603:23
Four L. and a Wren LEAR 460:4
hear the l. HOUS 390:19
larkspur l. listens TENN 764:9
Lars Porsena L. of Clusium MACA 483:3
lasciate L. OGNI SPERANZA DANT 249:7
lascivious l. gloating STOP 743:10
long, l. reign DEFO 255:13
lash blood drawn with the l. LINC 468:17
l. that whore SHAK 679:24
l. the age POPE 584:10
rum, sodomy, prayers, and the l. CHUR 216:4
lass every l. a queen KING 437:13
It came with a l. JAME 402:20
l. that loves a sailor DIBD 260:13
lies A l. unparalleled SHAK 658:4
lover and his l. SHAK 659:24
O, gie me the l. BURN 167:10
Sweet l. of Richmond Hill SONG 730:6
lasses Come l. and lads SONG 729:3
then she made the l. BURN 167:9
lassie I love a l. LAUD 454:6
love she's but a l. BURN 168:2
What can a young l. do BURN 169:9
last always the l. to know PROV 603:8
birds in l. year's nest PROV 612:1
cobbler stick to his l. PROV 605:20
Don't wait for the l. judgement CAMU 184:8
Free at l. EPIT 302:7
give unto this l. BIBL 96:19
has dawned is your l. HORA 386:17
Him first, him l. MILT 516:31
l. and best MILT 517:18
l. article of my creed GAND 329:6
l. best gift MILT 516:29
l. breath of Julius Caesar JEAN 404:18
L. came, and last did go MILT 513:5
l. day of an era past YELT 838:6
l. for ever CONR 234:25
l. gasp BIBL 92:21
l. gentleman in Europe LEVE 466:3
l. great Englishman TENN 765:2
l. my time CARL 187:6
L. night I dreamt OPEN 555:30
l. page is always latent WHAR 813:2
l. person who has sat on him HAIG 356:8
l. red leaf TENN 760:30
l. rose of summer MOOR 530:17
l. shall be first BIBL 96:17
l. state of that man BIBL 95:18
L.-supper-carved-on-a-peach-stone LANC 449:17
l. taste of sweets SHAK 694:18
l. thing I shall do LAST 455:8
l. thing one knows PASC 568:7
l. time I saw Paris HAMM 358:20
l. while they last DE G 255:27
l. words I should pronounce REYN 625:13
laughs l. PROV 602:7
laughs l., laughs longest PROV 602:29
live and l. CATU 194:21
Long foretold, long l. PROV 605:50
Look thy l. on all things lovely DE L 256:12
Nice guys finish l. DURO 286:7
no l. nor first BROW 157:13
this day as if thy l. KEN 433:1
To the l. syllable SHAK 685:22
Tristram Shandy did not l. JOHN 415:9
We were the l. romantics YEAT 835:11
world's l. night DONN 273:1
latch Cross-patch, Draw the l. NURS 547:17
latchet shoe's l. BIBL 101:9
late Better l. than never PROV 596:9
borrows from the l. man PROV 599:3
dread of being l. BETJ 71:8
five minutes too l. COWL 239:24

late (*cont.*):
l. into the night BYRO 179:4
never too l. to learn PROV 604:21
never too l. to mend PROV 604:22
not too l. to-morrow ARMS 25:16
No, you were l. LERN 465:4
offering even that too l. NEVI 541:13
rather l. for me LARK 452:12
This is a l. parrot MONT 529:6
Too l. came I AUGU 36:5
too l. into a world MUSS 537:13
years of human thought too l. LA B 446:18
latent l. in my first WHAR 813:2
later came l. in life ASQU 31:3
l. it would be bitter KIER 435:19
l. than you think SERV 654:24
lateral l. thinking DE B 254:6
latet *L. anguis in herba* VIRG 796:1
lath l. of wood BISM 116:16
Latin Devil knows L. KNOX 442:15
half Greek, half L. SCOT 650:5
he speaks L. SHAK 672:25
L. for a whopping ANST 22:16
L., ne of Greek SPEN 734:17
L. word for Tea BELL 64:11
No more L. ANON 18:2
small L. JONS 420:24
Then you understand L. FARQ 307:12
latrine mouth had been used as a l. AMIS 13:12
rotten seat of a l. FLAU 316:8
latrone *l. viator* JUVE 424:19
latter at the l. day BIBL 81:22
former and the l. BOOK 127:20
Lord blessed the l. end BIBL 82:5
laudamus *Te Deum l.* PRAY 592:7
laudant *L. illa* MART 497:24
laudate *L. Dominum, omnes gentes* BIBL 113:23
l. et superexaltate eum BIBL 114:2
laudator *l. temporis acti* HORA 386:2
laugh atheist-l.'s a poor exchange BURN 167:3
cannot make him l. SHAK 670:13
decent people l. [illegible]
dismissed with a l. HORA 389:22
do we not l. SHAK 687:30
horse-l. in the reader FIEL 310:11
l. all of the time LOOS 475:12
l. and sing BOOK 136:2
L. and the world laughs PROV 605:10
L., and the world laughs WILC 817:9
L. at all you trembled at COWP 241:8
l. at any mortal thing BYRO 177:4
l. at everything BEAU 58:9
l. at human actions SPIN 734:27
l. at live dragons TOLK 779:2
l. at them AUST 38:25
l. like a loon HARB 359:17
l. me to scorn BOOK 132:22
L. no man to scorn BIBL 91:21
l., to lie ASCH 30:4
l. to scorn SHAK 659:21
L. where we must POPE 585:5
l. with me, or at me STER 738:15
Let them l. that win PROV 605:22
loud l. that spoke GOLD 344:10
more unbecoming than to l. CONG 232:10
Others may be able to l. RHYS 625:16
sillier than a silly l. CATU 197:6
stupid will l. at him I-HS 398:18
time to l. BIBL 84:7
unextinguishable l. in heaven BROW 152:11
laughable very l. things JOHN 414:4
laughed first baby l. BARR 55:14
honest man is l. at HALI 358:1
l. at in the second NAPO 538:10
l. him into patience SHAK 657:1
l. with counterfeited glee GOLD 344:13
They all l. GERS 334:18
they l. consumedly FARQ 307:10
when he l. AUDE 33:26
laughing Happiness is no l. matter WHAT 813:8
hear you sweetly l. CATU 197:9
killed while l. KIPL 438:14
l. and jeering PEPY 573:2
l. devil BYRO 175:14
l. immoderately SMIT 725:12
l. is heard on the hill BLAK 120:19
l. queen HUNT 395:14
l. sexily SAPP 644:14
Minnehaha, L. Water LONG 474:13
most fun I ever had without l. ALLE 12:8
nothing worth l. at HAZL 365:10
laughs l. at lovers' perjuries TIBU 777:9
l. at lovers' perjury DRYD 282:8
l. at lovers' perjury PROV 604:45
l. best who PROV 602:7
l. last, laughs longest PROV 602:29
l. to see the green man HOFF 380:5
l. with a harvest JERR 407:5
laughter audible l. CHES 209:16
Even in l. BIBL 82:31
faculty of l. ADDI 5:16
gift of l. SABA 641:2
grail of l. CRAN 243:21
l. and ability DICK 266:19
l. and sorrow JOHN 410:14
l. and the love BELL 64:10
l. for a month SHAK 667:33
L. hath only a scornful SIDN 718:27
L. holding both his sides MILT 512:15
l. in a language GOLD 344:6
L. is nothing else HOBB 378:11
l. is pleasant PEAC 571:3
l. of a fool BIBL 84:13
L. . . . the most civilized music USTI 788:21
L. would be bereaved USTI 788:25
Laugh thy girlish l. WATS 805:2
mouth filled with l. BOOK 140:19
nothing more frightful than l. SAGA 641:9
Our sincerest l. SHEL 714:8
peals of l. POPE 583:2
present l. SHAK 701:10
weeping and the l. DOWS 277:6
weeping and with l. MACA 483:12
launch L. your vessel TENN 764:19
launched l. a thousand ships MARL 496:5
Laura Rose-cheeked L. CAMP 184:1
laureate became Poet L. TENN 767:16
laureateship offered the L. SCOT 652:15
laurel Apollo's l. bough MARL 496:8
Caesar's l. crown BLAK 118:3
l. for the perfect prime ROSS 634:7
that she might l. grow MARV 498:14
laurels Birds on box and l. SMAR 722:1
l. all are cut ANON 20:11
l. to paeans CICE 217:15
l. torn SMOL 726:15
Once more, O ye l. MILT 512:26
O ye l. OPEN 556:28
worth all your l. BYRO 179:6
lauriers *l. sont coupés* ANON 20:11
lava in its l. I still find WOOL 827:5
l. of the imagination BYRO 179:25
L. quod es sordidum LANG 451:2
lave Let the l. go by me STEV 742:25
lavender l., mints SHAK 703:16
L.'s blue NURS 549:2
Lavinia L., therefore must be loved SHAK 699:26
law according to the l. BIBL 90:5
against the l. for generals TRUM 784:8
army of unalterable l. MERE 505:20
become a universal l. KANT 425:14
books of l. JOHN 408:13
Born under one l. GREV 353:4
breaks the l. PLAT 578:1
built with stones of L. BLAK 119:19
but by the l. BIBL 105:3
chief l. CICE 217:12
child of l. BENT 66:16
Common L. of England HERB 371:21
Custom that is before all l. DANI 248:17
Custom, that unwritten l. D'AV 251:7
dead-level of l. and order TAWN 755:13
end of l. is LOCK 472:1
enonomic l. of motion MARX 499:16
Every land has its own l. PROV 599:28
fear of the L. JOYC 421:20
fence around the L. TALM 753:17
first is l. DRYD 281:19
from Jargon born to rescue L. LLOY 470:14
fulfilled the l. BIBL 105:20
God is thy l. MILT 516:21
government above the l. SCAR 646:11
had people not defied the l. SCAR 646:9
Hard cases make bad l. PROV 601:51
Hear my l. BOOK 137:3
He that neglects the L. TALM 753:20
I crave the l. SHAK 688:12
Ignorance of the l. PROV 603:43
Ignorance of the l. SELD 653:16
in l.'s grave study COKE 224:11
is a l. rational CHAP 202:16
it is of no force in l. COKE 224:6
judgement of the l. JACK 400:19
keep this l. BOOK 129:6
keystone of the rule of l. DENN 257:18
laid His hand on Moses' l. BLAK 118:16
l. and the prophets BIBL 94:6
l. can take a purse BUTL 172:16
l. doth give it SHAK 688:15
l. floats in a sea of ethics WARR 803:21
l. has made him equal DARR 250:12
l. is a ass DICK 264:19
L. is a bottomless pit ARBU 23:15
l. is above you DENN 257:17
L. is boldly BURR 169:13
l. is contrary to liberty BENT 66:21
l. is established SIDN 718:5
l. is such an ass CHAP 202:20
L. . . . is the perfection COKE 224:8
L. is the true embodiment GILB 337:12
l. is to be to restraint MILT 519:11
L.: It has honoured us WEBS 807:16
L. of Actions MAIN 491:11
L. of the Jungle KIPL 441:19
L. of the Yukon SERV 654:25
l. of thy mouth BOOK 140:8
l.'s delay SHAK 664:4
l. seems like a sort of maze MORT 533:8
L. to our selves MILT 517:16
l. to weed it out BACO 43:28
l. unto themselves BIBL 104:29
lesser breeds without the L. KIPL 440:5
life of the l. COKE 224:7
madhouse there exists no l. CLAR 218:10
majestic equality of the l. FRAN 322:15
make a fence around the L. TALM 753:11
make a scarecrow of the l. SHAK 686:4
moral l. within me KANT 425:12
Necessity has no l. PUBL 616:13
Necessity hath no l. CROM 245:17
Necessity knows no l. PROV 607:24
nine points of the l. PROV 609:31
No brilliance is needed in the l. MORT 533:11
Nor l., nor duty YEAT 836:10
not a l. at all ROBE 629:4
Nothing is l. POWE 590:22
No written l. more binding CATT 194:17
of a common l. JEFF 405:10
Of L. there can be no less HOOK 383:6
old father antick, the l. SHAK 667:18
one l. for all BURK 165:11
One l. for the rich PROV 608:45
One L., one Land KIPL 440:15
People crushed by l. BURK 164:27
perfection of our l. ANON 16:10
principle of the English l. DICK 261:4
purlieus of the L. ETHE 301:11
purlieus of the l. TENN 761:23

quillets of the l. SHAK 672:9
Seven hours to l. JONE 419:5
severity of the criminal l. PEEL 571:13
study of l. GIRA 340:8
sustained: by the L. TALM 753:12
this is the royal l. CORO 237:8
those by l. protected BURN 167:20
touching the l., a Pharisee BIBL 108:19
where no l. is BIBL 104:33
whole of the L. CROW 246:17
Who to himself is l. CHAP 202:14
windward of the l. CHUR 213:18
windy side of the l. SHAK 702:14
Wrest once the l. SHAK 688:13
lawful All things are l. for me BIBL 106:12
L. as eating SHAK 703:26
l. for me to do what I will BIBL 96:19
their l. occasions BOOK 142:5
lawk L. a mercy on me NURS 548:10
lawn bird-haunted English l. ARNO 26:19
Get your tanks off my l. WILS 822:1
l. about the shoulders thrown HERR 374:8
L. is full of south DICK 266:21
on the l. I lie in bed AUDE 34:16
saint in l. POPE 583:29
lawned l. areas with paving OFFI 554:14
lawns house with l. STEV 743:3
Lawrence L. was so unhappy TURN 785:13
laws are the l. of nature SHAW 706:18
arranges l. MACH 485:14
Bad l. BURK 164:28
bad or obnoxious l. GRAN 349:2
breaking of l. MORE 530:22
broke the l. of God and man EPIT 303:4
care who should make the l. FLET 317:22
dole Unequal l. TENN 767:8
dominion of l. PRIC 591:9
do with the l. HORS 390:3
facts governed by l. WHEW 813:13
giving heed unto her l. BIBL 91:14
government of l. ADAM 3:5
Government of l. and not of men FORD 319:13
Had l. not been D'AV 251:9
If l. are needed KHOM 435:13
l. and learning MANN 494:7
L. are generally found to be nets SHEN 715:7
L. are like cobwebs SWIF 747:14
L. are silent CICE 217:24
l. are their enemies BURK 164:27
L. grind the poor GOLD 345:10
L., like houses BURK 164:20
l. of God will be suspended SHAW 707:13
l. of most countries MILL 509:6
l. of Nature HUXL 397:15
l. of the land CHAR 203:4
l. or kings JOHN 411:12
l. or kings can cause GOLD 345:11
L. were made to be broken NORT 546:17
made so by l. BOLI 124:18
Nature, and Nature's l. POPE 584:9
neither l. made JOHN 407:9
New lords, new l. PROV 607:42
not a government of l. WEBS 807:14
not judges of l. PULT 617:1
observing God's l. ELEA 291:14
part of the l. of England HALE 357:3
planted thick with l. BOLT 124:20
prescribed l. to the learned DUPP 285:17
rather than obey the l. TOCQ 778:6
scientist's l. QUIN 619:5
scrutiny of the l. MONT 528:4
sweeps a room as for Thy l. HERB 372:14
their l. approve DRYD 281:25
two sorts of l. DIDE 267:4
Written l. ANAC 14:6
lawsuits engaged in l. NEWT 543:10
lawyer eye iv a l. DUNN 285:14
go to a l. GOGA 343:21
l. has no business JOHN 411:21
l. interprets the truth GIRA 340:8
l. tells me I may BURK 163:1
l. with his briefcase PUZO 618:6
own l. has a fool PROV 606:21
to a corporate l. COMM 230:9
lawyers crowd of l. WYCH 834:14
kill all the l. SHAK 672:21
l. can, with ease GAY 332:11
l. in the vacation SHAK 659:13
L. may revere FERG 308:16
l.' tongues PROV 598:10
two l. the battledores DICK 265:6
Woe unto you, l. BIBL 99:19
lay Cleric before, and L. behind BUTL 172:5
I l. me down to sleep PRAY 592:5
l. down his life BIBL 102:22
L. her i' the earth SHAK 666:26
l. me down in peace BOOK 131:21
l. mee downe BALL 51:12
L. on, Macduff SHAK 685:26
L.-overs for meddlers PROV 605:11
L. your sleeping head AUDE 34:8
layman neither cleric nor l. BERN 69:2
lays constructing tribal l. KIPL 439:4
l. it on with a trowel CONG 232:12
Lazarus certain beggar named L. BIBL 100:10
Come forth, L. JOYC 422:14
L. mystified HILL 376:15
lazy l. leaden-stepping hours MILT 514:3
l., long, lascivious DEFO 255:13
Long and l. PROV 605:48
LBJ All the way with L. POLI 581:2
Hey, L., how many kids POLI 581:14
lead blind l. the blind BIBL 95:29
child shall l. them BIBL 87:4
easy to l. BROU 151:14
evening l. CHUR 216:12
gold wes changyd into l. WYNT 834:16
l. a horticulture PARK 567:15
L., kindly Light NEWM 542:19
l. me in the right way BOOK 133:11
l. those that are with young BIBL 88:2
L. us, Heavenly Father EDME 289:3
l. us not into temptation BIBL 93:19
think we l. BYRO 179:10
When the blind l. the blind PROV 614:25
wherever it may l. DOST 276:9
leaden voice revives the l. strings CAMP 183:22
With l. foot JAGO 401:10
leader fanatic is a great l. BROU 151:18
I am their l. LEDR 461:15
l. of the enterprise VIRG 793:11
one people, one l. POLI 581:11
Take me to your l. CATC 196:22
test of a l. LIPP 470:2
leaders l. of a revolution CONR 234:23
leadership art of l. is saying no BLAI 117:8
leaf And I were like the l. SWIN 751:14
as an aspes l. CHAU 207:10
days are in the yellow l. BYRO 178:22
fade as a l. BIBL 89:7
Falls with the l. FLET 318:2
in tiny l. BROW 156:2
last red l. TENN 760:30
l., the bud, the flower SPEN 733:27
light as l. on lynde CHAU 205:10
sole remaining l. WORD 827:9
where the dead l. fell KEAT 427:23
wise man hide a l. CHES 211:6
yellow l. SHAK 685:17
league hadna sailed a l. BALL 50:12
Half a l. onward TENN 757:15
keep a l. till death SHAK 695:25
leak One l. will sink BUNY 161:11
leaks Little l. sink the ship PROV 605:39
lean could eat no l. NURS 548:23
if a man l. BIBL 80:28
l. and hungry look SHAK 674:16
l. as much to the contrary HALI 357:8
l. on one another BURK 164:20
l. over too far backward THUR 776:24
l. to wild extremes DURY 286:10
leaning l. all awry FITZ 314:19
leap giant l. for mankind ARMS 25:19
great l. in the dark VANB 789:7
l. as an hart BIBL 87:23
l. in the dark LAST 455:19
l. into the dark BROW 152:6
l. into the ocean HUME 394:14
l. over the wall BOOK 132:13
Look before you l. PROV 605:51
methinks it were an easy l. SHAK 667:26
leaped have I l. over a wall BIBL 79:12
leaping l. from place to place HARD 361:15
l. light AUDE 34:7
so long as there is no l. SURT 746:22
too broad for l. HOUS 391:8
Walking, and l. BIBL 103:19
learn but she can l. SHAK 688:4
craft so long to l. CHAU 206:28
don't want to l. SELL 654:2
l., and inwardly digest BOOK 127:22
l. how to be aged BLYT 123:4
l. in suffering SHEL 711:21
l. men from books DISR 270:32
l. the world CHES 209:9
l. to do nothing JOSE 421:11
L. to write well BUCK 159:16
L. to write well CLOS 222:17
live and l. POMF 580:5
Live and l. PROV 605:45
much desire to l. MILT 519:17
never too late to l. PROV 604:21
Never too old to l. PROV 607:39
People must l. to hate MAND 493:9
pleasure to l. CONF 231:3
We l. so little DAVI 251:15
while they teach, men l. SENE 654:18
learned been l. has been forgotten SKIN 721:17
l. anything from history HEGE 367:10
l. well how to obey THOM 771:3
L. without sense CHUR 214:9
loads of l. lumber POPE 585:2
much l. dust COWP 241:25
obscurity of a l. language GIBB 336:2
opinion with the l. CONG 232:16
prescribed laws to the l. DUPP 285:17
Things l. on earth BROW 157:2
this l. man MARL 496:8
learning alwayth a l. DICK 262:24
and in l. rules CRAB 243:1
a' the l. I desire BURN 167:4
attain good l. ASCH 30:1
commonwealth of l. LOCK 471:12
cry both arts and l. QUAR 618:22
deep l. little had he SPEN 734:17
enough of l. to misquote BYRO 178:1
Get l. BIBL 92:19
L. is better than house PROV 605:12
l. is most excellent PROV 614:20
l. lightly like a flower TENN 762:5
l. many things SOLO 727:8
l.'s crumbs BROW 155:27
L. teacheth more ASCH 30:5
L., that cobweb BUTL 172:6
L. will be cast BURK 163:25
little l. is a dangerous thing POPE 584:15
loyal body wanted l. TRAP 781:1
man of polite l. DEFO 254:11
much l. doth make thee mad BIBL 104:20
nonsense, and l. GOLD 345:17
not l. from history BLAI 117:9
of a state, l. BACO 44:21
of liberty, and of l. DISR 269:11
pleasures that go with l. SOCR 727:5
pursuit of l. LAO 452:2
rights in l.'s world EGER 289:15
royal road to l. PROV 612:17
scraps of l. YOUN 838:16
traitor to l. JOHN 407:14
twins of l. SHAK 673:24
Wear your l. CHES 209:14
Whence is thy l. GAY 332:6

learning (*cont.*):
will to l. ASCH 30:2
written for our l. BOOK 127:22
learnt easiest l. MILT 518:11
forgotten nothing and l. nothing DUMO 285:1
They have l. nothing TALL 753:7
lease summer's l. SHAK 704:9
leasehold l. for all LUCR 479:6
least faithful in that which is l. BIBL 100:9
l. government was the best FEIN 308:7
l. of all seeds BIBL 95:22
l. of these my brethren BIBL 97:13
leather nothing like l. PROV 612:18
leave for ever taking l. RILK 628:1
If you can't l. in a taxi FILM 311:13
Intreat me not to l. thee BIBL 78:12
L. all things behind BHAG 73:5
L. me, O Love SIDN 718:20
L. not a rack behind SHAK 699:6
L. not a stain BIBL 92:8
L. off first BIBL 92:6
l. spades alone SITW 721:4
l. the outcome CORN 236:16
l. the word of God BIBL 103:20
l. things alone you leave them CHES 211:11
l. without the King ELIZ 298:2
ready to l. MONT 527:7
shall a man l. his father BIBL 73:23
we asked none l. to love DONN 273:27
leaven l. leaveneth the whole lump BIBL 106:1
l. of malice BOOK 128:6
l. of malice and wickedness BIBL 106:2
leaves barren of l. SHAK 704:8
burning of the l. BINY 115:9
Crowned with calm l. SWIN 750:20
flaps its glad green l. HARD 361:6
her l. trimmed WALK 799:10
laughing l. of the tree SWIN 750:7
l. are falling SHEL 712:17
l. behind a part of oneself HARA 359:13
l. cover me SWIN 751:13
l. dead Are driven SHEL 712:12
l. fall early POUN 589:23
l. like light footfalls SHEL 712:11
l. of the tree BIBL 113:13
l. to a tree KEAT 431:2
l. to the trees HORA 389:6
Like that of l. HOME 382:2
noise among the l. KEAT 428:5
stipple l. with sun SACK 641:6
tender l. of hope SHAK 673:12
Thick as autumnal l. MILT 514:23
thou among the l. KEAT 429:9
withered l. ARNO 27:2
yellow l., or none SHAK 704:29
leaving L. his country FITZ 314:6
like the l. it SHAK 681:23
Lebanon cedared L. KEAT 427:13
cedars of L. BIBL 77:36
Lebens *L. goldner Baum* GOET 342:20
lecher small gilded fly Does l. SHAK 679:21
lecherous l. as a sparwe CHAU 205:3
rough and l. SHAK 678:6
lechery L., sir, it provokes SHAK 683:15
wars and l. SHAK 700:23
lectorem *L. delectando* HORA 386:3
lecture classic l., rich in sentiment TENN 765:12
l., love, in love's philosophy DONN 274:4
tried to l. *me* PAGL 563:5
lecturer requisite to a l. FARA 306:11
lectures l. or a little charity WHIT 815:16
led we are most l. BYRO 179:10
leek By this l. SHAK 672:3
lees drink Life to the l. TENN 767:9
wine on the l. BIBL 87:10
left better to be l. CONG 233:6
but of my l. hand MILT 519:23
everything is l. out JAME 403:4
goats on the l. BIBL 97:11
l. a lot o' little things KIPL 438:2
L. hand down a bit CATC 196:10
l.-handed marriage WOLL 825:22
l. thy first love BIBL 111:24
let not thy l. hand know BIBL 93:17
O let them be l. HOPK 384:10
other l. BIBL 97:6
something l. to treat MALL 492:5
leg does not resemble a l. APOL 23:1
here I leave my second l. HOOD 382:19
l. has often as much to do with it HUNT 395:19
l. you shall put into your breeches JOHN 413:14
lift a lawless l. BURN 167:13
my Julia's dainty l. HERR 374:18
legacy l. from a rich relative SMIT 724:2
legally accomplishing small things l. BALZ 53:1
lege *Tolle l.* AUGU 36:4
legend before your l. ever did JOHN 407:17
before your l. will JOHN 408:3
fables in the l. BACO 42:6
true l. STAL 736:4
leges *l. inter arma* CICE 217:24
legibility dawn of l. HAY 364:17
Legion My name is L. BIBL 98:5
legions give me back my l. AUGU 36:15
legislation imports and exports, l. ARIS 24:14
possess divine l. MEND 504:19
true basis of English l. GLAD 341:4
legislator l. of mankind JOHN 410:25
people is the true l. BURK 164:21
legislators idea of hereditary l. PAIN 563:23
unacknowledged l. SHEL 714:24
legitimate l. warfare NEWM 542:3
legs adorns my l. HOUS 390:5
any man's l. BOOK 141:25
born with your l. apart ORTO 558:4
cannon-ball took off his l. HOOD 382:18
dog's walking on his hinder l. JOHN 413:17
four bare l. in a bed PROV 612:4
Four l. good ORWE 558:6
If you could see my l. DICK 262:16
l. are as pillars of marble BIBL 85:21
loves to fold his l. JOHN 415:26
not for your bad l. ELIZ 297:2
on their own two l. CASS 193:11
stretches his l. PROV 599:42
use of his l. DICK 263:24
vast and trunkless l. SHEL 712:21
Walk under his huge l. SHAK 674:13
legunt *sed ista l.* MART 497:24
Leicester Farewell, L. Square JUDG 423:1
Here lies the Earl of L. EPIT 302:16
Leicestershire finest run in L. PAGE 563:1
leiden *L. oder triumphieren* GOET 343:5
leisure absence of l. to reflect HAVE 364:2
At l. married CONG 232:34
busiest have most l. PROV 596:42
conspicuous l. VEBL 791:3
detest at l. BYRO 177:21
fill l. intelligently RUSS 639:16
have l. to bother SHAW 709:7
Idle have the least l. PROV 603:10
improvement arises from l. JOHN 414:20
increased l. DISR 269:10
l. answers leisure SHAK 686:25
L. with honour CICE 217:26
life of l. MORE 531:1
luck in l. PROV 612:12
never at l. JOHN 415:26
opportunity of l. BIBL 92:11
polish it at l. DRYD 283:2
Politicians also have no l. ARIS 24:20
repent at l. PROV 606:31
When I have l. HILL 377:11
leman such l. BALL 52:4
lemon in the squeezing of a l. GOLD 345:20
l.-trees bloom GOET 343:12
lemons Oranges and l. NURS 550:4
lend l. me your ears SHAK 675:27
L. you money and lose PROV 605:14
men who l. LAMB 448:12
lender borrower, nor a l. be SHAK 662:12
lenders pen from l.' books SHAK 679:3
lendeth merciful, and l. BOOK 139:19
lendings Off, off, you l. SHAK 679:4
lends Three things I never l. SURT 746:20
length drags its dreary l. DICK 260:18
drags its slow l. POPE 584:21
in l. of days BIBL 81:16
l. and breadth BALL 50:14
L. begets loathing PROV 605:15
L. of days BIBL 82:8
what it lacks in l. FROS 326:2
lengthens As the day l. PROV 595:20
lengthy meaning of l. speech SCHI 648:14
Lenore angels name L. POE 579:16
Lent nearly as bad as L. BINC 115:6
lente *Festina l.* AUGU 36:16
L. currite noctis equi OVID 561:2
l., lente, currite MARL 496:7
leoni *vulpes aegroto cauta l.* HORA 386:12
Léonie Weep not for little L. GRAH 348:2
leopard l. change his spots BIBL 89:17
l. does not change COMP 230:16
l. does not change PROV 605:16
l. shall lie down BIBL 87:4
leopards three white l. sat ELIO 293:21
leper innocence is like a dumb l. GREE 351:24
wash the l.'s wounds TERE 768:9
leprosy skin was white as l. COLE 226:13
lerne gladly wolde he l. CHAU 204:20
Lesbia L. whom Catullus once loved CATU 197:10
L. with her sparrow MILL 509:15
Let us live, my L. CATU 197:2
My sweetest L. CAMP 183:21
lesbians l. often end up PAGL 563:4
Lesley bonnie L. BURN 166:19
less for nothing l. than thee DONN 273:22
had he pleased us l. ADDI 4:5
How l. what we may be BYRO 177:30
L. is a bore VENT 791:5
L. is more PROV 605:17
l. likely to fall GAY 332:3
L. than the dust HOPE 383:21
l. we love her PUSH 617:28
little l. BROW 155:18
more and more about l. and less BUTL 171:13
rather than be l. MILT 515:8
small Latin, and l. Greek JONS 420:24
you can't take *l.* CARR 189:19
lessen l. from day to day CARR 190:3
lesser l. breeds KIPL 440:5
l. to be chosen THOM 771:9
lessons l. to be drawn ELIZ 297:17
reason they're called l. CARR 190:3
lest L. we forget KIPL 440:3
let l. and hindered BOOK 128:1
L. my people go BIBL 75:35
L. my people go SONG 730:8
l. them all to my elder THOM 773:1
l. the sounds of music SHAK 688:21
L. us with a gladsome mind MILT 512:25
Lethe go not to L. KEAT 429:2
on L. wharf SHAK 662:28
waters of L. GINS 339:23
Lethean drunken of things L. SWIN 751:5
letter by speech than by l. BACO 43:21
don't think this is a l. RENO 624:15
how large a l. BIBL 107:24
huge wordy l. JUVE 424:20
l. by strange letter HEAN 366:8
l. from his wife CARR 191:28
l. killeth BIBL 107:5
l. to my love BALL 50:16
l. to the friends STEV 741:14
made this [l.] longer PASC 568:6
my l. to the world DICK 266:18
scarlet l. HAWT 364:13

Someone wants a l. ADVE 8:10
thou unnecessary l. SHAK 678:13
uncertain process of l.-writing ELIO 293:12
used to start a l. PLIN 579:1
very touch of the l. NIN 546:2
were reading a l. TALM 754:26
when he wrote a l. BACO 42:20
letters burn your l. ADAM 3:7
can't write l. BISH 116:3
L. for the rich AUDE 34:12
l. get in the wrong places MILN 511:5
l. in the grave JOHN 417:22
l., methinks, should be free OSBO 559:18
l. mingle souls DONN 274:22
L. of thanks AUDE 34:13
l. to a non-existent LEWI 466:23
like women's l. HAZL 365:4
nat the l. space CHAU 207:17
No arts; no l. HOBB 378:21
professor of French l. JOYC 422:16
than a man of l. STER 739:13
twenty-two fundamental l. SEFE 653:9
letting l. each other go RILK 628:2
lettuce eating too much l. POTT 588:19
letumque *L. Labosque* VIRG 794:20
levee Drove my Chevy to the l. MCLE 486:15
more alluring than a l. CONG 233:11
level l. of provincial existence ELIO 293:4
My life stands in the l. SHAK 703:6
Those who attempt to l. BURK 163:17
to one dead l. ev'ry mind POPE 580:22
leveller Death is the great l. PROV 598:2
levellers l. wish to level *down* JOHN 413:13
levelling cannot bear l. *up* JOHN 413:13
Leviathan L., called a commonwealth HOBB 378:12
L. Hugest of living creatures MILT 517:7
there is that L. BOOK 139:6
leviathan draw out l. BIBL 82:3
l. retrieving pebbles WELL 810:6
levity little judicious l. STEV 742:6
lewd certain l. fellows BIBL 104:4
Lewley bricks to L. BETJ 71:3
lex *Salus populi suprema l.* SELD 653:21
suprema est l. CICE 217:12
lexicographer *L.* A writer of dictionaries JOHN 409:10
wake a l. JOHN 409:6
lexicon Two men wrote a l. WATE 804:13
lexicons We are walking l. LIVE 470:8
liar answered 'Little L.' BELL 63:10
best l. BUTL 172:20
every man a l. BIBL 104:30
he is a l. BIBL 102:1
l. should be outlawed HALI 357:10
l. to have good memory PROV 605:24
penalty of a l. TALM 754:20
proved l. HAIL 356:11
She's like a l. SHAK 693:27
liars All men are l. BOOK 140:3
fears may be l. CLOU 223:3
Income Tax made more L. ROGE 631:19
l. and swearers SHAK 685:5
L. ought to have good memories SIDN 718:2
Poets . . . though l. HUME 395:5
prove the greatest l. DRAY 279:1
libation pouring a l. SOCR 727:6
libel excessive wealth a l. SHEL 714:19
greater the l. PROV 601:35
l. in a frown SWIF 749:9
libellum *novum l.* CATU 194:19
liber *L. scriptus* MISS 523:4
liberal as distinguished from the L. BIER 114:21
damned l. majority IBSE 398:5
either a little L. GILB 337:14
first L. leader STEE 736:14
is a l. education STEE 736:21
l. education BANK 53:8
l. is a conservative who WOLF 825:13
l. of another man's BACO 43:30
panted for a l. profession COLM 229:17
liberality liberality becomes a source BAED 45:18
liberals l. can understand BRUC 158:17
liberation l. of the human mind GOLD 344:5
Women's L. is just MEIR 503:12
liberavi *L. animam meam* BERN 69:3
libertas *Imperium et L.* DISR 269:22
L. et natale solum SWIF 749:28
Liberté *L.! Égalité* POLI 581:24
liberties give up their l. BURK 165:5
l. are taken in thy name GEOR 334:10
L. . . . depend on the silence HOBB 378:23
not to have l. PYM 618:8
libertine puffed and reckless l. SHAK 662:9
liberty ardour for l. PRIC 591:9
be light! said L. SHEL 711:11
Brightest in dungeons, L. BYRO 179:3
certainly destroys l. JOHN 416:27
chosen music, L. WORD 832:8
conceived in all l. LINC 468:13
contend for their l. HALI 357:20
contrary to l. BENT 66:21
dangers to l. lurk BRAN 146:20
delight with l. SPEN 734:16
desires in l. TOCQ 778:10
divests himself of natural l. LOCK 472:4
endanger the public l. ADAM 3:4
end to a woman's l. BURN 166:4
enemies of l. HUME 394:15
extremism in the defence of l. GOLD 345:33
full l. is not given COTT 238:2
given l. to man CURR 248:2
holy name of l. GAND 329:4
individual l. SALI 642:20
l. and equality ARIS 25:5
l. and prosperity JENY 406:11
l. and slavery CAMD 182:12
L. *and* Union WEBS 807:12
L. cannot be SUMN 746:6
L. cannot be preserved ADAM 3:12
l. cannot long exist BURK 162:15
L. consists in doing MILL 509:1
l. doesn't even go to the trouble BALZ 53:1
L. is liberty, not BERL 68:16
L. is precious LENI 463:13
L. is to faction MADI 489:2
L. is, to the lowest rank JOHN 409:2
L. is unfinished business ANON 17:7
L. means responsibility SHAW 708:17
L. not a means ACTO 1:15
l. of the individual MILL 508:21
l. of the press JUNI 423:12
l., or give me death HENR 371:3
l. plucks justice SHAK 686:1
L.'s a glorious feast BURN 167:20
L.'s in every blow BURN 168:8
L. to be saucy HALI 357:21
l. to gad abroad BIBL 92:1
l. to know, to utter MILT 519:18
L. too must be limited BURK 162:13
L., when it begins to take root WASH 804:10
l. which we can hope MILT 519:6
life, and l. JEFF 405:3
life, l. ANON 19:11
loudest yelps for l. JOHN 411:6
love is l. POPE 582:21
love of l. HAZL 365:8
mansion-house of l. MILT 519:16
notion of l. JOHN 412:25
of l., and of learning DISR 269:11
O l.! what crimes LAST 456:19
pinch the sea of its l. COTT 238:1
play not with my l. GODO 342:3
principate and l. TACI 752:6
proclaim l. to the captives BIBL 89:5
regulated l. BURK 163:12
right of l. TAFT 752:19
safeguards of l. FRAN 323:7
seek power and lose l. BACO 43:9
Shouted of l. LONG 474:10
so easy as l. ASTE 31:14
survival and the success of l. KENN 433:10
Sweet land of l. SMIT 724:16
symptom of constitutional l. GIBB 335:11
tree of l. JEFF 405:7
truth and l. SHEL 714:14
wait for l. MACA 481:16
what cannot be sold—l. GRAT 349:6
when they cry l. MILT 518:28
who ever gives, takes l. DONN 273:2
Wommen, of kynde, desiren l. CHAU 205:12
Liberty-Hall This is L., gentlemen GOLD 345:22
libraries circulating l. RUSK 638:18
l. of the Commons CHAN 202:8
library Alexandria's l. burned HUGH 393:5
choice of all my l. SHAK 700:1
circulating l. SHER 715:25
In his l. AUST 38:18
l. in every county town CARL 188:17
l. is thought in cold storage SAMU 643:12
lumber room of his l. DOYL 277:10
My l. Was dukedom SHAK 698:21
public l. BENN 65:10
public l. JOHN 410:21
sit in a l. FITZ 315:11
turn over half a l. JOHN 415:2
universe . . . others call the L. BORG 143:3
libro *Galeotto fu il l.* DANT 249:14
Libya L. about Cyrene BIBL 103:16
licence L. they mean MILT 518:28
l. to act like an asshole ZAPP 839:23
l. to print money THOM 775:24
love not freedom, but l. MILT 520:2
POETIC L. BANV 53:11
universal l. to be good COLE 224:16
license L. my roving hands DONN 272:16
licensed based upon l. premises O'BR 552:9
L. to kill MISQ 521:18
licentious l. passages GIBB 336:2
l. soldiery BURK 165:4
Licht *Mehr L.* LAST 456:15
lick enemies shall l. the dust BOOK 136:18
l. it into form BURT 170:5
licking finger l. good ADVE 7:32
licorice l. fields at Pontefract BETJ 70:15
Liddell right part wrote L. WATE 804:13
this is Mrs L. SPRI 735:9
Liddesdale Eskdale and L. SCOT 651:29
lids Drops his blue-fringèd l. COLE 225:11
with eternal l. apart KEAT 426:14
lie Bodies never l. DE M 257:1
can't tell a l. WASH 804:9
definition of a l. ANON 15:4
dost thou l. so low SHAK 675:19
Every word she writes is a l. MCCA 484:4
fain wald l. down BALL 51:1
fall victim to a big l. HITL 378:4
give the world the l. RALE 620:12
Here L. I EPIT 302:13
home to a l. POUN 589:16
House of the L. ZORO 841:15
if a l. may do thee grace SHAK 669:18
I l. down alone HOUS 390:11
I mean you l. SWIF 748:14
Is a dream a l. SPRI 735:13
leads you to believe a l. BLAK 118:14
l. diagonally in his bed STER 739:10
l. direct SHAK 659:26
l. even when it is inconvenient VIDA 792:12
l. follows PROU 594:9
L. FOLLOWS BY POST TELE 758:11
L. heavy on him, Earth EPIT 304:10
l. in cold obstruction SHAK 686:18
l. in the soul JOWE 421:12
l. that makes us realize truth PICA 576:5
l. that sinketh in BACO 44:17
l. through centuries BROW 155:14
l. which is part a truth TENN 759:6
l. will go round the world SPUR 735:14
L. with me BIBL 75:12
Live and l. reclined TENN 763:14
make your bed, so you must l. PROV 595:24
May l. till seven CLAR 219:16

lie (*cont.*):
mixture of a l. BACO 44:16
no worse l. JAME 404:3
obedient to their laws we l. EPIT 302:11
often a whole l. PROV 601:43
old L.: Dulce et decorum OWEN 562:8
possible to l. for the truth ADLE 6:4
readily can l. with art GAY 332:13
rule and dare not l. TENN 764:2
sent to l. abroad WOTT 833:6
that he should l. BIBL 76:29
undo the folded l. AUDE 35:2
what is a l. BYRO 177:17
when dead, l. as quietly EDWA 289:10
Whoever would l. usefully HERV 375:7
Who loves to l. with me SHAK 658:20
lieb *so herzlich l.* HEIN 368:8
lied because our fathers l. KIPL 438:8
l. to please the mob KIPL 438:13
lien have l. among the pots BOOK 136:7
lies Beats all the l. BLAK 118:1
believing their own l. ARBU 23:14
certain, and the rest is l. FITZ 314:13
delight is in l. BOOK 135:21
hear no l. PROV 595:27
Here l. a lady RANS 621:20
Here l. Groucho Marx EPIT 303:2
Here l. the Earl of Leicester EPIT 302:16
History is a pack of l. STUB 745:3
History, sir, will tell l. SHAW 707:1
l. a man who never lived THOM 775:1
l. are like the father SHAK 668:7
l. are often told in silence STEV 742:4
L. are the mortar WELL 810:12
l. as will lie in thy sheet SHAK 702:5
l. beneath your spell HOPE 383:20
l., damned lies and statistics DISR 271:8
l. it lives on and propagates FOSD 321:9
l. of tongue and pen CHES 210:8
make l. sound truthful ORWE 559:11
Matilda told such Dreadful L. BELL 63:9
produces l. like sand ANON 20:18
reality and l. COCT 223:16
spring of endless l. COWP 241:7
telling l. about the Democrats STEV 740:9
There l. the Doctor AUBR 32:11
though I know she l. SHAK 705:23
Truth exists, l. are invented BRAQ 147:3
truth to cover l. CONG 232:14
Without l. humanity FRAN 322:16
lieto *Chi vuol esser l. sia* MEDI 503:10
lieutenants God's l. upon earth JAME 402:14
life accounted his l. madness BIBL 91:11
actor's l. for me WASH 804:11
afternoon of human l. JUNG 423:10
all human l. is there ADVE 7:3
all human l. is there JAME 403:7
All L. death does end HOPK 384:13
All my past l. ROCH 630:9
all part of l.'s rich pageant MARS 497:18
All present l. BYRO 177:27
all the days of my l. BOOK 133:1
answers to the meaning of l. DAWK 253:5
as large as l. CARR 191:11
Bankrupt of l. DRYD 280:3
believe in l. DU B 284:1
believe in the l. to come BECK 59:12
best days of l. VIRG 796:20
better to enjoy l. JOHN 409:15
betwixt l. and death WORD 831:23
bitterness of l. CARR 191:28
book of l. BIBL 111:26
Book of L. begins WILD 818:26
brisking about the l. SMAR 722:6
careful of the single l. TENN 761:12
changing scenes of l. TATE 755:9
Chaos often breeds l. ADAM 2:19
Chief nourisher in l.'s feast SHAK 683:8
clinging to l. ARNO 28:14
contempt for l. VANE 789:16
content to manufacture l. BERN 68:19
count l. just a stuff BROW 156:10
criticism of l. ARNO 28:24
crown of l. BIBL 110:11
crown of l. BIBL 111:25
day-to-day business l. is LAFO 447:16
death after l. SPEN 733:22
death in l. ANON 17:22
death, nor l. BIBL 105:12
disease of modern l. ARNO 27:10
distinction of your l. TACI 752:11
Does thy l. destroy BLAK 121:7
doors to let out l. FLET 318:4
doors to let out l. MASS 501:6
drink L. to the lees TENN 767:9
drive l. into a corner THOR 776:12
escape the l.-sentence LAWR 458:24
essence of human l. MACD 484:17
essence of l. DAWK 253:3
everlasting l. BIBL 101:18
everlasting l. BIBL 101:30
evidence of l. after death SOPE 728:10
except my l. SHAK 663:14
fear love is to fear l. RUSS 639:18
fed full of l. LUCR 479:8
Fill me with l. anew HATC 363:17
findeth his l. BIBL 95:3
find l. in death COLE 225:10
finished A l. heroic MILT 518:24
following l. thro' creatures POPE 583:28
forfeit my l. BROW 152:2
for her l. he died STON 743:9
for l., not for lunch SAYI 647:24
former naughty l. BOOK 129:2
fountain of the water of l. BIBL 113:9
French for l.-jacket BARN 54:18
Friday I tasted l. DICK 266:21
from the dream of l. SHEL 710:23
Further sacrifice of l. DEV 259:5
gained in the university of l. BOTT 144:23
gave my l. for freedom EWER 305:11
genius into my l. WILD 819:9
give for his l. BIBL 80:37
giveth his l. for the sheep BIBL 102:6
giveth l. to the world BIBL 101:27
glory of this l. SHAK 699:16
golden tree of actual l. GOET 341:10
Good l. be now my task DRYD 281:18
great l. if you don't weaken BUCH 159:8
had a happy l. LAST 457:16
happy l. consist MART 498:3
hath a l. to live RAIN 620:6
His l. was gentle SHAK 677:4
honour and l. FRAN 323:1
hour of glorious l. MORD 530:21
Human l. BERN 69:9
human l. is, at the greatest TEMP 757:5
Human l. is everywhere JOHN 410:26
I bear a charmèd l. SHAK 685:24
if l. was bitter to thee SWIN 750:11
images of l. BERG 67:15
in l. as it is in ways BACO 41:19
in mourning for my l. CHEK 208:4
in our l. alone COLE 225:3
In the midst of l. BOOK 131:13
In the midst of l. MUMF 536:5
in the sea of l. ARNO 28:2
in this l. BIBL 106:21
Is it not *l.* BYRO 180:8
isn't l. a terrible thing THOM 772:18
I've had a wonderful l. LAST 457:6
jump the l. to come SHAK 682:8
lad of l. SHAK 671:12
lag-end of my l. SHAK 669:4
last of l. BROW 157:18
lay down his friends for his l. THOR 776:21
lay down his l. BIBL 102:22
lay down my l. CLOU 221:12
leadeth unto l. BIBL 94:8
Lead me from death to l. KUMA 446:5
L., a Fury slinging flame TENN 761:8
l. a glorious cycle of song PARK 567:1
l. all labour be TENN 763:13
l. and death BIBL 77:10
l., and liberty JEFF 405:3
l. and loves of a she-devil WELD 809:6
l. and power FOX 322:8
l. a series of images WARH 803:15
l. at a pin's fee SHAK 662:20
l. began by flickering out GONC 346:7
L. begins at forty PITK 576:18
L. begins at forty PROV 605:25
l., being weary SHAK 674:24
l. beyond life MILT 519:9
L. can little more supply POPE 585:4
l. eternal gave BYRO 174:4
L. exists in the universe JEAN 404:19
L. feeding death ALAB 9:14
L., force and beauty POPE 584:13
l. forget and death remember SWIN 751:10
L. for life BIBL 76:14
L., friends, is boring BERR 69:19
l. had been ruined BROO 151:4
l. has crept so long TENN 764:14
l. hath been one chain CLAR 218:8
L. imitates Art WILD 818:6
l. in another life ELIO 292:1
l. in miniature O'NE 554:21
l. in the village LEE 462:1
l. is 6 to 5 against RUNY 637:15
L. is a foreign language MORL 532:2
L. is a gamble STOP 743:20
L. is a great surprise NABO 537:19
L. is a horizontal fall COCT 223:17
L. is a jest EPIT 303:12
L. is all a VARIORUM BURN 167:21
L. is an incurable disease COWL 239:23
L. is an offensive WHIT 814:10
L. is a rainbow which YEVT 838:12
L. is a sexually SAYI 647:29
L. is as tedious SHAK 677:12
L. is a top GREV 353:3
L. is Colour and Warmth GREN 352:17
L. is doubt UNAM 787:6
L. is first boredom, then fear LARK 452:15
l. is given to none freehold LUCR 479:6
L. is just a bowl of cherries BROW 152:5
L. is just one damned HUBB 392:11
L. is made up of RICE 626:7
L. is mostly froth GORD 346:19
L. isn't finished CHEK 208:10
L. is real LONG 474:3
l. is short PROV 595:17
L. is short, the art long HIPP 377:15
L. is something to do LEBO 461:9
L. is the desert YOUN 839:15
L. is the other way round LODG 472:12
l. is the thing SMIT 724:12
L. is too much like a pathless wood FROS 325:14
L. is too precious ELIO 293:12
l. is very short TAYL 756:19
l. is washed BARZ 56:13
L. itself BROW 152:12
l., its enemy ANOU 22:10
L., Joy, Empire SHEL 713:16
L. levels all men SHAW 708:27
l., liberty ANON 19:11
l. like a box of chocolates FILM 312:2
L., like a dome SHEL 711:4
l. may perfect be JONS 420:21
l. might be put on parade EULA 301:18
l. more than meat BIBL 93:23
l. not about men DENE 257:7
L. not a series of gig lamps WOOL 826:14
l. of a man BIBL 74:20
l. of any important person PRIE 591:11
l. of his beast BIBL 82:25
l. of man, solitary, poor HOBB 378:21
l. of men on earth BEDE 60:19
l. of only one of them GODW 342:5
l. of the nation secure DOUG 277:2
l. of the world DOST 275:15
l. of wretchedness EURI 304:20
l. on the whole is far from gay LEAR 460:22
l. protracted JOHN 411:17

L. says: she did this BARN 55:1
L.'s better with POLI 581:25
L.'s but a walking shadow SHAK 685:22
l.'s dim windows BLAK 118:14
l.'s dull round SHEN 715:6
l. sentence goes on CONL 233:21
l.'s fitful fever SHAK 684:5
l.'s last scene JOHN 411:18
L.'s longing for itself GIBR 336:11
L.'s not just being alive MART 498:2
l. so fast doth fly DAVI 251:15
l.'s poor play is o'er POPE 585:25
l.'s story fills thirty-five pages ARNO 29:10
l. that breathes TENN 767:7
L., the shadow of death SWIN 750:9
L., the Universe and Everything ADAM 2:4
l. time's fool SHAK 669:12
l. to a dream MONT 528:3
L., to be sure, is nothing much HOUS 390:12
L. too short to stuff a mushroom CONR 235:3
l. unto the bitter in soul BIBL 81:6
l. was duty HOOP 383:8
L. well spent is long LEON 464:13
l. went through with death FORT 321:7
l. will be sour grapes ASHF 30:15
L. with its way MONS 526:11
L. without industry is guilt RUSK 638:8
l. without it were not ROWE 636:11
l. without theory DISR 270:7
L. would be tolerable LEWI 467:3
L. would be very pleasant SURT 747:2
L. would ring the bells GINS 339:19
live a l. half dead MILT 518:16
live out my l. talking VANZ 789:20
long as you have your l. JAME 402:25
looked at l. from both sides MITC 523:16
Lord and giver of l. BOOK 129:9
lost, except a little l. BYRO 178:21
love long l. better than figs SHAK 656:9
Mad from l.'s history HOOD 382:16
Man's l. BARN 55:10
matter of l. and death SHAN 706:6
measured out my l. with coffee spoons ELIO 295:6
medium of l. MANN 494:6
men confused with l. FRID 324:21
Mine honour is my l. SHAK 694:9
more a way of l. ANON 18:3
more of a l. CLAU 219:17
my l. is preserved BIBL 75:7
my l.'s a pain DAVI 251:17
My l. stands in the level SHAK 703:6
my l. to make you King CHAR 203:11
my l. upon a cast SHAK 697:1
my whole l., long or short ELIZ 297:14
nauseous draught of l. ROCH 630:8
no l. of a man CARL 187:11
No, no, no l. SHAK 680:14
not a L. at all GLAD 341:14
not a new form of l. DYSO 287:19
Nothing in his l. SHAK 681:23
Nothing in l. CORY 237:12
not in giving l. DE B 254:3
not one l. shall be destroyed TENN 761:10
not the men in my l. that counts WEST 812:4
not yet know about l. CONF 231:20
no wealth but l. RUSK 639:6
now my l. is done TICH 777:10
of man's l. a thing apart BYRO 176:7
O for a l. of sensations KEAT 430:22
one l. and one death BROW 156:9
one l. to lose LAST 456:8
one l. with another AKHM 9:7
one way in to l. SENE 654:19
only a l. of mistakes ELIO 292:16
only living l. O'NE 554:24
on the tree of l. MILT 516:11
Our end is L. MACN 488:17
our little l. SHAK 699:6
outer l. of telegrams FORS 320:17
paid the prices of l. GURN 355:3
pass my whole l. DICK 265:22
path of our l. DANT 249:6
path of our l. OPEN 556:4
Perfection of the l. YEAT 835:8
précis of l. FRIE 325:4
priceless gift of l. ROSE 633:20
pride of giving l. VICT 792:3
Pride of L. HARD 361:9
principal business of l. BUTL 172:18
really don't know l. at all MITC 523:16
Refraining from taking l. PALI 564:15
remaining years of l. MAND 493:8
remains of l. WALP 800:20
resurrection, and the l. BIBL 102:10
Reverence for L. SCHW 649:17
reward of labour is l. MORR 532:18
right to a dignified l. JOHN 407:11
river of water of l. BIBL 113:12
saving of l. must supersede TALM 754:4
science of l. BERN 69:7
seas of l., like wine TRAH 780:18
sech is l. DICK 263:10
sell the present l. KORA 444:8
shilling l. will give you AUDE 35:3
single l. doth well BACO 43:18
single page of our l. SAND 643:14
sketchy understanding of l. CRIC 245:2
slits the thin-spun l. MILT 513:3
space of l. between KEAT 426:15
spice of l. COWP 241:23
spirit giveth l. BIBL 107:5
stop a man's l. SENE 654:20
strenuous l. ROOS 633:4
Style is l. FLAU 316:16
such is L. DICK 262:22
take my l. FARQ 307:13
take my l. and all SHAK 688:16
take my l. from thee KIPL 441:3
taken over one's mortal l. LUCR 479:7
taking l. by the throat FROS 326:16
That l. so short CHAU 206:28
That which we call l. DONN 274:25
their l. was death ROSS 635:1
There is l., but not for you MORT 533:12
there is l. out there DAWK 253:6
There's the l. for ever STEV 742:25
they which he slew in his l. BIBL 78:8
third of my l. ALLE 12:18
this gives l. to thee SHAK 704:10
This l. is most jolly SHAK 659:5
this long disease, my l. POPE 583:4
Thou art my l. HERR 374:24
Thou art my l. QUAR 618:18
three-fourths of our l. ARNO 29:2
Time to taste l. BROW 155:32
tired of l. JOHN 415:24
took a man's l. with him CARL 187:14
torch of l. LUCR 479:4
Touch my l. TAGO 752:21
tree of l. BIBL 73:18
tree of l. BIBL 82:27
try to crowd out real l. FORS 321:2
turn over a new l. FLEM 317:13
upon the thorns of l. SHEL 712:16
value of l. MONT 527:10
view of l. DARW 250:22
voyage of their l. SHAK 676:28
walk in newness of l. BIBL 104:38
warm full blooded l. JOYC 422:15
Was my l. also OWEN 562:12
way, the truth, and the l. BIBL 102:18
well-written L. CARL 187:10
We should show l. CHEK 208:5
What a relaxed l. LUIS 479:10
What is l. ROST 635:13
What is l.? a frenzy CALD 181:5
What is this l. DAVI 252:8
what is your l. BIBL 110:21
What l. and death is CHAP 202:16
what l. is then to a man BIBL 92:7
wheel of l. run long STER 739:5
which tells of l. COLE 227:5
While there's l. PROV 614:43
whole l. shows in your face BACA 41:4
Wholesome of l. HORA 387:24
Who saw l. steadily ARNO 27:30
wine should l. employ GAY 331:17
With long l. BOOK 138:1
Without work, l. goes rotten CAMU 184:17
Woolworth l. hereafter NICO 544:23
write the l. of a man JOHN 414:13
years of my l. BIBL 75:20
you lived your l. JOHN 407:17
your longer l. ELIZ 297:3
life-blood l. of a master spirit MILT 519:9
lifeless virtue is l. PAST 569:4
life-lie Take the l. away IBSE 398:12
lifetime in their l. BELL 64:16
knowledge of a l. WHIS 813:21
l. of happiness SHAW 707:30
lift L. her with care HOOD 382:13
l. me as a wave SHEL 712:16
l. up mine eyes BOOK 140:12
L. up your heads BOOK 133:3
L. up your heart WESL 811:6
L. up your hearts BOOK 129:18
Lord, l. thou up BOOK 131:20
Lord l. up his countenance BIBL 76:24
lifting l. up of my hands BOOK 141:15
light armour of l. BIBL 105:21
armour of l. BOOK 127:21
as the shining l. BIBL 82:11
bathe the world in l. WORD 828:8
bear witness of that L. BIBL 101:5
between l. and darkness SIDD 718:1
blaze of living l. BYRO 175:20
brief crack of l. NABO 537:20
Buddha of Infinite L. MAHĀ 490:12
burning and a shining l. BIBL 101:23
certain Slant of l. DICK 266:16
children of l. BIBL 100:7
children of l. BOOK 130:9
Creature, which was L. BACO 44:32
crying for the l. TENN 761:11
dark is l. enough FRY 326:20
darkness rather than l. BIBL 101:19
day-labour, l. denied MILT 518:30
dim religious l. MILT 512:11
dying of the l. THOM 772:2
Endless L. ZORO 841:17
Even L. itself THOM 775:18
excess of l. GRAY 351:2
fierce l. which beats TENN 759:11
fire, to give them l. BIBL 76:5
For that celestial l. MILT 514:19
freedom is but a l. GUMI 354:19
From darkness lead me to L. UPAN 787:9
garmented in l. SHEL 714:16
Give me a l. HASK 363:16
gives a lovely l. MILL 509:11
giveth l. unto the eyes BOOK 132:16
God is L. BLAK 118:7
growing l. SHAK 672:27
hath the l. shined BIBL 86:28
how my l. is spent MILT 518:29
infinite ocean of l. FOX 322:7
into the world of l. VAUG 790:11
Jeanie with the l. brown hair FOST 321:16
know what l. is JOHN 415:19
Lead, kindly L. NEWM 542:19
leaping l. AUDE 34:7
Let's in new l. WALL 800:5
Let there be l. BIBL 73:10
Let there be l. BYRO 177:13
Let there be l. MARR 497:13
Let there be l. SHEL 711:11
Let your l. so shine BIBL 93:6
l. after smoke HORA 385:21
l., a glory COLE 225:4
l., and will aspire SHAK 705:29
l. at the end of the tunnel DICK 267:1
l. at the end of the tunnel LOWE 478:5
l. break forth BIBL 89:2
L. breaks where no sun THOM 772:9

light (*cont.*):
l. but the shadow BROW 152:12
L. come, light go PROV 605:27
l. dissolved in star-showers SHEL 713:29
l. excelleth darkness BIBL 84:6
l. fantastic round MILT 511:18
l. fantastic toe MILT 512:15
l. gleams an instant BECK 60:3
L. (God's eldest daughter) FULL 327:10
l. has gone out of our lives NEHR 540:5
l. in the darkness of mere being JUNG 423:7
l. in the dust SHEL 712:3
l. into bodies NEWT 543:4
l. is as darkness BIBL 81:13
l. is come BIBL 89:4
l. is sweet BIBL 84:31
l. is to painting BOUR 145:5
l. my fire MORR 532:22
l. of common day WORD 830:1
l. of evening, Lissadell YEAT 836:6
l. of his countenance BOOK 136:3
l. of jurisprudence CLOS 222:10
l. of Jurisprudence COKE 224:9
L. of Light BOOK 129:8
l. of Terewth DICK 261:2
L. of the heavens KORA 445:2
l. of the world BIBL 93:5
l. of thy countenance BOOK 131:20
l. of thy countenance BOOK 137:8
l. of thy Holy Spirit BOOK 128:9
l., shade, and perspective CONS 235:9
l. shineth in darkness BIBL 101:3
l. that never was WORD 828:2
l. to lighten the Gentiles BIBL 98:25
l. to shine upon the road COWP 240:21
l. to them that sit in darkness BIBL 98:18
l. unto my paths BOOK 140:9
l. within his own clear breast MILT 511:21
line of festal l. ARNO 27:8
Lonely and lost to l. BYRO 175:15
long l. shakes TENN 765:16
meditate on the lovely l. RIG 627:16
More l. LAST 456:15
move l. SORL 728:19
my l., and my salvation BOOK 133:18
neither heat nor l. WEBS 807:26
new l. of grace SMOL 726:14
noose of l. FITZ 314:7
once our brief l. has set CATU 197:2
once we lose this l. JONS 420:10
particles of l. BLAK 120:3
perpetual l. MISS 523:2
place of l. DISR 269:11
progeny of l. MILT 517:1
pure and endless l. VAUG 790:17
pure severity of perfect l. TENN 759:21
Put out the l. SHAK 693:22
reft the sonne his l. CHAU 205:13
ring of l. RAIN 620:8
seen a glorious l. SCOT 652:23
seen a great l. BIBL 86:28
set is our little l. CAMP 183:21
shew l. at Calais JOHN 413:16
silent as l. SMIT 726:9
soft! what l. SHAK 697:9
speed far faster than l. BULL 160:1
sudden gust of l. MOTI 534:5
sweetness and l. ARNO 28:8
sweetness and l. SWIF 747:12
Teach l. to counterfeit a gloom MILT 512:7
Thou art my l. QUAR 618:18
through the realms of l. GURN 355:5
thy l. and thy truth BOOK 134:10
tried to mend the Electric L. BELL 63:23
universal l. POPE 584:13
waited for the l. ROBI 629:15
Warmth and L. GREN 352:17
when my l. is low TENN 761:8
Wherefore is l. given BIBL 81:6
where sweetness and l. failed FORS 320:13
while the l. fails ELIO 294:19
Will l. only shine BERN 69:6
with a l. behind her GILB 339:12
with Thee l. BONH 125:8
Light Brigade Forward, the L. TENN 757:16
lighten let thy mercy l. upon us BOOK 126:2
L. our darkness BOOK 126:20
l. with celestial fire BOOK 142:7
lighter l. than vanity BUNY 161:1
lightest l. things swim at the top HALI 357:16
lightheaded l., variable men STEV 741:30
lighthouse Keeping a l. with his eyes CAMP 183:1
sitivation at the l. DICK 265:18
lighting l. devils BINC 115:4
lightly l. as it comth CHAU 206:8
l. skims the midge BETJ 70:9
unadvisedly, l., or wantonly BOOK 131:1
lightness unbearable l. of being KUND 446:6
lightning bottled l. DICK 264:6
Brief as the l. SHAK 689:5
chaos illuminated by l. WILD 818:7
from Jove the l. MANI 493:16
known the l.'s hour DAY- 253:12
l. and lashed rod HOPK 385:3
l. fall from heaven BIBL 99:9
L. never strikes PROV 605:28
loosed the fateful l. HOWE 391:15
Shakespeare by flashes of l. COLE 227:19
snatched the l. TURG 785:9
to keep the l. out ISHE 400:7
writing history with l. WILS 822:9
lights all-the-l.-on man REED 624:1
dimming of the l. NICO 545:1
Father of l. BIBL 110:12
Followed false l. DRYD 281:20
God made two great l. BIBL 73:13
l. are dim and low ORRE 557:14
l. around the door ROSS 635:8
may bear all l. SHAF 655:18
northern l. astream SMAR 722:13
Turn up the l. LAST 457:13
watching the tail l. CRAN 243:24
your l. burning BIBL 99:23
ligno *Regnavit a l. Deus* FORT 321:8
like but you'll l. it CATC 196:31
do just what you l. SHAW 707:11
don't l. this game CATC [illegible]
Do what you l. RABE 619:11
I am not made l. any ROUS 636:3
I'd l. to get away FROS 325:15
I L. Ike POLI 581:15
L. breeds like PROV 605:29
L. cures like MOTT 535:18
L. doth quit like SHAK 686:25
l. everyone else DE G 256:1
l. is not necessarily good BELL 62:21
l. it the least CHES 209:13
l., or at least tolerate TREV 781:10
l. this sort of thing LINC 469:3
l. what you get SHAW 708:31
L. will to like PROV 605:34
look upon his l. again SHAK 662:3
made me l. him less CONG 232:24
man I did not l. AUST 39:5
man you don't l. THOM 772:21
none of his friends l. him WILD 819:11
nothing *l.* it CARR 191:9
No wonder we l. them AMIS 13:18
very, very l. me STEV 742:14
wha's l. us TOAS 778:2
will much l. AUST 39:14
liked feeling that one is not l. SEI 653:11
l. it not, and died WOTT 833:3
l. whate'er She looked on BROW 156:25
wish to be l. RUSS 639:14
likely Not bloody l. SHAW 709:15
likeness any l. of any thing BIBL 76:8
in our image, after our l. BIBL 73:14
l. in the Torah KORA 445:11
l. of men BIBL 103:32
made in the l. of men. BIBL 108:16
likerous l. mouth CHAU 206:17
likes does what he l. to do GILL 339:14
likewise Go, and do thou l. BIBL 99:14
liking Being alone and l. it HASK 363:15
Friendships begin with l. ELIO 292:6
lost me in your l. SHAK 677:26
Not l. the person THOM 773:6
lilac Kew in l.-time NOYE 547:5
l. and the roses ARAG 23:11
l. is in bloom BROO 150:10
lilacs breeding L. ELIO 295:26
l. last in the dooryard WHIT 815:23
Lilian Airy, fairy L. TENN 762:21
lilies beauty lives though l. die FLEC 317:3
braids of l. knitting MILT 512:1
feedeth among the l. BIBL 85:12
few l. blow HOPK 384:9
give me l. in armfuls VIRG 795:2
kingcups, and loved l. SPEN 734:21
l. and languors SWIN 750:15
l. by the rivers BIBL 92:18
l. of the field BIBL 93:25
L. that fester SHAK 705:7
L. without MARV 498:22
Lotos and l. TENN 765:7
pale, lost l. DOWS 277:5
peacocks and l. RUSK 638:22
three l. in her hand ROSS 634:16
Lilliburlero bars of L. STER 738:20
L. Bullena-la WHAR 813:4
lilting About the l. house THOM 772:3
l., before dawn of day ELLI 298:9
lily across the l. leven BALL 52:1
Elaine, the l. maid TENN 759:25
folds the l. all her sweetness up TENN 766:3
l. of Florence LONG 473:18
l. of the valleys BIBL 85:9
l. on thy brow KEAT 428:8
l. rears its gouged face HILL 376:15
l.-white boys SONG 729:11
little l.-handed baronet TENN 766:7
paint the l. BYRO 176:24
paint the l. SHAK 677:15
pure as the l. LAUD 454:6
trembles to a l. DOBS 271:16
waved her l. hand GAY 332:22
with a poppy or a l. GILB 338:20
limb l. by limb MILT 519:13
on every airth a l. MONT 579:1
limbecks Distilled from l. SHAK 705:18
limber little child, a l. elf COLE 225:1
limbo l. large and broad MILT 516:5
limbs deck your lower l. in pants NASH 539:19
great smooth marbly l. BROW 155:13
life controls these l. VIRG 794:12
l. of a poet HORA 389:18
lime l.-tree bower my prison COLE 227:3
limestone l. quarried near YEAT 837:22
limit l. and isolate oneself GOET 343:16
quiet l. of the world TENN 766:16
limited Liberty too must be l. BURK 162:13
whizzed the L.— CRAN 243:24
limits l. of my language WITT 824:8
l. prescribed by the law LACL 447:7
stony l. SHAK 697:13
limns l. the water BACO 45:11
limousine All we want is a l. MACN 488:7
One perfect l. PARK 567:4
limp l. father of thousands JOYC 422:13
limpid stag in l. currents PHIL 575:10
Limpopo grey-green, greasy, L. KIPL 441:9
Lincoln I am a Ford, not a L. FORD 319:12
L. County Road or Armageddon DYLA 287:13
L. shovelled into the tombs SAND 643:19
L. went to New Orleans HUGH 392:19
Linden On L., when the sun CAMP 183:8
Linden Lea leän down low in L. BARN 55:6
line active l. on a walk KLEE 442:3
cancel half a l. FITZ 314:17
carved not a l. WOLF 825:5
combine to form a l. LIND 469:6
cut, the style, the l. LOES 473:2
direction of the right l. NEWT 543:6

full-resounding l. POPE 586:17
horizontal l. WHEW 813:14
l. is a fuse MAYA 502:16
l. is length without breadth EUCL 301:16
l. too labours POPE 584:23
l. upon line BIBL 87:13
l. will take us hours YEAT 835:2
lives along the l. POPE 585:15
problem of the colour l. DU B 284:2
thin red l. RUSS 640:13
through colour and l. MOND 526:2
lineaments l. of Gospel books ROYD 637:1
linen did not love clean l. JOHN 413:2
fair white l. cloth BOOK 129:3
In blanchèd l. KEAT 427:13
in l. like a gentleman JOHN 409:19
Love is like l. FLET 318:18
mad in white l. SHER 715:18
purple and fine l. BIBL 100:10
very fine l. BRUM 158:23
wash your l. STEV 742:21
liner L. she's a lady KIPL 439:11
lines face into more l. SHAK 702:7
I plant l. WALC 799:3
Just say the l. COWA 239:6
l. and colours POUS 590:7
l. are fallen unto me BOOK 132:9
l. like these CALV 182:2
l. (so loves) oblique MARV 498:11
liquid l. mellifluously bland BYRO 177:7
Prose is when all the l. BENT 67:1
six l. written RICH 627:10
town-crier spoke my l. SHAK 664:13
walk on the l. MILN 510:19
lingering alone sit l. here VAUG 790:11
l., with boiling oil GILB 338:12
lingua *Pange, l.* FORT 321:6
Pange, l. THOM 771:10
linguam *Et l. et mores* JUVE 424:9
linguistic l. philosophy RUSS 640:6
lining cloud has a silver l. PROV 599:21
There's a silver l. FORD 320:6
link weakest l. PROV 597:9
lin-lan-lone l. of evening bells TENN 758:18
linnet l. born within the cage TENN 761:3
linoleum shoot me through l. BANK 53:9
linsy-woolsy lawless l. brother BUTL 172:5
lion as a roaring l. BIBL 111:7
better than a dead l. PROV 605:47
bold as a l. BIBL 83:31
buttocked like a l. MALO 492:10
calf and the young l. BIBL 87:4
dead l. BIBL 84:20
desert l. ARNO 27:16
hungry l. roars SHAK 690:28
l. among ladies SHAK 689:29
l. and adder BOOK 137:23
L. and the Cock GOGA 343:23
l. and the unicorn NURS 549:3
l. shall eat straw BIBL 87:5
l. to frighten the wolves MACH 486:2
l. would cease to live THOM 771:15
March comes in like a l. PROV 606:28
mouse may help a l. PROV 607:13
nation that had l.'s heart CHUR 216:7
Rouse the l. SCOT 652:9
said to the sick l. HORA 386:12
Strong is the l. SMAR 722:10
To rouse a l. SHAK 667:25
wrath of the l. BLAK 119:20
lions l. do lack BOOK 133:21
L. led by donkeys MILI 508:11
l., or Vanity-Fair BUNY 161:13
l. roaring BOOK 139:5
my darling from the l. BOOK 133:24
on the other, l. PATM 569:21
soul is among l. BOOK 135:15
stronger than l. BIBL 79:2
We are two l. SHAK 675:11
lip 'twixt cup and l. PROV 612:27
lips ashes on the l. MOOR 530:19
beautiful l. in anger RIMB 628:13
Eternity was in our l. and eyes SHAK 656:16
ever at his l. KEAT 429:5
Is it Lombard's l. EWAR 305:10
keep the door of my l. BOOK 141:15
l. cannot fail BURG 162:5
l. drew near BYRO 176:15
l. have spoken SHEL 712:3
l. like a thread of scarlet BIBL 85:14
l. ne'er act the winning part HERR 374:10
l. of a strange woman BIBL 82:12
l. of dying men ARNO 27:17
l. of living men BUTL 173:2
l. of those that are asleep BIBL 86:6
l. once sanctified BROW 158:15
l. that laugh and hide SWIN 750:7
l., that they speak no guile BOOK 133:22
l. that touch liquor YOUN 839:16
moisten poor Jim's l. FARM 307:2
my Julia's l. do smile HERR 374:5
My l. are sealed BALD 49:10
My l. are sealed MISQ 522:4
never come out of a lady's l. FLEM 317:12
open my l. BOOK 135:9
O take those l. away SHAK 686:21
people of unclean l. BIBL 86:22
put my l. to it DICK 263:6
Read my l. BUSH 171:3
roses of thy l. LODG 472:18
round their narrow l. ROSS 635:1
saw their starved l. KEAT 428:13
shoot out their l. BOOK 132:22
touched thy l. BIBL 86:23
when I ope my l. SHAK 687:3
lipstick bears a l.'s traces MARV 499:9
liquefaction l. of her clothes HERR 375:4
liquid Cats, no less l. TESS 768:17
let their l. siftings fall ELIO 295:25
l. lines mellifluously bland BYRO 177:7
Thames is l. history BURN 166:5
liquor Good l., I stoutly maintain GOLD 345:17
lads for the l. HOUS 391:1
lips that touch l. YOUN 839:16
l. is quicker NASH 539:16
Livelier l. than the Muse HOUS 391:9
Love is that l. HERB 372:2
other spiritual l. BYRO 179:14
wanteth not l. BIBL 86:4
lirra Tirra l. TENN 762:18
lisped I l. in numbers POPE 583:3
Somwhat he l. CHAU 204:17
list I've got a little l. GILB 338:1
List, list, O, l. SHAK 662:24
snatched up the l. AKHM 9:11
listen Darkling I l. KEAT 429:13
good to l. ADVE 7:33
l. all day CARR 189:13
L., my children LONG 474:15
l. the more ZENO 840:1
only l. when I am unhappy SMIT 724:20
politicians have had to l. FITT 314:4
privilege of wisdom to l. HOLM 381:6
Stop-look-and-l. OFFI 554:12
world should l. then SHEL 714:9
listened he is not l. to TALM 754:20
listener l., who listens in the snow STEV 740:4
listeners L. never hear any good PROV 605:35
listening disease of not l. SHAK 669:23
l., lying in wait THOM 773:3
People hearing without l. SIMO 720:10
listeth wind bloweth where it l. BIBL 101:17
lit whole Fleet's l. up WOOD 826:9
literal say a l. God DONN 275:1
literary improving l. taste MCEL 485:5
l. and scientific ARNO 28:20
l. cooks MORE 530:23
l. man DICK 264:21
l. mornings AUDE 34:5
l. prejudices JOHN 410:4
l. productions GIBB 335:8
Never l. attempt HUME 395:3
Of all the l. scenes PRES 591:6
parole of l. men JOHN 416:21
unsuccessful l. man BELL 63:20
with St Paul are l. ARNO 28:27
literature almost invisible l. BALL 52:11
function of imaginative l. EMPS 300:8
great Cham of l. SMOL 726:16
Great l. is POUN 590:5
ideas to l. BOUR 145:5
in l., the oldest BULW 160:8
in the locks of l. TENN 767:19
itch of l. LOVE 477:3
life ruined by l. BROO 151:4
like their l. clear and cold LEWI 467:6
l. can and should do BYAT 173:5
L. cannot be the business SOUT 731:8
l. goes as freight GARC 329:12
l. is a drug BORR 143:11
L. is a luxury CHES 211:3
l. is more dependable BROD 149:5
l. is my mistress CHEK 208:14
L. is news POUN 590:3
L. mostly about having sex LODG 472:12
l. of *power* DE Q 258:12
L.'s always a good card BENN 66:10
l. seeks to communicate DE Q 258:9
l.'s performing flea O'CA 552:14
L. the orchestration of platitudes WILD 819:16
lover of l. SOUT 731:3
Philistine of genius in l. ARNO 29:4
profession of l. JOHN 411:3
province of l. MACA 482:17
Remarks are not l. STEI 737:5
rest is l. COLE 228:5
rest is l. VALÉ 789:1
superior man studies l. CONF 231:14
wash l. off ARTA 29:19
lites *inter vos tantas componere l.* VIRG 796:2
litigious l. lady NEWT 543:10
littérature *tout le reste est l.* VERL 791:7
little big words for l. matters JOHN 413:19
by l. and little BIBL 91:32
cry of the L. Peoples LE G 462:12
eat up the l. ones SHAK 694:7
Every l. helps PROV 599:29
Ev'ry day a l. death SOND 727:22
Go, l. bok CHAU 207:18
had a l. gun NURS 551:5
having too l. COMP 230:14
here a l., and there a little BIBL 87:13
hobgoblin of l. minds EMER 299:23
how l. the mind JOHN 415:1
how l. we think of the other TWAI 786:19
l. and loud PROV 605:48
L. boxes on the hillside REYN 625:14
l. creep through SHEN 715:7
L. drops of water CARN 189:2
L. Englanders ANON 17:9
l. fire kindleth BIBL 110:18
L. fish are sweet PROV 605:37
l. grey cells CHRI 212:15
l. learning is a dangerous thing POPE 584:15
little l. grave SHAK 695:14
Little man, l. man ELIZ 297:6
L. man, you've had a busy day SIGL 719:4
L. Miss Muffet NURS 549:7
l. more BROW 155:18
L. one! Oh, little one STEP 738:4
l. people pay taxes HELM 368:17
l. pot is soon hot PROV 605:41
l. saint HERR 374:21
l. seemed to him great MACA 482:6
l. ships of England GUED 354:10
L. strokes fell great oaks PROV 605:42
L. subject, little wit CARE 186:19
L. things please PROV 605:44
l. to say SKEL 721:9
l. volume, but large book CRAS 244:9
l. while BIBL 102:26

little (*cont.*):
l. woman who wrote LINC 469:4
Love me l. PROV 606:7
Man wants but l. GOLD 344:20
Many a l. PROV 606:22
no l. enemy PROV 612:16
offering Germany too l. NEVI 541:13
one of these l. ones BIBL 95:4
our l. life SHAK 699:6
Say l. and do much SHAM 706:4
She gives but l. YOUN 839:11
So l. done LAST 457:4
so l. done TENN 761:17
Thank heaven for l. girls LERN 465:8
this l. world SHAK 694:19
though she be but l. SHAK 690:7
too l. or too much BARR 55:12
very l. one MARR 497:16
wants that l. strong HOLM 381:9
with so l. stir WHIT 814:19
littleness For the long l. of life CORN 237:3
liturgy Popish l. PITT 576:24
Publick L. BOOK 125:11
live be, feel, l. HERD 373:21
Bid me to l. HERR 374:23
cannot l. with you MART 498:4
Can these bones l. BIBL 89:33
cease to l. ARNO 28:5
Come l. with me DONN 273:19
Come l. with me MARL 496:19
Come l. with me PROV 597:28
Could she not l. BYRO 174:4
dangerous to l. long THOM 771:6
Days are where we l. LARK 452:14
desires to l. long SWIF 749:2
Easy l. and quiet die SCOT 651:19
Eat to l. PROV 599:8
enable its citizens to l. WEIL 808:27
find out why we l. CHEK 208:10
forgets to l. LA B 446:16
Glad did I l. STEV 743:4
hast no more to l. SWIN 750:11
he isn't fit to l. KING 436:13
He shall l. BOOK 136:19
He shall l. by them TALM 754:7
he shall l. in them BIBL 76:22
He shall not l. SHAK 676:16
How can we l. like this INDI 399:1
how long I have to l. BOOK 133:29
If you don't l. it PARK 566:17
I joy to see My self now l. HERR 374:19
I l. not in myself BYRO 174:19
in him we l., and move BIBL 104:10
just shall l. by faith BIBL 104:26
know how to l. right HORA 387:10
let me l. to-night SHAK 693:24
Let us l., my Lesbia CATU 197:2
L. all you can JAME 402:25
l. and last CATU 194:21
l. and learn POMF 580:5
L. and learn PROV 605:45
L. and let live PROV 605:46
L. and lie reclined TENN 763:14
l. and take comfort WORD 832:12
l. a novel HARD 360:15
l. any longer in sin BIBL 104:37
L. a thousand years SHAK 675:20
l. beyond its income BUTL 172:23
l. by bread alone PROV 606:13
l. by sight BUNY 161:20
l. cleanly SHAK 669:19
l. dog is better PROV 605:47
l. in a fantasy world MURD 536:21
L. in despite of murder CHAP 202:15
l. in peace ARIS 24:19
l. in society ARIS 25:3
l. longest, see most PROV 612:35
l., not as we wish MENA 504:13
l. on this Crumpetty Tree LEAR 460:22
l. on your knees IBAR 398:3
l. or die wi' Charlie HOGG 380:13
l. past years again DRYD 281:3
l. their creeds GUES 354:14
l. this long BLAK 117:15
l. through someone else FRIE 324:23
L. till tomorrow COWP 240:14
l. to be over ninety ABBO 1:2
l. to do that MART 497:22
l. together as brothers KING 436:15
l. too long DANI 249:4
l. to please JOHN 411:11
l. to study BACO 44:31
l. under the shadow of a war SPEN 732:25
l., unseen, unknown POPE 586:25
l. well on nothing a year THAC 769:11
L. with yourself PERS 574:6
l. your life not as simple PAST 569:7
long as ye both shall l. BOOK 131:4
long to l. BOOK 126:15
Man is born to l. PAST 569:2
martyrdom to l. BROW 153:2
means whereby I l. SHAK 688:16
might as well l. PARK 567:6
mortal millions l. *alone* ARNO 28:2
must l. ARGE 24:6
nations how to l. MILT 519:20
never l. to be useless WESL 811:20
no man see me and l. BIBL 76:19
not l. to eat MOLI 524:17
Sacco's name will l. VANZ 789:19
see so much, nor l. so long SHAK 680:16
short time to l. BOOK 131:12
should bid thee l. TENN 766:2
sometimes l. apart SAKI 642:9
taught us how to l. TICK 777:11
Teach me to l. KEN 433:3
to l. dangerously NIET 545:16
to l. is Christ BIBL 108:14
To l. is like to love BUTL 172:27
To l. without him WOTT 833:3
to l. without labour TAWN 755:16
To l. with thee RALE 620:9
Too small to l. in ANON 19:8
turn and l. with animals WHIT 815:15
wanted to l. deep THOR 776:12
way they have to l. CATH 194:10
we bear to l. POPE 585:28
We l., as we dream CONR 234:11
We l. our lives RILK 628:1
wouldn't *l.* under Niagara CARL 188:20
would you l. for ever FRED 324:2
you shall l. by fame SPEN 733:4
lived Had we l. SCOT 650:9
I have l. long enough SHAK 685:17
I've l. inside myself DAVI 252:3
lies a man who never l. THOM 775:1
l. during the years around 1789 TALL 753:6
l. in social intercourse JOHN 414:13
l. light in the spring ARNO 26:7
Mr Holmes where *have* you l. DOYL 277:20
never loved, has never l. GAY 332:2
Never to have l. is best YEAT 836:3
say 'I have l.' HORA 388:23
lively l. Oracles of God CORO 237:8
true and l. Word BOOK 129:13
liver l. is on the right MOLI 525:9
L. of blaspheming Jew SHAK 684:19
l. spotted JONS 419:12
l.-wing of a fowl TENN 767:16
open and notorious evil l. BOOK 129:1
livered But I am pigeon-l. SHAK 663:29
liveries summer l. LANI 451:4
Liverpool folk that live in L. CHES 210:12
livers grave L. do in Scotland use WORD 831:13
livery in her sober l. all things clad MILT 516:19
shadowed l. SHAK 687:16
lives Careless talk costs l. OFFI 554:1
Clarissa l. RICH 627:4
Everything that l. BLAK 118:9
evil that men do l. SHAK 675:27
He l., he wakes SHEL 711:2
He that l. upon hope FRAN 323:12
he who l. more lives than one WILD 819:2
how he l. JOHN 414:5
how the other half l. PROV 608:41
in jeopardy of their l. BIBL 79:14
it's men's l. SCOT 651:17
light wind l. or dies KEAT 430:11
l. along the line POPE 585:15
l. by the sword PROV 602:30
l. come and go CONR 234:20
l. long who lives well PROV 602:8
l. of quiet desperation THOR 776:4
l. to eat SOCR 726:22
l. would grow together SWIN 751:14
make our l. sublime LONG 474:6
ninety l. have been taken MCGO 485:7
passing their l. together HUME 394:12
pleasant in their l. BIBL 79:2
their l. before SHAK 694:18
way to conduct our l. PLAT 578:6
woman who l. for others LEWI 466:19
liveth he that l. longest HENS 371:5
know that my redeemer l. BIBL 81:22
l. unto God BIBL 105:1
name l. for evermore BIBL 92:17
name l. for evermore EPIT 304:6
that l., and was dead BIBL 111:23
livid one l. smile WALP 801:21
living appointed for all l. BIBL 81:27
are you yet l. SHAK 690:34
book of the l. BOOK 136:13
Earned a precarious l. ANON 16:1
envy of the l. HOBB 379:5
even for the l. God BOOK 134:5
fever called 'l.' POE 579:14
fight for the l. JONE 419:2
fillest all things l. BOOK 141:20
for you to go on l. SOCR 727:2
get mine own l. BOOK 130:16
go on l. even after death FRAN 323:6
hands of the l. God BIBL 109:27
house is a machine for l. in LE C 461:13
land of the l. BIBL 88:18
language of the l. ELIO 294:13
life is not worth l. SOCR 727:1
L. and partly living ELIO 295:14
l. at this hour WORD 829:8
l. death MILT 518:16
l. dog BIBL 84:20
l. doll, everywhere you look PLAT 577:11
l. for one's diary AGAT 6:19
L. in history FITZ 315:19
l. in Philadelphia EPIT 303:5
L. is abnormal IONE 399:20
L. is an illness CHAM 201:5
L. is my job MONT 527:17
l. know No bounds SHIR 717:11
l. need charity ARNO 26:1
l. sacrifice BIBL 105:14
L.? The servants will do that VILL 792:18
l. to some purpose PAIN 564:7
l. up to it that is difficult THAC 768:19
long habit of l. BROW 153:3
machine for l. TOLS 779:13
more alone while l. CARR 189:5
more than the l. BIBL 84:9
nets to catch the l. WEBS 807:19
noble L. WORD 831:9
no l. of its own JENN 406:10
no l. people in it CHEK 208:5
no l. with thee ADDI 5:1
no man l. BOOK 141:17
not learning from but l. BLAI 117:9
Of health and l. SHAK 699:24
pain of l. ELIO 293:18
Plain l. and high thinking WORD 830:13
reasons for l. JUVE 424:18
respect to the l. VOLT 798:5
riotous l. BIBL 100:2
start by l. ANOU 22:12
Summer time an' the l. is easy HEYW 376:4
those who are l. BURK 163:29
too much love of l. SWIN 750:22

well and l. in Paris ANON 17:6
Who, l., had no roof HEYW 376:8
Why seek ye the l. BIBL 100:31
world does not owe us a l. PHIL 575:4
living-dead l. man SHAK 659:30
Livingstone Dr L., I presume STAN 736:6
livres *l. cadrent mal* MOLI 525:6
lizard L.'s leg SHAK 684:18
llama L. is a sort of fleecy goat BELL 63:20
Lloyd George L. knew my father ANON 17:11
lo L.! He comes WESL 811:8
L.! the poor Indian POPE 585:10
load l. and bless With fruit KEAT 430:8
L. every rift KEAT 431:23
loaf Half a l. is better PROV 601:41
l. with a field in the middle WILD 819:7
slice off a cut l. PROV 610:45
with a l. of bread FITZ 314:9
loafing cricket as organized l. TEMP 757:8
loan l. oft loses SHAK 662:12
loathe l. all things held CALL 181:16
loathing Length begets l. PROV 605:15
loaves five barley l. BIBL 101:25
lobster l. be any more ridiculous NERV 541:8
seen the mailed l. rise FRER 324:11
voice of the L. CARR 190:6
local little l. difficulties MACM 487:18
l., but prized elsewhere AUDE 35:5
l. habitation and a name SHAK 690:19
l. thing called Christianity HARD 360:8
locally act l. SAYI 648:5
Lochinvar young L. is come SCOT 651:7
loci *Geniumque l.* VIRG 795:4
lock broken the l. AUDE 34:18
l. o' his gowden hair BALL 52:5
why l. him in SHAW 708:12
locked hand that l. her up VAUG 790:15
locket Lucy L. lost NURS 549:11
locks in the l. of literature TENN 767:19
knotted and combinèd l. SHAK 662:25
l. were like the raven BURN 167:17
l. which are left you SOUT 730:21
never shake Thy gory l. SHAK 684:11
locksmiths Love laughs at l. PROV 606:5
locust hath the l. eaten BIBL 90:12
years that the l. hath eaten BIBL 90:13
locusts l. and wild honey BIBL 92:28
locuta *Roma l. est* AUGU 36:12
lodestar he was the l. LYDG 480:9
lodestone l. to the north DAVI 251:19
lodge as a l. in a garden BIBL 86:10
best to l. SHAK 702:8
l. Him in the manger ANON 19:19
lodged L. with me useless MILT 518:29
lodging Hard was their l. GART 330:12
lodgings l. in a head BUTL 171:23
pent up in frowzy l. SMOL 726:13
loft windy, untidy l. CANN 185:10
lofty great and l. things MONT 527:6
L. and sour SHAK 673:23
log big rotting l. WHIT 814:3
L.-cabin to White House THAY 770:15
logic Good, too, L., of course CLOU 221:17
l. and rhetoric BACO 44:8
l. of our times DAY- 253:14
nothing more than l. gates AUGA 35:20
overthrow of all his l. STEV 741:9
Second L. then ARIS 24:9
That's l. CARR 190:18
logical L. consequences HUXL 397:19
logically does not make them sound l. HALD 356:16
logs Tom bears l. SHAK 681:4
loin ungirt l. BROW 158:4
loins girded up his l. BIBL 80:1
Let your l. be girded BIBL 99:23
shudder in the l. engenders YEAT 836:15
thicker than my father's l. BIBL 79:21
Loire L. more than the Latin Tiber DU B 283:23
loitered l. my life away HAZL 365:6
loitering Alone and palely l. KEAT 428:7
palely l. OPEN 556:7
Lolita L., light of my life NABO 537:17
L., light of my life OPEN 556:1
Lombardy waveless plain of L. SHEL 712:4
London 1938 in L. MIDL 507:9
arch of L. Bridge MACA 482:10
best club in L. DICK 264:25
city much like L. SHEL 713:2
crowd flowed over L. Bridge ELIO 296:1
describes L. BAGE 47:22
foggy day in L. Town GERS 334:12
gazed at the L. skies BETJ 70:4
going to L. ELIO 293:1
gondola of L. DISR 270:20
in L. only is a trade DRYD 282:14
I've been to L. NURS 550:9
key of India is L. DISR 269:23
lies L.'s daughter THOM 772:12
L.: a nation DISR 270:19
L. Bridge is broken down NURS 549:10
L. doth pour out SHAK 672:1
L. is a fine town COLM 229:15
L. is a modern Babylon DISR 270:30
[L.] is become an overgrown SMOL 726:12
L. is to Paddington CANN 185:4
L. particular . . . A fog DICK 260:19
L., small and white and clean MORR 532:13
L. spread out in the sun LARK 453:8
L.'s towers BLAK 119:5
L., that great cesspool DOYL 278:4
L., that great sea SHEL 711:22
L., thou art of townes ANON 17:12
L., thou art the flower ANON 17:13
L. Transport diesel-engined FLAN 316:5
lungs of L. PITT 577:2
rainy Sunday in L. DE Q 258:7
tired of L. JOHN 415:24
vilest alleys in L. DOYL 277:9
with L.'s ghost GALV 329:1
Yankee Doodle came to L. COHA 224:1
lone From the l. shieling GALT 328:19
l. lorn creetur DICK 261:12
l. unhaunted place DONN 273:12
walking by his wild l. KIPL 441:7
loneliness bowery l. TENN 764:21
l. of the long-distance SILL 720:6
well of l. HALL 358:7
lonely All the l. people LENN 463:20
heart is a l. hunter BORR 144:10
mirrors are l. AUDE 34:20
None but the l. heart GOET 343:14
Only the l. ORBI 557:6
troubled with her l. life PEPY 573:3
lonesome on a l. road COLE 226:24
lonesomeness starlight lit my l. HARD 362:1
long be the day l. PROV 596:2
dangerous to live l. THOM 771:6
foot and a half l. HORA 385:17
For a l. time PROU 593:20
for such a l. time MOLI 525:1
fulfilled a l. time BIBL 91:10
How l. a time SHAK 694:12
how l. I have to live BOOK 133:29
How l. wilt thou forget me BOOK 132:4
if a man have l. hair BIBL 106:14
In the l. run KEYN 435:11
it hath very l. arms HALI 357:18
it sha'n't be l. CHES 209:1
lives l. who lives well PROV 602:8
live this l. BLAK 117:15
L. ago in Kentucky WARR 803:22
l., and lank, and brown COLE 226:16
L. and lazy PROV 605:48
l. and the short and the tall HUGH 392:16
l. as ye both shall live BOOK 131:4
l. day's task SHAK 657:13
l.-distance runner SILL 720:6
l. hot summer FILM 312:22
l. in city pent KEAT 430:16
L. is the way MILT 515:17
l., long thoughts LONG 473:23
l., long trail KING 436:19
l.-nosed Etruscans LAWR 458:7
l.-suffering, and of great goodness BOOK 138:18
l.-suffering, and very pitiful BIBL 91:16
l. time deid MOTT 535:3
l. way to Tipperary JUDG 423:1
l. week-end FORS 320:14
l., withdrawing roar ARNO 26:4
Lord, how l. BIBL 86:25
love me l. ANON 17:14
love me l. PROV 606:7
make a l. prologue BIBL 92:20
man goeth to his l. home BIBL 85:2
night of the l. knives HITL 378:5
Nor wants that little l. GOLD 344:20
So l. as men can breathe SHAK 704:10
story need be l. THOR 775:29
week is a l. time in politics WILS 821:16
With l. life BOOK 138:1
wooing not l. a-doing PROV 601:50
your way be l. CAVA 198:5
longa *Ars l., vita brevis* HIPP 377:15
longer living lasts l. ANOU 22:12
l. than the wave BALL 51:10
no l. my own METH 506:6
wished l. by its readers JOHN 418:14
your l. life ELIZ 297:3
longest laughs last, laughs l. PROV 602:29
live l., see most PROV 612:35
l. day and shortest night PROV 595:35
l. journey SHEL 711:9
l. way round PROV 605:49
longeth l. my soul after thee BOOK 134:5
my flesh also l. BOOK 135:24
longing cast a l. eye JEFF 405:9
desire and l. BOOK 137:11
hopeless l. ARNO 26:9
longings I have Immortal l. SHAK 657:28
longitude l. with no platitude FRY 326:23
longtemps *L., je me suis couché* PROU 593:20
look afraid to l. upon God BIBL 75:27
at the l. of him BOOK 139:7
cat may l. at a king PROV 597:7
dares not l. behind BLAI 117:6
dares not l. behind SHEL 715:4
direct him, where to l. DONN 272:7
do we l. for another BIBL 95:5
full l. at the worst HARD 361:13
Hit l. lak sparrer-grass HARR 362:14
I l. at the senators HALE 357:2
l. after our people LAST 455:13
l., and pass on DANT 249:8
L. as much like home FRY 326:24
l. at things in bloom HOUS 390:15
L. back in anger OSBO 560:1
L. before you leap PROV 605:51
L. for me by moonlight NOYE 547:7
l. forward to the trip STIN 743:8
L. in my face TRAI 780:19
l. in thy heart and write SIDN 718:9
l. no way but downwards BUNY 161:10
l. on and help LAWR 458:21
l. on both indifferently SHAK 674:8
L., stranger AUDE 34:6
l. the East End in the face ELIZ 298:1
L. thy last on all things lovely DE L 256:12
l. to his bond SHAK 687:28
L. to it LINC 468:10
l. to other people UNAM 787:8
l. to the end ANON 21:12
L. to your Moat HALI 358:3
l. upon a monkey CONG 233:19
l. upon his like again SHAK 662:3
l. upon thee BIBL 86:2
L. with thine ears SHAK 679:23
One cannot l. at this GOYA 347:12
row one way and l. another BURT 170:6
sit and l. at it for hours JERO 407:1
Stop-l.-and-listen OFFI 554:12
'Tis very sweet to l. KEAT 430:16

look (*cont.*):
We l. before and after SHEL 714:8
When I do l. on thee SIDN 718:21
looked If you l. away, you knew SERE 654:22
looked for a city BIBL 109:29
l. in this merciless glare WILL 820:19
l. upon Peter BIBL 100:24
more he l. inside MILN 510:11
She l. at me KEAT 428:10
lookers angels to be l. on BACO 41:16
L.-on see most PROV 606:1
looketh man l. on the outward BIBL 78:27
looking Here's l. at you FILM 311:10
keep l. over his shoulder BARU 56:12
l. at me like that ZOLA 840:14
l. back BIBL 99:7
l. one way, and rowing BUNY 161:3
l. together SAIN 641:13
May I be l. at you TIBU 777:7
no use l. beyond CHAM 200:12
someone may be l. MENC 504:17
stop other people from l. BLAC 116:20
looking glass cracked l. of a servant JOYC 422:8
smiles, As in a l. SHAK 702:33
suspension of the l. TATE 755:4
looking glasses plenty of l. ASHF 30:13
Women have served as l. WOOL 826:18
looks her l. went everywhere BROW 156:25
I have no proud l. BOOK 141:3
l. do menace heaven MARL 496:23
l. like a duck REUT 624:17
needs good l. TUCK 784:17
Stolen l. HUNT 395:16
woman as old as she l. PROV 606:14
loom labours of the l. DYER 286:14
she left the l. TENN 762:19
loon cream-faced l. SHAK 685:16
laugh like a l. HARB 359:17
looney janitor in a l.-bin WODE 824:18
L. Tunes, and squalid criminals REAG 623:6
loophole l. through which the pervert BRON 149:10
loose all hell broke l. MILT 516:28
Every which way but l. FILM 312:20
I let you l. WESL 811:18
L. his beard GRAY 350:3
l. the bands of Orion BIBL 81:34
l. the bands of wickedness BIBL 89:1
l. the seals BIBL 112:2
L. types of things WORD 832:10
man who should l. me LOWE 477:9
loosed l. our heart in tears ARNO 26:16
looted All has been l. AKHM 9:6
lops l. the mouldered branch TENN 759:7
loquendi *et ius et norma l.* HORA 385:15
loquitur *Cor ad cor l.* MOTT 535:5
Lorca L. was killed, singing READ 622:12
lord acceptable year of the L. BIBL 89:5
Admit l. SHAF 655:15
And I replied, 'My L.' HERB 372:8
belong unto the L. BIBL 77:9
by the hand of the L. BIBL 76:7
come, L. Jesus BIBL 113:16
coming of the L. HOWE 391:15
day which the l. hath made BOOK 140:6
dwell in the house of the L. BOOK 133:1
earth is the l.'s BIBL 106:13
earth is the L.'s BOOK 133:2
Everybody loves a l. PROV 599:39
glory of the L. BIBL 87:28
Go, and the L. be with thee BIBL 78:31
great l. BEAU 58:11
Great l. of all things POPE 585:20
house of the L. BOOK 140:14
kissing of my L. MARL 497:1
let a L. once own the happy lines POPE 584:25
L. and Father of mankind WHIT 816:5
L., deliver us BOOK 127:3
L., dismiss us BUCK 159:17
L., dost thou wash my feet BIBL 102:14
L. gave, and the Lord BIBL 80:36
L. has more truth yet ROBI 629:17
L., have mercy upon us BOOK 126:2
L. how it talk't BEAU 58:18
L., how long BIBL 86:25
L., I am coming LAUD 454:4
L. in His mercy CRAI 243:18
L. is a man of war BIBL 76:6
L. is gracious BIBL 110:27
L. is his name MONS 526:12
L. is in this place BIBL 75:2
L. is King BOOK 138:2
L. is my light BOOK 133:10
L. is my shepherd BOOK 132:26
L. is One SIDD 717:17
L. looketh on the heart BIBL 78:27
L. make his face shine BIBL 76:24
L. mighty in battle BOOK 133:3
L., now lettest thou BIBL 98:24
L. of all hopefulness STRU 745:2
L. of all the world SPEN 733:5
L. of himself WOTT 832:24
L. of hosts BOOK 133:4
L. Of life and death CRAS 244:6
l. of lords BIBL 113:3
L. of the Dance CART 192:16
l. of the foul and the brute COWP 242:17
L. our God is one Lord BIBL 77:6
L. Randal BALL 51:1
L., remember me BIBL 100:27
L.'s anointed temple SHAK 683:18
L. shall raise me up RALE 621:4
L.'s my shepherd SCOT 652:20
L. survives the rainbow LOWE 478:4
L. thy God BIBL 76:8
L. thy God is with thee BIBL 77:17
L., thy word abideth BAKE 48:12
l. to leggen in his bedde CHAU 205:26
L. Tomnoddy is thirty-four BROU 151:11
L. turned, and looked BIBL 100:24
L. was departed BIBL 78:6
L. watch between BIBL 75:5
L., what fools SHAK 690:5
L. will be there WHIT 815:17
L., ye know, is God KETH 434:11
Love is our L.'s meaning JULI 423:1
mouth of the L. BIBL 87:28
My L. and my God BIBL 103:5
My L. should take Frail flesh CROS 246:15
my L. Tomnoddy BARH 54:2
Name of the L. BOOK 140:7
nor the servant above his l. BIBL 94:35
nurture of the L. BOOK 131:2
O L., to what a state TERE 768:11
on the L.'s day BIBL 111:19
own thee L. PRAY 592:7
Praise the L. FORG 320:7
Prepare ye the way of the L. BIBL 92:27
Rejoice in the L. BIBL 108:23
Rejoice, the L. is King WESL 811:6
remembrance of his dying L. SPEN 733:13
saying 'L. Jones Dead' CHES 211:20
Seek ye the L. BIBL 88:21
sing the L.'s song BOOK 141:8
sought the L. aright BURN 166:23
soul doth magnify the L. BIBL 98:16
taken away my L. BIBL 102:40
those who love the L. HUNT 395:11
Up to a point, L. Copper WAUG 806:10
wait upon the Lord BIBL 88:5
way of the L. BIBL 87:28
we battle for the L. ROOS 633:9
Welcum the l. of lycht DOUG 276:12
what hour your L. doth come BIBL 97:7
when they crucified my L. SONG 730:7
Whom the L. loveth BIBL 110:3
wound thy l., thy king SHAK 698:12
lordliest l. in their wine MILT 518:21
lords admiring the House of L. BAGE 46:19
from the House of L. NORF 546:14
I made the carles l. JAME 402:18
l. have their pleasures MONT 528:9
L. in ermine ROBI 629:21
l. of human kind GOLD 345:9
l. o' the creation BURN 169:6
l. who lay ye low SHEL 713:25
l. whose parents were DEFO 255:14
l. will alway BARC 53:22
New l., new laws PROV 607:42
one of the l. of life LAWR 458:14
Scots l. at his feet BALL 51:17
wit among L. JOHN 412:13
with those L. I had gone so far MORE 531:9
lordships good enough for their l. ANON 19:6
lore l. its scholars need KEBL 432:6
volume of forgotten l. POE 579:15
lose cannot fear to l. ASTE 31:12
hurts to l. DOLE 272:2
if you l., you lose nothing PASC 568:16
is to l. it ORWE 559:14
l. her as a friend GLAD 341:16
l. his own soul BIBL 98:8
l. one parent WILD 817:16
l. the name of action SHAK 664:4
l. the war in an afternoon CHUR 216:20
l. to-morrow ARNO 27:9
l. what he never had WALT 802:22
l. what you never had PROV 615:39
nothing much to l. HOUS 390:12
nothing to l. CLOS 222:19
nothing to l. MARX 500:7
nothing to l. but our aitches ORWE 559:7
shall l. it BIBL 95:3
to l. thee were to lose MILT 517:20
way to l. him SHAK 656:14
we don't want to l. you RUBE 637:3
What you l. on the swings PROV 614:13
win or l. it all MONT 529:2
wins if he does not l. KISS 441:27
you l. a few PROV 616:8
losers both should l. be HERB 373:7
he shall be among the l. KORA 444:4
l. weepers PROV 600:20
no winners, but all are l. CHAM 200:16
loses l. his misery ARNO 27:12
Who l., and who wins SHAK 680:7
losest for fear thou l. all HERB 373:13
losing conduct of a l. party BURK 162:6
deem a l. gain SOUT 731:11
Hath but a l. office SHAK 669:21
l. everything Except DURC 286:1
l. one pleased Cato LUCA 478:13
l. trade BORR 143:11
l. your sight SASS 645:17
loss but from its l. YOUN 839:3
counted l. for Christ BIBL 108:20
deeper sense of her l. GASK 330:19
do our country l. SHAK 671:22
no great l. without PROV 612:29
One man's l. PROV 608:47
profit and l. ELIO 296:12
text was l. CUNN 247:17
lost All is l. save honour MISQ 521:1
All is not l. MILT 514:13
All love is l. DUNB 285:6
all was l. MILT 517:17
and we are l. PYRR 618:9
Are you l. daddy LARD 452:10
Balls will be l. always BERR 69:17
battles are l. WHIT 815:13
better to have fought and l. CLOU 223:1
better to have loved and l. PROV 613:6
better to have loved and l. TENN 761:4
country is l. WILL 820:1
Die in the l., lost fight CLOU 221:15
every day to be l. JOHN 417:19
everything is l. VOLT 798:8
found my sheep which was l. BIBL 99:33
France has not l. the war DE G 255:18
hesitates is l. PROV 602:27
Home of l. causes ARNO 28:15
I have l. a day TITU 777:16

I once was l. NEWT 543:13
land of l. content HOUS 391:5
let it be l. CATU 197:4
l. all the names JOHN 416:23
l. an empire ACHE 1:12
l. boyhood of Judas Æ 6:8
l. chord PROC 593:11
l. dog somewhere ANOU 22:13
l. evermore in the main TENN 766:13
l., except a little life BYRO 178:21
l. generation STEI 737:9
l. me in your liking SHAK 677:26
l. sheep BIBL 94:31
l., that is unsought CHAU 207:2
l. their mittens NURS 551:11
l. the only Playboy CLOS 222:18
l. the only Playboy SYNG 751:22
l. the world for love DRYD 282:9
l. traveller's dream BLAK 118:19
L., yesterday MANN 493:19
never l. till won CRAB 243:9
never to have l. at all BUTL 172:21
Next to a battle l. WELL 809:17
none of them is l. BIBL 102:28
nothing be l. BIBL 101:26
Not l. but gone before NORT 547:1
not l. but sent before CYPR 248:11
not that you won or l. RICE 626:3
OK. We l. MAJO 491:18
paradises we have l. PROU 594:10
they're l. to us MART 498:1
Though lovers be l. THOM 772:1
Vietnam was l. in MCLU 487:11
was l., and is found BIBL 100:6
what is l. in translation FROS 326:19
wherever we're l. FRY 326:24
who deliberates is l. ADDI 4:12
lot l. is fallen unto me BOOK 132:9
not a l. . . . but you'll like CATC 196:31
policeman's l. is not a happy one GILB 339:5
Remember L.'s wife BIBL 100:13
Lothario gay L. ROWE 636:9
lotos L. and lilies TENN 765:7
lots cast l. upon my vesture BOOK 132:25
lottery genetic l. comes up with PIML 576:7
judgement is a mere l. DRYD 283:8
l. is a taxation FIEL 310:3
L., with weekly pay-out ORWE 558:25
Marriage is a l. PROV 606:29
lotus jewelled l. throne MAHĀ 490:15
plucks the l. without TANT 755:2
Lou lady that's known as L. SERV 655:2
loud upon the l. cymbals BOOK 142:3
louder l. he talked of his honour EMER 299:15
loungers l. and idlers DOYL 278:4
lounging L. 'roun' en suffer'n' HARR 362:18
louse l. and a flea JOHN 417:4
l. in the locks of literature TENN 767:19
lousy *House Beautiful* is play l. PARK 567:10
L. but loyal SAYI 647:30
l. skin scabbed by cities BUNT 160:11
lout l.'s game WEST 812:9
Louvre You're the L. PORT 588:12
love Absence is to l. BUSS 171:6
acquainted with L. JOHN 412:16
Ah, l., let us be true ARNO 26:4
Ah! what is l. GREE 352:4
Alas! the l. of women BYRO 176:17
all did l. him once SHAK 676:3
all for l. SPEN 733:26
All l., all liking HERR 374:7
All l. at first BUTL 172:15
All l. is lost DUNB 285:6
All's fair in l. and war PROV 594:25
All that matters is l. and work FREU 324:18
Amazing l. WESL 810:20
and be my l. MARL 496:19
and be thy l. RALE 620:9
and L. the night DRYD 282:17
And yet I l. this false EPHE 300:18
Anxiety l.'s greatest killer NIN 546:3
Any kiddie in school can l. NASH 539:15
arms of my true l. TENN 764:11
as she did l. KEAT 428:10
as to l. a husband WYCH 834:12
bands of l. BIBL 90:11
be wise and eke to l. SPEN 734:20
be wise, and l. SHAK 700:13
bid me take l. easy YEAT 835:16
bring those who l. Thee TERE 768:11
brotherly l. continue BIBL 110:5
burned with l. VIRG 795:16
but one true l. BALL 52:6
came I to l. thee AUGU 36:5
cannot call it l. SHAK 665:15
cannot l. a woman so well ELIO 292:27
cantons of contemnèd l. SHAK 701:7
car'st not whom I l. DONN 273:2
caution in l. RUSS 639:15
Christ's particular l.'s sake BROW 157:23
come unto my l. SPEN 733:9
commonly called l. FIEL 310:9
constant l. deemed there SIDN 718:11
corner in the thing I l. SHAK 692:26
courage to l. TROL 782:6
course of true l. PROV 597:39
crime to l. too well POPE 582:17
cruel madness of l. TENN 763:23
dark secret l. BLAK 121:7
daughterly l. MORE 531:13
dearest l. in all the world RODG 631:4
Dear l., for nothing less DONN 273:22
Deep as first l. TENN 765:21
desire more l. and knowledge SHAK 658:9
doesn't l. a wall FROS 326:4
do not l. thee, Dr Fell BROW 152:7
earth could never living l. EPIT 302:16
Earth's the right place for l. FROS 325:15
end of l. should be HANN 359:10
every man's l. affair with America MAIL 491:2
experienced my greatest l. PROU 594:2
failures in l. MURD 536:17
faith and l. BIBL 109:9
fall in l. today GERS 334:13
fall in l. with me SHAK 659:16
Farewell, L. WYAT 834:1
fate of l. is BARR 55:12
fear casteth out l. CONN 234:3
fear l. is to fear life RUSS 639:18
fell in l. to the sound BENN 66:12
fit l. for gods MILT 517:15
flag and sign of l. SHAK 691:27
flowers and fruits of l. BYRO 178:22
food is l. and fame SHEL 711:10
food of l. OPEN 555:15
fool of l. HAZL 365:7
For ever wilt thou l. KEAT 428:24
for the l. he had to her BIBL 75:4
for us, it's l. BOUS 145:6
fou o' l. divine BURN 167:12
Friendship is L. BYRO 178:11
from the l. of God BIBL 105:12
gates unto my l. SPEN 733:8
Gather the rose of l. SPEN 734:1
gentleness And show of l. SHAK 674:6
gin l. be bonnie BALL 52:8
God is l., but LEE 461:19
God of l. HERB 373:14
God si L. FORS 321:3
good man's l. SHAK 659:15
got l. well weighed up AMIS 13:17
Greater l. hath no man BIBL 102:22
greater l. hath no man THOR 776:21
Greater l. than this JOYC 422:16
groans of l. to those of the dying LOWR 478:11
had a l. for Charlotte THAC 769:15
Hail, wedded l. MILT 516:25
half in l. KEAT 429:13
hate all that don't l. me FARQ 307:14
hate is conquered by l. PALI 565:17
have not all thy l. DONN 274:6
Hearts wound up with l. SPEN 732:22
heart whose l. is innocent BYRO 179:1
Hell is to l. no more BERN 68:21
He was all for l. DIBD 260:10
hidden l. of God WESL 811:9
hid in the heart of l. YEAT 836:23
hold l. out SHAK 697:13
hold so fast, as l. can do BURT 170:19
honeying and making l. SHAK 665:17
how can he l. God BIBL 111:15
How do I l. thee BROW 154:21
how I l. my country LAST 456:20
how l. constrained him DANT 249:13
How should I your true l. know SHAK 665:34
hurt us that we l. BEAU 58:15
I am sick of l. BIBL 85:19
I do not l. the man WATK 804:14
I don't l. you MART 497:23
If I can't l. Hitler MUST 537:15
If I l. you GOET 343:13
If it be l. indeed SHAK 656:7
if my l. were in my arms ANON 19:13
If this be not l. CONG 232:31
I hate and I l. CATU 197:19
I knew it was l. BYRO 179:7
I'll l. you AUDE 33:18
I l. a lass O'KE 553:7
I l. all waste SHEL 711:18
I l., and know not why EPHE 300:18
I l. but you alone BALL 51:6
I l. my work HILL 376:17
In l. alone we hate to find WALS 802:10
in l., and in debt BROM 149:6
in l. as in religion COWL 239:18
in l. to practise only this RILK 628:2
in l. when he marries BURN 165:24
in l. with a cold climate SOUT 731:7
in l. with his fetters BACO 42:1
in l. with night SHAK 697:29
in the world is l. BREN 147:22
I shall l. him JOHN 412:7
is not in l. SHAK 700:8
It's so simple, l. PRÉV 591:7
jealousy extinguishes l. MARG 495:9
joy of l. is too short MALO 492:11
King of l. BAKE 48:13
knew thee but to l. thee HALL 358:10
knowest that I l. thee BIBL 103:10
know Him, l. him CATE 194:5
labour of l. BIBL 109:7
Land that I l. BERL 68:7
lay aside long-cherished l. CATU 197:15
left thy first l. BIBL 111:24
let me l. DONN 273:21
Let me not l. Thee HERB 372:1
let me sow l. FRAN 323:5
Let's fall in l. PORT 588:7
letter to my l. BALL 50:16
let the warm L. in KEAT 429:19
Let those l. now ANON 21:8
let us live and l. CAMP 183:21
let us l. CATU 197:2
lightly turns to thoughts of l. TENN 762:22
little duty and less l. SHAK 672:12
live with me, and be my l. DONN 273:19
lost l. of mine SCOT 651:11
lost the world for l. DRYD 282:9
L., a child WROT 833:16
L., all alike DONN 274:15
L. alters not SHAK 705:17
l., an abject intercourse GOLD 345:13
L. and a cottage COLM 229:14
L. and a cough cannot PROV 606:2
l. and all its smart BEDD 60:14
l. and beauty fail ETHE 301:14
l. and be wise PROV 608:34
L. and delight therein DÜRE 286:4
L. and do what you will AUGU 36:9
l. and fame KEAT 430:19
L. and marriage BYRO 176:19
l. and murder will out CONG 232:13
L. and scandal FIEL 310:4

love (*cont.*):
l. a thing that can never go wrong PARK 567:1
L. bade me welcome HERB 372:22
L. be controlled by advice GAY 331:12
L. begets love PROV 606:3
l. be younger than thyself SHAK 701:19
l. boat has crashed LAST 456:13
L. built on beauty DONN 272:9
l. but only her BYRO 175:7
l. can find you at every time CHER 208:22
L. ceases to be a pleasure BEHN 62:7
l., cherish, and to obey BOOK 131:5
L. comes from blindness BUSS 171:5
L. comforteth like sunshine SHAK 706:1
L. conquers all things VIRG 796:12
l. Creation's final law TENN 761:14
L., curiosity, freckles, and doubt PARK 567:2
L. divine WESL 811:7
l. does not consist SAIN 641:13
L. doesn't just sit there LE G 462:14
L. doth to her eyes repair SHAK 702:29
l. Flames for a year LAMP 449:16
l. flies out of the window PROV 614:24
l. for any place ARNO 29:17
l. for Ireland CARS 192:4
L. goes toward love SHAK 697:16
l. grows diseased ETHE 301:12
L. guards the roses LODG 472:18
l. gushed from my heart COLE 226:19
l. had been sae ill to win BALL 52:9
l. has died for me to-day BALL 50:6
L. has pitched his mansion YEAT 835:13
l. he laughed to scorn SHAK 705:28
l. her, comfort her BOOK 131:4
l. her is a liberal education STEE 736:21
l. her till I die ANON 19:2
l. his country SHAK 675:26
l., I do not go DONN 274:13
L. (if such a thing there be) WINC 822:20
L. in a cold climate MITF 524:5
l. in a golden bowl BLAK 118:8
L. in a hut KEAT 428:15
L. in a palace KEAT 428:15
L. in desolation SHEL 710:21
L. in dying BARN 55:9
L.-in-idleness SHAK 689:23
L. in my bosom LODG 472:17
L., in the form CHAM 201:7
L. in this part of the world BYRO 180:5
L. is a boy BUTL 172:8
L. is a circle HERR 374:13
L. is a growing DONN 274:5
L. is ane fervent fire SCOT 650:3
L. is a passion HALI 357:7
L. is a spirit SHAK 705:29
l. is a thing below a man STER 739:9
L. is a universal migraine GRAV 349:15
l. is better than wine BIBL 85:6
L. is blind ANON 20:8
L. is blind PROV 606:4
l. is but discovery SOUT 730:10
l. is here to stay GERS 334:15
L. is he that alle thing CHAU 207:1
L. is just a system BARN 55:4
l. is liberty POPE 582:21
L. is like any other luxury TROL 783:13
L. is like linen FLET 318:18
L. is longer than the wave BALL 51:10
l. is Lord of all the world SPEN 733:5
l. is maister GOWE 347:10
l. is more cruel than lust SWIN 750:17
l. is mor than gold LYDG 480:12
L. is mutually feeding HEAD 366:1
L. is never defeated JOHN 408:5
L. is not love SHAK 678:1
L. is not love SHAK 705:15
l. is not secure CHES 210:3
l. is of a birth as rare MARV 498:10
L. is of the valley TENN 766:5
L. is only one JOHN 410:13
L. is our Lord's meaning JULI 423:4
l. is slight MARL 496:13
l. is strong as death BIBL 86:7
L. is that liquor HERB 372:2
L. is the delusion MENC 504:14
L. is the discovery of reality MURD 536:19
L. is the fart SUCK 745:9
L. is the fire SOUT 731:10
l. is the gift of oneself ANOU 22:11
L. is the greatest mercy WILB 817:8
l. is the keeping of her laws BIBL 91:14
L. is then our duty GAY 331:20
L. is the wisdom of the fool JOHN 418:10
l. is towards individuals SWIF 748:10
l. it cannot return ELIO 292:2
L. iz like the meazles BILL 115:2
L. just makes it safer ICE- 398:15
L. laughs at locksmiths PROV 606:5
L. looks not with the eyes SHAK 689:7
L. made me poet EPIT 303:14
L. makes them dance DAVI 251:19
L. makes the world go round PROV 606:6
L. means not ever having SEGA 653:10
l. me less GODO 342:3
L. me little ANON 17:14
L. me little PROV 606:7
L. me, love my dog PROV 606:8
l. men too little BURK 164:4
L.? most natural painkiller LAST 456:14
l., never strained HORA 387:23
l. not man the less BYRO 175:8
l. of Christ BIBL 107:28
l. of finished years ROSS 634:3
l. of friends BELL 64:10
l. of God is shed abroad BIBL 104:35
l. of liberty HAZL 365:8
l. of money BIBL 109:18
L. of our country GODW 342:6
l. of savages LERM 464:20
l. of Soul in the husband UPAN 787:11
l. of the people BURK 163:7
L. once possessed MILT 518:19
l. one another BIBL 105:20
l. one another or die AUDE 35:2
l. one maiden only TENN 759:20
l. one's country ANNA 15:2
L.-quarrels oft MILT [illegible]
L.'s a disease MACA 481:7
L.'s always seen COWL 239:16
l.'s a malady DRYD 282:7
L.'s a man of war HERB 372:10
l.'s a noble madness DRYD 280:25
l. Scotland better JOHN 409:20
L. seeketh not itself to please BLAK 121:1
L. seeketh only Self to please BLAK 121:2
l. seldom dies of hunger LENC 463:5
L. set you going PLAT 577:19
l.'s great artillery CRAS 244:10
L.'s harbinger MILT 517:25
l. she's but a lassie BURN 168:2
l. slights it BACO 42:23
L.'s like a red, red rose BURN 168:6
L.'s like the measles JERR 407:6
L.'s not Time's fool SHAK 705:16
l. someone is to isolate BAUD 57:14
L. sought is good SHAK 702:3
L.'s passives CRAS 244:4
l.'s philosophy DONN 274:4
L.'s pleasure lasts but a moment FLOR 318:20
l.'s proper exercise DAVI 251:18
l.'s sad satiety SHEL 714:7
l.'s the noblest frailty DRYD 281:27
L. still has something SEDL 653:2
L.'s tongue is in the eyes FLET 318:15
l.-story or an elopement DOYL 277:22
L. supports his reign SMAR 722:8
l.'s young dream MOOR 530:13
l. that asks no question SPRI 735:6
l. that can be reckoned SHAK 656:7
L. . . . That cordial drop ROCH 630:8
L. that dare not DOUG 276:11
L., that doth reign SURR 746:9
L. that endures for a breath SWIN 750:9
l. that moves the sun CLOS 222:2
l. that moves the sun DANT 250:5
L. that never told can be BLAK 120:11
l. the babe SHAK 682:17
L. the Beloved Republic FORS 321:5
l., the beloved Republic SWIN 751:1
L. the brotherhood BIBL 110:30
l. thee better after death BROW 154:22
l. thee in prose PRIO 592:10
L., the human form divine BLAK 120:15
l. the Lord thy God BIBL 96:24
l. the lovely bully SHAK 671:12
L. the sinner AUGU 36:11
L.-thirty, love-forty BETJ 71:6
l. those who love you VOLT 798:6
L., thou art absolute CRAS 244:6
l. thy neighbour BIBL 76:23
l. thy neighbour as thyself BIBL 96:24
L. thyself last SHAK 673:16
l. to hatred turned CONG 232:26
L. to the loveless shown CROS 246:15
l. toward thee BOOK 128:13
l. up groweth CHAU 207:20
L. was a terrible thing RHYS 625:19
l. was but a school WOTT 833:2
l. was passion's essence BYRO 174:20
l. were what the rose is SWIN 751:14
l. . . . whatever that may CHAR 203:17
l. what thou dost love HATC 363:17
L. will find a way PROV 606:9
l. will steer the stars RADO 620:4
l. will yield to business OVID 561:21
l. without the rhetoric STOP 743:17
L. with unconfinèd wings LOVE 476:12
L. wol nat been constreyned CHAU 205:11
l. you because I need you FROM 325:9
l. you just the same KIER 435:19
L. your enemies BIBL 99:4
L. you ten years before MARV 499:1
loving to l. AUGU 35:23
Make l. not war SAYI 647:31
making l. all year round BEAU 58:10
making l. to the Archbishop SHER 716:22
Man's l. is of man's life AMIS 13:16
Man's l. is of man's life BYRO 176:7
Man's l. of God MAIM 491:8
man, That l. my friend SHAK 676:9
man you l. to hate ADVE 7:42
man you l. to hate FILM 311:22
marriage without l. means CLAR 219:6
marry them for l. OSBO 559:20
may be crossed in l. SHER 715:19
Men l. in haste BYRO 177:21
met the L.-Talker CARB 185:18
ministers of L. COLE 226:1
money can't buy me l. LENN 463:19
more of l. than matrimony GOLD 345:29
Most people l. love PAST 569:3
music be the food of l. SHAK 700:26
My l. and I did meet BETJ 70:15
my l. and I did meet YEAT 835:16
My l. and I would lie HOUS 390:19
My l. for Heathcliff BRON 150:3
my l. is come to me ROSS 634:2
my l.'s in tune PROV 614:27
My only l. SHAK 697:8
My song is l. unknown CROS 246:15
needs must l. the highest TENN 759:22
Need we say it was not l. MILL 509:16
never l. a stranger BENS 66:14
never taint my l. SHAK 693:17
new l. may get WALS 802:9
no l. for such THOM 773:13
no lyves creature Withouten l. CHAU 207:7
none other I can l. TENN 759:28
not enough to make us l. SWIF 748:24
nothing but in l. BACO 43:15
not that I l. you less WALL 800:9
Now I know what L. is VIRG 796:9
Now with his l. CHAU 205:21
object of l. LAMB 448:10
of connubial l. MILT 516:24

office and affairs of l. SHAK 691:4
off with the old l. PROV 604:8
Of kindness and of l. WORD 829:2
O L.! has she done this LYLY 480:15
O L., O fire TENN 758:19
O lyric L. BROW 157:21
O my l. is slain DONN 272:14
one jot of former l. DRAY 279:3
one's absent love TROL 783:6
ones we choose to l. HARR 363:2
Only by l. can men see me BHAG 73:3
Only l. can apprehend RILK 627:19
onset and waning of l. LA B 446:14
opposite of l. WIES 816:15
our l. hath no decay DONN 273:18
over hir housbond as hir l. CHAU 206:22
pangs of disprized l. SHAK 664:4
passing the l. of women BIBL 79:3
path of true l. EWAR 305:9
perfect l. casteth out fear BIBL 111:14
philosopher of l. DRYD 281:33
Pity is akin to l. PROV 609:27
pluck the rose And l. it BROW 158:13
power and effect of l. BURT 170:18
presume too much upon my l. SHAK 676:22
price of l. was death DRAB 278:16
programmed to l. completely BAIN 48:9
putting L. away DICK 266:11
Queen's l. BALL 50:10
quick-eyed L., observing HERB 372:22
renewing is of l. EDWA 289:13
revolution where l. not allowed ANGE 14:18
right true end of l. DONN 272:11
same as for l. FROS 326:13
search for l. WALĘ 799:4
secret l. BIBL 83:28
Service and l. above all other DUNB 285:3
She never told her l. SHAK 701:24
shows of l. to other men SHAK 674:7
some l. but little policy SHAK 695:26
So true a fool is l. SHAK 704:22
sports of l. JONS 420:12
still their l. comes home to me LAWL 454:13
successful without l. TROL 781:19
support of the woman I l. EDWA 289:7
survive of us is l. LARK 452:13
sweet l.! was thought a crime BLAK 121:4
take our fill of l. BIBL 82:16
Tell l. it is but lust RALE 620:13
tell the laity our l. DONN 274:19
that they l. WALL 800:11
them that l. God BIBL 105:10
them which l. you BIBL 93:15
there are those who l. it WEBS 807:9
There is l. of course ANOU 22:10
there my l. will live CLAR 218:12
They l. indeed SIDN 718:14
They l. their land HALL 358:9
They l. us for it TENN 765:24
think my l. as rare SHAK 705:21
this spring of l. SHAK 702:26
those who l. the Lord HUNT 395:11
thought l. would adapt itself WALK 799:6
thought that l. would last AUDE 33:28
Through l., through hope WORD 831:16
thy sweet l. SHAK 704:15
time to l. BIBL 84:7
tired of L. BELL 63:16
'tis the hour of l. BYRO 177:2
To live is like to l. BUTL 172:27
to l. and be loved SAND 643:15
to l. and rapture's due ROCH 630:6
to l. is naturally mine DRAY 279:2
To manage l. BUTL 172:14
To see her is to l. her BURN 166:19
treason to our l. THOR 776:19
true l. hath my heart SIDN 718:8
true l. is a durable fire RALE 621:2
true l. is, it showeth DE P 258:4
'Twixt women's l., and men's DONN 273:17
unity, and godly l. BOOK 129:11
unlucky in l. PROV 606:10
vegetable l. should grow MARV 499:1
very few to l. WORD 831:19
vividly gifted in l. DUFF 284:10
was the song of l. ROSS 634:23
waters cannot quench l. BIBL 86:8
wayward is this foolish l. SHAK 702:25
well-nourished l. COLE 228:5
what is l. RALE 620:10
What is l. SHAK 701:10
What is L. SHEL 715:1
What l. I bore to thee WORD 828:25
What thing is l. PEEL 571:19
When l. congeals HART 363:5
When my l. swears SHAK 705:23
where I cannot l. BEHN 62:10
where l. is BIBL 82:36
where there is no l. BACO 43:1
who l., time is eternity VAN 789:15
who l. want wisdom SHEL 713:8
Whom the gods l. MENA 504:12
Whom the Gods l. PROV 615:3
Whom the gods l. die young BYRO 177:5
whom we l. most ABEL 1:4
wilder shores of l. BLAN 121:17
wi' L. o'ercome BURN 167:19
winds were l.-sick SHAK 656:23
wish I were in l. again HART 363:5
with my true l. RALE 621:1
withstand L.'s shock GOGA 343:23
woman's l. for us increases PUSH 617:28
woman wakes to l. TENN 760:5
Women who l. the same man BEER 61:15
Work is l. made visible GIBR 336:13
world and l. were young RALE 620:9
You can only l. one war GELL 333:2
You may give them your l. GIBR 336:11
'You must sit down,' says L. HERB 373:1
your true l.'s coming SHAK 701:9
loved all we l. of him SHEL 710:20
And the l. one BROW 157:1
better to have l. and lost BUTL 172:21
better to have l. and lost PROV 613:6
better to have l. and lost TENN 761:4
could l. thee, Dear LOVE 476:16
Dante, who l. well BROW 157:3
disciple whom Jesus l. BIBL 103:12
feared than l. MACH 485:16
God so l. the world BIBL 101:18
him I l. the most ANON 22:6
how much you were l. CAVA 198:4
idols I have l. FITZ 315:1
I have l. SUCK 745:10
I l. a lass WITH 824:2
I l. Ophelia SHAK 666:29
I l. thee once AYTO 40:9
I saw and l. GIBB 335:21
king l. his people WILL 820:3
Lavinia, therefore must be l. SHAK 699:26
l. by a girl TROL 782:28
l. by the gods PLAT 578:2
l. Caesar less SHAK 675:24
l. each other beyond belief HEIN 368:8
l. him so BROW 156:18
l. him too much RACI 619:15
l. not at first sight MARL 496:13
l. not at first sight SHAK 659:17
l. the doctrine DEFO 255:5
l. you, so I drew these tides LAWR 458:26
men who have l. them TROL 783:7
Might she have l. me BROW 156:15
never be by woman l. BLAK 117:20
never to have been l. CONG 233:6
she l. much BIBL 99:6
She who has never l. GAY 332:2
Solomon l. many strange women BIBL 79:20
thirst to be l. RHYS 625:17
thrice had I l. thee DONN 273:16
till we l. DONN 274:2
To be l. as to love FRAN 323:5
use him as though you l. him WALT 802:23
We l., sir BROW 155:22
who never l. before ANON 21:8
wish I l. the Human Race RALE 621:11
loveless Love to the l. shown CROS 246:15
loveliness Its l. increases KEAT 426:16
l. and perfection MILT 519:13
l. I never knew COLE 224:17
l. Needs not the foreign aid THOM 775:11
miracle of l. GILB 338:11
portion of the l. SHEL 711:3
weak from your l. BETJ 71:6
woman of shining l. YEAT 837:8
your l. KEAT 431:16
lovely altogether l. BIBL 85:21
Look thy last on all things l. DE L 256:12
l. and pleasant BIBL 79:2
L. and willing AUDE 34:5
l. at the beginning PALI 565:10
l. boy VIRG 795:17
L. enchanting language HERB 372:18
l. is the rose WORD 829:15
l. is thy dwelling-place SCOT 652:21
l. woman stoops to folly ELIO 296:11
l. woman stoops to folly GOLD 345:30
more l. and more temperate SHAK 704:9
My L. Horse LINE 469:12
once he made more l. SHEL 711:3
She has a l. face TENN 762:20
so be l. GRAV 349:14
That they might l. be CROS 246:15
what a l. war LITT 470:5
whatsoever things are l. BIBL 108:25
woods are l. FROS 326:12
wouldn't it be l. LERN 465:9
You have l. eyes CHEK 208:12
lover affliction taught a l. POPE 582:22
as true a l. SHAK 658:19
Beauty is the l.'s gift CONG 233:9
binds the l. SANS 644:7
dividing l. and lover SWIN 750:6
injured l.'s hell MILT 516:32
l. and his lass SHAK 659:24
l. and killer are mingled DOUG 276:16
l., and the poet SHAK 690:18
l. by lover YEAT 837:24
l. of my soul WESL 810:25
l.'s quarrel with the world FROS 326:3
l. stole my rose BURN 166:17
l. without indiscretion HARD 360:11
prove a l. SHAK 696:11
roaming l. CALL 181:16
satisfied with her l.'s mind TROL 783:6
she was a true l. MALO 492:13
sighed as a l. GIBB 335:22
some old l.'s ghost DONN 274:7
stroke your l. READ 622:17
truest l. MALO 492:15
what is left of a l. ROWL 636:12
Who could deceive a l. VIRG 794:11
woman loves her l. BYRO 176:18
woman says to her lusting l. CATU 197:12
lovers Journeys end in l. meeting SHAK 701:9
laughs at l.' perjuries OVID 561:6
laughs at l.' perjuries TIBU 777:9
laughs at l.' perjury PROV 604:45
l.' declarations AUDE 34:13
l.' perjury DRYD 282:8
L., to bed SHAK 690:27
l. were all untrue DRYD 282:18
make two l. happy POPE 586:23
old l. are soundest WEBS 808:6
quarrel of l. PROV 610:2
sleepless l. POPE 586:29
star-crossed l. SHAK 697:2
These l. fled away KEAT 427:16
Though l. be lost THOM 772:1
wonder if it's l. MULD 536:1
loves all her l. around her BYRO 178:9
all she l. is love BYRO 176:18
baggage l. me CONG 232:28
because God l. it JULI 423:2
die to that which one l. HARA 359:13
For who l. that MILT 518:28

loves (*cont.*):
He l. us not SHAK 685:4
kills the thing he l. WILD 818:32
lady l. Milk Tray ADVE 7:6
life and l. of a she-devil WELD 809:6
lines (so l.) oblique MARV 498:11
l. his wife as himself TALM 754:11
l. nothing but himself SOUT 731:4
l. the fox less SURT 746:19
l. what he is good at SHAD 655:12
no creature l. me SHAK 696:30
our l., must I remember them APOL 22:21
reigned with your l. ELIZ 297:4
son l. his sons TALM 754:16
soul that l. is happy GOET 342:13
their ain dear l. BALL 51:16
who l. me must have TENN 759:26
Who l. ya, baby CATC 196:28
woman whom nobody l. CORN 237:2
lovesome garden is a l. thing BROW 152:8
lovest l. thou me more BIBL 103:8
poor sinner, l. thou me COWP 240:19
loveth he that l. another BIBL 105:20
He that l. not BIBL 111:13
him whom my soul l. BIBL 85:13
prayeth well, who l. well COLE 226:27
whom the Lord l. BIBL 82:7
Whom the Lord l. BIBL 110:3
loving Can't help l. dat man HAMM 358:16
discharge for l. one MATL 501:14
For l., and for saying so DONN 274:17
heart be still as l. BYRO 179:4
I ain't had no l. NORW 547:2
l. and giving PROV 606:42
l. himself better than all COLE 227:7
l.-kindness and mercy BOOK 133:1
l. longest AUST 38:12
l. the land that has taught MOOR 530:7
l. to love AUGU 35:23
most l. mere folly SHAK 659:5
not l. you BAIN 48:8
savage l. has made me BECK 60:9
wickedness that hinders l. BROW 157:3
loving-kindness deeds of l. TALM 753:12
low dost thou lie so l. SHAK 675:19
exalted them of l. degree BIBL 98:17
Had me l. and had me down GERS 334:12
l. as where this earth ROSS 634:18
l. estate of his handmaiden BIBL 98:16
l. on whom assurance sits ELIO 296:10
l. opinion of himself TROL 782:23
Malice is of a l. stature HALI 357:18
Sweet and l. TENN 765:15
That l. man BROW 156:1
Too l. for envy COWL 239:14
upper station of l. life DEFO 254:18
lowbrow first militant l. BERL 68:18
Lowells L. talk to the Cabots BOSS 143:15
lower l. classes had such white CURZ 248:7
l. orders don't set us a good WILD 817:12
l. than the angels BOOK 131:27
l. than vermin BEVA 71:13
While there is a l. class DEBS 254:9
lowest l. and most dejected SHAK 679:13
take the l. room BIBL 99:24
lowlands Highlands and ye L. BALL 50:9
sails by the L. SONG 730:2
lowliness l. become mine inner clothing LITT 470:4
lowly l. air Of Seven Dials GILB 337:13
meek and l. in heart BIBL 95:9
loyal Lousy but l. SAYI 647:30
l. to his own career DALT 248:14
loyalties l. which centre upon number one CHUR 216:17
tragic conflict of l. HOWE 391:14
loyalty constitute l. BOSW 144:17
I want *l.* JOHN 408:18
learned body wanted l. TRAP 781:1
L. the Tory's secret weapon KILM 436:2
l. we feel to unhappiness GREE 351:19
LSD L.? Nothing much happened AUDE 35:17
L. reminds me of minks GRAV 349:22
PC is the L. of the '90s LEAR 461:1
Lucasta L., that bright northern star LOVE 476:10
lucem *ex fumo dare l.* HORA 385:21
lucid freqent l. intervals CERV 200:1
l. intervals BACO 44:26
l. intervals of life WORD 828:3
Lucifer falls like L. SHAK 673:13
L. arose MERE 505:20
L., son of the morning BIBL 87:7
L. that often warned them MILT 513:21
luck believes in l. STEA 736:13
devil's l. PROV 598:11
Fools for l. PROV 600:39
know about it [l.] HART 363:12
l. in leisure PROV 612:12
l. in odd numbers PROV 612:13
l. of my generation SHAW 710:2
l. of our name lost HORA 389:5
mother of good l. PROV 598:16
nae l. about the house MICK 507:2
watching his l. SERV 655:2
wished you good l. BOOK 140:7
luckless What l. apple MARV 499:6
lucky born l. than rich PROV 604:10
L. at cards PROV 606:10
l. if he gets out of it FILM 311:17
l. to be born WHIT 815:12
Third time l. PROV 612:39
lucrative so l. to cheat CLOU 222:26
lucre greedy of filthy l. BIBL 109:14
lucro *Fors dierum cumque dabit l.* HORA 387:20
lucury They knew l. MACA 481:12
Lucy L. ceased to be WORD 831:21
L. Locket lost NURS 549:11
Ludlow to L. come in HOUS 391:1
Luftwaffe With your L. PLAT 577:13
lug l. the guts SHAK 665:25
lugete *L., O Veneres* CATU 196:34
lugger Once aboard the l. MISQ 522:5
Luke honour unto L. Evangelist ROSS 635:3
lukewarm thou art l. BIBL 111:28
lukewarmness L. I account a sin COWL 239:18
lullaby dreamy l. GILB 337:21
I will sing a l. DEKK 256:6
Once in a l. HARB 359:18
lumber loads of learned l. POPE 585:2
l. of the schools SWIF 749:12
lumen *l. de lumine* MISS 520:17
luminous beating his l. wings ARNO 28:21
l. home of waters ARNO 27:19
with a l. nose LEAR 460:6
lump leaven leaveneth the whole l. BIBL 106:1
l. bred up in darkness KYD 446:9
L. the whole thing TWAI 786:14
poor in a l. is bad TENN 765:1
lumps l. in it STEP 738:3
luna great Lord of L. MACA 483:8
in the vats of l. MACA 483:4
sol et l. AUGU 36:1
lunae *Tacitae per amica silentia l.* VIRG 793:20
lunatic l., the lover SHAK 690:18
lunatics lunatic asylum run by l. LLOY 471:6
l. have taken charge ROWL 636:15
lunch cork out of my l. FIEL 310:19
for life, not for l. SAYI 647:24
no such thing as a free l. SAYI 648:4
unable to l. today PORT 588:8
luncheon Breakfast, supper, dinner, l. BROW 157:11
l. with a city friend BELL 63:25
take soup at l. CURZ 248:8
lungs dangerous to the l. JAME 402:12
from froth-corrupted l. OWEN 562:8
l. of London PITT 577:2
l. of the tobacconist JONS 419:12
Lupercal on the L. I thrice SHAK 676:2
lupus *L. est homo homini* PLAU 578:12
lurcher half l. and half cur COWP 242:4
lurching L. to rag-time tunes SASS 645:16
lure l. it back FITZ 314:17
l. this tassel-gentle SHAK 697:17
lurk dangers to liberty l. BRAN 146:20
l. outside GRAC 347:14
lurks l. a politician ARIS 24:13
luscious l. woodbine SHAK 689:25
lusisti *l. satis* HORA 387:10
lust Delight in l. PETR 574:18
despair rather than l. READ 622:14
fash'd wi' fleshly l. BURN 167:13
generous in mere l. ROCH 630:12
horrible that l. and rage YEAT 837:13
hutch of tasty l. HOPK 384:8
into ashes all my l. MARV 499:3
love is more cruel than l. SWIN 750:17
l. and calls it advertising LAHR 448:2
l. in action SHAK 705:19
l. of knowing FLEC 317:4
Men, when they l. GREE 352:3
Tell love it is but l. RALE 620:13
to l. after it LEWI 467:1
lustily sing praises l. unto him BOOK 133:19
lustre bright l. of a court CECI 199:6
Where is thy l. now SHAK 679:12
lusts Abstain from fleshly l. BIBL 110:29
fulfil the l. thereof BIBL 105:22
l. of the flesh BOOK 130:11
l. of your father BIBL 102:1
l. they do me leave VAUX 790:19
serve our present l. WITH 824:1
lust'st Thou hotly l. SHAK 679:24
lusty l. as an eagle BOOK 138:17
seye Of l. folk CHAU 206:19
lute Apollo's l. MILT 511:24
harp with the l. BOOK 137:9
l. and harp BOOK 135:17
l. is broken SHEL 712:3
l. its tones KEAT 427:1
Orpheus with his l. SHAK 673:9
pleasing of a l. SHAK 696:8
rift within the l. TENN 760:3
to her l. Corinna sings CAMP 183:22
lutes l. of amber HERR 375:5
Luther beyond what L. saw ROBI 629:18
lux *l. perpetua* MISS 523:2
luxuries and which l. WRIG 833:9
l. of life MOTL 534:8
luxury height of l. TENN 767:18
like any other l. TROL 783:13
Literature is a l. CHES 211:3
l., not a necessity ANTH 22:18
l. of doing good CRAB 243:8
l., peace BAUD 57:8
l. was doing good GART 330:12
mainly a l. BRIG 148:16
Morality is a costly l. ADAM 2:21
swinish l. of the rich MORR 532:19
trust people is a l. FORS 320:16
Lycidas L. is dead MILT 512:27
lying branch of the art of l. CORN 237:6
everyone else was l. GELD 332:26
express l. or falsehood SWIF 748:1
listening, l. in wait THOM 773:3
l., and slandering BOOK 130:15
l. down after CHIL 212:2
L. lips are abomination BIBL 82:26
L., on the other hand CAMU 184:15
l. till noon JOHN 411:23
One of you is l. PARK 567:8
smallest amount of l. BUTL 172:20
world is given to l. SHAK 669:17
Lyonnesse When I set out for L. HARD 362:1
lyre Make me thy l. SHEL 712:17
'Omer smote 'is bloomin' l. KIPL 440:20
lyres rhythmic tidal l. HARD 361:9
lyric among the l. poets HORA 387:13
good l. should be GERS 334:19

lyricis *me l. vatibus inseres* HORA 387:13

M dreaded four M's STRE 744:18
Ma M.'s out, Pa's out FLAN 316:3
Mab M., the Mistress-Fairy JONS 419:18
Queen M. hath been with SHAK 697:5
macaroni called it M. SONG 730:9
Macaulay as Tom M. MELB 503:17
M.'s few pages ELIO 293:15
Macavity M. WASN'T THERE ELIO 295:18
Macbeth had Lady M. KNIG 442:8
harm M. SHAK 684:22
Little Nell and Lady M. WOOL 827:7
M. does murder sleep SHAK 683:8
M. shall never vanquished be SHAK 685:2
M. shall sleep no more SHAK 683:9
night I appeared as M. HARG 362:6
MacCorley Rody M. goes to die CARB 186:2
Macduff Lay on, M. SHAK 685:26
M. was from his mother's womb SHAK 685:25
mace fool's bauble, the m. CROM 245:15
Macedonia Come over into M. BIBL 104:2
MacGregor Where M. sits PROV 614:38
Macheath jack-knife has M. BREC 147:17
Machiavel murderous M. SHAK 672:30
machine body is a m. TOLS 779:13
desiccated calculating m. BEVA 71:21
Ghost in the M. RYLE 640:20
house is a m. for living in LE C 461:13
m. for converting CARL 187:17
m. for turning the red wine DINE 267:20
pulse of the m. WORD 831:23
sausage m. CHRI 212:16
machinery Age of M. CARL 187:16
m. of the night GINS 339:20
machines M. have less problems WARH 803:16
their survival m. DAWK 253:4
whether m. think SKIN 721:16
macht *Arbeit m. frei* ANON 20:16
mackerel like rotten m. RAND 621:17
m. of the sea BALL 50:21
Not so the m. FRER 324:10
mackintosh bit of black m. WELB 809:3
mad All poets are m. BURT 170:7
bad and m. it was BROW 155:22
believed him m. BEAT 58:3
called me m. LEE 462:7
Don't get m., get even SAYI 647:13
glad m. brother's name SWIN 750:12
half of the nation is m. SMOL 726:11
heroically m. DRYD 280:15
Hieronimo is m. again KYD 446:12
house for fools and m. SWIF 749:26
M. about the boy COWA 238:14
m. all in God's keeping KIPL 441:15
m. all my life JOHN 411:24
m. and furious DOST 276:5
m. and savage master SOPH 728:16
M., bad, and dangerous LAMB 448:8
M. dogs and Englishmen COWA 238:15
m. north-north-west SHAK 663:21
M. world! mad kings SHAK 677:7
Make m. the guilty SHAK 663:28
make poor females m. SHAK 690:9
makes men m. SHAK 693:25
man is m. BYRO 179:21
men that God made m. CHES 210:2
much learning doth make thee m. BIBL 104:20
nobly wild, not m. HERR 374:16
O fool! I shall go m. SHAK 678:19
old, m., blind SHEL 713:28
O! let me not be m. SHAK 678:12
pleasure sure, In being m. DRYD 282:24
saint run m. POPE 586:12
some did count him m. BUNY 161:14
they first make m. PROV 615:4
We all are born m. BECK 60:2
when a heroine goes m. SHER 715:17
Whom the m. would destroy LEVI 466:9
world was m. SABA 641:2
madam globe-trotting M. YEAT 837:19
M. I may not call you ELIZ 297:11
madame Ah, m.! truly it's not right CRAN 243:23
madding Far from the m. crowd's GRAY 350:13
m. crowd BORR 144:5
made All things were m. by him BIBL 101:2
almost m. for each other SMIT 725:6
Begotten, not m. BOOK 129:8
day which the Lord hath m. BOOK 140:6
earth and the world were m. BOOK 137:17
fearfully and wonderfully m. BOOK 141:12
God m. and eaten BROW 155:14
Here's one I m. earlier CATC 195:23
he that hath m. us BOOK 138:13
he who m. the Lamb BLAK 121:10
I m. it FILM 311:1
Little Lamb who m. thee BLAK 120:17
m. heaven and earth BOOK 130:18
m., like bread LE G 462:14
m. me thus BIBL 105:13
man was m. to mourn BURN 167:25
not born but m. JERO 406:17
Who m. you CATE 194:5
Madeira M., m'dear FLAN 316:1
madeleine little piece of m. PROU 593:21
Madelon *Ce n'est que M.* BOUS 145:6
mademoiselle M. from Armenteers MILI 508:12
madhouse don't want m. EMPS 300:6
m. there exists no law CLAR 218:10
madhouses M., prisons CLAR 218:8
madman If a m. were to come JOHN 415:15
m. shakes a dead geranium ELIO 295:20
m. who thought he was COCT 223:18
madmen M. in authority KEYN 435:10
none but m. know DRYD 282:24
They were m. RENO 624:16
worst of m. POPE 586:12
madness accounted his life m. BIBL 91:11
cells of m. TENN 764:14
cruel m. of love TENN 763:23
define true m. SHAK 663:10
despondency and m. WORD 831:12
destroyed through m. GINS 339:20
devil's m.—War SERV 655:1
Even to m. SHAK 692:14
For that fine m. DRAY 279:6
harmonious m. SHEL 714:9
His flight was m. SHAK 685:3
inconceivable m. GONN 346:10
it is m. CONG 232:31
Like m. is the glory SHAK 699:16
love's a noble m. DRYD 280:25
m. is terrific WOOL 827:5
M.! Madness FILM 311:20
M. need not be all breakdown LAIN 448:5
m. of art JAME 403:8
m. of many POPE 587:15
m. of TV PAGL 563:2
m. their kings commit HORA 386:13
moon-struck m. MILT 517:24
no cure for this sort of m. SMIT 724:2
O! that way m. lies SHAK 678:27
Though this be m. SHAK 663:13
to m. near allied DRYD 280:2
very midsummer m. SHAK 702:10
Madonnas M. or Mary Magdalenes WILL 820:12
madrigal woeful stuff this m. would be POPE 584:25
maenad Of some fierce M. SHEL 712:13
maestro *m. di color che sanno* DANT 249:11
magazines graves of little m. PRES 591:6
Magdalen fourteen months at M. College GIBB 335:17
maggot create a m. MONT 528:2
maggots turmoil of a nest of m. BROO 150:18
magic daylight in upon m. BAGE 47:4
house rose like m. HARG 362:6
If this be m. SHAK 703:26
indistinguishable from m. CLAR 219:9
m. casements KEAT 429:14
m. in the web of it SHAK 693:6
m. of your fire TAGO 752:21
mistake medicine for m. SZAS 752:3
old black m. MERC 505:8
rough m. I here abjure SHAK 699:9
secret m. of numbers BROW 153:18
tell you what I want. M. WILL 820:20
tightness of the m. circle MACL 487:4
magical it is a m. event PRIE 591:12
Maginn bright, broken M. LOCK 472:11
magistrate m. corruptible ROBE 629:5
shocks the m. RUSS 640:1
magistri *iurare in verba m.* HORA 386:8
magna M. Charta is such a fellow COKE 224:13
M. est veritas, et praevalet BIBL 114:12
magnanimity M. in politics BURK 163:8
magnificat *M. anima mea Dominum* BIBL 114:3
magnificent mild and m. eye BROW 156:18
Mute and m. DRYD 282:26
magnifique *C'est m.* BOSQ 143:14
magnify m. thy holy Name BOOK 129:4
praise him, and m. him BOOK 126:5
soul doth m. the Lord BIBL 98:16
we m. thee BOOK 126:2
magnis *parva licet componere m.* VIRG 797:3
magpie swollen m. in a fitful sun POUN 589:22
magpies pair of m. fly HO 378:10
Maguire M. and his men KAVA 426:9
magus M. Zoroaster, my dead child SHEL 713:4
Mahomet mountain will not come to M. PROV 603:21
maid Being an old m. FERB 308:12
Can a m. forget her ornaments BIBL 89:10
espy a fair pretty m. SONG 729:15
fair, but frozen m. GARR 330:8
heard a m. sing SONG 729:4
I once was a m. BURN 167:18
m. and her wight HARD 361:17
m. is mine MISQ 522:5
m. is not dead BIBL 94:28
m. was in the garden NURS 550:18
m. whom there were few to praise WORD 831:19
man with a m. BIBL 83:36
many a m. MILT 512:21
my pretty m. NURS 551:20
neglected m. LEAP 460:2
She could not live a m. PEEL 571:20
maiden as the m.'s organ SHAK 701:3
god pursuing, the m. hid SWIN 750:7
love one m. only TENN 759:20
m. all forlorn NURS 551:7
m. meditation, fancy-free SHAK 689:23
m. of bashful fifteen SHER 716:14
pursued a m. SHEL 711:15
rare and radiant m. POE 579:16
maidenhead he rafte hire m. CHAU 206:21
maidenly So m., So womanly SKEL 721:10
maidens all the m. pretty COLM 229:15
lang may the m. sit BALL 51:16
laughter of comely m. DEV 259:6
m.' hearts SHAK 693:6
What m. loth KEAT 428:22
Young men and m. BOOK 142:1
maids fine ladies' m. HUGH 393:12
m. are May SHAK 659:20
malady Most incident to m. SHAK 703:18
Old m. biking ORWE 558:17
seven m. with seven mops CARR 190:19
Three little m. GILB 338:3
maidservants M., I hear people CARL 188:3
mail gets the m. through KEAT 426:13
mailed seen the m. lobster rise FRER 324:11

maimed M. us at the start YEAT 836:24
poor, and the m. BIBL 99:29
main lost evermore in the m. TENN 766:13
Maine As M. goes FARL 307:1
As M. goes POLI 581:5
mainspring m. perhaps of civilised SMIL 722:16
maintain m. mine own ways BIBL 81:17
maintained I m. myself THOR 776:7
maintenance art of motorcycle m. PIRS 576:16
maior *M. erat natu* LUCI 478:20
Maisie Proud M. is in the wood SCOT 651:26
maison *m. est une machine-* LE C 461:13
maistrye constreyned by m. CHAU 205:11
maîtresses *j'aurai des m.* GEOR 333:11
maize Plenty in the m. TENN 766:5
majesté *m. des souffrances* VIGN 792:15
majestic m. equality of the law FRAN 322:15
M. though in ruin MILT 515:14
majestical laid in bed m. SHAK 671:20
majesty appearance of Your M. BIBL 73:8
as his m. BIBL 91:17
earth of m. SHAK 694:19
Her M.'s Opposition BAGE 46:9
M.: of thy Glory BOOK 125:20
ride on in m. MILM 510:10
Thy M. how bright FABE 305:16
touching in its m. WORD 827:19
major change from m. to minor PORT 588:4
C M. BROW 155:1
Ground control to M. Tom BOWI 145:21
I was a m. part VIRG 793:17
modern M.-General GILB 339:3
With M. Major it had been all three HELL 368:14
majorities parliamentary m. BONA 125:2
majority against a tyrannical m. BALF 49:14
always in the m. KNOX 442:11
big enough m. TWAI 786:5
black m. rule SMIT 724:7
divine M. DICK 266:14
gone to join the m. PETR 574:15
m. are wrong DEBS 254:8
m. in a small part LYNC 480:19
m. is always the best repartee DISR 270:28
m. never has right IBSE 398:6
m. . . . one is enough DISR 270:11
silent m. NIXO 546:4
to the great m. YOUN 839:15
what the m. happen to like WHIT 814:15
will of the m. JEFF 405:11
majors live with scarlet M. SASS 645:15
makaris Chaucer, of m. flouir DUNB 285:5
make does not usually m. anything PHEL 575:2
If you don't m. mistakes PROV 603:30
m. all things new BIBL 113:8
m. an end JONS 421:3
M. do and mend OFFI 554:9
M. love not war SAYI 647:31
m. my day FILM 311:8
M. yourself necessary EMER 299:12
refuse to m. itself up TROL 782:2
Scotsman on the m. BARR 55:20
We cannot m. events ADAM 3:20
wrote M. IT NEW POUN 589:8
maker his M.'s image DRYD 279:18
kneel before the Lord our M. BOOK 138:6
m. and builder is God BIBL 109:29
M. of heaven and earth BOOK 126:10
M. of heaven and earth BOOK 129:8
more pure than his m. BIBL 81:8
sinneth before his M. BIBL 92:10
striveth with his m. BIBL 88:7
watch must have had a m. PALE 564:11
makes either m. me or fordoes me SHAK 693:21
makest What m. thou BIBL 88:7
making came the m. of man SWIN 750:8
take pleasure in m. NURS 547:15
ways of m. you talk CATC 196:26
malady love's a m. DRYD 282:7
m. Most incident to maids SHAK 703:18
m. of not marking SHAK 669:23
male Every modern m. BLY 123:2
M. and female BIBL 73:15
m. and the female BIBL 74:16
M. bonding TIGE 777:12
m., middle class, middle-aged STRE 744:18
m. of the species LAWR 458:8
more deadly than the m. KIPL 438:15
more deadly than the m. PROV 600:17
overcomes m. by tranquillity LAO 452:4
males compose Nothing but m. SHAK 682:18
Malherbe At last came M. BOIL 124:4
mali *Non ignara m.* VIRG 793:15
malice envy, hatred, and m. BOOK 127:4
leaven of m. BOOK 128:6
M. domestic SHAK 684:5
M. is of a low stature HALI 357:18
m. never was his aim SWIF 749:25
m., to breed causes JONS 420:14
m. toward none LINC 469:1
Much m. mingled DRYD 281:22
set down aught in m. SHAK 694:3
malicious God is subtle but not m. EINS 290:10
malignant part of Randolph that was not m. WAUG 806:20
malignity m. truly diabolical BURK 164:14
motiveless m. COLE 227:15
mallecho miching m. SHAK 664:22
Malmesey drowned in a barrel of M. FABY 305:23
malo *M. me Galatea petit* VIRG 795:20
malt ate the m. NURS 551:7
m. does more than Milton HOUS 391:9
Malvern on M. hilles LANG 450:16
mama M. may have HOLI 380:19
m. of dada FADI 306:2
maman *m. est morte* OPEN 555:8
mammas our m. bewitches BARB 53:18
mammon authentic m. than a bogus god MACN 488:6
God and m. BIBL 93:22
M. led them on MILT 515:3
m. of unrighteousness BIBL 100:8
pale M. pine POPE 583:21
serve God and M. PROV 615:44
mammoth m. but not fat TATE 755:4
mammy M., look at me LEWI 467:5
man against every m. BIBL 74:27
all that may become a m. SHAK 682:16
And the Lord God formed m. BIBL 73:17
animal called m. SWIF 748:10
another m., more wonderful FRID 324:21
any m.'s legs BOOK 141:25
apparel oft proclaims the m. SHAK 662:11
architectural m.-milliner RUSK 638:4
arms and the m. OPEN 555:3
arms and the m. VIRG 793:4
Arms, and the m. I sing DRYD 283:1
Arms and the m. I sing OPEN 555:4
arose as one m. BIBL 78:11
become the servant of a m. SHAW 707:8
better angel is a m. SHAK 705:24
between a m. who knew JOHN 413:25
Both m. and bird COLE 226:27
boy to do a m.'s job PROV 607:36
by m. came death BIBL 106:22
by m. shall his blood BIBL 74:21
call a m. *a good man* JOHN 417:8
came the making of m. SWIN 750:8
came to m.'s estate SHAK 702:22
Cannot a plain m. live SHAK 696:14
century of the common m. WALL 799:15
chief end of m. SHOR 717:15
childhood shows the m. MILT 518:7
come, but not the m. SCOT 651:24
contact with this Wild M. BLY 123:2
demolition of a m. LEVI 466:6
dominion [of the family] to the m. HOBB 379:2
Each m. for hymself CHAU 205:15
encompassed but one m. SHAK 674:15
entire m. that writes HUNT 395:19
Eustace is a m. no longer KING 437:15
ever tasted M. KIPL 441:12
every m. against every man HOBB 378:19
every m. and nation LOWE 477:15
Every m. for himself PROV 599:30
Every m. for himself PROV 599:31
Every m. for himself PROV 599:32
Every m. has a right JOHN 416:13
Every m. over forty SHAW 708:29
everyone has sat except a m. CUMM 247:7
extraordinary m. JOHN 417:9
father of the M. WORD 829:10
first m. BIBL 107:2
fit night out for m. or beast FIEL 310:20
for the sake of the m. HALI 357:15
from pig to m. CLOS 222:6
get out the m. POPE 580:22
get to the m. in the case KIPL 439:8
gives a meal m.-appeal ADVE 8:5
God has more right than m. JOHN 407:9
God is not a m. BIBL 76:29
good for inside of a m. PROV 612:21
Good Lord, what is m. BURN 168:9
good m. and a good citizen AUCT 33:9
Greater love hath no m. BIBL 102:22
Happy is the m. BOOK 140:22
He also created in m. TALM 754:23
helpless m. JOHN 411:19
He was a m. SHAK 662:3
He was her m. SONG 729:5
I am a worm, and no m. BOOK 132:22
I know myself a m. DAVI 251:17
I'm a m. of wealth JAGG 401:8
in m. there is nothing great HAMI 358:15
Isle of M. GIRA 340:4
It's that m. again NEWS 544:10
just the m. to do it BOLT 124:20
know a m. who can ADVE 7:10
large-hearted m. BROW 154:23
last strands of m. HOPK 384:2
last thing civilized by M. MERE 505:15
led to *perdition* by a m. WEST 812:18
let him pass for a m. SHAK 697:8
let no m. put asunder BOOK 131:7
Lord is a m. of war BIBL 76:6
Lord, what is m. CRAS 244:2
Love's a m. of war HERB 372:10
make a m. a woman PEMB 572:10
make m. in our image BIBL 73:14
makes a m. coloured HUGH 393:1
m. after his own heart BIBL 78:23
m. and a brother WEDG 808:21
m. and the hour YANC 834:19
M. and Wife BOOK 131:8
m. at the gate of the year HASK 363:16
M. being . . . by nature all free LOCK 472:3
M., biologically considered JAME 404:4
m. bites a dog BOGA 123:13
m. could ease a heart PARK 567:7
m. delights not me SHAK 663:18
M. did not make ARNO 26:15
M. didn't find the animals amusing NIET 545:11
M. disavows COWP 240:7
M. dreams of fame TENN 760:5
M., false man LEE 462:6
m. for all seasons WHIT 816:9
m. for others BONH 125:10
m. from animals OSLE 560:17
M. grows beyond his work STEI 737:10
M. hands on misery to man LARK 453:5
M. has created death YEAT 835:15
M. has Forever BROW 155:33
m. hath no preeminence BIBL 84:8
m. have the upper hand BOOK 132:1
m. hurrying along KEAT 431:13
M., I assure you MOLI 525:20
m. in his own proud esteem COWP 242:16
m. in nature PASC 568:9

M. is an embodied paradox COLT 230:5
M. is a noble animal BROW 153:10
M. is a tool-using animal CARL 188:10
M. is a useless passion SART 645:3
M. is born unto trouble BIBL 81:9
m. is but a devil STEV 741:8
M. is but earth DONN 275:11
m. is dead FROM 325:11
m. is man TENN 760:1
M. is man's A.B.C. QUAR 618:20
M. is Nature's sole mistake GILB 339:6
m. is of kin to the beasts BACO 42:8
M. is quite insane MONT 528:2
m. . . . is *so* in the way GASK 330:17
M. is something to be surpassed NIET 545:9
M. is still in arms ROCH 630:15
M. is the hunter TENN 765:24
M. is the interpreter of naure WHEW 813:15
M. is the master SWIN 751:3
M. is the measure PROT 593:18
M. is the measure PROV 606:16
m. is the only animal JEFF 405:4
M. is the Only Animal TWAI 786:9
M. is the only creature ORWE 558:5
M. is the shuttle VAUG 790:2
M. is to be held EDGE 288:17
m. made the town COWP 241:19
M. may not marry his Mother BOOK 142:15
m. not truly one STEV 741:13
m. of restless intellect HUXL 397:20
M.-of-war's 'er 'usband KIPL 439:11
M. owes his entire existence HEGE 367:11
M. partly is BROW 155:24
M. proposes PROV 606:18
m. proposes THOM 771:1
M., proud man SHAK 686:10
m. recovered of the bite GOLD 344:22
m. remains Sceptreless SHEL 713:14
m.'s a man for a' that BURN 167:7
m.'s desire is for the woman COLE 227:21
M.'s dominion BURN 168:23
m. sent from God BIBL 101:4
m.'s first disobedience MILT 514:7
m.'s first disobedience OPEN 556:5
m. shall have his mare SHAK 690:10
M. shall not live BIBL 92:32
m. shouldn't fool FAUL 308:2
M.'s inhumanity to man BURN 167:26
m.'s the gowd BURN 167:6
M. stole the fruit HERB 373:10
M.'s word is God in man TENN 759:12
m. that hath no music SHAK 688:25
M. that is born BIBL 81:18
M. that is born of a woman BOOK 131:12
m. that looks on glass HERB 372:13
m. that trusteth in him BOOK 133:20
M. the animal GOSS 347:6
M. wants but little GOLD 344:20
M. was by Nature CONG 232:29
M. was formed for society BLAC 117:1
M. was made for joy and woe BLAK 118:2
m. was made to mourn BURN 167:25
m. who has found himself out BARR 55:21
m. who has no office SHAW 707:16
m. who should loose me LOWE 477:9
m. who used to notice HARD 361:6
m. who would be king KIPL 441:16
M. will err GOET 342:14
m. will not merely endure FAUL 307:27
M. with all his noble qualities DARW 250:17
m. with a maid BIBL 83:36
m. write a better book EMER 300:3
m. you love to hate ADVE 7:42
m. you love to hate FILM 311:22
met a m. who wasn't there MEAR 503:3
moral centaur, m. and wife BYRO 177:10
more like a m. LERN 465:3
more wonderful than m. SOPH 728:14
mortal m. BIBL 81:8
mortal m. is a broomstick SWIF 748:12
My m. Friday DEFO 254:21
never done talking of M. FANO 306:7
new m. may be raised up BOOK 130:8
no m. ever shall put asunder SHAW 707:10
No m. hath seen God BIBL 101:8
no m. is wanted much EMER 299:26
no m. see me and live BIBL 76:19
No moon, no m. PROV 608:1
nor no m. ever loved SHAK 705:17
not m. for the sabbath BIBL 97:31
One m. in a thousand KIPL 440:11
one small step for a m. ARMS 25:19
only m. is vile HEBE 367:7
perfect M. BOOK 127:1
perilous to a m.'s honesty TROL 782:28
piece of work is a m. SHAK 663:18
plain, blunt m. SHAK 676:9
Reasonable M. HERB 371:21
repelled by m. INGE 399:6
right m. in the right place JEFF 406:4
said, ask a m. THAT 769:20
saw a m. this morning SHAW 709:29
shares m.'s smell HOPK 384:5
she was taken out of M. BIBL 73:22
single m. in possession OPEN 555:22
So much resemble m. COWP 240:22
Stand by your m. WYNE 834:15
standing by my m. CLIN 220:18
state of m. SHAK 673:12
strain of m.'s bred out SHAK 699:14
strange what a m. may do THAC 768:20
study of m. is man CHAR 204:2
Style is the m. BUFF 159:19
That is the m. BISM 116:17
that the m. should be alone BIBL 73:20
There was a little m. NURS 551:5
This bold bad m. SHAK 673:8
this M. and this Woman BOOK 130:22
This was a m. SHAK 677:4
Thou art the m. BIBL 79:6
Thou madest m. TENN 760:19
To cheat a m. is nothing GAY 331:21
To the m.-in-the-street AUDE 34:11
were m. But constant SHAK 702:30
What bloody m. SHAK 681:8
Whatever m. has done PROV 613:50
what is a m. PIND 576:11
What is m. BOOK 131:27
what is m. LENO 464:5
What m. has made of man WORD 829:7
what manner of m. he was BIBL 110:13
What m. thinks of changing TROL 783:2
What ought a m. to be IBSE 398:11
when a m. should marry BACO 43:20
When God at first made m. HERB 373:6
when I became a m. BIBL 106:16
which is m. SWIN 751:2
who kills a m. MILT 519:8
Who's master, who's m. SWIF 749:10
Whoso would be a m. EMER 299:22
woman was made for m. STAN 736:10
woman without a m. STEI 737:14
You'll be a M., my son KIPL 439:3
manage m. of a servile house WINC 822:22
m. without butter GOEB 342:9
managed disgracefully m. FIRB 313:7
not a free press but a m. RADC 620:3
management m. of a balance of power KISS 441:26
M. that wants to change TUSA 786:1
manager m. who gets the blame LINE 469:13
No m. ever got fired ADVE 8:4
managers m. of affairs of women KORA 444:6
managing kiss the M. Director WHIT 814:20
Manchester school of M. DISR 271:7
What M. says today PROV 614:4
mancipio *Vitaque m.* LUCR 479:6
Mandalay come you back to M. KIPL 439:12
road to M. KIPL 439:13
mandarin M. style CONN 233:27
mandate M. of Heaven CONF 231:6
royal m. ran BURN 167:5
Manderley dreamt I went to M. DU M 284:17
went to M. again OPEN 555:30
mandragora Give me to drink m. SHAK 656:18
mandrake frightful as a M. BYRO 179:21
Get with child a m. DONN 274:11
this quiet m. DONN 273:12
manes With draped m. HUGH 393:6
manger babe was born in a m. WHIT 814:19
in the rude m. lies MILT 513:19
laid him in a m. BIBL 98:20
lodge Him in the m. ANON 19:19
m. for his bed ALEX 11:10
mangle immense pecuniary m. DICK 265:22
mangrove held together by m. roots BISH 115:15
manhood ancient customs and its m. ENNI 300:15
harsh and embittered m. GOGO 344:1
m. an opportunity KEIL 432:10
M. a struggle DISR 270:3
M. taken by the Son NEWM 542:17
My m., long misled DRYD 281:20
touching his M. BOOK 127:1
manhoods hold their m. cheap SHAK 671:25
manibus *M. date lilia plenis* VIRG 795:2
manifesto first powerful plain m. SPEN 732:17
manifestoes in the party m. ROTH 635:21
manifold m. sins and wickedness BOOK 125:13
sundry and m. changes BOOK 128:7
manilla misery of m. folders ROET 631:7
mankind all m. BALL 51:6
countrymen are all m. GARR 330:10
crucify m. BRYA 159:3
Everything m. does JUVE 424:6
giant leap for m. ARMS 25:19
has not created m. TOCQ 778:12
hate, m. BYRO 174:18
How beauteous m. is SHAK 699:12
in th'original perused m. ARMS 25:14
legislator of m. JOHN 410:25
M. always sets itself MARX 499:14
m. and womankind BAHA 47:25
M. has done more damage COUS 238:7
M. is a dream PIND 576:11
M. is on the move SMUT 726:17
M. must put an end to war KENN 433:15
M.'s moral test KUND 446:7
no history of m. POPP 587:28
not in Asia, was m. born ARDR 23:20
one disillusion—m. KEYN 435:4
proper study of m. POPE 585:19
proper study of m. is books HUXL 396:18
ride m. EMER 299:8
school of m. BURK 164:24
manliness silent m. of grief GOLD 344:17
manly be a m. man MALO 492:9
than m. wise MARL 497:2
manna Exalted m. HERB 373:5
his tongue Dropped m. MILT 515:9
loathe our m. DRYD 282:4
m. of a day GREE 351:13
rained down m. BOOK 137:6
manned safeliest when with one man m. DONN 272:16
manner after the m. of men BIBL 106:24
all m. of thing JULI 423:3
All m. of thing shall be well ELIO 294:20
m. of his speech SHAK 656:22
to the m. born SHAK 662:17
manners As by his m. SPEN 734:11
bring good m. BURN 169:12
corrupt good m. BIBL 106:25
corrupt good m. PROV 599:44
English m. more frightening JARR 404:11
evil m. live in brass SHAK 673:22
for m.' sake BIBL 92:6
gentleness of your m. CLAI 218:5
good table m. MIKE 507:18
had very good m. SELL 654:6

manners (*cont.*):
lack of m. HATH 363:18
M. maketh man PROV 606:17
m. of a dancing master JOHN 412:14
m. of a Marquis GILB 339:7
Morals and m. CHAM 200:11
not men, but m. FIEL 310:1
Of m. gentle POPE 584:10
Oh, the m. CICE 217:19
Other times, other m. PROV 609:12
polished m. COWP 242:10
rectify m. MILT 519:12
soften m., but corrupt BYRO 178:6
thoughts and m. JOHN 410:25
Manningtree roasted M. ox SHAK 668:14
manoeuvre force with a m. TROT 783:19
manor sold a goodly m. for a song SHAK 656:4
manque *Un être seul vous m.* LAMA 448:6
mansion Back to its m. GRAY 350:10
everlasting m. SHAK 699:25
heavenly m., raging in the dark YEAT 835:8
Love has pitched his m. YEAT 835:13
m.-house of liberty MILT 519:16
My m. is MILT 511:12
mansions dolorous m. MILT 513:25
m. of the dead CRAB 242:27
many m. BIBL 102:17
mantle cast his m. upon him BIBL 80:4
green m. SHAK 679:6
her silver m. threw MILT 516:20
in russet m. clad SHAK 661:12
m. that covers all CERV 200:5
purple m. to the light RONS 632:7
twitched his m. blue MILT 513:13
mantled M. in mist AUDE 33:16
Mantovano salute thee, M. TENN 767:5
mantras M. and tantras TANT 755:1
Mantuan old M.! Who understandeth thee SHAK 680:25
manufacture content to m. life BERN 68:19
soul of every m. SMIL 722:16
manunkind this busy monster, m. CUMM 247:9
manure just what she lacks: m. GIDE 336:17
liquid m. from the West SOLZ 727:16
natural m. JEFF 405:7
manuscript youth's sweet-scented m. FITZ 315:2
many How m. things SOCR 726:20
makes so m. of them LINC 468:14
m. are called BIBL 96:21
m. are called PROV 606:25
M. hands make light work PROV 606:27
m.-headed monster POPE 586:19
m.-splendoured thing THOM 774:12
m. still must labour BYRO 175:13
m. ways out SENE 654:19
shed for you and for m. BOOK 129:22
So m. worlds TENN 761:17
so much owed by so m. to so few CHUR 215:12
we are m. BIBL 98:5
what are they among so m. BIBL 101:25
map in the new m. SHAK 702:7
m.-makers' colours BISH 115:17
m. me no maps FIEL 310:6
Roll up that m. PITT 577:7
use a larger m. SALI 642:15
mapmakers m. should place the Mississippi BELL 64:13
maps Geography is about M. BENT 67:2
in Afric-m. SWIF 749:16
m. on a small scale SALI 642:15
mar cannot m. ARNO 26:15
I m. on the other SKEL 721:13
marathon M. looks on the sea BYRO 176:26
trivial skirmish fought near M. GRAV 349:13
marble dreary m. halls CALV 182:6
dwelt in m. halls BUNN 160:10
Glowed on the m. ELIO 296:2
I am m.-constant SHAK 657:25
lasting m. seek WALL 800:4
left it m. AUGU 36:17
legs are as pillars of m. BIBL 85:21
m. index of a mind WORD 831:3
m., nor the gilded monuments SHAK 704:21
m. to retain BYRO 173:16
more than hard m. DU B 283:23
mould from m. living faces VIRG 795:1
placid m. HUNT 395:18
marbly great smooth m. limbs BROW 155:13
Marcellus M. exiled POPE 586:2
Tu M. eris VIRG 795:2
march Beware the ides of M. SHAK 674:4
boundary of the m. of a nation PARN 568:1
do not m. on Moscow MONT 528:13
droghte of M. CHAU 204:6
droghte of m. OPEN 556:25
ides of M. are come SHAK 675:14
in the front of M. TENN 758:21
Let us m. STEV 740:16
long majestic m. POPE 586:17
mad M. days MASE 500:14
m. as an alternative FITT 314:3
M. comes in like a lion PROV 606:28
M., march, Ettrick SCOT 651:29
m. my troops towards GRIM 353:15
m. of intellect SOUT 731:2
m. of mind PEAC 570:16
m. on their stomachs SELL 654:13
m. through rapine GLAD 341:5
m. towards it CALL 181:10
M., whan God first maked man CHAU 206:4
m. with sovereign tread BLOK 122:6
Men who m. away HARD 361:19
On the first of M. PROV 608:29
peck of M. dust PROV 609:21
So many mists in M. PROV 611:7
take The winds of M. SHAK 703:17
three hours' m. to dinner HAZL 365:23
marche *congrès ne m. pas* LIGN 468:1
marched m. breast forward BROW 155:4
M. them along BROW 156:21
Märchen *Ein M. aus alten Zeiten* HEIN 368:5
marches forced m., battles and death GARI 329:17
Funeral m. to the grave LONG 474:4
marching M. as to war BARI 54:13
m., charging feet JAGG 401:7
M. to the Promised Land BARI 54:14
M. where it likes ARNO 28:11
people m. on MORR 532:10
soul is m. on SONG 729:13
truth is m. on HOWE 391:15
mare brought him a Flanders m. HENR 370:11
grey m. is the better PROV 601:39
lend me your grey m. BALL 52:10
man shall have his m. SHAK 690:10
Money makes the m. to go PROV 607:4
qui trans m. currunt HORA 386:20
Margaret It's me, M. BLUM 122:9
M. you mourn for HOPK 384:19
Merry M. SKEL 721:11
marge page having an ample m. TENN 760:7
margerain With m. gentle SKEL 721:12
Margery See-saw, M. Daw NURS 550:16
margin abusive m. notes EDGE 288:18
m. too narrow FERM 309:1
Maria Aunt M. flung herself GRAH 348:2
Ave M. PRAY 592:1
Ave M.! 'tis the hour BYRO 177:2
ex M. Virgine MISS 520:18
Mariana this dejected M. SHAK 686:19
Marie I am M. of Roumania PARK 567:1
Maries Queen had four M. BALL 51:9
marigold m., that goes to bed SHAK 703:16
marijuana experimented with m. CLIN 221:4
mariner It is an ancient M. COLE 226:3
m. with the gentleman DRAK 278:19
mariners m., Souls that have toiled TENN 767:12
rest ye, brother m. TENN 763:15
Ye M. of England CAMP 183:18
marjoram savory, m. SHAK 703:16
mark man's distinctive m. BROW 155:24
m., or the name of the beast BIBL 112:21
m. upon Cain BIBL 74:11
M. well her bulwarks BOOK 134:26
m. what is done amiss BOOK 141:1
no drowning m. SHAK 698:16
not a m. ROST 635:12
press toward the m. BIBL 108:21
read, m., learn BOOK 127:22
would hit the m. LONG 473:13
market bought in the m. CLOU 221:18
enterprise of the m. ANON 15:20
Enthroned i' the m.-place SHAK 656:25
fast through the m. PROV 607:1
gathered in the m.-place CAVA 198:7
heart in the m.-place SHAK 691:18
marry a m.-gardener DICK 264:11
on m. research RODD 631:3
pig went to m. NURS 551:9
salutations in the m. BIBL 98:11
To m., to market NURS 551:14
Market Harborough AM IN M. TELE 758:1
marking malady of not m. SHAK 669:23
marks all manner of crooked m. EDGE 288:18
m. and scars I carry BUNY 161:18
m. of the beast HARD 360:13
marl Over the burning m. MILT 514:22
Marlborough Duke of M. MARL 495:15
From M.'s eyes JOHN 411:18
M.'s mighty soul ADDI 4:6
marmasyte Tullia's ape a m. ANON 16:16
marquis Abducted by a French M. GRAH 348:2
manners of a M. GILB 339:7
marred man that's m. SHAK 656:3
young man m. PROV 616:2
marriage blessings of m. SHAW 708:12
by way of m. FIEL 310:12
Chains do not hold a m. SIGN 719:5
count in any m. CLIN 221:3
Courtship to m. CONG 233:1
definition of m. SMIT 725:19
dictator before m. ELIO 292:17
drags the m. chain CLIN [illegible]
ended by a m. BYRO 176:21
every m. then is best in tune WATK 804:15
furnish forth the m. tables SHAK 662:1
get anywhere in a m. MURD 536:18
giving in m. BIBL 97:5
Hanging and m. FARQ 307:20
hear of a m. PROV 598:44
heart of m. is memories COSB 237:15
in companionship as in m. ADAM 2:14
In m., a man becomes slack STEV 741:26
joys of m. FORD 319:20
left-handed m. WOLL 825:22
live in a state of m. JOHN 414:12
long monotony of m. GIBB 336:8
Love and m. BYRO 176:19
M. a wonderful invention CONN 233:24
m. brings more joy EURI 304:16
m. for her was to be STAN 736:9
m. had always been her object AUST 38:20
M. has many pains JOHN 410:27
M. is a bribe WILD 819:15
M. is a lottery PROV 606:29
M. is a step so grave STEV 741:30
M. is like life STEV 742:1
M. is nothing but SELD 653:18
M. isn't a word FILM 311:24
M. is popular because SHAW 708:19
M. is the grave CAVE 198:12
M. is the waste-paper basket WEBB 807:2
M. I think SMIT 724:19
m. makes man and wife CONG 232:11
M. may often be a stormy lake PEAC 571:2
m. of true minds SHAK 705:15
m. on the rocks MERR 505:27
m. than a ministry BAGE 46:23

M., to women ANTH 22:18
m. without love means CLAR 219:6
more to m. than four PROV 612:4
nor are given in m. SWIF 748:26
party is like a m. MCIN 486:5
prevents a bad m. SHAK 701:4
primal m. blessing KEBL 432:7
Reading and m. MOLI 525:6
retrieve his fortunes by m. DICK 262:27
saying a m. 'failed' THOM 773:17
so bent on m. AUST 39:4
So that is m. WOOL 827:1
think there is any in m. GAY 331:22
three of us in this m. DIAN 260:5
value of m. DEV 259:13
wo that is in m. CHAU 206:15
marriages All the unhappy m. WODE 824:10
few happy m. ASTE 31:16
few m. are happy SWIF 748:28
happiest m. on earth DEV 259:10
have no more m. SHAK 664:9
M. are made in heaven PROV 606:30
M. would in general JOHN 415:11
most m. selling one's soul MACK 486:7
present at their m. TROL 783:7
There are good m. LA R 453:14
thousands of m. LARK 452:19
married At leisure m. CONG 232:34
before he m. SWIF 749:27
can't get m. at all FILM 312:9
delight we m. people have PEPY 573:10
Each thirteenth year he m. MERR 505:26
getting m. in the morning LERN 465:2
going to be m. GOLD 345:16
going to be m. STER 739:10
honest man who m. GOLD 345:25
if ever we had been m. GAY 331:11
If m. life were all that MILL 509:6
imprudently m. the barber FOOT 319:8
in every m. couple FIEL 309:15
In m. life three is company WILD 817:14
let us be m. LEAR 460:17
like other m. couples SAKI 642:9
m. beneath me ASTO 31:19
M., charming, chaste BYRO 175:29
m. me with a ring RAIN 620:8
m. past redemption DRYD 282:3
m. to a poem KEAT 431:15
m. to a single life CRAS 244:11
m.—to be the more together MACN 488:11
Miss will soon be m. HAYW 365:3
Mocks m. men SHAK 681:3
most m. man I ever saw WARD 803:8
One was never m. BURT 170:12
Reader, I m. him BRON 149:15
time we got m. CALL 181:14
Trade Unionism of the m. SHAW 708:11
well-bred as if we were not m. CONG 233:12
wench who is just m. GAY 331:13
when they got m. OPEN 555:5
when you m. me SHER 716:10
young man m. PROV 616:2
young man m. SHAK 656:3
marries in love when he m. BURN 165:24
m. without any consideration OSBO 559:19
signify whom one m. ROGE 631:16
When a man m. SHEL 712:1
marrow suck out all the m. THOR 776:12
marry advise no man to m. JOHN 418:13
better to m. than to burn BIBL 106:4
Can't get away to m. you LEIG 463:1
Doänt thou m. for munny TENN 764:23
find it in my heart to m. thee CONG 233:2
How can a bishop m. SMIT 725:16
m. a man who hates his mother BENN 66:11
m. a market-gardener DICK 264:11
m. a rich woman THAC 769:1
M. in haste PROV 606:31
M. in May PROV 606:32
m. Mr Collins AUST 38:19
M. my body to that dust KING 436:7
m. one another BUTL 172:22
m. whom she likes THAC 769:5
m. with his brother SHAK 665:13
may not m. his Mother BOOK 142:15
men we wanted to m. STEI 737:12
neither m., nor are given BIBL 96:23
never know who they may m. MITF 524:6
Never m. for money PROV 607:33
No artist should ever m. DELI 256:24
no woman should m. a teetotaller STEV 741:29
people people m. GILM 339:17
persons about to m. PUNC 617:2
Poets should never m. GONN 346:11
taken in when they m. AUST 37:24
than m. a man AUST 39:5
they neither m. SWIF 748:26
To m. is to domesticate STEV 742:2
when a man should m. BACO 43:20
while ye may, go m. HERR 375:3
Will you m. it PLAT 577:11
women m. off in haste ASTE 31:17
marrying m. in haste THOM 773:6
preventing men from m. TROL 783:12
Mars attack from M. SALI 643:3
Men are from M. GRAY 349:23
marshal m.'s baton LOUI 476:4
Martha M. was cumbered BIBL 99:15
martial m. airs of England WEBS 807:13
swashing and a m. outside SHAK 658:12
valiant and m. BACO 44:13
Martin Saint M.'s summer SHAK 672:7
Martini into a dry M. FILM 311:19
medium Vodka dry M. FLEM 317:9
Martinis Those dry M. ADE 5:21
martlet Like the m. SHAK 687:24
temple-haunting m. SHAK 682:7
martyr Glorious the m.'s gore SMAR 722:13
groan of the m.'s woe BLAK 119:1
if thow deye a m. CHAU 207:14
m. of the people CHAR 203:5
regarded as a m. KHOM 435:14
soul of a m. BAGE 46:2
martyrdom crown of m. WALP 801:20
M. is the test JOHN 416:13
m. must run its course AUDE 34:10
M. only way in which a man can SHAW 706:26
m. to live BROW 153:2
martyred shrouded oft our m. dead CONN 233:22
martyrs army of M. BOOK 125:20
blood of the m. PROV 596:31
graves of the m. STEV 742:24
love their m. DOST 276:2
no patience of m. THOM 771:15
stones and clouts make m. BROW 153:1
marvel m. at nothing HORA 386:18
m. my birthday away THOM 772:11
marvelled m. to see such things BOOK 134:24
marvellous Chatterton, the m. boy WORD 831:12
hath done m. things BOOK 138:9
m. demonstration FERM 309:1
m. in our eyes BOOK 140:6
towards the m. HUME 394:8
marvels all m. summèd lie SOUT 731:12
to credit m. HEAN 366:12
workest great marvels BOOK 126:17
Marx blame M. for what was done BENN 65:7
illegitimate child of Karl M. ATTL 32:4
in M.'s pages SCHU 649:12
Marxism more to Methodism than to M. PHIL 575:13
Marxist I am a M. SAYI 647:27
I am not a M. MARX 500:4
Marxiste *Je suis M.* SAYI 647:27
Mary Hail M. PRAY 592:1
M. Ambree BALL 51:5
M. had a little lamb HALE 357:4
M. hath chosen BIBL 99:16
M., quite contrary NURS 549:13
M.'s prayers FABE 305:15
M. was found in adulterous bed BLAK 118:15
one Hail M. DOYL 278:12
Where the lady M. is ROSS 634:20
winking M.-buds SHAK 660:21
Mary Jane *What* is the matter with M. MILN 510:20
Marylebone hanging garments of M. JOYC 421:19
Mary Magdalene cometh M. early BIBL 102:38
Mary Magdalenes Madonnas or M. WILL 820:12
masculine m. part, the poet in me BEHN 62:8
mask had a m. like Castlereagh SHEL 712:8
loathsome m. has fallen SHEL 713:14
m. that eats into the face UPDI 788:14
No m. like open truth CONG 232:14
masochistic m. form of exhibitionism OLIV 553:17
masons singing m. building SHAK 670:28
Where did the m. go BREC 147:20
masquerade m., a murdered peer ALCO 10:8
miss a m. POPE 587:4
truth in m. BYRO 177:17
mass activates the whole m. VIRG 794:22
blessed mutter of the m. BROW 155:14
listen to the B Minor M. TORK 779:17
M. is ended MISS 522:21
Meat and m. never hindered PROV 606:34
methods of m.-production LANC 449:18
Paris is well worth a m. HENR 370:6
rough and unordered m. OVID 561:12
two thousand years of m. HARD 361:8
Massachusetts denied in M. MILL 509:13
massacre not as sudden as a m. TWAI 786:6
masses bow, ye m. GILB 337:11
calling 'em the m. PRIE 591:14
huddled m. yearning LAZA 459:12
If it is for the m. SCHO 649:1
m. against the classes GLAD 341:8
m. conveying an emotion HEPW 371:6
m. get involved VOLT 798:8
sacrifices of M. BOOK 142:11
massy huge m. face MACA 481:13
mast m. Of some great admiral MILT 514:22
master allegiance to any m. HORA 386:8
be m. and win GOET 343:5
Caliban, Has a new m. SHAK 699:1
choice and m. spirits SHAK 675:20
Death is a m. from Germany CELA 199:10
disciple is not above his m. BIBL 94:35
dominion of the m. HUME 394:14
eye of a m. PROV 600:2
Jack as good as his m. PROV 604:42
Like m., like man PROV 605:31
love is m. GOWE 347:10
mad and savage m. SOPH 728:16
Man is the m. SWIN 751:3
m. a grief SHAK 691:13
M.-morality NIET 545:19
m. of his fate TENN 760:1
m. of my fate HENL 369:21
m. of the house cometh BIBL 98:13
m. of the Party HEAL 366:6
m. of those who know DANT 249:11
M., we have toiled BIBL 99:1
only the M. shall praise KIPL 440:19
presence of The M. THAC 768:22
slew his m. BIBL 80:25
This is our m. BROW 155:31
which is to be m. CARR 191:3
Who's m., who's man SWIF 749:10
Why eateth your M. BIBL 94:23
without m.-builders LOCK 471:12
masterly m. inactivity MACK 486:12
masterpiece Nature's great m. DONN 273:13

masterpieces in the midst of m. FRAN 322:17
masters anything but new m. HALI 357:20
ease of the m. SMIT 723:12
educate our m. LOWE 477:7
had two m. BEAV 59:7
m. of their fates SHAK 674:13
never wrong, the Old M. AUDE 34:9
people are the m. BURK 165:1
serve two m. BIBL 93:22
serve two m. PROV 607:47
spiritual pastors and m. BOOK 130:14
We are not the m. BLAI 117:12
We are the m. SHAW 709:27
We are the m. now MISQ 522:12
mastery m. of the thing HOPK 385:2
mastiff m.? the right hon. Gentleman's poodle LLOY 470:16
mastodons like m. bellowing WODE 824:19
masturbation Don't knock m. ALLE 12:9
m. of war RAE 620:5
sort of mental m. BYRO 180:10
match Honour is like a m. PAGN 563:6
lighted m. BROW 156:22
love m. was the only thing EDGE 288:14
m. the world above ZOHA 840:10
neuroses just don't m. MILL 509:24
matched m. us with His hour BROO 150:16
Thou wert never m. MALO 492:15
matches there he plays extravagant m. GILB 338:10
with that stick of m. MAND 493:11
matchless m. deed's achieved SMAR 722:13
matchwood m., immortal diamond HOPK 384:22
mate great artificer Made my m. STEV 742:22
mater *Stabat M. dolorosa* JACO 401:3
material bound by m. things CHUA 213:5
surpasses the m. OVID 561:13
materialism deteriorate into m. MOLT 525:23
materials I use simple m. LOWR 478:10
maternity m. a period of suffering STAN 736:9
mathematical m. heads ASCH 30:3
m. language GALI 328:13
of m. celebrity DOYL 277:17
mathematician appear as a pure m. JEAN 405:1
mathematics avoid pregnancy by resort to m. MENC 504:18
In m. you don't NEUM 541:11
knowledge in m. BACO 45:16
M. may be defined RUSS 639:19
M., rightly viewed RUSS 639:22
m., subtile BACO 44:8
mystical m. BROW 152:15
no place for ugly m. HARD 360:7
so like the m. WALT 802:12
used to love m. STEN 737:18
Matilda M. told such Dreadful Lies BELL 63:9
matrimony as that of m. TROL 782:10
critical period in m. HERB 371:19
in favour of m. AUST 39:12
joined together in holy M. BOOK 130:21
m. at its lowest STEV 741:27
more of love than m. GOLD 345:29
religion and m. CHES 209:3
safest in m. SHER 715:24
matron sober-suited m. SHAK 697:27
matter altering the position of m. RUSS 639:17
dislike the m. SHAK 656:22
Does it m. SASS 645:17
if it is it doesn't m. GILB 339:9
inditing of a good m. BOOK 134:13
m. enough to save BROW 156:16
m. out of place GRAY 349:24
M., the wickedest offspring ROCH 630:22
More m. with less art SHAK 663:11
root of the m. BIBL 81:23
speculations upon m. JOHN 410:6
sum of m. BACO 41:21
take away the m. BACO 43:32
this m. better in France STER 738:5
'twas no m. what he said BYRO 177:16
what does that m. GOET 343:13
What is M. PUNC 617:7
What is the m. with Mary Jane MILN 510:20
wretched m. and lame metre MILT 514:5
matters big words for little m. JOHN 413:19
else you do well m. ONAS 554:16
exercise myself in great m. BOOK 141:3
Nobody that m. MILL 509:9
What can I do that m. SPEN 732:25
Matthew M. Mark, Luke, and John PRAY 592:4
mattress crack it open on a m. MILL 509:20
mature M. love says FROM 325:9
m. women, *dancing* FRIE 325:5
maturing mind is m. late NASH 539:13
Maud into the garden, M. TENN 764:6
mausoleum as its m. AMIS 13:12
mawkish sweetly m. POPE 580:15
mawkishness thence proceeds m. KEAT 426:15
Max happened to M. and Moritz BUSC 170:23
incomparable M. SHAW 709:23
maxim just political m. HUME 395:4
M. Gun BELL 63:19
will that my m. KANT 425:14
maxima *mea m. culpa* MISS 520:11
may bring forth M. flowers PROV 595:15
darling buds of M. SHAK 704:9
fressh as is the month of M. CHAU 204:10
I'm to be Queen o' the M. TENN 764:18
maids are M. SHAK 659:20
Marry in M. PROV 606:32
matter for a M. morning SHAK 702:13
M. chickens come cheeping PROV 606:33
M. is a pious fraud LOWE 477:17
M. month flaps its leaves HARD 361:6
M.'s new-fangled mirth SHAK 680:19
M. to December ANDE 14:10
meadow in M. BABE 41:1
merry month of M. BALL 50:5
merry month of M. BALL 51:11
month of M. MALO 492:13
month of M. Is comen CHAU 206:24
moonlight-coloured m. SHEL 713:21
on a M. morning LANG 450:16
rose in M. CHAU 206:27
seventh of M. TROL 782:11
so many frosts in M. PROV 611:7
swarm in M. PROV 611:37
till M. be out PROV 607:25
what we m. be SHAK 666:2
will not when he m. PROV 602:18
world is white with M. TENN 759:16
Maya net of M. UPAN 788:4
maybe M., just maybe ADVE 7:44
maying let's go a-M. HERR 374:7
mayor tart who has married the M. BAXT 57:16
maypole away to the M. hie SONG 729:3
M. in the Strand BRAM 146:18
organ and the m. JORD 421:6
maypoles I sing of M. HERR 374:3
Mazda in the soul as Lord M. ZORO 841:13
M.-worshipper ZORO 841:7
maze like a sort of m. MORT 533:8
m. wherein affection RALE 620:11
mighty m. POPE 585:4
mazes accompany the m. SMAR 721:19
m. intricate MILT 517:3
MBEs M. and your knighthoods KEAT 426:12
McCarthyism M. is Americanism with MCCA 484:1
McGregor Mr M.'s garden POTT 588:20
McNamara M.'s War MCNA 488:3
me For you but not for m. MILI 508:13
M. Tarzan MISQ 522:2
now in the M. Decade WOLF 825:15
save thee and m. OWEN 562:2
meadow m. in May BABE 41:1
painted m. ADDI 4:21
meadows m. runnels KEAT 427:1
M. trim with daisies pied MILT 512:19
paint the m. SHAK 681:3
meal gives a m. man-appeal ADVE 8:5
handful of m. BIBL 79:26
mean admires m. things THAC 768:18
citizen of no m. city BIBL 104:15
depends what you m. by CATC 196:4
do a m. action STER 738:8
Down these m. streets CHAN 201:16
even if you don't m. it TRUM 784:9
for m. or no uses LOCK 471:14
Happy the golden m. MASS 501:4
having a m. Court BAGE 47:2
Know what I m., Harry BRUN 159:2
loves the golden m. HORA 388:7
no m. of death SHAK 675:20
nothing common did or m. MARV 498:19
poem should not m. but be MACL 487:3
say what you m. CARR 189:17
They may not m. to LARK 453:4
They m. well DISR 270:16
whatever that may m. CHAR 203:17
what we m., we say ARNO 26:3
Meander M.'s margent green MILT 511:19
meaner leave all m. things POPE 585:4
m. beauties of the night WOTT 833:1
only m. things ELIO 292:12
meanest m. of mankind POPE 586:3
meaning emptied of m. CAMU 184:14
Free from all m. DRYD 280:15
get at his m. RUSK 638:15
language charged with m. POUN 590:5
Love is our Lord's m. JULI 423:4
m. doesn't matter GILB 338:18
m. to afford CARY 193:5
mistake the m. WESL 811:17
plain m. SHAK 688:6
promises us m. BELL 64:15
richest without m. RUSK 638:20
take your m. BROW 158:5
teems with hidden m. GILB 339:8
To find its m. BROW 155:30
In some faint m. make pretence DRYD 281:36
What is the brief m. SCHI 646:14
within the m. of the Act ANON 18:7
meaningless almost m. ANON 18:20
meanings two m. packed up CARR 191:4
wrestle With words and m. ELIO 294:7
meanly all m. wrapped MILT 513:19
m. lose LINC 468:12
meanness land of m., sophistry BYRO 175:21
m. of opportunity ELIO 292:16
publish its m. THOR 776:12
means all m. are permitted DAWS 253:7
between ends and scarce m. ROBB 628:17
beyond our m. to pay DOST 275:18
by the best m. HUTC 396:14
die beyond my m. WILD 819:8
end cannot justify the m. HUXL 397:2
end justifies the m. BUSE 170:25
end justifies the m. PROV 599:12
end, never as m. KANT 425:18
Increased m. DISR 269:10
It m. everything RUSH 638:2
live within our m. WARD 803:6
m. all he says ADAM 3:2
m. just what I choose CARR 191:2
m. of grace BOOK 127:19
m. of rising JOHN 415:5
m. to do ill deeds SHAK 677:17
m. whereby I live SHAK 688:16
my m. may lie COWL 239:14
persons of small m. ELIO 293:10
politics by other m. CLAU 219:19
Private M. is dead SMIT 724:23
Whatever 'in love' m. DUFF 284:10
wills also the m. KANT 425:16
wills the m. PROV 602:34
Without m. BYRO 180:7

meant damned dots m. CHUR 214:17
knew what it m. BROW 158:16
knew what it m. KLOP 442:5
more is m. MILT 512:9
'w-a-t-e-r' m. the wonderful KELL 432:12
what he m. by that LOUI 476:6
measles Love's like the m. JERR 407:6
m. of the human race EINS 291:5
measure good m., pressed down BIBL 99:5
If you cannot m. it KELV 432:17
lead but one m. SCOT 651:11
leave to heaven the m. JOHN 411:20
Man is the m. PROV 606:16
m. in all things PROV 612:14
m. of all things PROT 593:18
m. of movement AUCT 33:15
m. of the universe SHEL 713:12
M. still for Measure SHAK 686:25
M. your mind's height BROW 157:4
serves to grace my m. PRIO 592:15
Shrunk to this little m. SHAK 675:19
strength beyond due m. EURI 305:1
With what m. ye mete BIBL 98:4
measured dance is a m. pace BACO 41:15
m. language lies TENN 760:24
m. out my life with coffee spoons ELIO 295:6
m. phrases WORD 831:13
measureless caverns m. to man COLE 225:20
over the m. whole LUCR 478:21
measures in short m. JONS 420:21
M. not men CANN 185:5
M. not men GOLD 345:15
Not men, but m. BURK 164:17
meat all manner of m. BOOK 139:13
appointed to buy the m. SELD 653:19
but He sends m. PROV 601:15
came forth m. BIBL 78:1
dish of m. is too good WALT 802:24
gavest m. or drink BALL 51:4
get m. without violence LAWS 459:5
givest them their m. BOOK 141:20
God sends m. PROV 601:17
have m. and cannot eat BURN 167:22
Heaven sends us good m. GARR 330:6
hungred, and ye gave me m. BIBL 97:12
life more than m. BIBL 93:23
M. and mass never hindered PROV 606:34
m. in the hall STEV 743:3
One man's m. PROV 608:48
On our m., and on us all HERR 374:2
Out-did the m. HERR 374:17
seek their m. from God BOOK 139:5
sent them m. enough BOOK 137:6
solid m. for men DRYD 283:13
taste my m. HERB 373:1
Upon what m. SHAK 674:14
meats funeral baked m. SHAK 662:1
Meaulnes call le grand M. ALAI 9:16
meazles Love iz like the m. BILL 115:2
mechanic m. part of wit ETHE 301:13
mechanical m. arts BACO 44:21
méchant *m. animal* MOLI 525:20
medal gold m. for poetry GRAV 349:19
m. for killing two men MATL 501:14
m. glitters CHUR 215:16
meddle Do not m. in the affairs TOLK 779:4
M. and muddle DERB 258:14
meddlers Lay-overs for m. PROV 605:11
meddles Minister that m. with art MELB 503:15
meddling fool will be m. BIBL 83:8
Medes M. and Persians BIBL 90:5
media exposed to the m. BOWI 145:22
m. is like an oil painting INGH 399:16
m. It sounds like STOP 743:13
medias *in m. res* HORA 386:1
mediator M. and Advocate BOOK 127:15
medical cocking their m. eyes DICK 266:2
in advance of m. thought WODE 824:20
Medici Miniver loved the M. ROBI 629:14
medicinal M. discovery AYRE 40:8
medicine desire to take m. OSLE 560:17
doeth good like a m. BIBL 83:4
ever m. thee SHAK 692:29
Grief is itself a m. COWP 239:28
it's late for m. OVID 561:20
m. for the sick SHAN 706:7
M. is my lawful wife CHEK 208:14
m. of life BIBL 91:20
m. the less SHAK 660:28
m. to heal their sickness BOOK 141:24
miserable have no other m. SHAK 686:15
mistake m. for magic SZAS 752:3
patent m. advertisement JERO 406:21
practise m. MOLI 525:9
Medicine Hat war-bonnet of M. BENÉ 64:23
medicines m. to make me love him SHAK 667:30
medicos m. marvelling RANS 621:20
medicus *plus sum quam m.* PLAU 578:14
medieval lily in your m. hand GILB 338:20
medio *M. de fonte leporum* LUCR 479:9
M. tutissimus ibis OVID 561:14
mediocre middle-aged and m. STRE 744:18
Some men are born m. HELL 368:14
Titles distinguish the m. SHAW 708:20
mediocribus *M. esse poetis* HORA 386:7
mediocritatem *Auream quisquis m.* HORA 388:7
mediocrity M. knows nothing higher DOYL 278:8
m. of her circumstances SMIT 723:14
m. of the apparatus TROT 783:18
m. thrust upon them HELL 368:14
meditate m. on the lovely light RIG 627:16
meditation abstracted m. JOHN 409:26
happy tone Of m. WORD 829:9
light with m. DUNN 285:12
m. of my heart BOOK 132:18
sage in m. found SHEL 713:30
meditations enter infinite m. MAHĀ 490:15
Mediterranean closer to the warm M. FRIE 325:7
M., where he lay SHEL 712:14
taken from the M. SHAF 655:14
medium insipid as a m. BURN 165:19
m. because nothing's well done ACE 1:9
m. is the message MCLU 487:8
Roast Beef, M. FERB 308:14
meek Blessed are the m. BIBL 93:3
borne his faculties so m. SHAK 682:10
m. and lowly in heart BIBL 95:9
m. and quiet spirit BIBL 111:2
m. shall inherit SMIT 724:1
M. wifehood is no part BROC 149:3
meekly m. kneeling BOOK 129:15
meet can never m. MARV 498:11
Extremes m. PROV 600:1
If I should m. thee BYRO 179:19
If we do m. again SHAK 676:30
make him an help m. BIBL 73:20
m. and right so to do BOOK 129:19
m. 'em on your way down MIZN 524:11
m. thee in that hollow vale KING 436:7
used to m. BROW 155:22
very m., right BOOK 129:20
When shall we three m. SHAK 681:6
Where dead men m. BUTL 173:2
meeting Journeys end in lovers m. SHAK 701:9
m. where it likes ARNO 28:11
meetings m. made December June TENN 761:26
meets than m. the ear MILT 512:9
méfiez-vous *Taisez-vous! M.* OFFI 554:13
megalith M.-still HUGH 393:6
melancholy as lovely m. FLET 318:6
black sun of m. NERV 541:7
busy to avoid m. BURT 170:2
charm in m. ROGE 631:15
green and yellow m. SHAK 701:24
Hence, loathèd M. MILT 512:12
inherited a vile m. JOHN 411:24
m. fit shall fall KEAT 429:4
m. god protect thee SHAK 701:22
M. has her sovran shrine KEAT 429:5
m., long ARNO 26:4
M. marked him for her own GRAY 350:14
m. of human reflections BAGE 47:13
m.'s child SHAK 676:32
moping m. MILT 517:24
Most musical, most m. MILT 512:6
Naught so sweet as M. BURT 170:1
Pale M. sate retired COLL 229:11
recipe for m. LAMB 448:24
soothe her m. GOLD 345:30
suck m. out of a song SHAK 658:21
this trick of m. SHAK 656:4
untroubled by m. BANV 53:10
villanous m. SHAK 678:7
what devil This m. is FORD 320:2
Melchisedech order of M. BOOK 139:17
meliora *Video m.* OVID 561:17
mellificatis *non vobis m. apes* VIRG 797:4
mellow m. fruitfulness KEAT 430:8
m. fruitfulness OPEN 556:14
too m. for me MONT 526:13
melodie Luve's like the m. BURN 168:6
melodies Heard m. are sweet KEAT 428:23
melodious Melting m. words HERR 375:5
some m. plot KEAT 429:6
melody ful of hevenyssh m. CHAU 207:19
M. is the essence MOZA 534:12
m. lingers BERL 68:10
m., which I've never ALAI 10:4
pretty girl is like a m. BERL 68:9
smale foweles maken m. CHAU 204:7
voice of m. BOOK 134:21
melons Stumbling on m. MARV 498:15
Melrose would'st view fair M. SCOT 650:16
melt earth shall m. away BOOK 134:19
Let Rome in Tiber m. SHAK 656:8
m. with ruth MILT 513:9
So let us m. DONN 274:19
solid flesh would m. SHAK 661:22
melted m. into air SHAK 699:6
M. to one vast Iris BYRO 174:25
melting like m. wax BOOK 132:24
M.-Pot where all the races ZANG 839:21
member every joint and m. MILT 519:13
I am not a m. of FLEM 317:15
m. of Christ BOOK 130:10
that will accept me as a m. MARX 499:11
members m. one of another BIBL 108:4
very m. incorporate BOOK 130:2
were all my m. written BOOK 141:13
membra *Etiam disiecti m. poetae* HORA 389:18
même *plus c'est la m. chose* KARR 426:1
meminisse *Forsan et haec olim m. iuvabit* VIRG 793:10
Nec me m. pigebit Elissae VIRG 794:12
memoirs M. are true and useful stars PEPY 573:16
write one's m. is to speak ill PÉTA 574:9
memor *Dum m. ipse me* VIRG 794:12
memorable that m. scene MARV 498:19
memorandum m. is written ACHE 1:14
memorial have no m. BIBL 92:17
out of the M. DICK 261:20
whole earth as their m. PERI 573:20
memorials there are no m. YEVT 838:9
memories dense melancholy of m. BABE 40:17
heart of marriage is m. COSB 237:15
m. are card-indexes CONN 234:2
m. are hunting horns APOL 22:20
M. are not shackles BENN 65:18
M. have three epochs AKHM 9:8
ought to have good m. SIDN 718:2
memory comes o'er my m. SHAK 693:8
faculty of m. DAVI 252:1
Fond M. brings the light MOOR 530:20
Footfalls echo in the m. ELIO 294:2
grand m. for forgetting STEV 741:6

memory (*cont.*):
His m. is going JOHN 417:2
liar to have good m. PROV 605:24
like a m. lost CLAR 218:15
m. be green SHAK 661:13
m. of a Macaulay BARR 56:3
m. of men BROW 153:8
m. of yesterday's pleasures DONN 275:9
m. remembers the happy things LOVE 477:1
m. revealed itself PROU 593:21
M. says: Want RICH 626:11
m. that only works backwards CARR 190:24
Midnight shakes the m. ELIO 295:20
mist of a m. PARI 566:16
my name and m. LAST 455:14
mystic chords of m. LINC 468:9
no force can abolish m. ROOS 633:1
No m. of having starred FROS 326:8
not intellect but rather m. LEON 464:12
Queen Elizabeth of most happy m. BIBL 73:7
sense them like a m. MOSE 534:4
silent m. of God GIBR 336:12
Some women'll stay in a man's m. KIPL 441:24
stepmother to m., oblivion JOHN 407:14
Thanks for the m. ROBI 629:10
thy tablets, M. ARNO 26:17
to his m. for his jests SHER 716:20
Vibrates in the m. SHEL 714:1
while m. holds a seat SHAK 662:32
men all m. are created equal ANON 19:11
all m. are rapists FREN 324:6
all things to all m. ANON 17:8
all things to all m. BIBL 106:9
best of m. PROV 595:47
between m. and women THUR 776:25
Bring forth m.-children SHAK 682:18
company of m. CHEK 208:19
conditions of m. BOOK 127:16
danger from all m. ADAM 3:4
daughters of m. BIBL 74:15
Destiny with M. for pieces FITZ 314:15
die like m. BOOK 137:10
finds too late that m. betray GOLD 345:30
fishers of m. BIBL 93:1
form Christian m. ARNO 29:13
generation of m. HOME 382:2
Good m. are scarce PROV 601:29
hell to m. AESC 6:9
how much m. hate them GREE 352:7
I eat m. PLAT 577:18
If m. could get pregnant KENN 433:5
If m. had to have babies DIAN 260:3
imprudently m. engage ASTE 31:16
innocent m., women, and children JEFF 406:2
in the catalogue ye go for m. SHAK 684:2
issue not towards m. BACO 43:7
learn m. from books DISR 270:32
life not about m. DENE 257:7
likeness of m. BIBL 103:32
looking upon m. as virtuous BOLI 124:18
Measures not m. CANN 185:5
m. and mountains meet BLAK 120:7
m. and nations behave wisely EBAN 287:20
M. are April when they woo SHAK 659:20
M. are but children DRYD 280:27
m. are created equal JEFF 405:3
M. are so honest LERN 465:3
M. are vile MONT 526:20
m. as trees, walking BIBL 98:7
M. at forty JUST 423:19
m. cannot help not loving you BAIN 48:8
m. confused with life FRID 324:21
m. don most harm LANG 450:18
M. don't know women TROL 782:9
M. drawn by worth PEMB 572:7
M. eat Hogs STEV 739:22
m. from the barn HOUS 391:1
m. have got love AMIS 13:17
M. have had every advantage AUST 38:11
M. have precedency BRAD 146:15
m. hurrying back MULD 536:1
m. in disguise ABSE 1:5
m. in shape and fashion ASCH 30:7
m. in women do require BLAK 120:9
men know so little of m. DU B 284:3
m., like satyrs MARL 496:9
M. lived like fishes SIDN 718:3
m. may come TENN 757:14
m. must work KING 437:12
M., my brothers TENN 763:2
m. naturally desire to know AUCT 33:10
m. naturally were born free MILT 520:3
m. of like passions BIBL 104:1
M. seldom make passes PARK 567:3
m.'s lack of manners HATH 363:18
M.! the only animal to fear LAWR 458:10
m. to some one quality DRAY 279:2
M. were deceivers ever SHAK 691:7
m. we wanted to marry STEI 737:12
M., when they lust GREE 352:3
m. who are discriminated MEIR 503:12
m. who have loved them TROL 783:7
M. who march away HARD 361:19
m. who will support me MELB 504:4
m. with the muck-rakes ROOS 633:7
m., women, and Herveys MONT 526:18
M. would be angels POPE 585:12
m. would be false LYLY 480:13
m. would be tyrants ADAM 1:18
Mocks married m. SHAK 681:3
more I see of m. ROLA 632:4
need of a world of m. BROW 157:6
not m., but manners FIEL 310:1
Not m., but measures BURK 164:17
not the m. in my life that counts WEST 812:4
power over m. WOLL 825:21
proper young m. BURN 167:18
Rejoiced they were na m. BURN 169:7
schemes o' mice an' m. BURN 168:24
State is a relation of m. WEBE 807:5
studied books than m. BACO 44:27
think all m. mortal YOUN 839:8
to m. French CHAR 203:16
transform M. into monsters FORD 320:2
trust themselves with m. SHAK 699:15
200,000 m. NAPU 539:1
two strong m. KIPL 438:5
very language of m. WORD 832:17
wealth accumulates, and m. decay GOLD 344:8
We are the hollow m. ELIO 294:24
What m. or gods KEAT 428:22
Women nicer than m. AMIS 13:18
menace m. to be defeated SCAR 646:11
mend Make do and m. OFFI 554:9
never too late to m. PROV 604:22
shine, and seek to m. DONN 272:24
we can't m. it CLOU 221:20
mendax *Splendide m.* HORA 388:20
mended all is m. SHAK 690:30
Least said, soonest m. PROV 605:13
nothing else but to be m. BUTL 171:24
mendicus *M. es* PLAU 578:14
mending ever want m. PROV 615:14
Mendip M.'s sunless caves MACA 482:18
mene m., tekel, upharsin BIBL 90:4
meningitis M. It was a word DEAN 253:18
menpleasers with eyeservice, as m. BIBL 108:11
mens *M. agitat molem* VIRG 794:22
M. sana in corpore sano JUVE 425:2
mensonge *m. suit* PROU 594:9
mental cease from m. fight BLAK 120:1
Freedom and slavery are m. states GAND 329:5
m. decay NICO 545:1
m. pleasure produced REYN 625:8
m. processes HALD 356:16
mention make m. of you always BIBL 104:24
m. of you in our prayers BIBL 109:7
never m. her BAYL 58:2
mentioned names to be m. AUST 38:24
mer *Poème De la M.* RIMB 628:7
Mercator *M.'s* North Poles CARR 191:22
mercenary m. and the prudent AUST 38:21
m. calling HOUS 390:9
merchandise mechanical arts and m. BACO 44:21
merchant like unto a m. man BIBL 95:23
m. shall hardly keep himself BIBL 92:2
m., to secure his treasure PRIO 592:15
merchantman monarchy is a m. AMES 13:8
mercies For his m. ay endure MILT 512:25
new m. I see CHIS 212:7
tender m. of the wicked BIBL 82:25
Thanks for m. past BUCK 159:17
merciful Blessed are the m. BIBL 93:3
God be m. ANON 21:10
God be m. BIBL 100:16
God be m. unto us BOOK 136:3
M. as constant GRAV 349:14
m., bashful TALM 754:12
m. eclipse GILB 337:8
m. one to another KORA 445:10
Name of God, the M. KORA 443:12
these were m. men BIBL 92:17
merciless black and m. things JAME 403:6
looked at in this m. glare WILL 820:19
mercury like feathered M. SHAK 668:30
m. sank AUDE 33:30
pick up m. with a fork LLOY 471:8
words of M. SHAK 681:5
mercy belle dame sans m. KEAT 427:14
big with m. COWP 240:17
Charity and M. DICK 263:4
compassion and m. BIBL 91:16
crowning m. CROM 245:13
everlasting m., Christ MASE 500:15
folks over to God's m. ELIO 291:23
God's gracious m. BOOK 131:10
Hae m. o' my soul EPIT 302:13
have m. and to forgive BOOK 127:15
have m. on you VILL 792:19
Have m. upon us BOOK 127:2
Justice with m. MILT 517:21
leaving m. to heaven FIEL 310:8
Lord, have m. upon us BOOK 126:2
Love is the greatest m. WILB 817:8
love m. BIBL 90:20
M. and truth BOOK 137:15
m. embraceth him BOOK 133:18
m. endureth for ever BOOK 141:6
M. has a human heart BLAK 120:15
M. I asked, mercy I found EPIT 303:15
m. I to others show POPE 587:13
M. . . . laboured much BUNY 161:15
m. to forgive DRYD 281:19
quality of m. SHAK 688:10
render The deeds of m. SHAK 688:11
shut the gates of m. GRAY 350:12
so good a grace As m. SHAK 686:8
so great is his m. BOOK 138:19
so is his m. BIBL 91:17
they shall obtain m. BIBL 93:3
wideness in God's m. FABE 305:18
merde *M.* CAMB 182:11
Meredith M., we're in CATC 196:12
merit how he esteems your m. COWP 240:5
m. for a bishopric WEST 812:20
m.'s all his own CHUR 214:11
m. wins the soul POPE 587:12
not their m. but our folly OSBO 559:20
What is m. PALM 566:9
merits not weighing our m. BOOK 130:1
mermaid Done at the M. BEAU 58:13
m. on a dolphin's back SHAK 689:22
M. Tavern KEAT 428:20
mermaids heard the m. singing ELIO 295:11
hear m. singing DONN 274:11
So many m., tended her SHAK 656:24

merrier more the m. PROV 607:8
merrily die all, die m. SHAK 669:1
m. hent the stile-a SHAK 703:12
m. meet in heaven MORE 531:13
Merrily, m. shall I live SHAK 699:11
Sing we m. BOOK 137:9
merriment m. of parsons JOHN 416:19
merry all their wars are m. CHES 210:2
always very m. SELL 654:11
be m. BIBL 84:19
eat, drink, and be m. BIBL 99:21
have such a m. day PEPY 573:14
Have they been m. SHAK 698:2
I am never m. SHAK 688:24
I am not m. SHAK 692:10
men are ever m. SHAK 670:11
M. and tragical SHAK 690:22
m. heart BIBL 82:35
m. heart doeth good BIBL 83:4
m. heart goes all the day SHAK 703:12
m. in hall PROV 604:20
m. monarch ROCH 630:17
m. month of May BALL 50:5
m. month of May BALL 51:11
m. old soul NURS 549:17
m. someris day CHAU 207:9
never a m. world SELD 653:20
never m. world in England SHAK 672:20
to-night we'll m. be SONG 729:2
with a m. noise BOOK 134:23
merrygoround It's no go the m. MACN 488:7
merses *M. profundo* HORA 389:4
Mesech constrained to dwell with M. BOOK 140:10
Meshach Shadrach, M., and Abed-nego BIBL 90:2
meshes Though its m. are wide LAO 452:6
mess accommodates the m. BECK 59:19
Another fine m. LAUR 454:8
In every m. I finds DIBD 260:12
m. of pottage BIBL 74:34
m. of pottage BIBL 82:36
m. we have made of things ELIO 293:25
message if there is a m. PAXM 570:11
medium is the m. MCLU 487:8
m. of your play BEHA 62:4
m. to Albert DISR 269:25
Publish your m. WESL 811:18
messager bisy larke, m. of day CHAU 205:17
messages m. should be delivered GOLD 346:6
messenger m.-boy Presidency SCHL 648:18
m. of Death SACK 641:4
M. of God KORA 445:3
M. of God KORA 445:10
M. with the guidance KORA 445:9
musician, if he's a m. HEND 369:17
only the M. of God KORA 444:15
messengers staying m. RILK 628:3
messing m. about in boats GRAH 348:7
met day and the way we m. SWIN 751:7
Hail, fellow, well m. SWIF 749:10
Ill m. by moonlight SHAK 689:19
m. together BOOK 137:15
m. us in your Son BOOK 130:2
M. you not with my true love RALE 621:1
We m. at nine LERN 465:4
metal Here's m. more attractive SHAK 664:20
Paradisal Imagineless m. THOM 774:16
with rich m. loaded SPEN 733:25
metamorphoses month of m. ARAG 23:11
metaphor whaling a universal m. LODG 472:14
metaphorical m. God DONN 275:1
metaphysic high As m. wit can fly BUTL 171:22
M. calls for aid on Sense POPE 582:12
metaphysical m. brothel for the emotions KOES 443:3
metaphysicians say of m. CHAM 201:8
metaphysics Explaining m. BYRO 175:25
M. is the finding BRAD 146:6
more towards m. DARW 251:3
mete With what measure ye m. BIBL 98:4
meteor cloud-encircled m. SHEL 711:23
hair Streamed, like a m. GRAY 350:3
Shone like a m. MILT 514:28
method yet there is m. in't SHAK 663:13
methodically elope m. GOLD 345:16
Methodism more to M. than to Marxism PHIL 575:13
Methodist morals of a M. GILB 339:7
methods You know my m. DOYL 278:2
methought M. I saw MILT 519:1
Methuselah days of M. BIBL 74:14
métier *c'est son m.* LAST 455:9
Mon m. et mon art MONT 527:17
metope o to be a m. CUMM 247:6
metre laws of God and man and m. EPIT 303:4
m. ballad-mongers SHAK 668:20
wretched m. and lame m. MILT 514:5
metrical m. composition WORD 832:18
metropolis m. of the empire COBB 223:11
mettle thy undaunted m. SHAK 682:18
metuant *Oderint, dum m.* ACCI 1:8
metus *M. et malesuada Fames* VIRG 794:20
meum *M. est propositum* ANON 21:10
meurt *La Garde m.* CAMB 182:11
mew be a kitten and cry m. SHAK 668:20
mewling infant, M. and puking SHAK 658:26
Mexico M., so far from God DIAZ 260:9
Mexique beyond the M. Bay MARV 498:9
mezzo *Nel m. del cammin* DANT 249:6
Nel m. del cammin OPEN 556:4
mice as long as it catches m. DENG 257:9
catches no m. PROV 597:6
Like little m. SUCK 745:8
m. will play PROV 614:26
schemes o' m. an' men BURN 168:24
than will catch m. PROV 604:48
Three blind m. NURS 551:10
Michael M. and his angels BIBL 112:19
Michelangelo designs by M. TWAI 786:14
M. left a proof YEAT 837:19
name of—M. REYN 625:13
Talking of M. ELIO 295:4
micher sun of heaven prove a m. SHAK 668:12
miching m. mallecho SHAK 664:22
Mickey Mouse M. could direct HYTN 398:2
You're M. PORT 588:12
mickle makes a m. PROV 606:22
Many a m. PROV 606:23
microbe M. is so very small BELL 63:21
microbes New sorts of m. DOST 276:5
on the antiquity of m. ANON 15:5
microscopic man a m. eye POPE 585:13
mid you in m.-air SOND 728:2
middenpit workshop, larder, m. BUNT 160:11
middle beginning, a m. ARIS 24:22
Heaven, a m. state MALL 492:5
life's m. state COWP 242:14
M. of Next Week CARR 192:1
M. Path PALI 565:11
m.-sized are alone entangled SHEN 715:7
m. way is none at all ADAM 3:6
mine was the m. state DEFO 254:18
people in the m. of the road BEVA 71:17
safely by the m. way OVID 561:14
Secret sits in the m. FROS 326:10
middle age dead centre of m. ADAM 2:7
enchantments of the M. BEER 61:13
last enchantments of the M. ARNO 28:15
reckless m. YEAT 836:22
middle-aged Grown m. WINT 823:11
Middle Ages go and live in the M. SMIT 724:22
M. ended in the 1950s HOBS 379:7
middle class great English m. ARNO 28:14
m. morality SHAW 709:13
M. people are apt SMIL 723:1
M. was quite prepared BELL 63:8
Philistines proper, or m. ARNO 28:10
sinking m. ORWE 559:7
than we of the m. suffer FRIE 325:6
middle classes bow, ye lower m. GILB 337:11
Middlesex acre in M. MACA 482:1
Rural M. again BETJ 70:17
midge lightly skims the m. BETJ 70:9
like a fretful m. ROSS 634:18
no bigger than a m.'s wing PROV 607:12
Midian host of M. BIBL 77:33
Midlands living in the M. BELL 64:6
midnight a-bed after m. SHAK 701:8
at m. speak with the Sun VAUG 790:4
black, and m. hags SHAK 684:21
budding morrow in m. KEAT 430:14
came upon a m. clear SEAR 652:24
cease upon the m. KEAT 429:13
Cerberus, and blackest M. MILT 512:12
chimes at m. SHAK 670:7
consumed the m. oil GAY 332:6
embalmer of the still m. KEAT 430:6
Holding hands at m. GERS 334:16
hour's sleep before m. PROV 608:44
iron tongue of m. SHAK 690:27
Let's mock the m. bell SHAK 657:6
M., a hotel bedroom READ 622:17
m. never come MARL 496:6
m. ride of Paul Revere LONG 474:15
M. shakes the memory ELIO 295:20
our m. oil QUAR 618:16
stroke of the m. hour NEHR 540:4
'Tis the year's m. DONN 274:8
upon a m. dreary POE 579:15
upon a m. pillow SHAK 658:19
Upon the m. hours KEAT 429:18
woes at m. rise LYLY 480:16
midst go up in the m. of thee BIBL 76:18
In the m. of life BOOK 131:13
there am I in the m. BIBL 96:10
midsummer high M. pomps ARNO 27:27
very m. madness SHAK 702:10
midway M. along the path DANT 249:6
M. along the path OPEN 556:4
midwife fairies' m. SHAK 697:5
midwinter In the bleak m. ROSS 634:5
mie *J'aime mieux ma m.* ANON 20:13
mieux *m. est l'ennemi du bien* VOLT 797:11
tout est au m. VOLT 797:5
might as our m. lessens ANON 21:15
Britons alone use 'M.' WAUG 806:15
counsel and m. BIBL 87:3
do it with thy m. BIBL 84:22
Exceeds man's m. SHAK 700:13
It m. have been HART 363:10
It m. have been WHIT 816:6
M. is right PROV 606:35
my name is M.-have-been ROSS 635:5
right makes m. LINC 468:7
Through the dear m. MILT 513:11
mightier make thee m. yet BENS 66:13
pen m. than the sword BULW 160:7
mightiest m. in the mightiest SHAK 688:10
mighty all that m. heart WORD 828:1
bringeth m. things to pass BOOK 140:5
how are the m. fallen BIBL 79:1
Lord m. in battle BOOK 133:3
Marlowe's m. line JONS 420:23
m. God BIBL 87:1
M. lak' a rose STAN 736:11
m. man is he LONG 474:19
m. man of valour BIBL 77:31
m. Poets in their misery WORD 831:14
m. working BOOK 131:14
Nimrod the m. hunter BIBL 74:23
put down the m. BIBL 98:17
rushing m. wind BIBL 103:15
things which are m. BIBL 105:29
thou art m. yet SHAK 677:1
through a m. hand BIBL 77:5

mignonne *M., allons voir* RONS 632:7
migraine Love is a universal m. GRAV 349:15
migrations all our m. GOLD 345:27
mild draw'd m. DICK 263:8
m. and magnificent eye BROW 156:18
prefer m. hale SURT 746:21
milder Not m. ARNO 27:1
mildest m. mannered man BYRO 176:23
mile compel thee to go a m. BIBL 93:13
miss is as good as a m. PROV 606:40
walked a crooked m. NURS 551:3
miles How many m. NURS 548:15
m. to go before I sleep FROS 326:12
milestones m. on the Dover Road DICK 262:26
militant Christ's Church m. BOOK 129:10
first m. lowbrow BERL 68:18
militants m. like cleaning women TRUF 784:1
militarism M. . . . is fetish worship TAWN 755:11
military entrust to m. men CLEM 220:9
m. divisions HAVE 364:4
M. force MCNA 488:5
m. man approaches SHAW 708:10
M. Two-step GREN 352:15
order and m. discipline MILI 508:5
milk Adversity's sweet m. SHAK 697:31
buy wine and m. BIBL 88:20
crying over spilt m. PROV 604:23
drunk the m. of Paradise COLE 225:25
end is moo, the other, m. NASH 539:9
flowing with m. and honey BIBL 75:28
Gin was mother's m. SHAW 709:14
his mother's m. SHAK 701:6
lady loves M. Tray ADVE 7:6
M. and then just as it comes BETJ 70:11
m. and the yoghurt TRIL 781:12
m. comes frozen home SHAK 681:4
m. is more likely BUTL 172:28
m. is so cheap PROV 615:6
m. my ewes and weep SHAK 703:23
m. of human kindness GUED 354:11
m. of human kindness SHAK 682:1
m. of the word BIBL 110:27
m. of the word BIBL 114:11
M.'s leap toward immortality FADI 306:1
M.-soup men call domestic PATM 569:20
m. the bull JOHN 413:10
m. the cow of the world WILB 817:5
m.-white steed BALL 51:20
Never cry over spilt m. FIEL 310:23
putting m. into babies CHUR 215:20
she gave him m. BIBL 77:28
take my m. for gall SHAK 682:3
trout in the m. THOR 775:27
weyveth m. and flessh CHAU 205:23
With m. and honey blessed NEAL 540:3
milka Drinka Pinta M. Day ADVE 7:17
milkmaid m. singeth blithe MILT 512:18
milky M. Way, the bird of Paradise HERB 373:5
steeped in stars, and m. RIMB 628:7
mill at the m. with slaves MILT 518:13
clappeth as a m. CHAU 205:9
forge and the m. HOUS 391:1
grist that comes to the m. PROV 594:23
m. cannot grind with PROV 606:36
neither a m. HUNT 396:9
old m. by the stream ARMS 25:13
mille *Da mi basia m.* CATU 197:3
millennium after the m. RAOU 622:2
Bunyan wanted the m. HILL 376:13
calico m. CARL 188:21
end of a m. promises HEWI 375:18
miller hackneyed jokes from M. BYRO 178:1
jolly m. BICK 114:14
milliner jewelled mass of m. TENN 763:24
million aiming at a m. BROW 156:1
Fifty m. Frenchmen MILI 508:7
m. deaths a statistic STAL 736:5
m. million spermatozoa HUXL 397:6
m. of the mouthless dead SORL 728:18
want to make a m. ANON 16:22
millionaire And an old-fashioned m. FISH 313:18
I am a M. SHAW 707:23
m. who bought it MCCA 483:18
silk hat on a Bradford m. ELIO 296:10
millions I will be m. EPIT 303:10
M. long for immortality ERTZ 301:6
m. of strange shadows SHAK 704:19
mortal m. live *alone* ARNO 28:2
multiplying m. O'SU 560:19
What m. died CAMP 183:15
mills dark Satanic m. BLAK 120:1
m. of God grind slowly LONG 474:8
m. of God grind slowly PROV 606:37
millstone m. round our necks DISR 268:16
m. were hanged about his neck BIBL 96:8
millstones Turned to m. SHEL 712:9
Milton malt does more than M. HOUS 391:9
M.! thou shouldst be living WORD 829:8
M. was for us BROW 156:18
morals hold Which M. held WORD 828:24
mute inglorious M. GRAY 350:11
mimic m. of the sun CRAN 243:22
miminy Francesca di Rimini, m. GILB 338:21
mimsy m. were the borogoves CARR 190:12
minarets Fretted with m. THWA 777:6
mince dined on m. LEAR 460:19
mind absence of m. SEEL 653:8
activity of his m. HUNT 395:18
all in the m. WOLF 825:9
And thou, my m. SIDN 718:20
at the end of the m. STEV 739:26
beat at your m. HECH 367:9
by the eternal m. WORD 830:3
Cast your m. on other days YEAT 837:21
change your m. AURE 37:7
[Charles] Sumner's m. ADAM 2:18
chords in the human m. DICK 261:1
Come back into my m. BELL 64:6
conformation of his m. MACA 482:6
conjunction of the m. MARV 498:11
could not make up his m. OLIV 553:15
dagger of the m. SHAK 682:21
damages his m. ANON 21:2
don't m. if I do CATC 195:26
empires of the m. CHUR 215:21
exists merely in the m. HUME 395:1
feeble, tiny m. JUVE 425:4
female m. IRWI 400:5
first destroys their m. DRYD 281:26
fool uttereth all his m. BIBL 83:33
forces of the m. PROU 594:11
frailty of the m. SHAD 655:11
frame of m. HORA 386:20
furnished with a m. so rare SHAK 660:18
generous and elevated m. JOHN 411:7
gentle m. by gentle deeds SPEN 734:11
Georgia on my m. GORR 347:4
give a sex to m. WOLL 825:17
hand the cutting edge of the m. BRON 149:8
has a m. and knows it SHAW 706:13
His m. his kingdom COWP 242:16
human m. in ruins DAVI 252:4
index of a feeling m. CRAB 243:10
infirmity of noble m. MILT 513:2
in m., body, or estate BOOK 127:18
In my m.'s eye SHAK 662:2
innocent and quiet m. STEV 741:28
in the m. of man WORD 829:5
Keep violence in the m. CLOS 222:16
know the m. of God HAWK 364:11
liberation of the human m. GOLD 344:5
love of the things of the m. PERI 573:19
Man's m. a mirror SOUT 731:12
man's unconquerable m. WORD 832:12
marble index of a m. WORD 831:3
march of m. PEAC 570:16
Measure your m.'s height BROW 157:4
m. and hand went together HEMI 369:8
m. and soul, according TENN 760:21
m. at peace BYRO 179:1
m. be a thoroughfare KEAT 431:19
m. can make Substance BYRO 177:32
m., did mind his grace ROYD 637:2
m. diseased BYRO 174:29
m. has mountains HOPK 384:12
M. has no sex MISQ 522:3
M. in its purest play WILB 817:6
m. is actually employed JOHN 415:1
m. is a very opal SHAK 701:22
m. is but a barren soil REYN 625:10
m. is clouded with a doubt TENN 760:17
m. is free DRAY 278:23
m. is its own place MILT 514:20
m. is like a mirror CHUA 213:7
m. is maturing late NASH 539:13
m. is not a bed AGAT 6:17
Mind, m. alone AKEN 9:4
m. moves upon silence YEAT 836:16
M. my bike CATC 196:13
m. of large general powers JOHN 409:27
M. of Man WORD 828:6
m. of winter STEV 740:4
m.'s construction SHAK 681:23
m. serene for contemplation GAY 332:14
m. shapes itself WOLL 825:23
m. the least of possessions WHIT 814:6
m. to me a kingdom is DYER 286:13
m. was that of Lord Beaverbrook ATTL 32:1
m. watches itself CAMU 184:3
m. which cannot bear MENG 504:20
m. which reveres details LEWI 467:9
m. will very generally refuse TROL 782:2
minister to a m. diseased SHAK 685:18
moved was their own m. HUI- 394:4
my m. a gap of danger HEAN 366:17
my m. forbids to crave DYER 286:13
My m. is stupefied VILL 792:17
My m. may lose its force BYRO 175:2
my m.'s unsworn EURI 304:19
noble m. DOYL 277:14
no blemish but the m. SHAK 702:17
no deeply thinking m. MELV 504:7
no female m. GILM 339:16
nothing great but m. HAMI 358:15
not in my perfect m. SHAK 680:4
no way out of the m. PLAT 577:12
ordinary m. WOOL 826:13
outlaw of his own dark m. BYRO 174:9
out of m. PROV 609:15
out of m. THOM 771:4
out of my m. OPEN 555:13
O! what a noble m. SHAK 664:10
padlock—on her m. PRIO 592:11
padlock on the m. POPE 580:19
persuaded in his own m. BIBL 105:24
prepare the m. of the country DISR 269:4
Reading is to the m. STEE 737:1
recesses in my m. BRON 149:14
remained, after his time, but m. SMIT 725:5
robs the m. BURK 163:10
sap the m. of the mind LEON 464:14
seen is merely their own m. MAHĀ 490:7
serve thee with a quiet m. BOOK 128:17
sex in the m. LAWR 458:9
so-called mortal m. EDDY 288:5
sound m. BIBL 109:20
sound m. JUVE 425:2
subsistence without a m. BERK 68:3
they're wrong. M. it FORS 320:20
this m. be in you BIBL 108:16
to one dead level ev'ry m. POPE 580:22
travel broadens the m. CHES 211:13
Travel broadens the m. PROV 613:16
turn thy m. to the Lord FOX 322:11
unbends the m. like them GAY 331:19
unseemly exposure of the m. HAZL 365:13
Until reeled the m. GIBB 336:9
What is M. PUNC 617:7
what one has in one's m. PROU 594:5
with all thy m. BIBL 96:24
without a m. BACO 42:6

mindful m. of him BOOK 131:27
minds comfortable m. CUMM 247:13
evil in young m. ARNO 29:16
fairly developed m. FORS 320:9
great empire and little m. BURK 163:8
Great m. think alike PROV 601:36
hearts and m. BIBL 108:24
marriage of true m. SHAK 705:15
M. are like parachutes DEWA 259:14
m. comprehend all things BYRO 177:8
M. innocent and quiet LOVE 476:14
M. like beds always made up WILL 821:1
m. made better ELIO 293:11
m. me o' departed joys BURN 166:18
m. of ordinary men BRON 149:10
please little m. PROV 605:44
spur of all great m. CHAP 202:23
weed their own m. WALP 801:9
mine all that's m. is thine BALL 50:19
but m. own SHAK 659:25
If they are m. or no HOUS 390:10
lovin' dat man of m. HAMM 358:16
m. own familiar friend BOOK 135:11
she is m. for life SPAR 731:18
So be m., as I yours GRAV 349:14
'Twas m., 'tis his SHAK 692:20
What thou art is m. MILT 517:20
with m. own BIBL 96:19
minefield grief is like a m. WARN 803:20
Life, if you're fat, is a m. MARG 495:8
miner Dwelt a m. MONT 529:4
mineral vegetable, animal, and m. GILB 339:3
miners like m.' coal dust BOOT 143:1
rugged m. poured to war MACA 482:18
Minerva owl of M. PAUL 570:8
mines m. reported in the fairway KIPL 439:16
mineworkers National Union of M. MACM 487:21
mingle In one spirit meet and m. SHEL 712:7
mining m.-claims BENÉ 64:23
minion morning's m. HOPK 385:1
minister As m. of the Crown PEEL 571:14
cheer the m. CANN 185:8
doobts aboot the m. PUNC 617:18
God help the M. MELB 503:15
m. going to run HEND 369:15
m. kiss'd the fiddler's wife BURN 168:3
m. to a mind diseased SHAK 685:18
M., whoever he at any time PAIN 564:3
m. who moves about CHOI 212:9
M. whose stubbornness JENK 406:8
spirit for my m. BYRO 175:7
Yes, M.! No, Minister CROS 246:13
ministered Angels came and m. BIBL 93:1
thousands m. unto him BIBL 90:6
ministering m. angel SHAK 666:26
m. angel thou SCOT 651:13
ministers Angels and m. of grace SHAK 662:18
grim Geneva m. AYTO 40:11
group of Cabinet M. CURZ 248:5
m. a flaming fire BOOK 139:1
m. decide THAT 770:9
m. of Christ BIBL 107:12
M. of State GILB 337:7
m. of the new testament BIBL 107:5
my actions are my m.' CHAR 203:14
passion-wingèd M. SHEL 710:16
teaching m. to consult SWIF 747:24
warning to all M. WALP 802:8
you murdering m. SHAK 682:3
ministries *Times* has made many m. BAGE 46:10
ministry marriage than a m. BAGE 46:23
m. of all the talents ANON 17:16
performs its secret m. COLE 225:12
secret m. of frost COLE 225:17
work of the m. BIBL 108:3
miniver M. loved the Medici ROBI 629:14
mink trick of wearing m. BALM 52:16
minks LSD reminds me of m. GRAV 349:22
Minnehaha M., Laughing Water LONG 474:13
minnows death for the m. TAWN 755:14
Triton of the m. SHAK 660:6
minor change from major to m. PORT 588:4
minorities M. . . . are almost always SMIT 726:3
minority m. possess their equal rights JEFF 405:11
m. who happen to be a majority LYNC 480:19
not enough to make a m. ALTM 13:1
minstrel M. Boy to the war MOOR 530:14
wandering m. I GILB 337:21
mint m. which coined our misery DRAY 279:5
m. with the hole ADVE 7:45
tithes of m. and cumin BIBL 96:26
mints lavender, m. SHAK 703:16
minuet constitutional m. SCAR 646:10
minute cannot cage the m. MACN 488:16
fill the unforgiving m. KIPL 439:3
first m., after noon DONN 274:5
good m. goes BROW 158:13
in m. particulars BLAK 119:2
sucker born every m. BARN 55:11
minutes famous for fifteen m. WARH 803:12
five m. too late COWL 239:24
have the seven m. COLL 229:3
m. hasten to their end SHAK 704:23
rate of sixty m. an hour LEWI 466:18
sixty diamond m. MANN 493:19
take care of m. CHES 209:12
white unblemished m. THOM 775:3
Mirabeau Under M. Bridge APOL 22:21
miracle m. in his own person HUME 394:9
m. of a youth EVEL 305:6
m. of our age CARE 186:4
m. of rare device COLE 225:22
seem a M. DONN 275:10
miracles age of m. PROV 594:19
age of m. hadn't passed GERS 334:12
miraculous most m. organ SHAK 664:1
Miranda Do you remember an Inn, M. BELL 64:7
mire cast into the m. BURK 163:25
m. and clay BOOK 133:31
Sow returns to her M. KIPL 438:20
mirk m., mirk night BALL 52:2
mirror in the rear m. RODD 631:3
live alone and smash his m. ANON 20:9
Man's mind a m. SOUT 731:12
mind is like a m. CHUA 213:7
m. cracked from side to side TENN 762:19
m. of alle curteisye CHAU 205:22
m. up to nature SHAK 664:16
novel is like a m. STEN 737:16
oppose a m. JONS 419:21
stand of m. bright HUI- 394:2
sunlit m. ABSE 1:7
mirrors m. and fatherhood are abominable BORG 143:6
m. are lonely AUDE 34:20
m. meant To glass the opulent HARD 361:9
m. of the gigantic shadows SHEL 714:24
m. of the sea are strewn FLEC 317:6
mirth betray me to your m. or hate FORD 320:3
I love such m. WALT 802:20
M. is like a flash ADDI 5:7
m.-subdual GISS 340:10
must borrow its m. WILC 817:9
Present m. SHAK 701:10
song of the birds for m. GURN 355:2
Than M. can do ANON 17:3
Who buys a minute's m. SHAK 704:1
misbeliever You call me m. SHAK 687:15
misce *M. stultitiam consiliis* HORA 389:11
mischance fil all this m. CHAU 206:5
mischief evil and m. BOOK 127:3
execute any m. CLAR 218:20
if m. befall him BIBL 75:17
In every deed of m. GIBB 335:12
intended m. against thee BOOK 132:20
it means m. SHAK 664:22
m. then into the world DRAY 279:5
m., thou art afoot SHAK 676:14
m. thou hast done NEWT 543:12
mother of m. PROV 607:12
no authority from God to do m. MAYH 502:20
punishment is m. BENT 66:20
Spectatress of the m. ROWE 636:10
what m. is in hand BYRO 177:7
mischiefs heap m. upon them BIBL 77:13
M. feed Like beasts JONS 420:15
misconceive hardly m. you BROW 158:5
misconduct no m. in anyone NELS 540:19
miscuit *qui m. utile dulci* HORA 386:3
misdoings these our m. BOOK 129:16
miserable make a man m. CHAR 203:8
Me m.! which way shall I fly MILT 516:9
M. comforters BIBL 81:19
m. have no other medicine SHAK 686:15
m. human being JAME 404:1
m. sinners BOOK 127:2
most m. things VIRG 793:17
of all men most m. BIBL 106:21
secret of being m. SHAW 709:7
so is it very m. TAYL 756:19
two people m. BUTL 172:22
miserande *Heu, m. puer* VIRG 795:2
miserere *m. nobis* MISS 522:19
miseria *Nella m.* DANT 249:12
miseries in shallows and in m. SHAK 676:28
m. of the world KEAT 427:18
miserrima *Quaeque ipse m. vidi* VIRG 793:17
miserum *Nec m. fieri* LUCR 479:7
misery bound in m. and iron BOOK 139:12
coined our m. DRAY 279:5
full of m. BOOK 131:12
great kick at m. LAWR 458:18
guilt and m. AUST 38:1
happiness and final m. MILT 515:19
loses his m. ARNO 27:12
Man hands on m. to man LARK 453:5
mighty Poets in their m. WORD 831:14
mine affliction and my m. BIBL 89:24
M. acquaints a man SHAK 698:33
m. is a battle gained WELL 809:17
M. loves company PROV 606:38
m. of being DRAB 278:15
m. of manilla folders ROET 631:7
m. which it is his duty LOWE 477:8
nothing but pure m. JOHN 416:16
Oppressed the m. CRAB 242:25
relation of distant m. GIBB 335:13
result m. DICK 261:19
splendid m. ROSS 634:14
to him that is in m. BIBL 81:6
vale of m. BOOK 137:12
when one is in m. DANT 249:12
misfits m., Looney Tunes, and criminals REAG 623:6
misfortune m. of our best friends LA R 453:21
m. to ourselves BIER 114:20
What a m. it is EDGE 288:16
misfortunes All the m. of men PASC 568:11
crimes and m. VOLT 797:18
crimes, follies, and m. GIBB 335:6
Few m. can befall MAUG 502:6
make m. more bitter BACO 43:25
M. never come singly PROV 606:39
m. of others LA R 453:12
talks of his m. JOHN 416:16
misgovernment cruelty, stupidity and m. GLAD 341:16
misguided m. men KING 436:17
mislaid afterwards m. PAST 569:6
mislead one to m. the public ASQU 31:6
misleading bound to be m. WATS 804:16
m. thoughts SPEN 732:6
misled most have been m. DRYD 281:24
mislike M. me not for my complexion SHAK 687:16

misnomer name of Epic's no m. BYRO 176:8
misquotation M. the privilege of the learned PEAR 571:9
misquote enough of learning to m. BYRO 178:1
misrepresentation some degree of m. ELIO 293:12
misrule Thirteen years of Tory m. POLI 581:30
miss calls her 'M.' CHES 210:19
little m. HUME 394:13
m. but a tree BLAM 121:15
m. for pleasure GAY 332:23
m. is as good as a mile PROV 606:40
M. not the discourse BIBL 91:22
M. respectably unmarried CART 192:10
never had you never m. PROV 614:15
never m. the water PROV 615:48
so might I m. BROW 156:15
missa *Ite m. est* MISS 522:21
missed m. the bus CHAM 201:2
m. the point completely ELIO 293:22
never would be m. GILB 338:1
No one would have m. her EPIT 303:1
Woman much m. HARD 361:21
misses m. family and friends EPIT 303:11
missing M. so much and so much CORN 237:2
mission m. workers came out too early RUNY 637:14
My m. is to pacify GLAD 340:17
sense of religious m. UPDI 788:17
missionaries eaten by m. SPOO 735:4
missionary I would eat a m. WILB 817:1
Mississippi place the m. BELL 64:13
singing of the M. HUGH 392:19
Missouri admit M. to the Union COBB 223:7
God has given us M. RAND 621:15
misspent thy m. time KEN 433:1
missus M., my Lord PUNC 617:17
mist air broke into a m. BROW 157:8
drizzling m. ASKE 30:20
Fuji through m. BASH 56:16
meanness, sophistry, and m. BYRO 175:21
m. and hum ARNO 27:18
m. in my face BROW 157:16
m. is dispelled GAY 331:18
mistake Among all forms of m. ELIO 292:19
made any such m. DICK 263:22
make a m. LA G 447:17
m. in the translation VANB 789:5
m. shall not be repeated EPIT 304:3
m. the meaning WESL 811:17
Nature's sole m. GILB 339:6
overlooks a m. HUXL 397:15
Shome m., shurely CATC 196:20
under a m. SWIF 748:14
mistaken possible you may be m. CROM 245:12
mistakes gives to their m. WILD 818:13
great men make m. CHUR 214:16
If he makes m. they must be covered CHUR 216:17
If you don't make m. PROV 603:30
just created like m. EMEC 299:4
knows some of the worst m. HEIS 368:11
make no m. CONR 234:19
man who makes no m. PHEL 575:2
search for our m. POPP 587:30
mistress Art is a jealous m. EMER 299:14
court a m. JONS 420:19
deck her m.' head BYRO 179:2
In ev'ry port a m. GAY 332:21
literature is my m. CHEK 208:14
m. I am ashamed to call you ELIZ 297:11
m. in my own KIPL 439:19
m. of herself POPE 583:16
m. of the Earl OPEN 555:20
m. of the Earl of Craven WILS 822:6
m. of the months SWIN 750:4
m. of the Party HEAL 366:6
m. or a friend SHEL 711:8
m. should be like WYCH 834:8
new m. now I chase LOVE 476:15
No casual m. TENN 761:16
O m. mine SHAK 701:9
teeming m. POPE 583:13
worst m. BACO 41:23
mistresses I shall have m. GEOR 333:11
m. with great smooth BROW 155:13
or your Lordship's m. WILK 819:19
Wives are young men's m. BACO 43:19
mists m. of righteous indignation MUGG 534:14
Season of m. KEAT 430:8
Season of m. OPEN 556:14
So many m. in March PROV 611:7
misty ful m. morwe CHAU 207:9
misunderstood people who remain m. TURG 785:8
To be great is to be m. EMER 299:24
truth m. JAME 404:3
misuse m., then cast their toys away COWP 240:8
misused m. words generate SPEN 732:6
mites threw in two m. BIBL 98:12
with m. of stars MAYA 502:15
Mithra M. of wide pastures ZORO 841:4
Mithridates M., he died old HOUS 391:10
mitre m. and a crown of martyrdom WALP 801:20
mittens lost their m. NURS 551:11
mix M. a little foolishness HORA 389:11
m. her with me SWIN 751:16
m. them with my brains OPIE 557:1
mixen Better wed over the m. PROV 596:14
mixture m. of a lie BACO 44:16
strange m. of blood CEÈV 244:21
Moab M. is my wash-pot BOOK 135:20
moan is not paid with m. THOM 774:3
made sweet m. KEAT 428:10
make delicious m. KEAT 429:18
m. of doves TENN 766:6
moanday m., tearsday, wailsday JOYC 421:20
moaning no m. of the bar TENN 757:18
moat Look to your M. HALI 358:3
moated at the m. grange SHAK 686:11
lonely m. grange TENN 763:19
mob do what the m. do DICK 265:5
lied to please the m. KIPL 438:13
M., Parliament, Rabble COBB 223:10
remonstrative whisper to a m. HUNT 396:4
supreme governors, the m. WALP 800:13
mock but to m. the kingdom PYM 618:8
m. at our accursed lot MCKA 486:6
m. on Voltaire BLAK 120:2
m. our eyes with air SHAK 657:12
mocked God is not m. BIBL 107:22
hand that m. them SHEL 712:22
mocker Wine is a m. BIBL 83:7
mocking great m. master DAVI 251:16
mockingbird kill a m. LEE 461:20
Out of the m.'s throat WHIT 815:6
mocks M. married men SHAK 681:3
model I am the very m. GILB 339:3
provide logical m. LÉVI 466:13
models Rules and m. HAZL 365:14
moderate m. income DURH 286:5
white m. devoted to order KING 436:12
moderation astonished at my own m. CLIV 221:9
M. in all things PROV 606:41
m. in everything HORA 389:15
m. in the pursuit of justice GOLD 345:33
m. in war is imbecility MACA 481:10
m. is a sort of treason BURK 162:11
perfect m. AUGU 36:10
playful m. in politics HUNT 396:4
term of m. BACO 41:24
modern disease of m. life ARNO 27:10
m. Babylon DISR 270:30
m. Major-General GILB 339:3
m. writers PLIN 578:15
writing a m. history RALE 621:6
moderns m. without contempt CHES 209:15
modest M.? My word, no REED 624:1
modified M. rapture GILB 338:5
modus *Est m. in rebus* HORA 389:15
moenia *flammantia m. mundi* LUCR 478:21
moins *m. des choses nouvelles* VOLT 797:6
mois *m. des floraisons* ARAG 23:11
mole go ask the m. BLAK 118:8
m. cinque-spotted SHAK 660:20
Well said, old m. SHAK 663:3
working like a m. HERB 372:19
molecule inhales one m. of it JEAN 404:18
molecules cells and associated m. CRIC 245:1
without understanding m. CRIC 245:2
molehills M. seem mountains COTT 237:16
moles *rudis indigestaque m.* OVID 561:12
moll King's M. Reno'd NEWS 544:12
Me and M. Maloney GRAV 349:8
Moloch great M., national sovereignty MEYE 506:14
M., horrid king MILT 514:24
mom place called M.'s ALGR 12:1
mome m. raths outgrabe CARR 190:12
moment Eternity was in that m. CONG 232:32
Every m. dies a man BABB 40:14
Exhaust the little m. BROO 151:5
impulse of the m. AUST 38:16
in a m. of time BIBL 98:28
m. dies a man TENN 767:13
m. in childhood GREE 351:23
m. of my greatness flicker ELIO 295:8
m. spent in Paradise SCHI 646:16
one brief shining m. LERN 465:1
momentary Beauty is m. in the mind STEV 740:2
pleasure is m. CHES 209:26
moments evanescent of m. JOYC 422:6
m. big as years KEAT 427:26
Wagner has lovely m. ROSS 635:10
momentum M. part of exhilaration LAHR 448:3
Mona M. did researches in original sin PLOM 579:4
monarch becomes The thronèd m. SHAK 688:10
hereditary m. was insane BAGE 46:13
make him a m. SHAK 693:20
merry m. ROCH 630:17
m. but would give his crown WALL 800:6
m. clothed with majesty COWP 242:16
m. of all I survey COWP 242:17
m. of the road FLAN 316:5
not so much a king as a M. SELL 654:11
relations with the M. BLAI 117:14
monarchical utility of m. power BOSW 144:17
monarchies elective m. GIBB 335:5
monarchs m. must obey DRYD 281:35
m. to choose favourites SWIF 747:24
Perplexes m. MILT 515:1
righteous m. BROO 150:6
monarchy absolute M. PAIN 563:12
constiutional m. BAGE 47:5
discontented under *m.* HOBB 379:1
essential to a true m. BAGE 46:4
m. and succession PAIN 563:13
M. is a labour-intensive WILS 822:5
m. is a merchantman AMES 13:8
M. is only SHEL 715:3
state of m. JAME 402:14
universal m. of wit CARE 186:7
US presidency a Tudor m. BURG 162:1
monasteries So much decay of m. SKEL 721:14
monastic Mild m. faces CLOU 221:14
Monday Born on M. NURS 550:19
going to do on M. YBAR 834:20

M.'s child NURS 549:14
M.'s child is fair PROV 606:42
monendo *delectando pariterque m.* HORA 386:3
Monet M. is only an eye CÉZA 200:9
money ain't got a barrel of m. WOOD 826:10
Bad m. drives out good PROV 595:30
bank will lend you m. HOPE 383:17
blessing that m. cannot buy WALT 802:26
Capitalism is using its m. CAST 193:15
corrupted by m. GREE 351:18
draining m. from the pockets SMIT 723:13
first thing to acquire is m. HORA 386:10
fool and his m. PROV 600:33
gay hym moore m. CHAU 205:6
getting m. JOHN 414:24
Give him the m., Barney CATC 195:16
given his m. upon usury BOOK 132:8
goä wheer m. is TENN 764:23
haven't got the m. RUTH 640:17
have to borrer the m. WARD 803:6
Having m. like being blonde QUAN 618:10
He had m. as well THAT 769:23
his private parts, his m. BUTL 172:29
Hollywood m. isn't money PARK 567:14
Honour, without m. RACI 620:2
if you can count your m. GETT 335:2
If you have m. you spend it KENN 434:1
licence to print m. THOM 775:24
listen to m. singing LARK 453:2
long enough to get m. from LEAC 459:16
love of m. BIBL 109:18
man without m. WYCH 834:14
m. answereth all things BIBL 84:26
m. can't buy me love LENN 463:19
M. couldn't buy friends MILL 510:7
M. doesn't talk, it swears DYLA 287:7
M. gives me pleasure BELL 63:16
m.-grabbing cronies HAGU 356:7
m. gushes into politics WHIT 814:9
m. has a power above BUTL 172:14
M. has no smell PROV 606:43
M. has no smell VESP 791:14
M. is indeed the most important SHAW 707:14
M. is like a sixth sense MAUG 502:4
M. is like muck BACO 43:33
M. . . . is none of the wheels HUME 394:11
M. isn't everything PROV 606:46
m. I spend on advertising LEVE 466:2
M. is power PROV 606:44
M. is the root PROV 606:45
M. is the sinews of love FARQ 307:18
M. is the true fuller's earth GAY 331:14
M. makes a man PROV 607:2
M. makes money PROV 607:3
M. makes the mare to go PROV 607:4
m. of fools HOBB 378:15
m. perish with thee BIBL 103:23
M. speaks sense BEHN 62:15
M. talks PROV 607:5
m. the sinews of war BACO 44:12
M. was exactly like sex BALD 49:2
m. was not time MERR 505:26
must put the m. in BULL 159:21
natural interest of m. MACA 481:19
Never marry for m. PROV 607:33
No m. RACI 620:1
No m., no Swiss PROV 607:49
no one shall work for m. KIPL 440:19
not spending m. alone EISE 291:8
only interested in m. SHAW 709:25
other people's m. RAND 621:18
Papa! What's m. DICK 262:10
pleasant it is to have m. CLOU 221:22
plenty of m. ANOU 22:7
poetry in m. GRAV 349:20
poor know that it is m. BREN 147:22
retreated back into their m. FITZ 315:13
rich man without m. USTI 788:23
rub up against m. RUNY 637:11
see what m. will do PEPY 573:13
somehow, make m. HORA 386:11
spent all the m. JOHN 416:23
Stealing m. is wrong AYER 40:5
they have more m. FITZ 315:6
They hired the m. COOL 236:4
time is m. FRAN 323:8
Time is m. PROV 613:2
to get all that m. CHES 211:19
unlimited m. CICE 217:23
use the m. for the poor PERÓ 573:23
Virtue does not come from m. SOCR 726:24
voice is full of m. FITZ 315:12
voter who uses his m. SAMU 643:13
way the m. goes MAND 493:6
What m. is better bestowed THAC 768:21
When you have m., it's sex DONL 272:5
Wherefore do ye spend m. BIBL 88:20
without m. and without price BIBL 88:20
worst moments into m. DONL 272:6
wrote, except for m. JOHN 415:17
You pays your m. PROV 616:5
You pays your m. PUNC 617:3
moneybag Aristocracy of the M. CARL 187:26
moneybags dream of m. SHAK 687:20
moneyless m. man goes fast PROV 607:1
moneys m. are for values BACO 41:14
mongoose motto of all the m. family KIPL 441:4
mongrels continent of energetic m. FISH 313:12
monk cowl does not make m. PROV 597:41
live as a m. JAIN 402:2
m. and a knight HENR 370:13
m. is still PALI 566:1
m. who shook the world MONT 528:15
monkey attack the m. BEVA 71:19
baboon and m. SHAK 699:14
descent from a m. WILB 817:2
higher the m. climbs PROV 602:39
look upon a m. CONG 233:19
make a m. of a man BENC 64:19
M. with lollipop paws LEAR 460:10
softly, catchee m. PROV 611:5
monkeys Cats and m. JAME 403:7
men and m. JENY 406:12
m. banging on typewriters WILE 819:17
m. strumming on typewriters EDDI 287:22
pay peanuts, get m. SAYI 647:21
three wise m. PROV 610:26
monks m. at Clonmacnoise HEAN 366:13
monogamous Woman m. JAME 404:6
monogamy M. is the same ANON 15:15
monologue m. is not a decision ATTL 32:6
monologues intersecting m. WEST 812:13
monopolists Men are m. MOOR 529:15
monopoly best of all m. profits HICK 376:9
m. stage of capitalism LENI 463:6
monotonous it becomes m. TROL 783:6
monotony in its swarthy m. HARD 360:16
long m. of marriage GIBB 336:8
Monroe M. Doctrine MONR 526:9
mouth of Marilyn M. MITT 524:10
monster become a m. NIET 545:17
blunt m. SHAK 669:20
green-eyed m. SHAK 692:21
many-headed m. POPE 586:19
m. horrendous VIRG 794:9
m. unto many BOOK 136:15
m., which the Blatant beast SPEN 734:10
m. whom I had created SHEL 710:8
new kind of m. HENR 370:13
overgrown m. SMOL 726:12
this busy m., manunkind CUMM 247:9
monsters reason produces m. GOYA 347:13
transform Men into m. FORD 320:2
monstrosity numerous piece of m. BROW 153:28
monstrous m. animal FIEL 310:13
m. carbuncle CHAR 203:18
M. carbuncles SPEN 732:15
m. regiment of women KNOX 442:10
this m. birth SHAK 692:8
Two evils, m. either one RANS 622:1
With m. head CHES 210:4
monstrum *M. horrendum* VIRG 794:9
montes *Parturient m.* HORA 385:20
Montezuma halls of M. MILI 508:8
who imprisoned M. MACA 482:7
month April is the cruellest m. ELIO 295:26
fressh as is the m. of May CHAU 204:10
little m. SHAK 661:26
merry m. of May BALL 50:5
merry m. of May BALL 51:11
m. in which the world bigan CHAU 206:4
m. of metamorphoses ARAG 23:11
m. of tension LESS 465:13
This is the m. MILT 513:17
months mistress of the m. SWIN 750:4
Montreal O God! O M. BUTL 173:3
monument ask for his M. BARH 54:1
corse, whose m. I am CONS 235:5
If you seek a m. EPIT 304:4
left some m. BURK 165:3
m. more lasting than bronze HORA 388:24
m. of the insufficiency JOHN 411:1
m. sticks like a fishbone LOWE 477:22
only m. the asphalt road ELIO 295:22
patience on a m. SHAK 701:24
shalt find thy m. SHAK 705:12
sonnet is a moment's m. ROSS 634:21
monumentum *Exegi m. aere perennius* HORA 388:24
Si m. requiris, circumspice EPIT 304:4
moo One end is m. NASH 539:9
moocow m. coming down along the road OPEN 556:9
moon and the m. winks SHAK 693:14
auld m. in her arm BALL 51:15
bay the m. SHAK 676:19
beneath a waning m. COLE 225:21
Beneath the visiting m. SHAK 657:19
by the light of the m. LEAR 460:19
cold fruitless m. SHAK 689:2
danced in the m. CART 192:16
Daughter of the M. LONG 474:11
defend the m. SALI 643:3
Devil M. in your eyes HARB 359:17
Don't let's ask for the m. FILM 311:3
fair as the m. BIBL 86:1
fleeting m. SHAK 657:25
glimpses of the m. SHAK 662:19
hornèd M. COLE 226:15
horned m. WORD 827:10
in the m.'s eclipse SHAK 684:19
isle, a sickle m. FLEC 317:6
i' the cold o' the m. BROW 155:19
It is the m. BURN 169:10
jumped over the m. NURS 548:12
like the m. CHEK 208:17
looking at the full m. GINS 339:21
minions of the m. SHAK 667:15
m. belongs to everyone DE S 259:3
m. be still as bright BYRO 179:4
m. by night BOOK 140:12
m. doth shine NURS 547:13
m. in lonely alleys CRAN 243:21
M., in the valley of Ajalon BIBL 77:22
m. is in the seventh house RADO 620:4
m.'s an arrant thief SHAK 699:22
m. shines bright SHAK 688:19
m. shone bright on Mrs Porter ELIO 296:7
m. under her feet BIBL 112:18
m. walks the night DE L 256:20
m. was full TENN 760:11
mortals call the M. SHEL 711:6
No m., no man PROV 608:1
O more than m. DONN 274:21
only a paper m. HARB 359:16
Only you beneath the m. PORT 588:10
owl does to the m. complain GRAY 350:7
roses across the m. MORR 532:15
sad steps, O M. SIDN 718:10
Shaped like the crescent-m. WORD 830:15

moon (*cont.*):
shine on, harvest m. NORW 547:2
shining to the quiet m. COLE 225:17
silent as the m. MILT 518:15
sun and m. AUGU 36:1
Sun and M. should doubt BLAK 118:4
sun and m. to stand TOAS 778:1
unmask her beauty to the m. SHAK 662:8
very error of the m. SHAK 693:25
voyage to the m. LARD 452:9
wan m. sets BURN 168:4
when the m. shall rise WOTT 833:1
when the m. was blood CHES 210:4
moonlight How sweet the m. sleeps SHAK 688:21
Ill met by m. SHAK 689:19
M. behind you COWA 238:18
of the soundless m. VIRG 793:20
visit it by the pale m. SCOT 650:16
Watch for me by m. NOYE 547:7
while there's m. and music BERL 68:8
moonlit Knocking on the m. door DE L 256:15
m. cedar ARNO 26:20
on the m. door OPEN 555:21
starlit or a m. dome YEAT 835:6
moons m. shall wax and wane no more WATT 805:18
moonshine everything as m. SCOT 652:17
find out m. SHAK 689:30
in pallid m. KEAT 427:8
Transcendental m. CARL 188:7
moonstruck m. madness MILT 517:24
moor M. has done his duty SCHI 648:16
m.-men win their hay BALL 50:7
moored island is m. only lightly BARR 56:1
moorish m., and wild, and knotty BRON 149:18
moose strong as a bull m. ROOS 633:12
mops seven maids with seven m. CARR 190:19
moral accounting for the m. sense CARL 187:15
attainment of m. good JOHN 407:11
Debasing the moral m. ELIO 292:15
detected in it by m. men ZOLA 841:1
drama onto the m. plane GIDE 336:16
Englishman thinks he is m. SHAW 708:6
Everything's got a m. CARR 189:21
form of m. effort LEAC 459:20
form of m. insurance BROD 149:5
good m. philosophy BACO 41:18
His m. pleases POPE 586:14
instrument of m. good SHEL 714:21
It *is* a m. issue NEWS 544:9
kind of m. eunuch SHEL 713:3
lower m. quality HARD 360:17
Mankind's m. test KUND 446:7
m. and intellectual MORE 531:4
m. as soon as one is unhappy PROU 594:3
m. disapproval AYER 40:5
m. evil and of good WORD 832:6
m. flabbiness JAME 404:5
m. imperative DIDI 267:10
M. indignation is jealousy WELL 810:17
m. is not preaching DIMN 267:16
m. law within me KANT 425:12
m. or an immoral book WILD 818:14
m. power strong as sexual CONF 231:18
m. principles please MENG 505:1
M. science is better occupied THOM 771:12
m. virtues CHES 209:20
nature of m. sciences COND 231:2
O m. Gower CHAU 207:22
party is a m. crusade WILS 821:13
people act on m. convictions EMPS 300:8
point a m. JOHN 411:16
religious and m. principles ARNO 29:14
settling the m. ADAM 2:15
stage in m. culture DARW 250:14
State m. case JEFF 405:6
till all are m. SPEN 732:10
Unfit to hear m. philosophy SHAK 700:10
moralist gave to the m. AYER 40:6
problem for the m. RUSS 639:11
sturdy m. JOHN 409:20
moralists delight to m. RUSS 639:26
distinguishes m. THAC 769:13
Leave those vain m. ROUS 636:6
We are perpetually m. JOHN 410:6
morality Absolute m. SPEN 732:3
Dr Johnson's m. HAWT 364:12
fits of m. MACA 481:18
for our best m. AUST 37:25
Goodbye, m. HERB 371:13
know about m. CAMU 184:16
may be called M. KANT 425:15
middle-class m. SHAW 709:13
M. expires POPE 582:13
m. for morality's sake COUS 238:6
M. in the novel LAWR 458:2
M. is a costly luxury ADAM 2:21
M. is the herd-instinct NIET 545:15
m. of art WILD 818:16
m. touched by emotion ARNO 29:1
national m. should have this SHAW 707:14
slave-m. NIET 545:19
some people talk of m. EDGE 288:10
system of m. HUME 395:8
What is m. WHIT 814:15
morally does nothing m. ELIO 293:14
morals either m. or principles GLAD 341:2
faith and m. hold WORD 828:24
Food first, then m. BREC 147:18
Have you no m. SHAW 709:12
lack of m. HATH 363:18
m. of a Methodist GILB 339:7
m. of a whore JOHN 412:14
pictured m. charm the mind EPIT 302:6
Why, man of m. COWL 239:11
morbo *Venienti occurrite m.* PERS 574:5
more For, I have m. DONN 273:6
I am m. BIBL 107:12
I want some m. DICK 264:13
Less is m. PROV 605:17
little m. BROW 155:18
m. and m. about less and less BUTL 171:13
m. equal than others ORWE 558:7
m. he has himself LAO 452:8
m. Piglet wasn't there MILN 510:11
m. than all NEWM 542:14
m. than Homer knew SWIF 749:15
m. than somewhat RUNY 637:12
m. the merrier PROV 607:8
m. things in heaven SHAK 663:4
M. will mean worse AMIS 13:20
m. you get PROV 607:9
Much would have m. PROV 607:15
no m. to say SHAK 700:25
O m. than moon DONN 274:21
take *m.* than nothing CARR 189:19
you get no m. of me DRAY 279:3
mores *Emollit m.* OVID 561:9
Et linguam et m. JUVE 424:9
O tempora, O m. CICE 217:19
morganatic m. alliance HARD 360:2
Morgen *M. sterb' ich* LESS 465:15
mori *In taberna m.* ANON 21:10
pro patria m. HORA 388:14
moriamur *M. et in media arma ruamus* VIRG 794:5
moriar *Non omnis m.* HORA 389:1
moribus *M. antiquis res* ENNI 300:15
morituri *Ave Caesar, m. te salutant* ANON 21:5
Moritz happened to Max and M. BUSC 170:23
morn But, look, the m. SHAK 661:12
Each m. a thousand roses FITZ 314:8
From m. to noon he fell MILT 515:5
m. Of bright carnations DRUM 279:15
new m. she saw not KEAT 428:3
Salute the happy m. BYRO 173:8
still m. went out MILT 513:12
this the happy m. MILT 513:17
morning arrested one fine m. OPEN 556:17
autumn arrives in the m. BOWE 145:11
before the m. watch BOOK 141:2
Come, lovely M. DAVI 252:9
danced in the m. CART 192:16
disasters in his m. face GOLD 344:13
Early in the m. HEBE 367:8
Early one m. SONG 729:4
evening and the m. BIBL 73:11
glad confident m. BROW 156:19
Good m., sir CATC 195:18
have the m. well-aired BRUM 158:22
In the m. it is green BOOK 137:18
joy cometh in the m. BOOK 133:15
Lucifer, son of the m. BIBL 87:7
many a glorious m. SHAK 704:17
m. after ADE 5:21
m. again in America POLI 581:19
m. cometh BIBL 87:8
M. dreams come true PROV 607:11
m. gilds the skies CASW 194:4
m. had been golden CHUR 216:12
M. has broken FARJ 306:15
M. in the bowl of night FITZ 314:7
m. light creaks down again SITW 720:21
m. of the world SHEL 710:19
m. rose KEAT 429:4
M.'s at seven BROW 157:12
m.'s minion HOPK 385:1
m. sow thy seed BIBL 84:30
m.'s war SHAK 672:27
Never m. wore TENN 760:26
New every m. KEBL 432:4
pay thy m. sacrifice KEN 432:18
scent the m. air SHAK 662:30
shining m. face SHAK 658:26
take you in the m. BALD 49:4
viewed the m. with alarm GERS 334:12
What a glorious m. ADAM 3:18
wings of the m. BOOK 141:11
won't go home till m. BUCK 159:18
mornings literary m. AUDE 34:5
Many bright m. VAUG 790:16
Mornington present of M. Crescent HARG 367:6
Morocco we're M. bound BURK 165:17
moron consumer isn't a m. OGIL 553:2
See the happy m. ANON 18:17
morphine m. or idealism JUNG 423:8
Morris M. Minor prototype NUFF 547:8
nine men's m. SHAK 689:20
morrow Eagerly I wished the m. POE 579:16
no thought for the m. BIBL 93:27
mors *Illi m. gravis incubat* SENE 654:21
Indignatio principis m. est MORE 531:10
M. aurem vellens VIRG 795:12
M. stupebit MISS 523:4
Mortalem vitam m. LUCR 479:7
Nil igitur m. LUCR 479:5
Pallida M. HORA 387:16
morsel I found you as a m. SHAK 657:5
morsels ice like m. BOOK 141:26
mort *La m. ne surprend* LA F 447:13
La m., sans phrases SIEY 719:2
mortal gathers all things m. SWIN 750:20
Her last disorder m. GOLD 344:21
laugh at any m. thing BYRO 177:4
m., and may err SHIR 717:10
m. men, mortal men SHAK 669:2
m. tongue GURN 355:5
shuffled off this m. coil SHAK 664:3
something m. LUCR 479:5
think all men m. YOUN 839:8
this m. life BOOK 127:21
this m. life BOOK 130:4
this m. must put on BIBL 107:3
mortality emblem of m. DISR 269:24
frail m. BACO 45:11
m. touches the heart VIRG 793:13
M. Weighs heavily on me KEAT 429:22

Old m. BROW 152:18
sad m. o'ersways SHAK 704:27
sepulchres of m. CREW 244:22
smells of m. SHAK 679:22
mortals good that m. know ADDI 4:22
not for m. ARMS 25:15
not in m. ADDI 4:9
startle Composing m. AUDE 33:17
what fools these m. be SHAK 690:5
mortar Lies are the m. WELL 810:12
mortifications m. and humiliations WALP 801:23
mortifying m. reflections CONG 233:19
Mortimer Are you Edmund M. SELL 654:7
mortis *Timor m. conturbat me* DUNB 285:4
morts *Il n'y a pas de m.* MAET 489:7
mortuus *Passer m. est* CATU 196:34
Moscow do not march on M. MONT 528:13
If I lived in M. CHEK 208:9
M.: those syllables PUSH 618:1
Moses From M. to Moses EPIT 302:8
Go down, M. SONG 730:8
greater than M. TALM 754:19
M. hid his face BIBL 75:27
sitting in M.' chair BLAK 118:16
Mosque from the Holy M. KORA 444:19
mosquito just another m. OKPI 553:11
moss gathers no m. PROV 610:16
miles of golden m. AUDE 33:27
mossy Happy field or m. cavern KEAT 428:20
violet by a m. stone WORD 831:20
mote m. that is in thy brother's eye BIBL 94:1
motes m. that people the sunbeams MILT 512:4
moth beetle, nor the death-m. KEAT 429:3
Both m. and flame ROET 631:11
candle singed the m. SHAK 687:26
Kill not the m. BLAK 117:21
like a m., the simple maid GAY 331:9
m. and rust doth corrupt BIBL 93:20
m. for the star SHEL 714:2
m. of peace SHAK 692:7
mother affectionate m. MAUG 502:6
all thy m.'s graces CORB 236:14
artist man and the m. woman SHAW 708:1
art thy m.'s glass SHAK 704:7
As is the m. BIBL 89:28
Behold thy m. BIBL 102:35
by our m.'s dust FORD 320:3
Can you hear me, m. CATC 195:7
Christ and his m. HOPK 384:21
church for his m. CYPR 248:10
father was frightened of his m. GEOR 334:6
for the m.'s sake COLE 227:2
France, m. of arts DU B 283:21
From whence his m. rose SEDL 653:2
gave her m. forty whacks ANON 17:10
Gentle Child of gentle M. DEAR 254:1
great sweet m. SWIN 751:16
happen to your m. WALK 799:5
have a beautiful m. WALK 799:9
heaviness of his m. BIBL 82:20
Honour thy father and thy m. BIBL 76:13
I arose a m. BIBL 77:26
joyful m. BOOK 139:20
leave his father and his m. BIBL 73:23
Like m., like daughter PROV 605:32
make love to the m. PROV 609:39
marry a man who hates his m. BENN 66:11
may not marry his M. BOOK 142:15
m. bids me bind HUNT 396:7
m. bore me in the southern wild BLAK 120:18
M. died today OPEN 555:8
m., do not cry FARM 307:2
M., give me the sun IBSE 398:8
m. laid her baby ALEX 11:10
m., make my bed BALL 50:6
M. needs something today JAGG 401:5
m. of all battles HUSS 396:13
m. of all treachery PAIS 564:8
M. OF HARLOTS BIBL 112:31
m. of invention PROV 607:23
m. of mankind MILT 514:10
m. of Parliaments BRIG 148:13
m. of sciences BACO 45:3
M. of the Free BENS 66:13
m. said I never should NURS 549:15
m.'s grief BRET 148:4
m.'s little helper JAGG 401:5
m.'s safeguard NAPO 538:13
m.'s yearning ELIO 292:1
m. taught me as a boy BERR 69:19
M. to dozens HERB 371:14
m. who talks about her own DISR 269:12
m. will be there HERB 371:11
murdered thy m. MALO 492:9
my father or my m. STER 738:13
my m. and my brethren BIBL 95:19
My m. groaned BLAK 121:3
my m. I see in myself FRID 324:20
never called me m. WOOD 826:7
O M. blest ALPH 12:22
O m., mother SHAK 660:16
plans to resemble: her m. BROO 151:2
recognize your m. VIRG 796:5
rob his m. FAUL 308:1
their Dacian m. BYRO 175:3
to make it well? My M. TAYL 756:12
Took great care of his M. MILN 510:16
Upon his m.'s grave WORD 830:17
mothers Come m. and fathers DYLA 287:16
happy m. made SHAK 697:4
m.-in-law and Wigan Pier BRID 148:6
m. of large families BELL 63:4
sorrows of the m. FREN 324:5
women become like their m. WILD 817:18
moths eaten by m. SITW 721:3
motion alteration of m. NEWT 543:6
Between the m. And the act ELIO 294:25
Devoid of sense and m. MILT 515:10
economic law of m. MARX 499:16
God ordered m. VAUG 790:2
m. of the wheels HUME 394:11
no m. has she now WORD 831:25
perpetual m. DICK 265:17
poetry in m. KAUF 426:5
poetry of m. GRAH 348:8
time's eternal m. FORD 320:5
uniform m. in a right line NEWT 543:5
motions secret m. BACO 45:1
motive m.-hunting of motiveless COLE 227:15
motives m. they act by ASTE 31:16
motley made myself a m. SHAK 705:13
M.'s the only wear SHAK 658:24
motor heart's stalled m. MAYA 502:18
motorcycle art of m. maintenance PIRS 576:16
motoribus Cincti Bis M. GODL 342:2
motto Be that my m. SWIF 749:22
mottoes m. on sundials POUN 589:13
motus *Hi m. animorum* VIRG 797:2
mould broke the m. ARIO 24:7
frozen in an out-of-date m. JENK 406:7
m. falls close ROSS 635:1
m. of a man's fortune BACO 42:32
m. them into an immortal MILT 519:13
moulded m. by the lips of man TENN 767:5
m. out of faults SHAK 686:26
mouldering many a m. heap GRAY 350:8
Moulmein old M. Pagoda KIPL 439:12
mount Mount, m., my soul SHAK 696:6
m. up with wings BIBL 88:5
Mount Abora Singing of M. COLE 225:24
mountain all my holy m. BIBL 87:5
alone on a great m. KILV 436:4
bare m. tops ARNO 28:25
Climb ev'ry m. HAMM 358:17
exceeding high m. BIBL 92:34
Flatter the m.-tops SHAK 704:17
from yonder m. height TENN 766:4
gone on the m. SCOT 650:13
go up to the m. KING 436:16
gross as a m. SHAK 668:7
In a m. greenery HART 363:7
into a high m. BIBL 98:28
misty m. tops SHAK 697:33
m. and hill BIBL 87:28
m. sheep are sweeter PEAC 571:5
M.'s slumberous voice SHEL 712:11
m. will not come to Mahomet PROV 603:21
say unto this m., Remove BIBL 96:6
trees, And the m.-tops SHAK 673:9
Up the airy m. ALLI 12:21
mountainous m. sports girl BETJ 71:2
mountains beautiful upon the m. BIBL 88:12
broke up the towering m. VIRG 796:16
Delectable M. BUNY 161:6
delights in m. CONF 231:13
Faith will move m. PROV 600:10
From the m. to the prairies BERL 68:7
like the tops of m. MACA 482:2
Make m. level SHAK 670:3
men and m. meet BLAK 120:7
m. also shall bring peace BOOK 136:17
m. are a feeling BYRO 174:19
M. are the beginning RUSK 638:12
m. by the winter sea TENN 760:10
m. gave back the sound WORD 827:11
m. look on Marathon BYRO 176:26
m. of Gilboa BIBL 79:1
M. of Mourne FREN 324:9
m. skipped like rams BOOK 139:21
m. were brought forth BOOK 137:17
M. will go into labour HORA 385:20
One of the m. WORD 832:8
river jumps over the m. AUDE 33:18
rocks of the m. BIBL 112:6
rose the m. BYRO 174:11
scale the icy m. MARL 496:21
so that I could remove m. BIBL 106:16
mountebank m. and his zany WALP 801:11
mourir *Partir c'est m. un peu* HARA 359:13
mourn Blessed are they that m. BIBL 93:3
comfort all that m. BIBL 89:5
countless thousands m. BURN 167:26
don't m. for me never EPIT 302:15
each will m. her own INGE 399:12
man was made to m. BURN 167:25
Margaret you m. for HOPK 384:19
M., hapless Caledonia SMOL 726:15
m. in prison MONT 526:17
m. with ever-returning spring WHIT 815:23
M., you powers of Charm CATU 196:34
No longer m. for me SHAK 704:28
now can never m. SHEL 711:1
sit and m. BALL 52:6
time to m. BIBL 84:7
Mourne Mountains of M. FREN 324:9
mourned we have m. unto you BIBL 95:7
Would have m. longer SHAK 661:26
mournful m. Ever weeping Paddington BLAK 118:21
mourning Don't waste time in m. LAST 456:10
great m. BIBL 92:25
in m. for my life CHEK 208:4
M. becomes Electra O'NE 554:22
oil of joy for m. BIBL 89:6
very deep m. AUST 39:6
widow bird sat m. SHEL 711:5
mouse appetit hath he to ete a m. CHAU 205:23
catch a m. or two GRAY 351:7
except that damned M. GEOR 334:4
free-born m. BARB 53:15
invention of a m. DISN 268:5
killing of a m. on Sunday BRAT 147:4
little m. will be born HORA 385:20
m. Kaught in a trappe CHAU 204:14
m. may help a lion PROV 607:13
m. ran up the clock NURS 548:14
Not a m. Shall disturb SHAK 690:29
Not a m. stirring SHAK 661:6
not even a m. MOOR 529:8

mouse (*cont.*):
One for the m. PROV 608:38
seen a m. go by the wal CHAU 205:23
mousetrap make a better m. EMER 300:3
The M. SHAK 664:24
mouth cometh out of the m. BIBL 95:28
door and bar for thy m. BIBL 92:4
Englishman to open his m. SHAW 709:10
fills the m. pleasantly JOIN 418:18
gift horse in the m. PROV 607:32
God be in my m. PRAY 592:3
God be in their m. BOOK 142:2
in my m. sweet as honey BIBL 112:17
Keep your m. shut OFFI 554:13
kisses of his m. BIBL 85:6
like chaff in my m. KEAT 431:22
m. as greet was CHAU 205:2
m. became the Brahmin RIG 627:18
m. filled with laughter BOOK 140:19
m. had been used as a latrine AMIS 13:12
m. is most sweet BIBL 85:21
m. is smoother than oil BIBL 82:12
m. of Marilyn Monroe MITT 524:10
m. of the dying day AUDE 33:30
m. of the Lord BIBL 87:28
m. of very babes BOOK 131:26
m. speaketh BIBL 95:13
my m. shall shew BOOK 135:9
My m. went across NERU 541:4
only one m. ZENO 840:1
opened not his m. BIBL 88:17
out of his m. BIBL 111:22
out of the m. of God BIBL 92:32
Out of thine own m. BIBL 100:17
purple-stainèd m. KEAT 429:8
shut m. catches no flies PROV 610:39
silver foot in his m. RICH 626:14
slap-dash down in the m. CONG 232:33
spew thee out of my m. BIBL 111:28
words of my m. BOOK 132:18
z is keeping your m. shut EINS 290:17
mouthful gold filling in a m. of decay OSBO 560:9
mouths God never sends m. PROV 601:15
made m. in a glass [illegible]
m., and speak not BOOK 139:23
m. of babes PROV 609:17
poet's m. be shut YEAT 836:21
pork please our m. MENG 505:1
stuffed their m. with gold BEVA 72:3
moutons *Revenons à ces m.* ANON 20:12
movable device of *M. Types* CARL 188:9
Paris is a m. feast HEMI 369:11
move But it does m. GALI 328:14
could m. a foot SUGE 745:13
feel the earth m. HEMI 369:10
great affair is to m. STEV 741:16
in him we live, and m. BIBL 104:10
let me breathe or m. FEAV 308:4
m. the earth ARCH 23:19
never should m. BOOK 139:1
whichever way you m. LUCA 478:17
moved earth be m. BOOK 134:18
I do not like being m. CLOU 221:13
king was much m. BIBL 79:11
m. about like the wind GERO 334:11
m. by what is not unusual ELIO 292:24
m. to folly by a noise LAWR 458:25
m. was their own mind HUI- 394:4
suffer thy foot to be m. BOOK 140:12
We shall not be m. POLI 582:6
movement measure of m. AUCT 33:15
right of free m. JOHN 407:11
mover arrive at a prime m. THOM 771:14
movere *Quieta m.* SALL 643:8
movers m. and shakers O'SH 560:11
moves If it m., salute it MILI 508:9
m. with its own organs SHAK 657:2
nothing m. in this world MAIN 491:12
moveth all that m. doth SPEN 734:13
movie could direct a m. HYTN 398:2
movies M. should have a beginning GODA 342:1
one thing that can kill the m. ROGE 631:18
pay to see bad m. GOLD 346:4
sexuality in the m. DENE 257:6
moving m. accident is not my trade WORD 828:19
m. finger writes FITZ 314:17
m. from hence to there SOCR 727:6
m. in opposite directions SMIT 725:19
m. toyshop of the heart POPE 586:30
Of m. accidents SHAK 691:33
mower m. whets his scythe MILT 512:18
Mozart Children are given M. SCHN 648:23
en famille, they play M. BART 56:6
M. and Salieri BARI 54:12
no female M. PAGL 563:3
when M. was my age LEHR 462:18
MP Being an M. ABBO 1:1
Being an M. PARR 568:4
MPs dull M. in close proximity GILB 337:16
When in that House M. divide GILB 337:15
Mrs *M.* respectably married CART 192:10
Ms *M.* means nudge, nudge CART 192:10
much how m. we think of ourselves TWAI 786:19
just so m., no more BROW 158:12
Missing so m. and so much CORN 237:2
M. as you said you were HARD 361:14
m. for my true-love BALL 52:6
m. to hear SKEL 721:9
M. would have more PROV 607:15
not m. for them to be COMP 230:13
Sing 'em m. MELB 503:13
so m. owed by so many to so few CHUR 215:12
so m. to do LAST 457:4
so m. to do TENN 761:17
too m. in anything BACO 42:16
too m. of a good thing PROV 615:25
muchness Much of a m. VANB 789:4
muck Money is like m. BACO 43:33
Where there's m. PROV 614:41
muckle makes a m. PROV 606:23
muckrake m. in his hand BUNY 161:10
muckrakes men with the m. ROOS 633:7
muckraking m. biographers BENN 66:3
mucus excretion of m. AURE 37:4
mud back in the m. AUGI 35:21
builds on m. MACH 486:1
crawled about in the m. BECK 59:27
filled up with m. SHAK 689:20
handful of m. against a wall BLUN 122:14
M.! Glorious mud FLAN 316:2
M.'s sister HOUS 390:5
muddle beginning, a m. LARK 453:9
Meddle and m. DERB 258:14
m. through BRIG 148:12
muddy almost always a m. horsepond PEAC 571:2
M., ill-seeming SHAK 698:13
m. understandings BURK 163:22
muero *Muero porque no m.* JOHN 407:15
Muffet Little Miss M. NURS 549:7
muffin M. and Crumpet DICK 263:16
mug graceful air and heavenly m. FLEM 317:18
Muhammad M. is not the father KORA 445:3
mulatto Grape is my m. mother HUGH 393:10
mule m. of politics DISR 270:4
Sicilian m. was to me GLAD 341:11
mules m. of politics POWE 591:1
mulier *m. formosa superne* HORA 385:10
mullets We will eat our m. JONS 419:9
Mulligan plump Buck M. OPEN 556:18
multiculturalism M. requires FINK 313:4
multiplication M. is vexation ANON 17:19
multiplicity m. of agreeable JOHN 413:22
multiply Be fruitful, and m. BIBL 73:16
Increase and m. BOOK 128:11
m. my signs and my wonders BIBL 75:33
multitude hoofs of a swinish m. BURK 163:25
m. is in the wrong DILL 267:15
m. of days JOHN 411:17
m. of sins BIBL 111:6
m. of the isles BOOK 138:8
m., that numerous piece BROW 153:28
m. the blind instruments GODW 342:6
m., the *hoi polloi* DRYD 283:8
m., which no man could number BIBL 112:7
multitudes I contain m. WHIT 815:18
m. in the valley of decision BIBL 90:15
Pestilence-stricken m. SHEL 712:12
Weeping, weeping m. ELIO 293:24
mum oafish louts remember M. BETJ 70:5
They fuck you up, your m. and dad LARK 453:4
mumble When in doubt, m. BORE 143:2
mumbled few m. cakes HUNT 396:2
mummy dyed in m. SHAK 693:6
munch m. on, crunch on BROW 157:11
mundane in this m. life MURA 536:14
mundi *peccata m.* MISS 522:19
Sic transit gloria m. ANON 21:13
mundus *pereat m.* MOTT 535:8
muneribus *deorum M. sapienter uti* HORA 389:10
muove *amor che m. il sole* DANT 250:5
Eppur si m. GALI 328:14
murder about a m. ORWE 558:10
battle and m. BOOK 127:6
commit a m. VAN 789:14
decided to m. his wife OPEN 555:26
do no m. BOOK 129:7
do not contrived m. SHAK 691:28
Don't they m. the people TROL 782:12
I met M. on the way SHEL 712:8
indulges himself in m. DE Q 258:11
I wanted to m. DOST 276:4
Killing no m. PROV 605:1
Killing no m. SEXB 655:4
Live in despite of m. CHAP 202:15
love and m. will out CONG 232:13
Macbeth does m. sleep SHAK 683:8
Most sacrilegious m. SHAK 683:18
most unnatural m. SHAK 662:26
m. by the law YOUN 838:20
m. by the throat LLOY 471:5
m. cannot be hid long SHAK 687:19
M. considered DE Q 258:10
m. into the home HITC 378:2
m., like talent LEWE 466:14
m. men everywhere FANO 306:7
M. most foul SHAK 662:27
m. respectable ORWE 559:11
M.'s out of tune SHAK 693:26
m. the thinker WESK 810:19
m., though it have no tongue SHAK 664:1
m. to dissect WORD 832:7
m. whiles I smile SHAK 672:29
M. will out PROV 607:16
M. wol out CHAU 206:3
m. yet is but fantastical SHAK 681:21
One m. made a villain PORT 588:13
Sooner m. an infant BLAK 119:24
stick to m. and leave art EPST 301:1
story is about not m. JAME 403:25
to m., for the truth ADLE 6:4
Vanity, like m., will out COWL 239:25
We hear war called m. MACD 485:1
withered m. SHAK 683:1
murdered Each one a m. self ROSS 635:2
m. peer ALCO 10:8
m. reputations CONG 233:3
Our royal master's m. SHAK 683:20
their m. man KEAT 428:2
murderer help the escaping m. STEV 741:9
honourable m. SHAK 694:2
m. for fancy prose style NABO 537:18
m. from the beginning BIBL 102:1
shoot your m. ACHE 1:10
tender m. BROW 155:9
thou art a m. MALO 492:9

murderers m., and idolaters BIBL 113:15
m. of Jewish children WIES 816:17
m. take the first step KARR 425:20
murderous m. hand a drowsy bench CRAB 243:17
murders most hideous of m. GISS 340:9
m. and assaults KOHL 443:8
murmur creeping m. SHAK 671:8
m. at his case COWP 240:9
m. of a summer's day ARNO 27:4
rustic m. of their bourg TENN 760:2
murmured m. in their tents BOOK 139:10
murmuring mazily m. TENN 764:21
m. of innumerable bees TENN 766:6
murmurs hollow m. died away COLL 229:12
In the m. SOND 727:22
m. of self-will BODE 123:9
Murphy M.'s Law SAYI 647:18
Murray slain the Earl of M. BALL 50:9
mus *nascetur ridiculus m.* HORA 385:20
muscle motion of a m. WORD 827:17
take the m. from bone ELIO 295:16
muscles M. better CUMM 247:12
muscular His Christianity was m. DISR 270:9
muse Can a m. of fire exist OLIV 553:18
every conqueror creates a M. WALL 800:8
grace my barren m. LANI 451:3
like a tenth m. ANON 16:15
Livelier liquor than the M. HOUS 391:9
M. but served to ease POPE 583:4
M. forbids to die HORA 389:8
m. in silence sings CLAR 218:12
M. invoked SWIF 749:14
M. of fire OPEN 556:6
m. on dromedary trots COLE 226:2
O! for a M. of fire SHAK 670:25
tenth American m. BRON 149:11
tenth M. TROL 783:10
Tragic M. first trod the stage POPE 586:27
Why does my M. only speak SMIT 724:20
mused m. a little space TENN 762:20
muses charm of all the M. TENN 767:4
house that serves the M. SAPP 644:16
M.' garden with pedantic weeds CARE 186:6
M. made write verse VIRG 796:11
M. sing of happy swains CRAB 243:12
museum ace caff with a nice m. ADVE 7:2
m. inside our heads LIVE 470:8
mushroom I am . . . a m. FORD 319:19
Life too short to stuff a m. CONR 235:3
m. of a night's growth DONN 275:7
m. rich civilian BYRO 179:16
supramundane m. LAUR 454:9
music accord all m. makes SIDN 718:21
aerial m.'s past SHEN 715:5
alive with the sound of m. HAMM 359:1
all kinds of m. BIBL 90:1
all m. is folk music ARMS 25:18
Beauty in m. IVES 400:11
beauty's Silent m. CAMP 184:1
body swayed to m. YEAT 835:3
built to m. TENN 759:18
but the m. there POPE 584:20
chosen m., liberty WORD 832:8
'classic' m. eliminates STRA 744:14
Classic m. is th'kind HUBB 392:13
come with your cold m. BROW 158:8
compulsion doth in m. lie MILT 511:9
condition of m. PATE 569:14
danceth without m. HERB 373:20
dance to the m. of time POWE 590:9
Darling of the m. halls SMIT 724:3
day the m. died MCLE 486:14
die in m. SHAK 693:29
essence of m. MOZA 534:12
Fading in m. SHAK 688:1
finds its food in m. LILL 468:3
Fled is that m. KEAT 429:16
From their own m. CAMP 184:2
frozen m. SCHE 646:13
Give me some m. SHAK 656:30
good m. CECI 199:5
how potent cheap m. is COWA 239:3
How sour sweet m. is SHAK 696:4
In sweet m. SHAK 673:10
I shall be made thy m. DONN 273:5
Let's face the m. and dance BERL 68:8
let the sounds of m. SHAK 688:21
Like softest m. SHAK 697:18
make the m. mute TENN 760:3
man that hath no m. SHAK 688:25
May make one m. TENN 760:21
meaning to m. COPL 236:10
most civilized m. USTI 788:21
M. alone with sudden charms CONG 233:16
M. and women PEPY 573:12
m. at the close SHAK 694:18
M. begins to atrophy POUN 590:2
m. be the food OPEN 555:15
m. be the food of love SHAK 700:26
M. breathing from her face BYRO 173:20
m. business is not MORR 533:5
m. by yonder springs THEO 770:17
M. has charms CONG 232:25
m. in the air ELGA 291:19
M. is essentially useless SANT 644:12
M. is feeling, then STEV 740:1
M. is your own experience PARK 566:17
m. of a *distant* drum FITZ 314:10
m. of a poem SYNG 751:21
m. of forfended spheres PATM 569:21
m. of men's lives SHAK 696:4
M. oft hath such a charm SHAK 686:22
m. of the Gospel FABE 305:17
m. of the spheres BROW 153:30
m. sent up to God BROW 154:25
M. shall untune the sky DRYD 282:23
m. that excels FISH 313:17
M. that gentlier on the spirit TENN 763:11
m. that I care to hear HOPK 384:7
m. the brandy of the damned SHAW 708:4
M., the greatest good ADDI 4:22
M., when soft voices die SHEL 714:1
My m. is best understood STRA 744:15
no m. in the nightingale SHAK 702:27
Of m. Dr Johnson used to say JOHN 418:12
passion cannot M. raise DRYD 282:21
perfected by m. CONF 231:17
practising your pastoral m. VIRG 795:13
real m. was sex DOYL 278:11
seduction of martial m. BURN 166:2
silence sank Like m. COLE 226:25
sound of soft m. DISR 270:34
still, sad m. WORD 829:5
Susanna's m. STEV 740:3
thou hast thy m. too KEAT 430:10
to m. lendeth SIDN 718:15
uproar's your only m. KEAT 430:25
We are the m. makers O'SH 560:11
when I hear sweet m. SHAK 688:24
worth expressing in m. DELI 256:23
musical found out m. tunes BIBL 92:15
Most m., most melancholy MILT 512:6
m. as is Apollo's lute MILT 511:24
m. Malcolm Sargent BEEC 61:2
Silence more m. ROSS 634:11
So m. a discord SHAK 690:15
musician dead, the sweet m. LONG 474:14
far below the m. LEON 464:19
m., if he's a messenger HEND 369:17
No better a m. SHAK 688:27
musing M. full sadly SPEN 733:21
M. in solitude WORD 828:5
peace, and lonely m. COLL 229:12
musk coming m.-rose KEAT 429:12
sweet m.-roses SHAK 689:25
musket Sam, pick up tha' m. HOLL 381:3
Muslim neither Hindu nor M. SIKH 720:4
Muslims named you M. KORA 445:1
zealous M. to execute KHOM 435:14
Muss *M. es sein* BEET 61:19
mussels gaping m., left CRAB 242:24
must forget because we m. ARNO 26:2
genius does what it m. BARI 54:12
It m. be BEET 61:19
Must! Is *m.* a word ELIZ 297:6
Needs m. PROV 607:26
This year, the m. shall foam MACA 483:4
What m. be, must be PROV 614:5
whispers low, *Thou m.* EMER 299:11
you m. go on BECK 59:20
mustard faith as a grain of m. seed BIBL 96:6
grain of m. seed BIBL 95:22
Pass the m. GILB 339:13
piece of beef and m. SHAK 698:10
mutabile *Varium et m. semper Femina* VIRG 794:13
mutability death, and m. SHEL 713:14
M. in them doth play SPEN 734:12
Nought may endure but M. SHEL 712:10
mutant *Caelum non animum m.* HORA 386:20
mutantur *spatio m.* LUCR 479:4
mutato *M. nomine de te* HORA 389:14
mutatus *Quantum mutatus ab illo* VIRG 794:2
mute M. and magnificent DRYD 282:26
m. recommendation PUBL 616:10
mutilate fold, spindle or m. SAYI 647:12
spindle or m. ANON 15:23
mutiny fear and m. SHAK 695:19
rise and m. SHAK 676:11
mutter blessed m. of the mass BROW 155:14
mutton make them into m.-pies CARR 191:14
mutual meet a m. heart THOM 775:17
M. cowardice JOHN 416:5
my m.-lorded him THAC 769:6
Orthodoxy or M.-doxy CARL 187:23
myriad Our *m.-minded* Shakespeare COLE 227:13
There died a m. POUN 589:17
myrrh bundle of m. BIBL 85:8
frankincense, and m. BIBL 92:23
myrtle m. and turkey AUST 37:26
m. tree BIBL 88:23
myrtles Ye m. brown MILT 512:16
Ye m. brown OPEN 556:28
myself I do not know m. GOET 343:18
If I am not for m. HILL 377:9
I celebrate m. WHIT 815:10
love him as m. BOOK 130:13
my mother I see in m. FRID 324:20
M. alone I seek to please GAY 332:12
such a thing as I m. SHAK 674:9
talking to m. BARN 55:5
thinking for m. GILB 338:28
When I give I give m. WHIT 815:16
mysteries most holy m. DION 268:4
m. in divinity BROW 153:15
m. of Hecate SHAK 677:23
m. of our religion HOBB 379:3
m. that are hidden HEIK 368:1
Stewards of the m. BIBL 105:31
mysterious moves in a m. way COWP 240:16
nothing m. or supernatural HUME 394:8
mystery burthen of the m. WORD 829:3
grasped the m. of the atom BRAD 146:10
heart of my m. SHAK 665:2
I shew you a m. BIBL 107:3
lose myself in a m. BROW 153:16
M., BABYLON THE GREAT BIBL 112:31
m. of the cross FORT 321:7
my tongue, the m. telling THOM 771:10
penetralium of m. KEAT 430:24
riddle wrapped in a m. CHUR 215:6
Your mystery, your m. SHAK 693:12
mystic m., wonderful TENN 759:13
mystical m. body of thy Son BOOK 130:2
m. mathematics BROW 152:15
m. way of Pythagoras BROW 153:18
myth m. not a fairy story RYLE 640:18
m. of democracy CROS 246:14
purpose of m. LÉVI 466:13
thing itself and not the m. RICH 626:10
mythologies Out of old m. YEAT 835:10

myths Science must begin with m. POPP 587:29
where m. Go when they die FENT 308:10

nabobs nattering n. AGNE 8:25
Naboth Ahab spake unto N. BIBL 80:7
nag gait of a shuffling n. SHAK 668:21
nagging N. is the repetition SUMM 746:5
naiad N. 'mid her reeds KEAT 427:24
nail blows his n. SHAK 681:4
I n. my pictures together SCHW 650:2
looks like a n. PROV 614:18
n. into his temples BIBL 77:25
One n. drives out PROV 609:1
thrusting The final n. BLOK 122:3
walks away with the n. LAWR 458:1
want of a n. PROV 600:41
nailing n. his colours FIEL 309:11
nails blowing of his n. SHAK 672:27
My n. are drove EPIT 303:16
n. bitten and pared MACA 481:13
nineteen hundred and forty n. SITW 721:2
print of the n. BIBL 103:3
three cloves like n. HEAT 367:4
with his n. he'll dig WEBS 808:14
naive n. domestic Burgundy THUR 776:26
n. forgive and forget SZAS 752:1
naked Half n., loving BYRO 176:16
left me n. to mine enemies SHAK 673:17
more enterprise In walking n. YEAT 835:10
my n. villainy SHAK 696:16
N., and ye clothed me BIBL 97:12
n. ape MORR 532:8
n. into the conference chamber BEVA 71:20
n. is the best disguise CONG 232:14
n. shingles of the world ARNO 26:4
N. they came TENN 765:7
n. to the hangman's noose HOUS 390:17
stark n. truth CLEL 220:8
starving hysterical n. GINS 339:20
When a' was n. SHAK 670:10
With n. foot WYAT 834:5
nakedness n. of the land BIBL 75:16
n. of the woman BLAK 119:20
not in utter n. WORD 829:20
namby-pamby N.'s little rhymes CARE 186:20

name above every n. BIBL 108:17
at the n. of Jesus BIBL 108:17
At the n. of Jesus NOEL 546:12
blot out his n. BIBL 111:26
Change the n. HORA 389:14
dare not speak its n. DOUG 276:11
deed without a n. SHAK 684:21
distain his n. BURN 167:24
fear my n. BIBL 90:25
filches from me my good n. SHAK 692:20
forgotten your n. SWIN 751:8
former n. Is heard no more MILT 517:4
gathered together in my n. BIBL 96:10
ghost of a great n. LUCA 478:14
gift of the divine N. SIKH 720:2
Give a dog a bad n. PROV 601:4
give them an everlasting n. BIBL 88:24
glory as an unsullied n. ELEA 291:14
glory in the n. of Briton GEOR 333:13
good n. BIBL 83:13
Grant that your n. remain SIKH 719:7
Halloo your n. SHAK 701:7
Hallowed be thy n. BIBL 93:19
his N. is great BOOK 137:1
his N. only is excellent BOOK 142:1
honour due unto his N. BOOK 138:7
I am become a n. TENN 767:9
I do not like her n. SHAK 659:12
ill n. is half hanged PROV 602:15
in a borrowed n. PRIO 592:15
In the n. of God, go AMER 13:7
In the n. of God, go CROM 245:14
In the N. of the Father MISS 520:8
In the N. of thy Lord KORA 445:17
its n. changed DANT 249:22
kept them in thy n. BIBL 102:28
king's n. SHAK 696:28
left a Corsair's n. BYRO 175:19
left a n. behind them BIBL 92:16
left the n. JOHN 411:16
Let me not n. it SHAK 693:22
liberties are taken in thy n. GEOR 334:10
local habitation and a n. SHAK 690:19
mark, or the n. of the beast BIBL 112:21
My Mary's n. to give CLAR 218:12
my n. and memory LAST 455:14
my n. is Jowett BEEC 61:9
My n. is Legion BIBL 98:5
My n. is Ozymandias SHEL 713:1
My n. is Used-to-was TRAI 780:19
My n. too will be linked OVID 561:8
my n. with a sign PARI 566:16
my new n. BIBL 111:27
my wife, and my n. SURT 746:20
n. Achilles assumed BROW 153:4
n. great in story BYRO 179:6
n. had been Edmund KEAT 431:20
n. is history THWA 777:6
n. is never heard BAYL 58:2
n. like yours CARR 190:26
n. liveth for ever SASS 645:23
n. liveth for evermore BIBL 92:17
n. liveth for evermore EPIT 304:6
n. made great HILL 377:8
n. of a man is a numbing blow MCLU 487:9
n. of God in vain BIBL 76:10
N. of God is sweet SIKH 719:9
N. of God, the Merciful KORA 443:12
n. of—Michael Angelo REYN 625:13
n. of the goddess SPEN 732:13
n. of the Lord BOOK 130:18
N. of the Lord BOOK 140:7
N. of the Lord BOOK 140:17
N. of the Lord our God BOOK 132:19
n. shall be called BIBL 87:1
n. the names AKHM 9:11
n. to all succeeding ages curst DRYD 279:21
n. upon the strand SPEN 733:4
n. we give the people FLER 317:21
n. were not so terrible SHAK [illegible]
no profit but the n. SHAK 665:29
nothing of a n. BYRO 175:12
one whose n. was writ EPIT 303:3
only differ in the n. CHUD 213:9
People you know, yet can't quite n. LARK 453:3
perfect N. of God SIKH 719:10
power of Jesus' N. PERR 574:1
prefer a self-made n. HAND 359:7
problem that has no n. FRIE 324:22
problem that has no n. FRIE 324:24
provides us with n. and nation BUNT 160:11
shakes up everyone's n. HORA 388:12
spared the n. SWIF 749:25
spell my n. right COHA 224:2
Stamps God's own n. COWP 241:15
state with the prettiest n. BISH 115:15
thy n., thy nature know WESL 811:2
trembled at the hideous n. MILT 515:24
unto thy N. give the praise BOOK 139:22
What's in a n. SHAK 697:12
what was done in his n. BENN 65:7
whispering its n. COCT 223:21
whistling of a n. POPE 586:3
Who gave you this N. BOOK 130:10
worshipped with spoken n. ZORO 841:4
worth an age without a n. MORD 530:21
writing our n. there HEAN 366:8
named N. is the mother LAO 451:5
n. you Muslims KORA 445:1
nameless intolerably n. names SASS 645:23
N. here for evermore POE 579:16
n. in worthy deeds BROW 153:7
N. is the origin LAO 451:5
n., unremembered, acts WORD 829:2
names Called him soft n. KEAT 429:13
called them by wrong n. BROW 155:11
calleth them all by their n. BOOK 141:24
commodity of good n. SHAK 667:19
confused things with their n. SART 645:6
forget men's n. SHAK 677:6
in love with American n. BENÉ 64:23
lost all the n. JOHN 416:23
man with three n. CROM 246:3
n. ignoble, born to be forgot COWP 240:25
N. Most Beautiful KORA 445:15
n. of all these particles FERM 309:2
n. of men TROL 783:4
n. of those who love HUNT 395:11
N. that should be CALV 182:3
n. to be mentioned AUST 38:24
No n., no pack-drill PROV 608:2
Not unholy n. DICK 263:4
naming N. of Cats ELIO 295:17
n. of parts REED 623:13
nap short n. at sermon ADDI 5:2
napalm smell of n. in the morning FILM 311:15
nape n. caught in his bill YEAT 836:14
Napoleon N. of crime DOYL 277:17
N.'s armies SELL 654:13
thinks he is N. CLEM 220:12
Napoleons Caesars and N. HUXL 397:3
narcotic n. be alcohol JUNG 423:8
narcotics Like dull n. TENN 760:24
Narragansett Where are the N. TECU 757:3
narration medium of n. MANN 494:6
n. always going backwards WALP 800:18
narrative descriptive n. EPHR 300:19
unconvincing n. GILB 338:13
narrow find the road n. MAIM 491:6
n. is the way BIBL 94:8
n.-souled people POPE 587:19
path is n. and difficult UPAN 788:2
saft and n. BALL 50:6
Nassau Stuart or N. PRIO 592:12
Nasticreechia N. Krorluppia LEAR 460:11
nastier how much n. I would be WAUG 806:23
nastiest n. thing in the nicest way GOLD 344:3
nasty as n. as himself SHAW 709:20
is a n. creature MOLI 525:20
man of n. ideas SWIF 749:3
n., brutish, and short HOBB 378:21
Something n. in the woodshed GIBB 336:7
natale Libertas et n. solum SWIF 749:28
nation AMERICA thus top n. SELL 654:16
boundary of the march of a n. PARN 568:1
broad mass of a n. HITL 378:4
can deprive a n. NAMI 538:6
create a n. Europe MONN 526:6
every man and n. LOWE 477:15
existence as a n. PITT 577:5
exterminate a n. SPOC 735:2
fate of a n. LONG 474:17
ghosts of a n. PEAR 571:8
holy n. BIBL 110:28
n. a le gouvernment MAIS 491:13
n. at his service POMP 580:7
n. expects to be ignorant JEFF 405:19
n. grieve DRYD 280:7
n. is not governed BURK 162:24
n., not a city DISR 270:19
n. of amateurs ROSE 633:17
n. of dancers EQUI 301:2
n. of shop-keepers ADAM 3:19
n. of shopkeepers NAPO 539:4
n. of shop-keepers PROV 599:15
n. of shopkeepers SMIT 723:10
N. once again DAVI 252:15
n. shall not lift up sword BIBL 86:13
n. shall rise BIBL 97:1
N. shall speak peace REND 624:13
N. spoke to a Nation KIPL 439:19
n. talking to itself MILL 510:3
n. that had lion's heart CHUR 216:7

n. which indulges toward another WASH 804:8
new n. LINC 468:13
No n. is fit WILS 822:10
No n. wanted it so much SWIF 749:26
no rainbow n. MAND 493:12
of the n.'s care PRIO 593:3
old and haughty n. MILT 511:15
one-third of a n. ill-housed ROOS 632:15
opt out of a n. LYNC 480:19
provides us with name and n. BUNT 160:11
rich and lazy n. KIPL 440:18
Righteousness exalteth a n. BIBL 82:33
single n. of brothers SCHI 648:17
small n. that stood alone DEV 259:7
so goes the n. POLI 581:5
Still better for the n. EPIT 303:1
terrorize a whole n. MURR 537:7
voice of a n. RUSS 640:9
what our N. stands for BETJ 70:13
while the n. is honest DOUG 277:2
national above n. prejudices NORT 546:15
n. debt HAMI 358:13
N. Debt is a very Good Thing SELL 654:12
n. dish no longer JEAN 404:16
n. flag SUMN 746:7
n. home for the Jewish people BALF 49:16
n. morality should have this SHAW 707:14
nationalism N. is an infantile sickness EINS 291:5
n. is a silly cock ALDI 10:11
nationalities n. of Europe ASQU 31:2
nationality n., language, religion JOYC 422:2
Other people have a n. BEHA 62:3
what n. he would prefer RHOD 625:15
nations belong to other n. GILB 339:1
belong to two different n. FOST 321:11
day of small n. CHAM 200:14
enrich unknowing n. DANI 249:3
Europe of n. DE G 255:24
father of many n. BIBL 104:34
fierce contending n. CLOS 222:9
formed Two N. DISR 270:25
friendship with all n. JEFF 405:13
gossip from all the n. AUDE 34:13
great n. acted like gangsters KUBR 446:4
hating all other n. GASK 330:21
healing of the n. BIBL 113:13
Let n. rage BISH 115:19
n. are as a drop BIBL 88:3
n. how to live MILT 519:20
N., like men BOLI 124:15
n. shall do him service BOOK 136:18
N. touch at their summits BAGE 46:20
n. under our feet BOOK 134:22
n. which have put mankind INGE 399:8
other n. and states draw aside GOGO 344:2
Other n. use 'force' WAUG 806:15
pedigree of n. JOHN 412:1
place among the n. EMME 300:4
Praise the Lord, all n. BIBL 113:23
rule n. by your government VIRG 795:1
smote divers n. BOOK 141:5
two great n. in the world TOCQ 778:15
Two n. DISR 270:23
two n. have been at war VOLT 797:7
two n. warring DURH 286:6
waits for the n. MIDR 507:11
native adieu! my n. shore BYRO 173:22
breathe his n. air POPE 586:24
by their n. shore COWP 240:23
in his n. place JOHN 414:11
more n. to the heart SHAK 661:15
my n. land SCOT 650:19
n. of the rocks JOHN 412:16
n. Of the very world SMAR 722:2
n. with the warmth KEAT 430:2
n. wood-notes wild MILT 512:24
our ideas about the n. LESS 465:12
rooms of thy n. country FULL 327:8
with his n. land EDGE 288:11
nativity At my n. SHAK 668:18
n. was under *ursa major* SHAK 678:6
nattering n. nabobs AGNE 8:25
natura *N. enim non imperatur* BACO 45:5
natural her colour is n. SHER 716:11
I do it more n. SHAK 701:12
interested in n. history SCOT 650:8
more than n. SHAK 663:20
n. and intrepid WALP 800:14
n. man has only two OSLE 560:16
n. party of government WILS 821:17
N. rights BENT 66:17
N. Selection DARW 250:18
N. selection a mechanism FISH 314:2
n., simple, affecting GOLD 345:3
n. to die BACO 42:24
so far from being n. JOHN 414:12
twice as n. CARR 191:11
wants the n. touch SHAK 685:4
naturalists n. observe, a flea SWIF 749:19
nature accordant with man's n. HARD 360:16
all animated n. COLE 225:8
Allow not n. more SHAK 678:17
Art is only N. HOLB 380:16
Arts at first from N. came LANI 451:3
arts of death outdoes N. SHAW 708:7
Auld n. swears BURN 167:9
better angels of our n. LINC 468:9
body, N. is POPE 585:16
book of n. GALI 328:13
By n. men are alike CONF 232:4
can drive out n. PROV 615:24
can't be N. CHUR 213:15
conquered human n. DICK 263:20
Constant, in N. were inconstancy COWL 239:17
course of N. YOUN 839:14
cruel works of n. DARW 251:1
[Death is] n.'s way ANON 15:22
debt of n. FABY 305:21
deposes Mother N. HUGH 393:11
does N. live COLE 225:3
do violence to own n. MENG 504:21
drive out n. HORA 386:19
education's, more than n.'s WINC 822:23
experiencing n. BAGE 47:11
Eye N.'s walks POPE 585:5
fair defect of n. MILT 517:23
fire of my n. BRON 149:14
frame of n. ADDI 4:23
from criticism to n. JOHN 410:14
fulfils great N.'s plan BURN 167:5
gay n. grieves SMAR 722:8
God and n. AUCT 33:4
Good painters imitate n. CERV 200:6
great n.'s second course SHAK 683:8
great wonders of N. ORCH 557:8
hand of N. GIBB 336:6
heartless, witless n. HOUS 390:10
hide the sparks of n. SHAK 660:25
How N. always does contrive GILB 337:14
human n. BAGE 47:14
human n. is finer KEAT 431:3
ignorance of n. HOLB 380:17
informed by the light of n. BACO 41:12
In n. there are neither INGE 399:14
in other words, N. SPIN 734:25
intellectual n. JOHN 410:6
interpreted n. as freely GIRA 340:8
interpreter of n. JOHN 410:25
interpreter of n. WHEW 813:15
Is N. felt WORD 828:3
It is a part of n. SPEN 732:7
Kind n. first doth cause DAVI 251:19
knowledge of n. WHEW 813:13
law of n. BURK 165:11
like N. to go no further LEIB 462:24
linger yet with n. BYRO 178:15
look on n., not as in the hour WORD 829:5
looks thro' N. POPE 586:4
made a gap in n. SHAK 656:25
man the less, but n. more BYRO 175:8
mere copier of n. REYN 625:5
mirror up to n. SHAK 664:16
more direct than does N. LEON 464:15
My n. is subdued SHAK 705:14
N. abhors a vacuum PROV 607:18
N. abhors a vacuum RABE 619:10
N. always desires AUCT 33:8
N., and Nature's laws POPE 584:9
n. by her mother wit SPEN 734:7
n. cannot be fooled FEYN 309:6
N. cannot be ordered BACO 45:5
N. does nothing in vain NEWT 543:3
N. does nothing uselessly ARIS 25:4
N. from her seat MILT 517:17
N. gives to each AUCT 33:7
N. had not befriended us CAVE 198:13
N. has not cure SMIT 724:2
n. her custom holds SHAK 666:15
n. I actually have DESC 258:19
N. in awe to him MILT 513:19
N. in him was almost lost COLL 229:13
N. in you stands SHAK 678:16
N. is always wise THUR 777:5
N. is a temple BAUD 57:7
N. is but a name COWP 242:8
n. is but art POPE 585:17
N. is creeping up WHIS 813:23
N. is dumb TURG 785:5
N. is not a temple TURG 785:1
n. is the art of God BROW 153:20
n. is tugging EMER 299:13
N. is usually wrong WHIS 813:19
n. itselfe cant endure FLEM 317:11
n., kindly bent to ease us SWIF 749:23
N. made her what she is BURN 166:19
n. made him ARIO 24:7
N., Mr Allnutt FILM 312:3
N. never makes LOCK 471:14
N. never set forth SIDN 718:22
N., obviously, hadn't TURG 784:19
n. of war HOBB 378:20
N., red in tooth and claw TENN 761:14
N.'s agreeable blunders COWL 239:26
N. say one thing BURK 164:8
N.'s decorations SMAR 722:1
N.'s great masterpiece DONN 273:13
n.'s handmaid art DRYD 280:28
n.'s journeymen SHAK 664:17
N.'s law BURN 167:25
N.'s social union BURN 168:23
N.'s sole mistake GILB 339:6
N.'s sweet restorer YOUN 839:2
n.'s way of telling you SAYI 647:9
N. that is above all art DANI 248:17
N. to advantage dressed POPE 584:18
n. to explore POPE 585:23
N. was degraded BLAK 117:16
N. wears one universal grin FIEL 310:14
n. yet remembers WORD 830:5
next to N. LAND 450:1
not n. CONS 235:7
observe n. OSLE 560:14
Of slower N. got the start DENH 257:13
O N.! we are thine WORD 828:4
One touch of n. SHAK 700:17
paint too much direct from n. GAUG 331:4
priketh hem n. CHAU 204:7
read N. DRYD 283:6
rest in N., not the God HERB 373:7
rest on N. fix COKE 224:11
Secretary of N. WALT 803:1
simply follow N. LAO 451:9
spark o' N.'s fire BURN 167:4
state of war by n. SWIF 749:18
state that n. hath provided LOCK 471:21
stuff that n. replaces it with WILL 820:16
sullenness against n. MILT 519:21
They perfect n. BACO 44:4
through n. to eternity SHAK 661:19
thy name, thy n. know WESL 811:2
Treat n. in terms CÉZA 200:8

nature (*cont.*):
Unerring N. POPE 584:13
various appearances of n. SMIT 723:3
violates the order of n. HERO 373:22
war of n. DARW 250:21
weakness of our mortal n. BOOK 128:10
whatever N. has in store FERM 309:3
Wise n. did never put BACO 45:7
naught it is n. BIBL 83:11
n. for your comfort CHES 210:1
naughtiness n. of thine heart BIBL 78:29
naughty former n. life BOOK 129:2
in a n. world SHAK 688:26
N. but nice FILM 312:23
nauseous n. draught of life ROCH 630:8
naval N. tradition CHUR 216:4
nave n. to the chaps SHAK 681:9
navel n. like a round goblet BIBL 86:4
navibus *n. atque Quadrigis* HORA 386:20
navies nations' airy n. TENN 763:3
our n. melt away KIPL 440:4
navita *N. de ventis* PROP 593:15
navy head of the N. CARS 192:6
n. nothing but rotten timber BURK 163:7
Ruler of the Queen's N. GILB 338:27
upon the n. CHAR 203:13
nay royal n. of England BLAC 117:3
your n., nay BIBL 110:23
Nazareth come out of N. BIBL 101:11
Nazis N. wanted war WAUG 806:16
Neaera tangles of N.'s hair MILT 513:2
Neanderthal N. skeleton HAWK 364:7
of N. man STRA 744:12
near come not n. to me BIBL 89:8
more n. the earth SHAK 693:25
n. in blood SHAK 683:22
N. is my kirtle PROV 607:21
N. is my shirt PROV 607:22
so n. and yet so far TENN 761:27
while he is n. BIBL 88:21
nearer little n. Spenser BASS 57:1
n. God's Heart in a garden GURN 355:2
N., my God, to thee ADAM 3:21
n. one Yet, than all other HOOD 382:14
n. than hands or feet TENN 759:10
n. the bone PROV 607:10
n. to him than the jugular KORA 445:13
n. you are to God WOTT 833:8
nearest n. and dearest enemy SHAK 668:27
nearly n. kept waiting LOUI 475:17
neat any good girl to be n. TAYL 756:11
N., but not gaudy WESL 812:1
Still to be n. JONS 419:19
Nebuchadnezzar N. the king BIBL 90:1
necessarily ain't n. so HEYW 376:3
Not n. conscription KING 437:2
necessary absolutely n. OCCA 552:15
if it is deemed n. BROW 152:2
journey *really* n. OFFI 554:7
little visible delight, but n. BRON 150:3
Make yourself n. EMER 299:12
n. evil BRAD 146:7
n. evil PAIN 563:11
n. evils JOHN 410:18
n. not to change FALK 306:6
n. to salvation BOOK 142:8
sometimes it is n. ADAM 2:9
very n. thing VOLT 798:1
necessities dispense with its n. MOTL 534:8
n. call out virtues ADAM 2:1
which were n. WRIG 833:9
necessity Cruel n. CROM 245:10
do not see the n. ARGE 24:6
door of n. DEFO 254:16
exceptional n. MILL 509:7
fiction is a n. CHES 211:3
grim N. SHAK 695:25
N. has no law PUBL 616:13
N. hath no law CROM 245:17
N. is a bad recommendation FIEL 310:5
N. is the mother PROV 607:23
N. is the plea PITT 577:3
N. knows no law PROV 607:24
N. makes an honest man DEFO 255:3
N. never made FRAN 323:10
no virtue like n. SHAK 694:15
pragmatic n. DIDI 267:10
stronger than N. EURI 304:18
villains by n. SHAK 678:5
neck and his n. brake BIBL 78:18
at last wrings its n. RUSS 639:23
break its n. VERL 791:9
had but one n. CALI 181:6
hanged about his n. BIBL 96:8
my n. is very short MORE 531:15
n. God made for other use HOUS 390:17
n. is as a tower of ivory BIBL 86:5
n. is like the tower BIBL 85:14
n. once broken WALS 802:9
Some chicken! Some n. CHUR 215:15
strecche forth the n. CHAU 206:6
neckcurls remember the n. ROET 631:8
necklace with our n. MAND 493:11
necklaces n. of gleaming fruit BABE 40:18
necks bowing our n. JERO 406:15
nectar comprehend a n. DICK 266:15
draws n. in a sieve COLE 227:6
lie beside their n. TENN 763:14
nectarine n., and curious peach MARV 498:15
need all ye n. to know KEAT 429:1
face of total n. BURR 169:15
friend in n. PROV 600:46
love you because I n. you FROM 325:9
n. in this life is ignorance TWAI 786:27
n. of a world of men BROW 157:6
not enough for everyone's n. BUCH 159:11
O reason not the n. SHAK 678:17
People who n. people MERR 505:25
Requires sorest n. DICK 266:15
things that people don't n. WARH 803:14
thy n. is greater SIDN 719:1
What can I want or n. HERB 373:14
Will you still n. me LENN 464:3
needed All I have n. CHIS 212:7
needful All that is n. WINK 823:8
needle eye of a n. BIBL 96:15
n, and the pen LEWI 467:2
n. better fits BRAD 146:14
Plying her n. and thread HOOD 382:20
upon a n.'s point CUDW 247:1
needs according to his n. MARX 499:15
my n. grow too fast WALK 799:6
N. must PROV 607:26
needy poor and n. BOOK 134:3
nefas *scire n.* HORA 387:21
negation n. of God GLAD 340:13
negative Europe the unfinished n. MCCA 484:2
N. Capability KEAT 430:24
n. waiting to be slipped WILS 821:11
prefers a n. peace KING 436:12
neglect n. of his duties THOM 774:19
Such sweet n. JONS 419:20
tender mercy is n. CRAB 243:17
this n. arises ADAM 1:19
neglected have his all n. JOHN 412:15
neglects He that n. the Law TALM 753:20
negotiate n. out of fear KENN 433:12
not here to n. TRIM 781:13
negotiating business of n. AHER 8:27
N. with de Valera LLOY 471:8
negotiation finish a difficult n. SALI 642:17
negotiis *procul n.* HORA 387:11
Negro drop of N. blood HUGH 393:1
life of the N. race DARR 250:12
N.'s great stumbling block KING 436:12
places where the average N. DAVI 252:12
Negroes drivers of n. JOHN 411:6
neiges *où sont les n. d'antan* VILL 793:1
neighbour done evil to his n. BOOK 132:7
do not do to your n. HILL 377:7
duty to my N. BOOK 130:12
duty towards my N. BOOK 130:13
guts into the n. room SHAK 665:25
love thy n. BIBL 76:23
love thy n. as thyself BIBL 96:24
make war upon a n. nation FAIR 306:4
n.'s house is on fire BURK 163:13
next-door n. for so many years SCOT 651:28
policy of the good n. ROOS 632:13
rob a n. MACA 481:8
thy n.'s house BIBL 76:13
thy n.'s house BIBL 83:20
To whom I am a n. SHAK 687:16
What a n. gets PROV 613:47
neighbourhood narrow into a n. JOHN 408:14
n. of voluntary spies AUST 38:6
neighbouring cynosure of n. eyes MILT 512:20
neighbours fences make good n. PROV 601:25
Good fences make good n. FROS 326:5
happening to our n. CHAM 200:15
have good n. ELIZ 296:25
in charity with your n. BOOK 129:15
relying upon his n. BAUD 57:12
sport for our n. AUST 38:25
will the n. say HARD 361:6
neighed n. after his neighbour's wife BIBL 89:11
Nell Little N. and Lady Macbeth WOOL 827:7
Pretty witty N. PEPY 573:7
Nellie N. Dean ARMS 25:13
Nelly Let not poor N. starve LAST 456:11
Nelson *N. touch* NELS 540:18
Nemo *N. me impune lacessit* MOTT 535:10
Neptune stands As N.'s park SHAK 660:23
Nereides gentlewomen, like the N. SHAK 656:24
nerve after the n. has been extracted ROWL 636:12
called a n. specialist WODE 824:18
creep through every n. BROW 158:8
do not lose my n. NEHR 540:6
in every n., and sinew JONS 419:21
n. o'er which do creep SHEL 711:20
nerves and the n. prick TENN 761:8
his vitals and his n. HUNT 395:19
Muscles better and n. more CUMM 247:12
n. Shall never tremble SHAK 684:12
nervous approaching n. breakdown RUSS 639:12
n. force into phrases CONR 235:1
they call it n. KEAT 432:2
nervousness only n. or death LEBO 461:8
nest birds in last year's n. PROV 612:1
fouls its own n. PROV 604:31
he makes his n. LODG 472:17
her soft and chilly n. KEAT 427:11
I have no n.-eggs LLOY 470:17
leaves his wat'ry n. D'AV 251:11
my n. is made TENN 765:23
n. of singing birds JOHN 412:6
n. where she may lay BOOK 137:11
theek our n. BALL 52:5
nests birds build n. VIRG 797:4
Birds in their little n. PROV 596:23
Birds in their little n. agree WATT 805:10
birds of the air have n. BIBL 94:19
built their n. in my beard LEAR 460:4
Made n. inside BROW 157:10
net All fish that comes to n. PROV 594:22
Heaven's n. is indeed vast LAO 452:6
I will let down the n. BIBL 99:1
laid a n. for my feet BOOK 135:16
n. is spread BIBL 82:6
n. is spread in the sight PROV 604:2
n. of Maya UPAN 788:4
play tennis with the n. down FROS 326:18
surfing the N. ELIZ 297:20
too old to rush up to the n. ADAM 2:7
nets holdeth fast the n. OXFO 562:16
into their own n. BOOK 141:16

Laws are generally found to be n. SHEN 715:7
n. to catch the living WEBS 807:19
time in making n. SWIF 748:28
try to fly by those n. JOYC 422:2
nettle gently touch a n. PROV 603:33
Out of this n., danger SHAK 667:35
Tender-handed stroke a n. HILL 376:11
nettles dust on the n. THOM 773:5
n. and brambles BIBL 87:20
overrun with n. WALP 801:9
network *N.* Anything reticulated JOHN 409:11
neuroses n. just don't match MILL 509:24
neurosis n. is a secret TYNA 787:3
N. is a way of avoiding TILL 777:13
thrombosis or n. DRAB 278:16
neurotics come to us from n. PROU 594:4
neuter aggressively n. BETJ 71:1
neutral studiously n. WILS 822:12
neutrality Armed n. is ineffectual WILS 822:14
Just for a word 'n.' BETH 70:3
N. helps the oppressor WIES 816:16
n. of an impartial judge BURK 165:12
neutralize White shall not n. BROW 157:26
neutrinos N., they are very small UPDI 788:15
never Better late than n. PROV 596:9
come no more, N., never SHAK 680:14
N. do to-day PUNC 617:5
N. explain FISH 313:15
N. explain HUBB 392:10
n. go to sea GILB 338:29
n. had it so good MACM 487:17
n. home came she KING 437:10
N. in the field of human conflict CHUR 215:12
N. is a long time PROV 607:30
N. knowingly undersold ADVE 8:2
N. on Sunday FILM 312:24
n. should move BOOK 139:1
n. so impatient BOOK 138:12
N. the time BROW 157:1
n. thought of thinking GILB 338:28
n. to have been loved CONG 233:6
N. to have lived is best YEAT 836:3
n. use a big, big D GILB 338:25
She who has n. loved GAY 332:2
This will n. do JEFF 406:5
We n. closed VAN 789:11
What, *n.* GILB 338:24
You n. can tell SHAW 709:21
nevermore Quoth the Raven, 'N.' POE 579:18
new All appeared n. TRAH 780:11
always old and always n. BROW 157:22
beginning of a n. month MANN 494:2
blessing of the N. BACO 42:3
Brave n. world BORR 144:1
called the N. World CANN 185:6
Emperor's n. clothes ANDE 14:8
Few n. truths have ever won BERL 68:17
find something n. VOLT 797:6
hear some n. thing BIBL 104:7
just a n. activity DYSO 287:19
make all things n. BIBL 113:8
make a n. acquaintance JOHN 417:19
make n. acquaintance JOHN 412:21
making n. enemies VOLT 798:15
my n. found land DONN 272:16
my n. name BIBL 111:27
n. and untried LINC 468:6
n.-bathed stars Emerge ARNO 27:19
N. brooms sweep clean PROV 607:41
n. deal for the American people ROOS 632:11
N. every morning KEBL 432:4
n. friend is as new wine BIBL 91:24
n. heaven and a new earth BIBL 113:7
n. heaven, new earth SHAK 656:7
new heavens and a n. earth BIBL 89:9
New Labour, n. danger POLI 581:26
N. lords, new laws PROV 607:42
n. man may be raised up BOOK 130:8
n. men, strange faces TENN 760:14
N. opinions are always suspected LOCK 471:11
n. race is sent down VIRG 796:4
n. stories are born RUSH 637:17
n. wine in old bottles PROV 615:29
n. wine into old bottles BIBL 94:26
n. world order BUSH 171:4
no n. thing under the sun BIBL 84:3
nothing n. in dying LAST 456:7
nothing n. under the sun PROV 612:20
O brave n. world SHAK 699:12
old lamps for n. ARAB 23:6
old offences of affections n. SHAK 705:13
on the nothing n. BECK 59:17
put on the n. man BIBL 109:4
require n. clothes THOR 776:6
shock of the n. DUNL 285:7
somehow always n. HEIN 368:6
something n. out of Africa PLIN 578:17
songs for ever n. KEAT 428:25
so quite n. a thing CUMM 247:12
Tell not as n. COWP 239:30
threshold of the n. WALL 800:5
unto the Lord a n. song BOOK 133:19
unto the Lord a n. song BOOK 138:9
we'll find the n. BAUD 57:10
What is n. cannot be true PROV 614:3
wrote MAKE IT N. POUN 589:8
Youth is something very n. CHAN 202:4
newborn use of a n. child FRAN 323:17
Newcastle made of N. coal WALP 800:22
newcomer O blithe n. WORD 832:9
New England most serious charge against N. KRUT 446:3
N. weather TWAI 786:26
newest n. kind of ways SHAK 670:17
n. works BULW 160:8
newness walk in n. of life BIBL 104:38
news bad n. infects SHAK 656:11
Bad n. travels fast PROV 595:31
bringer of unwelcome n. SHAK 669:21
get the n. to you TWAI 786:11
good n. from a far country BIBL 83:22
good n. from Ghent to Aix BROW 156:7
good n. yet to hear CHES 210:15
hear n. of home PROV 601:10
HERE IS THE N. HEAN 366:18
how much n. there is DOUG 276:20
Ill n. hath wings DRAY 278:22
it is an item of n. TALL 753:4
love of n. CRAB 243:4
n. and Prince of Peace FLET 318:13
n. into sausage factory PAXM 570:10
n. that's fit to print ADVE 7:4
news that STAYS n. POUN 590:3
n., the manna of a day GREE 351:13
No n. is good news PROV 608:3
only n. until he's read it WAUG 806:13
that is n. BOGA 123:13
told bad n. to American KEIL 432:11
What n. on the Rialto SHAK 687:11
New South Wales govern N. BELL 63:8
newspaper never to look into a n. SHER 715:13
n. and journalistic activity TOLS 779:15
N. editors TROL 783:4
n. is a nation talking MILL 510:3
newspapers n. I can't stand STOP 743:14
read the n. BEVA 72:2
writing for the n. LEWI 467:11
Newspeak whole aim of N. ORWE 558:23
newt Eye of n. SHAK 684:18
Newton another N., a new Donne HUXL 397:6
Let N. be POPE 584:9
N. at Peru WALP 801:3
N. in his garden AUDE 34:14
N.'s sleep BLAK 119:7
newts N., and blind-worms SHAK 689:27
New York California to the N. Island GUTH 355:7
gullet of N. MILL 510:1
New York, N. COMD 230:7
three o'clock in N. MIDL 507:9
next At forty-five, what n. LOWE 478:1
n. thing I do DIAN 260:6
n. to god america CUMM 247:4
n. to Nature LAND 450:1
nexus n. of man to man CARL 187:4
Niagara wouldn't *live* under N. CARL 188:20
Nibelungen N. is for the European LANG 450:13
nice all that's n. NURS 551:19
Naughty but n. FILM 312:23
N. but nubbly KIPL 441:12
N. guys finish last DURO 286:7
n. man is a man of nasty ideas SWIF 749:3
N. one, Cyril ADVE 8:3
n. to people on your way up MIZN 524:11
N. to see you CATC 196:14
N. work if you can get it GERS 334:16
thoroughly n. people PYM 618:7
Too n. for a statesman GOLD 345:1
nicely That'll do n. ADVE 7:5
nicens n. little boy OPEN 556:9
nicest nastiest thing in the n. way GOLD 344:3
niche your n. in creation HALL 358:8
Nicholas St N. soon would be there MOOR 529:8
nick improve the n. of time THOR 776:5
Satan, N., or Clootie BURN 166:6
nickname Every n. is a title PAIN 563:22
n. is the heaviest stone HAZL 365:12
Nicodemus N. saw such light VAUG 790:3
nidificatis *non vobis n. aves* VIRG 797:4
Nigeria daughter of N. EMEC 299:3
nigger n. of the world ONO 554:25
night acquainted with the n. FROS 325:13
after noon, is n. DONN 274:5
All n. long in the dark STEV 742:17
and Love the n. DRYD 282:17
armies clash by n. ARNO 26:5
bird of n. SHAK 674:22
black bat, n., has flown TENN 764:6
blue of the n. CROS 246:4
born to endless n. BLAK 118:6
borrower of the n. SHAK 684:1
breath Of the n.-wind ARNO 26:4
by n. in a pillar of fire BIBL 76:5
by Silvia in the n. SHAK 702:27
candles of the n. SHAK 688:29
carried His servant by n. KORA 444:19
certainly of N. THOM 775:21
Chaos and old N. MILT 514:29
cheek of n. SHAK 697:7
choose An everlasting n. DONN 273:4
city of dreadful n. THOM 775:20
Come, civil n. SHAK 697:27
come, dear n. CHAP 202:17
Come, thick n. SHAK 682:4
covered by the long n. HORA 389:9
curtain of the n. PUSH 618:3
dangers of this n. BOOK 126:20
dark and stormy n. OPEN 555:25
dark n. of the soul FITZ 315:14
dark n. of the soul MISQ 521:11
day brought back my n. MILT 519:2
Dear N.! this world's defeat VAUG 790:5
dog in the n.-time DOYL 277:18
dusky n. rides down the sky FIEL 309:16
endure for a n. BOOK 133:15
Every n. and alle BALL 51:2
face of n. is fair TENN 764:15
Farewell n. BUNY 161:17
fit n. out for man or beast FIEL 310:20
forests of the n. BLAK 121:8
gentle into that good n. THOM 772:2
go bump in the n. PRAY 592:2
goes of a n. SHER 716:11
hard day's n. LENN 463:22

night (*cont.*):
Harry in the n. SHAK 671:10
Hecate and the n. SHAK 677:23
honeyed middle of the n. KEAT 427:6
horror of a deep n. RACI 619:16
horses of the n. OVID 561:2
Illness is the n.-side SONT 728:9
in endless n. GRAY 351:2
infant crying in the n. TENN 761:11
in the collied n. SHAK 689:5
in the n.-season also BOOK 132:21
I pass, like n. COLE 226:26
it was n. CHAU 205:13
journey into n. O'NE 554:20
know his God by n. VAUG 790:3
language of the n. LE G 462:15
last out a n. in Russia SHAK 686:6
late into the n. BYRO 179:4
love-performing n. SHAK 697:26
lovers' tongues by n. SHAK 697:18
machinery of the n. GINS 339:20
making n. do penance WORD 831:4
Making n. hideous SHAK 662:19
many a bad n. NIET 545:18
meaner beauties of the n. WOTT 833:1
mirk, mirk n. BALL 52:2
moon by n. BOOK 140:12
moon walks the n. DE L 256:20
Morning in the bowl of n. FITZ 314:7
n. admits no ray DRYD 281:36
N. and day BALL 50:18
n. and day, brother BORR 143:9
N. and day, you PORT 588:10
n. before Christmas MOOR 529:8
N. brings counsel PROV 607:43
n. cometh BIBL 102:2
n. Darkens the streets MILT 514:27
n. has a thousand eyes BOUR 145:4
n. has been unruly SHAK 683:17
N. hath a thousand eyes LYLY 480:17
n. is far spent BIBL 105:21
N. Mail crossing the Border AUDE 34:12
N. makes no difference HERR 374:15
n. Of cloudless climes BYRO 178:24
n. of doubt BARI 54:14
n. of the long knives HITL 378:5
n. of time BROW 153:9
n. once more BECK 60:3
n.'s black agents SHAK 684:7
N.'s candles SHAK 697:33
n.'s starred face KEAT 430:18
n. stands like a black column BABE 40:18
n. starvation ADVE 7:27
n. succeeds thy little day EPIT 303:13
n.'s yawning peal SHAK 684:6
n. that he was betrayed BOOK 129:22
N., the shadow of light SWIN 750:9
n. to do with sleep MILT 511:17
n. will more than pay ARNO 26:9
one everlasting n. CATU 197:2
only for a n. WYCH 834:8
Out of the n. HENL 369:20
pass in the n. LONG 474:18
perfect day nor n. SHAK 672:27
perpetual n. JONS 420:10
Queen of silent n. BEST 70:2
returned on the previous n. BULL 160:1
revelry by n. BYRO 174:13
riding that n. LONG 474:17
rule the n. BIBL 73:13
Sable-vested N. MILT 515:26
shades of n. were falling LONG 473:16
sleep one ever-during n. CAMP 183:21
something of the n. WIDD 816:14
son of the sable N. DANI 249:1
Spirit of N. SHEL 714:11
Stay our all n. CHUR 214:2
such a n. as this SHAK 688:19
tender is the n. KEAT 429:11
terror by n. BOOK 137:22
that it may be n. BOOK 139:5
then silent n. MILT 516:22
there shall be no n. BIBL 113:11
This ae n. BALL 51:2
This is the n. SHAK 693:21
Through the dim n. SHEL 713:15
tire the n. in thought QUAR 618:16
toiled all the n. BIBL 99:1
toiling upward in the n. LONG 473:21
under the lonely n. VIRG 794:19
vile contagion of the n. SHAK 675:6
visited all n. COLE 225:18
watch in the n. BOOK 137:18
Watchman, what of the n. BIBL 87:8
weary N.'s decline BLAK 118:19
witching time of n. SHAK 665:5
womb of uncreated n. MILT 515:10
world's last n. DONN 273:1
nighted cast thy n. colour off SHAK 661:18
nightgown in his n. NURS 551:18
nightingale ah, the N. ARNO 26:20
brown bright n. SWIN 750:5
describing a n. ANON 21:14
newe abaysed n. CHAU 207:11
n., and not the lark SHAK 697:32
n., if she should sing SHAK 688:27
n. in the sycamore STEV 743:3
n. when May is past CARE 186:14
no music in the n. SHAK 702:27
ravished n. LYLY 480:16
roar you as 'twere any n. SHAK 689:13
nightingales n. are singing near ELIO 295:25
nightmare History is a n. JOYC 422:10
In the n. of the dark AUDE 34:2
long national n. is over FORD 319:13
nights chequerboard of n. and days FITZ 314:15
n. and feasts divine HORA 390:1
O ye N., and Days BOOK 126:6
nihil *Aut Caesar, aut n.* MOTT 535:2
N. est sine ratione LEIB 462:22
nil *N. actum credens* LUCA 478:15
N. admirari HORA 386:18
N. carborundum SAYI 647:33
N. desperandum HORA 387:18
N. posse creari LUCR 479:2
Nile my serpent of old N. SHAK 656:20
On the banks of the N. SHER 716:2
waters of the N. CARR 189:9
nimble Jack be n. NURS 548:22
nimini-pimini pronouncing to yourself n. BURG 162:5
Nimrod N. the mighty hunter BIBL 74:23
nine By the n. gods MACA 483:3
N. bean rows YEAT 836:11
N. days old NURS 550:6
n. men's morris SHAK 689:20
n. points of the law PROV 609:31
N. tailors make a man PROV 607:44
there be n. worthy CAXT 198:17
nineteen since n.-eighteen AHER 8:29
nineteenth n. century LAUR 454:10
nineties n. is a good time to die SPEN 733:1
ninety fears to speak of N.-Eight INGR 399:18
Leave the n. and nine BIBL 99:32
live to be over n. ABBO 1:2
nurse of n. years TENN 765:26
ninety-two I am n. EISE 291:12
Nineveh N. and Tyre KIPL 440:4
Quinquireme of N. MASE 500:13
Niobe Like N., all tears SHAK 661:26
nip n. him in the bud ROCH 630:3
nipping n. and an eager air SHAK 662:16
nipple behind the left n. DUNN 285:13
plucked my n. SHAK 682:17
nirvana called N. because PALI 565:4
lead all beings to n. MAHĀ 490:1
leads to N. PALI 565:11
nisi *N. Dominus* BIBL 113:24
N. Dominus frustra MOTT 535:11
nives *Diffugere n.* HORA 389:6
nix Sticks n. hick pix NEWS 544:14
no art of leadership is saying n. BLAI 117:8
everlasting N. CARL 188:14
I am also called N.-more ROSS 635:5
It's n. go the merrygoround MACN 488:7
land of the omnipotent N. BOLD 124:11
man who says n. CAMU 184:11
N. money RACI 620:1
n. more to say SHAK 700:25
N.! No! No THAT 770:11
N. sun—no moon HOOD 382:24
n. you always meant RUME 637:6
of Aye and N. NEWM 542:8
she said 'n.' ALLE 12:13
There is n. God BOOK 132:5
Noah gave N. the rainbow SONG 729:6
into N.'s ark COWP 241:11
N. he often said to his wife CHES 211:1
one poor N. HUXL 397:6
nobile *Par n. fratrum* HORA 389:23
nobility ancient n. BACO 43:22
flower of English n. ORDE 557:11
in others n. PAIN 563:21
N. has obligations LÉVI 466:10
N. is a graceful ornament BURK 163:30
N. of birth BACO 43:23
noble, save N. BYRO 174:1
order of n. BAGE 46:16
our old n. MANN 494:7
nobis *Non n., Domine* BIBL 113:22
noble Be n. to myself SHAK 657:22
days of the N. Savage BIKO 115:1
Do n. things KING 437:4
echo of a n. mind LONG 475:5
fredome is a n. thing BARB 53:21
Here all were n. BYRO 174:1
imagination, of n. grounds RUSK 638:9
Is this the n. nature SHAK 693:11
love's a n. madness DRYD 280:25
Man is a n. animal BROW 153:10
n. acts of chivalry CAXT 199:1
n. and nude and antique SWIN 750:14
n. grand book GASK 330:23
n. heart, that harbours SPEN 733:18
n. Living WORD 831:9
n. mind DOYL 277:14
n. savage ran DRYD 281:5
O! what a n. mind SHAK 664:10
silence is most n. SWIN 750:10
than a n. death EURI 304:20
What's brave, what's n. SHAK 657:20
nobleman king may make a n. BURK 165:14
Underrated N. GILB 337:5
nobleness allied with perfect n. ARNO 29:7
nobler Whether 'tis n. in the mind SHAK 664:3
nobles n. by the right MACA 481:17
n. with links of iron BOOK 142:2
noblesse *N. oblige* LÉVI 466:10
noblest honest man's the n. work BURN 166:26
n. of mankind CALV 182:7
n. prospect JOHN 413:6
n. Roman of them all SHAK 677:4
n. work of God POPE 586:1
n. work of man INGE 399:13
ruins of the n. man SHAK 675:21
nobly I am n. born DEKK 256:7
N., nobly Cape Saint Vincent BROW 156:4
n. save LINC 468:12
nobody care for n. BICK 114:15
n. came FILM 313:3
N. came GINS 339:19
n. comes BECK 59:25
n.'s going to stop 'em BERR 69:11
n.'s perfect FILM 312:9
n. walks much faster CARR 191:10
n. will come SAND 644:2
noctes *O n. cenaeque deum* HORA 390:1
noctis *currite n. equi* MARL 496:7
currite n. equi OVID 561:2
nod dwelt in the land of N. BIBL 74:12
n.'s as good as a wink PROV 607:46
Old N., the shepherd DE L 256:19

nodded n. with his darkish brows HOME 381:22
nods excellent Homer n. HORA 386:5
Homer sometimes n. PROV 602:44
it n. a little FARQ 307:21
N., and becks MILT 512:14
noes honest kersey n. SHAK 681:1
nohow for nothing. N. CARR 190:17
noire *triste et n.* BAUD 57:9
noise Go placidly amid the n. EHRM 290:5
happy n. to hear HOUS 390:19
little noiseless n. KEAT 428:5
loud n. at one end KNOX 442:16
make a cheerful n. BOOK 137:9
melt, and make no n. DONN 274:19
more n. they make POPE 587:19
moved to folly by a n. LAWR 458:25
n. is an effective means GOEB 342:10
n. like that of a water-mill SWIF 747:18
n., my dear ANON 18:1
n. of battle rolled TENN 760:10
Nursed amid her n. LAMB 448:25
so little n. LAWR 458:7
such n. that beast made MALO 492:10
those who make the n. BURK 163:26
till they make a n. CRAB 243:11
wi' flichterin' n. BURN 166:22
with a merry n. BOOK 134:23
noiseless little n. noise KEAT 428:5
n. tenor of their way GRAY 350:13
noises isle is full of n. SHAK 699:5
noisy into the n. crowd TAGO 753:1
n. years seem moments WORD 830:7
Nokomis wigwam of N. LONG 474:11
noli *N. me tangere* BIBL 114:10
nom de plume *n.* secures all ELIO 293:13
nomen *Omne capax movet urna n.* HORA 388:12
nominate n. a spade a spade JONS 419:23
nominated will not accept if n. SHER 717:3
nominative her n. case O'KE 553:7
nomine *In N. Patris* MISS 520:8
nominis *magni n. umbra* LUCA 478:14
non avoiding n.-being TILL 777:13
comes from n.-being LAO 451:14
no fury like a n.-combatant MONT 527:3
n.-being into utility LAO 451:8
n.-cooperation with evil GAND 329:7
N.-violence is the first article GAND 329:6
organization of n.-violence BAEZ 45:20
saturam n. scribere JUVE 424:3
nonconformist man must be a n. EMER 299:22
N. conscience WILD 818:11
nonconformity history of N. ORWE 559:4
none answer came there n. CARR 190:21
answer came there n. SCOT 650:10
answer made it n. SHAK 662:4
malice toward n. LINC 469:1
n. that doeth good BOOK 132:5
This is n. of I NURS 548:10
nonexistent obsolescent and n. BREN 147:25
nonsense His n. suits their nonsense CHAR 203:10
lump of clotted n. DRYD 283:14
n., and learning GOLD 345:17
n. upon stilts BENT 66:17
round the corner of n. COLE 227:26
your damned n. RICH 627:11
nook obscure n. for me BROW 157:5
noon amid the blaze of n. MILT 518:14
athwart the n. COLE 225:11
Far from the fiery n. KEAT 427:22
first minute, after n. DONN 274:5
lying till n. JOHN 411:23
returned before n. SAIN 641:10
When n. is past SHEL 711:17
noonday destroyeth in the n. BOOK 137:22
noose naked to the hangman's n. HOUS 390:17
n. of light FITZ 314:7
norfan N., both sides WELL 810:10
Norfolk bear him up the N. sky BETJ 70:7
Very flat, N. COWA 239:2
normal n. and easy JAME 403:12
we're n. OSBO 559:23
normalcy not nostrums but n. HARD 360:5
Norman like our N. King KIPL 438:3
simple faith than N. blood TENN 762:11
Normans If N. are disciplined WILL 819:21
N. are a race WILL 820:5
Noroway To N. o'er the faem BALL 51:14
north against the people of the N. LEE 462:9
Awake, O n. wind BIBL 85:17
beauties of the n. ADDI 4:11
heart of the N. is dead LAWR 458:22
He was my N., my South AUDE 33:28
mad n.-north-west SHAK 663:21
n. of my lady's opinion SHAK 702:4
N.-west passage STER 739:7
n. wind doth blow NURS 549:16
tender is the N. TENN 765:22
to us the near n. MENZ 505:3
triumph from the n. MACA 482:21
What answer from the N. KIPL 440:15
wild N.-easter KING 437:6
North African N. Empire GLAD 341:3
Northcliffe N. has sent for the King ANON 16:13
northern bright n. star LOVE 476:10
constant as the n. star SHAK 675:15
n. lights astream SMAR 722:13
N. reticence, the tight gag HEAN 366:19
Norval My name is N. HOME 381:17
nose at the end of his n. LEAR 460:17
cause of the human n. COLE 227:18
Cleopatra's n. been shorter PASC 568:12
cut off your n. PROV 598:34
great hook n. BLAK 118:10
hadde a semely n. CHAU 206:13
hateful to the n. JAME 402:12
Heaven stops the n. SHAK 693:14
insinuated n. WATS 805:3
jolly red n. BEAU 58:12
large n. is in fact the sign ROST 635:11
lifts his n. SWIF 749:8
n. and cheeks stand out DRYD 283:15
n. May ravage with impunity BROW 158:3
N. of Turk SHAK 684:19
n.-painting, sleep SHAK 683:15
n. was as sharp as a pen SHAK 671:3
not a n. at all WELL 810:14
plucks justice by the n. SHAK 686:1
run up your n. dead against BALD 49:12
That n. the hook BYRO 173:11
thirty inches from my n. AUDE 34:19
very shiny n. MARK 495:13
wipe a bloody n. GAY 332:9
with a luminous n. LEAR 460:6
noses Athwart men's n. SHAK 697:5
n. cast is of the roman FLEM 317:18
n. have they, and smell not BOOK 139:23
slightly flatter n. CONR 234:10
Where do the n. go HEMI 369:9
nosethirles n. blake were CHAU 205:2
nostalgia N. isn't what SAYI 647:34
nostalgie *n. de la boue* AUGI 35:21
noster *Pater n.* MISS 522:17
nostrils breathed into his n. BIBL 73:17
nostrums not n. but normalcy HARD 360:5
not find out what you are *n.* LOY 478:12
if this is n. PALI 565:6
n. I, but the wind LAWR 458:15
n.-incurious in God's handiwork BROW 155:27
N. so much a programme ANON 18:3
N. unto us, O Lord BOOK 139:22
n. wisely but too well SHAK 694:3
Thou shalt n. kill BIBL 76:13
notable meet a n. GERS 334:17
note living had no n. GIBB 336:4
longest suicide n. KAUF 426:3
n. I wanted JAME 403:12
only the n. of a bird SIMP 720:14
When found, make a n. DICK 262:13
notebook in a little n. LASK 454:2
Set in a n. SHAK 676:25
noted n. in thy book BOOK 135:13
notes N. are often necessary JOHN 410:18
n. I handle no better SCHN 648:22
n. like little fishes MACN 488:15
quality of the n. SCHN 648:23
right n. at the right time BACH 41:5
These rought n. SCOT 650:9
thick-warbled n. MILT 518:8
thinks two n. a song DAVI 252:5
too many n. JOSE 421:7
nothing better than n. PROV 611:8
brought n. into this world BIBL 109:17
but n. came BYRO 173:21
Caesar or n. MOTT 535:2
Death is n. to us EPIC 300:21
desired to know n. JOHN 414:28
doing n. COWP 241:13
do n. MELB 504:5
do n. for ever and ever EPIT 302:15
don't believe in n. CHES 211:22
drawing n. up COWP 241:26
Emperor has n. on ANDE 14:9
Emperors can do n. BREC 147:13
forgotten nothing and learnt n. DUMO 285:1
get something for n. PROV 615:46
gives to airy n. SHAK 690:19
good man to do n. MISQ 521:17
Goodness had n. to do with it WEST 812:5
has n. to do AUST 39:1
have not charity, I am n. BIBL 106:16
having n. BIBL 107:9
having n., yet hath all WOTT 832:24
I have done n. yet BRON 149:19
individually can do n. ALLE 12:7
I will say n. SHAK 678:24
labour of doing n. STEE 736:15
learn to do n. JOSE 421:11
let me have n. METH 506:6
live well on n. a year THAC 769:11
marvel at n. HORA 386:18
N. LOUI 476:3
N. ain't worth nothin' KRIS 446:2
N., and is nowhere LARK 452:17
n. a-year, paid quarterly SURT 747:6
N. begins THOM 774:3
N. beside remains SHEL 713:1
n. *better* CARR 191:9
N. can be created LUCR 479:2
n. can be required FIEL 309:19
n. can be sole or whole YEAT 835:13
N. comes of nothing PROV 608:10
n. could be finer GORD 347:1
n. extenuate SHAK 694:3
N. for nothing PROV 608:11
N. for nothink PUNC 617:11
n. happens AURE 37:3
N. happens BECK 59:25
N. in excess ANON 21:1
n. in his long career NEWS 544:17
n. in respect of infinite PASC 568:9
n. is But what is not SHAK 681:21
N. is ever done in this world SHAW 707:28
N. is here for tears MILT 518:25
N. is law POWE 590:22
N. is more dangerous ALAI 9:15
n. left remarkable SHAK 657:19
n. like leather PROV 612:18
N., like something, happens anywhere LARK 452:18
n. of a name BYRO 175:12
n. should be done for the first time CORN 237:4
N., thou elder brother ROCH 630:20
N. to be done BECK 59:21
N. to do but work KING 436:5
n. to do with the case GILB 338:14
n. to look backward to FROS 325:18
n. to say CAGE 181:1

nothing (*cont.*):
n. to say COLT 230:2
n. to what I could say CARR 190:2
n. to write about PLIN 579:1
n. to you BIBL 89:23
N. venture PROV 608:18
N. venture PROV 608:19
N. will come of nothing SHAK 677:22
on the n. new BECK 59:17
power over n. HERO 374:1
Prime Minister has n. to hide CHUR 215:22
resent having n. COMP 230:14
say n. HEAN 366:19
say n. PROV 602:35
Signifying n. SHAK 685:22
take *more* than n. CARR 189:19
Tar-baby ain't sayin' n. HARR 363:1
that he n. knows MILT 518:9
Thinking n. done LUCA 478:15
Think n. done ROGE 631:12
think of you with n. on MITC 523:10
those who do n. CONR 234:19
We strain at achieving n. HORA 386:20
without whom n. is strong BOOK 128:11
You ain't heard n. yet JOLS 418:20
nothingness never Pass into n. KEAT 426:16
N. haunts being SART 644:21
to n. do sink KEAT 430:19
nothings Invulnerable n. SHEL 710:23
notice escaped our n. CRIC 245:3
man who used to n. HARD 361:6
n. of my labours JOHN 412:17
notions General n. MONT 526:19
terrible n. of duty CLOU 221:13
notorious open and n. evil liver BOOK 129:1
nought n. did I in hate SHAK 694:2
n. shall make us rue SHAK 677:21
thing of n. CRAS 244:2
noun n., proper or improper FULL 327:4
nouns N. of number COBB 223:10
nourish n. all the world SHAK 680:28
N. thy children BIBL 91:2
n. us with all goodness BOOK 128:14
nourisher Chief n. in life's feast SHAK 683:8
nourishes n. them, incites them MONT 527:19
nouveau *trouver du n.* BAUD 57:10
nouvelles *moins des choses n.* VOLT 797:6
novel care for in a n. TROL 782:13
end of a n. TROL 782:4
given away by a n. KEAT 431:15
got the n. HILL 376:13
live a n. HARD 360:15
Morality in the n. LAWR 458:2
no more n.-writing HARD 362:2
n. can hardly be made interesting TROL 781:19
n. gets up and walks away LAWR 458:1
n. is an impression HARD 360:18
n. is balanced BELL 64:15
n. is like a mirror STEN 737:16
n. tells a story FORS 320:11
only a n. AUST 38:2
reading a n. ELIO 292:22
read in many a n. CALV 182:6
subject of a n. MURA 536:14
want to read a n. DISR 271:10
novelist only the n. can BREN 147:24
novelists great—the major n. LEAV 461:5
n. know their art proceeds BARN 55:2
n. treat sexual subjects GISS 340:9
novels ideal reader of my n. BURG 161:26
sex in yesterday's n. WELD 809:8
novelty This n. on earth MILT 517:23
November no leaves, no birds,— N. HOOD 382:25
N. at the gate PUSH 617:29
remember the Fifth of N. ANON 18:9
novo *N. cedat ritui* THOM 771:11
novum *Reddiderit iunctura n.* HORA 385:14
now If it be n. SHAK 667:3
If not n. when HILL 377:9
Leave N. for dogs BROW 155:33
Let those love n. ANON 21:8
N. fades the landscape GRAY 350:6
N. I lay me down to sleep PRAY 592:5
n. is the accepted time BIBL 107:8
N. more than ever KEAT 429:13
Right N. is better BINC 115:7
sees what is n. AURE 37:6
We are the masters n. MISQ 522:12
nowhere circumference is n. ANON 17:21
Eclipse first, the rest n. O'KE 553:9
not with you it is n. HÉLO 369:2
nowness n. of everything POTT 588:21
nowt say n. PROV 602:35
When in doubt, do n. PROV 614:21
noxious Of all n. animals KILV 436:3
nubbly Nice but n. KIPL 441:12
nuclear n. giants and ethical infants BRAD 146:11
nude keep one from going n. KING 436:5
noble and n. and antique SWIN 750:14
nudge nudge n., snap snap MONT 529:5
nugas *aliquid putare n.* CATU 194:20
nuisance not make himself a n. MILL 508:21
one n. for another nuisance ELLI 298:15
nuisances small n. of peace-time HAY 364:15
null splendidly n. TENN 763:21
nullius *N. addictus iurare* HORA 386:8
N. in verba MOTT 535:12
NUM against the Pope or the N. BALD 49:12
number best n. for a dinner party GULB 354:18
bigness of Avogadro's n. BENT 66:15
called the wrong n. THUR 776:27
forgotten as a nameless n. PAST 569:6
full of a n. of things STEV 742:12
half a n. of bees LONG 475:3
happiness of the greatest n. BENT 66:18
I am not a n. MCGO 485:8
multitude, which no man could n. BIBL 112:7
Not on the n. COWL 239:15
Nouns of n. COBB 223:10
n. of my days BOOK 133:29
n. of the beast BIBL 112:22
n. of your years MILT 527:10
n. our days BOOK 137:20
n. weight and measure BLAK 119:17
very interesting n. RAMA 621:13
numbered all n. BIBL 94:36
God hath n. thy kingdom BIBL 90:4
n. with the transgressors BIBL 88:19
numberless n. goings-on of life COLE 225:13
n. infinities DONN 272:20
thick and n. MILT 512:4
numbers add to golden n. DEKK 256:5
better than n. CROM 245:8
divinity in odd n. SHAK 689:1
greatest n. HUTC 396:15
I lisped in n. POPE 583:3
luck in odd n. PROV 612:13
Noting the n. of trains MAXW 502:12
n. that rocket the mind WILB 817:3
safety in n. PROV 612:23
secret magic of n. BROW 153:18
ten primordial n. SEFE 653:9
we got the n. MORR 532:21
numble live in a n. abode DICK 261:21
numbness drowsy n. OPEN 556:3
drowsy n. pains KEAT 429:6
numerical n. irrigation system AUGA 35:20
numerous n. piece of monstrosity BROW 153:28
numerus *Nos n. sumus* HORA 386:14
nun Come, pensive n. MILT 512:5
quiet as a n. WORD 828:23
nunc *et n., et semper* MISS 520:10
N. dimittis BIBL 114:5
N. est bibendum HORA 388:3
nunnery Get thee to a n. SHAK 664:6
n. Of thy chaste breast LOVE 476:15
nuns N. fret not at their convent's WORD 829:11
nuptials day set apart for her n. KELL 432:14
iteration of the n. CONG 233:14
Nuremberg prosecution at N. JACK 400:19
nurse always keep a-hold of N. BELL 63:7
baby beats the n. SHAK 686:1
Dear n. of arts SHAK 672:4
lull the babe at n. BYRO 178:7
n. of ninety years TENN 765:26
n. sleeps sweetly COWP 241:18
scratch the n. SHAK 702:25
sucks the n. asleep SHAK 658:3
what a n. should be NIGH 545:24
what the n. began DRYD 281:24
nursed n. a dear gazelle MOOR 530:18
n. the self-same hill MILT 512:29
nurseries n. of all vice FIEL 310:2
n. of heaven THOM 774:15
nursery century's cool n. AKHM 9:12
great n. of freemen SHIP 717:6
Kitchen-cabals, and n.-mishaps CRAB 242:22
nurses old men's n. BACO 43:19
nursing n. the unconquerable hope ARNO 27:11
nurture n. of the Lord BOOK 131:2
nut had a little n. tree NURS 548:17
spicy n.-brown ale MILT 512:22
nutmeg But a silver n. NURS 548:17
nuts gods send n. PROV 601:18
N. MCAU 483:17
where the n. come from THOM 771:16
nutshell bounded in a n. SHAK 663:17
nymph Not as a n. MARV 498:14
N., in thy orisons SHAK 664:5
n. shall break Diana's law POPE 587:4
nymphs to the N. VIRG 795:4

O Within this wooden O SHAK 670:26
oafish o. louts remember Mum BETJ 70:5
oafs muddied o. at the goals KIPL 439:6
oak ashes of an O. DONN 275:5
Beware of an o. PROV 596:16
English o. and holly HART 363:9
Heart of o. GARR 330:3
Jove's stout o. SHAK 699:9
juniper talks to the o. PAUL 570:7
O., and Ash, and Thorn KIPL 440:14
o.-cleaving. thunderbolts SHAK 678:21
o. is before the ash PROV 614:30
O. was round his breast HORA 387:15
o. would sprout in Derry HEAN 366:17
round that o. hangs PUSH 618:2
thunders from her native o. CAMP 183:19
oaks families last not three o. BROW 153:6
hews down o. with rushes SHAK 660:3
Little strokes fell great o. PROV 605:42
o. from little acorns PROV 601:37
O. that flourish LEWE 466:16
Tall o., branch-charmèd KEAT 427:27
oar heavy o. the pen is FLAU 316:10
oasis If O. are bigger than God CHIS 212:6
oatcakes o., and sulphur SMIT 725:13
oath cheats with an o. PLUT 579:9
good mouth-filling o. SHAK 668:25
Hire gretteste o. CHAU 204:12
man is not upon o. JOHN 415:7
oaths Judges must follow their o. ZOBE 840:7
o. are but words BUTL 172:9
o. are straws SHAK 671:4
soldier, Full of strange o. SHAK 659:1
oats feeds the horse enough o. GALB 328:9
O. A grain JOHN 409:12
Oaxen *rapidum cretae veniemus O.* VIRG 795:15
Obadiah O. Bind-their-kings MACA 482:20
obedience o. of planetary influence SHAK 678:5

o. to God BRAD 146:12
soldier is o. PROV 600:28
obedient o. to their laws we lie EPIT 302:11
penitent, and o. heart BOOK 125:13
Righteous women are o. KORA 444:7
obeisance made o. to my sheaf BIBL 75:9
obey cannot o. cannot command PROV 602:9
learned well how to o. THOM 771:3
love, cherish, and to o. BOOK 131:5
O. orders PROV 608:20
o. them HORS 390:3
To o. is better BIBL 78:25
woman to o. PEMB 572:7
obeyed o. as a son GIBB 335:22
right to be o. JOHN 407:9
She who must be o. HAGG 356:5
obeying except by o. BACO 45:5
obituary o. in serial form CRIS 245:5
your own o. BEHA 62:5
object My o. all sublime GILB 338:9
no o. worth its constancy SHEL 714:13
O. of Contempt AUST 37:23
see the o. ARNO 29:6
with his eye on the o. ARNO 29:5
objectification o. of feeling LANG 450:14
objectionable doubtless o. ANON 18:20
objective o. correlative ELIO 296:17
oblation o. of himself BOOK 129:21
oblations alms and o. BOOK 129:11
vain o. BIBL 86:11
obligation not always the sequel of o. JOHN 410:10
o. is a pain JOHN 410:20
o. which goes unrecognized WEIL 808:23
obligations Nobility has o. LÉVI 466:10
oblige *Noblesse o.* LÉVI 466:10
obliteration policy is o. BELL 62:22
oblivion formless ruin of o. SHAK 700:21
from place to place over o. HARD 361:15
iniquity of o. BROW 153:8
journey towards o. LAWR 458:12
mere o. SHAK 659:3
O! my o. is a very Antony SHAK 656:17
puts alms for o. SHAK 700:14
sank unwept into o. ELIO 292:16
stepmother to memory, o. JOHN 407:14
To cold o. SHEL 711:8
obnoxious I am o. BRAD 146:14
obscene Sailing on o. wings COLE 225:11
obscenity 'o.' not capable of exact definition RUSS 640:1
obscure become o. HORA 385:13
Deep and o. LAO 451:11
o. nook for me BROW 157:5
through the palpable o. MILT 515:16
obscurely o. bright BYRO 175:20
obscuri *Ibant o. sola sub nocte* VIRG 794:19
obscurity man from o. REYN 625:2
o. of a learned language GIBB 336:2
rise out of o. JUVE 424:12
obscurus *O. fio* HORA 385:13
obsequies solemnized their o. BROW 152:19
observance commended for their o. GIRA 340:6
observation common sense, and o. BROW 153:23
o. is concerned PAST 569:11
o. of facts COND 231:2
o. with extensive view JOHN 411:13
observe You see, but you do not o. DOYL 277:12
observed o. of all observers SHAK 664:10
o. the golden rule BLAK 120:4
observer for th'o.'s sake POPE 583:27
He is a great o. SHAK 674:17
keen o. of life AUDE 34:11
observeth o. the wind BIBL 84:29
obsolescence adolescence and o. LINK 469:15
planned o. STEV 739:17
obsolescent o. and nonexistent BREN 147:25
obsolete Either war is o. or men are FULL 327:3
obstinacy O. in a bad cause BROW 153:21
o. in a bad one STER 738:18
obstruct circumstances o. JUVE 424:12
obstruction consecrated o. BAGE 47:1
obtain o. effectually BOOK 128:19
obvious in obvious o. BALF 49:17
Occam O.'s Razor OCCA 552:15
occasion o. of all wars FOX 322:8
o.'s forelock watchful MILT 518:5
occasions o. do inform against me SHAK 665:30
their lawful o. BOOK 142:5
occidit *Occidit, o. Spes omnis* HORA 389:5
occupation cure for it is o. SHAW 709:7
diligent o. MORE 531:1
o. for an idle hour AUST 38:7
o. for an idle hour OPEN 556:16
Othello's o.'s gone SHAK 693:1
occupations let us love our o. DICK 261:7
occupy o. their business BOOK 139:14
occurred never to have o. BENT 67:7
ocean abandon the o. CLAY 220:1
all great Neptune's o. SHAK 683:11
all the O.'s sons DENH 257:11
cause the O. to attend BEST 70:2
day-star in the o. bed MILT 513:10
deep and dark blue O. BYRO 175:9
drop in the o. TERE 768:6
Earth when it is clearly O. CLAR 219:10
foliage of the o. SHEL 712:15
great o. of truth NEWT 543:11
In the o.'s bosom MARV 498:6
leap into the o. HUME 394:14
love you till the o. AUDE 33:18
mighty o. deep WHIT 815:1
o. as their road WALL 800:3
O. forbidding separation GRAT 349:7
o. has but one taste PALI 565:15
o. of darkness FOX 322:7
o. on a western beach LANG 450:11
O.'s child SHEL 712:6
o. sea BARN 55:8
O.'s nursling, Venice SHEL 712:5
On one side lay the O. TENN 760:11
on the vast o. HORA 387:19
Ransack the o. MARL 496:2
rivers with the o. SHEL 712:7
rolled the o. BYRO 174:11
rolling on of o. MORR 532:10
round o., and the living air WORD 829:5
seen the hungry o. SHAK 704:26
ship Upon a painted o. COLE 226:11
thou, vast o. MONT 528:16
oceanic his own o. mind COLE 227:27
oceans compendious o. CRAS 244:12
To the o. white with foam BERL 68:7
octavos o. fill a spacious plain CRAB 242:28
October O.'s strife GURN 355:3
O., that ambiguous month LESS 465:13
octopus dear o. SMIT 723:17
odd But not so o. BROW 152:9
divinity in o. numbers SHAK 689:1
God must think it exceedingly o. KNOX 442:14
How o. Of God EWER 305:12
It's an o. job MOLI 524:21
Nothing o. will do JOHN 415:9
oddfellow desperate o. society THOR 776:10
oddly eyes are o. made HAMM 359:5
odds facing fearful o. MACA 483:5
how am I to face the o. HOUS 390:7
what o. CRAS 244:13
oderint *O., dum metuant* ACCI 1:8
odi *O. et amo* CATU 197:19
O. profanum vulgus HORA 388:11
odious Comparisons are o. PROV 597:32
O.! in woollen POPE 584:3
odium lived in the o. BENT 67:4
odorous Comparisons are o. SHAK 691:14
odours golden vials full of o. BIBL 112:3
haste with o. sweet MILT 513:18
o. tangle DICK 266:21
Odysseus Like O., the President KEYN 435:5
Odyssey thunder of the O. LANG 450:11
oferēode *þæs o.* ANON 21:17
off I want to be o. it PAXM 570:11
O. with her head CARR 189:20
O. with his head CIBB 217:5
O. with his head SHAK 696:21
offence conscience void of o. BIBL 104:17
detest th'o. POPE 582:23
for a rock of o. BIBL 86:27
forgave the o. DRYD 281:10
I was like to give o. FROS 326:6
o. at a few faults HORA 386:4
o. inspires less horror GIBB 335:10
O! my o. is rank SHAK 665:7
only defence is in o. BALD 49:8
resented for an o. SWIF 748:20
What dire o. POPE 586:28
where the o. is SHAK 666:10
offences o. of my youth BOOK 133:5
old o. of affections new SHAK 705:13
offend coy and tender to o. HERB 373:15
doth o., when 'tis let loose SUCK 745:9
freedom to o. RUSH 637:18
offendar *non ego paucis O. maculis* HORA 386:4
offended him have I o. SHAK 675:26
not o. the king LAST 457:10
shadows have o. SHAK 690:30
offender hugged the o. DRYD 281:10
love th'o. POPE 582:23
offenders O. never pardon PROV 608:22
society o. GILB 338:1
offensive extremely o. SMIT 724:5
Life is an o. WHIT 814:10
offer close with the o. HUXL 397:13
o. he can't refuse PUZO 618:5
would refuse this o. SCOT 652:15
offering o. too little CANN 184:19
office for o. boys SALI 643:2
holding public o. ACHE 1:11
in his o. wait DODD 271:19
in o. but not in power LAMO 449:14
insignificant o. ADAM 3:9
insolence of o. SHAK 664:4
in which the o. is held HUXL 396:17
man unfit for o. FABI 305:20
no o. to go to SHAW 707:16
O. builds up a man BENN 65:6
o. going to run him HEND 369:15
o. of Prime Minister ASQU 31:4
o. party is not WHIT 814:20
receives the seals of o. ROSE 633:19
waters of o. TROL 782:5
Whichever party is in o. WILS 822:4
officer fear each bush an o. SHAK 673:4
o. and a gentleman MILI 508:3
official concept of the o. secret WEBE 807:8
This high o., all allow HERB 371:15
officialism Where there is o. FORS 321:1
officials o. are the servants GOWE 347:11
O. take different view ROTH 635:20
offspring Of human o. MILT 516:25
Time's noblest o. BERK 68:4
wickedest o. of thy race ROCH 630:22
oft as o. as ye shall drink it BOOK 129:22
by o. falling LATI 454:3
O. in danger WHIT 814:4
o. was thought POPE 584:18
often Vote early and vote o. MILE 507:21
Og O. the king of Basan BOOK 141:5
Ohioan black O. swan WRIG 833:13
Ohrmazd O. was on high ZORO 841:17
oil anointed my head with o. BOOK 133:1
consumed the midnight o. GAY 332:6
like an o. painting INGH 399:16
mix like o. and vinegar GAIN 327:18
o. controlling American soil DYLA 287:14
o. in a cruse BIBL 79:26

oil (*cont.*):
o. into their ears JONS 420:5
o. of gladness BOOK 134:14
o. of joy for mourning BIBL 89:6
o. to make him BOOK 139:3
O., vinegar, sugar GOLD 344:23
o. which renders HUME 394:11
smoother than o. BIBL 82:12
smoother than o. BOOK 135:12
sound of o. wells FISH 313:17
whose o. wellnigh would shine KORA 445:2
with boiling o. in it GILB 338:12
oiled in the o. wards KEAT 430:7
O. his way around the floor LERN 465:10
oily glib and o. art SHAK 677:25
ointment o. might have been sold BIBL 97:15
very precious o. BIBL 97:14
OK O. We lost MAJO 491:18
Okie O. means you're scum STEI 737:11
old adherence to the o. LINC 468:6
Any o. iron COLL 228:12
As with gladness men of o. DIX 271:13
attendance on my o. age YEAT 837:13
balance of the O. CANN 185:6
Being an o. maid FERB 308:12
being o. is having lighted rooms LARK 453:3
better than the Good O. Days BINC 115:7
blessing of the O. BACO 42:3
born from o. RUSH 637:17
boys of the o. Brigade WEAT 806:24
catch o. birds with chaff PROV 615:35
chilly and grown o. BROW 158:11
considered the days of o. BOOK 137:2
die before I get o. TOWN 780:3
died in a good o. age BIBL 80:30
Diseases and sad O. Age VIRG 794:20
dreary o. age VIRG 796:20
dressing o. words new SHAK 705:1
ere thou grow o. ROCH 630:19
foolish, fond o. man SHAK 680:4
good o. age BIBL 74:26
good o. Cause MILT 519:22
Growing o. a bad habit MAUR 502:9
Growing o. is like POWE 590:11
Grow o. along with me BROW 157:18
grow o. with a good grace STEE 736:18
hard sentences of o. BOOK 137:3
heart grows o. YEAT 837:10
HOW O. CARY GRANT TELE 758:7
I grow o. SOLO 727:8
I grow o. . . . I grow old ELIO 295:10
I'm growing o. LOUI 476:2
instead of o. ones PEEL 571:15
into a world too o. MUSS 537:13
lads that will never be o. HOUS 391:1
make an o. man young TENN 758:22
make me conservative when o. FROS 326:7
man is as o. as he feels PROV 606:14
man who reviews the o. CONF 231:7
Mithridates, he died o. HOUS 391:10
my folks were growing o. STEV 742:18
name thee O. Glory DRIV 279:12
Never too o. to learn PROV 607:39
no country for o. men YEAT 837:1
no fool like an o. fool PROV 612:28
no man would be o. SWIF 749:2
not yet so o. SHAK 688:4
now am not too o. BLUN 122:12
now am o. BOOK 133:26
off with the o. love PROV 604:8
o. Adam in this Child BOOK 130:8
o. age always fifteen years older BARU 56:10
O. Age, and Experience ROCH 630:14
O. Age a regret DISR 270:3
O.-age, a second child CHUR 213:23
o. age has brought to me STEP 737:20
O. age hath yet his honour TENN 767:12
O. age is the most unexpected TROT 783:15
o. age of cards POPE 583:15
O. age should burn THOM 772:2
o. age, the last gap but one WHIT 814:5
o. and faded MARL 495:15
O. and young STEV 741:24
o. before my time ROSS 634:7
o. black magic MERC 505:8
o. December's bareness SHAK 705:8
o. familiar faces LAMB 448:20
O. friends are best SELD 653:14
o. head on young shoulders PROV 615:42
o. heads on your young shoulders SPAR 731:17
o. in a second childhood ARIS 24:10
o. is better BIBL 99:2
O. King Cole NURS 549:17
o. lamps for new ARAB 23:6
o. Lie: Dulce et decorum OWEN 562:8
o., mad, blind SHEL 713:28
o. man does not care JOHN 413:23
o. man in a dry month ELIO 294:21
o. man in a hurry CHUR 214:15
o. man of Thermopylae LEAR 460:12
O. man river HAMM 358:22
o. man's darling PROV 596:5
o. man's wit may wander TENN 759:14
o. man upon a winter's night YEAT 836:21
o. man who said, 'Damn!' HARE 362:4
o. men and children BOOK 142:1
O. men and comets SWIF 749:4
o. men from the chimney corner SIDN 718:24
o. men must die PROV 616:3
o. men shall dream dreams BIBL 90:14
O. Mother Hubbard NURS 549:18
o. order changeth TENN 760:15
O. soldiers never die FOLE 318:24
o. too much WALP 800:24
o. truth receives a new WIGG 816:18
o., unhappy, far-off things WORD 832:3
o., wild, and incomprehensible man VICT 792:5
o. wine wholesomest WEBS 808:6
o. wood best to burn BACO 41:20
O, sir! you are o. SHAK 678:16
outrageous o. fellow HOYL 392:8
planned by o. men RICE 626:4
ruinous and o. SPEN 733:17
sad o. age TALL 753:9
Say I'm growing o. HUNT 395:15
shift an o. tree PROV 615:45
sing the o. songs CLAR 219:1
so o. a head SHAK 688:9
so o. a story HEIN 368:6
story always o. BROW 157:22
suppose an o. man decayed JOHN 417:2
teach an o. dog new tricks PROV 615:30
Tell me the o., old story HANK 359:9
that horror—the o. woman COLE 228:4
They shall grow not o. BINY 115:8
they were o. too MAUG 501:15
thinking of the o. 'un DICK 261:14
though an o. man JEFF 405:17
times begin to wax o. BIBL 91:3
too o. to rush up to the net ADAM 2:7
want an o.-fashioned house FISH 313:18
warn you not to grow o. KINN 437:20
wax o. as doth a garment BOOK 138:15
well an o. age is out DRYD 282:18
When I am an o. woman JOSE 421:10
when thou shalt be o. BIBL 103:11
when 'tis o. BALL 52:8
When you are very o. RONS 632:8
worn, and o. ROSS 634:6
you are o. and grey YEAT 837:23
You are o., Father William CARR 189:12
You are o., Father William SOUT 730:21
young can do for the o. SHAW 707:6
Young folks think o. folks PROV 616:1
older Another day o. TRAV 781:2
As we get o. REED 623:12
for us o. ones ELIZ 297:18
O. men declare war HOOV 383:13
o. than the rocks PATE 569:13
so much o. then DYLA 287:12
oldest o. hath borne most SHAK 680:16
o. rule in the book CARR 190:9
o. sins SHAK 670:17
olet *Pecunia non o.* VESP 791:14
oligarchy *aristocracy*, call it *o.* HOBB 379:1
olive children like the o.-branches BOOK 140:23
o., aloe, and maize TENN 758:14
Olivet purple brows of O. TENN 761:5
Olivia Cry out, 'O.!' SHAK 701:7
eyes did see O. SHAK 700:27
olla putrida what a clumsy *o.* LAWR 458:23
ologies instructed in the 'o.' CARL 188:3
olores *inter strepere anser o.* VIRG 796:11
Olympian O. bolts DISR 268:15
Olympus made great O. tremble HOME 381:22
O. on top of Ossa VIRG 796:16
Pelion on top of shady O. HORA 388:17
om end of o. is silence UPAN 788:8
Omega Alpha and O. BIBL 111:18
omelette fuss about an o. VOLT 798:14
make an o. without PROV 615:40
omen gods avert this o. CICE 217:22
Procul o. abesto OVID 561:3
This is the one best o. HOME 382:6
omens grievous o. SUTT 747:8
omitted O., all the voyage SHAK 676:28
omne *o. immensum peragravit* LUCR 478:21
omnes *Laudate Dominum, o. gentes* BIBL 113:23
omnia *Amor vincit o.* CHAU 204:15
non o. possumus omnes LUCI 478:20
Non o. possumus omnes VIRG 796:10
O. vincit Amor VIRG 796:12
omnibus man on the Clapham o. BOWE 145:18
Ninety-seven horse power o. FLAN 316:5
omnipotence proof of God's o. DEV 259:12
omnipotent land of the o. No BOLD 124:11
O. but friendless SHEL 713:11
omnis *Non o. moriar* HORA 389:1
omniscience o. his foible SMIT 726:5
omnium Duke of O. TROL 782:1
Onan into the sin of O. VOLT 798:7
once done but o. DONN 275:10
I was adored o. SHAK 701:16
oblation of himself o. offered BOOK 130:21
O. a—, always a— PROV 608:30
o. and future king MALO 492:16
o. in a great while PEPY 573:14
O. in royal David's city ALEX 11:10
O. more unto the breach SHAK 671:5
O. to every man LOWE 477:15
O. upon a time OPEN 556:8
through this world but o. GREL 352:14
You can only die o. PROV 615:26
one All for o., one for all DUMA 284:15
all is o. ZOHA 840:10
all things and I are o. CHUA 212:21
At o. fell swoop SHAK 685:8
But the O. was Me HUXL 397:6
doeth good, no not o. BOOK 132:5
encompassed but o. man SHAK 674:15
How to be o. up POTT 589:2
Long-expected o.-and-twenty JOHN 417:21
Lord is O. SIDD 717:17
loyalties which centre upon number o. CHUR 216:17
man not truly o. STEV 741:13
o. being is wanting LAMA 448:6
o. by one back FITZ 314:15
o. day in thy courts BOOK 137:13
o.-eyed man is king ERAS 301:4
o.-eyed yellow idol HAYE 365:2
O. flew east NURS 550:2
o. for my baby MERC 505:7
O. for sorrow PROV 608:37
O. for the mouse PROV 608:38
o. if by land LONG 474:16
O. in Three ALEX 11:11
o. man fewer METT 506:10

O. man shall have one vote CART 193:4
O. remains, the many change SHEL 711:4
o. thing at once SMIL 722:18
O., two, buckle NURS 550:3
ought to be Number O. CARR 190:9
she who but trifles with o. GAY 332:3
square root of minus o. BECK 60:8
Tao produced the O. LAO 451:15
When I was o.-and-twenty HOUS 390:18
oneself carefully at o. MOLI 525:12
Hell is o. ELIO 293:23
how to be o. MONT 527:15
onion o. atoms lurk SMIT 725:21
tears live in an o. SHAK 656:13
onions o., and eek lekes CHAU 205:4
only his o. begotten Son BIBL 101:18
It's the o. thing SAND 644:5
keep thee o. unto her BOOK 131:4
o. begotten of the Father BIBL 101:7
O. connect FORS 320:18
O. the lonely ORBI 557:6
To the o. begetter SHAK 704:4
only-begotten o. Son of God BOOK 129:8
onset o. and waning of love LA B 446:14
ontogeny o. recapitulates HAEC 355:12
onward O., Christian soldiers BARI 54:13
O. goes the pilgrim band BARI 54:14
ooze through the o. and slime SMIT 724:8
oozing feel it o. out SHER 716:8
O. charm from every pore LERN 465:10
Time like a last o. BECK 60:6
oozy sea-blooms and the o. woods SHEL 712:15
opal mind is a very o. SHAK 701:22
opals cream does look like o. JONS 419:9
open either shut or o. PROV 598:41
function when they are o. DEWA 259:14
great o. spaces MARQ 497:7
o. and notorious evil liver BOOK 129:1
o. any door PROV 601:21
O. covenants of peace WILS 822:17
o. my lips BOOK 135:9
O. not thine heart BIBL 91:23
O. rebuke BIBL 83:28
O. Sesame ARAB 23:7
o. the Kingdom of Heaven BOOK 126:1
O. the temple gates SPEN 733:8
O. to me, my sister BIBL 85:18
O., ye everlasting gates MILT 517:8
Secret thoughts and o. countenance ALBE 10:7
take to the o. road WHIT 815:20
opened bottle has just been o. HESI 375:14
opening essential o. sentences GREE 351:21
opera *Benedicite, omnia o. Domini* BIBL 114:2
language an o. is sung in APPL 23:3
o. ain't over SAYI 647:35
O. is when a guy gets stabbed GARD 329:15
operas German text of French o. WHAR 813:1
Soap o. sell MCEL 485:5
operatic so romantic, so o. PROU 594:7
operation end must direct the o. WOTT 833:5
operations o. which we can perform WHIT 814:17
opes *Fumum et o.* HORA 388:22
golden o., the iron shuts MILT 513:5
Magnas inter o. inops HORA 388:21
Ophelia I loved O. SHAK 666:29
opiate some dull o. KEAT 429:6
opiates best of o. SMIT 724:19
curing diverse maladies as o. SYDE 751:19
opinion approve a private o. HOBB 378:18
Backed his o. PRIO 593:1
by prevalent o. OLIV 553:14
fool gudgeon, this o. SHAK 687:4
form a clear o. BONH 125:9
Government and public o. SHAW 708:5
holds a good o. TROL 782:23
independent of public o. HEGE 367:16
man can brave o. STAË 735:18
man of common o. BAGE 46:1
north of my lady's o. SHAK 702:4
of his own o. still BUTL 172:12
o. and science HUME 394:17
o. he held once SHAK 675:4
o. in good men MILT 519:17
o. of himself BENN 66:4
o. one man entertains PALM 566:9
o. with the learned CONG 232:16
own o. still PROV 602:11
Party is organized o. DISR 268:22
plague of o. SHAK 700:18
poor itch of your o. SHAK 660:2
scorching world's o. FLET 318:7
supported by popular o. CATT 194:17
think the last o. right POPE 584:26
vagrant o. BIER 114:24
were of one o. MILL 508:19
whole climate of o. AUDE 33:29
opinions anger of men who have no o. CHES 211:5
anyone's o. but your own PERS 574:3
as many o. as people TERE 768:5
by men's o. FABI 305:20
conflict of o. JOHN 418:6
delivers his o. CICE 217:9
Golden o. SHAK 682:13
halt ye between two o. BIBL 79:27
killed with your hard o. SHAK 670:24
New o. are always suspected LOCK 471:11
public buys its o. BUTL 172:28
so bad as their o. MACK 486:11
so many o. PROV 611:6
Stiff in o. DRYD 280:9
opium o.-dose for keeping beasts KING 437:14
o. of the people MARX 499:13
o. that numbs the soul FLAU 316:9
subtle, and mighty o. DE Q 258:8
with an o. wand PAIN 564:3
opponents o. eventually die PLAN 577:10
opportunities one of those o. GLAD 341:7
opportunity also a matter of o. HIPP 377:17
God's o. PROV 606:19
Ireland's o. PROV 599:14
maximum of o. SHAW 708:19
meanness of o. ELIO 292:16
only requires o. ELIO 293:9
o. for achievement KEIL 432:10
o. is that wherein HIPP 377:16
O. makes a thief PROV 609:10
O. never knocks PROV 609:11
strong seducer, o. DRYD 281:7
unfettered o. MADA 488:20
when he had the o. ROWL 636:14
oppose o. everything DERB 258:13
opposing by o. end them SHAK 664:3
opposites o. are obviously absurd BOHR 124:3
opposition duty of an O. DERB 258:13
effective means of o. GOEB 342:10
formidable O. DISR 269:27
Her Majesty's O. BAGE 46:9
His Majesty's O. HOBH 379:6
O., on coming into power BAGE 46:18
oppressed let the o. go free BIBL 89:1
o., and he was afflicted BIBL 88:17
oppresseth enemy o. me BOOK 134:8
oppressing o. city BIBL 90:23
oppression behold o. BIBL 86:17
mad with o. TAYL 756:20
make o. bitter SHAK 663:29
violate would be o. JEFF 405:11
violence and o. SOLZ 727:14
oppressions o. of this earth SHEL 711:20
oppressor ends as an o. CAMU 184:13
Neutrality helps the o. WIES 816:16
o.'s wrong SHAK 664:4
opprobrium term of o. MOYN 534:11
opt o. out of a nation LYNC 480:19
optics o. of these eyes BROW 153:25
optima *O. quaeque dies miseris* VIRG 796:20
optimist o. is a guy MARQ 497:5
o. proclaims that we live CABE 180:13
optimistic o. for the moment BROD 149:4
opulent glass the o. HARD 361:9
opus *Hic o., hic labor est* VIRG 794:17
Iamque o. exegi OVID 561:19
superabat o. OVID 561:13
orabunt *O. causas melius* VIRG 795:1
oracle I am Sir O. SHAK 687:3
oracles earth's green o. SUTT 747:8
lively O. of God CORO 237:8
o. are dumb MILT 513:27
oracular use of my o. tongue SHER 716:1
oral o. contraception ALLE 12:13
orange clockwork o. BURG 161:24
in shades the o. bright MARV 498:7
of palm, of o.-blossom TENN 758:14
O. card CHUR 214:13
o. flower perfumes the bower SCOT 652:2
were an o.-tree HERB 372:15
oranges Coffee and o. STEV 740:5
O. and lemons NURS 550:4
orang-outang o. or the tiger BURK 165:3
orantes *Stabant o.* VIRG 794:21
oration studied as an o. OSBO 559:18
orator greatest o. HUME 394:13
I am no o., as Brutus is SHAK 676:9
o. ever made an impression BAGE 46:6
without an o. SHAK 703:30
orators first of o. MACA 481:11
play the o. MARL 496:22
oratory first in o. DEMO 257:4
orbed o. maiden SHEL 711:6
orbis *Si fractus illabatur o.* HORA 388:16
orbs from their o. shoots LODG 472:18
orchard on the o. bough BROW 156:2
orchards new-planted o. SHAK 676:12
orchestra golden rules for an o. BEEC 61:5
o. playing to the rich AUDE 33:20
orchestration o. of platitudes WILD 819:16
Orci *in faucibus O.* VIRG 794:20
ordained o. of God BIBL 105:19
'Tis so o. PRIO 593:4
order all in o. stand CRAB 242:28
all is in o. MANS 494:9
all that o. and beauty NEWT 543:3
began in o. BROW 152:15
best words in the best o. COLE 227:20
cannot bring o. MCNA 488:5
decently and in o. BIBL 106:18
defined by the word 'o.' METT 506:8
Father of O. ZORO 841:12
Good o. is the foundation BURK 164:6
harmony, o. or proportion BROW 153:30
I o. it done JUVE 424:15
more devoted to o. than justice KING 436:12
new world o. BUSH 171:4
not necessarily in that o. GODA 342:1
old o. changeth TENN 760:15
o. and beauty BAUD 57:8
o. breeds habit ADAM 2:19
o. in variety we see POPE 587:14
o. of Melchisedech BOOK 139:17
o. of the acts is planned PAST 569:7
o. of your going SHAK 684:13
O. reigns in Warsaw ANON 20:10
o. to a peopled kingdom SHAK 670:28
party of o. or stability MILL 508:20
prejudice of good o. MILI 508:5
put his household in o. BIBL 79:10
restoration of o. JAME 403:25
Set thine house in o. BIBL 87:25
social o. destroyed TOCQ 778:11
straining o. into tyranny GODW 342:8
They o., said I STER 738:5
violates the o. of nature HERO 373:22
war creates o. BREC 147:11
wretched rage for o. MAHO 490:19
ordered o. my goings BOOK 133:31
ordering o. of the universe ALFO 11:14
orders Almighty's o. to perform ADDI 4:7
don't obey no o. KIPL 438:11

orders (*cont.*):
gave them their o. WELL 810:3
Obey o. PROV 608:20
ordinary learn to see the o. BAIL 48:3
o. mind WOOL 826:13
o. one seem original HORA 385:14
see God in the o. things AWDR 39:20
warn you not to be o. KINN 437:20
ore dig the golden o. CRAB 243:15
Load your subject with o. KEAT 431:23
oremus *O.* MISS 520:14
organ as the maiden's o. SHAK 701:3
heaven's deep o. MILT 513:23
mellering to the o. DICK 264:23
one day at the o. PROC 593:12
o. and the maypole JORD 421:6
o. grinder is present BEVA 71:19
o. of public opinion DISR 268:15
o.-voice of England TENN 764:20
playing of the merry o. SONG 729:10
organic Be but o. harps COLE 225:8
form the key to o. life PAST 569:5
organization about the o. man WHYT 816:12
o. of forms CART 193:1
o. of hatreds ADAM 2:13
o. of idolatry SHAW 708:15
o. of non-violence BAEZ 45:20
organize Don't waste time mourning—o. LAST 456:10
o. her own immortality LASK 454:2
organized it's got to be o. HOCK 379:11
o. hypocrisy DISR 268:12
Party is o. opinion DISR 268:22
organizing Only an o. genius BEVA 71:12
organs Loud o., his glory BAKE 48:14
moves with its own o. SHAK 657:2
o. of beasts and fowls JOYC 422:12
other o. take their tone GLAD 340:14
orgasm o. has replaced the Cross MUGG 534:16
orgy o. looks particularly alluring MUGG 534:14
Oriens *equis O. adflavit* VIRG 796:15
orient corn was o. TRAH 780:13
origin Greek in its o. MAIN 491:12
stamp of his lowly o. DARW 250:17
original Behold the bright o. GAY 332:15
gone from o. righteousness BOOK 142:9
great and o. writer WORD 832:22
great O. frame ADDI 5:12
in th' o. perused mankind ARMS 25:14
nothing o. in me CAMP 183:17
ordinary one seem o. HORA 385:14
o. face HUI- 394:3
o. is unfaithful BORG 143:5
o. or instrumental HOBB 378:16
o. sin MELV 504:7
o. writer CHAT 204:4
returning to the o. LAO 451:12
saves o. thinking SAYE 646:6
To *women* their o. must owe COLL 228:8
originality man without o. SHAW 706:20
o. of your countenance CLAI 218:5
originals do not admire the o. PASC 568:10
few o. and many copies TOCQ 778:9
origins Consider your o. DANT 249:17
Orion bands of O. BIBL 81:34
O. plunges prone HOUS 390:11
orison mid his o. hears DYER 287:1
Orlando Run, run, O. SHAK 659:6
ornament deceived with o. SHAK 688:3
foreign aid of o. THOM 775:11
Nobility is a graceful o. BURK 163:30
o. of a meek and quiet spirit BIBL 111:2
o. to her profession BUNY 161:15
o. which truth doth give SHAK 704:20
respecting all o. RUSK 638:19
study's o. MIDD 507:6
woman's finest o. AUCT 33:14
ornaments Can a maid forget her o. BIBL 89:10
lieu of many o. SPEN 733:10
ornate o., and grotesque BAGE 47:24
Orontes Syrian O. JUVE 424:9
orphan defeat is an o. CIAN 217:3
failure is an o. PROV 611:32
O., both sides WELL 810:10
Orpheus O. with his lute SHAK 673:9
soul of O. sing MILT 512:8
orthodoxy O. is my doxy WARB 803:4
O. or My-doxy CARL 187:23
ortolans die eating o. DISR 270:34
Irish o. EDGE 288:12
Oscar assume that O. said it PARK 567:5
You will, O. WHIS 813:22
osprey o. to the fish SHAK 660:12
Ossa pile O. on Pelion VIRG 796:16
ossibus *ex o. ultor* VIRG 794:14
ostentation use rather than o. GIBB 335:8
ostentatious is not o. REYN 625:11
ostrich wings of an o. MACA 482:16
Othello O.'s occupation's gone SHAK 693:1
other either to o. BOOK 131:8
forsaking all o. BOOK 131:4
happens to *o.* people CART 192:9
I am not as o. men are BIBL 100:15
o. Eden SHAK 694:19
o. men's flowers MONT 528:5
o. people's children CLIN 221:2
o. person is feeling BURR 169:16
O. voices, other rooms CAPO 185:15
Were t'o. dear charmer away GAY 332:1
wonderful for o. people KERR 434:8
others Do unto o. as you would PROV 598:43
judging o. MOLI 525:12
man for o. BONH 125:10
woman who lives for o. LEWI 466:19
otherwise gods thought o. VIRG 794:6
would wish o. NEWS 544:17
otia *deus nobis haec o. fecit* VIRG 795:14
Otis Miss O. regrets PORT 588:8
otium *Cum dignitate o.* CICE 217:26
ought connected with an *o.* HUME 395:8
didn't o. never to have done it BEVI 72:12
hadn't o. to be HART 363:10
o. to have done BOOK 125:16
ounce o. of practice PROV 609:13
our O. Father BIBL 93:19
ours O. is the land MAYA 502:19
ourselves love of o. HAZL 365:8
not we o. BOOK 138:13
power of o. BOOK 128:4
remedies oft in o. do lie SHAK 656:1
ousel o. singing in the woods THOM 773:10
out cannot o.-vote them JOHN 415:27
counted them all o. HANR 359:11
get o. and get under CLAR 219:14
get o. while we're young SPRI 735:12
include me o. GOLD 346:1
left o. he would be dangerous MELB 503:16
many ways o. SENE 654:19
Mordre wol o. CHAU 206:3
O.-babying Wordsworth BULW 160:6
O., damned spot SHAK 685:9
o.-glittering Keats BULW 160:6
o.-herods Herod SHAK 664:14
o. it wente CHAU 207:13
o. of the body BIBL 107:15
O. of the deep BOOK 141:1
O. of this wood SHAK 690:4
Out, o., brief candle SHAK 685:22
O.-topping knowledge ARNO 27:13
o. with the Stuarts DISR 270:14
preserve thy going o. BOOK 140:13
truth is o. there CATC 196:23
will o.-argue them JOHN 415:27
outcast beweep my o. state SHAK 704:13
o. of the people BOOK 132:22
o. on the world HEWI 375:19
outcasts o. always mourn WILD 819:3
o. of Israel BOOK 141:24
outdated o. methods WILS 821:15
outdoor system of o. relief BRIG 148:11
outer o. life of telegrams FORS 320:17
outflows o. extinguished PALI 565:7
outgrabe mome raths o. CARR 190:12
outlaw attacks from o. states REAG 623:6
wandering o. BYRO 174:9
outlawed liar should be o. HALI 357:10
o. or exiled MAGN 489:12
outlive o. this powerful rhyme SHAK 704:21
outlived o. certain desires WOOL 827:2
outlives o. this day SHAK 671:23
outrage connive in civilised o. HEAN 366:15
mouth of o. SHAK 698:5
outrageous O. acts STEI 737:13
o. old fellow HOYL 392:8
outrageously o. virtuous STEE 736:19
outside just going o. LAST 456:1
just going o. MAHO 490:18
Kiss the book's o. COWP 240:4
o. of the text DERR 258:15
o. pissing in JOHN 408:19
outsoared hath o. the shadow SHEL 711:1
outstretched o. beneath the tree BLAK 121:6
outvoted they o. me LEE 462:7
outward American-o.-bound HOPK 385:4
In all her o. parts COWL 239:16
man looketh on the o. BIBL 78:27
on the o. wall SHAK 687:24
O. and the Inward KORA 445:14
o. and visible sign BOOK 130:17
O. be fair CHUR 214:1
o. show of things SPEN 734:14
o. shows SHAK 688:3
outwardly o. in our bodies BOOK 128:4
serve God both o. BAHY 48:1
Ovaltineys We are the O. ADVE 8:17
over ain't o. till it's over BERR 69:12
opera ain't o. SAYI 647:35
O. hill, over dale SHAK 689:16
oversexed, and o. here TRIN 781:16
O. the hills GAY 331:16
O. the hills and far away STEV 743:5
O. there COHA 223:22
O. the sea to Skye BOUL 145:2
They think it's all o. WOLS 826:6
tyranny be o. past BOOK 135:14
overbearing o. and offensive VICT 792:6
overbought thou hast o. So much CRAS 244:2
overcame I came, saw, and o. SHAK 670:12
overcoat my o. also RIMB 628:10
put on your o. LOWE 477:18
overcome Be not o. of evil BIBL 105:18
never o. them JUNG 423:6
o. the world BIBL 102:27
We shall o. POLI 582:7
overcomes Who o. By force MILT 515:2
overdo hadn't meant to o. it KEYE 435:2
overestimated o. the quality KEYE 435:2
overlook knowing what to o. JAME 404:2
overpaid grossly o. HERB 371:15
O., overfed, oversexed TRIN 781:16
overrated O., if you ask me MILN 511:7
oversexed o., and over here TRIN 781:16
overstated save by being o. BERL 68:17
overthrown o. some of you BIBL 90:18
overwhelm o. Myself in poesy KEAT 430:3
overwrought Spirits o. WORD 831:4
oves *Inter o.* MISS 523:6
Ovid O. has sweetly MONT 526:16
Venus clerk O. CHAU 206:23
ovo *Ab o.* HORA 389:17
owe o. God a death SHAK 670:8
O. no man anything BIBL 105:20
owed so much o. by so many to so few CHUR 215:12
owest o. God a death SHAK 669:7
oweth woman o. to her husband SHAK 698:14
owl bought an O. LEAR 460:10
fat greedy o. RICH 626:15

He respects O. MILN 510:13
mousing o. SHAK 683:23
O. and the Pussy-Cat LEAR 460:16
O., and the Waverley pen ADVE 8:13
o. does to the moon complain GRAY 350:7
o., for all his feathers KEAT 427:3
o., for all his feathers OPEN 556:13
o. of Minerva HEGE 367:15
o. of Minerva PAUL 570:8
o. that is in the desert BOOK 138:14
o. that shrieked SHAK 683:4
sings the staring o. SHAK 681:4
owlet o. Atheism COLE 225:11
owls companion to o. BIBL 81:28
couch when o. do cry SHAK 699:11
court for o. BIBL 87:20
eagle among blinking o. SHEL 711:23
TWO BLACK O. TELE 758:4
Two O. and a Hen LEAR 460:4
own All by my o.-alone HARR 362:15
at least it is my o. MUSS 537:10
but mine o. SHAK 659:25
his o. received him not BIBL 101:6
marked him for his o. WALT 803:2
money and a room of her o. WOOL 826:17
my words are my o. CHAR 203:14
only to those who o. one LIEB 467:19
recognize his o. ARNA 25:22
that which is mine o. SHAK 687:15
To each his o. ANON 20:17
owners if you break o. PROV 608:20
o. reap the gains COLL 228:7
ownership common o. ANON 19:9
ox brother to the o. MARK 495:12
eateth grass as an o. BIBL 81:38
eat straw like the o. BIBL 87:5
not covet his o. BIBL 76:13
one o. or one cow ANON 22:2
o. goeth to the slaughter BIBL 82:17
o. to wrath has moved BLAK 117:20
roasted Manningtree o. SHAK 668:14
stalled o. BIBL 82:36
stalled o. where hate PROV 596:3
oxen breath of the o. HAGG 356:4
great black o. YEAT 835:12
hundred pair of o. HOWE 391:17
Many o. are come about me BOOK 132:23
Who drives fat o. JOHN 417:13
with his own o. HORA 387:11
Oxenford Clerk there was of O. CHAU 204:18
Oxford academia in O. AUNG 36:19
clever men at O. GRAH 348:10
Half-Way House to Rome, O. PUNC 617:4
heart was with the O. men LETT 465:18
in O. made An art DRYD 282:14
Ipswich and O. SHAK 673:24
King to O. sent BROW 154:7
O. has made me insufferable BEER 61:11
O. is more attractive BAED 45:17
O. Street, stony-hearted DE Q 258:6
secret in the O. sense FRAN 323:20
sends his son to O. STEA 736:13
stagecoach from London to O. HAZL 365:20
To O. sent a troop TRAP 781:1
To the University of O. GIBB 335:17
oxlips o. and the nodding violet SHAK 689:25
Oxonian impertinent, being an O. FARQ 307:22
oxygen o. of publicity THAT 770:6
oyster eye that can open an o. WODE 824:15
first eat an o. SWIF 748:16
my o. knife HURS 396:11
o. may be crossed in love SHER 715:19
world is an o. MILL 509:20
world's mine o. SHAK 688:34
oysters Poverty and o. DICK 265:8
Ozymandias My name is O. SHEL 713:1

pace Creeps in this petty p. SHAK 685:22
dance is a measured p. BACO 41:15
nostra p. DANT 250:3
not afraid of 'the p.' SURT 746:22
p. that kills PROV 604:28
requiescant in p. MISS 523:7
pacem *dona nobis p.* MISS 522:19
paces open an oyster at sixty p. WODE 824:15
pacific repose of a p. station ADAM 2:1
stared at the P. KEAT 429:21
pacifist quietly p. peaceful WALK 799:8
pacify p. Ireland GLAD 340:17
pack changed the form of the p. TROT 783:16
p. and label men for God THOM 774:10
p., and take a train BROO 150:13
p. the cards BACO 42:18
p. up your troubles MILI 508:16
Pay, p., and follow BURT 169:20
running with the p. BUTL 171:17
whole p. of you SHAK 702:21
packages small p. PROV 595:48
packdrill No names, no p. PROV 608:2
packhorses p., And hollow pampered jades SHAK 669:32
Paddington Ever weeping P. BLAK 118:21
London is to P. CANN 185:4
paddling p. palms SHAK 702:33
paddocks Cold as p. HERR 374:2
paddy Come back, P. Reilly FREN 324:8
padlock p.—on her mind PRIO 592:11
p. on the mind POPE 580:19
Wedlock is a p. PROV 613:43
paeans laurels to p. CICE 217:15
paene *P. insularum* CATU 197:5
pagan p.—spoiled ZANG 839:20
P. suckled in a creed outworn WORD 832:16
page allowed P. 3 to develop MURD 537:2
foot of the first p. SAND 644:6
p. having an ample marge TENN 760:7
single p. of our life SAND 643:14
turn the p. BROW 155:16
pageant all part of life's rich p. MARS 497:18
p. of his bleeding heart ARNO 27:22
this insubstantial p. SHAK 699:6
pages life's story fills thirty-five p. ARNO 29:10
pagoda old Moulmein P. KIPL 439:12
paid attention must be p. MILL 509:21
Judas was p. POWE 590:16
p. the uttermost farthing BIBL 93:10
we ha' p. in full KIPL 440:9
well p. that is well satisfied SHAK 688:17
pain After great p. DICK 266:5
almost to amount to p. HUNT 396:6
any more p. BIBL 113:8
beneath the aromatic p. WINC 823:1
born in one another's p. THOM 774:3
cost Ceres all that p. MILT 516:14
cures all p. CLAR 218:11
Eternal P. ARNO 26:21
feel no p. ANON 16:21
gain, not p. OXFO 562:15
general drama of p. HARD 360:14
hark—what p. ARNO 26:20
I have no p., dear mother FARM 307:2
intermission of p. SELD 653:22
intoxication with p. BRON 149:10
Joy always came after p. APOL 22:21
long grief and p. TENN 764:11
more joy than p. EURI 304:16
my life's a p. DAVI 251:17
never inflicts p. NEWM 542:11
no greater p. DANT 249:12
No p., no gain PROV 608:5
No p., no palm PENN 572:13
obligation is a p. JOHN 410:20
Of p., darkness and cold BROW 157:17
old age and p. sneak up VIRG 796:20
Our Lady of P. SWIN 750:16
p. and anguish wring the brow SCOT 651:13
p. and grief BOOK 133:28
p. of a new idea BAGE 47:12
p. shall not be inflicted SPEN 732:3
p. to the bear MACA 482:14
physics p. SHAK 683:16
pleasure after p. DRYD 280:18
Pride feels no p. PROV 609:41
redress Of all my p. WYAT 834:3
rest from p. DRYD 281:29
rose in aromatic p. POPE 585:14
she hasn't a p. MILN 510:20
sure she felt no p. BROW 157:15
tender for another's p. GRAY 350:17
to another's p. COWP 241:28
travaileth in p. BIBL 105:9
turns to pleasing p. SPEN 734:4
unforgotten p. ROSS 635:4
vigil and all the p. SWIN 750:5
with no p. KEAT 429:13
without one p. TENN 763:18
With some p. is fraught SHEL 714:8
painful p. as the other BACO 42:24
p. pleasure SPEN 734:4
painkiller most natural p. LAST 456:14
pains capacity for taking p. PROV 601:3
double was his p. SPEN 733:23
let our p. be less BROM 149:7
Marriage has many p. JOHN 410:27
no gains without p. STEV 740:10
p. a man when 'tis kept close SUCK 745:9
p. of hell BOOK 140:1
pleasure in poetic p. COWP 241:22
turned round in whirl of p. JAIN 401:13
paint can't pick it up, p. it MILI 508:9
flinging a pot of p. RUSK 638:6
I p. with my prick MISQ 521:16
only showed the p. DRYD 281:12
p. 'em truest ADDI 4:8
p. objects as I think them PICA 576:2
p. on the face of Existence BYRO 180:2
p. the lily SHAK 677:15
p. the meadows SHAK 681:3
p. too much direct from nature GAUG 331:4
price of the p. VAN 789:18
should not p. the chair MUNC 536:13
throws aside his p.-pots HORA 385:17
wife needs no p. PROV 596:29
painted black as he is p. PROV 598:8
fears a p. devil SHAK 683:10
idle as a p. ship COLE 226:11
Lift not the p. veil SHEL 713:27
p. child of dirt POPE 583:9
p. clay SHAK 694:9
p. cunningly SPEN 733:17
p. her face BIBL 80:24
p. meadow ADDI 4:21
p. on the wall BROW 156:24
p. to look like iron BISM 116:16
p. to the eyes DOBS 271:16
took the p. thing BOCC 123:7
painter Farewell, great p. EPIT 302:6
great sculptor or p. RUSK 638:7
I am a p. SCHW 650:2
I, too, am a p. CORR 237:9
paintbrush in hands of p. PICA 575:15
ranks far below the p. LEON 464:19
scenes made me a p. CONS 235:6
tea-tray p. BLUN 122:14
writer or picture-p. LEWI 467:8
painters Good p. imitate nature CERV 200:6
P. and poets HORA 385:11
Poets like p. POPE 584:18
painting amateur p. in water-colour STEV 741:28
chapel I was p. MICH 506:15
essence of p. MOND 526:2
How vain p. is PASC 568:10
light is to p. BOUR 145:5
like an oil p. INGH 399:16
marvellous p. BACO 45:15
no matter what you're p. HOCK 379:11
on the unreal p. VIRG 793:13
p. and punctuality GAIN 327:18
P. became everything BROW 151:19
P. is saying 'Ta' SPEN 732:16
P. is silent poetry SIMO 720:13

painting (*cont.*):
p. not made to decorate PICA 575:16
poem is like a p. HORA 386:6
rudder of p. LEON 464:16
teachers of the Art of P. DÜRE 286:4
paintings I have heard of your p. SHAK 664:8
paints God p. the scenery HART 363:7
want to know a butcher p. BROW 157:27
pair Sleep on Blest p. MILT 516:26
Take a p. of sparkling eyes GILB 337:8
palace Be thine own p. DONN 274:23
chalice from the p. FILM 312:6
if his p. were in flames GODW 342:5
keepeth his p. BIBL 99:17
Love in a p. KEAT 428:15
p. and a prison on each hand BYRO 174:24
p. for a hermitage SHAK 695:14
p. is more than a house COLE 227:22
p. is not safe DISR 271:5
purple-linèd p. KEAT 428:16
straw cottage to a p. turns DYER 286:15
palaces dragons in their pleasant p. BIBL 87:6
gorgeous p. SHAK 699:6
pleasures and p. PAYN 570:14
plenteousness with thy p. BOOK 140:15
saw in sleep old p. SHEL 712:14
paladin starry p. BROW 158:1
Palaeozoic In the P. time SMIT 724:8
palate P., the hutch of tasty lust HOPK 384:8
steps down the p. OPEN 556:1
pale behold a p. horse BIBL 112:5
bond Which keeps me p. SHAK 684:7
P. as thy smock SHAK 693:31
P., beyond porch and portal SWIN 750:20
p. contented sort of discontent KEAT 428:17
p. fire she snatches SHAK 699:22
P. grew thy cheek BYRO 179:18
P. hands I loved HOPE 383:20
p.—is yet of gold CRAB 243:6
P. prime-roses SHAK 703:18
p., unripened beauties ADDI 4:11
p. young curate GILB 339:10
turned p. SOUT 731:6
whiter shade of p. REID 6[illegible]:7
Why so p. and wan SUCK 745:7
world grew p. JOHN 411:16
palely Alone and p. loitering KEAT 428:7
p. loitering OPEN 556:7
Palestine establishment in P. BALF 49:16
To sweeten P. RUME 637:5
paletot *Mon p. aussi* RIMB 628:10
paling piece-bright p. HOPK 384:21
Palladium P. of all the civil JUNI 423:12
pallida *P. Mors* HORA 387:16
Palliser Plantagenet P. TROL 782:1
pallor p. of girls' brows OWEN 562:7
palls everything p. ANON 20:15
palm bear the p. alone SHAK 674:12
has won it bear the p. MOTT 535:13
have an itching p. SHAK 676:18
No pain, no p. PENN 572:13
p. and southern pine TENN 758:14
p. at the end STEV 739:26
sweating p. to palm HUXL 397:7
Turner's p. as itchy SCOT 652:10
winning the p. HORA 386:9
win the p. MARV 498:13
palmae *sine pulvere p.* HORA 386:9
palmerworm p. hath left BIBL 90:12
palms other p. are won WORD 830:10
p. before my feet CHES 210:5
p. of her hands BIBL 80:27
palmy most high and p. state SHAK 661:9
palpable poem should be p. MACL 487:1
very p. hit SHAK 667:5
palsy p.-stricken, churchyard thing KEAT 427:7
paltry aged man is but a p. thing YEAT 837:2
Pam P., I adore you BETJ 71:2
pampered p. jades MARL 497:3
pamphleteer p. on guano TENN 766:7
pan great god P. BROW 154:20
P. did after Syrinx speed MARV 498:14
panachaea p., or polygony SPEN 734:3
panache *Mon p.* ROST 635:12
Pancras P. and Kentish-town BLAK 118:23
pancreas adorable p. KERR 434:9
pandemonium P., the high capital MILT 515:6
Pandora open that P.'s Box BEVI 72:11
panem *P. et circenses* JUVE 424:21
pange *P., lingua* FORT 321:6
P., lingua THOM 771:10
pangs bitter p. SOUT 731:14
panic p.'s in thy breastie BURN 168:22
wonderful p. HECH 367:9
Panjandrum grand P. himself FOOT 319:8
panoramic p. view of hell BYRO 176:8
pans If ifs and ands were pots and p. PROV 603:16
pansies p., that's for thoughts SHAK 666:7
pansy p. at my feet WORD 829:19
pantaloon lean and slippered p. SHAK 659:2
panteth As the hart p. BOOK 134:5
panther Black P. Party NEWT 543:2
panting For ever p. KEAT 428:26
p. heart of Rome WISE 823:16
pants As p. the hart TATE 755:8
deck your lower limbs in p. NASH 539:19
in fast thick p. COLE 225:21
Panzer P.-man, panzer-man PLAT 577:13
papa word P., besides DICK 263:1
papacy p. is not other HOBB 379:4
paparazzi p. dogs of war DENE 257:8
paper All reactionaries are p. tigers MAO 495:3
all the earth were p. LYLY 480:18
at a piece of tissue p. RUTH 640:16
built a p.-mill SHAK 672:24
By the evening p. MACN 488:11
he hath not eat p. SHAK 680:24
keep the p. work down ORTO 558:3
no more personality than a p. cup CHAN 201:13
only a p. moon HARB 359:16
p. appears dull STEE 736:20
p. hats and wooden swords USTI 7[illegible]:21
ran the p. for propaganda BEAV 59:4
scrap of p. BETH 70:3
sheet of p. SAUS 646:3
sheet of white p. SCOT 650:6
virtue of p. government BURK 162:21
worth the p. it is written on GOLD 346:3
papers He's got my p. PINT 576:12
turns over your p. LAVA 454:11
what I read in the p. ROGE 631:21
Papist P., yet a Calvinist EPIT 303:6
Paquin P. pull down POUN 589:21
parable open my mouth in a p. BOOK 137:3
parachutes Minds are like p. DEWA 259:14
parade life might be put on p. EULA 301:18
p. of riches SMIT 723:8
parades produce victory p. HOBS 379:8
paradisal P. Imagineless metal THOM 774:16
Paradise enjoy P. BECK 60:12
pass through P. COLE 227:9
paradise admit them to P. KORA 445:8
blundered into P. THOM 774:10
cannot catch the bird of p. KHRU 435:17
drunk the milk of P. COLE 225:25
eastern side beheld Of P. MILT 518:2
gadget-filled p. NIEB 545:6
Gates of P. BLAK 118:18
keys of P. DE Q 258:8
moment spent in P. SCHI 646:16
of a ruined P. SHEL 710:17
P. by way of Kensal Green CHES 210:15
P. of exiles SHEL 711:19
P. of Fools MILT 516:5
p. of four seas MARV 499:6
p. of women PROV 599:13
p. within thee MILT 517:28
paved p. MITC 523:15
rudiments of P. SOUT 728:21
weave A p. KEAT 427:17
wilderness is p. enow FITZ 314:9
with me in p. BIBL 100:28
paradises true p. are PROU 594:10
Two p. MARV 498:18
paradox Man is an embodied p. COLT 230:5
paragon p. of animals SHAK 663:18
parallel p. in the world above ZOHA 840:9
so truly p. MARV 498:11
parallelograms Princess of P. BYRO 179:22
parallels delves the p. SHAK 704:24
paralysed view of a p. cyclops HOCK 379:10
parameters five free p. GAMO 329:3
paranoid Only the p. survive GROV 354:8
parapets of the ancient p. RIMB 628:9
parasites p. or sub-parasites JONS 420:9
parcelled hardships p. within them BOLA 124:8
parcere *P. subiectis et debellare* VIRG 795:1
parch sun doth p. the green SURR 746:10
parchment bound in stale p. MERE 505:11
rotten p. bonds SHAK 694:19
should be made p. SHAK 672:22
parcus *P. deorum cultor* HORA 388:2
pardlike p. Spirit SHEL 710:21
pardon Alas but cannot p. AUDE 35:8
Bretful of p. CHAU 205:5
God may p. you ELIZ 297:5
God will p. me LAST 455:9
kiss of the sun for p. GURN 355:2
Offenders never p. PROV 608:22
P. all BUCK 159:17
p. and peace BOOK 128:17
P. me boy GORD 347:1
p., who have done the wrong DRYD 281:6
With a thousand Ta's and P.'s BETJ 70:17
pardoned praised than to be p. JONS 421:2
pardoning p. our offences BOOK 130:1
pardons P. him AUDE 34:3
parens king is truly *p. patriae* JAME 402:15
parent lose one p. WILD 817:16
one child makes you a p. FROS 325:12
p. of settlement BURK 163:15
p. who could see his boy LEAC 459:15
put any p. mad FLEM 317:10
smile for your p. VIRG 796:[illegible]
parenthood means valuing p. TOYN 780:6
parents begin by loving their p. WILD 818:27
bondage to p. WOLL 826:1
children inter their p. HERO 373:22
girl needs good p. TUCK 784:17
In mine it was the p. SLOV 721:18
Jewish man with p. alive ROTH 635:18
joys of p. BACO 43:24
lost to his p. BOWI 145:22
Of p. good SHAK 671:12
only illegitimate p. GLAD 340:11
Our p.' age HORA 388:19
p. kept me from children SPEN 732:20
P. love their children AUCT 33:12
p. obey their children EDWA 289:8
p. take more care CAVE 198:14
p. were the Lord knows who DEFO 255:14
produce bad p. MORS 533:7
sacrifice and p.' tears MILT 514:24
sharp and severe p. GREY 353:6
stranger to one of your p. AUST 38:19
sue its p. WATS 804:17
parentum *Aetas p.* HORA 388:19
parfit verray, p. gentil knyght CHAU 204:9
paries *p. cum proximus ardet* HORA 387:2
Paris after they've seen P. LEWI 467:4
Down and out in P. ORWE 558:11
go to P. APPL 23:4
Is P. burning HITL 378:9
king had given me P. ANON 20:13
last time I saw P. HAMM 358:20
P. is a movable feast HEMI 369:11
P. vaut bien une messe HENR 370:6
P. was French—and silent TUCH 784:16
they go to P. WILD 818:23

when they die go to P. PROV 601:22
without me P. would be taken ANON 20:6
parish all the world as my p. WESL 811:16
p. of rich women AUDE 33:31
pension from his p. RUSK 639:1
park come out to the ball p. BERR 69:11
gentleman's p. CONS 235:7
p., a policeman CHAP 202:9
Poisoning pigeons in the p. LEHR 462:17
wandering round a stately p. MAUG 501:16
within the new p. wall DUFF 284:7
parking put up a p. lot MITC 523:15
parks p. are the lungs of London PITT 577:2
parles their treasonous p. BROW 156:21
parley-voo Hinky, dinky, p. MILI 508:12
parliament build your House of P. WELL 810:5
crop-headed P. BROW 156:20
enables P. to do things SHAW 707:26
Irishmen in her P. BALF 49:15
minuet danced by P. SCAR 646:10
Mob, P., Rabble COBB 223:10
of [P.] BOOT 143:1
[p.] a lot of hard-faced men BALD 49:5
p. can do any thing PEMB 572:10
P. itself would not exist SCAR 646:9
P. of man TENN 763:3
P. speaking through reporters CARL 188:4
Rump P. SELL 654:10
parliamentarian safe pleasure for a p. CRIT 245:6
parliamentary old P. hand GLAD 341:6
p. eloquence CARL 188:6
parliaments mother of P. BRIG 148:13
parlour party in a p. WORD 830:16
walk into my p. HOWI 392:5
Parnassus my chief P. be SIDN 718:18
Parnell Poor P. JOYC 422:1
parochial he was p. JAME 403:5
parody devil's walking p. CHES 210:4
parole *p.* of literary men JOHN 416:21
paroles *confuses p.* BAUD 57:7
n'emploient les p. VOLT 797:10
parrot has become a p. PAIS 564:9
This is a late p. MONT 529:6
pars *Et quorum p. magna fui* VIRG 793:17
parsley P. seed goes nine PROV 609:18
parsnips butter no p. PROV 600:23
parson If P. lost his senses HODG 379:13
p. knows enough COWP 242:12
P. left off conjuring SELD 653:20
Whig in a p.'s gown JOHN 412:2
parsons merriment of p. JOHN 416:19
p. are the happiest men alive LLOY 470:13
P. are very like men CHES 209:6
p. do not care for truth STUB 745:3
part chosen that good p. BIBL 99:16
death p. thee and me BIBL 78:12
every man must play a p. SHAK 687:2
friends must p. PROV 595:46
Friends p. forever BASH 56:15
if we were ever to p. KIER 435:19
I was a major p. VIRG 793:17
leaves behind a p. of oneself HARA 359:13
let us kiss and p. DRAY 279:3
more willingly p. withal SHAK 663:14
My soul, bear thou thy p. GURN 355:6
p. at last without a kiss MORR 532:14
p. my garments BOOK 132:25
p. to tear a cat in SHAK 689:10
take your own p. BORR 143:13
we know in p. BIBL 106:16
What isn't p. of ourselves HESS 375:15
parted and his words are soon p. SHEN 715:8
Mine never shall be p. MILT 517:19
remember the way we p. SWIN 751:7
When we two p. BYRO 179:18
parterre nod on the p. POPE 583:25
Parthians P., and Medes BIBL 103:16
partial We grow more p. POPE 583:27
partiality neither anger nor p. TACI 752:12
particles names of all these p. FERM 309:2
p. of light BLAK 120:3
particular bright p. star SHAK 655:19
Did nothing in p. GILB 337:17
London p. . . . A fog DICK 260:19
particularities local customs, p. REYN 625:7
particulars generals than in p. HUME 394:17
in minute p. BLAK 119:2
parties Like other p. BYRO 180:3
P. must ever exist BURK 163:4
p. 'playing politics' WILS 822:8
warns the heads of p. ARBU 23:14
parting Ere the p. hour go by ARNO 26:17
In every p. ELIO 293:8
P. is all we know DICK 266:13
p. is such sweet sorrow SHAK 697:19
p. of the ways BIBL 89:31
p. was to die TENN 761:26
rive not more in p. SHAK 657:11
Speed the p. guest POPE 586:7
this p. was well made SHAK 676:30
partir *P. c'est mourir un peu* HARA 359:13
partisan inferior man is p. CONF 231:8
partitions thin p. DRYD 280:2
partly Living and p. living ELIO 295:14
partner look for a perfect p. WELD 809:7
partners change p. BERL 68:5
partridge Always p. ANON 20:14
p. sitteth on eggs BIBL 89:20
parts *dignified* p. BAGE 46:5
naming of p. REED 623:13
P. of it are excellent PUNC 617:22
p. of one stupendous whole POPE 585:16
plays many p. SHAK 658:25
refreshes the p. ADVE 7:25
save all the p. EHRL 290:3
want of p. JOHN 414:7
parturient *P. montes* HORA 385:20
party Collapse of Stout P. ANON 15:18
conduct of a losing p. BURK 162:6
curse to p.-strife WORD 828:3
educate our p. DISR 269:4
I believe that without p. DISR 269:8
in the p. manifestoes ROTH 635:21
invite to the last p. LEAR 461:2
master of the P. HEAL 366:6
natural p. of government WILS 821:17
nature of a political p. TROL 783:3
none was for a p. MACA 483:7
Not a select p. KEAT 431:19
not p. men NEWM 542:8
office p. is not WHIT 814:20
p. in a parlour WORD 830:16
p. is but a kind of conspiracy HALI 357:19
p. is like a marriage MCIN 486:5
P. is organized opinion DISR 268:22
p. like an old stagecoach WILS 822:3
p. not to be brought down HAIL 356:11
p. of order or stability MILL 508:20
p.'s over COMD 230:8
p.'s over CROS 246:7
P.-spirit, which at best is POPE 587:15
p. which comes nearest BAGE 47:18
passion and p. COLE 227:25
political p. in power SCAR 646:10
save the P. we love GAIT 328:1
sooner every p. breaks up AUST 37:17
spirit of p. WASH 804:7
Stick to your p. DISR 270:36
stupidest p. MILL 507:24
voted at my p.'s call GILB 338:28
Whichever p. is in office WILS 822:4
parva *p. licet componere magnis* VIRG 797:3
pasarán *No p.* IBAR 398:4
pass bringeth mighty things to p. BOOK 140:5
Do not p. go SAYI 647:17
let him p. for a man SHAK 687:8
let this cup p. BIBL 97:21
look, and p. on DANT 249:8
must come to p. BIBL 96:30
my words shall not p. BIBL 97:4
never P. into nothingness KEAT 426:16
O! let him p. SHAK 680:15
p., and turn again EMER 299:5
p. by me as the idle wind SHAK 676:23
p. for forty-three GILB 339:12
p. inn a crowd SWIF 748:4
p. in the night LONG 474:18
P. it on MORR 533:4
p. man's understanding BOOK 128:13
p. the ammunition FORG 320:7
P. the mustard GILB 339:13
p. through this world GREL 352:14
They shall not p. IBAR 398:4
They shall not p. MILI 508:10
with shining foot shall p. FITZ 315:3
passage fret a p. through FULL 327:11
long black p. STEV 742:15
North-west p. STER 739:7
p. from hand to hand SICK 717:16
p. which is particularly fine JOHN 414:22
passages foreign p. SHAK 694:14
imaginative or domestic p. KEAT 430:26
passed p. by on the other side BIBL 99:12
p. the time BECK 59:28
That p. over ANON 21:17
Timothy has p. EPIT 304:7
passer *de laisser p.* QUES 618:23
P. mortuus est CATU 196:34
passeront *Ils ne p. pas* MILI 508:10
passes beauty p. DE L 256:11
Everything p. ANON 20:15
Men seldom make p. PARK 567:3
p. the glory of the world ANON 21:13
passeth p. all understanding BIBL 108:24
p. knowledge BIBL 107:28
passi *O p. graviora* VIRG 793:9
passing did but see her p. by ANON 19:2
p.-bells for these who die OWEN 562:5
p. brave to be a king MARL 496:25
p. of a day SPEN 733:27
p. of the third floor JERO 406:19
p. the love of women BIBL 79:3
passion acknowledgement of a p. KELL 432:14
all p. spent MILT 518:26
commanding p. SHER 716:21
consumptive p. ETHE 301:12
Cows are my p. DICK 262:15
earthly p. turn LITT 470:3
Eternal P. ARNO 26:21
I have no p. for it JOHN 413:2
image of p. BART 56:7
In her first p. BYRO 176:18
inspire hopeless p. THAC 768:23
in such a p. about SHAW 709:28
love was p.'s essence BYRO 174:20
Man is a useless p. SART 645:3
most insipid p. ROCH 630:18
no good if a p. is in you BLAK 118:4
No p. so effectually BURK 163:10
of the tender p. PUSH 617:27
one p. and another STER 738:8
One p. doth expel another CHAP 202:19
our p. is our task JAME 403:8
O well-painted p. SHAK 693:10
P. always goes CHAN 202:2
P. and apathy MILT 515:19
p. and party COLE 227:25
p. and the power BYRO 174:11
p. cannot Music raise DRYD 282:21
p. could not shake SHAK 693:11
p. for hunting DICK 264:15
p. for words MOOR 530:4
p. in the human soul LILL 468:3
P., I see, is catching SHAK 675:23
P. makes the world go ICE- 398:15
p. or interest LOCK 471:20
p. shall have spent TENN 762:23
p.'s slave SHAK 664:18
p. turn into respect ETHE 301:14
prose and the p. FORS 320:18
remove p. by means of TANT 754:29

passion (*cont.*):
ruling p. conquers POPE 583:20
Search then the Ruling P. POPE 584:2
sick of an old p. DOWS 277:5
stubborn with his p. YEAT 835:4
vows his p. is infinite PARK 567:8
With all the p. EPHE 300:18
passionate full of p. intensity YEAT 837:5
passione *P. interdum movemur* THOM 771:7
passionless hopeless grief is p. BROW 154:17
P.?—no SHEL 713:14
passions acts from the p. DISR 270:6
concentrated p. HARD 361:4
diminishes commonplace p. LA R 453:18
experience of p. VOLT 798:2
his p. were expressed WALP 801:21
inferno of his p. JUNG 423:6
men of like p. BIBL 104:1
moderator of p. WALT 802:17
not his reason, but his p. STER 738:25
one of many p. JOHN 410:13
p. and resolutions HUME 394:13
p. are most like RALE 620:16
p. break not through PALI 565:18
p. come upon men EURI 305:1
p. of his fellow men HORA 388:15
slave of the p. HUME 395:6
two primal p. OSLE 560:16
passive p. and motionless CANN 185:7
passives Love's p. CRAS 244:4
Passover Christ our p. BIBL 106:2
come to our P. feast HAGG 355:13
it is the Lord's p. BIBL 76:1
passport My p.'s green HEAN 366:14
p. is sometimes asked for BAED 45:19
p. shall be made SHAK 671:23
password you-don't-know-the-p. WEIR 808:29
past always praising the p. SMIT 724:22
atone for our p. CHEK 208:3
call on p. and future O'NE 554:24
cannot remember the p. SANT 644:9
change the p. AGAT 6:20
dead P. bury its dead LONG 474:5
deeds of the p. DAVI 232:19
dote on p. achievement HAZL 365:16
funeral of the p. CLAR 218:17
Ghost of Christmas P. DICK 261:9
give me back my p. VIRG 795:6
God cannot alter the p. BUTL 172:17
lament the p. BURK 164:11
last day of an era p. YELT 838:6
live p. years again DRYD 281:3
looking forward to the p. OSBO 560:7
Many a woman has a p. WILD 818:9
neither repeat his p. AUDE 35:13
never become the p. BARK 54:15
nothing but the p. KEYN 435:7
nothing more than the p. BERG 67:16
p. as a watch BOOK 137:18
p., brittle with relics THOM 773:16
p. is a bucket of ashes SAND 644:1
p. is a foreign country HART 363:13
p. is a foreign country OPEN 556:11
p. is secure WEBS 807:10
p. is the only dead thing THOM 772:24
p. never dead FAUL 307:25
p. our dancing days SHAK 697:6
p., present and future EINS 291:4
plan the future by the p. BURK 162:9
Remembrance of things p. BORR 144:13
remembrance of things p. SHAK 704:16
soul of the whole P. CARL 187:29
things long p. SHAK 694:18
Things p. cannot be recalled PROV 612:37
Things p. redress SHAK 695:3
Time present and time p. ELIO 294:1
under the bloody p. AHER 8:28
upon the p. has power DRYD 282:33
Utopia is a blessed p. KISS 441:30
weary of the p. SHEL 711:14
What's p., and what's to come SHAK 700:21
What's p. is prologue SHAK 698:30
Who controls the p. ORWE 558:22
years that are p. BOOK 137:2
pastime take his p. therein BOOK 139:6
pastoral Cold P. KEAT 428:29
practising your p. music VIRG 795:13
pastors p. and teachers BIBL 108:3
P. she sends to help CHUR 213:21
some ungracious p. SHAK 662:9
spiritual p. and masters BOOK 130:14
pasture feed me in a green p. BOOK 132:26
people of his p. BOOK 138:6
sheep of his p. BOOK 138:13
pastures fresh woods, and p. new MILT 513:13
In p. green SCOT 652:20
Pipe me to p. HOPK 384:7
pat Now might I do it p. SHAK 665:8
P.-a-cake NURS 550:5
patch P. grief with proverbs SHAK 691:19
poor potsherd, p. HOPK 384:22
patches king of shreds and p. SHAK 665:19
thing of shreds and p. GILB 337:21
pate beat your p. POPE 582:25
p. of a politician SHAK 666:21
pâté de foie gras eating *p.* SMIT 726:4
pater *P. noster* MISS 522:17
paterna *buona imagine p.* DANT 249:16
P. rura HORA 387:11
paternal disclaim all my p. care SHAK 677:23
kindly p. image DANT 249:16
paternalism lessons of p. CLEV 220:15
paternoster No penny, no p. PROV 608:6
path beaten p. to his door EMER 300:3
Eightfold P. PALI 565:13
in the straight p. KORA 443:14
invisible p. PALI 565:19
long brown p. before me WHIT 815:20
Middle P. PALI 565:11
p. is narrow and difficult UPAN 788:2
p. of gold BROW 157:6
p. of the just BIBL 82:11
p. of true love EWAR 305:9
P. of Wickedness BALL 52:1
rough and thorny p. MONT 527:18
pathetic Is not p. WHIT 815:21
P. Fallacy RUSK 638:10
too p. for the feelings AUST 37:22
pathless pleasure in the p. woods BYRO 175:8
too much like a p. wood FROS 325:14
Truth is a p. land KRIS 445:22
pathos P., piety, courage FORS 320:23
paths all her p. are peace BIBL 82:9
all her p. are Peace SPRI 735:8
craggy p. of study JONS 420:7
light unto my p. BOOK 140:9
p. of glory GRAY 350:9
So many p. WILC 817:10
Thirty-two wondrous p. SEFE 653:9
pathway p. of a life unnoticed HORA 387:3
patience abuse our p. CICE 217:18
abusing of God's p. SHAK 688:32
aptitude for p. BUFF 159:20
burning p. RIMB 628:11
childhood had taught her p. COLE 228:3
deed, and eek hire p. CHAU 205:8
habits of peace and p. WALT 802:17
laughed him into p. SHAK 657:1
my p. is now at an end HITL 378:8
p., and shuffle the cards CERV 200:3
p. have her perfect work BIBL 110:10
P. is a virtue PROV 609:19
p. of Job BIBL 110:22
p. on a monument SHAK 701:24
p. to appreciate SANT 644:10
p. under their sufferings BOOK 127:18
p. will achieve BURK 164:3
pattern of all p. SHAK 678:24
preached up p. PRIO 593:1
preacheth p. HERB 372:5
weight in other people's p. UPDI 788:9
patient fury of a p. man DRYD 280:14
kill the p. BACO 43:3
not so p. SHAK 669:24
P. continuance BIBL 104:28
p. etherized upon a table ELIO 295:3
p. etherized upon a table LEWI 466:22
patiently take it p. BIBL 110:31
waited p. for the Lord BOOK 133:31
patients hurry his p. along MOLI 525:13
poets are their own p. THOM 773:12
patines p. of bright gold SHAK 688:22
patria Died some, pro p. POUN 589:16
pro p. mori HORA 388:14
sed pro p. NEWB 541:17
patriarchal wi' p. grace BURN 166:25
patrician This is the P. DONN 275:6
patrie *enfants de la p.* ROUG 636:1
patries *Europe des p.* DE G 255:24
patrimony all his p. SABA 641:2
patriot honest p., in the full tide JEFF 405:12
p. of the world CANN 185:1
p. yet, but was a fool DRYD 280:13
Such is the p.'s boast GOLD 345:7
patriotism knock the p. out of the human race SHAW 709:6
larger p. ROSE 633:16
P. in the female sex ADAM 2:2
P. is a lively sense ALDI 10:11
P. is not enough CAVE 198:10
P. is the last refuge JOHN 415:3
That kind of p. GASK 330:21
patriots all these country p. BYRO 173:12
blood of p. JEFF 405:7
P. are in the right WAUG 806:12
So to be p. BURK 164:19
True p. we CART 192:11
patron generous p. STEV 741:14
not a P., my Lord JOHN 412:17
p., and the jail JOHN 411:14
P. Commonly a wretch JOHN 409:13
patronage private p. ALBE 10:6
patrons great p. LUTY 480:7
patter rapid, unintelligible p. GILB 339:9
pattern Art is the imposing of a p. WHIT 814:16
Made him our p. BROW 156:18
p. informed by sensibility READ 622:11
p. of all patience SHAK 678:24
shewed as a p. SWIF 747:16
trace the p. WOOL 826:15
web, then, or the p. STEV 741:2
patterns weaves algebraic p. LOVE 476:9
What are p. for LOWE 477:9
paucity p. of human pleasures JOHN 418:9
Paul If Saint P.'s day be fair PROV 603:19
with St P. are literary ARNO 28:27
Pauli P. [exclusion] principle GAMO 329:2
pauper He's only a p. NOEL 546:13
pauperiem *Duramque callet p.* HORA 389:10
Indocilis p. pati HORA 387:12
paupertas *infelix p.* JUVE 424:11
pause dull it is to p. TENN 767:9
eine kleine P. LAST 456:18
I p. for a reply SHAK 675:26
p. in the day's occupations LONG 473:11
pauses happy p. BACO 44:26
p. between the notes SCHN 648:22
paved p. paradise MITC 523:15
streets are p. with gold COLM 229:15
pavement P. slippery ROBI 629:21
riches of heaven's p. MILT 515:3
pavilioned P. in splendour GRAN 348:15
paving lawned areas with p. OFFI 554:14
paw ear on its p. MAYA 502:15
paweth p. in the valley BIBL 81:35
pawn you p. your intelligence CUMM 247:5
pax *in terra p.* MISS 520:13
P. Domini MISS 522:18
P. Vobis BIBL 114:6
'P. vobiscum' will answer all SCOT 651:27
pay cannot p., let him pray PROV 602:10
Can't p., won't pay POLI 581:10

Crime doesn't p. SAYI 647:7
devil to p. ANON 16:11
Equal P. ANTH 22:17
I can p. for the damage CLOU 221:21
No cure, no p. PROV 607:45
Not a penny off the p. COOK 235:15
p. any price KENN 433:10
p. at the Greek Kalends AUGU 36:18
P. beforehand PROV 609:20
p. for by one and one KIPL 440:12
P. given to a state hireling JOHN 409:14
p. glad life's arrears BROW 157:17
P., pack, and follow BURT 169:20
p. us, pass us CHES 210:16
saved the sum of things for p. HOUS 390:9
sharper spur than p. GAY 332:7
two-thirds of a nation p. VOLT 798:10
unless you mean to p. them PROV 611:16
we are made to p. for FRIE 325:3
We won't p. FO 318:21
wonders what's to p. HOUS 390:8
paycock mornin' til night like a p. O'CA 552:11
paying P. the Dane-geld KIPL 440:18
price well worth p. LAMO 449:13
payment passes for current p. BURN 165:23
paynims three p., three Jews CAXT 198:17
pays p. the piper PROV 602:31
third time p. for all PROV 612:40
You p. your money PROV 616:5
You p. your money PUNC 617:3
PC P. is the LSD of the '90s LEAR 461:1
pea beautiful p.-green. boat LEAR 460:16
picking up a p. WELL 810:6
peace all her paths are p. BIBL 82:9
all her paths are P. SPRI 735:8
arch of p. morticed NICO 544:22
author of p. BOOK 126:12
banished p. SMOL 726:15
belong unto thy p. BIBL 100:19
blessing of p. BOOK 133:14
by judgement, and by p. TALM 753:14
call it p. TACI 752:9
came not to send p. BIBL 95:1
certain knot of p. SIDN 718:12
chastisement of our p. BIBL 88:17
[Christ] came and preached p. BIBL 107:25
cowardice keeps us in p. JOHN 416:5
for ever hold his p. BOOK 131:3
for p. like retarded pygmies PEAR 571:11
Give p. a chance LENN 463:21
goods are in p. BIBL 99:17
good war, or a bad p. FRAN 323:14
gospel of p. BIBL 108:13
Had Zimri p. BIBL 80:25
hard and bitter p. KENN 433:9
haunt of ancient P. TENN 765:10
his p. and quiet SHAK 692:14
If you want p. VEGE 791:4
I labour for p. BOOK 140:11
Imperishable p. HOUS 390:13
ingeminate the word *P.* CLAR 218:21
In His will is our p. DANT 250:3
inordinate demand for p. PEEL 571:16
In p.; goodwill CHUR 216:16
In p. there's nothing SHAK 671:5
instrument of Your p. FRAN 323:5
interest that keeps p. CROM 245:16
In the arts of p. SHAW 708:8
into the way of p. BIBL 98:18
in what p. a Christian can die LAST 457:3
Joy. P. PASC 569:1
just and lasting p. LINC 469:1
kneel for p. SHAK 698:15
lay me down in p. BOOK 131:21
Let p. fill our heart KUMA 446:5
Let us have p. GRAN 349:1
Let war yield to p. CICE 217:15
Love of p. COLL 229:12
luxury, p. BAUD 57:8
Make it a *green* p. DARN 250:10
makes a good p. HERB 373:19
make your p. with authority MORR 533:2
may not be a just p. IZET 400:12
moth of p. SHAK 692:7
mountains also shall bring p. BOOK 136:17
My p. is gone GOET 343:1
never stable p. COTT 238:2
news and Prince of P. FLET 318:13
no p. unto the wicked BIBL 88:10
Nor p. within SHEL 713:30
Nor shall this p. sleep SHAK 673:27
no such thing as inner p. LEBO 461:8
not a p. treaty FOCH 318:23
no way to p. MUST 537:16
on earth p. BIBL 98:22
Open covenants of p. WILS 822:17
ordered ways upon a state of p. VIRG 795:1
Over all the mountain tops is p. GOET 343:10
pardon and p. BOOK 128:17
p. above all earthly dignities SHAK 673:14
p. and propagation WALP 801:7
p. at the last NEWM 542:16
p. been as a river BIBL 88:9
P. be to this house BOOK 131:9
p. between equals WILS 822:13
P. be unto you BIBL 114:6
p. Built on complacency GAUN 331:5
P. cannot be built ADAM 2:11
p. cannot be maintained RUSS 640:10
P.; come away TENN 761:15
P., commerce JEFF 405:13
p. for our time CHAM 200:18
p. from freedom MALC 492:1
peaceful sloth, Not p. MILT 515:12
P. hath her victories MILT 519:4
p. I hope with honour DISR 269:18
P. I leave with you BIBL 102:21
p. in our time BOOK 126:11
p. in Shelley's mind SHEL 714:10
p. is a dream MOLT 525:23
P. is a very apoplexy SHAK 660:11
P. is indivisible LITV 470:6
P. is in the grave SHEL 713:9
P. is much more precious SADA 641:7
P. is poor reading HARD 360:9
'P.! it is I.' ANAT 14:7
P. its ten thousands PORT 588:14
P., *n.* In international affairs BIER 114:23
P. no longer a dream CLIN 221:7
P. nothing but slovenliness BREC 147:11
p. of God BIBL 108:24
p. of God JAME 402:17
p. of Jerusalem BOOK 140:15
p. of the double-bed CAMP 182:15
p. of thine ARNO 26:15
p. of wild things BERR 69:14
P. on earth WESL 810:22
p. on the earth SEAR 652:24
P.! Peace! Peace UPAN 787:19
P., perfect peace BICK 114:16
P., retrenchment, and reform BRIG 148:10
P., the human dress BLAK 120:15
p. there may be in silence EHRM 290:5
P. to corrupt MILT 517:26
P. to him that is far off BIBL 88:27
'P. upon earth!' was said HARD 361:8
p. which the world cannot give BOOK 126:19
p. will guide the planets RADO 620:4
p. with honour CHAM 200:18
people want p. so much EISE 291:10
plunging into a cold p. YELT 838:5
poor, and manglèd P. SHAK 672:4
potent advocates of p. GEOR 334:2
prefers a negative p. KING 436:12
Prince of P. WESL 810:23
publisheth p. BIBL 88:12
righteousness and p. BOOK 137:15
rust in p. SOUT 728:22
seek p., and ensue it BOOK 133:22
servant depart in p. BIBL 98:24
sing The merry songs of p. SHAK 673:26
slept in p. SHAK 673:19
So enamoured on p. CLAR 218:22
soft phrase of p. SHAK 691:31
speak p. unto nation REND 624:13
tell me p. has broken out BREC 147:15
than to make p. CLEM 220:11
that we may live in p. ARIS 24:19
there is no p. BIBL 89:14
thousand years of p. TENN 761:29
time of p. BIBL 84:7
time of p. SHAK 696:10
universal p. TENN 759:4
want p., prepare for war PROV 603:39
war and p. in 21st century KOHL 443:7
War is p. ORWE 558:21
What hast thou to do with p. BIBL 80:22
White P. FANS 306:10
peaceably living p. BIBL 92:15
p. if we can CLAY 220:2
so p. ordered BOOK 128:12
peaceful made this p. life for us VIRG 795:14
quietly pacifist p. WALK 799:8
peacefully p. towards its close DAWS 253:8
peacemakers Blessed are the p. BIBL 93:3
peach dare to eat a p. ELIO 295:11
Last-supper-carved-on-a-p.-stone LANC 449:17
nectarine, and curious p. MARV 498:15
woolly p. JONS 420:28
peaches What p. GINS 339:22
peacock Eyed like a p. KEAT 428:14
mornin' til night like a p. O'CA 552:11
pride of the p. BLAK 119:20
peacocks apes, and p. BIBL 79:19
p. and lilies RUSK 638:22
peak small things from the p. CHES 211:7
peal night's yawning p. SHAK 684:6
peanuts hate it as much as p. WELL 809:11
pay p., get monkeys SAYI 647:21
pear And a golden p. NURS 548:17
Here we go round the prickly p. ELIO 294:25
pearl barbaric p. and gold MILT 515:7
orient p. MARL 496:2
p. in every cowslip's ear SHAK 689:17
p. of great price BIBL 95:23
splendid p. SEXT 655:7
tears to p. he turned MARL 496:14
threw a p. away SHAK 694:3
pearls Give p. away HOUS 390:18
He who would search for p. DRYD 280:24
p. before swine BIBL 94:2
p. fetch a high price WHAT 813:11
p. roll in all directions ORCH 557:7
p. that were his eyes SHAK 698:27
p. upon an Ethiop's arm DYER 286:17
p. were strung JAME 403:3
throw p. to swine PROV 598:29
to sea for p. SMAR 722:3
pears Walnuts and p. PROV 613:37
Pearse Tom P. BALL 52:10
Pearsean P. ghost in the eye O'BR 552:6
peartree p. leaves and blooms HOPK 384:16
peasan toe of the p. SHAK 666:22
peasant I am a West Indian p. MCDO 485:3
p. and a philosopher JOHN 413:22
rogue and p. slave SHAK 663:26
peasantry p. its pack animal TROT 783:16
p., their country's pride GOLD 344:8
peasants cricket with their p. TREV 781:8
p. now Resign their pipes CRAB 243:12
pease P. porridge hot NURS 550:6
pebble smoother p. NEWT 543:11
wise man hide a p. CHES 211:6
pebbles leviathan retrieving p. WELL 810:6
peccata *p. mundi* MISS 522:19
peccator *Esto p.* LUTH 479:12
peccavi *P.*—I have Sindh WINK 823:10
peccavis *p. nimis cogitatione* MISS 520:11
pecker p. in my pocket JOHN 408:18
pectora *non mortalia p. cogis* VIRG 794:8
peculiar Chosen and made p. ground WATT 805:13
p. people BIBL 110:28
pecunia *P. non olet* VESP 791:14

pecuniary immense p. mangle DICK 265:22
pedant apothegmatical P. NASH 539:20
pedantic garden with p. weeds CARE 186:6
too p. for a gentleman CONG 232:23
pedantry P. is the dotage JACK 400:16
pedants learned p. much affect BUTL 171:20
peddle no shoddier than what they p. BECK 59:15
pede *nunc p. libero* HORA 388:3
pederasty Not flagellation, not p. RATT 622:6
pedestrians two classes of p. DEWA 259:15
pedigree languages are the p. JOHN 412:1
pee P., po, belly, bum, drawers FLAN 316:3
peel orange p. picked out RALE 621:12
p. me a grape WEST 812:3
peep Nevermore to p. again DE L 256:13
p. at such a world COWP 241:32
peepers where you get them p. MERC 505:6
peeping sun Came p. in at morn HOOD 382:21
peepshow ticket for the p. MACN 488:7
peer hath not left his p. MILT 512:27
many a p. of England HOUS 391:9
murdered p. ALCO 10:8
p. is exalted PAIN 563:21
reluctant p. BENN 65:4
peerage Charlemain with all his p. MILT 514:30
p., or Westminster Abbey NELS 540:14
should study the P. WILD 818:29
When I want a p. NORT 546:20
peerless Buddha, p. among men PALI 565:5
Here lies that p. paper peer EPIT 303:4
unveiled her p. light MILT 516:20
peers *flattery of one's p.* LODG 472:16
House of P. GILB 337:17
judgement of his p. MAGN 489:12
Lord in the P. BROU 151:11
peewees p. crying STEV 742:24
Pegasus thought it P. KEAT 430:4
peignoir Complacencies of the p. STEV 740:5
peine *Joie venait toujours après la p.* APOL 22:21
pelago *p. ratem* HORA 387:15
pelican bird is the p. MERR 506:1
p. in the wilderness BOOK 138:14
Pelion *P. imposuisse Olympo* HORA 388:17
pile Ossa on P. VIRG 796:16
pellet p. with the poison FILM 312:6
pellucid More p. streams WORD 829:1
Pemberley shades of P. AUST 38:23
pen Before my p. has gleaned KEAT 430:17
bite his p. SWIF 749:24
Biting my truant p. SIDN 718:9
books and p. I will apply WHIT 816:2
female p. ALCO 10:8
fingers held the p. COWP 240:24
glorious by my p. MONT 529:3
heavy oar the p. is FLAU 316:10
holding a p. DICK 263:24
mightier than the p. HOGB 380:10
My tongue is the p. BOOK 134:13
needle and the p. LEWI 467:2
nose was as sharp as a p. SHAK 671:3
pain to p. the book OXFO 562:16
p. has been in their hands AUST 38:11
p. in his hand JOHN 412:9
p. in his hand JOHN 416:15
p., in our age LEWE 466:15
p. is mightier PROV 609:22
p. is worse than the sword BURT 170:10
p. mightier than the sword BULW 160:7
scratching of a p. LOVE 477:3
squat p. rests HEAN 366:11
Waverley p. ADVE 8:13
woman's p. BOOT 142:19
woman that attempts the p. WINC 822:21
penalty p. of Adam SHAK 658:13
penance making night do p. WORD 831:4
pence eternal want of p. TENN 767:14
Take care of the p. LOWN 478:9
Take care of the p. PROV 611:38
pencil coloured p. long enough CHES 211:14
p. of the Holy Ghost BACO 42:4
pencils feel for their blue p. ESHE 301:7
p. and what-not MILN 511:7
sadness of p. ROET 631:7
Penelope true P. was Flaubert POUN 589:13
penetralium p. of mystery KEAT 430:24
peninsulas bright eye of p. CATU 197:5
penitent p., and obedient heart BOOK 125:13
p. drunkennesses RIMB 628:13
Restore thou them that are p. BOOK 125:17
penitus *p. toto divisos orbe* VIRG 795:15
pennant wind or the p. HUI- 394:4
pennies P. don't fall from heaven THAT 769:22
p. from heaven BURK 165:16
Pennsylvania leave the P. station GORD 347:1
penny bad p. always turns up PROV 595:32
In for a p. PROV 603:47
No p., no paternoster PROV 608:6
Not a p. off the pay COOK 235:15
One a p. NURS 550:1
one p. the worse BARH 54:6
p. plain and twopence coloured STEV 741:17
p. saved PROV 609:23
P. wise PROV 609:24
To turn a p. COWP 241:15
pens Let other p. dwell AUST 38:1
Penshurst Thou art not, P. JONS 420:27
pension hang your hat on a p. MACN 488:8
made his p. jingle COWP 242:18
p. from his parish RUSK 639:1
p. list of the republic CLEV 220:14
P. Pay given JOHN 409:14
spend my p. on brandy JOSE 421:10
pensions P. and Grenadiers STER 739:4
pensive Come, p. nun MILT 512:5
her p. soul COLL 229:11
vacant or in p. mood WORD 828:27
pent In the great city, p. COLE 225:15
pentagon P., that immense monument FRAN 323:10
penthouse his p. lid SHAK 681:12
Pentridge P. by the river BARN 55:7
peonies wealth of globèd p. KEAT 429:4
people afraid Of p. HAMM 359:5
All p. that on earth do dwell KETH 434:10
And the p. ANON 18:1
as if p. mattered SCHU 649:7
as many opinions as p. TERE 768:5
August for the p. AUDE 33:22
Before we were her p. FROS 326:1
bludgeoning of the p. WILD 819:6
builds on the p. MACH 486:1
by the p. PAGE 562:18
confidence of the p. CONF 231:22
debauch her p. JENY 406:11
die for the p. BIBL 102:12
dissolve the p. BREC 147:21
faces of p. going by PEPY 573:11
faith in the p. DICK 266:4
fiery, impulsive p. HOUS 391:12
fool all the p. LINC 469:5
full of p. BIBL 89:22
good of the p. CICE 217:12
I am myself the p. ROBE 629:2
indictment against an whole p. BURK 162:27
in favour of the p. BURK 164:12
is the *p.'s choice* SHER 715:22
I would be of the p. LA B 446:15
Let my p. go BIBL 75:35
Let my p. go SONG 730:8
Like p., like priest BIBL 90:9
Like p., like priest PROV 605:33
look after our p. LAST 455:13
love of the p. BURK 163:7
made for the p. WEBS 807:11
martyr of the p. CHAR 203:5
more than half the p. are right WHIT 814:2
Most p. ignore most poetry MITC 523:11
my p.'s happiness ELIZ 297:3
new p. takes the land CHES 210:17
no petty p. YEAT 838:2
Now, Sir, there are p. JOHN 416:18
one p., one leader POLI 581:11
only p. who count CLIN 221:3
opium of the p. MARX 499:13
p. are only human COMP 230:13
p. are the masters BLAI 117:12
p. are the masters BURK 165:1
p. arose as one BIBL 78:11
p. as a source of power SCAR 646:10
p. as base as itself PULI 616:21
p. don't do such things IBSE 398:9
p. govern themselves THIE 770:18
p. have spoken FITT 314:4
p. hurting people MAIL 491:3
p. imagine a vain thing BOOK 131:16
p. is grass BIBL 88:1
p. is the true legislator BURK 164:21
p. made the Constitution MARS 497:20
p. marching on MORR 532:10
p. of his pasture BOOK 138:6
p. overlaid with taxes BACO 44:13
People p., but books never die ROOS 633:1
p.'s prayer DRYD 280:5
P.'s Princess BLAI 117:13
p.'s voice is odd POPE 586:15
p. that read SHEN 715:9
p. that walked in darkness BIBL 86:28
p. went up into the city BIBL 77:20
p. who got there first USTI 788:22
People who need p. MERR 505:25
P. you know, yet can't quite name LARK 453:3
Power to the p. POLI 581:28
Privileged and the P. DISR 270:25
same as if they was p. DURE 286:3
save the p. ELLI 298:13
strength unto his p. BOOK 133:14
support of the p. CLEV 220:15
suppose the p. good ROBE 629:5
than the p. their king WILL 820:3
thy p. shall be my people BIBL 78:12
thy p. which call upon thee BOOK [illegible]
understanded of the p. BOOK 142:10
voice of the p. ALCU 10:10
voice of the p. PROV 613:35
we are the p. of England CHES 210:16
What is the city but the p. SHAK 660:7
world is bereft of p. LAMA 448:6
ye are the p. BIBL 81:15
peopled conquered and p. SEEL 653:8
peoples cry of the Little P. LE G 462:12
Peoria play in P. POLI 581:18
pepper peck of pickled p. NURS 550:7
Sergeant P. TYNA 787:2
per P. ME SI VA DANT 249:7
perceive p. and know BOOK 128:2
percentage reasonable p. BECK 59:23
perception Agent of all human P. COLE 227:11
doors of p. BLAK 119:28
gates of p. MAIM 491:7
no p., appellation MAHĀ 489:15
perchance To sleep: p. to dream SHAK 664:3
perdition led to *p.* by a man WEST 812:18
P. catch my soul SHAK 692:19
son of p. BIBL 102:28
perdrix *Toujours p.* ANON 20:14
pereat *p. mundus* MOTT 535:8
P., qui crastina curat VIRG 795:12
perenne *maneat p. saeclo* CATU 194:21
perennial Falsehood has a p. spring BURK 162:19
perennius *Exegi monumentum aere p.* HORA 388:24
perestroika restructuring [p.] GORB 346:17
started the process of p. GORB 346:18
pereunt *Qui nobis p.* MART 498:1

perfect being made p. BIBL 91:10
Be ye therefore p. BIBL 93:16
constant, he were p. SHAK 702:30
end of a p. day BOND 125:6
Entire and whole and p. SPRI 735:6
ever more p. eyes TEIL 757:4
If thou wilt be p. BIBL 96:13
life may p. be JONS 420:21
look for a p. partner WELD 809:7
made p. BIBL 110:4
made p. in weakness BIBL 107:17
nobody's p. FILM 312:9
None of us are p. WILD 817:21
Nothing is p. STEP 738:3
One p. rose PARK 567:4
patience have her p. work BIBL 110:10
p. democracy BURK 163:28
P. fear casteth out CONN 234:3
P. God BOOK 127:1
p. in this world DONN 275:9
p. Name of God SIKH 719:10
p. use of an imperfect medium WILD 818:16
p. woman; nobly planned WORD 831:24
Practice makes p. PROV 609:37
service is p. freedom BOOK 126:12
that which is p. is come BIBL 106:16
They p. nature BACO 44:4
this one is p. PALI 565:24
unto the p. day BIBL 82:11
perfected p. by music CONF 231:17
p. your religion KORA 444:16
woman is p. PLAT 577:15
perfectibility P. most unequivocal GODW 342:4
perfection Dead p., no more TENN 763:21
loveliness and p. MILT 519:13
p. is not the true basis GLAD 341:4
P. is the child HALL 358:6
p. of reason COKE 224:8
P. of the life YEAT 835:8
p. of wisdom MAHĀ 489:14
pictures of p. AUST 39:13
pursuit of p. ARNO 28:8
realise our p. WILD 818:3
road to p. JAIN 402:10
she did make defect p. SHAK 656:26
think of p. BURN 165:20
true p. SHAK 688:27
very pink of p. GOLD 345:19
What's come to p. BROW 157:2
perfections where all p. keep ANON 17:3
with his sweet p. caught ROYD 637:2
perfectly p. love thee BOOK 129:4
P. pure and good BROW 157:14
small, but p. formed COOP 236:6
perfide *ah, la p. Angleterre* BOSS 143:16
perfidious p. Albion XIMÉ 834:18
p. friends MEDI 503:9
perform Almighty's orders to p. ADDI 4:7
not able to p. BOOK 132:20
p. without thinking WHIT 814:17
zeal will p. this BIBL 87:2
performance all words And no p. MASS 501:5
insipid and tedious p. WALP 800:18
p., as he is now SHAK 673:21
p. every thing HUNT 396:1
p. keeps no day CAMP 184:2
so many years outlive p. SHAK 670:1
takes away the p. SHAK 683:15
performed vow be p. BOOK 135:26
performing aroma of p. seals HART 363:5
perfume curious p. AUBR 33:1
off'rings of p. SMAR 721:19
p. on the violet SHAK 677:15
perfumes No p. BRUM 158:23
p. of Arabia SHAK 685:11
perhaps grand P. BROW 155:8
P. it may turn out a sang BURN 167:1
seek a great p. LAST 455:20
Perigord truffles, P. POPE 582:11
peril p. in the fight CORN 236:15
those in p. on the sea WHIT 815:1
perilous dim and p. way WORD 828:11
perils defend us from all p. BOOK 126:20
in p. of waters BIBL 107:14
periods certain p. set SUCK 745:11
periphrastic p. study ELIO 294:7
perish England shall p. ELIZ 297:8
if I p., I perish BIBL 80:32
if it had to p. twice FROS 325:21
Let the day p. BIBL 81:3
Let them p. BOOK 131:23
money p. with thee BIBL 103:23
people p. BIBL 83:34
P. the thought CIBB 217:6
p. together as fools KING 436:15
p. with the sword BIBL 97:25
ready to p. BIBL 83:37
should not p. BIBL 101:18
single soul to p. TALM 753:10
speak again, and it will p. JOHN 411:5
They shall p. BOOK 138:15
They too shall p. LANG 450:10
though the world p. MOTT 535:8
To p. rather MILT 515:10
venal city ripe to p. SALL 643:10
world will p. BAKU 48:17
perished hope is p. BIBL 89:24
Now that love is p. MILL 509:16
p., each alone COWP 239:27
perishes nothing really p. BACO 41:21
What's come to perfection p. BROW 157:2
peritis *decede p.* HORA 387:10
perjured p. Clarence SHAK 696:18
perjuries laughs at lovers' p. OVID 561:6
laughs at lovers' p. TIBU 777:9
perjury laughs at lovers' p. PROV 604:45
lovers' p. DRYD 282:8
permanent Suffering is p. WORD 827:17
permission p. of all-ruling heaven MILT 514:18
permitted p. to make all the ballads FLET 317:22
pernicious his p. soul SHAK 693:28
most p. race SWIF 747:21
O most p. woman SHAK 663:1
P. weed COWP 240:2
perpendicular p. expression of horizontal SHAW 709:26
perpetua *lux p.* MISS 523:2
perpetual p. light MISS 523:2
p. motion DICK 265:17
p. night JONS 420:10
p. quarrel BURK 163:3
with p. motion SHAK 669:27
perplexed guide us when p. WINK 823:6
perplexes dull brain p. KEAT 429:11
persecute Why p. we him BIBL 81:23
persecuted I p. the church of God BIBL 106:19
merely because he is p. GOUL 347:8
persecutest Saul, why p. thou me BIBL 103:24
persecution no tyrannical p. THOM 771:15
P. is a bad and indirect way BROW 153:22
P. is not an original feature PAIN 563:24
P. produced its natural effect MACA 482:12
Religious p. BURK 165:6
some degree of p. SWIF 748:23
Persepolis through P. MARL 496:25
perseverance P., dear my lord SHAK 700:15
p. inn a good cause STER 738:18
persevere Give us grace to p. DEAR 254:1
persevering no dignity in p. in error PEEL 571:17
Persia here and in P. ARIS 24:18
Persian hate all that P. gear HORA 388:4
Persians Medes and P. BIBL 90:5
Truth-loving P. GRAV 349:13
Persicos *P. odi, puer, apparatus* HORA 388:4
persistence Hark, the dominant's p. BROW 158:6
take the place of p. COOL 236:5
person adornment of his p. THOM 774:19
frontier of my P. AUDE 34:19
most superior p. ANON 17:20
no more than a p. AUDE 33:29
P. from Porlock SMIT 724:25
p. on business from Porlock COLE 225:19
p. you and I took me for CARL 187:1
respect any p. BIBL 79:8
personal No p. consideration GRAN 349:3
P. isn't the same PRAT 591:2
P. relations FORS 320:17
warm p. gesture GALB 328:8
personalities meeting of two p. JUNG 423:9
p. of the two sexes MEAD 503:1
personality From 35 to 55, good p. TUCK 784:17
no more p. than a paper cup CHAN 201:13
value on the p. market FROM 325:10
persons confounding the P. BOOK 126:22
no respecter of p. BIBL 103:30
things, not in p. CURI 247:19
perspective light, shade, and p. CONS 235:9
P. is the bridle LEON 464:16
perspiration ninety-nine per cent p. EDIS 289:2
perspire Gladstone may p. CHUR 214:12
perspiring city of p. dreads RAPH 622:4
persuade p. a multitude HOOK 383:5
persuaded p. in his own mind BIBL 105:24
p. of them BIBL 109:30
persuaders hidden p. PACK 562:17
persuadest Almost thou p. me BIBL 104:22
persuading By p. others JUNI 423:14
p. me to it SHAK 699:23
persuasion P. is the resource GIBB 335:14
p. only is to work MILT 519:11
p. that a a thing is so BLAK 119:27
perturbation O polished p. SHAK 670:14
perturbations p. and calamities BACO 44:26
perturbed rest, p. spirit SHAK 663:6
Peru China to P. JOHN 411:13
perused in th'original p. mankind ARMS 25:14
perverse most p. creatures ADDI 5:6
P. and foolish BAKE 48:13
perversion War is the universal p. RAE 620:5
perversions of all the sexual p. HUXL 397:4
perversity p. of the human mind TROL 782:15
pervert loophole through which the p. BRON 149:10
pessimist know what a p. is SHAW 709:20
p. fears this is true CABE 180:13
p. waiting for rain COHE 224:4
pestered p. with a popinjay SHAK 667:23
pestilence breeds p. BLAK 119:14
p. and war MILT 515:23
p. that walketh in darkness BOOK 137:22
plague and p. NASH 539:23
purged the air of p. SHAK 700:27
pet p. theory of the universe EDDI 287:23
petal dropping a rose p. MARQ 497:11
Now sleeps the crimson p. TENN 766:3
O filigree p. THOM 774:16
petals peel all the p. off AYCK 40:3
P. on a wet, black bough POUN 589:18
petar Hoist with his own p. SHAK 665:24
Peter did outrun P. BIBL 102:39
government which robs P. SHAW 707:5
I'll call him P. SHAK 677:6
looked upon P. BIBL 100:24
P. Piper picked a peck NURS 550:7
P. wish himself within BYRO 179:14
Shock-headed P. HOFF 380:8
Simon P. saith unto them BIBL 103:7
Thou art P. BIBL 96:4
'twas P.'s drift SHEL 713:3
Where P. is AMBR 13:3

Petersburg P. the most abstract DOST 276:7
petis *Quod p. hic est* HORA 386:20
petitions desires and p. BOOK 126:18
petrifactions p. of a plodding brain BYRO 178:5
petrifies p. the feeling BURN 167:2
pets hate a word like 'p.' JENN 406:10
petticoat feet beneath her p. SUCK 745:8
keep down a single p. BYRO 180:9
out of the Realm in my p. ELIZ 296:24
petticoats hyena in p. WALP 801:14
pettiness something to expiate: a p. LAWR 458:14
petty Creeps in this p. pace SHAK 685:22
no p. people YEAT 838:2
we p. men SHAK 674:13
petulance P. is not sarcasm DISR 268:17
pews faith of those in the p. AUST 39:16
phagocytes stimulate the p. SHAW 707:3
phallic P. and ambrosial POUN 589:15
phantasma Like a p. SHAK 675:1
phantom grisly p. BEAT 58:5
p. of delight WORD 831:22
phantoms p. an unprofitable strife SHEL 710:23
Pharisee face of the P. BRON 149:13
touching the law, a P. BIBL 108:19
Pharisees drowns in the P.'s hypocrisy PAST 569:7
scribes and P. BIBL 93:8
scribes and P., hypocrites BIBL 96:26
pheasant roast p. with bread sauce SMIT 725:11
pheasants sup p.' eggs JONS 419:9
phenomena p. of the universe HUXL 397:15
phenomenon infant p. DICK 264:3
Phil fidgety P. HOFF 380:1
Philadelphia living in P. EPIT 303:5
philanthropist as a professed p. TROL 782:20
Philip from P. drunk ANON 15:11
not known me, P. BIBL 102:19
Philistine P. of genius in religion ARNO 29:4
run by a p. KAUF 426:4
Philistines Barbarians, P., and Populace ARNO 28:7
daughters of the P. BIBL 79:1
great apostle of the P. ARNO 28:19
P. be upon thee, Samson BIBL 78:5
P. proper ARNO 28:10
philistinism our yawning P. PRIT 593:9
P.!—We have not the expression ARNO 28:18
philologists P., who chase COWP 241:11
philology wakened by p. TOLK 779:5
philosopher in my time to be a p. EDWA 289:11
mend himself and others is a p. GOLD 345:24
Ovid, the soft p. DRYD 281:33
peasant and a p. JOHN 413:22
P.!—a fingering slave WORD 830:17
p. may preach GIBB 335:16
p.'s treatment WITT 824:4
some p. has said it CICE 217:10
understand by 'p.' NIET 545:13
philosophers little statesmen and p. EMER 299:23
p. and scholars PASC 569:1
p. have not maintained SWIF 747:24
separation of p. QUIN 619:6
philosophic bring the p. mind WORD 830:9
find the p. mind SMAR 722:8
philosophical European p. tradition WHIT 814:18
p. correctness AUST 39:18
poetry is something more p. ARIS 24:23
philosophies p. which are LEWI 467:14
philosophy bullied into a certain p. KEAT 430:26
divine p. MILT 511:24
dreamed of, in any p. HALD 356:15
dreamt of in your p. SHAK 663:4
faced with p. ELIO 292:20
false p. MILT 515:19
good moral p. BACO 41:18
History is p. DION 268:3
if p. could find it out SHAK 663:20
in p., we are concerned HEGE 367:13
linguistic p. RUSS 640:6
love's p. DONN 274:4
mere touch of cold p. KEAT 428:18
p. calls all in doubt DONN 272:7
p., grave BACO 44:8
p. inclineth man's mind BACO 42:7
P. is a battle WITT 824:3
P. is such an impertinently NEWT 543:10
P. is the replacement RYLE 640:19
P.? No; she too much rejects BYRO 177:29
p. paints its grey HEGE 367:15
p. quenches them VOLT 797:13
P., that leaned on Heav'n POPE 582:12
p. that this did BYRO 176:3
P.! the lumber SWIF 749:12
P. will clip KEAT 428:19
regions of p. HUME 395:2
religion and p. ARNO 28:22
study of P. SMIT 723:3
superstition to enslave a p. INGE 399:5
sweet milk, p. SHAK 697:31
Unfit to hear moral p. SHAK 700:10
Phlebas P. the Phoenician ELIO 296:12
Phoebus P. Apollo MERE 505:12
P., arise DRUM 279:14
P. 'gins arise SHAK 660:21
P. gins to shew SPEN 733:7
Phoenician Phlebas the P. ELIO 296:12
phoenix expect a p. hour DAY- 253:11
glory, like the p. BYRO 178:8
maiden p. SHAK 673:27
P. builds her spicy nest CARE 186:15
privilege of P. GRAC 347:15
phoenixes envy the pair of p. HO 378:10
phone answer the p. THUR 776:27
E.T. p. home FILM 311:5
never even made a p. call CHOM 212:13
P. for the fish-knives BETJ 70:10
photograph p. is a secret ARBU 23:13
photographer be a good p. BAIL [illegible]
p. is like the cod SHAW 709:24
photography mission of p. STEI 737:4
p. is all right HOCK 379:10
P. is truth GODA 341:20
p. of an event CART 193:1
phrase ancient Saxon p. LONG 473:19
p. and fame ARNO 28:5
p. becomes current HOLM 381:15
p. is born into the world BABE 40:15
phrases *La mort, sans p.* SIEY 719:2
nervous force into p. CONR 235:1
Taffeta p. SHAK 680:30
wonderful p. FRIE 325:4
phylacteries make broad their p. BIBL 96:25
Phyllida But P., my Phyllida DOBS 271:16
Phyllis P. is my only joy SEDL 653:4
phylogeny recapitulates p. HAEC 355:12
physic P. of Metaphysic begs defence POPE 582:12
Take p., pomp SHAK 679:1
Throw p. to the dogs SHAK 685:19
physical emotions lightly called p. COLE 228:2
p. illustration MAXW 502:13
physician death, the grand p. CLAR 218:11
died last night of my p. PRIO 593:2
hand of the p. BIBL 92:10
Honour a p. BIBL 92:9
need not a p. BIBL 94:24
P. art thou WORD 830:17
p. can bury his mistakes WRIG 833:10
P., heal thyself BIBL 98:29
P., heal thyself PROV 609:25
Tathagata, the great p. MAHĀ 490:10
than the p. SHAK 685:13
Time is the great p. DISR 270:15
physicians P. are like kings WEBS 808:3
P. of all men QUAR 618:21
P. of the Utmost Fame BELL 63:6
physicists p. have known sin OPPE 557:3
physics no democracy in p. ALVA 13:2
p. or stamp collecting RUTH 640:14
p. pain SHAK 683:16
pianist shoot the p. ANON 18:8
pianists no better than many p. SCHN 648:22
piano playing a p. in a brothel MUGG 535:21
pibble tiddle-taddle nor p.-pabble SHAK 671:13
Picardy Roses are flowering in P. WEAT 806:25
Picasso P. is a genius DALI 248:13
plastics, P., sunbathing WAUG 806:8
Piccadilly Goodbye, P. JUDG 423:1
walk down P. GILB 338:20
pick Sam, p. up tha' musket HOLL 381:3
See a pin and p. it up PROV 610:25
picker Karshish, the p.-up BROW 155:27
pickerel sidelong p. smile ROET 631:8
picket p.'s off duty forever BEER 61:18
picking keep my hands from p. BOOK 130:15
p. dewy apples VIRG 796:8
pickle weaned on a p. ANON 19:7
picklocks p. of biographers BENÉ 65:1
pickpockets crowd of p. WYCH 834:14
pickpurse no p. of another's wit SIDN 718:17
Pickwick P., the Owl ADVE 8:13
Pickwickian P. sense DICK 265:2
picnic Teddy Bears have their P. BRAT 147:5
pictoribus *P. atque poetis* HORA 385:11
pictura *Ut p. poesis* HORA 386:6
picture Before my face the p. SOUT 731:14
look Not on his p. JONS 420:18
no go the p. palace MACN 488:8
One p. is worth PROV 609:2
One p. is worth ten thousand BARN 54:16
p. of his father's face FLET 318:16
p. tells a story ADVE 7:19
p. tells a story PROV 599:37
p. to an original REYN 625:12
speaking p., with this end SIDN 718:23
your p. chases me RACI 619:19
pictured my friends p. within ELGA [illegible]
P. and written down BUSC 170:23
pictures all his p. faded BLAK 117:16
cutting all the p. out BELL 63:2
dead Are but as p. SHAK 683:10
furnish the p. HEAR 367:2
I nail my p. together SCHW 650:2
P. are for entertainment GOLD 346:6
p. aren't good enough CAPA 185:13
p. didn't have beginning POLL 580:3
p. do not sell VAN 789:18
p. for the page atone POPE 580:10
p. of perfection AUST 39:13
p. of silver BIBL 83:18
p. that got small FILM 312:15
sees more in my p. TURN 785:15
without p. or conversations CARR 189:7
picturesque p. and the beautiful PEAC 571:1
pie bakèd in this p. SHAK 700:2
Miss American P. MCLE 486:15
p. in the sky HILL 377:1
put into a p. POTT 588:20
piece p. of divinity in us BROW 154:3
pieces break them in p. BOOK 131:17
P. of eight STEV 741:20
thirty p. of silver BIBL 97:16
piecrust Promises, like p. PROV 609:44
pieman Simple Simon met a p. NURS 550:17
pierce his hand, and p. it BIBL 80:28
sword shall p. BIBL 98:26
pierced p. my hands and my feet BOOK 132:25
Pierian P. spring DRAY 279:7
taste not the P. spring POPE 584:15
pierides *Et me fecere poetam P.* VIRG 796:11
pies Bellamy's veal p. LAST 456:20

piety by natural p. WORD 829:10
in return for my p. CATU 197:17
nor all thy p. nor wit FITZ 314:17
p. more prone ALEX 11:13
True p. is this KORA 443:17
piffle p. before the wind ASHF 30:14
pig expect from a p. but a grunt PROV 613:49
from p. to man CLOS 222:6
happy for a month kill a p. PROV 603:41
p. got up and slowly walked away BURT 169:17
p. in a sausage TROL 783:14
p. is to the Irishman KOHL 443:9
p. went to market NURS 551:9
Stole a p. NURS 551:16
pigeon branded, p.-holed PRES 591:4
But I am p.-livered SHAK 663:29
Father, the Son, and the P. ANON 20:5
sweet kisses, p.-wise DIAN 260:8
pigeons casual flocks of p. STEV 740:6
P. on the grass STEI 737:6
Poisoning p. LEHR 462:17
piggesnye prymerole, a p. CHAU 205:26
piggy P.-wig stood LEAR 460:17
pigmy Fretted the p. body DRYD 279:21
pigs Epicurus' herd of p. HORA 386:17
P. treat us as equals CHUR 216:22
whether p. have wings CARR 190:20
pike freedom for the p. TAWN 755:14
Pilate jesting P. BACO 44:15
P. saith unto him BIBL 102:30
P. Washed his hands JAGG 401:8
Suffered under Pontius P. BOOK 126:10
water like P. GREE 351:15
pile Gaunt's embattled p. MACA 482:19
P. it high SAYI 648:1
p. Ossa on Pelion VIRG 796:16
P. the bodies high SAND 643:21
standst an ancient p. JONS 420:27
piled p. in large cities JEFF 405:8
pilfering quiet, p. CLAR 218:14
pilgrim Forth, p. CHAU 207:24
Onward goes the p. band BARI 54:14
p. oft At dead of night DYER 287:1
P. through this barren land WILL 820:8
To be a p. BUNY 161:16
pilgrimage beguile your p. FLEC 317:3
I'll take my p. RALE 620:15
proclaim the P. KORA 444:22
quiet p. CAMP 183:24
succeed me in my p. BUNY 161:18
pilgrimages longen folk to goon on p. CHAU 204:7
pilgrims land of the p. CUMM 247:4
Land of the p.' pride SMIT 724:16
Like p. to th'appointed place DRYD 282:11
p. on the earth BIBL 109:30
Pilgrim's Progress *Crusoe*, and *P.* JOHN 418:14
'P.', about a man TWAI 786:3
pill any p. can be swallowed TROL 782:5
Instruction is the p. RICH 627:9
little yellow p. JAGG 401:5
potion and his p. HERR 374:11
sleeping p. is white SEXT 655:7
women may take the p. THOM 773:9
pillar became a p. of salt BIBL 74:30
p. of a cloud BIBL 76:5
p. of fire BIBL 76:5
seemed A p. of state MILT 515:14
triple p. of the world SHAK 656:6
pillars hewn out her seven p. BIBL 82:18
not one of its p. ANON 16:14
p. bare like nude SPEN 732:23
p. of government BACO 43:31
seven p. of wisdom BORR 144:15
Pillicock P. sat on Pillicock-hill SHAK 679:2
pillow like a p. on a bed DONN 273:24
like the feather p. HAIG 356:8
softer p. than my heart BYRO 180:12
upon a midnight p. SHAK 658:19
upon the p.-hill STEV 742:13
pillows endless p. rise THOM 774:21
P. his chin MILT 513:28
pills mountebank who sold p. ADDI 5:19
p. and medicine DEAN 253:19
p. for the sick HOBB 379:3
pilot daring p. in extremity DRYD 280:1
Dropping the p. TENN 757:9
p. of the calm BAGE 46:12
p. of the Galilean lake MILT 513:5
See my p. face to face TENN 758:13
pilots P. of the purple twilight TENN 763:3
piminy Francesca di Rimini, miminy, p. GILB 338:21
Pimpernel demmed, elusive P. ORCZ 557:10
pimples scratching of p. on the body WOOL 827:3
pin life at a p.'s fee SHAK 662:20
p. up my hair with prose CONG 233:8
See a p. and pick it up PROV 610:25
siller p. BALL 52:9
sin to steal a p. PROV 604:30
with a little p. SHAK 695:11
pinch They brought one P. SHAK 659:30
pinching p. fingers SHAK 702:33
pine palm and southern p. TENN 758:14
p. for what is not SHEL 714:8
spray of Western p. HART 363:9
whisper of the p. THEO 770:17
pineapple p. of politeness SHER 715:26
pines lofty p. DRAY 279:5
pinguem *p. et nitidum bene* HORA 386:17
pinion imagination droops her p. BYRO 177:3
pinions with p. skim the air FRER 324:10
pink all this wonderful p. CART 193:3
very p. of courtesy SHAK 697:21
very p. of perfection GOLD 345:19
pinkly p. bursts the spray BETJ 70:16
pinko really p.-grey FORS 320:21
pinnace p. like a fluttered bird TENN 766:8
pinnacled p. dim SHEL 713:14
pinprick p. of eternity AURE 37:5
pins files of p. extend POPE 586:31
mixed with a packet of p. WELL 810:9
pinstripe come in a p. suit FEIN 308:6
pint p. of plain O'BR 552:10
p.—that's very nearly GALT 328:20
quart into a p. pot PROV 615:36
pinta Drinka P. Milka Day ADVE 7:17
pioneers are simply p. MURR 537:5
P.! O pioneers WHIT 815:7
pios *si qua p. respectant numina* VIRG 793:14
pious rarther p. ASHF 30:12
this p. morn KEAT 428:27
pipe p. a simple song WORD 828:19
p. Blown by surmises SHAK 669:20
P. me to pastures HOPK 384:7
p. might fall out FORS 320:10
p. of half-awakened birds TENN 765:21
p. with solemn interposing puff COWP 240:1
Thy small p. SHAK 701:3
piped We have p. unto you BIBL 95:7
piper pays the p. PROV 602:31
Peter P. picked a peck NURS 550:7
Tom he was a p.'s son NURS 551:15
Tom, Tom, the p.'s son NURS 551:16
pipes on their scrannel p. MILT 513:6
open the p. BYRD 173:6
What p. and timbrels KEAT 428:22
piping For ever p. songs KEAT 428:25
Helpless, naked, p. loud BLAK 121:3
P. songs of pleasant glee BLAK 120:12
weak p. time SHAK 696:10
Pippa P. passes BEER 61:12
pips until the p. squeak GEDD 332:25
pirate To be a P. King GILB 339:2
piscem *Desinat in p.* HORA 385:10
pismire p. is equally perfect WHIT 815:14
piss May'st thou ne'er p. ROCH 630:7
pitcher of warm p. GARN 330:1
pissing inside the tent p. out JOHN 408:19
pistol echo of a p.-shot DURR 286:8
I reach for my p. JOHS 418:17
p. in your pocket WEST 812:7
p. on the wall CHEK 208:21
p.-shot in the middle STEN 737:17
pun is a p. LAMB 448:17
when his p. misses fire GOLD 345:31
pistols Have you your p. WHIT 815:7
young ones carry p. SHAW 706:15
piston steam and p. stroke MORR 532:13
pistons black statement of p. SPEN 732:17
pit digged a p. before me BOOK 135:16
eagle know what is in the p. BLAK 118:8
He that diggeth a p. BIBL 84:24
Law is a bottomless p. ARBU 23:15
monster of the p. POPE 586:19
out of the horrible p. BOOK 133:31
sulphurous p. SHAK 679:22
pitch He that toucheth p. BIBL 91:27
imagination to the proper p. LACK 447:2
p. of grief HOPK 384:11
p. or direction HOPK 385:5
touches p. shall be defiled PROV 602:17
pitcher p. be broken at the fountain BIBL 85:2
p. will go to the well PROV 609:26
pitchers Little p. have large ears PROV 605:40
pitchfork drive out nature with a p. HORA 386:19
nature with a p. PROV 615:24
thrown on her with a p. SWIF 748:15
use my wit as a p. LARK 453:6
pith p. is in the postscript HAZL 365:4
pitied Better envied than p. PROV 596:6
pitieth p. his own children BOOK 138:19
pitiful God be p. BROW 154:16
long-suffering, and very p. BIBL 91:16
'twas wondrous p. SHAK 692:1
pitifulness p. of thy great mercy BOOK 127:15
pity by means of p. and fear ARIS 24:21
cherish p. BLAK 120:16
endure, then p. POPE 585:22
full of p. and concerned MAHĀ 489:16
no p. to myself SHAK 696:30
O source of p. MISS 523:5
P. a human face BLAK 120:15
p. beyond all telling YEAT 836:23
p. him afterwards JOHN 415:15
p. his ignorance DICK 264:1
P. is akin to love PROV 609:27
p. kills BALZ 52:18
p., like a naked new-born SHAK 682:11
p. never ceases to be shown DRYD 280:11
p. renneth soone CHAU 205:18
P. the reapers DUCK 284:4
p. this busy monster CUMM 247:9
Poetry is in the p. OWEN 562:3
saint took p. on COLE 226:17
seas of p. lie AUDE 34:2
she did p. them SHAK 692:2
some to have p. on me BOOK 136:11
some touch of p. SHAK 696:12
yet the p. of it, Iago SHAK 693:9
pix Sticks nix hick p. NEWS 544:14
place all in one p. BOIL 124:6
all other things give p. GAY 332:8
and the p. thereof BOOK 138:20
bourne of time and p. TENN 758:13
could have no p. BIBL 91:29
Ere time and p. were ROCH 630:21
exalt us unto the same p. BOOK 128:8
for one p. than another SOUT 731:4
for the sake of the p. HALI 357:15
genius of the p. POPE 583:23
Get p. and wealth POPE 586:10
Gratitude of p.-expectants WALP 802:7
his p. know him BIBL 81:11
In p. of strife CAST 193:13
keep in the same p. CARR 190:15
know the p. ELIO 294:17
lone unhaunted p. DONN 273:12
Lord is in this p. BIBL 75:2
Men in great p. BACO 43:8

place (*cont.*):
no p. to go WHIT 814:23
p. for everything PROV 609:28
p. in the sun BÜLO 160:4
p. in the sun WILH 819:18
P., that great object SMIT 723:4
p. within the meaning ANON 18:7
p. without power ROSE 633:15
prepare a p. for you BIBL 102:17
right man in the right p. JEFF 406:4
rising to great p. BACO 43:12
rising unto p. BACO 43:10
spirit of the p. VIRG 795:4
stand in the holy p. BIBL 97:2
thus with height of p. WOTT 833:4
till there be no p. BIBL 86:18
time and p. JOHN 410:25
time and p. for PROV 612:10
time and the p. BROW 157:1
Time, P. DRYD 283:4
woman's p. in the home PROV 615:15
placem *ut p. genus irritabile vatum* HORA 387:9
placeo *Quod spiro et p.* HORA 389:3
placere *Nulla p. diu carmina possunt* HORA 387:4
places All p., all airs BROW 153:27
all p. thou MILT 518:1
all p. were alike to him KIPL 441:6
father's fortunes, and his p. CORB 236:14
longest distance between two p. WILL 820:17
New p. you will not find CAVA 198:9
p. that the eye of heaven SHAK 694:15
P. where they sing BOOK 126:14
Proper words in proper p. SWIF 748:8
quietest p. HOUS 391:7
placidly Go p. amid the noise EHRM 290:5
plackets hand out of p. SHAK 679:3
placuisse *Principibus p. viris* HORA 386:22
plafond *lignes du p.* ÉLUA 299:2
plagiaire *l'état de p.* MUSS 537:10
plagiarism from one author, it's p. MIZN 524:12
plagiarist situation of the p MUSS 537:10
plagiarize P.! Let no one else's work LEHR 462:16
plague instruments to p. us SHAK 680:9
p. and pestilence NASH 539:23
p. come nigh thy dwelling BOOK 137:23
p. making us cruel PEPY 573:8
p. o' both your houses SHAK 697:23
p. the inventor SHAK 682:9
that's his p. BURT 170:12
plagues Great p. remain BOOK 133:18
of all p. DEFO 255:15
omit those two main p. BURT 170:9
plain apology for p.-speaking DICK 260:21
best p. set BACO 42:9
Books will speak p. BACO 42:17
Cannot a p. man live SHAK 696:14
darkling p. ARNO 26:5
divine p. face LAMB 449:4
Gromboolian p. LEAR 460:7
make it p. upon tables BIBL 90:22
Make thy way p. BOOK 131:22
making things p. HUXL 397:16
no p. women on television FORD 319:10
penny p. and twopence coloured STEV 741:17
pint of p. O'BR 552:10
p., blunt man SHAK 676:9
'p.' cooking cannot be entrusted MORP 532:5
p. Kate SHAK 698:7
P. living and high thinking WORD 830:13
p. meaning SHAK 688:6
p. Michael Faraday FARA 306:13
P. women he regarded ELIO 292:20
pricking on the p. SPEN 733:12
rough places p. BIBL 87:28
truth for p. people WESL 811:11
plainness Manifest p. LAO 451:10
perfect p. of speech ARNO 29:7
plains flowery p. of honour JONS 420:7
p. of windy Troy TENN 767:9
plaintive p. treble DISR 268:15
plaire *n'est pas de p.* MOLI 524:22
plaisir *P. d'amour* FLOR 318:20
plaister p. of the wall BIBL 90:3
plan by his p. of attack SASS 645:22
coherent p. to the universe HOYL 392:9
cunning p. CATC 195:28
not without a p. POPE 585:4
p. the future by the past BURK 162:9
rest on its original p. BURK 162:14
wagon of his 'P.' PAST 569:9
plane It's a p. ANON 16:7
only two emotions in a p. WELL 809:13
planes search me going into p. KEYE 434:17
planet born under a rhyming p. SHAK 691:22
hanging from a round p. EDDI 288:1
Jove's p. BROW 156:5
new p. swims into his ken KEAT 429:21
planetary p. influence SHAK 678:5
planets chronicle of the p. YEVT 838:11
people p. of its own BYRO 177:32
p. circle other suns POPE 585:6
p. in their stations MILT 517:8
plank landing on a p. EDDI 288:1
planned order of the acts is p. PAST 569:7
p. obsolescence STEV 739:17
planning p. is indispensable EISE 291:11
plans p. are useless EISE 291:11
plant Fame is no p. MILT 513:4
I p. lines WALC 799:3
p. for your heirs PROV 613:37
p. of rapid growth WASH 804:10
p. of slow growth PITT 576:21
Sensitive P. SHEL 713:22
That busy p. HERB 372:15
time to p. BIBL 84:7
What is a weed? A p. EMER 299:28
woman is not a potted p. WALK 799:10
Plantagenet where is P. CREW 244:22
plantation still working on a p. HOLI 380:21
planted I have p. BIBL 105:30
What our forefathers p. WITH 824:1
planter house of the p. CLAR 219:12
Ulsterman, of p. stock HEWI 378:1
planting p. my cabbages MONT 527:8
plants as the young p. BOOK 141:18
forced p. JOHN 416:14
He that p. trees FULL 327:12
p. suck in the earth COWL 239:10
talk to the p. CHAR 203:19
plasterer agog at the p. HEAN 366:8
plasters p., pills, and ointment LOCK 472:10
plastic cannot pass through p. JOHN 407:13
plastics p., Picasso, sunbathing WAUG 806:8
platinum bullets made of p. BELL 63:3
eyebrows made of p. FORS 320:8
platitude echo of a p. BIER 114:18
longitude with no p. FRY 326:23
p. is simply a truth repeated BALD 49:6
stroke a p. until it purrs MARQ 497:12
platitudes orchestration of p. WILD 819:16
Plato attachment à la P. GILB 338:19
be wrong with P. CICE 217:27
P. is dear to me ARIS 25:9
P.'s retirement MILT 518:8
P., thou reason'st well ADDI 4:16
p. told him: he couldn't CUMM 247:8
series of footnotes to P. WHIT 814:18
plaudits p. of the throng LONG 474:2
plausibly p. maintained BURR 169:13
play all the p., the insight BROW 155:3
All work and no p. PROV 595:6
better at a p. ANON 16:11
Better than a p. CHAR 203:7
boys late at their p. ARNO 27:2
cannot p. well BACO 42:18
children at p. MONT 527:11
come out to p. NURS 547:13
Did that p. of mine send out YEAT 836:17
Fair p.'s a jewel PROV 600:9
game at which two can p. BEER 61:16
Games people p. BERN 69:8
good p. needs no epilogue SHAK 659:29
holdeth children from p. SIDN 718:24
I could p. Ercles rarely SHAK 689:10
If you p. with fire PROV 603:35
Judge not the p. QUAR 618:15
Kings would not p. at COWP 242:5
let me not p. a woman SHAK 689:12
little victims p. GRAY 350:16
only to p. fair LABO 446:13
our p. is played out THAC 769:14
p. began to disgust EVEL 305:7
p. in Peoria POLI 581:18
P. it again, Sam FILM 311:12
P. it again, Sam MISQ 522:6
p. it over again LAMB 449:9
p.'s the thing SHAK 664:2
p. the game NEWB 541:18
p. the wantons SHAK 695:15
p. things as they are STEV 739:24
p. with my cat MONT 527:20
p. without a woman KYD 446:11
p. with souls BROW 156:16
p. with the gypsies NURS 549:15
presents you with a p. BOOT 142:19
rest of the p. PASC 568:14
rose up to p. BIBL 76:17
some foul p. SHAK 662:6
structure of a p. MILL 510:2
than see a p. BURT 170:17
very dull p. CONG 233:1
work, rest and p. ADVE 7:43
wouldst not p. false SHAK 682:1
written a damned p. REYN 625:2
y is p. EINS 290:17
Your p.'s hard to act CHEK 208:5
You would p. upon me SHAK 665:2
playbills time to read p. BURN 165:27
playboy lost the only P. SYNG 751:22
P. of the Western World CLOS 222:18
played He p. the King FIEL 309:10
p. our cards SCHE 646:12
p. the fool BIBL 78:37
playedst p. most foully for't SHAK 683:24
player as strikes the p. FITZ 314:16
p. on the other side HUXL 397:15
poor p., That struts SHAK 685:22
wrapped in a p.'s hide GREE 352:5
players men and women merely p. SHAK 658:25
P., Sir! I look JOHN 415:6
see the p. well bestowed SHAK 663:24
playing won on the p. fields WELL 810:1
work terribly hard at p. MORT 533:10
plays English p. are like VOLT 798:12
He that p. the king SHAK 663:19
loves no p. SHAK 674:18
Shaw's p. AGAT 6:15
plaything child's a p. LAMB 448:21
little p.-house WALP 800:15
p. of the boy BAGE 47:19
Plaza Toro Duke of P. GILB 337:5
plea Though justice be thy p. SHAK 688:11
without one p. ELLI 298:10
pleasance Youth is full of p. SHAK 703:27
pleasant abridgement of all that was p. GOLD 345:2
completed labours are p. CICE 217:11
do not find anything p. VOLT 797:6
green and p. bowers BLAK 119:5
green and p. land BLAK 120:1
in p. places BOOK 132:9
joyful and p. thing BOOK 141:24
Life would be very p. SURT 747:2
p. and clean work RUSK 638:16
p. it is to have money CLOU 221:22
P. to know Mr Lear LEAR 460:14
something p. happens MONT 528:18
that p. land BOOK 139:10
pleasantness ways are ways of p. BIBL 82:9

please can't p. everyone PROV 615:28
circumstance to p. us SWIF 749:23
do what I p. FRED 324:1
ladies to p. AUST 37:15
Little things p. PROV 605:44
live to p. JOHN 411:11
Myself alone I seek to p. GAY 332:12
never fails to p. SEDL 653:4
Nothing can p. many JOHN 410:11
only Self to p. BLAK 121:2
p. thee with my answer SHAK 688:7
p. the touchy breed of poets HORA 387:9
P. your eye PROV 609:29
those whom I wished to p. JOHN 412:20
To tax and to p. BURK 162:20
'twas natural to p. DRYD 279:19
pleased All seemed well p. MILT 517:2
consists in being p. HAZL 365:11
have p. leading men HORA 386:22
in whom I am well p. BIBL 92:31
more had p. us ADDI 4:5
p. not the million SHAK 663:23
p. with what he gets SHAK 658:22
pleases every prospect p. HEBE 367:7
pleaseth this age best p. me HERR 374:19
pleasing art of p. HAZL 365:11
method that I know of p. CHES 209:11
p. one intelligent man MAIM 491:6
turns to p. pain SPEN 734:4
pleasure aching P. nigh KEAT 429:5
Business before p. PROV 596:43
by their favourite p. VIRG 795:19
cabinet of p. HERB 373:2
doth ever add p. BACO 44:16
egg by p. laid COWP 241:4
fading p. SIDN 718:20
fine p. is not to do HOPK 385:8
fool bolts p. ANTR 22:19
For physical p. WAUG 806:17
for thy p. BIBL 112:1
full of p. CHAL 200:10
give p. MOLI 524:22
giving immediate p. WORD 832:19
go to my p., business WYCH 834:9
go to sea for p. PROV 602:22
greatest p. I know LAMB 449:7
great source of p. JOHN 409:25
Green p. or grey grief SWIN 751:14
harmless p. JOHN 410:8
heart with p. fills WORD 828:27
If they have p. BARC 53:22
if this is p. COWA 238:11
impression of p. BACO 41:6
I' the east my p. lies SHAK 656:29
left you for their p. BROW 158:7
little p. in the house MICK 507:2
lordly p.-house TENN 765:8
Love ceases to be a p. BEHN 62:7
make poetry and give p. HORA 389:3
meant by the p. of life TALL 753:6
miss for p. GAY 332:23
mixed profit with p. HORA 386:3
no p. in the strength BOOK 141:25
No p., nor no pain SEDL 653:1
No p. worth giving up AMIS 14:3
not in p. DRYD 281:29
on p. she was bent COWP 240:13
painful p. SPEN 734:4
pay a debt to p. ROCH 630:6
p. after pain DRYD 280:18
p. afterwards THAC 769:4
p. and repentance RALE 620:10
P. at the helm GRAY 350:5
p. in poetic pains COWP 241:22
p. in recalling CATU 197:14
p. in the pathless woods BYRO 175:8
P. is a thief DEFO 254:12
p. is momentary CHES 209:26
p. is not enhanced AUST 37:18
P. is nothing else SELD 653:22
p. lives in height TENN 766:4
p. me in his top-boots MARL 495:14
P. never is at home KEAT 427:20
p. of feeling FOST 321:13
p. of the fleeting year SHAK 705:8
P.'s a sin BYRO 176:6
p.'s done SCHI 730:10
P.'s for those who are bad YESE 838:8
p. so exquisite HUNT 396:6
p. sure, In being mad DRYD 282:24
p. to learn CONF 231:3
p. to the spectators MACA 482:14
p. was his business EDGE 288:15
privilege and p. GILB 337:7
read without p. JOHN 418:15
secondary p. STEN 737:15
Short p. SCOT 650:3
soul of p. BEHN 62:13
stately p.-dome decree COLE 225:20
suburbs Of your good p. SHAK 675:7
taking a little p. CHAR 203:8
to p. all they find GREE 351:14
type of a perfect p. WILD 818:19
Without one p. TENN 763:18
Youth and P. meet BYRO 174:14
pleasures all the p. prove MARL 496:19
celibacy has no p. JOHN 410:27
childish p. ALAI 9:16
deprive us of all the p. HAYW 365:3
English take their p. SULL 746:3
fool who delights in p. JAIN 401:13
hate the idle p. SHAK 696:11
here below for minor p. GRES 353:1
hypcrite in his p. JOHN 417:15
lords have their p. MONT 528:9
owes its p. COWP 241:28
paucity of human p. JOHN 418:9
p. and palaces PAYN 570:14
p. are like poppies BURN 168:13
p. of sense BHAG 72:19
p. of the senses ESHE 301:8
purest of human p. BACO 43:4
renounced those p. SOCR 727:5
some new p. prove DONN 273:19
Summers p. they are gone CLAR 218:18
tear our p. MARV 499:4
two supreme p. ROSE 633:19
understand the p. AUST 37:14
yesterday's p. DONN 275:9
pleats witty little p. BAIL 48:4
plebeian this the P. bran DONN 275:6
plebiscite justice by p. ZOBE 840:7
plectuntur *p. Achivi* HORA 386:13
pledge I will p. with mine JONS 420:20
p. allegiance BELL 62:24
pledged p. their troth BOOK 131:8
Pleiades influences of P. BIBL 81:34
Pleiads rainy P. wester HOUS 390:11
pleni *P. sunt coeli* MISS 520:21
plenteously p. bringing forth BOOK 128:20
plenteousness all things living with p. BOOK 141:20
p. with thy palaces BOOK 140:15
plenty but just had p. BURN 166:27
expectation of p. SHAK 683:13
here is God's p. DRYD 283:11
In delay there lies no p. SHAK 701:10
P. has made me poor OVID 561:15
P. in the maize TENN 766:5
Where P. smiles CRAB 243:15
pleuré *quelquefois p.* MUSS 537:12
pleut *il p. sa ville* VERL 791:11
pli *sans un p.* ROST 635:12
plie *Je p. et ne romps pas* LA F 447:10
taking their p. BURG 162:5
plight p. thee my troth BOOK 131:5
plods ploughman homeward p. GRAY 350:6
plot discerned in history a p. FISH 313:11
Gunpowder Treason and P. ANON 18:9
now the p. thickens BUCK 159:15
p. for a short story CHEK 208:7
p. is like COMP 230:18
Sonnet's scanty p. WORD 829:12
This blessèd p. SHAK 694:19
What is the p. good for BUCK 159:14
plots All my plays' p. CAVE 198:11
P., true or false DRYD 279:20
plotting most p. heart RICH 627:2
plough Behind his p. WORD 831:12
boy that driveth the p. TYND 787:4
plod behind the p. CRAB 243:12
p. my furrow alone ROSE 633:18
p. the fields CAMP 182:14
put his hand to the p. BIBL 99:7
wherefore p. SHEL 713:25
ploughed p. with my heifer BIBL 78:2
ploughman heavy p. snores SHAK 690:28
p. and professor JEFF 405:6
p. homeward plods GRAY 350:6
wrong even the poorest p. CHAR 203:3
ploughs p., ladies, bears CANN 185:10
ploughshare Soldiers of the p. RUSK 639:3
ploughshares swords into p. BIBL 86:13
plowers p. plowed upon my back BOOK 140:25
pluck I'll p. it down SHAK 672:30
p. it out BIBL 96:9
p. till time and times are done YEAT 837:12
plucked p. my nipple SHAK 682:17
plum biscuit, or confectionary p. COWP 240:26
buy a p. bun NURS 551:14
p. year, a dumb year PROV 597:14
pulled out a p. NURS 549:6
Some gave them p. cake NURS 549:3
plumage If you have bright p. CLAR 219:4
pities the p. PAIN 563:19
plumber choose to be a p. EINS 291:3
plumbers good p. NIXO 546:7
plume blast-beruffled p. HARD 361:11
Ruffles her pure cold p. TENN 760:18
tail was a p. LEON 464:10
plummet did ever p. sound SHAK 699:10
lie a leaden p. FORD 319:21
plump meet it p. ROCH 630:1
plums p. and orange peel RALE 621:12
plunder no man stop to p. MACA 483:2
What a place to p. MISQ 522:13
pluralism p. in social attitudes BOWI 145:23
plures *Abiit ad p.* PETR 574:15
plus *Il n'y a p. de Pyrénées* LOUI 476:1
P. ça change KARR 426:1
Plutonian Night's P. shore POE 579:17
plying a-p. up and down KIPL 439:11
Plymouth dreamin' arl the time o' P. Hoe NEWB 541:15
poacher old p. makes the best PROV 608:24
p. staggering MCCA 483:18
Pobble P. who has no toes LEAR 460:20
pocket guinea you have in your p. RUSK 639:2
gun in your p. WEST 812:7
hand in its breeches p. KEAT 431:1
in Britain, in your p. WILS 821:18
in each other's p. BIER 114:17
lost her p. NURS 549:11
not scruple to pick a p. DENN 258:1
pecker in my p. JOHN 408:18
picking his p. JOHN 408:11
put it in his p. SHAK 665:18
pockets hands in holey p. RIMB 628:10
in the p. of the people GLAD 341:15
jingle in his p. COWP 242:18
Shrouds have no p. PROV 610:38
young man feels his p. HOUS 390:8
poem begin a p. MCGO 485:11
being the author of that p. WOLF 825:7
drowsy frowzy p. BYRO 176:30
essentially the greatest p. WHIT 816:1
Every good p. is a bridge DAY- 253:15
figure a p. makes FROS 326:13
heroic p. of its sort CARL 187:11
himself to be a true p. MILT 519:5
long p. is a test KEAT 430:20
many beauties grace a p. HORA 386:4

poem *(cont.)*:
married to a p. KEAT 431:15
music of a p. SYNG 751:21
p. is like a painting HORA 386:6
p. lovely as a tree KILM 435:20
p. must ride on its own melting FROS 326:15
P. of the Sea RIMB 628:7
p. should be palpable MACL 487:1
p. should not mean but be MACL 487:3
p., whose subject CHAP 202:22
pretty p., Mr Pope BENT 67:10
write a p. after Auschwitz ADOR 6:7
poemata *Scribimus indocti doctique p.* HORA 387:6
poems no p. than bad poems LARK 453:11
P. are made by fools like me KILM 436:1
p. should be Clyde-built DUNN 285:10
we all scribble p. HORA 387:6
Poesie *P. des Lebens* GOET 343:7
poesis *Ut pictura p.* HORA 386:6
poesy call p. *vinum daemonum* BACO 41:17
heaven-bred p. SHAK 702:28
overwhelm Myself in p. KEAT 430:3
P. was ever thought BACO 41:11
viewless wings of P. KEAT 429:11
poet All a p. can do is warn OWEN 562:4
and the P.'s dream WORD 828:2
ask a p. to sing BOLD 124:12
business of a comic p. CONG 232:8
business of a p. JOHN 410:24
dreams of a p. JOHN 409:6
every fool is not a p. POPE 582:27
every p., in his kind SWIF 749:19
Fat-head p. that nobody reads CHES 210:7
flattery lost on p.'s ear SCOT 650:17
found no sacred p. ELIO 292:16
gentleman p. JOYC 422:11
grete p. of Ytaille CHAU 206:1
hate what every p. hates KAVA 426:11
have a p. able-bodied MACN 488:18
Honour the greatest p. DANT 249:10
Is this the great p. GARR 330:6
I was a p., I was young FLEC 317:7
lack their sacred p. HORA 389:9
Like a P. hidden SHEL 714:6
limbs of a p. HORA 387:10
lost on p.'s ear CLOS 222:8
Love made me p. EPIT 303:14
lover, and the p. SHAK 690:18
masculine part, the p. in me BEHN 62:8
modern p.'s fate HOOD 383:2
never be a p. DRYD 283:18
No p. ever interpreted GIRA 340:8
Not deep the P. sees ARNO 26:24
passionate heart of the p. TENN 763:22
P. and Saint COWL 239:21
p. and the dreamer KEAT 427:19
p. and the theme COWP 242:16
p. image aught so fair THOM 775:19
p. includes a critic SHEN 715:10
p. is like the prince BAUD 57:5
p. is the priest STEV 739:18
p. kings KEAT 430:5
p. ranks far below the painter LEON 464:19
p. seems most himself YEAT 837:26
p.'s eye, in a fine frenzy SHAK 690:19
p.'s gift is to soothe YESE 838:7
p.'s hope: to be AUDE 35:5
p.'s inward pride DAY- 253:12
p.'s mouth be shut YEAT 836:21
p.'s pen, all scorn BRAD 146:14
p. spewed up a good lump DRYD 283:14
p. stubborn with his passion YEAT 835:4
p.'s voice FAUL 307:28
p. will give up writing CELA 199:11
P. writes under one restriction WORD 832:19
poor p. named Clough SWIN 751:15
possess a p.'s brain DRAY 279:6
skilled p. PIND 576:9
starved p. LOCK 472:10
there is a p. indulging MAHO 490:19
Vex not thou the p.'s mind TENN 765:11
war p. whose right of honour GURN 355:3
was a true P. BLAK 119:11
what is left the p. here BYRO 176:27
poetae *Etiam disiecti membra p.* HORA 389:18
poète *poète est semblable* BAUD 57:5
poetic constitutes p. faith COLE 227:12
nurse for a p. child SCOT 651:2
P. Genius of my country BURN 169:11
P. Justice POPE 580:8
P. LICENCE BANV 53:11
poetical As to the p. character KEAT 431:10
claim to p. honours JOHN 410:4
poetis *Mediocribus esse p. Pictoribus atque p.* HORA 386:7
HORA 385:11
poetry best piece of p. JONS 420:17
bother about p. COCT 223:21
by no means rank p. BYRO 179:25
campaign in p. CUOM 247:18
car was p. and tragedy LEWI 467:7
cradled into p. by wrong SHEL 711:21
dead art Of p. POUN 589:12
deeper intimacy with p. NERU 541:5
drops into p. DICK 264:22
Emptied of its p. AUDE 34:2
give p. a proper flow BOIL 124:4
gold medal for p. GRAV 349:19
grand style arises in p. ARNO 29:8
I can repeat p. CARR 191:5
If p. comes not KEAT 431:2
Ireland hurt you into p. AUDE 33:31
It is not p. POPE 583:6
know it to be p. THOR 775:28
Language is fossil p. EMER 299:27
language of p. GRAY 351:6
mincing p. SHAK 668:21
misfortune of p. AUST 38:9
most p. ignores most people MITC 523:11
neither p. nor any thing else BYRO 180:10
p. administers to the effect SHEL 714:21
p. almost necessarily declines MACA 481:15
P. and Religion CARL 187:18
p. begins to atrophy POUN 590:2
p. happens between the ears DUNN 285:13
p. in money GRAV 349:20
p. in motion KAUF 426:5
P., in the most comprehensive HUNT 395:20
P. is a subject as precise FLAU 316:15
P. is at bottom ARNO 28:24
P. is a way FROS 326:10
[P.] is capable of saving us RICH 626:16
P. is certainly something more COLE 227:22
p. is eloquent painting SIMO 720:13
P. is in the pity OWEN 562:3
p. is more philosophical ARIS 24:23
P. is not most important THOM 772:22
P. is pre-eminently the medium FLAU 316:12
P. is the achievement SAND 644:3
P. is the breath WORD 832:21
P. is the record of the best SHEL 714:23
P. is the spontaneous overflow WORD 832:20
P. is the supreme fiction STEV 739:23
p. is very difficult MOOR 530:5
P. is what is lost FROS 326:19
P. is when some of them BENT 67:1
p. makes nothing happen AUDE 34:1
P. must be *as well written* POUN 590:6
p. of earth KEAT 429:23
p. of life GOET 343:7
p. of motion GRAH 348:8
p., prophecy, and religion RUSK 638:11
P.'s a mere drug FARQ 307:19
P.'s another word DURC 286:1
P. shall tune her sacred voice JOHN 411:8
P. should be great KEAT 431:1
P.'s the feverish fit WINC 822:20
p. = the *best* words COLE 227:20
P. there, is an art SIDN 718:23
P. Unearths from among the dead HILL 376:15
P. wants something DIDE 267:3
p., which is in Oxford DRYD 282:14
polar star of p. KEAT 430:20
quarrel with ourselves, p. YEAT 837:25
saying it and that is p. CAGE 181:1
saying so In whining p. DONN 274:17
She that with p. is won BUTL 172:7
significance of p. ISHE 400:9
Sir, what is p. JOHN 415:19
stimulated by p. CONF 231:17
That I make p. HORA 389:3
their p. is conceived ARNO 28:23
trying to say was p. OVID 561:23
turn to p. ARNO 28:22
We hate p. that has KEAT 431:1
What is p. RUSK 638:9
Writing a book of p. MARQ 497:11
poets All p. are mad BURT 170:7
amatory p. sing BYRO 177:7
for wits, then p. passed POPE 584:12
Greek, Latin p. CAVE 198:11
if there's room for p. BROW 154:10
impossible to hold the p. back GIRA 340:7
Irish p., learn your trade YEAT 837:20
mature p. steal ELIO 296:18
mighty P. in their misery WORD 831:14
No death has hurt p. more HEAN 367:1
only p. know COWP 241:22
Painters and p. HORA 385:11
pensive p. POPE 580:9
P. are the hierophants SHEL 714:24
p. are their own patients THOM 773:12
p. being second-rate HORA 386:7
p. bicycle-pump the human heart AMIS 13:16
P.' food is love SHEL 711:10
P. like painters POPE 584:18
P. must be *difficult* ELIO 296:21
p. only deliver a golden SIDN 718:22
P. should never marry GONN 346:11
P. that are sown WORD 828:7
P. that lasting marble seek WALL 800:4
P. . . . though liars HUME 395:5
p. took their golden age THOM 775:3
p. witty BACO 44:8
powerful p. of the century ELIO 296:20
prince of p. BYRO 176:29
romantic p. LEAP 460:1
Souls of p. dead KEAT 428:20
Tenderest of Roman p. TENN 758:20
theft in other p. DRYD 283:7
think all p. were Byronic COPE 236:9
Three p. in an age SWIF 749:13
touchy breed of p. HORA 387:9
We p. in our youth WORD 831:12
who wants p. at all HÖLD 380:18
worst of p. ranks CATU 197:8
youthful p. dream MILT 512:24
point Aloof from the entire p. SHAK 678:1
different p. of view NAPO 538:11
from p. to point TENN 763:4
p. a moral JOHN 411:16
p. his slow finger SHAK 693:13
still p. of the turning world ELIO 294:4
That was the p. ELIO 293:22
too fine a p. upon it DICK 260:21
upon a needle's p. CUDW 247:1
Up to a p., Lord Copper WAUG 806:10
You've hit the p. PLAU 578:14
points P. have no parts LIND 469:6
poising p. every weight MARV 498:12
poison another man's p. PROV 608:48
coward's weapon, p. FLET 318:19
food only a cover for p. BURK 164:15
got as far as p.-gas HARD 361:8
honey of p.-flowers TENN 763:23
if you p. us SHAK 687:30
p. in jest SHAK 664:24
p. the wells NEWM 542:3
p. the whole blood stream fills EMPS 300:7
p. wells MARL 496:17
put p. in your coffee CHUR 216:23
strongest p. ever known BLAK 118:3
tell them to drink the p. PLAT 578:3
Turning to p. KEAT 429:5

poisoned may have been p. FIEL 310:23
p. rat in a hole SWIF 748:11
taste like p. rubber LEON 464:9
poisoning P. pigeons LEHR 462:17
poisonous for its p. wine KEAT 429:2
p. reptiles to live in it GIRA 340:4
poisons p. all the rest WATT 805:4
well of p. GIRA 340:3
poke p. poor Billy GRAH 348:5
poker p. of whom every one is afraid MITF 524:4
pokers p. into true-love knots COLE 226:2
polar p. star of poetry KEAT 430:20
pole curses from p. to pole BLAK 118:16
from pole to p. COLE 226:20
From p. to pole THOM 775:7
top of the greasy p. DISR 271:2
polecat semi-house-trained p. FOOT 319:3
polemic don't watch BBC for p. SIMP 720:15
police among p. officers ORTO 558:3
citizen or the p. AUDE 35:2
friendship recognised by the p. STEV 741:27
p. can beat you SHAW 709:3
p. were to blame GRAN 348:14
policeman p. and a pretty girl CHAP 202:9
p.'s lot GILB 339:5
terrorist and the p. CONR 234:21
than a p. SALI 643:4
would not do for a p. NIGH 545:24
policemen P., like red squirrels ORTO 558:2
policy defend a bad p. SALI 643:5
English p. is to float SALI 642:14
home p.: I wage war CLEM 220:10
Honesty is the best p. PROV 602:45
Honesty is the best p. WHAT 813:10
If the p. isn't hurting MAJO 491:14
My [foreign] p. BEVI 72:10
national p. BRIA 148:5
p. of retaliation PARN 567:26
p. of the good neighbour ROOS 632:13
religion or p. RUSK 638:24
rugged brow of careful P. SPEN 733:6
some love but little p. SHAK 695:26
tyrants from p. BURK 163:24
polish contented to p. MORE 531:3
p. it at leisure DRYD 283:2
polished I p. up the handle GILB 338:27
O p. perturbation SHAK 670:14
p. corners of the temple BOOK 141:18
p. dry with pumice CATU 194:19
polite no allies to be p. to GEOR 334:7
p. meaningless words YEAT 835:18
time to be p. MONT 528:10
politeness glance of great p. BYRO 179:15
pineapple of p. SHER 715:26
p. of kings LOUI 476:5
p. of princes PROV 609:48
suave p. KNOX 442:12
political fear of P. Economy SELL 654:12
half your p. life THAT 770:1
healthy state of p. life MILL 508:20
highest p. end ACTO 1:15
I've kept p. diaries GEOG 333:8
my p. creed ADAM 3:11
nature of a p. party TROL 783:3
points to a p. career SHAW 707:27
p. animal ARIS 25:2
p. Cave of Adullam BRIG 148:14
p. consequences MANS 494:10
p. economist BAGE 47:9
p. genius TAYL 756:9
p. intriguer TROL 781:21
P. language . . . is designed ORWE 559:11
p. lives end in failure POWE 590:21
p. power of another LOCK 472:3
p. speech and writing ORWE 559:10
P. thought, in France ARON 29:18
p. will LYNN 480:21
Principles of P. Economy BENT 67:5
schemes of p. improvement JOHN 414:4
politician greatest art of a p. BOLI 124:19
like a scurvy p. SHAK 679:25
lurks a p. ARIS 24:13
makes the p. wise POPE 587:9
my life as a p. POWE 590:20
pate of a p. SHAK 666:21
p. is a man TRUM 784:5
p. is an arse upon CUMM 247:7
p. is a statesman who POMP 580:7
p. never believes what he says DE G 255:26
p. ought to sacrifice BURK 164:7
P.'s corpse BELL 63:14
p. to complain about POWE 590:18
p. tops his part GAY 332:13
p. urges them to rebel PERU 574:8
p. was a person LLOY 471:7
when a p. does get an idea MARQ 497:10
wise p. OLIV 553:14
politicians Conviction p. BANC 53:5
die for p. THOM 774:18
fault of our p. TROL 782:24
Old p. chew POPE 584:5
one of those p. TROL 782:8
P. also have no leisure ARIS 24:20
p. have had to listen FITT 314:4
p. hear the word 'culture' ESHE 301:7
P. often believe ROTH 635:20
too serious to be left to p. DE G 255:23
whole race of p. SWIF 747:22
politics Confound their p. SONG 729:8
continuation of p. CLAU 219:19
first part of p. MICH 506:16
From p., it was an easy step AUST 38:5
give his mind to p. SHAW 706:14
In p., if you want anything THAT 769:20
in p. the middle way ADAM 3:6
In p., there is no use CHAM 200:12
In p., what begins in fear COLE 227:24
invisible hand in p. FRIE 325:1
I taste no p. SMIT 725:8
language of p. DISR 268:19
Magnanimity in p. BURK 163:8
Modern p. ADAM 3:1
mule of p. DISR 270:4
no true friends in p. CLAR 219:2
parties 'playing p.' WILS 822:8
Philistine of genius in p. ARNO 29:4
playful moderation in p. HUNT 396:4
p. and equations EINS 291:6
P. and the fate CAMU 184:4
P. are now nothing more JOHN 415:5
P., as a practice ADAM 2:13
P. can only be KEEN 432:9
p. consists in ignoring facts ADAM 2:22
P., executive expression BRIT 149:1
p. grease TAWN 755:12
P. has got to be fun CLAR 219:5
P. in the middle STEN 737:17
P. is not the art GALB 328:11
p. is present history FREE 324:3
P. is the art of preventing VALÉ 789:3
P. is the Art of the Possible BUTL 171:16
P. is the chloroform GOGA 343:19
P. is the only profession STEV 741:4
P. is war without bloodshed MAO 495:1
p. like ours profess GREE 351:11
P. makes strange PROV 609:30
p. of happiness HUMP 395:9
p. of the left JENK 406:7
P. supposed to be REAG 623:3
P. too serious a matter DE G 255:23
practice of p. DISR 270:8
science of p. ARIS 24:16
secret of p. BISM 116:5
than it has with p. SHER 715:21
These are my p. STEV 741:8
week is a long time in p. WILS 821:16
will not close my p. FOX 322:6
zeal in p. JUNI 423:14
politique p. father JAME 402:15
Polka see me dance the P. GROS 354:2
polluted filthy and p. BIBL 90:23
Pemberley thus p. AUST 38:23
pollution engine of p., the dog SPAR 731:22
p. of democracy WHIT 814:9
Polly Little P. Flinders NURS 549:8
Our P. is a sad slut GAY 331:10
P. put the kettle on NURS 550:8
polyanthus p. of unnumbered dyes THOM 775:4
polygamous Man is p. JAME 404:6
polygamy chaste p. CARE 186:10
p. was made a sin DRYD 279:17
polygony panachaea, or p. SPEN 734:3
pomegranate from Browning some 'P.' BROW 154:18
piece of a p. BIBL 85:14
Pomeranian P. grenadier BISM 116:9
pomp bright p. ascended MILT 517:8
grinning at his p. SHAK 695:10
p. and plenty JOHN 417:21
p. and state BEAU 58:14
p. of pow'r GRAY 350:9
p. of waters DANI 248:16
p. of yesterday KIPL 440:4
Pride, p., and circumstance SHAK 692:30
Take physic, p. SHAK 679:1
tide of p. SHAK 671:20
Pompey Knew you not P. SHAK 674:3
P. the Great SHAK 671:13
pompous p. in the grave BROW 153:10
pomps high Midsummer p. ARNO 27:27
p. and vanity BOOK 130:11
pond have their stream and p. BROO 150:9
Old p., leap-splash BASH 56:17
ponder P. anew WINK 823:9
pondered p. them in her heart BIBL 98:23
ponies Five and twenty p. KIPL 440:8
wretched, blind, pit p. HODG 379:13
Pontefract licorice fields at P. BETJ 70:15
poo feel for the p. LAND 449:19
poodle in a p. parlour PARR 568:3
right hon. Gentleman's p. LLOY 470:16
pooh yawn, or 'P.' BYRO 177:27
pool flies over this p. SIKH 720:5
must first fill a p. BACO 43:18
Walk across my swimming p. RICE 626:8
pools p. are filled with water BOOK 137:12
Where the p. are bright HOGG 380:11
poop O p.-poop GRAH 348:9
poor annals of the p. GRAY 350:9
apt the p. are to be proud SHAK 702:1
Blessed are the p. BIBL 93:3
bring in hither the p. BIBL 99:29
congregation of the p. BOOK 136:21
cottages of the p. HORA 387:16
dare to be p. GAY 332:18
destruction of the p. BIBL 82:21
feed with the p. GARR 330:2
found'st me p. at first GOLD 344:19
give food to the p. CAMA 182:10
given to the p. BIBL 97:15
give to the p. BIBL 96:13
Good to the p. CARE 186:9
grind the faces of the p. BIBL 86:14
help the many who are p. KENN 433:11
how expensive it is to be p. BALD 48:19
inconvenient to be p. COWP 239:29
Laws grind the p. GOLD 345:10
let the p., and Thou HERB 373:16
live by robbing the p. SHAW 708:3
makes me p. indeed SHAK 692:20
murmuring p. CRAB 243:3
My countrymen Kiltartan's p. YEAT 836:9
no disgrace t'be p. HUBB 392:14
no peasant in my kingdom so p. HENR 370:4
not that men are p. DU B 284:3
open to the p. and the rich ANON 16:10
pastor for the p. ZORO 841:16
Plenty has made me p. OVID 561:15
p. always ye have BIBL 102:13
p. and needy BOOK 134:3
p. are Europe's blacks CHAM 201:9
p. but she was honest MILI 508:14
p. don't know that their function SART 645:8

poor (*cont.*):
p. get children KAHN 425:10
p. have cried SHAK 676:1
p. have no right RUSK 639:5
p. in a loomp is bad TENN 765:1
p. know that it is money BREN 147:22
P. little rich girl COWA 238:17
p. man at his gate ALEX 11:9
p. man had nothing BIBL 79:5
p. man loved the great MACA 483:7
p. man's dearest friend BURN 167:27
p. man slipped BIBL 91:29
p. soul sat sighing SHAK 693:18
p. who die SART 644:20
p. wot gets the blame MILI 508:14
propensity for being p. AUST 39:12
realize that he was p. USTI 788:23
Resolve not to be p. JOHN 416:27
RICH AND THE P. DISR 270:23
rich as well as the p. FRAN 322:15
rich on the p. JEFF 405:4
rich woman as a p. woman THAC 769:1
snatches senses from p. me CATU 197:9
so p. to do him reverence SHAK 676:4
steward for the p. POPE 583:21
Too p. for a bribe GRAY 351:5
undeserving p. SHAW 709:13
will be so p. ELIO 293:1
your tired, your p. LAZA 459:12
poorer for richer for p. BOOK 131:5
poorest p. he that is in England RAIN 620:6
p. man may in his cottage PITT 576:20
poorly P. (poor man) he lived FLET 318:17
pop P. goes the weasel MAND 493:6
pope against the P. or the NUM BALD 49:12
God bless our P. WISE 823:16
P.! How many divisions STAL 736:3
P. is quite satisfied MICH 506:15
striving with the P. PROV 604:19
to the P. afterwards TOAS 778:3
popery danger of P. ADDI 5:8
popinjay pestered with a p. SHAK 667:23
popish P. liturgy PITT 576:24
poplars p. are felled COWP 241:1
poppies fume of p. KEAT [illegible]
In Flanders p. the poppies blow MCCR 484:12
pleasures are like p. BURN 168:13
poppy not to wear a p. MCAL 481:4
p., nor mandragora SHAK 692:29
with a p. or a lily GILB 338:20
populace Barbarians, Philistines, and P. ARNO 28:7
clamours of the p. ADAM 3:3
give the name of P. ARNO 28:11
p. rise at once WHIT 815:9
popular loved to be p. JAME 403:21
strong p. feeling TROL 782:19
popularity every difficulty except p. WILD 819:10
population p., when unchecked MALT 493:3
talked of p. GOLD 345:25
populi *p., vox humbug* SHER 716:26
Salus p. CICE 217:12
Salus p. suprema lex SELD 653:21
Vox p. ALCU 10:10
porcelain dainty rogue in p. MERE 505:13
porcupines throw p. under you KHRU 435:18
pork p. please our mouths MENG 505:1
raw p. and opium BYRO 180:10
Porlock on business from P. COLE 225:19
Person from P. SMIT 724:25
pornographic p. show BLUN 122:14
pornography p. is really about SONT 728:6
p. of war RAE 620:5
P. the attempt to insult sex LAWR 458:3
porpentine quills upon the fretful p. SHAK 662:25
porpoise p. close behind us CARR 190:4
porridge consistency of cold p. TURI 785:10
healsome p. BURN 166:24
like cold p. SHAK 698:29
Pease p. hot NURS 550:6
sand in the p. COWA 238:11
Porson Wordsworth drunk and P. sober HOUS 391:11
port Any p. in a storm PROV 595:8
bent to make some p. ARNO 27:23
be p. if it could BENT 67:11
dissolved in p. POPE 580:16
In every p. a wife DIBD 260:12
In ev'ry p. a mistress GAY 332:21
little p. Had seldom seen CLOS 222:4
p., for men JOHN 416:8
p. is near WHIT 815:4
There lies the p. TENN 767:12
to which p. one is sailing SENE 654:17
portae *geminae Somni p.* VIRG 795:3
portal fiery p. of the east SHAK 695:12
fitful tracing of a p. STEV 740:2
porter devil-p. it no further SHAK 683:14
moon shone bright on Mrs P. ELIO 296:7
p. of hell-gate SHAK 683:13
Portia P. is Brutus' harlot SHAK 675:7
portion p. for foxes BOOK 135:25
p. of a good man's life WORD 829:2
their p. to drink BOOK 132:3
portmanteau like a p. CARR 191:4
portrait Every time I paint a p. SARG 644:17
p. of a blinking idiot SHAK 687:25
p. of the artist JOYC 421:22
styles of p. painting DICK 263:23
portraits put up and take down p. LICH 467:17
ports five p. of knowledge BROW 152:14
posies pocket full of p. NURS 550:13
position altering the p. of matter RUSS 639:17
only p. for women CARM 188:23
p. must be held to the last man HAIG 356:9
p. ridiculous CHES 209:26
positions p. of considerable emolument GAIS 327:19
positive ac-cent-tchu-ate the p. MERC 505:5
most p. men POPE 587:21
power of p. thinking PEAL 571:6
possess you may p. it GOET 342:16
possessed in order to be p. BURK 162:13
Love once p. [illegible]
much p. by death ELIO 296:16
p. his land BIBL 76:27
possessing p. all things BIBL 107:9
too dear for my p. SHAK 705:4
possession in the glad p. JONS 420:4
just p. of truth BROW 153:14
never your p. BROC 149:3
P. is nine points PROV 609:31
p. of them both KEAT 431:16
right, title, and p. BOOK 142:14
possessions All my p. LAST 455:2
behind the great p. JAME 403:6
he had great p. BIBL 96:14
he who has many p. HORA 389:10
least of p. WHIT 814:6
multitude of p. SMAR 722:4
possibilities improbable p. ARIS 25:1
possibility deny the p. of anything HUXL 398:1
p. of suicide CIOR 218:3
possible All things are p. with God PROV 595:4
all things p. BACO 45:1
art of the p. BISM 116:6
Art of the P. BUTL 171:16
art of the p. GALB 328:11
best of all p. worlds BRAD 146:7
if a thing is p. CALO 182:1
p. you may be mistaken CROM 245:12
realm of the p. PIND 576:10
something is p. CLAR 219:8
with God all things are p. BIBL 96:16
possidentem *p. multa* HORA 389:10
possum said the Honourable P. BERR 70:1
possumus *Non omnia p. omnes* VIRG 796:10
possunt *p., quia posse videntur* VIRG 794:15
post driving briskly in a p.-chaise JOHN 415:22
LIE FOLLOWS BY P. TELE 758:11
p. Allotted by the Gods TENN 763:17
P. coitum SAYI 648:2
p. of honour ADDI 4:15
p. of honour PROV 609:33
postage defrays the p. STEV 741:14
postal p. districts packed like squares of wheat LARK 453:8
posted p. presence of the watcher JAME 403:11
poster Kitchener is a great p. ASQU 31:7
p. a visual telegram CASS 193:9
posteri *Credite p.* HORA 388:10
posterity correspondent for p. BAGE 47:22
damage to p. WITH 824:1
go down to p. DISR 269:26
hope of p. POWE 591:1
looked upon by p. CLOS 222:12
look forward to p. BURK 163:16
P. as likely to be BROU 151:16
P. do something for us ADDI 5:17
Think of your p. ADAM 3:16
To evoke p. GRAV 349:16
trustees of P. DISR 270:26
write for p. ADE 5:20
postern p. door makes a thief PROV 609:32
Present has latched its p. HARD 361:6
posters P. of the sea and land SHAK 681:13
Posthumus Ah! P., the years SMAR 722:14
Post-Impressionist P. pictures BLUN 122:14
term P. WINT 823:12
postman p. always rings twice CAIN 181:2
think I am, a bloody p. BEHA 62:4
postmaster make him a p. HIND 377:13
posts fenced in with p. WINT 823:12
postscript but in her p. STEE 736:16
Here is yet a p. SHAK 701:30
most material in the p. BACO 42:20
pith is in the p. HAZL 365:4
postures lie down in clean p. FOWL 321:20
posy I made a p. HERB 372:21
pot chicken in every p. HOOV 383:11
chicken in his p. HENR 370:4
death in the p. BIBL 80:16
flinging a p. of paint RUSK [illegible]
Joan doth keel the p. SHAK 681:4
kettle and the earthen p. BIBL 91:28
Look at p. NASH 539:14
under a p. BIBL 84:13
watched p. never boils PROV 613:40
who the p. FITZ 314:20
potations dull and deep p. GIBB 335:18
potato bashful young p. GILB 338:19
p.-gatherers move KAVA 426:9
potent how p. cheap music is COWA 239:3
potion p. and his pill HERR 374:11
potions What p. have I drunk SHAK 705:18
Potomac All quiet along the P. BEER 61:18
quiet along the P. MCCL 484:7
potoribus *scribuntur aquae p.* HORA 387:4
pots have lien among the p. BOOK 136:7
potsherd Let the p. strive BIBL 88:7
poor p., patch HOPK 384:22
took him a p. BIBL 81:1
pottage mess of p. BIBL 74:34
potter hand then of the p. FITZ 314:19
p. and clay endure BROW 157:20
p. power over the clay BIBL 105:13
p.'s vessel BOOK 131:17
Who *is* the p., pray FITZ 314:20
pouch p. on side SHAK 659:2
poultry lives of the p. ELIO 292:9
pound in for a p. PROV 603:47
p. foolish PROV 609:24
p. here in Britain WILS 821:18
pounding Hard p. this WELL 809:16
pounds Give crowns and p. HOUS 390:18
how many p. JUVE 424:22
p. will take care LOWN 478:9
p. will take care of PROV 611:38

six hundred p. a-year SWIF 749:7
three hundred p. SHAK 688:35
two hundred p. a year BUTL 172:11
pour P. into our hearts BOOK 128:13
p. out my spirit BIBL 90:14
poured p. into his clothes WODE 824:25
p. out like water BOOK 132:24
pouring make in p. it out POPE 587:19
pours never rains but it p. PROV 604:29
poverty cost of setting him up in p. NAID 538:4
crime so shameful as p. FARQ 307:7
culture of p. FRIE 325:6
endure harsh p. HORA 389:10
Give me not p. DEFO 254:17
hunger and p. LARK 452:11
implication of dreary p. WEST 812:10
in his squadrons, P. FLAT 316:6
In honoured p. SHEL 714:14
In p., hunger, and dirt HOOD 382:28
misfortunes of p. JUVE 424:11
neither p. nor riches BIBL 83:35
P. a great evil AUST 39:4
p. and excess PENN 572:14
P. and oysters DICK 265:8
P. is a great enemy JOHN 416:27
P. is no disgrace PROV 609:34
P. is not a crime PROV 609:35
p.'s catching BEHN 62:14
represent p. as no evil JOHN 413:9
scorns our p. SHAK 672:16
struggled with p. BALD 48:19
their p. BIBL 82:21
Untaught to bear p. HORA 387:12
When p. comes in at the door PROV 614:24
worse than p. TRAH 780:17
worst of crimes is p. SHAW 707:21
powder food for p. SHAK 669:2
keep your p. dry BLAC 116:21
keep your p. dry PROV 610:1
when your p.'s runnin' low NEWB 541:14
powdered Still to be p. JONS 419:19
power absolute p. ADAM 3:11
acquisition of p. RUSS 640:2
All p. to the Soviets POLI 581:1
another name for absolute p. WORD 831:11
art is of such p. SHAK 698:25
balance of p. KISS 441:26
balance of p. NICO 544:22
because we had p. BENÉ 65:2
Black P. CARM 188:24
breathless, p. breathe forth SHAK 656:26
certainty of p. DAY- 253:12
coming into p. BAGE 46:18
conceive a dominant p. HARD 360:17
corridors of p. SNOW 726:18
defy P. SHEL 713:16
desire of p. HOBB 378:17
desires to have—P. BOUL 145:3
friend in p. ADAM 2:17
from our hands have p. WORD 831:16
good want p. SHEL 713:8
grace and p. BOOK 128:2
greater the p. BURK 164:25
have p. to hurt SHAK 705:6
have the p. to die TENN 767:2
Him the almighty p. MILT 514:11
his p. and his love GRAN 348:15
in office but not in p. LAMO 449:14
intoxicated with p. BURK 162:7
jaws of p. ADAM 3:13
Johnson's instinct for p. WHIT 814:8
Knowledge is p. PROV 605:7
knowledge itself is p. BACO 44:30
lies not in our p. MARL 496:12
life and p. FOX 322:8
literature of *p.* DE Q 258:12
live without a common p. HOBB 378:19
love of p. HAZL 365:8
maximal authority and minimal p. SZAS 751:23
Money is p. PROV 606:44
more contracted that p. is JOHN 415:30
no hopes but from p. BURK 164:27
not exempted from her p. HOOK 383:6
notions about a superior p. SWIF 747:10
only have p. over people SOLZ 727:10
or p. more BROM 149:7
outrun our spiritual p. KING 436:17
O wad some P. BURN 168:21
place without p. ROSE 633:15
political p. of another LOCK 472:3
P. a corrupter SHEL 714:19
p., and the glory BIBL 93:19
P. and War KIPL 438:6
p. belongeth unto God BOOK 135:23
p. can be rightfully exercised MILL 508:18
P. corrupts PROV 609:36
p. grows out of the barrel of a gun MAO 495:2
p. in the day of death BIBL 84:18
p. in trust DRYD 280:6
p. is a trust DISR 270:33
P. is given only DOST 276:3
P. is not a means ORWE 559:1
P. is so apt to be insolent HALI 357:21
P. is the great aphrodisiac KISS 441:28
p. of a man HOBB 378:16
p. of Jesus' Name PERR 574:1
p. of suppress NORT 546:19
p. of the crown BURK 164:13
p. of the written word CONR 234:17
p. over men WOLL 825:21
p. over nothing HERO 374:1
p. over other beings FOST 321:13
p. should always be distrusted JONE 419:4
P. tends to corrupt ACTO 1:16
p. that worketh BIBL 108:1
p. thrown away LESS 465:14
p. to act according to discretion LOCK 472:6
p. to be put forth CANN 185:7
p. to endanger ADAM 3:4
p. to tax MARS 497:19
P. to the people POLI 581:28
p. Which erring men call chance MILT 511:27
p. which stands on Privilege BELL 64:2
P. without responsibility KIPL 441:25
remain the slaves of p. WOLL 825:24
responsibility without p. STOP 743:12
Restored to life, and p. KEBL 432:4
rise to p. LUCR 479:3
seek p. and lose liberty BACO 43:9
seeks to communicate p. DE Q 258:9
selves have given a p. OSBO 559:21
shadow of some unseen P. SHEL 711:16
some great P. HUXL 397:13
strange p., After offence MILT 518:19
stripped of p. SCOT 651:4
supreme p. must be arbitrary HALI 357:14
take who have the p. WORD 831:17
Too weak for p. LEAP 460:2
Treasury is in p. WILS 822:4
unlimited p. ADAM 1:18
Unlimited p. PITT 576:22
upon the past has p. DRYD 282:33
utility of monarchical p. BOSW 144:17
want p. to execute JOHN 411:5
What p. have you got BENN 65:9
with Eternal God for p. TENN 765:6
powerful fear is that we are p. WILL 821:4
p. and free TOCQ 778:12
P. women only succeed LEE- 462:11
powerless p. to be born ARNO 27:21
powers acquaintance with ruling p. TALM 753:13
against p. BIBL 108:13
Headmasters have p. CHUR 216:13
high contracting p. BRIA 148:5
non-resistance to the higher p. MAYH 502:21
p. that be BIBL 105:19
principalities, nor p. BIBL 105:12
principalities, or p. BIBL 109:2
real separation of p. DENN 257:18
ultimate p. of the society JEFF 405:21
virtues, p. MILT 517:1
we lay waste our p. WORD 832:15
pox or of the p. WILK 819:19
practical p. intellectual STRO 745:1
we look at the p. GLAD 341:4
practice ounce of p. PROV 609:13
p. in being refused DIOG 268:2
P. makes perfect PROV 609:37
wear them out in p. BEAU 58:7
practices bloody principles and p. FOX 322:12
practise Go p. if you please BROW 157:23
never to p. either TWAI 786:8
p. in heaven BROW 157:2
P. what you preach PROV 609:38
p. without me SHER 715:16
practised making p. smiles SHAK 702:33
praemia *P. digna ferant* VIRG 793:14
praemitti *non amitti sed p.* CYPR 248:11
praestantissimum *Id quod est p.* CICE 217:26
praevalet *Magna est veritas, et p.* BIBL 114:12
prairies From the mountains to the p. BERL 68:7
praise against empty p. POPE 580:8
All p. to thee KEN 433:2
all song of p. is due SIDN 718:15
Apostles: p. thee BOOK 125:20
as is p. ASCH 30:2
chant hymns of p. ZORO 841:8
countryman must have p. BLYT 123:3
Damn with faint p. POPE 583:7
double was his p. SPEN 733:23
girded with p. GRAN 348:15
Give them not p. SORL 728:18
highest p. of God PROU 594:6
how to p. AUDE 34:4
husband's first p. BARB 53:19
idle smoke of p. DANI 249:2
is p. indeed MORT 534:1
lack tongues to p. SHAK 705:10
let his just p. be given WALT 803:3
little dust of p. TENN 761:19
man worthy of p. HORA 389:8
named thee but to p. HALL 358:10
oblique p. JOHN 416:3
Of p. a mere glutton GOLD 345:4
p. at morning POPE 584:26
P. belongs to God KORA 443:13
P. be to Nero's Neptune DYLA 287:4
p. 'em most ADDI 4:8
p. famous men BIBL 92:13
p. him, and magnify him BOOK 126:5
P., laud, and bless his name KETH 434:11
P. my soul LYTE 481:1
p. of ancient authors HOBB 379:5
p. of God AUGU 36:14
P. the child PROV 609:39
p. thee, God PRAY 592:7
P. the green earth BUNT 160:11
P. the Lord BOOK 138:16
P. the Lord FORG 320:7
P. the Lord, all nations BIBL 113:23
P. the Lord, for he is kind MILT 512:25
P. they that will HERR 374:19
p. those works MART 497:24
p. to Mount Sion BUNY 160:16
P. to the Holiest NEWM 542:18
P. to the Lord WINK 823:7
p. ye the Lord BAKE 48:14
Self-p. no recommendation PROV 610:29
shew thy p. BOOK 135:9
thank, p., laud, glorify HAGG 356:2
there were few to p. WORD 831:19
they only want p. MAUG 502:3
To their right p. SHAK 688:27
unto thy Name give the p. BOOK 139:22
utter all thy P. ADDI 5:10
We p. thee, O God BOOK 125:20
were no small p. MILT 518:4
praised everybody p. the Duke SOUT 730:13
God be p. BROW 154:16
happy when being p. BALF 50:3

praised (*cont.*):
more in him to be p. JONS 421:2
p., and got rid of CICE 218:2
p. him to his face TENN 766:12
p. his fleas YEAT 837:16
p. the dead BIBL 84:9
praiser p. of past times HORA 386:2
praises p. from the men COWL 239:20
p. those who follow HORA 389:12
These p. are not small HEYW 376:7
with faint p. WYCH 834:13
praising always p. the past SMIT 724:22
doing one's p. for oneself BUTL 172:19
P. all alike GAY 332:16
pram p. in the hall CONN 233:26
prata *sat p. biberunt* VIRG 796:3
prater pert, prim p. CHUR 214:7
pray as lief p. with Kit Smart JOHN 413:2
came to scoff, remained to p. GOLD 344:12
cannot pay, let him p. PROV 602:10
fervently do we p. LINC 468:17
I p. for the country HALE 357:2
nor p. with you SHAK 687:11
Often when I p. LEWI 466:23
p. all day long TALM 754:25
p., and not to faint BIBL 100:14
p. for her SHAK 680:23
P. for the dead JONE 419:2
p. for them LEE 462:9
P. for the repose of His soul ROLF 632:5
p. for you at St Paul's SMIT 726:1
p. in their distress BLAK 120:14
p. to Him BARN 55:5
P. without ceasing BIBL 109:10
p. you, master Lieutenant MORE 531:14
to Thee alone we p. KORA 443:14
Watch and p. BIBL 97:23
we do p. for mercy SHAK 688:11
We p. for peace GAUN 331:5
Work and p. HILL 377:1
prayed P. aloud AUBR 32:20
prayer Conservative Party at p. ROYD 636:16
Father, hear the p. WILL 821:6
Four spend in p. COKE 224:11
heard out the p. BOOK 135:26
homes of silent p. TENN 761:6
house of p. BIBL 88:25
house of p. BIBL 96:20
In p. the lips ne'er act HERR 374:10
lift up the hands in p. HOPK 385:6
man of p. SMAR 722:11
on a wing and a p. ADAM 4:1
One p. absorbs all others GLAD 341:9
people's p. DRYD 280:5
perfect p. LESS 465:16
p. at sinking of the sun KORA 444:20
p.is only answered TALM 754:10
p. never loses its value TALM 754:25
p. of a righteous man BIBL 110:24
p. reduces itself TURG 785:7
p. the Church's banquet HERB 373:4
things are wrought by p. TENN 760:16
'tis the hour of p. BYRO 177:2
wish for p. is a prayer BERN 68:20
prayers addicted to p. ASHF 30:12
among my p. HORA 389:24
Christopher Robin is saying his p. MILN 511:1
hear our p. BOOK 130:19
in my p. BIBL 104:24
mention of you in our p. BIBL 109:7
more zeal than holy p. CHUR 213:22
p. of saints BIBL 112:3
p. three hours a day POPE 584:7
recite one's p. TALM 754:26
three-mile p. BURN 169:3
prayeth p. well, who loveth well COLE 226:27
praying Amelia was p. for George THAC 769:9
No p. OTWA 560:23
now he is p. SHAK 665:8
past p. for SHAK 668:5
writing, or p. THOM 771:2
prays family that p. together SAYI 647:14
He p. but faintly SHAK 696:2
that faintly p. QUAR 618:19
preach could na p. for thinkin' o't BURN 168:3
Practise what you p. PROV 609:38
p. among the Gentiles BIBL 107:26
P. not because you have WHAT 813:7
p. the gospel BIBL 98:14
preached p. to death by wild curates SMIT 725:23
preacher Judge not the p. HERB 372:5
preachers best of all p. GUES 354:14
company of the p. BOOK 136:7
P. say, Do as I say SELD 653:24
preaching bad p. CECI 199:5
foolishness of p. BIBL 105:26
moral is not p. DIMN 267:16
woman's p. JOHN 413:17
precedency point of p. JOHN 417:4
precedent from p. LLOY 470:14
is a dangerous p. CORN 237:4
p. embalms a principle STOW 744:5
p. to precedent TENN 767:15
without p. ROUS 636:3
precept Example better than p. PROV 599:46
more efficacious than p. JOHN 410:28
p. must be upon precept BIBL 87:13
precepts icy p. of respect SHAK 699:21
We love the p. FARQ 307:16
precious Deserve the p. bane MILT 515:4
p. in our joys STER 738:12
so p. it must be rationed LENI 463:13
This p. stone SHAK 694:19
precipices from bogs and p. LOCK 472:1
p. show untrodden green KEAT 430:14
précis p. of life FRIE 325:4
precise when Art Is too p. HERR 374:8
precisely thinking too p. SHAK 665:32
predicament is the human p. QUIN 619:4
It is a p. BENN 65:22
predict enable us to p. events HAWK 364:9
only p. things after IONE 399:21
pre-eminence hath no p. BIBL 84:8
Lord hath the p. BOOK 140:5
prefaces Shaw's p. AGAT 6:15
preference invidious p. LAMB 448:10
special p. for beetles HALD 356:18
preferment knocking at P.'s door ARNO 27:5
preferred ought to be p. GODW 342:5
pregnancies P. are damaging SADE 641:8
pregnancy avoid p. by resort to mathematics MENC 504:18
pregnant elegant and p. texture STEV 741:2
If men could get p. KENN 433:5
p. bank swelled up DONN 273:24
prejudice P., *n.* A vagrant opinion BIER 114:24
p. of good order MILI 508:5
p. runs in favour of two DICK 263:18
Pride and p. BORR 144:12
PRIDE AND P. BURN 165:26
religious p. HUXL 397:20
prejudices above national p. NORT 546:15
deposit of p. EINS 291:1
Drive out p. FRED 323:21
it p. a man so SMIT 726:2
one of its own p. HEGE 367:16
p. and habits GIBB 335:16
p. to rest on WOLL 825:18
proprietor's p. SWAF 747:9
prelate religion without a p. BANC 53:4
prelaty yoke of p. MILT 519:24
premeditated abstract and p. city DOST 276:7
p. sins TALM 754:8
premier great p. BAGE 47:17
premises based upon licenced p. O'BR 552:9
prentice Her p. han' she tried BURN 167:9
preparation no p. is thought necessary STEV 741:4
prepare not to p. for life PAST 569:2
p. a place for you BIBL 102:17
p. for the worst PROV 602:48
p. to shed them now SHAK 676:6
P. VAULT FOR FUNERAL TELE 758:9
P. ye the way BIBL 87:28
P. ye the way of the Lord BIBL 92:27
prepared Be p. MOTT 535:4
favours only the p. PAST 569:11
p. for them that love thee BOOK 128:13
p. the dry land BOOK 138:6
world not yet p. DOYL 277:13
prerogative English subject's sole p. DRYD 282:27
exert his p. JOHN 411:4
p. of the harlot KIPL 441:25
last p. DRYD 281:19
p. of the eunuch STOP 743:12
rotten as P. BURK 164:13
that which is called p. LOCK 472:6
presagers dumb p. SHAK 704:12
presbyter New *P.* is but old *Priest* MILT 514:2
Presbytery let that [P.] go CHAR 203:9
prescription p. of a quick dip in bed WESL 811:23
presence away from thy p. BOOK 135:7
beautified with his p. BOOK 131:1
before his p. with a song BOOK 138:13
come before his p. BOOK 138:5
conspicuous by its p. RUSS 640:11
made better by their p. ELIO 293:11
posted p. of the watcher JAME 403:11
p. on the field WELL 809:19
present Act in the living P. LONG 474:5
All p. and correct MILI 508:2
characteristic of the p. age DISR 268:23
Eternally p. within all SIKH 719:13
know nothing but the p. KEYN 435:7
live in the p. CHEK 208:3
many as are here p. BOOK 125:14
no p. in Wales THOM 773:16
no redress for the p. DISR 270:1
No time like the p. MANL 493:17
No time like the p. PROV 608:8
past, p. and future EINS 291:4
perpetuates the p. DE B 254:5
p. contains nothing more BERG 67:16
P. has latched its postern HARD 361:6
p. in spirit BIBL 105:33
p. is an age of talkers HAZL 365:16
p. is an interlude O'NE 554:24
p. is the funeral CLAR 218:17
p. joys are more DRYD 281:23
p. laughter SHAK 701:10
p. moment MANN 494:3
p. of Mornington Crescent HARG 362:6
p., past, and future, sees BLAK 120:21
p. scorn BEHN 62:9
p., yes, we are in it LOWE 478:8
p. your front to the world MOLI 524:16
things p., nor things to come BIBL 105:12
Time p. and time past ELIO 294:1
un-birthday p. CARR 191:1
very p. help in trouble BOOK 134:18
What if this p. DONN 273:1
who controls the p. ORWE 558:22
présentez *P. toujours le devant* MOLI 524:16
presents bring p. BOOK 138:7
Christmas without any p. OPEN 555:11
give p. BOOK 136:18
P., I often say, endear Absents LAMB 448:11
preservation our creation, p. BOOK 127:19
p. of their property LOCK 472:5
Self-p. is first law PROV 610:30
preservative p. from want AUST 38:20
preserve do not p. myself ORTE 557:15
Dr Strabismus (Whom God P.) MORT 533:16
give and p. to our use BOOK 127:13
p. and enlarge freedom LOCK 472:1

p.'s full of stones BETJ 70:11
p. thy going out BOOK 140:13
preserved my life is p. BIBL 75:7
need not be p. OMAR 554:15
Union: it must be p. JACK 400:13
preserver Destroyer and p. SHEL 712:12
presidency cancer close to the P. DEAN 253:16
heart-beat from the P. STEV 740:13
I will seek the p. DOLE 272:1
messenger-boy P. SCHL 648:18
Teflon-coated P. SCHR 649:4
US p. a Tudor monarchy BURG 162:1
vice-p. isn't worth a pitcher GARN 330:1
president All the P. is TRUM 784:2
anybody could become P. DARR 250:13
any boy may become P. STEV 740:11
As P., I have no eyes LINC 469:2
going to be your next p. CART 192:13
nothing to hide from the P. CHUR 215:22
P. is a crook NIXO 546:6
P. of the Immortals CLOS 222:15
P. of the Immortals HARD 361:2
P. should not wear MCAL 481:4
P.'s spouse BUSH 171:1
rather be right than be P. CLAY 220:5
security around the p. MAIL 491:4
vote for the best P. PETE 574:11
We are the P.'s men KISS 441:29
When the P. does it NIXO 546:8
press be named P.-men ARNO 25:23
complain about the p. POWE 590:18
dead-born from the p. HUME 395:3
demagogic, corrupt p. PULI 616:21
freedom of the p. JEFF 405:14
Freedom of the p. guaranteed LIEB 467:19
Freedom of the p. in Britain SWAF 747:9
liberty of the p. JUNI 423:12
lose your temper with the P. PANK 566:11
not a free p. but a managed RADC 620:3
of our idolatry, the p. COWP 241:7
people from the p. TWAI 786:16
periodical p. TROL 783:10
popular p. is drinking MELL 504:6
power of the p. NORT 546:19
p. is ferocious DIAN 260:7
p. still hounded you JOHN 408:1
p. toward the mark BIBL 108:21
p. would kill her SPEN 732:11
to th' p. to trudge BRAD 146:13
with you on the free p. STOP 743:14
pressed p. down my soul BOOK 135:16
p. out of shape FROS 326:11
worth two p. men PROV 609:6
pressure Grace under p. HEMI 369:13
presume Dr Livingstone, I p. STAN 736:6
P. not that I am SHAK 670:23
p. too much upon my love SHAK 676:22
presumption amused by its p. THUR 776:26
presumptioun surquidrie and foul p. CHAU 206:30
prêt *toujours p. à partir* LA F 447:13
pretence to some faint meaning make p. DRYD 281:36
pretend We shall not p. NEWS 544:17
pretended p. friend is worse GAY 332:10
pretender blessing—the P. BYRO 173:10
James I, James II, and the Old P. GUED 354:12
pretending p. to be someone else PAQU 566:15
p. to extraordinary revelations BUTL 171:12
pretension p. is nothing HUNT 396:1
pretentious P. quotations FOWL 322:1
pretexts Tyrants seldom want p. BURK 162:8
pretio *Omnia Romae Cum p.* JUVE 424:13
pretty all my p. chickens SHAK 685:8
all the maidens p. COLM 229:15
He is a very p. weoman FLEM 317:18
It is a p. thing GREE 352:4
lived in a p. how town CUMM 247:3
my p. maid NURS 551:20
policeman and a p. girl CHAP 202:9
p. and proud PROV 605:48
p. girl is like a melody BERL 68:9
p. maids all in a row NURS 549:13
p. to see what money will do PEPY 573:13
P. witty Nell PEPY 573:7
Puts on his p. looks SHAK 677:11
sex object if you're p. GIOV 340:1
prevail I believe man will p. FAUL 307:27
truth, and shall p. BROO 151:10
prevailed they have not p. BOOK 140:25
prevarication last dyke of p. BURK 165:8
prevent not knowing how to p. them RUSS 640:8
P. us, O Lord BOOK 130:5
try to p. it MILN 511:8
preventing grace p. us BOOK 128:5
p. people from taking part VALÉ 789:3
prevention P. is better PROV 609:40
prey bent on his p. MILT 516:4
destined p. SHAW 708:2
drive a p. BALL 50:7
greater p. upon the less GREE 351:11
p. of the rich JEFF 405:4
roaring after their p. BOOK 139:5
to hast'ning ills a p. GOLD 344:8
yet a p. to all POPE 585:20
preys only one that p. JAME 404:4
Priam P.'s sons of Troy SURR 746:11
price bought it at any p. CLAR 218:22
Every man has his p. PROV 599:33
in Rome has its p. JUVE 424:13
love that pays the p. SPRI 735:6
pay any p. KENN 433:10
pearl of great p. BIBL 95:23
pearls fetch a high p. WHAT 813:11
p. is far above rubies BIBL 83:38
p. of admiralty KIPL 440:9
p. of a large turbot RUSK 638:17
p. of everything WILD 818:12
p. of justice BENN 66:6
p. of love was death DRAB 278:16
p. of the paint VAN 789:18
p. of wisdom BIBL 81:25
p. well worth paying LAMO 449:13
those men have their p. WALP 802:4
Too high a p. is asked DOST 275:18
What p. glory ANDE 14:11
without money and without p. BIBL 88:20
Wot p. Selvytion nah SHAW 707:25
prices contrivance to raise p. SMIT 723:7
High p. profit those CARR 191:27
paid the p. of life GURN 355:3
prick If you p. us SHAK 687:30
I paint with my p. MISQ 521:16
It is a p. PEEL 571:19
spur To p. the sides SHAK 682:12
pricking By the p. of my thumbs SHAK 684:20
p. on the plain SPEN 733:12
prickly *Here we go round the p. pear* ELIO 294:25
pricks kick against the p. BIBL 103:25
pride contempt on all my p. WATT 805:14
family p. is something GILB 337:22
here have P. and Truth YEAT 836:22
He that is low no p. BUNY 161:12
I know thy p. BIBL 78:29
lacks a proper p. MACD 484:16
look backward to with p. FROS 325:18
maiden p., adieu SHAK 691:11
p. and high disdain SCOT 650:15
P. and pleasure JOHN 417:21
P. and prejudice BORR 144:12
P. AND PREJUDICE BURN 165:26
p., cruelty, and ambition RALE 621:7
P. feels no pain PROV 609:41
P. goes before a fall PROV 609:42
P. goeth before destruction BIBL 82:38
P. in their port GOLD 345:9
P. of Life HARD 361:9
p. of the peacock BLAK 119:20
P. ruled my will NEWM 542:20
P. still is aiming at the blest POPE 585:12
p. that apes humility COLE 225:7
rank p., and haughtiness ADDI 4:10
save its p. MEYE 506:14
soldier's p. BROW 156:11
will her p. deflower SPEN 734:1
pridie day that hath no *p.* DONN 275:7
priest As a p. COWP 242:13
Delicate-handed p. TENN 764:1
fiddling p. COWP 241:2
great being a p. LINE 469:10
guts of the last p. DIDE 267:2
Like people, like p. BIBL 90:9
Like people, like p. PROV 605:33
listened to the p. BALL 51:8
New *Presbyter* is but old P. MILT 514:2
Once a p. PROV 608:31
p. continues DRYD 281:24
P. did offer Christ BOOK 142:11
p. doth reign MACA 483:1
P. for ever BOOK 139:17
p. of the invisible STEV 739:18
p. of the Muses HORA 388:11
p. persuades humble people PERU 574:8
religion from the p. GOLD 345:32
rid me of this turbulent p. HENR 370:9
'twixt the P. and Clerk HERR 374:15
visited by the p. SHAK 702:19
priestcraft ere p. did begin DRYD 279:17
priesthood royal p. BIBL 110:28
priestlike at their p. task KEAT 426:14
priests beheaded p. HENR 370:12
dominion of p. PRIC 591:9
P., and Deacons BOOK 127:9
p. by the imposition MACA 481:17
p. have been enemies HUME 394:15
p. on their way to bury BOCC 123:5
treen p. JEWE 407:8
with the guts of p. MESL 506:5
with women nor with p. SOUT 730:20
priggish p. schoolgirl GRIG 353:12
prigs p. and pedants DISR 268:21
prime arrive at a p. mover THOM 771:14
having lost but once your p. HERR 375:3
My p. of youth TICH 777:10
One's p. is elusive SPAR 731:19
spent my youthfu' p. BURN 169:8
Prime Minister best P. we have BUTL 171:14
buried the Unknown P. ASQU 31:5
HOW DARE YOU BECOME P. TELE 758:6
last British P. ADAM 2:10
model of a modern P. HENN 370:3
next P. but three BELL 63:8
No woman will be P. THAT 769:19
office of the P. ASQU 31:4
on the P.'s jet SELF 654:1
P. has nothing to hide CHUR 215:22
P. has resigned ANON 16:13
P. has to be a butcher BUTL 171:15
P. is like the banyan PATI 569:17
P. shuffling along HEAL 366:4
Prime Ministers Disraeli school of P. BLAI 117:14
P. and such as they GILB 337:9
P. are wedded SAKI 642:9
P. dissatisfied JENK 406:9
P. have never yet been CHUR 216:13
wild flowers, and P. BALD 49:7
primerole She was a p. CHAU 205:26
primeval forest p. LONG 473:14
primitive p. nothing ROCH 630:21
primordial bit of p. chaos WELL 810:14
primrose go the p. way SHAK 683:14
P. first born child FLET 318:8
p. path of dalliance SHAK 662:9
p. that forsaken dies MILT 513:8
soft silken p. MILT 513:15
withered p. BOLT 124:22
Primrose Hill P. and Saint John's Wood BLAK 118:22

primroses Pale p. SHAK 703:18
smiles, Wan as p. KEAT 427:2
prince Advise the p. ELIO 295:9
bless the P. of Wales LINL 469:16
danced with the P. of Wales FARJ 306:16
dominion of a p. HUME 394:14
draws sword against p. PROV 615:5
Good-night, sweet p. SHAK 667:12
Gorgon, P. of darkness SPEN 733:15
great p. in prison lies DONN 273:26
Hamlet without the P. SCOT 652:8
in a p. the virtue MASS 501:2
news and P. of Peace FLET 318:13
P. calls in the good old money LAMB 448:9
P. I am not DEKK 256:7
p. must be a fox MACH 486:2
p. of Aquitaine NERV 541:7
p. of darkness SHAK 679:7
p. of glory died WATT 805:14
P. of Peace BIBL 87:1
P. of Wales not a position BENN 65:22
p. sets himself up above the law MAYH 502:21
p. who begins early BAGE 47:6
p. who gets a reputation NAPO 538:10
safer for a p. MACH 485:16
send the companion a better p. SHAK 669:25
Who made thee a p. BIBL 75:23
princedoms p., virtues MILT 517:1
princes death of p. SHAK 675:9
inform his p. BOOK 139:9
like one of the p. BOOK 137:10
P. and lords may flourish GOLD 344:8
p. are come home again SHAK 677:21
p. in all lands BOOK 134:17
trust in p. BOOK 141:21
princess People's P. BLAI 117:13
P. leave the Englishwoman BISM 116:4
P. of Parallelograms BYRO 179:22
P. of Wales AUST 39:8
P. of Wales DOWD 277:4
principalities against p. BIBL 108:13
angels, nor p. BIBL 105:12
p., or powers BIBL 109:2
principate p. and liberty TACI 752:6
principibus *P. placuisse viris* HORA 386:22
principiis *P. obsta* OVID 561:20
principio *In p. erat Verbum* MISS 522:22
principis *Indignatio p. mors est* MORE 531:10
principle active P. WORD 828:14
does everything on p. SHAW 709:2
feel the p. of God FOX 322:11
little of the p. left REIT 624:8
precedent embalms a p. STOW 744:5
p. of all social progress FOUR 321:19
p. of the English law DICK 261:4
Protection is not a p. DISR 268:11
rebels from p. BURK 163:24
useful thing about a p. MAUG 501:17
principles bloody p. and practices FOX 322:12
Damn your p. DISR 270:36
denies the first p. AUCT 33:3
either morals or p. GLAD 341:2
embrace your Lordship's p. WILK 819:19
fundamental p. are thirteen MAIM 491:5
he has good p. JOHN 413:4
p. are the same JOHN 416:25
print *devils* must p. MOOR 530:8
eternity of p. WOOL 826:12
fit to p. ADVE 7:4
licence to p. money THOM 775:24
love a ballad in p. SHAK 703:21
p. My book HERR 375:1
p. of a man's naked foot DEFO 254:20
rambling brat (in p.) BRAD 146:13
say in p. ROBI 629:11
when you read the fine p. SEEG 653:7
printing caused p. to be used SHAK 672:24
Gunpowder, P. CARL 187:19
invented the art of p. CARL 188:9
p., gunpowder BACO 45:4
p. house in Hell BLAK 119:29
regulate p. MILT 519:12
printless clerical, p. toe BROO 150:12
set my p. feet MILT 512:2
with p. foot SHAK 699:8
priorities language of p. BEVA 71:14
p. have gone all wrong BEVA 72:1
prisca *Ut p. gens mortalium* HORA 387:11
prism his p., and silent face WORD 831:3
prunes and p. DICK 263:1
prison at home in p. WAUG 806:5
born in p. MALC 491:21
Come, let's away to p. SHAK 680:6
do not a p. make LOVE 476:14
forever p.-pent WOLF 825:8
great prince in p. lies DONN 273:26
grind in the p. house BIBL 78:7
hero from his p. AYTO 40:10
Home is the girl's p. SHAW 708:28
in p., and ye came unto me BIBL 97:12
is also a p. THOR 775:26
lime-tree bower my p. COLE 227:3
looseth men out of p. BOOK 141:22
mourn in p. MONT 526:17
only a p. CUST 248:9
opening of the p. BIBL 89:5
palace and a p. on each hand BYRO 174:24
p. and a smile WOTT 833:4
prison in a p. DICK 265:16
p. of his days AUDE 34:4
seeks to adorn its p. WOLL 825:23
Shades of the p.-house WORD 829:20
ship but a p. BURT 170:15
So cruel p. SURR 746:11
This p. where I live SHAK 696:3
while there is a soul in p. DEBS 254:9
world a vast p. WOLL 826:2
world not a 'p. house' ROBI 629:16
prisoner if the p. is happy SHAW 708:12
object to your being taken p. KITC 442:1
p. of the Lord BIBL 108:2
takes the reason p. SHAK 681:18
thoughts of a p. SOLZ 727:13
prisoners all p. and captives BOOK 127:11
p. call the sky WILD 818:31
p. in towns SITT 720:20
p. of addiction ILLI [illegible]
p. out of captivity BOOK 136:6
weapons of all p. COLE 228:3
prisons Madhouses, p. CLAR 218:8
P. are built with stones BLAK 119:19
privacy society of p. RAND 621:14
private at a p. view EDWA 289:5
consult our p. ends SWIF 749:23
fine and p. place MARV 499:3
Give me a p. station GAY 332:14
his p. parts BUTL 172:29
no p. life ELIO 292:8
P. faces in public places AUDE 34:15
p. life is a disgrace ANON 18:12
P. Means is dead SMIT 724:23
P. property is a necessary TAWN 755:15
p. station ADDI 4:15
p. will governs ROBE 629:3
sphere of p. life MELB 504:2
privates Faith, her p. SHAK 663:15
privilege Danger justified p. WAUG 806:16
inestimable p. of man SHEL 714:18
only extended p. HILL 376:12
power which stands on P. BELL 64:2
p. and pleasure GILB 337:7
p. I claim AUST 38:12
p. of seeing one another JENY 406:12
p. to breathe ELEA 291:16
privileged P. and the People DISR 270:25
p. to be very impertinent FARQ 307:22
They were p. children BROO 151:3
privileges stand for your p. HEMI 369:7
prize Bound for the p. SHAK 705:3
do not run for p. SORL 728:17
lawful p. GRAY 350:22
one receiveth the p. BIBL 106:10
yield the p. DRYD 280:23
prized local, but p. elsewhere AUDE 35:5
prizes glittering p. BORR 144:7
glittering p. SMIT 723:19
winners of the big p. ORWE 558:25
probabilities Human p. are not sufficient FAIR 306:4
probability p. is the very guide BUTL 171:9
probable P. impossibilities ARIS 25:1
probationary Eden's dread p. tree COWP 241:7
Probitas *P. laudatur et alget* JUVE 424:4
problem All in all he's a p. BURN 168:9
can't see the p. CHES 211:12
Houston, we've had a p. LOVE 477:2
part of the p. SAYI 647:22
p. is solved CHEK 208:16
p. of the colour line DU B 284:2
p.-solving minds KAUN 426:7
p. that has no name FRIE 324:22
p. that has no name FRIE 324:24
p. to be overcome KEIL 432:10
three-pipe p. DOYL 277:11
you're part of the p. CLEA 220:7
problems Machines have less p. WARH 803:16
p. as it can solve MARX 499:14
P. worthy of attack HEIN 368:2
procedure interstices of p. MAIN 491:11
proceed just works do p. BOOK 126:19
proceedeth p. from the Father BOOK 129:9
proceedings subsequent p. HART 363:11
procession torchlight p. O'SU 560:20
proclaims apparel oft p. the man SHAK 662:11
procrastination incivility and p. DE Q 258:11
p. is the art of MARQ 497:4
P. is the thief PROV 609:43
P. is the thief YOUN 839:6
procreant Always the p. urge WHIT 815:11
procreation p. of children BOOK 131:2
proctors prudes for p. TENN 765:12
procul *P. hinc, procul este* OVID 561:4
p. negotiis HORA 387:11
P. omen abesto OVID 561:3
P., o procul este VIRG 794:18
prodigal chariest maid is p. SHAK 662:8
p. of ease DRYD 280:3
p. weight SHAK 695:16
prodigies Africa and her p. BROW 153:19
produce p. it in God's name CARL 188:15
producing consumes without p. ORWE 558:5
product fraction of a p. CARL 188:15
production means of p. ANON 19:9
purpose of p. SMIT 723:11
productions literary p. GIBB 335:8
p. of time BLAK 119:16
products p. people really want NASH 539:14
profanation From sale and p. CHES 210:8
'Twere p. of our joys DONN 274:19
profane Coldly p. CRAB 243:2
Hence, ye p. COWL 239:13
p. and old wives' fables BIBL 109:15
P., erroneous, and vain BUTL 172:6
profaned desolated and p. GLAD 340:19
profani *procul este p.* VIRG 794:18
profanum *Odi p. vulgus* HORA 388:11
profess p. and call themselves BOOK 127:17
profession branches of a new p. TROL 783:11
charmed me from my p. SHAK 699:23
debtor to his p. BACO 41:26
discharge of any p. JOHN 415:1
most ancient p. KIPL 441:1
ornament to her p. BUNY 161:15
panted for a liberal p. COLM 229:17
second oldest p. REAG 623:3
professional p. is a man who can AGAT 6:18
P. men, they have no cares NASH 539:11
professionally P. he declines DICK 264:22

professions foot of the p. BLOM 122:7
p. are conspiracies SHAW 707:4
p. which are full THOR 776:8
some of all p. SHAK 683:14
professor called a *p. emeritus* LEAC 459:17
ploughman and p. JEFF 405:6
p. of French letters JOYC 422:16
profit count as p. every day HORA 387:20
inferior understands p. CONF 231:11
In labour there is p. BIBL 82:32
men write for p. WALP 801:8
mixed p. with pleasure HORA 386:3
no p. but the name SHAK 665:29
p. and loss ELIO 296:12
p. by the folly of others PLIN 578:18
To whose p. CICE 217:25
What p. hath a man BIBL 83:39
what shall it p. a man BIBL 98:8
profits best of all monopoly p. HICK 376:9
Civilization and p. COOL 236:1
little p. that an idle king TENN 767:8
nothing p. more MILT 517:11
profound p. truths recognized BOHR 124:3
profundis *De p. clamavi* BIBL 113:25
profundo *Merses p.* HORA 389:4
profusus *sui p.* SALL 643:7
prognostics P. do not always prove WALP 801:10
programme Not so much a p. ANON 18:3
programmed p. to love completely BAIN 48:9
progress Belief in p. BAUD 57:12
Congress makes no p. LIGN 468:1
conservatism and p. TROL 782:8
freedom and p. MADA 488:20
history of p. MACA 482:3
Humanity a work in p. WILL 820:14
no summer p. ANDR 14:15
party of p. or reform MILL 508:20
principle of all social p. FOUR 321:19
p. depends on unreasonable man SHAW 708:24
p. if a cannibal uses LEC 461:11
P. is a comfortable disease CUMM 247:9
p. is based upon BUTL 172:23
'p.' is ethical RUSS 640:5
P. is not an accident SPEN 732:7
P., man's distinctive mark BROW 155:24
p. of a deathless soul DONN 273:10
P. through technology ADVE 8:16
Reason and P. OSBO 560:6
Social P. began KIPL 438:20
social p., order, security JOHN 407:10
swell a p. ELIO 295:9
Time's thievish p. SHAK 705:2
truest type of p. ADDA 4:2
What we call 'p.' ELLI 298:15
progression Nothing in p. can rest BURK 162:14
there is no p. BLAK 119:9
progressive in a p. country DISR 269:5
p. societies MAIN 491:10
prohibition enacting P. HOOV 383:9
proie *à sa p. attachée* RACI 619:18
projections other figures in it Merely p. ELIO 293:23
projects fitter for new p. BACO 44:25
proletarian Sisyphus, p. CAMU 184:9
proletariat dictatorship of the p. MARX 500:3
prologue make a long p. BIBL 92:20
very witty p. CONG 233:1
What's past is p. SHAK 698:30
prologues happy p. SHAK 681:20
P. precede the piece GARR 330:7
Promethean true P. fire SHAK 680:26
promise broke no p. POPE 584:6
by p. BIBL 107:19
Eastern p. ADVE 7:20
eat the air, p.-crammed SHAK 664:19
ill keeper of p. BACO 42:13
P., large promise JOHN 409:18
p. made is a debt unpaid SERV 654:23
p. made not to dissever WYAT 834:4
this p. which has stood HAGG 355:14
Whose p. none relies on EPIT 302:14
promised Marching to the P. Land BARI 54:14
O Jesus, I have p. BODE 123:8
P. from eternal years CASW 194:3
reach the p. land CALL 181:10
seen the p. land KING 436:16
weird women p. SHAK 683:24
promises According to thy p. BOOK 125:17
have p. to keep FROS 326:12
leave his p. unfulfilled JOHN 411:5
p. and panaceas ROTH 635:21
P., like pie-crust PROV 609:44
p. were, as he then was SHAK 673:21
received the p. BIBL 109:30
Vote for the man who p. least BARU 56:11
young man of p. BALF 50:2
promising first call p. CONN 233:25
promontory sat upon a p. SHAK 689:22
See one p. BURT 170:11
Stretched like a p. MILT 517:7
promotion none will sweat but for p. SHAK 658:17
p. cometh neither from BOOK 136:22
p. to the blest DRYD 282:29
You'll get no p. HUGH 392:16
prone Orion plunges p. HOUS 390:11
position for women is p. CARM 188:23
pronounce better than they p. TWAI 786:13
could not frame to p. it BIBL 77:37
even to p. the word JOIN 418:18
pronounced p. the letter R AUBR 32:18
pronunciation p. Reigned tyrannically HEAN 366:18
proof America is the p. MCCA 484:2
Come time of p. GOOG 346:13
lapped in p. SHAK 681:10
p. of the pudding PROV 609:45
proofs p. of holy writ SHAK 692:28
Prooshans others may be P. DICK 263:7
prop p. To our infirmity WORD 831:2
propaganda on p. CORN 237:6
purely for p. BEAV 59:4
propagate likely to p. understanding JOHN 418:13
propagation peace and p. WALP 801:7
propensities natural p. BURK 164:23
propensity usual p. of mankind HUME 394:8
proper know our p. stations DICK 261:7
no p. time of day HOOD 382:24
noun, p. or improper FULL 327:4
p. man SHAK 689:14
P. words in proper places SWIF 748:8
p. young men BURN 167:18
properly never did anything p. LEAR 460:12
property degrees and kinds of p. MADI 489:3
dominion of p. GOLD 344:5
give me a little snug p. EDGE 288:10
makes it his p. LOCK 471:21
nature and p. BOOK 127:15
not p. but a trust FOX 322:4
preservation of their p. LOCK 472:5
preserve his p. LOCK 472:2
Private p. is a necessary TAWN 755:15
P. has its duties DRUM 279:13
p. is of greater value FRY 326:25
P. is theft PROU 593:19
p. of others SALL 643:7
p. of the rich RUSK 639:5
p. of thy fellow TALM 753:15
p. or honour MACH 486:3
p.-owning democracy SKEL 721:15
Propinquity and p. of blood SHAK 677:23
public p. JEFF 405:16
rank or p. JUNI 423:15
right of p. TAFT 752:19
Thieves respect p. CHES 211:8
through p. that we shall strike PANK 566:13
Where p. is in question SALI 642:20
prophecies not always prove p. WALP 801:10
p., they shall fail BIBL 106:16
verification of his own p. TROL 782:26
prophecy have the gift of p. BIBL 106:16
poetry, p., and religion RUSK 638:11
p. is the most gratuitous ELIO 292:19
prophesy man may p. SHAK 670:4
p. deceits BIBL 87:15
sons and daughters shall p. BIBL 90:14
prophet arise among you a p. BIBL 77:7
more than a p. BIBL 95:6
not as a p. MAND 493:8
p., his prophecy departs TALM 754:5
p. in Israel BIBL 80:17
p. is not without honour BIBL 95:24
p. not without honour PROV 609:46
p., to whose rapture THOM 775:19
p. who wishes to write HEIN 368:7
prophetic In her p. fury SHAK 693:6
O my p. soul SHAK 662:29
p. greeting SHAK 681:17
prophets Beware of false p. BIBL 94:9
Book, and the P. KORA 443:17
by the p. BIBL 109:25
ceased to pose as its p. POPP 587:25
fellowship of the P. BOOK 125:20
Is Saul also among the p. BIBL 78:21
knowledge from the p. SA'A 640:21
law and the p. BIBL 94:6
Men reject their p. DOST 276:2
p. and kings have desired BIBL 99:10
p. make sure of the event WALP 801:10
p. prophesy falsely BIBL 89:13
spake by the P. BOOK 129:9
propinquity P. and property of blood SHAK 677:23
proportion harmony, order or p. BROW 153:30
no p. kept SHAK 696:4
strangeness in the p. BACO 42:10
proportions by p. true MARV 498:12
proposes Man p. PROV 606:18
man p. THOM 771:1
proposition accept the p. AYER 40:4
copulations of p. HUME 395:8
expressing a genuine p. AYER 40:6
meaning of a p. SCHL 648:20
propositions General p. LOCK 471:13
propositum *Meum est p.* ANON 21:10
proprie *p. communia dicere* HORA 385:19
proprietor p.'s prejudices SWAF 747:9
propriety attention to p. WOLL 826:3
sole p. MILT 516:25
props p. to help him endure FAUL 307:28
prose All that is not p. MOLI 524:18
as well written as p. POUN 590:6
but p. run mad POPE 583:6
differs in nothing from p. GRAY 351:6
for p. and verse CARE 186:4
Good p. like a window-pane ORWE 558:8
govern in p. CUOM 247:18
harmony of p. DRYD 283:10
in p. or rhyme MILT 514:8
language of p. WORD 832:18
love others in p. PRIO 592:10
Meredith's a p. Browning WILD 817:26
nearest p. DRYD 282:15
Not verse now, only p. BROW 155:16
pin up my hair with p. CONG 233:8
p. and the passion FORS 320:18
P. is for ideas IBSE 398:13
p. is verse BYRO 178:3
P. is when all the lines BENT 67:1
P. was born yesterday FLAU 316:12
P. = words in their best order COLE 227:20
shut me up in p. DICK 266:17
speaking p. without knowing it MOLI 524:19
Stein's p.-song LEWI 467:12
Proserpine P. gathering flowers MILT 516:14
prospect every p. pleases HEBE 367:7
noblest p. JOHN 413:6
prospects undetermined p. ADDI 5:9

prosper I grow, I p. SHAK 678:4
sinners' ways p. HOPK 384:23
Treason doth never p. HARI 362:9
prosperity day of p. BIBL 84:16
jest's p. SHAK 681:2
liberty and p. JENY 406:11
man to han ben in p. CHAU 207:12
man who can stand p. CARL 188:2
P. doth best BACO 42:5
P. doth bewitch men WEBS 808:19
P. is the blessing BACO 42:3
prosperous make a nation p. BACO 45:14
prostitute doormat or a p. WEST 812:14
puff the p. away DRYD 282:34
prostitutes small nations like p. KUBR 446:4
prostitution banking and p. WRIG 833:11
P. Selling one's body MACK 486:7
prostrating bowing, p. KORA 445:11
protect p. a working-girl SMIT 723:18
p. the writer ACHE 1:14
protected must be p. ORTO 558:2
protection calls mutely for p. GREE 351:24
Grant me p. SIKH 719:11
mercy and p. BOOK 131:10
p. against war BEVI 72:9
P. is not a principle DISR 268:11
protector appoint to us a p. KORA 444:9
Friend and P. BARB 53:19
God, the p. BOOK 128:11
p. of the believers KORA 443:21
protest lady doth p. too much SHAK 664:23
Protestant Hitler attacked the P. church NIEM 545:8
I am the P. whore GWYN 355:8
live Thy P. to be HERR 374:23
preservation of the P. religion HAMP 359:6
P. counterpoint BEEC 61:6
p. ethic WEBE 807:3
P., if he wants aid DISR 270:18
P. Province of Ulster CARS 192:3
P. Religion CARL 187:19
P. with a horse BEHA 61:22
'tis a P. wind WHAR 813:5
Protestantism P., even the most cold BURK 162:26
Protestants in the hands of P. PUGI 616:19
religion of P. CHIL 212:3
Proteus sight of P. rising WORD 832:16
protoplasmal p. primordial globule GILB 337:22
protracted p. my work JOHN 412:20
p. woe JOHN 411:17
proud all the p. and mighty have DYER 286:16
apt the poor are to be p. SHAK 702:1
Death be not p. DONN 272:22
I have no p. looks BOOK 141:3
make death p. SHAK 657:20
makes him very p. MILN 511:3
mote ye lyve, and alle p. CHAU 207:5
p. and yet a wretched thing DAVI 251:17
proudest of the p. CHUR 214:7
p. if you'll be wise CHUD 213:10
p. in arms MILT 511:15
p. me no prouds SHAK 697:35
p. of the fact RUSS 639:10
scattered the p. BIBL 98:17
too p. for a wit GOLD 345:1
too p. to fight WILS 822:11
too p. to importune GRAY 351:5
prove chance to p. it MURR 537:6
I could p. everything PINT 576:12
O Lord, and p. me BOOK 133:7
P. all things BIBL 109:11
p. a lover SHAK 696:11
p. anything by figures CARL 187:2
p. me, and examine BOOK 141:14
p. our chance DRAY 279:9
to p. it I'm here CATC 196:6
proved God p. them BIBL 91:8
mighty soul was p. ADDI 4:6
p. me, and saw my works BOOK 138:6
p. most royally SHAK 667:14
you have p. to be HARD 361:14
proven worth proving can be p. TENN 757:10
Provence found it in P. WILL 821:3
proverb Israel shall be a p. BIBL 79:16
p. is one man's wit RUSS 640:12
proverbs Patch grief with p. SHAK 691:19
Solomon wrote the P. NAYL 539:24
proves exception p. the rule PROV 599:47
provide God will p. BIBL 74:32
goods the gods p. PROV 611:39
provided P. for DICK 262:3
providence assert eternal p. MILT 514:9
Behind a frowning p. COWP 240:18
inscrutable workings of P. SMIT 724:4
P. had sent a few men RUMB 637:4
P. has not created TOCQ 778:12
P. on the side PROV 609:47
p. so ordereth MATH 501:10
P. their guide MILT 518:3
way that P. dictates HITL 378:6
provident They are p. instead BOGA 123:12
province all knowledge to be my p. BACO 44:28
Ireland should be a p. GOOL 346:15
p. they have desolated GLAD 340:19
provinces defending those p. SMIT 723:14
provincial He was worse than p. JAME 403:5
level of p. existence ELIO 293:4
provincialism taken in p. HUXL 396:16
proving pleasure in p. their falseness DARW 250:15
provision p. for the flesh BIBL 105:22
provocation as in the p. BOOK 138:6
p. I have had POPE 586:21
provoke fathers, p. not BIBL 108:10
provoker Drink, sir, is a great p. SHAK 683:15
provokes No one p. me MOTT 535:10
proximus *paries cum p. ardet* HORA 387:2
prudence effect of p. on rascality SHAW 708:23
forced into p. AUST 38:8
P. bring thee back CHUR 214:2
P. is a rich, ugly BLAK 119:13
prudent mercenary and the p. AUST 38:21
prudes p. for proctors TENN 765:12
prudhomme *p. so grand* JOIN 418:18
prunes p. and prism DICK 263:1
pruninghooks spears into p. BIBL 86:13
prurient p. curiosity STOP 743:10
Prussia military domination of P. ASQU 31:2
national industry of P. MIRA 520:4
put P. on the Rhine ADEN 6:3
Prussian P., Or perhaps Ital-ian GILB 339:1
psalm echo of a p. PAST 569:10
practising the hundredth p. BYRO 179:17
p. of thanksgiving BOOK 138:10
Take the p. BOOK 137:9
psalmist sweet p. of Israel BIBL 79:13
psalms David wrote the P. NAYL 539:24
turned to holy p. PEEL 572:2
with p. BOOK 138:5
psaltery p., dulcimer BIBL 90:1
pseudopodium lonely p. SHIP 717:5
Psyche Your mournful P. KEAT 429:3
psychiatrist man who goes to a p. GOLD 346:5
psychic manifests all p. powers MAHĀ 490:15
psychopath p. is the furnace RAYM 622:9
psychosis Irish and the Jews have a p. BEHA 62:3
psychotherapy waste money on p. TORK 779:17
puberty p. assisted BYRO 176:3
pubic Hound that Caught the P. Hare BEHA 61:23
public as if I was a p. meeting VICT 792:7
assumes a p. trust JEFF 405:16
complainers for the p. BURK 162:17
consult the p. good SWIF 747:24
Desolation in immaculate p. places ROET 631:7
English p. school WAUG 806:5
excites the p. odium CLAY 220:3
expense of p. interests TAYL 756:17
for the p. good LOCK 472:6
glorified p. relations man TRUM 784:2
hand into the p. purse PEEL 571:18
I and the p. know AUDE 34:21
Nor p. men YEAT 836:10
one to mislead the p. ASQU 31:6
precedence over p. relations FEYN 309:6
Private faces in p. places AUDE 34:15
p. and merited disgrace STEV 742:7
p. be damned VAND 789:12
p. Prayer in the Church BOOK 142:10
p. rallies around an idea ASIM 30:18
p. scandal that constitutes MOLI 525:19
p. school accent LEAV 461:6
P. schools are the nurseries FIEL 310:2
P. schools 'tis public folly COWP 242:11
p. seldom forgive LAVA 454:12
p. thinks long JOHN 409:23
respect p. opinion RUSS 639:13
servants of the p. GOWE 347:11
sound Of p. scorn MILT 517:22
tell the p. which way SULZ 746:4
vexes p. men TENN 767:14
wider p. life ELIO 292:8
publican fawning p. SHAK 687:12
publicans even the p. BIBL 93:15
p. and sinners BIBL 94:23
publications previous p. HILB 376:10
publicity Any p. is good publicity PROV 595:9
bad p. BEHA 62:5
eternal p. BENN 66:6
oxygen of p. THAT 770:6
publish P. and be damned WELL 809:18
p. it not BIBL 79:1
p., right or wrong BYRO 177:33
P. your message WESL 811:18
published before this book is p. RUNC 637:9
publisher Barabbas was a p. CAMP 183:20
makes everybody a p. MCLU 487:12
publishers numerous p. ADE 5:20
p. are not women ROBI 629:11
publishing p. faster than think PAUL 570:6
Puck streak of P. HENL 369:19
pudding chieftain o' the p.-race BURN 168:20
Mrs Carter, could make a p. JOHN 412:8
proof of the p. PROV 609:45
p. and pie NURS 548:7
p. in his belly SHAK 668:14
solid p. POPE 580:8
Take away that p. CHUR 217:2
puddings like their English p. VOLT 798:12
puddle shining into a p. PROV 611:35
puerisque *Virginibus p. canto* HORA 388:11
puero *p. reverentia* JUVE 425:5
puff friends all united to p. SWIN 751:15
p. and get oneself puffed TROL 783:11
p.—and speak COWP 240:1
p. of a dunce GOLD 345:4
p. the prostitute away DRYD 282:34
puffs P., powders, patches POPE 586:31
pug O most charming p. FLEM 317:18
pugna *P. magna victi sumus* LIVY 470:11
puking infant, Mewling and p. SHAK 658:26
pulchrior *p. evenit* HORA 389:4
pull easier to p. down PROV 604:13
P. down thy vanity POUN 589:21
P. down thy VANITY POUN 589:22
puller p. down of kings SHAK 673:1
pulling Here p. down MARV 498:12
pulls p. a lady through MARQ 497:6
pulp p. my acquaintance TROL 783:14
p. so bitter THOM 774:7
pulpit faith of those in the p. AUST 39:16
such a bully p. ROOS 633:13
white glove p. REAG 623:2
pulsanda *P. tellus* HORA 388:3
pulse feeling a woman's p. STER 738:10
lost p. of feeling ARNO 26:3
My P., like a soft drum KING 436:8

p. begins to throb BRON 150:1
p. like a cannon EMER 299:16
p. of the machine WORD 831:23
two people with the one p. MACN 488:12
pulvere *sine p. palmae* HORA 386:9
pumice Beside a p. isle SHEL 712:14
polished dry with p. CATU 194:19
pumpkins early p. blow LEAR 460:5
pun make so vile a p. DENN 258:1
p. is a pistol LAMB 448:17
punch Some sipping p. WORD 830:16
punctuality painting and p. GAIN 327:18
P. is the politeness LOUI 476:5
P. is the politeness PROV 609:48
P. is the soul PROV 609:49
P. is the virtue of bores WAUG 806:19
punctuation concentrated on p. CORN 237:5
Punica *P. fide* SALL 643:11
punish God p. England FUNK 327:14
punished bodies to be p. PROV 597:37
p. everlastingly JOHN 417:11
[wickedness] is not p. COMP 230:17
punishing p. anyone who comes between SMIT 725:19
punishment cruel and unusual p. CONS 235:14
Does capital p. tend FRY 326:25
less horror than the p. GIBB 335:10
most terrible p. DOST 276:6
My p. is greater BIBL 74:10
object of p. MANN 493:18
p. fit the crime GILB 338:9
p. Is avarice JONS 420:6
p. is mischief BENT 66:20
p. is not for revenge FRY 326:26
restraint and p. MILT 519:11
suffer first p. CRAN 244:1
punishments charged with p. HENL 369:21
sanguinary p. PAIN 563:20
punk writings are p. ANON 16:20
punt better fun to p. than to be punted SAYE 646:5
punto *cinco en p. de la tarde* GARC 329:10
pupped down to Brighton and p. SMIT 725:24
puppets God, whose p. BROW 157:13
p. in a play of shadows BHAG 73:4
shut up the box and the p. THAC 769:14
puppy p.-dogs' tails NURS 551:19
purblind whining, p., wayward boy SHAK 680:22
purchase p. of my wealth JONS 420:4
purchased p. with money BIBL 103:23
purchasing not worth p. REED 624:4
pure as p. as snow SHAK 664:7
Blessed are the p. in heart BIBL 93:3
Blessed are the p. in heart KEBL 432:3
led a p. life CATU 197:16
Live p., speak true TENN 759:17
more p. than his maker BIBL 81:8
my heart is p. TENN 766:14
Perfectly p. and good BROW 157:14
P. and ready to mount DANT 250:2
p. as the driven slush BANK 53:7
p. as the lily LAUD 454:6
p. deeds of the Bodhisattvas SHAN 706:10
P. religion and undefiled BIBL 110:16
To the p. all things PROV 613:14
truth is rarely p. WILD 817:13
Unto the p. BIBL 109:24
whatsoever things are p. BIBL 108:25
pureness p. of living and truth BOOK 128:6
purest O P. of Creatures FABE 305:19
p. thing there is JONG 419:6
purgation p. of such emotions ARIS 24:21
purgatorial black, p. rails KEAT 427:4
purgatory no other p. but a woman BEAU 58:17
P. fire BALL 51:3
p. of servants PROV 599:13
purge I'll p., and leave sack SHAK 669:19
p. me with hyssop BOOK 135:6
purged p. the air of pestilence SHAK 700:27
purify p. My House KORA 444:22
p. the dialect of the tribe ELIO 294:16
puritan P. hated bear-baiting MACA 482:14
saw a P.-one BRAT 147:4
to the P. all things are impure LAWR 454:15
puritanism ecrudescence of P. RUSS 639:24
not P. but February KRUT 446:3
P. The haunting fear MENC 504:15
purity Except p. of heart DURC 286:1
Science lost its virgin p. GRAV 349:21
purlieus p. of the Law ETHE 301:11
p. of the law TENN 761:23
purling p. stream ADDI 4:21
to p. brooks POPE 584:7
purple colour p. WALK 799:11
deep p. falls PARI 566:16
in p. and gold BYRO 175:23
in the p. of Emperors KIPL 441:17
I shall wear p. JOSE 421:10
never saw a P. Cow BURG 162:2
p. and fine linen BIBL 100:10
p. brows of Olivet TENN 761:5
P. haze is in my brain HEND 369:16
p.-linèd palace KEAT 428:16
p. mantle to the light RONS 632:7
p. patch or two HORA 385:12
p.-stainèd mouth KEAT 429:8
p. testament SHAK 695:13
p. with love's wound SHAK 689:23
Ran p. to the sea MILT 514:26
purpose any p. perverts art CONS 235:10
creature hath a p. KEAT 431:13
embrace the p. of God TENN 764:17
fits thy p. AURE 36:22
for an Irish p. DAVI 252:20
Infirm of p. SHAK 683:10
My p. is, indeed SHAK 701:15
one increasing p. TENN 763:5
politics of p. HUMP 395:9
p. of his life CHEK 208:8
p. of human existence JUNG 423:7
Shake my fell p. SHAK 682:2
speak and p. not SHAK 677:25
time to every p. BIBL 84:7
working his p. out AING 9:3
purpureal p. gleams WORD 829:1
purpureus *P. Adsuitur pannus* HORA 385:12
purring p. at his heels BLAI 117:6
purrs p. like an epigram MARQ 497:12
purse as thy p. can buy SHAK 662:11
consumption of the p. SHAK 669:28
empty p. BRET 148:3
hand into the public p. PEEL 571:18
law can take a p. BUTL 172:16
silk p. out of sow's ear PROV 615:27
steals my p. SHAK 692:20
purses make heavy p. BACO 42:15
pursue fly it, it will p. JONS 420:19
or knowing it, p. DRYD 282:35
road he wishes to p. TALM 754:21
thing we all p. BEAU 58:16
pursued p. a maiden SHEL 711:15
you who are the p. SHAW 708:2
pursueth flee when no man p. BIBL 83:31
pursuing Faint, yet p. BIBL 77:35
still p. LONG 474:7
pursuit common p. LEAV 461:4
of that long p. THOM 774:9
p. of happiness ANON 19:11
p. of happiness JEFF 405:3
p. of perfection ARNO 28:8
p. of the uneatable WILD 818:24
What mad p. KEAT 428:22
pursy fatness of these p. times SHAK 665:21
purtenance with the p. thereof BIBL 75:39
purus *scelerisque p.* HORA 387:24
push one brave p. STEV 741:22
pushed and he p. LOGU 473:3
was he p. JAME 403:26
pussy I love little p. NURS 548:19
Owl and the P.-Cat LEAR 460:16
p. cat, where have you been NURS 550:9
P.'s in the well NURS 548:4
What a beautiful P. LEAR 460:16
put P. me to what you will METH 506:6
p. not your trust BOOK 141:21
p. on the new man BIBL 109:4
P. out the light SHAK 693:22
p. up with bad things TROL 782:22
up with which I will not p. CHUR 216:3
putrefaction preserve it from p. JOHN 417:16
puzzle Don't p. me STER 739:12
p. the devil BURN 168:9
Rule of Three doth p. me ANON 17:19
puzzles Nothing p. me more LAMB 449:1
pyjamas in p. for the heat LAWR 458:13
pylons P., those pillars bare SPEN 732:23
pyramid bottom of the economic p. ROOS 632:10
pyramids not like children but like p. FLAU 316:18
summit of these p. NAPO 538:8
Pyramus P. and Thisby SHAK 689:8
Pyrenees fleas that tease in the High P. BELL 64:8
P. are no more LOUI 476:1
pyres p. Of her salamandrine fires HARD 361:9
Pythagoras mystical way of P. BROW 153:18

quack potent q., long versed CRAB 243:17
quacks despicable q. JENY 406:11
quad No one about in the Q. KNOX 442:14
quadrangle triangle in a q. AUBR 32:14
quadrigis *Q. petimus bene vivere* HORA 386:20
quadrille q. in a sentry-box JAME 403:2
quadripedante *Q. putrem* VIRG 795:7
quadruped hairy q. DARW 250:16
quaffed jested, q., and swore DOYL 278:10
quaffing q., and unthinking DRYD 282:16
quail q. Whistle about us STEV 740:6
quailing No q., Mrs Gaskell BRON 150:5
quails we long for q. DRYD 282:4
quaint q. and curious war is HARD 361:18
quake q. to say they love SIDN 718:14
she gan to q. CHAU 207:10
qualification only great q. for CARS 192:6
qualis *Non sum q. eram* HORA 389:2
qualities great q. BAGE 46:11
Q. too elevated CHAM 201:6
such q. as would wear well GOLD 345:26
quality People of q. MOLI 525:15
persons of the best q. EVEL 305:5
q. of mercy SHAK 688:10
q. of the notes SCHN 648:23
to some one q. incline DRAY 279:2
qualms cold q. SOUT 731:14
Quangle-Wangle Quee Said the Q. LEAR 460:22
quanta *O q. qualia* ABEL 1:3
quantities ghosts of departed q. BERK 67:18
quantity *q.* of the notes SCHN 648:23
quantula *Q. sint hominum corpuscula* JUVE 425:1
quantum q. o' the sin BURN 167:2
quarks Three q. for Muster Mark JOYC 421:21
quarrel find q. in a straw SHAK 665:33
hath his q. just SHAK 672:17
justice of my q. ANON 17:1
lover's q. with the world FROS 326:3
no q. with the Viet Cong ALI 12:5
perpetual q. BURK 163:3
q. in a far away country CHAM 200:17
q. is now between light and darkness LAMB 449:11
q. of lovers PROV 610:2
q. with ourselves, poetry YEAT 837:25
takes one to make a q. INGE 399:7
two to make a q. PROV 604:40
very pretty q. SHER 716:7
quarrelled q. with my wife PEAC 571:4
quarrelling set them a q. HUME 395:2
surprised that they had been q. HUME 394:17

quarrels How many frivolous q. HUME 394:12
q. were hidden TRAH 780:12
q. with one's husband BONA 125:1
strained by nasty q. HORA 387:23
who in q. interpose GAY 332:9
quarry marked down q. SHAW 708:2
quart q. into a pint pot PROV 615:36
quarter for the remaining q. NAPO 538:14
quarterly nothing a-year, paid q. SURT 747:6
quarters awful q. of an hour ROSS 635:10
quarto beautiful q. page SHER 716:9
quartos q. their ordered ranks maintain CRAB 242:28
quatrains q. shovelled LOWE 478:7
quean flaunting, extravagant q. SHER 716:14
Quebec Long Live Free Q. DE G 255:28
queen Apparent q. MILT 516:20
Astarte, q. of heaven MILT 514:25
Cinara was my q. HORA 389:2
cold q. of England CHES 210:10
Ere you were Q. of Sheba SHIP 717:5
Famine Q. GONN 346:9
fought for Q. and Faith TENN 766:12
grace a summer q. SCOT 651:16
Hail holy q. PRAY 592:6
home life of our own dear Q. ANON 16:18
I have been to the Q. GLAD 341:11
I'm to be Q. o' the May TENN 764:18
Isabel the Q. MARL 496:10
laughing q. HUNT 395:14
Most Gracious Q. ANON 17:18
now our q. SHAK 661:14
Ocean's child, and then his q. SHEL 712:6
Q. and country THOM 774:18
Q. and huntress JONS 419:17
Q. had four Maries BALL 51:9
Q. has the quality PHIL 575:6
q. in a vesture of gold BOOK 134:15
q. in people's hearts DIAN 260:4
q. it no inch further SHAK 703:23
Q. must sign BAGE 47:3
q. of curds and cream SHAK 703:20
Q. of Hearts she made NURS 550:10
q. of Scots ELIZ 296:23
q. of Sheba BIBL 79:17
Q. of silent night BEST 70:2
Q. rose of the rosebud garden TENN 764:8
Q.'s luve BALL 50:10
q. was in the parlour NURS 550:18
Ruler of the Q.'s Navee GILB 338:27
to look at the q. NURS 550:9
To toast *The Q.* HEAN 366:14
weeping q. SHAK 695:18
your anointed Q. ELIZ 296:24
queens all the beautiful Q. DONN 275:7
all your acts are q. SHAK 703:19
Q. have died young NASH 539:22
Queensberry Duchess of Q. WALP 800:16
queer All the world is q. OWEN 562:2
here because we're q. BEHA 62:2
nowt so q. as folk PROV 612:33
q. sort of thing BARH 54:8
queerer universe q. than we suppose HALD 356:15
quem *Q. fugis* VIRG 795:18
quench q. all the fiery darts BIBL 108:13
shall he not q. BIBL 88:6
waters cannot q. love BIBL 86:8
quenched What hath q. them SHAK 683:3
querulous God's q. calling HUGH 393:7
quest to whose winding q. VAUG 790:2
questing passes the q. vole WAUG 806:11
q. beast MALO 492:10
question Answer to the Great Q. ADAM 2:4
ask an impertinent q. BRON 149:9
Ask a silly q. PROV 595:26
asked any clear q. CAMU 184:5
civil q. deserves PROV 597:22
mere asking of a q. FORS 320:22
not to q. other KIPL 438:4
Others abide our q. ARNO 27:13
q. is CARR 191:3
q. is absurd AUDE 35:10
q. why we died KIPL 438:8
secretly changed the Q. SELL 654:15
such a silly q. STER 738:14
that is the q. SHAK 664:3
To ask the hard q. AUDE 35:9
two sides to every q. PROV 612:3
what is the q. LAST 457:17
questioning Q. is not the mode JOHN 415:13
questionings for those obstinate q. WORD 830:6
questions *all* q. were stupid WEIS 809:1
answered three q. CARR 189:13
Ask no q. PROV 595:27
ask q. of those who cannot tell RALE 621:10
Fools ask q. PROV 600:37
puzzling q. BROW 153:4
q. the distempered part ELIO 294:10
queue orderly q. of one MIKE 507:20
quibble q. is to Shakespeare JOHN 410:15
quick Come! q. as you can DE L 256:8
Jack be q. NURS 548:22
judge the q. and the dead BOOK 126:10
q., and the dead DEWA 259:15
q. could never rest SURR 746:12
q. spirit SHAK 674:5
q. to blame AESC 6:12
quicken turn again, and q. us BOOK 137:14
quickeneth spirit that q. BIBL 101:31
quickly gives twice who gives q. PROV 602:5
It were done q. SHAK 682:8
Q. come, quickly go PROV 610:3
That thou doest, do q. BIBL 102:15
quickness q. of thought ASTE 31:13
quicksands q., and the rocks KEAT 431:9
Quicunque Q. vult BOOK 126:21
quiddities quips and thy q. SHAK 667:17
quidquid *Q. agunt homines* JUVE 424:6
quies *Tempus erat quo prima q.* VIRG 794:1
quiet All q. along the Potomac BEER 61:18
alone with the q. day JAME 403:16
Anythin' for a q. life DICK 265:18
Anything for a q. life MIDD 507:3
be q. and go a-Angling WALT 802:27
Easy live and q. die SCOT 651:19
Fie upon this q. life SHAK 668:2
harvest of a q. eye WORD 830:19
hath a q. mind VAUX 791:1
lain still and been q. BIBL 81:4
lives of q. desperation THOR 776:4
never have a q. world SHAW 709:6
O for this q. KEAT 432:1
q. along the Potomac MCCL 484:7
q. as a nun WORD 828:23
q. flows the Don SHOL 717:12
q. hours SHAK 669:4
q. life HICK 376:9
q. mind SURR 746:8
q. mind is worse TRAH 780:17
q. on the western front REMA 624:10
q., pilfering CLAR 218:14
Q. to quick bosoms BYRO 174:17
serve thee with a q. mind BOOK 128:17
sleepers in that q. earth CLOS 222:14
Study to be q. BIBL 109:8
quieta *Q. movere* SALL 643:8
quieten q. your enemy by talking CEAU 199:2
quieter q. retreat AURE 36:21
quietest q. places HOUS 391:7
quietly q. pacifist peaceful WALK 799:8
Q. shining COLE 225:17
quietness all godly q. BOOK 128:12
bride of q. OPEN 556:23
In q. and in confidence BIBL 87:16
unravished bride of q. KEAT 428:21
quietus q. make With a bare bodkin SHAK 664:4
quillets q. of the law SHAK 672:9
quills q. upon the fretful porpentine SHAK 662:25
quilts Soft q. on quilts THOM 774:21
quince slices of q. LEAR 460:19
quincunx q. of heaven BROW 152:14
quinquireme Q. of Nineveh MASE 500:13
quintessence q. of dust SHAK 663:18
quip q. modest SHAK 659:26
quips q. and thy quiddities SHAK 667:17
quires Q. and Places BOOK 126:14
quiring q. to the young-eyed cherubins SHAK 688:23
quis *q. custodiet ipsos Custodes* JUVE 424:16
quit may not q. the post TENN 763:17
q. for the next SHAK 670:9
Q. yourselves like men BIBL 78:17
quite not q. a gentleman ASHF 30:11
quiver hath his q. full BOOK 140:22
quo *Q. vadis* BIBL 114:7
quondam Q. was I WYAT 834:4
quotable eminently q. GERS 334:17
quotation always have a q. SAYE 646:6
considered worthy of q. COWA 239:8
Every q. contributes JOHN 409:5
get a happy q. anywhere HOLM 381:16
good q. book DAVI 252:1
q. what a speaker wants BENN 65:11
quotations heaps of q. DOUG 276:21
I hate q. EMER 300:1
opinion with q. PRIO 593:1
Pretentious q. FOWL 322:1
read books of q. CHUR 216:15
swathed himself in q. KIPL 441:17
quote devil can q. Scripture PROV 598:6
immortal as they q. YOUN 838:16
kill you if you q. it BURG 162:3
man is to q. him BENC 64:19
quoted elegies And q. odes TENN 765:12

R pronounced the letter R AUBR 32:18
rabbit gone to get a r. skin NURS 547:14
r. has a charming face ANON 18:12
r. in a snare STEP 738:4
rabble army would be a base r. BURK 163:7
Mob, Parliament, R. COBB 223:10
Rabelais soul of R. COLE 227:23
race Another r. hath been WORD 830:10
avails the sceptred r. LAND 450:3
born like the rest of my r. BLAK 119:8
melted into a new r. CREV 241:11
most pernicious r. SWIF 747:21
no matter what their r. WILL 821:8
No r. can prosper WASH 804:2
play the r. card SHAP 706:11
r. between education WELL 810:13
r. is not to the swift BIBL 84:23
r. is not to the swift PROV 610:4
r. is to the swift DAVI 251:13
r. that is set before us BIBL 110:2
r. that long in darkness SCOT 652:23
run out thy r. MILT 514:3
run the r. with Death JOHN 417:17
Run the straight r. MONS 526:11
they which run in a r. BIBL 106:10
unprotected r. CLAR 218:14
white r. *is* the cancer SONT 728:7
racer melodist to a fine r. MOZA 534:12
races darker to the lighter r. DU B 284:2
so-called white r. FORS 320:21
Some r. increase LUCR 479:4
two distinct r. LAMB 448:12
Rachel R. weeping BIBL 92:25
served seven years for R. BIBL 75:4
rack Leave not a r. behind SHAK 699:6
r. of a too easy chair POPE 580:25
r. of this tough world SHAK 680:15
racked r. with deep despair MILT 514:14
searched out and r. ORCH 557:9
racket all a German r. RIDL 627:15
r. of the female OSBO 560:4
rackets r. to these balls SHAK 670:29
rackrent pleased with Castle R. EDGE 289:1
radar This is the writer's r. HEMI 369:14

radiance Stains the white r. SHEL 711:4
radiances R. know him BERR 69:16
radical never dared be r. when young FROS 326:7
R. Chic . . . only radical in Style WOLF 825:16
radio had the r. on MONR 526:7
R. and television SARR 644:19
r. expands it WOGA 825:1
television and r. DEV 259:8
radish like a forked r. SHAK 670:10
r. and an egg COWP 242:2
raft discourse on dharma as a r. MAHĀ 490:4
Parable of the R. PALI 565:1
republic is a r. AMES 13:8
rag foul r.-and-bone shop YEAT 835:9
r. and a bone KIPL 440:16
r. blown by the wind WORD 827:9
Shakespeherian R. ELIO 296:5
rage die here in a r. SWIF 748:11
hard-favoured r. SHAK 671:5
heathen so furiously r. BOOK 131:16
Heaven has no r. CONG 232:26
Heaven in a r. BLAK 117:18
horrible that lust and r. YEAT 837:13
r. against the dying of the light THOM 772:2
r. of Caliban WILD 818:15
r. to live VANE 789:16
replete with too much r. SHAK 704:11
scholar in a r. KIPL 441:20
temp'ring virtuous r. POPE 584:10
wretched r. for order MAHO 490:19
writing increaseth r. DYER 286:12
rages weight of r. SPOO 735:3
ragged pair of r. claws ELIO 295:7
raggedness windowed r. SHAK 678:28
raging r. in the dark YEAT 835:8
r. of the sea BOOK 136:1
strong drink is r. BIBL 83:7
ragout fricassee, or a r. SWIF 748:13
rags are as filthy r. BIBL 89:7
r. and contempt BUNY 161:4
r. and tatters MOLI 525:4
r. of time DONN 274:15
ragtime R. . . . but when HUXL 397:7
raid R. BY DR JAMESON TELE 758:3
r. on the inarticulate ELIO 294:11
rail r. at me CONG 232:28
six young on the r. BROW 156:13
railing R. at life CHUR 213:23
railing for r. BIBL 111:4
railroad enterprised a r. RUSK 638:13
railway big r. station NABO 538:1
by r. timetables TAYL 756:6
R. termini FORS 320:15
with a r.-share CARR 191:25
raiment body than r. BIBL 93:23
man clothed in soft r. BIBL 95:6
rain abundance of r. BIBL 79:29
buried in the r. MILL 509:14
clouds and wind without r. BIBL 83:19
clouds return after the r. BIBL 85:2
command the r. PEPY 572:22
cries against the r. GASC 330:15
dead that the r. rains on PROV 596:26
drop of r. maketh a hole LATI 454:3
earth soaks up the r. COWL 239:10
fall like r. AUDE 35:11
February there be no r. PROV 603:17
gentle r. from heaven SHAK 688:10
glazed with r. water WILL 821:2
had outwept its r. SHEL 710:17
hard r.'s a gonna fall DYLA 287:6
Hath the r. a father BIBL 81:33
Jupiter the R.-giver TIBU 777:8
latter r. BOOK 127:20
like sunshine after r. SHAK 706:1
out of the caverns of r. SHEL 711:7
R. before seven PROV 610:5
r. in Spain LERN 465:6
r. is destroying his grain HERB 371:12
r. is on our lips SORL 728:17
r. is over and gone BIBL 85:10
r. it raineth every day SHAK 678:26
r. it raineth every day SHAK 702:22
r., it raineth on the just BOWE 145:20
r. of Dharma MAHĀ 490:9
R., rain, go away NURS 550:11
R.! Rain! Rain KEAT 431:4
sendeth r. BIBL 93:14
send my roots r. HOPK 384:24
small drops of r. BALL 52:6
small r. down can rain ANON 19:13
smell the dew and r. HERB 372:17
soft refreshing r. CAMP 182:14
Still falls the r. SITW 721:2
through the drizzling r. TENN 760:29
wailing of the r. LEDW 461:16
waiting for it to r. COHE 224:4
waiting for r. ELIO 294:21
wedding-cake in the r. AUDE 35:18
rainbow another hue Unto the r. SHAK 677:15
blessing of a r. ABSE 1:7
colours in r. BOOT 142:17
gave Noah the r. SONG 729:6
Lord survives the r. LOWE 478:4
melting r. AKEN 9:5
no r. nation MAND 493:12
r. and a cuckoo's song DAVI 252:6
r. coalition JACK 400:17
r. comes and goes WORD 829:15
R. gave thee birth DAVI 252:7
r. in the sky TENN 759:14
r. of the salt sand-wave KEAT 429:4
r. round about the throne BIBL 111:30
r.'s glory is shed SHEL 712:3
r. which includes black YEVT 838:12
Somewhere over the r. HARB 359:18
when I behold A r. WORD 829:10
rained r. down manna BOOK 137:6
raineth R. drop and staineth slop POUN 589:6
rainfall r. at morning STEV 742:21
raining if it's r., apologizes WELD 809:5
rains never r. but it pours PROV 604:29
r. pennies from heaven BURK 165:16
rainy r. day BIBL 83:30
R. days BASH 56:18
r. Pleiads wester HOUS 390:11
r. Sunday in London DE Q 258:7
strangers on a r. day SMAR 722:7
wish him a r. evening WALT 802:15
raise easier to r. the Devil PROV 604:14
Lord shall r. me up RALE 621:4
raised It is easily r. FIEL 310:3
r. not a stone WOLF 825:5
raising stop r. corn LEAS 461:3
raison *r. tonne en son cratère* POTT 589:5
rake r. in reading MONT 526:21
ram r. caught in a thicket BIBL 74:33
Rama In R. was there a voice BIBL 92:25
Ramadan month of R. KORA 443:18
ramas *Verdes r.* GARC 329:11
rambling r. brat (in print) BRAD 146:13
rampage On the R., Pip DICK 262:22
rampart corse to the r. WOLF 825:3
rams mountains skipped like r. BOOK 139:21
than the fat of r. BIBL 78:25
Ramsbottom Mr and Mrs R. EDGA 288:9
ran both r. together BIBL 102:39
r. before Ahab BIBL 80:1
they r. awa' MCLE 487:6
Who r. to help me TAYL 756:12
Randal Lord R. BALL 51:1
random word, at r. spoken SCOT 651:3
rangers Eight for the eight bold r. SONG 729:11
rank distinguished by r. JUNI 423:15
O! my offence is r. SHAK 665:7
r. is but the guinea's stamp BURN 167:6
r. me with whom you will METH 506:6
Things r. and gross SHAK 661:24
rankers Gentlemen-r. KIPL 438:17
ranks glittering r. MILT 513:22
In the r. of death MOOR 530:14
r. of Tuscany MACA 483:11
ransom world's r., blessèd Mary's Son SHAK 694:19
ransomed R., healed LYTE 481:1
rap r. at the ballot box CHIL 211:25
rape procrastinated r. PRIT 593:8
r.! a rape WEBS 808:12
r. isn't the worst thing WELD 809:10
you r. it DEGA 255:17
raped r. and speaks English ANON 15:10
when they were r. PAGL 563:5
Raphael draw like R. PICA 576:1
Raphaels talked of their R. GOLD 345:5
rapid r., unintelligible patter GILB 339:9
rapine march through r. GLAD 341:5
rapist r. bothers to buy a bottle DWOR 286:11
rapists all men are r. FREN 324:6
rapper to your son as a r. ICE 398:14
rappers first r. of Europe BJÖR 116:19
rapping r. at my chamber door POE 579:15
rapscallions kings is mostly r. TWAI 786:4
rapture first fine careless r. BROW 156:3
Modified r. GILB 338:5
thy r. move POPE 584:24
raptures high r. do infuse WALL 800:8
r. and roses SWIN 750:15
rara *R. avis* JUVE 424:14
rare man of culture r. GILB 338:17
O r. Ben Jonson EPIT 304:1
Rich and r. MOOR 530:16
was indeed a r. one WITH 824:2
rarely R., rarely, comest thou SHEL 713:24
rarer r. than the unicorn JONG 419:6
rari *r. nantes in gurgite vasto* VIRG 793:7
rascal rather be called a r. JOHN 415:20
you dirty r. NURS 548:20
rascality effect of prudence on r. SHAW 708:23
rascals R., would you live FRED 324:2
rash Her r. hand MILT 517:17
He was not r. GRAH 348:6
too r., too unadvised SHAK 697:15
Rasputin Like—like R. RHYS 625:19
Rast *Ohne Hast, aber ohne R.* GOET 343:15
rat Anyone can r. CHUR 215:1
Cat, the R., and Lovell COLL 228:9
creeps like a r. BOWE 145:13
giant r. of Sumatra DOYL 277:13
How now! a r. SHAK 665:12
poisoned r. in a hole SWIF 748:11
r. swimming *towards* CHUR 216:25
r. without a tail SHAK 681:11
smell a r. ROCH 630:3
You dirty r. MISQ 522:16
rate cannot r. me very high LACL 447:5
ratem *pelago r.* HORA 387:15
rathe r. primrose that forsaken dies MILT 513:8
ratio geometrical r. MALT 493:3
inverse r. HUXL 396:17
ratiocination pay with r. BUTL 171:18
rationabile *Sicut modo geniti infantes, r.* BIBL 114:11
rational call the r. soul LEIB 462:21
irrational is r. STEV 739:25
r. converse WOLL 825:20
What is r. is actual HEGE 367:14
rationed so precious it must be r. LENI 463:13
rats r.' alley ELIO 296:4
R.! They fought the dogs BROW 157:10
rattle education serves as a r. ARIS 25:8
hearing 'em r. a little FARQ 307:8
Pleased with a r. POPE 585:24
R. his bones NOEL 546:13
toy of man, his r. WOLL 825:19
rattlesnake thought he saw a R. CARR 192:1
raucle has a r. tongue BURN 166:13
ravage nose May r. with impunity BROW 158:3

ravaged R. and plundered MORR 532:23
raved as I r. and grew more fierce HERB 372:8
ravelling worn to a r. POTT 588:18
raven grim and ancient r. POE 579:17
Poe with this r. LOWE 477:13
r. himself is hoarse SHAK 682:2
r. o'er the infected house SHAK 693:8
saw a r. very high WORD 827:11
With r.'s feather SHAK 698:23
ravening r. wolves BIBL 94:9
ravens r. brought him bread BIBL 79:25
seen the r. flock AYTO 40:11
three r. BALL 52:3
turbulently, like r. PIND 576:9
ravish except you r. me DONN 272:25
ravished transported and r. TRAH 780:14
would have r. her FIEL 309:18
you have r. justice WEBS 808:12
ravishing dear r. thing BEHN 62:6
ravishment r. its sweet KEAT 427:1
ray r. of rays DICK 261:2
razor hew blocks with a r. POPE 587:17
mirror and a r. OPEN 556:18
Occam's R. OCCA 552:15
r. rusting PLAT 577:16
reach could not r. it SAPP 644:15
I r. for my pistol JOHS 418:17
man's r. should exceed BROW 155:2
My soul can r. BROW 154:21
other beers cannot r. ADVE 7:25
r. the brittle branches VIRG 796:8
r. the promised land CALL 181:10
things above his r. OVER 561:1
reaching r. forth BIBL 108:21
reaction can't get no girl r. JAGG 401:6
if there is any r. JUNG 423:9
opposed an equal r. NEWT 543:7
reactionaries All r. are paper tigers MAO 495:3
read Being r. to by a boy ELIO 294:21
bokes for to r. I me delyte CHAU 206:24
but r. these MART 497:24
cannot now r. a page WALP 802:8
did not r. any more DANT 249:14
fast as they can r. HALL [illegible]:17
has r. too widely PEAR 571:9
his books were r. BELL 64:4
In science, r. BULW 160:8
I r., and sigh HERB 371:24
I r. very hard JOHN 413:12
man ought to r. JOHN 413:7
Much had he r. ARMS 25:14
none can r. the text TENN 760:8
not r. Eliot, Auden RICH 626:18
Not that I ever r. them SHER 715:13
only news until he's r. it WAUG 806:13
others who can't r. CHUR 213:21
people that r. SHEN 715:9
people who can't r. ZAPP 839:24
r. a book before reviewing it SMIT 726:2
r., and censure HEMI 369:7
r. a nod, a shrug SWIF 749:9
r. any good books lately CATC 195:20
r. as much as other men AUBR 32:13
r. books *through* JOHN 414:21
r. in the train WILD 817:22
r., mark, learn BOOK 127:22
r., much of the night ELIO 295:27
R. my lips BUSH 171:3
R. not to contradict BACO 44:5
R. out my words FLEC 317:7
R. somewhat seldomer BROW 155:10
r. strange matters SHAK 682:5
r. the crystal BEVA 71:15
r. The Hunter's thoughts AUDE 33:24
r. the life of any important PRIE 591:11
r. without pleasure JOHN 418:15
superfluous to r. HILB 376:10
Take up and r. AUGU 36:4
want to r. a novel DISR 271:10
What do you r. SHAK 663:12
what I r. in the papers ROGE 631:21
What we used to r. CROS 246:8
who don't r. the books BYAT 173:5
whom they never r. CHUR 213:12
write, or r., or think WINC 822:22
reader common r. JOHN 410:4
delighting the r. HORA 386:3
half is with the r. CONR 234:26
Hypocrite r. BAUD 57:6
ideal r. of my novels BURG 161:26
ideal r. suffering from JOYC 421:18
no tears in the r. FROS 326:14
one r. in a hundred years KOES 443:5
R., I married him BRON 149:15
r. of the works of God COWP 241:27
r. seldom peruses ADDI 4:24
readers give their r. sleep POPE 580:9
Imaginative r. GRAV 349:18
r. better to enjoy JOHN 409:15
readeth he may run that r. it BIBL 90:22
readiness r. is all SHAK 667:3
reading careful of his r. LEWI 466:20
English r. public JOYC 422:19
get nowadays from r. GREE 351:22
health through r. RILK 628:5
he was r. AUGU 36:2
in the R.-room GISS 340:10
lie in a hot bath r. THOM 772:22
Like R., only farther FLEM 317:19
not worth r. AUST 37:20
Peace is poor r. HARD 360:9
pleasure in the r. QUAR 618:13
prefer r. SMIT 724:12
rake in r. MONT 526:21
R. and marriage MOLI 525:6
r., in order to write JOHN 415:2
r. is no more than STEN 737:15
R. isn't an occupation ORTO 558:3
r. is right JOHN 410:17
R. is to the mind STEE 737:1
R. maketh a full man BACO 44:7
r. of good books DESC 258:16
r. of such a book ASCH 30:8
r. or non-reading BYRO 180:9
r., or writing THOM 771:2
soul of r. STER 738:21
'twixt r. and bohea POPE 584:7
vile hard r. SHER 716:18
were r. a letter TALM 754:26
what is worth r. TREV 781:9
reads He r. much SHAK 674:17
Who r. Incessantly MILT 518:10
ready always r. to go LA F 447:13
conference a r. man BACO 44:7
fire when you are r. DEWE 259:16
gracious and r. help BOOK 130:4
necessity of being *r.* LINC 468:10
of a r. writer BOOK 134:13
R. to be any thing BROW 153:11
real home to a r. world TURK 785:11
Life is r. LONG 474:3
r. Simon Pure CENT 199:13
speechless r. BARZ 56:13
their world is the r. one ROTH 635:20
your r. nature HUI- 394:3
realism dislike of R. WILD 818:15
I don't want r. WILL 820:20
realistic make a 'r. decision' MCCA 484:3
reality art is but a vision of r. YEAT 835:22
bear very much r. ELIO 294:3
Between the idea And the r. ELIO 294:25
employs r. as little MOND 526:3
find r. MURD 536:21
in r. there are atoms DEMO 257:2
It is a r. CLIN 221:7
less in r. HUME 394:17
Love is the discovery of r. MURD 536:19
makes r. more bearable BYRO 177:29
other people's r. SONT 728:8
r. and lies COCT 223:16
R., as usual, beats CONR 235:2
R. goes bounding past COCK 223:14
r. take precedence FEYN 309:6
suffer r. to *suggest* BRON 149:20
to the r. EPIT 302:5
worth and spiritual r. HEGE 367:11
really as in itself it r. is ARNO 29:6
be a R. Useful Engine AWDR 39:19
what I r. really want ROWB 636:8
realm One r., one people POLI 581:11
this earth, this r. SHAK 694:19
realms r. of gold KEAT 429:20
r. of gold OPEN 556:2
through the r. of light GURN 355:5
whom three r. obey POPE 587:5
reap As you sow, so you r. PROV 595:25
neither do they r. BIBL 93:23
r. a character READ 622:16
r., if we faint not BIBL 107:23
r. in joy BOOK 140:20
r. the whirlwind BIBL 90:10
r. the whirlwind PROV 612:36
that shall he also r. BIBL 107:22
reaped should never be r. TRAH 780:13
reapers Pity the r. DUCK 284:4
r., reaping early TENN 762:14
reaping ever r. something new TENN 763:2
No, r. BOTT 144:22
r. where thou hast not sown BIBL 97:9
reaps another r. SHEL 713:26
rear r. the tender thought THOM 775:5
reason appear the better r. MILT 515:9
Blotting out r. GRAV 349:15
by their feelings than by r. ADAM 3:20
capability and god-like r. SHAK 665:31
conquers r. still POPE 583:20
discourse of r. SHAK 661:26
erring R.'s spite POPE 585:18
form of human r. LÉVI 466:12
Give you a r. SHAK 668:8
ideal of r. KANT 425:17
if it be against r. COKE 224:6
kills r. itself MILT 519:8
man who listens to R. SHAW 708:25
most sovereign r. SHAK 664:11
noble in r. SHAK 663:18
Nothing without a r. LEIB 462:22
not his r., but his passions STER 738:25
not r. and compare BLAK 118:20
O r. not the need SHAK 678:17
perfection of r. COKE [illegible]
pursue my r. BROW 153:16
R. always means GASK 330:20
r. and conscience PRIC 591:9
r., and justice BURK 163:1
R. and Progress OSBO 560:6
R. and the sciences LEIB 462:21
R., an *ignis fatuus* ROCH 630:13
r. can imagine TRAH 780:16
r. does buckle BACO 41:11
R. herself will respect GIBB 335:16
R., in her most exalted mood WORD 831:11
r. in the roasting PROV 612:22
r. is against it BUTL 172:27
R. is, and ought to be HUME 395:6
r. is insufficient HUME 394:9
R. is natural revelation LOCK 471:18
r. is our law MILT 517:16
r. is stifled BURK 162:12
R. is the life of the law COKE 224:7
r. knows nothing of PASC 568:17
r. produces monsters GOYA 347:13
R.'s ear ADDI 5:13
r. shall my heart direct ETHE 301:14
R. still keeps its throne FARQ 307:21
r. themselves out again SHAK 672:5
R. the natural image BONA 125:5
R. to rule DRYD 281:19
r. why I cannot tell BROW 152:7
render a r. BIBL 83:26
right deed for the wrong r. ELIO 295:15
show no r. can WATK 804:14
takes the r. prisoner SHAK 681:18
that is not r. POWE 590:22

Their's not to r. why TENN 757:16
triumph of human r. HAWK 364:11
ultimate r. of things LEIB 462:20
woman's r. SHAK 702:24
words clothed in r.'s garb MILT 515:12
reasonable of a r. soul BOOK 127:1
R. Man HERB 371:21
r. man adapts SHAW 708:24
They were r. people BROO 151:1
will must be r. JEFF 405:11
reasonableness sweet r. of Jesus ARNO 29:3
reasonably r. be expected to do WHAT 813:9
reasoning abstract r. HUME 394:7
cowards in r. SHAF 655:17
in dirt the r. engine ROCH 630:14
involved in r. VOLT 798:8
r., self-sufficing thing WORD 830:18
reasons finding of bad r. BRAD 146:6
five r. ALDR 11:2
Good r. must, of force SHAK 676:27
heart has its r. PASC 568:17
R. are not like garments ESSE 301:9
r. for living JUVE 424:18
r. for the rule change STRA 744:16
r. will certainly MANS 494:11
We want better r. RUSS 640:8
rebecks jocund r. sound MILT 512:21
rebel die like a true-blue r. LAST 456:10
experienced r., Time FLAT 316:6
I am *still* a r. BROW 152:4
R. without a cause FILM 313:1
still an Irish r. DUFF 284:11
What is a r. CAMU 184:11
rebellion little r. now and then JEFF 405:5
r. and revivalism THOM 773:7
r. is as the sin BIBL 78:26
R. lay in his way SHAK 669:5
R. to tyrants BRAD 146:12
R. to tyrants MOTT 535:15
r. was the certain consequence MANS 494:10
rum, Romanism, and r. BURC 161:21
rebellions everyday r. STEI 737:13
rebellious r. heart BIBL 89:12
rebels r. are our countrymen GRAN 348:18
subjects are r. BURK 163:24
reborn being r. therein MAHĀ 490:14
rebounds unless it r. JOHN 414:26
rebuke Open r. BIBL 83:28
r. hath broken my heart BOOK 136:11
r. the people BOOK 142:2
recall cannot r. their gifts TENN 767:1
takes wing beyond r. HORA 387:1
recalled once spoke can never be r. DILL 267:12
Things past cannot be r. PROV 612:37
recapitulates ontogeny r. HAEC 355:12
receipt r. of custom BIBL 94:22
receive better to give than to r. PROV 604:11
r. but what we give COLE 225:3
r. one such little child BIBL 96:8
than to r. BIBL 104:14
received Freely ye have r. BIBL 94:32
his own r. him not BIBL 101:6
receiver have left the r. off the hook KOES 443:4
r. is always thought CHES 209:2
receivers no r., no thieves PROV 603:24
receiveth Every one that asketh r. BIBL 94:4
receiving giving and r. of a Ring BOOK 131:8
receptacle r. for emotions PICA 575:17
recesses r. in my mind BRON 149:14
recession r. when your neighbour TRUM 784:6
spend way out of a r. CALL 181:9
recipes like r. in a cookbook STEW 743:6
r. that are always successful VALÉ 789:1
recirculation commodious vicus of r. JOYC 421:17
commodious vicus of r. OPEN 556:12
recited r. verses in writing BIBL 92:15
reckoned love that can be r. SHAK 656:7
reckoning at your own r. TROL 783:9
encounter my r. KORA 445:16
No r. made SHAK 662:31
sense of r. SHAK 671:21
reckonings Short r. PROV 610:37
recks r. not his own rede SHAK 662:9
recognize not r. me by my face TROL 781:17
only a trial if I r. it KAFK 425:7
recognized objects r. WORD 831:5
recommend tries to r. him JOHN 410:12
recompense r. is a pleasure JOHN 410:20
r. those who believe KORA 444:18
reconciles feasting r. everybody PEPY 573:9
reconciliation bridge of r. RUNC 637:7
silence and r. MACA 482:9
True r. does not MAND 493:10
reconstruct r. it there NEUR 541:12
record as fast as the world r. COLE 224:15
bound to r. it TURN 785:17
merely be the r. FAUL 307:28
put down in his r. ANON 22:2
r. of blissful old times BLAM 121:15
recordanti *r. benefacta priora* CATU 197:14
recording domesticate the R. Angel STEV 742:2
R. Angel, as he wrote it down STER 739:8
recover r. the use of his legs DICK 263:24
seldom or never r. SHAK 657:26
recovered may nought r. be CHAU 207:15
recreant soldier a mere r. SHAK 700:8
recrudescence r. of Puritanism RUSS 639:24
rectangular proceedings are quite r. BYRO 179:22
recte *Si possis r.* HORA 386:11
Vivere si r. nescis HORA 387:10
rectum one in the r. OSLE 560:15
recurret *usque r.* HORA 386:19
red As many r. herrings NURS 549:12
Better r. than dead POLI 581:6
blows so r. The rose FITZ 314:11
feel the r. in my mind DICK 266:21
gentlemen, In coats of r. DE L 256:14
give this cheek a little r. POPE 584:4
her lips' r. SHAK 705:20
jolly r. nose BEAU 58:12
keep the r. flag flying CONN 233:23
Luve's like a r., red rose BURN 168:6
Making the green one r. SHAK 683:11
my skin is r. SITT 720:18
Nor dim nor r. COLE 226:9
not even r. brick OSBO 560:5
people's flag is deepest r. CONN 233:22
Pluck a r. rose SHAK 672:11
raiment all r. MACA 482:21
r.-deer's herd BYRO 178:10
r. in tooth and claw TENN 761:14
r. men scalped each other MACA 481:8
R. sky at night PROV 610:6
r. wheel barrow WILL 821:2
rise with my r. hair PLAT 577:18
thin r. line RUSS 640:13
Thin r. line of 'eroes KIPL 440:13
wine when it is r. BIBL 83:16
wrists and fingers r. MACA 483:13
redbreast r. whistles KEAT 430:12
reddens sweet-apple r. SAPP 644:15
redder r. than the fyn coral CHAU 206:2
rede recks not his own r. SHAK 662:9
redeem R. thy mis-spent time KEN 433:1
redeemed r. Jerusalem BIBL 88:13
redeemer infant R. is laid HEBE 367:5
know that my r. liveth BIBL 81:22
O thou great R. WILL 820:8
Our blest R. AUBE 32:10
strength, and my r. BOOK 132:18
such a mighty R. MISS 523:8
To thee, R. NEAL 540:1
redeeming devastating or r. fires GONC 346:7
R. the time BIBL 108:8
redemption great r. from above MILT 513:17
married past r. DRYD 282:3
r.'s happy dawn CASW 194:3
redemptorem *meruit habere R.* MISS 523:8
redress r. Of all my pain WYAT 834:3
Things past r. SHAK 695:3
reds honour the indomitable R. DUNN 285:10
redtape r. talking-machine CARL 188:6
redwood r. forest to the Gulf Stream GUTH 355:7
reed bruised r. BIBL 80:28
bruised r. BIBL 88:6
but for a r. MARV 498:14
clasped a r. SHEL 711:15
he is a thinking r. PASC 568:18
into beauty like a r. LEWE 466:16
r. before the wind PROV 610:7
r. shaken with the wind BIBL 95:6
reeds floods over the r. PAST 569:8
in the r. by the river BROW 154:20
reeking r. into Cadiz Bay BROW 156:4
reel R. in a drunkard CHUR 214:2
They r. to and fro BOOK 139:15
reeled Until r. the mind GIBB 336:9
reels There's threesome r. BURN 166:29
referee having two you are a r. FROS 325:12
reference sensitive to frames of r. QUIN 619:6
references verify your r. ROUT 636:7
refine insert, r. SWIF 749:14
r. our language JOHN 410:22
refined disgust this r. age EVEL 305:7
Englishwoman is so r. SMIT 724:24
people of r. sentiments KELL 432:15
R. himself to soul DRYD 281:4
reflex r. of a star WORD 828:21
reform able to r. MORE 531:3
desire to r. ARNO 29:17
party of progress or r. MILL 508:20
Peace, retrenchment, and r. BRIG 148:10
r. or revolution BERL 68:14
r. the criminal FRY 326:26
sets about r. TOCQ 778:11
thunder for r. NEWS 544:15
reformation plotting some new r. DRYD 282:13
reforming of R. MILT 519:15
reformer r. is a guy who rides MIZN 524:13
reformers r. are bachelors MOOR 529:11
refraining R. from taking life PALI 564:15
refresh r. it when it was dry BOOK 127:20
refreshed r. with wine BOOK 137:7
refreshes r. the parts ADVE 7:25
refuge Dhamma as your r. PALI 564:18
easy to take r. in IBSE 398:10
God is thy r. BIBL 77:14
God of Jacob is our r. BOOK 134:19
gone to him as a r. PALI 564:14
hills are a r. BOOK 139:4
Patriotism is the last r. JOHN 415:3
r. from home life SHAW 709:22
thou hast been our r. BOOK 137:17
refusal great r. DANT 249:9
refuse offer he can't r. PUZO 618:5
r. of your teeming tents LAZA 459:12
r. to fight POLI 582:5
Which he did thrice r. SHAK 676:2
refused practice in being r. DIOG 268:2
stone which the builders r. BOOK 140:6
refuses sea r. no river PROV 610:23
refute I r. it *thus* JOHN 413:20
r. anyone who argues SA'A 640:21
r. a sneer PALE 564:12
regal someone that height look r. AMIE 13:10
regard least r. for SPEN 732:9
regarder *se r. soi-même* MOLI 525:12
regardless r. of their doom GRAY 350:16
regards r. that stand Aloof SHAK 678:1
regeneration baptism, a r. ELIO 291:22
reges *Quidquid delirant r.* HORA 386:13
regiment r. of women KNOX 442:10
regina *Salve, r.* PRAY 592:6

region Is this the r. MILT 514:19
r. of my song WORD 828:6
regions r. in your mind HABI 355:9
register r. of the crimes, follies GIBB 335:6
règle *grande r.* MOLI 524:22
regnavit *R. a ligno Deus* FORT 321:8
regnum *adveniat r. tuum* MISS 522:17
regret Old Age a r. DISR 270:3
r. can die TENN 761:20
vain r. ROSS 635:4
wild with all r. TENN 765:21
regrets congratulatory r. DISR 269:19
Miss Otis r. PORT 588:8
no r. VAUC 790:1
wild r., and the bloody sweats WILD 819:2
regrette *je ne r. rien* VAUC 790:1
Je r. l'Europe RIMB 628:9
regular Brought r. DICK 263:8
icily r. TENN 763:21
regularity genius and r. GAIN 327:18
R. and Decorum COOP 236:7
regulate r. printing MILT 519:12
regulated R. hatred HARD 360:4
regulations strong upon the R. Act WILD 818:33
regumque *R. turris* HORA 387:16
reheat cannot r. a soufflé MCCA 484:6
Reich *Ein R.* POLI 581:11
German R. is made BISM 116:13
reign begins early to r. BAGE 47:6
Better to r. in hell MILT 514:21
friendless is to r. SHEL 713:11
Long to r. over us SONG 729:7
Love, that doth r. SURR 746:9
r. of Chaos and old Night MILT 514:29
reigned if he had not r. TACI 752:15
r. with your loves ELIZ 297:4
reigning answered *'r.'* BENT 66:19
reigns king r. THIE 770:18
red blood r. SHAK 703:9
Reilly Come back, Paddy R. FREN 324:8
reindeer Herds of r. move AUDE 33:27
Red-Nosed R. MARK 495:13
reinforcement What r. we may gain MILT 514:17
reins try out my r. BOOK 133:7
reject stamped R. FIEL 309:13
rejected despised and r. BIBL 88:16
rejoice as men r. BIBL 86:28
desert shall r. BIBL 87:21
hills shall r. BOOK 136:2
let us heartily r. BOOK 138:5
Let us then r. ANON 21:9
may r. BOOK 135:6
Philistines r. BIBL 79:1
r. and be glad BOOK 140:6
r. at that news THAT 769:25
R. evermore BIBL 109:10
r. in Christ LUTH 479:12
R. in the Lord BIBL 108:23
r. the heart BOOK 132:16
R., the Lord is King WESL 811:6
R. with them BIBL 105:15
rejoiced R. they were na men BURN 169:7
spirit hath r. BIBL 98:16
rejoices poor heart that never r. PROV 604:5
rejoiceth r. as a giant BOOK 132:15
rejoicing home, r., brought me BAKE 48:13
r. with heaven MILT 519:21
relation cold r. BURK 164:5
nobody like a r. THAC 769:7
State is a r. of men WEBE 807:5
relations God's apology for r. KING 437:18
in personal r. RUSS 639:14
not have sexual r. CLIN 221:6
Personal r. FORS 320:17
relationship every human r. suffers FORS 321:1
r. that goes bad FAIT 306:5
r. that was not CLIN 221:8
Their r. consisted GUNN 355:1
relationships R., relationships FISH 313:10
relative set out one day in a r. way BULL 160:1
Success is r. ELIO 293:25
relaxed feel terribly r. DAYA 253:10
relaxes Bless r. BLAK 119:22
release called r. from bondage CHUA 213:5
Good-night. Ensured r. HOUS 390:13
relent make him once r. BUNY 161:16
make the gods above r. VIRG 795:5
relic Fair Greece! sad r. BYRO 174:5
like a holy r. WEBS 807:21
relics his r. are laid MOOR 530:15
with thise r. CHAU 205:6
relief death is rather a r. FITZ 315:4
For this r. much thanks SHAK 661:5
gave that thought r. WORD 829:16
r. of man's estate BACO 41:9
seek for kind r. BLAK 120:20
system of outdoor r. BRIG 148:11
relieve comfort and r. them BOOK 127:18
relieved By desperate appliances are r. SHAK 665:26
religio *Tantum r. potuit* LUCR 479:1
religion act of duty and r. OSBO 559:21
affront her r. JENY 406:11
all of the same r. DISR 270:12
another r. than Islam KORA 444:4
Art and R. are two roads BELL 62:19
As if R. were intended BUTL 171:24
As to r. PAIN 563:15
become a popular r. INGE 399:5
born for the sake of r. LAWS 459:2
brothels with bricks of r. BLAK 119:19
but of one r. SHAF 655:16
can't talk r. to SHAW 707:24
Christianity was the r. SWIF 748:23
concerned with r. TEMP 757:7
dominion of r. GOLD 344:5
establishment of r. CONS 235:12
Every dictator uses r. BHUT 73:6
feature of *any* r. PAIN 563:24
fox-hunting—the wisest r. HAIL 356:10
Freedom of r. JEFF 405:14
had only a little r. ANON 20:5
handmaid to r. BACO 41:18
impossibilities enough in r. BROW 153:15
increase in us true r. BOOK 100:14
in love as in r. COWL 239:18
innovation in r. MAEC 489:6
In their r. they are so uneven DEFO 255:10
just enough r. SWIF 748:24
Knight-errantry *is* r. CERV 199:18
matters of r. CHES 209:3
men's minds to r. BACO 42:7
more fierce in its r. NEWM 542:6
much wrong could r. induce LUCR 479:1
mysteries of our r. HOBB 379:3
No compulsion in r. KORA 443:20
no part of r. WESL 811:12
no r. but social WESL 811:10
on account of my r. BELL 64:12
One r. is as true BURT 170:22
only one r. SHAW 709:9
perfected your r. KORA 444:16
Philistine of genius in r. ARNO 29:4
Poetry and R. CARL 187:18
poetry, prophecy, and r. RUSK 638:11
politics as well as in r. JUNI 423:14
Pure r. and undefiled BIBL 110:16
r., and not atheism BURK 163:2
r. and philosophy ARNO 28:22
r., as a mere sentiment NEWM 542:7
r. at the lowest CHES 209:20
R. blushing POPE 582:13
r. but a childish toy MARL 496:15
r. for gentlemen CHAR 203:9
r. for religion's sake COUS 238:6
r. from the priest GOLD 345:32
r. has always been to me POTT 588:22
r. into after-dinner toasts TOAS 778:3
r. is allowed to invade MELB 504:2
R. is an all-important matter NAPO 538:13
R. is by no means CHES 209:4
r. is made MONT 527:19
r. is not circumambient FOST 321:12
r. is powerless to bestow FORB 319:9
R. is the sigh MARX 499:13
r. is to do good PAIN 564:5
r., justice, counsel BACO 43:31
r., knavery, and change BEHN 62:12
r. most prevalent BURK 162:26
r. of feeble minds BURK 164:1
r. of humanity PAIN 563:17
r. of Socialism BEVA 71:14
r. or policy RUSK 638:24
R.'s in the heart JERR 407:3
R. the frozen thought of men KRIS 445:21
r. weak SZAS 752:3
r. without a prelate BANC 53:4
r. without science is blind EINS 290:8
R.? Yes; but which BYRO 177:29
reproach to r. PENN 572:14
rum and true r. BYRO 176:11
some of r. EDGE 288:10
start your own r. ANON 16:22
system of r. PAIN 563:9
talks loudly against r. STER 738:25
That is my r. SHAW 707:23
that regards r. ADDI 5:11
They are for r. BUNY 161:4
too late to trust the old r. LOWE 478:6
tourism is their r. RUNC 637:8
true meaning of r. ARNO 29:1
true r. is Islam KORA 444:1
vice and r. SMIT 726:6
way to plant r. BROW 153:22
When I mention r. FIEL 310:7
religions R. are kept alive BREN 147:23
r. considered man as man TOCQ 778:8
sixty different r. CARA 185:17
they alone who found r. PROU 594:4
religiose r. And mystic DUNN 285:12
religious all r. revolution WEBE 807:7
but not r.-good HARD 361:3
dim r. light MILT 512:11
great r. art of the world CLAR 219:7
his r. opinions BUTL 172:29
hope I will be r. again FLEM 317:14
Old r. factions BURK 165:9
r. and moral principles ARNO 29:14
r. animal BURK 163:27
r. enquiries NEWM 542:10
R. persecution BURK 165:6
r. prejudice HUXL 397:20
seemeth to be r. BIBL 110:15
sense of r. mission UPDI 788:17
suspended my r. inquiries GIBB 335:20
with a r. book WOTT 832:23
relish one begins to have a r. HAYW 365:3
relished by which he is to be r. WORD 832:22
reluctance superstitious r. to sit JOHN 416:12
reluctant r. peer BENN 65:4
with r. feet LONG 473:22
rem *quocumque modo r.* HORA 386:11
R. tene CATO 194:16
remain fragments that r. BIBL 101:26
r. with you always BOOK 130:3
things have been, things r. CLOU 223:2
remains aught r. to do ROGE 631:12
r. of life WALP 800:20
remarkable anything r. about it PAST 569:3
nothing left r. SHAK 657:19
remarks R. are not literature STEI 737:5
said our r. before us DONA 272:3
remedies desperate r. PROV 598:5
r. oft in ourselves do lie SHAK 656:1
will not apply new r. BACO 43:14
remedy bestowed on mankind a r. SYDE 751:19
dangerous r. FAWK 308:3
Force is not a r. BRIG 148:15
My dog! what r. remains COWP 240:22
r. for everything except PROV 612:5
r. is death CHAM 201:5

r. is worse than the disease BACO 43:34
r. our *enemies* have chosen SHER 717:1
r. our own KYD 446:8
Things without all r. SHAK 684:4
'Tis a sharp r. RALE 621:8
remember Body, r. not only CAVA 198:4
cannot r. the past SANT 644:9
Do you r. an Inn, Miranda BELL 64:7
if thou wilt, r. ROSS 634:13
I r., I remember HOOD 382:21
I r. it well LERN 465:4
Lord, r. me BIBL 100:27
man to r. me RUNY 637:16
r. a happy time DANT 249:12
r. and be sad ROSS 634:9
r. even these things VIRG 793:10
r. for ever WARN 803:18
R. me ROSS 634:8
R. me TATE 755:7
R. me when I am dead DOUG 276:15
r. more than seven BELL 63:1
r. not past years NEWM 542:20
R. now thy Creator BIBL 85:2
r. sweet Alice ENGL 300:13
R. the Alamo SHER 716:25
r. the black wharves LONG 473:23
r. the children you got BROO 151:6
R. thee! Ay, thou poor ghost SHAK 662:32
r. the Fifth of November ANON 18:9
R. the sabbath day BIBL 76:11
r. the way we parted SWIN 751:7
r., whan it passed is CHAU 207:12
r. who I am VIRG 794:12
r. with advantages SHAK 671:24
thou r. and I forget SWIN 751:10
We will r. them BINY 115:8
what you can r. SELL 654:4
Yes; I r. Adlestrop THOM 772:23
yet never can, r. THOM 773:3
You must r. this HUPF 396:10
remembered blue r. hills HOUS 391:5
like to be r. POWE 590:19
r. around the world DISN 268:5
r. for a very long time MCGO 485:7
would have made myself r. KEAT 431:21
remembering R. without ceasing BIBL 109:7
remembrance arouse in them r. KORA 444:21
Do this in r. of me BOOK 129:22
everlasting r. BOOK 139:19
r. of a weeping queen SHAK 695:18
r. of his dying Lord SPEN 733:13
r. of them is grievous BOOK 129:16
R. of things past BORR 144:13
r. of things past SHAK 704:16
rosemary, that's for r. SHAK 666:7
Writ in r. more SHAK 694:18
remind R. me of you MARV 499:9
reminiscences R. make one feel SHAW 707:15
remission for the r. of sins BOOK 129:22
no r. BIBL 109:26
r. of pain or guilt BOOK 142:11
remnant smell my r. out HERB 372:21
remorse access and passage to r. SHAK 682:2
rather feel r. THOM 770:19
R. is surely the most wasteful FORS 320:19
R., the fatal egg COWP 241:4
R.! Those dry Martinis ADE 5:21
remorseful blabbing, and r. day SHAK 672:18
remote r. enquiries JOHN 409:26
removals household r. BAUD 57:11
Three r. are as bad PROV 612:47
remove owl of the R. RICH 626:15
R. not the ancient landmark BIBL 83:15
say unto this mountain, R. BIBL 96:6
remover with the r. to remove SHAK 705:15
Remus descendants of R. CATU 197:10
On the left side goes R. MACA 483:13
renard *Certain r. voulut* LA F 447:14
renascentur *Multa r.* HORA 385:15
render r. The deeds of mercy SHAK 688:11
R. to all their dues BIBL 105:20
R. unto Caesar BIBL 96:22
rendezvous My r. is appointed WHIT 815:17
r. with Death SEEG 653:5
renew r. a right spirit BOOK 135:7
r. their strength BIBL 88:5
R. your brilliance GRAC 347:15
renewal r. of love PROV 610:2
renewing r. is of love EDWA 289:13
Reno King's Moll R.'d NEWS 544:12
renounce I r. war FOSD 321:9
r. the devil BOOK 130:11
renouncing r. his body JAIN 402:4
renown O vain r. DANT 249:21
r. on scraps of learning YOUN 838:16
rent R. is that portion RICA 626:2
r. we pay for our room CLAY 220:6
That has not been r. YEAT 835:13
renunciation professors preach r. JAIN 401:17
repair friendship in constant r. JOHN 412:21
repairing begin r. his house WIND 823:3
repartee always the best r. DISR 270:28
repay I will r. BIBL 105:17
I will r. thee BIBL 99:13
Tiger well r. BELL 63:4
repeal r. of bad or obnoxious laws GRAN 349:2
repeat condemned to r. it SANT 644:9
Historians r. each other GUED 354:13
I can r. poetry CARR 191:5
images change as they r. WARH 803:15
neither r. his past AUDE 35:13
r. what we all know BELL 64:13
repeated mistake shall not be r. EPIT 304:3
simply a truth r. BALD 49:6
repeateth r. a matter BIBL 83:2
repeats History r. itself PROV 602:40
r. his words SHAK 677:11
repelled r. by man INGE 399:6
repent hope that they will r. MIDR 507:11
I do r. it SHAK 700:3
No follies to have to r. TAYL 756:14
r. at leisure PROV 606:31
r. in haste CONG 232:34
r. of my diets ALLE 12:19
R. ye BIBL 92:26
r. you of your sins BOOK 129:15
weak alone r. BYRO 175:16
repentance cool r. came SCOT 652:5
pleasure and r. RALE 620:10
R. and good works TALM 753:21
R. is but want of power DRYD 282:10
R. is so great TALM 754:8
R. is the virtue DRYD 281:28
R. on a Sunday night YBAR 834:20
sinners to r. BIBL 94:25
repente *Nemo r. fuit turpissimus* JUVE 424:8
repented strove, and much r. BYRO 176:4
repenteth Me r., said Merlin MALO 492:8
sinner that r. BIBL 100:1
repetition r. of unpalatable truths SUMM 746:5
repetitions vain r. BIBL 93:18
repetitious r. mechanism of the Universe WHIT 814:10
reply I pause for a r. SHAK 675:26
r. churlish SHAK 659:26
Their's not to make r. TENN 757:16
report believed our r. BIBL 88:14
of good r. BIBL 108:25
R. me and my cause SHAK 667:8
reporters speaking through r. CARL 188:4
reports Bring me no more r. SHAK 685:15
R. of my death TWAI 786:28
repose earned a night's r. LONG 474:20
last r. ANON 19:16
r. of a pacific station ADAM 2:1
stunned r. HILL 376:16
representation Taxation and r. CAMD 182:12
Taxation without r. OTIS 560:21
representations r. of general nature JOHN 410:11
similar r. DION 268:4
representative indignity of being your r. BELL 64:12
r. government DISR 270:27
Your r. owes you BURK 164:26
repress r. the speech ELIO 292:7
repression result of forced r. MILL 509:4
reproach r. a husband LA F 447:15
reproche *Chevalier sans peur et sans r.* ANON 20:4
reproof r. valiant SHAK 659:26
reproofs r. from authority BACO 43:11
reptile r. all the rest POPE 583:10
turn myself into a r. JOHN 412:23
republic aristocracy in a r. MITF 524:7
destroyed the R. DEV 259:5
England is a disguised r. BAGE 46:21
essence of the R. ROBE 629:6
Love the Beloved R. FORS 321:5
love, the beloved R. SWIN 751:1
r. is a raft AMES 13:8
sweet equal r. PAUL 570:7
republican on r. principles SHAW 709:2
surly r. JOHN 410:7
understood by r. government TOCQ 778:14
Republicans We are R. BURC 161:21
repugnant r. to the Word of God BOOK 142:10
repulsion Attraction and r. BLAK 119:9
repulsive Right but R. SELL 654:9
reputation disagreeables of r. ELIO 293:13
genius and good r. GERV 335:1
honour and r. JONS 420:7
of no r. BIBL 108:16
O! I have lost my r. SHAK 692:16
r. dies POPE 587:6
r. of five-and-twenty DRYD 282:2
r. through the world SHAK 694:19
r. which the world bestows DANT 249:22
Seeking the bubble r. SHAK 659:1
sold my r. for a song FITZ 315:1
spotless r. SHAK 694:9
wink a r. down SWIF 749:9
written out of r. BENT 67:9
reputations fuller's earth for r. GAY 331:14
home of ruined r. ELIO 292:14
murdered r. CONG 233:3
request No flowers, by r. AING 9:2
ruined at our own r. MORE 530:24
requiem *R. aeternam dona eis* MISS 523:2
requiescant *r. in pace* MISS 523:7
require thought 'e might r. KIPL 440:20
required nothing can be r. FIEL 309:19
soul shall be r. of thee BIBL 99:22
requisite r. in business ADDI 4:18
re-rat ingenuity to r. CHUR 215:1
res *in medias r.* HORA 386:1
r. age OVID 561:21
R. angusta domi JUVE 424:12
rescuers firing on the r. WOOL 827:6
research Basic r. is what BRAU 147:7
dignify by the name of r. LASK 454:1
r. is always incomplete PATT 570:4
r. the art of the soluble MEDA 503:6
steal from many, it's r. MIZN 524:12
resemblance from bearing any r. PROU 594:5
resemble least plans to r. BROO 151:2
So much r. man COWP 240:22
resentful state of r. coma LASK 454:1
resentment get up r. NEWM 542:2
reservations no mental r. LINC 468:8
reserved r. for some end CLIV 221:10
reservoir This year a r. POPE 583:21
residences Inns are not r. MOOR 530:1
resign Few die and none r. MISQ 521:12

resignation by r. none JEFF 405:15
well-bred r. TURG 785:3
resigned I am not r. MILL 509:10
more r. to CATH 194:10
Prime Minister has r. ANON 16:13
resist r. everything except temptation WILD 818:8
resistance break the r. STAL 736:1
line of least r. AMER 13:5
no length of r. BONA 125:2
r. of the Tolbooth-gate SCOT 651:25
resistible r. rise of Arturo Ui BREC 147:16
resolute bloody, bold, and r. SHAK 684:22
resolution native hue of r. SHAK 664:4
r. on reflection WALP 801:19
thought and r. TROL 783:8
what r. from despair MILT 514:17
resolutions great and mighty r. BUTL 172:4
passions and r. HUME 394:13
resolve Come, Firm R. BURN 168:25
R. not to be poor JOHN 416:27
R. to be thyself ARNO 27:12
resolved r. not to make ELIO 292:7
will soon be r. MARL 496:21
resolves R.; and re-resolves YOUN 839:7
resort it's your last r. PLAT 577:11
resource r.-and-sagacity KIPL 441:13
resources born to consume r. HORA 386:14
Have no Inner R. BERR 69:19
respect fail to get r. MACH 486:4
How I did r. you TROL 782:9
icy precepts of r. SHAK 699:21
neither doth God r. BIBL 79:8
outward r. AUST 37:12
owed the greatest r. JUVE 425:5
procuring r. JOHN 415:14
r. for the idea of God DUHA 284:12
r. of place, persons SHAK 701:13
r. to the living VOLT 798:5
R. was mingled with surprise SCOT 650:14
wind, Which I r. not SHAK 676:23
respectability r. and airconditioning BARA 53:13
save a shred of r. READ 622:10
respectable more r. he is SHAW 707:[illegible]
most devilish when r. BROW 154:12
Not one is r. or unhappy WHIT 815:15
those who aren't r. SAKI 642:3
respecter no r. of persons BIBL 103:30
respice *r. finem* ANON 21:12
respiration said it was artificial r. BURG 161:25
responsare *R. cupidinibus* HORA 390:2
responsibility In dreams begins r. YEAT 838:1
Liberty means r. SHAW 708:17
no sense of r. KNOX 442:16
Power without r. KIPL 441:25
r. without power STOP 743:12
responsible know who are r. PLAT 578:3
r. for such an absurd world DUHA 284:12
rest After dinner r. awhile PROV 594:18
all shall r. eternally SPEN 734:13
change is as good as a r. PROV 597:10
choose Their place of r. MILT 518:3
die or r. at last SHEL 711:14
dove found no r. BIBL 74:17
Everything was at r. TRAH 780:12
far, far better r. DICK 266:3
flee away, and be at r. BOOK 135:10
Grant them eternal r. MISS 523:2
holy r. NEWM 542:16
I will give you r. BIBL 95:9
no r. day or night BIBL 112:25
not to seek for r. IGNA 398:17
ordained no r. VAUG 790:2
peace and r. at last DOST 276:1
r. from their labours BIBL 112:26
R. in soft peace JONS 420:17
r. is literature COLE 228:5
r. is mere fine writing VERL 791:7
r. is silence SHAK 667:11
r. not day and night BIBL 111:32
R., rest, perturbèd spirit SHAK 663:6
r. upon thy holy hill BOOK 132:7
r. were little ones ELIZ 297:10
robs me of my r. LODG 472:17
Swift has sailed into his r. YEAT 837:15
take my r. BOOK 131:21
take no r. BOOK 132:21
talk about the r. of us ANON 19:4
weary be at r. BIBL 81:5
Without haste, but without r. GOET 343:15
work, r. and play ADVE 7:43
restaurant table at a good r. LEBO 461:10
rested r. the seventh day BIBL 76:12
resteth Wyatt r. here SURR 746:12
resting give us a r.-place WEIZ 809:2
restituit *cunctando r. rem* ENNI 300:16
restless heart is r. AUGU 35:22
rolls back the r. stone DUCK 284:5
restoration Church's R. BETJ 70:12
not revolution, but r. HARD 360:5
restore R. thou them that are penitent BOOK 125:17
restored r., forgiven LYTE 481:1
R. to life, and power KEBL 432:4
restorer Nature's sweet r. YOUN 839:2
restrain r. yourselves UPAN 787:16
restraint r. with which they write CAMP 183:2
restructuring r. [perestroika] GORB 346:17
rests until it r. in you AUGU 35:22
result r. happiness DICK 261:19
results quick and effective r. BULL 159:21
than for r. BAGE 47:7
resurrection by thy glorious R. BOOK 127:7
in the r. BIBL 96:23
on the Day of R. KORA 444:5
r., and the life BIBL 102:10
R. of the body BOOK 126:10
r. of the dead BIBL 106:22
r. of the dead BIBL 107:1
R. to eternal life BOOK 131:14
retained Him, they r. GERV 335:1
retaliation policy of r. PARN 567:26
retard r. what we cannot repel JOHN 409:7
retentive r. to the strength SHAK 674:24
reticence Northern r., the tight gag HEAN 366:19
R., in three volumes GLAD 341:14
reticulated *Network.* Anything r. JOHN 409:11
retired r. to their estates POPE 586:8
retirement there must be no r. HAIG 356:9
retort r. courteous SHAK 659:26
retreat absolute r. WINC 822:24
make an honourable r. SHAK 659:8
more untroubled r. AURE 36:21
noblest station is r. LYTT 481:3
not r. a single inch GARR 330:9
retreating Have you seen yourself r. NASH 539:19
my right is r. FOCH 318:22
retrenchment Peace, r., and reform BRIG 148:10
retrograde be not r. JONS 419:23
r. if it does not advance GIBB 335:15
retrorsum *nulla r.* HORA 386:12
return he shall not r. to me BIBL 79:7
I shall r. MACA 481:5
I will r. EPIT 303:10
not r. your blow SHAW 708:32
r. no more to his house BIBL 81:11
r., O Shulamite BIBL 86:2
r. unto God BIBL 85:2
Should I never r. MANS 494:9
state I came, r. VAUG 790:10
They shall not r. to us KIPL 439:15
unto dust shalt thou r. BIBL 74:7
whence I shall not r. BIBL 81:12
returned r. on the previous night BULL 160:1
returning R. were as tedious SHAK 684:15
returns r. to the sore tooth PROV 613:12
they say no one r. CATU 197:1
reveal like Nature, half r. TENN 760:23
r. Himself MILT 519:15
r. whatsoever He will KORA 445:6
revealed careless, when r. CENT 199:12
Lord shall be r. BIBL 87:28
nothing of r. religion MEND 504:19
revelation except by r. KORA 445:6
first hole is a r. MOOR 529:14
inspired by divine r. BACO 41:12
Reason is natural r. LOCK 471:18
revelations ends with R. WILD 818:26
extraordinary r. BUTL 171:12
offers stupendous r. HOFF 380:9
revelry r. by night BYRO 174:13
revels Our r. now are ended SHAK 699:6
r. long o' nights SHAK 675:13
What r. are in hand SHAK 690:21
revenge deaths become r. by morning MOTI 534:5
God's r. FOOT 319:6
gratitude is a species of r. JOHN 410:20
I will most horribly r. SHAK 672:3
man that studieth r. BACO 43:29
prone to anger and r. GIRA 340:5
Punishment is not for r. FRY 326:26
ranging for r. SHAK 675:22
r. for slight injuries MACH 485:15
R. herself went down TENN 766:13
R. his foul SHAK 662:26
R. is a dish PROV 610:8
r. is a kind of wild justice BACO 43:28
r. is always the pleasure JUVE 425:4
R. is sweet PROV 610:9
r. of the intellect upon art SONT 728:5
r.! Timotheus cries DRYD 280:22
R. triumphs over death BACO 42:23
shall we not r. SHAK 687:30
spur my dull r. SHAK 665:30
study of r. MILT 514:13
Sweet is r. BYRO 176:5
sweet r. grows harsh SHAK 693:26
tribal, intimate r. HEAN 366:15
with envy and r. MILT 514:10
revenged I'll be r. SHAK 702:21
revenges brings in his r. SHAK 702:20
revenons *R. à ces moutons* ANON 20:12
revenue standing r. BURK 163:3
Thrift is a great r. PROV 612:49
revenues bears a duke's r. SHAK 672:16
reverberation paucity of its r. MAIL 491:1
reverence In deeper r. praise WHIT 816:5
mystic r. BAGE 46:4
R. for Life SCHW 649:17
r. the King TENN 759:19
so poor to do him r. SHAK 676:4
reverends Wrong R. of every Order DICK 261:5
reveries r. so airy COWP 241:26
reversion r. in the sky POPE 582:18
review bad r. may spoil breakfast AMIS 14:2
your r. before me REGE 624:5
reviewers indolent r. TENN 764:22
R. are usually people who COLE 227:17
reviewing read a book before r. it SMIT 726:2
revisited r. ideas OLDF 553:12
revivalism rebellion and r. THOM 773:7
revivals history of r. BUTL 172:24
reviving r. the *castrati* REED 623:18
revolt It is a big r. LA R 453:23
r., disorder MORR 533:1
revolting r. and a rebellious heart BIBL 89:12
revolution After a r. HALI 357:12
after the r. AREN 24:3
age of r. JEFF 405:14
catalyst that sparks the r. DURY 286:10
crust over a volcano of r. ELLI 298:16
destroyed by a r. TOCQ 778:11
entered into this R. BROW 152:4
explain the French R. BAUD 57:11
French R. operated TOCQ 778:8
it is a big r. LA R 453:23
leaders of a r. CONR 234:23

not r., but restoration HARD 360:5
reform or r. BERL 68:14
R. a parent BURK 163:15
r. is the kicking down HEAN 366:21
R., like Saturn VERG 791:6
r. of rising expectations CLEV 220:16
r. of the times SHAK 670:3
r. where love not allowed ANGE 14:18
safeguard a r. ORWE 559:1
revolutionaries R. are more formalistic CALV 182:9
r. potential Tories ORWE 558:14
unmanageable r. DEV 259:9
revolutionary can't feel r. in a bathroom LINK 469:14
Every r. ends CAMU 184:13
forge his r. spirit GUEV 354:15
revolutionists age fatal to R. DESM 259:1
revolutions All modern r. CAMU 184:12
main cause of r. INGE 399:4
R. are not made PROV 610:10
R. have never lightened SHAW 708:14
r. never go backward SEWA 655:3
r. with rosewater HEAL 366:7
share in two r. PAIN 564:7
revolver resembles a r. FANO 306:8
revolving with the r. year SHEL 710:18
reward in no wise lose his r. BIBL 95:4
nothing for r. SPEN 733:26
not to ask for any r. IGNA 398:17
only r. of virtue EMER 299:17
taken r. against the innocent BOOK 132:8
Virtue is its own r. PROV 613:34
what r. have ye BIBL 93:15
Work not for a r. BHAG 72:18
rewarded of thee be plenteously r. BOOK 128:20
r. me evil for good BOOK 133:23
rewardest r. every man BOOK 135:23
rewards Crimes are their own r. FARQ 307:17
r. and Fairies CORB 236:11
rewrite is to r. it WILD 818:2
readers r. GRAV 349:18
rex *r. quondam* MALO 492:16
R. tremendae maiestatis MISS 523:5
Reynolds R. died BLAK 117:16
rhetoric aimless r. HUXL 397:20
Death, without r. SIEY 719:2
For r. he could not ope BUTL 171:19
logic and r. BACO 44:8
love without the r. STOP 743:17
quarrel with others, r. YEAT 837:25
rhetorician sophistical r. DISR 269:20
Rhine rolls the R. CALV 182:5
think of the R. BALD 49:9
rhinoceros armed r. SHAK 684:12
hide of a r. BARR 56:3
Rhodesia black majority rule in R. SMIT 724:7
rhubarb cold blancmange and r. tart KNOX 442:13
rhyme could not get a r. FLEM 317:18
I'm fond of r. BYRO 176:9
in prose or r. MILT 514:8
I r. for fun BURN 169:1
many a musèd r. KEAT 429:13
mere knack of r. CHUR 214:4
outlive this powerful r. SHAK 704:21
R. being . . . but the invention MILT 514:5
r. is a barrel MAYA 502:16
R. is the rock DRYD 280:16
R. still the most effective drum GIRA 340:7
r. themselves SHAK 672:5
r. the rudder is BUTL 172:3
still more tired of R. BELL 63:16
stringing blethers up to r. BURN 169:8
rhymed r. conversation GERS 334:19
rhymes Namby-pamby's little r. CARE 186:20
ring out my mournful r. TENN 761:29
rhyming bondage of r. MILT 514:6
born under a r. planet SHAK 691:22
r. mother-wits MARL 496:20
Thy drasty r. CHAU 206:14
rhythm I got r. GERS 334:14
sweet, soft, plenty r. MORT 533:17
rhythmic r. tidal lyres HARD 361:9
rhythmical r. grumbling ELIO 296:22
rhythms r. for bears to dance FLAU 316:7
Rialto What news on the R. SHAK 687:11
riband Just for a r. BROW 156:17
r. in the cap SHAK 666:11
ribbon blue r. of the turf DISR 270:17
changing a typewriter r. BENC 64:18
road was a r. of moonlight NOYE 547:6
ribbons r. rare HUNT 396:7
ribs he took one of his r. BIBL 73:21
Ribstone Pippin Right as a R. BELL 63:15
rice r. field, ocean BASH 56:14
r. pudding for dinner again MILN 510:20
rich Beauty too r. for use SHAK 697:7
born lucky than r. PROV 604:10
by chance grow r. THOM 773:1
certain r. man BIBL 100:10
feed with the r. JOHN 414:1
fell from the r. man's table BIBL 100:10
Grow r. in that SIDN 718:20
Isn't it r. SOND 728:2
live by robbing the r. SHAW 708:3
maketh haste to be r. BIBL 83:32
making Gay *r.* JOHN 410:3
man who dies . . . r. CARN 188:25
marry a r. woman THAC 769:1
neither r. nor rare POPE 583:5
never be too r. or too thin WIND 823:5
no sin, but to be r. SHAK 677:8
not really a r. man GETT 335:2
not r. enough REED 624:4
One law for the r. PROV 608:45
open to the poor and the r. ANON 16:10
orchestra playing to the r. AUDE 33:20
parish of r. women AUDE 33:31
Poor little r. girl COWA 238:17
potentiality of growing r. JOHN 416:20
R. and rare MOOR 530:16
R. AND THE POOR DISR 270:23
r. are covetous SMAR 722:4
r. are different from you and me FITZ 315:6
r. are the scum of the earth CHES 211:4
r. as well as the poor FRAN 322:15
r. beyond the dreams MOOR 529:10
r. enough to pay HEAL 366:2
r. get rich KAHN 425:10
r. have no right RUSK 639:5
r. he hath sent empty away BIBL 98:17
r. he hath sent empty away BIBL 114:4
r. in a more precious treasure MACA 481:17
r. in subjects DEFO 255:1
r. man has his ice PROV 610:11
r. man in his castle ALEX 11:9
r. man is fallen BIBL 91:29
r. man to enter BIBL 96:15
r. man without money USTI 788:23
R. men BIBL 92:15
r. men rule the law GOLD 345:10
r., not gaudy SHAK 662:11
r. on the poor JEFF 405:4
r., quiet, and infamous MACA 482:8
r. wage war SART 644:20
r. with forty pounds a year GOLD 344:11
r. wot gets the gravy MILI 508:14
save the few who are r. KENN 433:11
seems it r. to die KEAT 429:13
sincerely want to be r. CORN 236:19
something r. and strange SHAK 698:27
swinish luxury of the r. MORR 532:19
to get r. GELD 332:27
Richard put down R. SHAK 667:24
R.'s himself again CIBB 217:7
scowl on R. SHAK 695:27
richer for r. for poorer BOOK 131:5
R. than all his tribe SHAK 694:3
riches beggar amidst great r. HORA 388:21
chosen than great r. BIBL 83:13
deceitfulness of r. BIBL 95:21
embarrassment of r. ALLA 12:6
getteth r., and not by right BIBL 89:20
gives r. to those LUTH 480:5
gold or gret r. LYDG 480:12
heapeth up r. BOOK 133:30
Infinite r. MARL 496:16
in her left hand r. BIBL 82:8
looked upon r. SWIF 748:9
neither poverty nor r. BIBL 83:35
parade of r. SMIT 723:8
R. are a good handmaid BACO 41:23
R. are for spending BACO 42:29
r. grow in hell MILT 515:4
r. left, not got SURR 746:8
r. of heaven's pavement MILT 515:3
R., the dumb god JONS 420:3
titled for r. PEAR 571:10
unsearchable r. of Christ BIBL 107:26
When r. do abound GOOG 346:13
world's r., which dispersed lie HERB 373:6
richest r. without meaning RUSK 638:20
richly lady r. left SHAK 687:5
Richmond Sweet lass of R. Hill SONG 730:6
richness all in a rush With r. HOPK 384:16
Here's r. DICK 263:19
rid decorated, and got r. of CICE 218:2
never get r. of BARH 54:10
to be r. of thee CONG 233:2
riddance die and be a r. DICK 261:13
riddle dishcover the r. CARR 191:18
found out my r. BIBL 78:2
r. of the sands CHIL 212:1
r. of the world POPE 585:20
r. wrapped in a mystery CHUR 215:6
riddles R. lie here EPIT 303:6
ride if you cannot r. two horses MAXT 502:11
know how to r. BISM 116:7
R. a cock-horse NURS 550:12
r. in triumph MARL 496:25
r. of Paul Revere LONG 474:15
R. on! ride on in majesty MILM 510:10
She's got a ticket to r. LENN 464:2
way the ladies r. NURS 551:8
we r. them down TENN 765:24
ridentem *Dulce r.* HORA 388:1
rider r. and his horse SURT 747:7
rideret *r. Democritus* HORA 387:7
rides r. a tiger PROV 602:32
r. upon the storm COWP 240:16
rideth r. upon the heavens BOOK 136:6
ridicule adulation and r. LACL 447:3
r. in any subject SHAF 655:18
r. is the best test CHES 209:21
stand the test of r. SHAF 655:17
ridiculos *r. homines facit* JUVE 424:11
ridiculous heart of the r. MAHO 490:18
makes men r. JUVE 424:11
no spectacle so r. MACA 481:18
position r. CHES 209:26
r. and superficial MURA 536:15
r. excess SHAK 677:15
step above the r. PAIN 563:10
sublime to the r. NAPO 538:16
sublime to the r. PROV 600:49
ridiculus *nascetur r. mus* HORA 385:20
riding highwayman came r. NOYE 547:6
man goes r. by STEV 742:17
r. that night LONG 474:17
Ridley good comfort, Master R. LAST 455:4
rien *Ils n'ont r. appris* TALL 753:7
je ne regrette r. VAUC 790:1
R. LOUI 476:3
rifle r. all the breathing spring COLL 229:7
roll to your r. KIPL 440:22
rift loaded every r. SPEN 733:25
Load every r. KEAT 431:23
r. within the lute TENN 760:3
Rigby Eleanor R. LENN 463:20
riggish Bless her when she is r. SHAK 656:27

right All's r. with the world BROW 157:12
almost always in the r. SMIT 726:3
assert thy r. BARB 53:17
convinced that they are r. VAN 789:13
curst conceit o' bein' r. MACD 484:15
customer is always r. PROV 597:46
defend to the death your r. MISQ 521:14
Do r. and fear no man PROV 598:42
do what is r. HUXL 397:13
everyone is r. LA C 447:1
firmness in the r. LINC 469:1
foot standeth r. BOOK 133:9
forgive those who were r. MACL 487:5
grounded on just and r. MILT 517:11
heaven still guards the r. SHAK 695:5
if r., to be kept right SCHU 649:14
I had rather be r. CLAY 220:5
indefeasible, divine r. ADAM 3:12
individual r. TAFT 752:19
in itself what is r. VIRG 793:14
It must be r. CRAB 242:23
Jack — I'm all r. BONE 125:7
'just' or 'r.' PLAT 578:5
majority never has r. IBSE 398:6
Might is r. PROV 606:35
more than half the people are r. WHIT 814:2
my r. is retreating FOCH 318:22
never r. to do wrong SOCR 727:3
no more r. to consume SHAW 706:21
no r. in the circus MAXT 502:11
not all was r. CRAB 243:7
of all the earth do r. BIBL 74:29
of—them—is—r. KIPL 439:4
our country, r. or wrong DECA 254:10
questioned its r. to exist SCHU 649:8
renew a r. spirit BOOK 135:7
r., and our bounden duty BOOK 129:20
R. as a Ribstone Pippin BELL 63:15
R. but Repulsive SELL 654:9
r. can be determined HOBB 379:2
r. deed for the wrong reason ELIO 295:15
R. Divine of Kings POPE 580:20
r. hand of iniquity BOOK 141:18
r. hand of the Majesty BIBL 109:25
r. hands of fellowship BIBL 107:18
R. . . . is the child BENT 66:16
r. little, tight little Island DIBD 260:15
r. makes might LINC 468:7
r. man in the right place JEFF 406:4
r. notes at the right time BACH 41:5
r. of an excessive wrong BROW 157:24
r. of the ignorant man CARL 187:3
r. of trampling on them CHIL 211:24
r. part of the country FROS 326:17
r. that you have brought SHEL 714:18
r. there is none to dispute COWP 242:17
r. thought PALI 565:13
r. to a fair portion BURK 163:18
r. to be consulted BAGE 47:5
r. to be obeyed JOHN 407:9
r. to kill ADAM 2:9
r. which goes unrecognized WEIL 808:23
r. wrong TENN 759:17
scientists are probably r. ASIM 30:18
Self-government is our r. CASE 193:7
setting people r. MOOR 530:2
sheep on his r. hand BIBL 97:11
Sit thou on my r. hand BOOK 139:16
that which they will, is r. ADAM 2:15
that which was r. BIBL 78:9
thing which is r. BOOK 132:7
to be decorative and to do r. FIRB 313:5
To do a great r. SHAK 688:13
Two wrongs don't make a r. PROV 613:29
Two wrongs don't make a r. SZAS 752:4
Want to do r. RICH 626:11
Whatever IS, is R. POPE 585:18
What r. have they DICK 264:20
what's r. and fair HUGH 393:14
righteous godly, r., and sober life BOOK 125:17
have seen the r. forsaken BLUN 122:12
never the r. forsaken BOOK 133:26
not come to call the r. BIBL 94:25
prayer of a r. man BIBL 110:24
r. are bold BIBL 83:31
r. man BIBL 82:25
r. perisheth BIBL 88:26
r. shall be had BOOK 139:19
souls of the r. BIBL 91:8
righteousness breastplate of r. BIBL 108:13
clouds rain down r. BIBL 114:1
looked for r. BIBL 86:17
loved r., and hated iniquity BOOK 134:14
paths of r. SCOT 652:20
pursue r. PLAT 578:10
r. and peace BOOK 137:15
r. as the waves of the sea BIBL 88:9
R. exalteth a nation BIBL 82:33
r. hath not been forgotten BIBL 92:17
r. of the scribes BIBL 93:8
Sun of r. BIBL 90:25
Sun of R. WESL 810:23
superior understands r. CONF 231:11
thirst after r. BIBL 93:3
what r. really is ARNO 29:3
With r. shall he judge BOOK 138:11
righteousnesses r. are as filthy rags BIBL 89:7
rightful will to be r. JEFF 405:11
rights all your r. become CASE 193:8
as much r. as men TRUT 784:13
Bill of R. COMM 230:9
coloured men getting r. TRUT 784:14
duties as well as its r. DRUM 279:13
equal in dignity and r. ANON 15:6
extension of women's r. FOUR 321:19
from the South its dearest r. LEE 462:9
inalienable r. ROBE 629:4
intruder on r. of men WINC 822:21
Natural r. BENT 66:17
of his natural r. PRIE 592:9
r. are disregarded BROW 152:2
r. inherent and inalienable JEFF 405:3
r. in learning's world EGER 289:15
r. of an Englishman JUNI 423:12
r. of the smaller nationalities ASQU 31:2
'r.' of women NIGH 545:23
Stand up for your r. MARL 495:16
talked about equal r. JOHN 408:13
unalienable r. ANON 19:11
rigol from this golden r. SHAK 670:15
rigs Corn r., an' barley rigs BURN 167:16
rime extemporal god of r. SHAK 680:20
making beautiful old r. SHAK 705:9
r. was on the spray HARD 362:1
Rimmon in the house of R. BIBL 80:19
rind how shall taste the r. THOM 774:7
ring bright gold r. MOOR 530:16
giving and receiving of a R. BOOK 131:8
Like a great r. VAUG 790:17
not get the r. without the finger MIDD 507:4
now r. the bells WALP 802:3
One R. to rule them all TOLK 779:3
on his luminous r. TENN 765:9
only pretty r. time SHAK 659:24
R.-a-ring o'roses NURS 550:13
r. at the end of his nose LEAR 460:17
r. is worn away OVID 561:11
R. of bright water BORR 144:14
r. of bright water RAIN 620:8
R. out, wild bells TENN 761:28
R. out, ye crystal spheres MILT 513:23
r. the bells of Heaven HODG 379:13
sell for one shilling Your r. LEAR 460:18
small circle of a wedding-r. CIBB 217:4
wear the devil's gold r. PROV 601:6
What shall we do for a r. LEAR 460:17
With this R. I thee wed BOOK 131:6
Ring-Bo-Ree bottles of R. LEAR 460:10
ringleaders fling the r. ARNO 29:15
rings hands are as gold r. BIBL 85:21
postman always r. twice CAIN 181:2
riot r. is at bottom KING 436:18
riotous r. living BIBL 100:2
ripe Cherry r. CAMP 183:25
Soon r., soon rotten PROV 611:10
we r. and ripe SHAK 658:23
ripeness R. is all SHAK 680:5
ripening greatness is a-r. SHAK 673:12
white with our r. BERR 69:15
riper amuse his r. stage POPE 585:25
ripper no female Jack the R. PAGL 563:3
rise Created half to r. POPE 585:20
early to r. PROV 599:4
Early to r. THUR 777:1
fall to r. BROW 155:4
if the dead r. not BIBL 106:24
into this world to r. above FILM 312:3
Must r. at five CLAR 219:16
resistible r. of Arturo Ui BREC 147:16
r. against nation BIBL 97:1
r. and fight againe BALL 51:12
r. at ten thirty HARG 362:5
r. by other's fall SOUT 731:11
r. early JOHN 411:23
r. on stepping-stones TENN 760:22
r. out of obscurity JUVE 424:12
R. up, my love BIBL 85:10
r. with the lark BRET 148:2
stream cannot r. above PROV 611:28
risen floods are r. BOOK 138:3
rises sun also r. HEMI 369:12
rising from r. hope FOOT 319:4
means of r. JOHN 415:5
revolution of r. expectations CLEV 220:16
r. tide lifts all boats PROV 610:12
r. to great place BACO 43:12
r. up against us HAGG 355:14
risk life without r. LAHR 448:1
risks just one of the r. he takes STEV 740:11
risu *r. cognoscere matrem* VIRG 796:5
Solventur r. tabulae HORA 389:22
rites payens corsed olde r. CHAU 207:21
r. for which I love him SHAK 692:7
ritui *Novo cedat r.* THOM 771:11
Ritz open to all—like the R. MATH 501:12
rival craftsman's r. HESI 375:10
rivalry dead there is no r. MACA 481:20
rivals Jealousy of r. ADAM 1:19
Three for the r. SONG 729:11
rive soul and body r. not more SHAK 657:11
river Among the r. sallows KEAT 430:11
as in a r. HALI 357:16
black flowing r. HOOD 382:15
brook and r. meet LONG 473:22
daughter went through the r. BUNY 161:17
either side the r. lie TENN 762:12
even the weariest r. SWIN 750:22
Fame is like a r. BACO 43:26
House of Parliament upon the r. WELL 810:5
if I were a r. AKHM 9:7
in the reeds by the r. BROW 154:20
majestic r. ARNO 27:18
mingle with the r. SHEL 712:7
Ol' man r. HAMM 358:22
On the r.'s margin SMAR 721:19
Over the one-strand r. NURS 548:9
peace been as a r. BIBL 88:9
Pentridge by the r. BARN 55:7
r. at my garden's end SWIF 749:7
r. by the door STEV 743:3
r. in the tree DICK 266:21
r. Is a strong brown god ELIO 294:12
r. jumps over the mountains AUDE 33:18
r. of crystal light FIEL 309:9
r. of human industry TOCQ 778:18
r. of water of life BIBL 113:12
rook-racked, r.-rounded HOPK 384:4
see upon the r.'s reaches BLOK 122:3
Sleepless as the r. CRAN 243:25
twice into the same r. HERA 371:8
riverrun r., past Eve and Adam's JOYC 421:17
r., past Eve and Adam's OPEN 556:12

rivers as yet unknown r. VIRG 795:4
discourse of r. WALT 802:25
I've known r. HUGH 392:18
like r. grow cold MONT 526:16
R. and mountain-spring OAKL 552:5
r. cannot quench SHAK 673:2
r. dry up CHEK 208:11
r. in the south BOOK 140:20
r. like green ribbons TAYL 756:16
r. of blood JEFF 406:1
r. of Damascus BIBL 80:18
r. of water BIBL 87:19
r. run into the sea BIBL 84:1
rivulet neat r. of text SHER 716:9
road along the 'ard 'igh r. PUNC 617:8
And the r. below me STEV 743:1
braid, braid r. BALL 52:1
darksome r. CATU 197:1
Don't leave them on the r. GOGO 344:1
Follow the yellow brick r. HARB 359:19
Golden R. to Samarkand FLEC 317:4
Goodbye yellow brick r. JOHN 408:4
high r. JOHN 413:6
light to shine upon the r. COWP 240:21
on a lonesome r. COLE 226:24
one more for the r. MERC 505:7
on to the end of the r. LAUD 454:5
people in the middle of the r. BEVA 71:17
r. a thorny way CARB 186:1
r. he wishes to pursue TALM 754:21
r. of excess BLAK 119:12
R. to Heaven BALL 52:1
r. to hell is paved PROV 610:13
r. to the City of Emeralds BAUM 57:15
r. toward freedom MORR 533:1
r. to wealth TROL 782:10
r. up and the road down HERA 371:10
r. was a ribbon of moonlight NOYE 547:6
r. wind up-hill ROSS 634:12
rolling English r. CHES 210:13
royal r. to learning PROV 612:17
shut the r. through the woods KIPL 440:17
up the white r. ELIO 296:13
watched the ads and not the r. NASH 539:12
winding r. before me HAZL 365:23
ye'll tak' the high r. SONG 730:1
roads All r. lead to Rome PROV 594:24
By r. not adopted BETJ 71:7
How many r. DYLA 287:3
Two r. diverged FROS 326:9
where r. were bad LEE 462:2
without fear the lawless r. MUIR 535:22
roam don't know where to r. COLL 228:13
Everywhere I r. FOST 321:18
power to r. BYRO 174:11
sent to r. COWP 241:6
soar, but never r. WORD 832:11
Where'er I r. GOLD 345:6
roaming R. in the gloamin' LAUD 454:7
where are you r. SHAK 701:9
roar called upon to give the r. CHUR 216:7
die of that r. ELIO 292:23
long, withdrawing r. ARNO 26:4
r. of London's traffic CATC 196:17
r. their ribs out GILB 339:13
r. you as gently SHAK 689:13
roareth What is this that r. thus GODL 342:2
roaring r. after their prey BOOK 139:5
r. of the wind KEAT 431:11
roast in boiled and r. SMIT 725:8
In hell they'll r. thee BURN 168:18
R. beef and Yorkshire ORWE 558:10
R. Beef, Medium FERB 308:14
r. me in sulphur SHAK 694:1
r. their eggs BACO 44:23
roasting r. of eggs PROV 612:22
rob r. a lady of her fortune FIEL 310:12
r. his mother FAUL 308:1
robbed We was r. JACO 401:1
robber Barabbas was a r. BIBL 102:31
r.'s bundle SHEL 715:3
robbers in perils of r. BIBL 107:14
robbery In scandal, as in r. CHES 209:2
wrong and r. BOOK 135:22
robbing from r. he comes next DE Q 258:11
r. a bank BREC 147:19
r. of a foe CHUR 213:19
robe Give me my r. SHAK 657:28
judge's r. SHAK 686:8
like a giant's r. SHAK 685:14
shining r. of day THOM 775:18
white r. of churches RAOU 622:2
robes arrayed in white r. BIBL 112:9
r. ye weave SHEL 713:26
washed their r. BIBL 112:10
When all her r. are gone ANON 17:23
Robey R. the Darling of the music halls SMIT 724:3
robin bold R. Hood BALL 50:14
bonny sweet R. SHAK 666:8
Call for the r.-red-breast WEBS 808:13
R. and I are two honest men SHIP 717:7
r. and the wren PROV 610:14
R. Hood could brave PROV 610:15
r. red breast BLAK 117:18
R.'s not near KEPP 434:4
Sweet R. is in the bush SCOT 651:26
what will poor r. do NURS 549:16
Who killed Cock R. NURS 552:1
Robinson here's to you, Mrs R. SIMO 720:9
Robinson Crusoe *Don Quixote, R.* JOHN 418:14
robot r. may not injure a human ASIM 30:16
robotics Rules of R. ASIM 30:16
robots men may become r. FROM 325:11
robs government which r. Peter SHAW 707:5
robur *r. et aes triplex* HORA 387:15
rock Beside the jutting r. BYRO 178:10
for a r. of offence BIBL 86:27
founded upon a r. BIBL 94:12
from the Tarpeian r. ARNO 29:15
It is the Inchcape R. SOUT 730:17
I've gotten a r. BLAM 121:14
knew the perilous r. SOUT 730:16
like the R. of Gibraltar GAMO 329:2
Rhyme is the r. DRYD 280:16
R. journalism is people ZAPP 839:24
R. of Ages TOPL 779:16
Rock them, r. them, lullaby DEKK 256:6
ruled by the r. PROV 615:2
serpent upon a r. BIBL 83:36
set my feet upon the r. BOOK 133:31
Sex and drugs and r. and roll DURY 286:9
shadow of a great r. BIBL 87:19
tall r., The mountain WORD 829:4
upon this r. BIBL 96:4
rocked R. in the cradle of the deep WILL 819:20
r. the system ROBI 629:22
rocket numbers that r. the mind WILB 817:3
rose like a r. PAIN 563:18
Rockies R. may crumble GERS 334:15
rocking Brothers and sisters r. JOHN 408:7
cradle endlessly r. WHIT 815:6
r. a grown man BURK 162:14
rocking horse upon a r. KEAT 430:4
rocks eternal r. beneath BRON 150:3
hand that r. the cradle WALL 799:16
marriage on the r. MERR 505:27
native of the r. JOHN 412:16
older than the r. PATE 569:13
r., and stones, and trees WORD 831:25
R., caves, lakes, fens MILT 515:21
r. for the conies BOOK 139:4
r. of the mountains BIBL 112:6
R., torrents, gulfs BEAT 58:4
r. unscalable SHAK 660:23
seas roll over but the r. remain HERB 371:16
when r. are near WEBS 808:19
rod Aaron's r. BIBL 75:34
bruise them with a r. of iron BOOK 131:17
kiss the r. SHAK 702:25
lightning and lashed r. HOPK 385:3
r., which is the only instrument LOCK 472:7
shall come forth a r. BIBL 87:3
Spare the r. PROV 611:14
spare the r., and spoil the child BUTL 172:8
spareth his r. BIBL 82:30
thy r. and staff SCOT 652:20
thy r. and thy staff BOOK 133:1
rode r. madly off LEAC 459:19
r. upon the cherubims BOOK 132:11
roe like to a r. BIBL 86:9
roes breasts are like two young r. BIBL 85:14
rogue call r. and villain DRYD 283:15
dainty r. in porcelain MERE 505:13
r. and peasant slave SHAK 663:26
r.'s face CONG 232:17
rogues Four r. in buckram SHAK 668:5
roi *que le roi* SAYI 647:23
r. d'Yvetot BÉRA 67:14
Si le R. m'avait donné ANON 20:13
Roland *Childe R. to the Dark Tower* BROW 155:21
Child R. to the dark tower SHAK 679:9
roll drugs and rock and r. DURY 286:9
r. all our strength MARV 499:4
R. on, thou deep BYRO 175:9
R. up that map PITT 577:7
rolled bottoms of my trousers r. ELIO 295:10
roller r., pitch, and stumps LANG 450:10
rolling jus' keeps r. along HAMM 358:22
Like a r. stone DYLA 287:9
r. English road CHES 210:13
r. stone gathers PROV 610:16
rolls r. back the restless stone DUCK 284:5
r. it under his tongue HENR 370:15
Roman Before the R. came to Rye CHES 210:13
by a R. Valiantly vanquished SHAK 657:18
deceased R. Empire HOBB 379:4
fall of the R. empire STEV 740:21
found the R. nation VIRG 793:6
high R. fashion SHAK 657:20
I am a R. citizen CICE 217:21
make a R. holiday BYRO 175:3
more an antique R. SHAK 667:9
neither holy, nor R. VOLT 797:17
noblest R. of them all SHAK 677:4
noses cast is of the r. FLEM 317:18
R. and his trouble HOUS 391:3
R. for that FARQ 307:11
R., make your task to rule VIRG 795:1
R. meal . . . . . . a radish COWP 242:2
R. people CALI 181:6
R.-Saxon-Danish-Norman DEFO 255:12
R.'s life MACA 483:10
R. thought hath struck him SHAK 656:10
R. world is falling JERO 406:15
such a R. SHAK 676:19
sweet R. hand SHAK 702:9
Tenderest of R. poets TENN 758:20
would not be a R. SHAK 675:26
you R. writers PROP 593:17
Romana *stat R. virisque* ENNI 300:15
Roman Catholic R. Church MACA 482:10
romance any historical r. CLAR 219:15
fine r. with no kisses FIEL 310:16
learned r. AUST 38:8
music and love and r. BERL 68:8
not a little given to r. EVEL 305:4
symbols of a high r. KEAT 430:18
romances like r. read SUCK 745:6
Romanism rum, R., and rebellion BURC 161:21
Romans do as the R. do PROV 614:22
Friends, R., countrymen SHAK 675:27
R. call it stoicism ADDI 4:10
R. were like brothers MACA 483:7
romantic airline ticket to r. places MARV 499:9
Men are so r. WELD 809:7
once r. to burlesque BYRO 177:3
R. Ireland's dead and gone YEAT 837:9
'r.' music STRA 744:14

romantic (*cont.*):
r. poets LEAP 460:1
ruin that's r. GILB 338:16
Wrong but R. SELL 654:9
romanticism r. is disease GOET 343:17
romantics We were the last r. YEAT 835:11
Romanus *Civis R. sum* CICE 217:21
Civis R. sum PALM 566:3
Rome All roads lead to R. PROV 594:24
Bishop of R. BOOK 142:12
comen from R. al hoot CHAU 205:5
cruel men of R. SHAK 674:3
Everything in R. JUVE 424:13
from the Church of R. WOTT 833:8
grandeur that was R. POE 579:21
Half-Way House to R. PUNC 617:4
happy R., born when I CICE 218:1
hook-nosed fellow of R. SHAK 670:12
Let R. in Tiber melt SHAK 656:8
loved R. more SHAK 675:24
Men, I'm getting out of R. GARI 329:17
Now is it R. indeed SHAK 674:15
Oh R.! my country BYRO 174:27
palmy state of R. SHAK 661:9
panting heart of R. WISE 823:16
R., believe me CLOU 221:11
R. has spoken AUGU 36:12
R. hath lost her crown COLE 224:18
R. immortal GURN 355:3
R., in the height of her glory WEBS 807:13
R. shall stand BYRO 175:5
R.'s whitest day MACA 482:25
R., though her eagle WALL 800:7
R. was not built PROV 610:17
second at R. CAES 180:18
sitting at R. PROV 604:19
strangers of R. BIBL 103:16
time will doubt of R. BYRO 177:6
Treaty [of R.] DENN 257:16
voice of R. JONS 419:14
wealth and din of R. HORA 388:22
When I go to R. AMBR 13:4
When in R., do as PROV 614:22
Romeo wherefore art thou R. SHAK 697:11
romping r. of sturdy children DEFY 259:6
Romulus dregs of R. CICE 217:9
Ronsard *R. me célébrait* RONS 632:8
ronyon rump-fed r. SHAK 681:11
rood half a r. Of land SWIF 749:7
roof cat on a hot tin r. WILL 820:15
come under my r. BIBL 94:15
enter under my r. MISS 522:20
heavens my wide r.-tree AYTO 40:13
r. whirl around JONS 420:11
r.-wrecked; damps there drip HARD 361:7
this majestical r. SHAK 663:18
Who, living, had no r. HEYW 376:8
roofless through these r. halls SHEL 712:11
roofs tiles on the r. LUTH 479:14
rook r.-racked, river-rounded HOPK 384:4
When the last r. COLE 227:4
rooks r. are blown TENN 760:30
r. in families homeward go HARD 361:23
room about to enter a r. EDDI 288:1
All I want is a room LERN 465:9
always r. at the top PROV 612:8
always r. at the top WEBS 807:18
at ease in a r. PASC 568:11
Books do furnish a r. POWE 590:8
boys in the back r. LOES 473:1
cut out to make a r. LAO 451:8
Great hatred, little r. YEAT 836:24
How little r. Do we take up SHIR 717:11
In every grave make r. D'AV 251:8
into the next r. HOLL 381:2
just entering the r. BROU 151:18
large upper r. BIBL 100:21
little r. HOUS 390:15
make more r. BASS 57:1
money and a r. of her own WOOL 826:17
no r. for them in the inn BIBL 98:20
riches in a little r. MARL 496:16
r. at your head BALL 50:11
r. grows chilly GRAH 348:5
r. in my heart for thee ELLI 298:8
smallest r. of my house REGE 624:5
smoke-filled r. SIMP 720:16
struggle for r. MALT 493:4
sufficient r. BARN 55:8
taper to the outward r. DONN 273:8
wasn't r. to swing a cat DICK 262:5
rooms boys in the back r. BEAV 59:3
colder r. AUST 37:16
lighted r. inside your head LARK 453:3
Other voices, other r. CAPO 185:15
r. of thy native country FULL 327:8
Rooshans people . . . may be R. DICK 263:7
roost came home to r. MILL 510:2
come home to r. PROV 597:45
come home to r. SOUT 730:14
root axe is laid unto the r. BIBL 92:30
axe to the r. PAIN 563:20
begins to take r. WASH 804:10
eaten on the insane r. SHAK 681:18
Idleness is r. of all evil PROV 603:11
nips his r. SHAK 673:12
perced to the r. CHAU 204:6
perced to the r. OPEN 556:25
r. is ever in its grave HERB 373:17
r. of all evil BIBL 109:18
r. of all evil PROV 606:45
r. of heath BRON 149:18
r. of the matter BIBL 81:23
square r. of half a number LONG 475:3
roots drought is destroying his r. HERB 371:12
out of his r. BIBL 87:3
r. that can be pulled up ELIO 292:6
send my r. rain HOPK 384:24
rope by the r. we know JAME 402:26
fourfold r. of nerves HEAT 367:4
Give a man r. enough PROV 601:5
Never mention r. PROV 607:34
refuse to set his hand to a r. DRAK 278:19
sell us the r. MISQ 521:5
rorate *R., coeli* BIBL 114:1
rosa *r. Sera moretur* HORA 388:5
Rosalind No jewel is like R. SHAK 659:7
rose *allons voir si la r.* RONS 632:7
American beauty r. ROCK 630:23
beauty's r. SHAK 704:5
blossom as the r. BIBL 87:21
blows so red The r. FITZ 314:11
English unofficial r. BROO 150:11
expectancy and r. SHAK 664:10
fading r. CARE 186:13
fayr as is the r. CHAU 206:27
fire and the r. are one ELIO 294:20
fresh lap of the crimson r. SHAK 689:21
Gather therefore the r. SPEN 734:1
gave Ruth a r. AYCK 40:3
ghost of a r. BROW 152:16
Go, lovely r. WALL 800:2
Goodbye, England's r. JOHN 408:2
I know the colour r. ABSE 1:6
inimitable r. WINC 823:2
Into the r.-garden ELIO 294:2
I r., went forth WESL 810:21
labyrinthine buds the r. BROW 158:2
last r. of summer MOOR 530:17
late r. may yet linger HORA 388:5
lovely is the r. WORD 829:15
love were what the r. is SWIN 751:14
luver stole my r. BURN 166:17
Luve's like a red, red r. BURN 168:6
Mighty lak' a r. STAN 736:11
morning r. KEAT 429:4
no more desire a r. SHAK 680:19
No thorns go as deep as a r.'s SWIN 750:17
One perfect r. PARK 567:4
Pluck a red r. SHAK 672:11
pluck a white r. SHAK 672:10
pluck the r. BROW 158:13
Queen r. of the rosebud garden TENN 764:8
ravage with impunity a r. BROW 158:3
r. again from the dead BOOK 126:10
r. By any other name SHAK 697:12
R.-cheeked Laura CAMP 184:1
r. distilled SHAK 689:3
r. in aromatic pain POPE 585:14
r. in dark and evil days INGR 399:17
R. is a rose STEI 737:8
R. of all my days YEAT 837:17
r. of Sharon BIBL 85:9
r. of yesterday FITZ 314:8
r. Of youth SHAK 657:4
r.-red city BURG 162:4
r.-red sissy PLOM 579:5
R. shall fade DAVI 252:14
r. should shut KEAT 427:12
r.'s scent is bitterness THOM 774:2
R., thou art sick BLAK 121:7
r. to a pitch-black toad YESE 838:7
R., were you not PRIO 593:6
r. with all its sweetest leaves BYRO 177:28
r. without the thorn HERR 374:20
Roves back the r. DE L 256:9
secret and inviolate R. YEAT 837:7
sweet lovely r. SHAK 667:24
Sweet r., whose hue HERB 373:17
vanish with the r. FITZ 315:2
wavers to a r. DOBS 271:16
white r. of Scotland MACD 484:18
white r. weeps TENN 764:9
without thorn the r. MILT 516:13
yet a r. full-blown HERR 375:6
rosea *avertens r. cervice* VIRG 793:12
rosebud I did but touch the r. PHIL 575:11
R. is just a piece FILM 312:1
rosebuds crown ourselves with r. BIBL 91:6
Gather ye r. HERR 375:2
rosemary r. and rue SHAK 703:13
r., that's for remembrance SHAK 666:7
Rosencrantz R. and Guildenstern SHAK 667:13
roses ash the burnt r. leave ELIO 294:14
criticism with r. D'IS 271:11
days of wine and r. DOWS 277:7
Each morn a thousand r. FITZ 314:8
Everything's coming up r. SOND 728:1
fields where r. fade HOUS 391:8
flower of r. BIBL 92:10
Flung r., roses DOWS 277:5
Honey of r. HERB 372:18
let fall a shower of r. TERE 768:13
like my r. to see you SHER 716:23
lilac and the r. ARAG 23:11
not a bed of r. STEV 742:1
Plant thou no r. ROSS 634:13
raptures and r. SWIN 750:15
Ring-a-ring o'r. NURS 550:13
R. are flowering in Picardy WEAT 806:25
r. for the flush ROSS 634:7
R. have thorns SHAK 704:18
r. of thy lips LODG 472:18
roses, r., all the way BROW 157:7
r. within MARV 498:22
scent of the r. MOOR 530:11
smells like r. JOHN 408:18
soft as the r. BYRO 173:19
Treaties like girls and r. DE G 255:27
Two red r. MORR 532:15
rosewater made with r. PROV 610:10
revolutions with r. HEAL 366:7
rosy plain men have r. faces STEV 742:19
R.-fingered dawn HOME 382:10
r. morn long since SPEN 733:7
rot in cold obstruction and to r. SHAK 686:18
one to r. PROV 608:38
R. half a grain a day SHAK 693:28
r. in hospitals SOUT 728:22
we r. and rot SHAK 658:23
rote conned by r. SHAK 676:25
Rothschild R. and Baring GILB 337:20
rots Winter never r. PROV 615:11
rotted simply r. early NASH 539:13

rotten choice in r. apples PROV 611:2
good to feel r. YESE 838:8
hypocrite is really r. AREN 24:2
like r. mackerel RAND 621:17
r. apple injures PROV 610:18
r. boughs to climb WYAT 834:2
shines like r. wood RALE 620:12
Something is r. SHAK 662:22
Soon ripe, soon r. PROV 611:10
You r. swines CATC 196:32
rottenness r. begins in his conduct JEFF 405:9
r. of eighty years BYRO 179:12
r. of our civilization READ 622:10
rotting big r. log WHIT 814:3
rotundity r. o' the world SHAK 678:21
rotundus *teres, atque r.* HORA 390:2
rough al r. and long yherd CHAU 205:27
children who were r. SPEN 732:20
like a r. diamond DEFO 254:13
r. and lecherous SHAK 678:6
r. and ready man BROW 155:10
R.-hew them how we will SHAK 667:1
r. magic I here abjure SHAK 699:9
r. places plain BIBL 87:28
R. winds do shake SHAK 704:9
roughness r. breedeth hate BACO 43:11
roughs among his fellow r. DOYL 278:10
round flat pretending to be r. FORS 320:12
in that little r. FORD 320:4
into the r. hole SMIT 725:6
Love makes the world go r. PROV 606:6
made the r. world so sure BOOK 138:2
R. and round the circle ELIO 293:26
Round and r. the garden NURS 550:14
r. as a ball JULI 423:2
R. both the shires HOUS 390:19
r. earth's imagined corners DONN 272:20
r., fat, oily man THOM 774:23
R. the world ARNO 26:13
r. unvarnished tale SHAK 691:32
R. up the usual suspects FILM 311:21
said the world was r. GERS 334:18
roundabouts gain on the r. PROV 614:13
rounded polished and well-r. HORA 390:2
r. with a sleep SHAK 699:6
Roundheads R. (Right but Repulsive) SELL 654:9
rouse R. the lion SCOT 652:9
Rousseau ask Jean Jacques R. COWP 240:28
rout r. send forth a joyous shout MACA 482:21
routine care more for r. BAGE 47:7
rove r. as well as you BEHN 62:11
rover blood's a r. HOUS 390:16
roving go no more a-r. BYRO 179:4
row R. after row with strict impunity TATE 755:5
r. Of polished pillars JONS 420:27
r. one way and look another BURT 170:6
rowan r. leaves are dank BLOK 122:3
rowed All r. fast MISQ 521:2
rowing looking one way, and r. BUNY 161:3
Rowley 'Heigh-ho!' says R. NURS 548:6
royal If you have a R. Family PIML 576:7
needed no r. title SPEN 732:12
r. banners forward go FORT 321:7
r. captain of this ruined SHAK 671:9
r. priesthood BIBL 110:28
r. road to a knowledge MISQ 521:8
'r. road' to geometry EUCL 301:17
r. road to learning PROV 612:17
R. Society desires to confer FARA 306:13
r. throne of kings SHAK 694:19
this is the r. Law CORO 237:8
royalist more of a r. SAYI 647:23
royaliste *plus r.* SAYI 647:23
royally proved most r. SHAK 667:14
royalties entertain four r. SALI 642:17
royalty R. is a government BAGE 46:24
r. is to be reverenced BAGE 47:4
r. of Albion's king SHAK 672:15
R. the gold filling OSBO 560:9
R. will be strong BAGE 46:24
when you come to R. DISR 270:37
rub ay, there's the r. SHAK 664:3
r. up against money RUNY 637:11
rubber tast like poisoned r. LEON 464:9
rubbers look out for r. PROV 612:43
rubbish cast as r. to the void TENN 761:10
r. of an Adam SOUT 728:21
some of the r. LOCK 471:12
What r. BLÜC 122:8
rubble crushed by the r. SOLZ 727:15
rubies above r. BIBL 81:25
pearls away and r. HOUS 390:18
price is far above r. BIBL 83:38
R. unparagoned SHAK 660:19
rubs fog that r. its back ELIO 295:5
Leave no r. nor botches SHAK 684:3
rudder heart was to thy r. tied SHAK 657:3
rhyme the r. is BUTL 172:3
r. broke off BARN 55:2
r. of painting LEON 464:16
ruled by the r. PROV 615:2
ruddier r. than the cherry GAY 331:8
ruddy My beloved is white and r. BIBL 85:20
r., and beautiful BIBL 78:28
rude let's talk r. FLAN 316:3
R. am I in my speech SHAK 691:31
r. and wild BELL 63:12
r. heap, together hurled MARV 499:7
so r. to the good WORD 827:14
rudest r. work that tells a story RUSK 638:20
Rudolph R., the Red-Nosed MARK 495:13
rue nought shall make us r. SHAK 677:21
rosemary and r. SHAK 703:13
R., even for ruth SHAK 695:18
There's r. for you SHAK 666:8
ruffian father r. SHAK 668:14
menaces of a r. JOHN 414:23
ruffle r. up your spirits SHAK 676:11
ruffled r. feathers sex can EWAR 305:9
rugby R. Union which is THOM 773:7
rugged harsh cadence of a r. line DRYD 282:28
old r. cross BENN 65:14
r. verse I chose DRYD 282:15
steep and r. pathway WILL 821:6
system of r. individualism HOOV 383:10
rugs like a million bloody r. FITZ 315:15
Ruh *Meine R.' ist hin* GOET 343:1
Über allen Gipfeln Ist R.' GOET 343:10
Ruhm *Tat ist alles, nichts der R.* GOET 343:3
ruin God to r. has designed DRYD 281:26
hideous r. and combustion MILT 514:11
its r. didst not share DODI 271:21
Majestic though in r. MILT 515:14
Resolved to r. DRYD 280:4
roving's been my r. SONG 729:1
r. himself in twelve months GEOR 334:3
r. of all happiness BURN 165:25
R. seize thee GRAY 350:2
r. that Cromwell knocked about BEDF 60:20
r. that it feeds upon COWP 241:5
r. that's romantic GILB 338:16
r. upon ruin MILT 515:27
ruin—yet what r. BYRO 175:4
ruinae *Impavidum ferient r.* HORA 388:16
ruined home of r. reputations ELIO 292:14
O r. piece of nature SHAK 679:22
r. at our own request MORE 530:24
r. on the side BURK 164:23
r. sides of kings BEAU 58:14
They r. us DUNN 285:11
ruinous r. and old SPEN 733:17
R. inheritance GAIU 328:4
ruins human mind in r. DAVI 252:4
Of all r. DOYL 277:14
others' r. built SOUT 731:11
r. of the noblest man SHAK 675:21
r. would strike him unafraid HORA 388:16
shored against my r. ELIO 296:14
Ruislip Gaily into R. gardens BETJ 70:17
rule all be done by the r. SHAK 656:28
bear r. in their kingdoms BIBL 92:14
Be each man's r. TENN 759:4
Divide and r. PROV 598:20
exception proves the r. PROV 599:47
exception to every r. PROV 612:9
good old r. WORD 831:17
greatest r. of all MOLI 524:22
Ill can he r. the great SPEN 734:8
little r., a little sway DYER 286:16
make your r. BLAK 120:6
observed the golden r. BLAK 120:4
oldest r. in the book CARR 190:9
One Ring to r. them all TOLK 779:3
only infallible r. SURT 746:14
reasons for the r. change STRA 744:16
Reason to r. DRYD 281:19
rich men r. the law GOLD 345:10
R. I FEIN 308:5
R. I, on page I MONT 528:13
r. and dare not lie TENN 764:2
R., Britannia THOM 774:20
r. o'er freemen BROO 150:6
r. of speech HORA 385:15
r. the day BIBL 73:13
r. the state DRYD 280:4
You work, we r. DUNN 285:11
ruled r. by the rudder PROV 615:2
ruler choose a r. BAGE 46:17
r. and guide BOOK 128:11
r. in Israel BIBL 90:19
r. of all his substance BOOK 139:9
R. of the Queen's Navee GILB 338:27
rulers best r. LAO 451:9
conduct of their r. ADAM 3:12
R. have no authority MAYH 502:20
r., mostly knaves BIER 114:22
r. of the darkness BIBL 108:13
rules all the r. of art ADDI 5:18
break known r. CROM 245:17
by any hypercritical r. LINC 468:8
disregard of all the r. ORWE 559:8
Fallen by mistaken r. WINC 822:23
hand that r. the world WALL 799:16
keep making up these sex r. SALI 642:10
Nobody r. safely THOM 771:3
r. all the worlds UPAN 788:4
R. and models HAZL 365:14
R. of Robotics ASIM 30:16
r. of the game HUXL 397:15
r. the world PROV 601:45
taste or genius by r. REYN 625:6
two r. for design PUGI 616:15
wouldn't obey the r. BENN 65:21
ruleth r. his spirit BIBL 83:1
ruling r. passion conquers POPE 583:20
Search then the R. Passion POPE 584:2
rum r. and true religion BYRO 176:11
r., Romanism, and rebellion BURC 161:21
r., sodomy, prayers, and the lash CHUR 216:4
what a R. Go everything is WELL 810:11
rumble r. of a distant drum FITZ 314:10
R. thy bellyful SHAK 678:22
rumour distillation of r. CARL 187:22
R. is a pipe SHAK 669:20
R. not always wrong TACI 752:7
sound and r. MORR 532:10
rumours wars and r. of wars BIBL 96:30
rump r.-fed ronyon SHAK 681:11
R. Parliament SELL 654:10
run born to r. SPRI 735:12
enabled him to r. MACA 482:16
finest r. in Leicestershire PAGE 563:1
He can r. LOUI 476:7
he may r. that readeth it BIBL 90:22
In the long r. KEYN 435:11
makes the cup r. over PROV 605:9
Many a good r. SURT 746:17
never did r. smooth SHAK 689:4
Now Teddy must r. KENN 434:2
r. after two hares PROV 603:37

run (*cont.*):
R. and find out KIPL 441:4
r. from me and the child BALL 50:20
r. it down SWIF 749:17
r. over a cad CLOU 221:21
R., run, Orlando SHAK 659:6
r.-stealers flicker THOM 774:1
r. the race with Death JOHN 417:17
r. to and fro BIBL 90:8
r. with patience BIBL 110:2
r. with the hare PROV 615:43
shine, and r. to and fro BIBL 91:9
They get r. down BEVA 71:17
they which r. in a race BIBL 106:10
walk before we can r. PROV 613:46
we will make him r. MARV 499:4
What makes Sammy r. SCHU 649:5
runagates r. continue in scarceness BOOK 136:6
runaway curb a r. young star BYRO 179:11
r. Presidency SCHL 648:18
runcible ate with a r. spoon LEAR 460:19
R. Cat with crimson whiskers LEAR 460:21
weareth a r. hat LEAR 460:15
runic sort of R. rhyme POE 579:12
runnable r. stag DAVI 251:12
runnels r. pebble-stones KEAT 427:1
runner long-distance r. SILL 720:6
running all the r. *you* can do CARR 190:15
r. over BIBL 99:5
r. over with knowledge KEAT 431:12
r. with the pack BUTL 171:17
runs book, who r. may read KEBL 432:6
fights and r. away PROV 602:26
Rupert Prince R. DISR 268:9
R. of Debate BULW 160:5
R. of the Rhine MACA 482:22
rura *Paterna r.* HORA 387:11
rural Retirement, r. quiet THOM 775:6
r. spot HUNT 395:17
r. virtues leave GOLD 344:18
rus *R. in urbe* MART 498:5
rush fools r. in POPE 585:3
Fools r. in PROV 600:40
rushed r. into the field BYRO 174:15
rushes Green grow the r., O BURN 167:8
Green grow the r. O SONG 729:11
rushing r. mighty wind BIBL 103:15
russet plain r.-coated captain CROM 245:9
r. yeas SHAK 681:1
Russia forecast the action of R. CHUR 215:6
innocent R. squirmed AKHM 9:10
last out a night in R. SHAK 686:6
power of R. MITC 523:14
R. and British India SALI 642:15
R. an empire or democracy BRZE 159:6
R. has two generals NICH 543:17
Russian he might have been a R. GILB 339:1
R. knows only CHEK 208:18
Scratch a R. PROV 610:22
tumult in the R. heart PUSH 618:1
with a R. soul LERM 464:24
Russians R. and the Americans TOCQ 778:15
rust moth and r. doth corrupt BIBL 93:20
r. amid greenness MELV 504:9
r. in peace SOUT 728:22
r. unburnished, not to shine TENN 767:9
Tarnished with r. WILD 819:5
wear out than to r. out CUMB 247:2
wear out than to r. out PROV 596:13
which never taketh r. SIDN 718:20
rustic r. murmur of their bourg TENN 760:2
rusticity refined r. WORD 828:17
rustle r. in your dying throat FILM 312:14
rustling r. of the grass WORD 827:15
rusty grown r. BUTL 172:2
Ruth sad heart of R. KEAT 429:14
Rutherford R. was a disaster BULL 159:21
ruthless Ruin seize thee, r. King! GRAY 350:2
rye Before the Roman came to R. CHES 210:13
catcher in the r. BORR 144:3
catcher in the r. SALI 642:12
Comin thro' the r. BURN 166:20
fields of barley and of r. TENN 762:12
pocket full of r. NURS 550:18
r. reach to the chin PEEL 571:20

Saba kings of Arabia and S. BOOK 136:18
sabachthani Eli, Eli, lama s. BIBL 97:29
Sabaoth grant me that S.'s sight SPEN 734:13
Lord God of S. BOOK 125:20
sabbata *sunt illa s.* ABEL 1:3
Sabbath supersedes the S. TALM 754:4
sabbath born on the S. day NURS 549:14
Lord blest the s. day BIBL 76:12
Remember the s. day BIBL 76:11
S. eves BABE 40:17
s. was made for man BIBL 97:31
seventh day is the s. BIBL 76:11
sabbaths endless S. ABEL 1:3
saber *Con un no s. sabiendo* JOHN 407:16
Sabidi *Non amo te, S.* MART 497:23
sabiendo *Con un no saber s.* JOHN 407:16
sable paint the s. skies DRUM 279:14
S.-vested Night MILT 515:26
sabre keenness of his s. WALP 801:17
Sabrina S. fair MILT 512:1
Sacco S.'s name will live VANZ 789:19
sack I'll purge, and leave s. SHAK 669:19
intolerable deal of s. SHAK 668:17
s. and sugar SHAK 668:15
S. the lot FISH 313:14
sackbut flute, harp, s. BIBL 90:1
sacks Empty s. will never PROV 599:9
sacrament abortion would be a s. KENN 433:5
great S. revere THOM 771:11
take this holy S. BOOK 129:15
sacramental flesh was s. ROBI 629:20
sacraments minister the S. BOOK 142:10
S. hath Christ ordained BOOK 130:17
s. to a dying god CLOS 222:13
s. to a dying god HEIN 368:9
sacred feed his s. flame COLE 226:1
only s. thing FRAN 322:14
sacrifice approaching s. MILM 510:10
better than s. BIBL 78:25
blood Of human s. MILT 514:24
coming to the sacrifice KEAT 428:27
desirest no s. BOOK 135:9
evening s. BOOK 141:15
final s. SPRI 735:6
Further s. of life DEV 259:5
great pinnacle of S. LLOY 471:2
highest s. is ELEA 291:15
holy hush of ancient s. STEV 740:5
King refused a lesser s. MARY 500:9
living s. BIBL 105:14
one sweet s. SHAK 673:7
Passover s. HAGG 356:1
pay thy morning s. KEN 432:18
s. of God BOOK 135:9
s. other people SHAW 709:1
s. to God POPE 587:20
s. to the graces BURK 164:7
sufficient s. BOOK 129:21
Thine ancient S. KIPL 440:3
Too long a s. YEAT 835:20
turn delight into a s. HERB 372:4
sacrificed accuracy must be s. JOHN 409:1
be s. to expediency MAUG 501:17
slain and spent and s. SWIN 750:13
sacrificers s., but not butchers SHAK 675:2
sacrifices never forgive him for the s. MAUG 502:1
s. an hundred thousand WALP 801:6
such s., my Cordelia SHAK 680:8
sacrificial holy s. Lamb CONS 235:5
sacrilege consecrated s. DISR 269:7
sacrilegious Most s. murder SHAK 683:18
sad All my s. captains SHAK 657:6
all their songs are s. CHES 210:2
deliciously aged and s. SHAW 707:15
How s. and bad BROW 155:22
mine a s. one SHAK 687:2
of all s. words WHIT 816:6
remember and be s. ROSS 634:9
s. bad glad mad SWIN 750:12
s., black isle BAUD 57:9
s.-coloured sect HOOD 383:3
s. old age TALL 753:9
s. steps, O Moon SIDN 718:10
s. tale's best for winter SHAK 703:2
s. tires in a mile-a SHAK 703:12
s. vicissitude of things STER 739:16
So s., so fresh TENN 765:20
tell s. stories SHAK 695:9
too solemn s. SPEN 733:14
very s. to find BROW 158:5
When I am s. and weary MITC 523:10
why I am so s. HEIN 368:5
why I am so s. SHAK 687:1
world is s. and dreary FOST 321:18
saddening unvaried, s. sounds CRAB 242:25
sadder s. and a wiser man COLE 227:1
saddest telling the s. tale SHAK 689:18
tell of s. thought SHEL 714:8
saddle Boot, s., to horse BROW 155:15
Germany in the s. BISM 116:7
s. my horses SCOT 652:6
Things are in the s. EMER 299:8
saddled s. and bridled RUMB 637:4
s. his ass BIBL 79:10
sadly take their pleasures s. SULL 746:3
sadness diverter of s. WALT 802:17
Sweet though in s. SHEL 712:17
saeclum *Solvet s. in favilla* MISS 523:3
saecula *in s. saeculorum* MISS 520:10
saepibus *S. in nostris parvam* VIRG 796:8
safe Better be s. than sorry PROV 596:8
made s. for democracy WILS 822:15
S. bind, safe find PROV 610:19
s., but ne'er will reach DRYD 282:30
s. course for the defeated VIRG 794:5
S. is spelled D-U-L-L CLAR 219:5
s. lodging NEWM 542:16
s. side PROV 604:9
s. to be unpopular STEV 740:12
see me s. up MORE 531:14
thought it was s. ADVE [illegible]
To fly is s. COWP 241:30
will keep us s. JOHN 414:15
world s. for hypocrisy WOLF 825:10
safeguard s. of the West WORD 830:14
safeliest s. when with one man manned DONN 272:16
safely Thro' the world we s. go BLAK 118:2
safer Love just makes it s. ICE- 398:15
s. for a prince MACH 485:16
s. than a known way HASK 363:16
s. to be in a subordinate THOM 770:22
world s. for children LE G 462:13
safest when we are s. BROW 155:7
safety every man shall eat in s. SHAK 673:26
pluck this flower, s. SHAK 667:35
s. cometh from the Lord SCOT 652:22
s., honour, and welfare CHAR 203:13
s. in numbers PROV 612:23
s. is in our speed EMER 299:21
strike against public s. COOL 235:17
sagacity resource-and-s. KIPL 441:13
sagas frosty s. CRAN 243:19
peoples who memorized s. BJÖR 116:19
sage *ne surprend point le s.* LA F 447:13
Newton, childlike s. COWP 241:27
s. has the sun and moon CHUA 213:1
s., his wisdom departs TALM 754:5
sages all the s. can WORD 832:6
into s. and cranks QUIN 619:6
said all is done and s. VAUX 791:1
as if I had s. it myself SWIF 748:17
Everything has been s. LA B 446:18
fool hath s. in his heart BOOK 132:5
He himself s. CICE 217:13

if you want anything s. THAT 769:20
know who s. this THOM 770:21
Least s., soonest mended PROV 605:13
nobody had s. it before TWAI 786:17
not been s. before TERE 768:2
not know what they have s. CHUR 214:19
s. on both sides ADDI 5:3
s. our remarks before us DONA 272:3
what the soldier s. DICK 265:14
sail comes i' faith full s. CONG 233:7
in a sieve I'll thither s. SHAK 681:11
s. of his great verse SHAK 705:3
s. on, O Ship of State LONG 473:10
sea-mark of my utmost s. SHAK 693:30
sailed hadna s. a league BALL 50:12
I have s. the seas YEAT 837:3
s. away for a year and a day LEAR 460:17
Saturday s. from Bremen HOPK 385:4
you never s. with *me* JACK 400:15
sailing failing occurred in the s. CARR 191:23
S. over a cardboard sea HARB 359:16
s. to the strand BALL 51:16
to which port one is s. SENE 654:17
sailor Home is the s. STEV 743:4
lass that loves a s. DIBD 260:13
No man will be a s. JOHN 412:22
s.-boys were all up aloft SONG 729:15
Soldier, S. NURS 551:13
sailors children, s., and drunken men PROV 602:36
s. but men SHAK 687:10
s. who must rebuild NEUR 541:12
tell thee, s., when away GAY 332:21
sails Purple the s. SHAK 656:23
S. ripped, seams op'ning COWP 240:27
still the s. made on COLE 226:23
saint able to corrupt a s. SHAK 667:20
As with a s. SHAK 686:2
became a S. NEWM 542:14
call me a s. CAMA 182:10
England and S. George SHAK 671:6
greater the s. PROV 601:34
little s. HERR 374:21
make of me a s. CONG 233:17
my late espousèd s. MILT 519:1
neither s. nor sophist-led ARNO 26:6
No one, except a s. PÉGU 572:5
Poet and S. COWL 239:21
reel out a s. CHUR 214:2
s. in crape POPE 583:29
S. Martin's summer SHAK 672:7
s., *n.* A dead sinner BIER 114:25
s. or incarnation of Satan MADO 489:5
s. run mad POPE 586:12
s. took pity on COLE 226:17
seem a s. SHAK 696:16
Sloane turned secular s. BURC 161:23
Young s., old devil PROV 616:4
sainted thing enskyed and s. SHAK 686:2
saints Christ and His s. ANON 22:3
Communion of S. BOOK 126:10
death of his s. BOOK 140:4
fearful s. fresh courage take COWP 240:17
follow thy blessed S. BOOK 128:22
his lot is among the s. BIBL 91:11
least of all s. BIBL 107:26
Let the s. be joyful BOOK 142:2
prayers of s. BIBL 112:3
s. have dwelt secure WATT 805:19
s. immortal reign WATT 805:16
s. of this land GIRA 340:5
S. should be judged guilty ORWE 559:12
We are not s. BECK 60:1
saisons *Ô s.* RIMB 628:12
sake Art for art's s. CONS 235:10
Art for art's s. DIET 267:11
Christ's particular love's s. BROW 157:23
for his country's s. FITZ 314:6
loseth his life for my s. BIBL 95:3
That for my s. CROS 246:15
Saki like her, O S. FITZ 315:3
salad chicken s. JOHN 408:9
Our Garrick's a s. GOLD 344:23
s. days SHAK 656:21
s. from the brook COWP 242:9
salamandrine s. fires HARD 361:9
salary remembered that he had a s. GIBB 335:19
s. of the chief executive GALB 328:8
sales each equation would halve the s. HAWK 364:8
salesman Death of a s. MILL 509:19
s. is got to dream MILL 509:22
Salieri Mozart and S. BARI 54:12
salley by the s. gardens YEAT 835:16
sally make a sudden s. TENN 757:13
none like pretty S. CARE 186:21
salmon primordial as a s. WHIT 814:8
s. sing in the street AUDE 33:18
smoked s. and tinned WILS 822:2
saloon in the last chance s. MELL 504:6
salt adverbs the s. JAME 403:20
became a pillar of s. BIBL 74:30
grain of s. PLIN 578:19
Help you to s. PROV 602:38
how s. is the taste DANT 250:4
s. of the earth BIBL 93:4
s. rubbed into their wounds WEST 812:11
s. tides seawards flow ARNO 26:11
seasoned with s. BIBL 109:6
unplumbed, s., estranging sea ARNO 28:4
verge of the s. flood SHAK 699:25
Salteena S. was an elderly man ASHF 30:10
saltness sugar, and s. GOLD 344:23
salus *S. extra ecclesiam* AUGU 36:7
S. populi CICE 217:12
S. populi suprema lex SELD 653:21
salutant *Ave Caesar, morituri te s.* ANON 21:5
salutations s. in the market BIBL 98:11
salute If it moves, s. it MILI 508:9
S. one another BIBL 105:25
s. thee, Mantovano TENN 767:5
S. the happy morn BYRO 173:8
those about to die s. you ANON 21:5
salutes see if anyone s. it SAYI 647:28
salva *S. me* MISS 523:5
salvaged ships have been s. HALS 358:12
salvation bottle of s. RALE 620:15
cannot be s. CYPR 248:12
generally necessary to s. BOOK 130:17
hope of s. BIBL 109:9
my light, and my s. BOOK 133:10
necessary to s. BOOK 142:8
none of us Should see s. SHAK 688:11
no s. outside the church AUGU 36:7
Now is our s. nearer BIBL 105:21
now is the day of s. BIBL 107:8
publisheth s. BIBL 88:12
s. of Europe PITT 577:4
seeks her own s. SHAK 666:16
shew him my s. BOOK 138:1
strength of our s. BOOK 138:5
Visit us with thy s. WESL 811:7
Work out your own s. BIBL 108:18
Wot prawce s. nah SHAW 707:25
salve *S., regina* PRAY 592:6
Sam nephew of my Uncle S.'s COHA 224:1
Play it again, S. FILM 311:12
Play it again, S. MISQ 522:6
S., pick up tha' musket HOLL 381:3
Samaritan remember the Good S. THAT 769:23
Samarkand Golden Road to S. FLEC 317:4
silken S. KEAT 427:13
Samarra appointment with him in S. MAUG 502:5
same all say *the s.* MELB 504:1
but thou art the s. BOOK 138:15
Ever the s. MOTT 535:16
more they are the s. KARR 426:1
much the s. ANON 15:8
s. yesterday, and to day BIBL 110:7
would be all the s. DICK 263:22
you are the s. MART 498:4
samite Clothed in white s. TENN 759:13
Sammy What makes S. run SCHU 649:5
sampler girl shows her s. RUSK 639:8
Samson binding S. with withes HAMP 359:6
S. hath quit himself MILT 518:24
Samuel Lord called S. BIBL 78:14
sancta *s. simplicitas* JERO 406:14
sanctified s. by the wife BIBL 106:5
sanctify S. the Lord of hosts BIBL 86:27
sanctions Baldwin denouncing s. BEAV 59:1
sanctuary classes which need s. BALD 49:7
Cunning is the dark s. CHES 209:5
So much s.-breaking SKEL 721:14
sanctus *S., sanctus, sanctus* MISS 520:21
sand and a grain of s. WHIT 815:14
die upon the s. ARNO 27:16
house upon the s. BIBL 94:13
land of s. and ruin SWIN 751:18
Little grains of s. CARN 189:2
on the edge of the s. LEAR 460:19
quantities of s. CARR 190:19
s. against the wind BLAK 120:2
s. in the porridge COWA 238:11
s.-strewn caverns ARNO 26:12
world in a grain of s. BLAK 117:17
sandal s. shoon SHAK 665:34
sandals with s. grey MILT 513:12
sandbank no s., thrown up DAVI 252:18
sands Across the s. of Dee KING 437:9
Come unto these yellow s. SHAK 698:26
Footprints on the s. LONG 474:6
lone and level s. SHEL 713:1
on the s. with printless foot SHAK 699:8
riddle of the s. CHIL 212:1
s., ignoble things BEAU 58:14
s. upon the Red sea shore BLAK 120:3
sandwich ask for a watercress s. WILD 819:7
British Rail s. FIEL 309:13
cheaper than a prawn s. RATN 622:5
taste again that raw-onion s. BARN 55:3
sane if he was s. he had to fly HELL 368:13
San Francisco heart in S. CROS 246:10
sang morning stars s. BIBL 81:32
Perhaps it may turn out a s. BURN 167:1
s. a king out of three kingdoms WHAR 813:6
s. his didn't he CUMM 247:3
s. in my chains THOM 772:4
s. within the bloody wood ELIO 295:25
sanglots *Les s. longs* VERL 791:8
Sangreal story of the S. MALO 492:12
sanitary glorified s. engineer STRA 744:8
sanitas *S. sanitatum* MÉNA 504:11
sanitatum *Sanitas s.* MÉNA 504:11
sanity ain't no S. Claus FILM 311:18
sank s. my boat KENN 433:19
Sighted sub, s. same MASO 501:1
sano *Mens sana in corpore s.* JUVE 425:2
sans sans singer, and—s. End FITZ 314:12
S. teeth, sans eyes SHAK 659:3
sansculotte *bon S. Jésus* DESM 259:1
Santa Claus death or S. BERN 69:9
there is a S. CHUR 213:11
saoshyants truly shall be 's.' ZORO 841:14
sap dried the s. of my veins YEAT 836:2
world's whole s. is sunk DONN 274:9
sapere *s. aude* HORA 386:15
sapient s. head ARNO 28:5
s. sutlers ELIO 295:13
sapienti *Dictum s.* PLAU 578:13
sapless s. foliage of the ocean SHEL 712:15
saplings wind it plies the s. HOUS 391:2
sapphire purer s. melts TENN 764:5
sapphires ivory overlaid with s. BIBL 85:21
Sappho Where burning S. loved BYRO 176:25
Sarah ceased to be with S. BIBL 74:28
sardine jasper and a s. stone BIBL 111:30
sardines s. will be thrown CANT 185:12
Sargent musical Malcolm S. BEEC 61:2
Sarum had you upon S. plain SHAK 678:14
sash s. my father wore POLI 581:29

sashes one of his nice new s. GRAH 348:5
sassy I'm sickly but s. HARR 362:16
sat everyone has s. except a man CUMM 247:7
I s. down and wept BORR 144:2
S. and knotted SEDL 653:3
s. down under a juniper tree BIBL 80:2
s. too long here CROM 245:14
s. upon a promontory SHAK 689:22
we s. down and wept BOOK 141:7
Satan Auld Hornie, S. BURN 166:6
beat down S. BOOK 127:10
beheld S. BIBL 99:9
casting out S. by Satan SORL 728:20
Get thee behind me, S. BIBL 96:5
high capital Of S. MILT 515:6
Lord said unto S. BIBL 80:34
saint or incarnation of S. MADO 489:5
S. cast out Satan BIBL 98:1
S. exalted sat MILT 515:7
S. finds some mischief still WATT 805:6
S. met his ancient friend BYRO 179:16
S. seems to show GILB 337:1
S., so call him now MILT 517:4
S. stood Unterrified MILT 515:23
S., thou art but a dunce BLAK 118:19
Satanic dark S. mills BLAK 120:1
satellite With s. TV O'DO 553:1
satiable full of s. curtiosity KIPL 441:8
satiety love's sad s. SHEL 714:7
occasion of s. BACO 42:16
satin ease a heart like a s. gown PARK 567:7
mad in white s. SHER 715:18
satire hard not to write s. JUVE 424:3
let s. be my song BYRO 177:33
S., being levelled at all SWIF 748:20
s. indeed is entirely our own QUIN 619:8
S. is a sort of glass SWIF 747:11
S. is what closes Saturday KAUF 426:2
S. or sense POPE 583:9
s. out of time CHUR 214:4
satiric one s. touch SWIF 749:26
satirical sign of a s. wit AUBR 32:18
satirist bounding past the s. COCK 223:14
s. may laugh GIBB 335:16
second English S. HALL 358:5
satisfaction can't get no s. JAGG 401:6
give you s. GAY 331:22
murder, for my own s. DOST 276:4
satisfied can't be s. HUGH 393:2
Never s. with having WROT 833:16
well paid that is well s. SHAK 688:17
satisfies Where most she s. SHAK 656:27
satisfieth s. thy mouth BOOK 138:17
that which s. not BIBL 88:20
satisfy poorly s. our eyes WOTT 833:1
will I s. him BOOK 138:1
satisfying s. a voracious appetite FIEL 310:9
satura *S. quidem tota nostra est* QUIN 619:8
saturam *s. non scribere* JUVE 424:3
Saturday closes S. night KAUF 426:2
Glasgow Empire on a S. night DODD 271:18
S.'s child NURS 549:14
what he did on S. YBAR 834:20
Saturn grey-haired S. KEAT 427:22
Revolution, like S. VERG 791:6
while S. whirls TENN 765:9
Saturnia *redeunt S. regna* VIRG 796:4
Saturnus S., with his frosty face SACK 641:3
satyr Hyperion to a s. SHAK 661:25
satyrs men, like s. MARL 496:9
sauce Hunger is the best s. PROV 603:5
only one s. CARA 185:17
s. for the goose PROV 614:8
saucy with s. looks SHAK 680:18
Saul Is S. also among the prophets BIBL 78:21
name was S. BIBL 103:21
S. and Jonathan BIBL 79:2
S. hath slain his thousands BIBL 78:34
S. was consenting BIBL 103:22
S., why persecutest thou me BIBL 103:24
weep over S. BIBL 79:2
sausage news into s. factory PAXM 570:10
pig in a s. TROL 783:14
s. machine CHRI 212:16
savage days of the Noble S. BIKO 115:1
laws unto a s. race TENN 767:8
mad and s. master SOPH 728:16
noble s. ran DRYD 281:5
not allow it to be s. OVID 561:9
now the s. race CHUR 213:21
s. loving has made me BECK 60:9
s. wields his club HUXL 397:12
sooth a s. breast CONG 232:25
take some s. woman TENN 763:7
savaged s. by a dead sheep HEAL 366:3
savages love of s. LERM 464:20
save destroy the town to s. it ANON 17:4
exist in order to s. us DEV 259:12
God s. king Solomon BIBL 79:15
God s. the king SONG 729:7
helped s. the world KEYN 435:12
himself he cannot s. BIBL 97:28
rushed through life trying to s. ROGE 632:2
s. his soul BIBL 89:30
s. me MISS 523:5
Save me, oh, s. me CANN 185:3
s. one's own BROW 156:16
s. the people ELLI 298:13
s. the Union LINC 468:11
s. those that have no imagination SHAW 709:18
s. time BACO 42:28
S. us from our friends PROV 610:21
To s. your world AUDE 33:25
saved be s. in this World HALI 358:3
could have s. sixpence BECK 59:10
He s. others BIBL 97:28
only s. the world CHES 210:6
penny s. PROV 609:23
s. alive a whole world TALM 753:10
we are not s. BIBL 89:15
What must I do to be s. BIBL 104:3
Whosoever will be s. BOOK 126:21
youthful hose well s. SHAK 659:2
saving capable of s. us RICH 626:16
s. of life must supersede TALM 754:4
thy s. health BOOK 136:3
saviour because I am the S. JAIN 402:9
our S. dear BASS 56:21
S.'s birth is celebrated SHAK 661:11
s. spring to life BIBL 114:1
savoir *belle chose que de s.* MOLI 524:20
savory s., marjoram SHAK 703:16
savour keep Seeming and s. SHAK 703:13
salt have lost his s. BIBL 93:4
saw do not s. the air SHAK 664:13
He s., he sighed GAY 332:4
I came, I s., I conquered CAES 180:21
I came, s., and overcame SHAK 670:12
I s. and loved GIBB 335:21
Saxon ancient S. phrase LONG 473:19
say all s. *the same* MELB 504:1
anything good to s. LONG 475:8
could s. if I chose CARR 190:2
Do as I s. PROV 598:21
Do as I s. SELD 653:24
don't s. nothin' HAMM 358:22
Have something to s. ARNO 29:9
I s., before the morning BOOK 141:2
Lat thame s. MOTT 535:19
many things to s. unto you BIBL 102:25
more to s. when I am dead ROBI 629:12
no more to s. SHAK 700:25
nothing to s. CAGE 181:1
nothing to s. COLT 230:2
not much to s. COMP 230:19
not s. what one thinks EURI 305:3
not s. why and how WILS 822:6
S. I'm weary, say I'm sad HUNT 395:15
S. it ain't so ANON 18:14
S. it with flowers ADVE 8:8
S. little and do much SHAM 706:4
s. nowt PROV 602:35
s. only the word MISS 522:20
s. something GOOD 346:12
s. *something* about me COHA 224:2
s. the perfectly correct thing SHAW 707:11
s. what they please FRED 324:1
s. what you mean CARR 189:17
s. what you think TACI 752:14
see what I s. WALL 799:17
shall not s. much MATH 501:10
someone else has got to s. GASK 330:20
some s. that we wan MCLE 487:6
something to s. WHAT 813:7
what circumstances we s. it HAVE 364:3
whatever you s. HEAN 366:19
wink wink, s. no more MONT 529:5
saying For loving, and for s. so DONN 274:17
not worth s. BEAU 58:8
were s. yesterday LUIS 479:11
sayings s. are like women's letters HAZL 365:4
says not what he s. SMIT 724:15
What everybody s. PROV 613:51
What Manchester s. today PROV 614:4
Who s. A must say B PROV 615:1
scabbard threw away the s. CLAR 218:19
throw the s. away PROV 615:5
scabs Make yourselves s. SHAK 660:2
scaffold forever on the s. LOWE 477:16
s. and the doom AYTO 40:10
to a s. from a throne FANS 306:9
scale best s. for an experiment FISH 313:13
puts his thumb in the s. LAWR 458:2
sufficiently large s. SPEN 732:8
with her lifted s. POPE 580:8
scales someone is practising s. MACN 488:15
scallop s.-shell of quiet RALE 620:15
scallywags Women love s. BAIL 48:5
scaly s. horror of his folded tail MILT 513:26
scan gently s. your brother man BURN 166:8
scandal In s., as in robbery CHES 209:2
Love and s. FIEL 310:4
no s. like rags FARQ 307:7
s. by a woman of easy virtue HAIL 356:11
s. that constitutes offence MOLI 525:19
s. while you dine TENN 767:3
tea and s. CONG 232:9
scandalous s. and poor ROCH 630:17
scapegoat Let him go for a s. BIBL 76:21
scar wears their going like a s. DUNN 285:15
scarce Good men are s. PROV 601:29
scarceness runagates continue in s. BOOK 136:6
scare s. myself with my own desert FROS 325:20
those footprints s. me HORA 386:12
scarecrow make a s. of the law SHAK 686:4
scarecrows mechanized s. KAVA 426:9
s. of fools HUXL 397:19
scared always been s. of *you* PLAT 577:13
scarf S. up the tender eye SHAK 684:7
scarlet apes, though clothed in s. JONS 420:1
clad in silk or s. PROV 595:10
Cowards in s. GRAN 349:5
His sins were s. BELL 64:4
line of s. thread BIBL 77:18
lips like a thread of s. BIBL 85:14
raise the s. standard CONN 233:23
s. letter HAWT 364:13
s. soldiers AUDE 34:17
sins be as s. BIBL 86:12
wear his s. coat WILD 818:30
scars He jests at s. SHAK 697:9
marks and s. I carry BUNY 161:18
show his s. SHAK 671:24
scattered enemies be s. BOOK 136:5
s. the proud BIBL 98:17
scatterest thou s. them BOOK 137:18
scelerisque *s. purus* HORA 387:24

scene life's last s. JOHN 411:18
lofty s. be acted o'er SHAK 675:18
Speaks a new s. QUAR 618:15
scenery among savage s. HOFF 380:9
end of all natural s. RUSK 638:12
God paints the s. HART 363:7
S. is fine KEAT 431:3
s.'s divine CALV 182:5
talk to me about s. BECK 59:27
scenes behind your s. JOHN 412:10
s. where man hath never CLAR 218:16
scent s. of the roses MOOR 530:11
s. survives their close THOM 774:2
s. the fair annoys COWP 240:2
s. the morning air SHAK 662:30
sweetest flower for s. SHEL 713:23
sceptered s. isle SHAK 694:19
sceptic s. could inquire for BUTL 171:21
too much of a s. HUXL 398:1
scepticism lead to s. BERK 68:1
s. kept her SART 645:9
s. of the intellect NEWM 542:10
sceptre His the s. DIX 271:12
s. and the ball SHAK 671:20
sceptred avails the s. race LAND 450:3
sceptreless S., free SHEL 713:14
schemes best-laid s. PROV 596:1
s. of political improvement JOHN 414:4
s. o' mice an' men BURN 168:24
scherzando *S.! ma non troppo* GILB 337:4
schizoid s. self-alienation FROM 325:11
schizophrenic you are a s. SZAS 752:2
Schleswig-Holstein S. question PALM 566:8
scholar before a great s. LOCK 472:8
gentleman and s. BURN 169:5
He was a s. SHAK 673:23
mere s. DEFO 254:11
s. all Earth's volumes carry CHAP 202:24
s. in a rage KIPL 441:20
s.'s life assail JOHN 411:14
Soldier, s., horseman YEAT 836:8
scholars philosophers and s. PASC 569:1
S. and gentlemen WORD 831:6
S. dispute HORA 385:16
school At s. I never minded MORT 533:10
been to a good s. SAKI 642:6
destroy every grammar s. CROS 246:6
erecting a grammar s. SHAK 672:24
every s. knows it TAYL 756:18
Experience keeps dear s. PROV 599:50
goeth to s. BACO 44:14
learned about in s. JARR 404:10
love was but a s. WOTT 833:2
s. of Manchester DISR 271:7
s. of mankind BURK 164:24
s. of Stratford atte Bowe CHAU 204:13
sent to s. HUGH 393:13
tell tales out of s. PROV 607:38
Unwillingly to s. SHAK 658:26
vixen when she went to s. SHAK 690:7
went to s. without any boots BULM 160:3
schoolboy Every s. knows MACA 482:7
I see a s. YEAT 836:1
method that of a s. BLUN 122:14
Not the s. heat TENN 762:1
s.'s tip THAC 768:21
s. with a satchel BLAI 117:6
tell what every s. knows SWIF 749:8
whining s., with his satchel SHAK 658:26
schoolboys duly to delight s. JUVE 424:23
s. from their books SHAK 697:16
s. playing in the stream PEEL 571:20
schoolchildren What all s. learn AUDE 34:21
schoolgirl Pert as a s. GILB 338:3
priggish s. GRIG 353:12
s. complexion ADVE 7:38
schoolman no s.'s subtle art POPE 583:11
schoolmaster becoming a s. WAUG 806:4
s. is abroad BROU 151:13
so gentle a s. GREY 353:6
schoolmasters s. puzzle their brain GOLD 345:17
schoolrooms s. for 'the boy' COOK 235:16
schools banished from the s. CHUD 213:8
hundred s. of thought contend MAO 495:4
in our great s. JOHN 415:8
in the maze of s. POPE 584:11
lumber of the s. SWIF 749:12
Oh wrangling s. DONN 273:28
schooner It was the s. Hesperus LONG 475:1
sciatica S.: he cured it AUBR 32:19
science aim of s. BREC 147:9
All s. physics or stamp collecting RUTH 640:14
applications of s. PAST 569:12
beams of s. fall POPE 580:13
becoming s. fiction BALL 52:11
beginning of s. LEIB 462:20
countenance of all s. WORD 832:21
disease, not a s. MAIM 491:9
Dismal S. CARL 188:5
do s. in hell VAUG 790:18
essence of s. BRON 149:9
Fair S. frowned not GRAY 350:14
Geometry (which is the only s. HOBB 378:14
grand aim of all s. EINS 291:2
hand of s. AKEN 9:5
How s. dwindles YOUN 839:1
In s., read BULW 160:8
In s. the credit goes DARW 251:6
In s., we must be CURI 247:19
instrument of s. JOHN 409:4
investigated by s. ELIO 292:20
it is not s. KELV 432:17
no less true than s. DAY- 253:15
opinion and s. HUME 394:17
plundered this new s. MCEW 485:6
redefined the task of s. HAWK 364:9
s. and nature will have charms FARA 306:11
S. appears WORD 831:2
S. Fiction no more written ALDI 11:1
S. finds ANON 18:16
S. is an edged tool EDDI 288:3
s. is at a loss CHOM 212:12
S. is built up of facts POIN 580:2
S. is his forte SMIT 726:5
S. is nothing but trained HUXL 397:12
S. is organized knowledge SPEN 732:1
S. is part of culture GOUL 347:9
s. is satisfying the curiosity ARTS 29:20
s. is strong SZAS 752:3
s. is the right interpretation WHEW 813:15
S. lost its virgin purity GRAV 349:21
S. moves, but slowly TENN 763:4
S. must begin with myths POPP 587:29
S. offers best answers DAWK 253:5
s. of life BERN 69:7
s. of the tender passion PUSH 617:27
S. proceeds to destroy HUGH 393:11
s. reassures BRAQ 147:2
S. the aggregate of all VALÉ 789:1
s. which pretends to lay open SMIT 723:3
s. will appear incomplete ARNO 28:22
S. without religion is lame EINS 290:8
separation of state and s. FEYE 309:5
tragedy of S. HUXL 397:11
triumph of modern s. WAUG 806:20
true s. and study CHAR 204:2
science fiction S. writers foresee ASIM 30:17
sciences advancing the s. LOCK 471:12
bent on these s. ASCH 30:3
Books must follow s. BACO 45:6
mother of s. BACO 45:3
Reason and the s. LEIB 462:21
Small s. BAGE 47:19
scientific as if they were s. terms ARNO 28:27
Death was but a s. fact WILD 818:33
empirical s. system POPP 587:24
importance of s. work HILB 376:10
Jesus the most s. EDDY 288:4
know the s. names GILB 339:3
new s. truth PLAN 577:10
on the most s. principles PEAC 570:16
plunges into s. questions HUXL 397:20
s. faith's absurd BROW 155:26
s. opinion ARNO 28:20
s. power has outrun KING 436:17
S. truth MAXW 502:13
scientis *Signum s.* AUCT 33:13
scientist elderly s. states CLAR 219:8
exercise for a research s. LORE 475:15
not try to become a s. EINS 291:3
s.'s laws QUIN 619:5
s. thinks of a method PERU 574:8
s. were to cut his ear MEDA 503:5
scientists company of s. AUDE 35:14
s. are probably right ASIM 30:18
than most young s. MEDA 503:7
scire *s. nefas* HORA 387:21
scissor long, red-legged s.-man HOFF 380:3
scissors end up using s. HOCK 379:12
scoff fools, who came to s. GOLD 344:12
scoffer product of a s.'s pen WORD 828:10
scoffing S. his state SHAK 695:10
scold what a s. you are BULL 160:2
scones Over buttered s. ELIO 293:24
tea-cakes and s. BETJ 70:11
scope that man's s. SHAK 704:14
score time required to s. 500 COMP 230:10
scorer One Great S. RICE 626:3
scorn Disdain and s. SHAK 691:10
Laugh no man to s. BIBL 91:21
love he laughed to s. SHAK 705:28
s. is alluring CONG 233:10
S. not the Sonnet WORD 831:18
s. their bodies BAST 57:2
s. to change my state SHAK 704:15
s. which mocked the smart ARNO 27:22
sound Of public s. MILT 517:22
surmounted by s. CAMU 184:9
think foul s. ELIZ 296:27
thought s. BOOK 139:10
time of s. SHAK 693:13
very s. of men BOOK 132:22
what a deal of s. SHAK 702:2
scorned fury, like a woman s. CONG 232:26
was s. and died GAY 332:4
scornful dart not s. glances SHAK 698:12
only a s. tickling SIDN 718:27
seat of the s. BOOK 131:15
scorpions chastise you with s. BIBL 79:22
Scot Had Cain been S. CLEV 220:17
Scotch as a S. banker DAVI 252:2
inferior to the S. NORT 546:15
into a S. understanding SMIT 725:12
Mary, ma S. Bluebell LAUD 454:6
scotched s. the snake SHAK 684:4
Scotchman S. ever sees JOHN 413:6
Scotia chief of S.'s food BURN 166:24
old S.'s grandeur BURN 166:26
Scotland fair S.'s spear SCOT 651:15
fair S.'s strand BURN 167:15
flower of S. WILL 821:5
grave Livers do in S. use WORD 831:13
I do indeed come from S. JOHN 412:24
inferior sort of S. SMIT 725:7
in S. afore ye SONG 730:1
in S. supports the people JOHN 409:12
In S. we live between CRAW 244:18
of S. BYRO 175:21
our infinite S. MACD 484:14
S. a raucle tongue BURN 166:13
S. better than truth JOHN 409:20
S., land of the omnipotent No BOLD 124:11
Stands S. SHAK 685:6
white rose of S. MACD 484:18
Scots S. lords at his feet BALL 51:17
S., wha hae wi' Wallace bled BURN 168:7
six or seven dozen of S. SHAK 668:2
Scotsman S. on the make BARR 55:20
Scott half so flat as Walter S. ANON 18:6
wrong part wrote S. WATE 804:13
Scottish auld S. sang BURN 166:21
Scotty Beam me up, S. MISQ 521:4

scoundrel over forty is a s. SHAW 708:29
plea of the s. BLAK 119:2
refuge of a s. JOHN 415:3
to such a s. SWIF 748:9
scoured s. to nothing SHAK 669:27
scourge s. of small cords BIBL 101:15
scout s. 'em, and flout 'em SHAK 699:3
scowl s. on Richard SHAK 695:27
scrabble s. with all the vowels ELLI 298:7
scrannel on their s. pipes MILT 513:6
scrap s. of paper BETH 70:3
scrape s. himself withal BIBL 81:1
s. your strings darker CELA 199:9
scraps stolen the s. SHAK 680:29
scratch quick sharp s. BROW 156:22
S. a Russian PROV 610:22
S. the Christian ZANG 839:20
s. the nurse SHAK 702:25
scratching s. of a pen LOVE 477:3
s. of my finger HUME 395:7
s. of pimples on the body WOOL 827:3
scream as a last resort, s. SUGE 745:13
hilarity like a s. GREE 351:20
s. in a low voice BYRO 179:23
screw s. your courage SHAK 682:17
turn of the s. JAME 403:15
scribblative babblative and s. SOUT 731:1
scribble Always s., scribble, scribble GLOU 341:19
scrawl, and s. POPE 586:16
You who s. WYCH 834:13
scribbled by a s. name THOM 772:8
s. lines like fallen hopes HOPE 383:19
scribbling mob of s. women HAWT 364:14
s. fry YOUN 838:19
scribendi *S. cacoethes* JUVE 424:17
scribere *rapida s.* CATU 197:12
saturam non s. JUVE 424:3
scribes Beware of the s. BIBL 98:11
s. and Pharisees BIBL 93:8
s. and Pharisees, hypocrites BIBL 96:26
scribimus *S. indocti doctique poemata* HORA 387:6
scrip My s. of joy RALE 620:15
with s. and scrippage SHAK 657:8
scriptores *Cedite Romani s.* PROP 593:17
scripture better it in S. JAME 402:19
devil can cite S. SHAK 687:14
devil can quote S. PROV 598:6
Holy S. containeth BOOK 142:8
know more of the s. TYND 787:4
S. moveth us BOOK 125:13
scriptures all holy S. BOOK 127:22
Let us look at the s. SELD 653:13
S. in the hands PUGI 616:19
Search the s. BIBL 101:24
scroll charged with punishments the s. HENL 369:21
scrotumtightening s. sea JOYC 422:7
scroungy all s. and bearded CORS 237:10
scruple s. Of thinking too precisely SHAK 665:32
scrupulosity oriental s. JOHN 410:9
scrutamini *s. scripturas* SELD 653:13
scullion Away, you s. SHAK 669:29
sculptor great s. or painter RUSK 638:7
sculpture like that of s. RUSS 639:22
S. in stone MOOR 529:13
s. the true school of modesty PEAC 570:15
sculptured s. dead KEAT 427:4
scum Okie means you're s. STEI 737:11
rich are the s. of the earth CHES 211:4
s. of the earth WELL 809:20
scuttling S. across the floors of silent seas ELIO 295:7
Scylla S. and Charybdis NEWM 542:8
scythe mover whets his s. MILT 512:18
sighs like s. WALC 799:2
scythes last year's s. MELV 504:9
shaking s. at cannon HEAN 366:16
Scythia another group to S. VIRG 795:15
se *s. Iudice* JUVE 425:3
sea all the s. were ink LYLY 480:18
Alone on a wide wide s. COLE 226:17
around the glassy s. HEBE 367:8
as good fish in the s. PROV 611:45
As is the ribbed s.-sand COLE 226:16
as the waters cover the s. BIBL 87:5
beneath a rougher s. COWP 239:27
best thing is—the s. JERR 407:4
black s.-brute bulling MERW 506:3
boat on the rough s. HORA 387:15
burst Into that silent s. COLE 226:10
cloud out of the s. BIBL 79:30
cold grey stones, O S. TENN 757:11
complaining about the s. POWE 590:18
Death like a narrow s. WATT 805:17
deep, deep s. CONR 234:15
deeper than the s. BALL 51:10
dolorous midland s. SWIN 751:18
dominion of the s. COVE 238:8
Down to a sunless s. COLE 225:20
down to the s. again MASE 500:16
eating the s. ROBE 629:1
ebbing s. FORD 320:5
find another s. CAVA 198:9
flowing s. CUNN 247:15
forbear To teach the s. DONN 274:21
gaping wretches of the s. HUNT 395:13
garden front the s. SWIN 750:18
go to s. for pleasure PROV 602:22
gurly grew the s. BALL 50:12
having been at s. JOHN 415:28
headlong into the s. KEAT 431:9
He divided the s. BOOK 137:5
home from s. STEV 743:4
houses are all gone under the s. ELIO 294:8
if we gang to s. BALL 51:15
if Ye take away the s. KIPL 439:9
in a s. of glory SHAK 673:12
In a solitude of the s. HARD 361:9
in earth and air, And in the s. SMAR 722:11
in my chains like the s. THOM 772:4
in our s. of confusion GAMO 329:2
in perils in the s. BIBL 107:14
in the abysmal s. TENN 762:8
in the bottom of the s. SHAK 696:17
in the open s. UPDI 788:18
in the s. of life ARNO 28:2
Into a s. of dew FIEL 309:9
into the midst of the s. BOOK 134:18
like bathing in the s. LEIG 463:3
London, that great s. SHEL 711:22
looks s.-ward BROW 156:13
lover of men, the s. SWIN 751:16
machrel of the s. BALL 50:21
magic of the s. LONG 473:23
melts into the s. TENN 764:5
near to heaven by s. GILB 337:3
never go to s. GILB 338:29
of a sudden came the s. BROW 157:6
one is of the s. WORD 832:8
one s. to the other BOOK 136:18
one that goes To s. DONN 272:11
Over the s. to Skye STEV 742:23
over the summer s. TENN 766:10
Pieces of land and s. WALP 802:1
pinch the s. of its liberty COTT 238:1
Poem of the S. RIMB 628:7
Put out to s. MACN 488:17
Ran purple to the s. MILT 514:26
rude s. grew civil SHAK 689:22
sailed the wintry s. LONG 475:1
S., and hill, and wood COLE 225:13
s.-blooms and the oozy woods SHEL 712:15
s.-change in politics CALL 181:13
s. curling Star-climbed MERW 506:4
s.-fogs lap and cling KIPL 440:10
s. gave up the dead BIBL 113:6
s. hates a coward O'NE 554:23
s. is his BOOK 138:6
s. is not full BIBL 84:1
s. itself floweth in your veins TRAH 780:9
s.-mark of my utmost sail SHAK 693:30
S. of Faith ARNO 26:4
s. of glass BIBL 111:31
s. of glass BIBL 112:27
s. refuses no river PROV 610:23
s. saw that, and fled BOOK 139:21
S. shall give up her dead BOOK 142:6
s.! the sea! XENO 834:17
s. to shining sea BATE 57:4
s. was made his tomb BARN 55:8
see nothing but s. BACO 41:13
serpent-haunted s. FLEC 317:2
set in the silver s. SHAK 694:19
ship in the midst of the s. BIBL 83:36
sight of that immortal s. WORD 830:8
slowly towards the s. CHES 210:17
smiling surface of the s. PLUT 579:8
snotgreen s. JOYC 422:7
something of the s. SEDL 653:2
spouts out a s. MILT 517:7
spread like a green s. SHEL 712:4
stillness of the central s. TENN 762:4
strawberries grow in the s. NURS 549:12
suffer a s.-change SHAK 698:27
sweet Star of the S. FABE 305:19
there was no more s. BIBL 113:7
those in peril on the s. WHIT 815:1
thousand furlongs of s. SHAK 698:17
tossed them to the foaming s. LAWL 454:13
to the English that of the s. RICH 627:12
to the s. in ships BOOK 139:14
two if by s. LONG 474:16
unplumbed, salt, estranging s. ARNO 28:4
Upon the slimy s. COLE 226:12
uttermost parts of the s. BOOK 141:11
very much at s. CARS 192:6
walking on the s. BIBL 95:25
water in the rough rude s. SHAK 695:5
waves of the s. AESC 6:11
waves of the s. BOOK 138:3
waves on the great s. LUCR 479:3
went to s. LEAR 460:16
When I put out to s. TENN 757:18
Who hath desired the S. KIPL 440:7
who rush across the s. HORA 386:20
why the s. is boiling hot CARR 190:20
willing foe and s. room TOAS 778:5
Winds somewhere safe to s. SWIN 750:22
wrinkled s. beneath him TENN 758:17
your own s.-maws PROV 604:50
seagreen s. Incorruptible CARL 187:24
seagull I'm a s. CHEK 208:7
seagulls When s. follow a trawler CANT 185:12
seal opened the seventh s. BIBL 112:13
S. her sweet eyes ROSS 634:10
s. is not yet fixed BYRO 179:24
s. of the Holy One TALM 754:3
S. of the Prophets KORA 445:3
s. upon thine heart BIBL 86:7
S. up the mouth SHAK 698:5
sealed My lips are s. BALD 49:10
My lips are s. MISQ 522:4
sealing wax ships—and s. CARR 190:20
seals loose the s. BIBL 112:2
receives the s. of office ROSE 633:19
seam sew a fine s. NURS 547:18
seaman s. tells stories of winds PROP 593:15
seams Amusing little s. BAIL 48:4
sear fall'n into the s. SHAK 685:17
search active s. for truth LESS 465:17
in s. of an author PIRA 576:15
S. the scriptures BIBL 101:24
travels the world in s. MOOR 529:12
searched thou hast s. me out BOOK 141:9
will not be deep-s. SHAK 680:18
searching Canst thou by s. BIBL 81:14
seas dangers of the s. PARK 567:17
Draw not up s. DONN 274:21
foam Of perilous s. KEAT 429:14
hollow s., that roar MARV 498:8
multitudinous s. incarnadine SHAK 683:11
raging s. did roar SONG 729:15

Scuttling across the floors of silent s. ELIO 295:7
s. colder than the Hebrides FLEC 317:1
s. do laugh WEBS 808:19
s. of life, like wine TRAH 780:18
s. roll over but the rocks remain HERB 371:16
strange s. of thought WORD 831:3
such as pass on the s. BOOK 142:5
seashells She sells s. SULL 745:16
seashore boy on the s. NEWT 543:11
seasickness universal as s. SHAW 708:9
season by s. seasoned are SHAK 688:27
dry brain in a dry s. ELIO 294:23
In a summer s. LANG 450:15
in due s. BOOK 141:20
in s., out of season BIBL 109:22
man has every s. FOND 318:25
no s. knows, nor clime DONN 274:15
s. made for joys GAY 331:20
s. of all natures, sleep SHAK 684:16
s. of calm weather WORD 830:8
S. of mists KEAT 430:8
S. of mists OPEN 556:14
s. of snows and sins SWIN 750:6
there is a s. BIBL 84:7
time and s. AGES 8:23
word spoken in due s. BIBL 82:37
seasoned Like s. timber HERB 373:18
s. with salt BIBL 109:6
seasons four s. run their course CONF 232:6
lovers' s. run DONN 274:14
man for all s. BORR 144:11
man for all s. WHIT 816:9
O s., O castles RIMB 628:12
s. alter SHAK 689:21
s.' difference SHAK 658:13
s. shall be sweet COLE 225:16
s. such as these SHAK 678:28
vernal s. of the year MILT 519:21
seat Fasten your s.-belts FILM 311:6
into his s. SHAK 668:30
s. is the bosom of God HOOK 383:6
s. of Mars SHAK 694:19
s. of the scornful BOOK 131:15
seated looked wiser when he was s. KEYN 435:5
S. one day at the organ PROC 593:12
seats chief s. in the synagogues BIBL 96:25
fixed in our s. STEE 736:17
seawater salt s. passes TENN 760:31
seaworm s. crawls—grotesque HARD 361:9
seaworms Battening upon huge s. TENN 762:9
second for my s. race VAUG 790:7
grow a s. tongue MONT 527:4
Habit is s. nature AUCT 33:2
many s.-rate ones BEEC 61:7
my s. best bed SHAK 706:3
Nor s. he GRAY 351:2
no s. acts FITZ 315:16
no s. knows MILT 518:22
no s. spring PHIL 575:8
not a s. on the day COOK 235:15
s. at Rome CAES 180:18
s. best's a gay goodnight YEAT 836:3
s. childhood ARIS 24:10
s. childishness SHAK 659:3
s. oldest profession REAG 623:3
S. thoughts are best PROV 610:24
things have s. birth WORD 831:7
truth 24 times per s. GODA 341:20
when you come s. HILL 376:14
second-best anything but the s.-best LESS 465:11
secrecy S. the human dress BLAK 121:11
secret alms may be in s. BIBL 93:17
bread eaten in s. BIBL 82:19
ceases to be a s. BEHN 62:7
concept of the official s. WEBE 807:8
Et Vigny plus s. SAIN 641:10
girls that have no s. SPEN 732:23
gives charity in s. TALM 754:19
in s. sin CHUR 214:1
joys are s. BACO 43:24
knows the s. of God SIKH 719:14
know that's a s. CONG 232:19
neurosis is a s. TYNA 787:3
no s. so close SURT 747:7
not one s. concealed KORA 445:16
photograph is a s. ARBU 23:13
s. and inviolate Rose YEAT 837:7
s. anniversaries LONG 473:20
s., black, and midnight hags SHAK 684:21
s. in the Oxford sense FRAN 323:20
s. love BIBL 83:28
s. magic of numbers BROW 153:18
s. ministry of frost COLE 225:17
s. of politics BISM 116:5
s. of the long-nosed Etruscans LAWR 458:7
s. of the Lord KEBL 432:3
s. parts of Fortune SHAK 663:15
S. sits in the middle FROS 326:10
s. sports betwixt us twain DIAN 260:8
s. things BIBL 77:9
S. thoughts and open countenance ALBE 10:7
sin in s. MOLI 525:19
tender s. dwells BYRO 175:15
Three may keep a s. PROV 612:46
Vereker's s. JAME 403:3
secretary S. of Nature WALT 803:1
secretly entice thee s. BIBL 77:8
s., like wrongs hushed-up OWEN 562:10
secrets no s. are hid BOOK 129:4
privacy and tawdry s. LEAC 459:13
s. are edged tools DRYD 282:19
s. of heaven and earth SHEL 710:7
s. of th' abyss GRAY 351:2
S. with girls CRAB 243:11
throw their guilty s. PRIE 591:10
Trust not with s. LAVA 454:11
sect attached to that great s. SHEL 711:8
found them a s. MACA 482:12
into that ancient s. YEAT 837:14
loving his own s. COLE 227:7
paradise for a s. KEAT 427:17
sad-coloured s. HOOD 383:3
sectaries in a nation of s. DISR 270:5
sects diversity of s. SPEN 734:17
secular s. bird MILT 518:23
secure He is s. SHEL 711:1
past is s. WEBS 807:10
securities sooner trust to two s. CHES 209:20
security fear, otherwise styled s. MADA 488:22
make s. secure POPP 587:27
s. around the president MAIL 491:4
s. of Europe MITC 523:14
watchword is s. PITT 577:1
sedentary s. humour MONT 526:21
sedge s. has withered KEAT 428:7
seditione *de s. querentes* JUVE 424:7
seditions way to prevent s. BACO 43:32
seducer strong s., opportunity DRYD 281:7
seduction delusive s. BURN 166:2
In s., the rapist DWOR 286:11
sedulous played the s. ape STEV 741:7
see All that we s. POE 579:13
And for to s. CHAU 206:19
by my form did s. me MAHĀ 490:5
complain we cannot s. BERK 68:2
eyes which s. BIBL 99:10
hold, but cannot s. WESL 811:1
I'll s. you again COWA 238:13
In all things Thee to s. HERB 372:12
into the wilderness to s. BIBL 95:6
I s. a voice SHAK 690:25
I s., not feel COLE 225:2
I shall never s. KILM 435:20
I was blind, now I s. BIBL 102:4
last s. your father YEAM 835:1
like my roses to s. you SHER 716:23
live longest, s. most PROV 612:35
make you *s.* CONR 234:17
more people s. than weigh CHES 209:22
never let me s. PRIO 592:14
never s. him FLAU 316:17
never s. so much SHAK 680:16
Nice to s. you CATC 196:14
no man s. me and live BIBL 76:19
no man s. me more SHAK 673:11
not worth going to s. JOHN 416:10
one can s. rightly SAIN 641:12
Plenty to s. and hear JOYC 422:15
rather s. than be one BURG 162:2
s. and hear nothing THOM 773:3
s. another's woe BLAK 120:20
s. better days BEHN 62:12
s. beyond our bourn KEAT 430:15
s. me dance the Polka GROS 354:2
s. me sometime MISQ 522:15
S. no evil PROV 610:26
S. one promontory BURT 170:11
s. oursels as others see us BURN 168:21
S.-saw, Margery Daw NURS 550:16
s. the coloured counties HOUS 390:19
s. the goodness BOOK 133:12
s. the hours pass CIOR 218:4
s. the object ARNO 29:6
s. the things thou dost not SHAK 679:25
s. what I eat CARR 189:17
s. what I say WALL 799:17
s. with, not through, the eye BLAK 118:14
shall not s. me BIBL 102:26
taste and s. BOOK 133:20
they shall s. God BIBL 93:3
they shall s. our God KEBL 432:3
those who will not s. PROV 612:31
To s. her is to love her BURN 166:19
wait and s. ASQU 31:1
whatever you see LUCA 478:17
What the eye doesn't s. PROV 614:9
What you s. is what you get SAYI 648:9
yet I s. thee still SHAK 682:21
You s., but you do not observe DOYL 277:12
seed beareth forth good s. BOOK 140:20
blood of Christians is the s. TERT 768:15
Good s. makes good crop PROV 601:30
good s. on the land CAMP 182:14
lord will have the s. OXFO 562:15
No s. is sown IRWI 400:5
not one light s. KEAT 427:23
Parsley s. goes nine PROV 609:18
s. its harvest KEAT 427:1
s. of knowledge BACO 41:6
s. of what we know BERR 69:15
s.-time had my soul WORD 830:23
s. ye sow SHEL 713:26
sow thy s. BIBL 84:30
spring again from its s. SHEL 714:20
seeding One year's s. PROV 609:9
seeds into the s. of time SHAK 681:16
least of all s. BIBL 95:22
s. fell by the wayside BIBL 95:20
s. of the death of any state HOBB 378:24
wingèd s. SHEL 712:12
seedtime s. and harvest BIBL 74:19
seeing one way of s. RUSK 638:27
S. is believing PROV 610:27
s. what everybody has seen SZEN 752:5
very s. of God THOM 771:13
way of s. KEEN 432:9
seek All I s., the heaven above STEV 743:1
go s. the asses BIBL 78:20
If you s. a monument EPIT 304:4
Myself alone I s. to please GAY 332:12
s., and ye shall find BIBL 94:3
S. and ye shall find PROV 610:28
s. is find SMAR 722:11
S. not to know THOM 770:21
S. thou this soul of mine LITT 470:3
S. ye first the kingdom BIBL 93:26
S. ye the Lord BIBL 88:21
shall men s. death BIBL 112:15
sometime did me s. WYAT 834:5

seek (*cont.*):
strive, to s., to find TENN 767:12
We s. him here ORCZ 557:10
Who s., who hope, who love SIDN 718:19
Why s. ye the living BIBL 100:31
you would not s. me PASC 568:21
seeketh he that s. findeth BIBL 94:4
seeking s. asses found MILT 518:6
S., not in hope to THOM 773:15
Seelen *Zwei S. wohnen* GOET 342:17
seem Be what you would s. PROV 596:17
Let be be finale of s. STEV 739:21
that only s. SPEN 734:14
to s. active BONA 125:3
seemed well pleased, all s. MILT 517:2
seeming keep S. and savour SHAK 703:13
s. otherwise SHAK 692:10
seemly it is s. so to do KETH 434:11
seems I know not 's.' SHAK 661:20
s. too little or BARR 55:12
seen anybody here s. Kelly MURP 537:3
being s. for what one is DRAB 278:15
evidence of things not s. BIBL 109:28
God whom he hath not s. BIBL 111:15
Hast thou not s. WINK 823:8
having not s., ye love BIBL 110:25
I have s. God BIBL 75:7
I have s. war ROOS 632:14
needs only to be s. DRYD 281:17
No man hath s. God BIBL 101:8
not s., and yet have believed BIBL 103:6
s. and not heard PROV 597:18
s. is merely their own mind MAHĀ 490:7
s. one city slum AGNE 8:24
seen what I have s. SHAK 664:12
should be s. to be done HEWA 375:17
things have we s. BEAU 58:13
Too early s. unknown SHAK 697:8
when you've s. one Western WHIT 814:21
Who hath not s. thee KEAT 430:9
You've never s. this country PURD 617:25
sees s. and hears all we do PUNC 617:17
s. Dhamma sees me PALI 565:8
s. more in my pictures TURN 785:15
s. what is now [illegible]
seeth Lord s. not as man BIBL 78:27
segregation S. now WALL 799:14
Seine flows the S. APOL 22:21
Seinte Loy ooth was but by S. CHAU 204:12
seize s. the day HORA 387:22
s. the flow'r BURN 168:13
select each one should s. SHEL 711:8
Not a s. party KEAT 431:19
selection Natural S. DARW 250:18
Natural s. a mechanism FISH 314:2
self divided s. LAIN 448:4
exchange of s. and other SHAN 706:8
nature of s. PALI 565:7
only S. to please BLAK 121:2
s. is hateful PASC 568:20
S.-praise no recommendation PROV 610:29
S.-preservation is first law PROV 610:30
small hungry shivering s. ELIO 292:26
spirit is the true s. CICE 217:17
to thine own s. be true SHAK 662:13
self-assertion s. abroad WAUG 806:9
self-consumer s. of my woes CLAR 218:15
self-contempt S., well-grounded LEAV 461:7
self-control energy in s. JAIN 401:18
self-defence it was in s. MARL 496:1
self-denial S. is not a virtue SHAW 708:23
self-determination act of s. AHER 8:29
self-esteem proper measure of s. BENN 65:15
s., grounded on just MILT 517:11
self-evident s. beings NEWM 542:5
truths to be s. ANON 19:11
self-government S. is our right CASE 193:7
self-help spirit of s. SMIL 722:17
self-interest propelled by s. BAGE 46:3
selfish All sensible people are s. EMER 299:13
How small and s. is sorrow ELIZ 298:3
selfishness Reduce s. LAO 451:10
self-love but their s. SMIT 723:6
golden-calf of s. CARL 187:5
s. and social POPE 585:27
self-lovers nature of extreme s. BACO 44:23
self-made s. man is one who believes STEA 736:13
s. man may prefer HAND 359:7
self-preservation s. in the other JEFF 405:20
self-respect insult their s. TAWN 755:17
starves your s. PARR 568:4
self-righteousness S. is not religion BRON 149:13
self-sacrifice S. enables us SHAW 709:1
self-schooled S., self-scanned ARNO 27:14
self-slain As a god s. SWIN 750:19
self-slaughter fixed His canon 'gainst s. SHAK 661:22
self-sufficiency S. at home WAUG 806:9
self-sufficing reasoning, s. thing WORD 830:18
s. power of Solitude WORD 831:1
Selima pensive S. reclined GRAY 350:19
selkie s. in the sea BALL 50:17
Selkirk S. knew the plight KAVA 426:11
sell dreams to s. BEDD 60:18
I'll s. him LEAC 459:15
I s. here, Sir BOUL 145:3
mind to s. his house SWIF 747:16
Most people s. their souls SMIT 724:14
no man might buy or s. BIBL 112:21
One does not s. the earth CRAZ 244:19
s. in the dearest PROV 596:45
s. it cheap SAYI 648:1
s. Jack like soapflakes KENN 433:20
s., or deny, or delay MAGN 489:13
s. that thou hast BIBL 96:13
s. the present life KORA 444:8
to s. time TAWN 755:16
selling lives by s. something STEV 740:20
old firm, is s. out OSBO 560:6
S. off the family silver MISQ 522:7
sells s. eternity SHAK 704:1
seltzer weak hock and s. BETJ 70:4
semblable *Hypocrite lecteur,—mon s.* BAUD [illegible]
semblances outface it with their s. SHAK 658:12
semen no frozen s. ever read a story WILL 820:11
semi s.-house-trained polecat FOOT 319:3
seminaries s. of young ladies KNOX 442:17
seminary from a ladies' s. GILB 338:4
semita *Fallentis s. vitae* HORA 387:3
semper *et nunc, et s.* MISS 520:10
Quod ubique, quod s. VINC 793:3
S. aliquid novi PLIN 578:17
S. eadem MOTT 535:16
Sic s. tyrannis MOTT 535:17
senates s. hang upon thy tongue THOM 775:10
senator S., and a Democrat JOHN 408:10
senators I look at the s. HALE 357:2
s. burst with laughter AUDE 33:26
s. of mighty woods KEAT 427:27
teach his s. wisdom BOOK 139:9
send S. in the clowns SOND 728:3
s. me BIBL 86:24
sending s. down of the Book KORA 445:5
sends He s. out into EICH 290:6
senectus *Morbi tristisque S.* VIRG 794:20
sennights Weary s. SHAK 681:12
sensational s. to read in the train WILD 817:22
sensations easy prey to s. TREV 781:9
O for a life of s. KEAT 430:22
sense bind The wand'ring s. CONG 233:16
borrows all her rays from s. POPE 583:26
Common s. is not VOLT 797:12
curb the s. DRYD 281:4
deviates into s. DRYD 281:36
Devoid of s. and motion MILT 515:10
disease and want of s. ROCH 630:4
echo to the s. POPE 584:22
fountain of good s. DRYD 283:12
good s. and good taste LA B 446:17
it is not s. CHUR 213:15
Learned without s. CHUR 214:9
light of nature, s. ROCH 630:13
men of s. approve POPE 584:24
men of s. never tell SHAF 655:16
Money is like a sixth s. MAUG 502:4
motions of the s. SHAK 686:3
one grain of s. DRYD 281:8
pleasures of s. BHAG 72:19
Satire or s. POPE 583:9
s. for sense ALFR 11:15
s. is dim BEEC 61:8
servilely creeps after s. DRYD 282:30
Short gleams of s. CHUR 214:4
something more than good s. COLE 227:22
Take care of the s. CARR 190:1
talk s. to the American people STEV 740:10
want of s. DILL 267:14
senseless kind of s. wit WILB 817:6
worse than s. things SHAK 674:3
senses by your s. five BLAK 119:26
horses are the s. UPAN 788:1
If Parson lost his s. HODG 379:13
knowledge denied from s. SA'A 641:1
not enslaved by the s. TANT 755:2
pleasures of the s. ESHE 301:8
s. will never inform us SMIT 723:5
snatches away all the s. CATU 197:9
Unto our gentle s. SHAK 682:6
sensibilité equivalent to *s.* PALM 566:10
sensibility Dear s. STER 738:12
dissociation of s. ELIO 296:20
it is an immense s. JAME 403:9
pattern informed by s. READ 622:11
sensible All s. people are selfish EMER 299:13
be bold and be s. HORA 386:15
S. men DISR 270:12
s. of his natural rights PRIE 592:9
This s. warm motion SHAK 686:18
sensitive s. being WORD 831:10
S. Plant SHEL 713:22
try to be s. MURA 536:15
sensual Catholic and s. CHAN [illegible]
s. pleasure without vice JOHN 418:12
sensuality s., rebellion THOM 773:7
sent man s. from God BIBL 101:4
say I s. thee thither SHAK 673:5
s. before my time SHAK 696:9
sentence Give s. with me, O God BOOK 134:9
isn't a word . . . it's a s. FILM 311:24
life s. goes on CONL 233:21
Makes half a s. COWP 240:1
No! No! S. first CARR 190:10
recording the s. VILL 792:17
s. is enough PLAU 578:13
s. is factually significant AYER 40:4
sentenced s. to death in my absence BEHA 62:1
sentences Backward ran s. GIBB 336:9
essential opening s. GREE 351:21
half-finished s. EDGE 288:13
hard s. of old BOOK 137:3
sentiment corrupted by s. GREE 351:18
rich in s. TENN 765:12
S. is what I am not FLEM 317:16
sentiments *my own* s. BAGE 47:21
people of refined s. KELL 432:15
Them's my s. THAC 769:8
sentinel scarce worth the s. GOLD 345:28
S. of the grave TATE 755:6
sentinels s. to warn MARL 496:29
sentry quadrille in a s.-box JAME 403:2
stands a wingèd s. VAUG 790:6
separate able to s. us BIBL 105:12
can't s. peace MALC 492:1
s. and equal station JEFF 405:2
separated they cannot be s. SMIT 725:19

separately all hang s. FRAN 323:13
separateth s. very friends BIBL 83:2
separation impel them to the s. JEFF 405:2
prepare for a s. QUIN 619:3
prospect of an easy s. HUME 394:12
real s. of powers DENN 257:18
s., but fission and divorce SHIP 717:5
s. of state and science FEYE 309:5
that eternal s. STER 739:14
September days hath S. SAYI 648:6
S. blow soft PROV 610:31
When you reach S. ANDE 14:10
sepulchre first to the s. BIBL 102:39
living s. of life CLAR 218:17
No man knoweth of his s. BIBL 77:15
s. there by the sea POE 579:11
taken away from the s. BIBL 102:38
whited s. TROL 782:7
sepulchres s. BIBL 96:28
s. of mortality CREW 244:22
sepulcra *Per s. regionum* MISS 523:4
sequel natural s. AUST 38:8
sequestered one of those s. spots HARD 361:4
sera *rosa S. moretur* HORA 388:5
seraglio s. of eunuchs FOOT 319:1
seraphim bright s. in burning row MILT 511:11
sworded s. MILT 513:22
seraphims Above it stood the s. BIBL 86:21
one of the s. BIBL 86:23
seraphin Cherubin, and S. BOOK 125:20
sere Now my s. fancy BYRO 177:3
serene s., That men call age BROO 150:7
serenity called the s. of age BLIS 122:1
serf another man's s. HOME 382:11
serfdom abolish s. ALEX 11:7
sergeant S. Pepper TYNA 787:2
This fell s., death SHAK 667:7
serial obituary in s. form CRIS 245:5
serious joke's a very s. thing CHUR 213:20
Murder is a s. business OPEN 555:26
s. and the smirk DICK 263:23
s.-minded activity MONT 527:11
War is too s. CLEM 220:9
seriously S., though CATC 196:19
sermon honest and painful s. PEPY 572:20
Perhaps, turn out a s. BURN 167:1
rejected the S. on the Mount BRAD 146:10
who a s. flies HERB 372:4
sermons S. and soda-water BYRO 176:13
S. in stones SHAK 658:14
sero *S. te amavi* AUGU 36:5
serpent be the s. under't SHAK 682:5
biteth like a s. BIBL 83:16
infernal s. MILT 514:10
my s. of old Nile SHAK 656:20
Now the s. was more subtil BIBL 73:24
s. ate Eve HUGH 393:7
s. beguiled me BIBL 74:3
s., green in the mulberry bush TATE 755:6
s.-haunted sea FLEC 317:2
s. subtlest beast MILT 517:13
s. upon a rock BIBL 83:36
s., which is the Devil BIBL 113:4
sharper than a s.'s tooth DICK 264:27
sharper than a s.'s tooth SHAK 678:11
serpents wise as s. BIBL 94:34
servant as a humble s. MAND 493:8
become the s. of a man SHAW 707:8
born to be a s. TOCQ 778:10
carried His s. by night KORA 444:19
cracked lookingglass of a s. JOYC 422:8
Fire is a good s. PROV 600:25
form of a s. BIBL 108:16
good and faithful s. BIBL 97:8
Is thy s. a dog BIBL 80:21
judgement with thy s. BOOK 141:17
life of a s. of God NEWM 542:14
nor the s. above his lord BIBL 94:35
One s. worth a thousand gadgets SCHU 649:13
sent down on Our s. KORA 443:16
s. depart in peace BIBL 98:24
S. of God, well done MILT 517:5
s. of the Living God SMAR 722:5
s. shall have small BARC 53:22
s. to the devil SISS 720:17
s. with this clause HERB 372:14
thou wast a s. BIBL 77:5
thy s. heareth BIBL 78:15
well enough for a s. CONG 232:23
Wife and S. CHUD 213:9
Your s.'s cut in half GRAH 348:4
servants Between them and s. BARC 53:22
equality in the s.' hall BARR 55:13
purgatory of s. PROV 599:13
s. of the public GOWE 347:11
s. of the sovereign BACO 43:8
s. will do that for us VILL 792:18
wife or your s. to read GRIF 353:10
Women and s. most difficult CONF 232:7
Ye s. of the Lord DODD 271:19
serve Fleet in which we s. BOOK 142:4
left me to s. alone BIBL 99:15
love to s. my country GIBR 336:10
not yet able to s. man CONF 231:20
s. and lose GOET 343:5
s. Him in this world CATE 194:5
s. in the wars BOOK 142:13
s. thee with a quiet mind BOOK 128:17
s. the Lord with gladness BOOK 138:13
s. two masters BIBL 93:22
s. two masters PROV 607:47
s. your captives' need KIPL 440:21
than s. in heaven MILT 514:21
Thee only we s. KORA 443:14
They also s. MILT 518:30
will not s. if elected SHER 717:3
served first s. PROV 600:27
Had I but s. my God SHAK 673:17
s. her, perhaps mistakenly GLAD 341:12
s. to him course by course CHUR 215:5
well s. PROV 603:42
Worshipped and s. BIBL 104:27
Youth must be s. PROV 616:7
serveth as he that s. BIBL 100:22
service All s. ranks the same BROW 157:13
at the s. of the nation POMP 580:7
bounden duty and s. BOOK 130:1
devoted to your s. ELIZ 297:14
done the state some s. SHAK 694:3
Hacked with constant s. SOUT 728:22
No s. RACI 620:1
Pressed into s. FROS 326:11
S. and love above all other DUNB 285:3
s. is perfect freedom BOOK 126:12
s. of my love SPRI 735:6
s.? The rent we pay CLAY 220:6
serviettes kiddies have crumpled the s. BETJ 70:10
servile freed from s. bands WOTT 832:24
servilely s. creeps after sense DRYD 282:30
servility savage s. LOWE 477:21
serving cumbered about much s. BIBL 99:15
six honest s.-men KIPL 441:10
With s. still WYAT 834:3
servitude base laws of s. DRYD 281:5
Freedom and not s. BURK 163:2
servum *O imitatores, s. pecus* HORA 387:5
sesame Open S. ARAB 23:7
worm in a s. plant TALM 754:14
sesquipedalia *s. verba* HORA 385:17
sesquipedalian S. blackguard CLOU 221:16
sesquippledan S. verboojuice WELL 810:8
sessions s. of sweet silent thought SHAK 704:16
Sestos S. and Abydos of her breasts DONN 272:12
set play a s. SHAK 670:29
s. fair BENN 66:4
s. himself doggedly to it JOHN 412:11
S. me whereas the sun SURR 746:10
s. one slip of them SHAK 703:15
s. our sins from us BOOK 138:19
S. thine house in order BIBL 87:25
would not have s. out CAVA 198:6
Setebos my dam's god, S. SHAK 698:25
S., Setebos BROW 155:19
sets sun never s. NORT 546:16
setter Proud s. up SHAK 673:1
setting against a s. sun SHAK 699:17
s. people right MOOR 530:2
time is s. with me BURN 168:4
settle less will you s. to one KIPL 439:7
settlement parent of s. BURK 163:15
through the Act of S. RICE 626:6
seven acts being s. ages SHAK 658:25
first s. years SAYI 647:16
have the s. minutes COLL 229:3
hewn out her s. pillars BIBL 82:18
Jacob served s. years BIBL 75:4
Keep a thing s. years PROV 604:47
lowly air Of S. Dials GILB 337:13
man with s. wives NURS 547:11
Rain before s. PROV 610:5
remember more than s. BELL 63:1
s. churches BIBL 111:20
s. days are more than enough AUST 39:3
s. fat kine BIBL 75:13
s. feet of English ground HARO 362:11
s. golden candlesticks BIBL 111:21
s. maids with seven mops CARR 190:19
s.-stone weakling ADVE 7:36
S. types of ambiguity EMPS 300:9
Until seventy times s. BIBL 96:11
We are s. WORD 832:13
sevenfold s. gifts impart BOOK 142:7
seventeen Maud is not s. TENN 764:3
seventh moon is in the s. house RADO 620:4
opened the s. seal BIBL 112:13
rested the s. day BIBL 76:12
s. day is the sabbath BIBL 76:11
seventies s. started 21st century BOWI 145:23
seventy At s.-seven it is time JOHN 409:21
s. years young HOLM 381:11
Until s. times seven BIBL 96:11
sever kiss, and then we s. BURN 166:9
s. The chain CORY 237:12
severae *procul este, s.* OVID 561:4
several S. excuses HUXL 397:5
severance their s. ruled ARNO 28:3
severe man s. he was GOLD 344:13
to nothing but herself s. CARE 186:9
severity pure s. of perfect light TENN 759:21
Severity breedeth s. BACO 43:11
with its usual s. COLE 228:1
Severn S.'s right of maker GURN 355:4
thick on S. HOUS 391:2
twice a day the S. fills TENN 760:31
Seville these dogs of S. TENN 766:9
sew It can s., it can cook PLAT 577:11
s., sew, prick our fingers BROW 154:9
sewer midst of this putrid s. TOCQ 778:18
s. in a glass-bottomed boat MIZN 524:13
sewers houses thick and s. MILT 517:14
sewing job of s. on a button BROU 151:15
sex attempt to insult s. LAWR 458:3
because of my s. BEHN 62:8
Being a s. symbol WELC 809:4
call you darling after s. BARN 55:4
Continental people have s. life MIKE 507:19
contours of her s. WALK 799:10
dies from lack of s. ATWO 32:8
feathers s. can soothe EWAR 305:9
for my own s. AUST 38:12
give a s. to mind WOLL 825:17
have s. with a man WESL 811:24
if s. rears its ugly head AYCK 40:1
isn't s. but death SONT 728:6
Is s. dirty ALLE 12:10
men think. S., work FISH 313:10
Mind has no s. MISQ 522:3
Money was exactly like s. BALD 49:2
mostly about having s. LODG 472:12

sex (*cont.*):
no stronger than my s. SHAK 675:8
of s. ALLE 12:8
only unnatural s. act KINS 437:22
portray this [s.] relation ROBI 629:20
practically conceal its s. NASH 539:7
real music was s. DOYL 278:11
S. and drugs and rock and roll DURY 286:9
S. and taxes JONE 419:3
s. business isn't worth LAWR 459:1
s. in the mind LAWR 458:9
s. in yesterday's novels WELD 809:8
s. is a sublimation LODG 472:15
S. never an obsession BOY 146:4
s. object if you're pretty GIOV 340:1
S. something I really don't understand SALI 642:10
s. that brings forth DE B 254:3
S. was a competitive event GELD 332:26
s. without emotion PAGL 563:4
s. with someone I love ALLE 12:9
soft, unhappy s. BEHN 62:17
subordination of one s. MILL 509:3
weaker s. ALEX 11:13
When you have money, it's s. DONL 272:5
sexes personalities of the two s. MEAD 503:1
stronger, of the two s. GIBB 335:7
there are three s. SMIT 725:17
sexton s. tolled the bell HOOD 382:20
that bald s., Time SHAK 677:9
sexual car crash as a s. event BALL 52:12
draws so oddly with the s. GUNN 354:20
man's idea of his s. rights STAN 736:10
moral power strong as s. CONF 231:18
not have s. relations CLIN 221:6
of all the s. perversions HUXL 397:4
s. intercourse AURE 37:4
S. intercourse began LARK 452:12
s. subjects GISS 340:9
shock of s. astonishment WESL 811:23
sexuality relinquish their s. WOLF 825:2
s. in the movies DENE 257:6
sexually s. transmitted disease SAYI 647:29
shabby s. equipment ELIO 294:11
shackles Memories are not s. [illegible]
s. accidents SHAK 657:21
s. of government GOLD 344:5
shadblow Cowslip and s. CRAN 243:20
shade clutching the inviolable s. ARNO 27:11
elder brother even to s. ROCH 630:20
farewell to the s. COWP 241:1
gentlemen of the s. SHAK 667:15
his steadfast s. TENN 765:9
image of a s. SHEL 714:17
in a green s. MARV 498:16
in s. of Tempe sit SIDN 718:16
in the chequered s. MILT 512:21
let it sleep in the s. MOOR 530:15
light, s., and perspective CONS 235:9
sitting in the s. KIPL 438:19
sly s. of a Rural Dean BROO 150:12
sweeter s. To shepherds SHAK 672:28
whiter s. of pale REID 624:7
windings and such s. WINC 822:24
shades S. of the prison-house WORD 829:20
till the s. lengthen NEWM 542:16
shadow also casts a s. CHUR 215:16
but the s. of heaven MILT 516:33
cast their s. before PROV 597:29
days on the earth are as a s. BIBL 80:29
dream But of a s. CHAP 202:13
dream of a s. PIND 576:11
Falls the S. ELIO 294:25
fleeth also as a s. BIBL 81:18
Follow a s. JONS 420:19
in the s. of death BIBL 98:18
in the s. of the earth BROW 154:5
Life's but a walking s. SHAK 685:22
Like a vast s. moved VAUG 790:17
little s. that goes STEV 742:14
little s. that runs CROW 246:16
little s. that runs HAGG 356:4
live under the s. of a war SPEN 732:25
mere s. of death LAUD 454:4
S. cloaked from head to foot TENN 761:1
s. of a great rock BIBL 87:19
s. of death BIBL 81:12
s. of death BIBL 86:28
s. of death BOOK 139:12
s. of felicity WALL 800:10
s. of God BROW 152:12
s. of her even brows SPEN 733:24
s. of our night SHEL 711:1
s. of some unseen Power SHEL 711:16
s. of the sun RALE 620:11
s. of the Valois CHES 210:10
s. of thy Throne WATT 805:19
s. of turning BIBL 110:12
s. stands over us ALLI 12:20
s. will be shown NIET 545:14
Swift as a s. SHAK 689:5
through the s. VIRG 794:19
valley of the s. of death BOOK 133:1
walketh in a vain s. BOOK 133:30
shadowing employ any depth of s. DRYD 283:15
shadowless s. like Silence HOOD 382:26
shadows but s. SHAK 690:26
cold white s. WRIG 833:13
events cast their s. CAMP 183:10
From s. and types EPIT 302:5
half sick of s. TENN 762:15
Individuals pass like s. BURK 164:29
less liquid than their s. TESS 768:17
long s. on county grounds MAJO 491:16
millions of strange s. SHAK 704:19
Old sins cast long s. PROV 608:25
Our fatal s. FLET 318:5
puppets in a play of s. BHAG 73:4
see only their own s. PLAT 578:8
s. and twilights Æ 6:8
s. flee away BIBL 85:12
s. have offended SHAK 690:30
s., not substantial things SHIR 717:8
s. now so long do grow COTT 237:16
s. numberless KEAT 429:6
s. of the clouds WORD 827:15
s. of us men [illegible]
s. to-night SHAK 696:31
s. upon the sunbright walls WORD 827:13
Types and s. THOM 771:11
When the sun sets, s. LEE 462:3
Shadrach S., Meshach, and Abed-nego BIBL 90:2
shady s. trees BIBL 82:2
shaft Lie like a s. of light TENN 759:4
s., at random sent SCOT 651:3
shafts Its s. remain ROET 631:5
shoots s. divine LODG 472:18
shag common cormorant (or s.) ISHE 400:7
shaggy S., and lean COWP 242:4
shake Earth must s. HORA 388:3
only S.-scene in a country GREE 352:5
s. against the cold SHAK 704:29
s. hands with a king HALL 358:9
s. off the dust BIBL 94:33
s. their heads BOOK 132:22
this god did s. SHAK 674:11
shaken is never s. SHAK 705:15
S. and not stirred FLEM 317:9
s. me by the hand WESL 811:21
to be well s. COLM 229:20
shakers movers and s. O'SH 560:11
shakes s. his parting guest SHAK 700:16
s. so my single state SHAK 681:21
Shakespeare less S. he BROW 156:6
Our *myriad-minded* S. COLE 227:13
Our sweetest S. MILT 512:24
reproduce works of S. WILE 819:17
S., another Newton HUXL 397:6
S. by flashes of lightning COLE 227:19
S. is like bathing LEIG 463:8
S. is not more decidedly MACA 481:11
S. is of no age COLE 227:27
S. one gets AUST 37:27
S. unlocked his heart WORD 831:18
S. was of us BROW 156:18
S. would have grasped MCEW 485:6
She had read S. WELL 810:7
S.—the nearest thing OLIV 553:16
talk of my being like S. SCOT 652:14
When I read S. LAWR 458:16
When you do S. MIRR 520:5
Shakespearean Dogs are S. SCHW 649:15
That S. rag BUCK 159:12
Shakespeherian S. Rag ELIO 296:5
shaking entrusted to the s. hand VICT 792:5
fall without s. MONT 526:13
Shalimar loved beside the S. HOPE 383:20
shall mark you His absolute 's.' SHAK 660:6
picked the was of s. CUMM 247:11
shallow idle, s. things SHAK 702:11
S. brooks murmur SIDN 718:6
s. in himself MILT 518:10
s. murmur RALE 620:16
shallows in s. and in miseries SHAK 676:28
Shalott Lady of S. TENN 762:15
shalt Thou s. have no other gods BIBL 76:8
shame Ain't it all a bleedin' s. MILI 508:14
coward s. BURN 167:24
fruit of my vanity is s. PETR 574:12
glory is in their s. BIBL 108:22
mourn with her in s. EMEC 299:3
now bound in with s. SHAK 694:19
secret s. destroyed RICH 626:18
sense of some deathless s. WEBS 808:10
s. the devil PROV 611:44
s. unto him BIBL 106:14
terrible s. for me YOKO 838:13
waste of s. SHAK 705:19
shameful s. conquest of itself SHAK 694:19
shameless most s. thing BURK 163:28
What . . . can be more s. GODW 342:8
shames hold a candle to my s. SHAK 687:22
shamrock Apart from the s. MCAL 481:4
s. shine DAVI 252:14
Shandeism True *S.* STER 739:5
shank too wide For his shrunk s. SHAK 659:2
Shannon green banks of S. CAMP 183:7
shantih S. shantih ELIO 296:15
shape might be any s. CARR 190:26
pressed out of s. FROS 326:11
s. of things to come WELL 810:15
Take any s. but that SHAK 684:12
wrought me into s. FITZ 314:21
shaped s., sir, like itself SHAK 657:2
shapen s. in wickedness BOOK 135:5
shapes Change s. with Proteus SHAK 672:30
shaping s. spirit of imagination COLE 225:6
share all persons alike s. ARIS 25:5
all that I have I s. BOOK 131:6
greater s. of honour SHAK 671:22
its ruin didst not s. DODI 271:21
s. no one's ideas TURG 785:2
s. the transport WORD 832:5
shared trouble s. PROV 613:18
shares Fair s. for all POLI 581:12
s. are a penny GILB 337:20
shark s. has pretty teeth BREC 147:17
sharks s. circling, and waiting CLAR 219:2
Sharon rose of S. BIBL 85:9
sharp s. as a two-edged sword BIBL 82:12
so s. the conquerynge CHAU 206:28
'Tis a s. remedy RALE 621:8
sharpening s. my oyster knife HURS 396:11
sharper s. than a serpent's tooth DICK 264:27
s. than a serpent's tooth SHAK 678:11
s. the storm PROV 610:34
sharpers all your trade are s. DRYD 283:17
sharpness s. of death BOOK 126:1
sharps s. and flats BROW 157:10
shatter s. the vase MOOR 530:11
shaves s. and takes a train WHIT 813:24
Shaw S.'s plays AGAT 6:15
shawms trumpets also, and s. BOOK 138:10

she And then again S. does JAST 404:13
chaste, and unexpressive s. SHAK 659:6
life and loves of a s.-devil WELD 809:6
S. sells sea-shells SULL 745:16
S., she is dead DONN 272:8
S. who must be obeyed HAGG 356:5
S. who trifles with all GAY 332:3
That not impossible s. CRAS 244:15
sheaf made obeisance to my s. BIBL 75:9
shearers sheep before her s. BIBL 88:17
shears resembles a pair of s. SMIT 725:19
with th' abhorrèd s. MILT 513:3
sheathe s. the sword ASQU 31:2
sheaves bring his s. with him BOOK 140:20
s. of sacred fire CHAP 202:17
your s. stood BIBL 75:9
Sheba Another S. queen WITH 824:2
Ere you were Queen of S. SHIP 717:5
queen of S. BIBL 79:17
shed Burke under a s. JOHN 417:9
disused s. in Co. Wexford MAHO 490:20
prepare to s. them now SHAK 676:6
shall his blood be s. BIBL 74:21
s. for you and for many BOOK 129:22
s. innocent blood BIBL 89:3
shedding Without s. of blood BIBL 109:26
sheen s. is the sonne LANG 450:22
sheep Among the s. MISS 523:6
as s. going astray BIBL 111:1
bleating s. loses bite PROV 596:25
care of s. DYER 286:14
craved the life of a s. LA F 447:14
ensample to his s. CHAU 204:24
Feed my s. BIBL 103:9
folds shall be full of s. BOOK 136:2
found my s. which was lost BIBL 99:33
get back to these s. ANON 20:12
giveth his life for the s. BIBL 102:6
hanged for a s. PROV 608:49
has lost her s. NURS 549:4
hills like young s. BOOK 139:21
His silly s. COWP 241:3
hungry s. look up MILT 513:6
in s.'s clothing BIBL 94:9
keep s. and cows OSBO 559:17
like lost s. BOOK 125:15
like s. have gone astray BIBL 88:17
little black s. KIPL 438:17
looking on their silly s. SHAK 672:28
lost s. BIBL 94:31
mere s.-herding POUN 590:4
mountain s. are sweeter PEAC 571:5
old half-witted s. STEP 737:21
Other s. I have BIBL 102:8
savaged by a dead s. HEAL 366:3
s. bear fleeces VIRG 797:4
s. before her shearers BIBL 88:17
s.-bells and ship-bells KIPL 440:10
s. born carnivorous FAGU 306:3
s. in sheep's clothing CHUR 217:1
s. in sheep's clothing GOSS 347:7
s. of his hand BOOK 138:6
s. on his right hand BIBL 97:11
s.'s in the meadow NURS 549:5
s. that have not a shepherd BIBL 80:9
s., that were wont to be MORE 531:5
s. to pass resolutions INGE 399:7
sickly s. infects the flock WATT 805:4
teeth are like a flock of s. BIBL 85:14
two hundred years like a s. TIPU 777:15
sheeps s.' guts SHAK 691:6
sheet brought in the white s. GARC 329:10
England's winding s. BLAK 118:5
How at my s. THOM 772:6
s. knit at the four corners BIBL 103:28
s. were big enough SHAK 702:5
turn over the s. SAND 644:6
waters were his winding s. BARN 55:8
wet s. CUNN 247:15
sheets cool kindliness of s. BROO 150:8
s. with hay over JOHN 409:19
Shekinah rejoice in the S. ZOHA 840:11
shelf s. life of the modern TRIL 781:12
shell fired a 15-inch s. RUTH 640:16
gloomy s. ANON 17:22
prettier s. NEWT 543:11
thou s. of death MIDD 507:6
Shelley Burns, S., were with us BROW 156:18
did you once see S. BROW 156:23
peace in S.'s mind SHEL 714:10
shells choirs of wailing s. OWEN 562:6
shelter s. from the stormy blast WATT 805:19
shelves symmetry of s. LAMB 448:13
shepherd call you, S. ARNO 27:3
Dick the s. SHAK 681:4
God of love my S. is HERB 373:14
good s. BIBL 102:6
happy S. Boy WORD 829:18
like a s. BIBL 88:2
Lord is my s. BOOK 132:26
Lord's my s. SCOT 652:20
love a s. swain GREE 352:4
my s. is BAKE 48:13
Old Nod, the s. DE L 256:19
returned unto the S. BIBL 111:1
sheep that have not a s. BIBL 80:9
s., blowing of his nails SHAK 672:27
S., Corydon, burned with love VIRG 795:16
s. his sheep PROP 593:15
s.'s delight PROV 610:6
s. tells his tale MILT 512:18
shepherds s. abiding in the field BIBL 98:20
s. and butchers VOLT 798:3
s. call me also a poet VIRG 796:11
s. give a grosser name SHAK 666:13
s. watched their flocks TATE 755:10
sheriff I shot the s. MARL 496:1
Sheriffmuir at S. A battle MCLE 487:6
Sherman general (yes mam) s. CUMM 247:8
sherry s. flowing into second-rate whores PLOM 579:3
shibboleth Say now S. BIBL 77:37
shield broken was her s. SCOT 651:15
efforts to s. children ADDA 4:4
faith shall be my s. ASKE 30:20
lady in his s. TENN 762:16
Our S. and Defender GRAN 348:15
s. against retribution TALM 753:21
s. and buckler BOOK 137:21
S. of Abraham SIDD 717:18
s. of faith BIBL 108:13
trusty s. LUTH 480:2
shieling From the lone s. GALT 328:19
shift let me s. for myself MORE 531:14
s. in what the public wants CALL 181:13
shifted s. his trumpet GOLD 345:5
shilling sell for one s. Your ring LEAR 460:18
s. life will give you AUDE 35:3
shimmered Jeeves s. out WODE 824:11
shine Arise, s. BIBL 89:4
Boy you can gimme a s. GORD 347:1
Let your light so s. BIBL 93:6
Lord make his face s. BIBL 76:24
s. all through the sphere VAUG 790:15
s., and run to and fro BIBL 91:9
s. in company SWIF 749:1
s. on, harvest moon NORW 547:2
shiners Nine for the nine bright s. SONG 729:11
shines s. and stinks RAND 621:17
s. sae bright BURN 169:10
shingles naked s. of the world ARNO 26:4
shining I see it s. plain HOUS 391:5
s. from shook foil HOPK 384:5
s. into a puddle PROV 611:35
s. morning face SHAK 658:26
S. nowhere but in the dark VAUG 790:13
S. suspension CRAN 243:22
sun was s. everywhere GERS 334:12
with s. foot shall pass FITZ 315:3
woman of s. loveliness YEAT 837:8
ship all I ask is a tall s. MASE 500:16
being in a s. JOHN 412:22
build your s. of death LAWR 458:12
idle as a painted s. COLE 226:11
like a sinking s. WOOL 827:6
must rebuild their s. NEUR 541:12
one for the s. PROV 608:42
O S. of State LONG 473:10
sheep-bells and s.-bells KIPL 440:10
s., an isle FLEC 317:6
s. appeared in the air HEAN 366:13
s. has weathered every rack WHIT 815:4
s. I have got SONG 730:2
s. in a black storm WEBS 808:18
s. in the midst of the sea BIBL 83:36
S. me somewheres KIPL 439:14
s. on the sea GARC 329:11
s. substantial ASKE 30:20
s. was as still SOUT 730:15
s. would *not* travel CARR 191:23
Sink me the s., Master Gunner TENN 766:11
spoil the s. PROV 598:28
towards a sinking s. CHUR 216:25
What is a s. BURT 170:15
will sink a s. BUNY 161:11
woman and a s. ever want PROV 615:14
ships Hell to s. AESC 6:9
launched a thousand s. MARL 496:5
little s. of England GUED 354:10
move with the moving s. SWIN 751:17
mystery of the s. LONG 473:23
Of shoes—and s. CARR 190:20
S. are but boards SHAK 687:10
S., dim-discovered THOM 775:8
s. empty of men NICI 544:21
s. have been salvaged HALS 358:12
s. of the sea BOOK 134:25
s. sail like swans asleep FLEC 317:5
S. that pass in the night LONG 474:18
S., towers, domes WORD 827:19
something wrong with our bloody s. BEAT 58:6
Spanish s. of war TENN 766:8
stately s. go on TENN 757:12
There go the s. BOOK 139:6
to the sea in s. BOOK 139:14
we've got the s. HUNT 395:10
wooden wall is your s. THEM 770:16
shipwreck s. of time BACO 41:10
suffered s. BIBL 107:13
shire That s. which we may call DRAY 279:4
shires bugles calling from sad s. OWEN 562:6
Round both the s. HOUS 390:19
shirt Near is my s. PROV 607:22
Song of the S. HOOD 382:28
shirtsleeves From s. to PROV 600:48
shit chicken s. JOHN 408:9
s. in a silk stocking NAPO 539:6
s.-wiping stick MUMO 536:11
shock-proof s. detector HEMI 369:14
shiver praised and left to s. JUVE 424:4
tremble and s. HOOD 382:15
shoal bank and s. of time SHAK 682:8
s. of fools CONG 233:7
shoals s. of herring MACC 484:9
shock Future s. TOFF 779:1
S.-headed Peter HOFF 380:8
s. of the new DUNL 285:7
s. of your joy HUGH 393:9
s. them and keep them up to date SHAW 707:6
short, sharp s. GILB 338:6
sudden s. of joy BLIS 122:1
we shall s. them SHAK 677:21
shocked s. by this subject BOHR 124:1
shocking looked on as something s. PORT 588:2
shocks s. the magistrate RUSS 640:1
s. the mind of a child PAIN 563:9
thousand natural s. SHAK 664:3
twelve great s. of sound TENN 759:3
shod All s. with steel WORD 828:20
foot feel, being s. HOPK 384:5

shoddier no s. than what they peddle BECK 59:15
shoe Buckle my s. NURS 550:3
careless s.-string HERR 374:8
cast out my s. BOOK 135:20
embrace a woman's s. KRAU 445:19
If the s. fits PROV 603:22
I kiss his dirty s. SHAK 671:12
Into a left-hand s. CARR 191:15
lived in a s. NURS 551:6
s.'s latchet BIBL 101:9
want of a s. PROV 600:41
shoemaker s.'s son always PROV 610:35
shoes from the s. GOLD 345:32
shoes call for his old s. SELD 653:14
dead men's s. PROV 604:35
ere those s. were old SHAK 661:26
in cheap s. AMIE 13:9
mind it wipes its s. THOM 772:17
Of s.—and ships CARR 190:20
Put off thy s. BIBL 75:26
s. of his soldiers BAGE 46:14
s. that were not fellows DEFO 254:19
s. with broken high ideals MCGO 485:9
thy feet with s. BIBL 86:3
shoeshine riding on a smile and a s. MILL 509:22
shook earth s. BOOK 136:6
monk who s. the world MONT 528:15
more it's s. it shines HAMI 358:14
s. hands with time FORD 320:1
Ten days that s. the world REED 624:3
shoot can s., And can hit HERB 372:10
he shall s. higher SIDN 718:7
S., if you must WHIT 816:4
s. me in my absence BEHA 62:1
s. me through linoleum BANK 53:9
s. out their lips BOOK 132:22
s. the Hippopotamus BELL 63:3
s. the hippopotamus FORS 320:8
s. the pianist ANON 18:8
s. the sleepy, green-coat man HOFF 380:6
s. your murderer ACHE 1:10
They s. horses don't they MCCO 484:11
they shout and they s. INGE 399:3
You'd s. a fellow down HARD 361:18
young idea how to s. THOM 775:5
shooting s.-stars attend thee HERR 374:14
shoots green s. of recovery MISQ 521:13
man who s. him gets caught MAIL 491:4
shop ain't the s. for justice DICK 264:18
back to the s. LOCK 472:10
foul rag-and-bone s. YEAT 835:9
little back s. MONT 527:14
s. will keep you PROV 604:49
shopkeepers nation of s. ADAM 3:19
nation of s. NAPO 539:4
nation of s. PROV 599:15
nation of s. SMIT 723:10
shopocracy abuse the s. NORT 546:18
shopping main thing today is—s. MILL 509:23
shore adieu! my native s. BYRO 173:22
after-silence on the s. BYRO 178:21
for the further s. VIRG 794:21
high s. of this world SHAK 671:20
hugging the s. UPDI 788:10
impossible s. ARNO 27:23
kingdom of the s. SHAK 704:26
rapture on the lonely s. BYRO 175:8
s. Of the wide world KEAT 430:19
sounds by the s. YEAT 836:12
stayed upon the green s. KEAT 431:9
stretch from s. to shore WATT 805:18
To the other s. PAUL 570:9
unknown and silent s. LAMB 448:19
shored s. against my ruins ELIO 296:14
shoreless s. watery wild ARNO 28:2
shores around Desolate s. KEAT 430:1
betwixt their s. ARNO 28:4
on the s. of darkness KEAT 430:14
recognize my s. AKHM 9:7
wilder s. of love BLAN 121:17
shorewards great winds s. blow ARNO 26:11
shorn come home s. PROV 606:26
green grass s. BACO 43:5
priest all shaven and s. NURS 551:7
sheep that are even s. BIBL 85:14
tempers wind to s. lamb PROV 601:19
short Anger is a s. madness HORA 386:16
in a s. time BIBL 91:10
it is well it is s. TAYL 756:19
Life's s. span HORA 387:17
long and the s. and the tall HUGH 392:16
nasty, brutish, and s. HOBB 378:21
not S. DICK 264:10
s. horse soon curried PROV 610:36
s. in the story BIBL 92:20
s. notice, soon past PROV 605:50
s. of the glory of God BIBL 104:32
S. reckonings PROV 610:37
s., sharp shock GILB 338:6
s. time to live BOOK 131:12
s. way ASCH 30:6
Take s. views SMIT 725:14
That lyf so s. CHAU 206:28
while to make it s. THOR 775:29
shortcomings o'er its own s. LITT 470:4
shorter s. by the head ELIZ 296:26
time to make it s. PASC 568:6
shortest longest day and s. night PROV 595:35
s. way BACO 41:19
s. way home PROV 605:49
shorts Eat my s. CATC 195:11
khaki s. girl BETJ 71:2
shot be s. at HARD 362:2
Certain men the English s. YEAT 836:17
fired the s. BALL 50:18
I s. the sheriff MARL 496:1
s. at for sixpence a-day DIBD 260:11
s. heard round the world EMER 299:7
s. mine arrow SHAK 667:4
They've s. our fox BIRC 115:11
shotgun blew his head off with a s. BLY 122:15
shots of the best s. VOLT 798:4
take pot s. at you CLAR 219:4
shoulder giant's s. to mount on COLE 227:14
government shall be upon his s. BIBL 87:1
hifted it to another s. SHAW 708:14
keep looking over his s. BARU 56:12
left s.-blade GILB 338:11
shoulders Borne on our s. BROW 155:31
City of the Big S. SAND 643:18
from her s. did fall WYAT 834:6
grow beneath their s. SHAK 691:34
lawn about the s. HERR 374:8
old head on young s. PROV 615:42
on the s. of giants NEWT 543:9
on your young s. SPAR 731:17
s. held the sky suspended HOUS 390:9
s. of giants BERN 68:22
shout hardly a s. ARNO 27:2
shouted with a great s. BIBL 77:20
S. round me, let me hear WORD 829:18
s. that tore hell's concave MILT 514:29
S. with the largest DICK 265:5
they s. and they shoot INGE 399:3
shouted sons of God s. BIBL 81:32
shouting thunder and the s. BIBL 81:37
tumult and the s. KIPL 440:3
shovelled s. quatrains s. LOWE 478:7
shovelling S. white steam AUDE 34:12
show business like s. business BERL 68:11
learned not to s. it ALCO 10:9
make a s. themselves OVID 561:5
only a s. GOET 342:15
s. any just cause BOOK 131:3
s. business with blood BRUN 159:1
s. him my salvation BOOK 138:1
S. Must Go On GERS 334:21
s. our simple skill SHAK 690:23
s. that you have one CHES 209:14
s. the light BOOK 137:8
s. thy praise BOOK 135:9
shower abundant s. of curates BRON 149:16
coming s. SWIF 749:5
sweetness of a s. THOM 773:5
showers After sharpest s. LANG 450:22
April s. bring forth PROV 595:15
land never pleads for s. TIBU 777:8
S., and Dew BOOK 126:5
with his s. soote CHAU 204:6
with his s. soote OPEN 556:25
showery S., Flowery, Bowery ELLI 298:14
showeth true love is, it s. DE P 258:4
showing worth s. DANT 250:7
shows outward s. SHAK 688:3
shreds king of s. and patches SHAK 665:19
thing of s. and patches GILB 337:21
shrewd s. was that snatch BROW 155:12
shrewishly speaks very s. SHAK 701:6
Shrewsbury by S. clock SHAK 669:17
shriek hollow s. the steep MILT 513:27
short shrill s. COLL 229:8
shrieking Hooting and s. SHAK 674:22
s. and squeaking BROW 157:10
shrieks Not louder s. POPE 587:10
shrimp s. learns to whistle KHRU 435:15
s. of an author GRAY 351:8
shrimps s. to swim again JONS 419:9
shrine Erects a s. BYRO 178:2
fits a little s. HERR 374:21
shrined bower we s. to Tennyson HARD 361:7
shrines mouldering s. removed BYRO 174:2
shrink all the boards did s. COLE 226:12
never make thee s. BALL 51:4
shroud April s. KEAT 429:4
Fetch out no s. PUDN 616:14
heavy-shotted hammock s. TENN 760:27
stain the stiff dishonoured s. ELIO 295:25
striped s. THOM 773:8
whoever comes to s. me DONN 274:1
shrouds S. have no pockets PROV 610:38
shrug read a nod, a s. SWIF 749:9
with a patient s. SHAK 687:15
shrunk S. to this little measure SHAK 675:19
shudder s. at it beforehand DOST 276:6
s. in the loins engenders YEAT 836:15
shuffle All s. there YEAT 837:4
s. the cards CERV 200:3
shuffled s. off this mortal coil SHAK 664:3
Shulamite return, O S. BIBL 86:2
shun let me s. that SHAK 678:27
s. that wretched state CHUD 213:10
shut either s. or open PROV 598:41
gates of it shall not be s. BIBL 113:11
Men s. their doors SHAK 699:17
ought to be s. up JOHN 413:2
s. mouth catches no flies PROV 610:39
s. the door POPE 583:1
s. the stable-door PROV 604:36
S. up he explained LARD 452:10
shuts When one door s. PROV 614:23
shutter before her on a s. THAC 769:16
click the s. EISE 291:13
shuttered s. mansion FITZ 315:19
shutters close the s. fast COWP 241:31
shuttle Man is the s. VAUG 790:2
musical s. WHIT 815:6
swifter than a weaver's s. BIBL 81:10
shuttlecock Battledore and s. DICK 265:6
shy life has made me s. BERG 67:15
Once bitten, twice s. PROV 608:33
si *S. possis recte* HORA 386:11
Sibyl saw the S. at Cumae ROSS 635:9
Sibyllam *Nam S. quidem Cumis* PETR 574:16
Sicelides *S. Musae* VIRG 796:4
sick And I am s. at heart SHAK 661:5
but the daylight s. SHAK 688:28
Created s. GREV 353:4
devil was s. PROV 598:13
do not make me s. WHIT 815:15

do the s. no harm NIGH 545:22
extremely s. PRIO 593:6
half s. of shadows TENN 762:15
hired to watch the s. COWP 241:18
I am s., I must die NASH 539:22
I am s. of both JOHN 415:21
is Brutus s. SHAK 675:6
kingdom of the s. SONT 728:9
make him s. DONN 272:11
medicine for the s. SHAN 706:7
most s. and most healthy HA-L 357:5
Pass the s. bag, Alice CATC 196:18
Rose, thou art s. BLAK 121:7
s. and wicked AUST 39:13
s., and ye visited me BIBL 97:12
s. for home KEAT 429:14
s. hurry ARNO 27:10
s. in fortune SHAK 678:5
They are as s. SHAK 687:6
they that are s. BIBL 94:24
think we're s. WOLF 825:9
when he is s. JOHN 417:1
sickened s. at all triumphs CHUR 214:6
sickle isle, a s. moon FLEC 317:6
s. in the fruitful field BLAK 120:10
sickly I'm s. but sassy HARR 362:16
kind of s. smile HART 363:11
s. sheep infects the flock WATT 805:4
sickness age, grief, or s. KING 436:7
falling s. SHAK 674:20
in s. and in health BOOK 131:5
long s. Of health SHAK 699:24
medicine to heal their s. BOOK 141:24
s., or any other adversity BOOK 129:14
s. that destroyeth BOOK 137:22
Sid Tell S. ADVE 8:12
Sidcup get down to S. PINT 576:12
side bosom and half her s. COLE 224:20
Hear the other s. AUGU 36:8
my hand into his s. BIBL 103:3
on every s. BOOK 133:18
on our s. today MACA 483:2
on the other s. BUNY 161:19
on the s. of those ANOU 22:7
other s. of the hill WELL 809:22
over to the other s. REED 623:16
passed by on the other s. BIBL 99:12
S. by side WOOD 826:10
Which S. Are You On DYLA 287:4
which s. do they cheer for TEBB 757:2
Who is on my s. BIBL 80:26
sidelong s. would she bend KEAT 428:11
sidera *Sublimi feriam s. vertice* HORA 387:13
sides looked at life from both s. MITC 523:16
Norfan, both s. WELL 810:10
said on both s. ADDI 5:3
two s. to every question PROV 612:3
sidestreets down the s. GINS 339:21
siege envious s. SHAK 694:19
My s. is over VERT 791:12
She kept the s. HILL 376:16
Siegfried washing on the S. Line KENN 433:6
siesta Englishmen detest a s. COWA 238:15
sieve draws nectar in a s. COLE 227:6
in a s. I'll thither sail SHAK 681:11
went to sea in a S. LEAR 460:9
sifted s. a nation STOU 744:2
siftings let their liquid s. fall ELIO 295:25
sigh Born of the very s. KEAT 428:5
I s. the lack SHAK 704:16
I to s. for her SHAK 680:23
s. for thy repose WESL 811:9
s. in thanking BROW 154:8
s. is just a sigh HUPF 396:10
s. is the sword BLAK 119:1
s. like Tom o' Bedlam SHAK 678:7
s. no more, ladies SHAK 691:7
sighed S. and looked DRYD 280:21
S. and looked THOM 775:9
s. as a lover GIBB 335:22
s. his soul SHAK 688:19
sighing ability and S. DICK 266:19
poor soul sat s. SHAK 693:18
s. of a contrite heart BOOK 127:14
sighs on the Bridge of S. BYRO 174:24
world of s. SHAK 692:1
sight all very well at first s. SHAW 708:13
at first s. STEE 736:17
deprived of sight VIRG 794:9
evil in thy s. BOOK 135:4
giveth s. to the blind BOOK 141:22
in the s. of God BOOK 130:22
in the s. of the Lord BOOK 140:4
in thy s. BOOK 141:17
My dying s. BLOK 122:3
neatly out of s. CRAN 243:24
Out of s. PROV 609:15
out of s. THOM 771:4
s. of means SHAK 677:17
s. to dream of COLE 224:20
s. to make an old man young TENN 758:22
s. was often puzzled BOCC 123:7
thousand years in thy s. BOOK 137:18
To feeling as to s. SHAK 682:21
triple s. in blindness KEAT 430:14
sights few more impressive s. BARR 55:20
s. as youthful poets dream MILT 512:24
sign If only God would give some s. ALLE 12:15
if you s. this BRUG 158:20
In this s. shalt thou conquer CONS 235:11
Jews require a s. BIBL 105:27
outward and visible s. BOOK 130:17
Queen must s. BAGE 47:3
seeketh after a s. BIBL 95:15
signal do not see the s. NELS 540:15
Only a s. shown LONG 474:18
s.-elm ARNO 27:24
signals s. of the ancient flame DANT 250:1
signed hand that s. the paper THOM 772:7
I s. my death warrant COLL 229:2
What I have s. GRIF 353:8
significance s. of an event CART 193:1
s. of its own JUNG 423:10
signo *In hoc s. vinces* CONS 235:11
signposts s. to socialist Utopia CROS 246:5
signs merely conventional s. CARR 191:22
multiply my s. and my wonders BIBL 75:33
no 'white' or 'coloured' s. KENN 433:16
read s. of the times CHOI 212:9
s. and wonders BIBL 101:21
S. are the natural language SHAD 655:10
s. of the times BIBL 96:3
words are but the s. JOHN 409:4
Sikhs Grant to your S. SIKH 720:2
silence after-s. on the shore BYRO 178:21
answered best with s. JONS 420:8
but s. is golden PROV 611:17
chequered s. AKHM 9:12
clamour of s. TAGO 753:1
conspiracy of s. COMT 230:20
darkness again and a s. LONG 474:18
darkness and s. LEAR 460:7
Deep is the s. DRIN 279:11
easy step to s. AUST 38:5
end of OM is s. UPAN 788:8
eternal s. PASC 568:13
even darkness and s. KELL 432:13
flashes of s. SMIT 725:20
foster-child of s. KEAT 428:21
foster-child of s. OPEN 556:23
Gospel of S. MORL 532:3
Go to where the s. is GOOD 346:12
I kept s. BOOK 133:28
Indecency's conspiracy of s. SHAW 708:26
in that s. we the tempest DRYD 281:1
I shall state s. BECK 59:11
lies are often told in s. STEV 742:4
Lo! all in s. CRAB 242:28
mind moves upon s. YEAT 836:16
My gracious s., hail SHAK 660:5
Of the eternal S. WORD 830:7
other side of s. ELIO 292:23
period of s. on your part ATTL 32:2
rest is s. SHAK 667:11
shadowless like S. HOOD 382:26
sigh that s. heaves KEAT 428:5
s. all the airs MILT 519:12
S. alone is great VIGN 792:16
s. also does not ELIO 292:11
S. augmenteth grief DYER 286:12
s. deep as death CAMP 183:3
s., exile, and cunning JOYC 422:5
s. fell with the waking bird TENN 764:7
s. in heaven BIBL 112:13
s. in the hills TENN 760:31
S. is a woman's AUCT 33:14
S. is a woman's best PROV 610:40
S. is become his mother tongue GOLD 345:14
S. is deep as Eternity CARL 187:12
S. is golden PROV 610:41
s. is most noble SWIN 750:10
S. is the virtue BACO 41:25
S. like a cancer grows SIMO 720:10
S. means consent PROV 610:42
S. more musical ROSS 634:11
s. of a dream ROSS 634:3
s. of the law HOBB 378:23
s. sank Like music COLE 226:25
s. shroud such sin GILB 337:1
S., sing to me HOPK 384:7
s. surged softly backward DE L 256:17
S. that dreadful bell SHAK 692:15
S.! Voilà l'ennemi COND 231:1
small change of s. MERE 505:17
Sorrow and s. LONG 473:15
stain upon the s. BECK 60:7
Still-born S. FLEC 317:8
talent pour le s. CARL 187:28
Through the friendly s. VIRG 793:20
trembles into s. BYRO 175:15
twofold s. ROSS 634:23
visible s. ROSS 634:22
With s. and tears BYRO 179:19
world of s. EPIT 302:2
silenced because you have s. him MORL 532:4
silencing justified in s. MILL 508:19
silent All s., and all damned WORD 830:16
Grey s. fragments HUGH 393:6
impossible to be s. BURK 165:7
into the s. land ROSS 634:8
Laws are s. CICE 217:24
mornings are strangely s. CARS 192:7
one must be s. WITT 824:6
Paris was French—and s. TUCH 784:16
s. be AUDE 34:7
s. in seven languages BAGE 46:14
s. majority NIXO 546:4
s. manliness of grief GOLD 344:17
s. over Africa BROW 156:5
s. touches of time BURK 165:13
S., upon a peak CLOS 222:20
S., upon a peak in Darien KEAT 429:21
strong, s. man MORL 532:3
then s. night MILT 516:22
t is s. ASQU 31:8
unlocked her s. throat GIBB 336:4
why art thou s. CRAW 244:17
silentia *Tacitae per amica s. lunae* VIRG 793:20
silk breed the s. SHAK 693:6
clad in s. or scarlet PROV 595:10
he was shot s. STRA 744:6
make a s. purse MORT 533:13
make his couche of s. CHAU 205:23
shit in a s. stocking NAPO 539:6
s. hat on a Bradford millionaire ELIO 296:10
s. makes the difference FULL 327:13
s. purse out of sow's ear PROV 615:27
s. stockings JOHN 412:10
soft as s. remains HILL 376:11
worn with a s. hat EDWA 289:5
silken s. terms precise SHAK 680:30
s. tie SCOT 650:18

silks in fading s. compose WINC 823:2
in s. my Julia goes HERR 375:4
silkworm of s. size or immense MOOR 529:16
s. expend her yellow labours MIDD 507:8
silkworms s. droop BASH 56:18
sillier s. than a silly laugh CATU 197:6
silliest s. part of God's creation ROCH 630:18
s. woman can manage a clever man KIPL 441:18
silly Ask a s. question PROV 595:26
it's good to be s. HORA 389:11
s. twisted boy CATC 196:34
such a s. question STER 738:14
'tis very s. BYRO 176:24
You were s. like us AUDE 33:31
silvae *paulum s. super his* HORA 389:24
s. sint consule dignae VIRG 796:4
silvam *In s. . . . ligna feras* HORA 389:21
silvas *Habitarunt di quoque s.* VIRG 795:18
inter s. Academi HORA 387:8
silver About a s. lining COWA 238:20
all the Georgian s. MACM 488:1
Between their s. bars FLEC 317:6
bringing gold, and s. BIBL 79:19
cloud has a s. lining PROV 599:21
covered with s. wings BOOK 136:7
for a handful of s. BROW 156:17
gold and s. becks me SHAK 677:10
in her s. shoon DE L 256:20
pictures of s. BIBL 83:18
Selling off the family s. MISQ 522:7
S. and gold have I none BIBL 103:18
s. apples of the moon YEAT 837:12
s. cord be loosed BIBL 85:2
s. foot in his mouth RICH 626:14
s. link SCOT 650:18
s. pin BALL 52:9
s. plate on a coffin CURR 248:3
s., snarling trumpets KEAT 427:5
s.-sweet sound lovers' tongues SHAK 697:18
Speech is s. PROV 611:17
take s. or small change CHAM 201:6
There's a s. lining FORD 320:6
thirty pieces of s. BEVA 71:18
thirty pieces of s. BIBL 97:16
thousands of gold and s. BOOK 140:8
time hath to s. turned PEEL 572:1
silvery so s. is thy voice HERR 375:5
silvestrem *S. tenui Musam* VIRG 795:13
Silvia by S. in the night SHAK 702:27
Who is S. SHAK 702:29
similes play with s. WORD 832:10
similia *S. similibus curantur* MOTT 535:18
Simon real S. Pure CENT 199:13
Simple S. met a pieman NURS 550:17
simple and never s. WILD 817:13
ask the hard question is s. AUDE 35:9
beautiful and s. HENR 370:17
C'est tellement s. PRÉV 591:7
I'm a s. man LOWR 478:10
S. Simon met a pieman NURS 550:17
s. truth must be abused SHAK 696:14
smile with the s. GARR 330:2
too clear, too s. STEN 737:19
women are so s. SHAK 698:15
simplicitas *O sancta s.* HUSS 396:12
simplicity Cultivate s. LAMB 448:23
elegant s. STOW 744:4
Embrace s. LAO 451:10
holy s. JERO 406:14
O holy s. HUSS 396:12
Pity my s. WESL 810:26
s., a child POPE 584:10
s. of the three per cents DISR 270:13
simplify s. me when I'm dead DOUG 276:15
S., simplify THOR 776:13
Simpson I'm Bart S. CATC 196:1
simulacrum dark s. BROW 152:12
sin all the causes of s. JAIN 401:11
And the s. I impute BROW 158:4
bare the s. of many BIBL 88:19
beauty is only s. deep SAKI 642:5
brother s. against me BIBL 96:11
brought s. and death STAN 736:9
By that s. fell the angels SHAK 673:15
charity in s. SHAK 686:14
dark world of s. BICK 114:16
died unto s. once BIBL 105:1
dreadful record of s. DOYL 277:9
Excepting Original S. CAMP 183:17
fall into no s. BOOK 126:13
fall not in such s. GILB 337:2
go, and s. no more BIBL 101:34
go away and s. no more ANON 17:18
hate the s. AUGU 36:11
He that is without s. BIBL 101:33
Ignorance excuses from s. AUCT 33:5
I had not known s. BIBL 105:3
in secret s. CHUR 214:1
in s. hath my mother BOOK 135:5
keep us this day without s. BOOK 126:2
Lord imputeth no s. BOOK 133:17
lose the s. POPE 582:23
Lukewarmness I account a s. COWL 239:18
made almost a s. DRYD 281:4
My s., my soul NABO 537:17
My s., my soul OPEN 556:1
no s. but ignorance MARL 496:15
no s., but to be rich SHAK 677:8
not innocence but s. BROW 156:12
One s. will destroy BUNY 161:11
only one real s. LESS 465:11
original s. MELV 504:7
palace of sweet s. KEAT 428:16
physicists have known s. OPPE 557:3
quantum o' the s. BURN 167:2
rebellion is as the s. BIBL 78:26
researches in original s. PLOM 579:4
Shall we continue in s. BIBL 104:37
silence shroud such s. GILB 337:1
s. blows quite away HERB 373:12
s., death, and Hell BUNY 161:13
single venial s. NEWM 542:12
s. in secret MOLI 525:19
S. is behovely JULI 423:3
s. is ever before me BOOK 135:4
s. not BIBL 108:5
s. of public men TAYL 756:17
s.'s a pleasure BYRO 176:6
S.'s rotten trunk COWP 241:5
s. tends to be addictive AUDE 35:12
s. with caution CENT 199:12
s. ye do by two and two KIPL 440:12
Stand in awe, and s. not BOOK 131:19
taketh away the s. BIBL 101:10
triumph over death and s. SPEN 733:3
wages of s. is death BIBL 105:2
want of power to s. DRYD 282:10
we have no s. BIBL 111:11
what did he say about s. COOL 236:3
Where s. abounded BIBL 104:36
Which is my s. DONN 273:6
worst s. towards our fellow SHAW 706:25
Would you like to s. ANON 19:18
your s. will find you out BIBL 77:3
sincere Always be s. TRUM 784:9
be as wholly s. JUDA 422:23
be s. MENG 505:2
friend s. enough BULW 160:9
starkly s. RHYS 625:18
sincerely s. want to be rich CORN 236:19
sincerity Because of his s. COLL 229:4
be talked with in s. SHAK 686:2
s. is a dangerous thing WILD 818:5
unleavened bread of s. BIBL 106:2
Sindh I have S. WINK 823:10
sinecure no s. BYRO 180:5
sinews Money is the s. of love FARQ 307:18
money the s. of war BACO 44:12
s. of the soul FULL 327:9
s. of thy heart BLAK 121:9
s. of war CICE 217:23
Stiffen the s. SHAK 671:5
very s. of virtue WALT 802:18
sing Alleluia! s. to Jesus DIX 271:12
bygynneth to s. CHAU 207:11
can s. and won't sing PROV 605:36
celebrate myself, and s. myself WHIT 815:10
come, let us s. BOOK 138:5
do what men may s. PEMB 572:8
I'll s. you twelve O SONG 729:11
in thine heart to s. SWIN 751:9
I s. of brooks HERR 374:3
I s. the progress DONN 273:10
I, too, s. America HUGH 392:17
I will s. of the sun POUN 589:9
know ye s. well FLET 318:10
laugh and s. BOOK 136:2
never heard no horse s. ARMS 25:18
O s. unto God BOOK 134:21
people s. it BEAU 58:8
Places where they s. BOOK 126:14
Silence, s. to me HOPK 384:7
s. A faery's song KEAT 428:11
S. a song of sixpence NURS 550:18
S. before breakfast PROV 610:43
s. before him a new song HAGG 356:2
s. both high and low SHAK 701:9
S. 'em muck MELB 503:13
s. in a hempen string FLET 318:3
s. in the robber's face JUVE 424:19
s. like birds i' the cage SHAK 680:6
S. me a song STEV 742:23
S., my tongue FORT 321:6
S. no sad songs ROSS 634:13
s. praises unto his name BOOK 136:6
s. the ancient ways YEAT 837:17
s. the body electric WHIT 815:3
s. the Lord's song BOOK 141:8
s. the old songs CLAR 219:1
s. the sofa COWP 241:16
S. thou the songs of love GURN 355:6
s. to the harp BOOK 138:10
S. unto the Lord BOOK 133:19
s. unto the Lord BOOK !38:9
S. we merrily BOOK 137:9
S. whatever is well made YEAT 837:20
skilled to s. of time TENN 764:20
Soul clap its hands and s. YEAT 837:2
souls can s. openly SPEN 732:14
think that they will s. to me ELIO 295:11
thousand tongues to s. WESL 810:24
Who would not sing for S. MILT 512:27
world in ev'ry corner s. HERB [illegible]
singe it do s. yourself SHAK 673:6
S. my white head SHAK 678:21
singeing s. of the King of Spain's Beard DRAK 278:18
singer lived a s. in France SWIN 751:18
sans s., and—sans End FITZ 314:12
s. not the song BORR 144:16
s. of an empty day MORR 532:11
S. of sweet Colonus ARNO 27:30
singers well-known s. REED 623:18
singing angels all were s. BYRO 179:11
exercise of s. BYRD 173:6
have a s. face FLET 318:10
hear mermaids s. DONN 274:11
like a s. bird ROSS 634:1
listen to money s. LARK 453:2
Lorca was killed, s. READ 622:12
nest of s. birds JOHN 412:6
s. in the wilderness FITZ 314:9
s. in your genes BARR 56:2
s. masons building SHAK 670:28
s. of birds BIBL 85:10
s. of foolish and bawdy healths TURN 785:18
S. so rarely SCOT 651:26
s. still dost soar SHEL 714:4
s. to the praise AUGU 36:14
s. will never be done SASS 645:21
six little s.-boys BARH 54:4
suddenly burst out s. SASS 645:20
waves of thy sweet s. SHEL 713:13
single but a s. thought CLOS 222:23
come not s. spies SHAK 666:4

dies, in s. blessedness SHAK 689:3
he who continued s. GOLD 345:25
married to a s. life CRAS 244:11
Nothing in the world is s. SHEL 712:7
s. completed action BOIL 124:6
s. in the field WORD 832:2
s. life doth well BACO 43:18
s. man in possession AUST 38:14
s. man in possession OPEN 555:22
s. soul to perish TALM 753:10
S. women AUST 39:12
with a s. hair DRYD 282:36
singly Misfortunes never come s. PROV 606:39
sings fat lady s. SAYI 647:35
instead of bleeding, he s. GARD 329:15
s. each song twice over BROW 156:3
S. for his supper NURS 549:9
S. in the palm STEV 739:26
tell me what she s. WORD 832:3
why the caged bird s. DUNB 285:2
singular s. genius DIDE 267:8
s. in each particular SHAK 703:19
singularity S. is a clue DOYL 277:8
sinister strange and s. JAME 403:12
sink Little leaks s. the ship PROV 605:39
Not gross to s. SHAK 705:29
S. me the ship, Master Gunner TENN 766:11
sinking like a s. ship WOOL 827:6
that s. feeling ADVE 7:9
towards a s. ship CHUR 216:25
Sinn *Das kommt mir nicht aus dem S.* HEIN 368:5
sinned all have s. BIBL 104:32
More s. against than sinning SHAK 678:25
people s. against COMP 230:15
s. against heaven BIBL 100:4
s. exceedingly MISS 520:11
would have s. incessantly ROBI 629:14
sinner Be a s. LUTH 479:12
confessions of a justified s. HOGG 380:15
dead s. BIER 114:25
greater the s. PROV 601:34
Love the s. AUGU 36:11
Or I of her a s. CONG 233:17
poor s., lov'st thou me COWP 240:19
s. is at the heart PÉGU 572:5
s. that repenteth BIBL 100:1
to me a s. BIBL 100:16
who is that young s. HOUS 390:4
sinners early to catch any s. RUNY 637:14
favoured s. slain WESL 811:8
God and s. reconciled WESL 810:22
in the way of s. BOOK 131:15
miserable s. BOOK 127:2
publicans and s. BIBL 94:23
S.; of whom I am chief BIBL 109:13
s. to repentance BIBL 94:25
s.' ways prosper HOPK 384:23
sinneth s. before his Maker BIBL 92:10
sinning in good shape for more s. RUNY 637:14
More sinned against than s. SHAK 678:25
Sinns S. won in three years HEAL 366:7
sins Be all my s. remembered SHAK 664:5
chain of our s. BOOK 127:15
Compound for s. BUTL 172:1
covers a multitude of s. PROV 597:12
free from the bondage of s. BHAG 73:5
half the s. of mankind RUSS 639:11
Her s. are forgiven BIBL 99:6
His s. were scarlet BELL 64:4
manifold s. and wickedness BOOK 125:13
multitude of s. BIBL 111:6
not the s. of the fathers FREN 324:5
oldest s. SHAK 670:17
Old s. cast long shadows PROV 608:25
O remember not the s. BOOK 133:5
premeditated s. TALM 754:8
purged our s. BIBL 109:25
root of all s. JAME 402:11
set our s. from us BOOK 138:19
s. are attempts to fill WEIL 808:24
s. be as scarlet BIBL 86:12
s. of despair READ 622:14
s. of the fathers BOOK 129:5
s. or complaints TRAH 780:12
thinkin' on their s. BURN 167:11
ways of committing s. JAIN 402:6
who s. most SHAK 686:12
sint *S. ut sunt* CLEM 220:13
Sion captivity of S. BOOK 140:19
gracious unto S. BOOK 135:9
praised in S. BOOK 135:26
praise to Mount S. BUNY 160:16
remembered thee, O S. BOOK 141:7
Walk about S. BOOK 134:26
sir S.-come-spy-see BARH 54:1
sire S. of an immortal strain SHEL 710:14
Still from the s. SCOT 651:15
siren s. tears SHAK 705:18
sirens Blest pair of S. MILT 511:10
Sirmio S., bright eye CATU 197:5
Sisera fought against S. BIBL 77:27
sissy rose-red s. PLOM 579:5
sister done to our fair s. MORR 532:23
Had it been his s. EPIT 303:1
live a barren s. SHAK 689:2
my s. hath left me BIBL 99:15
my s., my spouse BIBL 85:16
no friend like a s. ROSS 634:4
Our sometime s. SHAK 661:14
s. and my sister's child COWP 240:12
s. throw up a lot WALK 799:5
s., thy first-begotten SWIN 751:11
trying to violate your s. STRA 744:9
sisterhood S. is powerful MORG 532:1
sisterly s. animosity SURT 747:4
sisters And so do his s. GILB 338:26
harmonious s. MILT 511:10
s. under their skins KIPL 439:8
twa s. sat in a bour BALL 50:8
weird s. SHAK 681:13
Sistine on the S. Chapel roof YEAT 837:19
Sisyphus imagine that S. is happy CAMU 184:10
like the torture of S. DE B 254:5
S., proletarian CAMU 184:9
sit Here I s., alone and sixty BENN 66:2
let us s. upon the ground SHAK 695:9
practically s. on it BISH 116:1
s. down on my botom FLEM 317:17
s. for a picture JOHN 416:12
S. thou on my right hand BOOK 139:16
So I did s. and eat HERB 373:1
Teach us to s. still ELIO 293:20
Though I s. down now DISR 268:6
sits I s. and thinks PUNC 617:24
Where MacGregor s. PROV 614:38
sitteth s. on the right hand of God BOOK 126:10
sitting A-s. on a gate CARR 191:13
cheap s. as standing PROV 604:7
find Thee s. careless KEAT 430:9
s. comfortably CATC 195:4
stay s. down CART 193:2
situation s. excellent FOCH 318:22
six on s. and sevene CHAU 207:14
Rode the s. hundred TENN 757:15
S. days shalt thou labour BIBL 76:11
s. honest serving-men KIPL 441:10
S. hundred threescore and six BIBL 112:22
s. little Singing-boys BARH 54:4
snowed for s. days THOM 772:13
sixpence bang—went s. PUNC 617:9
could have saved s. BECK 59:10
Finds s. in her shoe CORB 236:12
Nothing about s. BEVA 72:4
precious little for s. PUNC 617:11
Sing a song of s. NURS 550:18
s. given as change NESB 541:10
Whoso has s. CARL 188:11
sixpences two-and-forty s. JOHN 418:4
sixties found in the S. BURC 161:22
sixty Here I sit, alone and s. BENN 66:2
past S. it's the young AUDE 35:4
rate of s. minutes an hour LEWI 466:18
turned s. ALLE 12:18
When I'm s. four LENN 464:3
size one of ordinary s. LAND 450:8
sizzling advertiser's 's.' PRIE 591:16
skating S. across still water BLY 123:1
s. over thin ice EMER 299:21
skeletons s. copulating BEEC 61:3
Skiddaw S. saw the fire MACA 482:19
skies born under other s. LE C 461:14
danced the s. MAGE 489:8
man whose god is in the s. SHAW 708:22
paint the sable s. DRUM 279:14
soaring claim the s. FRER 324:11
thou climb'st the s. SIDN 718:10
virgin-daughter of the s. DRYD 282:29
watcher of the s. KEAT 429:21
skill Short Time and Little S. HARI 362:7
S. comes so slow DAVI 251:15
skilled S. or unskilled HORA 387:6
skimming S. our gable HEAN 366:8
skin ask the Gods for a thick s. TROL 782:27
beauty being only s.-deep KERR 434:9
Beauty only s. deep PROV 595:39
Can the Ethiopian change his s. BIBL 89:17
castle of my s. LAMM 449:12
cold s. sagging THOM 773:10
my s. is red SITT 720:18
nearer is my s. PROV 607:22
on his s. the swart flies DOUG 276:16
s. from the arm ELIO 295:16
s. is a different shade HAMM 359:5
s. of an innocent lamb SHAK 672:22
s. of my teeth BIBL 81:21
skull beneath the s. ELIO 296:16
thick s. a gift ADEN 6:2
throws her enamelled s. SHAK 689:26
skinny fear thy s. hand COLE 226:16
skins beauty of their s. TENN 765:24
sisters under their s. KIPL 439:8
such white s. CURZ 248:7
skip s. like a calf BOOK 133:13
skipped mountains s. like rams BOOK 139:21
skipper s. had taken his little daughter LONG 475:1
skirmish trivial s. fought near Marathon GRAV 349:13
skittles beer and s. CALV 182:4
beer and s. PROV 605:26
skivvies take a dozen s. MCGR 485:12
Skugg Here S. Lies snug EPIT 303:7
skull place of a s. BIBL 102:32
s., and the feet BIBL 80:27
s. beneath the skin ELIO 296:16
skuttle fish in mind of the s. ADDI 5:15
sky above, the vaulted s. CLAR 218:16
And the blue s. WORD 829:5
bowl we call The S. FITZ 314:18
clean the s. ELIO 295:16
clear blue s. over my head HAZL 365:23
climbin' clear up to the s. HAMM 358:21
diamond in the s. TAYL 756:13
ethereal s. ADDI 5:12
evening is spread out against the s. ELIO 295:3
If the s. falls PROV 603:23
Music shall untune the s. DRYD 282:23
pie in the s. HILL 377:1
prisoners call the s. WILD 818:31
Red s. at night PROV 610:6
rocking s. of '41 YEVT 838:10
shoulders held the s. suspended HOUS 390:9
s. and sea and land HOUS 390:13
s. changes SHAK 659:20
s. is darkening AUDE 35:11
s. is red BIBL 96:2
soars to math the s. PROC 593:10
to that equal s. POPE 585:11
triple-towered s. DAY- 253:11
upon the starry s. BLAK 118:23

sky (*cont.*):
wide and starry s. STEV 743:4
yon twelve-winded s. HOUS 391:4
Skye Over the sea to S. BOUL 145:2
Over the sea to S. STEV 742:23
skylark s. wounded in the wing BLAK 117:19
slacks girls in s. remember Dad BETJ 70:5
slag post-industrial s.-heap DRAB 278:14
slain Death, ere thou hast s. another EPIT 304:9
fifty thousand men s. WALP 802:5
fight and no be s. BURN 168:19
hurt but I am not s. BALL 51:12
law, chance, hath s. DONN 272:21
new-s. knight BALL 52:5
s. a thousand men BIBL 78:4
s. by a fair cruel maid SHAK 701:21
s. his thousands BIBL 78:34
s. in the way of God KORA 445:8
s., nor treated with violence JAIN 401:16
s. think he is slain EMER 299:5
Small s. body SWIN 751:11
slamming s. Doors BELL 63:11
S. their doors OSBO 560:4
slander angry at a s. JONS 419:15
one to s. you TWAI 786:11
slandered s. his neighbour BOOK 132:7
slandering lying, and s. BOOK 130:15
slang S. is a language SAND 644:4
slanged sneered and s. BELL 63:14
slant certain S. of light DICK 266:16
slap s.-up gal DICK 264:26
Slip, slop, s. OFFI 554:10
slapdash s. down in the mouth CONG 232:33
slashing s. article THAC 769:2
slate something off a s. KIPL 438:2
thoughts upon a s. HOOD 383:2
slaughter arrayed for mutual s. WORD 830:11
lamb to the s. BIBL 88:17
ox goeth to the s. BIBL 82:17
s. of plague, pestilence SHAW 708:7
s. will ensue CONG 232:30
through s. to a throne GRAY 350:12
Yet was thy s. small HARI 362:7
slave always the s. of the other LERM 464:21
Better be a s. BRON 149:17
female worker slave of that s. CONN 234:5
freedom to the s. LINC 468:12
freeing any s. LINC 468:11
half s. LINC 468:5
has been s. to thousands SHAK 692:20
makes the s. grow pleased ROCH 630:5
moment the s. resolves GAND 329:5
No s. is a slave to the same lengths MILL 509:5
passion's s. SHAK 664:18
Philosopher! a lingering s. WORD 830:17
s.-morality NIET 545:19
s. of the passions HUME 395:6
s.'s condition EURI 305:3
s. to its animosity WASH 804:8
S. to no sect POPE 586:4
womankind's in every state a s. EGER 289:14
wretched s. SHAK 671:20
young man's s. PROV 596:5
you were a Christian s. HENL 370:2
slavery Chains and s. BURN 168:7
chains Of heart-debasing s. GRAI 348:12
liberty and s. CAMD 182:12
life of white men is s. SITT 720:20
S. is SUMN 746:6
s. of the tea COBB 223:8
S. they can have BURK 163:5
sold off into s. TRUT 784:12
state of s. GILL 339:14
testimony against s. DOUG 277:1
wise and good in s. MACA 481:16
slaves Air for S. to breathe ANON 18:5
at the mill with s. MILT 518:13
Britons never will be s. THOM 774:20
creed of s. PITT 577:3
Englishmen never will be s. SHAW 708:5
freemen or s. WASH 804:4
have made our s. DARW 251:2
millions of royal s. GENE 333:5
no tsar, but the s. remain ZAMY 839:19
only freemen, are the only s. MASS 501:4
S. cannot breathe in England COWP 241:20
s., howe'er contented COWP 241:14
S. of the Lamp ARNO 25:23
s. that dig the golden ore CRAB 243:15
s. with weary footsteps SHEL 711:9
sons of former s. KING 436:14
wholly s. or wholly free DRYD 281:21
women are born s. ASTE 31:15
women born s. WOLL 826:2
slavish O imitators, you s. herd HORA 387:5
slay s. and slay and slay MACA 483:2
Though he s. me BIBL 81:17
slayer s. think he slays EMER 299:5
slew the s. MACA 483:1
slaying s. of a beautiful hypothesis HUXL 397:11
slays If any man thinks he s. UPAN 787:21
man thinks he s. BHAG 72:15
slayer think he s. EMER 299:5
sledge great s. drops in vain ROET 631:5
My s. and anvil EPIT 303:16
sleek S.-headed men SHAK 674:16
sleekit Wee, s., cow'rin' BURN 168:22
sleep all s. at last on the field MELV 504:9
as before, Love, —Only s. BROW 158:14
balmy s. YOUN 839:2
borders of s. THOM 773:2
Care-charmer S. DANI 249:1
Care-charming S. FLET 318:9
Come, s., O sleep SIDN 718:12
comfort in s. BROW 152:16
darkness brings not s. PUSH 618:3
Death and his brother S. SHEL 713:17
deep and dreamless s. BROO 151:9
deep s. of England ORWE 558:13
do I wake or s. KEAT 429:16
each day dies with s. HOPK 384:13
even as a s. BOOK 137:18
exposition of s. SHAK 690:13
fain I would s. BALL 50:11
first approach of s. BYRO 178:9
first s. ANON 19:16
from my mother's s. JARR 404:7
From s. and from damnation CHES 210:8
from the fields of s. WORD 829:17
God caused a deep s. BIBL 73:21
green ideas s. furiously CHOM 212:10
grey and full of s. YEAT 837:23
have I had in my s. SURT 746:17
have to go to s. LAST 456:6
him who invented s. CERV 200:5
hour's s. before midnight PROV 608:44
How s. the brave COLL 229:9
I lay me down to s. PRAY 592:5
In s. a king SHAK 705:5
in soot I s. BLAK 120:13
I shall s. SWIN 751:17
I s., but my heart waketh BIBL 85:18
I s. well MORT 534:2
lasting s. BEAU 58:16
like unwilling s. KEAT 429:22
little s. BIBL 82:14
Macbeth does murder s. SHAK 683:8
Macbeth shall s. no more SHAK 683:9
Me biful for to s. LANG 450:16
men who s. badly RUSS 639:10
miles to go before I s. FROS 326:12
Newton's s. BLAK 119:7
night to to with s. MILT 511:17
One short s. past DONN 272:23
put the world to s. MUIR 535:23
rounded with a s. SHAK 699:6
season of all natures, s. SHAK 684:16
Shake off this downy s. SHAK 683:19
She looks like s. SHAK 658:5
Six hours in s. COKE 224:11
Six hours s. for a man PROV 610:44
S. after toil SPEN 733:22
s. and a forgetting WORD 829:20
S.; and if life was bitter SWIN 750:11
s., and urine SHAK 683:15
s. between term and term SHAK 659:13
sleep, dear, s. BEDD 60:14
S. I can get nane BURN 166:15
s. is so deep CHAN 202:8
s. is sound indeed SHAK 670:15
S. is sweet BUNY 161:7
S.! it is a gentle thing COLE 226:20
S. no more SHAK 683:8
s. of a labouring man BIBL 84:12
S. on Blest pair MILT 516:26
s. one ever-during night CAMP 183:21
S. on (my Love!) KING 436:7
s. out this great gap of time SHAK 656:18
s. provides relief CHAM 201:5
S. shall neither night SHAK 681:12
s. so soundly SHAK 671:20
S. to wake BROW 155:4
s. under bridges FRAN 322:15
s. upon ale FARQ 307:5
slept an azure-lidded s. KEAT 427:13
Softer than s. TENN 765:10
some must s. SHAK 665:1
sons of Edward s. SHAK 696:23
such as s. o' nights SHAK 674:16
suffer nobody to s. ADDI 5:2
take their ease And s. SHAK 674:1
that sweet s. SHAK 692:29
Through s. and darkness KEBL 432:4
time enough to s. HOUS 390:16
time when first s. begins VIRG 794:1
To die: to s. SHAK 664:3
two gates of S. VIRG 795:3
uninvaded s. TENN 762:8
We shall not all s. BIBL 107:3
We shall not s. MCCR 484:13
We term s. a death BROW 154:4
when you can't get to s. LEBO 461:9
when you s. your remind me SASS 645:19
will not s. BOOK 140:12
sleeper never a quiet s. TENN 764:13
sleepers seven s. den DONN 274:2
s. in that quiet earth CLOS 222:14
sleepeth not dead, but s. BIBL 94:28
peradventure he s. BIBL 79:28
sleeping art thou s. there below NEWB 541:15
cursed him in s. BARH 54:5
fuss about s. together WAUG 806:17
Lay your s. head AUDE 34:8
Lest he find you s. BIBL 98:13
Let s. dogs lie PROV 605:18
like a S. Princess LAWR 458:20
s. and the dead SHAK 683:10
s., by a brother's hand SHAK 662:31
s. hound to wake CHAU 207:8
s. pill is white SEXT 655:7
s. under the desk GATE 331:2
s. with an elephant TRUD 783:23
waking s. MONT 528:3
sleepless S. as the river CRAN 243:25
s. soul that perished WORD 831:12
S. themselves POPE 580:9
s. with cold commemorative ROSS 635:6
sleeps Homer sometimes s. BYRO 177:1
it s. obedience PAIN 564:3
Now s. the crimson petal TENN 766:3
wakes or s. SHEL 710:22
while the world s. NEHR 540:4
sleepwalker assurance of a s. HITL 378:6
sleepy Contentment is a s. thing TRAH 780:17
I'm not s. DYLA 287:11
sleeve Ash on an old man's s. ELIO 294:14
heart upon my s. SHAK 691:24
lacy s. with vitriol WOOL 827:7
no further than your s. PROV 611:29
sleeves Americanism with its s. rolled MCCA 484:1

language that rolls up its s. SAND 644:4
Tie up my s. HUNT 396:7
sleight perceive a juggler's s. BUTL 172:10
slenderly s. known himself SHAK 678:2
slepen s. al the nyght with open ye CHAU 204:7
slept first fruits of them that s. BIBL 106:22
he thought I s. PATM 569:19
His saints s. ANON 22:3
I should have s. BIBL 81:4
s. with his fathers BIBL 79:24
Whilst Adam s. ANON 19:16
slew as he was ambitious, I s. him SHAK 675:25
dead which he s. at his death BIBL 78:8
s. his master BIBL 80:25
s. mighty kings BOOK 141:5
s. the slayer MACA 483:1
slice S. him where you like WODE 824:13
s. off a cut loaf PROV 610:45
slight Away, s. man SHAK 676:20
s. all that do FARQ 307:14
slime daubed it with s. BIBL 75:22
slimy hot s. channel CRAB 242:24
s. things did crawl COLE 226:12
thousand s. things COLE 226:18
slings s. and arrows SHAK 664:3
slip catch no s. by the way BUNY 160:17
enemies the s. for ever STER 738:17
many a s. 'twixt cup PROV 612:27
set one s. of them SHAK 703:15
s., slide, perish ELIO 294:5
S., slop, slap OFFI 554:10
slipper Old Mother S. Slopper NURS 549:19
s. and subtle knave SHAK 692:13
slippered lean and s. pantaloon SHAK 659:2
slippers in his golden s. BUNY 161:4
pair of s., sir BROW 154:9
slippery standing is s. BACO 43:10
slipping tail lights s. CRAN 243:24
slit S. your girl's KING 437:16
slits s. the thin-spun life MILT 513:3
slitty all be s.-eyed PHIL 575:5
sliver envious s. broke SHAK 666:14
Sloane S. turned secular saint BURC 161:23
sloe blacker than the s. CARB 185:18
slogans instead of principles, s. BENT 67:8
slogged s. up to Arras SASS 645:22
slop coffee and other s.-kettle COBB 223:8
Slip, s., slap OFFI 554:10
woman with a s.-pail HOPK 385:6
slopes butler's upper s. WODE 824:24
sloth my own amazing s. BISH 116:2
peaceful s., Not peace MILT 515:12
resty s. SHAK 660:27
Shake off dull s. KEN 432:18
time in studies is s. BACO 44:3
slouches S. towards Bethlehem YEAT 837:6
slough friendly bombs, fall on S. BETJ 71:4
s. was Despond BUNY 160:15
slovenliness Peace nothing but s. BREC 147:11
S. is no part of religion WESL 811:12
slow come he s. SCOT 651:6
comes ever s. DRAY 278:22
S. but sure PROV 611:1
s. of speech BIBL 75:31
Slow, s., fresh fount JONS 419:16
s. to anger BIBL 83:1
s. to speak BIBL 110:13
telling you to s. down ANON 15:22
telling you to s. down SAYI 647:9
Time is too s. VAN 789:15
slowly angel to pass, flying s. FIRB 313:6
Architecture acts the most s. DIMN 267:17
Make haste s. AUGU 36:16
Make haste s. PROV 606:11
mills of God grind s. LONG 474:8
mills of God grind s. PROV 606:37
Run s. OVID 561:2
Science moves, but s. TENN 763:4
twist s. in the wind EHRL 290:4
slugabed Get up, sweet S. HERR 374:6
sluggard foul s.'s comfort CARL 187:6
s. is wiser BIBL 83:26
thou s. BIBL 82:13
voice of the s. WATT 805:11
slughorn Dauntless the s. BROW 155:21
sluices Close the s. VIRG 796:3
sluicing browsing and s. WODE 824:23
slum seen one city s. AGNE 8:24
slumber little s. BIBL 82:14
neither s. nor sleep BOOK 140:12
s. did my spirit steal WORD 831:25
s. is more sweet than toil TENN 763:15
S.'s chain has bound me MOOR 530:20
to soothing s. seven JONE 419:5
slumbered you have but s. here SHAK 690:30
slumbers Golden s. kiss your eyes DEKK 256:6
has thou golden s. DEKK 256:5
slums gay intimacy of the s. WAUG 806:5
slurp s. into the barrels FISH 313:17
slush pure as the driven s. BANK 53:7
slut I am not a s. SHAK 659:14
sluts foul s. in dairies CORB 236:11
sly s. shade of a Rural Dean BROO 150:12
smacked I was s. out SELF 654:1
small between the s. and great COWP 242:14
big squadrons against the s. BUSS 171:7
both great and s. COLE 226:27
commonly thought s. WOOL 826:15
Correspondences like s.-clothes SMIT 725:25
day of s. nations CHAM 200:14
grind exceeding s. LONG 474:8
how s. the world is GROS 354:4
In s. proportions JONS 420:21
Microbe is so very s. BELL 63:21
pictures that got s. FILM 312:15
s. and full of holes BAIN 48:10
s., but perfectly formed COOP 236:6
s. college WEBS 807:9
S. is beautiful PROV 611:3
S. is beautiful SCHU 649:7
s. Latin JONS 420:24
s. packages PROV 595:48
s. states—Israel, Athens INGE 399:8
s.-talking world FRY 326:23
s. things with great VIRG 797:3
so s. a thing ARNO 26:7
speaks s. like a woman SHAK 688:31
Speech is the s. change MERE 505:17
still s. voice BIBL 80:3
that cannot reach the s. SPEN 734:8
they are very s. UPDI 788:15
Too s. to live in ANON 19:8
Town s.-talk flows CRAB 242:22
very s. the very great THAC 769:17
with s. men no great thing MILL 509:2
smaller s. fleas to bite 'em SWIF 749:19
s. than smallest atom UPAN 787:22
smallest s. amount of lying BUTL 172:20
s. room of my house REGE 624:5
smaragdine green ribbons s. TAYL 756:16
smart girls that are so s. CARE 186:21
love and all its s. BEDD 60:14
scorn which mocked the s. ARNO 27:22
s. for it BIBL 82:22
smash all s. and no grab NICO 545:4
English never s. in a face HALS 358:11
smashed s. it into because CUMM 247:11
s. up things and creatures FITZ 315:13
smatch some s. of honour SHAK 677:3
smattering s. of everything DICK 265:20
smell ancient and fish-like s. SHAK 698:31
I s. the blood SHAK 679:9
Money has no s. PROV 606:43
Money has no s. VESP 791:14
shares man's s. HOPK 384:5
s. and hideous hum GODL 342:2
s. a rat ROCH 630:3
s. of napalm in the morning FILM 311:15
s. too strong STER 738:22
sweet keen s. ROSS 635:8
Sweet s. of success FILM 313:4
smelleth s. the battle afar off BIBL 81:37
smells it s. to heaven SHAK 665:7
s. like roses JOHN 408:18
s. of mortality SHAK 679:22
smile Asians could still s. HEAD 365:24
call me that, s. WIST 823:17
Cambridge people rarely s. BROO 150:14
enchain him with a s. CARY 193:5
has a nice s. GROM 354:1
hear a s. CROS 246:11
Is it Colman's s. EWAR 305:10
kind of sickly s. HART 363:11
murder whiles I s. SHAK 672:29
my Julia's lips do s. HERR 374:5
one livid s. WALP 801:21
prison and a s. WOTT 833:4
riding on a s. and a shoeshine MILL 509:22
she did but s. WYAT 834:4
s., and be a villain SHAK 663:1
S. at us, pay us CHES 210:16
s. dwells a little longer CHAP 202:11
s. his face SHAK 702:7
s. his work to see BLAK 121:10
s. of accomplishment PLAT 577:15
s. of cosmic Cheshire cat HUXL 397:9
s. of fate DYER 286:16
s. on the face of the tiger ANON 18:10
s., smile, smile MILI 508:16
s. with the simple GARR 330:2
s. with the wise JOHN 414:1
tribute of a s. CLOS 222:8
vain tribute of a s. SCOT 650:17
why, we shall s. SHAK 676:30
your mother with a s. VIRG 796:5
smiled only the dead s. AKHM 9:9
Voltaire s. HUGO 394:1
smiler s. with the knyf CHAU 205:19
smiles charmed it with s. CARR 191:25
daggers in men's s. SHAK 683:22
greeted with s. BROO 151:3
making practised s. SHAK 702:33
robbed that s. SHAK 692:4
s., Wan as primroses KEAT 427:2
welcome ever s. SHAK 700:16
smilest Thou s. and art still ARNO 27:13
smiling hides a s. face COWP 240:18
S. at grief SHAK 701:24
s., damnèd villain SHAK 663:1
s., destructive man LEE 462:6
s. of Fortune COCK 223:12
s. surface of the sea PLUT 579:8
S. through her tears HOME 382:4
S. wonder of a day WRIG 833:14
smilingness Despair a s. assume BYRO 174:12
smirk serious and the s. DICK 263:23
smite ready to s. once MILT 513:7
s. all the firstborn BIBL 76:2
s. thee on thy right cheek BIBL 93:12
without hands to s. SWIN 750:9
smiteth to him that s. him BIBL 89:26
smith by naming him S. HOLM 381:7
Chuck it, S. CHES 209:28
s., a mighty man is he LONG 474:19
s. of his own fortune CLAU 219:18
Smithfield Canterbury or S. WALP 801:20
smithy village s. stands LONG 474:19
smitten bones are s. asunder BOOK 134:8
smock nearer is my s. PROV 607:21
smoke from the s. into the smother SHAK 658:10
Gossip is a sort of s. ELIO 292:3
have to s. more BAIN 48:10
her beloved s. LAMB 448:25
hills, they shall s. BOOK 139:7
idle s. of praise DANI 249:2
light after s. HORA 385:21
little s., in pallid moonshine KEAT 427:8
man who does not s. STEV 741:29
No s. without fire PROV 608:7

smoke (*cont.*):
rise then as s. to the sky CELA 199:9
s. and stir of this dim spot MILT 511:13
s. and wealth HORA 388:22
s.-filled room SIMP 720:16
S. gets in your eyes HARB 359:14
s. of their torment BIBL 112:25
Stygian s. JAME 402:12
watching people s. in old films WELD 809:8
smoked s. my first cigarette TOSC 780:1
s. salmon and tinned WILS 822:2
smokeless in the s. air WORD 827:19
smoking S. can seriously damage OFFI 554:11
s. flax BIBL 88:6
smoky burnt-out ends of s. days ELIO 295:19
smooth I am a s. man BIBL 74:37
knave with a s. tale WEBS 807:20
never did run s. PROV 597:39
never did run s. SHAK 689:4
s. the ice SHAK 677:15
s. things BIBL 87:15
smoother s. than oil BIBL 82:12
s. than oil BOOK 135:12
smote Israel s. him BIBL 76:27
s. divers nations BOOK 141:5
s. him thus SHAK 694:4
s. the king of Israel BIBL 80:11
s. them hip and thigh BIBL 78:3
smother from the smoke into the s. SHAK 658:10
smudge wears man's s. HOPK 384:5
smut S. detected in it ZOLA 841:1
snail creeping like s. SHAK 658:26
said a whiting to a s. CARR 190:4
seeing the s. DONN 274:23
s.'s on the thorn BROW 157:12
snake doth like a s. renew SHEL 711:12
like a wounded s. POPE 584:21
scotched the s. SHAK 684:4
s. came to my water-trough LAWR 458:13
s. hidden in the grass VIRG 796:1
s. throws her enamelled skin SHAK 689:26
snakes no s. to be met with JOHN 415:29
S. cut Fuga STEV 739:22
You spotted s. SHAK 689:27
snakeskin s.-titles BENÉ 64:23
snapper s.-up of unconsidered trifles SHAK 703:11
snare mockery, and a s. DENM 257:15
rabbit in a s. STEP 738:4
s. of the fowler BOOK 140:17
s. of the hunter BOOK 137:21
world's great s. SHAK 657:9
snares rain s. BOOK 132:3
s. of death BOOK 140:1
snaring s. the poor world CRAN 243:23
Snark S. *was* a Boojum CARR 191:26
snatch Shrewd was that s. BROW 155:12
s. Bookie Bob RUNY 637:13
s. me away FROS 325:15
snatched s. from Jove MANI 493:16
s. the lightning TURG 785:9
snatching s. his victuals from the table CHUR 215:5
sneaky snouty, s. mind NICO 545:2
sneer devil in his s. BYRO 175:14
refute a s. PALE 564:12
teach the rest to s. POPE 583:7
They s. at me FITZ 314:19
with solemn s. BYRO 174:21
sneering I was born s. GILB 337:22
sneeze like having a good s. LAWR 458:19
sneezed not to be s. at SCOT 652:15
sneezes beat him when he s. CARR 189:15
Coughs and s. OFFI 554:3
sneezing people s. ROBI 629:21
snicker hold my coat, and s. ELIO 295:8
vorpal blade went s.-snack CARR 190:13
snip S.! Snap! Snip HOFF 380:4
snipe so wet you could shoot s. off him POWE 590:10
snob admires mean things is a S. THAC 768:18
snobbery bereaved if s. died USTI 788:25
S. with Violence BENN 65:20
snobbish s. and vulgar VICT 792:6
snore s. upon the flint SHAK 660:27
snoring s., she disturbs COWP 241:18
snorted not one s. HUGH 393:6
Or s. we DONN 274:2
snotgreen s. sea JOYC 422:7
snout had as wise a s. on FERG 308:15
in a swine's s. BIBL 82:23
snouty s., sneaky mind NICO 545:2
snow amid the winter's s. CASW 194:3
architecture of the s. EMER 299:10
as white as s. BIBL 111:22
bloodless lay the untrodden s. CAMP 183:8
chaste as unsunned s. SHAK 660:22
congealed s. PARK 567:14
dark over the s. THOM 773:4
few acres of s. VOLT 797:7
first fall of s. PRIE 591:12
geese, like a s. cloud RANS 621:19
giveth s. like wool BOOK 141:26
Half-buried in the s. LONG 473:17
Ice and S. BOOK 126:6
I, this incessant s. DE L 256:18
last long streak of s. TENN 762:2
like the s. geese OKPI 553:11
listens in the s. STEV 740:4
little s.-white feet YEAT 835:16
naked in December s. SHAK 694:16
shivering in the s. SOUT 731:9
s. and vapours BOOK 141:27
s. before the summer sun TECU 757:3
s. came flying BRID 148:8
s. falling faintly JOYC 421:15
s. flutters down BLOK 122:4
s. in winter CAMP 182:14
s. of ferne yere CHAU 207:16
S. on snow ROSS 634:5
s. the leaves HOUS 391:2
used to be S. White WEST 812:8
we shall have s. NURS 549:16
white as s. BIBL 86:12
whiter than s. BOOK 135:6
wish a s. SHAK 680:19
wondrous strange s. SHAK 690:22
wrapped in wild s. BLOK 122:6
snowed s. for six days THOM 772:13
snowflake crown of s. pearls BLOK 122:6
snowflakes s. hurry PUSH 617:26
snows our Lady of the S. KIPL 439:19
s. have dispersed HORA 389:6
s. of yesteryear VILL 793:1
snowy S., Flowy, Blowy ELLI 298:14
snuff only took s. GOLD 345:5
You abuse s. COLE 227:18
snuffed s. out by an article BYRO 177:18
snug s. As a bug In a rug EPIT 303:7
s. little Island DIBD 260:15
so And s. do I HARD 361:22
if it was s., it might be CARR 190:18
soak expect a s. PROV 614:30
soaked s. to the skin COHE 224:4
soap made a s.-boiler costive WEBS 807:24
smiles and s. CARR 191:25
S. and education TWAI 786:6
S. operas sell MCEL 485:5
What! no s. FOOT 319:8
soapflakes sell Jack like s. KENN 433:20
soar creep as well as s. BURK 164:9
not to s. MACA 482:16
Two of the wise who s. WORD 832:11
soaring s. ever singest SHEL 714:4
soars s. to match the sky PROC 593:10
sob S., heavy world AUDE 33:16
sobbing a-sighing and a-s. NURS 552:1
sober at least not s. JOHN 411:24
Be s., be vigilant BIBL 111:7
compulsorily s. MAGE 489:10
godly, righteous, and s. life BOOK 125:17
go to bed s. FLET 318:2
s. me up FITZ 315:11
S., steadfast, and demure MILT 512:5
To-morrow we'll be s. SONG 729:2
to Philip s. ANON 15:11
Wordsworth drunk and Porson s. HOUS 391:11
sobs drawn-out s. VERL 791:8
social judge at once of the s. position TOCQ 778:16
no religion but s. WESL 811:10
self-love and s. POPE 585:27
s. and economic experiment HOOV 383:9
s. contract ROUS 636:4
S. Contract is nothing more WELL 810:12
s. progress, order, security JOHN 407:10
with a s. position ORWE 559:4
socialism Democracy and s. are means NEHR 540:7
religion of S. BEVA 71:14
S. can only arrive VIER 792:13
S. does not mean ORWE 559:5
s. would not lose its human face DUBČ 283:20
socialist build a s. society NYER 552:4
high-water mark of S. literature ORWE 559:6
signposts to s. Utopia CROS 246:5
typical S. ORWE 559:4
socialists s. throw it away CAST 193:15
We are all s. now HARC 360:1
society action of s. upon itself TOCQ 778:14
affluent s. GALB 328:5
bonds of civil s. LOCK 472:4
capital of polished s. BURK 163:30
consolidates s. JOHN 412:4
desperate oddfellow s. THOR 776:10
Great S. JOHN 408:15
happiness of s. ADAM 3:14
influence in s. LACL 447:3
in one s. WORD 830:24
live in s. ARIS 25:3
Man was formed for s. BLAC 117:1
moves about in s. CHOI 212:9
no letters; no s. HOBB 378:21
No s. can survive GING 339:18
no such thing as S. THAT 770:7
One great s. WORD 831:8
selects her own S. DICK 266:14
shape of s. ORWE 558:14
S. became my glittering bride WORD 828:12
s. distributes itself ARNO 28:7
s. founded on trash SAYE 646:4
S. is built on MAIL 491:3
S. is indeed a contract BURK 163:29
S. is now one polished horde BYRO 177:24
s. is wonderfully delightful WILD 818:28
S. needs to condemn MAJO 491:15
s. of privacy RAND 621:14
s. where it is safe to be STEV 740:12
s., with all its combinations BURK 163:18
s. would be a hell upon earth MILL 509:6
three for s. THOR 776:11
unfit a man for s. CHAM 201:6
sock hole in a s. EINS 291:7
Jonson's learnèd s. MILT 512:24
socket Burn to the s. WORD 828:9
sockets candles burn the s. HOUS 390:8
s. of fine gold BIBL 85:21
socks inability to put on your s. GONC 346:8
Socrates contradict S. SOCR 727:7
S., I shall not accuse you PLAT 578:3
Socratic S. manner is not a game BEER 61:16
sod under my head a s. BALL 50:14
withered in the s. BRON 149:12
soda Sermons and s.-water BYRO 176:13
wash their feet in s. water ELIO 296:7
sodden s. and unkind BELL 64:6
sodium discovered S. BENT 67:4
Sodom S. and Gomorrah BIBL 90:18
sodomy rum, s., prayers, and the lash CHUR 216:4

sods s. with our bayonets turning WOLF 825:4
sofa accomplished s. last COWP 241:17
Alternately on a S. AUST 37:22
sing the s. COWP 241:16
s. upholstered in panther skin PLOM 579:4
soft does not make us s. PERI 573:19
her s. and chilly nest KEAT 427:11
Ovid, the s. philosopher DRYD 281:33
s. and narrow BALL 50:6
s. answer BIBL 82:34
s. answer turneth PROV 611:4
s. as the dawn LOVE 477:4
s. as the dawn THUR 777:2
s. can wear away the hard TALM 754:22
s. phrase of peace SHAK 691:31
s. under-belly of Europe MISQ 522:8
s., unhappy sex BEHN 62:17
s. was the sun LANG 450:15
softer s. than butter BOOK 135:12
softest s. thing about him RUNY 637:13
softly Fair and s. PROV 600:7
go s. all my years BIBL 87:26
S. along the road DE L 256:19
s. and suddenly vanish CARR 191:24
S. come and softly go ORRE 557:14
Softly, s., catchee PROV 611:5
s. tread, said Christabel COLE 224:19
Tread s. YEAT 836:5
softness For s. she MILT 516:15
s. of my body will be guarded LOWE 477:9
whisper s. in chambers MILT 519:12
soggy s. little island UPDI 788:11
soil fertile s. BACO 45:14
Freedom's s. beneath our feet DRAK 278:21
grows in every s. BURK 163:5
powers of the s. RICA 626:2
regarding the s. as property THOR 776:1
s. Is bare now HOPK 384:5
s. which is soon exhausted REYN 625:10
tied to the s. HOME 382:11
sojourner discontented s. WORD 830:20
sojourners s., as were all our fathers BIBL 80:29
sol *s. et luna* AUGU 36:1
solace With s. and gladness SKEL 721:10
sold Never s. the truth TENN 765:6
ointment might have been s. BIBL 97:15
s. all that he had BIBL 95:23
s. his birthright BIBL 74:36
s. my reputation FITZ 315:1
what cannot be s.—liberty GRAT 349:6
soldier always tell an old s. SHAW 706:15
Ben Battle was a s. HOOD 382:18
British s. can stand up to SHAW 707:2
chocolate cream s. SHAW 706:16
death, who had the s. singled DOUG 276:16
Drinking is the soldier's s. DRYD 280:18
elder s., not a better SHAK 676:21
first duty of a s. PROV 600:28
For a s. I listed DIBD 260:11
German s. trying to violate STRA 744:9
go to your Gawd like a s. KIPL 440:22
greater freedom than the s. CAPA 185:14
great s.—of to-day BAGE 46:14
having been a s. JOHN 415:28
in the s. SHAK 686:11
iron-armed s. POLI 581:17
never expected a s. to think SHAW 706:27
s. a mere recreant SHAK 700:8
s. details his wounds PROP 593:15
s., Full of strange oaths SHAK 659:1
s. is better accommodated SHAK 670:5
s. is no more exempt STER 739:13
s. of the Great War EPIT 304:5
s. said isn't evidence PROV 614:10
S., Sailor NURS 551:13
S., scholar, horseman YEAT 836:8
s.'s life is terrible hard MILN 510:15
s.'s pole is fall'n SHAK 657:19
s.'s pride BROW 156:11
what the s. said DICK 265:14
soldiers believe the s. SALI 642:16
gives England her s. MERE 505:10
like s. may not quit TENN 763:17
Old s. never die FOLE 318:24
Old s. never die PROV 608:26
Onward, Christian s. BARI 54:13
our s. slighted QUAR 618:12
scarlet s. AUDE 34:17
S. are citizens of death's grey land SASS 645:18
s., mostly fools BIER 114:22
S. of Christ, arise WESL 811:4
S. of the ploughshare RUSK 639:3
S., this solitude DE L 256:18
s. under me BIBL 94:16
steel my s.' hearts SHAK 671:21
ten thousand s. SHAK 696:31
With twenty-six lead s. ANON 20:6
young Argentinian s. RUNC 637:7
soldiery Emperor's drunken s. YEAT 835:5
licentious s. BURK 165:4
sole *amor che muove il s.* DANT 250:5
nothing can be s. or whole YEAT 835:13
s. of her foot BIBL 74:17
solecism without a s. BROW 153:17
soleil *J'ai vu le s. bas* RIMB 628:8
s. d'Italie BANV 53:10
solemn Sapping a s. creed BYRO 174:21
upon our s. feast-day BOOK 137:9
soles *S. effugere atque abire sentit* MART 498:1
soliciting still-s. eye SHAK 677:26
solicitor only go to his s. DISR 270:18
solid s. for fluidity CHUR 215:3
solidity appearance of s. to pure wind ORWE 559:11
s. was knocked out LEAC 459:14
solitary Be not s. CLOS 222:5
ennui of a s. existence BONA 125:1
How doth the city sit s. BIBL 89:22
how s. they be ASCH 30:3
s., be not idle JOHN 416:11
s. confinement inside our own skins WILL 820:18
s. Highland lass! WORD 832:2
Their s. way CLOS 222:22
Their s. way MILT 518:3
till I am s. JOHN 412:17
waste And s. places SHEL 711:18
solitude bliss of s. WORD 828:27
delighted in s. BACO 42:34
each protects the s. RILK 628:4
feel his s. more keenly VALÉ 789:2
harmless s. MOLL 525:22
In s. What happiness MILT 517:9
Musing in s. WORD 828:5
one for s. THOR 776:11
seclusion and s. MONT 527:14
self-sufficing power of S. WORD 831:1
s. of the sea HARD 361:9
s. Through which we go DE L 256:18
solitudinem *S. faciunt pacem* TACI 752:9
Solomon all S.'s wisdom BIBL 79:17
anointed S. BIBL 79:15
felicities of S. BACO 42:4
greater than S. BIBL 95:16
S. Grundy NURS 550:19
S., I have vanquished JUST 424:2
S. in all his glory BIBL 93:25
S. loved many strange women BIBL 79:20
S. wrote the Proverbs NAYL 539:24
soluble art of the s. MEDA 503:6
solution can't see the s. CHES 211:12
conditions for its s. MARX 499:14
either part of the s. CLEA 220:7
final s. HEYD 376:2
heterosexual love no s. DURA 285:19
kind of s. CAVA 198:8
part of the s. SAYI 647:22
total s. GOER 342:12
solutions s. are not ASIM 30:17
solutus *S. omni faenore* HORA 387:11
solventur *S. risu tabulae* HORA 389:22
some fool s. of the people LINC 469:5
S. mishtake, shurely CATC 196:20
somebody brisk little s. BROW 155:6
life of s. else DAVI 252:3
When every one is s. GILB 337:10
someday S. I'll find you COWA 238:18
someone it was s. else ROGE 631:16
necessary to s. EMER 299:12
S. wants a letter ADVE 8:10
something get s. for nothing PROV 615:46
is that s. itself BECK 59:18
say *s.* about me COHA 224:2
s. completely different CATC 195:2
s. for Posterity ADDI 5:17
S. is better than PROV 611:8
S. must be done MISQ 522:9
s. of the night WIDD 816:14
S. should be done EDWA 289:6
s. to say WHAT 813:7
Time for a little s. MILN 511:4
was there s. CATC 195:18
sometime see me s. MISQ 522:15
woman is a s. thing HEYW 376:5
sometimes s. always RICH 627:11
somewhat more than s. RUNY 637:12
s. against thee BIBL 111:24
somewhere get s. else CARR 190:15
S. over the rainbow HARB 359:18
Somme S. is like the Holocaust BARK 54:15
son bear a s. BIBL 86:26
bear our s. KYD 446:10
be called thy s. BIBL 100:4
brought forth her firstborn s. BIBL 98:20
coming of the S. of Man BIBL 97:5
Epicurus owene s. CHAU 204:22
Fitzdotterel's eldest s. BROU 151:11
Forgive your s. JOYC 422:18
good idea—s. CATC 195:17
hateth his s. BIBL 82:30
his only begotten S. BIBL 101:18
if his s. ask bread BIBL 94:5
leichter of a fair s. ELIZ 296:23
Like father, like s. PROV 605:30
little s. into his bosom FLET 318:16
my s. was dead BIBL 100:6
O Absalom, my s., my son BIBL 79:11
s. loves his sons TALM 754:16
s. of Adam PRIO 592:12
s. of his old age BIBL 75:8
S. of man BIBL 94:19
S. of Morn in weary Night's decline BLAK 118:19
S. of Saint Louis FIRM 313:8
s. shall hear SCOT 651:15
s. till he gets him a wife PROV 607:17
s. was killed KIPL 438:14
Take now thy s. BIBL 74:31
This is my beloved S. BIBL 92:31
This is my s. TENN 767:11
unto us a s. is given BIBL 87:1
unto us by his S. BIBL 109:25
what's a s. KYD 446:9
wise s. BIBL 82:20
With a king's s. SURR 746:11
Woman, behold thy s. BIBL 102:35
younger s. gathered all together BIBL 100:2
your s.'s tender years JUVE 425:5
song after all an earthly s. TENN 761:15
all this for a s. CECI 199:7
ane end of ane old s. OGIL 553:3
Assist our s. GURN 355:5
auld Scotish s. BURN 166:21
becomes a sightless s. TENN 762:3
before his presence with a s. BOOK 138:13
beyond a s. or a billet ETHE 301:13
burthen of his s. BICK 114:15
carcase of an old s. THOM 773:16
frame my s. CHES 209:1
glorious s. of old SEAR 652:24
hate a s. that has sold BERL 68:13
in you my s. begins SIDN 718:15
let satire be my s. BYRO 177:33

song (*cont.*):
low lone s. CARP 189:4
made my s. a coat YEAT 835:10
my s. comes native KEAT 430:2
My s. is love unknown CROS 246:15
my s. would come OVID 561:23
old and antique s. SHAK 701:17
old s. of Percy and Douglas SIDN 718:26
On wings of s. HEIN 368:4
play a s. for me DYLA 287:11
region of my s. WORD 828:6
Sans wine, sans s. FITZ 314:12
sing the Lord's s. BOOK 141:8
sold a goodly manor for a s. SHAK 656:4
sold my reputation for a s. FITZ 315:1
s. charms the sense MILT 515:18
s. is ended BERL 68:10
S. made in lieu SPEN 733:10
s. of praise be sung POTT 588:16
s. of songs BIBL 85:6
s. of the birds for mirth GURN 355:2
S. of the Shirt HOOD 382:28
s. that echoes cheerly TENN 762:14
s. that found a path KEAT 429:14
s. that never ends GOET 342:19
s. the Syrens sang BROW 153:4
s. was wordless SASS 645:21
spur me into s. YEAT 837:13
start a s. VIRG 796:7
suck melancholy out of a s. SHAK 658:21
sung as it were a new s. BIBL 112:23
sung a s. of death BLAK 120:10
swallow-flights of s. TENN 761:7
thinks two notes a s. DAVI 252:5
Thy speech, thy s. JAME 402:22
till I end my s. SPEN 734:19
Time is our tedious s. MILT 514:1
trouble with a folk s. LAMB 449:9
unto the Lord a new s. BOOK 133:19
unto the Lord a new s. BOOK 138:9
was the s. of love ROSS 634:23
what they teach in s. SHEL 711:21
wine and s. LUTH 480:6
with the breeze of s. TENN 761:19
songs all their s. are sad CHES 210:2
For ever piping s. KEAT 428:23
I have s. of my own VIRG 796:11
lean and flashy s. MILT 513:6
Sing no sad s. ROSS 634:13
sing the old s. CLAR 219:1
Sing thou the s. of love GURN 355:6
S. consecrate to truth SHEL 714:14
s. never heard HORA 388:11
s. of Apollo SHAK 681:5
s. of expectation BARI 54:14
s. of gladness, praise SIKH 719:8
s. of peaceful Zion DIX 271:12
s. of pleasant glee BLAK 120:12
s. of Spring KEAT 430:10
s. were Ave Marys CORB 236:13
sweetest s. are those SHEL 714:8
these s. intendeth SIDN 718:15
with a few good s. FAIT 306:5
with s. beguile FLEC 317:3
sonitu *putrem s. quatit ungula* VIRG 795:7
sonnet Scorn not the S. WORD 831:18
s. is a moment's monument ROSS 634:21
S.'s scanty plot WORD 829:12
sonneteer starved hackney s. POPE 584:25
sonneter I shall turn s. SHAK 680:20
sonnets s. turned to holy psalms PEEL 572:2
written s. all his life BYRO 176:20
sons Bears all its s. away WATT 805:19
Clergymen's s. always PROV 597:24
cruel s. of Cain LE G 462:12
God's s. are things MADD 489:1
s. and daughters of Life GIBR 336:11
s. and daughters shall prophesy BIBL 90:14
s. Of Belial, flown with insolence MILT 514:27
s. of God BIBL 74:15
s. of God shouted BIBL 81:32
S. of the dark and bloody ground O'HA 553:6
s. of the morning HEBE 367:5
That our s. may grow up BOOK 141:18
soon short notice, s. past PROV 605:50
S., too soon SHEL 714:12
to Eve: Be s. THOM 774:6
sooner make an end the s. BACO 42:27
s. begun PROV 611:9
s. every party breaks up AUST 37:17
soot in s. I sleep BLAK 120:13
sophist neither saint nor s.-led ARNO 26:6
sophistry incline wits to s. BACO 44:29
s. and illusion HUME 394:7
s., cleaves close COWP 241:5
s. I can control ASTE 31:11
soporific lettuce is 's.' POTT 588:19
sops s. in wine SPEN 734:21
Sorbonne one day at the S. STEV 739:25
sorcerers s., and whoremongers BIBL 113:15
Sordello but the one 'S.' POUN 589:10
sore bear with a s. head MARR 497:15
we are s. let BOOK 128:1
sores dogs licked his s. BIBL 100:10
sorriness s. underlying the grandest things HARD 361:5
sorrow and the s. thereof MALO 492:11
any sorrow like unto my s. BIBL 89:23
ate his bread in s. GOET 343:11
bee of s. BABE 40:19
beguile thy s. SHAK 700:1
doubt and s. BARI 54:14
forgather wi' S. BURN 166:21
From my books surcease of s. POE 579:16
from s. to joy HAGG 356:2
Give s. words SHAK 685:7
glut thy s. KEAT 429:4
help you to s. PROV 602:38
How small and selfish is s. ELIZ 298:3
increaseth s. BIBL 84:5
In s. thou shalt bring forth BIBL 74:5
in trouble, s. BOOK 129:14
labour and s. BOOK 137:19
Labour without s. RUSK 638:23
Love's s. lasts all through life FLOR 318:20
more in s. than in anger SHAK 662:5
not be in s. too BLAK 120:20
not sure of s. SWIN 730:21
One for s. PROV 608:37
s. and sighing BIBL 87:24
S. and silence LONG 473:15
s. comes with years BROW 154:15
S. in all lands SUTT 747:8
S. is knowledge BYRO 178:13
S. is tranquillity remembered PARK 567:9
S. proud to be exalted ANON 17:3
s.'s crown of sorrow TENN 762:24
s. unforeseen PHIL 575:11
S., wilt thou live with me TENN 761:16
sphere of our s. SHEL 714:2
such sweet s. SHAK 697:19
thou climbing s. SHAK 678:15
water this s. SHAK 656:13
whipping S. driveth GREV 353:3
with s. to the grave BIBL 75:17
Write s. on the bosom SHAK 695:8
sorrowful heart is s. BIBL 82:31
He went away s. BIBL 96:14
way to the s. city DANT 249:7
sorrowing borrowing, goes a s. PROV 602:14
sorrows age, Disease, or s. CLOU 221:23
carried our s. BIBL 88:16
costly in our s. STER 738:12
Half the s. of women ELIO 292:7
man of s. BIBL 88:16
soothes his s. NEWT 543:15
s. are at an end GAY 331:13
s. of the mothers FREN 324:5
When s. come SHAK 666:4
sorry Better be safe than s. PROV 596:8
having to say you're s. SEGA 653:10
heartily s. BOOK 129:16
I'm s., now, I wrote it BURG 162:3
S. CAN'T COME TELE 758:11
S. for itself LAWR 458:11
that I shall be s. for SHAK 676:22
you'll be s. one day DUFF 284:9
sortem *nemo, quam sibi s.* HORA 389:12
sortir *l'en faire s.* LOUI 476:4
sorts all s. and conditions BOOK 127:16
takes all s. PROV 604:37
Sosostris Madame S. ELIO 295:29
sot *s. savant* MOLI 525:5
soteriological In s. terms FENT 308:9
soufflé cannot reheat a s. MCCA 484:6
sought Being, of all, least s. for CRAN 243:26
Love s. is good SHAK 702:3
many a thing I s. SHAK 704:16
never s. in vain BURN 166:23
s. it with thimbles CARR 191:25
soul adventures of his s. FRAN 322:17
assault and hurt the s. BOOK 128:4
believes in s. JAIN 401:11
bitterness of his s. BIBL 91:21
bitterness of my s. BIBL 87:26
brother's s. BARB 53:16
Call to the s. VAUG 790:14
call upon my s. SHAK 701:7
Calm s. of all things ARNO 26:15
captain of my s. HENL 369:21
casket of my s. KEAT 430:7
city of the s. BYRO 174:27
composed in the s. ARNO 28:23
confident concerning his s. SOCR 727:5
dark night of the s. FITZ 315:14
dark night of the s. MISQ 521:11
delivered my s. BOOK 140:2
depth of your s. ROUS 636:6
eager s., biting for anger FULL 327:11
engineers of the s. GORK 347:3
equal to the s.'s desires WORD 828:13
essence of a human s. CARL 188:18
every subject's s. SHAK 671:17
eyes are window of s. PROV 600:3
FIAT in my s. BEDD 60:16
fine point of his s. KEAT 430:23
fortitude the S. contains DICK 266:8
freed my s. BERN 69:3
from the s. itself COLE 225:4
from the S.'s eternity ROSS 634:21
give his own s. BOLT 124:21
God rest his s. SMIT 724:23
good for the s. PROV 597:34
half conceal the S. within TENN 760:23
Half my own s. HORA 387:14
Heart and s. do sing SIDN 718:21
Heaven take my s. SHAK 677:18
hurl my s. from heaven SHAK 693:31
hurt of my s. BOOK 135:25
I built my s. TENN 765:8
if I have a s. ANON 18:4
if your s. were BIBL 81:20
into my very s. SHAK 665:16
iron entered into his s. BOOK 139:8
leave my s. in hell BOOK 132:10
lie in the s. JOWE 421:12
life unto the bitter in s. BIBL 81:6
lift my s. to heaven SHAK 673:7
like an infant's s. TRAH 780:8
like s., my soul SHAK 661:3
longeth my s. after thee BOOK 134:5
lose his own s. BIBL 98:8
love of S. in the husband UPAN 787:11
lover of my s. WESL 810:25
Marlbro's mighty s. ADDI 4:6
mind and s., according TENN 760:21
My s., bear thou thy part GURN 355:6
My s. can reach BROW 154:21
My s. fleeth BOOK 141:2
My s. in agony COLE 226:17
my s. is white BLAK 120:18
My s., like to a ship WEBS 808:18
My s., there is a country VAUG 790:6
my unconquerable s. HENL 369:20
No coward s. is mine BRON 149:21
no s. to be damned THUR 777:4

not engineers of the s. KENN 433:18
One s. inhabiting two bodies ARIS 25:10
opium that numbs the s. FLAU 316:9
owe my s. to the company store TRAV 781:2
Perdition catch my s. SHAK 692:19
perfection of your s. SOCR 726:23
Poor intricated s. DONN 275:12
Pray for the repose of His s. ROLF 632:5
pray the Lord my s. to take PRAY 592:5
progress of a deathless s. DONN 273:10
prophetic s. SHAK 705:11
purest s. CARE 186:8
Refined himself to s. DRYD 281:4
retreat in his own s. AURE 36:21
save his s. BIBL 89:30
saves her s. BROW 155:9
selling one's s. MACK 486:7
sighed his s. SHAK 688:19
sinews of the s. FULL 327:9
s. above buttons COLM 229:17
S. and body part CRAS 244:14
s., a spirit FAUL 307:27
S. clap its hands and sing YEAT 837:2
s. doth magnify the Lord BIBL 98:16
s. has to itself decreed KEAT 430:3
s. he doth restore SCOT 652:20
s. in bliss SHAK 680:3
s. into the boughs MARV 498:17
s. is an enchanted boat SHEL 713:13
s. is Christ's abode KEBL 432:3
s. is form SPEN 734:15
s. is immortal PLAT 578:10
s. is immortal SOCR 727:4
s. is marching on SONG 729:13
s. is placed in the body DEFO 254:13
s. is under their blessed vault AKHM 9:8
S., leaving the body UPAN 787:14
s. of a man is born JOYC 422:2
s. of fire JOHN 411:15
s. of our dear brother BOOK 131:14
s. of pleasure BEHN 62:13
s. of Rabelais COLE 227:23
S. of the Age JONS 420:22
s. of the same stature MONT 527:6
s. of the whole Past CARL 187:29
s.'s dark cottage WALL 800:5
S. selects her own DICK 266:14
s. shall be required of thee BIBL 99:22
S. shall have her earthly freight WORD 830:4
s., sit thou QUAR 618:15
s. swooned slowly JOYC 421:15
S. that rises with us WORD 829:20
S., the body's guest RALE 620:12
S., the Inner Controller UPAN 787:13
S., thou hast much goods BIBL 99:21
s. to feel the flesh BRON 150:1
Stole many a man's s. JAGG 401:8
sweet and virtuous S. HERB 373:18
Tell out my s. BIBL 98:16
than that one s. NEWM 542:12
That S. is not this UPAN 787:15
this s. of mine LITT 470:3
this s.'s second inn DONN 273:12
through thy own s. BIBL 98:26
to an immortal s. VICT 792:3
try the s.'s strength BROW 156:10
tumult, of the s. WORD 828:28
two to bear my s. away PRAY 592:4
vale of s.-making KEAT 431:14
wake the s. by tender strokes POPE 586:27
war against the s. BIBL 110:29
What s. was his WORD 828:8
windows of the s. BLAK 118:14
with all thy s. BIBL 96:24
with a Russian s. LERM 464:24
with s. so dead SCOT 650:19
women have no s. ASTE 31:11
soulless when work is s. CAMU 184:17
souls Bishop of your s. BIBL 111:1
bodies but not their s. GIBR 336:11
common men have s. TAWN 755:17
damp s. of housemaids ELIO 295:12
engineers of human s. STAL 736:2
letters mingle s. DONN 274:22
Most people sell their s. SMIT 724:14
movements of s. VIRG 797:2
neglecting our s. WULF 833:18
open windows into men's s. ELIZ 297:9
Our s. exult BLAK 119:5
our waking s. DONN 274:3
play with s. BROW 156:16
price of s. JONS 420:3
pure lovers' s. descend DONN 273:26
s. did never kiss KEAT 427:1
s. do couch on flowers SHAK 657:14
s. mounting up to God ROSS 634:19
S. of poets dead KEAT 428:20
s. of the brave CLOU 221:15
s. of the righteous BIBL 91:8
s. out of men's bodies SHAK 691:6
s. to each other draw POPE 582:21
s. who dwell in night BLAK 118:7
sucks two s. DONN 273:27
they have no s. COKE 224:12
times that try men's s. PAIN 563:16
Two s. CLOS 222:23
Two s. dwell GOET 342:17
two virtuous s. BYRO 177:10
sound alive with the s. of music HAMM 359:1
all is not s. JONS 419:19
all things that give s. BAKE 48:14
commanded to be s. GREV 353:4
deep s. strikes BYRO 174:13
feeling, then, not s. STEV 740:1
fell in love to the s. BENN 66:12
form of s. words BIBL 109:21
from the tombs a doleful s. WATT 805:15
in a s. body JUVE 425:2
other half is not very s. SMOL 726:11
s. and fury SHAK 685:22
s. and rumour MORR 532:10
s. is gone out into all lands BOOK 132:15
s. me from my lowest note SHAK 665:2
s. mind BIBL 109:20
s. must seem an echo POPE 584:22
s. of abundance BIBL 79:29
s. of a great Amen PROC 593:13
s. of shallow foppery SHAK 687:21
s. of surprise BALL 52:15
s. of the trumpet BIBL 81:36
s. the back SAUS 646:3
s. were parted thence JONS 420:16
trumpet give an uncertain s. BIBL 106:17
what is that s. AUDE 34:17
soundbite s. all an interviewer BENN 65:11
soundest old lovers are s. WEBS 808:6
s. thing in England DOYL 277:21
sounding s. through the town BALL 50:10
Went s. on WORD 828:11
sounds better than it s. NYE 552:2
concord of sweet s. SHAK 688:25
let the s. of music SHAK 688:21
S. and sweet airs SHAK 699:5
s. will take care CARR 190:1
sweetest s. I'll ever hear RODG 631:4
soup blossom s. BASH 56:19
cake of portable s. BOSW 144:18
I won't have any s. today HOFF 379:17
licked the s. BROW 157:10
s. is chaos WARN 803:17
S. of the evening CARR 190:7
take s. at luncheon CURZ 248:8
soupe *Je vis de bonne s.* MOLI 525:3
sour How s. sweet music is SHAK 696:4
s. grapes BIBL 89:29
s. grapes and ashes ASHF 30:15
s., sober beverage BYRO 176:19
source God—the mighty s. SMAR 722:9
rise above its s. PROV 611:28
s. of little visible delight BRON 150:3
sourest sweetest things turn s. SHAK 705:7
south fickle is the S. TENN 765:22
full of the warm S. KEAT 429:8
go s. in the winter ELIO 295:27
hills of the S. Country BELL 64:6
I want to go s. LAWR 458:22
Lawn is full of s. DICK 266:21
nor yet from the s. BOOK 136:22
rivers in the s. BOOK 140:20
S. is avenged BOOT 142:16
s.-wind rushing warm TENN 763:3
wrest from the S. LEE 462:9
Yes, but not in the S. POTT 589:3
southern bore me in the s. wild BLAK 120:18
S. trees bear strange HOLI 380:20
souvenirs *s. sont cors de chasse* APOL 22:20
sovereign change for a s. NESB 541:10
civilities with my S. JOHN 413:24
has sixpence is s. CARL 188:11
Here lies our s. lord EPIT 302:14
he will have no s. COKE 224:13
S. has BAGE 47:5
s. Nation PAGE 562:18
s. oppresses his people JOHN 414:15
s. or state BACO 43:8
subject and a s. CHAR 203:4
to be a S. ELIZ 296:25
sovereignest s. that any man may have SKEL 721:9
sovereigns name ourselves its s. BYRO 178:14
what s. are doing NAPO 538:15
sovereignties addition of s. MONN 526:5
sovereignty s. is an artificial soul HOBB 378:12
s. of nature SHAK 660:12
sovereynetee Wommen desiren to have s. CHAU 206:22
soviet Communism is S. power LENI 463:10
S. Union has indeed FULB 327:2
soviets All power to the S. POLI 581:1
sow As you s., so you reap PROV 595:25
hath the s. by the right ear HENR 370:10
old s. that eats her farrow JOYC 422:3
shall not s. BIBL 84:29
silk purse out of s.'s ear PROV 615:27
S. dry and set wet PROV 611:11
s. in tears BOOK 140:20
s. may whistle PROV 611:12
S. returns to her Mire KIPL 438:20
s. the wind PROV 612:36
s. thy seed BIBL 84:30
they s. not BIBL 93:23
went forth to s. BIBL 95:20
sower s. went forth BIBL 95:20
soweth whatsoever a man s. BIBL 107:22
sown poets that are s. WORD 828:7
s. the wind BIBL 90:10
where thou hast not s. BIBL 97:9
Ye have s. much BIBL 90:24
space art of how to waste s. JOHN 408:22
Brahman is s. UPAN 787:17
cantos of unvanquished s. CRAN 243:19
filling the s. WEST 812:17
head outward into s. EDDI 288:1
Here is my s. SHAK 656:8
king of infinite s. SHAK 663:17
more s. where nobody is STEI 737:7
silent too as s. BYRO 177:31
S. is blue HEIS 368:12
S. isn't remote HOYL 392:7
s. of life between KEAT 426:15
time and s. LAMB 449:1
untrespassed sanctity of s. MAGE 489:9
spaces empty s. Between stars FROS 325:20
s. between the houses FENT 308:8
s. in your togetherness GIBR 336:12
vacant interstellar s. ELIO 294:9
spaceship regarding S. Earth FULL 327:5
spade call a s. a spade BURT 170:4
fiddle, sir, and s. SCOT 651:20
have never seen a s. WILD 817:23
nominate a s. a spade JONS 419:23
spades leave s. alone SITW 721:4
Let s. be trumps POPE 587:8
Spain castels thanne in S. CHAU 206:29
King of S.'s daughter NURS 548:17

Spain (*cont.*):
Lady of S. REAV 623:9
leave S. JUAN 422:22
not into the hands of S. TENN 766:11
permanence and unity of S. JUAN 422:21
spain rain in S. LERN 465:6
spake God s. once BOOK 135:23
no words he s. GILB 337:2
s. wisely BIBL 91:29
span but a s. DAVI 251:17
Contract into a s. HERB 373:6
Eternity shut in a s. CRAS 244:8
Less than a s. BACO 45:10
Spaniards not the power of the S. SCHU 649:6
S. seem wiser BACO 44:1
thrash the S. too DRAK 278:20
spanieled hearts That s. me SHAK 657:10
Spanish S. Ga-la-lee SONG 730:2
S. ships of war TENN 766:8
To God I speak S. CHAR 203:16
spare Brother can you s. a dime HARB 359:15
do in his s. time GILL 339:14
S. all I have FARQ 307:13
S. at the spigot PROV 611:13
s. man AUBR 32:16
s. the beechen tree CAMP 183:5
S. the rod PROV 611:14
s. those who have submitted VIRG 795:1
S. us all word of the weapons WILB 817:3
S. well and have to spend PROV 611:15
s. your country's flag WHIT 816:4
Woodman, s. that tree MORR 532:9
spared better s. a better man SHAK 669:15
sufferings which thou art s. ORCH 557:9
spares man that s. these stones EPIT 302:10
spareth s. his rod BIBL 82:30
spark shows a hasty s. SHAK 676:26
s. from heaven ARNO 27:7
s.-gap is mightier HOGB 380:10
s. of inextinguishable thought SHEL 714:22
s. of that ancient flame VIRG 794:10
s. o' Nature's fire BURN 167:4
Vital s. POPE 582:15
waitest for the s. from heaven ARNO 27:9
sparkle s. out among the fern TENN 757:13
They s. still SHAK 680:28
sparkles s. near the brim BYRO 174:10
sparkling s. in the sun CHAN 202:7
sparks Ashes and s. SHEL 712:18
as the s. fly upward BIBL 81:9
hide the s. of nature SHAK 660:25
s. among the stubble BIBL 91:9
sparrow am even as it were a s. BOOK 138:14
ef 'taint s.-grass HARR 362:14
fall of a s. SHAK 667:3
I, said the S. NURS 552:1
lecherous as a s. CHAU 205:3
Lesbia with her s. MILL 509:15
My lady's s. is dead CATU 196:34
or a s. fall POPE 585:8
s. alight upon my shoulder THOR 776:14
s. hath found her an house BOOK 137:11
s. should fly swiftly BEDE 60:19
sparrows five s. sold BIBL 99:20
of more value than many s. BIBL 94:36
pass through for the s. GALB 328:9
two s. sold BIBL 94:36
Spartan remnant of our S. dead BYRO 176:28
Spartans Go, tell the S. EPIT 302:11
speak all I think or s. WESL 811:3
Books will s. plain BACO 42:17
dare not s. its name DOUG 276:11
didn't s. up NIEM 545:8
difficult to s. BURK 165:7
fears to s. of Ninety-Eight INGR 399:18
grief that does not s. SHAK 685:7
I'll do't before I s. SHAK 677:25
I now s. for France DE G 255:19
I only s. right on SHAK 676:10
let him now s. BOOK 131:3
Let us not s. of them DANT 249:8
men shall s. well of you BIBL 99:3
neither s. they BOOK 139:23
one to s. THOR 776:18
province of knowledge to s. HOLM 381:6
slow to s. BIBL 110:13
s. afterwards PROV 612:38
s. and purpose not SHAK 677:25
speak, and to s. well JONS 421:4
s. as the common people do ASCH 30:9
s. as ye do BIBL 81:20
s. for Britain BOOT 142:20
S. for England AMER 13:6
s. for himself BIBL 102:3
s. ill of everybody except oneself PÉTA 574:9
s. ill of the dead PROV 607:37
s. in our tongues BIBL 103:16
S., Lord BIBL 78:15
S. low, if you speak love SHAK 691:3
s. no evil PROV 610:26
s. of eternity BROW 153:17
S. roughly CARR 189:15
S. softly ROOS 633:5
s. their minds BAGE 47:8
S. the speech SHAK 664:13
S. to Him thou TENN 759:10
s. to the wise PIND 576:9
s. unto them therof BOOK 140:11
S. unto us BIBL 87:15
s. when he is spoken to STEV 742:16
s. with their enemies BOOK 140:22
S. ye comfortably BIBL 87:27
stop and s. to you BROW 156:23
we shall s. of the somwhat CHAU 207:6
when I think, I must s. SHAK 659:10
whereof one cannot s. WITT 824:6
You were better s. first SHAK 659:19
speaker s. of fact PALI 564:20
speaketh s. things not to be spoken BIBL 91:29
speaking adepts in the s. trade CHUR 213:17
drowning their s. BROW 157:10
heard for their much s. BIBL 93:18
necessity for good s. TROL 782:25
People talking without s. SIMO 720:10
s. all their lives long MATH 501:10
s. picture, with this end SIDN 718:23
thy art of s. SHER 716:24
speaks He s. to Me VICT 792:7
hides one thing and s. another HOME 382:5
s. of a chair BISH 116:1
s. small like a woman SHAK 688:31
s. well of the bridge PROV 599:41
who s. does not know LAO 452:3
spear Bring me my s. BLAK 120:1
knappeth the s. in sunder BOOK 134:20
s., to equal which the tallest MILT 514:22
With a burning s. ANON 19:17
spearmen s. still made good SCOT 651:14
spears sheen of their s. BYRO 175:23
s. into pruninghooks BIBL 86:13
stars threw down their s. BLAK 121:10
special all s. cases CAMU 184:6
by s. grace BOOK 128:5
specials can't trust the 's.' COLL 228:13
species but a s. FIEL 310:1
characteristics of the human s. GODW 342:4
not the individual, but the s. JOHN 410:24
preys on its own s. JAME 404:4
specimen brick as a s. JOHN 410:12
spectacle great s. of life ELIO 292:26
no s. so ridiculous MACA 481:18
s. unto the world BIBL 105:32
spectacles pair of s. SHAK 700:19
s. of books DRYD 283:6
s. on nose SHAK 659:2
spectantia *Omnia te adversum s.* HORA 386:12
spectatress S. of the mischief ROWE 636:10
spectatum *S. veniunt* OVID 561:5
spectre pale, and s.-thin KEAT 429:10
s. of Communism MARX 500:5
spectres S. fly before it SMIL 723:2
speculate If you don't s. PROV 603:31
s. on the teachings SA'A 640:21
speculations s. and subtleties BROW 153:23
s. upon matter JOHN 410:6
speculative like a s. merchant BAGE 46:18
speech abridging the freedom of s. CONS 235:12
aspersion upon my parts of s. SHER 715:27
deal by s. BACO 43:21
forme of s. is chaunge CHAU 207:4
freedom of s. TWAI 786:8
freedom of the press's s. TWAI 786:16
function of s. to free BRAN 146:19
in one's s. LA R 453:20
little other use of their s. HALI 357:13
make a s. on conservation STEV 740:17
manner of his s. SHAK 656:22
meaning of lengthy s. SCHI 648:14
our concern was s. ELIO 294:16
perfect plainness of s. ARNO 29:7
quick of s. WINT 823:11
rule of s. HORA 385:15
slow of s. BIBL 75:31
Speak the s. SHAK 664:13
s. be alway with grace BIBL 109:6
s. bewrayeth thee BIBL 97:26
s. by Chamberlain BEVA 72:4
s. created thought SHEL 713:12
s. from Ernest Bevin FOOT 318:26
S. happens not to be STAË 735:19
s. is comely BIBL 85:14
s. is like a cracked kettle FLAU 316:7
S. is often barren ELIO 292:11
s. is shallow as Time CARL 187:12
S. is silver PROV 611:17
S. is the small change MERE 505:17
s. nor language BOOK 132:15
s. only to conceal VOLT 797:10
s. they have resolved ELIO 292:7
strange power of s. COLE 226:26
true use of s. GOLD 345:12
utterance, nor power of s. SHAK 676:10
verse is a measured s. BACO 41:15
wed itself with S. TENN 761:2
what manner of s. HOME 382:1
where s. is not HOBB 378:13
speeches all the easy s. CHES 210:8
s. were fine WALP 801:15
speechless from among the s. dead HILL 376:15
let it lie S. still EPIT 303:6
s. Christ SWIN 750:13
s. real BARZ 56:13
speechmaking practising s. JUVE 424:23
speed More haste, less s. PROV 607:6
our English S. CAVE 198:11
safety is in our s. EMER 299:21
S., bonnie boat BOUL 145:2
s. far faster than light BULL 160:1
s. glum heroes SASS 645:15
s. the going guest POPE 586:7
S. the parting guest POPE 586:7
Unsafe at any s. NADE 538:2
What good is s. KRAU 445:20
spell foreigners always s. better TWAI 786:13
lies beneath your s. HOPE 383:20
s. it with a "V" DICK 265:13
s. of great knowledge MAHĀ 490:3
S. TUESDAY MILN 510:13
utter inability to s. HAY 364:17
speller fancy of the s. DICK 265:13
wuss s. I know of WARD 803:5
spelling s. is Wobbly MILN 511:5
spem *s. nos vetat incohare* HORA 387:17
spend If you have money you s. it KENN 434:1
so wol we s. CHAU 206:8
Spare well and have to s. PROV 611:15
s. and God will send GASC 330:14
s. more time with my family FOWL 322:2
s. your way out CALL 181:9

whatever you have, s. less JOHN 416:27
whatsoever thou s. more BIBL 99:13
What you s., you have PROV 614:14
spending Getting and s. WORD 832:15
money-s. always 'vulgar' GASK 330:18
Riches are for s. BACO 42:29
S. again SHAK 705:1
s. other people's money RAND 621:18
Spens see Sir Patrick S. BALL 51:16
spent all passion s. MILT 518:26
s. all the money JOHN 416:23
What wee s., wee had EPIT 304:13
speranza LASCIATE OGNI S. DANT 249:7
sperare *salus victis nullam s.* VIRG 794:5
speraret *nec quid s. habebat* VIRG 795:16
speravi *In te Domine, s.* PRAY 592:8
spermatozoa million million s. HUXL 397:6
spes *Occidit, occidit S. omnis* HORA 389:5
spew bad ones s. it up CERV 200:6
s. thee out of my mouth BIBL 111:28
spewed s. up a good lump DRYD 283:14
sphere motion in one s. SHAK 669:11
shine all through the s. VAUG 790:15
s., the cone CÉZA 200:8
these walls thy s. DONN 274:16
they the s. DONN 273:25
yonder starry s. MILT 517:3
spheres Driv'n by the s. VAUG 790:17
music of forfended s. PATM 569:21
music of the s. BROW 153:30
Ring out, ye crystal s. MILT 513:23
spherical body is perfectly s. LEAR 460:15
spice s. of life COWP 241:23
Variety is the s. of life PROV 613:33
spices land of s. HERB 373:5
mountains of s. BIBL 86:9
No S. wanting HERR 374:22
s. thereof may flow out BIBL 85:17
spicy s. breezes Blow soft HEBE 367:7
s. nut-brown ale MILT 512:22
spider came a big s. NURS 549:7
kind of huge s.-web JAME 403:9
let the s. run alive PROV 603:40
like a s. catching them all DOST 276:4
said a s. to a fly HOWI 392:5
seen the s. SHAK 703:3
s. is sole denizen HARD 361:7
s.'s touch, how exquisitely fine POPE 585:15
s. trying to hide NERU 541:4
spiders like s.' webs ANAC 14:6
seen s. fly EDWA 289:9
s. in my bath ANON 18:2
s. marching through the air LOWE 478:2
Weaving s. come not SHAK 689:28
spies come not single s. SHAK 666:4
Instructed s. WOTT 833:2
voluntary s. AUST 38:6
Ye are s. BIBL 75:16
spigot Spare at the s. PROV 611:13
spill let them not s. me MACN 488:14
S. your guts at Wimbledon CONN 234:7
spilt as water s. on the ground BIBL 79:8
spin Go s., you jade SCOT 652:11
great world s. for ever TENN 763:9
neither do they s. BIBL 93:25
Sit by the fire and s. NURS 547:17
Sob, as you s. AUDE 33:16
s.-doctors in spin clinics BENN 65:12
ye whores, go s. PEMB 572:9
spinach I say it's s. WHIT 814:1
spindle fold, s. or mutilate SAYI 647:12
s. or mutilate ANON 15:23
spinis *s. de pluribus una* HORA 387:10
spinnage world of gammon and s. DICK 261:26
spinners long-legged s. SHAK 689:28
spinning at evening s. RONS 632:8
spinning-wheel wee bit s. BLAM 121:14
spinsters s. and the knitters SHAK 701:20
spires dreaming s. ARNO 27:25
grey s. of Oxford LETT 465:18
three steeple-house s. FOX 322:9
What s., what farms HOUS 391:5
Ye distant s. GRAY 350:15
spirit angry s.'s yell BEAT 58:5
Atman, the S. in man UPAN 787:10
Be thou a s. of health SHAK 662:18
blithe S. SHEL 714:3
body did contain a s. SHAK 669:13
bound in the s. BIBL 104:13
break a man's s. SHAW 706:23
'Brutus' will start a s. SHAK 674:14
but the same S. BIBL 106:15
by his S. BIBL 107:27
cabined ample S. ARNO 26:23
Come, Holy S. LANG 451:1
commend my s. BIBL 100:29
commend my s. BOOK 133:16
did my s. steal WORD 831:25
every pure and wise s. EMER 299:24
filled with the S. BIBL 108:9
forge his s. spirit GUEV 354:15
fruit of the S. BIBL 107:21
good s. or a bad AUBR 33:1
great s. gone SHAK 656:12
haughty s. BIBL 82:38
humble, tranquil s. DEKK 256:4
in the s. BIBL 111:19
Love is a s. SHAK 705:29
meek and quiet s. BIBL 111:2
nature of the s. LUCR 479:5
never approached my s. METT 506:12
no more s. in her BIBL 79:17
no s. can walk abroad SHAK 661:11
pardlike S. SHEL 710:21
poor in s. BIBL 93:3
pour out my s. BIBL 90:14
present in s. BIBL 105:33
quick s. SHAK 674:5
renew a right s. BOOK 135:7
retain the s. BIBL 84:18
ruleth his s. BIBL 83:1
sacramental of the s. ROBI 629:20
shaping s. of imagination COLE 225:6
s. and the letter PALI 565:10
s. burning but unbent BYRO 175:16
s. capable of compassion FAUL 307:27
s. giveth life BIBL 107:5
s. hath rejoiced BIBL 98:16
s. indeed is willing BIBL 97:23
s. in the woods WORD 829:13
s. is the true self CICE 217:17
s. leaves his mortal body BHAG 72:16
S. of adoption BIBL 105:7
s. of all knowledge WORD 832:21
S. of Delight SHEL 713:24
s. of Elijah BIBL 80:13
s. of fear BIBL 109:20
S. of God BIBL 73:10
s. of party WASH 804:7
S. of the Age HAZL 365:19
s. of the chainless mind BYRO 179:3
s. of the Lord BIBL 87:3
S. of the Lord God BIBL 89:5
s. of the place VIRG 795:4
s. passed before my face BIBL 81:7
s. shall return unto God BIBL 85:2
s. that always denies GOET 342:18
s. that quickeneth BIBL 101:31
S. wanders on to BHAG 72:14
s. within nourishes VIRG 794:22
S. with Spirit can meet TENN 759:10
stablish me with thy free S. BOOK 135:7
strength of his s. LUCR 478:21
strength of s. SHAK 674:24
take not thy holy S. BOOK 135:7
things of the S. BIBL 105:6
This grey s. yearning TENN 767:10
Thy s. walks abroad SHAK 677:1
troubled s. BOOK 135:9
unclean s. BIBL 95:17
vanity and vexation of s. BIBL 84:4
Wild S., which art moving SHEL 712:12
worship him in s. BIBL 101:20
wounded s. BIBL 83:5
spirits choice and master s. SHAK 675:20
drooping s. can raise COWL 239:20
insult to the s. RED 623:10
maketh his angels s. BOOK 139:1
ruffle up your s. SHAK 676:11
s. from the vasty deep SHAK 668:19
s. of just men BIBL 110:4
S. of well-shot woodcock BETJ 70:7
S. overwrought WORD 831:4
thousands of s. dancing CUDW 247:1
two primal S. ZORO 841:9
spiritu *Et cum s. tuo* MISS 520:7
spiritual approach the s. in art MOND 526:3
certain s. grandeur ELIO 292:16
found the s. cause EDDY 288:4
inward and s. grace BOOK 130:17
Millions of s. creatures MILT 516:23
Music is s. MORR 533:5
not being a s. people MANC 493:5
nothing in s. things DONN 275:9
other s. liquor BYRO 179:14
outrun our s. power KING 436:17
s. duties HOBY 379:9
spiritualist you are a s. SZAS 752:2
spiritualists convention of s. STOP 743:13
spiritus *dum s. hos regit artus* VIRG 794:12
Sancte S. LANG 451:1
S. intus alit VIRG 794:22
spiro *Quod s. et placeo* HORA 389:3
spit My friend may s. HERB 373:16
no gun, but I can s. AUDE 34:19
s. upon my Jewish gabardine SHAK 687:15
spite In S. of Everything ZIEG 840:3
s. your face PROV 598:34
spiteful like to write when I feel s. LAWR 458:19
spitting S. from lips BROW 158:15
Spitzbübin *S. war sie* HEIN 368:8
splash Old pond, leap-s. BASH 56:17
only get a s. PROV 614:30
splashed fear of being s. WALP 802:1
spleen wrong bias, s. GREE 351:12
splendeat *late qui s.* HORA 385:12
splendid by the vision s. WORD 830:1
having a s. Court BAGE 47:2
s. and a happy land GOLD 344:16
S. isolation NEWS 544:13
splendide *S. mendax* HORA 388:20
splendour Not in lone s. KEAT 426:14
Pavilioned in s. GRAN 348:15
s. borrows all her rays POPE 583:26
s. falls on castle walls TENN 765:16
s. in the grass WORD 830:9
Stung by the s. BROW 155:23
splendoured many-s. thing THOM 774:12
splintered s. the door AUDE 34:18
splinters teeth like s. CAUS 198:3
split care what a s. infinitive FOWL 321:21
Images s. the truth LEVE 466:4
make all s. SHAK 689:10
s. Ireland BRUG 158:20
when I s. an infinitive CHAN 201:18
spoil been the s. of me SHAK 668:28
divided the s. BOOK 136:7
divide the s. BIBL 86:28
s. it by trying to explain SHER 716:7
s. the broth PROV 613:13
s. the child PROV 611:14
s. the ship PROV 598:28
spoiled Better one house s. PROV 596:10
s. the Egyptians BIBL 76:4
s. the women's chats BROW 157:10
Story the s. child of art JAME 402:24
spoilers hands of s. BIBL 77:24
spoils belong the s. MARC 495:7
divideth his s. BIBL 99:17
spoke blood S. in her cheeks DONN 273:9
How well he s. STEV 740:16
s., and the world was made JOHN 411:5

spoken Lord hath s. BIBL 87:28
never have s. yet CHES 210:16
Rome has s. AUGU 36:12
s. of thee BOOK 137:16
s. unto us BIBL 109:25
word fitly s. BIBL 83:18
spongy Patrol the halls on s. shoes WILB 817:7
spontaneous S. joy and natural content YEAT 836:2
spoon ate with a runcible s. LEAR 460:19
have a long s. PROV 602:33
ran away with the s. NURS 548:12
trifle with the s. POPE 584:8
spoons counted our s. EMER 299:15
let us count our s. JOHN 413:8
world locks up its s. SHAW 708:10
sport amateur s. DOYL 277:21
Detested s. COWP 241:28
ended his s. with Tess CLOS 222:15
ended his s. with Tess HARD 361:2
kill us for their s. SHAK 679:15
owe to s. CAMU 184:16
Serious s. ORWE 559:8
s. for our neighbours AUST 38:25
s. of kings D'AV 251:10
s. of kings SOME 727:17
s. of kings SURT 746:16
S. that wrinkled Care derides MILT 512:15
s. with Amaryllis MILT 513:2
s. would be as tedious SHAK 667:22
sported s. on the green SOUT 730:11
sports mountainous s. girl BETJ 71:2
play Her cruel s. SPEN 734:12
s. of love JONS 420:12
sportsman fit to be called a s. SURT 746:17
spot fellows we put on the s. COLL 229:6
no s. in thee BIBL 85:15
Out, damned s. SHAK 685:9
sumpshous s. ASHF 30:13
Tip me the black s. STEV 741:19
with a s. I damn him SHAK 676:16
spotless All things were s. TRAH 780:12
spots change his s. PROV 605:16
leopard change his s. BIBL 89:17
s. rather a credit COMP 230:18
spotted wants to have been s. VIRG 795:20
You s. snakes SHAK 689:27
spouse in s. occasion to complain CENT 199:12
my sister, my s. BIBL 85:16
President's s. BUSH 171:1
shuts the s. Christ home HOPK 384:21
spout cataracts and hurricanoes s. SHAK 678:21
sprang s. to the stirrup BROW 156:8
spray pinkly bursts the s. BETJ 70:16
rime was on the s. HARD 362:1
singis on the s. DOUG 276:12
twirling in thy hand a withered s. ARNO 27:7
spread except it be s. BACO 43:33
Masters, s. yourselves SHAK 689:9
S. ALARM AND DESPONDENCY PENI 572:12
s. my dreams under your feet YEAT 836:5
sprightly first s. running DRYD 281:3
spring Alas, that s. should vanish FITZ 315:2
apparelled like the s. SHAK 694:6
azure sister of the s. SHEL 712:12
beckoning to his S. Queen JARR 404:9
bloom in the s. GILB 338:14
Blossom by blossom the s. SWIN 750:6
By chilly fingered s. KEAT 427:2
can S. be far behind SHEL 712:19
commonly called the s. COWP 242:19
easing the S. REED 623:14
Falsehood has a perennial s. BURK 162:19
first hour of s. BOWE 145:11
hounds of s. SWIN 750:5
In the s. a young man's fancy TENN 762:22
in the s. to follow SWIN 751:9
less quick to s. ARNO 27:29
lived light in the s. ARNO 26:7
new come s. SHAK 696:1
no second s. PHIL 575:8
No s., nor summer beauty DONN 272:10
not s. until you can plant PROV 604:24
only the right to s. FOND 318:25
Pierian s. DRAY 279:7
rifle all the breathing s. COLL 229:7
songs of S. KEAT 430:10
s. breaks through again COWA 238:13
S. Flow down the woods SACK 641:6
s. has kept in its folds ARAG 23:11
s. is wound up tight ANOU 22:8
s. now comes unheralded CARS 192:7
s. of business BAGE 46:7
s. of endless lies COWP 241:7
s. of light COLE 224:17
s. of the year BIBL 92:18
S. restores balmy warmth CATU 197:7
s. shut up, a fountain sealed BIBL 85:16
s. summer autumn winter CUMM 247:3
suddenly was changed to S. SHEL 713:19
Sweet lovers love the s. SHAK 659:24
Sweet s., full of sweet days HERB 373:17
this s. of love SHAK 702:26
with ever-returning s. WHIT 815:23
year's at the s. BROW 157:12
springe woodcock to mine own s. SHAK 667:6
springes s. to catch woodcocks SHAK 662:15
springlike limbs that fester are not s. ABSE 1:6
springs Fifty s. HOUS 390:15
many s., Many bright mornings VAUG 790:16
s. into the rivers BOOK 139:2
Wastes without s. CLAR 218:13
Where s. not fail HOPK 384:9
springtime Ballinderry in the s. FERG 308:17
Merry S.'s Harbinger FLET 318:8
sprite fleeting, wav'ring s. HADR 355:11
sprites s. and goblins SHAK 703:2
sprouting S. despondently at area gates ELIO 295:12
spun s. twelve ells ANON 22:5
spur Fame is the s. MILT 513:2
I have no s. SHAK 682:12
s. me into song YEAT 837:13
s. of all great minds CHAP 202:23
spurious s. brat, Tom Jones RICH 627:8
spurs this day to wynne his s. EDWA 289:4
win his s. EDWA 289:4
spy letters for a s. KIPL 440:8
s. out the land BIBL 76:25
s. who came in from the cold LE C 461:12
squad awkward s. fire over me LAST 455:11
squadrons big s. against the small BUSS 171:7
wingèd s. of the sky MILM 510:10
square I have not kept the s. SHAK 656:28
S. deal afterwards ROOS 633:6
s. on the hypotenuse GILB 339:4
s. person has squeezed himself SMIT 725:6
s. root of half a number LONG 475:3
squares on the lines or s. MILN 510:19
squash This s., this gentleman SHAK 703:1
squat s. like a toad MILT 516:27
s. pen rests HEAN 366:11
urban, s., and packed with guile BROO 150:14
squats s. on the hearthstone QUIL 619:2
squawking seven stars go s. AUDE 33:18
squeak s. and gibber SHAK 661:9
until the pips s. GEDD 332:25
squeaking shrieking and s. BROW 157:10
s. Cleopatra SHAK 657:24
s. wheel gets PROV 611:18
squeeze s. a right-hand foot CARR 191:15
squeezing in the s. of a lemon GOLD 345:20
squinch-owl jay-bird say ter der s. HARR 362:16
squint banish s. suspicion MILT 511:22
squire s. and his relations DICK 261:7
squires last sad s. ride CHES 210:17
squirrels Policemen, like red s. ORTO 558:2
stab do I s. at thee MELV 504:10
No iron can s. the heart BABE 40:16
saw him s. READ 622:13
stabant *S. orantes* VIRG 794:21
stabat *S. Mater dolorosa* JACO 401:3
stability party of order or s. MILL 508:20
s. or enlargement JOHN 409:5
stable born in a s. PROV 606:20
nothing s. in the world KEAT 430:25
stable-door shut the s. PROV 604:36
stables S. are the centre SHAW 707:12
stablish s. me with thy free Spirit BOOK 135:7
staff cockle hat and s. SHAK 665:34
I'll break my s. SHAK 699:10
s. of faith to walk upon RALE 620:15
thy rod and thy s. BOOK 133:1
trustest upon the s. BIBL 80:28
stag lean as a rutting S. BYRO 179:21
runnable s. DAVI 251:12
S. at Bay LEVI 466:8
s. in limpid currents PHIL 575:10
stage All the world's a s. SHAK 658:25
Don't put your daughter on the s. COWA 238:16
drown the s. with tears SHAK 663:28
get off the s. MAJO 491:19
leaves the s. SHAK 695:27
middle age of a s. BACO 44:21
On the s. GOLD 345:3
played upon a s. SHAK 702:12
s. where every man must play SHAK 687:2
this great s. of fools SHAK 680:1
traffick of our s. SHAK 697:3
wonder of our s. JONS 420:22
stagecoach party like an old s. WILS 822:3
s. from London to Oxford HAZL 365:20
stages four s. of man LINK 469:15
stagger s. like a drunken man BOOK 139:15
stagnant fen Of s. waters WORD 829:8
stagnation keeps life from s. BURN 165:18
stain bright s. on the vision GRAV 349:15
darkening like a s. AUDE 35:11
s. in thine honour BIBL [illegible]
s. the stiff dishonoured shroud ELIO 295:25
s. upon the silence BECK 60:7
world's slow s. SHEL 711:1
stained kick a hole in a s. glass window CHAN 201:12
s. with their own works BOOK 139:11
stains Innumerable of s. KEAT 427:9
s. the white radiance SHEL 711:4
washed the gory s. BYRO 178:10
stair by a winding s. BACO 43:12
falling from s. to stair BAYL 58:1
stairs another man's s. DANT 250:4
stake deep s. they have BURK 163:7
has his s.—his life CAPA 185:14
I am tied to the s. SHAK 679:11
s. driven through his heart O'BR 552:7
s. in the country WIND 823:4
what it is we have at s. PITT 577:5
stakeholder S. Economy BLAI 117:10
stale How weary, s., flat SHAK 661:23
Tho' s., not ripe POPE 580:15
staled S. are my thoughts DYER 286:12
Stalin guilt of S. GORB 346:16
S. himself rose TROT 783:18
Stalingrad cultural S. BALL 52:13
stalk Half asleep as they s. HARD 361:16
Men do not weigh the s. DANI 248:18
stalking like a s.-horse SHAK 659:28
s.-horse to error BOLI 124:13
s. in my chamber WYAT 834:5
stall Baby in an ox's s. BETJ 70:5
stalled heart's s. motor MAYA 502:18
s. ox BIBL 82:36
stallions bared teeth of s. CRAN 243:20

stamp but the guinea's s. BURN 167:6
physics or s. collecting RUTH 640:14
s. me back FITZ 314:21
stamps can lick the s. HIND 377:13
kill animals and stick in s. NICO 545:3
stand By uniting we s. DICK 266:23
can't s. the heat TRUM 784:3
firm spot on which to s. ARCH 23:19
Get up, s. up MARL 495:16
Here s. I LUTH 479:13
house divided cannot s. PROV 603:3
I will s. by GRIF 353:8
no time to s. and stare DAVI 252:8
s. and look at them WHIT 815:15
s. at the door, and knock BIBL 111:29
s. at the latter day BIBL 81:22
S. by thyself BIBL 89:8
S. by your man WYNE 834:15
s. in the holy place BIBL 97:2
s. in thy gates BOOK 140:14
s. on either hand MACA 483:6
s. on its own bottom PROV 599:38
s. out of my sun DIOG 268:1
s. secure ADDI 4:23
S. still MARL 496:6
s. up for bastards SHAK 678:4
s. up for Jesus DUFF 284:8
s. up for Jesus LAST 457:7
s. up to anything except SHAW 707:2
strengthen such as do s. BOOK 127:10
who only s. and wait MILT 518:30
who shall be able to s. BIBL 112:6
standard defending s. of living NIEM 545:7
float that s. sheet DRAK 278:21
raise the scarlet s. CONN 233:23
standards S. are always out of date BENN 65:19
standeth help s. in the Name BOOK 140:17
standing cheap sitting as s. PROV 604:7
mantle of the s. pool SHAK 679:6
ought to die s. LAST 455:12
s. by my man CLIN 220:18
St Andrews S. by the Northern LANG 450:9
stands s. about the woodland ride HOUS 390:14
S. Scotland SHAK 685:6
S. the Church clock BROO 150:15
sun now s. JOSE 421:8
stane heart o' s. BALL 51:19
star Being a s. has made it possible DAVI 252:12
bright northern s. LOVE 476:10
bright Occidental s. BIBL 73:7
bright particular s. SHAK 655:19
Bright s. KEAT 426:14
By a high s. our course MACN 488:17
catch a falling s. DONN 274:11
come back a s. FILM 312:13
constant as the northern s. SHAK 675:15
curb a runaway young s. BYRO 179:11
day s. arise BIBL 111:8
evening s. MILT 517:25
eve's one s. KEAT 427:22
great s. early drooped WHIT 815:23
guests s.-scattered FITZ 315:3
guiding s. CARS 192:5
guiding s. behold DIX 271:13
Hitch your wagon to a s. EMER 299:30
Knock at a s. HERR 374:4
light dissolved in s.-showers SHEL 713:29
like a falling s. MILT 515:5
loftiest s. SHEL 713:14
maidenliest s. SHAK 678:6
moth for the s. SHEL 714:2
O eastern s. SHAK 658:3
our life's s. WORD 829:20
reflex of a s. WORD 828:21
S. captains glow FLEC 317:1
S.-Chamber matter SHAK 688:30
s.-crossed lovers SHAK 697:2
s. differeth from another BIBL 106:26
S. for every State WINT 823:15
s. is called Wormwood BIBL 112:14
s.-led wizards MILT 513:18
S. of the east HEBE 367:5
s.-spangled banner KEY 434:16
s. to steer her by MASE 500:16
s. were confined VAUG 790:15
Sunset and evening s. TENN 757:18
sweet S. of the Sea FABE 305:19
There was a s. danced SHAK 691:5
twinkle, little s. TAYL 756:13
we have seen his s. BIBL 92:22
with one bright s. COLE 226:15
stardust We are s. MITC 523:17
stare indifference or frozen s. ELIO 292:21
never to s. at people BALF 49:17
no time to stand and s. DAVI 252:8
s. of the deer WILB 817:4
stony British s. TENN 764:4
upon the ground I se thee s. CHAU 206:12
starfighters see Black S. BLY 122:15
stark Molly S.'s a widow STAR 736:12
s. insensibility JOHN 412:5
starless s. and bible-black OPEN 556:24
starlight frosty s. ARNO 27:18
nae s. BALL 52:2
S. and dewdrop FOST 321:14
s. lit my lonesomeness HARD 362:1
starlit s. or a moonlit dome YEAT 835:6
starred No memory of having s. FROS 326:8
On a s. night MERE 505:20
starry beautiful evening, very s. WORD 827:10
entertain this s. stranger CRAS 244:7
her s. twain MILT 516:22
in her s. shade BYRO 178:15
s. dynamo GINS 339:20
s. paladin BROW 158:1
s. threshold of Jove's Court MILT 511:12
upon the s. sky BLAK 118:23
wide and s. sky STEV 743:4
stars all Danaë to the s. TENN 766:3
all the S. Hide MILT 516:7
As s., a fault of vision MAHĀ 490:6
certain s. shot madly SHAK 689:22
climb half-way to the s. CROS 246:10
crowned with the s. TRAH 780:9
crown of twelve s. BIBL 112:18
cut him out in little s. SHAK 697:29
day-blind s. BERR 69:14
didst the s. and sunbeams know ARNO 27:14
earnest s. KEAT 427:27
erratik s. CHAU 207:19
Far beyond the s. VAUG 790:6
heard it's in the s. PORT 588:11
heaventree of s. JOYC 422:17
imitate the s. celestial DAVI 251:21
in his right hand seven s. BIBL 111:22
journey-work of the s. WHIT 815:14
knowledge of the s. EDDI 288:2
like s. on the sea BYRO 175:23
Look at the s. HOPK 384:20
looking at the s. WILD 818:10
melt the s. FLAU 316:7
morning s. sang BIBL 81:32
new-bathed s. Emerge ARNO 27:19
not in our s. SHAK 674:13
of the months and s. SWIN 750:4
opposition of the s. MARV 498:11
power about The s. BUTL 172:14
puts the s. to flight FITZ 314:7
quench the s. YOUN 839:4
ready to mount to the s. DANT 250:2
same bright, patient s. KEAT 427:29
see the s. again DANT 249:18
Seven for the seven s. SONG 729:11
seven s. go squawking AUDE 33:18
shining of the s. TENN 760:9
silent s. go by BROO 151:9
s. above us SHAK 679:17
s. are old TAYL 756:15
s. begin to flicker PARI 566:16
s. came out TENN 766:10
s., garters, buttons MOOR 529:15
s. in her hair ROSS 634:16
s. in their courses BIBL 77:27
s. keep not their motion SHAK 669:11
s. move still MARL 496:7
s. of death AKHM 9:10
s. rush out COLE 226:14
S. scribble on our eyes CRAN 243:19
Stars, s. SHAK 703:25
s.' tennis-balls WEBS 808:5
s. threw down their spears BLAK 121:10
s. through the window pane KEAT 431:11
s. where no human race is FROS 325:20
s., which are the brain of heaven MERE 505:20
s. with deep amaze MILT 513:21
steeped in s. RIMB 628:7
strike the s. HORA 387:13
struggle to the s. MOTT 535:14
sun and other s. CLOS 222:2
sun and the other s. DANT 250:5
telleth the number of the s. BOOK 141:24
tell the s. as they rise VIRG 795:1
Tempt not the s. FORD 319:18
touch the s. SPEN 734:22
troops of s. COLE 225:18
useful s. PEPY 573:16
way to the s. VIRG 795:8
We have the s. FILM 311:3
with how splendid s. FLEC 317:6
with mites of s. MAYA 502:15
you chaste s. SHAK 693:22
Your chilly s. CORY 237:14
starshine s. at night STEV 742:20
starship voyages of the s. *Enterprise* RODD 631:1
start 'Brutus' will s. a spirit SHAK 674:14
end is where we s. from ELIO 294:18
s. from their spheres SHAK 662:25
s. together and finish BEEC 61:5
s. to the finish HORA 389:17
Stop it at the s. OVID 561:20
started arrive where we s. ELIO 294:17
s. like a guilty thing SHAK 661:10
s. so I'll finish CATC 196:7
s. to do something TALM 754:15
starter few thought he was a s. ATTL 32:3
Your s. for ten CATC 196:33
startle come down and s. AUDE 33:17
does not s. it KEAT 431:1
starts everything by s. DRYD 280:9
s. from where one stands LAO 452:5
starvation night s. ADVE 7:27
starve good men s. DRYD 281:8
Let not poor Nelly s. LAST 456:11
let our people s. NYER 552:3
s. a fever PROV 600:16
whom he helped to s. POPE 583:8
starved many are s. KING 436:20
s. poet LOCK 472:10
starves steed s. PROV 614:42
starving choice of working or s. JOHN 409:2
s. hysterical naked GINS 339:20
you have a s. population DISR 268:8
state all were for the s. MACA 483:7
Atlas of the s. COWP 241:9
bosom of a single s. DURH 286:6
change my s. SHAK 704:15
defrauding of the S. PENN 572:16
done the s. some service SHAK 694:3
first duty of a S. RUSK 638:25
Founding a firm s. MARV 498:12
glories of our blood and s. SHIR 717:8
Here's a s. of things GILB 338:8
I am the S. LOUI 475:16
in a free s. CAVO 198:15
In that s. I came VAUG 790:10
last s. of that man BIBL 95:18
mine was the middle s. DEFO 254:18
mock the air with idle s. GRAY 350:2
my glories and my s. SHAK 695:22
no harm come to the s. ANON 21:7

state (*cont.*):
no such thing as the S. AUDE 35:2
Only in the s. HEGE 367:11
O Ship of S. LONG 473:10
Our s. cannot be severed MILT 517:20
put the s. to rights ENNI 300:16
reinforcement of the S. CAMU 184:12
ruin of the S. BLAK 117:19
rule the s. DRYD 280:4
Scoffing his s. SHAK 695:10
separation of s. and science FEYE 309:5
sovereign or s. BACO 43:8
S. business is a cruel trade HALI 358:2
s. can exist CONF 231:22
S. for every Star WINT 823:15
s. has no place TRUD 783:21
S. in wonted manner keep JONS 419:17
S. is an instrument STAL 736:1
S. is a relation of men WEBE 807:5
S. is not 'abolished' ENGE 300:11
s. of life BOOK 130:16
s. to be endured JOHN 410:26
S. which dwarfs its men MILL 509:2
s. without the means BURK 163:14
s. with the prettiest name BISH 115:15
storms of s. SHAK 673:18
sun begins his s. MILT 512:17
to what a s. dost Thou bring TERE 768:11
usurped the powers of the s. GIBB 335:7
While the S. exists LENI 463:8
stately She is tall and s. TENN 764:3
S. as a galleon GREN 352:15
S. Homes of England COWA 238:19
s. homes of England HEMA 369:6
S., plump Buck Mulligan OPEN 556:18
with his s. stride MACA 483:8
statement black s. of pistons SPEN 732:17
s. that is quotable GERS 334:17
statements all previous s. inoperative ZIEG 840:4
states goodly s. and kingdoms KEAT 429:20
independent S. ADAM 3:8
indestructible S. CHAS 204:3
like to greater s. SUCK 745:11
many sovereign S. PAGE 567:18
rights of s. BROW 152:4
S., like men, have their growth LAND 450:7
s. unborn SHAK 675:18
Union of these S. WHIT 815:22
statesman chemist, fiddler, s. DRYD 280:9
constitutional s. BAGE 46:1
gift of any s. METT 506:7
he was a s. LLOY 471:7
requirement of a s. ACHE 1:13
set a s. right YEAT 836:21
s. is a politician TRUM 784:5
s. is a politician who POMP 580:7
s. must wait BISM 116:18
S., yet friend to Truth POPE 584:6
Too nice for a s. GOLD 345:1
statesmen faults of s. WALP 801:16
government of s. DISR 269:28
like great S. GAY 331:23
station antique s. BEER 61:13
By Grand Central S. BORR 144:2
her s. keeping JACO 401:3
private s. ADDI 4:15
stations know our proper s. DICK 261:7
statistic million deaths a s. STAL 736:5
statistical life is s. improbability DAWK 253:3
statistics experiment needs s. RUTH 640:15
lies, damned lies and s. DISR 271:8
uses s. as a drunken man LANG 450:12
We are just s. HORA 386:14
statuary form of s. ANON 16:9
statue like a marble s. SUGE 745:13
s. implicit in bronze ARIS 25:11
statues Ep's s. are junk ANON 16:20
stature cubit unto his s. BIBL 93:24
Malice is of a low s. HALI 357:18
of lofty s. EINH 290:7
status *from* S. MAIN 491:10
Human s. ought not to depend TEMP 757:6
status quo restored the s. SQUI 735:16
statutes keep my s. BIBL 76:22
s. of the Lord BOOK 132:16
staves comest to me with s. BIBL 78:33
stay here I s. MACM 487:13
If we can't s. here alive MONT 528:12
love is here to s. GERS 334:15
more care to s. SHAK 697:34
S. a little BACO 42:27
S. for me there KING 436:7
S. out all night CHUR 214:2
s. up all night BRYS 159:4
things to s. as they are LAMP 449:15
without thee here to s. MILT 518:1
staying s. messengers RILK 628:3
Tell the people I'm s. PEDR 571:12
stays never s. too long MACA 481:20
nothing s. HERA 371:7
s. together SAYI 647:14
stead in my soul's s. BIBL 81:20
steadfast s. as thou art KEAT 426:14
steady Full cup, s. hand PROV 601:2
One thought more s. FORD 320:5
S., boys, steady GARR 330:3
steak not the meat of the s. PRIE 591:16
steaks smell of s. in passageways ELIO 295:19
steal lest I s. DEFO 254:17
One man may s. a horse PROV 608:46
silently s. away LONG 473:12
sin to s. a pin PROV 604:30
s. a goose POLI 582:3
s. bread FRAN 322:15
s. from many, it's research MIZN 524:12
S. from the world POPE 586:25
s. more than a hundred men PUZO 618:6
s. my Basil-pot KEAT 428:4
s. my thunder DENN 258:3
s. the very teeth ARAB 23:10
thieves break through and s. BIBL 93:20
Thou shalt not s. BIBL 76:13
Thou shalt not s. CLOU 222:26
stealing For de little s. O'NE 554:18
hanged for s. horses HALI 357:22
his s. steps [illegible]
picking and s. BOOK 130:15
s. ducks ARAB 23:9
S. money is wrong AYER 40:5
steals s. my purse SHAK 692:20
s. something SHAK 692:4
stealth Do good by s. POPE 586:20
good action by s. LAMB 449:7
steam emply s. navigation LARD 452:9
Shovelling white s. AUDE 34:12
s.-engine in trousers SMIT 725:18
traces the s.-engine DISR 268:13
steamer s. breaking from the bay AUDE 34:5
s. from Harwich GILB 337:19
steamers little holiday s. PRIE 591:15
steaming wealth of s. phrases SCHU 649:12
steamy Throws up a s. column COWP 241:31
steed his s. was the best SCOT 651:7
milk-white s. BALL 51:20
set her on my pacing s. KEAT 428:11
s. starves PROV 614:42
s. That knows his rider BYRO 174:8
steeds mounting barbèd s. SHAK 696:8
steel All shod with s. WORD 828:20
clad in complete s. MILT 511:23
Give them the cold s. ARMI 25:12
hoops of s. SHAK 662:10
in complete s. SHAK 662:19
long divorce of s. SHAK 673:7
more than complete s. ANON 17:1
s. canisters hurtling about CASS 193:11
S. chambers HARD 361:9
S.-true and blade-straight STEV 742:22
with a line of s. RUSS 640:13
worthy of their s. SCOT 650:14
wounded surgeon plies the s. ELIO 294:10
steep s. and rugged pathway WILL 821:6
steeple lone religious s. CAMP 183:1
North Church s. REVE 624:18
three s.-house spires FOX 322:9
steeples dreary s. of Fermanagh CHUR 214:22
drenched our s. SHAK 678:21
s. far and near HOUS 390:19
steer s. their courses BUTL 172:3
Stein family S. ANON 16:20
stelle *muove il sole e l'altre s.* DANT 250:5
riveder le s. DANT 249:18
stem s. of Jesse BIBL 87:3
Stendhal great secret of S. GIDE 336:18
step first s. that is difficult DU D 284:6
first s. that is difficult PROV 604:26
One more s. along CART 192:17
one small s. for a man ARMS 25:19
One s. at a time PROV 609:3
one s. enough for me NEWM 542:19
To s. aside is human BURN 166:8
stepmother s. to memory, oblivion JOHN 407:14
stony-hearted s. DE Q 258:6
stepped in blood S. in SHAK 684:15
stepping rise on s.-stones TENN 760:22
s. westward WORD 832:4
s. where his comrade stood SCOT 651:14
steps sad s., O Moon SIDN 718:10
s. take hold on hell BIBL 82:12
uneasy s. Over the burning marl MILT 514:22
very long flight of s. GUIB 354:16
wandering s. and slow CLOS 222:22
wandering s. and slow MILT 518:3
sterbenden *einem s. Gotte* HEIN 368:9
sterile s. promontory SHAK 663:18
stern s. chase a long chase PROV 611:19
S. daughter of the voice of God WORD 830:12
sterner made of s. stuff SHAK 676:1
sternest s. knight MALO 492:15
steward backward s. POPE 583:21
commended the unjust s. BIBL 100:7
stewards S. of the mysteries BIBL 105:31
stewed S. in corruption SHAK 665:17
stick carry a big s. ROOS 633:5
fell like the s. PAIN 563:18
I shall s. SHAK 686:24
rattling of a s. inside ORWE 559:16
s. and a string SWIF 750:3
S. close to your desks GILB 338:29
s. more close than a brother KIPL 440:11
s. that he seizes TORR 779:18
s. to beat a dog PROV 604:16
tattered coat upon a s. YEAT 837:2
sticketh friend that s. closer BIBL 83:6
sticks handful of s. RICH 627:7
S. and stones PROV 611:20
S. nix hick pix NEWS 544:14
stiff woman can be proud and s. YEAT 835:13
stiffnecked thou art a s. people BIBL 76:18
stiffness too much s. in refusing BOOK 125:11
stigma Any s. to beat a dogma GUED 354:9
stile lame dog over a s. CHIL 212:4
still Because they liked me 's.' DICK 266:17
beside the s. waters BOOK 132:26
best be s. ARNO 26:14
be s. BOOK 131:19
Be s. and cool FOX 322:11
Be s. then, and know BOOK 134:20
do them s. DONN 273:6
heart is lying s. WORD 828:1
I'm s. here HOPE 383:18
monk is s. PALI 566:1
ship was as s. SOUT 730:15
S. crazy after all SIMO 720:11
S. falls the rain SITW 721:2
S. glides the Stream WORD 831:15
s. it is not we CHES 210:17
s. point of the turning world ELIO 294:4
s., sad music WORD 829:5
s. small voice BIBL 80:3

s. they gazed GOLD 344:15
s. tongue makes wise head PROV 611:21
s.-vexed Bermoothes SHAK 698:22
S. waters run deep PROV 611:22
s. we see thee lie BROO 151:9
'What gars ye rin sae s.?' ANON 18:15
stillness air a solemn s. holds GRAY 350:6
horrid s. first invades DRYD 281:1
modest s. and humility SHAK 671:5
present s. WARR 803:23
s. in the midst of chaos BELL 64:14
s. of the central sea TENN 762:4
stilly Oft, in the s. night MOOR 530:20
Stilton no end of S. Cheese LEAR 460:10
stilts nonsense upon s. BENT 66:17
stimulate s. the phagocytes SHAW 707:3
stimulation unnatural s. MILL 509:4
sting death, where is thy s. BIBL 107:4
it is a s. PEEL 571:19
s. like a bee ALI 12:4
s. you for your pains PROV 603:33
where is thy s.-a-ling-a-ling MILI 508:13
stingeth s. like an adder BIBL 83:16
stings s. in their tails BIBL 112:16
s., The crowd, and buzz COWL 239:19
s. you for your pains HILL 376:11
wanton s. SHAK 686:3
stink Fish and guests s. PROV 600:32
stinker Outrageous S. KIPL 441:23
stinks fish always s. PROV 600:31
that s. and stings POPE 583:9
worse it s. PROV 607:10
stir before you s. his fire PROV 616:6
more you s. it PROV 607:10
No s. in the air SOUT 730:15
No s. of air was there KEAT 427:23
smoke and s. of this dim spot MILT 511:13
s. men's blood SHAK 676:10
s. up undisputed matters SALL 643:8
S. up, we beseech thee BOOK 128:20
s. without great argument SHAK 665:33
stirbt er s. ab ENGE 300:11
stirred Shaken and not s. FLEM 317:9
something s. SIMP 720:14
stirring s. the fire AUST 38:17
stirrup foot already in the s. CERV 200:7
sprang to the s. BROW 156:8
s. and the ground EPIT 303:15
stirs Will that s. and urges HARD 361:10
stitch s. in time saves PROV 611:23
S.! stitch! stitch HOOD 382:28
stitches like so many s. RUSK 639:8
stitching s. and unstitching YEAT 835:2
St Ives going to S. NURS 547:11
St James ladies of S.'s DOBS 271:16
stock s. that scents the garden THOM 775:4
Woman s. is rising CHIL 211:25
stocking glimpse of s. PORT 588:2
silk s.'s hanging down SELL 654:6
stockings Golden s. GOGA 343:22
s. were hung MOOR 529:8
thy yellow s. SHAK 701:29
stocks hurt in the s. BOOK 139:8
stoic budge doctors of the s. fur MILT 511:28
stoical s. scheme of supplying SWIF 748:27
stoicism Romans call it s. ADDI 4:10
stole I wonder where you s. 'em SWIF 749:28
son of a bitch s. my watch FILM 312:8
S. many a man's soul JAGG 401:8
stolen had I s. the whole STEV 743:2
s., be your apples HUNT 395:16
S. fruit is sweet PROV 611:24
s. his wits away DE L 256:10
S. sweets are best CIBB 217:8
s. the scraps SHAK 680:29
S. waters are sweet BIBL 82:19
S. waters are sweet PROV 611:25
stoles nice white s. BARH 54:4
stolid S. and stunned MARK 495:12
stomach army marches on its s. NAPO 539:1
army marches on its s. PROV 595:16
burst s. like a cave DOUG 276:16
for thy s.'s sake BIBL 109:16
nor a stew-pan—but a *s.* HUNT 396:9
no s. to this fight SHAK 671:23
s. of a king ELIZ 296:27
s. of the country GLAD 340:14
s. sets us to work ELIO 292:13
through his s. PROV 613:41
stomacher bird with the red s. DONN 272:18
stomachs march on their s. SELL 654:13
stone against a s. BOOK 137:23
At his heels a s. SHAK 666:1
blossoming in s. LONG 473:18
bomb them back into the S. Age LEMA 463:4
brass, nor s., nor earth SHAK 704:27
bronze and s. RUNY 637:16
flung the s. FITZ 314:7
for a s. of stumbling BIBL 86:27
get blood from a s. PROV 615:37
give him a s. BIBL 94:5
give them the s. MONT 527:2
hollows out a s. OVID 561:11
jasper and a sardine s. BIBL 111:30
let him first cast a s. BIBL 101:33
Let them not make me a s. MACN 488:14
Like a rolling s. DYLA 287:9
like a s. wall BEE 61:1
look honestly like s. MOOR 529:13
make a s. of the heart YEAT 835:20
mighty angel took up a s. BIBL 113:1
nickname is the heaviest s. HAZL 365:12
not a s. Tell where I lie POPE 586:25
quiet as a s. KEAT 427:22
Raise the s. ANON 18:13
rolling s. gathers PROV 610:16
rolls back the restless s. DUCK 284:5
S.-dead hath no fellow PROV 611:26
s. taken away BIBL 102:38
s. the twenty-first BROW 155:20
s. to beauty grew EMER 299:9
S. walls do not a prison make LOVE 476:14
s. which he flings TORR 779:18
s. which the builders refused BOOK 140:6
sword out of this s. MALO 492:7
take the s. from stone ELIO 295:16
This precious s. SHAK 694:19
through a piece of s. MOOR 529:14
Turn but a s. THOM 774:12
Under every s. ARIS 24:13
under this little s. FANS 306:9
Virtue is like a rich s. BACO 42:9
wears away a s. PROV 597:36
stones chose him five smooth s. BIBL 78:32
Drive gently over the s. PROV 598:47
in pilèd s. MILT 513:14
man that spares these s. EPIT 302:10
move The s. of Rome SHAK 676:11
pile up s. WULF 833:18
scuttled under s. ROET 631:9
Sermons in s. SHAK 658:14
shouldn't throw s. PROV 612:42
Sticks and s. PROV 611:20
s. and clouts make martyrs BROW 153:1
s. will teach you BERN 69:1
s. would cry out BIBL 100:18
you are not s. SHAK 676:5
You buy land, you buy s. PROV 615:23
stony fell upon s. places BIBL 95:20
morre s. than a shore WILL 821:1
s. limits SHAK 697:13
S. outcrop of the Burren BETJ 70:14
stood should of s. in bed JACO 401:2
s. against the world SHAK 676:4
s. by me when I was crazy SHER 716:28
s. four-square to all the winds TENN 765:4
stools Between two s. PROV 596:15
necessity invented s. COWP 241:17
stoop dares to s. and take it DOST 276:3
stop come to the end: then s. CARR 190:8
could not s. for Death DICK 266:6
full s. at the right place BABE 40:16
kissing had to s. BROW 158:10
Might s. a hole SHAK 666:25
nobody's going to s. 'em BERR 69:11
so plain a s. SHAK 669:20
S. it at the start OVID 561:20
S.-look-and-listen OFFI 554:12
S. me and buy one ADVE 8:11
S. the world NEWL 542:1
s. to busy fools VAUG 790:5
wouldn't lift a finger to s. them LEDW 461:18
stoppeth s. one of three COLE 226:3
stops buck s. here TRUM 784:10
know my s. SHAK 665:2
storage thought in cold s. SAMU 643:12
store amid thy s. KEAT 430:9
in the s. we sell hope REVS 625:1
storehouse rich s. BACO 41:9
storey crack in your upper s. SMOL 726:14
storied S. of old MILT 511:25
stories beset him round With dismal s. BUNY 161:16
new s. are born RUSH 637:17
s. are there already BARR 56:2
S. to rede ar delitabill BARB 53:20
tell sad s. SHAK 695:9
stork S. from butter ADVE 7:11
storm After a s. comes a calm PROV 594:17
Any port in a s. PROV 595:8
carry you through the s. EWAR 305:10
coming s. GLAD 340:12
directs the s. ADDI 4:7
fled away into the s. KEAT 427:16
Head to the s. KIPL 439:5
pelting of this pitiless s. SHAK 678:28
pilot of the s. BAGE 46:12
rides upon the s. COWP 240:16
sharper the s. PROV 610:34
ship in a black s. WEBS 808:18
S. and stress KAUF 426:6
s.-clouds gather LEAR 460:8
S.-clouds whirl PUSH 617:26
swell before s. KIPL 440:7
wind and s. BOOK 141:27
Stormont Ulster Parliament at S. GEOR 334:1
storms He sought the s. DRYD 280:1
waves and s. BOOK 134:7
stormy dark and s. night OPEN 555:25
O s. peple CHAU 205:7
S. weather KOEH 443:2
to 'scape s. days DONN 273:4
story about you, that s. HORA 389:14
dreaming s. JARR 404:9
Have you thought of a s. SHEL 710:5
It's our *own* s. THUR 777:2
life's s. fills thirty-five pages ARNO 29:10
name great in s. BYRO 179:6
novel tells a s. FORS 320:11
One s. is good PROV 609:4
picture tells a s. ADVE 7:19
picture tells a s. PROV 599:37
plot for a short s. CHEK 208:7
read Richardson for the s. JOHN 414:17
short in the s. BIBL 92:20
so old a s. HEIN 368:6
s. always old BROW 157:22
s. and a byword WINT 823:14
s. chronicled MALO 492:12
s. need be long THOR 775:29
s. of our days RALE 621:4
S. the spoiled child of art JAME 402:24
tell my s. SHAK 667:10
tell you a s. NURS 548:18
work that tells a s. RUSK 638:20
stout Collapse of S. Party ANON 15:18
s. heart to stey brae PROV 609:50
St Pancras Towers of S. Station BEEC 61:4
St Paul's ruins of S. MACA 482:10
ruins of S. WALP 801:3
Say I am designing S. BENT 67:6
S. had slipped down SMIT 725:24
Strachan Sir Richard S. ANON 16:12
Strafford S., who was hurried hence EPIT 303:6

straight crooked shall be made s. BIBL 87:28
get it s. one day STEV 739:25
line which is accurately s. WHEW 813:14
make his paths s. BIBL 92:27
no s. thing KANT 425:19
nothing ever ran quite s. GALS 328:17
street which is called S. BIBL 103:26
unflexible as s. LOCK 471:19
strain s. at a gnat BIBL 96:27
s. of man's bred out SHAK 699:14
s., Time's eunuch HOPK 384:24
That s. again SHAK 700:26
train take the s. ADVE 7:40
Words s. ELIO 294:5
strait S. is the gate BIBL 94:8
straits echoing s. between us ARNO 28:2
strand fair Scotland's s. BURN 167:15
Maypole in the S. BRAM 146:18
name upon the s. SPEN 733:4
never alone with a S. ADVE 8:22
sailing to the s. BALL 51:16
walk down the S. HARG 362:5
walked along the S. JOHN 417:24
strands last s. of man HOPK 384:2
strange among the s. people BOOK 139:21
everything that looks s. PEPY 573:2
foul, s., and unnatural SHAK 662:27
hand of s. children BOOK 141:18
How s. it seems BROW 156:23
in a s. land BOOK 141:8
Let us be very s. CONG 233:12
millions of s. shadows SHAK 704:19
new and s. at first TRAH 780:11
new men, s. faces TENN 760:14
now wonder nyce and s. CHAU 207:4
something rich and s. SHAK 698:27
s. and sinister JAME 403:12
'S. friend,' I said OWEN 562:12
s. intelligence SHAK 681:17
stranger in a s. land BIBL 75:24
s. that one so young BYRO 176:3
too s. a hand SHAK 674:6
strangeness s. in the proportion BACO 42:10
stranger by a complete s. ANNE 15:3
entertain Him like a s. ANON 10:10
entertain this starry s. CRAS 244:7
gratitude of a s. TOCQ 778:16
I am a s. grown BURN 167:23
I am a s. here SHAK 694:20
I, a s. and afraid HOUS 390:7
I was a little s. TRAH 780:11
Look, s. AUDE 34:6
never love a s. BENS 66:14
s. and alone WOLF 825:8
s., and ye took me in BIBL 97:12
s.? 'Eave 'arf a brick PUNC 617:6
s. in a strange land BIBL 75:24
S. than fiction BYRO 177:26
s. than fiction PROV 613:19
s. to my heart and me SHAK 677:23
s. to one of your parents AUST 38:19
S., unless with bedroom eyes AUDE 34:19
surety for a s. BIBL 82:22
wiles of the s. NASH 539:10
You may see a s. HAMM 358:23
strangers careth for the s. BOOK 141:23
courteous to s. BACO 43:6
entertain s. BIBL 110:6
on the kindness of s. WILL 820:21
s. and pilgrims BIBL 109:30
s. in the Capitol HEWI 375:19
s. of Rome BIBL 103:16
s. on a rainy day SMAR 722:7
we are s. before thee BIBL 80:29
we may be better s. SHAK 659:11
strangled And s. her BROW 157:15
s. with the guts MESL 506:5
strangling s. in a string HOUS 390:17
S. is a very quiet death WEBS 808:4
Stratford atte Bowe scole of S. CHAU 204:13
strathspeys hornpipes and s. BURN 166:29
straw all things as s. dogs LAO 451:7
clutch at a s. PROV 598:48
Headpiece filled with s. ELIO 294:24
He gets the s. OXFO 562:15
last s. that breaks PROV 604:27
lion shall eat s. BIBL 87:5
make bricks without s. PROV 615:41
stumbles at a s. SPEN 734:22
Take a s. and throw it up SELD 653:17
strawberries s. grow in the sea NURS 549:12
S. swimming in the cream PEEL 571:20
strawberry Like s. wives ELIZ 297:10
of the s. BUTL 173:4
S. fields forever LENN 464:1
Strawberry Hill [S.] is WALP 800:15
strawed where thou hast not s. BIBL 97:9
straws oaths are s. SHAK 671:4
S. tell which way PROV 611:27
stray If with me you'd fondly s. GAY 331:16
what wonder if they s. COWP 241:3
strayed erred, and s. from thy ways BOOK 125:15
streak thin red s. RUSS 640:13
stream change horses in mid s. PROV 598:30
cool as a mountain s. ADVE 7:12
Fish have their s. BROO 150:9
like an ever-rolling s. WATT 805:19
long-legged fly upon the s. YEAT 836:16
old mill by the s. ARMS 25:13
purling s. ADDI 4:21
salt weed sways in the s. ARNO 26:12
Still glides the S. WORD 831:15
s. cannot rise above PROV 611:28
s. that leaps alive SMAR 721:19
streamers s. waving in the wind GAY 332:20
streams cold Companionable s. YEAT 837:24
Gilding pale s. SHAK 704:17
hart for cooling s. TATE 755:8
his crystàlline s. SHEL 712:14
More pellucid s. WORD 829:1
s. in the firmament MARL 496:7
s. of dotage flow JOHN 411:18
strebt *so lang er s.* GOET 342:14
street at the end of the s. MACN 488:10
don't do it in the s. CAMP 103:16
inability to cross the s. WOOL 827:2
jostling in the s. BLAK 120:7
live in a s. ELIO 293:1
long unlovely s. TENN 760:28
On the bald s. TENN 760:29
s. fighting man JAGG 401:7
s. of the city was gold BIBL 113:10
s. which is called Straight BIBL 103:26
sunny side of the s. FIEL 310:17
talking at s. corners VANZ 789:20
where the long s. roars TENN 762:4
streets children died in the s. AUDE 33:26
Down these mean s. CHAN 201:16
grass will grow in the s. HOOV 383:12
I walk the s. GALV 329:1
negro s. at dawn GINS 339:20
s. and lanes of the city BIBL 99:29
s. are paved with gold COLM 229:15
S. FLOODED TELE 758:10
s. that no longer exist FENT 308:8
strength as the s. of ten TENN 766:14
Ephraim also is the s. BOOK 135:19
Even if s. fail PROP 593:16
from s. to strength BOOK 137:12
giant's s. SHAK 686:9
girded himself with s. BOOK 138:2
His s. the more is BUNY 161:16
is their s. then BOOK 137:19
My s. and my hope BIBL 89:24
On which all s. depends SMAR 722:9
ordained s. BOOK 131:26
our hope and s. BOOK 134:18
rejoiceth in his s. BIBL 81:35
renew their s. BIBL 88:5
roll all our s. MARV 499:4
shall be your s. BIBL 87:16
s. and best security TROL 782:8
s. is lacking OVID 561:10
s. is made perfect BIBL 107:17
s. of an horse BOOK 141:25
s. of his spirit LUCR 478:21
s. of spirit SHAK 674:24
S. through joy POLI 581:21
s. unto his people BOOK 133:14
s. with his arm BIBL 98:17
S. without hands to smite SWIN 750:9
s. without insolence BYRO 179:20
Sun in his s. BIBL 73:8
that tower of s. TENN 765:4
tower of s. SHAK 696:28
try the soul's s. BROW 156:10
Union is s. PROV 613:31
yet would my s. be vain SIKH 719:7
strengthen bread to s. man's heart BOOK 139:3
S. me, O Lord SIKH 719:12
s. such as do stand BOOK 127:10
s. while one stands ROSS 634:4
S. ye the weak hands BIBL 87:22
strengtheneth Christ which s. me BIBL 109:1
strengthens s. our nerves BURK 164:2
strenua *S. nos exercet inertia* HORA 386:20
strenuous s. life ROOS 633:4
strepitumque *opes s. Romae* HORA 388:22
stress Storm and s. KAUF 426:6
stretch insight and the s. BROW 155:3
S. him out longer SHAK 680:15
s. the human frame SCAR 646:8
S. your arm no further PROV 611:29
stretched by a s. out arm BIBL 77:5
hand is s. out BIBL 86:20
things he s. TWAI 786:2
stretches s. his legs PROV 599:42
stricken I was a s. deer COWP 241:24
s. deer SHAK 665:1
well s. in age BIBL 74:28
stride At one s. comes the dark COLE 226:14
strides Tarquin's ravishing s. SHAK 683:1
strife double s. BACO 45:12
In place of s. CAST 193:13
Let there be no s. BIBL 74:24
man of s. BIBL 89:18
none was worth my s. LAND 450:1
Of that stern s. SCOT 651:15
step towards an end of s. GEOR 334:1
s. is o'er POTT 588:16
void of s. CHAL 200:10
strike in doubt, s. it out TWAI 786:24
s. against public safety COOL 235:17
S. him CALI 181:7
s. his father's crown SHAK 670:29
s. it in anger SHAW 708:21
s. it out JOHN 414:22
s. mine eyes JONS 419:20
s. not awry MORE 531:15
S. the tent LAST 457:5
S. while the iron PROV 611:30
thunder, S. flat SHAK 678:21
yet afraid to s. POPE 583:7
striker no s. BIBL 109:14
strikes as s. the player FITZ 314:16
Empire s. back FILM 312:19
s. the same place twice PROV 605:28
string end of a golden s. BLAK 119:3
one long yellow s. BROW 157:15
strangling in a s. HOUS 390:17
s. that ties SHEL 715:3
s. that ties them MONT 528:5
untune that s. SHAK 700:6
stringent s. execution GRAN 349:2
strings scrape your s. darker CELA 199:9
s. . . . in the human heart DICK 260:17
strip s. his sleeve SHAK 671:24
S. thine own back SHAK 679:24
stripe s. for stripe BIBL 76:14
striped s. like a zebra KEAT 428:14
s. shroud THOM 773:8

stripes forty s. save one BIBL 107:13
with his s. we are healed BIBL 88:17
stripling s. Thames ARNO 27:6
strive need'st not s. CLOU 222:24
s. on untiringly PALI 564:19
s., to seek, to find TENN 767:12
strives err while yet he s. GOET 342:14
striving s. evermore for these GREN 352:17
stroke greater s. astonisheth CONS 235:4
none so fast as s. MISQ 521:2
s. most dolorous MALO 492:8
s. of midnight ceases HOUS 390:11
strokes amorous of their s. SHAK 656:23
Different s. SAYI 647:10
strong all s. enough LA R 453:12
battle to the s. BIBL 84:23
battle to the s. DAVI 251:13
battle to the s. PROV 610:4
Be s. and of a good courage BIBL 77:17
keep the s. in awe SHAK 696:32
men be so s. BOOK 137:19
nature of s. people BONH 125:9
One still s. man TENN 764:2
only the S. shall thrive SERV 654:25
out of the s. BIBL 78:1
realize how s. she is REAG 623:1
river Is a s. brown god ELIO 294:12
Sorrow and silence are s. LONG 473:15
s. drink BIBL 83:37
s. drink is raging BIBL 83:7
s. in the arm PROV 615:21
S. is the lion SMAR 722:10
s. man armed BIBL 99:17
s. name of the Trinity ALEX 11:11
s., silent man MORL 532:3
wants that little s. HOLM 381:9
weak overcomes the s. LAO 452:7
without whom nothing is s. BOOK 128:11
stronger grows the s. STER 738:26
interest of the s. PLAT 578:5
no s. than my sex SHAK 675:8
on the side of the s. TACI 752:17
s. still, in earth and air SMAR 722:11
s. than lions BIBL 79:2
s. than Necessity EURI 304:18
strongest Wine is the s. BIBL 90:26
stronghold safe s. LUTH 480:2
strongly sin s. LUTH 479:12
strove s., and much repented BYRO 176:4
s. with none LAND 450:1
struck Diogenes s. the father BURT 170:21
I s. the board HERB 372:6
s. all of a heap SHER 715:20
s. regularly like gongs COWA 239:4
they s. at my life FOX 322:9
structure good s. in a winding stair HERB 372:20
struggle alarms of s. and flight ARNO 26:5
class s. MARX 500:3
gods themselves s. SCHI 648:13
Manhood a s. DISR 270:3
s. between the artist man SHAW 708:1
S. for Existence DARW 250:19
s. for room MALT 493:4
s. itself towards the heights CAMU 184:10
s. naught availeth CLOU 223:2
s. not of men ADAM 3:1
to-day the s. AUDE 35:7
What s. to escape KEAT 428:22
struggles history of class s. MARX 500:6
struggling her s. ceases PUSH 617:28
strumpet Into a s.'s fool SHAK 656:6
She was a s. HEIN 368:8
true; she is a s. SHAK 663:15
struts s. and frets his hour SHAK 685:22
s. his dames before MILT 512:16
Stuart S. or Nassau PRIO 592:12
Stuarts out with the S. DISR 270:14
stubble sparks among the s. BIBL 91:9
stubborn Facts are s. things PROV 600:5
faithless and s. generation BOOK 137:4
too s. and too strange SHAK 674:6
stubbornness self-righteous s. JENK 406:8
Stubbs S. butters Freeman ROGE 631:17
stuck 'Amen' S. in my throat SHAK 683:7
S. her with knives MORR 532:23
students not for the benefit of the s. SMIT 723:12
studied animal he s. less GOSS 347:6
s. books than men BACO 44:27
studies air of delightful s. MILT 520:1
Fred's s. ELIO 292:22
some particular s. DRYD 283:3
S. serve for delight BACO 44:2
too much time in s. BACO 44:3
studieth man that s. revenge BACO 43:29
studio *Sine ira et s.* TACI 752:12
studious S. let me sit THOM 775:16
S. of elegance GAY 332:12
S. of laborious ease COWP 241:29
studiously s. neutral WILS 822:12
study craggy paths of s. JONS 420:7
leisure, I will s. HILL 377:11
much s. is a weariness BIBL 85:4
not s. to live BACO 44:31
previous s. AUST 38:16
proper s. of mankind POPE 585:19
proper s. of mankind is books HUXL 396:18
S. is like the heaven's SHAK 680:18
s. of Greek literature GAIS 327:19
s. of man is man CHAR 204:2
s.'s ornament MIDD 507:6
S. to be quiet BIBL 109:8
studying I have been s. SHAK 696:3
stuff Life too short to s. a mushroom CONR 235:3
made of sterner s. SHAK 676:1
s. of life HOUS 391:4
unrefinèd s. of mine BRAD 146:16
Was there ever such s. GEOR 333:14
write such s. JOHN 417:3
stuffed We are the s. men ELIO 294:24
stuffs S. out his vacant garments SHAK 677:11
stultitiam *Misce s. consiliis* HORA 389:11
stumbles how the strong man s. ROOS 633:8
s. at a straw SPEN 734:22
stumbling for a stone of s. BIBL 86:27
s. through my soul GORE 347:2
stumbling-block unto the Jews a s. BIBL 105:28
stump mount the s. STEV 740:17
stumps roller, pitch, and s. LANG 450:10
stung S. by the splendour BROW 155:23
stupefying s. incense-smoke BROW 155:14
stupid *all* questions were s. WEIS 809:1
interesting . . . but s. CATC 196:24
It's the economy, s. POLI 581:20
most intelligent and most s. CONF 232:5
on the part of the s. WARN 803:19
s. enough to want it CHES 211:19
s. is doing something SHAW 706:19
s. neither forgive nor SZAS 752:1
stupidest s. party MILL 507:24
stupidity cruelty, s. and misgovernment GLAD 341:16
excess of s. JOHN 413:15
s. than depravity JOHN 414:7
With s. the gods themselves SCHI 648:13
stupidvision It is S. TOYN 780:7
Sturm *S. und Drang* KAUF 426:6
'stute small 's. fish KIPL 441:12
sty Over the nasty s. SHAK 665:17
Stygian In S. cave forlorn MILT 512:12
S. smoke JAME 402:12
style attain an English s. JOHN 409:24
cut, the s., the line LOES 473:2
definition of a s. SWIF 748:8
forges one's s. ZOLA 840:15
grand s. ARNO 29:8
has no real s. PICA 576:3
have his own s. MATH 501:8
How the s. refines POPE 584:25
Mandarin s. CONN 233:27
murderer for fancy prose s. NABO 537:18
only secret of s. ARNO 29:9
own towering s. CHES 211:16
see a natural s. PASC 568:8
s. cannot be too clear STEN 737:19
S. is life FLAU 316:16
S. is the dress of thought WESL 812:1
S. is the man BUFF 159:19
s. is the man PROV 611:31
that is s. STEV 741:2
with his eye on his s. ARNO 29:5
styles All s. are good VOLT 797:15
suave *S., mari magno* LUCR 479:3
sub Sighted s., sank same MASO 501:1
subdue chasten and s. WORD 829:5
s. all things to himself BOOK 131:14
s. the arrogant VIRG 795:1
s. the people BOOK 134:22
subdued My nature is s. SHAK 705:14
subhumanly s. ugly mate GREE 352:8
subiectis *Parcere s.* VIRG 795:1
subject Every s.'s duty SHAK 671:17
Grasp the s. CATO 194:16
honour is the s. SHAK 674:9
Little s., little wit CARE 186:19
shocked by this s. BOHR 124:1
s. and a sovereign CHAR 203:4
s. is not truth CHAP 202:22
s. of all verse EPIT 304:9
s. of a novel MURA 536:14
s. of conversation CHES 209:4
We know a s. ourselves JOHN 415:4
what it is to be a s. ELIZ 296:25
subjection bring it into s. BIBL 106:11
subjective any s. viewpoint CHUA 213:6
subjects good of s. DEFO 255:16
most important s. ARIS 24:14
rich in s. DEFO 255:1
s. are rebels BURK 163:24
sublimation sex is a s. LODG 472:15
sublime beauteous and s. AKEN 9:4
egotistical s. KEAT 431:10
essence of the true s. BYRO 178:3
heart of the ridiculous, the s. MAHO 490:18
My object all s. GILB 338:9
step above the s. PAIN 563:10
s. dashed to pieces COLE 227:26
s. to the ridiculous NAPO 538:16
s. to the ridiculous PROV 600:49
sublimity S. is the echo LONG 475:5
submerged s. tenth BOOT 142:18
submission appetite for s. ELIO 292:17
s. of men's actions HOBB 378:24
Yielded with coy s. MILT 516:16
submit Must he s. SHAK 695:14
s. myself BOOK 130:14
s. yourself CONR 234:16
subordinate in a s. position THOM 770:22
subordination s. of one sex MILL 509:3
subscribers list of s. JOHN 416:23
subsistence S. only increases MALT 493:3
s. without a mind BERK 68:3
subsisting human flesh s. BOOK 127:1
substance dividing the S. BOOK 126:22
eyes did see my s. BOOK 141:13
is the s. of men SWIN 751:2
mind can make S. BYRO 177:32
persons of some s. WIND 823:4
ruler of all his s. BOOK 139:9
s. from the common earth FITZ 314:21
s. of his house BIBL 86:8
s. of ten thousand soldiers SHAK 696:31
summed with all his s. CHAP 202:13
wasted his s. BIBL 100:2
What is your s. SHAK 704:19
substantial ship s. ASKE 30:20
substantive s. law MAIN 491:11
substitute no s. for victory MACA 481:6
substitutes Ours is the age of s. BENT 67:8
subterranean s. fields WORD 831:8

subtle God is s. but not malicious EINS 290:10
Now the serpent was more s. BIBL 73:24
slipper and s. knave SHAK 692:13
subtlest serpent s. beast MILT 517:13
subtleties speculations and s. BROW 153:23
s. of grace LOWE 478:7
subtlety brother came with s. BIBL 74:39
Human s. LEON 464:15
subtopia it will stick—s. NAIR 538:5
suburb new s. beyond the runway BETJ 70:8
suburbs In the south s. SHAK 702:8
s. Of your good pleasure SHAK 675:7
subversion Gracchi complaining about s. JUVE 424:7
subversive Whatever is funny is s. ORWE 559:13
subway in a New York s. STRA 744:12
succedaneum as a s. WORD 831:2
succeed How to s. in business MEAD 503:2
If at first you don't s. PROV 603:13
not going to s. MORT 533:12
possible to s. RENO 624:14
succeeds s. like success PROV 608:17
Whenever a friend s. VIDA 792:10
Where he s. CHUR 214:11
success bitch-goddess s. JAME 404:5
catch With his surcease s. SHAK 682:8
command s. ADDI 4:9
first requisite to s. SPEN 732:2
guarantee s. in war CHUR 215:13
If *A* is a s. in life EINS 290:17
no s. like failure DYLA 287:10
no very lively hope of s. SMIT 726:1
succeeds like s. PROV 608:17
S. has many fathers PROV 611:32
S. is counted sweetest DICK 266:15
S. is relative ELIO 293:25
s. is sure TWAI 786:27
Sweet smell of s. FILM 313:4
this ecstasy, is s. PATE 569:15
true s. is to labour STEV 741:25
wisdom to vulgar judgements—s. BURK 162:6
successful clever and the s. GREE 351:17
recipes that are always s. [illegible]
S. crimes alone DRYD 282:5
s. writer LEWI 467:8
whether s. or otherwise ADAM 3:17
succession monarchy and s. PAIN 563:13
successors dissatisfield with s. JENK 406:9
successus *Hos s. alit* VIRG 794:15
succour comfort and s. BOOK 129:14
such of s. is the kingdom of God BIBL 98:10
s. as I am BIBL 104:23
suck I have given s. SHAK 682:17
sucked s. on country pleasures DONN 274:2
sucker Never give a s. an even break FIEL 310:18
s. an even break PROV 607:29
s. born every minute BARN 55:11
sucking any s. dove SHAK 689:13
suckle s. fools SHAK 692:11
sucklings babes and s. BOOK 131:26
sucks as a weasel s. eggs SHAK 658:21
Sudan your 'ome in the S. KIPL 438:16
sudden followers of the S. HUI- 394:5
s. glory arising HOBB 378:11
s. thought BROW 155:23
to Dawn: Be s. THOM 774:6
too unadvised, too s. SHAK 697:15
suddenly s. became depraved JUVE 424:8
s. cast down BOOK 134:24
s., I saw you there GERS 334:12
Sudeten problem of the S. Germans HITL 378:8
sue Less used to s. SCOT 650:12
S. a beggar PROV 611:33
s. its parents WATS 804:17
sueños *Aun en s.* CALD 181:4
s., sueños son CALD 181:5
suet black s.-pudding LEWI 467:12
Suez East of S. KIPL 439:14
S.—a smash and grab raid NICO 545:4
S. Canal EDEN 288:8
suffer Better one s. DRYD 280:7
courage to s. TROL 782:6
Knows what I s. GOET 343:14
let's s. on the heights HUGO 393:17
nobody is going to s. KALD 425:11
s. a sea-change SHAK 698:27
s. fools gladly BIBL 107:11
s. for it BIBL 110:31
S. the little children BIBL 98:10
s. thy foot to be moved BOOK 140:12
s. thy Holy One BOOK 132:10
sufferance s. is the badge SHAK 687:15
suffered s. over *such* a woman HOME 381:23
S. under Pontius Pilate BOOK 126:10
sufferer was a s. DEKK 256:4
suffereth Charity s. long BIBL 106:16
suffering About s. they were never wrong AUDE 34:9
allay all the s. SHAN 706:7
atone for it by s. CHEK 208:3
Deep, unspeakable s. ELIO 291:22
healed of a s. PROU 594:8
learn in s. SHEL 711:21
Lounjun 'roun' en s. HARR 362:18
loved the s. many BENT 66:22
majesty of human s. VIGN 792:15
Noble Truth of S. PALI 565:12
not true that s. ennobles MAUG 501:19
put me to s. METH 506:6
s. from the particular disease JERO 406:21
S. is permanent WORD 827:17
This is s. PALI 564:16
Whatever s. is in store SHAN 706:10
sufferings patience under their s. BOOK 127:18
started a myriad s. HOME 381:20
s. for the Achaeans OPEN 555:1
s. which thou art spared ORCH 557:9
To each his s. GRAY 350:17
suffers does, not s. wrong SHEL 713:5
inform us of what he s. SMIT 723:5
suffice ice Is also great And would s. FROS 325:21
sufficiency elegant s. THOM 775:6
s. is of God BIBL 107:5
sufficient S. conscience to bother him LLOY 471:9
s. sacrifice BOOK 129:21
S. unto the day BIBL 93:27
S. unto the day PROV 611:34
whether he have s. BIBL 99:31
suffrance S. is a soverayn vertue LANG 450:19
sugar I must s. my hair CARR 190:6
no s. cane for miles HOLI 380:21
Oil, vinegar, s. GOLD 344:23
sack and s. SHAK 668:15
shower you with s. lumps LINE 469:12
S. and spice NURS 551:19
s. of literature JAME 403:20
sweetmeats and s.-plums TROL 782:4
suggest suffer reality to *s.* BRON 149:20
suicide alter the s. rate WHIT 816:3
convince me it wasn't s. LEON 464:7
infamous s. PLAT 577:16
it is s. MACD 485:1
longest s. note KAUF 426:3
not even s. STEV 742:2
possibility of s. CIOR 218:3
s. 25 years after his death BEAV 59:5
s. kills two people MILL 509:18
s. to be abroad BECK 59:9
thought of s. NIET 545:18
suicides s. have a special language SEXT 655:9
sui generis say I am *s.* LONG 473:8
suis *J'y s.* MACM 487:13
Suisse *point de S.* RACI 620:1
suit see ye wi' a s. on FERG 308:15
suitable s. case for treatment MERC 505:4
suitor think you are Ann's s. SHAW 708:2
suits s. of woe SHAK 661:21
sukebind s. hangs heavy GIBB 336:5
Sule Skerry home it is the S. BALL 50:17
sulk s. about having no boyfriend FIEL 309:12
sullen in his s. mind SPEN 733:21
S. and sad THOM 775:14
sulphur oat-cakes, and s. SMIT 725:13
sulphurous s. and thought-executing SHAK 678:21
sultry where the climate's s. BYRO 175:30
sum *Cogito, ergo s.* DESC 258:18
s. of matter BACO 41:21
With a great s. BIBL 104:16
Sumatra giant rat of S. DOYL 277:13
summer After many a s. TENN 766:16
As s. winds that creep SHEL 711:16
do when the s. is shed SWIN 751:9
ensure s. in England WALP 801:2
Eternal s. gilds them yet BYRO 176:25
fantastic s.'s heat SHAK 694:16
fly After s. merrily SHAK 699:11
guest of s. SHAK 682:7
if it takes all s. GRAN 348:17
In a s. season LANG 450:15
Indian S. of the heart WHIT 816:7
In s., quite the other way STEV 742:11
last rose of s. MOOR 530:17
like a s. birdcage WEBS 808:8
Like s. tempest TENN 765:26
long hot s. FILM 312:22
murmur of a s.'s day ARNO 27:4
No spring, nor s. beauty DONN 272:10
no s. progress ANDR 14:15
notice whether it's s. CHEK 208:9
one long bathing of a s.'s day WORD 830:22
over the s. sea TENN 766:10
Saint Martin's s. SHAK 672:7
see in a s.'s day SHAK 689:14
Singest of s. KEAT 429:6
s. afternoon JAME 403:23
s. eves by haunted streams MILT 512:24
S. has set in COLE 228:1
s. is ended BIBL 89:15
S. is icumen in ANON 18:22
s. liveries LANI 451:4
s.'s beauty yields SACK 641:3
s.'s green all girded up SHAK 704:8
S.'s joys are spoilt KEAT 427:21
s.'s lease SHAK 704:9
S. time and the livin' is easy HEYW 376:4
swallow does not make s. PROV 609:5
through the s. is not heard SHEL 711:17
thy eternal s. SHAK 704:10
to a s.'s day SHAK 704:9
trancèd s.-night KEAT 427:27
waken from his s. dreams SHEL 712:14
summers S. pleasures they are gone CLAR 218:18
summertime In s. on Bredon HOUS 390:19
summits Nations touch at their s. BAGE 46:20
summoner S. was ther CHAU 205:3
summons s. thee to heaven SHAK 683:2
Upon a fearful s. SHAK 661:10
summum *S. bonum* CICE 217:14
Sumner [Charles] S.'s mind ADAM 2:18
sumpshous s. spot ASHF 30:13
sun against a setting s. SHAK 699:17
all, except their s., is set BYRO 176:25
At the going down of the s. BINY 115:8
aweary of the s. SHAK 685:23
beauty of the s. SHAK 702:26
Before you let the s. in THOM 772:17
behold the s. BIBL 84:31
beneath another s. THOM 775:12
best s. we have WALP 800:22
black s. of melancholy NERV 541:7
blushing discontented s. SHAK 695:12
Born of the s. SPEN 732:19
bowled the s. TAYL 756:16

bride that s. shines on PROV 601:48
burnished s. SHAK 687:16
candle to the s. SIDN 718:4
candle to the s. YOUN 839:1
cannot make our s. Stand MARV 499:4
clear as the s. BIBL 86:1
countenance was as the s. BIBL 111:22
course of s. and stars ZORO 841:12
enjoyed the s. ARNO 26:7
especially Sir Brother S. FRAN 323:4
faded summer's s. BOLT 124:22
feel the s. BROW 154:14
flew between me and the s. BLUN 122:13
glorious S. uprist COLE 226:9
golden apples of the s. YEAT 837:12
Hath Britain all the s. SHAK 660:26
heat o' the s. SHAK 661:1
heaven's glorious s. SHAK 680:18
he beheld the s. WORD 828:8
hooting at the glorious s. COLE 225:11
I am too much i' the s. SHAK 661:17
I will sing of the s. POUN 589:9
Juliet is the s. SHAK 697:9
loves to live i' the s. SHAK 658:22
love that moves the s. CLOS 222:2
love that moves the s. DANT 250:5
maketh his sun to rise BIBL 93:14
maturing s. KEAT 430:8
Mother, give me the s. IBSE 398:8
never see the s. BROW 158:7
no new thing under the s. BIBL 84:3
nothing like the s. SHAK 705:20
nothing new under the s. PROV 612:20
no worship to the garish s. SHAK 697:29
old fool, unruly s. DONN 274:14
open face of the s. WESL 811:18
out in the midday s. COWA 238:15
place in the s. BÜLO 160:4
place in the s. WILH 819:18
places Under the s. HOUS 391:7
prayer at sinking of the s. KORA 444:20
ran the s. down with talk CALL 181:15
reign where'er the s. WATT 805:18
rising of the s. SONG 729:10
rising s. has first breathed VIRG 796:15
sacred radiance of the s. SHAK 677:23
seen the s. set RIMB 628:8
self-same s. SHAK 703:22
setting s. SHAK 694:18
shene is the s. LANG 450:22
shoots at the mid-day s. SIDN 718:7
soft was the s. LANG 450:15
speak with the S. VAUG 790:4
stand out of my s. DIOG 268:1
staring at the s. BELL 63:5
s. also rises HEMI 369:12
s. and moon AUGU 36:1
S. and Moon should doubt BLAK 118:4
s. and moon to stand TOAS 778:1
s. begins his state MILT 512:17
s. does not set SCHI 648:11
s. doth parch the green SURR 746:10
S.-girt city SHEL 712:6
s. go down on your anger PROV 607:31
s. go down upon your wrath BIBL 108:5
s. grows cold TAYL 756:15
s. has gone in SMIT 724:13
S. himself cannot forget ANON 19:1
S. in his strength BIBL 73:8
s. is laid to sleep JONS 419:17
s. is lost DONN 272:7
s. loses nothing PROV 611:35
s. loste his hewe CHAU 205:13
s. never sets NORT 546:16
s. now stands JOSE 421:8
s. of heaven prove a micher SHAK 668:12
S. of righteousness BIBL 90:25
S. of Righteousness WESL 810:23
s. of York SHAK 696:7
s. reigns supreme LE C 461:14
s. shall not burn thee BOOK 140:12
s. shone BECK 59:17
s. showing up the dust PERR 573:24
S.'s rim dips COLE 226:14
S., stand thou still BIBL 77:22
s. to me is dark MILT 518:15
S.-treader, life and light BROW 157:9
s. was shining everywhere GERS 334:12
S. wot won it NEWS 544:11
tired the s. with talking CORY 237:13
under the midday s. MILT 511:21
under the s. BIBL 83:39
Up roos the s. CHAU 205:20
watched the s. going down VAN 789:14
when the s. in bed MILT 513:28
when the s. rise BLAK 121:13
where no s. shines THOM 772:9
while the s. shines PROV 606:12
woman clothed with the s. BIBL 112:18
yet I saw no s. TICH 777:10
sunbeam Jesus wants me for a s. TALB 753:2
s. in a winter's day DYER 286:16
sunbeams didst the stars and s. know ARNO 27:14
people the s. MILT 512:4
s. out of cucumbers SWIF 747:23
sunbright upon the s. walls WORD 827:13
Sunday feeling of S. is the same RHYS 625:20
Here of a S. morning HOUS 390:19
killing of a mouse on S. BRAT 147:4
may be played on S. LEAC 459:20
Never on S. FILM 312:24
rainy S. afternoon ERTZ 301:6
rainy S. in London DE Q 258:7
She was the S. CLAR 219:13
S., bloody Sunday FILM 313:2
this is S. morning MACN 488:15
working week and S. best AUDE 33:28
Sundays begin a journey on S. SWIF 748:18
sundial s., and I make a botch BELL 64:3
sundry s. and manifold changes BOOK 128:7
sunflower S.! weary of time BLAK 120:22
sung He s. of God SMAR 722:9
s. as it were a new song BIBL 112:23
s. from noon to noon MORR 532:15
sunk s. beneath the wave COWP 240:23
sunless Down to a s. sea COLE 225:20
to the s. land WORD 828:15
sunlight s. on the garden MACN 488:16
sunnier s. side of doubt TENN 757:10
sunny Candlemas day be s. and bright PROV 603:14
leaps S. Jim ADVE 7:26
lived in a warm, s. climate COWA 239:1
s. pleasure-dome COLE 225:22
s. side of the street FIEL 310:17
sunrise Eternity's s. BLAK 120:8
suns light of setting s. WORD 829:5
planets circle other s. POPE 585:6
process of the s. TENN 763:5
S. can set and come CATU 197:2
S., that set JONS 420:10
sunset make a fine s. MADA 488:21
sail beyond the s. TENN 767:12
S. and evening star TENN 757:18
s. breezes shiver NEWB 541:16
s. of my life REAG 623:8
S. ran BROW 156:4
s.-seas ALDR 11:3
there's a s.-touch BROW 155:7
sunsets Autumn s. exquisitely dying HUXL 397:8
horror of s. PROU 594:7
sunshine Digressions are the s. STER 738:21
in the s. and with applause BUNY 161:4
like s. after rain SHAK 706:1
s. in the shady place SPEN 733:16
s. is a glorious birth WORD 829:15
s. of the heart CONS 235:8
s. to the sunless land WORD 828:15
sunt *Sint ut s.* CLEM 220:13
sup liveth longest doth but s. HENS 371:5
s. with my Lord Jesus Christ BRUC 158:19
superbos *et debellare s.* VIRG 795:1
superficial ridiculous and s. MURA 536:15
superfluities must have s. GAY 332:17
superfluity barren s. of words GART 330:13
superfluous in the poorest thing s. SHAK 678:17
nothing is s. LEON 464:15
s., a very necessary thing VOLT 798:1
s. in me ADAM 2:3
S., superfluous TURG 784:19
superhuman struggle for s. beauty GREE 352:8
superior being s. to time JOHN 410:25
embarrass the s. SHAW 708:20
most s. person ANON 17:20
no-one to be their *s.* TOCQ 778:17
notions about a s. power SWIF 747:10
s. man is broadminded CONF 231:8
S. people never make long visits MOOR 529:19
superman I teach you the s. NIET 545:9
It's S. ANON 16:7
supernatural nothing mysterious or s. HUME 394:8
s. source of evil CONR 234:24
superseded has not been s. LONG 475:4
superstition character of a s. CHOM 212:11
main source of s. RUSS 640:4
species of s. HUME 395:2
s. in avoiding superstition BACO 44:9
S. is the poetry of life GOET 343:7
S. is the religion BURK 164:1
s. sets the whole world VOLT 797:13
s. to enslave a philosophy INGE 399:5
superstitions end as s. HUXL 397:17
s. of the human mind VOLT 797:19
superstitious he is s. grown SHAK 675:4
in all things ye are too s. BIBL 104:8
more s., more bigoted NEWM 542:6
s. reluctance to sit JOHN 416:12
supped Hobson has s. MILT 514:4
s. full with horrors SHAK 685:21
supper after s. walk a mile PROV 594:18
consider s. as a turnpike EDWA 289:12
good s. at night ANST 22:14
Last-s.-carved-on-a-peach-stone LANC 449:17
leaned on his breast at s. BIBL 103:12
Sings for his s. NURS 549:9
S. of the Lord BOOK 130:17
suppliant s. for his own BYRO 178:19
thus the s. prays JOHN 411:17
supplications make our common s. BOOK 126:18
supplies just bought fresh s. BREC 147:15
support depend on the s. of Paul SHAW 707:5
help and s. of the woman EDWA 289:7
no invisible means of s. BUCH 159:9
s. him after SHAK 699:13
s. me when I am in the wrong MELB 504:4
s. of the people CLEV 220:15
s. of the whole COMP 230:18
s. us all the day long NEWM 542:16
swears that he will s. it JACK 400:14
visible means of s. BIER 114:24
supports s. with insolence JOHN 409:13
suppose universe queerer than we s. HALD 356:15
suppress power of s. NORT 546:19
supramundane s. mushroom LAUR 454:9
supreme in none s. ARNO 28:1
s. power must be arbitrary HALI 357:14
sups s. with the Devil PROV 602:33
surcease catch With his s. success SHAK 682:8
sure joy was never s. SWIN 750:21
made the round world so s. BOOK 138:2
Slow but s. PROV 611:1
What nobody is s. about BELL 63:22
surely Shome mishtake, s. CATC 196:20
surety s. for a stranger BIBL 82:22
surf s. floods over the reeds PAST 569:8
surface looks dingy on the s. PIRS 576:17

surfaces queen of s. DOWD 277:4
surfeit s. by eating of a lamprey FABY 305:22
s. of our own behaviour SHAK 678:5
s. with too much SHAK 687:6
surfing s. the Net ELIZ 297:20
We are s. food MACK 486:10
surge s. and thunder LANG 450:11
thine aëry s. SHEL 712:13
turbulent s. shall cover SHAK 699:25
surgeon not call the s. DICK 266:20
wounded s. plies the steel ELIO 294:10
surges s. lash the sounding shore POPE 584:23
surmise smothered in s. SHAK 681:21
with a wild s. KEAT 429:21
surprise get a big s. DIAN 260:6
Life is a great s. NABO 537:19
Live frugally on s. WALK 799:7
no little s. BARH 54:6
No s. for the writer FROS 326:14
Respect was mingled with s. SCOT 650:14
sound of s. BALL 52:15
wise man by s. LA F 447:13
surprised guilty thing s. WORD 830:6
S. by joy WORD 832:5
S. by unjust force MILT 511:27
surprises millions of s. HERB 373:11
S. are foolish things AUST 37:18
surquidry s. and foul presumpcioun CHAU 206:30
surrender die but do not s. CAMB 182:11
I s. to you GERO 334:11
No s. POLI 581:27
to Him we s. KORA 444:3
unconditional and immediate s. GRAN 348:16
we shall never s. CHUR 215:10
surrendered never s. her soul DEV 259:7
surroundings I plus my s. ORTE 557:15
sursum *S. corda* MISS 520:19
survey monarch of all I s. COWP 242:17
s. of all the world SHAK 669:12
s. the wondrous cross WATT 805:14
survival s. is all there is FULL 327:6
S. of the Fittest DARW 250:20
s. of the fittest SPEN 732:5
their s. machines DAWK 253:4
without victory, there is no s. CHUR 215:9
survive Dare hope to s. HUXL 397:6
expect to s. JEAN 404:17
know they can s. HART 363:3
Only the paranoid s. GROV 354:8
s. of us is love LARK 452:13
s. to consume VANE 789:17
survived I s. SIEY 719:3
survivors more the s.' affair MANN 494:5
old, old s. SHAW 710:2
Susan black-eyed S. came aboard GAY 332:20
susceptible s. to draughts WILD 817:21
suspect Always s. everybody DICK 264:12
makes a man s. much BACO 44:11
suspected New opinions are always s. LOCK 471:11
suspects Round up the usual s. FILM 311:21
suspended s. my religious inquiries GIBB 335:20
suspenders invention of s. SMIT 725:25
not forget the s. KIPL 441:11
suspension Shining s. CRAN 243:22
willing s. of disbelief COLE 227:12
suspicion above s. CAES 180:17
above s. PROV 596:46
against despots—s. DEMO 257:3
banish squint s. MILT 511:22
S. always haunts SHAK 673:4
s. that more than half WHIT 814:2
suspicions S. amongst thoughts BACO 44:10
Sussex S. won't be druv PROV 611:36
sustaining our s. corn SHAK 679:18
sutlers sapient s. ELIO 295:13
swaddling wrapped him in s. clothes BIBL 98:20
swagman Once a jolly s. PATE 569:16
swains all our s. commend her SHAK 702:29
swallow and the s. a nest BOOK 137:11
before the s. dares SHAK 703:17
O summer s. SWIN 751:11
speed of a s. BETJ 71:6
s. a camel BIBL 96:27
s. does not make summer PROV 609:5
s.-flights of song TENN 761:7
S., flying, flying South TENN 765:22
s. has set her six young BROW 156:13
S., my sister SWIN 751:9
s. the cow PROV 604:18
swallowed soon to be s. BLY 123:1
s. by way of *viaticum* GLAD 341:3
They had s. us up quick BOOK 140:16
swalloweth s. the ground BIBL 81:36
swallows gathering s. twitter KEAT 430:12
watching the s. WORD 827:13
swamp botanize in the s. CHES 211:15
swamps across primeval s. WODE 824:19
swan black Ohioan s. WRIG 833:13
I will play the s. SHAK 693:29
Leda's goose a s. ANON 16:16
like a sleeping s. SHEL 713:13
silver s. GIBB 336:4
some full-breasted s. TENN 760:18
so much as a black s. JUVE 424:14
Sweet S. of Avon JONS 420:26
this pale s. SHAK 704:3
Swanee down upon the S. River FOST 321:17
swanlike He makes a s. end SHAK 688:1
Swann no more talk of S. PROU 594:1
swans amongst tuneful s. VIRG 796:11
Dumb s., not chattering pies SIDN 718:14
I saw two s. SPEN 734:19
ships sail like s. asleep FLEC 317:5
s. are geese ARNO 26:14
s. of others are geese WALP 801:12
swap s. horses when crossing LINC 468:16
swarm s. in May PROV 611:37
S. over, death BETJ 71:4
swarthy in its s. monotony HARD 360:16
swashing s. and a martial outside [illegible]
swath thy hook Spares the next s. KEAT 430:9
sway little rule, a little s. DYER 286:16
swaying s. sound of the sea AUDE 34:7
sways So s. she level SHAK 701:18
swear And s. No where DONN 274:12
s. like a comfit-maker's wife SHAK 668:24
s. not at all BIBL 93:11
s. not by the moon SHAK 697:14
when very angry, s. TWAI 786:23
swearers and s. swear BURN 167:13
liars and s. SHAK 685:5
sweareth s. unto his neighbour BOOK 132:8
swearing let me alone for s. SHAK 702:15
swears Money doesn't talk, it s. DYLA 287:7
sweat Blood, s., and tear-wrung BYRO 173:13
blood, toil, tears and s. CHUR 215:7
die of a s. SHAK 670:24
In the s. of thy face BIBL 74:6
none will s. but for promotion SHAK 658:17
spend our midday s. QUAR 618:16
s. of an enseamèd bed SHAK 665:17
s. of its labourers EISE 291:8
work by the s. of his brow CHEK 208:8
sweating s. palm to palm HUXL 397:7
sweats Falstaff s. to death SHAK 667:34
wild regrets, and the bloody s. WILD 819:2
sweep Mountains of Mourne s. down FREN 324:9
s. his own door-step PROV 603:15
s. the dust SHAK 690:29
your chimneys I s. BLAK 120:13
sweeping S. up the Heart DICK 266:11
sweeps beats as it s. ADVE 7:30
s. a room as for Thy laws HERB 372:14
sweet All is not s. JONS 419:19
as a s. morsel HENR 370:15
buried in so s. a place SHEL 710:12
dead thing that smells s. THOM 772:24
Home, s. home PAYN 570:13
how it was s. BROW 155:22
How s. the moonlight sleeps SHAK 688:21
if TO-DAY be s. FITZ 314:14
in my mouth s. as honey BIBL 112:17
kiss me, s. and twenty SHAK 701:10
Life is very s. BORR 143:9
light is s. BIBL 84:31
Pyramus is a s.-faced man SHAK 689:14
seasons shall be s. COLE 225:16
Sleep is s. BUNY 161:7
So s. was ne'er so fatal SHAK 693:23
Stolen waters are s. BIBL 82:19
such s. sorrow SHAK 697:19
such s. thunder SHAK 690:15
suck on a boiled s. WESL 811:24
S. and low TENN 765:15
S. are the uses of adversity SHAK 658:14
s. as summer SHAK 673:23
S. day, so cool HERB 373:17
S. is revenge BYRO 176:5
s. is the whisper of the pine THEO 770:17
s. o' the year SHAK 703:9
s. peas, on tip-toe KEAT 428:6
s. reasonableness of Jesus ARNO 29:3
S. smell of success FILM 313:4
S., soft, plenty rhythm MORT 533:17
s. the name of Jesus NEWT 543:15
S. though in sadness SHEL 712:17
s. water and bitter BIBL 110:20
technically s. OPPE 557:4
Tell me not, s. LOVE 476:15
Things s. to taste SHAK 694:13
thy s. love SHAK 704:15
took s. counsel BOOK 135:11
wit enough to keep it s. JOHN 417:16
sweeteners s. of tea FIEL 310:4
sweeter mountain sheep are s. PEAC 571:5
s. also than honey BOOK 132:17
s. and a healthier one DOYL 277:21
s. than the berry GAY 331:8
those unheard Are s. KEAT 428:23
sweetest From the s. wine PROV [illegible]
Success is counted s. DICK 266:15
s. girl I know JUDG 423:1
s. sounds I'll ever hear RODG 631:4
sweetheart Blanch, and S. SHAK 679:10
Like the s. of the sun HOOD 382:27
sweetly Lalage, who laughs so s. HORA 388:1
sweetmeats pyramids of s. DRYD 283:13
s. and sugar-plums TROL 782:4
sweetness came forth s. BIBL 78:1
O how great the sum Of s. SMAR 722:7
s. and light ARNO 28:8
s. and light SWIF 747:12
s. of Anjou DU B 283:23
s. of a shower THOM 773:5
waste its s. GRAY 350:11
where s. and light failed FORS 320:13
sweets bag of boiled s. CRIT 245:6
brought'st Thy s. HERB 372:11
discandy, melt their s. SHAK 657:10
last taste of s. SHAK 694:18
Stolen s. HUNT 395:16
Stolen s. are best CIBB 217:8
s. compacted lie HERB 373:17
S. into your list HUNT 395:15
s. of place with power ROSE 633:15
S. to the sweet SHAK 666:27
sweetshop pressed to a s. window YEAT 836:1
swell deep sea s. ELIO 296:12
s. a progress ELIO 295:9
Thou s.! Thou witty HART 363:8
What a s. party PORT 588:11
swelling s. act SHAK 681:20
swept empty, s., and garnished BIBL 95:17
I s. the floor GILB 338:27
S. it for half a year CARR 190:19

swift Be s. to hear BIBL 110:13
Cousin S. DRYD 283:18
Love is s. of foot HERB 372:10
race is not to the s. BIBL 84:23
race is not to the s. PROV 610:4
race is to the s. DAVI 251:13
S. be thy flight SHEL 714:11
S. expires a driv'ler JOHN 411:18
swifter s. than a weaver's shuttle BIBL 81:10
s. than eagles BIBL 79:2
swiftness O s. never ceasing PEEL 572:1
swim learn how to s. PROV 598:35
swimmer s. in his agony BYRO 176:12
swimmers s. into cleanness leaping BROO 150:16
swimming Come softly s. SPEN 734:19
Odd figures s. VIRG 793:7
S. for his life GLAD 340:18
S. from tree to tree LOWE 478:2
s. in the air EDWA 289:9
s. under water FITZ 315:18
swindles all truly great s. HENR 370:17
swine husks that the s. did eat BIBL 100:3
in a s.'s snout BIBL 82:23
lady loved a s. NURS 551:4
Nor yet feed the s. NURS 547:18
pearls before s. BIBL 94:2
s. cheweth not the cud BIBL 76:20
throw pearls to s. PROV 598:29
turkeys, geese and s. PROV 608:28
whole herd of s. BIBL 94:21
swines You rotten s. CATC 196:32
swing ain't got that s. MILL 510:9
room to s. a cat SMOL 726:13
s. for it KING 437:16
S. low, sweet chariot SONG 730:4
s. our ungirded hips SORL 728:17
Swing, s. together CORY 237:11
want to s. a cat DICK 262:5
swings What you lose on the s. PROV 614:13
Swiss No money, no S. PROV 607:49
switching sanction of s. off EYRE 305:13
Swithun Saint S.'s day PROV 610:20
Switzerland I look upon S. SMIT 725:7
In S. they had FILM 311:16
S. is proud of this GIDE 336:17
swoons S. to a waltz HUXL 397:7
swoop all at one s. WEBS 808:7
At one fell s. SHAK 685:8
sword brave man with a s. WILD 818:32
but a s. BIBL 95:1
draws s. against prince PROV 615:5
edge of the s. BOOK 135:25
fallen by the edge of the s. BIBL 92:3
famous by my s. MONT 529:3
first drew the s. CLAR 218:19
His father's s. he has MOOR 530:14
I gave them a s. NIXO 546:9
lives by the s. PROV 602:30
make his s. BIBL 82:1
mightier than the s. PROV 609:22
My s., I give BUNY 161:18
nation shall not lift up s. BIBL 86:13
pen is worse than the s. BURT 170:10
pen mightier than the s. BULW 160:7
perish with the s. BIBL 97:25
put to the s. CROM 245:11
Put up thy s. BIBL 102:29
sharp as a two-edged s. BIBL 82:12
sheathe the s. ASQU 31:2
sigh is the s. BLAK 119:1
s., a horse, a shield LOVE 476:15
s. of a Norman Baron LEWE 466:15
s. out of this stone MALO 492:7
s. shall pierce BIBL 98:26
s. sleep in my hand BLAK 120:1
s. sung on the barren heath BLAK 120:10
s. the axis of the world DE G 255:29
s. was in the sheath COWP 240:24
terrible swift s. HOWE 391:15
two-edged s. BIBL 111:22
two-edged s. BOOK 142:2
watery if not flaming s. MARV 499:6
wield the s. of France DE G 255:20
with the edge of the s. BIBL 76:27
swords books are either dreams or s. LOWE 477:10
Keep up your bright s. SHAK 691:29
s. In our own proper entrails SHAK 677:1
s. into plowshares BIBL 86:13
s. shall play the orators MARL 496:22
ten thousand s. leapt BURK 163:20
yet they be very s. BOOK 135:12
swore armies s. terribly STER 739:1
My tongue s. EURI 304:19
when the son s. BURT 170:21
sworn had I so s. as you SHAK 682:17
sycamore nightingale in the s. STEV 743:3
sycophants s. and flatterers HARD 360:2
syllable chase A panting s. COWP 241:11
never used one s. JAY 404:15
To the last s. SHAK 685:22
syllables light s. leaped ROET 631:8
S. govern the world SELD 653:23
syllogism conclusion of your s. O'BR 552:9
sylph only s. I ever saw DICK 264:5
symbol Five for the s. at your door SONG 729:11
S. or energy ADAM 2:24
symboles *forêts de s.* BAUD 57:7
symbolic s. expression MAXW 502:13
symbolical works of women are s. BROW 154:9
symbols forests of s. BAUD 57:7
s. of a high romance KEAT 430:18
symmetry fearful s. BLAK 121:8
S. is tedious HUGO 393:19
s. of his body EINH 290:7
sympathies enlarge men's s. ELIO 293:14
sympathy give or take s. RHYS 625:18
messages of s. AYCK 40:2
secret s. SCOT 650:18
s. is cold GIBB 335:13
Tea and s. ANDE 14:12
symphony angelic s. MILT 513:23
Ninth S. will remain BAKU 48:17
s. like the world MAHL 490:17
symptoms hundred good s. POPE 587:23
synagogues chief seats in the s. BIBL 96:25
chief seats in the s. BIBL 98:11
syne For auld lang s. BURN 166:12
synod *S. of Cooks* JOHN 413:18
Syrens song the S. sang BROW 153:4
Syrian S. damsels to lament his fate MILT 514:26
S. Orontes JUVE 424:9
syrops lucent s. KEAT 427:13
system cannot be a true s. PAIN 563:9
must create a s. BLAK 118:20
rocked the s. ROBI 629:22
s. into system runs POPE 585:6
s. of Government GLAD 340:13
s. of outdoor relief BRIG 148:11
systems little s. have their day TENN 760:20
s. into ruin hurled POPE 585:8

T t is silent ASQU 31:8
ta saying 'T.' to God SPEN 732:16
tabby Demurest of the t. kind GRAY 350:19
tabernacle dwell in thy t. BOOK 132:7
t. were dissolved BIBL 107:7
tabernacles t. of thy grace SCOT 652:21
tabernas *pauperum t.* HORA 387:16
table behave mannerly at t. STEV 742:16
biforn his fader at the t. CHAU 204:11
cannot make a t. JOHN 413:3
fall from their masters' t. BIBL 96:1
fell from the rich man's t. BIBL 100:10
on a t.?—and under it BYRO 180:8
patient etherized upon a t. ELIO 295:3
prepare a t. before me BOOK 133:1
round about thy t. BOOK 140:23
T., at the Communion-time BOOK 129:3
takes the t. clean away BARN 55:10
tableau t. of crimes VOLT 797:18
tables make it plain upon t. BIBL 90:22
serve t. BIBL 103:20
tablet keep taking The T. THOM 773:9
tablets thy t., Memory ARNO 26:17
taboo t.'d by anxiety GILB 337:18
tabret bring hither the t. BOOK 137:9
tabulae *Solventur risu t.* HORA 389:22
tache *sans une t.* ROST 635:12
tactful t. in audacity COCT 223:19
tactics art of t. BAGE 46:14
tadpole When you were a t. SMIT 724:8
taedium vitae keep off the *t.* JOHN 412:25
taffeta doublet of changeable t. SHAK 701:22
T. phrases SHAK 680:30
Taffy T. was a Welshman NURS 551:1
tail choke on the t. PROV 604:18
Improve his shining t. CARR 189:9
more he shows his t. PROV 602:39
O! thereby hangs a t. SHAK 692:18
rat without a t. SHAK 681:11
scaly horror of his folded t. MILT 513:26
sensations of its "t." DISR 268:12
t. hangs down behind KIPL 441:5
t. that wagged WATS 805:3
t. was a plume LEON 464:10
treading on my t. CARR 190:4
tailor coat from the t. GOLD 345:32
ninth part even of a t. CARL 187:7
t. in Gloucester POTT 588:17
t. make thy doublet SHAK 701:22
Tinker, T. NURS 551:13
tailors eighteen t. CARL 188:16
Nine t. make a man PROV 607:44
tails bring their t. behind them NURS 549:4
stings in their t. BIBL 112:16
taint never t. my love SHAK 693:17
tainted t. wether of the flock SHAK 688:8
taisez-vous *T.! Méfiez-vous* OFFI 554:13
take big enough to t. away everything FORD 319:11
Give and t. fair play PROV 601:7
O t. those lips away SHAK 686:21
something people t. BALD 49:1
T. a pair of sparkling eyes GILB 337:8
t. a thing PROV 601:6
T., eat BIBL 97:18
T., eat, this is my Body BOOK 129:22
T. me to your leader CATC 196:22
t. my life FARQ 307:13
t. my life and all SHAK 688:16
t. not thy holy Spirit BOOK 135:7
T. now thy son BIBL 74:31
t. the nasty soup away HOFF 379:17
T. up the White Man's Burden KIPL 440:21
t. who have the power WORD 831:17
t. you in the morning BALD 49:4
taken Lord hath t. away BIBL 80:36
much is t., much abides TENN 767:12
One shall be t. BIBL 97:6
shall be t. away BIBL 97:10
she was t. out of Man BIBL 73:22
t. away my Lord BIBL 102:40
t. in when they marry AUST 37:24
When t. COLM 229:20
takes if it t. all summer GRAN 348:17
t. just like a woman DYLA 287:8
that it t. away BYRO 179:5
taketh t. away the sin BIBL 101:10
taking t. life by the throat FROS 326:16
we're t. over MORR 532:21
tale adorn a t. JOHN 411:16
fortunate for t.-tellers SCOT 652:1
had a t. to tell SCOT 650:9
honest t. SHAK 696:25
I could a t. unfold SHAK 662:25
mere t. of a tub WEBS 808:9
most tremendous t. of all BETJ 70:5
plain t. shall put you down SHAK 668:9
round unvarnished t. SHAK 691:32

tale (*cont.*):
sad t.'s best for winter SHAK 703:2
t. never loses in telling PROV 611:40
t. should be judicious COWP 239:30
t., sir, would cure deafness SHAK 698:20
t. Told by an idiot SHAK 685:22
t. which holdeth children SIDN 718:24
telling the saddest t. SHAK 689:18
Tell t. tit NURS 551:2
thereby hangs a t. SHAK 658:23
Trust the t. LAWR 458:4
twice-told t. SHAK 677:12
talent gifted t. acknowledged TURN 785:14
into my works is my t. WILD 819:9
Murder, like t. LEWE 466:14
no t. for writing BENC 64:21
sister of t. CHEK 208:15
T. develops in quiet places GOET 343:8
t. does what it can BARI 54:12
T. does what it can MERE 505:23
t. instantly recognizes genius DOYL 278:8
t. of a liar BYRO 180:6
t. pour le silence CARL 187:28
t. to amuse COWA 238:12
t. which is death to hide MILT 518:29
tomb of a mediocre t. SMIT 724:11
talents career open to the t. NAPO 539:3
If you have great t. REYN 625:4
ministry of all the t. ANON 17:16
virtue and t. JEFF 405:18
Whate'er the t. POPE 580:19
tales Dead men tell no t. PROV 597:50
idle t. BIBL 100:32
increased with t. BACO 42:22
tell t. out of school PROV 607:38
writing t. CONR 234:20
tali *t. auxilio nec defensoribus* VIRG 794:7
talk Careless t. costs lives OFFI 554:1
do not t. of ourselves TROL 782:14
good to t. ADVE 7:34
gotta use words when I t. to you ELIO 295:24
have out his t. JOHN 415:26
honest t. TENN 767:3
If you t. to God SZAS 752:2
I long to t. DONN 274:7
It can t., talk, talk PLAT 577:11
It would t. BEAU 58:18
let the people t. DANT 249:20
Money doesn't t., it swears DYLA 287:7
Most English t. JAME 403:2
no more t. of Swann PROU 594:1
No use to t. to me HOUS 390:18
people who can't t. ZAPP 839:24
ran the sun down with t. CALL 181:15
t. about the rest of us ANON 19:4
t. but a tinkling cymbal BACO 43:1
T. is cheap PROV 611:41
t. like a lady SHAW 709:11
t. of many things CARR 190:20
t. of the child TALM 754:9
T. of the Devil PROV 611:42
t. of wills SHAK 695:8
t. on for ever HAZL 365:5
t. six times BYRO 177:19
t. the less ZENO 840:1
t. too much DRYD 280:8
t. to the plants CHAR 203:19
Then he will t. LEE 462:4
They always t. PRIO 593:7
very easy to t. DICK 264:2
ways of making you t. CATC 196:26
we had a good t. BOSW 144:20
world may t. of hereafter COLL 228:10
talked I believe they t. of me FARQ 307:10
least t. about by men PERI 573:21
not being t. about WILD 818:17
t. like poor Poll GARR 330:4
t. of their Raphaels GOLD 345:5
t. shop ANON 16:15
t. with us by the way BIBL 100:34
talkers present is an age of t. HAZL 365:16
ten thousand t. DYLA 287:6
talking foolish t. BIBL 108:6
He is t. BIBL 79:28
know what we are t. about RUSS 639:19
leaves off t. BUTL 173:1
nation t. to itself MILL 510:3
People t. without speaking SIMO 720:10
quieten your enemy by t. CEAU 199:2
redtape t.-machine CARL 188:6
stop people t. ATTL 32:5
T. and eloquence JONS 421:4
t., Signior Benedick SHAK 690:34
t. to myself BARN 55:5
tired the sun with t. CORY 237:13
talks Money t. PROV 607:5
t. frankly only with his wife BABE 41:2
t. it so very fast FARQ 307:12
t. of Arthur's death SHAK 677:16
t. of his misfortunes JOHN 416:16
tall all I ask is a t. ship MASE 500:16
divinely t. TENN 758:16
exceeding t. men BACO 45:7
for this the clay grew t. OWEN 562:9
long and the short and the t. HUGH 392:16
t. as a crane SITW 720:21
'Tis a t. building CRAB 242:20
taller t. by almost the breadth SWIF 747:17
t. than other men HARO 362:11
Talmuds rotted T. of my childhood BABE 40:17
Tam T. was glorious BURN 168:12
tambourine Mr T. Man DYLA 287:11
play the t. DICK 264:5
tame tongue can no man t. BIBL 110:19
taming T. my wild heart SHAK 691:11
Tam Lin ken this night, T. BALL 51:19
tamper never want to t. AUDE 34:1
Tandy met wid Nappy T. POLI 581:16
tangere *Noli me t.* BIBL 114:10
tangle odors t. DICK 266:21
t. me no more WYAT 834:1
tangled t. web we weave SCOT 651:12
tangles t. of Neaera's hair MILT 513:2
tango Takes two to t. HOFF 379:15
takes two to t. PROV 604:41
tank T. come down the stalls SASS 645:16
tiger in your t. ADVE 8:7
tanks Get your t. off my lawn WILS 822:1
tanstaafl T. SAYI 648:4
tantae *T. molis erat* VIRG 793:6
tantras Mantras and t. TANT 755:1
tantum *T. ergo sacramentum* THOM 771:11
T. religio potuit LUCR 479:1
Tao not the eternal T. LAO 451:5
one is near T. CHUA 212:19
T. has reality and evidence CHUA 213:4
Therefore T. is great LAO 451:12
tap t. being turned off KIPL 441:21
tape boa constrictor as a t.-measure GOGA 343:21
taper Out went the t. KEAT 427:8
t. to the outward room DONN 273:8
with t. light To seek SHAK 677:15
tapestry earth in so rich t. SIDN 718:22
Turkey t. HOWE 391:16
tapping suddenly there came a t. POE 579:15
tar ha'porth of t. PROV 598:28
T.-baby ain't sayin' nuthin' HARR 363:1
T. water BERK 67:19
Tara through T.'s halls MOOR 530:12
when T. rose so high LAND 450:2
taratantara *t. dixit* ENNI 300:17
tarde *cinco en punto de la t.* GARC 329:10
tares but a field of t. TICH 777:10
t. of mine own brain BROW 153:23
tarnished neither t. nor afraid CHAN 201:16
Tarquin great house of T. MACA 483:3
T.'s ravishing strides SHAK 683:1
tarried too long he t. SWIF 749:27
too long we have t. LEAR 460:17
tarry Boatman, do not t. CAMP 183:11
t. till I come BIBL 103:13
why t. the wheels BIBL 77:30
You may for ever t. HERR 375:3
tarrying make no long t. BOOK 134:2
tart t. cathartic virtue EMER 299:18
t. who has married the Mayor BAXT 57:16
tartar find a T. PROV 610:22
T.'s lips SHAK 684:19
tarts action of two t. MACM 487:20
stole the t. NURS 550:10
Tarzan Me T. MISQ 522:2
task completed the t. TALM 754:15
long day's t. SHAK 657:13
thy worldly t. hast done SHAK 661:1
what he reads as a t. JOHN 413:7
with weary t. fordone SHAK 690:28
tasks have been my t. KOLL 443:10
tassel lure this t.-gentle SHAK 697:17
tassie fill it in a silver t. BURN 167:28
taste arbiter of t. TACI 752:13
bad t. HOPK 385:7
bad t. of the smoker ELIO 292:3
bouquet is better than the t. POTT 589:1
common sense and good t. SHAW 706:20
create the t. WORD 832:22
difference of t. in jokes ELIO 292:4
Every man to his t. PROV 599:35
forgot the t. of fears SHAK 685:21
ghastly good t. BETJ 71:10
good sense and good t. LA B 446:17
Good t. and humour MUGG 534:18
I did but t. a little honey BIBL 78:24
last t. of sweets SHAK 694:18
never t. who always drink PRIO 593:7
nobody has any t. for them VOLT 798:12
No! let me t. BROW 157:17
no t. when you married SHER 716:10
nothing for good t. TOLS 779:12
nowhere worse t. JOWE 421:13
ocean has but one t. PALI 565:15
t. and see BOOK 133:20
T. is the feminine FITZ 315:5
t. it but sparingly AUST 38:9
t. my Anno Domini FARQ 307:4
t. my meat HERB 373:1
t. or genius REYN 625:6
Things sweet to t. SHAK 694:12
undoubtedly wanted t. WALP 800:19
tasted books are to be t. BACO 44:6
so be ye have t. BIBL 110:27
tastes if it t. good, it's bad ASIM 30:19
no accounting for t. PROV 612:15
strongest t. were negative WAUG 806:8
T. differ PROV 611:43
t. greatly alter JOHN 413:23
tasting T. of Flora KEAT 429:7
Tat *T. ist alles, nichts der Ruhm* GOET 343:3
Tathagata called T. PALI 564:20
tattered t. coat upon a stick YEAT 837:2
wars have t. his ears HUGH 393:3
tatters rags and t. MOLI 525:4
taught afterward he t. CHAU 204:24
as if you t. them not POPE 585:1
Cristes loore He t. CHAU 205:1
got to be carefully t. HAMM 359:5
In them is plainest t. MILT 518:11
t. anything MOLI 525:15
t. by the enemy OVID 561:16
t. me first to beg SHAK 688:18
t. them as one having authority BIBL 94:14
t. to any purpose REYN 625:3
what we call highly t. ELIO 292:26
what we have t. her GAY 331:10
You t. me language SHAK 698:24
taunting grave, and not t. BACO 43:11
tavern hostess of the t. SHAK 667:16
in a t. drinking ANON 21:10
'So is the London T.' ANON 16:10
t. for his friends DOUG 276:19
t. in the town SONG 730:5
t. or inn JOHN 415:10
tax *Excise.* A hateful t. JOHN 409:9
I t. not you, you elements SHAK 678:22
power to t. MARS 497:19

soon be able to t. it FARA 306:14
To t. and to please BURK 162:20
taxation Inflation one form of t. FRIE 325:2
lottery is a t. FIEL 310:3
T. and representation CAMD 182:12
T. without representation OTIS 560:21
taxed world should be t. BIBL 98:19
taxes as true . . . as t. DICK 261:25
death and t. DEFO 254:15
death and t. FRAN 323:15
death and t. PROV 608:12
Death and t. and childbirth MITC 524:1
little people pay t. HELM 368:17
no new t. BUSH 171:3
overlaid with t. BACO 44:13
Sex and t. JONE 419:3
t. must fall upon agriculture GIBB 335:9
taxi If you can't leave in a t. FILM 311:13
t. throbbing waiting ELIO 296:8
taxi-cab look like a t. HUGH 392:15
taxing t. machine LOWE 477:8
Tay Bridge of the Silv'ry T. MCGO 485:7
tayl likerous t. CHAU 206:17
te *T. Deum laudamus* PRAY 592:7
tea and sometimes t. POPE 587:5
honey still for t. BROO 150:15
if this is t. PUNC 617:23
Latin word for T. BELL 64:11
Like having a cup of t. GALL 328:15
low-class t.-shops BRAM 146:17
shameless t.-drinker JOHN 409:22
slavery of the t. COBB 223:8
some sipping t. WORD 830:16
sweeteners of t. FIEL 310:4
Take some more t. CARR 189:19
T., although an Oriental CHES 210:20
t. and scandal CONG 232:9
T. and sympathy ANDE 14:12
t. for two CAES 180:14
t.'s out of the way REED 623:17
took t. and comfortable advice KEAT 431:9
We'll all have tea NURS 550:8
teabag woman is like a t. REAG 623:1
teach ability to t. AUCT 33:13
change the people who t. BYAT 173:5
Even while they t. SENE 654:18
gladly t. CHAU 204:20
no matter what you t. them JOHN 413:14
not t. his son a craft TALM 754:18
qualified to t. others CONF 231:7
t. Bloody instructions SHAK 682:9
t., convince, subdue AUBE 32:10
T. him how to live PORT 588:15
t. him rather to think SHEL 710:11
t. his senators wisdom BOOK 139:9
T. me, my God and King HERB 372:12
T. me thy way, O Lord BOOK 133:11
T. me to feel POPE 587:13
T. me to live KEN 433:3
t. taste or genius REYN 625:6
T. the free man AUDE 34:4
t. the torches SHAK 697:7
t. the young idea THOM 775:5
T. us to care ELIO 293:20
t. young babes SHAK 693:16
t. your grandmother PROV 598:38
to t. and delight SIDN 718:23
wants to t. SELL 654:2
what they t. in song SHEL 711:21
teacher closed fist of a t. PALI 564:17
Experience is best t. PROV 599:48
for the t.'s sake DEFO 255:5
for the t.'s sake FARQ 307:16
t. affects eternity ADAM 2:20
t. at a school AUST 39:5
t. is the most important GATE 331:3
t. should have maximal authority SZAS 751:23
teachers been their own t. REYN 625:3
governors, t. BOOK 130:14
rigorous t. ARNO 27:20
t. of the Art of Painting DÜRE 286:4
teaches experience t. TACI 752:18
he who cannot, t. PROV 602:24
He who cannot, t. SHAW 708:18
teachest Thou t. like a fool SHAK 656:14
teacheth t. more in one year ASCH 30:5
teaching follow mine own t. SHAK 687:7
t. nations how to live MILT 519:20
Wheel of T. PALI 565:24
teacup crack in the t. opens AUDE 33:19
teapot warming the t. MANS 494:8
tear dropped a t. upon the word STER 739:8
homage of a t. BYRO 174:3
No t.-floods DONN 274:19
shed a bitter t. CARR 190:19
shed one English t. MACA 482:24
some melodious t. MILT 512:28
t. each other's eyes WATT 805:9
T. him for his bad verses SHAK 676:15
t. is an intellectual thing BLAK 119:1
that divine t. HUGO 394:1
unanswerable t. BYRO 175:17
Wipe the t., baby dear WEST 812:21
without a t. DRYD 282:26
tears all thy t. FITZ 314:17
big t., for he wept SHEL 712:9
bitter t. to shed CORY 237:13
blood, toil, t. and sweat CHUR 215:7
brought me t. CALL 181:15
came her t. TENN 765:26
Come back in t. ROSS 634:3
crocodiles, that shed t. BACO 44:24
Drop, drop, slow t. FLET 318:13
enough of blood and t. RABI 619:14
even the altar sheds t. TALM 754:17
God will wipe away t. BIBL 87:11
heaven with their t. BLAK 121:10
Hence those t. TERE 768:1
I forbid my t. SHAK 666:15
If you have t. SHAK 676:6
iron t. down Pluto's cheek MILT 512:8
keep your t. PUDN 616:14
Like Niobe, all t. SHAK 661:26
loosed our heart in t. ARNO 26:16
mine eyes from t. BOOK 140:2
moistened it with t. KEAT 428:3
my salt t. JONS 419:16
No t. in the writer FROS 326:14
Nothing is here for t. MILT 518:25
now am full of t. YEAT 835:17
rich flames and hired t. BROW 152:19
sheddeth tender t. SPEN 733:19
shedding t. SHAK 695:15
Siren t. SHAK 705:18
Smiling through her t. HOME 382:4
sow in t. BOOK 140:20
t. I cannot hide HARB 359:14
T., idle tears TENN 765:19
t. into thy bottle BOOK 135:13
t. live in an onion SHAK 656:13
t. out the heart of it KNOW 442:9
t. shed for things VIRG 793:13
t. to pearl he turned MARL 496:14
these crocodile's t. BURT 170:20
this vale of t. PRAY 592:6
through my t. FLET 318:14
Time with a gift of t. SWIN 750:8
too deep for t. WORD 830:10
water my couch with my t. BOOK 131:24
whence no t. can win us HARD 361:19
wipe away all t. BIBL 112:12
wipe away all t. BIBL 113:8
With mine own t. SHAK 695:23
With silence and t. BYRO 179:19
tearsday moanday, t., wailsday JOYC 421:20
tease fleas that t. in the High Pyrenees BELL 64:8
t. us out of thought KEAT 428:29
teases Because he knows it t. CARR 189:15
tea tray t. in the sky CARR 189:18
t. painter BLUN 122:14
technically t. sweet OPPE 557:4
Technik *Vorsprung durch T.* ADVE 8:16
technology advanced t. is CLAR 219:9
Progress through t. ADVE 8:16
T. just a tool GATE 331:3
T. . . . the knack of so arranging FRIS 325:8
white heat of t. MISQ 522:14
tecum *Nec t. possum vivere* MART 498:4
T. habita PERS 574:6
Ted isn't it, T. LINE 469:10
teddy Like a t. bear NURS 550:14
Now T. must run KENN 434:2
T. Bears have their Picnic BRAT 147:5
tedious eloquence is t. PASC 568:19
t. and brief SHAK 690:22
t. as a twice-told tale SHAK 677:12
tedium road to t. FOWL 322:1
t. is the very basis of mourning HUGO 393:19
teeming gleaned my t. brain KEAT 430:17
teems t. with hidden meaning GILB 339:8
Tees for my lovelier T. MACA 482:23
teeth barrier of your t. HOME 382:1
cast into my t. SHAK 676:25
cast me in the t. BOOK 134:8
dig our graves with our t. SMIL 722:15
gnashing of t. BIBL 94:18
he's got iron t. GROM 354:1
is his front t. RUNY 637:13
keep their t. clean SHAK 660:4
makes my t. watter FLEM 317:13
old bitch gone in the t. POUN 589:17
shark has pretty t. BREC 147:17
skin of my t. BIBL 81:21
steal the very t. ARAB 23:10
t. are like a flock of sheep BIBL 85:14
t. are set on edge BIBL 89:29
t. are spears BOOK 135:15
t. like splinters CAUS 198:3
t. nothing on edge SHAK 668:21
those who have no t. PROV 601:18
untying with the t. BIER 114:19
teetotaller no woman should marry a t. STEV 741:29
only a beer t. SHAW 706:24
secret t. ORWE 559:4
Teflon T.-coated Presidency SCHR 649:4
tehee 'T.!' quod she CHAU 205:27
tekel mene, t., upharsin BIBL 90:4
telegram visual t. CASS 193:9
telegrams life of t. and anger FORS 320:17
Telemachus mine own T. TENN 767:11
telephones Tudor monarchy with t. BURG 162:1
telescope t. or hydrogen bomb LOVE 476:17
television daytime t. TOYN 780:7
I hate t. WELL 809:11
It's t., you see HOWE 392:3
no plain women on t. FORD 319:10
On t. I feel like MUGG 535:21
Radio and t. SARR 644:19
see bad t. for nothing GOLD 346:4
t. and radio DEV 259:8
t. as an agent EYRE 305:13
T. brought brutality MCLU 487:11
T. closer to reality PAGL 563:2
T. contracts imagination WOGA 825:1
T. has brought back murder HITC 378:2
T. has made dictatorship PERE 573:18
T. is for appearing on COWA 239:7
T. thrives on unreason DAY 253:9
T.? word is half Greek SCOT 650:5
tell closest friends won't t. you ADVE 7:18
Don't ask, don't t. NUNN 547:9
Go, t. the Spartans EPIT 302:11
I'll t. thee everything CARR 191:13
men of sense never t. SHAF 655:16
t. her she mustn't PUNC 617:12
T. it not in Gath BIBL 79:1
T. me not, Sweet LOVE 476:15
T. me the old, old story HANK 359:9
T. out my soul BIBL 98:16
t. sad stories SHAK 695:9
T. Sid ADVE 8:12
T. tale tit NURS 551:2

tell (*cont.*):
T. them I came DE L 256:16
t. them of us and say EPIT 304:14
t. the most heart-easing things KEAT 430:5
t. the towers thereof BOOK 134:26
telleth t. the number of the stars BOOK 141:24
telling I am t. you WHIS 813:16
pity beyond all t. YEAT 836:23
tale never loses in t. PROV 611:40
t. you something DUNM 285:8
Téméraire Fighting T. NEWB 541:16
temper enforce with t. GREN 352:18
including my t. NEHR 540:6
Keep me in t. SHAK 678:12
lose your t. with the Press PANK 566:11
only keep your t. STER 738:15
t. Justice with mercy MILT 517:21
truth that has lost its t. GIBR 336:14
uncertain t. AUST 38:15
temperance t. would be difficult JOHN 417:23
temperate more lovely and more t. SHAK 704:9
t. affords me none CARE 186:11
temperature acquire a t. SCHU 649:12
tempers God t. the wind STER 738:11
tempest Like summer t. TENN 765:26
rides out the t. BAUD 57:5
we the t. know DRYD 281:1
tempestas *Quo me cumque rapit t.* HORA 386:8
tempests looks on t. SHAK 705:15
nor sigh-t. move DONN 274:19
tempest-tost it shall be t. SHAK 681:12
tempête *hante la t.* BAUD 57:5
temple drove them all out of the t. BIBL 101:15
Lord's anointed t. SHAK 683:18
Nature is a t. BAUD 57:7
Open the t. gates SPEN 733:8
polished corners of the t. BOOK 141:18
t. of Delight KEAT 429:5
t. of silence MACA 482:9
t. of the Holy Ghost BIBL 106:3
train filled the t. BIBL 86:21
temples adapting Greek t. PUGI 616:21
my joyful t. bind WALL 800:6
nail into his t. BIBL 77:25
out of which they build t. KRIS 445:21
solemn t. SHAK 699:6
t. like a piece of a pomegranate BIBL 85:14
t. made with hands BIBL 104:9
t. of his gods MACA 483:5
tempora *O t., O mores* CICE 217:19
temporal pass through things t. BOOK 128:11
temporary force alone is but *t.* BURK 162:24
temps *O t.! suspend ton vol* LAMA 448:7
tempt T. me no more DAY- 253:12
T. not a desperate man SHAK 698:1
T. not the stars FORD 319:18
t. the Lord thy God BIBL 92:33
temptation endureth t. BIBL 110:11
enter not into t. BIBL 97:23
everything except t. WILD 818:8
exempt from t. LEWI 466:21
get the better of t. GRAH 347:17
last t. is the greatest treason ELIO 295:15
lead us not into t. BIBL 93:19
maximum of t. SHAW 708:19
power of t. TROL 783:8
resisting t. BECK 60:13
resisting t. KNOX 443:1
t. in the wilderness BOOK 138:6
t. to a rich and lazy nation KIPL 440:18
t. to be good BREC 147:8
under t. to it LOCK 471:20
yield to t. HOPE 383:15
temptations in spite of all t. GILB 339:1
protections against t. TWAI 786:10
t. both in wine and women KITC 441:31
through all t. BOOK 128:3
tempted one thing to be t. SHAK 686:5
your fathers t. me BOOK 138:6
tempter t. or the tempted SHAK 686:12
tempus *fugit inreparabile t.* VIRG 797:1
T. abire tibi est HORA 387:10
T. edax rerum OVID 561:18
T. erat quo prima quies VIRG 794:1
ten aren't no T. Commandments KIPL 439:14
as the strength of t. TENN 766:14
beat t. men who haven't SHAW 706:13
T. or twelve HOPK 384:1
T.-sixty-six and all that SELL 654:3
t. thousand BIBL 90:6
Your starter for t. CATC 196:33
tenantless graves stood t. SHAK 661:9
tenants T. of life's middle COWP 242:14
T. of the house ELIO 294:23
tendebantque *T. manus* VIRG 794:21
tender coy and t. to offend HERB 373:15
dark and true and t. TENN 765:22
I'll be irreproachably t. MAYA 502:14
t. for another's pain GRAY 350:17
t. is the night KEAT 429:11
t. mercies of the wicked BIBL 82:25
t. years of youth GOGO 344:1
tenderly Take her up t. HOOD 382:13
tenderness species of t. BYRO 179:24
Want of t. JOHN 414:7
tends t. and spares us LYTE 481:2
ténébreux *Je suis le t.* NERV 541:7
tenebricosum *iter t.* CATU 197:1
tenement Into a clayey t. CARE 186:8
t. or pelting farm SHAK 694:19
tennis Anyone for t. CATC 195:3
play t. with the net down FROS 326:18
stars' t.-balls WEBS 808:5
Tennyson bower we shrined to T. HARD 361:7
Lawn T. JOYC 422:11
tenor noiseless t. of their way GRAY 350:13
tent inside the t. pissing out JOHN 408:19
little t. of blue WILD 818:31
Strike the t. LAST 457:5
tenth like a t. muse ANON 16:15
submerged t. BOOT 142:18
t. Muse TROL 783:10
tents dwelling in t. BIBL 74:35
dwell in their t. BOOK 136:12
habitation among the t. of Kedar BOOK 140:10
Israel's t. do shine BLAK 120:3
murmured in their t. BOOK 139:10
stately t. of war MARL 496:20
t. have been struck SMUT 726:17
t. of Kedar BIBL 85:7
t. of ungodliness BOOK 137:13
t. their tents LONG 473:12
To your t., O Israel BIBL 79:23
ter *T. sunt conati imponere* VIRG 796:16
teres *t., atque rotundus* HORA 390:2
Terewth light of T. DICK 261:2
term sleep between term and t. SHAK 659:13
t. Invented to awe fools JONS 420:13
t. of moderation BACO 41:24
termagant o'erdoing T. SHAK 664:14
terminological t. inexactitude CHUR 214:18
terms come on perfect t. WHIT 815:17
come to t. with Him MOLI 525:18
happiest t. I have SHAK 669:18
terra *in t. pax* MISS 520:13
terrace t. walk SWIF 749:7
terrible appear most long and t. LEE 462:3
eyes became so t. BECK 60:11
isn't life a t. thing THOM 772:18
just the t. choice BROW 157:26
lend the eye a t. aspect SHAK 671:5
more t. SHAK 675:11
t. as an army BIBL 86:1
t. as hell MILT 515:22
t. beauty is born YEAT 835:19
T. is the temptation BREC 147:8
T. that old life of decency LOWE 477:20
t. to the enemy SHAK 669:27
would *not* be *t.* JOHN 413:19
terrified t. vague fingers YEAT 836:14
territorial last t. claim HITL 378:7
terror another t. to death LYND 480:20
boredom and t. WELL 809:13
From all that t. teaches CHES 210:8
new t. to death WETH 812:22
new t. to life TREE 781:6
no t., brother Toby STER 739:6
no t., Cassius, in your threats SHAK 676:23
no t. in a bang HITC 378:3
T. arises from a sense KING 437:3
t. by night BOOK 137:22
T. the human form divine BLAK 121:11
t. to the soul of Richard SHAK 696:31
t. to thyself BIBL 89:21
Thy t., O Christ, O God HOPK 385:3
victory in spite of all t. CHUR 215:9
terrorism subtle t. of words GAIT 328:3
trying to suppress t. SCHU 649:10
terrorist t. and the hijacker THAT 770:6
t. and the policeman CONR 234:21
terrorize t. a whole nation MURR 537:7
terrors little t. GAVA 331:7
new t. of Death ARBU 23:16
t. infants go through DRAB 278:13
t. of the earth SHAK 678:18
Tess ended his sport with T. HARD 361:2
test Beauty is the first t. HARD 360:7
cricket t. TEBB 757:2
No t. tube can breed love WILL 820:11
testament ministers of the new t. BIBL 107:5
purple t. SHAK 695:13
testicles requires t. VOLT 798:11
testify t. of me BIBL 101:24
testimonies Thy t., O Lord BOOK 138:3
testimony t. against slavery DOUG 277:1
t. to the whole world FOX 322:12
testing form of very virtue at the t. point LEWI 466:24
tetigisti *T. acu* PLAU 578:14
teutonophile unexaggeratedly t. LAMB 110:10
Tewkesbury Between T. and Stroudway GURN 355:4
text God takes a t. HERB 372:5
great t. in Galatians BROW 157:29
neat rivulet of t. SHER 716:9
of that t. a pulled hen CHAU 204:16
outside of the t. DERR 258:15
square of t. TENN 760:7
t. was loss CUNN 247:17
What is a t. course CROS 246:8
þaes *þ. oferēode* ANON 21:17
Thames clear T. bordered MORR 532:13
look, how T., enriched DANI 248:16
not of Gennesareth, but T. THOM 774:14
stripling T. ARNO 27:6
Sweet T., run softly SPEN 734:19
T. is between me and the Duchess WALP 800:16
T. is liquid history BURN 166:5
T., the most loved DENH 257:11
upon the banks of T. JONS 420:26
youthful T. ARNO 27:24
thank God, I t. thee BIBL 100:15
Now t. we all our God WINK 823:6
terrible thing, t. God THOM 772:18
t. heaven, fasting SHAK 659:15
T. me no thankings SHAK 697:35
t. the goodness and the grace TAYL 756:10
t. you for a Valentine LOCH 471:10
thanked When I'm not t. FIEL 310:15
thankful to be t. BOOK 141:24
thanking sigh in t. BROW 154:8
thankit let the Lord be t. BURN 167:22
thankless have a t. child SHAK 678:11
thanks deserve any t. CATU 197:13
gives you warmest t. CATU 197:8
give t. to God BIBL 109:7

give t. unto thee BOOK 129:20
give t. unto thee BOOK 141:12
give t. unto thee, O God BOOK 134:10
give t. unto the Lord BOOK 141:6
In everything give t. BIBL 109:10
return your t. BROW 158:15
T. for mercies past BUCK 159:17
T. for the memory ROBI 629:10
t. of a boy BEEC 61:8
to give t. is good SWIN 750:11
when he had given t. BOOK 129:22
thanksgiving before his presence with t. BOOK 138:5
shew the voice of t. BOOK 133:8
Tharsis Kings of T. BOOK 136:18
that man's a man for a' t. BURN 167:7
THOU ART T. UPAN 787:18
thatch round the t.-eaves run KEAT 430:8
worn the ancient t. TENN 763:19
thaw t. wind PROV 610:15
thcream I'll t. and thcream CROM 245:7
theatre As in a t. SHAK 695:27
I like the t. HART 363:6
shouting fire in a t. HOLM 381:14
t. of man's life BACO 41:16
t. of the world MARY 500:10
This House today is a t. BALD 49:11
theatres domes, t., temples WORD 827:19
theatrical t. writers SCOT 652:1
thee Dreamin' of t. WALL 799:13
save t. and me OWEN 562:2
theek t. our nest BALL 52:5
theft clever t. was praiseworthy SPEN 732:8
Property is t. PROU 593:19
t. in other poets DRYD 283:7
theist offer the t. AYER 40:6
them Lat t. say MOTT 535:19
theme Fools are my t. BYRO 177:33
it has no t. CHUR 217:2
t. For reason DONN 273:22
t. Too high doth seem GURN 355:5
themselves did not do things t. RAVE 622:8
laid violent hands upon t. BOOK 131:11
law unto t. BIBL 104:29
theologians believe the t. SALI 642:16
t. have employed ARNO 28:27
theology golden rule in t. MILT 519:14
schools of t. DIDE 267:7
theorem binomial t. GILB 339:4
Theorie *Grau ist alle T.* GOET 342:20
theories let our false t. die POPP 587:30
T. pass ROST 635:14
theorist t. could fit GAMO 329:3
theorize capital mistake to t. DOYL 278:5
theory All t., dear friend, is grey GOET 342:20
Died of a T. DAVI 252:11
life without t. DISR 270:7
sometimes t. MACA 482:17
t. against the second law EDDI 287:23
therapy T., tenth American muse BRON 149:11
there Because it's t. MALL 492:6
be t. when it happens ALLE 12:14
cry over me, T., there BOOK 136:14
I am not t. ANON 15:24
MACAVITY WASN'T T. ELIO 295:18
met a man who wasn't t. MEAR 503:3
Over t. COHA 223:22
T. but for the grace of God BRAD 146:5
thou art t. BOOK 141:11
Were you t. SONG 730:7
you were not t. HENR 370:5
thereby O! t. hangs a tail SHAK 692:18
therein all that t. is BOOK 133:2
thereof and the place t. BOOK 138:20
thermodynamics second law of t. EDDI 287:23
Thermopylae make a new T. BYRO 176:28
old man of T. LEAR 460:12
Thersites T.' body SHAK 660:29
they t. are not they WAUG 806:1
thick ask the Gods for a t. skin TROL 782:27
lay it on so t. BUTL 172:19
thcream till I'm t. CROM 245:7
t. and numberless MILT 512:4
t. on Severn HOUS 391:2
t. skin a gift ADEN 6:2
t. with corn BOOK 136:2
thickens now the plot t. BUCK 159:15
thicker History gets t. TAYL 756:5
little finger shall be t. BIBL 79:21
thicket ram caught in a t. BIBL 74:33
thief embrace the impenitent t. STEV 741:9
first cries stop t. CONG 232:20
Hang a t. when he's young PROV 601:46
he was a t. HEIN 368:8
honest t. BROW 155:9
I come as a t. BIBL 112:28
Opportunity makes a t. PROV 609:10
postern door makes a t. PROV 609:32
Set a t. to catch PROV 610:33
something from the t. SHAK 692:4
subtle t. of youth MILT 518:27
Taffy was a t. NURS 551:1
t. doth fear SHAK 673:4
t. of time YOUN 839:6
t. to business DEFO 254:12
this first grand t. MILT 516:11
thought as bad as the t. CHES 209:2
which is the t. SHAK 679:23
thieves den of t. BIBL 96:20
fell among t. BIBL 99:11
Her t. are never hung FERG 308:16
honour among t. PROV 612:11
knaves and t. SHAK 702:22
Little t. are hanged PROV 605:43
no receivers, no t. PROV 603:24
One of the t. BECK 59:23
t. break through and steal BIBL 93:20
T. respect property CHES 211:8
When t. fall out PROV 614:33
thievish Time's t. progress SHAK 705:2
thigh smote them hip and t. BIBL 78:3
thighs his t. the People RIG 627:18
Very different t. KEYE 435:1
thimbles sought it with t. CARR 191:25
thin become unnaturally t. WOLF 825:2
never be too rich or too t. WIND 823:5
pale and t. ones PLUT 579:7
t. ears devoured BIBL 75:14
t. man inside every fat man ORWE 558:9
t. one wildly signalling CONN 234:1
t. red line RUSS 640:13
T. red line of 'eroes KIPL 440:13
thine continue t. for ever BOOK 130:20
not my will, but t., be done BIBL 100:23
t. is the kingdom BIBL 93:19
thing draw the T. as he sees It KIPL 440:19
great To do that t. SHAK 657:21
ill-favoured t., sir SHAK 659:25
is it not *the t.* BYRO 180:8
one damned t. after another HUBB 392:11
one t. at once SMIL 722:18
play's the t. SHAK 664:2
Roman Conquest was a *Good T.* SELL 654:5
sort of t. they like LINC 469:3
that a t. is so BLAK 119:27
t. enskyed and sainted SHAK 686:2
t. itself and not the myth RICH 626:10
t. of beauty KEAT 426:16
t. of beauty OPEN 556:22
thingish Thing which seemed very T. MILN 510:14
things all t. through Christ BIBL 109:1
all t. to all men BIBL 106:9
confused t. with their names SART 645:6
from her loosening t. YEAT 836:14
God's sons are t. MADD 489:1
infection of t. gone LOWE 478:8
just one of those t. PORT 588:6
people don't do such t. IBSE 398:9
quick bright t. SHAK 689:6
tears shed for t. VIRG 793:13
T. ain't what they used to be PERS 574:7
T. are in the saddle EMER 299:8
t. are the sons of heaven JOHN 409:4
t. are wrought by prayer TENN 760:16
T. fall apart YEAT 837:5
t. in heaven and earth SHAK 663:4
t. that are not SHAK 676:32
t. they didn't know POUN 589:11
t. to come at large SHAK 700:9
think on these t. BIBL 108:25
Very excellent t. BOOK 137:16
think all I t. or speak WESL 811:3
attains to t. right JOHN 409:23
because I t. him so SHAK 702:24
can't make her t. PARK 567:15
comedy to those that t. WALP 801:5
don't t. I'll fall in love GERS 334:13
don't t. much of it LAST 456:4
Don't t. twice DYLA 287:5
don't t. you can't INGE 399:2
do something besides t. LOOS 475:10
easier to act than to t. AREN 24:4
fun you *t.* they had JONG 419:7
greatly t. POPE 582:18
Great minds t. alike PROV 601:36
Haply I t. on thee SHAK 704:15
hurts to t. HOUS 391:9
I can't t. for you DYLA 287:17
I t., therefore I am DESC 258:18
know what I t. WALL 799:17
might very well t. that CATC 196:30
more clearly than you t. BOHR 124:2
never expected a soldier to t. SHAW 706:27
not here to t. HERD 373:21
not so t. as you drunk SQUI 735:15
now—I t. it STEP 737:20
paint objects as I t. them PICA 576:2
people that t. SHEN 715:9
publishing faster than t. PAUL 570:6
spirit that would t. HUGO 393:21
t. alike who think at all PAIN 564:6
t. as wise men do ASCH 30:9
T. first and speak PROV 612:38
t. globally SAYI 648:5
T. like a wise man YEAT 838:3
t. like other people SHEL 710:11
t. of England SAYI 647:5
T. of your forefathers ADAM 3:16
t. only this of me BROO 150:17
t. only this of me OPEN 555:14
t. on these things BIBL 108:25
t. perhaps even less BROW 155:10
t. too little DRYD 280:8
t. what is true HUXL 397:13
t. what other people think YEAT 837:4
t. what you like TACI 752:14
t. with our wombs LUCE 478:19
t. without his hat BECK 59:26
t. yourself above BAGE 47:23
time to t. before I speak DARW 251:5
we've got to t. RUTH 640:17
Whatever you t. of your friend MIDR 507:12
what I must do then, t. now DONN 273:5
What the Bandar-log t. KIPL 441:2
when I t., I must speak SHAK 659:10
whether machines t. SKIN 721:16
who never t. PRIO 593:7
You know more than you t. SPOC 735:1
Young folks t. old folks PROV 616:1
young t. too little WALP 800:24
thinker murder the t. WESK 810:19
thinking ain't t. about it TROL 782:17
All t. for themselves GILB 337:16
can't prevent myself from t. SART 645:11
Every t. man ADAM 2:6
gentleman's way of t. ANON 21:10
he is a t. reed PASC 568:18
in t. to be spent VAUX 791:1
lateral t. DE B 254:6
modes of t. are different JOHN 416:25
much drinking, little t. SWIF 748:7
not t. accurately HOLM 381:15

thinking (*cont.*):
our modes of t. EINS 290:16
own way of t. NAPO 538:11
Plain living and high t. WORD 830:13
power of positive t. PEAL 571:6
saves original t. SAYE 646:6
song for t. hearts WORD 828:19
t. for myself GILB 338:28
T. is to me the greatest VANB 789:8
t. makes it so SHAK 663:16
t. man's crumpet MUIR 535:24
t. of the old 'un DICK 261:14
t. what nobody has thought SZEN 752:5
thinks as unhappy as one t. LA R 453:22
drinks beer, t. beer PROV 602:12
he t. no ill SHAK 704:22
He t. too much SHAK 674:16
If any man t. he slays UPAN 787:21
I sits and t. PUNC 617:24
man t. he slays BHAG 72:15
not say what one t. EURI 305:3
t. he knows everything SHAW 707:27
what she t. ROBI 629:11
third passing of the t. floor JERO 406:19
second and a t. time TALM 754:28
t. day he rose again BOOK 126:10
t. of my life ALLE 12:18
T. time lucky PROV 612:39
t. time pays for all PROV 612:40
t. who walks always ELIO 296:13
third-rate t. foreign conductors BEEC 61:7
thirst I t. BIBL 102:36
man can raise a t. KIPL 439:14
neither t. any more BIBL 112:11
offer you hunger, t. GARI 329:17
provocation of t. SWIF 748:2
shall never t. BIBL 101:28
soul is a t. for God BOOK 134:5
t. after righteousness BIBL 93:3
T. of wealth WINC 822:19
thirsteth every one that t. BIBL 88:20
thirsty cold waters to a t. soul BIBL 83:22
Drinking when we are not t. BEAU 58:10
t. and ye gave me drink BIBL 97:12
which I was t. BOOK 136:11
thirteen clocks were striking t. ORWE 558:19
striking t. OPEN 555:24
T. years of Tory misrule POLI 581:30
thirtieth t. year to heaven THOM 772:10
thirty At t. a man suspects YOUN 839:7
at t., the wit FRAN 323:11
brain is t. years old EISE 291:12
I am past t. ARNO 28:26
I shall soon be t. BRON 149:19
remained t.-five for years WILD 817:24
T. days hath SAYI 648:6
t. pieces of silver BEVA 71:18
t. pieces of silver BIBL 97:16
this T. happy breed of men SHAK 694:19
T. was a man SHAK 677:4
thistles figs of t. BIBL 94:10
Thomas On Saint T. the Divine PROV 608:28
ta'en true T. BALL 51:20
T., because thou hast seen BIBL 103:6
thorn creep under the t. PROV 596:16
Instead of the t. BIBL 88:23
left the t. wi' me BURN 166:17
Oak, and Ash, and T. KIPL 440:14
one t. out of many HORA 387:10
rose without the t. HERR 374:20
snail's on the t. BROW 157:12
t. in Charles's side FOX 322:3
t. in the flesh BIBL 107:16
t. removed by a thorn TANT 754:29
without t. the rose MILT 516:13
thorns crackling of t. BIBL 84:13
crown of t. BEVA 71:18
crown of t. BRYA 159:3
grapes of t. BIBL 94:10
some fell among t. BIBL 95:20
t. shall come up BIBL 87:20
upon the t. of life SHEL 712:16
thoroughfare t. for all thoughts KEAT 431:19
thou t. art not he or she WAUG 806:1
T. ART THAT UPAN 787:18
T. art the man BIBL 79:6
t. shalt have no other gods BIBL 76:8
T. swell! Thou witty HART 363:8
Through the T. a person becomes I BUBE 159:7
thought beautiful clean t. LAWR 458:6
Beyond the last t. STEV 739:26
bound of human t. TENN 767:10
by taking t. BIBL 93:24
carry all that t. HUNT 395:18
dress of t. JOHN 410:1
dress of t. POPE 584:19
enemy of t. CONR 234:18
father, Harry, to that t. SHAK 670:16
forced into a state of t. GALS 328:18
for want of t. DRYD 281:9
garment of t. CARL 188:12
gave that t. relief WORD 829:16
Grave without t. CHUR 214:3
harbours virtuous t. SPEN 733:18
he t. I slept PATM 569:19
inextinguishable t. SHEL 714:22
In the light of t. SHEL 714:6
life-blood of t. FLAU 316:16
Ministers of t. SHEL 710:16
modes of t. MILL 507:23
mystery beyond t. UPAN 788:7
My t. is *me* SART 645:11
never t. of thinking GILB 338:28
no t. for the morrow BIBL 93:27
oft was t. POPE 584:18
one that was never t. of BIBL 91:25
One t. more steady FORD 320:5
pale cast of t. SHAK 664:4
Perish the t. CIBB 217:6
put t. in a concentration camp ROOS 633:1
rear the tender t. THOM 775:5
Religion the frozen t. of men KRIS 445:21
right t. PALI 565:13
Roman t. hath struck him SHAK 656:10
seem a moment's t. YEAT 835:2
single grateful t. LESS 465:16
speech created t. SHEL 713:12
strange seas of t. WORD 831:3
sudden t. BROW 155:23
sweet silent t. SHAK 704:16
tease us out of t. KEAT 428:29
t. and resolution TROL 783:8
T. can with difficulty visit SHEL 715:4
t. charged with emotion GIDE 336:18
T. does not crush ROET 631:5
t.-executing fires SHAK 678:21
t. in cold storage SAMU 643:12
T. is free PROV 612:44
T. is free SHAK 699:3
T. is the child of Action DISR 270:32
t. is the front SAUS 646:3
t. is viscous ADAM 3:2
T. leapt out to wed TENN 761:2
T. shall be the harder ANON 21:15
t. so once; but now I know it EPIT 303:12
t.'s the slave of life SHAK 669:12
thought the t. BALL 50:18
t., word, and deed MISS 520:11
To a green t. MARV 498:16
very t. of Thee CASW 194:1
want of t. HOOD 382:22
what he t., he uttered HEMI 369:8
where a t. might grow MAHO 490:20
while, celestial t. VAUG 790:7
wish is father to the t. PROV 615:12
working-house of t. SHAK 672:1
years of human t. too late LA B 446:18
thoughtcrime t. literally impossible ORWE 558:23
thoughts all evil t. BOOK 128:4
As man's own t. WEBS 808:17
bring my t. to an end SMIT 724:25
Cleanse the t. of our hearts BOOK 129:4
conceal their t. VOLT 797:10
examine my t. BOOK 141:14
Good t. CAMP 183:24
Gored mine own t. SHAK 705:13
have bloody t. SHAK 699:7
Hunter's waking t. AUDE 33:24
in a shroud Of t. BYRO 174:23
in the t. of children LOCK 471:13
kills the t. SMIT 724:19
long, long t. LONG 473:23
misleading t. SPEN 732:6
my bloody t. SHAK 693:3
my t. are not your thoughts BIBL 88:22
ought to control our t. DARW 250:14
pansies, that's for t. SHAK 666:7
present t. build our life PALI 565:16
rather than of t. KEAT 430:22
Second t. are best PROV 610:24
secret t. ALBE 10:7
Staled are my t. DYER 286:12
thoroughfare for all t. KEAT 431:19
t. and manners JOHN 410:25
t. are legible in the eye ROYD 637:1
T., boundless, deep BYRO 177:31
t. of a prisoner SOLZ 727:13
t. of men are widened TENN 763:5
t. of other men COWP 242:6
t. that arise in me TENN 757:11
T., that breathe GRAY 351:3
T. that do often lie WORD 830:10
t. which I am alleged CHAR 204:1
t. within the breasts KORA 445:4
Words without t. SHAK 665:10
your love but not your t. GIBR 336:11
thousand better than a t. BOOK 137:13
blotted a t. JONS 421:2
cattle upon a t. hills BOOK 135:2
Death has a t. doors MASS 501:6
Empire lasts for a t. years CHUR 215:11
first t. days KENN 433:13
Give me a t. kisses CATU 197:3
had five t. a year THAC 769:12
night has a t. eyes BOUR 145:4
Night hath a t. eyes LYLY 480:17
not in a t. years SMIT 724:7
possessing ten t. eyes ZORO 841:4
ten t. BIBL 90:6
ten t. things LAO 451:15
t. ages in Thy sight WATT 805:19
t. doors open on to it SENE 654:20
t. shall fall BOOK 137:22
t. thousand slimy things COLE 226:18
t. tongues to sing WESL 810:24
t. years in thy sight BOOK 137:18
t. years of history GAIT 328:2
thousands limp father of t. JOYC 422:13
t. equally were meant SWIF 749:25
t. of gold and silver BOOK 140:8
thraldom single t. BACO 45:12
thrall Thee hath in t. KEAT 428:12
thread crimson t. of kinship PARK 567:20
line of scarlet t. BIBL 77:18
tied, With a silken t. KEAT 427:31
with a twined t. BURT 170:19
threadbare t., so worm-eaten FLAU 316:19
threads hundreds of tiny t. SIGN 719:5
threatened t., a lion CHAP 202:12
t. its life CARR 191:25
t. men live long PROV 612:45
threats no terror, Cassius, in your t. SHAK 676:23
something of t. KORA 444:21
t. unexecuted JOHN 411:5
three at t. years old LEON 464:18
confessing the T. PATR 570:2
divided into t. parts CAES 180:15
divided into t. parts OPEN 555:12
give him t. sides MONT 528:8
grant but t. BYRO 176:28
strike out t. BOIL 124:7
tell you t. times CARR 191:19
than T. in One DRYD 281:18

Though he was only t. MILN 510:16
T. acres and a cow POLI 582:1
T. bags full NURS 547:12
T. blind mice NURS 551:10
t. corners of the world SHAK 677:21
t. events in his life LA B 446:16
t. for a wedding PROV 608:37
t.-fourths of our life ARNO 29:2
t. gentlemen at once SHER 716:6
T. hours a day TROL 781:20
t. hundred pounds SHAK 688:35
T. in One ALEX 11:11
t. is a houseful SAYI 647:4
t. is company WILD 817:14
T. may keep a secret PROV 612:46
t. merry boys are we FLET 318:3
t. o'clock in the morning FITZ 315:14
t.-o-clock in the morning THOR 776:9
t. of us in this marriage DIAN 260:5
t.-pipe problem DOYL 277:11
t. ravens BALL 52:3
T. whole days together SUCK 745:10
T. wise men of Gotham NURS 551:12
two or t. are gathered BOOK 126:18
When shall we t. meet SHAK 681:6
where two or t. BIBL 96:10
threefold t. cord BIBL 84:10
way of superior man is t. CONF 231:23
threescore t. years and ten BOOK 137:19
threshold goes over the t. FULL 327:8
t. of the new WALL 800:5
threw t. him to a scaffold FANS 306:9
thrice deny me t. BIBL 97:19
T. is he armed SHAK 672:17
thrift T. is a great revenue PROV 612:49
Thrift, t., Horatio SHAK 662:1
thriftily men who left them t. KIPL 439:15
thriftless t. and hopeless DAVI 252:19
thrills t. the ear AUDE 34:17
thrive Bold knaves t. DRYD 281:8
He that would t. CLAR 219:16
Ill gotten goods never t. PROV 603:44
t. must first ask his wife PROV 602:19
throat 'Amen' Stuck in my t. SHAK 683:7
cut his t. before SWIF 749:27
fog in my t. BROW 157:16
have my t. cut EDGE 288:19
her little t. around BROW 157:15
if your t. 'tis hard to slit KING 437:16
in the city's t. LOWE 477:22
murder by the t. LLOY 471:5
rustle in your dying t. FILM 312:14
scuttled ship or cut a t. BYRO 176:23
So he has cut his t. BYRO 178:12
taking life by the t. FROS 326:16
unlocked her silent t. GIBB 336:4
your sweet dividing t. CARE 186:14
thrombosis like a t. DEAN 253:19
t. or neurosis DRAB 278:16
throne beats upon a t. TENN 759:11
behind the t. PITT 576:23
Bust outlasts the t. DOBS 271:14
fell before the t. BIBL 112:8
God's t. BIBL 93:11
High on a t. MILT 515:7
his the t. DIX 271:12
I saw a great white t. BIBL 113:5
like a burnished t. ELIO 296:2
like a burnished t. SHAK 656:23
living t. GRAY 351:2
Lord sitting upon a t. BIBL 86:21
One Land, one T. KIPL 440:15
rainbow round about the t. BIBL 111:30
round about the t. BIBL 111:31
royal t. of kings SHAK 694:19
shadow of thy T. WATT 805:19
stood before the t. BIBL 112:7
that sitteth upon the t. BIBL 112:6
t. he sits on SHAK 671:20
t. of bayonets INGE 399:9
t. of bayonets YELT 838:4
t. of Denmark SHAK 661:15
t. of the heavenly grace BOOK 125:14
T. sent word to a Throne KIPL 439:19
t. was like the fiery flame BIBL 90:6
t. *we* honour SHER 715:22
through slaughter to a t. GRAY 350:12
to a scaffold from a t. FANS 306:9
up to the T. KIPL 439:10
vacancy of the t. GIBB 335:5
thrones Not t. and crowns, but men ELLI 298:13
T., dominations MILT 517:1
t., or dominions BIBL 109:2
throng Leaving the tumultuous t. WORD 828:21
through let them go t. BOOK 137:5
live t. someone else FRIE 324:23
one who has gone t. it VIRG 795:11
read books *t.* JOHN 414:21
t. you but not from you GIBR 336:11
throw *can* t. it away TAWN 756:1
sister t. up a lot WALK 799:5
t. away SHAK 681:23
T. dirt enough PROV 612:50
t. out your dirty water PROV 598:39
who t. themselves away MENG 504:21
thrown All *this* t. away MARY 500:8
t. out, as good for nothing JOHN 412:3
thrush aged t. HARD 361:11
That's the wise t. BROW 156:3
t. replies SPEN 733:7
thrust guardsman's cut and t. HUXL 397:12
Thule *Ultima T.* VIRG 796:14
thumb puts his t. in the scale LAWR 458:2
t. each other's books RUSK 638:18
thumbs both his t. are off HOFF 380:4
By the pricking of my t. SHAK 684:20
Thummim Urim and the T. BIBL 76:15
thumps t. upon your back COWP 240:5
thunder as the voice of a great t. BIBL 112:23
dawn comes up like t. KIPL 439:13
dread rattling t. SHAK 699:9
falling houses t. JOHN 411:9
Glorious the t.'s roar SMAR 722:13
steal my t. DENN 258:3
such sweet t. SHAK 690:15
surge and t. LANG 450:11
t. for reform NEWS 544:15
T. is the voice of God MATH 501:11
T. like a mighty flood DIX 271:12
t. of the captains BIBL 81:37
voice like t. DAVI 252:17
thunderbolt like a t. he falls TENN 758:17
with a t. VIRG 796:16
thunderbolts Harmless t. PLIN 578:16
oak-cleaving t. SHAK 678:21
thunders t. from her native oak CAMP 183:19
Thursday T.'s child NURS 549:14
thus T. have I had thee SHAK 705:5
thusness reason of this t. WARD 803:9
thyme whereon the wild t. blows SHAK 689:25
wild t. and the gadding vine MILT 513:1
thyself beside t. BIBL 104:20
Tiber children to the T. MACA 483:13
pouring into the T. JUVE 424:9
River T. foaming POWE 590:15
T.! father Tiber MACA 483:10
T. foaming with much blood VIRG 794:16
Tiberius Coin, T. DOBS 271:14
Had T. been a cat ARNO 26:22
ticket return Him the t. DOST 275:18
She's got a t. to ride LENN 464:2
take a t. at Victoria BEVI 72:10
t. for the peepshow MACN 488:7
tickle if you t. us SHAK 687:30
T. and entertain us COWP 241:12
t. her with a hoe JERR 407:5
t. your catastrophe SHAK 669:29
tickled t. to death to go WEST 812:21
t. with a straw POPE 585:24
tickles t. this age ANON 16:16
tickling only a scornful t. SIDN 718:27
tiddle t.-taddle nor pibble-pabble SHAK 671:13
tide a going out with the t. DICK 262:4
But came the t. SPEN 733:4
call of the running t. MASE 500:17
filthy modern t. YEAT 837:14
full t. of human existence JOHN 414:27
Not this t. KIPL 439:17
rising t. lifts all boats PROV 610:12
tether time or t. BURN 168:14
t. in the affairs SHAK 676:28
t. in the affairs of women BYRO 177:11
Time and t. wait PROV 612:51
Treaty like an incoming t. DENN 257:16
Veer in the t. SWIN 751:17
view the lazy t. CRAB 242:24
With his full t. BEST 70:2
tides drew these t. of men LAWR 458:26
Push in their t. THOM 772:9
salt t. seawards flow ARNO 26:11
tidings bringeth good t. BIBL 88:12
good t. of great joy BIBL 98:21
who is truer in t. KORA 444:12
tidy Keep Britain t. OFFI 554:8
tie not fit to t. his brogues SCOT 652:14
tied t. and bound BOOK 127:15
t. to the soil HOME 382:11
tier t. upon tier BOCC 123:6
ties all the t. of humanity WESL 811:13
string that t. them MONT 528:5
tiger action of the t. SHAK 671:5
atom bomb is a paper t. MAO 495:3
egre as is a t. CHAU 205:9
Hyrcan t. SHAK 684:12
On a t. skin ANON 19:18
one poor t. PUNC 617:13
orang-outang or the t. BURK 165:3
O t.'s heart SHAK 672:26
rides a t. PROV 602:32
smile on the face of the t. ANON 18:10
t. in your tank ADVE 8:7
t.-moth's deep-damasked KEAT 427:9
t.'s heart wrapped GREE 352:5
T., Tyger BLAK 121:8
T. well repay BELL 63:4
two days like a t. TIPU 777:15
tigers tamed and shabby t. HODG 379:13
There *were* no t. ELIO 293:22
t. of wrath BLAK 119:21
t. which they dare not dismount CHUR 215:4
Tighe young Hamilton T. BARH 54:10
tight t. gag of place HEAN 366:19
t. little Island DIBD 260:15
tights played it in t. BEER 61:17
tile not red brick but white t. OSBO 560:5
tiles t. on the roofs LUTH 479:14
till Says Tweed to T. ANON 18:15
tilt ran at t. in France MARL 496:10
timber crooked t. of humanity KANT 425:19
Like seasoned t. HERB 373:18
navy nothing but rotten t. BURK 163:7
Timbuctoo plains of T. WILB 817:1
time abbreviation of t. GIBB 336:3
abysm of t. SHAK 698:19
act of t. BACO 43:22
Aghast the voice of T. DYER 287:1
All of the olden t. SONG 729:14
already t. to depart SOCR 727:2
annihilate but space and t. POPE 586:23
As t. goes by HUPF 396:10
bank and shoal of t. SHAK 682:8
beginning of t. USSH 788:20
being superior to t. JOHN 410:25
bid t. return SHAK 695:6
births of t. BACO 43:13
born out of due t. BIBL 106:19
bourne of t. and place TENN 758:13
but for all t. JONS 420:25
Cathedral t. ANON 15:16
child of T. HALL 358:6
chronicle of wasted t. SHAK 705:9
chronicles of the t. SHAK 663:24

time (*cont.*):
conjecture of a t. SHAK 671:8
Cormorant devouring T. SHAK 680:17
dance to the music of t. POWE 590:9
devote more t. FOWL 322:2
Ere t. and place were ROCH 630:21
Even such is T. RALE 621:4
experienced rebel, T. FLAT 316:6
find something to do with the t. ROGE 632:2
Fleet the t. carelessly SHAK 658:7
Fly envious T. MILT 514:3
for a moment of t. LAST 455:2
forefinger of all T. TENN 765:12
foremost files of t. TENN 763:8
good t. was had by all SMIT 724:18
half as old as T. BURG 162:4
half as old as T. ROGE 631:14
Healing is a matter of t. HIPP 377:17
How t. is slipping FITZ 314:14
Hurry up please it's t. ELIO 296:6
idea whose t. has come ANON 19:3
I forget all t. MILT 516:21
if you could kill t. THOR 776:3
improve the nick of t. THOR 776:5
instant of t. AURE 37:5
in the t. of trouble BOOK 134:3
into the seeds of t. SHAK 681:16
isn't this t. of year GOGA 343:20
I T.! arrest your flight LAMA 448:7
It saves t. CARR 190:14
Keeping t., time, time POE 579:12
last my t. CARL 187:6
leave exactly on t. MUSS 537:14
long t. with you BIBL 102:19
loved the t. too well CLAR 218:7
Love's not T.'s fool SHAK 705:16
may be some t. LAST 456:1
money was not t. MERR 505:26
mus'd on wasted t. BURN 169:8
my world as in my t. CHAU 206:18
night of t. BROW 153:9
no enemy but t. YEAT 836:7
no note of T. YOUN 839:3
No t. like the present MANL 493:17
No t. like the present PROV 608:8
now doth t. waste me SHAK 696:5
now is the accepted t. BIBL 107:8
O aching t. KEAT 427:26
old common arbitrator, T. SHAK 700:22
Old T. the clock-setter SHAK 677:9
Once upon a t. OPEN 556:8
on the sands of t. LONG 474:6
O t. too swift PEEL 572:1
passed the t. BECK 59:28
peace for our t. CHAM 200:18
peace in our t. BOOK 126:11
productions of t. BLAK 119:16
puzzles me more than t. LAMB 449:1
rags of t. DONN 274:15
ravages of t. HORA 388:19
recorded t. SHAK 685:22
Redeeming the t. BIBL 108:8
ringing grooves of t. TENN 763:9
save t. BACO 42:28
sent before my t. SHAK 696:9
she's on t. AUDE 34:12
shipwreck of t. BACO 41:10
shook hands with t. FORD 320:1
Short T. and Little Skill HARI 362:7
silent touches of t. BURK 165:13
speech is shallow as T. CARL 187:12
spend more t. with family THAT 770:10
stitch in t. saves PROV 611:23
strain, T.'s eunuch HOPK 384:24
Sun-flower! weary of t. BLAK 120:22
talk of killing t. BOUC 144:24
Tell t. it metes but motion RALE 620:13
tether t. or tide BURN 168:14
That t. of year SHAK 704:29
thief of t. PROV 609:43
thief of t. YOUN 839:6
This day T. winds BURN 168:10
T., a maniac scattering dust TENN 761:8
t. and place for PROV 612:10
t. and season AGES 8:23
T. and the hour SHAK 681:22
t. and the place BROW 157:1
t. and the present moment MANN 494:3
T. and tide wait PROV 612:51
t. and times are done YEAT 837:12
T. an endless song YEAT 836:13
t. by heart-throbs BAIL 48:6
t. cracks into furious flower BROO 151:7
t. creeps along JAGO 401:10
T. did beckon HERB 372:21
T. doth transfix SHAK 704:24
t. enough to sleep HOUS 390:16
T. flies PROV 612:52
T. for a little something MILN 511:4
t. for everything PROV 612:6
t. for such a word SHAK 685:22
t. for you to go HORA 387:10
t. has been properly spent TAYL 756:14
t. has come CARR 190:20
T. has no divisions MANN 494:2
T. has shaken me WESL 811:21
T. has three dimensions HOPK 385:5
T. has too much credit COMP 230:11
T. has transfigured them LARK 452:13
T. hath, my lord, a wallet SHAK 700:14
T. held me green THOM 772:4
T. in hours, days, years VAUG 790:17
T. is a great healer PROV 613:1
T. is a violent torrent AURE 37:1
t. is fleeing HORA 387:22
T. is fleeting LONG 474:4
t. is flying VIRG 797:1
T. is like a fashionable host SHAK 700:16
t. is money FRAN 323:8
t. is money HUGO 393:20
T. is money PROV 613:2
T. is on our side GLAD 340:16
T. is our tedious song MILT 514:1
t. is out of joint SHAK 663:7
t. is running out KOES 443:4
t. is setting with me BURN 168:4
T. is that wherein HIPP 377:16
t. is the greatest innovator BACO 43:14
T. is the great physician DISR 270:15
T. is the measure AUCT 33:15
t. is the medium MANN 494:6
T. is too slow VAN 789:15
T. like a last oozing BECK 60:6
T., like an ever-rolling stream WATT 805:19
T. makes these decay CARE 186:5
T., not Corydon ARNO 27:28
t. of asking BOOK 130:21
t. of our tribulation BOOK 127:8
T., Place DRYD 283:4
T. present and time past ELIO 294:1
t. remembered SWIN 750:6
t. runs MARL 496:7
t.'s arrow EDDI 287:21
t.'s deformity JONS 419:21
T.'s devouring hand BRAM 146:18
t.'s eternal motion FORD 320:5
T.'s fell hand SHAK 704:25
T.'s glory is to calm SHAK 704:2
T. shall throw a dart EPIT 304:9
T.'s iron feet MONT 528:16
T.'s noblest offspring BERK 68:4
T. spent on any item PARK 567:23
T. stays, *we* go DOBS 271:17
T.'s thievish progress SHAK 705:2
T.'s wheel runs back or stops BROW 157:20
T.'s wingèd chariot MARV 499:2
t. that shall surely be AING 9:3
T. that's lost BUCK 159:17
t., that takes survey SHAK 669:12
T., the avenger BYRO 175:1
T. the devourer OVID 561:18
t. the longest distance WILL 820:17
T. the subtle thief MILT 518:27
t. to be in earnest JOHN 409:21
t. to discover time GUIB 354:16
t. to every purpose BIBL 84:7
t. to read play-bills BURN 165:27
t. to think before I speak DARW 251:5
t. to win this game DRAK 278:20
T. travels in divers paces SHAK 659:13
T. was away and somewhere else MACN 488:12
t. was out of joint STRA 744:7
T. we may comprehend BROW 153:17
T. which destroys all things BHAG 73:2
t., which is the author BACO 41:7
t. will come DISR 268:6
t. will doubt of Rome BYRO 177:6
T. will run back MILT 513:24
T. will tell PROV 613:3
T. with a gift of tears SWIN 750:8
T. works wonders PROV 613:4
t. ylost CHAU 207:15
T., you old gipsy man HODG 379:14
T., you thief HUNT 395:15
to fill the t. available PARK 567:22
To it comes T. BARN 55:10
took t. to consider ASTE 31:17
to sell t. TAWN 755:16
to the church on t. LERN 465:2
trencher-friends, t.'s flies SHAK 699:18
triumphed over t. RALE 621:5
uncertain balance of proud t. GREE 352:2
unconscionable t. dying CHAR 203:15
unthinking t. DRYD 282:16
use your t. HERR 375:3
very good t. it was OPEN 556:9
waste of t. and effort VEBL 791:3
ways By which T. kills us SITW 721:7
When t. is broke SHAK 696:4
whips and scorns of t. SHAK 664:4
whirligig of t. SHAK 702:20
with his own t. AUST 39:1
womb of t. HEIN 368:10
world enough, and t. MARV 498:23
timely t. compliance FIEL 309:18
t. utterance WORD 829:16
timeo *t. Danaos et dona ferentes* VIRG 793:18
times bad t. just around COWA 238:20
best of t. OPEN 555:28
blissful old t. BLAM 121:15
coldness of the t. TENN 761:29
five t. did I say WORD 827:16
It was the best of t. DICK 265:21
my dear t.' waste SHAK 704:16
nature of the t. deceased SHAK 670:4
Oh, the t. CICE 217:19
one year's experience 30 t. CARR 189:6
Other t., other manners PROV 609:12
possibility of good t. BRAN 147:1
praiser of past t. HORA 386:2
signs of the t. BIBL 96:3
t. begin to wax old BIBL 91:3
T. change PROV 613:5
T. go by turns SOUT 731:13
T. has made many ministries BAGE 46:10
t. in which a genius ADAM 2:1
t. past HERR 374:19
t. that try men's souls PAIN 563:16
t. they are a-changin' DYLA 287:15
t. will not mend PARK 567:18
Top people take *The T.* ADVE 8:15
timet flagitium t. HORA 389:10
timetables by railway t. TAYL 756:6
timing t. of your death TACI 752:11
timor *T. mortis conturbat me* DUNB 285:4
Timothy T. has passed EPIT 304:7
T. Winters comes to school CAUS 198:3
tin cat on a hot t. roof WILL 820:15
cheap t. trays MASE 500:14
corrugated t. roof BEEC 61:3
tincture Actions receive their t. DEFO 255:6
t. in the blood DEFO 255:8
ting bells of Hell go t.-a-ling MILI 508:13
tingle ears shall t. BIBL 78:16
tingling It's t. fresh ADVE 7:35

tinker don't matter a t.'s cuss SHIN 717:4
T., Tailor NURS 551:13
to t. with his car MACN 488:15
tinkering rule of intelligent t. EHRL 290:3
tinkers no work for t.' hands PROV 603:16
tinklings t. lull the distant folds GRAY 350:6
tinned smoked salmon and t. WILS 822:2
t. sauce over BINC 115:5
tintinnabulation To the t. POE 579:12
tiny My t. watching eye DE L 256:21
Your t. hand is frozen GIAC 335:3
tip depends on the t. FILM 312:12
Within the nether t. COLE 226:15
Tippecanoe soldier of T. POLI 581:17
T. and Tyler, too POLI 582:2
Tipperary It's in T. TROL 782:12
long way to T. JUDG 423:1
notorious county of T. KOHL 443:8
tipple Fishes, that t. LOVE 476:13
tippled Have ye t. drink KEAT 428:20
tiptoe Dance t., bull BUNT 160:12
jocund day Stands t. SHAK 697:33
stand a t. SHAK 671:23
sweet peas, on t. KEAT 428:6
tired Give me your t., your poor LAZA 459:12
He was so t. ROLF 632:5
I'm t. LAST 456:6
Thou art t. ARNO 26:14
t. her head BIBL 80:24
t. of Bath AUST 38:3
t. of being a woman SEXT 655:5
t. of London JOHN 415:24
t. of Love BELL 63:16
t. of the world WALP 800:20
t. the sun with talking CORY 237:13
woman who always was t. EPIT 302:15
Tiresias T., old man with wrinkled dugs ELIO 296:9
tiresome except the t. VOLT 797:15
tiring T. thy wits DANI 249:2
Wooing, so t. MITF 524:8
tirra T. lirra TENN 762:18
tissue beautiful feminine t. HARD 360:19
Titan like thy glory, T. SHEL 713:16
titanic furniture on the deck of the T. MORT 533:18
inevitable the T. HAGU 356:6
T. sails at dawn DYLA 287:4
t. wars had groined OWEN 562:11
Tite *O T. tute Tati* ENNI 300:14
tithes t. of mint and cumin BIBL 96:26
Titian at heart about T. RUSK 638:28
title farcèd t. SHAK 671:20
feel his t. Hang loose SHAK 685:14
gained no t. POPE 584:6
needed no royal t. SPEN 732:12
right, t., and possession BOOK 142:14
t. from a better man I stole STEV 743:2
whatever t. suit thee BURN 166:6
titles rich for t. PEAR 571:10
their t. take CHAN 201:11
T. are but nick-namess PAIN 563:22
T. are shadows DEFO 255:16
T. are tinsel SHEL 714:19
T. distinguish the mediocre SHAW 708:20
t. thou hast given away SHAK 678:8
tittle t. tattle. prittle prattle BURN 166:3
titwillow Willow, t. GILB 338:15
Tityre *T., tu patulae recubans* VIRG 795:13
toad Give me your arm, old t. LARK 453:7
let the t. work LARK 453:6
like the t., ugly SHAK 658:14
not so old as the t. THOM 773:10
rather be a t. SHAK 692:26
rose to a pitch-black t. YESE 838:7
squat like a t. MILT 516:27
t. beneath the harrow KIPL 440:1
toads imaginary gardens with real t. MOOR 529:18
inconstant t. MONT 526:20
toast Let the t. pass SHER 716:14
My t. would be ADAM 3:17
never had a piece of t. PAYN 570:12
t. that pleased the most DIBD 260:13
toasted cheese—t., mostly STEV 741:21
his enemies, 'T.-cheese' CARR 191:21
tobacco divine t. were SPEN 734:3
For thy sake, T. LAMB 448:18
leave off t. LAMB 449:2
lives without t. MOLI 525:2
that tawney weed t. JONS 419:13
tobacconist lungs of the t. JONS 419:12
tocsin t. of the soul BYRO 177:9
today get where I am t. without CATC 195:24
if T. be sweet FITZ 314:14
I have lived t. DRYD 282:32
let us do something t. COLL 228:10
live t. MART 497:22
never jam t. CARR 190:23
standing here t. JOHN 408:12
t. I am fifty-five REED 623:12
T. if ye will hear BOOK 138:6
T. is the last day YELT 838:6
t. I suffer LESS 465:15
T. shalt thou be with me BIBL 100:28
t. the struggle AUDE 35:7
T. we have naming of parts REED 623:13
T. you; tomorrow me PROV 613:7
to-morrow as t. SHAK 702:31
we gave our t. EPIT 304:14
What Manchester says t. PROV 614:4
what you can do t. PROV 607:35
will not hang myself t. CHES 209:29
toe big t. ends up making a hole EINS 291:7
clerical, printless t. BROO 150:12
light fantastic t. MILT 512:15
t. of the peasant SHAK 666:22
toes Pobble who has no t. LEAR 460:20
toff Saunter along like a t. HARG 362:5
together all that believed were t. BIBL 103:17
keep them t. JOHN 414:12
lived comfortably so long t. GAY 331:11
persons acting t. ARAB 23:8
togetherness spaces in your t. GIBR 336:12
toil bleared, smeared with t. HOPK 384:5
blood, t., tears and sweat CHUR 215:7
day in t. QUAR 618:16
Death and T. VIRG 794:20
Double, double t. and trouble SHAK 684:17
Horny-handed sons of t. SALI 643:1
horny hands of t. LOWE 477:14
mock their useful t. GRAY 350:9
slumber is more sweet than t. TENN 763:15
strong t. of grace SHAK 658:5
they t. not BIBL 93:25
they waste their t. CLOS 222:8
t. after virtue LAMB 449:8
t. and not to seek for rest IGNA 398:17
T., envy, want JOHN 411:14
t. in other men's extremes KYD 446:8
unrequited t. LINC 468:17
with t. of breath COLE 225:10
toiled Master, we have t. BIBL 99:1
toiling t. upward in the night LONG 473:21
toils poorly recompense their t. COLL 228:7
token t. of a covenant BIBL 74:22
tokens Words are the t. BACO 41:14
Tolbooth-gate resistance of the T. SCOT 651:25
told half was not t. me BIBL 79:18
I t. you so EPIT 302:9
not what we were formerly t. BLUN 122:12
our fathers have t. us BOOK 134:12
phrase, 'I t. you so.' BYRO 177:25
plato t. him: he couldn't CUMM 247:8
t. my wrath BLAK 121:5
t. you from the beginning BIBL 88:4
Toledo T. trusty BUTL 172:2
tolerable Life would be t. LEWI 467:3
tolerance such a thing as t. WILS 822:16
T. the essential PHIL 575:6
tolerate like, or at least t. TREV 781:10
not to t. the intolerant POPP 587:26
tolerated women not merely t. AUNG 36:20
toleration t. produced mutual indulgence GIBB 335:4
toll T. for the brave COWP 240:23
t. me back from thee KEAT 429:15
tolle *T. lege* AUGU 36:4
tollis *t. peccata mundi* MISS 522:19
tolls For whom the bell t. BORR 144:6
for whom the bell t. DONN 275:3
Tom Ground control to Major T. BOWI 145:21
Poor T.'s a-cold SHAK 679:8
spurious brat, T. Jones RICH 627:8
T. he was a piper's son NURS 551:15
T. Pearse BALL 52:10
T., Tom, the piper's son NURS 551:16
Uncle T. Cobbleigh BALL 52:10
tomatoes babies in the t. GINS 339:22
tomb blossom on the t. CRAB 242:21
confined into a t. VAUG 790:15
empty in thy t. KING 436:7
fair Fidele's grassy t. COLL 229:7
in the silent t. WORD 832:5
like what it is—a t. SHEL 711:24
mother to the t. MACA 483:13
sea was made his t. BARN 55:8
tell the lover's t. THOM 772:6
this side the t. BYRO 174:12
threefold, fourfold t. BASS 57:1
t. by the side of the sea POE 579:11
t. of a mediocre talent SMIT 724:11
t. of wit CAVE 198:12
tombs from the t. a doleful sound WATT 805:15
in the cool t. SAND 643:19
t. of all regions MISS 523:4
tombstone end of the fight is a t. KIPL 439:18
t. where he lies LONG 474:1
written on its t. DAVI 252:11
tomcat t. lies stretched flat HUGH 393:3
Tommy Little T. Tucker NURS 549:9
T. this, an' Tommy that KIPL 440:13
Tomnoddy my Lord T. BARH 54:2
tomorrow Boast not thyself of t. BIBL 83:27
build our life of t. PALI 565:16
For your t. we gave EPIT 304:14
Here today—in next week t. GRAH 348:8
jam t. CARR 190:23
Jam t. PROV 604:43
Leave t. behind COWA 238:9
Never put off till t. PROV 607:35
no dividend from time's t. SASS 645:18
put off till t. PUNC 617:5
This, no t. hath DONN 273:18
Today you; t. me PROV 613:7
T., and to-morrow SHAK 685:22
t. as to-day SHAK 702:31
T. do thy worst DRYD 282:32
T. for the young AUDE 35:7
t. I die LESS 465:15
t. is another day CLOS 222:1
t. is another day MITC 524:3
T. is another day PROV 613:10
T. never comes PROV 613:11
t.'s life's too late MART 497:22
t. there's no knowing MEDI 503:10
t. to be brave ARMS 25:16
t. we shall die BIBL 87:9
T. we shall sail again HORA 387:19
Unborn T. FITZ 314:14
we thought was for t. BENN 65:5
what t. may bring HORA 387:20
tomtit little t. Sang GILB 338:15
tone t. of the company CHES 209:10
tones t. are remembered not SHEL 712:3
tongs taken with the t. BIBL 86:23
t. and the bones SHAK 690:11
tongue become his mother t. GOLD 345:14
between the t. and teeth DUNN 285:13
Bite out the t. ROBE 629:1

tongue (*cont.*):
bridleth not his t. BIBL 110:15
each carping t. BRAD 146:14
Englissh sweete upon his t. CHAU 204:17
eye, and such a t. SHAK 677:26
fallen by the t. BIBL 92:3
fellows of infinite t. SHAK 672:5
give dust a t. HERB 372:9
grow a second t. MONT 527:4
has a raucle t. BURN 166:13
him whose strenuous t. KEAT 429:5
his t. Dropped manna MILT 515:9
hold your t. DONN 273:21
I held my t. BOOK 133:28
I must hold my t. SHAK 661:28
in the vulgar t. BOOK 130:7
iron t. of midnight SHAK 690:27
Keep thy t. from evil BOOK 133:22
Kepe wel they t. CHAU 205:24
Let thy t. acquire TALM 754:2
lies of t. and pen CHES 210:8
Love's t. is in the eyes FLET 318:15
my t. could utter TENN 757:11
my t. from evil-speaking BOOK 130:15
My t. is the pen BOOK 134:13
My t. swore EURI 304:19
my t. the mystery telling THOM 771:10
nor t. to speak LENT 464:6
of a slow t. BIBL 75:31
our t. with joy BOOK 140:19
rolls it under his t. HENR 370:15
senates hang upon thy t. THOM 775:10
sharp t. IRVI 400:2
Sing, my t. FORT 321:6
still t. makes wise head PROV 611:21
tip of the t. OPEN 556:1
tip of the t. taking NABO 537:17
t. always returns PROV 613:12
t. a sharp sword BOOK 135:15
t. can no man tame BIBL 110:19
t. freezes into silence SAPP 644:14
t. In every wound SHAK 676:11
t. is the clapper SHAK 691:12
t. not understanded BOOK 142:10
t. of the dumb BIBL 87:22
t. shall be slit NURS 551:2
t. That Shakespeare spake WORD 828:24
t. to conceive SHAK 690:17
t. to persuade CLAR 218:20
t. with a tang SHAK 698:34
treasure of our t. DANI 249:3
use of my oracular t. SHER 716:1
voice and t. AUGU 36:2
while I held my t. BOOK 133:17
yield to the t. BIER 114:19
tongued t. with fire ELIO 294:13
tongueless t. vigil SWIN 750:5
tongues Hush your t. HORA 388:11
lack t. to praise SHAK 705:10
nor spoke with t. of gold RICH 626:13
speak in our t. BIBL 103:16
thousand t. to sing WESL 810:24
time in the t. SHAK 701:1
t. in trees SHAK 658:14
t. like as of fire BIBL 103:15
t. of dying men SHAK 694:17
t. of living flame AUBE 32:10
t. of men and of angels BIBL 106:16
t., they shall cease BIBL 106:16
t. were all broken DYLA 287:6
Walls have t. SWIF 749:20
tonic Hatred is a t. BALZ 52:18
tonight Not t., Josepehine NAPO 539:5
tons Sixteen t. TRAV 781:2
too T. kind, too kind NIGH 546:1
we are t. menny HARD 360:12
took 'E went an' t. KIPL 440:20
t. a man's life with him CARL 187:14
tool edged t. that grows keener IRVI 400:2
Man is a t.-making animal FRAN 323:16
Man is a t.-using animal CARL 188:10
Science is an edged t. EDDI 288:3
Technology just a t. GATE 331:3
tooled t. in a post-chaise BYRO 180:8
tools bad workman blames his t. PROV 595:33
Give us the t. CHUR 215:14
quarrel with their t. BYRO 176:9
secrets are edged t. DRYD 282:19
t. to him that can handle them CARL 187:13
Toome On the Bridge of T. CARB 186:2
tooth danger of her former t. SHAK 684:4
hadde alwey a coltes t. CHAU 206:20
red in t. and claw TENN 761:14
returns to the sore t. PROV 613:12
sharper than a serpent's t. SHAK 678:11
t. for tooth BIBL 76:14
where each t.-point goes KIPL 440.1
toothache endure the t. SHAK 691:20
Venerable Mother T. HEAT 367:4
toothpaste t. is out of the tube HALD 357:1
top always room at the t. PROV 612:8
always room at the t. WEBS 807:18
I shall die at the t. SWIF 750:2
Life is a t. GREV 353:3
t. of it reached to heaven BIBL 75:1
T. of the world FILM 311:1
T. people ADVE 8:15
t. thing in the world KEAT 431:17
You're the t. PORT 588:12
toper Lo! the poor t. CRAB 242:26
topics providing t. of amusement SWIF 747:10
two t., yourself and me JOHN 415:21
topless t. towers of Ilium MARL 496:5
topmost on the t. twig ROSS 634:15
topography T. displays no favourites BISH 115:17
Torah found in the T. ELEA 291:15
garments of the T. ZOHA 840:13
only through the T. ZOHA 840:8
T. are likened to fire MIDR 507:13
T., hard like iron TALM 754:22
T. in Edom MIDR 507:14
Turn it [T.] TALM 754:1
torch bright t. KEAT 429:19
t. borne in the wind CHAP 202:13
t. of life LUCR 479:4
t. passed to a new generation KENN 433:9
Truth, like a t. HAMI 358:14
we throw The t. MCCR 484:13
torches Lighting our little t. COKA 224:5
teach the t. SHAK 697:7
torchlight t. procession O'SU 560:20
Tories both *T.* BOSW 144:17
revolutionaries potential T. ORWE 558:14
T. born wicked ANON 17:15
T. own no argument BROW 154:7
torment measure of our t. KIPL 438:18
More grievous t. KEAT 428:15
most hateful t. for men HERO 374:1
no t. touch them BIBL 91:8
smoke of their t. BIBL 112:25
tormented cries of the t. MILL 510:6
tormenting t. the people NAPO 538:18
torments many t. lie CIBB 217:4
t. also may in length of time MILT 515:13
T. not moved ALAB 9:14
tornado set off a t. in Texas LORE 475:14
torpedo becomes a t. JOHN 412:9
torpedoes Damn the t. FARR 307:24
torrent Time is a violent t. AURE 37:1
t. of his fate JOHN 411:19
torrents t. of her myriad universe TENN 763:16
torrid t. or the frozen zone CARE 186:11
torso remain only a t. ERHA 301:5
tortoise How t.-like MARV 499:8
'T.' is a insect PUNC 617:10
torture tire T. and Time BYRO 175:2
t. one poor word DRYD 282:1
t. them, into believing NEWM 542:13
t. to death DOST 276:1
tortured T. with the telephone generator BLY 122:15
torturer t.'s horse scratches AUDE 34:10
Tory deep burning hatred for the T. Party BEVA 71:13
Loyalty the T.'s secret weapon KILM 436:2
my favourite T. FOOT 319:2
Thirteen years of T. misrule POLI 581:30
T. and Whig in turns SMIT 725:8
T. Corps d'Armée GLAD 341:1
T. men and Whig measures DISR 270:2
wise T. JOHN 416:25
tossed t. to and fro BIBL 108:3
you t. and gored BOSW 144:20
total t. solution GOER 342:12
totalitarianism under the name of t. GAND 329:4
totter t. into vogue WALP 800:21
totters Who t. forth SHEL 714:15
totus *et in se ipso t.* HORA 390:2
touch exquisite t. SCOT 652:12
gently t. a nettle PROV 603:33
little t. of Harry SHAK 671:10
Nelson t. NELS 540:18
nothing, Can t. him further SHAK 684:5
One t. of nature SHAK 700:17
puts it not unto the t. MONT 529:2
T.— for there is a spirit WORD 829:13
T. me not BIBL 103:2
T. not the cat SCOT 651:21
t. of earthly years WORD 831:25
t. the hills BOOK 139:7
very t. of the letter NIN 546:2
wants the natural t. SHAK 685:4
touched t. none that he did not adorn EPIT 303:17
t. thy lips BIBL 86:23
Who t. my clothes BIBL 98:6
touches silent t. of time BURK 165:13
t. of sweet harmony SHAK 688:21
Who t. this touches a man WHIT 815:8
toucheth He that t. pitch BIBL 91:27
tough in t. joints RUNY 637:12
T., and devilish sly DICK 262:9
t. get going KENN 433:21
T. on crime BLAI 117:7
When the going gets t. PROV 614:28
toughness T. doesn't have to come FEIN 308:6
tourism t. is their religion RUNC 637:8
What an odd thing t. is BRYS 159:5
tourist camera makes everyone a t. SONT 728:8
loathsome is the British t. KILV 436:3
t. of wars GELL 333:1
whisper to the t. BEER 61:13
tourmente *l'infini me t.* MUSS 537:11
tout *capable de t.* VOLT 798:13
T. passe ANON 20:15
toves slithy t. CARR 190:12
tower build a t. BIBL 99:31
Child Roland to the dark t. SHAK 679:9
fall'n at length that t. TENN 765:4
Fighting in the captain's t. DYLA 287:4
Giotto's t. LONG 473:18
Julius Caesar's ill-erected t. SHAK 695:24
prisoner in the T. FABY 305:23
to the Dark T. came BROW 155:21
t. of David BIBL 85:14
t. of nine storeys begins LAO 452:5
t. of strength SHAK 696:28
watchman on the lonely t. SCOT 651:4
with a t. and bells CRAB 242:20
with the blasted t. NERV 541:7
towered t. cities please us MILT 512:23
towering own t. style CHES 211:16
towers branchy between t. HOPK 384:4
cloud-capped t. SHAK 699:6
from a hundred t. TENN 759:3
tell the t. thereof BOOK 134:26
Whispering from her t. ARNO 28:15
ye antique t. GRAY 350:15

towery T. city HOPK 384:4
town Country in the t. MART 498:5
country t. is my detestation BURN 166:3
destroy the t. to save it ANON 17:4
directions to the t. SWIF 749:17
Dirty old t. MACC 484:8
every t. or city HOLM 381:5
haunted t. it is to me LANG 450:9
little t. by river KEAT 428:27
little t. of Bethlehem BROO 151:9
lived in a pretty how t. CUMM 247:3
man made the t. COWP 241:19
man made the t. PROV 601:13
never go down to the end of the t. MILN 510:16
retreat near the t. WYCH 834:8
sounding through the t. BALL 50:10
spreading of the hideous t. MORR 532:13
studies it in t. COWP 241:10
tavern in the t. SONG 730:5
t.-crier spoke my lines SHAK 664:13
way that takes the t. HERB 371:23
towns London, thou art of t. ANON 17:12
prisoners in t. SITT 720:20
Seven wealthy t. ANON 18:18
too long in country t. CATH 194:9
toy be the t. of man WOLL 825:19
foolish thing was but a t. SHAK 702:22
get a t. SHAK 704:1
toys brooches and t. STEV 742:20
Deceive boys with t. LYSA 480:22
misuse, then cast their t. away COWP 240:8
t. of age POPE 585:25
toyshop moving t. of the heart POPE 586:30
trace t. unusual things WINC 823:2
traces on winter's t. SWIN 750:5
tracing fitful t. of a portal STEV 740:2
track flying on our t. THOM 775:22
T. twenty nine GORD 347:1
tracks hungry on the t. CRAN 243:24
staring at its own t. MAND 493:14
tract left a little t. WILD 818:33
trade all is seared with t. HOPK 384:5
articles of t. ALBE 10:6
arts of t. DYER 286:14
autocrat: that's my t. CATH 194:12
Every man to his t. PROV 599:36
from the vulgar t. MARL 496:16
great t. BURK 162:18
in London only is a t. DRYD 282:14
in the way of t. COWP 241:15
Irish poets, learn you t. YEAT 837:20
It is his t. LAST 455:9
People of the same t. SMIT 723:7
There isn't any T. HERB 371:15
T. follows the flag PROV 613:15
t. to make tables JOHN 413:3
tricks in every t. PROV 612:2
Two of a t. never agree PROV 613:28
us that t. in love SHAK 656:30
War is the t. of kings DRYD 281:31
wheels of t. HUME 394:11
traders into the hands of t. GRAV 349:21
trades live by twa t. SCOT 651:20
tradesmen bow, ye t. GILB 337:11
trade unionism t. of the married SHAW 708:11
trade unionist British T. BEVI 72:7
trading t. on the blood LEE 462:10
tradition t. Approves CLOU 222:27
t. is a fence TALM 753:17
T. is entirely different STRA 744:13
T. means giving votes to CHES 211:9
t. objects to their being disqualified CHES 211:10
traditions those barbarous t. FINK 313:4
traduced t. Joseph K. OPEN 556:17
traffic Hushing the latest t. BRID 148:8
means of t. MARL 496:16
roar of London's t. CATC 196:17
trade and t. PUSH 618:3
t. of Jacob's ladder THOM 774:13
two hours' t. SHAK 697:3
trafficking permitted t. KORA 443:22
tragedies All t. are finished BYRO 176:21
t. of antiquity STOP 743:16
tragedy blustering about Imperial T. BROW 152:1
comedy is t. that happens CART 192:9
composition of a t. VOLT 798:11
convenient in t. ANOU 22:8
element of t. ELIO 292:24
Fate wrote her a t. BEER 61:17
first time as t. BARN 55:3
first time as t. MARX 500:1
go, litel myn t. CHAU 207:18
it is a t. AUST 37:20
I will write you a t. FITZ 315:10
out of it simply a t. WILD 818:28
That is their t. WILD 817:18
t., comedy, history SHAK 663:22
T. is clean ANOU 22:9
t. is thus a representation ARIS 24:21
t. of a man OLIV 553:15
t. of a man who has found BARR 55:21
t. of Science HUXL 397:11
t. of the age DU B 284:3
t. of the classical languages MADA 488:19
T. ought to be a great kick LAWR 458:18
t. to those that feel WALP 801:5
weak, washy way of true t. KAVA 426:10
what t. means STOP 743:19
You *may* abuse a t. JOHN 413:3
tragic I acted so t. HARG 362:6
t. consciousness FUEN 326:29
t. failure ELIO 292:16
T. Muse first trod the stage POPE 586:27
tragical Merry and t. SHAK 690:22
trahison *t. des clercs* BEND 64:22
trahit *T. sua quemque voluptas* VIRG 795:19
trail long, long t. KING 436:19
t. has its own stern code SERV 654:23
trailing t. clouds of glory WORD 829:20
train biggest electric t. set WELL 809:12
express-t. drew up there THOM 772:23
headlight of an oncoming t. DICK 267:1
light of the oncoming t. LOWE 478:5
like a runaway t. CONL 233:21
pack, and take a t. BROO 150:13
read in the t. WILD 817:22
Runs the red electric t. BETJ 70:17
rush in the t. THOM 775:22
shaves and takes a t. WHIT 813:24
Shaw is like a t. LEIG 463:3
t. filled the temple BIBL 86:21
t. is arriving on time MUSS 537:14
t. of events AMER 13:5
t. take the strain ADVE 7:40
T. up a child BIBL 83:14
waited for the t. TENN 759:1
trains Noting the numbers of t. MAXW 502:12
traitor hate the t. DANI 249:5
t. to learning JOHN 407:14
traitors fears do make us t. SHAK 685:3
form of our t. WEST 812:9
hate t. and the treason love DRYD 281:25
tram not even a bus, I'm a t. HARE 362:4
trammel t. up the consequence SHAK 682:8
tramp why the lady is a t. HART 363:6
trample t. the vices AUGU 36:13
trampling right of t. on them CHIL 211:24
trance fell into a t. BIBL 103:28
in mad t., strike SHEL 710:23
tranced t. summer-night KEAT 427:27
trances t. of the blast COLE 225:17
tranquil Farewell the t. mind SHAK 692:30
man of humanity is t. CONF 231:13
tranquillity chaos remembered in t. THUR 777:3
divine T. TENN 763:18
Fame and t. MONT 527:16
feeling of inward t. FORB 319:9
moments of t. VOLT 798:2
overcomes male by t. LAO 452:4
recollected in t. WORD 832:20
T. Base here ARMS 25:19
t. remembered in emotion PARK 567:9
tranquillized t. *Fifties* LOWE 477:23
transcendental of a t. kind GILB 338:18
T. moonshine CARL 188:7
transformed t. into a gigantic insect KAFK 425:9
transgression keeps himself from t. TALM 754:28
there is no t. BIBL 104:33
transgressions wounded for our t. BIBL 88:17
transgressors numbered with the t. BIBL 88:19
way of t. BIBL 82:28
transient t. is the smile DYER 286:16
T. lustre WRIG 833:14
transit *O quam cito gloria mundi* THOM 770:20
Sic t. gloria mundi ANON 21:13
transitory Action is t. WORD 827:17
this t. life BOOK 129:14
translate such as cannot write, t. DENH 257:14
t. Epictetus JOHN 412:8
translated bless thee! thou art t. SHAK 690:2
T. Daughter, come AUDE 33:17
t. into another tongue BIBL 91:15
t. into Italian WHAR 813:1
translation mistake in the t. VANB 789:5
t. is no translation SYNG 751:21
T. it is that openeth BIBL 73:9
t. of the Bible WHAT 813:12
t. thief MARV 499:5
unfaithful to the t. BORG 143:5
vanity of t. SHEL 714:20
what is lost in t. FROS 326:19
translations hold t. not unlike HOWE 391:16
transmigrates elements once out of it, it t. SHAK 657:2
transmit t. but do not create CONF 231:15
transmutations delighted with t. NEWT 543:4
transport share the t. WORD 832:5
transported t. and ravished TRAH 780:14
trapeze on the flying t. LEYB 467:15
trappings t. and the suits of woe SHAK 661:21
traps recognize the t. MACH 486:2
trash society founded on t. SAYE 646:4
steals t. SHAK 692:20
trauma Freaks born with their t. ARBU 23:12
traurig *ich so t. bin* HEIN 368:5
travail labour for my t. SHAK 700:4
travaileth t. in pain BIBL 105:9
travel books of t. ELIO 293:3
in a moment t. thither WORD 830:8
Men t. faster now CATH 194:7
obliged to t. again CHAR 203:12
preserve all that t. SWIF 748:18
real way to t. GRAH 348:8
T. broadens the mind PROV 613:16
t. broadens the mind; but CHES 211:13
t. by land or by water BOOK 127:11
t. for travel's sake STEV 741:16
t. from Dan to Beersheba STER 738:7
t. hopefully PROV 604:12
t. hopefully is a better thing STEV 741:25
t. in the direction of our fear BERR 69:18
T., in the younger sort BACO 44:14
T. light JUVE 424:19
T. them HABI 355:9
t. to see Englishmen STER 738:6
two classes of t. BENC 64:20
travelled care which way he t. BEAV 59:2
took the one less t. FROS 326:9
t. a good deal in Concord THOR 776:2
t. among unknown men WORD 828:25
traveller fellow t. ANON 19:1
good t. is one LIN 469:17
lost t.'s dream BLAK 118:19

traveller (*cont.*):
No t. returns SHAK 664:4
O thou T. unknown WESL 811:1
said the T. DE L 256:15
said the T. OPEN 555:21
spurs the lated t. SHAK 684:8
t. betwixt life and death WORD 831:23
t., by the faithful hound LONG 473:17
t. from an antique land SHEL 712:21
t. need have no scruple BAED 45:18
travellers t. must be content SHAK 658:18
travelling t. at twenty miles a second EDDI 288:1
T. is the ruin BURN 165:25
travels t. fastest PROV 602:23
t. the fastest KIPL 439:10
t. the world in search MOOR 529:12
trawler seagulls follow a t. CANT 185:12
tray T., Blanch SHAK 679:10
treachery fear their subjects' t. SHAK 672:28
killed with my own t. SHAK 667:6
mother of all t. PAIS 564:8
ready for any t. WILL 819:21
t. cannot trust JUNI 423:17
t. of the intellectuals BEND 64:22
t. or meanness DISR 270:31
tread Doth close behind him t. COLE 226:24
face with an undaunted t. STEV 742:15
May we t. rejoicingly WILL 821:6
so airy a tread TENN 764:10
softly t., said Christabel COLE 224:19
t. on classic ground ADDI 4:20
T. softly YEAT 836:5
t. the verge of Jordan WILL 820:9
Where'er you t. POPE 586:26
treason bloody t. flourished SHAK 676:8
condoned high t. DISR 269:7
[corporations] cannot commit t. COKE 224:12
Gunpowder T. and Plot ANON 18:9
hate traitors and the t. love DRYD 281:25
In trust I have found t. MISQ 521:15
last temptation is the greatest t. ELIO 295:15
love the t. DANI 249:5
moderation is a sort of t. BURK 162:11
none dare call it t. HARI 362:9
popular humanity is t. ADDI 4:13
t. a matter TALL 753:8
t. can but peep SHAK 666:6
T. has done his worst SHAK 684:5
t. is not owned DRYD 282:5
t., make the most of it HENR 371:1
t. of all clerks AUDE 33:21
t. to his country JOHN 409:14
t. to our love THOR 776:19
'Twixt t. and convenience EPIT 303:6
treasonous their t. parles BROW 156:21
treasons fit for t., stratagems SHAK 688:25
treasure liking his t. THOM 773:6
our hearts' t. ROCH 630:11
purest t. mortal times afford SHAK 694:9
stolen the t. CONG 232:20
t. in earthen vessels BIBL 107:6
t. in heaven BIBL 96:13
t. of our tongue DANI 249:3
t. to dispose ASTE 31:12
t. without measure SCOT 650:3
What trusty t. GRIM 353:14
Where your t. is BIBL 93:21
your chiefest t. BELL 63:2
treasures t. upon earth BIBL 93:20
treasury If the T. were to fill old bottles KEYN 435:9
our our T. Bench TROL 782:27
T. is in power WILS 822:4
T. is the spring BAGE 46:7
treble of the T. Bench DISR 268:15
treat t. 'em just the same DURE 286:3
t. if met where any bar is HARD 361:18
treaties T. like girls and roses DE G 255:27
treatise T. of Human Nature HUME 395:3
treatment suitable case for t. MERC 505:4
t. of a question WITT 824:4
treaty hand that signed the t. THOM 772:8
not a peace t. FOCH 318:23
T. emptied the British jails DAY- 253:13
T. like an incoming tide DENN 257:16
t. with Russia BISM 116:5
tree apple on the t. DICK 266:12
bare t. CANN 185:11
billboard lovely as a t. NASH 539:18
cut down a redwood t. STEV 740:17
falls far from t. PROV 595:14
finds that this t. KNOX 442:14
fool sees not the same t. BLAK 119:15
golden t. of actual life GOET 342:20
happy, happy t. KEAT 428:1
I must climb the t. HERB 373:10
in a green t. BIBL 100:25
in a t. did end their race MARV 498:14
leaves of the t. BIBL 113:13
miss but a t. BLAM 121:15
must climb the t. PROV 602:21
Of that forbidden t. MILT 514:7
only God can make a t. KILM 436:1
on the t. of life MILT 516:11
on this Crumpetty T. LEAR 460:22
outstretched beneath the t. BLAK 121:6
poem lovely as a t. KILM 435:20
revere that t. FERG 308:16
river in the t. DICK 266:21
shall be like that t. SWIF 750:2
she gave me of the t. BIBL 74:1
shift an old t. PROV 615:45
so is the t. inclined PROV 595:21
spare the beechen t. CAMP 183:5
Till the t. die SHAK 661:3
to my mind than a t. MORR 532:6
t. falls, so shall it lie PROV 595:18
t. in the front garden MUMO 536:12
t. is known by his fruit BIBL 95:12
t. is known by its fruit PROV 613:17
T. of Eternity UPAN 788:3
t. of knowledge BIBL 73:18
T. of Knowledge BYRO 178:13
t. of liberty JEFF 405:7
t. of life BIBL 73:18
t. of life BIBL 82:27
t. of the knowledge BIBL 73:19
t.'s inclined POPE 584:1
Under the greenwood t. SHAK 658:20
unfabled Incense t. DARL 250:9
Was there a t. COWL 239:22
where the t. falleth BIBL 84:28
wish I were a t. HERB 371:24
Woodman, spare that t. MORR 532:9
treefull t. of angels BENÉ 65:3
treen t. priests JEWE 407:8
trees all the t. are green KING 437:13
apple t. will never get across FROS 326:5
climbing t. in the Hesperides SHAK 680:27
die when the t. were green CLAR 218:7
harden like t. MONT 526:16
He that plants t. FULL 327:12
I like t. CATH 194:10
known by the t. CLAR 219:12
Loveliest of t. HOUS 390:14
men as t., walking BIBL 98:7
root of the t. BIBL 92:30
shady t. BIBL 82:2
stones, and t. WORD 831:25
sturdy t. so shattered SACK 641:3
tall ancestral t. HEMA 369:6
T. and stones will teach BERN 69:1
t., And the mountain-tops SHAK 673:9
t. bear strange fruit HOLI 380:20
t. of the Lord BOOK 139:3
t. that grow so fair KIPL 440:14
t. when I saw them first TRAH 780:14
upon the t. that are therein BOOK 141:7
When lofty t. I see SHAK 704:8
while some t. stand BROW 153:6
Trelawny And shall T. die HAWK 364:6
tremble earth shall tremble BOOK 139:7
made great Olympus t. HOME 381:22
t. for my country JEFF 406:3
trembled all you t. at before COWP 241:8
t. with fear ENGL 300:13
tremblers t. learned to trace GOLD 344:13
trembles t. as I do WELL 809:14
trembling every t. heart WESL 811:7
fear and t. BIBL 108:18
T., hoping POPE 582:15
T. in her soft KEAT 427:11
t. most, maintain a dignity WALP 801:19
t. seizes me SAPP 644:14
tremulous behind my t. stay HARD 361:6
trenchant t. blade BUTL 172:2
trencher t.-friends, time's flies SHAK 699:18
upon Dead Caesar's t. SHAK 657:5
trencherman very valiant t. SHAK 690:32
trenches dig deep t. SHAK 704:6
trespass t. there and go HOUS 390:10
trespasses forgive us our t. BOOK 125:18
tress little stolen t. YEAT 837:8
tresses blood-red t. BYRO 173:23
Fair t. man's imperial race POPE 587:2
triad no t. of vehicles MAHĀ 490:11
trial In the years of t. PAST 569:8
only a t. if I recognize it KAFK 425:7
t. by juries JEFF 405:14
T. by jury itself DENM 257:15
t. is by what is contrary MILT 519:10
triangle eternal t. ANON 16:2
t. in a quadrangle AUBR 32:14
triangles t. were to make a God MONT 528:8
tribal constructing t. lays KIPL 439:4
t., intimate revenge HEAN 366:15
tribalism pure t. FITT 314:3
tribe All that t. HORA 389:16
badge of all our t. SHAK 687:15
Our t.'s complicity HEAN 366:10
purify the dialect of the t. ELIO 294:16
Richer than all his t. SHAK 694:3
tribes thither the t. go up BOOK 140:14
two mighty t. BYRO 177:24
tribulation came out of great t. BIBL 112:10
time of our t. BOOK 127:8
ye shall have t. BIBL 102:27
tribute Hypocrisy is a t. LA R 453:15
to whom t. is due BIBL 105:20
trick conjuring t. with bones JENK 406:6
long t.'s over MASE 500:18
this t. of melancholy SHAK 656:4
to win the t. LABO 446:13
T. that everyone abhors BELL 63:11
t. the trickster LA F 447:11
t. worth two of that SHAK 667:28
win the t. HOYL 392:6
trickle T.-down theory GALB 328:9
tricks Frustrate their knavish t. SONG 729:8
teach an old dog new t. PROV 615:30
t. in every trade PROV 612:2
Women are like t. CONG 232:21
tried Christian ideal has not been t. CHES 211:17
she for a little t. WOTT 833:3
t. a little STEV 741:1
when he is t. BIBL 110:11
trifle careless t. SHAK 681:23
t. with the spoon POPE 584:8
trifles She who t. with all GAY 332:3
T. light as air SHAK 692:28
t. were worth something CATU 194:20
unconsidered t. SHAK 703:11
write t. with dignity JOHN 416:17
trigger want on the t. NEWS 544:19
triglyph now that t.'s here CUMM 247:6
trimmer innocent word *T.* HALI 357:8
trinity blessèd T. HEBE 367:8
invoking the T. PATR 570:2
name of the T. ALEX 11:11
one God in T. BOOK 126:22
trip Clunk, click, every t. OFFI 554:2
don't t. over the furniture COWA 239:6

forward to the t. STIN 743:8
from fearful t. WHIT 815:5
To t., trip it, trip it SONG 729:3
t. it as ye go MILT 512:15
triple t. bronze HORA 387:15
t. cord BURK 162:10
t. sight in blindness KEAT 430:14
t.-towered sky DAY- 253:11
t. utterance PALI 564:14
triplex *robur et aes t.* HORA 387:15
trippingly t. on the tongue SHAK 664:13
tripwire touch the t. WARN 803:20
triste jamais t. archy MARQ 497:8
t. et noire BAUD 57:9
tristesse *Adieu t.* ÉLUA 299:2
Tristram call him t. MALO 492:9
Tristram Shandy novel, called *T.* WALP 800:18
T. did not last JOHN 415:9
Triton T. blow his wreathèd horn WORD 832:16
T. of the minnows SHAK 660:6
triumph for evil to t. MISQ 521:17
glory in the t. CORN 236:15
our career and our t. VANZ 789:20
shall not see the t. DICK 266:1
t. and defeat LONG 474:2
t. and disaster KIPL 439:2
t. from the north MACA 482:21
T. in God above GURN 355:6
t. o'er the timid hare THOM 775:13
t. of hope over experience JOHN 414:10
t. of modern science WAUG 806:20
t. of the embalmer's art VIDA 792:11
t. over death and sin SPEN 733:3
uncircumcised t. BIBL 79:1
Victor's t. won POTT 588:16
triumphant With a t. noise WESL 811:5
with the t. sea SHAK 694:19
triumphs sickened at all t. CHUR 214:6
trivial rise from t. things POPE 586:28
such t. people LAWR 458:16
t. and the important POTT 588:21
t. and vulgar way BROW 153:29
T. personalities WOOL 826:12
t. round, the common task KEBL 432:5
trivialities contrast to t. BOHR 124:3
trod T. beside me, close HOUS 391:6
trodden quickly t. out SHAK 673:2
troika like a spirited *t.* GOGO 344:2
Trojan what T. 'orses will jump out BEVI 72:11
Trojans t. have suffered HOME 381:23
We T. are at an end VIRG 794:4
tromper *t. le trompeur* LA F 447:11
troops t. of error BROW 153:13
t. towards the sound GRIM 353:15
trope out there flew a t. BUTL 171:19
tropes ranged his t. PRIO 593:1
trophies among her cloudy t. KEAT 429:5
her weedy t. SHAK 666:14
remain as t. BROW 153:13
t. o'er the garden gates POPE 586:8
tropic Under the t. is our language WALL 800:12
trots who Time t. withal SHAK 659:13
trotting T. to the fair GRAV 349:8
trouble capacity of taking t. CARL 187:20
charm of powerful t. SHAK 684:18
Double, double toil and t. SHAK 684:17
full of t. BIBL 81:18
Gold? a transient, shining t. GRAI 348:11
Go t. younger hearts WYAT 834:2
have your t. doubled DEFO 255:2
help in time of t. ANON 15:4
in the time of t. BOOK 134:3
In t. and in joy TATE 755:9
in t., sorrow BOOK 129:14
it is not our t. MARQ 497:9
Man is born unto t. BIBL 81:9
Never t. trouble PROV 607:40
Roman and his t. HOUS 391:3
stranger to t. myself VIRG 793:15
There may be t. ahead BERL 68:8
there's t. brewing KNIG 442:6
took the t. to be born BEAU 58:11
t., black and bitter LAWL 454:14
t. enough of its own WILC 817:9
t. shared PROV 613:18
When in t., delegate BORE 143:2
women and care and t. WARD 803:11
wood's in t. HOUS 391:2
troubled be not t. BIBL 96:30
bridge over t. water SIMO 720:8
greatly t. by women JAIN 401:14
heart be t. BIBL 102:16
I am t. MOOR 530:3
to the t. air GRAY 350:3
t. spirit BOOK 135:9
t. with her lonely life PEPY 573:3
troubles against a sea of t. SHAK 664:3
From t. of the world HARV 363:14
got over all its t. JERO 406:20
meet t. half-way PROV 598:27
pack up your t. MILI 508:16
troublesome most t. creatures KELL 432:15
troubling wicked cease from t. BIBL 81:5
trousers bottoms of my t. rolled ELIO 295:10
cloud in t. MAYA 502:14
have your best t. on IBSE 398:7
steam-engine in t. SMIT 725:18
Wears any t. at all JAST 404:13
with his t. on NURS 548:3
trout t. in the milk THOR 775:27
Where the gray t. lies HOGG 380:11
trovato *è molto ben t.* SAYI 648:3
trowel lay it on with a t. DISR 270:37
lays it on with a t. CONG 232:12
With his t. point HEAN 366:8
Troy another T. for her to burn YEAT 836:20
from the shores of T. VIRG 793:4
Greece is fallen and T. COLE 224:18
heard T. doubted BYRO 177:6
night when T. was sacked ROWE 636:10
plains of windy T. TENN 767:9
Priam's sons of T. SURR 746:11
sacked T.'s sacred city HOME 382:9
sacked T.'s sacred city OPEN 556:20
when T. was sacked HALD 356:17
Where's T. BRAM 146:18
truant every t. knew GOLD 344:13
t. disposition SHAK 661:29
trucking Keep on t. CATC 196:9
trucks learn about t. AWDR 39:19
true Ah, love, let us be t. ARNO 26:4
always say what's t. STEV 742:16
always t. to you, darlin' PORT 588:1
And is it t. BETJ 70:5
as t. a lover SHAK 658:19
as t. . . . as taxes DICK 261:25
believe is not necessarily t. BELL 62:21
by the people as equally t. GIBB 335:4
can the devil speak t. SHAK 681:19
course of t. love SHAK 689:4
dark and t. and tender TENN 765:22
everybody says must be t. PROV 613:51
Faithful and T. BIBL 113:2
for the sake of the t. SAND 643:17
If it is not t. SAYI 648:3
If t., here only MILT 516:12
know what t. love is TENN 759:28
Let God be t. BIBL 104:30
like to be t. BACO 45:2
Live pure, speak t. TENN 759:17
long enough it *will* be t. BENN 66:9
much for my t.-love BALL 52:6
my shape as t. SHAK 678:3
not necessarily t. WILD 818:22
only things that are t. SHAW 706:22
Ring in the t. TENN 761:28
said t. things BROW 155:11
ta'en t. Thomas BALL 51:20
than that it be t. WHIT 814:11
think what is t. HUXL 397:13
three times is t. CARR 191:19
to itself do rest but t. SHAK 677:21
too wonderful to be t. FARA 306:12
to thine own self be t. SHAK 662:13
t. beginning SHAK 690:23
t. legend STAL 736:4
t. love hath my heart SIDN 718:8
t. to thyself BACO 44:22
t. word spoken in jest PROV 606:24
we are sure they are t. SHAK 703:21
What is new cannot be t. PROV 614:3
Whatsoever things are t. BIBL 108:25
what we are saying is t. RUSS 639:19
woman t. and fair DONN 274:12
You are not t. WILB 817:5
truer who is t. in tidings KORA 444:12
truest paint 'em t. ADDI 4:8
truffles t., Perigord POPE 582:11
trump at the last t. BIBL 107:3
sound of the t. BOOK 134:23
trumpet anon a t. sounds THOM 774:8
Blow t. TENN 759:16
Blow up the t. BOOK 137:9
Gideon blew a t. BIBL 77:32
great voice as of a t. BIBL 111:19
His t. shrill SPEN 733:2
shifted his t. GOLD 345:5
sound of the t. BIBL 77:20
than with a t. SIDN 718:26
t. give an uncertain sound BIBL 106:17
t. in terrible tones ENNI 300:17
t. shall be heard on high DRYD 282:23
t. shall sound BIBL 107:3
t.'s silver sound SCOT 651:5
t. will fling out MISS 523:4
trumpets kettle-drums and t. COLM 229:18
saith among the t. BIBL 81:37
silver, snarling t. KEAT 427:5
to the sound of t. SMIT 726:4
t. also, and shawms BOOK 138:10
t. came out brazenly LAWR 458:25
t. sounded for him BUNY 161:19
uplifted angel t. MILT 511:11
trumps Let spades be t. POPE 587:8
trunkless vast and t. legs SHEL 712:21
trust assumes a public t. JEFF 405:16
Because I don't t. him BREC 147:12
built An absolute t. SHAK 681:23
cheated than not to t. JOHN 410:19
except t. TAYL 756:4
I did t. in Christ WESL 811:15
In t. I have found treason MISQ 521:15
my sure t. is in thee BOOK 136:15
never t. experts SALI 642:16
Never t. the artist LAWR 458:4
not property but a t. FOX 322:4
no t. in the future HORA 387:22
power in t. DRYD 280:6
power is a t. DISR 270:33
put their t. in him BOOK 131:18
put thy t. in God BOOK 134:11
put your t. in God BLAC 116:21
Put your t. in God PROV 610:1
those that t. 'em WYCH 834:10
to mortality shall t. BACO 45:11
treachery cannot t. JUNI 423:17
t. in chariots BOOK 132:19
t. in God SMIT 725:14
t. in princes BOOK 141:21
t. in the flesh BIBL 108:19
t. me not at all TENN 760:4
T. none SHAK 671:4
T. not with secrets LAVA 454:11
T. one who has gone through it VIRG 795:11
t. people is a luxury FORS 320:16
t. themselves with men SHAK 699:15
t. was with the eternal MILT 515:8
yet will I t. in him BIBL 81:17
trusted friend, whom I t. BOOK 134:4
He t. in God BOOK 132:22
in thee have I t. BOOK 126:2
in which he t. BIBL 99:17

trusted (*cont.*):
not to be t. PROV 612:48
unfit to be t. CHES 209:24
trustest t. upon the staff BIBL 80:28
trusteth man that t. in him BOOK 133:20
trusting no t. appearances SHER 716:17
trustworthiness Carthaginian t. SALL 643:11
trusty that t. Achates carried VIRG 793:8
truth able to realize the T. HUI- 394:5
Art is not t. PICA 576:5
As t. will paint it CRAB 243:14
beautiful—is T. TOLS 779:10
Beauty is t. KEAT 429:1
Believing T. BELL 63:5
best test of t. CHES 209:21
bring t. to light SHAK 704:2
by t., by judgement TALM 753:14
cancels everything but t. HAZL 365:15
can tell you the t. MACH 486:4
can't get at the t. BREN 147:24
Christianity better than T. COLE 227:7
cinema is t. 24 times per second GODA 341:20
closing up t. to truth MILT 519:14
countenance of t. MILT 520:1
dared to speak the t. TROL 782:9
dearer still is t. ARIS 25:9
diminution of the love of t. JOHN 409:17
discover t. BACO 41:7
does not bellow the t. PÉGU 572:3
do not care for t. STUB 745:3
economical with the t. ARMS 25:20
economy of t. BURK 164:22
enemies of t. BROW 153:13
enemy of t. IBSE 398:5
fiction lags after t. BURK 162:23
fight for freedom and t. IBSE 398:7
follow t. too near RALE 621:6
fools tell t. PROV 597:16
forsake this t. ROSE 633:20
for Us and for T. ZORO 841:8
From delusion lead me to T. UPAN 787:9
give an air of t. HUME 395:5
greater the t. PROV 601:35
Great is T. BIBL 91:1
great is t. BROO 151:10
great ocean of t. NEWT 543:11
Half the t. is often PROV 601:43
heavenly t. imparts KEBL 432:6
here have Pride and T. YEAT 836:22
how many people know the t. WEST 812:16
Images split the t. LEVE 466:4
in His right hand all T. LESS 465:17
in possession of t. LOCK 471:16
inquiry of t. BACO 44:18
in spirit and in t. BIBL 101:20
irreconcilable foes to t. BUCK 159:13
is such a thing as t. BAGE 46:2
Is there in t. no beauty HERB 372:20
just possession of t. BROW 153:14
just tell the t. TRUM 784:4
keep t. safe in its hand TAGO 752:20
knew T. put to the worse MILT 519:19
know the t. at last EPIT 304:2
lawyer interprets the t. GIRA 340:8
least touch of t. BYRO 180:2
lie which is part a t. TENN 759:6
Lord has more t. yet ROBI 629:17
love of t. TENN 759:20
mainly he told the t. TWAI 786:2
May t. be embodied ZORO 841:11
Mercy and t. BOOK 137:15
mistook disenchantment for t. SART 645:5
neither T. nor Falsehood HOBB 378:13
Never sold the t. TENN 765:6
new scientific t. PLAN 577:10
noble end of glorious t. IRWI 400:6
Noble T. of Suffering PALI 565:12
No mask like open t. CONG 232:14
not maintained for the t. SWIF 747:24
not only t. RUSS 639:22
no t. in him BIBL 102:1
old t. receives a new WIGG 816:18
ornament which t. doth give SHAK 704:20
plain t. for plain people WESL 811:11
positive in error as in t. LOCK 471:19
possible to lie for the t. ADLE 6:4
rooted in t. HUNT 395:20
sad friends of T. MILT 519:13
Scotland better than t. JOHN 409:20
seal of Holy One is t. TALM 754:3
seekers after t. AUCT 33:11
seek for t. HORA 387:8
she is made of t. SHAK 705:23
should he even tell the t. TALM 754:20
simple t. must be abused SHAK 696:14
simply a t. repeated BALD 49:6
sincerity and t. BIBL 106:2
skulking T. to her old cavern POPE 582:12
speaketh the t. BOOK 132:7
spirit of t. BOOK 129:11
stark naked t. CLEL 220:8
Statesman, yet friend to T. POPE 584:6
stop telling the t. STEV 740:9
Stretch age's t. JONS 419:10
strife of T. with Falsehood LOWE 477:15
subject is not t. CHAP 202:22
Tell the t. and shame PROV 611:44
test of t. CRAB 242:23
that portion of t. LOCK 471:18
thy light and thy t. BOOK 134:10
trusted to speak the t. BALF 49:13
T. and honour CHAU 204:8
t. and liberty SHEL 714:14
t. and untruth BACO 42:34
T. beareth away the victory BIBL 90:26
t., beauty, and goodness WEIL 808:25
T. can never be told BLAK 119:25
T. exists, lies are invented BRAQ 147:3
T. forever on the scaffold LOWE 477:16
T. from his lips prevailed GOLD 344:12
T. has no special time SCHW 650:1
t. has such a face DRYD 281:17
t. in action DISR 268:14
t. in masquerade BYRO 177:17
t. in whores WRIG 833:15
t. in wine PROV 612:24
t. is always strange BYRO 177:26
T. is a pathless land KRIS 445:22
t. is marching on HOWE 391:15
T. is never undone ROET 631:5
t. is not in us BIBL 111:11
T. is now her painted toy YEAT 837:11
t. is out there CATC 196:23
t. is pulling its boots on SPUR 735:14
t. is rarely pure WILD 817:13
T. is stranger than PROV 613:19
T. is the cry BERK 67:20
t. is the first SAYI 648:10
t. is the hyeste thyng CHAU 205:14
T. is the most valuable thing TWAI 786:7
t., justice, and humanity GLAD 341:8
t., justice and the American way ANON 16:7
T. lies at the bottom PROV 613:20
t. lies somewhere COWP 240:10
T. lies within a little BOLI 124:16
T., like a torch HAMI 358:14
T., like the light, blinds CAMU 184:15
T.-loving Persians GRAV 349:13
t. makes men free AGAR 6:14
t. misunderstood JAME 404:3
t. not be impress'd HORA 389:13
T. not merely what we are thinking HAVE 364:3
t. of imagination KEAT 430:21
t. serve as a stalking-horse BOLI 124:13
t. shall be thy warrant RALE 620:12
t. shall make you free BIBL 101:35
T., Sir, is a cow JOHN 413:10
T. sits upon the lips ARNO 27:17
T. stands DONN 273:14
t. that has lost its temper GIBR 336:14
t. that's told with bad intent BLAK 118:1
t. thee shal delivere CHAU 207:24
t. then be thy dower SHAK 677:23
T., 'tis supposed SHAF 655:18
t. to the fact STEV 741:3
t. universally acknowledged AUST 38:14
t. universally acknowledged OPEN 555:22
T. was buried deep below DAVI 251:16
t. which you cannot contradict SOCR 727:7
T. will come to light SHAK 687:19
T. will out PROV 613:21
t. with gold she weighs POPE 580:8
t. within thy mind rehearse TENN 767:6
two to speak the t. THOR 776:18
ultimate t. NAGA 538:3
utter what he thinks t. JOHN 416:13
very few lovers of t. LOCK 471:17
War told me t. GURN 355:4
way, the t., and the life BIBL 102:18
wedded to the t. SAKI 642:9
we owe only t. VOLT 798:5
What is t. BACO 44:15
What is t. BIBL 102:30
white star of T. ARNO 27:20
truths all t. are half-truths WHIT 814:12
disagreeable t. BULW 160:9
eternal t. LEIB 462:21
fate of new t. HUXL 397:17
Few new t. have ever won BERL 68:17
Flat and flexible t. BROW 152:13
Irrationally held t. HUXL 397:18
profound t. recognized BOHR 124:3
repetition of unpalatable t. SUMM 746:5
t. begin as blasphemies SHAW 706:12
t. being in and out of favour FROS 325:16
t. he can impart WORD 830:19
T. that become old OUSP 560:25
t. that wake WORD 830:7
t. to be self-evident ANON 19:11
Two t. are told SHAK 681:20
We hold these t. JEFF 405:3
try can do till you t. PROV 615:47
t. him afterwards MOLI 525:14
T. me, O God BOOK 141:14
t. out my reins BOOK 133:7
t., try, try again PROV 603:13
We t. harder ADVE 0.10
trying I am t. to be SMIT 724:5
just goes on t. PICA 576:3
succeed in business without really t. MEAD 503:2
tsar no t., but the slaves remain ZAMY 839:19
T-shirt got the T. SAYI 647:1
tu *Et t., Brute?* SHAK 675:16
T.-whit, tu-who SHAK 681:4
tua *Nam t. res agitur* HORA 387:2
tub Every t. must stand PROV 599:38
mere tale of a t. WEBS 808:9
tuba *T. mirum spargens sonum* MISS 523:4
t. terribili sonitu ENNI 300:17
tube artificial inlet—a t. FOST 321:12
lovely t. of delight POTT 588:23
toothpaste is out of the t. HALD 357:1
tuberose sweet t. SHEL 713:23
tucker Little Tommy T. NURS 549:9
Tudor US presidency a T. monarchy BURG 162:1
tue *je te t.* CHAM 201:10
Tuesday spelling T. MILN 510:13
T.'s child NURS 549:14
tuffet Sat on a t. NURS 549:7
tug then comes the t. of war PROV 614:19
then was the t. of war LEE 462:5
tulgey whiffling through the t. wood CARR 190:13
tumble t. headlong down MARL 496:11
tumbled might is t. down COLE 224:18
tumbler t., and a corkscrew DICK 264:6
tumour aspirin for a brain t. CHAN 201:15
ripens in a t. ABSE 1:6
tumult depth, and not the t. WORD 828:28
t. and the shouting KIPL 440:3
t. and the shouting dies KNOX 442:13
t. dwindled to a calm BYRO 179:17

tun t. of man is thy companion SHAK 668:13
tune all the t. that he could play NURS 551:15
calls the t. PROV 602:31
dances to an ill t. PROV 602:16
good t. played on PROV 612:26
guy who could carry a t. EPIT 303:8
I t. the instrument DONN 273:5
keep thinkin'll turn into a t. HUBB 392:13
out of t. and harsh SHAK 664:11
sweetly play'd in t. BURN 168:6
turn on, t. in and drop out LEAR 460:23
tunes devil have all the best t. PROV 615:8
found out musical t. BIBL 92:15
have all the good t. HILL 377:3
Heft Of Cathedral T. DICK 266:16
t. of Handel SITW 721:8
tunnel back down the time t. KEAT 426:12
light at the end of the t. DICK 267:1
light at the end of the t. LOWE 478:5
some profound dull t. OWEN 562:11
tuppence wouldn't give you t. COLL 228:12
turbot (by way of t.) an archdeacon SMIT 725:10
price of a large t. RUSK 638:17
T., Sir WELB 809:3
turbulent rid me of this t. priest HENR 370:9
turd nat worth a t. CHAU 206:14
turf blue ribbon of the t. DISR 270:17
grass-green t. SHAK 666:1
Green be the t. above thee HALL 358:10
green t. beneath my feet HAZL 365:23
on the dappled t. WORD 832:10
Where heaves the t. GRAY 350:8
Turk French, or T. GILB 339:1
Nose of T. SHAK 684:19
turkey It *was* a t. DICK 261:11
myrtle and t. AUST 37:26
T., heresy, hops PROV 613:22
T. is a dying man NICH 543:16
turkeys kill all t., geese PROV 608:28
t. vote for Christmas CALL 181:12
Turkish English, not the T. court SHAK 670:19
Turks Let the T. now carry GLAD 340:19
turn and quickly t. away YEAT 836:3
Because I do not hope to t. ELIO 293:19
Even a worm will t. PROV 599:19
my t. now NELS 540:12
One good t. deserves PROV 608:40
pass, and t. again EMER 299:5
T. about is fair play PROV 613:23
t. again, and quicken us BOOK 137:14
t. down an empty glass FITZ 315:3
t. of the screw JAME 403:15
t. on, tune in and drop out LEAR 460:23
T. our captivity, O Lord BOOK 140:20
t. over a new life FLEM 317:13
t. over the sheet SAND 644:6
T. that off WILL 820:19
t. thee behind me BIBL 80:22
t. the page BROW 155:16
t. to him the other BIBL 93:12
T. up the lights LAST 457:13
T. us again, O God BOOK 137:8
turned having once t. round COLE 226:24
in case anything t. up DICK 261:18
Lord t. again BOOK 140:19
t. every one to his own way BIBL 88:17
t. from one's course FABI 305:20
t. out of the Realm ELIZ 296:24
Turner T.'s palm as itchy SCOT 652:10
turning gate where they're t. AUDE 34:18
lady's not for t. THAT 769:24
long lane that has no t. PROV 604:3
reached its t.-point TAYL 756:3
shadow of t. BIBL 110:12
still point of the t. world ELIO 294:4
t. one's worst moments DONL 272:6
turnip blood out of a t. MARR 497:14
candle in that great t. CHUR 216:5
rather Have a t. JOHN 418:8
turnpike consider supper as a t. EDWA 289:12
turns Times go by t. SOUT 731:13
Turpe *siquid T. paras* JUVE 425:5
turpissimus *Nemo repente fuit t.* JUVE 424:8
turret washed me out of the t. JARR 404:7
turrets half-glimpsèd t. THOM 774:8
her t. split the sky LAND 450:2
turtle soul of thy t.-dove BOOK 136:21
t. lives 'twixt plated decks NASH 539:7
voice of the t. BIBL 85:10
turya what is called *t.* UPAN 788:7
Tuscany ranks of T. MACA 483:11
Tusculum retirement at T. DICK 262:12
tush T., I shall never be BOOK 132:2
Tutankhamun T.'s tomb CART 193:3
TV blight has hit the T. industry STRE 744:18
by T. stupor SOLZ 727:14
T.—a clever contraction ACE 1:9
twa droon t. ANON 18:15
twain go with him t. BIBL 93:13
with t. he covered BIBL 86:21
twang melodious t. AUBR 33:1
twangs something t. and breaks MACN 488:10
tweed Says T. to Till ANON 18:15
Tweedledum 'Twixt T. and Tweedledee BYRO 173:9
twelve I had just turned t. VIRG 796:8
ruin himself in t. months GEOR 334:3
snowed for t. days THOM 772:13
Ten or t. HOPK 384:1
T. for the twelve apostles SONG 729:11
t. good men into a box BROU 151:12
t. great shocks of sound TENN 759:3
t. honest men have decided PULT 617:1
T. men are marching BLOK 122:4
twelvemonth run the t.'s length BURN 168:10
t. and a day BALL 52:6
twentieth close of the t. century HEWI 375:18
fill the twentieth t. LAUR 454:10
horror of the T. Century MAIL 491:1
language of the t. century BEVA 71:16
reality of the t. century BALL 52:11
t. century belongs to those TRUD 783:22
t. century have looked SCHL 648:19
t. century will be TOYN 780:5
twenty at T. I tried to vex AUDE 35:4
At t. years of age FRAN 323:11
first t. years SOUT 731:5
Let t. pass BROW 155:20
twenty-first started t. century BOWI 145:23
twenty-three chaste, and t. BYRO 175:29
twenty-twenty Hindsight is always t. WILD 819:14
twice gives t. who gives quickly PROV 602:5
He gives t. PUBL 616:11
it is t. blessed SHAK 688:10
must do t. as well as men WHIT 816:10
never knocks t. PROV 609:11
postman always rings t. CAIN 181:2
seldom forgive t. LAVA 454:12
t. as natural CARR 191:11
t. I have also heard BOOK 135:23
t. into the same river HERA 371:8
t.-told tale SHAK 677:12
twig as the t. is bent POPE 584:1
As the t. is bent PROV 595:21
t.'s having lashed across it FROS 325:14
twilight and t. grey MILT 516:19
beautiful t. CAMU 184:15
disastrous t. sheds MILT 515:1
fly by t. BACO 44:10
in the t. wait ROBI 629:13
t. dim with rose DE L 256:19
twilights shadows and t. Æ 6:8
twinkle Twinkle, t., little bat CARR 189:18
T., twinkle, little star TAYL 756:13
twinkling in the t. of an eye BIBL 107:3
t. of a bed-staff SHAD 655:13
twins every one bear t. BIBL 85:14
threw the t. she nursed GRAH 348:3
to have been born t. MADA 488:19
t. of learning SHAK 673:24
twirling t. in thy hand a withered spray ARNO 27:7
twist almost invisible t. BABE 40:15
death your vital t. shall sever DAVI 251:21
NO MORE T. POTT 588:18
t. slowly in the wind EHRL 290:4
t. the sinews of thy heart BLAK 121:9
twisted silly t. boy CATC 196:34
twitched t. his mantle blue MILT 513:13
two but truly t. STEV 741:13
Can t. walk together BIBL 90:16
game at which t. can play BEER 61:16
ride t. horses at once PROV 603:28
say that t. plus two make four ORWE 558:24
sweet t.-and-twenty BYRO 179:6
Takes t. to tango HOFF 379:15
takes t. to tango PROV 604:41
tea for t. CAES 180:14
There went in t. and two BIBL 74:16
twice t. be not four TURG 785:7
T. and two only NEWM 542:5
t. and two would continue to make WHIS 813:20
T. boys are half a boy PROV 613:25
t. by two in the ark LEVE 466:5
t. cultures SNOW 726:19
t. dogs are fighting PROV 614:44
t. ears of corn SWIF 747:22
t.-edged sword BIBL 111:22
t.-edged sword BOOK 142:2
t. for mirth PROV 608:37
t. glasses and two chairs MACN 488:12
t.-handed engine MILT 513:7
T. heads are better than one PROV 613:26
t. hours' traffick SHAK 697:3
t. hundred thousand men NAPO 539:2
T. is company PROV 613:27
t. is fun SAYI 647:4
T. nations DISR 270:23
t. o'clock in the morning NAPO 538:17
t. or three are gathered BOOK 126:18
t. people miserable BUTL 172:22
t. primal Spirits ZORO 841:9
t. ride on a horse PROV 603:25
t. things about the horse ROYD 636:17
t. things that will be believed TARK 755:3
t. to make a bargain PROV 604:39
t. to make a quarrel PROV 604:40
T. voices are there STEP 737:21
t. who are in it CLIN 221:3
We're number t. ADVE 8:18
where t. or three BIBL 96:10
with t. seeming bodies SHAK 690:6
twopence penny plain and t. coloured STEV 741:17
Tyburn damned T.-face CONG 232:17
tyger T., Tyger BLAK 121:8
tygers t. of wrath BLAK 119:21
Tyler Tippecanoe and T., too POLI 582:2
type careful of the t. TENN 761:12
wasn't even my t. PROU 594:2
types device of *Movable T.* CARL 188:9
From shadows and t. EPIT 302:5
Seven t. of ambiguity EMPS 300:9
T. and shadows THOM 771:11
typewriter changing a t. ribbon BENC 64:18
pen, pencil, and t. SCOT 650:6
t. separated me from NERU 541:5
typewriters banging on million t. WILE 819:17
monkeys strumming on t. EDDI 287:22
tyranne *tibi tanta t. tulisti* ENNI 300:14
tyrannical against a t. majority BALF 49:14
nothing more t. TROL 782:19
tyrannis *Sic semper t.* BOOT 142:16
Sic semper t. MOTT 535:17
tyrannous t. To use it like a giant SHAK 686:9
tyranny burden of t. SHAW 708:14
call it *t.* HOBB 379:1

tyranny (*cont.*):
conditions of t. AREN 24:4
Ecclesiastic t. DEFO 255:15
remedy in human nature against t. JOHN 414:15
straining order into t. GODW 342:8
t. be over-past BOOK 135:14
T. entrenches SHEL 715:2
t. had supplanted the law DUFF 284:11
T. is always better organized PÉGU 572:4
unnecessary t. RUSS 639:13
wage war against a monstrous t. CHUR 215:8
without representation is t. OTIS 560:21
worst sort of t. BURK 164:28
tyrant From t. duke SHAK 658:10
loses the king in the t. MAYH 502:21
No t. need fear till ARIS 25:7
O t. Titus Tatius ENNI 300:14
spurned a t.'s chain BARB 53:15
T. and Hector BARB 53:19
t. custom SHAK 692:6
t. of his fields withstood GRAY 350:11
t. of the mind DRYD 281:34
t. staring him in the face HORA 388:15
t.'s vein SHAK 689:11
t. whom I will not name WRIG 833:15
tyrants all men would be t. DEFO 255:8
argument of t. PITT 577:3
barbarity of t. SMIT 725:3
between t. and slaves GOLD 345:13
Kings will be t. BURK 163:24
men would be t. ADAM 1:18
patriots and t. JEFF 405:7
Rebellion to t. BRAD 146:12
Rebellion to t. MOTT 535:15
sceptre from t. TURG 785:9
t.' crests SHAK 705:12
T. seldom want pretexts BURK 162:8
Tyre men still call T. FLEC 317:5
Nineveh and T. KIPL 440:4
tyres concrete and t. LARK 452:16
Tyrian budded T. KEAT 429:17

ubi *U. Petrus, ibi ergo ecclesia* AMBR 13:3
ubique *Quod u., quod semper* VINC 793:3
ubiquities blazing u. EMER 300:2
Ucalegon U. burns very near VIRG 794:3
uffish in u. thought he stood CARR 190:13
ugly constancy to a bad, u. woman BYRO 179:13
Despised, if u. LEAP 460:2
good, the bad, and the u. FILM 312:21
never saw an u. thing CONS 235:9
no place for u. mathematics HARD 360:7
than to be u. WILD 818:21
u. fact HUXL 397:11
u., heavy and complex FLAU 316:20
Ullin Lord U.'s daughter CAMP 183:12
Ulster betrayal of U. CAIR 181:3
Protestant Province of U. CARS 192:3
to which U. will not go BONA 125:2
U. will fight CHUR 214:14
Ulsterman U., of planter stock HEWI 376:1
ulterioris *ripae u. amore* VIRG 794:21
ultima *U. Thule* VIRG 796:14
ultimate u. decency of things STEV 742:10
u. truth NAGA 538:3
ultio *voluptas U.* JUVE 425:4
ultrices *Luctus et u. posuere* VIRG 794:20
Ulva chief of U.'s isle CAMP 183:12
Ulysses Happy he who like U. DU B 283:22
umble so very 'u. DICK 261:23
umbra it is but *U. Mortis* LAUD 454:4
magni nominis u. LUCA 478:14
umbrage garden's u. mild SMAR 722:12
u. of the walls of Eden BYRO 173:21
umbrella shadow, an u. FLET 318:7
steals the just's u. BOWE 145:20
umbris *Ex u. et imaginibus* EPIT 302:5
umpire Chaos u. sits MILT 515:25
u., the pavilion cat LANG 450:10
una *spinis de pluribus u.* HORA 387:10
unable unwilling or u. WILL 821:1
unacceptable u. face of capitalism HEAT 367:3
unacknowledged u. legislators SHEL 714:24
unadvisedly u., lightly, or wantonly BOOK 131:1
unaffected Affecting to seem u. CONG 233:15
unafraid ruins would strike him u. HORA 388:16
unarm U., Eros SHAK 657:13
unattempted u. yet in prose or rhyme MILT 514:8
unattractive not against the u. GREE 351:17
unaware And I was u. HARD 361:12
Sees, some morning, u. BROW 156:2
unbearable in victory u. CHUR 216:10
u. lightness of being KUND 446:6
unbeatable In defeat u. CHUR 216:10
unbeautiful u. and have comfortable minds CUMM 247:13
unbecoming u. the character MILI 508:3
unbelief help thou mine u. BIBL 98:9
unbelievers Fire prepared for u. KORA 443:16
hard against the u. KORA 445:10
unbelieving u. husband BIBL 106:5
unbends u. the mind like them GAY 331:19
unbirthday u. present CARR 191:1
unborn u., not become PALI 565:21
Ventriloquizing for the u. GRAV 349:16
unbowed bloody, but u. HENL 369:20
unbroken part of u. stream HAWK 364:7
unbuild arise and u. it again SHEL 711:7
unburied bodies of u. men WEBS 808:13
unbutton Come; u. here SHAK 679:4
uncertain trumpet give an u. sound BIBL 106:17
U., coy, and hard to please SCOT 651:13
uncertainty limits set by the u. principle HAWK 364:9
uncharitableness from all u. BOOK 127:4
uncircumcised daughters of the u. BIBL 79:1
uncle My u. SHAK 662:29
u. me no uncle SHAK 695:1
U. Tom Cobbleigh BALL 52:10
unclean people of u. lips BIBL 86:22
u. spirit BIBL 95:17
u. to you BIBL 76:20
uncleanness all u. BIBL 96:28
Fornication, and all u. BIBL 108:6
unclouded u. blaze BYRO 175:20
unclubbable very u. man JOHN 413:21
unco Address to the u. guid BURN 166:7
uncoffined u., and unknown BYRO 175:10
uncomfortable thinks he is u. SHAW 708:6
unconditional u. and immediate surrender GRAN 348:16
unconfined with u. wings LOVE 476:12
unconquerable man's u. mind WORD 832:12
nursing the u. hope ARNO 27:11
u. will MILT 514:13
unconscionable u. time dying CHAR 203:15
unconscious knowledge of the u. FREU 324:13
knowledge of the u. MISQ 521:8
personal u. JUNG 423:5
unconsidered u. trifles SHAK 703:11
unconvincing bald and u. GILB 338:13
uncorrupt leadeth an u. life BOOK 132:7
uncouth His u. way MILT 515:16
U. unkist SPEN 734:23
uncreated one u. BOOK 126:23
uncreating U. word POPE 582:14
unction flattering u. SHAK 665:20
undefiled my love, my dove, my u. BIBL 85:18
Pure religion and u. BIBL 110:16
well of English u. SPEN 734:6
under employed as an u.-labourer LOCK 471:12
get out and get u. CLAR 219:14
go u. the earth BOOK 135:25
those that work u. them HALI 357:9
underachiever basically he's an u. ALLE 12:11
underbelly soft u. of Europe MISQ 522:8
u. of the Axis CHUR 215:18
underdogs Englishman among the u. WAUG 806:7
underground Johnny u. PUDN 616:14
undergrowth u. is part of the language EMPS 300:10
underlings ourselves, that we are u. SHAK 674:13
underneath U. the Arches FLAN 315:21
undersold Never knowingly u. ADVE 8:2
understand can anyone u. Ein ANON 16:20
child could u. FILM 312:11
criticize What you can't u. DYLA 287:16
doesn't u. the situation MURR 537:9
dogs who don't u. CALV 182:8
don't u. things NEUM 541:11
failed to u. BOHR 124:1
Grown-ups never u. anything SAIN 641:11
I do not u. FEYN 309:7
liberals can u. BRUC 158:17
little of what they u. GRAC 347:16
none could u. what she said BUNY 161:17
something I really don't u. SALI 642:10
thought I to u. this BOOK 136:20
to u. them SPIN 734:27
u. a little less MAJO 491:15
u. nothing CORN 236:18
u. one another CHAM 201:8
u. the country LESS 465:12
u. what is happening CHAM 200:15
we should not u. CONG 232:21
understanded tongue not u. BOOK 142:10
understandeth u. thee not SHAK 680:25
understanding candle of u. BIBL 91:4
declare, If thou hast u. BIBL 81:31
evidence against their own u. HALI 357:13
find you an u. JOHN 417:14
good u. BOOK 139:18
ignorant of his u. COLE 227:10
in length of days u. BIBL 81:16
likely to propagate u. JOHN 418:13
pass all u. JAME 402:17
passeth all u. BIBL 108:24
pass man's u. BOOK 128:13
sketchy u. of life CRIC 245:2
To be totally u. STAË 735:17
wisdom and u. BIBL 87:3
with all thy getting get u. BIBL 82:10
understandings muddy u. BURK 163:22
understands as he u. it JACK 400:14
he who understands u. DARW 251:3
world u. my language HAYD 364:18
understatement that was an u. MITC 523:12
understood hardest to be u. SHER 715:15
I have u. you DE G 255:21
music u. by children STRA 744:15
u., and not be believed BLAK 119:25
u. by others JACK 400:14
undertakers As u.—walk before GARR 330:7
like so many u. ADDI 4:19
undertaking no such u. has been received CHAM 201:1
underworld down to the U. VIRG 794:17
undeservedly books u. forgotten AUDE 35:15
undeserving u. poor SHAW 709:13
undevotional Dirty, dark, and u. VICT 792:4
undiscovered death, The u. country SHAK 664:4
undivided Alone and u. SHIP 717:5

undo For thee does she u. herself MIDD 507:8
u. the folded lie AUDE 35:2
u. this button SHAK 680:14
undone death had u. so many ELIO 296:1
I am u. BIBL 86:22
John Donne, Anne Donne, U. DONN 275:14
'tis we must be u. BEHN 62:9
We have left u. BOOK 125:16
What's done cannot be u. PROV 614:7
What's done cannot be u. SHAK 685:12
undress when I u. me FIEL 309:8
undulating u. throat BELL 63:20
uneasiness u. when being explained BALF 50:3
uneasy from u. dreams KAFK 425:9
U. lies the head SHAK 670:2
You are u. JACK 400:15
uneatable pursuit of the u. WILD 818:24
uneconomic shown it to be 'u.' SCHU 649:8
uneducated government by the u. CHES 211:21
u. man to read books CHUR 216:15
unemployed u. youth BAGE 46:22
unemployment leave it to u. KEYN 435:9
rising u. LAMO 449:13
unendurable which are unendurable LEWI 467:14
unequal equal division of u. earnings ELLI 298:12
unespied In the ocean's bosom u. MARV 498:6
unexamined u. life is not worth SOCR 727:1
unexpected Old age is the most u. TROT 783:15
u. always happens PROV 613:30
unexpectedness I call *u.* PEAC 571:1
unexplained you're u. as yet HALL 358:8
unextinguishable u. laugh in heaven BROW 152:11
unfabled u. Incense Tree DARL 250:9
unfaithful faith u. TENN 759:29
original is u. BORG 143:5
unfaithfulness U. in the house TALM 754:14
unfathomable u. deep forest THOM 773:2
unfathomed depth u. WESL 811:9
unfed houseless heads and u. sides SHAK 678:28
unfeeling u. for his own GRAY 350:17
unfeignedly them that u. love thee BOOK 128:22
unfinished Liberty is u. business ANON 17:7
unfit chosen from the u. ANON 15:19
chosen from the u. SAYI 647:6
u. to be trusted CHES 209:24
unforeseen certain but the u. PROV 608:13
unforgiveness alp of u. PLOM 579:2
unforgiving fill the u. minute KIPL 439:3
u. eye SHER 716:15
unfortunate u. man BOET 123:11
unfruitful becometh u. BIBL 95:21
unfurnished to be let u. BUTL 171:23
ungodliness tents of u. BOOK 137:13
ungodly because of the u. BOOK 133:25
counsel of the u. BOOK 131:15
hope of the u. BIBL 91:13
plagues remain for the u. BOOK 133:18
u. in great power BOOK 133:27
Upon the u. BOOK 132:3
ungraceful no more u. figure CECI 199:4
ungrammatical be a little u. FROS 326:17
ungratefulness call virtue there u. SIDN 718:11
unguem *Ad u. Factus homo* HORA 389:19
unguessed tread on Earth u. at ARNO 27:14
ungula *putrem sonitu quatit u.* VIRG 795:7
unhabitable no land u. THOR 776:20
unhanged three good men u. SHAK 668:3
unhappily bad end u. STOP 743:19
unhappiness loyalty we feel to u. GREE 351:19
prefer u. SANT 644:10
putting-off of u. GREE 351:16
u. develops the forces of the mind PROU 594:11
vocation of u. SIME 720:7
unhappy as u. as one thinks LA R 453:22
cannot be made u. LUCR 479:7
care for the u. VIRG 793:15
each u. family TOLS 779:6
I'm u. CHEK 208:4
Men who are u. RUSS 639:10
moral as soon as one is u. PROU 594:3
Not one is respectable or u. WHIT 815:15
only speak when she is u. SMIT 724:20
soft, u. sex BEHN 62:17
that of the u. WITT 824:9
think the great u. YOUN 838:17
u. can either give RHYS 625:18
u., far-off things WORD 832:3
U. the land that needs heroes BREC 147:10
unhasting Unresting, u. SMIT 726:9
unheard language of the u. KING 436:18
those u. Are sweeter KEAT 428:23
unholy sights u. MILT 512:12
unjust or u. SOCR 726:25
unhonoured Unwept, u. SCOT 651:1
unhouseled U., disappointed SHAK 662:31
unicorn like a young u. BOOK 133:13
lion and the u. NURS 549:3
rarer than the u. JONG 419:6
uniform good u. must work DICK 265:15
uniformity preferred before u. BACO 42:14
u. [of opinion] JEFF 406:2
uninitiated keep far off, you u. VIRG 794:18
uninspiring may be u. GEOR 334:5
unintelligible all this u. world WORD 829:3
rapid, u. patter GILB 339:9
uninterrupted work u. SITW 721:3
unintroduced u. neighbour ELIO 292:21
union Act of U. is there TRIM 781:14
Channel forbidding U. GRAT 349:7
determined to preserve this U. HOUS 391:12
devotion to the u. CARS 192:5
indestructible U. CHAS 204:3
Join the u. ANTH 22:17
key of the U. CLAY 220:4
Liberty *and* U. WEBS 807:12
O U., strong and great LONG 473:10
Our Federal U. JACK 400:13
our u. is perfect DICK 266:22
save the U. LINC 468:11
U. is strength PROV 613:31
u. of hands and hearts TAYL 756:21
U. of these States WHIT 815:22
U. will be dissolved COBB 223:7
unionists trades u. at heart JEVO 407:7
unions when Hitler attacked the u. NIEM 545:8
unit Misses an u. BROW 156:1
unite Workers of the world, u. CLOS 222:19
Workers of the world, u. MARX 500:7
united U. Colonies ADAM 3:8
U. we stand PROV 613:32
United States believe in the U. PAGE 562:18
close to the U. DIAZ 260:9
rise of the U. STEV 740:21
U. themselves WHIT 816:1
unities Three U. DRYD 283:4
u. are a completeness DICK 264:4
u. of time and place SCOT 652:1
uniting By u. we stand DICK 266:23
unity at u. in itself BOOK 140:14
dwell together in u. BOOK 141:4
Trinity in U. BOOK 126:22
truth, u., and concord BOOK 129:11
u. of our fatherland KOHL 443:6
u. of the empire BURK 163:6
u. of the faith BIBL 108:3
universal become a u. law KANT 425:14
kind of u. genius DRYD 283:3
one u. grin FIEL 310:14
Relaxed into a u. grin COWP 242:3
u. dovetailedness DICK 264:4
u. frame BACO 42:6
u. good POPE 585:17
u. monarchy of wit CARE 186:7
universe Architect of the U. JEAN 405:1
coherent plan to the u. HOYL 392:9
fact about the u. EINS 290:14
hell of a good u. next door CUMM 247:10
If the U. is hidden CHUA 213:3
knows the u. LA F 447:12
Life, the U. and Everything ADAM 2:4
measure of the u. SHEL 713:12
ordering of the u. ALFO 11:14
pet theory of the u. EDDI 287:23
Put back Thy u. JONE 418:21
repetitious mechanism of the U. WHIT 814:10
torrents of her myriad u. TENN 763:16
u. and I exist together CHUA 212:21
u. go to all the bother HAWK 364:10
u. is not hostile HOLM 381:4
u. is the plaything BAGE 47:19
u. . . . others call the Library BORG 143:3
u. queerer than we suppose HALD 356:15
u.'s existence is made known PENR 572:17
u. sleeps MAYA 502:15
u. was an illusion BORG 143:6
we and the u. exist HAWK 364:11
universities colleges and u. SMIT 723:12
U. incline wits to sophistry BACO 44:29
university able to get to a u. KINN 437:21
benefiting from u. AMIS 13:20
bred at an U. CONG 232:23
gained in the u. of life BOTT 144:23
God-sustaining U. GLAD 341:12
u. of Oxtail JOYC 422:16
u. of the air WILS 821:14
U. of these days CARL 188:1
U. should be DISR 269:11
We are the U. SPRI 735:9
unjust commended the u. steward BIBL 100:7
on the just and on the u. BIBL 93:14
u. or unholy SOCR 726:25
u. steals BOWE 145:20
unjustly teach to talk u. ARIS 24:9
unkind I am u. LOVE 476:15
sodden and u. BELL 64:6
unkindest most u. cut of all SHAK 676:7
unkindness u. may defeat my life SHAK 693:17
unking u. himself MAYH 502:21
unkist Uncouth u. SPEN 734:23
Unknowe, u., and lost CHAU 207:2
unknit u. that threatening SHAK 698:12
unknowable decide on the u. ZOBE 840:6
world u., we know THOM 774:11
unknowe U., unkist, and lost CHAU 207:2
unknowing cloud of u. ANON 15:17
u. and unknown BURN 167:23
unknown buried the U. Prime Minister ASQU 31:5
dies to himself u. SENE 654:21
forms of things u. SHAK 690:19
gates to the glorious and u. FORS 320:15
known and the u. PINT 576:13
live, unseen, u. POPE 586:25
My song is love u. CROS 246:15
She lived u. WORD 831:21
things u. POPE 585:1
Through the u. BAUD 57:10
to the u. god BIBL 104:8
travelled among u. men WORD 828:25
tread safely into the u. HASK 363:16
uncoffined, and u. BYRO 175:10
unknowing and u. BURN 167:23
u. and silent shore LAMB 448:19
u. is held to be glorious TACI 752:8
u. regions preserved ELIO 292:18
unmourned and u. HORA 389:9
unseen, unborn, u. FLEC 317:7
Woman is the great u. HARD 360:3
unlearned u. and uninformed AUST 39:10
unleavened u. bread BIBL 75:39
u. bread HAGG 356:1
u. bread of sincerity BIBL 106:2

unleaving Goldengrove u. HOPK 384:17
unlessoned u. girl SHAK 688:4
unlike through u. forms DION 268:4
u. any other FEIN 308:5
unloose not worthy to u. BIBL 101:9
unlovely long u. street TENN 760:28
unluckily good u. STOP 743:19
unlucky u. in love PROV 606:10
unmaking things are in the u. KING 437:3
unmanageable u. revolutionaries DEV 259:9
unmapped u. country ELIO 292:5
unmarried by their u. friends TROL 783:12
prime-roses, That die u. SHAK 703:18
unmask To u. falsehood SHAK 704:2
u. her beauty SHAK 662:8
unmeritable slight u. man SHAK 676:17
unmixed u. blessing HORA 388:9
unmourned u. and unknown HORA 389:9
unmuzzled come among you 'u.' GLAD 340:15
unnatural cruel, not u. SHAK 665:6
most u. murder SHAK 662:26
only u. sex act KINS 437:22
this u. scene SHAK 660:16
thoughts u. SHAK 692:22
unnecessary do the u. ANON 15:19
in u. matters BIBL 91:18
thou u. letter SHAK 678:13
to do the u. SAYI 647:6
unnoticed pathway of a life u. HORA 387:3
unofficial English u. rose BROO 150:11
unpalatable disastrous and the u. GALB 328:11
unparagoned Rubies u. SHAK 660:19
unparalleled lies A lass u. SHAK 658:4
unperson abolished, an u. ORWE 558:26
unpitied u., unreprieved MILT 515:11
unplayable another u. work SCHO 649:2
unpleasantness put up with u. NAPO 538:11
unplumbed u., salt, estranging sea ARNO 28:4
unpolicied great Caesar ass U. SHAK 658:2
unpolitical no such thing as an u. man MALA 491:20
unpopular safe to be u. STEV 740:12
unpremeditated u. art SHEL 714:3
u. verse MILT 517:12
unprepared Magnificently u. CORN 237:3
unprincipled sold by the u. CAPP 185:16
unprofitable flat, and u. SHAK 661:23
most idle and u. GIBB 335:17
unprofitably U. travelling WORD 830:21
unprotected u. race CLAR 218:14
unquiet be the earth never so u. BOOK 138:12
u. heart and brain TENN 760:24
unreality atmosphere of u. BAGE 47:8
unreason Television thrives on u. DAY 253:9
unreasonable progress depends on u. man SHAW 708:24
unrefined u. stuff of mine BRAD 146:16
unreflecting u. herd WORD 828:18
unregarded U. age SHAK 658:15
unreliable decrepit and u. OUSP 560:25
Even death is u. BECK 60:8
u. ally in the battle COHE 224:3
unremembered nameless, u., acts WORD 829:2
unremitting u. humanity BENN 66:1
unrequited what u. affection is DICK 262:16
unrest u. which men miscall delight SHEL 711:1
unresting U., unhasting SMIT 726:9
unrewarded Nothing went u. DRYD 280:10
unrighteousness mammon of u. BIBL 100:8
unruly old fool, u. sun DONN 274:14
u. evil BIBL 110:19
u. wills and affections BOOK 128:7
unsad U. and evere untrewe CHAU 205:7
unsafe U. at any speed NADE 538:2
unsatisfied leaves one u. WILD 818:19
unsayable say the u. RUSH 638:1
unscathed u. tourist of wars GELL 333:1
unseamed Till he u. him SHAK 681:9
unsearchable heart of kings is u. BIBL 83:17
u. riches of Christ BIBL 107:26
unseen born to blush u. GRAY 350:11
effect, itself u. REYN 625:11
God knows the U. KORA 445:4
Greet the u. BROW 155:5
O friend u. FLEC 317:7
Thou art u. SHEL 714:5
u. among us SHEL 711:16
u. things above HANK 359:9
walk the earth U. MILT 516:23
unsex U. me here SHAK 682:2
unshook u. amidst a bursting world POPE 583:2
unsifted like a green girl, U. SHAK 662:14
unsoiled delicately and u. CHUR 216:11
unsought lost, that is u. CHAU 207:2
unspeakable come to those u. joys BOOK 128:22
joy u. BIBL 110:25
speak the u. RUSH 638:1
u. in full pursuit WILD 818:24
unspotted keep himself u. BIBL 110:16
unstable U. as water BIBL 75:21
unsubstantial u. realms of Hades VIRG 794:19
unsung unhonoured, and u. SCOT 651:1
untalented product of the u. CAPP 185:16
untaught U. the noble end IRWI 400:6
untender So young, and so u. SHAK 677:23
unterrified Satan stood U. MILT 515:23
unthinking u. time DRYD 282:16
untilled land u. IRWI 400:5
untimely came I so u. forth WALL 800:10
U. ripped SHAK 685:25
unto give u. this last BIBL 96:19
u. us a child is born BIBL 87:1
untravelled Gleams that u. world TENN 767:9
untried difficult; and left u. CHES 211:17
new and u. LINC 468:6
untrodden among the u. ways WORD 831:19
through an u. forest MURR 537:5
untroubled u. where I lie CLAR 218:16
untrue man who's u. to his wife AUDE 34:11
Unsad and evere u. CHAU 205:7
untruth one wilful u. NEWM 542:12
truth and u. BACO 42:34
untune Music shall u. the sky DRYD 282:23
untwisted U. all the shining robe THOM 775:18
unusual cruel and u. punishment CONS 235:14
moved by what is not u. ELIO 292:24
unutterable looked u. things THOM 775:9
unvarnished round u. tale SHAK 691:32
unwanted feeling of being u. TERE 768:8
unwary all u. GILB 338:4
unwashed lean u. artificer SHAK 677:16
unwearied U. still, lover by lover YEAT 837:24
unwept U., unhonoured SCOT 651:1
Upon his watery bier U. MILT 512:28
unwholesome not u. AUST 37:13
unwilling committee is a group of the u. ANON 15:19
group of the u. SAYI 647:6
u. or unable WILL 821:1
unwillingly U. to school SHAK 658:26
unwise sight of the u. BIBL 91:8
to the wise, and to the u. BIBL 104:25
unworthiness for our u. we dare not BOOK 130:6
unwritten Custom, that u. law D'AV 251:7
up be u. betimes SHAK 701:8
Is notwithstanding u. SHAK 675:13
nice to people on your way u. MIZN 524:11
U. and down MAND 493:6
u. go we QUAR 618:22
U. Guards and at them WELL 809:15
u.-hill all the way ROSS 634:12
U., lad HOUS 390:16
U., Lord BOOK 132:1
U. to a point, Lord Copper WAUG 806:10
U. with your damned nonsense RICH 627:11
What goes u. must come down PROV 614:1
upharsin MENE, TEKEL, U. BIBL 90:4
upper butler's u. slopes WODE 824:24
large u. room BIBL 100:21
Like many of the U. Class BELL 63:24
man have the u. hand BOOK 132:1
prove the u. classes COWA 238:19
tempt the u. classes SMIT 723:18
u. station of low life DEFO 254:18
upright God hath made man u. BIBL 84:17
stand u. in the winds BOLT 124:20
that is, u. THOM 772:15
uprightness born with u. CONF 231:12
uprising mine u. BOOK 141:9
Our wakening and u. KEBL 432:4
uproar set all the city on an u. BIBL 104:4
u.'s your only music KEAT 430:25
upside turneth it u. down BOOK 141:23
world u. down BIBL 104:5
upstairs kicked u. HALI 358:4
u. into the world CONG 232:18
upstanding clean u. chap like you KING 437:16
upward Eternal Woman draws us u. GOET 343:4
Woman draws us u. CLOS 222:7
upwards car could go straight u. HOYL 392:7
uranium element u. may be turned EINS 290:15
urban u., squat, and packed with guile BROO 150:14
urbe *Rus in u.* MART 498:5
urge Always the procreant u. WHIT 815:11
u. for destruction BAKU 48:16
urges Will that stirs and u. HARD 361:10
Uricon ashes under U. HOUS 391:3
Urim U. and the Thummim BIBL 76:15
urinals graffiti in the u. GIDE 336:17
urine red wine of Shiraz into u. DINE 267:20
sleep, and u. SHAK 683:15
tang of faintly scented u. JOYC [illegible]
u. is congealed ice SHAK 686:20
urn darling in an u. CARE 186:12
loud-hissing u. COWP 241:31
Pit's long-broken u. WILD 819:3
storied u. GRAY 350:10
urna *Omne capax movet u. nomen* HORA 388:12
urns u. and sepulchres CREW 244:22
ursa major nativity was under *u.* SHAK 678:6
us Not unto u., O Lord BOOK 139:22
USA Born in the U. SPRI 735:10
usage if u. so choose HORA 385:15
use Beauty too rich for u. SHAK 697:7
let u. be preferred BACO 42:14
such as cannot u. them JONS 419:22
true u. of speech GOLD 345:12
u. alone that sanctifies POPE 583:26
u. a poor maiden so SONG 729:4
U. every man after his desert SHAK 663:25
u. him as though you loved him WALT 802:23
u. of a new-born child FRAN 323:17
u. rather than ostentation GIBB 335:8
worn away by u. OVID 561:11
used buy a u. car POLI 582:8
get u. to them NEUM 541:11
My name is U.-to-was TRAI 780:19
Things ain't what they u. to be PERS 574:7
useful be a Really U. Engine AWDR 39:19
know to be u. MORR 532:17
magistrate, as equally u. GIBB 335:4
some u. work THOM 771:2
way to what is u. COUS 238:6
useless absolutely, completely u. DOST 276:6
are the most u. RUSK 638:22
essentially u. SANT 644:12

Lodged with me u. MILT 518:29
never live to be u. WESL 811:20
plans are u. EISE 291:11
usquebae Wi' u., we'll face BURN 168:15
USSR Back in the U. LENN 463:18
usual Business carried on as u. CHUR 214:20
usura With u. hath no man a house POUN 589:7
usurp None can u. this height KEAT 427:18
usury forbidden u. KORA 443:22
given his money upon u. BOOK 132:8
u. is contrary to Scripture TAWN 755:16
usus *si volet u.* HORA 385:15
Uther romance of U.'s son MILT 514:30
uti *deorum Muneribus sapienter u.* HORA 389:10
utile *qui miscuit u. dulci* HORA 386:3
utility non-being into u. LAO 451:8
u. to its conditions SANT 644:12
Utopia Not in U. WORD 831:8
possibly be attained in U. GLAD 341:4
principality in U. MACA 482:1
signposts to socialist U. CROS 246:5
U. is a blessed past KISS 441:30
Utopias all the static U. INGE 399:4
utterance timely u. WORD 829:16
u. of the early gods KEAT 427:25
utterly should u. have fainted BOOK 133:12
uttermost u. parts of the sea BOOK 141:11
U-turn media catchphrase, the U. THAT 769:24

V with a "V" or a "W" DICK 265:13
vacancies v. to be obtained JEFF 405:15
vacancy another v. soon PRIE 591:17
vacant spoke the v. mind GOLD 344:10
Stuffs out his v. garments SHAK 677:11
V. heart and hand SCOT 651:19
v. interstellar spaces ELIO 294:9
v. or in pensive mood WORD 828:27
vacations No extras, no v. DICK 263:17
vacuous be absolutely v. CHUA 213:6
vacuum from behind the v. cleaner GREE 352:11
Nature abhors a v. PROV 607:18
Nature abhors a v. RABE 619:10
v. a hell of a lot better WILL 820:16
v. or space DESC 258:20
vadis *Quo v.* BIBL 114:7
vae *V. victis* LIVY 470:10
vagabond is a v. GOLD 345:24
vagabonds So many v. SKEL 721:14
vagrancy instructed v. ELIO 293:3
vague don't be v. ADVE 7:15
V. and eluding LAO 451:11
vagueness no hypocrisy and no v. STEN 737:18
vaguery V. in the Field OSBO 560:3
vain all is v. ROSS 635:4
deceive you with v. words BIBL 108:7
disquieteth himself in v. BOOK 133:30
knowledge that he lived in v. BYRO 174:12
name of God in v. BIBL 76:10
people imagine a v. thing BOOK 131:16
this man's religion is v. BIBL 110:15
v., ill-natured DEFO 255:11
V. man, said she SPEN 733:4
v. repetitions BIBL 93:18
V. the ambition of kings WEBS 807:19
V. wisdom all MILT 515:19
watchman waketh but in v. BOOK 140:21
vainglory land of v. BUNY 160:16
vainly V. begot GREV 353:4
v. men themselves amaze MARV 498:13
vale *ave atque v.* CATU 198:1
cool sequestered v. of life GRAY 350:13
in that hollow v. KING 436:7
shady sadness of a v. KEAT 427:22
this v. of tears PRAY 592:6
v. of misery BOOK 137:12
v. of soul-making KEAT 431:14
v. of years SHAK 692:25
valentine Hail, Bishop V. DONN 272:17
thank you for a V. LOCH 471:10
valere *sed v. vita est* MART 498:2
vales lily-silver'd v. POPE 580:23
thy hills and v. JAME 402:22
valet hero to his v. CORN 237:7
hero to his v. PROV 607:48
to his very v. seemed BYRO 173:15
valiant As he was v., I honour him SHAK 675:25
v. Jack Falstaff SHAK 668:16
v. never taste of death SHAK 675:10
valley great things from the v. CHES 211:7
How green was my v. LLEW 470:12
in the v. below SONG 729:4
in the v. of Death TENN 757:15
Love is of the v. TENN 766:5
multitudes in the v. of decision BIBL 90:15
paweth in the v. BIBL 81:35
V. and lowland, sing OAKL 552:5
v. full of bones BIBL 89:32
v. of Humiliation BUNY 160:17
v. of the shadow of death BOOK 133:1
v. shall be exalted BIBL 87:28
valleys down the v. wild BLAK 120:12
lily of the v. BIBL 85:9
v. also shall stand BOOK 136:2
v., groves, hills MARL 496:19
Vallombrosa V., where the Etrurian shades MILT 514:23
Valois shadow of the V. CHES 210:10
valorous childish v. MARL 497:2
valour better part of v. PROV 598:18
better part of v. SHAK 669:16
confused old age with v. LEON 464:8
For contemplation he and v. MILT 516:15
For v., is not love SHAK 680:27
men of great v. WILL 819:21
mighty man of v. BIBL 77:31
much care and v. SHAK 671:14
My v. is certainly going SHER 716:8
true v. see BUNY 161:16
valuable Truth is the most v. thing TWAI 786:7
value Four things of paramount v. JAIN 401:18
little v. of fortune STEE 737:2
Nothing has v. FORS 320:23
of more v. than many sparrows BIBL 94:36
prayer never loses its v. TALM 754:25
unsure of one's own v. FLAU 316:14
v. a virtuous LOCK 472:8
v. of life MONT 527:10
v. of nothing WILD 818:12
v. on the personality market FROM 325:10
V. yourselves CHUD 213:10
values authentic and pure v. WEIL 808:25
moneys are for v. BACO 41:14
Victorian v. THAT 770:3
van Follow the v. COLL 228:13
Vandyke V. is of the company LAST 457:15
vanish softly and suddenly v. CARR 191:24
v. with the rose FITZ 315:2
vanished This time it v. CARR 189:16
this v. being HAWK 364:7
touch of a v. hand TENN 757:12
v. before the white man TECU 757:3
v. like a dream CARL 187:29
vanisheth and then v. BIBL 110:21
vanishings Fallings from us, v. WORD 830:6
vanitas Ah! *V. Vanitatum* THAC 769:14
V. vanitatum BIBL 113:26
vanities bonfire of the v. WOLF 825:12
vanity all is v. BIBL 83:39
feeds your v. PARR 568:4
forbidden v. GREV 353:4
fruit of my v. PETR 574:12
lighter than v. BOOK 135:22
lions, or V.-Fair BUNY 161:13
mouth talketh of v. BOOK 141:18
name of the *Golden V.* SONG 730:2
name of V.-Fair BUNY 161:1
Oh, V. of vanities THAC 769:17
pomps and v. BOOK 130:11
Pull down thy v. POUN 589:21
Pull down thy v. POUN 589:22
revenge against v. FOOT 319:6
v. and vexation of spirit BIBL 84:4
v. in years SHAK 668:14
V. is as ill at ease ELIO 292:2
V., like murder, will out COWL 239:25
v. of human hopes JOHN 410:21
v. of others AUST 38:4
V. of vanities BIBL 83:39
v. the great passion SHER 716:21
ye that work v. BOOK 131:25
vanquish I will v. NEWM 542:4
vanquished I have v. thee JUST 424:2
Valiantly v. SHAK 657:18
vapour deceitful v. SMOL 726:14
I absorb the v. GLAD 341:13
It is even a v. BIBL 110:21
v. sometime like a bear SHAK 657:12
vapours congregation of v. SHAK 663:18
snow and v. BOOK 141:27
v. weep their burthen TENN 766:16
variable love prove likewise v. SHAK 697:14
variableness with whom is no v. BIBL 110:12
variation admitting any v. BOOK 125:11
variety order in v. we see POPE 587:14
source of pleasure is v. JOHN 409:25
stale Her infinite v. SHAK 656:27
V. is the soul BEHN 62:13
V. is the spice of life PROV 613:33
V.'s the very spice COWP 241:23
variorum Life is all a v. BURN 167:21
various constant as v. GRAV 349:14
man so v. DRYD 280:9
so be v. GRAV 349:14
varium *V. et mutabile semper Femina* VIRG 794:13
Varus V., give me back my legions AUGU 36:15
vase not a v. to be filled RABE 619:13
Sèvres v. in the hands WAUG 806:18
shatter the v. MOOR 530:11
vasty v. hall of death ARNO 26:23
vate *carent quia v. sacro* HORA 389:9
vats boilers and v. JOHN 416:20
purple in the v. TENN 766:5
vatum *genus irritabile v.* HORA 387:9
vaulted v. with such ease SHAK 668:30
vaulting V. ambition SHAK 682:12
V. the sea CRAN 243:25
vaunting V. aloud MILT 514:14
veal Bellamy's v. pies LAST 456:20
vécu *J'ai v.* SIEY 719:3
veels V. vithin veels DICK 265:16
Vega V. conspicuous overhead AUDE 34:16
vegetable v., animal, and mineral GILB 339:3
v. love should grow MARV 499:1
vegetarian v. leanings ORWE 559:4
vehicles no triad of v. MAHĀ 490:11
veil from behind a v. KORA 445:6
Lift not the painted v. SHEL 713:27
wrapped in a gauzy veil SHEL 714:15
vein not in the giving v. SHAK 696:22
than the jugular v. KORA 445:13
tyrant's v. SHAK 689:11
veins fury and the mire of human v. YEAT 835:6
In my v., in my bones ROET 631:6
jigging v. MARL 496:20
vellera *non vobis v. oves* VIRG 797:4
venal v. city ripe to perish SALL 643:10
venerable what v. creatures TRAH 780:15
Veneres *V. Cupidinesque* CATU 196:34
vengeance day of v. BIBL 89:5
stay the hands of v. JACK 400:19
sudden v. waits POPE 582:20
swift v. LANG 450:19

vengeance (*cont.*):
V., deep-brooding SCOT 650:15
V.! Forgyve be in nevere LANG 450:21
V. is mine BIBL 105:17
veni *V., Sancte Spiritus* LANG 451:1
V., vidi, vici CAES 180:21
veniam *v. petimusque damusque vicissim* HORA 385:11
Venice Ocean's nursling, V. SHEL 712:5
stood in V. BYRO 174:24
V.' pride is nought COLE 224:18
what V. earned BROW 158:9
venit *Benedictus qui v.* MISS 520:21
venite *v., adoremus Dominum* ANON 21:4
venomous no being so v. TROL 782:20
v. as the poison BOOK 135:18
vento *In v. et rapida* CATU 197:12
ventriloquizing V. for the unborn GRAV 349:16
venture drew a bow at a v. BIBL 80:11
Each v. Is a new beginning ELIO 294:11
Nothing v. PROV 608:18
Nothing v. PROV 608:19
ventured You have deeply v. BYRO 178:17
ventus *nullus suus v. est* SENE 654:17
Venus V. clerk Ovide CHAU 206:23
V. here will choose her dwelling DRYD 281:32
V., take my votive glass PRIO 592:14
V. tout entière RACI 619:18
women are from V. GRAY 349:23
ver *v. egelidos* CATU 197:7
vera *v. incessu patuit dea* VIRG 793:12
veracity tell us with v. GRAY 351:9
verb V. is God HUGO 393:16
v. not a noun FULL 327:4
word is the V. HUGO 393:16
verba *iurare in v. magistri* HORA 386:8
Nullius in v. MOTT 535:12
v. sequentur CATO 194:16
verbal v. contract isn't worth GOLD 346:3
verbo *sed tantum dic v.* MISS 522:20
verboojuice Sesquippledan v. WELL 810:8
verbosa *V. et grandis epistula* JUVE 424:20
v. rusticitas JERO 406:14
verbosity crude v. JERO 406:14
exuberance of his own v. DISR 269:20
verbrennt *wo man Bücher V.* HEIN 368:3
verbum *In principio erat V.* MISS 522:22
V. CARO FACTUM EST MISS 523:1
V. infans ANDR 14:14
V. sapienti PLAU 578:13
volat irrevocabile v. HORA 387:1
verde *V. que te quiero verde* GARC 329:11
verdict opportunity to pass their v. AHER 8:29
v. afterwards CARR 190:10
Vereker V.'s secret JAME 403:3
verge get to the v. DULL 284:13
verger erudite V. BARH 54:1
verifiability criterion of v. AYER 40:4
not the *v.* POPP 587:24
verification method of its v. SCHL 648:20
v. of his own prophecies TROL 782:26
verify v. your references ROUT 636:7
verily v., I say unto you BIBL 101:30
verisimilitude artistic v. GILB 338:13
fine isolated v. KEAT 430:24
veritas *magis amica v.* ARIS 25:9
Magna est v., et praevalet BIBL 114:12
veritatem *Ex umbris in v.* EPIT 302:5
vermilion V.-spotted, golden KEAT 428:14
vermin little odious v. SWIF 747:21
lower than v. BEVA 71:13
Vermont so goes V. FARL 307:1
vermouth gin and v. DEV 259:10
vernal from a v. wood WORD 832:6
v. seasons of the year MILT 519:21
vero *Se non è v.* SAYI 648:3
verre *je bois dans mon v.* MUSS 537:10
Versailles lady at the court of V. VOLT 798:9
verse accomplishment of v. WORD 828:7
all that is not v. MOLI 524:18
as soon write free v. FROS 326:18
book of v.—and Thou FITZ 314:9
by v. seek fame SIDN 718:19
could not v. immortal save BYRO 174:4
court others in v. PRIO 592:10
died to make v. free PRES 591:6
Doctors in v. THOM 773:12
each v. of thine HERR 374:17
for prose and v. CARE 186:4
French, whose v. GRAY 351:6
hoarse, rough v. POPE 584:23
incantation of this v. SHEL 712:18
indignation makes me write v. JUVE 424:5
Muses made write v. VIRG 796:11
No subject for immortal v. DAY- 253:14
Not v. now, only prose BROW 155:16
No v. can give pleasure HORA 387:4
Of all my v. STEV 743:2
rugged v. I chose DRYD 282:15
run them into v. DRYD 283:10
sail of his great v. SHAK 705:3
subject of all v. EPIT 304:9
turnings intricate of v. WORD 831:5
unpremeditated v. MILT 517:12
varying v. POPE 586:17
v. for visions IBSE 398:13
v. is a measured speech BACO 41:15
v. is merely prose BYRO 178:3
v. may find him HERB 372:4
v. the subject fit CARE 186:19
Voice, and V. MILT 511:10
with those in v. CONG 233:8
write it out in a v. YEAT 835:21
verses recited v. in writing BIBL 92:15
Tear him for his bad v. SHAK 676:15
versing relish v. HERB 372:17
versions hundred v. of it SHAW 709:9
versum *facit indignatio v.* JUVE 424:5
versus *temptabam dicere v.* OVID 561:23
vertigo butterflies of v. BECK 59:11
whirl around With the *v.* JONS 420:11
vertu *v. traitable* MOLI 525:10
verum *Ave v. corpus* ANON 21:6
quaerere v. HORA 387:8
very V. God of very God BOOK 129:8
V. interesting . . . but CATC 196:24
Vesper *accendit lumina V.* VIRG 796:15
vespers friars were singing v. GIBB 335:25
vessel gilded v. goes GRAY 350:5
one v. unto honour BIBL 105:13
potter's v. BOOK 131:17
remaining in a v. HUME 394:14
unto the weaker v. BIBL 111:3
v. with the pestle FILM 312:6
vessels Empty v. make PROV 599:10
treasure in earthen v. BIBL 107:6
vest body's v. aside MARV 498:17
Vestal blameless V.'s lost POPE 582:24
vestigia *quia me v. terrent* HORA 386:12
vestry see you in the v. SMIT 725:16
vesture as a v. BOOK 138:15
cast lots upon my v. BOOK 132:25
Mine outward v. be LITT 470:4
queen in a v. of gold BOOK 134:15
vex die to v. me MELB 503:14
V. not thou the poet's mind TENN 765:11
vexation Multiplication is v. ANON 17:19
of so infinite v. WEBS 808:17
vanity and v. of spirit BIBL 84:4
vexes other v. it KEAT 427:19
Vexilla *Vexilla regis prodeunt* FORT 321:7
vexing V. the dull ear SHAK 677:12
vials golden v. full of odours BIBL 112:3
viator *latrone v.* JUVE 424:19
vibrates V. in the memory SHEL 714:1
vibration brave v. each way free HERR 375:4
vicar V. of Bray SONG 729:12
vice any taint of v. SHAK 702:16
Art is v. DEGA 255:17
best discover v. BACO 42:5
bullied out of v. SURT 746:13
defence of liberty is no v. GOLD 345:33
end in sight was a v. BROW 158:4
English v. RATT 622:6
folly and v. TENN 763:22
Forgiveness of each v. BLAK 118:18
He lashed the v. SWIF 749:25
in a private man a v. MASS 501:2
in spreading V.'s snares CHUR 214:8
in the dust my v. is laid EPIT 303:16
not having been v. WALP 802:2
no v., but beggary SHAK 677:8
nurseries of all v. FIEL 310:2
of v. must pardon beg SHAK 665:21
old-gentlemanly v. BYRO 176:10
raptures and roses of v. SWIN 750:15
render v. serviceable BOLI 124:19
reverend v. SHAK 668:14
sanction V. BYRO 178:6
sensual pleasure without v. JOHN 418:12
v. and religion SMIT 726:6
V. came in always DEFO 254:16
V. is a monster POPE 585:22
V. is detestable BURN 165:21
v. of chastity VOLT 798:7
v. pays to virtue LA R 453:15
v. which is our own MONT 527:6
virtue and v. JOHN 413:8
vice-presidency of the v. ADAM 3:9
viceroy future V. must . . . not be VICT 792:6
V. has been forgotten NEHR 540:9
viceroys appointed you v. KORA 445:4
vices By hating v. too much BURK 164:4
ladder of our v. AUGU 36:13
most v. may be committed BOSW 144:21
our pleasant v. SHAK 680:9
redeemed his v. JONS 421:2
v. and follies of human kind CONG 232:8
v. and virtues of mankind TOCQ 777:17
v. with more zeal CHUR 213:22
virtues and not one's v. WEST 812:12
wipe out v. MONT 527:19
vicious didn't know what v. was [illegible]
expect a boy to be v. SAKI 642:6
Sid V. of the Sex Pistols DURC 286:2
yet more v. generation HORA 388:19
vicissitude sad v. of things STER 739:16
vicisti *V., Galilae* LAST 457:14
victa *sed v. Catoni* LUCA 478:13
victi *Pugna magna v. sumus* LIVY 470:11
victim felt like a v. WALP 801:18
first insults the v. CRAB 243:17
It marks a v. CLAY 220:3
oppressor, never the v. WIES 816:16
v. must be found GILB 338:1
v. of Parthenia's pride GAY 332:4
victims blame to its 'v.' SONT 728:4
gave its v. time to die GUIB 354:16
little v. play GRAY 350:16
They are its v. CONR 234:23
v. lie strewn around BOWE 145:10
v. of American Fascism ROSE 633:21
v. who respect their executioners SART 645:13
victis *Vae v.* LIVY 470:10
victor to the v. belong MARC 495:7
Victoria take a ticket at V. BEVI 72:10
Victorian stuffy V. family ORWE 558:16
V. values THAT 770:3
victories few sharp v. WAUG 806:12
Peace hath her v. MILT 519:4
proper use of v. POLY 580:4
victors are by v. undone DRYD 281:14
victorious ills o' life v. BURN 168:12
Send him v. SONG 729:7
victors v. are by victories undone DRYD 281:14
victory Dig for v. OFFI 554:4
Empire and V. SHEL 713:16
gotten himself the v. BOOK 138:9
grave, where is thy v. BIBL 107:4

great and glorious v. NELS 540:19
humanity after V. NELS 540:19
In v.; magnanimity CHUR 216:16
in v. unbearable CHUR 216:10
no substitute for v. MACA 481:6
not the v. but the contest COUB 238:3
One more such v. PYRR 618:9
peace without v. WILS 822:13
produce v. parades HOBS 379:8
smells like v. FILM 311:15
swallow up death in v. BIBL 87:11
Truth beareth away the v. BIBL 90:26
'twas a famous v. SOUT 730:13
v. by a woman WEST 812:18
V. has a hundred fathers CIAN 217:3
v. in spite of all terror CHUR 215:9
v. over oneself PALI 565:20
wallow in our v. PRES 591:5
victrix *V. causa deis placuit* LUCA 478:13
victuals please About their v. CALV 182:4
snatching his v. from the table CHUR 215:5
vida *¿Qué es la v.* CALD 181:5
vidders Be wery careful o' v. DICK 265:7
videri *salices et se cupit ante v.* VIRG 795:20
vidi *Ut v., ut perii* VIRG 796:8
Veni, v., vici CAES 180:21
vie *v. humaine commence* SART 645:10
vieillesse *Quelle triste v.* TALL 753:9
si v. pouvait ESTI 301:10
Vienna at the Congress of V. ADEN 6:3
V. is nothing METT 506:11
viento *Verde v.* GARC 329:11
Viet Cong no quarrel with the V. ALI 12:5
Vietnam since the V. war WHIT 814:3
To win in V. SPOC 735:2
V. as a war PILG 576:6
V. was lost in MCLU 487:11
view lends enchantment to the v. CAMP 183:13
motley to the v. SHAK 705:13
views Kipling and his v. AUDE 34:3
vigilance eternal v. CURR 248:2
vigilant Be sober, be v. BIBL 111:7
vigour she has a secret v. EMER 299:16
Viking Stir the V.'s blood KING 437:8
vile change our v. body BOOK 131:14
only man is v. HEBE 367:7
O v., Intolerable SHAK 698:11
Things base and v. SHAK 689:7
V., but viler George the Second LAND 450:4
vilest v. alleys in London DOYL 277:9
v. things Become themselves SHAK 656:27
village first in a v. CAES 180:18
image of a global v. MCLU 487:7
in a country v. AUST 39:9
life in the v. LEE 462:1
Some v.-Hampden GRAY 350:11
Sweet Auburn, loveliest v. GOLD 344:7
vegetate in a v. COLT 230:4
v. all declared GOLD 344:14
v. atheist brooding CHES 211:15
villages pleasant v. and farms MILT 517:14
villain determinèd to prove a v. SHAK 696:11
hungry, lean-faced v. SHAK 659:30
lecherous, kindless v. SHAK 663:30
One murder made a v. PORT 588:13
smiling, damnèd v. SHAK 663:1
villains Leave us our v. BENN 66:3
v. by necessity SHAK 678:5
villainy my naked v. SHAK 696:16
v. you teach me SHAK 687:31
Villiers Great V. lies POPE 583:22
vinces *In hoc signo v.* CONS 235:11
Vinci spell it V. TWAI 786:13
vincit *Omnia v. Amor* VIRG 796:12
vindicate v. the ways of God POPE 585:5
vine aloe, and maize and v. TENN 758:14
as the fruitful v. BOOK 140:23
best fits a little v. HERR 374:21
clusters of the v. MARV 498:15
foxlike in the v. TENN 766:5
gadding v. o'ergrown MILT 513:1
like the twining v. COLE 225:5
Under his own v. SHAK 673:26
v. about the elm DAVI 251:19
who will the v. destroy SHAK 704:1
vinegar gave me v. to drink BOOK 136:11
like v. from wine BYRO 176:19
like weak v. WELL 810:9
mix like oil and v. GAIN 327:18
more flies than v. PROV 602:46
Oil, v., sugar GOLD 344:23
on V. Hill HEAN 366:16
tartest v. PROV 601:1
vines advise his client to plant v. WRIG 833:10
bless With fruit the v. KEAT 430:8
foxes, that spoil the v. BIBL 85:11
vineyard Give me thy v. BIBL 80:7
v., which was in Jezreel BIBL 80:6
well-beloved hath a v. BIBL 86:15
who planteth a v. BIBL 106:8
vintage O, for a draught of v. KEAT 429:7
trampling out the v. HOWE 391:15
vinum call poesy *v. daemonum* BACO 41:17
violate v. would be oppression JEFF 405:11
violations no end to the v. BOWE 145:12
violence do v. to own nature MENG 504:21
get meat without v. LAWS 459:5
Keep v. in the mind CLOS 222:16
legitimate v. WEBE 807:5
not by v. LATI 454:3
organization of v. BAEZ 45:20
slain, nor treated with v. JAIN 401:16
Snobbery with V. BENN 65:20
source of all v. SART 645:12
Thus with v. BIBL 113:1
v. is necessary BROW 151:20
violent All v. feelings RUSK 638:10
laid v. hands upon themselves BOOK 131:11
violently v. if they must QUIN 619:3
violet At the v. hour ELIO 296:8
oxlips and the nodding v. SHAK 689:25
perfume on the v. SHAK 677:15
v. by a mossy stone WORD 831:20
v.-embroidered vale MILT 511:19
v. into a crucible SHEL 714:20
v. smells to him SHAK 671:15
v.'s reclining head DONN 273:24
violets By ashen roots the v. blow TENN 762:2
daisies pied and v. blue SHAK 681:3
Fast fading v. KEAT 429:12
I would give you some v. SHAK 666:8
Who are the v. now SHAK 696:1
violin v. so much wood and catgut PRIE 591:13
violins sobs of autumn's v. VERL 791:8
vipers O generation of v. BIBL 92:29
plays with his v. CELA 199:8
vir *Beatus v. qui timet Dominum* BIBL 113:21
vires *Quod si deficiant v.* PROP 593:16
Ut desint v. OVID 561:10
Virgil have just seen V. OVID 561:24
V., as he lay dying FLAU 316:14
V. at Mexico WALP 801:3
virgin In a V.'s womb once dwelling THOM 771:10
v.-choir KEAT 429:18
v. girls and boys HORA 388:11
v. goddess returns VIRG 796:4
V. had acted ADAM 2:24
V. is the possibility BRAN 147:1
v. mother born MILT 513:17
v. renowned for ever HORA 388:20
v. shall conceive BIBL 86:26
V. shrouded in snow BLAK 120:22
v. white integrity DONN 272:19
v., yet a bride CARE 186:10
was a v. once BLAK 118:19
withering on the v. thorn SHAK 689:3
virgined my true lip Hath v. it SHAK 660:14
Virginian I am not a V. HENR 371:2
virginibus *V. puerisque canto* HORA 388:11
virginity for my v. PRIO 593:6
little more v. TREE 781:4
long preserved v. MARV 499:3
v. could be a virtue VOLT 797:19
virgins holy v. in their ecstasies TENN 759:24
v. are soft BYRO 173:19
virgo *Iam redit et v.* VIRG 796:4
virisque *stat Romana v.* ENNI 300:15
virtuality voyager in v. TURK 785:11
virtue accommodating sort of v. MOLI 525:10
Assume a v. SHAK 665:22
best discover v. BACO 42:5
blundered on some v. unawares CHUR 214:8
call v. there ungratefulness SIDN 718:11
excellence or v. ARIS 24:17
Few men have v. to withstand WASH 804:5
flattered into v. SURT 746:13
follow v. and knowledge DANT 249:17
form of every v. at the testing point LEWI 466:24
governs his state by v. CONF 231:5
in a prince the v. MASS 501:2
instrument of v. MORE 531:1
is a soverayn v. LANG 450:19
lilies and languors of v. SWIN 750:15
Loss of v. in a female AUST 38:22
my v.'s guide MONT 526:14
no v. like necessity SHAK 694:15
O infinite v. SHAK 657:9
one v., and a thousand crimes BYRO 175:19
only reward of v. EMER 299:17
Patience is a v. PROV 609:19
really possesses v. LAO 451:13
recognize v. PERS 574:4
Self-denial is not a v. SHAW 708:23
stops the growth of v. WOLL 826:3
tart cathartic v. EMER 299:18
'tis some v. CONG 233:18
'tis some v. CONG 233:19
toil after v. LAMB 449:8
to the cause of v. BOLI 124:19
true v. of human beings MILL 509:7
very sinews of v. WALT 802:18
vice pays to v. LA R 453:15
virginity could be a v. VOLT 797:19
v. and talents JEFF 405:18
v. and vice JOHN 413:8
V. could see to do MILT 511:20
V. does not come from money SOCR 726:24
v. had gone out of him BIBL 98:6
V. is its own reward PROV 613:34
V. is like a rich stone BACO 42:9
v. is made of the vice VOLT 798:7
v. is the essence ROBE 629:6
V. is the fount MARL 496:27
V. itself of vice must SHAK 665:21
V. knows to a farthing WALP 802:2
V. may be assailed MILT 511:27
v. of bores WAUG 806:19
v. of fools BACO 41:25
V. she finds too painful POPE 583:14
V. shuns ease MONT 527:18
v. which requires GOLD 345:28
What is v. SHAW 708:11
without v. ROBE 629:8
woman of easy v. HAIL 356:11
Young men have more v. JOHN 413:11
virtues all the v. of Man BYRO 179:20
Curse on his v. ADDI 4:13
makes some v. impracticable JOHN 416:27
moral v. CHES 209:20
necessities call out v. ADAM 2:1
plant whose v. EMER 299:28
rural v. leave GOLD 344:18
vices and v. of mankind TOCQ 777:17
vices with his v. JONS 421:2
v. and not one's vices WEST 812:12
v. made or crimes DEFO 255:6
V. neglected CRAB 242:21
v. very kind PRIO 592:11
v. were his arts BURK 165:15
v. We write in water SHAK 673:22

virtues (*cont.*):
v. Will plead SHAK 682:10
world to hide v. in SHAK 701:2
virtuous because thou art v. SHAK 701:14
looking upon men as v. BOLI 124:18
men grow v. POPE 587:20
most v. man WALP 801:6
outrageously v. STEE 736:19
value a v. LOCK 472:8
v. woman BIBL 83:38
v. woman is a crown BIBL 82:24
virtute *Macte nova v.* VIRG 795:8
virus hear the v. humming DOTY 276:10
vis *V. consili expers mole* HORA 388:18
visibilium *v. omnium* MISS 520:16
visible all things v. and invisible BOOK 129:8
darkness v. MILT 514:12
it makes v. KLEE 442:2
outward and v. sign BOOK 130:17
representation of v. things LEON 464:19
Work is love made v. GIBR 336:13
vision art is but a v. of reality YEAT 835:22
Bedlam v. BYRO 180:10
Bright the v. MANT 494:12
by the v. splendid WORD 830:1
fabric of this v. SHAK 699:6
In v. beatific MILT 515:3
Saw the v. of the world TENN 763:3
single central v. BERL 68:15
Single v. and Newton's sleep BLAK 119:7
v. and the faculty WORD 828:7
v. flies SHEN 715:5
V. of Christ BLAK 118:10
V. or Imagination BLAK 121:12
v. thing BUSH 171:2
Was it a v. KEAT 429:16
Where there is no v. BIBL 83:34
Write the v. BIBL 90:22
young men's v. DRYD 280:5
visionary Whither is fled the v. gleam WORD 829:19
visioned V. One sees all PALI 565:5
visions Cecilia, appear in v. AUDE 33:17
lost in stormy v. SHEL 710:23
shades send deceptive v. VIRG 795:3
these v. did appear SHAK 690:30
verse for v. IBSE 398:13
what v. have I seen SHAK 690:14
young men shall see v. BIBL 90:14
visit Christ came to v. us BOOK 127:21
v. the fatherless and widows BIBL 110:16
visitation time of their v. BIBL 91:9
visited sick, and ye v. me BIBL 97:12
visitest thou v. him BOOK 131:27
visiting ordinary v.-card BAED 45:19
v. acquaintance SHER 716:4
v. the iniquity BIBL 76:9
visitor travel as a v. HORA 386:8
visits Superior people never make long v. MOOR 529:19
visual v. telegram CASS 193:9
vita *Ars longa, v. brevis* HIPP 377:15
cammin del nostra v. OPEN 556:4
cammin di nostra v. DANT 249:6
vitae *Integer v.* HORA 387:24
V. summa brevis HORA 387:17
vitai *v. lampada* LUCR 479:4
vital V. spark POPE 582:15
v. spirit BERG 67:17
vitality v. enough to preserve it JOHN 417:16
V. in a woman SHAW 707:32
vitam *Si v. puriter egi* CATU 197:16
vitriol sleeve with bottle of v. WOOL 827:7
vivacity v. of an idle man BAGE 47:17
vivam *sapientis dicere 'V.'* MART 497:22
vivamus *V., mea Lesbia* CATU 197:2
vive v. la bagatelle STER 738:9
vivendi *vitam v. perdere causas* JUVE 424:18
vivere *Nec tecum possum v.* MART 498:4
Quadrigis petimus bene v. HORA 386:20
vivid left the v. air signed SPEN 732:19
v. rather than happy LOVE 477:1
vivite *'v.' ait* VIRG 795:12
vivre *V.? les serviteurs feront cela* VILL 792:18
vixen v. when she went to school SHAK 690:7
vixi *Dixisse V.* HORA 388:23
vobis *Pax V.* BIBL 114:6
vobiscum *Dominus v.* MISS 520:7
sit semper v. MISS 522:18
vocabula *nunc sunt in honore v.* HORA 385:15
vocabulary v. of 'Bradshaw' DOYL 278:7
vocation As if his whole v. WORD 830:2
felt the v. CLOU 221:12
labour in his v. SHAK 667:21
test of a v. SMIT 724:10
v. of unhappiness SIME 720:7
worthy of the v. BIBL 108:2
vodka medium V. dry Martini FLEM 317:9
vogue totter into v. WALP 800:21
voi *Siete v. qui* DANT 249:15
voice All I have is a v. AUDE 35:2
daughter of the v. of God WORD 830:12
far-away tentative v. ALAI 10:4
followed me by my v. MAHĀ 490:5
great v. as of a trumpet BIBL 111:19
her v. the harmony HOOK 383:6
Her v. was ever soft SHAK 680:13
humble v. BOOK 125:14
I have lost my v. WEBS 808:20
inexhaustible v. FAUL 307:27
In Rama was there a v. BIBL 92:25
I see a v. SHAK 690:25
lift up your v. WESL 811:6
Lord, hear my v. BOOK 141:1
No v.; but oh COLE 226:25
Only a look and a v. LONG 474:18
people's v. is odd POPE 586:15
scream in a low v. BYRO 179:23
so silvery is thy v. HERR 375:5
sound of a v. that is still TENN 757:12
sound of his v. BENN 66:12
still small v. BIBL 80:3
supplicating v. JOHN 411:20
thou v. of my heart CRAW 244:17
Thunder is the v. of God MATH 501:11
tune her sacred v. JOHN 411:8
v. and nothing more ANON 21:14
V., and Verse MILT 511:10
v. as the sound of many waters BIBL 111:22
v. from heaven BIBL 112:23
v. is full of money FITZ 315:12
v. is Jacob's voice BIBL 74:38
V. is round me THOM 774:9
v. of a nation RUSS 640:9
V. of Doris Day FISH 313:17
v. of my beloved BIBL 85:18
v. of one crying BIBL 92:27
v. of Rome JONS 419:14
v. of the Bard BLAK 120:21
v. of the charmer BOOK 135:18
v. of the dead TENN 762:7
v. of the kingdom SWIF 747:13
v. of the Lobster CARR 190:6
v. of the Lord BOOK 133:13
v. of the Lord God BIBL 73:26
v. of the people ALCU 10:10
v. of the people PROV 613:35
v. of the sluggard WATT 805:11
v. of the turtle BIBL 85:10
v. of thy brother's blood BIBL 74:9
v. revives the leaden strings CAMP 183:22
v. so sweet JONS 420:16
v. that breathed o'er Eden KEBL 432:7
v. was that of Mr Churchill ATTL 32:1
v. will run KEAT 429:23
voices Ancestral v. prophesying war COLE 225:23
Other v., other rooms CAPO 185:15
Two v. are there STEP 737:21
Two V. are there WORD 832:8
v. of children BLAK 120:19
when soft v. die SHEL 714:1
void conscience v. of offence BIBL 104:17
habitation be v. BOOK 136:12
infinite V. PALI 565:19
No craving v. POPE 582:21
without form, and v. BIBL 73:10
voids attempts to fill v. WEIL 808:24
vol *suspend ton v.* LAMA 448:7
volat *v. irrevocabile verbum* HORA 387:1
volatile v. spirits SANT 644:10
volcano crust over a v. of revolution ELLI 298:16
dancing not on a v. FLAU 316:8
volcanoes range of exhausted v. DISR 269:9
v. burnt out BURK 165:9
vole passes the questing v. WAUG 806:11
volenti *V. non fit iniuria* ULPI 787:5
Volk *ein V.* POLI 581:11
Volkswagen V. parked in the gap MULD 536:1
volley v. of the sun WILB 817:8
v. we have just heard COLL 229:1
volo *Hoc v.* JUVE 424:15
volontade *E'n la sua v.* DANT 250:3
Voltaire V. in the Bastille DE G 256:2
voluisse *in magnis et v. sat est* PROP 593:16
volume in one v. octavo SMIT 725:5
In the v. of the book BOOK 134:1
take in our hand any v. HUME 394:7
volumes all Earth's v. CHAP 202:24
creators of odd v. LAMB 448:13
thirty fine v. MORL 532:3
whole v. in folio SHAK 680:20
voluntary Composing's not v. BIRT 115:14
v. spies AUST 38:6
voluntas *fiat v.* MISS 522:17
sit pro ratione v. JUVE 424:15
tamen est laudanda v. OVID 561:10
volunteer One v. is worth PROV 609:6
voluptas *Trahit sua quemque v.* VIRG 795:19
voluptuous V. as the first BYRO 178:9
vomit dog is turned to his own v. BIBL 111:10
dog returneth to his v. BIBL 83:24
Dog returns to his V. KIPL 438:20
dog returns to its v. PROV 598:24
returning to one's own v. POWE 590:17
Vorsprung *V. durch Technik* AUDI 8:16
votaress imperial v. SHAK 689:23
vote always v. *against* FIEL 310:22
brute v. BAGE 46:15
Don't buy a single v. more KENN 433:7
One man shall have one v. CART 193:4
turkeys v. for Christmas CALL 181:12
v. against somebody ADAM 2:8
V. early and vote often MILE 507:21
v. for the best President PETE 574:11
V. for the man who promises least BARU 56:11
v. just as their leaders tell 'em GILB 337:15
voted v. at my party's call GILB 338:28
v. cent per cent BYRO 173:13
voter Every intelligent v. ADAM 2:6
votes V. for women POLI 582:4
v. to get the things done SAMU 643:13
voting If v. changed anything LIVI 470:9
not the v. that's democracy STOP 743:11
votis *Hoc erat in v.* HORA 389:24
votive take my v. glass PRIO 592:14
vouchsafe V., O Lord: to keep us BOOK 126:2
voulu *Vous l'avez v.* MOLI 525:8
vow v. be performed BOOK 135:26
v. to thee, my country SPRI 735:6
vowels U green, O blue: v. RIMB 628:13
with all the v. missing ELLI 298:7
vows cancel all our v. DRAY 279:3
first v. sworn DIDE 267:5
pay my v. now BOOK 140:4
v. made in wine SHAK 659:16
vox *V. et praeterea nihil* ANON 21:14
v. humbug SHER 716:26
V. populi ALCU 10:10
voyage in for Hobbes's v. VANB 789:7
make the v. over VIRG 794:21
take my last v. LAST 455:19
v. not a harbour TOYN 780:4

v. of their life SHAK 676:28
v. to the moon LARD 452:9
voyages v. of the starship Enterprise RODD 631:1
voyaging V. through strange seas WORD 831:3
vulgar great v., and the small COWL 239:13
in the v. tongue BOOK 130:7
it's v. PUNC 617:14
let the v. stuff alone BELL 64:11
money-spending always 'v.' GASK 330:18
takes place with the v. BACO 41:24
trivial and v. way BROW 153:29
upon the v. with fine sense POPE 587:17
v. expression CONG 232:10
vulgarity human v. AMIS 14:4
vulpes *v. aegroto cauta leoni* HORA 386:12

W with a "V" or a "W" DICK 265:13
wabe gimble in the w. CARR 190:12
wade should I w. no more SHAK 684:15
waded w. in snow and much TURN 785:14
w. thro' red blude BALL 52:2
wafer men's faiths are w.-cakes SHAK 671:4
Waffen *Wehr und W.* LUTH 480:2
wag ambition to be a w. JOHN 418:3
W. as it will BYRO 173:7
Wood, the Weed, the W. RALE 620:17
wage give themselves for w. YEAT 836:22
home policy: I w. war CLEM 220:10
wager lost the w. SHAK 660:18
wagering w. that God is PASC 568:16
wages better w. and shorter hours ORWE 559:5
earneth w. BIBL 90:24
neither honours nor w. GARI 329:17
paid in full your w. KORA 444:5
ta'en thy w. SHAK 661:1
took their w. HOUS 390:9
w. of sin is death BIBL 105:2
wagged tail that w. WATS 805:3
Wagner W. has lovely moments ROSS 635:10
W.'s music NYE 552:2
wagon Hitch your w. to a star EMER 299:30
w. of his 'Plan' PAST 569:9
wail nothing to w. MILT 518:25
w. a week SHAK 704:1
w. my dear times' waste SHAK 704:16
wrynge, and w. CHAU 205:10
wailing w. for her demon-lover COLE 225:21
wains hangs heavy from the w. GIBB 336:5
wainscot In w. tubs DRAY 279:5
waist live about her w. SHAK 663:15
slender w. confined WALL 800:6
waistband roll the w. DUFF 284:9
waistcoat open your w. HUNT 396:3
yolk runs down the w. DICK 264:2
wait All things come to those who w. PROV 595:5
laid great w. for me BOOK 134:4
Time and tide w. PROV 612:51
too slow for those who w. VAN 789:15
w. and see ASQU 31:1
w. a wee BURN 169:10
w. for ever MACA 481:16
w. for what will come ROBI 629:13
wait upon the Lord BIBL 88:5
we won't w. ANON 19:12
who only stand and w. MILT 518:30
waited w. patiently for the Lord BOOK 133:31
waiter myself and a dam' good head w. GULB 354:18
waiting nearly kept w. LOUI 475:17
w. for Godot BECK 59:24
w. for something GRIF 353:11
w. for the Earl of Chatham ANON 16:12
W. for the end EMPS 300:5
w. means hurrying on MANN 494:3
w. seven hundred years COLL 229:3
w. somewhere for me RODG 631:4
What are we w. for CAVA 198:7
wake do I w. or sleep KEAT 429:16
slepyng hound to w. CHAU 207:8
w. in a fright BARH 54:5
W. now, my love SPEN 733:7
w. the soul by tender strokes POPE 586:27
W. up, England GEOR 333:16
we w. eternally DONN 272:23
waked You have w. me too soon WATT 805:11
wakening Our w. and uprising KEBL 432:4
wakes breed one work that w. HOPK 384:24
Hock-carts, wassails, w. HERR 374:3
w. or sleeps SHEL 710:22
w. them himself ADDI 5:2
What angel w. me SHAK 690:3
Wordsworth sometimes w. BYRO 177:1
waking w., no such matter SHAK 705:5
w. that kills us BROW 154:4
Wales bless the Prince of W. LINL 469:16
live ever in W. JAME 402:22
no present in W. THOM 773:16
Princess of W. AUST 39:8
Princess of W. DOWD 277:4
Side and W. Gate GURN 355:4
still parts of W. THOM 773:8
whole world . . . But for W. BOLT 124:21
walet His w., biforn him in his lappe CHAU 205:5
walk after supper w. a mile PROV 594:18
Can two w. together BIBL 90:16
closer w. with God COWP 240:21
machine that would w. APOL 23:1
men must w. POPE 586:9
never w. alone HAMM 359:4
no easy w.-over to freedom NEHR 540:8
not easy to w. on ways JAIN 402:8
take up thy bed, and w. BIBL 101:22
taking a w. that day OPEN 556:21
time to w. round me BALZ 53:3
upon which the people w. CRAZ 244:19
W. about Sion BOOK 134:26
w. abroad o' nights MARL 496:17
W. across my swimming pool RICE 626:8
w. a little faster CARR 190:4
w. before we can run PROV 613:46
W. cheerfully over the world FOX 322:10
w. circumspectly BIBL 108:8
w. humbly with thy God BIBL 90:20
w. in fear and dread COLE 226:24
w. in newness of life BIBL 104:38
w. o'er the western wave SHEL 714:11
w. on the wild side ALGR 11:16
w. the night SHAK 662:23
W. under his huge legs SHAK 674:13
W. upon England's mountains green BLAK 120:1
w. within the purlieus ETHE 301:11
w. ye BIBL 87:18
Where'er you w. POPE 586:26
Yea, though I w. BOOK 133:1
walked He w. by himself KIPL 441:6
people that w. in darkness BIBL 86:28
slowly w. away BURT 169:17
W. day and night LOGU 473:4
w. through the wilderness BUNY 160:14
w. through the wilderness OPEN 555:6
walkedst w. whither thou wouldest BIBL 103:11
walkers Six for the six proud w. SONG 729:11
walketh w. in a vain shadow BOOK 133:30
w. upon the wings BOOK 139:1
walking craves wary w. SHAK 674:25
empire w. very slowly FITZ 315:15
fingers do the w. ADVE 7:41
Lord God w. in the garden BIBL 73:26
men as trees, w. BIBL 98:7
W., and leaping BIBL 103:19
w. by his wild lone KIPL 441:7
w. every day COWL 239:22
w. in an air of glory VAUG 790:12
w. on the sea BIBL 95:25
w. up and down BIBL 80:34
wings prevent him from w. BAUD 57:5
walks Gibbon levelled w. COLM 229:18
left you all his w. SHAK 676:12
nobody w. much faster CARR 191:10
She w. in beauty BYRO 178:24
w. always beside you ELIO 296:13
w. put on their summer liveries LANI 451:4
wall against a w. of stone WILB 817:6
close the w. up SHAK 671:5
doesn't love a w. FROS 326:4
have I leaped over a w. BIBL 79:12
leap over the w. BOOK 132:13
like a stone w. BEE 61:1
look like a w. DUNN 285:14
on the outward w. SHAK 687:24
plaister of the w. BIBL 90:3
w. fell down flat BIBL 77:20
w. next door catches fire HORA 387:2
W. Street lays an egg NEWS 544:16
w. to a layman COMM 230:9
Watch the w., my darling KIPL 440:8
weakest go to the w. PROV 613:42
With our backs to the w. HAIG 356:9
Without a city w. ALEX 11:12
wooden w. is your ships THEM 770:16
Wallace hae wi' W. bled BURN 168:7
wallet Time hath, my lord, a w. SHAK 700:14
w. and a woeful end GASC 330:14
wallflower yellow w. THOM 775:4
walling What I was w. in FROS 326:6
wallow w. In glorious mud FLAN 316:2
w. in our victory PRES 591:5
walls angels on the w. MARL 496:29
not in w. NICI 544:21
Stone w. do not a prison make LOVE 476:14
these w. thy sphere DONN 274:16
Thy w. defaced BYRO 174:2
W. have ears PROV 613:36
W. have tongues SWIF 749:20
w. of Eden BYRO 173:21
w. of stone or brass COTT 238:1
within thy w. BOOK 140:15
wooden w. are the best COVE 238:8
walnut woman, dog, and w. tree PROV 615:13
walnuts W. and pears PROV 613:37
walrus Between them, W. and Carpenter LEVI 466:7
W. and the Carpenter CARR 190:19
Walsingham holy land Of W. RALE 621:1
waltz Swoons to a w. HUXL 397:7
zest goes out of a beautiful w. GREN 352:15
waltzing You'll come a-w., Matilda PATE 569:16
waly w., waly BALL 52:7
wan Why so pale and w. SUCK 745:7
wand on her w. she bore MOOR 530:16
wander love to w. CASS 193:10
Nor forced him w. CLEV 220:17
w. in the ways of men BURN 167:23
w. like a breeze COLE 225:15
Whither shall I w. NURS 548:8
will not w. more TENN 763:15
wandered w. far and wide HOME 382:9
w. far and wide OPEN 556:20
w. lonely as a cloud WORD 828:26
wanderer do not we, W., await it too ARNO 27:9
w. from the narrow way COWP 241:3
wandering but a w. voice WORD 832:9
by long w. ASCH 30:6
I'm just w. MURD 537:1
W. between two worlds ARNO 27:21
w. minstrel I GILB 337:21
w. outlaw BYRO 174:9
Werchynge and w. LANG 450:17
waning onset and w. of love LA B 446:14
want don't w. him MILN 510:12
feel the w. of it COLE 227:8
in w. of a wife AUST 38:14

want (*cont.*):
I shall not w. BOOK 132:26
I w. some more DICK 264:13
more you w. PROV 607:9
preservative from w. AUST 38:20
probably won't w. HOPE 383:14
Ring out the w. TENN 761:29
that people know what they w. MENC 504:16
third is freedom from w. ROOS 632:18
Though much I w. DYER 286:13
Toil, envy, w. JOHN 411:14
w. it the most CHES 209:13
w. no manner of thing BOOK 133:21
w. of a nail PROV 600:41
w. of decency DILL 267:14
W. one only of five giants BEVE 72:6
Waste not, w. not PROV 613:39
weep with w. TAYL 756:20
we w. it now MORR 532:23
What can I w. or need HERB 373:14
What does a woman w. FREU 324:17
what I really really w. ROWB 636:8
Wilful waste makes woeful w. PROV 615:10
wanted no man is w. much EMER 299:26
w. everything HAZL 365:6
w. nothing but death AUST 39:15
w. simply you HÉLO 369:1
wanting found w. BIBL 90:4
wanton do but w. in the South TENN 765:23
W. kittens make sober PROV 613:38
w. stings SHAK 686:3
wightly w. SHAK 680:23
wantonly unadvisedly, lightly, or w. BOOK 131:1
wantonness in clothes a w. HERR 374:8
wantons play the w. SHAK 695:15
wants Man w. but little GOLD 344:20
physical w. BAGE 46:6
provide for human *w.* BURK 163:19
scheme of supplying our w. SWIF 748:27
who w. poets at all HÖLD 380:18
wanwood worlds of w. leafmeal HOPK 384:18
war able to make w. with him BIBL 112:20
After each w. ATKI 31:20
ain't gonna be no w. MACM 487:18
All's fair in love and w. PROV 594:25
Ancestral voices prophesying w. COLE 225:23
another w. in Europe BISM 116:15
at w. with Germany CHAM 201:1
battle-plans of w. LUCR 479:3
better than to w.-war CHUR 216:6
blast of w. SHAK 671:5
bleeding w. SHAK 695:13
blood-red blossom of w. TENN 764:16
bungled, unwise w. PLOM 579:2
business of w. WELL 809:22
but it is not w. BOSQ 143:14
calamities of w. JOHN 409:17
clamour for w. PEEL 571:16
cold w. BARU 56:9
cold w. warrior THAT 769:21
condition which is called w. HOBB 378:19
Councils of w. never fight PROV 597:38
cruellest and most terrible w. LLOY 471:3
cudgel of the people's w. TOLS 779:12
day w. broke out CATC 195:8
delays are dangerous in w. DRYD 282:31
desolation of w. GEOR 334:2
determined without w. HOBB 379:2
devil's madness—w. SERV 655:1
done very well out of the w. BALD 49:5
Don John of Austria is going to the w. CHES 210:11
easier to make w. CLEM 220:11
Either w. is obsolete or men are FULL 327:3
enable it to make w. WEIL 808:27
endless w. still breed MILT 513:16
essence of w. is violence MACA 481:10
European w. might do it REDM 623:11
except the British W. Office SHAW 707:2
first invented w. MARL 496:24
First World W. had begun TAYL 756:6
France has not lost the w. DE G 255:18
furnish the w. HEAR 367:2
garland of the w. SHAK 657:19
gone wrong since the W. AMIS 13:11
Grim-visaged w. SHAK 696:8
guarantee success in w. CHUR 215:13
hand of w. SHAK 694:19
home policy: I wage w. CLEM 220:10
I am for w. RED 623:10
I am the tongue of w. VOZN 798:16
if someone gave a w. GINS 339:19
I hate w. ROOS 632:14
I have seen w. ROOS 632:14
Image of w. SOME 727:17
In a civil w. REED 623:16
in every w. they kill you in a new way ROGE 632:1
in the trade of w. SHAK 691:28
In w. it is necessary BONA 125:3
In w., no winners CHAM 200:16
In w.; resolution CHUR 216:16
in w. the two cardinal virtues HOBB 378:22
In w., three-quarters turns NAPO 538:14
I renounce w. FOSD 321:9
justifiable act of w. BELL 62:22
killed in the w. POWE 590:19
ladies declare w. on me LOUI 476:2
lead this people into w. WILS 822:16
Let me have w. SHAK 660:11
let slip the dogs of w. SHAK 675:22
Let w. yield to peace CICE 217:15
liking for w. BENN 65:17
live under the shadow of a w. SPEN 732:25
looks on w. as all glory SHER 717:2
Lord is a man of w. BIBL 76:6
lose the w. in an afternoon CHUR 216:20
made this great w. LINC 469:4
Make love not w. SAYI 647:31
makes a good w. HERB 373:19
make w. that we may live ARIS 24:19
Mankind must put an end to w. KENN 433:15
McNamara's W. MCNA 488:3
money the sinews of w. BACO 44:12
morning's w. SHAK 672:27
nature of w. HOBB 378:20
neither shall they learn w. BIBL 86:13
never met anyone who wasn't against w. LOW 477:6
never was a good w. FRAN 323:14
no declaration of w. EDEN 288:6
no discharge in that w. BIBL 84:18
No w., or battle's sound MILT 513:20
Older men declare w. HOOV 383:13
Only in w. MAND 493:15
page 1 of the book of w. MONT 528:13
paparazzi dogs of w. DENE 257:8
pattern called a w. LOWE 477:9
pestilence and w. MILT 515:23
Power and W. KIPL 438:6
prepare for w. VEGE 791:4
protection against w. BEVI 72:9
provoke a new civil w. JUAN 422:22
quaint and curious w. is HARD 361:18
race inured to w. WILL 820:5
recourse to w. BRIA 148:5
rich wage w. SART 644:20
seek no wider w. JOHN 408:16
seven days w. MUIR 535:23
silent in time of w. CICE 217:24
sinews of w. CICE 217:23
soon as w. is declared GIRA 340:7
stately tents of w. MARL 496:20
state of w. by nature SWIF 749:18
steel couch of w. SHAK 692:6
subject is W. OWEN 562:3
Suppose they gave a w. FILM 313:3
talk of a just w. SORL 728:20
tell us all about the w. SOUT 730:12
tempered by w. KENN 433:9
then comes the tug of w. PROV 614:19
they'll give a w. SAND 644:2
this is w. ADAM 2:3
This w. is an inconceivable madness GONN 346:10
time of w. BIBL 84:7
to full life by w. TOLK 779:5
to the w. is gone MOOR 530:14
To w. and arms LOVE 476:15
two nations have been at w. VOLT 797:7
used to w.'s alarms HOOD 382:18
Vietnam as a w. PILG 576:6
wage a pitiless w. GREE 351:17
wage no w. SOUT 730:20
wage w. against a monstrous tyranny CHUR 215:8
want peace, prepare for w. PROV 603:39
W. always finds a way BREC 147:14
w., an' a debt LOWE 477:12
w. and peace ARIS 24:14
w. and peace in 21st century KOHL 443:7
w. between men THUR 776:25
w. correspondent gets more CAPA 185:14
w. creates order BREC 147:11
w., dearth, age, agues DONN 272:21
w. has its laws NEWM 542:3
w. has used up words JAME 403:19
W. hath no fury MONT 527:3
W., he sung, is toil DRYD 280:20
w. in heaven BIBL 112:19
w. in his heart BOOK 135:12
w. is a necessary part MOLT 525:23
W. is capitalism with STOP 744:1
W. is continuation of politics CLAU 219:19
W. is hell, and all that HAY 364:15
w. is over GRAN 348:18
W. is peace ORWE 558:21
w. is politics with bloodshed MAO 495:1
w. is so terrible LEE 462:8
W. is the national industry MIRA 520:4
W. is the remedy SHER 717:1
W. is the trade of kings DRYD 281:31
W. is the universal perversion RAE 620:5
W. is too serious CLEM 220:9
W. its thousands slays PORT 588:14
W. makes good history HARD 360:9
w. of nature DARW 250:21
w. poet whose right of honour GURN 355:3
w.'s a game COWP 242:5
W.'s annals will cloud HARD 361:17
W.'s glorious art YOUN 838:20
w. situation HIRO 377:18
w. that drags on WAUG 806:12
w. that will end war WELL 810:16
w. that would not boil TAYL 756:8
W. the most exciting thing DAYA 253:10
W. told me truth GURN 355:4
W. to the knife PALA 564:10
w. to waste MILT 517:26
w. which existed in order to HOBS 379:8
W. will cease POLI 582:5
w. without its guilt SURT 746:16
waste of God, W. STUD 745:4
way of ending a w. ORWE 559:14
weapons of w. BIBL 79:3
We hear w. called murder MACD 485:1
we prepare for w. PEAR 571:11
what a lovely w. LITT 470:5
what did you do in the W. SAYI 647:8
When w. enters a country ANON 20:18
When w. is declared SAYI 648:10
win an atomic w. BRAD 146:9
win a w. is as disastrous CHRI 212:14
with himself at w. SHAK 674:7
without having won the w. YOKO 838:13
You can only love one w. GELL 333:2
warble W., child SHAK 680:21
warbler Attic w. pours GRAY 350:23
warder w. silent on the hill SCOT 651:5

wardrobe dalliance in the w. lies SHAK 670:30
open your w. WELD 809:9
wards W. in Jarndyce DICK 261:6
ware Breath's a w. HOUS 390:16
for the bed of W. SHAK 702:5
warfare Armed w. must be preceded ZINO 840:5
legitimate w. NEWM 542:3
w. is accomplished BIBL 87:27
Who goeth a w. BIBL 106:8
warlord concubine of a w. OPEN 555:7
warm For ever w. KEAT 428:26
lived in a w., sunny climate COWA 239:1
man who's w. to understand SOLZ 727:12
O! she's w. SHAK 703:26
too w. work, Hardy NELS 541:1
W. beds JOYC 422:15
w., but pure BYRO 178:4
w. kind world CORY 237:14
W. what is cold LANG 451:2
winters and keeps w. CARE 186:14
warmed heart strangely w. WESL 811:15
warming w. the teapot MANS 494:8
warmth awful load of w. KEAT 431:8
more w. SORL 728:19
native with the w. KEAT 430:2
Spring restores balmy w. CATU 197:7
vigorous w. DRYD 279:18
W. and Light GREN 352:17
yearned for w. and colour TENN 759:21
warn All a poet can do is w. OWEN 562:4
right to w. BAGE 47:5
w., to comfort, and command WORD 831:24
w. you not to be ordinary KINN 437:20
warning ruin in spite of w. JUDA 422:24
w. from another's wound JERO 406:13
w. to the world SHAK 704:28
With horrid w. KEAT 428:13
warp Weave the w. GRAY 350:4
warrant not a sufficient w. MILL 508:18
warring two nations w. DURH 286:6
W. in heaven MILT 516:8
warrior cold war w. THAT 769:21
great old w. LEON 464:8
Here lies a valiant w. EPIT 302:16
Home they brought her w. TENN 765:25
This is the happy w. READ 622:13
Who is the happy W. WORD 827:18
wars all their w. are merry CHES 210:2
came to an end all w. LLOY 471:3
end to the beginnings of all w. ROOS 633:3
History littered with the w. POWE 590:14
how do w. start KRAU 445:18
into any foreign w. ROOS 632:16
maketh w. to cease BOOK 134:20
My w. were global REED 623:15
not armaments that cause w. MADA 488:22
occasion of all w. FOX 322:8
serve in the w. BOOK 142:13
thousand w. of old TENN 761:29
tourist of w. GELL 333:1
w. and lechery SHAK 700:23
w. and rumours of wars BIBL 96:30
w. brought nothing about DRYD 282:18
w., horrible wars VIRG 794:16
w. planned by old men RICE 626:4
Warsaw Order reigns in W. ANON 20:10
warts w. and all MISQ 522:11
Warwick impudent and shameless W. SHAK 673:1
wary craves w. walking SHAK 674:25
was picked the w. of shall CUMM 247:11
Thinks what ne'er w. POPE 584:17
wash Bid them w. their faces SHAK 660:4
Lord, dost thou w. my feet BIBL 102:14
Moab is my w.-pot BOOK 135:20
thou shalt w. me BOOK 135:6
w. literature off ARTA 29:19
W. me throughly BOOK 135:4
w. my hands in innocency BOOK 133:8
w. one's dirty linen PROV 608:35
w. out a word of it FITZ 314:17
w. that man right outa HAMM 358:18
w. the balm SHAK 695:5
w. their feet in soda water ELIO 296:7
w. the wind ELIO 295:16
W. what is dirty LANG 451:2
will all w. off TURN 785:13
washed He w. himself JOHN 410:9
w. his hands BIBL 97:27
w. in the blood of the Lamb LIND 469:8
w. their robes BIBL 112:10
w.-up has-been DYLA 287:18
washerman w. removes the grime TANT 754:29
washes One hand w. the other PROV 608:43
Persil w. whiter ADVE 8:6
washing came up from the w. BIBL 85:14
country w. BRUM 158:23
taking in one another's w. ANON 16:1
w. on the Siegfried Line KENN 433:6
Where w. ain't done EPIT 302:15
Washington come to W. to be loved GRAM 348:13
Government at W. lives GARF 329:16
wasp everything about the w. THOM 772:14
wasps w. and hornets break through SWIF 747:14
wassails Hock-carts, w., wakes HERR 374:3
waste art of how to w. space JOHN 408:22
Don't w. time in mourning LAST 456:10
file your w. basket-paper BENN 65:10
Haste makes w. PROV 602:2
my dear times' w. SHAK 704:16
now doth time w. me SHAK 696:5
To what purpose is this w. BIBL 97:15
war to w. MILT 517:26
w. And solitary places SHEL 711:18
w. howling wilderness BIBL 77:11
W. not, want not PROV 613:39
w. of breath YEAT 836:10
w. of goods VEBL 791:3
w. of shame SHAK 705:19
w.-paper basket of the emotions WEBB 807:2
w. places of Jerusalem BIBL 88:13
w. remains and kills EMPS 300:7
we lay w. our powers WORD 832:15
What a w. DURY 286:10
Wilful w. makes woeful want PROV 615:10
world's perplexing w. BYRO 177:31
wasted spend on advertising is w. LEVE 466:2
w. his substance BIBL 100:2
wasteful clumsy, w., blundering DARW 251:1
wastes tossed them to the howling w. LAWL 454:13
W. without springs CLAR 218:13
watch before the morning w. BOOK 141:2
could ye not watch with me BIBL 97:22
done much better by a w. BELL 64:3
Fourteen angels w. WETT 812:23
hang on a w.-chain ANON 19:8
keeping w. above his own LOWE 477:16
keeping w. over their flock BIBL 98:20
knew how a w. was made JOHN 413:25
learning, like your w. CHES 209:14
like a fat gold w. PLAT 577:19
like little w. springs SPEN 732:22
my w. has stopped FILM 311:4
old w. chain COLL 228:12
Set a w., O Lord BOOK 141:15
some must w. SHAK 665:1
son of a bitch stole my w. FILM 312:8
W. and pray BIBL 97:23
W. and pray ELLI 298:11
w. a sailing cloud LIN 469:18
w. between me and thee BIBL 75:5
w. for her SHAK 680:23
w. in the night BOOK 137:18
w. must have had a maker PALE 564:11
w. not one another DONN 274:3
W. therefore BIBL 97:7
W. the wall, my darling KIPL 440:8
W. ye therefore BIBL 98:13
why not carry a w. TREE 781:5
watchdog w.'s voice that bayed GOLD 344:10
watched w. pot never boils PROV 613:40
watcher posted presence of the w. JAME 403:11
w. of the skies KEAT 429:21
watchful occasion's forelock w. MILT 518:5
w. at his gate DODD 271:19
watching BIG BROTHER IS W. YOU ORWE 558:20
My tiny w. eye DE L 256:21
watchmaker blind w. DAWK 253:1
watchman w. on the lonely tower SCOT 651:4
w. waketh but in vain BOOK 140:21
W., what of the night BIBL 87:8
watchmen w. that went about the city BIBL 85:19
watchword w. is security PITT 577:1
water as w. spilt on the ground BIBL 79:8
back in the w. ADVE 7:37
blackens all the w. ADDI 5:15
Blood thicker than w. PROV 596:30
bridge over troubled w. SIMO 720:8
Burned on the w. SHAK 656:23
By w. and the word STON 743:9
clear and sunny w. LONG 474:12
conscious w. saw its God CRAS 244:3
daughter of Earth and W. SHEL 711:7
delights in w. CONF 231:13
desireth the w.-brooks BOOK 134:5
Dirty w. will quench PROV 598:17
Don't go near the w. PROV 598:35
drawers of w. BIBL 77:21
drinkers of w. HORA 387:4
feet are always in the w. AMES 13:8
fountain of the w. of life BIBL 113:9
glass of pure w. MACD 484:17
go across salt w. DICK 265:23
green w. penetrates RIMB 628:6
hardly w. the ground BACO 43:18
He asked w. BIBL 77:28
I baptize with w. BIBL 101:9
if I were under w. KEAT 431:5
in the w. under the earth BIBL 76:8
King over the W. TOAS 778:4
Lay a great w. TENN 760:11
limns the w. BACO 45:11
Little drops of w. CARN 189:2
little w. clears us SHAK 683:12
Minnehaha, Laughing W. LONG 474:13
name was writ in w. EPIT 303:3
never miss the w. PROV 615:48
noise of the w.-pipes BOOK 134:7
No more w. SONG 729:6
poured out like w. BOOK 132:24
presence of still w. BERR 69:14
reached the calm of w. ADAM 2:18
ready by w. as by land ELST 298:17
Ring of bright w. BORR 144:14
ring of bright w. RAIN 620:8
river of w. of life BIBL 113:12
spring of ever-flowing w. HORA 389:24
sweet w. and bitter BIBL 110:20
take a horse to the w. PROV 615:33
Tar w. BERK 67:19
That stretch of w. PAUL 570:9
Too much of w. hast thou SHAK 666:15
travel by land or by w. BOOK 127:11
Unstable as w. BIBL 75:21
virtues We write in w. SHAK 673:22
walking on the w. THOM 774:14
w. and a crust KEAT 428:15
w. but the desert BYRO 174:28
w. hollows out OVID 561:11
w. in the rough rude sea SHAK 695:5
W. is best PIND 576:8
w. like Pilate GREE 351:15
'w.' meant the wonderful KELL 432:12
w. my couch with my tears BOOK 131:24
w. of affliction BIBL 80:10

water (*cont.*):
w. that is past PROV 606:36
w. this sorrow SHAK 656:13
W., water, everywhere COLE 226:12
w. what is dry LANG 451:2
weaker than w. LAO 452:7
We'll o'er the w. HOGG 380:13
where no w. is BOOK 135:24
where the w. goes CHES 211:1
wind and swift-flowing w. CATU 197:12
watercolour amateur painting in w. STEV 741:28
watercress ask for a w. sandwich WILD 819:7
watered Apollos w. BIBL 105:30
w. our houses in Helicon CHAP 202:18
watererd w. heaven with their tears BLAK 121:10
waterfall From the w. he named her LONG 474:13
watering w. mouth GASK 331:1
Waterloo Austerlitz and W. SAND 643:21
battle of W. WELL 810:1
battle of W. won ORWE 558:18
W.'s ensanguined plain ANON 18:6
world-earthquake, W. TENN 765:5
waterman great-grandfather was but a w. BUNY 161:3
watermelons down by the w. GINS 339:22
watermen w., that row one way BURT 170:6
watermill noise like that of a w. SWIF 747:18
waters all that move in the W. BOOK 126:9
as the voice of many w. BIBL 112:23
as the w. cover the sea BIBL 87:5
beside the still w. BOOK 132:26
By the w. of Babylon BOOK 141:7
By the w. of Babylon WALP 801:4
Cast thy bread upon the w. BIBL 84:27
cold w. to a thirsty soul BIBL 83:22
come ye to the w. BIBL 88:20
face of the w. BIBL 73:10
in great w. BOOK 139:14
in perils of w. BIBL 107:14
in the waste of w. VIRG 793:7
in the w. BOOK 139:1
knowledge of man is as the w. BACO 41:12
luminous home of w. ARNO 27:19
mighty w. rolling evermore WORD 830:8
moving w. KEAT 426:14
Once more upon the w. BYRO 174:8
pomp of w. DANI 248:16
quiet w. by SCOT 652:20
seething of the w. AURE 37:2
sitteth upon many w. BIBL 112:30
Still w. run deep PROV 611:22
Stolen w. are sweet BIBL 82:19
Stolen w. are sweet PROV 611:25
voice as the sound of many w. BIBL 111:22
w. cannot quench love BIBL 86:8
w. cover the sea AING 9:3
w. of affliction BIBL 87:17
w. of comfort BOOK 132:26
w. of Israel BIBL 80:18
w. of office TROL 782:5
W. on a starry night WORD 829:15
w. seeping upward ROET 631:6
W. that be above the Firmament BOOK 126:4
w. to stand on an heap BOOK 137:5
w. were his winding sheet BARN 55:8
watery crown the w. glade GRAY 350:15
shoreless w. wild ARNO 28:2
w. if not flaming sword MARV 499:6
Watson Elementary, my dear W. MISQ 521:9
Mr W., come here BELL 62:18
Wattle hear of Captain W. DIBD 260:10
waukin W. still and weary BURN 166:15
wave age is rocking the w. MAND 493:13
bind the restless w. WHIT 815:1
blue w. rolls nightly BYRO 175:23
bulling through w.-wrack MERW 506:3
cool, translucent w. MILT 512:1
great w. that echoes TENN 760:2
have grasped w. functions MCEW 485:6
lift me as a w. SHEL 712:16
longer than the w. BALL 51:10
upon an orient w. MILT 513:28
w. follows upon wave FISH 313:11
w.'s intenser day SHEL 712:14
waved w. her lily hand GAY 332:22
waveless w. plain of Lombardy SHEL 712:4
Waverley W. pen ADVE 8:13
waves chuckles of the w. AESC 6:11
floods lift up their w. BOOK 138:3
Him that walked the w. MILT 513:11
Like as the w. SHAK 704:23
little w. of Breffny GORE 347:2
longed-for dash of w. ARNO 27:19
lute-resounding w. POPE 580:24
noise of his w. BOOK 136:1
on which the w. break AURE 37:2
righteousness as the w. BIBL 88:9
w. and storms BOOK 134:7
w. and washèd it away SPEN 733:4
w. bound beneath me BYRO 174:8
w. of thy sweet singing SHEL 713:13
w. upon the shore SHEL 713:29
w. were always saying DICK 262:14
wild w. saying CARP 189:4
waving not w. but drowning SMIT 724:21
wax Hermes in the w. ARIS 25:11
hives with honey and w. SWIF 747:12
like melting w. BOOK 132:24
times begin to w. old BIBL 91:3
w. is preparing BYRO 179:24
w. old as doth a garment BOOK 138:15
W. to receive BYRO 173:16
waxworks If you think we're w. CARR 190:17
way all gone out of the w. BOOK 132:6
All the w. with LBJ POLI 581:2
broad is the w. BIBL 94:7
by w. of Beachy Head CHES 210:14
every one to his own w. BIBL 88:17
Every which w. FILM 312:20
flowers to strew Thy w. HERB 372:11
going the w. of all the earth BIBL 77:23
If w. to the Better there be HARD 361:13
In each thing give him w. SHAK 656:14
long w. to Tipperary JUDG 423:1
Love will find a w. PROV 606:9
make the W. great CONF 232:2
Make thy w. plain BOOK 131:22
more a w. of life ANON 18:3
no w. out of the mind PLAT 577:12
one w. in to life SENE 654:19
Prepare ye the w. of the Lord BIBL 92:27
Set your will on the W. CONF 231:16
shortest w. BACO 41:19
Teach me thy w., O Lord BOOK 133:11
there was a w. to Hell BUNY 161:8
This is the w. BIBL 87:18
Thou art my w. QUAR 618:18
thy w. may be known BOOK 136:3
War always finds a w. BREC 147:14
W. down upon the Swanee FOST 321:17
w. of a man with a maid BIBL 83:36
W. of our Master CONF 231:10
w. of seeing KEEN 432:9
w. of taking life FROS 326:16
w. of the Lord BIBL 87:28
w. of transgressors BIBL 82:28
W. that can be told of LAO 451:5
w., the truth, and the life BIBL 102:18
w. to dusty death SHAK 685:22
w. to the stars VIRG 795:8
whale's w. MASE 500:18
wilful man must have his w. PROV 615:9
will there's a w. PROV 614:40
your w. be long CAVA 198:5
ways in His w. with men TENN 760:9
in whose heart are thy w. BOOK 137:12
justify the w. of God MILT 514:9
keep thee in all thy w. BOOK 137:23
Let me count the w. BROW 154:21
maintain mine own w. BIBL 81:17
neither are your w. my ways BIBL 88:22
of the w. of God BIBL 82:1
parting of the w. BIBL 89:31
rough uneven w. SHAK 694:20
vindicate the w. of God POPE 585:5
wander in the w. of men BURN 167:23
w. are ways of pleasantness BIBL 82:9
w. be unconfined PRIO 592:11
w. of making you talk CATC 196:26
wayside seeds fell by the w. BIBL 95:20
wayward w. is this foolish love SHAK 702:25
we still it is not w. CHES 210:17
W. are seven WORD 832:13
W.'re here MILI 508:15
W. shall not pretend NEWS 544:17
weak concessions of the w. BURK 162:22
flesh is w. BIBL 97:23
found him w. in chemistry WELL 810:7
help the w.-hearted BOOK 127:10
Like all w. men MAUG 502:2
refuge of w. minds CHES 209:19
Strengthen ye the w. hands BIBL 87:22
virtue of w. minds DRYD 281:28
w. alone repent BYRO 175:16
w. always have to decide BONH 125:9
w. from your loveliness BETJ 71:6
w. in the head PROV 615:21
W. men must fall SHAK 695:5
w. overcomes the strong LAO 452:7
w. piping time SHAK 696:10
W. shall perish SERV 654:25
w. things of the world BIBL 105:29
weaken great life if you don't w. BUCH 159:8
weakening w. the will SPEN 732:24
weaker to the w. side inclined BUTL 172:13
unto the w. vessel BIBL 111:3
w. sex ALEX 11:13
weakest w. go to the wall PROV 613:42
w. kind of fruit SHAK 688:8
w. link PROV 597:9
weakling seven-stone w. ADVE 7:36
weakness made perfect in w. BIBL 107:17
makes our w. weaker BALZ 52:18
w. of our mortal nature BOOK 128:10
weal according to the common w. JAME 402:16
wealth acquisition of w. SOCR 726:23
consume w. without producing SHAW 706:21
excessive w. a libel SHEL 714:19
gave the little w. he had SWIF 749:26
get w. and place POPE 586:10
greater the w. GALB 328:7
health and w. HUNT 395:15
I'm a man of w. JAGG 401:8
in health and w. BOOK 126:15
insolence of w. JOHN 416:2
no increase in material w. TAWN 755:17
no w. but life RUSK 639:6
Outshone the w. of Ormuz MILT 515:7
prevents the rule of w. BAGE 46:16
promoting the w. BURK 163:9
purchase of my w. JONS 420:4
road to w. TROL 782:10
squandering w. DRYD 280:10
such w. brings SHAK 704:15
Thirst of w. WINC 822:19
w. accumulates, and men decay GOLD 344:8
w. and commerce MANN 494:7
w. and din of Rome HORA 388:22
w. around them makes them CRAB 243:15
w. a well-spent age CAMP 183:24
w. is a sacred thing FRAN 322:14
W. I seek not STEV 743:1
w. ye find SHEL 713:26
wealthy business of the w. man BELL 63:23
healthy, w., and wise PROV 599:4
some people are very w. ARIS 25:6
w. curlèd darlings SHAK 691:30
w. in a religious diving-bell FOST 321:12

weaned w. on a pickle ANON 19:7
were we not w. DONN 274:2
weapon art is not a w. KENN 433:18
bayonet is a w. POLI 581:4
held a w. BIBL 80:31
his w. wit EPIT 303:9
Innocence no earthly w. HILL 376:17
Loyalty the Tory's secret w. KILM 436:2
offensive and dangerous w. PICA 575:16
shield and w. LUTH 480:2
weapons books are w. ROOS 633:1
Clothes are our w. CART 192:8
fightings with outward w. FOX 322:12
Spare us all word of the w. WILB 817:3
w. of war BIBL 79:3
w. will be our words TRIM 781:15
wear w. BOOK 142:13
wear better to w. out CUMB 247:2
qualities as would w. well GOLD 345:26
w. him In my heart's core SHAK 664:18
w. of winning BELL 64:10
w. out than to rust out PROV 596:13
w. out to nought SHAK 679:22
w. them out in practice BEAU 58:7
what you are going to w. WELD 809:9
wearies you say it w. you SHAK 687:1
weariest even the w. river SWIN 750:22
weariness For w. of thee DONN 274:13
for w. of-walked LANG 450:16
much study is a w. BIBL 85:4
pale for w. SHEL 714:13
W. Can snore SHAK 660:27
w. May toss him to My breast HERB 373:8
w., the fever KEAT 429:9
w. treads on desire PETR 574:18
wearing w. armchairs tight about the hips WODE 824:22
w. o' the Green POLI 581:16
wherefore is he w. HOUS 390:4
wearisome miles and make them w. SHAK 694:20
wears so w. she to him SHAK 701:18
w. itself out HAZL 365:10
w. man's smudge HOPK 384:5
weary got the W. Blues HUGH 393:2
How w., stale, flat SHAK 661:23
not be w. in well doing BIBL 107:23
run, and not be w. BIBL 88:5
sae w. fu' o' care BURN 166:16
Waukin still and w. BURN 166:15
w. be at rest BIBL 81:5
w. of my groaning BOOK 131:24
w. warl goes round BLAM 121:14
w. wi' hunting BALL 51:1
with w. task fordone SHAK 690:28
weasel as a w. sucks eggs SHAK 658:21
Pop goes the w. MAND 493:6
w. under the cocktail cabinet PINT 576:14
w. word ROOS 633:11
weather blue unclouded w. TENN 762:17
Builds in the w. SHAK 687:24
care what the w. was like CHEK 208:9
first talk is of the w. JOHN 409:16
hard grey w. KING 437:7
Jolly boating w. CORY 237:11
most extraordinary w. GOGA 343:20
not in fine w. CLOU 221:17
sad or singing w. SWIN 751:14
Some are w.-wise FRAN 323:9
Stormy w. KOEH 443:2
w. gynneth clere CHAU 207:3
w. is always doing something TWAI 786:26
w. the cuckoo likes HARD 361:22
w. turned around THOM 772:11
will be fair w. BIBL 96:2
winter and rough w. SHAK 658:20
you won't hold up the w. MACN 488:9
weave tangled web we w. SCOT 651:12
W. the warp GRAY 350:4
weaver swifter than a w.'s shuttle BIBL 81:10
weaving my own hand's w. KEAT 427:31
web cool w. of language GRAV 349:12
magic in the w. of it SHAK 693:6
She left the w. TENN 762:19
tangled w. we weave SCOT 651:12
weaving of the w. HEIK 368:1
w., then, or the pattern STEV 741:2
wove a w. in childhood BRON 149:12
Webb W. from Dawley BETJ 71:3
webs By the dark w. YEAT 836:14
like spiders' w. ANAC 14:6
Webster Like W.'s Dictionary BURK 165:17
wed Better w. over the mixen PROV 596:14
December when they w. SHAK 659:20
for any good yeman to w. CHAU 205:26
I w. again CLAR 218:9
Som Cristen man shall w. me CHAU 206:16
think to w. it SHAK 655:19
w. the fair Ellen SCOT 651:9
With this Ring I thee w. BOOK 131:6
wedded Hail, w. love MILT 516:25
I have w. fyve CHAU 206:16
No w. man so hardy be CHAU 205:8
w. to calamity SHAK 697:30
w. to the truth SAKI 642:9
w. wife BOOK 131:4
wedding as she did her w. gown GOLD 345:26
earliest w.-day KEBL 432:7
face looks like a w.-cake AUDE 35:18
O God, and the w. CORS 237:10
One w. brings another PROV 609:7
small circle of a w.-ring CIBB 217:4
to a w. BIBL 99:24
w. clothes ADDI 5:14
w. dresses ready BYRO 177:19
W.-Guest here beat COLE 226:6
wedlock in holy w. BOOK 131:8
W., indeed, hath oft DAVI 251:14
W. is a padlock PROV 613:43
w.'s the devil BYRO 179:9
Wednesday W.'s child NURS 549:14
weds Egghead w. hourglass NEWS 544:4
wee cried, W.-wee-wee NURS 551:9
expectant w.-things BURN 166:22
W., sleekit, cow'rin' BURN 168:22
w. wifie waitin' MORR 533:3
W. Willie Winkie NURS 551:18
weed fat w. That rots itself SHAK 662:28
honey from the w. SHAK 671:11
Ignorance is an evil w. BEVE 72:5
law to w. it out BACO 43:28
Pernicious w. COWP 240:2
salt w. sways in the stream ARNO 26:12
w. that grows BURK 163:5
w. their own minds WALP 801:9
What is a w.? A plant EMER 299:28
Wood, the W., the Wag RALE 620:17
weeded W. and worn TENN 763:19
weeding seven years w. PROV 609:9
weeds all the idle w. SHAK 679:18
bred among the w. BROW 153:23
come up like w. WALK 799:6
coronet w. SHAK 666:14
grubbing w. from gravel paths KIPL 438:19
Ill w. grow apace PROV 603:45
Long live the w. HOPK 384:10
smell far worse than w. SHAK 705:7
W. are not supposed to grow LARK 453:1
w. spontaneous rise IRWI 400:5
week accomplished in a w. STEV 741:22
die in my w. JOPL 421:5
Middle of Next W. CARR 192:1
Sunday In every w. CLAR 219:13
wail a w. SHAK 704:1
w. after next CARR 191:16
w. a long time in politics WILS 821:16
w. of death DONN 274:25
weekend long w. FORS 320:14
w. starts here CATC 196:25
weep Doth w. full sore SPEN 733:19
fear of having to w. BEAU 58:9
If you want me to w. HORA 385:18
I may not w. BYRO 177:4
I w. for Adonais SHEL 710:13
make the angels w. SHAK 686:10
milk my ewes and w. SHAK 703:23
saw my lady w. ANON 17:3
scarcely cry 'w.! weep!' BLAK 120:13
She wolde w. CHAU 204:14
sit down and w. WALP 801:4
That he should w. for her SHAK 663:27
time to w. BIBL 84:7
w. and know why HOPK 384:18
w., and wrynge CHAU 205:10
w. and you weep alone PROV 605:10
W., and you weep alone WILC 817:9
W., children NERV 541:6
W. me not dead DONN 274:21
W. not for little Léonie GRAH 348:2
w. on your own grave GRAV 349:16
w. or she will die TENN 765:25
w. over Saul BIBL 79:2
weep with them that w. BIBL 105:15
W. you no more ANON 19:10
women must w. KING 437:12
weepers losers w. PROV 600:20
weepest Woman, why w. thou BIBL 103:1
weeping full cause of w. SHAK 678:19
goeth on his way w. BOOK 140:20
hear the children w. BROW 154:15
two w. motions CRAS 244:12
w. and gnashing BIBL 94:18
w. and the laughter DOWS 277:6
W. and watching GOET 343:11
w. and with laughter MACA 483:12
w. for her children BIBL 92:25
w. queen SHAK 695:18
weeps w. with loathing LITT 470:4
Weib *W. und Gesang* LUTH 480:6
Weibliche *Das Ewig-W.* CLOS 222:7
weigh more people see than w. CHES 209:22
w. and consider BACO 44:5
w. it down on one side HALI 357:8
w. thy words BIBL 92:4
weighed w. in the balances BIBL 90:4
weighing not w. our merits BOOK 130:1
weight bear the w. of Antony SHAK 656:19
heavy and the weary w. WORD 829:3
prodigal w. SHAK 695:16
w. in other people's patience UPDI 788:9
w. of rages SPOO 735:3
words are of less w. BACO 42:19
weights system of w. and measures NAPO 538:18
weilest *wo w. du* WAGN 798:18
Wein *W., Weib und Gesang* LUTH 480:6
weird w. sisters SHAK 681:13
w. women promised SHAK 683:24
welcome Advice is seldom w. CHES 209:13
be w. back again BURN 168:19
good evening, and w. CATC 195:21
Love bade me w. HERB 372:22
warmest w., at an inn SHEN 715:6
W., all wonders CRAS 244:8
w. day BUNY 161:17
w. ever smiles SHAK 700:16
W. the coming POPE 586:7
W. the sixte CHAU 206:16
W. to your gory bed BURN 168:7
welcomes w. at once all the world ANST 22:15
welcomest w. when they are gone SHAK 672:8
welfare anxious for its w. BURK 162:17
concerned with the w. MAHĀ 489:16
W. became a term MOYN 534:11
w. of this realm CHAR 203:13
welkin all the w. rings WESL 810:22
let the w. roar SHAK 669:32
well alive and w. ANON 17:6
all shall be w. ELIO 294:20
all shall be w. JULI 423:3
All's w. that ends well PROV 595:2
at the bottom of a w. PROV 613:20

well (*cont.*):
being w. MART 498:2
crown like a deep w. SHAK 695:21
deep as a w. SHAK 697:22
Didn't she do w. CATC 195:9
does himself extremely w. ANON 17:22
drink from every w. CALL 181:16
foolish thing w. done JOHN 414:19
handsome, w.-shaped. man AUBR 32:22
have the morning w.-aired BRUM 158:22
Is it w. with the child BIBL 80:15
It is not done w. JOHN 413:17
Let w. alone PROV 605:23
Like a w.-conducted person THAC 769:16
looking w. can't move her SUCK 745:7
men shall speak w. of you BIBL 99:3
never speaks w. of me CONG 232:28
not feeling very w. PUNC 617:20
not wisely but too w. SHAK 694:3
one of my w.-looking days GOLD 345:18
one who meant w. STEV 741:1
pitcher will go to the w. PROV 609:26
Pussy's in the w. NURS 548:4
rare as a w.-spent one CARL 187:10
sense of being w.-dressed FORB 319:9
shall be w. again ARNO 26:9
spent one whole day w. THOM 771:5
that's as w. said SWIF 748:17
till the w. runs dry PROV 615:48
use it for a w. BOOK 137:12
want a thing done w. PROV 603:38
want to do something w. BISH 116:2
W. begun is half done PROV 613:44
w.-beloved hath a vineyard BIBL 86:15
w.-born and unhappy woman ELIO 292:10
w.-bred as if we were not married CONG 233:12
w.-bred resignation TURG 785:3
W. done BIBL 97:8
W. done, David ADAM 2:12
w.-informed mind AUST 38:4
w. of English undefiled SPEN 734:6
w. of loneliness HALL 358:7
w. of love COLE 224:17
w. of poisons CIBB 110:3
w.-tuned cymbals BOOK 142:3
w.-written Life CARL 187:10
when ye do w. BIBL 110:31
would do very w. WALP 800:23
wellbeloved my w. unto me BIBL 85:8
Wellesley fat with W.'s glory BYRO 177:14
wells *poison the w.* NEWM 542:3
poison w. MARL 496:17
Welsh devil understands W. SHAK 668:23
W. as sweet as ditties SHAK 668:22
Welshman Taffy was a W. NURS 551:1
valour in this W. SHAK 671:14
Weltgeschichte *W. ist das Weltgericht* SCHI 648:15
wen great w. of all COBB 223:11
Wenceslas Good King W. NEAL 540:2
wench O ill-starred w. SHAK 693:31
w. is dead MARL 496:18
wenches many young w. OSBO 559:17
Wenlock On W. Edge HOUS 391:2
went He w. forth conquering BIBL 112:4
wept I sat down and w. BORR 144:2
Jesus w. BIBL 102:11
No one w. for the dead AGNO 8:26
sometimes w. MUSS 537:12
W. over her TENN 763:25
we sat down and w. BOOK 141:7
would have w. MALO 492:14
wert Which w., and art HEBE 367:8
Werther W. had a love for Charlotte THAC 769:15
west Cincinnatus of the W. BYRO 178:20
come out of the w. SCOT 651:7
daughter of the W. TENN 759:9
east is from the w. BOOK 138:19
East, w., home's best PROV 599:5
face neither East nor W. NKRU 546:11
gardens of the W. CONN 234:4
Go W., young man GREE 351:10
Go W., young man NEWS 544:7
liquid manure from the W. SOLZ 727:16
nor from the w. BOOK 136:22
O wild W. Wind SHEL 712:12
safeguard of the W. WORD 830:14
sailing away to the w. KING 437:11
travel due W. CARR 191:23
W. is West KIPL 438:5
W. of these out to seas FLEC 317:1
W.'s awake DAVI 252:17
where the W. begins CHAP 202:11
wester rainy Pleiads w. HOUS 390:11
western delivered by W. Union GOLD 346:6
Go to the w. gate ROBI 629:13
o'er the w. wave SHEL 714:11
Playboy of the W. World CLOS 222:18
Playboy of the W. World SYNG 751:22
quiet on the w. front REMA 624:10
spray of W. pine HART 363:9
W. is not only history LANG 450:13
When you've seen one W. WHIT 814:21
Wind of the w. sea TENN 765:15
Westerners W. have aggressive KAUN 426:7
West Indian I am a W. peasant MCDO 485:3
Westminster peerage, or W. Abbey NELS 540:14
westward stepping w. WORD 832:4
w., look, the land CLOU 223:4
W. the course of empire BERK 68:4
wet out of these w. clothes FILM 311:19
Sow dry and set w. PROV 611:11
so w. you could shoot snipe off him POWE 590:10
w. and wildness HOPK 384:10
w. sheet CUNN 247:15
would not w. her feet PROV 597:8
wether tainted w. of the flock SHAK 688:8
Wexford disused shed in Co. W. MAHO 490:20
whacks gave her mother forty w. ANON 17:10
whale prophet with the w. DICK 263:11
unconquering w. MELV 504:10
Very like a w. SHAK 665:3
whales great w. come sailing by ARNO 26:13
O ye W. BOOK 126:9
W. play WILL 820:6
whaleship w. was my Yale College MELV 504:8
whaling w. a universal metaphon LODG 472:14
whammy Labour's double w. POLI 581:23
wharves remember the black w. LONG 473:23
what for my own self w. am I HILL 377:9
He knew what's w. BUTL 171:22
W. and Why and When KIPL 441:10
W. is this BIBL 74:2
W. is to be done LENI 463:9
W.'s up, Doc CATC 196:27
why, or which, or w. LEAR 460:3
wheat belly like an heap of w. BIBL 86:4
orient and immortal w. TRAH 780:13
postal districts packed like squares of w. LARK 453:8
sleep among the w. CARR 191:14
w. from the chaff HUBB 392:12
wheel beneath thy Chariot w. HOPE 383:21
breaks a butterfly on a w. NEWS 544:18
butterfly upon a w. POPE 583:9
created the w. APOL 23:1
ever-whirling w. SPEN 734:12
in thy w. MARL 496:11
invented the w. NEME 541:3
red w. barrow WILL 821:2
round slippery w. DAVI 251:20
squeaking w. gets PROV 611:18
to make a w. LAO 451:8
w. broken at the cistern BIBL 85:2
w. of life run long STER 739:5
W. of Teaching PALI 565:24
wheels w. as burning fire BIBL 90:6
w. of black Marias AKHM 9:10
w. of trade HUME 394:11
why tarry the w. BIBL 77:30
when forgotten to say 'W.!' WODE 824:25
If not now w. HILL 377:9
w. a man should marry BACO 43:20
w. did you last see YEAM 835:1
W. you call me that WIST 823:17
whence w. came they BIBL 112:9
W. comest thou BIBL 80:20
w. cometh my help BOOK 140:12
w. did he whence LENO 464:5
w. it cometh BIBL 101:17
where fixed the w. and when HAWK 364:6
I knew not w. LONG 473:9
W. are you going BIBL 114:7
W. are you going to NURS 551:20
W. did you come from MACD 484:20
w. do they all come from LENN 463:20
W. is now thy God BOOK 134:8
w. is Plantagenet CREW 244:22
w. is your comforting HOPK 384:11
W. OUGHT I TO BE TELE 758:1
wherefore For every why he had a w. BUTL 171:21
w. art thou Romeo SHAK 697:11
W. does he why LENO 464:5
whereof w. one cannot speak WITT 824:6
whetstone no such w. ASCH 30:2
whiff w. of grapeshot CARL 187:21
whiffling w. through the tulgey wood CARR 190:13
Whig ascendancy of the W. party MACA 482:5
first W. was the Devil JOHN 416:4
hated a W. JOHN 418:5
Tory and W. in turns SMIT 725:8
Tory men and W. measures DISR 270:2
W. in any dress JOHN 412:2
wise W. JOHN 416:25
Whigs caught the W. bathing DISR 268:10
W. admit no force BROW 154:7
while little w. BIBL 102:26
whimper Not with a bang but a w. ELIO 294:26
whims w. of an egotist KEAT 430:26
whimsical say something w. LOVE 476:8
whin three w. bushes rode across KAVA 426:8
whine thin w. of hysteria DIDI 267:10
whining w., purblind, wayward boy SHAK 680:22
whip Do not forget the w. NIET 545:10
W.'s duty CANN 185:8
whipped w. the offending Adam SHAK 670:27
whippersnapper Critic and w. BROW 155:6
whipping w. Sorrow driveth GREV 353:3
who should 'scape w. SHAK 663:25
whips chastised you with w. BIBL 79:22
w. and scorns of time SHAK 664:4
whirligig w. of time SHAK 702:20
whirling by the w. rim BLAM 121:14
whirlwind Elijah went up by a w. BIBL 80:12
reap the w. BIBL 90:10
reap the w. PROV 612:36
Rides in the w. ADDI 4:7
w. hath blown DONN 275:6
whiskers Cat with crimson w. LEAR 460:21
whisky Freedom and W. BURN 166:14
give you a tot of w. HEAT 367:4
good old boys drinkin' w. MCLE 486:15
whisper remonstrative w. to a mob HUNT 396:4
what they w. there DANT 249:20
w. of a faction RUSS 640:9
w. of unseen wings THOM 773:11
w. softness in chambers MILT 519:12
w. to the tourist BEER 61:13
W. who dares MILN 511:1
whispered w. every where CONG 232:19

whispering just w. in her mouth MARX 499:10
w. its name COCT 223:21
w. sound COWP 241:1
whisperings keeps eternal w. KEAT 430:1
whispers what he w. SMIT 724:15
W. the o'er-fraught heart SHAK 685:7
whist ignorance of w. TALL 753:9
whistle hir joly w. wel ywet CHAU 206:11
I'd w. her off SHAK 692:23
shrimp learns to w. KHRU 435:15
sow may w. PROV 611:12
W. and she'll come FLET 318:11
w., an' I'll come BURN 168:5
You know how to w. FILM 311:25
whistled w. as he went DRYD 281:9
whistling w. half a dozen bars STER 738:20
w. woman and a crowing hen PROV 614:45
worth w. for PROV 604:4
white always goes into w. satin SHER 715:17
arrayed in w. robes BIBL 112:9
behold a w. horse BIBL 113:2
fat w. woman CORN 237:2
garment was w. as snow BIBL 90:6
hairs were w. like wool BIBL 111:22
I read w. BLAK 118:11
life of w. men SITT 720:20
lowest w. man JOHN 408:11
Many a head has turned w. MÜLL 536:4
My beloved is w. and ruddy BIBL 85:20
nor w. so very white CANN 185:2
no 'w.' or 'coloured' signs KENN 433:16
One w. foot PROV 609:8
pluck a w. rose SHAK 672:10
see the w. of their eyes PUTN 618:4
so-called w. races FORS 320:21
Some of my best friends are w. DURE 286:3
So purely w. SPEN 734:19
tupping your w. ewe SHAK 691:25
Two blacks don't make a w. PROV 613:24
up the w. road ELIO 296:13
want to be the w. man's brother KING 436:9
Wearing w. for Eastertide HOUS 390:14
w. and bristly beard SHAK 704:8
w. and hairless HERR 374:18
w. and sparkling CHAN 202:7
W. as an angel BLAK 120:18
w. as snow BIBL 86:12
w., celestial thought VAUG 790:7
w. Christmas BERL 68:12
w. cliffs I never more must see MACA 482:24
w. cliffs of Dover BURT 169:19
w.-collar people WHYT 816:12
w. flower of a blameless TENN 759:11
w. hairs SHAK 670:22
w. heat of technology MISQ 522:14
w. In a single night BYRO 178:23
w. in the blood of the Lamb BIBL 112:10
W. Man's Burden KIPL 440:21
w. men with horrible looks EQUI 301:3
w. owl in the belfry TENN 766:15
W. Peace FANS 306:10
w. race *is* the cancer SONT 728:7
W. shall not neutralize BROW 157:26
wild w. horses play ARNO 26:11
world is w. with May TENN 759:16
your w. hand WEBS 807:22
whited w. sepulchre TROL 782:7
w. sepulchres BIBL 96:28
Whitehall gentleman in W. JAY 404:14
White House Log-cabin to W. THAY 770:15
no whitewash at the W. NIXO 546:5
W. or home DOLE 272:1
whiter Persil washes w. ADVE 8:6
w. shade of pale REID 624:7
w. than snow BOOK 135:6
whitewash no w. at the White House NIXO 546:5
whither W. is he withering LENO 464:5
w. it goeth BIBL 101:17
whiting said a w. to a snail CARR 190:4
Whitman daintily dressed Walt W. CHES 211:15
no W. wanted BIRN 115:12
tonight, Walt W. GINS 339:21
understood Walt W. LODG 472:14
who O, w. am I CROS 246:15
tell me w. I am SHAK 678:9
W. am I going to be today WELD 809:9
W. dares wins MOTT 535:20
W. is on my side BIBL 80:26
W., or why, or which LEAR 460:3
w. the hell are you CATC 196:1
W.? Whom LENI 463:11
whole better than the w. PROV 601:42
faith hath made thee w. BIBL 94:27
greater than the w. HESI 375:11
had I stol'n the w. STEV 743:2
nothing can be sole or w. YEAT 835:13
seeing the w. RUSK 638:27
They that be w. BIBL 94:24
we shall be w. BOOK 137:8
w. man in himself HORA 390:2
wholesome out of his w. bed SHAK 675:6
whom W. are you ADE 6:1
Who? W. LENI 463:11
whooping out of all w. SHAK 659:9
whopping Latin for a w. ANST 22:16
whore cunning w. of Venice SHAK 693:15
Fortune's a right w. WEBS 808:7
I am the Protestant w. GWYN 355:8
I' the posture of a w. SHAK 657:24
judgement of the great w. BIBL 112:30
lash that w. SHAK 679:24
like a chaste w. MUGG 534:18
morals of a w. JOHN 412:14
Once a w. PROV 608:32
prisons, w.-shops CLAR 218:8
w. and the gambler BLAK 118:5
young man's w. JOHN 413:23
whoremongers sorcerers, and w. BIBL 113:15
whores second-rate w. PLOM 579:3
to work, ye w. PEMB 572:9
truth in w. WRIG 833:15
whoring went a w. BOOK 139:11
whose W. finger NEWS 544:19
whoso W. doeth these things BOOK 132:8
whosoever W. will be saved BOOK 126:21
why about the wasp, except w. THOM 772:14
but also w., to whom HAVE 364:3
can't tell you w. MART 497:23
finding only w. CUMM 247:11
For every w. he had a wherefore BUTL 171:21
W., Edward, tell me why WORD 827:16
W. not? Why not? Yeah LAST 457:19
Would this man ask w. AUDE 33:25
wibrated better not be w. DICK 260:17
wicked all the world w. BURK 164:14
August is a w. month O'BR 552:8
deceitful and w. man BOOK 134:9
desperately w. BIBL 89:19
fiery darts of the w. BIBL 108:13
no peace unto the w. BIBL 88:10
not that men are w. DU B 284:3
pretending to be w. WILD 817:20
sick and w. AUST 39:13
Something w. this way comes SHAK 684:20
tender mercies of the w. BIBL 82:25
Tories born w. ANON 17:15
what is more w. BALL 51:10
w. and moral CHUR 214:21
w. cease from troubling BIBL 81:5
w. flee BIBL 83:31
w. pack of cards ELIO 295:29
worse than w. PUNC 617:14
wickedness abhorrence for w. THAC 769:13
bands of w. BIBL 89:1
capable of every w. CONR 234:24
Hated w. BROW 157:3
malice and w. BOOK 128:6
manifold sins and w. BOOK 125:13
Path of W. BALL 52:1
shapen in w. BOOK 135:5
than human w. TAYL 756:7
turneth away from his w. BIBL 89:30
w. in high places BIBL 108:13
[w.] is not punished COMP 230:17
W. is the root ROBE 629:6
wicket flannelled fools at the w. KIPL 439:6
Widdicombe Fair want for to go to W. BALL 52:10
wide how w. also the east is BOOK 138:19
I am very w. BALZ 53:3
Poet sees, but w. ARNO 26:24
w. as a church door SHAK 697:22
W. is the gate BIBL 94:7
wideness w. in God's mercy FABE 305:18
wider seek no w. war JOHN 408:16
w. still and wider BENS 66:13
widow certain poor w. BIBL 98:12
fatherless and w. BOOK 141:23
French w. in every bedroom HOFF 380:9
Molly Stark's a w. STAR 736:12
old grey W.-maker KIPL 439:1
retired w. BAGE 46:22
virgin-w., and a *mourning bride* DRYD 282:12
w. bird sat mourning SHEL 711:5
w. of fifty SHER 716:14
W. The word consumes itself PLAT 577:20
widowhood comfortable estate of w. GAY 331:15
widows cause of the w. BOOK 136:6
devour w.' houses BIBL 98:11
fatherless children, and w. BOOK 127:12
These w., Sir ADDI 5:6
visit the fatherless and w. BIBL 110:16
w. whose husbands are alive BERN 69:5
wife after his neighbour's w. BIBL 89:11
as a w. is MILL 509:5
as his w. BRON 149:14
blind man's w. needs PROV 596:29
blind w. PROV 598:1
Brutus took to w. SHAK 675:8
Caesar's w. CAES 180:17
Caesar's w. PROV 596:46
cleave unto his w. BIBL 73:23
come in on the w.'s side LAMB 448:9
covet thy neighbour's w. BIBL 76:13
decided to murder his w. OPEN 555:26
Despair had a w. BUNY 161:5
divorces his first w. TALM 754:17
dwindle into a w. CONG 233:13
happy for a week take a w. PROV 603:41
have no w. BACO 45:12
his [Lot's] w. looked back BIBL 74:30
honour unto the w. BIBL 111:3
husband and w. FIEL 310:13
I'd have no w. CRAS 244:11
If I were your w. CHUR 216:23
I have a w. CONG 233:4
I have a w. LUCA 478:16
I have married a w. BIBL 99:28
in want of a w. AUST 38:14
in want of a w. OPEN 555:22
keeps up a w.'s spirits GAY 331:15
kick his w. out of bed SURT 746:17
kill a w. with kindness SHAK 698:9
lay down his w. for his friend JOYC 422:16
Like Caesar's w. ANON 17:8
look out for a w. SURT 747:3
love his w. as himself TALM 754:11
Man and W. BOOK 131:8
man who's untrue to his w. AUDE 34:11
Medicine is my lawful w. CHEK 208:14
moral centaur, man and w. BYRO 177:10
my sonne's w., Elizabeth INGE 399:12
my w., and my name SURT 746:20
My w., who, poor wretch PEPY 573:3
My w. won't let me LEIG 463:1
nobody's w. HERB 371:14
No casual mistress, but a w. TENN 761:16
Petrarch's w. BYRO 176:20

wife (*cont.*):
quarrelled with my w. PEAC 571:4
Remember Lot's w. BIBL 100:13
riding to and from his w. WHIT 813:24
she is your w. OGIL 553:2
some friend, not w. POPE 583:4
talks frankly only with his w. BABE 41:2
Thane of Fife had a w. SHAK 685:10
There's my w. SPRI 735:9
thrive must first ask his w. PROV 602:19
took from me my w. CLAR 218:9
to suit his w. TROL 783:2
true and honourable w. SHAK 675:7
wedded w. BOOK 131:4
What I need is a w. COLL 228:14
w. and children BACO 43:17
W. and Servant CHUD 213:9
w. for breed GAY 332:23
w. has ever taken SHAF 655:14
w. in bondage LEAP 460:2
w. is May WATK 804:15
w. or your servants to read GRIF 353:10
w. shall be as the fruitful vine BOOK 140:23
w. talks Greek JOHN 418:11
w. who looks out of door WELD 809:5
wind is my w. KEAT 431:11
with a w. SHAK 670:5
world and his w. ANST 22:15
young w. JONS 419:10
your w. and your dog HILL 376:14
wifehood Meek w. is no part BROC 149:3
wig w. with the scorched foretop MACA 481:13
Wigan mothers-in-law and W. Pier BRID 148:6
wights descriptions of the fairest w. SHAK 705:9
wigwam w. of Nokomis LONG 474:11
wild brought forth w. grapes BIBL 86:16
call of the w. LOND 473:5
gone w. into his grave SHAK 670:20
grew more fierce and w. HERB 372:8
never saw a w. thing LAWR 458:11
nobly w., not mad HERR 374:16
not a more fearful w. fowl SHAK 689:29
O Caledonia! stern and w. SCOT 651:2
peace of w. things BERR 69:14
three w. lads were we SCOT 651:23
walk on the w. side ALGR 11:16
waving his w. tail KIPL 441:7
w. geese are flighting KIPL 439:5
w. with all regret TENN 765:21
wilder w. shores of love BLAN 121:17
wilderness crieth in the w. BIBL 87:28
crying in the w. BIBL 92:27
day's journey into the w. BIBL 80:2
dwellings of the w. BOOK 136:2
grain into the w. STOU 744:2
in perils in the w. BIBL 107:14
in the w. BIBL 99:32
into the w. BIBL 76:21
into the w. to see BIBL 95:6
savage w. BURK 163:9
singing in the w. FITZ 314:9
temptation in the w. BOOK 138:6
They make a w. TACI 752:9
To the w. I wander ANON 19:17
walked through the w. OPEN 555:6
weeds and the w. HOPK 384:10
w. of idea BUTL 172:26
w. of this world BUNY 160:14
Women have no w. BOGA 123:12
world's wide w. WATT 805:13
wildness wet and w. HOPK 384:10
wilful w. man must have his way PROV 615:9
Wilhelmine little grandchild W. SOUT 730:11
will according to the common w. JAME 402:16
cause is in my w. SHAK 675:12
complies against his w. BUTL 172:12
complies against his w. PROV 602:11
death with one's w. JAIN 401:19
except a *good w.* KANT 425:13
general w. rules ROBE 629:3
Immanent W. HARD 361:10
In His w. is our peace DANT 250:3
knowing that we do Thy w. IGNA 398:17
know our w. is free JOHN 414:2
let my w. replace JUVE 424:15
not because we w. ARNO 26:2
not my w., but thine, be done BIBL 100:23
One single w. ROBE 629:7
political w. LYNN 480:21
resigning up one's w. OSBO 559:21
their w. ADAM 2:15
Thy w. be done BIBL 93:19
to have had the w. PROP 593:16
torrent of a woman's w. ANON 19:15
Where there's a w. PROV 614:40
w. against enjoyment HARD 361:1
W. in over-plus SHAK 705:22
w. in us is over-ruled MARL 496:12
w. most rank SHAK 692:22
w. not when he may PROV 602:18
w. of even common man CONF 231:19
w. of the majority JEFF 405:11
w. or decision CHOM 212:12
w. reigns FRAN 323:11
w. that my maxim KANT 425:14
w. to carry on LIPP 470:2
w. to go SHAK 697:34
W. you, won't you CARR 190:5
wind's w. LONG 473:23
wrote my w. across the sky LAWR 458:26
You w., Oscar WHIS 813:22
willed only a w. gentleness THOM 773:13
William You are old, Father W. CARR 189:12
Willie Wee W. Winkie NURS 551:18
willing Barkis is w. DICK 261:15
Lovely and w. AUDE 34:5
spirit indeed is w. BIBL 97:23
w. suspension of disbelief COLE 227:12
willingness w. is commendable OVID 561:10
willow green w. is my garland HEYW 376:6
Make me a w. cabin SHAK 701:7
Sing all a green w. SHAK 693:18
Stood Dido with a w. SHAK 688:20
w. grows aslant a brook SHAK 666:12
w. must be my garland SHAK 693:19
W., titwillow GILB 338:15
willows runs away into the w. VIRG 795:20
w. of the brook BIBL 82:2
w., old rotten planks CONS 235:6
W. whiten, aspens quiver TENN 762:13
wills talk of w. SHAK 695:8
w. the end PROV 602:34
wilt Do what thou w. CROW 246:17
Wimbledon Spill your guts at W. CONN 234:7
win can't w. them all PROV 615:32
From w. and lose MITC 523:16
Greetings, we w. LAST 455:17
know how to w. POLY 580:4
Let them laugh that w. PROV 605:22
spend it, and w. KENN 434:1
that's to w. MALR 492:18
To w. in Vietnam SPOC 735:2
w. an atomic war BRAD 146:9
w. a war is as disastrous CHRI 212:14
w. his spurs EDWA 289:4
W. just one for the Gipper GIPP 340:2
w. or lose it all MONT 529:2
would greatly w. BYRO 178:17
yet wouldst wrongly w. SHAK 682:1
You w. a few PROV 616:8
wince rather w. DICK 266:20
wind All-powerful as the w. AUBE 32:10
answer is blowin' in the w. DYLA 287:3
appearance of solidity to pure w. ORWE 559:11
as the idle w. SHAK 676:23
available with an east w. LOWE 477:18
Awake, O north w. BIBL 85:17
bleak w. of March HOOD 382:15
Blow, blow, thou winter w. SHAK 659:4
Blow, thou w. of God KING 437:8
boy's will is the w.'s LONG 473:23
brought forth the w. BIBL 87:12
candle in the w. JOHN 407:17
chiding of the winter's w. SHAK 658:13
clouds and w. without rain BIBL 83:19
east w. made flesh APPL 23:5
every w. of doctrine BIBL 108:3
feather for each w. SHAK 703:5
flare up in a w. FRAN 323:2
Freshly blows the w. WAGN 798:18
Frosty w. made moan ROSS 634:5
gentle w. does move BLAK 120:11
God tempers the w. STER 738:11
gone with the w. DOWS 277:5
hey, ho, the w. and the rain SHAK 678:26
His hammer of w. THOM 774:17
how the w. doth ramm POUN 589:6
ill w. that blows PROV 604:32
impatient as the w. WORD 832:5
let her down the w. SHAK 692:23
light w. lives or dies KEAT 430:11
like the w., that shifts DANT 249:22
Lord was not in the w. BIBL 80:3
moved about like the w. GERO 334:11
north w. doth blow NURS 549:16
not I, but the w. LAWR 458:15
Not with this w. blowing KIPL 439:17
no w. is favourable SENE 654:17
observeth the w. BIBL 84:29
O wild West W. SHEL 712:12
O w., the weder gynneth clere CHAU 207:3
piffle before the w. ASHF 30:14
rag blown by the w. WORD 827:9
reed before the w. PROV 610:7
reed shaken with the w. BIBL 95:6
rude w. Blows in your face SHAK 679:16
rushing mighty w. BIBL 103:15
sand against the w. BLAK 120:2
sown the w. BIBL 90:10
sow the w. PROV [illegible]
stood the w. for France DRAY 279:9
substance is but only w. WYAT 834:7
tempers w. to shorn lamb PROV 601:19
thaw w. PROV 610:15
'tis a Protestant w. WHAR 813:5
torch borne in the w. CHAP 202:13
twist slowly in the w. EHRL 290:4
Unhelped by any w. COLE 225:12
wash the w. ELIO 295:16
way the w. blows PROV 611:27
Western w. ANON 19:13
western w. was wild KING 437:9
Whenever the w. is high STEV 742:17
when the w. is southerly SHAK 663:21
wherever the w. takes me HORA 386:8
which way the w. is SELD 653:17
w. and storm BOOK 141:27
w. and swift-flowing water CATU 197:12
w. and the rain SHAK 702:22
w. and wave and oar TENN 763:15
w. blew due East CARR 191:23
w. bloweth where it listeth BIBL 101:17
w. blow the earth SHAK 678:20
w. doth blow BALL 52:6
w. extinguishes candles LA R 453:18
w. goeth over it BOOK 138:20
w. in that corner SHAK 691:8
w. is in the east PROV 614:31
w. is to fire BUSS 171:6
w. it into a ball BLAK 119:3
w. it plies the saplings HOUS 391:2
w. of change is blowing MACM 487:19
W. of the western sea TENN 765:15
w. or the pennant HUI- 394:4
w. plays up BLOK 122:4
w.'s feet shine SWIN 751:13
w.'s in the east DICK 260:20
w.'s like whetted knife MASE 500:18
wings of the w. BOOK 132:11

wings of the w. BOOK 139:1
Woord is but w. LYDG 480:11
windbags W. can be right FENT 308:11
winder w., a casement DICK 263:21
winding by a w. stair BACO 43:12
England's w. sheet BLAK 118:5
good structure in a w. stair HERB 372:20
have w. sheet DONN 274:24
waters were his w. sheet BARN 55:8
w.-sheet of Edward's GRAY 350:4
windings w. and such shade WINC 822:24
w. of the grove BEAT 58:5
window appears at a w. BEER 61:12
argument of the broken w. PANK 566:14
clapte the w. to CHAU 205:27
doggie in the w. MERR 505:24
eyes are w. of soul PROV 600:3
Good prose like a w.-pane ORWE 558:8
has not one w. JAME 403:11
kick a hole in a stained glass w. CHAN 201:12
kiss my ass in Macy's w. JOHN 408:18
little w. where the sun HOOD 382:21
looked out at a w. BIBL 80:24
openeth the w. BIBL 73:9
return through the w. FRED 323:21
rubs its back upon the w.-panes ELIO 295:5
through yonder w. breaks SHAK 697:9
throw it out of the w. BECK 59:16
Waits at the w. LENN 463:20
windows breaking of w. MORE 530:22
life's dim w. BLAK 118:14
open the w. of the Church JOHN 407:12
open w. into men's souls ELIZ 297:9
storied w. MILT 512:11
then the W. failed DICK 266:9
thought of high w. LARK 452:17
thus, Through w. DONN 274:14
without looking through w. LAO 452:1
winds all the w. of doctrine MILT 519:19
Blow, w., and crack SHAK 678:21
great w. shorewards blow ARNO 26:11
howling w. drive COWP 240:27
O ye W. of God BOOK 126:5
stormy w. did blow SONG 729:15
take The w. of March SHAK 703:17
w. are all composure SMAR 721:19
w. come to me WORD 829:17
w. do blow HERB 373:2
w. of heaven SHAK 661:25
w. that would blow BOLT 124:20
w. were love-sick SHAK 656:23
windscreen through the w. DUNM 285:8
windvane w. changabil huf puffe VIRG 794:13
windward w. of the law CHUR 213:18
windy w. side of the law SHAK 702:14
wine be not drunk with w. BIBL 108:9
best fits my little w. HERR 374:21
blood and w. WILD 818:30
Botticelli isn't a w. PUNC 617:21
buy w. and milk BIBL 88:20
can with w. dispense CRAB 242:26
castaway w.-pots CLOU 221:11
days of w. and roses DOWS 277:7
do crush their w. MARV 498:15
doesn't get into the w. CHES 211:1
Drinking the blude-red w. BALL 51:13
Drinking the blude-red w. OPEN 555:29
drink one cup of w. SCOT 651:11
drunk old w. BIBL 99:2
flask of w. FITZ 314:9
flown with insolence and w. MILT 514:27
From the sweetest w. PROV 601:1
Good w. needs no bush PROV 601:31
have w. and women BYRO 176:13
he drinks no w. SHAK 670:13
I as w. HERB 372:2
I'll not look for w. JONS 420:20
in w. we steep LOVE 476:13
kept the good w. BIBL 101:14
last companion, W. BELL 63:17
like generous w. Ferments BUTL 172:15
Like the best w. BIBL 86:6
Look not thou upon the w. BIBL 83:16
lordliest in their w. MILT 518:21
love is better than w. BIBL 85:6
mine host's Canary w. KEAT 428:20
new friend is as new w. BIBL 91:24
new w. in old bottles PROV 615:29
new w. into old bottles BIBL 94:26
Not given to w. BIBL 109:14
old w. wholesomest WEBS 808:6
out-did the frolic w. HERR 374:17
pint o' w. BURN 167:28
red sweet w. of youth BROO 150:7
red w. of Shiraz into urine DINE 267:20
refreshed with w. BOOK 137:7
rinsed with w. HOPK 384:8
Sans w., sans song FITZ 314:12
seas of life, like w. TRAH 780:18
take a glass of w. SHER 716:19
that is without w. BIBL 92:7
truth in w. PROV 612:24
vows made in w. SHAK 659:16
When the w. is in PROV 614:32
wholesome w. TENN 767:3
w. and women BURT 170:9
w. for thy stomach's sake BIBL 109:16
w. in rivers SCOT 651:23
w. is a good familiar creature SHAK 692:17
W. is a mocker BIBL 83:7
W. is the strongest BIBL 90:26
W. maketh merry BIBL 84:26
W., not water SANS 644:7
w. on the lees BIBL 87:10
w., reed as blood CHAU 205:4
w. that maketh glad BOOK 139:3
w. unto those of heavy hearts BIBL 83:37
w. with a merry heart BIBL 84:21
woman, w. and song LUTH 480:6
Women and w. GAY 331:17
wines Soused in high-country w. JONS 419:9
wing fanned by Conquest's crimson w. GRAY 350:2
flits by on leathern w. COLL 229:8
joy is ever on the w. MILT 518:12
knowst'ou w. from tail POUN 589:22
lark's on the w. BROW 157:12
never flew on one w. PROV 596:22
on a w. and a pray'r ADAM 4:1
so long on a broken w. TENN 764:14
winged Time's w. chariot MARV 499:2
w. life destroy BLAK 120:8
w. squadrons of the sky MILM 510:10
W. words HOME 381:21
wings beating his luminous w. ARNO 28:21
beating of his w. BRIG 148:9
Beteth his w. CHAU 205:11
brought beneath His w. MIDR 507:11
Clap her broad w. FRER 324:11
clip an Angel's w. KEAT 428:19
covered with silver w. BOOK 136:7
defend thee under his w. BOOK 137:21
dip Their w. in tears TENN 761:7
eagle's w., Unseen KEAT 427:28
envy birds their w. CLAR 218:10
giant's w. BAUD 57:5
great w. beating YEAT 836:14
Grief has no w. QUIL 619:2
healing in his w. BIBL 90:25
Ill news hath w. DRAY 278:22
Love without his w. BYRO 178:11
mount up with w. BIBL 88:5
O, for a horse with w. SHAK 660:24
on extended w. STEV 740:6
on laughter-silvered w. MAGE 489:8
On w. of song HEIN 368:4
own almighty w. KEN 433:2
shadow of thy w. BOOK 135:14
spread his w. on the blast BYRO 175:24
spreads her downy w. FANS 306:10
viewless w. of Poesy KEAT 429:11
Waft your w. together NURS 548:9
w. like a dove BOOK 135:10
w. of the morning BOOK 141:11
w. of the wind BOOK 132:11
w. of the wind BOOK 139:1
with ah! bright w. HOPK 384:6
wingy w. mysteries BROW 153:15
wink nod's as good as a w. PROV 607:46
w. a reputation down SWIF 749:9
wink w., say no more MONT 529:5
Winkie Wee Willie W. NURS 551:18
winners no w., but all are losers CHAM 200:16
winning act the w. part HERR 374:10
glory of the w. MERE 505:19
more fun w. DOLE 272:2
wear of w. BELL 64:10
w. cause pleased the gods LUCA 478:13
W. is everything HILL 376:14
w. isn't anything SAND 644:5
winnowing by the w. wind KEAT 430:9
wins Who dares w. MOTT 535:20
w. if he does not lose KISS 441:27
winter all the w. long SHAK 703:13
amid the w.'s snow CASW 194:3
by the w. sea TENN 760:10
English w. BYRO 177:23
furious w. blowing RANS 622:1
furious w.'s rages SHAK 661:1
go south in the w. ELIO 295:27
How like a w. SHAK 705:8
If W. comes SHEL 712:19
in the Middle of W. ADDI 5:4
In w. I get up at night STEV 742:11
It was the w. wild MILT 513:19
mind of w. STEV 740:4
my age is as a lusty w. SHAK 658:16
of autumn and w. cometh CLAR 218:18
old man upon a w.'s night YEAT 836:21
on w.'s traces SWIN 750:5
Our severest w. COWP 242:19
perils of w. TROL 782:11
sad tale's best for w. SHAK 703:2
something about w. CANN 185:11
summer or w. CHEK 208:9
very dead of W. ANDR 14:15
very dead of w. ELIO 294:27
W. Afternoons DICK 266:16
w. and rough weather SHAK 658:20
W. comes to rule the varied year THOM 775:14
W. is come and gone SHEL 710:18
W. is icummen in POUN 589:6
w. is past BIBL 85:10
W. lies too long CATH 194:9
W. never rots PROV 615:11
w. of discontent CALL 181:11
W. of discontent NEWS 544:20
w. of our discontent SHAK 696:7
w. of this year ALAI 10:2
w., plague and pestilence NASH 539:23
w.'s rains and ruins SWIN 750:6
W. suddenly was changed SHEL 713:19
wrathful w., 'proaching on SACK 641:3
winters When forty w. shall besiege SHAK 704:6
w. and keeps warm CARE 186:14
wipe *Gives it a w.* HOOD 383:2
Let me w. it first SHAK 679:22
w. away all tears BIBL 112:12
w. away all tears BIBL 113:8
wiped w. out of the book BOOK 136:13
wire Along the electric w. ANON 15:8
wires If hairs be w. SHAK 705:20
wisdom all men's w. RUSS 640:12
all Solomon's w. BIBL 79:17
apply our hearts unto w. BOOK 137:20
beginning of w. BOOK 139:18
contrivance of human w. BURK 163:19
door to infinite w. BREC 147:9
ends in w. FROS 326:13
evidences of our w. TROL 782:21
Experience father of w. PROV 599:49

wisdom (*cont.*):
Greeks seek after w. BIBL 105:27
his is a serene w. BHAG 72:19
How can he get w. BIBL 92:12
how little w. OXEN 562:14
infallible criterion of w. BURK 162:6
perfection of w. MAHĀ 489:14
price of w. BIBL 81:25
privilege of w. to listen HOLM 381:6
quintessence of w. JAIN 402:7
righteousness with w. PLAT 578:10
seven pillars of w. BORR 144:15
teach Eternal W. how to rule POPE 585:21
teach his senators w. BOOK 139:9
to the palace of w. BLAK 119:12
we had w. BENÉ 65:2
what is bettre than w. CHAU 205:25
where shall w. be found BIBL 81:24
w. and truth SOCR 726:23
w. and understanding BIBL 87:3
W. and Wit BRER 148:1
w. as many of us have TROL 783:8
w. be put in a silver rod BLAK 118:8
W. denotes the pursuing HUTC 396:14
W. excelleth folly BIBL 84:6
w. has no perplexities CONF 231:23
W. hath builded her house BIBL 82:18
w. in Edom MIDR 507:14
W. in minds attentive COWP 242:6
W. is humble COWP 242:7
W. is justified BIBL 95:8
W. is the principal thing BIBL 82:10
w. lingers TENN 763:6
w. of the crocodiles BACO 44:24
w. of the fool JOHN 418:10
W. say another BURK 164:8
w. shall die with you BIBL 81:15
w. we have lost in knowledge ELIO 295:21
With the ancient is w. BIBL 81:16
wise art of being w. JAME 404:2
Astrologers or three w. men LONG 475:6
beacons of w. men HUXL 397:19
become w. BIBL 92:11
being darkly w. POPE 585:19
be w. and eke to love [illegible] 734:20
be w., and love SHAK 700:13
Be w., be wise SOUT 730:10
Be w. to-day YOUN 839:5
Be w. with speed YOUN 838:18
confound the w. BIBL 105:29
consider her ways, and be w. BIBL 82:13
cunning men pass for w. BACO 42:21
deemed him wondrous w. BEAT 58:3
enough for the w. PLAU 578:13
errors of a w. man BLAK 120:6
follies of the w. JOHN 411:18
fool may give w. man PROV 600:35
fortunate than w. WEBS 808:16
Ful w. is he CHAU 205:29
have gone the few w. men LUIS 479:10
healthy, wealthy, and w. PROV 599:4
heard a w. man say HOUS 390:18
love and be w. PROV 608:34
man w. in his own conceit BIBL 83:25
more w. when he had JOHN 416:15
Nature is always w. THUR 777:5
Nor ever did a w. one EPIT 302:14
not always w. BIBL 81:29
only wretched are the w. PRIO 593:5
or a w. man LOCK 472:8
Penny w. PROV 609:24
proud if you'll be w. CHUD 213:10
smile with the w. JOHN 414:1
So w. so young SHAK 696:20
speak to the w. PIND 576:9
still tongue makes w. head PROV 611:21
teachings of the w. LUCR 479:3
than manly w. MARL 497:2
that a w. man sees BLAK 119:15
think as w. men do ASCH 30:9
Three w. men of Gotham NURS 551:12
'Tis folly to be w. GRAY 350:18
to the w., and to the unwise BIBL 104:25
What all the w. men promised MELB 504:3
wherefore thou be w. TENN 757:10
w. after the event PROV 604:15
w. as serpents BIBL 94:34
w. enough to play the fool SHAK 701:31
w. father that knows SHAK 687:18
w., for cure DRYD 281:13
w. forgive but do not forget SZAS 752:1
w. in his own conceit BIBL 83:23
w. in your own conceits BIBL 105:16
w. man or a fool BLAK 119:6
w. men from the east BIBL 92:22
w. son BIBL 82:20
w. want love SHEL 713:8
words of the w. BIBL 85:3
word to the w. is enough PROV 615:18
wisecrack w. that played Carnegie Hall LEVA 466:1
wisecracking w. and wit PARK 567:12
wisely Be w. worldly QUAR 618:17
nations behave w. EBAN 287:20
not w. but too well SHAK 694:3
spake w. BIBL 91:29
wiser French are w. BACO 44:1
guided by the w. CARL 187:3
he is w. today POPE 587:18
in their generation w. BIBL 100:7
looked w. when he was seated KEYN 435:5
not the w. grow POMF 580:5
sadder and a w. man COLE 227:1
w. by and by TENN 759:14
w. in his own conceit BIBL 83:26
wisest been noght w. men CHAU 206:10
first and w. of them MILT 518:9
Seems w., virtuousest MILT 517:10
w. and justest PLAT 578:4
w. fool in Christendom HENR 370:7
w. man can answer COLT 230:3
w. of all moral men DAVI 251:16
wish believe what they w. CAES 180:16
If otherwise w. I SHAW 709:29
live, not as we w. MENA 504:13
Whoever hath her w [illegible] 703:22
W. for prayer is a prayer BERN 68:20
w. I loved the Human Race RALE 621:11
w. is father to the thought PROV 615:12
w. I were in love again HART 363:5
w. was father, Harry SHAK 670:16
wishes compliance with my w. after reasonable discussion CHUR 216:19
exact to my w. EPIT 302:15
If w. were horses PROV 603:26
w. it were MALR 493:1
wist w., before I kist BALL 52:9
wit accepted w. has but to say GILB 339:13
age is in, the w. is out SHAK 691:15
at their w.'s end BOOK 139:15
at thirty, the w. FRAN 323:11
baiting place of w. SIDN 718:12
Brevity is the soul of w. PROV 596:39
Brevity is the soul of w. SHAK 663:9
but a little w. ANON 19:14
craves a kind of w. SHAK 701:31
Devise, w.; write, pen SHAK 680:20
fancy w. will come POPE 582:25
heart did do it, And not my w. EPIT 303:14
his weapon w. EPIT 303:9
His w. invites you COWP 240:3
How the w. brightens POPE 584:25
Impropriety is the soul of w. MAUG 501:18
In w., a man POPE 584:10
little tiny w. SHAK 678:26
mechanic part of w. ETHE 301:13
mingled with a little w. DRYD 281:22
nature by her mother w. SPEN 734:7
neither w., nor words SHAK 676:10
no free and splendid w. MILT 519:24
no pick-purse of another's w. SIDN 718:17
nor all thy piety nor w. FITZ 314:17
not his pointed w. POPE 586:14
o'erflowing of unbounded w. WINC 822:20
Old Mother W. DENH 257:13
only idea of w. SMIT 725:12
past the w. of man SHAK 690:16
proverb is one man's w. RUSS 640:12
ready and pleasant smooth w. AUBR 32:22
sharpen a good w. ASCH 30:2
shoots his w. SHAK 659:28
Some beams of w. DRYD 281:36
Staircase w. DIDE 267:6
steal their w. CAVE 198:11
takes more than w. LA B 446:19
tomb of w. CAVE 198:12
too proud for a w. GOLD 345:1
True w. is Nature POPE 584:18
universal monarchy of w. CARE 186:7
use my w. as a pitchfork LARK 453:6
Wisdom and W. BRER 148:1
w. among Lords JOHN 412:13
w. and humour AUST 38:2
w. enough to keep it sweet JOHN 417:16
W. has truth in it PARK 567:12
w. in all languages DRYD 283:5
w. is out PROV 614:32
W. is the epitaph NIET 545:20
w. its soul COLE 225:9
W. Makes such a wound SHEL 712:2
w.'s a feather POPE 586:1
W.'s empire EGER 289:15
w.'s the noblest frailty SHAD 655:11
W. will shine DRYD 282:28
w. with dunces POPE 580:18
witch Aroint thee, w. SHAK 681:11
witchcraft as the sin of w. BIBL 78:26
no w. charm thee SHAK 661:2
W. celebrates SHAK 683:1
w., there has been WALP 801:13
witches burnt at the stake as w. SMIT 724:22
Men feared w. BRAN 146:19
witching w. time of night SHAK 665:5
with He that is not w. me BIBL 95:10
I am w. you alway BIBL 97:30
Lord of hosts is w. us BOOK 134:19
withdrawing long, w. roar [illegible]
withdrawn yawn and be w. DURY 286:10
withdrew departed, he w. CICE 217:20
wither Age cannot w. her SHAK 656:27
w. and perish SMIT 726:10
w. slowly in thine arms TENN 766:16
withered are w. away COCK 223:13
dried up, and w. BOOK 137:18
O! w. is the garland SHAK 657:19
So w. and so wild SHAK 681:15
w. in the sod BRON 149:12
withereth grass w. BIBL 110:26
rose Fast w. too KEAT 428:8
withers *it w. away* ENGE 300:11
our w. are unwrung SHAK 664:25
within kingdom of God is w. you BIBL 100:12
oh, he never went w. COWL 239:16
that w. which passeth show SHAK 661:21
they that are w. DAVI 251:14
without forasmuch as w. thee BOOK 128:16
get where I am today w. CATC 195:24
I can do w. SOCR 726:20
no good thing w. thee BOOK 128:10
they that are w. DAVI 251:14
with you—or w. you MART 498:4
withstand w. in the evil day BIBL 108:13
witness bear false w. BIBL 76:13
bear w. of that Light BIBL 101:5
w. against you BIBL 77:4
witnesses cloud of w. BIBL 110:2
w. against mankind KORA 445:1
w. laid down their clothes BIBL 103:21
w. to the desolation of war GEOR 334:2
wits composed in their w. ARNO 28:23
for w., then poets passed POPE 584:12
Great w. DRYD 280:2
Great w. may sometimes POPE 584:14
homely w. SHAK 702:23
rhyming mother-w. MARL 496:20
stolen his w. away DE L 256:10

Tiring thy w. DANI 249:2
warming his five w. TENN 766:15
W. are gamecocks GAY 332:7
wittles live on broken w. DICK 261:16
witty dull men w. BACO 45:9
fancy myself mighty w. FARQ 307:21
It shall be w. CHES 209:1
of the w. devil GRAV 349:11
Thou swell! Thou w. HART 363:8
w. in myself SHAK 669:22
w. woman is a treasure MERE 505:9
wives And sklendre w. CHAU 205:9
divides the w. of aldermen SMIT 723:4
Husbands, love your w. BIBL 109:5
man with seven w. NURS 547:11
profane and old w.' fables BIBL 109:15
several chilled w. MERR 505:26
when they are w. SHAK 659:20
W. are young men's mistresses BACO 43:19
W. in the avocados GINS 339:22
wiving Hanging and w. PROV 601:47
wizards affairs of W. TOLK 779:4
star-led w. MILT 513:18
wobbly spelling is W. MILN 511:5
Wodehouse like W. dropping Jeeves WAUG 806:22
woe and all my w. GOLD 344:19
balm of w. SIDN 718:12
Companions of our w. WALS 802:10
deep, unutterable w. AYTO 40:12
discover sights of w. MILT 514:12
Europe made his w. her own ARNO 27:22
feel another's w. POPE 587:13
full of w. PROV 606:42
gave signs of w. MILT 517:17
oft in w. WHIT 814:4
protracted w. JOHN 411:17
see another's w. BLAK 120:20
song of w. TENN 761:15
source of softer w. SCOT 650:15
suits of w. SHAK 661:21
W. is me BIBL 86:22
w. that is in mariage CHAU 206:15
W. to her that is filthy BIBL 90:23
W. to the bloody city BIBL 90:21
W. to thee, O land BIBL 84:25
W. to the land SHAK 696:19
w. unto them BIBL 86:18
woes direful spring of w. OPEN 555:2
Of w. unnumbered POPE 586:6
self-consumer of my w. CLAR 218:15
What is the worst of w. BYRO 174:7
with old w. new wail SHAK 704:16
w. which Hope thinks infinite SHEL 713:16
wolf his sentinel, the w. SHAK 683:1
Hunger drives the w. PROV 603:4
keep the w. far thence WEBS 808:14
like the w. on the fold BYRO 175:23
no w. has ever craved LA F 447:14
w. behowls the moon SHAK 690:28
w. by the ears JEFF 405:20
w. of a different opinion INGE 399:7
w. shall dwell with the lamb BIBL 87:4
W. that shall keep it KIPL 441:19
w. to another man PLAU 578:12
wolfsbane twist W., tight-rooted KEAT 429:2
Wolsey W.'s home town NEWS 544:12
wolves eat like w. SHAK 671:7
frighten the w. MACH 486:2
howling of Irish w. SHAK 659:23
ravening w. BIBL 94:9
woman aren't I a w. TRUT 784:12
artist man and the mother w. SHAW 708:1
As you are w. GRAV 349:14
A w. sat HOOD 382:28
bad w. ADDI 4:17
beautiful w. on top HORA 385:10
bettre than a good w. CHAU 205:25
body of a weak and feeble w. ELIZ 296:27
born a w. EDGE 288:16
born of a w. BIBL 81:18
brawling w. BIBL 83:12
broken-hearted w. HAYE 365:2
business of a w.'s life SOUT 731:8
But what is w. COWL 239:26
called a w. in my own house WAUG 806:14
cannot love a w. so well ELIO 292:27
changeable always is w. VIRG 794:13
Christ wasn't a w. TRUT 784:13
Come to my w.'s breasts SHAK 682:3
contentious w. BIBL 83:30
could be a good w. THAC 769:12
dead w. bites not GRAY 350:1
dear deluding w. BURN 169:2
done, ask a w. THAT 769:20
Do you not know I am a w. SHAK 659:10
Each thought on the w. KING 437:11
embrace a w.'s shoe KRAU 445:19
end to a w.'s liberty BURN 166:4
Eternal W. draws us CLOS 222:7
Eternal W. draws us upward GOET 343:4
Every w. adores a Fascist PLAT 577:14
excellent thing in w. SHAK 680:13
fair w. without discretion BIBL 82:23
fat white w. CORN 237:2
Frailty, thy name is w. SHAK 661:26
fury, like a w. scorned CONG 232:26
greatest glory of a w. PERI 573:21
hair of a w. HOWE 391:17
Here lies a poor w. EPIT 302:15
honest w. of her word SHAK 687:27
I am a w. of the world SHAW 707:11
if a w. have long hair BIBL 106:14
I grant I am a w. SHAK 675:8
in a w. all defects excuse LANI 451:3
in a w.'s hide SHAK 672:26
inconstant w. GAY 332:19
injured w. BARB 53:17
In w.'s eye BYRO 175:17
Is to a w. DONN 273:20
just like a w. DYLA 287:8
large-brained w. BROW 154:23
leader of the enterprise a w. VIRG 793:11
let me not play a w. SHAK 689:12
Let us look for the w. DUMA 284:14
Like to a constant w. FORD 319:20
lips of a strange w. BIBL 82:12
little w. who wrote LINC 469:4
Love a w. ROCH 630:18
lovely w. HUNT 395:17
lovely w. stoops to folly GOLD 345:30
made he a w. BIBL 73:21
make a man a w. PEMB 572:10
Make a w. believe WEBS 807:20
man's desire is for the w. COLE 227:21
Man that is born of a w. BOOK 131:12
Many a w. has a past WILD 818:9
nakedness of the w. BLAK 119:20
never be by w. loved BLAK 117:20
never trust a w. WILD 818:25
never yet fair w. SHAK 678:23
no, nor w. neither SHAK 663:18
no other purgatory but a w. BEAU 58:17
No w. can be a beauty FARQ 307:9
no w. should marry a teetotaller STEV 741:29
No w. will be Prime Minister THAT 769:19
O most pernicious w. SHAK 663:1
One is not born a w. DE B 254:4
one of w. born SHAK 685:24
one young w. and another SHAW 707:29
only way for a w. SHAW 709:4
perfect w.; nobly planned WORD 831:24
play without a w. KYD 446:11
poor old w. RICH 627:7
post-chaise with a pretty w. JOHN 415:22
pretty w. as was ever seen BYRO 173:18
prime truth of w. CHES 211:18
semblative a w.'s part SHAK 701:3
she *is* a w. AUST 39:8
She is a w. SHAK 672:13
she's a w. RACI 619:17
she shall be called W. BIBL 73:22
shone one w. SWIN 751:18
sort of bloom on a w. BARR 55:19
stages in a w.'s life KELL 432:14
suffered over *such* a w. HOME 381:23
sweeter w. ne'er drew breath INGE 399:12
takes a very clever w. KIPL 441:18
take some savage w. TENN 763:7
that ever loved w. MALO 492:15
that horror—the old w. COLE 228:4
that one w. differs from another MENC 504:14
There was an old w. NURS 551:6
this Man and this W. BOOK 130:22
tired of being a w. SEXT 655:5
torrent of a w.'s will ANON 19:15
trapped in a w.'s body BOY 146:3
unbecoming to a w. WILD 818:11
victory by a w. WEST 812:18
virtuous w. BIBL 83:38
virtuous w. is a crown BIBL 82:24
Vitality in a w. SHAW 707:32
warst w. BALL 50:21
well-born and unhappy w. ELIO 292:10
What does a w. want FREU 324:17
What is a w. KIPL 439:1
when a w. appears GAY 331:18
where w. never smiled CLAR 218:16
whistling w. and a crowing hen PROV 614:45
who cheats a w. GAY 331:21
Why can't a w. be LERN 465:3
wicked w. liberty BIBL 92:1
wisest w. in Europe ELIO 295:29
witty w. is a treasure MERE 505:9
w. always a woman WOLL 825:20
w. and a ship ever want PROV 615:14
W., a pleasing but a short-lived LEAP 460:2
w. as old as she looks PROV 606:14
W., behold thy son BIBL 102:35
w. brought sin and death STAN 736:9
w. can be proud and stiff YEAT 835:13
w. can forgive a man MAUG 502:1
w. can hardly ever choose ELIO 292:12
w. clothed with the sun BIBL 112:18
w., coloured ill SHAK 705:24
w. dictates ELIO 292:17
w., dog, and walnut tree PROV 615:13
w. especially AUST 38:4
w. forget her sucking child BIBL 88:11
w. has given you her heart VANB 789:9
W.! in our hours of ease SCOT 651:13
w. in this humour SHAK 696:13
w. is a sometime thing HEYW 376:5
w. is his game TENN 765:24
w. is like a teabag REAG 623:1
w. is not a potted plant WALK 799:10
w. is so hard TENN 766:1
W. is the equal of man LOY 478:12
W. is the great unknown HARD 360:3
w., let her be as good ELIO 292:25
w. loves her lover BYRO 176:18
w. moved SHAK 698:13
W. much missed HARD 361:21
w. must have money WOOL 826:17
w. must submit to it STAË 735:18
w. must wear chains FARQ 307:8
w. of education AUST 39:4
w. of mean understanding AUST 38:15
w. of real genius FITZ 315:4
w. of shining loveliness YEAT 837:8
w. once was BALL 51:10
w. only the right to spring FOND 318:25
w. possessed of a common share ADAM 1:19
W.'s at best a contradiction POPE 583:17
w. says to her lusting lover CATU 197:12
w.'s best garment PROV 610:40
w. scorned PROV 602:37
W.'s cully made CONG 232:29
W.'s degradation STAN 736:10
w. seldom asks advice ADDI 5:14
w. seldom writes her mind STEE 736:16
w.'s finest ornament AUCT 33:14
w.'s friendship ever ends GAY 332:5
w.'s happiest knowledge MILT 516:21
w.'s noblest station LYTT 481:3

woman (*cont.*):
w. sober PEPY 573:4
w.'s pen BOOT 142:19
w.'s place in the home PROV 615:15
w.'s preaching JOHN 413:17
w.'s reason SHAK 702:24
W. stock is rising CHIL 211:25
w.'s whole existence BYRO 176:7
w.'s workhouse SHAW 708:28
w.'s work is never done PROV 615:16
w. take An elder SHAK 701:18
w. taken in adultery BIBL 101:32
w. that attempts the pen WINC 822:21
W. the nigger of the world ONO 554:25
w. think him an angel THAC 768:20
w. to define her feelings HARD 360:10
w. to obey PEMB 572:7
w. under her father's control LAWS 459:6
w. wakes to love TENN 760:5
w. was full of good works BIBL 103:27
W. was God's second blunder NIET 545:12
w. watches her body uneasily COHE 224:3
W., what have I to do BIBL 101:13
w. who deliberates ADDI 4:12
w. who did not care KIPL 440:16
w. who didn't appeal to me PROU 594:2
w. who lives for others LEWI 466:19
w. whom thou gavest BIBL 74:1
W., why weepest thou BIBL 103:1
W. will be the last thing MERE 505:15
w., wine and song LUTH 480:6
w. with a slop-pail HOPK 385:6
w. with fair opportunities THAC 769:5
w. without a man STEI 737:14
womanhead learnt that w. DONN 274:10
womanhood Heroic w. LONG 474:9
womankind mankind and w. BAHA 47:25
packs off its w. SHAW 708:10
think better of w. KEAT 431:7
w.'s in every state a slave EGER 289:14
womanly So maidenly, So w. SKEL 721:10
womb cloistered in thy dear w. DONN 273:7
from his mother's w. SHAK 685:25
fruit of thy w. PRAY 592:1
in our mother's w. DONN 274:24
O w.! O bely CHAU 206:7
teeming w. of royal kings SHAK 694:19
w. and bed of enormity JONS 419:11
w. of time HEIN 368:10
w. of uncreated night MILT 515:10
wombs think with our w. LUCE 478:19
women about the coloured w. TRUT 784:14
after the manner of w. BIBL 74:28
Alas! the love of w. BYRO 176:17
all these surplus w. RICH 626:17
American w. shoot FORS 320:8
between men and w. THUR 776:25
blessed art thou among w. BIBL 98:15
Certain w. should be struck COWA 239:4
Charming w. FARQ 307:16
choose your w. or linen PROV 607:27
claim our right as w. PANK 566:12
comfortable w. STRI 744:19
conduct of the w. MORE 531:2
dream of fair w. TENN 758:15
Equality for w. demands TOYN 780:6
especially to w. BYRO 176:5
Even w. and children SA'A 641:1
extension of w.'s rights FOUR 321:19
feelings of w. in a drawing-room WOOL 826:19
fight to get w. out GREE 352:11
freedom w. were supposed BURC 161:22
From w.'s eyes SHAK 680:26
From w.'s eyes SHAK 680:28
going to w. NIET 545:10
Good w. always think BROO 150:19
greatly troubled by w. JAIN 401:14
happiest w. ELIO 293:5
have wine and w. BYRO 176:13
hops, and w. DICK 265:3
how w. felt PAGL 563:5
if ye be kind towards w. KORA 444:14
I must have w. GAY 331:19
joined a w.'s group STEV 740:19
labour of w. in the house GILM 339:15
like w.'s letters HAZL 365:4
managers of affairs of w. KORA 444:6
man who doesn't know w. CHAN 202:1
many w., and many children JOHN 413:1
mature w., *dancing* FRIE 325:5
Men don't know w. TROL 782:9
men, w., and Herveys MONT 526:18
mere persons of w. MORE 531:4
mob of scribbling w. HAWT 364:14
Music and w. PEPY 573:12
no plain w. on television FORD 319:10
not w. truly then JONS 420:19
now called the nature of w. MILL 509:4
other w. cloy The appetites SHAK 656:27
our chilly w. BYRO 173:17
paradise of w. PROV 599:13
passing the love of w. BIBL 79:3
Plain w. he regarded ELIO 292:20
position for w. is prone CARM 188:23
Powerful w. only succeed LEE- 462:11
proper function of w. ELIO 293:6
publishers are not w. ROBI 629:11
regiment of w. KNOX 442:10
Righteous w. are obedient KORA 444:7
'rights' of w. NIGH 545:23
should w. be denied DEFO 254:14
simple w. only fit LEWI 467:2
Single w. AUST 39:12
Solomon loved many strange w. BIBL 79:20
Some w.'ll stay in a man's memory KIPL 441:24
sorrows of w. ELIO 292:7
spoiled the w.'s chats BROW 157:10
sung w. in three cities POUN 589:9
Though w. all above SHAK 679:22
tide in the affairs of w. BYRO 177:11
to w. as to men ANTH 22:18
to w. Italian CHAR 203:16
To w. their original must owe COLL 228:8
Votes for w. POLI 582:4
way with the w. DICK 265:15
weird w. promised SHAK 683:24
Whatever w. do WHIT 816:10
wine and w. BURT 170:9
With many w. I doubt TROL 782:18
with w. nor with priests SOUT 730:20
w. and care and trouble WARD 803:11
W., and Champagne BELL 64:2
w. and children could work SELL 654:14
W. and fortune WYCH 834:10
W. and Horses KIPL 438:6
W. and servants most difficult CONF 232:7
W. and wine GAY 331:17
W. are around all the time OSGO 560:13
W. are at once the boldest DEV 259:9
w. are born slaves ASTE 31:15
w. are from Venus GRAY 349:23
W. are like tricks CONG 232:21
w. are not educated CAVE 198:14
W. are only children CHES 209:17
W. are programmed to love BAIN 48:9
w. are so simple SHAK 698:15
W. are strongest BIBL 90:26
w.-authors COOP 236:7
w. become like their mothers WILD 817:18
w. become unnaturally thin WOLF 825:2
w. born slaves WOLL 826:2
w. cannot escape it GIBB 336:6
W. can't forgive failure CHEK 208:6
w. come and go ELIO 295:4
w. come out to cut up KIPL 440:22
w. come to see the show OVID 561:5
W. deprived of the company CHEK 208:19
W. desiren to have sovereynetee CHAU 206:22
W. do not find it difficult MACK 486:8
W. don't seem to think AMIS 13:17
W. enjoyed SUCK 745:6
w., God help us SAYE 646:7
W. have a positive moral sense ADAM 2:15
w. have no soul ASTE 31:11
W. have no wilderness BOGA 123:12
W. have served as looking-glasses WOOL 826:18
W. have very little idea GREE 352:7
w. in a state of ignorance KNOX 443:1
w. in furious secret rebellion SHAW 707:8
w. in men require BLAK 120:9
w. labouring of child BOOK 127:11
w. marry off in haste ASTE 31:17
w. marry them for love OSBO 559:20
w. must weep KING 437:12
w. need to be helped TRUT 784:12
W. never have young minds DELA 256:22
W. never look so well SURT 747:5
w. never so fair LYLY 480:13
W. nicer than men AMIS 13:18
w. not merely tolerated AUNG 36:20
W., of kynde, desiren libertee CHAU 205:12
W.—one half the human race BAGE 46:23
w. remain the slaves of power WOLL 825:24
W.'s Liberation is just MEIR 503:12
w. were first at the Cradle SAYE 646:7
W. what they are BRAD 146:15
w. . . . who are the lamps LAWS 459:7
W. who love the same man BEER 61:15
w. who write DURA 285:18
works of w. BROW 154:9
writ by w. CENT 199:15
you grim w. OVID 561:4
zeal of w. themselves MILL 509:8
won field is w. MORE 531:11
ground w. to-day ARNO 27:9
has w. it bear the palm MOTT 535:13
in this humour w. SHAK 696:13
I w. the count SOMO 727:19
never lost till w. CRAB 243:9
never w. fair lady PROV 600:6
not that you w. or lost RICE 626:3
not to have w. COUB 238:3
or you be w. SOUT 730:10
Sun wot w. it NEWS 544:11
Things w. are done SHAK 700:5
Where you will never w. BALL 50:13
woman, therefore may be w. SHAK 699:26
woman, therefore to be w. SHAK 672:13
wonder boneless w. CHUR 215:2
eyes to w. SHAK 705:10
great w. in heaven BIBL 112:18
I w. any man alive GAY 331:10
I w. by my troth DONN 274:2
knowledge and w. BACO 41:6
moon-washed apples of w. DRIN 279:11
One can only w. BENT 67:7
Smiling w. of a day WRIG 833:14
still the w. grew GOLD 344:15
To work a w. HERR 375:6
transcendent w. CARL 187:27
W. . . . and not any expectation SMIT 723:3
w. at the workmanship MILT 511:29
w. of our age DYER 286:12
w. of our stage JONS 420:22
w. that would be TENN 763:3
w. who's kissing her ADAM 2:5
wonderful God, how w. Thou art FABE 305:16
I've had a w. life LAST 457:6
many w. things SOPH 728:14
most w. wonderful SHAK 659:9
strange and w. TRAH 780:14
too w. and excellent BOOK 141:10
too w. for me BIBL 83:36
too w. to be true FARA 306:12
W., Counsellor BIBL 87:1
w. works of God BIBL 103:16
Yes, w. things CART 192:12
wonderfully fearfully and w. made BOOK 141:12
wonders Everything has its w. KELL 432:13
His w. to perform COWP 240:16

multiply my signs and my w. BIBL 75:33
signs and w. BIBL 101:21
Time works w. PROV 613:4
Welcome, all w. CRAS 244:8
w. in the deep BOOK 139:14
w. we seek without us BROW 153:19
W. will never cease PROV 615:17
wondrous all thy w. works BOOK 133:8
survey the w. cross WATT 805:14
won't administrative w. LYNN 480:21
if she w., she won't ANON 19:15
woo Come, w. me, woo me SHAK 659:18
Men are April when they w. SHAK 659:20
wood behind the little w. TENN 763:20
Bows down to w. and stone HEBE 367:7
bows down to w. and stone KIPL 438:11
cleave the w. ANON 18:13
deep and gloomy w. WORD 829:4
hewers of w. BIBL 77:21
In a dark w. I saw ROET 631:9
native w.-notes wild MILT 512:24
out of the w. PROV 598:36
Out of this w. SHAK 690:4
set out to plant a w. SWIF 749:7
w. of English bows DOYL 278:9
w.'s in trouble HOUS 391:2
W. the Weed, the Wag RALE 620:17
You are not w. SHAK 676:5
woodbine luscious w. SHAK 689:25
woodcock Spirits of well-shot w. BETJ 70:7
w. near the gin SHAK 701:26
w. to mine own springe SHAK 667:6
woodcocks springes to catch w. SHAK 662:15
wooden Sailed off in a w. shoe FIEL 309:9
with a w. leg DICK 264:21
Within this w. O SHAK 670:26
w. wall is your ships THEM 770:16
w. walls are the best COVE 238:8
woodland bit of w. HORA 389:24
stands about the w. ride HOUS 390:14
woodlanded by w. ways BETJ 71:7
woodlands About the w. I will go HOUS 390:15
woodman W., spare that tree MORR 532:9
w., spare the beechen tree CAMP 183:5
woods Enter these enchanted w. MERE 505:22
fresh w., and pastures new MILT 513:13
go down in the w. today BRAT 147:5
gods have lived in the w. VIRG 795:18
Love-whisp'ring w. POPE 580:24
never knew the summer w. TENN 761:3
once a road through the w. KIPL 440:17
pleasure in the pathless w. BYRO 175:8
senators of mighty w. KEAT 427:27
spirit in the w. WORD 829:13
We'll to the w. no more ANON 20:11
Wet Wild W. KIPL 441:7
w. against the world BLUN 122:11
w., and desert caves MILT 513:1
w. and groves WITH 824:1
w. are lovely FROS 326:12
w. decay and fall TENN 766:16
w. have ears PROV 600:18
w. More free from peril SHAK 658:13
w. of consular dignity VIRG 796:4
woodshed Something nasty in the w. GIBB 336:7
wooed therefore to be w. SHAK 672:13
woman, therefore may be w. SHAK 699:26
wooer knight to be their w. BALL 50:8
woof weave the w. GRAY 350:4
wooing my w. mind SHAK 681:1
w. not long a-doing PROV 601:50
W., so tiring MITF 524:8
would a-w. go NURS 548:6
wool giveth snow like w. BOOK 141:26
go out for w. PROV 606:26
hairs were white like w. BIBL 111:22
Have you any w. NURS 547:12
like the pure w. BIBL 90:6
Much cry and little w. PROV 607:14
Woolf afraid of Virginia W. ALBE 10:5
woollen Odious! in w. POPE 584:3
woolly w. peach JONS 420:28
Woolworth visit to W.'s BEVA 72:4
W. life hereafter NICO 544:23
Wooster half way through the W. series WAUG 806:22
Wops Huns or W. MITF 524:9
word action to the w. SHAK 664:15
be ye doers of the w. BIBL 110:14
By water and the w. STON 743:9
captive with a gentle w. CARY 193:5
choke the w. BIBL 95:21
cloudiness of a w. processor HEAN 366:20
comfort of thy holy W. BOOK 127:22
Englishman's w. PROV 599:17
engrafted w. BIBL 110:13
Every idle w. BIBL 95:14
Every w. she writes is a lie MCCA 484:4
every w. that proceedeth BIBL 92:32
flowering in a lonely w. TENN 767:4
fulfilling his w. BOOK 141:27
Greeks had a w. AKIN 9:13
honour? A w. SHAK 669:9
honour his own w. TENN 759:19
I kept my w. DE L 256:16
In the beginning was the W. BIBL 101:1
In the beginning was the W. OPEN 555:19
in w. mightier MILT 517:5
leave the w. of God BIBL 103:20
lies in one little w. SHAK 694:12
Lord gave the w. BOOK 136:7
Lord, thy w. abideth BAKE 48:12
milk of the w. BIBL 110:27
milk of the w. BIBL 114:11
nat o w. wol he faille CHAU 206:1
no w. in their language SWIF 748:1
out of his holy w. ROBI 629:17
packed up into one w. CARR 191:4
Perhaps we have not the w. ARNO 28:18
power of the written w. CONR 234:17
repugnant to the W. of God BOOK 142:10
single w. even may be SHEL 714:22
time for such a w. SHAK 685:22
To-day I pronounced a w. FLEM 317:12
torture one poor w. DRYD 282:1
truth of thy holy w. BOOK 129:11
understanding of thy W. BOOK 127:9
wash out a w. of it FITZ 314:17
weasel w. ROOS 633:11
what the w. did make it ELIZ 297:13
When *I* use a w. CARR 191:2
whose eternal W. MARR 497:13
w., at random spoken SCOT 651:3
w. fitly spoken BIBL 83:18
w. for word ALFR 11:15
w. is a lantern BOOK 140:9
W. is but wynd LYDG 480:11
w. is enough PLAU 578:13
w. is the Verb HUGO 393:16
w. of Caesar SHAK 676:4
w. spoken in due season BIBL 82:37
w. takes wing HORA 387:1
w. to the wise is enough PROV 615:18
W. was made flesh BIBL 101:7
W. WAS MADE FLESH MISS 523:1
W. without a word ANDR 14:14
wordless poem should be w. MACL 487:2
words Actions speak louder than w. PROV 594:14
all w. And no performance MASS 501:5
artillery of w. SWIF 749:11
barren superfluity of w. GART 330:13
big w. for little matters JOHN 413:19
But for your w. SHAK 676:29
coiner of sweet w. ARNO 27:15
comfortable w. BOOK 129:17
conceal a fact with w. MACH 485:13
confused w. BAUD 57:7
deceive you with vain w. BIBL 108:7
doctrines without w. LAO 451:6
dressing old w. new SHAK 705:1
Fair w. enough WYAT 834:7
fear those big w. JOYC 422:9
few w. of my own EDWA 289:7
find the w. to clothe CHUR 216:8
Fine w. PROV 600:23
food and not fine w. MOLI 525:3
fool and his w. SHEN 715:8
form of sound w. BIBL 109:21
four w. I write BOIL 124:7
frying pan of your w. FLAU 316:11
Give 'em w. JONS 420:5
Give sorrow w. SHAK 685:7
Good w. do not last long JOSE 421:9
good w., I think, were best SHAK 677:19
Good w. will not do LAMB 449:11
good w. with their mouth BOOK 135:21
gotta use w. when I talk to you ELIO 295:24
Hard w. break no bones PROV 601:52
heard w. that have been BEAU 58:13
He w. me, girls SHAK 657:22
His w. came feebly WORD 831:13
idiom of w. PRIO 592:13
In all his w. most wonderful NEWM 542:18
in w. deceiving MILT 513:27
kindest w. I'll ever know RODG 631:4
laid end to end w. LODG 472:14
let thy w. be few BIBL 84:11
may w. matter to you SMIT 724:6
Melting melodious w. HERR 375:5
misused w. generate SPEN 732:6
my w. among mankind SHEL 712:18
my w. are my own CHAR 203:14
my w. shall not pass BIBL 97:4
neither wit, nor w. SHAK 676:10
not even with w. BROO 151:1
no use indicting w. BECK 59:15
no w. he spake GILB 337:2
of all sad w. WHIT 816:6
passion for w. MOOR 530:4
poetry = the *best* w. COLE 227:20
polite meaningless w. YEAT 835:18
Proper w. in proper places SWIF 748:8
Rather than w. LARK 452:17
Read out my w. FLEC 317:7
repeats his w. SHAK 677:11
small coin of empty w. SAND 643:16
subtle terrorism of w. GAIT 328:3
threw w. like stones SPEN 732:20
Twist w. and meanings GAY 332:11
wall of w. BUTL 172:26
war has used up w. JAME 403:19
weapons will be our w. TRIM 781:15
weigh thy w. BIBL 92:4
wild and whirling w. SHAK 663:2
Winged w. HOME 381:21
Without relying upon w. MUMO 536:9
w. a foot and a half long HORA 385:17
w. are but the signs JOHN 409:4
w. are capable HAVE 364:4
W. are cheap CHAP 202:10
w. are emptied CAMU 184:14
W. are men's daughters MADD 489:1
w. are of less weight BACO 42:19
w. are slippery ADAM 3:2
w. are the daughters JOHN 409:4
W. are the tokens BACO 41:14
W. are wise men's counters HOBB 378:15
w. are words SHAK 692:5
w. but wind BUTL 172:9
w. clothed in reason's garb MILT 515:12
w. divide and rend SWIN 750:10
w. fail us AUST 39:17
w. firmly in their places RUSK 639:8
w. have undone the w. SELD 653:13
w., like Nature TENN 760:23
W. may be false SHAD 655:10
words, mere w. SHAK 700:24
w. move slow POPE 584:23
w. of his mouth BOOK 135:12
w. of Mercury SHAK 681:5
w. of my mouth BOOK 132:18
w. of the wise BIBL 85:3
w. of tongue and pen HART 363:10

words (*cont.*):
w. once spoke DILL 267:12
w. refuse before the crowd CLAR 218:12
w. seemed to them BIBL 100:32
w. so fair JONS 420:16
W. strain ELIO 294:5
w., that burn GRAY 351:3
w. tho That hadden pris CHAU 207:4
w. which express SHEL 714:24
w. will follow CATO 194:16
w. will never hurt me PROV 611:20
w. without knowledge BIBL 81:30
W. without thoughts SHAK 665:10
Words, w. or I shall burst FARQ 307:15
W., words, words SHAK 663:12
w. you couldn't say LEHR 462:19
worth ten thousand w. BARN 54:16
worth ten thousand w. PROV 609:2
wrestle With w. and meanings ELIO 294:7
yea, even from good w. BOOK 133:28
you can drug, with w. LOWE 477:10
Wordsworth what daffodils were for W. LARK 453:10
W. drunk and Porson sober HOUS 391:11
Wordsworthian W. or egotistical KEAT 431:10
work according to his w. BOOK 135:23
All that matters is love and w. FREU 324:18
All w. and no play PROV 595:6
as tedious as to w. SHAK 667:22
breed one w. that wakes HOPK 384:24
don't w. shan't eat PROV 603:32
Do the w. that's nearest KING 437:5
finished the w. OVID 561:19
goes to w. SAND 644:4
Go to w. on an egg ADVE 7:21
habit of persistent w. FLAU 316:9
hard and dirty w. RUSK 638:16
hard day's w. CHIL 212:2
has to w. to keep alive BELL 63:25
Her noblest w. she classes BURN 167:9
If any would not w. BIBL 109:12
I like w.: it fascinates me JERO 407:1
I love my w. HILL 376:17
immortality through my w. ALLE 12:17
in that w. does what he wants COLL 228:11
I want w. SHAK 668:2
left no immortal w. KEAT 431:21
let the toad w. LARK 453:6
looked for w. TEBB 757:1
Man grows beyond his w. STEI 737:10
Many hands make light w. PROV 606:27
men must w. KING 437:12
men think. Sex, w. FISH 313:10
men w. more and dispute less TAWN 755:15
Moor has done his w. SCHI 648:16
more w. than hands PROV 600:2
morning w. unequal ANON 22:5
my w. is done EPIT 303:16
never see half-done w. PROV 600:36
Nice w. if you can get it GERS 334:16
no one shall w. for money KIPL 440:19
Nothing to do but w. KING 436:5
not w. that kills PROV 604:25
of the life, or of the w. YEAT 835:8
patience have her perfect w. BIBL 110:10
piece of w. is a man SHAK 663:18
plenty of w. to do JERO 406:18
protracted my w. JOHN 412:20
six days' w., a world MILT 517:8
smile his w. to see BLAK 121:10
some useful w. THOM 771:2
stomach sets us to w. ELIO 292:13
sublimation of the w. instinct LODG 472:15
till our w. is done COLL 228:6
to w., ye whores PEMB 572:9
We w. in the dark JAME 403:8
when no man can w. BIBL 102:2
Without w., life goes rotten CAMU 184:17
woman's w. is never done PROV 615:16
W. and pray HILL 377:1
W. apace, apace DEKK 256:5
w. by the sweat of his brow CHEK 208:8
W. expands PARK 567:22
W. expands so as to fill PROV 615:19
w. for idle hands PROV 598:7
W. is love made visible GIBR 336:13
w. is never done DUCK 284:5
W. is of two kinds RUSS 639:17
w. is terribly important RUSS 639:12
W. is the call MORR 532:20
W. is the curse WILD 819:13
W. is *x* EINS 290:17
w. i' the earth SHAK 663:3
w. itself shall not be lost EPIT 302:1
W. liberates ANON 20:16
w. like a fiend THOM 772:19
W. not for a reward BHAG 72:18
w. of a useless character DOST 276:6
W. on, that you may possess GOET 342:16
W. out your own salvation BIBL 108:18
w., rest and play ADVE 7:43
w. stops, expenses CATO 194:15
w. terribly hard at playing MORT 533:10
w. together for good BIBL 105:10
W. to survive VANE 789:17
W. without hope COLE 227:6
wrought in the w. BIBL 80:31
You w., we rule DUNN 285:11
worked So on we w. ROBI 629:15
w. with my blood KOLL 443:11
yes it w. POLI 582:9
worker honours the w. TALM 754:13
w. at each end POLI 581:4
w. slave of capitalist society CONN 234:5
workers men the w. TENN 763:2
not the w. WHYT 816:12
organized w. of the country SHIN 717:4
secure for the w. ANON 19:9
W. all demand SERV 655:1
w. are perfectly free ENGE 300:12
W. of the world CLOS 222:19
W. of the world MARX 500:7
workhouse Christmas Day in the W. OPEN 555:23
woman's w. SHAW 708:28
working alwayth a w. DICK 262:24
choice of w. or starving JOHN 409:2
each for the joy of w. KIPL 440:19
in his w. time GILL 339:14
it isn't w. MAJO 491:14
killin' meself w. O'CA 552:11
kind of like w. BISH 116:3
Labour isn't w. POLI 581:22
mighty w. BOOK 131:14
protect a w.-girl SMIT 723:18
start their w. lives KIPL 438:19
this w.-day world SHAK 658:11
w. about six weeks a year THOR 776:7
W. and wandrynge LANG 450:17
w.-house of thought SHAK 672:1
w. like a dog LENN 463:22
working class into the w. ORWE 559:7
job w. parents want ABBO 1:1
of the w. ARNO 28:11
working classes worst fault of w. MORT 533:12
workings inscrutable w. of Providence SMIT 724:4
workman bad w. blames his tools PROV 595:33
workmanship wonder at the w. MILT 511:29
w. surpasses OVID 561:13
workmen Good w. never quarrel BYRO 176:9
works accepteth thy w. BIBL 84:21
according to their w. BIBL 113:6
all thy wondrous w. BOOK 133:8
all ye W. of the Lord BOOK 126:3
believe the w. BIBL 102:9
cast off the w. of darkness BIBL 105:21
devil and all his w. BOOK 130:11
Faith without w. BIBL 110:17
fruit of good w. BOOK 128:20
I know thy w. BIBL 111:28
in all our w. BOOK 130:5
into my w. is my talent WILD 819:9
Look on my w. SHEL 713:1
move immediately upon your w. GRAN 348:16
proved me, and saw my w. BOOK 138:6
seen the future and it w. STEF 737:3
stained with their own w. BOOK 139:11
their w. do follow them BIBL 112:26
through her w. gay nature SMAR 722:8
W. done least rapidly BROW 157:2
w. hard for its living PROV 606:42
w. of darkness BOOK 127:21
w. of women BROW 154:9
your good w. BIBL 93:6
workshop it's W. AMIS 13:11
nation may be its w. CHAM 200:13
not a temple but a w. TURG 785:1
w. of the world DISR 268:7
workshops busy w. BACO 45:14
world adventure in the w. of Aids PERK 573:22
All's right with the w. BROW 157:12
all the kingdoms of the w. BIBL 92:34
All the mighty w. WORD 829:6
all the sad w. needs WILC 817:10
All the w. is sad FOST 321:18
all the w. is young KING 437:13
All the w.'s a stage SHAK 658:25
all the w. was gay POPE 587:3
all this visible w. BYRO 178:14
along the W. I go CART 192:17
amidst a bursting w. POPE 583:2
and now a w. POPE 585:8
away from the whole w. VIRG 795:15
Berkeley destroyed this w. SMIT 725:5
bestride the narrow w. SHAK 674:13
Brave new w. BORR 144:1
breaks through from another w. GUMI 354:19
brought nothing into this w. BIBL 109:17
citizen of the w. BOSW 143:18
country in the w. PAIN 564:5
create my little w. BEDD 60:16
create the wondrous w. YOUN 839:10
dark w. of sin BICK 114:16
deceits of the w. BOOK 127:5
decide the fate of the w. DE G 255:22
destruction of the whole w. HUME 395:7
echoes round the w. TENN 760:2
ends of the w. BOOK 132:15
enjoy the w. aright TRAH 780:9
estate o' the w. SHAK 685:23
fashion of this w. BIBL 106:6
fit for this w. KEAT 430:23
fled From this vile w. SHAK 704:28
flood unto the w.'s end BOOK 136:18
foppery of the w. SHAK 678:5
frame of the w. BERK 68:3
funny old w. THAT 770:13
gain the whole w. BIBL 98:8
glory of the w. ANON 21:13
glory of this w. passes THOM 770:20
God so loved the w. BIBL 101:18
go out of this w. LAST 455:19
governs the whole w. OXEN 562:14
great wide w. EICH 290:6
great w. spin for ever TENN 763:9
grey silent w. HUGH 393:6
half-brother of the w. BAIL 48:7
happiness of the next w. BROW 153:2
have not loved the w. BYRO 174:22
hell of this w. BECK 60:12
her w. is brazen SIDN 718:22
Hog Butcher for the W. SAND 643:18
how small the w. is GROS 354:4
I have had my w. CHAU 206:18
immense w. of delight BLAK 119:26
in 1915 the old w. ended LAWR 457:21
in all the towns in all the w. FILM 312:4
in a naughty w. SHAK 688:26
In a w. I never made HOUS 390:7

infects the w. ARNO 27:1
interpreted the w. MARX 500:2
in the very w. WORD 831:8
into the w. alone CARR 189:5
journey to the w. below SOCR 727:5
knowledge of the w. CHES 209:7
know the w. YOUN 839:11
learn the w. CHES 209:9
light of the w. BIBL 93:5
limits of my w. WITT 824:8
Little Friend of all the W. KIPL 441:14
little w. made cunningly DONN 272:26
Look round the habitable w. DRYD 282:35
loosed upon the w. YEAT 837:5
lost the w. for love DRYD 282:9
Love makes the w. go round PROV 606:6
made the round w. so sure BOOK 138:2
Mad w.! mad kings SHAK 677:7
makes the whole w. kin SHAK 700:17
miseries of the w. KEAT 427:18
monk who shook the w. MONT 528:15
month in which the w. bigan CHAU 206:4
my letter to the w. DICK 266:18
new w. order BUSH 171:4
not as the w. giveth, give I BIBL 102:21
nourish all the w. SHAK 680:28
O brave new w. SHAK 699:12
observe a w. of variety FORD 320:4
Of the very w. he made SMAR 722:2
one half the w. fools JEFF 406:2
only saved the w. CHES 210:6
Our country is the w. GARR 330:10
out of the w. PROV 596:7
peace which the w. cannot give BOOK 126:19
put the w. to sleep MUIR 535:23
rack of this tough w. SHAK 680:15
responsible for such an absurd w. DUHA 284:12
rotundity o' the w. SHAK 678:21
Round the w. ARNO 26:13
saved alive a whole w. TALM 753:10
see how this w. goes SHAK 679:23
sees the w., Volumnius SHAK 677:2
six days' work, a w. MILT 517:8
small-talking w. FRY 326:23
snaring the poor w. CRAN 243:23
Sob, heavy w. AUDE 33:16
spectacle unto the w. BIBL 105:32
start of the majestic w. SHAK 674:12
still point of the turning w. ELIO 294:4
Stop the w. NEWL 542:1
Syllables govern the w. SELD 653:23
symphony like the w. MAHL 490:17
Ten days that shook the w. REED 624:3
Than this w. dreams of TENN 760:16
Their w. gives way MACN 488:10
There is a w. elsewhere SHAK 660:9
things of this w. MANN 494:1
this dark w. and wide MILT 518:29
This gewgaw w. DRYD 280:26
This w.'s no blot BROW 155:30
though the w. perish MOTT 535:8
three corners of the w. SHAK 677:21
through this w. but once GREL 352:14
tired of the w. WALP 800:20
Top of the w. FILM 311:1
triple pillar of the w. SHAK 656:6
untimely forth Into a w. WALL 800:10
unto the end of the w. BIBL 97:30
unto the w. SHAK 696:3
Wag as it will the w. BYRO 173:7
walls of the w. LUCR 478:21
warm kind w. CORY 237:14
way of coming into the w. SWIF 748:19
way the w. ends ELIO 294:26
We want the w. MORR 532:23
What a w. is this BOLI 124:17
What is the w. DE L 256:18
What is this w. CHAU 205:21
what it once was, the w. MARV 499:7
What would the w. be HOPK 384:10
whole w. is not sufficient QUAR 618:14
wilderness of the w. OPEN 555:6
wilderness of this w. BUNY 160:14
woods against the w. BLUN 122:11
words have undone the w. SELD 653:13
workshop of the w. DISR 268:7
w. and his wife ANST 22:15
w. and love were young RALE 620:9
w. at her feet AGAT 6:16
w. becoming like a lunatic asylum LLOY 471:6
w. but as the world SHAK 687:2
w. empty of people LAWR 458:6
w. enough, and time MARV 498:23
w. forgetting POPE 582:24
w. grew pale JOHN 411:16
w. has lost his youth BIBL 91:3
w. in a grain of sand BLAK 117:17
w. invisible THOM 774:11
w. is a comedy WALP 801:5
w. is an oyster MILL 509:20
w. is changing ELIZ 297:18
w. is charged HOPK 384:5
w. is disgracefully managed FIRB 313:7
w. is empty PALI 565:9
w. is everything that is the case WITT 824:7
w. is full of care WARD 803:11
w. is given over LE G 462:12
w. is not made MALR 493:1
w. is so full STEV 742:12
w. is still deceived SHAK 688:3
w. is too much with us WORD 832:15
w. is weary of the past SHEL 711:14
w. is white with May TENN 759:16
w. knew him not BIBL 101:6
w. may end tonight BROW 156:14
w. must be made safe WILS 822:15
w. of sighs SHAK 692:1
w. of silence EPIT 302:2
w. of the happy WITT 824:9
w.'s a bubble BACO 45:10
w. safe for hypocrisy WOLF 825:10
w.'s a jest STEP 737:20
w.'s an inn DRYD 282:11
w.'s at an end D'AV 251:8
w.'s great age begins anew SHEL 711:12
w.'s history SCHI 648:15
w. should be taxed BIBL 98:19
w. should break and fall HORA 388:16
w.'s in a state o' chassis O'CA 552:13
w.'s last night DONN 273:1
w.'s mine oyster SHAK 688:34
w.'s slow stain SHEL 711:1
w. surely is wide enough STER 738:24
w.'s whole sap is sunk DONN 274:9
w.'s worst wound SASS 645:23
w. upon him falsely smiled FANS 306:9
w. upside down BIBL 104:5
w. was all before them MILT 518:3
w. was not worthy BIBL 110:1
w. will be judged MISS 523:4
w. will end in fire FROS 325:21
w. will perish BAKU 48:17
w. without end BOOK 125:19
w. without end BOOK 137:17
w. would go round CARR 189:14
w. would smell like what it is SHEL 711:24
W., you have kept faith HARD 361:14
You live in a different w. DOYL 277:21
youth of the w. BACO 41:22
World Cups W. come only OSGO 560:13
worldly all my w. goods BOOK 131:6
be not w. wise QUAR 618:17
breath of w. men SHAK 695:5
clear from w. cares VAUX 791:1
weary of these w. bars SHAK 674:24
worlds best of all possible w. CABE 180:13
best of all possible w. PROV 595:1
best of all possible w. VOLT 797:5
destroyer of w. OPPE 557:2
number of w. is infinite ALEX 11:6
seek out w. unknown DRAY 279:5
Wandering between two w. ARNO 27:21
what w. away BROW 155:18
w. beyond this world's BYRO 177:31
w. of wanwood leafmeal HOPK 384:18
worm as for me, I am a w. BOOK 132:22
Beware, lest in the w. BARB 53:16
early bird catches w. PROV 599:2
Even a w. will turn PROV 599:19
fish with the w. SHAK 665:28
goes the same crooked w. THOM 772:6
I am but as a crushed w. PUNC 617:17
invisible w. BLAK 121:7
joy of the w. SHAK 657:27
laily w. BALL 50:21
sets foot upon a w. COWP 242:10
w. in a sesame plant TALM 754:14
w. i' the bud SHAK 701:24
w., the canker, and the grief BYRO 178:22
worms Among the hungry w. BALL 50:11
convocation of politic w. SHAK 665:27
diet of w. FENT 308:9
eaten of w. BIBL 103:31
Flies, w., and flowers WATT 805:7
Impaling w. COLM 229:19
set on me in W. LUTH 479:14
with vilest w. to dwell SHAK 704:28
w. destroy this body BIBL 81:22
w. shall try MARV 499:3
w. were hallowed SHAK 693:6
wormwood bitter as w. BIBL 82:12
star is called W. BIBL 112:14
w. and the gall BIBL 89:24
worn one so w. CRAB 243:6
When we're w. SOUT 728:22
worried may not be w. into being FROS 326:15
w. about Jim CATC 196:3
worry humanity has no w. CONF 231:23
kills, but w. PROV 604:25
worrying What's the use of w. MILI 508:16
W. the carcase THOM 773:16
worse Defend the bad against the w. DAY- 253:14
follow the w. OVID 561:17
for better for w. BOOK 131:5
For fear of finding something w. BELL 63:7
from w. to better HOOK 383:7
from w. to better JOHN 409:3
Go further and fare w. PROV 601:11
greater feeling to the w. SHAK 694:16
If my books had been any w. CHAN 201:17
is it something w. SPRI 735:13
make the w. appear MILT 515:9
Many w., better few LOCK 472:11
mean the W. one ARIS 24:9
might have been w. PROV 608:15
More will mean w. AMIS 13:20
one penny the w. BARH 54:6
w. than a crime BOUL 144:25
w. than the first BIBL 95:18
worst are no w. SHAK 690:26
worship earth doth w. thee BOOK 125:20
ignorantly w. BIBL 104:8
only object of w. ANON 15:7
O w. the King GRAN 348:15
O w. the Lord BOOK 138:7
second is freedom to w. ROOS 632:18
Some w. stones SIKH 719:14
various modes of w. GIBB 335:4
we w. thy Name BOOK 126:2
who w. the beast BIBL 112:25
with my body I thee w. BOOK 131:6
w. and fall down BOOK 138:6
w. her by years TENN 759:20
w. him in spirit BIBL 101:20
W. is transcendent wonder CARL 187:27
w. the Lord MONS 526:12
worshipped W. and served BIBL 104:27
worships w. in his way SMAR 722:5
worst best and the w. of this SWIN 751:8
did the w. to him ANON 22:6
full look at the w. HARD 361:13

worst (*cont.*):
good in the w. of us ANON 19:4
His w. is better HAZL 365:17
inn's w. room POPE 583:22
it was the w. of times DICK 265:21
knew the w. too young KIPL 438:18
know the w. BRAD 146:8
No w., there is none HOPK 384:11
prepare for the w. PROV 602:48
rape isn't the w. thing WELD 809:10
This is the w. SHAK 679:14
To-morrow do thy w. DRYD 282:32
When things are at the w. PROV 614:34
While the w. are full YEAT 837:5
world's w. wound SASS 645:23
w. form of Government CHUR 216:2
w. is death SHAK 695:7
w. is yet to come JOHN 408:21
w. of the company SWIF 748:5
w. of times OPEN 555:28
w. time of the year ANDR 14:15
w. time of the year ELIO 294:27
w. woman BALL 50:21
worth calculate the w. of a man FLAU 316:13
confident of their own w. AUNG 36:20
If a thing's w. doing PROV 603:12
more w. than his chambermaid GODW 342:5
nor words, nor w. SHAK 676:10
not w. going to see JOHN 416:10
not w. reading AUST 37:20
not w. the dust SHAK 679:16
trifles were w. something CATU 194:20
turned out w. anything SCOT 652:19
W. a guinea a box ADVE 8:21
w. a load of hay PROV 611:37
w. and spiritual reality HEGE 367:11
w. doing badly CHES 211:18
w. of a thing is what PROV 615:20
worthiness for the w. of thy Son BOOK 130:6
Worthington daughter on the stage, Mrs W. COWA 238:16
worthless this false, this w. man EPHE 300:18
worthy am no more w. BIBL 100:4
I am not w. MISS 522:20
labourer is w. of his hire BIBL 99:8
Lord I am not w. BIBL 94:15
nameless in w. deeds BROW 153:7
not w. to unloose BIBL 101:9
there be nine w. CAXT 198:17
world was not w. BIBL 110:1
w. of their steel SCOT 650:14
w. of the vocation BIBL 108:2
W. the Lamb that died WATT 805:12
w. to open the book BIBL 112:2
wotthehell w. archy MARQ 497:8
would evil which I w. not BIBL 105:4
He w., wouldn't he RICE 626:9
w. they should do unto me BOOK 130:13
wouldest whither thou w. not BIBL 103:11
wound Earth felt the w. MILT 517:17
heal me of my grievous w. TENN 760:17
Hearts w. up with love SPEN 732:22
help to w. itself SHAK 677:21
knife see not the w. SHAK 682:4
never felt a w. SHAK 697:9
not be whole of that w. MALO 492:8
purple with love's w. SHAK 689:23
tongue In every w. SHAK 676:11
warning from another's w. JERO 406:13
Willing to w. POPE 583:7
wit Makes such a w. SHEL 712:2
world's worst w. SASS 645:23
w. for wound BIBL 76:14
w. had been for Ireland LAST 457:20
w., not the bandage POTT 588:22
wounded escapes being w. PUGI 616:16
like a w. snake POPE 584:21
w. and left KIPL 440:22
w. for our transgressions BIBL 88:17
w. spirit BIBL 83:5
You're w. BROW 156:11
Wounded Knee Bury my heart at W. BENÉ 64:24
wounding w. heart CRAS 244:4
wounds bind up the nation's w. LINC 469:1
keeps his own w. green BACO 43:29
not to heed the w. IGNA 398:17
old w. bleed anew WALL 800:9
salt rubbed into their w. WEST 812:11
soldier details his w. PROP 593:15
These w. I had SHAK 671:24
w. of a friend BIBL 83:29
w. thou madest DANI 248:19
w. whose only bandage BYRO 178:10
woven w. them a garment AKHM 9:11
Wragg *W. is in custody* ARNO 28:16
wrangle shall we begin to w. ANON 18:19
wrap w. me in a gown HERB 371:23
wrapped all meanly w. MILT 513:19
w. him in swaddling clothes BIBL 98:20
wrath cometh the w. of God BIBL 108:7
day of his w. is come BIBL 112:6
day of w. MISS 523:3
dragon and his w. SHAK 677:24
Envy and w. BIBL 92:5
flee from the w. to come BIBL 92:29
grapes of w. BORR 144:9
grapes of w. HOWE 391:15
neither w. of Jove OVID 561:19
provoke not your children to w. BIBL 108:10
sun go down upon your w. BIBL 108:5
turneth away w. BIBL 82:34
turneth away w. PROV 611:4
tygers of w. BLAK 119:21
w. did end BLAK 121:5
w. of the Lamb BIBL 112:6
wreathed becks, and w. smiles MILT 512:14
wreaths laurel w. entwine HART 363:9
wreck on which thou art to w. DRYD 280:16
w. and not the story RICH 626:10
wrecks Vomits its w. SHEL 711:22
Wrekin W. heaves HOUS 391:2
wren Four Larks and a W. LEAR 460:4
hurt the little w. BLAK 117:20
Mr Christopher W. EVEL 305:6
musician than the w. SHAK 688:27
robin and the w. PROV 610:14
Sir Christopher W. BARH 54:1
Sir Christopher W. BENT 67:6
w. goes to't SHAK 679:21
youngest w. of nine SHAK 702:6
wrest W. once the law SHAK 688:13
wrestle w. not against flesh BIBL 108:13
w. With words and meanings ELIO 294:7
wrestled w. for perhaps too long HOWE 391:14
w. with him WALT 803:2
wrestles He that w. with us BURK 164:2
wrestling lay w. with (my God!) HOPK 384:3
W., I will not let thee go WESL 811:2
wretch w. that dares not die BURN 167:24
wretched all men hate the w. SHEL 710:9
only w. are the wise PRIO 593:5
proud and yet a w. thing DAVI 251:17
w. men are cradled SHEL 711:21
wretchedness O! the fierce w. SHAK 699:20
w. is irremediable EDGE 288:16
wretches feel what w. feel SHAK 679:1
How shall w. live GODL 342:2
Poor naked w. SHAK 678:28
wring soon w. their hands WALP 802:3
wrings at last w. its neck RUSS 639:23
wrinkle stamps the w. deeper BYRO 174:7
wrinkled w. sea beneath him TENN 758:17
wrinkles w. will devour NASH 539:21
wrinklies not because ageing w. STRA 744:17
wrist With gyves upon his w. HOOD 382:17
writ censure this mysterious w. DRYD 281:22
I never w. SHAK 705:17
name was w. in water EPIT 303:3
write angel should w. MOOR 530:8
baseness to w. fair SHAK 667:2
best to w. in wind CATU 197:12
compulsion to w. LARK 453:11
die while I w. PETR 574:13
difficult to w. MOOR 530:5
Ek gret effect men w. CHAU 207:17
four words I w. BOIL 124:7
great man can w. it WILD 818:1
hate all who w. WYCH 834:13
I w. of melancholy BURT 170:2
I w. one DISR 271:10
I w. them PUNC 617:15
Learn to w. well BUCK 159:16
Learn to w. well CLOS 222:17
like to w. when I feel spiteful LAWR 458:19
little more I have to w. HERR 374:12
look in thy heart and w. SIDN 718:9
love to w. them BISH 116:3
make me w. too much DANI 249:4
man ought to w. TROL 781:20
men w. for profit WALP 801:8
not enough for me to w. LYLY 480:18
nothing to w. about PLIN 579:1
people that w. SHEN 715:9
people who can't w. ZAPP 839:24
reading, in order to w. JOHN 415:2
restraint with which they w. CAMP 183:2
sit down to w. KEAT 431:18
sit down to w. SWIF 749:14
Some who can't w. CHUR 213:21
such as cannot w., translate DENH 257:14
things I w. about WOOL 827:5
those who cannot w. POPE 586:16
virtues We w. in water SHAK 673:22
whether I should w. HARI 362:7
women who w. DURA 285:18
w. about it AMIS 13:17
w. about it, Goddess POPE 580:21
w. all the books EDDI 287:22
w. and cypher too GOLD 344:14
w. at any time JOHN 412:11
w. every other day DOUG 276:20
w. for Antiquity LAMB 449:6
w. for posterity ADE 5:20
w. for the sake of writing KEAT 431:12
w. in a book BIBL 111:20
W. me as one HUNT 395:12
w., or read, or think WINC 822:22
W. sorrow on the bosom SHAK 695:8
w. such stuff JOHN 417:3
w. the life of a man JOHN 414:13
w. to the moment RICH 627:3
w. trifles with dignity JOHN 416:17
w. upon him BIBL 111:27
w. with ease SHER 716:18
writer best fame is a w.'s fame LEBO 461:10
damaging to a w. GREE 351:25
Epick w. with a k STEV 742:9
great and original w. WORD 832:22
I'm a w. WALC 799:3
in America the successful w. LEWI 467:8
knows whether the w. ADDI 4:24
loose, plain, rude w. BURT 170:4
modern hardback w. TRIL 781:12
more interested in the w. AMIS 14:4
No tears in the w. FROS 326:14
of a ready w. BOOK 134:13
original w. CHAT 204:4
things a w. is for RUSH 638:1
This is the w.'s radar HEMI 369:14
understand a w.'s ignorance COLE 227:10
was the book and w. DANT 249:14
w. must be as objective CHEK 208:13
w. must refuse SART 645:14
w.'s ambition should be KOES 443:5
w.'s only responsibility FAUL 308:1
w. who has finished JOIN 418:19
w., who said ATWO 32:9
writers dead w. are remote ELIO 296:19
modern w. PLIN 578:15
W., like teeth BAGE 47:10
writes entire man that w. HUNT 395:19
seldom w. mind STEE 736:16
w. as fast as they can read HAZL 365:17

w. in dust BACO 45:11
w. only half CONR 234:26
w. when it grows dark CELA 199:8
writing activity of w. STEN 737:15
any style of w. untouched EPIT 303:17
as I had in the w. QUAR 618:13
business of w. STEV 741:3
continue w. GARC 329:13
easy w.'s vile hard reading SHER 716:18
fairy kind of w. DRYD 281:30
Fine w. KEAT 431:17
get it in w. LEE 461:19
good w. FITZ 315:18
If w. did not exist SEI 653:12
incurable disease of w. JUVE 424:17
little point in w. AMIS 14:1
manner of w. [prose] MILT 519:23
no talent for w. BENC 64:21
obstacle to professional w. BENC 64:18
only end of w. JOHN 409:15
only possible w. CONR 235:1
This w. business MILN 511:7
thought *nothing* of her w. SITW 721:5
True ease in w. POPE 584:22
w. an exact man BACO 44:7
w. *at once* GIDE 336:18
w.? A way of escape GREE 351:26
w. in a language FLAU 316:19
w. increaseth rage DYER 286:12
w. in English JOYC 422:19
W. is not an amusing FERB 308:13
W. is not a profession SIME 720:7
W. is turning one's worst moments DONL 272:6
w. not *about* something BECK 59:18
w. of oure tonge CHAU 207:18
W., when properly managed STER 738:23
written anything may be w. TRAH 780:8
as well w. as prose POUN 590:6
being w. about BELL 64:16
I have w. BIBL 102:34
I have w. unto you BIBL 107:24
it is w. of me BOOK 134:1
power of the w. word CONR 234:17
well w., or badly written WILD 818:14
were all my members w. BOOK 141:13
w. a book JOWE 421:14
w. by mere man JOHN 418:14
w. exceptionally well HORA 385:14
w. out of reputation BENT 67:9
w. such volumes of stuff LEAR 460:14
w. without effort JOHN 418:15
wrong absent always in the w. PROV 602:28
absent are always in the w. DEST 259:2
Addison approved, Cannot be w. EPIT 304:12
all was w. CRAB 243:7
always in the w. DILL 267:15
as likely to be w. BROU 151:16
better to suffer w. JOHN 410:19
be w. with Plato CICE 217:27
both agree is w. CECI 199:3
called them by w. names BROW 155:11
called the w. number THUR 776:27
customer is never w. RITZ 628:14
different kinds of w. COMP 230:15
do a little w. SHAK 688:13
does, not suffers w. SHEL 713:5
Eating people is w. FLAN 316:4
English man in the w. SHAW 709:2
feel that something has gone w. POTT 589:2
Fifty million Frenchmen can't be w. MILI 508:7
gang a kennin w. BURN 166:8
generally w. MONT 526:19
Had anything been w. AUDE 35:10
he done her w. SONG 729:5
idea,—and that was w. DISR 270:24
If anything can go w. SAYI 647:18
if w., to be set right SCHU 649:14
in this world much w. FITZ 315:1
I was w. AUDE 33:28
keep himself from doing w. BIBL 92:2
king can do no w. BLAC 117:4
king can do no w. PROV 605:2
majority are w. DEBS 254:8
mind being w. AYER 40:7
much w. could religion induce LUCR 479:1
Nature is usually w. WHIS 813:19
never in the w. BURK 164:12
never w., the Old Masters AUDE 34:9
not always to be w. EDEN 288:7
only an accumulated w. CASE 193:8
our country, right or w. DECA 254:10
own he has been in the w. POPE 587:18
persist In doing w. SHAK 700:11
ran w. through all the land MUIR 535:22
requite w. with wrong SOCR 727:3
right deed for the w. reason ELIO 295:15
right of an excessive w. BROW 157:24
something w. with our bloody ships BEAT 58:6
that is a w. one JOHN 414:8
that which they reject, is w. ADAM 2:15
thought it w. to fight BELL 64:5
thou hast seen my w. BIBL 89:27
very probably w. CLAR 219:8
We were w. MCNA 488:4
When everyone is w. LA C 447:1
when I am in the w. MELB 504:4
W. but Wromantic SELL 654:9
w. decision isn't forever GALB 328:10
w. even the poorest ploughman CHAR 203:3
W. forever on the throne LOWE 477:16
W. from the start POUN 589:12
w. man the woman HARD 360:19
w. members in control ORWE 558:16
w. side of a tapestry HOWE 391:16
w. side of the door CHES 210:3
You w. me every way SHAK 676:21
wrongly yet wouldst w. win SHAK 682:1
wrongs like w. hushed-up OWEN 562:10
makes the people's w. his own DRYD 280:11
redressing human w. TENN 759:19
Two w. don't make a right PROV 613:29
Two w. don't make a right SZAS 752:4
wrote as I w. it HAND 359:8
w., except for money JOHN 415:17
w. like an angel GARR 330:4
w. over against the candlestick BIBL 90:3
wrought first he w. CHAU 204:24
What hath God w. BIBL 77:1
What hath God w. TELE 758:12
w. in the work BIBL 80:31
w. me into shape FITZ 314:21
wrung w. from speculations BROW 153:23
Wyatt W. resteth here SURR 746:12
Wye half the babbling w. TENN 760:31
Wykehamist rather dirty W. BETJ 71:9
Wynken W., Blynken, and Nod FIEL 309:9

X Generation X COUP 238:5
wouldn't give a XXXX ADVE 7:7
Xanadu In X. did Kubla Khan COLE 225:20
xerox X. makes everybody MCLU 487:12

Yale whaleship was my Y. College MELV 504:8
yang embrace the y. LAO 451:15
Yankee Y. Doodle SONG 730:9
Y. Doodle Dandy COHA 224:1
Yanks Y. are coming COHA 223:22
Yarrow dens o' Y. BALL 50:15
yawn everlasting y. POPE 580:25
y. and be withdrawn DURY 286:10
y., or 'Pooh' BYRO 177:27
yawning y. at a ball LERM 464:23
yawns Despair y. HUGO 393:19
Even the grave y. TREE 781:3
yawp sound my barbaric y. WHIT 815:19
ydrad ever was y. SPEN 733:14
of gods and men y. SPEN 734:10
yea Let your y. be yea BIBL 110:23
year acceptable y. of the Lord BIBL 89:5
cherry y., a merry year PROV 597:14
circle of the golden y. TENN 759:5
death-struck y. HOUS 391:6
in public once a y. GRAY 351:7
isn't this time of y. GOGA 343:20
man at the gate of the y. HASK 363:16
Next y. in Jerusalem HAGG 356:3
one y.'s experience 30 times CARR 189:6
One y.'s seeding PROV 609:9
pleasure of the fleeting y. SHAK 705:8
snow of ferne y. CHAU 207:16
That time of y. SHAK 704:29
thirtieth y. to heaven THOM 772:10
this time next y. REED 623:12
Thou crownest the y. BOOK 136:2
'Tis the y.'s midnight DONN 274:8
touch of earthly y. WORD 831:25
y. and the hour HORA 389:7
y. is dying TENN 761:28
y. of the Julian Calendar USSH 788:20
y.'s at the spring BROW 157:12
yearned Y. after by the wisest TENN 763:18
yearning man of y. thought ROSS 635:7
years after all these y. SIMO 720:11
Ah! Posthumus, the y. SMAR 722:14
bound him a thousand y. BIBL 113:4
days of the y. of my life BIBL 75:20
fears of all the y. BROO 151:9
five y. or fifty AURE 37:10
For him in after y. PUDN 616:14
Forty y. on BOWE 145:7
gave up the y. to be BROO 150:7
go softly all my y. BIBL 87:26
It may be for y. CRAW 244:17
Jacob served seven y. BIBL 75:4
love of finished y. ROSS 634:3
more than a hundred y. FROS 326:1
nor the y. condemn BINY 115:8
thousand y. in thy sight BOOK 137:18
threescore y. and ten BOOK 137:19
two hundred y. like a sheep TIPU 777:15
two thousand y. of hope WEIZ 809:2
vale of y. SHAK 692:25
y. are slipping by HORA 388:8
y. like great black oxen YEAT 835:12
y. of desolation JEFF 406:1
Y. steal Fire from the mind BYRO 174:10
y. that the locust hath eaten BIBL 90:13
y. to come YEAT 836:10
yeas russet y. SHAK 681:1
yell angry spirit's y. BEAT 58:5
yellow Come unto these y. sands SHAK 698:26
expend her yellow y. MIDD 507:8
falls into the y. Leaf BYRO 177:3
Follow the y. brick road HARB 359:19
Goodbye y. brick road JOHN 408:4
one long y. string BROW 157:15
paved with y. brick BAUM 57:15
sparkled on the y. field TENN 762:16
thy y. stockings SHAK 701:29
With a y. petticoat NURS 548:2
Y., and black, and pale SHEL 712:12
Y. God forever gazes HAYE 365:2
y. leaf SHAK 685:17
y. leaves, or none SHAK 704:29
y. like ripe corn ROSS 634:17
yelps loudest y. for liberty JOHN 411:6
yeoman did me y.'s service SHAK 667:2
yes getting the answer y. CAMU 184:5
I did say y. O at lightning HOPK 385:3
Y., but not in the South POTT 589:3
'Y.,' I answered you BROW 154:19
Y. it hurt POLI 582:9
Y., Minister! No, Minister CROS 246:13
Y., Virginia CHUR 213:11
y. you don't mean RUME 637:6
yesterday authority of the eternal y. WEBE 807:6
but as y. BOOK 137:18

yesterday (*cont.*):
but y. a King BYRO 178:18
dead Y. FITZ 314:14
give me y. JONE 418:21
keeping up with y. MARQ 497:4
O! call back y. SHAK 695:6
perhaps it was y. OPEN 555:8
rose of y. FITZ 314:8
same y., and to day BIBL 110:7
thoughts of y. PALI 565:16
were saying y. LUIS 479:11
y. doth not usher it in DONN 275:7
Y. I loved LESS 465:15
Y.'s men POLI 582:10
yesterdays all our y. SHAK 685:22
yesteryear snows of y. VILL 793:1
yet as y. there were none BOOK 141:13
but not y. AUGU 36:3
young man not y. BACO 43:20
yew Of true wood, of y. wood DOYL 278:9
slips of y. SHAK 684:19
YHVH image of Y. ZOHA 840:12
yid PUT THE ID BACK IN Y. ROTH 635:19
yield and not to y. TENN 767:12
just to y. to it GRAH 347:17
yin carry the y. LAO 451:15
yo Y.-ho-ho, and a bottle of rum STEV 741:18
yoga Y. is evenness of mind BHAG 72:18
yogi y. has gone to the root TANT 755:2
yoke bear the y. in his youth BIBL 89:25
break every y. BIBL 89:1
bull doth bear the y. SHAK 691:1
hath received our y. WALL 800:12
my y. is easy BIBL 95:9
y. of prelaty MILT 519:24
yoked y. with a lamb SHAK 676:26
yolk y. runs down the waistcoat DICK 264:2
Yonghy-Bonghy-Bó Lived the Y. LEAR 460:5
Yorick Alas, poor Y. SHAK 666:23
Yorkshire Y. born PROV 615:21
you cannot live with y. MART 498:4
For y. but not for me MILI 508:13
It could be y. ADVE 7:31
it was y. and me JAGG 401:9
wanted simply y. HÉLO 369:1
Y.'ll never walk HAMM 359:4
Y. too, Brutus CAES 180:22
Y.'ve got to be carefully taught HAMM 359:5
'Y.' your joys and sorrows CRIC 245:1
young artist as a y. man JOYC 421:22
as I was y. and easy THOM 772:3
before the y. had discovered MAUG 501:15
Being y. is overestimated QUAN 618:11
censor of the y. HORA 386:2
country of y. men EMER 299:32
crime of being a y. man PITT 576:19
defrauded y. KIPL 438:13
dies y. MENA 504:12
evil in y. minds ARNO 29:16
for ever y. KEAT 428:26
get out while we're y. SPRI 735:12
Gods love die y. PROV 615:3
good die y. PROV 601:24
Hang a thief when he's y. PROV 601:46
If I were y. MARL 495:15
I have been y. BLUN 122:12
I have been y. BOOK 133:26
I'll die y. BRUC 158:18
in the will of a y. gentleman ASCH 30:8
I was a poet, I was y. FLEC 317:7
knew the worst too y. KIPL 438:18
lead those that are with y. BIBL 88:2
look y. till forty DRYD 282:2
love's y. dream MOOR 530:13
make an old man y. TENN 758:22
Old and y. STEV 741:24
on your y. shoulders SPAR 731:17
O y., fresshe folkes CHAU 207:20
proper y. men BURN 167:18
resolute, the y. KIPL 439:15
seventy years y. HOLM 381:11
So wise so y. SHAK 696:20
so y. a body SHAK 688:9
So y., and so untender SHAK 677:23
too y. to fall asleep for ever SASS 645:19
too y. to take up golf ADAM 2:7
Unlike y. men SHAK 700:10
What can a y. lassie do BURN 169:9
what the world would call y. men PEEL 571:15
When thou wast y. BIBL 103:11
While we are y. ANON 21:9
Whom the gods love die y. BYRO 177:5
Women never have y. minds DELA 256:22
y. and foolish YEAT 835:16
y. and lusty BOOK 138:17
y. and sweating devil SHAK 693:4
y. are quick of speech WINT 823:11
Y. blood must have its course KING 437:13
y. can do for the old SHAW 707:6
Y. folks think old folks PROV 616:1
y., gifted and black HANS 359:12
Y., gifted and black IRVI 400:1
y. man married PROV 616:2
y. man married SHAK 656:3
y. man not yet BACO 43:20
y. man's slave PROV 596:5
y. man will be wiser TENN 759:14
Y. men and maidens BOOK 142:1
Y. men are fitter BACO 44:25
y. men glittering TRAH 780:15
Y. men have more virtue JOHN 413:11
Y. men may die PROV 616:3
y. men shall see visions BIBL 90:14
y. men's vision DRYD 280:5
y. men think it is HOUS 390:12
y. regard me as outrageous HOYL 392:8
Y. saint, old devil PROV 616:4
y. think too little WALP 800:24
y. was very heaven WORD 828:16
y. whom I hope to bother AUDE 35:4
y. wife JONS 419:10
younger love be y. than thyself SHAK 701:19
y. son gathered all together BIBL 100:2
Y. than she SHAK 697:4
y. than that now DYLA 207:12
youngster You're going out a y. FILM 312:13
yours never y., Augustus DICK 263:15
What I have done is y. SHAK 703:29
Y. till Hell freezes FISH 313:16
yourself DO IT Y. BARH 54:11
do it y. PROV 603:38
yourselve make honey not for y. VIRG 797:4
youth April of your y. HERB 371:22
bear the yoke in his y. BIBL 89:25
cap of y. SHAK 666:11
Crabbed age and y. SHAK 703:27
days of our y. BYRO 179:6
days of thy y. BIBL 85:2
evil from his y. BIBL 74:18
flattering y. defy ROCH 630:19
flourish set on y. SHAK 704:24
flower of their y. VIRG 796:7
from my y. up BOOK 140:24
How beautiful is y. MEDI 503:10
If y. knew ESTI 301:10
I have y. WEBS 807:21
In lusty y. SURR 746:10
in the days of thy y. BIBL 85:1
it is y. who must fight HOOV 383:13
many a y. MILT 512:21
miracle of a y. EVEL 305:6
My prime of y. TICH 777:10
noble y. did dress SHAK 669:31
offences of my y. BOOK 133:5
promises of y. JOHN 410:23
red sweet wine of y. BROO 150:7
remember my y. CONR 234:25
remembreth me Upon my y. CHAU 206:18
rose Of y. SHAK 657:4
seized my y. ARNO 27:20
shake their wicked sides at y. YEAT 836:22
sign of an ill-spent y. ROUP 636:2
spice-islands of Y. COLE 227:28
subtle thief of y. MILT 518:27
tender years of y. GOGO 344:1
things Y. needed not WORD 832:1
thoughts of y. are long LONG 473:23
To y. and age in common ARNO 28:6
unemployed y. BAGE 46:22
Where y. grows pale KEAT 429:10
With y. youth WYAT 834:2
world has lost his y. BIBL 91:3
Y. and Pleasure meet BYRO 174:14
y., I do adore thee SHAK 703:28
Y. is a blunder DISR 270:3
Y. is something very new CHAN 202:4
y. is the season of credulity PITT 576:21
Y. is vivid LOVE 477:1
Y. must be served PROV 616:7
Y. of a Nation DISR 270:26
y. of a state BACO 44:21
y. of England SHAK 670:30
y. of frolics POPE 583:15
y. of his generation FITZ 315:17
y. of labour GOLD 344:9
y. of the realm SHAK 672:24
y. of the world BACO 41:22
Y. on the prow GRAY 350:5
Y. pined away BLAK 120:22
y. replies, *I can* EMER 299:11
Y.'s a stuff SHAK 701:10
y.'s sweet-scented manuscript FITZ 315:2
Y.'s the season GAY 331:20
y. to fortune GRAY 350:14
y. to the gallows PAIN 564:4
y. unkind BAST 57:2
Y., what man's age is like DENH 257:12
Y., which is forgiven SHAW 708:30
Y. will be served BORR 143:12
Y. would be an ideal state ASQU 31:3
Yule green Y. makes PROV 601:38
yuppie y. version of bulimia EHRE 290:1
Yvetot king of Y. BÉRA 67:14

Zadok Z. the priest BIBL 79:15
Zaire Z. is the trigger FANO 306:8
zany mountebank and his z. WALP 801:11
Zanzibar count the cats in Z. THOR 776:15
Zarathustra follower of Z. ZORO 841:7
Zauber *Deine Z. binden wieder* SCHI 646:14
zeal all z., Mr Easy MARR 497:17
by men of z. BRAN 146:20
holy mistaken z. JUNI 423:14
not the slightest z. TALL 753:5
take it for z. THOM 771:7
Tell z. it wants devotion RALE 620:13
tempering bigot z. KNOX 442:12
z. of the Lord BIBL 87:2
z. of thine house BOOK 136:10
z. of women themselves MILL 509:8
zealous z. citizen BURK 164:5
zed Thou whoreson z. SHAK 678:13
Zen Z. and the art PIRS 576:16
zenith from the z. like a falling star MILT 515:5
zephyr Odes to every z. KING 437:6
Zephyrus Sweet breathing Z. SPEN 734:18
zest z. goes out of a beautiful waltz GREN 352:15
Zion daughter of Z. BIBL 86:10
songs of peaceful Z. DIX 271:12
Z., city of our God NEWT 543:14
Zionism Z., be it right or wrong BALF 49:18
zipless z. fuck JONG 419:6
Zitronen *Land, wo die Z. blühn* GOET 343:12
zone torrid or the frozen z. CARE 186:11
zoo human z. MORR 532:7
Zuleika Such was Z. BYRO 173:20
Zurich gnomes in Z. WILS 821:12